Funk & Wagnalls

Crossword Puzzle Word Finder

FUNK & WAGNALLS

Crossword Puzzle Word Finder

Edmund I. Schwartz
and Leon F. Landovitz

A Perigee Book

Perigee Books
are published by
The Putnam Publishing Group
200 Madison Avenue
New York, NY 10016

Published simultaneously in Canada by
General Publishing Co. Limited, Toronto

Library of Congress Cataloging-in-Publication Data

Schwartz, Edmund I.
Funk & Wagnalls crossword puzzle word finder.

Reprint. Originally published: New York :
Funk & Wagnalls, 1974.
1. Crossword puzzles—Glossaries, vocabularies, etc.
I. Landovitz, Leon F., date. II. Title.
III. Title: Funk and Wagnalls crossword puzzle word
finder. IV. Title: Crossword puzzle word finder.
GV1507.C7S24 1986 793.7′32′0321 85-16888
ISBN 0-399-51216-0

Reprinted by permission of Thomas Y. Crowell, Publishers.

Printed in the United States of America

2 3 4 5 6 7 8 9 10

CONTENTS

POSSET
POSSUM
POSTAL
POSTED
POSTER
POTAGE
POTASH
POTATO
POTBOY
POTEEN
POTENT
POTHER
POTION
POTPIE
POTSIE
POTTED
POTTER
POTTLE
POTTOS
POUCHY
POULTS
POUNCE
POUNDS
POURED
POURER
POUSTO
POUTED
POUTER
POWDER
POWELL
POWERS
POWTER
POWWOW
POYOUS

(1)

6

P•O•••

PEOPLE
PEORIA
PHOBIA
PHOCIS
PHOEBE
PHONED
PHONES
PHONEY
PHONIA
PHONIC
PHOOEY
PHOSPH
PHOTIC
PHOTON
PHOTOS
PLOUGH
PLOVER
PLOWED
PLOWER
POODLE
POOLED
POOPED
POORER
POORLY
PROBED
PROBER
PROBES
PROCNE

PROCTO
PROEMS
PROFIT
PROJET
PROLEG
PROLIX
PROMPT
PRONGS
PRONTO
PROOFS
PROPEL
PROPER
PROPYL
PROSED
PROSER
PROSES
PROSIT
PROTON
PROUST
PROVED
PROVEN
PROVER
PROVES
PROWLS
PTOSIS
PYOSIS

P••O••

PAEONS
PAGODA
PARODY
PAROLE
PATOIS
PAYOFF
PAYOLA
PEKOES
PELOPS
PELOTA
PEYOTE
PHLOEM
PHOOEY
PICOTS
PILOSE
PILOTS
PILOUS
PINOLE
PINONS
PITONS
PIVOTS
PODOUS
POMONA
POROUS
POYOUS
PRIORS
PRIORY
PROOFS
PUTOFF
PUTONS
PUTOUT
PYLONS
PYRONE
PYROPE

P•••O•

PALLOR
PARDON
PARGOS
PARLOR
PARROT
PARSON
PASTOR
PATHOL
PATHOS
PATIOS
PATROL
PATRON
PATTON
PAVIOR
PAVLOV
PEDROS
PEGTOP
PELION
PENGOS
PENNON
PEPLOS
PEQUOD
PEQUOT
PERIOD
PERRON
PERSON
PETROL
PHENOL
PHILOS
PHOTON
PHOTOS
PIANOS
PICTOR
PIGEON
PILLOW
PINGOS
PINION
PINTOS
PISTOL
PISTON
PLEXOR
PODSOL
PODZOL
POGROM
POISON
POMPOM
POMPON
PONTON
POTBOY
POTION
POTTOS
POWWOW
PRETOR
PRISON
PROTON
PUNTOS
PUTLOG
PYTHON

P••••O

PALAEO
PASHTO
PHLEBO

PHRENO
PHYLLO
PHYSIO
PIETRO
PLAGIO
PLASMO
PLEURO
PLUMBO
PLUVIO
PNEUMO
POMELO
PONCHO
POTATO
POUSTO
PRESTO
PROCTO
PRONTO
PSEUDO
PSYCHO
PUEBLO

•PO•••

APODAL
APOGEE
APOLLO
APOLOG
EPOCHS
EPODES
EPONYM
EPOPEE
SPOILS
SPOILT
SPOKED
SPOKEN
SPOKES
SPONGE
SPONGY
SPOOFS
SPOOKS
SPOOKY
SPOOLS
SPOONS
SPOONY
SPOORS
SPORED
SPORES
SPORTS
SPORTY
SPOTTY
SPOUSE
SPOUTS

•P•O••

APLOMB
APNOEA
APPOSE
APRONS
EPHODS
EPHORI
EPHORS
OPPOSE
SPOOFS
SPOOKS
SPOOKY

SPOOLS
SPOONS
SPOONY
SPOORS
SPROUT
UPBOWS
UPHOLD
UPMOST
UPROAR
UPROOT
UPROSE
UPTOWN

(3) **•P••O•**

APOLOG
EPILOG
EPIZOA
OPTION
SPIGOT
UPHROE
UPROOT
UPSHOT

(4)

•P•••O

APOLLO
SPERMO
SPHENO
SPLENO

••PO••

APPOSE
BIPODS
CAPONS
CAPOTE
COPOUT
CUPOLA
DEPORT
DEPOSE
DEPOTS
DIPODY
DIPOLE
EXPORT
EXPOSE
GIPONS
IMPORT
IMPOSE
IMPOST
JUPONS
KAPOKS
LIPOID
LIPOMA
MOPOKE
OPPOSE
REPORT
REPOSE
RIPOFF
RIPOST
SEPOYS
TIPOFF
VAPORI
VAPORS
YAPONS
YUPONS

••P•O•

CAPTOR
DEPLOY
DIPLOE
EMPLOY
HIPPOS
HYPNOS
LEPTON
NIPPON
OOPHOR
PEPLOS
SIPHON
TIPTOE
TIPTOP
TYPHON

••P••O

HEPATO
LAPARO
LEPIDO
NEPHRO
SAPPHO
TAPALO
TUPELO
TYPHLO

•••PO•

CAMPOS
COMPOS
COUPON
COWPOX
DESPOT
HIPPOS
HOOPOE
ISOPOD
MAYPOP
NIPPON
POMPOM
POMPON
SLIPON
STUPOR
TAMPON
TARPON
TEAPOT
TEAPOY
TEMPOS
TORPOR
TRIPOD
TRIPOS
UROPOD
WEAPON
YAUPON
YOUPON

•••P•O

ALEPPO
CRYPTO
GLYPTO
GRAPHO
LYMPHO
MORPHO
NYMPHO
SAPPHO
SCIPIO

HOW TO USE THIS BOOK

The *Word Finder* is designed to help you solve crossword puzzle sticklers solely through letters you have already filled in. Its system is based on the notion that when you are stumped by a partially completed answer you will be able to recognize the full word when you see it among a limited number of possible answers.

The format is simple and efficient. If you know any two letters of an answer with three to six letters (or one letter of a two-letter word) you will find here a list of words which fit that precise pattern of letters and blanks. The system is illustrated on the sample page opposite.

Assume that the clue is for a six-letter word meaning "choice" and that you are stuck after having gotten as far as • P • • O • by completing words that cross your answer. Then:

1. Use the tabs on the margins of the pages to flip quickly to the six-letter section.
2. Use the headings at the tops of the pages to riffle to the vicinity of lists with the letters P and O, in that order (the dots represent blank squares in the puzzle).
3. Find the list headed by the pattern of letters and blanks that matches the partially filled answer (• P • • O •).
4. With the clue "choice" in mind, you will easily recognize the only answer that fits: OPTION.

In each major section of the *Word Finder* the lists are organized under headings that run in strict alphabetical order (from AA • • • • to • • • • ZZ in the six-letter section). The complete sequence of P and O combinations in the six-letter section has the pattern:

PO • • • • P • O • • • P • • O • • P • • • O • P • • • • O	(P in the first position, O in positions two to six)
• PO • • • • P • O • • • P • • O • • P • • • O	(P in the second position, O in positions three to six)
• • PO • • • • P • O • • • P • • O	(P in the third position, O in positions four to six)
• • • PO • • • • P • O	(P in the fourth position, O in positions five and six)
• • • • PO	(P in the fifth position, O in the sixth)

If there are no answer words that fit a particular pattern of blanks and letters, that heading is simply omitted.

If you have filled in *more* than two letters of an answer having four to six letters, begin your search with the two letters that seem least likely to be used in combination, for at that position you will probably have to scan the fewest number of possible answers. If, for example, you know the letters W, E, and B in a six-letter word, the best starting place is probably the heading for the W and B pair, because these are less frequently used than E.

If you know only *one* letter in anything but a two-letter word, it is best to try to fill in one more letter by making attempts at crossing answers. Fill-ins with one letter can, of course, be found in the *Word Finder,* but the process is rather slow because the lists you need will be widely scattered, and the number of words you must scan will be large. All four-letter words with A in the second position, for example, will be found under the headings AA • •, BA • •, CA • •, etc., and all four-letter words with D in the third position are under the headings A • D •, B • D •, C • D •, and so on, throughout the alphabet.

If you have narrowed the search to several words, none of which you know, insert the possible answers successively on a trial basis, to see how they work with crossing answers. Frequently you can eliminate a word because it makes for an improbable combination of letters (for example, T Q or K B) in a crossing word.

When you are stumped by unfamiliar answer words, however, the quickest way to the solution is to look up the definitions of the "possibles." Although a great many of the entries in this book are defined in any good college-level dictionary, the *Word Finder* is especially designed to be used with the *Funk & Wagnalls Standard®*

College Dictionary. The two books, therefore, make the best possible companion volumes for puzzle solving: you can be sure that every entry in the *Word Finder* is defined in the *Standard College Dictionary;* with any other dictionary you may suffer some disappointments.

You will find that the system of the *Word Finder* works equally well for all types of crossword puzzles: standard, diagramless, and puns and anagrams. The book can be used also to fill out incomplete words in either part of double crostics; it can be used at leisure to bone up on the high-scoring words of crossword board games; and it is ideal for the trial-and-error approach to solving cryptograms. Fans of crossword-type sweepstakes contests will find it the perfect tool for constructing puzzles with words that have loads of high-point letters.

PREFACE

I am an ardent, albeit inconstant, lover of puzzles and games—crosswords, double crostics, Scrabble, chess, and bridge—going from one pastime to another as my mood dictates or the occasion demands. My wife is an equally fervent games enthusiast, but more discriminating and persevering. She detests cards but dotes on word games of every sort, and once started on a puzzle she will complete it by exhausting every resource—and, occasionally, my patience as well. This book owes its being largely, if obliquely, to one such demonstration of her persistence.

One afternoon we were sunning ourselves on the lawn, she deeply engrossed in the crossword puzzle of the Sunday *New York Times* and I in a novel, having sworn abstinence from puzzles until I had caught up on months of neglected reading. After an hour or so of silent effort my wife began the litany of the puzzle cultist: "What's a six-letter word for 'fabric'? It goes BLANK, A, BLANK, BLANK, S, BLANK." I took up the responses, with annoyance only occasionally tempered by the satisfaction of a correct answer quickly supplied (but not, on this occasion, D A M A S K). Finally, concentration on the novel shattered, I began to mull over the predicament familiar to all crossword fans—the impasse of the partially completed answer—and those ruminations at length led to the format you now see in the *Word Finder*.

What was needed, I saw, was a collection of lists of words that, regardless of meaning, would fit given patterns of letters and blanks such as the • A • • S • that had stumped my wife and me: anyone who could not *recall* that D A M A S K is a six-letter word for "fabric" would surely *recognize* the word in such a list. The notion seemed simple enough—picking a correct answer from a limited selection of possibles is far easier than dredging it up, unaided, from memory–but it gradually became clear that assembling such lists for innumerable combinations of letters and blanks would present monumental difficulties. My colleague, Dr. Landovitz, himself a long-suffering target of the "What's a . . . ?" type of question, became an eager and resourceful participant in the effort to solve the problems.

Dr. Landovitz and I first had to determine whether it was possible to make a compilation of such lists that would be comprehensive enough to be an effective tool for solving puzzles but limited enough to fit into a book about the size of a desk dictionary. Ultimately we concluded that to meet those specifications the lists must consist of words with two to six letters, and that words with three to six letters must be presented as partial answers with two letters known.

These two limitations represent a compromise between utility for the puzzle fan and compelling mathematics. Words of six letters or less comprise the great majority of answer words in even the most sophisticated crossword puzzles; and restricting the format to two known letters, we came to realize, actually improved the efficiency of the format in some ways.

Had we allowed for the widest range of possible answers, each word in every conceivable combination of letters and blanks (from one letter known to all but one letter known), the total compilation would have required a multi-volume set of books, and in this vast assemblage many individual lists would have been so long that they would be more discouraging than helpful. The "compelling mathematics" can be readily demonstrated.

With the total approach, each two-letter word would be processed into two incomplete forms (e.g., AT produces A • and • T), but at each increase in word length there would be a disproportionate increase in the number of incomplete words. Each three-letter word would produce six such entries (BAT produces B • •, BA •, B • T, • AT, • A •, and • • T). Each four-letter word would produce 14 entries, each five-letter word 30, and each six-letter word 62. Limiting the entries to forms with two letters known, however, reduces the number of combinations dramatically–from 62 to 15 for the six-letter words, for example. Even with this limited approach, the six-letter portion of the *Word Finder* has 514 pages; to accommodate the full range of 62 letter/blank combinations would have required more than 2,000 pages for this section alone, and it would have included many single lists that would have run on for pages. A list of the six-letter words with the pattern S • • • • • (one letter known, S in the first position), for example, would have contained more than 1,400 words; there would have been more than 3,000 with the pattern • • • • • S (one letter known, S in the sixth position).

Although the less comprehensive approach avoids such interminable lists, the puzzler who so desires can, in fact, find them here–but in disconnected series. All of the six-letter words that begin with S are offered under the headings S A • • • •, S C • • • •, S E • • • •, etc. (Note that headings beginning S B and S D are omitted because there are no words so spelled.) All six-letter words that end in S are covered in the lists headed A • • • • S, B • • • • S, C • • • • S, and so on, in sequence throughout the alphabet.

The decision to limit the entries to answers having two known letters does not work to the disadvantage of a puzzler who has filled in *more* letters; such a situation merely gives the user of the *Word Finder* a choice of starting places.

Once Dr. Landovitz and I had established the purely numerical dimensions of the project, there remained the matter of the source of the entries themselves. The source is significant bcause, while the book's system relies primarily upon the user's ability to recognize the answer that fits the clue, puzzles often contain obscure words, such as ZIBET, that may not be in the fan's everyday vocabulary. We knew that, inevitably, there would be times when the puzzler would have narrowed the choice to several words, all unfamiliar, and that in such cases the quickest route to the sole correct answer would be to look up definitions of the words. For the convenience of users, therefore, we concluded that the entries in the *Word Finder* should come from a single, comprehensive reference book.

It was not mere chance, then, that led us to seek Funk & Wagnalls as a prospective publisher; we knew that the firm's *Standard College Dictionary* had precisely those qualities that would make it a perfect companion volume for the *Word Finder*. It is an up-to-date and wide-ranging compilation which, unlike several other desk dictionaries, has practically all of its entries–including abbreviations and geographical and biographical entries–in a single alphabetical listing.

The *Word Finder*'s basic list of words, therefore, consists entirely of words of two to six letters in the *Funk & Wagnalls Standard College Dictionary*. (A great many of the definitions can, of course, be found in any recent "college" dictionary, but only the *Standard College Dictionary* has *all* of them.) We have included practically every type of word that is common fare in puzzles: foreign words as well as English; standard, informal, and slang words in every part of speech and every tense, number, and gender; variant spellings, abbreviations, acronyms, hyphenated words, and prefixes and suffixes; geographical names and the first and last names of people. We have excluded, for reasons of space, all phrases, and–because they are avoided by puzzle editors–words that are obscene, scatological, or racially offensive.

In the final stages of the development of the *Word Finder*, Dr. Landovitz and I had the able assistance of our editor at Funk & Wagnalls, Patrick Barrett, to guide us in achieving a format that is both efficient and easy to use.

Processing every word in the list to make entries with the right combinations of letters and blanks and assembling them into a logical sequence would have been, in other times, a tedious manual chore replete with opportunities for error. Fortunately, modern technology has provided us with a factotum for which no task is too onerous or difficult: the digital computer. The words were entered into a computer that was programmed to perform the sorting process and to produce a magnetic tape which, when fed to another electronic marvel, composed the pages you now see in the volume. Resolving the knotty problems of producing a book to solve puzzles has been a fascinating experience for my colleague and me. It has introduced us to several intriguing aspects of the structure of English words, avenues that we plan to investigate in more detail in the future.

Edmund I. Schwartz

2-LETTER WORDS

A•
AA
AB
AC
AD
AE
AF
AG
AH
AI
AL
AM
AN
AO
AP
AQ
AR
AS
AT
AU
AV
AW
AX
AY
AZ

•A
AA
BA
CA
DA
EA
FA
GA
HA
IA
JA
KA
LA
MA
NA
PA
RA
SA
TA
VA

B•
BA
BB
BC
BD
BE
BF
BG
BI
BJ
BK
BL
BM
BN
BO
BP
BR
BS
BT
BU
BV
BY
BZ

•B
AB
BB
CB
DB
FB
GB
HB
IB
KB
LB
MB
NB
OB
PB
QB
RB
SB
TB
WB
YB

C•
CA
CB
CC
CD
CE
CF
CG
CH
CI
CJ
CL
CM
CN
CO
CP
CQ
CR
CS
CT
CU
CY
CZ

•C
AC
BC
CC
DC
EC
FC
HC
IC
KC
LC
MC
NC
OC
PC
QC
RC
SC
TC
UC
VC
WC
XC

D•
DA
DB
DC
DD
DE
DF
DG
DH
DI
DL
DM
DN
DO
DP
DR
DS
DU
DV
DW
DX
DY
DZ

•D
AD
BD
CD
DD
ED
FD
GD
HD
ID
JD
KD
LD
MD
ND
OD
RD
SD
TD
VD
XD
YD

E•
EA
EC
ED
EE
EF
EG
EI
EL
EM
EN
EO
EP
ER
ES
ET
EU
EV
EX
EY

•E
AE
BE
CE
DE
EE
FE
GE
HE
IE
JE
LE
ME
NE
OE
RE
SE
TE
WE
XE
YE

F•
FA
FB
FC
FD
FE
FF
FI
FL
FM
FO
FP
FR
FS
FT
FV

•F
AF
BF
CF
DF
EF
FF
HF
IF
LF
MF
NF
OF
PF
RF
SF
WF
ZF

G•
GA
GB
GD
GE
GI
GK
GL
GM
GO
GP
GQ
GR
GS
GT
GU
GV

•G
AG
BG
CG
DG
EG
HG
IG
JG
KG
LG
MG
NG
OG
PG
SG
TG
VG

H•
HA
HB
HC
HD
HE
HF
HG
HH
HI
HJ
HL
HM
HO
HP
HQ
HR
HS
HT
HV
HW
HY

•H
AH
CH
DH
HH
LH
MH
NH
OH
PH
SH
TH
WH

I•
IA
IB
IC
ID
IE
IF
IG
IL
IM
IN
IO
IP
IQ
IR
IS
IT
IU

•I
AI
BI
CI
DI
EI
FI
GI
HI
LI
MI
NI
PI
RI
SI
TI
VI
WI
XI

J•
JA
JD
JE
JG
JL
JO
JP
JR
JS

2

JV
JY

•J
BJ
CJ
HJ
NJ
SJ

K•
KA
KB
KC
KD
KG
KL
KM
KN
KO
KP
KR
KS
KT
KV
KW
KY

•K
BK
GK
MK
OK
PK
UK
WK

L•
LA
LB
LC
LD
LE
LF
LG
LH
LI
LL
LM
LN
LO
LP
LS
LT
LU
LV
LY

•L
AL
BL
CL
DL
EL
FL
GL
HL
IL
JL
KL
LL
ML
OL
QL
SL
VL
WL
YL

M•
MA
MB
MC
MD
ME
MF
MG
MH
MI
MK
ML
MM
MN
MO
MP
MR
MS
MT
MU
MV
MW
MY

•M
AM
BM
CM
DM
EM
FM
GM
HM
IM
KM
LM
MM
NM
OM
PM
QM
RM
SM
WM

N•
NA
NB
NC
ND
NE
NF
NG
NH
NI
NJ
NM
NO
NS
NT
NU
NW
NY
NZ

•N
AN
BN
CN
DN
EN
IN
KN
LN
MN
ON
PN
RN
SN
TN
UN
VN
XN
ZN

O•
OB
OC
OD
OE
OF
OG
OH
OK
OL
OM
ON
OO
OP
OR
OS
OT
OX
OZ

•O
AO
BO
CO
DO
EO
FO
GO
HO
IO
JO
KO
LO
MO
NO
OO
PO
SO
TO
VO
WO

P•
PA
PB
PC
PF
PG
PH
PI
PK
PM
PN
PO
PP
PQ
PR
PS
PT
PU
PX
PY

•P
AP
BP
CP
DP
EP
FP
GP
HP
IP
JP
KP
LP
MP
OP
PP
QP
RP
SP
TP
UP
VP
XP

Q•
QB
QC
QL
QM
QP
QQ
QR
QS
QT
QU
QV

•Q
AQ
CQ
GQ
HQ
IQ
PQ
QQ
SQ

R•
RA
RB
RC
RD
RE
RF
RI
RM
RN
RP
RR
RS
RT
RU
RV
RW
RY

•R
AR
BR
CR
DR
ER
FR
GR
HR
IR
JR
KR
MR
OR
PR
QR
RR
SR
TR
UR
VR
YR
ZR

S•
SA
SB
SC
SD
SE
SF
SG
SH
SI
SJ
SL
SM
SN
SO
SP
SQ
SR
SS
ST
SV
SW
SY

•S
AS
BS
CS
DS
ES
FS
GS
HS
IS
JS
KS
LS
MS
NS
OS
PS
QS
RS
SS
TS
US
VS
WS
XS
YS
ZS

T•
TA
TB
TC
TD
TE
TG
TH
TI
TN
TO
TP
TR
TS
TT
TU
TV
TY

•T
AT
BT
CT
ET
FT
GT
HT
IT
KT
LT
MT
NT
OT
PT
QT
RT
ST
TT
UT
VT
WT
YT

U•
UC
UK
UN
UP
UR
US
UT
UX

•U
AU
BU
CU
DU
EU
GU
IU
LU
MU
NU
PU
QU
RU
TU

V•
VA
VC
VD
VG
VI
VL
VN
VO
VP
VR
VS
VT
VV

•V
AV
BV
DV
EV
FV
GV
HV
JV
KV
LV
MV
QV
RV
SV
TV
VV

W•
WB
WC
WE
WF
WH
WI
WK
WL
WM
WO
WS
WT

•W
AW
DW
HW
KW
MW
NW
RW
SW

X•
XC
XD
XE
XI
XN
XP
XS

•X
AX
DX
EX
OX
PX
UX

Y•
YB
YD
YE
YL
YR
YS
YT

•Y
AY
BY
CY
DY
EY
HY
JY
KY
LY
MY
NY
PY
RY
SY
TY

Z•
ZF
ZN
ZR
ZS

•Z
AZ
BZ
CZ
DZ
NZ
OZ

3-LETTER WORDS

AA•
AAA
AAF
AAL
AAR

A•A
AAA
ABA
ADA
AGA
AHA
AKA
ALA
AMA
ANA
ARA
ASA
AVA

•AA
AAA
BAA
FAA
NAA
TAA

AB•
ABA
ABC
ABE
ABS

A•B
AFB
ALB

•AB
BAB
CAB
DAB
GAB
JAB
KAB
LAB
MAB
NAB
TAB

AC•
ACC
ACE
ACT
ACU
ACY

A•C
ABC
ACC
ADC
AEC
AKC
ANC
ARC
ATC
AUC

•AC
LAC
MAC
SAC
WAC

AD•
ADA
ADC
ADD
ADE
ADJ
ADM
ADO
ADS
ADV
ADZ

A•D
ADD
AID
AND
ARD

•AD
BAD
CAD
DAD
FAD
GAD
HAD
LAD
MAD
PAD
RAD
SAD
TAD
WAD

AE•
AEC
AEF
AER
AES
AET

A•E
ABE
ACE
ADE
AGE
ALE
ANE
APE
ARE
ASE
ATE
AVE
AWE
AXE
AYE

•AE
BAE
CAE
GAE
MAE
NAE
RAE

AF•
AFB
AFG
AFL
AFR
AFT

A•F
AAF
AEF
ALF

•AF
AAF
CAF
OAF
RAF
WAF

AG•
AGA
AGE
AGO

A•G
AFG
ALG
AMG
ARG
AUG

•AG
BAG
DAG
FAG
GAG
HAG
JAG
LAG
NAG
RAG
SAG
TAG
WAG

AH•
AHA

A•H
APH
ASH

•AH
BAH
HAH
PAH
RAH
YAH

AI•
AID
AIL
AIM
AIN
AIR
AIS

A•I
ALI
AMI
ANI
AVI

A•J
ADJ

•AJ
RAJ
TAJ

AK•
AKA
AKC

A•K
ARK
ASK
AUK

•AK
DAK
OAK
YAK

AL•
ALA
ALB
ALE
ALF
ALG
ALI
ALL
ALP
ALS
ALT

A•L
AAL
AFL
AIL
ALL
AOL
AWL

•AL
AAL
CAL
DAL
GAL
HAL
IAL
KAL
MAL
PAL
SAL
VAL

AM•
AMA
AMG
AMI
AMP
AMT
AMU
AMY

A•M
ADM
AIM
ARM

•AM
CAM
DAM
EAM
FAM
GAM
HAM
JAM
LAM
NAM
PAM
RAM
SAM
TAM
YAM

AN•
ANA
ANC
AND
ANE
ANI
ANN
ANT
ANU
ANY

A•N
AIN
ANN
ARN
ASN
AWN

•AN
BAN
CAN
DAN
FAN
IAN
JAN
KAN
MAN
NAN
PAN
RAN
TAN
VAN
WAN

AO•
AOL

A•O
ADO
AGO
APO
AZO

•AO
FAO
GAO
LAO
MAO

AP•
APE
APH
APO
APR
APT

A•P
ALP
AMP
ASP

•AP
CAP
DAP
GAP
JAP
LAP
MAP
NAP
PAP
RAP
SAP
TAP
WAP
YAP

AR•
ARA
ARC
ARD
ARE
ARG
ARK
ARM
ARN
ARS
ART
ARV
ARY

A•R
AAR
AER
AFR
AIR

3

APR

•AR
AAR
BAR
CAR
DAR
EAR
FAR
GAR
JAR
LAR
MAR
OAR
PAR
SAR
TAR
UAR
WAR

AS•
ASA
ASE
ASH
ASK
ASN
ASP
ASS

A•S
ABS
ADS
AES
AIS
ALS
ARS
ASS
AUS
AYS

•AS
BAS
FAS
GAS
HAS
IAS
JAS
KAS
LAS
MAS
OAS
PAS
RAS
VAS
WAS

AT•
ATC
ATE

A•T
ACT
AET
AFT
ALT
AMT
ANT
APT
ART
AUT

•AT
BAT
CAT
EAT
FAT
GAT
HAT
JAT
LAT
MAT
NAT
OAT
PAT
RAT
SAT
TAT
VAT

AU•
AUC
AUG
AUK
AUS
AUT
AUX

A•U
ACU
AMU
ANU

•AU
EAU
TAU

AV•
AVA
AVE
AVI

A•V
ADV
ARV

•AV
BAV
CAV
NAV
TAV
VAV

AW•
AWE
AWL
AWN

•AW
CAW
DAW
HAW
JAW
LAW
MAW
PAW
RAW
SAW
TAW
UAW
YAW

AX•
AXE

A•X
AUX

•AX
FAX
LAX
MAX
PAX
SAX
TAX
WAX

AY•
AYE
AYS

A•Y
ACY
AMY
ANY
ARY

•AY
BAY
CAY
DAY
FAY
GAY
HAY
JAY
KAY
LAY
MAY
NAY
PAY
RAY
SAY
WAY
YAY

AZ•
AZO

A•Z
ADZ

BA•
BAA
BAB
BAD
BAE
BAG
BAH
BAN
BAR
BAS
BAT
BAV
BAY

B•A
BAA
BBA
BEA
BFA
BLA
BNA
BOA
BRA
BSA

•BA
ABA
BBA
DBA
FBA
MBA

BB•
BBA
BBC
BBL
BBS

B•B
BAB
BIB
BOB
BUB

•BB
EBB
OBB

BC•
BCE
BCG
BCL
BCP
BCS

B•C
BBC
BSC

•BC
ABC
BBC
CBC
NBC

B•D
BAD
BED
BID
BPD
BUD

•BD
CBD

BE•
BEA
BED
BEE
BEF
BEG
BEL
BEN
BES
BET
BEV
BEY

B•E
BAE
BCE
BEE
BME
BPE
BYE

•BE
ABE
DBE
GBE
NBE
SBE

BF•
BFA

B•F
BEF

B•G
BAG
BCG
BEG
BIG
BOG
BUG

B•H
BAH
BOH
BPH
BTH

BI•
BIB
BID
BIG
BIN
BIO
BIS
BIT

•BI
CBI
FBI
OBI
RBI

BL•
BLA
BLL
BLS

B•L
BBL
BCL
BEL
BLL
BOL
BUL

•BL
BBL
DBL

BM•
BME
BMR

B•M
BSM
BUM
BVM

•BM
HBM

BN•
BNA

B•N
BAN
BEN
BIN
BON
BUN

•BN
EBN
WBN

BO•
BOA
BOB
BOG
BOH
BOL
BON
BOO
BOP
BOT
BOW
BOX
BOY
BOZ

B•O
BIO
BOO

•BO
IBO

BP•
BPD
BPE
BPH

B•P
BCP
BOP

•BP
KBP
QBP

BR•
BRA

B•R
BAR
BMR
BUR

BS•
BSA
BSC
BSM
BSS

B•S
BAS
BBS
BCS
BES
BIS
BLS
BSS
BUS

•BS
ABS
BBS
CBS
EBS
LBS
NBS
OBS
TBS
WBS

BT•
BTH
BTU

B•T
BAT
BET
BIT
BOT
BUT

•BT
IBT

BU•
BUB
BUD
BUG
BUL
BUM
BUN
BUR
BUS
BUT
BUY

B•U
BTU

BV•
BVM

B•V
BAV
BEV

B•W
BOW

•BW
NBW
SBW

B•X
BOX

•BX
PBX

BY•
BYE

B•Y
BAY
BEY
BOY
BUY

B•Z
BOZ

CA•
CAB
CAD
CAE
CAF
CAL
CAM
CAN
CAP
CAR
CAT
CAV
CAW
CAY

C•A
CCA
CEA
CIA
CPA
CSA

•CA
CCA
FCA
GCA

CB•
CBC
CBD
CBI
CBS

C•B
CAB
COB
CUB

•CB
GCB
KCB
SCB

CC•
CCA
CCC

C•C
CBC
CCC
CIC
CSC

•CC
ACC
CCC
FCC
ICC

CD•
CDR

C•D
CAD
CBD
CID
COD
CUD

•CD
GCD
JCD
LCD
SCD

CE•
CEA
CEE
CEN
CER
CEY

C•E
CAE
CEE
CIE
CLE
CUE

•CE
ACE
BCE
ICE

CF•
CFI
CFM
CFS

C•F
CAF
CIF

CG•
CGH
CGM
CGS

C•G
CHG
COG

•CG
BCG
ECG

CH•
CHG
CHI
CHM

C•H
CGH
CPH

•CH
MCH

CI•
CIA
CIC
CID
CIE
CIF
CIO
CIR
CIS

C•I
CBI
CFI
CHI

•CI
SCI

•CK
OCK

CL•
CLE

C•L
CAL
COL
CPL

•CL
BCL
DCL
MCL

C•M
CAM
CFM
CGM
CHM
COM
CPM

•CM
DCM
LCM

CN•
CNO
CNS

C•N
CAN
CEN
CON
CTN

•CN
RCN

CO•
COB
COD
COG
COL
COM
CON
COO
COP
COR
COS
COT
COW
COX
COY
COZ

C•O
CIO
CNO
COO
CPO
CWO

•CO
NCO

CP•
CPA
CPH
CPL
CPM
CPO
CPS

C•P
CAP
COP
CUP

•CP
BCP
XCP

CR•
CRS
CRY

C•R
CAR
CDR
CER
CIR
COR
CUR

CS•
CSA
CSC
CST

C•S
CBS
CFS
CGS
CIS
CNS
COS
CPS
CRS
CTS

•CS
BCS
DCS
ICS
JCS
OCS

CT•
CTN
CTS

C•T
CAT
COT
CST
CUT
CWT
CYT

•CT
ACT
ECT
GCT
JCT
LCT
OCT
PCT
RCT

CU•
CUB
CUD
CUE
CUP
CUR
CUT

•CU
ACU
ECU

C•V
CAV

CW•
CWO
CWT

C•W
CAW
COW

•CW
ICW

C•X
COX

CY•
CYT

C•Y
CAY
CEY
COY
CRY

•CY
ACY
ICY

C•Z
COZ

DA•
DAB
DAD
DAG
DAK
DAL
DAM
DAN
DAP
DAR
DAW
DAY

D•A
DBA
DIA
DNA

•DA
ADA
FDA
IDA

DB•
DBA
DBE
DBL

D•B
DAB
DEB
DIB
DNB
DUB

•DB
EDB
PDB

DC•
DCL
DCM
DCS

D•C
DEC
DFC
DSC
DUC

•DC
ADC

DD•
DDS
DDT

D•D
DAD
DID
DMD
DOD
DUD

•DD
ADD
EDD
ODD
PDD

DE•
DEB
DEC
DEE
DEG
DEK
DEL
DEM
DEN
DEV
DEW
DEY

D•E
DBE
DEE
DIE
DME
DOE
DUE
DYE

•DE
ADE
IDE
ODE

DF•
DFC

D•F
DIF

D•G
DAG
DEG
DIG
DKG
DOG
DUG

D•H
DPH
DTH

•DH
EDH

DI•
DIA
DIB
DID
DIE
DIF
DIG
DIM
DIN
DIP
DIR
DIS
DIV

D•I
DUI

•DJ
ADJ

DK•
DKG
DKL
DKM
DKS

D•K
DAK
DEK

DL•
DLS

D•L
DAL
DBL
DCL
DEL
DKL
DOL

DM•
DMD
DME
DMZ

D•M
DAM
DCM
DEM
DIM
DKM
DOM
DSM
DVM

•DM
ADM
EDM

DN•
DNA
DNB

D•N
DAN
DEN
DIN
DON
DUN
DYN

DO•
DOD
DOE
DOG
DOL
DOM
DON
DOR
DOS
DOT
DOW
DOZ

D•O
DSO
DUO

•DO
ADO
EDO
UDO

DP•
DPH
DPW

D•P
DAP
DIP
DSP
DUP

•DP
EDP
NDP

DR•
DRY

D•R
DAR
DIR
DOR

•DR
CDR
SDR

DS•
DSC
DSM
DSO
DSP
DST

D•S
DCS
DDS
DIS
DKS
DLS
DOS
DYS

•DS
ADS
DDS
IDS
LDS
MDS
YDS

DT•
DTH

D•T
DDT
DOT
DST
DWT

•DT
DDT
EDT

DU•
DUB
DUC
DUD
DUE
DUG
DUI
DUN
DUO
DUP

DV•
DVM

D•V
DEV
DIV

•DV
ADV

DW•
DWT

D•W
DAW
DEW
DOW
DPW

DY•
DYE
DYN
DYS

D•Y
DAY
DEY
DRY

D•Z
DMZ
DOZ

•DZ
ADZ

EA•
EAM
EAR
EAT
EAU

E•A
ERA
ETA
EVA

•EA
BEA
CEA
KEA
LEA
PEA
REA
SEA
TEA
YEA

EB•
EBB
EBN
EBS

E•B
EBB
EDB
EIB

•EB
DEB
FEB
GEB
HEB
NEB
REB
SEB
WEB

EC•
ECG
ECT
ECU

E•C
EEC
ENC
ESC
ETC

•EC
AEC
DEC
EEC
REC
SEC

ED•
EDB
EDD
EDH
EDM
EDO
EDP
EDT

E•D
EDD
END

•ED
BED
FED
LED
MED
NED
OED
PED
QED
RED
TED
WED
ZED

EE•
EEC
EEG
EEL
EEN
EER
EES

E•E
EKE
ENE
ERE
ESE
EVE
EWE
EYE

•EE
BEE
CEE
DEE
FEE
GEE
JEE
LEE
NEE
PEE
SEE
TEE
VEE
WEE
ZEE

EF•
EFF
EFT

3

E•F EFF ELF EMF

•EF AEF BEF KEF QEF

EG• EGG EGO

E•G ECG EEG EGG EKG ENG ERG

•EG BEG DEG EEG KEG LEG MEG PEG REG TEG

E•H EDH ETH

EI• EIB EIN

E•I ELI EPI

•EI LEI PEI

EK• EKE EKG

E•K ELK

•EK DEK LEK

EL• ELF ELI ELK ELL ELM ELS ELY

E•L EEL ELL ENL

•EL BEL DEL EEL GEL MEL REL TEL

EM• EMF EMP EMS EMU

E•M EAM EDM ELM

•EM DEM FEM GEM HEM JEM LEM MEM REM

EN• ENC END ENE ENG ENL ENS ENT ENV

E•N EBN EEN EIN EON ERN

•EN BEN CEN DEN EEN FEN GEN HEN KEN LEN MEN PEN REN SEN TEN WEN XEN YEN ZEN

EO• EON EOS

E•O EDO EGO ETO EXO

•EO GEO LEO NEO

EP• EPI

E•P EDP EMP ESP

•EP HEP NEP PEP REP SEP YEP

E•Q ESQ

•EQ REQ SEQ

ER• ERA ERE ERG ERN ERR ERS ERV ERY

E•R EAR EER ERR EUR

•ER AER CER EER GER HER JER KER MER OER PER SER TER XER YER

ES• ESC ESE ESP ESQ ESS EST ESU

E•S EBS EES ELS EMS ENS EOS ERS ESS

•ES AES BES EES LES MES OES PES RES WES YES

ET• ETA ETC ETH ETO

E•T EAT ECT EDT EFT ENT EST EXT

•ET AET BET GET JET KET LET MET NET PET RET SET VET WET YET

EU• EUR

E•U EAU ECU EMU ESU

•EU FEU JEU LEU

EV• EVA EVE

E•V ENV ERV

•EV BEV DEV LEV MEV NEV REV

EW• EWE

•EW DEW FEW HEW JEW LEW MEW NEW PEW SEW YEW

EX• EXO EXT

•EX HEX LEX MEX REX SEX TEX VEX

EY• EYE

E•Y ELY ERY

•EY BEY CEY DEY FEY HEY KEY LEY

•EZ FEZ

FA• FAA FAD FAG FAM FAN FAO FAR FAS FAT FAX FAY

F•A FAA FBA FCA FDA FFA FHA FLA FPA FRA FWA

•FA BFA FFA

FB• FBA FBI

F•B FEB FIB FOB FRB

•FB AFB

FC• FCA FCC

F•C FCC FIC FPC FTC

•FC DFC IFC PFC RFC SFC

FD• FDA

F•D FAD FED FID

•FD MFD RFD

FE• FEB FED FEE FEM FEN FEU FEW FEY FEZ

F•E FEE FIE FOE

FF• FFA FFI FFV

•FF EFF OFF

F•G FAG FIG FOG

•FG AFG MFG PFG

FH• FHA

FI• FIB FIC FID FIE FIG FIN FIR FIT FIX

F•I FBI FFI FRI

•FI CFI FFI

FL• FLA FLO FLU FLY

F•L FUL

•FL AFL

F•M FAM FEM FPM

•FM CFM

F•N FAN FEN FIN FUN

FO• FOB FOE FOG FOP FOR FOX FOY

F•O FAO FLO FPO FRO

•FO UFO

FP• FPA FPC FPM FPO FPS

F•P FOP

FR• FRA FRB FRI FRO FRS FRY

F•R FAR FIR FOR FUR

•FR AFR

F•S FAS FPS FRS

•FS CFS IFS

FT• FTC

F•T FAT FIT

•FT AFT EFT OFT

FU• FUL FUN FUR

F•U FEU FLU

F•V FFV

•FV FFV

FW• FWA

F•W FEW

•FW VFW

F•X FAX FIX FOX

F•Y FAY FEY FLY FOY FRY

F•Z FEZ

GA• GAB GAD GAE GAG GAL GAM GAO GAP GAR GAS GAT GAY

G•A GCA GOA GSA

•GA AGA PGA

GB• GBE

G•B GAB

GCB
GEB
GIB
GOB

•GB
KGB

GC•
GCA
GCB
GCD
GCT

G•C
GMC
GSC
GTC

G•D
GAD
GCD
GID
GOD

•GD
SGD

GE•
GEB
GEE
GEL
GEM
GEN
GEO
GER
GET

G•E
GAE
GBE
GEE

•GE
AGE
LGE

G•G
GAG
GIG

•GG
EGG

GH•
GHQ

•GH
CGH
UGH

GI•
GIB
GID
GIG
GIL
GIN
GIP
GIS

G•I
GUI

•GK
NGK

G•L
GAL
GEL
GIL

GM•
GMC
GMT

G•M
GAM
GEM
GPM
GUM
GYM

•GM
CGM
MGM

GN•
GNP
GNU

G•N
GEN
GIN
GON
GUN
GYN

•GN
IGN

GO•
GOA
GOB
GOD
GON
GOO
GOP
GOT
GOV
GOY

G•O
GAO
GEO
GOO
GPO
GRO

•GO
AGO
EGO
GPU

GP•
GPM
GPO
GPU

G•P
GAP
GIP
GNP
GOP
GYP

G•Q
GHQ

GR•
GRO

G•R
GAR
GER
GYR

•GR
MGR

GS•
GSA
GSC

G•S
GAS
GIS
GUS

•GS
CGS

GT•
GTC

G•T
GAT
GCT
GET
GMT
GOT
GUT

•GT
HGT
SGT

GU•
GUI
GUM
GUN
GUS
GUT
GUY

G•U
GNU
GPU

G•V
GOV

GY•
GYM
GYN
GYP
GYR

G•Y
GAY
GOY
GUY

•GY
IGY

HA•
HAD
HAG
HAH
HAL
HAM
HAS
HAT
HAW
HAY

•HA
AHA
FHA
LHA
PHA

HB•
HBM

H•B
HEB
HOB
HUB

•HB
LHB
PHB
THB

•HC
PHC

H•D
HAD
HHD
HID
HOD

•HD
HHD
LHD
PHD
THD

HE•
HEB
HEM
HEN
HEP
HER
HEW
HEX
HEY

H•E
HIE
HOE
HUE

•HE
SHE
THE

•HF
SHF
UHF
VHF

HG•
HGT

H•G
HAG
HOG
HUG

•HG
CHG
MHG

HH•
HHD

H•H
HAH
HIH
HRH
HSH
HUH

HI•
HID
HIE
HIH
HIM
HIP
HIS
HIT

•HI
CHI
PHI
THI

HJ•
HJS

H•L
HAL
HOL
HYL

•HL
KHL
NHL

HM•
HMS

H•M
HAM
HBM
HEM
HIM
HSM
HUM

•HM
CHM
OHM

H•N
HEN
HON
HUN

HO•
HOB
HOD
HOE
HOG
HOL
HON
HOP
HOR
HOT
HOW
HOY

•HO
MHO
OHO
RHO
WHO

H•P
HEP
HIP
HOP
HYP

•HP
IHP

•HQ
GHQ

HR•
HRH
HRS

H•R
HER
HOR

•HR
WHR

HS•
HSH
HSM

H•S
HAS
HIS
HJS
HMS
HRS
HTS

•HS
IHS
OHS
PHS

HT•
HTS

H•T
HAT
HGT
HIT
HOT
HUT

HU•
HUB
HUE
HUG
HUH
HUM
HUN
HUT

H•W
HAW
HEW
HOW

H•X
HEX

HY•
HYL
HYP

H•Y
HAY
HEY
HOY

•HY
SHY
THY
WHY

IA•
IAL
IAN
IAS

I•A
IDA
ILA
INA
IPA
IRA
ITA

•IA
CIA
DIA
KIA
VIA

IB•
IBO
IBT

•IB
BIB
DIB
EIB
FIB
GIB
JIB
LIB
MIB
NIB
RIB
SIB

IC•
ICC
ICE
ICS
ICW
ICY

I•C
ICC
IFC
INC

•IC
CIC
FIC
SIC
TIC
VIC

ID•
IDA
IDE
IDS

I•D
IND
IOD
IUD

•ID
AID
BID
CID
DID
FID
GID
HID
KID
LID
MID
OID
RID
SID

I•E
ICE
IDE
IKE
ILE
INE
IRE
ISE
ITE
IVE

•IE
CIE
DIE
FIE
HIE
LIE
PIE
TIE
VIE

IF•
IFC
IFS

•IF
CIF
DIF

IG•
IGN
IGY

I•G
ING

•IG
BIG
DIG
FIG
GIG
JIG
MIG
PIG
RIG
WIG

IH•
IHP
IHS

I•H
ISH

•IH
HIH

IK•
IKE

I•K
ILK
INK
IRK

IL•
ILA
ILE
ILK
ILL
ILO
ILP
ILS

I•L
IAL
ILL

•IL
AIL
GIL
LIL
MIL
NIL
OIL
TIL
VIL

IM•
IMP

I•M
ISM
IUM

•IM
AIM
DIM
HIM
JIM
KIM
LIM
RIM
SIM
TIM
VIM

IN•
INA
INC
IND
INE
ING

3

INK
INN
INS
INT

I•N
IAN
IGN
INN
ION

•IN
AIN
BIN
DIN
EIN
FIN
GIN
KIN
LIN
PIN
SIN
TIN
VIN
WIN
YIN

IO•
IOD
ION
IOU
IOW

I•O
IBO
ILO
IRO
ISO
ITO

•IO
BIO
CIO
RIO

IP•
IPA

I•P
IHP
ILP
IMP

•IP
DIP
GIP
HIP
KIP
LIP
NIP
PIP
RIP
SIP
TIP

VIP
YIP
ZIP

•IQ
LIQ

IR•
IRA
IRE
IRK
IRO
IRS

I•R
ISR

•IR
AIR
CIR
DIR
FIR
MIR
SIR

IS•
ISE
ISH
ISM
ISO
ISR
IST

I•S
IAS
ICS
IDS
IFS
IHS
ILS
INS
IRS
ITS

•IS
AIS
BIS
CIS
DIS
GIS
HIS
MIS
PIS
SIS
TIS
VIS
WIS
XIS

IT•
ITA
ITE
ITO
ITS

ITY

I•T
IBT
INT
IST

•IT
BIT
FIT
HIT
KIT
LIT
NIT
OIT
PIT
RIT
SIT
TIT
WIT

IU•
IUD
IUM

I•U
IOU

•IU
PIU

IV•
IVE
IVY

•IV
DIV
VIV

IW•
IWW

I•W
ICW
IOW
IWW

•IX
FIX
MIX
NIX
PIX
SIX

I•Y
ICY
IGY
ITY
IVY

•IZ
LIZ
VIZ
WIZ

JA•
JAB
JAG
JAM
JAN
JAP
JAR
JAS
JAT
JAW
JAY

J•B
JAB
JIB
JOB

JC•
JCD
JCS
JCT

J•D
JCD

JE•
JEE
JEM
JER
JET
JEU
JEW

J•E
JEE
JOE

J•G
JAG
JIG
JOG
JUG

JI•
JIB
JIG
JIM

J•M
JAM
JEM
JIM

J•N
JAN
JON
JUN

JO•
JOB
JOE
JOG
JON
JOS

JOT
JOY

J•P
JAP

J•R
JAR
JER

J•S
JAS
JCS
JOS
JUS

•JS
HJS

J•T
JAT
JCT
JET
JOT
JUT

JU•
JUG
JUN
JUS
JUT

J•U
JEU

J•V
JWV

JW•
JWV

J•W
JAW
JEW

J•Y
JAY
JOY

KA•
KAB
KAL
KAN
KAS
KAY

K•A
KEA
KIA
KVA

•KA
AKA
OKA

KB•
KBP

K•B
KAB
KCB
KGB

KC•
KCB

•KC
AKC

K•D
KID

KE•
KEA
KEF
KEG
KEN
KER
KET
KEY

•KE
EKE
IKE

K•F
KEF

KG•
KGB

K•G
KEG

•KG
DKG
EKG
PKG

KH•
KHL

K•H
KWH

KI•
KIA
KID
KIM
KIN
KIP
KIT

•KI
SKI

KK•
KKK
KKT

K•K
KKK

•KK
KKK

K•L
KAL
KHL

•KL
DKL

K•M
KIM

•KM
DKM

K•N
KAN
KEN
KIN

KO•
KOP
KOR
KOS

•KO
TKO

K•P
KBP
KIP
KOP
KRP

KR•
KRP

K•R
KER
KOR

•KR
SKR
UKR

K•S
KAS
KOS

•KS
DKS
MKS
OKS

K•T
KET
KIT
KKT

•KT
KKT
MKT
QKT
SKT

•KU
PKU

KV•
KVA

KW•
KWH

K•Y
KAY
KEY

•KY
SKY

LA•
LAB
LAC
LAD
LAG
LAM
LAO
LAP
LAR
LAS
LAT
LAW
LAX
LAY

L•A
LEA
LHA

•LA
ALA
BLA
FLA
ILA
MLA

LB•
LBS

L•B
LAB
LHB
LIB
LLB
LOB

•LB
ALB
LLB

LC•
LCD

LCM
LCT

L•C
LAC

LD•
LDS

L•D
LAD
LCD
LED
LHD
LID
LLD
LSD
LTD

•LD
LLD
OLD

LE•
LEA
LED
LEE
LEG
LEI
LEK
LEM
LEN
LEO
LES
LET
LEU
LEV
LEW
LEX
LEY

L•E
LEE
LGE
LIE
LYE

•LE
ALE
CLE
ILE
OLE

•LF
ALF
ELF
VLF

LG•
LGE

L•G
LAG
LEG

LOG
LUG

•LG
ALG
MLG

LH•
LHA
LHB
LHD

L•H
LTH

LI•
LIB
LID
LIE
LIL
LIM
LIN
LIP
LIQ
LIT
LIZ

L•I
LEI

•LI
ALI
ELI

L•K
LEK

•LK
ELK
ILK

LL•
LLB
LLD
LLM

L•L
LIL

•LL
ALL
BLL
ELL
ILL

LM•
LMT

L•M
LAM
LCM
LEM
LIM
LLM

•LM
ELM
LLM

L•N
LEN
LIN

LO•
LOB
LOG
LOO
LOP
LOQ
LOT
LOU
LOW
LOX

L•O
LAO
LEO
LOO
LYO

•LO
FLO
ILO

LP•
LPS

L•P
LAP
LIP
LOP

•LP
ALP
ILP

L•Q
LIQ
LOQ

L•R
LAR

LS•
LSD
LSS

L•S
LAS
LBS
LDS
LES
LPS
LSS
LYS

•LS
ALS
BLS

DLS
ELS
ILS
MLS

LT•
LTD
LTH

L•T
LAT
LCT
LET
LIT
LMT
LOT

•LT
ALT
ULT

LU•
LUG
LUX

L•U
LEU
LOU

•LU
FLU

L•V
LEV

L•W
LAW
LEW
LOW

L•X
LAX
LEX
LOX
LUX

LY•
LYE
LYO
LYS

L•Y
LAY
LEY

•LY
ELY
FLY
PLY
SLY

L•Z
LIZ

MA•
MAB
MAC
MAD
MAE
MAL
MAN
MAO
MAP
MAR
MAS
MAT
MAW
MAX
MAY

M•A
MBA
MLA
MOA

•MA
AMA
OMA

MB•
MBA

M•B
MAB
MIB
MOB

MC•
MCH
MCL

M•C
MAC
MSC
MUC
MYC

•MC
GMC
QMC
SMC

MD•
MDS

M•D
MAD
MED
MFD
MID
MOD
MPD
MUD
MVD

•MD
DMD
VMD

ME•
MED
MEG
MEL
MEM
MEN
MER
MES
MET
MEV
MEW
MEX

M•E
MAE
MME
MOE
MPE

•ME
BME
DME
MME
OME

MF•
MFD
MFG

•MF
EMF

MG•
MGM
MGR

M•G
MEG
MFG
MHG
MIG
MLG
MUG

•MG
AMG
PMG
QMG

MH•
MHG
MHO

M•H
MCH
MPH

MI•
MIB
MID
MIG
MIL
MIR
MIS

MIX

M•I
MOI

•MI
AMI

MK•
MKS
MKT

•MK
WMK

ML•
MLA
MLG
MLS

M•L
MAL
MCL
MEL
MIL
MSL

MM•
MME

M•M
MEM
MGM
MOM
MUM

M•N
MAN
MEN
MON

MO•
MOA
MOB
MOD
MOE
MOI
MOM
MON
MOO
MOP
MOS
MOT
MOW

M•O
MAO
MHO
MOO
MYO

MP•
MPD
MPE

MPH

M•P
MAP
MOP

•MP
AMP
EMP
IMP

MR•
MRS

M•R
MAR
MER
MGR
MIR

•MR
BMR

MS•
MSC
MSL
MSS
MST

M•S
MAS
MDS
MES
MIS
MKS
MLS
MOS
MRS
MSS
MTS
MUS

•MS
EMS
HMS
RMS

MT•
MTS

M•T
MAT
MET
MKT
MOT
MST
MUT

•MT
AMT
GMT
LMT
UMT

MU•
MUC
MUD
MUG
MUM
MUS
MUT

•MU
AMU
EMU

MV•
MVD

M•V
MEV

M•W
MAW
MEW
MOW

•MW
UMW

M•X
MAX
MEX
MIX
MYX

MY•
MYC
MYO
MYX

M•Y
MAY

•MY
AMY

•MZ
DMZ

NA•
NAA
NAB
NAE
NAG
NAM
NAN
NAP
NAT
NAV
NAY

N•A
NAA
NRA
NSA

•NA
ANA
BNA
DNA
INA
RNA
UNA

NB•
NBC
NBE
NBS
NBW

N•B
NAB
NEB
NIB
NOB
NUB

•NB
DNB

NC•
NCO

N•C
NBC
NSC
NYC

•NC
ANC
ENC
INC

ND•
NDP

N•D
NED
NOD

•ND
AND
END
IND

NE•
NEB
NED
NEE
NEO
NEP
NET
NEV
NEW

N•E
NAE
NBE
NEE
NNE

•NE
ANE
ENE
INE
NNE
ONE

N•F
NSF

NG•
NGK

N•G
NAG
NOG

•NG
ENG
ING

NH•
NHL

N•H
NTH

NI•
NIB
NIL
NIP
NIT
NIX

•NI
ANI
ONI
UNI

N•K
NGK

•NK
INK

N•L
NHL
NIL

•NL
ENL

N•M
NAM
NOM

NN•
NNE
NNW

N•N
NAN
NON
NUN

•NN
ANN
INN

NO•
NOB
NOD
NOG
NOM
NON
NOR
NOS
NOT
NOV
NOW

N•O
NCO
NEO

•NO
CNO

NP•
NPT

N•P
NAP
NDP
NEP
NIP

•NP
GNP

NR•
NRA

N•R
NOR

•NR
RNR

NS•
NSA
NSC
NSF
NSW

N•S
NBS
NOS
NUS

•NS
CNS
ENS
INS

NT•
NTH

N•T NAT NET NIT NOT NPT NUT NWT

•NT ANT ENT INT ONT TNT

NU• NUB NUN NUS NUT

•NU ANU GNU

N•V NAV NEV NOV

•NV ENV

NW• NWT

N•W NBW NEW NNW NOW NSW

•NW NNW WNW

N•X NIX NYX

NY• NYC NYX

N•Y NAY

•NY ANY

OA• OAF OAK OAR OAS OAT

O•A OKA OMA OPA ORA OSA OVA OXA

•OA BOA GOA MOA ZOA

OB• OBB OBI OBS

O•B OBB ORB OSB

•OB BOB COB FOB GOB HOB JOB LOB MOB NOB ROB SOB

OC• OCK OCS OCT

O•C ORC OTC

•OC SOC TOC

OD• ODD ODE

O•D ODD OED OID OLD OSD

•OD COD DOD GOD HOD IOD MOD NOD POD ROD SOD TOD YOD

OE• OED OER OES

O•E ODE OLE OME ONE ORE OSE OWE

•OE DOE FOE HOE JOE MOE POE ROE TOE WOE ZOE

OF• OFF OFT

O•F OAF OFF OSF

•OG BOG COG DOG FOG HOG JOG LOG NOG TOG

OH• OHM OHO OHS

•OH BOH POH

OI• OID OIL OIT

O•I OBI ONI OUI OVI OWI

•OI MOI POI

OK• OKA OKS

O•K OAK OCK

•OK ROK

OL• OLD OLE

O•L OIL OWL

•OL AOL BOL COL DOL HOL POL SOL VOL

OM• OMA OME

O•M OHM

•OM COM DOM MOM NOM ROM SOM TOM YOM

ON• ONE ONI ONT

O•N OWN

•ON BON CON DON EON GON HON ION JON MON NON SON TON VON WON YON

O•O OHO ORO OTO OVO

•OO BOO COO GOO LOO MOO TOO WOO ZOO

OP• OPA OPS OPT OPY

O•P OSP

•OP BOP COP FOP GOP HOP KOP LOP MOP POP SOP TOP

•OQ LOQ

OR• ORA ORB ORC ORE ORO ORS ORY

O•R OAR OER OUR

•OR COR DOR FOR HOR KOR NOR TOR

OS• OSA OSB OSD OSE OSF OSP OSS

O•S OAS OBS OCS OES OHS OKS OPS ORS OSS OUS OZS

•OS COS DOS EOS JOS KOS MOS NOS SOS

OT• OTC OTO

O•T OAT OCT OFT OIT ONT OPT OUT

•OT BOT COT DOT GOT HOT JOT LOT MOT NOT POT ROT SOT TOT

OU• OUI OUR OUS OUT

•OU IOU LOU SOU YOU

OV• OVA OVI OVO

•OV GOV NOV

OW• OWE OWI OWL OWN

•OW BOW COW DOW HOW IOW LOW MOW NOW POW ROW SOW TOW VOW WOW YOW

OX• OXA OXY

•OX BOX COX FOX LOX POX SOX VOX

O•Y OPY ORY OXY

•OY BOY COY FOY GOY HOY JOY ROY SOY TOY

OZ• OZS

•OZ BOZ COZ DOZ

PA• PAD PAH PAL PAM PAN PAP PAR PAS PAT PAW PAX PAY

P•A PEA PGA PHA PTA

•PA CPA FPA IPA OPA SPA WPA

PB• PBX

P•B PDB PHB PUB

PC• PCT

P•C PFC PHC PPC

•PC FPC PPC

PD• PDB PDD

P•D PAD PDD PED PHD POD PPD

•PD BPD MPD PPD RPD

PE• PEA PED PEE PEG PEI PEN PEP PER PES PET PEW

P•E PEE PIE POE PRE PYE

•PE APE BPE MPE

PF• PFC PFG

P•F PSF

PG• PGA

P•G PEG PFG PIG PKG PMG PUG

PH• PHA PHB PHC PHD PHI PHS

P•H PAH POH

•PH APH BPH CPH DPH MPH

PI• PIE PIG PIN PIP PIS PIT PIU PIX

P•I PEI PHI POI PPI PSI

•PI EPI PPI

3

UPI

PK•
PKG
PKU

PL•
PLY

P•L
PAL
POL

•PL
CPL
QPL

PM•
PMG

P•M
PAM
PPM
PYM

•PM
CPM
FPM
GPM
PPM
RPM

P•N
PAN
PEN
PIN
PUN

PO•
POD
POE
POH
POI
POL
POP
POT
POW
POX

P•O
PRO
PTO
PYO

•PO
APO
CPO
FPO
GPO

PP•
PPC
PPD
PPI
PPM
PPS

P•P
PAP
PEP
PIP
POP
PUP

•PP
SPP

PR•
PRE
PRO
PRS
PRY

P•R
PAR
PER
PYR

•PR
APR

PS•
PSF
PSI
PSS
PST

P•S
PAS
PES
PHS
PIS
PPS
PRS
PSS

•PS
CPS
FPS
LPS
OPS
PPS
RPS
UPS

PT•
PTA
PTO

P•T
PAT
PCT
PET
PIT
POT
PST
PUT
PVT
PWT
PXT

•PT
APT
NPT
OPT

PU•
PUB
PUG
PUN
PUP
PUT

P•U
PIU
PKU

•PU
GPU
UPU

PV•
PVT

PW•
PWT

P•W
PAW
PEW
POW

•PW
DPW

PX•
PXT

P•X
PAX
PBX
PIX
POX
PYX

PY•
PYE
PYM
PYO
PYR
PYX

P•Y
PAY
PLY
PRY

•PY
OPY
SPY

Q•A
QUA

QB•
QBP

Q•C
QMC

Q•D
QED

QE•
QED
QEF

Q•F
QEF

Q•G
QMG

QK•
QKT

Q•L
QPL

QM•
QMC
QMG

Q•O
QTO

QP•
QPL

Q•P
QBP
QRP

QQ•
QQV

•QQ
SQQ

QR•
QRP

QT•
QTO

Q•T
QKT

QU•
QUA

Q•V
QQV

•QV
QQV

RA•
RAD
RAE
RAF
RAG
RAH
RAJ
RAM
RAN
RAP
RAS
RAT
RAW
RAY

R•A
REA
RNA
RSA

•RA
ARA
BRA
ERA
FRA
IRA
NRA
ORA
SRA

RB•
RBI

R•B
REB
RIB
ROB
RUB

•RB
FRB
ORB

RC•
RCN
RCT

R•C
REC
RFC

•RC
ARC
ORC

R•D
RAD
RED
RFD
RID
ROD
RPD

•RD
ARD

RE•
REA
REB
REC
RED
REG
REL
REM
REN
REP
REQ
RES
RET
REV
REX

R•E
RAE
ROE
RUE
RYE

•RE
ARE
ERE
IRE
ORE
PRE
URE

RF•
RFC
RFD

R•F
RAF

R•G
RAG
REG
RIG
RUG

•RG
ARG
ERG

RH•
RHO

R•H
RAH

•RH
HRH

RI•
RIB
RID
RIG
RIM
RIO
RIP
RIT

R•I
RBI

•RI
FRI
TRI

R•J
RAJ

R•K
ROK

•RK
ARK
IRK

R•L
REL

RM•
RMS

R•M
RAM
REM
RIM
ROM
RPM
RUM

•RM
ARM

RN•
RNA
RNR

R•N
RAN
RCN
REN
RUN

•RN
ARN
ERN
URN

RO•
ROB
ROD
ROE
ROK
ROM
ROT
ROW
ROY

R•O
RHO
RIO

•RO
FRO
GRO
IRO
ORO
PRO
SRO
URO

RP•
RPD
RPM
RPS

R•P
RAP
REP
RIP

•RP
KRP
QRP

R•Q
REQ

R•R
RNR

•RR
ERR

RS•
RSA
RSV

R•S
RAS
RES
RMS
RPS

•RS
ARS
CRS
ERS
FRS
HRS
IRS
MRS
ORS
PRS
YRS

R•T
RAT
RCT
RET
RIT
ROT
RUT

•RT
ART

RU•
RUB
RUE
RUG
RUM
RUN
RUT

R•V
REV
RSV

•RV
ARV
ERV

R•W
RAW
ROW

R•X
REX

RY•
RYE

R•Y
RAY
ROY

•RY
ARY
CRY
DRY
ERY
FRY
ORY
PRY
TRY
WRY

SA•
SAC
SAD
SAG
SAL
SAM
SAP
SAR
SAT
SAW
SAX
SAY

S•A
SEA
SPA
SRA
STA
SWA

•SA
ASA
BSA
CSA
GSA
NSA
OSA
RSA
USA

SB•
SBE
SBW

S•B
SCB
SEB
SIB
SOB
STB
SUB

•SB
OSB

SC•
SCB
SCD
SCI

S•C
SAC
SEC
SFC
SIC
SMC
SOC

•SC
BSC
CSC
DSC
ESC
GSC
MSC
NSC

SD•
SDR

S•D
SAD
SCD
SGD
SID
SOD
STD

•SD
LSD
OSD

3

SE•
SEA
SEB
SEC
SEE
SEN
SEP
SEQ
SER
SET
SEW
SEX

S•E
SBE
SEE
SHE
SSE
STE
SUE
SWE

•SE
ASE
ESE
ISE
OSE
SSE
USE

SF•
SFC

S•F
SHF

•SF
NSF
OSF
PSF

SG•
SGD
SGT

S•G
SAG
STG
SUG

SH•
SHE
SHF
SHY

•SH
ASH
HSH
ISH

SI•
SIB
SIC
SID
SIM
SIN
SIP
SIR
SIS
SIT
SIX

S•I
SCI
SKI

•SI
PSI

SK•
SKI
SKR
SKT
SKY

•SK
ASK

SL•
SLY

S•L
SAL
SOL
SYL

•SL
MSL

SM•
SMC

S•M
SAM
SIM
SOM
SSM
SUM
SYM

•SM
BSM
DSM
HSM
ISM
SSM

S•N
SEN
SIN
SON
SUN
SYN

•SN
ASN
USN

SO•
SOB
SOC
SOD
SOL
SOM
SON
SOP
SOS
SOT
SOU
SOW
SOX
SOY

S•O
SRO

•SO
DSO
ISO
USO

SP•
SPA
SPP
SPY

S•P
SAP
SEP
SIP
SOP
SPP
SUP

•SP
ASP
DSP
ESP
OSP
USP

SQ•
SQQ

S•Q
SEQ
SQQ

•SQ
ESQ

SR•
SRA
SRO

S•R
SAR
SDR
SER
SIR
SKR
SSR
STR
SUR
SYR

•SR
ISR
SSR

SS•
SSE
SSM
SSR
SSS
SST
SSW

S•S
SIS
SOS
SSS
SUS
SYS

•SS
ASS
BSS
ESS
LSS
MSS
OSS
PSS
SSS
USS

ST•
STA
STB
STD
STE
STG
STR
STU
STY

S•T
SAT
SET
SGT
SIT
SKT
SOT
SST

•ST
CST
DST
EST
IST
MST
PST
SST

SU•
SUB
SUE
SUG
SUM
SUN
SUP
SUR
SUS

S•U
SOU
STU

•SU
ESU
USU

•SV
RSV

SW•
SWA
SWE

S•W
SAW
SBW
SEW
SOW
SSW

•SW
NSW
SSW
USW
WSW

S•X
SAX
SEX
SIX
SOX

SY•
SYL
SYM
SYN
SYR
SYS

S•Y
SAY
SHY
SKY
SLY
SOY
SPY
STY

TA•
TAA
TAB
TAD
TAG
TAJ
TAM
TAN
TAP
TAR
TAT
TAU
TAV
TAW
TAX

T•A
TAA
TEA
TVA

•TA
ETA
ITA
PTA
STA

TB•
TBS

T•B
TAB
THB
TUB

•TB
STB

T•C
TIC
TOC

•TC
ATC
ETC
FTC
GTC
OTC

T•D
TAD
TED
THD
TOD

•TD
LTD
STD

TE•
TEA
TED
TEE
TEG
TEL
TEN
TER
TEX

T•E
TEE
THE
TIE
TOE

•TE
ATE
ITE
STE
UTE

T•G
TAG
TEG
TOG
TUG

•TG
STG

TH•
THB
THD
THE
THI
THY

•TH
BTH
DTH
ETH
LTH
NTH

TI•
TIC
TIE
TIL
TIM
TIN
TIP
TIS
TIT

T•I
THI
TRI
TWI

T•J
TAJ

TK•
TKO

T•L
TEL
TIL

T•M
TAM
TIM
TOM

TN•
TNT

T•N
TAN
TEN
TIN
TON
TUN

•TN
CTN

TO•
TOC
TOD
TOE
TOG
TOM
TON
TOO
TOP
TOR
TOT
TOW
TOY

T•O
TKO
TOO
TWO

•TO
ETO
ITO
OTO
PTO
QTO

T•P
TAP
TIP
TOP
TUP
TWP
TYP

TR•
TRI
TRY

T•R
TAR
TER
TOR

•TR
STR

T•S
TBS
TIS
TVS

•TS
CTS
HTS
ITS
MTS
UTS

T•T
TAT
TIT
TNT
TOT
TUT

TU•
TUB
TUG
TUN
TUP
TUT

T•U
TAU

•TU
BTU
STU

TV•
TVA
TVS

T•V
TAV

TW•
TWI
TWO
TWP
TWY

T•W
TAW
TOW

T•X
TAX
TEX

TY•
TYP

T•Y
THY
TOY
TRY
TWY

•TY
ITY
STY
XTY

UA•
UAR
UAW

U•A
UNA
USA

•UA
QUA

•UB
BUB
CUB
DUB
HUB
NUB
PUB
RUB
SUB
TUB

•UC
AUC
DUC
MUC
YUC

UD•
UDO

•UD
BUD
CUD
DUD
IUD
MUD

U•E
URE
USE
UTE

•UE
CUE
DUE
HUE
RUE
SUE

UF•
UFO

U•F
UHF

UG•
UGH

•UG
AUG
BUG
DUG
HUG

JUG
LUG
MUG
PUG
RUG
SUG
TUG
VUG

UH•
UHF

U•H
UGH

•UH
HUH

U•I
UNI
UPI

•UI
DUI
GUI
OUI

UK•
UKR

•UK
AUK
YUK

UL•
ULT

•UL
BUL
FUL
VUL

UM•
UMT
UMW

•UM
BUM
GUM
HUM
IUM
MUM
RUM
SUM

UN•
UNA
UNI

U•N
URN
USN

•UN
BUN
DUN
FUN
GUN
HUN
JUN
NUN
PUN
RUN
SUN
TUN

U•O
UDO
UFO
URO
USO

•UO
DUO

UP•
UPI
UPS
UPU

U•P
USP

•UP
CUP
DUP
PUP
SUP
TUP

UR•
URE
URN
URO

U•R
UAR
UKR

•UR
BUR
CUR
EUR
FUR
OUR
SUR

US•
USA
USE
USN
USO
USP
USS
USU
USW

U•S
UPS
USS
UTS

•US
AUS
BUS
GUS
JUS
MUS
NUS
OUS
SUS

UT•
UTE
UTS

U•T
ULT
UMT

•UT
AUT
BUT
CUT
GUT
HUT
JUT
MUT
NUT
OUT
PUT
RUT
TUT

U•U
UPU
USU

U•W
UAW
UMW
USW

•UX
AUX
LUX

•UY
BUY
GUY

VA•
VAL
VAN
VAS
VAT
VAV

V•A
VIA

•VA
AVA
EVA
KVA
OVA
TVA
WVA

V•C
VIC

V•D
VMD

•VD
MVD

VE•
VEE
VET
VEX

V•E
VEE
VIE

•VE
AVE
EVE
IVE

VF•
VFW

V•F
VHF
VLF

V•G
VUG

VH•
VHF

VI•
VIA
VIC
VIE
VIL
VIM
VIN
VIP
VIS
VIV
VIZ

•VI
AVI
OVI

VL•
VLF

V•L
VAL
VIL
VOL
VUL

VM•
VMD

V•M
VIM

•VM
BVM
DVM

V•N
VAN
VIN
VON

VO•
VOL
VON
VOW
VOX

•VO
OVO

V•P
VIP

V•S
VAS
VIS

•VS
TVS

V•T
VAT
VET

•VT
PVT

VU•
VUG
VUL

V•V
VAV
VIV

V•W
VFW
VOW

V•X
VEX
VOX

•VY
IVY

V•Z
VIZ

WA•
WAC
WAD
WAF
WAG
WAN
WAP
WAR
WAS
WAX
WAY

W•A
WPA
WVA

•WA
FWA
SWA

WB•
WBN
WBS

W•B
WEB

W•C
WAC

W•D
WAD
WED

WE•
WEB
WED
WEE
WEN
WES
WET

W•E
WEE
WOE
WYE

•WE
AWE
EWE
OWE
SWE

W•F
WAF

W•G
WAG

WIG

WH•
WHO
WHR
WHY

•WH
KWH

WI•
WIG
WIN
WIS
WIT
WIZ

•WI
OWI
TWI

W•K
WMK

•WL
AWL
OWL

WM•
WMK

WN•
WNW

W•N
WAN
WBN
WEN
WIN
WON

•WN
AWN
OWN

WO•
WOE
WON
WOO
WOW

W•O
WHO
WOO
WYO

•WO
CWO
TWO

WP•
WPA

W•P
WAP

•WP
TWP

WR•
WRY

W•R
WAR
WHR

WS•
WSW

W•S
WAS
WBS
WES
WIS

W•T
WET
WIT

•WT
CWT
DWT
NWT
PWT

WV•
WVA

•WV
JWV

W•W
WNW
WOW
WSW

•WW
IWW

W•X
WAX

WY•
WYE
WYO

W•Y
WAY
WHY
WRY

•WY
TWY

W•Z
WIZ

•XA
OXA

XC•
XCP

XE•
XEN
XER

•XE
AXE

XI•
XIS

X•L
XYL

X•N
XEN

•XO
EXO

X•P
XCP

X•R
XER

X•S
XIS

XT•
XTY

•XT
EXT
PXT

XY•
XYL

X•Y
XTY

•XY
OXY

YA•
YAH
YAK
YAM
YAP
YAW
YAY

Y•A
YEA

Y•C
YUC

•YC
MYC
NYC

YD•
YDS

Y•D
YOD

YE•
YEA
YEN
YEP
YER
YES
YET
YEW

•YE
AYE
BYE
DYE
EYE
LYE
PYE
RYE
WYE

•YG
ZYG

Y•H
YAH

YI•
YIN
YIP

Y•K
YAK
YUK

•YL
HYL
SYL
XYL

Y•M
YAM
YOM

•YM
GYM
PYM
SYM
ZYM

Y•N
YEN
YIN
YON

•YN
DYN
GYN
SYN

YO•
YOD
YOM
YON
YOU
YOW

•YO
LYO
MYO
PYO
WYO

Y•P
YAP
YEP
YIP

•YP
GYP

HYP
TYP

YR•
YRS

Y•R
YER

•YR
GYR
PYR
SYR

Y•S
YDS
YES
YRS

•YS
AYS
DYS
LYS
SYS

Y•T
YET

•YT
CYT

YU•
YUC
YUK

Y•U
YOU

Y•W
YAW
YEW

YOW

•YX
MYX
NYX
PYX

Y•Y
YAY

Z•A
ZOA

Z•D
ZED

ZE•
ZED
ZEE
ZEN

Z•E
ZEE
ZOE

Z•G
ZYG

ZI•
ZIP

Z•M
ZYM

Z•N
ZEN

ZO•
ZOA
ZOE
ZOO

Z•O
ZOO

•ZO
AZO

Z•P
ZIP

•ZS
OZS

ZY•
ZYG
ZYM

4-LETTER WORDS

AA••
AALS
AARE

A•A•
ABAS
ACAD
ADAH
ADAM
ADAR
ADAS
AFAR
AGAR
AGAS
AHAB
AJAR
AJAX
ALAE
ALAI
ALAN
ALAR
ALAS
AMAH
AMAS
ANAL
ANAM
ANAS
ANAT
ARAB
ARAD
ARAL
ARAM
ARAS
ASAS
AVAS
AWAY
AYAH
AZAN

A••A
ABBA
ACEA
ACTA
AGHA
AGRA
AIDA
ALBA
ALGA
ALMA
ALTA
ALVA
AMIA
ANNA
ANSA
ANTA
APIA
AQUA
AREA
ARIA
ASEA
ASIA
AURA

•AA•
BAAL
BAAS
HAAF
KAAS
MAAM
SAAR
TAAL
WAAC
WAAF

•A•A
BABA
BAIA
BAJA
CANA
CARA
CATA
DADA
DANA
DATA
FALA
GAEA
GAGA
GAIA
GALA
GAMA
GAYA
GAZA
HAHA
HAMA
IANA
JAVA
KAKA
KAMA
KANA
KAPA
KARA
KAVA
LAMA
LAVA
MAIA
MAMA
MANA
MAYA
NAHA
NAMA
NANA
NASA
PABA
PACA
PAPA
PARA
SAGA
SARA
TAPA
VARA
VASA

••AA
NCAA

AB••
ABAS
ABBA
ABBE
ABBR
ABBY
ABCS
ABED
ABEL
ABES
ABET
ABIB
ABIE
ABLE
ABLY
ABRI
ABUT

A•B•
ABBA
ABBE
ABBR
ABBY
ALBA
ALBS
AMBI
AMBO
AUBE

A••B
ABIB
AHAB
ARAB

•AB•
BABA
BABE
BABI
BABS
BABY
CABS
DABS
GABE
GABS
GABY
HABU
JABS
KABS
LABS
MABS
NABS
PABA
SABE
SABS
TABS
TABU

•A•B
BARB
CAMB
CARB
DARB
DAUB
GAMB
GARB
IADB
IAMB
JAMB
LAMB

••AB
AHAB
ARAB
BLAB
CRAB
DRAB
GRAB
JOAB
MOAB
SCAB
SLAB
STAB
SWAB

AC••
ACAD
ACCT
ACDC
ACEA
ACED
ACES
ACET
ACHE
ACID
ACME
ACNE
ACOU
ACRE
ACRO
ACTA
ACTH
ACTS

A•C•
ABCS
ACCT
ANCE
ANCY
ARCH
ARCS
ASCH
ASCI

A••C
ACDC
ALEC
APOC
ATIC
AVEC

•AC•
BACH
BACK
CACO
DACE
EACH
FACE
FACP
FACS
FACT
HACK
JACK
LACE
LACK
LACT
LACY
MACE
MACH
MACK
MACS
PACA
PACE
PACK
PACT
RACE
RACK
RACY
SACK
SACS
TACE
TACK
TACT
WACK
WACO
WACS
ZACH
ZACK

•A•C
CANC
LAIC
MARC
MASC
NARC
TALC
WAAC

••AC
WAAC

AD••
ADAH
ADAM
ADAR
ADAS
ADDS
ADDY
ADEN
ADIT
ADZE

A•D•
ACDC
ADDS
ADDY
AIDA
AIDE

AIDS
ALDO
ANDY

A••D
ABED
ACAD
ACED
ACID
AGED
AMID
APED
ARAD
ARID
AULD
AVID
AWED
AXED

•AD•
BADE
CADE
CADI
CADS
DADA
DADO
DADS
FADE
FADS
GADS
HADE
HADJ
IADB
JADE
KADI
LADE
LADS
LADY
MADE
MADS
PADS
RADS
SADE
SADI
TADS
WADE
WADI
WADS
WADY

•A•D
BALD
BAND
BARD
BAWD
CARD
GAUD
HAND
HARD
LAID
LAND
LARD
LAUD
MAID
MAUD
NARD
PAED
PAID
PARD
RAID
RAND
SAID
SAND
SARD
SAUD
WAND
WARD
YARD

••AD
ACAD
ARAD
BEAD
BRAD
CHAD
CLAD
DEAD
DUAD
DYAD
EGAD
GLAD
GOAD
GRAD
HEAD
LEAD
LOAD
MEAD
QUAD
READ
ROAD
SCAD
SHAD
THAD
TOAD
WOAD

AE••
AEON
AERI
AERO
AERY

A•E•
ABED
ABEL
ABES
ABET
ACEA
ACED
ACES
ACET
ADEN
AGED
AGES
AHEM
ALEC
ALEE
ALEF
ALES
ALEX
AMEN
AMER
AMES
ANEW
APED
APES
APEX
AREA
AREO
ARES
ASEA
AVEC
AVER
AVES
AWED
AWES
AXED
AXES
AYES

A••E
AARE
ABBE
ABIE
ABLE
ACHE
ACME
ACNE
ACRE
ADZE
AGUE
AIDE
ALAE
ALEE
ALOE
AMIE
ANCE
ANNE
ANTE
AONE
APSE
AUBE
AXLE
AYME

•AE•
CAEN
GAEA
GAEL
JAEN
MAES
PAED
RAES
TAEL

•A•E
AARE
BABE
BADE
BAKE
BALE
BANE
BARE
BASE
BATE
CADE
CAFE
CAGE
CAKE
CAME
CANE
CAPE
CARE
CASE
CAVE
DACE
DALE
DAME
DANE
DARE
DATE
DAVE
DAZE
EASE
FACE
FADE
FAKE
FAME
FARE
FATE
FAYE
FAZE
GABE
GAGE
GALE
GAME
GAPE
GATE
GAVE
GAZE
HADE
HAKE
HALE
HAME
HARE
HATE
HAVE
HAZE
JADE
JAKE
JANE
JAPE
KALE
KAME
KANE
KATE
LACE
LADE
LAFE
LAKE
LAME
LANE
LATE
LAVE
LAZE
MACE
MADE
MAGE
MAKE
MALE
MANE
MARE
MATE
MAZE
NAME
NAPE
NATE
NAVE
PACE
PAGE
PALE
PANE
PARE
PATE
PAVE
RACE
RAGE
RAKE
RALE
RAPE
RARE
RATE
RAVE
RAZE
SABE
SADE
SAFE
SAGE
SAKE
SALE
SAME
SANE
SATE
SAVE
TACE
TAKE
TALE
TAME
TAPE
TARE
VALE
VANE
VASE
WADE
WAGE
WAKE
WALE
WANE
WARE
WAVE
YALE

••AE
ALAE
BRAE
FRAE
IDAE
PRAE

AF••
AFAR
AFGH
AFRO

A•F•
ALFS

A••F
ALEF
ALIF

•AF•
BAFF
CAFE
DAFT
GAFF
HAFT
LAFE
OAFS
RAFF
RAFT
SAFE
TAFT
WAFS
WAFT

•A•F
BAFF
CALF
GAFF
HAAF
HALF
NAIF
RAFF
WAAF
WAIF
ZARF

••AF
DEAF
GRAF
HAAF
LEAF
LOAF
OLAF
USAF
WAAF
WRAF

AG••
AGAR
AGAS
AGED
AGES
AGHA
AGIO
AGNI
AGOG
AGON
AGRA
AGRO
AGUE

A•G•
AFGH
ALGA
ALGY
ARGO

A••G
AGOG

•AG•
BAGR
BAGS
CAGE
CAGY
DAGS
FAGS
GAGA
GAGE
GAGS
HAGI
HAGS
IAGO
JAGS
KAGU
LAGS
MAGE
MAGI
NAGS
PAGE
RAGE
RAGI
RAGS
SAGA
SAGE
SAGO
SAGS
SAGY
TAGS
VAGI
WAGE
WAGS

•A•G
BANG
DANG
FANG
GANG
HANG
LANG
PANG
RANG
SANG
TANG
VANG
YANG

••AG
BRAG
CRAG
DIAG
DRAG
FLAG
PEAG
PHAG
QUAG
SHAG
SLAG
SNAG
STAG
SWAG

AH••
AHAB
AHEM
AHOY

A•H•
ACHE
AGHA
ASHY

A••H
ACTH
ADAH
AFGH
ALPH
AMAH
ANKH
ANTH
ARCH
ASCH
AUTH
AYAH

•AH•
BAHT
HAHA
HAHN
HAHS
NAHA
OAHU

•A•H
BACH
BASH
BATH
CASH
CATH
DASH
EACH
GASH
GATH
HASH
HATH
KAPH
LASH
LATH
MACH
MASH
MATH
NASH
OATH
PATH
RASH
SASH
WASH
ZACH

••AH
ADAH
AMAH
AYAH
BLAH
LEAH
NOAH
OPAH
PTAH
SHAH
UTAH
YEAH

AI••
AIDA
AIDE
AIDS
AILS
AIMS
AINO
AINS
AINT
AINU
AIRS
AIRY

A•I•
ABIB
ABIE
ACID
ADIT
AGIO
AKIN
ALIF
ALIT
ALIX
AMIA
AMID
AMIE
AMIR
AMIS
ANIL
ANIM
ANIS
APIA
APIS
ARIA
ARID
ARIL
ARIZ
ASIA
ASIR
ATIC
AVID
AVIS
AXIL
AXIS
AYIN

A••I
ABRI
AERI
AGNI
ALAI
ALTI
AMBI
ANTI
AQUI
ASCI
ASTI
ATLI

•AI•
BAIA
BAIL
BAIT
CAIN
DAIS
FAIL
FAIN
FAIR
GAIA
GAIL
GAIN
GAIT
HAIK
HAIL
HAIR
JAIL
JAIN
KAIL
KAIN
LAIC
LAID
LAIN
LAIR
MAIA
MAID
MAIL
MAIM
MAIN
NAIF
NAIL
PAID
PAIL
PAIN
PAIR
RAID
RAIL
RAIN
SAID
SAIL
SAIS
TAIL
TAIN
VAIN
VAIR
WAIF
WAIL
WAIN
WAIT

•A•I
BABI
BALI
BANI
BARI
CADI
CALI
DALI
HAGI
KADI
KAKI
KALI
KAMI
LATI
MAGI
MALI
MANI
MAUI
NAZI
PALI
PARI
RAGI
RAKI
RAMI
RANI
SADI
SAKI
SARI
TAXI
VAGI
VARI
WADI

••AI
ALAI

AJ••
AJAR
AJAX

•AJ•
BAJA

•A•J
HADJ
MARJ

AK••
AKIN

A•K•
ANKH
ARKS
ASKS
AUKS

A••K
AMOK

•AK•
BAKE
BAKU
CAKE
DAKS
FAKE
HAKE
JAKE
KAKA
KAKI
LAKE
LAKY
MAKE
OAKS
RAKE
RAKI
SAKE
SAKI
TAKE
WAKE
YAKS

•A•K
BACK
BALK
BANK
BARK
BASK
CALK
CASK
DANK
DARK
DAWK
GAWK
HACK
HAIK
HANK
HARK
HAWK
JACK
LACK
LANK
LARK
MACK
MARK
MASK
PACK
PARK
RACK
RANK
SACK
SALK
SANK
SARK
SASK
SAUK
TACK
TALK
TANK
TASK
WACK
WALK
YANK
ZACK

••AK
BEAK
DHAK
DYAK
FLAK
LEAK
NDAK
PEAK
SDAK
SOAK
TEAK
WEAK

AL••
ALAE
ALAI
ALAN
ALAR
ALAS
ALBA
ALBS
ALDO
ALEC
ALEE
ALEF
ALES
ALEX
ALFS
ALGA
ALGY
ALIF
ALIT
ALIX
ALLO
ALLY
ALMA
ALMS
ALOE
ALOW
ALPH
ALPS
ALSO
ALTA
ALTI
ALTO
ALUM
ALVA
ALYS

A•L•
AALS
ABLE
ABLY
AILS
ALLO
ALLY
ATLI
AULD
AWLS
AXLE

A••L
ABEL
AMYL
ANAL
ANIL
ARAL
ARIL
ARYL
AWOL
AXIL

•AL•
AALS
BALD
BALE
BALI
BALK
BALL
BALM
BALT
CALF
CALI
CALK
CALL
CALM
CALX
DALE
DALI
FALA
FALL
GALA
GALE
GALL
GALS
HALE
HALF
HALL
HALO
HALS
HALT
KALE
KALI
LALL
MALE
MALI
MALL
MALT
PALE
PALI
PALL
PALM
PALP
PALS
PALY
RALE
RALL
SALE
SALK
SALT
TALC
TALE
TALK
TALL
VALE
VALS
WALE
WALK
WALL
WALT
YALE
YALU

•A•L
BAAL
BAIL
BALL
BAWL
CALL
CARL
CAUL
EARL
FAIL
FALL
FARL
GAEL
GAIL
GALL
GAOL
GAUL
HAIL
HALL
HAPL
HARL
HAUL
JAIL
JARL
KAIL
KARL
LALL
MAIL
MALL
MARL
MAUL
NAIL
NATL
PAIL
PALL
PAUL
PAWL
RAIL
RALL
SAIL
SAUL
TAAL
TAEL
TAIL
TALL
WAIL
WALL
WAUL
WAWL
YAWL

••AL
ANAL
ARAL
BAAL
COAL
DEAL
DIAL
DUAL
FOAL
GOAL
HEAL
HYAL
ICAL
ITAL
KCAL
MEAL
NEAL
OPAL
ORAL
OVAL
PEAL
REAL
RIAL
SEAL
SIAL
TAAL
TEAL
URAL
VEAL
VIAL
WEAL
ZEAL

AM••
AMAH
AMAS
AMBI
AMBO
AMEN
AMER
AMES
AMIA
AMID
AMIE
AMIR
AMIS
AMMO
AMOK
AMON
AMOS
AMOY
AMPS
AMTS
AMUR
AMUS
AMYL
AMYS

A•M•
ACME
AIMS
ALMA
ALMS
AMMO
ARMS
ARMY
ATMO
AYME

A••M
ADAM
AHEM
ALUM
ANAM
ANIM
ARAM
ARUM
ATOM

•AM•
CAMB
CAME

4

CAMP
CAMS
DAME
DAMN
DAMP
DAMS
FAME
GAMA
GAMB
GAME
GAMO
GAMP
GAMS
GAMY
HAMA
HAME
HAMS
IAMB
JAMB
JAMS
KAMA
KAME
KAMI
LAMA
LAMB
LAME
LAMP
LAMS
MAMA
NAMA
NAME
PAMS
RAMI
RAMP
RAMS
SAME
SAMP
SAMS
TAME
TAMP
TAMS
VAMP
YAMS

•A•M

BALM
BARM
CALM
FARM
HARM
MAAM
MAIM
PALM
WARM

••AM

ADAM
ANAM
ARAM
BEAM
CLAM
CRAM
DIAM
DRAM
EDAM
ELAM
EXAM
FLAM
FOAM
GRAM
GUAM
IMAM
LOAM
MAAM
PRAM
REAM
ROAM
SEAM
SHAM
SIAM
SLAM
SPAM
SWAM
TEAM
TRAM
WHAM

AN••

ANAL
ANAM
ANAS
ANAT
ANCE
ANCY
ANDY
ANEW
ANIL
ANIM
ANIS
ANKH
ANNA
ANNE
ANNO
ANNS
ANON
ANSA
ANTA
ANTE
ANTH
ANTI
ANTS
ANUS

A•N•

ACNE
AGNI
AINO
AINS
AINT
AINU
ANNA
ANNE
ANNO
ANNS
AONE
ARNO
ARNS
AUNT
AWNS
AWNY

A••N

ADEN
AEON
AGON
AKIN
ALAN
AMEN
AMON
ANON
ASSN
ATTN
AVON
AXON
AYIN
AZAN
AZON

•AN•

BAND
BANE
BANG
BANI
BANK
BANS
CANA
CANC
CANE
CANS
CANT
DANA
DANE
DANG
DANK
DANS
DANU
FANG
FANO
FANS
GANG
HAND
HANG
HANK
HANS
IANA
IANS
JANE
JANS
KANA
KANE
KANO
KANS
KANT
LAND
LANE
LANG
LANK
MANA
MANE
MANI
MANN
MANS
MANX
MANY
NANA
NANO
NANS
PANE
PANG
PANS
PANT
RAND
RANG
RANI
RANK
RANT
SAND
SANE
SANG
SANK
SANS
TANG
TANK
TANS
VANE
VANG
VANS
WAND
WANE
WANS
WANT
WANY
YANG
YANK
ZANY

•A•N

BARN
CAEN
CAIN
DAMN
DARN
DAWN
EARN
FAIN
FAUN
FAWN
GAIN
HAHN
JAEN
JAIN
KAIN
LAIN
LAWN
MAIN
MANN
PAIN
PAWN
RAIN
SAWN
TAIN
TARN
VAIN
WAIN
WARN
YARN
YAWN

••AN

ALAN
AZAN
BEAN
BRAN
CLAN
CYAN
DEAN
ELAN
EVAN
FLAN
FRAN
GMAN
GUAN
HWAN
IRAN
IVAN
JEAN
JOAN
JUAN
KHAN
LEAN
LOAN
MEAN
MOAN
OMAN
ORAN
PEAN
PLAN
ROAN
SCAN
SEAN
SHAN
SPAN
STAN
SWAN
THAN
URAN
WEAN
YEAN
YUAN
ZOAN

AO••

AONE

A•O•

ACOU
AEON
AGOG
AGON
AHOY
ALOE
ALOW
AMOK
AMON
AMOS
AMOY
ANON
APOC
ATOM
ATOP
ATOR
AVON
AVOW
AWOL
AXON
AZON
AZOV

A••O

ACRO
AERO
AFRO
AGIO
AGRO
AINO
ALDO
ALLO
ALSO
ALTO
AMBO
AMMO
ANNO
AREO
ARGO
ARNO
ATMO
ATTO
AUTO

•AO•

GAOL
LAOS
NAOS
TAOS

•A•O

BARO
CACO
CATO
DADO
FANO
FARO
GAMO
HALO
IAGO
JATO
KANO
KAYO
MAYO
NANO
NASO
NATO
PAVO
RATO
SAGO
TARO
VASO
WACO

••AO

LIAO

AP••

APED
APES
APEX
APIA
APIS
APOC
APSE
APUS

A•P•

ALPH
ALPS
AMPS
ASPS

A••P

ATOP

•AP•

BAPT
CAPE
CAPS
CAPT
DAPS
GAPE
GAPS
GAPY
HAPL
JAPE
KAPA
KAPH
LAPP
LAPS
MAPS
NAPE
NAPS
PAPA
PAPS
RAPE
RAPS
RAPT
SAPS
TAPA
TAPE
TAPS
WAPS
YAPS

•A•P

CAMP
CARP
DAMP
FACP
GAMP
GASP
HARP
HASP
LAMP
LAPP
PALP
RAMP
RASP
SAMP
TAMP
TARP
VAMP
WARP
WASP
YAUP
YAWP

••AP

CHAP
CLAP
CRAP
FLAP
FRAP
HEAP
LEAP
NEAP
REAP
SLAP
SNAP
SOAP
SWAP
TRAP
WHAP
WRAP

AQ••

AQUA
AQUI

••AQ

IRAQ

AR••

ARAB
ARAD
ARAL
ARAM
ARAS
ARCH
ARCS
AREA
AREO
ARES
ARGO
ARIA
ARID
ARIL
ARIZ
ARKS
ARMS
ARMY
ARNO
ARNS
ARTS
ARTY
ARUM
ARYL

A•R•

AARE
ABRI
ACRE
ACRO
AERI
AERO

4

AERY
AFRO
AGRA
AGRO
AIRS
AIRY
AURA
AWRY

A••R
ABBR
ADAR
AFAR
AGAR
AJAR
ALAR
AMER
AMIR
AMUR
ASIR
ASTR
ATOR
AVER

•AR•
AARE
BARB
BARD
BARE
BARI
BARK
BARM
BARN
BARO
BARS
BART
CARA
CARB
CARD
CARE
CARL
CARP
CARS
CART
CARY
DARB
DARE
DARK
DARN
DART
EARL
EARN
EARS
FARE
FARL
FARM
FARO
GARB
GARS
GARY
HARD
HARE
HARK
HARL
HARM
HARP
HART
HARZ
JARL
JARS
KARA
KARL
KARY
LARD
LARK
LARS
MARC
MARE
MARJ
MARK
MARL
MARS
MART
MARX
MARY
NARC
NARD
NARY
OARS
PARA
PARD
PARE
PARI
PARK
PARR
PARS
PART
RARE
SARA
SARD
SARI
SARK
TARE
TARN
TARO
TARP
TARS
TART
VARA
VARI
VARY
WARD
WARE
WARM
WARN
WARP
WARS
WART
WARY
YARD
YARN
ZARF

•A•R
BAGR
FAIR
GAUR
HAIR
LAIR
PAIR
PARR
SAAR
SAUR
TAUR
VAIR

••AR
ADAR
AFAR
AGAR
AJAR
ALAR
BEAR
BOAR
CHAR
CLAR
CZAR
DEAR
FEAR
GEAR
HEAR
HOAR
KNAR
LEAR
LIAR
NCAR
NEAR
OSAR
PEAR
REAR
ROAR
SAAR
SCAR
SEAR
SOAR
SPAR
STAR
TEAR
THAR
TSAR
TZAR
USAR
WEAR
YEAR
ZBAR

AS••
ASAS
ASCH
ASCI
ASEA
ASHY
ASIA
ASIR
ASKS
ASPS
ASSN
ASST
ASTI
ASTR

A•S•
ALSO
ANSA
APSE
ASSN
ASST
AUST

A••S
AALS
ABAS
ABCS
ABES
ACES
ACTS
ADAS
ADDS
AGAS
AGES
AIDS
AILS
AIMS
AINS
AIRS
ALAS
ALBS
ALES
ALFS
ALMS
ALPS
ALYS
AMAS
AMES
AMIS
AMOS
AMPS
AMTS
AMUS
AMYS
ANAS
ANIS
ANNS
ANTS
ANUS
APES
APIS
APUS
ARAS
ARCS
ARES
ARKS
ARMS
ARNS
ARTS
ASAS
ASKS
ASPS
AUKS
AVAS
AVES
AVIS
AWES
AWLS
AWNS
AXES
AXIS
AYES

•AS•
BASE
BASH
BASK
BASS
BAST
CASE
CASH
CASK
CASS
CAST
DASH
EASE
EAST
EASY
FAST
GASH
GASP
HASH
HASP
HAST
LASH
LASS
LAST
MASC
MASH
MASK
MASS
MAST
NASA
NASH
NASO
NAST
PASS
PAST
RASH
RASP
SASH
SASK
SASS
TASK
TASS
VASA
VASE
VASO
VAST
WASH
WASP
WAST

•A•S
AALS
BAAS
BABS
BAGS
BANS
BARS
BASS
BATS
BAYS
CABS
CADS
CAMS
CANS
CAPS
CARS
CASS
CATS
CAWS
CAYS
DABS
DADS
DAGS
DAIS
DAKS
DAMS
DANS
DAPS
DAWS
DAYS
EARS
EATS
FACS
FADS
FAGS
FANS
FATS
FAYS
GABS
GADS
GAGS
GALS
GAMS
GAPS
GARS
GATS
GAYS
HAGS
HAHS
HALS
HAMS
HANS
HATS
HAWS
HAYS
IANS
JABS
JAGS
JAMS
JANS
JARS
JAWS
JAYS
KAAS
KABS
KANS
KAYS
LABS
LADS
LAGS
LAMS
LAOS
LAPS
LARS
LASS
LAWS
LAYS
MABS
MACS
MADS
MAES
MANS
MAPS
MARS
MASS
MATS
MAWS
MAYS
NABS
NAGS
NANS
NAOS
NAPS
NATS
NAYS
OAFS
OAKS
OARS
OATS
PADS
PALS
PAMS
PANS
PAPS
PARS
PASS
PATS
PAWS
PAYS
RADS
RAES
RAGS
RAMS
RAPS
RATS
RAYS
SABS
SACS
SAGS
SAIS
SAMS
SANS
SAPS
SASS
SAWS
SAYS
TABS
TADS
TAGS
TAMS
TANS
TAOS
TAPS
TARS
TASS
TATS
TAUS
TAVS
TAWS
VALS
VANS
VATS
VAVS
WACS
WADS
WAFS
WAGS
WANS
WAPS
WARS
WAYS
YAKS
YAMS
YAPS
YAWS

••AS
ABAS
ADAS
AGAS
ALAS
AMAS
ANAS
ARAS
ASAS
AVAS
BAAS
BEAS
BIAS
BOAS
BRAS
DIAS
ERAS
ETAS
EVAS
EYAS
FRAS
GOAS
IDAS
INAS
IRAS
KAAS
KEAS
LEAS
MOAS
OKAS
PEAS
SEAS
SPAS
TEAS
UNAS
UPAS
XMAS
YEAS

AT••
ATIC
ATLI
ATMO
ATOM
ATOP
ATOR

ATTN
ATTO
ATTU
ATTY

A•T•
ACTA
ACTH
ACTS
ALTA
ALTI
ALTO
AMTS
ANTA
ANTE
ANTH
ANTI
ANTS
ARTS
ARTY
ASTI
ASTR
ATTN
ATTO
ATTU
ATTY
AUTH
AUTO

A••T
ABET
ABUT
ACCT
ACET
ADIT
AINT
ALIT
ANAT
ASST
AUNT
AUST

•AT•
BATE
BATH
BATS
BATT
CATA
CATH
CATO
CATS
DATA
DATE
EATS
FATE
FATS
GATE
GATH
GATS
GATT
HATE
HATH
HATS
JATO
KATE
LATE
LATH
LATI
MATE
MATH
MATS
MATT
NATE
NATL
NATO
NATS
OATH
OATS
PATE
PATH
PATS
RATE
RATO
RATS
SATE
TATS
VATS
WATT

•A•T
BAHT
BAIT
BALT
BAPT
BART
BAST
BATT
CANT
CAPT
CART
CAST
DAFT
DART
EAST
FACT
FAST
GAIT
GATT
HAFT
HALT
HART
HAST
KANT
LACT
LAST
MALT
MART
MAST
MATT
NAST
NAUT
PACT
PANT
PART
PAST
RAFT
RANT
RAPT
SALT
TACT
TAFT
TART
TAUT
VAST
WAFT
WAIT
WALT
WANT
WART
WAST
WATT

••AT
ANAT
BEAT
BLAT
BOAT
BRAT
CHAT
COAT
CRAT
DRAT
FEAT
FIAT
FLAT
FRAT
GHAT
GNAT
GOAT
GUAT
HEAT
KYAT
MEAT
MOAT
NEAT
PEAT
PLAT
SCAT
SEAT
SKAT
SLAT
SPAT
STAT
SWAT
TEAT
THAT
WHAT

AU••
AUBE
AUKS
AULD
AUNT
AURA
AUST
AUTH
AUTO

A•U•
ABUT
AGUE
ALUM
AMUR
AMUS
ANUS
APUS
AQUA
AQUI
ARUM

A••U
ACOU
AINU
ATTU

•AU•
CAUL
DAUB
EAUX
FAUN
GAUD
GAUL
GAUR
HAUL
LAUD
MAUD
MAUI
MAUL
NAUT
PAUL
SAUD
SAUK
SAUL
SAUR
TAUR
TAUS
TAUT
WAUL
YAUP

•A•U
BAKU
DANU
HABU
KAGU
OAHU
TABU
YALU

••AU
BEAU
ESAU
FRAU
LUAU
UNAU

AV••
AVAS
AVEC
AVER
AVES
AVID
AVIS
AVON
AVOW

A•V•
ALVA

A••V
AZOV

•AV•
CAVE
CAVY
DAVE
DAVY
GAVE
HAVE
JAVA
KAVA
LAVA
LAVE
NAVE
NAVY
PAVE
PAVO
RAVE
SAVE
TAVS
VAVS
WAVE
WAVY

••AV
OLAV
SLAV

AW••
AWAY
AWED
AWES
AWLS
AWNS
AWNY
AWOL
AWRY

A••W
ALOW
ANEW
AVOW

•AW•
BAWD
BAWL
CAWS
DAWK
DAWN
DAWS
FAWN
GAWK
HAWK
HAWS
JAWS
LAWN
LAWS
MAWS
PAWL
PAWN
PAWS
SAWN
SAWS
TAWS
WAWL
YAWL
YAWN
YAWP
YAWS

••AW
BRAW
CHAW
CLAW
CRAW
DRAW
FLAW
GNAW
SHAW
SKAW
SLAW
THAW

AX••
AXED
AXES
AXIL
AXIS
AXLE
AXON

A••X
AJAX
ALEX
ALIX
APEX

•AX•
TAXI
TAXY
WAXY

•A•X
CALX
EAUX
MANX
MARX

••AX
AJAX
COAX
FLAX
HOAX

AY••
AYAH
AYES
AYIN
AYME

A•Y•
ALYS
AMYL
AMYS
ARYL

A••Y
ABBY
ABLY
ADDY
AERY
AHOY
AIRY
ALGY
ALLY
AMOY
ANCY
ANDY
ARMY
ARTY
ASHY
ATTY
AWAY
AWNY
AWRY

•AY•
BAYS
CAYS
DAYS
FAYE
FAYS
GAYA
GAYS
HAYS
JAYS
KAYO
KAYS
LAYS
MAYA
MAYO
MAYS
NAYS
PAYS
RAYS
SAYS
WAYS

•A•Y
BABY
CAGY
CARY
CAVY
DAVY
EASY
GABY
GAMY
GAPY
GARY
HAZY
KARY
LACY
LADY
LAKY
LAZY
MANY
MARY
MAZY
NARY
NAVY
PALY
RACY
SAGY
TAXY
VARY
WADY
WANY
WARY
WAVY
WAXY
ZANY

••AY
AWAY
BRAY
CLAY
DDAY
DRAY
FLAY
FRAY
GRAY
OKAY
PLAY
PRAY
QUAY
SHAY
SLAY
SPAY
STAY
SWAY
TRAY
XRAY

AZ••
AZAN
AZON
AZOV

A•Z•
ADZE

A••Z
ARIZ

•AZ•
DAZE
FAZE
GAZA
GAZE
HAZE
HAZY
JAZZ
LAZE
LAZY
MAZE
MAZY
NAZI
RAZE
RAZZ

•A•Z
HARZ

JAZZ
RAZZ

••AZ
BRAZ
DIAZ
GRAZ

BA••
BAAL
BAAS
BABA
BABE
BABI
BABS
BABY
BACH
BACK
BADE
BAFF
BAGR
BAGS
BAHT
BAIA
BAIL
BAIT
BAJA
BAKE
BAKU
BALD
BALE
BALI
BALK
BALL
BALM
BALT
BAND
BANE
BANG
BANI
BANK
BANS
BAPT
BARB
BARD
BARE
BARI
BARK
BARM
BARN
BARO
BARS
BART
BASE
BASH
BASK
BASS
BAST
BATE
BATH
BATS
BATT
BAWD
BAWL
BAYS

B•A•
BAAL
BAAS
BEAD
BEAK
BEAM
BEAN
BEAR
BEAS
BEAT
BEAU
BIAS
BLAB
BLAH
BLAT
BOAR
BOAS
BOAT
BRAD
BRAE
BRAG
BRAN
BRAS
BRAT
BRAW
BRAY
BRAZ

B••A
BABA
BAIA
BAJA
BEMA
BETA
BOLA
BORA
BUNA

•BA•
ABAS
ZBAR

•B•A
ABBA
OBIA

••BA
ABBA
ALBA
BABA
CUBA
ELBA
ISBA
JUBA
PABA
REBA
TUBA

BB••
BBLS

B•B•
BABA
BABE
BABI
BABS
BABY
BIBB
BIBL
BIBS
BOBS
BUBO
BUBS

B••B
BARB
BIBB
BLAB
BLEB
BLOB
BOMB
BOOB
BULB

•BB•
ABBA
ABBE
ABBR
ABBY
EBBS

•B•B
ABIB

••BB
BIBB
COBB
IOBB

B•C•
BACH
BACK
BECK
BICE
BOCK
BUCK

B••C
BLOC
BSSC

•BC•
ABCS

B•D•
BADE
BEDE
BEDS
BIDE
BIDS
BLDG
BODE
BODY
BUDS

B••D
BALD
BAND
BARD
BAWD
BEAD
BEND
BIND
BIRD
BLED
BLVD
BOLD
BOND
BOYD
BRAD
BRED
BSED
BUND
BURD
BYRD

•B•D
ABED
IBID

BE••
BEAD
BEAK
BEAM
BEAN
BEAR
BEAS
BEAT
BEAU
BECK
BEDE
BEDS
BEEF
BEEN
BEEP
BEER
BEES
BEET
BEGS
BELG
BELL
BELS
BELT
BEMA
BEND
BENE
BENG
BENI
BENS
BENT
BERG
BERM
BERN
BERT
BESS
BEST
BETA
BETH
BETS
BEVS
BEVY
BEYS

B•E•
BEEF
BEEN
BEEP
BEER
BEES
BEET
BIER
BLEB
BLED
BLET
BLEW
BOER
BRED
BRER
BREV
BREW
BSED
BYES

B••E
BABE
BADE
BAKE
BALE
BANE
BARE
BASE
BATE
BEDE
BENE
BICE
BIDE
BIKE
BILE
BINE
BISE
BITE
BLUE
BODE
BOLE
BONE
BORE
BRAE
BRIE
BUTE
BYRE

•BE•
ABED
ABEL
ABES
ABET
EBEN
IBEX
OBEY

•B•E
ABBE
ABIE
ABLE
IBLE
OBOE

••BE
ABBE
AUBE
BABE
CUBE
ELBE
GABE
GIBE
HEBE
JIBE
JUBE
KIBE
KOBE
LOBE
ROBE
RUBE
SABE
TUBE

B•F•
BAFF
BIFF
BUFF

B••F
BAFF
BEEF
BIFF
BUFF

B•G•
BAGR
BAGS
BEGS
BOGS
BOGY
BUGS

B••G
BANG
BELG
BENG
BERG
BLDG
BONG
BRAG
BRIG
BULG
BUNG
BURG

B•H•
BAHT
BOHR
BUHL

B••H
BACH
BASH
BATH
BETH
BLAH
BOSH
BOTH
BUSH

BI••
BIAS
BIBB
BIBL
BIBS
BICE
BIDE
BIDS
BIER
BIFF
BIKE
BILE
BILK
BILL
BIND
BINE
BINS
BIOL
BION
BIRD
BIRL
BIRR
BISE
BITE
BITS
BITT

B•I•
BAIA
BAIL
BAIT
BLIP
BLIT
BOIL
BOIS
BRIE
BRIG
BRIM
BRIO
BRIT

B••I
BABI
BALI
BANI
BARI
BENI
BOVI

•BI•
ABIB
ABIE
IBID
IBIS
OBIA
OBIS
OBIT

•B•I
ABRI

••BI
AMBI
BABI
GOBI
SEBI

B•J•
BAJA

••BJ
SUBJ

B•K•
BAKE
BAKU
BIKE

B••K
BACK
BALK
BANK
BARK
BASK
BEAK
BECK
BILK
BOCK
BOOK
BOSK
BUCK
BULK
BUNK
BUSK

••BK
HDBK

BL••
BLAB
BLAH
BLAT
BLDG
BLEB
BLED
BLET
BLEW
BLIP
BLIT
BLOB
BLOC
BLOT
BLOW
BLUE
BLUR
BLVD

B•L•
BALD
BALE
BALI
BALK

BALL
BALM
BALT
BBLS
BELG
BELL
BELS
BELT
BILE
BILK
BILL
BOLA
BOLD
BOLE
BOLL
BOLO
BOLT
BULB
BULG
BULK
BULL

B••L
BAAL
BAIL
BALL
BAWL
BELL
BIBL
BILL
BIOL
BIRL
BOIL
BOLL
BOWL
BUHL
BULL
BURL

•BL•
ABLE
ABLY
BBLS
IBLE

•B•L
ABEL
OBOL

••BL
BIBL

BM••
BMUS

B•M•
BEMA
BOMB
BUMP
BUMS

B••M
BALM
BARM
BEAM
BERM
BOOM
BRIM
BROM

••BM
ICBM
IRBM

B•N•
BAND
BANE
BANG
BANI
BANK
BANS
BEND
BENE
BENG
BENI
BENS
BENT
BIND
BINE
BINS
BOND
BONE
BONG
BONN
BONY
BRNO
BUNA
BUND
BUNG
BUNK
BUNN
BUNS
BUNT

B••N
BARN
BEAN
BEEN
BERN
BION
BONN
BOON
BORN
BOSN
BRAN
BUNN
BURN

•B•N
EBEN
EBON

BO••
BOAR
BOAS
BOAT
BOBS
BOCK
BODE
BODY
BOER
BOGS
BOGY
BOHR
BOIL
BOIS
BOLA
BOLD
BOLE
BOLL
BOLO
BOLT
BOMB
BOND
BONE
BONG
BONN
BONY
BOOB
BOOK
BOOM
BOON
BOOR
BOOS
BOOT
BOPS
BORA
BORE
BORN
BORT
BOSH
BOSK
BOSN
BOSS
BOTH
BOTS
BOTT
BOUT
BOVI
BOWL
BOWS
BOYD
BOYS
BOZO

B•O•
BIOL
BION
BLOB
BLOC
BLOT
BLOW
BOOB
BOOK
BOOM
BOON
BOOR
BOOS
BOOT
BROM
BROO
BROW
BROZ
BUOY

B••O
BARO
BOLO
BOZO
BRIO
BRNO
BROO
BUBO

•BO•
EBON
OBOE
OBOL

•B•O
EBRO

••BO
AMBO
BUBO
GOBO
HOBO
LOBO
NEBO
SEBO
UMBO

B•P•
BAPT
BOPS

B••P
BEEP
BLIP
BUMP
BURP

BR••
BRAD
BRAE
BRAG
BRAN
BRAS
BRAT
BRAW
BRAY
BRAZ
BRED
BRER
BREV
BREW
BRIE
BRIG
BRIM
BRIO
BRIT
BRNO
BROM
BROO
BROW
BROZ
BRUT

B•R•
BARB
BARD
BARE
BARI
BARK
BARM
BARN
BARO
BARS
BART
BERG
BERM
BERN
BERT
BIRD
BIRL
BIRR
BORA
BORE
BORN
BORT
BURD
BURG
BURL
BURN
BURP
BURR
BURS
BURY
BYRD
BYRE

B••R
BAGR
BEAR
BEER
BIER
BIRR
BLUR
BOAR
BOER
BOHR
BOOR
BRER
BURR

•BR•
ABRI
EBRO

•B•R
ABBR
ZBAR

••BR
ABBR
FEBR
FIBR
HEBR
OMBR

BS••
BSED
BSSC

B•S•
BASE
BASH
BASK
BASS
BAST
BESS
BEST
BISE
BOSH
BOSK
BOSN
BOSS
BSSC
BUSH
BUSK
BUSS
BUST
BUSY

B••S
BAAS
BABS
BAGS
BANS
BARS
BASS
BATS
BAYS
BBLS
BEAS
BEDS
BEES
BEGS
BELS
BENS
BESS
BETS
BEVS
BEYS
BIAS
BIBS
BIDS
BINS
BITS
BMUS
BOAS
BOBS
BOGS
BOIS
BOOS
BOPS
BOSS
BOTS
BOWS
BOYS
BRAS
BUBS
BUDS
BUGS
BUMS
BUNS
BURS
BUSS
BUTS
BUYS
BYES

•B•S
ABAS
ABCS
ABES
BBLS
EBBS
IBIS
OBIS

••BS
ALBS
BABS
BIBS
BOBS
BUBS
CABS
COBS
CUBS
DABS
DEBS
DIBS
DUBS
EBBS
FIBS
FOBS
GABS
GIBS
GOBS
HOBS
HUBS
JABS
JIBS
JOBS
KABS
LABS
LOBS
MABS
MIBS
MOBS
NABS
NEBS
NIBS
NOBS
NUBS
ORBS
PUBS
REBS
RIBS
ROBS
RUBS
SABS
SIBS
SOBS
SUBS
TABS
TUBS
WEBS

B•T•
BATE
BATH
BATS
BATT
BETA
BETH
BETS
BITE
BITS
BITT
BOTH
BOTS
BOTT
BUTE
BUTS
BUTT

B••T
BAHT
BAIT
BALT
BAPT
BART
BAST
BATT
BEAT
BEET
BELT
BENT
BERT
BEST
BITT
BLAT
BLET
BLIT
BLOT
BOAT
BOLT
BOOT
BORT
BOTT
BOUT
BRAT
BRIT
BRUT
BUNT
BUST
BUTT

•B•T
ABET
ABUT
OBIT

••BT
DEBT

BU••
BUBO
BUBS
BUCK

BUDS
BUFF
BUGS
BUHL
BULB
BULG
BULK
BULL
BUMP
BUMS
BUNA
BUND
BUNG
BUNK
BUNN
BUNS
BUNT
BUOY
BURD
BURG
BURL
BURN
BURP
BURR
BURS
BURY
BUSH
BUSK
BUSS
BUST
BUSY
BUTE
BUTS
BUTT
BUYS
BUZZ

B•U•
BLUE
BLUR
BMUS
BOUT
BRUT

B••U
BAKU
BEAU

•BU•
ABUT

••BU
CEBU
HABU
TABU
ZEBU

B•V•
BEVS
BEVY
BLVD
BOVI

B••V
BREV

B•W•
BAWD
BAWL
BOWL
BOWS

B••W
BLEW
BLOW
BRAW
BREW
BROW

•B•X
IBEX

BY••
BYES
BYRD
BYRE

B•Y•
BAYS
BEYS
BOYD
BOYS
BUYS

B••Y
BABY
BEVY
BODY
BOGY
BONY
BRAY
BUOY
BURY
BUSY

•B•Y
ABBY
ABLY
OBEY

••BY
ABBY
BABY
DOBY
GABY
GOBY
RUBY
TOBY

B•Z•
BOZO
BUZZ

B••Z
BRAZ
BROZ
BUZZ

CA••
CABS
CACO
CADE
CADI
CADS
CAEN
CAFE
CAGE
CAGY
CAIN
CAKE
CALF
CALI
CALK
CALL
CALM
CALX
CAMB
CAME
CAMP
CAMS
CANA
CANC
CANE
CANS
CANT
CAPE
CAPS
CAPT
CARA
CARB
CARD
CARE
CARL
CARP
CARS
CART
CARY
CASE
CASH
CASK
CASS
CAST
CATA
CATH
CATO
CATS
CAUL
CAVE
CAVY
CAWS
CAYS

C•A•
CHAD
CHAP
CHAR
CHAT
CHAW
CLAD
CLAM
CLAN
CLAP
CLAR
CLAW
CLAY
COAL
COAT
COAX
CRAB
CRAG
CRAM
CRAP
CRAT
CRAW
CYAN
CZAR

C••A
CANA
CARA
CATA
CECA
CHIA
COCA
CODA
COLA
COMA
CORA
COXA
CUBA
CYMA

•CA•
ACAD
ICAL
KCAL
NCAA
NCAR
SCAB
SCAD
SCAN
SCAR
SCAT

•C•A
ACEA
ACTA
ECUA
NCAA
OCTA

••CA
CECA
COCA
DECA
FICA
INCA
MICA
PACA
PICA
SPCA
YMCA
YWCA

C•B•
CABS
CEBU
COBB
COBS
CUBA
CUBE
CUBS

C••B
CAMB
CARB
CHUB
CLUB
COBB
COMB
CRAB
CRIB
CURB

•CB•
ICBM

•C•B
SCAB

C•C•
CACO
CECA
COCA
COCK
COCO
CYCL

C••C
CANC
CHIC
CIRC
CONC

•CC•
ACCT
ECCL

•C•C
ACDC

••CC
SPCC

C•D•
CADE
CADI
CADS
CEDE
CIDE
CMDR
CODA
CODE
CODS
CODY
CUDS

C••D
CARD
CHAD
CHGD
CHID
CLAD
CLOD
COED
COLD
COND
CORD
CRUD
CUED
CURD

•CD•
ACDC

•C•D
ACAD
ACED
ACID
ICED
SCAD
SCUD

••CD
DECD

CE••
CEBU
CECA
CEDE
CEES
CEIL
CELE
CELL
CELT
CENE
CENO
CENT
CERE
CERO
CERT
CESS

C•E•
CAEN
CEES
CHEF
CHEM
CHES
CHET
CHEW
CHEZ
CLEF
CLEM
CLEO
CLEW
COED
COEF
COEL
CREE
CRES
CREW
CTEN
CUED
CUES

C••E
CADE
CAFE
CAGE
CAKE
CAME
CANE
CAPE
CARE
CASE
CAVE
CEDE
CELE
CENE
CERE
CIDE
CINE
CITE
CLUE
CODE
COKE
COLE
COME
CONE
COPE
CORE
COTE
COUE
COVE
CREE
CUBE
CULE
CURE
CUTE
CYME
CYTE

•CE•
ACEA
ACED
ACES
ACET
ICED
ICEL
ICES

•C•E
ACHE
ACME
ACNE
ACRE

••CE
ANCE
BICE
DACE
DICE
DUCE
ENCE
ESCE
FACE
FICE
LACE
LICE
LUCE
MACE
MICE
NICE
ONCE
PACE
PICE
PUCE
RACE
RICE
SICE
SYCE
TACE
VICE

C•F•
CAFE
CUFF

C••F
CALF
CHEF
CLEF
COEF
COIF
CONF
CORF
CUFF

C•G•
CAGE
CAGY
CHGD
CHGS
COGS

C••G
CHUG
CLOG
CONG
CRAG

••CG
USCG

CH••
CHAD
CHAP
CHAR
CHAT
CHAW
CHEF
CHEM
CHES
CHET
CHEW
CHEZ
CHGD
CHGS
CHIA
CHIC
CHID

CHIL
CHIN
CHIP
CHIR
CHIS
CHIT
CHOL
CHOP
CHOU
CHOW
CHUB
CHUG
CHUM
CHUR

C••H
CASH
CATH
COSH
CUSH

•CH•
ACHE
ECHO

•C•H
ACTH

••CH
ARCH
ASCH
BACH
DICH
EACH
ETCH
EXCH
FOCH
INCH
ITCH
LOCH
MACH
MICH
MUCH
OUCH
RICH
SUCH
WICH
ZACH

CI••
CIDE
CINE
CION
CIRC
CIST
CITE
CITY

C•I•
CAIN
CEIL
CHIA
CHIC
CHID
CHIL
CHIN
CHIP
CHIR
CHIS
CHIT
CLIO
CLIP
COIF
COIL
COIN
COIR
CRIB
CRIT

C••I
CADI
CALI

•CI•
ACID

••CI
ASCI
DECI
FOCI
FUCI
LOCI
MUCI

C••J
CLUJ
CONJ

•C•J
UCMJ

C•K•
CAKE
COKE

C••K
CALK
CASK
COCK
CONK
COOK
CORK
CUSK

••CK
BACK
BECK
BOCK
BUCK
COCK
DECK
DICK
DOCK
DUCK
GECK
GUCK
HACK
HECK
HICK
HOCK
JACK
JOCK
KECK
KICK
LACK
LICK
LOCK
LUCK
MACK
MOCK
MUCK
NECK
NICK
NOCK
PACK
PECK
PICK
POCK
PUCK
RACK
RICK
ROCK
RUCK
SACK
SICK
SOCK
SUCK
TACK
TICK
TUCK
VICK
WACK
WICK
ZACK

CL••
CLAD
CLAM
CLAN
CLAP
CLAR
CLAW
CLAY
CLEF
CLEM
CLEO
CLEW
CLIO
CLIP
CLOD
CLOG
CLON
CLOP
CLOT
CLOY
CLUB
CLUE
CLUJ

C•L•
CALF
CALI
CALK
CALL
CALM
CALX
CELE
CELL
CELT
COLA
COLD
COLE
COLL
COLO
COLS
COLT
COLY
CULE
CULL
CULM
CULT

C••L
CALL
CARL
CAUL
CEIL
CELL
CHIL
CHOL
COAL
COEL
COIL
COLL
COOL
COWL
CULL
CURL
CYCL

•C•L
ECCL
ECOL
ICAL
ICEL
KCAL
OCUL

••CL
CYCL
ECCL
ENCL
EXCL
INCL

CM••
CMDR

C•M•
CAMB
CAME
CAMP
CAMS
COMA
COMB
COME
COMM
COMO
COMP
COMR
CYMA
CYME
CYMO

C••M
CALM
CHEM
CHUM
CLAM
CLEM
COMM
CORM
COSM
CRAM
CULM

•CM•
ACME
RCMP
UCMJ

•C•M
ICBM
SCUM

C•N•
CANA
CANC
CANE
CANS
CANT
CENE
CENO
CENT
CINE
CONC
COND
CONE
CONF
CONG
CONJ
CONK
CONN
CONS
CONT
CONY

C••N
CAEN
CAIN
CHIN
CION
CLAN
CLON
COIN
CONN
COON
CORN
CTEN
CYAN

•CN•
ACNE

•C•N
ECON
ICON
SCAN

CO••
COAL
COAT
COAX
COBB
COBS
COCA
COCK
COCO
CODA
CODE
CODS
CODY
COED
COEF
COEL
COGS
COIF
COIL
COIN
COIR
COKE
COLA
COLD
COLE
COLL
COLO
COLS
COLT
COLY
COMA
COMB
COME
COMM
COMO
COMP
COMR
CONC
COND
CONE
CONF
CONG
CONJ
CONK
CONN
CONS
CONT
CONY
COOK
COOL
COON
COOP
COOS
COOT
COPE
COPR
COPS
COPT
COPY
CORA
CORD
CORE
CORF
CORK
CORM
CORN
CORP
COSH
COSM
COSS
COST
COTE
COTS
COUE
COUP
COVE
COWL
COWS
COXA
COZY

C•O•
CHOL
CHOP
CHOU
CHOW
CION
CLOD
CLOG
CLON
CLOP
CLOT
CLOY
COOK
COOL
COON
COOP
COOS
COOT
CROP
CROW

C••O
CACO
CATO
CENO
CERO
CLEO
CLIO
COCO
COLO
COMO
CRYO
CYMO
CYTO

•CO•
ACOU
ECOL
ECON
ICON
SCOP
SCOT
SCOW

•C•O
ACRO
ECHO
ECTO
OCTO

••CO
CACO
COCO
LOCO
MUCO
MYCO
PICO
POCO
TOCO
WACO

C•P•
CAPE
CAPS
CAPT
COPE
COPR
COPS
COPT
COPY
CUPR
CUPS

C••P
CAMP
CARP
CHAP
CHIP
CHOP
CLAP
CLIP
CLOP
COMP
COOP
CORP
COUP
CRAP
CROP
CUSP

•C•P
RCMP
SCOP
SCUP

••CP
FACP

CR••
CRAB
CRAG
CRAM
CRAP

CRAT
CRAW
CREE
CRES
CREW
CRIB
CRIT
CROP
CROW
CRUD
CRUS
CRUX
CRYO

C•R•
CARA
CARB
CARD
CARE
CARL
CARP
CARS
CART
CARY
CERE
CERO
CERT
CIRC
CORA
CORD
CORE
CORF
CORK
CORM
CORN
CORP
CURB
CURD
CURE
CURL
CURS
CURT

C••R
CHAR
CHIR
CHUR
CLAR
CMDR
COIR
COMR
COPR
CUPR
CZAR

•CR•
ACRE
ACRO
ECRU

•C•R
NCAR
SCAR

••CR
NECR
PICR

C•S•
CASE
CASH
CASK
CASS
CAST
CESS
CIST
COSH
COSM
COSS
COST
CUSH
CUSK
CUSP
CUSS
CYST

C••S
CABS
CADS
CAMS
CANS
CAPS
CARS
CASS
CATS
CAWS
CAYS
CEES
CESS
CHES
CHGS
CHIS
COBS
CODS
COGS
COLS
CONS
COOS
COPS
COSS
COTS
COWS
CRES
CRUS
CUBS
CUDS
CUES
CUPS
CURS
CUSS
CUTS

•C•S
ACES
ACTS
ECUS
ICES

••CS
ABCS
ARCS
FACS
FMCS
MACS
ORCS
SACS
SICS
TICS
WACS

CT••
CTEN

C•T•
CATA
CATH
CATO
CATS
CITE
CITY
COTE
COTS
CUTE
CUTS
CYTE
CYTO

C••T
CANT
CAPT
CART
CAST
CELT
CENT
CERT
CHAT
CHET
CHIT
CIST
CLOT
COAT
COLT
CONT
COOT
COPT
COST
CRAT
CRIT
CULT
CURT
CYST

•CT•
ACTA
ACTH
ACTS
ECTO
OCTA
OCTO

•C•T
ACCT

ACET
SCAT
SCOT
SCUT

••CT
ACCT
DUCT
FACT
HECT
LACT
NOCT
PACT
PICT
RECT
SECT
TACT

CU••
CUBA
CUBE
CUBS
CUDS
CUED
CUES
CUFF
CULE
CULL
CULM
CULT
CUPR
CUPS
CURB
CURD
CURE
CURL
CURS
CURT
CUSH
CUSK
CUSP
CUSS
CUTE
CUTS

C•U•
CAUL
CHUB
CHUG
CHUM
CHUR
CLUB
CLUE
CLUJ
COUE
COUP
CRUD
CRUS
CRUX

C••U
CEBU
CHOU

•CU•
ECUA
ECUS
OCUL
SCUD
SCUM
SCUP
SCUT

•C•U
ACOU
ECRU

C•V•
CAVE
CAVY
COVE

C•W•
CAWS
COWL
COWS

C••W
CHAW
CHEW
CHOW
CLAW
CLEW
CRAW
CREW
CROW

•C•W
SCOW

C•X•
COXA

C••X
CALX
COAX
CRUX

CY••
CYAN
CYCL
CYMA
CYME
CYMO
CYST
CYTE
CYTO

C•Y•
CAYS
CRYO

C••Y
CAGY
CARY
CAVY
CITY
CLAY

CLOY
CODY
COLY
CONY
COPY
COZY

••CY
ANCY
ENCY
LACY
LUCY
RACY
SECY

CZ••
CZAR

C•Z•
COZY

C••Z
CHEZ

DA••
DABS
DACE
DADA
DADO
DADS
DAFT
DAGS
DAIS
DAKS
DALE
DALI
DAME
DAMN
DAMP
DAMS
DANA
DANE
DANG
DANK
DANS
DANU
DAPS
DARB
DARE
DARK
DARN
DART
DASH
DATA
DATE
DAUB
DAVE
DAVY
DAWK
DAWN
DAWS
DAYS
DAZE

D•A•
DDAY
DEAD
DEAF
DEAL
DEAN
DEAR
DHAK
DIAG
DIAL
DIAM
DIAS
DIAZ
DRAB
DRAG
DRAM
DRAT
DRAW
DRAY
DUAD
DUAL
DYAD
DYAK

D••A
DADA
DANA
DATA
DECA
DEKA
DEVA
DITA
DIVA
DONA
DORA
DUMA
DURA
DYNA

•DA•
ADAH
ADAM
ADAR
ADAS
DDAY
EDAM
IDAE
IDAS
NDAK
SDAK

•D•A
EDDA
EDNA
IDEA
ODEA

••DA
AIDA
CODA
DADA
EDDA
LEDA
PODA

SODA
VEDA

D•B•
DABS
DEBS
DEBT
DIBS
DOBY
DUBS

D••B
DARB
DAUB
DRAB
DRIB
DRUB
DUMB

•DB•
HDBK

••DB
IADB

D•C•
DACE
DECA
DECD
DECI
DECK
DICE
DICH
DICK
DOCK
DUCE
DUCK
DUCT

D••C
DESC
DISC

•D•C
EDUC
FDIC
ODIC

••DC
ACDC

DD••
DDAY

D•D•
DADA
DADO
DADS
DIDO
DIDY
DODO
DUDE
DUDS

4

D••D
DEAD
DECD
DEED
DIED
DUAD
DYAD
DYED

•DD•
ADDS
ADDY
EDDA
EDDY
ODDS

••DD
KIDD
RUDD
SUDD
TODD

DE••
DEAD
DEAF
DEAL
DEAN
DEAR
DEBS
DEBT
DECA
DECD
DECI
DECK
DEED
DEEM
DEEP
DEER
DEES
DEFI
DEFT
DEFY
DEIL
DEKA
DEKE
DELE
DELF
DELL
DEME
DEMI
DEMO
DEMY
DENE
DENS
DENT
DENY
DEPT
DERM
DESC
DESK
DESL
DESS
DEUS
DEUT
DEVA
DEVI
DEVS
DEWS
DEWY
DEYS

D•E•
DEED
DEEM
DEEP
DEER
DEES
DIED
DIES
DIET
DOER
DOES
DREW
DUEL
DUES
DUET
DYED
DYER
DYES

D••E
DACE
DALE
DAME
DANE
DARE
DATE
DAVE
DAZE
DEKE
DELE
DEME
DENE
DICE
DIKE
DIME
DINE
DIRE
DIVE
DOGE
DOLE
DOME
DONE
DOPE
DOSE
DOTE
DOVE
DOZE
DUCE
DUDE
DUKE
DUNE
DUPE
DUSE
DYNE

•DE•
ADEN
EDEN
IDEA
IDEM
IDEO
IDES
ODEA
ODER
ODES

•D•E
ADZE
EDGE
EDIE
IDAE
IDLE

••DE
AIDE
BADE
BEDE
BIDE
BODE
CADE
CEDE
CIDE
CODE
DUDE
FADE
GIDE
HADE
HIDE
HYDE
JADE
JUDE
LADE
LODE
MADE
MODE
NIDE
NODE
NUDE
PEDE
RIDE
RODE
RUDE
SADE
SIDE
TIDE
TUDE
UNDE
VIDE
WADE
WIDE

D•F•
DAFT
DEFI
DEFT
DEFY
DOFF
DUFF

D••F
DEAF
DELF
DOFF
DOLF
DUFF

•DF•
IDFU

D•G•
DAGS
DIGS
DOGE
DOGS
DOGY
DUGS

D••G
DANG
DIAG
DING
DOUG
DRAG
DRUG
DUNG

•DG•
EDGE
EDGY

••DG
BLDG

DH••
DHAK
DHOW

D••H
DASH
DICH
DISH
DOTH

•DH•
EDHS

•D•H
ADAH

••DH
YODH

DI••
DIAG
DIAL
DIAM
DIAS
DIAZ
DIBS
DICE
DICH
DICK
DIDO
DIDY
DIED
DIES
DIET
DIGS
DIKE
DILI
DILL
DIME
DIMS
DINE
DING
DINO
DINS
DINT
DION
DIPL
DIPS
DIRE
DIRK
DIRT
DISC
DISH
DISK
DIST
DITA
DIVA
DIVE

D•I•
DAIS
DEIL
DOIT
DRIB
DRIP

D••I
DALI
DECI
DEFI
DEMI
DEVI
DILI

•DI•
ADIT
EDIE
EDIT
FDIC
IDIO
ODIC
ODIN
XDIV

••DI
CADI
KADI
LODI
MEDI
MIDI
MODI
NIDI
NUDI
PEDI
SADI
WADI

••DJ
HADJ

D•K•
DAKS
DEKA
DEKE
DIKE
DUKE

D••K
DANK
DARK
DAWK
DECK
DESK
DHAK
DICK
DIRK
DISK
DOCK
DUCK
DUNK
DUSK
DYAK

•D•K
HDBK
NDAK
SDAK

D•L•
DALE
DALI
DELE
DELF
DELL
DILI
DILL
DOLE
DOLF
DOLL
DOLS
DOLT
DULL
DULY

D••L
DEAL
DEIL
DELL
DESL
DIAL
DILL
DIPL
DOLL
DUAL
DUEL
DULL

•DL•
IDLE
IDLY

•D•L
IDOL
IDYL
ODYL

DM••
DMUS

D•M•
DAME
DAMN
DAMP
DAMS
DEME
DEMI
DEMO
DEMY
DIME
DIMS
DOME
DOMS
DUMA
DUMB
DUMP

D••M
DEEM
DERM
DIAM
DOOM
DORM
DRAM
DRUM

•D•M
ADAM
EDAM
EDOM
IDEM

D•N•
DANA
DANE
DANG
DANK
DANS
DANU
DENE
DENS
DENT
DENY
DINE
DING
DINO
DINS
DINT
DONA
DONE
DONS
DONT
DUNE
DUNG
DUNK
DUNS
DYNA
DYNE

D••N
DAMN
DARN
DAWN
DEAN
DION
DOON
DOWN

•DN•
EDNA

•D•N
ADEN
EDEN
ODIN

DO••
DOBY
DOCK
DODO
DOER
DOES
DOFF
DOGE
DOGS
DOGY
DOIT
DOLE
DOLF
DOLL
DOLS
DOLT
DOME
DOMS
DONA
DONE
DONS
DONT
DOOM
DOON
DOOR
DOPE
DOPY
DORA
DORM
DORR
DORS
DORY
DOSE
DOST
DOTE
DOTH
DOTS
DOTY
DOUG
DOUR
DOVE
DOWN
DOXY
DOZE

DOZY

D•O•
DHOW DION DOOM DOON DOOR DROP DUOS

D••O
DADO DEMO DIDO DINO DODO DURO

•DO•
EDOM IDOL ODOR UDOS

•D•O
IDEO IDIO

••DO
ALDO DADO DIDO DODO ENDO INDO IODO JUDO LIDO ORDO PEDO REDO TODO UNDO

D•P•
DAPS DEPT DIPL DIPS DOPE DOPY DUPE

D••P
DAMP DEEP DRIP DROP DUMP

DR••
DRAB DRAG DRAM DRAT DRAW DRAY DREW DRIB DRIP DROP DRUB DRUG DRUM

D•R•
DARB DARE DARK DARN DART DERM DIRE DIRK DIRT DORA DORM DORR DORS DORY DURA DURO DURR

D••R
DEAR DEER DOER DOOR DORR DOUR DURR DYER

•D•R
ADAR ODER ODOR

••DR
CMDR HYDR

D•S•
DASH DESC DESK DESL DESS DISC DISH DISK DIST DOSE DOST DUSE DUSK DUST

D••S
DABS DADS DAGS DAIS DAKS DAMS DANS DAPS DAWS DAYS DEBS DEES DENS DESS DEUS DEVS DEWS DEYS DIAS DIBS DIES DIGS DIMS DINS DIPS DMUS DOES DOGS DOLS DOMS DONS DORS DOTS DUBS DUDS DUES DUGS DUNS DUOS DYES

•D•S
ADAS ADDS EDHS IDAS IDES ODDS ODES UDOS

••DS
ADDS AIDS BEDS BIDS BUDS CADS CODS CUDS DADS DUDS ENDS FADS FIDS GADS GODS HODS KIDS LADS LIDS MADS MODS MUDS NEDS NODS ODDS PADS PHDS PODS RADS REDS RIDS RODS SIDS SODS SUDS TADS TEDS TODS WADS WEDS YODS ZEDS

D•T•
DATA DATE DITA DOTE DOTH DOTS DOTY DUTY

D••T
DAFT DART DEBT DEFT DENT DEPT DEUT DIET DINT DIRT DIST DOIT DOLT DONT DOST DRAT DUCT DUET DUST

•D•T
ADIT EDIT

DU••
DUAD DUAL DUBS DUCE DUCK DUCT DUDE DUDS DUEL DUES DUET DUFF DUGS DUKE DULL DULY DUMA DUMB DUMP DUNE DUNG DUNK DUNS DUOS DUPE DURA DURO DURR DUSE DUSK DUST DUTY

D•U•
DAUB DEUS DEUT DMUS DOUG DOUR DRUB DRUG DRUM

D••U
DANU

•DU•
EDUC

•D•U
IDFU

••DU
KUDU URDU

D•V•
DAVE DAVY DEVA DEVI DEVS DIVA DIVE DOVE

•D•V
XDIV

D•W•
DAWK DAWN DAWS DEWS DEWY DOWN

D••W
DHOW DRAW DREW

D•X•
DOXY

DY••
DYAD DYAK DYED DYER DYES DYNA DYNE

D•Y•
DAYS DEYS

D••Y
DAVY DDAY DEFY DEMY DENY DEWY DIDY DOBY DOGY DOPY DORY DOTY DOXY DOZY DRAY DULY DUTY

•DY•
IDYL ODYL

•D•Y
ADDY DDAY EDDY EDGY IDLY

••DY
ADDY ANDY BODY CODY DIDY EDDY JUDY LADY RUDY TIDY TODY UNDY WADY

D•Z•
DAZE DOZE DOZY

D••Z
DIAZ

•DZ•
ADZE

••DZ
LODZ

EA••
EACH EARL EARN EARS EASE EAST EASY EATS EAUX

E•A•
EDAM EGAD ELAM ELAN ERAS ESAU ETAS EVAN EVAS EXAM EYAS

E••A
ECUA EDDA EDNA ELBA ELIA ELLA ELSA ELVA EMIA EMMA ERMA ETNA ETTA EYRA EZRA

•EA•
BEAD BEAK BEAM BEAN BEAR BEAS BEAT BEAU DEAD DEAF DEAL DEAN DEAR FEAR FEAT GEAR HEAD HEAL HEAP HEAR HEAT JEAN KEAS LEAD LEAF LEAH LEAK LEAN LEAP LEAR LEAS MEAD MEAL MEAN MEAT NEAL NEAP NEAR NEAT PEAG PEAK PEAL PEAN PEAR PEAS PEAT READ REAL REAM REAP

REAR
SEAL
SEAM
SEAN
SEAR
SEAS
SEAT
TEAK
TEAL
TEAM
TEAR
TEAS
TEAT
VEAL
WEAK
WEAL
WEAN
WEAR
YEAH
YEAN
YEAR
YEAS
ZEAL

•E•A

BEMA
BETA
CECA
DECA
DEKA
DEVA
HEMA
HERA
HEXA
JENA
LEDA
LENA
LEVA
MEGA
MESA
META
NEMA
PERA
REBA
SERA
SETA
TELA
TERA
VEDA
VEGA
VELA
VENA
VERA
WEKA
ZETA

••EA

ACEA
AREA
ASEA
FLEA
GAEA
IDEA
ILEA
ODEA
PLEA
RHEA
SHEA
THEA
UREA
UVEA

EB••

EBBS
EBEN
EBON
EBRO

E•B•

EBBS
ELBA
ELBE

•EB•

CEBU
DEBS
DEBT
FEBR
HEBE
HEBR
NEBO
NEBS
REBA
REBS
SEBI
SEBO
WEBS
ZEBU

•E•B

HERB
KERB
SERB
VERB

••EB

BLEB
PLEB

EC••

ECCL
ECHO
ECOL
ECON
ECRU
ECTO
ECUA
ECUS

E•C•

EACH
ECCL
ENCE
ENCL
ENCY
ESCE
ETCH
EXCH
EXCL

E••C

EDUC
ELEC
EPIC
ERIC
EXEC

•EC•

BECK
CECA
DECA
DECD
DECI
DECK
GECK
HECK
HECT
KECK
NECK
NECR
PECK
RECT
SECT
SECY

•E•C

DESC
LEUC

••EC

ALEC
AVEC
ELEC
EXEC
SPEC

ED••

EDAM
EDDA
EDDY
EDEN
EDGE
EDGY
EDHS
EDIE
EDIT
EDNA
EDOM
EDUC

E•D•

EDDA
EDDY
ENDO
ENDS

E••D

EGAD
EKED
ENID
EXOD
EYED

•ED•

BEDE
BEDS
CEDE
LEDA
MEDI
NEDS
PEDE
PEDI
PEDO
REDO
REDS
TEDS
VEDA
WEDS
ZEDS

•E•D

BEAD
BEND
DEAD
DECD
DEED
FEED
FEND
FEOD
FEUD
GEED
GELD
HEAD
HEED
HELD
HERD
JEED
LEAD
LEND
LEUD
LEWD
MEAD
MELD
MEND
NEED
PEND
READ
REED
REND
SEED
SEND
TEED
TEND
VELD
VEND
WEED
WELD
WEND
ZEND

••ED

ABED
ACED
AGED
APED
AWED
AXED
BLED
BRED
BSED
COED
CUED
DEED
DIED
DYED
EKED
EYED
FEED
FLED
FRED
GEED
GIED
GLED
HEED
HIED
HOED
HUED
ICED
JEED
LIED
NEED
OKED
OWED
PAED
PIED
PLED
REED
RUED
SEED
SHED
SLED
SPED
SUED
TEED
TIED
TOED
USED
VIED
WEED

EE••

EELS
EELY
EENS
EERY

E•E•

EBEN
EDEN
EKED
EKES
ELEC
ELEM
ELEO
ELEV
EMEU
EPEE
EVEN
EVER
EVES
EWER
EWES
EXEC
EXES
EYED
EYES
EZEK

E••E

EASE
EDGE
EDIE
EIRE
ELBE
ELSE
ENCE
EPEE
ERIE
ERNE
ERSE
ESCE
ESTE
ETTE
EYRE

•EE•

BEEF
BEEN
BEEP
BEER
BEES
BEET
CEES
DEED
DEEM
DEEP
DEER
DEES
FEED
FEEL
FEES
FEET
GEED
GEEK
GEES
GEEZ
HEED
HEEL
JEED
JEEP
JEER
JEES
KEEF
KEEL
KEEN
KEEP
LEEK
LEER
LEES
LEET
MEEK
MEET
NEED
NEER
PEEK
PEEL
PEEN
PEEP
PEER
PEES
REED
REEF
REEK
REEL
SEED
SEEK
SEEM
SEEN
SEEP
SEER
SEES
TEED
TEEM
TEEN
TEES
VEER
VEES
WEED
WEEK
WEEP
ZEES

•E•E

BEDE
BENE
CEDE
CELE
CENE
CERE
DEKE
DELE
DEME
DENE
FEME
FETE
GENE
HEBE
HEME
HERE
JEFE
MERE
METE
NEVE
PEDE
PELE
PERE
PETE
RENE
RETE
SEME
SERE
TELE
WERE
ZEKE

••EE

ALEE
CREE
EPEE
FLEE
FREE
GHEE
GLEE
KLEE
KNEE
OGEE
SKEE
THEE
TREE
TYEE

EF••

EFFS
EFIK
EFTS

E•F•

EFFS

•EF•

DEFI
DEFT
DEFY
HEFT
JEFE
JEFF
KEFS
LEFT
WEFT

•E•F

BEEF
DEAF
DELF
JEFF
KEEF
KERF
LEAF
LEIF
PELF
REEF
SELF
SERF

••EF

ALEF
BEEF
CHEF
CLEF
COEF
FIEF
KEEF
LIEF
REEF
TREF
XREF

EG••

EGAD
EGGS
EGOS

E•G•
EDGE EDGY EGGS ENGR ERGO ERGS

•EG•
BEGS KEGS LEGS MEGA MEGS PEGS SEGO TEGS VEGA YEGG

•E•G
BELG BENG BERG PEAG YEGG

••EG
GREG SKEG

E•H•
ECHO EDHS ETHN ETHS

E••H
EACH ETCH EXCH

•EH•
JEHU LEHR

•E•H
BETH HETH LEAH MESH METH NEPH RESH SETH TETH YEAH ZEPH

EI••
EIRE

E•I•
EDIE EDIT EFIK ELIA ELIS EMIA EMIL EMIR EMIT ENID EPIC ERIC ERIE ERIK ERIN ERIS EVIL EXIT

E••I
EQUI ETUI

•EI•
CEIL DEIL HEIR LEIF LEIS MEIR NEIL REIN REIS VEIL VEIN WEIR ZEIN

•E•I
AERI BENI DECI DEFI DEMI DEVI HELI HEMI KEPI LEVI MEDI MENI NEVI PEDI PERI RENI SEBI SEMI SETI SEXI VENI YETI

•EJ•
SEJM

EK••
EKED EKES

E•K•
ELKS

E••K
EFIK ERIK EZEK

•EK•
DEKA DEKE LEKS WEKA ZEKE

•E•K
BEAK BECK DECK DESK GECK GEEK HECK JERK KECK LEAK LEEK LEUK MEEK NECK PEAK PECK PEEK PERK REEK SEEK TEAK WEAK WEEK YELK

••EK
EZEK GEEK LEEK MEEK PEEK REEK SEEK TREK WEEK

EL••
ELAM ELAN ELBA ELBE ELEC ELEM ELEO ELEV ELIA ELIS ELKS ELLA ELLS ELMS ELMY ELSA ELSE ELUL ELVA

E•L•
EELS EELY ELLA ELLS

E••L
EARL ECCL ECOL ELUL EMIL ENCL ENOL EVIL EXCL

•EL•
BELG BELL BELS BELT CELE CELL CELT DELE DELF DELL EELS EELY FELL FELT GELD GELS GELT HELD HELI HELL HELM HELP JELL KELP MELD MELS MELT NELL PELE PELF PELT RELY SELF SELL TELA TELE TELL TELO VELA VELD WELD WELL WELT YELK YELL YELP

•E•L
BELL CEIL CELL DEAL DEIL DELL DESL FEEL FELL GENL GEOL HEAL HEEL HELL HERL JELL KEEL MEAL MEWL NEAL NEIL NELL PEAL PEEL REAL REEL SEAL SELL TEAL TELL VEAL VEIL WEAL WELL YELL ZEAL

••EL
ABEL COEL DUEL FEEL FUEL GAEL HEEL ICEL JOEL KEEL KIEL KOEL MYEL NOEL PEEL PYEL REEL TAEL

EM••
EMEU EMIA EMIL EMIR EMIT EMMA EMMY EMUS

E•M•
ELMS ELMY EMMA EMMY ERMA

E••M
EDAM EDOM ELAM ELEM EXAM

•EM•
BEMA DEME DEMI DEMO DEMY FEME GEMS HEMA HEME HEMI HEMO HEMP HEMS JEMS LEMS MEMO MEMS NEMA REMS SEME SEMI TEMP

•E•M
BEAM BERM DEEM DERM GEOM GERM HELM REAM SEAM SEEM SEJM TEAM TEEM TERM

••EM
AHEM CHEM CLEM DEEM ELEM FLEM IDEM ITEM POEM SEEM SHEM STEM TEEM THEM

EN••
ENCE ENCL ENCY ENDO ENDS ENGR ENID ENOL ENOS ENTO ENVY

E•N•
EDNA EENS EONS ERNE ERNS ETNA

E••N
EARN EBEN EBON ECON EDEN ELAN ERIN ETHN ETON EVAN EVEN

•EN•
BEND BENE BENG BENI BENS BENT CENE CENO CENT DENE DENS DENT DENY EENS FEND FENS GENE GENL GENS GENT GENU GENY HENS JENA KENO KENS KENT LENA LEND LENO LENS LENT MEND MENI MENO MENT MENU OENO PEND PENN PENS PENT REND RENE RENI RENO RENT SEND SENT TEND TENN TENO TENS TENT VENA VEND VENI VENT WEND WENS WENT XENO YENS ZEND ZENO

•E•N
AEON BEAN

4

BEEN
BERN
DEAN
FERN
HEWN
JEAN
KEEN
KERN
LEAN
LEON
MEAN
NEON
PEAN
PEEN
PENN
PEON
REIN
SEAN
SEEN
SEWN
TEEN
TENN
TERN
VEIN
VERN
WEAN
YEAN
ZEIN

••EN
ADEN
AMEN
BEEN
CAEN
CTEN
EBEN
EDEN
EVEN
GLEN
GMEN
GWEN
JAEN
KEEN
LIEN
MIEN
OMEN
OPEN
OVEN
OWEN
OXEN
PEEN
PHEN
SEEN
STEN
TEEN
THEN
WHEN
WREN

EO••
EONS
EOUS

E•O•
EBON
ECOL
ECON
EDOM
EGOS
ENOL
ENOS
EPOS
EROS
ETON
EXOD

E••O
EBRO
ECHO
ECTO
ELEO
ENDO
ENTO
ERGO

•EO•
AEON
FEOD
GEOL
GEOM
KEOS
LEON
LEOS
MEOW
NEON
PEON

•E•O
AERO
CENO
CERO
DEMO
HEMO
HERO
KENO
KETO
LENO
LETO
LEVO
MEMO
MENO
MERO
MESO
NEBO
NERO
OENO
PEDO
PEPO
PESO
REDO
RENO
SEBO
SEGO
SERO
TELO
TENO
VETO
XENO
XERO
ZENO
ZERO

••EO
AREO
CLEO
ELEO
IDEO
ILEO
OLEO
RHEO
THEO

EP••
EPEE
EPIC
EPOS

E•P•
ESPY

•EP•
DEPT
HEPT
KEPI
KEPT
LEPT
NEPH
PEPO
PEPS
REPP
REPS
SEPT
WEPT
ZEPH

•E•P
BEEP
DEEP
HEAP
HELP
HEMP
JEEP
KEEP
KELP
LEAP
NEAP
PEEP
REAP
REPP
SEEP
TEMP
WEEP
YELP

••EP
BEEP
DEEP
JEEP
KEEP
PEEP
PREP
SEEP
SKEP
STEP
WEEP

EQ••
EQUI

•EQ•
SEQQ

•E•Q
SEQQ

••EQ
FREQ

ER••
ERAS
ERGO
ERGS
ERIC
ERIE
ERIK
ERIN
ERIS
ERMA
ERNE
ERNS
EROS
ERRS
ERSE
ERST

E•R•
EARL
EARN
EARS
EBRO
ECRU
EERY
EIRE
ERRS
EURY
EYRA
EYRE
EYRY
EZRA

E••R
EMIR
ENGR
EVER
EWER

•ER•
AERI
AERO
AERY
BERG
BERM
BERN
BERT
CERE
CERO
CERT
DERM
EERY
FERN
GERM
HERA
HERB
HERD
HERE
HERL
HERO
HERS
JERK
KERB
KERF
KERN
MERE
MERO
NERO
PERA
PERE
PERI
PERK
PERT
PERU
SERA
SERB
SERE
SERF
SERO
SERS
TERA
TERM
TERN
VERA
VERB
VERN
VERS
VERT
VERY
WERE
WERT
XERO
ZERO

•E•R
BEAR
BEER
DEAR
DEER
FEAR
FEBR
GEAR
HEAR
HEBR
HEIR
JEER
LEAR
LEER
LEHR
MEIR
METR
NEAR
NECR
NEER
NEUR
PEAR
PEER
PETR
REAR
SEAR
SEER
TEAR
TETR
VEER
WEAR
WEIR
YEAR

••ER
AMER
AVER
BEER
BIER
BOER
BRER
DEER
DOER
DYER
EVER
EWER
GOER
HIER
HOER
JEER
KIER
LEER
NEER
ODER
OMER
OVER
OYER
PEER
PIER
PTER
RUER
SEER
STER
SUER
TIER
USER
UTER
VEER
YMER
YSER

ES••
ESAU
ESCE
ESPY
ESTE

E•S•
EASE
EAST
EASY
ELSA
ELSE
ERSE
ERST

E••S
EARS
EATS
EBBS
ECUS
EDHS
EELS
EENS
EFFS
EFTS
EGGS
EGOS
EKES
ELIS
ELKS
ELLS
ELMS
EMUS
ENDS
ENOS
EONS
EOUS
EPOS
ERAS
ERGS
ERIS
ERNS
EROS
ERRS
ETAS
ETHS
EVAS
EVES
EWES
EXES
EYAS
EYES

•ES•
BESS
BEST
CESS
DESC
DESK
DESL
DESS
FESS
FEST
GEST
JESS
JEST
LESS
LEST
MESA
MESH
MESO
MESS
NESS
NEST
PESO
PEST
RESH
REST
TESS
TEST
VEST
WEST
ZEST

•E•S
BEAS
BEDS
BEES
BEGS
BELS
BENS
BESS
BETS
BEVS
BEYS
CEES
CESS
DEBS
DEES
DENS
DESS
DEUS
DEVS
DEWS
DEYS
EELS
EENS
FEES
FENS
FESS
FEUS
GEES
GELS
GEMS
GENS
GETS
HEMS
HENS
HERS
HEWS
JEES
JEMS
JESS
JETS
JEWS
KEAS
KEFS
KEGS
KENS
KEOS
KEYS
LEAS
LEES
LEGS
LEIS
LEKS
LEMS
LENS
LEOS

LESS LETS LEWS MEGS MELS MEMS MESS MEWS NEBS NEDS NESS NETS NEWS PEAS PEES PEGS PENS PEPS PETS PEWS REBS REDS REIS REMS REPS RETS REVS SEAS SEES SERS SETS SEWS TEAS TEDS TEES TEGS TENS TESS VEES VERS VETS WEBS WEDS WENS WETS YEAS YENS YEWS ZEDS ZEES ZEUS

••ES

ABES ACES AGES ALES AMES APES ARES AVES AWES AXES AYES BEES BYES CEES CHES CRES CUES DEES DIES DOES DUES DYES EKES EVES EWES EXES EYES FEES FOES GEES GOES HIES HOES HUES ICES IDES IKES IVES JEES JOES LEES LIES LUES LYES MAES MMES MOES NOES ODES ONES ORES OWES OYES PEES PIES PRES PYES RAES ROES RUES RYES SEES SUES TEES TIES TOES TUES USES UTES VEES VIES WOES WYES ZEES ZOES

ET••

ETAS ETCH ETHN ETHS ETNA ETON ETTA ETTE ETUI

E•T•

EATS ECTO EFTS ENTO ESTE ETTA ETTE

E••T

EAST EDIT EMIT ERST EXIT

•ET•

BETA BETH BETS FETE GETS HETH JETS KETO LETO LETS LETT META METE METH METR NETS PETE PETR PETS RETE RETS SETA SETH SETI SETS TETH TETR VETO VETS WETS YETI ZETA

•E•T

BEAT BEET BELT BENT BERT BEST CELT CENT CERT DEBT DEFT DENT DEPT DEUT FEAT FEET FELT FEST GELT GENT GEST HEAT HECT HEFT HEPT JEST KENT KEPT LEET LEFT LENT LEPT LEST LETT MEAT MEET MELT MENT NEAT NEST NEWT NEXT PEAT PELT PENT PERT PEST RECT RENT REST SEAT SECT SENT SEPT SEXT TEAT TENT TEST TEXT VENT VERT VEST WEFT WELT WENT WEPT WERT WEST ZEST

••ET

ABET ACET BEET BLET CHET DIET DUET FEET FRET HYET LEET MEET NYET POET STET SUET TRET WHET

EU••

EURY

E•U•

EAUX ECUA ECUS EDUC ELUL EMUS EOUS EQUI ETUI

E••U

ECRU EMEU ESAU

•EU•

DEUS DEUT FEUD FEUS JEUX LEUC LEUD LEUK NEUR ZEUS

•E•U

BEAU CEBU GENU JEHU MENU PERU ZEBU

••EU

EMEU LIEU

EV••

EVAN EVAS EVEN EVER EVES EVIL

E•V•

ELVA ENVY

E••V

ELEV

•EV•

BEVS BEVY DEVA DEVI DEVS LEVA LEVI LEVO LEVY NEVE NEVI REVS

••EV

BREV ELEV KIEV

EW••

EWER EWES

•EW•

DEWS DEWY HEWN HEWS JEWS LEWD LEWS MEWL MEWS NEWS NEWT PEWS SEWN SEWS YEWS

•E•W

MEOW

••EW

ANEW BLEW BREW CHEW CLEW CREW DREW FLEW GREW KNEW PHEW SHEW SKEW SLEW SMEW SPEW STEW THEW VIEW WHEW

EX••

EXAM EXCH EXCL EXEC EXES EXIT EXOD

E••X

EAUX

•EX•

HEXA NEXT SEXI SEXT SEXY TEXT

•E•X

JEUX

••EX

ALEX APEX FLEX IBEX ILEX

EY••

EYAS EYED EYES EYRA EYRE EYRY

E••Y

EASY EDDY EDGY EELY EERY ELMY EMMY ENCY ENVY ESPY EURY EYRY

•EY•

BEYS DEYS KEYS

•E•Y

AERY BEVY DEFY DEMY DENY DEWY EELY EERY GENY LEVY RELY SECY SEXY VERY

••EY

FREY GREY JOEY OBEY PREY THEY TREY UREY WHEY

EZ••

EZEK EZRA

•E•Z

GEEZ

••EZ

CHEZ GEEZ INEZ OYEZ SUEZ

FA••

FACE FACP FACS FACT FADE FADS FAGS FAIL FAIN

4

FAIR
FAKE
FALA
FALL
FAME
FANG
FANO
FANS
FARE
FARL
FARM
FARO
FAST
FATE
FATS
FAUN
FAWN
FAYE
FAYS
FAZE

F•A•
FEAR
FEAT
FIAT
FLAG
FLAK
FLAM
FLAN
FLAP
FLAT
FLAW
FLAX
FLAY
FOAL
FOAM
FRAE
FRAN
FRAP
FRAS
FRAT
FRAU
FRAY

F••A
FALA
FICA
FILA
FLEA
FNMA
FORA
FULA

•FA•
AFAR

••FA
SOFA
TUFA

F•B•
FEBR
FIBR
FIBS
FOBS

F••B
FLUB
FORB

F•C•
FACE
FACP
FACS
FACT
FICA
FICE
FMCS
FOCH
FOCI
FUCI

F••C
FDIC
FISC
FLOC

FD••
FDIC

F•D•
FADE
FADS
FIDS

F••D
FEED
FEND
FEOD
FEUD
FIND
FLED
FOLD
FOND
FOOD
FORD
FRED
FUND

FE••
FEAR
FEAT
FEBR
FEED
FEEL
FEES
FEET
FELL
FELT
FEME
FEND
FENS
FEOD
FERN
FESS
FEST
FETE
FEUD
FEUS

F•E•
FEED
FEEL
FEES
FEET
FIEF
FLEA
FLED
FLEE
FLEM
FLEW
FLEX
FOES
FRED
FREE
FREQ
FRET
FREY
FUEL

F••E
FACE
FADE
FAKE
FAME
FARE
FATE
FAYE
FAZE
FEME
FETE
FICE
FIFE
FILE
FINE
FIRE
FIVE
FLEE
FLOE
FLUE
FORE
FRAE
FREE
FROE
FUME
FUSE
FUZE
FYKE

••FE
CAFE
FIFE
JEFE
LAFE
LIFE
RIFE
RUFE
SAFE
WIFE

F•F•
FIFE

F••F
FIEF

•FF•
EFFS
IFFY

••FF
BAFF
BIFF
BUFF
CUFF
DOFF
DUFF
GAFF
GUFF
HUFF
JEFF
JIFF
LUFF
MIFF
MUFF
PUFF
RAFF
RIFF
RUFF
TIFF
TUFF

F•G•
FAGS
FIGS
FOGS
FOGY

F••G
FANG
FLAG
FLOG
FROG
FUNG

•FG•
AFGH

F•H•
FOHN

F••H
FISH
FOCH

•F•H
AFGH

FI••
FIAT
FIBR
FIBS
FICA
FICE
FIDS
FIEF
FIFE
FIGS
FIJI
FILA
FILE
FILL
FILM
FILS
FIND
FINE
FINK
FINN
FINS
FIRE
FIRM
FIRN
FIRS
FISC
FISH
FIST
FITS
FITZ
FIVE
FIZZ

F•I•
FAIL
FAIN
FAIR
FDIC
FLIP
FLIT
FOIL
FRIT

F••I
FIJI
FOCI
FUCI
FUJI

•FI•
EFIK

••FI
DEFI
HIFI
SUFI

F•J•
FIJI
FUJI

F•K•
FAKE
FYKE

F••K
FINK
FLAK
FOLK
FORK
FUNK

•F•K
EFIK

FL••
FLAG
FLAK
FLAM
FLAN
FLAP
FLAT
FLAW
FLAX
FLAY
FLEA
FLED
FLEE
FLEM
FLEW
FLEX
FLIP
FLIT
FLOC
FLOE
FLOG
FLOP
FLOR
FLOW
FLUB
FLUE
FLUO
FLUX

F•L•
FALA
FALL
FELL
FELT
FILA
FILE
FILL
FILM
FILS
FOLD
FOLK
FOLL
FULA
FULL

F••L
FAIL
FALL
FARL
FEEL
FELL
FILL
FOAL
FOIL
FOLL
FOOL
FOUL
FOWL
FUEL
FULL
FURL

FM••
FMCS

F•M•
FAME
FEME
FNMA
FUME
FUMY

F••M
FARM
FILM
FIRM
FLAM
FLEM
FOAM
FORM
FROM

FN••
FNMA

F•N•
FANG
FANO
FANS
FEND
FENS
FIND
FINE
FINK
FINN
FINS
FOND
FONT
FUND
FUNG
FUNK
FUNS

F••N
FAIN
FAUN
FAWN
FERN
FINN
FIRN
FLAN
FOHN
FRAN
FURN

FO••
FOAL
FOAM
FOBS
FOCH
FOCI
FOES
FOGS
FOGY
FOHN
FOIL
FOLD
FOLK
FOLL
FOND
FONT
FOOD
FOOL
FOOT
FOPS
FORA
FORB
FORD
FORE
FORK
FORM
FORT
FOSS
FOUL
FOUR
FOWL
FOXY
FOYS

F•O•
FEOD
FLOC
FLOE
FLOG
FLOP
FLOR
FLOW
FOOD
FOOL
FOOT
FROE
FROG
FROM
FROW

F••O
FANO
FARO
FLUO

•F•O
AFRO

F•P•
FOPS

F••P
FACP
FLAP
FLIP
FLOP
FRAP

F••Q
FREQ

FR••
FRAE
FRAN
FRAP

FRAS
FRAT
FRAU
FRAY
FRED
FREE
FREQ
FRET
FREY
FRIT
FROE
FROG
FROM
FROW

F•R•
FARE
FARL
FARM
FARO
FERN
FIRE
FIRM
FIRN
FIRS
FORA
FORB
FORD
FORE
FORK
FORM
FORT
FURL
FURN
FURS
FURY

F••R
FAIR
FEAR
FEBR
FIBR
FLOR
FOUR

•FR•
AFRO

•F•R
AFAR

F•S•
FAST
FESS
FEST
FISC
FISH
FIST
FOSS
FUSE
FUSS

F••S
FACS
FADS
FAGS
FANS
FATS
FAYS
FEES
FENS
FESS
FEUS
FIBS
FIDS
FIGS
FILS
FINS
FIRS
FITS
FMCS
FOBS
FOES
FOGS
FOPS
FOSS
FOYS
FRAS
FUNS
FURS
FUSS

•F•S
EFFS
EFTS

••FS
ALFS
EFFS
KEFS
OAFS
WAFS

F•T•
FATE
FATS
FETE
FITS
FITZ

F••T
FACT
FAST
FEAT
FEET
FELT
FEST
FIAT
FIST
FLAT
FLIT
FONT
FOOT
FORT
FRAT
FRET
FRIT

•FT•
EFTS

••FT
DAFT
DEFT
GIFT
HAFT
HEFT
LEFT
LIFT
LOFT
RAFT
RIFT
SIFT
SOFT
TAFT
TOFT
TUFT
WAFT
WEFT

FU••
FUCI
FUEL
FUJI
FULA
FULL
FUME
FUMY
FUND
FUNG
FUNK
FUNS
FURL
FURN
FURS
FURY
FUSE
FUSS
FUZE
FUZZ

F•U•
FAUN
FEUD
FEUS
FLUB
FLUE
FLUO
FLUX
FOUL
FOUR

F••U
FRAU

••FU
GIFU
IDFU

F•V•
FIVE

F•W•
FAWN
FOWL

F••W
FLAW
FLEW
FLOW
FROW

F•X•
FOXY

F••X
FLAX
FLEX
FLUX

FY••
FYKE

F•Y•
FAYE
FAYS
FOYS

F••Y
FLAY
FOGY
FOXY
FRAY
FREY
FUMY
FURY

•F•Y
IFFY

••FY
DEFY
IFFY

F•Z•
FAZE
FIZZ
FUZE
FUZZ

F••Z
FITZ
FIZZ
FUZZ

GA••
GABE
GABS
GABY
GADS
GAEA
GAEL
GAFF
GAGA
GAGE
GAGS
GAIA
GAIL
GAIN
GAIT
GALA
GALE
GALL
GALS
GAMA
GAMB
GAME
GAMO
GAMP
GAMS
GAMY
GANG
GAOL
GAPE
GAPS
GAPY
GARB
GARS
GARY
GASH
GASP
GATE
GATH
GATS
GATT
GAUD
GAUL
GAUR
GAVE
GAWK
GAYA
GAYS
GAZA
GAZE

G•A•
GEAR
GHAT
GLAD
GMAN
GNAT
GNAW
GOAD
GOAL
GOAS
GOAT
GRAB
GRAD
GRAF
GRAM
GRAY
GRAZ
GUAM
GUAN
GUAT

G••A
GAEA
GAGA
GAIA
GALA
GAMA
GAYA
GAZA
GIGA
GILA
GIZA
GOYA

•GA•
AGAR
AGAS
EGAD

•G•A
AGHA
AGRA

••GA
ALGA
GAGA
GIGA
INGA
MEGA
OLGA
RUGA
SAGA
TOGA
VEGA
YOGA
YUGA

G•B•
GABE
GABS
GABY
GIBE
GIBS
GOBI
GOBO
GOBS
GOBY

G••B
GAMB
GARB
GLIB
GLOB
GRAB
GRUB

G•C•
GECK
GUCK

G•D•
GADS
GIDE
GODS

G••D
GAUD
GEED
GELD
GIED
GILD
GIRD
GLAD
GLED
GOAD
GOLD
GOND
GOOD
GRAD
GRID

•G•D
AGED
EGAD

••GD
CHGD

GE••
GEAR
GECK
GEED
GEEK
GEES
GEEZ
GELD
GELS
GELT
GEMS
GENE
GENL
GENS
GENT
GENU
GENY
GEOL
GEOM
GERM
GEST
GETS

G•E•
GAEA
GAEL
GEED
GEEK
GEES
GEEZ
GHEE
GIED
GLED
GLEE
GLEN
GMEN
GOER
GOES
GREG
GREW
GREY
GWEN

G••E
GABE
GAGE
GALE
GAME
GAPE
GATE
GAVE
GAZE
GENE
GHEE
GIBE
GIDE
GIVE
GLEE
GLUE
GONE
GORE
GYRE

•GE•
AGED
AGES
OGEE

•G•E
AGUE
OGEE
OGLE
OGRE

••GE
CAGE
DOGE
EDGE
GAGE
HUGE
INGE
LOGE
MAGE
PAGE
RAGE
SAGE
URGE
WAGE

G•F•
GAFF
GIFT
GIFU
GUFF

G••F
GAFF
GOLF
GOOF
GRAF
GUFF
GULF

G•G•
GAGA
GAGE
GAGS
GIGA
GIGS

GOGH
GOGO

G••G
GANG
GONG
GREG
GRIG
GROG

•GG•
EGGS

•G•G
AGOG

••GG
NOGG
YEGG

GH••
GHAT
GHEE

G••H
GASH
GATH
GOGH
GOSH
GOTH
GUSH

•GH•
AGHA

••GH
AFGH
GOGH
HIGH
HUGH
NIGH
PUGH
SIGH
YOGH

GI••
GIBE
GIBS
GIDE
GIED
GIFT
GIFU
GIGA
GIGS
GILA
GILD
GILL
GILS
GILT
GIMP
GINK
GINS
GIPS
GIRD
GIRL
GIRO
GIRT
GIST
GIVE
GIZA

G•I•
GAIA
GAIL
GAIN
GAIT
GLIB
GLIM
GRID
GRIG
GRIM
GRIN
GRIP
GRIS
GRIT
GUIN

G••I
GOBI
GYRI

•GI•
AGIO

•G•I
AGNI
IGNI

••GI
HAGI
MAGI
RAGI
VAGI
YOGI

G••K
GAWK
GECK
GEEK
GINK
GOOK
GUCK

GL••
GLAD
GLED
GLEE
GLEN
GLIB
GLIM
GLOB
GLOT
GLOW
GLUE
GLUM
GLUT

G•L•
GALA
GALE
GALL
GALS
GELD
GELS
GELT
GILA
GILD
GILL
GILS
GILT
GOLD
GOLF
GULF
GULL
GULP

G••L
GAEL
GAIL
GALL
GAOL
GAUL
GENL
GEOL
GILL
GIRL
GOAL
GULL

•GL•
OGLE
UGLY

GM••
GMAN
GMEN

G•M•
GAMA
GAMB
GAME
GAMO
GAMP
GAMS
GAMY
GEMS
GIMP
GUMS
GYMN
GYMS

G••M
GEOM
GERM
GLIM
GLUM
GRAM
GRIM
GRUM
GUAM

GN••
GNAT
GNAW
GNUS

G•N•
GANG
GENE
GENL
GENS
GENT
GENU
GENY
GINK
GINS
GOND
GONE
GONG
GONO
GUNS
GYNO

G••N
GAIN
GLEN
GMAN
GMEN
GOON
GOWN
GRIN
GUAN
GUIN
GWEN
GWYN
GYMN

•GN•
AGNI
IGNI

•G•N
AGON

••GN
LIGN
SIGN

GO••
GOAD
GOAL
GOAS
GOAT
GOBI
GOBO
GOBS
GOBY
GODS
GOER
GOES
GOGH
GOGO
GOLD
GOLF
GOND
GONE
GONG
GONO
GOOD
GOOF
GOOK
GOON
GOOP
GORE
GORY
GOSH
GOTH
GOUT
GOVT
GOWN
GOYA

G•O•
GAOL
GEOL
GEOM
GLOB
GLOT
GLOW
GOOD
GOOF
GOOK
GOON
GOOP
GROG
GROT
GROW
GYOR

G••O
GAMO
GIRO
GOBO
GOGO
GONO
GYNO
GYRO

•GO•
AGOG
AGON
EGOS

•G•O
AGIO
AGRO

••GO
ARGO
ERGO
GOGO
HUGO
IAGO
LOGO
SAGO
SEGO
TOGO
ZYGO

G•P•
GAPE
GAPS
GAPY
GIPS
GYPS

G••P
GAMP
GASP
GIMP
GOOP
GRIP
GULP

•GP•
OGPU

GR••
GRAB
GRAD
GRAF
GRAM
GRAY
GRAZ
GREG
GREW
GREY
GRID
GRIG
GRIM
GRIN
GRIP
GRIS
GRIT
GROG
GROT
GROW
GRUB
GRUM

G•R•
GARB
GARS
GARY
GERM
GIRD
GIRL
GIRO
GIRT
GORE
GORY
GURU
GYRE
GYRI
GYRO

G••R
GAUR
GEAR
GOER
GYOR

•GR•
AGRA
AGRO
OGRE

•G•R
AGAR

••GR
BAGR
ENGR
HYGR
MSGR
NIGR

G•S•
GASH
GASP
GEST
GIST
GOSH
GUSH
GUST

G••S
GABS
GADS
GAGS
GALS
GAMS
GAPS
GARS
GATS
GAYS
GEES
GELS
GEMS
GENS
GETS
GIBS
GIGS
GILS
GINS
GIPS
GNUS
GOAS
GOBS
GODS
GOES
GRIS
GUMS
GUNS
GUTS
GUYS
GYMS
GYPS

•G•S
AGAS
AGES
EGGS
EGOS

••GS
BAGS
BEGS
BOGS
BUGS
CHGS
COGS
DAGS
DIGS
DOGS
DUGS
EGGS
ERGS
FAGS
FIGS
FOGS
GAGS
GIGS
HAGS
HOGS
HUGS
JAGS
JIGS
JOGS
JUGS
KEGS
LAGS
LEGS
LOGS
LUGS
MEGS
MIGS
MUGS
NAGS
NOGS
PEGS
PIGS
PUGS
RAGS
RIGS
RUGS
SAGS
TAGS
TEGS
TOGS
TUGS
VUGS
WAGS
WIGS

G•T•
GATE
GATH
GATS
GATT
GETS
GOTH
GUTS

G••T
GAIT
GATT
GELT
GENT

GEST
GHAT
GIFT
GILT
GIRT
GIST
GLOT
GLUT
GNAT
GOAT
GOUT
GOVT
GRIT
GROT
GUAT
GUST

••GT
MSGT

GU••
GUAM
GUAN
GUAT
GUCK
GUFF
GUIN
GULF
GULL
GULP
GUMS
GUNS
GURU
GUSH
GUST
GUTS
GUYS

G•U•
GAUD
GAUL
GAUR
GLUE
GLUM
GLUT
GNUS
GOUT
GRUB
GRUM

G••U
GENU
GIFU
GURU

•GU•
AGUE

•G•U
OGPU

••QU
KAGU

G•V•
GAVE
GIVE
GOVT

GW••
GWEN
GWYN

G•W•
GAWK
GOWN

G••W
GLOW
GNAW
GREW
GROW

GY••
GYMN
GYMS
GYNO
GYOR
GYPS
GYRE
GYRI
GYRO

G•Y•
GAYA
GAYS
GOYA
GUYS
GWYN

G••Y
GABY
GAMY
GAPY
GARY
GENY
GOBY
GORY
GRAY
GREY

•G•Y
UGLY

••GY
ALGY
BOGY
CAGY
DOGY
EDGY
FOGY
LOGY
ORGY
POGY
SAGY

G•Z•
GAZA
GAZE
GIZA

G••Z
GEEZ
GRAZ

HA••
HAAF
HABU
HACK
HADE
HADJ
HAFT
HAGI
HAGS
HAHA
HAHN
HAHS
HAIK
HAIL
HAIR
HAKE
HALE
HALF
HALL
HALO
HALS
HALT
HAMA
HAME
HAMS
HAND
HANG
HANK
HANS
HAPL
HARD
HARE
HARK
HARL
HARM
HARP
HART
HARZ
HASH
HASP
HAST
HATE
HATH
HATS
HAUL
HAVE
HAWK
HAWS
HAYS
HAZE
HAZY

H•A•
HAAF
HEAD
HEAL
HEAP
HEAR
HEAT
HOAR
HOAX
HWAN
HYAL

H••A
HAHA
HAMA
HEMA
HERA
HEXA
HORA
HULA
HUPA
HYLA

•HA•
AHAB
CHAD
CHAP
CHAR
CHAT
CHAW
DHAK
GHAT
KHAN
PHAG
SHAD
SHAG
SHAH
SHAM
SHAN
SHAW
SHAY
THAD
THAN
THAR
THAT
THAW
WHAM
WHAP
WHAT

•H•A
CHIA
RHEA
SHEA
THEA
WHOA

••HA
AGHA
HAHA
NAHA
YMHA
YWHA

H•B•
HABU
HDBK
HEBE
HEBR
HOBO
HOBS
HUBS

H••B
HERB

•H•B
AHAB
CHUB

H•C•
HACK
HECK
HECT
HICK
HOCK

•H•C
CHIC

HD••
HDBK

H•D•
HADE
HADJ
HIDE
HODS
HYDE
HYDR

H••D
HAND
HARD
HEAD
HEED
HELD
HERD
HIED
HIND
HOED
HOLD
HOND
HOOD
HUED

•HD•
PHDS

•H•D
CHAD
CHGD
CHID
SHAD
SHED
SHOD
THAD
THUD

HE••
HEAD
HEAL
HEAP
HEAR
HEAT
HEBE
HEBR
HECK
HECT
HEED
HEEL
HEFT
HEIR
HELD
HELI
HELL
HELM
HELP
HEMA
HEME
HEMI
HEMO
HEMP
HEMS
HENS
HEPT
HERA
HERB
HERD
HERE
HERL
HERO
HERS
HETH
HEWN
HEWS
HEXA

H•E•
HEED
HEEL
HIED
HIER
HIES
HOED
HOER
HOES
HUED
HUES
HYET

H••E
HADE
HAKE
HALE
HAME
HARE
HATE
HAVE
HAZE
HEBE
HEME
HERE
HIDE
HIKE
HIRE
HIVE
HOLE
HOME
HONE
HOPE
HOSE
HOVE
HOWE
HUGE
HUME
HYDE

•HE•
AHEM
CHEF
CHEM
CHES
CHET
CHEW
CHEZ
GHEE
PHEN
PHEW
RHEA
RHEO
SHEA
SHED
SHEM
SHEW
THEA
THEE
THEM
THEN
THEO
THEW
THEY
WHEN
WHET
WHEW
WHEY

•H•E
GHEE
SHOE
THEE

••HE
ACHE

H•F•
HAFT
HEFT
HIFI
HUFF

H••F
HAAF
HALF
HOOF
HUFF

•H•F
CHEF

H•G•
HAGI
HAGS
HIGH
HOGS
HUGE
HUGH
HUGO
HUGS
HYGR

H••G
HANG
HONG
HUNG

•HG•
CHGD
CHGS

•H•G
CHUG
PHAG
SHAG
THUG
WHIG

H•H•
HAHA
HAHN
HAHS

H••H
HASH
HATH
HETH
HIGH
HUGH
HUSH

•H•H
SHAH
YHWH

HI••
HICK
HIDE
HIED
HIER
HIES
HIFI
HIGH
HIKE
HILL
HILO
HILT
HIND
HINT
HIPP
HIPS
HIRE
HISS
HIST
HITS

4

HIVE

H•I•
HAIK
HAIL
HAIR
HEIR
HRIP

H••I
HAGI
HELI
HEMI
HIFI
HOPI

•HI•
CHIA
CHIC
CHID
CHIL
CHIN
CHIP
CHIR
CHIS
CHIT
OHIO
PHIL
PHIS
RHIN
RHIZ
SHIM
SHIN
SHIP
SHIV
THIN
THIO
THIS
WHIG
WHIM
WHIN
WHIP
WHIR
WHIT
WHIZ

••HI
OPHI

H••J
HADJ

H•K•
HAKE
HIKE

H••K
HACK
HAIK
HANK
HARK
HAWK
HDBK
HECK
HICK
HOCK
HONK
HOOK
HULK
HUNK
HUSK

•H•K
DHAK

H•L•
HALE
HALF
HALL
HALO
HALS
HALT
HELD
HELI
HELL
HELM
HELP
HILL
HILO
HILT
HOLD
HOLE
HOLM
HOLO
HOLY
HULA
HULK
HULL
HYLA
HYLO

H••L
HAIL
HALL
HAPL
HARL
HAUL
HEAL
HEEL
HELL
HERL
HILL
HOWL
HULL
HURL
HYAL

•H•L
CHIL
CHOL
PHIL
PHYL
SHUL

••HL
BUHL
KOHL

H•M•
HAMA
HAME
HAMS
HEMA
HEME
HEMI
HEMO
HEMP
HEMS
HOME
HOMO
HOMS
HUME
HUMP
HUMS
HYMN

H••M
HARM
HELM
HOLM

•HM•
OHMS

•H•M
AHEM
CHEM
CHUM
SHAM
SHEM
SHIM
THEM
WHAM
WHIM
WHOM

H•N•
HAND
HANG
HANK
HANS
HENS
HIND
HINT
HOND
HONE
HONG
HONK
HUNG
HUNK
HUNS
HUNT

H••N
HAHN
HEWN
HORN
HWAN
HYMN

•H•N
CHIN
KHAN
PHEN
PHON
RHIN
SHAN
SHIN
SHUN
THAN
THEN
THIN
WHEN
WHIN

••HN
ETHN
FOHN
HAHN
JOHN

HO••
HOAR
HOAX
HOBO
HOBS
HOCK
HODS
HOED
HOER
HOES
HOGS
HOLD
HOLE
HOLM
HOLO
HOLY
HOME
HOMO
HOMS
HOND
HONE
HONG
HONK
HOOD
HOOF
HOOK
HOOP
HOOT
HOPE
HOPI
HOPS
HORA
HORN
HORT
HOSE
HOST
HOUR
HOVE
HOWE
HOWL
HOYS

H•O•
HOOD
HOOF
HOOK
HOOP
HOOT

H••O
HALO
HEMO
HERO
HILO
HOBO
HOLO
HOMO
HUGO
HYLO
HYPO

•HO•
AHOY
CHOL
CHOP
CHOU
CHOW
DHOW
MHOS
PHON
PHOT
RHOS
SHOD
SHOE
SHOO
SHOP
SHOT
SHOW
THOR
THOU
WHOA
WHOM
WHOP

•H•O
OHIO
RHEO
SHOO
THEO
THIO

••HO
ECHO
SOHO

H•P•
HAPL
HEPT
HIPP
HIPS
HOPE
HOPI
HOPS
HUPA
HYPO

H••P
HARP
HASP
HEAP
HELP
HEMP
HIPP
HOOP
HRIP
HUMP

•H•P
CHAP
CHIP
CHOP
SHIP
SHOP
WHAP
WHIP
WHOP

HR••
HRIP

H•R•
HARD
HARE
HARK
HARL
HARM
HARP
HART
HARZ
HERA
HERB
HERD
HERE
HERL
HERO
HERS
HIRE
HORA
HORN
HORT
HURL
HURT

H••R
HAIR
HEAR
HEBR
HEIR
HIER
HOAR
HOER
HOUR
HYDR
HYGR

•HR•
THRU

•H•R
CHAR
CHIR
CHUR
THAR
THOR
WHIR

••HR
BOHR
LEHR
RUHR

H•S•
HASH
HASP
HAST
HISS
HIST
HOSE
HOST
HUSH
HUSK

H••S
HAGS
HAHS
HALS
HAMS
HANS
HATS
HAWS
HAYS
HEMS
HENS
HERS
HEWS
HIES
HIPS
HISS
HITS
HOBS
HODS
HOES
HOGS
HOMS
HOPS
HOYS
HUBS
HUES
HUGS
HUMS
HUNS
HUTS

•H•S
CHES
CHGS
CHIS
MHOS
OHMS
PHDS
PHIS
RHOS
THIS
THUS
WHYS

••HS
EDHS
ETHS
HAHS

H•T•
HATE
HATH
HATS
HETH
HITS
HUTS

H••T
HAFT
HALT
HART
HAST
HEAT
HECT
HEFT
HEPT
HILT
HINT
HIST
HOOT
HORT
HOST
HUNT
HURT
HYET

•H•T
CHAT
CHET
CHIT
GHAT
PHOT
PHYT
SHOT
SHUT
THAT
WHAT
WHET
WHIT

••HT
BAHT

HU••
HUBS
HUED
HUES
HUFF
HUGE
HUGH
HUGO
HUGS
HULA
HULK
HULL
HUME
HUMP
HUMS

HUNG
HUNK
HUNS
HUNT
HUPA
HURL
HURT
HUSH
HUSK
HUTS

H•U•
HAUL
HOUR

H••U
HABU

•HU•
CHUB
CHUG
CHUM
CHUR
SHUL
SHUN
SHUT
THUD
THUG
THUS

•H•U
CHOU
THOU
THRU

••HU
JEHU
OAHU

H•V•
HAVE
HIVE
HOVE

•H•V
SHIV

HW••
HWAN

H•W•
HAWK
HAWS
HEWN
HEWS
HOWE
HOWL

•HW•
YHWH

•H•W
CHAW
CHEW
CHOW
DHOW
PHEW
SHAW
SHEW
SHOW
THAW
THEW
WHEW

H•X•
HEXA

H••X
HOAX

HY••
HYAL
HYDE
HYDR
HYET
HYGR
HYLA
HYLO
HYMN
HYPO

H•Y•
HAYS
HOYS

H••Y
HAZY
HOLY

•HY•
PHYL
PHYT
WHYS

•H•Y
AHOY
SHAY
THEY
WHEY

••HY
ASHY

H•Z•
HAZE
HAZY

H••Z
HARZ

•H•Z
CHEZ
RHIZ
WHIZ

IA••
IADB
IAGO
IAMB
IANA
IANS

I•A•
ICAL
IDAE
IDAS
IMAM
INAS
IRAN
IRAQ
IRAS
ITAL
IVAN

I••A
IANA
IDEA
ILEA
ILIA
INCA
INGA
INIA
IONA
IOTA
IOWA
IRMA
ISBA
IXIA

•IA•
BIAS
DIAG
DIAL
DIAM
DIAS
DIAZ
FIAT
LIAO
LIAR
RIAL
SIAL
SIAM
VIAL

•I•A
AIDA
DITA
DIVA
FICA
FILA
GIGA
GILA
GIZA
KIVA
LILA
LIMA
LIRA
LISA
LIZA
MICA
MINA
NINA
NIPA
NITA
PICA
PIKA
PIMA
PINA
PITA
RITA
SIMA
SIVA
TINA
VINA
VISA
VITA
VIVA

••IA
AMIA
APIA
ARIA
ASIA
BAIA
CHIA
ELIA
EMIA
GAIA
ILIA
INIA
IXIA
MAIA
OBIA
OPIA
URIA
USIA

IB••
IBEX
IBID
IBIS
IBLE

I•B•
ICBM
IOBB
IRBM
ISBA

I••B
IADB
IAMB
IOBB

•IB•
BIBB
BIBL
BIBS
DIBS
FIBR
FIBS
GIBE
GIBS
JIBE
JIBS
KIBE
MIBS
NIBS
RIBS
SIBS

•I•B
BIBB
LIMB

••IB
ABIB
CRIB
DRIB
GLIB

IC••
ICAL
ICBM
ICED
ICEL
ICES
ICON

I•C•
INCA
INCH
INCL
ITCH

•IC•
BICE
DICE
DICH
DICK
FICA
FICE
HICK
KICK
LICE
LICK
MICA
MICE
MICH
NICE
NICK
PICA
PICE
PICK
PICO
PICR
PICT
RICE
RICH
RICK
SICE
SICK
SICS
TICK
TICS
VICE
VICK
WICH
WICK

•I•C
CIRC
DISC
FISC
MISC
PISC
VISC
WISC
ZINC

••IC
ATIC
CHIC
EPIC
ERIC
FDIC
LAIC
ODIC
OTIC
PYIC
URIC
ZOIC

ID••
IDAE
IDAS
IDEA
IDEM
IDEO
IDES
IDFU
IDIO
IDLE
IDLY
IDOL
IDYL

I•D•
IADB
INDO
IODO

I••D
IBID
ICED
IMID
IRID

•ID•
AIDA
AIDE
AIDS
BIDE
BIDS
CIDE
DIDO
DIDY
FIDS
GIDE
HIDE
KIDD
KIDS
LIDO
LIDS
MIDI
NIDE
NIDI
RIDE
RIDS
SIDE
SIDS
TIDE
TIDY
VIDE
WIDE

•I•D
BIND
BIRD
DIED
FIND
GIED
GILD
GIRD
HIED
HIND
KIDD
KIND
LIED
LIND
MILD
MIND
PIED
RIND
TIED
VIED
WILD
WIND

••ID
ACID
AMID
ARID
AVID
CHID
ENID
GRID
IBID
IMID
IRID
LAID
MAID
OVID
PAID
QUID
RAID
SAID
SKID
SLID
VOID

I•E•
IBEX
ICED
ICEL
ICES
IDEA
IDEM
IDEO
IDES
IKES
ILEA
ILEO
ILEX
INEZ
ITEM
IVES

I••E
IBLE
IDAE
IDLE
ILSE
INGE
ISLE

•IE•
BIER
DIED
DIES
DIET
FIEF
GIED
HIED
HIER
HIES
KIEL
KIER
KIEV
LIED
LIEF
LIEN
LIES
LIEU
MIEN
PIED
PIER
PIES
TIED
TIER
TIES
VIED
VIES
VIEW

•I•E
AIDE
BICE
BIDE
BIKE
BILE
BINE
BISE
BITE
CIDE
CINE
CITE
DICE
DIKE
DIME
DINE
DIRE

DIVE EIRE FICE FIFE FILE FINE FIRE FIVE GIBE GIDE GIVE HIDE HIKE HIRE HIVE JIBE JIVE KIBE KINE KITE LICE LIFE LIKE LIME LINE LIRE LITE LIVE MICE MIKE MILE MIME MINE MIRE MISE MITE NICE NIDE NIKE NILE NINE NIUE PICE PIKE PILE PINE PIPE RICE RIDE RIFE RILE RIME RIPE RISE RITE RIVE SICE SIDE SINE SIRE SITE SIZE TIDE TILE TIME TINE TIRE VICE VIDE VILE VINE VISE VIVE WIDE WIFE WILE WINE WIPE WIRE WISE WIVE YIPE

••IE

ABIE AMIE BRIE EDIE ERIE OKIE

IF••

IFFY

I•F•

IDFU IFFY

•IF•

BIFF FIFE GIFT GIFU HIFI JIFF LIFE LIFT MIFF RIFE RIFF RIFT SIFT TIFF WIFE

•I•F

BIFF FIEF JIFF LIEF MIFF RIFF TIFF

••IF

ALIF COIF LEIF NAIF WAIF

IG••

IGNI

I•G•

IAGO INGA INGE

•IG•

DIGS FIGS GIGA GIGS HIGH JIGS LIGN MIGS NIGH NIGR PIGS RIGS SIGH SIGN WIGS

•I•G

DIAG DING KING LING MING PING RING SING TING WING ZING

••IG

BRIG GRIG OLIG ORIG PRIG SWIG TRIG TWIG WHIG

I••H

INCH ITCH

•I•H

DICH DISH FISH HIGH KITH LITH MICH NIGH PISH PITH RICH SIGH SIKH WICH WISH WITH XIPH

I•I•

IBID IBIS IDIO ILIA IMID IMIN INIA INIT IRID IRIS ISIS IXIA

I••I

IGNI IMPI INRI

•I•I

DILI FIJI HIFI KIWI MIDI MIMI MINI NIDI NISI PILI SITI TIKI TITI VINI

•IJ•

FIJI

IK••

IKES IKON

I•K•

INKS INKY IRKS

•IK•

BIKE DIKE HIKE LIKE MIKE NIKE PIKA PIKE SIKH TIKI

•I•K

BILK DICK DIRK DISK FINK GINK HICK JINK KICK KINK KIRK LICK LINK MILK MINK NICK PICK PINK RICK RINK RISK SICK SILK SINK TICK VICK WICK WINK

••IK

EFIK ERIK HAIK

IL••

ILEA ILEO ILEX ILIA ILLS ILLY ILSE ILUS

I•L•

IBLE IDLE IDLY ILLS ILLY INLY ISLE

I••L

ICAL ICEL IDOL IDYL INCL ITAL ITOL

•IL•

AILS BILE BILK BILL DILI DILL FILA FILE FILL FILM FILS GILA GILD GILL GILS GILT HILL HILO HILT JILL JILT KILL KILN KILO KILT LILA LILS LILT LILY MILD MILE MILK MILL MILO MILS MILT NILE OILS OILY PILE PILI PILL RILE RILL SILK SILL SILO SILT TILE TILL TILT VILE VILL WILD WILE WILL WILT WILY

•I•L

BIBL BILL BIOL BIRL DIAL DILL DIPL FILL GILL GIRL HILL JILL KIEL KILL MILL PILL RIAL RILL SIAL SILL TILL VIAL VILL VIOL WILL

••IL

ANIL ARIL AXIL BAIL BOIL CEIL CHIL COIL DEIL EMIL EVIL FAIL FOIL GAIL HAIL JAIL KAIL MAIL MOIL NAIL NEIL NOIL PAIL PHIL RAIL ROIL SAIL SOIL TAIL TOIL VEIL WAIL

IM••

IMAM IMID IMIN IMMY IMPI IMPS

I•M•

IAMB IMMY IRMA ISMS

I••M

ICBM IDEM IMAM IRBM ITEM

•IM•

AIMS DIME DIMS GIMP JIMS LIMA LIMB LIME LIMN LIMP LIMY MIME MIMI PIMA PIMP RIME RIMS RIMY SIMA SIMP SIMS TIME TIMS

•I•M

DIAM FILM FIRM SIAM

••IM

ANIM BRIM GLIM GRIM MAIM PRIM SHIM SKIM SLIM SWIM TRIM WHIM

IN••
INAS
INCA
INCH
INCL
INDO
INEZ
INGA
INGE
INIA
INIT
INKS
INKY
INLY
INNS
INRI
INSP
INST
INTO

I•N•
IANA
IANS
IGNI
INNS
IONA
IONS
ISNT

I••N
ICON
IKON
IMIN
IRAN
IRON
IVAN

•IN•
AINO
AINS
AINT
AINU
BIND
BINE
BINS
CINE
DINE
DING
DINO
DINS
DINT
FIND
FINE
FINK
FINN
FINS
GINK
GINS
HIND
HINT
JINK
JINN
JINX
KIND
KINE
KING
KINK
KINO
LIND
LINE
LING
LINK
LINT
LINY
LINZ
MINA
MIND
MINE
MING
MINI
MINK
MINN
MINT
MINX
NINA
NINE
OINO
PINA
PINE
PING
PINK
PINS
PINT
PINY
RIND
RING
RINK
SINE
SING
SINK
SINO
SINS
TINA
TINE
TING
TINS
TINT
TINY
VINA
VINE
VINI
VINO
VINY
WIND
WINE
WING
WINK
WINO
WINS
WINY
XINT
ZINC
ZING

•I•N
BION
CION
DION
FINN
FIRN
JINN
KILN
LIEN
LIGN
LIMN
LION
MIEN
MINN
PION
SIGN
SION
TION
XION
ZION

••IN
AKIN
AYIN
CAIN
CHIN
COIN
ERIN
FAIN
GAIN
GRIN
GUIN
IMIN
JAIN
JOIN
KAIN
LAIN
LOIN
MAIN
ODIN
PAIN
PYIN
RAIN
REIN
RHIN
RUIN
SHIN
SKIN
SPIN
TAIN
THIN
TWIN
VAIN
VEIN
WAIN
WHIN
ZEIN

IO••
IOBB
IODO
IONA
IONS
IOTA
IOUS
IOWA

I•O•
ICON
IDOL
IKON
IRON
ITOL
IVOR

I••O
IAGO
IDEO
IDIO
ILEO
INDO
INTO
IODO

•IO•
BIOL
BION
CION
DION
LION
PION
RIOT
SION
TION
VIOL
XION
ZION

•I•O
AINO
DIDO
DINO
GIRO
HILO
KILO
KINO
LIAO
LIDO
LIPO
MILO
MISO
OINO
PICO
SILO
SINO
SITO
TIRO
TITO
VINO
WINO

••IO
AGIO
BRIO
CLIO
IDIO
OHIO
OLIO
THIO
TRIO

I•P•
IMPI
IMPS

I••P
INSP

•IP•
DIPL
DIPS
GIPS
HIPP
HIPS
KIPS
LIPO
LIPS
NIPA
NIPS
PIPE
PIPS
PIPY
RIPE
RIPS
SIPS
TIPS
VIPS
WIPE
XIPH
YIPE
YIPS
ZIPS

•I•P
GIMP
HIPP
LIMP
LISP
PIMP
SIMP
WISP

••IP
BLIP
CHIP
CLIP
DRIP
FLIP
GRIP
HRIP
QUIP
SHIP
SKIP
SLIP
SNIP
TRIP
WHIP

I••Q
IRAQ

IR••
IRAN
IRAQ
IRAS
IRBM
IRID
IRIS
IRKS
IRMA
IRON

I•R•
INRI

I••R
IVOR

•IR•
AIRS
AIRY
BIRD
BIRL
BIRR
CIRC
DIRE
DIRK
DIRT
EIRE
FIRE
FIRM
FIRN
FIRS
GIRD
GIRL
GIRO
GIRT
HIRE
KIRK
LIRA
LIRE
MIRE
MIRS
MIRV
SIRE
SIRS
TIRE
TIRO
WIRE
WIRY

•I•R
BIER
BIRR
FIBR
HIER
KIER
LIAR
NIGR
NITR
PICR
PIER
TIER
VITR

••IR
AMIR
ASIR
CHIR
COIR
EMIR
FAIR
HAIR
HEIR
LAIR
MEIR
MUIR
PAIR
SPIR
STIR
VAIR
WEIR
WHIR
YMIR

IS••
ISBA
ISIS
ISLE
ISMS
ISNT

I•S•
ILSE
INSP
INST

I••S
IANS
IBIS
ICES
IDAS
IDES
IKES
ILLS
ILUS
IMPS
INAS
INKS
INNS
IONS
IOUS
IRAS
IRIS
IRKS
ISIS
ISMS
ITYS
IVES
IVYS

•IS•
BISE
CIST
DISC
DISH
DISK
DIST
FISC
FISH
FIST
GIST
HISS
HIST
KISS
LISA
LISP
LIST
MISC
MISE
MISO
MISS
MIST
NISI
PISC
PISH
RISE
RISK
VISA
VISC
VISE
WISC
WISE
WISH
WISP

•I•S
AIDS
AILS
AIMS
AINS
AIRS
BIAS
BIBS
BIDS
BINS
BITS
DIAS
DIBS
DIES
DIGS
DIMS
DINS
DIPS
FIBS
FIDS
FIGS
FILS
FINS
FIRS
FITS
GIBS
GIGS
GILS
GINS
GIPS
HIES
HIPS
HISS
HITS
JIBS
JIGS
JIMS
KIDS
KIPS
KISS
KITS

4

LIDS
LIES
LILS
LIPS
MIBS
MIGS
MILS
MIRS
MISS
NIBS
NIPS
NITS
OILS
PIES
PIGS
PINS
PIPS
PITS
PIUS
RIBS
RIDS
RIGS
RIMS
RIPS
SIBS
SICS
SIDS
SIMS
SINS
SIPS
SIRS
SITS
TICS
TIES
TIMS
TINS
TIPS
TITS
VIES
VIPS
WIGS
WINS
WITS
YIPS
ZIPS

••IS
AMIS
ANIS
APIS
AVIS
AXIS
BOIS
CHIS
DAIS
ELIS
ERIS
GRIS
IBIS
IRIS
ISIS
KRIS
LEIS
LOIS
LUIS
OBIS
OSIS
OTIS
PHIS
PSIS
REIS
SAIS
SKIS
THIS
TRIS

IT••
ITAL
ITCH
ITEM
ITOL
ITYS

I•T•
INTO
IOTA

I••T
INIT
INST
ISNT

•IT•
BITE
BITS
BITT
CITE
CITY
DITA
FITS
FITZ
HITS
KITE
KITH
KITS
LITE
LITH
MITE
MITT
NITA
NITR
NITS
PITA
PITH
PITS
PITT
PITY
RITA
RITE
SITE
SITI
SITO
SITS
TITI
TITO
TITS
VITA
VITR
WITH
WITS

•I•T
AINT
BITT
CIST
DIET
DINT
DIRT
DIST
FIAT
FIST
GIFT
GILT
GIRT
GIST
HILT
HINT
HIST
JILT
KILT
LIFT
LILT
LINT
LIST
MILT
MINT
MIST
MITT
MIXT
PICT
PINT
PITT
RIFT
RIOT
SIFT
SILT
TILT
TINT
WILT
XINT

••IT
ADIT
ALIT
BAIT
BLIT
BRIT
CHIT
CRIT
DOIT
EDIT
EMIT
EXIT
FLIT
FRIT
GAIT
GRIT
INIT
KNIT
OBIT
OMIT
QUIT
SKIT
SLIT
SMIT
SNIT
SPIT
SUIT
TWIT
UNIT
WAIT
WHIT
WRIT

I•U•
ILUS
IOUS

I••U
IDFU

•IU•
NIUE
PIUS

•I•U
AINU
GIFU
KIVU
LIEU

IV••
IVAN
IVES
IVOR
IVYS

•IV•
DIVA
DIVE
FIVE
GIVE
HIVE
JIVE
KIVA
KIVU
LIVE
RIVE
SIVA
TIVY
VIVA
VIVE
WIVE

•I•V
KIEV
MIRV

••IV
SHIV
XDIV

I•W•
IOWA

•IW•
KIWI

•I•W
VIEW

IX••
IXIA

I••X
IBEX
ILEX

•IX•
MIXT
PIXY

•I•X
JINX
MINX

••IX
ALIX
TRIX

I•Y•
IDYL
ITYS
IVYS

I••Y
IDLY
IFFY
ILLY
IMMY
INKY
INLY
IZZY

•I•Y
AIRY
CITY
DIDY
LILY
LIMY
LINY
OILY
PINY
PIPY
PITY
PIXY
RIMY
SIZY
TIDY
TINY
TIVY
VINY
WILY
WINY
WIRY

IZ••
IZZY

I•Z•
IZZY

I••Z
INEZ

•IZ•
FIZZ
GIZA
LIZA
PIZZ
SIZE
SIZY

•I•Z
DIAZ
FITZ
FIZZ
LINZ
PIZZ

••IZ
ARIZ
LUIZ
QUIZ
RHIZ
WHIZ

JA••
JABS
JACK
JADE
JAEN
JAGS
JAIL
JAIN
JAKE
JAMB
JAMS
JANE
JANS
JAPE
JARL
JARS
JATO
JAVA
JAWS
JAYS
JAZZ

J•A•
JEAN
JOAB
JOAN
JUAN

J••A
JAVA
JENA
JUBA
JURA

•JA•
AJAR
AJAX

••JA
BAJA
SOJA

J•B•
JABS
JIBE
JIBS
JOBS
JUBA
JUBE

J••B
JAMB
JOAB

J•C•
JACK
JOCK

J••C
JUNC

J•D•
JADE
JUDE
JUDO
JUDY

J••D
JEED

JE••
JEAN
JEED
JEEP
JEER
JEES
JEFE
JEFF
JEHU
JELL
JEMS
JENA
JERK
JESS
JEST
JETS
JEUX
JEWS

J•E•
JAEN
JEED
JEEP
JEER
JEES
JOEL
JOES
JOEY

J••E
JADE
JAKE
JANE
JAPE
JEFE
JIBE
JIVE
JOKE
JOSE
JOVE
JUBE
JUDE
JULE
JUNE
JUTE

J•F•
JEFE
JEFF
JIFF

J••F
JEFF
JIFF

J•G•
JAGS
JIGS
JOGS
JUGS

J••G
JUNG

J•H•
JEHU
JOHN

J••H
JOSH

JI••
JIBE
JIBS
JIFF
JIGS
JILL
JILT
JIMS
JINK
JINN
JINX
JIVE

J•I•
JAIL
JAIN
JOIN

••JI
FIJI
FUJI

J•J•
JUJU

J•K•
JAKE
JOKE

J••K
JACK
JERK
JINK
JOCK
JUNK

J•L•
JELL
JILL
JILT
JOLO
JOLT
JULE
JULY

J••L
JAIL
JARL
JELL
JILL
JOEL
JOWL

J•M•
JAMB
JAMS
JEMS
JIMS
JUMP

••JM
SEJM

J•N•
JANE
JANS
JENA
JINK
JINN
JINX
JONS
JUNC
JUNE
JUNG
JUNK
JUNO

J••N
JAEN
JAIN
JEAN
JINN
JOAN
JOHN
JOIN
JUAN

JO••
JOAB
JOAN
JOBS
JOCK
JOEL
JOES
JOEY
JOGS
JOHN
JOIN
JOKE
JOLO
JOLT
JONS
JOSE
JOSH
JOSS
JOTS
JOVE
JOWL
JOYS

J••O
JATO
JOLO
JUDO
JUNO

J•P•
JAPE

J••P
JEEP
JUMP

J•R•
JARL
JARS
JERK
JURA
JURY

J••R
JEER

•J•R
AJAR

J•S•
JESS
JEST
JOSE
JOSH
JOSS
JUST

J••S
JABS
JAGS
JAMS
JANS
JARS
JAWS
JAYS
JEES
JEMS
JESS
JETS
JEWS
JIBS
JIGS
JIMS
JOBS
JOES
JOGS
JONS
JOSS
JOTS
JOYS
JUGS
JUTS

J•T•
JATO
JETS
JOTS
JUTE
JUTS

J••T
JEST
JILT
JOLT
JUST

JU••
JUAN
JUBA
JUBE
JUDE
JUDO
JUDY
JUGS
JUJU
JULE
JULY
JUMP
JUNC
JUNE
JUNG
JUNK
JUNO
JURA
JURY
JUST
JUTE
JUTS

J•U•
JEUX

J••U
JEHU
JUJU

••JU
JUJU

J•V•
JAVA
JIVE
JOVE

J•W•
JAWS
JEWS
JOWL

J••X
JEUX
JINX

•J•X
AJAX

J•Y•
JAYS
JOYS

J••Y
JOEY
JUDY
JULY
JURY

J•Z•
JAZZ

J••Z
JAZZ

KA••
KAAS
KABS
KADI
KAGU
KAIL
KAIN
KAKA
KAKI
KALE
KALI
KAMA
KAME
KAMI
KANA
KANE
KANO
KANS
KANT
KAPA
KAPH
KARA
KARL
KARY
KATE
KAVA
KAYO
KAYS

K•A•
KAAS
KCAL
KEAS
KHAN
KNAR
KYAT

K••A
KAKA
KAMA
KANA
KAPA
KARA
KAVA
KIVA
KOLA
KURA

•KA•
OKAS
OKAY
SKAT
SKAW

•K•A
OKLA
OKRA
SKUA

••KA
DEKA
KAKA
PIKA
WEKA

K•B•
KABS
KIBE
KOBE

K••B
KERB
KNOB

KC••
KCAL

K•C•
KECK
KICK

K•D•
KADI
KIDD
KIDS
KUDU

K••D
KIDD
KIND
KURD

•K•D
EKED
NKVD
OKED
SKID

KE••
KEAS
KECK
KEEF
KEEL
KEEN
KEEP
KEFS
KEGS
KELP
KENO
KENS
KENT
KEOS
KEPI
KEPT
KERB
KERF
KERN
KETO
KEYS

K•E•
KEEF
KEEL
KEEN
KEEP
KIEL
KIER
KIEV
KLEE
KNEE
KNEW
KOEL

K••E
KALE
KAME
KANE
KATE
KIBE
KINE
KITE
KLEE
KNEE
KOBE
KURE

•KE•
EKED
EKES
IKES
OKED
SKEE
SKEG
SKEP
SKEW

•K•E
OKIE
SKEE
SKYE

••KE
BAKE
BIKE
CAKE
COKE
DEKE
DIKE
DUKE
FAKE
FYKE
HAKE
HIKE
JAKE
JOKE
LAKE
LIKE
LUKE
MAKE
MIKE
MOKE
NIKE
PIKE
POKE
PUKE
RAKE
SAKE
SOKE
TAKE
TYKE
WAKE
WOKE
YOKE
ZEKE

K•F•
KEFS

K••F
KEEF
KERF

K•G•
KAGU
KEGS

K••G
KING

•K•G
SKEG

KH••
KHAN

K•H•
KOHL

K••H
KAPH
KITH
KOPH

••KH
ANKH
SIKH

KI••
KIBE
KICK
KIDD
KIDS
KIEL
KIER
KIEV
KILL
KILN
KILO
KILT
KIND
KINE
KING
KINK
KINO
KIPS
KIRK
KISS
KITE
KITH
KITS
KIVA
KIVU
KIWI

K•I•
KAIL
KAIN
KNIT
KRIS

K••I
KADI
KAKI
KALI
KAMI
KEPI
KIWI

•KI•
AKIN
OKIE
SKID
SKIM
SKIN
SKIP
SKIS
SKIT

••KI
KAKI
RAKI
SAKI
TIKI

KK••
KKTP

4

K•K•
KAKA
KAKI

K••K
KECK
KICK
KINK
KIRK
KOOK

KL••
KLEE

K•L•
KALE
KALI
KELP
KILL
KILN
KILO
KILT
KOLA

K••L
KAIL
KARL
KCAL
KEEL
KIEL
KILL
KOEL
KOHL

•KL•
OKLA
WKLY

K•M•
KAMA
KAME
KAMI

•K•M
SKIM

KN••
KNAR
KNEE
KNEW
KNIT
KNOB
KNOP
KNOT
KNOW
KNOX
KNUR

K•N•
KANA
KANE
KANO
KANS
KANT
KENO
KENS
KENT
KIND
KINE
KING
KINK
KINO

K••N
KAIN
KEEN
KERN
KHAN
KILN

•K•N
AKIN
IKON
SKIN

KO••
KOBE
KOEL
KOHL
KOLA
KOOK
KOPH
KOPS
KORS
KOTO

K•O•
KEOS
KNOB
KNOP
KNOT
KNOW
KNOX
KOOK

K••O
KANO
KAYO
KENO
KETO
KILO
KINO
KOTO

•KO•
IKON

K•P•
KAPA
KAPH
KEPI
KEPT
KIPS
KOPH
KOPS

K••P
KEEP
KELP
KKTP
KNOP

•K•P
KKTP
SKEP
SKIP

KR••
KRIS

K•R•
KARA
KARL
KARY
KERB
KERF
KERN
KIRK
KORS
KURA
KURD
KURE
KURT

K••R
KIER
KNAR
KNUR

•KR•
OKRA

K•S•
KISS

K••S
KAAS
KABS
KANS
KAYS
KEAS
KEFS
KEGS
KENS
KEOS
KEYS
KIDS
KIPS
KISS
KITS
KOPS
KORS
KRIS

•K•S
EKES
IKES
OKAS
SKIS

••KS
ARKS
ASKS
AUKS
DAKS
ELKS
INKS
IRKS
LEKS
OAKS
YAKS
YUKS

K•T•
KATE
KETO
KITE
KITH
KITS
KKTP
KOTO

K••T
KANT
KENT
KEPT
KILT
KNIT
KNOT
KURT
KYAT

•KT•
KKTP

•K•T
SKAT
SKIT

KU••
KUDU
KURA
KURD
KURE
KURT

K•U•
KNUR

K••U
KAGU
KIVU
KUDU

•KU•
SKUA

••KU
BAKU

K•V•
KAVA
KIVA
KIVU

K••V
KIEV

•KV•
NKVD

K•W•
KIWI

K••W
KNEW
KNOW

•K•W
SKAW
SKEW

K••X
KNOX

KY••
KYAT

K•Y•
KAYO
KAYS
KEYS

K••Y
KARY

•KY•
SKYE

•K•Y
OKAY
WKLY

••KY
INKY
LAKY
POKY
SUKY

LA••
LABS
LACE
LACK
LACT
LACY
LADE
LADS
LADY
LAFE
LAGS
LAIC
LAID
LAIN
LAIR
LAKE
LAKY
LALL
LAMA
LAMB
LAME
LAMP
LAMS
LAND
LANE
LANG
LANK
LAOS
LAPP
LAPS
LARD
LARK
LARS
LASH
LASS
LAST
LATE
LATH
LATI
LAUD
LAVA
LAVE
LAWN
LAWS
LAYS
LAZE
LAZY

L•A•
LEAD
LEAF
LEAH
LEAK
LEAN
LEAP
LEAR
LEAS
LIAO
LIAR
LOAD
LOAF
LOAM
LOAN
LUAU

L••A
LAMA
LAVA
LEDA
LENA
LEVA
LILA
LIMA
LIRA
LISA
LIZA
LOLA
LUNA
LUTA
LYRA

•LA•
ALAE
ALAI
ALAN
ALAR
ALAS
BLAB
BLAH
BLAT
CLAD
CLAM
CLAN
CLAP
CLAR
CLAW
CLAY
ELAM
ELAN
FLAG
FLAK
FLAM
FLAN
FLAP
FLAT
FLAW
FLAX
FLAY
GLAD
OLAF
OLAV
PLAN
PLAT
PLAY
SLAB
SLAG
SLAM
SLAP
SLAT
SLAV
SLAW
SLAY

•L•A
ALBA
ALGA
ALMA
ALTA
ALVA
ELBA
ELIA
ELLA
ELSA
ELVA
FLEA
ILEA
ILIA
OLGA
OLLA
PLEA
ULNA

••LA
BOLA
COLA
ELLA
FALA
FILA
FULA
GALA
GILA
HULA
HYLA
KOLA
LILA
LOLA
OKLA
OLLA
SOLA
TELA
TOLA
VELA
ZOLA

L•B•
LABS
LOBE
LOBO
LOBS

L••B
LAMB
LIMB

•LB•
ALBA
ALBS
ELBA
ELBE

•L•B
BLAB
BLEB
BLOB
CLUB
FLUB
GLIB
GLOB
NLRB
PLEB
SLAB
SLOB
SLUB

••LB
BULB

L•C•
LACE
LACK
LACT
LACY
LICE
LICK
LOCH
LOCI
LOCK
LOCO
LUCE
LUCK
LUCY

L••C
LAIC
LEUC

•L•C
ALEC
BLOC
ELEC
FLOC

••LC
TALC

L•D•
LADE
LADS
LADY
LEDA
LIDO
LIDS
LODE
LODI
LODZ

L••D
LAID
LAND
LARD
LAUD
LEAD
LEND
LEUD
LEWD
LIED
LIND
LOAD
LORD
LOUD

•LD•
ALDO
BLDG

•L•D
BLED
BLVD
CLAD
CLOD
FLED
GLAD
GLED
PLED
PLOD
SLED
SLID

••LD
AULD
BALD
BOLD
COLD
FOLD
GELD
GILD
GOLD
HELD
HOLD
MELD
MILD
MOLD
SOLD
TOLD
VELD
WELD
WILD
WOLD

LE••
LEAD
LEAF
LEAH
LEAK
LEAN
LEAP
LEAR
LEAS
LEDA
LEEK
LEER
LEES
LEET
LEFT
LEGS
LEHR
LEIF
LEIS
LEKS
LEMS
LENA
LEND
LENO
LENS
LENT
LEON
LEOS
LEPT
LESS
LEST
LETO
LETS
LETT
LEUC
LEUD
LEUK
LEVA
LEVI
LEVO
LEVY
LEWD
LEWS

L•E•
LEEK
LEER
LEES
LEET
LIED
LIEF
LIEN
LIES
LIEU
LUES
LYES

L••E
LACE
LADE
LAFE
LAKE
LAME
LANE
LATE
LAVE
LAZE
LICE
LIFE
LIKE
LIME
LINE
LIRE
LITE
LIVE
LOBE
LODE
LOGE
LOME
LONE
LOPE
LORE
LOSE
LOVE
LUCE
LUKE
LUNE
LURE
LUTE
LUXE
LYLE
LYRE
LYSE
LYTE
LYZE

•LE•
ALEC
ALEE
ALEF
ALES
ALEX
BLEB
BLED
BLET
BLEW
CLEF
CLEM
CLEO
CLEW
ELEC
ELEM
ELEO
ELEV
FLEA
FLED
FLEE
FLEM
FLEW
FLEX
GLED
GLEE
GLEN
ILEA
ILEO
ILEX
KLEE
OLEO
PLEA
PLEB
PLED
SLED
SLEW

•L•E
ALAE
ALEE
ALOE
BLUE
CLUE
ELBE
ELSE
FLEE
FLOE
FLUE
GLEE
GLUE
ILSE
KLEE
MLLE
SLOE
SLUE

••LE
ABLE
AXLE
BALE
BILE
BOLE
CELE
COLE
CULE
DALE
DELE
DOLE
FILE
GALE
HALE
HOLE
IBLE
IDLE
ISLE
JULE
KALE
LYLE
MALE
MILE
MLLE
MOLE
MULE
NILE
OGLE
ORLE
PALE
PELE
PILE
POLE
PULE
PYLE
RALE
RILE
ROLE
RULE
SALE
SOLE
TALE
TELE
TILE
TOLE
TULE
VALE
VILE
VOLE
WALE
WILE
YALE
YULE

L•F•
LAFE
LEFT
LIFE
LIFT
LOFT
LUFF

L••F
LEAF
LEIF
LIEF
LOAF
LOOF
LUFF

•LF•
ALFS

•L•F
ALEF
ALIF
CLEF
OLAF

••LF
CALF
DELF
DOLF
GOLF
GULF
HALF
PELF
ROLF
SELF
WOLF

L•G•
LAGS
LEGS
LIGN
LOGE
LOGO
LOGS
LOGY
LUGS

L••G
LANG
LING
LONG
LUNG

•LG•
ALGA
ALGY
OLGA

•L•G
BLDG
CLOG
FLAG
FLOG
OLIG
PLUG
SLAG
SLOG
SLUG

••LG
BELG
BULG

L•H•
LEHR

L••H
LASH
LATH
LEAH
LITH
LOCH
LOTH
LUSH
LUTH

•L•H
ALPH
BLAH

LI••
LIAO
LIAR
LICE
LICK
LIDO
LIDS
LIED
LIEF
LIEN
LIES
LIEU
LIFE
LIFT
LIGN
LIKE
LILA
LILS
LILT
LILY
LIMA
LIMB
LIME
LIMN
LIMP
LIMY
LIND
LINE
LING
LINK
LINT
LINY
LINZ
LION
LIPO
LIPS
LIRA
LIRE
LISA
LISP
LIST
LITE
LITH
LIVE
LIZA

L•I•
LAIC
LAID
LAIN
LAIR
LEIF
LEIS
LOIN
LOIS
LUIS
LUIZ

L••I
LATI
LEVI
LOCI
LODI
LUNI
LYSI

•LI•
ALIF
ALIT
ALIX
BLIP
BLIT
CLIO
CLIP
ELIA
ELIS
FLIP
FLIT
GLIB
GLIM
ILIA
OLIG
OLIO
SLID
SLIM
SLIP
SLIT

•L•I
ALAI
ALTI

••LI
ATLI
BALI
CALI
DALI
DILI
HELI
KALI
MALI
PALI
PILI
SOLI

•L•J
CLUJ

L•K•
LAKE
LAKY
LEKS
LIKE
LUKE

L••K
LACK
LANK
LARK
LEAK
LEEK
LEUK
LICK
LINK
LOCK
LOOK
LUCK
LURK

•LK•
ELKS

•L•K
FLAK

••LK
BALK

BILK
BULK
CALK
FOLK
HULK
MILK
POLK
SALK
SILK
SULK
TALK
WALK
YELK
YOLK

L•L•
LALL
LILA
LILS
LILT
LILY
LOLA
LOLL
LULL
LULU
LYLE

L••L
LALL
LOLL
LULL

•LL•
ALLO
ALLY
ELLA
ELLS
ILLS
ILLY
MLLE
OLLA
OLLY

•L•L
ELUL

••LL
BALL
BELL
BILL
BOLL
BULL
CALL
CELL
COLL
CULL
DELL
DILL
DOLL
DULL
FALL
FELL
FILL
FOLL
FULL
GALL
GILL
GULL
HALL
HELL
HILL
HULL
JELL
JILL
KILL
LALL
LOLL
LULL
MALL
MILL
MOLL
MULL
NELL
NULL
PALL
PILL
POLL
PULL
RALL
RILL
ROLL
SELL
SILL
TALL
TELL
TILL
TOLL
VILL
WALL
WELL
WILL
YELL

L•M•
LAMA
LAMB
LAME
LAMP
LAMS
LEMS
LIMA
LIMB
LIME
LIMN
LIMP
LIMY
LOME
LUMP

L••M
LOAM
LOOM

•LM•
ALMA
ALMS
ELMS
ELMY

•L•M
ALUM
CLAM
CLEM
ELAM
ELEM
FLAM
FLEM
GLIM
GLUM
PLUM
SLAM
SLIM
SLUM

••LM
BALM
CALM
CULM
FILM
HELM
HOLM
PALM

L•N•
LAND
LANE
LANG
LANK
LENA
LEND
LENO
LENS
LENT
LIND
LINE
LING
LINK
LINT
LINY
LINZ
LONE
LONG
LUNA
LUNE
LUNG
LUNI
LUNT
LYNN
LYNX

L••N
LAIN
LAWN
LEAN
LEON
LIEN
LIGN
LIMN
LION
LOAN
LOIN
LOON
LYNN

•LN•
ULNA

•L•N
ALAN
CLAN
CLON
ELAN
FLAN
GLEN
PLAN

••LN
KILN

LO••
LOAD
LOAF
LOAM
LOAN
LOBE
LOBO
LOBS
LOCH
LOCI
LOCK
LOCO
LODE
LODI
LODZ
LOFT
LOGE
LOGO
LOGS
LOGY
LOIN
LOIS
LOLA
LOLL
LOME
LONE
LONG
LOOF
LOOK
LOOM
LOON
LOOP
LOOS
LOOT
LOPE
LOPS
LORD
LORE
LORY
LOSE
LOSS
LOST
LOTH
LOTS
LOTT
LOUD
LOUP
LOUR
LOUT
LOVE
LOWS

L•O•
LAOS
LEON
LEOS
LION
LOOF
LOOK
LOOM
LOON
LOOP
LOOS
LOOT

L••O
LENO
LETO
LEVO
LIAO
LIDO
LIPO
LOBO
LOCO
LOGO

•LO•
ALOE
ALOW
BLOB
BLOC
BLOT
BLOW
CLOD
CLOG
CLON
CLOP
CLOT
CLOY
FLOC
FLOE
FLOG
FLOP
FLOR
FLOW
GLOB
GLOT
GLOW
PLOD
PLOP
PLOT
PLOW
PLOY
SLOB
SLOE
SLOG
SLOP
SLOT
SLOW

•L•O
ALDO
ALLO
ALSO
ALTO
CLEO
CLIO
ELEO
FLUO
ILEO
OLEO
OLIO

••LO
ALLO
BOLO
COLO
HALO
HILO
HOLO
HYLO
JOLO
KILO
MILO
POLO
SILO
SOLO
TELO
XYLO

L•P•
LAPP
LAPS
LEPT
LIPO
LIPS
LOPE
LOPS

L••P
LAMP
LAPP
LEAP
LIMP
LISP
LOOP
LOUP
LUMP

•LP•
ALPH
ALPS

•L•P
BLIP
CLAP
CLIP
CLOP
FLAP
FLIP
FLOP
PLOP
SLAP
SLIP
SLOP

••LP
GULP
HELP
KELP
PALP
PULP
YELP

L•R•
LARD
LARK
LARS
LIRA
LIRE
LORD
LORE
LORY
LURE
LURK
LYRA
LYRE

L••R
LAIR
LEAR
LEER
LEHR
LIAR
LOUR

•LR•
NLRB

•L•R
ALAR
BLUR
CLAR
FLOR
SLUR

L•S•
LASH
LASS
LAST
LESS
LEST
LISA
LISP
LIST
LOSE
LOSS
LOST
LUSH
LUST
LYSE
LYSI

L••S
LABS
LADS
LAGS
LAMS
LAOS
LAPS
LARS
LASS
LAWS
LAYS
LEAS
LEES
LEGS
LEIS
LEKS
LEMS
LENS
LEOS
LESS
LETS
LEWS
LIDS
LIES
LILS
LIPS
LOBS
LOGS
LOIS
LOOS
LOPS
LOSS
LOTS
LOWS
LUES
LUGS
LUIS
LYES

•LS•
ALSO
ELSA
ELSE
ILSE

•L•S
ALAS
ALBS
ALES
ALFS
ALMS
ALPS
ALYS
ELIS
ELKS
ELLS
ELMS
ILLS
ILUS
PLUS

••LS
AALS
AILS
AWLS
BBLS
BELS
COLS
DOLS
EELS
ELLS

FILS
GALS
GELS
GILS
HALS
ILLS
LILS
MELS
MILS
OILS
OWLS
PALS
SOLS
VALS
VOLS

L•T•
LATE
LATH
LATI
LETO
LETS
LETT
LITE
LITH
LOTH
LOTS
LOTT
LUTA
LUTE
LUTH
LYTE

L••T
LACT
LAST
LEET
LEFT
LENT
LEPT
LEST
LETT
LIFT
LILT
LINT
LIST
LOFT
LOOT
LOST
LOTT
LOUT
LUNT
LUST

•LT•
ALTA
ALTI
ALTO

•L•T
ALIT
BLAT
BLET
BLIT
BLOT
CLOT
FLAT
FLIT
GLOT
GLUT
PLAT
PLOT
SLAT
SLIT
SLOT
SLUT

••LT
BALT
BELT
BOLT
CELT
COLT
CULT
DOLT
FELT
GELT
GILT
HALT
HILT
JILT
JOLT
KILT
LILT
MALT
MELT
MILT
MOLT
MULT
PELT
SALT
SILT
TILT
VOLT
WALT
WELT
WILT

LU••
LUAU
LUCE
LUCK
LUCY
LUES
LUFF
LUGS
LUIS
LUIZ
LUKE
LULL
LULU
LUMP
LUNA
LUNE
LUNG
LUNI
LUNT
LURE
LURK
LUSH
LUST
LUTA
LUTE
LUTH
LUXE

L•U•
LAUD
LEUC
LEUD
LEUK
LOUD
LOUP
LOUR
LOUT

L••U
LIEU
LUAU
LULU

•LU•
ALUM
BLUE
BLUR
CLUB
CLUE
CLUJ
ELUL
FLUB
FLUE
FLUO
FLUX
GLUE
GLUM
GLUT
ILUS
PLUG
PLUM
PLUS
SLUB
SLUE
SLUG
SLUM
SLUR
SLUT

••LU
LULU
SULU
TOLU
YALU
ZULU

L•V•
LAVA
LAVE
LEVA
LEVI
LEVO
LEVY
LIVE
LOVE

•LV•
ALVA
BLVD
ELVA

•L•V
ELEV
OLAV
SLAV

L•W•
LAWN
LAWS
LEWD
LEWS
LOWS

•L•W
ALOW
BLEW
BLOW
CLAW
CLEW
FLAW
FLEW
FLOW
GLOW
PLOW
SLAW
SLEW
SLOW

L•X•
LUXE

L••X
LYNX

•L•X
ALEX
ALIX
FLAX
FLEX
FLUX
ILEX

••LX
CALX

LY••
LYES
LYLE
LYNN
LYNX
LYRA
LYRE
LYSE
LYSI
LYTE
LYZE

L•Y•
LAYS

L••Y
LACY
LADY
LAKY
LAZY
LEVY
LILY
LIMY
LINY
LOGY
LORY
LUCY

•LY•
ALYS

•L•Y
ALGY
ALLY
CLAY
CLOY
ELMY
FLAY
ILLY
OLLY
PLAY
PLOY
SLAY

••LY
ABLY
ALLY
COLY
DULY
EELY
HOLY
IDLY
ILLY
INLY
JULY
LILY
MOLY
OILY
OLLY
ONLY
PALY
POLY
RELY
UGLY
WILY
WKLY

L•Z•
LAZE
LAZY
LIZA
LYZE

L••Z
LINZ
LODZ
LUIZ

MA••
MAAM
MABS
MACE
MACH
MACK
MACS
MADE
MADS
MAES
MAGE
MAGI
MAIA
MAID
MAIL
MAIM
MAIN
MAKE
MALE
MALI
MALL
MALT
MAMA
MANA
MANE
MANI
MANN
MANS
MANX
MANY
MAPS
MARC
MARE
MARJ
MARK
MARL
MARS
MART
MARX
MARY
MASC
MASH
MASK
MASS
MAST
MATE
MATH
MATS
MATT
MAUD
MAUI
MAUL
MAWS
MAYA
MAYO
MAYS
MAZE
MAZY

M•A•
MAAM
MEAD
MEAL
MEAN
MEAT
MOAB
MOAN
MOAS
MOAT

M••A
MAIA
MAMA
MANA
MAYA
MEGA
MESA
META
MICA
MINA
MONA
MORA
MOXA
MYNA
MYRA

•MA•
AMAH
AMAS
GMAN
IMAM
OMAN
XMAS

•M•A
AMIA
EMIA
EMMA
YMCA
YMHA

••MA
ALMA
BEMA
COMA
CYMA
DUMA
EMMA
ERMA
FNMA
GAMA
HAMA
HEMA
IRMA
KAMA
LAMA
LIMA
MAMA
NAMA
NEMA
NOMA
PIMA
PUMA
ROMA
SIMA
SOMA
USMA
YUMA

M•B•
MABS
MIBS
MOBS

M••B
MOAB

•MB•
AMBI
AMBO
OMBR
UMBO

••MB
BOMB
CAMB
COMB
DUMB
GAMB
IAMB
JAMB
LAMB
LIMB
NUMB
TOMB
WOMB

M•C•
MACE
MACH
MACK
MACS
MICA
MICE
MICH
MOCK
MUCH
MUCI
MUCK
MUCO
MYCO

M••C
MARC
MASC
MISC

•MC•
FMCS
YMCA

••MC
USMC

M•D•
MADE
MADS
MEDI
MIDI
MODE

4

MODI
MODS
MUDS

M••D
MAID
MAUD
MEAD
MELD
MEND
MILD
MIND
MOLD
MOOD

•MD•
CMDR

•M•D
AMID
IMID

ME••
MEAD
MEAL
MEAN
MEAT
MEDI
MEEK
MEET
MEGA
MEGS
MEIR
MELD
MELS
MELT
MEMO
MEMS
MEND
MENI
MENO
MENT
MENU
MEOW
MERE
MERO
MESA
MESH
MESO
MESS
META
METE
METH
METR
MEWL
MEWS

M•E•
MAES
MEEK
MEET
MIEN
MMES
MOES

MYEL

M••E
MACE
MADE
MAGE
MAKE
MALE
MANE
MARE
MATE
MAZE
MERE
METE
MICE
MIKE
MILE
MIME
MINE
MIRE
MISE
MITE
MLLE
MODE
MOKE
MOLE
MOPE
MORE
MOSE
MOTE
MOUE
MOVE
MULE
MUSE
MUTE

•ME•
AMEN
AMER
AMES
EMEU
GMEN
MMES
OMEN
OMER
SMEW
YMER

•M•E
AMIE

••ME
ACME
AYME
CAME
COME
CYME
DAME
DEME
DIME
DOME
FAME
FEME
FUME

GAME
HAME
HEME
HOME
HUME
KAME
LAME
LIME
LOME
MIME
NAME
NOME
POME
RIME
ROME
SAME
SEME
SOME
TAME
TIME
TOME
ZYME

M•F•
MIFF
MUFF

M••F
MIFF
MUFF

M•G•
MAGE
MAGI
MEGA
MEGS
MIGS
MSGR
MSGT
MUGS

M••G
MING

•M•G
SMOG
SMUG

MH••
MHOS

M••H
MACH
MASH
MATH
MESH
METH
MICH
MOTH
MSTH
MUCH
MUSH
MYTH

•MH•
YMHA

•M•H
AMAH

MI••
MIBS
MICA
MICE
MICH
MIDI
MIEN
MIFF
MIGS
MIKE
MILD
MILE
MILK
MILL
MILO
MILS
MILT
MIME
MIMI
MINA
MIND
MINE
MING
MINI
MINK
MINN
MINT
MINX
MIRE
MIRS
MIRV
MISC
MISE
MISO
MISS
MIST
MITE
MITT
MIXT

M•I•
MAIA
MAID
MAIL
MAIM
MAIN
MEIR
MOIL
MUIR

M••I
MAGI
MALI
MANI
MAUI
MEDI
MENI
MIDI

MIMI
MINI
MODI
MUCI
MYRI

•MI•
AMIA
AMID
AMIE
AMIR
AMIS
EMIA
EMIL
EMIR
EMIT
IMID
IMIN
OMIT
SMIT
YMIR

•M•I
AMBI
IMPI
OMNI

••MI
DEMI
HEMI
KAMI
MIMI
RAMI
SEMI

M••J
MARJ

••MJ
UCMJ

M•K•
MAKE
MIKE
MOKE

M••K
MACK
MARK
MASK
MEEK
MILK
MINK
MOCK
MONK
MUCK
MUSK

•M•K
AMOK
OMSK

ML••
MLLE

M•L•
MALE
MALI
MALL
MALT
MELD
MELS
MELT
MILD
MILE
MILK
MILL
MILO
MILS
MILT
MLLE
MOLD
MOLE
MOLL
MOLT
MOLY
MULE
MULL
MULT

M••L
MAIL
MALL
MARL
MAUL
MEAL
MEWL
MILL
MOIL
MOLL
MULL
MYEL

•M•L
AMYL
EMIL

MM••
MMES

M•M•
MAMA
MEMO
MEMS
MIME
MIMI
MOMS
MUMM
MUMS

M••M
MAAM
MAIM
MUMM

•MM•
AMMO
EMMA
EMMY

IMMY

•M•M
IMAM

••MM
COMM
MUMM

M•N•
MANA
MANE
MANI
MANN
MANS
MANX
MANY
MEND
MENI
MENO
MENT
MENU
MINA
MIND
MINE
MING
MINI
MINK
MINN
MINT
MINX
MONA
MONK
MONO
MONS
MONT
MYNA

M••N
MAIN
MANN
MEAN
MIEN
MINN
MOAN
MOON
MORN
MOWN
MUON

•MN•
OMNI

•M•N
AMEN
AMON
GMAN
GMEN
IMIN
OMAN
OMEN

••MN
DAMN

GYMN
HYMN
LIMN

MO••
MOAB
MOAN
MOAS
MOAT
MOBS
MOCK
MODE
MODI
MODS
MOES
MOIL
MOKE
MOLD
MOLE
MOLL
MOLT
MOLY
MOMS
MONA
MONK
MONO
MONS
MONT
MOOD
MOON
MOOR
MOOS
MOOT
MOPE
MOPS
MORA
MORE
MORN
MORO
MORS
MORT
MOSE
MOSS
MOST
MOTE
MOTH
MOTS
MOTT
MOUE
MOVE
MOWN
MOWS
MOXA

M•O•
MEOW
MHOS
MOOD
MOON
MOOR
MOOS
MOOT
MUON

4

M••O
MAYO
MEMO
MENO
MERO
MESO
MILO
MISO
MONO
MORO
MUCO
MYCO
MYXO

•MO•
AMOK
AMON
AMOS
AMOY
SMOG

•M•O
AMBO
AMMO
UMBO

••MO
AMMO
ATMO
COMO
CYMO
DEMO
GAMO
HEMO
HOMO
MEMO
NOMO
SUMO
ZYMO

M•P•
MAPS
MOPE
MOPS

•MP•
AMPS
IMPI
IMPS

••MP
BUMP
CAMP
COMP
DAMP
DUMP
GAMP
GIMP
HEMP
HUMP
JUMP
LAMP
LIMP
LUMP
PIMP
POMP
PUMP
RAMP
RCMP
ROMP
RUMP
SAMP
SIMP
SUMP
TAMP
TEMP
VAMP

M•R•
MARC
MARE
MARJ
MARK
MARL
MARS
MART
MARX
MARY
MERE
MERO
MIRE
MIRS
MIRV
MORA
MORE
MORN
MORO
MORS
MORT
MYRA
MYRI

M••R
MEIR
METR
MOOR
MSGR
MUIR

•M•R
AMER
AMIR
AMUR
CMDR
EMIR
OMBR
OMER
YMER
YMIR

••MR
COMR

MS••
MSGR
MSGT
MSTH
MSTS

M•S•
MASC
MASH
MASK
MASS
MAST
MESA
MESH
MESO
MESS
MISC
MISE
MISO
MISS
MIST
MOSE
MOSS
MOST
MUSE
MUSH
MUSK
MUSS
MUST

M••S
MABS
MACS
MADS
MAES
MANS
MAPS
MARS
MASS
MATS
MAWS
MAYS
MEGS
MELS
MEMS
MESS
MEWS
MHOS
MIBS
MIGS
MILS
MIRS
MISS
MMES
MOAS
MOBS
MODS
MOES
MOMS
MONS
MOOS
MOPS
MORS
MOSS
MOTS
MOWS
MSTS
MUDS
MUGS
MUMS
MUSS
MUTS

•MS•
OMSK

•M•S
AMAS
AMES
AMIS
AMOS
AMPS
AMTS
AMUS
AMYS
BMUS
DMUS
EMUS
FMCS
IMPS
MMES
UMTS
XMAS

••MS
AIMS
ALMS
ARMS
BUMS
CAMS
DAMS
DIMS
DOMS
ELMS
GAMS
GEMS
GUMS
GYMS
HAMS
HEMS
HOMS
HUMS
ISMS
JAMS
JEMS
JIMS
LAMS
LEMS
MEMS
MOMS
MUMS
OHMS
PAMS
RAMS
REMS
RIMS
RUMS
SAMS
SIMS
SUMS
TAMS
TIMS
TOMS
USMS
YAMS

M•T•
MATE
MATH
MATS
MATT
META
METE
METH
METR
MITE
MITT
MOTE
MOTH
MOTS
MOTT
MSTH
MSTS
MUTE
MUTS
MUTT
MYTH

M••T
MALT
MART
MAST
MATT
MEAT
MEET
MELT
MENT
MILT
MINT
MIST
MITT
MIXT
MOAT
MOLT
MONT
MOOT
MORT
MOST
MOTT
MSGT
MULT
MUST
MUTT

•MT•
AMTS
UMTS

•M•T
EMIT
OMIT
SMIT
SMUT

MU••
MUCH
MUCI
MUCK
MUCO
MUDS
MUFF
MUGS
MUIR
MULE
MULL
MULT
MUMM
MUMS
MUON
MUSE
MUSH
MUSK
MUSS
MUST
MUTE
MUTS
MUTT

M•U•
MAUD
MAUI
MAUL
MOUE

M••U
MENU

•MU•
AMUR
AMUS
BMUS
DMUS
EMUS
SMUG
SMUT

•M•U
EMEU

M•V•
MOVE

M••V
MIRV

M•W•
MAWS
MEWL
MEWS
MOWN
MOWS

M••W
MEOW

•M•W
SMEW

M•X•
MIXT
MOXA
MYXO

M••X
MANX
MARX
MINX

MY••
MYCO
MYEL
MYNA
MYRA
MYRI
MYTH
MYXO

M•Y•
MAYA
MAYO
MAYS

M••Y
MANY
MARY
MAZY
MOLY

•MY•
AMYL
AMYS

•M•Y
AMOY
EMMY
IMMY

••MY
ARMY
DEMY
ELMY
EMMY
FUMY
GAMY
IMMY
LIMY
NOMY
RIMY
TOMY

M•Z•
MAZE
MAZY

NA••
NABS
NAGS
NAHA
NAIF
NAIL
NAMA
NAME
NANA
NANO
NANS
NAOS
NAPE
NAPS
NARC
NARD
NARY
NASA
NASH
NASO
NAST
NATE
NATL
NATO
NATS
NAUT
NAVE
NAVY
NAYS
NAZI

N•A•
NCAA
NCAR
NDAK
NEAL
NEAP
NEAR
NEAT
NOAH

N••A
NAHA
NAMA
NANA
NASA
NCAA
NEMA
NINA
NIPA
NITA
NOMA
NONA
NORA
NOVA

•NA•
ANAL
ANAM
ANAS
ANAT
GNAT
GNAW
INAS
KNAR
SNAG
SNAP
UNAS
UNAU

•N•A
ANNA
ANSA
ANTA
FNMA
INCA
INGA

INIA

••NA
ANNA
BUNA
CANA
DANA
DONA
DYNA
EDNA
ETNA
IANA
IONA
JENA
KANA
LENA
LUNA
MANA
MINA
MONA
MYNA
NANA
NINA
NONA
PINA
PUNA
TINA
TUNA
ULNA
USNA
VENA
VINA

N•B•
NABS
NEBO
NEBS
NIBS
NOBS
NUBS

N••B
NLRB
NUMB

•N•B
KNOB
SNOB
SNUB

NC••
NCAA
NCAR

N•C•
NECK
NECR
NICE
NICK
NOCK
NOCT

N••C
NARC

•NC•
ANCE
ANCY
ENCE
ENCL
ENCY
INCA
INCH
INCL
ONCE

••NC
CANC
CONC
JUNC
ZINC

ND••
NDAK

N•D•
NEDS
NIDE
NIDI
NODE
NODS
NUDE
NUDI

N••D
NARD
NEED
NKVD

•ND•
ANDY
ENDO
ENDS
INDO
UNDE
UNDO
UNDY

•N•D
ENID

••ND
BAND
BEND
BIND
BOND
BUND
COND
FEND
FIND
FOND
FUND
GOND
HAND
HIND
HOND
KIND
LAND
LEND
LIND
MEND
MIND
PEND
POND
RAND
REND
RIND
RYND
SAND
SEND
TEND
VEND
WAND
WEND
WIND
YOND
ZEND

NE••
NEAL
NEAP
NEAR
NEAT
NEBO
NEBS
NECK
NECR
NEDS
NEED
NEER
NEIL
NELL
NEMA
NEON
NEPH
NERO
NESS
NEST
NETS
NEUR
NEVE
NEVI
NEWS
NEWT
NEXT

N•E•
NEED
NEER
NOEL
NOES
NYET

N••E
NAME
NAPE
NATE
NAVE
NEVE
NICE
NIDE
NIKE
NILE
NINE
NIUE
NODE
NOME
NONE
NOPE
NOSE
NOTE
NUDE

•NE•
ANEW
INEZ
KNEE
KNEW
ONES

•N•E
ANCE
ANNE
ANTE
ENCE
INGE
KNEE
ONCE
SNYE
UNDE

••NE
ACNE
ANNE
AONE
BANE
BENE
BINE
BONE
CANE
CENE
CINE
CONE
DANE
DENE
DINE
DONE
DUNE
DYNE
ERNE
FINE
GENE
GONE
HONE
JANE
JUNE
KANE
KINE
LANE
LINE
LONE
LUNE
MANE
MINE
NINE
NONE
PANE
PINE
PONE
RENE
RUNE
SANE
SINE
SONE
SYNE
TINE
TONE
TUNE
VANE
VINE
WANE
WINE
ZONE

N••F
NAIF

••NF
CONF

N•G•
NAGS
NIGH
NIGR
NOGG
NOGS

N••G
NOGG

•NG•
ENGR
INGA
INGE

•N•G
SNAG
SNUG

••NG
BANG
BENG
BONG
BUNG
CONG
DANG
DING
DUNG
FANG
FUNG
GANG
GONG
HANG
HONG
HUNG
JUNG
KING
LANG
LING
LONG
LUNG
MING
PANG
PING
PUNG
RANG
RING
RUNG
SANG
SING
SONG
SUNG
TANG
TING
TONG
VANG
WING
YANG
ZING

N•H•
NAHA

N••H
NASH
NEPH
NIGH
NOAH

•N•H
ANKH
ANTH
INCH

NI••
NIBS
NICE
NICK
NIDE
NIDI
NIGH
NIGR
NIKE
NILE
NINA
NINE
NIPA
NIPS
NISI
NITA
NITR
NITS
NIUE

N•I•
NAIF
NAIL
NEIL
NOIL

N••I
NAZI
NEVI
NIDI
NISI
NUDI

•NI•
ANIL
ANIM
ANIS
ENID
INIA
INIT
KNIT
SNIP
SNIT
UNIT

•N•I
ANTI
INRI

••NI
AGNI
BANI
BENI
IGNI
LUNI
MANI
MENI
MINI
OMNI
RANI
RENI
TONI
VENI
VINI

••NJ
CONJ

NK••
NKVD

N•K•
NIKE

N••K
NDAK
NECK
NICK
NOCK
NOOK

•NK•
ANKH
INKS
INKY

••NK
BANK
BUNK
CONK
DANK
DUNK
FINK
FUNK
GINK
HANK
HONK
HUNK
JINK
JUNK
KINK
LANK
LINK
MINK
MONK
PINK
PUNK
RANK
RINK
SANK
SINK
SUNK
TANK
WINK
YANK

NL••
NLRB

N•L•
NELL
NILE
NULL

N••L
NAIL
NATL
NEAL
NEIL
NELL
NOEL
NOIL
NULL

•NL•
INLY
ONLY

•N•L
ANAL
ANIL
ENCL
ENOL
INCL

••NL
GENL

N•M•
NAMA
NAME
NEMA
NOMA
NOME
NOMO
NOMY
NUMB

N••M
NORM

•NM•
FNMA

•N•M
ANAM
ANIM

N•N•
NANA
NANO
NANS
NINA
NINE
NONA
NONE
NUNS

N••N
NEON
NOON
NORN
NOUN

•NN•
ANNA
ANNE
ANNO
ANNS
INNS

•N•N
ANON

••NN
BONN
BUNN
CONN
FINN
JINN
LYNN
MANN
MINN
PENN
SUNN
TENN

NO••
NOAH
NOBS
NOCK
NOCT
NODE
NODS
NOEL
NOES
NOGG
NOGS
NOIL
NOMA
NOME
NOMO
NOMY
NONA
NONE
NOOK
NOON
NOPE
NORA
NORM
NORN
NOSE
NOSO
NOSY
NOTE
NOTO
NOUN
NOVA
NOWS

N•O•
NAOS
NEON
NOOK
NOON

N••O
NANO
NASO
NATO
NEBO
NERO
NOMO
NOSO
NOTO

•NO•
ANON
ENOL
ENOS
KNOB
KNOP
KNOT
KNOW
KNOX
SNOB
SNOT
SNOW

•N•O
ANNO
ENDO
ENTO
INDO
INTO
ONTO
UNDO
UNTO

••NO
AINO
ANNO
ARNO
BRNO
CENO
DINO
FANO
GONO
GYNO
JUNO
KANO
KENO
KINO
LENO
MENO
MONO
NANO
OENO
OINO
RENO
SINO
TENO
TONO
VINO
WINO
XENO
ZENO

N•P•
NAPE
NAPS
NEPH
NIPA
NIPS
NOPE

N••P
NEAP

•N•P
INSP
KNOP
SNAP
SNIP

N•R•
NARC
NARD
NARY
NERO
NLRB
NORA
NORM
NORN

N••R
NCAR
NEAR
NECR
NEER
NEUR
NIGR
NITR

•NR•
INRI

•N•R
ENGR
KNAR
KNUR

••NR
USNR

N•S•
NASA
NASH
NASO
NAST
NESS
NEST
NISI
NOSE
NOSO
NOSY

N••S
NABS
NAGS
NANS
NAOS
NAPS
NATS
NAYS
NEBS
NEDS
NESS
NETS
NEWS
NIBS
NIPS
NITS
NOBS
NODS
NOES
NOGS
NOWS
NUBS
NUNS
NUTS

•NS•
ANSA
INSP
INST

•N•S
ANAS
ANIS
ANNS
ANTS
ANUS
ENDS
ENOS
GNUS
INAS
INKS
INNS
ONES
ONUS
UNAS

••NS
AINS
ANNS
ARNS
AWNS
BANS
BENS
BINS
BUNS
CANS
CONS
DANS
DENS
DINS
DONS
DUNS
EENS
EONS
ERNS
FANS
FENS
FINS
FUNS
GENS
GINS
GUNS
HANS
HENS
HUNS
IANS
INNS
IONS
JANS
JONS
KANS
KENS
LENS
MANS
MONS
NANS
NUNS
OWNS
PANS
PENS
PINS
PONS
PUNS
RUNS
SANS
SINS
SONS
SUNS
TANS
TENS
TINS
TONS
TUNS
URNS
VANS
WANS
WENS
WINS
YENS

N•T•
NATE
NATL
NATO
NATS
NETS
NITA
NITR
NITS
NOTE
NOTO
NUTS

N••T
NAST
NAUT
NEAT
NEST
NEWT
NEXT
NOCT
NYET

•NT•
ANTA
ANTE
ANTH
ANTI
ANTS
ENTO
INTO
ONTO
UNTO
XNTY

•N•T
ANAT
GNAT
INIT
INST
KNIT
KNOT
SNIT
SNOT
UNIT

••NT
AINT
AUNT
BENT
BUNT
CANT
CENT
CONT
DENT
DINT
DONT
FONT
GENT
HINT
HUNT
ISNT
KANT
KENT
LENT
LINT
LUNT
MENT
MINT
MONT
PANT
PENT
PINT
PUNT
RANT
RENT
RUNT
SENT
TENT
TINT
VENT
WANT
WENT
WONT
XINT

NU••
NUBS
NUDE
NUDI
NULL
NUMB
NUNS
NUTS

N•U•
NAUT
NEUR
NIUE
NOUN

•NU•
ANUS
GNUS
KNUR
ONUS
SNUB
SNUG

•N•U
UNAU

••NU
AINU
DANU
GENU
MENU

N•V•
NAVE
NAVY
NEVE
NEVI
NKVD
NOVA

•NV•
ENVY

N•W•
NEWS
NEWT
NOWS

•N•W
ANEW
GNAW
KNEW
KNOW
SNOW

N•X•
NEXT

•N•X
KNOX
ONYX
PNYX

••NX
JINX
LYNX
MANX
MINX

NY••
NYET

N•Y•
NAYS

N••Y
NARY
NAVY
NOMY
NOSY

•NY•
ONYX
PNYX
SNYE

•N•Y
ANCY
ANDY
ENCY
ENVY
INKY
INLY
ONLY
UNDY
XNTY

••NY
AWNY
BONY
CONY
DENY
GENY
LINY
MANY
PINY
PONY

PUNY
TINY
TONY
VINY
WANY
WINY
ZANY

N•Z•
NAZI

•N•Z
INEZ

••NZ
LINZ

OA••
OAFS
OAHU
OAKS
OARS
OATH
OATS

O•A•
OKAS
OKAY
OLAF
OLAV
OMAN
OPAH
OPAL
ORAL
ORAN
OSAR
OVAL

O••A
OBIA
OCTA
ODEA
OKLA
OKRA
OLGA
OLLA
OPIA
OSSA

•OA•
BOAR
BOAS
BOAT
COAL
COAT
COAX
FOAL
FOAM
GOAD
GOAL
GOAS
GOAT
HOAR
HOAX
JOAB
JOAN
LOAD
LOAF
LOAM
LOAN
MOAB
MOAN
MOAS
MOAT
NOAH
ROAD
ROAM
ROAN
ROAR
SOAK
SOAP
SOAR
TOAD
WOAD
ZOAN

•O•A
BOLA
BORA
COCA
CODA
COLA
COMA
CORA
COXA
DONA
DORA
FORA
GOYA
HORA
IONA
IOTA
IOWA
KOLA
LOLA
MONA
MORA
MOXA
NOMA
NONA
NORA
NOVA
PODA
ROMA
ROSA
ROTA
SODA
SOFA
SOJA
SOLA
SOMA
SORA
SOYA
TOGA
TOLA
VORA
YOGA
ZOLA

••OA
PROA
STOA
WHOA

OB••
OBEY
OBIA
OBIS
OBIT
OBOE
OBOL

O•B•
OMBR
ORBS

•OB•
BOBS
COBB
COBS
DOBY
FOBS
GOBI
GOBO
GOBS
GOBY
HOBO
HOBS
IOBB
JOBS
KOBE
LOBE
LOBO
LOBS
MOBS
NOBS
ROBE
ROBS
SOBS
TOBY

•O•B
BOMB
BOOB
COBB
COMB
FORB
IOBB
JOAB
MOAB
SORB
TOMB
WOMB

••OB
BLOB
BOOB
GLOB
KNOB
SLOB
SNOB

OC••
OCTA
OCTO
OCUL

O•C•
ONCE
ORCS
OUCH

O••C
ODIC
OTIC

•OC•
BOCK
COCA
COCK
COCO
DOCK
FOCH
FOCI
HOCK
JOCK
LOCH
LOCI
LOCK
LOCO
MOCK
NOCK
NOCT
POCK
POCO
ROCK
SOCK
TOCO

•O•C
CONC
ROTC
ZOIC

••OC
APOC
BLOC
FLOC

OD••
ODDS
ODEA
ODER
ODES
ODIC
ODIN
ODOR
ODYL

O•D•
ODDS
ORDO

O••D
OKED
OVID
OWED

•OD•
BODE
BODY
CODA
CODE
CODS
CODY
DODO
GODS
HODS
IODO
LODE
LODI
LODZ
MODE
MODI
MODS
NODE
NODS
PODA
PODS
RODE
RODS
SODA
SODS
TODD
TODO
TODS
TODY
YODH
YODS

•O•D
BOLD
BOND
BOYD
COED
COLD
COND
CORD
FOLD
FOND
FOOD
FORD
GOAD
GOLD
GOND
GOOD
HOED
HOLD
HOND
HOOD
LOAD
LORD
LOUD
MOLD
MOOD
POND
POOD
ROAD
ROOD
SOLD
TOAD
TODD
TOED
TOLD
VOID
WOAD
WOLD
WOOD
WORD
YOND

••OD
CLOD
EXOD
FEOD
FOOD
GOOD
HOOD
MOOD
PLOD
POOD
PROD
QUOD
ROOD
SHOD
TROD
WOOD

OE••
OENO

O•E•
OBEY
ODEA
ODER
ODES
OGEE
OKED
OLEO
OMEN
OMER
ONES
OPEN
ORES
OVEN
OVER
OWED
OWEN
OWES
OXEN
OYER
OYES
OYEZ

O••E
OBOE
OGEE
OGLE
OGRE
OKIE
ONCE
OOZE
ORLE
OSTE
OUSE

•OE•
BOER
COED
COEF
COEL
DOER
DOES
FOES
GOER
GOES
HOED
HOER
HOES
JOEL
JOES
JOEY
KOEL
MOES
NOEL
NOES
POEM
POET
ROES
TOED
TOES
WOES
ZOES

•O•E
AONE
BODE
BOLE
BONE
BORE
CODE
COKE
COLE
COME
CONE
COPE
CORE
COTE
COUE
COVE
DOGE
DOLE
DOME
DONE
DOPE
DOSE
DOTE
DOVE
DOZE
FORE
GONE
GORE
HOLE
HOME
HONE
HOPE
HOSE
HOVE
HOWE
JOKE
JOSE
JOVE
KOBE
LOBE
LODE
LOGE
LOME
LONE
LOPE
LORE
LOSE
LOVE
MODE
MOKE
MOLE
MOPE
MORE
MOSE
MOTE
MOUE
MOVE
NODE
NOME
NONE
NOPE
NOSE
NOTE
OOZE
POKE
POLE
POME
PONE
POPE
PORE
POSE
ROBE
RODE
ROLE
ROME
ROPE
ROSE
ROTE
ROUE
ROVE
SOKE
SOLE
SOME
SONE
SORE
TOLE
TOME
TONE
TOPE
TORE
TOTE
VOLE
VORE
VOTE
WOKE
WORE
WOVE
YOKE

YORE
ZONE

••OE
ALOE
FLOE
FROE
OBOE
SHOE
SLOE

O•F•
OAFS

O••F
OLAF

•OF•
DOFF
LOFT
SOFA
SOFT
TOFT

•O•F
COEF
COIF
CONF
CORF
DOFF
DOLF
GOLF
GOOF
HOOF
LOAF
LOOF
POUF
ROLF
ROOF
WOLF
WOOF

••OF
GOOF
HOOF
LOOF
PROF
ROOF
WOOF

OG••
OGEE
OGLE
OGPU
OGRE

O•G•
OLGA
ORGY

O••G
OLIG
ORIG

•OG•
BOGS
BOGY
COGS
DOGE
DOGS
DOGY
FOGS
FOGY
GOGH
GOGO
HOGS
JOGS
LOGE
LOGO
LOGS
LOGY
NOGG
NOGS
POGY
TOGA
TOGO
TOGS
YOGA
YOGH
YOGI

•O•G
BONG
CONG
DOUG
GONG
HONG
LONG
NOGG
SONG
TONG

••OG
AGOG
CLOG
FLOG
FROG
GROG
SLOG
SMOG

OH••
OHIO
OHMS

O•H•
OAHU
OPHI

O••H
OATH
OPAH
ORTH
OUCH

•OH•
BOHR
FOHN
JOHN
KOHL
SOHO

•O•H
BOSH
BOTH
COSH
DOTH
FOCH
GOGH
GOSH
GOTH
JOSH
KOPH
LOCH
LOTH
MOTH
NOAH
POOH
POSH
TOPH
TOSH
YODH
YOGH

••OH
POOH

OI••
OILS
OILY
OINO

O•I•
OBIA
OBIS
OBIT
ODIC
ODIN
OHIO
OKIE
OLIG
OLIO
OMIT
OPIA
ORIG
OSIS
OTIC
OTIS
OVID

O••I
OMNI
OPHI
OSSI

•OI•
BOIL
BOIS
COIF
COIL
COIN
COIR
DOIT
FOIL
JOIN
LOIN
LOIS
MOIL
NOIL
ROIL
SOIL
TOIL
VOID
ZOIC

•O•I
BOVI
FOCI
GOBI
HOPI
LOCI
LODI
MODI
SOLI
SORI
TONI
TOPI
TORI
TOTI
YOGI

•OJ•
SOJA

•O•J
CONJ

OK••
OKAS
OKAY
OKED
OKIE
OKLA
OKRA

O•K•
OAKS

O••K
OMSK

•OK•
COKE
JOKE
MOKE
POKE
POKY
SOKE
WOKE
YOKE

•O•K
BOCK
BOOK
BOSK
COCK
CONK
COOK
CORK
DOCK
FOLK
FORK
GOOK
HOCK
HONK
HOOK
JOCK
KOOK
LOCK
LOOK
MOCK
MONK
NOCK
NOOK
POCK
POLK
PORK
ROCK
ROOK
SOAK
SOCK
TOOK
WORK
YOLK
YORK

••OK
AMOK
BOOK
COOK
GOOK
HOOK
KOOK
LOOK
NOOK
ROOK
TOOK

OL••
OLAF
OLAV
OLEO
OLGA
OLIG
OLIO
OLLA
OLLY

O•L•
OGLE
OILS
OILY
OKLA
OLLA
OLLY
ONLY
ORLE
OWLS

O••L
OBOL
OCUL
ODYL
OPAL
ORAL
OVAL

•OL•
BOLA
BOLD
BOLE
BOLL
BOLO
BOLT
COLA
COLD
COLE
COLL
COLO
COLS
COLT
COLY
DOLE
DOLF
DOLL
DOLS
DOLT
FOLD
FOLK
FOLL
GOLD
GOLF
HOLD
HOLE
HOLM
HOLO
HOLY
JOLO
JOLT
KOLA
LOLA
LOLL
MOLD
MOLE
MOLL
MOLT
MOLY
POLE
POLK
POLL
POLO
POLY
ROLE
ROLF
ROLL
SOLA
SOLD
SOLE
SOLI
SOLO
SOLS
TOLA
TOLD
TOLE
TOLL
TOLU
VOLE
VOLS
VOLT
WOLD
WOLF
YOLK
ZOLA

•O•L
BOIL
BOLL
BOWL
COAL
COEL
COIL
COLL
COOL
COWL
DOLL
FOAL
FOIL
FOLL
FOOL
FOUL
FOWL
GOAL
HOWL
JOEL
JOWL
KOEL
KOHL
LOLL
MOIL
MOLL
NOEL
NOIL
POLL
POOL
ROIL
ROLL
ROTL
SOIL
SOUL
TOIL
TOLL
TOOL
WOOL
YOWL
ZOOL

••OL
AWOL
BIOL
CHOL
COOL
ECOL
ENOL
FOOL
GAOL
GEOL
IDOL
ITOL
OBOL
POOL
STOL
TOOL
VIOL
VTOL
WOOL
ZOOL

OM••
OMAN
OMBR
OMEN
OMER
OMIT
OMNI
OMSK

O•M•
OHMS

O••M
OVUM

•OM•
BOMB
COMA
COMB
COME
COMM
COMO
COMP
COMR
DOME
DOMS
HOME
HOMO
HOMS
LOME
MOMS
NOMA
NOME
NOMO
NOMY
POME
POMP
ROMA
ROME
ROMP
SOMA
SOME
TOMB
TOME
TOMS
TOMY
WOMB

•O•M
BOOM
COMM
CORM
COSM
DOOM

DORM FOAM FORM HOLM LOAM LOOM NORM POEM ROAM ROOM WORM ZOOM

••OM

ATOM BOOM BROM DOOM EDOM FROM GEOM LOOM PROM ROOM WHOM ZOOM

ON••

ONCE ONES ONLY ONTO ONUS ONYX

O•N•

OENO OINO OMNI OWNS

O••N

ODIN OMAN OMEN OPEN ORAN OVEN OWEN OXEN OXON

•ON•

AONE BOND BONE BONG BONN BONY CONC COND CONE CONF CONG CONJ CONK CONN CONS CONT CONY DONA DONE DONS DONT EONS FOND FONT GOND GONE GONG GONO HOND HONE HONG HONK IONA IONS JONS LONE LONG MONA MONK MONO MONS MONT NONA NONE POND PONE PONS PONY SONE SONG SONS TONE TONG TONI TONO TONS TONY WONT YOND ZONE

•O•N

BONN BOON BORN BOSN COIN CONN COON CORN DOON DOWN FOHN GOON GOWN HORN JOAN JOHN JOIN LOAN LOIN LOON MOAN MOON MORN MOWN NOON NORN NOUN POON PORN ROAN SOON SOWN TOON TORN TOWN WORN ZOAN ZOON

••ON

AEON AGON AMON ANON AVON AXON AZON BION BOON CION CLON COON DION DOON EBON ECON ETON GOON ICON IKON IRON LEON LION LOON MOON MUON NEON NOON OXON PEON PHON PION POON PRON SION SOON TION TOON TRON UPON XION ZION ZOON

OO••

OOZE OOZY

O•O•

OBOE OBOL ODOR OXON

O••O

OCTO OENO OHIO OINO OLEO OLIO ONTO ORDO OTTO

•OO•

BOOB BOOK BOOM BOON BOOR BOOS BOOT COOK COOL COON COOP COOS COOT DOOM DOON DOOR FOOD FOOL FOOT GOOD GOOF GOOK GOON GOOP HOOD HOOF HOOK HOOP HOOT KOOK LOOF LOOK LOOM LOON LOOP LOOS LOOT MOOD MOON MOOR MOOS MOOT NOOK NOON POOD POOH POOL POON POOP POOR ROOD ROOF ROOK ROOM ROOT SOON SOOT TOOK TOOL TOON TOOT WOOD WOOF WOOL WOOS ZOOL ZOOM ZOON ZOOS

•O•O

BOLO BOZO COCO COLO COMO DODO GOBO GOGO GONO HOBO HOLO HOMO IODO JOLO KOTO LOBO LOCO LOGO MONO MORO NOMO NOSO NOTO POCO POLO SOHO SOLO SOSO TOCO TODO TOGO TONO TOPO TOYO YOYO

••OO

BROO SHOO

OP••

OPAH OPAL OPEN OPHI OPIA OPSY OPTS OPUS

O•P•

OGPU

•OP•

BOPS COPE COPR COPS COPT COPY DOPE DOPY FOPS HOPE HOPI HOPS KOPH KOPS LOPE LOPS MOPE MOPS NOPE POPE POPS ROPE ROPY SOPS TOPE TOPH TOPI TOPO TOPS

•O•P

COMP COOP CORP COUP GOOP HOOP LOOP LOUP POMP POOP ROMP ROUP SOAP SOUP

••OP

ATOP CHOP CLOP COOP CROP DROP FLOP GOOP HOOP KNOP LOOP PLOP POOP PROP SCOP SHOP SLOP STOP TROP WHOP

OR••

ORAL ORAN ORBS ORCS ORDO ORES ORGY ORIG ORLE ORTH ORYX

O•R•

OARS OGRE OKRA OURS

O••R

ODER ODOR OMBR OMER OSAR OVER OYER

•OR•

BORA BORE BORN BORT CORA CORD CORE CORF CORK CORM CORN CORP DORA DORM DORR DORS DORY FORA FORB FORD FORE FORK FORM FORT GORE GORY HORA HORN HORT KORS LORD LORE LORY MORA MORE MORN MORO MORS MORT NORA NORM NORN PORE PORK PORN PORT RORY SORA SORB SORE SORI SORT TORE TORI TORN TORS TORT TORY VORA VORE WORD WORE WORK WORM WORN WORT YORE YORK

•O•R
BOAR
BOER
BOHR
BOOR
COIR
COMR
COPR
DOER
DOOR
DORR
DOUR
FOUR
GOER
HOAR
HOER
HOUR
LOUR
MOOR
POOR
POUR
ROAR
SOAR
SOUR
TOUR
YOUR

••OR
ATOR
BOOR
DOOR
FLOR
GYOR
IVOR
MOOR
ODOR
POOR
SPOR
THOR

OS••
OSAR
OSIS
OSSA
OSSI
OSTE

O•S•
OMSK
OPSY
OSSA
OSSI
OUSE
OUST

O••S
OAFS
OAKS
OARS
OATS
OBIS
ODDS
ODES
OHMS
OILS
OKAS
ONES
ONUS
OPTS
OPUS
ORBS
ORCS
ORES
OSIS
OTIS
OURS
OUTS
OWES
OWLS
OWNS
OYES

•OS•
BOSH
BOSK
BOSN
BOSS
COSH
COSM
COSS
COST
DOSE
DOST
FOSS
GOSH
HOSE
HOST
JOSE
JOSH
JOSS
LOSE
LOSS
LOST
MOSE
MOSS
MOST
NOSE
NOSO
NOSY
POSE
POSH
POST
POSY
ROSA
ROSE
ROSS
ROSY
SOSO
TOSH
TOSS

•O•S
BOAS
BOBS
BOGS
BOIS
BOOS
BOPS
BOSS
BOTS
BOWS
BOYS
COBS
CODS
COGS
COLS
CONS
COOS
COPS
COSS
COTS
COWS
DOES
DOGS
DOLS
DOMS
DONS
DORS
DOTS
EONS
EOUS
FOBS
FOES
FOGS
FOPS
FOSS
FOYS
GOAS
GOBS
GODS
GOES
HOBS
HODS
HOES
HOGS
HOMS
HOPS
HOYS
IONS
IOUS
JOBS
JOES
JOGS
JONS
JOSS
JOTS
JOYS
KOPS
KORS
LOBS
LOGS
LOIS
LOOS
LOPS
LOSS
LOTS
LOWS
MOAS
MOBS
MODS
MOES
MOMS
MONS
MOOS
MOPS
MORS
MOSS
MOTS
MOWS
NOBS
NODS
NOES
NOGS
NOWS
PODS
PONS
POPS
POTS
POWS
ROBS
RODS
ROES
ROSS
ROTS
ROWS
ROYS
SOBS
SODS
SOLS
SONS
SOPS
SOTS
SOUS
SOWS
SOYS
TODS
TOES
TOGS
TOMS
TONS
TOPS
TORS
TOSS
TOTS
TOWS
TOYS
VOLS
VOWS
WOES
WOOS
WOWS
YODS
YOWS
ZOES
ZOOS

••OS
AMOS
BOOS
COOS
DUOS
EGOS
ENOS
EPOS
EROS
KEOS
LAOS
LEOS
LOOS
MHOS
MOOS
NAOS
PROS
RHOS
TAOS
TWOS
UDOS
WOOS
ZOOS

OT••
OTIC
OTIS
OTTO

O•T•
OATH
OATS
OCTA
OCTO
ONTO
OPTS
ORTH
OSTE
OTTO
OUTS

O••T
OBIT
OMIT
OUST

•OT•
BOTH
BOTS
BOTT
COTE
COTS
DOTE
DOTH
DOTS
DOTY
GOTH
IOTA
JOTS
KOTO
LOTH
LOTS
LOTT
MOTE
MOTH
MOTS
MOTT
NOTE
NOTO
POTS
ROTA
ROTC
ROTE
ROTL
ROTS
SOTS
TOTE
TOTI
TOTS
VOTE

•O•T
BOAT
BOLT
BOOT
BORT
BOTT
BOUT
COAT
COLT
CONT
COOT
COPT
COST
DOIT
DOLT
DONT
DOST
FONT
FOOT
FORT
GOAT
GOUT
GOVT
HOOT
HORT
HOST
JOLT
LOFT
LOOT
LOST
LOTT
LOUT
MOAT
MOLT
MONT
MOOT
MORT
MOST
MOTT
NOCT
POET
PORT
POST
POUT
ROOT
ROUT
SOFT
SOOT
SORT
TOFT
TOOT
TORT
TOUT
VOLT
WONT
WORT

••OT
BLOT
BOOT
CLOT
COOT
FOOT
GLOT
GROT
HOOT
KNOT
LOOT
MOOT
PHOT
PLOT
PROT
RIOT
ROOT
RYOT
SCOT
SHOT
SLOT
SNOT
SOOT
SPOT
TOOT
TROT

OU••
OUCH
OURS
OUSE
OUST
OUTS

O•U•
OCUL
ONUS
OPUS
OVUM

O••U
OAHU
OGPU

•OU•
BOUT
COUE
COUP
DOUG
DOUR
EOUS
FOUL
FOUR
GOUT
HOUR
IOUS
LOUD
LOUP
LOUR
LOUT
MOUE
NOUN
POUF
POUR
POUT
ROUE
ROUP
ROUT
ROUX
SOUL
SOUP
SOUR
SOUS
TOUR
TOUT
YOUR

•O•U
TOLU

••OU
ACOU
CHOU
THOU

OV••
OVAL
OVEN
OVER
OVID
OVUM

O••V
OLAV

•OV•
BOVI
COVE
DOVE
GOVT
HOVE
JOVE
LOVE
MOVE
NOVA
ROVE
WOVE

••OV
AZOV

OW••
OWED
OWEN
OWES
OWLS
OWNS

•OW•
BOWL
BOWS
COWL
COWS
DOWN
FOWL
GOWN
HOWE
HOWL

IOWA
JOWL
LOWS
MOWN
MOWS
NOWS
POWS
ROWS
SOWN
SOWS
TOWN
TOWS
VOWS
WOWS
YOWL
YOWS

••OW
ALOW
AVOW
BLOW
BROW
CHOW
CROW
DHOW
FLOW
FROW
GLOW
GROW
KNOW
MEOW
PLOW
PROW
SCOW
SHOW
SLOW
SNOW
STOW

OX••
OXEN
OXON

O••X
ONYX
ORYX

•OX•
COXA
DOXY
FOXY
MOXA
ROXY

•O•X
COAX
HOAX
ROUX

••OX
KNOX

OY••
OYER
OYES
OYEZ

O•Y•
ODYL
ONYX
ORYX

O••Y
OBEY
OILY
OKAY
OLLY
ONLY
OOZY
OPSY
ORGY

•OY•
BOYD
BOYS
FOYS
GOYA
HOYS
JOYS
ROYS
SOYA
SOYS
TOYO
TOYS
YOYO

•O•Y
BODY
BOGY
BONY
CODY
COLY
CONY
COPY
COZY
DOBY
DOGY
DOPY
DORY
DOTY
DOXY
DOZY
FOGY
FOXY
GOBY
GORY
HOLY
JOEY
LOGY
LORY
MOLY
NOMY
NOSY
OOZY
POGY
POKY
POLY
PONY
POSY
ROPY
RORY
ROSY
ROXY
TOBY
TODY
TOMY
TONY
TORY

••OY
AHOY
AMOY
BUOY
CLOY
PLOY
TROY

O•Z•
OOZE
OOZY

O••Z
OYEZ

•OZ•
BOZO
COZY
DOZE
DOZY
OOZE
OOZY

•O•Z
LODZ

••OZ
BROZ

PA••
PABA
PACA
PACE
PACK
PACT
PADS
PAED
PAGE
PAID
PAIL
PAIN
PAIR
PALE
PALI
PALL
PALM
PALP
PALS
PALY
PAMS
PANE
PANG
PANS
PANT
PAPA
PAPS
PARA
PARD
PARE
PARI
PARK
PARR
PARS
PART
PASS
PAST
PATE
PATH
PATS
PAUL
PAVE
PAVO
PAWL
PAWN
PAWS
PAYS

P•A•
PEAG
PEAK
PEAL
PEAN
PEAR
PEAS
PEAT
PHAG
PLAN
PLAT
PLAY
PRAE
PRAM
PRAY
PTAH

P••A
PABA
PACA
PAPA
PARA
PERA
PICA
PIKA
PIMA
PINA
PITA
PLEA
PODA
PROA
PUMA
PUNA
PUPA

•PA•
OPAH
OPAL
SPAM
SPAN
SPAR
SPAS
SPAT
SPAY
UPAS

•P•A
APIA
OPIA
SPCA

••PA
HUPA
KAPA
NIPA
PAPA
PUPA
TAPA

P•B•
PABA
PUBS

P••B
PLEB

P•C•
PACA
PACE
PACK
PACT
PECK
PICA
PICE
PICK
PICO
PICR
PICT
POCK
POCO
PUCE
PUCK

P••C
PISC
PYIC

•PC•
SPCA
SPCC

•P•C
APOC
EPIC
SPCC
SPEC

P•D•
PADS
PEDE
PEDI
PEDO
PHDS
PODA
PODS

P••D
PAED
PAID
PARD
PEND
PIED
PLED
PLOD
POND
POOD
PROD

•P•D
APED
SPED
SPUD

PE••
PEAG
PEAK
PEAL
PEAN
PEAR
PEAS
PEAT
PECK
PEDE
PEDI
PEDO
PEEK
PEEL
PEEN
PEEP
PEER
PEES
PEGS
PELE
PELF
PELT
PEND
PENN
PENS
PENT
PEON
PEPO
PEPS
PERA
PERE
PERI
PERK
PERT
PERU
PESO
PEST
PETE
PETR
PETS
PEWS

P•E•
PAED
PEEK
PEEL
PEEN
PEEP
PEER
PEES
PHEN
PHEW
PIED
PIER
PIES
PLEA
PLEB
PLED
POEM
POET
PREP
PRES
PREY
PTER
PYEL
PYES

P••E
PACE
PAGE
PALE
PANE
PARE
PATE
PAVE
PEDE
PELE
PERE
PETE
PICE
PIKE
PILE
PINE
PIPE
POKE
POLE
POME
PONE
POPE
PORE
POSE
PRAE
PRUE
PUCE
PUKE
PULE
PURE
PYLE
PYRE

•PE•
APED
APES
APEX
EPEE
OPEN
SPEC
SPED
SPEW

•P•E
APSE
EPEE

••PE
CAPE
COPE
DOPE
DUPE
GAPE
HOPE
JAPE
LOPE
MOPE
NAPE
NOPE
PIPE
POPE
RAPE
RIPE
ROPE
SUPE
TAPE
TOPE
TYPE
WIPE
YIPE

P•F•
PUFF

P••F
PELF
POUF
PROF
PUFF

P•G•
PAGE
PEGS
PIGS
POGY
PUGH
PUGS

P••G
PANG
PEAG
PHAG
PING
PLUG
PRIG
PUNG

PH••
PHAG
PHDS
PHEN
PHEW
PHIL
PHIS
PHON
PHOT
PHYL

4

PHYT

P••H
PATH
PISH
PITH
POOH
POSH
PTAH
PUGH
PUSH

•PH•
OPHI

•P•H
OPAH

••PH
ALPH
KAPH
KOPH
NEPH
TOPH
XIPH
ZEPH

PI••
PICA
PICE
PICK
PICO
PICR
PICT
PIED
PIER
PIES
PIGS
PIKA
PIKE
PILE
PILI
PILL
PIMA
PIMP
PINA
PINE
PING
PINK
PINS
PINT
PINY
PION
PIPE
PIPS
PIPY
PISC
PISH
PITA
PITH
PITS
PITT
PITY
PIUS
PIXY
PIZZ

P•I•
PAID
PAIL
PAIN
PAIR
PHIL
PHIS
PRIG
PRIM
PSIS
PYIC
PYIN

P••I
PALI
PARI
PEDI
PERI
PILI
PURI

•PI•
APIA
APIS
EPIC
OPIA
SPIN
SPIR
SPIT

•P•I
OPHI

••PI
HOPI
IMPI
KEPI
TOPI
TUPI

P•K•
PIKA
PIKE
POKE
POKY
PUKE

P••K
PACK
PARK
PEAK
PECK
PEEK
PERK
PICK
PINK
POCK
POLK
PORK
PUCK
PUNK

PL••
PLAN
PLAT
PLAY
PLEA
PLEB
PLED
PLOD
PLOP
PLOT
PLOW
PLOY
PLUG
PLUM
PLUS

P•L•
PALE
PALI
PALL
PALM
PALP
PALS
PALY
PELE
PELF
PELT
PILE
PILI
PILL
POLE
POLK
POLL
POLO
POLY
PULE
PULL
PULP
PYLE

P••L
PAIL
PALL
PAUL
PAWL
PEAL
PEEL
PHIL
PHYL
PILL
POLL
POOL
PULL
PURL
PYEL

•P•L
OPAL

••PL
DIPL
HAPL

P•M•
PAMS
PIMA
PIMP
POME
POMP
PUMA
PUMP

P••M
PALM
PLUM
POEM
PRAM
PRIM
PROM

•P•M
SPAM

PN••
PNYX

P•N•
PANE
PANG
PANS
PANT
PEND
PENN
PENS
PENT
PINA
PINE
PING
PINK
PINS
PINT
PINY
POND
PONE
PONS
PONY
PUNA
PUNG
PUNK
PUNS
PUNT
PUNY

P••N
PAIN
PAWN
PEAN
PEEN
PENN
PEON
PHEN
PHON
PION
PLAN
POON
PORN
PRON
PYIN

•P•N
OPEN
SPAN
SPIN
SPUN
UPON

PO••
POCK
POCO
PODA
PODS
POEM
POET
POGY
POKE
POKY
POLE
POLK
POLL
POLO
POLY
POME
POMP
POND
PONE
PONS
PONY
POOD
POOH
POOL
POON
POOP
POOR
POPE
POPS
PORE
PORK
PORN
PORT
POSE
POSH
POST
POSY
POTS
POUF
POUR
POUT
POWS

P•O•
PEON
PHON
PHOT
PION
PLOD
PLOP
PLOT
PLOW
PLOY
POOD
POOH
POOL
POON
POOP
POOR
PROA
PROD
PROF
PROM
PRON
PROP
PROS
PROT
PROW

P••O
PAVO
PEDO
PEPO
PESO
PICO
POCO
POLO
PYRO

•PO•
APOC
EPOS
SPOR
SPOT
UPON

••PO
HYPO
LIPO
PEPO
TOPO
TYPO

P•P•
PAPA
PAPS
PEPO
PEPS
PIPE
PIPS
PIPY
POPE
POPS
PUPA
PUPS

P••P
PALP
PEEP
PIMP
PLOP
POMP
POOP
PREP
PROP
PULP
PUMP

••PP
HIPP
LAPP
REPP
SUPP

•PQ•
SPQR

PR••
PRAE
PRAM
PRAY
PREP
PRES
PREY
PRIG
PRIM
PROA
PROD
PROF
PROM
PRON
PROP
PROS
PROT
PROW
PRUE

P•R•
PARA
PARD
PARE
PARI
PARK
PARR
PARS
PART
PERA
PERE
PERI
PERK
PERT
PERU
PORE
PORK
PORN
PORT
PURE
PURI
PURL
PURR
PYRE
PYRO

P••R
PAIR
PARR
PEAR
PEER
PETR
PICR
PIER
POOR
POUR
PTER
PURR

•PR•
SPRY

•P•R
SPAR
SPIR
SPOR
SPQR
SPUR

••PR
COPR
CUPR

PS••
PSIS

P•S•
PASS
PAST
PESO
PEST
PISC
PISH
POSE
POSH
POST
POSY
PUSH
PUSS

P••S
PADS
PALS
PAMS
PANS
PAPS
PARS
PASS
PATS
PAWS
PAYS
PEAS
PEES
PEGS
PENS
PEPS
PETS
PEWS
PHDS
PHIS
PIES
PIGS
PINS
PIPS
PITS
PIUS
PLUS
PODS
PONS

4

POPS
POTS
POWS
PRES
PROS
PSIS
PUBS
PUGS
PUNS
PUPS
PUSS
PUTS
PYES

•PS•
APSE
OPSY

•P•S
APES
APIS
APUS
EPOS
OPTS
OPUS
SPAS
UPAS

••PS
ALPS
AMPS
ASPS
BOPS
CAPS
COPS
CUPS
DAPS
DIPS
FOPS
GAPS
GIPS
GYPS
HIPS
HOPS
IMPS
KIPS
KOPS
LAPS
LIPS
LOPS
MAPS
MOPS
NAPS
NIPS
PAPS
PEPS
PIPS
POPS
PUPS
RAPS
REPS
RIPS
SAPS
SIPS
SOPS
SUPS
TAPS
TIPS
TOPS
TUPS
VIPS
WAPS
YAPS
YIPS
ZIPS

PT••
PTAH
PTER

P•T•
PATE
PATH
PATS
PETE
PETR
PETS
PITA
PITH
PITS
PITT
PITY
POTS
PUTS
PUTT

P••T
PACT
PANT
PART
PAST
PEAT
PELT
PENT
PERT
PEST
PHOT
PHYT
PICT
PINT
PITT
PLAT
PLOT
POET
PORT
POST
POUT
PROT
PUNT
PUTT

•PT•
OPTS

•P•T
SPAT
SPIT
SPOT

••PT
BAPT
CAPT
COPT
DEPT
HEPT
KEPT
LEPT
RAPT
SEPT
SUPT
WEPT

PU••
PUBS
PUCE
PUCK
PUFF
PUGH
PUGS
PUKE
PULE
PULL
PULP
PUMA
PUMP
PUNA
PUNG
PUNK
PUNS
PUNT
PUNY
PUPA
PUPS
PURE
PURI
PURL
PURR
PUSH
PUSS
PUTS
PUTT

P•U•
PAUL
PIUS
PLUG
PLUM
PLUS
POUF
POUR
POUT
PRUE

P••U
PERU

•PU•
APUS
OPUS
SPUD
SPUN
SPUR

••PU
OGPU

P•V•
PAVE
PAVO

P•W•
PAWL
PAWN
PAWS
PEWS
POWS

P••W
PHEW
PLOW
PROW

•P•W
SPEW

P•X•
PIXY

P••X
PNYX

•P•X
APEX

PY••
PYEL
PYES
PYIC
PYIN
PYLE
PYRE
PYRO

P•Y•
PAYS
PHYL
PHYT
PNYX

P••Y
PALY
PINY
PIPY
PITY
PIXY
PLAY
PLOY
POGY
POKY
POLY
PONY
POSY
PRAY
PREY
PUNY

•P•Y
OPSY
SPAY
SPRY

••PY
COPY
DOPY
ESPY
GAPY
PIPY
ROPY

P•Z•
PIZZ

P••Z
PIZZ

Q•A•
QUAD
QUAG
QUAY

•Q•A
AQUA

Q••D
QUAD
QUID
QUOD

Q••G
QUAG

Q•I•
QUID
QUIP
QUIT
QUIZ

•Q•I
AQUI
EQUI

Q•O•
QUOD

Q••P
QUIP

••QQ
SEQQ

••QR
SPQR

Q••T
QUIT

QU••
QUAD
QUAG
QUAY
QUID
QUIP
QUIT
QUIZ
QUOD

•QU•
AQUA
AQUI
EQUI

Q••Y
QUAY

Q••Z
QUIZ

RA••
RACE
RACK
RACY
RADS
RAES
RAFF
RAFT
RAGE
RAGI
RAGS
RAID
RAIL
RAIN
RAKE
RAKI
RALE
RALL
RAMI
RAMP
RAMS
RAND
RANG
RANI
RANK
RANT
RAPE
RAPS
RAPT
RARE
RASH
RASP
RATE
RATO
RATS
RAVE
RAYS
RAZE
RAZZ

R•A•
READ
REAL
REAM
REAP
REAR
RIAL
ROAD
ROAM
ROAN
ROAR

R••A
REBA
RHEA
RITA
ROMA
ROSA
ROTA
RUGA

•RA•
ARAB
ARAD
ARAL
ARAM
ARAS
BRAD
BRAE
BRAG
BRAN
BRAS
BRAT
BRAW
BRAY
BRAZ
CRAB
CRAG
CRAM
CRAP
CRAT
CRAW
DRAB
DRAG
DRAM
DRAT
DRAW
DRAY
ERAS
FRAE
FRAN
FRAP
FRAS
FRAT
FRAU
FRAY
GRAB
GRAD
GRAF
GRAM
GRAY
GRAZ
IRAN
IRAQ
IRAS
ORAL
ORAN
PRAE
PRAM
PRAY
TRAM
TRAP
TRAY
URAL
URAN
WRAF
WRAP
XRAY

•R•A
AREA
ARIA
ERMA
IRMA
PROA
UREA
URIA

••RA
AGRA
AURA
BORA
CARA
CORA
DORA
DURA
EYRA
EZRA
FORA
HERA
HORA
JURA
KARA
KURA
LIRA
LYRA
MORA
MYRA
NORA
OKRA
PARA
PERA
SARA
SERA
SORA
SURA
TERA
VARA
VERA
VORA

R•B•
REBA
REBS
RIBS
ROBE
ROBS
RUBE
RUBS
RUBY

•RB•
IRBM
ORBS

•R•B
ARAB
CRAB
CRIB
DRAB
DRIB
DRUB
GRAB
GRUB

••RB
BARB
CARB
CURB
DARB
FORB
GARB
HERB
KERB
NLRB
SERB
SORB
VERB

RC••
RCMP

R•C•
RACE
RACK
RACY
RECT
RICE
RICH
RICK
ROCK
RUCK

R••C
ROTC

•RC•
ARCH
ARCS
ORCS

•R•C
ERIC
URIC

••RC
CIRC
MARC
NARC

R•D•
RADS
REDO
REDS
RIDE
RIDS
RODE
RODS
RUDD
RUDE
RUDY

R••D
RAID
RAND
READ
REED
REND
RIND
ROAD
ROOD
RUDD
RUED
RYND

•RD•
ORDO
URDU

•R•D
ARAD
ARID
BRAD
BRED
CRUD
FRED
GRAD
GRID
IRID
PROD
TROD

••RD
BARD
BIRD
BURD
BYRD
CARD
CORD
CURD
FORD
GIRD
HARD
HERD
KURD
LARD
LORD
NARD
PARD
SARD
SURD
WARD
WORD
YARD

RE••
READ
REAL
REAM
REAP
REAR
REBA
REBS
RECT
REDO
REDS
REED
REEF
REEK
REEL
REIN
REIS
RELY
REMS
REND
RENE
RENI
RENO
RENT
REPP
REPS
RESH
REST
RETE
RETS
REVS

R•E•
RAES
REED
REEF
REEK
REEL
RHEA
RHEO
ROES
RUED
RUER
RUES
RYES

R••E
RACE
RAGE
RAKE
RALE
RAPE
RARE
RATE
RAVE
RAZE
RENE
RETE
RICE
RIDE
RIFE
RILE
RIME
RIPE
RISE
RITE
RIVE
ROBE
RODE
ROLE
ROME
ROPE
ROSE
ROTE
ROUE
ROVE
RUBE
RUDE
RUFE
RULE
RUNE
RUSE

•RE•
AREA
AREO
ARES
BRED
BRER
BREV
BREW
CREE
CRES
CREW
DREW
FRED
FREE
FREQ
FRET
FREY
GREG
GREW
GREY
ORES
PREP
PRES
PREY
TREE
TREF
TREK
TRET
TREY
UREA
UREY
WREN
XREF

•R•E
BRAE
BRIE
CREE
ERIE
ERNE
ERSE
FRAE
FREE
FROE
ORLE
PRAE
PRUE
TREE
TRUE
URGE

••RE
AARE
ACRE
BARE
BORE
BYRE
CARE
CERE
CORE
CURE
DARE
DIRE
EIRE
EYRE
FARE
FIRE
FORE
GORE
GYRE
HARE
HERE
HIRE
KURE
LIRE
LORE
LURE
LYRE
MARE
MERE
MIRE
MORE
OGRE
PARE
PERE
PORE
PURE
PYRE
RARE
SERE
SIRE
SORE
SURE
TARE
TIRE
TORE
TYRE
VORE
WARE
WERE
WIRE
WORE
YORE

R•F•
RAFF
RAFT
RIFE
RIFF
RIFT
RUFE
RUFF

R••F
RAFF
REEF
RIFF
ROLF
ROOF
RUFF

•R•F
GRAF
PROF
TREF
WRAF
XREF

••RF
CORF
KERF
SERF
SURF
TURF
ZARF

R•G•
RAGE
RAGI
RAGS
RIGS
RUGA
RUGS

R••G
RANG
RING
RUNG

•RG•
ARGO
ERGO
ERGS
ORGY
URGE

•R•G
BRAG
BRIG
CRAG
DRAG
DRUG
FROG
GREG
GRIG
GROG
ORIG
PRIG
TRIG

••RG
BERG
BURG
SURG

RH••
RHEA
RHEO
RHIN
RHIZ
RHOS

R•H•
RUHR

R••H
RASH
RESH
RICH
RUSH
RUTH

•R•H
ARCH
ORTH

RI••
RIAL
RIBS
RICE
RICH
RICK
RIDE
RIDS
RIFE
RIFF
RIFT
RIGS
RILE
RILL
RIME
RIMS
RIMY
RIND
RING
RINK
RIOT
RIPE
RIPS
RISE
RISK
RITA
RITE
RIVE

R•I•
RAID
RAIL
RAIN
REIN
REIS
RHIN
RHIZ
ROIL
RUIN

R••I
RAGI
RAKI
RAMI
RANI
RENI

•RI•
ARIA
ARID
ARIL
ARIZ
BRIE
BRIG
BRIM
BRIO
BRIT
CRIB
CRIT
DRIB
DRIP
ERIC
ERIE
ERIK
ERIN
ERIS
FRIT
GRID
GRIG
GRIM
GRIN
GRIP
GRIS
GRIT
HRIP
IRID
IRIS
KRIS
ORIG
PRIG
PRIM
TRIG
TRIM
TRIO
TRIP
TRIS
TRIX
URIA
URIC
WRIT

••RI
ABRI
AERI
BARI
GYRI
INRI
MYRI
PARI
PERI
PURI
SARI
SORI
TORI
VARI

••RJ
MARJ

R•K•
RAKE
RAKI

R••K
RACK
RANK
REEK
RICK
RINK
RISK
ROCK
ROOK
RUCK
RUSK

•RK•
ARKS
IRKS

•R•K
ERIK
TREK
TRUK

••RK
BARK
CORK
DARK
DIRK
FORK
HARK
JERK
KIRK
LARK
LURK
MARK
PARK
PERK
PORK
SARK
TURK
WORK
YORK

R•L•
RALE
RALL
RELY
RILE
RILL
ROLE
ROLF
ROLL
RULE

R••L
RAIL
RALL
REAL
REEL
RIAL
RILL
ROIL
ROLL
ROTL

•RL•
ORLE

•R•L
ARAL
ARIL
ARYL
ORAL
URAL

••RL
BIRL
BURL
CARL
CURL
EARL
FARL
FURL
GIRL
HARL
HERL
HURL
JARL
KARL
MARL
PURL

R•M•
RAMI
RAMP
RAMS
RCMP
REMS
RIME
RIMS
RIMY
ROMA
ROME
ROMP
RUMP
RUMS

R••M
REAM
ROAM
ROOM

•RM•
ARMS
ARMY
ERMA
IRMA

•R•M
ARAM
ARUM
BRIM
BROM
CRAM
DRAM
DRUM
FROM
GRAM
GRIM
GRUM
IRBM
PRAM
PRIM
PROM
TRAM
TRIM

••RM
BARM
BERM
CORM
DERM
DORM
FARM
FIRM
FORM
GERM
HARM
NORM
TERM
WARM
WORM

R•N•
RAND
RANG
RANI
RANK
RANT
REND
RENE
RENI
RENO
RENT
RIND
RING
RINK
RUNE
RUNG
RUNS
RUNT
RYND

R••N
RAIN
REIN
RHIN
ROAN
RUIN

•RN•
ARNO
ARNS
BRNO
ERNE
ERNS
URNS

•R•N
BRAN
ERIN
FRAN
GRIN
IRAN
IRON
ORAN
PRON
TRON
URAN
WREN

••RN
BARN
BERN
BORN
BURN
CORN
DARN
EARN
FERN
FIRN
FURN
HORN
KERN
MORN
NORN
PORN
TARN
TERN
TORN
TURN
VERN
WARN
WORN
YARN

RO••
ROAD
ROAM
ROAN
ROAR
ROBE
ROBS
ROCK
RODE
RODS
ROES
ROIL
ROLE
ROLF
ROLL
ROMA
ROME
ROMP
ROOD
ROOF
ROOK
ROOM
ROOT
ROPE
ROPY
RORY
ROSA
ROSE
ROSS
ROSY
ROTA
ROTC
ROTE
ROTL
ROTS
ROUE
ROUP
ROUT
ROUX
ROVE
ROWS
ROXY
ROYS

R•O•
RHOS
RIOT
ROOD
ROOF
ROOK
ROOM
ROOT
RYOT

R••O
RATO
REDO
RENO
RHEO

•RO•
BROM
BROO
BROW
BROZ
CROP
CROW
DROP
EROS
FROE
FROG
FROM
FROW
GROG
GROT
GROW
IRON
PROA
PROD
PROF
PROM
PRON
PROP
PROS
PROT
PROW
TROD
TRON
TROP
TROT
TROY

•R•O
AREO
ARGO
ARNO
BRIO
BRNO
BROO
CRYO
ERGO
ORDO
TRIO

••RO
ACRO
AERO
AFRO
AGRO
BARO
CERO
DURO
EBRO
FARO
GIRO
GYRO
HERO
MERO
MORO
NERO
PYRO
SERO
TARO
TIRO
TYRO
XERO
ZERO

R•P•
RAPE
RAPS
RAPT
REPP
REPS
RIPE
RIPS
ROPE
ROPY

R••P
RAMP
RASP
RCMP
REAP
REPP
ROMP
ROUP
RSVP
RUMP

•R•P
CRAP
CROP
DRIP
DROP
FRAP
GRIP
HRIP
PREP
PROP
TRAP
TRIP
TROP
WRAP

••RP
BURP
CARP
CORP
HARP
TARP
WARP

•R•Q
FREQ
IRAQ

R•R•
RARE
RORY

R••R
REAR
ROAR
RUER
RUHR

•RR•
ERRS

•R•R
BRER

••RR
BIRR
BURR
DORR
DURR
PARR
PURR

RS••
RSVP

R•S•
RASH
RASP
RESH
REST
RISE
RISK
ROSA
ROSE
ROSS
ROSY
RUSE
RUSH
RUSK
RUSS
RUST

R••S
RADS
RAES
RAGS
RAMS
RAPS
RATS
RAYS
REBS
REDS
REIS
REMS
REPS
RETS
REVS
RHOS
RIBS
RIDS
RIGS
RIMS
RIPS
ROBS
RODS
ROES
ROSS
ROTS
ROWS
ROYS
RUBS
RUES
RUGS
RUMS
RUNS
RUSS
RUTS
RYES

•RS•
ERSE
ERST

•R•S
ARAS
ARCS
ARES
ARKS
ARMS
ARNS
ARTS
BRAS
CRES
CRUS
ERAS
ERGS
ERIS
ERNS
EROS
ERRS
FRAS
GRIS
IRAS
IRIS
IRKS
KRIS
ORBS
ORCS

ORES
PRES
PROS
TRIS
URNS
URUS
XRTS

••RS
AIRS
BARS
BURS
CARS
CURS
DORS
EARS
ERRS
FIRS
FURS
GARS
HERS
JARS
KORS
LARS
MARS
MIRS
MORS
OARS
OURS
PARS
SERS
SIRS
TARS
TORS
VERS
WARS

R•T•
RATE
RATO
RATS
RETE
RETS
RITA
RITE
ROTA
ROTC
ROTE
ROTL
ROTS
RUTH
RUTS

R••T
RAFT
RANT
RAPT
RECT
RENT
REST
RIFT
RIOT
ROOT
ROUT
RUNT
RUST
RYOT

•RT•
ARTS
ARTY
ORTH
XRTS

•R•T
BRAT
BRIT
BRUT
CRAT
CRIT
DRAT
ERST
FRAT
FRET
FRIT
GRIT
GROT
PROT
TRET
TROT
WRIT

••RT
BART
BERT
BORT
CART
CERT
CURT
DART
DIRT
FORT
GIRT
HART
HORT
HURT
KURT
MART
MORT
PART
PERT
PORT
SORT
TART
TORT
VERT
WART
WERT
WORT

RU••
RUBE
RUBS
RUBY
RUCK
RUDD
RUDE
RUDY
RUED
RUER
RUES
RUFE
RUFF
RUGA
RUGS
RUHR
RUIN
RULE
RUMP
RUMS
RUNE
RUNG
RUNS
RUNT
RUSE
RUSH
RUSK
RUSS
RUST
RUTH
RUTS

R•U•
ROUE
ROUP
ROUT
ROUX

•RU•
ARUM
BRUT
CRUD
CRUS
CRUX
DRUB
DRUG
DRUM
GRUB
GRUM
PRUE
TRUE
TRUK
URUS

•R•U
FRAU
URDU

••RU
ECRU
GURU
PERU
THRU

R•V•
RAVE
REVS
RIVE
ROVE
RSVP

•R•V
BREV

••RV
MIRV

R•W•
ROWS

•R•W
BRAW
BREW
BROW
CRAW
CREW
CROW
DRAW
DREW
FROW
GREW
GROW
PROW

R•X•
ROXY

R••X
ROUX

•R•X
CRUX
ORYX
TRIX

••RX
MARX

RY••
RYES
RYND
RYOT

R•Y•
RAYS
ROYS

R••Y
RACY
RELY
RIMY
ROPY
RORY
ROSY
ROXY
RUBY
RUDY

•RY•
ARYL
CRYO
ORYX

•R•Y
ARMY
ARTY
BRAY
DRAY
FRAY
FREY
GRAY
GREY
ORGY
PRAY
PREY
TRAY
TREY
TROY
UREY
XRAY

••RY
AERY
AIRY
AWRY
BURY
CARY
DORY
EERY
EURY
EYRY
FURY
GARY
GORY
JURY
KARY
LORY
MARY
NARY
RORY
SPRY
TORY
VARY
VERY
WARY
WIRY

R•Z•
RAZE
RAZZ

R••Z
RAZZ
RHIZ

•R•Z
ARIZ
BRAZ
BROZ
GRAZ

••RZ
HARZ

SA••
SAAR
SABE
SABS
SACK
SACS
SADE
SADI
SAFE
SAGA
SAGE
SAGO
SAGS
SAGY
SAID
SAIL
SAIS
SAKE
SAKI
SALE
SALK
SALT
SAME
SAMP
SAMS
SAND
SANE
SANG
SANK
SANS
SAPS
SARA
SARD
SARI
SARK
SASH
SASK
SASS
SATE
SAUD
SAUK
SAUL
SAUR
SAVE
SAWN
SAWS
SAYS

S•A•
SAAR
SCAB
SCAD
SCAN
SCAR
SCAT
SDAK
SEAL
SEAM
SEAN
SEAR
SEAS
SEAT
SHAD
SHAG
SHAH
SHAM
SHAN
SHAW
SHAY
SIAL
SIAM
SKAT
SKAW
SLAB
SLAG
SLAM
SLAP
SLAT
SLAV
SLAW
SLAY
SNAG
SNAP
SOAK
SOAP
SOAR
SPAM
SPAN
SPAR
SPAS
SPAT
SPAY
STAB
STAG
STAN
STAR
STAT
STAY
SWAB
SWAG
SWAM
SWAN
SWAP
SWAT
SWAY

S••A
SAGA
SARA
SERA
SETA
SHEA
SIMA
SIVA
SKUA
SODA
SOFA
SOJA
SOLA
SOMA
SORA
SOYA
SPCA
STOA
SURA
SUVA

•SA•
ASAS
ESAU
OSAR
TSAR
USAF
USAR

•S•A
ASEA
ASIA
ISBA
OSSA
USIA
USMA
USNA

••SA
ANSA
ELSA
LISA
MESA
NASA
OSSA
ROSA
VASA
VISA

S•B•
SABE
SABS
SEBI
SEBO
SIBS
SOBS
SUBJ
SUBS

S••B
SCAB
SERB
SLAB
SLOB
SLUB
SNOB
SNUB
SORB
STAB
STUB
SWAB

•SB•
ISBA

SC••
SCAB
SCAD
SCAN
SCAR
SCAT
SCOP
SCOT
SCOW
SCUD
SCUM
SCUP
SCUT

S•C•
SACK

SACS SECT SECY SICE SICK SICS SOCK SPCA SPCC SUCH SUCK SYCE

S••C

SPCC SPEC

•SC•

ASCH ASCI ESCE USCG

•S•C

BSSC USMC

••SC

BSSC DESC DISC FISC MASC MISC PISC VISC WISC

SD••

SDAK

S•D•

SADE SADI SIDE SIDS SODA SODS SUDD SUDS

S••D

SAID SAND SARD SAUD SCAD SCUD SEED SEND SHAD SHED SHOD SKID SLED SLID SOLD SPED SPUD STUD SUDD SUED SURD

•S•D

BSED USED

SE••

SEAL SEAM SEAN SEAR SEAS SEAT SEBI SEBO SECT SECY SEED SEEK SEEM SEEN SEEP SEER SEES SEGO SEJM SELF SELL SEME SEMI SEND SENT SEPT SEQQ SERA SERB SERE SERF SERO SERS SETA SETH SETI SETS SEWN SEWS SEXI SEXT SEXY

S•E•

SEED SEEK SEEM SEEN SEEP SEER SEES SHEA SHED SHEM SHEW SKEE SKEG SKEP SKEW SLED SLEW SMEW SPEC SPED SPEW STEM STEN STEP STER STET STEW SUED SUER SUES SUET SUEZ

S••E

SABE SADE SAFE SAGE SAKE SALE SAME SANE SATE SAVE SEME SERE SHOE SICE SIDE SINE SIRE SITE SIZE SKEE SKYE SLOE SLUE SNYE SOKE SOLE SOME SONE SORE SUPE SURE SYCE SYNE

•SE•

ASEA BSED USED USER USES YSER

•S•E

ESCE ESTE ISLE OSTE

••SE

APSE BASE BISE CASE DOSE DUSE EASE ELSE ERSE FUSE HOSE ILSE JOSE LOSE LYSE MISE MOSE MUSE NOSE OUSE POSE RISE ROSE RUSE VASE VISE WISE

S•F•

SAFE SIFT SOFA SOFT SUFI

S••F

SELF SERF SURF

•S•F

USAF

S•G•

SAGA SAGE SAGO SAGS SAGY SEGO SIGH SIGN

S••G

SANG SHAG SING SKEG SLAG SLOG SLUG SMOG SMUG SNAG SNUG SONG STAG SUNG SURG SWAG SWIG

•SG•

MSGR MSGT

•S•G

USCG

SH••

SHAD SHAG SHAH SHAM SHAN SHAW SHAY SHEA SHED SHEM SHEW SHIM SHIN SHIP SHIV SHOD SHOE SHOO SHOP SHOT SHOW SHUL SHUN SHUT

S•H•

SOHO

S••H

SASH SETH SHAH SIGH SIKH SUCH

•SH•

ASHY

•S•H

ASCH MSTH

••SH

BASH BOSH BUSH CASH COSH CUSH DASH DISH FISH GASH GOSH GUSH HASH HUSH JOSH LASH LUSH MASH MESH MUSH NASH PISH POSH PUSH RASH RESH RUSH SASH TOSH TUSH WASH WISH

SI••

SIAL SIAM SIBS SICE SICK SICS SIDE SIDS SIFT SIGH SIGN SIKH SILK SILL SILO SILT SIMA SIMP SIMS SINE SING SINK SINO SINS SION SIPS SIRE SIRS SITE SITI SITO SITS SIVA SIZE SIZY

S•I•

SAID SAIL SAIS SHIM SHIN SHIP SHIV SKID SKIM SKIN SKIP SKIS SKIT SLID SLIM SLIP SLIT SMIT SNIP SNIT SOIL SPIN SPIR SPIT STIR SUIT SWIG SWIM

S••I

SADI SAKI SARI SEBI SEMI SETI SEXI SITI SOLI SORI SUFI

•SI•

ASIA ASIR ISIS OSIS PSIS USIA

•S•I

ASCI ASTI OSSI

••SI

LYSI NISI OSSI

S•J•

SEJM SOJA

S••J

SUBJ

SK••

SKAT SKAW SKEE SKEG SKEP SKEW SKID SKIM SKIN SKIP SKIS SKIT SKUA SKYE

S•K•

SAKE SAKI SIKH SOKE SUKY

S••K

SACK SALK SANK SARK SASK SAUK SDAK SEEK SICK SILK SINK SOAK SOCK SUCK SULK SUNK

•SK•

ASKS

••SK
BASK
BOSK
BUSK
CASK
CUSK
DESK
DISK
DUSK
HUSK
MASK
MUSK
OMSK
RISK
RUSK
SASK
TASK
TUSK

SL••
SLAB
SLAG
SLAM
SLAP
SLAT
SLAV
SLAW
SLAY
SLED
SLEW
SLID
SLIM
SLIP
SLIT
SLOB
SLOE
SLOG
SLOP
SLOT
SLOW
SLUB
SLUE
SLUG
SLUM
SLUR
SLUT

S•L•
SALE
SALK
SALT
SELF
SELL
SILK
SILL
SILO
SILT
SOLA
SOLD
SOLE
SOLI
SOLO
SOLS
SULK
SULU

S••L
SAIL
SAUL
SEAL
SELL
SHUL
SIAL
SILL
SOIL
SOUL
STOL

•SL•
ISLE

••SL
DESL

SM••
SMEW
SMIT
SMOG
SMUG
SMUT

S•M•
SAME
SAMP
SAMS
SEME
SEMI
SIMA
SIMP
SIMS
SOMA
SOME
SUMO
SUMP
SUMS

S••M
SCUM
SEAM
SEEM
SEJM
SHAM
SHEM
SHIM
SIAM
SKIM
SLAM
SLIM
SLUM
SPAM
STEM
STUM
SWAM
SWIM
SWUM

•SM•
ISMS
USMA
USMC
USMS

••SM
COSM

SN••
SNAG
SNAP
SNIP
SNIT
SNOB
SNOT
SNOW
SNUB
SNUG
SNYE

S•N•
SAND
SANE
SANG
SANK
SANS
SEND
SENT
SINE
SING
SINK
SINO
SINS
SONE
SONG
SONS
SUNG
SUNK
SUNN
SUNS
SYNE

S••N
SAWN
SCAN
SEAN
SEEN
SEWN
SHAN
SHIN
SHUN
SIGN
SION
SKIN
SOON
SOWN
SPAN
SPIN
SPUN
STAN
STEN
STUN
SUNN
SWAN

•SN•
ISNT
USNA
USNR

•S•N
ASSN

••SN
ASSN
BOSN

SO••
SOAK
SOAP
SOAR
SOBS
SOCK
SODA
SODS
SOFA
SOFT
SOHO
SOIL
SOJA
SOKE
SOLA
SOLD
SOLE
SOLI
SOLO
SOLS
SOMA
SOME
SONE
SONG
SONS
SOON
SOOT
SOPS
SORA
SORB
SORE
SORI
SORT
SOSO
SOTS
SOUL
SOUP
SOUR
SOUS
SOWN
SOWS
SOYA
SOYS

S•O•
SCOP
SCOT
SCOW
SHOD
SHOE
SHOO
SHOP
SHOT
SHOW
SION
SLOB
SLOE
SLOG
SLOP
SLOT
SLOW
SMOG
SNOB
SNOT
SNOW
SOON
SOOT
SPOR
SPOT
STOA
STOL
STOP
STOW

S••O
SAGO
SEBO
SEGO
SERO
SHOO
SILO
SINO
SITO
SOHO
SOLO
SOSO
SUMO

••SO
ALSO
MESO
MISO
NASO
NOSO
PESO
SOSO
VASO

SP••
SPAM
SPAN
SPAR
SPAS
SPAT
SPAY
SPCA
SPCC
SPEC
SPED
SPEW
SPIN
SPIR
SPIT
SPOR
SPOT
SPQR
SPRY
SPUD
SPUN
SPUR

S•P•
SAPS
SEPT
SIPS
SOPS
SUPE
SUPP
SUPS
SUPT

S••P
SAMP
SCOP
SCUP
SEEP
SHIP
SHOP
SIMP
SKEP
SKIP
SLAP
SLIP
SLOP
SNAP
SNIP
SOAP
SOUP
STEP
STOP
SUMP
SUPP
SWAP

•SP•
ASPS
ESPY

•S•P
RSVP

••SP
CUSP
GASP
HASP
INSP
LISP
RASP
WASP
WISP

S•Q•
SEQQ
SPQR

S••Q
SEQQ

S•R•
SARA
SARD
SARI
SARK
SERA
SERB
SERE
SERF
SERO
SERS
SIRE
SIRS
SORA
SORB
SORE
SORI
SORT
SPRY
SURA
SURD
SURE
SURF
SURG

S••R
SAAR
SAUR
SCAR
SEAR
SEER
SLUR
SOAR
SOUR
SPAR
SPIR
SPOR
SPQR
SPUR
STAR
STER
STIR
SUER

•S•R
ASIR
ASTR
MSGR
OSAR
TSAR
USAR
USER
USNR
USSR
YSER

••SR
USSR

S•S•
SASH
SASK
SASS
SOSO

S••S
SABS
SACS
SAGS
SAIS
SAMS
SANS
SAPS
SASS
SAWS
SAYS
SEAS
SEES
SERS
SETS
SEWS
SIBS
SICS
SIDS
SIMS
SINS
SIPS
SIRS
SITS
SKIS
SOBS
SODS
SOLS
SONS
SOPS
SOTS
SOUS
SOWS
SOYS
SPAS
STUS
SUBS
SUDS
SUES
SUMS
SUNS
SUPS

•SS•
ASSN
ASST
BSSC
OSSA
OSSI
USSR

•S•S
ASAS
ASKS
ASPS
ISIS
ISMS
MSTS
OSIS
PSIS
USES
USMS

4

••SS
BASS
BESS
BOSS
BUSS
CASS
CESS
COSS
CUSS
DESS
FESS
FOSS
FUSS
HISS
JESS
JOSS
KISS
LASS
LESS
LOSS
MASS
MESS
MISS
MOSS
MUSS
NESS
PASS
PUSS
ROSS
RUSS
SASS
TASS
TESS
TOSS

ST••
STAB
STAG
STAN
STAR
STAT
STAY
STEM
STEN
STEP
STER
STET
STEW
STIR
STOA
STOL
STOP
STOW
STUB
STUD
STUM
STUN
STUS
STYX

S•T•
SATE
SETA
SETH
SETI
SETS
SITE
SITI
SITO
SITS
SOTS

S••T
SALT
SCAT
SCOT
SCUT
SEAT
SECT
SENT
SEPT
SEXT
SHOT
SHUT
SIFT
SILT
SKAT
SKIT
SLAT
SLIT
SLOT
SLUT
SMIT
SMUT
SNIT
SNOT
SOFT
SOOT
SORT
SPAT
SPIT
SPOT
STAT
STET
SUET
SUIT
SUPT
SWAT

•ST•
ASTI
ASTR
ESTE
MSTH
MSTS
OSTE

•S•T
ASST
ISNT
MSGT

••ST
ASST
AUST
BAST
BEST
BUST
CAST
CIST
COST
CYST
DIST
DOST
DUST
EAST
ERST
FAST
FEST
FIST
GEST
GIST
GUST
HAST
HIST
HOST
INST
JEST
JUST
LAST
LEST
LIST
LOST
LUST
MAST
MIST
MOST
MUST
NAST
NEST
OUST
PAST
PEST
POST
REST
RUST
TEST
VAST
VEST
WAST
WEST
XYST
ZEST

SU••
SUBJ
SUBS
SUCH
SUCK
SUDD
SUDS
SUED
SUER
SUES
SUET
SUEZ
SUFI
SUIT
SUKY
SULK
SULU
SUMO
SUMP
SUMS
SUNG
SUNK
SUNN
SUNS
SUPE
SUPP
SUPS
SUPT
SURA
SURD
SURE
SURF
SURG
SUVA
SUZY

S•U•
SAUD
SAUK
SAUL
SAUR
SCUD
SCUM
SCUP
SCUT
SHUL
SHUN
SHUT
SKUA
SLUB
SLUE
SLUG
SLUM
SLUR
SLUT
SMUG
SMUT
SNUB
SNUG
SOUL
SOUP
SOUR
SOUS
SPUD
SPUN
SPUR
STUB
STUD
STUM
STUN
STUS
SWUM

S••U
SULU

•S•U
ESAU

S•V•
SAVE
SIVA
SUVA

S••V
SHIV
SLAV

•SV•
RSVP

SW••
SWAB
SWAG
SWAM
SWAN
SWAP
SWAT
SWAY
SWIG
SWIM
SWUM

S•W•
SAWN
SAWS
SEWN
SEWS
SOWN
SOWS

S••W
SCOW
SHAW
SHEW
SHOW
SKAW
SKEW
SLAW
SLEW
SLOW
SMEW
SNOW
SPEW
STEW
STOW

S•X•
SEXI
SEXT
SEXY

S••X
STYX

SY••
SYCE
SYNE

S•Y•
SAYS
SKYE
SNYE
SOYA
SOYS
STYX

S••Y
SAGY
SECY
SEXY
SHAY
SIZY
SLAY
SPAY
SPRY
STAY
SUKY
SUZY
SWAY

•S•Y
ASHY
ESPY

••SY
BUSY
EASY
NOSY
OPSY
POSY
ROSY

S•Z•
SIZE
SIZY
SUZY

S••Z
SUEZ

TA••
TAAL
TABS
TABU
TACE
TACK
TACT
TADS
TAEL
TAFT
TAGS
TAIL
TAIN
TAKE
TALC
TALE
TALK
TALL
TAME
TAMP
TAMS
TANG
TANK
TANS
TAOS
TAPA
TAPE
TAPS
TARE
TARN
TARO
TARP
TARS
TART
TASK
TASS
TATS
TAUR
TAUS
TAUT
TAVS
TAWS
TAXI
TAXY

T•A•
TAAL
TEAK
TEAL
TEAM
TEAR
TEAS
TEAT
THAD
THAN
THAR
THAT
THAW
TOAD
TRAM
TRAP
TRAY
TSAR
TZAR

T••A
TAPA
TELA
TERA
THEA
TINA
TOGA
TOLA
TUBA
TUFA
TUNA

•TA•
ETAS
ITAL
PTAH
STAB
STAG
STAN
STAR
STAT
STAY
UTAH

•T•A
ETNA
ETTA
STOA

••TA
ACTA
ALTA
ANTA
BETA
CATA
DATA
DITA
ETTA
IOTA
LUTA
META
NITA
OCTA
PITA
RITA
ROTA
SETA
VITA
ZETA

T•B•
TABS
TABU
TOBY
TUBA
TUBE
TUBS

T••B
TOMB

•T•B
STAB
STUB

T•C•
TACE
TACK
TACT
TICK
TICS
TOCO
TUCK

T••C
TALC

•TC•
ETCH
ITCH

•T•C
ATIC
OTIC

••TC
ROTC

T•D•
TADS
TEDS
TIDE
TIDY

TODD
TODO
TODS
TODY
TUDE

T••D
TEED
TEND
THAD
THUD
TIED
TOAD
TODD
TOED
TOLD
TROD

•T•D
STUD

TE••
TEAK
TEAL
TEAM
TEAR
TEAS
TEAT
TEDS
TEED
TEEM
TEEN
TEES
TEGS
TELA
TELE
TELL
TELO
TEMP
TEND
TENN
TENO
TENS
TENT
TERA
TERM
TERN
TESS
TEST
TETH
TETR
TEXT

T•E•
TAEL
TEED
TEEM
TEEN
TEES
THEA
THEE
THEM
THEN
THEO
THEW
THEY
TIED
TIER
TIES
TOED
TOES
TREE
TREF
TREK
TRET
TREY
TUES
TYEE

T••E
TACE
TAKE
TALE
TAME
TAPE
TARE
TELE
THEE
TIDE
TILE
TIME
TINE
TIRE
TOLE
TOME
TONE
TOPE
TORE
TOTE
TREE
TRUE
TUBE
TUDE
TULE
TUNE
TYEE
TYKE
TYPE
TYRE

•TE•
CTEN
ITEM
PTER
STEM
STEN
STEP
STER
STET
STEW
UTER
UTES

•T•E
ETTE

••TE
ANTE
BATE
BITE
BUTE
CITE
COTE
CUTE
CYTE
DATE
DOTE
ESTE
ETTE
FATE
FETE
GATE
HATE
JUTE
KATE
KITE
LATE
LITE
LUTE
LYTE
MATE
METE
MITE
MOTE
MUTE
NATE
NOTE
OSTE
PATE
PETE
RATE
RETE
RITE
ROTE
SATE
SITE
TOTE
VOTE

T•F•
TAFT
TIFF
TOFT
TUFA
TUFF
TUFT

T••F
TIFF
TREF
TUFF
TURF

T•G•
TAGS
TEGS
TOGA
TOGO
TOGS
TUGS

T••G
TANG
THUG
TING
TONG
TRIG
TWIG

•T•G
STAG

TH••
THAD
THAN
THAR
THAT
THAW
THEA
THEE
THEM
THEN
THEO
THEW
THEY
THIN
THIO
THIS
THOR
THOU
THRU
THUD
THUG
THUS

T••H
TETH
TOPH
TOSH
TUSH

•TH•
ETHN
ETHS

•T•H
ETCH
ITCH
PTAH
UTAH

••TH
ACTH
ANTH
AUTH
BATH
BETH
BOTH
CATH
DOTH
GATH
GOTH
HATH
HETH
KITH
LATH
LITH
LOTH
LUTH
MATH
METH
MOTH
MSTH
MYTH
OATH
ORTH
PATH
PITH
RUTH
SETH
TETH
WITH

TI••
TICK
TICS
TIDE
TIDY
TIED
TIER
TIES
TIFF
TIKI
TILE
TILL
TILT
TIME
TIMS
TINA
TINE
TING
TINS
TINT
TINY
TION
TIPS
TIRE
TIRO
TITI
TITO
TITS
TIVY

T•I•
TAIL
TAIN
THIN
THIO
THIS
TOIL
TRIG
TRIM
TRIO
TRIP
TRIS
TRIX
TWIG
TWIN
TWIT

T••I
TAXI
TIKI
TITI
TONI
TOPI
TORI
TOTI
TUPI

•TI•
ATIC
OTIC
OTIS
STIR

•T•I
ATLI
ETUI

••TI
ALTI
ANTI
ASTI
LATI
SETI
SITI
TITI
TOTI
YETI

T•K•
TAKE
TIKI
TYKE

T••K
TACK
TALK
TANK
TASK
TEAK
TICK
TOOK
TREK
TRUK
TUCK
TURK
TUSK

T•L•
TALC
TALE
TALK
TALL
TELA
TELE
TELL
TELO
TILE
TILL
TILT
TOLA
TOLD
TOLE
TOLL
TOLU
TULE

T••L
TAAL
TAEL
TAIL
TALL
TEAL
TELL
TILL
TOIL
TOLL
TOOL

•TL•
ATLI

•T•L
ITAL
ITOL
STOL
VTOL

••TL
NATL
ROTL

T•M•
TAME
TAMP
TAMS
TEMP
TIME
TIMS
TOMB
TOME
TOMS
TOMY

T••M
TEAM
TEEM
TERM
THEM
TRAM
TRIM

•TM•
ATMO

•T•M
ATOM
ITEM
STEM
STUM

T•N•
TANG
TANK
TANS
TEND
TENN
TENO
TENS
TENT
TINA
TINE
TING
TINS
TINT
TINY
TONE
TONG
TONI
TONO
TONS
TONY
TUNA
TUNE
TUNS

T••N
TAIN
TARN
TEEN
TENN
TERN
THAN
THEN
THIN
TION
TOON
TORN
TOWN
TRON
TURN
TWIN

•TN•
ETNA

•T•N
ATTN
CTEN
ETHN
ETON
STAN
STEN
STUN

••TN
ATTN

TO••
TOAD
TOBY
TOCO
TODD
TODO
TODS
TODY
TOED
TOES
TOFT
TOGA

4

TOGO TOGS TOIL TOLA TOLD TOLE TOLL TOLU TOMB TOME TOMS TOMY TONE TONG TONI TONO TONS TONY TOOK TOOL TOON TOOT TOPE TOPH TOPI TOPO TOPS TORE TORI TORN TORS TORT TORY TOSH TOSS TOTE TOTI TOTS TOUR TOUT TOWN TOWS TOYO TOYS

T•O•

TAOS THOR THOU TION TOOK TOOL TOON TOOT TROD TRON TROP TROT TROY TWOS

T••O

TARO TELO TENO THEO THIO TIRO TITO TOCO TODO TOGO TONO TOPO TOYO TRIO TYPO TYRO

•TO•

ATOM ATOP ATOR ETON ITOL STOA STOL STOP STOW VTOL

•T•O

ATMO ATTO OTTO

••TO

ALTO ATTO AUTO CATO CYTO ECTO ENTO INTO JATO KETO KOTO LETO NATO NOTO OCTO ONTO OTTO RATO SITO TITO UNTO VETO

T•P•

TAPA TAPE TAPS TIPS TOPE TOPH TOPI TOPO TOPS TUPI TUPS TYPE TYPO

T••P

TAMP TARP TEMP TRAP TRIP TROP

•T•P

ATOP STEP STOP

••TP

KKTP

TR••

TRAM TRAP TRAY TREE TREF TREK TRET TREY TRIG TRIM TRIO TRIP TRIS TRIX TROD TRON TROP TROT TROY TRUE TRUK

T•R•

TARE TARN TARO TARP TARS TART TERA TERM TERN THRU TIRE TIRO TORE TORI TORN TORS TORT TORY TURF TURK TURN TYRE TYRO

T••R

TAUR TEAR TETR THAR THOR TIER TOUR TSAR TZAR

•T•R

ATOR PTER STAR STER STIR UTER

••TR

ASTR METR NITR PETR TETR VITR

TS••

TSAR

T•S•

TASK TASS TESS TEST TOSH TOSS TUSH TUSK

T••S

TABS TADS TAGS TAMS TANS TAOS TAPS TARS TASS TATS TAUS TAVS TAWS TEAS TEDS TEES TEGS TENS TESS THIS THUS TICS TIES TIMS TINS TIPS TITS TODS TOES TOGS TOMS TONS TOPS TORS TOSS TOTS TOWS TOYS TRIS TUBS TUES TUGS TUNS TUPS TWOS

•T•S

ETAS ETHS ITYS OTIS STUS UTES

••TS

ACTS AMTS ANTS ARTS BATS BETS BITS BOTS BUTS CATS COTS CUTS DOTS EATS EFTS FATS FITS GATS GETS GUTS HATS HITS HUTS JETS JOTS JUTS KITS LETS LOTS MATS MOTS MSTS MUTS NATS NETS NITS NUTS OATS OPTS OUTS PATS PETS PITS POTS PUTS RATS RETS ROTS RUTS SETS SITS SOTS TATS TITS TOTS UMTS VATS VETS WETS WITS XRTS

T•T•

TATS TETH TETR TITI TITO TITS TOTE TOTI TOTS TUTU

T••T

TACT TAFT TART TAUT TEAT TENT TEST TEXT THAT TILT TINT TOFT TOOT TORT TOUT TRET TROT TUFT TWIT

•TT•

ATTN ATTO ATTU ATTY ETTA ETTE OTTO

•T•T

STAT STET

••TT

BATT BITT BOTT BUTT GATT LETT LOTT MATT MITT MOTT MUTT PITT PUTT WATT

TU••

TUBA TUBE TUBS TUCK TUDE TUES TUFA TUFF TUFT TUGS TULE TUNA TUNE TUNS TUPI TUPS TURF TURK TURN TUSH TUSK TUTU

T•U•

TAUR TAUS TAUT THUD THUG THUS TOUR TOUT TRUE TRUK

T••U

TABU THOU THRU TOLU TUTU

•TU•

ETUI STUB STUD STUM STUN STUS

•T•U

ATTU

••TU

ATTU TUTU

T•V•

TAVS TIVY

TW••

TWIG TWIN TWIT TWOS

T•W•

TAWS TOWN TOWS

T••W

THAW THEW

•T•W

STEW STOW

T•X•

TAXI TAXY TEXT

T••X

TRIX

•T•X

STYX

TY••
TYEE
TYKE
TYPE
TYPO
TYRE
TYRO

T•Y•
TOYO
TOYS

T••Y
TAXY
THEY
TIDY
TINY
TIVY
TOBY
TODY
TOMY
TONY
TORY
TRAY
TREY
TROY

•TY•
ITYS
STYX

•T•Y
ATTY
STAY

••TY
ARTY
ATTY
CITY
DOTY
DUTY
PITY
XNTY

TZ••
TZAR

••TZ
FITZ

U•A•
UNAS
UNAU
UPAS
URAL
URAN
USAF
USAR
UTAH

U••A
ULNA
UREA
URIA
USIA
USMA
USNA
UVEA

•UA•
DUAD
DUAL
GUAM
GUAN
GUAT
JUAN
LUAU
QUAD
QUAG
QUAY
YUAN

•U•A
AURA
BUNA
CUBA
DUMA
DURA
FULA
HULA
HUPA
JUBA
JURA
KURA
LUNA
LUTA
PUMA
PUNA
PUPA
RUGA
SURA
SUVA
TUBA
TUFA
TUNA
YUGA
YUMA

••UA
AQUA
ECUA
SKUA

U•B•
UMBO

•UB•
AUBE
BUBO
BUBS
CUBA
CUBE
CUBS
DUBS
HUBS
JUBA
JUBE
NUBS
PUBS
RUBE
RUBS
RUBY
SUBJ
SUBS
TUBA
TUBE
TUBS

•U•B
BULB
CURB
DUMB
NUMB

••UB
CHUB
CLUB
DAUB
DRUB
FLUB
GRUB
SLUB
SNUB
STUB

UC••
UCMJ

U•C•
USCG

U••C
URIC
USMC

•UC•
BUCK
DUCE
DUCK
DUCT
FUCI
GUCK
LUCE
LUCK
LUCY
MUCH
MUCI
MUCK
MUCO
OUCH
PUCE
PUCK
RUCK
SUCH
SUCK
TUCK

•U•C
JUNC

••UC
EDUC
LEUC

UD••
UDOS

U•D•
UNDE
UNDO
UNDY
URDU

U••D
USED

•UD•
BUDS
CUDS
DUDE
DUDS
JUDE
JUDO
JUDY
KUDU
MUDS
NUDE
NUDI
RUDD
RUDE
RUDY
SUDD
SUDS
TUDE

•U•D
AULD
BUND
BURD
CUED
CURD
DUAD
FUND
HUED
KURD
QUAD
QUID
QUOD
RUDD
RUED
SUDD
SUED
SURD

••UD
CRUD
FEUD
GAUD
LAUD
LEUD
LOUD
MAUD
SAUD
SCUD
SPUD
STUD
THUD

U•E•
UREA
UREY
USED
USER
USES
UTER
UTES
UVEA

U••E
UNDE
URGE

•UE•
CUED
CUES
DUEL
DUES
DUET
FUEL
HUED
HUES
LUES
RUED
RUER
RUES
SUED
SUER
SUES
SUET
SUEZ
TUES

•U•E
AUBE
BUTE
CUBE
CULE
CURE
CUTE
DUCE
DUDE
DUKE
DUNE
DUPE
DUSE
FUME
FUSE
FUZE
HUGE
HUME
JUBE
JUDE
JULE
JUNE
JUTE
KURE
LUCE
LUKE
LUNE
LURE
LUTE
LUXE
MULE
MUSE
MUTE
NUDE
OUSE
PUCE
PUKE
PULE
PURE
RUBE
RUDE
RUFE
RULE
RUNE
RUSE
SUPE
SURE
TUBE
TUDE
TULE
TUNE
YULE

••UE
AGUE
BLUE
CLUE
COUE
FLUE
GLUE
MOUE
NIUE
PRUE
ROUE
SLUE
TRUE

U••F
USAF

•UF•
BUFF
CUFF
DUFF
GUFF
HUFF
LUFF
MUFF
PUFF
RUFE
RUFF
SUFI
TUFA
TUFF
TUFT

•U•F
BUFF
CUFF
DUFF
GUFF
GULF
HUFF
LUFF
MUFF
PUFF
RUFF
SURF
TUFF
TURF

••UF
POUF

UG••
UGLY

U•G•
URGE

U••G
USCG

•UG•
BUGS
DUGS
HUGE
HUGH
HUGO
HUGS
JUGS
LUGS
MUGS
PUGH
PUGS
RUGA
RUGS
TUGS
VUGS
YUGA

•U•G
BULG
BUNG
BURG
DUNG
FUNG
HUNG
JUNG
LUNG
PUNG
QUAG
RUNG
SUNG
SURG

••UG
CHUG
DOUG
DRUG
PLUG
SLUG
SMUG
SNUG
THUG

U••H
UTAH

•UH•
BUHL
RUHR

•U•H
AUTH
BUSH
CUSH
GUSH
HUGH
HUSH
LUSH
LUTH
MUCH
MUSH
OUCH
PUGH
PUSH
RUSH
RUTH
SUCH
TUSH

U•I•
UNIT
URIA
URIC
USIA

•UI•
GUIN
LUIS
LUIZ
MUIR
QUID
QUIP
QUIT
QUIZ
RUIN
SUIT

•U•I
FUCI
FUJI
LUNI
MUCI
NUDI
PURI
SUFI
TUPI

••UI
AQUI
EQUI
ETUI
MAUI

U••J
UCMJ

•UJ•
FUJI
JUJU

•U•J
SUBJ

••UJ
CLUJ

•UK•
AUKS
DUKE
LUKE
PUKE
SUKY
YUKS

•U•K
BUCK
BULK
BUNK
BUSK
CUSK
DUCK
DUNK
DUSK
FUNK
GUCK
HULK
HUNK
HUSK
JUNK
LUCK
LURK
MUCK
MUSK
PUCK
PUNK
RUCK
RUSK
SUCK
SULK
SUNK
TUCK
TURK
TUSK

••UK
LEUK
SAUK
TRUK

UL••
ULNA

U•L•
UGLY

U••L
URAL

•UL•
AULD
BULB
BULG
BULK
BULL
CULE
CULL
CULM
CULT
DULL
DULY
FULA
FULL
GULF
GULL
GULP
HULA
HULK
HULL
JULE
JULY
LULL
LULU
MULE
MULL
MULT
NULL
PULE
PULL
PULP
RULE
SULK
SULU
TULE
YULE
ZULU

•U•L
BUHL
BULL
BURL
CULL
CURL
DUAL
DUEL
DULL
FUEL
FULL
FURL
GULL
HULL
HURL
LULL
MULL
NULL
PULL
PURL

••UL
CAUL
ELUL
FOUL
GAUL
HAUL
MAUL
OCUL
PAUL
SAUL
SHUL
SOUL
WAUL

UM••
UMBO
UMTS

U•M•
UCMJ
USMA
USMC
USMS

•UM•
BUMP
BUMS
DUMA
DUMB
DUMP
FUME
FUMY
GUMS
HUME
HUMP
HUMS
JUMP
LUMP
MUMM
MUMS
NUMB
PUMA
PUMP
RUMP
RUMS
SUMO
SUMP
SUMS
YUMA

•U•M
CULM
GUAM
MUMM

••UM
ALUM
ARUM
CHUM
DRUM
GLUM
GRUM
OVUM
PLUM
SCUM
SLUM
STUM
SWUM

UN••
UNAS
UNAU
UNDE
UNDO
UNDY
UNIT
UNTO

U•N•
ULNA
URNS
USNA
USNR

U••N
UPON
URAN

•UN•
AUNT
BUNA
BUND
BUNG
BUNK
BUNN
BUNS
BUNT
DUNE
DUNG
DUNK
DUNS
FUND
FUNG
FUNK
FUNS
GUNS
HUNG
HUNK
HUNS
HUNT
JUNC
JUNE
JUNG
JUNK
JUNO
LUNA
LUNE
LUNG
LUNI
LUNT
NUNS
PUNA
PUNG
PUNK
PUNS
PUNT
PUNY
RUNE
RUNG
RUNS
RUNT
SUNG
SUNK
SUNN
SUNS
TUNA
TUNE
TUNS

•U•N
BUNN
BURN
FURN
GUAN
GUIN
JUAN
MUON
RUIN
SUNN
TURN
YUAN

••UN
FAUN
NOUN
SHUN
SPUN
STUN

U•O•
UDOS
UPON

U••O
UMBO
UNDO
UNTO

•UO•
BUOY
DUOS
MUON
QUOD

•U•O
AUTO
BUBO
DURO
HUGO
JUDO
JUNO
MUCO
SUMO

••UO
FLUO

UP••
UPAS
UPON

•UP•
CUPR
CUPS
DUPE
HUPA
PUPA
PUPS
SUPE
SUPP
SUPS
SUPT
TUPI
TUPS

•U•P
BUMP
BURP
CUSP
DUMP
GULP
HUMP
JUMP
LUMP
PULP
PUMP
QUIP
RUMP
SUMP
SUPP

••UP
COUP
LOUP
ROUP
SCUP
SOUP
YAUP

UR••
URAL
URAN
URDU
UREA
UREY
URGE
URIA
URIC
URNS
URUS

U••R
USAR
USER
USNR
USSR
UTER

•UR•
AURA
BURD
BURG
BURL
BURN
BURP
BURR
BURS
BURY
CURB
CURD
CURE
CURL
CURS
CURT
DURA
DURO
DURR
EURY
FURL
FURN
FURS
FURY
GURU
HURL
HURT
JURA
JURY
KURA
KURD
KURE
KURT
LURE
LURK
OURS
PURE
PURI
PURL
PURR
SURA
SURD
SURE
SURF
SURG
TURF
TURK
TURN

•U•R
BURR
CUPR
DURR
MUIR
PURR
RUER
RUHR
SUER

••UR
AMUR
BLUR
CHUR
DOUR
FOUR
GAUR
HOUR
KNUR
LOUR
NEUR
POUR
SAUR
SLUR
SOUR
SPUR
TAUR
TOUR
YOUR

US••
USAF
USAR
USCG
USED
USER
USES
USIA
USMA
USMC
USMS
USNA
USNR
USSR

U•S•
USSR

U••S
UDOS
UMTS
UNAS
UPAS
URNS
URUS
USES
USMS
UTES

•US•
AUST
BUSH
BUSK
BUSS
BUST
BUSY
CUSH
CUSK
CUSP
CUSS
DUSE
DUSK
DUST
FUSE
FUSS
GUSH
GUST
HUSH
HUSK
JUST
LUSH
LUST
MUSE
MUSH
MUSK
MUSS
MUST
OUSE
OUST
PUSH
PUSS
RUSE
RUSH
RUSK

RUSS
RUST
TUSH
TUSK

•U•S
AUKS
BUBS
BUDS
BUGS
BUMS
BUNS
BURS
BUSS
BUTS
BUYS
CUBS
CUDS
CUES
CUPS
CURS
CUSS
CUTS
DUBS
DUDS
DUES
DUGS
DUNS
DUOS
FUNS
FURS
FUSS
GUMS
GUNS
GUTS
GUYS
HUBS
HUES
HUGS
HUMS
HUNS
HUTS
JUGS
JUTS
LUES
LUGS
LUIS
MUDS
MUGS
MUMS
MUSS
MUTS
NUBS
NUNS
NUTS
OURS
OUTS
PUBS
PUGS
PUNS
PUPS
PUSS
PUTS
RUBS
RUES
RUGS
RUMS
RUNS
RUSS
RUTS
SUBS
SUDS
SUES
SUMS
SUNS
SUPS
TUBS
TUES
TUGS
TUNS
TUPS
VUGS
YUKS

••US
AMUS
ANUS
APUS
BMUS
CRUS
DEUS
DMUS
ECUS
EMUS
EOUS
FEUS
GNUS
ILUS
IOUS
ONUS
OPUS
PIUS
PLUS
SOUS
STUS
TAUS
THUS
URUS
ZEUS

UT••
UTAH
UTER
UTES

U•T•
UMTS
UNTO

U••T
UNIT

•UT•
AUTH
AUTO
BUTE
BUTS
BUTT
CUTE
CUTS
DUTY
GUTS
HUTS
JUTE
JUTS
LUTA
LUTE
LUTH
MUTE
MUTS
MUTT
NUTS
OUTS
PUTS
PUTT
RUTH
RUTS
TUTU

•U•T
AUNT
AUST
BUNT
BUST
BUTT
CULT
CURT
DUCT
DUET
DUST
GUAT
GUST
HUNT
HURT
JUST
KURT
LUNT
LUST
MULT
MUST
MUTT
OUST
PUNT
PUTT
QUIT
RUNT
RUST
SUET
SUIT
SUPT
TUFT

••UT
ABUT
BOUT
BRUT
DEUT
GLUT
GOUT
LOUT
NAUT
POUT
ROUT
SCUT
SHUT
SLUT
SMUT
TAUT
TOUT

U•U•
URUS

U••U
UNAU
URDU

•U•U
GURU
JUJU
KUDU
LUAU
LULU
SULU
TUTU
ZULU

UV••
UVEA

•UV•
SUVA

•UX•
LUXE

••UX
CRUX
EAUX
FLUX
JEUX
ROUX

U••Y
UGLY
UNDY
UREY

•UY•
BUYS
GUYS

•U•Y
BUOY
BURY
BUSY
DULY
DUTY
EURY
FUMY
FURY
JUDY
JULY
JURY
LUCY
PUNY
QUAY
RUBY
RUDY
SUKY
SUZY

•UZ•
BUZZ
FUZE
FUZZ
SUZY

•U•Z
BUZZ
FUZZ
LUIZ
QUIZ
SUEZ

VA••
VAGI
VAIN
VAIR
VALE
VALS
VAMP
VANE
VANG
VANS
VARA
VARI
VARY
VASA
VASE
VASO
VAST
VATS
VAVS

V•A•
VEAL
VIAL

V••A
VARA
VASA
VEDA
VEGA
VELA
VENA
VERA
VINA
VISA
VITA
VIVA
VORA

•VA•
AVAS
EVAN
EVAS
IVAN
OVAL

•V•A
UVEA

••VA
ALVA
DEVA
DIVA
ELVA
JAVA
KAVA
KIVA
LAVA
LEVA
NOVA
SIVA
SUVA
VIVA

V••B
VERB

V•C•
VICE
VICK

V••C
VISC

•V•C
AVEC

V•D•
VEDA
VIDE

V••D
VELD
VEND
VIED
VOID

•V•D
AVID
OVID

••VD
BLVD
NKVD

VE••
VEAL
VEDA
VEER
VEES
VEGA
VEIL
VEIN
VELA
VELD
VENA
VEND
VENI
VENT
VERA
VERB
VERN
VERS
VERT
VERY
VEST
VETO
VETS

V•E•
VEER
VEES
VIED
VIES
VIEW

V••E
VALE
VANE
VASE
VICE
VIDE
VILE
VINE
VISE
VIVE
VOLE
VORE
VOTE

•VE•
AVEC
AVER
AVES
EVEN
EVER
EVES
IVES
OVEN
OVER
UVEA

••VE
CAVE
COVE
DAVE
DIVE
DOVE
FIVE
GAVE
GIVE
HAVE
HIVE
HOVE
JIVE
JOVE
LAVE
LIVE
LOVE
MOVE
NAVE
NEVE
PAVE
RAVE
RIVE
ROVE
SAVE
VIVE
WAVE
WIVE
WOVE

V•G•
VAGI
VEGA
VUGS

V••G
VANG

VI••
VIAL
VICE
VICK
VIDE
VIED
VIES
VIEW
VILE
VILL
VINA
VINE
VINI
VINO
VINY
VIOL
VIPS
VISA
VISC
VISE
VITA
VITR
VIVA
VIVE

V•I•
VAIN
VAIR
VEIL
VEIN
VOID

V••I
VAGI
VARI
VENI
VINI

•VI•
AVID
AVIS
EVIL
OVID

••VI
BOVI
DEVI
LEVI

4

NEVI

V••K
VICK

V•L•
VALE
VALS
VELA
VELD
VILE
VILL
VOLE
VOLS
VOLT

V••L
VEAL
VEIL
VIAL
VILL
VIOL
VTOL

•V•L
EVIL
OVAL

V•M•
VAMP

•V•M
OVUM

V•N•
VANE
VANG
VANS
VENA
VEND
VENI
VENT
VINA
VINE
VINI
VINO
VINY

V••N
VAIN
VEIN
VERN

•V•N
AVON
EVAN
EVEN
IVAN
OVEN

VO••
VOID
VOLE
VOLS
VOLT
VORA
VORE
VOTE
VOWS

V•O•
VIOL
VTOL

V••O
VASO
VETO
VINO

•VO•
AVON
AVOW
IVOR

••VO
LEVO
PAVO

V•P•
VIPS

V••P
VAMP

••VP
RSVP

V•R•
VARA
VARI
VARY
VERA
VERB
VERN
VERS
VERT
VERY
VORA
VORE

V••R
VAIR
VEER
VITR

•V•R
AVER
EVER
IVOR
OVER

V•S•
VASA
VASE
VASO
VAST
VEST
VISA
VISC
VISE

V••S
VALS
VANS
VATS
VAVS
VEES
VERS
VETS
VIES
VIPS
VOLS
VOWS
VUGS

•V•S
AVAS
AVES
AVIS
EVAS
EVES
IVES
IVYS

••VS
BEVS
DEVS
REVS
TAVS
VAVS

VT••
VTOL

V•T•
VATS
VETO
VETS
VITA
VITR
VOTE

V••T
VAST
VENT
VERT
VEST
VOLT

••VT
GOVT

VU••
VUGS

•VU•
OVUM

••VU
KIVU

V•V•
VAVS
VIVA
VIVE

V•W•
VOWS

V••W
VIEW

•V•W
AVOW

V••Y
VARY
VERY
VINY

•VY•
IVYS

••VY
BEVY
CAVY
DAVY
ENVY
LEVY
NAVY
TIVY
WAVY

WA••
WAAC
WAAF
WACK
WACO
WACS
WADE
WADI
WADS
WADY
WAFS
WAFT
WAGE
WAGS
WAIF
WAIL
WAIN
WAIT
WAKE
WALE
WALK
WALL
WALT
WAND
WANE
WANS
WANT
WANY
WAPS
WARD
WARE
WARM
WARN
WARP
WARS
WART
WARY
WASH
WASP
WAST
WATT
WAUL
WAVE
WAVY
WAWL
WAXY
WAYS

W•A•
WAAC
WAAF
WEAK
WEAL
WEAN
WEAR
WHAM
WHAP
WHAT
WOAD
WRAF
WRAP

W••A
WEKA
WHOA

•WA•
AWAY
HWAN
SWAB
SWAG
SWAM
SWAN
SWAP
SWAT
SWAY

•W•A
YWCA
YWHA

••WA
IOWA

W•B•
WEBS

W••B
WOMB

•W•B
SWAB

W•C•
WACK
WACO
WACS
WICH
WICK

W••C
WAAC
WISC

•WC•
YWCA

W•D•
WADE
WADI
WADS
WADY
WEDS
WIDE

W••D
WAND
WARD
WEED
WELD
WEND
WILD
WIND
WOAD
WOLD
WOOD
WORD

•W•D
AWED
OWED

••WD
BAWD
LEWD

WE••
WEAK
WEAL
WEAN
WEAR
WEBS
WEDS
WEED
WEEK
WEEP
WEFT
WEIR
WEKA
WELD
WELL
WELT
WEND
WENS
WENT
WEPT
WERE
WERT
WEST
WETS

W•E•
WEED
WEEK
WEEP
WHEN
WHET
WHEW
WHEY
WOES
WREN
WYES

W••E
WADE
WAGE
WAKE
WALE
WANE
WARE
WAVE
WERE
WIDE
WIFE
WILE
WINE
WIPE
WIRE
WISE
WIVE
WOKE
WORE
WOVE

•WE•
AWED
AWES
EWER
EWES
GWEN
OWED
OWEN
OWES

••WE
HOWE

W•F•
WAFS
WAFT
WEFT
WIFE

W••F
WAAF
WAIF
WOLF
WOOF
WRAF

W•G•
WAGE
WAGS
WIGS

W••G
WHIG
WING

•W•G
SWAG
SWIG
TWIG

WH••
WHAM
WHAP
WHAT
WHEN
WHET
WHEW
WHEY
WHIG
WHIM
WHIN
WHIP
WHIR
WHIT
WHIZ
WHOA
WHOM
WHOP
WHYS

W••H
WASH
WICH
WISH
WITH

•WH•
YWHA

••WH
YHWH

WI••
WICH
WICK
WIDE
WIFE
WIGS
WILD
WILE
WILL
WILT
WILY
WIND
WINE
WING
WINK
WINO
WINS
WINY
WIPE
WIRE
WIRY
WISC
WISE

WISH
WISP
WITH
WITS
WIVE

W•I•
WAIF
WAIL
WAIN
WAIT
WEIR
WHIG
WHIM
WHIN
WHIP
WHIR
WHIT
WHIZ
WRIT

W••I
WADI

•WI•
SWIG
SWIM
TWIG
TWIN
TWIT

••WI
KIWI

WK••
WKLY

W•K•
WAKE
WEKA
WOKE

W••K
WACK
WALK
WEAK
WEEK
WICK
WINK
WORK

••WK
DAWK
GAWK
HAWK

W•L•
WALE
WALK
WALL
WALT
WELD
WELL
WELT
WILD
WILE
WILL
WILT
WILY
WKLY
WOLD
WOLF

W••L
WAIL
WALL
WAUL
WAWL
WEAL
WELL
WILL
WOOL

•WL•
AWLS
OWLS

•W•L
AWOL

••WL
BAWL
BOWL
COWL
FOWL
HOWL
JOWL
MEWL
PAWL
WAWL
YAWL
YOWL

W•M•
WOMB

W••M
WARM
WHAM
WHIM
WHOM
WORM

•W•M
SWAM
SWIM
SWUM

W•N•
WAND
WANE
WANS
WANT
WANY
WEND
WENS
WENT
WIND
WINE
WING
WINK
WINO
WINS
WINY
WONT

W••N
WAIN
WARN
WEAN
WHEN
WHIN
WORN
WREN

•WN•
AWNS
AWNY
OWNS

•W•N
GWEN
GWYN
HWAN
OWEN
SWAN
TWIN

••WN
DAWN
DOWN
FAWN
GOWN
HEWN
LAWN
MOWN
PAWN
SAWN
SEWN
SOWN
TOWN
YAWN

WO••
WOAD
WOES
WOKE
WOLD
WOLF
WOMB
WONT
WOOD
WOOF
WOOL
WOOS
WORD
WORE
WORK
WORM
WORN
WORT
WOVE
WOWS

W•O•
WHOA
WHOM
WHOP
WOOD
WOOF
WOOL
WOOS

W••O
WACO
WINO

•WO•
AWOL
TWOS

W•P•
WAPS
WEPT
WIPE

W••P
WARP
WASP
WEEP
WHAP
WHIP
WHOP
WISP
WRAP

•W•P
SWAP

••WP
YAWP

WR••
WRAF
WRAP
WREN
WRIT

W•R•
WARD
WARE
WARM
WARN
WARP
WARS
WART
WARY
WERE
WERT
WIRE
WIRY
WORD
WORE
WORK
WORM
WORN
WORT

W••R
WEAR
WEIR
WHIR

•WR•
AWRY

•W•R
EWER

W•S•
WASH
WASP
WAST
WEST
WISC
WISE
WISH
WISP

W••S
WACS
WADS
WAFS
WAGS
WANS
WAPS
WARS
WAYS
WEBS
WEDS
WENS
WETS
WHYS
WIGS
WINS
WITS
WOES
WOOS
WOWS
WYES

•W•S
AWES
AWLS
AWNS
EWES
OWES
OWLS
OWNS
TWOS

••WS
BOWS
CAWS
COWS
DAWS
DEWS
HAWS
HEWS
JAWS
JEWS
LAWS
LEWS
LOWS
MAWS
MEWS
MOWS
NEWS
NOWS
PAWS
PEWS
POWS
ROWS
SAWS
SEWS
SOWS
TAWS
TOWS
VOWS
WOWS
YAWS
YEWS
YOWS

W•T•
WATT
WETS
WITH
WITS

W••T
WAFT
WAIT
WALT
WANT
WART
WAST
WATT
WEFT
WELT
WENT
WEPT
WERT
WEST
WHAT
WHET
WHIT
WILT
WONT
WORT
WRIT

•W•T
SWAT
TWIT

••WT
NEWT

W•U•
WAUL

•WU•
SWUM

W•V•
WAVE
WAVY
WIVE
WOVE

W•W•
WAWL
WOWS

W••W
WHEW

W•X•
WAXY

WY••
WYES

W•Y•
WAYS
WHYS

W••Y
WADY
WANY
WARY
WAVY
WAXY
WHEY
WILY
WINY
WIRY
WKLY

•WY•
GWYN

•W•Y
AWAY
AWNY
AWRY
SWAY

••WY
DEWY

W••Z
WHIZ

X•A•
XMAS
XRAY

•XA•
EXAM

•X•A
IXIA

••XA
COXA
HEXA
MOXA

•XC•
EXCH
EXCL

•X•C
EXEC

XD••
XDIV

•X•D
AXED
EXOD

XE••
XENO
XERO

X•E•
XREF

•XE•
AXED
AXES
EXEC
EXES
OXEN

•X•E
AXLE

••XE
LUXE

X••F
XREF

X••H
XIPH

•X•H
EXCH

XI••
XINT
XION
XIPH

X•I•
XDIV

•XI•
AXIL
AXIS
EXIT
IXIA

••XI
SEXI
TAXI

X•L•
XYLO

•XL•
AXLE

•X•L
AXIL
EXCL

XM••
XMAS

•X•M
EXAM

XN••
XNTY

X•N•
XENO
XINT

X••N
XION

•X•N
AXON
OXEN
OXON

X•O•
XION

X••O
XENO
XERO
XYLO

•XO•
AXON
EXOD
OXON

••XO
MYXO

X•P•
XIPH

XR••
XRAY
XREF
XRTS

X•R•
XERO

X•S•
XYST

X••S
XMAS
XRTS

•X•S
AXES
AXIS
EXES

X•T•
XNTY
XRTS

X••T
XINT
XYST

•X•T
EXIT

••XT
MIXT
NEXT
SEXT
TEXT

X••V
XDIV

XY••
XYLO
XYST

X••Y
XNTY
XRAY

••XY
DOXY
FOXY
PIXY
ROXY
SEXY
TAXY
WAXY

YA••
YAKS
YALE
YALU
YAMS
YANG
YANK
YAPS
YARD
YARN
YAUP
YAWL
YAWN
YAWP
YAWS

Y•A•
YEAH
YEAN
YEAR
YEAS
YUAN

Y••A
YMCA
YMHA
YOGA
YUGA
YUMA
YWCA
YWHA

•YA•
AYAH
CYAN
DYAD
DYAK
EYAS
HYAL
KYAT

•Y•A
CYMA
DYNA
EYRA
HYLA
LYRA
MYNA
MYRA

••YA
GAYA
GOYA
MAYA
SOYA

Y•C•
YMCA
YWCA

•YC•
CYCL
MYCO
SYCE

•Y•C
PYIC

Y•D•
YODH
YODS

Y••D
YARD
YOND

•YD•
HYDE
HYDR

•Y•D
BYRD
DYAD
DYED
EYED
RYND

••YD
BOYD

YE••
YEAH
YEAN
YEAR
YEAS
YEGG
YELK
YELL
YELP
YENS
YETI
YEWS

Y•E•
YMER
YSER

Y••E
YALE
YIPE
YOKE
YORE
YULE

•YE•
AYES
BYES
DYED
DYER
DYES
EYED
EYES
HYET
LYES
MYEL
NYET
OYER
OYES
OYEZ
PYEL
PYES
RYES
TYEE
WYES

•Y•E
AYME
BYRE
CYME
CYTE
DYNE
EYRE
FYKE
GYRE
HYDE
LYLE
LYRE
LYSE
LYTE
LYZE
PYLE
PYRE
SYCE
SYNE
TYEE
TYKE
TYPE
TYRE
ZYME

••YE
FAYE
SKYE
SNYE

Y•G•
YEGG
YOGA
YOGH
YOGI
YUGA

Y••G
YANG
YEGG

•YG•
HYGR
ZYGO

YH••
YHWH

Y•H•
YMHA
YWHA

Y••H
YEAH
YHWH
YODH
YOGH

•Y•H
AYAH
MYTH

YI••
YIPE
YIPS

Y•I•
YMIR

Y••I
YETI
YOGI

•YI•
AYIN
PYIC
PYIN

•Y•I
GYRI
LYSI
MYRI

Y•K•
YAKS
YOKE
YUKS

Y••K
YANK
YELK
YOLK
YORK

•YK•
FYKE
TYKE

•Y•K
DYAK

Y•L•
YALE
YALU
YELK
YELL
YELP
YOLK
YULE

Y••L
YAWL
YELL
YOWL

•YL•
HYLA
HYLO
LYLE
PYLE
XYLO

•Y•L
CYCL
HYAL
MYEL
PYEL

••YL
AMYL
ARYL
IDYL
ODYL
PHYL

YM••
YMCA
YMER
YMHA
YMIR

Y•M•
YAMS
YUMA

•YM•
AYME
CYMA
CYME
CYMO
GYMN
GYMS
HYMN
ZYME
ZYMO

Y•N•
YANG
YANK
YENS
YOND

Y••N
YARN
YAWN
YEAN
YUAN

•YN•
DYNA
DYNE
GYNO
LYNN
LYNX
MYNA
RYND
SYNE

•Y•N
AYIN
CYAN
GYMN
HYMN
LYNN
PYIN

••YN
GWYN

YO••
YODH
YODS
YOGA
YOGH
YOGI
YOKE
YOLK
YOND
YORE
YORK
YOUR
YOWL
YOWS
YOYO

Y••O
YOYO

•YO•
GYOR
RYOT

•Y•O
CYMO
CYTO
GYNO
GYRO
HYLO
HYPO
MYCO
MYXO
PYRO
TYPO
TYRO
XYLO
ZYGO
ZYMO

••YO
CRYO
KAYO
MAYO
TOYO
YOYO

Y•P•
YAPS
YIPE
YIPS

Y••P
YAUP
YAWP
YELP

•YP•
GYPS
HYPO
TYPE
TYPO

Y•R•
YARD
YARN
YORE
YORK

Y••R
YEAR
YMER
YMIR
YOUR
YSER

•YR•
BYRD
BYRE
EYRA
EYRE
EYRY
GYRE
GYRI

GYRO
LYRA
LYRE
MYRA
MYRI
PYRE
PYRO
TYRE
TYRO

•Y•R
DYER
GYOR
HYDR
HYGR
OYER

YS••
YSER

Y••S
YAKS
YAMS
YAPS
YAWS
YEAS
YENS
YEWS
YIPS
YODS
YOWS
YUKS

•YS•
CYST
LYSE
LYSI
XYST

•Y•S
AYES
BYES
DYES
EYAS
EYES
GYMS
GYPS
LYES
OYES
PYES
RYES
WYES

••YS
ALYS
AMYS
BAYS
BEYS
BOYS
BUYS
CAYS
DAYS
DEYS
FAYS
FOYS
GAYS
GUYS
HAYS
HOYS
ITYS
IVYS
JAYS
JOYS
KAYS
KEYS
LAYS
MAYS
NAYS
PAYS
RAYS
ROYS
SAYS
SOYS
TOYS
WAYS
WHYS

Y•T•
YETI

•YT•
CYTE
CYTO
LYTE
MYTH

•Y•T
CYST
HYET
KYAT
NYET
RYOT
XYST

••YT
PHYT

YU••
YUAN
YUGA
YUKS
YULE
YUMA

Y•U•
YAUP
YOUR

Y••U
YALU

YW••
YWCA
YWHA

Y•W•
YAWL
YAWN
YAWP
YAWS
YEWS
YHWH
YOWL
YOWS

•YX•
MYXO

•Y•X
LYNX

••YX
ONYX
ORYX
PNYX
STYX

Y•Y•
YOYO

•Y•Y
EYRY

•YZ•
LYZE

•Y•Z
OYEZ

ZA••
ZACH
ZACK
ZANY
ZARF

Z•A•
ZBAR
ZEAL
ZOAN

Z••A
ZETA
ZOLA

•ZA•
AZAN
CZAR
TZAR

•Z•A
EZRA

••ZA
GAZA
GIZA
LIZA

ZB••
ZBAR

Z•B•
ZEBU

Z•C•
ZACH
ZACK

Z••C
ZINC
ZOIC

Z•D•
ZEDS

Z••D
ZEND

ZE••
ZEAL
ZEBU
ZEDS
ZEES
ZEIN
ZEKE
ZEND
ZENO
ZEPH
ZERO
ZEST
ZETA
ZEUS

Z•E•
ZEES
ZOES

Z••E
ZEKE
ZONE
ZYME

•ZE•
EZEK

••ZE
ADZE
DAZE
DOZE
FAZE
FUZE
GAZE
HAZE
LAZE
LYZE
MAZE
OOZE
RAZE
SIZE

Z••F
ZARF

Z•G•
ZYGO

Z••G
ZING

Z••H
ZACH
ZEPH

ZI••
ZINC
ZING
ZION
ZIPS

Z•I•
ZEIN
ZOIC

••ZI
NAZI

Z•K•
ZEKE

Z••K
ZACK

•Z•K
EZEK

Z•L•
ZOLA
ZULU

Z••L
ZEAL
ZOOL

Z•M•
ZYME
ZYMO

Z••M
ZOOM

Z•N•
ZANY
ZEND
ZENO
ZINC
ZING
ZONE

Z••N
ZEIN
ZION
ZOAN
ZOON

•Z•N
AZAN
AZON

ZO••
ZOAN
ZOES
ZOIC
ZOLA
ZONE
ZOOL
ZOOM
ZOON
ZOOS

Z•O•
ZION
ZOOL
ZOOM
ZOON
ZOOS

Z••O
ZENO
ZERO
ZYGO
ZYMO

•ZO•
AZON
AZOV

••ZO
BOZO

Z•P•
ZEPH
ZIPS

Z•R•
ZARF
ZERO

Z••R
ZBAR

•ZR•
EZRA

•Z•R
CZAR
TZAR

Z•S•
ZEST

Z••S
ZEDS
ZEES
ZEUS
ZIPS
ZOES
ZOOS

Z•T•
ZETA

Z••T
ZEST

ZU••
ZULU

Z•U•
ZEUS

Z••U
ZEBU
ZULU

•Z•V
AZOV

ZY••
ZYGO
ZYME
ZYMO

Z••Y
ZANY

•Z•Y
IZZY

••ZY
COZY
DOZY
HAZY
IZZY
LAZY
MAZY
OOZY
SIZY
SUZY

•ZZ•
IZZY

••ZZ
BUZZ
FIZZ
FUZZ
JAZZ
PIZZ
RAZZ

5-LETTER WORDS

AA•••
AALII
AARON

A•A••
ABACA
ABACI
ABACK
ABAFT
ABASE
ABASH
ABATE
ADAGE
ADAHS
ADAMS
ADAPT
AGAIN
AGAMA
AGANA
AGAPE
AGATE
AGAVE
AGAZE
ALACK
ALAMO
ALANS
ALARM
ALARY
ALATE
AMAHS
AMAIN
AMASS
AMATI
AMAZE
APACE
APART
AQABA
ARABS
ARABY
ATAXY
AVAIL
AVARS
AVAST
AWAIT
AWAKE
AWARD
AWARE
AWASH
AYAHS
AZANS

A••A•
ABBAS
ABEAM
ABRAM
ACEAE
ACEAN
ADDAX
ADMAN
AETAT
AGHAS
AHEAD
AIDAS
ALBAN
ALBAS
ALCAN
ALDAN
ALGAE
ALGAL
ALIAS
ALLAH
ALLAN
ALLAY
ALMAH
ALMAS
ALTAI
ALTAR
ALTAS
ALVAN
ALWAY
AMIAS
AMMAN
ANEAR
ANLAS
ANNAL
ANNAM
ANNAS
ANSAE
ANTAE
ANZAC
APEAK
APIAN
APPAL
AQUAE
AQUAS
AREAE
AREAL
AREAS
ARGAL
ARIAN
ARIAS
ARPAD
ARRAN
ARRAS
ARRAY
ARVAL
ARYAN
ASCAP
ASIAN
ASSAI
ASSAM
ASSAY
ASWAN
ATLAS
ATMAN
ATTAR
AUDAD
AURAE
AURAL
AURAS
AVIAN
AXIAL
AXMAN

A•••A
ABACA
ABOMA
ACCRA
ADELA
ADYTA
AECIA
AEMIA
AFTRA
AGAMA
AGANA
AGORA
ALEXA
ALGIA
ALOHA
ALPHA
ALULA
AMEBA
AMNIA
ANIMA
ANITA
ANTRA
AORTA
APNEA
AQABA
ARECA
ARENA
ARICA
AROMA
ARUBA
ASPCA
ASYLA
ATRIA

•AA••
BAAED
KAABA
NAACP

•A•A•
BABAR
BABAS
BAHAI
BALAS
BANAL
BANAT
BASAL
BATAN
CABAL
CACAO
CANAD
CANAL
CARAS
CARAT
DAGAN
DAKAR
DAMAN
DANAE
DAVAO
FARAD
FATAL
FAYAL
GALAS
GALAX
HAHAS
HAMAL
HARAR
JALAP
JAPAN
KAKAS
KALAT
KARAT
KAUAI
KAVAS
KAYAK
KAZAN
LAGAN
LAMAS
LANAI
LAOAG
LAPAR
LAVAS
LAZAR
MACAO
MACAW
MADAM
MAHAN
MALAC
MALAR
MALAY
MAMAS
MARAT
MAYAN
MAYAS
NAIAD
NANAS
NASAL
NATAL
NAVAL
NAVAR
NAWAB
PACAS
PAEAN
PAGAN
PALAE
PAPAL
PAPAS
PAPAW
PARAS
PAVAN
QATAR
RADAR
RAJAB
RAJAH
RATAL
RAYAH
SABAH
SAGAS
SALAD
SAMAR
SARAH
SARAN
SARAS
SATAN
TATAR
VARAS
WATAP

•A••A
BALSA
BANDA
BARCA
BASRA
CALLA
CANEA
CANNA
CAPUA
CARLA
CAUCA
DACCA
DACHA
DACIA
FANGA
FAUNA
GALEA
GAMMA
HAIDA
HAIFA
HAMZA
HANNA
JAFFA
JAINA
KAABA
KAFKA
KAPPA
KARMA
LABIA
LABRA
LAIKA
LAMIA
LARVA
LAURA
MAFIA
MAGDA
MAGMA
MAMBA
MAMMA
MANIA
MANNA
MANTA
MARIA
MARTA
MAURA
NAHUA
PADUA
PAISA
PALEA
PANDA
PAPUA
PARKA
PASHA
PASTA
PAULA
SABRA
SACRA
SAIGA
SALPA
SAMBA

SAMOA
SAUNA
TAFIA
TAIGA
TAMPA
TANKA
TATRA
TAZZA
VACUA
WALLA
WANDA
YALTA
ZAMIA

••AA•
CRAAL
GRAAL
ISAAC
KRAAL

••A•A
ABACA
AGAMA
AGANA
AQABA
BEATA
BRAVA
BRAZA
BWANA
CEARA
CLARA
DIANA
DRAMA
DRAVA
DUALA
GHANA
GRAMA
GUAVA
JUANA
KAABA
KLARA
KOALA
LHASA
LIANA
LLAMA
OMAHA
OMASA
PLAYA
PLAZA
RIATA
SCAPA
TIARA

AB•••
ABACA
ABACI
ABACK
ABAFT
ABASE
ABASH
ABATE
ABBAS
ABBES
ABBEY
ABBIE
ABBOT
ABBYS
ABEAM
ABELE
ABELS
ABETS
ABHOR
ABIBS
ABIDE
ABIEL
ABIES
ABLER
ABNER
ABODE
ABOHM
ABOMA
ABOMB
ABORT
ABOUT
ABOVE
ABRAM
ABRIS
ABUSE
ABUTS
ABYSM
ABYSS

A•B••
ABBAS
ABBES
ABBEY
ABBIE
ABBOT
ABBYS
ALBAN
ALBAS
ALBEE
ALBIN
ALBUM
AMBER
AMBIT
AMBLE
AMBOS
AMBRY
ARBOR

A••B•
ABIBS
ADOBE
ALIBI
AMEBA
AQABA
ARABS
ARABY
ARUBA

A•••B
ABOMB
ACERB
ADLIB
ARDEB

•AB••
BABAR
BABAS
BABEL
BABER
BABES
BABOO
BABUL
CABAL
CABBY
CABER
CABIN
CABLE
CABOB
CABOT
FABLE
GABBY
GABES
GABLE
GABON
GABYS
HABIT
HABUS
JABEZ
JABOT
KABOB
KABUL
LABEL
LABIA
LABIO
LABOR
LABRA
MABEL
NABOB
PABLO
RABBI
RABIC
RABID
SABAH
SABED
SABER
SABES
SABIN
SABLE
SABOT
SABRA
TABBY
TABES
TABID
TABLE
TABOO
TABOR

•A•B•
BARBS
CABBY
CARBO
DAUBS
DAUBY
GABBY
GAMBS
GARBS
IAMBI
IAMBS
JAMBS
KAABA
LAMBS
MAMBA
MAMBO
MAYBE
RABBI
SAMBA
SAMBO
TABBY

•A••B
CABOB
CALEB
CARIB
CAROB
JACOB
JAKOB
KABOB
NABOB
NAWAB
RAJAB
SAHEB
SAHIB

••AB•
AQABA
ARABS
ARABY
BLABS
CRABS
DRABS
GRABS
KAABA
SCABS
SLABS
STABS
SWABS

•••AB
NAWAB
RAJAB
SQUAB

AC•••
ACCEL
ACCRA
ACEAE
ACEAN
ACERB
ACETO
ACHED
ACHES
ACIDS
ACING
ACINI
ACITY
ACOCK
ACORN
ACOUO
ACRED
ACRES
ACRID
ACTED
ACTIN
ACTOR
ACUTE

A•C••
ACCEL
ACCRA
AECIA
ALCAN
ANCON
ARCED
ARCHI
ARCHY
ARCUS
ASCAP
ASCOT
ASCUS

A••C•
ABACA
ABACI
ABACK
ACOCK
AITCH
ALACK
ALECK
ALECS
ALICE
ALYCE
AMICE
AMUCK
APACE
ARECA
ARICA
ASPCA

A•••C
ADUNC
ANTIC
ANZAC
AREIC
ASPIC
ASSOC
ATTIC
AULIC
AURIC
AZOIC
AZTEC

•AC••
BACCI
BACKS
BACON
CACAO
CACHE
CACTI
DACCA
DACES
DACHA
DACIA
FACED
FACER
FACES
FACET
FACTS
HACKS
JACKS
JACKY
JACOB
LACED
LACES
LACKS
LACTO
MACAO
MACAW
MACED
MACER
MACES
MACHY
MACKS
MACLE
MACON
MACRO
NACRE
PACAS
PACED
PACER
PACES
PACHY
PACKS
PACTS
RACED
RACER
RACES
RACKS
SACKS
SACRA
SACRO
TACET
TACHY
TACIT
TACKS
TACKY
VACUA
WACKE
WACKS
WACKY
YACHT

•A•C•
BACCI
BARCA
BATCH
CALCI
CASCO
CATCH
CAUCA
DACCA
DANCE
FANCY
FARCE
FARCY
HANCE
HATCH
LANCE
LARCH
LATCH
MANCY
MARCH
MARCO
MARCS
MATCH
NAACP
NANCY
NARCO
PARCH
PASCH
PATCH
RANCE
RANCH
RATCH
SARCO
SAUCE
SAUCY
TALCS
WATCH

•A••C
BARIC
BASIC
DARIC
GAMIC
HAVOC
MAGIC
MALAC
MALIC
MANIC
PANIC
RABIC
SALIC
VARIC
VATIC

••AC•
ABACA
ABACI
ABACK
ALACK
APACE
BEACH
BLACK
BRACE
BRACT
CLACK
COACH
CRACK
CRACY
DRACO
ENACT
EPACT
EXACT
FLACK
GLACE
GRACE
GUACO
KNACK
LEACH
LOACH
NAACP
ORACH
PEACE
PEACH
PLACE
PLACK
POACH
QUACK
REACH
REACT
ROACH
SHACK
SLACK
SMACK
SNACK
SPACE
STACK
STACY
TEACH
TRACE
TRACH
TRACK
TRACT
WHACK
WRACK

••A•C
BLANC
FRANC
GLAUC
ISAAC

•••AC
ANZAC
ILEAC
ILIAC
ISAAC
LILAC
MALAC
SERAC
SUMAC

AD•••
ADAGE
ADAHS
ADAMS
ADAPT
ADDAX
ADDED
ADDER
ADDIE
ADDLE
ADDYS
ADEEM
ADELA
ADELE
ADENI
ADENO
ADEPT
ADIEU
ADIOS
ADITS
ADLER
ADLIB
ADMAN
ADMEN
ADMIN
ADMIT

ADMIX
ADOBE
ADOLF
ADOPT
ADORE
ADORN
ADULT
ADUNC
ADUST
ADYTA
ADZES

A•D••

ADDAX
ADDED
ADDER
ADDIE
ADDLE
ADDYS
AEDES
AIDAS
AIDED
AIDER
AIDES
ALDAN
ALDEN
ALDER
ALDIS
ALDOL
ALDOS
ALDUS
ANDES
ANDRE
ANDRO
ANDYS
ARDEB
ARDEN
ARDOR
AUDAD
AUDEN
AUDIO
AUDIT
AYDIN

A••D•

ABIDE
ABODE
ACIDS
AMIDE
AMIDO
ANODE
ASIDE

A•••D

ACHED
ACRED
ACRID
ACTED
ADDED
AHEAD
AIDED
AILED
AIMED
AIRED
ALGID
ALMUD
ALOUD
AMEND
ANTED
APHID
ARCED
ARMED
AROID
ARPAD
ASKED
AUDAD
AVOID
AWARD
AWNED
AXLED

•AD••

BADEN
BADGE
BADLY
CADDO
CADDY
CADES
CADET
CADGE
CADIS
CADIZ
CADRE
DADDY
EADIE
FADDY
FADED
FADES
GADID
HADED
HADES
HADJI
JADED
JADES
KADIS
LADED
LADEN
LADES
LADIN
LADLE
MADAM
MADGE
MADLY
NADER
NADIR
PADDY
PADRE
PADUA
RADAR
RADII
RADIO
RADIX
RADON
SADHU
SADIE
SADLY
VADUZ
WADDY
WADED
WADER
WADES

•A•D•

BALDR
BANDA
BANDS
BANDY
BARDE
BARDS
BAWDS
BAWDY
CADDO
CADDY
CANDY
CARDI
CARDS
DADDY
DANDY
FADDY
GAUDI
GAUDS
GAUDY
HAIDA
HANDS
HANDY
HARDS
HARDY
HAYDN
KANDY
LANDS
LARDS
LARDY
LAUDS
MAGDA
MAHDI
MAIDS
MANDY
MAUDE
MAUDS
NARDS
PADDY
PAEDO
PANDA
PANDY
PARDS
RAIDS
RANDS
RANDY
SANDS
SANDY
TARDY
WADDY
WALDO
WANDA
WANDS
WARDS
YARDS

•A••D

BAAED
BAIRD
BAKED
BALED
BARED
BASED
BATED
BAYED
CAGED
CAIRD
CAKED
CANAD
CANED
CARED
CASED
CAVED
CAWED
DARED
DATED
DAVID
DAZED
EARED
EASED
FACED
FADED
FAKED
FAMED
FARAD
FARED
FATED
FAXED
FAYED
FAZED
GADID
GAGED
GAMED
GAPED
GATED
GAZED
HADED
HALED
HALID
HATED
HAWED
HAYED
HAZED
JADED
JARED
JAWED
LACED
LADED
LAIRD
LAKED
LAMED
LAVED
LAWED
LAZED
MACED
MANED
MATED
MAUND
MAZED
NAIAD
NAKED
NAMED
OARED
PACED
PAGED
PALED
PARED
PAVED
PAWED
PAYED
RABID
RACED
RAGED
RAKED
RAPED
RAPID
RATED
RAVED
RAYED
RAZED
SABED
SALAD
SAPID
SATED
SAVED
SAWED
SAYID
TABID
TAMED
TAPED
TARED
TAWED
TAXED
VALID
VANED
VAPID
WADED
WAGED
WAKED
WALED
WANED
WAVED
WAXED
YAWED

••AD•

BEADS
BEADY
BLADE
BRADS
BRADY
DUADS
DYADS
EVADE
GLADE
GLADS
GOADS
GRADE
GRADS
HEADS
HEADY
KHADI
LEADS
LEADY
LOADS
MEADS
QUADS
READS
READY
ROADS
SCADS
SHADE
SHADY
SPADE
THADS
THADY
TOADS
TOADY
TRADE
TSADE
WOADS

••A•D

AWARD
BAAED
BEARD
BLAND
BOARD
BRAID
BRAND
CHARD
ELAND
FRAUD
GLAND
GRAND
GUARD
HEARD
HOARD
PLAID
ROALD
SCALD
SCAND
SHARD
SKALD
STAID
STAND
SWARD
VIAND
WEALD
WOALD

•••AD

AHEAD
ARPAD
AUDAD
BREAD
BROAD
CANAD
CYCAD
DREAD
DRYAD
FARAD
GONAD
HEXAD
ILIAD
JIHAD
KNEAD
MONAD
NAIAD
NOMAD
OCTAD
OREAD
PLEAD
SALAD
SQUAD
STEAD
TREAD
TRIAD

AE•••

AECIA
AEDES
AEGIR
AEGIS
AEMIA
AEONS
AERIE
AESIR
AESOP
AETAT

A•E••

ABEAM
ABELE
ABELS
ABETS
ACEAE
ACEAN
ACERB
ACETO
ADEEM
ADELA
ADELE
ADENI
ADENO
ADEPT
AGENT
AHEAD
AKENE
ALECK
ALECS
ALEFS
ALEPH
ALERT
ALEUT
ALEXA
AMEBA
AMEND
AMENS
AMENT
ANEAR
ANEMO
ANENT
APEAK
APERY
AREAE
AREAL
AREAS
ARECA
AREIC
ARENA
ARENT
ARETE
AVENS
AVERS
AVERT
AVERY

A••E•

ABBES
ABBEY
ABIEL
ABIES
ABLER
ABNER
ACCEL
ACHED
ACHES
ACRED
ACRES
ACTED
ADDED
ADDER
ADEEM
ADIEU
ADLER
ADMEN
ADZES
AEDES
AFTER
AGGER
AGLEE
AGLET
AGLEY
AGNES
AGREE
AGUES
AIDED
AIDER
AIDES
AIKEN
AILED
AIMED
AIMEE
AIRED
ALBEE
ALDEN
ALDER
ALGER
ALIEN
ALLEN
ALLEY
ALOES
ALTER
AMBER
AMIEL
AMIES
ANDES
ANGEL
ANGER
ANNES
ANNEX
ANSEL
ANTED
ANTES
APNEA
APPEL
APSES
ARCED
ARDEB

ARDEN
ARIEL
ARIES
ARLES
ARMED
ARMET
ARPEN
ARSES
ARTEL
ARTER
ASHEN
ASHER
ASHES
ASKED
ASKER
ASKEW
ASPEN
ASPER
ASSES
ASSET
ASTER
AUDEN
AUGER
AUREI
AURES
AWNED
AXLED
AXLES
AXMEN
AZTEC

A•••E

ABASE
ABATE
ABBIE
ABELE
ABIDE
ABODE
ABOVE
ABUSE
ACEAE
ACUTE
ADAGE
ADDIE
ADDLE
ADELE
ADOBE
ADORE
AERIE
AFIRE
AGAPE
AGATE
AGAVE
AGAZE
AGGIE
AGILE
AGLEE
AGREE
AIMEE
AISLE
AISNE
AKENE
ALATE
ALBEE
ALGAE
ALGIE
ALICE
ALIKE
ALINE
ALIVE
ALLIE
ALONE
ALYCE
AMAZE
AMBLE
AMICE
AMIDE
AMINE
AMOLE
AMPLE
AMUSE
ANDRE
ANGLE
ANILE
ANIME
ANISE
ANKLE
ANNIE
ANODE
ANSAE
ANTAE
APACE
APPLE
AQUAE
AREAE
ARETE
ARGUE
ARISE
ARNIE
AROSE
ARTIE
ASIDE
ATIVE
ATONE
AURAE
AWAKE
AWARE
AWOKE
AXILE
AXONE
AZINE
AZOLE
AZOTE
AZURE

•AE••

GAELS
PAEAN
PAEDO
PAEON
TAELS

•A•E•

BAAED
BABEL
BABER
BABES
BADEN
BAGEL
BAKED
BAKER
BAKES
BALED
BALER
BALES
BARED
BARER
BARES
BASED
BASEL
BASES
BATED
BATES
BAYED
CABER
CADES
CADET
CAFES
CAGED
CAGES
CAGEY
CAKED
CAKES
CALEB
CAMEL
CAMEO
CAMES
CANEA
CANED
CANER
CANES
CAPEK
CAPER
CAPES
CAPET
CARED
CARER
CARES
CARET
CAREY
CASED
CASES
CATER
CAVED
CAVES
CAWED
DACES
DALES
DAMES
DANES
DARED
DARER
DARES
DATED
DATER
DATES
DAVES
DAVEY
DAZED
DAZES
EAGER
EARED
EASED
EASEL
EASES
EATEN
EATER
EAVES
FACED
FACER
FACES
FACET
FADED
FADES
FAKED
FAKER
FAKES
FAMED
FARED
FARER
FARES
FATED
FATES
FAXED
FAXES
FAYED
FAYES
FAZED
FAZES
GABES
GAGED
GAGER
GAGES
GALEA
GALEN
GALES
GAMED
GAMES
GANEF
GAPED
GAPER
GAPES
GASES
GATED
GATES
GAVEL
GAYER
GAZED
GAZER
GAZES
HADED
HADES
HAKES
HALED
HALER
HALES
HAMES
HAREM
HARES
HATED
HATER
HATES
HAVEN
HAWED
HAYED
HAYES
HAZED
HAZEL
HAZER
HAZES
JABEZ
JADED
JADES
JAKES
JAMES
JANES
JANET
JAPES
JARED
JAWED
KAMES
KAMET
KAREN
KATES
LABEL
LACED
LACES
LADED
LADEN
LADES
LAGER
LAKED
LAKER
LAKES
LAMED
LAMER
LAMES
LANES
LAPEL
LARES
LASER
LATER
LATEX
LAVED
LAVER
LAVES
LAWED
LAXER
LAYER
LAZED
LAZES
MABEL
MACED
MACER
MACES
MAGES
MAKER
MAKES
MALES
MAMEY
MANED
MANES
MANET
MARES
MASER
MATED
MATEO
MATES
MATEY
MAZED
MAZER
MAZES
NADER
NAKED
NAMED
NAMER
NAMES
NAPES
NARES
NATES
NAVEL
NAVES
OAKEN
OARED
OASES
OATEN
OATES
OAVES
PACED
PACER
PACES
PAGED
PAGES
PALEA
PALED
PALEO
PALER
PALES
PALEY
PANEL
PANES
PAPEN
PAPER
PARED
PAREN
PARER
PARES
PAREU
PATEN
PATER
PATES
PAVED
PAVER
PAVES
PAWED
PAWER
PAYED
PAYEE
PAYER
RACED
RACER
RACES
RAGED
RAGEE
RAGES
RAKED
RAKEE
RAKER
RAKES
RALES
RANEE
RAPED
RAPES
RARER
RATED
RATEL
RATER
RATES
RAVED
RAVEL
RAVEN
RAVER
RAVES
RAWER
RAYED
RAZED
RAZEE
RAZES
SABED
SABER
SABES
SAFER
SAFES
SAGER
SAGES
SAHEB
SAKER
SAKES
SALEM
SALEP
SALES
SAMEK
SANER
SATED
SATES
SAVED
SAVER
SAVES
SAWED
SAWER
SAXES
SAYER
TABES
TACET
TAKEN
TAKER
TAKES
TALER
TALES
TAMED
TAMER
TAMES
TANEY
TAPED
TAPER
TAPES
TARED
TARES
TAWED
TAWER
TAXED
TAXER
TAXES
VALES
VALET
VANED
VANES
VASES
WADED
WADER
WADES
WAFER
WAGED
WAGER
WAGES
WAKED
WAKEN
WAKES
WALED
WALER
WALES
WANED
WANES
WANEY
WARES
WATER
WAVED
WAVER
WAVES
WAVEY
WAXED
WAXEN
WAXES
XAXES
YAGER
YAMEN
YAWED
YAXES

•A••E

BADGE
BAIZE
BARDE
BARGE
BARYE
BASLE
BASTE
BATHE
BAUME
CABLE
CACHE
CADGE
CADRE
CALPE
CALVE
CANOE
CARTE
CARVE
CASTE
CAUSE
CAVIE
DANAE
DANCE
DANTE
DAVIE
EADIE
EAGLE
EAGRE
EARLE
FABLE
FALSE
FARCE

FARLE
GABLE
GAFFE
GASPE
GAUGE
GAUZE
GAVLE
HAGUE
HALLE
HALVE
HANCE
HANSE
HARTE
HASTE
HAWSE
JAMIE
KATIE
LADLE
LANCE
LAPSE
LARGE
LATHE
MACLE
MADGE
MAINE
MAIZE
MAMIE
MANGE
MANSE
MAPLE
MARGE
MARIE
MARNE
MASSE
MATTE
MAUDE
MAUVE
MAYBE
NACRE
NAIVE
NAPPE
PADRE
PAINE
PAISE
PALAE
PARSE
PASSE
PASTE
PAUSE
PAYEE
RAGEE
RAISE
RAKEE
RAMIE
RANCE
RANEE
RANGE
RAPHE
RAZEE
SABLE
SADIE
SALVE
SAUCE
SAUTE
TABLE
TAHOE
TASTE
TAUPE
VAGUE
VALUE
VALVE
VARVE
WACKE
WAIVE
WASTE
WAYNE
YAHVE
ZAIRE

••AE•

BAAED
BRAES
CHAET
ELAEO

••A•E

ABASE
ABATE
ADAGE
AGAPE
AGATE
AGAVE
AGAZE
ALATE
AMAZE
APACE
AWAKE
AWARE
BLADE
BLAKE
BLAME
BLARE
BLASE
BLAZE
BRACE
BRAGE
BRAHE
BRAKE
BRAVE
BRAZE
CEASE
CHAFE
CHAPE
CHARE
CHASE
CLARE
CRAKE
CRANE
CRAPE
CRATE
CRAVE
CRAZE
DEANE
DIANE
DRAKE
DRAPE
DRAVE
DUANE
ELATE
ENATE
ERASE
ETAPE
EVADE
FEASE
FLAKE
FLAME
FLARE
FRAME
GLACE
GLADE
GLARE
GLAZE
GRACE
GRADE
GRAPE
GRATE
GRAVE
GRAZE
HEAVE
IMAGE
INANE
IRATE
KNAVE
LEASE
LEAVE
LIANE
ORATE
OSAGE
OVATE
PEACE
PEASE
PHAGE
PHANE
PHASE
PIAVE
PLACE
PLANE
PLATE
PRATE
QUAKE
RHAGE
SCALE
SCAPE
SCARE
SHADE
SHAKE
SHALE
SHAME
SHAPE
SHARE
SHAVE
SKATE
SLAKE
SLATE
SLAVE
SMAZE
SNAKE
SNARE
SPACE
SPADE
SPARE
SPATE
STAGE
STAKE
STALE
STARE
STATE
STAVE
SUAVE
SWAGE
SWALE
TEASE
THANE
TRACE
TRADE
TRAVE
TSADE
UKASE
URATE
USAGE
WEAVE
WHALE

•••AE

ACEAE
ALGAE
ANSAE
ANTAE
AQUAE
AREAE
AURAE
COMAE
COXAE
CYMAE
DANAE
HORAE
MINAE
MORAE
NOVAE
PALAE
PUPAE
RUGAE
SETAE
STOAE
TELAE
TOGAE
ULNAE
VENAE
VITAE

AF•••

AFFIX
AFIRE
AFOOT
AFOUL
AFROS
AFTER
AFTRA

A•F••

AFFIX
AWFUL

A••F•

ABAFT
ALEFS
ALIFS
ALOFT

A•••F

ADOLF
ALOOF

•AF••

BAFFS
BAFFY
CAFES
DAFFY
GAFFE
GAFFS
HAFIZ
HAFTS
JAFFA
KAFKA
MAFIA
RAFTS
SAFER
SAFES
TAFFY
TAFIA
WAFER
WAFTS

•A•F•

BAFFS
BAFFY
BANFF
DAFFY
GAFFE
GAFFS
HAIFA
JAFFA
TAFFY
WAIFS
ZARFS

•A••F

BANFF
CALIF
GANEF

••AF•

ABAFT
CHAFE
CHAFF
CRAFT
DRAFF
DRAFT
GRAFT
KRAFT
LEAFS
LEAFY
LOAFS
OLAFS
QUAFF
SHAFT
SNAFU
STAFF
USAFI

••A•F

CHAFF
DRAFF
DWARF
QUAFF
SCARF
STAFF
WHARF

•••AF

PILAF
SHEAF

AG•••

AGAIN
AGAMA
AGANA
AGAPE
AGATE
AGAVE
AGAZE
AGENT
AGGER
AGGIE
AGHAS
AGILE
AGING
AGIOS
AGIST
AGLEE
AGLET
AGLEY
AGLOW
AGNES
AGNIS
AGONY
AGORA
AGREE
AGUES

A•G••

AEGIR
AEGIS
AGGER
AGGIE
ALGAE
ALGAL
ALGER
ALGIA
ALGID
ALGIE
ALGIN
ALGOL
ALGOR
ALGUM
ALGYS
ANGEL
ANGER
ANGIO
ANGLE
ANGLO
ANGRY
ANGST
ANGUS
ARGAL
ARGIL
ARGOL
ARGON
ARGOS
ARGOT
ARGUE
ARGUS
AUGER
AUGHT
AUGUR

A••G•

ADAGE
ALIGN
AMIGO

A•••G

ACING
AGING
ALMUG
ALONG
AMONG
APING
AWING
AXING

•AG••

BAGEL
BAGGY
CAGED
CAGES
CAGEY
DAGAN
EAGER
EAGLE
EAGRE
FAGOT
GAGED
GAGER
GAGES
HAGIO
HAGUE
JAGGS
JAGGY
KAGUS
LAGAN
LAGER
LAGOS
MAGDA
MAGES
MAGIC
MAGMA
MAGNI
MAGOT
MAGUS
PAGAN
PAGED
PAGES
RAGED
RAGEE
RAGES
RAGGY
SAGAS
SAGER
SAGES
SAGOS
SAGUM
VAGIN
VAGUE
VAGUS
WAGED
WAGER
WAGES
WAGON
YAGER

•A•G•

BADGE
BAGGY
BANGS
BARGE
CADGE
CARGO
DANGS
FANGA
FANGS
FARGO
FAUGH
GANGS
GAUGE
HANGS
JAGGS
JAGGY
LARGE
LARGO
LAUGH
MADGE
MANGE
MANGO
MANGY
MARGE
MARGO
PANGS
PARGO
RAGGY
RANGE
RANGY
SAIGA
TAIGA
TANGO
TANGS
TANGY
VANGS
WAUGH

•A••G

LAOAG

••AG•

ADAGE
BRAGE
BRAGI
BRAGS
CRAGS
DRAGS
FLAGS
IMAGE

IMAGO
OSAGE
PHAGE
PHAGO
PHAGY
PLAGI
QUAGS
RHAGE
RHAGY
SHAGS
SLAGS
SNAGS
STAGE
STAGS
STAGY
SWAGE
SWAGS
TRAGI
USAGE

••A•G

BHANG
CHANG
CLANG
CRAIG
LIANG
ORANG
SLANG
SPANG
TWANG
WHANG

•••AG

LAOAG
SCRAG
SPRAG

AH•••

AHEAD

A•H••

ABHOR
ACHED
ACHES
AGHAS
APHID
APHIS
ASHEN
ASHER
ASHES
ASHUR
ATHOS

A••H•

ABOHM
ADAHS
ALOHA
ALPHA
ALPHY
AMAHS
AMPHI
AMPHR
ANKHS
ANTHO
ARCHI
ARCHY
ARTHR
AUGHT
AYAHS

A•••H

ABASH
AITCH
ALEPH
ALLAH
ALMAH
AMISH
APISH
AWASH
AZOTH

•AH••

BAHAI
BAHTS
HAHAS
MAHAN
MAHDI
NAHUA
NAHUM
SAHEB
SAHIB
TAHOE
WAHOO
YAHOO
YAHVE

•A•H•

BATHE
BATHO
BATHS
BATHY
CACHE
CATHY
DACHA
DASHY
KAPHS
KATHY
LATHE
LATHS
LATHY
MACHY
MASHY
OATHS
PACHY
PASHA
PATHO
PATHS
PATHY
RAPHE
SADHU
TACHY
WASHY
YACHT

•A••H

BARTH
BATCH
CATCH
EARTH
FAITH
FAUGH
GARTH
HARSH
HATCH
LARCH
LATCH
LAUGH
MARCH
MARSH
MATCH
PARCH
PASCH
PATCH
RAJAH
RALPH
RANCH
RATCH
RAYAH
SABAH
SARAH
WATCH
WAUGH
XANTH

••AH•

ADAHS
AMAHS
AYAHS
BLAHS
BRAHE
IDAHO
NOAHS
OMAHA
OPAHS
PRAHU
SHAHS
SPAHI

••A•H

ABASH
AWASH
BEACH
BRASH
CLASH
COACH
CRASH
DEATH
FLASH
GNASH
GRAPH
HEATH
LEACH
LEASH
LOACH
LOATH
NEATH
ORACH
PEACH
PLASH
POACH
QUASH
REACH
ROACH
SLASH
SMASH
SNATH
STAPH
STASH
SWASH
SWATH
TEACH
TRACH
TRASH
WRATH

•••AH

ALLAH
ALMAH
DINAH
EPHAH
JONAH
JUDAH
KEDAH
LOTAH
MICAH
NORAH
RAJAH
RAYAH
SABAH
SARAH
SELAH
SHIAH
SUBAH
SURAH
TORAH
URIAH

AI•••

AIDAS
AIDED
AIDER
AIDES
AIKEN
AILED
AIMED
AIMEE
AINOS
AINUS
AIRED
AISLE
AISNE
AITCH

A•I••

ABIBS
ABIDE
ABIEL
ABIES
ACIDS
ACING
ACINI
ACITY
ADIEU
ADIOS
ADITS
AFIRE
AGILE
AGING
AGIOS
AGIST
ALIAS
ALIBI
ALICE
ALIEN
ALIFS
ALIGN
ALIKE
ALINE
ALIVE
AMIAS
AMICE
AMIDE
AMIDO
AMIEL
AMIES
AMIGO
AMINE
AMINO
AMIRS
AMISH
AMISS
AMITY
ANILE
ANILS
ANIMA
ANIME
ANION
ANISE
ANISO
ANITA
APIAN
APING
APISH
ARIAN
ARIAS
ARICA
ARIEL
ARIES
ARILS
ARION
ARISE
ARIUM
ARIUS
ASIAN
ASIDE
ATILT
ATION
ATIVE
AVIAN
AVION
AVISO
AWING
AXIAL
AXILE
AXILS
AXING
AXIOM
AYINS
AZINE

A••I•

AALII
ABBIE
ABRIS
ACRID
ACTIN
ADDIE
ADLIB
ADMIN
ADMIT
ADMIX
AECIA
AEGIR
AEGIS
AEMIA
AERIE
AESIR
AFFIX
AGAIN
AGGIE
AGNIS
ALBIN
ALDIS
ALGIA
ALGID
ALGIE
ALGIN
ALLIE
ALLIS
ALOIN
ALOIS
ALUIN
ALVIN
ALWIN
AMAIN
AMBIT
AMNIA
ANGIO
ANNIE
ANTIC
ANTIS
ANVIL
ANZIO
APHID
APHIS
APRIL
APSIS
AREIC
ARGIL
ARNIE
AROID
ARRIS
ARSIS
ARTIE
ASPIC
ASPIS
ASTIR
ATRIA
ATRIP
ATTIC
ATTIS
AUDIO
AUDIT
AULIC
AULIS
AURIC
AURIS
AUXIL
AUXIN
AVAIL
AVOID
AVOIR
AWAIT
AYDIN
AZOIC

A•••I

AALII
ABACI
ACINI
ADENI
ALIBI
ALTAI
AMATI
AMPHI
ARCHI
ASSAI
AUREI

•AI••

BAILS
BAIRD
BAIRN
BAITS
BAIZE
CAIRD
CAIRN
CAIRO
DAILY
DAIRY
DAISY
FAILS
FAINT
FAIRS
FAIRY
FAITH
GAILS
GAILY
GAINS
GAITS
HAIDA
HAIFA
HAIKS
HAIKU
HAILS
HAIRS
HAIRY
HAITI
JAILS
JAINA
JAINS
LAIKA
LAIRD
LAIRS
LAITY
MAIDS
MAILS
MAIMS
MAINE
MAINS
MAINZ
MAIZE
NAIAD
NAILS
NAIVE
PAILS
PAINE
PAINS
PAINT
PAIRS
PAISA
PAISE
RAIDS
RAILS
RAINS
RAINY
RAISE
SAIGA
SAILS
SAINT
TAIGA
TAILS
TAINO
TAINS
TAINT
VAIRS
WAIFS
WAILS
WAINS
WAIST
WAITS
WAIVE
ZAIRE

•A•I•

AALII
BARIC
BARIT
BASIC
BASIL
BASIN
BASIS
BATIK
CABIN
CADIS
CADIZ
CALIF
CALIX
CANIS
CARIB
CAVIE
CAVIL
DACIA
DARIC
DAVID
DAVIE
DAVIS
DAVIT
EADIE
FAKIR
GADID
GAMIC

GAMIN
HABIT
HAFIZ
HAGIO
HAKIM
HALID
IASIS
JAMIE
KADIS
KAKIS
KAMIK
KATIE
LABIA
LABIO
LADIN
LAMIA
LAPIN
LAPIS
LATIN
MAFIA
MAGIC
MALIC
MAMIE
MANIA
MANIC
MARIA
MARIE
MATIN
MAVIS
MAXIM
NADIR
NARIS
NAZIS
OASIS
PANIC
PARIS
PATIO
PAVIS
RABIC
RABID
RADII
RADIO
RADIX
RAMIE
RANIS
RAPID
RATIO
SABIN
SADIE
SAHIB
SALIC
SAPID
SARIS
SASIN
SATIN
SAVIN
SAYID
TABID
TACIT
TAFIA
TAMIS
TANIS
TAPIR
TAPIS
TAXIS
VAGIN
VALID
VANIR
VAPID
VARIC
VARIO
VARIX
VATIC
XAXIS
YAXIS
ZAMIA
ZAYIN

•A••I

AALII
BACCI
BAHAI
BASSI
CACTI
CALCI
CALLI
CAMPI
CAPRI
CARDI
CARPI
GAUDI
HADJI
HAITI
HANOI
IAMBI
KAUAI
KAURI
LANAI
MAGNI
MAHDI
MAORI
MATRI
NAOMI
PALMI
PALPI
PAPPI
PARSI
PATRI
RABBI
RADII
SALMI
TARSI

••AI•

AGAIN
AMAIN
AVAIL
AWAIT
BLAIN
BRAID
BRAIL
BRAIN
CHAIN
CHAIR
CLAIM
CRAIG
DRAIN
ELAIN
ELAIO
FLAIL
FLAIR
FRAIL
GLAIR
GRAIL
GRAIN
KRAIT
PLAID
PLAIN
PLAIT
QUAIL
SLAIN
SNAIL
SPAIN
SPAIT
STAID
STAIN
STAIR
SWAIL
SWAIN
TRAIL
TRAIN
TRAIT
TWAIN
VMAIL

••A•I

ABACI
AMATI
BRAGI
COATI
CRANI
GHAZI
GRANI
IRAQI
KHADI
KHAKI
MIAMI
OKAPI
PLAGI
PLANI
QUASI
SCAPI
SPAHI
SWAMI
TRAGI
USAFI

•••AI

ALTAI
ASSAI
BAHAI
DOUAI
KAUAI
LANAI
LITAI
SERAI
SINAI

A•J••

ANJOU

•AJ••

CAJON
CAJUN
MAJOR
RAJAB
RAJAH
SAJOU

•A•J•

BANJO
HADJI

AK•••

AKENE
AKRON

A•K••

AIKEN
ALKYL
ANKHS
ANKLE
ANKUS
ASKED
ASKER
ASKEW

A••K•

ALIKE
AWAKE
AWOKE

A•••K

ABACK
ACOCK
ALACK
ALECK
AMUCK
APEAK

•AK••

BAKED
BAKER
BAKES
CAKED
CAKES
DAKAR
FAKED
FAKER
FAKES
FAKIR
HAKES
HAKIM
JAKES
JAKOB
KAKAS
KAKIS
LAKED
LAKER
LAKES
MAKER
MAKES
NAKED
OAKEN
OAKUM
RAKED
RAKEE
RAKER
RAKES
SAKER
SAKES
TAKEN
TAKER
TAKES
WAKED
WAKEN
WAKES

•A•K•

BACKS
BALKS
BALKY
BANKS
BARKS
BARKY
BASKS
CALKS
CASKS
DAWKS
GAWKS
GAWKY
HACKS
HAIKS
HAIKU
HANKS
HARKS
HAWKS
JACKS
JACKY
KAFKA
LACKS
LAIKA
LANKY
LARKS
MACKS
MARKS
MASKS
PACKS
PARKA
PARKS
RACKS
RANKS
SACKS
SARKS
TACKS
TACKY
TALKS
TANKA
TANKS
TASKS
WACKE
WACKS
WACKY
WALKS
YANKS

•A••K

BATIK
CAPEK
CAULK
KAMIK
KAPOK
KAYAK
SAMEK
TALUK

••AK•

AWAKE
BEAKS
BLAKE
BRAKE
BRAKY
CRAKE
DHAKS
DRAKE
FLAKE
FLAKY
KHAKI
LEAKS
LEAKY
PEAKS
QUAKE
QUAKY
SHAKE
SHAKO
SHAKY
SLAKE
SNAKE
SNAKY
SOAKS
STAKE
TEAKS

••A•K

ABACK
ALACK
BLACK
BLANK
CHALK
CLACK
CLANK
CLARK
CRACK
CRANK
DRANK
FLACK
FLANK
FLASK
FRANK
KNACK
OZARK
PLACK
PLANK
PRANK
QUACK
QUARK
SHACK
SHANK
SHARK
SLACK
SMACK
SNACK
SNARK
SPANK
SPARK
STACK
STALK
STANK
STARK
SWANK
THANK
TRACK
WHACK
WRACK

•••AK

APEAK
BLEAK
BREAK
CLOAK
CREAK
CROAK
FREAK
KAYAK
KODAK
KULAK
SNEAK
SPEAK
STEAK
TWEAK
UMIAK
WREAK

AL•••

ALACK
ALAMO
ALANS
ALARM
ALARY
ALATE
ALBAN
ALBAS
ALBEE
ALBIN
ALBUM
ALCAN
ALDAN
ALDEN
ALDER
ALDIS
ALDOL
ALDOS
ALDUS
ALECK
ALECS
ALEFS
ALEPH
ALERT
ALEUT
ALEXA
ALGAE
ALGAL
ALGER
ALGIA
ALGID
ALGIE
ALGIN
ALGOL
ALGOR
ALGUM
ALGYS
ALIAS
ALIBI
ALICE
ALIEN
ALIFS
ALIGN
ALIKE
ALINE
ALIVE
ALKYL
ALLAH
ALLAN
ALLAY
ALLEN
ALLEY
ALLIE
ALLIS
ALLOT
ALLOW
ALLOY
ALLYL
ALMAH
ALMAS
ALMUD
ALMUG
ALOES
ALOFT
ALOHA
ALOIN
ALOIS
ALONE
ALONG
ALOOF
ALOUD
ALPHA
ALPHY
ALTAI
ALTAR
ALTAS
ALTER
ALTON
ALTOS
ALUIN
ALULA
ALUMS
ALVAN
ALVIN
ALWAY
ALWIN
ALYCE

A•L••

AALII
ABLER
ADLER
ADLIB
AGLEE
AGLET
AGLEY
AGLOW

AILED
ALLAH
ALLAN
ALLAY
ALLEN
ALLEY
ALLIE
ALLIS
ALLOT
ALLOW
ALLOY
ALLYL
ANLAS
ARLES
ATLAS
AULIC
AULIS
AXLED
AXLES

A••L•

ABELE
ABELS
ADDLE
ADELA
ADELE
ADOLF
ADULT
AGILE
AISLE
ALULA
AMBLE
AMOLE
AMPLE
AMPLY
AMYLO
AMYLS
ANGLE
ANGLO
ANILE
ANILS
ANKLE
APPLE
APPLY
APTLY
ARILS
ASYLA
ATILT
ATOLL
AXILE
AXILS
AZOLE

A•••L

ABIEL
ACCEL
AFOUL
ALDOL
ALGAL
ALGOL
ALKYL
ALLYL
AMIEL
AMPUL
ANGEL
ANNAL
ANNUL
ANSEL
ANVIL
APPAL
APPEL
APRIL
AREAL
ARGAL
ARGIL
ARGOL
ARIEL
ARTEL
ARVAL
ATOLL
AURAL
AUSTL
AUXIL
AVAIL
AWFUL
AXIAL

•AL••

AALII
BALAS
BALDR
BALED
BALER
BALES
BALKS
BALKY
BALLS
BALMS
BALMY
BALSA
BALTS
CALCI
CALEB
CALIF
CALIX
CALKS
CALLA
CALLI
CALLS
CALMS
CALPE
CALVE
CALYX
DALES
DALLY
FALLS
FALSE
GALAS
GALAX
GALEA
GALEN
GALES
GALLS
GALOP
HALED
HALER
HALES
HALID
HALLE
HALLS
HALOS
HALTS
HALVE
JALAP
KALAT
LALLS
MALAC
MALAR
MALAY
MALES
MALIC
MALLS
MALTS
MALTY
PALAE
PALEA
PALED
PALEO
PALER
PALES
PALEY
PALLS
PALMI
PALMS
PALMY
PALPI
PALSY
RALES
RALLY
RALPH
SALAD
SALEM
SALEP
SALES
SALIC
SALLY
SALMI
SALOL
SALON
SALPA
SALTS
SALTY
SALUS
SALVE
SALVO
TALCS
TALER
TALES
TALKS
TALLY
TALON
TALOS
TALUK
TALUS
VALES
VALET
VALID
VALOR
VALUE
VALVE
WALDO
WALED
WALER
WALES
WALKS
WALLA
WALLS
WALLY
WALTS
WALTZ
YALTA

•A•L•

BADLY
BAILS
BALLS
BASLE
BAWLS
CABLE
CALLA
CALLI
CALLS
CARLA
CARLO
CARLS
CAULK
CAULS
DAILY
DALLY
EAGLE
EARLE
EARLS
EARLY
FABLE
FAILS
FALLS
FARLE
FARLS
FATLY
FAULT
GABLE
GAELS
GAILS
GAILY
GALLS
GAOLS
GAULS
GAVLE
GAYLY
HAILS
HALLE
HALLS
HAPLO
HAPLY
HARLS
HAULM
HAULS
JAILS
JARLS
KARLS
LADLE
LALLS
LAXLY
MACLE
MADLY
MAILS
MALLS
MANLY
MAPLE
MARLS
MARLY
MAULS
NAILS
PABLO
PAILS
PALLS
PAOLO
PAULA
PAULO
PAULS
PAWLS
RAILS
RALLY
RAWLY
SABLE
SADLY
SAILS
SALLY
SAULS
SAULT
TABLE
TAELS
TAILS
TALLY
VAULT
WAILS
WALLA
WALLS
WALLY
WANLY
WAULS
WAWLS
YAWLS

•A••L

BABEL
BABUL
BAGEL
BANAL
BASAL
BASEL
BASIL
CABAL
CAMEL
CANAL
CAROL
CAVIL
EASEL
FATAL
FAYAL
GAVEL
HAMAL
HAZEL
KABUL
KAROL
LABEL
LAPEL
MABEL
NASAL
NATAL
NAVAL
NAVEL
PANEL
PAPAL
PAROL
RAOUL
RATAL
RATEL
RAVEL
SALOL

••AL•

BIALY
CHALK
COALS
DEALS
DEALT
DIALS
DOALL
DUALA
EXALT
FOALS
GOALS
HEALS
HYALO
ITALS
ITALY
KOALA
MEALS
MEALY
NEALS
OPALS
ORALS
OVALS
PEALS
PSALM
QUALM
REALM
REALS
RIALS
ROALD
SCALD
SCALE
SCALL
SCALP
SCALY
SEALS
SHALE
SHALL
SHALT
SHALY
SIALO
SKALD
SMALL
SMALT
SPALL
STALE
STALK
STALL
SWALE
TEALS
URALS
VIALS
WEALD
WEALS
WHALE
WOALD

••A•L

AVAIL
BRAIL
BRAWL
CRAAL
CRAWL
DOALL
DRAWL
FLAIL
FRAIL
GNARL
GRAAL
GRAIL
KRAAL
MIAUL
PEARL
QUAIL
SCALL
SHALL
SHAWL
SMALL
SNAIL
SNARL
SPALL
STALL
SWAIL
TRAIL
TRAWL
VMAIL

•••AL

ALGAL
ANNAL
APPAL
AREAL
ARGAL
ARVAL
AURAL
AXIAL
BANAL
BASAL
BINAL
BUBAL
CABAL
CANAL
CECAL
CIDAL
COMAL
COPAL
CORAL
COXAL
CRAAL
DECAL
DEDAL
DOTAL
DUCAL
DURAL
EQUAL
FATAL
FAYAL
FECAL
FERAL
FETAL
FINAL
FOCAL
FUGAL
GORAL
GRAAL
GYRAL
HAMAL
HEMAL
HORAL
IDEAL
ILEAL
JUGAL
JURAL
KRAAL
LEGAL
LOCAL
LOYAL
MEDAL
MEGAL
METAL
MODAL
MOLAL
MORAL
MURAL
NASAL
NATAL
NAVAL
NEPAL
NIVAL
NODAL
NOPAL
OFFAL
PAPAL
PEDAL
PENAL
PETAL
PHIAL
PICAL
PIPAL
RATAL
REGAL
RENAL
RIVAL
RIYAL
ROYAL
RURAL
SEPAL
SERAL
SHOAL
SISAL
SKOAL
STEAL
SURAL
TICAL
TIDAL
TONAL
TOTAL
TRIAL
TUBAL
UREAL
USUAL

UVEAL
UXMAL
VENAL
VIRAL
VITAL
VOCAL
WHEAL
ZONAL

AM•••

AMAHS
AMAIN
AMASS
AMATI
AMAZE
AMBER
AMBIT
AMBLE
AMBOS
AMBRY
AMEBA
AMEND
AMENS
AMENT
AMIAS
AMICE
AMIDE
AMIDO
AMIEL
AMIES
AMIGO
AMINE
AMINO
AMIRS
AMISH
AMISS
AMITY
AMMAN
AMMON
AMNIA
AMOLE
AMONG
AMOUR
AMPHI
AMPHR
AMPLE
AMPLY
AMPUL
AMUCK
AMUSE
AMYLO
AMYLS

A•M••

ADMAN
ADMEN
ADMIN
ADMIT
ADMIX
AEMIA
AIMED
AIMEE
ALMAH
ALMAS
ALMUD
ALMUG
AMMAN
AMMON
ARMED
ARMET
ARMOR
ATMAN
AXMAN
AXMEN

A••M•

ABOMA
ABOMB
ADAMS
AGAMA
ALAMO
ALUMS
ANEMO
ANIMA
ANIME
AROMA
ARUMS
ATOMS

A•••M

ABEAM
ABOHM
ABRAM
ABYSM
ADEEM
ALARM
ALBUM
ALGUM
ANNAM
ARIUM
ASSAM
AURUM
AXIOM

•AM••

CAMEL
CAMEO
CAMES
CAMPI
CAMPO
CAMPS
CAMPY
CAMUS
DAMAN
DAMES
DAMNS
DAMON
DAMPS
FAMED
GAMBS
GAMED
GAMES
GAMIC
GAMIN
GAMMA
GAMPS
GAMUT
HAMAL
HAMES
HAMMY
HAMZA
IAMBI
IAMBS
JAMBS
JAMES
JAMIE
KAMES
KAMET
KAMIK
LAMAS
LAMBS
LAMED
LAMER
LAMES
LAMIA
LAMPS
MAMAS
MAMBA
MAMBO
MAMEY
MAMIE
MAMMA
MAMMY
NAMED
NAMER
NAMES
RAMIE
RAMMY
RAMPS
RAMUS
SAMAR
SAMBA
SAMBO
SAMEK
SAMMY
SAMOA
SAMOS
TAMED
TAMER
TAMES
TAMIS
TAMPA
TAMPS
VAMPS
WAMUS
YAMEN
YAMUN
ZAMIA

•A•M•

BALMS
BALMY
BARMY
BAUME
CALMS
FARMS
GAMMA
HAMMY
HARMS
KARMA
MAGMA
MAIMS
MAMMA
MAMMY
NAOMI
PALMI
PALMS
PALMY
RAMMY
SALMI
SAMMY
WARMS

•A••M

CAROM
DATUM
FANUM
HAKIM
HAREM
HAULM
MADAM
MAXIM
NAHUM
OAKUM
SAGUM
SALEM

••AM•

ADAMS
AGAMA
ALAMO
BEAMS
BEAMY
BLAME
CHAMP
CLAMP
CLAMS
CRAMP
CRAMS
DRAMA
DRAMS
EXAMS
FLAME
FLAMS
FLAMY
FOAMS
FOAMY
FRAME
GRAMA
GRAMS
IMAMS
LLAMA
LOAMS
LOAMY
MIAMI
PRAMS
REAMS
ROAMS
SCAMP
SEAMS
SEAMY
SHAME
SHAMS
SLAMS
STAMP
SWAMI
SWAMP
TEAMS
TRAMP
TRAMS
WHAMS

••A•M

ALARM
CHARM
CHASM
CLAIM
INARM
PLASM
PSALM
QUALM
REALM
REARM
SHAWM
SPASM
SWARM
UNARM

•••AM

ABEAM
ABRAM
ANNAM
ASSAM
BREAM
CERAM
CREAM
DREAM
FLEAM
GLEAM
HBEAM
HIRAM
IBEAM
IHRAM
ISLAM
JORAM
MADAM
NIZAM
PRIAM
SCRAM
STEAM
ZBEAM

AN•••

ANCON
ANDES
ANDRE
ANDRO
ANDYS
ANEAR
ANEMO
ANENT
ANGEL
ANGER
ANGIO
ANGLE
ANGLO
ANGRY
ANGST
ANGUS
ANILE
ANILS
ANIMA
ANIME
ANION
ANISE
ANISO
ANITA
ANJOU
ANKHS
ANKLE
ANKUS
ANLAS
ANNAL
ANNAM
ANNAS
ANNES
ANNEX
ANNIE
ANNOY
ANNUL
ANODE
ANSAE
ANSEL
ANTAE
ANTED
ANTES
ANTHO
ANTIC
ANTIS
ANTON
ANTRA
ANVIL
ANZAC
ANZIO

A•N••

ABNER
AGNES
AGNIS
AINOS
AINUS
AMNIA
ANNAL
ANNAM
ANNAS
ANNES
ANNEX
ANNIE
ANNOY
ANNUL
APNEA
ARNIE
AUNTS
AUNTY
AWNED

A••N•

ACING
ACINI
ADENI
ADENO
ADUNC
AEONS
AGANA
AGENT
AGING
AGONY
AISNE
AKENE
ALANS
ALINE
ALONE
ALONG
AMEND
AMENS
AMENT
AMINE
AMINO
AMONG
ANENT
APING
ARENA
ARENT
ASSNS
ATONE
ATONY
AVENS
AWING
AXING
AXONE
AXONS
AYINS
AZANS
AZINE
AZONS

A•••N

AARON
ACEAN
ACORN
ACTIN
ADMAN
ADMEN
ADMIN
ADORN
AGAIN
AIKEN
AKRON
ALBAN
ALBIN
ALCAN
ALDAN
ALDEN
ALGIN
ALIEN
ALIGN
ALLAN
ALLEN
ALOIN
ALTON
ALUIN
ALVAN
ALVIN
ALWIN
AMAIN
AMMAN
AMMON
ANCON
ANION
ANTON
APIAN
APRON
ARDEN
ARGON
ARIAN
ARION
ARPEN
ARRAN
ARSON
ARYAN
ASHEN
ASIAN
ASPEN
ASTON
ASWAN
ATION
ATMAN
AUDEN
AUXIN
AVIAN
AVION
AXMAN
AXMEN
AYDIN

•AN••

BANAL
BANAT
BANDA
BANDS
BANDY
BANFF
BANGS
BANJO
BANKS
BANNS
BANTU
CANAD
CANAL
CANDY
CANEA
CANED
CANER
CANES
CANIS
CANNA
CANNY
CANOE
CANON
CANSO
CANST
CANTO
CANTS
DANAE
DANCE
DANDY
DANES
DANGS
DANNY
DANTE
FANCY
FANGA

FANGS
FANNY
FANON
FANOS
FANUM
GANEF
GANGS
HANCE
HANDS
HANDY
HANGS
HANKS
HANNA
HANOI
HANSE
JANES
JANET
JANOS
JANUS
KANDY
LANAI
LANCE
LANDS
LANES
LANKY
MANCY
MANDY
MANED
MANES
MANET
MANGE
MANGO
MANGY
MANIA
MANIC
MANLY
MANNA
MANOR
MANSE
MANTA
MANUS
NANAS
NANCY
NANNY
PANDA
PANDY
PANEL
PANES
PANGS
PANIC
PANSY
PANTO
PANTS
PANTY
RANCE
RANCH
RANDS
RANDY
RANEE
RANGE
RANGY
RANIS
RANKS
RANTS
SANDS
SANDY
SANER
TANEY
TANGO
TANGS
TANGY
TANIS
TANKA
TANKS
TANSY
TANTO
VANED
VANES
VANGS
VANIR
WANDA
WANDS
WANED
WANES
WANEY
WANLY
WANTS
XANTH
YANKS

•A•N•
BANNS
BARNS
CANNA
CANNY
DAMNS
DANNY
DARNS
DAUNT
DAWNS
EARNS
FAINT
FANNY
FAUNA
FAUNS
FAWNS
GAINS
GAUNT
HANNA
HASNT
HAUNT
JAINA
JAINS
JAUNT
LAWNS
LAWNY
MAGNI
MAINE
MAINS
MAINZ
MANNA
MARNE
MAUND
NANNY
PAINE
PAINS
PAINT
PAWNS
RAINS
RAINY
SAINT
SAUNA
TAINO
TAINS
TAINT
TARNS
TAUNT
TAWNY
VAUNT
WAINS
WARNS
WASNT
WAYNE
YARNS
YAWNS

•A••N
AARON
BACON
BADEN
BAIRN
BARON
BASIN
BATAN
BATON
CABIN
CAIRN
CAJON
CAJUN
CANON
CAPON
DAGAN
DAMAN
DAMON
EATEN
FANON
GABON
GALEN
GAMIN
GATUN
HAVEN
HAYDN
JAPAN
JASON
KAREN
KAZAN
LADEN
LADIN
LAGAN
LAPIN
LATIN
MACON
MAHAN
MASON
MATIN
MAYAN
OAKEN
OATEN
PAEAN
PAEON
PAGAN
PAPEN
PAREN
PATEN
PAVAN
RADON
RAVEN
RAYON
SABIN
SALON
SARAN
SASIN
SATAN
SATIN
SAVIN
SAXON
TAKEN
TALON
VAGIN
WAGON
WAKEN
WAXEN
YAMEN
YAMUN
YAPON
ZAYIN

••AN•
AGANA
ALANS
AZANS
BEANO
BEANS
BHANG
BLANC
BLAND
BLANK
BRAND
BRANS
BRANT
BWANA
CHANG
CHANT
CLANG
CLANK
CLANS
CRANE
CRANI
CRANK
CYANO
DEANE
DEANS
DIANA
DIANE
DRANK
DUANE
ELAND
EVANS
FLANK
FLANS
FRANC
FRANK
FRANZ
GHANA
GIANT
GLAND
GLANS
GRAND
GRANI
GRANO
GRANT
GUANO
GUANS
INANE
IVANS
JEANS
JOANS
JUANA
JUANS
KHANS
LEANS
LEANT
LIANA
LIANE
LIANG
LLANO
LOANS
MEANS
MEANT
MEANY
MOANS
ORANG
PEANS
PHANE
PHANY
PIANO
PLANE
PLANI
PLANK
PLANO
PLANS
PLANT
PRANK
QUANT
RIANT
ROANS
SCAND
SCANS
SCANT
SEANS
SHANK
SHANS
SHANT
SLANG
SLANT
SPANG
SPANK
SPANS
STAND
STANK
STANS
SWANK
SWANS
THANE
THANK
TRANS
TWANG
URANO
VIAND
WEANS
WHANG
YEANS

••A•N
AGAIN
AMAIN
BLAIN
BRAIN
BRAWN
CHAIN
DRAIN
DRAWN
ELAIN
GNAWN
GRAIN
LEARN
PLAIN
PRAWN
SHAUN
SHAWN
SLAIN
SPAIN
SPAWN
STAIN
SWAIN
TRAIN
TWAIN
YEARN

•••AN
ACEAN
ADMAN
ALBAN
ALCAN
ALDAN
ALLAN
ALVAN
AMMAN
APIAN
ARIAN
ARRAN
ARYAN
ASIAN
ASWAN
ATMAN
AVIAN
AXMAN
BATAN
BEGAN
BOGAN
BRIAN
BRYAN
BURAN
CLEAN
COHAN
CUBAN
DAGAN
DAMAN
DEWAN
DIVAN
DIWAN
EGEAN
ELMAN
ETHAN
FURAN
GLEAN
GROAN
HEMAN
HOGAN
HOKAN
HONAN
HUMAN
HUNAN
ICIAN
ILIAN
INCAN
JAPAN
KAZAN
KORAN
KUBAN
LAGAN
LIGAN
LORAN
LYMAN
MAHAN
MAYAN
MEGAN
MELAN
MILAN
MOSAN
NISAN
OCEAN
ORGAN
OSCAN
OSMAN
PAEAN
PAGAN
PAVAN
PECAN
PEKAN
PIMAN
PUSAN
PYRAN
QUEAN
REDAN
REGAN
REMAN
RENAN
RERAN
ROMAN
ROWAN
SARAN
SATAN
SEDAN
SIVAN
SKEAN
SOLAN
SUDAN
SUSAN
TITAN
TOLAN
TOMAN
UHLAN
UNMAN
URBAN
WIGAN
WITAN
WODAN
WOMAN
WOTAN
XTIAN
XYLAN

AO•••
AORTA

A•O••
ABODE
ABOHM
ABOMA
ABOMB
ABORT
ABOUT
ABOVE
ACOCK
ACORN
ACOUO
ADOBE
ADOLF
ADOPT
ADORE
ADORN
AEONS
AFOOT
AFOUL
AGONY
AGORA
ALOES
ALOFT
ALOHA
ALOIN
ALOIS
ALONE
ALONG
ALOOF
ALOUD
AMOLE
AMONG
AMOUR
ANODE
APORT
AROID
AROMA
AROSE
ATOLL
ATOMS
ATONE
ATONY
ATORY
AVOID
AVOIR
AVOWS
AWOKE
AXONE
AXONS
AZOIC
AZOLE
AZONS
AZOTE
AZOTH

5

A••O•
AARON
ABBOT
ABHOR
ACTOR
ADIOS
AESOP
AFOOT
AFROS
AGIOS
AGLOW
AINOS
AKRON
ALDOL
ALDOS
ALGOL
ALGOR
ALLOT
ALLOW
ALLOY
ALOOF
ALTON
ALTOS
AMBOS
AMMON
ANCON
ANION
ANJOU
ANNOY
ANTON
APRON
ARBOR
ARDOR
ARGOL
ARGON
ARGOS
ARGOT
ARION
ARMOR
ARROW
ARSON
ASCOT
ASSOC
ASTON
ASTOR
ATHOS
ATION
AUTOS
AVION
AXIOM

A•••O
ACETO
ACOUO
ADENO
ALAMO
AMIDO
AMIGO
AMINO
AMYLO
ANDRO
ANEMO
ANGIO
ANGLO
ANISO
ANTHO
ANZIO
ASTRO
AUDIO
AVISO

•AO••
GAOLS
LAOAG
MAORI
NAOMI
PAOLO
RAOUL

•A•O•
AARON
BABOO
BACON
BARON
BATON
BAYOU
CABOB
CABOT
CAJON
CANOE
CANON
CAPON
CAROB
CAROL
CAROM
DAMON
FAGOT
FANON
FANOS
FAVOR
GABON
GALOP
GAVOT
HALOS
HANOI
HAVOC
JABOT
JACOB
JAKOB
JANOS
JASON
JATOS
KABOB
KAPOK
KAROL
KAYOS
KAZOO
LABOR
LAGOS
MACON
MAGOT
MAJOR
MANOR
MASON
MAYOR
NABOB
PAEON
PAROL
RADON
RAYON
RAZOR
SABOT
SAGOS
SAJOU
SALOL
SALON
SAMOA
SAMOS
SAPOR
SAVOR
SAVOY
SAXON
TABOO
TABOR
TAHOE
TALON
TALOS
TAROS
TAROT
VALOR
VAPOR
WAGON
WAHOO
YAHOO
YAPON

•A••O
BABOO
BANJO
BASSO
BATHO
CACAO
CADDO
CAIRO
CAMEO
CAMPO
CANSO
CANTO
CARBO
CARGO
CARLO
CARPO
CARYO
CASCO
DATTO
DAVAO
FARGO
HAGIO
HAPLO
IATRO
KARYO
KAZOO
LABIO
LACTO
LARGO
LASSO
MACAO
MACRO
MAMBO
MANGO
MARCO
MARGO
MASTO
MATEO
MATZO
NARCO
PABLO
PAEDO
PALEO
PANTO
PAOLO
PARGO
PATHO
PATIO
PAULO
RADIO
RATIO
SACRO
SALVO
SAMBO
SAPRO
SARCO
SARTO
SAURO
SAYSO
TABOO
TAINO
TANGO
TANTO
TARSO
TASSO
TAURO
TAUTO
VARIO
VARRO
WAHOO
WALDO
YAHOO

••AO•
CHAOS

••A•O
ALAMO
BEANO
BRAVO
CLARO
CYANO
DIAZO
DRACO
ELAEO
ELAIO
ERATO
GRANO
GUACO
GUANO
HYALO
IDAHO
IMAGO
LLANO
PHAGO
PIANO
PLANO
PLATO
SCATO
SEATO
SHAKO
SIALO
SLAVO
STATO
URANO

•••AO
CACAO
DAVAO
MACAO

AP•••
APACE
APART
APEAK
APERY
APHID
APHIS
APIAN
APING
APISH
APNEA
APORT
APPAL
APPEL
APPLE
APPLY
APRIL
APRON
APSES
APSIS
APTLY

A•P••
ALPHA
ALPHY
AMPHI
AMPHR
AMPLE
AMPLY
AMPUL
APPAL
APPEL
APPLE
APPLY
ARPAD
ARPEN
ASPCA
ASPEN
ASPER
ASPIC
ASPIS

A••P•
ADAPT
ADEPT
ADOPT
AGAPE
ALEPH

A•••P
AESOP
ASCAP
ATRIP

•AP••
CAPEK
CAPER
CAPES
CAPET
CAPON
CAPRI
CAPUA
CAPUT
GAPED
GAPER
GAPES
GAPPY
HAPLO
HAPLY
HAPPY
JAPAN
JAPES
KAPHS
KAPOK
KAPPA
KAPUT
LAPAR
LAPEL
LAPIN
LAPIS
LAPPS
LAPSE
MAPLE
NAPES
NAPPE
NAPPY
PAPAL
PAPAS
PAPAW
PAPEN
PAPER
PAPPI
PAPPY
PAPUA
RAPED
RAPES
RAPHE
RAPID
SAPID
SAPOR
SAPPY
SAPRO
TAPED
TAPER
TAPES
TAPIR
TAPIS
VAPID
VAPOR
YAPON

•A•P•
CALPE
CAMPI
CAMPO
CAMPS
CAMPY
CARPI
CARPO
CARPS
DAMPS
GAMPS
GAPPY
GASPE
GASPS
HAPPY
HARPS
HARPY
HASPS
KAPPA
LAMPS
LAPPS
NAPPE
NAPPY
PALPI
PAPPI
PAPPY
RALPH
RAMPS
RASPS
RASPY
SALPA
SAPPY
TAMPA
TAMPS
TARPS
TAUPE
VAMPS
WARPS
WASPS
WASPY
YAUPS
YAWPS

•A••P
GALOP
JALAP
NAACP
SALEP
WATAP

••AP•
ADAPT
AGAPE
CHAPE
CHAPS
CHAPT
CLAPS
CRAPE
CRAPS
DRAPE
ETAPE
FLAPS
FRAPS
GRAPE
GRAPH
GRAPY
HEAPS
INAPT
LEAPS
LEAPT
NEAPS
OKAPI
REAPS
SCAPA
SCAPE
SCAPI
SHAPE
SLAPS
SNAPS
SOAPS
SOAPY
STAPH
SWAPS
TRAPS
UNAPT
WHAPS
WRAPS
WRAPT

••A•P
CHAMP
CLAMP
CLASP
CRAMP
GRASP
NAACP
SCALP
SCAMP
SCARP
SCAUP
SHARP
STAMP
SWAMP
TRAMP

•••AP
ASCAP
CHEAP
DOVAP
JALAP
RECAP
SCRAP
STRAP
UNCAP
WATAP

AQ•••
AQABA
AQUAE
AQUAS

••AQ•
IRAQI

AR•••
ARABS
ARABY
ARBOR
ARCED
ARCHI
ARCHY
ARCUS
ARDEB
ARDEN
ARDOR

AREAE
AREAL
AREAS
ARECA
AREIC
ARENA
ARENT
ARETE
ARGAL
ARGIL
ARGOL
ARGON
ARGOS
ARGOT
ARGUE
ARGUS
ARIAN
ARIAS
ARICA
ARIEL
ARIES
ARILS
ARION
ARISE
ARIUM
ARIUS
ARLES
ARMED
ARMET
ARMOR
ARNIE
AROID
AROMA
AROSE
ARPAD
ARPEN
ARRAN
ARRAS
ARRAY
ARRIS
ARROW
ARSES
ARSIS
ARSON
ARTEL
ARTER
ARTHR
ARTIE
ARUBA
ARUMS
ARVAL
ARYAN

A•R••

AARON
ABRAM
ABRIS
ACRED
ACRES
ACRID
AERIE
AFROS
AGREE
AIRED
AKRON
AORTA
APRIL
APRON
ARRAN
ARRAS
ARRAY
ARRIS
ARROW
ATRIA
ATRIP
AURAE
AURAL
AURAS
AUREI
AURES
AURIC
AURIS
AURUM

A••R•

ABORT
ACCRA
ACERB
ACORN
ADORE
ADORN
AFIRE
AFTRA
AGORA
ALARM
ALARY
ALERT
AMBRY
AMIRS
ANDRE
ANDRO
ANGRY
ANTRA
APART
APERY
APORT
ASTRO
ATORY
AVARS
AVERS
AVERT
AVERY
AWARD
AWARE
AZURE

A•••R

ABHOR
ABLER
ABNER
ACTOR
ADDER
ADLER
AEGIR
AESIR
AFTER
AGGER
AIDER
ALDER
ALGER
ALGOR
ALTAR
ALTER
AMBER
AMOUR
AMPHR
ANEAR
ANGER
ARBOR
ARDOR
ARMOR
ARTER
ARTHR
ASHER
ASHUR
ASKER
ASPER
ASSYR
ASTER
ASTIR
ASTOR
ATTAR
AUGER
AUGUR
AVOIR

•AR••

AARON
BARBS
BARCA
BARDE
BARDS
BARED
BARER
BARES
BARGE
BARIC
BARIT
BARKS
BARKY
BARMY
BARNS
BARON
BARRY
BARTH
BARYE
CARAS
CARAT
CARBO
CARDI
CARDS
CARED
CARER
CARES
CARET
CAREY
CARGO
CARIB
CARLA
CARLO
CARLS
CAROB
CAROL
CAROM
CARPI
CARPO
CARPS
CARRY
CARTE
CARTS
CARVE
CARYO
CARYS
DARED
DARER
DARES
DARIC
DARNS
DARTS
EARED
EARLE
EARLS
EARLY
EARNS
EARTH
FARAD
FARCE
FARCY
FARED
FARER
FARES
FARGO
FARLE
FARLS
FARMS
GARBS
GARTH
GARYS
HARAR
HARDS
HARDY
HAREM
HARES
HARKS
HARLS
HARMS
HARPS
HARPY
HARRY
HARSH
HARTE
HARTS
HARTZ
JARED
JARLS
KARAT
KAREN
KARLS
KARMA
KAROL
KARYO
LARCH
LARDS
LARDY
LARES
LARGE
LARGO
LARKS
LARRY
LARVA
MARAT
MARCH
MARCO
MARCS
MARES
MARGE
MARGO
MARIA
MARIE
MARKS
MARLS
MARLY
MARNE
MARRY
MARSH
MARTA
MARTS
MARTY
NARCO
NARDS
NARES
NARIS
OARED
PARAS
PARCH
PARDS
PARED
PAREN
PARER
PARES
PAREU
PARGO
PARIS
PARKA
PARKS
PAROL
PARRS
PARRY
PARSE
PARSI
PARTS
PARTY
RARER
SARAH
SARAN
SARAS
SARCO
SARIS
SARKS
SARTO
TARDY
TARED
TARES
TARNS
TAROS
TAROT
TARPS
TARRY
TARSI
TARSO
TARTS
VARAS
VARIC
VARIO
VARIX
VARRO
VARUS
VARVE
WARDS
WARES
WARMS
WARNS
WARPS
WARTS
WARTY
YARDS
YARNS
ZARFS

•A•R•

BAIRD
BAIRN
BARRY
BASRA
CADRE
CAIRD
CAIRN
CAIRO
CAPRI
CARRY
DAIRY
EAGRE
FAIRS
FAIRY
GAURS
HAIRS
HAIRY
HARRY
IATRO
IATRY
KAURI
KAURY
LABRA
LAIRD
LAIRS
LARRY
LATRY
LAURA
MACRO
MAORI
MARRY
MATRI
MAURA
NACRE
NAURU
PADRE
PAIRS
PARRS
PARRY
PATRI
SABRA
SACRA
SACRO
SAPRO
SAURO
SAURY
TARRY
TATRA
TAURO
VAIRS
VARRO
ZAIRE

•A••R

BABAR
BABER
BAKER
BALDR
BALER
BARER
CABER
CANER
CAPER
CARER
CATER
DAKAR
DARER
DATER
EAGER
EATER
FACER
FAKER
FAKIR
FARER
FAVOR
GAGER
GAPER
GASTR
GAYER
GAZER
HALER
HARAR
HATER
HAZER
LABOR
LAGER
LAKER
LAMER
LAPAR
LASER
LATER
LAVER
LAXER
LAYER
LAZAR
MACER
MAJOR
MAKER
MALAR
MANOR
MASER
MAYOR
MAZER
NADER
NADIR
NAMER
NAVAR
PACER
PALER
PAPER
PARER
PATER
PAVER
PAWER
PAYER
QATAR
RACER
RADAR
RAKER
RARER
RATER
RAVER
RAWER
RAZOR
SABER
SAFER
SAGER
SAKER
SAMAR
SANER
SAPOR
SATYR
SAVER
SAVOR
SAWER
SAYER
TABOR
TAKER
TALER
TAMER
TAPER
TAPIR
TATAR
TAWER
TAXER
VALOR
VANIR
VAPOR
WADER
WAFER
WAGER
WALER
WATER
WAVER
YAGER

••AR•

ALARM
ALARY
APART
AVARS
AWARD
AWARE
BEARD
BEARS
BLARE
BOARD
BOARS
CEARA
CHARD
CHARE
CHARM

5

CHARS
CHART
CHARY
CLARA
CLARE
CLARK
CLARO
CLARY
CZARS
DEARS
DEARY
DIARY
DWARF
FEARS
FLARE
GEARS
GLARE
GLARY
GNARL
GUARD
HEARD
HEARS
HEART
HOARD
HOARY
INARM
KLARA
KNARS
LEARN
LIARS
NEARS
OVARY
OZARK
PEARL
PEARS
PEARY
QUARK
QUART
REARM
REARS
ROARS
SCARE
SCARF
SCARP
SCARS
SCARY
SEARS
SHARD
SHARE
SHARK
SHARP
SMART
SNARE
SNARK
SNARL
SOARS
SPARE
SPARK
SPARS
STARE
STARK
STARS
START
SWARD
SWARM
SWART
TEARS
TEARY
TIARA
TSARS
TZARS
UNARM
WEARS
WEARY
WHARF
YEARN
YEARS
ZBARS

••A•R

CHAIR
FLAIR
GLAIR
STAIR

•••AR

ALTAR
ANEAR
ATTAR
BABAR
BIHAR
BLEAR
BOLAR
BOYAR
BRIAR
CEDAR
CESAR
CIGAR
CLEAR
CYMAR
DAKAR
DEBAR
DINAR
DONAR
DREAR
EDGAR
EGGAR
ELGAR
EMBAR
FEUAR
FILAR
FRIAR
GULAR
HARAR
IYYAR
LAPAR
LAZAR
LOBAR
LUNAR
MALAR
MOLAR
NAVAR
NOPAR
OSCAR
PILAR
POLAR
QATAR
RADAR
SAMAR
SHEAR
SIMAR
SITAR
SIZAR
SMEAR
SOLAR
SONAR
SOWAR
SPEAR
SUGAR
SWEAR
TATAR
ULNAR
UNBAR
VELAR
VICAR
VOLAR

AS•••

ASCAP
ASCOT
ASCUS
ASHEN
ASHER
ASHES
ASHUR
ASIAN
ASIDE
ASKED
ASKER
ASKEW
ASPCA
ASPEN
ASPER
ASPIC
ASPIS
ASSAI
ASSAM
ASSAY
ASSES
ASSET
ASSNS
ASSOC
ASSTS
ASSYR
ASTER
ASTIR
ASTON
ASTOR
ASTRO
ASWAN
ASYLA
ASYUT

A•S••

AESIR
AESOP
AISLE
AISNE
ANSAE
ANSEL
APSES
APSIS
ARSES
ARSIS
ARSON
ASSAI
ASSAM
ASSAY
ASSES
ASSET
ASSNS
ASSOC
ASSTS
ASSYR
AUSTL

A••S•

ABASE
ABASH
ABUSE
ABYSM
ABYSS
ADUST
AGIST
AMASS
AMISH
AMISS
AMUSE
ANGST
ANISE
ANISO
APISH
ARISE
AROSE
AVAST
AVISO
AWASH

A•••S

ABBAS
ABBES
ABBYS
ABELS
ABETS
ABIBS
ABIES
ABRIS
ABUTS
ABYSS
ACHES
ACIDS
ACRES
ADAHS
ADAMS
ADDYS
ADIOS
ADITS
ADZES
AEDES
AEGIS
AEONS
AFROS
AGHAS
AGIOS
AGNES
AGNIS
AGUES
AIDAS
AIDES
AINOS
AINUS
ALANS
ALBAS
ALDIS
ALDOS
ALDUS
ALECS
ALEFS
ALGYS
ALIAS
ALIFS
ALLIS
ALMAS
ALOES
ALOIS
ALTAS
ALTOS
ALUMS
AMAHS
AMASS
AMBOS
AMENS
AMIAS
AMIES
AMIRS
AMISS
AMYLS
ANDES
ANDYS
ANGUS
ANILS
ANKHS
ANKUS
ANLAS
ANNAS
ANNES
ANTES
ANTIS
APHIS
APSES
APSIS
AQUAS
ARABS
ARCUS
AREAS
ARGOS
ARGUS
ARIAS
ARIES
ARILS
ARIUS
ARLES
ARRAS
ARRIS
ARSES
ARSIS
ARUMS
ASCUS
ASHES
ASPIS
ASSES
ASSNS
ASSTS
ATHOS
ATLAS
ATOMS
ATTIS
ATTYS
AULIS
AUNTS
AURAS
AURES
AURIS
AUTOS
AVARS
AVENS
AVERS
AVOWS
AXILS
AXLES
AXONS
AYAHS
AYINS
AZANS
AZONS

•AS••

BASAL
BASED
BASEL
BASES
BASIC
BASIL
BASIN
BASIS
BASKS
BASLE
BASRA
BASSI
BASSO
BASTE
CASCO
CASED
CASES
CASKS
CASTE
CASTS
CASUS
DASHY
EASED
EASEL
EASES
FASTS
GASES
GASPE
GASPS
GASSY
GASTR
HASNT
HASPS
HASTE
HASTY
IASIS
JASON
JASSY
LASER
LASSO
LASTS
MASER
MASHY
MASKS
MASON
MASSE
MASSY
MASTO
MASTS
NASAL
NASTY
OASES
OASIS
PASCH
PASHA
PASSE
PASSY
PASTA
PASTE
PASTS
PASTY
RASPS
RASPY
SASIN
SASSY
TASKS
TASSO
TASTE
TASTY
VASES
VASTY
WASHY
WASNT
WASPS
WASPY
WASTE

•A•S•

BALSA
BASSI
BASSO
CANSO
CANST
CAUSE
DAISY
FALSE
FAUST
GASSY
GAUSS
HANSE
HARSH
HAWSE
JASSY
LAPSE
LASSO
MANSE
MARSH
MASSE
MASSY
MATSU
MAYST
PAISA
PAISE
PALSY
PANSY
PARSE
PARSI
PASSE
PASSY
PATSY
PAUSE
RAISE
SASSY
SAYSO
TANSY
TARSI
TARSO
TASSO
WAIST

•A••S

BABAS
BABES
BACKS
BAFFS
BAHTS
BAILS
BAITS
BAKES
BALAS
BALES
BALKS
BALLS
BALMS
BALTS
BANDS
BANGS
BANKS
BANNS
BARBS
BARDS
BARES
BARKS
BARNS
BASES
BASIS
BASKS
BATES
BATHS
BAWDS
BAWLS
CADES
CADIS
CAFES
CAGES
CAKES
CALKS
CALLS
CALMS
CAMES
CAMPS
CAMUS
CANES
CANIS
CANTS

CAPES
CARAS
CARDS
CARES
CARLS
CARPS
CARTS
CARYS
CASES
CASKS
CASTS
CASUS
CAULS
CAVES
DACES
DALES
DAMES
DAMNS
DAMPS
DANES
DANGS
DARES
DARNS
DARTS
DATES
DAUBS
DAVES
DAVIS
DAVYS
DAWKS
DAWNS
DAZES
EARLS
EARNS
EASES
EAVES
FACES
FACTS
FADES
FAILS
FAIRS
FAKES
FALLS
FANGS
FANOS
FARES
FARLS
FARMS
FASTS
FATES
FAUNS
FAVUS
FAWNS
FAXES
FAYES
FAZES
GABES
GABYS
GAELS
GAFFS
GAGES
GAILS
GAINS
GAITS
GALAS
GALES
GALLS
GAMBS
GAMES
GAMPS
GANGS
GAOLS
GAPES
GARBS
GARYS
GASES
GASPS
GATES
GAUDS
GAULS
GAURS
GAUSS
GAWKS
GAZES
HABUS
HACKS
HADES
HAFTS
HAHAS
HAIKS
HAILS
HAIRS
HAKES
HALES
HALLS
HALOS
HALTS
HAMES
HANDS
HANGS
HANKS
HARDS
HARES
HARKS
HARLS
HARMS
HARPS
HARTS
HASPS
HATES
HAULS
HAWKS
HAYES
HAZES
IAMBS
IASIS
JACKS
JADES
JAGGS
JAILS
JAINS
JAKES
JAMBS
JAMES
JANES
JANOS
JANUS
JAPES
JARLS
JATOS
KADIS
KAGUS
KAKAS
KAKIS
KAMES
KAPHS
KARLS
KATES
KAVAS
KAYOS
LACES
LACKS
LADES
LAGOS
LAIRS
LAKES
LALLS
LAMAS
LAMBS
LAMES
LAMPS
LANDS
LANES
LAPIS
LAPPS
LARDS
LARES
LARKS
LASTS
LATHS
LAUDS
LAVAS
LAVES
LAWNS
LAZES
MACES
MACKS
MAGES
MAGUS
MAIDS
MAILS
MAIMS
MAINS
MAKES
MALES
MALLS
MALTS
MAMAS
MANES
MANUS
MARCS
MARES
MARKS
MARLS
MARTS
MASKS
MASTS
MATES
MATTS
MAUDS
MAULS
MAVIS
MAYAS
MAZES
NAILS
NAMES
NANAS
NAPES
NARDS
NARES
NARIS
NATES
NAVES
NAZIS
OASES
OASIS
OATES
OATHS
OAVES
PACAS
PACES
PACKS
PACTS
PAGES
PAILS
PAINS
PAIRS
PALES
PALLS
PALMS
PANES
PANGS
PANTS
PAPAS
PARAS
PARDS
PARES
PARIS
PARKS
PARRS
PARTS
PASTS
PATES
PATHS
PAULS
PAVES
PAVIS
PAWLS
PAWNS
RACES
RACKS
RAFTS
RAGES
RAIDS
RAILS
RAINS
RAKES
RALES
RAMPS
RAMUS
RANDS
RANIS
RANKS
RANTS
RAPES
RASPS
RATES
RAVES
RAZES
SABES
SACKS
SAFES
SAGAS
SAGES
SAGOS
SAILS
SAKES
SALES
SALTS
SALUS
SAMOS
SANDS
SARAS
SARIS
SARKS
SATES
SAULS
SAVES
SAXES
TABES
TACKS
TAELS
TAILS
TAINS
TAKES
TALCS
TALES
TALKS
TALOS
TALUS
TAMES
TAMIS
TAMPS
TANGS
TANIS
TANKS
TAPES
TAPIS
TARES
TARNS
TAROS
TARPS
TARTS
TASKS
TAXES
TAXIS
VAGUS
VAIRS
VALES
VAMPS
VANES
VANGS
VARAS
VARUS
VASES
WACKS
WADES
WAFTS
WAGES
WAIFS
WAILS
WAINS
WAITS
WAKES
WALES
WALKS
WALLS
WALTS
WAMUS
WANDS
WANES
WANTS
WARDS
WARES
WARMS
WARNS
WARPS
WARTS
WASPS
WATTS
WAULS
WAVES
WAWLS
WAXES
XAXES
XAXIS
YANKS
YARDS
YARNS
YAUPS
YAWLS
YAWNS
YAWPS
YAXES
YAXIS
ZARFS

••AS•

ABASE
ABASH
AMASS
AVAST
AWASH
BEAST
BLASE
BLAST
BOAST
BRASH
BRASS
CEASE
CHASE
CHASM
CLASH
CLASP
CLASS
COAST
CRASH
CRASS
ERASE
FEASE
FEAST
FLASH
FLASK
GLASS
GNASH
GRASP
GRASS
KVASS
LEASE
LEASH
LEAST
LHASA
OMASA
PEASE
PHASE
PHASY
PLASH
PLASM
PLAST
PLASY
QUASH
QUASI
QUASS
ROAST
SLASH
SMASH
SPASM
STASH
SWASH
TEASE
TOAST
TRASH
TRASS
UKASE
YEAST

••A•S

ADAHS
ADAMS
ALANS
AMAHS
AMASS
ARABS
AVARS
AYAHS
AZANS
BEADS
BEAKS
BEAMS
BEANS
BEARS
BEATS
BEAUS
BLABS
BLAHS
BLATS
BOARS
BOATS
BRADS
BRAES
BRAGS
BRANS
BRASS
BRATS
BRAYS
CHAOS
CHAPS
CHARS
CHATS
CHAWS
CLAMS
CLANS
CLAPS
CLASS
CLAWS
CLAYS
COALS
COATS
CRABS
CRAGS
CRAMS
CRAPS
CRASS
CRAWS
CZARS
DEALS
DEANS
DEARS
DHAKS
DIALS
DRABS
DRAGS
DRAMS
DRAWS
DRAYS
DUADS
DYADS
EVANS
EXAMS
FEARS
FEATS
FIATS
FLAGS
FLAMS
FLANS
FLAPS
FLATS
FLAWS
FLAYS
FOALS
FOAMS
FRAPS
FRATS
FRAYS
GEARS
GHATS
GLADS
GLANS
GLASS
GNATS
GNAWS
GOADS
GOALS
GOATS
GRABS
GRADS
GRAMS
GRASS
GRAYS
GUANS
HEADS
HEALS

HEAPS
HEARS
HEATS
IMAMS
ITALS
IVANS
JEANS
JOANS
JUANS
KEATS
KHANS
KNARS
KVASS
KYATS
LEADS
LEAFS
LEAKS
LEANS
LEAPS
LIARS
LOADS
LOAFS
LOAMS
LOANS
LUAUS
MEADS
MEALS
MEANS
MEATS
MOANS
MOATS
NEALS
NEAPS
NEARS
NOAHS
OKAYS
OLAFS
OLAVS
OPAHS
OPALS
ORALS
OVALS
PEAKS
PEALS
PEANS
PEARS
PEATS
PLANS
PLATS
PLAYS
PRAMS
PRAYS
QUADS
QUAGS
QUASS
QUAYS
READS
REALS
REAMS
REAPS
REARS
RIALS
ROADS
ROAMS

ROANS
ROARS
SCABS
SCADS
SCANS
SCARS
SCATS
SEALS
SEAMS
SEANS
SEARS
SEATS
SHAGS
SHAHS
SHAMS
SHANS
SHAWS
SHAYS
SLABS
SLAGS
SLAMS
SLAPS
SLATS
SLAVS
SLAWS
SLAYS
SNAGS
SNAPS
SOAKS
SOAPS
SOARS
SPANS
SPARS
SPATS
SPAYS
STABS
STAGS
STANS
STARS
STAYS
SWABS
SWAGS
SWANS
SWAPS
SWATS
SWAYS
TEAKS
TEALS
TEAMS
TEARS
TEATS
THADS
THAWS
TOADS
TRAMS
TRANS
TRAPS
TRASS
TRAYS
TSARS
TZARS
UNAUS
URALS
VIALS

WEALS
WEANS
WEARS
WHAMS
WHAPS
WOADS
WRAPS
XRAYS
YEANS
YEARS
YEATS
ZBARS

•••AS

ABBAS
AGHAS
AIDAS
ALBAS
ALIAS
ALMAS
ALTAS
AMIAS
ANLAS
ANNAS
AQUAS
AREAS
ARIAS
ARRAS
ATLAS
AURAS
BABAS
BALAS
BETAS
BOLAS
CARAS
CHIAS
COCAS
CODAS
COLAS
COMAS
CORAS
DEGAS
DEVAS
DITAS
DIVAS
DONAS
DORAS
DUMAS
EDDAS
EDNAS
ELIAS
ELLAS
ELSAS
ELVAS
EMMAS
ENEAS
ERMAS
ETNAS
ETTAS
EYRAS
EZRAS
FLEAS
GALAS
GIGAS

HAHAS
HORAS
HULAS
HYLAS
IDEAS
INCAS
IOTAS
IRMAS
ISBAS
IXIAS
JONAS
JUBAS
JUDAS
KAKAS
KAVAS
KIVAS
KOLAS
LAMAS
LAVAS
LENAS
LILAS
LIRAS
LISAS
LITAS
LIZAS
LOLAS
MAMAS
MAYAS
MESAS
METAS
MICAS
MIDAS
MINAS
MONAS
MORAS
MOXAS
MYNAS
MYRAS
NANAS
NINAS
NIPAS
NOMAS
NONAS
NORAS
NOVAS
OKRAS
OLGAS
OLLAS
PACAS
PAPAS
PARAS
PICAS
PIKAS
PIMAS
PINAS
PITAS
PLEAS
PROAS
PSOAS
PUMAS
PUNAS
RHEAS
RITAS
ROSAS

ROTAS
SAGAS
SARAS
SHEAS
SILAS
SKUAS
SODAS
SOFAS
SOJAS
SORAS
SOYAS
STOAS
SURAS
TEXAS
TINAS
TOGAS
TOLAS
TOMAS
TREAS
TROAS
TUBAS
TUNAS
ULNAS
UVEAS
VARAS
VERAS
VINAS
VISAS
WEKAS
YUGAS
ZETAS

AT•••

ATAXY
ATHOS
ATILT
ATION
ATIVE
ATLAS
ATMAN
ATOLL
ATOMS
ATONE
ATONY
ATORY
ATRIA
ATRIP
ATTAR
ATTIC
ATTIS
ATTYS

A•T••

ACTED
ACTIN
ACTOR
AETAT
AFTER
AFTRA
AITCH
ALTAI
ALTAR
ALTAS
ALTER

ALTON
ALTOS
ANTAE
ANTED
ANTES
ANTHO
ANTIC
ANTIS
ANTON
ANTRA
APTLY
ARTEL
ARTER
ARTHR
ARTIE
ASTER
ASTIR
ASTON
ASTOR
ASTRO
ATTAR
ATTIC
ATTIS
ATTYS
AUTOS
AZTEC

A••T•

ABATE
ABETS
ABUTS
ACETO
ACITY
ACUTE
ADITS
ADYTA
AGATE
ALATE
AMATI
AMITY
ANITA
AORTA
ARETE
ASSTS
AUNTS
AUNTY
AUSTL
AZOTE
AZOTH

A•••T

ABAFT
ABBOT
ABORT
ABOUT
ADAPT
ADEPT
ADMIT
ADOPT
ADULT
ADUST
AETAT
AFOOT
AGENT

AGIST
AGLET
ALERT
ALEUT
ALLOT
ALOFT
AMBIT
AMENT
ANENT
ANGST
APART
APORT
ARENT
ARGOT
ARMET
ASCOT
ASSET
ASYUT
ATILT
AUDIT
AUGHT
AVAST
AVERT
AWAIT

•AT••

BATAN
BATCH
BATED
BATES
BATHE
BATHO
BATHS
BATHY
BATIK
BATON
BATTY
CATCH
CATER
CATHY
CATTY
DATED
DATER
DATES
DATTO
DATUM
EATEN
EATER
FATAL
FATED
FATES
FATLY
FATTY
GATED
GATES
GATUN
HATCH
HATED
HATER
HATES
HATTY
IATRO
IATRY
JATOS

KATES
KATHY
KATIE
LATCH
LATER
LATEX
LATHE
LATHS
LATHY
LATIN
LATRY
MATCH
MATED
MATEO
MATES
MATEY
MATIN
MATRI
MATSU
MATTE
MATTS
MATTY
MATZO
NATAL
NATES
NATTY
OATEN
OATES
OATHS
PATCH
PATEN
PATER
PATES
PATHO
PATHS
PATHY
PATIO
PATRI
PATSY
PATTY
QATAR
RATAL
RATCH
RATED
RATEL
RATER
RATES
RATIO
RATTY
SATAN
SATED
SATES
SATIN
SATYR
TATAR
TATRA
VATIC
WATAP
WATCH
WATER
WATTS

•A•T•

BAHTS

5

BAITS
BALTS
BANTU
BARTH
BASTE
BATTY
CACTI
CANTO
CANTS
CARTE
CARTS
CASTE
CASTS
CATTY
DANTE
DARTS
DATTO
EARTH
FACTS
FAITH
FASTS
FATTY
GAITS
GARTH
GASTR
HAFTS
HAITI
HALTS
HARTE
HARTS
HARTZ
HASTE
HASTY
HATTY
LACTO
LAITY
LASTS
MALTS
MALTY
MANTA
MARTA
MARTS
MARTY
MASTO
MASTS
MATTE
MATTS
MATTY
NASTY
NATTY
PACTS
PANTO
PANTS
PANTY
PARTS
PARTY
PASTA
PASTE
PASTS
PASTY
PATTY
RAFTS
RANTS
RATTY
SALTS
SALTY
SARTO
SAUTE
TANTO
TARTS
TASTE
TASTY
TAUTO
VASTY
WAFTS
WAITS
WALTS
WALTZ
WANTS
WARTS
WARTY
WASTE
WATTS
XANTH
YALTA

•A••T

BANAT
BARIT
CABOT
CADET
CANST
CAPET
CAPUT
CARAT
CARET
DAUNT
DAVIT
FACET
FAGOT
FAINT
FAULT
FAUST
GAMUT
GAUNT
GAVOT
HABIT
HASNT
HAUNT
JABOT
JANET
JAUNT
KALAT
KAMET
KAPUT
KARAT
MAGOT
MANET
MARAT
MAYST
PAINT
SABOT
SAINT
SAULT
TACET
TACIT
TAINT
TAROT
TAUNT
VALET
VAULT
VAUNT
WAIST
WASNT
YACHT

••AT•

ABATE
AGATE
ALATE
AMATI
BEATA
BEATS
BLATS
BOATS
BRATS
CHATS
COATI
COATS
CRATE
DEATH
ELATE
ENATE
ERATO
FEATS
FIATS
FLATS
FRATS
GHATS
GNATS
GOATS
GRATE
HEATH
HEATS
IRATE
KEATS
KYATS
LOATH
MEATS
MEATY
MOATS
NEATH
ORATE
OVATE
PEATS
PEATY
PLATE
PLATO
PLATS
PLATY
PRATE
RIATA
SCATO
SCATS
SEATO
SEATS
SKATE
SLATE
SLATS
SLATY
SNATH
SPATE
SPATS
STATE
STATO
SWATH
SWATS
TEATS
URATE
WRATH
WYATT
YEATS

••A•T

ABAFT
ADAPT
APART
AVAST
AWAIT
BEAST
BEAUT
BLAST
BOAST
BRACT
BRANT
CHAET
CHANT
CHAPT
CHART
COAST
CRAFT
DEALT
DRAFT
ENACT
EPACT
EXACT
EXALT
FEAST
GHAUT
GIANT
GRAFT
GRANT
HEART
INAPT
KRAFT
KRAIT
KRAUT
LEANT
LEAPT
LEAST
MEANT
PLAIT
PLANT
PLAST
QUANT
QUART
REACT
RIANT
ROAST
SCANT
SHAFT
SHALT
SHANT
SLANT
SMALT
SMART
SPAIT
START
SWART
TOAST
TRACT
TRAIT
UNAPT
WRAPT
WYATT
YEAST

•••AT

AETAT
BANAT
BEGAT
BLEAT
BLOAT
CARAT
CERAT
CHEAT
CLEAT
CROAT
DUCAT
EBOAT
ECLAT
FLOAT
GLOAT
GREAT
GROAT
HEMAT
HEPAT
HERAT
JURAT
KALAT
KARAT
KERAT
MARAT
MURAT
NEMAT
PLEAT
SEBAT
SHOAT
SOMAT
SPLAT
SPRAT
SQUAT
STOAT
STRAT
SWEAT
TERAT
TREAT
UBOAT
UNHAT
WHEAT

AU•••

AUDAD
AUDEN
AUDIO
AUDIT
AUGER
AUGHT
AUGUR
AULIC
AULIS
AUNTS
AUNTY
AURAE
AURAL
AURAS
AUREI
AURES
AURIC
AURIS
AURUM
AUSTL
AUTOS
AUXIL
AUXIN

A•U••

ABUSE
ABUTS
ACUTE
ADULT
ADUNC
ADUST
AGUES
ALUIN
ALULA
ALUMS
AMUCK
AMUSE
AQUAE
AQUAS
ARUBA
ARUMS
AZURE

A••U•

ABOUT
ACOUO
AFOUL
AINUS
ALBUM
ALDUS
ALEUT
ALGUM
ALMUD
ALMUG
ALOUD
AMOUR
AMPUL
ANGUS
ANKUS
ANNUL
ARCUS
ARGUE
ARGUS
ARIUM
ARIUS
ASCUS
ASHUR
ASYUT
AUGUR
AURUM
AWFUL

A•••U

ADIEU
ANJOU

•AU••

BAUME
CAUCA
CAULK
CAULS
CAUSE
DAUBS
DAUBY
DAUNT
FAUGH
FAULT
FAUNA
FAUNS
FAUST
GAUDI
GAUDS
GAUDY
GAUGE
GAULS
GAUNT
GAURS
GAUSS
GAUZE
GAUZY
HAULM
HAULS
HAUNT
JAUNT
KAUAI
KAURI
KAURY
LAUDS
LAUGH
LAURA
MAUDE
MAUDS
MAULS
MAUND
MAURA
MAUVE
NAURU
PAULA
PAULO
PAULS
PAUSE
SAUCE
SAUCY
SAULS
SAULT
SAUNA
SAURO
SAURY
SAUTE
TAUNT
TAUPE
TAURO
TAUTO
VAULT
VAUNT
WAUGH
WAULS
YAUPS

•A•U•

BABUL
CAJUN
CAMUS
CAPUA
CAPUT
CASUS
DATUM
FANUM
FAVUS
GAMUT
GATUN
HABUS
HAGUE
JANUS
KABUL
KAGUS
KAPUT
MAGUS
MANUS
NAHUA
NAHUM
OAKUM
PADUA
PAPUA
RAMUS
RAOUL
SAGUM
SALUS
TALUK
TALUS
VACUA
VADUZ
VAGUE
VAGUS
VALUE
VARUS
WAMUS
YAMUN

•A••U

BANTU
BAYOU
HAIKU
MATSU
NAURU
PAREU
SADHU
SAJOU

••AU•

BEAUS
BEAUT
BEAUX
FRAUD
GHAUT
GLAUC
KRAUT
LUAUS
MIAUL
SCAUP

SHAUN
UNAUS

••A•U
PRAHU
SNAFU

AV•••
AVAIL
AVARS
AVAST
AVENS
AVERS
AVERT
AVERY
AVIAN
AVION
AVISO
AVOID
AVOIR
AVOWS

A•V••
ALVAN
ALVIN
ANVIL
ARVAL

A••V•
ABOVE
AGAVE
ALIVE
ATIVE

•AV••
CAVED
CAVES
CAVIE
CAVIL
DAVAO
DAVES
DAVEY
DAVID
DAVIE
DAVIS
DAVIT
DAVYS
EAVES
FAVOR
FAVUS
GAVEL
GAVLE
GAVOT
HAVEN
HAVOC
KAVAS
LAVAS
LAVED
LAVER
LAVES
MAVIS
NAVAL
NAVAR
NAVEL
NAVES
NAVVY
OAVES
PAVAN
PAVED
PAVER
PAVES
PAVIS
RAVED
RAVEL
RAVEN
RAVER
RAVES
SAVED
SAVER
SAVES
SAVIN
SAVOR
SAVOY
SAVVY
WAVED
WAVER
WAVES
WAVEY

•A•V•
CALVE
CARVE
HALVE
LARVA
MAUVE
NAIVE
NAVVY
SALVE
SALVO
SAVVY
VALVE
VARVE
WAIVE
YAHVE

••AV•
AGAVE
BRAVA
BRAVE
BRAVO
CRAVE
DRAVA
DRAVE
GRAVE
GRAVY
GUAVA
HEAVE
HEAVY
KNAVE
LEAVE
LEAVY
OLAVS
PEAVY
PIAVE
SHAVE
SLAVE
SLAVO
SLAVS
STAVE
SUAVE
TRAVE
WEAVE

AW•••
AWAIT
AWAKE
AWARD
AWARE
AWASH
AWFUL
AWING
AWNED
AWOKE

A•W••
ALWAY
ALWIN
ASWAN

A••W•
AVOWS

A•••W
AGLOW
ALLOW
ARROW
ASKEW

•AW••
BAWDS
BAWDY
BAWLS
CAWED
DAWKS
DAWNS
FAWNS
GAWKS
GAWKY
HAWED
HAWKS
HAWSE
JAWED
LAWED
LAWNS
LAWNY
NAWAB
PAWED
PAWER
PAWLS
PAWNS
RAWER
RAWLY
SAWED
SAWER
TAWED
TAWER
TAWNY
WAWLS
YAWED
YAWLS
YAWNS
YAWPS

•A••W
MACAW
PAPAW

••AW•
BRAWL
BRAWN
CHAWS
CLAWS
CRAWL
CRAWS
DRAWL
DRAWN
DRAWS
FLAWS
FLAWY
GNAWN
GNAWS
PRAWN
SHAWL
SHAWM
SHAWN
SHAWS
SLAWS
SPAWN
THAWS
TRAWL

•••AW
BYLAW
INLAW
MACAW
PAPAW
PSHAW
SQUAW
STRAW

AX•••
AXIAL
AXILE
AXILS
AXING
AXIOM
AXLED
AXLES
AXMAN
AXMEN
AXONE
AXONS

A•X••
AUXIL
AUXIN

A••X•
ALEXA
ATAXY

A•••X
ADDAX
ADMIX
AFFIX
ANNEX

•AX••
FAXED
FAXES
LAXER
LAXLY
MAXIM
SAXES
SAXON
TAXED
TAXER
TAXES
TAXIS
WAXED
WAXEN
WAXES
XAXES
XAXIS
YAXES
YAXIS

•A••X
CALIX
CALYX
GALAX
LATEX
RADIX
VARIX

••AX•
ATAXY
BRAXY
FLAXY

••A•X
BEAUX

•••AX
ADDAX
BORAX
GALAX
HYRAX
RELAX

AY•••
AYAHS
AYDIN
AYINS

A•Y••
ABYSM
ABYSS
ADYTA
ALYCE
AMYLO
AMYLS
ARYAN
ASYLA
ASYUT

A••Y•
ABBYS
ADDYS
ALGYS
ALKYL
ALLYL
ANDYS
ASSYR
ATTYS

A•••Y
ABBEY
ACITY
AGLEY
AGONY
ALARY
ALLAY
ALLEY
ALLOY
ALPHY
ALWAY
AMBRY
AMITY
AMPLY
ANGRY
ANNOY
APERY
APPLY
APTLY
ARABY
ARCHY
ARRAY
ASSAY
ATAXY
ATONY
ATORY
AUNTY
AVERY

•AY••
BAYED
BAYOU
FAYAL
FAYED
FAYES
GAYER
GAYLY
HAYDN
HAYED
HAYES
KAYAK
KAYOS
LAYER
MAYAN
MAYAS
MAYBE
MAYOR
MAYST
PAYED
PAYEE
PAYER
RAYAH
RAYED
RAYON
SAYER
SAYID
SAYSO
WAYNE
ZAYIN

•A•Y•
BARYE
CALYX
CARYO
CARYS
DAVYS
GABYS
GARYS
KARYO
SATYR

•A••Y
BADLY
BAFFY
BAGGY
BALKY
BALMY
BANDY
BARKY
BARMY
BARRY
BATHY
BATTY
BAWDY
CABBY
CADDY
CAGEY
CAMPY
CANDY
CANNY
CAREY
CARRY
CATHY
CATTY
DADDY
DAFFY
DAILY
DAIRY
DAISY
DALLY
DANDY
DANNY
DASHY
DAUBY
DAVEY
EARLY
FADDY
FAIRY
FANCY
FANNY
FARCY
FATLY
FATTY
GABBY
GAILY
GAPPY
GASSY
GAUDY
GAUZY
GAWKY
GAYLY
HAIRY
HAMMY
HANDY
HAPLY
HAPPY
HARDY
HARPY
HARRY
HASTY
HATTY
IATRY
JACKY
JAGGY
JASSY
JAZZY
KANDY
KATHY
KAURY
LAITY
LANKY
LARDY
LARRY
LATHY
LATRY
LAWNY
LAXLY
MACHY
MADLY
MALAY
MALTY
MAMEY
MAMMY
MANCY
MANDY
MANGY
MANLY
MARLY
MARRY
MARTY
MASHY
MASSY
MATEY
MATTY
NANCY
NANNY
NAPPY
NASTY
NATTY
NAVVY
PACHY
PADDY
PALEY
PALMY
PALSY
PANDY
PANSY
PANTY
PAPPY
PARRY
PARTY
PASSY
PASTY
PATHY
PATSY
PATTY
RAGGY
RAINY

RALLY
RAMMY
RANDY
RANGY
RASPY
RATTY
RAWLY
SADLY
SALLY
SALTY
SAMMY
SANDY
SAPPY
SASSY
SAUCY
SAURY
SAVOY
SAVVY
TABBY
TACHY
TACKY
TAFFY
TALLY
TANEY
TANGY
TANSY
TARDY
TARRY
TASTY
TAWNY
VASTY
WACKY
WADDY
WALLY
WANEY
WANLY
WARTY
WASHY
WASPY
WAVEY

••AY•
BRAYS
CLAYS
DRAYS
FLAYS
FRAYS
GRAYS
OKAYS
PLAYA
PLAYS
PRAYS
QUAYS
SHAYS
SLAYS
SPAYS
STAYS
SWAYS
TRAYS
XRAYS

••A•Y
ALARY
ARABY
ATAXY
BEADY
BEAMY
BIALY
BRADY
BRAKY
BRAXY
CHARY
CLARY
CRACY
CRAZY
DEARY
DIARY
FLAKY
FLAMY
FLAWY
FLAXY
FOAMY
GLARY
GLAZY
GRAPY
GRAVY
HEADY
HEAVY
HOARY
ITALY
LEADY
LEAFY
LEAKY
LEAVY
LOAMY
MEALY
MEANY
MEATY
OVARY
PEARY
PEATY
PEAVY
PHAGY
PHANY
PHASY
PLASY
PLATY
QUAKY
READY
RHAGY
SCALY
SCARY
SEAMY
SHADY
SHAKY
SHALY
SLATY
SNAKY
SOAPY
STACY
STAGY
TEARY
THADY
TOADY
WEARY

•••AY
ALLAY
ALWAY
ARRAY
ASSAY
BELAY
BYWAY
DECAY
DELAY
DOUAY
EMBAY
ESSAY
FORAY
INLAY
MALAY
MORAY
NOWAY
RELAY
REPAY
SPLAY
SPRAY
STRAY
TODAY
TOKAY
UNLAY
UNSAY

AZ•••
AZANS
AZINE
AZOIC
AZOLE
AZONS
AZOTE
AZOTH
AZTEC
AZURE

A•Z••
ADZES
ANZAC
ANZIO

A••Z•
AGAZE
AMAZE

•AZ••
DAZED
DAZES
FAZED
FAZES
GAZED
GAZER
GAZES
HAZED
HAZEL
HAZER
HAZES
JAZZY
KAZAN
KAZOO
LAZAR
LAZED
LAZES
MAZED
MAZER
MAZES
NAZIS
RAZED
RAZEE
RAZES
RAZOR
TAZZA

•A•Z•
BAIZE
GAUZE
GAUZY
HAMZA
JAZZY
MAIZE
MATZO
TAZZA

•A••Z
CADIZ
HAFIZ
HARTZ
JABEZ
MAINZ
VADUZ
WALTZ

••AZ•
AGAZE
AMAZE
BLAZE
BRAZA
BRAZE
CRAZE
CRAZY
DIAZO
GHAZI
GLAZE
GLAZY
GRAZE
PLAZA
SMAZE

••A•Z
FRANZ

•••AZ
HEJAZ
IGNAZ
TOPAZ

BA•••
BAAED
BABAR
BABAS
BABEL
BABER
BABES
BABOO
BABUL
BACCI
BACKS
BACON
BADEN
BADGE
BADLY
BAFFS
BAFFY
BAGEL
BAGGY
BAHAI
BAHTS
BAILS
BAIRD
BAIRN
BAITS
BAIZE
BAKED
BAKER
BAKES
BALAS
BALDR
BALED
BALER
BALES
BALKS
BALKY
BALLS
BALMS
BALMY
BALSA
BALTS
BANAL
BANAT
BANDA
BANDS
BANDY
BANFF
BANGS
BANJO
BANKS
BANNS
BANTU
BARBS
BARCA
BARDE
BARDS
BARED
BARER
BARES
BARGE
BARIC
BARIT
BARKS
BARKY
BARMY
BARNS
BARON
BARRY
BARTH
BARYE
BASAL
BASED
BASEL
BASES
BASIC
BASIL
BASIN
BASIS
BASKS
BASLE
BASRA
BASSI
BASSO
BASTE
BATAN
BATCH
BATED
BATES
BATHE
BATHO
BATHS
BATHY
BATIK
BATON
BATTY
BAUME
BAWDS
BAWDY
BAWLS
BAYED
BAYOU

B•A••
BAAED
BEACH
BEADS
BEADY
BEAKS
BEAMS
BEAMY
BEANO
BEANS
BEARD
BEARS
BEAST
BEATA
BEATS
BEAUS
BEAUT
BEAUX
BHANG
BIALY
BLABS
BLACK
BLADE
BLAHS
BLAIN
BLAKE
BLAME
BLANC
BLAND
BLANK
BLARE
BLASE
BLAST
BLATS
BLAZE
BOARD
BOARS
BOAST
BOATS
BRACE
BRACT
BRADS
BRADY
BRAES
BRAGE
BRAGI
BRAGS
BRAHE
BRAID
BRAIL
BRAIN
BRAKE
BRAKY
BRAND
BRANS
BRANT
BRASH
BRASS
BRATS
BRAVA
BRAVE
BRAVO
BRAWL
BRAWN
BRAXY
BRAYS
BRAZA
BRAZE
BWANA

B••A•
BABAR
BABAS
BAHAI
BALAS
BANAL
BANAT
BASAL
BATAN
BEGAN
BEGAT
BELAY
BETAS
BIHAR
BINAL
BLEAK
BLEAR
BLEAT
BLOAT
BOGAN
BOLAR
BOLAS
BORAX
BOYAR
BREAD
BREAK
BREAM
BRIAN
BRIAR
BROAD
BRYAN
BUBAL
BURAN
BYLAW
BYWAY

B•••A
BALSA
BANDA
BARCA
BASRA
BEATA
BEIRA
BELGA
BELLA
BERTA
BEULA
BIOTA
BOHEA
BRAVA
BRAZA
BREDA
BULLA
BURMA
BURSA
BWANA

•BA••
ABACA
ABACI
ABACK
ABAFT
ABASE
ABASH
ABATE
ZBARS

•B•A•
ABBAS
ABEAM
ABRAM
EBOAT
HBEAM
IBEAM
UBOAT
ZBEAM

•B••A
ABACA
ABOMA

••BA•
ABBAS
ALBAN
ALBAS
BABAR
BABAS
BUBAL
CABAL
CUBAN
DEBAR
EMBAR
EMBAY
ISBAS
JUBAS
KUBAN

LOBAR
SABAH
SEBAT
SUBAH
TUBAL
TUBAS
UNBAR
URBAN

••B•A
COBIA
COBRA
DOBLA
DOBRA
LABIA
LABRA
LIBRA
LIBYA
NUBIA
SABRA
TIBIA
UMBRA
ZEBRA

•••BA
AMEBA
AQABA
ARUBA
CEIBA
CHIBA
KAABA
MAMBA
RUMBA
SAMBA
SCUBA
SHEBA
YERBA

B•B••
BABAR
BABAS
BABEL
BABER
BABES
BABOO
BABUL
BEBOP
BIBBS
BIBLE
BOBBY
BUBAL
BUBER

B••B•
BARBS
BEEBE
BIBBS
BILBO
BLABS
BLEBS
BLOBS
BOBBY
BOMBE
BOMBS
BOOBS
BOOBY
BRIBE
BULBS
BUSBY

B•••B
BLURB

•BB••
ABBAS
ABBES
ABBEY
ABBIE
ABBOT
ABBYS
EBBED

•B•B•
ABIBS

•B••B
ABOMB
HBOMB

••BB•
BIBBS
BOBBY
CABBY
COBBS
CUBBY
DEBBY
DOBBY
GABBY
HOBBS
HOBBY
LIBBY
LOBBY
NOBBY
NUBBY
RABBI
TABBY
TUBBY
WEBBY

••B•B
CABOB
CUBEB
KABOB
NABOB

B•C••
BACCI
BACKS
BACON
BECKS
BECKY
BICES
BOCHE
BUCKO
BUCKS

B••C•
BACCI
BARCA
BATCH
BEACH
BEECH
BELCH
BENCH
BIRCH
BITCH
BLACK
BLOCK
BLOCS
BOSCH
BOTCH
BRACE
BRACT
BRICE
BRICK
BRUCE
BRYCE
BUNCH
BUNCO

B•••C
BARIC
BASIC
BLANC
BORIC
BRONC

•B•C•
ABACA
ABACI
ABACK

••B•C
CUBIC
PUBIC
RABIC
REBEC
XEBEC
ZEBEC

B•D••
BADEN
BADGE
BADLY
BEDEW
BEDIM
BIDDY
BIDED
BIDES
BIDET
BLDGS
BODED
BODES
BUDDY
BUDGE

B••D•
BALDR
BANDA
BANDS
BANDY
BARDE
BARDS
BAWDS
BAWDY
BEADS
BEADY
BENDS
BENDY
BIDDY
BINDS
BIRDS
BLADE
BONDS
BOYDS
BRADS
BRADY
BREDA
BRIDE
BUDDY
BUNDE
BUNDS
BURDS

B•••D
BAAED
BAIRD
BAKED
BALED
BARED
BASED
BATED
BAYED
BEARD
BIDED
BIFID
BIPED
BIPOD
BLAND
BLEED
BLEND
BLIND
BLOND
BLOOD
BLUED
BOARD
BODED
BONED
BOOED
BORED
BOUND
BOVID
BOWED
BOXED
BRAID
BRAND
BREAD
BREED
BROAD
BROOD
BUILD
BUSED

•B•D•
ABIDE
ABODE

•B••D
EBBED

••B•D
CUBED
EBBED
EMBED
GIBED
IMBED
JIBED
LOBED
ORBED
RABID
ROBED
SABED
TABID
TUBED

BE•••
BEACH
BEADS
BEADY
BEAKS
BEAMS
BEAMY
BEANO
BEANS
BEARD
BEARS
BEAST
BEATA
BEATS
BEAUS
BEAUT
BEAUX
BEBOP
BECKS
BECKY
BEDEW
BEDIM
BEEBE
BEECH
BEEFS
BEEFY
BEEPS
BEERS
BEERY
BEETS
BEFIT
BEFOG
BEGAN
BEGAT
BEGET
BEGIN
BEGOT
BEGUM
BEGUN
BEIGE
BEING
BEIRA
BELAY
BELCH
BELEM
BELGA
BELIE
BELLA
BELLE
BELLS
BELLY
BELOW
BELTS
BENCH
BENDS
BENDY
BENES
BENET
BENIN
BENJY
BENNE
BENNY
BENUE
BERET
BERGS
BERME
BERMS
BERNE
BERRY
BERTA
BERTH
BERTS
BERTY
BERYL
BESET
BESOM
BESOT
BESSY
BESTS
BETAS
BETEL
BETHS
BETON
BETSY
BETTE
BETTY
BEULA
BEVEL
BEVIN
BEZEL

B•E••
BEEBE
BEECH
BEEFS
BEEFY
BEEPS
BEERS
BEERY
BEETS
BIERS
BLEAK
BLEAR
BLEAT
BLEBS
BLEED
BLEND
BLENT
BLESS
BLEST
BMEWS
BOERS
BREAD
BREAK
BREAM
BREDA
BREED
BRENT
BREST
BREVE
BREVI
BREWS

B••E•
BAAED
BABEL
BABER
BABES
BADEN
BAGEL
BAKED
BAKER
BAKES
BALED
BALER
BALES
BARED
BARER
BARES
BASED
BASEL
BASES
BATED
BATES
BAYED
BEDEW
BEGET
BELEM
BENES
BENET
BERET
BESET
BETEL
BEVEL
BEZEL
BICES
BIDED
BIDES
BIDET
BIKES
BILES
BINES
BINET
BIPED
BISES
BITER
BITES
BIZET
BLEED
BLUED
BLUER
BLUES
BLUET
BODED
BODES
BOGEY
BOHEA
BOLES
BONED
BONER
BONES
BOOED
BORED
BORER
BORES
BOWED
BOWEL
BOWER
BOXED
BOXER
BOXES
BRAES
BREED
BRIEF
BRIER
BUBER
BUSED
BUSES
BUYER
BYRES

B•••E
BADGE
BAIZE
BARDE
BARGE
BARYE
BASLE
BASTE
BATHE
BAUME
BEEBE
BEIGE
BELIE
BELLE
BENNE
BENUE
BERME
BERNE
BETTE
BIBLE
BILGE
BINGE
BIRLE
BLADE
BLAKE
BLAME
BLARE
BLASE
BLAZE
BLOKE
BOCHE
BOGIE
BOGLE
BOISE
BOMBE
BONZE
BOONE

BOOZE
BORNE
BOULE
BOUSE
BOWIE
BOWSE
BOYLE
BOYNE
BRACE
BRAGE
BRAHE
BRAKE
BRAVE
BRAZE
BREVE
BRIBE
BRICE
BRIDE
BRINE
BROKE
BROME
BRUCE
BRUME
BRUTE
BRYCE
BUDGE
BUGLE
BULGE
BUNDE
BURKE
BURSE
BUTTE

•BE••
ABEAM
ABELE
ABELS
ABETS
HBEAM
IBEAM
OBESE
OBEYS
ZBEAM

•B•E•
ABBES
ABBEY
ABIEL
ABIES
ABLER
ABNER
EBBED
IBSEN
OBOES

•B••E
ABASE
ABATE
ABBIE
ABELE
ABIDE
ABODE
ABOVE
ABUSE
OBESE
TBONE

••BE•
ABBES
ABBEY
ALBEE
AMBER
BABEL
BABER
BABES
BUBER
CABER
CUBEB
CUBED
CUBES
EBBED
EMBED
EMBER
FIBER
GABES
GIBED
GIBER
GIBES
IMBED
JABEZ
JIBED
JIBES
JUBES
KIBEI
KIBES
LABEL
LIBEL
LIBER
LOBED
LOBES
MABEL
NOBEL
OMBER
ORBED
PUBES
REBEC
REBEL
ROBED
ROBES
RUBES
SABED
SABER
SABES
SOBER
TABES
TEBET
TIBER
TIBET
TUBED
TUBER
TUBES
UMBEL
UMBER
VIBES
WEBER
XEBEC
ZEBEC
ZIBET

••B•E
ABBIE
ALBEE
AMBLE
BIBLE
CABLE
COBLE
DOBIE
DUBHE
FABLE
GABLE
IMBUE
NOBLE
OMBRE
ROBLE
RUBLE
SABLE
TABLE

•••BE
ADOBE
BEEBE
BOMBE
BRIBE
GLEBE
GLOBE
GREBE
MAYBE
NIOBE
PHEBE
PHOBE
PLEBE
PROBE
TRIBE

B•F••
BAFFS
BAFFY
BEFIT
BEFOG
BIFFS
BIFFY
BIFID
BUFFI
BUFFO
BUFFS
BUFFY

B••F•
BAFFS
BAFFY
BANFF
BEEFS
BEEFY
BIFFS
BIFFY
BLUFF
BUFFI
BUFFO
BUFFS
BUFFY

B•••F
BANFF
BLUFF
BRIEF

•B•F•
ABAFT

B•G••
BAGEL
BAGGY
BEGAN
BEGAT
BEGET
BEGIN
BEGOT
BEGUM
BEGUN
BIGHT
BIGLY
BIGOT
BOGAN
BOGEY
BOGGY
BOGIE
BOGLE
BOGOR
BOGUS
BUGGY
BUGLE

B••G•
BADGE
BAGGY
BANGS
BARGE
BEIGE
BELGA
BERGS
BILGE
BILGY
BINGE
BINGO
BLDGS
BLIGH
BOGGY
BONGO
BONGS
BOUGH
BRAGE
BRAGI
BRAGS
BRIGS
BUDGE
BUGGY
BULGE
BULGY
BUNGS
BURGH
BURGS

B•••G
BEFOG
BEING
BHANG
BOURG
BRING

••B•G
DEBUG

BH•••
BHANG

B•H••
BAHAI
BAHTS
BIHAR
BOHEA
BOHOL

B••H•
BATHE
BATHO
BATHS
BATHY
BETHS
BIGHT
BLAHS
BOCHE
BRAHE
BUSHY

B•••H
BARTH
BATCH
BEACH
BEECH
BELCH
BENCH
BERTH
BIRCH
BIRTH
BITCH
BLIGH
BLUSH
BOOTH
BOSCH
BOTCH
BOUGH
BRASH
BROTH
BRUSH
BUNCH
BURGH

•BH••
ABHOR

•B•H•
ABOHM

•B••H
ABASH

••BH•
DUBHE

••B•H
SABAH
SUBAH

BI•••
BIALY
BIBBS
BIBLE
BICES
BIDDY
BIDED
BIDES
BIDET
BIERS
BIFFS
BIFFY
BIFID
BIGHT
BIGLY
BIGOT
BIHAR
BIJOU
BIKES
BIKOL
BILBO
BILES
BILGE
BILGY
BILKS
BILLS
BILLY
BINAL
BINDS
BINES
BINET
BINGE
BINGO
BINIT
BIOTA
BIPED
BIPOD
BIRCH
BIRDS
BIRLE
BIRLS
BIRRS
BIRTH
BISES
BISON
BITCH
BITER
BITES
BITTS
BIZET

B•I••
BAILS
BAIRD
BAIRN
BAITS
BAIZE
BEIGE
BEING
BEIRA
BLIGH
BLIMP
BLIND
BLINK
BLIPS
BLISS
BLITZ
BOILS
BOISE
BRIAN
BRIAR
BRIBE
BRICE
BRICK
BRIDE
BRIEF
BRIER
BRIGS
BRILL
BRIMS
BRINE
BRING
BRINK
BRINY
BRISK
BUILD
BUILT

B••I•
BARIC
BARIT
BASIC
BASIL
BASIN
BASIS
BATIK
BEDIM
BEFIT
BEGIN
BELIE
BENIN
BEVIN
BIFID
BINIT
BLAIN
BLOIS
BOGIE
BONIN
BORIC
BORIS
BOVID
BOWIE
BRAID
BRAIL
BRAIN
BROIL
BRUIN
BRUIT
BURIN

B•••I
BACCI
BAHAI
BASSI
BRAGI
BREVI
BUFFI
BYSSI

•BI••
ABIBS
ABIDE
ABIEL
ABIES
OBITS

•B•I•
ABBIE
ABRIS

•B••I
ABACI
OBOLI

••BI•
ABBIE
ALBIN
AMBIT
CABIN
COBIA
CUBIC
CUBIT
DEBIT
DOBIE
HABIT
LABIA
LABIO
NUBIA
ORBIT
PUBIC
PUBIS
RABIC
RABID
ROBIN
SABIN
SYBIL
TABID
TIBIA

••B•I
FEBRI
KIBEI
RABBI

•••BI
ALIBI
IAMBI
KRUBI
LIMBI
NIMBI
ORIBI
RABBI
ZOMBI

B•J••
BIJOU

B••J•
BANJO
BENJY

5

B•K••
BAKED
BAKER
BAKES
BIKES
BIKOL

B••K•
BACKS
BALKS
BALKY
BANKS
BARKS
BARKY
BASKS
BEAKS
BECKS
BECKY
BILKS
BLAKE
BLOKE
BOOKS
BOSKS
BOSKY
BRAKE
BRAKY
BROKE
BUCKO
BUCKS
BULKS
BULKY
BUNKO
BUNKS
BURKE
BUSKS

B•••K
BATIK
BLACK
BLANK
BLEAK
BLINK
BLOCK
BREAK
BRICK
BRINK
BRISK
BROOK
BRUSK

•B••K
ABACK

BL•••
BLABS
BLACK
BLADE
BLAHS
BLAIN
BLAKE
BLAME
BLANC
BLAND
BLANK
BLARE
BLASE
BLAST
BLATS
BLAZE
BLDGS
BLEAK
BLEAR
BLEAT
BLEBS
BLEED
BLEND
BLENT
BLESS
BLEST
BLIGH
BLIMP
BLIND
BLINK
BLIPS
BLISS
BLITZ
BLOAT
BLOBS
BLOCK
BLOCS
BLOIS
BLOKE
BLOND
BLOOD
BLOOM
BLOTS
BLOWN
BLOWS
BLOWY
BLUED
BLUER
BLUES
BLUET
BLUFF
BLUNT
BLURB
BLURS
BLURT
BLUSH

B•L••
BALAS
BALDR
BALED
BALER
BALES
BALKS
BALKY
BALLS
BALMS
BALMY
BALSA
BALTS
BELAY
BELCH
BELEM
BELGA
BELIE
BELLA
BELLE
BELLS
BELLY
BELOW
BELTS
BILBO
BILES
BILGE
BILGY
BILKS
BILLS
BILLY
BOLAR
BOLAS
BOLES
BOLLS
BOLOS
BOLTS
BOLUS
BULBS
BULGE
BULGY
BULKS
BULKY
BULLA
BULLS
BULLY
BYLAW

B••L•
BADLY
BAILS
BALLS
BASLE
BAWLS
BELLA
BELLE
BELLS
BELLY
BEULA
BIALY
BIBLE
BIGLY
BILLS
BILLY
BIRLE
BIRLS
BOGLE
BOILS
BOLLS
BOULE
BOWLS
BOYLE
BRILL
BUGLE
BUILD
BUILT
BULLA
BULLS
BULLY
BURLS
BURLY

B•••L
BABEL
BABUL
BAGEL
BANAL
BASAL
BASEL
BASIL
BERYL
BETEL
BEVEL
BEZEL
BIKOL
BINAL
BOHOL
BOWEL
BRAIL
BRAWL
BRILL
BROIL
BUBAL
BUTYL

•BL••
ABLER

•B•L•
ABELE
ABELS
OBOLI
UBOLT

•B••L
ABIEL

••BL•
AMBLE
BIBLE
CABLE
COBLE
DOBLA
FABLE
GABLE
NOBLE
NOBLY
PABLO
ROBLE
RUBLE
SABLE
TABLE

••B•L
BABEL
BABUL
BUBAL
CABAL
CIBOL
KABUL
LABEL
LIBEL
MABEL
NOBEL
REBEL
SIBYL
SYBIL
TOBOL
TUBAL
UMBEL

BM•••
BMEWS

B•M••
BOMBE
BOMBS
BUMPS
BUMPY

B••M•
BALMS
BALMY
BARMY
BAUME
BEAMS
BEAMY
BERME
BERMS
BLAME
BLIMP
BOOMS
BRIMS
BROME
BROMO
BRUME
BURMA

B•••M
BEDIM
BEGUM
BELEM
BESOM
BLOOM
BOSOM
BREAM
BROOM
BUXOM

•B•M•
ABOMA
ABOMB
HBOMB

•B••M
ABEAM
ABOHM
ABRAM
ABYSM
HBEAM
IBEAM
ZBEAM

••B•M
ALBUM
SEBUM

B•N••
BANAL
BANAT
BANDA
BANDS
BANDY
BANFF
BANGS
BANJO
BANKS
BANNS
BANTU
BENCH
BENDS
BENDY
BENES
BENET
BENIN
BENJY
BENNE
BENNY
BENUE
BINAL
BINDS
BINES
BINET
BINGE
BINGO
BINIT
BONDS
BONED
BONER
BONES
BONGO
BONGS
BONIN
BONNY
BONUS
BONZE
BUNCH
BUNCO
BUNDE
BUNDS
BUNGS
BUNKO
BUNKS
BUNNS
BUNNY
BUNTS

B••N•
BANNS
BARNS
BEANO
BEANS
BEING
BENNE
BENNY
BERNE
BHANG
BLANC
BLAND
BLANK
BLEND
BLENT
BLIND
BLINK
BLOND
BLUNT
BONNY
BOONE
BOONS
BORNE
BORNU
BOUND
BOYNE
BRAND
BRANS
BRANT
BRENT
BRINE
BRING
BRINK
BRINY
BRONC
BRONX
BRUNO
BRUNT
BUNNS
BUNNY
BURNS
BURNT
BWANA

B•••N
BACON
BADEN
BAIRN
BARON
BASIN
BATAN
BATON
BEGAN
BEGIN
BEGUN
BENIN
BETON
BEVIN
BISON
BLAIN
BLOWN
BOGAN
BONIN
BORON
BOSUN
BOURN
BRAIN
BRAWN
BRIAN
BROWN
BRUIN
BRYAN
BURAN
BURIN
BYRON

•BN••
ABNER

•B•N•
EBONS
EBONY
TBONE

•B••N
IBSEN

••B•N
ALBAN
ALBIN
CABIN
CUBAN
GABON
KUBAN
ROBIN
SABIN
URBAN

BO•••
BOARD
BOARS
BOAST
BOATS
BOBBY
BOCHE
BODED
BODES
BOERS
BOGAN
BOGEY
BOGGY
BOGIE
BOGLE
BOGOR
BOGUS
BOHEA
BOHOL
BOILS
BOISE
BOLAR
BOLAS
BOLES
BOLLS
BOLOS
BOLTS
BOLUS
BOMBE
BOMBS
BONDS
BONED
BONER
BONES
BONGO
BONGS
BONIN
BONNY
BONUS
BONZE
BOOBS
BOOBY
BOOED
BOOKS
BOOMS
BOONE
BOONS

BOORS
BOOST
BOOTH
BOOTS
BOOTY
BOOZE
BOOZY
BORAX
BORED
BORER
BORES
BORIC
BORIS
BORNE
BORNU
BORON
BORTS
BORTY
BORTZ
BOSCH
BOSKS
BOSKY
BOSOM
BOSSY
BOSUN
BOTCH
BOTTS
BOUGH
BOULE
BOUND
BOURG
BOURN
BOUSE
BOUSY
BOUTS
BOVID
BOWED
BOWEL
BOWER
BOWIE
BOWLS
BOWSE
BOXED
BOXER
BOXES
BOYAR
BOYDS
BOYLE
BOYNE
BOZOS

B•O••
BIOTA
BLOAT
BLOBS
BLOCK
BLOCS
BLOIS
BLOKE
BLOND
BLOOD
BLOOM
BLOTS
BLOWN
BLOWS
BLOWY
BOOBS
BOOBY
BOOED
BOOKS
BOOMS
BOONE
BOONS
BOORS
BOOST
BOOTH
BOOTS
BOOTY
BOOZE
BOOZY
BROAD
BROIL
BROKE
BROME
BROMO
BRONC
BRONX
BROOD
BROOK
BROOM
BROOS
BROTH
BROWN
BROWS
BUOYS

B••O•
BABOO
BACON
BARON
BATON
BAYOU
BEBOP
BEFOG
BEGOT
BELOW
BESOM
BESOT
BETON
BIGOT
BIJOU
BIKOL
BIPOD
BISON
BLOOD
BLOOM
BOGOR
BOHOL
BOLOS
BORON
BOSOM
BOZOS
BROOD
BROOK
BROOM
BROOS
BUXOM
BYRON

B•••O
BABOO
BANJO
BASSO
BATHO
BEANO
BILBO
BINGO
BONGO
BRAVO
BROMO
BRUNO
BUCKO
BUFFO
BUNCO
BUNKO
BURRO

•BO••
ABODE
ABOHM
ABOMA
ABOMB
ABORT
ABOUT
ABOVE
EBOAT
EBONS
EBONY
HBOMB
OBOES
OBOLI
TBONE
UBOAT
UBOLT

•B•O•
ABBOT
ABHOR

••BO•
ABBOT
AMBOS
ARBOR
BABOO
BEBOP
CABOB
CABOT
CIBOL
ELBOW
EMBOW
GABON
GOBOS
HOBOS
JABOT
KABOB
LABOR
LOBOS
NABOB
OXBOW
ROBOT
SABOT
TABOO
TABOR
TOBOL
UMBOS
UPBOW

••B•O
BABOO
FIBRO
LABIO
OMBRO
PABLO
TABOO

•••BO
BILBO
CARBO
COMBO
GUMBO
JUMBO
LIMBO
MAMBO
SAMBO
TURBO

B•P••
BIPED
BIPOD

B••P•
BEEPS
BLIPS
BUMPS
BUMPY
BURPS

B•••P
BEBOP
BLIMP

••B•P
BEBOP

BR•••
BRACE
BRACT
BRADS
BRADY
BRAES
BRAGE
BRAGI
BRAGS
BRAHE
BRAID
BRAIL
BRAIN
BRAKE
BRAKY
BRAND
BRANS
BRANT
BRASH
BRASS
BRATS
BRAVA
BRAVE
BRAVO
BRAWL
BRAWN
BRAXY
BRAYS
BRAZA
BRAZE
BREAD
BREAK
BREAM
BREDA
BREED
BRENT
BREST
BREVE
BREVI
BREWS
BRIAN
BRIAR
BRIBE
BRICE
BRICK
BRIDE
BRIEF
BRIER
BRIGS
BRILL
BRIMS
BRINE
BRING
BRINK
BRINY
BRISK
BROAD
BROIL
BROKE
BROME
BROMO
BRONC
BRONX
BROOD
BROOK
BROOM
BROOS
BROTH
BROWN
BROWS
BRUCE
BRUIN
BRUIT
BRUME
BRUNO
BRUNT
BRUSH
BRUSK
BRUTE
BRYAN
BRYCE

B•R••
BARBS
BARCA
BARDE
BARDS
BARED
BARER
BARES
BARGE
BARIC
BARIT
BARKS
BARKY
BARMY
BARNS
BARON
BARRY
BARTH
BARYE
BERET
BERGS
BERME
BERMS
BERNE
BERRY
BERTA
BERTH
BERTS
BERTY
BERYL
BIRCH
BIRDS
BIRLE
BIRLS
BIRRS
BIRTH
BORAX
BORED
BORER
BORES
BORIC
BORIS
BORNE
BORNU
BORON
BORTS
BORTY
BORTZ
BURAN
BURDS
BURGH
BURGS
BURIN
BURKE
BURLS
BURLY
BURMA
BURNS
BURNT
BURPS
BURRO
BURRS
BURRY
BURSA
BURSE
BURST
BYRES
BYRON

B••R•
BAIRD
BAIRN
BARRY
BASRA
BEARD
BEARS
BEERS
BEERY
BEIRA
BERRY
BIERS
BIRRS
BLARE
BLURB
BLURS
BLURT
BOARD
BOARS
BOERS
BOORS
BOURG
BOURN
BURRO
BURRS
BURRY

B•••R
BABAR
BABER
BAKER
BALDR
BALER
BARER
BIHAR
BITER
BLEAR
BLUER
BOGOR
BOLAR
BONER
BORER
BOWER
BOXER
BOYAR
BRIAR
BRIER
BUBER
BUYER

•BR••
ABRAM
ABRIS

•B•R•
ABORT
ZBARS

•B••R
ABHOR
ABLER
ABNER

••BR•
AMBRY
COBRA
DOBRA
EMBRY
FEBRI
FIBRO
LABRA
LIBRA
OMBRE
OMBRO
SABRA
UMBRA
ZEBRA

••B•R
AMBER
ARBOR
BABAR
BABER
BUBER
CABER
DEBAR
EMBAR
EMBER
FIBER
GIBER
LABOR
LIBER
LOBAR
OMBER
SABER
SOBER
TABOR
TIBER
TUBER
UMBER
UNBAR
WEBER

B•S••
BASAL
BASED
BASEL
BASES
BASIC
BASIL
BASIN
BASIS
BASKS
BASLE
BASRA
BASSI
BASSO
BASTE
BESET
BESOM
BESOT
BESSY
BESTS
BISES
BISON
BOSCH
BOSKS

BOSKY
BOSOM
BOSSY
BOSUN
BUSBY
BUSED
BUSES
BUSHY
BUSKS
BUSTS
BYSSI

B••S•

BALSA
BASSI
BASSO
BEAST
BESSY
BETSY
BLASE
BLAST
BLESS
BLEST
BLISS
BLUSH
BOAST
BOISE
BOOST
BOSSY
BOUSE
BOUSY
BOWSE
BRASH
BRASS
BREST
BRISK
BRUSH
BRUSK
BURSA
BURSE
BURST
BYSSI

B•••S

BABAS
BABES
BACKS
BAFFS
BAHTS
BAILS
BAITS
BAKES
BALAS
BALES
BALKS
BALLS
BALMS
BALTS
BANDS
BANGS
BANKS
BANNS
BARBS
BARDS
BARES
BARKS
BARNS
BASES
BASIS
BASKS
BATES
BATHS
BAWDS
BAWLS
BEADS
BEAKS
BEAMS
BEANS
BEARS
BEATS
BEAUS
BECKS
BEEFS
BEEPS
BEERS
BEETS
BELLS
BELTS
BENDS
BENES
BERGS
BERMS
BERTS
BESTS
BETAS
BETHS
BIBBS
BICES
BIDES
BIERS
BIFFS
BIKES
BILES
BILKS
BILLS
BINDS
BINES
BIRDS
BIRLS
BIRRS
BISES
BITES
BITTS
BLABS
BLAHS
BLATS
BLDGS
BLEBS
BLESS
BLIPS
BLISS
BLOBS
BLOCS
BLOIS
BLOTS
BLOWS
BLUES
BLURS
BMEWS
BOARS
BOATS
BODES
BOERS
BOGUS
BOILS
BOLAS
BOLES
BOLLS
BOLOS
BOLTS
BOLUS
BOMBS
BONDS
BONES
BONGS
BONUS
BOOBS
BOOKS
BOOMS
BOONS
BOORS
BOOTS
BORES
BORIS
BORTS
BOSKS
BOTTS
BOUTS
BOWLS
BOXES
BOYDS
BOZOS
BRADS
BRAES
BRAGS
BRANS
BRASS
BRATS
BRAYS
BREWS
BRIGS
BRIMS
BROOS
BROWS
BUCKS
BUFFS
BULBS
BULKS
BULLS
BUMPS
BUNDS
BUNGS
BUNKS
BUNNS
BUNTS
BUOYS
BURDS
BURGS
BURLS
BURNS
BURPS
BURRS
BUSES
BUSKS
BUSTS
BUTTS
BYRES

•BS••

IBSEN

•B•S•

ABASE
ABASH
ABUSE
ABYSM
ABYSS
OBESE

•B••S

ABBAS
ABBES
ABBYS
ABELS
ABETS
ABIBS
ABIES
ABRIS
ABUTS
ABYSS
EBONS
OBEYS
OBITS
OBOES
ZBARS

••B•S

ABBAS
ABBES
ABBYS
ALBAS
AMBOS
BABAS
BABES
BIBBS
COBBS
CUBES
DEBTS
GABES
GABYS
GIBES
GOBOS
GOBYS
HABUS
HOBBS
HOBOS
ISBAS
JIBES
JUBAS
JUBES
KIBES
LOBES
LOBOS
PUBES
PUBIS
REBUS
ROBES
RUBES
RUBYS
SABES
TABES
TOBYS
TUBAS
TUBES
UMBOS
VIBES
ZEBUS

•••BS

ABIBS
ARABS
BARBS
BIBBS
BLABS
BLEBS
BLOBS
BOMBS
BOOBS
BULBS
CHUBS
CLUBS
COBBS
COMBS
CRABS
CRIBS
CURBS
DAUBS
DRABS
DRIBS
DRUBS
FLUBS
FORBS
GAMBS
GARBS
GLOBS
GRABS
GRUBS
HERBS
HOBBS
IAMBS
JAMBS
KERBS
KNOBS
LAMBS
LIMBS
NUMBS
PLEBS
SCABS
SERBS
SLABS
SLOBS
SLUBS
SNOBS
SNUBS
SORBS
STABS
STUBS
SWABS
TOMBS
VERBS
WOMBS

B•T••

BATAN
BATCH
BATED
BATES
BATHE
BATHO
BATHS
BATHY
BATIK
BATON
BATTY
BETAS
BETEL
BETHS
BETON
BETSY
BETTE
BETTY
BITCH
BITER
BITES
BITTS
BOTCH
BOTTS
BUTTE
BUTTS
BUTYL

B••T•

BAHTS
BAITS
BALTS
BANTU
BARTH
BASTE
BATTY
BEATA
BEATS
BEETS
BELTS
BERTA
BERTH
BERTS
BERTY
BESTS
BETTE
BETTY
BIOTA
BIRTH
BITTS
BLATS
BLITZ
BLOTS
BOATS
BOLTS
BOOTH
BOOTS
BOOTY
BORTS
BORTY
BORTZ
BOTTS
BOUTS
BRATS
BROTH
BRUTE
BUNTS
BUSTS
BUTTE
BUTTS

B•••T

BANAT
BARIT
BEAST
BEAUT
BEFIT
BEGAT
BEGET
BEGOT
BENET
BERET
BESET
BESOT
BIDET
BIGHT
BIGOT
BINET
BINIT
BIZET
BLAST
BLEAT
BLENT
BLEST
BLOAT
BLUET
BLUNT
BLURT
BOAST
BOOST
BRACT
BRANT
BRENT
BREST
BRUIT
BRUNT
BUILT
BURNT
BURST

•B•T•

ABATE
ABETS
ABUTS
OBITS

•B••T

ABAFT
ABBOT
ABORT
ABOUT
EBOAT
UBOAT
UBOLT

••BT•

DEBTS

••B•T

ABBOT
AMBIT
CABOT
CUBIT
DEBIT
DEBUT
HABIT
JABOT
ORBIT
REBUT
ROBOT
SABOT
SEBAT
TEBET
TIBET
ZIBET

•••BT

DOUBT

BU•••

BUBAL
BUBER
BUCKO
BUCKS
BUDDY
BUDGE
BUFFI
BUFFO
BUFFS
BUFFY
BUGGY
BUGLE
BUILD
BUILT
BULBS
BULGE
BULGY
BULKS
BULKY
BULLA
BULLS
BULLY
BUMPS
BUMPY
BUNCH
BUNCO
BUNDE
BUNDS
BUNGS
BUNKO
BUNKS
BUNNS
BUNNY
BUNTS
BUOYS
BURAN
BURDS
BURGH
BURGS

BURIN
BURKE
BURLS
BURLY
BURMA
BURNS
BURNT
BURPS
BURRO
BURRS
BURRY
BURSA
BURSE
BURST
BUSBY
BUSED
BUSES
BUSHY
BUSKS
BUSTS
BUTTE
BUTTS
BUTYL
BUXOM
BUYER

B•U••
BAUME
BEULA
BLUED
BLUER
BLUES
BLUET
BLUFF
BLUNT
BLURB
BLURS
BLURT
BLUSH
BOUGH
BOULE
BOUND
BOURG
BOURN
BOUSE
BOUSY
BOUTS
BRUCE
BRUIN
BRUIT
BRUME
BRUNO
BRUNT
BRUSH
BRUSK
BRUTE

B••U•
BABUL
BEAUS
BEAUT
BEAUX
BEGUM
BEGUN
BENUE
BOGUS
BOLUS
BONUS
BOSUN

B•••U
BANTU
BAYOU
BIJOU
BORNU

•BU••
ABUSE
ABUTS

•B•U•
ABOUT

••BU•
ALBUM
BABUL
DEBUG
DEBUT
HABUS
IMBUE
KABUL
REBUS
REBUT
SEBUM
ZEBUS

B•V••
BEVEL
BEVIN
BOVID

B••V•
BRAVA
BRAVE
BRAVO
BREVE
BREVI

•B•V•
ABOVE

BW•••
BWANA

B•W••
BAWDS
BAWDY
BAWLS
BOWED
BOWEL
BOWER
BOWIE
BOWLS
BOWSE
BYWAY

B••W•
BLOWN
BLOWS
BLOWY
BMEWS
BRAWL
BRAWN
BREWS
BROWN
BROWS

B•••W
BEDEW
BELOW
BYLAW

••B•W
ELBOW
EMBOW
OXBOW
UPBOW

B•X••
BOXED
BOXER
BOXES
BUXOM

B••X•
BRAXY

B•••X
BEAUX
BORAX
BRONX

BY•••
BYLAW
BYRES
BYRON
BYSSI
BYWAY

B•Y••
BAYED
BAYOU
BOYAR
BOYDS
BOYLE
BOYNE
BRYAN
BRYCE
BUYER

B••Y•
BARYE
BERYL
BRAYS
BUOYS
BUTYL

B•••Y
BADLY
BAFFY
BAGGY
BALKY
BALMY
BANDY
BARKY
BARMY
BARRY
BATHY
BATTY
BAWDY
BEADY
BEAMY
BECKY
BEEFY
BEERY
BELAY
BELLY
BENDY
BENJY
BENNY
BERRY
BERTY
BESSY
BETSY
BETTY
BIALY
BIDDY
BIFFY
BIGLY
BILGY
BILLY
BLOWY
BOBBY
BOGEY
BOGGY
BONNY
BOOBY
BOOTY
BOOZY
BORTY
BOSKY
BOSSY
BOUSY
BRADY
BRAKY
BRAXY
BRINY
BUDDY
BUFFY
BUGGY
BULGY
BULKY
BULLY
BUMPY
BUNNY
BURLY
BURRY
BUSBY
BUSHY
BYWAY

•BY••
ABYSM
ABYSS

•B•Y•
ABBYS
OBEYS

•B••Y
ABBEY
EBONY

••BY•
ABBYS
GABYS
GOBYS
LIBYA
RUBYS
SIBYL
TOBYS

••B•Y
ABBEY
AMBRY
BOBBY
CABBY
CUBBY
DEBBY
DOBBY
EMBAY
EMBRY
GABBY
HOBBY
LIBBY
LOBBY
NOBBY
NOBLY
NUBBY
TABBY
TUBBY
WEBBY

•••BY
ARABY
BOBBY
BOOBY
BUSBY
CABBY
CUBBY
DAUBY
DEBBY
DERBY
DOBBY
FLYBY
GABBY
HERBY
HOBBY
LIBBY
LOBBY
LOOBY
NOBBY
NUBBY
RUGBY
TABBY
TUBBY
WEBBY
WOMBY

B•Z••
BEZEL
BIZET
BOZOS

B••Z•
BAIZE
BLAZE
BONZE
BOOZE
BOOZY
BRAZA
BRAZE

B•••Z
BLITZ
BORTZ

••B•Z
JABEZ

CA•••
CABAL
CABBY
CABER
CABIN
CABLE
CABOB
CABOT
CACAO
CACHE
CACTI
CADDO
CADDY
CADES
CADET
CADGE
CADIS
CADIZ
CADRE
CAFES
CAGED
CAGES
CAGEY
CAIRD
CAIRN
CAIRO
CAJON
CAJUN
CAKED
CAKES
CALCI
CALEB
CALIF
CALIX
CALKS
CALLA
CALLI
CALLS
CALMS
CALPE
CALVE
CALYX
CAMEL
CAMEO
CAMES
CAMPI
CAMPO
CAMPS
CAMPY
CAMUS
CANAD
CANAL
CANDY
CANEA
CANED
CANER
CANES
CANIS
CANNA
CANNY
CANOE
CANON
CANSO
CANST
CANTO
CANTS
CAPEK
CAPER
CAPES
CAPET
CAPON
CAPRI
CAPUA
CAPUT
CARAS
CARAT
CARBO
CARDI
CARDS
CARED
CARER
CARES
CARET
CAREY
CARGO
CARIB
CARLA
CARLO
CARLS
CAROB
CAROL
CAROM
CARPI
CARPO
CARPS
CARRY
CARTE
CARTS
CARVE
CARYO
CARYS
CASCO
CASED
CASES
CASKS
CASTE
CASTS
CASUS
CATCH
CATER
CATHY
CATTY
CAUCA
CAULK
CAULS
CAUSE
CAVED
CAVES
CAVIE
CAVIL
CAWED

C•A••
CEARA
CEASE
CHAET
CHAFE
CHAFF
CHAIN
CHAIR
CHALK
CHAMP
CHANG
CHANT
CHAOS
CHAPE
CHAPS
CHAPT
CHARD
CHARE
CHARM
CHARS
CHART
CHARY
CHASE
CHASM
CHATS
CHAWS
CLACK
CLAIM
CLAMP
CLAMS
CLANG
CLANK
CLANS
CLAPS
CLARA
CLARE
CLARK
CLARO
CLARY
CLASH
CLASP
CLASS
CLAWS
CLAYS
COACH
COALS
COAST
COATI
COATS

CRAAL
CRABS
CRACK
CRACY
CRAFT
CRAGS
CRAIG
CRAKE
CRAMP
CRAMS
CRANE
CRANI
CRANK
CRAPE
CRAPS
CRASH
CRASS
CRATE
CRAVE
CRAWL
CRAWS
CRAZE
CRAZY
CYANO
CZARS

C••A•

CABAL
CACAO
CANAD
CANAL
CARAS
CARAT
CECAL
CEDAR
CERAM
CERAT
CESAR
CHEAP
CHEAT
CHIAS
CIDAL
CIGAR
CLEAN
CLEAR
CLEAT
CLOAK
COCAS
CODAS
COHAN
COLAS
COMAE
COMAL
COMAS
COPAL
CORAL
CORAS
COXAE
COXAL
CRAAL
CREAK
CREAM
CROAK
CROAT
CUBAN
CYCAD
CYMAE
CYMAR

C•••A

CALLA
CANEA
CANNA
CAPUA
CARLA
CAUCA
CEARA
CEIBA
CELIA
CELLA
CERIA
CHELA
CHIBA
CHINA
CHITA
CHUFA
CILIA
CIRCA
CITRA
CLARA
COBIA
COBRA
COCOA
COLZA
COMMA
CONGA
COPRA
CORIA
COSTA
COTTA
CRURA
CULPA
CURIA

•CA••

SCABS
SCADS
SCALD
SCALE
SCALL
SCALP
SCALY
SCAMP
SCAND
SCANS
SCANT
SCAPA
SCAPE
SCAPI
SCARE
SCARF
SCARP
SCARS
SCARY
SCATO
SCATS
SCAUP

•C•A•

ACEAE
ACEAN
ECLAT
ICIAN
OCEAN
OCTAD
SCRAG
SCRAM
SCRAP

•C••A

ACCRA
OCREA
SCAPA
SCHWA
SCUBA
SCUTA

••CA•

ALCAN
ASCAP
CACAO
CECAL
COCAS
CYCAD
DECAL
DECAY
DUCAL
DUCAT
FECAL
FOCAL
INCAN
INCAS
LOCAL
MACAO
MACAW
MICAH
MICAS
OSCAN
OSCAR
PACAS
PECAN
PICAL
PICAS
RECAP
TICAL
UNCAP
VICAR
VOCAL

••C•A

ACCRA
AECIA
COCOA
DACCA
DACHA
DACIA
DICTA
LUCCA
LUCIA
LYCEA
MECCA
MICRA
MOCHA
NUCHA
PUCKA
RECTA
SACRA
VACUA
YUCCA

•••CA

ABACA
ARECA
ARICA
ASPCA
BARCA
CAUCA
CIRCA
DACCA
ERICA
LORCA
LUCCA
MECCA
MUSCA
PLICA
SPICA
THECA
UTICA
YUCCA

C•B••

CABAL
CABBY
CABER
CABIN
CABLE
CABOB
CABOT
CIBOL
COBBS
COBIA
COBLE
COBRA
CUBAN
CUBBY
CUBEB
CUBED
CUBES
CUBIC
CUBIT

C••B•

CABBY
CARBO
CEIBA
CHIBA
CHUBS
CLUBS
COBBS
COMBO
COMBS
CRABS
CRIBS
CUBBY
CURBS

C•••B

CABOB
CALEB
CARIB
CAROB
CLIMB
COOMB
CRUMB
CUBEB

•C•B•

SCABS
SCUBA

•C••B

ACERB
SCRUB

••C•B

JACOB

C•C••

CACAO
CACHE
CACTI
CECAL
CECIL
CECUM
COCAS
COCCI
COCKS
COCKY
COCOA
COCOS
CYCAD
CYCLE
CYCLO

C••C•

CALCI
CASCO
CATCH
CAUCA
CHECK
CHICK
CHICO
CHOCK
CHUCK
CINCH
CIRCA
CIRCE
CISCO
CLACK
CLICK
CLOCK
CLUCK
COACH
COCCI
CONCH
COUCH
CRACK
CRACY
CRECY
CRICK
CROCE
CROCI
CROCK
CRUCI
CULCH
CURCH
CUTCH
CZECH

C•••C

CERIC
CIVIC
COLIC
COMIC
CONIC
COSEC
CRESC
CUBIC
CUSEC
CYNIC

•CC••

ACCEL
ACCRA
MCCOY
OCCUR

•C•C•

ACOCK

••CC•

BACCI
COCCI
DACCA
LUCCA
MECCA
SECCO
YUCCA

••C•C

ENCYC

C•D••

CADDO
CADDY
CADES
CADET
CADGE
CADIS
CADIZ
CADRE
CEDAR
CEDED
CEDES
CIDAL
CIDER
CODAS
CODED
CODES
CODEX
CUDDY

C••D•

CADDO
CADDY
CANDY
CARDI
CARDS
CHIDE
CINDY
CLODS
CLYDE
COEDS
COLDS
COMDR
COMDT
CORDS
CREDO
CRUDE
CUDDY
CURDS
CURDY

C•••D

CAGED
CAIRD
CAKED
CANAD
CANED
CARED
CASED
CAVED
CAWED
CEDED
CERED
CHARD
CHILD
CHORD
CITED
CLOUD
CLUED
CODED
COKED
CONED
CONTD
COOED
COPED
CORED
COULD
COVED
COWED
COXED
CREED
CRIED
CROWD
CUBED
CUPID
CURED
CYCAD

•C•D•

ACIDS
SCADS
SCUDI
SCUDO
SCUDS

•C••D

ACHED
ACRED
ACRID
ACTED
OCTAD
SCALD
SCAND
SCEND
SCOLD
SCROD

••C•D

ARCED
CYCAD
DICED
FACED
LACED
LUCID
MACED
MUCID
PACED
RACED
RICED

CE•••

CEARA
CEASE
CECAL
CECIL
CECUM
CEDAR
CEDED
CEDES
CEIBA
CEILS
CELIA
CELIE
CELLA
CELLO
CELLS
CELOM
CELTS
CENIS
CENSE
CENTI
CENTO
CENTR
CENTS
CEORL
CERAM
CERAT
CERED
CERES
CERIA
CERIC
CEROS
CESAR
CESTI
CETUS

C•E••

CHEAP
CHEAT

CHECK
CHEEK
CHEEP
CHEER
CHEFS
CHELA
CHEMI
CHEMO
CHERT
CHESS
CHEST
CHETH
CHETS
CHEVY
CHEWS
CHEWY
CLEAN
CLEAR
CLEAT
CLEFS
CLEFT
CLEMS
CLEON
CLERK
CLEWS
COEDS
COELE
COELO
COENO
CREAK
CREAM
CRECY
CREDO
CREED
CREEK
CREEL
CREEP
CREES
CREME
CREON
CREPE
CREPT
CRESC
CRESS
CREST
CRETE
CREWE
CREWS
CTENO
CZECH

C••E•
CABER
CADES
CADET
CAFES
CAGED
CAGES
CAGEY
CAKED
CAKES
CALEB
CAMEL
CAMEO
CAMES
CANEA
CANED
CANER
CANES
CAPEK
CAPER
CAPES
CAPET
CARED
CARER
CARES
CARET
CAREY
CASED
CASES
CATER
CAVED
CAVES
CAWED
CEDED
CEDES
CERED
CERES
CHAET
CHEEK
CHEEP
CHEER
CHIEF
CIDER
CIMEX
CITED
CITES
CIVET
CLUED
CLUES
CODED
CODES
CODEX
COKED
COKES
COLES
COMER
COMES
COMET
CONED
CONES
CONEY
COOED
COOEE
COOER
COOEY
COPED
COPES
CORED
CORER
CORES
COSEC
COTES
COVED
COVER
COVES
COVET
COVEY
COWED
COWER
COXED
COXES
COZEN
CREED
CREEK
CREEL
CREEP
CREES
CRIED
CRIER
CRIES
CRUEL
CRUET
CUBEB
CUBED
CUBES
CULET
CUPEL
CURED
CURER
CURES
CUSEC
CUTER
CUTEY
CYMES

C•••E
CABLE
CACHE
CADGE
CADRE
CALPE
CALVE
CANOE
CARTE
CARVE
CASTE
CAUSE
CAVIE
CEASE
CELIE
CENSE
CHAFE
CHAPE
CHARE
CHASE
CHIDE
CHILE
CHIME
CHINE
CHIVE
CHLOE
CHOKE
CHOLE
CHORE
CHOSE
CHUTE
CHYLE
CHYME
CIRCE
CLARE
CLIME
CLINE
CLIVE
CLONE
CLOSE
CLOVE
CLYDE
COBLE
COELE
COMAE
COMTE
CONGE
CONTE
COOEE
COPSE
CORSE
COUPE
COXAE
CRAKE
CRANE
CRAPE
CRATE
CRAVE
CRAZE
CREME
CREPE
CRETE
CREWE
CRIME
CROCE
CRONE
CRORE
CROZE
CRUDE
CRUSE
CURIE
CURSE
CURVE
CUTIE
CYCLE
CYMAE

•CE••
ACEAE
ACEAN
ACERB
ACETO
OCEAN
SCEND
SCENE
SCENT

•C•E•
ACCEL
ACHED
ACHES
ACRED
ACRES
ACTED
ICIER
OCHER
OCREA
OCTET
SCREE
SCREW

•C••E
ACEAE
ACUTE
ECOLE
SCALE
SCAPE
SCARE
SCENE
SCONE
SCOPE
SCORE
SCREE
SCUTE

••CE•
ACCEL
ARCED
BICES
DACES
DICED
DICER
EMCEE
EXCEL
FACED
FACER
FACES
FACET
FECES
FICES
LACED
LACES
LUCES
LYCEA
LYCEE
MACED
MACER
MACES
NICER
PACED
PACER
PACES
PUCES
RACED
RACER
RACES
RICED
RICER
RICES
SICES
SYCEE
SYCES
TACET
ULCER
VICES
VOCES

••C•E
BOCHE
CACHE
CYCLE
EMCEE
FICHE
LOCKE
LUCRE
LYCEE
MACLE
NACRE
NICHE
RUCHE
SOCLE
SUCRE
SYCEE
TYCHE
UNCLE
WACKE

•••CE
ALICE
ALYCE
AMICE
APACE
BRACE
BRICE
BRUCE
BRYCE
CIRCE
CROCE
DANCE
DEICE
DEUCE
DOLCE
DULCE
DUNCE
EDUCE
FARCE
FENCE
FORCE
GLACE
GRACE
HANCE
HENCE
JOYCE
JUICE
LANCE
MINCE
NIECE
NONCE
OUNCE
PEACE
PENCE
PIECE
PLACE
PONCE
PRICE
RANCE
SAUCE
SINCE
SLICE
SPACE
SPICE
TRACE
TRICE
TRUCE
TWICE
VINCE
VOICE
WINCE

C•F••
CAFES
CUFFS

C••F•
CHAFE
CHAFF
CHEFS
CHUFA
CLEFS
CLEFT
CLIFF
COIFS
CORFU
CRAFT
CROFT
CUFFS

C•••F
CALIF
CHAFF
CHIEF
CLIFF

•C•F•
SCIFI
SCOFF
SCUFF

•C••F
SCARF
SCOFF
SCUFF
SCURF

C•G••
CAGED
CAGES
CAGEY
CIGAR
COGON

C••G•
CADGE
CARGO
CHUGS
CLOGS
COIGN
CONGA
CONGE
CONGO
CORGI
COUGH
CRAGS

C•••G
CHANG
CLANG
CLING
CLUNG
CRAIG
CUING

•C••G
ACING
ICING
SCRAG

CH•••
CHAET
CHAFE
CHAFF
CHAIN
CHAIR
CHALK
CHAMP
CHANG
CHANT
CHAOS
CHAPE
CHAPS
CHAPT
CHARD
CHARE
CHARM
CHARS
CHART
CHARY
CHASE
CHASM
CHATS
CHAWS
CHEAP
CHEAT
CHECK
CHEEK
CHEEP
CHEER
CHEFS
CHELA
CHEMI
CHEMO
CHERT
CHESS
CHEST
CHETH
CHETS
CHEVY
CHEWS
CHEWY
CHIAS
CHIBA
CHICK
CHICO
CHIDE
CHIEF
CHILD
CHILE
CHILI
CHILL
CHILO
CHIME
CHINA
CHINE
CHINK
CHINO
CHINS

5

CHIOS
CHIPS
CHIRM
CHIRO
CHIRP
CHIRR
CHITA
CHITS
CHIVE
CHLOE
CHLOR
CHOCK
CHOIR
CHOKE
CHOKY
CHOLE
CHOPS
CHORD
CHORE
CHORO
CHOSE
CHOWS
CHRIS
CHROM
CHRON
CHRYS
CHUBS
CHUCK
CHUFA
CHUGS
CHUMP
CHUMS
CHUNK
CHURL
CHURN
CHURR
CHUTE
CHYLE
CHYME

C•H••

COHAN

C••H•

CACHE
CATHY
CUSHY

C•••H

CATCH
CHETH
CINCH
CLASH
CLOTH
COACH
CONCH
COUCH
COUGH
CRASH
CRUSH
CUISH
CULCH
CURCH
CUTCH
CZECH

•CH••

ACHED
ACHES
ECHIN
ICHOR
OCHER
OCHRY
SCHIZ
SCHMO
SCHWA

•C••H

SCYPH

••CH•

ARCHI
ARCHY
BOCHE
CACHE
DACHA
DICHO
DUCHY
FICHE
FICHU
ITCHY
LICHT
LOCHS
MACHY
MOCHA
NICHE
NUCHA
ORCHI
PACHY
RUCHE
TACHY
TECHN
TYCHE
VICHY
YACHT

••C•H

MICAH

•••CH

AITCH
BATCH
BEACH
BEECH
BELCH
BENCH
BIRCH
BITCH
BOSCH
BOTCH
BUNCH
CATCH
CINCH
COACH
CONCH
COUCH
CULCH
CURCH
CUTCH
CZECH
DITCH
DUTCH
ENOCH
EPOCH
ERICH
FETCH
FILCH
FINCH
FITCH
GULCH
HATCH
HITCH
HOOCH
HUNCH
HUTCH
KENCH
KERCH
KETCH
LARCH
LATCH
LEACH
LEECH
LOACH
LUNCH
LURCH
LYNCH
MARCH
MATCH
MILCH
MITCH
MOOCH
MOUCH
MULCH
MUNCH
NOTCH
ORACH
PARCH
PASCH
PATCH
PEACH
PERCH
PINCH
PITCH
POACH
POOCH
PORCH
POUCH
PSYCH
PUNCH
RANCH
RATCH
REACH
REICH
RETCH
ROACH
ROTCH
STICH
TEACH
TENCH
TOUCH
TRACH
TRICH
VETCH
VOUCH
WATCH
WELCH
WENCH
WHICH
WINCH
WITCH

CI•••

CIBOL
CIDAL
CIDER
CIGAR
CILIA
CIMEX
CINCH
CINDY
CIONS
CIRCA
CIRCE
CIRRI
CIRRO
CISCO
CISSY
CISTS
CITED
CITES
CITRA
CIVET
CIVIC
CIVIL

C•I••

CAIRD
CAIRN
CAIRO
CEIBA
CEILS
CHIAS
CHIBA
CHICK
CHICO
CHIDE
CHIEF
CHILD
CHILE
CHILI
CHILL
CHILO
CHIME
CHINA
CHINE
CHINK
CHINO
CHINS
CHIOS
CHIPS
CHIRM
CHIRO
CHIRP
CHIRR
CHITA
CHITS
CHIVE
CLICK
CLIFF
CLIMB
CLIME
CLINE
CLING
CLINK
CLINO
CLINT
CLIOS
CLIPS
CLIVE
COIFS
COIGN
COILS
COINS
CRIBS
CRICK
CRIED
CRIER
CRIES
CRIME
CRIMP
CRISP
CUING
CUISH

C••I•

CABIN
CADIS
CADIZ
CALIF
CALIX
CANIS
CARIB
CAVIE
CAVIL
CECIL
CELIA
CELIE
CENIS
CERIA
CERIC
CHAIN
CHAIR
CHOIR
CHRIS
CILIA
CIVIC
CIVIL
CLAIM
COBIA
COLIC
COLIN
COMIC
CONIC
CONIO
CORIA
CRAIG
CROIX
CUBIC
CUBIT
CUMIN
CUPID
CURIA
CURIE
CURIO
CUTIE
CUTIN
CUTIS
CYLIX
CYNIC
CYRIL

C•••I

CACTI
CALCI
CALLI
CAMPI
CAPRI
CARDI
CARPI
CENTI
CESTI
CHEMI
CHILI
CIRRI
COATI
COCCI
CORGI
CRANI
CROCI
CRUCI
CULTI
CURVI
CYMRI
CYSTI

•CI••

ACIDS
ACING
ACINI
ACITY
ICIAN
ICIER
ICILY
ICING
SCIFI
SCION

•C•I•

ACRID
ACTIN
ECHIN
SCHIZ
SCRIM
SCRIP

•C••I

ACINI
ICOSI
SCAPI
SCIFI
SCUDI

••CI•

AECIA
CECIL
DACIA
DECIM
FECIT
LICIT
LUCIA
LUCID
MUCID
MUCIN
ORCIN
RICIN
SOCIO
TACIT

••C•I

ARCHI
BACCI
CACTI
COCCI
NOCTI
NYCTI
ORCHI
RECTI

•••CI

ABACI
BACCI
CALCI
COCCI
CROCI
CRUCI
DISCI
MERCI
PISCI
SULCI
VINCI

C•J••

CAJON
CAJUN

C•K••

CAKED
CAKES
COKED
COKES

C••K•

CALKS
CASKS
CHOKE
CHOKY
COCKS
COCKY
CONKS
COOKS
COOKY
CORKS
CORKY
CRAKE
CUSKS

C•••K

CAPEK
CAULK
CHALK
CHECK
CHEEK
CHICK
CHINK
CHOCK
CHUCK
CHUNK
CLACK
CLANK
CLARK
CLERK
CLICK
CLINK
CLOAK
CLOCK
CLUCK
CRACK
CRANK
CREAK
CREEK
CRICK
CROAK
CROCK
CROOK

•C••K

ACOCK

••CK•

BACKS
BECKS
BECKY
BUCKO
BUCKS
COCKS
COCKY
DECKS
DICKS
DICKY
DOCKS
DUCKS
DUCKY
GECKO
GECKS
HACKS
HICKS
HOCKS
JACKS
JACKY
JOCKO
KECKS
KICKS
LACKS
LICKS
LOCKE
LOCKS
LUCKY
MACKS
MICKY
MOCKS
MUCKS
MUCKY

NECKS
NICKS
NICKY
NOCKS
PACKS
PECKS
PICKS
POCKS
POCKY
PUCKA
PUCKS
RACKS
RICKS
RICKY
ROCKS
ROCKY
RUCKS
SACKS
SICKS
SOCKS
SUCKS
TACKS
TACKY
TICKS
TUCKS
VICKS
VICKY
WACKE
WACKS
WACKY
WICKS

•••CK

ABACK
ACOCK
ALACK
ALECK
AMUCK
BLACK
BLOCK
BRICK
CHECK
CHICK
CHOCK
CHUCK
CLACK
CLICK
CLOCK
CLUCK
CRACK
CRICK
CROCK
DIRCK
FLACK
FLECK
FLICK
FLOCK
FROCK
HOICK
KNACK
KNOCK
PLACK
PLUCK
PRICK
QUACK
QUICK
SHACK
SHOCK
SHUCK
SLACK
SLICK
SMACK
SMOCK
SNACK
SNICK
SPECK
STACK
STICK
STOCK
STUCK
THICK
TRACK
TRICK
TRUCK
VNECK
WHACK
WRACK
WRECK

CL•••

CLACK
CLAIM
CLAMP
CLAMS
CLANG
CLANK
CLANS
CLAPS
CLARA
CLARE
CLARK
CLARO
CLARY
CLASH
CLASP
CLASS
CLAWS
CLAYS
CLEAN
CLEAR
CLEAT
CLEFS
CLEFT
CLEMS
CLEON
CLERK
CLEWS
CLICK
CLIFF
CLIMB
CLIME
CLINE
CLING
CLINK
CLINO
CLINT
CLIOS
CLIPS
CLIVE
CLOAK
CLOCK
CLODS
CLOGS
CLONE
CLONS
CLOPS
CLOSE
CLOTH
CLOTS
CLOUD
CLOUT
CLOVE
CLOWN
CLOYS
CLUBS
CLUCK
CLUED
CLUES
CLUMP
CLUNG
CLUNY
CLYDE

C•L••

CALCI
CALEB
CALIF
CALIX
CALKS
CALLA
CALLI
CALLS
CALMS
CALPE
CALVE
CALYX
CELIA
CELIE
CELLA
CELLO
CELLS
CELOM
CELTS
CHLOE
CHLOR
CILIA
COLAS
COLDS
COLES
COLIC
COLIN
COLLY
COLON
COLOR
COLTS
COLZA
CULCH
CULET
CULLS
CULMS
CULPA
CULTI
CULTS
CYLIX

C••L•

CABLE
CALLA
CALLI
CALLS
CARLA
CARLO
CARLS
CAULK
CAULS
CEILS
CELLA
CELLO
CELLS
CHALK
CHELA
CHILD
CHILE
CHILI
CHILL
CHILO
CHOLE
CHYLE
COALS
COBLE
COELE
COELO
COILS
COLLY
COOLS
COULD
COWLS
COYLY
CULLS
CURLS
CURLY
CYCLE
CYCLO

C•••L

CABAL
CAMEL
CANAL
CAROL
CAVIL
CECAL
CECIL
CEORL
CHILL
CHURL
CIBOL
CIDAL
CIVIL
COMAL
COPAL
CORAL
COXAL
CRAAL
CRAWL
CREEL
CRUEL
CUPEL
CYRIL

•CL••

ECLAT

•C•L•

ECOLE
ICILY
OCULO
SCALD
SCALE
SCALL
SCALP
SCALY
SCOLD
SCULL
SCULP

•C••L

ACCEL
OCTYL
SCALL
SCOWL
SCULL

••CL•

CYCLE
CYCLO
MACLE
SOCLE
UNCLE

••C•L

ACCEL
CECAL
CECIL
DECAL
DUCAL
EXCEL
FECAL
FOCAL
LOCAL
PICAL
PICUL
TICAL
VOCAL

C•M••

CAMEL
CAMEO
CAMES
CAMPI
CAMPO
CAMPS
CAMPY
CAMUS
CIMEX
COMAE
COMAL
COMAS
COMBO
COMBS
COMDR
COMDT
COMER
COMES
COMET
COMIC
COMMA
COMPO
COMTE
CUMIN
CYMAE
CYMAR
CYMES
CYMRI
CYMRY

C••M•

CALMS
CHAMP
CHEMI
CHEMO
CHIME
CHUMP
CHUMS
CHYME
CLAMP
CLAMS
CLEMS
CLIMB
CLIME
CLUMP
COMMA
COOMB
CORMS
COSMO
CRAMP
CRAMS
CREME
CRIME
CRIMP
CRUMB
CRUMP
CULMS

C•••M

CAROM
CECUM
CELOM
CERAM
CHARM
CHASM
CHIRM
CHROM
CLAIM
CREAM

•C•M•

SCAMP
SCHMO
SCUMS

•C••M

SCRAM
SCRIM
SCRUM

••C•M

CECUM
DECIM

C•N••

CANAD
CANAL
CANDY
CANEA
CANED
CANER
CANES
CANIS
CANNA
CANNY
CANOE
CANON
CANSO
CANST
CANTO
CANTS
CENIS
CENSE
CENTI
CENTO
CENTR
CENTS
CINCH
CINDY
CONCH
CONED
CONES
CONEY
CONGA
CONGE
CONGO
CONIC
CONIO
CONKS
CONNY
CONTD
CONTE
CONTO
CONTR
CONUS
CYNIC

C••N•

CANNA
CANNY
CHANG
CHANT
CHINA
CHINE
CHINK
CHINO
CHINS
CHUNK
CIONS
CLANG
CLANK
CLANS
CLINE
CLING
CLINK
CLINO
CLINT
CLONE
CLONS
CLUNG
CLUNY
COENO
COINS
CONNY
COONS
CORNS
CORNU
CORNY
COUNT
CRANE
CRANI
CRANK
CRONE
CRONY
CTENO
CUING
CYANO

C•••N

CABIN
CAIRN
CAJON
CAJUN
CANON
CAPON
CHAIN
CHRON
CHURN
CLEAN
CLEON
CLOWN
COGON
COHAN
COIGN
COLIN
COLON
COZEN
CREON
CROON
CROWN
CUBAN
CUMIN
CUTIN

•C•N•

ACING
ACINI
ICING
ICONO
ICONS
SCAND
SCANS
SCANT
SCEND
SCENE
SCENT
SCONE

5

•C••N
ACEAN
ACORN
ACTIN
ECHIN
ICIAN
OCEAN
SCION
SCORN

••C•N
ALCAN
ANCON
BACON
INCAN
MACON
MUCIN
ORCIN
OSCAN
PECAN
RICIN
TECHN

CO•••
COACH
COALS
COAST
COATI
COATS
COBBS
COBIA
COBLE
COBRA
COCAS
COCCI
COCKS
COCKY
COCOA
COCOS
CODAS
CODED
CODES
CODEX
COEDS
COELE
COELO
COENO
COGON
COHAN
COIFS
COIGN
COILS
COINS
COKED
COKES
COLAS
COLDS
COLES
COLIC
COLIN
COLLY
COLON
COLOR
COLTS
COLZA
COMAE
COMAL
COMAS
COMBO
COMBS
COMDR
COMDT
COMER
COMES
COMET
COMIC
COMMA
COMPO
COMTE
CONCH
CONED
CONES
CONEY
CONGA
CONGE
CONGO
CONIC
CONIO
CONKS
CONNY
CONTD
CONTE
CONTO
CONTR
CONUS
COOED
COOEE
COOER
COOEY
COOKS
COOKY
COOLS
COOMB
COONS
COOPS
COOPT
COOTS
COPAL
COPED
COPES
COPRA
COPRO
COPSE
COPTS
CORAL
CORAS
CORDS
CORED
CORER
CORES
CORFU
CORGI
CORIA
CORKS
CORKY
CORMS
CORNS
CORNU
CORNY
COROT
CORPS
CORSE
COSEC
COSMO
COSTA
COSTO
COSTS
COTES
COTTA
COUCH
COUGH
COULD
COUNT
COUPE
COUPS
COURT
COVED
COVER
COVES
COVET
COVEY
COWED
COWER
COWLS
COWRY
COXAE
COXAL
COXED
COXES
COYLY
COYPU
COZEN

C•O••
CEORL
CHOCK
CHOIR
CHOKE
CHOKY
CHOLE
CHOPS
CHORD
CHORE
CHORO
CHOSE
CHOWS
CIONS
CLOAK
CLOCK
CLODS
CLOGS
CLONE
CLONS
CLOPS
CLOSE
CLOTH
CLOTS
CLOUD
CLOUT
CLOVE
CLOWN
CLOYS
COOED
COOEE
COOER
COOEY
COOKS
COOKY
COOLS
COOMB
COONS
COOPS
COOPT
COOTS
CROAK
CROAT
CROCE
CROCI
CROCK
CROFT
CROIX
CRONE
CRONY
CROOK
CROON
CROPS
CRORE
CROSS
CROUP
CROWD
CROWN
CROWS
CROZE

C••O•
CABOB
CABOT
CAJON
CANOE
CANON
CAPON
CAROB
CAROL
CAROM
CELOM
CEROS
CHAOS
CHIOS
CHLOE
CHLOR
CHROM
CHRON
CIBOL
CLEON
CLIOS
COCOA
COCOS
COGON
COLON
COLOR
COROT
CREON
CROOK
CROON
CRUOR

C•••O
CACAO
CADDO
CAIRO
CAMEO
CAMPO
CANSO
CANTO
CARBO
CARGO
CARLO
CARPO
CARYO
CASCO
CELLO
CENTO
CHEMO
CHICO
CHILO
CHINO
CHIRO
CHORO
CIRRO
CISCO
CLARO
CLINO
COELO
COENO
COMBO
COMPO
CONGO
CONIO
CONTO
COPRO
COSMO
COSTO
CREDO
CTENO
CUPRO
CURIO
CUSSO
CYANO
CYCLO
CYSTO

•CO••
ACOCK
ACORN
ACOUO
ECOLE
ICONO
ICONS
ICOSI
SCOFF
SCOLD
SCONE
SCOOP
SCOOT
SCOPE
SCOPS
SCOPY
SCORE
SCORN
SCOTO
SCOTS
SCOTT
SCOUR
SCOUT
SCOWL
SCOWS

•C•O•
ACTOR
ICHOR
MCCOY
SCION
SCOOP
SCOOT
SCROD

•C••O
ACETO
ACOUO
ICONO
OCULO
SCATO
SCHMO
SCOTO
SCUDO

••CO•
ANCON
ASCOT
BACON
COCOA
COCOS
DECOR
DECOY
JACOB
LOCOS
MACON
MCCOY
PECOS
PICOT

••C•O
BUCKO
CACAO
CYCLO
DICHO
GECKO
HECTO
JOCKO
LACTO
MACAO
MACRO
MICRO
MUCRO
NECRO
NYCTO
PICRO
RECTO
SACRO
SECCO
SOCIO

•••CO
BUNCO
CASCO
CHICO
CISCO
DRACO
GLYCO
GRECO
GUACO
JUNCO
LEUCO
MARCO
NARCO
PHYCO
SARCO
SECCO
TURCO
URICO

C•P••
CAPEK
CAPER
CAPES
CAPET
CAPON
CAPRI
CAPUA
CAPUT
COPAL
COPED
COPES
COPRA
COPRO
COPSE
COPTS
CUPEL
CUPID
CUPRO

C••P•
CALPE
CAMPI
CAMPO
CAMPS
CAMPY
CARPI
CARPO
CARPS
CHAPE
CHAPS
CHAPT
CHIPS
CHOPS
CLAPS
CLIPS
CLOPS
COMPO
COOPS
COOPT
CORPS
COUPE
COUPS
COYPU
CRAPE
CRAPS
CREPE
CREPT
CROPS
CRYPT
CULPA
CUSPS

C•••P
CHAMP
CHEAP
CHEEP
CHIRP
CHUMP
CLAMP
CLASP
CLUMP
CRAMP
CREEP
CRIMP
CRISP
CROUP
CRUMP
CUTUP

•C•P•
SCAPA
SCAPE
SCAPI
SCOPE
SCOPS
SCOPY
SCUPS
SCYPH

•C••P
SCALP
SCAMP
SCARP
SCAUP
SCOOP
SCRAP
SCRIP
SCULP

••C•P
ASCAP
RECAP
UNCAP

•••CP
NAACP

CR•••
CRAAL
CRABS
CRACK
CRACY
CRAFT
CRAGS
CRAIG
CRAKE
CRAMP
CRAMS
CRANE
CRANI

CRANK
CRAPE
CRAPS
CRASH
CRASS
CRATE
CRAVE
CRAWL
CRAWS
CRAZE
CRAZY
CREAK
CREAM
CRECY
CREDO
CREED
CREEK
CREEL
CREEP
CREES
CREME
CREON
CREPE
CREPT
CRESC
CRESS
CREST
CRETE
CREWE
CREWS
CRIBS
CRICK
CRIED
CRIER
CRIES
CRIME
CRIMP
CRISP
CROAK
CROAT
CROCE
CROCI
CROCK
CROFT
CROIX
CRONE
CRONY
CROOK
CROON
CROPS
CRORE
CROSS
CROUP
CROWD
CROWN
CROWS
CROZE
CRUCI
CRUDE
CRUEL
CRUET
CRUMB
CRUMP
CRUOR
CRURA
CRUSE
CRUSH
CRUST
CRYPT

C•R••

CARAS
CARAT
CARBO
CARDI
CARDS
CARED
CARER
CARES
CARET
CAREY
CARGO
CARIB
CARLA
CARLO
CARLS
CAROB
CAROL
CAROM
CARPI
CARPO
CARPS
CARRY
CARTE
CARTS
CARVE
CARYO
CARYS
CERAM
CERAT
CERED
CERES
CERIA
CERIC
CEROS
CHRIS
CHROM
CHRON
CHRYS
CIRCA
CIRCE
CIRRI
CIRRO
CORAL
CORAS
CORDS
CORED
CORER
CORES
CORFU
CORGI
CORIA
CORKS
CORKY
CORMS
CORNS
CORNU
CORNY
COROT
CORPS
CORSE
CURBS
CURCH
CURDS
CURDY
CURED
CURER
CURES
CURIA
CURIE
CURIO
CURLS
CURLY
CURRY
CURSE
CURST
CURVE
CURVI
CYRIL
CYRUS

C••R•

CADRE
CAIRD
CAIRN
CAIRO
CAPRI
CARRY
CEARA
CEORL
CHARD
CHARE
CHARM
CHARS
CHART
CHARY
CHERT
CHIRM
CHIRO
CHIRP
CHIRR
CHORD
CHORE
CHORO
CHURL
CHURN
CHURR
CIRRI
CIRRO
CITRA
CLARA
CLARE
CLARK
CLARO
CLARY
CLERK
COBRA
COPRA
COPRO
COURT
COWRY
CRORE
CRURA
CUPRO
CURRY
CYMRI
CYMRY
CZARS

C•••R

CABER
CANER
CAPER
CARER
CATER
CEDAR
CENTR
CESAR
CHAIR
CHEER
CHIRR
CHLOR
CHOIR
CHURR
CIDER
CIGAR
CLEAR
COLOR
COMDR
COMER
CONTR
COOER
CORER
COVER
COWER
CRIER
CRUOR
CURER
CUTER
CYMAR

•CR••

ACRED
ACRES
ACRID
OCREA
SCRAG
SCRAM
SCRAP
SCREE
SCREW
SCRIM
SCRIP
SCROD
SCRUB
SCRUM

•C•R•

ACCRA
ACERB
ACORN
OCHRY
SCARE
SCARF
SCARP
SCARS
SCARY
SCORE
SCORN
SCURF

•C••R

ACTOR
ICHOR
ICIER
OCCUR
OCHER
SCOUR

••CR•

ACCRA
DECRY
LUCRE
MACRO
MICRA
MICRO
MUCRO
NACRE
NECRO
PICRO
SACRA
SACRO
SUCRE

••C•R

DECOR
DICER
FACER
INCUR
MACER
NICER
OCCUR
OSCAR
PACER
RACER
RECUR
RICER
ULCER
VICAR

•••CR

USMCR

C•S••

CASCO
CASED
CASES
CASKS
CASTE
CASTS
CASUS
CESAR
CESTI
CISCO
CISSY
CISTS
COSEC
COSMO
COSTA
COSTO
COSTS
CUSEC
CUSHY
CUSKS
CUSPS
CUSSO
CYSTI
CYSTO
CYSTS

C••S•

CANSO
CANST
CAUSE
CEASE
CENSE
CHASE
CHASM
CHESS
CHEST
CHOSE
CISSY
CLASH
CLASP
CLASS
CLOSE
COAST
COPSE
CORSE
CRASH
CRASS
CRESC
CRESS
CREST
CRISP
CROSS
CRUSE
CRUSH
CRUST
CUISH
CURSE
CURST
CUSSO

C•••S

CADES
CADIS
CAFES
CAGES
CAKES
CALKS
CALLS
CALMS
CAMES
CAMPS
CAMUS
CANES
CANIS
CANTS
CAPES
CARAS
CARDS
CARES
CARLS
CARPS
CARTS
CARYS
CASES
CASKS
CASTS
CASUS
CAULS
CAVES
CEDES
CEILS
CELLS
CELTS
CENIS
CENTS
CERES
CEROS
CETUS
CHAOS
CHAPS
CHARS
CHATS
CHAWS
CHEFS
CHESS
CHETS
CHEWS
CHIAS
CHINS
CHIOS
CHIPS
CHITS
CHOPS
CHOWS
CHRIS
CHRYS
CHUBS
CHUGS
CHUMS
CIONS
CISTS
CITES
CLAMS
CLANS
CLAPS
CLASS
CLAWS
CLAYS
CLEFS
CLEMS
CLEWS
CLIOS
CLIPS
CLODS
CLOGS
CLONS
CLOPS
CLOTS
CLOYS
CLUBS
CLUES
COALS
COATS
COBBS
COCAS
COCKS
COCOS
CODAS
CODES
COEDS
COIFS
COILS
COINS
COKES
COLAS
COLDS
COLES
COLTS
COMAS
COMBS
COMES
CONES
CONKS
CONUS
COOKS
COOLS
COONS
COOPS
COOTS
COPES
COPTS
CORAS
CORDS
CORES
CORKS
CORMS
CORNS
CORPS
COSTS
COTES
COUPS
COVES
COWLS
COXES
CRABS
CRAGS
CRAMS
CRAPS
CRASS
CRAWS
CREES
CRESS
CREWS
CRIBS
CRIES
CROPS
CROSS
CROWS
CUBES
CUFFS
CULLS
CULMS
CULTS
CURBS
CURDS
CURES
CURLS
CUSKS

CUSPS
CUTIS
CYMES
CYRUS
CYSTS
CZARS

•C•S•
ICOSI

•C••S
ACHES
ACIDS
ACRES
ICONS
ICTUS
SCABS
SCADS
SCANS
SCARS
SCATS
SCOPS
SCOTS
SCOWS
SCUDS
SCUMS
SCUPS
SCUTS

••C•S
ARCUS
ASCUS
BACKS
BECKS
BICES
BUCKS
COCAS
COCKS
COCOS
DACES
DECKS
DICKS
DOCKS
DUCKS
DUCTS
FACES
FACTS
FECES
FICES
FOCUS
FUCUS
GECKS
HACKS
HICKS
HOCKS
HOCUS
INCAS
INCUS
JACKS
KECKS
KICKS
LACES
LACKS
LICKS
LOCHS
LOCKS
LOCOS
LOCUS
LUCES
LUCYS
MACES
MACKS
MICAS
MOCKS
MUCKS
MUCUS
NECKS
NICKS
NOCKS
ORCUS
PACAS
PACES
PACKS
PACTS
PECKS
PECOS
PICAS
PICKS
PICTS
POCKS
PUCES
PUCKS
RACES
RACKS
RICES
RICKS
ROCKS
RUCKS
SACKS
SECTS
SICES
SICKS
SOCKS
SUCKS
SYCES
TACKS
TICKS
TUCKS
VICES
VICKS
VOCES
WACKS
WICKS

•••CS
ALECS
BLOCS
DISCS
EPICS
ERICS
EXECS
FISCS
FLOCS
MARCS
SPECS
TALCS
ZINCS

CT•••
CTENO

C•T••
CATCH
CATER
CATHY
CATTY
CETUS
CITED
CITES
CITRA
COTES
COTTA
CUTCH
CUTER
CUTEY
CUTIE
CUTIN
CUTIS
CUTTY
CUTUP

C••T•
CACTI
CANTO
CANTS
CARTE
CARTS
CASTE
CASTS
CATTY
CELTS
CENTI
CENTO
CENTR
CENTS
CESTI
CHATS
CHETH
CHETS
CHITA
CHITS
CHUTE
CISTS
CLOTH
CLOTS
COATI
COATS
COLTS
COMTE
CONTD
CONTE
CONTO
CONTR
COOTS
COPTS
COSTA
COSTO
COSTS
COTTA
CRATE
CRETE
CULTI
CULTS
CUTTY
CYSTI
CYSTO
CYSTS

C•••T
CABOT
CADET
CANST
CAPET
CAPUT
CARAT
CARET
CERAT
CHAET
CHANT
CHAPT
CHART
CHEAT
CHERT
CHEST
CIVET
CLEAT
CLEFT
CLINT
CLOUT
COAST
COMDT
COMET
COOPT
COROT
COUNT
COURT
COVET
CRAFT
CREPT
CREST
CROAT
CROFT
CRUET
CRUST
CRYPT
CUBIT
CULET
CURST

•CT••
ACTED
ACTIN
ACTOR
ICTUS
OCTAD
OCTET
OCTYL

•C•T•
ACETO
ACITY
ACUTE
SCATO
SCATS
SCOTO
SCOTS
SCOTT
SCUTA
SCUTE
SCUTS

•C••T
ECLAT
OCTET
SCANT
SCENT
SCOOT
SCOTT
SCOUT

••CT•
CACTI
DICTA
DUCTS
FACTS
HECTO
LACTO
NOCTI
NYCTI
NYCTO
PACTS
PICTS
RECTA
RECTI
RECTO
SECTS

••C•T
ASCOT
DUCAT
FACET
FECIT
LICHT
LICIT
PICOT
TACET
TACIT
UNCUT
YACHT

•••CT
BRACT
EDICT
EDUCT
EJECT
ELECT
ENACT
EPACT
ERECT
ERUCT
EVICT
EXACT
MULCT
PROCT
REACT
TINCT
TRACT
VISCT

CU•••
CUBAN
CUBBY
CUBEB
CUBED
CUBES
CUBIC
CUBIT
CUDDY
CUFFS
CUING
CUISH
CULCH
CULET
CULLS
CULMS
CULPA
CULTI
CULTS
CUMIN
CUPEL
CUPID
CUPRO
CURBS
CURCH
CURDS
CURDY
CURED
CURER
CURES
CURIA
CURIE
CURIO
CURLS
CURLY
CURRY
CURSE
CURST
CURVE
CURVI
CUSEC
CUSHY
CUSKS
CUSPS
CUSSO
CUTCH
CUTER
CUTEY
CUTIE
CUTIN
CUTIS
CUTTY
CUTUP

C•U••
CAUCA
CAULK
CAULS
CAUSE
CHUBS
CHUCK
CHUFA
CHUGS
CHUMP
CHUMS
CHUNK
CHURL
CHURN
CHURR
CHUTE
CLUBS
CLUCK
CLUED
CLUES
CLUMP
CLUNG
CLUNY
COUCH
COUGH
COULD
COUNT
COUPE
COUPS
COURT
CRUCI
CRUDE
CRUEL
CRUET
CRUMB
CRUMP
CRUOR
CRURA
CRUSE
CRUSH
CRUST

C••U•
CAJUN
CAMUS
CAPUA
CAPUT
CASUS
CECUM
CETUS
CLOUD
CLOUT
CONUS
CROUP
CUTUP
CYRUS

C•••U
CORFU
CORNU
COYPU

•CU••
ACUTE
OCULO
SCUBA
SCUDI
SCUDO
SCUDS
SCUFF
SCULL
SCULP
SCUMS
SCUPS
SCURF
SCUTA
SCUTE
SCUTS

•C•U•
ACOUO
ICTUS
OCCUR
SCAUP
SCOUR
SCOUT
SCRUB
SCRUM

••CU•
ARCUS
ASCUS
CECUM
FOCUS
FUCUS
HOCUS
INCUR
INCUS
LOCUS
MUCUS
OCCUR
ORCUS
PICUL
RECUR
UNCUT
VACUA

••C•U
FICHU

C•V••
CAVED
CAVES
CAVIE
CAVIL
CIVET
CIVIC
CIVIL
COVED
COVER
COVES
COVET
COVEY

C••V•
CALVE
CARVE
CHEVY
CHIVE
CLIVE
CLOVE
CRAVE
CURVE
CURVI

C•W••
CAWED
COWED

5

COWER
COWLS
COWRY

C••W•
CHAWS
CHEWS
CHEWY
CHOWS
CLAWS
CLEWS
CLOWN
CRAWL
CRAWS
CREWE
CREWS
CROWD
CROWN
CROWS

•C•W•
SCHWA
SCOWL
SCOWS

•C••W
SCREW

••C•W
MACAW

C•X••
COXAE
COXAL
COXED
COXES

C•••X
CALIX
CALYX
CIMEX
CODEX
CROIX
CYLIX

CY•••
CYANO
CYCAD
CYCLE
CYCLO
CYLIX
CYMAE
CYMAR
CYMES
CYMRI
CYMRY
CYNIC
CYRIL
CYRUS
CYSTI
CYSTO
CYSTS

C•Y••
CHYLE
CHYME
CLYDE
COYLY
COYPU
CRYPT

C••Y•
CALYX
CARYO
CARYS
CHRYS
CLAYS
CLOYS

C•••Y
CABBY
CADDY
CAGEY
CAMPY
CANDY
CANNY
CAREY
CARRY
CATHY
CATTY
CHARY
CHEVY
CHEWY
CHOKY
CINDY
CISSY
CLARY
CLUNY
COCKY
COLLY
CONEY
CONNY
COOEY
COOKY
CORKY
CORNY
COVEY
COWRY
COYLY
CRACY
CRAZY
CRECY
CRONY
CUBBY
CUDDY
CURDY
CURLY
CURRY
CUSHY
CUTEY
CUTTY
CYMRY

•CY••
SCYPH

•C•Y•
OCTYL

•C••Y
ACITY
ICILY
MCCOY
OCHRY
SCALY
SCARY
SCOPY

••CY•
ENCYC
LUCYS

••C•Y
ARCHY
BECKY
COCKY
DECAY
DECOY
DECRY
DICKY
DUCHY
DUCKY
ITCHY
JACKY
LUCKY
MACHY
MCCOY
MICKY
MUCKY
NICKY
PACHY
POCKY
RICKY
ROCKY
TACHY
TACKY
VICHY
VICKY
WACKY

•••CY
CRACY
CRECY
DULCY
FANCY
FARCY
JUICY
MANCY
MERCY
NANCY
PERCY
SAUCY
SPICY
STACY
ZINCY

CZ•••
CZARS
CZECH

C•Z••
COZEN

C••Z•
COLZA
CRAZE
CRAZY
CROZE

C•••Z
CADIZ

•C••Z
SCHIZ

DA•••
DACCA
DACES
DACHA
DACIA
DADDY
DAFFY
DAGAN
DAILY
DAIRY
DAISY
DAKAR
DALES
DALLY
DAMAN
DAMES
DAMNS
DAMON
DAMPS
DANAE
DANCE
DANDY
DANES
DANGS
DANNY
DANTE
DARED
DARER
DARES
DARIC
DARNS
DARTS
DASHY
DATED
DATER
DATES
DATTO
DATUM
DAUBS
DAUBY
DAUNT
DAVAO
DAVES
DAVEY
DAVID
DAVIE
DAVIS
DAVIT
DAVYS
DAWKS
DAWNS
DAZED
DAZES

D•A••
DEALS
DEALT
DEANE
DEANS
DEARS
DEARY
DEATH
DHAKS
DIALS
DIANA
DIANE
DIARY
DIAZO
DOALL
DRABS
DRACO
DRAFF
DRAFT
DRAGS
DRAIN
DRAKE
DRAMA
DRAMS
DRANK
DRAPE
DRAVA
DRAVE
DRAWL
DRAWN
DRAWS
DRAYS
DUADS
DUALA
DUANE
DWARF
DYADS

D••A•
DAGAN
DAKAR
DAMAN
DANAE
DAVAO
DEBAR
DECAL
DECAY
DEDAL
DEGAS
DELAY
DEVAS
DEWAN
DINAH
DINAR
DITAS
DIVAN
DIVAS
DIWAN
DONAR
DONAS
DORAS
DOTAL
DOUAI
DOUAY
DOVAP
DREAD
DREAM
DREAR
DRYAD
DUCAL
DUCAT
DUMAS
DURAL

D•••A
DACCA
DACHA
DACIA
DELIA
DELLA
DELTA
DERMA
DIANA
DICTA
DINKA
DOBLA
DOBRA
DOGMA
DONNA
DORSA
DOURA
DRAMA
DRAVA
DUALA
DULIA
DURRA
DVINA
DYULA

•DA••
ADAGE
ADAHS
ADAMS
ADAPT
IDAHO

•D•A•
ADDAX
ADMAN
EDDAS
EDGAR
EDNAS
IDEAL
IDEAS

•D••A
ADELA
ADYTA
EDEMA
EDINA

••DA•
ADDAX
AIDAS
ALDAN
AUDAD
CEDAR
CIDAL
CODAS
DEDAL
EDDAS
JUDAH
JUDAS
KEDAH
KODAK
MADAM
MEDAL
MIDAS
MODAL
NODAL
PEDAL
RADAR
REDAN
SEDAN
SODAS
SUDAN
TIDAL
TODAY
WODAN

••D•A
HEDDA
HYDRA
INDIA
INDRA
JIDDA
JUDEA
LYDDA
LYDIA
MEDEA
MEDIA
OIDEA
PADUA
PODIA
PYDNA
VODKA

•••DA
BANDA
BREDA
FREDA
GERDA
GILDA
GOUDA
HAIDA
HEDDA
HILDA
HULDA
JIDDA
LINDA
LYDDA
MAGDA
OUIDA
PANDA
RHODA
THEDA
TILDA
TRUDA
WANDA

D•B••
DEBAR
DEBBY
DEBIT
DEBTS
DEBUG
DEBUT
DOBBY
DOBIE
DOBLA
DOBRA
DUBHE

D••B•
DAUBS
DAUBY
DEBBY
DERBY
DOBBY
DOUBT
DRABS
DRIBS
DRUBS

D•••B
DEMOB
DENEB

•D•B•
ADOBE

•D••B
ADLIB

••D•B
ARDEB

D•C••
DACCA
DACES
DACHA
DACIA
DECAL
DECAY
DECIM
DECKS
DECOR
DECOY
DECRY
DICED
DICER
DICHO
DICKS
DICKY
DICTA
DOCKS
DUCAL
DUCAT
DUCHY
DUCKS
DUCKY

DUCTS

D••C•
DACCA
DANCE
DEICE
DEUCE
DIRCK
DISCI
DISCS
DITCH
DOLCE
DRACO
DULCE
DULCY
DUNCE
DUTCH

D•••C
DARIC
DODEC
DOMIC
DORIC

•D•C•
EDICT
EDUCE
EDUCT

•D••C
ADUNC
EDDIC

••D•C
DODEC
EDDIC
INDIC
IODIC
MEDIC
MEDOC
PUDIC
VEDIC

D•D••
DADDY
DEDAL
DIDNT
DIDOS
DIDST
DODEC
DODGE
DODOS
DUDES

D••D•
DADDY
DANDY
DEEDS
DENDR
DIODE
DOWDY
DUADS
DYADS

D•••D
DARED
DATED
DAVID
DAZED
DEKED
DELED
DEWED
DICED
DIKED
DINED
DIVED
DOLED
DOMED
DOPED
DOSED
DOTED
DOZED
DREAD
DRIED
DRUID
DRYAD
DUPED

•DD••
ADDAX
ADDED
ADDER
ADDIE
ADDLE
ADDYS
EDDAS
EDDIC
EDDIE
ODDER
ODDLY
UDDER

•D••D
ADDED
EDGED
EDRED
IDLED

••DD•
BIDDY
BUDDY
CADDO
CADDY
CUDDY
DADDY
FADDY
GIDDY
HEDDA
JIDDA
KIDDY
LYDDA
MIDDY
MUDDY
NEDDY
NODDY
PADDY
RODDY
RUDDS
RUDDY
TEDDY
TODDS
TODDY
WADDY
WIDDY

••D•D
ADDED
AIDED
AUDAD
BIDED
BODED
CEDED
CODED
ENDED
FADED
GADID
HADED
JADED
LADED
NIDED
REDID
SIDED
TIDED
UNDID
WADED

DE•••
DEALS
DEALT
DEANE
DEANS
DEARS
DEARY
DEATH
DEBAR
DEBBY
DEBIT
DEBTS
DEBUG
DEBUT
DECAL
DECAY
DECIM
DECKS
DECOR
DECOY
DECRY
DEDAL
DEEDS
DEEMS
DEEPS
DEFER
DEFIS
DEFOE
DEGAS
DEGUM
DEICE
DEIFY
DEIGN
DEISM
DEIST
DEITY
DEKED
DEKES
DELAY
DELED
DELES
DELFT
DELHI
DELIA
DELLA
DELLS
DELOS
DELTA
DELVE
DEMES
DEMIT
DEMOB
DEMON
DEMOS
DEMUR
DENDR
DENEB
DENES
DENIM
DENIS
DENNY
DENSE
DENTI
DENTO
DENTS
DENYS
DEOXY
DEPOT
DEPTH
DERBY
DEREK
DERMA
DERMO
DERRY
DESEX
DESKS
DETER
DEUCE
DEVAS
DEVIL
DEVON
DEWAN
DEWED
DEWEY
DEXTR

D•E••
DEEDS
DEEMS
DEEPS
DIEGO
DIENE
DIETS
DOERS
DOEST
DOETH
DREAD
DREAM
DREAR
DREGS
DRESS
DREST
DREWS
DUELS
DUETS
DWELL
DWELT
DYERS

D••E•
DACES
DALES
DAMES
DANES
DARED
DARER
DARES
DATED
DATER
DATES
DAVES
DAVEY
DAZED
DAZES
DEFER
DEKED
DEKES
DELED
DELES
DEMES
DENEB
DENES
DEREK
DESEX
DETER
DEWED
DEWEY
DICED
DICER
DIKED
DIKER
DIKES
DIMER
DIMES
DINED
DINER
DINES
DIRER
DIVED
DIVER
DIVES
DIZEN
DODEC
DOGES
DOLED
DOLES
DOMED
DOMES
DONEE
DOPED
DOPES
DOPEY
DOSED
DOSER
DOSES
DOTED
DOTER
DOTES
DOVER
DOVES
DOWEL
DOWER
DOYEN
DOZED
DOZEN
DOZES
DRIED
DRIER
DRIES
DRYER
DUDES
DUKES
DUNES
DUPED
DUPER
DUPES
DURER
DYNES

D•••E
DANAE
DANCE
DANTE
DAVIE
DEANE
DEFOE
DEICE
DELVE
DENSE
DEUCE
DHOLE
DIANE
DIENE
DIODE
DIONE
DIRGE
DIXIE
DOBIE
DODGE
DOGIE
DOLCE
DONEE
DONNE
DOUSE
DOWSE
DOYLE
DRAKE
DRAPE
DRAVE
DRIVE
DROME
DRONE
DROVE
DRUPE
DRUSE
DUANE
DUBHE
DULCE
DULSE
DUNCE
DUPLE

•DE••
ADEEM
ADELA
ADELE
ADENI
ADENO
ADEPT
EDEMA
IDEAL
IDEAS
ODEON
ODETS
ODEUM

•D•E•
ADDED
ADDER
ADEEM
ADIEU
ADLER
ADMEN
ADZES
EDGED
EDGES
EDIES
EDRED
IDLED
IDLER
IDLES
ODDER
UDDER

•D••E
ADAGE
ADDIE
ADDLE
ADELE
ADOBE
ADORE
EDDIE
EDILE
EDUCE
ODYLE

••DE•
ADDED
ADDER
AEDES
AIDED
AIDER
AIDES
ALDEN
ALDER
ANDES
ARDEB
ARDEN
AUDEN
BADEN
BEDEW
BIDED
BIDES
BIDET
BODED
BODES
CADES
CADET
CEDED
CEDES
CIDER
CODED
CODES
CODEX
DODEC
DUDES
EIDER
ELDER
EMDEN
ENDED
FADED
FADES
FIDEL
HADED
HADES
HIDER
HIDES
INDEX
JADED
JADES
JUDEA
JUDEO
JUDES
LADED
LADEN
LADES
LODEN
LODES
MEDEA
MODEL
MODES
NADER
NIDED
NIDES
NODES
NUDES
ODDER
OIDEA
OLDEN
OLDER
ORDER
PEDES
RIDER
RIDES
RODEO
RUDER
SEDER
SIDED
SIDER
SIDES
TIDED
TIDES
UDDER
UNDEE
UNDER
VIDEO

WADED
WADER
WADES
WIDEN
WIDER
WODEN
YODEL

••D•E
ADDIE
ADDLE
ANDRE
BADGE
BUDGE
CADGE
CADRE
DODGE
EADIE
EDDIE
ENDUE
FUDGE
HEDGE
HODGE
INDUE
JUDGE
KEDGE
LADLE
LEDGE
LODGE
MADGE
MIDGE
NUDGE
PADRE
RIDGE
SADIE
SEDGE
SIDLE
UNDEE
UNDUE
WEDGE

•••DE
ABIDE
ABODE
AMIDE
ANODE
ASIDE
BARDE
BLADE
BRIDE
BUNDE
CHIDE
CLYDE
CRUDE
DIODE
ELIDE
ELUDE
EPODE
ERODE
ETUDE
EVADE
EXUDE
GEODE
GLADE
GLEDE
GLIDE
GRADE
GRIDE
GUIDE
HORDE
IMIDE
MAUDE
MONDE
OXIDE
PRIDE
PRUDE
SHADE
SLIDE
SNIDE
SPADE
SPODE
SUEDE
SWEDE
TILDE
TRADE
TSADE

D•F••
DAFFY
DEFER
DEFIS
DEFOE
DOFFS
DUFFS

D••F•
DAFFY
DEIFY
DELFT
DOFFS
DRAFF
DRAFT
DRIFT
DUFFS

D•••F
DRAFF
DWARF

•D•F•
EDIFY

•D••F
ADOLF

D•G••
DAGAN
DEGAS
DEGUM
DIGIT
DOGES
DOGGY
DOGIE
DOGMA

D••G•
DANGS
DEIGN
DIEGO
DINGO
DINGS
DINGY
DIRGE
DODGE
DOGGY
DOUGH
DOUGS
DRAGS
DREGS
DRUGS
DUNGS
DUNGY

D•••G
DEBUG
DOING
DYING

•DG••
EDGAR
EDGED
EDGES

•D•G•
ADAGE

••DG•
BADGE
BLDGS
BUDGE
CADGE
DODGE
FUDGE
HEDGE
HEDGY
HODGE
JUDGE
KEDGE
LEDGE
LEDGY
LODGE
MADGE
MIDGE
NUDGE
PODGY
PUDGY
RIDGE
RIDGY
SEDGE
SEDGY
WEDGE
WEDGY

DH•••
DHAKS
DHOLE
DHOTI
DHOWS

D••H•
DACHA
DASHY
DELHI
DICHO
DUBHE
DUCHY

D•••H
DEATH
DEPTH
DINAH
DITCH
DOETH
DOLPH
DOUGH
DUTCH

•D•H•
ADAHS
IDAHO

•D••H
EDITH

••DH•
SADHU
YODHS

••D•H
JUDAH
KEDAH
WIDTH

DI•••
DIALS
DIANA
DIANE
DIARY
DIAZO
DICED
DICER
DICHO
DICKS
DICKY
DICTA
DIDNT
DIDOS
DIDST
DIEGO
DIENE
DIETS
DIGIT
DIJON
DIKED
DIKER
DIKES
DIMER
DIMES
DIMLY
DINAH
DINAR
DINED
DINER
DINES
DINGO
DINGS
DINGY
DINKA
DINKY
DINTS
DIODE
DIONE
DIPLO
DIPPY
DIRCK
DIRER
DIRGE
DIRKS
DIRTY
DISCI
DISCS
DISKO
DISKS
DITAS
DITCH
DITTO
DITTY
DIVAN
DIVAS
DIVED
DIVER
DIVES
DIVOT
DIVVY
DIWAN
DIXIE
DIXIT
DIZEN
DIZZY

D•I••
DAILY
DAIRY
DAISY
DEICE
DEIFY
DEIGN
DEISM
DEIST
DEITY
DOILY
DOING
DOITS
DRIBS
DRIED
DRIER
DRIES
DRIFT
DRILL
DRILY
DRINK
DRIPS
DRIPT
DRIVE
DVINA
DYING

D••I•
DACIA
DARIC
DAVID
DAVIE
DAVIS
DAVIT
DEBIT
DECIM
DEFIS
DELIA
DEMIT
DENIM
DENIS
DEVIL
DIGIT
DIXIE
DIXIT
DOBIE
DOGIE
DOMIC
DORIC
DORIS
DRAIN
DROIT
DRUID
DULIA

D•••I
DELHI
DENTI
DHOTI
DISCI
DORSI
DOUAI
DUOMI

•DI••
ADIEU
ADIOS
ADITS
EDICT
EDIES
EDIFY
EDILE
EDINA
EDITH
EDITS
IDIOM
IDIOT
ODIUM

•D•I•
ADDIE
ADLIB
ADMIN
ADMIT
ADMIX
EDDIC
EDDIE
EDWIN

•D••I
ADENI

••DI•
ADDIE
ALDIS
AUDIO
AUDIT
AYDIN
BEDIM
CADIS
CADIZ
EADIE
EDDIC
EDDIE
GADID
INDIA
INDIC
IODIC
KADIS
LADIN
LYDIA
MEDIA
MEDIC
MEDIO
NADIR
PODIA
PUDIC
RADII
RADIO
RADIX
REDID
RODIN
SADIE
UNDID
VEDIC

••D•I
HADJI
INDRI
RADII

•••DI
CARDI
GAUDI
GONDI
HINDI
KHADI
MAHDI
SCUDI
SOLDI
VERDI

D•J••
DIJON

••DJ•
HADJI

D•K••
DAKAR
DEKED
DEKES
DIKED
DIKER
DIKES
DUKES

D••K•
DAWKS
DECKS
DESKS
DHAKS
DICKS
DICKY
DINKA
DINKY
DIRKS
DISKO
DISKS
DOCKS
DRAKE
DUCKS
DUCKY
DUNKS
DUSKS
DUSKY

D•••K
DEREK
DIRCK
DRANK
DRINK
DRUNK

••DK•
VODKA

••D•K
KODAK

D•L••
DALES
DALLY
DELAY
DELED
DELES
DELFT
DELHI
DELIA
DELLA
DELLS
DELOS
DELTA
DELVE
DOLCE
DOLED
DOLES
DOLLS
DOLLY
DOLOR
DOLPH
DOLTS
DULCE
DULCY
DULIA
DULLS
DULLY
DULSE

D••L•
DAILY

DALLY
DEALS
DEALT
DELLA
DELLS
DHOLE
DIALS
DIMLY
DIPLO
DOALL
DOBLA
DOILY
DOLLS
DOLLY
DOOLY
DOYLE
DOYLY
DRILL
DRILY
DROLL
DRYLY
DUALA
DUELS
DULLS
DULLY
DUPLE
DWELL
DWELT
DYULA

D•••L
DECAL
DEDAL
DEVIL
DOALL
DOTAL
DOWEL
DRAWL
DRILL
DROLL
DROOL
DUCAL
DURAL
DWELL

•DL••
ADLER
ADLIB
IDLED
IDLER
IDLES

•D•L•
ADDLE
ADELA
ADELE
ADOLF
ADULT
EDILE
IDOLS
IDYLL
IDYLS
ODDLY
ODYLE

•D••L
IDEAL
IDYLL

••DL•
ADDLE
BADLY
GODLY
LADLE
MADLY
ODDLY
REDLY
SADLY
SIDLE

••D•L
ALDOL
CIDAL
DEDAL
FIDEL
IODOL
MEDAL
MODAL
MODEL
NODAL
PEDAL
TIDAL
YODEL

D•M••
DAMAN
DAMES
DAMNS
DAMON
DAMPS
DEMES
DEMIT
DEMOB
DEMON
DEMOS
DEMUR
DIMER
DIMES
DIMLY
DOMED
DOMES
DOMIC
DUMAS
DUMMY
DUMPS
DUMPY

D••M•
DEEMS
DERMA
DERMO
DOGMA
DOOMS
DORMS
DORMY
DRAMA
DRAMS
DROME
DRUMS
DUMMY
DUOMI
DUOMO

D•••M
DATUM
DECIM
DEGUM
DEISM
DENIM
DREAM
DURUM

•DM••
ADMAN
ADMEN
ADMIN
ADMIT
ADMIX

•D•M•
ADAMS
EDEMA

•D••M
ADEEM
IDIOM
ODEUM
ODIUM

••D•M
BEDIM
MADAM
SEDUM
SODOM

D•N••
DANAE
DANCE
DANDY
DANES
DANGS
DANNY
DANTE
DENDR
DENEB
DENES
DENIM
DENIS
DENNY
DENSE
DENTI
DENTO
DENTS
DENYS
DINAH
DINAR
DINED
DINER
DINES
DINGO
DINGS
DINGY
DINKA
DINKY
DINTS
DONAR
DONAS
DONEE
DONNA
DONNE
DONOR
DONTS
DUNCE
DUNES
DUNGS
DUNGY
DUNKS
DYNES

D••N•
DAMNS
DANNY
DARNS
DAUNT
DAWNS
DEANE
DEANS
DENNY
DIANA
DIANE
DIDNT
DIENE
DIONE
DOING
DONNA
DONNE
DOWNS
DOWNY
DRANK
DRINK
DRONE
DRUNK
DUANE
DVINA
DYING

D•••N
DAGAN
DAMAN
DAMON
DEIGN
DEMON
DEVON
DEWAN
DIJON
DIVAN
DIWAN
DIZEN
DOORN
DOYEN
DOZEN
DRAIN
DRAWN
DROWN

•DN••
EDNAS

•D•N•
ADENI
ADENO
ADUNC
EDINA
ODONT

•D••N
ADMAN
ADMEN
ADMIN
ADORN
EDWIN
ODEON

••DN•
DIDNT
PYDNA

••D•N
ALDAN
ALDEN
ARDEN
AUDEN
AYDIN
BADEN
EMDEN
LADEN
LADIN
LODEN
OLDEN
RADON
REDAN
RODIN
SEDAN
SIDON
SUDAN
WIDEN
WODAN
WODEN

•••DN
HAYDN

DO•••
DOALL
DOBBY
DOBIE
DOBLA
DOBRA
DOCKS
DODEC
DODGE
DODOS
DOERS
DOEST
DOETH
DOFFS
DOGES
DOGGY
DOGIE
DOGMA
DOILY
DOING
DOITS
DOLCE
DOLED
DOLES
DOLLS
DOLLY
DOLOR
DOLPH
DOLTS
DOMED
DOMES
DOMIC
DONAR
DONAS
DONEE
DONNA
DONNE
DONOR
DONTS
DOOLY
DOOMS
DOORN
DOORS
DOPED
DOPES
DOPEY
DORAS
DORIC
DORIS
DORMS
DORMY
DORRS
DORSA
DORSI
DORSO
DORUS
DOSED
DOSER
DOSES
DOTAL
DOTED
DOTER
DOTES
DOTTY
DOUAI
DOUAY
DOUBT
DOUGH
DOUGS
DOURA
DOUSE
DOVAP
DOVER
DOVES
DOWDY
DOWEL
DOWER
DOWNS
DOWNY
DOWRY
DOWSE
DOYEN
DOYLE
DOYLY
DOZED
DOZEN
DOZES

D•O••
DEOXY
DHOLE
DHOTI
DHOWS
DIODE
DIONE
DOOLY
DOOMS
DOORN
DOORS
DROIT
DROLL
DROME
DRONE
DROOL
DROOP
DROPS
DROPT
DROSS
DROVE
DROWN
DUOMI
DUOMO

D••O•
DAMON
DECOR
DECOY
DEFOE
DELOS
DEMOB
DEMON
DEMOS
DEPOT
DEVON
DIDOS
DIJON
DIVOT
DODOS
DOLOR
DONOR
DROOL
DROOP
DUROS

D•••O
DATTO
DAVAO
DENTO
DERMO
DIAZO
DICHO
DIEGO
DINGO
DIPLO
DISKO
DITTO
DORSO
DRACO
DUOMO

•DO••
ADOBE
ADOLF
ADOPT
ADORE
ADORN
IDOLS
ODONT
ODORS

•D•O•
ADIOS
IDIOM
IDIOT
ODEON

•D••O
ADENO
IDAHO

••DO•
ALDOL
ALDOS
ARDOR
DIDOS
DODOS
ENDOW
FEDOR
INDOW
IODOL
KUDOS
MEDOC
RADON
SIDON
SODOM
SUDOR
TODOS
TUDOR
WIDOW

••D•O
ANDRO
AUDIO
CADDO
HYDRO
JUDEO
MEDIO
PEDRO
RADIO
RODEO
VIDEO

•••DO
AMIDO
CADDO
CREDO
GUIDO
IMIDO
IRIDO
MISDO
OUTDO
PAEDO

RONDO
SCUDO
SOLDO
UREDO
WALDO

D•P••
DEPOT
DEPTH
DIPLO
DIPPY
DOPED
DOPES
DOPEY
DUPED
DUPER
DUPES
DUPLE

D••P•
DAMPS
DEEPS
DIPPY
DOLPH
DRAPE
DRIPS
DRIPT
DROPS
DROPT
DRUPE
DUMPS
DUMPY

D•••P
DOVAP
DROOP

•D•P•
ADAPT
ADEPT
ADOPT

DR•••
DRABS
DRACO
DRAFF
DRAFT
DRAGS
DRAIN
DRAKE
DRAMA
DRAMS
DRANK
DRAPE
DRAVA
DRAVE
DRAWL
DRAWN
DRAWS
DRAYS
DREAD
DREAM
DREAR
DREGS
DRESS
DREST
DREWS
DRIBS
DRIED
DRIER
DRIES
DRIFT
DRILL
DRILY
DRINK
DRIPS
DRIPT
DRIVE
DROIT
DROLL
DROME
DRONE
DROOL
DROOP
DROPS
DROPT
DROSS
DROVE
DROWN
DRUBS
DRUGS
DRUID
DRUMS
DRUNK
DRUPE
DRURY
DRUSE
DRYAD
DRYER
DRYLY

D•R••
DARED
DARER
DARES
DARIC
DARNS
DARTS
DERBY
DEREK
DERMA
DERMO
DERRY
DIRCK
DIRER
DIRGE
DIRKS
DIRTY
DORAS
DORIC
DORIS
DORMS
DORMY
DORRS
DORSA
DORSI
DORSO
DORUS
DURAL
DURER
DUROS
DURRA
DURUM

D••R•
DAIRY
DEARS
DEARY
DECRY
DERRY
DIARY
DOBRA
DOERS
DOORN
DOORS
DORRS
DOURA
DOWRY
DRURY
DURRA
DWARF
DYERS

D•••R
DAKAR
DARER
DATER
DEBAR
DECOR
DEFER
DEMUR
DENDR
DETER
DEXTR
DICER
DIKER
DIMER
DINAR
DINER
DIRER
DIVER
DOLOR
DONAR
DONOR
DOSER
DOTER
DOVER
DOWER
DREAR
DRIER
DRYER
DUPER
DURER

•DR••
EDRED

•D•R•
ADORE
ADORN
ODORS

•D••R
ADDER
ADLER
EDGAR
IDLER
ODDER
UDDER

••DR•
ANDRE
ANDRO
CADRE
HYDRA
HYDRO
INDRA
INDRI
PADRE
PEDRO

••D•R
ADDER
AIDER
ALDER
ARDOR
CEDAR
CIDER
EIDER
ELDER
FEDOR
HIDER
NADER
NADIR
ODDER
OLDER
ORDER
RADAR
RIDER
RUDER
SEDER
SIDER
SUDOR
TUDOR
UDDER
UNDER
WADER
WIDER

•••DR
BALDR
COMDR
DENDR

D•S••
DASHY
DESEX
DESKS
DISCI
DISCS
DISKO
DISKS
DOSED
DOSER
DOSES
DUSKS
DUSKY
DUSTS
DUSTY

D••S•
DAISY
DEISM
DEIST
DENSE
DIDST
DOEST
DORSA
DORSI
DORSO
DOUSE
DOWSE
DRESS
DREST
DROSS
DRUSE
DULSE

D•••S
DACES
DALES
DAMES
DAMNS
DAMPS
DANES
DANGS
DARES
DARNS
DARTS
DATES
DAUBS
DAVES
DAVIS
DAVYS
DAWKS
DAWNS
DAZES
DEALS
DEANS
DEARS
DEBTS
DECKS
DEEDS
DEEMS
DEEPS
DEFIS
DEGAS
DEKES
DELES
DELLS
DELOS
DEMES
DEMOS
DENES
DENIS
DENTS
DENYS
DESKS
DEVAS
DHAKS
DHOWS
DIALS
DICKS
DIDOS
DIETS
DIKES
DIMES
DINES
DINGS
DINTS
DIRKS
DISCS
DISKS
DITAS
DIVAS
DIVES
DOCKS
DODOS
DOERS
DOFFS
DOGES
DOITS
DOLES
DOLLS
DOLTS
DOMES
DONAS
DONTS
DOOMS
DOORS
DOPES
DORAS
DORIS
DORMS
DORRS
DORUS
DOSES
DOTES
DOUGS
DOVES
DOWNS
DOZES
DRABS
DRAGS
DRAMS
DRAWS
DRAYS
DREGS
DRESS
DREWS
DRIBS
DRIES
DRIPS
DROPS
DROSS
DRUBS
DRUGS
DRUMS
DUADS
DUCKS
DUCTS
DUDES
DUELS
DUETS
DUFFS
DUKES
DULLS
DUMAS
DUMPS
DUNES
DUNGS
DUNKS
DUPES
DUROS
DUSKS
DUSTS
DYADS
DYERS
DYNES

•D•S•
ADUST

•D••S
ADAHS
ADAMS
ADDYS
ADIOS
ADITS
ADZES
EDDAS
EDGES
EDIES
EDITS
EDNAS
IDEAS
IDLES
IDOLS
IDYLS
ODETS
ODORS

••DS•
DIDST
MIDST
SUDSY

••D•S
ADDYS
AEDES
AIDAS
AIDES
ALDIS
ALDOS
ALDUS
ANDES
ANDYS
BIDES
BLDGS
BODES
CADES
CADIS
CEDES
CODAS
CODES
DIDOS
DODOS
DUDES
EDDAS
FADES
HADES
HIDES
INDUS
JADES
JUDAS
JUDES
JUDYS
KADIS
KUDOS
KUDUS
LADES
LODES
MIDAS
MODES
MODUS
NIDES
NIDUS
NODES
NODUS
NUDES
PEDES
RIDES
RUDDS
RUDYS
SIDES
SODAS
TIDES
TODDS
TODOS
WADES
YODHS

•••DS
ACIDS
BANDS
BARDS
BAWDS
BEADS
BENDS
BINDS
BIRDS
BONDS
BOYDS
BRADS
BUNDS
BURDS
CARDS
CLODS
COEDS
COLDS
CORDS
CURDS
DEEDS
DUADS
DYADS
ENIDS
FEEDS
FENDS
FEODS
FEUDS
FINDS
FOLDS

FOODS
FORDS
FREDS
FUNDS
GAUDS
GELDS
GILDS
GIRDS
GLADS
GLEDS
GOADS
GOLDS
GOODS
GRADS
GRIDS
HANDS
HARDS
HEADS
HEEDS
HERDS
HINDS
HOLDS
HOODS
HURDS
IMIDS
KINDS
LANDS
LARDS
LAUDS
LEADS
LENDS
LEUDS
LOADS
LORDS
MAIDS
MAUDS
MEADS
MELDS
MENDS
MINDS
MOLDS
MOODS
NARDS
NEEDS
PARDS
PENDS
PLODS
PONDS
POODS
PRODS
QUADS
QUIDS
QUODS
RAIDS
RANDS
READS
REEDS
RENDS
RINDS
ROADS
ROODS
RUDDS
RYNDS
SANDS
SCADS
SCUDS
SEEDS
SENDS
SHEDS
SKIDS
SLEDS
SPUDS
STUDS
SURDS
TENDS
THADS
THUDS
TOADS
TODDS
VELDS
VENDS
VOIDS
WANDS
WARDS
WEEDS
WELDS
WENDS
WILDS
WINDS
WOADS
WOLDS
WOODS
WORDS
YARDS

D•T••

DATED
DATER
DATES
DATTO
DATUM
DETER
DITAS
DITCH
DITTO
DITTY
DOTAL
DOTED
DOTER
DOTES
DOTTY
DUTCH

D••T•

DANTE
DARTS
DATTO
DEATH
DEBTS
DEITY
DELTA
DENTI
DENTO
DENTS
DEPTH
DEXTR
DHOTI
DICTA
DIETS
DINTS
DIRTY
DITTO
DITTY
DOETH
DOITS
DOLTS
DONTS
DOTTY
DUCTS
DUETS
DUSTS
DUSTY

D•••T

DAUNT
DAVIT
DEALT
DEBIT
DEBUT
DEIST
DELFT
DEMIT
DEPOT
DIDNT
DIDST
DIGIT
DIVOT
DIXIT
DOEST
DOUBT
DRAFT
DREST
DRIFT
DRIPT
DROIT
DROPT
DUCAT
DWELT

•D•T•

ADITS
ADYTA
EDITH
EDITS
ODETS

•D••T

ADAPT
ADEPT
ADMIT
ADOPT
ADULT
ADUST
EDICT
EDUCT
IDIOT
ODONT

••DT•

WIDTH

••D•T

AUDIT
BIDET
CADET
DIDNT
DIDST
MIDST

•••DT

COMDT
VELDT

DU•••

DUADS
DUALA
DUANE
DUBHE
DUCAL
DUCAT
DUCHY
DUCKS
DUCKY
DUCTS
DUDES
DUELS
DUETS
DUFFS
DUKES
DULCE
DULCY
DULIA
DULLS
DULLY
DULSE
DUMAS
DUMMY
DUMPS
DUMPY
DUNCE
DUNES
DUNGS
DUNGY
DUNKS
DUOMI
DUOMO
DUPED
DUPER
DUPES
DUPLE
DURAL
DURER
DUROS
DURRA
DURUM
DUSKS
DUSKY
DUSTS
DUSTY
DUTCH

D•U••

DAUBS
DAUBY
DAUNT
DEUCE
DOUAI
DOUAY
DOUBT
DOUGH
DOUGS
DOURA
DOUSE
DRUBS
DRUGS
DRUID
DRUMS
DRUNK
DRUPE
DRURY
DRUSE
DYULA

D••U•

DATUM
DEBUG
DEBUT
DEGUM
DEMUR
DORUS
DURUM

•DU••

ADULT
ADUNC
ADUST
EDUCE
EDUCT

•D•U•

ODEUM
ODIUM

•D••U

ADIEU

••DU•

ALDUS
ENDUE
INDUE
INDUS
KUDUS
MODUS
NIDUS
NODUS
PADUA
SEDUM
UNDUE
VADUZ

••D•U

SADHU

•••DU

HINDU
PERDU

DV•••

DVINA

D•V••

DAVAO
DAVES
DAVEY
DAVID
DAVIE
DAVIS
DAVIT
DAVYS
DEVAS
DEVIL
DEVON
DIVAN
DIVAS
DIVED
DIVER
DIVES
DIVOT
DIVVY
DOVAP
DOVER
DOVES

D••V•

DELVE
DIVVY
DRAVA
DRAVE
DRIVE
DROVE

DW•••

DWARF
DWELL
DWELT

D•W••

DAWKS
DAWNS
DEWAN
DEWED
DEWEY
DIWAN
DOWDY
DOWEL
DOWER
DOWNS
DOWNY
DOWRY
DOWSE

D••W•

DHOWS
DRAWL
DRAWN
DRAWS
DREWS
DROWN

•DW••

EDWIN

••D•W

BEDEW
ENDOW
INDOW
WIDOW

D•X••

DEXTR
DIXIE
DIXIT

D••X•

DEOXY

D•••X

DESEX

•D••X

ADDAX
ADMIX

••D•X

ADDAX
CODEX
INDEX
RADIX

DY•••

DYADS
DYERS
DYING
DYNES
DYULA

D•Y••

DOYEN
DOYLE
DOYLY
DRYAD
DRYER
DRYLY

D••Y•

DAVYS
DENYS
DRAYS

D•••Y

DADDY
DAFFY
DAILY
DAIRY
DAISY
DALLY
DANDY
DANNY
DASHY
DAUBY
DAVEY
DEARY
DEBBY
DECAY
DECOY
DECRY
DEIFY
DEITY
DELAY
DENNY
DEOXY
DERBY
DERRY
DEWEY
DIARY
DICKY
DIMLY
DINGY
DINKY
DIPPY
DIRTY
DITTY
DIVVY
DIZZY
DOBBY
DOGGY
DOILY
DOLLY
DOOLY
DOPEY
DORMY
DOTTY
DOUAY
DOWDY
DOWNY
DOWRY
DOYLY
DRILY
DRURY
DRYLY
DUCHY
DUCKY
DULCY
DULLY
DUMMY
DUMPY
DUNGY
DUSKY
DUSTY

•DY••

ADYTA
IDYLL
IDYLS
ODYLE

•D•Y•

ADDYS

•D••Y

EDIFY
ODDLY

••DY•

ADDYS
ANDYS
JUDYS
RUDYS

••D•Y

BADLY
BIDDY

5

BUDDY
CADDY
CUDDY
DADDY
FADDY
GIDDY
GODLY
HEDGY
KIDDY
LEDGY
MADLY
MIDDY
MUDDY
NEDDY
NODDY
ODDLY
PADDY
PODGY
PUDGY
REDLY
RIDGY
RODDY
RUDDY
SADLY
SEDGY
SUDSY
TEDDY
TODAY
TODDY
WADDY
WEDGY
WIDDY

•••DY

BANDY
BAWDY
BEADY
BENDY
BIDDY
BRADY
BUDDY
CADDY
CANDY
CINDY
CUDDY
CURDY
DADDY
DANDY
DOWDY
FADDY
FUNDY
GAUDY
GIDDY
GOODY
HANDY
HARDY
HEADY
HOWDY
KANDY
KIDDY
LARDY
LEADY
MANDY
MIDDY
MOLDY
MOODY
MUDDY
NEDDY
NEEDY
NODDY
PADDY
PANDY
RANDY
READY
REEDY
RODDY
ROWDY
RUDDY
SANDY
SEEDY
SHADY
STUDY
TARDY
TEDDY
THADY
TOADY
TODDY
TRUDY
WADDY
WEEDY
WENDY
WIDDY
WINDY
WOODY
WORDY

D•Z••

DAZED
DAZES
DIZEN
DIZZY
DOZED
DOZEN
DOZES

D••Z•

DIAZO
DIZZY

•DZ••

ADZES

••D•Z

CADIZ
VADUZ

EA•••

EADIE
EAGER
EAGLE
EAGRE
EARED
EARLE
EARLS
EARLY
EARNS
EARTH
EASED
EASEL
EASES
EATEN
EATER
EAVES

E•A••

ELAEO
ELAIN
ELAIO
ELAND
ELATE
ENACT
ENATE
EPACT
ERASE
ERATO
ETAPE
EVADE
EVANS
EXACT
EXALT
EXAMS

E••A•

EBOAT
ECLAT
EDDAS
EDGAR
EDNAS
EGEAN
EGGAR
ELGAR
ELIAS
ELLAS
ELMAN
ELSAS
ELVAS
EMBAR
EMBAY
EMMAS
ENEAS
EPHAH
EQUAL
ERMAS
ESSAY
ETHAN
ETNAS
ETTAS
EYRAS
EZRAS

E•••A

EDEMA
EDINA
ELENA
ELIZA
ENEMA
ENNEA
ENTIA
ERICA
ERIKA
ETYMA
EVITA
EXTRA

•EA••

BEACH
BEADS
BEADY
BEAKS
BEAMS
BEAMY
BEANO
BEANS
BEARD
BEARS
BEAST
BEATA
BEATS
BEAUS
BEAUT
BEAUX
CEARA
CEASE
DEALS
DEALT
DEANE
DEANS
DEARS
DEARY
DEATH
FEARS
FEASE
FEAST
FEATS
GEARS
HEADS
HEADY
HEALS
HEAPS
HEARD
HEARS
HEART
HEATH
HEATS
HEAVE
HEAVY
JEANS
KEATS
LEACH
LEADS
LEADY
LEAFS
LEAFY
LEAKS
LEAKY
LEANS
LEANT
LEAPS
LEAPT
LEARN
LEASE
LEASH
LEAST
LEAVE
LEAVY
MEADS
MEALS
MEALY
MEANS
MEANT
MEANY
MEATS
MEATY
NEALS
NEAPS
NEARS
NEATH
PEACE
PEACH
PEAKS
PEALS
PEANS
PEARL
PEARS
PEARY
PEASE
PEATS
PEATY
PEAVY
REACH
REACT
READS
READY
REALM
REALS
REAMS
REAPS
REARM
REARS
SEALS
SEAMS
SEAMY
SEANS
SEARS
SEATO
SEATS
TEACH
TEAKS
TEALS
TEAMS
TEARS
TEARY
TEASE
TEATS
WEALD
WEALS
WEANS
WEARS
WEARY
WEAVE
YEANS
YEARN
YEARS
YEAST
YEATS

•E•A•

AETAT
BEGAN
BEGAT
BELAY
BETAS
CECAL
CEDAR
CERAM
CERAT
CESAR
DEBAR
DECAL
DECAY
DEDAL
DEGAS
DELAY
DEVAS
DEWAN
FECAL
FERAL
FETAL
FEUAR
HEJAZ
HEMAL
HEMAN
HEMAT
HEPAT
HERAT
HEXAD
KEDAH
KERAT
LEGAL
LENAS
MEDAL
MEGAL
MEGAN
MELAN
MESAS
METAL
METAS
NEMAT
NEPAL
PECAN
PEDAL
PEKAN
PENAL
PETAL
RECAP
REDAN
REGAL
REGAN
RELAX
RELAY
REMAN
RENAL
RENAN
REPAY
RERAN
SEBAT
SEDAN
SELAH
SEPAL
SERAC
SERAI
SERAL
SETAE
TELAE
TERAT
TEXAS
VELAR
VENAE
VENAL
VERAS
WEKAS
ZETAS

•E••A

AECIA
AEMIA
BEATA
BEIRA
BELGA
BELLA
BERTA
BEULA
CEARA
CEIBA
CELIA
CELLA
CERIA
DELIA
DELLA
DELTA
DERMA
GEMMA
GENOA
GENUA
GERDA
HEDDA
HEKLA
HELGA
HEMIA
HENNA
HEPTA
HERMA
KENYA
LEHUA
LEILA
LEMMA
LEONA
LEORA
LEPTA
MECCA
MEDEA
MEDIA
MENSA
PELLA
PENNA
PENTA
PEPLA
RECTA
REGMA
RETIA
RETTA
SELMA
SENNA
SEPIA
SEPTA
SERRA
TERRA
TESLA
TESTA
TETRA
VERNA
VESTA
XENIA
YERBA
ZEBRA

••EA•

ABEAM
ACEAE
ACEAN
AHEAD
ANEAR
APEAK
AREAE
AREAL
AREAS
BLEAK
BLEAR
BLEAT
BREAD
BREAK
BREAM
CHEAP
CHEAT
CLEAN
CLEAR
CLEAT
CREAK
CREAM
DREAD
DREAM
DREAR
EGEAN
ENEAS
FLEAM
FLEAS
FREAK
GLEAM
GLEAN
GREAT
HBEAM
IBEAM
IDEAL
IDEAS
ILEAC
ILEAL
KNEAD
OCEAN
OREAD
PAEAN
PLEAD
PLEAS
PLEAT
QUEAN
RHEAS
SHEAF
SHEAR
SHEAS
SKEAN
SMEAR
SNEAK
SPEAK

5

SPEAR
STEAD
STEAK
STEAL
STEAM
SWEAR
SWEAT
TREAD
TREAS
TREAT
TWEAK
UREAL
UVEAL
UVEAS
WHEAL
WHEAT
WREAK
ZBEAM

••E•A

ADELA
ALEXA
AMEBA
ARECA
ARENA
BREDA
CHELA
EDEMA
ELENA
ENEMA
FREDA
FRENA
FREYA
GRETA
HYENA
OMEGA
OPERA
PIETA
PLENA
PRESA
SHEBA
THECA
THEDA
THETA
ULEMA

•••EA

APNEA
BOHEA
CANEA
ENNEA
FOVEA
GALEA
HOSEA
JUDEA
KOREA
LYCEA
MEDEA
OCREA
OIDEA
PALEA
PILEA
RHOEA
RRHEA
TINEA

EB•••

EBBED
EBOAT
EBONS
EBONY

E•B••

EBBED
ELBOW
EMBAR
EMBAY
EMBED
EMBER
EMBOW
EMBRY

E•••B

EXURB

•EB••

BEBOP
DEBAR
DEBBY
DEBIT
DEBTS
DEBUG
DEBUT
FEBRI
REBEC
REBEL
REBUS
REBUT
SEBAT
SEBUM
TEBET
WEBBY
WEBER
XEBEC
ZEBEC
ZEBRA
ZEBUS

•E•B•

BEEBE
CEIBA
DEBBY
DERBY
HERBS
HERBY
KERBS
SERBS
VERBS
WEBBY
YERBA

•E••B

DEMOB
DENEB

••EB•

AMEBA
BEEBE
BLEBS
GLEBE
GREBE
PHEBE
PLEBE
PLEBS
SHEBA

••E•B

ACERB

•••EB

ARDEB
CALEB
CUBEB
DENEB
HOREB
PHLEB
SAHEB

EC•••

ECHIN
ECLAT
ECOLE

E•C••

EMCEE
ENCYC
EXCEL

E••C•

EDICT
EDUCE
EDUCT
EJECT
ELECT
ENACT
ENOCH
EPACT
EPICS
EPOCH
ERECT
ERICA
ERICH
ERICS
ERUCT
EVICT
EXACT
EXECS

E•••C

EDDIC
ENCYC
EOLIC
ETHIC

•EC••

AECIA
BECKS
BECKY
CECAL
CECIL
CECUM
DECAL
DECAY
DECIM
DECKS
DECOR
DECOY
DECRY
FECAL
FECES
FECIT
GECKO
GECKS
HECTO
KECKS
MECCA
NECKS
NECRO
PECAN
PECKS
PECOS
RECAP
RECTA
RECTI
RECTO
RECUR
SECCO
SECTS
TECHN

•E•C•

BEACH
BEECH
BELCH
BENCH
DEICE
DEUCE
FENCE
FETCH
HENCE
KENCH
KERCH
KETCH
LEACH
LEECH
LEUCO
MECCA
MERCI
MERCY
PEACE
PEACH
PENCE
PERCH
PERCY
REACH
REACT
REICH
RETCH
SECCO
TEACH
TENCH
VETCH
WELCH
WENCH

•E••C

CERIC
GENIC
HELIC
HEMIC
MEDIC
MEDOC
MELIC
MESIC
REBEC
RELIC
SERAC
TELIC
VEDIC
VESIC
XEBEC
XERIC
ZEBEC

••EC•

ALECK
ALECS
ARECA
BEECH
CHECK
CRECY
CZECH
EJECT
ELECT
ERECT
EXECS
FLECK
GRECO
LEECH
NIECE
PIECE
SPECK
SPECS
THECA
VNECK
WRECK

••E•C

AREIC
CRESC
ILEAC
OLEIC

•••EC

AZTEC
COSEC
CUSEC
DODEC
GYNEC
REBEC
XEBEC
ZEBEC

ED•••

EDDAS
EDDIC
EDDIE
EDEMA
EDGAR
EDGED
EDGES
EDICT
EDIES
EDIFY
EDILE
EDINA
EDITH
EDITS
EDNAS
EDRED
EDUCE
EDUCT
EDWIN

E•D••

EADIE
EDDAS
EDDIC
EDDIE
EIDER
ELDER
EMDEN
ENDED
ENDOW
ENDUE

E••D•

ELIDE
ELUDE
ENIDS
EPODE
ERODE
ETUDE
EVADE
EXUDE

E•••D

EARED
EASED
EBBED
EDGED
EDRED
EGGED
ELAND
EMBED
EMEND
ENDED
EPHOD
ERRED

•ED••

AEDES
BEDEW
BEDIM
CEDAR
CEDED
CEDES
DEDAL
FEDOR
HEDDA
HEDGE
HEDGY
KEDAH
KEDGE
LEDGE
LEDGY
MEDAL
MEDEA
MEDIA
MEDIC
MEDIO
MEDOC
NEDDY
PEDAL
PEDES
PEDRO
REDAN
REDID
REDLY
SEDAN
SEDER
SEDGE
SEDGY
SEDUM
TEDDY
VEDIC
WEDGE
WEDGY

•E•D•

BEADS
BEADY
BENDS
BENDY
DEEDS
DENDR
FEEDS
FENDS
FEODS
FEUDS
GELDS
GEODE
GERDA
HEADS
HEADY
HEDDA
HEEDS
HERDS
LEADS
LEADY
LENDS
LEUDS
MEADS
MELDS
MENDS
NEDDY
NEEDS
NEEDY
PENDS
PERDU
READS
READY
REEDS
REEDY
RENDS
SEEDS
SEEDY
SENDS
TEDDY
TENDS
VELDS
VELDT
VENDS
VERDI
WEEDS
WEEDY
WELDS
WENDS
WENDY

•E••D

BEARD
CEDED
CERED
DEKED
DELED
DEWED
FELID
FETED
FEUED
GELID
GEOID
HEARD
HEROD
HEWED
HEXAD
HEXED
KEYED
LEPID
METED
MEWED
REDID
SERED
SEWED
SEXED
TEPID
VEXED
WEALD
WEIRD

••ED•

BREDA
COEDS
CREDO
DEEDS
FEEDS
FREDA
FREDS
GLEDE
GLEDS
HEEDS
NEEDS
NEEDY
PAEDO
REEDS
REEDY
SEEDS
SEEDY
SHEDS
SLEDS

SUEDE
SWEDE
THEDA
UREDO
WEEDS
WEEDY

••E•D

AHEAD
AMEND
BLEED
BLEND
BREAD
BREED
CREED
DREAD
EMEND
FIELD
FIEND
FJELD
FREED
FREUD
GREED
KNEAD
KNEED
OREAD
PLEAD
PSEUD
SCEND
SHERD
SKEED
SPEED
SPEND
STEAD
STEED
TREAD
TREED
TREND
TWEED
UPEND
WIELD
YIELD

•••ED

ACHED
ACRED
ACTED
ADDED
AIDED
AILED
AIMED
AIRED
ANTED
ARCED
ARMED
ASKED
AWNED
AXLED
BAAED
BAKED
BALED
BARED
BASED
BATED
BAYED
BIDED
BIPED
BLEED
BLUED
BODED
BONED
BOOED
BORED
BOWED
BOXED
BREED
BUSED
CAGED
CAKED
CANED
CARED
CASED
CAVED
CAWED
CEDED
CERED
CITED
CLUED
CODED
COKED
CONED
COOED
COPED
CORED
COVED
COWED
COXED
CREED
CRIED
CUBED
CURED
DARED
DATED
DAZED
DEKED
DELED
DEWED
DICED
DIKED
DINED
DIVED
DOLED
DOMED
DOPED
DOSED
DOTED
DOZED
DRIED
DUPED
EARED
EASED
EBBED
EDGED
EDRED
EGGED
EMBED
ENDED
ERRED
FACED
FADED
FAKED
FAMED
FARED
FATED
FAXED
FAYED
FAZED
FETED
FEUED
FIFED
FILED
FINED
FIRED
FIXED
FLIED
FOXED
FREED
FRIED
FUMED
FUSED
FUZED
GAGED
GAMED
GAPED
GATED
GAZED
GIBED
GLUED
GORED
GREED
GUYED
HADED
HALED
HATED
HAWED
HAYED
HAZED
HEWED
HEXED
HIKED
HIRED
HIVED
HOLED
HOMED
HONED
HOPED
HOSED
IDLED
IMBED
INKED
INNED
IRKED
ISLED
IVIED
JADED
JARED
JAWED
JIBED
JOKED
JOYED
KEYED
KITED
KNEED
LACED
LADED
LAKED
LAMED
LAVED
LAWED
LAZED
LIKED
LIMED
LINED
LIVED
LOBED
LOOED
LOPED
LOVED
LOWED
LURED
LUTED
LYSED
MACED
MANED
MATED
MAZED
METED
MEWED
MIMED
MINED
MIRED
MIXED
MOOED
MOPED
MOVED
MOWED
MUSED
MUTED
NAKED
NAMED
NIDED
NIXED
NOSED
NOTED
OARED
OGLED
OILED
OOZED
OPTED
ORBED
OUTED
OWNED
PACED
PAGED
PALED
PARED
PAVED
PAWED
PAYED
PIKED
PILED
PINED
PIPED
PLIED
POKED
POLED
PORED
POSED
PRIED
PUKED
PULED
RACED
RAGED
RAKED
RAPED
RATED
RAVED
RAYED
RAZED
RICED
RILED
RIMED
RIVED
ROBED
ROPED
ROSED
ROVED
ROWED
RULED
SABED
SATED
SAVED
SAWED
SERED
SEWED
SEXED
SHIED
SHRED
SIDED
SIRED
SIZED
SKEED
SKIED
SLUED
SOLED
SOWED
SPEED
SPIED
STEED
STIED
TAMED
TAPED
TARED
TAWED
TAXED
TIDED
TILED
TIMED
TINED
TIRED
TONED
TOPED
TOTED
TOWED
TOYED
TREED
TRIED
TRUED
TUBED
TUNED
TWEED
TYPED
UNWED
UPPED
URGED
VANED
VEXED
VISED
VOTED
VOWED
WADED
WAGED
WAKED
WALED
WANED
WAVED
WAXED
WILED
WINED
WIPED
WIRED
WISED
WIVED
WOOED
WOWED
WRIED
YAWED
YOKED
YOWED
ZONED

EE•••

EERIE

E•E••

EDEMA
EGEAN
EGEST
EJECT
ELECT
ELEGY
ELEMI
ELENA
EMEER
EMEND
EMERY
EMEUS
ENEAS
ENEMA
ENEMY
EPEES
ERECT
EVENS
EVENT
EVERT
EVERY
EWERS
EXECS
EXERT

E••E•

EAGER
EARED
EASED
EASEL
EASES
EATEN
EATER
EAVES
EBBED
EDGED
EDGES
EDIES
EDRED
EGGED
EGGER
EGRET
EIDER
ELAEO
ELDER
ELLEN
ELMER
ELVER
ELVES
EMBED
EMBER
EMCEE
EMDEN
EMEER
EMMER
EMMET
ENDED
ENNEA
ENTER
EPEES
ERIES
ERNES
ERRED
ERSES
ESHER
ESKER
ESSEN
ESSES
ESSEX
ESTER
ETHEL
ETHER
EULER
EXCEL
EXPEL

E•••E

EADIE
EAGLE
EAGRE
EARLE
ECOLE
EDDIE
EDILE
EDUCE
EERIE
EFFIE
ELATE
ELIDE
ELISE
ELITE
ELLIE
ELOPE
ELSIE
ELUDE
EMCEE
EMILE
EMMIE
EMOTE
ENATE
ENDUE
ENSUE
EPODE
ERASE
ERNIE
ERODE
EROSE
ESQUE
ESSIE
ETAPE
ETTIE
ETUDE
EVADE
EVOKE
EXILE
EXUDE
EYRIE

•EE••

BEEBE
BEECH
BEEFS
BEEFY
BEEPS
BEERS
BEERY
BEETS
DEEDS
DEEMS
DEEPS
FEEDS
FEELS
FEEZE
GEEKS
GEESE
GEEST
HEEDS
HEELS
JEEPS
JEERS
KEEFS
KEELS
KEENS
KEEPS
KEEVE
LEECH
LEEKS
LEERS
LEERY
LEETS
MEETS
NEEDS
NEEDY
PEEKS
PEELS
PEENS
PEEPS

PEERS PEEVE REEDS REEDY REEFS REEFY REEKS REEKY REELS REEVE SEEDS SEEDY SEEKS SEEMS SEEPS SEERS TEEMS TEENS TEENY TEETH VEERS VEERY WEEDS WEEDY WEEKS WEEMS WEENY WEEPS WEEPY WEEST

•E•E•

AEDES BEDEW BEGET BELEM BENES BENET BERET BESET BETEL BEVEL BEZEL CEDED CEDES CERED CERES DEFER DEKED DEKES DELED DELES DEMES DENEB DENES DEREK DESEX DETER DEWED DEWEY FECES FEMES FETED FETES FEUED FEVER FEWER GENES GENET HEGEL HELEN HEMEN HEWED HEWER HEXED HEXES JEFES JEREZ JEWEL KERES KEVEL KEYED LEGER LEGES LENES LEPER LEVEE LEVEL LEVEN LEVER MEDEA MELEE MENES METED METER METES MEWED NEGEV NEVER NEWEL NEWER PEDES PELEE PERES PETER PETES PEWEE REBEC REBEL REFER REGES REMEX RENEE RENES RENEW REPEL RESET RETEM REVEL REVET SEDER SELEN SEMEN SERED SERES SEVEN SEVER SEWED SEWER SEXED SEXES TEBET TEHEE TELEG TELEO TELEX TENET TEPEE VEXED VEXER VEXES WEBER XEBEC YEMEN YESES ZEBEC ZEKES

•E••E

AERIE BEEBE BEIGE BELIE BELLE BENNE BENUE BERME BERNE BETTE CEASE CELIE CENSE DEANE DEFOE DEICE DELVE DENSE DEUCE EERIE FEASE FEEZE FEMME FENCE FESSE GEESE GENIE GENRE GEODE HEAVE HEDGE HELLE HELVE HENCE JESSE KEDGE KEEVE LEASE LEAVE LEDGE LETHE LEVEE LEWIE LEYTE MELEE MERGE MERLE MEROE MESNE MEUSE NERVE NEUME PEACE PEASE PEEVE PEKOE PELEE PENCE PERSE PEWEE REEVE RENEE RENTE REVUE SEDGE SEINE SEIZE SENSE SERGE SERVE SETAE TEASE TEHEE TELAE TEMPE TENSE TEPEE TERSE VENAE VENUE VERGE VERNE VERSE VERVE WEAVE WEDGE

••EE•

ADEEM BLEED BREED CHEEK CHEEP CHEER CREED CREEK CREEL CREEP CREES EMEER EPEES FLEER FLEES FLEET FREED FREER FREES GLEES GLEET GREED GREEK GREEN GREET KNEED KNEEL KNEES OGEES PREEN QUEEN QUEER SHEEN SHEEP SHEER SHEET SKEED SKEES SKEET SLEEK SLEEP SLEET SNEER SPEED STEED STEEL STEEP STEER SWEEP SWEET TREED TREES TWEED TWEEN TWEET TYEES WHEEL

••E•E

ABELE ACEAE ADELE AKENE AREAE ARETE BEEBE BREVE COELE CREME CREPE CRETE CREWE DIENE FEEZE FRERE GEESE GLEBE GLEDE GREBE IRENE ISERE KEEVE LIEGE NIECE OBESE OXEYE PEEVE PHEBE PIECE PLEBE QUEUE REEVE SCENE SIEGE SIEVE STELE STERE STEVE SUEDE SWEDE THEME THERE THESE WHERE

•••EE

AGLEE AGREE AIMEE ALBEE COOEE DONEE EMCEE FUSEE FUZEE LEVEE LYCEE MELEE PAYEE PELEE PEWEE PUREE RAGEE RAKEE RANEE RAZEE RENEE RUPEE SCREE SPREE SYCEE TEHEE TEPEE THREE UNDEE YOGEE

EF•••

EFFIE

E•F••

EFFIE ELFIN

E••F•

EDIFY

•EF••

BEFIT BEFOG DEFER DEFIS DEFOE HEFTS HEFTY JEFES JEFFS LEFTS LEFTY REFER REFIT WEFTS

•E•F•

BEEFS BEEFY DEIFY DELFT FEOFF JEFFS KEEFS KERFS LEAFS LEAFY LEIFS PELFS REEFS REEFY REIFY SERFS

•E••F

FEOFF SERIF

••EF•

ALEFS BEEFS BEEFY CHEFS CLEFS CLEFT FIEFS KEEFS REEFS REEFY THEFT

••E•F

SHEAF SHELF

•••EF

BRIEF CHIEF GANEF GRIEF THIEF UNREF

EG•••

EGEAN EGEST EGGAR EGGED EGGER EGRET EGYPT

E•G••

EAGER EAGLE EAGRE EDGAR EDGED EDGES EGGAR EGGED EGGER EIGHT ELGAR ELGIN ERGOT

E••G•

ELEGY

E•••G

EKING EWING EYING

•EG••

AEGIR AEGIS BEGAN BEGAT BEGET BEGIN BEGOT BEGUM BEGUN DEGAS DEGUM HEGEL LEGAL LEGER LEGES LEGGY LEGIT MEGAL MEGAN NEGEV NEGRO NEGUS PEGGY REGAL REGAN REGES REGIN REGMA SEGNI SEGNO SEGOS

YEGGS

•E•G•
BEIGE
BELGA
BERGS
DEIGN
FEIGN
HEDGE
HEDGY
HELGA
KEDGE
LEDGE
LEDGY
LEGGY
LEIGH
MERGE
NEIGH
PEGGY
PENGO
REIGN
SEDGE
SEDGY
SERGE
VERGE
WEDGE
WEDGY
WEIGH
YEGGS

•E••G
BEFOG
BEING
DEBUG
TELEG

••EG•
DIEGO
DREGS
ELEGY
GREGO
GREGS
LIEGE
OMEGA
PLEGY
SIEGE
SKEGS

•••EG
GRIEG
TELEG
UNPEG

E•H••
ECHIN
EPHAH
EPHOD
EPHOR
ESHER
ETHAN
ETHEL
ETHER
ETHIC
ETHNO
ETHOS
ETHYL

E••H•
EIGHT
ELIHU

E•••H
EARTH
EDITH
ENOCH
EPHAH
EPOCH
ERICH

•EH••
JEHUS
LEHRS
LEHUA
NEHRU
TEHEE

•E•H•
BETHS
DELHI
LETHE
MESHY
METHO
NEPHO
NEPHR
SETHS
TECHN
TETHS

•E••H
BEACH
BEECH
BELCH
BENCH
BERTH
DEATH
DEPTH
FETCH
HEATH
KEDAH
KEITH
KENCH
KERCH
KETCH
LEACH
LEASH
LEECH
LEIGH
NEATH
NEIGH
PEACH
PERCH
PERTH
REACH
REICH
RETCH
SELAH
TEACH
TEETH
TENCH
TENTH
VETCH
WEIGH
WELCH
WELSH
WENCH

••EH•
FOEHN

••E•H
ALEPH
BEECH
CHETH
CZECH
DOETH
FLESH
FRESH
LEECH
STETH
TEETH

•••EH
HOPEH
HUPEH

EI•••
EIDER
EIGHT

E•I••
EDICT
EDIES
EDIFY
EDILE
EDINA
EDITH
EDITS
EKING
ELIAS
ELIDE
ELIHU
ELIOT
ELISE
ELITE
ELIZA
EMILE
EMILS
EMILY
EMIRS
EMITS
ENIDS
EPICS
ERICA
ERICH
ERICS
ERIES
ERIKA
ERIKS
EVICT
EVILS
EVITA
EWING
EXILE
EXIST
EXITS
EYING

E••I•
EADIE
ECHIN
EDDIC
EDDIE
EDWIN
EERIE
EFFIE
ELAIN
ELAIO
ELFIN
ELGIN
ELLIE
ELLIS
ELOIN
ELSIE
ELVIN
ELWIN
EMMIE
ENTIA
EOLIC
EOSIN
EQUIP
ERNIE
ERWIN
ESSIE
ETHIC
ETTIE
ETUIS
EYRIE

E•••I
ELEMI
ENNUI

•EI••
BEIGE
BEING
BEIRA
CEIBA
CEILS
DEICE
DEIFY
DEIGN
DEISM
DEIST
DEITY
FEIGN
FEINT
FEIST
HEIRS
HEIST
KEITH
LEIFS
LEIGH
LEILA
NEIGH
NEILS
REICH
REIFY
REIGN
REIMS
REINS
SEINE
SEISM
SEIZE
VEILS
VEINS
VEINY
WEIGH
WEIRD
WEIRS

•E•I•
AECIA
AEGIR
AEGIS
AEMIA
AERIE
AESIR
BEDIM
BEFIT
BEGIN
BELIE
BENIN
BEVIN
CECIL
CELIA
CELIE
CENIS
CERIA
CERIC
DEBIT
DECIM
DEFIS
DELIA
DEMIT
DENIM
DENIS
DEVIL
EERIE
FECIT
FELID
FELIX
FETID
GELID
GENIC
GENIE
GENII
GEOID
HELIC
HELIO
HELIX
HEMIA
HEMIC
HEMIN
KEPIS
KEVIN
LEGIT
LENIN
LENIS
LEPID
LEVIS
LEWIE
LEWIS
MEDIA
MEDIC
MEDIO
MELIC
MERIT
MESIC
METIS
NEVIL
PEKIN
PEPIN
PERIL
PERIS
PETIT
PEWIT
REDID
REFIT
REGIN
RELIC
REMIT
RENIN
RESIN
RETIA
SEPIA
SERIF
SERIN
TELIC
TEPID
VEDIC
VESIC
VEXIL
XENIA
XERIC
YETIS

•E••I
CENTI
CESTI
DELHI
DENTI
FEBRI
FERMI
FERRI
GENII
HENRI
MERCI
NEURI
PELVI
PENNI
PETRI
PETTI
RECTI
SEGNI
SEPTI
SERAI
TEMPI
TERRI
VERDI
VERMI

••EI•
AREIC
OLEIC
OLEIN
ONEIR
SHEIK
SKEIN
STEIN
THEIR
TIEIN

••E•I
ADENI
BREVI
CHEMI
ELEMI
FLEXI
UTERI

•••EI
AUREI
ISSEI
KIBEI
NISEI
PILEI

EJ•••
EJECT

E•J••
ENJOY

•EJ••
HEJAZ

•E•J•
BENJY

EK•••
EKING

E•K••
ESKER

E••K•
ERIKA
ERIKS
EVOKE

•EK••
DEKED
DEKES
HEKLA
HEKTO
PEKAN
PEKIN
PEKOE
WEKAS
ZEKES

•E•K•
BEAKS
BECKS
BECKY
DECKS
DESKS
GECKO
GECKS
GEEKS
JERKS
JERKY
KECKS
LEAKS
LEAKY
LEEKS
LEUKO
NECKS
PEAKS
PECKS
PEEKS
PERKS
PERKY
PESKY
REEKS
REEKY
SEEKS
TEAKS
WEEKS
YELKS

•E••K
DEREK

••EK•
GEEKS
LEEKS
PEEKS
REEKS
REEKY
SEEKS
TREKS
WEEKS

••E•K
ALECK
APEAK
BLEAK
BREAK
CHECK
CHEEK
CLERK
CREAK
CREEK
FLECK
FREAK
GREEK
SHEIK
SLEEK
SNEAK
SPEAK
SPECK
STEAK
TWEAK
VNECK
WHELK
WREAK
WRECK

•••EK
CAPEK
CHEEK

5

CREEK
DEREK
GREEK
KOPEK
SAMEK
SLEEK

EL•••
ELAEO
ELAIN
ELAIO
ELAND
ELATE
ELBOW
ELDER
ELECT
ELEGY
ELEMI
ELENA
ELFIN
ELGAR
ELGIN
ELIAS
ELIDE
ELIHU
ELIOT
ELISE
ELITE
ELIZA
ELLAS
ELLEN
ELLIE
ELLIS
ELMAN
ELMER
ELOIN
ELOPE
ELSAS
ELSIE
ELTON
ELUDE
ELVAS
ELVER
ELVES
ELVIN
ELWIN

E•L••
ECLAT
ELLAS
ELLEN
ELLIE
ELLIS
EOLIC
EULER

E••L•
EAGLE
EARLE
EARLS
EARLY
ECOLE
EDILE
EMILE
EMILS
EMILY
ENOLS
EVILS
EXALT
EXILE
EXULT

E•••L
EASEL
EQUAL
ETHEL
ETHYL
EXCEL
EXPEL
EXTOL

•EL••
BELAY
BELCH
BELEM
BELGA
BELIE
BELLA
BELLE
BELLS
BELLY
BELOW
BELTS
CELIA
CELIE
CELLA
CELLO
CELLS
CELOM
CELTS
DELAY
DELED
DELES
DELFT
DELHI
DELIA
DELLA
DELLS
DELOS
DELTA
DELVE
FELID
FELIX
FELLS
FELLY
FELON
FELTS
GELDS
GELID
HELEN
HELGA
HELIC
HELIO
HELIX
HELLE
HELLO
HELLS
HELMS
HELOT
HELPS
HELVE
JELLO
JELLS
JELLY
KELPS
MELAN
MELDS
MELEE
MELIC
MELON
MELTS
NELLS
NELLY
PELEE
PELFS
PELLA
PELLY
PELON
PELTS
PELVI
RELAX
RELAY
RELIC
SELAH
SELEN
SELLS
SELMA
TELAE
TELEG
TELEO
TELEX
TELIC
TELLS
TELLY
VELAR
VELDS
VELDT
VELUM
WELCH
WELDS
WELLS
WELSH
WELTS
YELKS
YELLS
YELPS

•E•L•
BELLA
BELLE
BELLS
BELLY
BEULA
CEILS
CELLA
CELLO
CELLS
DEALS
DEALT
DELLA
DELLS
FEELS
FELLS
FELLY
HEALS
HEELS
HEKLA
HELLE
HELLO
HELLS
HERLS
JELLO
JELLS
JELLY
KEELS
LEILA
MEALS
MEALY
MERLE
MEWLS
NEALS
NEILS
NELLS
NELLY
NEWLY
PEALS
PEELS
PELLA
PELLY
PEPLA
REALM
REALS
REDLY
REELS
REPLY
SEALS
SELLS
TEALS
TELLS
TELLY
TESLA
VEILS
WEALD
WEALS
WELLS
WETLY
YELLS

•E••L
BERYL
BETEL
BEVEL
BEZEL
CECAL
CECIL
CEORL
DECAL
DEDAL
DEVIL
FECAL
FERAL
FETAL
HEGEL
HEMAL
HEXYL
JEWEL
KEVEL
LEGAL
LEVEL
MEDAL
MEGAL
METAL
NEPAL
NEVIL
NEWEL
PEARL
PEDAL
PENAL
PERIL
PETAL
REBEL
REGAL
RENAL
REPEL
REVEL
SEOUL
SEPAL
SERAL
VENAL
VEXIL

••EL•
ABELE
ABELS
ADELA
ADELE
CHELA
COELE
COELO
DUELS
DWELL
DWELT
FEELS
FIELD
FJELD
FUELS
GAELS
HEELS
JOELS
KEELS
KNELL
KNELT
KOELS
MYELO
NOELS
PEELS
PYELO
QUELL
REELS
SHELF
SHELL
SMELL
SMELT
SNELL
SPELL
SPELT
STELE
SWELL
TAELS
WHELK
WHELM
WHELP
WIELD
YIELD

••E•L
AREAL
CREEL
DWELL
IDEAL
ILEAL
KNEEL
KNELL
QUELL
SHELL
SHEOL
SMELL
SNELL
SPELL
STEAL
STEEL
SWELL
UREAL
UVEAL
WHEAL
WHEEL

•••EL
ABIEL
ACCEL
AMIEL
ANGEL
ANSEL
APPEL
ARIEL
ARTEL
BABEL
BAGEL
BASEL
BETEL
BEVEL
BEZEL
BOWEL
CAMEL
CREEL
CRUEL
CUPEL
DOWEL
EASEL
ETHEL
EXCEL
EXPEL
FIDEL
FUSEL
GAVEL
GIMEL
GRUEL
HAZEL
HEGEL
HOTEL
HOVEL
IMPEL
JEWEL
JUREL
KEVEL
KNEEL
LABEL
LAPEL
LEVEL
LIBEL
MABEL
MODEL
MOREL
MOTEL
NAVEL
NEWEL
NIGEL
NOBEL
NOVEL
ORIEL
OUSEL
OUZEL
PANEL
PINEL
RATEL
RAVEL
REBEL
REPEL
REVEL
RIGEL
ROWEL
SOREL
SPIEL
STEEL
TOWEL
UMBEL
URIEL
VOWEL
WHEEL
YODEL
YOKEL

EM•••
EMBAR
EMBAY
EMBED
EMBER
EMBOW
EMBRY
EMCEE
EMDEN
EMEER
EMEND
EMERY
EMEUS
EMILE
EMILS
EMILY
EMIRS
EMITS
EMMAS
EMMER
EMMET
EMMIE
EMMYS
EMORY
EMOTE
EMPTY

E•M••
ELMAN
ELMER
EMMAS
EMMER
EMMET
EMMIE
EMMYS
ERMAS

E••M•
EDEMA
ELEMI
ENEMA
ENEMY
ETYMA
EXAMS

E•••M
ENTOM
EPSOM

•EM••
AEMIA
DEMES
DEMIT
DEMOB
DEMON
DEMOS
DEMUR
FEMES
FEMME
FEMTO
FEMUR
GEMMA
GEMMY
GEMOT
HEMAL
HEMAN
HEMAT
HEMEN
HEMIA
HEMIC
HEMIN
HEMPS
HEMPY
JEMMY
LEMMA
LEMON
LEMUR
MEMOS
NEMAT
REMAN
REMEX
REMIT
REMUS
SEMEN
TEMPE
TEMPI
TEMPO
TEMPT
YEMEN

•E•M•
BEAMS
BEAMY
BERME
BERMS
DEEMS
DERMA
DERMO
FEMME
FERMI
GEMMA
GEMMY
GERMS
HELMS
HERMA
JEMMY
LEMMA
NEUME
REAMS
REGMA
REIMS
SEAMS
SEAMY
SEEMS
SELMA
TEAMS
TEEMS
TERMS
VERMI
WEEMS

•E••M
BEDIM
BEGUM
BELEM
BESOM
CECUM
CELOM
CERAM
DECIM
DEGUM
DEISM
DENIM
REALM
REARM
RETEM
SEBUM
SEDUM
SEISM
SERUM
VELUM
VENOM

••EM•
ANEMO
CHEMI
CHEMO
CLEMS
CREME
DEEMS
EDEMA
ELEMI
ENEMA
ENEMY
ITEMS
POEMS
SEEMS
STEMS
TEEMS
THEME
ULEMA
WEEMS

••E•M
ABEAM
ADEEM
BREAM
CREAM
DREAM
FLEAM
GLEAM
HBEAM
IBEAM
ILEUM
ODEUM
PNEUM
RHEUM
SPERM
STEAM
THERM
WHELM
ZBEAM

•••EM
ADEEM
BELEM
GOLEM
HAREM
PROEM
RETEM
SALEM
TOTEM
XYLEM
YQUEM

EN•••
ENACT
ENATE
ENCYC
ENDED
ENDOW
ENDUE
ENEAS
ENEMA
ENEMY
ENIDS
ENJOY
ENNEA
ENNUI
ENOCH
ENOLS
ENSUE
ENTER
ENTIA
ENTOM
ENTRY
ENVOY

E•N••
EDNAS
ENNEA
ENNUI
ERNES
ERNIE
ERNST
ETNAS

E••N•
EARNS
EBONS
EBONY
EDINA
EKING
ELAND
ELENA
EMEND
ETHNO
EVANS
EVENS
EVENT
EWING
EYING

E•••N
EATEN
ECHIN
EDWIN
EGEAN
ELAIN
ELFIN
ELGIN
ELLEN
ELMAN
ELOIN
ELTON
ELVIN
ELWIN
EMDEN
EOSIN
ERWIN
ESSEN
ETHAN

•EN••
BENCH
BENDS
BENDY
BENES
BENET
BENIN
BENJY
BENNE
BENNY
BENUE
CENIS
CENSE
CENTI
CENTO
CENTR
CENTS
DENDR
DENEB
DENES
DENIM
DENIS
DENNY
DENSE
DENTI
DENTO
DENTS
DENYS
FENCE
FENDS
FENNY
GENES
GENET
GENIC
GENIE
GENII
GENOA
GENRE
GENRO
GENTS
GENUA
GENUS
HENCE
HENNA
HENRI
HENRY
JENNY
KENCH
KENNY
KENTS
KENYA
LENAS
LENDS
LENES
LENIN
LENIS
LENNY
LENOS
LENTO
LENTS
MENDS
MENES
MENSA
MENUS
PENAL
PENCE
PENDS
PENGO
PENNA
PENNI
PENNY
PENTA
RENAL
RENAN
RENDS
RENEE
RENES
RENEW
RENIN
RENTE
RENTS
SENDS
SENNA
SENOR
SENSE
TENCH
TENDS
TENET
TENON
TENOR
TENSE
TENTH
TENTS
VENAE
VENAL
VENDS
VENOM
VENTS
VENUE
VENUS
WENCH
WENDS
WENDY
WENNY
XENIA
XENON

•E•N•
AEONS
BEANO
BEANS
BEING
BENNE
BENNY
BERNE
DEANE
DEANS
DENNY
FEINT
FENNY
FERNS
FERNY
HENNA
JEANS
JENNY
KEENS
KENNY
KERNS
LEANS
LEANT
LENNY
LEONA
LEONS
MEANS
MEANT
MEANY
MESNE
PEANS
PEENS
PENNA
PENNI
PENNY
PEONS
PEONY
REINS
SEANS
SEGNI
SEGNO
SEINE
SENNA
TEENS
TEENY
TERNS
VEINS
VEINY
VERNA
VERNE
VERNS
WEANS
WEENY
WENNY
YEANS

•E••N
BEGAN
BEGIN
BEGUN
BENIN
BETON
BEVIN
DEIGN
DEMON
DEVON
DEWAN
FEIGN
FELON
HELEN
HEMAN
HEMEN
HEMIN
HERON
KEVIN
LEARN
LEMON
LENIN
LEVEN
MEGAN
MELAN
MELON
MESON
PECAN
PEKAN
PEKIN
PELON
PEPIN
PERON
REDAN
REGAN
REGIN
REIGN
REMAN
RENAN
RENIN
RERAN
RERUN
RESIN
SEDAN
SELEN
SEMEN
SERIN
SETON
SEVEN
TECHN
TENON
TETON
XENON
YEARN
YEMEN

••EN•
ADENI
ADENO
AGENT
AKENE
AMEND
AMENS
AMENT
ANENT
ARENA
ARENT
AVENS
BLEND
BLENT
BRENT
COENO
CTENO
DIENE
ELENA
EMEND
EVENS
EVENT
FIEND
FRENA
GHENT
GLENN
GLENS
GWENN
GWENS
HYENA
IRENE
KEENS
LIENS
MIENS
OMENS
OPENS
OVENS
OWENS
PEENS
PHENO
PLENA
SCEND
SCENE
SCENT
SPEND
SPENT
STENO
TEENS
TEENY
TREND
TRENT
ULENT
UPEND
WEENY
WHENS
WRENS

••E•N
ACEAN
CLEAN
CLEON
CREON
EGEAN
FOEHN
FREON
GLEAN
GLENN
GREEN
GWENN
OCEAN
ODEON
OLEIN
PAEAN
PAEON
PREEN
QUEAN
QUEEN
QUERN
SHEEN
SHEWN
SKEAN
SKEIN
STEIN
STERN
TIEIN
TWEEN

•••EN
ADMEN
AIKEN
ALDEN
ALIEN
ALLEN
ARDEN
ARPEN
ASHEN
ASPEN
AUDEN
AXMEN
BADEN
COZEN
DIZEN
DOYEN
DOZEN
EATEN
ELLEN
EMDEN
ESSEN
GALEN
GIVEN
GREEN
HAVEN
HELEN
HEMEN
HYMEN
IBSEN
ILMEN
KAREN
LADEN
LEVEN
LIKEN

LIMEN
LINEN
LIVEN
LODEN
LUMEN
NUMEN
OAKEN
OATEN
OFTEN
OLDEN
PAPEN
PAREN
PATEN
PHREN
PREEN
QUEEN
RAVEN
RIPEN
RISEN
RIVEN
ROUEN
ROWEN
RUMEN
SELEN
SEMEN
SEVEN
SHEEN
SIREN
SPHEN
SPLEN
TAKEN
TOKEN
TWEEN
VIMEN
VIXEN
WAKEN
WAXEN
WIDEN
WIZEN
WODEN
WOKEN
WOMEN
WOVEN
YAMEN
YEMEN

EO•••
EOLIC
EOSIN

E•O••
EBOAT
EBONS
EBONY
ECOLE
ELOIN
ELOPE
EMORY
EMOTE
ENOCH
ENOLS
EPOCH
EPODE
EPOXY
ERODE
EROSE
EVOKE

E••O•
ELBOW
ELIOT
ELTON
EMBOW
ENDOW
ENJOY
ENTOM
ENVOY
EPHOD
EPHOR
EPSOM
ERGOT
ERROR
ESTOP
ETHOS
EXTOL

E•••O
ELAEO
ELAIO
ERATO
ETHNO

•EO••
AEONS
CEORL
DEOXY
FEODS
FEOFF
GEODE
GEOID
LEONA
LEONS
LEORA
MEOWS
PEONS
PEONY
SEOUL

•E•O•
AESOP
BEBOP
BEFOG
BEGOT
BELOW
BESOM
BESOT
BETON
CELOM
CEROS
DECOR
DECOY
DEFOE
DELOS
DEMOB
DEMON
DEMOS
DEPOT
DEVON
FEDOR
FELON
FETOR
GEMOT
GENOA
HELOT
HEROD
HERON
LEMON
LENOS
LEROY
MEDOC
MELON
MEMOS
MEROE
MESON
NEROS
PECOS
PEKOE
PELON
PEPOS
PERON
PESOS
SEGOS
SENOR
SEPOY
SEROW
SETON
TENON
TENOR
TETON
VENOM
XENON
XEROX
ZEROS

•E••O
BEANO
CELLO
CENTO
DENTO
DERMO
FEMTO
FERRO
GECKO
GENRO
GESSO
HECTO
HEKTO
HELIO
HELLO
JELLO
LENTO
LEPTO
LEUCO
LEUKO
MEDIO
METHO
METRO
MEZZO
NECRO
NEGRO
NEPHO
NEURO
PEDRO
PENGO
PETRO
PETTO
RECTO
RETRO
SEATO
SECCO
SEGNO
SEPTO
SERVO
SETTO
TELEO
TEMPO
VERSO

••EO•
CLEON
CREON
FREON
ODEON
PAEON
SHEOL

••E•O
ACETO
ADENO
ANEMO
CHEMO
COELO
COENO
CREDO
CTENO
DIEGO
GRECO
GREGO
HIERO
HYETO
MYELO
PAEDO
PHENO
PIEZO
PTERO
PYELO
STENO
UREDO
UTERO

•••EO
CAMEO
ELAEO
HOMEO
JUDEO
MATEO
OSTEO
PALEO
RODEO
ROMEO
TELEO
VIDEO
VIREO

EP•••
EPACT
EPEES
EPHAH
EPHOD
EPHOR
EPICS
EPOCH
EPODE
EPOXY
EPSOM

E•P••
EMPTY
EXPEL

E••P•
EGYPT
ELOPE
ERUPT
ETAPE

E•••P
EQUIP
ESTOP

•EP••
DEPOT
DEPTH
HEPAT
HEPTA
KEPIS
LEPER
LEPID
LEPSY
LEPTA
LEPTO
LEPUS
NEPAL
NEPHO
NEPHR
PEPIN
PEPLA
PEPOS
PEPPY
PEPYS
REPAY
REPEL
REPLY
SEPAL
SEPIA
SEPOY
SEPTA
SEPTI
SEPTO
SEPTS
TEPEE
TEPID

•E•P•
BEEPS
DEEPS
HEAPS
HELPS
HEMPS
HEMPY
JEEPS
KEEPS
KELPS
LEAPS
LEAPT
NEAPS
PEEPS
PEPPY
REAPS
SEEPS
TEMPE
TEMPI
TEMPO
TEMPT
WEEPS
WEEPY
YELPS

•E••P
AESOP
BEBOP
GETUP
LETUP
RECAP
SETUP

••EP•
ADEPT
ALEPH
BEEPS
CREPE
CREPT
DEEPS
INEPT
JEEPS
KEEPS
PEEPS
SEEPS
SKEPS
SLEPT
STEPS
SWEPT
WEEPS
WEEPY

••E•P
CHEAP
CHEEP
CREEP
SHEEP
SLEEP
STEEP
SWEEP
TIEUP
TWERP
WHELP

•••EP
CHEEP
CREEP
JULEP
SALEP
SHEEP
SLEEP
STEEP
SWEEP

EQ•••
EQUAL
EQUIP

E•Q••
ESQUE

ER•••
ERASE
ERATO
ERECT
ERGOT
ERICA
ERICH
ERICS
ERIES
ERIKA
ERIKS
ERMAS
ERNES
ERNIE
ERNST
ERODE
EROSE
ERRED
ERROR
ERSES
ERUCT
ERUPT
ERWIN

E•R••
EARED
EARLE
EARLS
EARLY
EARNS
EARTH
EDRED
EERIE
EGRET
ERRED
ERROR
EURUS
EYRAS
EYRIE
EZRAS

E••R•
EAGRE
EMBRY
EMERY
EMIRS
EMORY
ENTRY
EVERT
EVERY
EWERS
EXERT
EXTRA
EXURB

E•••R
EAGER
EATER
EDGAR
EGGAR
EGGER
EIDER
ELDER
ELGAR
ELMER
ELVER
EMBAR
EMBER
EMEER
EMMER
ENTER
EPHOR
ERROR
ESHER
ESKER
ESTER
ETHER
EULER

•ER••
AERIE
BERET
BERGS
BERME
BERMS
BERNE
BERRY
BERTA
BERTH
BERTS
BERTY
BERYL
CERAM
CERAT
CERED
CERES
CERIA
CERIC
CEROS
DERBY
DEREK
DERMA
DERMO
DERRY
EERIE
FERAL
FERMI
FERNS
FERNY
FERRI
FERRO
FERRY
GERDA
GERMS
GERRY
GERTY
HERAT
HERBS
HERBY

HERDS
HERLS
HERMA
HEROD
HERON
HERTZ
JEREZ
JERKS
JERKY
JERRY
KERAT
KERBS
KERCH
KERES
KERFS
KERNS
KERRY
LEROY
MERCI
MERCY
MERGE
MERIT
MERLE
MEROE
MERRY
NEROS
NERVE
NERVY
PERCH
PERCY
PERDU
PERES
PERIL
PERIS
PERKS
PERKY
PERON
PERRY
PERSE
PERTH
RERAN
RERUN
SERAC
SERAI
SERAL
SERBS
SERED
SERES
SERFS
SERGE
SERIF
SERIN
SEROW
SERRA
SERUM
SERVE
SERVO
TERAT
TERMS
TERNS
TERRA
TERRI
TERRY
TERSE
VERAS
VERBS
VERDI
VERGE
VERMI
VERNA
VERNE
VERNS
VERSE
VERSO
VERST
VERTU
VERVE
XERIC
XEROX
XERUS
YERBA
ZEROS

•E•R•

BEARD
BEARS
BEERS
BEERY
BEIRA
BERRY
CEARA
CEORL
DEARS
DEARY
DECRY
DERRY
FEARS
FEBRI
FERRI
FERRO
FERRY
GEARS
GENRE
GENRO
GERRY
HEARD
HEARS
HEART
HEIRS
HENRI
HENRY
JEERS
JERRY
JEWRY
KERRY
LEARN
LEERS
LEERY
LEHRS
LEORA
MERRY
METRO
METRY
NEARS
NECRO
NEGRO
NEHRU
NEURI
NEURO
PEARL
PEARS
PEARY
PEDRO
PEERS
PERRY
PETRI
PETRO
REARM
REARS
RETRO
RETRY
SEARS
SEERS
SERRA
TEARS
TEARY
TERRA
TERRI
TERRY
TETRA
VEERS
VEERY
WEARS
WEARY
WEIRD
WEIRS
YEARN
YEARS
ZEBRA

•E••R

AEGIR
AESIR
CEDAR
CENTR
CESAR
DEBAR
DECOR
DEFER
DEMUR
DENDR
DETER
DEXTR
FEDOR
FEMUR
FETOR
FEUAR
FEVER
FEWER
HEWER
LEGER
LEMUR
LEPER
LEVER
METER
NEPHR
NEVER
NEWER
PETER
RECUR
REFER
SEDER
SENOR
SEVER
SEWER
TENOR
VELAR
VEXER
WEBER

••ER•

ACERB
ALERT
APERY
AVERS
AVERT
AVERY
BEERS
BEERY
BIERS
BOERS
CHERT
CLERK
DOERS
DYERS
EMERY
EVERT
EVERY
EWERS
EXERT
FIERY
FRERE
GOERS
HIERO
HOERS
INERT
ISERE
JEERS
KIERS
LEERS
LEERY
OMERS
ONERY
OPERA
OVERT
OYERS
PEERS
PIERS
PTERO
QUERN
QUERY
RUERS
SEERS
SHERD
SPERM
STERE
STERN
SUERS
THERE
THERM
TIERS
TWERP
USERS
UTERI
UTERO
VEERS
VEERY
WHERE

••E•R

ANEAR
BLEAR
CHEER
CLEAR
DREAR
EMEER
FLEER
FREER
ONEIR
QUEER
SHEAR
SHEER
SIEUR
SMEAR
SNEER
SPEAR
STEER
SWEAR
THEIR

•••ER

ABLER
ABNER
ADDER
ADLER
AFTER
AGGER
AIDER
ALDER
ALGER
ALTER
AMBER
ANGER
ARTER
ASHER
ASKER
ASPER
ASTER
AUGER
BABER
BAKER
BALER
BARER
BITER
BLUER
BONER
BORER
BOWER
BOXER
BRIER
BUBER
BUYER
CABER
CANER
CAPER
CARER
CATER
CHEER
CIDER
COMER
COOER
CORER
COVER
COWER
CRIER
CURER
CUTER
DARER
DATER
DEFER
DETER
DICER
DIKER
DIMER
DINER
DIRER
DIVER
DOSER
DOTER
DOVER
DOWER
DRIER
DRYER
DUPER
DURER
EAGER
EATER
EGGER
EIDER
ELDER
ELMER
ELVER
EMBER
EMEER
EMMER
ENTER
ESHER
ESKER
ESTER
ETHER
EULER
FACER
FAKER
FARER
FEVER
FEWER
FIBER
FIFER
FILER
FINER
FIRER
FIVER
FIXER
FLEER
FLIER
FLYER
FOYER
FREER
FRIER
FRYER
GAGER
GAPER
GAYER
GAZER
GIBER
GIVER
GONER
HALER
HATER
HAZER
HEWER
HIDER
HIKER
HIRER
HOMER
HOVER
HUGER
HYPER
ICIER
IDLER
INFER
INKER
INNER
INTER
JOKER
KHMER
LAGER
LAKER
LAMER
LASER
LATER
LAVER
LAXER
LAYER
LEGER
LEPER
LEVER
LIBER
LIFER
LINER
LITER
LIVER
LONER
LOPER
LOSER
LOVER
LOWER
LUGER
LURER
MACER
MAKER
MASER
MAZER
METER
MILER
MIMER
MINER
MISER
MITER
MIXER
MOPER
MOVER
MOWER
NADER
NAMER
NEVER
NEWER
NICER
NIGER
NITER
NOTER
OCHER
ODDER
OFFER
OGLER
OILER
OLDER
OMBER
ORDER
ORMER
OSIER
OSLER
OTHER
OTTER
OUTER
OWNER
PACER
PALER
PAPER
PARER
PATER
PAVER
PAWER
PAYER
PETER
PIKER
PINER
PIPER
PLIER
POKER
POSER
POWER
PRIER
PRYER
PULER
PURER
QUEER
RACER
RAKER
RARER
RATER
RAVER
RAWER
REFER
RICER
RIDER
RIMER
RIPER
RISER
RIVER
ROGER
ROVER
ROWER
RUDER
RULER
SABER
SAFER
SAGER
SAKER
SANER
SAVER
SAWER

SAYER
SEDER
SEVER
SEWER
SHEER
SHIER
SHOER
SHYER
SIDER
SKIER
SLIER
SLYER
SNEER
SOBER
SORER
SOWER
SPIER
STEER
SUMER
SUPER
SURER
TAKER
TALER
TAMER
TAPER
TAWER
TAXER
TIBER
TIGER
TILER
TIMER
TITER
TONER
TOPER
TOTER
TOWER
TOYER
TRIER
TRUER
TUBER
TUNER
TYLER
UDDER
ULCER
UMBER
UNDER
UPPER
USHER
UTHER
UTTER
VEXER
VILER
VIPER
VOMER
VOTER
VOWER
WADER
WAFER
WAGER
WALER
WATER
WAVER
WEBER
WIDER
WIPER
WIRER
WISER
WIVER
WOOER
WRIER
WRYER
YAGER

ES•••

ESHER
ESKER
ESQUE
ESSAY
ESSEN
ESSES
ESSEX
ESSIE
ESTER
ESTOP

E•S••

EASED
EASEL
EASES
ELSAS
ELSIE
ENSUE
EOSIN
EPSOM
ERSES
ESSAY
ESSEN
ESSES
ESSEX
ESSIE

E••S•

EGEST
ELISE
ERASE
ERNST
EROSE
EXIST

E•••S

EARLS
EARNS
EASES
EAVES
EBONS
EDDAS
EDGES
EDIES
EDITS
EDNAS
ELIAS
ELLAS
ELLIS
ELSAS
ELVAS
ELVES
EMEUS
EMILS
EMIRS
EMITS
EMMAS
EMMYS
ENEAS
ENIDS
ENOLS
EPEES
EPICS
ERICS
ERIES
ERIKS
ERMAS
ERNES
ERSES
ESSES
ETHOS
ETNAS
ETTAS
ETUIS
EURUS
EVANS
EVENS
EVILS
EWERS
EXAMS
EXECS
EXITS
EYRAS
EZRAS

•ES••

AESIR
AESOP
BESET
BESOM
BESOT
BESSY
BESTS
CESAR
CESTI
DESEX
DESKS
FESSE
GESSO
JESSE
JESSY
JESTS
JESUS
MESAS
MESHY
MESIC
MESNE
MESON
MESSY
NESTS
PESKY
PESOS
PESTS
RESET
RESIN
RESTS
TESLA
TESTA
TESTS
TESTY
VESIC
VESTA
VESTS
YESES
ZESTS
ZESTY

•E•S•

BEAST
BESSY
BETSY
CEASE
CENSE
DEISM
DEIST
DENSE
FEASE
FEAST
FEIST
FESSE
GEESE
GEEST
GESSO
HEIST
JESSE
JESSY
LEASE
LEASH
LEAST
LEPSY
MENSA
MESSY
MEUSE
NEWSY
PEASE
PERSE
SEISM
SENSE
TEASE
TENSE
TERSE
VERSE
VERSO
VERST
WEEST
WELSH
YEAST

•E••S

AEDES
AEGIS
AEONS
BEADS
BEAKS
BEAMS
BEANS
BEARS
BEATS
BEAUS
BECKS
BEEFS
BEEPS
BEERS
BEETS
BELLS
BELTS
BENDS
BENES
BERGS
BERMS
BERTS
BESTS
BETAS
BETHS
CEDES
CEILS
CELLS
CELTS
CENIS
CENTS
CERES
CEROS
CETUS
DEALS
DEANS
DEARS
DEBTS
DECKS
DEEDS
DEEMS
DEEPS
DEFIS
DEGAS
DEKES
DELES
DELLS
DELOS
DEMES
DEMOS
DENES
DENIS
DENTS
DENYS
DESKS
DEVAS
FEARS
FEATS
FECES
FEEDS
FEELS
FELLS
FELTS
FEMES
FENDS
FEODS
FERNS
FETES
FETUS
FEUDS
GEARS
GECKS
GEEKS
GELDS
GENES
GENTS
GENUS
GERMS
HEADS
HEALS
HEAPS
HEARS
HEATS
HEEDS
HEELS
HEFTS
HEIRS
HELLS
HELMS
HELPS
HEMPS
HERBS
HERDS
HERLS
HEXES
JEANS
JEEPS
JEERS
JEFES
JEFFS
JEHUS
JELLS
JERKS
JESTS
JESUS
KEATS
KECKS
KEEFS
KEELS
KEENS
KEEPS
KELPS
KENTS
KEPIS
KERBS
KERES
KERFS
KERNS
LEADS
LEAFS
LEAKS
LEANS
LEAPS
LEEKS
LEERS
LEETS
LEFTS
LEGES
LEHRS
LEIFS
LENAS
LENDS
LENES
LENIS
LENOS
LENTS
LEONS
LEPUS
LETTS
LEUDS
LEVIS
LEWIS
MEADS
MEALS
MEANS
MEATS
MEETS
MELDS
MELTS
MEMOS
MENDS
MENES
MENUS
MEOWS
MESAS
METAS
METES
METIS
MEWLS
NEALS
NEAPS
NEARS
NECKS
NEEDS
NEGUS
NEILS
NELLS
NEROS
NESTS
NEVUS
NEWTS
NEXUS
PEAKS
PEALS
PEANS
PEARS
PEATS
PECKS
PECOS
PEDES
PEEKS
PEELS
PEENS
PEEPS
PEERS
PELFS
PELTS
PENDS
PEONS
PEPOS
PEPYS
PERES
PERIS
PERKS
PESOS
PESTS
PETES
READS
REALS
REAMS
REAPS
REARS
REBUS
REEDS
REEFS
REEKS
REELS
REGES
REIMS
REINS
REMUS
RENDS
RENES
RENTS
RESTS
SEALS
SEAMS
SEANS
SEARS
SEATS
SECTS
SEEDS
SEEKS
SEEMS
SEEPS
SEERS
SEGOS
SELLS
SENDS
SEPTS
SERBS
SERES
SERFS
SETHS
SEXES
TEAKS
TEALS
TEAMS
TEARS
TEATS
TEEMS
TEENS
TELLS
TENDS
TENTS
TERMS
TERNS
TESTS
TETHS
TEXAS
TEXTS
VEERS
VEILS
VEINS
VELDS
VENDS
VENTS
VENUS
VERAS
VERBS
VERNS
VESTS
VEXES
WEALS
WEANS
WEARS
WEEDS
WEEKS
WEEMS

WEEPS
WEFTS
WEIRS
WEKAS
WELDS
WELLS
WELTS
WENDS
XERUS
YEANS
YEARS
YEATS
YEGGS
YELKS
YELLS
YELPS
YESES
YETIS
ZEBUS
ZEKES
ZEROS
ZESTS
ZETAS

••ES•

BLESS
BLEST
BREST
CHESS
CHEST
CRESC
CRESS
CREST
DOEST
DRESS
DREST
EGEST
FLESH
FRESH
GEESE
GEEST
GUESS
GUEST
LOESS
OBESE
POESY
PRESA
PRESS
PREST
QUEST
THESE
TRESS
WEEST
WREST

••E•S

ABELS
ABETS
ALECS
ALEFS
AMENS
AREAS
AVENS
AVERS
BEEFS
BEEPS
BEERS
BEETS
BIERS
BLEBS
BLESS
BMEWS
BOERS
BREWS
CHEFS
CHESS
CHETS
CHEWS
CLEFS
CLEMS
CLEWS
COEDS
CREES
CRESS
CREWS
DEEDS
DEEMS
DEEPS
DIETS
DOERS
DREGS
DRESS
DREWS
DUELS
DUETS
DYERS
EMEUS
ENEAS
EPEES
EVENS
EWERS
EXECS
FEEDS
FEELS
FIEFS
FLEAS
FLEES
FLEWS
FREDS
FREES
FRETS
FUELS
GAELS
GEEKS
GLEDS
GLEES
GLENS
GOERS
GREGS
GREYS
GUESS
GWENS
HEEDS
HEELS
HOERS
IDEAS
ILEUS
ITEMS
JEEPS
JEERS
JOELS
JOEYS
KEEFS
KEELS
KEENS
KEEPS
KIERS
KNEES
KOELS
LEEKS
LEERS
LEETS
LIENS
LOESS
MEETS
MIENS
NEEDS
NOELS
OBEYS
ODETS
OGEES
OMENS
OMERS
OPENS
OVENS
OWENS
OYERS
PEEKS
PEELS
PEENS
PEEPS
PEERS
PIERS
PLEAS
PLEBS
POEMS
POETS
PRESS
PREYS
REEDS
REEFS
REEKS
REELS
RHEAS
RUERS
SEEDS
SEEKS
SEEMS
SEEPS
SEERS
SHEAS
SHEDS
SHEWS
SKEES
SKEGS
SKEPS
SKEWS
SLEDS
SLEWS
SMEWS
SPECS
SPEWS
STEMS
STEPS
STETS
STEWS
SUERS
TAELS
TEEMS
TEENS
THEWS
TIERS
TREAS
TREES
TREKS
TRESS
TREYS
TYEES
USERS
UVEAS
VEERS
VIEWS
WEEDS
WEEKS
WEEMS
WEEPS
WHENS
WHETS
WHEYS
WRENS

•••ES

ABBES
ABIES
ACHES
ACRES
ADZES
AEDES
AGNES
AGUES
AIDES
ALOES
AMIES
ANDES
ANNES
ANTES
APSES
ARIES
ARLES
ARSES
ASHES
ASSES
AURES
AXLES
BABES
BAKES
BALES
BARES
BASES
BATES
BENES
BICES
BIDES
BIKES
BILES
BINES
BISES
BITES
BLUES
BODES
BOLES
BONES
BORES
BOXES
BRAES
BUSES
BYRES
CADES
CAFES
CAGES
CAKES
CAMES
CANES
CAPES
CARES
CASES
CAVES
CEDES
CERES
CITES
CLUES
CODES
COKES
COLES
COMES
CONES
COPES
CORES
COTES
COVES
COXES
CREES
CRIES
CUBES
CURES
CYMES
DACES
DALES
DAMES
DANES
DARES
DATES
DAVES
DAZES
DEKES
DELES
DEMES
DENES
DIKES
DIMES
DINES
DIVES
DOGES
DOLES
DOMES
DOPES
DOSES
DOTES
DOVES
DOZES
DRIES
DUDES
DUKES
DUNES
DUPES
DYNES
EASES
EAVES
EDGES
EDIES
ELVES
EPEES
ERIES
ERNES
ERSES
ESSES
FACES
FADES
FAKES
FARES
FATES
FAXES
FAYES
FAZES
FECES
FEMES
FETES
FICES
FIFES
FILES
FINES
FIRES
FIVES
FIXES
FLEES
FLIES
FLOES
FLUES
FORES
FOXES
FREES
FRIES
FROES
FUMES
FUSES
FUZES
FYKES
GABES
GAGES
GALES
GAMES
GAPES
GASES
GATES
GAZES
GENES
GIBES
GILES
GIVES
GLEES
GLUES
GORES
GULES
GYRES
HADES
HAKES
HALES
HAMES
HARES
HATES
HAYES
HAZES
HEXES
HIDES
HIKES
HIRES
HIVES
HOLES
HOMES
HONES
HOPES
HOSES
IDLES
ISLES
IVIES
JADES
JAKES
JAMES
JANES
JAPES
JEFES
JIBES
JOKES
JOLES
JONES
JUBES
JUDES
JULES
JUNES
JUTES
KAMES
KATES
KERES
KIBES
KITES
KNEES
LACES
LADES
LAKES
LAMES
LANES
LARES
LAVES
LAZES
LEGES
LENES
LIKES
LIMES
LINES
LIVES
LOBES
LODES
LOGES
LOPES
LORES
LOSES
LOVES
LUCES
LUNES
LURES
LUTES
LUXES
LYLES
LYRES
LYSES
MACES
MAGES
MAKES
MALES
MANES
MARES
MATES
MAZES
MENES
METES
MIKES
MILES
MIMES
MINES
MIRES
MISES
MITES
MIXES
MLLES
MODES
MOKES
MOLES
MOPES
MORES
MOSES
MOTES
MOUES
MOVES
MULES
MUSES
MUTES
MYLES
NAMES
NAPES
NARES
NATES
NAVES
NIDES
NINES
NIXES
NODES
NONES
NOSES
NOTES
NUDES
OASES
OATES
OAVES
OBOES
OGEES
OGLES
OGRES
OKIES
OOZES
ORLES
PACES
PAGES

PALES
PANES
PARES
PATES
PAVES
PEDES
PERES
PETES
PIKES
PILES
PINES
PIPES
PLIES
POKES
POLES
POMES
PONES
POPES
PORES
POSES
PRIES
PUBES
PUCES
PUKES
PULES
PYRES
PYXES
RACES
RAGES
RAKES
RALES
RAPES
RATES
RAVES
RAZES
REGES
RENES
RICES
RIDES
RILES
RIMES
RISES
RITES
RIVES
ROBES
ROLES
ROPES
ROSES
ROUES
ROVES
RUBES
RULES
RUNES
RUSES
SABES
SAFES
SAGES
SAKES
SALES
SATES
SAVES
SAXES
SERES
SEXES
SHOES
SICES
SIDES
SINES
SIRES
SITES
SIXES
SIZES
SKEES
SKIES
SLOES
SLUES
SNYES
SOKES
SOLES
SONES
SORES
SPIES
STIES
SUPES
SYCES
TABES
TAKES
TALES
TAMES
TAPES
TARES
TAXES
TIDES
TILES
TIMES
TINES
TIRES
TOLES
TOMES
TONES
TOPES
TOTES
TREES
TRIES
TRUES
TUBES
TULES
TUNES
TYEES
TYKES
TYPES
URGES
VALES
VANES
VASES
VEXES
VIBES
VICES
VINES
VIRES
VISES
VOCES
VOLES
VOTES
WADES
WAGES
WAKES
WALES
WANES
WARES
WAVES
WAXES
WILES
WINES
WIPES
WIRES
WISES
WIVES
WRIES
XAXES
YAXES
YESES
YIPES
YOKES
YPRES
YULES
ZEKES
ZONES

ET•••

ETAPE
ETHAN
ETHEL
ETHER
ETHIC
ETHNO
ETHOS
ETHYL
ETNAS
ETTAS
ETTIE
ETUDE
ETUIS
ETYMA

E•T••

EATEN
EATER
ELTON
ENTER
ENTIA
ENTOM
ENTRY
ESTER
ESTOP
ETTAS
ETTIE
EXTOL
EXTRA

E••T•

EARTH
EDITH
EDITS
ELATE
ELITE
EMITS
EMOTE
EMPTY
ENATE
ERATO
EVITA
EXITS

E•••T

EBOAT
ECLAT
EDICT
EDUCT
EGEST
EGRET
EGYPT
EIGHT
EJECT
ELECT
ELIOT
EMMET
ENACT
EPACT
ERECT
ERGOT
ERNST
ERUCT
ERUPT
EVENT
EVERT
EVICT
EXACT
EXALT
EXERT
EXIST
EXULT

•ET••

AETAT
BETAS
BETEL
BETHS
BETON
BETSY
BETTE
BETTY
CETUS
DETER
FETAL
FETCH
FETED
FETES
FETID
FETOR
FETUS
GETUP
HETTY
JETTY
KETCH
LETHE
LETTS
LETTY
LETUP
METAL
METAS
METED
METER
METES
METHO
METIS
METRO
METRY
NETTY
PETAL
PETER
PETES
PETIT
PETRI
PETRO
PETTI
PETTO
PETTY
RETCH
RETEM
RETIA
RETRO
RETRY
RETTA
SETAE
SETHS
SETON
SETTO
SETUP
TETHS
TETON
TETRA
VETCH
WETLY
YETIS
ZETAS

•E•T•

BEATA
BEATS
BEETS
BELTS
BERTA
BERTH
BERTS
BERTY
BESTS
BETTE
BETTY
CELTS
CENTI
CENTO
CENTR
CENTS
CESTI
DEATH
DEBTS
DEITY
DELTA
DENTI
DENTO
DENTS
DEPTH
DEXTR
FEATS
FELTS
FEMTO
GENTS
GERTY
HEATH
HEATS
HECTO
HEFTS
HEFTY
HEKTO
HEPTA
HERTZ
HETTY
JESTS
JETTY
KEATS
KEITH
KENTS
LEETS
LEFTS
LEFTY
LENTO
LENTS
LEPTA
LEPTO
LETTS
LETTY
LEYTE
MEATS
MEATY
MEETS
MELTS
NEATH
NESTS
NETTY
NEWTS
PEATS
PEATY
PELTS
PENTA
PERTH
PESTS
PETTI
PETTO
PETTY
RECTA
RECTI
RECTO
RENTE
RENTS
RESTS
RETTA
SEATO
SEATS
SECTS
SEPTA
SEPTI
SEPTO
SEPTS
SETTO
TEATS
TEETH
TENTH
TENTS
TESTA
TESTS
TESTY
TEXTS
VENTS
VERTU
VESTA
VESTS
WEFTS
WELTS
YEATS
ZESTS
ZESTY

•E••T

AETAT
BEAST
BEAUT
BEFIT
BEGAT
BEGET
BEGOT
BENET
BERET
BESET
BESOT
CERAT
DEALT
DEBIT
DEBUT
DEIST
DELFT
DEMIT
DEPOT
FEAST
FECIT
FEINT
FEIST
GEEST
GEMOT
GENET
HEART
HEIST
HELOT
HEMAT
HEPAT
HERAT
KERAT
LEANT
LEAPT
LEAST
LEGIT
MEANT
MERIT
NEMAT
PETIT
PEWIT
REACT
REBUT
REFIT
REMIT
RESET
REVET
SEBAT
TEBET
TEMPT
TENET
TERAT
VELDT
VERST
WEEST
YEAST

••ET•

ABETS
ACETO
ARETE
BEETS
CHETH
CHETS
CRETE
DIETS
DOETH
DUETS
FRETS
GRETA
HYETO
LEETS
MEETS
ODETS
PIETA
PIETY
POETS
STETH
STETS
SUETY
TEETH
THETA
WHETS

••E•T

ADEPT
AGENT
ALERT
ALEUT
AMENT
ANENT
ARENT
AVERT
BLEAT
BLENT
BLEST
BRENT
BREST
CHEAT
CHERT
CHEST
CLEAT
CLEFT
CREPT
CREST
DOEST
DREST
DWELT
EGEST
EJECT
ELECT
ERECT
EVENT
EVERT
EXERT
FLEET
GEEST

GHENT
GLEET
GREAT
GREET
GUEST
INEPT
INERT
KNELT
LIEUT
OVERT
PLEAT
PREST
QUEST
SCENT
SHEET
SKEET
SLEET
SLEPT
SMELT
SPELT
SPENT
SWEAT
SWEET
SWEPT
THEFT
TREAT
TRENT
TWEET
ULENT
WEEST
WHEAT
WREST

•••ET
AGLET
ARMET
ASSET
BEGET
BENET
BERET
BESET
BIDET
BINET
BIZET
BLUET
CADET
CAPET
CARET
CHAET
CIVET
COMET
COVET
CRUET
CULET
EGRET
EMMET
FACET
FILET
FLEET
GENET
GLEET
GREET
INLET
INSET
ISLET
JANET
KAMET
LUNET
MANET
MONET
OCTET
ONSET
OWLET
PIPET
PUGET
QUIET
RESET
REVET
RIVET
SHEET
SKEET
SLEET
SWEET
TACET
TEBET
TENET
TIBET
TWEET
UPSET
VALET
ZIBET

EU•••
EULER
EURUS

E•U••
EDUCE
EDUCT
ELUDE
EQUAL
EQUIP
ERUCT
ERUPT
ETUDE
ETUIS
EXUDE
EXULT
EXURB

E••U•
EMEUS
ENDUE
ENNUI
ENSUE
ESQUE
EURUS

E•••U
ELIHU

•EU••
BEULA
DEUCE
FEUAR
FEUDS
FEUED
LEUCO
LEUDS
LEUKO
MEUSE
NEUME
NEURI
NEURO

•E•U•
BEAUS
BEAUT
BEAUX
BEGUM
BEGUN
BENUE
CECUM
CETUS
DEBUG
DEBUT
DEGUM
DEMUR
FEMUR
FETUS
GENUA
GENUS
GETUP
JEHUS
JESUS
LEHUA
LEMUR
LEPUS
LETUP
MENUS
NEGUS
NEVUS
NEXUS
REBUS
REBUT
RECUR
REMUS
RERUN
REVUE
SEBUM
SEDUM
SEOUL
SERUM
SETUP
VELUM
VENUE
VENUS
XERUS
ZEBUS

•E••U
NEHRU
PERDU
VERTU

••EU•
ALEUT
EMEUS
FREUD
ILEUM
ILEUS
LIEUT
ODEUM
PNEUM
PSEUD
QUEUE
RHEUM
SIEUR
TIEUP

•••EU
ADIEU
PAREU

EV•••
EVADE
EVANS
EVENS
EVENT
EVERT
EVERY
EVICT
EVILS
EVITA
EVOKE

E•V••
EAVES
ELVAS
ELVER
ELVES
ELVIN
ENVOY

•EV••
BEVEL
BEVIN
DEVAS
DEVIL
DEVON
FEVER
KEVEL
KEVIN
LEVEE
LEVEL
LEVEN
LEVER
LEVIS
NEVER
NEVIL
NEVUS
REVEL
REVET
REVUE
SEVEN
SEVER

•E•V•
DELVE
HEAVE
HEAVY
HELVE
KEEVE
LEAVE
LEAVY
NERVE
NERVY
PEAVY
PEEVE
PELVI
REEVE
SERVE
SERVO
VERVE
WEAVE

•E••V
NEGEV

••EV•
BREVE
BREVI
CHEVY
KEEVE
PEEVE
REEVE
SIEVE
STEVE

•••EV
NEGEV

EW•••
EWERS
EWING

E•W••
EDWIN
ELWIN
ERWIN

E•••W
ELBOW
EMBOW
ENDOW

•EW••
DEWAN
DEWED
DEWEY
FEWER
HEWED
HEWER
JEWEL
JEWRY
LEWIE
LEWIS
MEWED
MEWLS
NEWEL
NEWER
NEWLY
NEWSY
NEWTS
PEWEE
PEWIT
SEWED
SEWER

•E•W•
MEOWS

•E••W
BEDEW
BELOW
RENEW
SEROW

••EW•
BMEWS
BREWS
CHEWS
CHEWY
CLEWS
CREWE
CREWS
DREWS
FLEWS
SHEWN
SHEWS
SKEWS
SLEWS
SMEWS
SPEWS
STEWS
THEWS
THEWY
VIEWS
VIEWY

•••EW
ASKEW
BEDEW
RENEW
SCREW
SHREW
SINEW
STREW
THREW
UNMEW

EX•••
EXACT
EXALT
EXAMS
EXCEL
EXECS
EXERT
EXILE
EXIST
EXITS
EXPEL
EXTOL
EXTRA
EXUDE
EXULT
EXURB

E••X•
EPOXY

E•••X
ESSEX

•EX••
DEXTR
HEXAD
HEXED
HEXES
HEXYL
NEXUS
SEXED
SEXES
TEXAS
TEXTS
VEXED
VEXER
VEXES
VEXIL

•E•X•
DEOXY

•E••X
BEAUX
DESEX
FELIX
HELIX
RELAX
REMEX
TELEX
XEROX

••EX•
ALEXA
FLEXI
PREXY

•••EX
ANNEX
CIMEX
CODEX
DESEX
ESSEX
INDEX
LATEX
MUREX
PYREX
REMEX
SILEX
TELEX
UNSEX

EY•••
EYING
EYRAS
EYRIE

E•Y••
EGYPT
ETYMA

E••Y•
EMMYS
ENCYC
ETHYL

E•••Y
EARLY
EBONY
EDIFY
ELEGY
EMBAY
EMBRY
EMERY
EMILY
EMORY
EMPTY
ENEMY
ENJOY
ENTRY
ENVOY
EPOXY
ESSAY
EVERY

•EY••
KEYED
LEYTE

•E•Y•
BERYL
DENYS
HEXYL
KENYA
PEPYS

•E••Y
BEADY
BEAMY
BECKY
BEEFY
BEERY
BELAY
BELLY
BENDY
BENJY
BENNY
BERRY
BERTY
BESSY
BETSY
BETTY
DEARY
DEBBY
DECAY
DECOY
DECRY
DEIFY
DEITY
DELAY
DENNY
DEOXY
DERBY
DERRY
DEWEY
FELLY
FENNY
FERNY
FERRY
GEMMY

GERRY
GERTY
HEADY
HEAVY
HEDGY
HEFTY
HEMPY
HENRY
HERBY
HETTY
JELLY
JEMMY
JENNY
JERKY
JERRY
JESSY
JETTY
JEWRY
KENNY
KERRY
LEADY
LEAFY
LEAKY
LEAVY
LEDGY
LEERY
LEFTY
LEGGY
LENNY
LEPSY
LEROY
LETTY
MEALY
MEANY
MEATY
MERCY
MERRY
MESHY
MESSY
METRY
NEDDY
NEEDY
NELLY
NERVY
NETTY
NEWLY
NEWSY
PEARY
PEATY
PEAVY
PEGGY
PELLY
PENNY
PEONY
PEPPY
PERCY
PERKY
PERRY
PESKY
PETTY
READY
REDLY
REEDY
REEFY
REEKY
REIFY
RELAY
REPAY
REPLY
RETRY
SEAMY
SEDGY
SEEDY
SEPOY
TEARY
TEDDY
TEENY
TELLY
TERRY
TESTY
VEERY
VEINY
WEARY
WEBBY
WEDGY
WEEDY
WEENY
WEEPY
WENDY
WENNY
WETLY
ZESTY

••EY•
FREYA
GREYS
JOEYS
OBEYS
OXEYE
PREYS
TREYS
WHEYS

••E•Y
APERY
AVERY
BEEFY
BEERY
CHEVY
CHEWY
CRECY
ELEGY
EMERY
ENEMY
EVERY
FIERY
LEERY
NEEDY
ONERY
PIETY
PLEGY
POESY
PREXY
QUERY
REEDY
REEFY
REEKY
SEEDY
SUETY
TEENY
THEWY
VEERY
VIEWY
WEEDY
WEENY
WEEPY

•••EY
ABBEY
AGLEY
ALLEY
BOGEY
CAGEY
CAREY
CONEY
COOEY
COVEY
CUTEY
DAVEY
DEWEY
DOPEY
GLUEY
GOOEY
HOLEY
HOMEY
HONEY
HOOEY
LIMEY
LINEY
MAMEY
MATEY
MIKEY
MONEY
MOSEY
MULEY
NOSEY
PALEY
PINEY
POGEY
POKEY
RILEY
SKYEY
TANEY
WANEY
WAVEY

EZ•••
EZRAS

E••Z•
ELIZA

•EZ••
BEZEL
MEZZO

•E•Z•
FEEZE
MEZZO
SEIZE

•E••Z
HEJAZ
HERTZ
JEREZ

••EZ•
FEEZE
PIEZO

•••EZ
JABEZ
JEREZ

FA•••
FABLE
FACED
FACER
FACES
FACET
FACTS
FADDY
FADED
FADES
FAGOT
FAILS
FAINT
FAIRS
FAIRY
FAITH
FAKED
FAKER
FAKES
FAKIR
FALLS
FALSE
FAMED
FANCY
FANGA
FANGS
FANNY
FANON
FANOS
FANUM
FARAD
FARCE
FARCY
FARED
FARER
FARES
FARGO
FARLE
FARLS
FARMS
FASTS
FATAL
FATED
FATES
FATLY
FATTY
FAUGH
FAULT
FAUNA
FAUNS
FAUST
FAVOR
FAVUS
FAWNS
FAXED
FAXES
FAYAL
FAYED
FAYES
FAZED
FAZES

F•A••
FEARS
FEASE
FEAST
FEATS
FIATS
FLACK
FLAGS
FLAIL
FLAIR
FLAKE
FLAKY
FLAME
FLAMS
FLAMY
FLANK
FLANS
FLAPS
FLARE
FLASH
FLASK
FLATS
FLAWS
FLAWY
FLAXY
FLAYS
FOALS
FOAMS
FOAMY
FRAIL
FRAME
FRANC
FRANK
FRANZ
FRAPS
FRATS
FRAUD
FRAYS

F••A•
FARAD
FATAL
FAYAL
FECAL
FERAL
FETAL
FEUAR
FILAR
FINAL
FLEAM
FLEAS
FLOAT
FOCAL
FORAY
FREAK
FRIAR
FUGAL
FURAN

F•••A
FANGA
FAUNA
FIONA
FLORA
FOLIA
FOSSA
FOVEA
FREDA
FRENA
FREYA

•F•A•
OFFAL

•F••A
AFTRA

••FA•
OFFAL
SOFAS

••F•A
INFRA
JAFFA
KAFKA
KUFRA
MAFIA
SOFIA
SOFTA
TAFIA

•••FA
CHUFA
HAIFA
JAFFA
SOLFA
SULFA

F•B••
FABLE
FEBRI
FIBER
FIBRO

F••B•
FLUBS
FLYBY
FORBS

F•C••
FACED
FACER
FACES
FACET
FACTS
FECAL
FECES
FECIT
FICES
FICHE
FICHU
FOCAL
FOCUS
FUCUS

F••C•
FANCY
FARCE
FARCY
FENCE
FETCH
FILCH
FINCH
FISCS
FITCH
FLACK
FLECK
FLICK
FLOCK
FLOCS
FORCE
FROCK

F•••C
FOLIC
FRANC

••F•C
SUFIC

F•D••
FADDY
FADED
FADES
FEDOR
FIDEL
FUDGE

F••D•
FADDY
FEEDS
FENDS
FEODS
FEUDS
FINDS
FOLDS
FOODS
FORDS
FREDA
FREDS
FUNDS
FUNDY

F•••D
FACED
FADED
FAKED
FAMED
FARAD
FARED
FATED
FAXED
FAYED
FAZED
FELID
FETED
FETID
FEUED
FIELD
FIEND
FIFED
FILED
FINED
FIORD
FIRED
FIXED
FJELD
FJORD
FLIED
FLOOD
FLOYD
FLUID
FOUND
FOXED
FRAUD
FREED
FREUD
FRIED
FROND
FUMED
FUSED
FUZED

••F•D
BIFID
FIFED

FE•••
FEARS
FEASE
FEAST
FEATS
FEBRI
FECAL
FECES
FECIT
FEDOR
FEEDS
FEELS
FEEZE
FEIGN
FEINT
FEIST
FELID
FELIX
FELLS
FELLY
FELON
FELTS
FEMES
FEMME
FEMTO
FEMUR
FENCE
FENDS

FENNY
FEODS
FEOFF
FERAL
FERMI
FERNS
FERNY
FERRI
FERRO
FERRY
FESSE
FETAL
FETCH
FETED
FETES
FETID
FETOR
FETUS
FEUAR
FEUDS
FEUED
FEVER
FEWER

F•E••
FEEDS
FEELS
FEEZE
FIEFS
FIELD
FIEND
FIERY
FJELD
FLEAM
FLEAS
FLECK
FLEER
FLEES
FLEET
FLESH
FLEWS
FLEXI
FOEHN
FREAK
FREDA
FREDS
FREED
FREER
FREES
FRENA
FREON
FRERE
FRESH
FRETS
FREUD
FREYA
FUELS

F••E•
FACED
FACER
FACES
FACET
FADED
FADES
FAKED
FAKER
FAKES
FAMED
FARED
FARER
FARES
FATED
FATES
FAXED
FAXES
FAYED
FAYES
FAZED
FAZES
FECES
FEMES
FETED
FETES
FEUED
FEVER
FEWER
FIBER
FICES
FIDEL
FIFED
FIFER
FIFES
FILED
FILER
FILES
FILET
FINED
FINER
FINES
FIRED
FIRER
FIRES
FIVER
FIVES
FIXED
FIXER
FIXES
FLEER
FLEES
FLEET
FLIED
FLIER
FLIES
FLOES
FLUES
FLYER
FORES
FOVEA
FOXED
FOXES
FOYER
FREED
FREER
FREES
FRIED
FRIER
FRIES
FROES
FRYER
FUMED
FUMES
FUSED
FUSEE
FUSEL
FUSES
FUZED
FUZEE
FUZES
FYKES

F•••E
FABLE
FALSE
FARCE
FARLE
FEASE
FEEZE
FEMME
FENCE
FESSE
FICHE
FIQUE
FLAKE
FLAME
FLARE
FLUKE
FLUME
FLUTE
FORCE
FORGE
FORTE
FOSSE
FRAME
FRERE
FRISE
FROZE
FUDGE
FUGLE
FUGUE
FURZE
FUSEE
FUZEE

•F•E•
AFTER
OFFER
OFTEN

•F••E
AFIRE
EFFIE

••FE•
CAFES
DEFER
FIFED
FIFER
FIFES
INFER
JEFES
LIFER
OFFER
REFER
SAFER
SAFES
WAFER

••F•E
DEFOE
EFFIE
GAFFE
RIFLE

•••FE
CHAFE
GAFFE
KNIFE
ROLFE

F•F••
FIFED
FIFER
FIFES
FIFTH
FIFTY

F••F•
FEOFF
FIEFS
FLUFF

F•••F
FEOFF
FLUFF

•FF••
AFFIX
EFFIE
OFFAL
OFFER

••FF•
BAFFS
BAFFY
BIFFS
BIFFY
BUFFI
BUFFO
BUFFS
BUFFY
CUFFS
DAFFY
DOFFS
DUFFS
GAFFE
GAFFS
HUFFS
HUFFY
JAFFA
JEFFS
JIFFS
JIFFY
LUFFS
MIFFS
MIFFY
MUFFS
PUFFS
PUFFY
RIFFS
RUFFS
TAFFY
TIFFS

•••FF
BANFF
BLUFF
CHAFF
CLIFF
DRAFF
FEOFF
FLUFF
GRUFF
QUAFF
SCOFF
SCUFF
SKIFF
SNIFF
SNUFF
STAFF
STIFF
STUFF
WHIFF

F•G••
FAGOT
FIGHT
FOGGY
FUGAL
FUGIO
FUGLE
FUGUE

F••G•
FANGA
FANGS
FARGO
FAUGH
FEIGN
FLAGS
FLOGS
FOGGY
FORGE
FORGO
FRIGG
FROGS
FUDGE
FUNGI
FUNGO

F•••G
FLING
FLONG
FLUNG
FRIGG

••F•G
BEFOG

F••H•
FICHE
FICHU
FIGHT
FISHY
FOEHN

F•••H
FAITH
FAUGH
FETCH
FIFTH
FILCH
FILTH
FINCH
FIRTH
FITCH
FLASH
FLESH
FLUSH
FORTH
FRESH
FRITH
FROSH
FROTH
FURTH

••F•H
FIFTH

FI•••
FIATS
FIBER
FIBRO
FICES
FICHE
FICHU
FIDEL
FIEFS
FIELD
FIEND
FIERY
FIFED
FIFER
FIFES
FIFTH
FIFTY
FIGHT
FIJIS
FILAR
FILCH
FILED
FILER
FILES
FILET
FILLS
FILLY
FILMS
FILMY
FILTH
FILUM
FINAL
FINCH
FINDS
FINED
FINER
FINES
FINIS
FINKS
FINNS
FINNY
FIONA
FIORD
FIQUE
FIRED
FIRER
FIRES
FIRMS
FIRNS
FIRRY
FIRST
FIRTH
FISCS
FISHY
FISTS
FITCH
FITLY
FIVER
FIVES
FIXED
FIXER
FIXES
FIZZY

F•I••
FAILS
FAINT
FAIRS
FAIRY
FAITH
FEIGN
FEINT
FEIST
FLICK
FLIED
FLIER
FLIES
FLING
FLINT
FLIPS
FLIRT
FLITS
FOILS
FOISM
FOIST
FRIAR
FRIED
FRIER
FRIES
FRIGG
FRILL
FRIML
FRISE
FRISK
FRITH
FRITS
FRITZ
FRIZZ

F••I•
FAKIR
FECIT
FELID
FELIX
FETID
FIJIS
FINIS
FLAIL
FLAIR
FLUID
FOLIA
FOLIC
FOLIO
FRAIL
FRUIT
FUGIO
FUSIL
FUZIL

F•••I
FEBRI
FERMI
FERRI
FLEXI
FORLI
FUNGI

•FI••
AFIRE

•F•I•
AFFIX
EFFIE

••FI•
AFFIX
BEFIT
BIFID
DEFIS
EFFIE
ELFIN
HAFIZ
HIFIS
INFIX
MAFIA
REFIT
SOFIA
SUFIC
SUFIS
TAFIA
UNFIT
UNFIX

••F•I
BUFFI
MUFTI

•••FI
BUFFI
SCIFI
USAFI

5

FJ•••
FJELD
FJORD

F•J••
FIJIS

F•K••
FAKED
FAKER
FAKES
FAKIR
FYKES

F••K•
FINKS
FLAKE
FLAKY
FLUKE
FLUKY
FOLKS
FORKS
FUNKS
FUNKY

F•••K
FLACK
FLANK
FLASK
FLECK
FLICK
FLOCK
FLUNK
FRANK
FREAK
FRISK
FROCK

••FK•
KAFKA

FL•••
FLACK
FLAGS
FLAIL
FLAIR
FLAKE
FLAKY
FLAME
FLAMS
FLAMY
FLANK
FLANS
FLAPS
FLARE
FLASH
FLASK
FLATS
FLAWS
FLAWY
FLAXY
FLAYS
FLEAM
FLEAS
FLECK
FLEER
FLEES
FLEET
FLESH
FLEWS
FLEXI
FLICK
FLIED
FLIER
FLIES
FLING
FLINT
FLIPS
FLIRT
FLITS
FLOAT
FLOCK
FLOCS
FLOES
FLOGS
FLONG
FLOOD
FLOOR
FLOPS
FLORA
FLOSS
FLOUR
FLOUT
FLOWN
FLOWS
FLOYD
FLUBS
FLUES
FLUFF
FLUID
FLUKE
FLUKY
FLUME
FLUMP
FLUNG
FLUNK
FLUOR
FLUSH
FLUTE
FLUTY
FLYBY
FLYER

F•L••
FALLS
FALSE
FELID
FELIX
FELLS
FELLY
FELON
FELTS
FILAR
FILCH
FILED
FILER
FILES
FILET
FILLS
FILLY
FILMS
FILMY
FILTH
FILUM
FOLDS
FOLIA
FOLIC
FOLIO
FOLKS
FOLLY
FULLS
FULLY

F••L•
FABLE
FAILS
FALLS
FARLE
FARLS
FATLY
FAULT
FEELS
FELLS
FELLY
FIELD
FILLS
FILLY
FITLY
FJELD
FOALS
FOILS
FOLLY
FOOLS
FORLI
FOULS
FOWLS
FRILL
FUELS
FUGLE
FULLS
FULLY
FURLS

F•••L
FATAL
FAYAL
FECAL
FERAL
FETAL
FIDEL
FINAL
FLAIL
FOCAL
FRAIL
FRILL
FRIML
FUGAL
FUSEL
FUSIL
FUZIL

•F••L
AFOUL
OFFAL

••FL•
RIFLE

••F•L
AWFUL
OFFAL

F•M••
FAMED
FEMES
FEMME
FEMTO
FEMUR
FUMED
FUMES

F••M•
FARMS
FEMME
FERMI
FILMS
FILMY
FIRMS
FLAME
FLAMS
FLAMY
FLUME
FLUMP
FOAMS
FOAMY
FORMS
FRAME
FRIML
FRUMP

F•••M
FANUM
FILUM
FLEAM
FOISM
FORUM

F•N••
FANCY
FANGA
FANGS
FANNY
FANON
FANOS
FANUM
FENCE
FENDS
FENNY
FINAL
FINCH
FINDS
FINED
FINER
FINES
FINIS
FINKS
FINNS
FINNY
FONTS
FUNDS
FUNDY
FUNGI
FUNGO
FUNKS
FUNKY
FUNNY

F••N•
FAINT
FANNY
FAUNA
FAUNS
FAWNS
FEINT
FENNY
FERNS
FERNY
FIEND
FINNS
FINNY
FIONA
FIRNS
FLANK
FLANS
FLING
FLINT
FLONG
FLUNG
FLUNK
FOUND
FOUNT
FRANC
FRANK
FRANZ
FRENA
FROND
FRONT
FUNNY

F•••N
FANON
FEIGN
FELON
FLOWN
FOEHN
FREON
FROWN
FURAN

•F••N
OFTEN

••F•N
ELFIN

FO•••
FOALS
FOAMS
FOAMY
FOCAL
FOCUS
FOEHN
FOGGY
FOILS
FOISM
FOIST
FOLDS
FOLIA
FOLIC
FOLIO
FOLKS
FOLLY
FONTS
FOODS
FOOLS
FOOTS
FOOTY
FORAY
FORBS
FORCE
FORDS
FORES
FORGE
FORGO
FORKS
FORLI
FORMS
FORTE
FORTH
FORTS
FORTY
FORUM
FOSSA
FOSSE
FOULS
FOUND
FOUNT
FOURS
FOVEA
FOWLS
FOXED
FOXES
FOYER

F•O••
FEODS
FEOFF
FIONA
FIORD
FJORD
FLOAT
FLOCK
FLOCS
FLOES
FLOGS
FLONG
FLOOD
FLOOR
FLOPS
FLORA
FLOSS
FLOUR
FLOUT
FLOWN
FLOWS
FLOYD
FOODS
FOOLS
FOOTS
FOOTY
FROCK
FROES
FROGS
FROND
FRONT
FROSH
FROST
FROTH
FROWN
FROWS
FROZE

F••O•
FAGOT
FANON
FANOS
FAVOR
FEDOR
FELON
FETOR
FLOOD
FLOOR
FLUOR
FREON
FSTOP
FUROR

F•••O
FARGO
FEMTO
FERRO
FIBRO
FOLIO
FORGO
FUGIO
FUNGO

•FO••
AFOOT
AFOUL

•F•O•
AFOOT
AFROS

••FO•
BEFOG
DEFOE

••F•O
BUFFO

•••FO
BUFFO
SULFO

F••P•
FLAPS
FLIPS
FLOPS
FRAPS

F•••P
FLUMP
FRUMP
FSTOP

F•Q••
FIQUE

FR•••
FRAIL
FRAME
FRANC
FRANK
FRANZ
FRAPS
FRATS
FRAUD
FRAYS
FREAK
FREDA
FREDS
FREED
FREER
FREES
FRENA
FREON
FRERE
FRESH
FRETS
FREUD
FREYA
FRIAR
FRIED
FRIER
FRIES
FRIGG
FRILL
FRIML
FRISE
FRISK
FRITH
FRITS
FRITZ
FRIZZ
FROCK
FROES
FROGS
FROND
FRONT
FROSH
FROST
FROTH
FROWN
FROWS
FROZE
FRUIT
FRUMP
FRYER

F•R••
FARAD
FARCE
FARCY
FARED
FARER
FARES
FARGO
FARLE
FARLS
FARMS
FERAL
FERMI
FERNS
FERNY
FERRI
FERRO
FERRY
FIRED
FIRER
FIRES
FIRMS
FIRNS
FIRRY
FIRST
FIRTH
FORAY
FORBS
FORCE
FORDS
FORES
FORGE
FORGO
FORKS
FORLI
FORMS
FORTE
FORTH
FORTS
FORTY
FORUM
FURAN
FURLS
FUROR
FURRY
FURTH
FURZE
FURZY

F••R•
FAIRS
FAIRY
FEARS
FEBRI
FERRI
FERRO
FERRY
FIBRO
FIERY
FIORD
FIRRY
FJORD
FLARE
FLIRT
FLORA
FOURS
FRERE
FURRY

F•••R
FACER
FAKER
FAKIR
FARER
FAVOR
FEDOR
FEMUR
FETOR
FEUAR
FEVER
FEWER
FIBER
FIFER
FILAR
FILER
FINER
FIRER
FIVER
FIXER
FLAIR
FLEER
FLIER
FLOOR
FLOUR
FLUOR
FLYER
FOYER
FREER
FRIAR
FRIER
FRYER
FUROR

•FR••
AFROS

•F•R•
AFIRE
AFTRA

•F••R
AFTER
OFFER

••FR•
INFRA
KUFRA

••F•R
DEFER
FIFER
INFER
LIFER
OFFER
REFER
SAFER
WAFER

FS•••
FSTOP

F•S••
FASTS
FESSE
FISCS
FISHY
FISTS
FOSSA
FOSSE
FUSED
FUSEE
FUSEL
FUSES
FUSIL
FUSSY
FUSTY

F••S•
FALSE
FAUST
FEASE
FEAST
FEIST
FESSE
FIRST
FLASH
FLASK
FLESH
FLOSS
FLUSH
FOISM
FOIST
FOSSA
FOSSE
FRESH
FRISE
FRISK
FROSH
FROST
FUSSY

F•••S
FACES
FACTS
FADES
FAILS
FAIRS
FAKES
FALLS
FANGS
FANOS
FARES
FARLS
FARMS
FASTS
FATES
FAUNS
FAVUS
FAWNS
FAXES
FAYES
FAZES
FEARS
FEATS
FECES
FEEDS
FEELS
FELLS
FELTS
FEMES
FENDS
FEODS
FERNS
FETES
FETUS
FEUDS
FIATS
FICES
FIEFS
FIFES
FIJIS
FILES
FILLS
FILMS
FINDS
FINES
FINIS
FINKS
FINNS
FIRES
FIRMS
FIRNS
FISCS
FISTS
FIVES
FIXES
FLAGS
FLAMS
FLANS
FLAPS
FLATS
FLAWS
FLAYS
FLEAS
FLEES
FLEWS
FLIES
FLIPS
FLITS
FLOCS
FLOES
FLOGS
FLOPS
FLOSS
FLOWS
FLUBS
FLUES
FOALS
FOAMS
FOCUS
FOILS
FOLDS
FOLKS
FONTS
FOODS
FOOLS
FOOTS
FORBS
FORDS
FORES
FORKS
FORMS
FORTS
FOULS
FOURS
FOWLS
FOXES
FRAPS
FRATS
FRAYS
FREDS
FREES
FRETS
FRIES
FRITS
FROES
FROGS
FROWS
FUCUS
FUELS
FULLS
FUMES
FUNDS
FUNKS
FURLS
FUSES
FUZES
FYKES

•F••S
AFROS

••F•S
BAFFS
BIFFS
BUFFS
CAFES
CUFFS
DEFIS
DOFFS
DUFFS
FIFES
GAFFS
GIFTS
HAFTS
HEFTS
HIFIS
HUFFS
JEFES
JEFFS
JIFFS
LEFTS
LIFTS
LOFTS
LUFFS
MIFFS
MUFFS
PUFFS
RAFTS
RIFFS
RIFTS
RUFFS
RUFUS
SAFES
SIFTS
SOFAS
SUFIS
TIFFS
TOFTS
TUFTS
WAFTS
WEFTS

•••FS
ALEFS
ALIFS
BAFFS
BEEFS
BIFFS
BUFFS
CHEFS
CLEFS
COIFS
CUFFS
DOFFS
DUFFS
FIEFS
GAFFS
GOLFS
GOOFS
GULFS
HOOFS
HUFFS
JEFFS
JIFFS
KEEFS
KERFS
LEAFS
LEIFS
LOAFS
LOOFS
LUFFS
MIFFS
MUFFS
OLAFS
PELFS
POUFS
PROFS
PUFFS
REEFS
RIFFS
ROLFS
ROOFS
RUFFS
SERFS
SURFS
TIFFS
TURFS
WAIFS
WOLFS
WOOFS
ZARFS

F•T••
FATAL
FATED
FATES
FATLY
FATTY
FETAL
FETCH
FETED
FETES
FETID
FETOR
FETUS
FITCH
FITLY
FSTOP

F••T•
FACTS
FAITH
FASTS
FATTY
FEATS
FELTS
FEMTO
FIATS
FIFTH
FIFTY
FILTH
FIRTH
FISTS
FLATS
FLITS
FLUTE
FLUTY
FONTS
FOOTS
FOOTY
FORTE
FORTH
FORTS
FORTY
FRATS
FRETS
FRITH
FRITS
FRITZ
FROTH
FURTH
FUSTY

F•••T
FACET
FAGOT
FAINT
FAULT
FAUST
FEAST
FECIT
FEINT
FEIST
FIGHT
FILET
FIRST
FLEET
FLINT
FLIRT
FLOAT
FLOUT
FOIST
FOUNT
FRONT
FROST
FRUIT

•FT••
AFTER
AFTRA
OFTEN

•F••T
AFOOT

••FT•
FIFTH
FIFTY
GIFTS
HAFTS
HEFTS
HEFTY
LEFTS
LEFTY
LIFTS
LOFTS
LOFTY
MUFTI
NIFTY
RAFTS
RIFTS
SIFTS
SOFTA
SOFTY
TOFTS
TUFTS
TUFTY
WAFTS
WEFTS

••F•T
BEFIT
REFIT
UNFIT

•••FT
ABAFT
ALOFT
CLEFT
CRAFT
CROFT
DELFT
DRAFT
DRIFT
GRAFT
KRAFT
SHAFT
SHIFT
SWIFT
THEFT

5

FU•••

FUCUS FUDGE FUELS FUGAL FUGIO FUGLE FUGUE FULLS FULLY FUMED FUMES FUNDS FUNDY FUNGI FUNGO FUNKS FUNKY FUNNY FURAN FURLS FUROR FURRY FURTH FURZE FURZY FUSED FUSEE FUSEL FUSES FUSIL FUSSY FUSTY FUZED FUZEE FUZES FUZIL FUZZY

F•U••

FAUGH FAULT FAUNA FAUNS FAUST FEUAR FEUDS FEUED FLUBS FLUES FLUFF FLUID FLUKE FLUKY FLUME FLUMP FLUNG FLUNK FLUOR FLUSH FLUTE FLUTY FOULS FOUND FOUNT FOURS FRUIT FRUMP

F••U•

FANUM FAVUS FEMUR FETUS FILUM FIQUE FLOUR FLOUT FOCUS FORUM FRAUD FREUD FUCUS FUGUE

F•••U

FICHU

•F•U•

AFOUL

••FU•

AWFUL RUFUS

•••FU

CORFU SNAFU

F•V••

FAVOR FAVUS FEVER FIVER FIVES FOVEA

F•W••

FAWNS FEWER FOWLS

F••W•

FLAWS FLAWY FLEWS FLOWN FLOWS FROWN FROWS

F•X••

FAXED FAXES FIXED FIXER FIXES FOXED FOXES

F••X•

FLAXY FLEXI

F•••X

FELIX

•F••X

AFFIX

••F•X

AFFIX INFIX UNFIX

FY•••

FYKES

F•Y••

FAYAL FAYED FAYES FLYBY FLYER FOYER FRYER

F••Y•

FLAYS FLOYD FRAYS FREYA

F•••Y

FADDY FAIRY FANCY FANNY FARCY FATLY FATTY FELLY FENNY FERNY FERRY FIERY FIFTY FILLY FILMY FINNY FIRRY FISHY FITLY FIZZY FLAKY FLAMY FLAWY FLAXY FLUKY FLUTY FLYBY FOAMY FOGGY FOLLY FOOTY FORAY FORTY FULLY FUNDY FUNKY FUNNY FURRY FURZY FUSSY FUSTY FUZZY

••F•Y

BAFFY BIFFY BUFFY DAFFY FIFTY HEFTY HUFFY JIFFY LEFTY LOFTY MIFFY NIFTY PUFFY SOFTY TAFFY TUFTY

•••FY

BAFFY BEEFY BIFFY BUFFY DAFFY DEIFY EDIFY GOOFY HUFFY JIFFY LEAFY MIFFY PUFFY REEFY REIFY SURFY TAFFY TURFY UNIFY

F•Z••

FAZED FAZES FIZZY FUZED FUZEE FUZES FUZIL FUZZY

F••Z•

FEEZE FIZZY FRIZZ FROZE FURZE FURZY FUZZY

F•••Z

FRANZ FRITZ FRIZZ

••F•Z

HAFIZ

GA•••

GABBY GABES GABLE GABON GABYS GADID GAELS GAFFE GAFFS GAGED GAGER GAGES GAILS GAILY GAINS GAITS GALAS GALAX GALEA GALEN GALES GALLS GALOP GAMBS GAMED GAMES GAMIC GAMIN GAMMA GAMPS GAMUT GANEF GANGS GAOLS GAPED GAPER GAPES GAPPY GARBS GARTH GARYS GASES GASPE GASPS GASSY GASTR GATED GATES GATUN GAUDI GAUDS GAUDY GAUGE GAULS GAUNT GAURS GAUSS GAUZE GAUZY GAVEL GAVLE GAVOT GAWKS GAWKY GAYER GAYLY GAZED GAZER GAZES

G•A••

GEARS GHANA GHATS GHAUT GHAZI GIANT GLACE GLADE GLADS GLAIR GLAND GLANS GLARE GLARY GLASS GLAUC GLAZE GLAZY GNARL GNASH GNATS GNAWN GNAWS GOADS GOALS GOATS GRAAL GRABS GRACE GRADE GRADS GRAFT GRAIL GRAIN GRAMA GRAMS GRAND GRANI GRANO GRANT GRAPE GRAPH GRAPY GRASP GRASS GRATE GRAVE GRAVY GRAYS GRAZE GUACO GUANO GUANS GUARD GUAVA

G••A•

GALAS GALAX GIGAS GLEAM GLEAN GLOAT GONAD GORAL GRAAL GREAT GROAN GROAT GULAR GYRAL

G•••A

GALEA GAMMA GEMMA GENOA GENUA GERDA GHANA GILDA GONIA GOTHA GOUDA GRAMA GRETA GUAVA GUMMA GUSTA GUTTA

•GA••

AGAIN AGAMA AGANA AGAPE AGATE AGAVE AGAZE

•G•A•

AGHAS EGEAN EGGAR IGNAZ

•G••A

AGAMA AGANA AGORA

••GA•

ALGAE ALGAL ARGAL BEGAN BEGAT BOGAN CIGAR DAGAN DEGAS EDGAR EGGAR ELGAR FUGAL GIGAS HOGAN JUGAL LAGAN LEGAL LIGAN MEGAL MEGAN OLGAS ORGAN PAGAN REGAL REGAN RUGAE SAGAS SUGAR TOGAE TOGAS WIGAN YUGAS

••G•A

ALGIA DOGMA LOGIA MAGDA MAGMA REGMA SIGMA

•••GA

BELGA CONGA FANGA HELGA LINGA OMEGA SAIGA TAIGA TONGA VIRGA VOLGA

G•B••
GABBY
GABES
GABLE
GABON
GABYS
GIBED
GIBER
GIBES
GOBOS
GOBYS

G••B•
GABBY
GAMBS
GARBS
GLEBE
GLOBE
GLOBS
GRABS
GREBE
GRUBS
GUMBO

••GB•
RUGBY

G•C••
GECKO
GECKS

G••C•
GLACE
GLYCO
GRACE
GRECO
GUACO
GULCH

G•••C
GAMIC
GENIC
GLAUC
GYNEC

••G•C
LOGIC
MAGIC
YOGIC

G•D••
GADID
GIDDY
GODLY

G••D•
GAUDI
GAUDS
GAUDY
GELDS
GEODE
GERDA
GIDDY
GILDA
GILDS
GIRDS
GLADE
GLADS
GLEDE
GLEDS
GLIDE
GOADS
GOLDS
GONDI
GOODS
GOODY
GOUDA
GRADE
GRADS
GRIDE
GRIDS
GUIDE
GUIDO

G•••D
GADID
GAGED
GAMED
GAPED
GATED
GAZED
GELID
GEOID
GIBED
GLAND
GLUED
GONAD
GORED
GOURD
GRAND
GREED
GRIND
GUARD
GUILD
GUYED

•G••D
EGGED
OGLED

••GD•
MAGDA

••G•D
ALGID
CAGED
EDGED
EGGED
GAGED
PAGED
RAGED
RIGID
URGED
WAGED

GE•••
GEARS
GECKO
GECKS
GEEKS
GEESE
GEEST
GELDS
GELID
GEMMA
GEMMY
GEMOT
GENES
GENET
GENIC
GENIE
GENII
GENOA
GENRE
GENRO
GENTS
GENUA
GENUS
GEODE
GEOID
GERDA
GERMS
GERRY
GERTY
GESSO
GETUP

G•E••
GAELS
GEEKS
GEESE
GEEST
GHENT
GLEAM
GLEAN
GLEBE
GLEDE
GLEDS
GLEES
GLEET
GLENN
GLENS
GOERS
GREAT
GREBE
GRECO
GREED
GREEK
GREEN
GREET
GREGO
GREGS
GRETA
GREYS
GUESS
GUEST
GWENN
GWENS

G••E•
GABES
GAGED
GAGER
GAGES
GALEA
GALEN
GALES
GAMED
GAMES
GANEF
GAPED
GAPER
GAPES
GASES
GATED
GATES
GAVEL
GAYER
GAZED
GAZER
GAZES
GENES
GENET
GIBED
GIBER
GIBES
GILES
GIMEL
GIVEN
GIVER
GIVES
GLEES
GLEET
GLUED
GLUES
GLUEY
GOLEM
GONER
GOOEY
GORED
GORES
GREED
GREEK
GREEN
GREET
GRIEF
GRIEG
GRUEL
GULES
GUYED
GYNEC
GYRES

G•••E
GABLE
GAFFE
GASPE
GAUGE
GAUZE
GAVLE
GEESE
GENIE
GENRE
GEODE
GIGUE
GLACE
GLADE
GLARE
GLAZE
GLEBE
GLEDE
GLIDE
GLOBE
GLOVE
GLOZE
GLUME
GNOME
GOOSE
GORGE
GORSE
GOUGE
GRACE
GRADE
GRAPE
GRATE
GRAVE
GRAZE
GREBE
GRIDE
GRIME
GRIPE
GROPE
GROVE
GRUME
GUIDE
GUILE
GUISE

•GE••
AGENT
EGEAN
EGEST
OGEES

•G•E•
AGGER
AGLEE
AGLET
AGLEY
AGNES
AGREE
AGUES
EGGED
EGGER
EGRET
OGEES
OGLED
OGLER
OGLES
OGRES

•G••E
AGAPE
AGATE
AGAVE
AGAZE
AGGIE
AGILE
AGLEE
AGREE
OGIVE

••GE•
AGGER
ALGER
ANGEL
ANGER
AUGER
BAGEL
BEGET
BOGEY
CAGED
CAGES
CAGEY
DOGES
EAGER
EDGED
EDGES
EGGED
EGGER
GAGED
GAGER
GAGES
HEGEL
HUGER
LAGER
LEGER
LEGES
LOGES
LUGER
MAGES
NEGEV
NIGEL
NIGER
PAGED
PAGES
POGEY
PUGET
RAGED
RAGEE
RAGES
REGES
RIGEL
ROGER
SAGER
SAGES
TIGER
URGED
URGES
WAGED
WAGER
WAGES
YAGER
YOGEE

••G•E
AGGIE
ALGAE
ALGIE
ANGLE
ARGUE
BOGIE
BOGLE
BUGLE
DOGIE
EAGLE
EAGRE
FUGLE
FUGUE
GIGUE
HAGUE
LOGUE
RAGEE
ROGUE
RUGAE
TOGAE
TOGUE
VAGUE
VOGUE
YOGEE

•••GE
ADAGE
BADGE
BARGE
BEIGE
BILGE
BINGE
BRAGE
BUDGE
BULGE
CADGE
CONGE
DIRGE
DODGE
FORGE
FUDGE
GAUGE
GORGE
GOUGE
HEDGE
HINGE
HODGE
IMAGE
JORGE
JUDGE
KEDGE
LARGE
LEDGE
LIEGE
LODGE
LUNGE
MADGE
MANGE
MARGE
MERGE
MIDGE
NUDGE
OSAGE
PHAGE
PURGE
RANGE
RHAGE
RIDGE
ROUGE
SEDGE
SERGE
SIEGE
SINGE
STAGE
SURGE
SWAGE
SYNGE
TINGE
USAGE
VERGE
VIRGE
WEDGE

G•F••
GAFFE
GAFFS
GIFTS

G••F•
GAFFE
GAFFS
GOLFS
GOOFS
GOOFY
GRAFT
GRUFF
GULFS

G•••F
GANEF
GRIEF
GRUFF

G•G••
GAGED
GAGER
GAGES
GIGAS
GIGOT
GIGUE
GOGOL

G••G•
GANGS
GAUGE
GONGS
GORGE
GOUGE
GREGO
GREGS

G•••G
GIING
GOING
GRIEG

•GG••
AGGER
AGGIE
EGGAR
EGGED
EGGER

•G••G
AGING

5

••GG•
BAGGY
BOGGY
BUGGY
DOGGY
FOGGY
JAGGS
JAGGY
LEGGY
MUGGY
NOGGS
PEGGY
PIGGY
RAGGY
RIGGS
SOGGY
VUGGY
YEGGS

•••GG
FRIGG

GH•••
GHANA
GHATS
GHAUT
GHAZI
GHENT
GHOST
GHOUL

G••H•
GOTHA
GOTHS
GUSHY

G•••H
GARTH
GIRTH
GLYPH
GNASH
GRAPH
GULCH

•GH••
AGHAS

••GH•
AUGHT
BIGHT
EIGHT
FIGHT
HIGHS
HUGHS
LIGHT
MIGHT
NIGHT
OUGHT
RIGHT
SIGHS
SIGHT
TIGHT
WIGHT
YOGHS

•••GH
BLIGH
BOUGH
BURGH
COUGH
DOUGH
FAUGH
LAUGH
LEIGH
LOUGH
NEIGH
ROUGH
SOUGH
THIGH
TOUGH
WAUGH
WEIGH

GI•••
GIANT
GIBED
GIBER
GIBES
GIDDY
GIFTS
GIGAS
GIGOT
GIGUE
GIING
GILDA
GILDS
GILES
GILLS
GIMEL
GIMPS
GIMPY
GINKS
GINNY
GIPON
GIPSY
GIRDS
GIRLS
GIROS
GIRTH
GIRTS
GISMO
GISTS
GIVEN
GIVER
GIVES
GIZMO

G•I••
GAILS
GAILY
GAINS
GAITS
GIING
GLIDE
GLIMS
GLINT
GOING
GRIDE
GRIDS
GRIEF
GRIEG
GRILL
GRIME
GRIMM
GRIND
GRINS
GRIPE
GRIPS
GRIPT
GRIST
GRITS
GUIDE
GUIDO
GUILD
GUILE
GUILT
GUISE

G••I•
GADID
GAMIC
GAMIN
GELID
GENIC
GENIE
GENII
GEOID
GLAIR
GONIA
GONIO
GOYIM
GRAIL
GRAIN
GROIN

G•••I
GAUDI
GENII
GHAZI
GONDI
GORKI
GRANI

•GI••
AGILE
AGING
AGIOS
AGIST
OGIVE

•G•I•
AGAIN
AGGIE
AGNIS

••GI•
AEGIR
AEGIS
AGGIE
ALGIA
ALGID
ALGIE
ALGIN
ANGIO
ARGIL
BEGIN
BOGIE
DIGIT
DOGIE
ELGIN
FUGIO
HAGIO
LEGIT
LOGIA
LOGIC
MAGIC
REGIN
RIGID
SIGIL
VAGIN
VIGIL
YOGIC
YOGIN
YOGIS

••G•I
LIGNI
MAGNI
NIGRI
SEGNI

•••GI
BRAGI
CORGI
FUNGI
LONGI
LUIGI
LUNGI
PLAGI
TRAGI

G••K•
GAWKS
GAWKY
GECKO
GECKS
GEEKS
GINKS
GOOKS
GORKI
GORKY

G•••K
GREEK

GL•••
GLACE
GLADE
GLADS
GLAIR
GLAND
GLANS
GLARE
GLARY
GLASS
GLAUC
GLAZE
GLAZY
GLEAM
GLEAN
GLEBE
GLEDE
GLEDS
GLEES
GLEET
GLENN
GLENS
GLIDE
GLIMS
GLINT
GLOAT
GLOBE
GLOBS
GLOOM
GLORY
GLOSS
GLOST
GLOVE
GLOWS
GLOZE
GLUED
GLUES
GLUEY
GLUME
GLUTS
GLYCO
GLYPH

G•L••
GALAS
GALAX
GALEA
GALEN
GALES
GALLS
GALOP
GELDS
GELID
GILDA
GILDS
GILES
GILLS
GOLDS
GOLEM
GOLFS
GOLLY
GULAR
GULCH
GULES
GULFS
GULLS
GULLY
GULPS

G••L•
GABLE
GAELS
GAILS
GAILY
GALLS
GAOLS
GAULS
GAVLE
GAYLY
GILLS
GIRLS
GOALS
GODLY
GOLLY
GRILL
GUILD
GUILE
GUILT
GULLS
GULLY

G•••L
GAVEL
GHOUL
GIMEL
GNARL
GOGOL
GORAL
GRAAL
GRAIL
GRILL
GROWL
GRUEL
GYRAL

•GL••
AGLEE
AGLET
AGLEY
AGLOW
IGLOO
OGLED
OGLER
OGLES

•G•L•
AGILE

••GL•
ANGLE
ANGLO
BIGLY
BOGLE
BUGLE
EAGLE
FUGLE

••G•L
ALGAL
ALGOL
ANGEL
ARGAL
ARGIL
ARGOL
BAGEL
FUGAL
GOGOL
HEGEL
JUGAL
LEGAL
MEGAL
MOGUL
NIGEL
REGAL
RIGEL
SIGIL
VIGIL
VOGUL

G•M••
GAMBS
GAMED
GAMES
GAMIC
GAMIN
GAMMA
GAMPS
GAMUT
GEMMA
GEMMY
GEMOT
GIMEL
GIMPS
GIMPY
GUMBO
GUMMA
GUMMY
GYMNO

G••M•
GAMMA
GEMMA
GEMMY
GERMS
GISMO
GIZMO
GLIMS
GLUME
GNOME
GNOMY
GRAMA
GRAMS
GRIME
GRIMM
GRUME
GUMMA
GUMMY

G•••M
GLEAM
GLOOM
GOLEM
GOYIM
GRIMM
GROOM

•G•M•
AGAMA

••GM•
DOGMA
MAGMA
PIGMY
PYGMY
REGMA
SIGMA

••G•M
ALGUM
BEGUM
DEGUM
SAGUM

GN•••
GNARL
GNASH
GNATS
GNAWN
GNAWS
GNOME
GNOMY

G•N••
GANEF
GANGS
GENES
GENET
GENIC
GENIE
GENII
GENOA
GENRE
GENRO
GENTS
GENUA
GENUS
GINKS
GINNY
GONAD
GONDI
GONER
GONGS
GONIA
GONIO
GUNNY
GYNEC

G••N•
GAINS
GAUNT
GHANA
GHENT
GIANT
GIING
GINNY
GLAND
GLANS
GLENN
GLENS
GLINT
GOING
GOONS
GOWNS
GRAND
GRANI
GRANO
GRANT
GRIND

GRINS
GRUNT
GUANO
GUANS
GUNNY
GWENN
GWENS
GWYNS
GYMNO

G•••N
GABON
GALEN
GAMIN
GATUN
GIPON
GIVEN
GLEAN
GLENN
GNAWN
GRAIN
GREEN
GROAN
GROIN
GROWN
GWENN
GYRON

•GN••
AGNES
AGNIS
IGNAZ

•G•N•
AGANA
AGENT
AGING
AGONY

•G••N
AGAIN
EGEAN

••GN•
LIGNI
LIGNO
MAGNI
SEGNI
SEGNO
SIGNS

••G•N
ALGIN
ARGON
BEGAN
BEGIN
BEGUN
BOGAN
COGON
DAGAN
ELGIN
HOGAN
LAGAN
LIGAN
MEGAN
ORGAN
PAGAN
REGAN
REGIN
VAGIN
WAGON
WIGAN
YOGIN

•••GN
ALIGN
COIGN
DEIGN
FEIGN
REIGN

GO•••
GOADS
GOALS
GOATS
GOBOS
GOBYS
GODLY
GOERS
GOGOL
GOING
GOLDS
GOLEM
GOLFS
GOLLY
GONAD
GONDI
GONER
GONGS
GONIA
GONIO
GOODS
GOODY
GOOEY
GOOFS
GOOFY
GOOKS
GOONS
GOOSE
GOOSY
GORAL
GORED
GORES
GORGE
GORKI
GORKY
GORSE
GORSY
GOTHA
GOTHS
GOUDA
GOUGE
GOURD
GOUTY
GOVTS
GOWNS
GOYIM

G•O••
GAOLS
GEODE
GEOID
GHOST
GHOUL
GLOAT
GLOBE
GLOBS
GLOOM
GLORY
GLOSS
GLOST
GLOVE
GLOWS
GLOZE
GNOME
GNOMY
GOODS
GOODY
GOOEY
GOOFS
GOOFY
GOOKS
GOONS
GOOSE
GOOSY
GROAN
GROAT
GROIN
GROOM
GROPE
GROSS
GROSZ
GROTS
GROUP
GROUT
GROVE
GROWL
GROWN
GROWS

G••O•
GABON
GALOP
GAVOT
GEMOT
GENOA
GIGOT
GIPON
GIROS
GLOOM
GOBOS
GOGOL
GROOM
GYRON
GYROS

G•••O
GECKO
GENRO
GESSO
GISMO
GIZMO
GLYCO
GONIO
GRANO
GRECO
GREGO
GUACO
GUANO
GUIDO
GUMBO
GUSTO
GYMNO

•GO••
AGONY
AGORA

•G•O•
AGIOS
AGLOW
IGLOO

•G••O
IGLOO

••GO•
ALGOL
ALGOR
ARGOL
ARGON
ARGOS
ARGOT
BEGOT
BIGOT
BOGOR
COGON
ERGOT
FAGOT
GIGOT
GOGOL
HUGOS
INGOT
LAGOS
LOGOS
MAGOT
RIGOR
SAGOS
SEGOS
VIGOR
WAGON

••G•O
ANGIO
ANGLO
FUGIO
HAGIO
HYGRO
LIGNO
NEGRO
SEGNO

•••GO
AMIGO
BINGO
BONGO
CARGO
CONGO
DIEGO
DINGO
FARGO
FORGO
FUNGO
GREGO
IMAGO
INIGO
JINGO
LARGO
LINGO
MANGO
MARGO
MUNGO
OLIGO
OUTGO
PARGO
PENGO
PHAGO
PINGO
SORGO
TANGO
TRIGO
VIRGO
VULGO

G•P••
GAPED
GAPER
GAPES
GAPPY
GIPON
GIPSY
GUPPY
GYPSY

G••P•
GAMPS
GAPPY
GASPE
GASPS
GIMPS
GIMPY
GLYPH
GRAPE
GRAPH
GRAPY
GRIPE
GRIPS
GRIPT
GROPE
GULPS
GUPPY

G•••P
GALOP
GETUP
GRASP
GROUP

•G•P•
AGAPE
EGYPT

GR•••
GRAAL
GRABS
GRACE
GRADE
GRADS
GRAFT
GRAIL
GRAIN
GRAMA
GRAMS
GRAND
GRANI
GRANO
GRANT
GRAPE
GRAPH
GRAPY
GRASP
GRASS
GRATE
GRAVE
GRAVY
GRAYS
GRAZE
GREAT
GREBE
GRECO
GREED
GREEK
GREEN
GREET
GREGO
GREGS
GRETA
GREYS
GRIDE
GRIDS
GRIEF
GRIEG
GRILL
GRIME
GRIMM
GRIND
GRINS
GRIPE
GRIPS
GRIPT
GRIST
GRITS
GROAN
GROAT
GROIN
GROOM
GROPE
GROSS
GROSZ
GROTS
GROUP
GROUT
GROVE
GROWL
GROWN
GROWS
GRUBS
GRUEL
GRUFF
GRUME
GRUNT

G•R••
GARBS
GARTH
GARYS
GERDA
GERMS
GERRY
GERTY
GIRDS
GIRLS
GIROS
GIRTH
GIRTS
GORAL
GORED
GORES
GORGE
GORKI
GORKY
GORSE
GORSY
GURUS
GYRAL
GYRES
GYRON
GYROS
GYRUS

G••R•
GAURS
GEARS
GENRE
GENRO
GERRY
GLARE
GLARY
GLORY
GNARL
GOERS
GOURD
GUARD

G•••R
GAGER
GAPER
GASTR
GAYER
GAZER
GIBER
GIVER
GLAIR
GONER
GULAR

•GR••
AGREE
EGRET
OGRES

•G•R•
AGORA

•G••R
AGGER
EGGAR
EGGER
OGLER

••GR•
ANGRY
EAGRE
HYGRO
NEGRO
NIGRI

••G•R
AEGIR
AGGER
ALGER
ALGOR
ANGER
AUGER
AUGUR
BOGOR
CIGAR
EAGER
EDGAR
EGGAR
EGGER
ELGAR
GAGER
HUGER
LAGER
LEGER
LUGER
NIGER
RIGOR
ROGER
SAGER
SUGAR
TIGER
VIGOR
WAGER
YAGER

G•S••
GASES
GASPE
GASPS
GASSY
GASTR
GESSO
GISMO
GISTS
GUSHY
GUSTA
GUSTO
GUSTS
GUSTY

5

G••S•
GASSY GAUSS GEESE GEEST GESSO GHOST GIPSY GLASS GLOSS GLOST GNASH GOOSE GOOSY GORSE GORSY GRASP GRASS GRIST GROSS GROSZ GUESS GUEST GUISE GUTSY GYPSY

G•••S
GABES GABYS GAELS GAFFS GAGES GAILS GAINS GAITS GALAS GALES GALLS GAMBS GAMES GAMPS GANGS GAOLS GAPES GARBS GARYS GASES GASPS GATES GAUDS GAULS GAURS GAUSS GAWKS GAZES GEARS GECKS GEEKS GELDS GENES GENTS GENUS GERMS GHATS GIBES GIFTS GIGAS GILDS GILES GILLS GIMPS GINKS GIRDS GIRLS GIROS GIRTS GISTS GIVES GLADS GLANS GLASS GLEDS GLEES GLENS GLIMS GLOBS GLOSS GLOWS GLUES GLUTS GNATS GNAWS GOADS GOALS GOATS GOBOS GOBYS GOERS GOLDS GOLFS GONGS GOODS GOOFS GOOKS GOONS GORES GOTHS GOVTS GOWNS GRABS GRADS GRAMS GRASS GRAYS GREGS GREYS GRIDS GRINS GRIPS GRITS GROSS GROTS GROWS GRUBS GUANS GUESS GULES GULFS GULLS GULPS GURUS GUSTS GWENS GWYNS GYRES GYROS GYRUS

•G•S•
AGIST EGEST

•G••S
AGHAS AGIOS AGNES AGNIS AGUES OGEES OGLES OGRES

••GS•
ANGST

••G•S
AEGIS ALGYS ANGUS ARGOS ARGUS BOGUS CAGES DEGAS DOGES EDGES GAGES GIGAS HIGHS HUGHS HUGOS JAGGS KAGUS LAGOS LEGES LOGES LOGOS MAGES MAGUS NEGUS NOGGS OLGAS PAGES RAGES REGES RIGGS SAGAS SAGES SAGOS SEGOS SIGHS SIGNS TOGAS URGES VAGUS WAGES YEGGS YOGHS YOGIS YUGAS

•••GS
BANGS BERGS BLDGS BONGS BRAGS BRIGS BUNGS BURGS CHUGS CLOGS CRAGS DANGS DINGS DOUGS DRAGS DREGS DRUGS DUNGS FANGS FLAGS FLOGS FROGS GANGS GONGS GREGS HANGS HONGS JAGGS KINGS LINGS LONGS LUNGS NOGGS PANGS PINGS PLUGS PRIGS PUNGS QUAGS RIGGS RINGS RUNGS SHAGS SINGS SKEGS SLAGS SLOGS SLUGS SMOGS SNAGS SNUGS SONGS STAGS SWAGS SWIGS TANGS THUGS TINGS TONGS TRIGS TWIGS VANGS WHIGS WINGS YEGGS ZINGS

G•T••
GATED GATES GATUN GETUP GOTHA GOTHS GUTSY GUTTA

G••T•
GAITS GARTH GASTR GENTS GERTY GHATS GIFTS GIRTH GIRTS GISTS GLUTS GNATS GOATS GOUTY GOVTS GRATE GRETA GRITS GROTS GUSTA GUSTO GUSTS GUSTY GUTTA

G•••T
GAMUT GAUNT GAVOT GEEST GEMOT GENET GHAUT GHENT GHOST GIANT GIGOT GLEET GLINT GLOAT GLOST GRAFT GRANT GREAT GREET GRIPT GRIST GROAT GROUT GRUNT GUEST GUILT

•G•T•
AGATE

•G••T
AGENT AGIST AGLET EGEST EGRET EGYPT

••G•T
ANGST ARGOT AUGHT BEGAT BEGET BEGOT BIGHT BIGOT DIGIT EIGHT ERGOT FAGOT FIGHT GIGOT INGOT LEGIT LIGHT MAGOT MIGHT NIGHT OUGHT PUGET RIGHT SIGHT TIGHT WIGHT

GU•••
GUACO GUANO GUANS GUARD GUAVA GUESS GUEST GUIDE GUIDO GUILD GUILE GUILT GUISE GULAR GULCH GULES GULFS GULLS GULLY GULPS GUMBO GUMMA GUMMY GUNNY GUPPY GURUS GUSHY GUSTA GUSTO GUSTS GUSTY GUTSY GUTTA GUYED

G•U••
GAUDI GAUDS GAUDY GAUGE GAULS GAUNT GAURS GAUSS GAUZE GAUZY GLUED GLUES GLUEY GLUME GLUTS GOUDA GOUGE GOURD GOUTY GRUBS GRUEL GRUFF GRUME GRUNT

G••U•
GAMUT GATUN GENUA GENUS GETUP GHAUT GHOUL GIGUE GLAUC GROUP GROUT GURUS GYRUS

•GU••
AGUES

••GU•
ALGUM ANGUS ARGUE ARGUS AUGUR BEGUM BEGUN BOGUS DEGUM FUGUE GIGUE HAGUE KAGUS LOGUE MAGUS MOGUL NEGUS ROGUE SAGUM TOGUE VAGUE VAGUS VOGUE VOGUL

G•V••
GAVEL GAVLE GAVOT GIVEN GIVER GIVES GOVTS

G••V•
GLOVE GRAVE GRAVY GROVE GUAVA

•G•V•
AGAVE OGIVE

••G•V
NEGEV

GW•••
GWENN GWENS GWYNS

G•W••
GAWKS GAWKY GOWNS

G••W•
GLOWS
GNAWN
GNAWS
GROWL
GROWN
GROWS

•G••W
AGLOW

G•••X
GALAX

GY•••
GYMNO
GYNEC
GYPSY
GYRAL
GYRES
GYRON
GYROS
GYRUS

G•Y••
GAYER
GAYLY
GLYCO
GLYPH
GOYIM
GUYED
GWYNS

G••Y•
GABYS
GARYS
GOBYS
GRAYS
GREYS

G•••Y
GABBY
GAILY
GAPPY
GASSY
GAUDY
GAUZY
GAWKY
GAYLY
GEMMY
GERRY
GERTY
GIDDY
GIMPY
GINNY
GIPSY
GLARY
GLAZY
GLORY
GLUEY
GNOMY
GODLY
GOLLY
GOODY
GOOEY
GOOFY
GOOSY
GORKY
GORSY
GOUTY
GRAPY
GRAVY
GULLY
GUMMY
GUNNY
GUPPY
GUSHY
GUSTY
GUTSY
GYPSY

•GY••
EGYPT

•G••Y
AGLEY
AGONY

••GY•
ALGYS

••G•Y
ANGRY
BAGGY
BIGLY
BOGEY
BOGGY
BUGGY
CAGEY
DOGGY
FOGGY
JAGGY
LEGGY
MUGGY
PEGGY
PIGGY
PIGMY
POGEY
PYGMY
RAGGY
RUGBY
SOGGY
VUGGY

•••GY
BAGGY
BILGY
BOGGY
BUGGY
BULGY
DINGY
DOGGY
DUNGY
ELEGY
FOGGY
HEDGY
JAGGY
LEDGY
LEGGY
MANGY
MUGGY
OLOGY
PEGGY
PHAGY
PIGGY
PLEGY
PODGY
PORGY
PUDGY
RAGGY
RANGY
RHAGY
RIDGY
SEDGY
SOGGY
STAGY
STOGY
SURGY
TANGY
VUGGY
WEDGY
WINGY

G•Z••
GAZED
GAZER
GAZES
GIZMO

G••Z•
GAUZE
GAUZY
GHAZI
GLAZE
GLAZY
GLOZE
GRAZE

G•••Z
GROSZ

•G•Z•
AGAZE

•G••Z
IGNAZ

HA•••
HABIT
HABUS
HACKS
HADED
HADES
HADJI
HAFIZ
HAFTS
HAGIO
HAGUE
HAHAS
HAIDA
HAIFA
HAIKS
HAIKU
HAILS
HAIRS
HAIRY
HAITI
HAKES
HAKIM
HALED
HALER
HALES
HALID
HALLE
HALLS
HALOS
HALTS
HALVE
HAMAL
HAMES
HAMMY
HAMZA
HANCE
HANDS
HANDY
HANGS
HANKS
HANNA
HANOI
HANSE
HAPLO
HAPLY
HAPPY
HARAR
HARDS
HARDY
HAREM
HARES
HARKS
HARLS
HARMS
HARPS
HARPY
HARRY
HARSH
HARTE
HARTS
HARTZ
HASNT
HASPS
HASTE
HASTY
HATCH
HATED
HATER
HATES
HATTY
HAULM
HAULS
HAUNT
HAVEN
HAVOC
HAWED
HAWKS
HAWSE
HAYDN
HAYED
HAYES
HAZED
HAZEL
HAZER
HAZES

H•A••
HEADS
HEADY
HEALS
HEAPS
HEARD
HEARS
HEART
HEATH
HEATS
HEAVE
HEAVY
HOARD
HOARY
HYALO

H••A•
HAHAS
HAMAL
HARAR
HBEAM
HEJAZ
HEMAL
HEMAN
HEMAT
HEPAT
HERAT
HEXAD
HIRAM
HOGAN
HOKAN
HONAN
HORAE
HORAL
HORAS
HULAS
HUMAN
HUNAN
HYLAS
HYRAX

H•••A
HAIDA
HAIFA
HAMZA
HANNA
HEDDA
HEKLA
HELGA
HEMIA
HENNA
HEPTA
HERMA
HILDA
HOSEA
HULDA
HYDRA
HYENA
HYPHA

•HA••
BHANG
CHAET
CHAFE
CHAFF
CHAIN
CHAIR
CHALK
CHAMP
CHANG
CHANT
CHAOS
CHAPE
CHAPS
CHAPT
CHARD
CHARE
CHARM
CHARS
CHART
CHARY
CHASE
CHASM
CHATS
CHAWS
DHAKS
GHANA
GHATS
GHAUT
GHAZI
KHADI
KHAKI
KHANS
LHASA
PHAGE
PHAGO
PHAGY
PHANE
PHANY
PHASE
PHASY
RHAGE
RHAGY
SHACK
SHADE
SHADY
SHAFT
SHAGS
SHAHS
SHAKE
SHAKO
SHAKY
SHALE
SHALL
SHALT
SHALY
SHAME
SHAMS
SHANK
SHANS
SHANT
SHAPE
SHARD
SHARE
SHARK
SHARP
SHAUN
SHAVE
SHAWL
SHAWM
SHAWN
SHAWS
SHAYS
THADS
THADY
THANE
THANK
THAWS
WHACK
WHALE
WHAMS
WHANG
WHAPS
WHARF

•H•A•
AHEAD
CHEAP
CHEAT
CHIAS
IHRAM
PHIAL
RHEAS
SHEAF
SHEAR
SHEAS
SHIAH
SHOAL
SHOAT
UHLAN
WHEAL
WHEAT

•H••A
CHELA
CHIBA
CHINA
CHITA
CHUFA
GHANA
LHASA
PHILA
PHYLA
RHODA
RHOEA
SHEBA
THECA
THEDA
THETA
THUJA

••HA•
AGHAS
BAHAI
BIHAR
COHAN
EPHAH
ETHAN
HAHAS
JIHAD
MAHAN
PSHAW
UNHAT

••H•A
BOHEA
LEHUA
NAHUA
RRHEA
SCHWA

•••HA
ALOHA
ALPHA
DACHA
GOTHA
HYPHA
MOCHA
NUCHA
OMAHA
PASHA

HB•••
HBEAM
HBOMB

H•B••
HABIT
HABUS
HOBBS
HOBBY
HOBOS

H••B•
HERBS
HERBY
HOBBS
HOBBY

H•••B
HBOMB
HOREB

•H•B•
CHIBA
CHUBS
PHEBE
PHOBE
SHEBA

•H••B
PHLEB
RHOMB
RHUMB
SHRUB
THROB
THUMB

5

••H•B
SAHEB
SAHIB

H•C••
HACKS
HECTO
HICKS
HOCKS
HOCUS

H••C•
HANCE
HATCH
HENCE
HITCH
HOICK
HOOCH
HUNCH
HUTCH

H•••C
HAVOC
HELIC
HEMIC
HUMIC

•H•C•
CHECK
CHICK
CHICO
CHOCK
CHUCK
PHYCO
SHACK
SHOCK
SHUCK
THECA
THICK
WHACK
WHICH

•H••C
OHMIC

••H•C
ETHIC

H•D••
HADED
HADES
HADJI
HEDDA
HEDGE
HEDGY
HIDER
HIDES
HODGE
HYDRA
HYDRO

H••D•
HAIDA
HANDS
HANDY
HARDS
HARDY
HAYDN
HEADS
HEADY
HEDDA
HEEDS
HERDS
HILDA
HINDI
HINDS
HINDU
HOLDS
HOODS
HORDE
HOWDY
HULDA
HURDS

H•••D
HADED
HALED
HALID
HATED
HAWED
HAYED
HAZED
HEARD
HEROD
HEWED
HEXAD
HEXED
HIKED
HIRED
HIVED
HOARD
HOLED
HOMED
HONED
HOPED
HOSED
HOUND
HUMID
HYOID

•H•D•
CHIDE
KHADI
RHODA
SHADE
SHADY
SHEDS
THADS
THADY
THEDA
THUDS

•H••D
AHEAD
CHARD
CHILD
CHORD
KHOND
SHARD
SHERD
SHIED
SHRED
THIRD

••HD•
MAHDI

••H•D
ACHED
APHID
EPHOD
JIHAD

HE•••
HEADS
HEADY
HEALS
HEAPS
HEARD
HEARS
HEART
HEATH
HEATS
HEAVE
HEAVY
HECTO
HEDDA
HEDGE
HEDGY
HEEDS
HEELS
HEFTS
HEFTY
HEGEL
HEIRS
HEIST
HEJAZ
HEKLA
HEKTO
HELEN
HELGA
HELIC
HELIO
HELIX
HELLE
HELLO
HELLS
HELMS
HELOT
HELPS
HELVE
HEMAL
HEMAN
HEMAT
HEMEN
HEMIA
HEMIC
HEMIN
HEMPS
HEMPY
HENCE
HENNA
HENRI
HENRY
HEPAT
HEPTA
HERAT
HERBS
HERBY
HERDS
HERLS
HERMA
HEROD
HERON
HERTZ
HETTY
HEWED
HEWER
HEXAD
HEXED
HEXES
HEXYL

H•E••
HBEAM
HEEDS
HEELS
HIERO
HOERS
HYENA
HYETO

H••E•
HADED
HADES
HAKES
HALED
HALER
HALES
HAMES
HAREM
HARES
HATED
HATER
HATES
HAVEN
HAWED
HAYED
HAYES
HAZED
HAZEL
HAZER
HAZES
HEGEL
HELEN
HEMEN
HEWED
HEWER
HEXED
HEXES
HIDER
HIDES
HIKED
HIKER
HIKES
HIRED
HIRER
HIRES
HIVED
HIVES
HOLED
HOLES
HOLEY
HOMED
HOMEO
HOMER
HOMES
HOMEY
HONED
HONES
HONEY
HOOEY
HOPED
HOPEH
HOPES
HOREB
HOSEA
HOSED
HOSES
HOTEL
HOVEL
HOVER
HUGER
HUPEH
HYMEN
HYPER

H•••E
HAGUE
HALLE
HALVE
HANCE
HANSE
HARTE
HASTE
HAWSE
HEAVE
HEDGE
HELLE
HELVE
HENCE
HINGE
HODGE
HOOKE
HORAE
HORDE
HORSE
HOUSE
HOWIE
HOYLE

•HE••
AHEAD
CHEAP
CHEAT
CHECK
CHEEK
CHEEP
CHEER
CHEFS
CHELA
CHEMI
CHEMO
CHERT
CHESS
CHEST
CHETH
CHETS
CHEVY
CHEWS
CHEWY
GHENT
PHEBE
PHENO
RHEAS
RHEUM
SHEAF
SHEAR
SHEAS
SHEBA
SHEDS
SHEEN
SHEEP
SHEER
SHEET
SHEIK
SHELF
SHELL
SHEOL
SHERD
SHEWN
SHEWS
THECA
THEDA
THEFT
THEIR
THEME
THERE
THERM
THESE
THETA
THEWS
THEWY
WHEAL
WHEAT
WHEEL
WHELK
WHELM
WHELP
WHENS
WHERE
WHETS
WHEYS

•H•E•
CHAET
CHEEK
CHEEP
CHEER
CHIEF
KHMER
PHLEB
PHREN
RHOEA
SHEEN
SHEEP
SHEER
SHEET
SHIED
SHIER
SHOER
SHOES
SHRED
SHREW
SHYER
THIEF
THREE
THREW
WHEEL

•H••E
CHAFE
CHAPE
CHARE
CHASE
CHIDE
CHILE
CHIME
CHINE
CHIVE
CHLOE
CHOKE
CHOLE
CHORE
CHOSE
CHUTE
CHYLE
CHYME
DHOLE
PHAGE
PHANE
PHASE
PHEBE
PHILE
PHOBE
PHONE
PHORE
PHYLE
PHYRE
PHYTE
RHAGE
RHINE
RHONE
RHYME
SHADE
SHAKE
SHALE
SHAME
SHAPE
SHARE
SHAVE
SHINE
SHIRE
SHIVE
SHONE
SHORE
SHOTE
SHOVE
SHUTE
THANE
THEME
THERE
THESE
THINE
THOLE
THOSE
THREE
THULE
THYME
WHALE
WHERE
WHILE
WHINE
WHITE
WHOLE
WHORE
WHOSE

••HE•
ACHED
ACHES
ASHEN
ASHER
ASHES
BOHEA
ESHER
ETHEL
ETHER
OCHER
OTHER
RRHEA
SAHEB
SPHEN
TEHEE
USHER
UTHER

••H•E
TAHOE
TEHEE
YAHVE

•••HE
BATHE
BOCHE
BRAHE
CACHE
DUBHE
FICHE
LATHE
LETHE
LITHE
NICHE
RAPHE
RUCHE
TITHE
TYCHE
WITHE

H•F••
HAFIZ
HAFTS

HEFTS
HEFTY
HIFIS
HUFFS
HUFFY

H••F•
HAIFA
HOOFS
HUFFS
HUFFY

•H•F•
CHAFE
CHAFF
CHEFS
CHUFA
SHAFT
SHIFT
THEFT
WHIFF

•H••F
CHAFF
CHIEF
SHEAF
SHELF
THIEF
WHARF
WHIFF

H•G••
HAGIO
HAGUE
HEGEL
HIGHS
HOGAN
HUGER
HUGHS
HUGOS
HYGRO

H••G•
HANGS
HEDGE
HEDGY
HELGA
HINGE
HODGE
HONGS

H•••G
HYING

•H•G•
CHUGS
PHAGE
PHAGO
PHAGY
RHAGE
RHAGY
SHAGS
THIGH
THUGS
WHIGS

•H••G
BHANG
CHANG
SHRUG
THING
THONG
WHANG

HH•••
HHOUR

H•H••
HAHAS

H••H•
HIGHS
HUGHS
HYPHA

H•••H
HARSH
HATCH
HEATH
HITCH
HOOCH
HOPEH
HUMPH
HUNCH
HUPEH
HUTCH

•H•H•
SHAHS

•H••H
CHETH
SHIAH
SHUSH
THIGH
THOTH
WHICH
WHISH

••H•H
EPHAH

HI•••
HICKS
HIDER
HIDES
HIERO
HIFIS
HIGHS
HIKED
HIKER
HIKES
HILDA
HILLS
HILLY
HILTS
HILUM
HINDI
HINDS
HINDU
HINGE
HINNY
HINTS
HIPPO
HIRAM
HIRED
HIRER
HIRES
HISTO
HITCH
HIVED
HIVES

H•I••
HAIDA
HAIFA
HAIKS
HAIKU
HAILS
HAIRS
HAIRY
HAITI
HEIRS
HEIST
HOICK
HOIST
HYING

H••I•
HABIT
HAFIZ
HAGIO
HAKIM
HALID
HELIC
HELIO
HELIX
HEMIA
HEMIC
HEMIN
HIFIS
HOWIE
HUMIC
HUMID
HYOID

H•••I
HADJI
HAITI
HANOI
HENRI
HINDI
HOURI

•HI••
CHIAS
CHIBA
CHICK
CHICO
CHIDE
CHIEF
CHILD
CHILE
CHILI
CHILL
CHILO
CHIME
CHINA
CHINE
CHINK
CHINO
CHINS
CHIOS
CHIPS
CHIRM
CHIRO
CHIRP
CHIRR
CHITA
CHITS
CHIVE
PHIAL
PHILA
PHILE
PHILO
PHILS
PHILY
PHIPS
RHINE
RHINO
RHIZO
SHIAH
SHIED
SHIER
SHIFT
SHILL
SHILY
SHIMS
SHINE
SHINS
SHINY
SHIPS
SHIRE
SHIRK
SHIRR
SHIRT
SHIVE
SHIVS
THICK
THIEF
THIGH
THINE
THING
THINK
THINS
THIOL
THIRD
WHICH
WHIFF
WHIGS
WHILE
WHIMS
WHINE
WHINS
WHINY
WHIPS
WHIPT
WHIRL
WHIRS
WHISH
WHISK
WHIST
WHITE
WHITS

•H•I•
CHAIN
CHAIR
CHOIR
CHRIS
OHMIC
SHEIK
THEIR

•H••I
CHEMI
CHILI
DHOTI
GHAZI
KHADI
KHAKI
PHYSI
SHOJI

••HI•
APHID
APHIS
ECHIN
ETHIC
NIHIL
OPHIO
SAHIB
SCHIZ

••H•I
BAHAI
MAHDI

•••HI
AMPHI
ARCHI
DELHI
ORCHI
SPAHI
TOPHI
XIPHI

H•J••
HEJAZ

H••J•
HADJI

•H•J•
SHOJI
THUJA

H•K••
HAKES
HAKIM
HEKLA
HEKTO
HIKED
HIKER
HIKES
HOKAN
HOKUM

H••K•
HACKS
HAIKS
HAIKU
HANKS
HARKS
HAWKS
HICKS
HOCKS
HONKS
HOOKE
HOOKS
HOOKY
HULKS
HULKY
HUNKS
HUNKY
HUSKS
HUSKY

H•••K
HOICK

•H•K•
CHOKE
CHOKY
DHAKS
KHAKI
SHAKE
SHAKO
SHAKY

•H••K
CHALK
CHECK
CHEEK
CHICK
CHINK
CHOCK
CHUCK
CHUNK
SHACK
SHANK
SHARK
SHEIK
SHIRK
SHOCK
SHOOK
SHUCK
THANK
THICK
THINK
WHACK
WHELK
WHISK

H•L••
HALED
HALER
HALES
HALID
HALLE
HALLS
HALOS
HALTS
HALVE
HELEN
HELGA
HELIC
HELIO
HELIX
HELLE
HELLO
HELLS
HELMS
HELOT
HELPS
HELVE
HILDA
HILLS
HILLY
HILTS
HILUM
HOLDS
HOLED
HOLES
HOLEY
HOLLY
HOLMS
HULAS
HULDA
HULKS
HULKY
HULLS
HYLAS

H••L•
HAILS
HALLE
HALLS
HAPLO
HAPLY
HARLS
HAULM
HAULS
HEALS
HEELS
HEKLA
HELLE
HELLO
HELLS
HERLS
HILLS
HILLY
HOLLY
HOTLY
HOWLS
HOYLE
HULLS
HURLS
HURLY
HYALO

H•••L
HAMAL
HAZEL
HEGEL
HEMAL
HEXYL
HORAL
HOTEL
HOVEL

•HL••
CHLOE
CHLOR
PHLEB
PHLOX
UHLAN

•H•L•
CHALK
CHELA
CHILD
CHILE
CHILI
CHILL
CHILO
CHOLE
CHYLE
DHOLE
PHILA
PHILE
PHILO
PHILS
PHILY
PHYLA
PHYLE
PHYLL
PHYLO
SHALE
SHALL
SHALT
SHALY
SHELF
SHELL
SHILL
SHILY
SHULS
SHYLY
THOLE
THULE
WHALE
WHELK
WHELM
WHELP
WHILE
WHOLE

•H••L
CHILL
CHURL
GHOUL
PHIAL

PHYLL
SHALL
SHAWL
SHELL
SHEOL
SHILL
SHOAL
SHORL
THIOL
WHEAL
WHEEL
WHIRL
WHORL

••HL•
MUHLY

••H•L
BOHOL
ETHEL
ETHYL
NIHIL

H•M••
HAMAL
HAMES
HAMMY
HAMZA
HEMAL
HEMAN
HEMAT
HEMEN
HEMIA
HEMIC
HEMIN
HEMPS
HEMPY
HOMED
HOMEO
HOMER
HOMES
HOMEY
HUMAN
HUMIC
HUMID
HUMOR
HUMPH
HUMPS
HUMPY
HUMUS
HYMEN
HYMNS

H••M•
HAMMY
HARMS
HBOMB
HELMS
HERMA
HOLMS

H•••M
HAKIM
HAREM
HAULM
HBEAM
HILUM
HIRAM
HOKUM

•HM••
KHMER
OHMIC

•H•M•
CHAMP
CHEMI
CHEMO
CHIME
CHUMP
CHUMS
CHYME
RHOMB
RHUMB
RHYME
SHAME
SHAMS
SHIMS
THEME
THUMB
THUMP
THYME
THYMY
WHAMS
WHIMS

•H••M
CHARM
CHASM
CHIRM
CHROM
IHRAM
RHEUM
SHAWM
THERM
THRUM
WHELM

••HM•
SCHMO

••H•M
NAHUM

•••HM
ABOHM

H•N••
HANCE
HANDS
HANDY
HANGS
HANKS
HANNA
HANOI
HANSE
HENCE
HENNA
HENRI
HENRY
HINDI
HINDS
HINDU
HINGE
HINNY
HINTS
HONAN
HONED
HONES
HONEY
HONGS
HONKS
HONOR
HUNAN
HUNCH
HUNKS
HUNKY
HUNTS

H••N•
HANNA
HASNT
HAUNT
HENNA
HINNY
HORNS
HORNY
HOUND
HYENA
HYING
HYMNS
HYPNO

H•••N
HAVEN
HAYDN
HELEN
HEMAN
HEMEN
HEMIN
HERON
HOGAN
HOKAN
HONAN
HUMAN
HUNAN
HURON
HYMEN
HYSON

•H•N•
BHANG
CHANG
CHANT
CHINA
CHINE
CHINK
CHINO
CHINS
CHUNK
GHANA
GHENT
KHANS
KHOND
PHANE
PHANY
PHENO
PHONE
PHONO
PHONY
RHINE
RHINO
RHONE
SHANK
SHANS
SHANT
SHINE
SHINS
SHINY
SHONE
SHUNS
SHUNT
THANE
THANK
THINE
THING
THINK
THINS
THONG
WHANG
WHENS
WHINE
WHINS
WHINY

•H••N
CHAIN
CHRON
CHURN
PHREN
SHAUN
SHAWN
SHEEN
SHEWN
SHORN
SHOWN
THORN
UHLAN

••HN•
ETHNO
JOHNS

••H•N
ASHEN
COHAN
ECHIN
ETHAN
MAHAN
SPHEN

•••HN
FOEHN
TECHN

HO•••
HOARD
HOARY
HOBBS
HOBBY
HOBOS
HOCKS
HOCUS
HODGE
HOERS
HOGAN
HOICK
HOIST
HOKAN
HOKUM
HOLDS
HOLED
HOLES
HOLEY
HOLLY
HOLMS
HOMED
HOMEO
HOMER
HOMES
HOMEY
HONAN
HONED
HONES
HONEY
HONGS
HONKS
HONOR
HOOCH
HOODS
HOOEY
HOOFS
HOOKE
HOOKS
HOOKY
HOOPS
HOOTS
HOPED
HOPEH
HOPES
HORAE
HORAL
HORAS
HORDE
HOREB
HORNS
HORNY
HORSE
HORST
HORSY
HORUS
HOSEA
HOSED
HOSES
HOSTS
HOTEL
HOTLY
HOUND
HOURI
HOURS
HOUSE
HOVEL
HOVER
HOWDY
HOWIE
HOWLS
HOYLE

H•O••
HBOMB
HHOUR
HOOCH
HOODS
HOOEY
HOOFS
HOOKE
HOOKS
HOOKY
HOOPS
HOOTS
HYOID

H••O•
HALOS
HANOI
HAVOC
HELOT
HEROD
HERON
HOBOS
HONOR
HUGOS
HUMOR
HURON
HYPOS
HYSON

H•••O
HAGIO
HAPLO
HECTO
HEKTO
HELIO
HELLO
HIERO
HIPPO
HISTO
HOMEO
HYALO
HYDRO
HYETO
HYGRO
HYPNO
HYPSO

•HO••
CHOCK
CHOIR
CHOKE
CHOKY
CHOLE
CHOPS
CHORD
CHORE
CHORO
CHOSE
CHOWS
DHOLE
DHOTI
DHOWS
GHOST
GHOUL
HHOUR
KHOND
PHOBE
PHONE
PHONO
PHONY
PHORE
PHOTO
PHOTS
RHODA
RHOEA
RHOMB
RHONE
SHOAL
SHOAT
SHOCK
SHOER
SHOES
SHOJI
SHONE
SHOOK
SHOOS
SHOOT
SHOPS
SHORE
SHORL
SHORN
SHORT
SHOTE
SHOTS
SHOUT
SHOVE
SHOWN
SHOWS
SHOWY
THOLE
THONG
THORN
THORP
THOSE
THOTH
WHOLE
WHOOP
WHOPS
WHORE
WHORL
WHORT
WHOSE
WHOSO

•H•O•
CHAOS
CHIOS
CHLOE
CHLOR
CHROM
CHRON
PHLOX
SHEOL
SHOOK
SHOOS
SHOOT
THIOL
THROB
THROW
WHOOP

•H••O
CHEMO
CHICO
CHILO
CHINO
CHIRO
CHORO
PHAGO
PHENO
PHILO
PHONO
PHOTO
PHYCO
PHYLO
PHYTO
RHINO
RHIZO
SHAKO
THYRO
WHOSO

••HO•
ABHOR
ATHOS
BOHOL
EPHOD
EPHOR
ETHOS
ICHOR
TAHOE
WAHOO
YAHOO

••H•O
ETHNO
OPHIO
SCHMO
WAHOO
YAHOO

•••HO
ANTHO
BATHO
DICHO
IDAHO
LITHO
METHO
MYTHO
NEPHO
ORTHO
PATHO

H•P••
HAPLO
HAPLY
HAPPY
HEPAT
HEPTA
HIPPO
HOPED
HOPEH
HOPES
HUPEH
HYPER
HYPHA
HYPNO
HYPOS
HYPSO

H••P•
HAPPY
HARPS
HARPY
HASPS
HEAPS
HELPS
HEMPS
HEMPY
HIPPO
HOOPS
HUMPH
HUMPS
HUMPY

•H•P•
CHAPE
CHAPS
CHAPT
CHIPS
CHOPS
PHIPS
SHAPE
SHIPS
SHOPS
WHAPS
WHIPS
WHIPT
WHOPS

•H••P
CHAMP
CHEAP
CHEEP
CHIRP
CHUMP
SHARP
SHEEP
THORP
THUMP
WHELP
WHOOP

H•R••
HARAR
HARDS
HARDY
HAREM
HARES
HARKS
HARLS
HARMS
HARPS
HARPY
HARRY
HARSH
HARTE
HARTS
HARTZ
HERAT
HERBS
HERBY
HERDS
HERLS
HERMA
HEROD
HERON
HERTZ
HIRAM
HIRED
HIRER
HIRES
HORAE
HORAL
HORAS
HORDE
HOREB
HORNS
HORNY
HORSE
HORST
HORSY
HORUS
HURDS
HURLS
HURLY
HURON
HURRY
HURTS
HYRAX

H••R•
HAIRS
HAIRY
HARRY
HEARD
HEARS
HEART
HEIRS
HENRI
HENRY
HIERO
HOARD
HOARY
HOERS
HOURI
HOURS
HURRY
HYDRA
HYDRO
HYGRO

H•••R
HALER
HARAR
HATER
HAZER
HEWER
HHOUR
HIDER
HIKER
HIRER
HOMER
HONOR
HOVER
HUGER
HUMOR
HYPER

•HR••
CHRIS
CHROM
CHRON
CHRYS
IHRAM
PHREN
SHRED
SHREW
SHRUB
SHRUG
THREE
THREW
THROB
THROW
THRUM

•H•R•
CHARD
CHARE
CHARM
CHARS
CHART
CHARY
CHERT
CHIRM
CHIRO
CHIRP
CHIRR
CHORD
CHORE
CHORO
CHURL
CHURN
CHURR
PHORE
PHYRE
SHARD
SHARE
SHARK
SHARP
SHERD
SHIRE
SHIRK
SHIRR
SHIRT
SHORE
SHORL
SHORN
SHORT
THERE
THERM
THIRD
THORN
THORP
THURS
THYRO
WHARF
WHERE
WHIRL
WHIRS
WHORE
WHORL
WHORT

•H••R
CHAIR
CHEER
CHIRR
CHLOR
CHOIR
CHURR
HHOUR
KHMER
SHEAR
SHEER
SHIER
SHIRR
SHOER
SHYER
THEIR

••HR•
LEHRS
NEHRU
OCHRY

••H•R
ABHOR
ASHER
ASHUR
BIHAR
EPHOR
ESHER
ETHER
ICHOR
MOHUR
OCHER
OTHER
USHER
UTHER

•••HR
AMPHR
ARTHR
NEPHR

H•S••
HASNT
HASPS
HASTE
HASTY
HISTO
HOSEA
HOSED
HOSES
HOSTS
HUSKS
HUSKY
HUSSY
HYSON

H••S•
HANSE
HARSH
HAWSE
HEIST
HOIST
HORSE
HORST
HORSY
HOUSE
HUSSY
HYPSO

H•••S
HABUS
HACKS
HADES
HAFTS
HAHAS
HAIKS
HAILS
HAIRS
HAKES
HALES
HALLS
HALOS
HALTS
HAMES
HANDS
HANGS
HANKS
HARDS
HARES
HARKS
HARLS
HARMS
HARPS
HARTS
HASPS
HATES
HAULS
HAWKS
HAYES
HAZES
HEADS
HEALS
HEAPS
HEARS
HEATS
HEEDS
HEELS
HEFTS
HEIRS
HELLS
HELMS
HELPS
HEMPS
HERBS
HERDS
HERLS
HEXES
HICKS
HIDES
HIFIS
HIGHS
HIKES
HILLS
HILTS
HINDS
HINTS
HIRES
HIVES
HOBBS
HOBOS
HOCKS
HOCUS
HOERS
HOLDS
HOLES
HOLMS
HOMES
HONES
HONGS
HONKS
HOODS
HOOFS
HOOKS
HOOPS
HOOTS
HOPES
HORAS
HORNS
HORUS
HOSES
HOSTS
HOURS
HOWLS
HUFFS
HUGHS
HUGOS
HULAS
HULKS
HULLS
HUMPS
HUMUS
HUNKS
HUNTS
HURDS
HURLS
HURTS
HUSKS
HYLAS
HYMNS
HYPOS

•H•S•
CHASE
CHASM
CHESS
CHEST
CHOSE
GHOST
LHASA
PHASE
PHASY
PHYSI
SHUSH
THESE
THOSE
WHISH
WHISK
WHIST
WHOSE
WHOSO

•H••S
CHAOS
CHAPS
CHARS
CHATS
CHAWS
CHEFS
CHESS
CHETS
CHEWS
CHIAS
CHINS
CHIOS
CHIPS
CHITS
CHOPS
CHOWS
CHRIS
CHRYS
CHUBS
CHUGS
CHUMS
DHAKS
DHOWS
GHATS
KHANS
PHILS
PHIPS
PHOTS
RHEAS
SHAGS
SHAHS
SHAMS
SHANS
SHAWS
SHAYS
SHEAS
SHEDS
SHEWS
SHIMS
SHINS
SHIPS
SHIVS
SHOES
SHOOS
SHOPS
SHOTS
SHOWS
SHULS
SHUNS
SHUTS
THADS
THAWS
THEWS
THINS
THUDS
THUGS
THURS
WHAMS
WHAPS
WHENS
WHETS
WHEYS
WHIGS
WHIMS
WHINS
WHIPS
WHIRS
WHITS
WHOPS

••H•S
ACHES
AGHAS
APHIS
ASHES
ATHOS
BAHTS
ETHOS
HAHAS
JEHUS
JOHNS
LEHRS

•••HS
ADAHS
AMAHS
ANKHS
AYAHS
BATHS
BETHS
BLAHS
GOTHS
HIGHS
HUGHS
KAPHS
LATHS
LOCHS
MOTHS
MYTHS
NOAHS
OATHS
OPAHS
PATHS
PITHS
RUTHS
SETHS
SHAHS
SIGHS
SIKHS

TETHS
USPHS
YODHS
YOGHS

H•T••
HATCH
HATED
HATER
HATES
HATTY
HETTY
HITCH
HOTEL
HOTLY
HUTCH

H••T•
HAFTS
HAITI
HALTS
HARTE
HARTS
HARTZ
HASTE
HASTY
HATTY
HEATH
HEATS
HECTO
HEFTS
HEFTY
HEKTO
HEPTA
HERTZ
HETTY
HILTS
HINTS
HISTO
HOOTS
HOSTS
HUNTS
HURTS
HYETO

H•••T
HABIT
HASNT
HAUNT
HEART
HEIST
HELOT
HEMAT
HEPAT
HERAT
HOIST
HORST

•H•T•
CHATS
CHETH
CHETS
CHITA
CHITS
CHUTE
DHOTI
GHATS
PHOTO
PHOTS
PHYTE
PHYTO
SHOTE
SHOTS
SHUTE
SHUTS
THETA
THOTH
WHETS
WHITE
WHITS

•H••T
CHAET
CHANT
CHAPT
CHART
CHEAT
CHERT
CHEST
GHAUT
GHENT
GHOST
SHAFT
SHALT
SHANT
SHEET
SHIFT
SHIRT
SHOAT
SHOOT
SHORT
SHOUT
SHUNT
THEFT
WHEAT
WHIPT
WHIST
WHORT

••HT•
BAHTS

••H•T
UNHAT

•••HT
AUGHT
BIGHT
EIGHT
FIGHT
LICHT
LIGHT
MIGHT
NIGHT
OUGHT
RIGHT
SIGHT
TIGHT
WIGHT
YACHT

HU•••
HUFFS
HUFFY
HUGER
HUGHS
HUGOS
HULAS
HULDA
HULKS
HULKY
HULLS
HUMAN
HUMIC
HUMID
HUMOR
HUMPH
HUMPS
HUMPY
HUMUS
HUNAN
HUNCH
HUNKS
HUNKY
HUNTS
HUPEH
HURDS
HURLS
HURLY
HURON
HURRY
HURTS
HUSKS
HUSKY
HUSSY
HUTCH

H•U••
HAULM
HAULS
HAUNT
HOUND
HOURI
HOURS
HOUSE

H••U•
HABUS
HAGUE
HHOUR
HILUM
HOCUS
HOKUM
HORUS
HUMUS

H•••U
HAIKU
HINDU

•HU••
CHUBS
CHUCK
CHUFA
CHUGS
CHUMP
CHUMS
CHUNK
CHURL
CHURN
CHURR
CHUTE
RHUMB
SHUCK
SHULS
SHUNS
SHUNT
SHUSH
SHUTE
SHUTS
THUDS
THUGS
THUJA
THULE
THUMB
THUMP
THURS

•H•U•
GHAUT
GHOUL
HHOUR
RHEUM
SHAUN
SHOUT
SHRUB
SHRUG
THRUM

••HU•
ASHUR
JEHUS
LEHUA
MOHUR
NAHUA
NAHUM

••H•U
NEHRU

•••HU
ELIHU
FICHU
PRAHU
SADHU

H•V••
HAVEN
HAVOC
HIVED
HIVES
HOVEL
HOVER

H••V•
HALVE
HEAVE
HEAVY
HELVE

•H•V•
CHEVY
CHIVE
SHAVE
SHIVE
SHIVS
SHOVE

••HV•
YAHVE

H•W••
HAWED
HAWKS
HAWSE
HEWED
HEWER
HOWDY
HOWIE
HOWLS

•H•W•
CHAWS
CHEWS
CHEWY
CHOWS
DHOWS
SHAWL
SHAWM
SHAWN
SHAWS
SHEWN
SHEWS
SHOWN
SHOWS
SHOWY
THAWS
THEWS
THEWY

•H••W
SHREW
THREW
THROW

••HW•
SCHWA

••H•W
PSHAW

H•X••
HEXAD
HEXED
HEXES
HEXYL

H•••X
HELIX
HYRAX

•H••X
PHLOX

HY•••
HYALO
HYDRA
HYDRO
HYENA
HYETO
HYGRO
HYING
HYLAS
HYMEN
HYMNS
HYOID
HYPER
HYPHA
HYPNO
HYPOS
HYPSO
HYRAX
HYSON

H•Y••
HAYDN
HAYED
HAYES
HOYLE

H••Y•
HEXYL

H•••Y
HAIRY
HAMMY
HANDY
HAPLY
HAPPY
HARDY
HARPY
HARRY
HASTY
HATTY
HEADY
HEAVY
HEDGY
HEFTY
HEMPY
HENRY
HERBY
HETTY
HILLY
HINNY
HOARY
HOBBY
HOLEY
HOLLY
HOMEY
HONEY
HOOEY
HOOKY
HORNY
HORSY
HOTLY
HOWDY
HUFFY
HULKY
HUMPY
HUNKY
HURLY
HURRY
HUSKY
HUSSY

•HY••
CHYLE
CHYME
PHYCO
PHYLA
PHYLE
PHYLL
PHYLO
PHYRE
PHYSI
PHYTE
PHYTO
RHYME
SHYER
SHYLY
THYME
THYMY
THYRO

•H•Y•
CHRYS
SHAYS
WHEYS

•H••Y
CHARY
CHEVY
CHEWY
CHOKY
PHAGY
PHANY
PHASY
PHILY
PHONY
RHAGY
SHADY
SHAKY
SHALY
SHILY
SHINY
SHOWY
SHYLY
THADY
THEWY
THYMY
WHINY

••HY•
ETHYL

••H•Y
MUHLY
OCHRY

•••HY
ALPHY
ARCHY
BATHY
BUSHY
CATHY
CUSHY
DASHY
DUCHY
FISHY
GUSHY
ITCHY
KATHY
LATHY
MACHY
MASHY
MESHY
MOTHY
MUSHY
PACHY
PATHY
PITHY
PUSHY
RUSHY
SOPHY
TACHY
VICHY
WASHY
WITHY

H•Z••
HAZED
HAZEL
HAZER
HAZES

H••Z•
HAMZA

H•••Z
HAFIZ
HARTZ
HEJAZ
HERTZ

•H•Z•
GHAZI
RHIZO

••H•Z
SCHIZ

IA•••
IAMBI
IAMBS
IASIS
IATRO
IATRY

I•A••
IDAHO
IMAGE
IMAGO
IMAMS

INANE
INAPT
INARM
IRAQI
IRATE
ISAAC
ITALS
ITALY
IVANS

I••A•
IBEAM
ICIAN
IDEAL
IDEAS
IGNAZ
IHRAM
ILEAC
ILEAL
ILIAC
ILIAD
ILIAN
INCAN
INCAS
INLAW
INLAY
IOTAS
IRMAS
ISAAC
ISBAS
ISLAM
IXIAS
IYYAR

I•••A
ILONA
INDIA
INDRA
INFRA
INTRA
IONIA

•IA••
BIALY
DIALS
DIANA
DIANE
DIARY
DIAZO
FIATS
GIANT
LIANA
LIANE
LIANG
LIARS
MIAMI
MIAUL
PIANO
PIAVE
RIALS
RIANT
RIATA
SIALO
TIARA
VIALS
VIAND

•I•A•
AIDAS
BIHAR
BINAL
CIDAL
CIGAR
DINAH
DINAR
DITAS
DIVAN
DIVAS
DIWAN
FILAR
FINAL
GIGAS
HIRAM
JIHAD
KIVAS
LIGAN
LILAC
LILAS
LIRAS
LISAS
LITAI
LITAS
LIZAS
MICAH
MICAS
MIDAS
MILAN
MINAE
MINAS
NINAS
NIPAS
NISAN
NIVAL
NIZAM
PICAL
PICAS
PIKAS
PILAF
PILAR
PIMAN
PIMAS
PINAS
PIPAL
PITAS
RITAS
RIVAL
RIYAL
SILAS
SIMAR
SINAI
SISAL
SITAR
SIVAN
SIZAR
TICAL
TIDAL
TINAS
TITAN
VICAR
VINAS
VIRAL
VISAS
VITAE
VITAL
WIGAN
WITAN

•I••A
BIOTA
CILIA
CIRCA
CITRA
DIANA
DICTA
DINKA
FIONA
GILDA
HILDA
JIDDA
KIOWA
LIANA
LIBRA
LIBYA
LINDA
LINGA
LIVIA
MICRA
MILIA
MINNA
MIRZA
OIDEA
PIETA
PILEA
PINNA
PINTA
PIZZA
RIATA
SIGMA
SILVA
SITKA
TIARA
TIBIA
TILDA
TINEA
VILLA
VIOLA
VIRGA
VISTA
VITTA
WILLA
WILMA
WIRRA

••IA•
ALIAS
AMIAS
APIAN
ARIAN
ARIAS
ASIAN
AVIAN
AXIAL
BRIAN
BRIAR
CHIAS
ELIAS
FRIAR
ICIAN
ILIAC
ILIAD
ILIAN
IXIAS
NAIAD
PHIAL
PRIAM
SHIAH
TRIAD
TRIAL
UMIAK
URIAH
XTIAN

••I•A
ANIMA
ANITA
ARICA
BEIRA
CEIBA
CHIBA
CHINA
CHITA
DVINA
EDINA
ELIZA
ERICA
ERIKA
EVITA
HAIDA
HAIFA
JAINA
LAIKA
LEILA
LUISA
MOIRA
ORIYA
OUIDA
OUIJA
PAISA
PHILA
PLICA
PRIMA
SAIGA
SPICA
TAIGA
TRINA
UTICA
VOILA

•••IA
AECIA
AEMIA
ALGIA
AMNIA
ATRIA
CELIA
CERIA
CILIA
COBIA
CORIA
CURIA
DACIA
DELIA
DULIA
ENTIA
FOLIA
GONIA
HEMIA
INDIA
IONIA
JULIA
LABIA
LAMIA
LIVIA
LOGIA
LUCIA
LYDIA
MAFIA
MANIA
MARIA
MEDIA
MILIA
MYRIA
NORIA
NUBIA
OPSIA
OSTIA
PODIA
RETIA
SEPIA
SOFIA
SONIA
STRIA
SYRIA
TAFIA
TIBIA
XENIA
ZAMIA

IB•••
IBEAM
IBSEN

I•B••
IMBED
IMBUE
ISBAS

I••B•
IAMBI
IAMBS

•IB••
BIBBS
BIBLE
CIBOL
FIBER
FIBRO
GIBED
GIBER
GIBES
JIBED
JIBES
KIBEI
KIBES
LIBBY
LIBEL
LIBER
LIBRA
LIBYA
SIBYL
TIBER
TIBET
TIBIA
VIBES
ZIBET

•I•B•
BIBBS
BILBO
LIBBY
LIMBI
LIMBO
LIMBS
NIMBI
NIOBE

••IB•
ABIBS
ALIBI
BRIBE
CEIBA
CHIBA
CRIBS
DRIBS
ORIBI
TRIBE

••I•B
CLIMB

•••IB
ADLIB
CARIB
SAHIB
SQUIB

IC•••
ICHOR
ICIAN
ICIER
ICILY
ICING
ICONO
ICONS
ICOSI
ICTUS

I•C••
INCAN
INCAS
INCUR
INCUS
ITCHY

I•••C
ILEAC
ILIAC
INDIC
IODIC
IONIC
ISAAC
ISTIC

•IC••
BICES
DICED
DICER
DICHO
DICKS
DICKY
DICTA
FICES
FICHE
FICHU
HICKS
KICKS
LICHT
LICIT
LICKS
MICAH
MICAS
MICKY
MICRA
MICRO
NICER
NICHE
NICKS
NICKY
PICAL
PICAS
PICKS
PICOT
PICRO
PICTS
PICUL
RICED
RICER
RICES
RICIN
RICKS
RICKY
SICES
SICKS
TICAL
TICKS
VICAR
VICES
VICHY
VICKS
VICKY
WICKS

•I•C•
AITCH
BIRCH
BITCH
CINCH
CIRCA
CIRCE
CISCO
DIRCK
DISCI
DISCS
DITCH
FILCH
FINCH
FISCS
FITCH
HITCH
MILCH
MINCE
MITCH
NIECE
PIECE
PINCH
PISCI
PITCH
SINCE
TINCT
VINCE
VINCI
VISCT
WINCE
WINCH
WITCH
ZINCS
ZINCY

•I••C
CIVIC
LILAC
MIMIC
SILIC
VINIC

••IC•
ALICE
AMICE
ARICA
BRICE
BRICK
CHICK
CHICO
CLICK
CRICK
DEICE
EDICT
EPICS
ERICA
ERICH
ERICS
EVICT
FLICK
HOICK
JUICE
JUICY
PLICA
PRICE
PRICK
QUICK
REICH
SLICE

5

SLICK
SNICK
SPICA
SPICE
SPICY
STICH
STICK
THICK
TRICE
TRICH
TRICK
TWICE
URICO
UTICA
VOICE
WHICH

••I•C
ILIAC

•••IC
ANTIC
AREIC
ASPIC
ATTIC
AULIC
AURIC
AZOIC
BARIC
BASIC
BORIC
CERIC
CIVIC
COLIC
COMIC
CONIC
CUBIC
CYNIC
DARIC
DOMIC
DORIC
EDDIC
EOLIC
ETHIC
FOLIC
GAMIC
GENIC
HELIC
HEMIC
HUMIC
INDIC
IODIC
IONIC
ISTIC
LOGIC
LYRIC
LYTIC
MAGIC
MALIC
MANIC
MEDIC
MELIC
MESIC
MIMIC
MUSIC
OHMIC
OLEIC
OPTIC
OSMIC
PANIC
PUBIC
PUDIC
PUNIC
RABIC
RELIC
RUNIC
SALIC
SILIC
SONIC
STOIC
SUFIC
TELIC
TONIC
TOPIC
TORIC
TOXIC
TUNIC
VARIC
VATIC
VEDIC
VESIC
VINIC
XERIC
YOGIC

ID•••
IDAHO
IDEAL
IDEAS
IDIOM
IDIOT
IDLED
IDLER
IDLES
IDOLS
IDYLL
IDYLS

I•D••
INDEX
INDIA
INDIC
INDOW
INDRA
INDRI
INDUE
INDUS
IODIC
IODOL

I••D•
IMIDE
IMIDO
IMIDS
IRIDO

I•••D
IDLED
ILIAD
IMBED
INKED
INNED
IRKED
ISLED
IVIED

•ID••
AIDAS
AIDED
AIDER
AIDES
BIDDY
BIDED
BIDES
BIDET
CIDAL
CIDER
DIDNT
DIDOS
DIDST
EIDER
FIDEL
GIDDY
HIDER
HIDES
JIDDA
KIDDY
MIDAS
MIDDY
MIDGE
MIDST
NIDED
NIDES
NIDUS
OIDEA
RIDER
RIDES
RIDGE
RIDGY
SIDED
SIDER
SIDES
SIDLE
SIDON
TIDAL
TIDED
TIDES
VIDEO
WIDDY
WIDEN
WIDER
WIDOW
WIDTH

•I•D•
BIDDY
BINDS
BIRDS
CINDY
DIODE
FINDS
GIDDY
GILDA
GILDS
GIRDS
HILDA
HINDI
HINDS
HINDU
JIDDA
KIDDY
KINDS
LINDA
MIDDY
MINDS
MISDO
RINDS
TILDA
TILDE
WIDDY
WILDS
WINDS
WINDY

•I••D
AIDED
AILED
AIMED
AIRED
BIDED
BIFID
BIPED
BIPOD
CITED
DICED
DIKED
DINED
DIVED
FIELD
FIEND
FIFED
FILED
FINED
FIORD
FIRED
FIXED
GIBED
HIKED
HIRED
HIVED
JIBED
JIHAD
KITED
LIKED
LIMED
LINED
LIPID
LIVED
LIVID
MIMED
MINED
MIRED
MIXED
NIDED
NIXED
OILED
PIKED
PILED
PINED
PIPED
RICED
RIGID
RILED
RIMED
RIVED
SIDED
SIRED
SIZED
TIDED
TILED
TIMED
TIMID
TINED
TIRED
VIAND
VISED
VIVID
WIELD
WILED
WINED
WIPED
WIRED
WISED
WIVED
YIELD

••ID•
ABIDE
ACIDS
AMIDE
AMIDO
ASIDE
BRIDE
CHIDE
ELIDE
ENIDS
GLIDE
GRIDE
GRIDS
GUIDE
GUIDO
HAIDA
IMIDE
IMIDO
IMIDS
IRIDO
MAIDS
OUIDA
OXIDE
PRIDE
QUIDS
RAIDS
SKIDS
SLIDE
SNIDE
VOIDS

••I•D
BAIRD
BLIND
BUILD
CAIRD
CHILD
CRIED
DRIED
FLIED
FRIED
GRIND
GUILD
ILIAD
IVIED
LAIRD
NAIAD
PLIED
POIND
PRIED
SHIED
SKIED
SPIED
STIED
THIRD
TRIAD
TRIED
WEIRD
WRIED

•••ID
ACRID
ALGID
APHID
AROID
AVOID
BIFID
BOVID
BRAID
CUPID
DAVID
DRUID
FELID
FETID
FLUID
GADID
GELID
GEOID
HALID
HUMID
HYOID
LEPID
LIPID
LIVID
LUCID
LURID
MUCID
MYOID
OVOID
PLAID
PLOID
PYOID
RABID
RAPID
REDID
RIGID
SAPID
SAYID
SOLID
SQUID
STAID
TABID
TEPID
TIMID
TUMID
UNDID
VALID
VAPID
VIVID
ZOOID

I•E••
IBEAM
IDEAL
IDEAS
ILEAC
ILEAL
ILEUM
ILEUS
INEPT
INERT
IRENE
ISERE
ITEMS

I••E•
IBSEN
ICIER
IDLED
IDLER
IDLES
ILMEN
IMBED
IMPEL
INDEX
INFER
INKED
INKER
INLET
INNED
INNER
INSET
INTER
IRKED
ISLED
ISLES
ISLET
ISSEI
IVIED
IVIES

I•••E
IMAGE
IMBUE
IMIDE
IMINE
INANE
INDUE
INKLE
INURE
IRATE
IRENE
IRONE
ISERE
ISSUE
ISTLE
IXTLE

•IE••
BIERS
DIEGO
DIENE
DIETS
FIEFS
FIELD
FIEND
FIERY
HIERO
KIERS
LIEGE
LIENS
LIEUT
MIENS
NIECE
PIECE
PIERS
PIETA
PIETY
PIEZO
SIEGE
SIEUR
SIEVE
TIEIN
TIERS
TIEUP
VIEWS
VIEWY
WIELD
YIELD

•I•E•
AIDED
AIDER
AIDES
AIKEN
AILED
AIMED
AIMEE
AIRED
BICES
BIDED
BIDES
BIDET
BIKES
BILES
BINES
BINET
BIPED
BISES
BITER
BITES
BIZET
CIDER
CIMEX
CITED
CITES

CIVET
DICED
DICER
DIKED
DIKER
DIKES
DIMER
DIMES
DINED
DINER
DINES
DIRER
DIVED
DIVER
DIVES
DIZEN
EIDER
FIBER
FICES
FIDEL
FIFED
FIFER
FIFES
FILED
FILER
FILES
FILET
FINED
FINER
FINES
FIRED
FIRER
FIRES
FIVER
FIVES
FIXED
FIXER
FIXES
GIBED
GIBER
GIBES
GILES
GIMEL
GIVEN
GIVER
GIVES
HIDER
HIDES
HIKED
HIKER
HIKES
HIRED
HIRER
HIRES
HIVED
HIVES
JIBED
JIBES
KIBEI
KIBES
KITED
KITES
LIBEL
LIBER
LIFER
LIKED
LIKEN
LIKES
LIMED
LIMEN
LIMES
LIMEY
LINED
LINEN
LINER
LINES
LINEY
LITER
LIVED
LIVEN
LIVER
LIVES
MIKES
MIKEY
MILER
MILES
MIMED
MIMER
MIMES
MINED
MINER
MINES
MIRED
MIRES
MISER
MISES
MITER
MITES
MIXED
MIXER
MIXES
NICER
NIDED
NIDES
NIGEL
NIGER
NINES
NISEI
NITER
NIXED
NIXES
OIDEA
OILED
OILER
PIKED
PIKER
PIKES
PILEA
PILED
PILEI
PILES
PINED
PINEL
PINER
PINES
PINEY
PIPED
PIPER
PIPES
PIPET
RICED
RICER
RICES
RIDER
RIDES
RIGEL
RILED
RILES
RILEY
RIMED
RIMER
RIMES
RIPEN
RIPER
RISEN
RISER
RISES
RITES
RIVED
RIVEN
RIVER
RIVES
RIVET
SICES
SIDED
SIDER
SIDES
SILEX
SINES
SINEW
SIRED
SIREN
SIRES
SITES
SIXES
SIZED
SIZES
TIBER
TIBET
TIDED
TIDES
TIGER
TILED
TILER
TILES
TIMED
TIMER
TIMES
TINEA
TINED
TINES
TIRED
TIRES
TITER
VIBES
VICES
VIDEO
VILER
VIMEN
VINES
VIPER
VIREO
VIRES
VISED
VISES
VIXEN
WIDEN
WIDER
WILED
WILES
WINED
WINES
WIPED
WIPER
WIPES
WIRED
WIRER
WIRES
WISED
WISER
WISES
WIVED
WIVER
WIVES
WIZEN
YIPES
ZIBET

•I••E

AIMEE
AISLE
AISNE
BIBLE
BILGE
BINGE
BIRLE
CIRCE
DIANE
DIENE
DIODE
DIONE
DIRGE
DIXIE
FICHE
FIQUE
GIGUE
HINGE
LIANE
LIEGE
LISLE
LITHE
LIVRE
MIDGE
MINAE
MINCE
NICHE
NIECE
NIOBE
NIXIE
PIAVE
PIECE
PIQUE
PIXIE
RIDGE
RIFLE
RINSE
SIDLE
SIEGE
SIEVE
SINCE
SINGE
SIXTE
TILDE
TINGE
TITHE
TITLE
VINCE
VIRGE
VITAE
WINCE
WINZE
WITHE
WITTE

••IE•

ABIEL
ABIES
ADIEU
ALIEN
AMIEL
AMIES
ARIEL
ARIES
BRIEF
BRIER
CHIEF
CRIED
CRIER
CRIES
DRIED
DRIER
DRIES
EDIES
ERIES
FLIED
FLIER
FLIES
FRIED
FRIER
FRIES
GRIEF
GRIEG
ICIER
IVIED
IVIES
OKIES
ORIEL
OSIER
PLIED
PLIER
PLIES
PRIED
PRIER
PRIES
QUIET
SHIED
SHIER
SKIED
SKIER
SKIES
SLIER
SPIED
SPIEL
SPIER
SPIES
STIED
STIES
THIEF
TRIED
TRIER
TRIES
URIEL
WRIED
WRIER
WRIES

••I•E

ABIDE
AFIRE
AGILE
ALICE
ALIKE
ALINE
ALIVE
AMICE
AMIDE
AMINE
ANILE
ANIME
ANISE
ARISE
ASIDE
ATIVE
AXILE
AZINE
BAIZE
BEIGE
BOISE
BRIBE
BRICE
BRIDE
BRINE
CHIDE
CHILE
CHIME
CHINE
CHIVE
CLIME
CLINE
CLIVE
CRIME
DEICE
DRIVE
EDILE
ELIDE
ELISE
ELITE
EMILE
EXILE
FRISE
GLIDE
GRIDE
GRIME
GRIPE
GUIDE
GUILE
GUISE
IMIDE
IMINE
JUICE
KNIFE
KOINE
LOIRE
LUISE
MAINE
MAIZE
MOIRE
NAIVE
NOISE
OGIVE
OLIVE
OPINE
OVINE
OXIDE
OXIME
PAINE
PAISE
PHILE
POISE
PRICE
PRIDE
PRIME
PRIZE
QUIRE
QUITE
RAISE
RHINE
SEINE
SEIZE
SHINE
SHIRE
SHIVE
SKIVE
SLICE
SLIDE
SLIME
SMILE
SMITE
SNIDE
SNIPE
SPICE
SPIKE
SPILE
SPINE
SPIRE
SPITE
STILE
STIPE
SUITE
SWINE
SWIPE
THINE
TOILE
TRIBE
TRICE
TRINE
TRIPE
TRITE
TWICE
TWINE
UNITE
URINE
UTILE
VOICE
VOILE
WAIVE
WHILE
WHINE
WHITE
WRITE
ZAIRE

•••IE

ABBIE
ADDIE
AERIE
AGGIE
ALGIE
ALLIE
ANNIE
ARNIE
ARTIE
BELIE
BOGIE
BOWIE
CAVIE
CELIE
CURIE
CUTIE
DAVIE
DIXIE
DOBIE
DOGIE
EADIE
EDDIE
EERIE
EFFIE
ELLIE
ELSIE
EMMIE
ERNIE
ESSIE
ETTIE
EYRIE
GENIE
HOWIE
JAMIE
JOSIE
JULIE
KATIE
LEWIE
MAMIE
MARIE
MOVIE
MOXIE
NIXIE
OLLIE
PIXIE
PYXIE
RAMIE
SADIE
SUSIE

UNTIE

I•F••
INFER
INFIX
INFRA

•IF••
BIFFS
BIFFY
BIFID
FIFED
FIFER
FIFES
FIFTH
FIFTY
GIFTS
HIFIS
JIFFS
JIFFY
LIFER
LIFTS
MIFFS
MIFFY
NIFTY
RIFFS
RIFLE
RIFTS
SIFTS
TIFFS

•I•F•
BIFFS
BIFFY
FIEFS
JIFFS
JIFFY
MIFFS
MIFFY
RIFFS
TIFFS

•I••F
PILAF

••IF•
ALIFS
CLIFF
COIFS
DEIFY
DRIFT
EDIFY
HAIFA
KNIFE
LEIFS
REIFY
SCIFI
SHIFT
SKIFF
SNIFF
STIFF
SWIFT
UNIFY
WAIFS
WHIFF

••I•F
BRIEF
CHIEF
CLIFF
GRIEF
SKIFF
SNIFF
STIFF
THIEF
WHIFF

•••IF
CALIF
MOTIF
SERIF

IG•••
IGLOO
IGNAZ

I•G••
INGOT

I••G•
IMAGE
IMAGO
INIGO

I•••G
ICING

•IG••
BIGHT
BIGLY
BIGOT
CIGAR
DIGIT
EIGHT
FIGHT
GIGAS
GIGOT
GIGUE
HIGHS
LIGAN
LIGHT
LIGNI
LIGNO
MIGHT
NIGEL
NIGER
NIGHT
NIGRI
PIGGY
PIGMY
RIGEL
RIGGS
RIGHT
RIGID
RIGOR
SIGHS
SIGHT
SIGIL
SIGMA
SIGNS
TIGER
TIGHT
VIGIL
VIGOR
WIGAN
WIGHT

•I•G•
BILGE
BILGY
BINGE
BINGO
DIEGO
DINGO
DINGS
DINGY
DIRGE
HINGE
JINGO
KINGS
LIEGE
LINGA
LINGO
LINGS
MIDGE
PIGGY
PINGO
PINGS
RIDGE
RIDGY
RIGGS
RINGS
SIEGE
SINGE
SINGS
TINGE
TINGS
VIRGA
VIRGE
VIRGO
WINGS
WINGY
ZINGS

•I••G
GIING
LIANG

••IG•
ALIGN
AMIGO
BEIGE
BLIGH
BRIGS
COIGN
DEIGN
FEIGN
FRIGG
INIGO
LEIGH
LUIGI
NEIGH
OLIGO
PRIGS
REIGN
SAIGA
SWIGS
TAIGA
THIGH
TRIGO
TRIGS
TWIGS
WEIGH
WHIGS

••I•G
ACING
AGING
APING
AWING
AXING
BEING
BRING
CLING
CUING
DOING
DYING
EKING
EWING
EYING
FLING
FRIGG
GIING
GOING
GRIEG
HYING
ICING
LYING
OKING
OWING
RUING
SLING
STING
SUING
SWING
THING
TYING
USING
VYING
WRING

•••IG
CRAIG
SPRIG
UNRIG

IH•••
IHRAM

I•H••
ICHOR

I••H•
IDAHO
ITCHY

I•••H
IRISH

•IH••
BIHAR
JIHAD
NIHIL

•I•H•
BIGHT
DICHO
EIGHT
FICHE
FICHU
FIGHT
FISHY
HIGHS
LICHT
LIGHT
LITHE
LITHO
MIGHT
NICHE
NIGHT
PITHS
PITHY
RIGHT
SIGHS
SIGHT
SIKHS
TIGHT
TITHE
VICHY
WIGHT
WITHE
WITHY
XIPHI

•I••H
AITCH
BIRCH
BIRTH
BITCH
CINCH
DINAH
DITCH
FIFTH
FILCH
FILTH
FINCH
FIRTH
FITCH
GIRTH
HITCH
MICAH
MILCH
MIRTH
MITCH
NINTH
PINCH
PITCH
SIXTH
TILTH
WIDTH
WINCH
WITCH

••IH•
ELIHU

••I•H
AMISH
APISH
BLIGH
CUISH
EDITH
ERICH
FAITH
FRITH
IRISH
KEITH
LEIGH
NEIGH
REICH
SHIAH
SMITH
STICH
SWISH
THIGH
TRICH
URIAH
WEIGH
WHICH
WHISH

I•I••
ICIAN
ICIER
ICILY
ICING
IDIOM
IDIOT
ILIAC
ILIAD
ILIAN
ILIUM
IMIDE
IMIDO
IMIDS
IMINE
IMINO
INIGO
INION
IRIDO
IRISH
ITION
IVIED
IVIES
IXIAS
IXION

I••I•
IASIS
IMMIX
INDIA
INDIC
INFIX
IODIC
IONIA
IONIC
IRVIN
IRWIN
ISTIC

I•••I
IAMBI
ICOSI
INDRI
IRAQI
ISSEI

•II••
GIING

•I•I•
BIFID
BINIT
CILIA
CIVIC
CIVIL
DIGIT
DIXIE
DIXIT
FIJIS
FINIS
HIFIS
KININ
KIRIN
KIWIS
LICIT
LIMIT
LININ
LIPID
LIVIA
LIVID
MILIA
MIMIC
MIMIR
MIMIS
MINIM
NIHIL
NIXIE
PILIS
PIPIT
PIXIE
RICIN
RIGID
SIGIL
SILIC
SITIN
TIBIA
TIEIN
TIKIS
TIMID
TITIS
VIGIL
VINIC
VISIT
VIVID
VIZIR

•I••I
CIRRI
DISCI
HINDI
JINNI
KIBEI
LIGNI
LIMBI
LIPPI
LITAI
MIAMI
MILLI
NIGRI
NIMBI
NISEI
NITRI
PILEI
PINNI
PISCI
SINAI
VILLI
VINCI
VITRI
XIPHI

••I•I
ACINI
ALIBI
CHILI
HAITI
LUIGI
ORIBI
PRIMI
SCIFI
SPINI

•••II
AALII
GENII
RADII
TORII

•IJ••
BIJOU
DIJON
FIJIS

••IJ•
OUIJA

IK•••
IKONS

I•K••
INKED
INKER
INKLE
IRKED

•IK••
AIKEN
BIKES
BIKOL
DIKED

DIKER
DIKES
HIKED
HIKER
HIKES
LIKED
LIKEN
LIKES
MIKES
MIKEY
PIKAS
PIKED
PIKER
PIKES
SIKHS
TIKIS

•I•K•
BILKS
DICKS
DICKY
DINKA
DINKY
DIRKS
DISKO
DISKS
FINKS
GINKS
HICKS
JINKS
KICKS
KINKS
KINKY
KIRKS
LICKS
LINKS
MICKY
MILKS
MILKY
MINKS
NICKS
NICKY
PICKS
PINKS
PINKY
RICKS
RICKY
RINKS
RISKS
RISKY
SICKS
SILKS
SILKY
SINKS
SITKA
TICKS
VICKS
VICKY
WICKS
WINKS
ZINKY

•I••K
DIRCK
KIOSK
MINSK

••IK•
ALIKE
ERIKA
ERIKS
HAIKS
HAIKU
LAIKA
SPIKE
SPIKY

••I•K
BLINK
BRICK
BRINK
BRISK
CHICK
CHINK
CLICK
CLINK
CRICK
DRINK
FLICK
FRISK
HOICK
PRICK
PRINK
QUICK
QUIRK
SHIRK
SKINK
SLICK
SLINK
SMIRK
SNICK
STICK
STINK
STIRK
THICK
THINK
TRICK
UMIAK
WHISK

•••IK
BATIK
KAMIK
RURIK
SHEIK
TUPIK

IL•••
ILEAC
ILEAL
ILEUM
ILEUS
ILIAC
ILIAD
ILIAN
ILIUM
ILLUS
ILMEN
ILONA

I•L••
IDLED
IDLER
IDLES
IGLOO
ILLUS
INLAW
INLAY
INLET
ISLAM
ISLED
ISLES
ISLET

I••L•
ICILY
IDOLS
IDYLL
IDYLS
IMPLY
INKLE
ISTLE
ITALS
ITALY
IXTLE

I•••L
IDEAL
IDYLL
ILEAL
IMPEL
IODOL

•IL••
AILED
BILBO
BILES
BILGE
BILGY
BILKS
BILLS
BILLY
CILIA
FILAR
FILCH
FILED
FILER
FILES
FILET
FILLS
FILLY
FILMS
FILMY
FILTH
FILUM
GILDA
GILDS
GILES
GILLS
HILDA
HILLS
HILLY
HILTS
HILUM
JILLS
JILTS
KILLS
KILNS
KILOS
KILTS
KILTY
LILAC
LILAS
LILLY
LILTS
LILYS
MILAN
MILCH
MILER
MILES
MILIA
MILKS
MILKY
MILLI
MILLS
MILLY
MILTS
OILED
OILER
PILAF
PILAR
PILEA
PILED
PILEI
PILES
PILIS
PILLS
PILOT
RILED
RILES
RILEY
RILLS
SILAS
SILEX
SILIC
SILKS
SILKY
SILLS
SILLY
SILOS
SILTS
SILTY
SILVA
TILDA
TILDE
TILED
TILER
TILES
TILLS
TILLY
TILTH
TILTS
VILER
VILLA
VILLI
VILLS
WILDS
WILED
WILES
WILLA
WILLS
WILLY
WILMA
WILTS

•I•L•
AISLE
BIALY
BIBLE
BIGLY
BILLS
BILLY
BIRLE
BIRLS
DIALS
DIMLY
DIPLO
FIELD
FILLS
FILLY
FITLY
GILLS
GIRLS
HILLS
HILLY
JILLS
KILLS
LILLY
LISLE
MILLI
MILLS
MILLY
PILLS
RIALS
RIFLE
RILLS
SIALO
SIDLE
SILLS
SILLY
TILLS
TILLY
TITLE
VIALS
VILLA
VILLI
VILLS
VIOLA
VIOLS
WIELD
WILLA
WILLS
WILLY
YIELD

•I••L
BIKOL
BINAL
CIBOL
CIDAL
CIVIL
FIDEL
FINAL
GIMEL
LIBEL
MIAUL
NIGEL
NIHIL
NIVAL
PICAL
PICUL
PINEL
PIPAL
RIGEL
RIVAL
RIYAL
SIBYL
SIGIL
SISAL
TICAL
TIDAL
VIGIL
VINYL
VIRAL
VITAL

••IL•
AGILE
ANILE
ANILS
ARILS
ATILT
AXILE
AXILS
BAILS
BOILS
BRILL
BUILD
BUILT
CEILS
CHILD
CHILE
CHILI
CHILL
CHILO
COILS
DAILY
DOILY
DRILL
DRILY
EDILE
EMILE
EMILS
EMILY
EVILS
EXILE
FAILS
FOILS
FRILL
GAILS
GAILY
GRILL
GUILD
GUILE
GUILT
HAILS
ICILY
JAILS
LEILA
MAILS
MOILS
NAILS
NEILS
PAILS
PHILA
PHILE
PHILO
PHILS
PHILY
POILU
QUILL
QUILT
RAILS
ROILS
ROILY
SAILS
SHILL
SHILY
SKILL
SLILY
SMILE
SOILS
SPILE
SPILL
SPILT
STILE
STILL
STILT
SWILL
TAILS
TOILE
TOILS
TRILL
TWILL
UTILE
VEILS
VOILA
VOILE
WAILS
WHILE

••I•L
ABIEL
AMIEL
ARIEL
AXIAL
BRILL
CHILL
DRILL
FRILL
FRIML
GRILL
ORIEL
PHIAL
QUILL
SHILL
SKILL
SPIEL
SPILL
STILL
SWILL
SWIRL
THIOL
TRIAL
TRILL
TRIOL
TWILL
TWIRL
URIEL
WHIRL

•••IL
ANVIL
APRIL
ARGIL
AUXIL
AVAIL
BASIL
BRAIL
BROIL
CAVIL
CECIL
CIVIL
CYRIL
DEVIL
FLAIL
FRAIL
FUSIL
FUZIL
GRAIL
NEVIL
NIHIL
PERIL
PUPIL
QUAIL
SIGIL
SNAIL
SPOIL
SWAIL
SYBIL
TRAIL
UNTIL
VEXIL
VIGIL
VMAIL
ZORIL

IM•••
IMAGE
IMAGO
IMAMS
IMBED
IMBUE
IMIDE
IMIDO
IMIDS
IMINE
IMINO
IMMIX
IMPEL
IMPLY

5

I•M••
IAMBI
IAMBS
ILMEN
IMMIX
IRMAS

I••M•
IMAMS
ITEMS

I•••M
IBEAM
IDIOM
IHRAM
ILEUM
ILIUM
INARM
ISLAM

•IM••
AIMED
AIMEE
CIMEX
DIMER
DIMES
DIMLY
GIMEL
GIMPS
GIMPY
JIMMY
LIMBI
LIMBO
LIMBS
LIMED
LIMEN
LIMES
LIMEY
LIMIT
LIMNS
LIMPS
MIMED
MIMER
MIMES
MIMIC
MIMIR
MIMIS
NIMBI
PIMAN
PIMAS
PIMPS
RIMED
RIMER
RIMES
SIMAR
SIMON
SIMPS
TIMED
TIMER
TIMES
TIMID
TIMMY
VIMEN

•I•M•
FILMS
FILMY
FIRMS
GISMO
GIZMO
JIMMY
MIAMI
PIGMY
SIGMA
TIMMY
WILMA

•I••M
FILUM
HILUM
HIRAM
MINIM
NIZAM

••IM•
ANIMA
ANIME
BLIMP
BRIMS
CHIME
CLIMB
CLIME
CRIME
CRIMP
FRIML
GLIMS
GRIME
GRIMM
MAIMS
OXIME
PRIMA
PRIME
PRIMI
PRIMO
PRIMP
PRIMS
REIMS
SHIMS
SKIMO
SKIMP
SKIMS
SLIME
SLIMS
SLIMY
STIMY
SWIMS
TRIMS
WHIMS

••I•M
ARIUM
AXIOM
CHIRM
DEISM
FOISM
GRIMM
IDIOM
ILIUM
ODIUM
OPIUM
PRIAM
PRISM
SEISM

•••IM
BEDIM
CLAIM
DECIM
DENIM
GOYIM
HAKIM
MAXIM
MINIM
PURIM
SCRIM

IN•••
INANE
INAPT
INARM
INCAN
INCAS
INCUR
INCUS
INDEX
INDIA
INDIC
INDOW
INDRA
INDRI
INDUE
INDUS
INEPT
INERT
INFER
INFIX
INFRA
INGOT
INIGO
INION
INKED
INKER
INKLE
INLAW
INLAY
INLET
INNED
INNER
INPUT
INSET
INTER
INTRA
INTRO
INURE
INURN

I•N••
IGNAZ
INNED
INNER
IONIA
IONIC

I••N•
ICING
ICONO
ICONS
IKONS
ILONA
IMINE
IMINO
INANE
IRENE
IRONE
IRONS
IRONY
IVANS

I•••N
IBSEN
ICIAN
ILIAN
ILMEN
INCAN
INION
INURN
IRVIN
IRWIN
ITION
IXION

•IN••
AINOS
AINUS
BINAL
BINDS
BINES
BINET
BINGE
BINGO
BINIT
CINCH
CINDY
DINAH
DINAR
DINED
DINER
DINES
DINGO
DINGS
DINGY
DINKA
DINKY
DINTS
FINAL
FINCH
FINDS
FINED
FINER
FINES
FINIS
FINKS
FINNS
FINNY
GINKS
GINNY
HINDI
HINDS
HINDU
HINGE
HINNY
HINTS
JINGO
JINKS
JINNI
JINNY
KINDS
KINGS
KININ
KINKS
KINKY
LINDA
LINED
LINEN
LINER
LINES
LINEY
LINGA
LINGO
LINGS
LININ
LINKS
LINTY
LINUS
MINAE
MINAS
MINCE
MINDS
MINED
MINER
MINES
MINIM
MINKS
MINNA
MINOR
MINOS
MINSK
MINTS
MINUS
NINAS
NINES
NINNY
NINTH
NINUS
PINAS
PINCH
PINED
PINEL
PINER
PINES
PINEY
PINGO
PINGS
PINKS
PINKY
PINNA
PINNI
PINON
PINTA
PINTO
PINTS
PINUP
RINDS
RINGS
RINKS
RINSE
SINAI
SINCE
SINES
SINEW
SINGE
SINGS
SINKS
SINUS
TINAS
TINCT
TINEA
TINED
TINES
TINGE
TINGS
TINNY
TINTS
VINAS
VINCE
VINCI
VINES
VINIC
VINNY
VINYL
WINCE
WINCH
WINDS
WINDY
WINED
WINES
WINGS
WINGY
WINKS
WINOS
WINZE
ZINCS
ZINCY
ZINGS
ZINKY

•I•N•
AISNE
CIONS
DIANA
DIANE
DIDNT
DIENE
DIONE
FIEND
FINNS
FINNY
FIONA
FIRNS
GIANT
GIING
GINNY
HINNY
JINNI
JINNY
KILNS
LIANA
LIANE
LIANG
LIENS
LIGNI
LIGNO
LIMNS
LIONS
MIENS
MINNA
NINNY
PIANO
PINNA
PINNI
PIONS
RIANT
SIGNS
TINNY
VIAND
VINNY

•I••N
AIKEN
BISON
DIJON
DIVAN
DIWAN
DIZEN
GIPON
GIVEN
KININ
KIRIN
LIGAN
LIKEN
LIMEN
LINEN
LININ
LIVEN
MILAN
NISAN
NITON
NIXON
PIMAN
PINON
PITON
RICIN
RIPEN
RISEN
RIVEN
SIDON
SIMON
SIREN
SITIN
SIVAN
TIEIN
TITAN
VIMEN
VIXEN
WIDEN
WIGAN
WITAN
WIZEN
ZIRON

••IN•
ACING
ACINI
AGING
ALINE
AMINE
AMINO
APING
AWING
AXING
AYINS
AZINE
BEING
BLIND
BLINK
BRINE
BRING
BRINK
BRINY
CHINA
CHINE
CHINK
CHINO
CHINS
CLINE
CLING
CLINK
CLINO
CLINT
COINS
CUING
DOING
DRINK
DVINA
DYING
EDINA
EKING
EWING
EYING
FAINT
FEINT
FLING
FLINT
GAINS
GIING
GLINT
GOING
GRIND
GRINS
HYING
ICING
IMINE
IMINO
JAINA
JAINS
JOINS
JOINT
KOINE
LOINS
LYING
MAINE
MAINS
MAINZ
OKING

OPINE
OVINE
OWING
PAINE
PAINS
PAINT
PLINY
POIND
POINT
PRINK
PRINT
QUINT
RAINS
RAINY
REINS
RHINE
RHINO
RUING
RUINS
SAINT
SEINE
SHINE
SHINS
SHINY
SKINK
SKINS
SLING
SLINK
SPINE
SPINI
SPINS
SPINY
STING
STINK
STINT
SUING
SUINT
SWINE
SWING
TAINO
TAINS
TAINT
THINE
THING
THINK
THINS
TRINA
TRINE
TWINE
TWINS
TYING
URINE
URINO
USING
VEINS
VEINY
VYING
WAINS
WHINE
WHINS
WHINY
WRING

••I•N

ALIEN
ALIGN
ANION
APIAN
ARIAN
ARION
ASIAN
ATION
AVIAN
AVION
BAIRN
BRIAN
CAIRN
COIGN
DEIGN
FEIGN
ICIAN
ILIAN
INION
ITION
IXION
ONION
ORION
REIGN
SCION
UNION
XTIAN

•••IN

ACTIN
ADMIN
AGAIN
ALBIN
ALGIN
ALOIN
ALUIN
ALVIN
ALWIN
AMAIN
AUXIN
AYDIN
BASIN
BEGIN
BENIN
BEVIN
BLAIN
BONIN
BRAIN
BRUIN
BURIN
CABIN
CHAIN
COLIN
CUMIN
CUTIN
DRAIN
ECHIN
EDWIN
ELAIN
ELFIN
ELGIN
ELOIN
ELVIN
ELWIN
EOSIN
ERWIN
GAMIN
GRAIN
GROIN
HEMIN
IRVIN
IRWIN
KEVIN
KININ
KIRIN
LADIN
LAPIN
LATIN
LENIN
LININ
LYSIN
MATIN
MUCIN
OLEIN
ORCIN
ORPIN
PEKIN
PEPIN
PLAIN
QUOIN
REGIN
RENIN
RESIN
RICIN
ROBIN
RODIN
ROSIN
RUNIN
SABIN
SASIN
SATIN
SAVIN
SERIN
SITIN
SKEIN
SLAIN
SOZIN
SPAIN
STAIN
STEIN
SWAIN
TIEIN
TOXIN
TRAIN
TURIN
TWAIN
UNPIN
VAGIN
YOGIN
ZAYIN

IO•••

IODIC
IODOL
IONIA
IONIC
IOTAS

I•O••

ICONO
ICONS
ICOSI
IDOLS
IKONS
ILONA
IRONE
IRONS
IRONY
IVORY

I••O•

ICHOR
IDIOM
IDIOT
IGLOO
INDOW
INGOT
INION
IODOL
ITION
IXION

I•••O

IATRO
ICONO
IDAHO
IGLOO
IMAGO
IMIDO
IMINO
INIGO
INTRO
IRIDO

•IO••

BIOTA
CIONS
DIODE
DIONE
FIONA
FIORD
KIOSK
KIOWA
LIONS
NIOBE
PIONS
PIOUS
RIOTS
SIOUX
VIOLA
VIOLS

•I•O•

AINOS
BIGOT
BIJOU
BIKOL
BIPOD
BISON
CIBOL
DIDOS
DIJON
DIVOT
GIGOT
GIPON
GIROS
KILOS
MINOR
MINOS
NITON
NIXON
PICOT
PILOT
PINON
PITON
PIVOT
RIGOR
SIDON
SILOS
SIMON
TIROS
VIGOR
VISOR
VIZOR
WIDOW
WINOS
ZIRON

•I••O

BILBO
BINGO
CIRRO
CISCO
DIAZO
DICHO
DIEGO
DINGO
DIPLO
DISKO
DITTO
FIBRO
GISMO
GIZMO
HIERO
HIPPO
HISTO
JINGO
LIGNO
LIMBO
LINGO
LITHO
MICRO
MISDO
NITRO
PIANO
PICRO
PIEZO
PINGO
PINTO
SIALO
VIDEO
VIREO
VIRGO

••IO•

ADIOS
AGIOS
ANION
ARION
ATION
AVION
AXIOM
CHIOS
CLIOS
ELIOT
IDIOM
IDIOT
INION
ITION
IXION
OLIOS
ONION
ORION
PRIOR
SCION
THIOL
TRIOL
TRIOS
UNION

••I•O

AMIDO
AMIGO
AMINO
ANISO
AVISO
CAIRO
CHICO
CHILO
CHINO
CHIRO
CLINO
GUIDO
IMIDO
IMINO
INIGO
IRIDO
OLIGO
ONIRO
PHILO
PRIMO
QUITO
RHINO
RHIZO
SKIMO
SPIRO
TAINO
TRIGO
URICO
URINO

•••IO

ANGIO
ANZIO
AUDIO
CONIO
CURIO
ELAIO
FOLIO
FUGIO
GONIO
HAGIO
HELIO
JULIO
LABIO
MEDIO
OPHIO
PATIO
POLIO
RADIO
RATIO
SOCIO
TOKIO
VARIO

I•P••

IMPEL
IMPLY
INPUT

I••P•

INAPT
INEPT

•IP••

BIPED
BIPOD
DIPLO
DIPPY
GIPON
GIPSY
HIPPO
LIPID
LIPPI
LIPPY
NIPAS
NIPPY
PIPAL
PIPED
PIPER
PIPES
PIPET
PIPIT
RIPEN
RIPER
TIPPY
TIPSY
VIPER
WIPED
WIPER
WIPES
XIPHI
YIPES
ZIPPY

•I•P•

DIPPY
GIMPS
GIMPY
HIPPO
LIMPS
LIPPI
LIPPY
LISPS
NIPPY
PIMPS
SIMPS
TIPPY
WISPS
WISPY
ZIPPY

•I••P

MIXUP
PINUP
SIRUP
TIEUP

••IP•

BLIPS
CHIPS
CLIPS
DRIPS
DRIPT
FLIPS
GRIPE
GRIPS
GRIPT
PHIPS
QUIPS
QUIPU
SHIPS
SKIPS
SLIPS
SLIPT
SNIPE
SNIPS
STIPE
SWIPE
TRIPE
TRIPS
WHIPS
WHIPT

••I•P

BLIMP
CHIRP
CRIMP
CRISP
PRIMP
SKIMP
TWIRP

•••IP

ATRIP
EQUIP
OXLIP
SCRIP
STRIP
TULIP
UNRIP

I••Q•

IRAQI

•IQ••

FIQUE
PIQUE

IR•••
IRAQI
IRATE
IRENE
IRIDO
IRISH
IRKED
IRMAS
IRONE
IRONS
IRONY
IRVIN
IRWIN

I•R••
IHRAM

I••R•
IATRO
IATRY
INARM
INDRA
INDRI
INERT
INFRA
INTRA
INTRO
INURE
INURN
ISERE
IVORY

I•••R
ICHOR
ICIER
IDLER
INCUR
INFER
INKER
INNER
INTER
IYYAR

•IR••
AIRED
BIRCH
BIRDS
BIRLE
BIRLS
BIRRS
BIRTH
CIRCA
CIRCE
CIRRI
CIRRO
DIRCK
DIRER
DIRGE
DIRKS
DIRTY
FIRED
FIRER
FIRES
FIRMS
FIRNS
FIRRY
FIRST
FIRTH
GIRDS
GIRLS
GIROS
GIRTH
GIRTS
HIRAM
HIRED
HIRER
HIRES
KIRIN
KIRKS
LIRAS
MIRED
MIRES
MIRTH
MIRZA
SIRED
SIREN
SIRES
SIRUP
TIRED
TIRES
TIROS
VIRAL
VIREO
VIRES
VIRGA
VIRGE
VIRGO
VIRTU
VIRUS
WIRED
WIRER
WIRES
WIRRA
ZIRON

•I•R•
BIERS
BIRRS
CIRRI
CIRRO
CITRA
DIARY
FIBRO
FIERY
FIORD
FIRRY
HIERO
KIERS
LIARS
LIBRA
LIVRE
MICRA
MICRO
NIGRI
NITRI
NITRO
PICRO
PIERS
TIARA
TIERS
VITRI
WIRRA

•I••R
AIDER
BIHAR
BITER
CIDER
CIGAR
DICER
DIKER
DIMER
DINAR
DINER
DIRER
DIVER
EIDER
FIBER
FIFER
FILAR
FILER
FINER
FIRER
FIVER
FIXER
GIBER
GIVER
HIDER
HIKER
HIRER
LIBER
LIFER
LINER
LITER
LIVER
MILER
MIMER
MIMIR
MINER
MINOR
MISER
MITER
MIXER
NICER
NIGER
NITER
OILER
PIKER
PILAR
PINER
PIPER
RICER
RIDER
RIGOR
RIMER
RIPER
RISER
RIVER
SIDER
SIEUR
SIMAR
SITAR
SIZAR
TIBER
TIGER
TILER
TIMER
TITER
VICAR
VIGOR
VILER
VIPER
VISOR
VIZIR
VIZOR
WIDER
WIPER
WIRER
WISER
WIVER

••IR•
AFIRE
AMIRS
BAIRD
BAIRN
BEIRA
CAIRD
CAIRN
CAIRO
CHIRM
CHIRO
CHIRP
CHIRR
DAIRY
EMIRS
FAIRS
FAIRY
FLIRT
HAIRS
HAIRY
HEIRS
LAIRD
LAIRS
LOIRE
MOIRA
MOIRE
ONIRO
PAIRS
QUIRE
QUIRK
QUIRT
SHIRE
SHIRK
SHIRR
SHIRT
SKIRR
SKIRT
SMIRK
SPIRE
SPIRO
SPIRT
SPIRY
STIRK
STIRS
SWIRL
THIRD
TWIRL
TWIRP
VAIRS
WEIRD
WEIRS
WHIRL
WHIRS
ZAIRE

••I•R
BRIAR
BRIER
CHIRR
CRIER
DRIER
FLIER
FRIAR
FRIER
ICIER
OSIER
PLIER
PRIER
PRIOR
SHIER
SHIRR
SKIER
SKIRR
SLIER
SPIER
TRIER
WRIER

•••IR
AEGIR
AESIR
ASTIR
AVOIR
CHAIR
CHOIR
FAKIR
FLAIR
GLAIR
MIMIR
NADIR
ONEIR
STAIR
TAPIR
THEIR
VANIR
VIZIR

IS•••
ISAAC
ISBAS
ISERE
ISLAM
ISLED
ISLES
ISLET
ISSEI
ISSUE
ISTIC
ISTLE

I•S••
IASIS
IBSEN
INSET
ISSEI
ISSUE

I••S•
ICOSI
IRISH

I•••S
IAMBS
IASIS
ICONS
ICTUS
IDEAS
IDLES
IDOLS
IDYLS
IKONS
ILEUS
ILLUS
IMAMS
IMIDS
INCAS
INCUS
INDUS
IOTAS
IRMAS
IRONS
ISBAS
ISLES
ITALS
ITEMS
IVANS
IVIES
IXIAS
IZZYS

•IS••
AISLE
AISNE
BISES
BISON
CISCO
CISSY
CISTS
DISCI
DISCS
DISKO
DISKS
FISCS
FISHY
FISTS
GISMO
GISTS
HISTO
LISAS
LISLE
LISPS
LISTS
LISZT
MISDO
MISER
MISES
MISSY
MISTS
MISTY
NISAN
NISEI
NISUS
PISCI
RISEN
RISER
RISES
RISKS
RISKY
RISUS
SISAL
SISSY
VISAS
VISCT
VISED
VISES
VISIT
VISOR
VISTA
WISED
WISER
WISES
WISPS
WISPY

•I•S•
CISSY
DIDST
FIRST
GIPSY
KIOSK
MIDST
MINSK
MISSY
RINSE
SISSY
TIPSY

•I••S
AIDAS
AIDES
AINOS
AINUS
BIBBS
BICES
BIDES
BIERS
BIFFS
BIKES
BILES
BILKS
BILLS
BINDS
BINES
BIRDS
BIRLS
BIRRS
BISES
BITES
BITTS
CIONS
CISTS
CITES
DIALS
DICKS
DIDOS
DIETS
DIKES
DIMES
DINES
DINGS
DINTS
DIRKS
DISCS
DISKS
DITAS
DIVAS
DIVES
FIATS
FICES
FIEFS
FIFES
FIJIS
FILES
FILLS
FILMS
FINDS
FINES
FINIS
FINKS
FINNS
FIRES
FIRMS
FIRNS
FISCS
FISTS
FIVES
FIXES
GIBES
GIFTS
GIGAS
GILDS
GILES
GILLS
GIMPS
GINKS
GIRDS
GIRLS
GIROS
GIRTS
GISTS
GIVES
HICKS
HIDES
HIFIS
HIGHS
HIKES
HILLS
HILTS
HINDS
HINTS
HIRES
HIVES

JIBES
JIFFS
JILLS
JILTS
JINKS
KIBES
KICKS
KIERS
KILLS
KILNS
KILOS
KILTS
KINDS
KINGS
KINKS
KIRKS
KITES
KIVAS
KIWIS
LIARS
LICKS
LIENS
LIFTS
LIKES
LILAS
LILTS
LILYS
LIMBS
LIMES
LIMNS
LIMPS
LINES
LINGS
LINKS
LINUS
LIONS
LIRAS
LISAS
LISPS
LISTS
LITAS
LIVES
LIZAS
MICAS
MIDAS
MIENS
MIFFS
MIKES
MILES
MILKS
MILLS
MILTS
MIMES
MIMIS
MINAS
MINDS
MINES
MINKS
MINOS
MINTS
MINUS
MIRES
MISES
MISTS
MITES
MITTS
MIXES
NICKS
NIDES
NIDUS
NINAS
NINES
NINUS
NIPAS
NISUS
NIXES
PICAS
PICKS
PICTS
PIERS
PIKAS
PIKES
PILES
PILIS
PILLS
PIMAS
PIMPS
PINAS
PINES
PINGS
PINKS
PINTS
PIONS
PIOUS
PIPES
PITAS
PITHS
RIALS
RICES
RICKS
RIDES
RIFFS
RIFTS
RIGGS
RILES
RILLS
RIMES
RINDS
RINGS
RINKS
RIOTS
RISES
RISKS
RISUS
RITAS
RITES
RIVES
SICES
SICKS
SIDES
SIFTS
SIGHS
SIGNS
SIKHS
SILAS
SILKS
SILLS
SILOS
SILTS
SIMPS
SINES
SINGS
SINKS
SINUS
SIRES
SITES
SITUS
SIXES
SIZES
TICKS
TIDES
TIERS
TIFFS
TIKIS
TILES
TILLS
TILTS
TIMES
TINAS
TINES
TINGS
TINTS
TIRES
TIROS
TITIS
TITUS
VIALS
VIBES
VICES
VICKS
VIEWS
VILLS
VINAS
VINES
VIOLS
VIRES
VIRUS
VISAS
VISES
WICKS
WILDS
WILES
WILLS
WILTS
WINDS
WINES
WINGS
WINKS
WINOS
WIPES
WIRES
WISES
WISPS
WIVES
YIPES
ZINCS
ZINGS

••IS•

AGIST
AMISH
AMISS
ANISE
ANISO
APISH
ARISE
AVISO
BLISS
BOISE
BRISK
CRISP
CUISH
DAISY
DEISM
DEIST
ELISE
EXIST
FEIST
FOISM
FOIST
FRISE
FRISK
GRIST
GUISE
HEIST
HOIST
IRISH
JOIST
LUISA
LUISE
MOIST
NOISE
NOISY
PAISA
PAISE
POISE
PRISM
RAISE
SEISM
SWISH
SWISS
TWIST
WAIST
WHISH
WHISK
WHIST
WRIST

••I•S

ABIBS
ABIES
ACIDS
ADIOS
ADITS
AGIOS
ALIAS
ALIFS
AMIAS
AMIES
AMIRS
AMISS
ANILS
ARIAS
ARIES
ARILS
ARIUS
AXILS
AYINS
BAILS
BAITS
BLIPS
BLISS
BOILS
BRIGS
BRIMS
CEILS
CHIAS
CHINS
CHIOS
CHIPS
CHITS
CLIOS
CLIPS
COIFS
COILS
COINS
CRIBS
CRIES
DOITS
DRIBS
DRIES
DRIPS
EDIES
EDITS
ELIAS
EMILS
EMIRS
EMITS
ENIDS
EPICS
ERICS
ERIES
ERIKS
EVILS
EXITS
FAILS
FAIRS
FLIES
FLIPS
FLITS
FOILS
FRIES
FRITS
GAILS
GAINS
GAITS
GLIMS
GRIDS
GRINS
GRIPS
GRITS
HAIKS
HAILS
HAIRS
HEIRS
IMIDS
IVIES
IXIAS
JAILS
JAINS
JOINS
KNITS
LAIRS
LEIFS
LOINS
MAIDS
MAILS
MAIMS
MAINS
MOILS
NAILS
NEILS
OBITS
OKIES
OLIOS
OMITS
PAILS
PAINS
PAIRS
PHILS
PHIPS
PLIES
PRIES
PRIGS
PRIMS
QUIDS
QUIPS
QUITS
RAIDS
RAILS
RAINS
REIMS
REINS
ROILS
RUINS
SAILS
SHIMS
SHINS
SHIPS
SHIVS
SKIDS
SKIES
SKIMS
SKINS
SKIPS
SKITS
SLIMS
SLIPS
SLITS
SNIPS
SOILS
SPIES
SPINS
SPITS
STIES
STIRS
SUITS
SWIGS
SWIMS
SWISS
TAILS
TAINS
THINS
TOILS
TRIES
TRIGS
TRIMS
TRIOS
TRIPS
TWIGS
TWINS
TWITS
UNITS
VAIRS
VEILS
VEINS
VOIDS
WAIFS
WAILS
WAINS
WAITS
WEIRS
WHIGS
WHIMS
WHINS
WHIPS
WHIRS
WHITS
WRIES
WRITS

•••IS

ABRIS
AEGIS
AGNIS
ALDIS
ALLIS
ALOIS
ANTIS
APHIS
APSIS
ARRIS
ARSIS
ASPIS
ATTIS
AULIS
AURIS
BASIS
BLOIS
BORIS
CADIS
CANIS
CENIS
CHRIS
CUTIS
DAVIS
DEFIS
DENIS
DORIS
ELLIS
ETUIS
FIJIS
FINIS
HIFIS
IASIS
KADIS
KAKIS
KEPIS
KIWIS
LAPIS
LENIS
LEVIS
LEWIS
LORIS
LOUIS
LYSIS
MAVIS
METIS
MIMIS
NARIS
NAZIS
OASIS
OPSIS
ORNIS
ORRIS
PARIS
PAVIS
PERIS
PILIS
PUBIS
PYXIS
RANIS
SARIS
SUFIS
TAMIS
TANIS
TAPIS
TAXIS
TIKIS
TITIS
TONIS
TOPIS
TUNIS
TUPIS
XAXIS
YAXIS
YETIS
YOGIS

IT•••

ITALS
ITALY
ITCHY
ITEMS
ITION

I•T••

IATRO
IATRY
ICTUS
INTER
INTRA
INTRO
IOTAS
ISTIC
ISTLE
IXTLE

I••T•

IRATE

I•••T
IDIOT
INAPT
INEPT
INERT
INGOT
INLET
INPUT
INSET
ISLET

•IT••
AITCH
BITCH
BITER
BITES
BITTS
CITED
CITES
CITRA
DITAS
DITCH
DITTO
DITTY
FITCH
FITLY
HITCH
KITED
KITES
KITTY
LITAI
LITAS
LITER
LITHE
LITHO
MITCH
MITER
MITES
MITTS
NITER
NITON
NITRI
NITRO
NITTY
PITAS
PITCH
PITHS
PITHY
PITON
RITAS
RITES
RITZY
SITAR
SITES
SITIN
SITKA
SITUS
TITAN
TITER
TITHE
TITIS
TITLE
TITUS
VITAE
VITAL
VITRI
VITTA
WITAN
WITCH
WITHE
WITHY
WITTE
WITTY

•I•T•
BIOTA
BIRTH
BITTS
CISTS
DICTA
DIETS
DINTS
DIRTY
DITTO
DITTY
FIATS
FIFTH
FIFTY
FILTH
FIRTH
FISTS
GIFTS
GIRTH
GIRTS
GISTS
HILTS
HINTS
HISTO
JILTS
KILTS
KILTY
KITTY
LIFTS
LILTS
LINTY
LISTS
MILTS
MINTS
MIRTH
MISTS
MISTY
MITTS
NIFTY
NINTH
NITTY
PICTS
PIETA
PIETY
PINTA
PINTO
PINTS
RIATA
RIFTS
RIOTS
SIFTS
SILTS
SILTY
SIXTE
SIXTH
SIXTY
TILTH
TILTS
TINTS
VIRTU
VISTA
VITTA
WIDTH
WILTS
WITTE
WITTY

•I••T
BIDET
BIGHT
BIGOT
BINET
BINIT
BIZET
CIVET
DIDNT
DIDST
DIGIT
DIVOT
DIXIT
EIGHT
FIGHT
FILET
FIRST
GIANT
GIGOT
LICHT
LICIT
LIEUT
LIGHT
LIMIT
LISZT
MIDST
MIGHT
NIGHT
PICOT
PILOT
PIPET
PIPIT
PIVOT
RIANT
RIGHT
RIVET
SIGHT
TIBET
TIGHT
TINCT
VISCT
VISIT
WIGHT
ZIBET

••IT•
ACITY
ADITS
AMITY
ANITA
BAITS
BLITZ
CHITA
CHITS
DEITY
DOITS
EDITH
EDITS
ELITE
EMITS
EVITA
EXITS
FAITH
FLITS
FRITH
FRITS
FRITZ
GAITS
GRITS
HAITI
KEITH
KNITS
LAITY
OBITS
OMITS
OSITY
QUITE
QUITO
QUITS
SKITS
SLITS
SMITE
SMITH
SPITE
SPITS
SPITZ
SUITE
SUITS
TRITE
TWITS
UNITE
UNITS
UNITY
WAITS
WHITE
WHITS
WRITE
WRITS

••I•T
AGIST
ATILT
BUILT
CLINT
DEIST
DRIFT
DRIPT
EDICT
ELIOT
EVICT
EXIST
FAINT
FEINT
FEIST
FLINT
FLIRT
FOIST
GLINT
GRIPT
GRIST
GUILT
HEIST
HOIST
IDIOT
JOINT
JOIST
MOIST
PAINT
POINT
PRINT
QUIET
QUILT
QUINT
QUIRT
SAINT
SHIFT
SHIRT
SKIRT
SLIPT
SPILT
SPIRT
STILT
STINT
SUINT
SWIFT
TAINT
TWIST
TWIXT
WAIST
WHIPT
WHIST
WRIST

•••IT
ADMIT
AMBIT
AUDIT
AWAIT
BARIT
BEFIT
BINIT
BRUIT
CUBIT
DAVIT
DEBIT
DEMIT
DIGIT
DIXIT
DROIT
FECIT
FRUIT
HABIT
KRAIT
LEGIT
LICIT
LIMIT
MERIT
ORBIT
PETIT
PEWIT
PIPIT
PLAIT
POSIT
QUOIT
REFIT
REMIT
SPAIT
SPLIT
SPRIT
TACIT
TRAIT
UNFIT
UNLIT
VISIT
VOMIT

I•U••
INURE
INURN

I••U•
ICTUS
ILEUM
ILEUS
ILIUM
ILLUS
IMBUE
INCUR
INCUS
INDUE
INDUS
INPUT
ISSUE

•I•U•
AINUS
FILUM
FIQUE
GIGUE
HILUM
LIEUT
LINUS
MIAUL
MINUS
MIXUP
NIDUS
NINUS
NISUS
PICUL
PINUP
PIOUS
PIQUE
RISUS
SIEUR
SINUS
SIOUX
SIRUP
SITUS
TIEUP
TITUS
VIRUS

•I••U
BIJOU
FICHU
HINDU
VIRTU

••IU•
ARIUM
ARIUS
ILIUM
ODIUM
OPIUM

••I•U
ADIEU
ELIHU
HAIKU
POILU
QUIPU

IV•••
IVANS
IVIED
IVIES
IVORY

I•V••
IRVIN

•IV••
CIVET
CIVIC
CIVIL
DIVAN
DIVAS
DIVED
DIVER
DIVES
DIVOT
DIVVY
FIVER
FIVES
GIVEN
GIVER
GIVES
HIVED
HIVES
KIVAS
LIVED
LIVEN
LIVER
LIVES
LIVIA
LIVID
LIVRE
NIVAL
PIVOT
RIVAL
RIVED
RIVEN
RIVER
RIVES
RIVET
SIVAN
VIVID
WIVED
WIVER
WIVES

•I•V•
DIVVY
PIAVE
SIEVE
SILVA

••IV•
ALIVE
ATIVE
CHIVE
CLIVE
DRIVE
NAIVE
OGIVE
OLIVE
PRIVY
SHIVE
SHIVS
SKIVE
WAIVE

I•W••
IRWIN

I•••W
INDOW
INLAW

•IW••
DIWAN
KIWIS

•I•W•
KIOWA
VIEWS
VIEWY

•I••W
SINEW
WIDOW

IX•••
IXIAS
IXION
IXTLE

I•••X
IMMIX
INDEX
INFIX

•IX••
DIXIE
DIXIT
FIXED
FIXER
FIXES
MIXED
MIXER

MIXES
MIXUP
NIXED
NIXES
NIXIE
NIXON
PIXIE
SIXES
SIXTE
SIXTH
SIXTY
VIXEN

•I••X
CIMEX
SILEX
SIOUX

••IX•
TRIXY
TWIXT

•••IX
ADMIX
AFFIX
CALIX
CROIX
CYLIX
FELIX
HELIX
IMMIX
INFIX
KYLIX
RADIX
UNFIX
VARIX

IY•••
IYYAR

I•Y••
IDYLL
IDYLS
IYYAR

I••Y•
IZZYS

I•••Y
IATRY
ICILY
IMPLY
INLAY
IRONY
ITALY
ITCHY
IVORY

•IY••
RIYAL

•I•Y•
LIBYA
LILYS
SIBYL
VINYL

•I••Y
BIALY
BIDDY
BIFFY
BIGLY
BILGY
BILLY
CINDY
CISSY
DIARY
DICKY
DIMLY
DINGY
DINKY
DIPPY
DIRTY
DITTY
DIVVY
DIZZY
FIERY
FIFTY
FILLY
FILMY
FINNY
FIRRY
FISHY
FITLY
FIZZY
GIDDY
GIMPY
GINNY
GIPSY
HILLY
HINNY
JIFFY
JIMMY
JINNY
KIDDY
KILTY
KINKY
KITTY
LIBBY
LILLY
LIMEY
LINEY
LINTY
LIPPY
LIZZY
MICKY
MIDDY
MIFFY
MIKEY
MILKY
MILLY
MISSY
MISTY
NICKY
NIFTY
NINNY
NIPPY
NITTY
PIETY
PIGGY
PIGMY
PINEY
PINKY
PITHY
RICKY
RIDGY
RILEY
RISKY
RITZY
SILKY
SILLY
SILTY
SISSY
SIXTY
TILLY
TIMMY
TINNY
TIPPY
TIPSY
TIZZY
VICHY
VICKY
VIEWY
VINNY
WIDDY
WILLY
WINDY
WINGY
WISPY
WITHY
WITTY
ZINCY
ZINKY
ZIPPY

••IY•
ORIYA

••I•Y
ACITY
AMITY
BRINY
DAILY
DAIRY
DAISY
DEIFY
DEITY
DOILY
DRILY
EDIFY
EMILY
FAIRY
GAILY
HAIRY
ICILY
JUICY
LAITY
NOISY
OSITY
PHILY
PLINY
PRIVY
RAINY
REIFY
ROILY
SHILY
SHINY
SLILY
SLIMY
SPICY
SPIKY
SPINY
SPIRY
STIMY
TRIXY
UNIFY
UNITY
VEINY
WHINY

IZ•••
IZZYS

I•Z••
IZZYS

I•••Z
IGNAZ

•IZ••
BIZET
DIZEN
DIZZY
FIZZY
GIZMO
LIZAS
LIZZY
NIZAM
PIZZA
SIZAR
SIZED
SIZES
TIZZY
VIZIR
VIZOR
WIZEN

•I•Z•
DIAZO
DIZZY
FIZZY
LISZT
LIZZY
MIRZA
PIEZO
PIZZA
RITZY
TIZZY
WINZE

••IZ•
BAIZE
ELIZA
FRIZZ
MAIZE
PRIZE
RHIZO
SEIZE

••I•Z
BLITZ
FRITZ
FRIZZ
MAINZ
SPITZ

•••IZ
CADIZ
HAFIZ
SCHIZ

JA•••
JABEZ
JABOT
JACKS
JACKY
JACOB
JADED
JADES
JAFFA
JAGGS
JAGGY
JAILS
JAINA
JAINS
JAKES
JAKOB
JALAP
JAMBS
JAMES
JAMIE
JANES
JANET
JANOS
JANUS
JAPAN
JAPES
JARED
JARLS
JASON
JASSY
JATOS
JAUNT
JAWED
JAZZY

J•A••
JEANS
JOANS
JUANA
JUANS

J••A•
JALAP
JAPAN
JIHAD
JONAH
JONAS
JORAM
JUBAS
JUDAH
JUDAS
JUGAL
JURAL
JURAT

J•••A
JAFFA
JAINA
JIDDA
JOSUA
JUANA
JUDEA
JULIA
JUMNA
JUNTA
JURUA
JUXTA

••JA•
HEJAZ
RAJAB
RAJAH
SOJAS

•••JA
OUIJA
THUJA

J•B••
JABEZ
JABOT
JIBED
JIBES
JUBAS
JUBES

J••B•
JAMBS
JUMBO

J•••B
JACOB
JAKOB

••J•B
RAJAB

J•C••
JACKS
JACKY
JACOB
JOCKO

J••C•
JOYCE
JUICE
JUICY
JUNCO

•J•C•
EJECT

J•D••
JADED
JADES
JIDDA
JUDAH
JUDAS
JUDEA
JUDEO
JUDES
JUDGE
JUDYS

J••D•
JIDDA

J•••D
JADED
JARED
JAWED
JIBED
JIHAD
JOKED
JOYED

•J••D
FJELD
FJORD
NJORD

JE•••
JEANS
JEEPS
JEERS
JEFES
JEFFS
JEHUS
JELLO
JELLS
JELLY
JEMMY
JENNY
JEREZ
JERKS
JERKY
JERRY
JESSE
JESSY
JESTS
JESUS
JETTY
JEWEL
JEWRY

J•E••
JEEPS
JEERS
JOELS
JOEYS

J••E•
JABEZ
JADED
JADES
JAKES
JAMES
JANES
JANET
JAPES
JARED
JAWED
JEFES
JEREZ
JEWEL
JIBED
JIBES
JOKED
JOKER
JOKES
JOLES
JONES
JOYED
JUBES
JUDEA
JUDEO
JUDES
JULEP
JULES
JUNES
JUREL
JUTES

J•••E
JAMIE
JESSE
JORGE
JOSIE
JOSUE
JOULE
JOYCE
JUDGE
JUICE
JULIE

•JE••
EJECT
FJELD

•••JE
KOPJE

J•F••
JAFFA
JEFES
JEFFS
JIFFS
JIFFY

J••F•
JAFFA
JEFFS
JIFFS
JIFFY

J•G••
JAGGS
JAGGY
JUGAL

5

J••G•
JAGGS
JAGGY
JINGO
JORGE
JUDGE

J•H••
JEHUS
JIHAD
JOHNS

J•••H
JONAH
JUDAH

••J•H
RAJAH

JI•••
JIBED
JIBES
JIDDA
JIFFS
JIFFY
JIHAD
JILLS
JILTS
JIMMY
JINGO
JINKS
JINNI
JINNY

J•I••
JAILS
JAINA
JAINS
JOINS
JOINT
JOIST
JUICE
JUICY

J••I•
JAMIE
JOSIE
JULIA
JULIE
JULIO

J•••I
JINNI

••JI•
FIJIS

•••JI
HADJI
SHOJI

J•J••
JUJUS

J•K••
JAKES
JAKOB
JOKED
JOKER
JOKES

J••K•
JACKS
JACKY
JERKS
JERKY
JINKS
JOCKO
JUNKS
JUNKY

J•L••
JALAP
JELLO
JELLS
JELLY
JILLS
JILTS
JOLES
JOLLY
JOLTS
JOLTY
JULEP
JULES
JULIA
JULIE
JULIO
JULYS

J••L•
JAILS
JARLS
JELLO
JELLS
JELLY
JILLS
JOELS
JOLLY
JOULE
JOWLS

J•••L
JEWEL
JUGAL
JURAL
JUREL

•J•L•
FJELD

J•M••
JAMBS
JAMES
JAMIE
JEMMY
JIMMY
JUMBO
JUMNA
JUMPS
JUMPY

J••M•
JEMMY
JIMMY

J•••M
JORAM
JORUM

J•N••
JANES
JANET
JANOS
JANUS
JENNY
JINGO
JINKS
JINNI
JINNY
JONAH
JONAS
JONES
JONNY
JUNCO
JUNES
JUNKS
JUNKY
JUNTA

J••N•
JAINA
JAINS
JAUNT
JEANS
JENNY
JINNI
JINNY
JOANS
JOHNS
JOINS
JOINT
JONNY
JUANA
JUANS
JUMNA

J•••N
JAPAN
JASON
JOTUN
JUPON

••J•N
CAJON
CAJUN
DIJON

JO•••
JOANS
JOCKO
JOELS
JOEYS
JOHNS
JOINS
JOINT
JOIST
JOKED
JOKER
JOKES
JOLES
JOLLY
JOLTS
JOLTY
JONAH
JONAS
JONES
JONNY
JORAM
JORGE
JORUM
JOSIE
JOSUA
JOSUE
JOTUN
JOULE
JOUST
JOWLS
JOYCE
JOYED

J••O•
JABOT
JACOB
JAKOB
JANOS
JASON
JATOS
JUPON
JUROR

J•••O
JELLO
JINGO
JOCKO
JUDEO
JULIO
JUMBO
JUNCO

•JO••
FJORD
NJORD

••JO•
ANJOU
BIJOU
CAJON
DIJON
ENJOY
MAJOR
SAJOU

•••JO
BANJO

J•P••
JAPAN
JAPES
JUPON

J••P•
JEEPS
JUMPS
JUMPY

J•••P
JALAP
JULEP

J•R••
JARED
JARLS
JEREZ
JERKS
JERKY
JERRY
JORAM
JORGE
JORUM
JURAL
JURAT
JUREL
JUROR
JURUA

J••R•
JEERS
JERRY
JEWRY

J•••R
JOKER
JUROR

•J•R•
FJORD
NJORD

••J•R
MAJOR

J•S••
JASON
JASSY
JESSE
JESSY
JESTS
JESUS
JOSIE
JOSUA
JOSUE
JUSTS

J••S•
JASSY
JESSE
JESSY
JOIST
JOUST

J•••S
JACKS
JADES
JAGGS
JAILS
JAINS
JAKES
JAMBS
JAMES
JANES
JANOS
JANUS
JAPES
JARLS
JATOS
JEANS
JEEPS
JEERS
JEFES
JEFFS
JEHUS
JELLS
JERKS
JESTS
JESUS
JIBES
JIFFS
JILLS
JILTS
JINKS
JOANS
JOELS
JOEYS
JOHNS
JOINS
JOKES
JOLES
JOLTS
JONAS
JONES
JOWLS
JUANS
JUBAS
JUBES
JUDAS
JUDES
JUDYS
JUJUS
JULES
JULYS
JUMPS
JUNES
JUNKS
JUSTS
JUTES

••J•S
FIJIS
JUJUS
SOJAS

J•T••
JATOS
JETTY
JOTUN
JUTES

J••T•
JESTS
JETTY
JILTS
JOLTS
JOLTY
JUNTA
JUSTS
JUXTA

J•••T
JABOT
JANET
JAUNT
JOINT
JOIST
JOUST
JURAT

•J••T
EJECT

JU•••
JUANA
JUANS
JUBAS
JUBES
JUDAH
JUDAS
JUDEA
JUDEO
JUDES
JUDGE
JUDYS
JUGAL
JUICE
JUICY
JUJUS
JULEP
JULES
JULIA
JULIE
JULIO
JULYS
JUMBO
JUMNA
JUMPS
JUMPY
JUNCO
JUNES
JUNKS
JUNKY
JUNTA
JUPON
JURAL
JURAT
JUREL
JUROR
JURUA
JUSTS
JUTES
JUXTA

J•U••
JAUNT
JOULE
JOUST

J••U•
JANUS
JEHUS
JESUS
JORUM
JOSUA
JOSUE
JOTUN
JUJUS
JURUA

••JU•
CAJUN
JUJUS

••J•U
ANJOU
BIJOU
SAJOU

J•W••
JAWED
JEWEL
JEWRY
JOWLS

J•X••
JUXTA

J•Y••
JOYCE
JOYED

J••Y•
JOEYS
JUDYS
JULYS

J•••Y
JACKY
JAGGY
JASSY
JAZZY
JELLY
JEMMY
JENNY
JERKY
JERRY
JESSY
JETTY
JEWRY
JIFFY
JIMMY
JINNY
JOLLY
JOLTY
JONNY

JUICY
JUMPY
JUNKY

••J•Y
ENJOY

•••JY
BENJY

J•Z••
JAZZY

J••Z•
JAZZY

J•••Z
JABEZ
JEREZ

••J•Z
HEJAZ

KA•••
KAABA
KABOB
KABUL
KADIS
KAFKA
KAGUS
KAKAS
KAKIS
KALAT
KAMES
KAMET
KAMIK
KANDY
KAPHS
KAPOK
KAPPA
KAPUT
KARAT
KAREN
KARLS
KARMA
KAROL
KARYO
KATES
KATHY
KATIE
KAUAI
KAURI
KAURY
KAVAS
KAYAK
KAYOS
KAZAN
KAZOO

K•A••
KAABA
KEATS
KHADI
KHAKI
KHANS
KLARA
KNACK
KNARS
KNAVE
KOALA
KRAAL
KRAFT
KRAIT
KRAUT
KVASS
KYATS

K••A•
KAKAS
KALAT
KARAT
KAUAI
KAVAS
KAYAK
KAZAN
KEDAH
KERAT
KIVAS
KNEAD
KODAK
KOLAS
KORAN
KRAAL
KUBAN
KULAK

K•••A
KAABA
KAFKA
KAPPA
KARMA
KENYA
KIOWA
KLARA
KOALA
KONYA
KOREA
KRONA
KUFRA

•KA••
OKAPI
OKAYS
SKALD
SKATE
UKASE

•K•A•
OKRAS
SKEAN
SKOAL
SKUAS

••KA•
DAKAR
HOKAN
KAKAS
PEKAN
PIKAS
TOKAY
WEKAS

••K•A
HEKLA
PUKKA

•••KA
DINKA
ERIKA
KAFKA
LAIKA
PARKA
POLKA
PUCKA
PUKKA
PUNKA
SITKA
STUKA
TANKA
VODKA

K•B••
KABOB
KABUL
KIBEI
KIBES
KUBAN

K••B•
KAABA
KERBS
KNOBS
KRUBI

K•••B
KABOB

••K•B
JAKOB

K•C••
KECKS
KICKS

K••C•
KENCH
KERCH
KETCH
KNACK
KNOCK

K•D••
KADIS
KEDAH
KEDGE
KIDDY
KODAK
KUDOS
KUDUS

K••D•
KANDY
KHADI
KIDDY
KINDS

K•••D
KEYED
KHOND
KITED
KNEAD
KNEED

•K•D•
SKIDS

•K••D
SKALD
SKEED
SKIED

••K•D
ASKED
BAKED
CAKED
COKED
DEKED
DIKED
FAKED
HIKED
INKED
IRKED
JOKED
LAKED
LIKED
NAKED
PIKED
POKED
PUKED
RAKED
WAKED
YOKED

KE•••
KEATS
KECKS
KEDAH
KEDGE
KEEFS
KEELS
KEENS
KEEPS
KEEVE
KEITH
KELPS
KENCH
KENNY
KENTS
KENYA
KEPIS
KERAT
KERBS
KERCH
KERES
KERFS
KERNS
KERRY
KETCH
KEVEL
KEVIN
KEYED

K•E••
KEEFS
KEELS
KEENS
KEEPS
KEEVE
KIERS
KNEAD
KNEED
KNEEL
KNEES
KNELL
KNELT
KOELS

K••E•
KAMES
KAMET
KAREN
KATES
KERES
KEVEL
KEYED
KHMER
KIBEI
KIBES
KITED
KITES
KNEED
KNEEL
KNEES
KOPEK
KOREA

K•••E
KATIE
KEDGE
KEEVE
KNAVE
KNIFE
KOINE
KOPJE
KRONE

•KE••
AKENE
SKEAN
SKEED
SKEES
SKEET
SKEGS
SKEIN
SKEPS
SKEWS

•K•E•
OKIES
SKEED
SKEES
SKEET
SKIED
SKIER
SKIES
SKYEY

•K••E
AKENE
SKATE
SKIVE
UKASE

••KE•
AIKEN
ASKED
ASKER
ASKEW
BAKED
BAKER
BAKES
BIKES
CAKED
CAKES
COKED
COKES
DEKED
DEKES
DIKED
DIKER
DIKES
DUKES
ESKER
FAKED
FAKER
FAKES
FYKES
HAKES
HIKED
HIKER
HIKES
INKED
INKER
IRKED
JAKES
JOKED
JOKER
JOKES
LAKED
LAKER
LAKES
LIKED
LIKEN
LIKES
MAKER
MAKES
MIKES
MIKEY
MOKES
NAKED
OAKEN
PIKED
PIKER
PIKES
POKED
POKER
POKES
POKEY
PUKED
PUKES
RAKED
RAKEE
RAKER
RAKES
SAKER
SAKES
SOKES
TAKEN
TAKER
TAKES
TOKEN
TYKES
WAKED
WAKEN
WAKES
WOKEN
YOKED
YOKEL
YOKES
ZEKES

••K•E
ANKLE
INKLE
PEKOE
RAKEE

•••KE
ALIKE
AWAKE
AWOKE
BLAKE
BLOKE
BRAKE
BROKE
BURKE
CHOKE
CRAKE
DRAKE
EVOKE
FLAKE
FLUKE
HOOKE
LOCKE
QUAKE
SHAKE
SLAKE
SMOKE
SNAKE
SPIKE
SPOKE
STAKE
STOKE
WACKE

K•F••
KAFKA
KUFRA

K••F•
KEEFS
KERFS
KNIFE
KRAFT

K•••F
KLOOF

•K•F•
SKIFF

•K••F
SKIFF

K•G••
KAGUS

K••G•
KEDGE
KINGS

•K•G•
SKEGS

•K••G
EKING
OKING

KH•••
KHADI
KHAKI
KHANS
KHMER
KHOND

K••H•
KAPHS
KATHY

K•••H
KEDAH
KEITH
KENCH
KERCH
KETCH

••KH•
ANKHS
SIKHS

KI•••
KIBEI
KIBES
KICKS
KIDDY
KIERS
KILLS
KILNS
KILOS
KILTS
KILTY
KINDS
KINGS

KININ
KINKS
KINKY
KIOSK
KIOWA
KIRIN
KIRKS
KITED
KITES
KITTY
KIVAS
KIWIS

K•I••
KEITH
KNIFE
KNITS
KOINE

K••I•
KADIS
KAKIS
KAMIK
KATIE
KEPIS
KEVIN
KININ
KIRIN
KIWIS
KRAIT
KYLIX

K•••I
KAUAI
KAURI
KHADI
KHAKI
KIBEI
KRUBI

•KI••
EKING
OKIES
OKING
SKIDS
SKIED
SKIER
SKIES
SKIFF
SKILL
SKIMO
SKIMP
SKIMS
SKINK
SKINS
SKIPS
SKIRR
SKIRT
SKITS
SKIVE

•K•I•
SKEIN

•K••I
OKAPI

••KI•
FAKIR
HAKIM
KAKIS
PEKIN
TIKIS
TOKIO

•••KI
GORKI
KHAKI
TURKI

K••J•
KOPJE

K•K••
KAKAS
KAKIS

K••K•
KAFKA
KECKS
KHAKI
KICKS
KINKS
KINKY
KIRKS
KOOKS
KOOKY

K•••K
KAMIK
KAPOK
KAYAK
KIOSK
KNACK
KNOCK
KODAK
KOPEK
KULAK
KURSK

•K••K
SKINK
SKULK
SKUNK

••KK•
PUKKA

KL•••
KLARA
KLOOF

K•L••
KALAT
KELPS
KILLS
KILNS
KILOS
KILTS
KILTY
KOLAS
KULAK
KYLIX

K••L•
KARLS
KEELS
KILLS
KNELL
KNELT
KNOLL
KOALA
KOELS

K•••L
KABUL
KAROL
KEVEL
KNEEL
KNELL
KNOLL
KNURL
KRAAL

•K•L•
SKALD
SKILL
SKULK
SKULL

•K••L
SKILL
SKOAL
SKULL

••KL•
ANKLE
HEKLA
INKLE

••K•L
ALKYL
BIKOL
YOKEL

K•M••
KAMES
KAMET
KAMIK
KHMER

K••M•
KARMA

•K•M•
SKIMO
SKIMP
SKIMS

••K•M
HAKIM
HOKUM
OAKUM

KN•••
KNACK
KNARS
KNAVE
KNEAD
KNEED
KNEEL
KNEES
KNELL
KNELT
KNIFE
KNITS
KNOBS
KNOCK
KNOLL
KNOPS
KNOSP
KNOTS
KNOUT
KNOWN
KNOWS
KNURL
KNURS

K•N••
KANDY
KENCH
KENNY
KENTS
KENYA
KINDS
KINGS
KININ
KINKS
KINKY
KONYA

K••N•
KEENS
KENNY
KERNS
KHANS
KHOND
KILNS
KOINE
KRONA
KRONE

K•••N
KAREN
KAZAN
KEVIN
KININ
KIRIN
KNOWN
KORAN
KORUN
KUBAN

•K•N•
AKENE
EKING
IKONS
OKING
SKINK
SKINS
SKUNK

•K••N
AKRON
SKEAN
SKEIN

••K•N
AIKEN
HOKAN
LIKEN
OAKEN
PEKAN
PEKIN
TAKEN
TOKEN
WAKEN
WOKEN
YUKON

KO•••
KOALA
KODAK
KOELS
KOINE
KOLAS
KONYA
KOOKS
KOOKY
KOPEK
KOPJE
KORAN
KOREA
KORUN
KOTOS

K•O••
KHOND
KIOSK
KIOWA
KLOOF
KNOBS
KNOCK
KNOLL
KNOPS
KNOSP
KNOTS
KNOUT
KNOWN
KNOWS
KOOKS
KOOKY
KRONA
KRONE
KYOTO

K••O•
KABOB
KAPOK
KAROL
KAYOS
KAZOO
KILOS
KLOOF
KOTOS
KUDOS

K•••O
KARYO
KAZOO
KYOTO

•KO••
IKONS
SKOAL

•K•O•
AKRON

•K••O
SKIMO

••KO•
BIKOL
JAKOB
PEKOE
YUKON

••K•O
HEKTO
TOKIO
TOKYO

•••KO
BUCKO
BUNKO
DISKO
GECKO
JOCKO
LEUKO
SHAKO

K•P••
KAPHS
KAPOK
KAPPA
KAPUT
KEPIS
KOPEK
KOPJE

K••P•
KAPPA
KEEPS
KELPS
KNOPS
KRUPP

K•••P
KNOSP
KRUPP

•K•P•
OKAPI
SKEPS
SKIPS

•K••P
SKIMP

KR•••
KRAAL
KRAFT
KRAIT
KRAUT
KRONA
KRONE
KRUBI
KRUPP

K•R••
KARAT
KAREN
KARLS
KARMA
KAROL
KARYO
KERAT
KERBS
KERCH
KERES
KERFS
KERNS
KERRY
KIRIN
KIRKS
KORAN
KOREA
KORUN
KURSK
KURUS

K••R•
KAURI
KAURY
KERRY
KIERS
KLARA
KNARS
KNURL
KNURS
KUFRA

K•••R
KHMER

•KR••
AKRON
OKRAS

•K•R•
SKIRR
SKIRT

•K••R
SKIER
SKIRR

••K•R
ASKER
BAKER
DAKAR
DIKER
ESKER
FAKER
FAKIR
HIKER
INKER
JOKER
LAKER
MAKER
PIKER
POKER
RAKER
SAKER
TAKER

K••S•
KIOSK
KNOSP
KURSK
KVASS

K•••S
KADIS
KAGUS
KAKAS
KAKIS
KAMES
KAPHS
KARLS
KATES
KAVAS
KAYOS
KEATS
KECKS
KEEFS
KEELS
KEENS
KEEPS
KELPS
KENTS
KEPIS
KERBS
KERES
KERFS
KERNS
KHANS
KIBES
KICKS
KIERS
KILLS
KILNS
KILOS
KILTS
KINDS
KINGS
KINKS
KIRKS
KITES
KIVAS
KIWIS

KNARS
KNEES
KNITS
KNOBS
KNOPS
KNOTS
KNOWS
KNURS
KOELS
KOLAS
KOOKS
KOTOS
KUDOS
KUDUS
KURUS
KVASS
KYATS

•K•S•
UKASE

•K••S
IKONS
OKAYS
OKIES
OKRAS
SKEES
SKEGS
SKEPS
SKEWS
SKIDS
SKIES
SKIMS
SKINS
SKIPS
SKITS
SKUAS

••K•S
ANKHS
ANKUS
BAKES
BIKES
CAKES
COKES
DEKES
DIKES
DUKES
FAKES
FYKES
HAKES
HIKES
JAKES
JOKES
KAKAS
KAKIS
LAKES
LIKES
MAKES
MIKES
MOKES
PIKAS
PIKES
POKES
PUKES
RAKES
SAKES
SIKHS
SOKES
TAKES
TIKIS
TYKES
WAKES
WEKAS
YOKES
ZEKES

•••KS
BACKS
BALKS
BANKS
BARKS
BASKS
BEAKS
BECKS
BILKS
BOOKS
BOSKS
BUCKS
BULKS
BUNKS
BUSKS
CALKS
CASKS
COCKS
CONKS
COOKS
CORKS
CUSKS
DAWKS
DECKS
DESKS
DHAKS
DICKS
DIRKS
DISKS
DOCKS
DUCKS
DUNKS
DUSKS
ERIKS
FINKS
FOLKS
FORKS
FUNKS
GAWKS
GECKS
GEEKS
GINKS
GOOKS
HACKS
HAIKS
HANKS
HARKS
HAWKS
HICKS
HOCKS
HONKS
HOOKS
HULKS
HUNKS
HUSKS
JACKS
JERKS
JINKS
JUNKS
KECKS
KICKS
KINKS
KIRKS
KOOKS
LACKS
LARKS
LEAKS
LEEKS
LICKS
LINKS
LOCKS
LOOKS
LURKS
MACKS
MARKS
MASKS
MILKS
MINKS
MOCKS
MONKS
MUCKS
MUSKS
NECKS
NICKS
NOCKS
NOOKS
PACKS
PARKS
PEAKS
PECKS
PEEKS
PERKS
PICKS
PINKS
POCKS
PUCKS
PUNKS
RACKS
RANKS
REEKS
RICKS
RINKS
RISKS
ROCKS
ROOKS
RUCKS
RUSKS
SACKS
SARKS
SEEKS
SICKS
SILKS
SINKS
SOAKS
SOCKS
SUCKS
SULKS
TACKS
TALKS
TANKS
TASKS
TEAKS
TICKS
TREKS
TUCKS
TURKS
TUSKS
VICKS
WACKS
WALKS
WEEKS
WICKS
WINKS
WORKS
YANKS
YELKS
YOLKS

K•T••
KATES
KATHY
KATIE
KETCH
KITED
KITES
KITTY
KOTOS

K••T•
KEATS
KEITH
KENTS
KILTS
KILTY
KITTY
KNITS
KNOTS
KYATS
KYOTO

K•••T
KALAT
KAMET
KAPUT
KARAT
KERAT
KNELT
KNOUT
KRAFT
KRAIT
KRAUT

•K•T•
SKATE
SKITS

•K••T
SKEET
SKIRT

••KT•
HEKTO

KU•••
KUBAN
KUDOS
KUDUS
KUFRA
KULAK
KURSK
KURUS

K•U••
KAUAI
KAURI
KAURY
KNURL
KNURS
KRUBI
KRUPP

K••U•
KABUL
KAGUS
KAPUT
KNOUT
KORUN
KRAUT
KUDUS
KURUS

•KU••
SKUAS
SKULK
SKULL
SKUNK

••KU•
ANKUS
HOKUM
OAKUM

•••KU
HAIKU

KV•••
KVASS

K•V••
KAVAS
KEVEL
KEVIN
KIVAS

K••V•
KEEVE
KNAVE

•K•V•
SKIVE

K•W••
KIWIS

K••W•
KIOWA
KNOWN
KNOWS

•K•W•
SKEWS

••K•W
ASKEW

K•••X
KYLIX

KY•••
KYATS
KYLIX
KYOTO

K•Y••
KAYAK
KAYOS
KEYED

K••Y•
KARYO
KENYA
KONYA

K•••Y
KANDY
KATHY
KAURY
KENNY
KERRY
KIDDY
KILTY
KINKY
KITTY
KOOKY

•KY••
SKYEY

•K•Y•
OKAYS

•K••Y
SKYEY

••KY•
ALKYL
TOKYO

••K•Y
MIKEY
POKEY
TOKAY

•••KY
BALKY
BARKY
BECKY
BOSKY
BRAKY
BULKY
CHOKY
COCKY
COOKY
CORKY
DICKY
DINKY
DUCKY
DUSKY
FLAKY
FLUKY
FUNKY
GAWKY
GORKY
HOOKY
HULKY
HUNKY
HUSKY
JACKY
JERKY
JUNKY
KINKY
KOOKY
LANKY
LEAKY
LUCKY
MICKY
MILKY
MUCKY
MURKY
MUSKY
NICKY
PERKY
PESKY
PINKY
POCKY
PORKY
PUNKY
QUAKY
REEKY
RICKY
RISKY
ROCKY
ROOKY
SHAKY
SILKY
SMOKY
SNAKY
SPIKY
SULKY
TACKY
VICKY
WACKY
YOLKY
ZINKY

K•Z••
KAZAN
KAZOO

LA•••
LABEL
LABIA
LABIO
LABOR
LABRA
LACED
LACES
LACKS
LACTO
LADED
LADEN
LADES
LADIN
LADLE
LAGAN
LAGER
LAGOS
LAIKA
LAIRD
LAIRS
LAITY
LAKED
LAKER
LAKES
LALLS
LAMAS
LAMBS
LAMED
LAMER
LAMES
LAMIA
LAMPS
LANAI
LANCE
LANDS
LANES
LANKY
LAOAG
LAPAR
LAPEL
LAPIN
LAPIS
LAPPS
LAPSE
LARCH
LARDS
LARDY
LARES
LARGE
LARGO
LARKS
LARRY
LARVA
LASER
LASSO
LASTS
LATCH
LATER
LATEX
LATHE
LATHS
LATHY
LATIN
LATRY
LAUDS
LAUGH

5

LAURA
LAVAS
LAVED
LAVER
LAVES
LAWED
LAWNS
LAWNY
LAXER
LAXLY
LAYER
LAZAR
LAZED
LAZES

L•A••

LEACH
LEADS
LEADY
LEAFS
LEAFY
LEAKS
LEAKY
LEANS
LEANT
LEAPS
LEAPT
LEARN
LEASE
LEASH
LEAST
LEAVE
LEAVY
LHASA
LIANA
LIANE
LIANG
LIARS
LLAMA
LLANO
LOACH
LOADS
LOAFS
LOAMS
LOAMY
LOANS
LOATH
LUAUS

L••A•

LAGAN
LAMAS
LANAI
LAOAG
LAPAR
LAVAS
LAZAR
LEGAL
LENAS
LIGAN
LILAC
LILAS
LIRAS
LISAS
LITAI
LITAS
LIZAS
LOBAR
LOCAL
LOLAS
LORAN
LOTAH
LOYAL
LUNAR
LYMAN

L•••A

LABIA
LABRA
LAIKA
LAMIA
LARVA
LAURA
LEHUA
LEILA
LEMMA
LEONA
LEORA
LEPTA
LHASA
LIANA
LIBRA
LIBYA
LINDA
LINGA
LIVIA
LLAMA
LOGIA
LORCA
LORNA
LOTTA
LUCCA
LUCIA
LUISA
LYCEA
LYDDA
LYDIA
LYSSA
LYTTA

•LA••

ALACK
ALAMO
ALANS
ALARM
ALARY
ALATE
BLABS
BLACK
BLADE
BLAHS
BLAIN
BLAKE
BLAME
BLANC
BLAND
BLANK
BLARE
BLASE
BLAST
BLATS
BLAZE
CLACK
CLAIM
CLAMP
CLAMS
CLANG
CLANK
CLANS
CLAPS
CLARA
CLARE
CLARK
CLARO
CLARY
CLASH
CLASP
CLASS
CLAWS
CLAYS
ELAEO
ELAIN
ELAIO
ELAND
ELATE
FLACK
FLAGS
FLAIL
FLAIR
FLAKE
FLAKY
FLAME
FLAMS
FLAMY
FLANK
FLANS
FLAPS
FLARE
FLASH
FLASK
FLATS
FLAWS
FLAWY
FLAXY
FLAYS
GLACE
GLADE
GLADS
GLAIR
GLAND
GLANS
GLARE
GLARY
GLASS
GLAUC
GLAZE
GLAZY
KLARA
LLAMA
LLANO
OLAFS
OLAVS
PLACE
PLACK
PLAGI
PLAID
PLAIN
PLAIT
PLANE
PLANI
PLANK
PLANO
PLANS
PLANT
PLASH
PLASM
PLAST
PLASY
PLATE
PLATO
PLATS
PLATY
PLAYA
PLAYS
PLAZA
SLABS
SLACK
SLAGS
SLAIN
SLAKE
SLAMS
SLANG
SLANT
SLAPS
SLASH
SLATE
SLATS
SLATY
SLAVE
SLAVO
SLAVS
SLAWS
SLAYS

•L•A•

ALBAN
ALBAS
ALCAN
ALDAN
ALGAE
ALGAL
ALIAS
ALLAH
ALLAN
ALLAY
ALMAH
ALMAS
ALTAI
ALTAR
ALTAS
ALVAN
ALWAY
BLEAK
BLEAR
BLEAT
BLOAT
CLEAN
CLEAR
CLEAT
CLOAK
ELGAR
ELIAS
ELLAS
ELMAN
ELSAS
ELVAS
FLEAM
FLEAS
FLOAT
GLEAM
GLEAN
GLOAT
ILEAC
ILEAL
ILIAC
ILIAD
ILIAN
OLGAS
OLLAS
PLEAD
PLEAS
PLEAT
ULNAE
ULNAR
ULNAS

•L••A

ALEXA
ALGIA
ALOHA
ALPHA
ALULA
CLARA
ELENA
ELIZA
FLORA
ILONA
KLARA
LLAMA
PLAYA
PLAZA
PLENA
PLICA
ULEMA
ULTRA

••LA•

ALLAH
ALLAN
ALLAY
ANLAS
ATLAS
BALAS
BELAY
BOLAR
BOLAS
BYLAW
COLAS
DELAY
ECLAT
ELLAS
FILAR
GALAS
GALAX
GULAR
HULAS
HYLAS
INLAW
INLAY
ISLAM
JALAP
KALAT
KOLAS
KULAK
LILAC
LILAS
LOLAS
MALAC
MALAR
MALAY
MELAN
MILAN
MOLAL
MOLAR
OLLAS
PALAE
PILAF
PILAR
POLAR
RELAX
RELAY
SALAD
SELAH
SILAS
SOLAN
SOLAR
SPLAT
SPLAY
TELAE
TOLAN
TOLAS
UHLAN
UNLAY
VELAR
VOLAR
XYLAN

••L•A

BALSA
BELGA
BELLA
BULLA
CALLA
CELIA
CELLA
CILIA
COLZA
CULPA
DELIA
DELLA
DELTA
DULIA
FOLIA
GALEA
GILDA
HELGA
HILDA
HULDA
JULIA
MILIA
PALEA
PELLA
PILEA
POLKA
SALPA
SELMA
SILVA
SOLFA
SULFA
SYLVA
TILDA
TULSA
VILLA
VOLGA
VOLTA
VOLVA
VULVA
WALLA
WILLA
WILMA
YALTA

•••LA

ADELA
ALULA
ASYLA
BELLA
BEULA
BULLA
CALLA
CARLA
CELLA
CHELA
DELLA
DOBLA
DUALA
DYULA
HEKLA
KOALA
LEILA
PAULA
PELLA
PEPLA
PHILA
PHYLA
TESLA
UVULA
VILLA
VIOLA
VOILA
WALLA
WILLA

L•B••

LABEL
LABIA
LABIO
LABOR
LABRA
LIBBY
LIBEL
LIBER
LIBRA
LIBYA
LOBAR
LOBBY
LOBED
LOBES
LOBOS

L••B•

LAMBS
LIBBY
LIMBI
LIMBO
LIMBS
LOBBY
LOOBY

•LB••

ALBAN
ALBAS
ALBEE
ALBIN
ALBUM
ELBOW

•L•B•

ALIBI
BLABS
BLEBS
BLOBS
CLUBS
FLUBS
FLYBY
GLEBE
GLOBE
GLOBS
PLEBE
PLEBS
SLABS
SLOBS
SLUBS

•L••B

BLURB
CLIMB
PLUMB

••LB•

BILBO
BULBS

••L•B

ADLIB
CALEB
PHLEB

L•C••

LACED
LACES
LACKS

LACTO
LICHT
LICIT
LICKS
LOCAL
LOCHS
LOCKE
LOCKS
LOCOS
LOCUS
LUCCA
LUCES
LUCIA
LUCID
LUCKY
LUCRE
LUCYS
LYCEA
LYCEE

L••C•
LANCE
LARCH
LATCH
LEACH
LEECH
LEUCO
LOACH
LORCA
LUCCA
LUNCH
LURCH
LYNCH

L•••C
LILAC
LOGIC
LYRIC
LYTIC

•LC••
ALCAN
ULCER

•L•C•
ALACK
ALECK
ALECS
ALICE
ALYCE
BLACK
BLOCK
BLOCS
CLACK
CLICK
CLOCK
CLUCK
ELECT
FLACK
FLECK
FLICK
FLOCK
FLOCS
GLACE
GLYCO
PLACE
PLACK
PLICA
PLUCK
SLACK
SLICE
SLICK

•L••C
BLANC
GLAUC
ILEAC
ILIAC
OLEIC

••LC•
BELCH
CALCI
CULCH
DOLCE
DULCE
DULCY
FILCH
GULCH
MILCH
MULCH
MULCT
SULCI
TALCS
WELCH

••L•C
AULIC
COLIC
EOLIC
FOLIC
HELIC
LILAC
MALAC
MALIC
MELIC
RELIC
SALIC
SILIC
TELIC

L•D••
LADED
LADEN
LADES
LADIN
LADLE
LEDGE
LEDGY
LODEN
LODES
LODGE
LYDDA
LYDIA

L••D•
LANDS
LARDS
LARDY
LAUDS
LEADS
LEADY
LENDS
LEUDS
LINDA
LOADS
LORDS
LYDDA

L•••D
LACED
LADED
LAIRD
LAKED
LAMED
LAVED
LAWED
LAZED
LEPID
LIKED
LIMED
LINED
LIPID
LIVED
LIVID
LLOYD
LOBED
LOOED
LOPED
LOVED
LOWED
LUCID
LURED
LURID
LUTED
LYSED

•LD••
ALDAN
ALDEN
ALDER
ALDIS
ALDOL
ALDOS
ALDUS
BLDGS
ELDER
OLDEN
OLDER

•L•D•
BLADE
CLODS
CLYDE
ELIDE
ELUDE
GLADE
GLADS
GLEDE
GLEDS
GLIDE
PLODS
SLEDS
SLIDE

•L••D
ALGID
ALMUD
ALOUD
BLAND
BLEED
BLEND
BLIND
BLOND
BLOOD
BLUED
CLOUD
CLUED
ELAND
FLIED
FLOOD
FLOYD
FLUID
GLAND
GLUED
ILIAD
LLOYD
PLAID
PLEAD
PLIED
PLOID
SLOYD
SLUED

••LD•
BALDR
COLDS
FOLDS
GELDS
GILDA
GILDS
GOLDS
HILDA
HOLDS
HULDA
MELDS
MOLDS
MOLDY
SOLDI
SOLDO
TILDA
TILDE
VELDS
VELDT
WALDO
WELDS
WILDS
WOLDS

••L•D
AILED
AXLED
BALED
DELED
DOLED
FELID
FILED
GELID
HALED
HALID
HOLED
IDLED
ISLED
OGLED
OILED
PALED
PILED
POLED
PULED
RILED
RULED
SALAD
SOLED
SOLID
TILED
VALID
WALED
WILED

•••LD
BUILD
CHILD
COULD
FIELD
FJELD
GUILD
MOULD
ROALD
SCALD
SCOLD
SKALD
WEALD
WIELD
WOALD
WORLD
WOULD
YIELD

LE•••
LEACH
LEADS
LEADY
LEAFS
LEAFY
LEAKS
LEAKY
LEANS
LEANT
LEAPS
LEAPT
LEARN
LEASE
LEASH
LEAST
LEAVE
LEAVY
LEDGE
LEDGY
LEECH
LEEKS
LEERS
LEERY
LEETS
LEFTS
LEFTY
LEGAL
LEGER
LEGES
LEGGY
LEGIT
LEHRS
LEHUA
LEIFS
LEIGH
LEILA
LEMMA
LEMON
LEMUR
LENAS
LENDS
LENES
LENIN
LENIS
LENNY
LENOS
LENTO
LENTS
LEONA
LEONS
LEORA
LEPER
LEPID
LEPSY
LEPTA
LEPTO
LEPUS
LEROY
LETHE
LETTS
LETTY
LETUP
LEUCO
LEUDS
LEUKO
LEVEE
LEVEL
LEVEN
LEVER
LEVIS
LEWIE
LEWIS
LEYTE

L•E••
LEECH
LEEKS
LEERS
LEERY
LEETS
LIEGE
LIENS
LIEUT
LOESS

L••E•
LABEL
LACED
LACES
LADED
LADEN
LADES
LAGER
LAKED
LAKER
LAKES
LAMED
LAMER
LAMES
LANES
LAPEL
LARES
LASER
LATER
LATEX
LAVED
LAVER
LAVES
LAWED
LAXER
LAYER
LAZED
LAZES
LEGER
LEGES
LENES
LEPER
LEVEE
LEVEL
LEVEN
LEVER
LIBEL
LIBER
LIFER
LIKED
LIKEN
LIKES
LIMED
LIMEN
LIMES
LIMEY
LINED
LINEN
LINER
LINES
LINEY
LITER
LIVED
LIVEN
LIVER
LIVES
LOBED
LOBES
LODEN
LODES
LOGES
LONER
LOOED
LOPED
LOPER
LOPES
LORES
LOSER
LOSES
LOVED
LOVER
LOVES
LOWED
LOWER
LUCES
LUGER
LUMEN
LUNES
LUNET
LURED
LURER
LURES
LUTED
LUTES
LUXES
LYCEA
LYCEE
LYLES
LYRES
LYSED
LYSES

L•••E
LADLE
LANCE
LAPSE
LARGE
LATHE
LEASE
LEAVE
LEDGE
LETHE
LEVEE
LEWIE
LEYTE
LIANE
LIEGE
LISLE
LITHE
LIVRE
LOCKE
LODGE
LOGUE
LOIRE
LOOSE
LOUPE
LOUSE
LUCRE
LUISE
LUNGE
LYCEE

•LE••
ALECK
ALECS
ALEFS
ALEPH
ALERT

ALEUT
ALEXA
BLEAK
BLEAR
BLEAT
BLEBS
BLEED
BLEND
BLENT
BLESS
BLEST
CLEAN
CLEAR
CLEAT
CLEFS
CLEFT
CLEMS
CLEON
CLERK
CLEWS
ELECT
ELEGY
ELEMI
ELENA
FLEAM
FLEAS
FLECK
FLEER
FLEES
FLEET
FLESH
FLEWS
FLEXI
GLEAM
GLEAN
GLEBE
GLEDE
GLEDS
GLEES
GLEET
GLENN
GLENS
ILEAC
ILEAL
ILEUM
ILEUS
OLEIC
OLEIN
PLEAD
PLEAS
PLEAT
PLEBE
PLEBS
PLEGY
PLENA
SLEDS
SLEEK
SLEEP
SLEET
SLEPT
SLEWS
ULEMA
ULENT

•L•E•

ALBEE
ALDEN
ALDER
ALGER
ALIEN
ALLEN
ALLEY
ALOES
ALTER
BLEED
BLUED
BLUER
BLUES
BLUET
CLUED
CLUES
ELAEO
ELDER
ELLEN
ELMER
ELVER
ELVES
FLEER
FLEES
FLEET
FLIED
FLIER
FLIES
FLOES
FLUES
FLYER
GLEES
GLEET
GLUED
GLUES
GLUEY
ILMEN
MLLES
OLDEN
OLDER
PLIED
PLIER
PLIES
SLEEK
SLEEP
SLEET
SLIER
SLOES
SLUED
SLUES
SLYER
ULCER

•L••E

ALATE
ALBEE
ALGAE
ALGIE
ALICE
ALIKE
ALINE
ALIVE
ALLIE
ALONE
ALYCE
BLADE
BLAKE
BLAME
BLARE
BLASE
BLAZE
BLOKE
CLARE
CLIME
CLINE
CLIVE
CLONE
CLOSE
CLOVE
CLYDE
ELATE
ELIDE
ELISE
ELITE
ELLIE
ELOPE
ELSIE
ELUDE
FLAKE
FLAME
FLARE
FLUKE
FLUME
FLUTE
GLACE
GLADE
GLARE
GLAZE
GLEBE
GLEDE
GLIDE
GLOBE
GLOVE
GLOZE
GLUME
OLIVE
OLLIE
PLACE
PLANE
PLATE
PLEBE
PLUME
SLAKE
SLATE
SLAVE
SLICE
SLIDE
SLIME
SLOPE
ULNAE
ULOSE

••LE•

ABLER
ADLER
AGLEE
AGLET
AGLEY
AILED
ALLEN
ALLEY
ARLES
AXLED
AXLES
BALED
BALER
BALES
BELEM
BILES
BOLES
CALEB
COLES
CULET
DALES
DELED
DELES
DOLED
DOLES
ELLEN
EULER
FILED
FILER
FILES
FILET
GALEA
GALEN
GALES
GILES
GOLEM
GULES
HALED
HALER
HALES
HELEN
HOLED
HOLES
HOLEY
IDLED
IDLER
IDLES
INLET
ISLED
ISLES
ISLET
JOLES
JULEP
JULES
LYLES
MALES
MELEE
MILER
MILES
MLLES
MOLES
MULES
MULEY
MYLES
OGLED
OGLER
OGLES
OILED
OILER
ORLES
OSLER
OWLET
PALEA
PALED
PALEO
PALER
PALES
PALEY
PELEE
PHLEB
PILEA
PILED
PILEI
PILES
POLED
POLES
PULED
PULER
PULES
RALES
RILED
RILES
RILEY
ROLES
RULED
RULER
RULES
SALEM
SALEP
SALES
SELEN
SILEX
SOLED
SOLES
SPLEN
TALER
TALES
TELEG
TELEO
TELEX
TILED
TILER
TILES
TOLES
TULES
TYLER
VALES
VALET
VILER
VOLES
WALED
WALER
WALES
WILED
WILES
XYLEM
YULES

••L•E

AGLEE
ALLIE
BELIE
BELLE
BILGE
BULGE
CALPE
CALVE
CELIE
CHLOE
DELVE
DOLCE
DULCE
DULSE
ELLIE
FALSE
HALLE
HALVE
HELLE
HELVE
JULIE
MELEE
OLLIE
PALAE
PELEE
PULSE
ROLFE
SALVE
SOLVE
TELAE
TILDE
TULLE
VALUE
VALVE

•••LE

ABELE
ADDLE
ADELE
AGILE
AISLE
AMBLE
AMOLE
AMPLE
ANGLE
ANILE
ANKLE
APPLE
AXILE
AZOLE
BASLE
BELLE
BIBLE
BIRLE
BOGLE
BOULE
BOYLE
BUGLE
CABLE
CHILE
CHOLE
CHYLE
COBLE
COELE
CYCLE
DHOLE
DOYLE
DUPLE
EAGLE
EARLE
ECOLE
EDILE
EMILE
EXILE
FABLE
FARLE
FUGLE
GABLE
GAVLE
GUILE
HALLE
HELLE
HOYLE
INKLE
ISTLE
IXTLE
JOULE
LADLE
LISLE
MACLE
MAPLE
MERLE
NOBLE
ODYLE
OVULE
PHILE
PHYLE
RIFLE
ROBLE
RUBLE
SABLE
SCALE
SHALE
SIDLE
SMILE
SOCLE
SPILE
STALE
STELE
STILE
STOLE
STYLE
SWALE
TABLE
THOLE
THULE
TITLE
TOILE
TULLE
UNCLE
UTILE
VOILE
WHALE
WHILE
WHOLE

L•F••

LEFTS
LEFTY
LIFER
LIFTS
LOFTS
LOFTY
LUFFS

L••F•

LEAFS
LEAFY
LEIFS
LOAFS
LOOFS
LUFFS

•LF••

ELFIN

•L•F•

ALEFS
ALIFS
ALOFT
BLUFF
CLEFS
CLEFT
CLIFF
FLUFF
OLAFS

•L••F

ALOOF
BLUFF
CLIFF
FLUFF
KLOOF

••LF•

DELFT
GOLFS
GULFS
PELFS
ROLFE
ROLFS
SOLFA
SULFA
SULFO
WOLFS

••L•F

CALIF
PILAF

•••LF

ADOLF
SHELF

L•G••

LAGAN
LAGER
LAGOS
LEGAL
LEGER
LEGES
LEGGY
LEGIT
LIGAN
LIGHT

LIGNI
LIGNO
LOGES
LOGIA
LOGIC
LOGOS
LOGUE
LUGER

L••G•
LARGE
LARGO
LAUGH
LEDGE
LEDGY
LEGGY
LEIGH
LIEGE
LINGA
LINGO
LINGS
LODGE
LONGI
LONGS
LOUGH
LUIGI
LUNGE
LUNGI
LUNGS

L•••G
LAOAG
LIANG
LYING

•LG••
ALGAE
ALGAL
ALGER
ALGIA
ALGID
ALGIE
ALGIN
ALGOL
ALGOR
ALGUM
ALGYS
ELGAR
ELGIN
OLGAS

•L•G•
ALIGN
BLDGS
BLIGH
CLOGS
ELEGY
FLAGS
FLOGS
OLIGO
OLOGY
PLAGI
PLEGY
PLUGS
SLAGS
SLOGS
SLUGS

•L••G
ALMUG
ALONG
CLANG
CLING
CLUNG
FLING
FLONG
FLUNG
SLANG
SLING
SLUNG

••LG•
BELGA
BILGE
BILGY
BULGE
BULGY
HELGA
VOLGA
VULGO

••L•G
TELEG

LH•••
LHASA

L•H••
LEHRS
LEHUA

L••H•
LATHE
LATHS
LATHY
LETHE
LICHT
LIGHT
LITHE
LITHO
LOCHS

L•••H
LARCH
LATCH
LAUGH
LEACH
LEASH
LEECH
LEIGH
LOACH
LOATH
LOTAH
LOUGH
LUNCH
LURCH
LYMPH
LYNCH

•L•H•
ALOHA
ALPHA
ALPHY
BLAHS
ELIHU

•L••H
ALEPH
ALLAH
ALMAH
BLIGH
BLUSH
CLASH
CLOTH
FLASH
FLESH
FLUSH
GLYPH
PLASH
PLUSH
SLASH
SLOSH
SLOTH
SLUSH

••LH•
DELHI

••L•H
ALLAH
BELCH
CULCH
DOLPH
FILCH
FILTH
GULCH
MILCH
MULCH
RALPH
ROLPH
SELAH
SYLPH
TILTH
WELCH
WELSH

LI•••
LIANA
LIANE
LIANG
LIARS
LIBBY
LIBEL
LIBER
LIBRA
LIBYA
LICHT
LICIT
LICKS
LIEGE
LIENS
LIEUT
LIFER
LIFTS
LIGAN
LIGHT
LIGNI
LIGNO
LIKED
LIKEN
LIKES
LILAC
LILAS
LILLY
LILTS
LILYS
LIMBI
LIMBO
LIMBS
LIMED
LIMEN
LIMES
LIMEY
LIMIT
LIMNS
LIMPS
LINDA
LINED
LINEN
LINER
LINES
LINEY
LINGA
LINGO
LINGS
LININ
LINKS
LINTY
LINUS
LIONS
LIPID
LIPPI
LIPPY
LIRAS
LISAS
LISLE
LISPS
LISTS
LISZT
LITAI
LITAS
LITER
LITHE
LITHO
LIVED
LIVEN
LIVER
LIVES
LIVIA
LIVID
LIVRE
LIZAS
LIZZY

L•I••
LAIKA
LAIRD
LAIRS
LAITY
LEIFS
LEIGH
LEILA
LOINS
LOIRE
LUIGI
LUISA
LUISE
LYING

L••I•
LABIA
LABIO
LADIN
LAMIA
LAPIN
LAPIS
LATIN
LEGIT
LENIN
LENIS
LEPID
LEVIS
LEWIE
LEWIS
LICIT
LIMIT
LININ
LIPID
LIVIA
LIVID
LOGIA
LOGIC
LORIS
LOUIS
LUCIA
LUCID
LURID
LYDIA
LYRIC
LYSIN
LYSIS
LYTIC

L•••I
LANAI
LIGNI
LIMBI
LIPPI
LITAI
LONGI
LUIGI
LUNGI

•LI••
ALIAS
ALIBI
ALICE
ALIEN
ALIFS
ALIGN
ALIKE
ALINE
ALIVE
BLIGH
BLIMP
BLIND
BLINK
BLIPS
BLISS
BLITZ
CLICK
CLIFF
CLIMB
CLIME
CLINE
CLING
CLINK
CLINO
CLINT
CLIOS
CLIPS
CLIVE
ELIAS
ELIDE
ELIHU
ELIOT
ELISE
ELITE
ELIZA
FLICK
FLIED
FLIER
FLIES
FLING
FLINT
FLIPS
FLIRT
FLITS
GLIDE
GLIMS
GLINT
ILIAC
ILIAD
ILIAN
ILIUM
OLIGO
OLIOS
OLIVE
PLICA
PLIED
PLIER
PLIES
PLINY
SLICE
SLICK
SLIDE
SLIER
SLILY
SLIME
SLIMS
SLIMY
SLING
SLINK
SLIPS
SLIPT
SLITS

•L•I•
ALBIN
ALDIS
ALGIA
ALGID
ALGIE
ALGIN
ALLIE
ALLIS
ALOIN
ALOIS
ALUIN
ALVIN
ALWIN
BLAIN
BLOIS
CLAIM
ELAIN
ELAIO
ELFIN
ELGIN
ELLIE
ELLIS
ELOIN
ELSIE
ELVIN
ELWIN
FLAIL
FLAIR
FLUID
GLAIR
OLEIC
OLEIN
OLLIE
PLAID
PLAIN
PLAIT
PLOID
SLAIN

•L••I
ALIBI
ALTAI
ELEMI
FLEXI
PLAGI
PLANI
PLURI
PLUVI

••LI•
AALII
ADLIB
ALLIE
ALLIS
AULIC
AULIS
BELIE
CALIF
CALIX
CELIA
CELIE
CILIA
COLIC
COLIN
CYLIX
DELIA
DULIA
ELLIE
ELLIS
EOLIC
FELID
FELIX
FOLIA
FOLIC
FOLIO
GELID
HALID
HELIC
HELIO
HELIX
JULIA
JULIE
JULIO
KYLIX
MALIC
MELIC
MILIA
OLLIE
OXLIP
PILIS
POLIO
RELIC
SALIC
SILIC
SOLID
SPLIT
TELIC
TULIP
UNLIT
VALID

••L•I
AALII
CALCI
CALLI
CULTI
DELHI
MILLI
MULTI
PALMI
PALPI
PELVI
PILEI
SALMI
SOLDI
SULCI
VILLI
VOLTI

•••LI
CALLI
CHILI
FORLI
MILLI
OBOLI

OVOLI
STYLI
VILLI

L•K••
LAKED
LAKER
LAKES
LIKED
LIKEN
LIKES

L••K•
LACKS
LAIKA
LANKY
LARKS
LEAKS
LEAKY
LEEKS
LEUKO
LICKS
LINKS
LOCKE
LOCKS
LOOKS
LUCKY
LURKS

•LK••
ALKYL

•L•K•
ALIKE
BLAKE
BLOKE
FLAKE
FLAKY
FLUKE
FLUKY
SLAKE

•L••K
ALACK
ALECK
BLACK
BLANK
BLEAK
BLINK
BLOCK
CLACK
CLANK
CLARK
CLERK
CLICK
CLINK
CLOAK
CLOCK
CLUCK
FLACK
FLANK
FLASK
FLECK
FLICK
FLOCK
FLUNK
PLACK
PLANK
PLUCK
PLUNK
SLACK
SLEEK
SLICK
SLINK
SLUNK

••LK•
BALKS
BALKY
BILKS
BULKS
BULKY
CALKS
FOLKS
HULKS
HULKY
MILKS
MILKY
POLKA
SILKS
SILKY
SULKS
SULKY
TALKS
WALKS
YELKS
YOLKS
YOLKY

••L•K
KULAK
TALUK

•••LK
CAULK
CHALK
SKULK
STALK
WHELK

LL•••
LLAMA
LLANO
LLOYD

L•L••
LALLS
LILAC
LILAS
LILLY
LILTS
LILYS
LOLAS
LOLLS
LOLLY
LULLS
LULUS
LYLES

L••L•
LADLE
LALLS
LAXLY
LEILA
LILLY
LISLE
LOLLS
LOLLY
LOWLY
LULLS

L•••L
LABEL
LAPEL
LEGAL
LEVEL
LIBEL
LOCAL
LOYAL
LYSOL

•LL••
ALLAH
ALLAN
ALLAY
ALLEN
ALLEY
ALLIE
ALLIS
ALLOT
ALLOW
ALLOY
ALLYL
ELLAS
ELLEN
ELLIE
ELLIS
ILLUS
MLLES
OLLAS
OLLIE

•L•L•
ALULA
SLILY
SLYLY

•L••L
ALDOL
ALGAL
ALGOL
ALKYL
ALLYL
FLAIL
ILEAL

••LL•
BALLS
BELLA
BELLE
BELLS
BELLY
BILLS
BILLY
BOLLS
BULLA
BULLS
BULLY
CALLA
CALLI
CALLS
CELLA
CELLO
CELLS
COLLY
CULLS
DALLY
DELLA
DELLS
DOLLS
DOLLY
DULLS
DULLY
FALLS
FELLS
FELLY
FILLS
FILLY
FOLLY
FULLS
FULLY
GALLS
GILLS
GOLLY
GULLS
GULLY
HALLE
HALLS
HELLE
HELLO
HELLS
HILLS
HILLY
HOLLY
HULLS
JELLO
JELLS
JELLY
JILLS
JOLLY
KILLS
LALLS
LILLY
LOLLS
LOLLY
LULLS
MALLS
MILLI
MILLS
MILLY
MOLLS
MOLLY
MULLS
NELLS
NELLY
PALLS
PELLA
PELLY
PILLS
POLLS
POLLY
PULLS
RALLY
RILLS
ROLLO
ROLLS
SALLY
SELLS
SILLS
SILLY
SULLY
TALLY
TELLS
TELLY
TILLS
TILLY
TOLLS
TULLE
TULLY
VILLA
VILLI
VILLS
WALLA
WALLS
WALLY
WELLS
WILLA
WILLS
WILLY
YELLS

••L•L
ALLYL
MOLAL
SALOL
TOLYL
XYLOL
XYLYL

•••LL
ATOLL
BRILL
CHILL
DOALL
DRILL
DROLL
DWELL
FRILL
GRILL
IDYLL
KNELL
KNOLL
PHYLL
QUELL
QUILL
SCALL
SCULL
SHALL
SHELL
SHILL
SKILL
SKULL
SMALL
SMELL
SNELL
SPALL
SPELL
SPILL
STALL
STILL
STULL
SWELL
SWILL
TRILL
TROLL
TWILL

L•M••
LAMAS
LAMBS
LAMED
LAMER
LAMES
LAMIA
LAMPS
LEMMA
LEMON
LEMUR
LIMBI
LIMBO
LIMBS
LIMED
LIMEN
LIMES
LIMEY
LIMIT
LIMNS
LIMPS
LUMEN
LUMPS
LUMPY
LYMAN
LYMPH

L••M•
LEMMA
LLAMA
LOAMS
LOAMY
LOOMS

•LM••
ALMAH
ALMAS
ALMUD
ALMUG
ELMAN
ELMER
ILMEN

•L•M•
ALAMO
ALUMS
BLAME
BLIMP
CLAMP
CLAMS
CLEMS
CLIMB
CLIME
CLUMP
ELEMI
FLAME
FLAMS
FLAMY
FLUME
FLUMP
GLIMS
GLUME
LLAMA
PLUMB
PLUME
PLUMP
PLUMS
PLUMY
SLAMS
SLIME
SLIMS
SLIMY
SLUMP
SLUMS
ULEMA

•L••M
ALARM
ALBUM
ALGUM
BLOOM
CLAIM
FLEAM
GLEAM
GLOOM
ILEUM
ILIUM
PLASM

••LM•
BALMS
BALMY
CALMS
CULMS
FILMS
FILMY
HELMS
HOLMS
PALMI
PALMS
PALMY
PULMO
SALMI
SELMA
WILMA

••L•M
BELEM
CELOM
FILUM
GOLEM
HILUM
ISLAM
SALEM
VELUM
XYLEM

•••LM
HAULM
PSALM
QUALM
REALM
WHELM

L•N••
LANAI
LANCE
LANDS
LANES
LANKY
LENAS
LENDS
LENES
LENIN
LENIS
LENNY
LENOS
LENTO
LENTS
LINDA
LINED
LINEN
LINER
LINES
LINEY
LINGA
LINGO
LINGS
LININ
LINKS
LINTY
LINUS
LONER
LONGI
LONGS
LUNAR
LUNCH
LUNES
LUNET
LUNGE
LUNGI
LUNGS
LUNTS
LYNCH
LYNNS

L••N•
LAWNS
LAWNY
LEANS
LEANT
LENNY
LEONA
LEONS
LIANA
LIANE

LIANG
LIENS
LIGNI
LIGNO
LIMNS
LIONS
LLANO
LOANS
LOINS
LOONS
LOONY
LORNA
LYING
LYNNS
LYONS

L•••N

LADEN
LADIN
LAGAN
LAPIN
LATIN
LEARN
LEMON
LENIN
LEVEN
LIGAN
LIKEN
LIMEN
LINEN
LININ
LIVEN
LODEN
LORAN
LUMEN
LUZON
LYMAN
LYSIN

•LN••

ULNAE
ULNAR
ULNAS

•L•N•

ALANS
ALINE
ALONE
ALONG
BLANC
BLAND
BLANK
BLEND
BLENT
BLIND
BLINK
BLOND
BLUNT
CLANG
CLANK
CLANS
CLINE
CLING
CLINK
CLINO
CLINT
CLONE
CLONS
CLUNG
CLUNY
ELAND
ELENA
FLANK
FLANS
FLING
FLINT
FLONG
FLUNG
FLUNK
GLAND
GLANS
GLENN
GLENS
GLINT
ILONA
LLANO
PLANE
PLANI
PLANK
PLANO
PLANS
PLANT
PLENA
PLINY
PLUNK
SLANG
SLANT
SLING
SLINK
SLUNG
SLUNK
ULENT

•L••N

ALBAN
ALBIN
ALCAN
ALDAN
ALDEN
ALGIN
ALIEN
ALIGN
ALLAN
ALLEN
ALOIN
ALTON
ALUIN
ALVAN
ALVIN
ALWIN
BLAIN
BLOWN
CLEAN
CLEON
CLOWN
ELAIN
ELFIN
ELGIN
ELLEN
ELMAN
ELOIN
ELTON
ELVIN
ELWIN
FLOWN
GLEAN
GLENN
ILIAN
ILMEN
OLDEN
OLEIN
PLAIN
SLAIN

••LN•

KILNS

••L•N

ALLAN
ALLEN
COLIN
COLON
ELLEN
FELON
GALEN
HELEN
MELAN
MELON
MILAN
NYLON
ORLON
PELON
PYLON
SALON
SELEN
SOLAN
SOLON
SPLEN
TALON
TOLAN
UHLAN
XYLAN

LO•••

LOACH
LOADS
LOAFS
LOAMS
LOAMY
LOANS
LOATH
LOBAR
LOBBY
LOBED
LOBES
LOBOS
LOCAL
LOCHS
LOCKE
LOCKS
LOCOS
LOCUS
LODEN
LODES
LODGE
LOESS
LOFTS
LOFTY
LOGES
LOGIA
LOGIC
LOGOS
LOGUE
LOINS
LOIRE
LOLAS
LOLLS
LOLLY
LONER
LONGI
LONGS
LOOBY
LOOED
LOOFS
LOOKS
LOOMS
LOONS
LOONY
LOOPS
LOOSE
LOOTS
LOPED
LOPER
LOPES
LOPPY
LORAN
LORCA
LORDS
LORES
LORIS
LORNA
LORRY
LOSER
LOSES
LOTAH
LOTOS
LOTTA
LOTTO
LOTTY
LOTUS
LOUGH
LOUIS
LOUPE
LOUPS
LOURS
LOUSE
LOUSY
LOUTS
LOVED
LOVER
LOVES
LOWED
LOWER
LOWLY
LOYAL

L•O••

LAOAG
LEONA
LEONS
LEORA
LIONS
LLOYD
LOOBY
LOOED
LOOFS
LOOKS
LOOMS
LOONS
LOONY
LOOPS
LOOSE
LOOTS
LYONS

L••O•

LABOR
LAGOS
LEMON
LENOS
LEROY
LOBOS
LOCOS
LOGOS
LOTOS
LUXOR
LUZON
LYSOL

L•••O

LABIO
LACTO
LARGO
LASSO
LENTO
LEPTO
LEUCO
LEUKO
LIGNO
LIMBO
LINGO
LITHO
LLANO
LOTTO

•LO••

ALOES
ALOFT
ALOHA
ALOIN
ALOIS
ALONE
ALONG
ALOOF
ALOUD
BLOAT
BLOBS
BLOCK
BLOCS
BLOIS
BLOKE
BLOND
BLOOD
BLOOM
BLOTS
BLOWN
BLOWS
BLOWY
CLOAK
CLOCK
CLODS
CLOGS
CLONE
CLONS
CLOPS
CLOSE
CLOTH
CLOTS
CLOUD
CLOUT
CLOVE
CLOWN
CLOYS
ELOIN
ELOPE
FLOAT
FLOCK
FLOCS
FLOES
FLOGS
FLONG
FLOOD
FLOOR
FLOPS
FLORA
FLOSS
FLOUR
FLOUT
FLOWN
FLOWS
FLOYD
GLOAT
GLOBE
GLOBS
GLOOM
GLORY
GLOSS
GLOST
GLOVE
GLOWS
GLOZE
ILONA
KLOOF
LLOYD
OLOGY
PLODS
PLOID
PLOPS
PLOTS
PLOWS
PLOYS
SLOBS
SLOES
SLOGS
SLOOP
SLOPE
SLOPS
SLOSH
SLOTH
SLOTS
SLOWS
SLOYD
ULOSE
ULOUS
ZLOTY

•L•O•

ALDOL
ALDOS
ALGOL
ALGOR
ALLOT
ALLOW
ALLOY
ALOOF
ALTON
ALTOS
BLOOD
BLOOM
CLEON
CLIOS
ELBOW
ELIOT
ELTON
FLOOD
FLOOR
FLUOR
GLOOM
KLOOF
OLIOS
SLOOP

•L••O

ALAMO
CLARO
CLINO
ELAEO
ELAIO
GLYCO
LLANO
OLIGO
PLANO
PLATO
PLUTO
SLAVO

••LO•

AGLOW
ALLOT
ALLOW
ALLOY
BELOW
BOLOS
CELOM
CHLOE
CHLOR
COLON
COLOR
DELOS
DOLOR
FELON
GALOP
HALOS
HELOT
IGLOO
KILOS
MELON
NYLON
ORLON
ORLOP
PELON
PHLOX
PILOT
PYLON
SALOL
SALON
SILOS
SOLON
SOLOS
TALON
TALOS
VALOR
XYLOL

••L•O

BILBO
CELLO
FOLIO
HELIO
HELLO
IGLOO
JELLO
JULIO
MOLTO
PALEO
POLIO
PULMO
ROLLO
SALVO
SOLDO
SULFO
TELEO
VULGO
WALDO

•••LO

AMYLO
ANGLO
CARLO
CELLO
CHILO
COELO
CYCLO
DIPLO
HAPLO
HELLO
HYALO
JELLO
MYELO
OCULO
OVOLO
PABLO

PAOLO
PAULO
PHILO
PHYLO
PYELO
ROLLO
SIALO
STYLO

L•P••
LAPAR
LAPEL
LAPIN
LAPIS
LAPPS
LAPSE
LEPER
LEPID
LEPSY
LEPTA
LEPTO
LEPUS
LIPID
LIPPI
LIPPY
LOPED
LOPER
LOPES
LOPPY
LUPUS

L••P•
LAMPS
LAPPS
LEAPS
LEAPT
LIMPS
LIPPI
LIPPY
LISPS
LOOPS
LOPPY
LOUPE
LOUPS
LUMPS
LUMPY
LYMPH

L•••P
LETUP

•LP••
ALPHA
ALPHY

•L•P•
ALEPH
BLIPS
CLAPS
CLIPS
CLOPS
ELOPE
FLAPS
FLIPS
FLOPS
GLYPH
PLOPS
SLAPS
SLEPT
SLIPS
SLIPT
SLOPE
SLOPS

•L••P
BLIMP
CLAMP
CLASP
CLUMP
FLUMP
PLUMP
SLEEP
SLOOP
SLUMP
SLURP

••LP•
CALPE
CULPA
DOLPH
GULPS
HELPS
KELPS
PALPI
PULPS
PULPY
RALPH
ROLPH
SALPA
SYLPH
YELPS

••L•P
GALOP
JALAP
JULEP
ORLOP
OXLIP
POLYP
SALEP
TULIP

•••LP
SCALP
SCULP
WHELP

L•R••
LARCH
LARDS
LARDY
LARES
LARGE
LARGO
LARKS
LARRY
LARVA
LEROY
LIRAS
LORAN
LORCA
LORDS
LORES
LORIS
LORNA
LORRY
LURCH
LURED
LURER
LURES
LURID
LURKS
LYRES
LYRIC

L••R•
LABRA
LAIRD
LAIRS
LARRY
LATRY
LAURA
LEARN
LEERS
LEERY
LEHRS
LEORA
LIARS
LIBRA
LIVRE
LOIRE
LORRY
LOURS
LUCRE

L•••R
LABOR
LAGER
LAKER
LAMER
LAPAR
LASER
LATER
LAVER
LAXER
LAYER
LAZAR
LEGER
LEMUR
LEPER
LEVER
LIBER
LIFER
LINER
LITER
LIVER
LOBAR
LONER
LOPER
LOSER
LOVER
LOWER
LUGER
LUNAR
LURER
LUXOR

•L•R•
ALARM
ALARY
ALERT
BLARE
BLURB
BLURS
BLURT
CLARA
CLARE
CLARK
CLARO
CLARY
CLERK
FLARE
FLIRT
FLORA
GLARE
GLARY
GLORY
KLARA
PLURI
SLURP
SLURS
ULTRA

•L••R
ALDER
ALGER
ALGOR
ALTAR
ALTER
BLEAR
BLUER
CLEAR
ELDER
ELGAR
ELMER
ELVER
FLAIR
FLEER
FLIER
FLOOR
FLOUR
FLUOR
FLYER
GLAIR
OLDER
PLIER
SLIER
SLYER
ULCER
ULNAR

••L•R
ABLER
ADLER
BALDR
BALER
BOLAR
CHLOR
COLOR
DOLOR
EULER
FILAR
FILER
GULAR
HALER
IDLER
MALAR
MILER
MOLAR
OGLER
OILER
OSLER
PALER
PILAR
POLAR
PULER
RULER
SOLAR
TALER
TILER
TYLER
VALOR
VELAR
VILER
VOLAR
WALER

L•S••
LASER
LASSO
LASTS
LISAS
LISLE
LISPS
LISTS
LISZT
LOSER
LOSES
LUSTS
LUSTY
LYSED
LYSES
LYSIN
LYSIS
LYSOL
LYSSA

L••S•
LAPSE
LASSO
LEASE
LEASH
LEAST
LEPSY
LHASA
LOESS
LOOSE
LOUSE
LOUSY
LUISA
LUISE
LYSSA

L•••S
LACES
LACKS
LADES
LAGOS
LAIRS
LAKES
LALLS
LAMAS
LAMBS
LAMES
LAMPS
LANDS
LANES
LAPIS
LAPPS
LARDS
LARES
LARKS
LASTS
LATHS
LAUDS
LAVAS
LAVES
LAWNS
LAZES
LEADS
LEAFS
LEAKS
LEANS
LEAPS
LEEKS
LEERS
LEETS
LEFTS
LEGES
LEHRS
LEIFS
LENAS
LENDS
LENES
LENIS
LENOS
LENTS
LEONS
LEPUS
LETTS
LEUDS
LEVIS
LEWIS
LIARS
LICKS
LIENS
LIFTS
LIKES
LILAS
LILTS
LILYS
LIMBS
LIMES
LIMNS
LIMPS
LINES
LINGS
LINKS
LINUS
LIONS
LIRAS
LISAS
LISPS
LISTS
LITAS
LIVES
LIZAS
LOADS
LOAFS
LOAMS
LOANS
LOBES
LOBOS
LOCHS
LOCKS
LOCOS
LOCUS
LODES
LOESS
LOFTS
LOGES
LOGOS
LOINS
LOLAS
LOLLS
LONGS
LOOFS
LOOKS
LOOMS
LOONS
LOOPS
LOOTS
LOPES
LORDS
LORES
LORIS
LOSES
LOTOS
LOTUS
LOUIS
LOUPS
LOURS
LOUTS
LOVES
LUAUS
LUCES
LUCYS
LUFFS
LULLS
LULUS
LUMPS
LUNES
LUNGS
LUNTS
LUPUS
LURES
LURKS
LUSTS
LUTES
LUXES
LYLES
LYNNS
LYONS
LYRES
LYSES
LYSIS

•LS••
ELSAS
ELSIE

•L•S•
BLASE
BLAST
BLESS
BLEST
BLISS
BLUSH
CLASH
CLASP
CLASS
CLOSE
ELISE
FLASH
FLASK
FLESH
FLOSS
FLUSH
GLASS
GLOSS
GLOST
PLASH
PLASM
PLAST
PLASY
PLUSH
SLASH
SLOSH
SLUSH
ULOSE

•L••S
ALANS
ALBAS
ALDIS
ALDOS
ALDUS
ALECS
ALEFS
ALGYS
ALIAS
ALIFS
ALLIS
ALMAS
ALOES
ALOIS
ALTAS
ALTOS
ALUMS
BLABS
BLAHS
BLATS

BLDGS
BLEBS
BLESS
BLIPS
BLISS
BLOBS
BLOCS
BLOIS
BLOTS
BLOWS
BLUES
BLURS
CLAMS
CLANS
CLAPS
CLASS
CLAWS
CLAYS
CLEFS
CLEMS
CLEWS
CLIOS
CLIPS
CLODS
CLOGS
CLONS
CLOPS
CLOTS
CLOYS
CLUBS
CLUES
ELIAS
ELLAS
ELLIS
ELSAS
ELVAS
ELVES
FLAGS
FLAMS
FLANS
FLAPS
FLATS
FLAWS
FLAYS
FLEAS
FLEES
FLEWS
FLIES
FLIPS
FLITS
FLOCS
FLOES
FLOGS
FLOPS
FLOSS
FLOWS
FLUBS
FLUES
GLADS
GLANS
GLASS
GLEDS
GLEES
GLENS
GLIMS
GLOBS
GLOSS
GLOWS
GLUES
GLUTS
ILEUS
ILLUS
MLLES
OLAFS
OLAVS
OLGAS
OLIOS
OLLAS
PLANS
PLATS
PLAYS
PLEAS
PLEBS
PLIES
PLODS
PLOPS
PLOTS
PLOWS
PLOYS
PLUGS
PLUMS
SLABS
SLAGS
SLAMS
SLAPS
SLATS
SLAVS
SLAWS
SLAYS
SLEDS
SLEWS
SLIMS
SLIPS
SLITS
SLOBS
SLOES
SLOGS
SLOPS
SLOTS
SLOWS
SLUBS
SLUES
SLUGS
SLUMS
SLURS
SLUTS
ULNAS
ULOUS

••LS•

BALSA
DULSE
FALSE
PALSY
PULSE
TULSA
WELSH

••L•S

ALLIS
ANLAS
ARLES
ATLAS
AULIS
AXLES
BALAS
BALES
BALKS
BALLS
BALMS
BALTS
BELLS
BELTS
BILES
BILKS
BILLS
BOLAS
BOLES
BOLLS
BOLOS
BOLTS
BOLUS
BULBS
BULKS
BULLS
CALKS
CALLS
CALMS
CELLS
CELTS
COLAS
COLDS
COLES
COLTS
CULLS
CULMS
CULTS
DALES
DELES
DELLS
DELOS
DOLES
DOLLS
DOLTS
DULLS
ELLAS
ELLIS
FALLS
FELLS
FELTS
FILES
FILLS
FILMS
FOLDS
FOLKS
FULLS
GALAS
GALES
GALLS
GELDS
GILDS
GILES
GILLS
GOLDS
GOLFS
GULES
GULFS
GULLS
GULPS
HALES
HALLS
HALOS
HALTS
HELLS
HELMS
HELPS
HILLS
HILTS
HOLDS
HOLES
HOLMS
HULAS
HULKS
HULLS
HYLAS
IDLES
ILLUS
ISLES
JELLS
JILLS
JILTS
JOLES
JOLTS
JULES
JULYS
KELPS
KILLS
KILNS
KILOS
KILTS
KOLAS
LALLS
LILAS
LILTS
LILYS
LOLAS
LOLLS
LULLS
LULUS
LYLES
MALES
MALLS
MALTS
MELDS
MELTS
MILES
MILKS
MILLS
MILTS
MLLES
MOLDS
MOLES
MOLLS
MOLTS
MULES
MULLS
MYLES
NELLS
OGLES
OLLAS
ORLES
PALES
PALLS
PALMS
PELFS
PELTS
PILES
PILIS
PILLS
POLES
POLLS
PULES
PULLS
PULPS
RALES
RILES
RILLS
ROLES
ROLFS
ROLLS
RULES
SALES
SALTS
SALUS
SELLS
SILAS
SILKS
SILLS
SILOS
SILTS
SOLES
SOLOS
SOLUS
SULKS
SULUS
TALCS
TALES
TALKS
TALOS
TALUS
TELLS
TILES
TILLS
TILTS
TOLAS
TOLES
TOLLS
TULES
VALES
VELDS
VILLS
VOLES
VOLTS
WALES
WALKS
WALLS
WALTS
WELDS
WELLS
WELTS
WILDS
WILES
WILLS
WILTS
WOLDS
WOLFS
YELKS
YELLS
YELPS
YOLKS
YULES
ZULUS

•••LS

ABELS
AMYLS
ANILS
ARILS
AXILS
BAILS
BALLS
BAWLS
BELLS
BILLS
BIRLS
BOILS
BOLLS
BOWLS
BULLS
BURLS
CALLS
CARLS
CAULS
CEILS
CELLS
COALS
COILS
COOLS
COWLS
CULLS
CURLS
DEALS
DELLS
DIALS
DOLLS
DUELS
DULLS
EARLS
EMILS
ENOLS
EVILS
FAILS
FALLS
FARLS
FEELS
FELLS
FILLS
FOALS
FOILS
FOOLS
FOULS
FOWLS
FUELS
FULLS
FURLS
GAELS
GAILS
GALLS
GAOLS
GAULS
GILLS
GIRLS
GOALS
GULLS
HAILS
HALLS
HARLS
HAULS
HEALS
HEELS
HELLS
HERLS
HILLS
HOWLS
HULLS
HURLS
IDOLS
IDYLS
ITALS
JAILS
JARLS
JELLS
JILLS
JOELS
JOWLS
KARLS
KEELS
KILLS
KOELS
LALLS
LOLLS
LULLS
MAILS
MALLS
MARLS
MAULS
MEALS
MEWLS
MILLS
MOILS
MOLLS
MULLS
NAILS
NEALS
NEILS
NELLS
NOELS
OPALS
ORALS
OVALS
PAILS
PALLS
PAULS
PAWLS
PEALS
PEELS
PHILS
PILLS
POLLS
POOLS
PULLS
PURLS
RAILS
REALS
REELS
RIALS
RILLS
ROILS
ROLLS
SAILS
SAULS
SEALS
SELLS
SHULS
SILLS
SOILS
SOULS
TAELS
TAILS
TEALS
TELLS
TILLS
TOILS
TOLLS
TOOLS
URALS
VEILS
VIALS
VILLS
VIOLS
WAILS
WALLS
WAULS
WAWLS
WEALS
WELLS
WILLS
WOOLS
YAWLS
YELLS
YOWLS

L•T••

LATCH
LATER
LATEX
LATHE
LATHS
LATHY
LATIN
LATRY
LETHE
LETTS
LETTY
LETUP
LITAI
LITAS
LITER
LITHE
LITHO
LOTAH
LOTOS

LOTTA LOTTO LOTTY LOTUS LUTED LUTES LYTIC LYTTA

L••T•

LACTO LAITY LASTS LEETS LEFTS LEFTY LENTO LENTS LEPTA LEPTO LETTS LETTY LEYTE LIFTS LILTS LINTY LISTS LOATH LOFTS LOFTY LOOTS LOTTA LOTTO LOTTY LOUTS LUNTS LUSTS LUSTY LYTTA

L•••T

LEANT LEAPT LEAST LEGIT LICHT LICIT LIEUT LIGHT LIMIT LISZT LUNET

•LT••

ALTAI ALTAR ALTAS ALTER ALTON ALTOS ELTON ULTRA

•L•T•

ALATE BLATS BLITZ BLOTS CLOTH CLOTS ELATE ELITE FLATS FLITS FLUTE FLUTY GLUTS PLATE PLATO PLATS PLATY PLOTS PLUTO SLATE SLATS SLATY SLITS SLOTH SLOTS SLUTS ZLOTY

•L••T

ALERT ALEUT ALLOT ALOFT BLAST BLEAT BLENT BLEST BLOAT BLUET BLUNT BLURT CLEAT CLEFT CLINT CLOUT ELECT ELIOT FLEET FLINT FLIRT FLOAT FLOUT GLEET GLINT GLOAT GLOST PLAIT PLANT PLAST PLEAT SLANT SLEET SLEPT SLIPT ULENT

••LT•

BALTS BELTS BOLTS CELTS COLTS CULTI CULTS DELTA DOLTS FELTS FILTH HALTS HILTS JILTS JOLTS JOLTY KILTS KILTY LILTS MALTS MALTY MELTS MILTS MOLTO MOLTS MULTI PELTS SALTS SALTY SILTS SILTY TILTH TILTS VOLTA VOLTI VOLTS WALTS WALTZ WELTS WILTS YALTA

••L•T

AGLET ALLOT CULET DELFT ECLAT FILET HELOT INLET ISLET KALAT MULCT OWLET PILOT SPLAT SPLIT UNLIT VALET VELDT

•••LT

ADULT ATILT BUILT DEALT DWELT EXALT EXULT FAULT GUILT KNELT MOULT POULT QUILT SAULT SHALT SMALT SMELT SMOLT SPELT SPILT STILT UBOLT VAULT

LU•••

LUAUS LUCCA LUCES LUCIA LUCID LUCKY LUCRE LUCYS LUFFS LUGER LUIGI LUISA LUISE LULLS LULUS LUMEN LUMPS LUMPY LUNAR LUNCH LUNES LUNET LUNGE LUNGI LUNGS LUNTS LUPUS LURCH LURED LURER LURES LURID LURKS LUSTS LUSTY LUTED LUTES LUXES LUXOR LUZON

L•U••

LAUDS LAUGH LAURA LEUCO LEUDS LEUKO LOUGH LOUIS LOUPE LOUPS LOURS LOUSE LOUSY LOUTS

L••U•

LEHUA LEMUR LEPUS LETUP LIEUT LINUS LOCUS LOGUE LOTUS LUAUS LULUS LUPUS

•LU••

ALUIN ALULA ALUMS BLUED BLUER BLUES BLUET BLUFF BLUNT BLURB BLURS BLURT BLUSH CLUBS CLUCK CLUED CLUES CLUMP CLUNG CLUNY ELUDE FLUBS FLUES FLUFF FLUID FLUKE FLUKY FLUME FLUMP FLUNG FLUNK FLUOR FLUSH FLUTE FLUTY GLUED GLUES GLUEY GLUME GLUTS PLUCK PLUGS PLUMB PLUME PLUMP PLUMS PLUMY PLUNK PLURI PLUSH PLUTO PLUVI SLUBS SLUED SLUES SLUGS SLUMP SLUMS SLUNG SLUNK SLURP SLURS SLUSH SLUTS

•L•U•

ALBUM ALDUS ALEUT ALGUM ALMUD ALMUG ALOUD CLOUD CLOUT FLOUR FLOUT GLAUC ILEUM ILEUS ILIUM ILLUS ULOUS

•L••U

ELIHU

••LU•

BOLUS FILUM HILUM ILLUS LULUS SALUS SOLUS SULUS TALUK TALUS VALUE VELUM ZULUS

•••LU

POILU

L•V••

LAVAS LAVED LAVER LAVES LEVEE LEVEL LEVEN LEVER LEVIS LIVED LIVEN LIVER LIVES LIVIA LIVID LIVRE LOVED LOVER LOVES

L••V•

LARVA LEAVE LEAVY

•LV••

ALVAN ALVIN ELVAS ELVER ELVES ELVIN

•L•V•

ALIVE CLIVE CLOVE GLOVE OLAVS OLIVE PLUVI SLAVE SLAVO SLAVS

••LV•

CALVE DELVE HALVE HELVE PELVI SALVE SALVO SILVA SOLVE SYLVA VALVE VOLVA VULVA

L•W••

LAWED LAWNS LAWNY LEWIE LEWIS LOWED LOWER LOWLY

•LW••

ALWAY ALWIN ELWIN

•L•W•

BLOWN BLOWS BLOWY CLAWS CLEWS CLOWN FLAWS FLAWY FLEWS FLOWN FLOWS GLOWS PLOWS SLAWS SLEWS SLOWS

•L••W

ALLOW ELBOW

••L•W

AGLOW ALLOW BELOW BYLAW INLAW

L•X••

LAXER LAXLY LUXES LUXOR

L•••X

LATEX

•L•X•
ALEXA FLAXY FLEXI

••L•X
CALIX CALYX CYLIX FELIX GALAX HELIX KYLIX PHLOX RELAX SILEX TELEX

LY•••
LYCEA LYCEE LYDDA LYDIA LYING LYLES LYMAN LYMPH LYNCH LYNNS LYONS LYRES LYRIC LYSED LYSES LYSIN LYSIS LYSOL LYSSA LYTIC LYTTA

L•Y••
LAYER LEYTE LOYAL

L••Y•
LIBYA LILYS LLOYD LUCYS

L•••Y
LAITY LANKY LARDY LARRY LATHY LATRY LAWNY LAXLY LEADY LEAFY LEAKY LEAVY LEDGY LEERY LEFTY LEGGY LENNY LEPSY LEROY LETTY LIBBY LILLY LIMEY LINEY LINTY LIPPY LIZZY LOAMY LOBBY LOFTY LOLLY LOOBY LOONY LOPPY LORRY LOTTY LOUSY LOWLY LUCKY LUMPY LUSTY

•LY••
ALYCE CLYDE FLYBY FLYER GLYCO GLYPH SLYER SLYLY

•L•Y•
ALGYS ALKYL ALLYL CLAYS CLOYS FLAYS FLOYD LLOYD PLAYA PLAYS PLOYS SLAYS SLOYD

•L••Y
ALARY ALLAY ALLEY ALLOY ALPHY ALWAY BLOWY CLARY CLUNY ELEGY FLAKY FLAMY FLAWY FLAXY FLUKY FLUTY FLYBY GLARY GLAZY GLORY GLUEY OLOGY PLASY PLATY PLEGY PLINY PLUMY SLATY SLILY SLIMY SLYLY ZLOTY

••LY•
ALLYL CALYX JULYS LILYS POLYP TOLYL XYLYL

••L•Y
AGLEY ALLAY ALLEY ALLOY BALKY BALMY BELAY BELLY BILGY BILLY BULGY BULKY BULLY COLLY DALLY DELAY DOLLY DULCY DULLY FELLY FILLY FILMY FOLLY FULLY GOLLY GULLY HILLY HOLEY HOLLY HULKY INLAY JELLY JOLLY JOLTY KILTY LILLY LOLLY MALAY MALTY MILKY MILLY MOLDY MOLLY MULEY NELLY PALEY PALMY PALSY PELLY POLLY PULPY RALLY RELAY RILEY SALLY SALTY SILKY SILLY SILTY SPLAY SULKY SULLY TALLY TELLY TILLY TULLY UNLAY WALLY WILLY YOLKY

•••LY
AMPLY APPLY APTLY BADLY BELLY BIALY BIGLY BILLY BULLY BURLY COLLY COYLY CURLY DAILY DALLY DIMLY DOILY DOLLY DOOLY DOYLY DRILY DRYLY DULLY EARLY EMILY FATLY FELLY FILLY FITLY FOLLY FULLY GAILY GAYLY GODLY GOLLY GULLY HAPLY HILLY HOLLY HOTLY HURLY ICILY IMPLY ITALY JELLY JOLLY LAXLY LILLY LOLLY LOWLY MADLY MANLY MARLY MEALY MILLY MOLLY MUHLY NELLY NEWLY NOBLY ODDLY PELLY PHILY POLLY RALLY RAWLY REDLY REPLY ROILY SADLY SALLY SCALY SHALY SHILY SHYLY SILLY SLILY SLYLY SULLY SURLY TALLY TELLY TILLY TRULY TULLY WALLY WANLY WETLY WILLY WOOLY WRYLY

L•Z••
LAZAR LAZED LAZES LIZAS LIZZY LUZON

L••Z•
LISZT LIZZY

•L•Z•
BLAZE ELIZA GLAZE GLAZY GLOZE PLAZA

•L••Z
BLITZ

••LZ•
COLZA

••L•Z
WALTZ

MA•••
MABEL MACAO MACAW MACED MACER MACES MACHY MACKS MACLE MACON MACRO MADAM MADGE MADLY MAFIA MAGDA MAGES MAGIC MAGMA MAGNI MAGOT MAGUS MAHAN MAHDI MAIDS MAILS MAIMS MAINE MAINS MAINZ MAIZE MAJOR MAKER MAKES MALAC MALAR MALAY MALES MALIC MALLS MALTS MALTY MAMAS MAMBA MAMBO MAMEY MAMIE MAMMA MAMMY MANCY MANDY MANED MANES MANET MANGE MANGO MANGY MANIA MANIC MANLY MANNA MANOR MANSE MANTA MANUS MAORI MAPLE MARAT MARCH MARCO MARCS MARES MARGE MARGO MARIA MARIE MARKS MARLS MARLY MARNE MARRY MARSH MARTA MARTS MARTY MASER MASHY MASKS MASON MASSE MASSY MASTO MASTS MATCH MATED MATEO MATES MATEY MATIN MATRI MATSU MATTE MATTS MATTY MATZO MAUDE MAUDS MAULS MAUND MAURA MAUVE MAVIS MAXIM MAYAN MAYAS MAYBE MAYOR MAYST MAZED MAZER MAZES

M•A••
MEADS MEALS MEALY MEANS MEANT MEANY MEATS MEATY MIAMI MIAUL MOANS MOATS

M••A•
MACAO MACAW MADAM MAHAN MALAC MALAR MALAY MAMAS MARAT MAYAN MAYAS MEDAL MEGAL MEGAN MELAN MESAS METAL

5

METAS
MICAH
MICAS
MIDAS
MILAN
MINAE
MINAS
MODAL
MOLAL
MOLAR
MONAD
MONAS
MORAE
MORAL
MORAS
MORAY
MOSAN
MOXAS
MURAL
MURAT
MYNAS
MYRAS

M•••A

MAFIA
MAGDA
MAGMA
MAMBA
MAMMA
MANIA
MANNA
MANTA
MARIA
MARTA
MAURA
MECCA
MEDEA
MEDIA
MENSA
MICRA
MILIA
MINNA
MIRZA
MOCHA
MOIRA
MORNA
MURRA
MUSCA
MYOMA
MYRIA
MYRNA

•MA••

AMAHS
AMAIN
AMASS
AMATI
AMAZE
IMAGE
IMAGO
IMAMS
OMAHA
OMASA
SMACK
SMALL
SMALT
SMART
SMASH
SMAZE
VMAIL

•M•A•

AMIAS
AMMAN
EMBAR
EMBAY
EMMAS
SMEAR
UMIAK

•M••A

AMEBA
AMNIA
OMAHA
OMASA
OMEGA
UMBRA

••MA•

ADMAN
ALMAH
ALMAS
AMMAN
ATMAN
AXMAN
COMAE
COMAL
COMAS
CYMAE
CYMAR
DAMAN
DUMAS
ELMAN
EMMAS
ERMAS
HAMAL
HEMAL
HEMAN
HEMAT
HUMAN
IRMAS
LAMAS
LYMAN
MAMAS
NEMAT
NOMAD
NOMAS
OSMAN
PIMAN
PIMAS
PUMAS
REMAN
ROMAN
SAMAR
SIMAR
SOMAT
SUMAC
TOMAN
TOMAS
UNMAN
UXMAL
WOMAN

••M•A

AEMIA
COMMA
GAMMA
GEMMA
GUMMA
HAMZA
HEMIA
JUMNA
LAMIA
LEMMA
MAMBA
MAMMA
RUMBA
SAMBA
SAMOA
TAMPA
ZAMIA

•••MA

ABOMA
AGAMA
ANIMA
AROMA
BURMA
COMMA
DERMA
DOGMA
DRAMA
EDEMA
ENEMA
ETYMA
GAMMA
GEMMA
GRAMA
GUMMA
HERMA
KARMA
LEMMA
LLAMA
MAGMA
MAMMA
MYOMA
NORMA
PRIMA
REGMA
SELMA
SIGMA
STOMA
TRYMA
ULEMA
WILMA

M•B••

MABEL

M••B•

MAMBA
MAMBO
MAYBE

•MB••

AMBER
AMBIT
AMBLE
AMBOS
AMBRY
EMBAR
EMBAY
EMBED
EMBER
EMBOW
EMBRY
IMBED
IMBUE
OMBER
OMBRE
OMBRO
UMBEL
UMBER
UMBOS
UMBRA

•M•B•

AMEBA

••MB•

BOMBE
BOMBS
COMBO
COMBS
GAMBS
GUMBO
IAMBI
IAMBS
JAMBS
JUMBO
LAMBS
LIMBI
LIMBO
LIMBS
MAMBA
MAMBO
NIMBI
NUMBS
RUMBA
SAMBA
SAMBO
TOMBS
WOMBS
WOMBY
ZOMBI

••M•B

DEMOB

•••MB

ABOMB
CLIMB
COOMB
CRUMB
HBOMB
PLUMB
RHOMB
RHUMB
THUMB

MC•••

MCCOY

M•C••

MACAO
MACAW
MACED
MACER
MACES
MACHY
MACKS
MACLE
MACON
MACRO
MCCOY
MECCA
MICAH
MICAS
MICKY
MICRA
MICRO
MOCHA
MOCKS
MUCID
MUCIN
MUCKS
MUCKY
MUCRO
MUCUS

M••C•

MANCY
MARCH
MARCO
MARCS
MATCH
MECCA
MERCI
MERCY
MILCH
MINCE
MITCH
MOOCH
MOUCH
MULCH
MULCT
MUNCH
MUSCA

M•••C

MAGIC
MALAC
MALIC
MANIC
MEDIC
MEDOC
MELIC
MESIC
MIMIC
MUSIC

•MC••

EMCEE

•M•C•

AMICE
AMUCK
SMACK
SMOCK

••MC•

USMCR

••M•C

COMIC
DOMIC
GAMIC
HEMIC
HUMIC
MIMIC
OHMIC
OSMIC
SUMAC

M•D••

MADAM
MADGE
MADLY
MEDAL
MEDEA
MEDIA
MEDIC
MEDIO
MEDOC
MIDAS
MIDDY
MIDGE
MIDST
MODAL
MODEL
MODES
MODUS
MUDDY

M••D•

MAGDA
MAHDI
MAIDS
MANDY
MAUDE
MAUDS
MEADS
MELDS
MENDS
MIDDY
MINDS
MISDO
MOLDS
MOLDY
MONDE
MOODS
MOODY
MUDDY

M•••D

MACED
MANED
MATED
MAUND
MAZED
METED
MEWED
MIMED
MINED
MIRED
MIXED
MONAD
MOOED
MOPED
MOULD
MOVED
MOWED
MUCID
MUSED
MUTED
MYOID

•MD••

EMDEN

•M•D•

AMIDE
AMIDO
IMIDE
IMIDO
IMIDS

•M••D

AMEND
EMBED
EMEND
IMBED

••MD•

COMDR
COMDT

••M•D

AIMED
ALMUD
ARMED
DOMED
FAMED
FUMED
GAMED
HOMED
HUMID
LAMED
LIMED
MIMED
NAMED
NOMAD
RIMED
TAMED
TIMED
TIMID
TUMID

ME•••

MEADS
MEALS
MEALY
MEANS
MEANT
MEANY
MEATS
MEATY
MECCA
MEDAL
MEDEA
MEDIA
MEDIC
MEDIO
MEDOC
MEETS
MEGAL
MEGAN
MELAN
MELDS
MELEE
MELIC
MELON
MELTS
MEMOS
MENDS
MENES
MENSA
MENUS
MEOWS
MERCI
MERCY
MERGE
MERIT
MERLE
MEROE
MERRY
MESAS
MESHY
MESIC
MESNE
MESON
MESSY
METAL
METAS
METED
METER
METES
METHO
METIS
METRO
METRY
MEUSE
MEWED
MEWLS
MEZZO

M•E••

MEETS
MIENS
MYELO

5

M••E•
MABEL
MACED
MACER
MACES
MAGES
MAKER
MAKES
MALES
MAMEY
MANED
MANES
MANET
MARES
MASER
MATED
MATEO
MATES
MATEY
MAZED
MAZER
MAZES
MEDEA
MELEE
MENES
METED
METER
METES
MEWED
MIKES
MIKEY
MILER
MILES
MIMED
MIMER
MIMES
MINED
MINER
MINES
MIRED
MIRES
MISER
MISES
MITER
MITES
MIXED
MIXER
MIXES
MLLES
MODEL
MODES
MOKES
MOLES
MONET
MONEY
MOOED
MOPED
MOPER
MOPES
MOREL
MORES
MOSES
MOSEY
MOTEL
MOTES
MOUES
MOVED
MOVER
MOVES
MOWED
MOWER
MULES
MULEY
MUREX
MUSED
MUSES
MUTED
MUTES
MYLES

M•••E
MACLE
MADGE
MAINE
MAIZE
MAMIE
MANGE
MANSE
MAPLE
MARGE
MARIE
MARNE
MASSE
MATTE
MAUDE
MAUVE
MAYBE
MELEE
MERGE
MERLE
MEROE
MESNE
MEUSE
MIDGE
MINAE
MINCE
MOIRE
MONDE
MONTE
MOORE
MOOSE
MORAE
MORSE
MOUSE
MOVIE
MOXIE
MURRE
MYOPE

•ME••
AMEBA
AMEND
AMENS
AMENT
BMEWS
EMEER
EMEND
EMERY
EMEUS
OMEGA
OMENS
OMERS
SMEAR
SMELL
SMELT
SMEWS

•M•E•
AMBER
AMIEL
AMIES
EMBED
EMBER
EMCEE
EMDEN
EMEER
EMMER
EMMET
IMBED
IMPEL
OMBER
UMBEL
UMBER

•M••E
AMAZE
AMBLE
AMICE
AMIDE
AMINE
AMOLE
AMPLE
AMUSE
EMCEE
EMILE
EMMIE
EMOTE
IMAGE
IMBUE
IMIDE
IMINE
OMBRE
SMAZE
SMILE
SMITE
SMOKE
SMOTE

••ME•
ADMEN
AIMED
AIMEE
ARMED
ARMET
AXMEN
CAMEL
CAMEO
CAMES
CIMEX
COMER
COMES
COMET
CYMES
DAMES
DEMES
DIMER
DIMES
DOMED
DOMES
ELMER
EMMER
EMMET
FAMED
FEMES
FUMED
FUMES
GAMED
GAMES
GIMEL
HAMES
HEMEN
HOMED
HOMEO
HOMER
HOMES
HOMEY
HYMEN
ILMEN
JAMES
KAMES
KAMET
KHMER
LAMED
LAMER
LAMES
LIMED
LIMEN
LIMES
LIMEY
LUMEN
MAMEY
MIMED
MIMER
MIMES
NAMED
NAMER
NAMES
NUMEN
ORMER
POMES
REMEX
RIMED
RIMER
RIMES
ROMEO
RUMEN
SAMEK
SEMEN
SUMER
TAMED
TAMER
TAMES
TIMED
TIMER
TIMES
TOMES
UNMEW
VIMEN
VOMER
WOMEN
YAMEN
YEMEN

••M•E
AIMEE
BOMBE
COMAE
COMTE
CYMAE
EMMIE
FEMME
JAMIE
MAMIE
RAMIE
SOMME
TEMPE

•••ME
ANIME
BAUME
BERME
BLAME
BROME
BRUME
CHIME
CHYME
CLIME
CREME
CRIME
DROME
FEMME
FLAME
FLUME
FRAME
GLUME
GNOME
GRIME
GRUME
NEUME
OXIME
PLUME
PRIME
RHYME
SHAME
SLIME
SOMME
SPUME
STOME
THEME
THYME

M•F••
MAFIA
MIFFS
MIFFY
MUFFS
MUFTI

M••F•
MIFFS
MIFFY
MUFFS

M•••F
MOTIF

M•G••
MAGDA
MAGES
MAGIC
MAGMA
MAGNI
MAGOT
MAGUS
MEGAL
MEGAN
MIGHT
MOGUL
MUGGY

M••G•
MADGE
MANGE
MANGO
MANGY
MARGE
MARGO
MERGE
MIDGE
MUGGY
MUNGO

•M•G•
AMIGO
IMAGE
IMAGO
OMEGA
SMOGS

•M••G
AMONG

••M•G
ALMUG

M•H••
MAHAN
MAHDI
MOHUR
MUHLY

M••H•
MACHY
MASHY
MESHY
METHO
MIGHT
MOCHA
MOTHS
MOTHY
MUSHY
MYTHO
MYTHS

M•••H
MARCH
MARSH
MATCH
MICAH
MILCH
MIRTH
MITCH
MONTH
MOOCH
MORPH
MOUCH
MOUTH
MULCH
MUNCH
MYRRH

•M•H•
AMAHS
AMPHI
AMPHR
OMAHA

•M••H
AMISH
SMASH
SMITH

••M•H
ALMAH
HUMPH
LYMPH
NYMPH
OOMPH

MI•••
MIAMI
MIAUL
MICAH
MICAS
MICKY
MICRA
MICRO
MIDAS
MIDDY
MIDGE
MIDST
MIENS
MIFFS
MIFFY
MIGHT
MIKES
MIKEY
MILAN
MILCH
MILER
MILES
MILIA
MILKS
MILKY
MILLI
MILLS
MILLY
MILTS
MIMED
MIMER
MIMES
MIMIC
MIMIR
MIMIS
MINAE
MINAS
MINCE
MINDS
MINED
MINER
MINES
MINIM
MINKS
MINNA
MINOR
MINOS
MINSK
MINTS
MINUS
MIRED
MIRES
MIRTH
MIRZA
MISDO
MISER
MISES
MISSY
MISTS
MISTY
MITCH
MITER
MITES
MITTS
MIXED
MIXER
MIXES
MIXUP

M•I••
MAIDS
MAILS
MAIMS
MAINE
MAINS
MAINZ
MAIZE
MOILS
MOIRA
MOIRE
MOIST

M••I•
MAFIA
MAGIC
MALIC
MAMIE
MANIA
MANIC
MARIA
MARIE
MATIN
MAVIS

5

MAXIM
MEDIA
MEDIC
MEDIO
MELIC
MERIT
MESIC
METIS
MILIA
MIMIC
MIMIR
MIMIS
MINIM
MOTIF
MOVIE
MOXIE
MUCID
MUCIN
MUSIC
MYOID
MYRIA

M•••I
MAGNI
MAHDI
MAORI
MATRI
MERCI
MIAMI
MILLI
MUFTI
MULTI

•MI••
AMIAS
AMICE
AMIDE
AMIDO
AMIEL
AMIES
AMIGO
AMINE
AMINO
AMIRS
AMISH
AMISS
AMITY
EMILE
EMILS
EMILY
EMIRS
EMITS
IMIDE
IMIDO
IMIDS
IMINE
IMINO
OMITS
SMILE
SMIRK
SMITE
SMITH
UMIAK

•M•I•
AMAIN
AMBIT
AMNIA
EMMIE
IMMIX
VMAIL

•M••I
AMATI
AMPHI

••MI•
ADMIN
ADMIT
ADMIX
AEMIA
COMIC
CUMIN
DEMIT
DOMIC
EMMIE
GAMIC
GAMIN
HEMIA
HEMIC
HEMIN
HUMIC
HUMID
IMMIX
JAMIE
KAMIK
LAMIA
LIMIT
MAMIE
MIMIC
MIMIR
MIMIS
OHMIC
OSMIC
RAMIE
REMIT
TAMIS
TIMID
TUMID
VOMIT
ZAMIA

••M•I
CAMPI
CYMRI
IAMBI
LIMBI
NIMBI
SOMNI
TEMPI
ZOMBI

•••MI
CHEMI
DUOMI
ELEMI
FERMI
MIAMI
NAOMI
PALMI
PRIMI
SALMI
SWAMI
VERMI

M•J••
MAJOR

M•K••
MAKER
MAKES
MIKES
MIKEY
MOKES

M••K•
MACKS
MARKS
MASKS
MICKY
MILKS
MILKY
MINKS
MOCKS
MONKS
MUCKS
MUCKY
MURKY
MUSKS
MUSKY

M•••K
MINSK

•M•K•
SMOKE
SMOKY

•M••K
AMUCK
SMACK
SMIRK
SMOCK
UMIAK

••M•K
KAMIK
SAMEK

ML•••
MLLES

M•L••
MALAC
MALAR
MALAY
MALES
MALIC
MALLS
MALTS
MALTY
MELAN
MELDS
MELEE
MELIC
MELON
MELTS
MILAN
MILCH
MILER
MILES
MILIA
MILKS
MILKY
MILLI
MILLS
MILLY
MILTS
MLLES
MOLAL
MOLAR
MOLDS
MOLDY
MOLES
MOLLS
MOLLY
MOLTO
MOLTS
MULCH
MULCT
MULES
MULEY
MULLS
MULTI
MYLES

M••L•
MACLE
MADLY
MAILS
MALLS
MANLY
MAPLE
MARLS
MARLY
MAULS
MEALS
MEALY
MERLE
MEWLS
MILLI
MILLS
MILLY
MOILS
MOLLS
MOLLY
MOULD
MOULT
MUHLY
MULLS
MYELO

M•••L
MABEL
MEDAL
MEGAL
METAL
MIAUL
MODAL
MODEL
MOGUL
MOLAL
MORAL
MOREL
MOTEL
MURAL

•M•L•
AMBLE
AMOLE
AMPLE
AMPLY
AMYLO
AMYLS
EMILE
EMILS
EMILY
IMPLY
SMALL
SMALT
SMELL
SMELT
SMILE
SMOLT

•M••L
AMIEL
AMPUL
IMPEL
SMALL
SMELL
UMBEL
VMAIL

••ML•
DIMLY

••M•L
CAMEL
COMAL
GIMEL
HAMAL
HEMAL
UXMAL

•••ML
FRIML

M•M••
MAMAS
MAMBA
MAMBO
MAMEY
MAMIE
MAMMA
MAMMY
MEMOS
MIMED
MIMER
MIMES
MIMIC
MIMIR
MIMIS
MOMUS
MUMMS
MUMMY
MUMPS

M••M•
MAGMA
MAIMS
MAMMA
MAMMY
MIAMI
MUMMS
MUMMY
MYOMA

M•••M
MADAM
MAXIM
MINIM

•MM••
AMMAN
AMMON
EMMAS
EMMER
EMMET
EMMIE
EMMYS
IMMIX

•M•M•
IMAMS

••MM•
COMMA
DUMMY
FEMME
GAMMA
GEMMA
GEMMY
GUMMA
GUMMY
HAMMY
JEMMY
JIMMY
LEMMA
MAMMA
MAMMY
MUMMS
MUMMY
RAMMY
RUMMY
SAMMY
SOMME
TIMMY
TOMMY
YUMMY

•••MM
GRIMM

M•N••
MANCY
MANDY
MANED
MANES
MANET
MANGE
MANGO
MANGY
MANIA
MANIC
MANLY
MANNA
MANOR
MANSE
MANTA
MANUS
MENDS
MENES
MENSA
MENUS
MINAE
MINAS
MINCE
MINDS
MINED
MINER
MINES
MINIM
MINKS
MINNA
MINOR
MINOS
MINSK
MINTS
MINUS
MONAD
MONAS
MONDE
MONET
MONEY
MONKS
MONTE
MONTH
MONTY
MUNCH
MUNGO
MUNRO
MYNAS

M••N•
MAGNI
MAINE
MAINS
MAINZ
MANNA
MARNE
MAUND
MEANS
MEANT
MEANY
MESNE
MIENS
MINNA
MOANS
MOONS
MOONY
MORNA
MORNS
MOUNT
MUONS
MYRNA

M•••N
MACON
MAHAN
MASON
MATIN
MAYAN
MEGAN
MELAN
MELON
MESON
MILAN
MORON
MOSAN
MOURN
MUCIN
MYRON

•MN••
AMNIA

•M•N•
AMEND
AMENS
AMENT
AMINE
AMINO
AMONG
EMEND
IMINE
IMINO
OMENS

•M••N
AMAIN
AMMAN
AMMON
EMDEN

••MN•
DAMNS
GYMNO
HYMNS
JUMNA
LIMNS
SOMNI

••M•N
ADMAN
ADMEN
ADMIN
AMMAN
AMMON
ATMAN
AXMAN
AXMEN

5

CUMIN
DAMAN
DAMON
DEMON
ELMAN
GAMIN
HEMAN
HEMEN
HEMIN
HUMAN
HYMEN
ILMEN
LEMON
LIMEN
LUMEN
LYMAN
NUMEN
OSMAN
PIMAN
REMAN
ROMAN
RUMEN
SEMEN
SIMON
TOMAN
UNMAN
VIMEN
WOMAN
WOMEN
YAMEN
YAMUN
YEMEN

MO•••
MOANS
MOATS
MOCHA
MOCKS
MODAL
MODEL
MODES
MODUS
MOGUL
MOHUR
MOILS
MOIRA
MOIRE
MOIST
MOKES
MOLAL
MOLAR
MOLDS
MOLDY
MOLES
MOLLS
MOLLY
MOLTO
MOLTS
MOMUS
MONAD
MONAS
MONDE
MONET
MONEY
MONKS
MONTE
MONTH
MONTY
MOOCH
MOODS
MOODY
MOOED
MOONS
MOONY
MOORE
MOORS
MOOSE
MOPED
MOPER
MOPES
MORAE
MORAL
MORAS
MORAY
MOREL
MORES
MORNA
MORNS
MORON
MOROS
MORPH
MORRO
MORSE
MORTS
MORTY
MOSAN
MOSES
MOSEY
MOSSO
MOSSY
MOTEL
MOTES
MOTHS
MOTHY
MOTIF
MOTOR
MOTTO
MOUCH
MOUES
MOULD
MOULT
MOUNT
MOURN
MOUSE
MOUSY
MOUTH
MOVED
MOVER
MOVES
MOVIE
MOWED
MOWER
MOXAS
MOXIE

M•O••
MAORI
MEOWS
MOOCH
MOODS
MOODY
MOOED
MOONS
MOONY
MOORE
MOORS
MOOSE
MUONS
MYOID
MYOMA
MYOPE
MYOPY

M••O•
MACON
MAGOT
MAJOR
MANOR
MASON
MAYOR
MCCOY
MEDOC
MELON
MEMOS
MEROE
MESON
MINOR
MINOS
MORON
MOROS
MOTOR
MYRON

M•••O
MACAO
MACRO
MAMBO
MANGO
MARCO
MARGO
MASTO
MATEO
MATZO
MEDIO
METHO
METRO
MEZZO
MICRO
MISDO
MOLTO
MORRO
MOSSO
MOTTO
MUCRO
MUNGO
MUNRO
MYELO
MYTHO

•MO••
AMOLE
AMONG
AMOUR
EMORY
EMOTE
SMOCK
SMOGS
SMOKE
SMOKY
SMOLT
SMOTE

•M•O•
AMBOS
AMMON
EMBOW
UMBOS

•M••O
AMIDO
AMIGO
AMINO
AMYLO
IMAGO
IMIDO
IMINO
OMBRO

••MO•
AMMON
ARMOR
DAMON
DEMOB
DEMON
DEMOS
GEMOT
HUMOR
LEMON
MEMOS
RUMOR
SAMOA
SAMOS
SIMON
TUMOR

••M•O
CAMEO
CAMPO
COMBO
COMPO
FEMTO
GUMBO
GYMNO
HOMEO
JUMBO
LIMBO
MAMBO
ROMEO
SAMBO
TEMPO

•••MO
ALAMO
ANEMO
BROMO
CHEMO
COSMO
DERMO
DUOMO
GISMO
GIZMO
PRIMO
PULMO
SCHMO
SKIMO

M•P••
MAPLE
MOPED
MOPER
MOPES

M••P•
MORPH
MUMPS
MYOPE
MYOPY

M•••P
MIXUP

•MP••
AMPHI
AMPHR
AMPLE
AMPLY
AMPUL
EMPTY
IMPEL
IMPLY

••MP•
BUMPS
BUMPY
CAMPI
CAMPO
CAMPS
CAMPY
COMPO
DAMPS
DUMPS
DUMPY
GAMPS
GIMPS
GIMPY
HEMPS
HEMPY
HUMPH
HUMPS
HUMPY
JUMPS
JUMPY
LAMPS
LIMPS
LUMPS
LUMPY
LYMPH
MUMPS
NYMPH
OOMPH
PIMPS
PUMPS
RAMPS
ROMPS
RUMPS
SIMPS
SUMPS
TAMPA
TAMPS
TEMPE
TEMPI
TEMPO
TEMPT
VAMPS

•••MP
BLIMP
CHAMP
CHUMP
CLAMP
CLUMP
CRAMP
CRIMP
CRUMP
FLUMP
FRUMP
PLUMP
PRIMP
SCAMP
SKIMP
SLUMP
STAMP
STOMP
STUMP
SWAMP
THUMP
TRAMP
TRUMP

M•R••
MARAT
MARCH
MARCO
MARCS
MARES
MARGE
MARGO
MARIA
MARIE
MARKS
MARLS
MARLY
MARNE
MARRY
MARSH
MARTA
MARTS
MARTY
MERCI
MERCY
MERGE
MERIT
MERLE
MEROE
MERRY
MIRED
MIRES
MIRTH
MIRZA
MORAE
MORAL
MORAS
MORAY
MOREL
MORES
MORNA
MORNS
MORON
MOROS
MORPH
MORRO
MORSE
MORTS
MORTY
MURAL
MURAT
MUREX
MURKY
MURRA
MURRE
MURRY
MYRAS
MYRIA
MYRNA
MYRON
MYRRH

M••R•
MACRO
MAORI
MARRY
MATRI
MAURA
MERRY
METRO
METRY
MICRA
MICRO
MOIRA
MOIRE
MOORE
MOORS
MORRO
MOURN
MUCRO
MUNRO
MURRA
MURRE
MURRY
MYRRH

M•••R
MACER
MAJOR
MAKER
MALAR
MANOR
MASER
MAYOR
MAZER
METER
MILER
MIMER
MIMIR
MINER
MINOR
MISER
MITER
MIXER
MOHUR
MOLAR
MOPER
MOTOR
MOVER
MOWER

•M•R•
AMBRY
AMIRS
EMBRY
EMERY
EMIRS
EMORY
OMBRE
OMBRO
OMERS
SMART
SMIRK
UMBRA

•M••R
AMBER
AMOUR
AMPHR
EMBAR
EMBER
EMEER
EMMER
OMBER
SMEAR
UMBER

••MR•
CYMRI
CYMRY

••M•R
ARMOR
COMDR
COMER
CYMAR
DEMUR
DIMER
ELMER
EMMER
FEMUR
HOMER
HUMOR
KHMER
LAMER
LEMUR
MIMER

MIMIR
NAMER
ORMER
RIMER
RUMOR
SAMAR
SIMAR
SUMER
TAMER
TIMER
TUMOR
USMCR
VOMER

M•S••

MASER
MASHY
MASKS
MASON
MASSE
MASSY
MASTO
MASTS
MESAS
MESHY
MESIC
MESNE
MESON
MESSY
MISDO
MISER
MISES
MISSY
MISTS
MISTY
MOSAN
MOSES
MOSEY
MOSSO
MOSSY
MUSCA
MUSED
MUSES
MUSHY
MUSIC
MUSKS
MUSKY
MUSSY
MUSTS
MUSTY

M••S•

MANSE
MARSH
MASSE
MASSY
MATSU
MAYST
MENSA
MESSY
MEUSE
MIDST
MINSK
MISSY
MOIST
MOOSE
MORSE
MOSSO
MOSSY
MOUSE
MOUSY
MUSSY

M•••S

MACES
MACKS
MAGES
MAGUS
MAIDS
MAILS
MAIMS
MAINS
MAKES
MALES
MALLS
MALTS
MAMAS
MANES
MANUS
MARCS
MARES
MARKS
MARLS
MARTS
MASKS
MASTS
MATES
MATTS
MAUDS
MAULS
MAVIS
MAYAS
MAZES
MEADS
MEALS
MEANS
MEATS
MEETS
MELDS
MELTS
MEMOS
MENDS
MENES
MENUS
MEOWS
MESAS
METAS
METES
METIS
MEWLS
MICAS
MIDAS
MIENS
MIFFS
MIKES
MILES
MILKS
MILLS
MILTS
MIMES
MIMIS
MINAS
MINDS
MINES
MINKS
MINOS
MINTS
MINUS
MIRES
MISES
MISTS
MITES
MITTS
MIXES
MLLES
MOANS
MOATS
MOCKS
MODES
MODUS
MOILS
MOKES
MOLDS
MOLES
MOLLS
MOLTS
MOMUS
MONAS
MONKS
MOODS
MOONS
MOORS
MOPES
MORAS
MORES
MORNS
MOROS
MORTS
MOSES
MOTES
MOTHS
MOUES
MOVES
MOXAS
MUCKS
MUCUS
MUFFS
MULES
MULLS
MUMMS
MUMPS
MUONS
MUSES
MUSKS
MUSTS
MUTES
MUTTS
MYLES
MYNAS
MYRAS
MYTHS

•M•S•

AMASS
AMISH
AMISS
AMUSE
OMASA
SMASH

•M••S

AMAHS
AMASS
AMBOS
AMENS
AMIAS
AMIES
AMIRS
AMISS
AMYLS
BMEWS
EMEUS
EMILS
EMIRS
EMITS
EMMAS
EMMYS
IMAMS
IMIDS
OMENS
OMERS
OMITS
SMEWS
SMOGS
SMUTS
UMBOS

••M•S

ALMAS
BOMBS
BUMPS
CAMES
CAMPS
CAMUS
COMAS
COMBS
COMES
CYMES
DAMES
DAMNS
DAMPS
DEMES
DEMOS
DIMES
DOMES
DUMAS
DUMPS
EMMAS
EMMYS
ERMAS
FEMES
FUMES
GAMBS
GAMES
GAMPS
GIMPS
HAMES
HEMPS
HOMES
HUMPS
HUMUS
HYMNS
IAMBS
IRMAS
JAMBS
JAMES
JUMPS
KAMES
LAMAS
LAMBS
LAMES
LAMPS
LIMBS
LIMES
LIMNS
LIMPS
LUMPS
MAMAS
MEMOS
MIMES
MIMIS
MOMUS
MUMMS
MUMPS
NAMES
NOMAS
NUMBS
PIMAS
PIMPS
POMES
PUMAS
PUMPS
RAMPS
RAMUS
REMUS
RIMES
ROMPS
RUMPS
SAMOS
SIMPS
SUMPS
TAMES
TAMIS
TAMPS
TIMES
TOMAS
TOMBS
TOMES
VAMPS
WAMUS
WOMBS

•••MS

ADAMS
ALUMS
ARUMS
ATOMS
BALMS
BEAMS
BERMS
BOOMS
BRIMS
CALMS
CHUMS
CLAMS
CLEMS
CORMS
CRAMS
CULMS
DEEMS
DOOMS
DORMS
DRAMS
DRUMS
EXAMS
FARMS
FILMS
FIRMS
FLAMS
FOAMS
FORMS
GERMS
GLIMS
GRAMS
HARMS
HELMS
HOLMS
IMAMS
ITEMS
LOAMS
LOOMS
MAIMS
MUMMS
NORMS
PALMS
PLUMS
POEMS
PRAMS
PRIMS
PROMS
REAMS
REIMS
ROAMS
ROOMS
SCUMS
SEAMS
SEEMS
SHAMS
SHIMS
SKIMS
SLAMS
SLIMS
SLUMS
STEMS
STUMS
SWIMS
TEAMS
TEEMS
TERMS
TRAMS
TRIMS
WARMS
WEEMS
WHAMS
WHIMS
WORMS
ZOOMS

M•T••

MATCH
MATED
MATEO
MATES
MATEY
MATIN
MATRI
MATSU
MATTE
MATTS
MATTY
MATZO
METAL
METAS
METED
METER
METES
METHO
METIS
METRO
METRY
MITCH
MITER
MITES
MITTS
MOTEL
MOTES
MOTHS
MOTHY
MOTIF
MOTOR
MOTTO
MUTED
MUTES
MUTTS
MYTHO
MYTHS

M••T•

MALTS
MALTY
MANTA
MARTA
MARTS
MARTY
MASTO
MASTS
MATTE
MATTS
MATTY
MEATS
MEATY
MEETS
MELTS
MILTS
MINTS
MIRTH
MISTS
MISTY
MITTS
MOATS
MOLTO
MOLTS
MONTE
MONTH
MONTY
MORTS
MORTY
MOTTO
MOUTH
MUFTI
MULTI
MUSTS
MUSTY
MUTTS

M•••T

MAGOT
MANET
MARAT
MAYST
MEANT
MERIT
MIDST
MIGHT
MOIST
MONET
MOULT
MOUNT
MULCT
MURAT

•M•T•

AMATI
AMITY
EMITS
EMOTE
EMPTY
OMITS
SMITE
SMITH
SMOTE
SMUTS

•M••T

AMBIT
AMENT
EMMET
SMALT
SMART
SMELT
SMOLT

••MT•

COMTE
FEMTO

••M•T

ADMIT
ARMET
COMDT
COMET
DEMIT

EMMET
GAMUT
GEMOT
HEMAT
KAMET
LIMIT
NEMAT
REMIT
SOMAT
TEMPT
VOMIT

MU•••
MUCID
MUCIN
MUCKS
MUCKY
MUCRO
MUCUS
MUDDY
MUFFS
MUFTI
MUGGY
MUHLY
MULCH
MULCT
MULES
MULEY
MULLS
MULTI
MUMMS
MUMMY
MUMPS
MUNCH
MUNGO
MUNRO
MUONS
MURAL
MURAT
MUREX
MURKY
MURRA
MURRE
MURRY
MUSCA
MUSED
MUSES
MUSHY
MUSIC
MUSKS
MUSKY
MUSSY
MUSTS
MUSTY
MUTED
MUTES
MUTTS
MUZZY

M•U••
MAUDE
MAUDS
MAULS
MAUND
MAURA
MAUVE
MEUSE
MOUCH
MOUES
MOULD
MOULT
MOUNT
MOURN
MOUSE
MOUSY
MOUTH

M••U•
MAGUS
MANUS
MENUS
MIAUL
MINUS
MIXUP
MODUS
MOGUL
MOHUR
MOMUS
MUCUS

M•••U
MATSU

•MU••
AMUCK
AMUSE
SMUTS

•M•U•
AMOUR
AMPUL
EMEUS
IMBUE

••MU•
ALMUD
ALMUG
CAMUS
DEMUR
FEMUR
GAMUT
HUMUS
LEMUR
MOMUS
RAMUS
REMUS
WAMUS
YAMUN

M•V••
MAVIS
MOVED
MOVER
MOVES
MOVIE

M••V•
MAUVE

M•W••
MEWED
MEWLS
MOWED
MOWER

M••W•
MEOWS

M•••W
MACAW

•M•W•
BMEWS
SMEWS

•M••W
EMBOW

••M•W
UNMEW

M•X••
MAXIM
MIXED
MIXER
MIXES
MIXUP
MOXAS
MOXIE

M•••X
MUREX

•M••X
IMMIX

••M•X
ADMIX
CIMEX
IMMIX
REMEX

MY•••
MYELO
MYLES
MYNAS
MYOID
MYOMA
MYOPE
MYOPY
MYRAS
MYRIA
MYRNA
MYRON
MYRRH
MYTHO
MYTHS

M•Y••
MAYAN
MAYAS
MAYBE
MAYOR
MAYST

M•••Y
MACHY
MADLY
MALAY
MALTY
MAMEY
MAMMY
MANCY
MANDY
MANGY
MANLY
MARLY
MARRY
MARTY
MASHY
MASSY
MATEY
MATTY
MCCOY
MEALY
MEANY
MEATY
MERCY
MERRY
MESHY
MESSY
METRY
MICKY
MIDDY
MIFFY
MIKEY
MILKY
MILLY
MISSY
MISTY
MOLDY
MOLLY
MONEY
MONTY
MOODY
MOONY
MORAY
MORTY
MOSEY
MOSSY
MOTHY
MOUSY
MUCKY
MUDDY
MUGGY
MUHLY
MULEY
MUMMY
MURKY
MURRY
MUSHY
MUSKY
MUSSY
MUSTY
MUZZY
MYOPY

•MY••
AMYLO
AMYLS

•M•Y•
EMMYS

•M••Y
AMBRY
AMITY
AMPLY
EMBAY
EMBRY
EMERY
EMILY
EMORY
EMPTY
IMPLY
SMOKY

••MY•
EMMYS

••M•Y
BUMPY
CAMPY
CYMRY
DIMLY
DUMMY
DUMPY
GEMMY
GIMPY
GUMMY
HAMMY
HEMPY
HOMEY
HUMPY
JEMMY
JIMMY
JUMPY
LIMEY
LUMPY
MAMEY
MAMMY
MUMMY
RAMMY
RUMMY
SAMMY
TIMMY
TOMMY
WOMBY
YUMMY

•••MY
BALMY
BARMY
BEAMY
DORMY
DUMMY
ENEMY
FILMY
FLAMY
FOAMY
GEMMY
GNOMY
GUMMY
HAMMY
JEMMY
JIMMY
LOAMY
MAMMY
MUMMY
PALMY
PIGMY
PLUMY
PYGMY
RAMMY
ROOMY
RUMMY
SAMMY
SEAMY
SLIMY
SPUMY
STIMY
STOMY
STYMY
THYMY
TIMMY
TOMMY
WORMY
YUMMY

M•Z••
MAZED
MAZER
MAZES
MEZZO
MUZZY

M••Z•
MAIZE
MATZO
MEZZO
MIRZA
MUZZY

M•••Z
MAINZ

•M•Z•
AMAZE
SMAZE

••MZ•
HAMZA

NA•••
NAACP
NABOB
NACRE
NADER
NADIR
NAHUA
NAHUM
NAIAD
NAILS
NAIVE
NAKED
NAMED
NAMER
NAMES
NANAS
NANCY
NANNY
NAOMI
NAPES
NAPPE
NAPPY
NARCO
NARDS
NARES
NARIS
NASAL
NASTY
NATAL
NATES
NATTY
NAURU
NAVAL
NAVAR
NAVEL
NAVES
NAVVY
NAWAB
NAZIS

N•A••
NAACP
NEALS
NEAPS
NEARS
NEATH
NOAHS

N••A•
NAIAD
NANAS
NASAL
NATAL
NAVAL
NAVAR
NAWAB
NEMAT
NEPAL
NINAS
NIPAS
NISAN
NIVAL
NIZAM
NODAL
NOMAD
NOMAS
NONAS
NOPAL
NOPAR
NORAH
NORAS
NOVAE
NOVAS
NOWAY

N•••A
NAHUA
NORIA
NORMA
NUBIA
NUCHA

•NA••
ENACT
ENATE
GNARL
GNASH
GNATS
GNAWN
GNAWS
INANE
INAPT
INARM
KNACK
KNARS
KNAVE
SNACK
SNAFU
SNAGS
SNAIL
SNAKE
SNAKY
SNAPS
SNARE
SNARK
SNARL
SNATH
UNAPT
UNARM
UNAUS

•N•A•
ANEAR
ANLAS
ANNAL
ANNAM
ANNAS
ANSAE
ANTAE
ANZAC
ENEAS
INCAN
INCAS
INLAW
INLAY
KNEAD
SNEAK
UNBAR
UNCAP
UNHAT
UNLAY
UNMAN
UNSAY

•N••A
ANIMA
ANITA
ANTRA
ENEMA

ENNEA
ENTIA
INDIA
INDRA
INFRA
INTRA

••NA•

ANNAL
ANNAM
ANNAS
BANAL
BANAT
BINAL
CANAD
CANAL
DANAE
DINAH
DINAR
DONAR
DONAS
EDNAS
ETNAS
FINAL
GONAD
HONAN
HUNAN
IGNAZ
JONAH
JONAS
LANAI
LENAS
LUNAR
MINAE
MINAS
MONAD
MONAS
MYNAS
NANAS
NINAS
NONAS
PENAL
PINAS
PUNAS
RENAL
RENAN
SINAI
SONAR
TINAS
TONAL
TUNAS
ULNAE
ULNAR
ULNAS
VENAE
VENAL
VINAS
ZONAL

••N•A

AMNIA
APNEA
BANDA
CANEA
CANNA
CONGA
DINKA
DONNA
ENNEA
FANGA
GENOA
GENUA
GONIA
HANNA
HENNA
IONIA
JUNTA
KENYA
KONYA
LINDA
LINGA
MANIA
MANNA
MANTA
MENSA
MINNA
PANDA
PENNA
PENTA
PINNA
PINTA
PUNKA
SENNA
SONIA
SONYA
SUNNA
TANKA
TINEA
TONGA
WANDA
XENIA

•••NA

AGANA
ARENA
BWANA
CANNA
CHINA
DIANA
DONNA
DVINA
EDINA
ELENA
FAUNA
FIONA
FRENA
GHANA
HANNA
HENNA
HYENA
ILONA
JAINA
JUANA
JUMNA
KRONA
LEONA
LIANA
LORNA
MANNA
MINNA
MORNA
MYRNA
PENNA
PINNA
PLENA
PYDNA
SAUNA
SENNA
SUNNA
TRINA
TRONA
VERNA

N•B••

NABOB
NOBBY
NOBEL
NOBLE
NOBLY
NUBBY
NUBIA

N••B•

NIMBI
NIOBE
NOBBY
NUBBY
NUMBS

N•••B

NABOB
NAWAB

•NB••

UNBAR

•N•B•

KNOBS
SNOBS
SNUBS

••N•B

DENEB

N•C••

NACRE
NECKS
NECRO
NICER
NICHE
NICKS
NICKY
NOCKS
NOCTI
NUCHA
NYCTI
NYCTO

N••C•

NAACP
NANCY
NARCO
NIECE
NONCE
NOTCH

•NC••

ANCON
ENCYC
INCAN
INCAS
INCUR
INCUS
UNCAP
UNCLE
UNCUT

•N•C•

ENACT
ENOCH
KNACK
KNOCK
SNACK
SNICK
VNECK

•N••C

ANTIC
ANZAC
ENCYC
INDIC

••NC•

BENCH
BUNCH
BUNCO
CINCH
CONCH
DANCE
DUNCE
FANCY
FENCE
FINCH
HANCE
HENCE
HUNCH
JUNCO
KENCH
LANCE
LUNCH
LYNCH
MANCY
MINCE
MUNCH
NANCY
NONCE
OUNCE
PENCE
PINCH
PONCE
PUNCH
RANCE
RANCH
SINCE
TENCH
TINCT
VINCE
VINCI
WENCH
WINCE
WINCH
ZINCS
ZINCY

••N•C

CONIC
CYNIC
GENIC
GYNEC
IONIC
MANIC
PANIC
PUNIC
RUNIC
SONIC
TONIC
TUNIC
VINIC

•••NC

ADUNC
BLANC
BRONC
FRANC

N•D••

NADER
NADIR
NEDDY
NIDED
NIDES
NIDUS
NODAL
NODDY
NODES
NODUS
NUDES
NUDGE

N••D•

NARDS
NEDDY
NEEDS
NEEDY
NODDY

N•••D

NAIAD
NAKED
NAMED
NIDED
NIXED
NJORD
NOMAD
NOSED
NOTED

•ND••

ANDES
ANDRE
ANDRO
ANDYS
ENDED
ENDOW
ENDUE
INDEX
INDIA
INDIC
INDOW
INDRA
INDRI
INDUE
INDUS
UNDEE
UNDER
UNDID
UNDUE

•N•D•

ANODE
ENIDS
SNIDE

•N••D

ANTED
ENDED
INKED
INNED
KNEAD
KNEED
SNOOD
UNDID
UNWED

••ND•

BANDA
BANDS
BANDY
BENDS
BENDY
BINDS
BONDS
BUNDE
BUNDS
CANDY
CINDY
DANDY
DENDR
FENDS
FINDS
FUNDS
FUNDY
GONDI
HANDS
HANDY
HINDI
HINDS
HINDU
KANDY
KINDS
LANDS
LENDS
LINDA
MANDY
MENDS
MINDS
MONDE
PANDA
PANDY
PENDS
PONDS
RANDS
RANDY
RENDS
RINDS
RONDO
RYNDS
SANDS
SANDY
SENDS
TENDS
VENDS
WANDA
WANDS
WENDS
WENDY
WINDS
WINDY

••N•D

AWNED
BONED
CANAD
CANED
CONED
CONTD
DINED
FINED
GONAD
HONED
INNED
LINED
MANED
MINED
MONAD
OWNED
PINED
SYNOD
TINED
TONED
TUNED
VANED
WANED
WINED
ZONED

•••ND

AMEND
BLAND
BLEND
BLIND
BLOND
BOUND
BRAND
ELAND
EMEND
FIEND
FOUND
FROND
GLAND
GRAND
GRIND
HOUND
KHOND
MAUND
POIND
POUND
ROUND
SCAND
SCEND
SOUND
SPEND
STAND
TREND
UPEND
VIAND
WOUND

NE•••

NEALS
NEAPS
NEARS
NEATH
NECKS
NECRO
NEDDY
NEEDS
NEEDY
NEGEV
NEGRO
NEGUS
NEHRU
NEIGH
NEILS
NELLS
NELLY
NEMAT
NEPAL
NEPHO
NEPHR
NEROS
NERVE
NERVY
NESTS
NETTY
NEUME
NEURI
NEURO
NEVER
NEVIL
NEVUS
NEWEL
NEWER
NEWLY
NEWSY
NEWTS
NEXUS

N•E••

NEEDS
NEEDY
NIECE

NOELS

N••E•
NADER
NAKED
NAMED
NAMER
NAMES
NAPES
NARES
NATES
NAVEL
NAVES
NEGEV
NEVER
NEWEL
NEWER
NICER
NIDED
NIDES
NIGEL
NIGER
NINES
NISEI
NITER
NIXED
NIXES
NOBEL
NODES
NONES
NOSED
NOSES
NOSEY
NOTED
NOTER
NOTES
NOVEL
NUDES
NUMEN

N•••E
NACRE
NAIVE
NAPPE
NERVE
NEUME
NICHE
NIECE
NIOBE
NIXIE
NOBLE
NOISE
NONCE
NOOSE
NORSE
NOVAE
NUDGE
NURSE

•NE••
ANEAR
ANEMO
ANENT
ENEAS
ENEMA
ENEMY
INEPT
INERT
KNEAD
KNEED
KNEEL
KNEES
KNELL
KNELT
ONEIR
ONERY
PNEUM
SNEAK
SNEER
SNELL
VNECK

•N•E•
ANDES
ANGEL
ANGER
ANNES
ANNEX
ANSEL
ANTED
ANTES
ENDED
ENNEA
ENTER
INDEX
INFER
INKED
INKER
INLET
INNED
INNER
INSET
INTER
KNEED
KNEEL
KNEES
ONSET
SNEER
SNYES
UNDEE
UNDER
UNMEW
UNPEG
UNREF
UNSEX
UNWED

•N••E
ANDRE
ANGLE
ANILE
ANIME
ANISE
ANKLE
ANNIE
ANODE
ANSAE
ANTAE
ENATE
ENDUE
ENSUE
GNOME
INANE
INDUE
INKLE
INURE
KNAVE
KNIFE
SNAKE
SNARE
SNIDE
SNIPE
SNORE
UNCLE
UNDEE
UNDUE
UNITE
UNTIE

••NE•
ABNER
AGNES
ANNES
ANNEX
APNEA
AWNED
BENES
BENET
BINES
BINET
BONED
BONER
BONES
CANEA
CANED
CANER
CANES
CONED
CONES
CONEY
DANES
DENEB
DENES
DINED
DINER
DINES
DONEE
DUNES
DYNES
ENNEA
ERNES
FINED
FINER
FINES
GANEF
GENES
GENET
GONER
GYNEC
HONED
HONES
HONEY
INNED
INNER
JANES
JANET
JONES
JUNES
LANES
LENES
LINED
LINEN
LINER
LINES
LINEY
LONER
LUNES
LUNET
MANED
MANES
MANET
MENES
MINED
MINER
MINES
MONET
MONEY
NINES
NONES
OWNED
OWNER
PANEL
PANES
PINED
PINEL
PINER
PINES
PINEY
PONES
RANEE
RENEE
RENES
RENEW
RUNES
SANER
SINES
SINEW
SONES
TANEY
TENET
TINEA
TINED
TINES
TONED
TONER
TONES
TUNED
TUNER
TUNES
VANED
VANES
VINES
WANED
WANES
WANEY
WINED
WINES
ZONED
ZONES

••N•E
ANNIE
ARNIE
BENNE
BENUE
BINGE
BONZE
BUNDE
CANOE
CENSE
CONGE
CONTE
DANAE
DANCE
DANTE
DENSE
DONEE
DONNE
DUNCE
ERNIE
FENCE
GENIE
GENRE
HANCE
HANSE
HENCE
HINGE
LANCE
LUNGE
MANGE
MANSE
MINAE
MINCE
MONDE
MONTE
NONCE
OUNCE
PENCE
PONCE
RANCE
RANEE
RANGE
RENEE
RENTE
RINSE
SENSE
SINCE
SINGE
SYNGE
TENSE
TINGE
ULNAE
VENAE
VENUE
VINCE
WINCE
WINZE

•••NE
AISNE
AKENE
ALINE
ALONE
AMINE
ATONE
AXONE
AZINE
BENNE
BERNE
BOONE
BORNE
BOYNE
BRINE
CHINE
CLINE
CLONE
CRANE
CRONE
DEANE
DIANE
DIENE
DIONE
DONNE
DRONE
DUANE
IMINE
INANE
IRENE
IRONE
KOINE
KRONE
LIANE
MAINE
MARNE
MESNE
OPINE
OVINE
OZONE
PAINE
PHANE
PHONE
PLANE
PRONE
PRUNE
RHINE
RHONE
SCENE
SCONE
SEINE
SHINE
SHONE
SPINE
STONE
SWINE
TBONE
THANE
THINE
TRINE
TWINE
URINE
VERNE
WAYNE
WHINE

N•F••
NIFTY

•NF••
INFER
INFIX
INFRA
UNFIT
UNFIX

•N•F•
KNIFE
SNAFU
SNIFF
SNUFF
UNIFY

•N••F
SNIFF
SNUFF
UNREF

••NF•
BANFF

••N•F
BANFF
GANEF

N•G••
NEGEV
NEGRO
NEGUS
NIGEL
NIGER
NIGHT
NIGRI
NOGGS

N••G•
NEIGH
NOGGS
NUDGE

•NG••
ANGEL
ANGER
ANGIO
ANGLE
ANGLO
ANGRY
ANGST
ANGUS
INGOT

•N•G•
INIGO
SNAGS
SNUGS

•N••G
UNPEG
UNRIG

••NG•
BANGS
BINGE
BINGO
BONGO
BONGS
BUNGS
CONGA
CONGE
CONGO
DANGS
DINGO
DINGS
DINGY
DUNGS
DUNGY
FANGA
FANGS
FUNGI
FUNGO
GANGS
GONGS
HANGS
HINGE
HONGS
JINGO
KINGS
LINGA
LINGO
LINGS
LONGI
LONGS
LUNGE
LUNGI
LUNGS
MANGE
MANGO
MANGY
MUNGO
PANGS
PENGO
PINGO
PINGS
PUNGS
RANGE
RANGY
RINGS
RUNGS
SINGE
SINGS
SONGS
SYNGE
TANGO
TANGS
TANGY
TINGE
TINGS
TONGA
TONGS
VANGS
WINGS
WINGY
ZINGS

•••NG
ACING
AGING
ALONG
AMONG
APING
AWING
AXING
BEING
BHANG
BRING
CHANG
CLANG
CLING
CLUNG
CUING
DOING
DYING
EKING
EWING
EYING
FLING
FLONG
FLUNG
GIING
GOING
HYING
ICING
LIANG
LYING
OKING
ORANG
OWING
PRONG
RUING
SLANG
SLING
SLUNG
SPANG
STING
STUNG
SUING
SWING
SWUNG
THING
THONG
TWANG
TYING
USING
VYING
WHANG
WRING
WRONG
WRUNG
YOUNG

N•H••
NAHUA
NAHUM
NEHRU
NIHIL

N••H•
NEPHO
NEPHR
NICHE
NIGHT
NOAHS
NUCHA

N•••H
NEATH
NEIGH
NINTH
NORAH
NORTH
NOTCH
NYMPH

•NH••
UNHAT

•N•H•
ANKHS
ANTHO

•N••H
ENOCH
GNASH
SNATH

••N•H
BENCH
BUNCH
CINCH
CONCH
DINAH
FINCH
HUNCH
JONAH
KENCH
LUNCH
LYNCH
MONTH
MUNCH
NINTH
PINCH
PUNCH
RANCH
TENCH
TENTH
WENCH
WINCH
XANTH

NI•••
NICER
NICHE
NICKS
NICKY
NIDED
NIDES
NIDUS
NIECE
NIFTY
NIGEL
NIGER
NIGHT
NIGRI
NIHIL
NIMBI
NINAS
NINES
NINNY
NINTH
NINUS
NIOBE
NIPAS
NIPPY
NISAN
NISEI
NISUS
NITER
NITON
NITRI
NITRO
NITTY
NIVAL
NIXED
NIXES
NIXIE
NIXON
NIZAM

N•I••
NAIAD
NAILS
NAIVE
NEIGH
NEILS
NOISE
NOISY

N••I•
NADIR
NARIS
NAZIS
NEVIL
NIHIL
NIXIE
NORIA
NUBIA

N•••I
NAOMI
NEURI
NIGRI
NIMBI
NISEI
NITRI
NOCTI
NYCTI

•NI••
ANILE
ANILS
ANIMA
ANIME
ANION
ANISE
ANISO
ANITA
ENIDS
INIGO
INION
KNIFE
KNITS
ONION
ONIRO
SNICK
SNIDE
SNIFF
SNIPE
SNIPS
UNIFY
UNION
UNITE
UNITS
UNITY

•N•I•
ANGIO
ANNIE
ANTIC
ANTIS
ANVIL
ANZIO
ENTIA
INDIA
INDIC
INFIX
ONEIR
SNAIL
UNDID
UNFIT
UNFIX
UNLIT
UNPIN
UNRIG
UNRIP
UNTIE
UNTIL

•N••I
ENNUI
INDRI

••NI•
AGNIS
AMNIA
ANNIE
ARNIE
BENIN
BINIT
BONIN
CANIS
CENIS
CONIC
CONIO
CYNIC
DENIM
DENIS
ERNIE
FINIS
GENIC
GENIE
GENII
GONIA
GONIO
IONIA
IONIC
KININ
LENIN
LENIS
LININ
MANIA
MANIC
MINIM
ORNIS
PANIC
PUNIC
RANIS
RENIN
RUNIC
RUNIN
SONIA
SONIC
TANIS
TONIC
TONIS
TUNIC
TUNIS
VANIR
VINIC
XENIA

••N•I
CENTI
DENTI
ENNUI
FUNGI
GENII
GONDI
HANOI
HENRI
HINDI
JINNI
LANAI
LONGI
LUNGI
PENNI
PINNI
SINAI
SUNNI
VINCI

•••NI
ACINI
ADENI
CRANI
GRANI
JINNI
LIGNI
MAGNI
PENNI
PINNI
PLANI
SEGNI
SOMNI
SPINI
SUNNI

NJ•••
NJORD

•NJ••
ANJOU
ENJOY

••NJ•
BANJO
BENJY

N•K••
NAKED

N••K•
NECKS
NICKS
NICKY
NOCKS
NOOKS

•NK••
ANKHS
ANKLE
ANKUS
INKED
INKER
INKLE

•N•K•
SNAKE
SNAKY

•N••K
KNACK
KNOCK
SNACK
SNARK
SNEAK
SNICK
SNOOK
VNECK

••NK•
BANKS
BUNKO
BUNKS
CONKS
DINKA
DINKY
DUNKS
FINKS
FUNKS
FUNKY
GINKS
HANKS
HONKS
HUNKS
HUNKY
JINKS
JUNKS
JUNKY
KINKS
KINKY
LANKY
LINKS
MINKS
MONKS
PINKS
PINKY
PUNKA
PUNKS
PUNKY
RANKS
RINKS
SINKS
TANKA
TANKS
WINKS
YANKS
ZINKY

••N•K
MINSK

•••NK
BLANK
BLINK
BRINK
CHINK
CHUNK
CLANK
CLINK
CRANK
DRANK
DRINK
DRUNK
FLANK
FLUNK
FRANK
PLANK
PLUNK
PRANK
PRINK
SHANK
SKINK
SKUNK
SLINK
SLUNK
SPANK
SPUNK
STANK
STINK
STUNK
SWANK
THANK
THINK
TRUNK

N•L••
NELLS
NELLY
NYLON

N••L•
NAILS
NEALS
NEILS
NELLS
NELLY
NEWLY
NOBLE
NOBLY
NOELS

N•••L
NASAL
NATAL
NAVAL
NAVEL
NEPAL
NEVIL
NEWEL
NIGEL
NIHIL
NIVAL
NOBEL
NODAL
NOPAL
NOVEL

•NL••
ANLAS
INLAW
INLAY
INLET
UNLAY
UNLIT

•N•L•
ANGLE
ANGLO
ANILE
ANILS
ANKLE
ENOLS
INKLE
KNELL
KNELT
KNOLL
SNELL
UNCLE

•N••L
ANGEL
ANNAL
ANNUL
ANSEL
ANVIL
GNARL
KNEEL
KNELL
KNOLL
KNURL
SNAIL
SNARL
SNELL
UNTIL

••NL•
MANLY
WANLY

••N•L
ANNAL
ANNUL
BANAL
BINAL
CANAL
FINAL
PANEL
PENAL
PINEL
RENAL
TONAL
VENAL
VINYL
ZONAL

N•M••
NAMED
NAMER
NAMES
NEMAT
NIMBI
NOMAD
NOMAS
NUMBS
NUMEN
NYMPH

N••M•
NAOMI
NEUME
NORMA
NORMS

N•••M
NAHUM
NIZAM

•NM••
UNMAN
UNMEW

•N•M•
ANEMO
ANIMA
ANIME
ENEMA
ENEMY
GNOME
GNOMY

•N••M
ANNAM
ENTOM
INARM
PNEUM
UNARM

••N•M
ANNAM
DENIM
FANUM
MINIM
VENOM

N•N••
NANAS
NANCY
NANNY
NINAS
NINES
NINNY
NINTH
NINUS
NONAS
NONCE
NONES

N••N•
NANNY
NINNY
NOONS
NORNS
NOUNS

N•••N
NISAN
NITON
NIXON
NUMEN
NYLON

•NN••
ANNAL
ANNAM
ANNAS
ANNES
ANNEX
ANNIE
ANNOY
ANNUL
ENNEA
ENNUI
INNED
INNER

•N•N•
ANENT
INANE

•N••N
ANCON
ANION
ANTON
GNAWN
INCAN
INION
INURN
KNOWN
ONION
UNION
UNMAN
UNPIN

••NN•
BANNS
BENNE
BENNY
BONNY
BUNNS
BUNNY
CANNA
CANNY
CONNY
DANNY
DENNY
DONNA
DONNE
FANNY
FENNY
FINNS
FINNY
FUNNY
GINNY
GUNNY
HANNA
HENNA
HINNY
JENNY
JINNI
JINNY
JONNY
KENNY
LENNY
LYNNS
MANNA
MINNA
NANNY
NINNY
PENNA
PENNI
PENNY
PINNA
PINNI
RONNY
SENNA
SONNY
SUNNA
SUNNI
SUNNS
SUNNY
TINNY
TUNNY
VINNY
WENNY

••N•N
BENIN
BONIN
CANON
FANON
HONAN
HUNAN
KININ
LENIN
LINEN
LININ
PINON
RENAN
RENIN
RUNIN
RUNON
TENON
XENON

•••NN
GLENN
GWENN

NO•••
NOAHS
NOBBY
NOBEL
NOBLE
NOBLY
NOCKS
NOCTI
NODAL
NODDY
NODES
NODUS
NOELS
NOGGS
NOISE
NOISY
NOMAD
NOMAS
NONAS
NONCE
NONES
NOOKS
NOONS
NOOSE
NOPAL
NOPAR
NORAH
NORAS
NORIA
NORMA
NORMS
NORNS
NORSE
NORTH
NOSED
NOSES
NOSEY
NOTCH
NOTED
NOTER
NOTES
NOUNS
NOVAE
NOVAS
NOVEL
NOWAY

N•O••
NAOMI
NIOBE
NJORD
NOOKS
NOONS
NOOSE

N••O•
NABOB
NEROS
NITON
NIXON
NYLON

N•••O
NARCO
NECRO
NEGRO
NEPHO
NEURO
NITRO
NYCTO

•NO••
ANODE
ENOCH
ENOLS
GNOME
GNOMY
KNOBS
KNOCK
KNOLL
KNOPS
KNOSP
KNOTS
KNOUT
KNOWN
KNOWS
SNOBS
SNOOD
SNOOK
SNOOP
SNOOT
SNORE
SNORT
SNOTS
SNOUT
SNOWS
SNOWY

•N•O•
ANCON
ANION
ANJOU
ANNOY
ANTON
ENDOW
ENJOY
ENTOM
ENVOY
INDOW
INGOT
INION
ONION
SNOOD
SNOOK
SNOOP
SNOOT
UNION

•N••O
ANDRO
ANEMO
ANGIO
ANGLO
ANISO
ANTHO
ANZIO
INIGO
INTRO
ONIRO

••NO•
AINOS
ANNOY
CANOE
CANON
DONOR
FANON
FANOS
GENOA
HANOI
HONOR
JANOS
LENOS
MANOR
MINOR
MINOS
PINON
RUNON
SENOR
SYNOD
TENON
TENOR
VENOM
WINOS
XENON

••N•O
BANJO
BINGO
BONGO
BUNCO
BUNKO
CANSO
CANTO
CENTO
CONGO
CONIO
CONTO
DENTO
DINGO
FUNGO
GENRO
GONIO
JINGO
JUNCO
LENTO
LINGO
MANGO
MUNGO
MUNRO
PANTO
PENGO
PINGO
PINTO
PUNTO
RONDO
TANGO
TANTO

•••NO
ADENO
AMINO
BEANO
BRUNO
CHINO
CLINO
COENO
CTENO
CYANO
ETHNO
GRANO
GUANO
GYMNO
HYPNO
ICONO
IMINO
LIGNO
LLANO
PHENO
PHONO
PIANO
PLANO
PORNO
RHINO
SEGNO
STENO
TAINO
URANO
URINO

N•P••
NAPES
NAPPE
NAPPY
NEPAL
NEPHO
NEPHR
NIPAS
NIPPY
NOPAL
NOPAR

N••P•
NAPPE
NAPPY
NEAPS
NIPPY
NYMPH

N•••P
NAACP

•NP••
INPUT
UNPEG
UNPIN

•N•P•
INAPT
INEPT
KNOPS
SNAPS
SNIPE
SNIPS
UNAPT

•N••P
KNOSP
SNOOP
UNCAP
UNRIP

••N•P
PINUP
SUNUP

N•R••
NARCO
NARDS
NARES
NARIS
NEROS
NERVE
NERVY
NORAH
NORAS
NORIA
NORMA
NORMS
NORNS
NORSE
NORTH
NURSE

N••R•
NACRE
NAURU
NEARS
NECRO
NEGRO
NEHRU
NEURI
NEURO
NIGRI
NITRI
NITRO
NJORD

N•••R
NADER
NADIR
NAMER
NAVAR
NEPHR
NEVER
NEWER
NICER
NIGER
NITER
NOPAR
NOTER

•NR••
UNREF
UNRIG
UNRIP

•N•R•
ANDRE
ANDRO
ANGRY
ANTRA
ENTRY
GNARL
INARM
INDRA
INDRI
INERT
INFRA
INTRA
INTRO
INURE
INURN
KNARS
KNURL
KNURS
ONERY
ONIRO
SNARE
SNARK
SNARL
SNORE
SNORT
UNARM

•N••R
ANEAR
ANGER
ENTER
INCUR
INFER
INKER
INNER
INTER
ONEIR
SNEER
UNBAR
UNDER

••NR•
GENRE
GENRO
HENRI
HENRY
MUNRO

••N•R
ABNER
BONER
CANER
CENTR
CONTR
DENDR
DINAR
DINER
DONAR
DONOR
FINER
GONER
HONOR
INNER
LINER
LONER
LUNAR
MANOR
MINER
MINOR
OWNER
PINER
SANER
SENOR
SONAR
TENOR
TONER
TUNER
ULNAR
VANIR

N•S••
NASAL
NASTY
NESTS
NISAN
NISEI
NISUS
NOSED
NOSES
NOSEY

N••S•
NEWSY
NOISE
NOISY
NOOSE
NORSE
NURSE

N•••S
NAILS
NAMES
NANAS
NAPES
NARDS
NARES
NARIS
NATES
NAVES
NAZIS
NEALS
NEAPS
NEARS
NECKS
NEEDS
NEGUS
NEILS
NELLS
NEROS
NESTS
NEVUS
NEWTS
NEXUS
NICKS
NIDES
NIDUS
NINAS
NINES
NINUS
NIPAS
NISUS
NIXES
NOAHS
NOCKS
NODES
NODUS
NOELS
NOGGS
NOMAS
NONAS
NONES
NOOKS
NOONS
NORAS
NORMS
NORNS
NOSES
NOTES
NOUNS
NOVAS
NUDES
NUMBS

•NS••
ANSAE
ANSEL
ENSUE
INSET
ONSET
UNSAY
UNSEX

•N•S•
ANGST
ANISE
ANISO
GNASH
KNOSP

•N••S
ANDES
ANDYS
ANGUS
ANILS
ANKHS
ANKUS
ANLAS
ANNAS
ANNES
ANTES
ANTIS
ENEAS
ENIDS
ENOLS
GNATS
GNAWS
INCAS
INCUS
INDUS
KNARS
KNEES
KNITS
KNOBS
KNOPS
KNOTS
KNOWS
KNURS
SNAGS
SNAPS
SNIPS
SNOBS
SNOTS
SNOWS
SNUBS
SNUGS
SNYES
UNAUS
UNITS

••NS•
CANSO
CANST
CENSE
DENSE
ERNST
HANSE
MANSE
MENSA
MINSK
PANSY
RINSE
SENSE
TANSY
TENSE

••N•S
AGNES
AGNIS
AINOS
AINUS
ANNAS
ANNES
AUNTS
BANDS
BANGS
BANKS
BANNS
BENDS
BENES
BINDS
BINES
BONDS
BONES
BONGS
BONUS
BUNDS
BUNGS
BUNKS
BUNNS
BUNTS
CANES
CANIS
CANTS
CENIS
CENTS
CONES
CONKS
CONUS
DANES
DANGS
DENES
DENIS
DENTS
DENYS
DINES
DINGS
DINTS
DONAS
DONTS
DUNES
DUNGS
DUNKS
DYNES
EDNAS
ERNES
ETNAS
FANGS
FANOS
FENDS
FINDS
FINES
FINIS
FINKS
FINNS
FONTS
FUNDS
FUNKS
GANGS
GENES
GENTS
GENUS
GINKS
GONGS
HANDS
HANGS
HANKS
HINDS
HINTS
HONES
HONGS
HONKS
HUNKS
HUNTS
JANES
JANOS
JANUS
JINKS
JONAS
JONES
JUNES
JUNKS
KENTS
KINDS
KINGS
KINKS
LANDS
LANES
LENAS
LENDS
LENES
LENIS
LENOS
LENTS
LINES
LINGS
LINKS
LINUS
LONGS
LUNES
LUNGS
LUNTS
LYNNS
MANES
MANUS
MENDS
MENES
MENUS
MINAS
MINDS
MINES
MINKS
MINOS
MINTS
MINUS
MONAS
MONKS
MYNAS
NANAS
NINAS
NINES
NINUS
NONAS
NONES
ORNIS
PANES
PANGS
PANTS
PENDS
PINAS
PINES
PINGS
PINKS
PINTS
PONDS
PONES
PUNAS
PUNGS
PUNKS
PUNTS
RANDS
RANIS
RANKS
RANTS
RENDS
RENES
RENTS
RINDS
RINGS
RINKS
RUNES
RUNGS
RUNTS
RYNDS
SANDS
SENDS
SINES
SINGS
SINKS
SINUS
SONES
SONGS
SUNNS
TANGS
TANIS
TANKS
TENDS
TENTS
TINAS
TINES
TINGS
TINTS
TONES
TONGS
TONIS
TONUS
TONYS
TUNAS
TUNES
TUNIS
ULNAS
VANES
VANGS
VENDS
VENTS
VENUS
VINAS
VINES
WANDS
WANES
WANTS
WENDS
WINDS
WINES
WINGS
WINKS
WINOS
YANKS
ZINCS
ZINGS
ZONES

•••NS
AEONS
ALANS
AMENS
ASSNS
AVENS
AXONS
AYINS
AZANS
AZONS
BANNS
BARNS
BEANS
BOONS
BRANS
BUNNS
BURNS
CHINS
CIONS
CLANS
CLONS
COINS
COONS
CORNS
DAMNS
DARNS
DAWNS
DEANS
DOWNS
EARNS
EBONS
EVANS
EVENS
FAUNS
FAWNS
FERNS
FINNS
FIRNS
FLANS
GAINS
GLANS
GLENS
GOONS
GOWNS
GRINS
GUANS
GWENS
GWYNS
HORNS
HYMNS
ICONS
IKONS
IRONS
IVANS
JAINS
JEANS
JOANS
JOHNS
JOINS
JUANS
KEENS
KERNS
KHANS
KILNS
LAWNS
LEANS
LEONS
LIENS
LIMNS
LIONS
LOANS
LOINS
LOONS
LYNNS
LYONS

5

MAINS
MEANS
MIENS
MOANS
MOONS
MORNS
MUONS
NOONS
NORNS
NOUNS
OMENS
OPENS
OVENS
OWENS
PAINS
PAWNS
PEANS
PEENS
PEONS
PIONS
PLANS
POONS
RAINS
REINS
ROANS
RUINS
SCANS
SEANS
SHANS
SHINS
SHUNS
SIGNS
SKINS
SPANS
SPINS
STANS
STUNS
SUNNS
SWANS
TAINS
TARNS
TEENS
TERNS
THINS
TOWNS
TRANS
TURNS
TWINS
VEINS
VERNS
WAINS
WARNS
WEANS
WHENS
WHINS
WRENS
YARNS
YAWNS
YEANS
ZOONS

N•T••
NATAL
NATES
NATTY
NETTY
NITER
NITON
NITRI
NITRO
NITTY
NOTCH
NOTED
NOTER
NOTES
NUTTY

N••T•
NASTY
NATTY
NEATH
NESTS
NETTY
NEWTS
NIFTY
NINTH
NITTY
NOCTI
NORTH
NUTTY
NYCTI
NYCTO

N•••T
NEMAT
NIGHT

•NT••
ANTAE
ANTED
ANTES
ANTHO
ANTIC
ANTIS
ANTON
ANTRA
ENTER
ENTIA
ENTOM
ENTRY
INTER
INTRA
INTRO
UNTIE
UNTIL

•N•T•
ANITA
ENATE
GNATS
KNITS
KNOTS
SNATH
SNOTS
UNITE
UNITS
UNITY

•N••T
ANENT
ANGST
ENACT
INAPT
INEPT
INERT
INGOT
INLET
INPUT
INSET
KNELT
KNOUT
ONSET
SNOOT
SNORT
SNOUT
UNAPT
UNCUT
UNFIT
UNHAT
UNLIT

••NT•
AUNTS
AUNTY
BANTU
BUNTS
CANTO
CANTS
CENTI
CENTO
CENTR
CENTS
CONTD
CONTE
CONTO
CONTR
DANTE
DENTI
DENTO
DENTS
DINTS
DONTS
FONTS
GENTS
HINTS
HUNTS
JUNTA
KENTS
LENTO
LENTS
LINTY
LUNTS
MANTA
MINTS
MONTE
MONTH
MONTY
NINTH
PANTO
PANTS
PANTY
PENTA
PINTA
PINTO
PINTS
PUNTO
PUNTS
PUNTY
RANTS
RENTE
RENTS
RUNTS
RUNTY
TANTO
TENTH
TENTS
TINTS
VENTS
WANTS
XANTH

••N•T
BANAT
BENET
BINET
BINIT
CANST
ERNST
GENET
JANET
LUNET
MANET
MONET
TENET
TINCT

•••NT
AGENT
AMENT
ANENT
ARENT
BLENT
BLUNT
BRANT
BRENT
BRUNT
BURNT
CHANT
CLINT
COUNT
DAUNT
DIDNT
EVENT
FAINT
FEINT
FLINT
FOUNT
FRONT
GAUNT
GHENT
GIANT
GLINT
GRANT
GRUNT
HASNT
HAUNT
JAUNT
JOINT
LEANT
MEANT
MOUNT
ODONT
PAINT
PLANT
POINT
PRINT
QUANT
QUINT
RIANT
SAINT
SCANT
SCENT
SHANT
SHUNT
SLANT
SPENT
STINT
STUNT
SUINT
TAINT
TAUNT
TRENT
ULENT
VAUNT
WASNT

NU•••
NUBBY
NUBIA
NUCHA
NUDES
NUDGE
NUMBS
NUMEN
NURSE
NUTTY

N•U••
NAURU
NEUME
NEURI
NEURO
NOUNS

N••U•
NAHUA
NAHUM
NEGUS
NEVUS
NEXUS
NIDUS
NINUS
NISUS
NODUS

N•••U
NAURU
NEHRU

•NU••
INURE
INURN
KNURL
KNURS
SNUBS
SNUFF
SNUGS

•N•U•
ANGUS
ANKUS
ANNUL
ENDUE
ENNUI
ENSUE
INCUR
INCUS
INDUE
INDUS
INPUT
KNOUT
PNEUM
SNOUT
UNAUS
UNCUT
UNDUE

•N••U
ANJOU
SNAFU

••NU•
AINUS
ANNUL
BENUE
BONUS
CONUS
ENNUI
FANUM
GENUA
GENUS
JANUS
LINUS
MANUS
MENUS
MINUS
NINUS
PINUP
SINUS
SUNUP
TONUS
VENUE
VENUS

••N•U
BANTU
HINDU

•••NU
BORNU
CORNU

N•V••
NAVAL
NAVAR
NAVEL
NAVES
NAVVY
NEVER
NEVIL
NEVUS
NIVAL
NOVAE
NOVAS
NOVEL

N••V•
NAIVE
NAVVY
NERVE
NERVY

N•••V
NEGEV

•NV••
ANVIL
ENVOY

•N•V•
KNAVE

N•W••
NAWAB
NEWEL
NEWER
NEWLY
NEWSY
NEWTS
NOWAY

•NW••
UNWED

•N•W•
GNAWN
GNAWS
KNOWN
KNOWS
SNOWS
SNOWY

•N••W
ENDOW
INDOW
INLAW
UNMEW

••N•W
RENEW
SINEW

N•X••
NEXUS
NIXED
NIXES
NIXIE
NIXON

•N••X
ANNEX
INDEX
INFIX
UNFIX
UNSEX

••N•X
ANNEX

•••NX
BRONX

NY•••
NYCTI
NYCTO
NYLON
NYMPH

N•••Y
NANCY
NANNY
NAPPY
NASTY
NATTY
NAVVY
NEDDY
NEEDY
NELLY
NERVY
NETTY
NEWLY
NEWSY
NICKY
NIFTY
NINNY
NIPPY
NITTY
NOBBY
NOBLY
NODDY
NOISY
NOSEY
NOWAY
NUBBY
NUTTY

•NY••
SNYES

•N•Y•
ANDYS
ENCYC

•N••Y
ANGRY
ANNOY
ENEMY
ENJOY
ENTRY
ENVOY

GNOMY
INLAY
ONERY
SNAKY
SNOWY
UNIFY
UNITY
UNLAY
UNSAY

••NY•
DENYS
KENYA
KONYA
SONYA
TONYS
VINYL

••N•Y
ANNOY
AUNTY
BANDY
BENDY
BENJY
BENNY
BONNY
BUNNY
CANDY
CANNY
CINDY
CONEY
CONNY
DANDY
DANNY
DENNY
DINGY
DINKY
DUNGY
FANCY
FANNY
FENNY
FINNY
FUNDY
FUNKY
FUNNY
GINNY
GUNNY
HANDY
HENRY
HINNY
HONEY
HUNKY
JENNY
JINNY
JONNY
JUNKY
KANDY
KENNY
KINKY
LANKY
LENNY
LINEY
LINTY
MANCY
MANDY
MANGY
MANLY
MONEY
MONTY
NANCY
NANNY
NINNY
PANDY
PANSY
PANTY
PENNY
PINEY
PINKY
PUNKY
PUNTY
RANDY
RANGY
RONNY
RUNTY
SANDY
SONNY
SUNNY
TANEY
TANGY
TANSY
TINNY
TUNNY
VINNY
WANEY
WANLY
WENDY
WENNY
WINDY
WINGY
ZINCY
ZINKY

•••NY
AGONY
ATONY
BENNY
BONNY
BRINY
BUNNY
CANNY
CLUNY
CONNY
CORNY
CRONY
DANNY
DENNY
DOWNY
EBONY
FANNY
FENNY
FERNY
FINNY
FUNNY
GINNY
GUNNY
HINNY
HORNY
IRONY
JENNY
JINNY
JONNY
KENNY
LAWNY
LENNY
LOONY
MEANY
MOONY
NANNY
NINNY
PENNY
PEONY
PHANY
PHONY
PLINY
RAINY
RONNY
SHINY
SONNY
SPINY
STONY
SUNNY
TAWNY
TEENY
TINNY
TUNNY
VEINY
VINNY
WEENY
WENNY
WHINY

N•Z••
NAZIS
NIZAM

•NZ••
ANZAC
ANZIO

••NZ•
BONZE
WINZE

••N•Z
IGNAZ

•••NZ
FRANZ
MAINZ

OA•••
OAKEN
OAKUM
OARED
OASES
OASIS
OATEN
OATES
OATHS
OAVES

O•A••
OKAPI
OKAYS
OLAFS
OLAVS
OMAHA
OMASA
OPAHS
OPALS
ORACH
ORALS
ORANG
ORATE
OSAGE
OVALS
OVARY
OVATE
OZARK

O••A•
OCEAN
OCTAD
OFFAL
OKRAS
OLGAS
OLLAS
OREAD
ORGAN
OSCAN
OSCAR
OSMAN

O•••A
OCREA
OIDEA
OMAHA
OMASA
OMEGA
OPERA
OPSIA
ORIYA
OSTIA
OUIDA
OUIJA

•OA••
BOARD
BOARS
BOAST
BOATS
COACH
COALS
COAST
COATI
COATS
DOALL
FOALS
FOAMS
FOAMY
GOADS
GOALS
GOATS
HOARD
HOARY
JOANS
KOALA
LOACH
LOADS
LOAFS
LOAMS
LOAMY
LOANS
LOATH
MOANS
MOATS
NOAHS
POACH
ROACH
ROADS
ROALD
ROAMS
ROANS
ROARS
ROAST
SOAKS
SOAPS
SOAPY
SOARS
TOADS
TOADY
TOAST
WOADS
WOALD

•O•A•
BOGAN
BOLAR
BOLAS
BORAX
BOYAR
COCAS
CODAS
COHAN
COLAS
COMAE
COMAL
COMAS
COPAL
CORAL
CORAS
COXAE
COXAL
DONAR
DONAS
DORAS
DOTAL
DOUAI
DOUAY
DOVAP
FOCAL
FORAY
GONAD
GORAL
HOGAN
HOKAN
HONAN
HORAE
HORAL
HORAS
IOTAS
JONAH
JONAS
JORAM
KODAK
KOLAS
KORAN
LOBAR
LOCAL
LOLAS
LORAN
LOTAH
LOYAL
MODAL
MOLAL
MOLAR
MONAD
MONAS
MORAE
MORAL
MORAS
MORAY
MOSAN
MOXAS
NODAL
NOMAD
NOMAS
NONAS
NOPAL
NOPAR
NORAH
NORAS
NOVAE
NOVAS
NOWAY
POLAR
ROMAN
ROSAS
ROTAS
ROWAN
ROYAL
SODAS
SOFAS
SOJAS
SOLAN
SOLAR
SOMAT
SONAR
SORAS
SOWAR
SOYAS
TODAY
TOGAE
TOGAS
TOKAY
TOLAN
TOLAS
TOMAN
TOMAS
TONAL
TOPAZ
TORAH
TOTAL
VOCAL
VOLAR
WODAN
WOMAN
WOTAN
ZONAL

•O••A
AORTA
BOHEA
COBIA
COBRA
COCOA
COLZA
COMMA
CONGA
COPRA
CORIA
COSTA
COTTA
DOBLA
DOBRA
DOGMA
DONNA
DORSA
DOURA
FOLIA
FOSSA
FOVEA
GONIA
GOTHA
GOUDA
HOSEA
IONIA
JOSUA
KOALA
KONYA
KOREA
LOGIA
LORCA
LORNA
LOTTA
MOCHA
MOIRA
MORNA
NORIA
NORMA
PODIA
POLKA
SOFIA
SOFTA
SOLFA
SONIA
SONYA
SOUSA
TONGA
VODKA
VOILA
VOLGA
VOLTA
VOLVA

••OA•
BLOAT
BROAD
CLOAK
CROAK
CROAT
EBOAT
FLOAT
GLOAT
GROAN
GROAT
LAOAG
PROAS
PSOAS
SHOAL
SHOAT
SKOAL
STOAE
STOAS
STOAT
TROAS
UBOAT

••O•A
ABOMA
AGORA
ALOHA
AROMA
BIOTA
FIONA
FLORA
ILONA
KIOWA
KRONA
LEONA
LEORA
MYOMA
QUOTA
RHODA
RHOEA
STOMA
TRONA
VIOLA

•••OA
COCOA
GENOA
SAMOA

OB•••
OBESE
OBEYS
OBITS
OBOES
OBOLI

O•B••
OMBER
OMBRE
OMBRO
ORBED
ORBIT
OXBOW

O••B•
ORIBI

•OB••
BOBBY
COBBS
COBIA
COBLE
COBRA
DOBBY
DOBIE
DOBLA
DOBRA
GOBOS
GOBYS
HOBBS
HOBBY
HOBOS
LOBAR
LOBBY
LOBED
LOBES
LOBOS
NOBBY
NOBEL
NOBLE
NOBLY
ROBED
ROBES
ROBIN
ROBLE
ROBOT
SOBER
TOBOL
TOBYS

•O•B•
BOBBY
BOMBE
BOMBS
BOOBS
BOOBY
COBBS
COMBO
COMBS
DOBBY
DOUBT
FORBS
HOBBS
HOBBY
LOBBY
LOOBY
NOBBY
SORBS
TOMBS
WOMBS
WOMBY
ZOMBI

•O••B
COOMB
HOREB

••OB•
ADOBE
BLOBS
BOOBS
BOOBY
GLOBE
GLOBS
KNOBS
LOOBY
NIOBE
PHOBE
PROBE
SLOBS
SNOBS

••O•B
ABOMB
COOMB
HBOMB
RHOMB

•••OB
CABOB
CAROB
DEMOB
JACOB
JAKOB
KABOB
NABOB
THROB

OC•••
OCCUR
OCEAN
OCHER
OCHRY
OCREA
OCTAD
OCTET
OCTYL
OCULO

O•C••
OCCUR
ORCHI
ORCIN
ORCUS
OSCAN
OSCAR

O••C•
ORACH
OUNCE

O•••C
OHMIC
OLEIC
OPTIC
OSMIC

•OC••
BOCHE
COCAS
COCCI
COCKS
COCKY
COCOA
COCOS
DOCKS
FOCAL
FOCUS
HOCKS
HOCUS
JOCKO
LOCAL
LOCHS
LOCKE
LOCKS
LOCOS
LOCUS
MOCHA
MOCKS
NOCKS
NOCTI
POCKS
POCKY
ROCKS
ROCKY
SOCIO
SOCKS
SOCLE
VOCAL
VOCES

•O•C•
BOSCH
BOTCH
COACH
COCCI
CONCH
COUCH
DOLCE
FORCE
HOICK
HOOCH
JOYCE
LOACH
LORCA
MOOCH
MOUCH
NONCE
NOTCH
POACH
PONCE
POOCH
PORCH
POUCH
ROACH
ROTCH
TOUCH
VOICE
VOUCH

•O••C
BORIC
COLIC
COMIC
CONIC
COSEC
DODEC
DOMIC
DORIC
EOLIC
FOLIC
IODIC
IONIC
LOGIC
SONIC
TONIC
TOPIC
TORIC
TOXIC
YOGIC

••OC•
ACOCK
BLOCK
BLOCS
CHOCK
CLOCK
CROCE
CROCI
CROCK
ENOCH
EPOCH
FLOCK
FLOCS
FROCK
HOOCH
KNOCK
MOOCH
POOCH
PROCT
SHOCK
SMOCK
STOCK

••O•C
AZOIC
BRONC
STOIC

•••OC
ASSOC
HAVOC
MEDOC

OD•••
ODDER
ODDLY
ODEON
ODETS
ODEUM
ODIUM
ODONT
ODORS
ODYLE

O•D••
ODDER
ODDLY
OIDEA
OLDEN
OLDER
ORDER

O••D•
OUIDA
OUTDO
OXIDE

O•••D
OARED
OCTAD
OGLED
OILED
OOZED
OPTED
ORBED
OREAD
OUTED
OVOID
OWNED

•OD••
BODED
BODES
CODAS
CODED
CODES
CODEX
DODEC
DODGE
DODOS
GODLY
HODGE
IODIC
IODOL
KODAK
LODEN
LODES
LODGE
MODAL
MODEL
MODES
MODUS
NODAL
NODDY
NODES
NODUS
PODGY
PODIA
RODDY
RODEO
RODIN
SODAS
SODOM
TODAY
TODDS
TODDY
TODOS
VODKA
WODAN
WODEN
YODEL
YODHS

•O•D•
BONDS
BOYDS
COEDS
COLDS
COMDR
COMDT
CORDS
DOWDY
FOLDS
FOODS
FORDS
GOADS
GOLDS
GONDI
GOODS
GOODY
GOUDA
HOLDS
HOODS
HORDE
HOWDY
LOADS
LORDS
MOLDS
MOLDY
MONDE
MOODS
MOODY
NODDY
PONDS
POODS
ROADS
RODDY
RONDO
ROODS
ROWDY
SOLDI
SOLDO
TOADS
TOADY
TODDS
TODDY
VOIDS
WOADS
WOLDS
WOODS
WOODY
WORDS
WORDY

•O••D
BOARD
BODED
BONED
BOOED
BORED
BOUND
BOVID
BOWED
BOXED
CODED
COKED
CONED
CONTD
COOED
COPED
CORED
COULD
COVED
COWED
COXED
DOLED
DOMED
DOPED
DOSED
DOTED
DOZED
FOUND
FOXED
GONAD
GORED
GOURD
HOARD
HOLED
HOMED
HONED
HOPED
HOSED
HOUND
JOKED
JOYED
LOBED
LOOED
LOPED
LOVED
LOWED
MONAD
MOOED
MOPED
MOULD
MOVED
MOWED
NOMAD
NOSED
NOTED
OOZED
POIND
POKED
POLED
PORED
POSED
POUND
ROALD
ROBED
ROPED
ROSED
ROUND
ROVED
ROWED
SOLED
SOLID
SOUND
SOWED
TONED
TOPED
TOTED
TOWED
TOYED
VOTED
VOWED
WOALD
WOOED
WORLD
WOULD
WOUND
WOWED
YOKED
YOWED
ZONED
ZOOID

••OD•
ABODE
ANODE
CLODS
DIODE
EPODE
ERODE
FEODS
FOODS
GEODE
GOODS
GOODY
HOODS
MOODS
MOODY
PLODS
POODS
PRODS
QUODS
RHODA
RODS
SPODE
WOODS
WOODY

••O•D
ALOUD
AROID
AVOID
BLOND
BLOOD
BOOED
BROAD
BROOD
CHORD
CLOUD
COOED
CROWD
FIORD
FJORD
FLOOD
FLOYD
FROND
GEOID
HYOID
KHOND
LLOYD
LOOED
MOOED
MYOID
NJORD
OVOID
PLOID

5

PROUD
PYOID
SCOLD
SLOYD
SNOOD
STOOD
SWORD
WOOED
ZOOID

•••OD

BIPOD
BLOOD
BROOD
EPHOD
FLOOD
HEROD
SCROD
SNOOD
STOOD
SYNOD

O•E••

OBESE
OBEYS
OCEAN
ODEON
ODETS
ODEUM
OGEES
OLEIC
OLEIN
OMEGA
OMENS
OMERS
ONEIR
ONERY
OPENS
OPERA
OREAD
OVENS
OVERT
OWENS
OXEYE
OYERS

O••E•

OAKEN
OARED
OASES
OATEN
OATES
OAVES
OBOES
OCHER
OCREA
OCTET
ODDER
OFFER
OFTEN
OGEES
OGLED
OGLER
OGLES
OGRES
OIDEA
OILED
OILER
OKIES
OLDEN
OLDER
OMBER
ONSET
OOZED
OOZES
OPTED
ORBED
ORDER
ORIEL
ORLES
ORMER
OSIER
OSLER
OSTEO
OTHER
OTTER
OUSEL
OUTED
OUTER
OUZEL
OWLET
OWNED
OWNER

O•••E

OBESE
ODYLE
OGIVE
OLIVE
OLLIE
OMBRE
OPINE
ORATE
OSAGE
OUNCE
OUTRE
OVATE
OVINE
OVULE
OXEYE
OXIDE
OXIME
OZONE

•OE••

BOERS
COEDS
COELE
COELO
COENO
DOERS
DOEST
DOETH
FOEHN
GOERS
HOERS
JOELS
JOEYS
KOELS
LOESS
NOELS
POEMS
POESY
POETS

•O•E•

BODED
BODES
BOGEY
BOHEA
BOLES
BONED
BONER
BONES
BOOED
BORED
BORER
BORES
BOWED
BOWEL
BOWER
BOXED
BOXER
BOXES
CODED
CODES
CODEX
COKED
COKES
COLES
COMER
COMES
COMET
CONED
CONES
CONEY
COOED
COOEE
COOER
COOEY
COPED
COPES
CORED
CORER
CORES
COSEC
COTES
COVED
COVER
COVES
COVET
COVEY
COWED
COWER
COXED
COXES
COZEN
DODEC
DOGES
DOLED
DOLES
DOMED
DOMES
DONEE
DOPED
DOPES
DOPEY
DOSED
DOSER
DOSES
DOTED
DOTER
DOTES
DOVER
DOVES
DOWEL
DOWER
DOYEN
DOZED
DOZEN
DOZES
FORES
FOVEA
FOXED
FOXES
FOYER
GOLEM
GONER
GOOEY
GORED
GORES
HOLED
HOLES
HOLEY
HOMED
HOMEO
HOMER
HOMES
HOMEY
HONED
HONES
HONEY
HOOEY
HOPED
HOPEH
HOPES
HOREB
HOSEA
HOSED
HOSES
HOTEL
HOVEL
HOVER
JOKED
JOKER
JOKES
JOLES
JONES
JOYED
KOPEK
KOREA
LOBED
LOBES
LODEN
LODES
LOGES
LONER
LOOED
LOPED
LOPER
LOPES
LORES
LOSER
LOSES
LOVED
LOVER
LOVES
LOWED
LOWER
MODEL
MODES
MOKES
MOLES
MONET
MONEY
MOOED
MOPED
MOPER
MOPES
MOREL
MORES
MOSES
MOSEY
MOTEL
MOTES
MOUES
MOVED
MOVER
MOVES
MOWED
MOWER
NOBEL
NODES
NONES
NOSED
NOSES
NOSEY
NOTED
NOTER
NOTES
NOVEL
OOZED
OOZES
POGEY
POKED
POKER
POKES
POKEY
POLED
POLES
POMES
PONES
POPES
PORED
PORES
POSED
POSER
POSES
POWER
ROBED
ROBES
RODEO
ROGER
ROLES
ROMEO
ROPED
ROPES
ROSED
ROSES
ROUEN
ROUES
ROVED
ROVER
ROVES
ROWED
ROWEL
ROWEN
ROWER
SOBER
SOKES
SOLED
SOLES
SONES
SOREL
SORER
SORES
SOWED
SOWER
TOKEN
TOLES
TOMES
TONED
TONER
TONES
TOPED
TOPER
TOPES
TOTED
TOTEM
TOTER
TOTES
TOWED
TOWEL
TOWER
TOYED
TOYER
VOCES
VOLES
VOMER
VOTED
VOTER
VOTES
VOWED
VOWEL
VOWER
WODEN
WOKEN
WOMEN
WOOED
WOOER
WOVEN
WOWED
YODEL
YOGEE
YOKED
YOKEL
YOKES
YOWED
ZONED
ZONES

•O••E

BOCHE
BOGIE
BOGLE
BOISE
BOMBE
BONZE
BOONE
BOOZE
BORNE
BOULE
BOUSE
BOWIE
BOWSE
BOYLE
BOYNE
COBLE
COELE
COMAE
COMTE
CONGE
CONTE
COOEE
COPSE
CORSE
COUPE
COXAE
DOBIE
DODGE
DOGIE
DOLCE
DONEE
DONNE
DOUSE
DOWSE
DOYLE
FORCE
FORGE
FORTE
FOSSE
GOOSE
GORGE
GORSE
GOUGE
HODGE
HOOKE
HORAE
HORDE
HORSE
HOUSE
HOWIE
HOYLE
JORGE
JOSIE
JOSUE
JOULE
JOYCE
KOINE
KOPJE
LOCKE
LODGE
LOGUE
LOIRE
LOOSE
LOUPE
LOUSE
MOIRE
MONDE
MONTE
MOORE
MOOSE
MORAE
MORSE
MOUSE
MOVIE
MOXIE
NOBLE
NOISE
NONCE
NOOSE
NORSE
NOVAE
POISE
PONCE
POSSE
ROBLE
ROGUE
ROLFE
ROQUE
ROUGE
ROUSE
ROUTE
SOCLE
SOLVE
SOMME
SOUSE
TOGAE
TOGUE
TOILE
TOQUE
TORTE
VOGUE
VOICE
VOILE
WORSE
YOGEE
YOURE
YOUVE

••OE•

ALOES
BOOED
COOED
COOEE
COOER
COOEY
FLOES
FROES
GOOEY
HOOEY
LOOED

MOOED OBOES PROEM RHOEA SHOER SHOES SLOES WOOED WOOER

••O•E

ABODE ABOVE ADOBE ADORE ALONE AMOLE ANODE AROSE ATONE AWOKE AXONE AZOLE AZOTE BLOKE BOONE BOOZE BROKE BROME CHOKE CHOLE CHORE CHOSE CLONE CLOSE CLOVE COOEE CROCE CRONE CRORE CROZE DHOLE DIODE DIONE DROME DRONE DROVE ECOLE ELOPE EMOTE EPODE ERODE EROSE EVOKE FROZE GEODE GLOBE GLOVE GLOZE GNOME GOOSE GROPE GROVE HOOKE IRONE KRONE LOOSE MOORE MOOSE MYOPE NIOBE NOOSE OZONE PHOBE PHONE PHORE PROBE PRONE PROSE PROVE QUOTE RHONE SCONE SCOPE SCORE SHONE SHORE SHOTE SHOVE SLOPE SMOKE SMOTE SNORE SPODE SPOKE SPORE STOAE STOKE STOLE STOME STONE STOPE STORE STOVE STOWE SWORE TBONE THOLE THOSE TROPE TROVE ULOSE WHOLE WHORE WHOSE WROTE

•••OE

CANOE CHLOE DEFOE MEROE PEKOE TAHOE

OF•••

OFFAL OFFER OFTEN

O•F••

OFFAL OFFER

O••F•

OLAFS

•OF••

DOFFS LOFTS LOFTY SOFAS SOFIA SOFTA SOFTY TOFTS

•O•F•

COIFS CORFU DOFFS GOLFS GOOFS GOOFY HOOFS LOAFS LOOFS POUFS ROLFE ROLFS ROOFS SOLFA WOLFS WOOFS

•O••F

MOTIF

••OF•

ALOFT CROFT FEOFF GOOFS GOOFY HOOFS LOOFS PROFS ROOFS SCOFF WOOFS

••O•F

ADOLF ALOOF FEOFF KLOOF PROOF SCOFF SPOOF

•••OF

ALOOF KLOOF PROOF SPOOF

OG•••

OGEES OGIVE OGLED OGLER OGLES OGRES

O•G••

OLGAS ORGAN OUGHT

O••G•

OLIGO OLOGY OMEGA OSAGE OUTGO

O•••G

OKING ORANG OWING

•OG••

BOGAN BOGEY BOGGY BOGIE BOGLE BOGOR BOGUS COGON DOGES DOGGY DOGIE DOGMA FOGGY GOGOL HOGAN LOGES LOGIA LOGIC LOGOS LOGUE MOGUL NOGGS POGEY ROGER ROGUE SOGGY TOGAE TOGAS TOGUE VOGUE VOGUL YOGEE YOGHS YOGIC YOGIN YOGIS

•O•G•

BOGGY BONGO BONGS BOUGH COIGN CONGA CONGE CONGO CORGI COUGH DODGE DOGGY DOUGH DOUGS FOGGY FORGE FORGO GONGS GORGE GOUGE HODGE HONGS JORGE LODGE LONGI LONGS LOUGH NOGGS PODGY PORGY ROUGE ROUGH SOGGY SONGS SORGO SOUGH TONGA TONGS TOUGH VOLGA

•O••G

BOURG DOING GOING YOUNG

••OG•

CLOGS FLOGS FROGS OLOGY SLOGS SMOGS STOGY

••O•G

ALONG AMONG FLONG LAOAG PRONG THONG WRONG

•••OG

BEFOG

OH•••

OHMIC

O•H••

OCHER OCHRY OPHIO OTHER

O••H•

OATHS OMAHA OPAHS ORCHI ORTHO OUGHT

O•••H

OOMPH ORACH

•OH••

BOHEA BOHOL COHAN JOHNS MOHUR

•O•H•

BOCHE FOEHN GOTHA GOTHS LOCHS MOCHA MOTHS MOTHY NOAHS SOPHY TOPHI YODHS YOGHS

•O••H

BOOTH BOSCH BOTCH BOUGH COACH CONCH COUCH COUGH DOETH DOLPH DOUGH FORTH HOOCH HOPEH JONAH LOACH LOATH LOTAH LOUGH MONTH MOOCH MORPH MOUCH MOUTH NORAH NORTH NOTCH OOMPH POACH POOCH PORCH POUCH ROACH ROLPH ROTCH ROUGH SOUGH SOUTH TOOTH TORAH TOUCH TOUGH VOUCH WORTH YOUTH

••OH•

ABOHM ALOHA

••O•H

AZOTH BOOTH BROTH CLOTH ENOCH EPOCH FROSH FROTH HOOCH MOOCH POOCH QUOTH SLOSH SLOTH THOTH TOOTH TROPH TROTH

OI•••

OIDEA OILED OILER

O•I••

OBITS ODIUM OGIVE OKIES OKING OLIGO OLIOS OLIVE OMITS ONION ONIRO OPINE OPIUM ORIBI ORIEL ORION ORIYA OSIER OSITY OUIDA OUIJA OVINE OWING OXIDE OXIME

O••I•

OASIS OHMIC OLEIC OLEIN OLLIE ONEIR OPHIO OPSIA OPSIS OPTIC ORBIT ORCIN ORNIS ORPIN ORRIS OSMIC OSTIA OVOID OXLIP

O•••I

OBOLI OKAPI ORCHI ORIBI OVOLI

•OI••

BOILS BOISE COIFS COIGN COILS COINS DOILY DOING

5

DOITS
FOILS
FOISM
FOIST
GOING
HOICK
HOIST
JOINS
JOINT
JOIST
KOINE
LOINS
LOIRE
MOILS
MOIRA
MOIRE
MOIST
NOISE
NOISY
POILU
POIND
POINT
POISE
ROILS
ROILY
SOILS
TOILE
TOILS
VOICE
VOIDS
VOILA
VOILE

•O•I•

BOGIE
BONIN
BORIC
BORIS
BOVID
BOWIE
COBIA
COLIC
COLIN
COMIC
CONIC
CONIO
CORIA
DOBIE
DOGIE
DOMIC
DORIC
DORIS
EOLIC
EOSIN
FOLIA
FOLIC
FOLIO
GONIA
GONIO
GOYIM
HOWIE
IODIC
IONIA
IONIC
JOSIE
LOGIA
LOGIC
LORIS
LOUIS
MOTIF
MOVIE
MOXIE
NORIA
PODIA
POLIO
POSIT
ROBIN
RODIN
ROSIN
SOCIO
SOFIA
SOLID
SONIA
SONIC
SOZIN
TOKIO
TONIC
TONIS
TOPIC
TOPIS
TORIC
TORII
TOXIC
TOXIN
VOMIT
YOGIC
YOGIN
YOGIS
ZOOID
ZORIL

•O••I

COATI
COCCI
CORGI
DORSI
DOUAI
FORLI
GONDI
GORKI
HOURI
LONGI
NOCTI
SOLDI
SOMNI
TOPHI
TORII
TORSI
VOLTI
ZOMBI

••OI•

ALOIN
ALOIS
AROID
AVOID
AVOIR
AZOIC
BLOIS
BROIL
CHOIR
CROIX
DROIT
ELOIN
GEOID
GROIN
HYOID
MYOID
OVOID
PLOID
PYOID
QUOIN
QUOIT
SPOIL
STOIC
ZOOID

••O•I

CROCI
DHOTI
DUOMI
ICOSI
MAORI
NAOMI
OBOLI
OVOLI
SHOJI

•••OI

HANOI

O••J•

OUIJA

•OJ••

SOJAS

•O•J•

KOPJE

••OJ•

SHOJI

OK•••

OKAPI
OKAYS
OKIES
OKING
OKRAS

O•K••

OAKEN
OAKUM

O•••K

OZARK

•OK••

COKED
COKES
HOKAN
HOKUM
JOKED
JOKER
JOKES
MOKES
POKED
POKER
POKES
POKEY
SOKES
TOKAY
TOKEN
TOKIO
TOKYO
WOKEN
YOKED
YOKEL
YOKES

•O•K•

BOOKS
BOSKS
BOSKY
COCKS
COCKY
CONKS
COOKS
COOKY
CORKS
CORKY
DOCKS
FOLKS
FORKS
GOOKS
GORKI
GORKY
HOCKS
HONKS
HOOKE
HOOKS
HOOKY
JOCKO
KOOKS
KOOKY
LOCKE
LOCKS
LOOKS
MOCKS
MONKS
NOCKS
NOOKS
POCKS
POCKY
POLKA
PORKY
ROCKS
ROCKY
ROOKS
ROOKY
SOAKS
SOCKS
VODKA
WORKS
YOLKS
YOLKY

•O••K

HOICK
KODAK
KOPEK
TORSK

••OK•

AWOKE
BLOKE
BOOKS
BROKE
CHOKE
CHOKY
COOKS
COOKY
EVOKE
GOOKS
HOOKE
HOOKS
HOOKY
KOOKS
KOOKY
LOOKS
NOOKS
ROOKS
ROOKY
SMOKE
SMOKY
SPOKE
STOKE

••O•K

ACOCK
BLOCK
BROOK
CHOCK
CLOAK
CLOCK
CROAK
CROCK
CROOK
FLOCK
FROCK
KIOSK
KNOCK
SHOCK
SHOOK
SMOCK
SNOOK
SPOOK
STOCK
STOOK
STORK

•••OK

BROOK
CROOK
KAPOK
SHOOK
SNOOK
SPOOK
STOOK

OL•••

OLAFS
OLAVS
OLDEN
OLDER
OLEIC
OLEIN
OLGAS
OLIGO
OLIOS
OLIVE
OLLAS
OLLIE
OLOGY

O•L••

OGLED
OGLER
OGLES
OILED
OILER
OLLAS
OLLIE
ORLES
ORLON
ORLOP
OSLER
OWLET
OXLIP

O••L•

OBOLI
OCULO
ODDLY
ODYLE
OPALS
ORALS
OVALS
OVOLI
OVOLO
OVULE

O•••L

OCTYL
OFFAL
ORIEL
OUSEL
OUZEL

•OL••

BOLAR
BOLAS
BOLES
BOLLS
BOLOS
BOLTS
BOLUS
COLAS
COLDS
COLES
COLIC
COLIN
COLLY
COLON
COLOR
COLTS
COLZA
DOLCE
DOLED
DOLES
DOLLS
DOLLY
DOLOR
DOLPH
DOLTS
EOLIC
FOLDS
FOLIA
FOLIC
FOLIO
FOLKS
FOLLY
GOLDS
GOLEM
GOLFS
GOLLY
HOLDS
HOLED
HOLES
HOLEY
HOLLY
HOLMS
JOLES
JOLLY
JOLTS
JOLTY
KOLAS
LOLAS
LOLLS
LOLLY
MOLAL
MOLAR
MOLDS
MOLDY
MOLES
MOLLS
MOLLY
MOLTO
MOLTS
POLAR
POLED
POLES
POLIO
POLKA
POLLS
POLLY
POLYP
ROLES
ROLFE
ROLFS
ROLLO
ROLLS
ROLPH
SOLAN
SOLAR
SOLDI
SOLDO
SOLED
SOLES
SOLFA
SOLID
SOLON
SOLOS
SOLUS
SOLVE
TOLAN
TOLAS
TOLES
TOLLS
TOLYL
VOLAR
VOLES
VOLGA
VOLTA
VOLTI
VOLTS
VOLVA
WOLDS
WOLFS
YOLKS
YOLKY

•O•L•

BOGLE
BOILS
BOLLS
BOULE
BOWLS
BOYLE
COALS
COBLE
COELE
COELO
COILS
COLLY
COOLS
COULD
COWLS
COYLY
DOALL
DOBLA
DOILY
DOLLS
DOLLY
DOOLY
DOYLE
DOYLY
FOALS
FOILS
FOLLY
FOOLS
FORLI
FOULS
FOWLS
GOALS
GODLY
GOLLY
HOLLY
HOTLY
HOWLS
HOYLE
JOELS

JOLLY
JOULE
JOWLS
KOALA
KOELS
LOLLS
LOLLY
LOWLY
MOILS
MOLLS
MOLLY
MOULD
MOULT
NOBLE
NOBLY
NOELS
POILU
POLLS
POLLY
POOLS
POULT
ROALD
ROBLE
ROILS
ROILY
ROLLO
ROLLS
SOCLE
SOILS
SOULS
TOILE
TOILS
TOLLS
TOOLS
VOILA
VOILE
WOALD
WOOLS
WOOLY
WORLD
WOULD
YOWLS

•O••L

BOHOL
BOWEL
COMAL
COPAL
CORAL
COXAL
DOALL
DOTAL
DOWEL
FOCAL
GOGOL
GORAL
HORAL
HOTEL
HOVEL
IODOL
LOCAL
LOYAL
MODAL
MODEL
MOGUL
MOLAL
MORAL
MOREL
MOTEL
NOBEL
NODAL
NOPAL
NOVEL
ROWEL
ROYAL
SOREL
SOTOL
TOBOL
TOLYL
TONAL
TOTAL
TOWEL
VOCAL
VOGUL
VOWEL
YODEL
YOKEL
ZONAL
ZORIL

••OL•

ADOLF
AMOLE
ATOLL
AZOLE
CHOLE
COOLS
DHOLE
DOOLY
DROLL
ECOLE
ENOLS
FOOLS
GAOLS
IDOLS
KNOLL
OBOLI
OVOLI
OVOLO
PAOLO
POOLS
SCOLD
SMOLT
STOLE
THOLE
TOOLS
TROLL
UBOLT
VIOLA
VIOLS
WHOLE
WOOLS
WOOLY

••O•L

AFOUL
ATOLL
BROIL
CEORL
DROLL
DROOL
GHOUL
GROWL
KNOLL
PROWL
RAOUL
SCOWL
SEOUL
SHOAL
SHORL
SKOAL
SPOIL
SPOOL
STOOL
TROLL
WHORL

•••OL

ALDOL
ALGOL
ARGOL
BIKOL
BOHOL
CAROL
CIBOL
DROOL
EXTOL
GOGOL
IODOL
KAROL
LYSOL
PAROL
SALOL
SHEOL
SOTOL
SPOOL
STOOL
THIOL
TOBOL
TRIOL
TYROL
XYLOL

OM•••

OMAHA
OMASA
OMBER
OMBRE
OMBRO
OMEGA
OMENS
OMERS
OMITS

O•M••

OHMIC
OOMPH
ORMER
OSMAN
OSMIC

O••M•

OXIME

O•••M

OAKUM
ODEUM
ODIUM
OPIUM

•OM••

BOMBE
BOMBS
COMAE
COMAL
COMAS
COMBO
COMBS
COMDR
COMDT
COMER
COMES
COMET
COMIC
COMMA
COMPO
COMTE
DOMED
DOMES
DOMIC
HOMED
HOMEO
HOMER
HOMES
HOMEY
MOMUS
NOMAD
NOMAS
OOMPH
POMES
ROMAN
ROMEO
ROMPS
SOMAT
SOMME
SOMNI
TOMAN
TOMAS
TOMBS
TOMES
TOMMY
VOMER
VOMIT
WOMAN
WOMBS
WOMBY
WOMEN
ZOMBI

•O•M•

BOOMS
COMMA
COOMB
CORMS
COSMO
DOGMA
DOOMS
DORMS
DORMY
FOAMS
FOAMY
FORMS
HOLMS
LOAMS
LOAMY
LOOMS
NORMA
NORMS
POEMS
ROAMS
ROOMS
ROOMY
SOMME
TOMMY
WORMS
WORMY
ZOOMS

•O••M

BOSOM
FOISM
FORUM
GOLEM
GOYIM
HOKUM
JORAM
JORUM
SODOM
TOTEM

••OM•

ABOMA
ABOMB
AROMA
ATOMS
BOOMS
BROME
BROMO
COOMB
DOOMS
DROME
DUOMI
DUOMO
GNOME
GNOMY
HBOMB
LOOMS
MYOMA
NAOMI
PROMS
RHOMB
ROOMS
ROOMY
STOMA
STOME
STOMP
STOMY
ZOOMS

••O•M

ABOHM
BLOOM
BROOM
GLOOM
GROOM
PROEM
STORM

•••OM

AXIOM
BESOM
BLOOM
BOSOM
BROOM
BUXOM
CAROM
CELOM
CHROM
ENTOM
EPSOM
GLOOM
GROOM
IDIOM
SODOM
VENOM

ON•••

ONEIR
ONERY
ONION
ONIRO
ONSET

O•N••

ORNIS
OUNCE
OWNED
OWNER

O••N•

ODONT
OKING
OMENS
OPENS
OPINE
ORANG
OVENS
OVINE
OWENS
OWING
OZONE

O•••N

OAKEN
OATEN
OCEAN
ODEON
OFTEN
OLDEN
OLEIN
ONION
ORCIN
ORGAN
ORION
ORLON
ORPIN
OSCAN
OSMAN

•ON••

BONDS
BONED
BONER
BONES
BONGO
BONGS
BONIN
BONNY
BONUS
BONZE
CONCH
CONED
CONES
CONEY
CONGA
CONGE
CONGO
CONIC
CONIO
CONKS
CONNY
CONTD
CONTE
CONTO
CONTR
CONUS
DONAR
DONAS
DONEE
DONNA
DONNE
DONOR
DONTS
FONTS
GONAD
GONDI
GONER
GONGS
GONIA
GONIO
HONAN
HONED
HONES
HONEY
HONGS
HONKS
HONOR
IONIA
IONIC
JONAH
JONAS
JONES
JONNY
KONYA
LONER
LONGI
LONGS
MONAD
MONAS
MONDE
MONET
MONEY
MONKS
MONTE
MONTH
MONTY
NONAS
NONCE
NONES
PONCE
PONDS
PONES
RONDO
RONNY
SONAR
SONES
SONGS
SONIA
SONIC
SONNY
SONYA
TONAL
TONED
TONER
TONES
TONGA
TONGS
TONIC
TONIS
TONUS
TONYS
ZONAL
ZONED
ZONES

•O•N•

BONNY
BOONE
BOONS
BORNE
BORNU
BOUND
BOYNE
COENO
COINS
CONNY
COONS
CORNS
CORNU
CORNY
COUNT
DOING
DONNA
DONNE
DOWNS
DOWNY
FOUND
FOUNT
GOING
GOONS
GOWNS

HORNS
HORNY
HOUND
JOANS
JOHNS
JOINS
JOINT
JONNY
KOINE
LOANS
LOINS
LOONS
LOONY
LORNA
MOANS
MOONS
MOONY
MORNA
MORNS
MOUNT
NOONS
NORNS
NOUNS
POIND
POINT
POONS
PORNO
POUND
ROANS
RONNY
ROUND
SOMNI
SONNY
SOUND
TOWNS
WOUND
YOUNG
ZOONS

•O••N

BOGAN
BONIN
BORON
BOSUN
BOURN
COGON
COHAN
COIGN
COLIN
COLON
COZEN
DOORN
DOYEN
DOZEN
EOSIN
FOEHN
HOGAN
HOKAN
HONAN
JOTUN
KORAN
KORUN
LODEN
LORAN
MORON
MOSAN
MOURN
ROBIN
RODIN
ROMAN
ROSIN
ROUEN
ROWAN
ROWEN
SOLAN
SOLON
SOZIN
TOKEN
TOLAN
TOMAN
TOXIN
TOYON
WODAN
WODEN
WOKEN
WOMAN
WOMEN
WOTAN
WOVEN
YOGIN

••ON•

AEONS
AGONY
ALONE
ALONG
AMONG
ATONE
ATONY
AXONE
AXONS
AZONS
BLOND
BOONE
BOONS
BRONC
BRONX
CIONS
CLONE
CLONS
COONS
CRONE
CRONY
DIONE
DRONE
EBONS
EBONY
FIONA
FLONG
FROND
FRONT
GOONS
ICONO
ICONS
IKONS
ILONA
IRONE
IRONS
IRONY
KHOND
KRONA
KRONE
LEONA
LEONS
LIONS
LOONS
LOONY
LYONS
MOONS
MOONY
MUONS
NOONS
ODONT
OZONE
PEONS
PEONY
PHONE
PHONO
PHONY
PIONS
POONS
PRONE
PRONG
RHONE
SCONE
SHONE
STONE
STONY
TBONE
THONG
TRONA
WRONG
ZOONS

••O•N

ACORN
ADORN
ALOIN
BLOWN
BROWN
CLOWN
CROON
CROWN
DOORN
DROWN
ELOIN
FLOWN
FROWN
GROAN
GROIN
GROWN
KNOWN
QUOIN
SCORN
SHORN
SHOWN
SPOON
SWOON
SWORN
THORN

•••ON

AARON
AKRON
ALTON
AMMON
ANCON
ANION
ANTON
APRON
ARGON
ARION
ARSON
ASTON
ATION
AVION
BACON
BARON
BATON
BETON
BISON
BORON
BYRON
CAJON
CANON
CAPON
CHRON
CLEON
COGON
COLON
CREON
CROON
DAMON
DEMON
DEVON
DIJON
ELTON
FANON
FELON
FREON
GABON
GIPON
GYRON
HERON
HURON
HYSON
INION
ITION
IXION
JASON
JUPON
LEMON
LUZON
MACON
MASON
MELON
MESON
MORON
MYRON
NITON
NIXON
NYLON
ODEON
ONION
ORION
ORLON
PAEON
PELON
PERON
PINON
PITON
PUTON
PYLON
RADON
RAYON
RUNON
SALON
SAXON
SCION
SETON
SIDON
SIMON
SOLON
SPOON
SWOON
TALON
TENON
TETON
TOYON
UNION
WAGON
XENON
YAPON
YUKON
YUPON
ZIRON

OO•••

OOMPH
OOZED
OOZES

O•O••

OBOES
OBOLI
ODONT
ODORS
OLOGY
OVOID
OVOLI
OVOLO
OZONE

O••O•

ODEON
OLIOS
ONION
ORION
ORLON
ORLOP
OTTOS
OXBOW

O•••O

OCULO
OLIGO
OMBRO
ONIRO
OPHIO
ORTHO
OSTEO
OUTDO
OUTGO
OVOLO

•OO••

BOOBS
BOOBY
BOOED
BOOKS
BOOMS
BOONE
BOONS
BOORS
BOOST
BOOTH
BOOTS
BOOTY
BOOZE
BOOZY
COOED
COOEE
COOER
COOEY
COOKS
COOKY
COOLS
COOMB
COONS
COOPS
COOPT
COOTS
DOOLY
DOOMS
DOORN
DOORS
FOODS
FOOLS
FOOTS
FOOTY
GOODS
GOODY
GOOEY
GOOFS
GOOFY
GOOKS
GOONS
GOOSE
GOOSY
HOOCH
HOODS
HOOEY
HOOFS
HOOKE
HOOKS
HOOKY
HOOPS
HOOTS
KOOKS
KOOKY
LOOBY
LOOED
LOOFS
LOOKS
LOOMS
LOONS
LOONY
LOOPS
LOOSE
LOOTS
MOOCH
MOODS
MOODY
MOOED
MOONS
MOONY
MOORE
MOORS
MOOSE
NOOKS
NOONS
NOOSE
POOCH
POODS
POOLS
POONS
POOPO
POOPS
ROODS
ROOFS
ROOKS
ROOKY
ROOMS
ROOMY
ROOST
ROOTS
ROOTY
SOOTS
SOOTY
TOOLS
TOOTH
TOOTS
WOODS
WOODY
WOOED
WOOER
WOOFS
WOOLS
WOOLY
WOOZY
ZOOID
ZOOMS
ZOONS

•O•O•

BOGOR
BOHOL
BOLOS
BORON
BOSOM
BOZOS
COCOA
COCOS
COGON
COLON
COLOR
COROT
DODOS
DOLOR
DONOR
GOBOS
GOGOL
HOBOS
HONOR
IODOL
KOTOS
LOBOS
LOCOS
LOGOS
LOTOS
MORON
MOROS
MOTOR
POYOU
ROBOT
ROTOR
SODOM
SOLON
SOLOS
SOPOR
SOTOL
TOBOL
TODOS
TOYON
TOYOS
YOYOS

•O••O

BONGO
COELO
COENO
COMBO
COMPO
CONGO
CONIO
CONTO
COPRO
COSMO
COSTO
DORSO
FOLIO
FORGO
GONIO
HOMEO
JOCKO
LOTTO
MOLTO
MORRO
MOSSO
MOTTO
POLIO
POOPO
PORNO
POTTO
RODEO
ROLLO
ROMEO
RONDO
SOCIO
SOLDO
SORGO

TOKIO
TOKYO
TORSO

••OO•
AFOOT
ALOOF
BLOOD
BLOOM
BROOD
BROOK
BROOM
BROOS
CROOK
CROON
DROOL
DROOP
FLOOD
FLOOR
GLOOM
GROOM
KLOOF
PROOF
SCOOP
SCOOT
SHOOK
SHOOS
SHOOT
SLOOP
SNOOD
SNOOK
SNOOP
SNOOT
SPOOF
SPOOK
SPOOL
SPOON
SPOOR
STOOD
STOOK
STOOL
STOOP
SWOON
SWOOP
TROOP
WHOOP

••O•O
ACOUO
BROMO
CHORO
DUOMO
ICONO
KYOTO
OVOLO
PAOLO
PHONO
PHOTO
POOPO
PROTO
PROVO
SCOTO
SPORO
WHOSO

•••OO
BABOO
IGLOO
KAZOO
TABOO
WAHOO
YAHOO

OP•••
OPAHS
OPALS
OPENS
OPERA
OPHIO
OPINE
OPIUM
OPSIA
OPSIS
OPTED
OPTIC

O•P••
ORPIN

O••P•
OKAPI
OOMPH

O•••P
ORLOP
OXLIP

•OP••
COPAL
COPED
COPES
COPRA
COPRO
COPSE
COPTS
DOPED
DOPES
DOPEY
HOPED
HOPEH
HOPES
KOPEK
KOPJE
LOPED
LOPER
LOPES
LOPPY
MOPED
MOPER
MOPES
NOPAL
NOPAR
POPES
POPPY
ROPED
ROPES
SOPHY
SOPOR
SOPPY

TOPAZ
TOPED
TOPER
TOPES
TOPHI
TOPIC
TOPIS
TOPSY

•O•P•
COMPO
COOPS
COOPT
CORPS
COUPE
COUPS
COYPU
DOLPH
HOOPS
LOOPS
LOPPY
LOUPE
LOUPS
MORPH
OOMPH
POOPO
POOPS
POPPY
ROLPH
ROMPS
ROUPY
SOAPS
SOAPY
SOPPY
SOUPS
SOUPY

•O••P
DOVAP
POLYP

••OP•
ADOPT
CHOPS
CLOPS
COOPS
COOPT
CROPS
DROPS
DROPT
ELOPE
FLOPS
GROPE
HOOPS
KNOPS
LOOPS
MYOPE
MYOPY
PLOPS
POOPO
POOPS
PROPS
SCOPE
SCOPS

SCOPY
SHOPS
SLOPE
SLOPS
STOPE
STOPS
STOPT
TROPE
TROPH
WHOPS

••O•P
CROUP
DROOP
GROUP
KNOSP
SCOOP
SLOOP
SNOOP
STOMP
STOOP
STOUP
SWOOP
THORP
TROOP
WHOOP

•••OP
AESOP
BEBOP
DROOP
ESTOP
FSTOP
GALOP
ORLOP
SCOOP
SLOOP
SNOOP
STOOP
STROP
SWOOP
TROOP
WHOOP

•OQ••
ROQUE
TOQUE

OR•••
ORACH
ORALS
ORANG
ORATE
ORBED
ORBIT
ORCHI
ORCIN
ORCUS
ORDER
OREAD
ORGAN
ORIBI
ORIEL
ORION

ORIYA
ORLES
ORLON
ORLOP
ORMER
ORNIS
ORPIN
ORRIS
ORTHO

O•R••
OARED
OCREA
OGRES
OKRAS
ORRIS

O••R•
OCHRY
ODORS
OMBRE
OMBRO
OMERS
ONERY
ONIRO
OPERA
OUTRE
OVARY
OVERT
OYERS
OZARK

O•••R
OCCUR
OCHER
ODDER
OFFER
OGLER
OILER
OLDER
OMBER
ONEIR
ORDER
ORMER
OSCAR
OSIER
OSLER
OTHER
OTTER
OUTER
OWNER

•OR••
AORTA
BORAX
BORED
BORER
BORES
BORIC
BORIS
BORNE
BORNU
BORON
BORTS

BORTY
BORTZ
CORAL
CORAS
CORDS
CORED
CORER
CORES
CORFU
CORGI
CORIA
CORKS
CORKY
CORMS
CORNS
CORNU
CORNY
COROT
CORPS
CORSE
DORAS
DORIC
DORIS
DORMS
DORMY
DORRS
DORSA
DORSI
DORSO
DORUS
FORAY
FORBS
FORCE
FORDS
FORES
FORGE
FORGO
FORKS
FORLI
FORMS
FORTE
FORTH
FORTS
FORTY
FORUM
GORAL
GORED
GORES
GORGE
GORKI
GORKY
GORSE
GORSY
HORAE
HORAL
HORAS
HORDE
HOREB
HORNS
HORNY
HORSE
HORST
HORSY
HORUS

JORAM
JORGE
JORUM
KORAN
KOREA
KORUN
LORAN
LORCA
LORDS
LORES
LORIS
LORNA
LORRY
MORAE
MORAL
MORAS
MORAY
MOREL
MORES
MORNA
MORNS
MORON
MOROS
MORPH
MORRO
MORSE
MORTS
MORTY
NORAH
NORAS
NORIA
NORMA
NORMS
NORNS
NORSE
NORTH
PORCH
PORED
PORES
PORGY
PORKY
PORNO
PORTS
SORAS
SORBS
SOREL
SORER
SORES
SORGO
SORRY
SORTS
SORUS
TORAH
TORIC
TORII
TORSI
TORSK
TORSO
TORTE
TORTS
TORUS
WORDS
WORDY
WORKS

WORLD
WORMS
WORMY
WORRY
WORSE
WORST
WORTH
WORTS
ZORIL

•O•R•
BOARD
BOARS
BOERS
BOORS
BOURG
BOURN
COBRA
COPRA
COPRO
COURT
COWRY
DOBRA
DOERS
DOORN
DOORS
DORRS
DOURA
DOWRY
FOURS
GOERS
GOURD
HOARD
HOARY
HOERS
HOURI
HOURS
LOIRE
LORRY
LOURS
MOIRA
MOIRE
MOORE
MOORS
MORRO
MOURN
POURS
ROARS
SOARS
SORRY
SOURS
TOURS
WORRY
YOURE
YOURS

•O••R
BOGOR
BOLAR
BONER
BORER
BOWER
BOXER
BOYAR

COLOR
COMDR
COMER
CONTR
COOER
CORER
COVER
COWER
DOLOR
DONAR
DONOR
DOSER
DOTER
DOVER
DOWER
FOYER
GONER
HOMER
HONOR
HOVER
JOKER
LOBAR
LONER
LOPER
LOSER
LOVER
LOWER
MOHUR
MOLAR
MOPER
MOTOR
MOVER
MOWER
NOPAR
NOTER
POKER
POLAR
POSER
POWER
ROGER
ROTOR
ROVER
ROWER
SOBER
SOLAR
SONAR
SOPOR
SORER
SOWAR
SOWER
TONER
TOPER
TOTER
TOWER
TOYER
VOLAR
VOMER
VOTER
VOWER
WOOER

••OR•
ABORT
ACORN
ADORE
ADORN
AGORA
APORT
ATORY
BOORS
CEORL
CHORD
CHORE
CHORO
CRORE
DOORN
DOORS
EMORY
FIORD
FJORD
FLORA
GLORY
IVORY
LEORA
MAORI
MOORE
MOORS
NJORD
ODORS
PHORE
SCORE
SCORN
SHORE
SHORL
SHORN
SHORT
SNORE
SNORT
SPORE
SPORO
SPORT
STORE
STORK
STORM
STORY
SWORD
SWORE
SWORN
THORN
THORP
WHORE
WHORL
WHORT

••O•R
AMOUR
AVOIR
CHOIR
COOER
FLOOR
FLOUR
HHOUR
SCOUR
SHOER
SPOOR
WOOER

•••OR
ABHOR
ACTOR
ALGOR
ARBOR
ARDOR
ARMOR
ASTOR
BOGOR
CHLOR
COLOR
CRUOR
DECOR
DOLOR
DONOR
EPHOR
ERROR
FAVOR
FEDOR
FETOR
FLOOR
FLUOR
FUROR
HONOR
HUMOR
ICHOR
JUROR
LABOR
LUXOR
MAJOR
MANOR
MAYOR
MINOR
MOTOR
PRIOR
RAZOR
RIGOR
ROTOR
RUMOR
SAPOR
SAVOR
SENOR
SOPOR
SPOOR
SUDOR
TABOR
TENOR
TUDOR
TUMOR
TUTOR
VALOR
VAPOR
VIGOR
VISOR
VIZOR

OS•••
OSAGE
OSCAN
OSCAR
OSIER
OSITY
OSLER
OSMAN
OSMIC
OSTEO
OSTIA

O•S••
OASES
OASIS
ONSET
OPSIA
OPSIS
OUSEL
OUSTS

O••S•
OBESE
OMASA

O•••S
OASES
OASIS
OATES
OATHS
OAVES
OBEYS
OBITS
OBOES
ODETS
ODORS
OGEES
OGLES
OGRES
OKAYS
OKIES
OKRAS
OLAFS
OLAVS
OLGAS
OLIOS
OLLAS
OMENS
OMERS
OMITS
OOZES
OPAHS
OPALS
OPENS
OPSIS
ORALS
ORCUS
ORLES
ORNIS
ORRIS
OTTOS
OUSTS
OVALS
OVENS
OWENS
OYERS

•OS••
BOSCH
BOSKS
BOSKY
BOSOM
BOSSY
BOSUN
COSEC
COSMO
COSTA
COSTO
COSTS
DOSED
DOSER
DOSES
EOSIN
FOSSA
FOSSE
HOSEA
HOSED
HOSES
HOSTS
JOSIE
JOSUA
JOSUE
LOSER
LOSES
MOSAN
MOSES
MOSEY
MOSSO
MOSSY
NOSED
NOSES
NOSEY
POSED
POSER
POSES
POSIT
POSSE
POSTS
ROSAS
ROSED
ROSES
ROSIN

•O•S•
BOAST
BOISE
BOOST
BOSSY
BOUSE
BOUSY
BOWSE
COAST
COPSE
CORSE
DOEST
DORSA
DORSI
DORSO
DOUSE
DOWSE
FOISM
FOIST
FOSSA
FOSSE
GOOSE
GOOSY
GORSE
GORSY
HOIST
HORSE
HORST
HORSY
HOUSE
JOIST
JOUST
LOESS
LOOSE
LOUSE
LOUSY
MOIST
MOOSE
MORSE
MOSSO
MOSSY
MOUSE
MOUSY
NOISE
NOISY
NOOSE
NORSE
POESY
POISE
POSSE
POTSY
ROAST
ROOST
ROUSE
ROUST
SOUSA
SOUSE
TOAST
TOPSY
TORSI
TORSK
TORSO
WORSE
WORST

•O••S
BOARS
BOATS
BODES
BOERS
BOGUS
BOILS
BOLAS
BOLES
BOLLS
BOLOS
BOLTS
BOLUS
BOMBS
BONDS
BONES
BONGS
BONUS
BOOBS
BOOKS
BOOMS
BOONS
BOORS
BOOTS
BORES
BORIS
BORTS
BOSKS
BOTTS
BOUTS
BOWLS
BOXES
BOYDS
BOZOS
COALS
COATS
COBBS
COCAS
COCKS
COCOS
CODAS
CODES
COEDS
COIFS
COILS
COINS
COKES
COLAS
COLDS
COLES
COLTS
COMAS
COMBS
COMES
CONES
CONKS
CONUS
COOKS
COOLS
COONS
COOPS
COOTS
COPES
COPTS
CORAS
CORDS
CORES
CORKS
CORMS
CORNS
CORPS
COSTS
COTES
COUPS
COVES
COWLS
COXES
DOCKS
DODOS
DOERS
DOFFS
DOGES
DOITS
DOLES
DOLLS
DOLTS
DOMES
DONAS
DONTS
DOOMS
DOORS
DOPES
DORAS
DORIS
DORMS
DORRS
DORUS
DOSES
DOTES
DOUGS
DOVES
DOWNS
DOZES
FOALS
FOAMS
FOCUS
FOILS
FOLDS
FOLKS
FONTS
FOODS
FOOLS
FOOTS
FORBS
FORDS
FORES
FORKS
FORMS
FORTS
FOULS
FOURS
FOWLS
FOXES
GOADS
GOALS
GOATS
GOBOS
GOBYS
GOERS
GOLDS
GOLFS
GONGS
GOODS
GOOFS
GOOKS
GOONS
GORES
GOTHS
GOVTS
GOWNS
HOBBS
HOBOS
HOCKS
HOCUS
HOERS
HOLDS
HOLES
HOLMS
HOMES
HONES

5

HONGS HONKS HOODS HOOFS HOOKS HOOPS HOOTS HOPES HORAS HORNS HORUS HOSES HOSTS HOURS HOWLS IOTAS JOANS JOELS JOEYS JOHNS JOINS JOKES JOLES JOLTS JONAS JONES JOWLS KOELS KOLAS KOOKS KOTOS LOADS LOAFS LOAMS LOANS LOBES LOBOS LOCHS LOCKS LOCOS LOCUS LODES LOESS LOFTS LOGES LOGOS LOINS LOLAS LOLLS LONGS LOOFS LOOKS LOOMS LOONS LOOPS LOOTS LOPES LORDS LORES LORIS LOSES LOTOS LOTUS LOUIS

LOUPS LOURS LOUTS LOVES MOANS MOATS MOCKS MODES MODUS MOILS MOKES MOLDS MOLES MOLLS MOLTS MOMUS MONAS MONKS MOODS MOONS MOORS MOPES MORAS MORES MORNS MOROS MORTS MOSES MOTES MOTHS MOUES MOVES MOXAS NOAHS NOCKS NODES NODUS NOELS NOGGS NOMAS NONAS NONES NOOKS NOONS NORAS NORMS NORNS NOSES NOTES NOUNS NOVAS OOZES POCKS POEMS POETS POKES POLES POLLS POMES PONDS PONES POODS POOLS POONS

POOPS POPES PORES PORTS POSES POSTS POUFS POURS POUTS POWYS ROADS ROAMS ROANS ROARS ROBES ROCKS ROILS ROLES ROLFS ROLLS ROMPS ROODS ROOFS ROOKS ROOMS ROOTS ROPES ROSAS ROSES ROTAS ROUES ROUTS ROVES SOAKS SOAPS SOARS SOCKS SODAS SOFAS SOILS SOJAS SOKES SOLES SOLOS SOLUS SONES SONGS SOOTS SORAS SORBS SORES SORTS SORUS SOULS SOUPS SOURS SOYAS TOADS TOBYS TODDS TODOS TOFTS TOGAS TOILS

TOLAS TOLES TOLLS TOMAS TOMBS TOMES TONES TONGS TONIS TONUS TONYS TOOLS TOOTS TOPES TOPIS TORTS TORUS TOTES TOURS TOUTS TOWNS TOYOS VOCES VOIDS VOLES VOLTS VOTES WOADS WOLDS WOLFS WOMBS WOODS WOOFS WOOLS WORDS WORKS WORMS WORTS YODHS YOGHS YOGIS YOKES YOLKS YOURS YOWLS YOYOS ZONES ZOOMS ZOONS

••OS•

AROSE BOOST CHOSE CLOSE CROSS DROSS EROSE FLOSS FROSH FROST GHOST GLOSS GLOST GOOSE GOOSY GROSS GROSZ ICOSI KIOSK KNOSP LOOSE MOOSE NOOSE PROSE PROSY ROOST SLOSH STOSS THOSE ULOSE WHOSE WHOSO

••O•S

AEONS ALOES ALOIS ATOMS AVOWS AXONS AZONS BLOBS BLOCS BLOIS BLOTS BLOWS BOOBS BOOKS BOOMS BOONS BOORS BOOTS BROOS BROWS BUOYS CHOPS CHOWS CIONS CLODS CLOGS CLONS CLOPS CLOTS CLOYS COOKS COOLS COONS COOPS COOTS CROPS CROSS CROWS DHOWS DOOMS DOORS DROPS DROSS EBONS ENOLS FEODS FLOCS FLOES FLOGS FLOPS FLOSS FLOWS FOODS FOOLS FOOTS FROES FROGS FROWS GAOLS GLOBS GLOSS GLOWS GOODS GOOFS GOOKS GOONS GROSS GROTS GROWS HOODS HOOFS HOOKS HOOPS HOOTS ICONS IDOLS IKONS IRONS KNOBS KNOPS KNOTS KNOWS KOOKS LEONS LIONS LOOFS LOOKS LOOMS LOONS LOOPS LOOTS LYONS MEOWS MOODS MOONS MOORS MUONS NOOKS NOONS OBOES ODORS PEONS PHOTS PIONS PIOUS PLODS PLOPS PLOTS PLOWS PLOYS POODS POOLS POONS POOPS PROAS PRODS PROFS PROMS PROPS PROWS PSOAS QUODS RIOTS ROODS ROOFS ROOKS ROOMS ROOTS RYOTS SCOPS SCOTS SCOWS SHOES SHOOS SHOPS SHOTS SHOWS SLOBS SLOES SLOGS SLOPS SLOTS SLOWS SMOGS SNOBS SNOTS SNOWS SOOTS SPOTS STOAS STOPS STOSS STOWS TOOLS TOOTS TROAS TROTS ULOUS VIOLS WHOPS WOODS WOOFS WOOLS ZOOMS ZOONS

•••OS

ADIOS AFROS AGIOS AINOS ALDOS ALTOS AMBOS ARGOS ATHOS AUTOS BOLOS BOZOS BROOS CEROS CHAOS CHIOS CLIOS COCOS DELOS DEMOS DIDOS DODOS DUROS ETHOS FANOS GIROS GOBOS GYROS HALOS HOBOS HUGOS HYPOS JANOS JATOS KAYOS KILOS KOTOS KUDOS LAGOS LENOS LOBOS LOCOS LOGOS LOTOS MEMOS MINOS MOROS NEROS OLIOS OTTOS PECOS PEPOS PESOS SAGOS SAMOS SEGOS SHOOS SILOS SOLOS TALOS TAROS TIROS TODOS TOYOS TRIOS TYPOS TYROS UMBOS

WINOS
YOYOS
ZEROS

OT•••
OTHER
OTTER
OTTOS

O•T••
OATEN
OATES
OATHS
OCTAD
OCTET
OCTYL
OFTEN
OPTED
OPTIC
ORTHO
OSTEO
OSTIA
OTTER
OTTOS
OUTDO
OUTED
OUTER
OUTGO
OUTRE

O••T•
OBITS
ODETS
OMITS
ORATE
OSITY
OUSTS
OVATE

O•••T
OCTET
ODONT
ONSET
ORBIT
OUGHT
OVERT
OWLET

•OT••
BOTCH
BOTTS
COTES
COTTA
DOTAL
DOTED
DOTER
DOTES
DOTTY
GOTHA
GOTHS
HOTEL
HOTLY
IOTAS
JOTUN
KOTOS
LOTAH
LOTOS
LOTTA
LOTTO
LOTTY
LOTUS
MOTEL
MOTES
MOTHS
MOTHY
MOTIF
MOTOR
MOTTO
NOTCH
NOTED
NOTER
NOTES
POTSY
POTTO
POTTY
ROTAS
ROTCH
ROTOR
SOTOL
TOTAL
TOTED
TOTEM
TOTER
TOTES
VOTED
VOTER
VOTES
WOTAN

•O•T•
AORTA
BOATS
BOLTS
BOOTH
BOOTS
BOOTY
BORTS
BORTY
BORTZ
BOTTS
BOUTS
COATI
COATS
COLTS
COMTE
CONTD
CONTE
CONTO
CONTR
COOTS
COPTS
COSTA
COSTO
COSTS
COTTA
DOETH
DOITS
DOLTS
DONTS
DOTTY
FONTS
FOOTS
FOOTY
FORTE
FORTH
FORTS
FORTY
GOATS
GOUTY
GOVTS
HOOTS
HOSTS
JOLTS
JOLTY
LOATH
LOFTS
LOFTY
LOOTS
LOTTA
LOTTO
LOTTY
LOUTS
MOATS
MOLTO
MOLTS
MONTE
MONTH
MONTY
MORTS
MORTY
MOTTO
MOUTH
NOCTI
NORTH
POETS
PORTS
POSTS
POTTO
POTTY
POUTS
ROOTS
ROOTY
ROUTE
ROUTS
SOFTA
SOFTY
SOOTS
SOOTY
SORTS
SOUTH
TOFTS
TOOTH
TOOTS
TORTE
TORTS
TOUTS
VOLTA
VOLTI
VOLTS
WORTH
WORTS
YOUTH

•O••T
BOAST
BOOST
COAST
COMDT
COMET
COOPT
COROT
COUNT
COURT
COVET
DOEST
DOUBT
FOIST
FOUNT
HOIST
HORST
JOINT
JOIST
JOUST
MOIST
MONET
MOULT
MOUNT
POINT
POSIT
POULT
ROAST
ROBOT
ROOST
ROUST
SOMAT
TOAST
VOMIT
WORST

••OT•
AZOTE
AZOTH
BIOTA
BLOTS
BOOTH
BOOTS
BOOTY
BROTH
CLOTH
CLOTS
COOTS
DHOTI
EMOTE
FOOTS
FOOTY
FROTH
GROTS
HOOTS
KNOTS
KYOTO
LOOTS
PHOTO
PHOTS
PLOTS
PROTO
QUOTA
QUOTE
QUOTH
RIOTS
ROOTS
ROOTY
RYOTS
SCOTO
SCOTS
SCOTT
SHOTE
SHOTS
SLOTH
SLOTS
SMOTE
SNOTS
SOOTS
SOOTY
SPOTS
THOTH
TOOTH
TOOTS
TROTH
TROTS
WROTE
ZLOTY

••O•T
ABORT
ABOUT
ADOPT
AFOOT
ALOFT
APORT
BLOAT
BOOST
CLOUT
COOPT
CROAT
CROFT
DROIT
DROPT
EBOAT
FLOAT
FLOUT
FRONT
FROST
GHOST
GLOAT
GLOST
GROAT
GROUT
KNOUT
ODONT
PROCT
QUOIT
ROOST
SCOOT
SCOTT
SCOUT
SHOAT
SHOOT
SHORT
SHOUT
SMOLT
SNOOT
SNORT
SNOUT
SPORT
SPOUT
STOAT
STOPT
STOUT
TROUT
UBOAT
UBOLT
WHORT

•••OT
ABBOT
AFOOT
ALLOT
ARGOT
ASCOT
BEGOT
BESOT
BIGOT
CABOT
COROT
DEPOT
DIVOT
ELIOT
ERGOT
FAGOT
GAVOT
GEMOT
GIGOT
HELOT
IDIOT
INGOT
JABOT
MAGOT
PICOT
PILOT
PIVOT
ROBOT
SABOT
SCOOT
SHOOT
SNOOT
TAROT

OU•••
OUGHT
OUIDA
OUIJA
OUNCE
OUSEL
OUSTS
OUTDO
OUTED
OUTER
OUTGO
OUTRE
OUZEL

O•U••
OCULO
OVULE

O••U•
OAKUM
OCCUR
ODEUM
ODIUM
OPIUM
ORCUS

•OU••
BOUGH
BOULE
BOUND
BOURG
BOURN
BOUSE
BOUSY
BOUTS
COUCH
COUGH
COULD
COUNT
COUPE
COUPS
COURT
DOUAI
DOUAY
DOUBT
DOUGH
DOUGS
DOURA
DOUSE
FOULS
FOUND
FOUNT
FOURS
GOUDA
GOUGE
GOURD
GOUTY
HOUND
HOURI
HOURS
HOUSE
JOULE
JOUST
LOUGH
LOUIS
LOUPE
LOUPS
LOURS
LOUSE
LOUSY
LOUTS
MOUCH
MOUES
MOULD
MOULT
MOUNT
MOURN
MOUSE
MOUSY
MOUTH
NOUNS
POUCH
POUFS
POULT
POUND
POURS
POUTS
ROUEN
ROUES
ROUGE
ROUGH
ROUND
ROUPY
ROUSE
ROUST
ROUTE
ROUTS
SOUGH
SOULS
SOUND
SOUPS
SOUPY
SOURS
SOUSA
SOUSE
SOUTH
TOUCH
TOUGH
TOURS
TOUTS
VOUCH
WOULD
WOUND
YOUNG
YOURE
YOURS
YOUTH
YOUVE

•O•U•
BOGUS
BOLUS
BONUS
BOSUN
CONUS
DORUS
FOCUS
FORUM
HOCUS
HOKUM
HORUS
JORUM
JOSUA
JOSUE
JOTUN
KORUN
LOCUS
LOGUE
LOTUS
MODUS
MOGUL
MOHUR
MOMUS
NODUS
ROGUE
ROQUE

SOLUS
SORUS
TOGUE
TONUS
TOQUE
TORUS
VOGUE
VOGUL

•O••U
BORNU
CORFU
CORNU
COYPU
POILU
POYOU

••OU•
ABOUT
ACOUO
AFOUL
ALOUD
AMOUR
CLOUD
CLOUT
CROUP
FLOUR
FLOUT
GHOUL
GROUP
GROUT
HHOUR
KNOUT
PIOUS
PROUD
RAOUL
SCOUR
SCOUT
SEOUL
SHOUT
SIOUX
SNOUT
SPOUT
STOUP
STOUT
TROUT
ULOUS

•••OU
ANJOU
BAYOU
BIJOU
POYOU
SAJOU

OV•••
OVALS
OVARY
OVATE
OVENS
OVERT
OVINE
OVOID
OVOLI
OVOLO
OVULE

O•V••
OAVES

O••V•
OGIVE
OLAVS
OLIVE

•OV••
BOVID
COVED
COVER
COVES
COVET
COVEY
DOVAP
DOVER
DOVES
FOVEA
GOVTS
HOVEL
HOVER
LOVED
LOVER
LOVES
MOVED
MOVER
MOVES
MOVIE
NOVAE
NOVAS
NOVEL
ROVED
ROVER
ROVES
WOVEN

•O•V•
SOLVE
VOLVA
YOUVE

••OV•
ABOVE
CLOVE
DROVE
GLOVE
GROVE
PROVE
PROVO
SHOVE
STOVE
TROVE

OW•••
OWENS
OWING
OWLET
OWNED
OWNER

O•••W
OXBOW

•OW••
BOWED
BOWEL
BOWER
BOWIE
BOWLS
BOWSE
COWED
COWER
COWLS
COWRY
DOWDY
DOWEL
DOWER
DOWNS
DOWNY
DOWRY
DOWSE
FOWLS
GOWNS
HOWDY
HOWIE
HOWLS
JOWLS
LOWED
LOWER
LOWLY
MOWED
MOWER
NOWAY
POWER
POWYS
ROWAN
ROWDY
ROWED
ROWEL
ROWEN
ROWER
SOWAR
SOWED
SOWER
TOWED
TOWEL
TOWER
TOWNS
VOWED
VOWEL
VOWER
WOWED
YOWED
YOWLS

••OW•
AVOWS
BLOWN
BLOWS
BLOWY
BROWN
BROWS
CHOWS
CLOWN
CROWD
CROWN
CROWS
DHOWS
DROWN
FLOWN
FLOWS
FROWN
FROWS
GLOWS
GROWL
GROWN
GROWS
KIOWA
KNOWN
KNOWS
MEOWS
PLOWS
PROWL
PROWS
SCOWL
SCOWS
SHOWN
SHOWS
SHOWY
SLOWS
SNOWS
SNOWY
STOWE
STOWS

•••OW
AGLOW
ALLOW
ARROW
BELOW
ELBOW
EMBOW
ENDOW
INDOW
OXBOW
SEROW
THROW
UPBOW
WIDOW

OX•••
OXBOW
OXEYE
OXIDE
OXIME
OXLIP

•OX••
BOXED
BOXER
BOXES
COXAE
COXAL
COXED
COXES
FOXED
FOXES
MOXAS
MOXIE
TOXIC
TOXIN

•O••X
BORAX
CODEX

••OX•
DEOXY
EPOXY
PROXY

••O•X
BRONX
CROIX
SIOUX

•••OX
PHLOX
XEROX

OY•••
OYERS

O•Y••
ODYLE

O••Y•
OBEYS
OCTYL
OKAYS
ORIYA
OXEYE

O•••Y
OCHRY
ODDLY
OLOGY
ONERY
OSITY
OVARY

•OY••
BOYAR
BOYDS
BOYLE
BOYNE
COYLY
COYPU
DOYEN
DOYLE
DOYLY
FOYER
GOYIM
HOYLE
JOYCE
JOYED
LOYAL
POYOU
ROYAL
SOYAS
TOYED
TOYER
TOYON
TOYOS
YOYOS

•O•Y•
GOBYS
JOEYS
KONYA
POLYP
POWYS
SONYA
TOBYS
TOKYO
TOLYL
TONYS

•O••Y
BOBBY
BOGEY
BOGGY
BONNY
BOOBY
BOOTY
BOOZY
BORTY
BOSKY
BOSSY
BOUSY
COCKY
COLLY
CONEY
CONNY
COOEY
COOKY
CORKY
CORNY
COVEY
COWRY
COYLY
DOBBY
DOGGY
DOILY
DOLLY
DOOLY
DOPEY
DORMY
DOTTY
DOUAY
DOWDY
DOWNY
DOWRY
DOYLY
FOAMY
FOGGY
FOLLY
FOOTY
FORAY
FORTY
GODLY
GOLLY
GOODY
GOOEY
GOOFY
GOOSY
GORKY
GORSY
GOUTY
HOARY
HOBBY
HOLEY
HOLLY
HOMEY
HONEY
HOOEY
HOOKY
HORNY
HORSY
HOTLY
HOWDY
JOLLY
JOLTY
JONNY
KOOKY
LOAMY
LOBBY
LOFTY
LOLLY
LOOBY
LOONY
LOPPY
LORRY
LOTTY
LOUSY
LOWLY
MOLDY
MOLLY
MONEY
MONTY
MOODY
MOONY
MORAY
MORTY
MOSEY
MOSSY
MOTHY
MOUSY
NOBBY
NOBLY
NODDY
NOISY
NOSEY
NOWAY
POCKY
PODGY
POESY
POGEY
POKEY
POLLY
POPPY
PORGY
PORKY
POTSY
POTTY
ROCKY
RODDY
ROILY
RONNY
ROOKY
ROOMY
ROOTY
ROUPY
ROWDY
SOAPY
SOFTY
SOGGY
SONNY
SOOTY
SOPHY
SOPPY
SORRY
SOUPY
TOADY
TODAY
TODDY
TOKAY
TOMMY
TOPSY
WOMBY
WOODY
WOOLY
WOOZY
WORDY
WORMY
WORRY
YOLKY

••OY•
BUOYS
CLOYS
FLOYD
LLOYD
PLOYS
SLOYD

••O•Y
AGONY
ATONY
ATORY
BLOWY
BOOBY
BOOTY
BOOZY
CHOKY
COOEY
COOKY
CRONY
DEOXY
DOOLY
EBONY
EMORY
EPOXY
FOOTY
GLORY
GNOMY
GOODY
GOOEY
GOOFY
GOOSY
HOOEY
HOOKY
IRONY
IVORY

KOOKY
LOOBY
LOONY
MOODY
MOONY
MYOPY
OLOGY
PEONY
PHONY
PROSY
PROXY
ROOKY
ROOMY
ROOTY
SCOPY
SHOWY
SMOKY
SNOWY
SOOTY
STOGY
STOMY
STONY
STORY
WOODY
WOOLY
WOOZY
ZLOTY

•••OY
ALLOY
ANNOY
DECOY
ENJOY
ENVOY
LEROY
MCCOY
SAVOY
SEPOY

OZ•••
OZARK
OZONE

O•Z••
OOZED
OOZES
OUZEL

•OZ••
BOZOS
COZEN
DOZED
DOZEN
DOZES
OOZED
OOZES
SOZIN

•O•Z•
BONZE
BOOZE
BOOZY
COLZA
WOOZY

•O••Z
BORTZ
TOPAZ

••OZ•
BOOZE
BOOZY
CROZE
FROZE
GLOZE
WOOZY

••O•Z
GROSZ

PA•••
PABLO
PACAS
PACED
PACER
PACES
PACHY
PACKS
PACTS
PADDY
PADRE
PADUA
PAEAN
PAEDO
PAEON
PAGAN
PAGED
PAGES
PAILS
PAINE
PAINS
PAINT
PAIRS
PAISA
PAISE
PALAE
PALEA
PALED
PALEO
PALER
PALES
PALEY
PALLS
PALMI
PALMS
PALMY
PALPI
PALSY
PANDA
PANDY
PANEL
PANES
PANGS
PANIC
PANSY
PANTO
PANTS
PANTY
PAOLO
PAPAL
PAPAS
PAPAW
PAPEN
PAPER
PAPPI
PAPPY
PAPUA
PARAS
PARCH
PARDS
PARED
PAREN
PARER
PARES
PAREU
PARGO
PARIS
PARKA
PARKS
PAROL
PARRS
PARRY
PARSE
PARSI
PARTS
PARTY
PASCH
PASHA
PASSE
PASSY
PASTA
PASTE
PASTS
PASTY
PATCH
PATEN
PATER
PATES
PATHO
PATHS
PATHY
PATIO
PATRI
PATSY
PATTY
PAULA
PAULO
PAULS
PAUSE
PAVAN
PAVED
PAVER
PAVES
PAVIS
PAWED
PAWER
PAWLS
PAWNS
PAYED
PAYEE
PAYER

P•A••
PEACE
PEACH
PEAKS
PEALS
PEANS
PEARL
PEARS
PEARY
PEASE
PEATS
PEATY
PEAVY
PHAGE
PHAGO
PHAGY
PHANE
PHANY
PHASE
PHASY
PIANO
PIAVE
PLACE
PLACK
PLAGI
PLAID
PLAIN
PLAIT
PLANE
PLANI
PLANK
PLANO
PLANS
PLANT
PLASH
PLASM
PLAST
PLASY
PLATE
PLATO
PLATS
PLATY
PLAYA
PLAYS
PLAZA
POACH
PRAHU
PRAMS
PRANK
PRATE
PRAWN
PRAYS
PSALM

P••A•
PACAS
PAEAN
PAGAN
PALAE
PAPAL
PAPAS
PAPAW
PARAS
PAVAN
PECAN
PEDAL
PEKAN
PENAL
PETAL
PHIAL
PICAL
PICAS
PIKAS
PILAF
PILAR
PIMAN
PIMAS
PINAS
PIPAL
PITAS
PLEAD
PLEAS
PLEAT
POLAR
PRIAM
PROAS
PSHAW
PSOAS
PUMAS
PUNAS
PUPAE
PUSAN
PYRAN

P•••A
PADUA
PAISA
PALEA
PANDA
PAPUA
PARKA
PASHA
PASTA
PAULA
PELLA
PENNA
PENTA
PEPLA
PHILA
PHYLA
PIETA
PILEA
PINNA
PINTA
PIZZA
PLAYA
PLAZA
PLENA
PLICA
PODIA
POLKA
PRESA
PRIMA
PUCKA
PUKKA
PUNKA
PYDNA

•PA••
APACE
APART
EPACT
OPAHS
OPALS
SPACE
SPADE
SPAHI
SPAIN
SPAIT
SPALL
SPANG
SPANK
SPANS
SPARE
SPARK
SPARS
SPASM
SPATE
SPATS
SPAWN
SPAYS

•P•A•
APEAK
APIAN
APPAL
EPHAH
SPEAK
SPEAR
SPLAT
SPLAY
SPRAG
SPRAT
SPRAY

•P••A
APNEA
OPERA
OPSIA
SPICA

••PA•
APPAL
ARPAD
COPAL
HEPAT
JAPAN
LAPAR
NEPAL
NIPAS
NOPAL
NOPAR
PAPAL
PAPAS
PAPAW
PIPAL
PUPAE
REPAY
SEPAL
TOPAZ

••P•A
ALPHA
ASPCA
CAPUA
COPRA
HEPTA
HYPHA
KAPPA
LEPTA
PAPUA
PEPLA
SEPIA
SEPTA
SUPRA

•••PA
CULPA
KAPPA
SALPA
SCAPA
STUPA
TAMPA

P•B••
PABLO
PUBES
PUBIC
PUBIS

P••B•
PHEBE
PHOBE
PLEBE
PLEBS
PROBE

P•••B
PHLEB
PLUMB

•PB••
UPBOW

P•C••
PACAS
PACED
PACER
PACES
PACHY
PACKS
PACTS
PECAN
PECKS
PECOS
PICAL
PICAS
PICKS
PICOT
PICRO
PICTS
PICUL
POCKS
POCKY
PUCES
PUCKA
PUCKS

P••C•
PARCH
PASCH
PATCH
PEACE
PEACH
PENCE
PERCH
PERCY
PHYCO
PIECE
PINCH
PISCI
PITCH
PLACE
PLACK
PLICA
PLUCK
POACH
PONCE
POOCH
PORCH
POUCH
PRICE
PRICK
PROCT
PSYCH
PUNCH

P•••C
PANIC
PUBIC
PUDIC
PUNIC

•P•C•
APACE
EPACT
EPICS
EPOCH
SPACE
SPECK
SPECS
SPICA
SPICE
SPICY

•P••C
OPTIC

••PC•
ASPCA

••P•C
ASPIC
TOPIC

P•D••
PADDY
PADRE
PADUA

PEDAL
PEDES
PEDRO
PODGY
PODIA
PUDGY
PUDIC
PYDNA

P••D•
PADDY
PAEDO
PANDA
PANDY
PARDS
PENDS
PERDU
PLODS
PONDS
POODS
PRIDE
PRODS
PRUDE

P•••D
PACED
PAGED
PALED
PARED
PAVED
PAWED
PAYED
PIKED
PILED
PINED
PIPED
PLAID
PLEAD
PLIED
PLOID
POIND
POKED
POLED
PORED
POSED
POUND
PRIED
PROUD
PSEUD
PUKED
PULED
PYOID

•P•D•
EPODE
SPADE
SPODE
SPUDS

•P••D
APHID
EPHOD
OPTED
SPEED
SPEND
SPIED
UPEND
UPPED

••P•D
ARPAD
BIPED
BIPOD
COPED
CUPID
DOPED
DUPED
GAPED
HOPED
LEPID
LIPID
LOPED
MOPED
PIPED
RAPED
RAPID
ROPED
SAPID
TAPED
TEPID
TOPED
TYPED
UPPED
VAPID
WIPED

PE•••
PEACE
PEACH
PEAKS
PEALS
PEANS
PEARL
PEARS
PEARY
PEASE
PEATS
PEATY
PEAVY
PECAN
PECKS
PECOS
PEDAL
PEDES
PEDRO
PEEKS
PEELS
PEENS
PEEPS
PEERS
PEEVE
PEGGY
PEKAN
PEKIN
PEKOE
PELEE
PELFS
PELLA
PELLY
PELON
PELTS
PELVI
PENAL
PENCE
PENDS
PENGO
PENNA
PENNI
PENNY
PENTA
PEONS
PEONY
PEPIN
PEPLA
PEPOS
PEPPY
PEPYS
PERCH
PERCY
PERDU
PERES
PERIL
PERIS
PERKS
PERKY
PERON
PERRY
PERSE
PERTH
PESKY
PESOS
PESTS
PETAL
PETER
PETES
PETIT
PETRI
PETRO
PETTI
PETTO
PETTY
PEWEE
PEWIT

P•E••
PAEAN
PAEDO
PAEON
PEEKS
PEELS
PEENS
PEEPS
PEERS
PEEVE
PHEBE
PHENO
PIECE
PIERS
PIETA
PIETY
PIEZO
PLEAD
PLEAS
PLEAT
PLEBE
PLEBS
PLEGY
PLENA
PNEUM
POEMS
POESY
POETS
PREEN
PRESA
PRESS
PREST
PREXY
PREYS
PSEUD
PTERO
PYELO

P••E•
PACED
PACER
PACES
PAGED
PAGES
PALEA
PALED
PALEO
PALER
PALES
PALEY
PANEL
PANES
PAPEN
PAPER
PARED
PAREN
PARER
PARES
PAREU
PATEN
PATER
PATES
PAVED
PAVER
PAVES
PAWED
PAWER
PAYED
PAYEE
PAYER
PEDES
PELEE
PERES
PETER
PETES
PEWEE
PHLEB
PHREN
PIKED
PIKER
PIKES
PILEA
PILED
PILEI
PILES
PINED
PINEL
PINER
PINES
PINEY
PIPED
PIPER
PIPES
PIPET
PLIED
PLIER
PLIES
POGEY
POKED
POKER
POKES
POKEY
POLED
POLES
POMES
PONES
POPES
PORED
PORES
POSED
POSER
POSES
POWER
PREEN
PRIED
PRIER
PRIES
PROEM
PRYER
PUBES
PUCES
PUGET
PUKED
PUKES
PULED
PULER
PULES
PUREE
PURER
PYRES
PYREX
PYXES

P•••E
PADRE
PAINE
PAISE
PALAE
PARSE
PASSE
PASTE
PAUSE
PAYEE
PEACE
PEASE
PEEVE
PEKOE
PELEE
PENCE
PERSE
PEWEE
PHAGE
PHANE
PHASE
PHEBE
PHILE
PHOBE
PHONE
PHORE
PHYLE
PHYRE
PHYTE
PIAVE
PIECE
PIQUE
PIXIE
PLACE
PLANE
PLATE
PLEBE
PLUME
POISE
PONCE
POSSE
PRATE
PRICE
PRIDE
PRIME
PRIZE
PROBE
PRONE
PROSE
PROVE
PRUDE
PRUNE
PULSE
PUPAE
PUREE
PURGE
PURSE
PYXIE

•PE••
APEAK
APERY
EPEES
OPENS
OPERA
SPEAK
SPEAR
SPECK
SPECS
SPEED
SPELL
SPELT
SPEND
SPENT
SPERM
SPEWS
UPEND

•P•E•
APNEA
APPEL
APSES
EPEES
OPTED
SPEED
SPHEN
SPIED
SPIEL
SPIER
SPIES
SPLEN
SPREE
UPPED
UPPER
UPSET
YPRES

•P••E
APACE
APPLE
EPODE
OPINE
SPACE
SPADE
SPARE
SPATE
SPICE
SPIKE
SPILE
SPINE
SPIRE
SPITE
SPODE
SPOKE
SPORE
SPREE
SPRUE
SPUME

••PE•
APPEL
ARPEN
ASPEN
ASPER
BIPED
CAPEK
CAPER
CAPES
CAPET
COPED
COPES
CUPEL
DOPED
DOPES
DOPEY
DUPED
DUPER
DUPES
EXPEL
GAPED
GAPER
GAPES
HOPED
HOPEH
HOPES
HUPEH
HYPER
IMPEL
JAPES
KOPEK
LAPEL
LEPER
LOPED
LOPER
LOPES
MOPED
MOPER
MOPES
NAPES
PAPEN
PAPER
PIPED
PIPER
PIPES
PIPET
POPES
RAPED
RAPES
REPEL
RIPEN
RIPER
ROPED
ROPES
RUPEE
SUPER
SUPES
TAPED
TAPER
TAPES
TEPEE
TOPED
TOPER
TOPES
TYPED
TYPES
UNPEG
UPPED
UPPER
VIPER
WIPED
WIPER
WIPES
YIPES

••P•E
AMPLE
APPLE
COPSE
DUPLE
KOPJE
LAPSE
MAPLE
NAPPE
PUPAE
RAPHE
RUPEE

TEPEE

•••PE
AGAPE
CALPE
CHAPE
COUPE
CRAPE
CREPE
DRAPE
DRUPE
ELOPE
ETAPE
GASPE
GRAPE
GRIPE
GROPE
LOUPE
MYOPE
NAPPE
SCAPE
SCOPE
SHAPE
SLOPE
SNIPE
STIPE
STOPE
STUPE
SWIPE
TAUPE
TEMPE
TRIPE
TROPE

P•F••
PUFFS
PUFFY

P••F•
PELFS
POUFS
PROFS
PUFFS
PUFFY

P•••F
PILAF
PROOF

•P••F
SPOOF

P•G••
PAGAN
PAGED
PAGES
PEGGY
PIGGY
PIGMY
POGEY
PUGET
PYGMY

P••G•
PANGS
PARGO
PEGGY
PENGO
PHAGE
PHAGO
PHAGY
PIGGY
PINGO
PINGS
PLAGI
PLEGY
PLUGS
PODGY
PORGY
PRIGS
PUDGY
PUNGS
PURGE

P•••G
PRONG

•P••G
APING
SPANG
SPRAG
SPRIG

••P•G
UNPEG

PH•••
PHAGE
PHAGO
PHAGY
PHANE
PHANY
PHASE
PHASY
PHEBE
PHENO
PHIAL
PHILA
PHILE
PHILO
PHILS
PHILY
PHIPS
PHLEB
PHLOX
PHOBE
PHONE
PHONO
PHONY
PHORE
PHOTO
PHOTS
PHREN
PHYCO
PHYLA
PHYLE
PHYLL
PHYLO
PHYRE
PHYSI
PHYTE
PHYTO

P•H••
PSHAW

P••H•
PACHY
PASHA
PATHO
PATHS
PATHY
PITHS
PITHY
PRAHU
PUSHY

P•••H
PARCH
PASCH
PATCH
PEACH
PERCH
PERTH
PINCH
PITCH
PLASH
PLUSH
POACH
POOCH
PORCH
POUCH
PSYCH
PUNCH

•PH••
APHID
APHIS
EPHAH
EPHOD
EPHOR
OPHIO
SPHEN

•P•H•
OPAHS
SPAHI

•P••H
APISH
EPHAH
EPOCH

••PH•
ALPHA
ALPHY
AMPHI
AMPHR
HYPHA
KAPHS
NEPHO
NEPHR
RAPHE
SOPHY
TOPHI
USPHS
XIPHI

••P•H
DEPTH
HOPEH
HUPEH

•••PH
ALEPH
DOLPH
GLYPH
GRAPH
HUMPH
LYMPH
MORPH
NYMPH
OOMPH
RALPH
ROLPH
SCYPH
STAPH
SYLPH
TROPH

PI•••
PIANO
PIAVE
PICAL
PICAS
PICKS
PICOT
PICRO
PICTS
PICUL
PIECE
PIERS
PIETA
PIETY
PIEZO
PIGGY
PIGMY
PIKAS
PIKED
PIKER
PIKES
PILAF
PILAR
PILEA
PILED
PILEI
PILES
PILIS
PILLS
PILOT
PIMAN
PIMAS
PIMPS
PINAS
PINCH
PINED
PINEL
PINER
PINES
PINEY
PINGO
PINGS
PINKS
PINKY
PINNA
PINNI
PINON
PINTA
PINTO
PINTS
PINUP
PIONS
PIOUS
PIPAL
PIPED
PIPER
PIPES
PIPET
PIPIT
PIQUE
PISCI
PITAS
PITCH
PITHS
PITHY
PITON
PIVOT
PIXIE
PIZZA

P•I••
PAILS
PAINE
PAINS
PAINT
PAIRS
PAISA
PAISE
PHIAL
PHILA
PHILE
PHILO
PHILS
PHILY
PHIPS
PLICA
PLIED
PLIER
PLIES
PLINY
POILU
POIND
POINT
POISE
PRIAM
PRICE
PRICK
PRIDE
PRIED
PRIER
PRIES
PRIGS
PRIMA
PRIME
PRIMI
PRIMO
PRIMP
PRIMS
PRINK
PRINT
PRIOR
PRISM
PRIVY
PRIZE

P••I•
PANIC
PARIS
PATIO
PAVIS
PEKIN
PEPIN
PERIL
PERIS
PETIT
PEWIT
PILIS
PIPIT
PIXIE
PLAID
PLAIN
PLAIT
PLOID
PODIA
POLIO
POSIT
PUBIC
PUBIS
PUDIC
PUNIC
PUPIL
PURIM
PYOID
PYXIE
PYXIS

P•••I
PALMI
PALPI
PAPPI
PARSI
PATRI
PELVI
PENNI
PETRI
PETTI
PHYSI
PILEI
PINNI
PISCI
PLAGI
PLANI
PLURI
PLUVI
PRIMI

•PI••
APIAN
APING
APISH
EPICS
OPINE
OPIUM
SPICA
SPICE
SPICY
SPIED
SPIEL
SPIER
SPIES
SPIKE
SPIKY
SPILE
SPILL
SPILT
SPINE
SPINI
SPINS
SPINY
SPIRE
SPIRO
SPIRT
SPIRY
SPITE
SPITS
SPITZ

•P•I•
APHID
APHIS
APRIL
APSIS
OPHIO
OPSIA
OPSIS
OPTIC
SPAIN
SPAIT
SPLIT
SPOIL
SPRIG
SPRIT

•P••I
SPAHI
SPINI

••PI•
ASPIC
ASPIS
CUPID
KEPIS
LAPIN
LAPIS
LEPID
LIPID
ORPIN
PEPIN
PIPIT
PUPIL
RAPID
SAPID
SEPIA
TAPIR
TAPIS
TEPID
TOPIC
TOPIS
TUPIK
TUPIS
UNPIN
VAPID

••P•I
AMPHI
CAPRI
LIPPI
PAPPI
SEPTI
TOPHI
XIPHI

•••PI
CAMPI
CARPI
LIPPI
OKAPI
PALPI
PAPPI
SCAPI
TEMPI

••PJ•
KOPJE

P•K••
PEKAN
PEKIN
PEKOE
PIKAS
PIKED
PIKER
PIKES
POKED
POKER
POKES
POKEY
PUKED
PUKES
PUKKA

P••K•
PACKS
PARKA
PARKS
PEAKS
PECKS
PEEKS
PERKS
PERKY
PESKY

PICKS
PINKS
PINKY
POCKS
POCKY
POLKA
PORKY
PUCKA
PUCKS
PUKKA
PUNKA
PUNKS
PUNKY

P•••K
PLACK
PLANK
PLUCK
PLUNK
PRANK
PRICK
PRINK

•P•K•
SPIKE
SPIKY
SPOKE

•P••K
APEAK
SPANK
SPARK
SPEAK
SPECK
SPOOK
SPUNK

••P•K
CAPEK
KAPOK
KOPEK
TUPIK

PL•••
PLACE
PLACK
PLAGI
PLAID
PLAIN
PLAIT
PLANE
PLANI
PLANK
PLANO
PLANS
PLANT
PLASH
PLASM
PLAST
PLASY
PLATE
PLATO
PLATS
PLATY
PLAYA
PLAYS
PLAZA
PLEAD
PLEAS
PLEAT
PLEBE
PLEBS
PLEGY
PLENA
PLICA
PLIED
PLIER
PLIES
PLINY
PLODS
PLOID
PLOPS
PLOTS
PLOWS
PLOYS
PLUCK
PLUGS
PLUMB
PLUME
PLUMP
PLUMS
PLUMY
PLUNK
PLURI
PLUSH
PLUTO
PLUVI

P•L••
PALAE
PALEA
PALED
PALEO
PALER
PALES
PALEY
PALLS
PALMI
PALMS
PALMY
PALPI
PALSY
PELEE
PELFS
PELLA
PELLY
PELON
PELTS
PELVI
PHLEB
PHLOX
PILAF
PILAR
PILEA
PILED
PILEI
PILES
PILIS
PILLS
PILOT
POLAR
POLED
POLES
POLIO
POLKA
POLLS
POLLY
POLYP
PULED
PULER
PULES
PULLS
PULMO
PULPS
PULPY
PULSE
PYLON

P••L•
PABLO
PAILS
PALLS
PAOLO
PAULA
PAULO
PAULS
PAWLS
PEALS
PEELS
PELLA
PELLY
PEPLA
PHILA
PHILE
PHILO
PHILS
PHILY
PHYLA
PHYLE
PHYLL
PHYLO
PILLS
POILU
POLLS
POLLY
POOLS
POULT
PSALM
PULLS
PURLS
PYELO

P•••L
PANEL
PAPAL
PAROL
PEARL
PEDAL
PENAL
PERIL
PETAL
PHIAL
PHYLL
PICAL
PICUL
PINEL
PIPAL
PROWL
PUPIL

•PL••
SPLAT
SPLAY
SPLEN
SPLIT

•P•L•
APPLE
APPLY
APTLY
OPALS
SPALL
SPELL
SPELT
SPILE
SPILL
SPILT

•P••L
APPAL
APPEL
APRIL
SPALL
SPELL
SPIEL
SPILL
SPOIL
SPOOL

••PL•
AMPLE
AMPLY
APPLE
APPLY
DIPLO
DUPLE
HAPLO
HAPLY
IMPLY
MAPLE
PEPLA
REPLY

••P•L
AMPUL
APPAL
APPEL
COPAL
CUPEL
EXPEL
IMPEL
LAPEL
NEPAL
NOPAL
PAPAL
PIPAL
PUPIL
REPEL
SEPAL

P•M••
PIMAN
PIMAS
PIMPS
POMES
PUMAS
PUMPS

P••M•
PALMI
PALMS
PALMY
PIGMY
PLUMB
PLUME
PLUMP
PLUMS
PLUMY
POEMS
PRAMS
PRIMA
PRIME
PRIMI
PRIMO
PRIMP
PRIMS
PROMS
PULMO
PYGMY

P•••M
PLASM
PNEUM
PRIAM
PRISM
PROEM
PSALM
PURIM

•P•M•
SPUME
SPUMY

•P••M
EPSOM
OPIUM
SPASM
SPERM

PN•••
PNEUM

P•N••
PANDA
PANDY
PANEL
PANES
PANGS
PANIC
PANSY
PANTO
PANTS
PANTY
PENAL
PENCE
PENDS
PENGO
PENNA
PENNI
PENNY
PENTA
PINAS
PINCH
PINED
PINEL
PINER
PINES
PINEY
PINGO
PINGS
PINKS
PINKY
PINNA
PINNI
PINON
PINTA
PINTO
PINTS
PINUP
PONCE
PONDS
PONES
PUNAS
PUNCH
PUNGS
PUNIC
PUNKA
PUNKS
PUNKY
PUNTO
PUNTS
PUNTY

P••N•
PAINE
PAINS
PAINT
PAWNS
PEANS
PEENS
PENNA
PENNI
PENNY
PEONS
PEONY
PHANE
PHANY
PHENO
PHONE
PHONO
PHONY
PIANO
PINNA
PINNI
PIONS
PLANE
PLANI
PLANK
PLANO
PLANS
PLANT
PLENA
PLINY
PLUNK
POIND
POINT
POONS
PORNO
POUND
PRANK
PRINK
PRINT
PRONE
PRONG
PRUNE
PYDNA

P•••N
PAEAN
PAEON
PAGAN
PAPEN
PAREN
PATEN
PAVAN
PECAN
PEKAN
PEKIN
PELON
PEPIN
PERON
PHREN
PIMAN
PINON
PITON
PLAIN
PRAWN
PREEN
PUSAN
PUTON
PYLON
PYRAN

•PN••
APNEA

•P•N•
APING
OPENS
OPINE
SPANG
SPANK
SPANS
SPEND
SPENT
SPINE
SPINI
SPINS
SPINY
SPUNK
UPEND

•P••N
APIAN
APRON
SPAIN
SPAWN
SPHEN
SPLEN
SPOON
SPURN

••PN•
HYPNO

••P•N
ARPEN
ASPEN
CAPON
GIPON
JAPAN
JUPON
LAPIN
ORPIN
PAPEN
PEPIN
RIPEN
UNPIN
YAPON
YUPON

PO•••
POACH
POCKS
POCKY
PODGY
PODIA
POEMS
POESY
POETS
POGEY
POILU
POIND
POINT
POISE
POKED
POKER
POKES
POKEY
POLAR
POLED
POLES
POLIO
POLKA
POLLS
POLLY
POLYP
POMES
PONCE
PONDS
PONES
POOCH

POODS
POOLS
POONS
POOPO
POOPS
POPES
POPPY
PORCH
PORED
PORES
PORGY
PORKY
PORNO
PORTS
POSED
POSER
POSES
POSIT
POSSE
POSTS
POTSY
POTTO
POTTY
POUCH
POUFS
POULT
POUND
POURS
POUTS
POWER
POWYS
POYOU

P•O••

PAOLO
PEONS
PEONY
PHOBE
PHONE
PHONO
PHONY
PHORE
PHOTO
PHOTS
PIONS
PIOUS
PLODS
PLOID
PLOPS
PLOTS
PLOWS
PLOYS
POOCH
POODS
POOLS
POONS
POOPO
POOPS
PROAS
PROBE
PROCT
PRODS
PROEM
PROFS
PROMS
PRONE
PRONG
PROOF
PROPS
PROSE
PROSY
PROTO
PROUD
PROVE
PROVO
PROWL
PROWS
PROXY
PSOAS
PYOID

P••O•

PAEON
PAROL
PECOS
PEKOE
PELON
PEPOS
PERON
PESOS
PHLOX
PICOT
PILOT
PINON
PITON
PIVOT
POYOU
PRIOR
PROOF
PUTON
PYLON

P•••O

PABLO
PAEDO
PALEO
PANTO
PAOLO
PARGO
PATHO
PATIO
PAULO
PEDRO
PENGO
PETRO
PETTO
PHAGO
PHENO
PHILO
PHONO
PHOTO
PHYCO
PHYLO
PHYTO
PIANO
PICRO
PIEZO
PINGO
PINTO
PLANO
PLATO
PLUTO
POLIO
POOPO
PORNO
POTTO
PRIMO
PROTO
PROVO
PTERO
PULMO
PUNTO
PYELO

•PO••

APORT
EPOCH
EPODE
EPOXY
SPODE
SPOIL
SPOKE
SPOOF
SPOOK
SPOOL
SPOON
SPOOR
SPORE
SPORO
SPORT
SPOTS
SPOUT

•P•O•

APRON
EPHOD
EPHOR
EPSOM
SPOOF
SPOOK
SPOOL
SPOON
SPOOR
UPBOW

•P••O

OPHIO
SPIRO
SPORO

••PO•

BIPOD
CAPON
DEPOT
GIPON
HYPOS
JUPON
KAPOK
PEPOS
SAPOR
SEPOY
SOPOR
TYPOS
VAPOR
YAPON
YUPON

••P•O

COPRO
CUPRO
DIPLO
HAPLO
HIPPO
HYPNO
HYPSO
LEPTO
NEPHO
SAPRO
SEPTO

•••PO

CAMPO
CARPO
COMPO
HIPPO
POOPO
TEMPO

P•P••

PAPAL
PAPAS
PAPAW
PAPEN
PAPER
PAPPI
PAPPY
PAPUA
PEPIN
PEPLA
PEPOS
PEPPY
PEPYS
PIPAL
PIPED
PIPER
PIPES
PIPET
PIPIT
POPES
POPPY
PUPAE
PUPIL
PUPPY

P••P•

PALPI
PAPPI
PAPPY
PEEPS
PEPPY
PHIPS
PIMPS
PLOPS
POOPO
POOPS
POPPY
PROPS
PULPS
PULPY
PUMPS
PUPPY

P•••P

PINUP
PLUMP
POLYP
PRIMP
PUTUP

•PP••

APPAL
APPEL
APPLE
APPLY
UPPED
UPPER

••PP•

DIPPY
GAPPY
GUPPY
HAPPY
HIPPO
KAPPA
LAPPS
LIPPI
LIPPY
LOPPY
NAPPE
NAPPY
NIPPY
PAPPI
PAPPY
PEPPY
POPPY
PUPPY
SAPPY
SOPPY
TIPPY
ZIPPY

•••PP

KRUPP

P•Q••

PIQUE

PR•••

PRAHU
PRAMS
PRANK
PRATE
PRAWN
PRAYS
PREEN
PRESA
PRESS
PREST
PREXY
PREYS
PRIAM
PRICE
PRICK
PRIDE
PRIED
PRIER
PRIES
PRIGS
PRIMA
PRIME
PRIMI
PRIMO
PRIMP
PRIMS
PRINK
PRINT
PRIOR
PRISM
PRIVY
PRIZE
PROAS
PROBE
PROCT
PRODS
PROEM
PROFS
PROMS
PRONE
PRONG
PROOF
PROPS
PROSE
PROSY
PROTO
PROUD
PROVE
PROVO
PROWL
PROWS
PROXY
PRUDE
PRUNE
PRYER

P•R••

PARAS
PARCH
PARDS
PARED
PAREN
PARER
PARES
PAREU
PARGO
PARIS
PARKA
PARKS
PAROL
PARRS
PARRY
PARSE
PARSI
PARTS
PARTY
PERCH
PERCY
PERDU
PERES
PERIL
PERIS
PERKS
PERKY
PERON
PERRY
PERSE
PERTH
PHREN
PORCH
PORED
PORES
PORGY
PORKY
PORNO
PORTS
PUREE
PURER
PURGE
PURIM
PURLS
PURRS
PURSE
PURSY
PYRAN
PYRES
PYREX

P••R•

PADRE
PAIRS
PARRS
PARRY
PATRI
PEARL
PEARS
PEARY
PEDRO
PEERS
PERRY
PETRI
PETRO
PHORE
PHYRE
PICRO
PIERS
PLURI
POURS
PTERO
PURRS

P•••R

PACER
PALER
PAPER
PARER
PATER
PAVER
PAWER
PAYER
PETER
PIKER
PILAR
PINER
PIPER
PLIER
POKER
POLAR
POSER
POWER
PRIER
PRIOR
PRYER
PULER
PURER

•PR••

APRIL
APRON
SPRAG
SPRAT
SPRAY
SPREE
SPRIG
SPRIT
SPRUE
YPRES

•P•R•

APART
APERY
APORT
OPERA
SPARE
SPARK
SPARS
SPERM
SPIRE
SPIRO
SPIRT
SPIRY
SPORE
SPORO
SPORT
SPURN
SPURS
SPURT

•P••R

EPHOR
SPEAR
SPIER
SPOOR
UPPER

••PR•

CAPRI
COPRA
COPRO
CUPRO
SAPRO
SUPRA

••P•R
AMPHR
ASPER
CAPER
DUPER
GAPER
HYPER
LAPAR
LEPER
LOPER
MOPER
NEPHR
NOPAR
PAPER
PIPER
RIPER
SAPOR
SOPOR
SUPER
TAPER
TAPIR
TOPER
UPPER
VAPOR
VIPER
WIPER

PS•••
PSALM
PSEUD
PSHAW
PSOAS
PSYCH

P•S••
PASCH
PASHA
PASSE
PASSY
PASTA
PASTE
PASTS
PASTY
PESKY
PESOS
PESTS
PISCI
POSED
POSER
POSES
POSIT
POSSE
POSTS
PUSAN
PUSHY
PUSSY

P••S•
PAISA
PAISE
PALSY
PANSY
PARSE
PARSI
PASSE
PASSY
PATSY
PAUSE
PEASE
PERSE
PHASE
PHASY
PHYSI
PLASH
PLASM
PLAST
PLASY
PLUSH
POESY
POISE
POSSE
POTSY
PRESA
PRESS
PREST
PRISM
PROSE
PROSY
PULSE
PURSE
PURSY
PUSSY

P•••S
PACAS
PACES
PACKS
PACTS
PAGES
PAILS
PAINS
PAIRS
PALES
PALLS
PALMS
PANES
PANGS
PANTS
PAPAS
PARAS
PARDS
PARES
PARIS
PARKS
PARRS
PARTS
PASTS
PATES
PATHS
PAULS
PAVES
PAVIS
PAWLS
PAWNS
PEAKS
PEALS
PEANS
PEARS
PEATS
PECKS
PECOS
PEDES
PEEKS
PEELS
PEENS
PEEPS
PEERS
PELFS
PELTS
PENDS
PEONS
PEPOS
PEPYS
PERES
PERIS
PERKS
PESOS
PESTS
PETES
PHILS
PHIPS
PHOTS
PICAS
PICKS
PICTS
PIERS
PIKAS
PIKES
PILES
PILIS
PILLS
PIMAS
PIMPS
PINAS
PINES
PINGS
PINKS
PINTS
PIONS
PIOUS
PIPES
PITAS
PITHS
PLANS
PLATS
PLAYS
PLEAS
PLEBS
PLIES
PLODS
PLOPS
PLOTS
PLOWS
PLOYS
PLUGS
PLUMS
POCKS
POEMS
POETS
POKES
POLES
POLLS
POMES
PONDS
PONES
POODS
POOLS
POONS
POOPS
POPES
PORES
PORTS
POSES
POSTS
POUFS
POURS
POUTS
POWYS
PRAMS
PRAYS
PRESS
PREYS
PRIES
PRIGS
PRIMS
PROAS
PRODS
PROFS
PROMS
PROPS
PROWS
PSOAS
PUBES
PUBIS
PUCES
PUCKS
PUFFS
PUKES
PULES
PULLS
PULPS
PUMAS
PUMPS
PUNAS
PUNGS
PUNKS
PUNTS
PURLS
PURRS
PUTTS
PYRES
PYXES
PYXIS

•PS••
APSES
APSIS
EPSOM
OPSIA
OPSIS
UPSET

•P•S•
APISH
SPASM

•P••S
APHIS
APSES
APSIS
EPEES
EPICS
OPAHS
OPALS
OPENS
OPSIS
SPANS
SPARS
SPATS
SPAYS
SPECS
SPEWS
SPIES
SPINS
SPITS
SPOTS
SPUDS
SPURS
YPRES

••PS•
COPSE
GIPSY
GYPSY
HYPSO
LAPSE
LEPSY
TIPSY
TOPSY

••P•S
ASPIS
CAPES
COPES
COPTS
DOPES
DUPES
GAPES
HOPES
HYPOS
JAPES
KAPHS
KEPIS
LAPIS
LAPPS
LEPUS
LOPES
LUPUS
MOPES
NAPES
NIPAS
PAPAS
PEPOS
PEPYS
PIPES
POPES
RAPES
ROPES
SEPTS
SUPES
TAPES
TAPIS
TOPES
TOPIS
TUPIS
TYPES
TYPOS
USPHS
WIPES
YIPES

•••PS
BEEPS
BLIPS
BUMPS
BURPS
CAMPS
CARPS
CHAPS
CHIPS
CHOPS
CLAPS
CLIPS
CLOPS
COOPS
CORPS
COUPS
CRAPS
CROPS
CUSPS
DAMPS
DEEPS
DRIPS
DROPS
DUMPS
FLAPS
FLIPS
FLOPS
FRAPS
GAMPS
GASPS
GIMPS
GRIPS
GULPS
HARPS
HASPS
HEAPS
HELPS
HEMPS
HOOPS
HUMPS
JEEPS
JUMPS
KEEPS
KELPS
KNOPS
LAMPS
LAPPS
LEAPS
LIMPS
LISPS
LOOPS
LOUPS
LUMPS
MUMPS
NEAPS
PEEPS
PHIPS
PIMPS
PLOPS
POOPS
PROPS
PULPS
PUMPS
QUIPS
RAMPS
RASPS
REAPS
ROMPS
RUMPS
SCOPS
SCUPS
SEEPS
SHIPS
SHOPS
SIMPS
SKEPS
SKIPS
SLAPS
SLIPS
SLOPS
SNAPS
SNIPS
SOAPS
SOUPS
STEPS
STOPS
SUMPS
SWAPS
TAMPS
TARPS
TRAPS
TRIPS
VAMPS
WARPS
WASPS
WEEPS
WHAPS
WHIPS
WHOPS
WISPS
WRAPS
YAUPS
YAWPS
YELPS

PT•••
PTERO

P•T••
PATCH
PATEN
PATER
PATES
PATHO
PATHS
PATHY
PATIO
PATRI
PATSY
PATTY
PETAL
PETER
PETES
PETIT
PETRI
PETRO
PETTI
PETTO
PETTY
PITAS
PITCH
PITHS
PITHY
PITON
POTSY
POTTO
POTTY
PUTON
PUTTS
PUTTY
PUTUP

P••T•
PACTS
PANTO
PANTS
PANTY
PARTS
PARTY
PASTA
PASTE
PASTS
PASTY
PATTY
PEATS
PEATY
PELTS
PENTA
PERTH
PESTS
PETTI
PETTO
PETTY
PHOTO
PHOTS
PHYTE
PHYTO
PICTS
PIETA
PIETY
PINTA
PINTO
PINTS
PLATE
PLATO
PLATS
PLATY
PLOTS
PLUTO
POETS
PORTS

POSTS
POTTO
POTTY
POUTS
PRATE
PROTO
PUNTO
PUNTS
PUNTY
PUTTS
PUTTY

P•••T
PAINT
PETIT
PEWIT
PICOT
PILOT
PIPET
PIPIT
PIVOT
PLAIT
PLANT
PLAST
PLEAT
POINT
POSIT
POULT
PREST
PRINT
PROCT
PUGET

•PT••
APTLY
OPTED
OPTIC

•P•T•
SPATE
SPATS
SPITE
SPITS
SPITZ
SPOTS

•P••T
APART
APORT
EPACT
SPAIT
SPELT
SPENT
SPILT
SPIRT
SPLAT
SPLIT
SPORT
SPOUT
SPRAT
SPRIT
SPURT
UPSET

••PT•
COPTS
DEPTH
EMPTY
HEPTA
LEPTA
LEPTO
SEPTA
SEPTI
SEPTO
SEPTS

••P•T
CAPET
CAPUT
DEPOT
HEPAT
INPUT
KAPUT
PIPET
PIPIT

•••PT
ADAPT
ADEPT
ADOPT
CHAPT
COOPT
CREPT
CRYPT
DRIPT
DROPT
EGYPT
ERUPT
GRIPT
INAPT
INEPT
LEAPT
SLEPT
SLIPT
STOPT
SWEPT
TEMPT
UNAPT
WHIPT
WRAPT

PU•••
PUBES
PUBIC
PUBIS
PUCES
PUCKA
PUCKS
PUDGY
PUDIC
PUFFS
PUFFY
PUGET
PUKED
PUKES
PUKKA
PULED
PULER
PULES
PULLS
PULMO
PULPS
PULPY
PULSE
PUMAS
PUMPS
PUNAS
PUNCH
PUNGS
PUNIC
PUNKA
PUNKS
PUNKY
PUNTO
PUNTS
PUNTY
PUPAE
PUPIL
PUPPY
PUREE
PURER
PURGE
PURIM
PURLS
PURRS
PURSE
PURSY
PUSAN
PUSHY
PUSSY
PUTON
PUTTS
PUTTY
PUTUP

P•U••
PAULA
PAULO
PAULS
PAUSE
PLUCK
PLUGS
PLUMB
PLUME
PLUMP
PLUMS
PLUMY
PLUNK
PLURI
PLUSH
PLUTO
PLUVI
POUCH
POUFS
POULT
POUND
POURS
POUTS
PRUDE
PRUNE

P••U•
PADUA
PAPUA
PICUL
PINUP
PIOUS
PIQUE
PNEUM
PROUD
PSEUD
PUTUP

P•••U
PAREU
PERDU
POILU
POYOU
PRAHU

•PU••
SPUDS
SPUME
SPUMY
SPUNK
SPURN
SPURS
SPURT

•P•U•
OPIUM
SPOUT
SPRUE

••PU•
AMPUL
CAPUA
CAPUT
INPUT
KAPUT
LEPUS
LUPUS
PAPUA

•••PU
COYPU
QUIPU

P•V••
PAVAN
PAVED
PAVER
PAVES
PAVIS
PIVOT

P••V•
PEAVY
PEEVE
PELVI
PIAVE
PLUVI
PRIVY
PROVE
PROVO

P•W••
PAWED
PAWER
PAWLS
PAWNS
PEWEE
PEWIT
POWER
POWYS

P••W•
PLOWS
PRAWN
PROWL
PROWS

P•••W
PAPAW
PSHAW

•P•W•
SPAWN
SPEWS

•P••W
UPBOW

••P•W
PAPAW

P•X••
PIXIE
PYXES
PYXIE
PYXIS

P••X•
PREXY
PROXY

P•••X
PHLOX
PYREX

•P•X•
EPOXY

PY•••
PYDNA
PYELO
PYGMY
PYLON
PYOID
PYRAN
PYRES
PYREX
PYXES
PYXIE
PYXIS

P•Y••
PAYED
PAYEE
PAYER
PHYCO
PHYLA
PHYLE
PHYLL
PHYLO
PHYRE
PHYSI
PHYTE
PHYTO
POYOU
PRYER
PSYCH

P••Y•
PEPYS
PLAYA
PLAYS
PLOYS
POLYP
POWYS
PRAYS
PREYS

P•••Y
PACHY
PADDY
PALEY
PALMY
PALSY
PANDY
PANSY
PANTY
PAPPY
PARRY
PARTY
PASSY
PASTY
PATHY
PATSY
PATTY
PEARY
PEATY
PEAVY
PEGGY
PELLY
PENNY
PEONY
PEPPY
PERCY
PERKY
PERRY
PESKY
PETTY
PHAGY
PHANY
PHASY
PHILY
PHONY
PIETY
PIGGY
PIGMY
PINEY
PINKY
PITHY
PLASY
PLATY
PLEGY
PLINY
PLUMY
POCKY
PODGY
POESY
POGEY
POKEY
POLLY
POPPY
PORGY
PORKY
POTSY
POTTY
PREXY
PRIVY
PROSY
PROXY
PUDGY
PUFFY
PULPY
PUNKY
PUNTY
PUPPY
PURSY
PUSHY
PUSSY
PUTTY
PYGMY

•P•Y•
SPAYS

•P••Y
APERY
APPLY
APTLY
EPOXY
SPICY
SPIKY
SPINY
SPIRY
SPLAY
SPRAY
SPUMY

••PY•
PEPYS

••P•Y
ALPHY
AMPLY
APPLY
DIPPY
DOPEY
EMPTY
GAPPY
GIPSY
GUPPY
GYPSY
HAPLY
HAPPY
IMPLY
LEPSY
LIPPY
LOPPY
NAPPY
NIPPY
PAPPY
PEPPY
POPPY
PUPPY
REPAY
REPLY
SAPPY
SEPOY
SOPHY
SOPPY
TIPPY
TIPSY
TOPSY
ZIPPY

•••PY
BUMPY
CAMPY
DIPPY
DUMPY
GAPPY
GIMPY
GRAPY
GUPPY
HAPPY
HARPY
HEMPY
HUMPY
JUMPY
LIPPY
LOPPY
LUMPY
MYOPY
NAPPY
NIPPY
PAPPY
PEPPY
POPPY
PULPY
PUPPY
RASPY
ROUPY
SAPPY
SCOPY
SOAPY
SOPPY
SOUPY
TIPPY
WASPY
WEEPY
WISPY
ZIPPY

P•Z••
PIZZA

P••Z•
PIEZO

5

PIZZA
PLAZA
PRIZE

•P••Z
SPITZ

••P•Z
TOPAZ

QA•••
QATAR

Q•A••
QUACK
QUADS
QUAFF
QUAGS
QUAIL
QUAKE
QUAKY
QUALM
QUANT
QUARK
QUART
QUASH
QUASI
QUASS
QUAYS

Q••A•
QATAR
QUEAN

Q•••A
QUOTA

•QA••
AQABA

•Q•A•
AQUAE
AQUAS
EQUAL
SQUAB
SQUAD
SQUAT
SQUAW

•Q••A
AQABA

•Q•B•
AQABA

•Q••B
SQUAB
SQUIB

Q••C•
QUACK
QUICK

Q••D•
QUADS
QUIDS
QUODS

•Q••D
SQUAD
SQUID

Q•E••
QUEAN
QUEEN
QUEER
QUELL
QUERN
QUERY
QUEST
QUEUE

Q••E•
QUEEN
QUEER
QUIET

Q•••E
QUAKE
QUEUE
QUIRE
QUITE
QUOTE

•Q•E•
YQUEM

•Q••E
AQUAE

••Q•E
ESQUE
FIQUE
PIQUE
ROQUE
TOQUE
TUQUE

Q••F•
QUAFF

Q•••F
QUAFF

Q••G•
QUAGS

Q•••H
QUASH
QUOTH

Q•I••
QUICK
QUIDS
QUIET
QUILL
QUILT
QUINT
QUIPS
QUIPU
QUIRE
QUIRK
QUIRT
QUITE
QUITO
QUITS

Q••I•
QUAIL
QUOIN
QUOIT

Q•••I
QUASI

•Q•I•
EQUIP
SQUIB
SQUID

•••QI
IRAQI

Q••K•
QUAKE
QUAKY

Q•••K
QUACK
QUARK
QUICK
QUIRK

Q••L•
QUALM
QUELL
QUILL
QUILT

Q•••L
QUAIL
QUELL
QUILL

•Q••L
EQUAL

Q•••M
QUALM

•Q••M
YQUEM

Q••N•
QUANT
QUINT

Q•••N
QUEAN
QUEEN
QUERN
QUOIN

Q•O••
QUODS
QUOIN
QUOIT
QUOTA
QUOTE
QUOTH

Q•••O
QUITO

Q••P•
QUIPS
QUIPU

•Q••P
EQUIP

Q••R•
QUARK
QUART
QUERN
QUERY
QUIRE
QUIRK
QUIRT

Q•••R
QATAR
QUEER

Q••S•
QUASH
QUASI
QUASS
QUEST

Q•••S
QUADS
QUAGS
QUASS
QUAYS
QUIDS
QUIPS
QUITS
QUODS

•Q••S
AQUAS

Q•T••
QATAR

Q••T•
QUITE
QUITO
QUITS
QUOTA
QUOTE
QUOTH

Q•••T
QUANT
QUART
QUEST
QUIET
QUILT
QUINT
QUIRT
QUOIT

•Q••T
SQUAT

QU•••
QUACK
QUADS
QUAFF
QUAGS
QUAIL
QUAKE
QUAKY
QUALM
QUANT
QUARK
QUART
QUASH
QUASI
QUASS
QUAYS
QUEAN
QUEEN
QUEER
QUELL
QUERN
QUERY
QUEST
QUEUE
QUICK
QUIDS
QUIET
QUILL
QUILT
QUINT
QUIPS
QUIPU
QUIRE
QUIRK
QUIRT
QUITE
QUITO
QUITS
QUODS
QUOIN
QUOIT
QUOTA
QUOTE
QUOTH

Q••U•
QUEUE

Q•••U
QUIPU

•QU••
AQUAE
AQUAS
EQUAL
EQUIP
SQUAB
SQUAD
SQUAT
SQUAW
SQUIB
SQUID
YQUEM

••QU•
ESQUE
FIQUE
PIQUE
ROQUE
TOQUE
TUQUE

•Q••W
SQUAW

Q••Y•
QUAYS

Q•••Y
QUAKY
QUERY

RA•••
RABBI
RABIC
RABID
RACED
RACER
RACES
RACKS
RADAR
RADII
RADIO
RADIX
RADON
RAFTS
RAGED
RAGEE
RAGES
RAGGY
RAIDS
RAILS
RAINS
RAINY
RAISE
RAJAB
RAJAH
RAKED
RAKEE
RAKER
RAKES
RALES
RALLY
RALPH
RAMIE
RAMMY
RAMPS
RAMUS
RANCE
RANCH
RANDS
RANDY
RANEE
RANGE
RANGY
RANIS
RANKS
RANTS
RAOUL
RAPED
RAPES
RAPHE
RAPID
RARER
RASPS
RASPY
RATAL
RATCH
RATED
RATEL
RATER
RATES
RATIO
RATTY
RAVED
RAVEL
RAVEN
RAVER
RAVES
RAWER
RAWLY
RAYAH
RAYED
RAYON
RAZED
RAZEE
RAZES
RAZOR

R•A••
REACH
REACT
READS
READY
REALM
REALS
REAMS
REAPS
REARM
REARS
RHAGE
RHAGY
RIALS
RIANT
RIATA
ROACH
ROADS
ROALD
ROAMS
ROANS
ROARS
ROAST

R••A•
RADAR
RAJAB
RAJAH
RATAL
RAYAH
RECAP
REDAN
REGAL
REGAN
RELAX
RELAY
REMAN
RENAL
RENAN
REPAY
RERAN
RHEAS
RITAS
RIVAL
RIYAL
ROMAN
ROSAS
ROTAS
ROWAN
ROYAL
RUGAE
RURAL

R•••A
RECTA
REGMA
RETIA
RETTA
RHODA
RHOEA
RIATA
RRHEA
RUMBA

•RA••
ARABS
ARABY
BRACE
BRACT
BRADS
BRADY
BRAES
BRAGE
BRAGI
BRAGS
BRAHE
BRAID
BRAIL
BRAIN
BRAKE
BRAKY
BRAND
BRANS
BRANT

5

BRASH
BRASS
BRATS
BRAVA
BRAVE
BRAVO
BRAWL
BRAWN
BRAXY
BRAYS
BRAZA
BRAZE
CRAAL
CRABS
CRACK
CRACY
CRAFT
CRAGS
CRAIG
CRAKE
CRAMP
CRAMS
CRANE
CRANI
CRANK
CRAPE
CRAPS
CRASH
CRASS
CRATE
CRAVE
CRAWL
CRAWS
CRAZE
CRAZY
DRABS
DRACO
DRAFF
DRAFT
DRAGS
DRAIN
DRAKE
DRAMA
DRAMS
DRANK
DRAPE
DRAVA
DRAVE
DRAWL
DRAWN
DRAWS
DRAYS
ERASE
ERATO
FRAIL
FRAME
FRANC
FRANK
FRANZ
FRAPS
FRATS
FRAUD
FRAYS
GRAAL
GRABS
GRACE
GRADE
GRADS
GRAFT
GRAIL
GRAIN
GRAMA
GRAMS
GRAND
GRANI
GRANO
GRANT
GRAPE
GRAPH
GRAPY
GRASP
GRASS
GRATE
GRAVE
GRAVY
GRAYS
GRAZE
IRAQI
IRATE
KRAAL
KRAFT
KRAIT
KRAUT
ORACH
ORALS
ORANG
ORATE
PRAHU
PRAMS
PRANK
PRATE
PRAWN
PRAYS
TRACE
TRACH
TRACK
TRACT
TRADE
TRAGI
TRAIL
TRAIN
TRAIT
TRAMP
TRAMS
TRANS
TRAPS
TRASH
TRASS
TRAVE
TRAWL
TRAYS
URALS
URANO
URATE
WRACK
WRAPS
WRAPT
WRATH
XRAYS

•R•A•

AREAE
AREAL
AREAS
ARGAL
ARIAN
ARIAS
ARPAD
ARRAN
ARRAS
ARRAY
ARVAL
ARYAN
BREAD
BREAK
BREAM
BRIAN
BRIAR
BROAD
BRYAN
CRAAL
CREAK
CREAM
CROAK
CROAT
DREAD
DREAM
DREAR
DRYAD
ERMAS
FREAK
FRIAR
GRAAL
GREAT
GROAN
GROAT
IRMAS
KRAAL
OREAD
ORGAN
PRIAM
PROAS
TREAD
TREAS
TREAT
TRIAD
TRIAL
TROAS
URBAN
UREAL
URIAH
WREAK

•R••A

ARECA
ARENA
ARICA
AROMA
ARUBA
BRAVA
BRAZA
BREDA
CRURA
DRAMA
DRAVA
ERICA
ERIKA
FREDA
FRENA
FREYA
GRAMA
GRETA
KRONA
ORIYA
PRESA
PRIMA
RRHEA
TRINA
TRONA
TRUDA
TRYMA

••RA•

ABRAM
ARRAN
ARRAS
ARRAY
AURAE
AURAL
AURAS
BORAX
BURAN
CARAS
CARAT
CERAM
CERAT
CORAL
CORAS
DORAS
DURAL
EYRAS
EZRAS
FARAD
FERAL
FORAY
FURAN
GORAL
GYRAL
HARAR
HERAT
HIRAM
HORAE
HORAL
HORAS
HYRAX
IHRAM
JORAM
JURAL
JURAT
KARAT
KERAT
KORAN
LIRAS
LORAN
MARAT
MORAE
MORAL
MORAS
MORAY
MURAL
MURAT
MYRAS
NORAH
NORAS
OKRAS
PARAS
PYRAN
RERAN
RURAL
SARAH
SARAN
SARAS
SCRAG
SCRAM
SCRAP
SERAC
SERAI
SERAL
SORAS
SPRAG
SPRAT
SPRAY
STRAP
STRAT
STRAW
STRAY
SURAH
SURAL
SURAS
TERAT
TORAH
VARAS
VERAS
VIRAL

••R•A

AORTA
ATRIA
BARCA
BERTA
BURMA
BURSA
CARLA
CERIA
CIRCA
CORIA
CURIA
DERMA
DORSA
DURRA
GERDA
HERMA
JURUA
KARMA
KOREA
LARVA
LORCA
LORNA
MARIA
MARTA
MIRZA
MORNA
MURRA
MYRIA
MYRNA
NORIA
NORMA
OCREA
PARKA
SERRA
STRIA
SYRIA
TERRA
VERNA
VIRGA
WIRRA
YERBA

•••RA

ACCRA
AFTRA
AGORA
ANTRA
BASRA
BEIRA
CEARA
CITRA
CLARA
COBRA
COPRA
CRURA
DOBRA
DOURA
DURRA
EXTRA
FLORA
HYDRA
INDRA
INFRA
INTRA
KLARA
KUFRA
LABRA
LAURA
LEORA
LIBRA
MAURA
MICRA
MOIRA
MURRA
OPERA
SABRA
SACRA
SERRA
SUPRA
SUTRA
TATRA
TERRA
TETRA
TIARA
ULTRA
UMBRA
WIRRA
ZEBRA

R•B••

RABBI
RABIC
RABID
REBEC
REBEL
REBUS
REBUT
ROBED
ROBES
ROBIN
ROBLE
ROBOT
RUBES
RUBLE
RUBYS

R••B•

RABBI
RUGBY
RUMBA

R•••B

RAJAB
RHOMB
RHUMB

•RB••

ARBOR
ORBED
ORBIT
URBAN

•R•B•

ARABS
ARABY
ARUBA
BRIBE
CRABS
CRIBS
DRABS
DRIBS
DRUBS
GRABS
GREBE
GRUBS
KRUBI
ORIBI
PROBE
TRIBE

•R••B

ARDEB
CRUMB

••RB•

BARBS
CARBO
CURBS
DERBY
FORBS
GARBS
HERBS
HERBY
KERBS
SERBS
SORBS
TURBO
VERBS
YERBA

••R•B

CARIB
CAROB
HOREB
SCRUB
SHRUB
THROB

•••RB

ACERB
BLURB
EXURB

R•C••

RACED
RACER
RACES
RACKS
RECAP
RECTA
RECTI
RECTO
RECUR
RICED
RICER
RICES
RICIN
RICKS
RICKY
ROCKS
ROCKY
RUCHE
RUCKS

R••C•

RANCE
RANCH
RATCH
REACH
REACT
REICH
RETCH
ROACH
ROTCH

R•••C

RABIC
REBEC
RELIC
RUNIC

•RC••

ARCED
ARCHI
ARCHY
ARCUS
ORCHI

5

ORCIN
ORCUS

•R•C•
ARECA
ARICA
BRACE
BRACT
BRICE
BRICK
BRUCE
BRYCE
CRACK
CRACY
CRECY
CRICK
CROCE
CROCI
CROCK
CRUCI
DRACO
ERECT
ERICA
ERICH
ERICS
ERUCT
FROCK
GRACE
GRECO
ORACH
PRICE
PRICK
PROCT
TRACE
TRACH
TRACK
TRACT
TRICE
TRICH
TRICK
TRUCE
TRUCK
URICO
WRACK
WRECK

•R••C
AREIC
BRONC
CRESC
FRANC

••RC•
BARCA
BIRCH
CIRCA
CIRCE
CURCH
DIRCK
FARCE
FARCY
FORCE
KERCH
LARCH
LORCA
LURCH
MARCH
MARCO
MARCS
MERCI
MERCY
NARCO
PARCH
PERCH
PERCY
PORCH
SARCO
TURCO

••R•C
AURIC
BARIC
BORIC
CERIC
DARIC
DORIC
LYRIC
SERAC
TORIC
VARIC
XERIC

R•D••
RADAR
RADII
RADIO
RADIX
RADON
REDAN
REDID
REDLY
RIDER
RIDES
RIDGE
RIDGY
RODDY
RODEO
RODIN
RUDDS
RUDDY
RUDER
RUDYS

R••D•
RAIDS
RANDS
RANDY
READS
READY
REEDS
REEDY
RENDS
RHODA
RINDS
ROADS
RODDY
RONDO
ROODS
ROWDY
RUDDS
RUDDY
RYNDS

R•••D
RABID
RACED
RAGED
RAKED
RAPED
RAPID
RATED
RAVED
RAYED
RAZED
REDID
RICED
RIGID
RILED
RIMED
RIVED
ROALD
ROBED
ROPED
ROSED
ROUND
ROVED
ROWED
RULED

•RD••
ARDEB
ARDEN
ARDOR
ORDER

•R•D•
BRADS
BRADY
BREDA
BRIDE
CREDO
CRUDE
ERODE
FREDA
FREDS
GRADE
GRADS
GRIDE
GRIDS
IRIDO
PRIDE
PRODS
PRUDE
TRADE
TRUDA
TRUDY
UREDO

•R••D
ARCED
ARMED
AROID
ARPAD
BRAID
BRAND
BREAD
BREED
BROAD
BROOD
CREED
CRIED
CROWD
DREAD
DRIED
DRUID
DRYAD
ERRED
FRAUD
FREED
FREUD
FRIED
FROND
GRAND
GREED
GRIND
IRKED
ORBED
OREAD
PRIED
PROUD
TREAD
TREED
TREND
TRIAD
TRIED
TRUED
URGED
WRIED

••RD•
BARDE
BARDS
BIRDS
BURDS
CARDI
CARDS
CORDS
CURDS
CURDY
FORDS
GERDA
GIRDS
HARDS
HARDY
HERDS
HORDE
HURDS
LARDS
LARDY
LORDS
NARDS
PARDS
PERDU
SURDS
TARDY
VERDI
WARDS
WORDS
WORDY
YARDS

••R•D
ACRED
ACRID
AIRED
BARED
BORED
CARED
CERED
CORED
CURED
DARED
EARED
EDRED
ERRED
FARAD
FARED
FIRED
GORED
HEROD
HIRED
JARED
LURED
LURID
MIRED
OARED
PARED
PORED
SCROD
SERED
SHRED
SIRED
TARED
TIRED
WIRED
WORLD

•••RD
AWARD
BAIRD
BEARD
BOARD
CAIRD
CHARD
CHORD
FIORD
FJORD
GOURD
GUARD
HEARD
HOARD
LAIRD
NJORD
SHARD
SHERD
SWARD
SWORD
THIRD
WEIRD

RE•••
REACH
REACT
READS
READY
REALM
REALS
REAMS
REAPS
REARM
REARS
REBEC
REBEL
REBUS
REBUT
RECAP
RECTA
RECTI
RECTO
RECUR
REDAN
REDID
REDLY
REEDS
REEDY
REEFS
REEFY
REEKS
REEKY
REELS
REEVE
REFER
REFIT
REGAL
REGAN
REGES
REGIN
REGMA
REICH
REIFY
REIGN
REIMS
REINS
RELAX
RELAY
RELIC
REMAN
REMEX
REMIT
REMUS
RENAL
RENAN
RENDS
RENEE
RENES
RENEW
RENIN
RENTE
RENTS
REPAY
REPEL
REPLY
RERAN
RERUN
RESET
RESIN
RESTS
RETCH
RETEM
RETIA
RETRO
RETRY
RETTA
REVEL
REVET
REVUE

R•E••
REEDS
REEDY
REEFS
REEFY
REEKS
REEKY
REELS
REEVE
RHEAS
RHEUM
RUERS

R••E•
RACED
RACER
RACES
RAGED
RAGEE
RAGES
RAKED
RAKEE
RAKER
RAKES
RALES
RANEE
RAPED
RAPES
RARER
RATED
RATEL
RATER
RATES
RAVED
RAVEL
RAVEN
RAVER
RAVES
RAWER
RAYED
RAZED
RAZEE
RAZES
REBEC
REBEL
REFER
REGES
REMEX
RENEE
RENES
RENEW
REPEL
RESET
RETEM
REVEL
REVET
RHOEA
RICED
RICER
RICES
RIDER
RIDES
RIGEL
RILED
RILES
RILEY
RIMED
RIMER
RIMES
RIPEN
RIPER
RISEN
RISER
RISES
RITES
RIVED
RIVEN
RIVER
RIVES
RIVET
ROBED
ROBES
RODEO
ROGER
ROLES
ROMEO
ROPED
ROPES
ROSED
ROSES
ROUEN
ROUES
ROVED
ROVER
ROVES
ROWED
ROWEL
ROWEN
ROWER
RRHEA
RUBES
RUDER
RULED
RULER
RULES
RUMEN
RUNES
RUPEE
RUSES

R•••E
RAGEE
RAISE
RAKEE
RAMIE

5

RANCE
RANEE
RANGE
RAPHE
RAZEE
REEVE
RENEE
RENTE
REVUE
RHAGE
RHINE
RHONE
RHYME
RIDGE
RIFLE
RINSE
ROBLE
ROGUE
ROLFE
ROQUE
ROUGE
ROUSE
ROUTE
RUBLE
RUCHE
RUGAE
RUPEE

•RE••

AREAE
AREAL
AREAS
ARECA
AREIC
ARENA
ARENT
ARETE
BREAD
BREAK
BREAM
BREDA
BREED
BRENT
BREST
BREVE
BREVI
BREWS
CREAK
CREAM
CRECY
CREDO
CREED
CREEK
CREEL
CREEP
CREES
CREME
CREON
CREPE
CREPT
CRESC
CRESS
CREST
CRETE
CREWE
CREWS
DREAD
DREAM
DREAR
DREGS
DRESS
DREST
DREWS
ERECT
FREAK
FREDA
FREDS
FREED
FREER
FREES
FRENA
FREON
FRERE
FRESH
FRETS
FREUD
FREYA
GREAT
GREBE
GRECO
GREED
GREEK
GREEN
GREET
GREGO
GREGS
GRETA
GREYS
IRENE
OREAD
PREEN
PRESA
PRESS
PREST
PREXY
PREYS
TREAD
TREAS
TREAT
TREED
TREES
TREKS
TREND
TRENT
TRESS
TREYS
UREAL
UREDO
WREAK
WRECK
WRENS
WREST

•R•E•

ARCED
ARDEB
ARDEN
ARIEL
ARIES
ARLES
ARMED
ARMET
ARPEN
ARSES
ARTEL
ARTER
BRAES
BREED
BRIEF
BRIER
CREED
CREEK
CREEL
CREEP
CREES
CRIED
CRIER
CRIES
CRUEL
CRUET
DRIED
DRIER
DRIES
DRYER
ERIES
ERNES
ERRED
ERSES
FREED
FREER
FREES
FRIED
FRIER
FRIES
FROES
FRYER
GREED
GREEK
GREEN
GREET
GRIEF
GRIEG
GRUEL
IRKED
ORBED
ORDER
ORIEL
ORLES
ORMER
PREEN
PRIED
PRIER
PRIES
PROEM
PRYER
RRHEA
TREED
TREES
TRIED
TRIER
TRIES
TRUED
TRUER
TRUES
URGED
URGES
URIEL
WRIED
WRIER
WRIES
WRYER

•R••E

AREAE
ARETE
ARGUE
ARISE
ARNIE
AROSE
ARTIE
BRACE
BRAGE
BRAHE
BRAKE
BRAVE
BRAZE
BREVE
BRIBE
BRICE
BRIDE
BRINE
BROKE
BROME
BRUCE
BRUME
BRUTE
BRYCE
CRAKE
CRANE
CRAPE
CRATE
CRAVE
CRAZE
CREME
CREPE
CRETE
CREWE
CRIME
CROCE
CRONE
CRORE
CROZE
CRUDE
CRUSE
DRAKE
DRAPE
DRAVE
DRIVE
DROME
DRONE
DROVE
DRUPE
DRUSE
ERASE
ERNIE
ERODE
EROSE
FRAME
FRERE
FRISE
FROZE
GRACE
GRADE
GRAPE
GRATE
GRAVE
GRAZE
GREBE
GRIDE
GRIME
GRIPE
GROPE
GROVE
GRUME
IRATE
IRENE
IRONE
KRONE
ORATE
PRATE
PRICE
PRIDE
PRIME
PRIZE
PROBE
PRONE
PROSE
PROVE
PRUDE
PRUNE
TRACE
TRADE
TRAVE
TRIBE
TRICE
TRINE
TRIPE
TRITE
TROPE
TROVE
TRUCE
URATE
URINE
WRITE
WROTE

••RE•

ACRED
ACRES
AGREE
AIRED
AUREI
AURES
BARED
BARER
BARES
BERET
BORED
BORER
BORES
BYRES
CARED
CARER
CARES
CARET
CAREY
CERED
CERES
CORED
CORER
CORES
CURED
CURER
CURES
DARED
DARER
DARES
DEREK
DIRER
DURER
EARED
EDRED
EGRET
ERRED
FARED
FARER
FARES
FIRED
FIRER
FIRES
FORES
GORED
GORES
GYRES
HAREM
HARES
HIRED
HIRER
HIRES
HOREB
JARED
JEREZ
JUREL
KAREN
KERES
KOREA
LARES
LORES
LURED
LURER
LURES
LYRES
MARES
MIRED
MIRES
MOREL
MORES
MUREX
NARES
OARED
OCREA
OGRES
PARED
PAREN
PARER
PARES
PAREU
PERES
PHREN
PORED
PORES
PUREE
PURER
PYRES
PYREX
RARER
SCREE
SCREW
SERED
SERES
SHRED
SHREW
SIRED
SIREN
SIRES
SOREL
SORER
SORES
SPREE
STREW
SURER
TARED
TARES
THREE
THREW
TIRED
TIRES
UNREF
VIREO
VIRES
WARES
WIRED
WIRER
WIRES
YPRES

••R•E

AERIE
AGREE
AURAE
BARDE
BARGE
BARYE
BERME
BERNE
BIRLE
BORNE
BURKE
BURSE
CARTE
CARVE
CIRCE
CORSE
CURIE
CURSE
CURVE
DIRGE
EARLE
EERIE
EYRIE
FARCE
FARLE
FORCE
FORGE
FORTE
FURZE
GORGE
GORSE
HARTE
HORAE
HORDE
HORSE
JORGE
LARGE
MARGE
MARIE
MARNE
MERGE
MERLE
MEROE
MORAE
MORSE
MURRE
NERVE
NORSE
NURSE
PARSE
PERSE
PUREE
PURGE
PURSE
SCREE
SERGE
SERVE
SPREE
SPRUE
SURGE
TERSE
THREE
TORTE
VARVE
VERGE
VERNE
VERSE
VERVE
VIRGE
WORSE

•••RE

ADORE
AFIRE
ANDRE
AWARE
AZURE
BLARE
CADRE
CHARE
CHORE
CLARE
CRORE
EAGRE
FLARE

FRERE
GENRE
GLARE
INURE
ISERE
LIVRE
LOIRE
LUCRE
MOIRE
MOORE
MURRE
NACRE
OMBRE
OUTRE
PADRE
PHORE
PHYRE
QUIRE
SCARE
SCORE
SHARE
SHIRE
SHORE
SNARE
SNORE
SPARE
SPIRE
SPORE
STARE
STERE
STORE
SUCRE
SWORE
THERE
WHERE
WHORE
YOURE
ZAIRE

R•F••
RAFTS
REFER
REFIT
RIFFS
RIFLE
RIFTS
RUFFS
RUFUS

R••F•
REEFS
REEFY
REIFY
RIFFS
ROLFE
ROLFS
ROOFS
RUFFS

•R•F•
CRAFT
CROFT
DRAFF
DRAFT
DRIFT
GRAFT
GRUFF
KRAFT
PROFS

•R••F
BRIEF
DRAFF
GRIEF
GRUFF
PROOF

••RF•
CORFU
KERFS
SERFS
SURFS
SURFY
TURFS
TURFY
ZARFS

••R•F
SERIF
UNREF

•••RF
DWARF
SCARF
SCURF
WHARF

R•G••
RAGED
RAGEE
RAGES
RAGGY
REGAL
REGAN
REGES
REGIN
REGMA
RIGEL
RIGGS
RIGHT
RIGID
RIGOR
ROGER
ROGUE
RUGAE
RUGBY

R••G•
RAGGY
RANGE
RANGY
REIGN
RHAGE
RHAGY
RIDGE
RIDGY
RIGGS
RINGS
ROUGE
ROUGH
RUNGS

R•••G
RUING

•RG••
ARGAL
ARGIL
ARGOL
ARGON
ARGOS
ARGOT
ARGUE
ARGUS
ERGOT
ORGAN
URGED
URGES

•R•G•
BRAGE
BRAGI
BRAGS
BRIGS
CRAGS
DRAGS
DREGS
DRUGS
FRIGG
FROGS
GREGO
GREGS
PRIGS
TRAGI
TRIGO
TRIGS

•R••G
BRING
CRAIG
FRIGG
GRIEG
ORANG
PRONG
WRING
WRONG
WRUNG

••RG•
BARGE
BERGS
BURGH
BURGS
CARGO
CORGI
DIRGE
FARGO
FORGE
FORGO
GORGE
JORGE
LARGE
LARGO
MARGE
MARGO
MERGE
PARGO
PORGY
PURGE
SERGE
SORGO
SURGE
SURGY
VERGE
VIRGA
VIRGE
VIRGO

••R•G
SCRAG
SHRUG
SPRAG
SPRIG
UNRIG

•••RG
BOURG

RH•••
RHAGE
RHAGY
RHEAS
RHEUM
RHINE
RHINO
RHIZO
RHODA
RHOEA
RHOMB
RHONE
RHUMB
RHYME

R•H••
RRHEA

R••H•
RAPHE
RIGHT
RUCHE
RUSHY
RUTHS

R•••H
RAJAH
RALPH
RANCH
RATCH
RAYAH
REACH
REICH
RETCH
ROACH
ROLPH
ROTCH
ROUGH

•RH••
RRHEA

•R•H•
ARCHI
ARCHY
ARTHR
BRAHE
ORCHI
ORTHO
PRAHU

•R••H
BRASH
BROTH
BRUSH
CRASH
CRUSH
ERICH
FRESH
FRITH
FROSH
FROTH
GRAPH
IRISH
ORACH
TRACH
TRASH
TRICH
TROPH
TROTH
TRUTH
URIAH
WRATH

••R•H
BARTH
BERTH
BIRCH
BIRTH
BURGH
CURCH
EARTH
FIRTH
FORTH
FURTH
GARTH
GIRTH
HARSH
KERCH
LARCH
LURCH
MARCH
MARSH
MIRTH
MORPH
MYRRH
NORAH
NORTH
PARCH
PERCH
PERTH
PORCH
SARAH
SURAH
TORAH
WORTH

•••RH
MYRRH

RI•••
RIALS
RIANT
RIATA
RICED
RICER
RICES
RICIN
RICKS
RICKY
RIDER
RIDES
RIDGE
RIDGY
RIFFS
RIFLE
RIFTS
RIGEL
RIGGS
RIGHT
RIGID
RIGOR
RILED
RILES
RILEY
RILLS
RIMED
RIMER
RIMES
RINDS
RINGS
RINKS
RINSE
RIOTS
RIPEN
RIPER
RISEN
RISER
RISES
RISKS
RISKY
RISUS
RITAS
RITES
RITZY
RIVAL
RIVED
RIVEN
RIVER
RIVES
RIVET
RIYAL

R•I••
RAIDS
RAILS
RAINS
RAINY
RAISE
REICH
REIFY
REIGN
REIMS
REINS
RHINE
RHINO
RHIZO
ROILS
ROILY
RUING
RUINS

R••I•
RABIC
RABID
RADII
RADIO
RADIX
RAMIE
RANIS
RAPID
RATIO
REDID
REFIT
REGIN
RELIC
REMIT
RENIN
RESIN
RETIA
RICIN
RIGID
ROBIN
RODIN
ROSIN
RUNIC
RUNIN
RURIK

R•••I
RABBI
RADII
RECTI

•RI••
ARIAN
ARIAS
ARICA
ARIEL
ARIES
ARILS
ARION
ARISE
ARIUM
ARIUS
BRIAN
BRIAR
BRIBE
BRICE
BRICK
BRIDE
BRIEF
BRIER
BRIGS
BRILL
BRIMS
BRINE
BRING
BRINK
BRINY
BRISK
CRIBS
CRICK
CRIED
CRIER
CRIES
CRIME
CRIMP
CRISP
DRIBS
DRIED
DRIER
DRIES
DRIFT
DRILL
DRILY
DRINK
DRIPS
DRIPT
DRIVE
ERICA
ERICH
ERICS
ERIES
ERIKA
ERIKS
FRIAR
FRIED
FRIER
FRIES
FRIGG
FRILL
FRIML
FRISE
FRISK
FRITH
FRITS
FRITZ
FRIZZ
GRIDE
GRIDS
GRIEF
GRIEG
GRILL
GRIME
GRIMM
GRIND
GRINS
GRIPE
GRIPS
GRIPT
GRIST
GRITS
IRIDO
IRISH

ORIBI
ORIEL
ORION
ORIYA
PRIAM
PRICE
PRICK
PRIDE
PRIED
PRIER
PRIES
PRIGS
PRIMA
PRIME
PRIMI
PRIMO
PRIMP
PRIMS
PRINK
PRINT
PRIOR
PRISM
PRIVY
PRIZE
TRIAD
TRIAL
TRIBE
TRICE
TRICH
TRICK
TRIED
TRIER
TRIES
TRIGO
TRIGS
TRILL
TRIMS
TRINA
TRINE
TRIOL
TRIOS
TRIPE
TRIPS
TRITE
TRIXY
URIAH
URICO
URIEL
URINE
URINO
WRIED
WRIER
WRIES
WRING
WRIST
WRITE
WRITS

•R•I•

AREIC
ARGIL
ARNIE
AROID
ARRIS
ARSIS
ARTIE
BRAID
BRAIL
BRAIN
BROIL
BRUIN
BRUIT
CRAIG
CROIX
DRAIN
DROIT
DRUID
ERNIE
ERWIN
FRAIL
FRUIT
GRAIL
GRAIN
GROIN
IRVIN
IRWIN
KRAIT
ORBIT
ORCIN
ORNIS
ORPIN
ORRIS
TRAIL
TRAIN
TRAIT

•R••I

ARCHI
BRAGI
BREVI
CRANI
CROCI
CRUCI
GRANI
IRAQI
KRUBI
ORCHI
ORIBI
PRIMI
TRAGI

••RI•

ABRIS
ACRID
AERIE
APRIL
ARRIS
ATRIA
ATRIP
AURIC
AURIS
BARIC
BARIT
BORIC
BORIS
BURIN
CARIB
CERIA
CERIC
CHRIS
CORIA
CURIA
CURIE
CURIO
CYRIL
DARIC
DORIC
DORIS
EERIE
EYRIE
KIRIN
LORIS
LURID
LYRIC
MARIA
MARIE
MERIT
MYRIA
NARIS
NORIA
ORRIS
PARIS
PERIL
PERIS
PURIM
RURIK
SARIS
SCRIM
SCRIP
SERIF
SERIN
SPRIG
SPRIT
STRIA
STRIP
SYRIA
TORIC
TORII
TURIN
UNRIG
UNRIP
VARIC
VARIO
VARIX
XERIC
ZORIL

••R•I

AUREI
CARDI
CARPI
CIRRI
CORGI
CURVI
DORSI
FERMI
FERRI
FORLI
GORKI
MERCI
PARSI
SERAI
TARSI
TERRI
TORII
TORSI
TURKI
VERDI
VERMI

•••RI

CAPRI
CIRRI
CYMRI
FEBRI
FERRI
HENRI
HOURI
INDRI
KAURI
MAORI
MATRI
NEURI
NIGRI
NITRI
PATRI
PETRI
PLURI
TERRI
UTERI
VITRI

R•J••

RAJAB
RAJAH

R•K••

RAKED
RAKEE
RAKER
RAKES

R••K•

RACKS
RANKS
REEKS
REEKY
RICKS
RICKY
RINKS
RISKS
RISKY
ROCKS
ROCKY
ROOKS
ROOKY
RUCKS
RUSKS

R•••K

RURIK

•RK••

IRKED

•R•K•

BRAKE
BRAKY
BROKE
CRAKE
DRAKE
ERIKA
ERIKS
TREKS

•R••K

BREAK
BRICK
BRINK
BRISK
BROOK
BRUSK
CRACK
CRANK
CREAK
CREEK
CRICK
CROAK
CROCK
CROOK
DRANK
DRINK
DRUNK
FRANK
FREAK
FRISK
FROCK
GREEK
PRANK
PRICK
PRINK
TRACK
TRICK
TRUCK
TRUNK
WRACK
WREAK
WRECK

••RK•

BARKS
BARKY
BURKE
CORKS
CORKY
DIRKS
FORKS
GORKI
GORKY
HARKS
JERKS
JERKY
KIRKS
LARKS
LURKS
MARKS
MURKY
PARKA
PARKS
PERKS
PERKY
PORKY
SARKS
TURKI
TURKS
WORKS

••R•K

DEREK
DIRCK
KURSK
RURIK
TORSK

•••RK

CLARK
CLERK
OZARK
QUARK
QUIRK
SHARK
SHIRK
SMIRK
SNARK
SPARK
STARK
STIRK
STORK

R•L••

RALES
RALLY
RALPH
RELAX
RELAY
RELIC
RILED
RILES
RILEY
RILLS
ROLES
ROLFE
ROLFS
ROLLO
ROLLS
ROLPH
RULED
RULER
RULES

R••L•

RAILS
RALLY
RAWLY
REALM
REALS
REDLY
REELS
REPLY
RIALS
RIFLE
RILLS
ROALD
ROBLE
ROILS
ROILY
ROLLO
ROLLS
RUBLE

R•••L

RAOUL
RATAL
RATEL
RAVEL
REBEL
REGAL
RENAL
REPEL
REVEL
RIGEL
RIVAL
RIYAL
ROWEL
ROYAL
RURAL

•RL••

ARLES
ORLES
ORLON
ORLOP

•R•L•

ARILS
BRILL
DRILL
DRILY
DROLL
DRYLY
FRILL
GRILL
ORALS
TRILL
TROLL
TRULY
URALS
WRYLY

•R••L

AREAL
ARGAL
ARGIL
ARGOL
ARIEL
ARTEL
ARVAL
BRAIL
BRAWL
BRILL
BROIL
CRAAL
CRAWL
CREEL
CRUEL
DRAWL
DRILL
DROLL
DROOL
FRAIL
FRILL
FRIML
GRAAL
GRAIL
GRILL
GROWL
GRUEL
KRAAL
ORIEL
PROWL
TRAIL
TRAWL
TRIAL
TRILL
TRIOL
TROLL
UREAL
URIEL

••RL•

BIRLE
BIRLS
BURLS
BURLY
CARLA
CARLO
CARLS
CURLS
CURLY
EARLE
EARLS
EARLY
FARLE
FARLS
FORLI
FURLS
GIRLS
HARLS
HERLS
HURLS
HURLY
JARLS
KARLS
MARLS
MARLY
MERLE
PURLS
SURLY
WORLD

••R•L

APRIL
AURAL
BERYL
CAROL
CORAL
CYRIL
DURAL
FERAL
GORAL
GYRAL

5

HORAL
JURAL
JUREL
KAROL
MORAL
MOREL
MURAL
PAROL
PERIL
RURAL
SERAL
SOREL
SURAL
TYROL
VIRAL
ZORIL

•••RL
CEORL
CHURL
GNARL
KNURL
PEARL
SHORL
SNARL
SWIRL
TWIRL
WHIRL
WHORL

R•M••
RAMIE
RAMMY
RAMPS
RAMUS
REMAN
REMEX
REMIT
REMUS
RIMED
RIMER
RIMES
ROMAN
ROMEO
ROMPS
RUMBA
RUMEN
RUMMY
RUMOR
RUMPS

R••M•
RAMMY
REAMS
REGMA
REIMS
RHOMB
RHUMB
RHYME
ROAMS
ROOMS
ROOMY
RUMMY

R•••M
REALM
REARM
RETEM
RHEUM

•RM••
ARMED
ARMET
ARMOR
ERMAS
IRMAS
ORMER

•R•M•
AROMA
ARUMS
BRIMS
BROME
BROMO
BRUME
CRAMP
CRAMS
CREME
CRIME
CRIMP
CRUMB
CRUMP
DRAMA
DRAMS
DROME
DRUMS
FRAME
FRIML
FRUMP
GRAMA
GRAMS
GRIME
GRIMM
GRUME
PRAMS
PRIMA
PRIME
PRIMI
PRIMO
PRIMP
PRIMS
PROMS
TRAMP
TRAMS
TRIMS
TRUMP
TRYMA

•R••M
ARIUM
BREAM
BROOM
CREAM
DREAM
GRIMM
GROOM
PRIAM
PRISM
PROEM

••RM•
BARMY
BERME
BERMS
BURMA
CORMS
DERMA
DERMO
DORMS
DORMY
FARMS
FERMI
FIRMS
FORMS
GERMS
HARMS
HERMA
KARMA
NORMA
NORMS
TERMS
VERMI
WARMS
WORMS
WORMY

••R•M
ABRAM
AURUM
CAROM
CERAM
CHROM
DURUM
FORUM
HAREM
HIRAM
IHRAM
JORAM
JORUM
PURIM
SCRAM
SCRIM
SCRUM
SERUM
STRUM
THRUM

•••RM
ALARM
CHARM
CHIRM
INARM
REARM
SPERM
STORM
SWARM
THERM
UNARM

R•N••
RANCE
RANCH
RANDS
RANDY
RANEE
RANGE
RANGY
RANIS
RANKS
RANTS
RENAL
RENAN
RENDS
RENEE
RENES
RENEW
RENIN
RENTE
RENTS
RINDS
RINGS
RINKS
RINSE
RONDO
RONNY
RUNES
RUNGS
RUNIC
RUNIN
RUNON
RUNTS
RUNTY
RYNDS

R••N•
RAINS
RAINY
REINS
RHINE
RHINO
RHONE
RIANT
ROANS
RONNY
ROUND
RUING
RUINS

R•••N
RADON
RAVEN
RAYON
REDAN
REGAN
REGIN
REIGN
REMAN
RENAN
RENIN
RERAN
RERUN
RESIN
RICIN
RIPEN
RISEN
RIVEN
ROBIN
RODIN
ROMAN
ROSIN
ROUEN
ROWAN
ROWEN
RUMEN
RUNIN
RUNON

•RN••
ARNIE
ERNES
ERNIE
ERNST
ORNIS

•R•N•
ARENA
ARENT
BRAND
BRANS
BRANT
BRENT
BRINE
BRING
BRINK
BRINY
BRONC
BRONX
BRUNO
BRUNT
CRANE
CRANI
CRANK
CRONE
CRONY
DRANK
DRINK
DRONE
DRUNK
FRANC
FRANK
FRANZ
FRENA
FROND
FRONT
GRAND
GRANI
GRANO
GRANT
GRIND
GRINS
GRUNT
IRENE
IRONE
IRONS
IRONY
KRONA
KRONE
ORANG
PRANK
PRINK
PRINT
PRONE
PRONG
PRUNE
TRANS
TREND
TRENT
TRINA
TRINE
TRONA
TRUNK
URANO
URINE
URINO
WRENS
WRING
WRONG
WRUNG

•R••N
ARDEN
ARGON
ARIAN
ARION
ARPEN
ARRAN
ARSON
ARYAN
BRAIN
BRAWN
BRIAN
BROWN
BRUIN
BRYAN
CREON
CROON
CROWN
DRAIN
DRAWN
DROWN
ERWIN
FREON
FROWN
GRAIN
GREEN
GROAN
GROIN
GROWN
IRVIN
IRWIN
ORCIN
ORGAN
ORION
ORLON
ORPIN
PRAWN
PREEN
TRAIN
URBAN

••RN•
BARNS
BERNE
BORNE
BORNU
BURNS
BURNT
CORNS
CORNU
CORNY
DARNS
EARNS
FERNS
FERNY
FIRNS
HORNS
HORNY
KERNS
LORNA
MARNE
MORNA
MORNS
MYRNA
NORNS
PORNO
TARNS
TERNS
TURNS
VERNA
VERNE
VERNS
WARNS
YARNS

••R•N
AARON
AKRON
APRON
ARRAN
BARON
BORON
BURAN
BURIN
BYRON
CHRON
FURAN
GYRON
HERON
HURON
KAREN
KIRIN
KORAN
KORUN
LORAN
MORON
MYRON
PAREN
PERON
PHREN
PYRAN
RERAN
RERUN
SARAN
SERIN
SIREN
TURIN
ZIRON

•••RN
ACORN
ADORN
BAIRN
BOURN
CAIRN
CHURN
DOORN
INURN
LEARN
MOURN
QUERN
SCORN
SHORN
SPURN
STERN
SWORN
THORN
UTURN
YEARN

RO•••
ROACH
ROADS
ROALD
ROAMS
ROANS
ROARS
ROAST
ROBED
ROBES
ROBIN
ROBLE
ROBOT
ROCKS
ROCKY
RODDY
RODEO
RODIN
ROGER
ROGUE
ROILS
ROILY
ROLES
ROLFE
ROLFS
ROLLO
ROLLS
ROLPH
ROMAN
ROMEO
ROMPS
RONDO
RONNY
ROODS
ROOFS
ROOKS
ROOKY
ROOMS
ROOMY
ROOST
ROOTS
ROOTY
ROPED

ROPES ROQUE ROSAS ROSED ROSES ROSIN ROTAS ROTCH ROTOR ROUEN ROUES ROUGE ROUGH ROUND ROUPY ROUSE ROUST ROUTE ROUTS ROVED ROVER ROVES ROWAN ROWDY ROWED ROWEL ROWEN ROWER ROYAL

R•O••

RAOUL RHODA RHOEA RHOMB RHONE RIOTS ROODS ROOFS ROOKS ROOKY ROOMS ROOMY ROOST ROOTS ROOTY RYOTS

R••O•

RADON RAYON RAZOR RIGOR ROBOT ROTOR RUMOR RUNON

R•••O

RADIO RATIO RECTO RETRO RHINO RHIZO RODEO ROLLO ROMEO RONDO RUSSO

•RO••

AROID AROMA AROSE BROAD BROIL BROKE BROME BROMO BRONC BRONX BROOD BROOK BROOM BROOS BROTH BROWN BROWS CROAK CROAT CROCE CROCI CROCK CROFT CROIX CRONE CRONY CROOK CROON CROPS CRORE CROSS CROUP CROWD CROWN CROWS CROZE DROIT DROLL DROME DRONE DROOL DROOP DROPS DROPT DROSS DROVE DROWN ERODE EROSE FROCK FROES FROGS FROND FRONT FROSH FROST FROTH FROWN FROWS FROZE GROAN GROAT GROIN GROOM GROPE GROSS GROSZ GROTS GROUP GROUT GROVE GROWL GROWN GROWS IRONE IRONS IRONY KRONA KRONE PROAS PROBE PROCT PRODS PROEM PROFS PROMS PRONE PRONG PROOF PROPS PROSE PROSY PROTO PROUD PROVE PROVO PROWL PROWS PROXY TROAS TROLL TRONA TROOP TROPE TROPH TROTH TROTS TROUT TROVE WRONG WROTE

•R•O•

ARBOR ARDOR ARGOL ARGON ARGOS ARGOT ARION ARMOR ARROW ARSON BROOD BROOK BROOM BROOS CREON CROOK CROON CRUOR DROOL DROOP ERGOT ERROR FREON GROOM ORION ORLON ORLOP PRIOR PROOF TRIOL TRIOS TROOP

•R••O

BRAVO BROMO BRUNO CREDO DRACO ERATO GRANO GRECO GREGO IRIDO ORTHO PRIMO PROTO PROVO TRIGO URANO UREDO URICO URINO

••RO•

AARON AFROS AKRON APRON ARROW BARON BORON BYRON CAROB CAROL CAROM CEROS CHROM CHRON COROT DUROS ERROR FUROR GIROS GYRON GYROS HEROD HERON HURON JUROR KAROL LEROY MEROE MORON MOROS MYRON NEROS PAROL PERON SCROD SEROW STROP TAROS TAROT THROB THROW TIROS TYROL TYROS XEROX ZEROS ZIRON

••R•O

BURRO CARBO CARGO CARLO CARPO CARYO CIRRO CURIO DERMO DORSO FARGO FERRO FORGO KARYO LARGO MARCO MARGO MORRO NARCO PARGO PORNO SARCO SARTO SERVO SORGO TARSO TORSO TURBO TURCO VARIO VARRO VERSO VIREO VIRGO

•••RO

ANDRO ASTRO BURRO CAIRO CHIRO CHORO CIRRO CLARO COPRO CUPRO FERRO FIBRO GENRO HIERO HYDRO HYGRO IATRO INTRO MACRO METRO MICRO MORRO MUCRO MUNRO NECRO NEGRO NEURO NITRO OMBRO ONIRO PEDRO PETRO PICRO PTERO RETRO SACRO SAPRO SAURO SPIRO SPORO TAURO THYRO UTERO VARRO

R•P••

RAPED RAPES RAPHE RAPID REPAY REPEL REPLY RIPEN RIPER ROPED ROPES RUPEE

R••P•

RALPH RAMPS RASPS RASPY REAPS ROLPH ROMPS ROUPY RUMPS

R•••P

RECAP

•RP••

ARPAD ARPEN ORPIN

•R•P•

CRAPE CRAPS CREPE CREPT CROPS CRYPT DRAPE DRIPS DRIPT DROPS DROPT DRUPE ERUPT FRAPS GRAPE GRAPH GRAPY GRIPE GRIPS GRIPT GROPE KRUPP PROPS TRAPS TRIPE TRIPS TROPE TROPH WRAPS WRAPT

•R••P

CRAMP CREEP CRIMP CRISP CROUP CRUMP DROOP FRUMP GRASP GROUP KRUPP ORLOP PRIMP TRAMP TROOP TRUMP

••RP•

BURPS CARPI CARPO CARPS CORPS HARPS HARPY MORPH TARPS WARPS

••R•P

ATRIP SCRAP SCRIP SIRUP STRAP STRIP STROP SYRUP UNRIP

•••RP

CHIRP SCARP SHARP SLURP THORP TWERP TWIRP USURP

R•Q••

ROQUE

•R•Q•

IRAQI

RR•••

RRHEA

R•R••

RARER RERAN RERUN RURAL RURIK

R••R•

REARM REARS RETRO RETRY ROARS RUERS

R•••R

RACER

5

RADAR
RAKER
RARER
RATER
RAVER
RAWER
RAZOR
RECUR
REFER
RICER
RIDER
RIGOR
RIMER
RIPER
RISER
RIVER
ROGER
ROTOR
ROVER
ROWER
RUDER
RULER
RUMOR

•RR••
ARRAN
ARRAS
ARRAY
ARRIS
ARROW
ERRED
ERROR
ORRIS

•R•R•
CRORE
CRURA
DRURY
FRERE

•R••R
ARBOR
ARDOR
ARMOR
ARTER
ARTHR
BRIAR
BRIER
CRIER
CRUOR
DREAR
DRIER
DRYER
ERROR
FREER
FRIAR
FRIER
FRYER
ORDER
ORMER
PRIER
PRIOR
PRYER
TRIER
TRUER
WRIER
WRYER

••RR•
BARRY
BERRY
BIRRS
BURRO
BURRS
BURRY
CARRY
CIRRI
CIRRO
CURRY
DERRY
DORRS
DURRA
FERRI
FERRO
FERRY
FIRRY
FURRY
GERRY
HARRY
HURRY
JERRY
KERRY
LARRY
LORRY
MARRY
MERRY
MORRO
MURRA
MURRE
MURRY
MYRRH
PARRS
PARRY
PERRY
PURRS
SERRA
SORRY
TARRY
TERRA
TERRI
TERRY
VARRO
WIRRA
WORRY

••R•R
BARER
BORER
CARER
CORER
CURER
DARER
DIRER
DURER
ERROR
FARER
FIRER
FUROR
HARAR
HIRER
JUROR
LURER
PARER
PURER
RARER
SORER
SURER
WIRER

•••RR
CHIRR
CHURR
SHIRR
SKIRR

R•S••
RASPS
RASPY
RESET
RESIN
RESTS
RISEN
RISER
RISES
RISKS
RISKY
RISUS
ROSAS
ROSED
ROSES
ROSIN
RUSES
RUSHY
RUSKS
RUSSO
RUSTS
RUSTY

R••S•
RAISE
RINSE
ROAST
ROOST
ROUSE
ROUST
RUSSO

R•••S
RACES
RACKS
RAFTS
RAGES
RAIDS
RAILS
RAINS
RAKES
RALES
RAMPS
RAMUS
RANDS
RANIS
RANKS
RANTS
RAPES
RASPS
RATES
RAVES
RAZES
READS
REALS
REAMS
REAPS
REARS
REBUS
REEDS
REEFS
REEKS
REELS
REGES
REIMS
REINS
REMUS
RENDS
RENES
RENTS
RESTS
RHEAS
RIALS
RICES
RICKS
RIDES
RIFFS
RIFTS
RIGGS
RILES
RILLS
RIMES
RINDS
RINGS
RINKS
RIOTS
RISES
RISKS
RISUS
RITAS
RITES
RIVES
ROADS
ROAMS
ROANS
ROARS
ROBES
ROCKS
ROILS
ROLES
ROLFS
ROLLS
ROMPS
ROODS
ROOFS
ROOKS
ROOMS
ROOTS
ROPES
ROSAS
ROSES
ROTAS
ROUES
ROUTS
ROVES
RUBES
RUBYS
RUCKS
RUDDS
RUDYS
RUERS
RUFFS
RUFUS
RUINS
RULES
RUMPS
RUNES
RUNGS
RUNTS
RUSES
RUSKS
RUSTS
RUTHS
RYNDS
RYOTS

•RS••
ARSES
ARSIS
ARSON
ERSES

•R•S•
ARISE
AROSE
BRASH
BRASS
BREST
BRISK
BRUSH
BRUSK
CRASH
CRASS
CRESC
CRESS
CREST
CRISP
CROSS
CRUSE
CRUSH
CRUST
DRESS
DREST
DROSS
DRUSE
ERASE
ERNST
EROSE
FRESH
FRISE
FRISK
FROSH
FROST
GRASP
GRASS
GRIST
GROSS
GROSZ
IRISH
PRESA
PRESS
PREST
PRISM
PROSE
PROSY
TRASH
TRASS
TRESS
TRUSS
TRUST
TRYST
WREST
WRIST

•R••S
ARABS
ARCUS
AREAS
ARGOS
ARGUS
ARIAS
ARIES
ARILS
ARIUS
ARLES
ARRAS
ARRIS
ARSES
ARSIS
ARUMS
BRADS
BRAES
BRAGS
BRANS
BRASS
BRATS
BRAYS
BREWS
BRIGS
BRIMS
BROOS
BROWS
CRABS
CRAGS
CRAMS
CRAPS
CRASS
CRAWS
CREES
CRESS
CREWS
CRIBS
CRIES
CROPS
CROSS
CROWS
DRABS
DRAGS
DRAMS
DRAWS
DRAYS
DREGS
DRESS
DREWS
DRIBS
DRIES
DRIPS
DROPS
DROSS
DRUBS
DRUGS
DRUMS
ERICS
ERIES
ERIKS
ERMAS
ERNES
ERSES
FRAPS
FRATS
FRAYS
FREDS
FREES
FRETS
FRIES
FRITS
FROES
FROGS
FROWS
GRABS
GRADS
GRAMS
GRASS
GRAYS
GREGS
GREYS
GRIDS
GRINS
GRIPS
GRITS
GROSS
GROTS
GROWS
GRUBS
IRMAS
IRONS
ORALS
ORCUS
ORLES
ORNIS
ORRIS
PRAMS
PRAYS
PRESS
PREYS
PRIES
PRIGS
PRIMS
PROAS
PRODS
PROFS
PROMS
PROPS
PROWS
TRAMS
TRANS
TRAPS
TRASS
TRAYS
TREAS
TREES
TREKS
TRESS
TREYS
TRIES
TRIGS
TRIMS
TRIOS
TRIPS
TROAS
TROTS
TRUES
TRUSS
URALS
URGES
WRAPS
WRENS
WRIES
WRITS
XRAYS

••RS•
BURSA
BURSE
BURST
CORSE
CURSE
CURST
DORSA
DORSI
DORSO
FIRST
GORSE
GORSY
HARSH
HORSE
HORST
HORSY
KURSK
MARSH
MORSE
NORSE
NURSE
PARSE
PARSI
PERSE
PURSE
PURSY
TARSI
TARSO
TERSE
TORSI
TORSK
TORSO
VERSE
VERSO
VERST

WORSE
WORST

••R•S

ABRIS
ACRES
AFROS
ARRAS
ARRIS
AURAS
AURES
AURIS
BARBS
BARDS
BARES
BARKS
BARNS
BERGS
BERMS
BERTS
BIRDS
BIRLS
BIRRS
BORES
BORIS
BORTS
BURDS
BURGS
BURLS
BURNS
BURPS
BURRS
BYRES
CARAS
CARDS
CARES
CARLS
CARPS
CARTS
CARYS
CERES
CEROS
CHRIS
CHRYS
CORAS
CORDS
CORES
CORKS
CORMS
CORNS
CORPS
CURBS
CURDS
CURES
CURLS
CYRUS
DARES
DARNS
DARTS
DIRKS
DORAS
DORIS
DORMS
DORRS
DORUS
DUROS
EARLS
EARNS
EURUS
EYRAS
EZRAS
FARES
FARLS
FARMS
FERNS
FIRES
FIRMS
FIRNS
FORBS
FORDS
FORES
FORKS
FORMS
FORTS
FURLS
GARBS
GARYS
GERMS
GIRDS
GIRLS
GIROS
GIRTS
GORES
GURUS
GYRES
GYROS
GYRUS
HARDS
HARES
HARKS
HARLS
HARMS
HARPS
HARTS
HERBS
HERDS
HERLS
HIRES
HORAS
HORNS
HORUS
HURDS
HURLS
HURTS
JARLS
JERKS
KARLS
KERBS
KERES
KERFS
KERNS
KIRKS
KURUS
LARDS
LARES
LARKS
LIRAS
LORDS
LORES
LORIS
LURES
LURKS
LYRES
MARCS
MARES
MARKS
MARLS
MARTS
MIRES
MORAS
MORES
MORNS
MOROS
MORTS
MYRAS
NARDS
NARES
NARIS
NEROS
NORAS
NORMS
NORNS
OGRES
OKRAS
ORRIS
PARAS
PARDS
PARES
PARIS
PARKS
PARRS
PARTS
PERES
PERIS
PERKS
PORES
PORTS
PURLS
PURRS
PYRES
SARAS
SARIS
SARKS
SERBS
SERES
SERFS
SIRES
SORAS
SORBS
SORES
SORTS
SORUS
SURAS
SURDS
SURFS
TARES
TARNS
TAROS
TARPS
TARTS
TERMS
TERNS
TIRES
TIROS
TORTS
TORUS
TURFS
TURKS
TURNS
TYROS
VARAS
VARUS
VERAS
VERBS
VERNS
VIRES
VIRUS
WARDS
WARES
WARMS
WARNS
WARPS
WARTS
WIRES
WORDS
WORKS
WORMS
WORTS
XERUS
YARDS
YARNS
YPRES
ZARFS
ZEROS

•••RS

AMIRS
AVARS
AVERS
BEARS
BEERS
BIERS
BIRRS
BLURS
BOARS
BOERS
BOORS
BURRS
CHARS
CZARS
DEARS
DOERS
DOORS
DORRS
DYERS
EMIRS
EWERS
FAIRS
FEARS
FOURS
GAURS
GEARS
GOERS
HAIRS
HEARS
HEIRS
HOERS
HOURS
JEERS
KIERS
KNARS
KNURS
LAIRS
LEERS
LEHRS
LIARS
LOURS
MOORS
NEARS
ODORS
OMERS
OYERS
PAIRS
PARRS
PEARS
PEERS
PIERS
POURS
PURRS
REARS
ROARS
RUERS
SCARS
SEARS
SEERS
SLURS
SOARS
SOURS
SPARS
SPURS
STARS
STIRS
SUERS
TEARS
THURS
TIERS
TOURS
TSARS
TZARS
USERS
VAIRS
VEERS
WEARS
WEIRS
WHIRS
YEARS
YOURS
ZBARS

R•T••

RATAL
RATCH
RATED
RATEL
RATER
RATES
RATIO
RATTY
RETCH
RETEM
RETIA
RETRO
RETRY
RETTA
RITAS
RITES
RITZY
ROTAS
ROTCH
ROTOR
RUTHS
RUTTY

R••T•

RAFTS
RANTS
RATTY
RECTA
RECTI
RECTO
RENTE
RENTS
RESTS
RETTA
RIATA
RIFTS
RIOTS
ROOTS
ROOTY
ROUTE
ROUTS
RUNTS
RUNTY
RUSTS
RUSTY
RUTTY
RYOTS

R•••T

REACT
REBUT
REFIT
REMIT
RESET
REVET
RIANT
RIGHT
RIVET
ROAST
ROBOT
ROOST
ROUST

•RT••

ARTEL
ARTER
ARTHR
ARTIE
ORTHO

•R•T•

ARETE
BRATS
BROTH
BRUTE
CRATE
CRETE
ERATO
FRATS
FRETS
FRITH
FRITS
FRITZ
FROTH
GRATE
GRETA
GRITS
GROTS
IRATE
ORATE
PRATE
PROTO
TRITE
TROTH
TROTS
TRUTH
URATE
WRATH
WRITE
WRITS
WROTE

•R••T

ARENT
ARGOT
ARMET
BRACT
BRANT
BRENT
BREST
BRUIT
BRUNT
CRAFT
CREPT
CREST
CROAT
CROFT
CRUET
CRUST
CRYPT
DRAFT
DREST
DRIFT
DRIPT
DROIT
DROPT
ERECT
ERGOT
ERNST
ERUCT
ERUPT
FRONT
FROST
FRUIT
GRAFT
GRANT
GREAT
GREET
GRIPT
GRIST
GROAT
GROUT
GRUNT
KRAFT
KRAIT
KRAUT
ORBIT
PREST
PRINT
PROCT
TRACT
TRAIT
TREAT
TRENT
TROUT
TRUST
TRYST
WRAPT
WREST
WRIST

••RT•

AORTA
BARTH
BERTA
BERTH
BERTS
BERTY
BIRTH
BORTS
BORTY
BORTZ
CARTE
CARTS
DARTS
DIRTY
EARTH
FIRTH
FORTE
FORTH
FORTS
FORTY
FURTH
GARTH
GERTY
GIRTH
GIRTS
HARTE
HARTS
HARTZ
HERTZ
HURTS
MARTA
MARTS
MARTY
MIRTH
MORTS
MORTY
NORTH
PARTS
PARTY
PERTH

PORTS
SARTO
SORTS
TARTS
TORTE
TORTS
VERTU
VIRTU
WARTS
WARTY
WORTH
WORTS

••R•T
BARIT
BERET
BURNT
BURST
CARAT
CARET
CERAT
COROT
CURST
EGRET
FIRST
HERAT
HORST
JURAT
KARAT
KERAT
MARAT
MERIT
MURAT
SPRAT
SPRIT
STRAT
STRUT
TAROT
TERAT
VERST
WORST

•••RT
ABORT
ALERT
APART
APORT
AVERT
BLURT
CHART
CHERT
COURT
EVERT
EXERT
FLIRT
HEART
INERT
OVERT
QUART
QUIRT
SHIRT
SHORT
SKIRT
SMART
SNORT
SPIRT
SPORT
SPURT
START
SWART
WHORT

RU•••
RUBES
RUBLE
RUBYS
RUCHE
RUCKS
RUDDS
RUDDY
RUDER
RUDYS
RUERS
RUFFS
RUFUS
RUGAE
RUGBY
RUING
RUINS
RULED
RULER
RULES
RUMBA
RUMEN
RUMMY
RUMOR
RUMPS
RUNES
RUNGS
RUNIC
RUNIN
RUNON
RUNTS
RUNTY
RUPEE
RURAL
RURIK
RUSES
RUSHY
RUSKS
RUSSO
RUSTS
RUSTY
RUTHS
RUTTY

R•U••
RHUMB
ROUEN
ROUES
ROUGE
ROUGH
ROUND
ROUPY
ROUSE
ROUST
ROUTE
ROUTS

R••U•
RAMUS
RAOUL
REBUS
REBUT
RECUR
REMUS
RERUN
REVUE
RHEUM
RISUS
ROGUE
ROQUE
RUFUS

•RU••
ARUBA
ARUMS
BRUCE
BRUIN
BRUIT
BRUME
BRUNO
BRUNT
BRUSH
BRUSK
BRUTE
CRUCI
CRUDE
CRUEL
CRUET
CRUMB
CRUMP
CRUOR
CRURA
CRUSE
CRUSH
CRUST
DRUBS
DRUGS
DRUID
DRUMS
DRUNK
DRUPE
DRURY
DRUSE
ERUCT
ERUPT
FRUIT
FRUMP
GRUBS
GRUEL
GRUFF
GRUME
GRUNT
KRUBI
KRUPP
PRUDE
PRUNE
TRUCE
TRUCK
TRUDA
TRUDY
TRUED
TRUER
TRUES
TRULY
TRUMP
TRUNK
TRUSS
TRUST
TRUTH
WRUNG

•R•U•
ARCUS
ARGUE
ARGUS
ARIUM
ARIUS
CROUP
FRAUD
FREUD
GROUP
GROUT
KRAUT
ORCUS
PROUD
TROUT

•R••U
PRAHU

••RU•
AURUM
CYRUS
DORUS
DURUM
EURUS
FORUM
GURUS
GYRUS
HORUS
JORUM
JURUA
KORUN
KURUS
RERUN
SCRUB
SCRUM
SERUM
SHRUB
SHRUG
SIRUP
SORUS
SPRUE
STRUM
STRUT
SYRUP
THRUM
TORUS
VARUS
VIRUS
XERUS

••R•U
BORNU
CORFU
CORNU
PAREU
PERDU
VERTU
VIRTU

•••RU
NAURU
NEHRU

R•V••
RAVED
RAVEL
RAVEN
RAVER
RAVES
REVEL
REVET
REVUE
RIVAL
RIVED
RIVEN
RIVER
RIVES
RIVET
ROVED
ROVER
ROVES

R••V•
REEVE

•RV••
ARVAL
IRVIN

•R•V•
BRAVA
BRAVE
BRAVO
BREVE
BREVI
CRAVE
DRAVA
DRAVE
DRIVE
DROVE
GRAVE
GRAVY
GROVE
PRIVY
PROVE
PROVO
TRAVE
TROVE

••RV•
CARVE
CURVE
CURVI
LARVA
NERVE
NERVY
SERVE
SERVO
VARVE
VERVE

R•W••
RAWER
RAWLY
ROWAN
ROWDY
ROWED
ROWEL
ROWEN
ROWER

R•••W
RENEW

•RW••
ERWIN
IRWIN

•R•W•
BRAWL
BRAWN
BREWS
BROWN
BROWS
CRAWL
CRAWS
CREWE
CREWS
CROWD
CROWN
CROWS
DRAWL
DRAWN
DRAWS
DREWS
DROWN
FROWN
FROWS
GROWL
GROWN
GROWS
PRAWN
PROWL
PROWS
TRAWL

•R••W
ARROW

••R•W
ARROW
SCREW
SEROW
SHREW
STRAW
STREW
THREW
THROW

R•••X
RADIX
RELAX
REMEX

•R•X•
BRAXY
PREXY
PROXY
TRIXY

•R••X
BRONX
CROIX

••R•X
BORAX
HYRAX
MUREX
PYREX
VARIX
XEROX

RY•••
RYNDS
RYOTS

R•Y••
RAYAH
RAYED
RAYON
RHYME
RIYAL
ROYAL

R••Y•
RUBYS
RUDYS

R•••Y
RAGGY
RAINY
RALLY
RAMMY
RANDY
RANGY
RASPY
RATTY
RAWLY
READY
REDLY
REEDY
REEFY
REEKY
REIFY
RELAY
REPAY
REPLY
RETRY
RHAGY
RICKY
RIDGY
RILEY
RISKY
RITZY
ROCKY
RODDY
ROILY
RONNY
ROOKY
ROOMY
ROOTY
ROUPY
ROWDY
RUDDY
RUGBY
RUMMY
RUNTY
RUSHY
RUSTY
RUTTY

•RY••
ARYAN
BRYAN
BRYCE
CRYPT
DRYAD
DRYER
DRYLY
FRYER
PRYER
TRYMA
TRYST
WRYER
WRYLY

•R•Y•
BRAYS
DRAYS
FRAYS
FREYA
GRAYS
GREYS
ORIYA
PRAYS
PREYS
TRAYS
TREYS
XRAYS

•R••Y
ARABY
ARCHY
ARRAY
BRADY
BRAKY
BRAXY
BRINY
CRACY
CRAZY
CRECY
CRONY
DRILY
DRURY
DRYLY
GRAPY
GRAVY
IRONY
PREXY

PRIVY
PROSY
PROXY
TRIXY
TRUDY
TRULY
WRYLY

••RY•

BARYE
BERYL
CARYO
CARYS
CHRYS
GARYS
KARYO

••R•Y

ARRAY
BARKY
BARMY
BARRY
BERRY
BERTY
BORTY
BURLY
BURRY
CAREY
CARRY
CORKY
CORNY
CURDY
CURLY
CURRY
DERBY
DERRY
DIRTY
DORMY
EARLY
FARCY
FERNY
FERRY
FIRRY
FORAY
FORTY
FURRY
FURZY
GERRY
GERTY
GORKY
GORSY
HARDY
HARPY
HARRY
HERBY
HORNY
HORSY
HURLY
HURRY
JERKY
JERRY
KERRY
LARDY
LARRY
LEROY
LORRY
MARLY
MARRY
MARTY
MERCY
MERRY
MORAY
MORTY
MURKY
MURRY
NERVY
PARRY
PARTY
PERCY
PERKY
PERRY
PORGY
PORKY
PURSY
SORRY
SPRAY
STRAY
SURFY
SURGY
SURLY
TARDY
TARRY
TERRY
TURFY
WARTY
WORDY
WORMY
WORRY

•••RY

ALARY
AMBRY
ANGRY
APERY
ATORY
AVERY
BARRY
BEERY
BERRY
BURRY
CARRY
CHARY
CLARY
COWRY
CURRY
CYMRY
DAIRY
DEARY
DECRY
DERRY
DIARY
DOWRY
DRURY
EMBRY
EMERY
EMORY
ENTRY
EVERY
FAIRY
FERRY
FIERY
FIRRY
FURRY
GERRY
GLARY
GLORY
HAIRY
HARRY
HENRY
HOARY
HURRY
IATRY
IVORY
JERRY
JEWRY
KAURY
KERRY
LARRY
LATRY
LEERY
LORRY
MARRY
MERRY
METRY
MURRY
OCHRY
ONERY
OVARY
PARRY
PEARY
PERRY
QUERY
RETRY
SAURY
SCARY
SORRY
SPIRY
STORY
TARRY
TEARY
TERRY
USURY
VEERY
WEARY
WORRY

R•Z••

RAZED
RAZEE
RAZES
RAZOR

R••Z•

RHIZO
RITZY

•R•Z•

BRAZA
BRAZE
CRAZE
CRAZY
CROZE
FRIZZ
FROZE
GRAZE
PRIZE

•R••Z

FRANZ
FRITZ
FRIZZ
GROSZ

••RZ•

FURZE
FURZY
MIRZA

••R•Z

BORTZ
HARTZ
HERTZ
JEREZ

SA•••

SABAH
SABED
SABER
SABES
SABIN
SABLE
SABOT
SABRA
SACKS
SACRA
SACRO
SADHU
SADIE
SADLY
SAFER
SAFES
SAGAS
SAGER
SAGES
SAGOS
SAGUM
SAHEB
SAHIB
SAIGA
SAILS
SAINT
SAJOU
SAKER
SAKES
SALAD
SALEM
SALEP
SALES
SALIC
SALLY
SALMI
SALOL
SALON
SALPA
SALTS
SALTY
SALUS
SALVE
SALVO
SAMAR
SAMBA
SAMBO
SAMEK
SAMMY
SAMOA
SAMOS
SANDS
SANDY
SANER
SAPID
SAPOR
SAPPY
SAPRO
SARAH
SARAN
SARAS
SARCO
SARIS
SARKS
SARTO
SASIN
SASSY
SATAN
SATED
SATES
SATIN
SATYR
SAUCE
SAUCY
SAULS
SAULT
SAUNA
SAURO
SAURY
SAUTE
SAVED
SAVER
SAVES
SAVIN
SAVOR
SAVOY
SAVVY
SAWED
SAWER
SAXES
SAXON
SAYER
SAYID
SAYSO

S•A••

SCABS
SCADS
SCALD
SCALE
SCALL
SCALP
SCALY
SCAMP
SCAND
SCANS
SCANT
SCAPA
SCAPE
SCAPI
SCARE
SCARF
SCARP
SCARS
SCARY
SCATO
SCATS
SCAUP
SEALS
SEAMS
SEAMY
SEANS
SEARS
SEATO
SEATS
SHACK
SHADE
SHADY
SHAFT
SHAGS
SHAHS
SHAKE
SHAKO
SHAKY
SHALE
SHALL
SHALT
SHALY
SHAME
SHAMS
SHANK
SHANS
SHANT
SHAPE
SHARD
SHARE
SHARK
SHARP
SHAUN
SHAVE
SHAWL
SHAWM
SHAWN
SHAWS
SHAYS
SIALO
SKALD
SKATE
SLABS
SLACK
SLAGS
SLAIN
SLAKE
SLAMS
SLANG
SLANT
SLAPS
SLASH
SLATE
SLATS
SLATY
SLAVE
SLAVO
SLAVS
SLAWS
SLAYS
SMACK
SMALL
SMALT
SMART
SMASH
SMAZE
SNACK
SNAFU
SNAGS
SNAIL
SNAKE
SNAKY
SNAPS
SNARE
SNARK
SNARL
SNATH
SOAKS
SOAPS
SOAPY
SOARS
SPACE
SPADE
SPAHI
SPAIN
SPAIT
SPALL
SPANG
SPANK
SPANS
SPARE
SPARK
SPARS
SPASM
SPATE
SPATS
SPAWN
SPAYS
STABS
STACK
STACY
STAFF
STAGE
STAGS
STAGY
STAID
STAIN
STAIR
STAKE
STALE
STALK
STALL
STAMP
STAND
STANK
STANS
STAPH
STARE
STARK
STARS
START
STASH
STATE
STATO
STAVE
STAYS
SUAVE
SWABS
SWAGE
SWAGS
SWAIL
SWAIN
SWALE
SWAMI
SWAMP
SWANK
SWANS
SWAPS
SWARD
SWARM
SWART
SWASH
SWATH
SWATS
SWAYS

S••A•

SABAH
SAGAS
SALAD
SAMAR
SARAH
SARAN
SARAS
SATAN
SCRAG
SCRAM
SCRAP
SEBAT
SEDAN
SELAH
SEPAL
SERAC
SERAI
SERAL
SETAE
SHEAF
SHEAR
SHEAS
SHIAH
SHOAL
SHOAT
SILAS
SIMAR
SINAI
SISAL
SITAR
SIVAN
SIZAR
SKEAN
SKOAL

SKUAS
SMEAR
SNEAK
SODAS
SOFAS
SOJAS
SOLAN
SOLAR
SOMAT
SONAR
SORAS
SOWAR
SOYAS
SPEAK
SPEAR
SPLAT
SPLAY
SPRAG
SPRAT
SPRAY
SQUAB
SQUAD
SQUAT
SQUAW
STEAD
STEAK
STEAL
STEAM
STOAE
STOAS
STOAT
STRAP
STRAT
STRAW
STRAY
SUBAH
SUDAN
SUGAR
SUMAC
SURAH
SURAL
SURAS
SUSAN
SWEAR
SWEAT

S•••A
SABRA
SACRA
SAIGA
SALPA
SAMBA
SAMOA
SAUNA
SCAPA
SCHWA
SCUBA
SCUTA
SELMA
SENNA
SEPIA
SEPTA
SERRA
SHEBA
SIGMA
SILVA
SITKA
SOFIA
SOFTA
SOLFA
SONIA
SONYA
SOUSA
SPICA
STOMA
STRIA
STUKA
STUPA
SULFA
SUNNA
SUPRA
SUTRA
SYLVA
SYRIA

•SA••
ISAAC
OSAGE
PSALM
TSADE
TSARS
USAFI
USAGE

•S•A•
ASCAP
ASIAN
ASSAI
ASSAM
ASSAY
ASWAN
ESSAY
ISAAC
ISBAS
ISLAM
OSCAN
OSCAR
OSMAN
PSHAW
PSOAS
USUAL

•S••A
ASPCA
ASYLA
OSTIA

••SA•
ANSAE
ASSAI
ASSAM
ASSAY
BASAL
CESAR
ELSAS
ESSAY
LISAS
MESAS
MOSAN
NASAL
NISAN
PUSAN
ROSAS
SISAL
SUSAN
UNSAY
VISAS

••S•A
BASRA
COSTA
FOSSA
GUSTA
HOSEA
JOSUA
LYSSA
MUSCA
OPSIA
PASHA
PASTA
TESLA
TESTA
VESTA
VISTA

•••SA
BALSA
BURSA
DORSA
FOSSA
LHASA
LUISA
LYSSA
MENSA
OMASA
PAISA
PRESA
SOUSA
TULSA

S•B••
SABAH
SABED
SABER
SABES
SABIN
SABLE
SABOT
SABRA
SEBAT
SEBUM
SIBYL
SOBER
SUBAH
SYBIL

S••B•
SAMBA
SAMBO
SCABS
SCUBA
SERBS
SHEBA
SLABS
SLOBS
SLUBS
SNOBS
SNUBS
SORBS
STABS
STUBS
SWABS

S•••B
SAHEB
SAHIB
SCRUB
SHRUB
SQUAB
SQUIB

•SB••
ISBAS

••SB•
BUSBY

SC•••
SCABS
SCADS
SCALD
SCALE
SCALL
SCALP
SCALY
SCAMP
SCAND
SCANS
SCANT
SCAPA
SCAPE
SCAPI
SCARE
SCARF
SCARP
SCARS
SCARY
SCATO
SCATS
SCAUP
SCEND
SCENE
SCENT
SCHIZ
SCHMO
SCHWA
SCIFI
SCION
SCOFF
SCOLD
SCONE
SCOOP
SCOOT
SCOPE
SCOPS
SCOPY
SCORE
SCORN
SCOTO
SCOTS
SCOTT
SCOUR
SCOUT
SCOWL
SCOWS
SCRAG
SCRAM
SCRAP
SCREE
SCREW
SCRIM
SCRIP
SCROD
SCRUB
SCRUM
SCUBA
SCUDI
SCUDO
SCUDS
SCUFF
SCULL
SCULP
SCUMS
SCUPS
SCURF
SCUTA
SCUTE
SCUTS
SCYPH

S•C••
SACKS
SACRA
SACRO
SECCO
SECTS
SICES
SICKS
SOCIO
SOCKS
SOCLE
SUCKS
SUCRE
SYCEE
SYCES

S••C•
SARCO
SAUCE
SAUCY
SECCO
SHACK
SHOCK
SHUCK
SINCE
SLACK
SLICE
SLICK
SMACK
SMOCK
SNACK
SNICK
SPACE
SPECK
SPECS
SPICA
SPICE
SPICY
STACK
STACY
STICH
STICK
STOCK
STUCK
SULCI

S•••C
SALIC
SERAC
SILIC
SONIC
STOIC
SUFIC
SUMAC

•SC••
ASCAP
ASCOT
ASCUS
OSCAN
OSCAR

•S•C•
ASPCA
PSYCH
USMCR

•S••C
ASPIC
ASSOC
ISAAC
ISTIC
OSMIC

••SC•
BOSCH
CASCO
CISCO
DISCI
DISCS
FISCS
MUSCA
PASCH
PISCI
VISCT

••S•C
ASSOC
BASIC
COSEC
CUSEC
MESIC
MUSIC
VESIC

•••SC
CRESC

S•D••
SADHU
SADIE
SADLY
SEDAN
SEDER
SEDGE
SEDGY
SEDUM
SIDED
SIDER
SIDES
SIDLE
SIDON
SODAS
SODOM
SUDAN
SUDOR
SUDSY

S••D•
SANDS
SANDY
SCADS
SCUDI
SCUDO
SCUDS
SEEDS
SEEDY
SENDS
SHADE
SHADY
SHEDS
SKIDS
SLEDS
SLIDE
SNIDE
SOLDI
SOLDO
SPADE
SPODE
SPUDS
STUDS
STUDY
SUEDE
SURDS
SWEDE

S•••D
SABED
SALAD
SAPID
SATED
SAVED
SAWED
SAYID
SCALD
SCAND
SCEND
SCOLD
SCROD
SERED
SEWED
SEXED
SHARD
SHERD
SHIED
SHRED
SIDED
SIRED
SIZED
SKALD
SKEED
SKIED
SLOYD
SLUED
SNOOD
SOLED
SOLID
SOUND
SOWED
SPEED
SPEND
SPIED
SQUAD
SQUID
STAID
STAND
STEAD
STEED
STIED
STOOD
SWARD
SWORD
SYNOD

•S•D•
ASIDE
TSADE

•S••D
ASKED
ISLED
PSEUD

••SD•
MISDO

••S•D
BASED
BUSED
CASED
DOSED
EASED
FUSED
HOSED
LYSED
MUSED
NOSED
POSED
ROSED
VISED
WISED

SE•••

SEALS
SEAMS
SEAMY
SEANS
SEARS
SEATO
SEATS
SEBAT
SEBUM
SECCO
SECTS
SEDAN
SEDER
SEDGE
SEDGY
SEDUM
SEEDS
SEEDY
SEEKS
SEEMS
SEEPS
SEERS
SEGNI
SEGNO
SEGOS
SEINE
SEISM
SEIZE
SELAH
SELEN
SELLS
SELMA
SEMEN
SENDS
SENNA
SENOR
SENSE
SEOUL
SEPAL
SEPIA
SEPOY
SEPTA
SEPTI
SEPTO
SEPTS
SERAC
SERAI
SERAL
SERBS
SERED
SERES
SERFS
SERGE
SERIF
SERIN
SEROW
SERRA
SERUM
SERVE
SERVO
SETAE
SETHS
SETON
SETTO
SETUP
SEVEN
SEVER
SEWED
SEWER
SEXED
SEXES

S•E••

SCEND
SCENE
SCENT
SEEDS
SEEDY
SEEKS
SEEMS
SEEPS
SEERS
SHEAF
SHEAR
SHEAS
SHEBA
SHEDS
SHEEN
SHEEP
SHEER
SHEET
SHEIK
SHELF
SHELL
SHEOL
SHERD
SHEWN
SHEWS
SIEGE
SIEUR
SIEVE
SKEAN
SKEED
SKEES
SKEET
SKEGS
SKEIN
SKEPS
SKEWS
SLEDS
SLEEK
SLEEP
SLEET
SLEPT
SLEWS
SMEAR
SMELL
SMELT
SMEWS
SNEAK
SNEER
SNELL
SPEAK
SPEAR
SPECK
SPECS
SPEED
SPELL
SPELT
SPEND
SPENT
SPERM
SPEWS
STEAD
STEAK
STEAL
STEAM
STEED
STEEL
STEEP
STEER
STEIN
STELE
STEMS
STENO
STEPS
STERE
STERN
STETH
STETS
STEVE
STEWS
SUEDE
SUERS
SUETY
SWEAR
SWEAT
SWEDE
SWEEP
SWEET
SWELL
SWEPT

S••E•

SABED
SABER
SABES
SAFER
SAFES
SAGER
SAGES
SAHEB
SAKER
SAKES
SALEM
SALEP
SALES
SAMEK
SANER
SATED
SATES
SAVED
SAVER
SAVES
SAWED
SAWER
SAXES
SAYER
SCREE
SCREW
SEDER
SELEN
SEMEN
SERED
SERES
SEVEN
SEVER
SEWED
SEWER
SEXED
SEXES
SHEEN
SHEEP
SHEER
SHEET
SHIED
SHIER
SHOER
SHOES
SHRED
SHREW
SHYER
SICES
SIDED
SIDER
SIDES
SILEX
SINES
SINEW
SIRED
SIREN
SIRES
SITES
SIXES
SIZED
SIZES
SKEED
SKEES
SKEET
SKIED
SKIER
SKIES
SKYEY
SLEEK
SLEEP
SLEET
SLIER
SLOES
SLUED
SLUES
SLYER
SNEER
SNYES
SOBER
SOKES
SOLED
SOLES
SONES
SOREL
SORER
SORES
SOWED
SOWER
SPEED
SPHEN
SPIED
SPIEL
SPIER
SPIES
SPLEN
SPREE
STEED
STEEL
STEEP
STEER
STIED
STIES
STREW
SUMER
SUPER
SUPES
SURER
SWEEP
SWEET
SYCEE
SYCES

S•••E

SABLE
SADIE
SALVE
SAUCE
SAUTE
SCALE
SCAPE
SCARE
SCENE
SCONE
SCOPE
SCORE
SCREE
SCUTE
SEDGE
SEINE
SEIZE
SENSE
SERGE
SERVE
SETAE
SHADE
SHAKE
SHALE
SHAME
SHAPE
SHARE
SHAVE
SHINE
SHIRE
SHIVE
SHONE
SHORE
SHOTE
SHOVE
SHUTE
SIDLE
SIEGE
SIEVE
SINCE
SINGE
SIXTE
SKATE
SKIVE
SLAKE
SLATE
SLAVE
SLICE
SLIDE
SLIME
SLOPE
SMAZE
SMILE
SMITE
SMOKE
SMOTE
SNAKE
SNARE
SNIDE
SNIPE
SNORE
SOCLE
SOLVE
SOMME
SOUSE
SPACE
SPADE
SPARE
SPATE
SPICE
SPIKE
SPILE
SPINE
SPIRE
SPITE
SPODE
SPOKE
SPORE
SPREE
SPRUE
SPUME
STAGE
STAKE
STALE
STARE
STATE
STAVE
STELE
STERE
STEVE
STILE
STIPE
STOAE
STOKE
STOLE
STOME
STONE
STOPE
STORE
STOVE
STOWE
STUPE
STYLE
SUAVE
SUCRE
SUEDE
SUITE
SURGE
SUSIE
SWAGE
SWALE
SWEDE
SWINE
SWIPE
SWORE
SYCEE
SYNGE

•SE••

ISERE
PSEUD
USERS

•S•E•

ASHEN
ASHER
ASHES
ASKED
ASKER
ASKEW
ASPEN
ASPER
ASSES
ASSET
ASTER
ESHER
ESKER
ESSEN
ESSES
ESSEX
ESTER
ISLED
ISLES
ISLET
ISSEI
OSIER
OSLER
OSTEO
USHER

•S••E

ASIDE
ESQUE
ESSIE
ISERE
ISSUE
ISTLE
OSAGE
TSADE
USAGE

••SE•

ANSEL
APSES
ARSES
ASSES
ASSET
BASED
BASEL
BASES
BESET
BISES
BUSED
BUSES
CASED
CASES
COSEC
CUSEC
DESEX
DOSED
DOSER
DOSES
EASED
EASEL
EASES
ERSES
ESSEN
ESSES
ESSEX
FUSED
FUSEE
FUSEL
FUSES
GASES
HOSEA
HOSED
HOSES
IBSEN
INSET
ISSEI
LASER
LOSER
LOSES
LYSED
LYSES
MASER
MISER
MISES
MOSES
MOSEY
MUSED
MUSES
NISEI
NOSED
NOSES
NOSEY
OASES
ONSET
OUSEL
POSED
POSER
POSES
RESET
RISEN
RISER
RISES
ROSED
ROSES
RUSES
UNSEX
UPSET
VASES
VISED

VISES
WISED
WISER
WISES
YESES

••S•E
AISLE
AISNE
ANSAE
BASLE
BASTE
CASTE
ELSIE
ENSUE
ESSIE
FESSE
FOSSE
FUSEE
GASPE
HASTE
ISSUE
JESSE
JOSIE
JOSUE
LISLE
MASSE
MESNE
PASSE
PASTE
POSSE
SUSIE
TASTE
WASTE

•••SE
ABASE
ABUSE
AMUSE
ANISE
ARISE
AROSE
BLASE
BOISE
BOUSE
BOWSE
BURSE
CAUSE
CEASE
CENSE
CHASE
CHOSE
CLOSE
COPSE
CORSE
CRUSE
CURSE
DENSE
DOUSE
DOWSE
DRUSE
DULSE
ELISE
ERASE
EROSE
FALSE
FEASE
FESSE
FOSSE
FRISE
GEESE
GOOSE
GORSE
GUISE
HANSE
HAWSE
HORSE
HOUSE
JESSE
LAPSE
LEASE
LOOSE
LOUSE
LUISE
MANSE
MASSE
MEUSE
MOOSE
MORSE
MOUSE
NOISE
NOOSE
NORSE
NURSE
OBESE
PAISE
PARSE
PASSE
PAUSE
PEASE
PERSE
PHASE
POISE
POSSE
PROSE
PULSE
PURSE
RAISE
RINSE
ROUSE
SENSE
SOUSE
TEASE
TENSE
TERSE
THESE
THOSE
UKASE
ULOSE
VERSE
WHOSE
WORSE

S•F••
SAFER
SAFES
SIFTS
SOFAS
SOFIA
SOFTA
SOFTY
SUFIC
SUFIS

S••F•
SCIFI
SCOFF
SCUFF
SERFS
SHAFT
SHIFT
SKIFF
SNAFU
SNIFF
SNUFF
SOLFA
STAFF
STIFF
STUFF
SULFA
SULFO
SURFS
SURFY
SWIFT

S•••F
SCARF
SCOFF
SCUFF
SCURF
SERIF
SHEAF
SHELF
SKIFF
SNIFF
SNUFF
SPOOF
STAFF
STIFF
STUFF

•S•F•
USAFI

S•G••
SAGAS
SAGER
SAGES
SAGOS
SAGUM
SEGNI
SEGNO
SEGOS
SIGHS
SIGHT
SIGIL
SIGMA
SIGNS
SOGGY
SUGAR

S••G•
SAIGA
SEDGE
SEDGY
SERGE
SHAGS
SIEGE
SINGE
SINGS
SKEGS
SLAGS
SLOGS
SLUGS
SMOGS
SNAGS
SNUGS
SOGGY
SONGS
SORGO
SOUGH
STAGE
STAGS
STAGY
STOGY
SURGE
SURGY
SWAGE
SWAGS
SWIGS
SYNGE

S•••G
SCRAG
SHRUG
SLANG
SLING
SLUNG
SPANG
SPRAG
SPRIG
STING
STUNG
SUING
SWING
SWUNG

•S•G•
OSAGE
USAGE

•S••G
USING

SH•••
SHACK
SHADE
SHADY
SHAFT
SHAGS
SHAHS
SHAKE
SHAKO
SHAKY
SHALE
SHALL
SHALT
SHALY
SHAME
SHAMS
SHANK
SHANS
SHANT
SHAPE
SHARD
SHARE
SHARK
SHARP
SHAUN
SHAVE
SHAWL
SHAWM
SHAWN
SHAWS
SHAYS
SHEAF
SHEAR
SHEAS
SHEBA
SHEDS
SHEEN
SHEEP
SHEER
SHEET
SHEIK
SHELF
SHELL
SHEOL
SHERD
SHEWN
SHEWS
SHIAH
SHIED
SHIER
SHIFT
SHILL
SHILY
SHIMS
SHINE
SHINS
SHINY
SHIPS
SHIRE
SHIRK
SHIRR
SHIRT
SHIVE
SHIVS
SHOAL
SHOAT
SHOCK
SHOER
SHOES
SHOJI
SHONE
SHOOK
SHOOS
SHOOT
SHOPS
SHORE
SHORL
SHORN
SHORT
SHOTE
SHOTS
SHOUT
SHOVE
SHOWN
SHOWS
SHOWY
SHRED
SHREW
SHRUB
SHRUG
SHUCK
SHULS
SHUNS
SHUNT
SHUSH
SHUTE
SHUTS
SHYER
SHYLY

S•H••
SAHEB
SAHIB
SCHIZ
SCHMO
SCHWA
SPHEN

S••H•
SADHU
SETHS
SHAHS
SIGHS
SIGHT
SIKHS
SOPHY
SPAHI

S•••H
SABAH
SARAH
SCYPH
SELAH
SHIAH
SHUSH
SIXTH
SLASH
SLOSH
SLOTH
SLUSH
SMASH
SMITH
SNATH
SOUGH
SOUTH
STAPH
STASH
STETH
STICH
SUBAH
SURAH
SWASH
SWATH
SWISH
SYLPH

•SH••
ASHEN
ASHER
ASHES
ASHUR
ESHER
PSHAW
USHER

•S•H•
USPHS

•S••H
PSYCH

••SH•
BUSHY
CUSHY
DASHY
FISHY
GUSHY
MASHY
MESHY
MUSHY
PASHA
PUSHY
RUSHY
WASHY

••S•H
BOSCH
PASCH

•••SH
ABASH
AMISH
APISH
AWASH
BLUSH
BRASH
BRUSH
CLASH
CRASH
CRUSH
CUISH
FLASH
FLESH
FLUSH
FRESH
FROSH
GNASH
HARSH
IRISH
LEASH
MARSH
PLASH
PLUSH
QUASH
SHUSH
SLASH
SLOSH
SLUSH
SMASH
STASH
SWASH
SWISH
TRASH
WELSH
WHISH

SI•••
SIALO
SIBYL
SICES
SICKS
SIDED
SIDER
SIDES
SIDLE
SIDON
SIEGE
SIEUR
SIEVE
SIFTS
SIGHS
SIGHT
SIGIL
SIGMA
SIGNS
SIKHS
SILAS
SILEX
SILIC
SILKS
SILKY
SILLS
SILLY
SILOS
SILTS
SILTY
SILVA
SIMAR
SIMON
SIMPS
SINAI
SINCE
SINES
SINEW
SINGE
SINGS
SINKS
SINUS
SIOUX
SIRED
SIREN
SIRES
SIRUP
SISAL
SISSY
SITAR
SITES

SITIN
SITKA
SITUS
SIVAN
SIXES
SIXTE
SIXTH
SIXTY
SIZAR
SIZED
SIZES

S•I••

SAIGA
SAILS
SAINT
SCIFI
SCION
SEINE
SEISM
SEIZE
SHIAH
SHIED
SHIER
SHIFT
SHILL
SHILY
SHIMS
SHINE
SHINS
SHINY
SHIPS
SHIRE
SHIRK
SHIRR
SHIRT
SHIVE
SHIVS
SKIDS
SKIED
SKIER
SKIES
SKIFF
SKILL
SKIMO
SKIMP
SKIMS
SKINK
SKINS
SKIPS
SKIRR
SKIRT
SKITS
SKIVE
SLICE
SLICK
SLIDE
SLIER
SLILY
SLIME
SLIMS
SLIMY
SLING
SLINK
SLIPS
SLIPT
SLITS
SMILE
SMIRK
SMITE
SMITH
SNICK
SNIDE
SNIFF
SNIPE
SNIPS
SOILS
SPICA
SPICE
SPICY
SPIED
SPIEL
SPIER
SPIES
SPIKE
SPIKY
SPILE
SPILL
SPILT
SPINE
SPINI
SPINS
SPINY
SPIRE
SPIRO
SPIRT
SPIRY
SPITE
SPITS
SPITZ
STICH
STICK
STIED
STIES
STIFF
STILE
STILL
STILT
STIMY
STING
STINK
STINT
STIPE
STIRK
STIRS
SUING
SUINT
SUITE
SUITS
SWIFT
SWIGS
SWILL
SWIMS
SWINE
SWING
SWIPE
SWIRL
SWISH
SWISS

S••I•

SABIN
SADIE
SAHIB
SALIC
SAPID
SARIS
SASIN
SATIN
SAVIN
SAYID
SCHIZ
SCRIM
SCRIP
SEPIA
SERIF
SERIN
SHEIK
SIGIL
SILIC
SITIN
SKEIN
SLAIN
SNAIL
SOCIO
SOFIA
SOLID
SONIA
SONIC
SOZIN
SPAIN
SPAIT
SPLIT
SPOIL
SPRIG
SPRIT
SQUIB
SQUID
STAID
STAIN
STAIR
STEIN
STOIC
STRIA
STRIP
SUFIC
SUFIS
SUSIE
SWAIL
SWAIN
SYBIL
SYRIA

S•••I

SALMI
SCAPI
SCIFI
SCUDI
SEGNI
SEPTI
SERAI
SHOJI
SINAI
SOLDI
SOMNI
SPAHI
SPINI
STYLI
SULCI
SUNNI
SWAMI

•SI••

ASIAN
ASIDE
OSIER
OSITY
USING

•S•I•

ASPIC
ASPIS
ASTIR
ESSIE
ISTIC
OSMIC
OSTIA

•S••I

ASSAI
ISSEI
USAFI

••SI•

AESIR
APSIS
ARSIS
BASIC
BASIL
BASIN
BASIS
ELSIE
EOSIN
ESSIE
FUSIL
IASIS
JOSIE
LYSIN
LYSIS
MESIC
MUSIC
OASIS
OPSIA
OPSIS
POSIT
RESIN
ROSIN
SASIN
SUSIE
VESIC
VISIT

••S•I

ASSAI
BASSI
BYSSI
CESTI
CYSTI
DISCI
ISSEI
NISEI
PISCI

•••SI

BASSI
BYSSI
DORSI
ICOSI
PARSI
PHYSI
QUASI
TARSI
TORSI

S•J••

SAJOU
SOJAS

S••J•

SHOJI

SK•••

SKALD
SKATE
SKEAN
SKEED
SKEES
SKEET
SKEGS
SKEIN
SKEPS
SKEWS
SKIDS
SKIED
SKIER
SKIES
SKIFF
SKILL
SKIMO
SKIMP
SKIMS
SKINK
SKINS
SKIPS
SKIRR
SKIRT
SKITS
SKIVE
SKOAL
SKUAS
SKULK
SKULL
SKUNK
SKYEY

S•K••

SAKER
SAKES
SIKHS
SOKES

S••K•

SACKS
SARKS
SEEKS
SHAKE
SHAKO
SHAKY
SICKS
SILKS
SILKY
SINKS
SITKA
SLAKE
SMOKE
SMOKY
SNAKE
SNAKY
SOAKS
SOCKS
SPIKE
SPIKY
SPOKE
STAKE
STOKE
STUKA
SUCKS
SULKS
SULKY

S•••K

SAMEK
SHACK
SHANK
SHARK
SHEIK
SHIRK
SHOCK
SHOOK
SHUCK
SKINK
SKULK
SKUNK
SLACK
SLEEK
SLICK
SLINK
SLUNK
SMACK
SMIRK
SMOCK
SNACK
SNARK
SNEAK
SNICK
SNOOK
SPANK
SPARK
SPEAK
SPECK
SPOOK
SPUNK
STACK
STALK
STANK
STARK
STEAK
STICK
STINK
STIRK
STOCK
STOOK
STORK
STUCK
STUNK
SWANK

•SK••

ASKED
ASKER
ASKEW
ESKER

••SK•

BASKS
BOSKS
BOSKY
BUSKS
CASKS
CUSKS
DESKS
DISKO
DISKS
DUSKS
DUSKY
HUSKS
HUSKY
MASKS
MUSKS
MUSKY
PESKY
RISKS
RISKY
RUSKS
TASKS
TUSKS

•••SK

BRISK
BRUSK
FLASK
FRISK
KIOSK
KURSK
MINSK
TORSK
WHISK

SL•••

SLABS
SLACK
SLAGS
SLAIN
SLAKE
SLAMS
SLANG
SLANT
SLAPS
SLASH
SLATE
SLATS
SLATY
SLAVE
SLAVO
SLAVS
SLAWS
SLAYS
SLEDS
SLEEK
SLEEP
SLEET
SLEPT
SLEWS
SLICE
SLICK
SLIDE
SLIER
SLILY
SLIME
SLIMS
SLIMY
SLING
SLINK
SLIPS
SLIPT
SLITS
SLOBS
SLOES
SLOGS
SLOOP
SLOPE
SLOPS
SLOSH
SLOTH
SLOTS
SLOWS
SLOYD
SLUBS
SLUED
SLUES
SLUGS
SLUMP
SLUMS
SLUNG
SLUNK
SLURP
SLURS
SLUSH
SLUTS
SLYER
SLYLY

S•L••

SALAD
SALEM
SALEP
SALES
SALIC
SALLY
SALMI
SALOL
SALON
SALPA

SALTS
SALTY
SALUS
SALVE
SALVO
SELAH
SELEN
SELLS
SELMA
SILAS
SILEX
SILIC
SILKS
SILKY
SILLS
SILLY
SILOS
SILTS
SILTY
SILVA
SOLAN
SOLAR
SOLDI
SOLDO
SOLED
SOLES
SOLFA
SOLID
SOLON
SOLOS
SOLUS
SOLVE
SPLAT
SPLAY
SPLEN
SPLIT
SULCI
SULFA
SULFO
SULKS
SULKY
SULLY
SULUS
SYLPH
SYLVA

S••L•

SABLE
SADLY
SAILS
SALLY
SAULS
SAULT
SCALD
SCALE
SCALL
SCALP
SCALY
SCOLD
SCULL
SCULP
SEALS
SELLS
SHALE
SHALL
SHALT
SHALY
SHELF
SHELL
SHILL
SHILY
SHULS
SHYLY
SIALO
SIDLE
SILLS
SILLY
SKALD
SKILL
SKULK
SKULL
SLILY
SLYLY
SMALL
SMALT
SMELL
SMELT
SMILE
SMOLT
SNELL
SOCLE
SOILS
SOULS
SPALL
SPELL
SPELT
SPILE
SPILL
SPILT
STALE
STALK
STALL
STELE
STILE
STILL
STILT
STOLE
STULL
STYLE
STYLI
STYLO
SULLY
SURLY
SWALE
SWELL
SWILL

S•••L

SALOL
SCALL
SCOWL
SCULL
SEOUL
SEPAL
SERAL
SHALL
SHAWL
SHELL
SHEOL
SHILL
SHOAL
SHORL
SIBYL
SIGIL
SISAL
SKILL
SKOAL
SKULL
SMALL
SMELL
SNAIL
SNARL
SNELL
SOREL
SOTOL
SPALL
SPELL
SPIEL
SPILL
SPOIL
SPOOL
STALL
STEAL
STEEL
STILL
STOOL
STULL
SURAL
SWAIL
SWELL
SWILL
SWIRL
SYBIL

•SL••

ISLAM
ISLED
ISLES
ISLET
OSLER

•S•L•

ASYLA
ISTLE
PSALM

•S••L

USUAL

••SL•

AISLE
BASLE
LISLE
TESLA

••S•L

ANSEL
AUSTL
BASAL
BASEL
BASIL
EASEL
FUSEL
FUSIL
LYSOL
NASAL
OUSEL
SISAL

SM•••

SMACK
SMALL
SMALT
SMART
SMASH
SMAZE
SMEAR
SMELL
SMELT
SMEWS
SMILE
SMIRK
SMITE
SMITH
SMOCK
SMOGS
SMOKE
SMOKY
SMOLT
SMOTE
SMUTS

S•M••

SAMAR
SAMBA
SAMBO
SAMEK
SAMMY
SAMOA
SAMOS
SEMEN
SIMAR
SIMON
SIMPS
SOMAT
SOMME
SOMNI
SUMAC
SUMER
SUMPS

S••M•

SALMI
SAMMY
SCAMP
SCHMO
SCUMS
SEAMS
SEAMY
SEEMS
SELMA
SHAME
SHAMS
SHIMS
SIGMA
SKIMO
SKIMP
SKIMS
SLAMS
SLIME
SLIMS
SLIMY
SLUMP
SLUMS
SOMME
SPUME
SPUMY
STAMP
STEMS
STIMY
STOMA
STOME
STOMP
STOMY
STUMP
STUMS
STYMY
SWAMI
SWAMP
SWIMS

S•••M

SAGUM
SALEM
SCRAM
SCRIM
SCRUM
SEBUM
SEDUM
SEISM
SERUM
SHAWM
SODOM
SPASM
SPERM
STEAM
STORM
STRUM
SWARM

•SM••

OSMAN
OSMIC
USMCR

•S••M

ASSAM
ISLAM
PSALM

••SM•

COSMO
GISMO

••S•M

ASSAM
BESOM
BOSOM
EPSOM

•••SM

ABYSM
CHASM
DEISM
FOISM
PLASM
PRISM
SEISM
SPASM

SN•••

SNACK
SNAFU
SNAGS
SNAIL
SNAKE
SNAKY
SNAPS
SNARE
SNARK
SNARL
SNATH
SNEAK
SNEER
SNELL
SNICK
SNIDE
SNIFF
SNIPE
SNIPS
SNOBS
SNOOD
SNOOK
SNOOP
SNOOT
SNORE
SNORT
SNOTS
SNOUT
SNOWS
SNOWY
SNUBS
SNUFF
SNUGS
SNYES

S•N••

SANDS
SANDY
SANER
SENDS
SENNA
SENOR
SENSE
SINAI
SINCE
SINES
SINEW
SINGE
SINGS
SINKS
SINUS
SONAR
SONES
SONGS
SONIA
SONIC
SONNY
SONYA
SUNNA
SUNNI
SUNNS
SUNNY
SUNUP
SYNGE
SYNOD

S••N•

SAINT
SAUNA
SCAND
SCANS
SCANT
SCEND
SCENE
SCENT
SCONE
SEANS
SEGNI
SEGNO
SEINE
SENNA
SHANK
SHANS
SHANT
SHINE
SHINS
SHINY
SHONE
SHUNS
SHUNT
SIGNS
SKINK
SKINS
SKUNK
SLANG
SLANT
SLING
SLINK
SLUNG
SLUNK
SOMNI
SONNY
SOUND
SPANG
SPANK
SPANS
SPEND
SPENT
SPINE
SPINI
SPINS
SPINY
SPUNK
STAND
STANK
STANS
STENO
STING
STINK
STINT
STONE
STONY
STUNG
STUNK
STUNS
STUNT
SUING
SUINT
SUNNA
SUNNI
SUNNS
SUNNY
SWANK
SWANS
SWINE
SWING
SWUNG

S•••N

SABIN
SALON
SARAN
SASIN
SATAN
SATIN
SAVIN
SAXON
SCION
SCORN
SEDAN
SELEN
SEMEN
SERIN
SETON
SEVEN
SHAUN
SHAWN
SHEEN
SHEWN
SHORN
SHOWN
SIDON
SIMON
SIREN
SITIN
SIVAN
SKEAN
SKEIN
SLAIN
SOLAN
SOLON
SOZIN
SPAIN
SPAWN
SPHEN
SPLEN
SPOON
SPURN
STAIN
STEIN
STERN

SUDAN
SUSAN
SWAIN
SWOON
SWORN

•S•N•
ASSNS
USING

•S••N
ASHEN
ASIAN
ASPEN
ASTON
ASWAN
ESSEN
OSCAN
OSMAN

••SN•
AISNE
ASSNS
HASNT
MESNE
WASNT

••S•N
ARSON
BASIN
BISON
BOSUN
EOSIN
ESSEN
HYSON
IBSEN
JASON
LYSIN
MASON
MESON
MOSAN
NISAN
PUSAN
RESIN
RISEN
ROSIN
SASIN
SUSAN

SO•••
SOAKS
SOAPS
SOAPY
SOARS
SOBER
SOCIO
SOCKS
SOCLE
SODAS
SODOM
SOFAS
SOFIA
SOFTA
SOFTY
SOGGY
SOILS
SOJAS
SOKES
SOLAN
SOLAR
SOLDI
SOLDO
SOLED
SOLES
SOLFA
SOLID
SOLON
SOLOS
SOLUS
SOLVE
SOMAT
SOMME
SOMNI
SONAR
SONES
SONGS
SONIA
SONIC
SONNY
SONYA
SOOTS
SOOTY
SOPHY
SOPOR
SOPPY
SORAS
SORBS
SOREL
SORER
SORES
SORGO
SORRY
SORTS
SORUS
SOTOL
SOUGH
SOULS
SOUND
SOUPS
SOUPY
SOURS
SOUSA
SOUSE
SOUTH
SOWAR
SOWED
SOWER
SOYAS
SOZIN

S•O••
SCOFF
SCOLD
SCONE
SCOOP
SCOOT
SCOPE
SCOPS
SCOPY
SCORE
SCORN
SCOTO
SCOTS
SCOTT
SCOUR
SCOUT
SCOWL
SCOWS
SEOUL
SHOAL
SHOAT
SHOCK
SHOER
SHOES
SHOJI
SHONE
SHOOK
SHOOS
SHOOT
SHOPS
SHORE
SHORL
SHORN
SHORT
SHOTE
SHOTS
SHOUT
SHOVE
SHOWN
SHOWS
SHOWY
SIOUX
SKOAL
SLOBS
SLOES
SLOGS
SLOOP
SLOPE
SLOPS
SLOSH
SLOTH
SLOTS
SLOWS
SLOYD
SMOCK
SMOGS
SMOKE
SMOKY
SMOLT
SMOTE
SNOBS
SNOOD
SNOOK
SNOOP
SNOOT
SNORE
SNORT
SNOTS
SNOUT
SNOWS
SNOWY
SOOTS
SOOTY
SPODE
SPOIL
SPOKE
SPOOF
SPOOK
SPOOL
SPOON
SPOOR
SPORE
SPORO
SPORT
SPOTS
SPOUT
STOAE
STOAS
STOAT
STOCK
STOGY
STOIC
STOKE
STOLE
STOMA
STOME
STOMP
STOMY
STONE
STONY
STOOD
STOOK
STOOL
STOOP
STOPE
STOPS
STOPT
STORE
STORK
STORM
STORY
STOSS
STOUP
STOUT
STOVE
STOWE
STOWS
SWOON
SWOOP
SWORD
SWORE
SWORN

S••O•
SABOT
SAGOS
SAJOU
SALOL
SALON
SAMOA
SAMOS
SAPOR
SAVOR
SAVOY
SAXON
SCION
SCOOP
SCOOT
SCROD
SEGOS
SENOR
SEPOY
SEROW
SETON
SHEOL
SHOOK
SHOOS
SHOOT
SIDON
SILOS
SIMON
SLOOP
SNOOD
SNOOK
SNOOP
SNOOT
SODOM
SOLON
SOLOS
SOPOR
SOTOL
SPOOF
SPOOK
SPOOL
SPOON
SPOOR
STOOD
STOOK
STOOL
STOOP
STROP
SUDOR
SWOON
SWOOP
SYNOD

S•••O
SACRO
SALVO
SAMBO
SAPRO
SARCO
SARTO
SAURO
SAYSO
SCATO
SCHMO
SCOTO
SCUDO
SEATO
SECCO
SEGNO
SEPTO
SERVO
SETTO
SHAKO
SIALO
SKIMO
SLAVO
SOCIO
SOLDO
SORGO
SPIRO
SPORO
STATO
STENO
STYLO
SULFO

•SO••
PSOAS

•S•O•
ASCOT
ASSOC
ASTON
ASTOR
ESTOP
FSTOP

•S••O
ASTRO
OSTEO

••SO•
AESOP
ARSON
ASSOC
BESOM
BESOT
BISON
BOSOM
EPSOM
HYSON
JASON
LYSOL
MASON
MESON
PESOS
VISOR

••S•O
BASSO
CASCO
CISCO
COSMO
COSTO
CUSSO
CYSTO
DISKO
GESSO
GISMO
GUSTO
HISTO
LASSO
MASTO
MISDO
MOSSO
RUSSO
TASSO

•••SO
ANISO
AVISO
BASSO
CANSO
CUSSO
DORSO
GESSO
HYPSO
LASSO
MOSSO
RUSSO
SAYSO
TARSO
TASSO
TORSO
VERSO
WHOSO

SP•••
SPACE
SPADE
SPAHI
SPAIN
SPAIT
SPALL
SPANG
SPANK
SPANS
SPARE
SPARK
SPARS
SPASM
SPATE
SPATS
SPAWN
SPAYS
SPEAK
SPEAR
SPECK
SPECS
SPEED
SPELL
SPELT
SPEND
SPENT
SPERM
SPEWS
SPHEN
SPICA
SPICE
SPICY
SPIED
SPIEL
SPIER
SPIES
SPIKE
SPIKY
SPILE
SPILL
SPILT
SPINE
SPINI
SPINS
SPINY
SPIRE
SPIRO
SPIRT
SPIRY
SPITE
SPITS
SPITZ
SPLAT
SPLAY
SPLEN
SPLIT
SPODE
SPOIL
SPOKE
SPOOF
SPOOK
SPOOL
SPOON
SPOOR
SPORE
SPORO
SPORT
SPOTS
SPOUT
SPRAG
SPRAT
SPRAY
SPREE
SPRIG
SPRIT
SPRUE
SPUDS
SPUME
SPUMY
SPUNK
SPURN
SPURS
SPURT

S•P••
SAPID
SAPOR
SAPPY
SAPRO
SEPAL
SEPIA
SEPOY
SEPTA
SEPTI
SEPTO
SEPTS
SOPHY
SOPOR
SOPPY
SUPER
SUPES
SUPRA

S••P•
SALPA
SAPPY
SCAPA
SCAPE
SCAPI
SCOPE
SCOPS

SCOPY
SCUPS
SCYPH
SEEPS
SHAPE
SHIPS
SHOPS
SIMPS
SKEPS
SKIPS
SLAPS
SLEPT
SLIPS
SLIPT
SLOPE
SLOPS
SNAPS
SNIPE
SNIPS
SOAPS
SOAPY
SOPPY
SOUPS
SOUPY
STAPH
STEPS
STIPE
STOPE
STOPS
STOPT
STUPA
STUPE
SUMPS
SWAPS
SWEPT
SWIPE
SYLPH

S•••P

SALEP
SCALP
SCAMP
SCARP
SCAUP
SCOOP
SCRAP
SCRIP
SCULP
SETUP
SHARP
SHEEP
SIRUP
SKIMP
SLEEP
SLOOP
SLUMP
SLURP
SNOOP
STAMP
STEEP
STOMP
STOOP
STOUP
STRAP
STRIP
STROP
STUMP
SUNUP
SWAMP
SWEEP
SWOOP
SYRUP

•SP••

ASPCA
ASPEN
ASPER
ASPIC
ASPIS
USPHS

•S••P

ASCAP
ESTOP
FSTOP
USURP

••SP•

CUSPS
GASPE
GASPS
HASPS
LISPS
RASPS
RASPY
WASPS
WASPY
WISPS
WISPY

••S•P

AESOP

•••SP

CLASP
CRISP
GRASP
KNOSP

SQ•••

SQUAB
SQUAD
SQUAT
SQUAW
SQUIB
SQUID

•SQ••

ESQUE

S•R••

SARAH
SARAN
SARAS
SARCO
SARIS
SARKS
SARTO
SCRAG
SCRAM
SCRAP
SCREE
SCREW
SCRIM
SCRIP
SCROD
SCRUB
SCRUM
SERAC
SERAI
SERAL
SERBS
SERED
SERES
SERFS
SERGE
SERIF
SERIN
SEROW
SERRA
SERUM
SERVE
SERVO
SHRED
SHREW
SHRUB
SHRUG
SIRED
SIREN
SIRES
SIRUP
SORAS
SORBS
SOREL
SORER
SORES
SORGO
SORRY
SORTS
SORUS
SPRAG
SPRAT
SPRAY
SPREE
SPRIG
SPRIT
SPRUE
STRAP
STRAT
STRAW
STRAY
STREW
STRIA
STRIP
STROP
STRUM
STRUT
SURAH
SURAL
SURAS
SURDS
SURER
SURFS
SURFY
SURGE
SURGY
SURLY
SYRIA
SYRUP

S••R•

SABRA
SACRA
SACRO
SAPRO
SAURO
SAURY
SCARE
SCARF
SCARP
SCARS
SCARY
SCORE
SCORN
SCURF
SEARS
SEERS
SERRA
SHARD
SHARE
SHARK
SHARP
SHERD
SHIRE
SHIRK
SHIRR
SHIRT
SHORE
SHORL
SHORN
SHORT
SKIRR
SKIRT
SLURP
SLURS
SMART
SMIRK
SNARE
SNARK
SNARL
SNORE
SNORT
SOARS
SORRY
SOURS
SPARE
SPARK
SPARS
SPERM
SPIRE
SPIRO
SPIRT
SPIRY
SPORE
SPORO
SPORT
SPURN
SPURS
SPURT
STARE
STARK
STARS
START
STERE
STERN
STIRK
STIRS
STORE
STORK
STORM
STORY
SUCRE
SUERS
SUPRA
SUTRA
SWARD
SWARM
SWART
SWIRL
SWORD
SWORE
SWORN

S•••R

SABER
SAFER
SAGER
SAKER
SAMAR
SANER
SAPOR
SATYR
SAVER
SAVOR
SAWER
SAYER
SCOUR
SEDER
SENOR
SEVER
SEWER
SHEAR
SHEER
SHIER
SHIRR
SHOER
SHYER
SIDER
SIEUR
SIMAR
SITAR
SIZAR
SKIER
SKIRR
SLIER
SLYER
SMEAR
SNEER
SOBER
SOLAR
SONAR
SOPOR
SORER
SOWAR
SOWER
SPEAR
SPIER
SPOOR
STAIR
STEER
SUDOR
SUGAR
SUMER
SUPER
SURER
SWEAR

•S•R•

ASTRO
ISERE
TSARS
USERS
USURP
USURY

•S••R

ASHER
ASHUR
ASKER
ASPER
ASSYR
ASTER
ASTIR
ASTOR
ESHER
ESKER
ESTER
OSCAR
OSIER
OSLER
USHER
USMCR

••SR•

BASRA

••S•R

AESIR
ASSYR
CESAR
DOSER
GASTR
LASER
LOSER
MASER
MISER
POSER
RISER
VISOR
WISER

S•S••

SASIN
SASSY
SISAL
SISSY
SUSAN
SUSIE

S••S•

SASSY
SAYSO
SEISM
SENSE
SHUSH
SISSY
SLASH
SLOSH
SLUSH
SMASH
SOUSA
SOUSE
SPASM
STASH
STOSS
SUDSY
SWASH
SWISH
SWISS

S•••S

SABES
SACKS
SAFES
SAGAS
SAGES
SAGOS
SAILS
SAKES
SALES
SALTS
SALUS
SAMOS
SANDS
SARAS
SARIS
SARKS
SATES
SAULS
SAVES
SAXES
SCABS
SCADS
SCANS
SCARS
SCATS
SCOPS
SCOTS
SCOWS
SCUDS
SCUMS
SCUPS
SCUTS
SEALS
SEAMS
SEANS
SEARS
SEATS
SECTS
SEEDS
SEEKS
SEEMS
SEEPS
SEERS
SEGOS
SELLS
SENDS
SEPTS
SERBS
SERES
SERFS
SETHS
SEXES
SHAGS
SHAHS
SHAMS
SHANS
SHAWS
SHAYS
SHEAS
SHEDS
SHEWS
SHIMS
SHINS
SHIPS
SHIVS
SHOES
SHOOS
SHOPS
SHOTS
SHOWS
SHULS
SHUNS
SHUTS
SICES
SICKS
SIDES
SIFTS
SIGHS
SIGNS
SIKHS
SILAS
SILKS
SILLS
SILOS
SILTS
SIMPS
SINES
SINGS
SINKS
SINUS
SIRES
SITES
SITUS
SIXES
SIZES
SKEES
SKEGS
SKEPS
SKEWS
SKIDS
SKIES

SKIMS
SKINS
SKIPS
SKITS
SKUAS
SLABS
SLAGS
SLAMS
SLAPS
SLATS
SLAVS
SLAWS
SLAYS
SLEDS
SLEWS
SLIMS
SLIPS
SLITS
SLOBS
SLOES
SLOGS
SLOPS
SLOTS
SLOWS
SLUBS
SLUES
SLUGS
SLUMS
SLURS
SLUTS
SMEWS
SMOGS
SMUTS
SNAGS
SNAPS
SNIPS
SNOBS
SNOTS
SNOWS
SNUBS
SNUGS
SNYES
SOAKS
SOAPS
SOARS
SOCKS
SODAS
SOFAS
SOILS
SOJAS
SOKES
SOLES
SOLOS
SOLUS
SONES
SONGS
SOOTS
SORAS
SORBS
SORES
SORTS
SORUS
SOULS
SOUPS
SOURS
SOYAS
SPANS
SPARS
SPATS
SPAYS
SPECS
SPEWS
SPIES
SPINS
SPITS
SPOTS
SPUDS
SPURS
STABS
STAGS
STANS
STARS
STAYS
STEMS
STEPS
STETS
STEWS
STIES
STIRS
STOAS
STOPS
STOSS
STOWS
STUBS
STUDS
STUMS
STUNS
SUCKS
SUERS
SUFIS
SUITS
SULKS
SULUS
SUMPS
SUNNS
SUPES
SURAS
SURDS
SURFS
SUZYS
SWABS
SWAGS
SWANS
SWAPS
SWATS
SWAYS
SWIGS
SWIMS
SWISS
SYCES

•SS••

ASSAI
ASSAM
ASSAY
ASSES
ASSET
ASSNS
ASSOC
ASSTS
ASSYR
ESSAY
ESSEN
ESSES
ESSEX
ESSIE
ISSEI
ISSUE

•S••S

ASCUS
ASHES
ASPIS
ASSES
ASSNS
ASSTS
ESSES
ISBAS
ISLES
PSOAS
TSARS
USERS
USPHS

••SS•

BASSI
BASSO
BESSY
BOSSY
BYSSI
CISSY
CUSSO
FESSE
FOSSA
FOSSE
FUSSY
GASSY
GESSO
HUSSY
JASSY
JESSE
JESSY
LASSO
LYSSA
MASSE
MASSY
MESSY
MISSY
MOSSO
MOSSY
MUSSY
PASSE
PASSY
POSSE
PUSSY
RUSSO
SASSY
SISSY
TASSO

••S•S

APSES
APSIS
ARSES
ARSIS
ASSES
ASSNS
ASSTS
BASES
BASIS
BASKS
BESTS
BISES
BOSKS
BUSES
BUSKS
BUSTS
CASES
CASKS
CASTS
CASUS
CISTS
COSTS
CUSKS
CUSPS
CYSTS
DESKS
DISCS
DISKS
DOSES
DUSKS
DUSTS
EASES
ELSAS
ERSES
ESSES
FASTS
FISCS
FISTS
FUSES
GASES
GASPS
GISTS
GUSTS
HASPS
HOSES
HOSTS
HUSKS
IASIS
JESTS
JESUS
JUSTS
LASTS
LISAS
LISPS
LISTS
LOSES
LUSTS
LYSES
LYSIS
MASKS
MASTS
MESAS
MISES
MISTS
MOSES
MUSES
MUSKS
MUSTS
NESTS
NISUS
NOSES
OASES
OASIS
OPSIS
OUSTS
PASTS
PESOS
PESTS
POSES
POSTS
RASPS
RESTS
RISES
RISKS
RISUS
ROSAS
ROSES
RUSES
RUSKS
RUSTS
TASKS
TESTS
TUSKS
VASES
VESTS
VISAS
VISES
WASPS
WISES
WISPS
XYSTS
YESES
ZESTS

•••SS

ABYSS
AMASS
AMISS
BLESS
BLISS
BRASS
CHESS
CLASS
CRASS
CRESS
CROSS
DRESS
DROSS
FLOSS
GAUSS
GLASS
GLOSS
GRASS
GROSS
GUESS
KVASS
LOESS
PRESS
QUASS
STOSS
SWISS
TRASS
TRESS
TRUSS

ST•••

STABS
STACK
STACY
STAFF
STAGE
STAGS
STAGY
STAID
STAIN
STAIR
STAKE
STALE
STALK
STALL
STAMP
STAND
STANK
STANS
STAPH
STARE
STARK
STARS
START
STASH
STATE
STATO
STAVE
STAYS
STEAD
STEAK
STEAL
STEAM
STEED
STEEL
STEEP
STEER
STEIN
STELE
STEMS
STENO
STEPS
STERE
STERN
STETH
STETS
STEVE
STEWS
STICH
STICK
STIED
STIES
STIFF
STILE
STILL
STILT
STIMY
STING
STINK
STINT
STIPE
STIRK
STIRS
STOAE
STOAS
STOAT
STOCK
STOGY
STOIC
STOKE
STOLE
STOMA
STOME
STOMP
STOMY
STONE
STONY
STOOD
STOOK
STOOL
STOOP
STOPE
STOPS
STOPT
STORE
STORK
STORM
STORY
STOSS
STOUP
STOUT
STOVE
STOWE
STOWS
STRAP
STRAT
STRAW
STRAY
STREW
STRIA
STRIP
STROP
STRUM
STRUT
STUBS
STUCK
STUDS
STUDY
STUFF
STUKA
STULL
STUMP
STUMS
STUNG
STUNK
STUNS
STUNT
STUPA
STUPE
STYLE
STYLI
STYLO
STYMY

S•T••

SATAN
SATED
SATES
SATIN
SATYR
SETAE
SETHS
SETON
SETTO
SETUP
SITAR
SITES
SITIN
SITKA
SITUS
SOTOL
SUTRA

S••T•

SALTS
SALTY
SARTO
SAUTE
SCATO
SCATS
SCOTO
SCOTS
SCOTT
SCUTA
SCUTE
SCUTS
SEATO
SEATS
SECTS
SEPTA
SEPTI
SEPTO
SEPTS
SETTO
SHOTE
SHOTS
SHUTE
SHUTS
SIFTS
SILTS
SILTY
SIXTE
SIXTH
SIXTY
SKATE
SKITS
SLATE
SLATS
SLATY
SLITS
SLOTH
SLOTS
SLUTS
SMITE
SMITH
SMOTE

SMUTS
SNATH
SNOTS
SOFTA
SOFTY
SOOTS
SOOTY
SORTS
SOUTH
SPATE
SPATS
SPITE
SPITS
SPITZ
SPOTS
STATE
STATO
STETH
STETS
SUETY
SUITE
SUITS
SWATH
SWATS

S•••T

SABOT
SAINT
SAULT
SCANT
SCENT
SCOOT
SCOTT
SCOUT
SEBAT
SHAFT
SHALT
SHANT
SHEET
SHIFT
SHIRT
SHOAT
SHOOT
SHORT
SHOUT
SHUNT
SIGHT
SKEET
SKIRT
SLANT
SLEET
SLEPT
SLIPT
SMALT
SMART
SMELT
SMOLT
SNOOT
SNORT
SNOUT
SOMAT
SPAIT
SPELT
SPENT
SPILT
SPIRT
SPLAT
SPLIT
SPORT
SPOUT
SPRAT
SPRIT
SPURT
SQUAT
START
STILT
STINT
STOAT
STOPT
STOUT
STRAT
STRUT
STUNT
SUINT
SWART
SWEAT
SWEET
SWEPT
SWIFT

•ST••

ASTER
ASTIR
ASTON
ASTOR
ASTRO
ESTER
ESTOP
FSTOP
ISTIC
ISTLE
OSTEO
OSTIA

•S•T•

ASSTS
OSITY

•S••T

ASCOT
ASSET
ASYUT
ISLET

••ST•

ASSTS
AUSTL
BASTE
BESTS
BUSTS
CASTE
CASTS
CESTI
CISTS
COSTA
COSTO
COSTS
CYSTI
CYSTO
CYSTS
DUSTS
DUSTY
FASTS
FISTS
FUSTY
GASTR
GISTS
GUSTA
GUSTO
GUSTS
GUSTY
HASTE
HASTY
HISTO
HOSTS
JESTS
JUSTS
LASTS
LISTS
LUSTS
LUSTY
MASTO
MASTS
MISTS
MISTY
MUSTS
MUSTY
NASTY
NESTS
OUSTS
PASTA
PASTE
PASTS
PASTY
PESTS
POSTS
RESTS
RUSTS
RUSTY
TASTE
TASTY
TESTA
TESTS
TESTY
VASTY
VESTA
VESTS
VISTA
WASTE
XYSTS
ZESTS
ZESTY

••S•T

ASSET
BESET
BESOT
HASNT
INSET
LISZT
ONSET
POSIT
RESET
UPSET
VISCT
VISIT
WASNT

•••ST

ADUST
AGIST
ANGST
AVAST
BEAST
BLAST
BLEST
BOAST
BOOST
BREST
BURST
CANST
CHEST
COAST
CREST
CRUST
CURST
DEIST
DIDST
DOEST
DREST
EGEST
ERNST
EXIST
FAUST
FEAST
FEIST
FIRST
FOIST
FROST
GEEST
GHOST
GLOST
GRIST
GUEST
HEIST
HOIST
HORST
JOIST
JOUST
LEAST
MAYST
MIDST
MOIST
PLAST
PREST
QUEST
ROAST
ROOST
ROUST
TOAST
TRUST
TRYST
TWIST
VERST
WAIST
WEEST
WHIST
WORST
WREST
WRIST
YEAST

SU•••

SUAVE
SUBAH
SUCKS
SUCRE
SUDAN
SUDOR
SUDSY
SUEDE
SUERS
SUETY
SUFIC
SUFIS
SUGAR
SUING
SUINT
SUITE
SUITS
SULCI
SULFA
SULFO
SULKS
SULKY
SULLY
SULUS
SUMAC
SUMER
SUMPS
SUNNA
SUNNI
SUNNS
SUNNY
SUNUP
SUPER
SUPES
SUPRA
SURAH
SURAL
SURAS
SURDS
SURER
SURFS
SURFY
SURGE
SURGY
SURLY
SUSAN
SUSIE
SUTRA
SUZYS

S•U••

SAUCE
SAUCY
SAULS
SAULT
SAUNA
SAURO
SAURY
SAUTE
SCUBA
SCUDI
SCUDO
SCUDS
SCUFF
SCULL
SCULP
SCUMS
SCUPS
SCURF
SCUTA
SCUTE
SCUTS
SHUCK
SHULS
SHUNS
SHUNT
SHUSH
SHUTE
SHUTS
SKUAS
SKULK
SKULL
SKUNK
SLUBS
SLUED
SLUES
SLUGS
SLUMP
SLUMS
SLUNG
SLUNK
SLURP
SLURS
SLUSH
SLUTS
SMUTS
SNUBS
SNUFF
SNUGS
SOUGH
SOULS
SOUND
SOUPS
SOUPY
SOURS
SOUSA
SOUSE
SOUTH
SPUDS
SPUME
SPUMY
SPUNK
SPURN
SPURS
SPURT
SQUAB
SQUAD
SQUAT
SQUAW
SQUIB
SQUID
STUBS
STUCK
STUDS
STUDY
STUFF
STUKA
STULL
STUMP
STUMS
STUNG
STUNK
STUNS
STUNT
STUPA
STUPE
SWUNG

S••U•

SAGUM
SALUS
SCAUP
SCOUR
SCOUT
SCRUB
SCRUM
SEBUM
SEDUM
SEOUL
SERUM
SETUP
SHAUN
SHOUT
SHRUB
SHRUG
SIEUR
SINUS
SIOUX
SIRUP
SITUS
SNOUT
SOLUS
SORUS
SPOUT
SPRUE
STOUP
STOUT
STRUM
STRUT
SULUS
SUNUP
SYRUP

S•••U

SADHU
SAJOU
SNAFU

•SU••

USUAL
USURP
USURY

•S•U•

ASCUS
ASHUR
ASYUT
ESQUE
ISSUE
PSEUD

••SU•

BOSUN
CASUS
ENSUE
ISSUE
JESUS
JOSUA
JOSUE
NISUS
RISUS

•••SU

MATSU

S•V••

SAVED
SAVER
SAVES
SAVIN
SAVOR
SAVOY
SAVVY
SEVEN
SEVER
SIVAN

S••V•

SALVE
SALVO
SAVVY
SERVE
SERVO
SHAVE
SHIVE
SHIVS
SHOVE
SIEVE
SILVA
SKIVE
SLAVE
SLAVO
SLAVS
SOLVE
STAVE
STEVE
STOVE
SUAVE
SYLVA

SW•••

SWABS
SWAGE
SWAGS
SWAIL
SWAIN
SWALE
SWAMI
SWAMP

SWANK
SWANS
SWAPS
SWARD
SWARM
SWART
SWASH
SWATH
SWATS
SWAYS
SWEAR
SWEAT
SWEDE
SWEEP
SWEET
SWELL
SWEPT
SWIFT
SWIGS
SWILL
SWIMS
SWINE
SWING
SWIPE
SWIRL
SWISH
SWISS
SWOON
SWOOP
SWORD
SWORE
SWORN
SWUNG

S•W••

SAWED
SAWER
SEWED
SEWER
SOWAR
SOWED
SOWER

S••W•

SCHWA
SCOWL
SCOWS
SHAWL
SHAWM
SHAWN
SHAWS
SHEWN
SHEWS
SHOWN
SHOWS
SHOWY
SKEWS
SLAWS
SLEWS
SLOWS
SMEWS
SNOWS
SNOWY
SPAWN
SPEWS
STEWS
STOWE
STOWS

S•••W

SCREW
SEROW
SHREW
SINEW
SQUAW
STRAW
STREW

•SW••

ASWAN

•S••W

ASKEW
PSHAW

S•X••

SAXES
SAXON
SEXED
SEXES
SIXES
SIXTE
SIXTH
SIXTY

S•••X

SILEX
SIOUX

•S••X

ESSEX

••S•X

DESEX
ESSEX
UNSEX

SY•••

SYBIL
SYCEE
SYCES
SYLPH
SYLVA
SYNGE
SYNOD
SYRIA
SYRUP

S•Y••

SAYER
SAYID
SAYSO
SCYPH
SHYER
SHYLY
SKYEY
SLYER
SLYLY
SNYES
SOYAS
STYLE
STYLI
STYLO
STYMY

S••Y•

SATYR
SHAYS
SIBYL
SLAYS
SLOYD
SONYA
SPAYS
STAYS
SUZYS
SWAYS

S•••Y

SADLY
SALLY
SALTY
SAMMY
SANDY
SAPPY
SASSY
SAUCY
SAURY
SAVOY
SAVVY
SCALY
SCARY
SCOPY
SEAMY
SEDGY
SEEDY
SEPOY
SHADY
SHAKY
SHALY
SHILY
SHINY
SHOWY
SHYLY
SILKY
SILLY
SILTY
SISSY
SIXTY
SKYEY
SLATY
SLILY
SLIMY
SLYLY
SMOKY
SNAKY
SNOWY
SOAPY
SOFTY
SOGGY
SONNY
SOOTY
SOPHY
SOPPY
SORRY
SOUPY
SPICY
SPIKY
SPINY
SPIRY
SPLAY
SPRAY
SPUMY
STACY
STAGY
STIMY
STOGY
STOMY
STONY
STORY
STRAY
STUDY
STYMY
SUDSY
SUETY
SULKY
SULLY
SUNNY
SURFY
SURGY
SURLY

•SY••

ASYLA
ASYUT
PSYCH

•S•Y•

ASSYR

•S••Y

ASSAY
ESSAY
OSITY
USURY

••SY•

ASSYR

••S•Y

ASSAY
BESSY
BOSKY
BOSSY
BUSBY
BUSHY
CISSY
CUSHY
DASHY
DUSKY
DUSTY
ESSAY
FISHY
FUSSY
FUSTY
GASSY
GUSHY
GUSTY
HASTY
HUSKY
HUSSY
JASSY
JESSY
LUSTY
MASHY
MASSY
MESHY
MESSY
MISSY
MISTY
MOSEY
MOSSY
MUSHY
MUSKY
MUSSY
MUSTY
NASTY
NOSEY
PASSY
PASTY
PESKY
PUSHY
PUSSY
RASPY
RISKY
RUSHY
RUSTY
SASSY
SISSY
TASTY
TESTY
UNSAY
VASTY
WASHY
WASPY
WISPY
ZESTY

•••SY

BESSY
BETSY
BOSSY
BOUSY
CISSY
DAISY
FUSSY
GASSY
GIPSY
GOOSY
GORSY
GUTSY
GYPSY
HORSY
HUSSY
JASSY
JESSY
LEPSY
LOUSY
MASSY
MESSY
MISSY
MOSSY
MOUSY
MUSSY
NEWSY
NOISY
PALSY
PANSY
PASSY
PATSY
PHASY
PLASY
POESY
POTSY
PROSY
PURSY
PUSSY
SASSY
SISSY
SUDSY
TANSY
TIPSY
TOPSY

S•Z••

SIZAR
SIZED
SIZES
SOZIN
SUZYS

S••Z•

SEIZE
SMAZE

S•••Z

SCHIZ
SPITZ

••SZ•

LISZT

•••SZ

GROSZ

TA•••

TABBY
TABES
TABID
TABLE
TABOO
TABOR
TACET
TACHY
TACIT
TACKS
TACKY
TAELS
TAFFY
TAFIA
TAHOE
TAIGA
TAILS
TAINO
TAINS
TAINT
TAKEN
TAKER
TAKES
TALCS
TALER
TALES
TALKS
TALLY
TALON
TALOS
TALUK
TALUS
TAMED
TAMER
TAMES
TAMIS
TAMPA
TAMPS
TANEY
TANGO
TANGS
TANGY
TANIS
TANKA
TANKS
TANSY
TANTO
TAPED
TAPER
TAPES
TAPIR
TAPIS
TARDY
TARED
TARES
TARNS
TAROS
TAROT
TARPS
TARRY
TARSI
TARSO
TARTS
TASKS
TASSO
TASTE
TASTY
TATAR
TATRA
TAUNT
TAUPE
TAURO
TAUTO
TAWED
TAWER
TAWNY
TAXED
TAXER
TAXES
TAXIS
TAZZA

T•A••

TEACH
TEAKS
TEALS
TEAMS
TEARS
TEARY
TEASE
TEATS
THADS
THADY
THANE
THANK
THAWS
TIARA
TOADS
TOADY
TOAST
TRACE
TRACH
TRACK
TRACT
TRADE
TRAGI
TRAIL
TRAIN
TRAIT
TRAMP
TRAMS
TRANS
TRAPS
TRASH
TRASS
TRAVE
TRAWL
TRAYS
TSADE
TSARS
TWAIN
TWANG
TZARS

T••A•

TATAR
TELAE
TERAT
TEXAS
TICAL
TIDAL
TINAS
TITAN
TODAY
TOGAE
TOGAS
TOKAY
TOLAN
TOLAS
TOMAN
TOMAS
TONAL
TOPAZ
TORAH
TOTAL
TREAD

TREAS
TREAT
TRIAD
TRIAL
TROAS
TUBAL
TUBAS
TUNAS
TWEAK

T•••A
TAFIA
TAIGA
TAMPA
TANKA
TATRA
TAZZA
TERRA
TESLA
TESTA
TETRA
THECA
THEDA
THETA
THUJA
TIARA
TIBIA
TILDA
TINEA
TONGA
TRINA
TRONA
TRUDA
TRYMA
TULSA

•TA••
ATAXY
ETAPE
ITALS
ITALY
STABS
STACK
STACY
STAFF
STAGE
STAGS
STAGY
STAID
STAIN
STAIR
STAKE
STALE
STALK
STALL
STAMP
STAND
STANK
STANS
STAPH
STARE
STARK
STARS
START
STASH
STATE
STATO
STAVE
STAYS

•T•A•
ATLAS
ATMAN
ATTAR
ETHAN
ETNAS
ETTAS
STEAD
STEAK
STEAL
STEAM
STOAE
STOAS
STOAT
STRAP
STRAT
STRAW
STRAY
XTIAN

•T••A
ATRIA
ETYMA
STOMA
STRIA
STUKA
STUPA
UTICA

••TA•
AETAT
ALTAI
ALTAR
ALTAS
ANTAE
ATTAR
BATAN
BETAS
DITAS
DOTAL
ETTAS
FATAL
FETAL
IOTAS
LITAI
LITAS
LOTAH
METAL
METAS
NATAL
OCTAD
PETAL
PITAS
QATAR
RATAL
RITAS
ROTAS
SATAN
SETAE
SITAR
TATAR
TITAN
TOTAL
VITAE
VITAL
WATAP
WITAN
WOTAN
ZETAS

••T•A
AFTRA
ANTRA
CITRA
COTTA
ENTIA
EXTRA
GOTHA
GUTTA
INTRA
LOTTA
LYTTA
OSTIA
RETIA
RETTA
SITKA
SUTRA
TATRA
TETRA
ULTRA
VITTA

•••TA
ADYTA
ANITA
AORTA
BEATA
BERTA
BIOTA
CHITA
COSTA
COTTA
DELTA
DICTA
EVITA
GRETA
GUSTA
GUTTA
HEPTA
JUNTA
JUXTA
LEPTA
LOTTA
LYTTA
MANTA
MARTA
PASTA
PENTA
PIETA
PINTA
QUOTA
RECTA
RETTA
RIATA
SCUTA
SEPTA
SOFTA
TESTA
THETA
VESTA
VISTA
VITTA
VOLTA
YALTA

TB•••
TBONE

T•B••
TABBY
TABES
TABID
TABLE
TABOO
TABOR
TEBET
TIBER
TIBET
TIBIA
TOBOL
TOBYS
TUBAL
TUBAS
TUBBY
TUBED
TUBER
TUBES

T••B•
TABBY
TOMBS
TRIBE
TUBBY
TURBO

T•••B
THROB
THUMB

•T•B•
STABS
STUBS

T•C••
TACET
TACHY
TACIT
TACKS
TACKY
TECHN
TICAL
TICKS
TUCKS
TYCHE

T••C•
TALCS
TEACH
TENCH
THECA
THICK
TINCT
TOUCH
TRACE
TRACH
TRACK
TRACT
TRICE
TRICH
TRICK
TRUCE
TRUCK
TURCO
TWICE

T•••C
TELIC
TONIC
TOPIC
TORIC
TOXIC
TUNIC

•TC••
ITCHY

•T•C•
STACK
STACY
STICH
STICK
STOCK
STUCK
UTICA

•T••C
ATTIC
ETHIC
STOIC

••TC•
AITCH
BATCH
BITCH
BOTCH
CATCH
CUTCH
DITCH
DUTCH
FETCH
FITCH
HATCH
HITCH
HUTCH
KETCH
LATCH
MATCH
MITCH
NOTCH
PATCH
PITCH
RATCH
RETCH
ROTCH
VETCH
WATCH
WITCH

••T•C
ANTIC
ATTIC
AZTEC
ISTIC
LYTIC
OPTIC
VATIC

T•D••
TEDDY
TIDAL
TIDED
TIDES
TODAY
TODDS
TODDY
TODOS
TUDOR

T••D•
TARDY
TEDDY
TENDS
THADS
THADY
THEDA
THUDS
TILDA
TILDE
TOADS
TOADY
TODDS
TODDY
TRADE
TRUDA
TRUDY
TSADE

T•••D
TABID
TAMED
TAPED
TARED
TAWED
TAXED
TEPID
THIRD
TIDED
TILED
TIMED
TIMID
TINED
TIRED
TONED
TOPED
TOTED
TOWED
TOYED
TREAD
TREED
TREND
TRIAD
TRIED
TRUED
TUBED
TUMID
TUNED
TWEED
TYPED

•T•D•
ETUDE
STUDS
STUDY

•T••D
STAID
STAND
STEAD
STEED
STIED
STOOD

••TD•
OUTDO

••T•D
ACTED
ANTED
BATED
CITED
DATED
DOTED
FATED
FETED
FETID
GATED
HATED
KITED
LUTED
MATED
METED
MUTED
NOTED
OCTAD
OPTED
OUTED
RATED
SATED
TOTED
VOTED

•••TD
CONTD

TE•••
TEACH
TEAKS
TEALS
TEAMS
TEARS
TEARY
TEASE
TEATS
TEBET
TECHN
TEDDY
TEEMS
TEENS
TEENY
TEETH
TEHEE
TELAE
TELEG
TELEO
TELEX
TELIC
TELLS
TELLY
TEMPE
TEMPI
TEMPO
TEMPT
TENCH
TENDS
TENET
TENON
TENOR
TENSE
TENTH
TENTS
TEPEE
TEPID
TERAT
TERMS
TERNS
TERRA
TERRI
TERRY
TERSE
TESLA
TESTA
TESTS
TESTY
TETHS
TETON
TETRA
TEXAS
TEXTS

T•E••
TAELS
TEEMS
TEENS
TEENY
TEETH
THECA
THEDA
THEFT
THEIR
THEME
THERE

THERM THESE THETA THEWS THEWY TIEIN TIERS TIEUP TREAD TREAS TREAT TREED TREES TREKS TREND TRENT TRESS TREYS TWEAK TWEED TWEEN TWEET TWERP TYEES

T••E•

TABES TACET TAKEN TAKER TAKES TALER TALES TAMED TAMER TAMES TANEY TAPED TAPER TAPES TARED TARES TAWED TAWER TAXED TAXER TAXES TEBET TEHEE TELEG TELEO TELEX TENET TEPEE THIEF THREE THREW TIBER TIBET TIDED TIDES TIGER TILED TILER TILES TIMED TIMER TIMES TINEA TINED TINES TIRED TIRES TITER TOKEN TOLES TOMES TONED TONER TONES TOPED TOPER TOPES TOTED TOTEM TOTER TOTES TOWED TOWEL TOWER TOYED TOYER TREED TREES TRIED TRIER TRIES TRUED TRUER TRUES TUBED TUBER TUBES TULES TUNED TUNER TUNES TWEED TWEEN TWEET TYEES TYKES TYLER TYPED TYPES

T•••E

TABLE TAHOE TASTE TAUPE TBONE TEASE TEHEE TELAE TEMPE TENSE TEPEE TERSE THANE THEME THERE THESE THINE THOLE THOSE THREE THULE THYME TILDE TINGE TITHE TITLE TOGAE TOGUE TOILE TOQUE TORTE TRACE TRADE TRAVE TRIBE TRICE TRINE TRIPE TRITE TROPE TROVE TRUCE TSADE TULLE TUQUE TWICE TWINE TYCHE

•TE••

CTENO ITEMS PTERO STEAD STEAK STEAL STEAM STEED STEEL STEEP STEER STEIN STELE STEMS STENO STEPS STERE STERN STETH STETS STEVE STEWS UTERI UTERO

•T•E•

ETHEL ETHER OTHER OTTER STEED STEEL STEEP STEER STIED STIES STREW UTHER UTTER

•T••E

ATIVE ATONE ETAPE ETTIE ETUDE STAGE STAKE STALE STARE STATE STAVE STELE STERE STEVE STILE STIPE STOAE STOKE STOLE STOME STONE STOPE STORE STOVE STOWE STUPE STYLE UTILE

••TE•

ACTED AFTER ALTER ANTED ANTES ARTEL ARTER ASTER AZTEC BATED BATES BETEL BITER BITES CATER CITED CITES COTES CUTER CUTEY DATED DATER DATES DETER DOTED DOTER DOTES EATEN EATER ENTER ESTER FATED FATES FETED FETES GATED GATES HATED HATER HATES HOTEL INTER JUTES KATES KITED KITES LATER LATEX LITER LUTED LUTES MATED MATEO MATES MATEY METED METER METES MITER MITES MOTEL MOTES MUTED MUTES NATES NITER NOTED NOTER NOTES OATEN OATES OCTET OFTEN OPTED OSTEO OTTER OUTED OUTER PATEN PATER PATES PETER PETES RATED RATEL RATER RATES RETEM RITES SATED SATES SITES TITER TOTED TOTEM TOTER TOTES UTTER VOTED VOTER VOTES WATER

••T•E

ANTAE ARTIE BATHE BETTE BUTTE CUTIE ETTIE ISTLE IXTLE KATIE LATHE LETHE LITHE MATTE OUTRE SETAE TITHE TITLE UNTIE VITAE WITHE WITTE

•••TE

ABATE ACUTE AGATE ALATE ARETE AZOTE BASTE BETTE BRUTE BUTTE CARTE CASTE CHUTE COMTE CONTE CRATE CRETE DANTE ELATE ELITE EMOTE ENATE FLUTE FORTE GRATE HARTE HASTE IRATE LEYTE MATTE MONTE ORATE OVATE PASTE PHYTE PLATE PRATE QUITE QUOTE RENTE ROUTE SAUTE SCUTE SHOTE SHUTE SIXTE SKATE SLATE SMITE SMOTE SPATE SPITE STATE SUITE TASTE TORTE TRITE UNITE URATE WASTE WHITE WITTE WRITE WROTE

T•F••

TAFFY TAFIA TIFFS TOFTS TUFTS TUFTY

T••F•

TAFFY THEFT TIFFS TURFS TURFY

T•••F

THIEF

•T•F•

STAFF STIFF STUFF

•T••F

STAFF STIFF STUFF

••T•F

MOTIF

T•G••

TIGER TIGHT TOGAE TOGAS TOGUE

T••G•

TAIGA TANGO TANGS TANGY THIGH THUGS TINGE TINGS TONGA TONGS TOUGH TRAGI TRIGO TRIGS TWIGS

T•••G

TELEG THING THONG TWANG TYING

•T•G•

STAGE STAGS STAGY STOGY

•T••G

STING STUNG

••TG•

OUTGO

TH•••

THADS THADY THANE THANK THAWS THECA

THEDA
THEFT
THEIR
THEME
THERE
THERM
THESE
THETA
THEWS
THEWY
THICK
THIEF
THIGH
THINE
THING
THINK
THINS
THIOL
THIRD
THOLE
THONG
THORN
THORP
THOSE
THOTH
THREE
THREW
THROB
THROW
THRUM
THUDS
THUGS
THUJA
THULE
THUMB
THUMP
THURS
THYME
THYMY
THYRO

T•H••
TAHOE
TEHEE

T••H•
TACHY
TECHN
TETHS
TIGHT
TITHE
TOPHI
TYCHE

T•••H
TEACH
TEETH
TENCH
TENTH
THIGH
THOTH
TILTH
TOOTH
TORAH
TOUCH
TOUGH
TRACH
TRASH
TRICH
TROPH
TROTH
TRUTH

•TH••
ATHOS
ETHAN
ETHEL
ETHER
ETHIC
ETHNO
ETHOS
ETHYL
OTHER
UTHER

•T•H•
ITCHY

•T••H
STAPH
STASH
STETH
STICH

••TH•
ANTHO
ARTHR
BATHE
BATHO
BATHS
BATHY
BETHS
CATHY
GOTHA
GOTHS
KATHY
LATHE
LATHS
LATHY
LETHE
LITHE
LITHO
METHO
MOTHS
MOTHY
MYTHO
MYTHS
OATHS
ORTHO
PATHO
PATHS
PATHY
PITHS
PITHY
RUTHS
SETHS
TETHS
TITHE
WITHE
WITHY

••T•H
AITCH
BATCH
BITCH
BOTCH
CATCH
CUTCH
DITCH
DUTCH
FETCH
FITCH
HATCH
HITCH
HUTCH
KETCH
LATCH
LOTAH
MATCH
MITCH
NOTCH
PATCH
PITCH
RATCH
RETCH
ROTCH
VETCH
WATCH
WITCH

•••TH
AZOTH
BARTH
BERTH
BIRTH
BOOTH
BROTH
CHETH
CLOTH
DEATH
DEPTH
DOETH
EARTH
EDITH
FAITH
FIFTH
FILTH
FIRTH
FORTH
FRITH
FROTH
FURTH
GARTH
GIRTH
HEATH
KEITH
LOATH
MIRTH
MONTH
MOUTH
NEATH
NINTH
NORTH
PERTH
QUOTH
SIXTH
SLOTH
SMITH
SNATH
SOUTH
STETH
SWATH
TEETH
TENTH
THOTH
TILTH
TOOTH
TROTH
TRUTH
WIDTH
WORTH
WRATH
XANTH
YOUTH

TI•••
TIARA
TIBER
TIBET
TIBIA
TICAL
TICKS
TIDAL
TIDED
TIDES
TIEIN
TIERS
TIEUP
TIFFS
TIGER
TIGHT
TIKIS
TILDA
TILDE
TILED
TILER
TILES
TILLS
TILLY
TILTH
TILTS
TIMED
TIMER
TIMES
TIMID
TIMMY
TINAS
TINCT
TINEA
TINED
TINES
TINGE
TINGS
TINNY
TINTS
TIPPY
TIPSY
TIRED
TIRES
TIROS
TITAN
TITER
TITHE
TITIS
TITLE
TITUS
TIZZY

T•I••
TAIGA
TAILS
TAINO
TAINS
TAINT
THICK
THIEF
THIGH
THINE
THING
THINK
THINS
THIOL
THIRD
TOILE
TOILS
TRIAD
TRIAL
TRIBE
TRICE
TRICH
TRICK
TRIED
TRIER
TRIES
TRIGO
TRIGS
TRILL
TRIMS
TRINA
TRINE
TRIOL
TRIOS
TRIPE
TRIPS
TRITE
TRIXY
TWICE
TWIGS
TWILL
TWINE
TWINS
TWIRL
TWIRP
TWIST
TWITS
TWIXT
TYING

T••I•
TABID
TACIT
TAFIA
TAMIS
TANIS
TAPIR
TAPIS
TAXIS
TELIC
TEPID
THEIR
TIBIA
TIEIN
TIKIS
TIMID
TITIS
TOKIO
TONIC
TONIS
TOPIC
TOPIS
TORIC
TORII
TOXIC
TOXIN
TRAIL
TRAIN
TRAIT
TULIP
TUMID
TUNIC
TUNIS
TUPIK
TUPIS
TURIN
TWAIN

T•••I
TARSI
TEMPI
TERRI
TOPHI
TORII
TORSI
TRAGI
TURKI
TUTTI

•TI••
ATILT
ATION
ATIVE
ITION
STICH
STICK
STIED
STIES
STIFF
STILE
STILL
STILT
STIMY
STING
STINK
STINT
STIPE
STIRK
STIRS
UTICA
UTILE
XTIAN

•T•I•
ATRIA
ATRIP
ATTIC
ATTIS
ETHIC
ETTIE
ETUIS
STAID
STAIN
STAIR
STEIN
STOIC
STRIA
STRIP

•T••I
STYLI
UTERI

••TI•
ACTIN
ANTIC
ANTIS
ARTIE
ASTIR
ATTIC
ATTIS
BATIK
CUTIE
CUTIN
CUTIS
ENTIA
ETTIE
FETID
ISTIC
KATIE
LATIN
LYTIC
MATIN
METIS
MOTIF
OPTIC
OSTIA
PATIO
PETIT
RATIO
RETIA
SATIN
SITIN
TITIS
UNTIE
UNTIL
VATIC
YETIS

••T•I
ALTAI
LITAI
MATRI
NITRI
PATRI
PETRI
PETTI
TUTTI
VITRI

•••TI
AMATI
CACTI
CENTI
CESTI
COATI
CULTI
CYSTI
DENTI
DHOTI
HAITI
MUFTI
MULTI
NOCTI
NYCTI
PETTI
RECTI
SEPTI
TUTTI
VOLTI

T••J•
THUJA

T•K••
TAKEN
TAKER
TAKES
TIKIS
TOKAY
TOKEN
TOKIO
TOKYO
TYKES

T••K•
TACKS
TACKY
TALKS
TANKA
TANKS
TASKS
TEAKS
TICKS
TREKS
TUCKS
TURKI
TURKS
TUSKS

T•••K
TALUK
THANK

THICK
THINK
TORSK
TRACK
TRICK
TRUCK
TRUNK
TUPIK
TWEAK

•T•K•
STAKE
STOKE
STUKA

•T••K
STACK
STALK
STANK
STARK
STEAK
STICK
STINK
STIRK
STOCK
STOOK
STORK
STUCK
STUNK

••TK•
SITKA

••T•K
BATIK

T•L••
TALCS
TALER
TALES
TALKS
TALLY
TALON
TALOS
TALUK
TALUS
TELAE
TELEG
TELEO
TELEX
TELIC
TELLS
TELLY
TILDA
TILDE
TILED
TILER
TILES
TILLS
TILLY
TILTH
TILTS
TOLAN
TOLAS
TOLES
TOLLS
TOLYL
TULES
TULIP
TULLE
TULLY
TULSA
TYLER

T••L•
TABLE
TAELS
TAILS
TALLY
TEALS
TELLS
TELLY
TESLA
THOLE
THULE
TILLS
TILLY
TITLE
TOILE
TOILS
TOLLS
TOOLS
TRILL
TROLL
TRULY
TULLE
TULLY
TWILL

T•••L
THIOL
TICAL
TIDAL
TOBOL
TOLYL
TONAL
TOTAL
TOWEL
TRAIL
TRAWL
TRIAL
TRILL
TRIOL
TROLL
TUBAL
TWILL
TWIRL
TYROL

•TL••
ATLAS

•T•L•
ATILT
ATOLL
ITALS
ITALY
STALE
STALK
STALL
STELE
STILE
STILL
STILT
STOLE
STULL
STYLE
STYLI
STYLO
UTILE

•T••L
ATOLL
ETHEL
ETHYL
STALL
STEAL
STEEL
STILL
STOOL
STULL

••TL•
APTLY
FATLY
FITLY
HOTLY
ISTLE
IXTLE
TITLE
WETLY

••T•L
ARTEL
BETEL
BUTYL
DOTAL
EXTOL
FATAL
FETAL
HOTEL
METAL
MOTEL
NATAL
OCTYL
PETAL
RATAL
RATEL
SOTOL
TOTAL
UNTIL
VITAL

•••TL
AUSTL

T•M••
TAMED
TAMER
TAMES
TAMIS
TAMPA
TAMPS
TEMPE
TEMPI
TEMPO
TEMPT
TIMED
TIMER
TIMES
TIMID
TIMMY
TOMAN
TOMAS
TOMBS
TOMES
TOMMY
TUMID
TUMOR

T••M•
TEAMS
TEEMS
TERMS
THEME
THUMB
THUMP
THYME
THYMY
TIMMY
TOMMY
TRAMP
TRAMS
TRIMS
TRUMP
TRYMA

T•••M
THERM
THRUM
TOTEM

•TM••
ATMAN

•T•M•
ATOMS
ETYMA
ITEMS
STAMP
STEMS
STIMY
STOMA
STOME
STOMP
STOMY
STUMP
STUMS
STYMY

•T••M
STEAM
STORM
STRUM

••T•M
DATUM
ENTOM
RETEM
TOTEM

T•N••
TANEY
TANGO
TANGS
TANGY
TANIS
TANKA
TANKS
TANSY
TANTO
TENCH
TENDS
TENET
TENON
TENOR
TENSE
TENTH
TENTS
TINAS
TINCT
TINEA
TINED
TINES
TINGE
TINGS
TINNY
TINTS
TONAL
TONED
TONER
TONES
TONGA
TONGS
TONIC
TONIS
TONUS
TONYS
TUNAS
TUNED
TUNER
TUNES
TUNIC
TUNIS
TUNNY

T••N•
TAINO
TAINS
TAINT
TARNS
TAUNT
TAWNY
TBONE
TEENS
TEENY
TERNS
THANE
THANK
THINE
THING
THINK
THINS
THONG
TINNY
TOWNS
TRANS
TREND
TRENT
TRINA
TRINE
TRONA
TRUNK
TUNNY
TURNS
TWANG
TWINE
TWINS
TYING

T•••N
TAKEN
TALON
TECHN
TENON
TETON
THORN
TIEIN
TITAN
TOKEN
TOLAN
TOMAN
TOXIN
TOYON
TRAIN
TURIN
TWAIN
TWEEN

•TN••
ETNAS

•T•N•
ATONE
ATONY
CTENO
ETHNO
STAND
STANK
STANS
STENO
STING
STINK
STINT
STONE
STONY
STUNG
STUNK
STUNS
STUNT

•T••N
ATION
ATMAN
ETHAN
ITION
STAIN
STEIN
STERN
UTURN
XTIAN

••T•N
ACTIN
ALTON
ANTON
ASTON
BATAN
BATON
BETON
CUTIN
EATEN
ELTON
GATUN
JOTUN
LATIN
MATIN
NITON
OATEN
OFTEN
PATEN
PITON
PUTON
SATAN
SATIN
SETON
SITIN
TETON
TITAN
WITAN
WOTAN

TO•••
TOADS
TOADY
TOAST
TOBOL
TOBYS
TODAY
TODDS
TODDY
TODOS
TOFTS
TOGAE
TOGAS
TOGUE
TOILE
TOILS
TOKAY
TOKEN
TOKIO
TOKYO
TOLAN
TOLAS
TOLES
TOLLS
TOLYL
TOMAN
TOMAS
TOMBS
TOMES
TOMMY
TONAL
TONED
TONER
TONES
TONGA
TONGS
TONIC
TONIS
TONUS
TONYS
TOOLS
TOOTH
TOOTS
TOPAZ
TOPED
TOPER
TOPES
TOPHI
TOPIC
TOPIS
TOPSY
TOQUE
TORAH
TORIC
TORII
TORSI
TORSK
TORSO
TORTE
TORTS
TORUS
TOTAL
TOTED
TOTEM
TOTER
TOTES
TOUCH
TOUGH
TOURS
TOUTS
TOWED
TOWEL
TOWER
TOWNS
TOXIC
TOXIN
TOYED
TOYER
TOYON
TOYOS

T•O••
TBONE
THOLE
THONG
THORN
THORP
THOSE
THOTH

TOOLS
TOOTH
TOOTS
TROAS
TROLL
TRONA
TROOP
TROPE
TROPH
TROTH
TROTS
TROUT
TROVE

T••O•
TABOO
TABOR
TAHOE
TALON
TALOS
TAROS
TAROT
TENON
TENOR
TETON
THIOL
THROB
THROW
TIROS
TOBOL
TODOS
TOYON
TOYOS
TRIOL
TRIOS
TROOP
TUDOR
TUMOR
TUTOR
TYPOS
TYROL
TYROS

T•••O
TABOO
TAINO
TANGO
TANTO
TARSO
TASSO
TAURO
TAUTO
TELEO
TEMPO
THYRO
TOKIO
TOKYO
TORSO
TRIGO
TURBO
TURCO

•TO••
ATOLL
ATOMS
ATONE
ATONY
ATORY
STOAE
STOAS
STOAT
STOCK
STOGY
STOIC
STOKE
STOLE
STOMA
STOME
STOMP
STOMY
STONE
STONY
STOOD
STOOK
STOOL
STOOP
STOPE
STOPS
STOPT
STORE
STORK
STORM
STORY
STOSS
STOUP
STOUT
STOVE
STOWE
STOWS

•T•O•
ATHOS
ATION
ETHOS
ITION
OTTOS
STOOD
STOOK
STOOL
STOOP
STROP

•T••O
CTENO
ETHNO
PTERO
STATO
STENO
STYLO
UTERO

••TO•
ACTOR
ALTON
ALTOS
ANTON
ASTON
ASTOR
AUTOS
BATON
BETON
ELTON
ENTOM
ESTOP
EXTOL
FETOR
FSTOP
JATOS
KOTOS
LOTOS
MOTOR
NITON
OTTOS
PITON
PUTON
ROTOR
SETON
SOTOL
TETON
TUTOR

••T•O
ANTHO
ASTRO
BATHO
DATTO
DITTO
IATRO
INTRO
LITHO
LOTTO
MATEO
MATZO
METHO
METRO
MOTTO
MYTHO
NITRO
ORTHO
OSTEO
OUTDO
OUTGO
PATHO
PATIO
PETRO
PETTO
POTTO
RATIO
RETRO
SETTO

•••TO
ACETO
CANTO
CENTO
CONTO
COSTO
CYSTO
DATTO
DENTO
DITTO
ERATO
FEMTO
GUSTO
HECTO
HEKTO
HISTO
HYETO
KYOTO
LACTO
LENTO
LEPTO
LOTTO
MASTO
MOLTO
MOTTO
NYCTO
PANTO
PETTO
PHOTO
PHYTO
PINTO
PLATO
PLUTO
POTTO
PROTO
PUNTO
QUITO
RECTO
SARTO
SCATO
SCOTO
SEATO
SEPTO
SETTO
STATO
TANTO
TAUTO

T•P••
TAPED
TAPER
TAPES
TAPIR
TAPIS
TEPEE
TEPID
TIPPY
TIPSY
TOPAZ
TOPED
TOPER
TOPES
TOPHI
TOPIC
TOPIS
TOPSY
TUPIK
TUPIS
TYPED
TYPES
TYPOS

T••P•
TAMPA
TAMPS
TARPS
TAUPE
TEMPE
TEMPI
TEMPO
TEMPT
TIPPY
TRAPS
TRIPE
TRIPS
TROPE
TROPH

T•••P
THORP
THUMP
TIEUP
TRAMP
TROOP
TRUMP
TULIP
TWERP
TWIRP

•T•P•
ETAPE
STAPH
STEPS
STIPE
STOPE
STOPS
STOPT
STUPA
STUPE

•T••P
ATRIP
STAMP
STEEP
STOMP
STOOP
STOUP
STRAP
STRIP
STROP
STUMP

••T•P
CUTUP
ESTOP
FSTOP
GETUP
LETUP
PUTUP
SETUP
WATAP

T•Q••
TOQUE
TUQUE

TR•••
TRACE
TRACH
TRACK
TRACT
TRADE
TRAGI
TRAIL
TRAIN
TRAIT
TRAMP
TRAMS
TRANS
TRAPS
TRASH
TRASS
TRAVE
TRAWL
TRAYS
TREAD
TREAS
TREAT
TREED
TREES
TREKS
TREND
TRENT
TRESS
TREYS
TRIAD
TRIAL
TRIBE
TRICE
TRICH
TRICK
TRIED
TRIER
TRIES
TRIGO
TRIGS
TRILL
TRIMS
TRINA
TRINE
TRIOL
TRIOS
TRIPE
TRIPS
TRITE
TRIXY
TROAS
TROLL
TRONA
TROOP
TROPE
TROPH
TROTH
TROTS
TROUT
TROVE
TRUCE
TRUCK
TRUDA
TRUDY
TRUED
TRUER
TRUES
TRULY
TRUMP
TRUNK
TRUSS
TRUST
TRUTH
TRYMA
TRYST

T•R••
TARDY
TARED
TARES
TARNS
TAROS
TAROT
TARPS
TARRY
TARSI
TARSO
TARTS
TERAT
TERMS
TERNS
TERRA
TERRI
TERRY
TERSE
THREE
THREW
THROB
THROW
THRUM
TIRED
TIRES
TIROS
TORAH
TORIC
TORII
TORSI
TORSK
TORSO
TORTE
TORTS
TORUS
TURBO
TURCO
TURFS
TURFY
TURIN
TURKI
TURKS
TURNS
TYROL
TYROS

T••R•
TARRY
TATRA
TAURO
TEARS
TEARY
TERRA
TERRI
TERRY
TETRA
THERE
THERM
THIRD
THORN
THORP
THURS
THYRO
TIARA
TIERS
TOURS
TSARS
TWERP
TWIRL
TWIRP
TZARS

T•••R
TABOR
TAKER
TALER
TAMER
TAPER
TAPIR
TATAR
TAWER
TAXER
TENOR
THEIR
TIBER
TIGER
TILER
TIMER
TITER
TONER
TOPER
TOTER
TOWER
TOYER
TRIER
TRUER
TUBER
TUDOR
TUMOR
TUNER
TUTOR
TYLER

•TR••
ATRIA
ATRIP
STRAP
STRAT
STRAW
STRAY
STREW
STRIA
STRIP
STROP
STRUM
STRUT

•T•R•

ATORY PTERO STARE STARK STARS START STERE STERN STIRK STIRS STORE STORK STORM STORY UTERI UTERO UTURN

•T••R

ATTAR ETHER OTHER OTTER STAIR STEER UTHER UTTER

••TR•

AFTRA ANTRA ASTRO CITRA ENTRY EXTRA IATRO IATRY INTRA INTRO LATRY MATRI METRO METRY NITRI NITRO OUTRE PATRI PETRI PETRO RETRO RETRY SUTRA TATRA TETRA ULTRA VITRI

••T•R

ACTOR AFTER ALTAR ALTER ARTER ARTHR ASTER ASTIR ASTOR ATTAR BITER CATER CUTER DATER DETER DOTER EATER ENTER ESTER FETOR HATER INTER LATER LITER METER MITER MOTOR NITER NOTER OTTER OUTER PATER PETER QATAR RATER ROTOR SATYR SITAR TATAR TITER TOTER TUTOR UTTER VOTER WATER

•••TR

CENTR CONTR DEXTR GASTR

TS•••

TSADE TSARS

T•S••

TASKS TASSO TASTE TASTY TESLA TESTA TESTS TESTY TUSKS

T••S•

TANSY TARSI TARSO TASSO TEASE TENSE TERSE THESE THOSE TIPSY TOAST TOPSY TORSI TORSK TORSO TRASH TRASS TRESS TRUSS TRUST TRYST TULSA TWIST

T•••S

TABES TACKS TAELS TAILS TAINS TAKES TALCS TALES TALKS TALOS TALUS TAMES TAMIS TAMPS TANGS TANIS TANKS TAPES TAPIS TARES TARNS TAROS TARPS TARTS TASKS TAXES TAXIS TEAKS TEALS TEAMS TEARS TEATS TEEMS TEENS TELLS TENDS TENTS TERMS TERNS TESTS TETHS TEXAS TEXTS THADS THAWS THEWS THINS THUDS THUGS THURS TICKS TIDES TIERS TIFFS TIKIS TILES TILLS TILTS TIMES TINAS TINES TINGS TINTS TIRES TIROS TITIS TITUS TOADS TOBYS TODDS TODOS TOFTS TOGAS TOILS TOLAS TOLES TOLLS TOMAS TOMBS TOMES TONES TONGS TONIS TONUS TONYS TOOLS TOOTS TOPES TOPIS TORTS TORUS TOTES TOURS TOUTS TOWNS TOYOS TRAMS TRANS TRAPS TRASS TRAYS TREAS TREES TREKS TRESS TREYS TRIES TRIGS TRIMS TRIOS TRIPS TROAS TROTS TRUES TRUSS TSARS TUBAS TUBES TUCKS TUFTS TULES TUNAS TUNES TUNIS TUPIS TURFS TURKS TURNS TUSKS TUTUS TWIGS TWINS TWITS TYEES TYKES TYPES TYPOS TYROS TZARS

•T•S•

STASH STOSS

•T••S

ATHOS ATLAS ATOMS ATTIS ATTYS ETHOS ETNAS ETTAS ETUIS ITALS ITEMS OTTOS STABS STAGS STANS STARS STAYS STEMS STEPS STETS STEWS STIES STIRS STOAS STOPS STOSS STOWS STUBS STUDS STUMS STUNS

••TS•

BETSY GUTSY MATSU PATSY POTSY

••T•S

ALTAS ALTOS ANTES ANTIS ATTIS ATTYS AUTOS BATES BATHS BETAS BETHS BITES BITTS BOTTS BUTTS CETUS CITES COTES CUTIS DATES DITAS DOTES ETTAS FATES FETES FETUS GATES GOTHS HATES ICTUS IOTAS JATOS JUTES KATES KITES KOTOS LATHS LETTS LITAS LOTOS LOTUS LUTES MATES MATTS METAS METES METIS MITES MITTS MOTES MOTHS MUTES MUTTS MYTHS NATES NOTES OATES OATHS OTTOS PATES PATHS PETES PITAS PITHS PUTTS RATES RITAS RITES ROTAS RUTHS SATES SETHS SITES SITUS TETHS TITIS TITUS TOTES TUTUS VOTES WATTS YETIS ZETAS

•••TS

ABETS ABUTS ADITS ASSTS AUNTS BAHTS BAITS BALTS BEATS BEETS BELTS BERTS BESTS BITTS BLATS BLOTS BOATS BOLTS BOOTS BORTS BOTTS BOUTS BRATS BUNTS BUSTS BUTTS CANTS CARTS CASTS CELTS CENTS CHATS CHETS CHITS CISTS CLOTS COATS COLTS COOTS COPTS COSTS CULTS CYSTS DARTS DEBTS DENTS DIETS DINTS DOITS DOLTS DONTS DUCTS DUETS DUSTS EDITS EMITS EXITS FACTS FASTS FEATS FELTS FIATS FISTS FLATS FLITS FONTS FOOTS FORTS FRATS FRETS FRITS GAITS GENTS GHATS GIFTS GIRTS GISTS GLUTS GNATS GOATS GOVTS GRITS GROTS GUSTS HAFTS HALTS HARTS HEATS HEFTS HILTS

HINTS
HOOTS
HOSTS
HUNTS
HURTS
JESTS
JILTS
JOLTS
JUSTS
KEATS
KENTS
KILTS
KNITS
KNOTS
KYATS
LASTS
LEETS
LEFTS
LENTS
LETTS
LIFTS
LILTS
LISTS
LOFTS
LOOTS
LOUTS
LUNTS
LUSTS
MALTS
MARTS
MASTS
MATTS
MEATS
MEETS
MELTS
MILTS
MINTS
MISTS
MITTS
MOATS
MOLTS
MORTS
MUSTS
MUTTS
NESTS
NEWTS
OBITS
ODETS
OMITS
OUSTS
PACTS
PANTS
PARTS
PASTS
PEATS
PELTS
PESTS
PHOTS
PICTS
PINTS
PLATS
PLOTS
POETS
PORTS
POSTS
POUTS
PUNTS
PUTTS
QUITS
RAFTS
RANTS
RENTS
RESTS
RIFTS
RIOTS
ROOTS
ROUTS
RUNTS
RUSTS
RYOTS
SALTS
SCATS
SCOTS
SCUTS
SEATS
SECTS
SEPTS
SHOTS
SHUTS
SIFTS
SILTS
SKITS
SLATS
SLITS
SLOTS
SLUTS
SMUTS
SNOTS
SOOTS
SORTS
SPATS
SPITS
SPOTS
STETS
SUITS
SWATS
TARTS
TEATS
TENTS
TESTS
TEXTS
TILTS
TINTS
TOFTS
TOOTS
TORTS
TOUTS
TROTS
TUFTS
TWITS
UNITS
VENTS
VESTS
VOLTS
WAFTS
WAITS
WALTS
WANTS
WARTS
WATTS
WEFTS
WELTS
WHETS
WHITS
WILTS
WORTS
WRITS
XYSTS
YEATS
ZESTS

T•T••

TATAR
TATRA
TETHS
TETON
TETRA
TITAN
TITER
TITHE
TITIS
TITLE
TITUS
TOTAL
TOTED
TOTEM
TOTER
TOTES
TUTOR
TUTTI
TUTTY
TUTUS

T••T•

TANTO
TARTS
TASTE
TASTY
TAUTO
TEATS
TEETH
TENTH
TENTS
TESTA
TESTS
TESTY
TEXTS
THETA
THOTH
TILTH
TILTS
TINTS
TOFTS
TOOTH
TOOTS
TORTE
TORTS
TOUTS
TRITE
TROTH
TROTS
TRUTH
TUFTS
TUFTY
TUTTI
TUTTY
TWITS

T•••T

TACET
TACIT
TAINT
TAROT
TAUNT
TEBET
TEMPT
TENET
TERAT
THEFT
TIBET
TIGHT
TINCT
TOAST
TRACT
TRAIT
TREAT
TRENT
TROUT
TRUST
TRYST
TWEET
TWIST
TWIXT

•TT••

ATTAR
ATTIC
ATTIS
ATTYS
ETTAS
ETTIE
OTTER
OTTOS
UTTER

•T•T•

STATE
STATO
STETH
STETS

•T••T

ATILT
START
STILT
STINT
STOAT
STOPT
STOUT
STRAT
STRUT
STUNT

••TT•

BATTY
BETTE
BETTY
BITTS
BOTTS
BUTTE
BUTTS
CATTY
COTTA
CUTTY
DATTO
DITTO
DITTY
DOTTY
FATTY
GUTTA
HATTY
HETTY
JETTY
KITTY
LETTS
LETTY
LOTTA
LOTTO
LOTTY
LYTTA
MATTE
MATTS
MATTY
MITTS
MOTTO
MUTTS
NATTY
NETTY
NITTY
NUTTY
PATTY
PETTI
PETTO
PETTY
POTTO
POTTY
PUTTS
PUTTY
RATTY
RETTA
RUTTY
SETTO
TUTTI
TUTTY
VITTA
WATTS
WITTE
WITTY

••T•T

AETAT
OCTET
PETIT

•••TT

SCOTT
WYATT

TU•••

TUBAL
TUBAS
TUBBY
TUBED
TUBER
TUBES
TUCKS
TUDOR
TUFTS
TUFTY
TULES
TULIP
TULLE
TULLY
TULSA
TUMID
TUMOR
TUNAS
TUNED
TUNER
TUNES
TUNIC
TUNIS
TUNNY
TUPIK
TUPIS
TUQUE
TURBO
TURCO
TURFS
TURFY
TURIN
TURKI
TURKS
TURNS
TUSKS
TUTOR
TUTTI
TUTTY
TUTUS

T•U••

TAUNT
TAUPE
TAURO
TAUTO
THUDS
THUGS
THUJA
THULE
THUMB
THUMP
THURS
TOUCH
TOUGH
TOURS
TOUTS
TRUCE
TRUCK
TRUDA
TRUDY
TRUED
TRUER
TRUES
TRULY
TRUMP
TRUNK
TRUSS
TRUST
TRUTH

T••U•

TALUK
TALUS
THRUM
TIEUP
TITUS
TOGUE
TONUS
TOQUE
TORUS
TROUT
TUQUE
TUTUS

•TU••

ETUDE
ETUIS
STUBS
STUCK
STUDS
STUDY
STUFF
STUKA
STULL
STUMP
STUMS
STUNG
STUNK
STUNS
STUNT
STUPA
STUPE
UTURN

•T•U•

STOUP
STOUT
STRUM
STRUT

••TU•

CETUS
CUTUP
DATUM
FETUS
GATUN
GETUP
ICTUS
JOTUN
LETUP
LOTUS
PUTUP
SETUP
SITUS
TITUS
TUTUS

••T•U

MATSU

•••TU

BANTU
VERTU
VIRTU

T••V•

TRAVE
TROVE

•T•V•

ATIVE
STAVE
STEVE
STOVE

TW•••

TWAIN
TWANG
TWEAK
TWEED
TWEEN
TWEET
TWERP
TWICE
TWIGS
TWILL
TWINE
TWINS
TWIRL
TWIRP
TWIST
TWITS
TWIXT

T•W••

TAWED
TAWER
TAWNY
TOWED
TOWEL
TOWER
TOWNS

T••W•

THAWS
THEWS
THEWY
TRAWL

T•••W

THREW
THROW

•T•W•

STEWS
STOWE
STOWS

•T••W

STRAW
STREW

T•X••
TAXED
TAXER
TAXES
TAXIS
TEXAS
TEXTS
TOXIC
TOXIN

T••X•
TRIXY
TWIXT

T•••X
TELEX

•T•X•
ATAXY

••T•X
LATEX

TY•••
TYCHE
TYEES
TYING
TYKES
TYLER
TYPED
TYPES
TYPOS
TYROL
TYROS

T•Y••
THYME
THYMY
THYRO
TOYED
TOYER
TOYON
TOYOS
TRYMA
TRYST

T••Y•
TOBYS
TOKYO
TOLYL
TONYS
TRAYS
TREYS

T•••Y
TABBY
TACHY
TACKY
TAFFY
TALLY
TANEY
TANGY
TANSY
TARDY
TARRY
TASTY
TAWNY
TEARY
TEDDY
TEENY
TELLY
TERRY
TESTY
THADY
THEWY
THYMY
TILLY
TIMMY
TINNY
TIPPY
TIPSY
TIZZY
TOADY
TODAY
TODDY
TOKAY
TOMMY
TOPSY
TRIXY
TRUDY
TRULY
TUBBY
TUFTY
TULLY
TUNNY
TURFY
TUTTY

•TY••
ETYMA
STYLE
STYLI
STYLO
STYMY

•T•Y•
ATTYS
ETHYL
STAYS

•T••Y
ATAXY
ATONY
ATORY
ITALY
ITCHY
STACY
STAGY
STIMY
STOGY
STOMY
STONY
STORY
STRAY
STUDY
STYMY

••TY•
ATTYS
BUTYL
OCTYL
SATYR

••T•Y
APTLY
BATHY
BATTY
BETSY
BETTY
CATHY
CATTY
CUTEY
CUTTY
DITTY
DOTTY
ENTRY
FATLY
FATTY
FITLY
GUTSY
HATTY
HETTY
HOTLY
IATRY
JETTY
KATHY
KITTY
LATHY
LATRY
LETTY
LOTTY
MATEY
MATTY
METRY
MOTHY
NATTY
NETTY
NITTY
NUTTY
PATHY
PATSY
PATTY
PETTY
PITHY
POTSY
POTTY
PUTTY
RATTY
RETRY
RITZY
RUTTY
TUTTY
WETLY
WITHY
WITTY

•••TY
ACITY
AMITY
AUNTY
BATTY
BERTY
BETTY
BOOTY
BORTY
CATTY
CUTTY
DEITY
DIRTY
DITTY
DOTTY
DUSTY
EMPTY
FATTY
FIFTY
FLUTY
FOOTY
FORTY
FUSTY
GERTY
GOUTY
GUSTY
HASTY
HATTY
HEFTY
HETTY
JETTY
JOLTY
KILTY
KITTY
LAITY
LEFTY
LETTY
LINTY
LOFTY
LOTTY
LUSTY
MALTY
MARTY
MATTY
MEATY
MISTY
MONTY
MORTY
MUSTY
NASTY
NATTY
NETTY
NIFTY
NITTY
NUTTY
OSITY
PANTY
PARTY
PASTY
PATTY
PEATY
PETTY
PIETY
PLATY
POTTY
PUNTY
PUTTY
RATTY
ROOTY
RUNTY
RUSTY
RUTTY
SALTY
SILTY
SIXTY
SLATY
SOFTY
SOOTY
SUETY
TASTY
TESTY
TUFTY
TUTTY
UNITY
VASTY
WARTY
WITTY
ZESTY
ZLOTY

TZ•••
TZARS

T•Z••
TAZZA
TIZZY

T••Z•
TAZZA
TIZZY

T•••Z
TOPAZ

••TZ•
MATZO
RITZY

•••TZ
BLITZ
BORTZ
FRITZ
HARTZ
HERTZ
SPITZ
WALTZ

U•A••
UKASE
UNAPT
UNARM
UNAUS
URALS
URANO
URATE
USAFI
USAGE

U••A•
UBOAT
UHLAN
ULNAE
ULNAR
ULNAS
UMIAK
UNBAR
UNCAP
UNHAT
UNLAY
UNMAN
UNSAY
URBAN
UREAL
URIAH
USUAL
UVEAL
UVEAS
UXMAL

U•••A
ULEMA
ULTRA
UMBRA
UTICA
UVULA

•UA••
DUADS
DUALA
DUANE
GUACO
GUANO
GUANS
GUARD
GUAVA
JUANA
JUANS
LUAUS
QUACK
QUADS
QUAFF
QUAGS
QUAIL
QUAKE
QUAKY
QUALM
QUANT
QUARK
QUART
QUASH
QUASI
QUASS
QUAYS
SUAVE

•U•A•
AUDAD
AURAE
AURAL
AURAS
BUBAL
BURAN
CUBAN
DUCAL
DUCAT
DUMAS
DURAL
FUGAL
FURAN
GULAR
HULAS
HUMAN
HUNAN
JUBAS
JUDAH
JUDAS
JUGAL
JURAL
JURAT
KUBAN
KULAK
LUNAR
MURAL
MURAT
PUMAS
PUNAS
PUPAE
PUSAN
QUEAN
RUGAE
RURAL
SUBAH
SUDAN
SUGAR
SUMAC
SURAH
SURAL
SURAS
SUSAN
TUBAL
TUBAS
TUNAS
YUGAS

•U••A
BULLA
BURMA
BURSA
CULPA
CURIA
DUALA
DULIA
DURRA
GUAVA
GUMMA
GUSTA
GUTTA
HULDA
JUANA
JUDEA
JULIA
JUMNA
JUNTA
JURUA
JUXTA
KUFRA
LUCCA
LUCIA
LUISA
MURRA
MUSCA
NUBIA
NUCHA
OUIDA
OUIJA
PUCKA
PUKKA
PUNKA
QUOTA
RUMBA
SULFA
SUNNA
SUPRA
SUTRA
TULSA
VULVA
YUCCA

••UA•
AQUAE
AQUAS
DOUAI
DOUAY
EQUAL
FEUAR
KAUAI
SKUAS
SQUAB
SQUAD
SQUAT
SQUAW
USUAL

••U•A
ALULA
ARUBA
BEULA
CAUCA
CHUFA
CRURA
DOURA
DYULA
FAUNA
GOUDA
LAURA
MAURA
PAULA
SAUNA
SCUBA
SCUTA
SOUSA
STUKA
STUPA
THUJA
TRUDA
UVULA

•••UA
CAPUA
GENUA
JOSUA
JURUA
LEHUA
NAHUA
PADUA

PAPUA
VACUA

UB•••
UBOAT
UBOLT

U•B••
UMBEL
UMBER
UMBOS
UMBRA
UNBAR
UPBOW
URBAN

•UB••
BUBAL
BUBER
CUBAN
CUBBY
CUBEB
CUBED
CUBES
CUBIC
CUBIT
DUBHE
JUBAS
JUBES
KUBAN
NUBBY
NUBIA
PUBES
PUBIC
PUBIS
RUBES
RUBLE
RUBYS
SUBAH
TUBAL
TUBAS
TUBBY
TUBED
TUBER
TUBES

•U•B•
BULBS
BUSBY
CUBBY
CURBS
GUMBO
JUMBO
NUBBY
NUMBS
RUGBY
RUMBA
TUBBY
TURBO

•U••B
CUBEB

••UB•
ARUBA
CHUBS
CLUBS
DAUBS
DAUBY
DOUBT
DRUBS
FLUBS
GRUBS
KRUBI
SCUBA
SLUBS
SNUBS
STUBS

••U•B
BLURB
CRUMB
EXURB
PLUMB
RHUMB
SQUAB
SQUIB
THUMB

•••UB
SCRUB
SHRUB

U•C••
ULCER
UNCAP
UNCLE
UNCUT

U••C•
URICO
USMCR
UTICA

•UC••
BUCKO
BUCKS
DUCAL
DUCAT
DUCHY
DUCKS
DUCKY
DUCTS
FUCUS
LUCCA
LUCES
LUCIA
LUCID
LUCKY
LUCRE
LUCYS
MUCID
MUCIN
MUCKS
MUCKY
MUCRO
MUCUS
NUCHA
PUCES
PUCKA
PUCKS
RUCHE
RUCKS
SUCKS
SUCRE
TUCKS
YUCCA

•U•C•
BUNCH
BUNCO
CULCH
CURCH
CUTCH
DULCE
DULCY
DUNCE
DUTCH
GUACO
GULCH
HUNCH
HUTCH
JUICE
JUICY
JUNCO
LUCCA
LUNCH
LURCH
MULCH
MULCT
MUNCH
MUSCA
OUNCE
PUNCH
QUACK
QUICK
SULCI
TURCO
YUCCA

•U••C
AULIC
AURIC
CUBIC
CUSEC
HUMIC
MUSIC
PUBIC
PUDIC
PUNIC
RUNIC
SUFIC
SUMAC
TUNIC

••UC•
AMUCK
BRUCE
CAUCA
CHUCK
CLUCK
COUCH
CRUCI
DEUCE
EDUCE
EDUCT
ERUCT
LEUCO
MOUCH
PLUCK
POUCH
SAUCE
SAUCY
SHUCK
STUCK
TOUCH
TRUCE
TRUCK
VOUCH

••U•C
ADUNC

•••UC
GLAUC

UD•••
UDDER

U•D••
UDDER
UNDEE
UNDER
UNDID
UNDUE

U••D•
UREDO

U•••D
UNDID
UNWED
UPEND
UPPED
URGED

•UD••
AUDAD
AUDEN
AUDIO
AUDIT
BUDDY
BUDGE
CUDDY
DUDES
FUDGE
JUDAH
JUDAS
JUDEA
JUDEO
JUDES
JUDGE
JUDYS
KUDOS
KUDUS
MUDDY
NUDES
NUDGE
PUDGY
PUDIC
RUDDS
RUDDY
RUDER
RUDYS
SUDAN
SUDOR
SUDSY
TUDOR

•U•D•
BUDDY
BUNDE
BUNDS
BURDS
CUDDY
CURDS
CURDY
DUADS
FUNDS
FUNDY
GUIDE
GUIDO
HULDA
HURDS
MUDDY
OUIDA
OUTDO
QUADS
QUIDS
QUODS
RUDDS
RUDDY
SUEDE
SURDS

•U••D
AUDAD
BUILD
BUSED
CUBED
CUPID
CURED
DUPED
FUMED
FUSED
FUZED
GUARD
GUILD
GUYED
HUMID
LUCID
LURED
LURID
LUTED
MUCID
MUSED
MUTED
OUTED
PUKED
PULED
RULED
TUBED
TUMID
TUNED

••UD•
CRUDE
ELUDE
ETUDE
EXUDE
FEUDS
GAUDI
GAUDS
GAUDY
GOUDA
LAUDS
LEUDS
MAUDE
MAUDS
PRUDE
SCUDI
SCUDO
SCUDS
SPUDS
STUDS
STUDY
THUDS
TRUDA
TRUDY

••U•D
BLUED
BOUND
CLUED
COULD
DRUID
FEUED
FLUID
FOUND
GLUED
GOURD
HOUND
MAUND
MOULD
POUND
ROUND
SLUED
SOUND
SQUAD
SQUID
TRUED
WOULD
WOUND

•••UD
ALMUD
ALOUD
CLOUD
FRAUD
FREUD
PROUD
PSEUD

U•E••
ULEMA
ULENT
UPEND
UREAL
UREDO
USERS
UTERI
UTERO
UVEAL
UVEAS

U••E•
UDDER
ULCER
UMBEL
UMBER
UNDEE
UNDER
UNMEW
UNPEG
UNREF
UNSEX
UNWED
UPPED
UPPER
UPSET
URGED
URGES
URIEL
USHER
UTHER
UTTER

U•••E
UKASE
ULNAE
ULOSE
UNCLE
UNDEE
UNDUE
UNITE
UNTIE
URATE
URINE
USAGE
UTILE

•UE••
DUELS
DUETS
FUELS
GUESS
GUEST
QUEAN
QUEEN
QUEER
QUELL
QUERN
QUERY
QUEST
QUEUE
RUERS
SUEDE
SUERS
SUETY

•U•E•
AUDEN
AUGER
AUREI
AURES
BUBER
BUSED
BUSES
BUYER
CUBEB
CUBED
CUBES
CULET
CUPEL
CURED
CURER
CURES
CUSEC
CUTER
CUTEY
DUDES
DUKES
DUNES
DUPED
DUPER
DUPES
DURER
EULER
FUMED
FUMES
FUSED
FUSEE
FUSEL
FUSES
FUZED
FUZEE
FUZES
GULES
GUYED
HUGER
HUPEH
JUBES
JUDEA
JUDEO
JUDES
JULEP
JULES
JUNES
JUREL
JUTES
LUCES
LUGER
LUMEN
LUNES
LUNET
LURED
LURER
LURES
LUTED
LUTES
LUXES

MULES
MULEY
MUREX
MUSED
MUSES
MUTED
MUTES
NUDES
NUMEN
OUSEL
OUTED
OUTER
OUZEL
PUBES
PUCES
PUGET
PUKED
PUKES
PULED
PULER
PULES
PUREE
PURER
QUEEN
QUEER
QUIET
RUBES
RUDER
RULED
RULER
RULES
RUMEN
RUNES
RUPEE
RUSES
SUMER
SUPER
SUPES
SURER
TUBED
TUBER
TUBES
TULES
TUNED
TUNER
TUNES
YULES

•U••E

AURAE
BUDGE
BUGLE
BULGE
BUNDE
BURKE
BURSE
BUTTE
CURIE
CURSE
CURVE
CUTIE
DUANE
DUBHE
DULCE
DULSE
DUNCE
DUPLE
FUDGE
FUGLE
FUGUE
FURZE
FUSEE
FUZEE
GUIDE
GUILE
GUISE
JUDGE
JUICE
JULIE
LUCRE
LUISE
LUNGE
MURRE
NUDGE
NURSE
OUNCE
OUTRE
PULSE
PUPAE
PUREE
PURGE
PURSE
QUAKE
QUEUE
QUIRE
QUITE
QUOTE
RUBLE
RUCHE
RUGAE
RUPEE
SUAVE
SUCRE
SUEDE
SUITE
SURGE
SUSIE
TULLE
TUQUE

••UE•

AGUES
BLUED
BLUER
BLUES
BLUET
CLUED
CLUES
CRUEL
CRUET
FEUED
FLUES
GLUED
GLUES
GLUEY
GRUEL
MOUES
ROUEN
ROUES
SLUED
SLUES
TRUED
TRUER
TRUES
YQUEM

••U•E

ABUSE
ACUTE
AMUSE
AQUAE
AZURE
BAUME
BOULE
BOUSE
BRUCE
BRUME
BRUTE
CAUSE
CHUTE
COUPE
CRUDE
CRUSE
DEUCE
DOUSE
DRUPE
DRUSE
EDUCE
ELUDE
ETUDE
EXUDE
FLUKE
FLUME
FLUTE
GAUGE
GAUZE
GLUME
GOUGE
GRUME
HOUSE
INURE
JOULE
LOUPE
LOUSE
MAUDE
MAUVE
MEUSE
MOUSE
NEUME
OVULE
PAUSE
PLUME
PRUDE
PRUNE
ROUGE
ROUSE
ROUTE
SAUCE
SAUTE
SCUTE
SHUTE
SOUSE
SPUME
STUPE
TAUPE
THULE
TRUCE
YOURE
YOUVE

•••UE

ARGUE
BENUE
ENDUE
ENSUE
ESQUE
FIQUE
FUGUE
GIGUE
HAGUE
IMBUE
INDUE
ISSUE
JOSUE
LOGUE
PIQUE
QUEUE
REVUE
ROGUE
ROQUE
SPRUE
TOGUE
TOQUE
TUQUE
UNDUE
VAGUE
VALUE
VENUE
VOGUE

U•F••

UNFIT
UNFIX

U••F•

UNIFY
USAFI

U•••F

UNREF

•UF••

BUFFI
BUFFO
BUFFS
BUFFY
CUFFS
DUFFS
HUFFS
HUFFY
KUFRA
LUFFS
MUFFS
MUFTI
PUFFS
PUFFY
RUFFS
RUFUS
SUFIC
SUFIS
TUFTS
TUFTY

•U•F•

BUFFI
BUFFO
BUFFS
BUFFY
CUFFS
DUFFS
GULFS
HUFFS
HUFFY
LUFFS
MUFFS
PUFFS
PUFFY
QUAFF
RUFFS
SULFA
SULFO
SURFS
SURFY
TURFS
TURFY

•U••F

QUAFF

••UF•

BLUFF
CHUFA
FLUFF
GRUFF
POUFS
SCUFF
SNUFF
STUFF

••U•F

BLUFF
FLUFF
GRUFF
SCUFF
SCURF
SNUFF
STUFF

U•G••

URGED
URGES

U••G•

USAGE

U•••G

UNPEG
UNRIG
USING

•UG••

AUGER
AUGHT
AUGUR
BUGGY
BUGLE
FUGAL
FUGIO
FUGLE
FUGUE
HUGER
HUGHS
HUGOS
JUGAL
LUGER
MUGGY
OUGHT
PUGET
RUGAE
RUGBY
SUGAR
VUGGY
YUGAS

•U•G•

BUDGE
BUGGY
BULGE
BULGY
BUNGS
BURGH
BURGS
DUNGS
DUNGY
FUDGE
FUNGI
FUNGO
JUDGE
LUIGI
LUNGE
LUNGI
LUNGS
MUGGY
MUNGO
NUDGE
OUTGO
PUDGY
PUNGS
PURGE
QUAGS
RUNGS
SURGE
SURGY
VUGGY
VULGO

•U••G

CUING
RUING
SUING

••UG•

BOUGH
CHUGS
COUGH
DOUGH
DOUGS
DRUGS
FAUGH
GAUGE
GOUGE
LAUGH
LOUGH
PLUGS
ROUGE
ROUGH
SLUGS
SNUGS
SOUGH
THUGS
TOUGH
WAUGH

••U•G

BOURG
CLUNG
FLUNG
SLUNG
STUNG
SWUNG
WRUNG
YOUNG

•••UG

ALMUG
DEBUG
SHRUG

UH•••

UHLAN

U•H••

UNHAT
USHER
UTHER

U••H•

USPHS

U•••H

URIAH

•UH••

MUHLY

•U•H•

AUGHT
BUSHY
CUSHY
DUBHE
DUCHY
GUSHY
HUGHS
MUSHY
NUCHA
OUGHT
PUSHY
RUCHE
RUSHY
RUTHS

•U••H

BUNCH
BURGH
CUISH
CULCH
CURCH
CUTCH
DUTCH
FURTH
GULCH
HUMPH
HUNCH
HUPEH
HUTCH
JUDAH
LUNCH
LURCH
MULCH
MUNCH
PUNCH
QUASH
QUOTH
SUBAH
SURAH

••U•H

BLUSH
BOUGH
BRUSH
COUCH
COUGH
CRUSH
DOUGH
FAUGH
FLUSH
LAUGH
LOUGH
MOUCH
MOUTH
PLUSH
POUCH
ROUGH
SHUSH
SLUSH
SOUGH
SOUTH
TOUCH
TOUGH
TRUTH
VOUCH
WAUGH
YOUTH

U•I••

UMIAK
UNIFY
UNION
UNITE
UNITS
UNITY
URIAH

URICO
URIEL
URINE
URINO
USING
UTICA
UTILE

U••I•
UNDID
UNFIT
UNFIX
UNLIT
UNPIN
UNRIG
UNRIP
UNTIE
UNTIL

U•••I
USAFI
UTERI

•UI••
BUILD
BUILT
CUING
CUISH
GUIDE
GUIDO
GUILD
GUILE
GUILT
GUISE
JUICE
JUICY
LUIGI
LUISA
LUISE
OUIDA
OUIJA
QUICK
QUIDS
QUIET
QUILL
QUILT
QUINT
QUIPS
QUIPU
QUIRE
QUIRK
QUIRT
QUITE
QUITO
QUITS
RUING
RUINS
SUING
SUINT
SUITE
SUITS

•U•I•
AUDIO
AUDIT
AULIC
AULIS
AURIC
AURIS
AUXIL
AUXIN
BURIN
CUBIC
CUBIT
CUMIN
CUPID
CURIA
CURIE
CURIO
CUTIE
CUTIN
CUTIS
DULIA
FUGIO
FUSIL
FUZIL
HUMIC
HUMID
JULIA
JULIE
JULIO
LUCIA
LUCID
LURID
MUCID
MUCIN
MUSIC
NUBIA
PUBIC
PUBIS
PUDIC
PUNIC
PUPIL
PURIM
QUAIL
QUOIN
QUOIT
RUNIC
RUNIN
RURIK
SUFIC
SUFIS
SUSIE
TULIP
TUMID
TUNIC
TUNIS
TUPIK
TUPIS
TURIN

•U••I
AUREI
BUFFI
CULTI
CURVI
DUOMI
FUNGI
LUIGI
LUNGI
MUFTI
MULTI
QUASI
SULCI
SUNNI
TURKI
TUTTI

••UI•
ALUIN
BRUIN
BRUIT
DRUID
EQUIP
ETUIS
FLUID
FRUIT
LOUIS
SQUIB
SQUID

••U•I
CRUCI
DOUAI
GAUDI
HOURI
KAUAI
KAURI
KRUBI
NEURI
PLURI
PLUVI
SCUDI

•••UI
ENNUI

•UJ••
JUJUS

•U•J•
OUIJA

••UJ•
THUJA

UK•••
UKASE

U•••K
UMIAK

•UK••
DUKES
PUKED
PUKES
PUKKA
YUKON

•U•K•
BUCKO
BUCKS
BULKS
BULKY
BUNKO
BUNKS
BURKE
BUSKS
CUSKS
DUCKS
DUCKY
DUNKS
DUSKS
DUSKY
FUNKS
FUNKY
HULKS
HULKY
HUNKS
HUNKY
HUSKS
HUSKY
JUNKS
JUNKY
LUCKY
LURKS
MUCKS
MUCKY
MURKY
MUSKS
MUSKY
PUCKA
PUCKS
PUKKA
PUNKA
PUNKS
PUNKY
QUAKE
QUAKY
RUCKS
RUSKS
SUCKS
SULKS
SULKY
TUCKS
TURKI
TURKS
TUSKS

•U••K
KULAK
KURSK
QUACK
QUARK
QUICK
QUIRK
RURIK
TUPIK

••UK•
FLUKE
FLUKY
LEUKO
STUKA

••U•K
AMUCK
BRUSK
CAULK
CHUCK
CHUNK
CLUCK
DRUNK
FLUNK
PLUCK
PLUNK
SHUCK
SKULK
SKUNK
SLUNK
SPUNK
STUCK
STUNK
TRUCK
TRUNK

•••UK
TALUK

UL•••
ULCER
ULEMA
ULENT
ULNAE
ULNAR
ULNAS
ULOSE
ULOUS
ULTRA

U•L••
UHLAN
UNLAY
UNLIT

U••L•
UBOLT
UNCLE
URALS
UTILE
UVULA

U•••L
UMBEL
UNTIL
UREAL
URIEL
USUAL
UVEAL
UXMAL

•UL••
AULIC
AULIS
BULBS
BULGE
BULGY
BULKS
BULKY
BULLA
BULLS
BULLY
CULCH
CULET
CULLS
CULMS
CULPA
CULTI
CULTS
DULCE
DULCY
DULIA
DULLS
DULLY
DULSE
EULER
FULLS
FULLY
GULAR
GULCH
GULES
GULFS
GULLS
GULLY
GULPS
HULAS
HULDA
HULKS
HULKY
HULLS
JULEP
JULES
JULIA
JULIE
JULIO
JULYS
KULAK
LULLS
LULUS
MULCH
MULCT
MULES
MULEY
MULLS
MULTI
PULED
PULER
PULES
PULLS
PULMO
PULPS
PULPY
PULSE
RULED
RULER
RULES
SULCI
SULFA
SULFO
SULKS
SULKY
SULLY
SULUS
TULES
TULIP
TULLE
TULLY
TULSA
VULGO
VULVA
YULES
ZULUS

•U•L•
BUGLE
BUILD
BUILT
BULLA
BULLS
BULLY
BURLS
BURLY
CULLS
CURLS
CURLY
DUALA
DUELS
DULLS
DULLY
DUPLE
FUELS
FUGLE
FULLS
FULLY
FURLS
GUILD
GUILE
GUILT
GULLS
GULLY
HULLS
HURLS
HURLY
LULLS
MUHLY
MULLS
PULLS
PURLS
QUALM
QUELL
QUILL
QUILT
RUBLE
SULLY
SURLY
TULLE
TULLY

•U••L
AURAL
AUSTL
AUXIL
BUBAL
BUTYL
CUPEL
DUCAL
DURAL
FUGAL
FUSEL
FUSIL
FUZIL
JUGAL
JURAL
JUREL
MURAL
OUSEL
OUZEL
PUPIL
QUAIL
QUELL
QUILL
RURAL
SURAL
TUBAL

••UL•
ADULT
ALULA
BEULA
BOULE
CAULK
CAULS
COULD
DYULA
EXULT
FAULT
FOULS
GAULS
HAULM
HAULS
JOULE
MAULS
MOULD
MOULT
OCULO
OVULE
PAULA
PAULO
PAULS
POULT
SAULS
SAULT
SCULL
SCULP
SHULS
SKULK
SKULL
SOULS
STULL
THULE
TRULY
UVULA
VAULT
WAULS
WOULD

••U•L
CHURL
CRUEL
EQUAL
GRUEL

KNURL
SCULL
SKULL
STULL
USUAL

•••UL
AFOUL
AMPUL
ANNUL
AWFUL
BABUL
GHOUL
KABUL
MIAUL
MOGUL
PICUL
RAOUL
SEOUL
VOGUL

UM•••
UMBEL
UMBER
UMBOS
UMBRA
UMIAK

U•M••
UNMAN
UNMEW
USMCR
UXMAL

U••M•
ULEMA

U•••M
UNARM

•UM••
BUMPS
BUMPY
CUMIN
DUMAS
DUMMY
DUMPS
DUMPY
FUMED
FUMES
GUMBO
GUMMA
GUMMY
HUMAN
HUMIC
HUMID
HUMOR
HUMPH
HUMPS
HUMPY
HUMUS
JUMBO
JUMNA
JUMPS
JUMPY
LUMEN
LUMPS
LUMPY
MUMMS
MUMMY
MUMPS
NUMBS
NUMEN
PUMAS
PUMPS
RUMBA
RUMEN
RUMMY
RUMOR
RUMPS
SUMAC
SUMER
SUMPS
TUMID
TUMOR
YUMMY

•U•M•
BURMA
CULMS
DUMMY
DUOMI
DUOMO
GUMMA
GUMMY
MUMMS
MUMMY
PULMO
RUMMY
YUMMY

•U••M
AURUM
BUXOM
DURUM
PURIM
QUALM

••UM•
ALUMS
ARUMS
BAUME
BRUME
CHUMP
CHUMS
CLUMP
CRUMB
CRUMP
DRUMS
FLUME
FLUMP
FRUMP
GLUME
GRUME
NEUME
PLUMB
PLUME
PLUMP
PLUMS
PLUMY
RHUMB
SCUMS
SLUMP
SLUMS
SPUME
SPUMY
STUMP
STUMS
THUMB
THUMP
TRUMP

••U•M
HAULM
YQUEM

•••UM
ALBUM
ALGUM
ARIUM
AURUM
BEGUM
CECUM
DATUM
DEGUM
DURUM
FANUM
FILUM
FORUM
HILUM
HOKUM
ILEUM
ILIUM
JORUM
NAHUM
OAKUM
ODEUM
ODIUM
OPIUM
PNEUM
RHEUM
SAGUM
SCRUM
SEBUM
SEDUM
SERUM
STRUM
THRUM
VELUM

UN•••
UNAPT
UNARM
UNAUS
UNBAR
UNCAP
UNCLE
UNCUT
UNDEE
UNDER
UNDID
UNDUE
UNFIT
UNFIX
UNHAT
UNIFY
UNION
UNITE
UNITS
UNITY
UNLAY
UNLIT
UNMAN
UNMEW
UNPEG
UNPIN
UNREF
UNRIG
UNRIP
UNSAY
UNSEX
UNTIE
UNTIL
UNWED

U•N••
ULNAE
ULNAR
ULNAS

U••N•
ULENT
UPEND
URANO
URINE
URINO
USING

U•••N
UHLAN
UNION
UNMAN
UNPIN
URBAN
UTURN

•UN••
AUNTS
AUNTY
BUNCH
BUNCO
BUNDE
BUNDS
BUNGS
BUNKO
BUNKS
BUNNS
BUNNY
BUNTS
DUNCE
DUNES
DUNGS
DUNGY
DUNKS
FUNDS
FUNDY
FUNGI
FUNGO
FUNKS
FUNKY
FUNNY
GUNNY
HUNAN
HUNCH
HUNKS
HUNKY
HUNTS
JUNCO
JUNES
JUNKS
JUNKY
JUNTA
LUNAR
LUNCH
LUNES
LUNET
LUNGE
LUNGI
LUNGS
LUNTS
MUNCH
MUNGO
MUNRO
OUNCE
PUNAS
PUNCH
PUNGS
PUNIC
PUNKA
PUNKS
PUNKY
PUNTO
PUNTS
PUNTY
RUNES
RUNGS
RUNIC
RUNIN
RUNON
RUNTS
RUNTY
SUNNA
SUNNI
SUNNS
SUNNY
SUNUP
TUNAS
TUNED
TUNER
TUNES
TUNIC
TUNIS
TUNNY

•U•N•
BUNNS
BUNNY
BURNS
BURNT
CUING
DUANE
FUNNY
GUANO
GUANS
GUNNY
JUANA
JUANS
JUMNA
MUONS
QUANT
QUINT
RUING
RUINS
SUING
SUINT
SUNNA
SUNNI
SUNNS
SUNNY
TUNNY
TURNS

•U••N
AUDEN
AUXIN
BURAN
BURIN
CUBAN
CUMIN
CUTIN
FURAN
HUMAN
HUNAN
HURON
JUPON
KUBAN
LUMEN
LUZON
MUCIN
NUMEN
PUSAN
PUTON
QUEAN
QUEEN
QUERN
QUOIN
RUMEN
RUNIN
RUNON
SUDAN
SUSAN
TURIN
YUKON
YUPON

••UN•
ADUNC
BLUNT
BOUND
BRUNO
BRUNT
CHUNK
CLUNG
CLUNY
COUNT
DAUNT
DRUNK
FAUNA
FAUNS
FLUNG
FLUNK
FOUND
FOUNT
GAUNT
GRUNT
HAUNT
HOUND
JAUNT
MAUND
MOUNT
NOUNS
PLUNK
POUND
PRUNE
ROUND
SAUNA
SHUNS
SHUNT
SKUNK
SLUNG
SLUNK
SOUND
SPUNK
STUNG
STUNK
STUNS
STUNT
SWUNG
TAUNT
TRUNK
VAUNT
WOUND
WRUNG
YOUNG

••U•N
ALUIN
BOURN
BRUIN
CHURN
INURN
MOURN
ROUEN
SPURN
UTURN

•••UN
BEGUN
BOSUN
CAJUN
GATUN
JOTUN
KORUN
RERUN
SHAUN
YAMUN

U•O••
UBOAT
UBOLT
ULOSE
ULOUS

U••O•
UMBOS
UNION
UPBOW

U•••O
URANO
UREDO
URICO
URINO
UTERO

•UO••
BUOYS
DUOMI
DUOMO
MUONS
QUODS
QUOIN
QUOIT
QUOTA
QUOTE
QUOTH

•U•O•
AUTOS
BUXOM
DUROS
FUROR
HUGOS
HUMOR
HURON
JUPON
JUROR
KUDOS
LUXOR
LUZON
PUTON
RUMOR
RUNON
SUDOR
TUDOR
TUMOR
TUTOR
YUKON
YUPON

•U••O
AUDIO
BUCKO
BUFFO
BUNCO
BUNKO
BURRO
CUPRO
CURIO
CUSSO
DUOMO

FUGIO
FUNGO
GUACO
GUANO
GUIDO
GUMBO
GUSTO
JUDEO
JULIO
JUMBO
JUNCO
MUCRO
MUNGO
MUNRO
OUTDO
OUTGO
PULMO
PUNTO
QUITO
RUSSO
SULFO
TURBO
TURCO
VULGO

••UO•
CRUOR
FLUOR

••U•O
BRUNO
LEUCO
LEUKO
NEURO
OCULO
PAULO
PLUTO
SAURO
SCUDO
TAURO
TAUTO

•••UO
ACOUO

UP•••
UPBOW
UPEND
UPPED
UPPER
UPSET

U•P••
UNPEG
UNPIN
UPPED
UPPER
USPHS

U••P•
UNAPT

U•••P
UNCAP
UNRIP
USURP

•UP••
CUPEL
CUPID
CUPRO
DUPED
DUPER
DUPES
DUPLE
GUPPY
HUPEH
JUPON
LUPUS
PUPAE
PUPIL
PUPPY
RUPEE
SUPER
SUPES
SUPRA
TUPIK
TUPIS
YUPON

•U•P•
BUMPS
BUMPY
BURPS
CULPA
CUSPS
DUMPS
DUMPY
GULPS
GUPPY
HUMPH
HUMPS
HUMPY
JUMPS
JUMPY
LUMPS
LUMPY
MUMPS
PULPS
PULPY
PUMPS
PUPPY
QUIPS
QUIPU
RUMPS
SUMPS

•U••P
CUTUP
JULEP
PUTUP
SUNUP
TULIP

••UP•
COUPE
COUPS
DRUPE
ERUPT
KRUPP
LOUPE
LOUPS
ROUPY
SCUPS
SOUPS
SOUPY
STUPA
STUPE
TAUPE
YAUPS

••U•P
CHUMP
CLUMP
CRUMP
EQUIP
FLUMP
FRUMP
KRUPP
PLUMP
SCULP
SLUMP
SLURP
STUMP
THUMP
TRUMP
USURP

•••UP
CROUP
CUTUP
GETUP
GROUP
LETUP
MIXUP
PINUP
PUTUP
SCAUP
SETUP
SIRUP
STOUP
SUNUP
SYRUP
TIEUP

•UQ••
TUQUE

UR•••
URALS
URANO
URATE
URBAN
UREAL
UREDO
URGED
URGES
URIAH
URICO
URIEL
URINE
URINO

U•R••
UNREF
UNRIG
UNRIP

U••R•
ULTRA
UMBRA
UNARM
USERS
USURP
USURY
UTERI
UTERO
UTURN

U•••R
UDDER
ULCER
ULNAR
UMBER
UNBAR
UNDER
UPPER
USHER
USMCR
UTHER
UTTER

•UR••
AURAE
AURAL
AURAS
AUREI
AURES
AURIC
AURIS
AURUM
BURAN
BURDS
BURGH
BURGS
BURIN
BURKE
BURLS
BURLY
BURMA
BURNS
BURNT
BURPS
BURRO
BURRS
BURRY
BURSA
BURSE
BURST
CURBS
CURCH
CURDS
CURDY
CURED
CURER
CURES
CURIA
CURIE
CURIO
CURLS
CURLY
CURRY
CURSE
CURST
CURVE
CURVI
DURAL
DURER
DUROS
DURRA
DURUM
EURUS
FURAN
FURLS
FUROR
FURRY
FURTH
FURZE
FURZY
GURUS
HURDS
HURLS
HURLY
HURON
HURRY
HURTS
JURAL
JURAT
JUREL
JUROR
JURUA
KURSK
KURUS
LURCH
LURED
LURER
LURES
LURID
LURKS
MURAL
MURAT
MUREX
MURKY
MURRA
MURRE
MURRY
NURSE
PUREE
PURER
PURGE
PURIM
PURLS
PURRS
PURSE
PURSY
RURAL
RURIK
SURAH
SURAL
SURAS
SURDS
SURER
SURFS
SURFY
SURGE
SURGY
SURLY
TURBO
TURCO
TURFS
TURFY
TURIN
TURKI
TURKS
TURNS

•U•R•
BURRO
BURRS
BURRY
CUPRO
CURRY
DURRA
FURRY
GUARD
HURRY
KUFRA
LUCRE
MUCRO
MUNRO
MURRA
MURRE
MURRY
OUTRE
PURRS
QUARK
QUART
QUERN
QUERY
QUIRE
QUIRK
QUIRT
RUERS
SUCRE
SUERS
SUPRA
SUTRA

•U••R
AUGER
AUGUR
BUBER
BUYER
CURER
CUTER
DUPER
DURER
EULER
FUROR
GULAR
HUGER
HUMOR
JUROR
LUGER
LUNAR
LURER
LUXOR
OUTER
PULER
PURER
QUEER
RUDER
RULER
RUMOR
SUDOR
SUGAR
SUMER
SUPER
SURER
TUBER
TUDOR
TUMOR
TUNER
TUTOR

••UR•
AZURE
BLURB
BLURS
BLURT
BOURG
BOURN
CHURL
CHURN
CHURR
COURT
CRURA
DOURA
DRURY
EXURB
FOURS
GAURS
GOURD
HOURI
HOURS
INURE
INURN
KAURI
KAURY
KNURL
KNURS
LAURA
LOURS
MAURA
MOURN
NAURU
NEURI
NEURO
PLURI
POURS
SAURO
SAURY
SCURF
SLURP
SLURS
SOURS
SPURN
SPURS
SPURT
TAURO
THURS
TOURS
USURP
USURY
UTURN
YOURE
YOURS

••U•R
BLUER
CHURR
CRUOR
FEUAR
FLUOR
TRUER

•••UR
AMOUR
ASHUR
AUGUR
DEMUR
FEMUR
FLOUR
HHOUR
INCUR
LEMUR
MOHUR
OCCUR
RECUR
SCOUR
SIEUR

US•••
USAFI
USAGE
USERS
USHER
USING
USMCR
USPHS
USUAL
USURP
USURY

U•S••
UNSAY
UNSEX
UPSET

U••S•
UKASE
ULOSE

U•••S
ULNAS
ULOUS
UMBOS
UNAUS
UNITS
URALS
URGES
USERS
USPHS

UVEAS

•US••
AUSTL
BUSBY
BUSED
BUSES
BUSHY
BUSKS
BUSTS
CUSEC
CUSHY
CUSKS
CUSPS
CUSSO
DUSKS
DUSKY
DUSTS
DUSTY
FUSED
FUSEE
FUSEL
FUSES
FUSIL
FUSSY
FUSTY
GUSHY
GUSTA
GUSTO
GUSTS
GUSTY
HUSKS
HUSKY
HUSSY
JUSTS
LUSTS
LUSTY
MUSCA
MUSED
MUSES
MUSHY
MUSIC
MUSKS
MUSKY
MUSSY
MUSTS
MUSTY
OUSEL
OUSTS
PUSAN
PUSHY
PUSSY
RUSES
RUSHY
RUSKS
RUSSO
RUSTS
RUSTY
SUSAN
SUSIE
TUSKS

•U•S•
BURSA
BURSE
BURST
CUISH
CURSE
CURST
CUSSO
DULSE
FUSSY
GUESS
GUEST
GUISE
GUTSY
HUSSY
KURSK
LUISA
LUISE
MUSSY
NURSE
PULSE
PURSE
PURSY
PUSSY
QUASH
QUASI
QUASS
QUEST
RUSSO
SUDSY
TULSA

•U••S
AULIS
AUNTS
AURAS
AURES
AURIS
AUTOS
BUCKS
BUFFS
BULBS
BULKS
BULLS
BUMPS
BUNDS
BUNGS
BUNKS
BUNNS
BUNTS
BUOYS
BURDS
BURGS
BURLS
BURNS
BURPS
BURRS
BUSES
BUSKS
BUSTS
BUTTS
CUBES
CUFFS
CULLS
CULMS
CULTS
CURBS
CURDS
CURES
CURLS
CUSKS
CUSPS
CUTIS
DUADS
DUCKS
DUCTS
DUDES
DUELS
DUETS
DUFFS
DUKES
DULLS
DUMAS
DUMPS
DUNES
DUNGS
DUNKS
DUPES
DUROS
DUSKS
DUSTS
EURUS
FUCUS
FUELS
FULLS
FUMES
FUNDS
FUNKS
FURLS
FUSES
FUZES
GUANS
GUESS
GULES
GULFS
GULLS
GULPS
GURUS
GUSTS
HUFFS
HUGHS
HUGOS
HULAS
HULKS
HULLS
HUMPS
HUMUS
HUNKS
HUNTS
HURDS
HURLS
HURTS
HUSKS
JUANS
JUBAS
JUBES
JUDAS
JUDES
JUDYS
JUJUS
JULES
JULYS
JUMPS
JUNES
JUNKS
JUSTS
JUTES
KUDOS
KUDUS
KURUS
LUAUS
LUCES
LUCYS
LUFFS
LULLS
LULUS
LUMPS
LUNES
LUNGS
LUNTS
LUPUS
LURES
LURKS
LUSTS
LUTES
LUXES
MUCKS
MUCUS
MUFFS
MULES
MULLS
MUMMS
MUMPS
MUONS
MUSES
MUSKS
MUSTS
MUTES
MUTTS
NUDES
NUMBS
OUSTS
PUBES
PUBIS
PUCES
PUCKS
PUFFS
PUKES
PULES
PULLS
PULPS
PUMAS
PUMPS
PUNAS
PUNGS
PUNKS
PUNTS
PURLS
PURRS
PUTTS
QUADS
QUAGS
QUASS
QUAYS
QUIDS
QUIPS
QUITS
QUODS
RUBES
RUBYS
RUCKS
RUDDS
RUDYS
RUERS
RUFFS
RUFUS
RUINS
RULES
RUMPS
RUNES
RUNGS
RUNTS
RUSES
RUSKS
RUSTS
RUTHS
SUCKS
SUERS
SUFIS
SUITS
SULKS
SULUS
SUMPS
SUNNS
SUPES
SURAS
SURDS
SURFS
SUZYS
TUBAS
TUBES
TUCKS
TUFTS
TULES
TUNAS
TUNES
TUNIS
TUPIS
TURFS
TURKS
TURNS
TUSKS
TUTUS
YUGAS
YULES
ZULUS

••US•
ABUSE
ADUST
AMUSE
BLUSH
BOUSE
BOUSY
BRUSH
BRUSK
CAUSE
CRUSE
CRUSH
CRUST
DOUSE
DRUSE
FAUST
FLUSH
GAUSS
HOUSE
JOUST
LOUSE
LOUSY
MEUSE
MOUSE
MOUSY
PAUSE
PLUSH
ROUSE
ROUST
SHUSH
SLUSH
SOUSA
SOUSE
TRUSS
TRUST

••U•S
ABUTS
AGUES
ALUMS
AQUAS
ARUMS
BLUES
BLURS
BOUTS
CAULS
CHUBS
CHUGS
CHUMS
CLUBS
CLUES
COUPS
DAUBS
DOUGS
DRUBS
DRUGS
DRUMS
ETUIS
FAUNS
FEUDS
FLUBS
FLUES
FOULS
FOURS
GAUDS
GAULS
GAURS
GAUSS
GLUES
GLUTS
GRUBS
HAULS
HOURS
KNURS
LAUDS
LEUDS
LOUIS
LOUPS
LOURS
LOUTS
MAUDS
MAULS
MOUES
NOUNS
PAULS
PLUGS
PLUMS
POUFS
POURS
POUTS
ROUES
ROUTS
SAULS
SCUDS
SCUMS
SCUPS
SCUTS
SHULS
SHUNS
SHUTS
SKUAS
SLUBS
SLUES
SLUGS
SLUMS
SLURS
SLUTS
SMUTS
SNUBS
SNUGS
SOULS
SOUPS
SOURS
SPUDS
SPURS
STUBS
STUDS
STUMS
STUNS
THUDS
THUGS
THURS
TOURS
TOUTS
TRUES
TRUSS
WAULS
YAUPS
YOURS

•••US
AINUS
ALDUS
ANGUS
ANKUS
ARCUS
ARGUS
ARIUS
ASCUS
BEAUS
BOGUS
BOLUS
BONUS
CAMUS
CASUS
CETUS
CONUS
CYRUS
DORUS
EMEUS
EURUS
FAVUS
FETUS
FOCUS
FUCUS
GENUS
GURUS
GYRUS
HABUS
HOCUS
HORUS
HUMUS
ICTUS
ILEUS
ILLUS
INCUS
INDUS
JANUS
JEHUS
JESUS
JUJUS
KAGUS
KUDUS
KURUS
LEPUS
LINUS
LOCUS
LOTUS
LUAUS
LULUS
LUPUS
MAGUS
MANUS
MENUS
MINUS
MODUS
MOMUS
MUCUS
NEGUS
NEVUS
NEXUS
NIDUS
NINUS
NISUS
NODUS
ORCUS
PIOUS
RAMUS
REBUS
REMUS
RISUS
RUFUS
SALUS

SINUS
SITUS
SOLUS
SORUS
SULUS
TALUS
TITUS
TONUS
TORUS
TUTUS
ULOUS
UNAUS
VAGUS
VARUS
VENUS
VIRUS
WAMUS
XERUS
ZEBUS
ZULUS

UT•••
UTERI
UTERO
UTHER
UTICA
UTILE
UTTER
UTURN

U•T••
ULTRA
UNTIE
UNTIL
UTTER

U••T•
UNITE
UNITS
UNITY
URATE

U•••T
UBOAT
UBOLT
ULENT
UNAPT
UNCUT
UNFIT
UNHAT
UNLIT
UPSET

•UT••
AUTOS
BUTTE
BUTTS
BUTYL
CUTCH
CUTER
CUTEY
CUTIE
CUTIN
CUTIS
CUTTY
CUTUP
DUTCH
GUTSY
GUTTA
HUTCH
JUTES
LUTED
LUTES
MUTED
MUTES
MUTTS
NUTTY
OUTDO
OUTED
OUTER
OUTGO
OUTRE
PUTON
PUTTS
PUTTY
PUTUP
RUTHS
RUTTY
SUTRA
TUTOR
TUTTI
TUTTY
TUTUS

•U•T•
AUNTS
AUNTY
AUSTL
BUNTS
BUSTS
BUTTE
BUTTS
CULTI
CULTS
CUTTY
DUCTS
DUETS
DUSTS
DUSTY
FURTH
FUSTY
GUSTA
GUSTO
GUSTS
GUSTY
GUTTA
HUNTS
HURTS
JUNTA
JUSTS
JUXTA
LUNTS
LUSTS
LUSTY
MUFTI
MULTI
MUSTS
MUSTY
MUTTS
NUTTY
OUSTS
PUNTO
PUNTS
PUNTY
PUTTS
PUTTY
QUITE
QUITO
QUITS
QUOTA
QUOTE
QUOTH
RUNTS
RUNTY
RUSTS
RUSTY
RUTTY
SUETY
SUITE
SUITS
TUFTS
TUFTY
TUTTI
TUTTY

•U••T
AUDIT
AUGHT
BUILT
BURNT
BURST
CUBIT
CULET
CURST
DUCAT
GUEST
GUILT
JURAT
LUNET
MULCT
MURAT
OUGHT
PUGET
QUANT
QUART
QUEST
QUIET
QUILT
QUINT
QUIRT
QUOIT
SUINT

••UT•
ABUTS
ACUTE
BOUTS
BRUTE
CHUTE
FLUTE
FLUTY
GLUTS
GOUTY
LOUTS
MOUTH
PLUTO
POUTS
ROUTE
ROUTS
SAUTE
SCUTA
SCUTE
SCUTS
SHUTE
SHUTS
SLUTS
SMUTS
SOUTH
TAUTO
TOUTS
TRUTH
YOUTH

••U•T
ADULT
ADUST
BLUET
BLUNT
BLURT
BRUIT
BRUNT
COUNT
COURT
CRUET
CRUST
DAUNT
DOUBT
EDUCT
ERUCT
ERUPT
EXULT
FAULT
FAUST
FOUNT
FRUIT
GAUNT
GRUNT
HAUNT
JAUNT
JOUST
MOULT
MOUNT
POULT
ROUST
SAULT
SHUNT
SPURT
SQUAT
STUNT
TAUNT
TRUST
VAULT
VAUNT

•••UT
ABOUT
ALEUT
ASYUT
BEAUT
CAPUT
CLOUT
DEBUT
FLOUT
GAMUT
GHAUT
GROUT
INPUT
KAPUT
KNOUT
KRAUT
LIEUT
REBUT
SCOUT
SHOUT
SNOUT
SPOUT
STOUT
STRUT
TROUT
UNCUT

U•U••
USUAL
USURP
USURY
UTURN
UVULA

U••U•
ULOUS
UNAUS
UNCUT
UNDUE

•U•U•
AUGUR
AURUM
CUTUP
DURUM
EURUS
FUCUS
FUGUE
GURUS
HUMUS
JUJUS
JURUA
KUDUS
KURUS
LUAUS
LULUS
LUPUS
MUCUS
PUTUP
QUEUE
RUFUS
SULUS
SUNUP
TUQUE
TUTUS
ZULUS

•U••U
QUIPU

••U•U
NAURU

UV•••
UVEAL
UVEAS
UVULA

•U•V•
CURVE
CURVI
GUAVA
SUAVE
VULVA

••UV•
MAUVE
PLUVI
YOUVE

U•W••
UNWED

U•••W
UNMEW
UPBOW

••U•W
SQUAW

UX•••
UXMAL

U•••X
UNFIX
UNSEX

•UX••
AUXIL
AUXIN
BUXOM
JUXTA
LUXES
LUXOR

•U••X
MUREX

•••UX
BEAUX
SIOUX

U•••Y
UNIFY
UNITY
UNLAY
UNSAY
USURY

•UY••
BUYER
GUYED

•U•Y•
BUOYS
BUTYL
JUDYS
JULYS
LUCYS
QUAYS
RUBYS
RUDYS
SUZYS

•U••Y
AUNTY
BUDDY
BUFFY
BUGGY
BULGY
BULKY
BULLY
BUMPY
BUNNY
BURLY
BURRY
BUSBY
BUSHY
CUBBY
CUDDY
CURDY
CURLY
CURRY
CUSHY
CUTEY
CUTTY
DUCHY
DUCKY
DULCY
DULLY
DUMMY
DUMPY
DUNGY
DUSKY
DUSTY
FULLY
FUNDY
FUNKY
FUNNY
FURRY
FURZY
FUSSY
FUSTY
FUZZY
GULLY
GUMMY
GUNNY
GUPPY
GUSHY
GUSTY
GUTSY
HUFFY
HULKY
HUMPY
HUNKY
HURLY
HURRY
HUSKY
HUSSY
JUICY
JUMPY
JUNKY
LUCKY
LUMPY
LUSTY
MUCKY
MUDDY
MUGGY
MUHLY
MULEY
MUMMY
MURKY
MURRY
MUSHY
MUSKY
MUSSY
MUSTY
MUZZY
NUBBY
NUTTY
PUDGY
PUFFY
PULPY
PUNKY
PUNTY
PUPPY
PURSY
PUSHY
PUSSY
PUTTY
QUAKY
QUERY
RUDDY
RUGBY
RUMMY
RUNTY
RUSHY
RUSTY
RUTTY
SUDSY
SUETY
SULKY
SULLY
SUNNY
SURFY
SURGY
SURLY
TUBBY
TUFTY
TULLY
TUNNY
TURFY
TUTTY
VUGGY
YUMMY

••U•Y
BOUSY
CLUNY

DAUBY
DOUAY
DRURY
FLUKY
FLUTY
GAUDY
GAUZY
GLUEY
GOUTY
KAURY
LOUSY
MOUSY
PLUMY
ROUPY
SAUCY
SAURY
SOUPY
SPUMY
STUDY
TRUDY
TRULY
USURY

•UZ••
FUZED
FUZEE
FUZES
FUZIL
FUZZY
LUZON
MUZZY
OUZEL
SUZYS

•U•Z•
FURZE
FURZY
FUZZY
MUZZY

••UZ•
GAUZE
GAUZY

•••UZ
VADUZ

VA•••
VACUA
VADUZ
VAGIN
VAGUE
VAGUS
VAIRS
VALES
VALET
VALID
VALOR
VALUE
VALVE
VAMPS
VANED
VANES
VANGS
VANIR
VAPID
VAPOR
VARAS
VARIC
VARIO
VARIX
VARRO
VARUS
VARVE
VASES
VASTY
VATIC
VAULT
VAUNT

V•A••
VIALS
VIAND
VMAIL

V••A•
VARAS
VELAR
VENAE
VENAL
VERAS
VICAR
VINAS
VIRAL
VISAS
VITAE
VITAL
VOCAL
VOLAR

V•••A
VACUA
VERNA
VESTA
VILLA
VIOLA
VIRGA
VISTA
VITTA
VODKA
VOILA
VOLGA
VOLTA
VOLVA
VULVA

•VA••
AVAIL
AVARS
AVAST
EVADE
EVANS
IVANS
KVASS
OVALS
OVARY
OVATE

•V•A•
AVIAN
UVEAL
UVEAS

•V••A
DVINA
EVITA
UVULA

••VA•
ALVAN
ARVAL
DAVAO
DEVAS
DIVAN
DIVAS
DOVAP
ELVAS
KAVAS
KIVAS
LAVAS
NAVAL
NAVAR
NIVAL
NOVAE
NOVAS
PAVAN
RIVAL
SIVAN

••V•A
FOVEA
LIVIA

•••VA
BRAVA
DRAVA
GUAVA
LARVA
SILVA
SYLVA
VOLVA
VULVA

V•B••
VIBES

V••B•
VERBS

V•C••
VACUA
VICAR
VICES
VICHY
VICKS
VICKY
VOCAL
VOCES

V••C•
VETCH
VINCE
VINCI
VISCT
VNECK
VOICE
VOUCH

V•••C
VARIC
VATIC
VEDIC
VESIC
VINIC

•V•C•
EVICT

••V•C
CIVIC
HAVOC

V•D••
VADUZ
VEDIC
VIDEO
VODKA

V••D•
VELDS
VELDT
VENDS
VERDI
VOIDS

V•••D
VALID
VANED
VAPID
VEXED
VIAND
VISED
VIVID
VOTED
VOWED

•V•D•
EVADE

•V••D
AVOID
IVIED
OVOID

••V•D
BOVID
CAVED
COVED
DAVID
DIVED
HIVED
LAVED
LIVED
LIVID
LOVED
MOVED
PAVED
RAVED
RIVED
ROVED
SAVED
VIVID
WAVED
WIVED

VE•••
VEDIC
VEERS
VEERY
VEILS
VEINS
VEINY
VELAR
VELDS
VELDT
VELUM
VENAE
VENAL
VENDS
VENOM
VENTS
VENUE
VENUS
VERAS
VERBS
VERDI
VERGE
VERMI
VERNA
VERNE
VERNS
VERSE
VERSO
VERST
VERTU
VERVE
VESIC
VESTA
VESTS
VETCH
VEXED
VEXER
VEXES
VEXIL

V•E••
VEERS
VEERY
VIEWS
VIEWY
VNECK

V••E•
VALES
VALET
VANED
VANES
VASES
VEXED
VEXER
VEXES
VIBES
VICES
VIDEO
VILER
VIMEN
VINES
VIPER
VIREO
VIRES
VISED
VISES
VIXEN
VOCES
VOLES
VOMER
VOTED
VOTER
VOTES
VOWED
VOWEL
VOWER

V•••E
VAGUE
VALUE
VALVE
VARVE
VENAE
VENUE
VERGE
VERNE
VERSE
VERVE
VINCE
VIRGE
VITAE
VOGUE
VOICE
VOILE

•VE••
AVENS
AVERS
AVERT
AVERY
EVENS
EVENT
EVERT
EVERY
OVENS
OVERT
UVEAL
UVEAS

•V•E•
IVIED
IVIES

•V••E
EVADE
EVOKE
OVATE
OVINE
OVULE

••VE•
BEVEL
CAVED
CAVES
CIVET
COVED
COVER
COVES
COVET
COVEY
DAVES
DAVEY
DIVED
DIVER
DIVES
DOVER
DOVES
EAVES
ELVER
ELVES
FEVER
FIVER
FIVES
FOVEA
GAVEL
GIVEN
GIVER
GIVES
HAVEN
HIVED
HIVES
HOVEL
HOVER
KEVEL
LAVED
LAVER
LAVES
LEVEE
LEVEL
LEVEN
LEVER
LIVED
LIVEN
LIVER
LIVES
LOVED
LOVER
LOVES
MOVED
MOVER
MOVES
NAVEL
NAVES
NEVER
NOVEL
OAVES
PAVED
PAVER
PAVES
RAVED
RAVEL
RAVEN
RAVER
RAVES
REVEL
REVET
RIVED
RIVEN
RIVER
RIVES
RIVET
ROVED
ROVER
ROVES
SAVED
SAVER
SAVES
SEVEN
SEVER
WAVED
WAVER
WAVES
WAVEY
WIVED
WIVER
WIVES
WOVEN

••V•E
CAVIE
DAVIE
GAVLE
LEVEE
LIVRE
MOVIE
NOVAE
REVUE

•••VE
ABOVE
AGAVE
ALIVE
ATIVE
BRAVE
BREVE
CALVE
CARVE
CHIVE
CLIVE
CLOVE
CRAVE
CURVE
DELVE
DRAVE
DRIVE
DROVE
GLOVE
GRAVE
GROVE
HALVE
HEAVE
HELVE
KEEVE
KNAVE
LEAVE
MAUVE

NAIVE
NERVE
OGIVE
OLIVE
PEEVE
PIAVE
PROVE
REEVE
SALVE
SERVE
SHAVE
SHIVE
SHOVE
SIEVE
SKIVE
SLAVE
SOLVE
STAVE
STEVE
STOVE
SUAVE
TRAVE
TROVE
VALVE
VARVE
VERVE
WAIVE
WEAVE
YAHVE
YOUVE

V•G••
VAGIN
VAGUE
VAGUS
VIGIL
VIGOR
VOGUE
VOGUL
VUGGY

V••G•
VANGS
VERGE
VIRGA
VIRGE
VIRGO
VOLGA
VUGGY
VULGO

V•••G
VYING

V••H•
VICHY

V•••H
VETCH
VOUCH

VI•••
VIALS
VIAND
VIBES
VICAR
VICES
VICHY
VICKS
VICKY
VIDEO
VIEWS
VIEWY
VIGIL
VIGOR
VILER
VILLA
VILLI
VILLS
VIMEN
VINAS
VINCE
VINCI
VINES
VINIC
VINNY
VINYL
VIOLA
VIOLS
VIPER
VIRAL
VIREO
VIRES
VIRGA
VIRGE
VIRGO
VIRTU
VIRUS
VISAS
VISCT
VISED
VISES
VISIT
VISOR
VISTA
VITAE
VITAL
VITRI
VITTA
VIVID
VIXEN
VIZIR
VIZOR

V•I••
VAIRS
VEILS
VEINS
VEINY
VOICE
VOIDS
VOILA
VOILE
VYING

V••I•
VAGIN
VALID
VANIR
VAPID
VARIC
VARIO
VARIX
VATIC
VEDIC
VESIC
VEXIL
VIGIL
VINIC
VISIT
VIVID
VIZIR
VMAIL
VOMIT

V•••I
VERDI
VERMI
VILLI
VINCI
VITRI
VOLTI

•VI••
AVIAN
AVION
AVISO
DVINA
EVICT
EVILS
EVITA
IVIED
IVIES
OVINE

•V•I•
AVAIL
AVOID
AVOIR
OVOID

•V••I
OVOLI

••VI•
ALVIN
ANVIL
BEVIN
BOVID
CAVIE
CAVIL
CIVIC
CIVIL
DAVID
DAVIE
DAVIS
DAVIT
DEVIL
ELVIN
IRVIN
KEVIN
LEVIS
LIVIA
LIVID
MAVIS
MOVIE
NEVIL
PAVIS
SAVIN
VIVID

•••VI
BREVI
CURVI
PELVI
PLUVI

V••K•
VICKS
VICKY
VODKA

V•••K
VNECK

•V•K•
EVOKE

V•L••
VALES
VALET
VALID
VALOR
VALUE
VALVE
VELAR
VELDS
VELDT
VELUM
VILER
VILLA
VILLI
VILLS
VOLAR
VOLES
VOLGA
VOLTA
VOLTI
VOLTS
VOLVA
VULGO
VULVA

V••L•
VAULT
VEILS
VIALS
VILLA
VILLI
VILLS
VIOLA
VIOLS
VOILA
VOILE

V•••L
VENAL
VEXIL
VIGIL
VINYL
VIRAL
VITAL
VMAIL
VOCAL
VOGUL
VOWEL

•V•L•
EVILS
OVALS
OVOLI
OVOLO
OVULE
UVULA

•V••L
AVAIL
UVEAL

••VL•
GAVLE

••V•L
ANVIL
ARVAL
BEVEL
CAVIL
CIVIL
DEVIL
GAVEL
HOVEL
KEVEL
LEVEL
NAVAL
NAVEL
NEVIL
NIVAL
NOVEL
RAVEL
REVEL
RIVAL

VM•••
VMAIL

V•M••
VAMPS
VIMEN
VOMER
VOMIT

V••M•
VERMI

V•••M
VELUM
VENOM

VN•••
VNECK

V•N••
VANED
VANES
VANGS
VANIR
VENAE
VENAL
VENDS
VENOM
VENTS
VENUE
VENUS
VINAS
VINCE
VINCI
VINES
VINIC
VINNY
VINYL

V••N•
VAUNT
VEINS
VEINY
VERNA
VERNE
VERNS
VIAND
VINNY
VYING

V•••N
VAGIN
VIMEN
VIXEN

•V•N•
AVENS
DVINA
EVANS
EVENS
EVENT
IVANS
OVENS
OVINE

•V••N
AVIAN
AVION

••V•N
ALVAN
ALVIN
BEVIN
DEVON
DIVAN
ELVIN
GIVEN
HAVEN
IRVIN
KEVIN
LEVEN
LIVEN
PAVAN
RAVEN
RIVEN
SAVIN
SEVEN
SIVAN
WOVEN

VO•••
VOCAL
VOCES
VODKA
VOGUE
VOGUL
VOICE
VOIDS
VOILA
VOILE
VOLAR
VOLES
VOLGA
VOLTA
VOLTI
VOLTS
VOLVA
VOMER
VOMIT
VOTED
VOTER
VOTES
VOUCH
VOWED
VOWEL
VOWER

V•O••
VIOLA
VIOLS

V••O•
VALOR
VAPOR
VENOM
VIGOR
VISOR
VIZOR

V•••O
VARIO
VARRO
VERSO
VIDEO
VIREO
VIRGO
VULGO

•VO••
AVOID
AVOIR
AVOWS
EVOKE
IVORY
OVOID
OVOLI
OVOLO

•V•O•
AVION

•V••O
AVISO
OVOLO

••VO•
DEVON
DIVOT
ENVOY
FAVOR
GAVOT
HAVOC
PIVOT
SAVOR
SAVOY

••V•O
DAVAO

•••VO
BRAVO
PROVO
SALVO
SERVO
SLAVO

V•P••
VAPID
VAPOR
VIPER

V••P•
VAMPS

••V•P
DOVAP

V•R••
VARAS
VARIC
VARIO
VARIX
VARRO
VARUS
VARVE
VERAS
VERBS
VERDI
VERGE
VERMI
VERNA
VERNE
VERNS
VERSE
VERSO
VERST
VERTU
VERVE

VIRAL
VIREO
VIRES
VIRGA
VIRGE
VIRGO
VIRTU
VIRUS

V••R•
VAIRS
VARRO
VEERS
VEERY
VITRI

V•••R
VALOR
VANIR
VAPOR
VELAR
VEXER
VICAR
VIGOR
VILER
VIPER
VISOR
VIZIR
VIZOR
VOLAR
VOMER
VOTER
VOWER

•V•R•
AVARS
AVERS
AVERT
AVERY
EVERT
EVERY
IVORY
OVARY
OVERT

•V••R
AVOIR

••VR•
LIVRE

••V•R
COVER
DIVER
DOVER
ELVER
FAVOR
FEVER
FIVER
GIVER
HOVER
LAVER
LEVER
LIVER
LOVER
MOVER
NAVAR
NEVER
PAVER
RAVER
RIVER
ROVER
SAVER
SAVOR
SEVER
WAVER
WIVER

V•S••
VASES
VASTY
VESIC
VESTA
VESTS
VISAS
VISCT
VISED
VISES
VISIT
VISOR
VISTA

V••S•
VERSE
VERSO
VERST

V•••S
VAGUS
VAIRS
VALES
VAMPS
VANES
VANGS
VARAS
VARUS
VASES
VEERS
VEILS
VEINS
VELDS
VENDS
VENTS
VENUS
VERAS
VERBS
VERNS
VESTS
VEXES
VIALS
VIBES
VICES
VICKS
VIEWS
VILLS
VINAS
VINES
VIOLS
VIRES
VIRUS
VISAS
VISES
VOCES
VOIDS
VOLES
VOLTS
VOTES

•V•S•
AVAST
AVISO
KVASS

•V••S
AVARS
AVENS
AVERS
AVOWS
EVANS
EVENS
EVILS
IVANS
IVIES
KVASS
OVALS
OVENS
UVEAS

••V•S
CAVES
COVES
DAVES
DAVIS
DAVYS
DEVAS
DIVAS
DIVES
DOVES
EAVES
ELVAS
ELVES
FAVUS
FIVES
GIVES
GOVTS
HIVES
KAVAS
KIVAS
LAVAS
LAVES
LEVIS
LIVES
LOVES
MAVIS
MOVES
NAVES
NEVUS
NOVAS
OAVES
PAVES
PAVIS
RAVES
RIVES
ROVES
SAVES
WAVES
WIVES

•••VS
OLAVS
SHIVS
SLAVS

V•T••
VATIC
VETCH
VITAE
VITAL
VITRI
VITTA
VOTED
VOTER
VOTES

V••T•
VASTY
VENTS
VERTU
VESTA
VESTS
VIRTU
VISTA
VITTA
VOLTA
VOLTI
VOLTS

V•••T
VALET
VAULT
VAUNT
VELDT
VERST
VISCT
VISIT
VOMIT

•V•T•
EVITA
OVATE

•V••T
AVAST
AVERT
EVENT
EVERT
EVICT
OVERT

••VT•
GOVTS

••V•T
CIVET
COVET
DAVIT
DIVOT
GAVOT
PIVOT
REVET
RIVET

VU•••
VUGGY
VULGO
VULVA

V•U••
VAULT
VAUNT
VOUCH

V••U•
VACUA
VADUZ
VAGUE
VAGUS
VALUE
VARUS
VELUM
VENUE
VENUS
VIRUS
VOGUE
VOGUL

V•••U
VERTU
VIRTU

•VU••
OVULE
UVULA

••VU•
FAVUS
NEVUS
REVUE

V•V••
VIVID

V••V•
VALVE
VARVE
VERVE
VOLVA
VULVA

••VV•
DIVVY
NAVVY
SAVVY

V•W••
VOWED
VOWEL
VOWER

V••W•
VIEWS
VIEWY

•V•W•
AVOWS

V•X••
VEXED
VEXER
VEXES
VEXIL
VIXEN

V•••X
VARIX

VY•••
VYING

V••Y•
VINYL

V•••Y
VASTY
VEERY
VEINY
VICHY
VICKY
VIEWY
VINNY
VUGGY

•V••Y
AVERY
EVERY
IVORY
OVARY

••VY•
DAVYS

••V•Y
COVEY
DAVEY
DIVVY
ENVOY
NAVVY
SAVOY
SAVVY
WAVEY

•••VY
CHEVY
DIVVY
GRAVY
HEAVY
LEAVY
NAVVY
NERVY
PEAVY
PRIVY
SAVVY

V•Z••
VIZIR
VIZOR

V•••Z
VADUZ

WA•••
WACKE
WACKS
WACKY
WADDY
WADED
WADER
WADES
WAFER
WAFTS
WAGED
WAGER
WAGES
WAGON
WAHOO
WAIFS
WAILS
WAINS
WAIST
WAITS
WAIVE
WAKED
WAKEN
WAKES
WALDO
WALED
WALER
WALES
WALKS
WALLA
WALLS
WALLY
WALTS
WALTZ
WAMUS
WANDA
WANDS
WANED
WANES
WANEY
WANLY
WANTS
WARDS
WARES
WARMS
WARNS
WARPS
WARTS
WARTY
WASHY
WASNT
WASPS
WASPY
WASTE
WATAP
WATCH
WATER*
WATTS
WAUGH
WAULS
WAVED
WAVER
WAVES
WAVEY
WAWLS
WAXED
WAXEN
WAXES
WAYNE

W•A••
WEALD
WEALS
WEANS
WEARS
WEARY
WEAVE
WHACK
WHALE
WHAMS
WHANG
WHAPS
WHARF
WOADS
WOALD
WRACK
WRAPS
WRAPT
WRATH
WYATT

W••A•
WATAP
WEKAS
WHEAL
WHEAT
WIGAN
WITAN
WODAN
WOMAN
WOTAN
WREAK

W•••A
WALLA
WANDA
WILLA
WILMA
WIRRA

•WA••
AWAIT
AWAKE
AWARD
AWARE
AWASH
BWANA
DWARF
SWABS
SWAGE
SWAGS

SWAIL
SWAIN
SWALE
SWAMI
SWAMP
SWANK
SWANS
SWAPS
SWARD
SWARM
SWART
SWASH
SWATH
SWATS
SWAYS
TWAIN
TWANG

•W•A•
SWEAR
SWEAT
TWEAK

•W••A
BWANA

••WA•
ALWAY
ASWAN
BYWAY
DEWAN
DIWAN
NAWAB
NOWAY
ROWAN
SOWAR

•••WA
KIOWA
SCHWA

W•B••
WEBBY
WEBER

W••B•
WEBBY
WOMBS
WOMBY

•W•B•
SWABS

••W•B
NAWAB

W•C••
WACKE
WACKS
WACKY
WICKS

W••C•
WATCH
WELCH
WENCH
WHACK
WHICH
WINCE
WINCH
WITCH
WRACK
WRECK

•W•C•
TWICE

W•D••
WADDY
WADED
WADER
WADES
WEDGE
WEDGY
WIDDY
WIDEN
WIDER
WIDOW
WIDTH
WODAN
WODEN

W••D•
WADDY
WALDO
WANDA
WANDS
WARDS
WEEDS
WEEDY
WELDS
WENDS
WENDY
WIDDY
WILDS
WINDS
WINDY
WOADS
WOLDS
WOODS
WOODY
WORDS
WORDY

W•••D
WADED
WAGED
WAKED
WALED
WANED
WAVED
WAXED
WEALD
WEIRD
WIELD
WILED
WINED
WIPED
WIRED
WISED
WIVED
WOALD
WOOED
WORLD
WOULD
WOUND
WOWED
WRIED

•W•D•
SWEDE

•W••D
AWARD
AWNED
OWNED
SWARD
SWORD
TWEED

••WD•
BAWDS
BAWDY
DOWDY
HOWDY
ROWDY

••W•D
BOWED
CAWED
COWED
DEWED
HAWED
HEWED
JAWED
LAWED
LOWED
MEWED
MOWED
PAWED
ROWED
SAWED
SEWED
SOWED
TAWED
TOWED
UNWED
VOWED
WOWED
YAWED
YOWED

•••WD
CROWD

WE•••
WEALD
WEALS
WEANS
WEARS
WEARY
WEAVE
WEBBY
WEBER
WEDGE
WEDGY
WEEDS
WEEDY
WEEKS
WEEMS
WEENY
WEEPS
WEEPY
WEEST
WEFTS
WEIGH
WEIRD
WEIRS
WEKAS
WELCH
WELDS
WELLS
WELSH
WELTS
WENCH
WENDS
WENDY
WENNY
WETLY

W•E••
WEEDS
WEEDY
WEEKS
WEEMS
WEENY
WEEPS
WEEPY
WEEST
WHEAL
WHEAT
WHEEL
WHELK
WHELM
WHELP
WHENS
WHERE
WHETS
WHEYS
WIELD
WREAK
WRECK
WRENS
WREST

W••E•
WADED
WADER
WADES
WAFER
WAGED
WAGER
WAGES
WAKED
WAKEN
WAKES
WALED
WALER
WALES
WANED
WANES
WANEY
WARES
WATER
WAVED
WAVER
WAVES
WAVEY
WAXED
WAXEN
WAXES
WEBER
WHEEL
WIDEN
WIDER
WILED
WILES
WINED
WINES
WIPED
WIPER
WIPES
WIRED
WIRER
WIRES
WISED
WISER
WISES
WIVED
WIVER
WIVES
WIZEN
WODEN
WOKEN
WOMEN
WOOED
WOOER
WOVEN
WOWED
WRIED
WRIER
WRIES
WRYER

W•••E
WACKE
WAIVE
WASTE
WAYNE
WEAVE
WEDGE
WHALE
WHERE
WHILE
WHINE
WHITE
WHOLE
WHORE
WHOSE
WINCE
WINZE
WITHE
WITTE
WORSE
WRITE
WROTE

•WE••
DWELL
DWELT
EWERS
GWENN
GWENS
OWENS
SWEAR
SWEAT
SWEDE
SWEEP
SWEET
SWELL
SWEPT
TWEAK
TWEED
TWEEN
TWEET
TWERP

•W•E•
AWNED
OWLET
OWNED
OWNER
SWEEP
SWEET
TWEED
TWEEN
TWEET

•W••E
AWAKE
AWARE
AWOKE
SWAGE
SWALE
SWEDE
SWINE
SWIPE
SWORE
TWICE
TWINE

••WE•
BOWED
BOWEL
BOWER
CAWED
COWED
COWER
DEWED
DEWEY
DOWEL
DOWER
FEWER
HAWED
HEWED
HEWER
JAWED
JEWEL
LAWED
LOWED
LOWER
MEWED
MOWED
MOWER
NEWEL
NEWER
PAWED
PAWER
PEWEE
POWER
RAWER
ROWED
ROWEL
ROWEN
ROWER
SAWED
SAWER
SEWED
SEWER
SOWED
SOWER
TAWED
TAWER
TOWED
TOWEL
TOWER
UNWED
VOWED
VOWEL
VOWER
WOWED
YAWED
YOWED

••W•E
BOWIE
BOWSE
DOWSE
HAWSE
HOWIE
LEWIE
PEWEE

•••WE
CREWE
STOWE

W•F••
WAFER
WAFTS
WEFTS

W••F•
WAIFS
WHIFF
WOLFS
WOOFS

W•••F
WHARF
WHIFF

•WF••
AWFUL

•W•F•
SWIFT

•W••F
DWARF

W•G••
WAGED
WAGER
WAGES
WAGON
WIGAN
WIGHT

W••G•
WAUGH
WEDGE
WEDGY
WEIGH
WHIGS
WINGS
WINGY

W•••G
WHANG
WRING
WRONG
WRUNG

•W•G•
SWAGE
SWAGS
SWIGS
TWIGS

•W••G
AWING
EWING
OWING
SWING
SWUNG
TWANG

WH•••
WHACK
WHALE
WHAMS
WHANG
WHAPS
WHARF
WHEAL
WHEAT
WHEEL
WHELK
WHELM
WHELP
WHENS

WHERE
WHETS
WHEYS
WHICH
WHIFF
WHIGS
WHILE
WHIMS
WHINE
WHINS
WHINY
WHIPS
WHIPT
WHIRL
WHIRS
WHISH
WHISK
WHIST
WHITE
WHITS
WHOLE
WHOOP
WHOPS
WHORE
WHORL
WHORT
WHOSE
WHOSO

W•H••

WAHOO

W••H•

WASHY
WIGHT
WITHE
WITHY

W•••H

WATCH
WAUGH
WEIGH
WELCH
WELSH
WENCH
WHICH
WHISH
WIDTH
WINCH
WITCH
WORTH
WRATH

•W••H

AWASH
SWASH
SWATH
SWISH

WI•••

WICKS
WIDDY
WIDEN
WIDER
WIDOW
WIDTH
WIELD
WIGAN
WIGHT
WILDS
WILED
WILES
WILLA
WILLS
WILLY
WILMA
WILTS
WINCE
WINCH
WINDS
WINDY
WINED
WINES
WINGS
WINGY
WINKS
WINOS
WINZE
WIPED
WIPER
WIPES
WIRED
WIRER
WIRES
WIRRA
WISED
WISER
WISES
WISPS
WISPY
WITAN
WITCH
WITHE
WITHY
WITTE
WITTY
WIVED
WIVER
WIVES
WIZEN

W•I••

WAIFS
WAILS
WAINS
WAIST
WAITS
WAIVE
WEIGH
WEIRD
WEIRS
WHICH
WHIFF
WHIGS
WHILE
WHIMS
WHINE
WHINS
WHINY
WHIPS
WHIPT
WHIRL
WHIRS
WHISH
WHISK
WHIST
WHITE
WHITS
WRIED
WRIER
WRIES
WRING
WRIST
WRITE
WRITS

•WI••

AWING
EWING
OWING
SWIFT
SWIGS
SWILL
SWIMS
SWINE
SWING
SWIPE
SWIRL
SWISH
SWISS
TWICE
TWIGS
TWILL
TWINE
TWINS
TWIRL
TWIRP
TWIST
TWITS
TWIXT

•W•I•

AWAIT
SWAIL
SWAIN
TWAIN

•W••I

SWAMI

••WI•

ALWIN
BOWIE
EDWIN
ELWIN
ERWIN
HOWIE
IRWIN
KIWIS
LEWIE
LEWIS
PEWIT

W•K••

WAKED
WAKEN
WAKES
WEKAS
WOKEN

W••K•

WACKE
WACKS
WACKY
WALKS
WEEKS
WICKS
WINKS
WORKS

W•••K

WHACK
WHELK
WHISK
WRACK
WREAK
WRECK

•W•K•

AWAKE
AWOKE

•W••K

SWANK
TWEAK

••WK•

DAWKS
GAWKS
GAWKY
HAWKS

W•L••

WALDO
WALED
WALER
WALES
WALKS
WALLA
WALLS
WALLY
WALTS
WALTZ
WELCH
WELDS
WELLS
WELSH
WELTS
WILDS
WILED
WILES
WILLA
WILLS
WILLY
WILMA
WILTS
WOLDS
WOLFS

W••L•

WAILS
WALLA
WALLS
WALLY
WANLY
WAULS
WAWLS
WEALD
WEALS
WELLS
WETLY
WHALE
WHELK
WHELM
WHELP
WHILE
WHOLE
WIELD
WILLA
WILLS
WILLY
WOALD
WOOLS
WOOLY
WORLD
WOULD
WRYLY

W•••L

WHEAL
WHEEL
WHIRL
WHORL

•WL••

OWLET

•W•L•

DWELL
DWELT
SWALE
SWELL
SWILL
TWILL

•W••L

AWFUL
DWELL
SWAIL
SWELL
SWILL
SWIRL
TWILL
TWIRL

••WL•

BAWLS
BOWLS
COWLS
FOWLS
HOWLS
JOWLS
LOWLY
MEWLS
NEWLY
PAWLS
RAWLY
WAWLS
YAWLS
YOWLS

••W•L

BOWEL
DOWEL
JEWEL
NEWEL
ROWEL
TOWEL
VOWEL

•••WL

BRAWL
CRAWL
DRAWL
GROWL
PROWL
SCOWL
SHAWL
TRAWL

W•M••

WAMUS
WOMAN
WOMBS
WOMBY
WOMEN

W••M•

WARMS
WEEMS
WHAMS
WHIMS
WILMA
WORMS
WORMY

W•••M

WHELM

•W•M•

SWAMI
SWAMP
SWIMS

•W••M

SWARM

•••WM

SHAWM

W•N••

WANDA
WANDS
WANED
WANES
WANEY
WANLY
WANTS
WENCH
WENDS
WENDY
WENNY
WINCE
WINCH
WINDS
WINDY
WINED
WINES
WINGS
WINGY
WINKS
WINOS
WINZE

W••N•

WAINS
WARNS
WASNT
WAYNE
WEANS
WEENY
WENNY
WHANG
WHENS
WHINE
WHINS
WHINY
WOUND
WRENS
WRING
WRONG
WRUNG

W•••N

WAGON
WAKEN
WAXEN
WIDEN
WIGAN
WITAN
WIZEN
WODAN
WODEN
WOKEN
WOMAN
WOMEN
WOTAN
WOVEN

•WN••

AWNED
OWNED
OWNER

•W•N•

AWING
BWANA
EWING
GWENN
GWENS
GWYNS
OWENS
OWING
SWANK
SWANS
SWINE
SWING
SWUNG
TWANG
TWINE
TWINS

•W••N

GWENN
SWAIN
SWOON
SWORN
TWAIN
TWEEN

••WN•

DAWNS
DOWNS
DOWNY
FAWNS
GOWNS
LAWNS
LAWNY
PAWNS
TAWNY
TOWNS
YAWNS

••W•N

ALWIN
ASWAN
DEWAN
DIWAN
EDWIN
ELWIN
ERWIN
IRWIN
ROWAN
ROWEN

•••WN

BLOWN
BRAWN
BROWN
CLOWN
CROWN
DRAWN
DROWN
FLOWN
FROWN
GNAWN
GROWN
KNOWN
PRAWN
SHAWN
SHEWN
SHOWN
SPAWN

WO•••
WOADS
WOALD
WODAN
WODEN
WOKEN
WOLDS
WOLFS
WOMAN
WOMBS
WOMBY
WOMEN
WOODS
WOODY
WOOED
WOOER
WOOFS
WOOLS
WOOLY
WOOZY
WORDS
WORDY
WORKS
WORLD
WORMS
WORMY
WORRY
WORSE
WORST
WORTH
WORTS
WOTAN
WOULD
WOUND
WOVEN
WOWED

W•O••
WHOLE
WHOOP
WHOPS
WHORE
WHORL
WHORT
WHOSE
WHOSO
WOODS
WOODY
WOOED
WOOER
WOOFS
WOOLS
WOOLY
WOOZY
WRONG
WROTE

W••O•
WAGON
WAHOO
WHOOP
WIDOW
WINOS

W•••O
WAHOO
WALDO
WHOSO

•WO••
AWOKE
SWOON
SWOOP
SWORD
SWORE
SWORN

•W•O•
SWOON
SWOOP

W•P••
WIPED
WIPER
WIPES

W••P•
WARPS
WASPS
WASPY
WEEPS
WEEPY
WHAPS
WHIPS
WHIPT
WHOPS
WISPS
WISPY
WRAPS
WRAPT

W•••P
WATAP
WHELP
WHOOP

•W•P•
SWAPS
SWEPT
SWIPE

•W••P
SWAMP
SWEEP
SWOOP
TWERP
TWIRP

••WP•
YAWPS

WR•••
WRACK
WRAPS
WRAPT
WRATH
WREAK
WRECK
WRENS
WREST
WRIED
WRIER
WRIES
WRING
WRIST
WRITE
WRITS
WRONG
WROTE
WRUNG
WRYER
WRYLY

W•R••
WARDS
WARES
WARMS
WARNS
WARPS
WARTS
WARTY
WIRED
WIRER
WIRES
WIRRA
WORDS
WORDY
WORKS
WORLD
WORMS
WORMY
WORRY
WORSE
WORST
WORTH
WORTS

W••R•
WEARS
WEARY
WEIRD
WEIRS
WHARF
WHERE
WHIRL
WHIRS
WHORE
WHORL
WHORT
WIRRA
WORRY

W•••R
WADER
WAFER
WAGER
WALER
WATER
WAVER
WEBER
WIDER
WIPER
WIRER
WISER
WIVER
WOOER
WRIER
WRYER

•W•R•
AWARD
AWARE
DWARF
EWERS
SWARD
SWARM
SWART
SWIRL
SWORD
SWORE
SWORN
TWERP
TWIRL
TWIRP

•W••R
OWNER
SWEAR

••WR•
COWRY
DOWRY
JEWRY

••W•R
BOWER
COWER
DOWER
FEWER
HEWER
LOWER
MOWER
NEWER
PAWER
POWER
RAWER
ROWER
SAWER
SEWER
SOWAR
SOWER
TAWER
TOWER
VOWER

W•S••
WASHY
WASNT
WASPS
WASPY
WASTE
WISED
WISER
WISES
WISPS
WISPY

W••S•
WAIST
WEEST
WELSH
WHISH
WHISK
WHIST
WHOSE
WHOSO
WORSE
WORST
WREST
WRIST

W•••S
WACKS
WADES
WAFTS
WAGES
WAIFS
WAILS
WAINS
WAITS
WAKES
WALES
WALKS
WALLS
WALTS
WAMUS
WANDS
WANES
WANTS
WARDS
WARES
WARMS
WARNS
WARPS
WARTS
WASPS
WATTS
WAULS
WAVES
WAWLS
WAXES
WEALS
WEANS
WEARS
WEEDS
WEEKS
WEEMS
WEEPS
WEFTS
WEIRS
WEKAS
WELDS
WELLS
WELTS
WENDS
WHAMS
WHAPS
WHENS
WHETS
WHEYS
WHIGS
WHIMS
WHINS
WHIPS
WHIRS
WHITS
WHOPS
WICKS
WILDS
WILES
WILLS
WILTS
WINDS
WINES
WINGS
WINKS
WINOS
WIPES
WIRES
WISES
WISPS
WIVES
WOADS
WOLDS
WOLFS
WOMBS
WOODS
WOOFS
WOOLS
WORDS
WORKS
WORMS
WORTS
WRAPS
WRENS
WRIES
WRITS

•W•S•
AWASH
SWASH
SWISH
SWISS
TWIST

•W••S
EWERS
GWENS
GWYNS
OWENS
SWABS
SWAGS
SWANS
SWAPS
SWATS
SWAYS
SWIGS
SWIMS
SWISS
TWIGS
TWINS
TWITS

••WS•
BOWSE
DOWSE
HAWSE
NEWSY

••W•S
BAWDS
BAWLS
BOWLS
COWLS
DAWKS
DAWNS
DOWNS
FAWNS
FOWLS
GAWKS
GOWNS
HAWKS
HOWLS
JOWLS
KIWIS
LAWNS
LEWIS
MEWLS
NEWTS
PAWLS
PAWNS
POWYS
TOWNS
WAWLS
YAWLS
YAWNS
YAWPS
YOWLS

•••WS
AVOWS
BLOWS
BMEWS
BREWS
BROWS
CHAWS
CHEWS
CHOWS
CLAWS
CLEWS
CRAWS
CREWS
CROWS
DHOWS
DRAWS
DREWS
FLAWS
FLEWS
FLOWS
FROWS
GLOWS
GNAWS
GROWS
KNOWS
MEOWS
PLOWS
PROWS
SCOWS
SHAWS
SHEWS
SHOWS
SKEWS
SLAWS
SLEWS
SLOWS
SMEWS
SNOWS
SPEWS
STEWS
STOWS
THAWS
THEWS
VIEWS

W•T••
WATAP
WATCH
WATER
WATTS
WETLY
WITAN
WITCH
WITHE
WITHY
WITTE
WITTY
WOTAN

W••T•
WAFTS
WAITS
WALTS
WALTZ
WANTS
WARTS
WARTY
WASTE
WATTS
WEFTS
WELTS
WHETS
WHITE
WHITS
WIDTH
WILTS
WITTE
WITTY
WORTH
WORTS
WRATH
WRITE
WRITS
WROTE
WYATT

W•••T
WAIST
WASNT
WEEST
WHEAT
WHIPT
WHIST
WHORT

WIGHT
WORST
WRAPT
WREST
WRIST
WYATT

•W•T•
SWATH
SWATS
TWITS

•W••T
AWAIT
DWELT
OWLET
SWART
SWEAT
SWEET
SWEPT
SWIFT
TWEET
TWIST
TWIXT

••WT•
NEWTS

••W•T
PEWIT

W•U••
WAUGH
WAULS
WOULD
WOUND
WRUNG

W••U•
WAMUS

•WU••
SWUNG

•W•U•
AWFUL

W•V••
WAVED
WAVER
WAVES
WAVEY
WIVED
WIVER
WIVES
WOVEN

W••V•
WAIVE
WEAVE

W•W••
WAWLS
WOWED

W•••W
WIDOW

W•X••
WAXED
WAXEN
WAXES

•W•X•
TWIXT

WY•••
WYATT

W•Y••
WAYNE
WRYER
WRYLY

W••Y•
WHEYS

W•••Y
WACKY
WADDY
WALLY
WANEY
WANLY
WARTY
WASHY
WASPY
WAVEY
WEARY
WEBBY
WEDGY
WEEDY
WEENY
WEEPY
WENDY
WENNY
WETLY
WHINY
WIDDY
WILLY
WINDY
WINGY
WISPY
WITHY
WITTY
WOMBY
WOODY
WOOLY
WOOZY
WORDY
WORMY
WORRY
WRYLY

•WY••
GWYNS

•W•Y•
SWAYS

••WY•
POWYS

••W•Y
ALWAY
BAWDY
BYWAY
COWRY
DEWEY
DOWDY
DOWNY
DOWRY
GAWKY
HOWDY
JEWRY
LAWNY
LOWLY
NEWLY
NEWSY
NOWAY
RAWLY
ROWDY
TAWNY

•••WY
BLOWY
CHEWY
FLAWY
SHOWY
SNOWY
THEWY
VIEWY

W•Z••
WIZEN

W••Z•
WINZE
WOOZY

W•••Z
WALTZ

XA•••
XANTH
XAXES
XAXIS

X•A••
XRAYS

X••A•
XTIAN
XYLAN

X•••A
XENIA

•XA••
EXACT
EXALT
EXAMS

•X•A•
AXIAL
AXMAN
IXIAS
UXMAL

•X••A
EXTRA

••XA•
COXAE
COXAL
HEXAD
MOXAS
TEXAS

••X•A
JUXTA

•••XA
ALEXA

X•B••
XEBEC

•XB••
OXBOW

•X••B
EXURB

X•••C
XEBEC
XERIC

•XC••
EXCEL

•X•C•
EXACT
EXECS

••X•C
TOXIC

•X•D•
EXUDE
OXIDE

•X••D
AXLED

••X•D
BOXED
COXED
FAXED
FIXED
FOXED
HEXAD
HEXED
MIXED
NIXED
SEXED
TAXED
VEXED
WAXED

XE•••
XEBEC
XENIA
XENON
XERIC
XEROX
XERUS

X••E•
XAXES
XEBEC
XYLEM

•XE••
EXECS
EXERT
OXEYE

•X•E•
AXLED
AXLES
AXMEN
EXCEL
EXPEL

•X••E
AXILE
AXONE
EXILE
EXUDE
IXTLE
OXEYE
OXIDE
OXIME

••XE•
BOXED
BOXER
BOXES
COXED
COXES
FAXED
FAXES
FIXED
FIXER
FIXES
FOXED
FOXES
HEXED
HEXES
LAXER
LUXES
MIXED
MIXER
MIXES
NIXED
NIXES
PYXES
SAXES
SEXED
SEXES
SIXES
TAXED
TAXER
TAXES
VEXED
VEXER
VEXES
VIXEN
WAXED
WAXEN
WAXES
XAXES
YAXES

••X•E
COXAE
DIXIE
MOXIE
NIXIE
PIXIE
PYXIE
SIXTE

•X••G
AXING

X••H•
XIPHI

X•••H
XANTH

••X•H
SIXTH

XI•••
XIPHI

X•I••
XTIAN

X••I•
XAXIS
XENIA
XERIC

X•••I
XIPHI

•XI••
AXIAL
AXILE
AXILS
AXING
AXIOM
EXILE
EXIST
EXITS
IXIAS
IXION
OXIDE
OXIME

•X•I•
OXLIP

••XI•
AUXIL
AUXIN
DIXIE
DIXIT
MAXIM
MOXIE
NIXIE
PIXIE
PYXIE
PYXIS
TAXIS
TOXIC
TOXIN
VEXIL
XAXIS
YAXIS

•••XI
FLEXI

X•L••
XYLAN
XYLEM
XYLOL
XYLYL

X•••L
XYLOL
XYLYL

•XL••
AXLED
AXLES
OXLIP

•X•L•
AXILE
AXILS
EXALT
EXILE
EXULT
IXTLE

•X••L
AXIAL
EXCEL
EXPEL
EXTOL
UXMAL

••XL•
LAXLY

••X•L
AUXIL
COXAL
HEXYL
VEXIL

X•••M
XYLEM

•XM••
AXMAN
AXMEN
UXMAL

•X•M•
EXAMS
OXIME

•X••M
AXIOM

••X•M
BUXOM
MAXIM

X•N••
XANTH
XENIA
XENON

X•••N
XENON
XTIAN
XYLAN

•X•N•
AXING
AXONE
AXONS

•X••N
AXMAN
AXMEN
IXION

••X•N
AUXIN
NIXON
SAXON
TOXIN
VIXEN
WAXEN

X••O•
XENON
XEROX
XYLOL

•XO••
AXONE
AXONS

•X•O•
AXIOM
EXTOL
IXION
OXBOW

••XO•
BUXOM

LUXOR
NIXON
SAXON

X•P••
XIPHI

•XP••
EXPEL

•X••P
OXLIP

••X•P
MIXUP

XR•••
XRAYS

X•R••
XERIC
XEROX
XERUS

•X•R•
EXERT
EXTRA
EXURB

••X•R
BOXER
DEXTR
FIXER
LAXER
LUXOR
MIXER
TAXER
VEXER

X•S••
XYSTS

X•••S
XAXES
XAXIS
XERUS
XRAYS
XYSTS

•X•S•
EXIST

•X••S
AXILS
AXLES
AXONS
EXAMS
EXECS
EXITS
IXIAS

••X•S
BOXES
COXES
FAXES
FIXES
FOXES
HEXES
LUXES
MIXES
MOXAS
NEXUS
NIXES
PYXES
PYXIS
SAXES
SEXES
SIXES
TAXES
TAXIS
TEXAS
TEXTS
VEXES
WAXES
XAXES
XAXIS
YAXES
YAXIS

XT•••
XTIAN

X••T•
XANTH
XYSTS

•XT••
EXTOL
EXTRA
IXTLE

•X•T•
EXITS

•X••T
EXACT
EXALT
EXERT
EXIST
EXULT

••XT•
DEXTR
JUXTA
SIXTE
SIXTH
SIXTY
TEXTS

••X•T
DIXIT

•••XT
TWIXT

X••U•
XERUS

•XU••
EXUDE
EXULT
EXURB

••XU•
MIXUP
NEXUS

•X••W
OXBOW

X•X••
XAXES
XAXIS

X•••X
XEROX

XY•••
XYLAN
XYLEM
XYLOL
XYLYL
XYSTS

X••Y•
XRAYS
XYLYL

•X•Y•
OXEYE

••XY•
HEXYL

••X•Y
LAXLY
SIXTY

•••XY
ATAXY
BRAXY
DEOXY
EPOXY
FLAXY
PREXY
PROXY
TRIXY

YA•••
YACHT
YAGER
YAHOO
YAHVE
YALTA
YAMEN
YAMUN
YANKS
YAPON
YARDS
YARNS
YAUPS
YAWED
YAWLS
YAWNS
YAWPS
YAXES
YAXIS

Y•A••
YEANS
YEARN
YEARS
YEAST
YEATS

Y••A•
YUGAS

Y•••A
YALTA
YERBA
YUCCA

•YA••
AYAHS
CYANO
DYADS
HYALO
KYATS
WYATT

•Y•A•
BYLAW
BYWAY
CYCAD
CYMAE
CYMAR
EYRAS
GYRAL
HYLAS
HYRAX
IYYAR
LYMAN
MYNAS
MYRAS
PYRAN
XYLAN

•Y••A
DYULA
HYDRA
HYENA
HYPHA
LYCEA
LYDDA
LYDIA
LYSSA
LYTTA
MYOMA
MYRIA
MYRNA
PYDNA
SYLVA
SYRIA

••YA•
ARYAN
BOYAR
BRYAN
DRYAD
FAYAL
IYYAR
KAYAK
LOYAL
MAYAN
MAYAS
RAYAH
RIYAL
ROYAL
SOYAS

••Y•A
ADYTA
ASYLA
ETYMA
PHYLA
TRYMA

•••YA
FREYA
KENYA
KONYA
LIBYA
ORIYA
PLAYA
SONYA

Y••B•
YERBA

•YB••
SYBIL

••YB•
FLYBY
MAYBE

Y•C••
YACHT
YUCCA

Y••C•
YUCCA

Y•••C
YOGIC

•YC••
CYCAD
CYCLE
CYCLO
LYCEA
LYCEE
NYCTI
NYCTO
SYCEE
SYCES
TYCHE

•Y•C•
LYNCH

•Y••C
CYNIC
GYNEC
LYRIC
LYTIC

••YC•
ALYCE
BRYCE
GLYCO
JOYCE
PHYCO
PSYCH

•••YC
ENCYC

Y•D••
YODEL
YODHS

Y••D•
YARDS

Y•••D
YAWED
YIELD
YOKED
YOWED

•YD••
AYDIN
HYDRA
HYDRO
LYDDA
LYDIA
PYDNA

•Y•D•
DYADS
LYDDA
RYNDS

•Y••D
CYCAD
HYOID
LYSED
MYOID
PYOID
SYNOD
TYPED

••YD•
BOYDS
CLYDE
HAYDN

••Y•D
BAYED
DRYAD
FAYED
GUYED
HAYED
JOYED
KEYED
PAYED
RAYED
SAYID
TOYED

•••YD
FLOYD
LLOYD
SLOYD

YE•••
YEANS
YEARN
YEARS
YEAST
YEATS
YEGGS
YELKS
YELLS
YELPS
YEMEN
YERBA
YESES
YETIS

Y•E••
YIELD

Y••E•
YAGER
YAMEN
YAWED
YAXES
YEMEN
YESES
YIPES
YODEL
YOGEE
YOKED
YOKEL
YOKES
YOWED
YPRES
YQUEM
YULES

Y•••E
YAHVE
YOGEE
YOURE
YOUVE

•YE••
DYERS
HYENA
HYETO
MYELO
OYERS
PYELO
TYEES

•Y•E•
BYRES
CYMES
DYNES
FYKES
GYNEC
GYRES
HYMEN
HYPER
LYCEA
LYCEE
LYLES
LYRES
LYSED
LYSES
MYLES
PYRES
PYREX
PYXES
SYCEE
SYCES
TYEES
TYKES
TYLER
TYPED
TYPES
XYLEM

•Y••E
CYCLE
CYMAE
EYRIE
LYCEE
MYOPE
PYXIE
SYCEE
SYNGE
TYCHE

••YE•
BAYED
BUYER
DOYEN
DRYER
FAYED
FAYES
FLYER
FOYER
FRYER
GAYER
GUYED
HAYED
HAYES
JOYED
KEYED
LAYER
PAYED
PAYEE
PAYER
PRYER
RAYED
SAYER
SHYER
SKYEY

SLYER
SNYES
TOYED
TOYER
WRYER

••Y•E
ALYCE
BOYLE
BOYNE
BRYCE
CHYLE
CHYME
CLYDE
DOYLE
HOYLE
JOYCE
LEYTE
MAYBE
ODYLE
PAYEE
PHYLE
PHYRE
PHYTE
RHYME
STYLE
THYME
WAYNE

•••YE
BARYE
OXEYE

Y•G••
YAGER
YEGGS
YOGEE
YOGHS
YOGIC
YOGIN
YOGIS
YUGAS

Y••G•
YEGGS

Y•••G
YOUNG

•YG••
HYGRO
PYGMY

•Y•G•
SYNGE

•Y••G
DYING
EYING
HYING
LYING
TYING
VYING

Y•H••
YAHOO
YAHVE

Y••H•
YACHT
YODHS
YOGHS

Y•••H
YOUTH

•Y•H•
AYAHS
HYPHA
MYTHO
MYTHS
TYCHE

•Y••H
LYMPH
LYNCH
MYRRH
NYMPH
SYLPH

••Y•H
GLYPH
PSYCH
RAYAH
SCYPH

YI•••
YIELD
YIPES

Y••I•
YAXIS
YETIS
YOGIC
YOGIN
YOGIS

•YI••
AYINS
DYING
EYING
HYING
LYING
TYING
VYING

•Y•I•
AYDIN
CYLIX
CYNIC
CYRIL
EYRIE
HYOID
KYLIX
LYDIA
LYRIC
LYSIN
LYSIS
LYTIC
MYOID
MYRIA
PYOID
PYXIE
PYXIS
SYBIL
SYRIA

•Y••I
BYSSI
CYMRI
CYSTI
NYCTI

••YI•
GOYIM
SAYID
ZAYIN

••Y•I
PHYSI
STYLI

Y•K••
YOKED
YOKEL
YOKES
YUKON

Y••K•
YANKS
YELKS
YOLKS
YOLKY

•YK••
FYKES
TYKES

••Y•K
KAYAK

Y•L••
YALTA
YELKS
YELLS
YELPS
YOLKS
YOLKY
YULES

Y••L•
YAWLS
YELLS
YIELD
YOWLS

Y•••L
YODEL
YOKEL

•YL••
BYLAW
CYLIX
HYLAS
KYLIX
LYLES
MYLES
NYLON
PYLON
SYLPH
SYLVA
TYLER
XYLAN
XYLEM
XYLOL
XYLYL

•Y•L•
CYCLE
CYCLO
DYULA
HYALO
MYELO
PYELO

•Y••L
CYRIL
GYRAL
LYSOL
SYBIL
TYROL
XYLOL
XYLYL

••YL•
AMYLO
AMYLS
ASYLA
BOYLE
CHYLE
COYLY
DOYLE
DOYLY
DRYLY
GAYLY
HOYLE
IDYLL
IDYLS
ODYLE
PHYLA
PHYLE
PHYLL
PHYLO
SHYLY
SLYLY
STYLE
STYLI
STYLO
WRYLY

••Y•L
FAYAL
IDYLL
LOYAL
PHYLL
RIYAL
ROYAL

•••YL
ALKYL
ALLYL
BERYL
BUTYL
ETHYL
HEXYL
OCTYL
SIBYL
TOLYL
VINYL
XYLYL

Y•M••
YAMEN
YAMUN
YEMEN
YUMMY

Y••M•
YUMMY

Y•••M
YQUEM

•YM••
CYMAE
CYMAR
CYMES
CYMRI
CYMRY
GYMNO
HYMEN
HYMNS
LYMAN
LYMPH
NYMPH

•Y•M•
MYOMA
PYGMY

•Y••M
XYLEM

••YM•
CHYME
ETYMA
RHYME
STYMY
THYME
THYMY
TRYMA

••Y•M
ABYSM
GOYIM

Y•N••
YANKS

Y••N•
YARNS
YAWNS
YEANS
YOUNG

Y•••N
YAMEN
YAMUN
YAPON
YEARN
YEMEN
YOGIN
YUKON
YUPON

•YN••
CYNIC
DYNES
GYNEC
LYNCH
LYNNS
MYNAS
RYNDS
SYNGE
SYNOD

•Y•N•
AYINS
CYANO
DYING
EYING
GYMNO
HYENA
HYING
HYMNS
HYPNO
LYING
LYNNS
LYONS
MYRNA
PYDNA
TYING
VYING

•Y••N
AYDIN
BYRON
GYRON
HYMEN
HYSON
LYMAN
LYSIN
MYRON
NYLON
PYLON
PYRAN
XYLAN

••YN•
BOYNE
GWYNS
WAYNE

••Y•N
ARYAN
BRYAN
DOYEN
HAYDN
MAYAN
RAYON
TOYON
ZAYIN

YO•••
YODEL
YODHS
YOGEE
YOGHS
YOGIC
YOGIN
YOGIS
YOKED
YOKEL
YOKES
YOLKS
YOLKY
YOUNG
YOURE
YOURS
YOUTH
YOUVE
YOWED
YOWLS
YOYOS

Y••O•
YAHOO
YAPON
YOYOS
YUKON
YUPON

Y•••O
YAHOO

•YO••
HYOID
KYOTO
LYONS
MYOID
MYOMA
MYOPE
MYOPY
PYOID
RYOTS

•Y•O•
BYRON
GYRON
GYROS
HYPOS
HYSON
LYSOL
MYRON
NYLON
PYLON
SYNOD
TYPOS
TYROL
TYROS
XYLOL

•Y••O
CYANO
CYCLO
CYSTO
GYMNO
HYALO
HYDRO
HYETO
HYGRO
HYPNO
HYPSO
KYOTO
MYELO
MYTHO
NYCTO
PYELO

••YO•
BAYOU
KAYOS
MAYOR
POYOU
RAYON
TOYON
TOYOS
YOYOS

••Y•O
AMYLO
GLYCO
PHYCO
PHYLO
PHYTO
SAYSO
STYLO
THYRO

•••YO
CARYO
KARYO
TOKYO

YP•••
YPRES

Y•P••
YAPON
YIPES
YUPON

Y••P•
YAUPS
YAWPS
YELPS

•YP••
GYPSY
HYPER
HYPHA

5

HYPNO
HYPOS
HYPSO
TYPED
TYPES
TYPOS

•Y•P•
LYMPH
MYOPE
MYOPY
NYMPH
SYLPH

•Y••P
SYRUP

••YP•
COYPU
CRYPT
EGYPT
GLYPH
SCYPH

•••YP
POLYP

YQ•••
YQUEM

Y•R••
YARDS
YARNS
YERBA
YPRES

Y••R•
YEARN
YEARS
YOURE
YOURS

Y•••R
YAGER

•YR••
BYRES
BYRON
CYRIL
CYRUS
EYRAS
EYRIE
GYRAL
GYRES
GYRON
GYROS
GYRUS
HYRAX
LYRES
LYRIC
MYRAS
MYRIA
MYRNA
MYRON
MYRRH
PYRAN
PYRES
PYREX
SYRIA
SYRUP
TYROL
TYROS

•Y•R•
CYMRI
CYMRY
DYERS
HYDRA
HYDRO
HYGRO
MYRRH
OYERS

•Y••R
CYMAR
HYPER
IYYAR
TYLER

••YR•
PHYRE
THYRO

••Y•R
BOYAR
BUYER
DRYER
FLYER
FOYER
FRYER
GAYER
IYYAR
LAYER
MAYOR
PAYER
PRYER
SAYER
SHYER
SLYER
TOYER
WRYER

•••YR
ASSYR
SATYR

Y•S••
YESES

Y••S•
YEAST

Y•••S
YANKS
YARDS
YARNS
YAUPS
YAWLS
YAWNS
YAWPS
YAXES
YAXIS
YEANS
YEARS
YEATS
YEGGS
YELKS
YELLS
YELPS
YESES
YETIS
YIPES
YODHS
YOGHS
YOGIS
YOKES
YOLKS
YOURS
YOWLS
YOYOS
YPRES
YUGAS
YULES

•YS••
BYSSI
CYSTI
CYSTO
CYSTS
HYSON
LYSED
LYSES
LYSIN
LYSIS
LYSOL
LYSSA
XYSTS

•Y•S•
BYSSI
GYPSY
HYPSO
LYSSA

•Y••S
AYAHS
AYINS
BYRES
CYMES
CYRUS
CYSTS
DYADS
DYERS
DYNES
EYRAS
FYKES
GYRES
GYROS
GYRUS
HYLAS
HYMNS
HYPOS
KYATS
LYLES
LYNNS
LYONS
LYRES
LYSES
LYSIS
MYLES
MYNAS
MYRAS
MYTHS
OYERS
PYRES
PYXES
PYXIS
RYNDS
RYOTS
SYCES
TYEES
TYKES
TYPES
TYPOS
TYROS
XYSTS

••YS•
ABYSM
ABYSS
MAYST
PHYSI
SAYSO
TRYST

••Y•S
ABYSS
AMYLS
BOYDS
FAYES
GWYNS
HAYES
IDYLS
KAYOS
MAYAS
SNYES
SOYAS
TOYOS
YOYOS

•••YS
ABBYS
ADDYS
ALGYS
ANDYS
ATTYS
BRAYS
BUOYS
CARYS
CHRYS
CLAYS
CLOYS
DAVYS
DENYS
DRAYS
EMMYS
FLAYS
FRAYS
GABYS
GARYS
GOBYS
GRAYS
GREYS
IZZYS
JOEYS
JUDYS
JULYS
LILYS
LUCYS
OBEYS
OKAYS
PEPYS
PLAYS
PLOYS
POWYS
PRAYS
PREYS
QUAYS
RUBYS
RUDYS
SHAYS
SLAYS
SPAYS
STAYS
SUZYS
SWAYS
TOBYS
TONYS
TRAYS
TREYS
WHEYS
XRAYS

Y•T••
YETIS

Y••T•
YALTA
YEATS
YOUTH

Y•••T
YACHT
YEAST

•YT••
LYTIC
LYTTA
MYTHO
MYTHS

•Y•T•
CYSTI
CYSTO
CYSTS
HYETO
KYATS
KYOTO
LYTTA
NYCTI
NYCTO
RYOTS
WYATT
XYSTS

•Y••T
WYATT

••YT•
ADYTA
LEYTE
PHYTE
PHYTO

••Y•T
ASYUT
CRYPT
EGYPT
MAYST
TRYST

YU•••
YUCCA
YUGAS
YUKON
YULES
YUMMY
YUPON

Y•U••
YAUPS
YOUNG
YOURE
YOURS
YOUTH
YOUVE
YQUEM

Y••U•
YAMUN

•YU••
DYULA

•Y•U•
CYRUS
GYRUS
SYRUP

••YU•
ASYUT

••Y•U
BAYOU
COYPU
POYOU

Y••V•
YAHVE
YOUVE

•Y•V•
SYLVA

Y•W••
YAWED
YAWLS
YAWNS
YAWPS
YOWED
YOWLS

•YW••
BYWAY

•Y••W
BYLAW

Y•X••
YAXES
YAXIS

•YX••
PYXES
PYXIE
PYXIS

•Y••X
CYLIX
HYRAX
KYLIX
PYREX

•••YX
CALYX

Y•Y••
YOYOS

Y•••Y
YOLKY
YUMMY

•YY••
IYYAR

•Y•Y•
XYLYL

•Y••Y
BYWAY
CYMRY
GYPSY
MYOPY
PYGMY

••Y•Y
COYLY
DOYLY
DRYLY
FLYBY
GAYLY
SHYLY
SKYEY
SLYLY
STYMY
THYMY
WRYLY

ZA•••
ZAIRE
ZAMIA
ZARFS
ZAYIN

Z•A••
ZBARS

Z••A•
ZBEAM
ZETAS
ZONAL

Z•••A
ZAMIA
ZEBRA

•ZA••
AZANS
CZARS
OZARK
TZARS

•Z•A•
EZRAS

••ZA•
ANZAC
KAZAN
LAZAR
LIZAS
NIZAM
SIZAR

••Z•A
PIZZA
TAZZA

•••ZA
BRAZA
COLZA
ELIZA
HAMZA
MIRZA
PIZZA
PLAZA
TAZZA

ZB•••
ZBARS
ZBEAM

Z•B••
ZEBEC
ZEBRA
ZEBUS
ZIBET

Z••B•
ZOMBI

Z••C•
ZINCS

5

ZINCY

Z•••C
ZEBEC

•Z•C•
CZECH

•Z••C
AZOIC
AZTEC

••Z•C
ANZAC

Z•••D
ZONED
ZOOID

••Z•D
DAZED
DOZED
FAZED
FUZED
GAZED
HAZED
LAZED
MAZED
OOZED
RAZED
SIZED

ZE•••
ZEBEC
ZEBRA
ZEBUS
ZEKES
ZEROS
ZESTS
ZESTY
ZETAS

Z•E••
ZBEAM

Z••E•
ZEBEC
ZEKES
ZIBET
ZONED
ZONES

Z•••E
ZAIRE

•ZE••
CZECH

•Z•E•
AZTEC

•Z••E
AZINE
AZOLE
AZOTE
AZURE
OZONE

••ZE•
ADZES
BEZEL
BIZET
COZEN
DAZED
DAZES
DIZEN
DOZED
DOZEN
DOZES
FAZED
FAZES
FUZED
FUZEE
FUZES
GAZED
GAZER
GAZES
HAZED
HAZEL
HAZER
HAZES
LAZED
LAZES
MAZED
MAZER
MAZES
OOZED
OOZES
OUZEL
RAZED
RAZEE
RAZES
SIZED
SIZES
WIZEN

••Z•E
FUZEE
RAZEE

•••ZE
AGAZE
AMAZE
BAIZE
BLAZE
BONZE
BOOZE
BRAZE
CRAZE
CROZE
FEEZE
FROZE
FURZE
GAUZE
GLAZE
GLOZE
GRAZE
MAIZE
PRIZE
SEIZE
SMAZE
WINZE

Z••F•
ZARFS

Z••G•
ZINGS

•Z••H
AZOTH
CZECH

ZI•••
ZIBET
ZINCS
ZINCY
ZINGS
ZINKY
ZIPPY
ZIRON

Z•I••
ZAIRE

Z••I•
ZAMIA
ZAYIN
ZOOID
ZORIL

Z•••I
ZOMBI

•ZI••
AZINE

•Z•I•
AZOIC

••ZI•
ANZIO
FUZIL
NAZIS
SOZIN
VIZIR

•••ZI
GHAZI

Z•K••
ZEKES

Z••K•
ZINKY

•Z••K
OZARK

ZL•••
ZLOTY

Z•L••
ZULUS

Z•••L
ZONAL
ZORIL

•Z•L•
AZOLE

••Z•L
BEZEL
FUZIL
HAZEL
OUZEL

Z•M••
ZAMIA
ZOMBI

Z••M•
ZOOMS

Z•••M
ZBEAM

••ZM•
GIZMO

••Z•M
NIZAM

Z•N••
ZINCS
ZINCY
ZINGS
ZINKY
ZONAL
ZONED
ZONES

Z••N•
ZOONS

Z•••N
ZAYIN
ZIRON

•Z•N•
AZANS
AZINE
AZONS
OZONE

••Z•N
COZEN
DIZEN
DOZEN
KAZAN
LUZON
SOZIN
WIZEN

ZO•••
ZOMBI
ZONAL
ZONED
ZONES
ZOOID
ZOOMS
ZOONS
ZORIL

Z•O••
ZLOTY
ZOOID
ZOOMS
ZOONS

Z••O•
ZEROS
ZIRON

•ZO••
AZOIC
AZOLE
AZONS
AZOTE
AZOTH
OZONE

••ZO•
BOZOS
KAZOO
LUZON
RAZOR
VIZOR

••Z•O
ANZIO
GIZMO
KAZOO
MEZZO

•••ZO
DIAZO
MATZO
MEZZO
PIEZO
RHIZO

Z•P••
ZIPPY

Z••P•
ZIPPY

Z•R••
ZARFS
ZEROS
ZIRON
ZORIL

Z••R•
ZAIRE
ZBARS
ZEBRA

•ZR••
EZRAS

•Z•R•
AZURE
CZARS
OZARK
TZARS

••Z•R
GAZER
HAZER
LAZAR
MAZER
RAZOR
SIZAR
VIZIR
VIZOR

Z•S••
ZESTS
ZESTY

Z•••S
ZARFS
ZBARS
ZEBUS
ZEKES
ZEROS
ZESTS
ZETAS
ZINCS
ZINGS
ZONES
ZOOMS
ZOONS
ZULUS

•Z••S
AZANS
AZONS
CZARS
EZRAS
IZZYS
TZARS

••Z•S
ADZES
BOZOS
DAZES
DOZES
FAZES
FUZES
GAZES
HAZES
IZZYS
LAZES
LIZAS
MAZES
NAZIS
OOZES
RAZES
SIZES
SUZYS

Z•T••
ZETAS

Z••T•
ZESTS
ZESTY
ZLOTY

Z•••T
ZIBET

•ZT••
AZTEC

•Z•T•
AZOTE
AZOTH

••Z•T
BIZET

•••ZT
LISZT

ZU•••
ZULUS

Z••U•
ZEBUS
ZULUS

•ZU••
AZURE

Z•Y••
ZAYIN

Z•••Y
ZESTY
ZINCY
ZINKY
ZIPPY
ZLOTY

•Z•Y•
IZZYS

••ZY•
IZZYS
SUZYS

••Z•Y
DIZZY
FIZZY
FUZZY
JAZZY
LIZZY
MUZZY
TIZZY

•••ZY
BOOZY
CRAZY
DIZZY
FIZZY
FURZY
FUZZY
GAUZY
GLAZY
JAZZY
LIZZY
MUZZY
RITZY
TIZZY
WOOZY

•ZZ••
IZZYS

••ZZ•
DIZZY
FIZZY
FUZZY
JAZZY
LIZZY
MEZZO
MUZZY
PIZZA
TAZZA
TIZZY

•••ZZ
FRIZZ

5

6-LETTER WORDS

AA••••
AACHEN
AALAND
AALIIS
AARONS

A•A•••
ABACAS
ABACUS
ABASED
ABASER
ABASES
ABATED
ABATER
ABATES
ABATIS
ABATOR
ACACIA
ACADIA
ACAJOU
ACARID
ADAGES
ADAGIO
ADAPTS
AEACUS
AGAMAS
AGAMIC
AGAPAE
AGARIC
AGATES
AGATHA
AGAVES
ALAMOS
ALARIC
ALARMS
ALARUM
ALASKA
ALATED
AMADOU
AMANDA
AMATOL
AMAZED
AMAZES
AMAZON
ANABAS
ANADEM
ANALOG
ANANKE
ANATTO
APACHE
APATHY
ARABEL
ARABIA
ARABIC
ARABLE
ARAGON
ARANTA
ARARAT
ARAWAK
ASARUM
ATABAL
ATAMAN
ATAVIC
ATAXIA
ATAXIC
AVAILS
AVALON
AVATAR
AWAITS
AWAKED
AWAKEN
AWAKES
AWARDS
AZALEA
AZAZEL

A••A••
AALAND
ABBACY
ABLAUT
ABLAZE
ABOARD
ABRADE
ABRAMS
ABWATT
ACHAEA
ACHAIA
ACKACK
ACUATE
ADDAMS
ADNATE
AERATE
AFFAIR
AFLAME
AFRAID
AFRAME
AGHAST
AGLAIA
AGNAIL
AGNATE
AGRAFE
ALBANY
ALBATA
ALCAIC
ALFAKI
ALKALI
ALKANE
ALLANS
ALLAYS
ALMAHS
ALPACA
ALSACE
ALTAIC
ALTAIR
ALTARS
ALVANS
ALWAYS
AMBAGE
AMBARI
AMBARY
ANGARY
ANKARA
ANLACE
ANLAGE
ANNALS
ANSATE
APIARY
APPALL
APPALS
ARCADE
ARCANE
ARGALI
ARGALS
ARIANS
ARMADA
ARMAGH
ARMAND
ARNAUD
ARRACK
ARRANT
ARRAYS
ARYANS
ASGARD
ASIANS
ASKANT
ASLANT
ASSAIL
ASSAIS
ASSAYS
ATTACH
ATTACK
ATTAIN
ATTARS
AUBADE
AUDADS
AURATE
AVIARY
AVIATE
AWEARY
AYEAYE
AYMARA
AZRAEL

A•••A•
ABACAS
ABIJAH
ABOMAS
ABORAL
ABROAD
ACETAL
ACTUAL
ADONAI
ADRIAN
AECIAL
AEGEAN
AENEAS
AERIAL
AFFRAY
AFGHAN
AFLOAT
AGAMAS
AGAPAE
AGLEAM
AGORAE
AGORAS
AIDMAN
AIRMAN
AIRWAY
AJOWAN
ALEGAR
ALIDAD
ALPHAS
ALULAE
ALULAR
AMEBAE
AMEBAS
AMORAL
AMYTAL
ANABAS
ANDEAN
ANIMAL
ANIMAS
ANITAS
ANNEAL
ANNUAL
ANORAK
ANTIAR
ANURAN
ANYWAY
AORTAE
AORTAL
AORTAS
AOUDAD
APICAL
APNEAL
APODAL
APPEAL
APPEAR
APPIAN
ARARAT
ARAWAK
ARECAS
ARENAS
AROMAS
ARREAR
ASHLAR
ASHMAN
ASTRAL
ASTRAY
ATABAL
ATAMAN
ATONAL
ATRIAL
AUGEAN

6

AVATAR
AVOWAL
AXEMAN

A••••A

ABOLLA
ABULIA
ACACIA
ACADIA
ACEDIA
ACHAEA
ACHAIA
AEOLIA
AFRICA
AFTOSA
AGATHA
AGENDA
AGLAIA
AHIMSA
ALASKA
ALBATA
ALEXIA
ALICIA
ALMIRA
ALPACA
ALTHEA
ALUMNA
ALVINA
AMANDA
AMELIA
AMENRA
AMOEBA
AMRITA
ANCONA
ANDREA
ANEMIA
ANGELA
ANGINA
ANGLIA
ANGOLA
ANGORA
ANITRA
ANKARA
ANOXIA
ANTHEA
ANTLIA
APHTHA
APNOEA
APULIA
AQUILA
ARABIA
ARANTA
ARBELA
AREOLA
ARISTA
ARMADA
ARNICA
ARROBA
ARUNTA
ASTHMA
ATAXIA
ATHENA
ATTICA
ATTILA
AURIGA
AURORA
AVESTA
AXILLA
AYESHA
AYMARA
AZALEA

•AA•••

BAAING
BAALIM
KAASES
LAAGER

•A•A••

AALAND
BAGASS
BAHAIS
BAHAMA
BALAAM
BALATA
BAMAKO
BANANA
BASALT
BATAAN
BAYARD
CABALA
CABALS
CABANA
CACAOS
CALAIS
CALASH
CAMASS
CANAAN
CANADA
CANALS
CANAPE
CANARD
CANARY
CARACK
CARAFE
CARATE
CARATS
CASABA
CASALS
CASAVA
CATALO
DAMAGE
DAMANS
DAMASK
DANAID
DANAUS
DATARY
FACADE
FARADS
GALACT
GALAXY
GARAGE
GAWAIN
GAZABO
HAMALS
HAMAUL
HARASS
HAVANA
HAWAII
HAZARD
JACANA
JALAPS
JAPANS
KABAKA
KABAYA
KAKAPO
KAMALA
KANAKA
KARATE
KARATS
KAVASS
KAYAKS
LANAIS
LANATE
LAPARO
LAVABO
LAVAGE
LAZARS
MACACO
MACAWS
MADAME
MADAMS
MALACO
MALADY
MALAGA
MALATE
MALAWI
MALAYA
MALAYS
MANAGE
MANANA
MARACA
MARAUD
NAGANA
NAIADS
NAPALM
NASALS
NATANT
NAVAHO
NAVAJO
NAWABS
PAEANS
PAGANS
PAJAMA
PALACE
PALAEO
PALATE
PANADA
PANAMA
PAPACY
PAPAIN
PAPAWS
PAPAYA
PARADE
PARANG
PARAPH
PAVANS
RADARS
RAJABS
RAJAHS
RATALS
RAVAGE
RAYAHS
SAFARI
SAHARA
SALAAM
SALADS
SALAMI
SALARY
SAMARA
SARAHS
SARAPE
SATANG
SATARA
SAVAGE
SAVANT
TABARD
TAMALE
TAPALO
TATARS
VACANT
VACATE
VAGARY
VASARI
WABASH
WAHABI
WATAPE
WATAPS
ZANANA

•A••A•

BADMAN
BAGDAD
BAGMAN
BAIKAL
BALAAM
BALKAN
BALLAD
BALSAM
BALSAS
BALZAC
BANIAN
BANTAM
BANYAN
BANZAI
BAOBAB
BARMAN
BASHAW
BASRAH
BATAAN
BATEAU
BATMAN
CABMAN
CAESAR
CAFTAN
CAIMAN
CALCAR
CALLAO
CALLAS
CALPAC
CANAAN
CANCAN
CANNAE
CANNAS
CANVAS
CAPIAS
CARLAS
CARMAN
CARNAL
CARPAL
CASBAH
CASHAW
CASPAR
CASUAL
CATHAY
CAUDAD
CAUDAL
CAUSAL
CAVEAT
CAVIAR
CAYMAN
DACHAS
DACHAU
DAEDAL
DAGMAR
DALLAS
DAMMAR
DARDAN
EARLAP
EARWAX
FABIAN
FACIAL
FALLAL
FANGAS
FANTAN
FAUCAL
FAUNAE
FAUNAL
FAUNAS
GALEAE
GALWAY
GALYAK
GAMMAS
GASBAG
GASMAN
GASPAR
GAVIAL
HALLAH
HAMMAL
HAMZAS
HANGAR
HANNAH
HANNAS
HARLAN
HARTAL
HAWHAW
HAZZAN
JACKAL
JAGUAR
JAINAS
KALIAN
KALPAK
KANSAN
KANSAS
KAPPAS
KARMAS
KARNAK
KASPAR
LABIAL
LACTAM
LAMIAE
LAMIAS
LAMMAS
LAMPAD
LAMPAS
LANDAU
LARIAT
LARVAE
LARVAL
LASCAR
LAURAE
LAURAS
LAYDAY
LAYMAN
MADCAP
MADMAN
MADRAS
MAENAD
MAGYAR
MAMBAS
MAMMAE
MAMMAL
MAMMAS
MANDAN
MANIAC
MANIAS
MANTAS
MANUAL
MARGAY
MARIAN
MARIAS
MARTAS
MAUMAU
MAYDAY
MAYHAP
NARIAL
NARWAL
NASIAL
NASSAU
NATHAN
PALEAE
PALLAS
PALMAR
PAMPAS
PANDAS
PAPUAN
PARCAE
PARIAH
PARIAN
PARKAS
PARLAY
PARRAL
PASCAL
PASHAS
PASTAS
PATHAN
PAULAS
PAWPAW
PAXWAX
PAYDAY
RACIAL
RADIAL
RADIAN
RAGLAN

RAGMAN
RAGTAG
RANDAL
RANDAN
RAPHAE
RASCAL
RATTAN
SABBAT
SABEAN
SABRAS
SACRAL
SAGGAR
SAIGAS
SAIPAN
SALAAM
SALPAS
SAMBAS
SAMIAN
SAMOAN
SAMPAN
SANDAL
SANGAR
SANJAK
SANSAR
SAPHAR
SARSAR
SASHAY
SATRAP
SAUNAS
TAIGAS
TAIWAN
TAMBAC
TAMPAN
TAMTAM
TANKAS
TARMAC
TARNAL
TARSAL
TARTAN
TARTAR
TARZAN
TASMAN
TAZZAS
VALVAL
VALVAR
VANDAL
VANMAN
VASSAL
WALLAH
WALLAS
WANDAS
WARSAW
WAYLAY
YASMAK
ZAFFAR
ZAMIAS

•A•••A
BAHAMA
BALATA
BALBOA
BANANA
BARYTA
CABALA
CABANA
CAEOMA
CALESA
CAMERA
CAMILA
CANADA
CANULA
CAPITA
CARINA
CASABA
CASAVA
CASSIA
CATENA
CAYUGA
DAGOBA
DAHLIA
DAKOTA
DATURA
FACULA
FANEGA
FARINA
FASCIA
FATIMA
GALENA
GAMBIA
HAVANA
JACANA
JARINA
KABAKA
KABAYA
KALMIA
KAMALA
KANAKA
LACUNA
LADOGA
LAMBDA
LAMINA
LATRIA
LATVIA
MACULA
MADURA
MALAGA
MALAYA
MALTHA
MANANA
MANILA
MANTUA
MARACA
MARCIA
MARINA
MARKKA
MARSHA
MARTHA
MASORA
MAZUMA
NAGANA
NAGOYA
NASHUA
NAUSEA
PAGODA
PAJAMA
PAMELA
PANADA
PANAMA
PAPAYA
PAPULA
PATHIA
PATINA
PAYOLA
RADULA
RAFFIA
RAMONA
SABINA
SAHARA
SALIVA
SALVIA
SAMARA
SANDRA
SATARA
TACOMA
TAENIA
VAGINA
VARUNA
YAKIMA
ZAMBIA
ZANANA
ZAREBA

••AA••
CRAALS
ISAACS
KRAALS

••A•A•
ABACAS
AGAMAS
AGAPAE
ANABAS
ARARAT
ARAWAK
ATABAL
ATAMAN
AVATAR
BIAXAL
BRAZAS
BWANAS
CLARAS
COAXAL
CRAVAT
DIANAS
DRAMAS
FRACAS
GRAHAM
GUAVAS
ISAIAH
KOALAS
LIANAS
LLAMAS
PLAGAL
PLANAR
PLATAN
PLAYAS
PLAZAS
QUAPAW
QUASAR
RIATAS
SCALAR
SCARAB
SEAMAN
SEAWAN
SEAWAY
SHAMAN
STALAG
STATAL
SWARAJ
THANAT
TIARAS
UTAHAN
VEADAR

••A••A
ACACIA
ACADIA
AGATHA
ALASKA
AMANDA
ARABIA
ARANTA
ATAXIA
AZALEA
BIANCA
BRAHMA
CHACMA
CHAETA
CRANIA
DHARMA
DHARNA
EXACTA
FLAVIA
JOANNA
LUANDA
MIASMA
PHAGIA
PHASIA
PIAZZA
PLASIA
PLASMA
PRAVDA
QUAGGA
QUANTA
RWANDA
SHASTA
SPARTA
SRADHA
STADIA
STANZA
THALIA
TRAUMA
UGANDA
URANIA

•••AA•
BALAAM
BATAAN
CANAAN
SALAAM

•••A•A
ACHAEA
ACHAIA
AGLAIA
ALBATA
ALPACA
ANKARA
ARMADA
AYMARA
BAHAMA
BALATA
BANANA
BEMATA
CABALA
CABANA
CANADA
CASABA
CASAVA
CICADA
CICALA
CLOACA
ERRATA
ESPANA
GEMARA
GOTAMA
GUIANA
GUYANA
HAVANA
IGUANA
IMPALA
INDABA
ITHACA
JACANA
JUDAEA
KABAKA
KABAYA
KAMALA
KANAKA
KERALA
MALAGA
MALAYA
MANANA
MARACA
NAGANA
NEVADA
ORGANA
OTTAVA
OTTAWA
PAJAMA
PANADA
PANAMA
PAPAYA
PIRANA
POSADA
PURANA
ROXANA
SAHARA
SAMARA
SATARA
SOMATA
SONATA
SQUAMA
STRATA
TIRANA
ZANANA
ZENANA

AB••••
ABACAS
ABACUS
ABASED
ABASER
ABASES
ABATED
ABATER
ABATES
ABATIS
ABATOR
ABBACY
ABBESS
ABBEYS
ABBIES
ABBOTS
ABDUCT
ABELES
ABHORS
ABIDED
ABIDER
ABIDES
ABIJAH
ABJECT
ABJURE
ABLAUT
ABLAZE
ABLEST
ABLOOM
ABLUSH
ABNERS
ABOARD
ABODES
ABOHMS
ABOLLA
ABOMAS
ABOMBS
ABORAL
ABORTS
ABOUND
ABRADE
ABRAMS
ABROAD
ABRUPT
ABSENT
ABSORB
ABSURD
ABULIA
ABUSED
ABUSER
ABUSES
ABVOLT
ABWATT
ABYDOS
ABYSMS

A•B•••
ABBACY
ABBESS
ABBEYS
ABBIES
ABBOTS
ALBANY
ALBATA
ALBEDO
ALBEIT

6

ALBERT
ALBINO
ALBION
ALBITE
ALBUMS
AMBAGE
AMBARI
AMBARY
AMBERS
AMBERY
AMBITS
AMBLED
AMBLER
AMBLES
AMBUSH
ARBELA
ARBORI
ARBORS
ARBUTE
ASBURY
AUBADE
AUBREY
AUBURN

A••B••

ADOBES
ALIBIS
ALIBLE
AMEBAE
AMEBAS
AMEBIC
ANABAS
ANUBIS
ARABEL
ARABIA
ARABIC
ARABLE
ATABAL

A•••B•

ABOMBS
ADLIBS
AEROBE
AKIMBO
AMOEBA
ARDEBS
ARROBA

A••••B

ABSORB
ADSORB
ADVERB
APLOMB

•AB•••

BABBIE
BABBLE
BABIED
BABIES
BABISM
BABIST
BABITE
BABOON
BABOOS
BABULS
CABALA
CABALS
CABANA
CABINS
CABLED
CABLES
CABLET
CABMAN
CABMEN
CABOBS
DABBED
DABBER
DABBLE
FABIAN
FABLED
FABLER
FABLES
FABRIC
GABBED
GABBER
GABBLE
GABBRO
GABION
GABLED
GABLES
HABILE
HABITS
JABBED
JABBER
JABIRU
JABOTS
KABAKA
KABAYA
KABIKI
KABOBS
KABUKI
LABELS
LABIAL
LABILE
LABIUM
LABORS
LABOUR
LABRET
LABRUM
MABELS
NABBED
NABOBS
RABBET
RABBIS
RABBIT
RABBLE
RABIES
SABBAT
SABEAN
SABERS
SABINA
SABINE
SABINS
SABLES
SABOTS
SABRAS
TABARD
TABLED
TABLES
TABLET
TABOOS
TABORS
WABASH
WABBLE
WABBLY
YABBER

•A•B••

BABBIE
BABBLE
BALBOA
BAMBOO
BAOBAB
BARBED
BARBEL
BARBER
BARBET
BARBIE
BAUBLE
CAMBER
CARBON
CARBOY
CASBAH
DABBED
DABBER
DABBLE
DAUBED
DAUBER
DAUBRY
GABBED
GABBER
GABBLE
GABBRO
GAMBIA
GAMBIR
GAMBIT
GAMBLE
GAMBOL
GARBED
GARBLE
GASBAG
HAGBUT
HARBIN
HARBOR
HATBOX
IAMBIC
IAMBUS
JABBED
JABBER
LAMBDA
LAMBED
LAMBIE
MAMBAS
MAMBOS
MARBLE
NABBED
RABBET
RABBIS
RABBIT
RABBLE
RAMBLE
SABBAT
SAMBAS
SAMBOS
SAMBUR
TAMBAC
WABBLE
WABBLY
WAMBLE
WAMBLY
WARBLE
YABBER
ZAMBIA

•A••B•

CABOBS
CALEBS
CARIBE
CARIBS
CAROBS
CASABA
DAGOBA
DANUBE
GAZABO
GAZEBO
JACOBS
KABOBS
LAVABO
NABOBS
NAWABS
RAJABS
SAHEBS
SAHIBS
WAHABI
ZAREBA

•A•••B

BAOBAB

••AB••

ANABAS
ARABEL
ARABIA
ARABIC
ARABLE
ATABAL
CHABUK
CRABBY
DOABLE
DRABLY
ENABLE
FLABBY
GRABEN
ISABEL
LIABLE
SCABBY
SEABEE
SHABBY
STABLE
SUABLE
UNABLE
USABLE
USABLY
VIABLE

••A•B•

CRABBY
CRAMBO
FLABBY
FLAMBE
NEARBY
SCABBY
SHABBY

••A••B

SCARAB

•••AB•

CASABA
GAZABO
INDABA
LAVABO
NAWABS
RAJABS
SQUABS
WAHABI

•••A•B

BEDAUB
BICARB

••••AB

BAOBAB
CONFAB
PREFAB
PUNJAB
SCARAB
SERDAB

AC••••

ACACIA
ACADIA
ACAJOU
ACARID
ACCEDE
ACCENT
ACCEPT
ACCESS
ACCORD
ACCOST
ACCRUE
ACCUSE
ACEDIA
ACEOUS
ACETAL
ACETIC
ACETUM
ACETYL
ACHAEA
ACHAIA
ACHENE
ACHING
ACIDIC
ACIDLY
ACINUS
ACIOUS
ACKACK
ACNODE
ACORNS
ACQUIT
ACROSS
ACTING
ACTINI
ACTINO
ACTION
ACTIUM
ACTIVE
ACTORS
ACTUAL
ACUATE
ACUITY
ACUMEN

A•C•••

AACHEN
ACCEDE
ACCENT
ACCEPT
ACCESS
ACCORD
ACCOST
ACCRUE
ACCUSE
AECIAL
AECIUM
ALCAIC
ALCOTT
ALCOVE
ALCUIN
ANCHOR
ANCONA
ANCONE
ARCADE
ARCANE
ARCHED
ARCHEO
ARCHER
ARCHES
ARCHIE
ARCHIL
ARCHLY
ARCHON
ARCHYS
ARCING
ARCKED
ARCTIC
ASCEND
ASCENT
ASCOTS

A••C••

ABACAS
ABACUS
ACACIA
AEACUS
AFLCIO
ALECTO
ALICES
ALICIA
AMICES
APACHE
APICAL
APICES

6

ARECAS
AVOCET

A•••C•

ABBACY
ABDUCT
ABJECT
ACKACK
ADDICT
ADDUCE
ADDUCT
ADVICE
AFFECT
AFRICA
AGENCY
ALMUCE
ALPACA
ALSACE
AMERCE
ANLACE
ANTICS
APERCU
APIECE
ARNICA
ARRACK
ASPECT
ASPICS
ATTACH
ATTACK
ATTICA
ATTICS
AVOUCH
AZTECS

A••••C

ACETIC
ACIDIC
ADIPIC
ADONIC
AEOLIC
AGAMIC
AGARIC
AGONIC
ALARIC
ALCAIC
ALTAIC
AMEBIC
AMIDIC
AMYLIC
ANEMIC
ANGLIC
ANODIC
ANOMIC
ANOXIC
AORTIC
APNEIC
ARABIC
ARCTIC
ATAVIC
ATAXIC
ATOMIC
ATONIC
AZONIC
AZOTIC

•AC•••

AACHEN
BACHED
BACHES
BACKED
BACKER
CACAOS
CACHED
CACHES
CACHET
CACHOU
CACKLE
CACTUS
DACHAS
DACHAU
DACOIT
DACRON
DACTYL
FACADE
FACERS
FACETS
FACIAL
FACIES
FACILE
FACING
FACTOR
FACULA
HACKED
HACKEE
HACKER
HACKIE
HACKLE
JACANA
JACKAL
JACKED
JACKET
JACKIE
JACKYS
JACOBS
LACHES
LACIER
LACILY
LACING
LACKED
LACKEY
LACTAM
LACTIC
LACUNA
MACACO
MACAWS
MACERS
MACING
MACKLE
MACLES
MACRON
MACULA
MACULE
PACERS
PACIFY
PACING
PACKED
PACKER
PACKET
RACEME
RACERS
RACHEL
RACHIS
RACIAL
RACIER
RACILY
RACINE
RACING
RACISM
RACIST
RACKED
RACKER
RACKET
RACOON
SACHEM
SACHET
SACKED
SACKER
SACRAL
SACRED
SACRUM
TACKED
TACKER
TACKEY
TACKLE
TACOMA
TACTIC
VACANT
VACATE
VACUUM
YACHTS

•A•C••

BAUCIS
CAECUM
CALCAR
CALCES
CALCIC
CANCAN
CANCEL
CANCER
CARCEL
CATCHY
CAUCUS
DANCED
DANCER
DANCES
FALCON
FARCED
FARCER
FARCES
FASCES
FASCIA
FAUCAL
FAUCES
FAUCET
GARCON
GASCON
GAUCHE
GAUCHO
HANCES
LANCED
LANCER
LANCES
LANCET
LASCAR
MADCAP
MANCHU
MARCEL
MARCIA
MARCOS
MARCUS
MASCON
MASCOT
NANCYS
PARCAE
PARCEL
PASCAL
PATCHY
RANCHO
RANCID
RANCOR
RASCAL
SAUCED
SAUCER
SAUCES
TALCED
TALCUM

•A••C•

BARUCH
BASICS
CALICO
CANUCK
CARACK
DARICS
GALACT
HAUNCH
JANICE
LAUNCE
LAUNCH
MACACO
MALACO
MALICE
MARACA
NAUTCH
PALACE
PANICE
PANICS
PAPACY
PAUNCH
VARICO

•A•••C

BALTIC
BALZAC
BARDIC
CALCIC
CALPAC
CAPRIC
CARPIC
FABRIC
GAELIC
GALLIC
GARLIC
IAMBIC
IATRIC
LACTIC
MANIAC
MANIOC
MANTIC
MASTIC
NASTIC
PARSEC
SAITIC
TACTIC
TAMBAC
TANNIC
TANREC
TARMAC

••AC••

ABACAS
ABACUS
ACACIA
AEACUS
APACHE
BEACHY
BEACON
BLACKS
BRACED
BRACER
BRACES
BRACHI
BRACHY
BRACTS
CHACMA
CLACKS
CRACKS
CRACKY
CRACOW
DEACON
DRACHM
ENACTS
EPACTS
EXACTA
EXACTS
FIACRE
FLACKS
FLACON
FRACAS
GLACES
GLACIS
GRACED
GRACES
GUACOS
KNACKS
LEACHY
NIACIN
ORACHS
ORACLE
PEACHY
PLACED
PLACER
PLACES
PLACET
PLACID
PLACKS
POACHY
QUACKS
REACTS
SHACKO
SHACKS
SLACKS
SMACKS
SNACKS
SPACED
SPACER
SPACES
STACIE
STACKS
STACTE
STACYS
TEACUP
TRACED
TRACER
TRACES
TRACHE
TRACHY
TRACKS
TRACTS
WHACKS
WRACKS

••A•C•

BIANCA
BLANCH
BRANCH
CHALCO
CHANCE
CHANCY
CRATCH
EPARCH
EXARCH
FIANCE
FIASCO
FRANCE
FRANCK
FRANCO
FRANCS
GLANCE
GLAUCO
GRAECO
INARCH
ISAACS
NUANCE
PLAICE
PLANCH
PLANCK
PRANCE
SCARCE
SEANCE
SEARCH
SNATCH
STANCE
STANCH
STARCH
SWATCH
THATCH
TRANCE
USANCE

••A••C

AGAMIC
AGARIC
ALARIC

ARABIC
ATAVIC
ATAXIC
CYANIC
DYADIC
ENATIC
ITALIC
OXALIC
PHASIC
SIALIC
SLAVIC
STATIC
TRAGIC
URALIC
URANIC
VIATIC

•••AC•
ABBACY
ACKACK
ALPACA
ALSACE
ANLACE
ARRACK
ATTACH
ATTACK
BLEACH
BONACI
BREACH
BROACH
CARACK
CLOACA
CURACY
DEFACE
DETACH
EFFACE
ENFACE
ENLACE
GALACT
HIJACK
HORACE
IGNACE
IMPACT
INLACE
INTACT
ISAACS
ITHACA
LEGACY
LILACS
LUNACY
MACACO
MALACO
MARACA
MENACE
PALACE
PAPACY
PESACH
PIRACY
PLEACH
POMACE
PREACH
REDACT
RUBACE
SERACS
SOLACE
SUMACS
TENACE
THWACK
UNLACE
UNPACK
VIVACE

•••A•C
ALCAIC
ALTAIC
EDDAIC
JUDAIC
MOSAIC
ROMAIC
VEDAIC

••••AC
BALZAC
CALPAC
CELIAC
COGNAC
CORSAC
IPECAC
MANIAC
MICMAC
OVISAC
SENLAC
SYRIAC
TAMBAC
TARMAC
THORAC
TOMBAC
ZODIAC

AD••••
ADAGES
ADAGIO
ADAPTS
ADDAMS
ADDEND
ADDERS
ADDICT
ADDING
ADDLED
ADDLES
ADDUCE
ADDUCT
ADEEMS
ADENIS
ADEPTS
ADHERE
ADIEUS
ADIEUX
ADIPIC
ADJOIN
ADJURE
ADJUST
ADLIBS
ADMIRE
ADMITS
ADMIXT
ADNATE
ADNOUN
ADOBES
ADOLPH
ADONAI
ADONIC
ADONIS
ADOPTS
ADORED
ADORER
ADORES
ADORNS
ADRIAN
ADRIEN
ADRIFT
ADROIT
ADSORB
ADULTS
ADVENT
ADVERB
ADVERT
ADVICE
ADVISE
ADYTUM

A•D•••
ABDUCT
ADDAMS
ADDEND
ADDERS
ADDICT
ADDING
ADDLED
ADDLES
ADDUCE
ADDUCT
AEDILE
AIDERS
AIDING
AIDMAN
AIDMEN
ALDERS
ALDINE
ALDOSE
ALDOUS
ANDEAN
ANDREA
ANDREI
ANDRES
ANDREW
ARDEBS
ARDENT
ARDORS
AUDADS
AUDILE
AUDITS
AUDREY

A••D••
ABIDED
ABIDER
ABIDES
ABODES
ABYDOS
ACADIA
ACEDIA
ACIDIC
ACIDLY
AGEDLY
AIRDRY
ALIDAD
ALUDEL
AMADOU
AMIDES
AMIDIC
AMIDIN
AMIDOL
AMIDST
ANADEM
ANODES
ANODIC
AOUDAD
APODAL
ARIDLY
ASIDES
AVIDIN
AVIDLY

A•••D•
ABRADE
ACCEDE
ACNODE
AGENDA
ALBEDO
ALLUDE
ALMUDE
ALMUDS
AMANDA
AMENDS
APHIDS
ARCADE
ARMADA
AROIDS
AUBADE
AUDADS
AVOIDS
AWARDS

A••••D
AALAND
ABASED
ABATED
ABIDED
ABOARD
ABOUND
ABROAD
ABSURD
ABUSED
ACARID
ACCORD
ADDEND
ADDLED
ADORED
AENEID
AERIED
AFFORD
AFIELD
AFRAID
AGREED
AISLED
ALATED
ALFRED
ALGOID
ALIDAD
ALINED
ALIPED
ALLIED
ALMOND
AMAZED
AMBLED
AMUSED
ANGLED
ANTEED
AOUDAD
APPEND
ARCHED
ARCKED
ARGUED
ARMAND
ARNAUD
ARNOLD
AROUND
ASCEND
ASGARD
ASTRID
ATONED
ATTEND
AUGEND
AUTOED
AVOWED
AWAKED
AXSEED

•AD•••
BADGED
BADGER
BADGES
BADMAN
BADMEN
CADDIE
CADDIS
CADENT
CADETS
CADGED
CADGER
CADGES
CADMUS
CADRES
DADDLE
DADOES
FADEIN
FADING
GADDED
GADDER
GADFLY
GADGET
GADOID
HADING
JADING
JADISH
LADDER
LADDIE
LADIES
LADING
LADINO
LADLED
LADLER
LADLES
LADOGA
MADAME
MADAMS
MADCAP
MADDED
MADDEN
MADDER
MADEUP
MADGES
MADMAN
MADMEN
MADRAS
MADRID
MADURA
MADURO
NADINE
NADIRS
PADDED
PADDLE
PADDYS
PADRES
RADARS
RADDLE
RADIAL
RADIAN
RADIOS
RADISH
RADIUM
RADIUS
RADOME
RADULA
SADDEN
SADDER
SADDLE
SADHUS
SADIES
SADISM
SADIST
VADOSE
WADDED
WADDLE
WADDLY
WADERS
WADIES
WADING
WADSET

•A•D••
BAGDAD
BALDER
BALDLY
BANDED
BANDIT
BARDED
BARDES
BARDIC
BAWDRY
CADDIE
CADDIS
CAMDEN

CANDID
CANDLE
CANDOR
CARDED
CARDER
CARDIO
CAUDAD
CAUDAL
CAUDEX
CAUDLE
DADDLE
DAEDAL
DANDER
DANDLE
DARDAN
DAWDLE
GADDED
GADDER
GANDER
GANDHI
GARDEN
HAGDON
HAMDEN
HANDED
HANDEL
HANDLE
HARDEN
HARDER
HARDLY
LADDER
LADDIE
LANDAU
LANDED
LANDER
LARDED
LARDER
LARDON
LAUDED
LAUDER
LAYDAY
MADDED
MADDEN
MADDER
MAIDEN
MANDAN
MANDYS
MARDUK
MAUDES
MAYDAY
PADDED
PADDLE
PADDYS
PANDAS
PANDER
PARDON
PAYDAY
RADDLE
RAIDED
RAIDER
RANDAL
RANDAN
RANDOM
SADDEN
SADDER
SADDLE
SANDAL
SANDED
SANDER
SANDHI
SANDRA
SANDYS
TANDEM
TAWDRY
VANDAL
WADDED
WADDLE
WADDLY
WALDOS
WANDAS
WANDER
WANDLE
WARDED
WARDEN
WARDER
YARDED

•A••D•

CANADA
DAVIDS
FACADE
FARADS
HAIRDO
HALIDE
HALIDS
LAIRDS
LAMBDA
LAMEDS
LAREDO
MALADY
MAUNDS
MAUNDY
NAIADS
PAGODA
PANADA
PARADE
PARODY
RAPIDS
SALADS

•A•••D

AALAND
BABIED
BACHED
BACKED
BADGED
BAFFED
BAGDAD
BAGGED
BAILED
BAITED
BALKED
BALLAD
BALLED
BANDED
BANGED
BANKED
BANNED
BARBED
BARDED
BARGED
BARKED
BARRED
BASHED
BASKED
BASTED
BATHED
BATTED
BAWLED
BAYARD
CABLED
CACHED
CADGED
CALKED
CALLED
CALMED
CALVED
CAMPED
CANARD
CANDID
CANNED
CANOED
CANTED
CAPPED
CARDED
CARPED
CARTED
CARVED
CASHED
CATTED
CAUDAD
CAUSED
DABBED
DAMMED
DAMNED
DAMPED
DANAID
DANCED
DANGED
DAPPED
DARNED
DARTED
DASHED
DAUBED
DAWNED
EARNED
FABLED
FAGGED
FAILED
FAIRED
FANGED
FANNED
FARCED
FARMED
FASTED
FATTED
FAWNED
GABBED
GABLED
GADDED
GADOID
GAFFED
GAGGED
GAINED
GAITED
GALLED
GANGED
GANOID
GAPPED
GARBED
GASHED
GASPED
GASSED
GAUGED
GAWKED
HACKED
HAILED
HAIRED
HALOID
HALTED
HALVED
HAMMED
HANDED
HANGED
HARKED
HARMED
HAROLD
HARPED
HASHED
HASPED
HASTED
HATRED
HATTED
HAULED
HAWKED
HAZARD
JABBED
JACKED
JAGGED
JAILED
JAMMED
JARRED
JAZZED
KAYOED
LACKED
LADLED
LAGGED
LAIRED
LALLED
LAMBED
LAMMED
LAMPAD
LAMPED
LANCED
LANDED
LAPPED
LAPSED
LARDED
LARKED
LASHED
LASTED
LATHED
LAUDED
MADDED
MADRID
MAENAD
MAILED
MAIMED
MALLED
MALTED
MANNED
MAPPED
MARAUD
MARKED
MARLED
MARRED
MASHED
MASKED
MASSED
MASTED
MATTED
MAULED
NABBED
NAGGED
NAILED
NAPPED
PACKED
PADDED
PAINED
PAIRED
PALLED
PALLID
PALMED
PANNED
PANTED
PARKED
PARSED
PARTED
PASSED
PASTED
PATTED
PAUSED
PAWNED
RACKED
RAFTED
RAGGED
RAIDED
RAILED
RAINED
RAISED
RAMMED
RAMPED
RAMROD
RANCID
RANGED
RANKED
RANTED
RAPPED
RASPED
RATTED
RAZEED
RAZZED
SACKED
SACRED
SAGGED
SAILED
SALPID
SALTED
SALVED
SANDED
SAPPED
SASHED
SASSED
SAUCED
TABARD
TABLED
TACKED
TAGGED
TAILED
TALCED
TALKED
TALMUD
TAMPED
TANGED
TANKED
TANNED
TAPPED
TARRED
TASKED
TASTED
TATTED
TAXIED
VALUED
VALVED
VAMPED
VARIED
VATTED
WADDED
WAFTED
WAGGED
WAIFED
WAILED
WAITED
WAIVED
WALKED
WALLED
WANNED
WANTED
WAPPED
WARDED
WARMED
WARNED
WARPED
WARRED
WASHED
WASTED
WAULED
WAWLED
YAKKED
YANKED
YAPPED
YARDED
YAUPED
YAWLED
YAWNED
YAWPED

••AD••

ACADIA
AMADOU
ANADEM
BEADED
BEADLE
BLADED
BLADES

CRADLE
DEADEN
DEADLY
DIADEM
DYADIC
EVADED
EVADER
EVADES
GLADES
GLADLY
GLADYS
GOADED
GRADED
GRADER
GRADES
GRADIN
GRADUS
HEADED
HEADER
HEADON
HYADES
ISADOR
LEADED
LEADEN
LEADER
LEADIN
LOADED
LOADER
MEADOW
QUADRI
READER
SEADOG
SHADED
SHADES
SHADOW
SPADED
SPADER
SPADES
SPADIX
SRADHA
STADIA
THADDY
THADYS
TRADED
TRADER
TRADES
TSADES
VEADAR
WOADED

••A•D•
AMANDA
AWARDS
BEARDS
BOARDS
BRAIDS
BRANDS
BRANDY
CHARDS
CLAUDE
ELANDS
FRAUDS
GLANDS
GUARDS
HOARDS
LUANDA
PLAIDS
PRAVDA
ROALDS
RWANDA
SCALDS
SHARDS
SKALDS
STANDS
SWARDS
THADDY
UGANDA
VIANDS
WEALDS
WOALDS

••A••D
ABASED
ABATED
ACARID
ALATED
AMAZED
AWAKED
BEADED
BEAKED
BEAMED
BEANED
BEARED
BIASED
BLADED
BLAMED
BLARED
BLAZED
BOATED
BRACED
BRAKED
BRAVED
BRAYED
BRAZED
CEASED
CHAFED
CHARED
CHASED
CHAWED
CLAWED
CLAYED
COALED
COATED
COAXED
CRANED
CRAPED
CRATED
CRAVED
CRAZED
CYANID
DIALED
DRAPED
DRAYED
ELATED
ERASED
EVADED
FEARED
FEASED
FLAKED
FLAMED
FLARED
FLAWED
FLAYED
FOALED
FOAMED
FRAMED
FRAYED
GEARED
GLARED
GLAZED
GNAWED
GOADED
GRACED
GRADED
GRATED
GRAVED
GRAVID
GRAYED
GRAZED
HEADED
HEALED
HEAPED
HEATED
HEAVED
HOAXED
LEADED
LEAFED
LEAKED
LEANED
LEAPED
LEASED
LEAVED
LOADED
LOAFED
LOAMED
LOANED
MOANED
MOATED
NEARED
OKAYED
ORATED
PEAKED
PEALED
PHASED
PLACED
PLACID
PLANED
PLATED
PLAYED
PRATED
PRAYED
QUAKED
REAMED
REAPED
REARED
ROAMED
ROARED
SCALED
SCARED
SEALED
SEAMED
SEARED
SEATED
SHADED
SHALED
SHAMED
SHAPED
SHARED
SHAVED
SKATED
SLAKED
SLATED
SLAVED
SNAKED
SNARED
SOAKED
SOAPED
SOARED
SPACED
SPADED
SPARED
SPAYED
STAGED
STAKED
STALED
STARED
STATED
STAVED
STAYED
SWAGED
SWAYED
TEAMED
TEARED
TEASED
THAWED
TRACED
TRADED
VIALED
WEANED
WEAVED
WHALED
WOADED
XRAYED
YEANED

•••AD•
ABRADE
ARCADE
ARMADA
AUBADE
AUDADS
BREADS
BROADS
CANADA
CICADA
CYCADS
DECADE
DORADO
DREADS
DRYADS
FACADE
FARADS
GONADS
HEXADS
INVADE
JIHADS
KNEADS
MALADY
MIKADO
MILADY
MONADS
NAIADS
NEVADA
NOMADS
OCTADS
OREADS
PANADA
PARADE
PESADE
PLEADS
POMADE
POSADA
REMADE
SALADS
SQUADS
STEADY
TIRADE
TREADS
TRIADS
TULADI
UNLADE
UNMADE

•••A•D
AALAND
ABOARD
AFRAID
ARMAND
ARNAUD
ASGARD
BAYARD
BOYARD
CANARD
COWARD
DANAID
DEMAND
DONALD
ECHARD
EDUARD
EDWARD
ERRAND
EXPAND
GERALD
GERARD
HAZARD
HERALD
HOLARD
HOWARD
INLAID
INLAND
INWARD
ISLAND
IZZARD
LIGAND
LIZARD
MARAUD
ONWARD
OSWALD
PETARD
POLAND
REGARD
REMAND
REPAID
REPAND
RETARD
REWARD
RIBALD
RITARD
ROBAND
ROLAND
RONALD
SEWARD
SOLAND
STRAND
TABARD
TOGAED
TOWARD
UNHAND
UNLAID
UNPAID
UNSAID
UPLAND
UPWARD
UTGARD
VISAED
VISARD
VIZARD
WIZARD

••••AD
ABROAD
ALIDAD
AOUDAD
BAGDAD
BALLAD
BEHEAD
BYROAD
CAUDAD
CONRAD
DOODAD
DORSAD
ENNEAD
FORBAD
GILEAD
HEPTAD
INROAD
KONRAD
LAMPAD
MAENAD
MYRIAD
OGDOAD
PENTAD
PLEIAD
RELOAD
SINBAD
SPREAD
TETRAD
THREAD
UNCLAD
UNLEAD
UNLOAD
UNREAD

6

AE••••
AEACUS
AECIAL
AECIUM
AEDILE
AEETES
AEGEAN
AEGEUS
AENEAS
AENEID
AEOLIA
AEOLIC
AEOLIS
AEOLUS
AERATE
AERIAL
AERIED
AERIES
AERIFY
AEROBE
AERUGO
AETHER

A•E•••
ABELES
ACEDIA
ACEOUS
ACETAL
ACETIC
ACETUM
ACETYL
ADEEMS
ADENIS
ADEPTS
AEETES
AGEDLY
AGEING
AGENCY
AGENDA
AGENTS
AKENES
ALECTO
ALEGAR
ALEPHS
ALEPPO
ALERTS
ALEUTS
ALEXIA
ALEXIN
ALEXIS
AMEBAE
AMEBAS
AMEBIC
AMELIA
AMELIE
AMENDS
AMENRA
AMENTS
AMERCE
ANEMIA
ANEMIC
ANERGY
APERCU
APEXES
ARECAS
ARENAS
AREOLA
ARETES
AREZZO
AVENGE
AVENUE
AVERNO
AVERSE
AVERTS
AVERYS
AVESTA
AWEARY
AWEIGH
AWEING
AXEMAN
AXEMEN
AYEAYE
AYESHA

A••E••
ABBESS
ABBEYS
ABJECT
ABLEST
ABNERS
ABSENT
ACCEDE
ACCENT
ACCEPT
ACCESS
ACHENE
ADDEND
ADDERS
ADEEMS
ADHERE
ADIEUS
ADIEUX
ADVENT
ADVERB
ADVERT
AEGEAN
AEGEUS
AENEAS
AENEID
AFFECT
AFIELD
AFRESH
AGGERS
AGLEAM
AGLETS
AGREED
AGREES
AIDERS
AILEEN
ALBEDO
ALBEIT
ALBERT
ALDERS
ALIENS
ALKENE
ALLEGE
ALLELE
ALLENS
ALLEYS
ALTERS
AMBERS
AMBERY
AMIENS
AMOEBA
AMPERE
ANDEAN
ANGELA
ANGELO
ANGELS
ANGERS
ANNEAL
ANSELM
ANTEED
ANTERO
APIECE
APNEAL
APNEIC
APPEAL
APPEAR
APPELS
APPEND
ARBELA
ARDEBS
ARDENT
ARGENT
ARIELS
ARLEEN
ARLENE
ARMETS
ARPENS
ARPENT
ARREAR
ARREST
ARTELS
ARTERY
ASCEND
ASCENT
ASKERS
ASLEEP
ASPECT
ASPENS
ASPERS
ASSENT
ASSERT
ASSESS
ASSETS
ASTERI
ASTERN
ASTERO
ASTERS
ATHENA
ATHENE
ATHENS
ATREUS
ATTEND
ATTEST
AUGEAN
AUGEND
AUGERS
AUREUS
AWLESS
AXSEED
AZTECS

A•••E•
AACHEN
ABASED
ABASER
ABASES
ABATED
ABATER
ABATES
ABBIES
ABELES
ABIDED
ABIDER
ABIDES
ABODES
ABUSED
ABUSER
ABUSES
ACHAEA
ACUMEN
ADAGES
ADDLED
ADDLES
ADOBES
ADORED
ADORER
ADORES
ADRIEN
AEETES
AERIED
AERIES
AETHER
AGATES
AGAVES
AGONES
AGREED
AGREES
AIDMEN
AIGLET
AILEEN
AIRIER
AIRMEN
AISLED
AISLES
AKENES
ALATED
ALFRED
ALICES
ALINED
ALINES
ALIPED
ALLIED
ALLIES
ALTHEA
ALUDEL
AMAZED
AMAZES
AMBLED
AMBLER
AMBLES
AMICES
AMIDES
AMOLES
AMULET
AMUSED
AMUSER
AMUSES
ANADEM
ANDREA
ANDREI
ANDRES
ANDREW
ANGLED
ANGLER
ANGLES
ANISES
ANKLES
ANKLET
ANNIES
ANODES
ANSWER
ANTEED
ANTHEA
ANTHEM
ANTHER
ANTLER
ANUSES
APEXES
APICES
APNOEA
APOGEE
APPLES
ARABEL
ARCHED
ARCHEO
ARCHER
ARCHES
ARCKED
ARETES
ARGUED
ARGUER
ARGUES
ARISEN
ARISES
ARLEEN
ARMIES
ARMLET
ARNIES
ARTIES
ASHIER
ASHLEY
ASHMEN
ASIDES
ASLEEP
ATONED
ATONER
ATONES
ATTLEE
AUBREY
AUDREY
AUKLET
AUSPEX
AUSTEN
AUSTER
AUTOED
AVOCET
AVOWED
AVOWER
AWAKED
AWAKEN
AWAKES
AXEMEN
AXONES
AXSEED
AZALEA
AZAZEL
AZINES
AZOLES
AZORES
AZRAEL
AZURES

A••••E
ABJURE
ABLAZE
ABRADE
ACCEDE
ACCRUE
ACCUSE
ACHENE
ACNODE
ACTIVE
ACUATE
ADDUCE
ADHERE
ADJURE
ADMIRE
ADNATE
ADVICE
ADVISE
AEDILE
AERATE
AEROBE
AFLAME
AFRAME
AGAPAE
AGNATE
AGOGUE
AGORAE
AGRAFE
ALBITE
ALCOVE
ALDINE
ALDOSE
ALIBLE
ALKANE
ALKENE
ALKYNE
ALLEGE
ALLELE
ALLUDE
ALLURE
ALMUCE
ALMUDE
ALPINE
ALSACE
ALSIKE
ALULAE
ALVINE
AMBAGE
AMEBAE

AMELIE
AMERCE
AMPERE
AMPULE
ANANKE
ANCONE
ANLACE
ANLAGE
ANOMIE
ANSATE
ANYONE
AORTAE
APACHE
APIECE
APLITE
APOGEE
APPOSE
ARABLE
ARBUTE
ARCADE
ARCANE
ARCHIE
ARGIVE
ARGYLE
ARIOSE
ARLENE
ARLINE
ARMURE
AROUSE
ARRIVE
ARSINE
ASHORE
ASLOPE
ASPIRE
ASSIZE
ASSUME
ASSURE
ASTUTE
ATHENE
ATHOME
ATTIRE
ATTLEE
ATTUNE
AUBADE
AUDILE
AUGITE
AUNTIE
AURATE
AVENGE
AVENUE
AVERSE
AVIATE
AWHILE
AXLIKE
AYEAYE

•AE•••

CAECUM
CAEOMA
CAESAR
DAEDAL
DAEMON
FAEROE
GAELIC
JAEGER
MAENAD
NAEVUS
PAEANS
PAEONS
TAENIA

•A•E••

BAGELS
BAKERS
BAKERY
BALEEN
BALERS
BAREGE
BARELY
BAREST
BASELY
BATEAU
BAYEUX
CADENT
CADETS
CALEBS
CALESA
CAMELS
CAMEOS
CAMERA
CANERS
CAPERS
CAREEN
CAREER
CARERS
CARESS
CARETS
CASEFY
CASEIN
CASERN
CATENA
CATERS
CAVEAT
CAVEIN
CAVELL
CAVERN
DALETH
DARERS
DATERS
DAVEYS
EASELS
EATERS
FACERS
FACETS
FADEIN
FAKERS
FAKERY
FANEGA
FARERS
GAGERS
GAIETY
GALEAE
GALENA
GAMELY
GAMETE
GAMETO
GANEFS
GAPERS
GAVELS
GAYEST
GAYETY
GAZEBO
GAZERS
HALERS
HAREMS
HATERS
HAVENS
HAVENT
HAZELS
HAZERS
JANETS
KARENS
LABELS
LAGERS
LAKERS
LAMEDS
LAMELY
LAMENT
LAMEST
LAPELS
LAREDO
LASERS
LATEEN
LATELY
LATENT
LATEST
LAVERS
LAXEST
LAYERS
MABELS
MACERS
MADEUP
MAKERS
MAKEUP
MAMEYS
MANEGE
MASERS
MATEOS
MATEYS
MAYEST
MAZERS
NAMELY
NAMERS
NAPERY
NAVELS
PACERS
PALEAE
PALELY
PALEST
PAMELA
PANELS
PAPERS
PAPERY
PARENS
PARENT
PARERS
PAREUS
PATENS
PATENT
PATERS
PAVERS
PAWERS
PAYEES
PAYERS
RACEME
RACERS
RAKERS
RANEES
RAREFY
RARELY
RAREST
RATELS
RATERS
RAVELS
RAVENS
RAVERS
RAWEST
RAZEED
RAZEES
SABEAN
SABERS
SAFELY
SAFEST
SAFETY
SAGELY
SAGEST
SAHEBS
SAKERS
SANELY
SANEST
SATEEN
SAVERS
SAWERS
SAYERS
TAKEIN
TAKERS
TAKEUP
TALENT
TALERS
TAMERS
TAMEST
TAPERS
TAVERN
TAWERS
TAXEME
TAXERS
VALERY
VALETS
WADERS
WAFERS
WAGERS
WAKENS
WALERS
WATERS
WATERY
WAVERS
WAVEYS
YAGERS
YAMENS
ZAREBA

•A••E•

AACHEN
BABIED
BABIES
BACHED
BACHES
BACKED
BACKER
BADGED
BADGER
BADGES
BADMEN
BAFFED
BAGGED
BAGMEN
BAILED
BAILEE
BAILER
BAILEY
BAITED
BAITER
BALDER
BALEEN
BALKED
BALLED
BALLET
BANDED
BANGED
BANKED
BANKER
BANNED
BANNER
BANTER
BARBED
BARBEL
BARBER
BARBET
BARDED
BARDES
BARGED
BARGEE
BARGES
BARKED
BARKER
BARLEY
BARMEN
BARNEY
BARRED
BARREL
BARREN
BARRET
BARTER
BARYES
BASHED
BASHES
BASKED
BASKET
BASSES
BASSET
BASTED
BASTES
BATHED
BATHER
BATMEN
BATTED
BATTEN
BATTER
BAWLED
BAWLER
BAXTER
CABLED
CABLES
CABLET
CABMEN
CACHED
CACHES
CACHET
CADGED
CADGER
CADGES
CADRES
CAGIER
CAHIER
CALCES
CALKED
CALKER
CALLED
CALLER
CALMED
CALMER
CALVED
CALVES
CALXES
CAMBER
CAMDEN
CAMLET
CAMPED
CAMPER
CANCEL
CANCER
CANKER
CANNED
CANNEL
CANNER
CANNES
CANOED
CANOES
CANTED
CANTER
CAPPED
CAPPER
CARCEL
CARDED
CARDER
CAREEN
CAREER
CARIES
CARMEL
CARMEN
CARPED
CARPEL
CARPER
CARPET
CARREL
CARTED
CARTEL
CARTER
CARTES
CARVED
CARVEL
CARVEN
CARVER
CARVES

6

CASHED
CASHES
CASHEW
CASKET
CASPER
CASTER
CASTES
CATHER
CATTED
CAUDEX
CAULES
CAUSED
CAUSER
CAUSES
CAVIES
DABBED
DABBER
DADOES
DAGGER
DAISES
DALLES
DAMMED
DAMMER
DAMNED
DAMPED
DAMPEN
DAMPER
DAMSEL
DANCED
DANCER
DANCES
DANDER
DANGED
DANGER
DANIEL
DANKER
DAPPED
DAPPER
DARIEN
DARKEN
DARKER
DARNED
DARNEL
DARTED
DARTER
DASHED
DASHER
DASHES
DAUBED
DAUBER
DAVIES
DAWNED
EAGLES
EAGLET
EARLES
EARNED
EARNER
EASIER
EASTER
FABLED
FABLER
FABLES
FACIES
FAGGED
FAILED
FAIRED
FAIRER
FALLEN
FALLER
FALSER
FALTER
FANGED
FANJET
FANNED
FANNER
FARCED
FARCER
FARCES
FARLES
FARLEY
FARMED
FARMER
FASCES
FASTED
FASTEN
FASTER
FATHER
FATTED
FATTEN
FATTER
FAUCES
FAUCET
FAUVES
FAWKES
FAWNED
FAWNER
GABBED
GABBER
GABLED
GABLES
GADDED
GADDER
GADGET
GAFFED
GAFFER
GAFFES
GAGGED
GAGGER
GAINED
GAINER
GAITED
GAITER
GALLED
GALLEY
GAMIER
GAMMER
GANDER
GANGED
GANGER
GANGES
GANNET
GAOLER
GAPPED
GARBED
GARDEN
GARGET
GARNER
GARNET
GARRET
GARTER
GASHED
GASHES
GASKET
GASMEN
GASPED
GASPER
GASSED
GASSES
GATHER
GAUGED
GAUGER
GAUGES
GAUZES
GAWKED
HACKED
HACKEE
HACKER
HAILED
HAILER
HAIRED
HALLEL
HALLEY
HALOES
HALSEY
HALTED
HALTER
HALVED
HALVES
HAMDEN
HAMLET
HAMMED
HAMMER
HAMPER
HANCES
HANDED
HANDEL
HANGED
HANGER
HANKER
HANSEL
HAPPEN
HARDEN
HARDER
HARKED
HARKEN
HARLEM
HARLEY
HARMED
HARPED
HARPER
HARVEY
HASHED
HASHES
HASLET
HASPED
HASSEL
HASTED
HASTEN
HASTES
HATRED
HATTED
HATTER
HAULED
HAULER
HAUSEN
HAWKED
HAWKER
HAWSER
HAWSES
HAZIER
JABBED
JABBER
JACKED
JACKET
JAEGER
JAGGED
JAILED
JAILER
JAMIES
JAMMED
JAPHET
JARRED
JARVEY
JASPER
JAYVEE
JAZZED
JAZZER
JAZZES
KAASES
KAISER
KATIES
KAYOED
LAAGER
LABRET
LACHES
LACIER
LACKED
LACKEY
LADDER
LADIES
LADLED
LADLER
LADLES
LAGGED
LAGGER
LAIRED
LAKIER
LALLED
LAMBED
LAMMED
LAMPED
LANCED
LANCER
LANCES
LANCET
LANDED
LANDER
LANKER
LANNER
LAPPED
LAPPER
LAPPET
LAPSED
LAPSER
LAPSES
LARDED
LARDER
LARGER
LARKED
LARKER
LASHED
LASHER
LASHES
LASSES
LASTED
LASTER
LASTEX
LATEEN
LATHED
LATHER
LATHES
LATTEN
LATTER
LAUDED
LAUDER
LAUREL
LAWYER
LAYMEN
LAZIER
MACLES
MADDED
MADDEN
MADDER
MADGES
MADMEN
MAGNET
MAGUEY
MAHLER
MAIDEN
MAILED
MAILER
MAIMED
MAIMER
MAIZES
MALLED
MALLEE
MALLET
MALTED
MAMIES
MAMMET
MANGER
MANNED
MANNER
MANSES
MANTEL
MANTES
MANUEL
MAPLES
MAPPED
MARCEL
MARGES
MARIES
MARKED
MARKER
MARKET
MARLED
MARRED
MARRER
MARTEN
MARVEL
MASHED
MASHER
MASHES
MASKED
MASKEG
MASKER
MASSED
MASSES
MASTED
MASTER
MATTED
MATTEO
MATTER
MATTES
MAUDES
MAULED
MAULER
MAUSER
MAUVES
MAYHEM
MAZIER
NABBED
NAGGED
NAGGER
NAILED
NANTES
NAOSES
NAPIER
NAPLES
NAPPED
NAPPER
NAPPES
NASSER
NAUSEA
NAVIES
OAKLEY
PACKED
PACKER
PACKET
PADDED
PADRES
PAINED
PAIRED
PALAEO
PALLED
PALLET
PALMED
PALMER
PALTER
PAMPER
PANDER
PANNED
PANTED
PANZER
PARCEL
PARGET
PARIES
PARKED
PARKER
PARLEY
PARREL
PARSEC
PARSED
PARSEE

PARSES
PARTED
PASSED
PASSEE
PASSER
PASSES
PASTED
PASTEL
PASTER
PASTES
PATTED
PATTEN
PATTER
PAUKER
PAUPER
PAUSED
PAUSER
PAUSES
PAWNED
PAWNEE
PAWNER
PAYEES
RABBET
RABIES
RACHEL
RACIER
RACKED
RACKER
RACKET
RAFTED
RAFTER
RAGGED
RAGMEN
RAIDED
RAIDER
RAILED
RAINED
RAISED
RAISER
RAISES
RAMIES
RAMMED
RAMMER
RAMPED
RANEES
RANGED
RANGER
RANGES
RANKED
RANKER
RANTED
RANTER
RAPIER
RAPPED
RAPPEE
RAPPEL
RAPPER
RASHER
RASHES
RASPED
RASPER
RATHER
RATTED
RATTEN
RATTER
RAZEED
RAZEES
RAZZED
RAZZES
SABLES
SACHEM
SACHET
SACKED
SACKER
SACRED
SADDEN
SADDER
SADIES
SAGGED
SAGGER
SAGIER
SAILED
SAILER
SALLET
SALTED
SALTER
SALVED
SALVER
SALVES
SAMIEL
SAMLET
SAMUEL
SANDED
SANDER
SANGER
SANIES
SANSEI
SAPPED
SAPPER
SASHED
SASHES
SASSED
SASSES
SATEEN
SAUCED
SAUCER
SAUCES
SAUGER
SAUREL
SAUTES
SAWYER
TABLED
TABLES
TABLET
TACKED
TACKER
TACKEY
TAGGED
TAGGER
TAILED
TAIPEI
TALCED
TALKED
TALKER
TALLER
TAMPED
TAMPER
TANDEM
TANGED
TANKED
TANKER
TANNED
TANNER
TANREC
TAPPED
TAPPER
TAPPET
TARGET
TARRED
TARTER
TASKED
TASSEL
TASSET
TASTED
TASTER
TASTES
TATLER
TATTED
TATTER
TAUPES
TAUTEN
TAUTER
TAXIED
VAGUER
VAINER
VALLEY
VALUED
VALUES
VALVED
VALVES
VAMPED
VANMEN
VARIED
VARIER
VARIES
VARLET
VARVES
VASTER
VATTED
WADDED
WADIES
WADSET
WAFTED
WAFTER
WAGGED
WAGNER
WAIFED
WAILED
WAILER
WAITED
WAITER
WAIVED
WAIVER
WAIVES
WALKED
WALKER
WALLED
WALLET
WALTER
WANDER
WANNED
WANNER
WANTED
WANTER
WAPPED
WARDED
WARDEN
WARDER
WARIER
WARMED
WARMER
WARNED
WARNER
WARPED
WARPER
WARRED
WARREN
WASHED
WASHER
WASHES
WASTED
WASTER
WASTES
WAULED
WAVIER
WAVIES
WAWLED
WAXIER
WAYNES
XAVIER
YABBER
YAHVEH
YAHWEH
YAKKED
YAMMER
YANKED
YANKEE
YAPPED
YARDED
YAUPED
YAWLED
YAWNED
YAWNER
YAWPED
YAWPER
ZAFFER
ZANIER
ZANIES

•A•••E

BABBIE
BABBLE
BABITE
BAFFLE
BAILEE
BAILIE
BANGLE
BARBIE
BAREGE
BARGEE
BARITE
BARMIE
BARQUE
BASQUE
BATTLE
BATTUE
BAUBLE
CACKLE
CADDIE
CAIQUE
CAJOLE
CAMISE
CANAPE
CANDLE
CANGUE
CANINE
CANNAE
CANNIE
CANTLE
CANUTE
CAPOTE
CARAFE
CARATE
CARIBE
CAROLE
CARRIE
CASQUE
CASSIE
CASTLE
CATTIE
CATTLE
CAUDLE
CAVITE
CAYUSE
DABBLE
DADDLE
DAMAGE
DANDLE
DANGLE
DANITE
DANUBE
DAPHNE
DAPPLE
DARKLE
DARTLE
DATIVE
DAWDLE
DAZZLE
FACADE
FACILE
FAEROE
FAILLE
FAMINE
FANNIE
FAUNAE
GABBLE
GAGGLE
GALEAE
GALORE
GAMBLE
GAMETE
GANGUE
GARAGE
GARBLE
GARGLE
GAUCHE
HABILE
HACKEE
HACKIE
HACKLE
HAGGLE
HALIDE
HALITE
HAMITE
HANDLE
HASSLE
HATTIE
JACKIE
JANGLE
JANICE
JAYVEE
KARATE
KATHIE
LABILE
LADDIE
LAGUNE
LAHORE
LAMBIE
LAMIAE
LANATE
LANOSE
LAOTSE
LARINE
LARVAE
LASSIE
LAUNCE
LAURAE
LAURIE
LAVAGE
MACKLE
MACULE
MADAME
MAGGIE
MAGPIE
MAIGRE
MAISIE
MAITRE
MALATE
MALGRE
MALICE
MALINE
MALLEE
MAMMAE
MANAGE
MANEGE
MANGLE
MANQUE
MANTLE
MANURE
MARBLE
MARGIE
MARINE
MARQUE
MARTHE
MASHIE
MASQUE
MATTIE
MATURE
MAXINE
MAXIXE
NADINE
NAPPIE
NARINE
NATIVE

6

NATURE
PADDLE
PAIUTE
PALACE
PALATE
PALEAE
PANICE
PANTIE
PAPULE
PARADE
PARCAE
PAROLE
PARSEE
PARURE
PASSEE
PATINE
PAVISE
PAWNEE
RABBLE
RACEME
RACINE
RADDLE
RADOME
RAFFLE
RAMBLE
RAMOSE
RANKLE
RAPHAE
RAPINE
RAPPEE
RATINE
RATITE
RATTLE
RAVAGE
RAVINE
SABINE
SADDLE
SALINE
SALOME
SALUTE
SAMITE
SAMPLE
SARAPE
SARTRE
SATIRE
SAVAGE
TACKLE
TAILLE
TAMALE
TANGLE
TATTLE
TAXEME
TAXITE
VACATE
VADOSE
VALISE
WABBLE
WADDLE
WAFFLE
WAGGLE
WAHINE
WALLIE
WAMBLE
WANDLE
WANGLE
WARBLE
WATAPE
WATTLE
YANKEE
ZAFFRE

••AE••

CHAETA
CHAETO
GRAECO
QUAERE
URAEUS

••A•E•

ABASED
ABASER
ABASES
ABATED
ABATER
ABATES
ADAGES
AGATES
AGAVES
ALATED
AMAZED
AMAZES
ANADEM
ARABEL
AWAKED
AWAKEN
AWAKES
AZALEA
AZAZEL
BEADED
BEAKED
BEAKER
BEAMED
BEANED
BEARED
BEARER
BEATEN
BEATER
BEAVER
BIASED
BIASES
BLADED
BLADES
BLAMED
BLAMES
BLARED
BLARES
BLAZED
BLAZER
BLAZES
BOATED
BRACED
BRACER
BRACES
BRAKED
BRAKES
BRAVED
BRAVER
BRAVES
BRAYED
BRAYER
BRAZED
BRAZEN
BRAZER
BRAZES
CEASED
CEASES
CHAFED
CHAFER
CHAFES
CHALEH
CHALET
CHAPEL
CHAPES
CHARED
CHARES
CHASED
CHASER
CHASES
CHAWED
CLARES
CLARET
CLAWED
CLAYED
CLAYEY
COALED
COALER
COATED
COAXED
COAXER
COAXES
CRAKES
CRANED
CRANES
CRAPED
CRAPES
CRATED
CRATER
CRATES
CRAVED
CRAVEN
CRAVER
CRAVES
CRAZED
CRAZES
DEADEN
DEAFEN
DEALER
DEARER
DIADEM
DIALED
DIALER
DIANES
DIAPER
DRAGEE
DRAKES
DRAPED
DRAPER
DRAPES
DRAWEE
DRAWER
DRAYED
ELATED
ELATER
ELATES
ENAMEL
ENATES
ERASED
ERASER
ERASES
ETAPES
EVADED
EVADER
EVADES
EXAMEN
EYASES
FEARED
FEARER
FEASED
FEASES
FLAKED
FLAKER
FLAKES
FLAMED
FLAMEN
FLAMES
FLARED
FLARES
FLAWED
FLAXEN
FLAXES
FLAYED
FLAYER
FOALED
FOAMED
FRAMED
FRAMER
FRAMES
FRATER
FRAUEN
FRAYED
GEARED
GLACES
GLADES
GLARED
GLARES
GLAZED
GLAZER
GLAZES
GNAWED
GNAWER
GOADED
GOATEE
GRABEN
GRACED
GRACES
GRADED
GRADER
GRADES
GRAPES
GRATED
GRATER
GRATES
GRAVED
GRAVEL
GRAVEN
GRAVER
GRAVES
GRAYED
GRAYER
GRAZED
GRAZER
GRAZES
HEADED
HEADER
HEALED
HEALER
HEAPED
HEARER
HEATED
HEATER
HEAVED
HEAVEN
HEAVER
HEAVES
HOAXED
HOAXER
HOAXES
HYADES
IMAGES
IMARET
ISABEL
JUAREZ
KAASES
KNAVES
KRAKEN
LAAGER
LEADED
LEADEN
LEADER
LEAFED
LEAKED
LEANED
LEANER
LEAPED
LEAPER
LEASED
LEASES
LEAVED
LEAVEN
LEAVER
LEAVES
LIANES
LOADED
LOADER
LOAFED
LOAFER
LOAMED
LOANED
LOAVES
MEAGER
MEANER
MOANED
MOATED
NEARED
NEARER
NEATER
OCASEY
OKAYED
ONAGER
ORATED
ORATES
PEAHEN
PEAKED
PEALED
PEASEN
PEASES
PEAVEY
PHASED
PHASES
PLACED
PLACER
PLACES
PLACET
PLANED
PLANER
PLANES
PLANET
PLATED
PLATEN
PLATER
PLATES
PLAYED
PLAYER
PRATED
PRATER
PRATES
PRAYED
PRAYER
QUAKED
QUAKER
QUAKES
QUAVER
READER
REALES
REAMED
REAMER
REAPED
REAPER
REARED
REARER
ROAMED
ROAMER
ROARED
ROARER
SCALED
SCALER
SCALES
SCAPES
SCARED
SCARER
SCARES
SEABEE
SEALED
SEALER
SEAMED
SEAMEN
SEAMER
SEAPEN
SEARED
SEATED
SHADED
SHADES
SHAKEN
SHAKER

SHAKES
SHALED
SHALES
SHAMED
SHAMES
SHAPED
SHAPEN
SHAPER
SHAPES
SHARED
SHARER
SHARES
SHAVED
SHAVEN
SHAVER
SHAVES
SKATED
SKATER
SKATES
SLAKED
SLAKES
SLATED
SLATER
SLATES
SLAVED
SLAVER
SLAVES
SLAYER
SMAZES
SNAKED
SNAKES
SNARED
SNARER
SNARES
SOAKED
SOAKER
SOAPED
SOARED
SOARER
SPACED
SPACER
SPACES
SPADED
SPADER
SPADES
SPARED
SPARER
SPARES
SPATES
SPAYED
STAGED
STAGER
STAGES
STAGEY
STAKED
STAKES
STALED
STALER
STALES
STAMEN
STAPES
STARED
STARER
STARES
STASES
STATED
STATER
STATES
STAVED
STAVES
STAYED
STAYER
SWAGED
SWAGES
SWALES
SWANEE
SWAYED
TEAMED
TEARED
TEASED
TEASEL
TEASER
TEASES
THALES
THAMES
THANES
THAWED
THAYER
TRACED
TRACER
TRACES
TRADED
TRADER
TRADES
TRAVEL
TRAVES
TSADES
UKASES
UPASES
USAGES
VIALED
WEAKEN
WEAKER
WEANED
WEANER
WEARER
WEASEL
WEAVED
WEAVER
WEAVES
WHALED
WHALER
WHALES
WOADED
XRAYED
YEANED

••A••E

AGAPAE
ANANKE
APACHE
ARABLE
BEADLE
BEAGLE
BEANIE
BRAISE
BRAIZE
BRAQUE
CHAISE
CHANCE
CHANGE
CHARGE
CHASSE
CHASTE
CLAIRE
CLAQUE
CLAUDE
CLAUSE
COARSE
CRADLE
DEARIE
DOABLE
DRAGEE
DRAWEE
ECARTE
ELAINE
ELAPSE
ELAYNE
ENABLE
FIACRE
FIANCE
FLAMBE
FLANGE
FRAISE
FRANCE
FRAPPE
GLANCE
GOALIE
GOATEE
GRANGE
HEARSE
HEAUME
HOARSE
JEANNE
JOANNE
LEAGUE
LIABLE
LOATHE
MEALIE
MEANIE
NUANCE
OPAQUE
ORACLE
ORANGE
PIAFFE
PLAGUE
PLAICE
PLAQUE
PLATTE
PRAGUE
PRAISE
PRANCE
QUAERE
QUARTE
QUATRE
SCARCE
SCATHE
SEABEE
SEANCE
SNATHE
SPARGE
SPARSE
SPATHE
STABLE
STACIE
STACTE
STANCE
STAPLE
STARVE
STATUE
SUABLE
SWANEE
SWATHE
TRACHE
TRANCE
UNABLE
USABLE
USANCE
VIABLE
WHARVE
WRASSE

•••AE•

ACHAEA
AZRAEL
ISRAEL
JUDAEA
JUDAEO
PALAEO
TOGAED
VISAED

•••A•E

ABLAZE
ABRADE
ACUATE
ADNATE
AERATE
AFLAME
AFRAME
AGNATE
AGRAFE
ALKANE
ALSACE
AMBAGE
ANLACE
ANLAGE
ANSATE
ARCADE
ARCANE
AUBADE
AURATE
AVIATE
AYEAYE
BECAME
BEHAVE
BERATE
BETAKE
BEWARE
BORAGE
BORANE
BORATE
BUTANE
BYLANE
BYNAME
CANAPE
CARAFE
CARATE
CERATE
CESARE
CETANE
CLEAVE
COMATE
COWAGE
CREASE
CREATE
CUBAGE
CURARE
CURATE
DAMAGE
DEBASE
DEBATE
DECADE
DECANE
DECARE
DEFACE
DEFAME
DEGAGE
DEGAME
DEKARE
DILATE
DOGAPE
DONATE
DOSAGE
DOTAGE
EFFACE
EMPALE
ENCAGE
ENCASE
ENFACE
ENGAGE
ENLACE
ENRAGE
EQUATE
ERGATE
ESCAPE
ESTATE
ETHANE
EXHALE
FACADE
FEMALE
FINALE
FIXATE
FORAGE
GARAGE
GREASE
GREAVE
GYRATE
HECATE
HEXANE
HOMAGE
HORACE
HUMANE
IDEATE
IGNACE
IMPALE
INCAGE
INCASE
INHALE
INLACE
INMATE
INNATE
INSANE
INTAKE
INVADE
IODATE
JUGATE
KARATE
KINASE
LANATE
LAVAGE
LEGATE
LENAPE
LIGATE
LINAGE
LIPASE
LOBATE
LOCALE
LOCATE
LOVAGE
LUNATE
LUXATE
MADAME
MALATE
MANAGE
MENACE
MENAGE
METAGE
MILAGE
MIRAGE
MOHAVE
MOJAVE
MORALE
MUTATE
NEGATE
NONAGE
OBLATE
OCTANE
OCTAVE
OHMAGE
OLEATE
OPIATE
ORNATE
PALACE
PALATE
PARADE
PEDATE
PELAGE
PESADE
PHRASE
PILATE
PIPAGE
PIRATE
PLEASE
POMACE
POMADE
POTAGE
PUPATE
RAVAGE
REBATE
REGALE
RELATE
REMADE
REMAKE

RESALE
RETAKE
ROTATE
ROXANE
RRHAGE
RUBACE
RUGATE
SARAPE
SAVAGE
SCRAPE
SEDATE
SENATE
SERAPE
SESAME
SEWAGE
SHEAVE
SLEAVE
SOCAGE
SOLACE
SPLAKE
SQUARE
STRAFE
STRAKE
TAMALE
TENACE
TIRADE
TISANE
TOWAGE
TUBATE
ULLAGE
UNCAGE
UNLACE
UNLADE
UNMADE
UNMAKE
UNSAFE
UPDATE
UPTAKE
URBANE
UREASE
VACATE
VELATE
VISAGE
VIVACE
VOYAGE
WATAPE
ZONATE
ZOUAVE
ZYMASE

••••AE
AGAPAE
AGORAE
ALULAE
AMEBAE
AORTAE
BULLAE
BURSAE
CANNAE
CELLAE
CHELAE
COSTAE
COTTAE
CURIAE
FAUNAE
FLORAE
FOSSAE
FOVEAE
GALEAE
GEMMAE
GUTTAE
HERMAE
HYDRAE
HYPHAE
LAMIAE
LARVAE
LAURAE
LIBRAE
LYTTAE
MAMMAE
MEDIAE
MUSCAE
NUCHAE
OCREAE
PALEAE
PARCAE
PENNAE
PHYLAE
PINNAE
PLICAE
RAPHAE
SILVAE
SPICAE
STELAE
STRIAE
SUNDAE
SYLVAE
TESTAE
THEBAE
THECAE
TIBIAE
UMBRAE
UVULAE
VITTAE
VULVAE

AF••••
AFFAIR
AFFECT
AFFIRM
AFFLUX
AFFORD
AFFRAY
AFGHAN
AFIELD
AFLAME
AFLCIO
AFLOAT
AFRAID
AFRAME
AFRESH
AFRICA
AFTOSA

A•F•••
AFFAIR
AFFECT
AFFIRM
AFFLUX
AFFORD
AFFRAY
ALFAKI
ALFONS
ALFRED

A••F••
ARMFUL
ARTFUL

A•••F•
ADRIFT
AERIFY
AGRAFE
ARGUFY

•AF•••
BAFFED
BAFFIN
BAFFLE
CAFTAN
DAFTLY
FAFNIR
GAFFED
GAFFER
GAFFES
KAFFIR
OAFISH
RAFFIA
RAFFLE
RAFTED
RAFTER
SAFARI
SAFELY
SAFEST
SAFETY
WAFERS
WAFFLE
WAFTED
WAFTER
ZAFFAR
ZAFFER
ZAFFIR
ZAFFRE

•A•F••
BAFFED
BAFFIN
BAFFLE
BARFLY
DAYFLY
EARFUL
GADFLY
GAFFED
GAFFER
GAFFES
HATFUL
JARFUL
KAFFIR
LAPFUL
LAWFUL
MANFUL
RAFFIA
RAFFLE
SAWFLY
VATFUL
WAFFLE
WAIFED
ZAFFAR
ZAFFER
ZAFFIR
ZAFFRE

•A••F•
BASIFY
CALIFS
CARAFE
CASEFY
FAROFF
GANEFS
LAYOFF
NAZIFY
PACIFY
PAYOFF
RAMIFY
RAREFY
RATIFY
SALIFY
TARIFF

•A•••F
FAROFF
LAYOFF
MASSIF
PAYOFF
TARIFF

••AF••
CHAFED
CHAFER
CHAFES
CHAFFS
CHAFFY
CRAFTS
CRAFTY
DEAFEN
DEAFLY
DRAFFS
DRAFFY
DRAFTS
DRAFTY
GRAFTS
LEAFED
LOAFED
LOAFER
PIAFFE
QUAFFS
SHAFTS
SNAFUS
STAFFS

••A•F•
CHAFFS
CHAFFY
DRAFFS
DRAFFY
DWARFS
PIAFFE
QUAFFS
SCARFS
STAFFS
WHARFS

•••AF•
AGRAFE
CARAFE
PILAFS
SCLAFF
STRAFE
UNSAFE

•••A•F
BEHALF
SCLAFF

••••AF
GUSTAF

AG••••
AGAMAS
AGAMIC
AGAPAE
AGARIC
AGATES
AGATHA
AGAVES
AGEDLY
AGEING
AGENCY
AGENDA
AGENTS
AGGERS
AGHAST
AGISTS
AGLAIA
AGLEAM
AGLETS
AGNAIL
AGNATE
AGOGUE
AGONES
AGONIC
AGORAE
AGORAS
AGOUTI
AGOUTY
AGRAFE
AGREED
AGREES
AGUISH

A•G•••
AEGEAN
AEGEUS
AFGHAN
AGGERS
AIGLET
ALGOID
ANGARY
ANGELA
ANGELO
ANGELS
ANGERS
ANGINA
ANGKOR
ANGLED
ANGLER
ANGLES
ANGLIA
ANGLIC
ANGOLA
ANGORA
ARGALI
ARGALS
ARGENT
ARGIVE
ARGOSY
ARGOTS
ARGUED
ARGUER
ARGUES
ARGUFY
ARGYLE
ARGYLL
ASGARD
AUGEAN
AUGEND
AUGERS
AUGHTS
AUGITE
AUGURS
AUGURY
AUGUST

A••G••
ADAGES
ADAGIO
AGOGUE
ALEGAR
ALIGHT
ALIGNS
AMIGOS
APOGEE
ARAGON
ARIGHT

A•••G•
AERUGO
ALLEGE
AMBAGE
ANERGY
ANLAGE
ARMAGH
ASSIGN
AURIGA
AVENGE
AWEIGH

A••••G
ACHING
ACTING
ADDING
AGEING
AIDING
AILING

6

AIMING
AIRING
ANALOG
APOLOG
ARCING
ARMING
ASKING
AWEING
AWNING

•AG•••
BAGASS
BAGDAD
BAGELS
BAGGED
BAGMAN
BAGMEN
BAGNIO
CAGIER
CAGILY
CAGING
DAGGER
DAGMAR
DAGOBA
EAGLES
EAGLET
FAGGED
FAGGOT
FAGOTS
GAGERS
GAGGED
GAGGER
GAGGLE
GAGING
HAGBUT
HAGDON
HAGGIS
HAGGLE
JAGGED
JAGUAR
LAGERS
LAGGED
LAGGER
LAGOON
LAGUNE
MAGGIE
MAGGOT
MAGNET
MAGNUM
MAGOTS
MAGPIE
MAGUEY
MAGYAR
NAGANA
NAGGED
NAGGER
NAGOYA
PAGANS
PAGING
PAGODA
RAGGED
RAGING
RAGLAN
RAGMAN
RAGMEN
RAGOUT
RAGTAG
SAGELY
SAGEST
SAGGAR
SAGGED
SAGGER
SAGIER
TAGGED
TAGGER
VAGARY
VAGINA
VAGINO
VAGUER
WAGERS
WAGGED
WAGGLE
WAGGLY
WAGGON
WAGING
WAGNER
WAGONS
YAGERS

•A•G••
BADGED
BADGER
BADGES
BAGGED
BANGED
BANGLE
BANGOR
BANGUI
BANGUP
BARGED
BARGEE
BARGES
CADGED
CADGER
CADGES
CANGUE
CARGOS
CATGUT
CAUGHT
DAGGER
DANGED
DANGER
DANGLE
FAGGED
FAGGOT
FANGAS
FANGED
GADGET
GAGGED
GAGGER
GAGGLE
GANGED
GANGER
GANGES
GANGLI
GANGUE
GARGET
GARGLE
GAUGED
GAUGER
GAUGES
HAGGIS
HAGGLE
HANGAR
HANGED
HANGER
HANGUP
JAEGER
JAGGED
JANGLE
JARGON
LAAGER
LAGGED
LAGGER
LANGUR
LARGER
LARGOS
LAUGHS
MADGES
MAGGIE
MAGGOT
MAIGRE
MALGRE
MANGER
MANGLE
MANGOS
MARGAY
MARGES
MARGIE
MARGIN
MARGOS
MARGOT
NAGGED
NAGGER
NAUGHT
PARGET
PARGOS
RAGGED
RANGED
RANGER
RANGES
SAGGAR
SAGGED
SAGGER
SAIGAS
SAIGON
SANGAR
SANGER
SÁNGUI
SARGON
SAUGER
TAGGED
TAGGER
TAIGAS
TANGED
TANGLE
TANGLY
TANGOS
TARGET
TAUGHT
VALGUS
WAGGED
WAGGLE
WAGGLY
WAGGON
WANGLE

•A••G•
BAREGE
CAYUGA
DAMAGE
FANEGA
GARAGE
LADOGA
LANUGO
LAVAGE
MALAGA
MALIGN
MANAGE
MANEGE
RAVAGE
SAVAGE

•A•••G
BAAING
BAKING
BALING
BARING
BARONG
BASING
BATING
BAYING
CAGING
CAKING
CANING
CARING
CASING
CAVING
CAWING
DANZIG
DARING
DATING
DAZING
EALING
EARING
EARWIG
EASING
EATING
FACING
FADING
FAKING
FARING
FATING
FAXING
FAYING
FAZING
GAGING
GAMING
GAPING
GASBAG
GATING
GAZING
HADING
HALING
HATING
HAVING
HAWING
HAYING
HAZING
JADING
JAWING
KALONG
LACING
LADING
LAKING
LAMING
LARYNG
LAVING
LAWING
LAYING
LAZING
MACING
MAKING
MASKEG
MATING
MAYING
MAZING
NAMING
OARING
PACING
PAGING
PALING
PARANG
PARING
PAVING
PAWING
PAYING
RACING
RAGING
RAGTAG
RAKING
RAPING
RARING
RATING
RAVING
RAYING
RAZING
SARONG
SATANG
SATING
SAVING
SAWING
SAYING
TAKING
TAMING
TAPING
TARING
TAWING
TAXING
WADING
WAGING
WAKING
WALING
WANING
WAVING
WAXING
YAWING

••AG••
ADAGES
ADAGIO
ARAGON
BEAGLE
CRAGGY
DRAGEE
DRAGON
FLAGGY
FLAGON
IMAGES
LAAGER
LEAGUE
MEAGER
ONAGER
ONAGRI
PHAGIA
PLAGAL
PLAGIO
PLAGUE
PLAGUY
PRAGUE
QUAGGA
QUAGGY
SHAGGY
SLAGGY
SNAGGY
STAGED
STAGER
STAGES
STAGEY
STAGGY
SWAGED
SWAGES
TRAGIC
TRAGUS
USAGES

••A•G•
CHANGE
CHANGS
CHARGE
CLANGS
CRAGGY
CRAIGS
FLAGGY
FLANGE
GRANGE
ORANGE
ORANGS
QUAGGA
QUAGGY
SHAGGY
SLAGGY
SLANGY
SNAGGY
SPARGE
STAGGY
TWANGS
TWANGY
UBANGI
WHANGS

••A••G
ANALOG
BAAING

6

DIALOG
QUAHOG
SEADOG
STALAG

•••AG•
AMBAGE
ANLAGE
ARMAGH
BORAGE
COWAGE
CUBAGE
DAMAGE
DEGAGE
DOSAGE
DOTAGE
ENCAGE
ENGAGE
ENRAGE
FORAGE
GARAGE
HOMAGE
INCAGE
LAVAGE
LINAGE
LOVAGE
MALAGA
MANAGE
MENAGE
METAGE
MILAGE
MIRAGE
NONAGE
OHMAGE
PELAGE
PIPAGE
POTAGE
RAVAGE
RRHAGE
RRHAGY
SAVAGE
SCRAGS
SEWAGE
SOCAGE
SPRAGS
TOBAGO
TOWAGE
ULLAGE
UNCAGE
VIRAGO
VISAGE
VOYAGE

•••A•G
PARANG
PINANG
SATANG
SPRANG

••••AG
GASBAG
RAGTAG
STALAG
WIGWAG

ZIGZAG

AH••••
AHIMSA

A•H•••
ABHORS
ACHAEA
ACHAIA
ACHENE
ACHING
ADHERE
AGHAST
APHIDS
APHTHA
ASHIER
ASHLAR
ASHLEY
ASHMAN
ASHMEN
ASHORE
ATHENA
ATHENE
ATHENS
ATHOME
AWHILE
AWHIRL

A••H••
AACHEN
ABOHMS
AETHER
AFGHAN
ALPHAS
ALPHYL
ALTHEA
AMPHRS
ANCHOR
ANTHEA
ANTHEM
ANTHER
ANYHOW
ARCHED
ARCHEO
ARCHER
ARCHES
ARCHIE
ARCHIL
ARCHLY
ARCHON
ARCHYS
ARTHRO
ARTHUR
ASTHMA
AUGHTS
AUTHOR

A•••H•
AGATHA
ALEPHS
ALIGHT
ALMAHS
APACHE
APATHY
APHTHA
ARIGHT
AYESHA

A••••H
ABIJAH
ABLUSH
ADOLPH
AFRESH
AGUISH
AMBUSH
ARMAGH
ATTACH
AVOUCH
AWEIGH

•AH•••
BAHAIS
BAHAMA
CAHIER
DAHLIA
DAHOON
LAHORE
MAHLER
MAHOUT
NAHUMS
SAHARA
SAHEBS
SAHIBS
WAHABI
WAHINE
WAHOOS
YAHOOS
YAHVEH
YAHWEH

•A•H••
AACHEN
BACHED
BACHES
BASHAW
BASHED
BASHES
BATHED
BATHER
BATHOS
CACHED
CACHES
CACHET
CACHOU
CARHOP
CASHAW
CASHED
CASHES
CASHEW
CASHOO
CATHAY
CATHER
CATHYS
DACHAS
DACHAU
DAPHNE
DASHED
DASHER
DASHES
FATHER
FATHOM
GASHED
GASHES
GATHER
HASHED
HASHES
HAWHAW
JAPHET
KATHIE
KATHYS
LACHES
LASHED
LASHER
LASHES
LATHED
LATHER
LATHES
MASHED
MASHER
MASHES
MASHIE
MAYHAP
MAYHEM
NASHUA
NATHAN
PASHAS
PASHTO
PATHAN
PATHIA
PATHOL
PATHOS
RACHEL
RACHIS
RAPHAE
RAPHIS
RASHER
RASHES
RASHLY
RATHER
SACHEM
SACHET
SADHUS
SAPHAR
SASHAY
SASHED
SASHES
VASHTI
WASHED
WASHER
WASHES
YACHTS

•A••H•
CANTHI
CATCHY
CAUGHT
EARTHS
EARTHY
FAITHS
GANDHI
GAUCHE
GAUCHO
LAUGHS
MALTHA
MANCHU
MARSHA
MARSHY
MARTHA
MARTHE
NAUGHT
NAVAHO
PATCHY
RAJAHS
RALPHS
RANCHO
RAYAHS
SAMSHU
SANDHI
SAPPHO
SARAHS
TAUGHT
XANTHO

•A•••H
BANISH
BARUCH
BASRAH
CALASH
CALIPH
CASBAH
DALETH
DANISH
FAMISH
GALOSH
GARISH
HALLAH
HANNAH
HAUNCH
JADISH
LATISH
LAUNCH
LAVISH
NAUTCH
OAFISH
PALISH
PARAPH
PARIAH
PARISH
PAUNCH
RADISH
RAKISH
RAVISH
RAWISH
SALISH
VANISH
WABASH
WALLAH
WARMTH
YAHVEH
YAHWEH

••AH••
BRAHMA
BRAHMS
GRAHAM
PEAHEN

QUAHOG
SPAHIS
UTAHAN

••A•H•
AGATHA
APACHE
APATHY
BEACHY
BRACHI
BRACHY
BRASHY
DEATHS
DEATHY
DRACHM
FLASHY
GNATHO
GRAPHO
GRAPHS
GRAPHY
HEATHS
HEATHY
LEACHY
LOATHE
ORACHS
PEACHY
PLASHY
POACHY
SCATHE
SNATHE
SNATHS
SPATHE
SRADHA
SWATHE
SWATHS
TRACHE
TRACHY
TRASHY
WRATHY

••A••H
BLANCH
BRANCH
CHALEH
CRATCH
DEARTH
EPARCH
EXARCH
HEALTH
HEARTH
INARCH
ISAIAH
PLANCH
SEARCH
SNATCH
STANCH
STARCH
SWARTH
SWATCH
THATCH
WEALTH
WRAITH

6

•••AH•
ALMAHS
DINAHS
EPHAHS
JONAHS
JUDAHS
LOTAHS
NAVAHO
RAJAHS
RAYAHS
SARAHS
SUBAHS
SURAHS
TORAHS

•••A•H
ARMAGH
ATTACH
BLEACH
BREACH
BREATH
BROACH
BYPATH
CALASH
DETACH
PARAPH
PESACH
PLEACH
POTASH
PREACH
REHASH
SERAPH
SHEATH
SIWASH
SPLASH
SQUASH
TERAPH
THRASH
WABASH
WREATH

••••AH
ABIJAH
BASRAH
BEULAH
CASBAH
CHETAH
COPRAH
ELIJAH
FELLAH
GULLAH
HALLAH
HANNAH
HOOKAH
HOWDAH
HURRAH
ISAIAH
JOSIAH
JUBBAH
KEDDAH
KIBLAH
LOOFAH
MOLLAH
MOOLAH
MULLAH
NULLAH
PARIAH
PISGAH
PURDAH
RUPIAH
SUNNAH
TOBIAH
TUSSAH
WALLAH
WHIDAH
WHYDAH
ZILLAH

AI••••
AIDERS
AIDING
AIDMAN
AIDMEN
AIGLET
AILEEN
AILING
AIMING
AIRDRY
AIRIER
AIRILY
AIRING
AIRMAN
AIRMEN
AIRWAY
AISLED
AISLES

A•I•••
ABIDED
ABIDER
ABIDES
ABIJAH
ACIDIC
ACIDLY
ACINUS
ACIOUS
ADIEUS
ADIEUX
ADIPIC
AFIELD
AGISTS
AHIMSA
AKIMBO
ALIBIS
ALIBLE
ALICES
ALICIA
ALIDAD
ALIENS
ALIGHT
ALIGNS
ALINED
ALINES
ALIPED
ALISON
AMICES
AMIDES
AMIDIC
AMIDIN
AMIDOL
AMIDST
AMIENS
AMIGOS
ANILIN
ANIMAL
ANIMAS
ANIMUS
ANIONS
ANISES
ANITAS
ANITRA
APIARY
APICAL
APICES
APIECE
ARIANS
ARIDLY
ARIELS
ARIGHT
ARIOSE
ARIOSO
ARIOUS
ARISEN
ARISES
ARISTA
ARISTO
ASIANS
ASIDES
AVIARY
AVIATE
AVIDIN
AVIDLY
AVISOS
AXILLA
AXIOMS
AZINES

A••I••
AALIIS
ABBIES
ACHING
ACTING
ACTINI
ACTINO
ACTION
ACTIUM
ACTIVE
ACUITY
ADDICT
ADDING
ADLIBS
ADMIRE
ADMITS
ADMIXT
ADRIAN
ADRIEN
ADRIFT
ADVICE
ADVISE
AECIAL
AECIUM
AEDILE
AERIAL
AERIED
AERIES
AERIFY
AFFIRM
AFRICA
AGEING
AGUISH
AIDING
AILING
AIMING
AIRIER
AIRILY
AIRING
ALBINO
ALBION
ALBITE
ALDINE
ALLIED
ALLIES
ALLIUM
ALMIRA
ALPINE
ALSIKE
ALUINO
ALUINS
ALVINA
ALVINE
AMBITS
AMNION
AMRITA
ANGINA
ANNIES
ANOINT
ANTIAR
ANTICS
ANVILS
AORIST
APHIDS
APLITE
APPIAN
APRILS
AQUILA
ARCING
ARGIVE
ARLINE
ARMIES
ARMING
ARNICA
ARNIES
AROIDS
ARRIVE
ARSINE
ARTIES
ARTIST
ASHIER
ASKING
ASPICS
ASPIRE
ASSIGN
ASSISI
ASSIST
ASSIZE
ATRIAL
ATRIUM
ATTICA
ATTICS
ATTILA
ATTIRE
AUDILE
AUDITS
AUGITE
AURIGA
AURIST
AUTISM
AUXINS
AVAILS
AVOIDS
AWAITS
AWEIGH
AWEING
AWHILE
AWHIRL
AWNING
AXLIKE

A•••I•
AALIIS
ABATIS
ABULIA
ACACIA
ACADIA
ACARID
ACEDIA
ACETIC
ACHAIA
ACIDIC
ACQUIT
ADAGIO
ADENIS
ADIPIC
ADJOIN
ADONIC
ADONIS
ADROIT
AENEID
AEOLIA
AEOLIC
AEOLIS
AFFAIR
AFLCIO
AFRAID
AGAMIC
AGARIC
AGLAIA
AGNAIL
AGONIC
ALARIC
ALBEIT
ALCAIC
ALCUIN
ALEXIA
ALEXIN
ALEXIS
ALGOID
ALIBIS
ALICIA
ALTAIC
ALTAIR
ALUMIN
AMEBIC
AMELIA
AMELIE
AMIDIC
AMIDIN
AMYLIC
ANEMIA
ANEMIC
ANGLIA
ANGLIC
ANILIN
ANODIC
ANOMIC
ANOMIE
ANOXIA
ANOXIC
ANTLIA
ANTRIM
ANUBIS
AORTIC
APNEIC
APULIA
ARABIA
ARABIC
ARCHIE
ARCHIL
ARCTIC
ARMPIT
ARTOIS
ASSAIL
ASSAIS
ASTRID
ATAVIC
ATAXIA
ATAXIC
ATOMIC
ATONIC
ATTAIN
AUNTIE
AUSTIN
AVIDIN
AZONIC
AZOTIC

A••••I
ACTINI
ADONAI
AGOUTI
ALFAKI
ALKALI
ALUMNI
AMBARI
ANDREI
ARBORI
ARGALI
ASSISI
ASTERI

•AI•••
BAIKAL
BAILED
BAILEE

6

BAILER
BAILEY
BAILIE
BAILOR
BAIRNS
BAITED
BAITER
CAIMAN
CAIQUE
CAIRNS
DAIMIO
DAIMON
DAIMYO
DAINTY
DAISES
DAISYS
FAILED
FAILLE
FAINTS
FAIRED
FAIRER
FAIRLY
FAITHS
GAIETY
GAINED
GAINER
GAINLY
GAITED
GAITER
HAILED
HAILER
HAIRDO
HAIRED
JAILED
JAILER
JAILOR
JAINAS
JAIPUR
KAISER
LAIRDS
LAIRED
MAIDEN
MAIGRE
MAILED
MAILER
MAIMED
MAIMER
MAINLY
MAISIE
MAISON
MAITRE
MAIZES
NAIADS
NAILED
PAINED
PAINTS
PAINTY
PAIRED
PAIUTE
RAIDED
RAIDER
RAILED
RAINED
RAISED
RAISER
RAISES
RAISIN
SAIGAS
SAIGON
SAILED
SAILER
SAILOR
SAINTS
SAIPAN
SAITIC
TAIGAS
TAILED
TAILLE
TAILOR
TAINOS
TAINTS
TAIPEI
TAIWAN
VAINER
VAINLY
WAIFED
WAILED
WAILER
WAISTS
WAITED
WAITER
WAIVED
WAIVER
WAIVES

•A•I••

AALIIS
BAAING
BABIED
BABIES
BABISM
BABIST
BABITE
BAKING
BALING
BANIAN
BANISH
BARING
BARITE
BARIUM
BASICS
BASIFY
BASILS
BASING
BASINS
BASION
BATIKS
BATING
BAYING
CABINS
CAGIER
CAGILY
CAGING
CAHIER
CAKING
CALICO
CALIFS
CALIPH
CAMILA
CAMION
CAMISE
CANINE
CANING
CAPIAS
CAPITA
CARIBE
CARIBS
CARIES
CARINA
CARING
CASING
CASINO
CATION
CAVIAR
CAVIES
CAVILS
CAVING
CAVITE
CAVITY
CAWING
DANIEL
DANISH
DANITE
DARICS
DARIEN
DARING
DARIUS
DATING
DATIVE
DAVIDS
DAVIES
DAVITS
DAZING
EALING
EARING
EASIER
EASILY
EASING
EATING
FABIAN
FACIAL
FACIES
FACILE
FACING
FADING
FAKING
FAKIRS
FAMILY
FAMINE
FAMISH
FANION
FARINA
FARING
FATIMA
FATING
FAXING
FAYING
FAZING
GABION
GAGING
GALIOT
GAMIER
GAMILY
GAMING
GAMINS
GAPING
GARISH
GATING
GAVIAL
GAZING
HABILE
HABITS
HADING
HAKIMS
HALIDE
HALIDS
HALING
HALITE
HAMITE
HATING
HAVING
HAWING
HAYING
HAZIER
HAZILY
HAZING
JABIRU
JADING
JADISH
JAMIES
JANICE
JARINA
JAWING
KABIKI
KALIAN
KALIUM
KAMIKS
KATIES
KATION
LABIAL
LABILE
LABIUM
LACIER
LACILY
LACING
LADIES
LADING
LADINO
LAKIER
LAKING
LAMIAE
LAMIAS
LAMINA
LAMING
LAPINS
LARIAT
LARINE
LATINS
LATISH
LAVING
LAVISH
LAWING
LAXITY
LAYING
LAZIER
LAZILY
LAZING
MACING
MAKING
MALICE
MALIGN
MALINE
MAMIES
MANIAC
MANIAS
MANILA
MANIOC
MANITO
MANITU
MAOISM
MAOIST
MARIAN
MARIAS
MARIES
MARINA
MARINE
MARION
MARIST
MATING
MATINS
MAXIMS
MAXINE
MAXIXE
MAYING
MAZIER
MAZILY
MAZING
NADINE
NADIRS
NAMING
NANISM
NAPIER
NARIAL
NARINE
NASIAL
NASION
NATION
NATIVE
NAVIES
NAZIFY
NAZISM
OAFISH
OARING
PACIFY
PACING
PAGING
PALING
PALISH
PANICE
PANICS
PAPIST
PARIAH
PARIAN
PARIES
PARING
PARISH
PARITY
PATINA
PATINE
PATIOS
PAVING
PAVIOR
PAVISE
PAWING
PAYING
RABIES
RACIAL
RACIER
RACILY
RACINE
RACING
RACISM
RACIST
RADIAL
RADIAN
RADIOS
RADISH
RADIUM
RADIUS
RAGING
RAKING
RAKISH
RAMIES
RAMIFY
RAPIDS
RAPIER
RAPINE
RAPING
RAPIST
RARING
RARITY
RATIFY
RATINE
RATING
RATION
RATIOS
RATITE
RAVINE
RAVING
RAVISH
RAWISH
RAYING
RAZING
SABINA
SABINE
SABINS
SADIES
SADISM
SADIST
SAGIER
SAHIBS
SALIFY
SALINE
SALISH
SALIVA
SAMIAN
SAMIEL
SAMITE
SANIES
SANITY
SASINS
SATING
SATINS
SATINY

6

SATIRE
SAVING
SAVINS
SAVIOR
SAWING
SAYING
TAKING
TALION
TAMING
TANIST
TAOISM
TAOIST
TAPING
TAPIRS
TARIFF
TARING
TAWING
TAXIED
TAXING
TAXITE
VAGINA
VAGINO
VALISE
VANISH
VANITY
VARICO
VARIED
VARIER
VARIES
VASILI
WADIES
WADING
WAGING
WAHINE
WAKIKI
WAKING
WALING
WANING
WANION
WAPITI
WARIER
WARILY
WAVIER
WAVIES
WAVILY
WAVING
WAXIER
WAXING
XAVIER
YAKIMA
YAWING
ZAMIAS
ZANIER
ZANIES
ZAYINS

•A••I•

AALIIS
BAALIM
BABBIE
BAFFIN
BAGNIO
BAHAIS
BAILIE
BALTIC
BANDIT
BARBIE
BARDIC
BARMIE
BARRIO
BATTIK
BAUCIS
CADDIE
CADDIS
CALAIS
CALCIC
CALVIN
CANDID
CANNIE
CAPLIN
CAPRIC
CARDIO
CARPIC
CARRIE
CASEIN
CASSIA
CASSIE
CASSIS
CATKIN
CATLIN
CATNIP
CATTIE
CAULIS
CAVEIN
DACOIT
DAHLIA
DAIMIO
DAKOIT
DANAID
DANZIG
DARWIN
EARWIG
FABRIC
FADEIN
FAFNIR
FANNIE
FASCIA
GADOID
GAELIC
GALLIC
GAMBIA
GAMBIR
GAMBIT
GANOID
GARLIC
GASKIN
GAWAIN
HACKIE
HAGGIS
HALOID
HARBIN
HARMIN
HATPIN
HATTIE
HAWAII
IAMBIC
IATRIC
JACKIE
JARVIS
KAFFIR
KALMIA
KAMSIN
KAOLIN
KATHIE
KAURIS
LACTIC
LADDIE
LAMBIE
LANAIS
LASSIE
LATRIA
LATVIA
LAURIE
MADRID
MAGGIE
MAGPIE
MAISIE
MANTIC
MANTIS
MAORIS
MAQUIS
MARCIA
MARGIE
MARGIN
MARLIN
MARTIN
MARVIN
MASHIE
MASSIF
MASTIC
MATRIX
MATTIE
NAOMIS
NAPKIN
NAPPIE
NASTIC
PALLID
PANTIE
PAPAIN
PARSIS
PARVIS
PASSIM
PASTIL
PATHIA
PATOIS
PAULIN
RABBIS
RABBIT
RACHIS
RAFFIA
RAISIN
RANCID
RAPHIS
RATLIN
SAITIC
SALMIS
SALPID
SALVIA
TACTIC
TAENIA
TAKEIN
TANNIC
TANNIN
VALOIS
WALLIE
WALLIS
WALVIS
ZAFFIR
ZAMBIA

•A•••I

BANGUI
BANZAI
CANTHI
GANDHI
GANGLI
HAWAII
KABIKI
KABUKI
LAZULI
MALAWI
SAFARI
SALAMI
SALUKI
SANDHI
SANGUI
SANSEI
SATORI
TAIPEI
VAPORI
VASARI
VASHTI
VASILI
WAHABI
WAKIKI
WAPITI
WATUSI

••AI••

AVAILS
AWAITS
BAAING
BLAINS
BRAIDS
BRAILS
BRAINS
BRAINY
BRAISE
BRAIZE
CHAINS
CHAIRS
CHAISE
CLAIMS
CLAIRE
CRAIGS
DRAINS
ELAINE
FLAILS
FLAIRS
FRAILS
FRAISE
GLAIRS
GLAIRY
GRAINS
GRAINY
ISAIAH
KRAITS
PLAICE
PLAIDS
PLAINS
PLAINT
PLAITS
PRAISE
QUAILS
QUAINT
SNAILS
SPAITS
STAINS
STAIRS
SWAILS
SWAINS
TRAILS
TRAINS
TRAITS
WRAITH

••A•I•

ABATIS
ACACIA
ACADIA
ACARID
ADAGIO
AGAMIC
AGARIC
ALARIC
ARABIA
ARABIC
ATAVIC
ATAXIA
ATAXIC
BAALIM
BEANIE
BRAZIL
COATIS
CRANIA
CRANIO
CRASIS
CYANIC
CYANID
CYANIN
DEARIE
DIAZIN
DYADIC
ENATIC
FLAVIA
FLAVIN
GLACIS
GOALIE
GRADIN
GRATIS
GRAVID
GUANIN
IRAQIS
ITALIC
KHAKIS
LEADIN
MEALIE
MEANIE
NIACIN
OKAPIS
OXALIC
OXALIS
PHAGIA
PHASIA
PHASIC
PHASIS
PLACID
PLAGIO
PLASIA
PLASIS
PRAXIS
SIALIC
SLAVIC
SPADIX
SPAHIS
SPAVIN
STACIE
STADIA
STALIN
STAMIN
STASIS
STATIC
SWAMIS
THALIA
TRAGIC
URALIC
URANIA
URANIC
VIATIC

••A••I

BRACHI
GHARRI
ONAGRI
QUADRI
SCAMPI
SMALTI
UBANGI

•••AI•

ACHAIA
AFFAIR
AFRAID
AGLAIA
AGNAIL
ALCAIC
ALTAIC
ALTAIR
ASSAIL
ASSAIS
ATTAIN
BAHAIS
BEWAIL
CALAIS
COCAIN
DANAID
DERAIL
DERAIN
DETAIL
DETAIN
DOMAIN
ECLAIR
EDDAIC
ENTAIL

6

FUSAIN
GAWAIN
HAWAII
IMPAIR
INLAID
JEZAIL
JUDAIC
KUWAIT
LANAIS
LORAIN
MIDAIR
MOHAIR
MOSAIC
OBTAIN
ORDAIN
OXTAIL
PAPAIN
PETAIN
REGAIN
REMAIN
REPAID
REPAIR
RETAIL
RETAIN
ROMAIC
SERAIS
SPRAIN
STRAIN
STRAIT
UNFAIR
UNHAIR
UNLAID
UNPAID
UNSAID
VEDAIC

•••A•I
ALFAKI
ALKALI
AMBARI
ARGALI
BIHARI
BONACI
HAWAII
MALAWI
PEDATI
SAFARI
SALAMI
SOUARI
STRATI
TULADI
VASARI
WAHABI

••••AI
ADONAI
BANZAI
BONSAI
HERMAI
NILGAI

AJ••••
AJOWAN

A•J•••
ABJECT
ABJURE
ADJOIN
ADJURE
ADJUST

A••J••
ABIJAH
ACAJOU

•AJ•••
CAJOLE
CAJUNS
MAJORS
PAJAMA
RAJABS
RAJAHS
RAJPUT
SAJOUS

•A•J••
BANJOS
FANJET
SANJAK

•A••J•
NAVAJO

••AJ••
ACAJOU

••A••J
SWARAJ

•••AJ•
NAVAJO

••••AJ
SWARAJ

AK••••
AKENES
AKIMBO

A•K•••
ACKACK
ALKALI
ALKANE
ALKENE
ALKYLS
ALKYNE
ANKARA
ANKLES
ANKLET
ANKYLO
ASKANT
ASKERS
ASKING
AUKLET

A••K••
ANGKOR
ARCKED

AWAKED
AWAKEN
AWAKES

A•••K•
ALASKA
ALFAKI
ALSIKE
ANANKE
AXLIKE

A••••K
ACKACK
ANORAK
ARAWAK
ARRACK
ATTACK

•AK•••
BAKERS
BAKERY
BAKING
CAKING
DAKOIT
DAKOTA
FAKERS
FAKERY
FAKING
FAKIRS
HAKIMS
KAKAPO
LAKERS
LAKIER
LAKING
MAKERS
MAKEUP
MAKING
OAKLEY
RAKERS
RAKING
RAKISH
SAKERS
TAKEIN
TAKERS
TAKEUP
TAKING
WAKENS
WAKIKI
WAKING
YAKIMA
YAKKED

•A•K••
BACKED
BACKER
BAIKAL
BALKAN
BALKED
BANKED
BANKER
BARKED
BARKER
BASKED
BASKET
CACKLE
CALKED
CALKER
CANKER
CASKET
CATKIN
DANKER
DANKLY
DARKEN
DARKER
DARKLE
DARKLY
FAWKES
GASKET
GASKIN
GAWKED
HACKED
HACKEE
HACKER
HACKIE
HACKLE
HANKER
HARKED
HARKEN
HAWKED
HAWKER
JACKAL
JACKED
JACKET
JACKIE
JACKYS
LACKED
LACKEY
LANKER
LANKLY
LARKED
LARKER
MACKLE
MARKED
MARKER
MARKET
MARKKA
MARKUP
MASKED
MASKEG
MASKER
NAPKIN
PACKED
PACKER
PACKET
PARKAS
PARKED
PARKER
PAUKER
RACKED
RACKER
RACKET
RANKED
RANKER
RANKLE
RANKLY
SACKED
SACKER
TACKED
TACKER
TACKEY
TACKLE
TALKED
TALKER
TANKAS
TANKED
TANKER
TASKED
VALKYR
WALKED
WALKER
WALKON
WALKUP
YAKKED
YANKED
YANKEE

•A••K•
BAMAKO
BATIKS
CAULKS
KABAKA
KABIKI
KABUKI
KAMIKS
KANAKA
KAPOKS
KAYAKS
MARKKA
SALUKI
WAKIKI

•A•••K
BARTOK
BATTIK
CANUCK
CARACK
DAMASK
GALYAK
KALPAK
KARNAK
MARDUK
SANJAK
YASMAK

••AK••
AWAKED
AWAKEN
AWAKES
BEAKED
BEAKER
BRAKED
BRAKES
CRAKES
DRAKES
FLAKED
FLAKER
FLAKES
KHAKIS
KRAKEN
LEAKED
PEAKED
QUAKED
QUAKER
QUAKES
SHAKEN
SHAKER
SHAKES
SHAKOS
SLAKED
SLAKES
SNAKED
SNAKES
SOAKED
SOAKER
STAKED
STAKES
WEAKEN
WEAKER
WEAKLY

••A•K•
ALASKA
ANANKE
BLACKS
BLANKS
CHALKS
CHALKY
CLACKS
CLANKS
CRACKS
CRACKY
CRANKS
CRANKY
FLACKS
FLANKS
FLASKS
FRANKS
KNACKS
PLACKS
PLANKS
PRANKS
QUACKS
QUARKS
SHACKO
SHACKS
SHANKS
SHARKS
SLACKS
SMACKS
SNACKS
SPANKS
SPARKS
STACKS
STALKS
STALKY
SWANKY
THANKS
TRACKS
WHACKS
WRACKS

••A••K
ARAWAK
CHABUK
FRANCK
PLANCK

6

•••AK•
ALFAKI
BAMAKO
BETAKE
BLEAKS
BREAKS
CLOAKS
CREAKS
CREAKY
CROAKS
CROAKY
FREAKS
FREAKY
INTAKE
KABAKA
KANAKA
KAYAKS
KODAKS
KULAKS
REMAKE
RETAKE
SNEAKS
SNEAKY
SPEAKS
SPLAKE
STEAKS
STRAKE
TWEAKS
TWEAKY
UMIAKS
UNMAKE
UPTAKE
WREAKS

•••A•K
ACKACK
ARRACK
ATTACK
BYTALK
CARACK
DAMASK
DEBARK
EMBANK
EMBARK
HIJACK
IMBARK
IMPARK
MOHAWK
NEWARK
REMARK
SHRANK
SQUAWK
THWACK
UNMASK
UNPACK

••••AK
ANORAK
ARAWAK
DVORAK
GALYAK
KALPAK
KARNAK
KODIAK
OOMIAK
SANJAK
SCREAK
SLOVAK
SQUEAK
STREAK
YASMAK

AL••••
ALAMOS
ALARIC
ALARMS
ALARUM
ALASKA
ALATED
ALBANY
ALBATA
ALBEDO
ALBEIT
ALBERT
ALBINO
ALBION
ALBITE
ALBUMS
ALCAIC
ALCOTT
ALCOVE
ALCUIN
ALDERS
ALDINE
ALDOSE
ALDOUS
ALECTO
ALEGAR
ALEPHS
ALEPPO
ALERTS
ALEUTS
ALEXIA
ALEXIN
ALEXIS
ALFAKI
ALFONS
ALFRED
ALGOID
ALIBIS
ALIBLE
ALICES
ALICIA
ALIDAD
ALIENS
ALIGHT
ALIGNS
ALINED
ALINES
ALIPED
ALISON
ALKALI
ALKANE
ALKENE
ALKYLS
ALKYNE
ALLANS
ALLAYS
ALLEGE
ALLELE
ALLENS
ALLEYS
ALLIED
ALLIES
ALLIUM
ALLOTS
ALLOUT
ALLOWS
ALLOYS
ALLUDE
ALLURE
ALLYLS
ALMAHS
ALMIRA
ALMOND
ALMOST
ALMUCE
ALMUDE
ALMUDS
ALONSO
ALONZO
ALPACA
ALPHAS
ALPHYL
ALPINE
ALSACE
ALSIKE
ALTAIC
ALTAIR
ALTARS
ALTERS
ALTHEA
ALUDEL
ALUINO
ALUINS
ALULAE
ALULAR
ALUMIN
ALUMNA
ALUMNI
ALVANS
ALVINA
ALVINE
ALWAYS

A•L•••
AALAND
AALIIS
ABLAUT
ABLAZE
ABLEST
ABLOOM
ABLUSH
ADLIBS
AFLAME
AFLCIO
AFLOAT
AGLAIA
AGLEAM
AGLETS
AILEEN
AILING
ALLANS
ALLAYS
ALLEGE
ALLELE
ALLENS
ALLEYS
ALLIED
ALLIES
ALLIUM
ALLOTS
ALLOUT
ALLOWS
ALLOYS
ALLUDE
ALLURE
ALLYLS
ANLACE
ANLAGE
APLITE
APLOMB
ARLEEN
ARLENE
ARLINE
ASLANT
ASLEEP
ASLOPE
AWLESS
AXLIKE

A••L••
ABELES
ABOLLA
ABULIA
ADDLED
ADDLES
ADOLPH
ADULTS
AEOLIA
AEOLIC
AEOLIS
AEOLUS
AFFLUX
AIGLET
AISLED
AISLES
ALULAE
ALULAR
AMBLED
AMBLER
AMBLES
AMELIA
AMELIE
AMOLES
AMULET
AMYLIC
AMYLUM
ANALOG
ANGLED
ANGLER
ANGLES
ANGLIA
ANGLIC
ANILIN
ANKLES
ANKLET
ANTLER
ANTLIA
APOLLO
APOLOG
APPLES
APULIA
ARMLET
ASHLAR
ASHLEY
ASYLUM
ATOLLS
ATTLEE
AUKLET
AVALON
AXILLA
AZALEA
AZOLES

A•••L•
ABOLLA
ABVOLT
ACIDLY
AEDILE
AFIELD
AGEDLY
AIRILY
ALIBLE
ALKALI
ALKYLS
ALLELE
ALLYLS
AMPULE
AMPULS
ANGELA
ANGELO
ANGELS
ANGOLA
ANKYLO
ANNALS
ANNULS
ANSELM
ANVILS
APOLLO
APPALL
APPALS
APPELS
APRILS
AQUILA
ARABLE
ARBELA
ARCHLY
AREOLA
ARGALI
ARGALS
ARGYLE
ARGYLL
ARIDLY
ARIELS
ARNOLD
ARTELS
ATOLLS
ATTILA
AUDILE
AVAILS
AVIDLY
AWHILE
AXILLA

A••••L
ABORAL
ACETAL
ACETYL
ACTUAL
AECIAL
AERIAL
AGNAIL
ALPHYL
ALUDEL
AMATOL
AMIDOL
AMORAL
AMYTAL
ANIMAL
ANNEAL
ANNUAL
AORTAL
APICAL
APNEAL
APODAL
APPALL
APPEAL
ARABEL
ARCHIL
ARGYLL
ARMFUL
ARTFUL
ASSAIL
ASTRAL
ATABAL
ATONAL
ATRIAL
AVOWAL
AWHIRL
AZAZEL
AZRAEL

•AL•••
AALAND
AALIIS
BALAAM
BALATA
BALBOA
BALDER
BALDLY
BALEEN
BALERS
BALING
BALKAN
BALKED
BALLAD
BALLED
BALLET
BALLOT
BALSAM
BALSAS
BALTIC
BALZAC

6

CALAIS
CALASH
CALCAR
CALCES
CALCIC
CALEBS
CALESA
CALICO
CALIFS
CALIPH
CALKED
CALKER
CALLAO
CALLAS
CALLED
CALLER
CALLOW
CALLUS
CALMED
CALMER
CALMLY
CALORY
CALPAC
CALVED
CALVES
CALVIN
CALXES
DALETH
DALLAS
DALLES
DALTON
EALING
FALCON
FALLAL
FALLEN
FALLER
FALLOW
FALSER
FALTER
GALACT
GALAXY
GALEAE
GALENA
GALIOT
GALLED
GALLEY
GALLIC
GALLON
GALLOP
GALLUP
GALLUS
GALOOT
GALOPS
GALORE
GALOSH
GALWAY
GALYAK
HALERS
HALIDE
HALIDS
HALING
HALITE
HALLAH
HALLEL
HALLEY
HALLOO
HALLOW
HALLUX
HALOES
HALOID
HALSEY
HALTED
HALTER
HALUTZ
HALVED
HALVES
JALAPS
JALOPY
KALIAN
KALIUM
KALMIA
KALONG
KALPAK
LALLED
MALACO
MALADY
MALAGA
MALATE
MALAWI
MALAYA
MALAYS
MALGRE
MALICE
MALIGN
MALINE
MALLED
MALLEE
MALLET
MALLOW
MALORY
MALTED
MALTHA
PALACE
PALAEO
PALATE
PALEAE
PALELY
PALEST
PALING
PALISH
PALLAS
PALLED
PALLET
PALLID
PALLOR
PALMAR
PALMED
PALMER
PALPUS
PALTER
PALTRY
RALPHS
SALAAM
SALADS
SALAMI
SALARY
SALIFY
SALINE
SALISH
SALIVA
SALLET
SALLOW
SALLYS
SALMIS
SALMON
SALOME
SALONS
SALOON
SALOOP
SALPAS
SALPID
SALTED
SALTER
SALUKI
SALUTE
SALVED
SALVER
SALVES
SALVIA
SALVOR
SALVOS
TALCED
TALCUM
TALENT
TALERS
TALION
TALKED
TALKER
TALLER
TALLOW
TALMUD
TALONS
VALERY
VALETS
VALGUS
VALISE
VALKYR
VALLEY
VALOIS
VALUED
VALUES
VALVAL
VALVAR
VALVED
VALVES
WALDOS
WALERS
WALING
WALKED
WALKER
WALKON
WALKUP
WALLAH
WALLAS
WALLED
WALLET
WALLIE
WALLIS
WALLOP
WALLOW
WALLYS
WALNUT
WALRUS
WALTER
WALTON
WALVIS

•A•L••

BAALIM
BAILED
BAILEE
BAILER
BAILEY
BAILIE
BAILOR
BALLAD
BALLED
BALLET
BALLOT
BARLEY
BAWLED
BAWLER
CABLED
CABLES
CABLET
CALLAO
CALLAS
CALLED
CALLER
CALLOW
CALLUS
CAMLET
CAPLIN
CARLAS
CARLOS
CATLIN
CAULES
CAULIS
CAULKS
DAHLIA
DALLAS
DALLES
EAGLES
EAGLET
EARLAP
EARLES
FABLED
FABLER
FABLES
FAILED
FAILLE
FALLAL
FALLEN
FALLER
FALLOW
FARLES
FARLEY
FAULTS
FAULTY
GABLED
GABLES
GAELIC
GALLED
GALLEY
GALLIC
GALLON
GALLOP
GALLUP
GALLUS
GAOLER
GARLIC
HAILED
HAILER
HALLAH
HALLEL
HALLEY
HALLOO
HALLOW
HALLUX
HAMLET
HARLAN
HARLEM
HARLEY
HARLOT
HASLET
HAULED
HAULER
HAULMY
JAILED
JAILER
JAILOR
KAOLIN
LADLED
LADLER
LADLES
LALLED
MACLES
MAHLER
MAILED
MAILER
MALLED
MALLEE
MALLET
MALLOW
MAPLES
MARLED
MARLIN
MAULED
MAULER
NAILED
NAPLES
OAKLEY
PALLAS
PALLED
PALLET
PALLID
PALLOR
PARLAY
PARLEY
PARLOR
PAULAS
PAULIN
PAULUS
PAVLOV
RAGLAN
RAILED
RATLIN
SABLES
SAILED
SAILER
SAILOR
SALLET
SALLOW
SALLYS
SAMLET
SAULTS
TABLED
TABLES
TABLET
TAILED
TAILLE
TAILOR
TALLER
TALLOW
TATLER
TAYLOR
VALLEY
VARLET
VAULTS
WAILED
WAILER
WALLAH
WALLAS
WALLED
WALLET
WALLIE
WALLIS
WALLOP
WALLOW
WALLYS
WAULED
WAWLED
WAYLAY
YAWLED

•A••L•

BABBLE
BABULS
BAFFLE
BAGELS
BALDLY
BANGLE
BARELY
BARFLY
BASALT
BASELY
BASILS
BATTLE
BAUBLE
CABALA
CABALS
CACKLE
CAGILY
CAJOLE
CALMLY
CAMELS
CAMILA
CANALS
CANDLE
CANTLE
CANULA
CAROLE
CAROLS
CASALS

CASTLE
CATALO
CATTLE
CAUDLE
CAVELL
CAVILS
DABBLE
DADDLE
DAFTLY
DAMPLY
DANDLE
DANGLE
DANKLY
DAPPLE
DARKLE
DARKLY
DARTLE
DAWDLE
DAYFLY
DAZZLE
EASELS
EASILY
FACILE
FACULA
FAILLE
FAIRLY
FAMILY
GABBLE
GADFLY
GAGGLE
GAINLY
GAMBLE
GAMELY
GAMILY
GANGLI
GARBLE
GARGLE
GAVELS
HABILE
HACKLE
HAGGLE
HAMALS
HANDLE
HARDLY
HAROLD
HASSLE
HAZELS
HAZILY
JANGLE
KAMALA
LABELS
LABILE
LACILY
LAMELY
LANKLY
LAPELS
LASTLY
LATELY
LAZILY
LAZULI
MABELS
MACKLE
MACULA
MACULE
MAINLY
MANGLE
MANILA
MANTLE
MARBLE
MAZILY
NAMELY
NAPALM
NASALS
NAVELS
PADDLE
PALELY
PAMELA
PANELS
PAPULA
PAPULE
PAROLE
PARTLY
PAYOLA
RABBLE
RACILY
RADDLE
RADULA
RAFFLE
RAMBLE
RANKLE
RANKLY
RAOULS
RARELY
RASHLY
RATALS
RATELS
RATTLE
RATTLY
RAVELS
SADDLE
SAFELY
SAGELY
SAMPLE
SANELY
SAWFLY
TACKLE
TAILLE
TAMALE
TANGLE
TANGLY
TAPALO
TARTLY
TATTLE
TAUTLY
VAINLY
VASILI
VASTLY
WABBLE
WABBLY
WADDLE
WADDLY
WAFFLE
WAGGLE
WAGGLY
WAMBLE
WAMBLY
WANDLE
WANGLE
WARBLE
WARILY
WARMLY
WATTLE
WAVILY

•A•••L

BAIKAL
BARBEL
BARREL
CANCEL
CANNEL
CARCEL
CARMEL
CARNAL
CARPAL
CARPEL
CARREL
CARTEL
CARVEL
CASUAL
CAUDAL
CAUSAL
CAVELL
DACTYL
DAEDAL
DAMSEL
DANIEL
DARNEL
EARFUL
FACIAL
FALLAL
FAUCAL
FAUNAL
GAMBOL
GAVIAL
HALLEL
HAMAUL
HAMMAL
HANDEL
HANSEL
HARTAL
HASSEL
HATFUL
JACKAL
JARFUL
LABIAL
LAPFUL
LARVAL
LAUREL
LAWFUL
MAMMAL
MANFUL
MANTEL
MANUAL
MANUEL
MARCEL
MARVEL
NARIAL
NARWAL
NASIAL
PARCEL
PARRAL
PARREL
PASCAL
PASTEL
PASTIL
PATHOL
PATROL
RACHEL
RACIAL
RADIAL
RANDAL
RAPPEL
RASCAL
SACRAL
SAMIEL
SAMUEL
SANDAL
SANTOL
SAUREL
TARNAL
TARSAL
TASSEL
VALVAL
VANDAL
VASSAL
VATFUL

••AL••

ANALOG
AVALON
AZALEA
BAALIM
BIALYS
CHALCO
CHALEH
CHALET
CHALKS
CHALKY
COALED
COALER
DEALER
DIALED
DIALER
DIALOG
DOALLS
EXALTS
FEALTY
FOALED
GOALIE
HEALED
HEALER
HEALTH
ICALLY
ITALIC
KOALAS
MEALIE
ORALLY
OVALLY
OXALIC
OXALIS
PEALED
PSALMS
QUALMS
QUALMY
REALES
REALLY
REALMS
REALTY
RIALTO
ROALDS
SCALAR
SCALDS
SCALED
SCALER
SCALES
SCALPS
SEALED
SEALER
SHALED
SHALES
SIALIC
SKALDS
SLALOM
SMALLS
SMALTI
SMALTO
SPALLS
STALAG
STALED
STALER
STALES
STALIN
STALKS
STALKY
STALLS
SWALES
THALES
THALIA
URALIC
VIALED
WEALDS
WEALTH
WHALED
WHALER
WHALES
WOALDS
ZEALOT

••A•L•

ARABLE
AVAILS
BEADLE
BEAGLE
BRAILS
BRAWLS
CRAALS
CRADLE
CRAWLS
CRAWLY
DEADLY
DEAFLY
DEARLY
DOABLE
DOALLS
DRABLY
DRAWLS
DRAWLY
ENABLE
FLAILS
FLATLY
FRAILS
GLADLY
GNARLS
GNARLY
GRAYLY
ICALLY
KRAALS
LEANLY
LIABLE
MEANLY
MEASLY
MIAULS
NEARLY
NEATLY
ORACLE
ORALLY
OVALLY
PEARLS
PEARLY
QUAILS
REALLY
SHAWLS
SMALLS
SNAILS
SNARLS
SNARLY
SPALLS
STABLE
STALLS
STAPLE
SUABLE
SWAILS
TRAILS
TRAWLS
UNABLE
USABLE
USABLY
VIABLE
WEAKLY
YEARLY

••A••L

AMATOL
ARABEL
ATABAL
AZAZEL
BIAXAL
BRAZIL
CHAPEL
COAXAL
ENAMEL
GRAVEL
ISABEL
PLAGAL
STATAL
TEASEL
TRAVEL
URANYL
WEASEL

•••AL•

ALKALI
ANNALS
APPALL

APPALS
ARGALI
ARGALS
BASALT
BECALM
BEFALL
BEHALF
BUBALS
BYTALK
CABALA
CABALS
CANALS
CASALS
CATALO
CICALA
COBALT
COPALM
CORALS
CRAALS
DECALS
DESALT
DONALD
EMBALM
EMPALE
ENDALL
EQUALS
EXHALE
FEMALE
FINALE
FINALS
GERALD
GORALS
HAMALS
HERALD
IDEALS
IMBALM
IMPALA
IMPALE
INHALE
INWALL
KAMALA
KERALA
KRAALS
LOCALE
LOCALS
MEDALS
MEGALO
METALS
MORALE
MORALS
MURALS
NAPALM
NASALS
NOBALL
NOPALS
OSWALD
PEDALS
PETALS
PHIALS
RATALS
RECALL
REGALE
RESALE
RIBALD
RIVALS
RIYALS
ROBALO
RONALD
ROYALS
SEPALS
SEWALL
SHOALS
SHOALY
SQUALL
STEALS
TAMALE
TAPALO
THRALL
TICALS
TOTALS
TRIALS
TYBALT
VITALS
VOCALS
WHEALS

•••A•L

AGNAIL
APPALL
ASSAIL
AZRAEL
BEFALL
BEWAIL
DERAIL
DETAIL
ENDALL
ENTAIL
HAMAUL
INHAUL
INWALL
ISRAEL
JEZAIL
NOBALL
OXTAIL
RECALL
RETAIL
SCRAWL
SEWALL
SPRAWL
SQUALL
THRALL

••••AL

ABORAL
ACETAL
ACTUAL
AECIAL
AERIAL
AMORAL
AMYTAL
ANIMAL
ANNEAL
ANNUAL
AORTAL
APICAL
APNEAL
APODAL
APPEAL
ASTRAL
ATABAL
ATONAL
ATRIAL
AVOWAL
BAIKAL
BELIAL
BENGAL
BIAXAL
BOREAL
BRIDAL
BROMAL
BRUMAL
BRUTAL
BUCCAL
BURIAL
BURSAL
CARNAL
CARPAL
CASUAL
CAUDAL
CAUSAL
CENTAL
CEREAL
CHORAL
CITRAL
COAXAL
COCCAL
COEVAL
CORRAL
COSTAL
CRURAL
CUNEAL
CURIAL
CYMBAL
DAEDAL
DENIAL
DENTAL
DERMAL
DISMAL
DISTAL
DORSAL
DOSSAL
EPICAL
ESPIAL
FACIAL
FALLAL
FAUCAL
FAUNAL
FECIAL
FERIAL
FESTAL
FETIAL
FEUDAL
FILIAL
FINIAL
FISCAL
FLORAL
FOETAL
FONTAL
FORMAL
FOVEAL
FRUGAL
FUNGAL
GAVIAL
GENIAL
GINGAL
GLOBAL
GOORAL
HAMMAL
HARTAL
HEDRAL
HERBAL
HIEMAL
HYETAL
HYMNAL
HYPHAL
JACKAL
JINGAL
JOVIAL
LABIAL
LARVAL
LETHAL
LINEAL
LUTEAL
MAMMAL
MANUAL
MEDIAL
MENIAL
MENSAL
MENTAL
MESCAL
MESIAL
MISKAL
MISSAL
MITRAL
MORTAL
MUTUAL
NARIAL
NARWAL
NASIAL
NEURAL
NORMAL
NOUNAL
ORDEAL
OSTEAL
PARRAL
PASCAL
PENIAL
PENPAL
PINEAL
PINNAL
PLAGAL
PLURAL
PORTAL
POSTAL
PRIMAL
RACIAL
RADIAL
RANDAL
RASCAL
RECTAL
REGNAL
RENTAL
REVEAL
RHINAL
RICTAL
RITUAL
SACRAL
SANDAL
SENDAL
SEPTAL
SERIAL
SERVAL
SEXUAL
SIGNAL
SOCIAL
SPINAL
SPIRAL
SPITAL
SQUEAL
STATAL
TARNAL
TARSAL
TERGAL
THECAL
THENAL
TIBIAL
TIMBAL
TINCAL
TRIBAL
TRINAL
TROPAL
TUSSAL
UNCIAL
UNGUAL
UNREAL
UNSEAL
URINAL
VALVAL
VANDAL
VASSAL
VENIAL
VERBAL
VERNAL
VESTAL
VISUAL
VULVAL
WITHAL
ZOONAL

AM••••

AMADOU
AMANDA
AMATOL
AMAZED
AMAZES
AMAZON
AMBAGE
AMBARI
AMBARY
AMBERS
AMBERY
AMBITS
AMBLED
AMBLER
AMBLES
AMBUSH
AMEBAE
AMEBAS
AMEBIC
AMELIA
AMELIE
AMENDS
AMENRA
AMENTS
AMERCE
AMICES
AMIDES
AMIDIC
AMIDIN
AMIDOL
AMIDST
AMIENS
AMIGOS
AMNION
AMOEBA
AMOLES
AMORAL
AMOUNT
AMOURS
AMPERE
AMPHRS
AMPULE
AMPULS
AMRITA
AMULET
AMUSED
AMUSER
AMUSES
AMYLIC
AMYLUM
AMYTAL

A•M•••

ADMIRE
ADMITS
ADMIXT
AIMING
ALMAHS
ALMIRA
ALMOND
ALMOST
ALMUCE
ALMUDE
ALMUDS
ARMADA
ARMAGH
ARMAND
ARMETS
ARMFUL
ARMIES
ARMING
ARMLET
ARMORS
ARMORY
ARMPIT
ARMURE
AYMARA

A••M••

ABOMAS
ABOMBS
ACUMEN
AGAMAS
AGAMIC

AHIMSA
AIDMAN
AIDMEN
AIRMAN
AIRMEN
AKIMBO
ALAMOS
ALUMIN
ALUMNA
ALUMNI
ANEMIA
ANEMIC
ANIMAL
ANIMAS
ANIMUS
ANOMIC
ANOMIE
AROMAS
ASHMAN
ASHMEN
ATAMAN
ATOMIC
AXEMAN
AXEMEN

A•••M•
ABOHMS
ABRAMS
ABYSMS
ADDAMS
ADEEMS
AFLAME
AFRAME
ALARMS
ALBUMS
APLOMB
ASSUME
ASTHMA
ATHOME
AUTUMN
AXIOMS

A••••M
ABLOOM
ACETUM
ACTIUM
ADYTUM
AECIUM
AFFIRM
AGLEAM
ALARUM
ALLIUM
AMYLUM
ANADEM
ANONYM
ANSELM
ANTHEM
ANTRIM
ANTRUM
ASARUM
ASYLUM
ATRIUM
AUTISM

•AM•••
BAMAKO
BAMBOO
CAMASS
CAMBER
CAMDEN
CAMELS
CAMEOS
CAMERA
CAMILA
CAMION
CAMISE
CAMLET
CAMPED
CAMPER
CAMPOS
CAMPUS
DAMAGE
DAMANS
DAMASK
DAMMAR
DAMMED
DAMMER
DAMNED
DAMPED
DAMPEN
DAMPER
DAMPLY
DAMSEL
DAMSON
FAMILY
FAMINE
FAMISH
FAMOUS
GAMBIA
GAMBIR
GAMBIT
GAMBLE
GAMBOL
GAMELY
GAMETE
GAMETO
GAMIER
GAMILY
GAMING
GAMINS
GAMMAS
GAMMER
GAMMON
GAMOUS
GAMUTS
HAMALS
HAMAUL
HAMDEN
HAMITE
HAMLET
HAMMAL
HAMMED
HAMMER
HAMPER
HAMZAS
IAMBIC
IAMBUS
JAMIES

JAMMED
KAMALA
KAMIKS
KAMSIN
LAMBDA
LAMBED
LAMBIE
LAMEDS
LAMELY
LAMENT
LAMEST
LAMIAE
LAMIAS
LAMINA
LAMING
LAMMAS
LAMMED
LAMPAD
LAMPAS
LAMPED
MAMBAS
MAMBOS
MAMEYS
MAMIES
MAMMAE
MAMMAL
MAMMAS
MAMMET
MAMMON
NAMELY
NAMERS
NAMING
PAMELA
PAMPAS
PAMPER
RAMBLE
RAMIES
RAMIFY
RAMMED
RAMMER
RAMONA
RAMOSE
RAMOUS
RAMPED
RAMROD
RAMSON
SAMARA
SAMBAS
SAMBOS
SAMBUR
SAMIAN
SAMIEL
SAMITE
SAMLET
SAMMYS
SAMOAN
SAMPAN
SAMPLE
SAMSHU
SAMSON
SAMUEL
TAMALE
TAMBAC
TAMERS

TAMEST
TAMING
TAMPAN
TAMPED
TAMPER
TAMPON
TAMTAM
VAMPED
WAMBLE
WAMBLY
WAMMUS
WAMPUM
WAMPUS
YAMENS
YAMMER
YAMUNS
ZAMBIA
ZAMIAS

•A•M••
BADMAN
BADMEN
BAGMAN
BAGMEN
BARMAN
BARMEN
BARMIE
BATMAN
BATMEN
CABMAN
CABMEN
CADMUS
CAIMAN
CALMED
CALMER
CALMLY
CARMAN
CARMEL
CARMEN
CAYMAN
DAEMON
DAGMAR
DAIMIO
DAIMON
DAIMYO
DAMMAR
DAMMED
DAMMER
FARMED
FARMER
GAMMAS
GAMMER
GAMMON
GASMAN
GASMEN
HAMMAL
HAMMED
HAMMER
HARMED
HARMIN
HAYMOW
JAMMED
KALMIA
KARMAS

LAMMAS
LAMMED
LAYMAN
LAYMEN
MADMAN
MADMEN
MAIMED
MAIMER
MAMMAE
MAMMAL
MAMMAS
MAMMET
MAMMON
MARMOT
MAUMAU
NAOMIS
PALMAR
PALMED
PALMER
RAGMAN
RAGMEN
RAMMED
RAMMER
SALMIS
SALMON
SAMMYS
TALMUD
TARMAC
TASMAN
VANMAN
VANMEN
WAMMUS
WARMED
WARMER
WARMLY
WARMTH
WARMUP
YAMMER
YASMAK

•A••M•
BAHAMA
CAEOMA
CAROMS
FANUMS
FATIMA
HAKIMS
HAREMS
HAULMY
MADAME
MADAMS
MAXIMS
MAZUMA
NAHUMS
PAJAMA
PANAMA
RACEME
RADOME
SALAMI
SALOME
TACOMA
TAXEME
YAKIMA

•A•••M
BAALIM
BABISM
BALAAM
BALSAM
BANTAM
BARIUM
BARNUM
CAECUM
FANTOM
FATHOM
HANSOM
HARLEM
KALIUM
LABIUM
LABRUM
LACTAM
MAGNUM
MAOISM
MAYHEM
NANISM
NAPALM
NAZISM
PASSIM
RACISM
RADIUM
RANDOM
RANSOM
SACHEM
SACRUM
SADISM
SALAAM
TALCUM
TAMTAM
TANDEM
TAOISM
VACUUM
WAMPUM

••AM••
AGAMAS
AGAMIC
ALAMOS
ATAMAN
BEAMED
BLAMED
BLAMES
CHAMMY
CHAMPS
CLAMMY
CLAMOR
CLAMPS
CRAMBO
CRAMPS
DRAMAS
ENAMEL
ENAMOR
EXAMEN
FLAMBE
FLAMED
FLAMEN
FLAMES
FOAMED
FRAMED

6

FRAMER
FRAMES
LLAMAS
LOAMED
REAMED
REAMER
ROAMED
ROAMER
SCAMPI
SCAMPS
SEAMAN
SEAMED
SEAMEN
SEAMER
SEAMUS
SHAMAN
SHAMED
SHAMES
SHAMMY
SHAMUS
STAMEN
STAMIN
STAMPS
SWAMIS
SWAMPS
SWAMPY
TEAMED
THAMES
TRAMPS
WHAMMY

••A•M•

ALARMS
BRAHMA
BRAHMS
CHACMA
CHAMMY
CHARMS
CHASMS
CLAIMS
CLAMMY
DHARMA
HEAUME
INARMS
MIASMA
PLASMA
PLASMO
PSALMS
QUALMS
QUALMY
REALMS
REARMS
SHAMMY
SHAWMS
SMARMY
SPASMS
SWARMS
TRAUMA
WHAMMY

••A••M

ALARUM
ANADEM
ASARUM
BAALIM
DIADEM
DIATOM
DRACHM
GRAHAM
OMASUM
SLALOM

•••AM•

ABRAMS
ADDAMS
AFLAME
AFRAME
BAHAMA
BECAME
BIGAMY
BREAMS
BYNAME
CREAMS
CREAMY
DECAMP
DEFAME
DEGAME
DIGAMY
DREAMS
DREAMT
DREAMY
DYNAMO
ENCAMP
FLEAMS
GLEAMS
GLEAMY
GOTAMA
HBEAMS
HIRAMS
IBEAMS
IHRAMS
INFAMY
JORAMS
MADAME
MADAMS
PAJAMA
PANAMA
REVAMP
SALAMI
SCRAMS
SESAME
SQUAMA
STEAMS
STEAMY
ZBEAMS

•••A•M

BALAAM
BECALM
CHIASM
COPALM
DISARM
EMBALM
IMBALM
NAPALM
ORGASM
SALAAM

••••AM

AGLEAM
BALAAM
BALSAM
BANTAM
BEDLAM
BELDAM
DIRHAM
DURHAM
ENGRAM
GOTHAM
GRAHAM
JETSAM
LACTAM
LOGJAM
MIRIAM
PUTNAM
SALAAM
SCREAM
STREAM
TAMTAM
UNSEAM
WIGWAM

AN••••

ANABAS
ANADEM
ANALOG
ANANKE
ANATTO
ANCHOR
ANCONA
ANCONE
ANDEAN
ANDREA
ANDREI
ANDRES
ANDREW
ANEMIA
ANEMIC
ANERGY
ANGARY
ANGELA
ANGELO
ANGELS
ANGERS
ANGINA
ANGKOR
ANGLED
ANGLER
ANGLES
ANGLIA
ANGLIC
ANGOLA
ANGORA
ANILIN
ANIMAL
ANIMAS
ANIMUS
ANIONS
ANISES
ANITAS
ANITRA
ANKARA
ANKLES
ANKLET
ANKYLO
ANLACE
ANLAGE
ANNALS
ANNEAL
ANNIES
ANNOYS
ANNUAL
ANNULS
ANODES
ANODIC
ANOINT
ANOMIC
ANOMIE
ANONYM
ANORAK
ANOXIA
ANOXIC
ANSATE
ANSELM
ANSWER
ANTEED
ANTERO
ANTHEA
ANTHEM
ANTHER
ANTIAR
ANTICS
ANTLER
ANTLIA
ANTONS
ANTONY
ANTRIM
ANTRUM
ANUBIS
ANURAN
ANUSES
ANVILS
ANYHOW
ANYONE
ANYWAY

A•N•••

ABNERS
ACNODE
ADNATE
ADNOUN
AENEAS
AENEID
AGNAIL
AGNATE
AMNION
ANNALS
ANNEAL
ANNIES
ANNOYS
ANNUAL
ANNULS
APNEAL
APNEIC
APNOEA
ARNAUD
ARNICA
ARNIES
ARNOLD
AUNTIE
AWNING

A••N••

ACINUS
ADENIS
ADONAI
ADONIC
ADONIS
AGENCY
AGENDA
AGENTS
AGONES
AGONIC
AKENES
ALINED
ALINES
ALONSO
ALONZO
AMANDA
AMENDS
AMENRA
AMENTS
ANANKE
ANONYM
ARANTA
ARENAS
ARUNTA
ATONAL
ATONED
ATONER
ATONES
ATONIC
AVENGE
AVENUE
AXONES
AZINES
AZONIC

A•••N•

AALAND
AARONS
ABOUND
ABSENT
ACCENT
ACHENE
ACHING
ACORNS
ACTING
ACTINI
ACTINO
ADDEND
ADDING
ADORNS
ADVENT
AGEING
AIDING
AILING
AIMING
AIRING
ALBANY
ALBINO
ALDINE
ALFONS
ALIENS
ALIGNS
ALKANE
ALKENE
ALKYNE
ALLANS
ALLENS
ALMOND
ALPINE
ALUINO
ALUINS
ALUMNA
ALUMNI
ALVANS
ALVINA
ALVINE
AMIENS
AMOUNT
ANCONA
ANCONE
ANGINA
ANIONS
ANOINT
ANTONS
ANTONY
ANYONE
APPEND
APRONS
ARCANE
ARCING
ARDENT
ARGENT
ARIANS
ARLENE
ARLINE
ARMAND
ARMING
AROUND
ARPENS
ARPENT
ARRANT
ARSINE
ARYANS
ASCEND
ASCENT
ASIANS
ASKANT
ASKING
ASLANT
ASPENS
ASSENT
ATHENA
ATHENE
ATHENS
ATTEND
ATTUNE
AUGEND
AUXINS
AVERNO
AWEING
AWNING

A••••N
AACHEN
ACTION
ACUMEN
ADJOIN
ADNOUN
ADRIAN
ADRIEN
AEGEAN
AFGHAN
AIDMAN
AIDMEN
AILEEN
AIRMAN
AIRMEN
AJOWAN
ALBION
ALCUIN
ALEXIN
ALISON
ALUMIN
AMAZON
AMIDIN
AMNION
ANDEAN
ANILIN
ANURAN
APPIAN
ARAGON
ARCHON
ARISEN
ARLEEN
ASHMAN
ASHMEN
ASSIGN
ASTERN
ATAMAN
ATTAIN
ATTORN
AUBURN
AUGEAN
AUSTEN
AUSTIN
AUTUMN
AVALON
AVIDIN
AWAKEN
AXEMAN
AXEMEN

•AN•••
BANANA
BANDED
BANDIT
BANGED
BANGLE
BANGOR
BANGUI
BANGUP
BANIAN
BANISH
BANJOS
BANKED
BANKER
BANNED
BANNER
BANTAM
BANTER
BANTUS
BANYAN
BANZAI
CANAAN
CANADA
CANALS
CANAPE
CANARD
CANARY
CANCAN
CANCEL
CANCER
CANDID
CANDLE
CANDOR
CANERS
CANGUE
CANINE
CANING
CANKER
CANNAE
CANNAS
CANNED
CANNEL
CANNER
CANNES
CANNIE
CANNON
CANNOT
CANOED
CANOES
CANONS
CANOPY
CANSOS
CANTED
CANTER
CANTHI
CANTLE
CANTON
CANTOR
CANTOS
CANTUS
CANUCK
CANULA
CANUTE
CANVAS
CANYON
DANAID
DANAUS
DANCED
DANCER
DANCES
DANDER
DANDLE
DANGED
DANGER
DANGLE
DANIEL
DANISH
DANITE
DANKER
DANKLY
DANNYS
DANTON
DANUBE
DANZIG
FANEGA
FANGAS
FANGED
FANION
FANJET
FANNED
FANNER
FANNIE
FANNYS
FANONS
FANTAN
FANTOM
FANUMS
GANDER
GANDHI
GANEFS
GANGED
GANGER
GANGES
GANGLI
GANGUE
GANNET
GANOID
GANTRY
HANCES
HANDED
HANDEL
HANDLE
HANGAR
HANGED
HANGER
HANGUP
HANKER
HANNAH
HANNAS
HANSEL
HANSOM
JANETS
JANGLE
JANICE
KANAKA
KANSAN
KANSAS
LANAIS
LANATE
LANCED
LANCER
LANCES
LANCET
LANDAU
LANDED
LANDER
LANGUR
LANKER
LANKLY
LANNER
LANOSE
LANUGO
MANAGE
MANANA
MANCHU
MANDAN
MANDYS
MANEGE
MANFUL
MANGER
MANGLE
MANGOS
MANIAC
MANIAS
MANILA
MANIOC
MANITO
MANITU
MANNED
MANNER
MANORS
MANQUE
MANSES
MANTAS
MANTEL
MANTES
MANTIC
MANTIS
MANTLE
MANTUA
MANUAL
MANUEL
MANURE
NANCYS
NANISM
NANTES
PANADA
PANAMA
PANDAS
PANDER
PANELS
PANICE
PANICS
PANNED
PANSYS
PANTED
PANTIE
PANTRY
PANZER
RANCHO
RANCID
RANCOR
RANDAL
RANDAN
RANDOM
RANEES
RANGED
RANGER
RANGES
RANKED
RANKER
RANKLE
RANKLY
RANSOM
RANTED
RANTER
SANDAL
SANDED
SANDER
SANDHI
SANDRA
SANDYS
SANELY
SANEST
SANGAR
SANGER
SANGUI
SANIES
SANITY
SANJAK
SANNUP
SANSAR
SANSEI
SANTOL
TANDEM
TANGED
TANGLE
TANGLY
TANGOS
TANIST
TANKAS
TANKED
TANKER
TANNED
TANNER
TANNIC
TANNIN
TANREC
VANDAL
VANISH
VANITY
VANMAN
VANMEN
WANDAS
WANDER
WANDLE
WANGLE
WANING
WANION
WANNED
WANNER
WANTED
WANTER
WANTON
XANTHO
YANKED
YANKEE
ZANANA
ZANIER
ZANIES

•A•N••
BAGNIO
BANNED
BANNER
BARNEY
BARNUM
CANNAE
CANNAS
CANNED
CANNEL
CANNER
CANNES
CANNIE
CANNON
CANNOT
CARNAL
CATNIP
DAINTY
DAMNED
DANNYS
DARNED
DARNEL
DAUNTS
DAWNED
EARNED
EARNER
FAFNIR
FAINTS
FANNED
FANNER
FANNIE
FANNYS
FAUNAE
FAUNAL
FAUNAS
FAUNUS
FAWNED
FAWNER
GAINED
GAINER
GAINLY
GANNET
GARNER
GARNET
HANNAH
HANNAS
HAUNCH
HAUNTS
JAINAS
JAUNTS
JAUNTY
KARNAK
LANNER
LAUNCE
LAUNCH
MAENAD
MAGNET
MAGNUM
MAINLY
MANNED
MANNER
MAUNDS
MAUNDY
PAINED
PAINTS
PAINTY
PANNED
PAUNCH
PAWNED
PAWNEE
PAWNER
RAINED
SAINTS

SANNUP
SAUNAS
TAENIA
TAINOS
TAINTS
TANNED
TANNER
TANNIC
TANNIN
TARNAL
TAUNTS
VAINER
VAINLY
VAUNTS
WAGNER
WALNUT
WANNED
WANNER
WARNED
WARNER
WAYNES
YAWNED
YAWNER

•A••N•

AALAND
AARONS
BAAING
BAIRNS
BAKING
BALING
BANANA
BARING
BARONG
BARONS
BARONY
BASING
BASINS
BATING
BATONS
BAYING
CABANA
CABINS
CADENT
CAGING
CAIRNS
CAJUNS
CAKING
CANINE
CANING
CANONS
CAPONS
CARINA
CARING
CASING
CASINO
CATENA
CAVING
CAWING
DAMANS
DAPHNE
DARING
DATING
DAZING
EALING
EARING
EASING
EATING
FACING
FADING
FAKING
FAMINE
FANONS
FARINA
FARING
FATING
FAXING
FAYING
FAZING
GAGING
GALENA
GAMING
GAMINS
GAPING
GATING
GAZING
HADING
HALING
HATING
HAVANA
HAVENS
HAVENT
HAVING
HAWING
HAYING
HAZING
JACANA
JADING
JAPANS
JARINA
JASONS
JAWING
KALONG
KARENS
LACING
LACUNA
LADING
LADINO
LAGUNE
LAKING
LAMENT
LAMINA
LAMING
LAPINS
LARINE
LARYNG
LARYNX
LATENT
LATINS
LAVING
LAWING
LAYING
LAZING
MACING
MAKING
MALINE
MANANA
MARINA
MARINE
MASONS
MATING
MATINS
MAXINE
MAYING
MAZING
NADINE
NAGANA
NAMING
NARINE
NATANT
OARING
PACING
PAEANS
PAEONS
PAGANS
PAGING
PALING
PARANG
PARENS
PARENT
PARING
PATENS
PATENT
PATINA
PATINE
PAVANS
PAVING
PAWING
PAYING
RACINE
RACING
RAGING
RAKING
RAMONA
RAPINE
RAPING
RARING
RATINE
RATING
RAVENS
RAVINE
RAVING
RAYING
RAYONS
RAZING
SABINA
SABINE
SABINS
SALINE
SALONS
SARONG
SASINS
SATANG
SATING
SATINS
SATINY
SAVANT
SAVING
SAVINS
SAWING
SAXONS
SAXONY
SAYING
TAKING
TALENT
TALONS
TAMING
TAPING
TARING
TAWING
TAXING
VACANT
VAGINA
VAGINO
VARUNA
WADING
WAGING
WAGONS
WAHINE
WAKENS
WAKING
WALING
WANING
WAVING
WAXING
YAMENS
YAMUNS
YAPONS
YAWING
ZANANA
ZAYINS

•A•••N

AACHEN
BABOON
BADMAN
BADMEN
BAFFIN
BAGMAN
BAGMEN
BALEEN
BALKAN
BANIAN
BANYAN
BARMAN
BARMEN
BARREN
BARTON
BARYON
BASION
BATAAN
BATMAN
BATMEN
BATTEN
CABMAN
CABMEN
CAFTAN
CAIMAN
CALVIN
CAMDEN
CAMION
CANAAN
CANCAN
CANNON
CANTON
CANYON
CAPLIN
CARBON
CAREEN
CARMAN
CARMEN
CARSON
CARTON
CARVEN
CASEIN
CASERN
CATION
CATKIN
CATLIN
CAVEIN
CAVERN
CAYMAN
DACRON
DAEMON
DAHOON
DAIMON
DALTON
DAMPEN
DAMSON
DANTON
DARDAN
DARIEN
DARKEN
DARWIN
DAWSON
DAYTON
EASTON
FABIAN
FADEIN
FALCON
FALLEN
FANION
FANTAN
FASTEN
FATTEN
GABION
GALLON
GAMMON
GARCON
GARDEN
GASCON
GASKIN
GASMAN
GASMEN
GASTON
GAWAIN
HAGDON
HAMDEN
HAPPEN
HARBIN
HARDEN
HARKEN
HARLAN
HARMIN
HASTEN
HATPIN
HAUSEN
HAZZAN
JARGON
KALIAN
KAMSIN
KANSAN
KAOLIN
KATION
LAGOON
LARDON
LATEEN
LATTEN
LAYMAN
LAYMEN
MACRON
MADDEN
MADMAN
MADMEN
MAIDEN
MAISON
MALIGN
MAMMON
MANDAN
MARGIN
MARIAN
MARION
MARLIN
MAROON
MARTEN
MARTIN
MARVIN
MASCON
MATRON
NAPKIN
NASION
NATHAN
NATION
NATRON
PAPAIN
PAPUAN
PARDON
PARIAN
PARSON
PATHAN
PATRON
PATTEN
PATTON
PAULIN
RACOON
RADIAN
RAGLAN
RAGMAN
RAGMEN
RAISIN
RAMSON
RANDAN
RATION
RATLIN
RATOON
RATTAN
RATTEN
SABEAN
SADDEN
SAIGON
SAIPAN
SALMON
SALOON
SAMIAN

6

SAMOAN
SAMPAN
SAMSON
SARGON
SATEEN
SATURN
TAIWAN
TAKEIN
TALION
TAMPAN
TAMPON
TANNIN
TARPON
TARTAN
TARZAN
TASMAN
TAUTEN
TAVERN
VANMAN
VANMEN
WAGGON
WALKON
WALTON
WANION
WANTON
WARDEN
WARREN
WATSON
YAUPON

••AN••

AMANDA
ANANKE
ARANTA
BEANED
BEANIE
BIANCA
BLANCH
BLANKS
BRANCH
BRANDS
BRANDY
BRANNY
BRANTS
BWANAS
CHANCE
CHANCY
CHANGE
CHANGS
CHANTS
CHANTY
CLANGS
CLANKS
CRANED
CRANES
CRANIA
CRANIO
CRANKS
CRANKY
CRANNY
CYANIC
CYANID
CYANIN
DIANAS
DIANES
ELANDS
FIANCE
FLANGE
FLANKS
FRANCE
FRANCK
FRANCO
FRANCS
FRANKS
GIANTS
GLANCE
GLANDS
GRANGE
GRANNY
GRANTS
GUANIN
GUANOS
JEANNE
JOANNA
JOANNE
LEANED
LEANER
LEANLY
LEANTO
LIANAS
LIANES
LLANOS
LOANED
LUANDA
MEANER
MEANIE
MEANLY
MOANED
NUANCE
ORANGE
ORANGS
PEANUT
PIANOS
PLANAR
PLANCH
PLANCK
PLANED
PLANER
PLANES
PLANET
PLANKS
PLANTS
PRANCE
PRANKS
QUANTA
QUANTS
RWANDA
SCANTY
SEANCE
SHANKS
SHANTY
SLANGY
SLANTS
SPANKS
STANCE
STANCH
STANDS
STANZA
SWANEE
SWANKY
THANAT
THANES
THANKS
TRANCE
TRANSP
TWANGS
TWANGY
UBANGI
UGANDA
URANIA
URANIC
URANUS
URANYL
USANCE
VIANDS
WEANED
WEANER
WHANGS
YEANED

••A•N•

BAAING
BLAINS
BRAINS
BRAINY
BRANNY
BRAWNY
CHAINS
CRANNY
DHARNA
DRAINS
ELAINE
ELAYNE
FLAUNT
GRAINS
GRAINY
GRANNY
JEANNE
JOANNA
JOANNE
LEARNS
LEARNT
PLAINS
PLAINT
PRAWNS
QUAINT
SPAWNS
STAINS
SWAINS
TRAINS
YEARNS

••A••N

AMAZON
ARAGON
ATAMAN
AVALON
AWAKEN
BEACON
BEATEN
BLAZON
BRAZEN
CHARON
CRAVEN
CRAYON
CYANIN
DEACON
DEADEN
DEAFEN
DIAZIN
DRAGON
EXAMEN
FLACON
FLAGON
FLAMEN
FLAVIN
FLAXEN
FRAUEN
GRABEN
GRADIN
GRAVEN
GUANIN
HEADON
HEAVEN
KLAXON
KRAKEN
LEADEN
LEADIN
LEAVEN
NIACIN
PEAHEN
PEASEN
PLATAN
PLATEN
REASON
SEAMAN
SEAMEN
SEAPEN
SEASON
SEAWAN
SHAKEN
SHAMAN
SHAPEN
SHARON
SHAVEN
SPAVIN
STALIN
STAMEN
STAMIN
UTAHAN
WEAKEN
WEAPON

•••AN•

AALAND
ALBANY
ALKANE
ALLANS
ALVANS
ARCANE
ARIANS
ARMAND
ARRANT
ARYANS
ASIANS
ASKANT
ASLANT
BANANA
BEZANT
BOGANS
BORANE
BOTANY
BRYANT
BURANS
BUTANE
BYLANE
CABANA
CETANE
CLEANS
CUBANS
CYRANO
DAMANS
DECANE
DECANT
DEDANS
DEMAND
DEWANS
DIVANS
DIWANS
EMBANK
ERRAND
ERRANT
ESPANA
ETHANE
ETHANS
EXPAND
EXTANT
GIGANT
GITANO
GLEANS
GROANS
GUIANA
GUYANA
HAVANA
HEXANE
HOGANS
HUMANE
HUMANS
IGUANA
INFANT
INLAND
INSANE
ISLAND
JACANA
JAPANS
JOHANN
JURANT
LEVANT
LIGAND
LITANY
MANANA
MELANO
MUTANT
NAGANA
NATANT
OCEANS
OCTANE
OCTANT
ORGANA
ORGANO
ORGANS
OSCANS
PAEANS
PAGANS
PARANG
PAVANS
PECANS
PEDANT
PEKANS
PINANG
PIRANA
PLIANT
POLAND
PURANA
PYRANS
QUEANS
RECANT
REDANS
REMAND
REMANS
REPAND
ROBAND
ROLAND
ROMANS
ROMANY
ROWANS
ROXANA
ROXANE
SATANG
SAVANT
SECANT
SEDANS
SEJANT
SHRANK
SKEANS
SOLAND
SOLANO
SOLANS
SONANT
SPRANG
STRAND
SUSANS
TENANT
TETANY
TIRANA
TISANE
TITANS
TOMANS
TRUANT
TYRANT
UNHAND
UNMANS
UPLAND
URBANE
VACANT
VOLANT
WIGANS
XYLANS
ZANANA
ZENANA

•••A•N

ATTAIN
BATAAN

CANAAN
COCAIN
DERAIN
DETAIN
DOMAIN
FUSAIN
GAWAIN
IMPAWN
JOHANN
LORAIN
OBTAIN
ORDAIN
PAPAIN
PETAIN
REGAIN
REMAIN
RETAIN
SPRAIN
STRAIN

••••AN
ADRIAN
AEGEAN
AFGHAN
AIDMAN
AIRMAN
AJOWAN
ANDEAN
ANURAN
APPIAN
ASHMAN
ATAMAN
AUGEAN
AXEMAN
BADMAN
BAGMAN
BALKAN
BANIAN
BANYAN
BARMAN
BATAAN
BATMAN
BEDPAN
BEMEAN
BEMOAN
BHUTAN
BOWMAN
BROGAN
BUNYAN
BUSMAN
CABMAN
CAFTAN
CAIMAN
CANAAN
CANCAN
CARMAN
CAYMAN
CORBAN
COWMAN
CRETAN
DARDAN
DECCAN
DEEWAN
DELIAN
DEMEAN
DESMAN
DOLMAN
DORIAN
DUNCAN
DURBAN
DURIAN
EOLIAN
EONIAN
FABIAN
FANTAN
FENIAN
FEZZAN
FIJIAN
FIRMAN
FOEMAN
GASMAN
GERMAN
GIBRAN
GUNMAN
HARLAN
HAZZAN
HERMAN
HETMAN
ICEMAN
INDIAN
INSPAN
IONIAN
JORDAN
JOVIAN
JUDEAN
JULIAN
KALIAN
KANSAN
KOREAN
LAYMAN
LEGMAN
LIBYAN
LILIAN
LONGAN
LUCIAN
MADMAN
MANDAN
MARIAN
MECCAN
MEDIAN
MERMAN
MESIAN
MINOAN
MORGAN
NATHAN
NORMAN
NUBIAN
OHIOAN
OILCAN
ORIGAN
ORPHAN
OSSIAN
OUTMAN
OUTRAN
PAPUAN
PARIAN
PATHAN
PENMAN
PITMAN
PLATAN
PTISAN
RADIAN
RAGLAN
RAGMAN
RANDAN
RATTAN
RODMAN
SABEAN
SAIPAN
SAMIAN
SAMOAN
SAMPAN
SEAMAN
SEAWAN
SEXTAN
SHAMAN
SHORAN
SILVAN
SIMIAN
SIOUAN
SKYMAN
SLOGAN
SOCMAN
STEFAN
STEPAN
SULTAN
SYLVAN
SYRIAN
TAIWAN
TAMPAN
TARTAN
TARZAN
TASMAN
TITIAN
TREPAN
TROJAN
TRUMAN
TURBAN
TUSCAN
TYMPAN
UTAHAN
VANMAN
VIVIAN
VULCAN
WYSTAN
YEOMAN

AO••••
AORIST
AORTAE
AORTAL
AORTAS
AORTIC
AOUDAD

A•O•••
ABOARD
ABODES
ABOHMS
ABOLLA
ABOMAS
ABOMBS
ABORAL
ABORTS
ABOUND
ACORNS
ADOBES
ADOLPH
ADONAI
ADONIC
ADONIS
ADOPTS
ADORED
ADORER
ADORES
ADORNS
AEOLIA
AEOLIC
AEOLIS
AEOLUS
AGOGUE
AGONES
AGONIC
AGORAE
AGORAS
AGOUTI
AGOUTY
AJOWAN
ALONSO
ALONZO
AMOEBA
AMOLES
AMORAL
AMOUNT
AMOURS
ANODES
ANODIC
ANOINT
ANOMIC
ANOMIE
ANONYM
ANORAK
ANOXIA
ANOXIC
APODAL
APOGEE
APOLLO
APOLOG
AROIDS
AROMAS
AROUND
AROUSE
ATOLLS
ATOMIC
ATONAL
ATONED
ATONER
ATONES
ATONIC
AVOCET
AVOIDS
AVOUCH
AVOWAL
AVOWED
AVOWER
AXONES
AZOLES
AZONIC
AZORES
AZOTIC

A••O••
AARONS
ABBOTS
ABHORS
ABLOOM
ABROAD
ABSORB
ABVOLT
ACCORD
ACCOST
ACEOUS
ACIOUS
ACNODE
ACROSS
ACTORS
ADJOIN
ADNOUN
ADROIT
ADSORB
AEROBE
AFFORD
AFLOAT
AFTOSA
ALCOTT
ALCOVE
ALDOSE
ALDOUS
ALFONS
ALGOID
ALLOTS
ALLOUT
ALLOWS
ALLOYS
ALMOND
ALMOST
ANCONA
ANCONE
ANGOLA
ANGORA
ANIONS
ANNOYS
ANTONS
ANTONY
ANYONE
APLOMB
APNOEA
APPOSE
APRONS
ARBORI
ARBORS
ARDORS
AREOLA
ARGOSY
ARGOTS
ARIOSE
ARIOSO
ARIOUS
ARMORS
ARMORY
ARNOLD
ARROBA
ARROWS
ARROYO
ARTOIS
ASCOTS
ASHORE
ASLOPE
ASSORT
ATHOME
ATTORN
AURORA
AUROUS
AUTOED
AXIOMS

A•••O•
ABATOR
ABLOOM
ABYDOS
ACAJOU
ACTION
ALAMOS
ALBION
ALISON
AMADOU
AMATÔL
AMAZON
AMIDOL
AMIGOS
AMNION
ANALOG
ANCHOR
ANGKOR
ANYHOW
APOLOG
ARAGON
ARCHON
AUTHOR
AVALON
AVISOS

A••••O
ACTINO
ADAGIO
AERUGO
AFLCIO
AKIMBO
ALBEDO
ALBINO
ALECTO
ALEPPO
ALONSO
ALONZO
ALUINO
ANATTO
ANGELO
ANKYLO
ANTERO
APOLLO
ARCHEO
AREZZO
ARIOSO
ARISTO

6

ARROYO
ARTHRO
ARTURO
ASTERO
AUSTRO
AVERNO

•AO•••

BAOBAB
GAOLER
KAOLIN
LAOTSE
MAOISM
MAOIST
MAORIS
NAOMIS
NAOSES
RAOULS
TAOISM
TAOIST

•A•O••

AARONS
BABOON
BABOOS
BARONG
BARONS
BARONY
BATONS
BAYOUS
CABOBS
CAEOMA
CAJOLE
CALORY
CANOED
CANOES
CANONS
CANOPY
CAPONS
CAPOTE
CAROBS
CAROLE
CAROLS
CAROMS
CAVORT
DACOIT
DADOES
DAGOBA
DAHOON
DAKOIT
DAKOTA
FAGOTS
FAMOUS
FANONS
FAROFF
FAROUT
FAVORS
GADOID
GALOOT
GALOPS
GALORE
GALOSH
GAMOUS
GANOID
GAVOTS
HALOES
HALOID
HAROLD
JABOTS
JACOBS
JALOPY
JASONS
KABOBS
KALONG
KAPOKS
KAYOED
KAZOOS
LABORS
LABOUR
LADOGA
LAGOON
LAHORE
LANOSE
LAYOFF
LAYOUT
MAGOTS
MAHOUT
MAJORS
MALORY
MANORS
MAROON
MASONS
MASORA
MAYORS
NABOBS
NAGOYA
PAEONS
PAGODA
PARODY
PAROLE
PATOIS
PAYOFF
PAYOLA
RACOON
RADOME
RAGOUT
RAMONA
RAMOSE
RAMOUS
RATOON
RAYONS
RAZORS
SABOTS
SAJOUS
SALOME
SALONS
SALOON
SALOOP
SAMOAN
SARONG
SATORI
SAVORS
SAVORY
SAXONS
SAXONY
TABOOS
TABORS
TACOMA
TALONS
TAROTS
VADOSE
VALOIS
VAPORI
VAPORS
WAGONS
WAHOOS
WAYOUT
YAHOOS
YAPONS

•A••O•

BABOON
BABOOS
BAILOR
BALBOA
BALLOT
BAMBOO
BANGOR
BANJOS
BARROW
BARTOK
BARTON
BARYON
BASION
BASSOS
BATHOS
CACAOS
CACHOU
CALLOW
CAMEOS
CAMION
CAMPOS
CANDOR
CANNON
CANNOT
CANSOS
CANTON
CANTOR
CANTOS
CANYON
CAPTOR
CARBON
CARBOY
CARGOS
CARHOP
CARLOS
CARROT
CARSON
CARTON
CASHOO
CASTOR
CATION
DACRON
DAEMON
DAHOON
DAIMON
DALTON
DAMSON
DANTON
DARROW
DATTOS
DAWSON
DAYTON
EASTON
FACTOR
FAEROE
FAGGOT
FALCON
FALLOW
FANION
FANTOM
FARROW
FATHOM
GABION
GALIOT
GALLON
GALLOP
GALOOT
GAMBOL
GAMMON
GARCON
GASCON
GASTON
HAGDON
HALLOO
HALLOW
HANSOM
HARBOR
HARLOT
HARROW
HATBOX
HAYMOW
JAILOR
JARGON
KARROO
KATION
KAZOOS
LAGOON
LARDON
LARGOS
LASSOS
MACRON
MAGGOT
MAISON
MALLOW
MAMBOS
MAMMON
MANGOS
MANIOC
MARCOS
MARGOS
MARGOT
MARION
MARMOT
MAROON
MARROW
MASCON
MASCOT
MATEOS
MATRON
MATZOS
MATZOT
MAYPOP
NARROW
NASION
NATION
NATRON
PALLOR
PARDON
PARGOS
PARLOR
PARROT
PARSON
PASTOR
PATHOL
PATHOS
PATIOS
PATROL
PATRON
PATTON
PAVIOR
PAVLOV
RACOON
RADIOS
RAMROD
RAMSON
RANCOR
RANDOM
RANSOM
RATION
RATIOS
RATOON
SAIGON
SAILOR
SALLOW
SALMON
SALOON
SALOOP
SALVOR
SALVOS
SAMBOS
SAMSON
SANTOL
SARGON
SARTOR
SAVIOR
TABOOS
TAILOR
TAINOS
TALION
TALLOW
TAMPON
TANGOS
TARPON
TATTOO
TAYLOR
WAGGON
WAHOOS
WALDOS
WALKON
WALLOP
WALLOW
WALTON
WANION
WANTON
WATSON
YAHOOS
YARROW
YAUPON

•A•••O

BAGNIO
BAMAKO
BAMBOO
BARRIO
BASUTO
CALICO
CALLAO
CARDIO
CARUSO
CASHOO
CASINO
CASTRO
CATALO
DAIMIO
DAIMYO
GABBRO
GAMETO
GASTRO
GAUCHO
GAZABO
GAZEBO
HAIRDO
HALLOO
KAKAPO
KARROO
LADINO
LANUGO
LAPARO
LAREDO
LAVABO
MACACO
MADURO
MALACO
MANITO
MATTEO
NAVAHO
NAVAJO
PALAEO
PASHTO
RANCHO
SAPPHO
TAPALO
TATTOO
VAGINO
VARICO
XANTHO

••AO••

GIAOUR

••A•O•

ABATOR
ACAJOU
ALAMOS
AMADOU
AMATOL
AMAZON
ANALOG
ARAGON
AVALON
BEACON
BLAZON
BRAVOS

BRAZOS
CHARON
CLAMOR
CLAROS
CRACOW
CRAYON
DEACON
DIALOG
DIATOM
DRAGON
ENAMOR
FLACON
FLAGON
FLAVOR
GUACOS
GUANOS
HEADON
ISADOR
KLAXON
LLANOS
MEADOW
ORATOR
PIANOS
QUAHOG
REASON
REAVOW
SEADOG
SEASON
SHADOW
SHAKOS
SHARON
SLALOM
STATOR
TEAPOT
TEAPOY
VIATOR
WEAPON
ZEALOT

••A••O
ADAGIO
ANATTO
BLASTO
CHAETO
CHALCO
CRAMBO
CRANIO
FIASCO
FRANCO
GLAUCO
GNATHO
GRAECO
GRAPHO
LEANTO
PLAGIO
PLASMO
QUARTO
RIALTO
SHACKO
SMALTO
STAURO

•••AO•
CACAOS

•••A•O
BAMAKO
CATALO
CERATO
CYRANO
DORADO
DYNAMO
GAZABO
GITANO
HEMATO
HEPATO
JUDAEO
KAKAPO
KERATO
LAPARO
LAVABO
LEGATO
MACACO
MALACO
MEGALO
MELANO
MIKADO
NAVAHO
NAVAJO
NEMATO
OCTAVO
ORGANO
PALAEO
POTATO
REBATO
ROBALO
RUBATO
SOLANO
SOMATO
TAPALO
TERATO
TOBAGO
TOMATO
VIRAGO

••••AO
BILBAO
CALLAO

AP••••
APACHE
APATHY
APERCU
APEXES
APHIDS
APHTHA
APIARY
APICAL
APICES
APIECE
APLITE
APLOMB
APNEAL
APNEIC
APNOEA
APODAL
APOGEE
APOLLO
APOLOG
APPALL
APPALS
APPEAL
APPEAR
APPELS
APPEND
APPIAN
APPLES
APPOSE
APRILS
APRONS
APULIA

A•P•••
ALPACA
ALPHAS
ALPHYL
ALPINE
AMPERE
AMPHRS
AMPULE
AMPULS
APPALL
APPALS
APPEAL
APPEAR
APPELS
APPEND
APPIAN
APPLES
APPOSE
ARPENS
ARPENT
ASPECT
ASPENS
ASPERS
ASPICS
ASPIRE

A••P••
ADAPTS
ADEPTS
ADIPIC
ADOPTS
AGAPAE
ALEPHS
ALEPPO
ALIPED
ARMPIT
AUSPEX

A•••P•
ABRUPT
ACCEPT
ADOLPH
ALEPPO
ASLOPE

A••••P
ASLEEP

•AP•••
CAPERS
CAPIAS
CAPITA
CAPLIN
CAPONS
CAPOTE
CAPPED
CAPPER
CAPRIC
CAPTOR
DAPHNE
DAPPED
DAPPER
DAPPLE
GAPERS
GAPING
GAPPED
HAPPEN
JAPANS
JAPHET
KAPOKS
KAPPAS
LAPARO
LAPELS
LAPFUL
LAPINS
LAPPED
LAPPER
LAPPET
LAPSED
LAPSER
LAPSES
LAPSUS
MAPLES
MAPPED
NAPALM
NAPERY
NAPIER
NAPKIN
NAPLES
NAPPED
NAPPER
NAPPES
NAPPIE
PAPACY
PAPAIN
PAPAWS
PAPAYA
PAPERS
PAPERY
PAPIST
PAPPUS
PAPUAN
PAPULA
PAPULE
RAPHAE
RAPHIS
RAPIDS
RAPIER
RAPINE
RAPING
RAPIST
RAPPED
RAPPEE
RAPPEL
RAPPER
SAPHAR
SAPPED
SAPPER
SAPPHO
TAPALO
TAPERS
TAPING
TAPIRS
TAPPED
TAPPER
TAPPET
VAPORI
VAPORS
WAPITI
WAPPED
YAPONS
YAPPED

•A•P••
CALPAC
CAMPED
CAMPER
CAMPOS
CAMPUS
CAPPED
CAPPER
CARPAL
CARPED
CARPEL
CARPER
CARPET
CARPIC
CARPUS
CASPAR
CASPER
DAMPED
DAMPEN
DAMPER
DAMPLY
DAPPED
DAPPER
DAPPLE
GAPPED
GASPAR
GASPED
GASPER
HAMPER
HAPPEN
HARPED
HARPER
HASPED
HATPIN
JAIPUR
JASPER
KALPAK
KAPPAS
KASPAR
LAMPAD
LAMPAS
LAMPED
LAPPED
LAPPER
LAPPET
MAGPIE
MAPPED
MAYPOP
NAPPED
NAPPER
NAPPES
NAPPIE
PALPUS
PAMPAS
PAMPER
PAPPUS
PAUPER
PAWPAW
RAJPUT
RALPHS
RAMPED
RAPPED
RAPPEE
RAPPEL
RAPPER
RASPED
RASPER
SAIPAN
SALPAS
SALPID
SAMPAN
SAMPLE
SAPPED
SAPPER
SAPPHO
TAIPEI
TAMPAN
TAMPED
TAMPER
TAMPON
TAPPED
TAPPER
TAPPET
TARPON
TAUPES
VAMPED
WAMPUM
WAMPUS
WAPPED
WARPED
WARPER
YAPPED
YAUPED
YAUPON
YAWPED
YAWPER

•A••P•
CALIPH
CANAPE
CANOPY
GALOPS
JALAPS
JALOPY
KAKAPO
PARAPH
SARAPE
WATAPE
WATAPS

6

•A•••P
BANGUP
CARHOP
CATNIP
CATSUP
EARLAP
GALLOP
GALLUP
HANGUP
LARRUP
MADCAP
MADEUP
MAKEUP
MARKUP
MAYHAP
MAYPOP
SALOOP
SANNUP
SATRAP
TAKEUP
WALKUP
WALLOP
WARMUP

••AP••
ADAPTS
AGAPAE
CHAPEL
CHAPES
CRAPED
CRAPES
DIAPER
DRAPED
DRAPER
DRAPES
ELAPSE
ETAPES
FRAPPE
GRAPES
GRAPHO
GRAPHS
GRAPHY
HEAPED
LEAPED
LEAPER
OKAPIS
QUAPAW
REAPED
REAPER
SCAPES
SEAPEN
SHAPED
SHAPEN
SHAPER
SHAPES
SNAPPY
SOAPED
STAPES
STAPLE
TEAPOT
TEAPOY
WEAPON
WRAPUP

••A•P•
CHAMPS
CLAMPS
CLASPS
CRAMPS
FRAPPE
GRASPS
SCALPS
SCAMPI
SCAMPS
SCARPS
SCAUPS
SHARPS
SNAPPY
STAMPS
SWAMPS
SWAMPY
TRAMPS

••A••P
TEACUP
TRANSP
WRAPUP

•••AP•
CANAPE
DOGAPE
ENRAPT
ESCAPE
JALAPS
KAKAPO
LENAPE
PARAPH
RECAPS
SARAPE
SCRAPE
SCRAPS
SERAPE
SERAPH
STRAPS
TERAPH
UNCAPS
WATAPE
WATAPS

•••A•P
DECAMP
ENCAMP
ESCARP
REVAMP

••••AP
BURLAP
DEWLAP
EARLAP
ENTRAP
ENWRAP
HUBCAP
ICECAP
INWRAP
KIDNAP
MADCAP
MAYHAP
MISHAP
MOBCAP
MUDCAP
REDCAP
RIPRAP
SATRAP
SKYCAP
TOECAP
UNSNAP
UNWRAP

AQ••••
AQUILA

A•Q•••
ACQUIT

•AQ•••
MAQUIS

•A•Q••
BARQUE
BASQUE
CAIQUE
CASQUE
MANQUE
MARQUE
MASQUE

••AQ••
BRAQUE
CLAQUE
IRAQIS
OPAQUE
PLAQUE

AR••••
ARABEL
ARABIA
ARABIC
ARABLE
ARAGON
ARANTA
ARARAT
ARAWAK
ARBELA
ARBORI
ARBORS
ARBUTE
ARCADE
ARCANE
ARCHED
ARCHEO
ARCHER
ARCHES
ARCHIE
ARCHIL
ARCHLY
ARCHON
ARCHYS
ARCING
ARCKED
ARCTIC
ARDEBS
ARDENT
ARDORS
ARECAS
ARENAS
AREOLA
ARETES
AREZZO
ARGALI
ARGALS
ARGENT
ARGIVE
ARGOSY
ARGOTS
ARGUED
ARGUER
ARGUES
ARGUFY
ARGYLE
ARGYLL
ARIANS
ARIDLY
ARIELS
ARIGHT
ARIOSE
ARIOSO
ARIOUS
ARISEN
ARISES
ARISTA
ARISTO
ARLEEN
ARLENE
ARLINE
ARMADA
ARMAGH
ARMAND
ARMETS
ARMFUL
ARMIES
ARMING
ARMLET
ARMORS
ARMORY
ARMPIT
ARMURE
ARNAUD
ARNICA
ARNIES
ARNOLD
AROIDS
AROMAS
AROUND
AROUSE
ARPENS
ARPENT
ARRACK
ARRANT
ARRAYS
ARREAR
ARREST
ARRIVE
ARROBA
ARROWS
ARROYO
ARSINE
ARTELS
ARTERY
ARTFUL
ARTHRO
ARTHUR
ARTIES
ARTIST
ARTOIS
ARTURO
ARUNTA
ARYANS

A•R•••
AARONS
ABRADE
ABRAMS
ABROAD
ABRUPT
ACROSS
ADRIAN
ADRIEN
ADRIFT
ADROIT
AERATE
AERIAL
AERIED
AERIES
AERIFY
AEROBE
AERUGO
AFRAID
AFRAME
AFRESH
AFRICA
AGRAFE
AGREED
AGREES
AIRDRY
AIRIER
AIRILY
AIRING
AIRMAN
AIRMEN
AIRWAY
AMRITA
AORIST
AORTAE
AORTAL
AORTAS
AORTIC
APRILS
APRONS
ARRACK
ARRANT
ARRAYS
ARREAR
ARREST
ARRIVE
ARROBA
ARROWS
ARROYO
ATREUS
ATRIAL
ATRIUM
AURATE
AUREUS
AURIGA
AURIST
AURORA
AUROUS
AZRAEL

A••R••
ABORAL
ABORTS
ACARID
ACCRUE
ACORNS
ADORED
ADORER
ADORES
ADORNS
AFFRAY
AGARIC
AGORAE
AGORAS
ALARIC
ALARMS
ALARUM
ALERTS
ALFRED
AMERCE
AMORAL
ANDREA
ANDREI
ANDRES
ANDREW
ANERGY
ANORAK
ANTRIM
ANTRUM
ANURAN
APERCU
ARARAT
ASARUM
ASTRAL
ASTRAY
ASTRID
AUBREY
AUDREY
AVERNO
AVERSE
AVERTS
AVERYS
AWARDS
AZORES
AZURES

A•••R•
ABHORS
ABJURE
ABNERS
ABOARD
ABSORB
ABSURD
ACCORD
ACTORS
ADDERS

6

ADHERE
ADJURE
ADMIRE
ADSORB
ADVERB
ADVERT
AFFIRM
AFFORD
AGGERS
AIDERS
AIRDRY
ALBERT
ALDERS
ALLURE
ALMIRA
ALTARS
ALTERS
AMBARI
AMBARY
AMBERS
AMBERY
AMENRA
AMOURS
AMPERE
AMPHRS
ANGARY
ANGERS
ANGORA
ANITRA
ANKARA
ANTERO
APIARY
ARBORI
ARBORS
ARDORS
ARMORS
ARMORY
ARMURE
ARTERY
ARTHRO
ARTURO
ASBURY
ASGARD
ASHORE
ASKERS
ASPERS
ASPIRE
ASSERT
ASSORT
ASSURE
ASTERI
ASTERN
ASTERO
ASTERS
ATTARS
ATTIRE
ATTORN
AUBURN
AUGERS
AUGURS
AUGURY
AURORA
AUSTRO
AVIARY
AWEARY
AWHIRL
AYMARA

A••••R

ABASER
ABATER
ABATOR
ABIDER
ABUSER
ADORER
AETHER
AFFAIR
AIRIER
ALEGAR
ALTAIR
ALULAR
AMBLER
AMUSER
ANCHOR
ANGKOR
ANGLER
ANSWER
ANTHER
ANTIAR
ANTLER
APPEAR
ARCHER
ARGUER
ARREAR
ARTHUR
ASHIER
ASHLAR
ATONER
AUSTER
AUTHOR
AVATAR
AVOWER

•AR•••

AARONS
BARBED
BARBEL
BARBER
BARBET
BARBIE
BARDED
BARDES
BARDIC
BAREGE
BARELY
BAREST
BARFLY
BARGED
BARGEE
BARGES
BARING
BARITE
BARIUM
BARKED
BARKER
BARLEY
BARMAN
BARMEN
BARMIE
BARNEY
BARNUM
BARONG
BARONS
BARONY
BARQUE
BARRED
BARREL
BARREN
BARRET
BARRIO
BARROW
BARRYS
BARTER
BARTOK
BARTON
BARUCH
BARYES
BARYON
BARYTA
CARACK
CARAFE
CARATE
CARATS
CARBON
CARBOY
CARCEL
CARDED
CARDER
CARDIO
CAREEN
CAREER
CARERS
CARESS
CARETS
CARGOS
CARHOP
CARIBE
CARIBS
CARIES
CARINA
CARING
CARLAS
CARLOS
CARMAN
CARMEL
CARMEN
CARNAL
CAROBS
CAROLE
CAROLS
CAROMS
CARPAL
CARPED
CARPEL
CARPER
CARPET
CARPIC
CARPUS
CARREL
CARRIE
CARROT
CARSON
CARTED
CARTEL
CARTER
CARTES
CARTON
CARUSO
CARVED
CARVEL
CARVEN
CARVER
CARVES
DARDAN
DARERS
DARICS
DARIEN
DARING
DARIUS
DARKEN
DARKER
DARKLE
DARKLY
DARNED
DARNEL
DARROW
DARTED
DARTER
DARTLE
DARWIN
EARFUL
EARING
EARLAP
EARLES
EARNED
EARNER
EARTHS
EARTHY
EARWAX
EARWIG
FARADS
FARCED
FARCER
FARCES
FARERS
FARINA
FARING
FARLES
FARLEY
FARMED
FARMER
FAROFF
FAROUT
FARROW
GARAGE
GARBED
GARBLE
GARCON
GARDEN
GARGET
GARGLE
GARISH
GARLIC
GARNER
GARNET
GARRET
GARTER
HARASS
HARBIN
HARBOR
HARDEN
HARDER
HARDLY
HAREMS
HARKED
HARKEN
HARLAN
HARLEM
HARLEY
HARLOT
HARMED
HARMIN
HAROLD
HARPED
HARPER
HARROW
HARRYS
HARTAL
HARVEY
JARFUL
JARGON
JARINA
JARRED
JARVEY
JARVIS
KARATE
KARATS
KARENS
KARMAS
KARNAK
KARROO
LARDED
LARDER
LARDON
LAREDO
LARGER
LARGOS
LARIAT
LARINE
LARKED
LARKER
LARRUP
LARRYS
LARVAE
LARVAL
LARYNG
LARYNX
MARACA
MARAUD
MARBLE
MARCEL
MARCIA
MARCOS
MARCUS
MARDUK
MARGAY
MARGES
MARGIE
MARGIN
MARGOS
MARGOT
MARIAN
MARIAS
MARIES
MARINA
MARINE
MARION
MARIST
MARKED
MARKER
MARKET
MARKKA
MARKUP
MARLED
MARLIN
MARMOT
MAROON
MARQUE
MARRED
MARRER
MARROW
MARSHA
MARSHY
MARTAS
MARTEN
MARTHA
MARTHE
MARTIN
MARTYR
MARTYS
MARVEL
MARVIN
NARIAL
NARINE
NARROW
NARWAL
OARING
PARADE
PARANG
PARAPH
PARCAE
PARCEL
PARDON
PARENS
PARENT
PARERS
PAREUS
PARGET
PARGOS
PARIAH
PARIAN
PARIES
PARING
PARISH
PARITY
PARKAS
PARKED
PARKER
PARLAY
PARLEY
PARLOR
PARODY
PAROLE
PARRAL

PARREL
PARROT
PARSEC
PARSED
PARSEE
PARSES
PARSIS
PARSON
PARTED
PARTLY
PARURE
PARVIS
RAREFY
RARELY
RAREST
RARING
RARITY
SARAHS
SARAPE
SARGON
SARONG
SARSAR
SARTOR
SARTRE
TARGET
TARIFF
TARING
TARMAC
TARNAL
TAROTS
TARPON
TARRED
TARSAL
TARSUS
TARTAN
TARTAR
TARTER
TARTLY
TARZAN
VARICO
VARIED
VARIER
VARIES
VARLET
VARUNA
VARVES
WARBLE
WARDED
WARDEN
WARDER
WARIER
WARILY
WARMED
WARMER
WARMLY
WARMTH
WARMUP
WARNED
WARNER
WARPED
WARPER
WARRED
WARREN
WARSAW
YARDED
YARROW
ZAREBA

•A•R••

BAIRNS
BARRED
BARREL
BARREN
BARRET
BARRIO
BARROW
BARRYS
BASRAH
CADRES
CAIRNS
CAPRIC
CARREL
CARRIE
CARROT
DACRON
DARROW
FABRIC
FAEROE
FAIRED
FAIRER
FAIRLY
FARROW
GARRET
HAIRDO
HAIRED
HARROW
HARRYS
HATRED
IATRIC
JARRED
KARROO
KAURIS
LABRET
LABRUM
LAIRDS
LAIRED
LARRUP
LARRYS
LATRIA
LAURAE
LAURAS
LAUREL
LAURIE
MACRON
MADRAS
MADRID
MAORIS
MARRED
MARRER
MARROW
MATRIX
MATRON
NARROW
NATRON
PADRES
PAIRED
PARRAL
PARREL
PARROT
PATROL
PATRON
RAMROD
SABRAS
SACRAL
SACRED
SACRUM
SATRAP
SAUREL
SAURUS
TANREC
TARRED
TAURUS
WALRUS
WARRED
WARREN
YARROW

•A••R•

BAKERS
BAKERY
BALERS
BAWDRY
BAYARD
CALORY
CAMERA
CANARD
CANARY
CANERS
CAPERS
CARERS
CASERN
CASTRO
CATERS
CAVERN
CAVORT
DARERS
DATARY
DATERS
DATURA
DAUBRY
EATERS
FACERS
FAKERS
FAKERY
FAKIRS
FARERS
FAVORS
GABBRO
GAGERS
GALORE
GANTRY
GAPERS
GASTRO
GAZERS
HALERS
HATERS
HAZARD
HAZERS
JABIRU
LABORS
LAGERS
LAHORE
LAKERS
LAPARO
LASERS
LAVERS
LAYERS
LAZARS
MACERS
MADURA
MADURO
MAIGRE
MAITRE
MAJORS
MAKERS
MALGRE
MALORY
MANORS
MANURE
MASERS
MASORA
MATURE
MAYORS
MAZERS
NADIRS
NAMERS
NAPERY
NATURE
PACERS
PALTRY
PANTRY
PAPERS
PAPERY
PARERS
PARURE
PASTRY
PATERS
PAVERS
PAWERS
PAYERS
RACERS
RADARS
RAKERS
RATERS
RAVERS
RAZORS
SABERS
SAFARI
SAHARA
SAKERS
SALARY
SAMARA
SANDRA
SARTRE
SATARA
SATIRE
SATORI
SATURN
SATYRS
SAVERS
SAVORS
SAVORY
SAWERS
SAYERS
TABARD
TABORS
TAKERS
TALERS
TAMERS
TAPERS
TAPIRS
TATARS
TAVERN
TAWDRY
TAWERS
TAXERS
VAGARY
VALERY
VAPORI
VAPORS
VASARI
WADERS
WAFERS
WAGERS
WALERS
WATERS
WATERY
WAVERS
YAGERS
ZAFFRE

•A•••R

BACKER
BADGER
BAILER
BAILOR
BAITER
BALDER
BANGOR
BANKER
BANNER
BANTER
BARBER
BARKER
BARTER
BATHER
BATTER
BAWLER
BAXTER
CADGER
CAESAR
CAGIER
CAHIER
CALCAR
CALKER
CALLER
CALMER
CAMBER
CAMPER
CANCER
CANDOR
CANKER
CANNER
CANTER
CANTOR
CAPPER
CAPTOR
CARDER
CAREER
CARPER
CARTER
CARVER
CASPAR
CASPER
CASTER
CASTOR
CATHER
CAUSER
CAVIAR
DABBER
DAGGER
DAGMAR
DAMMAR
DAMMER
DAMPER
DANCER
DANDER
DANGER
DANKER
DAPPER
DARKER
DARTER
DASHER
DAUBER
EARNER
EASIER
EASTER
FABLER
FACTOR
FAFNIR
FAIRER
FALLER
FALSER
FALTER
FANNER
FARCER
FARMER
FASTER
FATHER
FATTER
FAWNER
GABBER
GADDER
GAFFER
GAGGER
GAINER
GAITER
GAMBIR
GAMIER
GAMMER
GANDER
GANGER
GAOLER
GARNER
GARTER
GASPAR
GASPER
GATHER
GAUGER
HACKER
HAILER
HALTER
HAMMER
HAMPER

HANGAR
HANGER
HANKER
HARBOR
HARDER
HARPER
HATTER
HAULER
HAWKER
HAWSER
HAZIER
JABBER
JAEGER
JAGUAR
JAILER
JAILOR
JAIPUR
JASPER
JAZZER
KAFFIR
KAISER
KASPAR
LAAGER
LABOUR
LACIER
LADDER
LADLER
LAGGER
LAKIER
LANCER
LANDER
LANGUR
LANKER
LANNER
LAPPER
LAPSER
LARDER
LARGER
LARKER
LASCAR
LASHER
LASTER
LATHER
LATTER
LAUDER
LAWYER
LAZIER
MADDER
MAGYAR
MAHLER
MAILER
MAIMER
MANGER
MANNER
MARKER
MARRER
MARTYR
MASHER
MASKER
MASTER
MATTER
MAULER
MAUSER
MAZIER
NAGGER
NAPIER
NAPPER
NASSER
PACKER
PALLOR
PALMAR
PALMER
PALTER
PAMPER
PANDER
PANZER
PARKER
PARLOR
PASSER
PASTER
PASTOR
PATTER
PAUKER
PAUPER
PAUSER
PAVIOR
PAWNER
RACIER
RACKER
RAFTER
RAIDER
RAISER
RAMMER
RANCOR
RANGER
RANKER
RANTER
RAPIER
RAPPER
RASHER
RASPER
RATHER
RATTER
SACKER
SADDER
SAGGAR
SAGGER
SAGIER
SAILER
SAILOR
SALTER
SALVER
SALVOR
SAMBUR
SANDER
SANGAR
SANGER
SANSAR
SAPHAR
SAPPER
SARSAR
SARTOR
SAUCER
SAUGER
SAVIOR
SAWYER
TACKER
TAGGER
TAILOR
TALKER
TALLER
TAMPER
TANKER
TANNER
TAPPER
TARTAR
TARTER
TASTER
TATLER
TATTER
TAUTER
TAYLOR
VAGUER
VAINER
VALKYR
VALVAR
VARIER
VASTER
WAFTER
WAGNER
WAILER
WAITER
WAIVER
WALKER
WALTER
WANDER
WANNER
WANTER
WARDER
WARIER
WARMER
WARNER
WARPER
WASHER
WASTER
WAVIER
WAXIER
XAVIER
YABBER
YAMMER
YAWNER
YAWPER
ZAFFAR
ZAFFER
ZAFFIR
ZANIER

••AR••

ACARID
AGARIC
ALARIC
ALARMS
ALARUM
ARARAT
ASARUM
AWARDS
BEARDS
BEARED
BEARER
BLARED
BLARES
BOARDS
CHARDS
CHARED
CHARES
CHARGE
CHARMS
CHARON
CHARRY
CHARTS
CLARAS
CLARES
CLARET
CLAROS
COARSE
DEARER
DEARIE
DEARLY
DEARTH
DHARMA
DHARNA
DWARFS
ECARTE
EPARCH
EXARCH
FEARED
FEARER
FLARED
FLARES
GEARED
GHARRI
GHARRY
GLARED
GLARES
GNARLS
GNARLY
GUARDS
HEARER
HEARSE
HEARST
HEARTH
HEARTS
HEARTY
HOARDS
HOARSE
ICARUS
IMARET
INARCH
INARMS
JUAREZ
KNARRY
LEARNS
LEARNT
NEARBY
NEARED
NEARER
NEARLY
PEARLS
PEARLY
QUARKS
QUARRY
QUARTE
QUARTO
QUARTS
QUARTZ
REARED
REARER
REARMS
ROARED
ROARER
SCARAB
SCARCE
SCARED
SCARER
SCARES
SCARFS
SCARPS
SEARCH
SEARED
SHARDS
SHARED
SHARER
SHARES
SHARKS
SHARON
SHARPS
SMARMY
SMARTS
SNARED
SNARER
SNARES
SNARLS
SNARLY
SOARED
SOARER
SPARED
SPARER
SPARES
SPARGE
SPARKS
SPARRY
SPARSE
SPARTA
STARCH
STARED
STARER
STARES
STARRY
STARTS
STARVE
SWARAJ
SWARDS
SWARMS
SWARTH
SWARTY
TEARED
TIARAS
WEARER
WHARFS
WHARVE
YEARLY
YEARNS

••A•R•

CHAIRS
CHARRY
CLAIRE
FIACRE
FLAIRS
GHARRI
GHARRY
GLAIRS
GLAIRY
KNARRY
ONAGRI
QUADRI
QUAERE
QUARRY
QUATRE
SPARRY
STAIRS
STARRY
STAURO

••A••R

ABASER
ABATER
ABATOR
AVATAR
BEAKER
BEARER
BEATER
BEAVER
BLAZER
BRACER
BRAVER
BRAYER
BRAZER
CHAFER
CHASER
CLAMOR
COALER
COAXER
CRATER
CRAVER
DEALER
DEARER
DIALER
DIAPER
DRAPER
DRAWER
ELATER
ENAMOR
ERASER
EVADER
FEARER
FLAKER
FLAVOR
FLAYER
FRAMER
FRATER
GIAOUR
GLAZER
GNAWER
GRADER
GRATER
GRAVER
GRAYER
GRAZER
HEADER
HEALER
HEARER
HEATER
HEAVER

HOAXER
ISADOR
LAAGER
LEADER
LEANER
LEAPER
LEAVER
LOADER
LOAFER
MEAGER
MEANER
NEARER
NEATER
ONAGER
ORATOR
PLACER
PLANAR
PLANER
PLATER
PLAYER
PRATER
PRAYER
QUAKER
QUASAR
QUAVER
READER
REAMER
REAPER
REARER
ROAMER
ROARER
SCALAR
SCALER
SCARER
SEALER
SEAMER
SHAKER
SHAPER
SHARER
SHAVER
SKATER
SLATER
SLAVER
SLAYER
SNARER
SOAKER
SOARER
SPACER
SPADER
SPARER
STAGER
STALER
STARER
STATER
STATOR
STAYER
TEASER
THAYER
TRACER
TRADER
VEADAR
VIATOR
WEAKER
WEANER
WEARER
WEAVER
WHALER

•••AR•

ABOARD
ALTARS
AMBARI
AMBARY
ANGARY
ANKARA
APIARY
ASGARD
ATTARS
AVIARY
AWEARY
AYMARA
BAYARD
BEWARE
BICARB
BIHARI
BINARY
BLEARS
BLEARY
BOYARD
BOYARS
BRIARS
CANARD
CANARY
CEDARS
CESARE
CIGARS
CLEARS
COWARD
CURARE
CYMARS
DATARY
DEBARK
DEBARS
DECARE
DEKARE
DENARY
DEPART
DINARS
DISARM
DREARY
ECHARD
EDGARS
EDUARD
EDWARD
EGGARS
EMBARK
EMBARS
ESCARP
FEUARS
FRIARS
FRIARY
GEMARA
GERARD
GOCART
GOKART
HAZARD
HILARY
HOBART
HOLARD
HORARY
HOWARD
IMBARK
IMPARK
IMPART
INWARD
IZZARD
LAPARO
LAZARS
LIZARD
MOLARS
MOZART
NEWARK
NOTARY
ONWARD
OSCARS
PETARD
RADARS
REGARD
REMARK
RETARD
REWARD
RITARD
ROSARY
ROTARY
SAFARI
SAHARA
SALARY
SAMARA
SATARA
SENARY
SEWARD
SHEARS
SIMARS
SITARS
SIZARS
SMEARS
SMEARY
SONARS
SOUARI
SOWARS
SPEARS
SQUARE
STUART
SUDARY
SUGARS
SUGARY
SWEARS
TABARD
TATARS
THWART
TOWARD
UNBARS
UNWARY
UPWARD
UTGARD
VAGARY
VASARI
VICARS
VISARD
VIZARD
VOTARY
WIZARD
ZONARY

•••A•R

AFFAIR
ALTAIR
ECLAIR
IMPAIR
MIDAIR
MOHAIR
REPAIR
UNFAIR
UNHAIR

••••AR

ALEGAR
ALULAR
ANTIAR
APPEAR
ARREAR
ASHLAR
AVATAR
BEGGAR
BEZOAR
BOXCAR
BULBAR
BULGAR
BURSAR
CAESAR
CALCAR
CASPAR
CAVIAR
CELLAR
COLLAR
COSTAR
COTTAR
COUGAR
DAGMAR
DAMMAR
DEODAR
DISBAR
DOGEAR
DOLLAR
DUNBAR
DURBAR
ENDEAR
ESCHAR
FOLIAR
FULMAR
GASPAR
GUITAR
GUNNAR
HANGAR
HUSSAR
INSTAR
ISHTAR
ISOBAR
JAGUAR
KASPAR
LASCAR
LINEAR
LUMBAR
MAGYAR
MEDLAR
MORTAR
MUGGAR
NECTAR
OCULAR
OVULAR
PALMAR
PILLAR
PINDAR
PLANAR
POPLAR
PREWAR
PULSAR
QUASAR
REHEAR
SAGGAR
SANGAR
SANSAR
SAPHAR
SARSAR
SCALAR
SECPAR
SEGGAR
SHIKAR
SHOFAR
SIRDAR
STELAR
STYLAR
TARTAR
THENAR
TROCAR
TUSSAR
UNBEAR
UPROAR
UVULAR
VALVAR
VEADAR
VULGAR
VULVAR
WEIMAR
ZAFFAR

AS••••

ASARUM
ASBURY
ASCEND
ASCENT
ASCOTS
ASGARD
ASHIER
ASHLAR
ASHLEY
ASHMAN
ASHMEN
ASHORE
ASIANS
ASIDES
ASKANT
ASKERS
ASKING
ASLANT
ASLEEP
ASLOPE
ASPECT
ASPENS
ASPERS
ASPICS
ASPIRE
ASSAIL
ASSAIS
ASSAYS
ASSENT
ASSERT
ASSESS
ASSETS
ASSIGN
ASSISI
ASSIST
ASSIZE
ASSORT
ASSUME
ASSURE
ASTERI
ASTERN
ASTERO
ASTERS
ASTHMA
ASTRAL
ASTRAY
ASTRID
ASTUTE
ASYLUM

A•S•••

ABSENT
ABSORB
ABSURD
ADSORB
AISLED
AISLES
ALSACE
ALSIKE
ANSATE
ANSELM
ANSWER
ARSINE
ASSAIL
ASSAIS
ASSAYS
ASSENT
ASSERT
ASSESS
ASSETS
ASSIGN
ASSISI
ASSIST
ASSIZE
ASSORT
ASSUME
ASSURE
AUSPEX
AUSTEN
AUSTER
AUSTIN
AUSTRO
AXSEED

A••S••

ABASED
ABASER

ABASES
ABUSED
ABUSER
ABUSES
ABYSMS
AGISTS
ALASKA
ALISON
AMUSED
AMUSER
AMUSES
ANISES
ANUSES
ARISEN
ARISES
ARISTA
ARISTO
AVESTA
AVISOS
AYESHA

A•••S•

ABBESS
ABLEST
ABLUSH
ACCESS
ACCOST
ACCUSE
ACROSS
ADJUST
ADVISE
AFRESH
AFTOSA
AGHAST
AGUISH
AHIMSA
ALDOSE
ALMOST
ALONSO
AMBUSH
AMIDST
AORIST
APPOSE
ARGOSY
ARIOSE
ARIOSO
AROUSE
ARREST
ARTIST
ASSESS
ASSISI
ASSIST
ATTEST
AUGUST
AURIST
AUTISM
AVERSE
AWLESS

A••••S

AALIIS
AARONS
ABACAS
ABACUS
ABASES
ABATES
ABATIS
ABBESS
ABBEYS
ABBIES
ABBOTS
ABELES
ABHORS
ABIDES
ABNERS
ABODES
ABOHMS
ABOMAS
ABOMBS
ABORTS
ABRAMS
ABUSES
ABYDOS
ABYSMS
ACCESS
ACEOUS
ACINUS
ACIOUS
ACORNS
ACROSS
ACTORS
ADAGES
ADAPTS
ADDAMS
ADDERS
ADDLES
ADEEMS
ADENIS
ADEPTS
ADIEUS
ADLIBS
ADMITS
ADOBES
ADONIS
ADOPTS
ADORES
ADORNS
ADULTS
AEACUS
AEETES
AEGEUS
AENEAS
AEOLIS
AEOLUS
AERIES
AGAMAS
AGATES
AGAVES
AGENTS
AGGERS
AGISTS
AGLETS
AGONES
AGORAS
AGREES
AIDERS
AISLES
AKENES
ALAMOS
ALARMS
ALBUMS
ALDERS
ALDOUS
ALEPHS
ALERTS
ALEUTS
ALEXIS
ALFONS
ALIBIS
ALICES
ALIENS
ALIGNS
ALINES
ALKYLS
ALLANS
ALLAYS
ALLENS
ALLEYS
ALLIES
ALLOTS
ALLOWS
ALLOYS
ALLYLS
ALMAHS
ALMUDS
ALPHAS
ALTARS
ALTERS
ALUINS
ALVANS
ALWAYS
AMAZES
AMBERS
AMBITS
AMBLES
AMEBAS
AMENDS
AMENTS
AMICES
AMIDES
AMIENS
AMIGOS
AMOLES
AMOURS
AMPHRS
AMPULS
AMUSES
ANABAS
ANDRES
ANGELS
ANGERS
ANGLES
ANIMAS
ANIMUS
ANIONS
ANISES
ANITAS
ANKLES
ANNALS
ANNIES
ANNOYS
ANNULS
ANODES
ANTICS
ANTONS
ANUBIS
ANUSES
ANVILS
AORTAS
APEXES
APHIDS
APICES
APPALS
APPELS
APPLES
APRILS
APRONS
ARBORS
ARCHES
ARCHYS
ARDEBS
ARDORS
ARECAS
ARENAS
ARETES
ARGALS
ARGOTS
ARGUES
ARIANS
ARIELS
ARIOUS
ARISES
ARMETS
ARMIES
ARMORS
ARNIES
AROIDS
AROMAS
ARPENS
ARRAYS
ARROWS
ARTELS
ARTIES
ARTOIS
ARYANS
ASCOTS
ASIANS
ASIDES
ASKERS
ASPENS
ASPERS
ASPICS
ASSAIS
ASSAYS
ASSESS
ASSETS
ASTERS
ATHENS
ATOLLS
ATONES
ATREUS
ATTARS
ATTICS
AUDADS
AUDITS
AUGERS
AUGHTS
AUGURS
AUREUS
AUROUS
AUXINS
AVAILS
AVERTS
AVERYS
AVISOS
AVOIDS
AWAITS
AWAKES
AWARDS
AWLESS
AXIOMS
AXONES
AZINES
AZOLES
AZORES
AZTECS
AZURES

•AS•••

BASALT
BASELY
BASHAW
BASHED
BASHES
BASICS
BASIFY
BASILS
BASING
BASINS
BASION
BASKED
BASKET
BASQUE
BASRAH
BASSES
BASSET
BASSOS
BASTED
BASTES
BASUTO
CASABA
CASALS
CASAVA
CASBAH
CASEFY
CASEIN
CASERN
CASHAW
CASHED
CASHES
CASHEW
CASHOO
CASING
CASINO
CASKET
CASPAR
CASPER
CASQUE
CASSIA
CASSIE
CASSIS
CASTER
CASTES
CASTLE
CASTOR
CASTRO
CASUAL
DASHED
DASHER
DASHES
EASELS
EASIER
EASILY
EASING
EASTER
EASTON
FASCES
FASCIA
FASTED
FASTEN
FASTER
GASBAG
GASCON
GASHED
GASHES
GASKET
GASKIN
GASMAN
GASMEN
GASPAR
GASPED
GASPER
GASSED
GASSES
GASTON
GASTRO
HASHED
HASHES
HASLET
HASPED
HASSEL
HASSLE
HASTED
HASTEN
HASTES
JASONS
JASPER
KASPAR
LASCAR
LASERS
LASHED
LASHER
LASHES
LASSES
LASSIE
LASSOS
LASTED
LASTER
LASTEX
LASTLY
MASCON
MASCOT
MASERS
MASHED

MASHER
MASHES
MASHIE
MASKED
MASKEG
MASKER
MASONS
MASORA
MASQUE
MASSED
MASSES
MASSIF
MASTED
MASTER
MASTIC
NASALS
NASHUA
NASIAL
NASION
NASSAU
NASSER
NASTIC
PASCAL
PASHAS
PASHTO
PASSED
PASSEE
PASSER
PASSES
PASSIM
PASSUS
PASTAS
PASTED
PASTEL
PASTER
PASTES
PASTIL
PASTOR
PASTRY
RASCAL
RASHER
RASHES
RASHLY
RASPED
RASPER
SASHAY
SASHED
SASHES
SASINS
SASSED
SASSES
TASKED
TASMAN
TASSEL
TASSET
TASTED
TASTER
TASTES
VASARI
VASHTI
VASILI
VASSAL
VASTER
VASTLY
WASHED
WASHER
WASHES
WASTED
WASTER
WASTES
YASMAK

•A•S••

BALSAM
BALSAS
BASSES
BASSET
BASSOS
CAESAR
CANSOS
CARSON
CASSIA
CASSIE
CASSIS
CATSUP
CAUSAL
CAUSED
CAUSER
CAUSES
DAISES
DAISYS
DAMSEL
DAMSON
DAWSON
FALSER
GASSED
GASSES
HALSEY
HANSEL
HANSOM
HASSEL
HASSLE
HAUSEN
HAWSER
HAWSES
KAASES
KAISER
KAMSIN
KANSAN
KANSAS
LAPSED
LAPSER
LAPSES
LAPSUS
LASSES
LASSIE
LASSOS
MAISIE
MAISON
MANSES
MARSHA
MARSHY
MASSED
MASSES
MASSIF
MAUSER
NAOSES
NASSAU
NASSER
NAUSEA
PANSYS
PARSEC
PARSED
PARSEE
PARSES
PARSIS
PARSON
PASSED
PASSEE
PASSER
PASSES
PASSIM
PASSUS
PATSYS
PAUSED
PAUSER
PAUSES
RAISED
RAISER
RAISES
RAISIN
RAMSON
RANSOM
SAMSHU
SAMSON
SANSAR
SANSEI
SARSAR
SASSED
SASSES
TARSAL
TARSUS
TASSEL
TASSET
VASSAL
WADSET
WAISTS
WARSAW
WATSON

•A••S•

BABISM
BABIST
BAGASS
BANISH
BAREST
CALASH
CALESA
CAMASS
CAMISE
CARESS
CARUSO
CAYUSE
DAMASK
DANISH
FAMISH
GALOSH
GARISH
GAYEST
HARASS
JADISH
KAVASS
LAMEST
LANOSE
LAOTSE
LATEST
LATISH
LAVISH
LAXEST
MAOISM
MAOIST
MARIST
MAYEST
NANISM
NAZISM
OAFISH
PALEST
PALISH
PAPIST
PARISH
PAVISE
RACISM
RACIST
RADISH
RAKISH
RAMOSE
RAPIST
RAREST
RAVISH
RAWEST
RAWISH
SADISM
SADIST
SAFEST
SAGEST
SALISH
SANEST
TAMEST
TANIST
TAOISM
TAOIST
VADOSE
VALISE
VANISH
WABASH
WATUSI

•A•••S

AALIIS
AARONS
BABIES
BABOOS
BABULS
BACHES
BADGES
BAGASS
BAGELS
BAHAIS
BAIRNS
BAKERS
BALERS
BALSAS
BANJOS
BANTUS
BARDES
BARGES
BARONS
BARRYS
BARYES
BASHES
BASICS
BASILS
BASINS
BASSES
BASSOS
BASTES
BATHOS
BATIKS
BATONS
BAUCIS
BAYOUS
CABALS
CABINS
CABLES
CABOBS
CACAOS
CACHES
CACTUS
CADDIS
CADETS
CADGES
CADMUS
CADRES
CAIRNS
CAJUNS
CALAIS
CALCES
CALEBS
CALIFS
CALLAS
CALLUS
CALVES
CALXES
CAMASS
CAMELS
CAMEOS
CAMPOS
CAMPUS
CANALS
CANERS
CANNAS
CANNES
CANOES
CANONS
CANSOS
CANTOS
CANTUS
CANVAS
CAPERS
CAPIAS
CAPONS
CARATS
CARERS
CARESS
CARETS
CARGOS
CARIBS
CARIES
CARLAS
CARLOS
CAROBS
CAROLS
CAROMS
CARPUS
CARTES
CARVES
CASALS
CASHES
CASSIS
CASTES
CATERS
CATHYS
CAUCUS
CAULES
CAULIS
CAULKS
CAUSES
CAVIES
CAVILS
DACHAS
DADOES
DAISES
DAISYS
DALLAS
DALLES
DAMANS
DANAUS
DANCES
DANNYS
DARERS
DARICS
DARIUS
DASHES
DATERS
DATTOS
DAUNTS
DAVEYS
DAVIDS
DAVIES
DAVITS
EAGLES
EARLES
EARTHS
EASELS
EATERS
FABLES
FACERS
FACETS
FACIES
FAGOTS
FAINTS
FAITHS
FAKERS
FAKIRS
FAMOUS
FANGAS
FANNYS
FANONS
FANUMS
FARADS
FARCES
FARERS
FARLES
FASCES

FAUCES
FAULTS
FAUNAS
FAUNUS
FAUVES
FAVORS
FAWKES
GABLES
GAFFES
GAGERS
GALLUS
GALOPS
GAMINS
GAMMAS
GAMOUS
GAMUTS
GANEFS
GANGES
GAPERS
GASHES
GASSES
GAUGES
GAUZES
GAVELS
GAVOTS
GAZERS
HABITS
HAGGIS
HAKIMS
HALERS
HALIDS
HALOES
HALVES
HAMALS
HAMZAS
HANCES
HANNAS
HARASS
HAREMS
HARRYS
HASHES
HASTES
HATERS
HATTYS
HAUNTS
HAVENS
HAWSES
HAZELS
HAZERS
IAMBUS
JABOTS
JACKYS
JACOBS
JAINAS
JALAPS
JAMIES
JANETS
JAPANS
JARVIS
JASONS
JAUNTS
JAZZES
KAASES
KABOBS
KAMIKS
KANSAS
KAPOKS
KAPPAS
KARATS
KARENS
KARMAS
KATHYS
KATIES
KAURIS
KAVASS
KAYAKS
KAZOOS
LABELS
LABORS
LACHES
LADIES
LADLES
LAGERS
LAIRDS
LAKERS
LAMEDS
LAMIAS
LAMMAS
LAMPAS
LANAIS
LANCES
LAPELS
LAPINS
LAPSES
LAPSUS
LARGOS
LARRYS
LASERS
LASHES
LASSES
LASSOS
LATHES
LATINS
LAUGHS
LAURAS
LAVERS
LAYERS
LAZARS
MABELS
MACAWS
MACERS
MACLES
MADAMS
MADGES
MADRAS
MAGOTS
MAIZES
MAJORS
MAKERS
MALAYS
MAMBAS
MAMBOS
MAMEYS
MAMIES
MAMMAS
MANDYS
MANGOS
MANIAS
MANORS
MANSES
MANTAS
MANTES
MANTIS
MAORIS
MAPLES
MAQUIS
MARCOS
MARCUS
MARGES
MARGOS
MARIAS
MARIES
MARTAS
MARTYS
MASERS
MASHES
MASONS
MASSES
MATEOS
MATEYS
MATINS
MATTES
MATZOS
MAUDES
MAUNDS
MAUVES
MAXIMS
MAYORS
MAZERS
NABOBS
NADIRS
NAEVUS
NAHUMS
NAIADS
NAMERS
NANCYS
NANTES
NAOMIS
NAOSES
NAPLES
NAPPES
NASALS
NAVELS
NAVIES
NAWABS
PACERS
PADDYS
PADRES
PAEANS
PAEONS
PAGANS
PAINTS
PALLAS
PALPUS
PAMPAS
PANDAS
PANELS
PANICS
PANSYS
PAPAWS
PAPERS
PAPPUS
PARENS
PARERS
PAREUS
PARGOS
PARIES
PARKAS
PARSES
PARSIS
PARVIS
PASHAS
PASSES
PASSUS
PASTAS
PASTES
PATENS
PATERS
PATHOS
PATIOS
PATOIS
PATSYS
PAULAS
PAULUS
PAUSES
PAVANS
PAVERS
PAWERS
PAYEES
PAYERS
RABBIS
RABIES
RACERS
RACHIS
RADARS
RADIOS
RADIUS
RAISES
RAJABS
RAJAHS
RAKERS
RALPHS
RAMIES
RAMOUS
RANEES
RANGES
RAOULS
RAPHIS
RAPIDS
RASHES
RATALS
RATELS
RATERS
RATIOS
RAVELS
RAVENS
RAVERS
RAYAHS
RAYONS
RAZEES
RAZORS
RAZZES
SABERS
SABINS
SABLES
SABOTS
SABRAS
SADHUS
SADIES
SAHEBS
SAHIBS
SAIGAS
SAINTS
SAJOUS
SAKERS
SALADS
SALLYS
SALMIS
SALONS
SALPAS
SALVES
SALVOS
SAMBAS
SAMBOS
SAMMYS
SANDYS
SANIES
SARAHS
SASHES
SASINS
SASSES
SATINS
SATYRS
SAUCES
SAULTS
SAUNAS
SAURUS
SAUTES
SAVERS
SAVINS
SAVORS
SAWERS
SAXONS
SAYERS
TABLES
TABOOS
TABORS
TAIGAS
TAINOS
TAINTS
TAKERS
TALERS
TALONS
TAMERS
TANGOS
TANKAS
TAPERS
TAPIRS
TAROTS
TARSUS
TASTES
TATARS
TAUNTS
TAUPES
TAURUS
TAWERS
TAXERS
TAZZAS
VALETS
VALGUS
VALOIS
VALUES
VALVES
VAPORS
VARIES
VARVES
VAULTS
VAUNTS
WADERS
WADIES
WAFERS
WAGERS
WAGONS
WAHOOS
WAISTS
WAIVES
WAKENS
WALDOS
WALERS
WALLAS
WALLIS
WALLYS
WALRUS
WALVIS
WAMMUS
WAMPUS
WANDAS
WASHES
WASTES
WATAPS
WATERS
WAVERS
WAVEYS
WAVIES
WAYNES
YACHTS
YAGERS
YAHOOS
YAMENS
YAMUNS
YAPONS
ZAMIAS
ZANIES
ZAYINS

••AS••

ABASED
ABASER
ABASES
ALASKA
BEASTS
BIASED
BIASES
BLASTO
BLASTS
BOASTS
BRASHY
BRASSY
CEASED
CEASES
CHASED
CHASER
CHASES
CHASMS

CHASSE
CHASTE
CLASPS
CLASSY
COASTS
CRASIS
ERASED
ERASER
ERASES
EYASES
FEASED
FEASES
FEASTS
FIASCO
FLASHY
FLASKS
GLASSY
GRASPS
GRASSY
KAASES
LEASED
LEASES
MEASLY
MIASMA
OCASEY
OMASUM
PEASEN
PEASES
PHASED
PHASES
PHASIA
PHASIC
PHASIS
PLASHY
PLASIA
PLASIS
PLASMA
PLASMO
PLASTY
QUASAR
REASON
ROASTS
SEASON
SHASTA
SPASMS
STASES
STASIS
TEASED
TEASEL
TEASER
TEASES
TOASTS
TRASHY
UKASES
UPASES
WEASEL
WRASSE
YEASTS
YEASTY

••A•S•

BRAISE
BRASSY
CHAISE
CHASSE
CLASSY
CLAUSE
COARSE
ELAPSE
FRAISE
GLASSY
GRASSY
HEARSE
HEARST
HOARSE
PRAISE
SPARSE
TRANSP
WRASSE

••A••S

ABACAS
ABACUS
ABASES
ABATES
ABATIS
ADAGES
ADAPTS
AEACUS
AGAMAS
AGATES
AGAVES
ALAMOS
ALARMS
AMAZES
ANABAS
AVAILS
AWAITS
AWAKES
AWARDS
BEARDS
BEASTS
BEAUTS
BIALYS
BIASES
BLACKS
BLADES
BLAINS
BLAMES
BLANKS
BLARES
BLASTS
BLAZES
BOARDS
BOASTS
BRACES
BRACTS
BRAHMS
BRAIDS
BRAILS
BRAINS
BRAKES
BRANDS
BRANTS
BRAVES
BRAVOS
BRAWLS
BRAZAS
BRAZES
BRAZOS
BWANAS
CEASES
CHAFES
CHAFFS
CHAINS
CHAIRS
CHALKS
CHAMPS
CHANGS
CHANTS
CHAPES
CHARDS
CHARES
CHARMS
CHARTS
CHASES
CHASMS
CLACKS
CLAIMS
CLAMPS
CLANGS
CLANKS
CLARAS
CLARES
CLAROS
CLASPS
COASTS
COATIS
COAXES
CRAALS
CRACKS
CRAFTS
CRAIGS
CRAKES
CRAMPS
CRANES
CRANKS
CRAPES
CRASIS
CRATES
CRAVES
CRAWLS
CRAZES
DEATHS
DIANAS
DIANES
DOALLS
DRAFFS
DRAFTS
DRAINS
DRAKES
DRAMAS
DRAPES
DRAWLS
DWARFS
ELANDS
ELATES
ENACTS
ENATES
EPACTS
ERASES
ETAPES
EVADES
EXACTS
EXALTS
EYASES
FEASES
FEASTS
FLACKS
FLAILS
FLAIRS
FLAKES
FLAMES
FLANKS
FLARES
FLASKS
FLATUS
FLAXES
FRACAS
FRAILS
FRAMES
FRANCS
FRANKS
FRAUDS
GHAUTS
GIANTS
GLACES
GLACIS
GLADES
GLADYS
GLAIRS
GLANDS
GLARES
GLAZES
GNARLS
GRACES
GRADES
GRADUS
GRAFTS
GRAINS
GRANTS
GRAPES
GRAPHS
GRASPS
GRATES
GRATIS
GRAVES
GRAZES
GUACOS
GUANOS
GUARDS
GUAVAS
HEARTS
HEATHS
HEAVES
HIATUS
HOARDS
HOAXES
HYADES
ICARUS
IMAGES
INARMS
IRAQIS
ISAACS
KAASES
KHAKIS
KNACKS
KNAVES
KOALAS
KRAALS
KRAITS
LEARNS
LEASES
LEAVES
LIANAS
LIANES
LLAMAS
LLANOS
LOAVES
MEATUS
MIAULS
OKAPIS
ORACHS
ORANGS
ORATES
OXALIS
PEARLS
PEASES
PHASES
PHASIS
PIANOS
PLACES
PLACKS
PLAIDS
PLAINS
PLAITS
PLANES
PLANKS
PLANTS
PLASIS
PLATES
PLAYAS
PLAZAS
PRANKS
PRATES
PRAWNS
PRAXIS
PSALMS
QUACKS
QUAFFS
QUAILS
QUAKES
QUALMS
QUANTS
QUARKS
QUARTS
REACTS
REALES
REALMS
REARMS
RIATAS
ROALDS
ROASTS
SCALDS
SCALES
SCALPS
SCAMPS
SCAPES
SCARES
SCARFS
SCARPS
SCAUPS
SEAMUS
SHACKS
SHADES
SHAFTS
SHAKES
SHAKOS
SHALES
SHAMES
SHAMUS
SHANKS
SHAPES
SHARDS
SHARES
SHARKS
SHARPS
SHAVES
SHAWLS
SHAWMS
SKALDS
SKATES
SLACKS
SLAKES
SLANTS
SLATES
SLAVES
SMACKS
SMALLS
SMARTS
SMAZES
SNACKS
SNAFUS
SNAILS
SNAKES
SNARES
SNARLS
SNATHS
SPACES
SPADES
SPAHIS
SPAITS
SPALLS
SPANKS
SPARES
SPARKS
SPASMS
SPATES
SPAWNS
STACKS
STACYS
STAFFS
STAGES
STAINS
STAIRS
STAKES
STALES
STALKS
STALLS
STAMPS
STANDS
STAPES
STARES
STARTS

STASES
STASIS
STATES
STATUS
STAVES
SWAGES
SWAILS
SWAINS
SWALES
SWAMIS
SWAMPS
SWARDS
SWARMS
SWATHS
TEASES
THADYS
THALES
THAMES
THANES
THANKS
TIARAS
TOASTS
TRACES
TRACKS
TRACTS
TRADES
TRAGUS
TRAILS
TRAINS
TRAITS
TRAMPS
TRAVES
TRAWLS
TSADES
TWANGS
UKASES
UPASES
URAEUS
URANUS
USAGES
VIANDS
WEALDS
WEAVES
WHACKS
WHALES
WHANGS
WHARFS
WOALDS
WRACKS
YEARNS
YEASTS

•••AS•

AGHAST
BAGASS
BREAST
BYPASS
BYPAST
CALASH
CAMASS
CHIASM
CREASE
CREASY
DAMASK
DEBASE
DICAST
DYNAST
ENCASE
GREASE
GREASY
HARASS
INCASE
KAVASS
KINASE
LIPASE
MEGASS
MORASS
OBLAST
ORGASM
PHRASE
PLEASE
POTASH
QUEASY
RECAST
REHASH
REPASS
REPAST
SIWASH
SPLASH
SQUASH
STRASS
THRASH
UNEASY
UNMASK
UPCAST
UREASE
WABASH
ZYMASE

•••A•S

ABRAMS
ADDAMS
ALLANS
ALLAYS
ALMAHS
ALTARS
ALVANS
ALWAYS
ANNALS
APPALS
ARGALS
ARIANS
ARRAYS
ARYANS
ASIANS
ASSAIS
ASSAYS
ATTARS
AUDADS
BAGASS
BAHAIS
BELAYS
BLEAKS
BLEARS
BLEATS
BLOATS
BOGANS
BOYARS
BREADS
BREAKS
BREAMS
BRIARS
BROADS
BUBALS
BURANS
BYLAWS
BYPASS
BYWAYS
CABALS
CACAOS
CALAIS
CAMASS
CANALS
CARATS
CASALS
CEDARS
CHEATS
CHIAUS
CIGARS
CLEANS
CLEARS
CLEATS
CLOAKS
CORALS
CRAALS
CREAKS
CREAMS
CROAKS
CROATS
CUBANS
CYCADS
CYMARS
DAMANS
DANAUS
DEBARS
DECALS
DECAYS
DEDANS
DELAYS
DEWANS
DINAHS
DINARS
DIVANS
DIWANS
DREADS
DREAMS
DRYADS
DUCATS
EBOATS
EDGARS
EGGARS
EMBARS
EMBAYS
EPHAHS
EQUALS
ESSAYS
ETHANS
FARADS
FEUARS
FINALS
FLEAMS
FLOATS
FORAYS
FREAKS
FRIARS
GLEAMS
GLEANS
GLOATS
GONADS
GORALS
GREATS
GROANS
GROATS
HAMALS
HARASS
HBEAMS
HEXADS
HIRAMS
HOGANS
HUMANS
IBEAMS
IDEALS
IHRAMS
INLAWS
INLAYS
ISAACS
JALAPS
JAPANS
JIHADS
JONAHS
JORAMS
JUDAHS
JURATS
KARATS
KAVASS
KAYAKS
KNEADS
KODAKS
KRAALS
KULAKS
LANAIS
LAZARS
LILACS
LOCALS
LOTAHS
MACAWS
MADAMS
MALAYS
MEDALS
MEGASS
METALS
MOLARS
MONADS
MORALS
MORASS
MORAYS
MURALS
NAIADS
NASALS
NAWABS
NOMADS
NOPALS
NOWAYS
OCEANS
OCTADS
OREADS
ORGANS
OSCANS
OSCARS
PAEANS
PAGANS
PAPAWS
PAVANS
PECANS
PEDALS
PEKANS
PETALS
PHIALS
PILAFS
PLEADS
PLEATS
PSHAWS
PYRANS
QUEANS
RADARS
RAJABS
RAJAHS
RATALS
RAYAHS
RECAPS
REDANS
RELAYS
REMANS
REPASS
REPAYS
RIVALS
RIYALS
ROMANS
ROWANS
ROYALS
SALADS
SARAHS
SCRAGS
SCRAMS
SCRAPS
SEBATS
SEDANS
SEPALS
SERACS
SERAIS
SHEARS
SHOALS
SHOATS
SIMARS
SITARS
SIZARS
SKEANS
SMEARS
SNEAKS
SOLANS
SONARS
SOWARS
SPEAKS
SPEARS
SPLATS
SPLAYS
SPRAGS
SPRATS
SPRAYS
SQUABS
SQUADS
SQUATS
SQUAWS
STEAKS
STEALS
STEAMS
STOATS
STRAPS
STRASS
STRAWS
STRAYS
SUBAHS
SUGARS
SUMACS
SURAHS
SUSANS
SWEARS
SWEATS
TATARS
TICALS
TITANS
TOMANS
TORAHS
TOTALS
TREADS
TREATS
TRIADS
TRIALS
TWEAKS
UBOATS
UMIAKS
UNBARS
UNCAPS
UNHATS
UNLAYS
UNMANS
UNSAYS
VICARS
VITALS
VOCALS
WATAPS
WHEALS
WHEATS
WIGANS
WREAKS
XYLANS
ZBEAMS

••••AS

ABACAS
ABOMAS
AENEAS
AGAMAS
AGORAS
ALPHAS
AMEBAS
ANABAS
ANIMAS
ANITAS
AORTAS
ARECAS
ARENAS
AROMAS
BALSAS

BELGAS
BELLAS
BEULAS
BOREAS
BRAZAS
BURSAS
BWANAS
CALLAS
CANNAS
CANVAS
CAPIAS
CARLAS
CEIBAS
CELIAS
CHELAS
CHUFAS
CLARAS
COBIAS
COBRAS
COCOAS
COLZAS
COMMAS
CONGAS
COTTAS
CUTLAS
DACHAS
DALLAS
DELIAS
DELLAS
DELTAS
DERMAS
DIANAS
DIPSAS
DOBLAS
DOBRAS
DOGMAS
DONNAS
DRAMAS
ELENAS
ELIZAS
ENEMAS
EVITAS
EXTRAS
FANGAS
FAUNAS
FLORAS
FRACAS
FREDAS
GAMMAS
GILDAS
GRETAS
GUAVAS
GUMMAS
HAMZAS
HANNAS
HELLAS
HENNAS
HILDAS
HYDRAS
HYENAS
JAINAS
JOSIAS
JULIAS
JUNTAS
KANSAS
KAPPAS
KARMAS
KOALAS
LAMIAS
LAMMAS
LAMPAS
LAURAS
LEHUAS
LEMMAS
LEONAS
LIANAS
LIBRAS
LINDAS
LINGAS
LIVIAS
LLAMAS
LUCIAS
LYDIAS
MADRAS
MAMBAS
MAMMAS
MANIAS
MANTAS
MARIAS
MARTAS
MECCAS
MOIRAS
MYRNAS
NORIAS
NORMAS
NUBIAS
OMEGAS
OPERAS
PALLAS
PAMPAS
PANDAS
PARKAS
PASHAS
PASTAS
PAULAS
PELIAS
PIZZAS
PLAYAS
PLAZAS
POLKAS
PRESAS
PUNKAS
QUOTAS
RHODAS
RIATAS
RUMBAS
SABRAS
SAIGAS
SALPAS
SAMBAS
SAUNAS
SCHWAS
SCUBAS
SENNAS
SEPIAS
SIGMAS
SILVAS
SOFTAS
SONIAS
SONYAS
STUPAS
SUTRAS
SYLVAS
TAIGAS
TANKAS
TAZZAS
THEDAS
THETAS
THOMAS
THUJAS
TIARAS
TIBIAS
TOBIAS
ULEMAS
UMBRAS
UVULAS
VERNAS
VESTAS
VILLAS
VIOLAS
VIRGAS
VISTAS
VODKAS
VOLVAS
WALLAS
WANDAS
WILMAS
YERBAS
YUCCAS
ZAMIAS
ZEBRAS

AT••••

ATABAL
ATAMAN
ATAVIC
ATAXIA
ATAXIC
ATHENA
ATHENE
ATHENS
ATHOME
ATOLLS
ATOMIC
ATONAL
ATONED
ATONER
ATONES
ATONIC
ATREUS
ATRIAL
ATRIUM
ATTACH
ATTACK
ATTAIN
ATTARS
ATTEND
ATTEST
ATTICA
ATTICS
ATTILA
ATTIRE
ATTLEE
ATTORN
ATTUNE

A•T•••

ACTING
ACTINI
ACTINO
ACTION
ACTIUM
ACTIVE
ACTORS
ACTUAL
AETHER
AFTOSA
ALTAIC
ALTAIR
ALTARS
ALTERS
ALTHEA
ANTEED
ANTERO
ANTHEA
ANTHEM
ANTHER
ANTIAR
ANTICS
ANTLER
ANTLIA
ANTONS
ANTONY
ANTRIM
ANTRUM
ARTELS
ARTERY
ARTFUL
ARTHRO
ARTHUR
ARTIES
ARTIST
ARTOIS
ARTURO
ASTERI
ASTERN
ASTERO
ASTERS
ASTHMA
ASTRAL
ASTRAY
ASTRID
ASTUTE
ATTACH
ATTACK
ATTAIN
ATTARS
ATTEND
ATTEST
ATTICA
ATTICS
ATTILA
ATTIRE
ATTLEE
ATTORN
ATTUNE
AUTHOR
AUTISM
AUTOED
AUTUMN
AZTECS

A••T••

ABATED
ABATER
ABATES
ABATIS
ABATOR
ACETAL
ACETIC
ACETUM
ACETYL
ADYTUM
AEETES
AGATES
AGATHA
ALATED
AMATOL
AMYTAL
ANATTO
ANITAS
ANITRA
AORTAE
AORTAL
AORTAS
AORTIC
APATHY
APHTHA
ARCTIC
ARETES
AUNTIE
AUSTEN
AUSTER
AUSTIN
AUSTRO
AVATAR
AZOTIC

A•••T•

ABBOTS
ABORTS
ABWATT
ACUATE
ACUITY
ADAPTS
ADEPTS
ADMITS
ADNATE
ADOPTS
ADULTS
AERATE
AGENTS
AGISTS
AGLETS
AGNATE
AGOUTI
AGOUTY
ALBATA
ALBITE
ALCOTT
ALECTO
ALERTS
ALEUTS
ALLOTS
AMBITS
AMENTS
AMRITA
ANATTO
ANSATE
APLITE
ARANTA
ARBUTE
ARGOTS
ARISTA
ARISTO
ARMETS
ARUNTA
ASCOTS
ASSETS
ASTUTE
AUDITS
AUGHTS
AUGITE
AURATE
AVERTS
AVESTA
AVIATE
AWAITS

A••••T

ABDUCT
ABJECT
ABLAUT
ABLEST
ABRUPT
ABSENT
ABVOLT
ABWATT
ACCENT
ACCEPT
ACCOST
ACQUIT
ADDICT
ADDUCT
ADJUST
ADMIXT
ADRIFT
ADROIT
ADVENT
ADVERT
AFFECT
AFLOAT
AGHAST
AIGLET
ALBEIT
ALBERT
ALCOTT
ALIGHT
ALLOUT
ALMOST
AMIDST
AMOUNT
AMULET
ANKLET

ANOINT
AORIST
ARARAT
ARDENT
ARGENT
ARIGHT
ARMLET
ARMPIT
ARPENT
ARRANT
ARREST
ARTIST
ASCENT
ASKANT
ASLANT
ASPECT
ASSENT
ASSERT
ASSIST
ASSORT
ATTEST
AUGUST
AUKLET
AURIST
AVOCET

•AT•••

BATAAN
BATEAU
BATHED
BATHER
BATHOS
BATIKS
BATING
BATMAN
BATMEN
BATONS
BATTED
BATTEN
BATTER
BATTIK
BATTLE
BATTUE
CATALO
CATCHY
CATENA
CATERS
CATGUT
CATHAY
CATHER
CATHYS
CATION
CATKIN
CATLIN
CATNIP
CATSUP
CATTED
CATTIE
CATTLE
DATARY
DATERS
DATING
DATIVE
DATTOS
DATURA
EATERS
EATING
FATHER
FATHOM
FATIMA
FATING
FATTED
FATTEN
FATTER
GATHER
GATING
HATBOX
HATERS
HATFUL
HATING
HATPIN
HATRED
HATTED
HATTER
HATTIE
HATTYS
IATRIC
KATHIE
KATHYS
KATIES
KATION
LATEEN
LATELY
LATENT
LATEST
LATHED
LATHER
LATHES
LATINS
LATISH
LATRIA
LATTEN
LATTER
LATVIA
MATEOS
MATEYS
MATING
MATINS
MATRIX
MATRON
MATTED
MATTEO
MATTER
MATTES
MATTIE
MATURE
MATZOS
MATZOT
NATANT
NATHAN
NATION
NATIVE
NATRON
NATURE
PATCHY
PATENS
PATENT
PATERS
PATHAN
PATHIA
PATHOL
PATHOS
PATINA
PATINE
PATIOS
PATOIS
PATROL
PATRON
PATSYS
PATTED
PATTEN
PATTER
PATTON
RATALS
RATELS
RATERS
RATHER
RATIFY
RATINE
RATING
RATION
RATIOS
RATITE
RATLIN
RATOON
RATTAN
RATTED
RATTEN
RATTER
RATTLE
RATTLY
SATANG
SATARA
SATEEN
SATING
SATINS
SATINY
SATIRE
SATORI
SATRAP
SATURN
SATYRS
TATARS
TATLER
TATTED
TATTER
TATTLE
TATTOO
VATFUL
VATTED
WATAPE
WATAPS
WATERS
WATERY
WATSON
WATTLE
WATUSI

•A•T••

BAITED
BAITER
BALTIC
BANTAM
BANTER
BANTUS
BARTER
BARTOK
BARTON
BASTED
BASTES
BATTED
BATTEN
BATTER
BATTIK
BATTLE
BATTUE
BAXTER
CACTUS
CAFTAN
CANTED
CANTER
CANTHI
CANTLE
CANTON
CANTOR
CANTOS
CANTUS
CAPTOR
CARTED
CARTEL
CARTER
CARTES
CARTON
CASTER
CASTES
CASTLE
CASTOR
CASTRO
CATTED
CATTIE
CATTLE
DACTYL
DAFTLY
DALTON
DANTON
DARTED
DARTER
DARTLE
DATTOS
DAYTON
EARTHS
EARTHY
EASTER
EASTON
FACTOR
FAITHS
FALTER
FANTAN
FANTOM
FASTED
FASTEN
FASTER
FATTED
FATTEN
FATTER
GAITED
GAITER
GANTRY
GARTER
GASTON
GASTRO
HALTED
HALTER
HARTAL
HASTED
HASTEN
HASTES
HATTED
HATTER
HATTIE
HATTYS
LACTAM
LACTIC
LAOTSE
LASTED
LASTER
LASTEX
LASTLY
LATTEN
LATTER
MAITRE
MALTED
MALTHA
MANTAS
MANTEL
MANTES
MANTIC
MANTIS
MANTLE
MANTUA
MARTAS
MARTEN
MARTHA
MARTHE
MARTIN
MARTYR
MARTYS
MASTED
MASTER
MASTIC
MATTED
MATTEO
MATTER
MATTES
MATTIE
NANTES
NASTIC
NAUTCH
PALTER
PALTRY
PANTED
PANTIE
PANTRY
PARTED
PARTLY
PASTAS
PASTED
PASTEL
PASTER
PASTES
PASTIL
PASTOR
PASTRY
PATTED
PATTEN
PATTER
PATTON
RAFTED
RAFTER
RAGTAG
RANTED
RANTER
RATTAN
RATTED
RATTEN
RATTER
RATTLE
RATTLY
SAITIC
SALTED
SALTER
SANTOL
SARTOR
SARTRE
SAUTES
TACTIC
TAMTAM
TARTAN
TARTAR
TARTER
TARTLY
TASTED
TASTER
TASTES
TATTED
TATTER
TATTLE
TATTOO
TAUTEN
TAUTER
TAUTLY
VASTER
VASTLY
VATTED
WAFTED
WAFTER
WAITED
WAITER
WALTER
WALTON
WANTED
WANTER
WANTON
WASTED
WASTER
WASTES
WATTLE
XANTHO

•A••T•

BABITE
BALATA
BARITE
BARYTA

BASUTO
CADETS
CANUTE
CAPITA
CAPOTE
CARATE
CARATS
CARETS
CAVITE
CAVITY
DAINTY
DAKOTA
DALETH
DANITE
DAUNTS
DAVITS
FACETS
FAGOTS
FAINTS
FAULTS
FAULTY
GAIETY
GAMETE
GAMETO
GAMUTS
GAVOTS
GAYETY
HABITS
HALITE
HALUTZ
HAMITE
HAUNTS
JABOTS
JANETS
JAUNTS
JAUNTY
KARATE
KARATS
LANATE
LAXITY
MAGOTS
MALATE
MANITO
MANITU
PAINTS
PAINTY
PAIUTE
PALATE
PARITY
PASHTO
RARITY
RATITE
SABOTS
SAFETY
SAINTS
SALUTE
SAMITE
SANITY
SAULTS
TAINTS
TAROTS
TAUNTS
TAXITE
VACATE
VALETS
VANITY
VASHTI
VAULTS
VAUNTS
WAISTS
WAPITI
WARMTH
YACHTS

•A•••T

BABIST
BALLET
BALLOT
BANDIT
BARBET
BAREST
BARRET
BASALT
BASKET
BASSET
CABLET
CACHET
CADENT
CAMLET
CANNOT
CARPET
CARROT
CASKET
CATGUT
CAUGHT
CAVEAT
CAVORT
DACOIT
DAKOIT
EAGLET
FAGGOT
FANJET
FAROUT
FAUCET
GADGET
GALACT
GALIOT
GALOOT
GAMBIT
GANNET
GARGET
GARNET
GARRET
GASKET
GAYEST
HAGBUT
HAMLET
HARLOT
HASLET
HAVENT
JACKET
JAPHET
LABRET
LAMENT
LAMEST
LANCET
LAPPET
LARIAT
LATENT
LATEST
LAXEST
LAYOUT
MAGGOT
MAGNET
MAHOUT
MALLET
MAMMET
MAOIST
MARGOT
MARIST
MARKET
MARMOT
MASCOT
MATZOT
MAYEST
NATANT
NAUGHT
PACKET
PALEST
PALLET
PAPIST
PARENT
PARGET
PARROT
PATENT
RABBET
RABBIT
RACIST
RACKET
RAGOUT
RAJPUT
RAPIST
RAREST
RAWEST
SABBAT
SACHET
SADIST
SAFEST
SAGEST
SALLET
SAMLET
SANEST
SAVANT
TABLET
TALENT
TAMEST
TANIST
TAOIST
TAPPET
TARGET
TASSET
TAUGHT
VACANT
VARLET
WADSET
WALLET
WALNUT
WAYOUT

••AT••

ABATED
ABATER
ABATES
ABATIS
ABATOR
AGATES
AGATHA
ALATED
AMATOL
ANATTO
APATHY
AVATAR
BEATEN
BEATER
BOATED
CHATTY
COATED
COATIS
CRATCH
CRATED
CRATER
CRATES
DEATHS
DEATHY
DIATOM
ELATED
ELATER
ELATES
ENATES
ENATIC
FLATLY
FLATUS
FRATER
GNATHO
GOATEE
GRATED
GRATER
GRATES
GRATIS
HEATED
HEATER
HEATHS
HEATHY
HIATUS
LOATHE
MEATUS
MOATED
NEATER
NEATLY
ORATED
ORATES
ORATOR
PLATAN
PLATED
PLATEN
PLATER
PLATES
PLATTE
PRATED
PRATER
PRATES
QUATRE
RIATAS
SCATHE
SEATED
SKATED
SKATER
SKATES
SLATED
SLATER
SLATES
SNATCH
SNATHE
SNATHS
SPATES
SPATHE
STATAL
STATED
STATER
STATES
STATIC
STATOR
STATUE
STATUS
SWATCH
SWATHE
SWATHS
THATCH
VIATIC
VIATOR
WRATHY

••A•T•

ADAPTS
ANATTO
ARANTA
AWAITS
BEASTS
BEAUTS
BEAUTY
BLASTO
BLASTS
BOASTS
BRACTS
BRANTS
CHAETA
CHAETO
CHANTS
CHANTY
CHARTS
CHASTE
CHATTY
COASTS
CRAFTS
CRAFTY
DEARTH
DRAFTS
DRAFTY
ECARTE
ENACTS
EPACTS
EXACTA
EXACTS
EXALTS
FEALTY
FEASTS
GHAUTS
GIANTS
GRAFTS
GRANTS
HEALTH
HEARTH
HEARTS
HEARTY
KRAITS
LEANTO
PLAITS
PLANTS
PLASTY
PLATTE
QUANTA
QUANTS
QUARTE
QUARTO
QUARTS
QUARTZ
REACTS
REALTY
RIALTO
ROASTS
SCANTY
SHAFTS
SHANTY
SHASTA
SLANTS
SMALTI
SMALTO
SMARTS
SPAITS
SPARTA
STACTE
STARTS
SWARTH
SWARTY
TOASTS
TRACTS
TRAITS
WEALTH
WRAITH
YEASTS
YEASTY

••A••T

ARARAT
CHALET
CLARET
CRAVAT
FLAUNT
HEARST
IMARET
LEARNT
PEANUT
PLACET
PLAINT
PLANET
QUAINT
TEAPOT
THANAT
ZEALOT

•••AT•

ABWATT
ACUATE
ADNATE

6

AERATE
AGNATE
ALBATA
ANSATE
AURATE
AVIATE
BALATA
BEMATA
BERATE
BLEATS
BLOATS
BORATE
BREATH
BYPATH
CARATE
CARATS
CERATE
CERATO
CHEATS
CLEATS
COMATE
CREATE
CROATS
CURATE
DEBATE
DILATE
DONATE
DUCATS
EBOATS
EQUATE
ERGATE
ERRATA
ERSATZ
ESTATE
FIXATE
FLOATS
FLOATY
GLOATS
GREATS
GROATS
GYRATE
HECATE
HEMATO
HEPATO
IDEATE
INMATE
INNATE
IODATE
JUGATE
JURATS
KARATE
KARATS
KERATO
LANATE
LEGATE
LEGATO
LIGATE
LOBATE
LOCATE
LUNATE
LUXATE
MALATE
MUTATE
NEGATE
NEMATO
OBLATE
OLEATE
OPIATE
ORNATE
PALATE
PEDATE
PEDATI
PILATE
PIRATE
PLEATS
POTATO
PUPATE
REBATE
REBATO
RELATE
ROTATE
RUBATO
RUGATE
SEBATS
SEDATE
SENATE
SHEATH
SHOATS
SOMATA
SOMATO
SONATA
SPLATS
SPRATS
SQUATS
STOATS
STRATA
STRATI
SWEATS
SWEATY
TERATO
TOMATO
TREATS
TREATY
TUBATE
UBOATS
UNHATS
UPDATE
VACATE
VELATE
WHEATS
WREATH
ZONATE

•••A•T

ABLAUT
ABWATT
AGHAST
ARRANT
ASKANT
ASLANT
BASALT
BEZANT
BREAST
BRYANT
BYPAST
COBALT
DECANT
DEPART
DESALT
DICAST
DREAMT
DYNAST
ENRAPT
ERRANT
EXTANT
GALACT
GIGANT
GOCART
GOKART
HOBART
IMPACT
IMPART
INFANT
INTACT
JURANT
KUWAIT
LEVANT
MOZART
MUTANT
NATANT
OBLAST
OCTANT
PEDANT
PLIANT
RECANT
RECAST
REDACT
REPAST
SAVANT
SECANT
SEJANT
SONANT
STRAIT
STUART
TENANT
THWART
TRUANT
TYBALT
TYRANT
UMLAUT
UPCAST
VACANT
VOLANT

••••AT

AFLOAT
ARARAT
BOBCAT
CAVEAT
CILIAT
CLIMAT
COMBAT
CRAVAT
CUSHAT
DEFEAT
DERMAT
FORMAT
GUTTAT
HEREAT
LARIAT
LOQUAT
MUSCAT
NOUGAT
ORGEAT
OUTSAT
REHEAT
REPEAT
RESEAT
SABBAT
SEURAT
SHEBAT
SNOCAT
STOMAT
THANAT
THREAT
THROAT
TOMCAT
UNSEAT
UPBEAT
WOMBAT

AU••••

AUBADE
AUBREY
AUBURN
AUDADS
AUDILE
AUDITS
AUDREY
AUGEAN
AUGEND
AUGERS
AUGHTS
AUGITE
AUGURS
AUGURY
AUGUST
AUKLET
AUNTIE
AURATE
AUREUS
AURIGA
AURIST
AURORA
AUROUS
AUSPEX
AUSTEN
AUSTER
AUSTIN
AUSTRO
AUTHOR
AUTISM
AUTOED
AUTUMN
AUXINS

A•U•••

ABULIA
ABUSED
ABUSER
ABUSES
ACUATE
ACUITY
ACUMEN
ADULTS
AGUISH
ALUDEL
ALUINO
ALUINS
ALULAE
ALULAR
ALUMIN
ALUMNA
ALUMNI
AMULET
AMUSED
AMUSER
AMUSES
ANUBIS
ANURAN
ANUSES
AOUDAD
APULIA
AQUILA
ARUNTA
AZURES

A••U••

ABDUCT
ABJURE
ABLUSH
ABOUND
ABRUPT
ABSURD
ACCUSE
ACQUIT
ACTUAL
ADDUCE
ADDUCT
ADJURE
ADJUST
AERUGO
AGOUTI
AGOUTY
ALBUMS
ALCUIN
ALEUTS
ALLUDE
ALLURE
ALMUCE
ALMUDE
ALMUDS
AMBUSH
AMOUNT
AMOURS
AMPULE
AMPULS
ANNUAL
ANNULS
ARBUTE
ARGUED
ARGUER
ARGUES
ARGUFY
ARMURE
AROUND
AROUSE
ARTURO
ASBURY
ASSUME
ASSURE
ASTUTE
ATTUNE
AUBURN
AUGURS
AUGURY
AUGUST
AUTUMN
AVOUCH

A•••U•

ABACUS
ABLAUT
ACCRUE
ACEOUS
ACETUM
ACINUS
ACIOUS
ACTIUM
ADIEUS
ADIEUX
ADNOUN
ADYTUM
AEACUS
AECIUM
AEGEUS
AEOLUS
AFFLUX
AGOGUE
ALARUM
ALDOUS
ALLIUM
ALLOUT
AMYLUM
ANIMUS
ANTRUM
ARIOUS
ARMFUL
ARNAUD
ARTFUL
ARTHUR
ASARUM
ASYLUM
ATREUS
ATRIUM
AUREUS
AUROUS
AVENUE

A••••U

ACAJOU
AMADOU
APERCU

•AU•••

BAUBLE
BAUCIS
CAUCUS
CAUDAD
CAUDAL
CAUDEX
CAUDLE
CAUGHT
CAULES

CAULIS
CAULKS
CAUSAL
CAUSED
CAUSER
CAUSES
DAUBED
DAUBER
DAUBRY
DAUNTS
FAUCAL
FAUCES
FAUCET
FAULTS
FAULTY
FAUNAE
FAUNAL
FAUNAS
FAUNUS
FAUVES
GAUCHE
GAUCHO
GAUGED
GAUGER
GAUGES
GAUZES
HAULED
HAULER
HAULMY
HAUNCH
HAUNTS
HAUSEN
JAUNTS
JAUNTY
KAURIS
LAUDED
LAUDER
LAUGHS
LAUNCE
LAUNCH
LAURAE
LAURAS
LAUREL
LAURIE
MAUDES
MAULED
MAULER
MAUMAU
MAUNDS
MAUNDY
MAUSER
MAUVES
NAUGHT
NAUSEA
NAUTCH
PAUKER
PAULAS
PAULIN
PAULUS
PAUNCH
PAUPER
PAUSED
PAUSER
PAUSES
SAUCED
SAUCER
SAUCES
SAUGER
SAULTS
SAUNAS
SAUREL
SAURUS
SAUTES
TAUGHT
TAUNTS
TAUPES
TAURUS
TAUTEN
TAUTER
TAUTLY
VAULTS
VAUNTS
WAULED
YAUPED
YAUPON

•A•U••

BABULS
BARUCH
BASUTO
CAJUNS
CANUCK
CANULA
CANUTE
CARUSO
CASUAL
CAYUGA
CAYUSE
DANUBE
DATURA
FACULA
FANUMS
GAMUTS
HALUTZ
JAGUAR
KABUKI
LACUNA
LAGUNE
LANUGO
LAZULI
MACULA
MACULE
MADURA
MADURO
MAGUEY
MANUAL
MANUEL
MANURE
MAQUIS
MATURE
MAZUMA
NAHUMS
NATURE
PAIUTE
PAPUAN
PAPULA
PAPULE
PARURE
RADULA
RAOULS
SALUKI
SALUTE
SAMUEL
SATURN
VACUUM
VAGUER
VALUED
VALUES
VARUNA
WATUSI
YAMUNS

•A••U•

BANGUI
BANGUP
BANTUS
BARIUM
BARNUM
BARQUE
BASQUE
BATTUE
BAYEUX
BAYOUS
CACTUS
CADMUS
CAECUM
CAIQUE
CALLUS
CAMPUS
CANGUE
CANTUS
CARPUS
CASQUE
CATGUT
CATSUP
CAUCUS
DANAUS
DARIUS
EARFUL
FAMOUS
FAROUT
FAUNUS
GALLUP
GALLUS
GAMOUS
GANGUE
HAGBUT
HALLUX
HAMAUL
HANGUP
HATFUL
IAMBUS
JAIPUR
JARFUL
KALIUM
LABIUM
LABOUR
LABRUM
LANGUR
LAPFUL
LAPSUS
LARRUP
LAWFUL
LAYOUT
MADEUP
MAGNUM
MAHOUT
MAKEUP
MANFUL
MANQUE
MANTUA
MARAUD
MARCUS
MARDUK
MARKUP
MARQUE
MASQUE
NAEVUS
NASHUA
PALPUS
PAPPUS
PAREUS
PASSUS
PAULUS
RADIUM
RADIUS
RAGOUT
RAJPUT
RAMOUS
SACRUM
SADHUS
SAJOUS
SAMBUR
SANGUI
SANNUP
SAURUS
TAKEUP
TALCUM
TALMUD
TARSUS
TAURUS
VACUUM
VALGUS
VATFUL
WALKUP
WALNUT
WALRUS
WAMMUS
WAMPUM
WAMPUS
WARMUP
WAYOUT

•A•••U

BATEAU
CACHOU
DACHAU
JABIRU
LANDAU
MANCHU
MANITU
MAUMAU
NASSAU
SAMSHU

••AU••

BEAUTS
BEAUTY
CLAUDE
CLAUSE
FLAUNT
FRAUDS
FRAUEN
GHAUTS
GLAUCO
HEAUME
MIAULS
SCAUPS
STAURO
TRAUMA

••A•U•

ABACUS
AEACUS
ALARUM
ASARUM
BRAQUE
CHABUK
CLAQUE
FLATUS
GIAOUR
GRADUS
HIATUS
ICARUS
LEAGUE
MEATUS
OMASUM
OPAQUE
PEANUT
PLAGUE
PLAGUY
PLAQUE
PRAGUE
SEAMUS
SHAMUS
SNAFUS
STATUE
STATUS
TEACUP
TRAGUS
URAEUS
URANUS
WRAPUP

••A••U

ACAJOU
AMADOU

•••AU•

ABLAUT
ARNAUD
BEDAUB
CHIAUS
DANAUS
HAMAUL
INHAUL
MARAUD
UMLAUT

••••AU

BATEAU
BUREAU
COTEAU
DACHAU
DESSAU
JUNEAU
LANDAU
MAUMAU
MOREAU
NASSAU
RESEAU

AV••••

AVAILS
AVALON
AVATAR
AVENGE
AVENUE
AVERNO
AVERSE
AVERTS
AVERYS
AVESTA
AVIARY
AVIATE
AVIDIN
AVIDLY
AVISOS
AVOCET
AVOIDS
AVOUCH
AVOWAL
AVOWED
AVOWER

A•V•••

ABVOLT
ADVENT
ADVERB
ADVERT
ADVICE
ADVISE
ALVANS
ALVINA
ALVINE
ANVILS

A••V••

AGAVES
ATAVIC

A•••V•

ACTIVE
ALCOVE
ARGIVE
ARRIVE

•AV•••

CAVEAT
CAVEIN
CAVELL
CAVERN
CAVIAR

6

CAVIES
CAVILS
CAVING
CAVITE
CAVITY
CAVORT
DAVEYS
DAVIDS
DAVIES
DAVITS
FAVORS
GAVELS
GAVIAL
GAVOTS
HAVANA
HAVENS
HAVENT
HAVING
KAVASS
LAVABO
LAVAGE
LAVERS
LAVING
LAVISH
NAVAHO
NAVAJO
NAVELS
NAVIES
PAVANS
PAVERS
PAVING
PAVIOR
PAVISE
PAVLOV
RAVAGE
RAVELS
RAVENS
RAVERS
RAVINE
RAVING
RAVISH
SAVAGE
SAVANT
SAVERS
SAVING
SAVINS
SAVIOR
SAVORS
SAVORY
TAVERN
WAVERS
WAVEYS
WAVIER
WAVIES
WAVILY
WAVING
XAVIER

•A•V••
CALVED
CALVES
CALVIN
CANVAS
CARVED
CARVEL
CARVEN
CARVER
CARVES
FAUVES
HALVED
HALVES
HARVEY
JARVEY
JARVIS
JAYVEE
LARVAE
LARVAL
LATVIA
MARVEL
MARVIN
MAUVES
NAEVUS
PARVIS
SALVED
SALVER
SALVES
SALVIA
SALVOR
SALVOS
VALVAL
VALVAR
VALVED
VALVES
VARVES
WAIVED
WAIVER
WAIVES
WALVIS
YAHVEH

•A••V•
CASAVA
DATIVE
NATIVE
SALIVA

•A•••V
PAVLOV

••AV••
AGAVES
ATAVIC
BEAVER
BRAVED
BRAVER
BRAVES
BRAVOS
CRAVAT
CRAVED
CRAVEN
CRAVER
CRAVES
FLAVIA
FLAVIN
FLAVOR
GRAVED
GRAVEL
GRAVEN
GRAVER
GRAVES
GRAVID
GUAVAS
HEAVED
HEAVEN
HEAVER
HEAVES
KNAVES
LEAVED
LEAVEN
LEAVER
LEAVES
LOAVES
PEAVEY
PRAVDA
QUAVER
REAVOW
SHAVED
SHAVEN
SHAVER
SHAVES
SLAVED
SLAVER
SLAVES
SLAVIC
SPAVIN
STAVED
STAVES
TRAVEL
TRAVES
WEAVED
WEAVER
WEAVES

••A•V•
STARVE
WHARVE

•••AV•
BEHAVE
CASAVA
CLEAVE
GREAVE
MOHAVE
MOJAVE
OCTAVE
OCTAVO
OTTAVA
SHEAVE
SLEAVE
ZOUAVE

••••AV
GUSTAV

AW••••
AWAITS
AWAKED
AWAKEN
AWAKES
AWARDS
AWEARY
AWEIGH
AWEING
AWHILE
AWHIRL
AWLESS
AWNING

A•W•••
ABWATT
ALWAYS

A••W••
AIRWAY
AJOWAN
ANSWER
ANYWAY
ARAWAK
AVOWAL
AVOWED
AVOWER

A•••W•
ALLOWS
ARROWS

A••••W
ANDREW
ANYHOW

•AW•••
BAWDRY
BAWLED
BAWLER
CAWING
DAWDLE
DAWNED
DAWSON
FAWKES
FAWNED
FAWNER
GAWAIN
GAWKED
HAWAII
HAWHAW
HAWING
HAWKED
HAWKER
HAWSER
HAWSES
JAWING
LAWFUL
LAWING
LAWYER
NAWABS
PAWERS
PAWING
PAWNED
PAWNEE
PAWNER
PAWPAW
RAWEST
RAWISH
SAWERS
SAWFLY
SAWING
SAWYER
TAWDRY
TAWERS
TAWING
WAWLED
YAWING
YAWLED
YAWNED
YAWNER
YAWPED
YAWPER

•A•W••
DARWIN
EARWAX
EARWIG
GALWAY
NARWAL
PAXWAX
TAIWAN
YAHWEH

•A••W•
MACAWS
MALAWI
PAPAWS

•A•••W
BARROW
BASHAW
CALLOW
CASHAW
CASHEW
DARROW
FALLOW
FARROW
HALLOW
HARROW
HAWHAW
HAYMOW
MALLOW
MARROW
NARROW
PAWPAW
SALLOW
TALLOW
WALLOW
WARSAW
YARROW

••AW••
ARAWAK
BRAWLS
BRAWNY
CHAWED
CLAWED
CRAWLS
CRAWLY
DRAWEE
DRAWER
DRAWLS
DRAWLY
FLAWED
GNAWED
GNAWER
PRAWNS
SEAWAN
SEAWAY
SHAWLS
SHAWMS
SPAWNS
THAWED
TRAWLS

••A••W
CRACOW
MEADOW
QUAPAW
REAVOW
SHADOW

•••AW•
BYLAWS
IMPAWN
INLAWS
MACAWS
MALAWI
MOHAWK
OTTAWA
PAPAWS
PSHAWS
SCRAWL
SPRAWL
SQUAWK
SQUAWS
STRAWS
STRAWY

••••AW
BASHAW
CASHAW
CUSHAW
GEWGAW
GUFFAW
HAWHAW
HEEHAW
JIGSAW
OUTLAW
PAWPAW
QUAPAW
RIPSAW
SEESAW
UNDRAW
WARSAW

AX••••
AXEMAN
AXEMEN
AXILLA
AXIOMS
AXLIKE
AXONES
AXSEED

A•X•••
AUXINS

6

A••X••
ALEXIA
ALEXIN
ALEXIS
ANOXIA
ANOXIC
APEXES
ATAXIA
ATAXIC

A•••X•
ADMIXT

A••••X
ADIEUX
AFFLUX
AUSPEX

•AX•••
BAXTER
FAXING
LAXEST
LAXITY
MAXIMS
MAXINE
MAXIXE
PAXWAX
SAXONS
SAXONY
TAXEME
TAXERS
TAXIED
TAXING
TAXITE
WAXIER
WAXING

•A•X••
CALXES

•A••X•
GALAXY
MAXIXE

•A•••X
BAYEUX
CAUDEX
EARWAX
HALLUX
HATBOX
LARYNX
LASTEX
MATRIX
PAXWAX

••AX••
ATAXIA
ATAXIC
BIAXAL
COAXAL
COAXED
COAXER
COAXES
FLAXEN
FLAXES
HOAXED
HOAXER
HOAXES
KLAXON
PRAXIS

••A••X
SPADIX

•••AX•
GALAXY

••••AX
CLIMAX
EARWAX
FORNAX
PAXWAX
PICKAX
POLEAX
SMILAX
STORAX
SURTAX
SYNTAX
THORAX

AY••••
AYEAYE
AYESHA
AYMARA

A•Y•••
ABYDOS
ABYSMS
ADYTUM
AMYLIC
AMYLUM
AMYTAL
ANYHOW
ANYONE
ANYWAY
ARYANS
ASYLUM

A••Y••
ALKYLS
ALKYNE
ALLYLS
ANKYLO
ARGYLE
ARGYLL

A•••Y•
ABBEYS
ACETYL
ALLAYS
ALLEYS
ALLOYS
ALPHYL
ALWAYS
ANNOYS
ANONYM
ARCHYS
ARRAYS
ARROYO
ASSAYS
AVERYS
AYEAYE

A••••Y
ABBACY
ACIDLY
ACUITY
AERIFY
AFFRAY
AGEDLY
AGENCY
AGOUTY
AIRDRY
AIRILY
AIRWAY
ALBANY
AMBARY
AMBERY
ANERGY
ANGARY
ANTONY
ANYWAY
APATHY
APIARY
ARCHLY
ARGOSY
ARGUFY
ARIDLY
ARMORY
ARTERY
ASBURY
ASHLEY
ASTRAY
AUBREY
AUDREY
AUGURY
AVIARY
AVIDLY
AWEARY

•AY•••
BAYARD
BAYEUX
BAYING
BAYOUS
CAYMAN
CAYUGA
CAYUSE
DAYFLY
DAYTON
FAYING
GAYEST
GAYETY
HAYING
HAYMOW
JAYVEE
KAYAKS
KAYOED
LAYDAY
LAYERS
LAYING
LAYMAN
LAYMEN
LAYOFF
LAYOUT
MAYDAY
MAYEST
MAYHAP
MAYHEM
MAYING
MAYORS
MAYPOP
PAYDAY
PAYEES
PAYERS
PAYING
PAYOFF
PAYOLA
RAYAHS
RAYING
RAYONS
SAYERS
SAYING
TAYLOR
WAYLAY
WAYNES
WAYOUT
ZAYINS

•A•Y••
BANYAN
BARYES
BARYON
BARYTA
CANYON
GALYAK
LARYNG
LARYNX
LAWYER
MAGYAR
SATYRS
SAWYER

•A••Y•
BARRYS
CATHYS
DACTYL
DAIMYO
DAISYS
DANNYS
DAVEYS
FANNYS
HARRYS
HATTYS
JACKYS
KABAYA
KATHYS
LARRYS
MALAYA
MALAYS
MAMEYS
MANDYS
MARTYR
MARTYS
MATEYS
NAGOYA
NANCYS
PADDYS
PANSYS
PAPAYA
PATSYS
SALLYS
SAMMYS
SANDYS
VALKYR
WALLYS
WAVEYS

•A•••Y
BAILEY
BAKERY
BALDLY
BARELY
BARFLY
BARLEY
BARNEY
BARONY
BASELY
BASIFY
BAWDRY
CAGILY
CALMLY
CALORY
CANARY
CANOPY
CARBOY
CASEFY
CATCHY
CATHAY
CAVITY
DAFTLY
DAINTY
DAMPLY
DANKLY
DARKLY
DATARY
DAUBRY
DAYFLY
EARTHY
EASILY
FAIRLY
FAKERY
FAMILY
FARLEY
FAULTY
GADFLY
GAIETY
GAINLY
GALAXY
GALLEY
GALWAY
GAMELY
GAMILY
GANTRY
GAYETY
HALLEY
HALSEY
HARDLY
HARLEY
HARVEY
HAULMY
HAZILY
JALOPY
JARVEY
JAUNTY
LACILY
LACKEY
LAMELY
LANKLY
LASTLY
LATELY
LAXITY
LAYDAY
LAZILY
MAGUEY
MAINLY
MALADY
MALORY
MARGAY
MARSHY
MAUNDY
MAYDAY
MAZILY
NAMELY
NAPERY
NAZIFY
OAKLEY
PACIFY
PAINTY
PALELY
PALTRY
PANTRY
PAPACY
PAPERY
PARITY
PARLAY
PARLEY
PARODY
PARTLY
PASTRY
PATCHY
PAYDAY
RACILY
RAMIFY
RANKLY
RAREFY
RARELY
RARITY
RASHLY
RATIFY
RATTLY
SAFELY
SAFETY
SAGELY
SALARY
SALIFY
SANELY
SANITY
SASHAY
SATINY
SAVORY
SAWFLY
SAXONY
TACKEY

6

TANGLY
TARTLY
TAUTLY
TAWDRY
VAGARY
VAINLY
VALERY
VALLEY
VANITY
VASTLY
WABBLY
WADDLY
WAGGLY
WAMBLY
WARILY
WARMLY
WATERY
WAVILY
WAYLAY

••AY••
BRAYED
BRAYER
CLAYED
CLAYEY
CRAYON
DRAYED
ELAYNE
FLAYED
FLAYER
FRAYED
GRAYED
GRAYER
GRAYLY
OKAYED
PLAYAS
PLAYED
PLAYER
PRAYED
PRAYER
SLAYER
SPAYED
STAYED
STAYER
SWAYED
THAYER
XRAYED

••A•Y•
BIALYS
GLADYS
STACYS
THADYS
URANYL

••A••Y
APATHY
BEACHY
BEAUTY
BRACHY
BRAINY
BRANDY
BRANNY
BRASHY
BRASSY
BRAWNY
CHAFFY
CHALKY
CHAMMY
CHANCY
CHANTY
CHARRY
CHATTY
CLAMMY
CLASSY
CLAYEY
CRABBY
CRACKY
CRAFTY
CRAGGY
CRANKY
CRANNY
CRAWLY
DEADLY
DEAFLY
DEARLY
DEATHY
DRABLY
DRAFFY
DRAFTY
DRAWLY
FEALTY
FLABBY
FLAGGY
FLASHY
FLATLY
GHARRY
GLADLY
GLAIRY
GLASSY
GNARLY
GRAINY
GRANNY
GRAPHY
GRASSY
GRAYLY
HEARTY
HEATHY
ICALLY
KNARRY
LEACHY
LEANLY
MEANLY
MEASLY
NEARBY
NEARLY
NEATLY
OCASEY
ORALLY
OVALLY
PEACHY
PEARLY
PEAVEY
PLAGUY
PLASHY
PLASTY
POACHY
QUAGGY
QUALMY
QUARRY
REALLY
REALTY
SCABBY
SCANTY
SEAWAY
SHABBY
SHAGGY
SHAMMY
SHANTY
SLAGGY
SLANGY
SMARMY
SNAGGY
SNAPPY
SNARLY
SPARRY
STAGEY
STAGGY
STALKY
STARRY
SWAMPY
SWANKY
SWARTY
TEAPOY
THADDY
TRACHY
TRASHY
TWANGY
USABLY
WEAKLY
WHAMMY
WRATHY
YEARLY
YEASTY

•••AY•
ALLAYS
ALWAYS
ARRAYS
ASSAYS
AYEAYE
BELAYS
BYWAYS
DECAYS
DELAYS
EMBAYS
ESSAYS
FORAYS
INLAYS
KABAYA
MALAYA
MALAYS
MORAYS
NOWAYS
PAPAYA
RELAYS
REPAYS
SPLAYS
SPRAYS
STRAYS
UNLAYS
UNSAYS

•••A•Y
ABBACY
ALBANY
AMBARY
ANGARY
APIARY
AVIARY
AWEARY
BIGAMY
BINARY
BLEARY
BOTANY
CANARY
CREAKY
CREAMY
CREASY
CROAKY
CURACY
DATARY
DENARY
DIGAMY
DREAMY
DREARY
FLOATY
FREAKY
FRIARY
GALAXY
GLEAMY
GREASY
HILARY
HORARY
INFAMY
LEGACY
LITANY
LUNACY
MALADY
MILADY
NOTARY
PAPACY
PIRACY
QUEASY
ROMANY
ROSARY
ROTARY
RRHAGY
SALARY
SENARY
SHOALY
SLEAZY
SMEARY
SNEAKY
STEADY
STEAMY
STRAWY
SUDARY
SUGARY
SWEATY
TETANY
TREATY
TWEAKY
UNEASY
UNWARY
VAGARY
VOTARY
ZONARY

••••AY
AFFRAY
AIRWAY
ANYWAY
ASTRAY
BENDAY
BETRAY
BISCAY
BOMBAY
BYPLAY
CATHAY
COGWAY
CORDAY
CULLAY
DEFRAY
DISMAY
ESTRAY
FRIDAY
GALWAY
HEYDAY
HOORAY
HURRAY
KEYWAY
LAYDAY
LEEWAY
MARGAY
MAYDAY
MIDDAY
MIDWAY
MILLAY
MISLAY
MONDAY
MURRAY
NORWAY
ONEWAY
OUTLAY
PARLAY
PAYDAY
PREPAY
REDBAY
REPLAY
RUNWAY
SASHAY
SEAWAY
SKYWAY
SUBWAY
SUNDAY
TWOWAY
WAYLAY

AZ••••
AZALEA
AZAZEL
AZINES
AZOLES
AZONIC
AZORES
AZOTIC
AZRAEL
AZTECS
AZURES

A••Z••
AMAZED
AMAZES
AMAZON
AREZZO
AZAZEL

A•••Z•
ABLAZE
ALONZO
AREZZO
ASSIZE

•AZ•••
DAZING
DAZZLE
FAZING
GAZABO
GAZEBO
GAZERS
GAZING
HAZARD
HAZELS
HAZERS
HAZIER
HAZILY
HAZING
HAZZAN
JAZZED
JAZZER
JAZZES
KAZOOS
LAZARS
LAZIER
LAZILY
LAZING
LAZULI
MAZERS
MAZIER
MAZILY
MAZING
MAZUMA
NAZIFY
NAZISM
RAZEED
RAZEES
RAZING
RAZORS
RAZZED
RAZZES
TAZZAS

•A•Z••
BALZAC
BANZAI
DANZIG
DAZZLE
GAUZES
HAMZAS
HAZZAN
JAZZED
JAZZER
JAZZES
MAIZES

MATZOS
MATZOT
PANZER
RAZZED
RAZZES
TARZAN
TAZZAS

•A•••Z
HALUTZ

••AZ••
AMAZED
AMAZES
AMAZON
AZAZEL
BLAZED
BLAZER
BLAZES
BLAZON
BRAZAS
BRAZED
BRAZEN
BRAZER
BRAZES
BRAZIL
BRAZOS
CRAZED
CRAZES
DIAZIN
GLAZED
GLAZER
GLAZES
GRAZED
GRAZER
GRAZES
PIAZZA
PLAZAS
SMAZES

••A•Z•
BRAIZE
PIAZZA
STANZA

••A••Z
JUAREZ
QUARTZ

•••AZ•
ABLAZE
SLEAZY

•••A•Z
ERSATZ

BA••••
BAAING
BAALIM
BABBIE
BABBLE
BABIED
BABIES
BABISM
BABIST
BABITE
BABOON
BABOOS
BABULS
BACHED
BACHES
BACKED
BACKER
BADGED
BADGER
BADGES
BADMAN
BADMEN
BAFFED
BAFFIN
BAFFLE
BAGASS
BAGDAD
BAGELS
BAGGED
BAGMAN
BAGMEN
BAGNIO
BAHAIS
BAHAMA
BAIKAL
BAILED
BAILEE
BAILER
BAILEY
BAILIE
BAILOR
BAIRNS
BAITED
BAITER
BAKERS
BAKERY
BAKING
BALAAM
BALATA
BALBOA
BALDER
BALDLY
BALEEN
BALERS
BALING
BALKAN
BALKED
BALLAD
BALLED
BALLET
BALLOT
BALSAM
BALSAS
BALTIC
BALZAC
BAMAKO
BAMBOO
BANANA
BANDED
BANDIT
BANGED
BANGLE
BANGOR
BANGUI
BANGUP
BANIAN
BANISH
BANJOS
BANKED
BANKER
BANNED
BANNER
BANTAM
BANTER
BANTUS
BANYAN
BANZAI
BAOBAB
BARBED
BARBEL
BARBER
BARBET
BARBIE
BARDED
BARDES
BARDIC
BAREGE
BARELY
BAREST
BARFLY
BARGED
BARGEE
BARGES
BARING
BARITE
BARIUM
BARKED
BARKER
BARLEY
BARMAN
BARMEN
BARMIE
BARNEY
BARNUM
BARONG
BARONS
BARONY
BARQUE
BARRED
BARREL
BARREN
BARRET
BARRIO
BARROW
BARRYS
BARTER
BARTOK
BARTON
BARUCH
BARYES
BARYON
BARYTA
BASALT
BASELY
BASHAW
BASHED
BASHES
BASICS
BASIFY
BASILS
BASING
BASINS
BASION
BASKED
BASKET
BASQUE
BASRAH
BASSES
BASSET
BASSOS
BASTED
BASTES
BASUTO
BATAAN
BATEAU
BATHED
BATHER
BATHOS
BATIKS
BATING
BATMAN
BATMEN
BATONS
BATTED
BATTEN
BATTER
BATTIK
BATTLE
BATTUE
BAUBLE
BAUCIS
BAWDRY
BAWLED
BAWLER
BAXTER
BAYARD
BAYEUX
BAYING
BAYOUS

B•A•••
BAAING
BAALIM
BEACHY
BEACON
BEADED
BEADLE
BEAGLE
BEAKED
BEAKER
BEAMED
BEANED
BEANIE
BEARDS
BEARED
BEARER
BEASTS
BEATEN
BEATER
BEAUTS
BEAUTY
BEAVER
BIALYS
BIANCA
BIASED
BIASES
BIAXAL
BLACKS
BLADED
BLADES
BLAINS
BLAMED
BLAMES
BLANCH
BLANKS
BLARED
BLARES
BLASTO
BLASTS
BLAZED
BLAZER
BLAZES
BLAZON
BOARDS
BOASTS
BOATED
BRACED
BRACER
BRACES
BRACHI
BRACHY
BRACTS
BRAHMA
BRAHMS
BRAIDS
BRAILS
BRAINS
BRAINY
BRAISE
BRAIZE
BRAKED
BRAKES
BRANCH
BRANDS
BRANDY
BRANNY
BRANTS
BRAQUE
BRASHY
BRASSY
BRAVED
BRAVER
BRAVES
BRAVOS
BRAWLS
BRAWNY
BRAYED
BRAYER
BRAZAS
BRAZED
BRAZEN
BRAZER
BRAZES
BRAZIL
BRAZOS
BWANAS

B••A••
BAGASS
BAHAIS
BAHAMA
BALAAM
BALATA
BAMAKO
BANANA
BASALT
BATAAN
BAYARD
BECALM
BECAME
BEDAUB
BEFALL
BEHALF
BEHAVE
BELAYS
BEMATA
BERATE
BETAKE
BEWAIL
BEWARE
BEZANT
BICARB
BIGAMY
BIHARI
BINARY
BLEACH
BLEAKS
BLEARS
BLEARY
BLEATS
BLOATS
BOGANS
BONACI
BORAGE
BORANE
BORATE
BOTANY
BOYARD
BOYARS
BREACH
BREADS
BREAKS
BREAMS
BREAST
BREATH
BRIARS
BROACH
BROADS
BRYANT
BUBALS
BURANS
BUTANE
BYLANE
BYLAWS
BYNAME
BYPASS
BYPAST
BYPATH

6

BYTALK
BYWAYS

B•••A•
BADMAN
BAGDAD
BAGMAN
BAIKAL
BALAAM
BALKAN
BALLAD
BALSAM
BALSAS
BALZAC
BANIAN
BANTAM
BANYAN
BANZAI
BAOBAB
BARMAN
BASHAW
BASRAH
BATAAN
BATEAU
BATMAN
BEDLAM
BEDPAN
BEGGAR
BEHEAD
BELDAM
BELGAS
BELIAL
BELLAS
BEMEAN
BEMOAN
BENDAY
BENGAL
BETRAY
BEULAH
BEULAS
BEZOAR
BHUTAN
BIAXAL
BILBAO
BISCAY
BOBCAT
BOMBAY
BONSAI
BOREAL
BOREAS
BOWMAN
BOXCAR
BRAZAS
BRIDAL
BROGAN
BROMAL
BRUMAL
BRUTAL
BUCCAL
BULBAR
BULGAR
BULLAE
BUNYAN
BUREAU
BURIAL
BURLAP
BURSAE
BURSAL
BURSAR
BURSAS
BUSMAN
BWANAS
BYPLAY
BYROAD

B••••A
BAHAMA
BALATA
BALBOA
BANANA
BARYTA
BELUGA
BEMATA
BENITA
BERTHA
BIANCA
BODEGA
BOGOTA
BORGIA
BRAHMA
BREGMA
BRENDA
BUCKRA
BUDDHA

•BA•••
ABACAS
ABACUS
ABASED
ABASER
ABASES
ABATED
ABATER
ABATES
ABATIS
ABATOR
UBANGI

•B•A••
ABBACY
ABLAUT
ABLAZE
ABOARD
ABRADE
ABRAMS
ABWATT
EBOATS
HBEAMS
IBEAMS
OBLAST
OBLATE
OBTAIN
UBOATS
ZBEAMS

•B••A•
ABACAS
ABIJAH
ABOMAS
ABORAL
ABROAD

•B•••A
ABOLLA
ABULIA
IBERIA

••BA••
ABBACY
ALBANY
ALBATA
AMBAGE
AMBARI
AMBARY
AUBADE
BUBALS
CABALA
CABALS
CABANA
COBALT
CUBAGE
CUBANS
DEBARK
DEBARS
DEBASE
DEBATE
EMBALM
EMBANK
EMBARK
EMBARS
EMBAYS
HOBART
IMBALM
IMBARK
KABAKA
KABAYA
LOBATE
NOBALL
REBATE
REBATO
RIBALD
ROBALO
ROBAND
RUBACE
RUBATO
SEBATS
SUBAHS
TABARD
TOBAGO
TUBATE
TYBALT
UNBARS
URBANE
WABASH

••B•A•
BOBCAT
CABMAN
COBIAS
COBRAS
DOBLAS
DOBRAS
FABIAN
GIBRAN
HUBCAP
JUBBAH
KIBLAH
LABIAL
LIBRAE
LIBRAS
LIBYAN
MOBCAP
NUBIAN
NUBIAS
SABBAT
SABEAN
SABRAS
SUBWAY
TIBIAE
TIBIAL
TIBIAS
TOBIAH
TOBIAS
UMBRAE
UMBRAS
UNBEAR
UPBEAT
ZEBRAS

••B••A
ALBATA
ARBELA
CABALA
CABANA
EUBOEA
FIBULA
KABAKA
KABAYA
NEBULA
ROBBIA
SABINA

•••BA•
AMEBAE
AMEBAS
ANABAS
ATABAL
BAOBAB
BILBAO
BOMBAY
BULBAR
CASBAH
CEIBAS
COMBAT
CORBAN
CYMBAL
DISBAR
DUNBAR
DURBAN
DURBAR
FORBAD
GASBAG
GLOBAL
HERBAL
ISOBAR
JUBBAH
LUMBAR
MAMBAS
REDBAY
RUMBAS
SABBAT
SAMBAS
SCUBAS
SHEBAT
SINBAD
TAMBAC
THEBAE
TIMBAL
TOMBAC
TRIBAL
TURBAN
VERBAL
WOMBAT
YERBAS

•••B•A
ARABIA
BALBOA
GAMBIA
JERBOA
LAMBDA
LISBOA
OJIBWA
PHOBIA
ROBBIA
SERBIA
TERBIA
ZAMBIA

••••BA
AMOEBA
ARROBA
CASABA
DAGOBA
HECUBA
INDABA
RHUMBA
YORUBA
ZAREBA

B•B•••
BABBIE
BABBLE
BABIED
BABIES
BABISM
BABIST
BABITE
BABOON
BABOOS
BABULS
BIBBED
BIBBER
BIBLES
BIBLIO
BOBBED
BOBBER
BOBBIE
BOBBIN
BOBBLE
BOBBYS
BOBCAT
BUBALS
BUBBLE
BUBBLY
BUBOES
BYBLOW

B••B••
BABBIE
BABBLE
BALBOA
BAMBOO
BAOBAB
BARBED
BARBEL
BARBER
BARBET
BARBIE
BAUBLE
BEDBUG
BERBER
BIBBED
BIBBER
BILBAO
BLEBBY
BOBBED
BOBBER
BOBBIE
BOBBIN
BOBBLE
BOBBYS
BOMBAY
BOMBED
BOMBER
BOMBES
BONBON
BOOBOO
BRIBED
BRIBER
BRIBES
BUBBLE
BUBBLY
BULBAR
BULBEL
BULBIL
BULBUL
BUMBLE
BURBLE
BURBOT
BYEBYE

B•••B•
BLEBBY
BLOWBY
BLURBS

B••••B
BAOBAB
BEDAUB
BENUMB
BICARB

•BB•••
ABBACY
ABBESS
ABBEYS
ABBIES
ABBOTS
EBBING

•B••B•
ABOMBS
HBOMBS

•B•••B
ABSORB

••BB••
BABBIE
BABBLE
BIBBED
BIBBER
BOBBED
BOBBER
BOBBIE
BOBBIN
BOBBLE
BOBBYS
BUBBLE
BUBBLY
COBBLE
DABBED
DABBER
DABBLE
DEBBYS
DIBBED
DIBBER
DIBBLE
DOBBER
DOBBIN
DUBBED
DUBBIN
DYBBUK
FIBBED
FIBBER
FOBBED
GABBED
GABBER
GABBLE
GABBRO
GIBBED
GIBBER
GIBBET
GIBBON
GOBBET
GOBBLE
HOBBES
HOBBLE
HUBBUB
JABBED
JABBER
JIBBED
JIBBER
JOBBED
JOBBER
JUBBAH
LIBBYS
LOBBED
LUBBER
MOBBED
MOBBER
NABBED
NIBBED
NIBBLE
NOBBLE
NUBBIN
NUBBLE
NUBBLY
PEBBLE
PEBBLY
RABBET
RABBIS
RABBIT
RABBLE
RIBBED
RIBBON
ROBBED
ROBBER
ROBBIA
ROBBIE
RUBBED
RUBBER
RUBBLE
SABBAT
SOBBED
TUBBED
TUBBER
WABBLE
WABBLY
WEBBED
WOBBLE
WOBBLY
YABBER

••B•B•
CABOBS
CUBEBS
IMBIBE
KABOBS
NABOBS

••B••B
COBWEB
HOBNOB
HUBBUB
SUBDEB
SUBURB

•••BB•
BLEBBY
CHUBBY
CRABBY
FLABBY
GRUBBY
SCABBY
SHABBY
STUBBY

•••B•B
BAOBAB

HUBBUB

B•C•••
BACHED
BACHES
BACKED
BACKER
BECALM
BECAME
BECKED
BECKET
BECKON
BECKYS
BECOME
BICARB
BICEPS
BICKER
BICORN
BOCCIE
BUCCAL
BUCKED
BUCKER
BUCKET
BUCKLE
BUCKRA

B••C••
BAUCIS
BEACHY
BEACON
BISCAY
BLACKS
BLOCKS
BLOCKY
BOBCAT
BOCCIE
BOTCHY
BOUCLE
BOXCAR
BRACED
BRACER
BRACES
BRACHI
BRACHY
BRACTS
BRECHT
BRICKS
BRUCES
BUCCAL
BUNCHE
BUNCHY
BUNCOS

B•••C•
BARUCH
BASICS
BEDECK
BIANCA
BIERCE
BISECT
BLANCH
BLEACH
BLENCH
BLOTCH
BODICE
BONACI
BORSCH
BOUNCE
BOUNCY
BRANCH
BREACH
BREECH
BROACH
BRONCO
BRONCS
BROOCH
BRUNCH

B••••C
BALTIC
BALZAC
BARDIC
BELGIC
BELLOC
BIOTIC
BROMIC
BUSTIC

•B•C••
ABACAS
ABACUS
IBICES

•B••C•
ABBACY
ABDUCT
ABJECT
OBJECT
OBTECT

••BC••
BOBCAT
HUBCAP
MOBCAP

••B•C•
ABBACY
LUBECK
REBECS
RUBACE
XEBECS
ZEBECK
ZEBECS

••B••C
FABRIC
PUBLIC
RUBRIC

•••B•C
AMEBIC
ARABIC
CHEBEC
IAMBIC
LIMBIC
QUEBEC
TAMBAC
TOMBAC

B•D•••
BADGED
BADGER
BADGES
BADMAN
BADMEN
BEDAUB
BEDBUG
BEDDED
BEDDER
BEDECK
BEDEWS
BEDIMS
BEDLAM
BEDPAN
BEDRID
BEDUIN
BIDDEN
BIDDER
BIDETS
BIDING
BODEGA
BODICE
BODIED
BODIES
BODILY
BODING
BODKIN
BUDDED
BUDDER
BUDDHA
BUDDLE
BUDGED
BUDGES
BUDGET
BUDGIE

B••D••
BAGDAD
BALDER
BALDLY
BANDED
BANDIT
BARDED
BARDES
BARDIC
BAWDRY
BEADED
BEADLE
BEDDED
BEDDER
BELDAM
BENDAY
BENDEE
BENDER
BIDDEN
BIDDER
BINDER
BIRDIE
BLADED
BLADES
BOLDER
BOLDLY
BONDED
BONDER
BOODLE
BORDEL
BORDER
BRIDAL
BRIDES
BRIDGE
BRIDIE
BRIDLE
BUDDED
BUDDER
BUDDHA
BUDDLE
BUNDLE
BURDEN
BURDIE

B•••D•
BEARDS
BESIDE
BETIDE
BIPEDS
BIPODS
BLEEDS
BLENDE
BLENDS
BLINDS
BLONDE
BLONDS
BLOODS
BLOODY
BOARDS
BOLIDE
BORIDE
BOUNDS
BRAIDS
BRANDS
BRANDY
BREADS
BREEDS
BRENDA
BROADS
BROODS
BROODY
BUILDS

B••••D
BABIED
BACHED
BACKED
BADGED
BAFFED
BAGDAD
BAGGED
BAILED
BAITED
BALKED
BALLAD
BALLED
BANDED
BANGED
BANKED
BANNED
BARBED

6

BARDED
BARGED
BARKED
BARRED
BASHED
BASKED
BASTED
BATHED
BATTED
BAWLED
BAYARD
BEADED
BEAKED
BEAMED
BEANED
BEARED
BECKED
BEDDED
BEDRID
BEEFED
BEEPED
BEGGED
BEGIRD
BEHEAD
BEHELD
BEHIND
BEHOLD
BELIED
BELLED
BELTED
BESTED
BETTED
BEYOND
BIASED
BIBBED
BIFFED
BIFOLD
BILGED
BILKED
BILLED
BINNED
BIRLED
BIRRED
BITTED
BLADED
BLAMED
BLARED
BLAZED
BOATED
BOBBED
BODIED
BOGGED
BOILED
BOLLED
BOLTED
BOMBED
BONDED
BONGED
BOOKED
BOOMED
BOOTED
BOOZED
BOPPED
BOSSED

BOUSED
BOWLED
BOWSED
BOYARD
BRACED
BRAKED
BRAVED
BRAYED
BRAZED
BREWED
BRIBED
BRIGID
BRINED
BUCKED
BUDDED
BUDGED
BUFFED
BUGGED
BUGLED
BULGED
BULKED
BUMMED
BUMPED
BUNGED
BUNKED
BUNTED
BUOYED
BURIED
BURKED
BURLED
BURNED
BURPED
BURRED
BUSHED
BUSIED
BUSSED
BUSTED
BUTTED
BUZZED
BYROAD
BYWORD

•BD•••

ABDUCT

•B•D••

ABIDED
ABIDER
ABIDES
ABODES
ABYDOS
IBIDEM

•B••D•

ABRADE

•B•••D

ABASED
ABATED
ABIDED
ABOARD
ABOUND
ABROAD
ABSURD
ABUSED
OBEYED
OBTUND

••BD••

SUBDEB
SUBDUE

••B•D•

ALBEDO
AUBADE
EMBEDS
EMBODY
IMBEDS
IMBODY
LIBIDO

••B••D

AMBLED
BABIED
BIBBED
BOBBED
CABLED
CEBOID
CUBOID
DABBED
DIBBED
DUBBED
FABLED
FIBBED
FOBBED
GABBED
GABLED
GIBBED
HYBRID
IMBUED
INBRED
JABBED
JIBBED
JOBBED
KOBOLD
LOBBED
MOBBED
NABBED
NIBBED
RIBALD
RIBBED
ROBAND
ROBBED
RUBBED
SOBBED
TABARD
TABLED
TUBBED
UNBEND
UNBIND
UNBRED
WEBBED

•••BD•

LAMBDA

•••B•D

BARBED
BIBBED
BOBBED
BOMBED
BRIBED
COMBED
CURBED
DABBED
DAUBED
DIBBED
DUBBED
FIBBED
FOBBED
FORBAD
FORBID
GABBED
GARBED
GIBBED
GLOBED
HOTBED
JABBED
JIBBED
JOBBED
LAMBED
LIMBED
LOBBED
MOBBED
MORBID
NABBED
NIBBED
NUMBED
OUTBID
PROBED
REDBUD
RIBBED
ROBBED
RUBBED
SINBAD
SOBBED
TOMBED
TUBBED
TURBID
WEBBED
WOMBED

BE••••

BEACHY
BEACON
BEADED
BEADLE
BEAGLE
BEAKED
BEAKER
BEAMED
BEANED
BEANIE
BEARDS
BEARED
BEARER
BEASTS
BEATEN
BEATER
BEAUTS
BEAUTY
BEAVER
BECALM
BECAME
BECKED
BECKET
BECKON
BECKYS
BECOME
BEDAUB
BEDBUG
BEDDED
BEDDER
BEDECK
BEDEWS
BEDIMS
BEDLAM
BEDPAN
BEDRID
BEDUIN
BEEFED
BEEPED
BEETLE
BEEVES
BEFALL
BEFELL
BEFITS
BEFOGS
BEFOOL
BEFORE
BEFOUL
BEGETS
BEGGAR
BEGGED
BEGINS
BEGIRD
BEGIRT
BEGUIN
BEGUMS
BEHALF
BEHAVE
BEHEAD
BEHELD
BEHEST
BEHIND
BEHOLD
BEHOOF
BEHOVE
BEIGES
BEINGS
BEIRUT
BELAYS
BELDAM
BELFRY
BELGAS
BELGIC
BELIAL
BELIED
BELIEF
BELIER
BELIES
BELIZE
BELLAS
BELLED
BELLES
BELLOC
BELLOW
BELOIT
BELONG
BELTED
BELUGA
BEMATA
BEMEAN
BEMIRE
BEMOAN
BEMUSE
BENDAY
BENDEE
BENDER
BENGAL
BENIGN
BENITA
BENITO
BENJYS
BENNES
BENNET
BENNYS
BENTON
BENUMB
BENZOL
BENZYL
BERATE
BERBER
BEREFT
BERETS
BERGEN
BERING
BERLIN
BERMES
BERNEY
BERNIE
BERTHA
BERTHE
BERTHS
BERTIE
BERYLS
BESEEM
BESETS
BESIDE
BESOMS
BESOTS
BESSIE
BESSYS
BESTED
BESTIR
BESTOW
BETAKE
BETELS
BETHEL
BETIDE
BETISE
BETONY
BETOOK
BETRAY
BETSYS
BETTED
BETTER
BETTES
BETTOR
BETTYS

6

BEULAH
BEULAS
BEVELS
BEVIES
BEWAIL
BEWARE
BEYOND
BEZANT
BEZELS
BEZOAR

B•E•••

BEEFED
BEEPED
BEETLE
BEEVES
BIERCE
BLEACH
BLEAKS
BLEARS
BLEARY
BLEATS
BLEBBY
BLEEDS
BLENCH
BLENDE
BLENDS
BLENNY
BREACH
BREADS
BREAKS
BREAMS
BREAST
BREATH
BRECHT
BREECH
BREEDS
BREEZE
BREEZY
BREGMA
BREMEN
BRENDA
BRENTS
BRETON
BREVES
BREVET
BREWED
BREWER
BREWIS
BYEBYE

B••E••

BAGELS
BAKERS
BAKERY
BALEEN
BALERS
BAREGE
BARELY
BAREST
BASELY
BATEAU
BAYEUX
BEDECK
BEDEWS
BEFELL
BEGETS
BEHEAD
BEHELD
BEHEST
BEMEAN
BEREFT
BERETS
BESEEM
BESETS
BETELS
BEVELS
BEZELS
BICEPS
BIDETS
BIPEDS
BIREME
BISECT
BITERS
BLEEDS
BLUELY
BLUEST
BLUETS
BODEGA
BOGEYS
BOLERO
BOLEYN
BONERS
BOREAL
BOREAS
BORERS
BOWELS
BOWERS
BOWERY
BOXERS
BREECH
BREEDS
BREEZE
BREEZY
BRIEFS
BRIERS
BRIERY
BUREAU
BUYERS

B•••E•

BABIED
BABIES
BACHED
BACHES
BACKED
BACKER
BADGED
BADGER
BADGES
BADMEN
BAFFED
BAGGED
BAGMEN
BAILED
BAILEE
BAILER
BAILEY
BAITED
BAITER
BALDER
BALEEN
BALKED
BALLED
BALLET
BANDED
BANGED
BANKED
BANKER
BANNED
BANNER
BANTER
BARBED
BARBEL
BARBER
BARBET
BARDED
BARDES
BARGED
BARGEE
BARGES
BARKED
BARKER
BARLEY
BARMEN
BARNEY
BARRED
BARREL
BARREN
BARRET
BARTER
BARYES
BASHED
BASHES
BASKED
BASKET
BASSES
BASSET
BASTED
BASTES
BATHED
BATHER
BATMEN
BATTED
BATTEN
BATTER
BAWLED
BAWLER
BAXTER
BEADED
BEAKED
BEAKER
BEAMED
BEANED
BEARED
BEARER
BEATEN
BEATER
BEAVER
BECKED
BECKET
BEDDED
BEDDER
BEEFED
BEEPED
BEEVES
BEGGED
BEIGES
BELIED
BELIEF
BELIER
BELIES
BELLED
BELLES
BELTED
BENDEE
BENDER
BENNES
BENNET
BERBER
BERGEN
BERMES
BERNEY
BESEEM
BESTED
BETHEL
BETTED
BETTER
BETTES
BEVIES
BIASED
BIASES
BIBBED
BIBBER
BIBLES
BICKER
BIDDEN
BIDDER
BIFFED
BIFLEX
BIGGER
BILGED
BILGES
BILKED
BILKER
BILLED
BILLET
BINDER
BINGES
BINNED
BIOGEN
BIRLED
BIRLES
BIRRED
BISTER
BITTED
BITTEN
BITTER
BLADED
BLADES
BLAMED
BLAMES
BLARED
BLARES
BLAZED
BLAZER
BLAZES
BLOKES
BLOWER
BOATED
BOBBED
BOBBER
BODIED
BODIES
BOGGED
BOGIES
BOGLES
BOILED
BOILER
BOLDER
BOLLED
BOLTED
BOLTER
BOMBED
BOMBER
BOMBES
BONDED
BONDER
BONGED
BONIER
BONNET
BONZER
BONZES
BOOKED
BOOMED
BOOTED
BOOTEE
BOOZED
BOOZER
BOOZES
BOPPED
BORDEL
BORDER
BORNEO
BOSHES
BOSKET
BOSSED
BOSSES
BOTHER
BOULES
BOUSED
BOUSES
BOWLED
BOWLEG
BOWLER
BOWMEN
BOWSED
BOWSES
BOWYER
BRACED
BRACER
BRACES
BRAKED
BRAKES
BRAVED
BRAVER
BRAVES
BRAYED
BRAYER
BRAZED
BRAZEN
BRAZER
BRAZES
BREMEN
BREVES
BREVET
BREWED
BREWER
BRIBED
BRIBER
BRIBES
BRIDES
BRINED
BRINES
BROKEN
BROKER
BROMES
BRUCES
BRUGES
BRUMES
BRUNEI
BRUNET
BRUTES
BUBOES
BUCKED
BUCKER
BUCKET
BUDDED
BUDDER
BUDGED
BUDGES
BUDGET
BUFFED
BUFFER
BUFFET
BUGGED
BUGGER
BUGLED
BUGLER
BUGLES
BULBEL
BULGED
BULGER
BULGES
BULKED
BULLET
BUMMED
BUMMER
BUMPED
BUMPER
BUNGED
BUNKED
BUNKER
BUNSEN
BUNTED
BUOYED
BURDEN
BURGEE
BURGER
BURIED
BURIES
BURKED
BURKES
BURLED

6

BURLER
BURLEY
BURNED
BURNER
BURNET
BURPED
BURRED
BURSES
BUSHED
BUSHEL
BUSHES
BUSIED
BUSIES
BUSMEN
BUSSED
BUSSES
BUSTED
BUSTER
BUTLER
BUTTED
BUTTER
BUTTES
BUZZED
BUZZER
BUZZES

B••••E

BABBIE
BABBLE
BABITE
BAFFLE
BAILEE
BAILIE
BANGLE
BARBIE
BAREGE
BARGEE
BARITE
BARMIE
BARQUE
BASQUE
BATTLE
BATTUE
BAUBLE
BEADLE
BEAGLE
BEANIE
BECAME
BECOME
BEETLE
BEFORE
BEHAVE
BEHOVE
BELIZE
BEMIRE
BEMUSE
BENDEE
BERATE
BERNIE
BERTHE
BERTIE
BESIDE
BESSIE
BETAKE
BETIDE
BETISE
BEWARE
BIERCE
BILLIE
BIRDIE
BIREME
BISQUE
BLENDE
BLITHE
BLONDE
BLOUSE
BLUNGE
BOBBIE
BOBBLE
BOCCIE
BODICE
BOGGLE
BOLIDE
BONNIE
BOODLE
BOOKIE
BOOTEE
BOOTIE
BORAGE
BORANE
BORATE
BORIDE
BOTTLE
BOUCLE
BOUFFE
BOUGIE
BOUNCE
BOURNE
BOURSE
BOVINE
BRAISE
BRAIZE
BRAQUE
BREEZE
BRIDGE
BRIDIE
BRIDLE
BROGUE
BRONTE
BRONZE
BROWSE
BRUISE
BUBBLE
BUCKLE
BUDDLE
BUDGIE
BULLAE
BUMBLE
BUNCHE
BUNDLE
BUNGLE
BURBLE
BURDIE
BURGEE
BURGLE
BURSAE
BUSTLE
BUTANE
BYEBYE
BYGONE
BYLANE
BYLINE
BYNAME

•BE•••

ABELES
HBEAMS
IBEAMS
IBERIA
IBEXES
OBELUS
OBERON
OBEYED
OBEYER
ZBEAMS

•B•E••

ABBESS
ABBEYS
ABJECT
ABLEST
ABNERS
ABSENT
OBJECT
OBSESS
OBTECT
OBTEST
OBVERT
UBIETY

•B••E•

ABASED
ABASER
ABASES
ABATED
ABATER
ABATES
ABBIES
ABELES
ABIDED
ABIDER
ABIDES
ABODES
ABUSED
ABUSER
ABUSES
IBEXES
IBICES
IBIDEM
IBISES
OBEYED
OBEYER
TBONES

•B•••E

ABJURE
ABLAZE
ABRADE
OBLATE
OBLIGE
OBTUSE

••BE••

ABBESS
ABBEYS
ALBEDO
ALBEIT
ALBERT
AMBERS
AMBERY
ARBELA
CUBEBS
CYBELE
EGBERT
ELBERT
EMBEDS
EMBERS
FIBERS
GIBERS
HUBERT
IMBEDS
KIBEIS
LABELS
LIBELS
LUBECK
MABELS
OSBERT
REBECS
REBELS
ROBERT
RUBENS
SABEAN
SABERS
SOBERS
TUBERS
UMBELS
UMBERS
UNBEAR
UNBELT
UNBEND
UNBENT
UPBEAT
WEBERS
XEBECS
ZEBECK
ZEBECS
ZIBETH
ZIBETS

••B•E•

ABBIES
AMBLED
AMBLER
AMBLES
AUBREY
BABIED
BABIES
BIBBED
BIBBER
BIBLES
BOBBED
BOBBER
BUBOES
CABLED
CABLES
CABLET
CABMEN
COBLES
COBWEB
DABBED
DABBER
DIBBED
DIBBER
DOBBER
DOBIES
DUBBED
EMBLEM
EUBOEA
FABLED
FABLER
FABLES
FIBBED
FIBBER
FOBBED
GABBED
GABBER
GABLED
GABLES
GIBBED
GIBBER
GIBBET
GIBLET
GOBBET
GOBIES
GOBLET
HEBREW
HOBBES
HOBOES
IMBUED
IMBUES
INBRED
JABBED
JABBER
JIBBED
JIBBER
JOBBED
JOBBER
LABRET
LOBBED
LUBBER
MOBBED
MOBBER
NABBED
NIBBED
RABBET
RABIES
RIBBED
ROBBED
ROBBER
ROBLES
RUBBED
RUBBER
RUBIES
RUBLES
SABLES
SOBBED
SUBDEB
SUBLET
SUBTER
TABLED
TABLES
TABLET
TOBIES
TUBBED
TUBBER
UMBLES
UNBRED
WEBBED
YABBER

••B••E

ALBITE
AMBAGE
ARBUTE
AUBADE
BABBIE
BABBLE
BABITE
BOBBIE
BOBBLE
BUBBLE
COBBLE
CUBAGE
CYBELE
DABBLE
DEBASE
DEBATE
DIBBLE
EMBRUE
GABBLE
GOBBLE
HABILE
HOBBLE
IMBIBE
IMBRUE
LABILE
LIBRAE
LOBATE
LOBULE
MOBILE
NIBBLE
NOBBLE
NUBBLE
NUBILE
PEBBLE
RABBLE
REBATE
REBUKE
RIBOSE
ROBBIE
RUBACE
RUBBLE
SABINE
SUBDUE
SUBTLE
TIBIAE
TUBATE
TUBULE
UMBRAE
URBANE
WABBLE
WOBBLE

6

•••BE•
ADOBES
ARABEL
BARBED
BARBEL
BARBER
BARBET
BERBER
BIBBED
BIBBER
BOBBED
BOBBER
BOMBED
BOMBER
BOMBES
BRIBED
BRIBER
BRIBES
BULBEL
CAMBER
CHEBEC
COMBED
COMBER
CORBEL
CUMBER
CURBED
DABBED
DABBER
DAUBED
DAUBER
DIBBED
DIBBER
DOBBER
DUBBED
FERBER
FIBBED
FIBBER
FOBBED
GABBED
GABBER
GARBED
GHEBER
GIBBED
GIBBER
GIBBET
GLEBES
GLOBED
GLOBES
GOBBET
GOOBER
GRABEN
GREBES
HOBBES
HOTBED
ISABEL
ISOBEL
JABBED
JABBER
JIBBED
JIBBER
JOBBED
JOBBER
KHYBER
LAMBED
LIMBED
LIMBER
LOBBED
LUBBER
LUMBER
MEMBER
MOBBED
MOBBER
NABBED
NIBBED
NUMBED
NUMBER
PLEBES
PROBED
PROBER
PROBES
QUEBEC
RABBET
REUBEN
RIBBED
ROBBED
ROBBER
RUBBED
RUBBER
SEABEE
SOBBED
SOMBER
THEBES
TIMBER
TOMBED
TRIBES
TUBBED
TUBBER
WEBBED
WILBER
WOMBED
YABBER

•••B•E
ALIBLE
AMEBAE
ARABLE
BABBIE
BABBLE
BARBIE
BAUBLE
BOBBIE
BOBBLE
BUBBLE
BUMBLE
BURBLE
BYEBYE
COBBLE
DABBLE
DIBBLE
DOABLE
DOUBLE
EDIBLE
ENABLE
FEEBLE
FIMBLE
FOIBLE
FUMBLE
GABBLE
GAMBLE
GARBLE
GOBBLE
HOBBLE
HOMBRE
HUMBLE
JUMBLE
LAMBIE
LIABLE
MARBLE
MUMBLE
NIBBLE
NIMBLE
NOBBLE
NUBBLE
PEBBLE
RABBLE
RAMBLE
ROBBIE
ROUBLE
RUBBLE
RUMBLE
SEABEE
STABLE
SUABLE
THEBAE
TIMBRE
TREBLE
TUMBLE
UNABLE
USABLE
VIABLE
WABBLE
WAMBLE
WARBLE
WIMBLE
WOBBLE
ZOMBIE

••••BE
AEROBE
CARIBE
DANUBE
ENROBE
FLAMBE
IMBIBE
JUJUBE
PHOEBE
SCRIBE

B•F•••
BAFFED
BAFFIN
BAFFLE
BEFALL
BEFELL
BEFITS
BEFOGS
BEFOOL
BEFORE
BEFOUL
BIFFED
BIFFIN
BIFLEX
BIFOLD
BIFORM
BUFFED
BUFFER
BUFFET

B••F••
BAFFED
BAFFIN
BAFFLE
BARFLY
BEEFED
BELFRY
BIFFED
BIFFIN
BLUFFS
BOTFLY
BOUFFE
BOWFIN
BUFFED
BUFFER
BUFFET

B•••F•
BASIFY
BEREFT
BLUFFS
BOUFFE
BRIEFS

B••••F
BEHALF
BEHOOF
BELIEF

••B•F•
REBUFF

••B••F
REBUFF

B•G•••
BAGASS
BAGDAD
BAGELS
BAGGED
BAGMAN
BAGMEN
BAGNIO
BEGETS
BEGGAR
BEGGED
BEGINS
BEGIRD
BEGIRT
BEGUIN
BEGUMS
BIGAMY
BIGGER
BIGGIN
BIGHTS
BIGOTS
BIGWIG
BOGANS
BOGEYS
BOGGED
BOGGLE
BOGIES
BOGLES
BOGOTA
BUGGED
BUGGER
BUGLED
BUGLER
BUGLES
BYGONE

B••G••
BADGED
BADGER
BADGES
BAGGED
BANGED
BANGLE
BANGOR
BANGUI
BANGUP
BARGED
BARGEE
BARGES
BEAGLE
BEGGAR
BEGGED
BEIGES
BELGAS
BELGIC
BENGAL
BERGEN
BIGGER
BIGGIN
BILGED
BILGES
BINGES
BIOGEN
BLIGHT
BOGGED
BOGGLE
BONGED
BONGOS
BORGIA
BOUGHS
BOUGHT
BOUGIE
BREGMA
BRIGHT
BRIGID
BROGAN
BROGUE
BRUGES
BUDGED
BUDGES
BUDGET
BUDGIE
BUGGED
BUGGER
BULGAR
BULGED
BULGER
BULGES
BUNGED
BUNGLE
BURGEE
BURGER
BURGHS
BURGLE
BURGOO
BURGOS

B•••G•
BAREGE
BEFOGS
BEINGS
BELUGA
BENIGN
BLUNGE
BODEGA
BORAGE
BOURGS
BRIDGE
BRINGS

B••••G
BAAING
BAKING
BALING
BARING
BARONG
BASING
BATING
BAYING
BEDBUG
BELONG
BERING
BIDING
BIGWIG
BITING
BLUING
BODING
BONING
BOOING
BORING
BOWING
BOWLEG
BOXING
BUSING
BUYING

•B••G•
OBLIGE
UBANGI

•B•••G
EBBING
OBLONG

••B•G•
AMBAGE
CUBAGE
DEBUGS
RUBIGO
TOBAGO

••B••G
CUBING
EBBING
GIBING
JIBING
ORBING
ROBING
TUBING

•••B•G
BEDBUG
DORBUG
GASBAG
HUMBUG
REDBUG

BH••••
BHUTAN

B•H•••
BAHAIS
BAHAMA
BEHALF
BEHAVE
BEHEAD
BEHELD
BEHEST
BEHIND
BEHOLD
BEHOOF
BEHOVE
BIHARI

B••H••
BACHED
BACHES
BASHAW
BASHED
BASHES
BATHED
BATHER
BATHOS
BETHEL
BIGHTS
BISHOP
BOOHOO
BOSHES
BOTHER
BRAHMA
BRAHMS
BUSHED
BUSHEL
BUSHES

B•••H•
BEACHY
BERTHA
BERTHE
BERTHS
BIRTHS
BLIGHT
BLITHE
BOOTHS
BOTCHY
BOUGHS
BOUGHT
BRACHI
BRACHY
BRASHY
BRECHT
BRIGHT
BROTHS
BRUSHY
BUDDHA
BUNCHE
BUNCHY
BURGHS

B••••H
BANISH
BARUCH
BASRAH
BEULAH
BLANCH
BLEACH
BLENCH
BLOTCH
BLUISH
BORSCH
BOYISH
BRANCH
BREACH
BREATH
BREECH
BROACH
BROOCH
BRUNCH
BYPATH

•BH•••
ABHORS

•B•H••
ABOHMS

•B•••H
ABIJAH
ABLUSH

••B•H•
SUBAHS

••B••H
AMBUSH
JUBBAH
KIBLAH
KIBOSH
TOBIAH
WABASH
ZIBETH

•••B•H
CASBAH
JUBBAH

BI••••
BIALYS
BIANCA
BIASED
BIASES
BIAXAL
BIBBED
BIBBER
BIBLES
BIBLIO
BICARB
BICEPS
BICKER
BICORN
BIDDEN
BIDDER
BIDETS
BIDING
BIERCE
BIFFED
BIFFIN
BIFLEX
BIFOLD
BIFORM
BIGAMY
BIGGER
BIGGIN
BIGHTS
BIGOTS
BIGWIG
BIHARI
BIJOUX
BIKINI
BIKOLS
BILBAO
BILGED
BILGES
BILITY
BILKED
BILKER
BILLED
BILLET
BILLIE
BILLON
BILLOW
BILLYS
BILOXI
BINARY
BINDER
BINGES
BINITS
BINNED
BIOGEN
BIOPSY
BIOSIS
BIOTIC
BIOTIN
BIPEDS
BIPODS
BIRDIE
BIREME
BIRLED
BIRLES
BIRRED
BIRTHS
BISCAY
BISECT
BISHOP
BISQUE
BISTER
BISTRO
BITERS
BITING
BITTED
BITTEN
BITTER

B•I•••
BAIKAL
BAILED
BAILEE
BAILER
BAILEY
BAILIE
BAILOR
BAIRNS
BAITED
BAITER
BEIGES
BEINGS
BEIRUT
BLIGHT
BLIMPS
BLINDS
BLINKS
BLINTZ
BLITHE
BOILED
BOILER
BRIARS
BRIBED
BRIBER
BRIBES
BRICKS
BRIDAL
BRIDES
BRIDGE
BRIDIE
BRIDLE
BRIEFS
BRIERS
BRIERY
BRIGHT
BRIGID
BRILLS
BRINED
BRINES
BRINGS
BRINKS
BRISKS
BRITON
BUILDS

B••I••
BAAING
BABIED
BABIES
BABISM
BABIST
BABITE
BAKING
BALING
BANIAN
BANISH
BARING
BARITE
BARIUM
BASICS
BASIFY
BASILS
BASING
BASINS
BASION
BATIKS
BATING
BAYING
BEDIMS
BEFITS
BEGINS
BEGIRD
BEGIRT
BEHIND
BELIAL
BELIED
BELIEF
BELIER
BELIES
BELIZE
BEMIRE
BENIGN
BENITA
BENITO
BERING
BESIDE
BETIDE
BETISE
BEVIES
BIDING
BIKINI
BILITY
BINITS
BITING
BLAINS
BLUING
BLUISH
BODICE
BODIED
BODIES
BODILY
BODING
BOGIES
BOLIDE
BONIER
BONING
BONITO
BOOING
BORIDE
BORING
BOVINE
BOWING
BOXING
BOYISH
BRAIDS
BRAILS
BRAINS
BRAINY
BRAISE
BRAIZE
BROILS
BRUINS
BRUISE
BRUITS
BUNION
BURIAL
BURIED
BURIES
BURINS
BUSIED
BUSIES
BUSILY
BUSING
BUYING
BYLINE

B•••I•
BAALIM
BABBIE
BAFFIN
BAGNIO
BAHAIS
BAILIE
BALTIC
BANDIT
BARBIE
BARDIC
BARMIE
BARRIO
BATTIK
BAUCIS
BEANIE
BEDRID
BEDUIN
BEGUIN
BELGIC
BELOIT
BERLIN
BERNIE
BERTIE
BESSIE
BESTIR
BEWAIL
BIBLIO
BIFFIN
BIGGIN
BIGWIG
BILLIE
BIOSIS
BIOTIC
BIOTIN
BIRDIE
BOBBIE
BOBBIN
BOCCIE
BODKIN
BOLLIX
BONNIE
BOOKIE
BOOTIE
BORGIA

6

BOUGIE
BOWFIN
BRAZIL
BREWIS
BRIDIE
BRIGID
BROMIC
BUDGIE
BULBIL
BUMKIN
BURDIE
BUSKIN
BUSTIC

B••••I
BANGUI
BANZAI
BIHARI
BIKINI
BILOXI
BONACI
BONSAI
BORZOI
BRACHI
BRUNEI

•BI•••
ABIDED
ABIDER
ABIDES
ABIJAH
IBICES
IBIDEM
IBISES
OBIISM
UBIETY

•B•I••
ABBIES
EBBING
OBIISM
OBLIGE
OBOIST

•B••I•
ABATIS
ABULIA
IBERIA
OBTAIN

•B•••I
UBANGI

••BI••
ABBIES
ALBINO
ALBION
ALBITE
AMBITS
BABIED
BABIES
BABISM
BABIST
BABITE
CABINS
COBIAS
CUBING
CUBISM
CUBIST
CUBITS
DEBITS
DOBIES
EBBING
ERBIUM
FABIAN
GABION
GIBING
GOBIES
HABILE
HABITS
IMBIBE
JABIRU
JIBING
KABIKI
KIBITZ
LABIAL
LABILE
LABIUM
LIBIDO
MOBILE
MOBIUS
NUBIAN
NUBIAS
NUBILE
ORBING
ORBITS
RABIES
REBILL
ROBING
ROBINS
RUBIES
RUBIGO
SABINA
SABINE
SABINS
SUBITO
SYBILS
TIBIAE
TIBIAL
TIBIAS
TOBIAH
TOBIAS
TOBIES
TUBING
UNBIND

••B•I•
ALBEIT
BABBIE
BIBLIO
BOBBIE
BOBBIN
CEBOID
CUBOID
DEBRIS
DOBBIN
DUBBIN
DUBLIN
FABRIC
FIBRIL
FIBRIN
GOBLIN
HUBRIS
HYBRID
HYBRIS
KIBEIS
LUBLIN
NUBBIN
PUBLIC
RABBIS
RABBIT
ROBBIA
ROBBIE
RUBRIC
SUBMIT
VIBRIO

••B••I
AMBARI
ARBORI
EMBOLI
KABIKI
KABUKI

•••BI•
ALIBIS
AMEBIC
ANUBIS
ARABIA
ARABIC
BABBIE
BARBIE
BOBBIE
BOBBIN
BULBIL
DOBBIN
DUBBIN
FORBID
GAMBIA
GAMBIR
GAMBIT
GERBIL
GLOBIN
HARBIN
HENBIT
IAMBIC
KRUBIS
LAMBIE
LIMBIC
MORBID
NUBBIN
ORIBIS
OUTBID
PHOBIA
RABBIS
RABBIT
ROBBIA
ROBBIE
SERBIA
TERBIA
TIDBIT
TURBID
TURBIT
TWIBIL
TWOBIT
ZAMBIA
ZOMBIE
ZOMBIS

•••B•I
CIMBRI

••••BI
EPHEBI
INCUBI
RHOMBI
WAHABI

B•J•••
BIJOUX

B••J••
BANJOS
BENJYS

•BJ•••
ABJECT
ABJURE
OBJECT

•B•J••
ABIJAH

B•K•••
BAKERS
BAKERY
BAKING
BIKINI
BIKOLS

B••K••
BACKED
BACKER
BAIKAL
BALKAN
BALKED
BANKED
BANKER
BARKED
BARKER
BASKED
BASKET
BEAKED
BEAKER
BECKED
BECKET
BECKON
BECKYS
BICKER
BILKED
BILKER
BLOKES
BODKIN
BOOKED
BOOKIE
BOSKET
BRAKED
BRAKES
BROKEN
BROKER
BUCKED
BUCKER
BUCKET
BUCKLE
BUCKRA
BULKED
BUMKIN
BUNKED
BUNKER
BUNKUM
BURKED
BURKES
BUSKIN

B•••K•
BAMAKO
BATIKS
BETAKE
BLACKS
BLANKS
BLEAKS
BLINKS
BLOCKS
BLOCKY
BREAKS
BRICKS
BRINKS
BRISKS
BROOKS

B••••K
BARTOK
BATTIK
BEDECK
BETOOK
BYTALK
BYWORK

••B•K•
KABAKA
KABIKI
KABUKI
REBUKE

••B••K
DEBARK
DEBUNK
DYBBUK
EMBANK
EMBARK
IMBARK
LUBECK
ZEBECK

•••B•K
CHABUK
DYBBUK

BL••••
BLACKS
BLADED
BLADES
BLAINS
BLAMED
BLAMES
BLANCH
BLANKS
BLARED
BLARES
BLASTO
BLASTS
BLAZED
BLAZER
BLAZES
BLAZON
BLEACH
BLEAKS
BLEARS
BLEARY
BLEATS
BLEBBY
BLEEDS
BLENCH
BLENDE
BLENDS
BLENNY
BLIGHT
BLIMPS
BLINDS
BLINKS
BLINTZ
BLITHE
BLOATS
BLOCKS
BLOCKY
BLOKES
BLONDE
BLONDS
BLOODS
BLOODY
BLOOMS
BLOOMY
BLOTCH
BLOUSE
BLOWBY
BLOWER
BLOWUP
BLOWZY
BLUELY
BLUEST
BLUETS
BLUFFS
BLUING
BLUISH
BLUNGE
BLUNTS
BLURBS
BLURRY
BLURTS

B•L•••
BALAAM
BALATA
BALBOA

6

BALDER
BALDLY
BALEEN
BALERS
BALING
BALKAN
BALKED
BALLAD
BALLED
BALLET
BALLOT
BALSAM
BALSAS
BALTIC
BALZAC
BELAYS
BELDAM
BELFRY
BELGAS
BELGIC
BELIAL
BELIED
BELIEF
BELIER
BELIES
BELIZE
BELLAS
BELLED
BELLES
BELLOC
BELLOW
BELOIT
BELONG
BELTED
BELUGA
BILBAO
BILGED
BILGES
BILITY
BILKED
BILKER
BILLED
BILLET
BILLIE
BILLON
BILLOW
BILLYS
BILOXI
BOLDER
BOLDLY
BOLERO
BOLEYN
BOLIDE
BOLLED
BOLLIX
BOLSON
BOLTED
BOLTER
BULBAR
BULBEL
BULBIL
BULBUL
BULGAR
BULGED
BULGER
BULGES
BULKED
BULLAE
BULLET
BYLANE
BYLAWS
BYLINE

B••L••
BAALIM
BAILED
BAILEE
BAILER
BAILEY
BAILIE
BAILOR
BALLAD
BALLED
BALLET
BALLOT
BARLEY
BAWLED
BAWLER
BEDLAM
BELLAS
BELLED
BELLES
BELLOC
BELLOW
BERLIN
BEULAH
BEULAS
BIALYS
BIBLES
BIBLIO
BIFLEX
BILLED
BILLET
BILLIE
BILLON
BILLOW
BILLYS
BIRLED
BIRLES
BOGLES
BOILED
BOILER
BOLLED
BOLLIX
BOULES
BOWLED
BOWLEG
BOWLER
BRILLS
BRULOT
BUGLED
BUGLER
BUGLES
BUILDS
BULLAE
BULLET
BURLAP
BURLED
BURLER
BURLEY
BUTLER
BYBLOW
BYPLAY

B•••L•
BABBLE
BABULS
BAFFLE
BAGELS
BALDLY
BANGLE
BARELY
BARFLY
BASALT
BASELY
BASILS
BATTLE
BAUBLE
BEADLE
BEAGLE
BECALM
BEETLE
BEFALL
BEFELL
BEHALF
BEHELD
BEHOLD
BERYLS
BETELS
BEVELS
BEZELS
BIFOLD
BIKOLS
BLUELY
BOBBLE
BODILY
BOGGLE
BOLDLY
BOODLE
BOTFLY
BOTTLE
BOUCLE
BOWELS
BRAILS
BRAWLS
BRIDLE
BRILLS
BROILS
BUBALS
BUBBLE
BUBBLY
BUCKLE
BUDDLE
BUMBLE
BUNDLE
BUNGLE
BURBLE
BURGLE
BUSILY
BUSTLE
BYTALK

B••••L
BAIKAL
BARBEL
BARREL
BEFALL
BEFELL
BEFOOL
BEFOUL
BELIAL
BENGAL
BENZOL
BENZYL
BETHEL
BEWAIL
BIAXAL
BORDEL
BOREAL
BRAZIL
BRIDAL
BROMAL
BRUMAL
BRUTAL
BUCCAL
BULBEL
BULBIL
BULBUL
BURIAL
BURSAL
BUSHEL

•BL•••
ABLAUT
ABLAZE
ABLEST
ABLOOM
ABLUSH
OBLAST
OBLATE
OBLIGE
OBLONG

•B•L••
ABELES
ABOLLA
ABULIA
OBELUS
OBOLUS
UBOLTS

•B••L•
ABOLLA
ABVOLT

•B•••L
ABORAL

••BL••
AMBLED
AMBLER
AMBLES
BIBLES
BIBLIO
BYBLOW
CABLED
CABLES
CABLET
COBLES
DOBLAS
DOBLON
DUBLIN
EMBLEM
FABLED
FABLER
FABLES
GABLED
GABLES
GIBLET
GOBLET
GOBLIN
KIBLAH
LUBLIN
PUBLIC
ROBLES
RUBLES
SABLES
SUBLET
TABLED
TABLES
TABLET
UMBLES

••B•L•
ARBELA
BABBLE
BABULS
BOBBLE
BUBALS
BUBBLE
BUBBLY
CABALA
CABALS
CIBOLS
COBALT
COBBLE
CYBELE
DABBLE
DIBBLE
EMBALM
EMBOLI
FIBULA
GABBLE
GOBBLE
HABILE
HOBBLE
IMBALM
KOBOLD
LABELS
LABILE
LIBELS
LOBULE
MABELS
MOBILE
NEBULA
NIBBLE
NOBALL
NOBBLE
NUBBLE
NUBBLY
NUBILE
PEBBLE
PEBBLY
RABBLE
REBELS
REBILL
RIBALD
ROBALO
RUBBLE
SIBYLS
SUBTLE
SUBTLY
SYBILS
TUBULE
TYBALT
UMBELS
UNBELT
UNBOLT
WABBLE
WABBLY
WOBBLE
WOBBLY

••B••L
FIBRIL
LABIAL
NOBALL
REBILL
TIBIAL

•••BL•
ALIBLE
ARABLE
BABBLE
BAUBLE
BOBBLE
BUBBLE
BUBBLY
BUMBLE
BURBLE
COBBLE
DABBLE
DIBBLE
DOABLE
DOUBLE
DOUBLY
DRABLY
DUMBLY
EDIBLE
ENABLE
FEEBLE
FIMBLE
FOIBLE
FUMBLE
GABBLE
GAMBLE
GARBLE
GLIBLY
GOBBLE
HOBBLE
HUMBLE
HUMBLY
JUMBLE
LIABLE

MARBLE
MUMBLE
NIBBLE
NIMBLE
NOBBLE
NUBBLE
NUBBLY
NUMBLY
PEBBLE
PEBBLY
PUEBLO
RABBLE
RAMBLE
ROUBLE
RUBBLE
RUMBLE
STABLE
SUABLE
TREBLE
TUMBLE
UNABLE
USABLE
USABLY
VIABLE
WABBLE
WABBLY
WAMBLE
WAMBLY
WARBLE
WIMBLE
WOBBLE
WOBBLY

•••B•L

ARABEL
ATABAL
BARBEL
BULBEL
BULBIL
BULBUL
CORBEL
CYMBAL
DIOBOL
GAMBOL
GERBIL
GLOBAL
HERBAL
ISABEL
ISOBEL
SYMBOL
TIMBAL
TRIBAL
TWIBIL
VERBAL

B•M•••

BAMAKO
BAMBOO
BEMATA
BEMEAN
BEMIRE
BEMOAN
BEMUSE
BOMBAY
BOMBED
BOMBER
BOMBES
BUMBLE
BUMKIN
BUMMED
BUMMER
BUMPED
BUMPER

B••M••

BADMAN
BADMEN
BAGMAN
BAGMEN
BARMAN
BARMEN
BARMIE
BATMAN
BATMEN
BEAMED
BERMES
BLAMED
BLAMES
BLIMPS
BOOMED
BOWMAN
BOWMEN
BREMEN
BROMAL
BROMES
BROMIC
BRUMAL
BRUMES
BUMMED
BUMMER
BUSMAN
BUSMEN

B•••M•

BAHAMA
BECAME
BECOME
BEDIMS
BEGUMS
BENUMB
BESOMS
BIGAMY
BIREME
BLOOMS
BLOOMY
BOSOMS
BRAHMA
BRAHMS
BREAMS
BREGMA
BROOMS
BROOMY
BYNAME

B••••M

BAALIM
BABISM
BALAAM
BALSAM
BANTAM
BARIUM
BARNUM
BECALM
BEDLAM
BELDAM
BESEEM
BIFORM
BOTTOM
BUNKUM

•B•M••

ABOMAS
ABOMBS
HBOMBS

•B••M•

ABOHMS
ABRAMS
ABYSMS
HBEAMS
IBEAMS
ZBEAMS

•B•••M

ABLOOM
IBIDEM
OBIISM

••BM••

CABMAN
CABMEN
SUBMIT

••B•M•

ALBUMS

••B••M

BABISM
CUBISM
EMBALM
EMBLEM
ERBIUM
IMBALM
LABIUM
LABRUM

B•N•••

BANANA
BANDED
BANDIT
BANGED
BANGLE
BANGOR
BANGUI
BANGUP
BANIAN
BANISH
BANJOS
BANKED
BANKER
BANNED
BANNER
BANTAM
BANTER
BANTUS
BANYAN
BANZAI
BENDAY
BENDEE
BENDER
BENGAL
BENIGN
BENITA
BENITO
BENJYS
BENNES
BENNET
BENNYS
BENTON
BENUMB
BENZOL
BENZYL
BINARY
BINDER
BINGES
BINITS
BINNED
BONACI
BONBON
BONDED
BONDER
BONERS
BONGED
BONGOS
BONIER
BONING
BONITO
BONNET
BONNIE
BONNYS
BONSAI
BONZER
BONZES
BUNCHE
BUNCHY
BUNCOS
BUNDLE
BUNGED
BUNGLE
BUNION
BUNKED
BUNKER
BUNKUM
BUNSEN
BUNTED
BUNYAN
BYNAME

B••N••

BAGNIO
BANNED
BANNER
BARNEY
BARNUM
BEANED
BEANIE
BEINGS
BENNES
BENNET
BENNYS
BERNEY
BERNIE
BIANCA
BINNED
BLANCH
BLANKS
BLENCH
BLENDE
BLENDS
BLENNY
BLINDS
BLINKS
BLINTZ
BLONDE
BLONDS
BLUNGE
BLUNTS
BONNET
BONNIE
BONNYS
BORNEO
BOUNCE
BOUNCY
BOUNDS
BOUNTY
BRANCH
BRANDS
BRANDY
BRANNY
BRANTS
BRENDA
BRENTS
BRINED
BRINES
BRINGS
BRINKS
BRONCO
BRONCS
BRONTE
BRONZE
BRONZY
BRUNCH
BRUNEI
BRUNET
BRUNOS
BURNED
BURNER
BURNET
BWANAS

B•••N•

BAAING
BAIRNS
BAKING
BALING
BANANA
BARING
BARONG
BARONS
BARONY
BASING
BASINS
BATING
BATONS
BAYING
BEGINS
BEHIND
BELONG
BERING
BETONY
BEYOND
BEZANT
BIDING
BIKINI
BITING
BLAINS
BLENNY
BLUING
BODING
BOGANS
BONING
BOOING
BORANE
BORING
BOTANY
BOURNE
BOURNS
BOVINE
BOWING
BOXING
BRAINS
BRAINY
BRANNY
BRAWNY
BROWNS
BRUINS
BRYANT
BRYONY
BURANS
BURINS
BUSING
BUTANE
BUYING
BYGONE
BYLANE
BYLINE

B••••N

BABOON
BADMAN
BADMEN
BAFFIN
BAGMAN
BAGMEN
BALEEN
BALKAN
BANIAN
BANYAN
BARMAN
BARMEN
BARREN
BARTON
BARYON
BASION

BATAAN
BATMAN
BATMEN
BATTEN
BEACON
BEATEN
BECKON
BEDPAN
BEDUIN
BEGUIN
BEMEAN
BEMOAN
BENIGN
BENTON
BERGEN
BERLIN
BHUTAN
BICORN
BIDDEN
BIFFIN
BIGGIN
BILLON
BIOGEN
BIOTIN
BITTEN
BLAZON
BOBBIN
BODKIN
BOLEYN
BOLSON
BONBON
BOSTON
BOWFIN
BOWMAN
BOWMEN
BRAZEN
BREMEN
BRETON
BRITON
BROGAN
BROKEN
BUMKIN
BUNION
BUNSEN
BUNYAN
BURDEN
BUSKIN
BUSMAN
BUSMEN
BUTTON

•BN•••

ABNERS

•B•N••

TBONES
UBANGI

•B••N•

ABOUND
ABSENT
EBBING
OBLONG
OBTUND

•B•••N

OBERON
OBTAIN

••BN••

COBNUT
HOBNOB

••B•N•

ALBANY
ALBINO
CABANA
CABINS
CUBANS
CUBING
DEBUNK
EBBING
EMBANK
GIBING
JIBING
ORBING
ROBAND
ROBING
ROBINS
RUBENS
SABINA
SABINE
SABINS
TUBING
UNBEND
UNBENT
UNBIND
URBANE

••B••N

ALBION
AUBURN
BABOON
BOBBIN
CABMAN
CABMEN
DOBBIN
DOBLON
DOBSON
DUBBIN
DUBLIN
FABIAN
FIBRIN
GABION
GIBBON
GIBRAN
GIBSON
GOBLIN
HEBRON
INBORN
LIBYAN
LUBLIN
NUBBIN
NUBIAN
OSBORN
REBORN
RIBBON
ROBSON
SABEAN
SUBORN
UNBORN

•••B•N

BOBBIN
BONBON
CARBON
CORBAN
DOBBIN
DUBBIN
DURBAN
GIBBON
GLOBIN
GRABEN
HARBIN
LISBON
NUBBIN
REUBEN
RIBBON
TURBAN

BO••••

BOARDS
BOASTS
BOATED
BOBBED
BOBBER
BOBBIE
BOBBIN
BOBBLE
BOBBYS
BOBCAT
BOCCIE
BODEGA
BODICE
BODIED
BODIES
BODILY
BODING
BODKIN
BOGANS
BOGEYS
BOGGED
BOGGLE
BOGIES
BOGLES
BOGOTA
BOILED
BOILER
BOLDER
BOLDLY
BOLERO
BOLEYN
BOLIDE
BOLLED
BOLLIX
BOLSON
BOLTED
BOLTER
BOMBAY
BOMBED
BOMBER
BOMBES
BONACI
BONBON
BONDED
BONDER
BONERS
BONGED
BONGOS
BONIER
BONING
BONITO
BONNET
BONNIE
BONNYS
BONSAI
BONZER
BONZES
BOOBOO
BOODLE
BOOHOO
BOOING
BOOKED
BOOKIE
BOOMED
BOOSTS
BOOTED
BOOTEE
BOOTHS
BOOTIE
BOOZED
BOOZER
BOOZES
BOPPED
BORAGE
BORANE
BORATE
BORDEL
BORDER
BOREAL
BOREAS
BORERS
BORGIA
BORIDE
BORING
BORNEO
BORROW
BORSCH
BORZOI
BOSHES
BOSKET
BOSOMS
BOSSED
BOSSES
BOSTON
BOTANY
BOTCHY
BOTFLY
BOTHER
BOTTLE
BOTTOM
BOUCLE
BOUFFE
BOUGHS
BOUGHT
BOUGIE
BOULES
BOUNCE
BOUNCY
BOUNDS
BOUNTY
BOURGS
BOURNE
BOURNS
BOURSE
BOUSED
BOUSES
BOVINE
BOWELS
BOWERS
BOWERY
BOWFIN
BOWING
BOWLED
BOWLEG
BOWLER
BOWMAN
BOWMEN
BOWSED
BOWSES
BOWWOW
BOWYER
BOXCAR
BOXERS
BOXING
BOYARD
BOYARS
BOYISH

B•O•••

BAOBAB
BIOGEN
BIOPSY
BIOSIS
BIOTIC
BIOTIN
BLOATS
BLOCKS
BLOCKY
BLOKES
BLONDE
BLONDS
BLOODS
BLOODY
BLOOMS
BLOOMY
BLOTCH
BLOUSE
BLOWBY
BLOWER
BLOWUP
BLOWZY
BOOBOO
BOODLE
BOOHOO
BOOING
BOOKED
BOOKIE
BOOMED
BOOSTS
BOOTED
BOOTEE
BOOTHS
BOOTIE
BOOZED
BOOZER
BOOZES
BROACH
BROADS
BROGAN
BROGUE
BROILS
BROKEN
BROKER
BROMAL
BROMES
BROMIC
BRONCO
BRONCS
BRONTE
BRONZE
BRONZY
BROOCH
BROODS
BROODY
BROOKS
BROOMS
BROOMY
BROTHS
BROWNS
BROWSE
BUOYED

B••O••

BABOON
BABOOS
BARONG
BARONS
BARONY
BATONS
BAYOUS
BECOME
BEFOGS
BEFOOL
BEFORE
BEFOUL
BEHOLD
BEHOOF
BEHOVE
BELOIT
BELONG
BEMOAN
BESOMS
BESOTS
BETONY
BETOOK
BEYOND
BICORN
BIFOLD
BIFORM
BIGOTS
BIJOUX
BIKOLS
BILOXI

BIPODS
BLOODS
BLOODY
BLOOMS
BLOOMY
BOGOTA
BOSOMS
BROOCH
BROODS
BROODY
BROOKS
BROOMS
BROOMY
BRYONY
BUBOES
BYGONE
BYROAD
BYWORD
BYWORK

B•••O•
BABOON
BABOOS
BAILOR
BALBOA
BALLOT
BAMBOO
BANGOR
BANJOS
BARROW
BARTOK
BARTON
BARYON
BASION
BASSOS
BATHOS
BEACON
BECKON
BEFOOL
BEHOOF
BELLOC
BELLOW
BENTON
BENZOL
BESTOW
BETOOK
BETTOR
BILLON
BILLOW
BISHOP
BLAZON
BOLSON
BONBON
BONGOS
BOOBOO
BOOHOO
BORROW
BORZOI
BOSTON
BOTTOM
BOWWOW
BRAVOS
BRAZOS
BRETON
BRITON
BRULOT
BRUNOS
BUNCOS
BUNION
BURBOT
BURGOO
BURGOS
BURROS
BURROW
BUTTON
BYBLOW

B••••O
BAGNIO
BAMAKO
BAMBOO
BARRIO
BASUTO
BENITO
BIBLIO
BILBAO
BISTRO
BLASTO
BOLERO
BONITO
BOOBOO
BOOHOO
BORNEO
BRONCO
BURGOO

•BO•••
ABOARD
ABODES
ABOHMS
ABOLLA
ABOMAS
ABOMBS
ABORAL
ABORTS
ABOUND
EBOATS
HBOMBS
OBOIST
OBOLUS
TBONES
UBOATS
UBOLTS

•B•O••
ABBOTS
ABHORS
ABLOOM
ABROAD
ABSORB
ABVOLT
OBLONG

•B••O•
ABATOR
ABLOOM
ABYDOS
OBERON

••BO••
ABBOTS
ARBORI
ARBORS
BABOON
BABOOS
BUBOES
CABOBS
CEBOID
CIBOLS
CUBOID
ELBOWS
EMBODY
EMBOLI
EMBOSS
EMBOWS
EUBOEA
HOBOES
IMBODY
INBORN
JABOTS
KABOBS
KIBOSH
KOBOLD
LABORS
LABOUR
NABOBS
OSBORN
OXBOWS
REBORN
REBOZO
RIBOSE
ROBOTS
SABOTS
SUBORN
TABOOS
TABORS
UNBOLT
UNBORN
UPBOWS

••B•O•
ALBION
BABOON
BABOOS
BYBLOW
DEBTOR
DOBLON
DOBSON
GABION
GIBBON
GIBSON
HEBRON
HOBNOB
RIBBON
ROBSON
TABOOS

••B••O
ALBEDO
ALBINO
BIBLIO
EMBRYO
GABBRO
LIBIDO
REBATO
REBOZO
ROBALO
RUBATO
RUBIGO
SUBITO
TOBAGO
VIBRIO

•••BO•
BALBOA
BAMBOO
BONBON
BOOBOO
BURBOT
CARBON
CARBOY
COMBOS
COWBOY
DIOBOL
FOGBOW
GAMBOL
GIBBON
GUMBOS
HARBOR
HATBOX
HOTBOX
ICEBOX
JERBOA
LISBOA
LISBON
LOWBOY
MAMBOS
OVIBOS
POTBOY
RIBBON
SAMBOS
SUNBOW
SYMBOL
TOMBOY
TURBOT

•••B•O
BAMBOO
BILBAO
BOOBOO
GABBRO
PUEBLO

••••BO
AKIMBO
CRAMBO
GAZABO
GAZEBO
LAVABO
PHLEBO
PLUMBO

B•P•••
BIPEDS
BIPODS
BOPPED
BYPASS
BYPAST
BYPATH
BYPLAY

B••P••
BEDPAN
BEEPED
BIOPSY
BOPPED
BUMPED
BUMPER
BURPED

B•••P•
BICEPS
BLIMPS

B••••P
BANGUP
BISHOP
BLOWUP
BURLAP

•B••P•
ABRUPT

••B••P
HUBCAP
MOBCAP

B••Q••
BARQUE
BASQUE
BISQUE
BRAQUE

BR••••
BRACED
BRACER
BRACES
BRACHI
BRACHY
BRACTS
BRAHMA
BRAHMS
BRAIDS
BRAILS
BRAINS
BRAINY
BRAISE
BRAIZE
BRAKED
BRAKES
BRANCH
BRANDS
BRANDY
BRANNY
BRANTS
BRAQUE
BRASHY
BRASSY
BRAVED
BRAVER
BRAVES
BRAVOS
BRAWLS
BRAWNY
BRAYED
BRAYER
BRAZAS
BRAZED
BRAZEN
BRAZER
BRAZES
BRAZIL
BRAZOS
BREACH
BREADS
BREAKS
BREAMS
BREAST
BREATH
BRECHT
BREECH
BREEDS
BREEZE
BREEZY
BREGMA
BREMEN
BRENDA
BRENTS
BRETON
BREVES
BREVET
BREWED
BREWER
BREWIS
BRIARS
BRIBED
BRIBER
BRIBES
BRICKS
BRIDAL
BRIDES
BRIDGE
BRIDIE
BRIDLE
BRIEFS
BRIERS
BRIERY
BRIGHT
BRIGID
BRILLS
BRINED
BRINES
BRINGS
BRINKS
BRISKS
BRITON
BROACH
BROADS
BROGAN
BROGUE
BROILS
BROKEN
BROKER
BROMAL
BROMES

6

BROMIC
BRONCO
BRONCS
BRONTE
BRONZE
BRONZY
BROOCH
BROODS
BROODY
BROOKS
BROOMS
BROOMY
BROTHS
BROWNS
BROWSE
BRUCES
BRUGES
BRUINS
BRUISE
BRUITS
BRULOT
BRUMAL
BRUMES
BRUNCH
BRUNEI
BRUNET
BRUNOS
BRUSHY
BRUTAL
BRUTES
BRUTUS
BRYANT
BRYONY

B•R•••

BARBED
BARBEL
BARBER
BARBET
BARBIE
BARDED
BARDES
BARDIC
BAREGE
BARELY
BAREST
BARFLY
BARGED
BARGEE
BARGES
BARING
BARITE
BARIUM
BARKED
BARKER
BARLEY
BARMAN
BARMEN
BARMIE
BARNEY
BARNUM
BARONG
BARONS
BARONY
BARQUE
BARRED
BARREL
BARREN
BARRET
BARRIO
BARROW
BARRYS
BARTER
BARTOK
BARTON
BARUCH
BARYES
BARYON
BARYTA
BERATE
BERBER
BEREFT
BERETS
BERGEN
BERING
BERLIN
BERMES
BERNEY
BERNIE
BERTHA
BERTHE
BERTHS
BERTIE
BERYLS
BIRDIE
BIREME
BIRLED
BIRLES
BIRRED
BIRTHS
BORAGE
BORANE
BORATE
BORDEL
BORDER
BOREAL
BOREAS
BORERS
BORGIA
BORIDE
BORING
BORNEO
BORROW
BORSCH
BORZOI
BURANS
BURBLE
BURBOT
BURDEN
BURDIE
BUREAU
BURGEE
BURGER
BURGHS
BURGLE
BURGOO
BURGOS
BURIAL
BURIED
BURIES
BURINS
BURKED
BURKES
BURLAP
BURLED
BURLER
BURLEY
BURNED
BURNER
BURNET
BURPED
BURRED
BURROS
BURROW
BURSAE
BURSAL
BURSAR
BURSAS
BURSES
BURSTS
BYROAD

B••R••

BAIRNS
BARRED
BARREL
BARREN
BARRET
BARRIO
BARROW
BARRYS
BASRAH
BEARDS
BEARED
BEARER
BEDRID
BEIRUT
BETRAY
BIERCE
BIRRED
BLARED
BLARES
BLURBS
BLURRY
BLURTS
BOARDS
BORROW
BOURGS
BOURNE
BOURNS
BOURSE
BURRED
BURROS
BURROW

B•••R•

BAKERS
BAKERY
BALERS
BAWDRY
BAYARD
BEFORE
BEGIRD
BEGIRT
BELFRY
BEMIRE
BEWARE
BICARB
BICORN
BIFORM
BIHARI
BINARY
BISTRO
BITERS
BLEARS
BLEARY
BLURRY
BOLERO
BONERS
BORERS
BOWERS
BOWERY
BOXERS
BOYARD
BOYARS
BRIARS
BRIERS
BRIERY
BUCKRA
BUYERS
BYWORD
BYWORK

B••••R

BACKER
BADGER
BAILER
BAILOR
BAITER
BALDER
BANGOR
BANKER
BANNER
BANTER
BARBER
BARKER
BARTER
BATHER
BATTER
BAWLER
BAXTER
BEAKER
BEARER
BEATER
BEAVER
BEDDER
BEGGAR
BELIER
BENDER
BERBER
BESTIR
BETTER
BETTOR
BEZOAR
BIBBER
BICKER
BIDDER
BIGGER
BILKER
BINDER
BISTER
BITTER
BLAZER
BLOWER
BOBBER
BOILER
BOLDER
BOLTER
BOMBER
BONDER
BONIER
BONZER
BOOZER
BORDER
BOTHER
BOWLER
BOWYER
BOXCAR
BRACER
BRAVER
BRAYER
BRAZER
BREWER
BRIBER
BROKER
BUCKER
BUDDER
BUFFER
BUGGER
BUGLER
BULBAR
BULGAR
BULGER
BUMMER
BUMPER
BUNKER
BURGER
BURLER
BURNER
BURSAR
BUSTER
BUTLER
BUTTER
BUZZER

•BR•••

ABRADE
ABRAMS
ABROAD
ABRUPT

•B•R••

ABORAL
ABORTS
IBERIA
OBERON

•B••R•

ABHORS
ABJURE
ABNERS
ABOARD
ABSORB
ABSURD
OBVERT

•B•••R

ABASER
ABATER
ABATOR
ABIDER
ABUSER
OBEYER

••BR••

AUBREY
COBRAS
DEBRIS
DOBRAS
ELBRUS
EMBRUE
EMBRYO
FABRIC
FIBRIL
FIBRIN
GIBRAN
HEBREW
HEBRON
HUBRIS
HYBRID
HYBRIS
IMBRUE
INBRED
LABRET
LABRUM
LIBRAE
LIBRAS
RUBRIC
SABRAS
UMBRAE
UMBRAS
UNBRED
VIBRIO
ZEBRAS

••B•R•

ALBERT
AMBARI
AMBARY
AMBERS
AMBERY
ARBORI
ARBORS
ASBURY
AUBURN
DEBARK
DEBARS
EGBERT
ELBERT
EMBARK
EMBARS
EMBERS
FIBERS
GABBRO

GIBERS
HOBART
HUBERT
IMBARK
INBORN
JABIRU
LABORS
OSBERT
OSBORN
REBORN
ROBERT
SABERS
SOBERS
SUBORN
SUBURB
TABARD
TABORS
TUBERS
UMBERS
UNBARS
UNBORN
WEBERS

••B••R

AMBLER
BIBBER
BOBBER
DABBER
DEBTOR
DIBBER
DOBBER
FABLER
FIBBER
GABBER
GIBBER
JABBER
JIBBER
JOBBER
LABOUR
LUBBER
MOBBER
ROBBER
RUBBER
SUBTER
TUBBER
UNBEAR
YABBER

•••BR•

CIMBRI
DAUBRY
GABBRO
HOMBRE
TIMBRE

•••B•R

BARBER
BERBER
BIBBER
BOBBER
BOMBER
BRIBER
BULBAR
CAMBER
COMBER
CUMBER
DABBER
DAUBER
DIBBER
DISBAR
DOBBER
DUNBAR
DURBAR
FERBER
FIBBER
GABBER
GAMBIR
GHEBER
GIBBER
GOOBER
HARBOR
ISOBAR
JABBER
JIBBER
JOBBER
KHYBER
LIMBER
LUBBER
LUMBAR
LUMBER
MEMBER
MOBBER
NUMBER
PROBER
ROBBER
RUBBER
SAMBUR
SOMBER
TIMBER
TUBBER
WILBER
WILBUR
YABBER

B•S•••

BASALT
BASELY
BASHAW
BASHED
BASHES
BASICS
BASIFY
BASILS
BASING
BASINS
BASION
BASKED
BASKET
BASQUE
BASRAH
BASSES
BASSET
BASSOS
BASTED
BASTES
BASUTO
BESEEM
BESETS
BESIDE
BESOMS
BESOTS
BESSIE
BESSYS
BESTED
BESTIR
BESTOW
BISCAY
BISECT
BISHOP
BISQUE
BISTER
BISTRO
BOSHES
BOSKET
BOSOMS
BOSSED
BOSSES
BOSTON
BUSHED
BUSHEL
BUSHES
BUSIED
BUSIES
BUSILY
BUSING
BUSKIN
BUSMAN
BUSMEN
BUSSED
BUSSES
BUSTED
BUSTER
BUSTIC
BUSTLE
BYSSUS

B••S••

BALSAM
BALSAS
BASSES
BASSET
BASSOS
BEASTS
BESSIE
BESSYS
BETSYS
BIASED
BIASES
BIOSIS
BLASTO
BLASTS
BOASTS
BOLSON
BONSAI
BOOSTS
BORSCH
BOSSED
BOSSES
BOUSED
BOUSES
BOWSED
BOWSES
BRASHY
BRASSY
BRISKS
BRUSHY
BUNSEN
BURSAE
BURSAL
BURSAR
BURSAS
BURSES
BURSTS
BUSSED
BUSSES
BYSSUS

B•••S•

BABISM
BABIST
BAGASS
BANISH
BAREST
BEHEST
BEMUSE
BETISE
BIOPSY
BLOUSE
BLUEST
BLUISH
BOURSE
BOYISH
BRAISE
BRASSY
BREAST
BROWSE
BRUISE
BYPASS
BYPAST

B••••S

BABIES
BABOOS
BABULS
BACHES
BADGES
BAGASS
BAGELS
BAHAIS
BAIRNS
BAKERS
BALERS
BALSAS
BANJOS
BANTUS
BARDES
BARGES
BARONS
BARRYS
BARYES
BASHES
BASICS
BASILS
BASINS
BASSES
BASSOS
BASTES
BATHOS
BATIKS
BATONS
BAUCIS
BAYOUS
BEARDS
BEASTS
BEAUTS
BECKYS
BEDEWS
BEDIMS
BEEVES
BEFITS
BEFOGS
BEGETS
BEGINS
BEGUMS
BEIGES
BEINGS
BELAYS
BELGAS
BELIES
BELLAS
BELLES
BENJYS
BENNES
BENNYS
BERETS
BERMES
BERTHS
BERYLS
BESETS
BESOMS
BESOTS
BESSYS
BETELS
BETSYS
BETTES
BETTYS
BEULAS
BEVELS
BEVIES
BEZELS
BIALYS
BIASES
BIBLES
BICEPS
BIDETS
BIGHTS
BIGOTS
BIKOLS
BILGES
BILLYS
BINGES
BINITS
BIOSIS
BIPEDS
BIPODS
BIRLES
BIRTHS
BITERS
BLACKS
BLADES
BLAINS
BLAMES
BLANKS
BLARES
BLASTS
BLAZES
BLEAKS
BLEARS
BLEATS
BLEEDS
BLENDS
BLIMPS
BLINDS
BLINKS
BLOATS
BLOCKS
BLOKES
BLONDS
BLOODS
BLOOMS
BLUETS
BLUFFS
BLUNTS
BLURBS
BLURTS
BOARDS
BOASTS
BOBBYS
BODIES
BOGANS
BOGEYS
BOGIES
BOGLES
BOMBES
BONERS
BONGOS
BONNYS
BONZES
BOOSTS
BOOTHS
BOOZES
BOREAS
BORERS
BOSHES
BOSOMS
BOSSES
BOUGHS
BOULES
BOUNDS
BOURGS
BOURNS
BOUSES
BOWELS
BOWERS
BOWSES
BOXERS
BOYARS
BRACES
BRACTS
BRAHMS
BRAIDS
BRAILS
BRAINS
BRAKES

BRANDS
BRANTS
BRAVES
BRAVOS
BRAWLS
BRAZAS
BRAZES
BRAZOS
BREADS
BREAKS
BREAMS
BREEDS
BRENTS
BREVES
BREWIS
BRIARS
BRIBES
BRICKS
BRIDES
BRIEFS
BRIERS
BRILLS
BRINES
BRINGS
BRINKS
BRISKS
BROADS
BROILS
BROMES
BRONCS
BROODS
BROOKS
BROOMS
BROTHS
BROWNS
BRUCES
BRUGES
BRUINS
BRUITS
BRUMES
BRUNOS
BRUTES
BRUTUS
BUBALS
BUBOES
BUDGES
BUGLES
BUILDS
BULGES
BUNCOS
BURANS
BURGHS
BURGOS
BURIES
BURINS
BURKES
BURROS
BURSAS
BURSES
BURSTS
BUSHES
BUSIES
BUSSES
BUTTES
BUYERS
BUZZES
BWANAS
BYLAWS
BYPASS
BYSSUS
BYWAYS

•BS•••

ABSENT
ABSORB
ABSURD
OBSESS

•B•S••

ABASED
ABASER
ABASES
ABUSED
ABUSER
ABUSES
ABYSMS
IBISES

•B••S•

ABBESS
ABLEST
ABLUSH
OBIISM
OBLAST
OBOIST
OBSESS
OBTEST
OBTUSE

•B•••S

ABACAS
ABACUS
ABASES
ABATES
ABATIS
ABBESS
ABBEYS
ABBIES
ABBOTS
ABELES
ABHORS
ABIDES
ABNERS
ABODES
ABOHMS
ABOMAS
ABOMBS
ABORTS
ABRAMS
ABUSES
ABYDOS
ABYSMS
EBOATS
HBEAMS
HBOMBS
IBEAMS
IBEXES
IBICES
IBISES
OBELUS
OBOLUS
OBSESS
TBONES
UBOATS
UBOLTS
ZBEAMS

••BS••

DOBSON
GIBSON
ROBSON

••B•S•

ABBESS
AMBUSH
BABISM
BABIST
CUBISM
CUBIST
DEBASE
EMBOSS
KIBOSH
RIBOSE
ROBUST
WABASH

••B••S

ABBESS
ABBEYS
ABBIES
ABBOTS
ALBUMS
AMBERS
AMBITS
AMBLES
ARBORS
BABIES
BABOOS
BABULS
BIBLES
BOBBYS
BUBALS
BUBOES
CABALS
CABINS
CABLES
CABOBS
CIBOLS
COBIAS
COBLES
COBRAS
CUBANS
CUBEBS
CUBITS
DEBARS
DEBBYS
DEBITS
DEBRIS
DEBUGS
DEBUTS
DOBIES
DOBLAS
DOBRAS
ELBOWS
ELBRUS
EMBARS
EMBAYS
EMBEDS
EMBERS
EMBOSS
EMBOWS
FABLES
FIBERS
GABLES
GIBERS
GOBIES
HABITS
HOBBES
HOBOES
HUBRIS
HYBRIS
IMBEDS
IMBUES
JABOTS
KABOBS
KIBEIS
LABELS
LABORS
LIBBYS
LIBELS
LIBRAS
MABELS
MOBIUS
NABOBS
NUBIAS
ORBITS
OXBOWS
RABBIS
RABIES
REBECS
REBELS
REBUTS
ROBINS
ROBLES
ROBOTS
RUBENS
RUBIES
RUBLES
SABERS
SABINS
SABLES
SABOTS
SABRAS
SEBATS
SIBYLS
SOBERS
SUBAHS
SYBILS
TABLES
TABOOS
TABORS
TIBIAS
TOBIAS
TOBIES
TUBERS
UMBELS
UMBERS
UMBLES
UMBRAS
UNBARS
UPBOWS
WEBERS
XEBECS
ZEBECS
ZEBRAS
ZIBETS

•••B•S

ADOBES
ALIBIS
AMEBAS
ANABAS
ANUBIS
BOBBYS
BOMBES
BRIBES
CEIBAS
COMBOS
DEBBYS
DOUBTS
EREBUS
FLYBYS
GLEBES
GLOBES
GREBES
GUMBOS
HOBBES
IAMBUS
KRUBIS
LIBBYS
LIMBUS
MAMBAS
MAMBOS
NIMBUS
ORIBIS
OVIBOS
PLEBES
PROBES
RABBIS
RUMBAS
SAMBAS
SAMBOS
SCUBAS
THEBES
TRIBES
YERBAS
ZOMBIS

••••BS

ABOMBS
ADLIBS
ARDEBS
BLURBS
CABOBS
CALEBS
CARIBS
CAROBS
CLIMBS
COOMBS
CRUMBS
CUBEBS
DEMOBS
EXURBS
HBOMBS
JACOBS
KABOBS
NABOBS
NAWABS
PLUMBS
RAJABS
RHUMBS
SAHEBS
SAHIBS
SCRUBS
SHRUBS
SQUABS
SQUIBS
THROBS
THUMBS

B•T•••

BATAAN
BATEAU
BATHED
BATHER
BATHOS
BATIKS
BATING
BATMAN
BATMEN
BATONS
BATTED
BATTEN
BATTER
BATTIK
BATTLE
BATTUE
BETAKE
BETELS
BETHEL
BETIDE
BETISE
BETONY
BETOOK
BETRAY
BETSYS
BETTED
BETTER
BETTES
BETTOR
BETTYS
BITERS
BITING
BITTED
BITTEN
BITTER
BOTANY
BOTCHY
BOTFLY
BOTHER
BOTTLE
BOTTOM
BUTANE
BUTLER

BUTTED
BUTTER
BUTTES
BUTTON
BYTALK

B••T••
BAITED
BAITER
BALTIC
BANTAM
BANTER
BANTUS
BARTER
BARTOK
BARTON
BASTED
BASTES
BATTED
BATTEN
BATTER
BATTIK
BATTLE
BATTUE
BAXTER
BEATEN
BEATER
BEETLE
BELTED
BENTON
BERTHA
BERTHE
BERTHS
BERTIE
BESTED
BESTIR
BESTOW
BETTED
BETTER
BETTES
BETTOR
BETTYS
BHUTAN
BIOTIC
BIOTIN
BIRTHS
BISTER
BISTRO
BITTED
BITTEN
BITTER
BLITHE
BLOTCH
BOATED
BOLTED
BOLTER
BOOTED
BOOTEE
BOOTHS
BOOTIE
BOSTON
BOTTLE
BOTTOM
BRETON
BRITON
BROTHS
BRUTAL
BRUTES
BRUTUS
BUNTED
BUSTED
BUSTER
BUSTIC
BUSTLE
BUTTED
BUTTER
BUTTES
BUTTON

B•••T•
BABITE
BALATA
BARITE
BARYTA
BASUTO
BEASTS
BEAUTS
BEAUTY
BEFITS
BEGETS
BEMATA
BENITA
BENITO
BERATE
BERETS
BESETS
BESOTS
BIDETS
BIGHTS
BIGOTS
BILITY
BINITS
BLASTO
BLASTS
BLEATS
BLINTZ
BLOATS
BLUETS
BLUNTS
BLURTS
BOASTS
BOGOTA
BONITO
BOOSTS
BORATE
BOUNTY
BRACTS
BRANTS
BREATH
BRENTS
BRONTE
BRUITS
BURSTS
BYPATH

B••••T
BABIST
BALLET
BALLOT
BANDIT
BARBET
BAREST
BARRET
BASALT
BASKET
BASSET
BECKET
BEGIRT
BEHEST
BEIRUT
BELOIT
BENNET
BEREFT
BEZANT
BILLET
BISECT
BLIGHT
BLUEST
BOBCAT
BONNET
BOSKET
BOUGHT
BREAST
BRECHT
BREVET
BRIGHT
BRULOT
BRUNET
BRYANT
BUCKET
BUDGET
BUFFET
BULLET
BURBOT
BURNET
BYPAST

•BT•••
OBTAIN
OBTECT
OBTEST
OBTUND
OBTUSE

•B•T••
ABATED
ABATER
ABATES
ABATIS
ABATOR

•B••T•
ABBOTS
ABORTS
ABWATT
EBOATS
OBLATE
UBIETY
UBOATS
UBOLTS

•B•••T
ABDUCT
ABJECT
ABLAUT
ABLEST
ABRUPT
ABSENT
ABVOLT
ABWATT
OBJECT
OBLAST
OBOIST
OBTECT
OBTEST
OBVERT

••BT••
DEBTOR
SUBTER
SUBTLE
SUBTLY

••B•T•
ABBOTS
ALBATA
ALBITE
AMBITS
ARBUTE
BABITE
CUBITS
DEBATE
DEBITS
DEBUTS
HABITS
JABOTS
KIBITZ
LOBATE
ORBITS
REBATE
REBATO
REBUTS
ROBOTS
RUBATO
SABOTS
SEBATS
SUBITO
TUBATE
ZIBETH
ZIBETS

••B••T
ALBEIT
ALBERT
BABIST
BOBCAT
CABLET
COBALT
COBNUT
CUBIST
EGBERT
ELBERT
GIBBET
GIBLET
GOBBET
GOBLET
HOBART
HUBERT
LABRET
OSBERT
RABBET
RABBIT
ROBERT
ROBUST
SABBAT
SUBLET
SUBMIT
TABLET
TYBALT
UNBELT
UNBENT
UNBOLT
UPBEAT

•••BT•
DOUBTS

•••B•T
BARBET
BURBOT
COMBAT
GAMBIT
GIBBET
GOBBET
HAGBUT
HENBIT
KRUBUT
RABBET
RABBIT
SABBAT
SHEBAT
TIDBIT
TURBIT
TURBOT
TWOBIT
WOMBAT

BU••••
BUBALS
BUBBLE
BUBBLY
BUBOES
BUCCAL
BUCKED
BUCKER
BUCKET
BUCKLE
BUCKRA
BUDDED
BUDDER
BUDDHA
BUDDLE
BUDGED
BUDGES
BUDGET
BUDGIE
BUFFED
BUFFER
BUFFET
BUGGED
BUGGER
BUGLED
BUGLER
BUGLES
BUILDS
BULBAR
BULBEL
BULBIL
BULBUL
BULGAR
BULGED
BULGER
BULGES
BULKED
BULLAE
BULLET
BUMBLE
BUMKIN
BUMMED
BUMMER
BUMPED
BUMPER
BUNCHE
BUNCHY
BUNCOS
BUNDLE
BUNGED
BUNGLE
BUNION
BUNKED
BUNKER
BUNKUM
BUNSEN
BUNTED
BUNYAN
BUOYED
BURANS
BURBLE
BURBOT
BURDEN
BURDIE
BUREAU
BURGEE
BURGER
BURGHS
BURGLE
BURGOO
BURGOS
BURIAL
BURIED
BURIES
BURINS
BURKED
BURKES
BURLAP
BURLED
BURLER
BURLEY
BURNED
BURNER
BURNET
BURPED
BURRED

6

BURROS
BURROW
BURSAE
BURSAL
BURSAR
BURSAS
BURSES
BURSTS
BUSHED
BUSHEL
BUSHES
BUSIED
BUSIES
BUSILY
BUSING
BUSKIN
BUSMAN
BUSMEN
BUSSED
BUSSES
BUSTED
BUSTER
BUSTIC
BUSTLE
BUTANE
BUTLER
BUTTED
BUTTER
BUTTES
BUTTON
BUYERS
BUYING
BUZZED
BUZZER
BUZZES

B•U•••
BAUBLE
BAUCIS
BEULAH
BEULAS
BHUTAN
BLUELY
BLUEST
BLUETS
BLUFFS
BLUING
BLUISH
BLUNGE
BLUNTS
BLURBS
BLURRY
BLURTS
BOUCLE
BOUFFE
BOUGHS
BOUGHT
BOUGIE
BOULES
BOUNCE
BOUNCY
BOUNDS
BOUNTY
BOURGS
BOURNE
BOURNS
BOURSE
BOUSED
BOUSES
BRUCES
BRUGES
BRUINS
BRUISE
BRUITS
BRULOT
BRUMAL
BRUMES
BRUNCH
BRUNEI
BRUNET
BRUNOS
BRUSHY
BRUTAL
BRUTES
BRUTUS

B••U••
BABULS
BARUCH
BASUTO
BEAUTS
BEAUTY
BEDUIN
BEGUIN
BEGUMS
BELUGA
BEMUSE
BENUMB
BLOUSE

B•••U•
BANGUI
BANGUP
BANTUS
BARIUM
BARNUM
BARQUE
BASQUE
BATTUE
BAYEUX
BAYOUS
BEDAUB
BEDBUG
BEFOUL
BEIRUT
BIJOUX
BISQUE
BLOWUP
BRAQUE
BROGUE
BRUTUS
BULBUL
BUNKUM
BYSSUS

B••••U
BATEAU
BUREAU

•BU•••
ABULIA
ABUSED
ABUSER
ABUSES

•B•U••
ABDUCT
ABJURE
ABLUSH
ABOUND
ABRUPT
ABSURD
OBTUND
OBTUSE

•B••U•
ABACUS
ABLAUT
OBELUS
OBOLUS

••BU••
ALBUMS
AMBUSH
ARBUTE
ASBURY
AUBURN
BABULS
DEBUGS
DEBUNK
DEBUTS
FIBULA
IMBUED
IMBUES
KABUKI
LOBULE
NEBULA
REBUFF
REBUKE
REBUTS
ROBUST
SUBURB
TUBULE

••B•U•
COBNUT
DYBBUK
ELBRUS
EMBRUE
ERBIUM
HUBBUB
IMBRUE
LABIUM
LABOUR
LABRUM
MOBIUS
SUBDUE

••B••U
JABIRU

•••BU•
BEDBUG
BULBUL
CHABUK
DORBUG
DYBBUK
EREBUS
HAGBUT
HUBBUB
HUMBUG
IAMBUS
KRUBUT
LIMBUS
NIMBUS
REDBUD
REDBUG
SAMBUR
WILBUR

B•V•••
BEVELS
BEVIES
BOVINE

B••V••
BEAVER
BEEVES
BRAVED
BRAVER
BRAVES
BRAVOS
BREVES
BREVET

B•••V•
BEHAVE
BEHOVE

•BV•••
ABVOLT
OBVERT

BW••••
BWANAS

B•W•••
BAWDRY
BAWLED
BAWLER
BEWAIL
BEWARE
BOWELS
BOWERS
BOWERY
BOWFIN
BOWING
BOWLED
BOWLEG
BOWLER
BOWMAN
BOWMEN
BOWSED
BOWSES
BOWWOW
BOWYER
BYWAYS
BYWORD
BYWORK

B••W••
BIGWIG
BLOWBY
BLOWER
BLOWUP
BLOWZY
BOWWOW
BRAWLS
BRAWNY
BREWED
BREWER
BREWIS
BROWNS
BROWSE

B•••W•
BEDEWS
BYLAWS

B••••W
BARROW
BASHAW
BELLOW
BESTOW
BILLOW
BORROW
BOWWOW
BURROW
BYBLOW

•BW•••
ABWATT

••BW••
COBWEB
SUBWAY

••B•W•
ELBOWS
EMBOWS
OXBOWS
UPBOWS

••B••W
BYBLOW
HEBREW

•••BW•
OJIBWA

•••B•W
FOGBOW
SUNBOW

B•X•••
BAXTER
BOXCAR
BOXERS
BOXING

B••X••
BIAXAL

B•••X•
BILOXI

B••••X
BAYEUX
BIFLEX
BIJOUX
BOLLIX

•B•X••
IBEXES

•••B•X
HATBOX
HOTBOX
ICEBOX

BY••••
BYBLOW
BYEBYE
BYGONE
BYLANE
BYLAWS
BYLINE
BYNAME
BYPASS
BYPAST
BYPATH
BYPLAY
BYROAD
BYSSUS
BYTALK
BYWAYS
BYWORD
BYWORK

B•Y•••
BAYARD
BAYEUX
BAYING
BAYOUS
BEYOND
BOYARD
BOYARS
BOYISH
BRYANT
BRYONY
BUYERS
BUYING

B••Y••
BANYAN
BARYES
BARYON
BARYTA
BERYLS
BOWYER
BRAYED
BRAYER
BUNYAN
BUOYED

B•••Y•
BARRYS
BECKYS
BELAYS
BENJYS
BENNYS
BENZYL
BESSYS
BETSYS
BETTYS
BIALYS
BILLYS
BOBBYS
BOGEYS
BOLEYN
BONNYS
BYEBYE
BYWAYS

B••••Y
BAILEY
BAKERY
BALDLY
BARELY
BARFLY
BARLEY
BARNEY
BARONY
BASELY
BASIFY
BAWDRY
BEACHY
BEAUTY
BELFRY
BENDAY
BERNEY
BETONY
BETRAY
BIGAMY
BILITY
BINARY
BIOPSY
BISCAY
BLEARY
BLEBBY
BLENNY
BLOCKY
BLOODY
BLOOMY
BLOWBY
BLOWZY
BLUELY
BLURRY
BODILY
BOLDLY
BOMBAY
BOTANY
BOTCHY
BOTFLY
BOUNCY
BOUNTY
BOWERY
BRACHY
BRAINY
BRANDY
BRANNY
BRASHY
BRASSY
BRAWNY
BREEZY
BRIERY
BRONZY
BROODY
BROOMY
BRUSHY
BRYONY
BUBBLY
BUNCHY
BURLEY
BUSILY
BYPLAY

•BY•••
ABYDOS
ABYSMS

•B•Y••
OBEYED
OBEYER

•B••Y•
ABBEYS

•B•••Y
ABBACY
UBIETY

••BY••
LIBYAN
SIBYLS

••B•Y•
ABBEYS
BOBBYS
DEBBYS
EMBAYS
EMBRYO
KABAYA
LIBBYS

••B••Y
ABBACY
ALBANY
AMBARY
AMBERY
ASBURY
AUBREY
BUBBLY
EMBODY
IMBODY
NUBBLY
PEBBLY
SUBTLY
SUBWAY
WABBLY
WOBBLY

•••BY•
BOBBYS
BYEBYE
DEBBYS
FLYBYS
LIBBYS

•••B•Y
BLEBBY
BOMBAY
BUBBLY
CARBOY
CHUBBY
COWBOY
CRABBY
DAUBRY
DOUBLY
DRABLY
DUMBLY
FLABBY
GLIBLY
GRUBBY
HUMBLY
LOWBOY
NUBBLY
NUMBLY
PEBBLY
POTBOY
REDBAY
SCABBY
SHABBY
STUBBY
TOMBOY
USABLY
WABBLY
WAMBLY
WOBBLY

••••BY
BLEBBY
BLOWBY
CHUBBY
CRABBY
CRUMBY
FLABBY
GOODBY
GRUBBY
HEREBY
NEARBY
SCABBY
SHABBY
SHELBY
STUBBY

B•Z•••
BEZANT
BEZELS
BEZOAR
BUZZED
BUZZER
BUZZES

B••Z••
BALZAC
BANZAI
BENZOL
BENZYL
BLAZED
BLAZER
BLAZES
BLAZON
BONZER
BONZES
BOOZED
BOOZER
BOOZES
BORZOI
BRAZAS
BRAZED
BRAZEN
BRAZER
BRAZES
BRAZIL
BRAZOS
BUZZED
BUZZER
BUZZES

B•••Z•
BELIZE
BLOWZY
BRAIZE
BREEZE
BREEZY
BRONZE
BRONZY

B••••Z
BLINTZ

•B••Z•
ABLAZE

••B•Z•
REBOZO

••B••Z
KIBITZ

CA••••
CABALA
CABALS
CABANA
CABINS
CABLED
CABLES
CABLET
CABMAN
CABMEN
CABOBS
CACAOS
CACHED
CACHES
CACHET
CACHOU
CACKLE
CACTUS
CADDIE
CADDIS
CADENT
CADETS
CADGED
CADGER
CADGES
CADMUS
CADRES
CAECUM
CAEOMA
CAESAR
CAFTAN
CAGIER
CAGILY
CAGING
CAHIER
CAIMAN
CAIQUE
CAIRNS
CAJOLE
CAJUNS
CAKING
CALAIS
CALASH
CALCAR
CALCES
CALCIC
CALEBS
CALESA
CALICO
CALIFS
CALIPH
CALKED
CALKER
CALLAO
CALLAS
CALLED
CALLER
CALLOW
CALLUS
CALMED
CALMER
CALMLY
CALORY
CALPAC
CALVED
CALVES
CALVIN
CALXES
CAMASS
CAMBER
CAMDEN
CAMELS
CAMEOS
CAMERA
CAMILA
CAMION
CAMISE
CAMLET
CAMPED
CAMPER
CAMPOS
CAMPUS
CANAAN
CANADA
CANALS
CANAPE
CANARD
CANARY
CANCAN
CANCEL
CANCER
CANDID
CANDLE
CANDOR
CANERS
CANGUE
CANINE
CANING
CANKER
CANNAE
CANNAS
CANNED
CANNEL
CANNER
CANNES
CANNIE
CANNON
CANNOT
CANOED
CANOES
CANONS
CANOPY
CANSOS
CANTED
CANTER
CANTHI
CANTLE
CANTON
CANTOR
CANTOS
CANTUS
CANUCK
CANULA
CANUTE
CANVAS
CANYON
CAPERS
CAPIAS
CAPITA
CAPLIN
CAPONS
CAPOTE
CAPPED
CAPPER
CAPRIC
CAPTOR
CARACK
CARAFE
CARATE
CARATS
CARBON
CARBOY
CARCEL
CARDED
CARDER
CARDIO
CAREEN

6

CAREER
CARERS
CARESS
CARETS
CARGOS
CARHOP
CARIBE
CARIBS
CARIES
CARINA
CARING
CARLAS
CARLOS
CARMAN
CARMEL
CARMEN
CARNAL
CAROBS
CAROLE
CAROLS
CAROMS
CARPAL
CARPED
CARPEL
CARPER
CARPET
CARPIC
CARPUS
CARREL
CARRIE
CARROT
CARSON
CARTED
CARTEL
CARTER
CARTES
CARTON
CARUSO
CARVED
CARVEL
CARVEN
CARVER
CARVES
CASABA
CASALS
CASAVA
CASBAH
CASEFY
CASEIN
CASERN
CASHAW
CASHED
CASHES
CASHEW
CASHOO
CASING
CASINO
CASKET
CASPAR
CASPER
CASQUE
CASSIA
CASSIE
CASSIS
CASTER
CASTES
CASTLE
CASTOR
CASTRO
CASUAL
CATALO
CATCHY
CATENA
CATERS
CATGUT
CATHAY
CATHER
CATHYS
CATION
CATKIN
CATLIN
CATNIP
CATSUP
CATTED
CATTIE
CATTLE
CAUCUS
CAUDAD
CAUDAL
CAUDEX
CAUDLE
CAUGHT
CAULES
CAULIS
CAULKS
CAUSAL
CAUSED
CAUSER
CAUSES
CAVEAT
CAVEIN
CAVELL
CAVERN
CAVIAR
CAVIES
CAVILS
CAVING
CAVITE
CAVITY
CAVORT
CAWING
CAYMAN
CAYUGA
CAYUSE

C•A•••

CEASED
CEASES
CHABUK
CHACMA
CHAETA
CHAETO
CHAFED
CHAFER
CHAFES
CHAFFS
CHAFFY
CHAINS
CHAIRS
CHAISE
CHALCO
CHALEH
CHALET
CHALKS
CHALKY
CHAMMY
CHAMPS
CHANCE
CHANCY
CHANGE
CHANGS
CHANTS
CHANTY
CHAPEL
CHAPES
CHARDS
CHARED
CHARES
CHARGE
CHARMS
CHARON
CHARRY
CHARTS
CHASED
CHASER
CHASES
CHASMS
CHASSE
CHASTE
CHATTY
CHAWED
CLACKS
CLAIMS
CLAIRE
CLAMMY
CLAMOR
CLAMPS
CLANGS
CLANKS
CLAQUE
CLARAS
CLARES
CLARET
CLAROS
CLASPS
CLASSY
CLAUDE
CLAUSE
CLAWED
CLAYED
CLAYEY
COALED
COALER
COARSE
COASTS
COATED
COATIS
COAXAL
COAXED
COAXER
COAXES
CRAALS
CRABBY
CRACKS
CRACKY
CRACOW
CRADLE
CRAFTS
CRAFTY
CRAGGY
CRAIGS
CRAKES
CRAMBO
CRAMPS
CRANED
CRANES
CRANIA
CRANIO
CRANKS
CRANKY
CRANNY
CRAPED
CRAPES
CRASIS
CRATCH
CRATED
CRATER
CRATES
CRAVAT
CRAVED
CRAVEN
CRAVER
CRAVES
CRAWLS
CRAWLY
CRAYON
CRAZED
CRAZES
CYANIC
CYANID
CYANIN

C••A••

CABALA
CABALS
CABANA
CACAOS
CALAIS
CALASH
CAMASS
CANAAN
CANADA
CANALS
CANAPE
CANARD
CANARY
CARACK
CARAFE
CARATE
CARATS
CASABA
CASALS
CASAVA
CATALO
CEDARS
CERATE
CERATO
CESARE
CETANE
CHEATS
CHIASM
CHIAUS
CICADA
CICALA
CIGARS
CLEANS
CLEARS
CLEATS
CLEAVE
CLOACA
CLOAKS
COBALT
COCAIN
COMATE
COPALM
CORALS
COWAGE
COWARD
CRAALS
CREAKS
CREAKY
CREAMS
CREAMY
CREASE
CREASY
CREATE
CROAKS
CROAKY
CROATS
CUBAGE
CUBANS
CURACY
CURARE
CURATE
CYCADS
CYMARS
CYRANO

C•••A•

CABMAN
CAESAR
CAFTAN
CAIMAN
CALCAR
CALLAO
CALLAS
CALPAC
CANAAN
CANCAN
CANNAE
CANNAS
CANVAS
CAPIAS
CARLAS
CARMAN
CARNAL
CARPAL
CASBAH
CASHAW
CASPAR
CASUAL
CATHAY
CAUDAD
CAUDAL
CAUSAL
CAVEAT
CAVIAR
CAYMAN
CEIBAS
CELIAC
CELIAS
CELLAE
CELLAR
CENTAL
CEREAL
CHELAE
CHELAS
CHETAH
CHORAL
CHUFAS
CILIAT
CITRAL
CLARAS
CLIMAT
CLIMAX
COAXAL
COBIAS
COBRAS
COCCAL
COCOAS
COEVAL
COGNAC
COGWAY
COLLAR
COLZAS
COMBAT
COMMAS
CONFAB
CONGAS
CONRAD
COPRAH
CORBAN
CORDAY
CORRAL
CORSAC
COSTAE
COSTAL
COSTAR
COTEAU
COTTAE
COTTAR
COTTAS
COUGAR
COWMAN
CRAVAT
CRETAN
CRURAL
CULLAY
CUNEAL
CURIAE
CURIAL
CUSHAT
CUSHAW
CUTLAS

CYMBAL

C••••A
CABALA
CABANA
CAEOMA
CALESA
CAMERA
CAMILA
CANADA
CANULA
CAPITA
CARINA
CASABA
CASAVA
CASSIA
CATENA
CAYUGA
CEDULA
CENTRA
CESURA
CHACMA
CHAETA
CHOLLA
CHOREA
CHROMA
CICADA
CICALA
CINEMA
CITOLA
CLOACA
CODEIA
CONCHA
CONTRA
COPPRA
COPULA
CORNEA
CORNUA
CORONA
CORYZA
COWPEA
CRANIA
CREUSA
CRIMEA
CUESTA
CUPOLA

•CA•••
ACACIA
ACADIA
ACAJOU
ACARID
ECARTE
ICALLY
ICARUS
OCASEY
SCABBY
SCALAR
SCALDS
SCALED
SCALER
SCALES
SCALPS
SCAMPI
SCAMPS
SCANTY
SCAPES
SCARAB
SCARCE
SCARED
SCARER
SCARES
SCARFS
SCARPS
SCATHE
SCAUPS

•C•A••
ACHAEA
ACHAIA
ACKACK
ACUATE
ECHARD
ECLAIR
OCEANS
OCTADS
OCTANE
OCTANT
OCTAVE
OCTAVO
SCLAFF
SCRAGS
SCRAMS
SCRAPE
SCRAPS
SCRAWL

•C••A•
ACETAL
ACTUAL
ICECAP
ICEMAN
OCREAE
OCULAR
SCALAR
SCARAB
SCHWAS
SCREAK
SCREAM
SCUBAS

•C•••A
ACACIA
ACADIA
ACEDIA
ACHAEA
ACHAIA
ECZEMA
SCHEMA
SCLERA
SCORIA
SCOTIA
SCYLLA

••CA••
ALCAIC
ARCADE
ARCANE
BECALM
BECAME
BICARB
CACAOS
CICADA
CICALA
COCAIN
CYCADS
DECADE
DECALS
DECAMP
DECANE
DECANT
DECARE
DECAYS
DICAST
DUCATS
ENCAGE
ENCAMP
ENCASE
ESCAPE
ESCARP
FACADE
GOCART
HECATE
INCAGE
INCASE
JACANA
LOCALE
LOCALS
LOCATE
MACACO
MACAWS
OSCANS
OSCARS
PECANS
RECALL
RECANT
RECAPS
RECAST
SECANT
SOCAGE
TICALS
UNCAGE
UNCAPS
UPCAST
VACANT
VACATE
VICARS
VOCALS

••C•A•
AECIAL
BUCCAL
COCCAL
COCOAS
DACHAS
DACHAU
DECCAN
ESCHAR
FACIAL
FECIAL
JACKAL
LACTAM
LUCIAN
LUCIAS
MECCAN
MECCAS
MICMAC
NECTAR
NUCHAE
PICKAX
RACIAL
RECTAL
RICTAL
SACRAL
SECPAR
SOCIAL
SOCMAN
UNCIAL
UNCLAD
YUCCAS

••C••A
ANCONA
BUCKRA
CICADA
CICALA
ENCINA
FACULA
FECULA
HECUBA
ISCHIA
JACANA
LACUNA
LOCHIA
MACULA
MUCOSA
TACOMA
VICUNA

•••CA•
ABACAS
APICAL
ARECAS
BISCAY
BOBCAT
BOXCAR
BUCCAL
CALCAR
CANCAN
COCCAL
DECCAN
DUNCAN
EPICAL
FAUCAL
FISCAL
FRACAS
HUBCAP
ICECAP
IPECAC
LASCAR
MADCAP
MECCAN
MECCAS
MESCAL
MOBCAP
MUDCAP
MUSCAE
MUSCAT
OILCAN
PARCAE
PASCAL
PLICAE
RASCAL
REDCAP
SKYCAP
SNOCAT
SPICAE
THECAE
THECAL
TINCAL
TOECAP
TOMCAT
TROCAR
TUSCAN
VULCAN
YUCCAS

•••C•A
ACACIA
ALICIA
CHACMA
CONCHA
EJECTA
EXACTA
FASCIA
FULCRA
MARCIA
MERCIA

••••CA
AFRICA
ALPACA
ARNICA
ATTICA
BIANCA
CLOACA
DODECA
ITHACA
LORICA
MARACA
MONICA
MYRICA
SENECA
SILICA
TUNICA
VESICA
VOMICA

C•B•••
CABALA
CABALS
CABANA
CABINS
CABLED
CABLES
CABLET
CABMAN
CABMEN
CABOBS
CEBOID
CIBOLS
COBALT
COBBLE
COBIAS
COBLES
COBNUT
COBRAS
COBWEB
CUBAGE
CUBANS
CUBEBS
CUBING
CUBISM
CUBIST
CUBITS
CUBOID
CYBELE

C••B••
CAMBER
CARBON
CARBOY
CASBAH
CEIBAS
CHABUK
CHEBEC
CHUBBY
CIMBRI
COBBLE
COMBAT
COMBED
COMBER
COMBOS
CORBAN
CORBEL
COWBOY
CRABBY
CUMBER
CURBED
CYMBAL

C•••B•
CABOBS
CALEBS
CARIBE
CARIBS
CAROBS
CASABA
CHUBBY
CLIMBS
COOMBS
CRABBY
CRAMBO
CRUMBS
CRUMBY
CUBEBS

C••••B
CHERUB
COBWEB
CONFAB
CORYMB

6

•C•B••
ICEBOX
SCABBY
SCUBAS

•C••B•
SCABBY
SCRIBE
SCRUBS

•C•••B
SCARAB

••C•B•
HECUBA
INCUBI
JACOBS

••C••B
BICARB

C•C•••
CACAOS
CACHED
CACHES
CACHET
CACHOU
CACKLE
CACTUS
CECILE
CECILS
CECILY
CICADA
CICALA
CICELY
CICERO
COCAIN
COCCAL
COCCID
COCCUS
COCCYX
COCHIN
COCKED
COCKER
COCKLE
COCKUP
COCOAS
COCOON
CUCKOO
CYCADS
CYCLED
CYCLER
CYCLES
CYCLIC

C••C••
CAECUM
CALCAR
CALCES
CALCIC
CANCAN
CANCEL
CANCER
CARCEL
CATCHY
CAUCUS
CHACMA
CHECKS
CHICHI
CHICKS
CHICLE
CHICOS
CHOCKS
CHUCKS
CIRCLE
CIRCUM
CIRCUS
CISCOS
CLACKS
CLICHE
CLICKS
CLOCHE
CLOCKS
CLUCKS
COCCAL
COCCID
COCCUS
COCCYX
CONCHA
CONCHS
CONCHY
CONCUR
CRACKS
CRACKY
CRACOW
CRECHE
CRICKS
CROCKS
CROCUS
CRUCES
CZECHS

C•••C•
CALICO
CANUCK
CARACK
CHALCO
CHANCE
CHANCY
CHINCH
CHOICE
CHURCH
CILICE
CIVICS
CLENCH
CLINCH
CLOACA
CLUTCH
COERCE
COMICS
CONICS
CRATCH
CROTCH
CROUCH
CRUNCH
CRUTCH
CULTCH
CURACY
CYNICS

C••••C
CALCIC
CALPAC
CAPRIC
CARPIC
CEDRIC
CELIAC
CELTIC
CHEBEC
CHORIC
CHYMIC
CITRIC
CLERIC
CLINIC
CLONIC
COGNAC
COPTIC
CORSAC
COSMIC
CRETIC
CRITIC
CUPRIC
CYANIC
CYCLIC
CYMRIC
CYSTIC

•CC•••
ACCEDE
ACCENT
ACCEPT
ACCESS
ACCORD
ACCOST
ACCRUE
ACCUSE
ECCLES
OCCULT
OCCUPY
OCCURS

•C•C••
ACACIA
ICECAP
ICICLE

•C••C•
ACKACK
OCLOCK
SCARCE
SCHICK
SCONCE
SCORCH
SCOTCH
SCUTCH

•C•••C
ACETIC
ACIDIC
ECHOIC
ICONIC
SCENIC

••CC••
BOCCIE
BUCCAL
COCCAL
COCCID
COCCUS
COCCYX
DECCAN
HICCUP
MECCAN
MECCAS
SOCCER
SUCCOR
YUCCAS

••C•C•
DECOCT
ENCYCL
MACACO
ROCOCO
UNCOCK

••C••C
ALCAIC
ARCTIC
CYCLIC
HECTIC
LACTIC
MICMAC
PECTIC
PICNIC
PICRIC
TACTIC

•••CC•
STUCCO

•••C•C
CALCIC
IPECAC
ZINCIC

C•D•••
CADDIE
CADDIS
CADENT
CADETS
CADGED
CADGER
CADGES
CADMUS
CADRES
CEDARS
CEDING
CEDRIC
CEDULA
CIDERS
CODDER
CODDLE
CODEIA
CODEIN
CODGER
CODIFY
CODING
CUDDIE
CUDDLE
CUDDLY
CUDGEL

C••D••
CADDIE
CADDIS
CAMDEN
CANDID
CANDLE
CANDOR
CARDED
CARDER
CARDIO
CAUDAD
CAUDAL
CAUDEX
CAUDLE
CHIDED
CHIDER
CHIDES
CINDER
CINDYS
CLODDY
CLYDES
CODDER
CODDLE
COLDER
COLDLY
CONDOM
CONDOR
CORDAY
CORDED
CORDER
CORDON
CRADLE
CREDIT
CREDOS
CRUDER
CUDDIE
CUDDLE
CUDDLY
CURDED
CURDLE

C•••D•
CANADA
CHARDS
CHONDR
CHORDS
CICADA
CLAUDE
CLODDY
CLOUDS
CLOUDY
COMEDO
COMEDY
CORODY
CREEDS
CROWDS
CYCADS

C••••D
CABLED
CACHED
CADGED
CALKED
CALLED
CALMED
CALVED
CAMPED
CANARD
CANDID
CANNED
CANOED
CANTED
CAPPED
CARDED
CARPED
CARTED
CARVED
CASHED
CATTED
CAUDAD
CAUSED
CEASED
CEBOID
CEILED
CENSED
CHAFED
CHARED
CHASED
CHAWED
CHEWED
CHIDED
CHIMED
CHOKED
CITIED
CLAWED
CLAYED
CLERID
CLEWED
CLOSED
CLOYED
COALED
COATED
COAXED
COCCID
COCKED
COGGED
COIFED
COILED
COINED
COMBED
CONKED
CONNED
CONOID
CONRAD
COOEED
COOKED
COOLED
COOPED
COPIED
COPPED
CORDED
CORKED

6

CORNED
COSHED
COSTED
COWARD
COWLED
CRANED
CRAPED
CRATED
CRAVED
CRAZED
CREPED
CROWED
CUBOID
CUFFED
CULLED
CULMED
CUPPED
CURBED
CURDED
CURLED
CURSED
CURVED
CUSPED
CUSPID
CUSSED
CYANID
CYCLED
CYMOID

•C•D••
ACADIA
ACEDIA
ACIDIC
ACIDLY

•C••D•
ACCEDE
ACNODE
OCTADS
SCALDS
SCENDS
SCOLDS
SCRODS

•C•••D
ACARID
ACCORD
ECHARD
ECHOED
SCALED
SCARED
SCORED
SCREED

••C•D•
ACCEDE
ARCADE
CICADA
CYCADS
DECADE
DECIDE
DECODE
ENCODE
ESCUDO
EXCIDE
FACADE
RECEDE
SECEDE

••C••D
ACCORD
ARCHED
ARCKED
ASCEND
BACHED
BACKED
BECKED
BUCKED
CACHED
COCCID
COCKED
CYCLED
DECKED
DOCKED
DUCKED
EMCEED
ETCHED
EUCLID
EXCEED
FECUND
FUCOID
HACKED
HOCKED
INCHED
ITCHED
JACKED
JOCUND
KECKED
KICKED
LACKED
LICKED
LOCKED
LOCOED
MOCKED
MUCKED
MUCOID
NECKED
NICHED
NICKED
NOCKED
ORCHID
PACKED
PECKED
PICKED
RACKED
RECORD
RICKED
ROCKED
RUCKED
SACKED
SACRED
SECOND
SECUND
SICKED
SOCKED
SOCRED
SUCKED
TACKED
TICKED
TUCKED
UNCLAD
WICKED

•••C•D
BRACED
COCCID
DANCED
DEICED
DEUCED
EDUCED
FARCED
FENCED
FORCED
GRACED
LANCED
MINCED
PIECED
PLACED
PLACID
PRICED
RANCID
SAUCED
SLICED
SPACED
SPICED
TALCED
TOMCOD
TRACED
TRICED
VISCID
VOICED
WINCED
ZINCED

CE••••
CEASED
CEASES
CEBOID
CECILE
CECILS
CECILY
CEDARS
CEDING
CEDRIC
CEDULA
CEIBAS
CEILED
CELERY
CELIAC
CELIAS
CELLAE
CELLAR
CELLOS
CELTIC
CEMENT
CENSED
CENSER
CENSES
CENSOR
CENSUS
CENTAL
CENTER
CENTOS
CENTRA
CENTRI
CENTRO
CEORLS
CERATE
CERATO
CEREAL
CEREUS
CERING
CERIPH
CERISE
CERITE
CERIUM
CERMET
CEROUS
CERTES
CERUSE
CERVIX
CESARE
CESIUM
CESTUS
CESURA
CETANE
CEYLON

C•E•••
CAECUM
CAEOMA
CAESAR
CHEATS
CHEBEC
CHECKS
CHEEKS
CHEEKY
CHEEPS
CHEERS
CHEERY
CHEESE
CHEESY
CHEGOE
CHEILO
CHEIRO
CHELAE
CHELAS
CHEOPS
CHERRY
CHERUB
CHERYL
CHESTS
CHESTY
CHETAH
CHEWED
CHEWER
CLEANS
CLEARS
CLEATS
CLEAVE
CLEFTS
CLEIST
CLENCH
CLEOME
CLERGY
CLERIC
CLERID
CLERKS
CLEVER
CLEVIS
CLEWED
COELOM
COEMPT
COERCE
COEVAL
CREAKS
CREAKY
CREAMS
CREAMY
CREASE
CREASY
CREATE
CRECHE
CREDIT
CREDOS
CREEDS
CREEKS
CREELS
CREEPS
CREEPY
CREESE
CREMES
CRENEL
CREOLE
CREPED
CREPES
CRESOL
CRESTS
CRETAN
CRETIC
CRETIN
CREUSA
CREWEL
CUESTA
CZECHS

C••E••
CADENT
CADETS
CALEBS
CALESA
CAMELS
CAMEOS
CAMERA
CANERS
CAPERS
CAREEN
CAREER
CARERS
CARESS
CARETS
CASEFY
CASEIN
CASERN
CATENA
CATERS
CAVEAT
CAVEIN
CAVELL
CAVERN
CELERY
CEMENT
CEREAL
CEREUS
CHAETA
CHAETO
CHEEKS
CHEEKY
CHEEPS
CHEERS
CHEERY
CHEESE
CHEESY
CHIEFS
CICELY
CICERO
CIDERS
CINEMA
CINEOL
CIVETS
CLIENT
CODEIA
CODEIN
COGENT
COHERE
COLEUS
COMEDO
COMEDY
COMELY
COMEON
COMERS
COMETS
CONEYS
COOEED
COOEES
COOERS
COOEYS
CORERS
COTEAU
COVERS
COVERT
COVETS
COVEYS
COWERS
COZENS
CREEDS
CREEKS
CREELS
CREEPS
CREEPY
CREESE
CRIERS
CRUETS
CUBEBS
CULETS
CUNEAL
CUPELS
CURERS
CUTELY
CUTEST
CUTEYS
CYBELE
CYMENE
CYRENE

6

C•••E•

CABLED
CABLES
CABLET
CABMEN
CACHED
CACHES
CACHET
CADGED
CADGER
CADGES
CADRES
CAGIER
CAHIER
CALCES
CALKED
CALKER
CALLED
CALLER
CALMED
CALMER
CALVED
CALVES
CALXES
CAMBER
CAMDEN
CAMLET
CAMPED
CAMPER
CANCEL
CANCER
CANKER
CANNED
CANNEL
CANNER
CANNES
CANOED
CANOES
CANTED
CANTER
CAPPED
CAPPER
CARCEL
CARDED
CARDER
CAREEN
CAREER
CARIES
CARMEL
CARMEN
CARPED
CARPEL
CARPER
CARPET
CARREL
CARTED
CARTEL
CARTER
CARTES
CARVED
CARVEL
CARVEN
CARVER
CARVES
CASHED
CASHES
CASHEW
CASKET
CASPER
CASTER
CASTES
CATHER
CATTED
CAUDEX
CAULES
CAUSED
CAUSER
CAUSES
CAVIES
CEASED
CEASES
CEILED
CENSED
CENSER
CENSES
CENTER
CERMET
CERTES
CHAFED
CHAFER
CHAFES
CHALEH
CHALET
CHAPEL
CHAPES
CHARED
CHARES
CHASED
CHASER
CHASES
CHAWED
CHEBEC
CHEWED
CHEWER
CHIDED
CHIDER
CHIDES
CHIMED
CHIMER
CHIMES
CHINES
CHISEL
CHIVES
CHLOES
CHOKED
CHOKER
CHOKES
CHOLER
CHOREA
CHOREO
CHORES
CHOSEN
CHUTES
CINDER
CIPHER
CITHER
CITIED
CITIES
CIVIES
CLARES
CLARET
CLAWED
CLAYED
CLAYEY
CLEVER
CLEWED
CLIMES
CLINES
CLIVES
CLONES
CLOSED
CLOSER
CLOSES
CLOSET
CLOVEN
CLOVER
CLOVES
CLOYED
CLYDES
CLYPEI
COALED
COALER
COATED
COAXED
COAXER
COAXES
COBLES
COBWEB
COCKED
COCKER
CODDER
CODGER
COFFEE
COFFER
COGGED
COIFED
COILED
COILER
COINED
COINER
COLDER
COLIES
COLLET
COLTER
COMBED
COMBER
COMPEL
CONFER
CONGER
CONGES
CONIES
CONKED
CONNED
CONNER
CONTES
CONVEX
CONVEY
COOEED
COOEES
COOKED
COOKER
COOKEY
COOLED
COOLER
COOPED
COOPER
COPIED
COPIER
COPIES
COPLEY
COPPED
COPPER
COPSES
COQUET
CORBEL
CORDED
CORDER
CORKED
CORKER
CORNEA
CORNED
CORNEL
CORNER
CORNET
CORSES
CORSET
CORTES
CORTEX
CORTEZ
CORVEE
CORVES
COSHED
COSHER
COSHES
COSSES
COSSET
COSTED
COTTER
COULEE
COUPES
COWLED
COWMEN
COWPEA
COWPER
COZIER
COZIES
CRAKES
CRANED
CRANES
CRAPED
CRAPES
CRATED
CRATER
CRATES
CRAVED
CRAVEN
CRAVER
CRAVES
CRAZED
CRAZES
CREMES
CRENEL
CREPED
CREPES
CREWEL
CRIMEA
CRIMES
CRISES
CRONES
CRORES
CROWED
CROZER
CROZES
CRUCES
CRUDER
CRUSES
CRUSET
CRUXES
CUDGEL
CUFFED
CULLED
CULLER
CULLET
CULMED
CULVER
CUMBER
CUNNER
CUPPED
CUPPER
CURBED
CURDED
CURFEW
CURIES
CURLED
CURLER
CURLEW
CURSED
CURSES
CURVED
CURVES
CURVET
CUSPED
CUSSED
CUSSES
CUSTER
CUTIES
CUTLER
CUTLET
CUTTER
CYCLED
CYCLER
CYCLES
CYGNET
CYPHER

C••••E

CACKLE
CADDIE
CAIQUE
CAJOLE
CAMISE
CANAPE
CANDLE
CANGUE
CANINE
CANNAE
CANNIE
CANTLE
CANUTE
CAPOTE
CARAFE
CARATE
CARIBE
CAROLE
CARRIE
CASQUE
CASSIE
CASTLE
CATTIE
CATTLE
CAUDLE
CAVITE
CAYUSE
CECILE
CELLAE
CERATE
CERISE
CERITE
CERUSE
CESARE
CETANE
CHAISE
CHANCE
CHANGE
CHARGE
CHASSE
CHASTE
CHEESE
CHEGOE
CHELAE
CHICLE
CHIGOE
CHOICE
CHOOSE
CHROME
CILICE
CINQUE
CIRCLE
CIRQUE
CISSIE
CLAIRE
CLAQUE
CLAUDE
CLAUSE
CLEAVE
CLEOME
CLICHE
CLIQUE
CLOCHE
CLOTHE
COARSE
COBBLE
COCKLE
CODDLE
COERCE
COFFEE
COFFLE
COHERE
COHUNE
COLINE
COLLIE
COLURE
COMATE
COMMIE

6

COMOSE
CONNIE
CONTRE
COOKIE
COOLIE
COOTIE
CORPSE
CORVEE
COSINE
COSTAE
COTTAE
COULEE
COUPLE
COURSE
COWAGE
COWRIE
COYOTE
CRADLE
CREASE
CREATE
CRECHE
CREESE
CREOLE
CRINGE
CROSSE
CROUPE
CRUISE
CRUSOE
CUBAGE
CUDDIE
CUDDLE
CUISSE
CUPULE
CURARE
CURATE
CURDLE
CURIAE
CURULE
CUTTLE
CYBELE
CYMENE
CYMOSE
CYRENE

•CE•••
ACEDIA
ACEOUS
ACETAL
ACETIC
ACETUM
ACETYL
ECESIS
ICEBOX
ICECAP
ICEMAN
ICEMEN
OCEANS
OCELOT
SCENDS
SCENES
SCENIC
SCENTS

•C•E••
ACCEDE
ACCENT
ACCEPT
ACCESS
ACHENE
ECZEMA
ICIEST
OCHERS
OCHERY
OCREAE
OCTETS
SCHEMA
SCHEME
SCLERA
SCLERO
SCREAK
SCREAM
SCREED
SCREEN
SCREWS
SCREWY
YCLEPT

•C••E•
ACHAEA
ACUMEN
ECCLES
ECHOED
ECHOER
ECHOES
ECOLES
ICEMEN
OCASEY
SCALED
SCALER
SCALES
SCAPES
SCARED
SCARER
SCARES
SCENES
SCOLEX
SCONES
SCOPES
SCORED
SCORER
SCORES
SCOTER
SCREED
SCREEN
SCUTES

•C•••E
ACCEDE
ACCRUE
ACCUSE
ACHENE
ACNODE
ACTIVE
ACUATE
ECARTE
ECTYPE
ICICLE
OCREAE
OCTANE
OCTAVE
SCARCE
SCATHE
SCHEME
SCONCE
SCRAPE
SCRIBE
SCRIVE
SCURVE
SCYTHE

••CE••
ACCEDE
ACCENT
ACCEPT
ACCESS
ASCEND
ASCENT
BICEPS
CICELY
CICERO
DECEIT
DECENT
DECERN
DICERS
DOCENT
EMCEED
EMCEES
EOCENE
ESCENT
EXCEED
EXCELS
EXCEPT
EXCESS
FACERS
FACETS
INCEPT
INCEST
LUCENT
LYCEES
LYCEUM
MACERS
MICELL
MYCETE
NICELY
NICEST
NICETY
NOCENT
ORCEIN
PACERS
RACEME
RACERS
RECEDE
RECENT
RECEPT
RECESS
RICERS
SECEDE
SECERN
SYCEES
ULCERS

••C•E•
AACHEN
ARCHED
ARCHEO
ARCHER
ARCHES
ARCKED
BACHED
BACHES
BACKED
BACKER
BECKED
BECKET
BICKER
BUCKED
BUCKER
BUCKET
CACHED
CACHES
CACHET
COCKED
COCKER
CYCLED
CYCLER
CYCLES
DECKED
DECKEL
DECKER
DECREE
DICKER
DICKEY
DOCKED
DOCKER
DOCKET
DUCKED
DUCKER
ECCLES
EMCEED
EMCEES
ESCHEW
ETCHED
ETCHER
ETCHES
EXCEED
FACIES
FICHES
HACKED
HACKEE
HACKER
HICKEY
HOCKED
HOCKEY
INCHED
INCHES
ITCHED
ITCHES
JACKED
JACKET
JOCKEY
KECKED
KICKED
KICKER
KUCHEN
LACHES
LACIER
LACKED
LACKEY
LECHER
LICHEE
LICHEN
LICKED
LOCKED
LOCKER
LOCKET
LOCOED
LUCIEN
LYCEES
MACLES
MICHEL
MICKEY
MOCKED
MOCKER
MUCKED
MUCKER
NECKED
NICHED
NICHES
NICKED
NICKEL
NICKER
NOCKED
PACKED
PACKER
PACKET
PECKED
PECKER
PECTEN
PICKED
PICKER
PICKET
POCKET
PUCKER
RACHEL
RACIER
RACKED
RACKER
RACKET
RICHER
RICHES
RICKED
RICKEY
ROCHET
ROCKED
ROCKER
ROCKET
RUCHES
RUCKED
SACHEM
SACHET
SACKED
SACKER
SACRED
SECKEL
SECRET
SICKED
SICKEN
SICKER
SOCCER
SOCKED
SOCKET
SOCLES
SOCMEN
SOCRED
SUCKED
SUCKER
SUCRES
SYCEES
TACKED
TACKER
TACKEY
TICKED
TICKER
TICKET
TUCKED
TUCKER
UNCLES
WICHES
WICKED
WICKER
WICKET

••C••E
ACCEDE
ACCRUE
ACCUSE
ALCOVE
ANCONE
ARCADE
ARCANE
ARCHIE
BECAME
BECOME
BOCCIE
BUCKLE
CACKLE
CECILE
COCKLE
DECADE
DECANE
DECARE
DECIDE
DECILE
DECKLE
DECODE
DECREE
DICKIE
DOCILE
ENCAGE
ENCASE
ENCODE
ENCORE
EOCENE
ESCAPE
EUCHRE
EXCIDE
EXCISE
EXCITE
EXCUSE
FACADE
FACILE
FICKLE
FOCSLE

6

HACKEE
HACKIE
HACKLE
HECATE
HECKLE
HUCKLE
INCAGE
INCASE
INCISE
INCITE
INCOME
INCUSE
JACKIE
JOCOSE
KECKLE
LICHEE
LOCALE
LOCATE
LUCILE
LUCITE
MACKLE
MACULE
MUCOSE
MYCETE
NICOLE
NUCHAE
OOCYTE
OSCINE
OSCULE
PICKLE
RACEME
RACINE
RECEDE
RECIPE
RECITE
RECUSE
RICHIE
ROCKNE
SECEDE
SECURE
SICKLE
SOCAGE
SUCKLE
TACKLE
TICKLE
UNCAGE
VACATE

•••CE•
ALICES
AMICES
APICES
AVOCET
BRACED
BRACER
BRACES
BRUCES
CALCES
CANCEL
CANCER
CARCEL
CRUCES
DANCED
DANCER
DANCES
DEICED
DEICER
DEICES
DEUCED
DEUCES
DULCET
DUNCES
EDUCED
EDUCES
FARCED
FARCER
FARCES
FASCES
FAUCES
FAUCET
FENCED
FENCER
FENCES
FORCED
FORCER
FORCES
GLACES
GRACED
GRACES
GROCER
HANCES
IBICES
JOYCES
JUICER
JUICES
LANCED
LANCER
LANCES
LANCET
MARCEL
MERCER
MINCED
MINCER
MINCES
NIECES
OUNCES
PARCEL
PENCEL
PIECED
PIECER
PIECES
PISCES
PLACED
PLACER
PLACES
PLACET
PRICED
PRICES
SAUCED
SAUCER
SAUCES
SLICED
SLICER
SLICES
SOCCER
SPACED
SPACER
SPACES
SPICED
SPICER
SPICES
TALCED
TERCEL
TERCET
TEUCER
TRACED
TRACER
TRACES
TRICED
TRICES
TRUCES
UNICEF
VINCES
VOICED
VOICES
WINCED
WINCER
WINCES
WINCEY
ZINCED

•••C•E
APACHE
BOCCIE
BOUCLE
BUNCHE
CHICLE
CIRCLE
CLICHE
CLOCHE
CRECHE
DOUCHE
DULCIE
FESCUE
FIACRE
FLECHE
GAUCHE
ICICLE
MISCUE
MUSCAE
MUSCLE
ORACLE
PARCAE
PLICAE
PROCNE
PSYCHE
RESCUE
ROSCOE
ROTCHE
ROUCHE
SEICHE
SIECLE
SPECIE
SPICAE
STACIE
STACTE
THECAE
TOUCHE
TRACHE
TROCHE

••••CE
ADDUCE
ADVICE
ALMUCE
ALSACE
AMERCE
ANLACE
APIECE
BIERCE
BODICE
BOUNCE
CHANCE
CHOICE
CILICE
COERCE
DEDUCE
DEFACE
DEVICE
EFFACE
ENFACE
ENLACE
ENTICE
EUNICE
EVINCE
FELICE
FIANCE
FIERCE
FLEECE
FRANCE
GLANCE
GREECE
HORACE
IGNACE
INDUCE
INLACE
JANICE
JOUNCE
LAUNCE
MALICE
MENACE
NOTICE
NOVICE
NUANCE
OFFICE
ORRICE
PALACE
PANICE
PEIRCE
PIERCE
PLAICE
POLICE
POMACE
POUNCE
PRANCE
PRINCE
PUMICE
QUINCE
REDUCE
RUBACE
SCARCE
SCONCE
SEANCE
SEDUCE
SLUICE
SOLACE
SOURCE
SPLICE
SPRUCE
STANCE
TENACE
THENCE
THRICE
TIERCE
TRANCE
ULENCE
UNLACE
USANCE
VELOCE
VENICE
VIVACE
WHENCE

C•F•••
CAFTAN
COFFEE
COFFER
COFFIN
COFFLE
CUFFED

C••F••
CHAFED
CHAFER
CHAFES
CHAFFS
CHAFFY
CHUFAS
CLEFTS
CLIFFS
CLIFFY
COFFEE
COFFER
COFFIN
COFFLE
COIFED
COMFIT
CONFAB
CONFER
CRAFTS
CRAFTY
CROFTS
CUFFED
CUPFUL
CURFEW

C•••F•
CALIFS
CARAFE
CASEFY
CHAFFS
CHAFFY
CHIEFS
CLIFFS
CLIFFY
CODIFY
CUTOFF

C••••F
CUTOFF

•C•F••
SCOFFS
SCUFFS

•C••F•
SCARFS
SCLAFF
SCOFFS
SCRUFF
SCUFFS
SCURFY

•C•••F
SCLAFF
SCRUFF

••C•F•
PACIFY

•••C•F
UNICEF

C•G•••
CAGIER
CAGILY
CAGING
CIGARS
COGENT
COGGED
COGNAC
COGWAY
CYGNET
CYGNUS

C••G••
CADGED
CADGER
CADGES
CANGUE
CARGOS
CATGUT
CAUGHT
CHEGOE
CHIGOE
CLOGGY
CODGER
COGGED
COIGNS
CONGAS
CONGER
CONGES
CONGOU
CORGIS
COUGAR
COUGHS
CRAGGY
CUDGEL

C•••G•
CAYUGA
CHANGE

6

CHANGS
CHARGE
CHOUGH
CLANGS
CLERGY
CLINGS
CLINGY
CLOGGY
CLOUGH
COLUGO
COSIGN
COWAGE
CRAGGY
CRAIGS
CRINGE
CUBAGE

C••••G
CAGING
CAKING
CANING
CARING
CASING
CAVING
CAWING
CEDING
CERING
CITING
CLUING
CODING
COKING
COMING
CONING
COOING
COPING
CORING
COVING
COWING
COXING
CRYING
CUBING
CURING

•C••G•
ICINGS
SCRAGS

•C•••G
ACHING
ACTING

••C•G•
ENCAGE
INCAGE
SOCAGE
UNCAGE

••C••G
ARCING
DICING
FACING
LACING
MACING
PACING
RACING
RICING

CH••••
CHABUK
CHACMA
CHAETA
CHAETO
CHAFED
CHAFER
CHAFES
CHAFFS
CHAFFY
CHAINS
CHAIRS
CHAISE
CHALCO
CHALEH
CHALET
CHALKS
CHALKY
CHAMMY
CHAMPS
CHANCE
CHANCY
CHANGE
CHANGS
CHANTS
CHANTY
CHAPEL
CHAPES
CHARDS
CHARED
CHARES
CHARGE
CHARMS
CHARON
CHARRY
CHARTS
CHASED
CHASER
CHASES
CHASMS
CHASSE
CHASTE
CHATTY
CHAWED
CHEATS
CHEBEC
CHECKS
CHEEKS
CHEEKY
CHEEPS
CHEERS
CHEERY
CHEESE
CHEESY
CHEGOE
CHEILO
CHEIRO
CHELAE
CHELAS
CHEOPS
CHERRY
CHERUB
CHERYL
CHESTS
CHESTY
CHETAH
CHEWED
CHEWER
CHIASM
CHIAUS
CHICHI
CHICKS
CHICLE
CHICOS
CHIDED
CHIDER
CHIDES
CHIEFS
CHIGOE
CHILLS
CHILLY
CHIMED
CHIMER
CHIMES
CHINCH
CHINES
CHINKS
CHINKY
CHINTZ
CHIPPY
CHIRMS
CHIRON
CHIRPS
CHIRRS
CHISEL
CHITIN
CHITON
CHITTY
CHIVES
CHLOES
CHLORO
CHOCKS
CHOICE
CHOIRS
CHOKED
CHOKER
CHOKES
CHOLER
CHOLLA
CHONDR
CHOOSE
CHOOSY
CHOPIN
CHOPPY
CHORAL
CHORDS
CHOREA
CHOREO
CHORES
CHORIC
CHORUS
CHOSEN
CHOUGH
CHRISM
CHRIST
CHROMA
CHROME
CHROMO
CHRONO
CHRYSO
CHUBBY
CHUCKS
CHUFAS
CHUMMY
CHUMPS
CHUNKS
CHUNKY
CHURCH
CHURLS
CHURNS
CHURRS
CHUTES
CHYMIC

C•H•••
CAHIER
COHERE
COHORT
COHOSH
COHUNE

C••H••
CACHED
CACHES
CACHET
CACHOU
CARHOP
CASHAW
CASHED
CASHES
CASHEW
CASHOO
CATHAY
CATHER
CATHYS
CIPHER
CITHER
COCHIN
COSHED
COSHER
COSHES
CUSHAT
CUSHAW
CYPHER

C•••H•
CANTHI
CATCHY
CAUGHT
CHICHI
CLICHE
CLOCHE
CLOTHE
CLOTHO
CLOTHS
CONCHA
CONCHS
CONCHY
COUGHS
CRECHE
CZECHS

C••••H
CALASH
CALIPH
CASBAH
CERIPH
CHALEH
CHETAH
CHINCH
CHOUGH
CHURCH
CLENCH
CLINCH
CLOUGH
CLUTCH
COHOSH
COPRAH
COYISH
CRATCH
CROTCH
CROUCH
CRUNCH
CRUTCH
CULTCH

•CH•••
ACHAEA
ACHAIA
ACHENE
ACHING
ECHARD
ECHINI
ECHINO
ECHOED
ECHOER
ECHOES
ECHOIC
ICHTHY
OCHERS
OCHERY
SCHEMA
SCHEME
SCHICK
SCHISM
SCHIST
SCHIZO
SCHMOS
SCHOOL
SCHORL
SCHUIT
SCHUSS
SCHWAS

•C••H•
ICHTHY
SCATHE
SCYPHI
SCYPHO
SCYTHE

•C•••H
SCORCH
SCOTCH
SCUTCH

••CH••
AACHEN
ANCHOR
ARCHED
ARCHEO
ARCHER
ARCHES
ARCHIE
ARCHIL
ARCHLY
ARCHON
ARCHYS
BACHED
BACHES
CACHED
CACHES
CACHET
CACHOU
COCHIN
DACHAS
DACHAU
ESCHAR
ESCHEW
ETCHED
ETCHER
ETCHES
EUCHRE
FICHES
FICHUS
INCHED
INCHES
INCHON
ISCHIA
ITCHED
ITCHES
KUCHEN
LACHES
LECHER
LICHEE
LICHEN
LOCHIA
MICHEL
NICHED
NICHES
NUCHAE
ORCHID
ORCHIL
ORCHIO
ORCHIS
RACHEL
RACHIS
RICHER
RICHES
RICHIE
RICHLY
ROCHET
RUCHES
SACHEM
SACHET
TECHNO
TUCHUN

6

URCHIN
WICHES
YACHTS
ZECHIN

•••CH•
APACHE
BEACHY
BOTCHY
BRACHI
BRACHY
BRECHT
BUNCHE
BUNCHY
CATCHY
CHICHI
CLICHE
CLOCHE
CONCHA
CONCHS
CONCHY
CRECHE
CZECHS
DOUCHE
DRACHM
EPOCHS
ERICHS
FLECHE
GAUCHE
GAUCHO
LEACHY
MANCHU
ORACHS
PATCHY
PEACHY
PITCHY
POACHY
PONCHO
POUCHY
PSYCHE
PSYCHO
PUNCHY
RANCHO
REECHO
REICHS
ROTCHE
ROUCHE
SEICHE
TETCHY
TOUCHE
TOUCHY
TRACHE
TRACHY
TRICHI
TRICHO
TROCHE

••••CH
ATTACH
AVOUCH
BARUCH
BLANCH
BLEACH
BLENCH
BLOTCH
BORSCH
BRANCH
BREACH
BREECH
BROACH
BROOCH
BRUNCH
CHINCH
CHURCH
CLENCH
CLINCH
CLUTCH
CRATCH
CROTCH
CROUCH
CRUNCH
CRUTCH
CULTCH
DETACH
DRENCH
ENRICH
EPARCH
EUNUCH
EXARCH
FETICH
FLENCH
FLETCH
FLINCH
FLITCH
FRENCH
GROUCH
HAUNCH
HOOTCH
INARCH
KIRSCH
KITSCH
LAUNCH
MOLOCH
MUNICH
NAUTCH
PAUNCH
PESACH
PLANCH
PLEACH
PREACH
PUTSCH
QUITCH
SCORCH
SCOTCH
SCUTCH
SEARCH
SKETCH
SLOUCH
SMIRCH
SMOOCH
SMUTCH
SNATCH
SNITCH
SPEECH
STANCH
STARCH
STENCH
STITCH
SWATCH
SWITCH
THATCH
TRENCH
TWITCH
WRENCH
WRETCH
ZURICH

CI••••
CIBOLS
CICADA
CICALA
CICELY
CICERO
CIDERS
CIGARS
CILIAT
CILICE
CILIUM
CIMBRI
CINDER
CINDYS
CINEMA
CINEOL
CINQUE
CIPHER
CIRCLE
CIRCUM
CIRCUS
CIRQUE
CIRRUS
CISCOS
CISSIE
CISSYS
CITHER
CITIED
CITIES
CITING
CITOLA
CITRAL
CITRIC
CITRON
CITRUS
CIVETS
CIVICS
CIVIES
CIVISM

C•I•••
CAIMAN
CAIQUE
CAIRNS
CEIBAS
CEILED
CHIASM
CHIAUS
CHICHI
CHICKS
CHICLE
CHICOS
CHIDED
CHIDER
CHIDES
CHIEFS
CHIGOE
CHILLS
CHILLY
CHIMED
CHIMER
CHIMES
CHINCH
CHINES
CHINKS
CHINKY
CHINTZ
CHIPPY
CHIRMS
CHIRON
CHIRPS
CHIRRS
CHISEL
CHITIN
CHITON
CHITTY
CHIVES
CLICHE
CLICKS
CLIENT
CLIFFS
CLIFFY
CLIMAT
CLIMAX
CLIMBS
CLIMES
CLINCH
CLINES
CLINGS
CLINGY
CLINIC
CLINKS
CLINTS
CLIQUE
CLIQUY
CLIVES
COIFED
COIGNS
COILED
COILER
COINED
COINER
CRICKS
CRIERS
CRIMEA
CRIMES
CRIMPS
CRIMPY
CRINGE
CRINUM
CRISES
CRISIS
CRISPS
CRISPY
CRITIC
CUISSE

C••I••
CABINS
CAGIER
CAGILY
CAGING
CAHIER
CAKING
CALICO
CALIFS
CALIPH
CAMILA
CAMION
CAMISE
CANINE
CANING
CAPIAS
CAPITA
CARIBE
CARIBS
CARIES
CARINA
CARING
CASING
CASINO
CATION
CAVIAR
CAVIES
CAVILS
CAVING
CAVITE
CAVITY
CAWING
CECILE
CECILS
CECILY
CEDING
CELIAC
CELIAS
CERING
CERIPH
CERISE
CERITE
CERIUM
CESIUM
CHAINS
CHAIRS
CHAISE
CHEILO
CHEIRO
CHOICE
CHOIRS
CHRISM
CHRIST
CILIAT
CILICE
CILIUM
CITIED
CITIES
CITING
CIVICS
CIVIES
CIVISM
CLAIMS
CLAIRE
CLEIST
CLUING
COBIAS
CODIFY
CODING
COKING
COLIES
COLINE
COLINS
COMICS
COMING
COMITY
CONICS
CONIES
CONING
CONIUM
COOING
COPIED
COPIER
COPIES
COPING
CORING
CORIUM
COSIGN
COSINE
COVING
COWING
COXING
COYISH
COZIER
COZIES
COZILY
CRAIGS
CRUISE
CRYING
CUBING
CUBISM
CUBIST
CUBITS
CUMINS
CURIAE
CURIAL
CURIES
CURING
CURIOS
CURIUM
CUTIES
CUTINS
CYNICS
CYRILS

C•••I•
CADDIE
CADDIS
CALAIS
CALCIC
CALVIN
CANDID
CANNIE
CAPLIN
CAPRIC
CARDIO
CARPIC
CARRIE
CASEIN
CASSIA

6

CASSIE
CASSIS
CATKIN
CATLIN
CATNIP
CATTIE
CAULIS
CAVEIN
CEBOID
CEDRIC
CELTIC
CERVIX
CHITIN
CHOPIN
CHORIC
CHYMIC
CISSIE
CITRIC
CLERIC
CLERID
CLEVIS
CLINIC
CLONIC
CLOVIS
COATIS
COCAIN
COCCID
COCHIN
CODEIA
CODEIN
COFFIN
COLLIE
COMFIT
COMMIE
COMMIT
COMMIX
CONNIE
CONOID
CONTIN
COOKIE
COOLIE
COOTIE
COPTIC
CORGIS
CORTIN
COSMIC
COUSIN
COWRIE
CRANIA
CRANIO
CRASIS
CREDIT
CRETIC
CRETIN
CRISIS
CRITIC
CROJIK
CUBOID
CUDDIE
CULLIS
CUPRIC
CURTIS
CUSPID
CUSPIS
CYANIC
CYANID
CYANIN
CYCLIC
CYMLIN
CYMOID
CYMRIC
CYPRIN
CYSTIC

C••••I
CANTHI
CENTRI
CHICHI
CIMBRI
CLYPEI

•CI•••
ACIDIC
ACIDLY
ACINUS
ACIOUS
ICICLE
ICIEST
ICINGS
SCIONS
SCIPIO

•C•I••
ACHING
ACTING
ACTINI
ACTINO
ACTION
ACTIUM
ACTIVE
ACUITY
ECHINI
ECHINO
SCHICK
SCHISM
SCHIST
SCHIZO
SCRIBE
SCRIMP
SCRIPS
SCRIPT
SCRIVE

•C••I•
ACACIA
ACADIA
ACARID
ACEDIA
ACETIC
ACHAIA
ACIDIC
ACQUIT
ECESIS
ECHOIC
ECLAIR
ICONIC
SCENIC
SCHUIT
SCIPIO
SCORIA
SCOTIA

•C•••I
ACTINI
ECHINI
OCTOPI
OCTROI
SCAMPI
SCYPHI

••CI••
AECIAL
AECIUM
ARCING
CECILE
CECILS
CECILY
DECIDE
DECILE
DICING
DOCILE
ENCINA
EXCIDE
EXCISE
EXCITE
FACIAL
FACIES
FACILE
FACING
FECIAL
INCISE
INCITE
LACIER
LACILY
LACING
LUCIAN
LUCIAS
LUCIEN
LUCILE
LUCITE
LUCIUS
MACING
OSCINE
PACIFY
PACING
RACIAL
RACIER
RACILY
RACINE
RACING
RACISM
RACIST
RECIPE
RECITE
RICING
SICILY
SOCIAL
UNCIAL

••C•I•
ALCAIC
ALCUIN
ARCHIE
ARCHIL
ARCTIC
BOCCIE
COCAIN
COCCID
COCHIN
CYCLIC
DACOIT
DECEIT
DICKIE
EUCLID
FUCOID
HACKIE
HECTIC
ISCHIA
JACKIE
LACTIC
LOCHIA
MUCOID
ORCEIN
ORCHID
ORCHIL
ORCHIO
ORCHIS
PECTIC
PECTIN
PICNIC
PICRIC
RACHIS
RECOIL
RICHIE
TACTIC
TOCSIN
UNCOIL
URCHIN
VICTIM
ZECHIN

••C••I
INCUBI

•••CI•
ACACIA
AFLCIO
ALICIA
BAUCIS
BOCCIE
CALCIC
COCCID
DULCIE
ELICIT
FASCIA
GLACIS
MARCIA
MERCIA
NIACIN
NUNCIO
PENCIL
PHOCIS
PLACID
PRECIS
RANCID
SPECIE
STACIE
VISCID
ZINCIC

•••C•I
BRACHI
CHICHI
TRICHI

••••CI
BONACI

C•J•••
CAJOLE
CAJUNS

C••J••
CROJIK

•C•J••
ACAJOU

C•K•••
CAKING
COKING

C••K••
CACKLE
CALKED
CALKER
CANKER
CASKET
CATKIN
CHOKED
CHOKER
CHOKES
COCKED
COCKER
COCKLE
COCKUP
CONKED
COOKED
COOKER
COOKEY
COOKIE
CORKED
CORKER
CRAKES
CUCKOO

C•••K•
CAULKS
CHALKS
CHALKY
CHECKS
CHEEKS
CHEEKY
CHICKS
CHINKS
CHINKY
CHOCKS
CHUCKS
CHUNKS
CHUNKY
CLACKS
CLANKS
CLERKS
CLICKS
CLINKS
CLOAKS
CLOCKS
CLUCKS
CRACKS
CRACKY
CRANKS
CRANKY
CREAKS
CREAKY
CREEKS
CRICKS
CROAKS
CROAKY
CROCKS
CROOKS

C••••K
CANUCK
CARACK
CHABUK
CROJIK

•CK•••
ACKACK

•C•••K
ACKACK
OCLOCK
SCHICK
SCREAK

••CK••
ARCKED
BACKED
BACKER
BECKED
BECKET
BECKON
BECKYS
BICKER
BUCKED
BUCKER
BUCKET
BUCKLE
BUCKRA
CACKLE
COCKED
COCKER
COCKLE
COCKUP
CUCKOO
DECKED
DECKEL
DECKER
DECKLE
DICKER
DICKEY
DICKIE
DOCKED

6

DOCKER
DOCKET
DUCKED
DUCKER
FICKLE
GECKOS
HACKED
HACKEE
HACKER
HACKIE
HACKLE
HECKLE
HICKEY
HICKOK
HOCKED
HOCKEY
HUCKLE
JACKAL
JACKED
JACKET
JACKIE
JACKYS
JOCKEY
JOCKOS
KECKED
KECKLE
KICKED
KICKER
LACKED
LACKEY
LICKED
LOCKED
LOCKER
LOCKET
LOCKUP
MACKLE
MICKEY
MICKYS
MOCKED
MOCKER
MOCKUP
MUCKED
MUCKER
NECKED
NICKED
NICKEL
NICKER
NICKYS
NOCKED
PACKED
PACKER
PACKET
PECKED
PECKER
PICKAX
PICKED
PICKER
PICKET
PICKLE
PICKUP
POCKET
PUCKER
RACKED
RACKER

RACKET
RECKON
RICKED
RICKEY
RICKYS
ROCKED
ROCKER
ROCKET
ROCKNE
RUCKED
RUCKUS
SACKED
SACKER
SECKEL
SICKED
SICKEN
SICKER
SICKLE
SICKLY
SOCKED
SOCKET
SUCKED
SUCKER
SUCKLE
TACKED
TACKER
TACKEY
TACKLE
TICKED
TICKER
TICKET
TICKLE
TUCKED
TUCKER
VICKYS
WICKED
WICKER
WICKET

••C••K

HICKOK
UNCOCK
UNCORK

•••CK•

BLACKS
BLOCKS
BLOCKY
BRICKS
CHECKS
CHICKS
CHOCKS
CHUCKS
CLACKS
CLICKS
CLOCKS
CLUCKS
CRACKS
CRACKY
CRICKS
CROCKS
FLACKS
FLECKS
FLICKS

FLOCKS
FLOCKY
FROCKS
HOICKS
KNACKS
KNOCKS
PLACKS
PLUCKS
PLUCKY
PRICKS
QUACKS
SHACKO
SHACKS
SHOCKS
SHUCKS
SLACKS
SLICKS
SMACKS
SMOCKS
SNACKS
SNICKS
SPECKS
STACKS
STICKS
STICKY
STOCKS
STOCKY
TRACKS
TRICKS
TRICKY
TRUCKS
VNECKS
WHACKS
WRACKS
WRECKS
YOICKS
ZINCKY

••••CK

ACKACK
ARRACK
ATTACK
BEDECK
CANUCK
CARACK
FRANCK
HIJACK
KOPECK
LUBECK
MOHOCK
OCLOCK
PLANCK
SCHICK
SHTICK
STRICK
STRUCK
THWACK
UNCOCK
UNLOCK
UNPACK
UNPICK
ZEBECK

CL••••

CLACKS
CLAIMS
CLAIRE
CLAMMY
CLAMOR
CLAMPS
CLANGS
CLANKS
CLAQUE
CLARAS
CLARES
CLARET
CLAROS
CLASPS
CLASSY
CLAUDE
CLAUSE
CLAWED
CLAYED
CLAYEY
CLEANS
CLEARS
CLEATS
CLEAVE
CLEFTS
CLEIST
CLENCH
CLEOME
CLERGY
CLERIC
CLERID
CLERKS
CLEVER
CLEVIS
CLEWED
CLICHE
CLICKS
CLIENT
CLIFFS
CLIFFY
CLIMAT
CLIMAX
CLIMBS
CLIMES
CLINCH
CLINES
CLINGS
CLINGY
CLINIC
CLINKS
CLINTS
CLIQUE
CLIQUY
CLIVES
CLOACA
CLOAKS
CLOCHE
CLOCKS
CLODDY
CLOGGY
CLONES
CLONIC
CLONUS

CLOSED
CLOSER
CLOSES
CLOSET
CLOTHE
CLOTHO
CLOTHS
CLOTTY
CLOUDS
CLOUDY
CLOUGH
CLOUTS
CLOVEN
CLOVER
CLOVES
CLOVIS
CLOWNS
CLOYED
CLUCKS
CLUING
CLUMPS
CLUMPY
CLUMSY
CLUTCH
CLYDES
CLYPEI

C•L•••

CALAIS
CALASH
CALCAR
CALCES
CALCIC
CALEBS
CALESA
CALICO
CALIFS
CALIPH
CALKED
CALKER
CALLAO
CALLAS
CALLED
CALLER
CALLOW
CALLUS
CALMED
CALMER
CALMLY
CALORY
CALPAC
CALVED
CALVES
CALVIN
CALXES
CELERY
CELIAC
CELIAS
CELLAE
CELLAR
CELLOS
CELTIC
CHLOES
CHLORO

CILIAT
CILICE
CILIUM
COLDER
COLDLY
COLEUS
COLIES
COLINE
COLINS
COLLAR
COLLET
COLLIE
COLLOP
COLONS
COLONY
COLORS
COLOUS
COLTER
COLUGO
COLUMN
COLURE
COLZAS
CULETS
CULLAY
CULLED
CULLER
CULLET
CULLIS
CULMED
CULTCH
CULTUS
CULVER

C••L••

CABLED
CABLES
CABLET
CALLAO
CALLAS
CALLED
CALLER
CALLOW
CALLUS
CAMLET
CAPLIN
CARLAS
CARLOS
CATLIN
CAULES
CAULIS
CAULKS
CEILED
CELLAE
CELLAR
CELLOS
CEYLON
CHALCO
CHALEH
CHALET
CHALKS
CHALKY
CHELAE
CHELAS
CHILLS

6

CHILLY
CHOLER
CHOLLA
COALED
COALER
COBLES
COELOM
COILED
COILER
COLLAR
COLLET
COLLIE
COLLOP
COOLED
COOLER
COOLIE
COOLLY
COPLEY
COULEE
COWLED
CULLAY
CULLED
CULLER
CULLET
CULLIS
CURLED
CURLER
CURLEW
CUTLAS
CUTLER
CUTLET
CYCLED
CYCLER
CYCLES
CYCLIC
CYMLIN

C•••L•
CABALA
CABALS
CACKLE
CAGILY
CAJOLE
CALMLY
CAMELS
CAMILA
CANALS
CANDLE
CANTLE
CANULA
CAROLE
CAROLS
CASALS
CASTLE
CATALO
CATTLE
CAUDLE
CAVELL
CAVILS
CECILE
CECILS
CECILY
CEDULA
CEORLS
CHEILO
CHICLE
CHILLS
CHILLY
CHOLLA
CHURLS
CIBOLS
CICALA
CICELY
CIRCLE
CITOLA
COBALT
COBBLE
COCKLE
CODDLE
COFFLE
COLDLY
COMELY
COMPLY
COOLLY
COPALM
COPULA
CORALS
COSTLY
COUPLE
COZILY
CRAALS
CRADLE
CRAWLS
CRAWLY
CREELS
CREOLE
CUDDLE
CUDDLY
CUPELS
CUPOLA
CUPULE
CURDLE
CURTLY
CURULE
CUTELY
CUTTLE
CYBELE
CYRILS

C••••L
CANCEL
CANNEL
CARCEL
CARMEL
CARNAL
CARPAL
CARPEL
CARREL
CARTEL
CARVEL
CASUAL
CAUDAL
CAUSAL
CAVELL
CENTAL
CEREAL
CHAPEL
CHERYL
CHISEL
CHORAL
CINEOL
CITRAL
COAXAL
COCCAL
COEVAL
COMPEL
CONSUL
CORBEL
CORNEL
CORRAL
COSTAL
CRENEL
CRESOL
CREWEL
CRURAL
CUDGEL
CUNEAL
CUPFUL
CURIAL
CYMBAL

•CL•••
ECLAIR
OCLOCK
SCLAFF
SCLERA
SCLERO
YCLEPT

•C•L••
ECCLES
ECOLES
ICALLY
OCELOT
OCULAR
SCALAR
SCALDS
SCALED
SCALER
SCALES
SCALPS
SCOLDS
SCOLEX
SCULLS
SCULPT
SCYLLA

•C••L•
ACIDLY
ICALLY
ICICLE
OCCULT
SCOWLS
SCROLL
SCULLS
SCYLLA

•C•••L
ACETAL
ACETYL
ACTUAL
SCHOOL
SCHORL
SCRAWL
SCROLL

••CL••
CYCLED
CYCLER
CYCLES
CYCLIC
ECCLES
EUCLID
MACLES
SOCLES
UNCLAD
UNCLES

••C•L•
ARCHLY
BECALM
BUCKLE
CACKLE
CECILE
CECILS
CECILY
CICALA
CICELY
COCKLE
DECALS
DECILE
DECKLE
DOCILE
EXCELS
FACILE
FACULA
FECULA
FICKLE
FOCSLE
HACKLE
HECKLE
HUCKLE
KECKLE
LACILY
LOCALE
LOCALS
LUCILE
MACKLE
MACULA
MACULE
MICELL
NICELY
NICOLE
OCCULT
OSCULE
PICKLE
PICULS
RACILY
RECALL
RICHLY
SICILY
SICKLE
SICKLY
SUCKLE
TACKLE
TICALS
TICKLE
VOCALS

••C••L
AECIAL
ARCHIL
BUCCAL
COCCAL
DACTYL
DECKEL
ENCYCL
FACIAL
FECIAL
JACKAL
MICELL
MICHEL
NICKEL
ORCHIL
RACHEL
RACIAL
RECALL
RECOIL
RECTAL
RICTAL
SACRAL
SECKEL
SOCIAL
UNCIAL
UNCOIL
UNCURL

•••CL•
BOUCLE
CHICLE
CIRCLE
ICICLE
MUSCLE
ORACLE
SIECLE

•••C•L
APICAL
BUCCAL
CANCEL
CARCEL
COCCAL
EPICAL
FAUCAL
FISCAL
GLYCOL
MARCEL
MESCAL
PARCEL
PASCAL
PENCEL
PENCIL
RASCAL
TERCEL
THECAL
TINCAL

••••CL
ENCYCL

C•M•••
CAMASS
CAMBER
CAMDEN
CAMELS
CAMEOS
CAMERA
CAMILA
CAMION
CAMISE
CAMLET
CAMPED
CAMPER
CAMPOS
CAMPUS
CEMENT
CIMBRI
COMATE
COMBAT
COMBED
COMBER
COMBOS
COMEDO
COMEDY
COMELY
COMEON
COMERS
COMETS
COMFIT
COMICS
COMING
COMITY
COMMAS
COMMIE
COMMIT
COMMIX
COMMON
COMOSE
COMOUS
COMPEL
COMPLY
COMPOS
CUMBER
CUMINS
CYMARS
CYMBAL
CYMENE
CYMLIN
CYMOID
CYMOSE
CYMOUS
CYMRIC

C••M••
CABMAN
CABMEN
CADMUS
CAIMAN
CALMED
CALMER
CALMLY
CARMAN
CARMEL
CARMEN

6

CAYMAN
CERMET
CHAMMY
CHAMPS
CHIMED
CHIMER
CHIMES
CHUMMY
CHUMPS
CHYMIC
CLAMMY
CLAMOR
CLAMPS
CLIMAT
CLIMAX
CLIMBS
CLIMES
CLUMPS
CLUMPY
CLUMSY
COEMPT
COMMAS
COMMIE
COMMIT
COMMIX
COMMON
COOMBS
COSMIC
COSMOS
COWMAN
COWMEN
CRAMBO
CRAMPS
CREMES
CRIMEA
CRIMES
CRIMPS
CRIMPY
CRUMBS
CRUMBY
CRUMMY
CRUMPS
CULMED

C•••M•
CAEOMA
CAROMS
CHACMA
CHAMMY
CHARMS
CHASMS
CHIRMS
CHROMA
CHROME
CHROMO
CHUMMY
CINEMA
CLAIMS
CLAMMY
CLEOME
COLUMN
CORYMB
CREAMS
CREAMY
CRUMMY

C••••M
CAECUM
CERIUM
CESIUM
CHIASM
CHRISM
CILIUM
CIRCUM
CIVISM
COELOM
CONDOM
CONIUM
COPALM
CORIUM
CRINUM
CUBISM
CUPRUM
CURIUM
CUSTOM

•C•M••
ACUMEN
ICEMAN
ICEMEN
SCAMPI
SCAMPS
SCHMOS
SCUMMY

•C••M•
ECTOMY
ECZEMA
SCHEMA
SCHEME
SCRAMS
SCRIMP
SCRUMS
SCUMMY

•C•••M
ACETUM
ACTIUM
SCHISM
SCREAM
SCUTUM

••CM••
MICMAC
SOCMAN
SOCMEN

••C•M•
BECAME
BECOME
DECAMP
ENCAMP
INCOME
RACEME
TACOMA

••C••M
AECIUM
BECALM
DICTUM
LACTAM
LYCEUM
RACISM
RECTUM
SACHEM
SACRUM
VACUUM
VICTIM

•••CM•
CHACMA

•••C•M
CAECUM
CIRCUM
DRACHM
NONCOM
TALCUM

C•N•••
CANAAN
CANADA
CANALS
CANAPE
CANARD
CANARY
CANCAN
CANCEL
CANCER
CANDID
CANDLE
CANDOR
CANERS
CANGUE
CANINE
CANING
CANKER
CANNAE
CANNAS
CANNED
CANNEL
CANNER
CANNES
CANNIE
CANNON
CANNOT
CANOED
CANOES
CANONS
CANOPY
CANSOS
CANTED
CANTER
CANTHI
CANTLE
CANTON
CANTOR
CANTOS
CANTUS
CANUCK
CANULA
CANUTE
CANVAS
CANYON
CENSED
CENSER
CENSES
CENSOR
CENSUS
CENTAL
CENTER
CENTOS
CENTRA
CENTRI
CENTRO
CINDER
CINDYS
CINEMA
CINEOL
CINQUE
CONCHA
CONCHS
CONCHY
CONCUR
CONDOM
CONDOR
CONEYS
CONFAB
CONFER
CONGAS
CONGER
CONGES
CONGOU
CONICS
CONIES
CONING
CONIUM
CONKED
CONNED
CONNER
CONNIE
CONOID
CONRAD
CONSUL
CONTES
CONTIN
CONTOS
CONTRA
CONTRE
CONVEX
CONVEY
CONVOY
CUNEAL
CUNNER
CYNICS

C••N••
CANNAE
CANNAS
CANNED
CANNEL
CANNER
CANNES
CANNIE
CANNON
CANNOT
CARNAL
CATNIP
CHANCE
CHANCY
CHANGE
CHANGS
CHANTS
CHANTY
CHINCH
CHINES
CHINKS
CHINKY
CHINTZ
CHONDR
CHUNKS
CHUNKY
CLANGS
CLANKS
CLENCH
CLINCH
CLINES
CLINGS
CLINGY
CLINIC
CLINKS
CLINTS
CLONES
CLONIC
CLONUS
COBNUT
COGNAC
COINED
COINER
CONNED
CONNER
CONNIE
CORNEA
CORNED
CORNEL
CORNER
CORNET
CORNUA
CORNUS
COUNTS
COUNTY
CRANED
CRANES
CRANIA
CRANIO
CRANKS
CRANKY
CRANNY
CRENEL
CRINGE
CRINUM
CRONES
CRONUS
CRUNCH
CUNNER
CYANIC
CYANID
CYANIN
CYGNET
CYGNUS

C•••N•
CABANA
CABINS
CADENT
CAGING
CAIRNS
CAJUNS
CAKING
CANINE
CANING
CANONS
CAPONS
CARINA
CARING
CASING
CASINO
CATENA
CAVING
CAWING
CEDING
CEMENT
CERING
CETANE
CHAINS
CHRONO
CHURNS
CITING
CLEANS
CLIENT
CLOWNS
CLUING
CODING
COGENT
COHUNE
COIGNS
COKING
COLINE
COLINS
COLONS
COLONY
COMING
CONING
COOING
COPING
CORING
CORONA
COSINE
COVING
COWING
COXING
COZENS
CRANNY
CROONS
CROWNS
CRYING
CUBANS
CUBING
CUMINS
CURING
CUTINS
CYMENE
CYRANO
CYRENE

6

C••••N
CABMAN
CABMEN
CAFTAN
CAIMAN
CALVIN
CAMDEN
CAMION
CANAAN
CANCAN
CANNON
CANTON
CANYON
CAPLIN
CARBON
CAREEN
CARMAN
CARMEN
CARSON
CARTON
CARVEN
CASEIN
CASERN
CATION
CATKIN
CATLIN
CAVEIN
CAVERN
CAYMAN
CEYLON
CHARON
CHIRON
CHITIN
CHITON
CHOPIN
CHOSEN
CITRON
CLOVEN
COCAIN
COCHIN
COCOON
CODEIN
COFFIN
COLUMN
COMEON
COMMON
CONTIN
CORBAN
CORDON
CORTIN
COSIGN
COTTON
COUPON
COUSIN
COWMAN
COWMEN
CRAVEN
CRAYON
CRETAN
CRETIN
CROTON
CYANIN
CYMLIN
CYPRIN

•CN•••
ACNODE

•C•N••
ACINUS
ICINGS
ICONIC
SCANTY
SCENDS
SCENES
SCENIC
SCENTS
SCONCE
SCONES

•C••N•
ACCENT
ACHENE
ACHING
ACORNS
ACTING
ACTINI
ACTINO
ECHINI
ECHINO
OCEANS
OCTANE
OCTANT
SCIONS
SCORNS

•C•••N
ACTION
ACUMEN
ICEMAN
ICEMEN
SCREEN

••CN••
PICNIC

••C•N•
ACCENT
ANCONA
ANCONE
ARCANE
ARCING
ASCEND
ASCENT
DECANE
DECANT
DECENT
DICING
DOCENT
ENCINA
EOCENE
ESCENT
FACING
FECUND
JACANA
JOCUND
LACING
LACUNA
LUCENT
MACING
NOCENT
OSCANS
OSCINE
PACING
PECANS
RACINE
RACING
RECANT
RECENT
RICING
ROCKNE
SECANT
SECOND
SECUND
TECHNO
VACANT
VICUNA

••C••N
AACHEN
ALCUIN
ARCHON
BECKON
BICORN
COCAIN
COCHIN
COCOON
DACRON
DECCAN
DECERN
INCHON
KUCHEN
LICHEN
LUCIAN
LUCIEN
MACRON
MECCAN
MICRON
ORCEIN
PECTEN
PECTIN
RACOON
RECKON
SECERN
SICKEN
SOCMAN
SOCMEN
TOCSIN
TUCHUN
TUCSON
TYCOON
URCHIN
ZECHIN

•••CN•
PROCNE

•••C•N
BEACON
CANCAN
DEACON
DECCAN
DUNCAN
FALCON
FLACON
GARCON
GASCON
MASCON
MECCAN
NIACIN
OILCAN
TUSCAN
VULCAN
ZIRCON

CO••••
COALED
COALER
COARSE
COASTS
COATED
COATIS
COAXAL
COAXED
COAXER
COAXES
COBALT
COBBLE
COBIAS
COBLES
COBNUT
COBRAS
COBWEB
COCAIN
COCCAL
COCCID
COCCUS
COCCYX
COCHIN
COCKED
COCKER
COCKLE
COCKUP
COCOAS
COCOON
CODDER
CODDLE
CODEIA
CODEIN
CODGER
CODIFY
CODING
COELOM
COEMPT
COERCE
COEVAL
COFFEE
COFFER
COFFIN
COFFLE
COGENT
COGGED
COGNAC
COGWAY
COHERE
COHORT
COHOSH
COHUNE
COIFED
COIGNS
COILED
COILER
COINED
COINER
COKING
COLDER
COLDLY
COLEUS
COLIES
COLINE
COLINS
COLLAR
COLLET
COLLIE
COLLOP
COLONS
COLONY
COLORS
COLOUS
COLTER
COLUGO
COLUMN
COLURE
COLZAS
COMATE
COMBAT
COMBED
COMBER
COMBOS
COMEDO
COMEDY
COMELY
COMEON
COMERS
COMETS
COMFIT
COMICS
COMING
COMITY
COMMAS
COMMIE
COMMIT
COMMIX
COMMON
COMOSE
COMOUS
COMPEL
COMPLY
COMPOS
CONCHA
CONCHS
CONCHY
CONCUR
CONDOM
CONDOR
CONEYS
CONFAB
CONFER
CONGAS
CONGER
CONGES
CONGOU
CONICS
CONIES
CONING
CONIUM
CONKED
CONNED
CONNER
CONNIE
CONOID
CONRAD
CONSUL
CONTES
CONTIN
CONTOS
CONTRA
CONTRE
CONVEX
CONVEY
CONVOY
COOEED
COOEES
COOERS
COOEYS
COOING
COOKED
COOKER
COOKEY
COOKIE
COOLED
COOLER
COOLIE
COOLLY
COOMBS
COOPED
COOPER
COOPTS
COOTIE
COPALM
COPIED
COPIER
COPIES
COPING
COPLEY
COPOUT
COPPED
COPPER
COPPRA
COPRAH
COPSES
COPTIC
COPULA
COQUET
CORALS
CORBAN
CORBEL
CORDAY
CORDED
CORDER
CORDON
CORERS
CORGIS
CORING
CORIUM

CORKED
CORKER
CORNEA
CORNED
CORNEL
CORNER
CORNET
CORNUA
CORNUS
CORODY
CORONA
CORPSE
CORPUS
CORRAL
CORSAC
CORSES
CORSET
CORTES
CORTEX
CORTEZ
CORTIN
CORVEE
CORVES
CORVUS
CORYMB
CORYZA
COSHED
COSHER
COSHES
COSIGN
COSINE
COSMIC
COSMOS
COSSES
COSSET
COSTAE
COSTAL
COSTAR
COSTED
COSTLY
COTEAU
COTTAE
COTTAR
COTTAS
COTTER
COTTON
COUGAR
COUGHS
COULEE
COUNTS
COUNTY
COUPES
COUPLE
COUPON
COURSE
COURTS
COUSIN
COVERS
COVERT
COVETS
COVEYS
COVING
COWAGE
COWARD
COWBOY
COWERS
COWING
COWLED
COWMAN
COWMEN
COWPEA
COWPER
COWPOX
COWRIE
COXING
COYISH
COYOTE
COYPUS
COZENS
COZIER
COZIES
COZILY

C•O•••

CEORLS
CHOCKS
CHOICE
CHOIRS
CHOKED
CHOKER
CHOKES
CHOLER
CHOLLA
CHONDR
CHOOSE
CHOOSY
CHOPIN
CHOPPY
CHORAL
CHORDS
CHOREA
CHOREO
CHORES
CHORIC
CHORUS
CHOSEN
CHOUGH
CLOACA
CLOAKS
CLOCHE
CLOCKS
CLODDY
CLOGGY
CLONES
CLONIC
CLONUS
CLOSED
CLOSER
CLOSES
CLOSET
CLOTHE
CLOTHO
CLOTHS
CLOTTY
CLOUDS
CLOUDY
CLOUGH
CLOUTS
CLOVEN
CLOVER
CLOVES
CLOVIS
CLOWNS
CLOYED
COOEED
COOEES
COOERS
COOEYS
COOING
COOKED
COOKER
COOKEY
COOKIE
COOLED
COOLER
COOLIE
COOLLY
COOMBS
COOPED
COOPER
COOPTS
COOTIE
CROAKS
CROAKY
CROATS
CROCKS
CROCUS
CROFTS
CROJIK
CRONES
CRONUS
CROOKS
CROONS
CRORES
CROSSE
CROTCH
CROTON
CROUCH
CROUPE
CROUPS
CROUPY
CROWDS
CROWED
CROWNS
CROZER
CROZES

C••O••

CABOBS
CAEOMA
CAJOLE
CALORY
CANOED
CANOES
CANONS
CANOPY
CAPONS
CAPOTE
CAROBS
CAROLE
CAROLS
CAROMS
CAVORT
CEBOID
CEROUS
CHEOPS
CHLOES
CHLORO
CHOOSE
CHOOSY
CHROMA
CHROME
CHROMO
CHRONO
CIBOLS
CITOLA
CLEOME
COCOAS
COCOON
COHORT
COHOSH
COLONS
COLONY
COLORS
COLOUS
COMOSE
COMOUS
CONOID
COPOUT
CORODY
CORONA
COYOTE
CREOLE
CROOKS
CROONS
CUBOID
CUPOLA
CUTOFF
CUTOUT
CYMOID
CYMOSE
CYMOUS

C•••O•

CACAOS
CACHOU
CALLOW
CAMEOS
CAMION
CAMPOS
CANDOR
CANNON
CANNOT
CANSOS
CANTON
CANTOR
CANTOS
CANYON
CAPTOR
CARBON
CARBOY
CARGOS
CARHOP
CARLOS
CARROT
CARSON
CARTON
CASHOO
CASTOR
CATION
CELLOS
CENSOR
CENTOS
CEYLON
CHARON
CHEGOE
CHICOS
CHIGOE
CHIRON
CHITON
CINEOL
CISCOS
CITRON
CLAMOR
CLAROS
COCOON
COELOM
COLLOP
COMBOS
COMEON
COMMON
COMPOS
CONDOM
CONDOR
CONGOU
CONTOS
CONVOY
CORDON
COSMOS
COTTON
COUPON
COWBOY
COWPOX
CRACOW
CRAYON
CREDOS
CRESOL
CROTON
CRUSOE
CUCKOO
CURIOS
CUSSOS
CUSTOM
CUSTOS

C••••O

CALICO
CALLAO
CARDIO
CARUSO
CASHOO
CASINO
CASTRO
CATALO
CENTRO
CERATO
CHAETO
CHALCO
CHEILO
CHEIRO
CHLORO
CHOREO
CHROMO
CHRONO
CHRYSO
CICERO
CLOTHO
COLUGO
COMEDO
CRAMBO
CRANIO
CRYPTO
CUCKOO
CYRANO

•CO•••

ACORNS
ECOLES
ICONIC
SCOFFS
SCOLDS
SCOLEX
SCONCE
SCONES
SCOOPS
SCOOTS
SCOPES
SCOPUS
SCORCH
SCORED
SCORER
SCORES
SCORIA
SCORNS
SCOTCH
SCOTER
SCOTIA
SCOTTS
SCOURS
SCOUTS
SCOWLS

•C•O••

ACCORD
ACCOST
ACEOUS
ACIOUS
ACNODE
ACROSS
ACTORS
ECHOED
ECHOER
ECHOES
ECHOIC
ECTOMY
OCLOCK
OCTOPI
SCHOOL
SCHORL
SCIONS
SCOOPS
SCOOTS
SCRODS
SCROLL

SCROOP

•C••O•
ACAJOU
ACTION
ICEBOX
OCELOT
OCTROI
SCHMOS
SCHOOL
SCROOP

•C•••O
ACTINO
ECHINO
OCTAVO
SCHIZO
SCIPIO
SCLERO
SCYPHO

••CO••
ACCORD
ACCOST
ALCOTT
ALCOVE
ANCONA
ANCONE
ASCOTS
BECOME
BICORN
COCOAS
COCOON
DACOIT
DECOCT
DECODE
DECORS
DECOYS
ENCODE
ENCORE
ESCORT
FUCOID
FUCOUS
INCOME
INCORP
JACOBS
JOCOSE
LOCOED
MUCOID
MUCOSA
MUCOSE
MUCOUS
NICOLE
PICOTS
RACOON
RECOIL
RECORD
RECOUP
ROCOCO
SECOND
TACOMA
TYCOON
UNCOCK
UNCOIL
UNCORK
WICOPY

••C•O•
ANCHOR
ARCHON
BECKON
CACAOS
CACHOU
COCOON
CUCKOO
DACRON
DOCTOR
ESCROW
FACTOR
GECKOS
HECTOR
HICKOK
INCHON
JOCKOS
LECTOR
LICTOR
MACRON
MICRON
PICTOR
RACOON
RECKON
RECTOR
RECTOS
SECTOR
SUCCOR
TUCSON
TYCOON
VECTOR
VICTOR

••C••O
ARCHEO
CICERO
CUCKOO
ESCUDO
MACACO
ORCHIO
ROCOCO
TECHNO

•••CO•
BEACON
BUNCOS
CHICOS
CISCOS
CRACOW
DEACON
FALCON
FLACON
GARCON
GASCON
GLYCOL
GUACOS
JUNCOS
MARCOS
MASCON
MASCOT
MOSCOW
NONCOM
RANCOR
ROSCOE
SUCCOR
TOMCOD
TRICOT
TURCOS
ZIRCON

•••C•O
AFLCIO
ALECTO
GAUCHO
NUNCIO
PONCHO
PROCTO
PSYCHO
RANCHO
REECHO
SHACKO
STUCCO
TRICHO

••••CO
BRONCO
CALICO
CHALCO
ENRICO
FIASCO
FRANCO
FRESCO
GLAUCO
GRAECO
GYNECO
HELICO
MACACO
MALACO
MEDICO
MEJICO
MEXICO
ROCOCO
SILICO
STUCCO
UNESCO
VARICO
VESICO

C•P•••
CAPERS
CAPIAS
CAPITA
CAPLIN
CAPONS
CAPOTE
CAPPED
CAPPER
CAPRIC
CAPTOR
CIPHER
COPALM
COPIED
COPIER
COPIES
COPING
COPLEY
COPOUT
COPPED
COPPER
COPPRA
COPRAH
COPSES
COPTIC
COPULA
CUPELS
CUPFUL
CUPOLA
CUPPED
CUPPER
CUPRIC
CUPRUM
CUPULE
CYPHER
CYPRIN
CYPRUS

C••P••
CALPAC
CAMPED
CAMPER
CAMPOS
CAMPUS
CAPPED
CAPPER
CARPAL
CARPED
CARPEL
CARPER
CARPET
CARPIC
CARPUS
CASPAR
CASPER
CHAPEL
CHAPES
CHIPPY
CHOPIN
CHOPPY
CLYPEI
COMPEL
COMPLY
COMPOS
COOPED
COOPER
COOPTS
COPPED
COPPER
COPPRA
CORPSE
CORPUS
COUPES
COUPLE
COUPON
COWPEA
COWPER
COWPOX
COYPUS
CRAPED
CRAPES
CREPED
CREPES
CRYPTO
CRYPTS
CUPPED
CUPPER
CUSPED
CUSPID
CUSPIS

C•••P•
CALIPH
CANAPE
CANOPY
CERIPH
CHAMPS
CHEEPS
CHEOPS
CHIPPY
CHIRPS
CHOPPY
CHUMPS
CLAMPS
CLASPS
CLUMPS
CLUMPY
COEMPT
CRAMPS
CREEPS
CREEPY
CRIMPS
CRIMPY
CRISPS
CRISPY
CROUPE
CROUPS
CROUPY
CRUMPS
CUTUPS

C••••P
CARHOP
CATNIP
CATSUP
COCKUP
COLLOP

•C•P••
SCAPES
SCIPIO
SCOPES
SCOPUS
SCYPHI
SCYPHO

•C••P•
ACCEPT
ECTYPE
OCCUPY
OCTOPI
SCALPS
SCAMPI
SCAMPS
SCARPS
SCAUPS
SCOOPS
SCRAPE
SCRAPS
SCRIPS
SCRIPT
SCULPT
YCLEPT

•C•••P
ICECAP
SCRIMP
SCROOP

••CP••
SECPAR

••C•P•
ACCEPT
BICEPS
ESCAPE
EXCEPT
INCEPT
OCCUPY
RECAPS
RECEPT
RECIPE
UNCAPS
WICOPY

••C••P
COCKUP
DECAMP
ENCAMP
ESCARP
HICCUP
INCORP
LOCKUP
MOCKUP
PICKUP
RECOUP

•••C•P
EYECUP
HICCUP
HUBCAP
ICECAP
MADCAP
MOBCAP
MUDCAP
REDCAP
SKYCAP
TEACUP
TOECAP

C•Q•••
COQUET

C••Q••
CAIQUE
CASQUE
CINQUE
CIRQUE
CLAQUE

CLIQUE
CLIQUY

•CQ•••
ACQUIT

CR••••
CRAALS
CRABBY
CRACKS
CRACKY
CRACOW
CRADLE
CRAFTS
CRAFTY
CRAGGY
CRAIGS
CRAKES
CRAMBO
CRAMPS
CRANED
CRANES
CRANIA
CRANIO
CRANKS
CRANKY
CRANNY
CRAPED
CRAPES
CRASIS
CRATCH
CRATED
CRATER
CRATES
CRAVAT
CRAVED
CRAVEN
CRAVER
CRAVES
CRAWLS
CRAWLY
CRAYON
CRAZED
CRAZES
CREAKS
CREAKY
CREAMS
CREAMY
CREASE
CREASY
CREATE
CRECHE
CREDIT
CREDOS
CREEDS
CREEKS
CREELS
CREEPS
CREEPY
CREESE
CREMES
CRENEL
CREOLE
CREPED
CREPES
CRESOL
CRESTS
CRETAN
CRETIC
CRETIN
CREUSA
CREWEL
CRICKS
CRIERS
CRIMEA
CRIMES
CRIMPS
CRIMPY
CRINGE
CRINUM
CRISES
CRISIS
CRISPS
CRISPY
CRITIC
CROAKS
CROAKY
CROATS
CROCKS
CROCUS
CROFTS
CROJIK
CRONES
CRONUS
CROOKS
CROONS
CRORES
CROSSE
CROTCH
CROTON
CROUCH
CROUPE
CROUPS
CROUPY
CROWDS
CROWED
CROWNS
CROZER
CROZES
CRUCES
CRUDER
CRUETS
CRUISE
CRUMBS
CRUMBY
CRUMMY
CRUMPS
CRUNCH
CRURAL
CRUSES
CRUSET
CRUSOE
CRUSTS
CRUSTY
CRUTCH
CRUXES
CRYING
CRYPTO
CRYPTS

C•R•••
CARACK
CARAFE
CARATE
CARATS
CARBON
CARBOY
CARCEL
CARDED
CARDER
CARDIO
CAREEN
CAREER
CARERS
CARESS
CARETS
CARGOS
CARHOP
CARIBE
CARIBS
CARIES
CARINA
CARING
CARLAS
CARLOS
CARMAN
CARMEL
CARMEN
CARNAL
CAROBS
CAROLE
CAROLS
CAROMS
CARPAL
CARPED
CARPEL
CARPER
CARPET
CARPIC
CARPUS
CARREL
CARRIE
CARROT
CARSON
CARTED
CARTEL
CARTER
CARTES
CARTON
CARUSO
CARVED
CARVEL
CARVEN
CARVER
CARVES
CERATE
CERATO
CEREAL
CEREUS
CERING
CERIPH
CERISE
CERITE
CERIUM
CERMET
CEROUS
CERTES
CERUSE
CERVIX
CHRISM
CHRIST
CHROMA
CHROME
CHROMO
CHRONO
CHRYSO
CIRCLE
CIRCUM
CIRCUS
CIRQUE
CIRRUS
CORALS
CORBAN
CORBEL
CORDAY
CORDED
CORDER
CORDON
CORERS
CORGIS
CORING
CORIUM
CORKED
CORKER
CORNEA
CORNED
CORNEL
CORNER
CORNET
CORNUA
CORNUS
CORODY
CORONA
CORPSE
CORPUS
CORRAL
CORSAC
CORSES
CORSET
CORTES
CORTEX
CORTEZ
CORTIN
CORVEE
CORVES
CORVUS
CORYMB
CORYZA
CURACY
CURARE
CURATE
CURBED
CURDED
CURDLE
CURERS
CURFEW
CURIAE
CURIAL
CURIES
CURING
CURIOS
CURIUM
CURLED
CURLER
CURLEW
CURSED
CURSES
CURTIS
CURTLY
CURTSY
CURULE
CURVED
CURVES
CURVET
CYRANO
CYRENE
CYRILS

C••R••
CADRES
CAIRNS
CAPRIC
CARREL
CARRIE
CARROT
CEDRIC
CEORLS
CHARDS
CHARED
CHARES
CHARGE
CHARMS
CHARON
CHARRY
CHARTS
CHERRY
CHERUB
CHERYL
CHIRMS
CHIRON
CHIRPS
CHIRRS
CHORAL
CHORDS
CHOREA
CHOREO
CHORES
CHORIC
CHORUS
CHURCH
CHURLS
CHURNS
CHURRS
CIRRUS
CITRAL
CITRIC
CITRON
CITRUS
CLARAS
CLARES
CLARET
CLAROS
CLERGY
CLERIC
CLERID
CLERKS
COARSE
COBRAS
COERCE
CONRAD
COPRAH
CORRAL
COURSE
COURTS
COWRIE
CRORES
CRURAL
CUPRIC
CUPRUM
CYMRIC
CYPRIN
CYPRUS

C•••R•
CALORY
CAMERA
CANARD
CANARY
CANERS
CAPERS
CARERS
CASERN
CASTRO
CATERS
CAVERN
CAVORT
CEDARS
CELERY
CENTRA
CENTRI
CENTRO
CESARE
CESURA
CHAIRS
CHARRY
CHEERS
CHEERY
CHEIRO
CHERRY
CHIRRS
CHLORO
CHOIRS
CHURRS
CICERO
CIDERS
CIGARS
CIMBRI
CLAIRE
CLEARS
COHERE
COHORT
COLORS
COLURE
COMERS

CONTRA
CONTRE
COOERS
COPPRA
CORERS
COVERS
COVERT
COWARD
COWERS
CRIERS
CURARE
CURERS
CYMARS

C••••R
CADGER
CAESAR
CAGIER
CAHIER
CALCAR
CALKER
CALLER
CALMER
CAMBER
CAMPER
CANCER
CANDOR
CANKER
CANNER
CANTER
CANTOR
CAPPER
CAPTOR
CARDER
CAREER
CARPER
CARTER
CARVER
CASPAR
CASPER
CASTER
CASTOR
CATHER
CAUSER
CAVIAR
CELLAR
CENSER
CENSOR
CENTER
CHAFER
CHASER
CHEWER
CHIDER
CHIMER
CHOKER
CHOLER
CHONDR
CINDER
CIPHER
CITHER
CLAMOR
CLEVER
CLOSER
CLOVER
COALER
COAXER
COCKER
CODDER
CODGER
COFFER
COILER
COINER
COLDER
COLLAR
COLTER
COMBER
CONCUR
CONDOR
CONFER
CONGER
CONNER
COOKER
COOLER
COOPER
COPIER
COPPER
CORDER
CORKER
CORNER
COSHER
COSTAR
COTTAR
COTTER
COUGAR
COWPER
COZIER
CRATER
CRAVER
CROZER
CRUDER
CULLER
CULVER
CUMBER
CUNNER
CUPPER
CURLER
CUSTER
CUTLER
CUTTER
CYCLER
CYPHER

•CR•••
ACROSS
OCREAE
SCRAGS
SCRAMS
SCRAPE
SCRAPS
SCRAWL
SCREAK
SCREAM
SCREED
SCREEN
SCREWS
SCREWY
SCRIBE
SCRIMP
SCRIPS
SCRIPT
SCRIVE
SCRODS
SCROLL
SCROOP
SCRUBS
SCRUFF
SCRUMS

•C•R••
ACARID
ACCRUE
ACORNS
ECARTE
ICARUS
OCTROI
SCARAB
SCARCE
SCARED
SCARER
SCARES
SCARFS
SCARPS
SCORCH
SCORED
SCORER
SCORES
SCORIA
SCORNS
SCURFY
SCURRY
SCURVE
SCURVY

•C••R•
ACCORD
ACTORS
ECHARD
OCCURS
OCHERS
OCHERY
SCHORL
SCLERA
SCLERO
SCOURS
SCURRY

•C•••R
ECHOER
ECLAIR
OCULAR
SCALAR
SCALER
SCARER
SCORER
SCOTER

••CR••
ACCRUE
DACRON
DECREE
ESCROW
MACRON
MICRON
PICRIC
SACRAL
SACRED
SACRUM
SECRET
SOCRED
SUCRES

••C•R•
ACCORD
BICARB
BICORN
BUCKRA
CICERO
DECARE
DECERN
DECORS
DECURY
DICERS
ENCORE
ESCARP
ESCORT
EUCHRE
FACERS
GOCART
INCORP
INCURS
MACERS
OCCURS
OSCARS
PACERS
RACERS
RECORD
RECURS
RICERS
SECERN
SECURE
ULCERS
UNCORK
UNCURL
VICARS

••C••R
ANCHOR
ARCHER
BACKER
BICKER
BUCKER
COCKER
CYCLER
DECKER
DICKER
DOCKER
DOCTOR
DUCKER
ESCHAR
ETCHER
FACTOR
HACKER
HECTOR
KICKER
LACIER
LECHER
LECTOR
LICTOR
LOCKER
MOCKER
MUCKER
NECTAR
NICKER
PACKER
PECKER
PICKER
PICTOR
PUCKER
RACIER
RACKER
RECTOR
RICHER
ROCKER
SACKER
SECPAR
SECTOR
SICKER
SOCCER
SUCCOR
SUCKER
TACKER
TICKER
TUCKER
VECTOR
VICTOR
WICKER

•••CR•
DESCRY
FIACRE
FULCRA
OUTCRY

•••C•R
BOXCAR
BRACER
CALCAR
CANCER
CONCUR
DANCER
DEICER
ELECTR
FARCER
FENCER
FORCER
GROCER
JUICER
LANCER
LASCAR
MERCER
MINCER
PIECER
PLACER
RANCOR
SAUCER
SLICER
SOCCER
SPACER
SPICER
SUCCOR
TEUCER
TRACER
TROCAR
WINCER

C•S•••
CASABA
CASALS
CASAVA
CASBAH
CASEFY
CASEIN
CASERN
CASHAW
CASHED
CASHES
CASHEW
CASHOO
CASING
CASINO
CASKET
CASPAR
CASPER
CASQUE
CASSIA
CASSIE
CASSIS
CASTER
CASTES
CASTLE
CASTOR
CASTRO
CASUAL
CESARE
CESIUM
CESTUS
CESURA
CISCOS
CISSIE
CISSYS
COSHED
COSHER
COSHES
COSIGN
COSINE
COSMIC
COSMOS
COSSES
COSSET
COSTAE
COSTAL
COSTAR
COSTED
COSTLY
CUSHAT
CUSHAW
CUSPED
CUSPID
CUSPIS
CUSSED
CUSSES
CUSSOS
CUSTER
CUSTOM

CUSTOS
CYSTIC

C••S••

CAESAR
CANSOS
CARSON
CASSIA
CASSIE
CASSIS
CATSUP
CAUSAL
CAUSED
CAUSER
CAUSES
CEASED
CEASES
CENSED
CENSER
CENSES
CENSOR
CENSUS
CHASED
CHASER
CHASES
CHASMS
CHASSE
CHASTE
CHESTS
CHESTY
CHISEL
CHOSEN
CISSIE
CISSYS
CLASPS
CLASSY
CLOSED
CLOSER
CLOSES
CLOSET
COASTS
CONSUL
COPSES
CORSAC
CORSES
CORSET
COSSES
COSSET
COUSIN
CRASIS
CRESOL
CRESTS
CRISES
CRISIS
CRISPS
CRISPY
CROSSE
CRUSES
CRUSET
CRUSOE
CRUSTS
CRUSTY
CUESTA
CUISSE
CURSED
CURSES
CUSSED
CUSSES
CUSSOS

C•••S•

CALASH
CALESA
CAMASS
CAMISE
CARESS
CARUSO
CAYUSE
CERISE
CERUSE
CHAISE
CHASSE
CHEESE
CHEESY
CHIASM
CHOOSE
CHOOSY
CHRISM
CHRIST
CHRYSO
CIVISM
CLASSY
CLAUSE
CLEIST
CLUMSY
COARSE
COHOSH
COMOSE
CORPSE
COURSE
COYISH
CREASE
CREASY
CREESE
CREUSA
CROSSE
CRUISE
CUBISM
CUBIST
CUISSE
CURTSY
CUTEST
CYMOSE

C••••S

CABALS
CABINS
CABLES
CABOBS
CACAOS
CACHES
CACTUS
CADDIS
CADETS
CADGES
CADMUS
CADRES
CAIRNS
CAJUNS
CALAIS
CALCES
CALEBS
CALIFS
CALLAS
CALLUS
CALVES
CALXES
CAMASS
CAMELS
CAMEOS
CAMPOS
CAMPUS
CANALS
CANERS
CANNAS
CANNES
CANOES
CANONS
CANSOS
CANTOS
CANTUS
CANVAS
CAPERS
CAPIAS
CAPONS
CARATS
CARERS
CARESS
CARETS
CARGOS
CARIBS
CARIES
CARLAS
CARLOS
CAROBS
CAROLS
CAROMS
CARPUS
CARTES
CARVES
CASALS
CASHES
CASSIS
CASTES
CATERS
CATHYS
CAUCUS
CAULES
CAULIS
CAULKS
CAUSES
CAVIES
CAVILS
CEASES
CECILS
CEDARS
CEIBAS
CELIAS
CELLOS
CENSES
CENSUS
CENTOS
CEORLS
CEREUS
CEROUS
CERTES
CESTUS
CHAFES
CHAFFS
CHAINS
CHAIRS
CHALKS
CHAMPS
CHANGS
CHANTS
CHAPES
CHARDS
CHARES
CHARMS
CHARTS
CHASES
CHASMS
CHEATS
CHECKS
CHEEKS
CHEEPS
CHEERS
CHELAS
CHEOPS
CHESTS
CHIAUS
CHICKS
CHICOS
CHIDES
CHIEFS
CHILLS
CHIMES
CHINES
CHINKS
CHIRMS
CHIRPS
CHIRRS
CHIVES
CHLOES
CHOCKS
CHOIRS
CHOKES
CHORDS
CHORES
CHORUS
CHUCKS
CHUFAS
CHUMPS
CHUNKS
CHURLS
CHURNS
CHURRS
CHUTES
CIBOLS
CIDERS
CIGARS
CINDYS
CIRCUS
CIRRUS
CISCOS
CISSYS
CITIES
CITRUS
CIVETS
CIVICS
CIVIES
CLACKS
CLAIMS
CLAMPS
CLANGS
CLANKS
CLARAS
CLARES
CLAROS
CLASPS
CLEANS
CLEARS
CLEATS
CLEFTS
CLERKS
CLEVIS
CLICKS
CLIFFS
CLIMBS
CLIMES
CLINES
CLINGS
CLINKS
CLINTS
CLIVES
CLOAKS
CLOCKS
CLONES
CLONUS
CLOSES
CLOTHS
CLOUDS
CLOUTS
CLOVES
CLOVIS
CLOWNS
CLUCKS
CLUMPS
CLYDES
COASTS
COATIS
COAXES
COBIAS
COBLES
COBRAS
COCCUS
COCOAS
COIGNS
COLEUS
COLIES
COLINS
COLONS
COLORS
COLOUS
COLZAS
COMBOS
COMERS
COMETS
COMICS
COMMAS
COMOUS
COMPOS
CONCHS
CONEYS
CONGAS
CONGES
CONICS
CONIES
CONTES
CONTOS
COOEES
COOERS
COOEYS
COOMBS
COOPTS
COPIES
COPSES
CORALS
CORERS
CORGIS
CORNUS
CORPUS
CORSES
CORTES
CORVES
CORVUS
COSHES
COSMOS
COSSES
COTTAS
COUGHS
COUNTS
COUPES
COURTS
COVERS
COVETS
COVEYS
COWERS
COYPUS
COZENS
COZIES
CRAALS
CRACKS
CRAFTS
CRAIGS
CRAKES
CRAMPS
CRANES
CRANKS
CRAPES
CRASIS
CRATES
CRAVES
CRAWLS
CRAZES
CREAKS
CREAMS
CREDOS
CREEDS
CREEKS
CREELS
CREEPS
CREMES
CREPES

CRESTS
CRICKS
CRIERS
CRIMES
CRIMPS
CRISES
CRISIS
CRISPS
CROAKS
CROATS
CROCKS
CROCUS
CROFTS
CRONES
CRONUS
CROOKS
CROONS
CRORES
CROUPS
CROWDS
CROWNS
CROZES
CRUCES
CRUETS
CRUMBS
CRUMPS
CRUSES
CRUSTS
CRUXES
CRYPTS
CUBANS
CUBEBS
CUBITS
CULETS
CULLIS
CULTUS
CUMINS
CUPELS
CURERS
CURIES
CURIOS
CURSES
CURTIS
CURVES
CUSPIS
CUSSES
CUSSOS
CUSTOS
CUTEYS
CUTIES
CUTINS
CUTLAS
CUTUPS
CYCADS
CYCLES
CYGNUS
CYMARS
CYMOUS
CYNICS
CYPRUS
CYRILS
CZECHS

•C•S••

ECESIS
OCASEY

•C••S•

ACCESS
ACCOST
ACCUSE
ACROSS
ICIEST
SCHISM
SCHIST
SCHUSS

•C•••S

ACCESS
ACEOUS
ACINUS
ACIOUS
ACORNS
ACROSS
ACTORS
ECCLES
ECESIS
ECHOES
ECOLES
ICARUS
ICINGS
OCCURS
OCEANS
OCHERS
OCTADS
OCTETS
SCALDS
SCALES
SCALPS
SCAMPS
SCAPES
SCARES
SCARFS
SCARPS
SCAUPS
SCENDS
SCENES
SCENTS
SCHMOS
SCHUSS
SCHWAS
SCIONS
SCOFFS
SCOLDS
SCONES
SCOOPS
SCOOTS
SCOPES
SCOPUS
SCORES
SCORNS
SCOTTS
SCOURS
SCOUTS
SCOWLS
SCRAGS
SCRAMS
SCRAPS
SCREWS
SCRIPS
SCRODS
SCRUBS
SCRUMS
SCUBAS
SCUFFS
SCULLS
SCUTES

••CS••

FOCSLE
TOCSIN
TUCSON

••C•S•

ACCESS
ACCOST
ACCUSE
DICAST
ENCASE
ENCYST
EXCESS
EXCISE
EXCUSE
INCASE
INCEST
INCISE
INCUSE
JOCOSE
LOCUST
MUCOSA
MUCOSE
NICEST
RACISM
RACIST
RECAST
RECESS
RECUSE
UPCAST

••C••S

ACCESS
ARCHES
ARCHYS
ASCOTS
BACHES
BECKYS
BICEPS
CACAOS
CACHES
CACTUS
CECILS
COCCUS
COCOAS
CYCADS
CYCLES
DACHAS
DECALS
DECAYS
DECORS
DECOYS
DICERS
DUCATS
ECCLES
EMCEES
ETCHES
EXCELS
EXCESS
FACERS
FACETS
FACIES
FICHES
FICHUS
FUCOUS
GECKOS
INCHES
INCURS
ITCHES
JACKYS
JACOBS
JOCKOS
LACHES
LOCALS
LUCIAS
LUCIUS
LYCEES
MACAWS
MACERS
MACLES
MECCAS
MICKYS
MUCOUS
NICHES
NICKYS
OCCURS
ORCHIS
OSCANS
OSCARS
PACERS
PECANS
PICOTS
PICULS
RACERS
RACHIS
RECAPS
RECESS
RECTOS
RECTUS
RECURS
RICERS
RICHES
RICKYS
RICTUS
RUCHES
RUCKUS
SOCLES
SUCRES
SYCEES
TICALS
ULCERS
UNCAPS
UNCLES
VICARS
VICKYS
VOCALS
WICHES
YACHTS
YUCCAS

•••C•S

ABACAS
ABACUS
AEACUS
ALICES
AMICES
APICES
ARECAS
BAUCIS
BLACKS
BLOCKS
BRACES
BRACTS
BRICKS
BRUCES
BUNCOS
CALCES
CAUCUS
CHECKS
CHICKS
CHICOS
CHOCKS
CHUCKS
CIRCUS
CISCOS
CLACKS
CLICKS
CLOCKS
CLUCKS
COCCUS
CONCHS
CRACKS
CRICKS
CROCKS
CROCUS
CRUCES
CZECHS
DANCES
DEICES
DEUCES
DISCUS
DUNCES
EDICTS
EDUCES
EDUCTS
EJECTS
ELECTS
ENACTS
EPACTS
EPOCHS
ERECTS
ERICHS
ERUCTS
EVICTS
EXACTS
FARCES
FASCES
FAUCES
FENCES
FLACKS
FLECKS
FLICKS
FLOCKS
FORCES
FRACAS
FROCKS
GLACES
GLACIS
GRACES
GUACOS
HANCES
HOICKS
IBICES
IOLCUS
JOYCES
JUICES
JUNCOS
KNACKS
KNOCKS
LANCES
MARCOS
MARCUS
MECCAS
MINCES
MULCTS
NANCYS
NIECES
ORACHS
OUNCES
PERCYS
PHOCIS
PIECES
PISCES
PLACES
PLACKS
PLUCKS
PRECIS
PRICES
PRICKS
QUACKS
REACTS
REICHS
SAUCES
SHACKS
SHOCKS
SHUCKS
SLACKS
SLICES
SLICKS
SMACKS
SMOCKS
SNACKS
SNICKS
SPACES
SPECKS
SPICES
STACKS
STACYS
STICKS
STOCKS
SULCUS
TINCTS
TRACES
TRACKS
TRACTS

6

TRICES
TRICKS
TRUCES
TRUCKS
TURCOS
VINCES
VISCUS
VNECKS
VOICES
WHACKS
WINCES
WRACKS
WRECKS
YOICKS
YUCCAS

••••CS
ANTICS
ASPICS
ATTICS
AZTECS
BASICS
BRONCS
CIVICS
COMICS
CONICS
CYNICS
DARICS
ETHICS
FRANCS
ISAACS
LILACS
LYRICS
MEDICS
MIMICS
OPTICS
PANICS
REBECS
RELICS
SERACS
STOICS
SUMACS
TONICS
TOPICS
TUNICS
XEBECS
ZEBECS

C•T•••
CATALO
CATCHY
CATENA
CATERS
CATGUT
CATHAY
CATHER
CATHYS
CATION
CATKIN
CATLIN
CATNIP
CATSUP
CATTED
CATTIE
CATTLE
CETANE
CITHER
CITIED
CITIES
CITING
CITOLA
CITRAL
CITRIC
CITRON
CITRUS
COTEAU
COTTAE
COTTAR
COTTAS
COTTER
COTTON
CUTELY
CUTEST
CUTEYS
CUTIES
CUTINS
CUTLAS
CUTLER
CUTLET
CUTOFF
CUTOUT
CUTTER
CUTTLE
CUTUPS

C••T••
CACTUS
CAFTAN
CANTED
CANTER
CANTHI
CANTLE
CANTON
CANTOR
CANTOS
CANTUS
CAPTOR
CARTED
CARTEL
CARTER
CARTES
CARTON
CASTER
CASTES
CASTLE
CASTOR
CASTRO
CATTED
CATTIE
CATTLE
CELTIC
CENTAL
CENTER
CENTOS
CENTRA
CENTRI
CENTRO
CERTES
CESTUS
CHATTY
CHETAH
CHITIN
CHITON
CHITTY
CHUTES
CLOTHE
CLOTHO
CLOTHS
CLOTTY
CLUTCH
COATED
COATIS
COLTER
CONTES
CONTIN
CONTOS
CONTRA
CONTRE
COOTIE
COPTIC
CORTES
CORTEX
CORTEZ
CORTIN
COSTAE
COSTAL
COSTAR
COSTED
COSTLY
COTTAE
COTTAR
COTTAS
COTTER
COTTON
CRATCH
CRATED
CRATER
CRATES
CRETAN
CRETIC
CRETIN
CRITIC
CROTCH
CROTON
CRUTCH
CULTCH
CULTUS
CURTIS
CURTLY
CURTSY
CUSTER
CUSTOM
CUSTOS
CUTTER
CUTTLE
CYSTIC

C•••T•
CADETS
CANUTE
CAPITA
CAPOTE
CARATE
CARATS
CARETS
CAVITE
CAVITY
CERATE
CERATO
CERITE
CHAETA
CHAETO
CHANTS
CHANTY
CHARTS
CHASTE
CHATTY
CHEATS
CHESTS
CHESTY
CHINTZ
CHITTY
CIVETS
CLEATS
CLEFTS
CLINTS
CLOTTY
CLOUTS
COASTS
COMATE
COMETS
COMITY
COOPTS
COUNTS
COUNTY
COURTS
COVETS
COYOTE
CRAFTS
CRAFTY
CREATE
CRESTS
CROATS
CROFTS
CRUETS
CRUSTS
CRUSTY
CRYPTO
CRYPTS
CUBITS
CUESTA
CULETS
CURATE

C••••T
CABLET
CACHET
CADENT
CAMLET
CANNOT
CARPET
CARROT
CASKET
CATGUT
CAUGHT
CAVEAT
CAVORT
CEMENT
CERMET
CHALET
CHRIST
CILIAT
CLARET
CLEIST
CLIENT
CLIMAT
CLOSET
COBALT
COBNUT
COEMPT
COGENT
COHORT
COLLET
COMBAT
COMFIT
COMMIT
COPOUT
COQUET
CORNET
CORSET
COSSET
COVERT
CRAVAT
CREDIT
CRUSET
CUBIST
CULLET
CURVET
CUSHAT
CUTEST
CUTLET
CUTOUT
CYGNET

•CT•••
ACTING
ACTINI
ACTINO
ACTION
ACTIUM
ACTIVE
ACTORS
ACTUAL
ECTOMY
ECTYPE
OCTADS
OCTANE
OCTANT
OCTAVE
OCTAVO
OCTETS
OCTOPI
OCTROI

•C•T••
ACETAL
ACETIC
ACETUM
ACETYL
ICHTHY
SCATHE
SCOTCH
SCOTER
SCOTIA
SCOTTS
SCUTCH
SCUTES
SCUTUM
SCYTHE

•C••T•
ACUATE
ACUITY
ECARTE
OCTETS
SCANTY
SCENTS
SCOOTS
SCOTTS
SCOUTS

•C•••T
ACCENT
ACCEPT
ACCOST
ACQUIT
ICIEST
OCCULT
OCELOT
OCTANT
SCHIST
SCHUIT
SCRIPT
SCULPT
YCLEPT

••CT••
ARCTIC
CACTUS
DACTYL
DICTUM
DOCTOR
FACTOR
HECTIC
HECTOR
LACTAM
LACTIC
LECTOR
LICTOR
NECTAR
PECTEN
PECTIC
PECTIN
PICTOR
RECTAL
RECTOR
RECTOS
RECTUM
RECTUS
RICTAL
RICTUS
SECTOR
TACTIC
VECTOR

6

VICTIM
VICTOR

••C•T•
ALCOTT
ASCOTS
DUCATS
EXCITE
FACETS
HECATE
INCITE
LOCATE
LUCITE
MYCETE
NICETY
OOCYTE
PICOTS
RECITE
VACATE
YACHTS

••C••T
ACCENT
ACCEPT
ACCOST
ALCOTT
ASCENT
BECKET
BUCKET
CACHET
DACOIT
DECANT
DECEIT
DECENT
DECOCT
DICAST
DOCENT
DOCKET
ENCYST
ESCENT
ESCORT
EXCEPT
GOCART
INCEPT
INCEST
JACKET
LOCKET
LOCUST
LUCENT
NICEST
NOCENT
OCCULT
PACKET
PICKET
POCKET
RACIST
RACKET
RECANT
RECAST
RECENT
RECEPT
ROCHET
ROCKET
SACHET
SECANT
SECRET
SOCKET
TICKET
UPCAST
VACANT
WICKET

•••CT•
ALECTO
BRACTS
EDICTS
EDUCTS
EJECTA
EJECTS
ELECTR
ELECTS
ENACTS
EPACTS
ERECTS
ERUCTS
EVICTS
EXACTA
EXACTS
MULCTS
PROCTO
REACTS
STACTE
TINCTS
TRACTS

•••C•T
AVOCET
BOBCAT
BRECHT
DULCET
ELICIT
FAUCET
LANCET
MASCOT
MUSCAT
PLACET
SNOCAT
TERCET
TOMCAT
TRICOT

••••CT
ABDUCT
ABJECT
ADDICT
ADDUCT
AFFECT
ASPECT
BISECT
DECOCT
DEDUCT
DEFECT
DEJECT
DELICT
DEPICT
DETECT
DIRECT
EFFECT
EXPECT
EXSECT
GALACT
IMPACT
INDICT
INDUCT
INFECT
INJECT
INSECT
INTACT
OBJECT
OBTECT
REDACT
REJECT
RELICT
RESECT
SELECT
STRICT

CU••••
CUBAGE
CUBANS
CUBEBS
CUBING
CUBISM
CUBIST
CUBITS
CUBOID
CUCKOO
CUDDIE
CUDDLE
CUDDLY
CUDGEL
CUESTA
CUFFED
CUISSE
CULETS
CULLAY
CULLED
CULLER
CULLET
CULLIS
CULMED
CULTCH
CULTUS
CULVER
CUMBER
CUMINS
CUNEAL
CUNNER
CUPELS
CUPFUL
CUPOLA
CUPPED
CUPPER
CUPRIC
CUPRUM
CUPULE
CURACY
CURARE
CURATE
CURBED
CURDED
CURDLE
CURERS
CURFEW
CURIAE
CURIAL
CURIES
CURING
CURIOS
CURIUM
CURLED
CURLER
CURLEW
CURSED
CURSES
CURTIS
CURTLY
CURTSY
CURULE
CURVED
CURVES
CURVET
CUSHAT
CUSHAW
CUSPED
CUSPID
CUSPIS
CUSSED
CUSSES
CUSSOS
CUSTER
CUSTOM
CUSTOS
CUTELY
CUTEST
CUTEYS
CUTIES
CUTINS
CUTLAS
CUTLER
CUTLET
CUTOFF
CUTOUT
CUTTER
CUTTLE
CUTUPS

C•U•••
CAUCUS
CAUDAD
CAUDAL
CAUDEX
CAUDLE
CAUGHT
CAULES
CAULIS
CAULKS
CAUSAL
CAUSED
CAUSER
CAUSES
CHUBBY
CHUCKS
CHUFAS
CHUMMY
CHUMPS
CHUNKS
CHUNKY
CHURCH
CHURLS
CHURNS
CHURRS
CHUTES
CLUCKS
CLUING
CLUMPS
CLUMPY
CLUMSY
CLUTCH
COUGAR
COUGHS
COULEE
COUNTS
COUNTY
COUPES
COUPLE
COUPON
COURSE
COURTS
COUSIN
CRUCES
CRUDER
CRUETS
CRUISE
CRUMBS
CRUMBY
CRUMMY
CRUMPS
CRUNCH
CRURAL
CRUSES
CRUSET
CRUSOE
CRUSTS
CRUSTY
CRUTCH
CRUXES

C••U••
CAJUNS
CANUCK
CANULA
CANUTE
CARUSO
CASUAL
CAYUGA
CAYUSE
CEDULA
CERUSE
CESURA
CHOUGH
CLAUDE
CLAUSE
CLOUDS
CLOUDY
CLOUGH
CLOUTS
COHUNE
COLUGO
COLUMN
COLURE
COPULA
COQUET
CREUSA
CROUCH
CROUPE
CROUPS
CROUPY
CUPULE
CURULE
CUTUPS

C•••U•
CACTUS
CADMUS
CAECUM
CAIQUE
CALLUS
CAMPUS
CANGUE
CANTUS
CARPUS
CASQUE
CATGUT
CATSUP
CAUCUS
CENSUS
CEREUS
CERIUM
CEROUS
CESIUM
CESTUS
CHABUK
CHERUB
CHIAUS
CHORUS
CILIUM
CINQUE
CIRCUM
CIRCUS
CIRQUE
CIRRUS
CITRUS
CLAQUE
CLIQUE
CLIQUY
CLONUS
COBNUT
COCCUS
COCKUP
COLEUS
COLOUS
COMOUS
CONCUR
CONIUM
CONSUL
COPOUT
CORIUM
CORNUA
CORNUS
CORPUS
CORVUS
COYPUS
CRINUM

6

CROCUS
CRONUS
CULTUS
CUPFUL
CUPRUM
CURIUM
CUTOUT
CYGNUS
CYMOUS
CYPRUS

C••••U
CACHOU
CONGOU
COTEAU

•CU•••
ACUATE
ACUITY
ACUMEN
OCULAR
SCUBAS
SCUFFS
SCULLS
SCULPT
SCUMMY
SCURFY
SCURRY
SCURVE
SCURVY
SCUTCH
SCUTES
SCUTUM

•C•U••
ACCUSE
ACQUIT
ACTUAL
OCCULT
OCCUPY
OCCURS
SCAUPS
SCHUIT
SCHUSS
SCOURS
SCOUTS
SCRUBS
SCRUFF
SCRUMS

•C••U•
ACCRUE
ACEOUS
ACETUM
ACINUS
ACIOUS
ACTIUM
ICARUS
SCOPUS
SCUTUM

•C•••U
ACAJOU

••CU••
ACCUSE
ALCUIN
DECURY
ESCUDO
EXCUSE
FACULA
FECULA
FECUND
HECUBA
INCUBI
INCURS
INCUSE
JOCUND
LACUNA
LOCUST
MACULA
MACULE
OCCULT
OCCUPY
OCCURS
OSCULE
PICULS
RECURS
RECUSE
SECUND
SECURE
UNCURL
VACUUM
VICUNA

••C•U•
ACCRUE
AECIUM
CACTUS
COCCUS
COCKUP
DICTUM
FICHUS
FUCOUS
HICCUP
LOCKUP
LUCIUS
LYCEUM
MOCKUP
MUCOUS
PICKUP
RECOUP
RECTUM
RECTUS
RICTUS
RUCKUS
SACRUM
TUCHUN
VACUUM

••C••U
CACHOU
DACHAU

•••CU•
ABACUS
AEACUS
CAECUM
CAUCUS
CIRCUM
CIRCUS
COCCUS
CONCUR
CROCUS
DISCUS
EYECUP
FESCUE
HICCUP
IOLCUS
MARCUS
MISCUE
RESCUE
SULCUS
TALCUM
TEACUP
VISCUS

•••C•U
MANCHU

••••CU
APERCU

C•V•••
CAVEAT
CAVEIN
CAVELL
CAVERN
CAVIAR
CAVIES
CAVILS
CAVING
CAVITE
CAVITY
CAVORT
CIVETS
CIVICS
CIVIES
CIVISM
COVERS
COVERT
COVETS
COVEYS
COVING

C••V••
CALVED
CALVES
CALVIN
CANVAS
CARVED
CARVEL
CARVEN
CARVER
CARVES
CERVIX
CHIVES
CLEVER
CLEVIS
CLIVES
CLOVEN
CLOVER
CLOVES
CLOVIS
COEVAL
CONVEX
CONVEY
CONVOY
CORVEE
CORVES
CORVUS
CRAVAT
CRAVED
CRAVEN
CRAVER
CRAVES
CULVER
CURVED
CURVES
CURVET

C•••V•
CASAVA
CLEAVE

•C••V•
ACTIVE
OCTAVE
OCTAVO
SCRIVE
SCURVE
SCURVY

••C•V•
ALCOVE

C•W•••
CAWING
COWAGE
COWARD
COWBOY
COWERS
COWING
COWLED
COWMAN
COWMEN
COWPEA
COWPER
COWPOX
COWRIE

C••W••
CHAWED
CHEWED
CHEWER
CLAWED
CLEWED
CLOWNS
COBWEB
COGWAY
CRAWLS
CRAWLY
CREWEL
CROWDS
CROWED
CROWNS

C••••W
CALLOW
CASHAW
CASHEW
CRACOW
CURFEW
CURLEW
CUSHAW

•C•W••
SCHWAS
SCOWLS

•C••W•
SCRAWL
SCREWS
SCREWY

••C•W•
MACAWS

••C••W
ESCHEW
ESCROW

•••C•W
CRACOW
MOSCOW

C•X•••
COXING

C••X••
CALXES
COAXAL
COAXED
COAXER
COAXES
CRUXES

C••••X
CAUDEX
CERVIX
CLIMAX
COCCYX
COMMIX
CONVEX
CORTEX
COWPOX

•C•••X
ICEBOX
SCOLEX

••C••X
COCCYX
PICKAX

•••C•X
COCCYX

CY••••
CYANIC
CYANID
CYANIN
CYBELE
CYCADS
CYCLED
CYCLER
CYCLES
CYCLIC
CYGNET
CYGNUS
CYMARS
CYMBAL
CYMENE
CYMLIN
CYMOID
CYMOSE
CYMOUS
CYMRIC
CYNICS
CYPHER
CYPRIN
CYPRUS
CYRANO
CYRENE
CYRILS
CYSTIC

C•Y•••
CAYMAN
CAYUGA
CAYUSE
CEYLON
CHYMIC
CLYDES
CLYPEI
COYISH
COYOTE
COYPUS
CRYING
CRYPTO
CRYPTS

C••Y••
CANYON
CHRYSO
CLAYED
CLAYEY
CLOYED
CORYMB
CORYZA
CRAYON

C•••Y•
CATHYS
CHERYL
CINDYS
CISSYS
COCCYX
CONEYS
COOEYS
COVEYS
CUTEYS

C••••Y
CAGILY

6

CALMLY
CALORY
CANARY
CANOPY
CARBOY
CASEFY
CATCHY
CATHAY
CAVITY
CECILY
CELERY
CHAFFY
CHALKY
CHAMMY
CHANCY
CHANTY
CHARRY
CHATTY
CHEEKY
CHEERY
CHEESY
CHERRY
CHESTY
CHILLY
CHINKY
CHIPPY
CHITTY
CHOOSY
CHOPPY
CHUBBY
CHUMMY
CHUNKY
CICELY
CLAMMY
CLASSY
CLAYEY
CLERGY
CLIFFY
CLINGY
CLIQUY
CLODDY
CLOGGY
CLOTTY
CLOUDY
CLUMPY
CLUMSY
CODIFY
COGWAY
COLDLY
COLONY
COMEDY
COMELY
COMITY
COMPLY
CONCHY
CONVEY
CONVOY
COOKEY
COOLLY
COPLEY
CORDAY
CORODY
COSTLY
COUNTY
COWBOY
COZILY
CRABBY
CRACKY
CRAFTY
CRAGGY
CRANKY
CRANNY
CRAWLY
CREAKY
CREAMY
CREASY
CREEPY
CRIMPY
CRISPY
CROAKY
CROUPY
CRUMBY
CRUMMY
CRUSTY
CUDDLY
CULLAY
CURACY
CURTLY
CURTSY
CUTELY

•CY•••

SCYLLA
SCYPHI
SCYPHO
SCYTHE

•C•Y••

ECTYPE

•C••Y•

ACETYL

•C•••Y

ACIDLY
ACUITY
ECTOMY
ICALLY
ICHTHY
OCASEY
OCCUPY
OCHERY
SCABBY
SCANTY
SCREWY
SCUMMY
SCURFY
SCURRY
SCURVY

••CY••

ENCYCL
ENCYST
OOCYTE

••C•Y•

ARCHYS
BECKYS
COCCYX
DACTYL
DECAYS
DECOYS
JACKYS
MICKYS
NICKYS
RICKYS
VICKYS

••C••Y

ARCHLY
CECILY
CICELY
DECURY
DICKEY
HICKEY
HOCKEY
JOCKEY
LACILY
LACKEY
MICKEY
NICELY
NICETY
OCCUPY
PACIFY
RACILY
RICHLY
RICKEY
SICILY
SICKLY
TACKEY
WICOPY

•••CY•

COCCYX
NANCYS
PERCYS
STACYS

•••C•Y

BEACHY
BISCAY
BLOCKY
BOTCHY
BRACHY
BUNCHY
CATCHY
CONCHY
CRACKY
DESCRY
FLOCKY
LEACHY
OUTCRY
PATCHY
PEACHY
PITCHY
PLUCKY
POACHY
POUCHY
PUNCHY
STICKY
STOCKY
TETCHY
TOUCHY
TRACHY
TRICKY
WINCEY
ZINCKY

••••CY

ABBACY
AGENCY
BOUNCY
CHANCY
CURACY
FLEECY
IDIOCY
LEGACY
LUNACY
PAPACY
PIRACY
POLICY
QUINCY

CZ••••

CZECHS

C•Z•••

COZENS
COZIER
COZIES
COZILY

C••Z••

COLZAS
CRAZED
CRAZES
CROZER
CROZES

C•••Z•

CORYZA

C••••Z

CHINTZ
CORTEZ

•CZ•••

ECZEMA

•C••Z•

SCHIZO

DA••••

DABBED
DABBER
DABBLE
DACHAS
DACHAU
DACOIT
DACRON
DACTYL
DADDLE
DADOES
DAEDAL
DAEMON
DAFTLY
DAGGER
DAGMAR
DAGOBA
DAHLIA
DAHOON
DAIMIO
DAIMON
DAIMYO
DAINTY
DAISES
DAISYS
DAKOIT
DAKOTA
DALETH
DALLAS
DALLES
DALTON
DAMAGE
DAMANS
DAMASK
DAMMAR
DAMMED
DAMMER
DAMNED
DAMPED
DAMPEN
DAMPER
DAMPLY
DAMSEL
DAMSON
DANAID
DANAUS
DANCED
DANCER
DANCES
DANDER
DANDLE
DANGED
DANGER
DANGLE
DANIEL
DANISH
DANITE
DANKER
DANKLY
DANNYS
DANTON
DANUBE
DANZIG
DAPHNE
DAPPED
DAPPER
DAPPLE
DARDAN
DARERS
DARICS
DARIEN
DARING
DARIUS
DARKEN
DARKER
DARKLE
DARKLY
DARNED
DARNEL
DARROW
DARTED
DARTER
DARTLE
DARWIN
DASHED
DASHER
DASHES
DATARY
DATERS
DATING
DATIVE
DATTOS
DATURA
DAUBED
DAUBER
DAUBRY
DAUNTS
DAVEYS
DAVIDS
DAVIES
DAVITS
DAWDLE
DAWNED
DAWSON
DAYFLY
DAYTON
DAZING
DAZZLE

D•A•••

DEACON
DEADEN
DEADLY
DEAFEN
DEAFLY
DEALER
DEARER
DEARIE
DEARLY
DEARTH
DEATHS
DEATHY
DHARMA
DHARNA
DIADEM
DIALED
DIALER
DIALOG
DIANAS
DIANES
DIAPER
DIATOM
DIAZIN
DOABLE
DOALLS
DRABLY
DRACHM
DRAFFS
DRAFFY
DRAFTS
DRAFTY
DRAGEE

6

DRAGON
DRAINS
DRAKES
DRAMAS
DRAPED
DRAPER
DRAPES
DRAWEE
DRAWER
DRAWLS
DRAWLY
DRAYED
DWARFS
DYADIC

D••A••
DAMAGE
DAMANS
DAMASK
DANAID
DANAUS
DATARY
DEBARK
DEBARS
DEBASE
DEBATE
DECADE
DECALS
DECAMP
DECANE
DECANT
DECARE
DECAYS
DEDANS
DEFACE
DEFAME
DEGAGE
DEGAME
DEKARE
DELAYS
DEMAND
DENARY
DEPART
DERAIL
DERAIN
DESALT
DETACH
DETAIL
DETAIN
DEWANS
DICAST
DIGAMY
DILATE
DINAHS
DINARS
DISARM
DIVANS
DIWANS
DOGAPE
DOMAIN
DONALD
DONATE
DORADO
DOSAGE

DOTAGE
DREADS
DREAMS
DREAMT
DREAMY
DREARY
DRYADS
DUCATS
DYNAMO
DYNAST

D•••A•
DACHAS
DACHAU
DAEDAL
DAGMAR
DALLAS
DAMMAR
DARDAN
DECCAN
DEEWAN
DEFEAT
DEFRAY
DELIAN
DELIAS
DELLAS
DELTAS
DEMEAN
DENIAL
DENTAL
DEODAR
DERMAL
DERMAS
DERMAT
DESMAN
DESSAU
DEWLAP
DIANAS
DIPSAS
DIRHAM
DISBAR
DISMAL
DISMAY
DISTAL
DOBLAS
DOBRAS
DOGEAR
DOGMAS
DOLLAR
DOLMAN
DONNAS
DOODAD
DORIAN
DORSAD
DORSAL
DOSSAL
DRAMAS
DUNBAR
DUNCAN
DURBAN
DURBAR
DURHAM
DURIAN
DVORAK

D••••A
DAGOBA
DAHLIA
DAKOTA
DATURA
DHARMA
DHARNA
DHURNA
DODECA
DUENNA

•DA•••
ADAGES
ADAGIO
ADAPTS

•D•A••
ADDAMS
ADNATE
EDDAIC
EDGARS
EDUARD
EDWARD
IDEALS
IDEATE

•D••A•
ADONAI
ADRIAN

•D•••A
EDWINA
GDYNIA
ODESSA
ODYNIA

••DA••
ADDAMS
AUDADS
BEDAUB
CEDARS
DEDANS
EDDAIC
ENDALL
INDABA
IODATE
JUDAEA
JUDAEO
JUDAHS
JUDAIC
KODAKS
MADAME
MADAMS
MEDALS
MIDAIR
ORDAIN
PEDALS
PEDANT
PEDATE
PEDATI
RADARS
REDACT
REDANS
SEDANS

SEDATE
SUDARY
UPDATE
VEDAIC

••D•A•
AIDMAN
ANDEAN
BADMAN
BEDLAM
BEDPAN
ENDEAR
HEDRAL
HYDRAE
HYDRAS
INDIAN
JUDEAN
KEDDAH
KIDNAP
KODIAK
LYDIAS
MADCAP
MADMAN
MADRAS
MEDIAE
MEDIAL
MEDIAN
MEDLAR
MIDDAY
MIDWAY
MUDCAP
OGDOAD
ORDEAL
RADIAL
RADIAN
REDBAY
REDCAP
RODMAN
UNDRAW
VODKAS
ZODIAC

••D••A
ANDREA
BODEGA
BUDDHA
CEDULA
CODEIA
DODECA
EIDOLA
EUDORA
FEDORA
GODIVA
INDABA
JUDAEA
LADOGA
MADURA
MEDUSA
RADULA
REDOWA

•••DA•
ALIDAD
AOUDAD

APODAL
BAGDAD
BELDAM
BENDAY
BRIDAL
CAUDAD
CAUDAL
CORDAY
DAEDAL
DARDAN
DEODAR
DOODAD
FEUDAL
FREDAS
FRIDAY
GILDAS
HEYDAY
HILDAS
HOWDAH
JORDAN
KEDDAH
LANDAU
LAYDAY
LINDAS
MANDAN
MAYDAY
MIDDAY
MONDAY
PANDAS
PAYDAY
PINDAR
PURDAH
RANDAL
RANDAN
RHODAS
SANDAL
SENDAL
SERDAB
SIRDAR
SUNDAE
SUNDAY
THEDAS
VANDAL
VEADAR
WANDAS
WHIDAH
WHYDAH

•••D•A
ACADIA
ACEDIA
BUDDHA
EXEDRA
SANDRA
SRADHA
STADIA
TUNDRA

••••DA
AGENDA
AMANDA
ARMADA
BRENDA
CANADA

CICADA
FRIEDA
LAMBDA
LUANDA
NEVADA
ONEIDA
PAGODA
PANADA
POSADA
PRAVDA
REMUDA
RESEDA
RWANDA
UGANDA

D•B•••
DABBED
DABBER
DABBLE
DEBARK
DEBARS
DEBASE
DEBATE
DEBBYS
DEBITS
DEBRIS
DEBTOR
DEBUGS
DEBUNK
DEBUTS
DIBBED
DIBBER
DIBBLE
DOBBER
DOBBIN
DOBIES
DOBLAS
DOBLON
DOBRAS
DOBSON
DUBBED
DUBBIN
DUBLIN
DYBBUK

D••B••
DABBED
DABBER
DABBLE
DAUBED
DAUBER
DAUBRY
DEBBYS
DIBBED
DIBBER
DIBBLE
DIOBOL
DISBAR
DOABLE
DOBBER
DOBBIN
DORBUG
DOUBLE
DOUBLY

6

DOUBTS
DRABLY
DUBBED
DUBBIN
DUMBLY
DUNBAR
DURBAN
DURBAR
DYBBUK

D•••B•
DAGOBA
DANUBE
DEMOBS

•D•B••
ADOBES
EDIBLE

•D••B•
ADLIBS

•D•••B
ADSORB
ADVERB

••DB••
BEDBUG
REDBAY
REDBUD
REDBUG
TIDBIT

••D•B•
ARDEBS
INDABA

••D••B
BEDAUB
MIDRIB

•••DB•
GOODBY

•••D•B
SERDAB
SUBDEB

D•C•••
DACHAS
DACHAU
DACOIT
DACRON
DACTYL
DECADE
DECALS
DECAMP
DECANE
DECANT
DECARE
DECAYS
DECCAN
DECEIT
DECENT
DECERN
DECIDE
DECILE
DECKED
DECKEL
DECKER
DECKLE
DECOCT
DECODE
DECORS
DECOYS
DECREE
DECURY
DICAST
DICERS
DICING
DICKER
DICKEY
DICKIE
DICTUM
DOCENT
DOCILE
DOCKED
DOCKER
DOCKET
DOCTOR
DUCATS
DUCKED
DUCKER

D••C••
DANCED
DANCER
DANCES
DEACON
DECCAN
DEICED
DEICER
DEICES
DESCRY
DEUCED
DEUCES
DISCUS
DOUCHE
DRACHM
DULCET
DULCIE
DUNCAN
DUNCES

D•••C•
DARICS
DECOCT
DEDUCE
DEDUCT
DEFACE
DEFECT
DEJECT
DELICT
DEPICT
DETACH
DETECT
DEVICE
DIRECT
DODECA
DRENCH

D••••C
DEIFIC
DERMIC
DYADIC

•D•C••
EDICTS
EDUCED
EDUCES
EDUCTS

•D••C•
ADDICT
ADDUCE
ADDUCT
ADVICE
IDIOCY

•D•••C
ADIPIC
ADONIC
EDDAIC

••DC••
MADCAP
MUDCAP
REDCAP

••D•C•
ABDUCT
ADDICT
ADDUCE
ADDUCT
BEDECK
BODICE
DEDUCE
DEDUCT
DODECA
INDICT
INDUCE
INDUCT
MEDICO
MEDICS
REDACT
REDUCE
SEDUCE

••D••C
CEDRIC
EDDAIC
HYDRIC
JUDAIC
VEDAIC
ZODIAC

•••D•C
ACIDIC
AMIDIC
ANODIC
BARDIC
DYADIC
GEODIC
HERDIC
IRIDIC
NORDIC
RHODIC
SYNDIC

D•D•••
DADDLE
DADOES
DEDANS
DEDUCE
DEDUCT
DIDDLE
DIDIES
DIDOES
DODDER
DODECA
DODGED
DODGER
DODGES
DODOES
DUDEEN
DUDISH
DUDLEY

D••D••
DADDLE
DAEDAL
DANDER
DANDLE
DARDAN
DAWDLE
DEADEN
DEADLY
DEEDED
DENDRI
DENDRO
DEODAR
DIADEM
DIDDLE
DIKDIK
DIODES
DODDER
DOODAD
DOODLE
DREDGE
DRUDGE
DRYDEN
DUNDEE
DUODEN
DYADIC

D•••D•
DAVIDS
DECADE
DECIDE
DECODE
DELUDE
DEMODE
DENUDE
DERIDE
DIPODY
DIRNDL
DIVIDE
DORADO
DREADS
DRUIDS
DRYADS

D••••D
DABBED
DAMMED
DAMNED
DAMPED
DANAID
DANCED
DANGED
DAPPED
DARNED
DARTED
DASHED
DAUBED
DAWNED
DECKED
DEEDED
DEEMED
DEFEND
DEFIED
DEICED
DELVED
DEMAND
DENIED
DENNED
DENTED
DEPEND
DESMID
DEUCED
DEVOID
DIALED
DIBBED
DIETED
DIMMED
DINGED
DINNED
DINTED
DIPPED
DIRKED
DISHED
DOCKED
DODGED
DOFFED
DOGGED
DOLLED
DONALD
DONNED
DOODAD
DOOMED
DORSAD
DOTTED
DOUSED
DOWNED
DOWSED
DRAPED
DRAYED
DRONED
DROVED
DUBBED
DUCKED
DUELED
DULLED
DUMPED
DUNGED
DUNKED
DUNNED
DUSKED
DUSTED

•DD•••
ADDAMS
ADDEND
ADDERS
ADDICT
ADDING
ADDLED
ADDLES
ADDUCE
ADDUCT
EDDAIC
EDDIES
ODDEST
ODDITY
UDDERS

•D•••D
ADDEND
ADDLED
ADORED
EDITED
EDMOND
EDMUND
EDUARD
EDUCED
EDWARD

••DD••
BEDDED
BEDDER
BIDDEN
BIDDER
BUDDED
BUDDER
BUDDHA
BUDDLE
CADDIE
CADDIS
CODDER
CODDLE
CUDDIE
CUDDLE
CUDDLY
DADDLE
DIDDLE
DODDER
FIDDLE
FODDER
FUDDLE
GADDED
GADDER
HEDDLE
HIDDEN
HODDEN

6

HUDDLE
KEDDAH
KIDDED
KIDDER
KIDDIE
LADDER
LADDIE
LIDDED
MADDED
MADDEN
MADDER
MEDDLE
MIDDAY
MIDDEN
MIDDLE
MUDDED
MUDDER
MUDDLE
NODDED
NODDER
NODDLE
PADDED
PADDLE
PADDYS
PEDDLE
PIDDLE
PODDED
PUDDLE
PUDDLY
RADDLE
REDDEN
REDDER
REDDLE
REDDOG
RIDDED
RIDDEN
RIDDLE
RODDYS
RUDDER
RUDDLE
SADDEN
SADDER
SADDLE
SIDDUR
SODDED
SODDEN
SUDDEN
TEDDED
TEDDER
TEDDYS
TODDLE
WADDED
WADDLE
WADDLY
WEDDED
WIDDIE

••D•D•
AUDADS
IODIDE

••D••D
ADDEND
ADDLED
BADGED
BEDDED
BEDRID
BODIED
BUDDED
BUDGED
CADGED
DODGED
ELDRED
ENDUED
FUDGED
GADDED
GADOID
HEDGED
INDEED
INDUED
JUDGED
KEDGED
KIDDED
LADLED
LIDDED
LODGED
MADDED
MADRID
MUDDED
NODDED
NUDGED
OGDOAD
PADDED
PODDED
REDBUD
RIDDED
RIDGED
SIDLED
SODDED
TEDDED
TIDIED
WADDED
WEDDED
WEDGED

•••DD•
CLODDY
FREDDY
SHODDY
THADDY

•••D•D
ABIDED
ALIDAD
AOUDAD
BAGDAD
BANDED
BARDED
BEADED
BEDDED
BLADED
BONDED
BUDDED
CANDID
CARDED
CAUDAD
CHIDED
CORDED
CURDED
DEEDED
DOODAD
ELIDED
ELUDED
ERODED
EVADED
EXUDED
FENDED
FEUDED
FOLDED
FORDED
FUNDED
GADDED
GELDED
GILDED
GIRDED
GLIDED
GOADED
GRADED
GRIDED
GUIDED
HANDED
HEADED
HEEDED
HERDED
HOODED
HORDED
KIDDED
LANDED
LARDED
LAUDED
LEADED
LIDDED
LOADED
LORDED
MADDED
MELDED
MENDED
MINDED
MISDID
MOLDED
MUDDED
NEEDED
NODDED
OUTDID
PADDED
PENDED
PODDED
PRIDED
RAIDED
REEDED
RENDED
RIDDED
SANDED
SEEDED
SHADED
SODDED
SORDID
SPADED
TEDDED
TENDED
TRADED
VENDED
VOIDED
WADDED
WARDED
WEDDED
WEEDED
WELDED
WENDED
WINDED
WOADED
WOODED
WORDED
YARDED

DE••••
DEACON
DEADEN
DEADLY
DEAFEN
DEAFLY
DEALER
DEARER
DEARIE
DEARLY
DEARTH
DEATHS
DEATHY
DEBARK
DEBARS
DEBASE
DEBATE
DEBBYS
DEBITS
DEBRIS
DEBTOR
DEBUGS
DEBUNK
DEBUTS
DECADE
DECALS
DECAMP
DECANE
DECANT
DECARE
DECAYS
DECCAN
DECEIT
DECENT
DECERN
DECIDE
DECILE
DECKED
DECKEL
DECKER
DECKLE
DECOCT
DECODE
DECORS
DECOYS
DECREE
DECURY
DEDANS
DEDUCE
DEDUCT
DEEDED
DEEMED
DEEPEN
DEEPER
DEEPLY
DEEWAN
DEFACE
DEFAME
DEFEAT
DEFECT
DEFEND
DEFERS
DEFIED
DEFIER
DEFIES
DEFILE
DEFINE
DEFORM
DEFRAY
DEFTER
DEFTLY
DEGAGE
DEGAME
DEGREE
DEGUMS
DEGUST
DEHORN
DEICED
DEICER
DEICES
DEIFIC
DEIGNS
DEISTS
DEJECT
DEKARE
DEKING
DELAYS
DELETE
DELIAN
DELIAS
DELICT
DELIUS
DELLAS
DELPHI
DELTAS
DELUDE
DELUGE
DELUXE
DELVED
DELVER
DELVES
DEMAND
DEMEAN
DEMIES
DEMISE
DEMITS
DEMOBS
DEMODE
DEMONO
DEMONS
DEMOTE
DEMURE
DEMURS
DENARY
DENDRI
DENDRO
DENGUE
DENIAL
DENIED
DENIER
DENIES
DENIMS
DENISE
DENNED
DENNIS
DENNYS
DENOTE
DENSER
DENTAL
DENTED
DENTIL
DENTIN
DENUDE
DENVER
DEODAR
DEPART
DEPEND
DEPICT
DEPLOY
DEPORT
DEPOSE
DEPOTS
DEPTHS
DEPUTE
DEPUTY
DERAIL
DERAIN
DEREKS
DERIDE
DERIVE
DERMAL
DERMAS
DERMAT
DERMIC
DERRIS
DESALT
DESCRY
DESERT
DESIGN
DESIRE
DESIST
DESMAN
DESMID
DESOXY
DESPOT
DESSAU
DETACH
DETAIL
DETAIN
DETECT
DETENT
DETERS
DETEST
DETOUR
DEUCED
DEUCES
DEVEIN
DEVEST
DEVICE

6

DEVILS
DEVISE
DEVOID
DEVOIR
DEVOTE
DEVOUR
DEVOUT
DEWANS
DEWIER
DEWITT
DEWLAP
DEXTER
DEXTRO

D•E•••

DAEDAL
DAEMON
DEEDED
DEEMED
DEEPEN
DEEPER
DEEPLY
DEEWAN
DIEPPE
DIESEL
DIESES
DIESIS
DIETED
DIETER
DOESNT
DREADS
DREAMS
DREAMT
DREAMY
DREARY
DREDGE
DREGGY
DRENCH
DRESSY
DUELED
DUELER
DUELLO
DUENNA
DWELLS
DYEING

D••E••

DALETH
DARERS
DATERS
DAVEYS
DECEIT
DECENT
DECERN
DEFEAT
DEFECT
DEFEND
DEFERS
DEJECT
DELETE
DEMEAN
DEPEND
DEREKS
DESERT
DETECT
DETENT
DETERS
DETEST
DEVEIN
DEVEST
DICERS
DIGEST
DIMERS
DINERO
DINERS
DIRECT
DIRELY
DIREST
DIVERS
DIVERT
DIVEST
DIZENS
DOCENT
DODECA
DOGEAR
DONEES
DONETS
DOREEN
DOSERS
DOTERS
DOWELS
DOWERS
DOWERY
DOYENS
DOZENS
DRIERS
DRIEST
DRYERS
DRYEST
DUDEEN
DUPERS
DUPERY
DURESS

D•••E•

DABBED
DABBER
DADOES
DAGGER
DAISES
DALLES
DAMMED
DAMMER
DAMNED
DAMPED
DAMPEN
DAMPER
DAMSEL
DANCED
DANCER
DANCES
DANDER
DANGED
DANGER
DANIEL
DANKER
DAPPED
DAPPER
DARIEN
DARKEN
DARKER
DARNED
DARNEL
DARTED
DARTER
DASHED
DASHER
DASHES
DAUBED
DAUBER
DAVIES
DAWNED
DEADEN
DEAFEN
DEALER
DEARER
DECKED
DECKEL
DECKER
DECREE
DEEDED
DEEMED
DEEPEN
DEEPER
DEFIED
DEFIER
DEFIES
DEFTER
DEGREE
DEICED
DEICER
DEICES
DELVED
DELVER
DELVES
DEMIES
DENIED
DENIER
DENIES
DENNED
DENSER
DENTED
DENVER
DEUCED
DEUCES
DEWIER
DEXTER
DHOLES
DIADEM
DIALED
DIALER
DIANES
DIAPER
DIBBED
DIBBER
DICKER
DICKEY
DIDIES
DIDOES
DIESEL
DIESES
DIETED
DIETER
DIFFER
DIGGER
DIMMED
DIMMER
DINGED
DINGEY
DINKEY
DINNED
DINNER
DINTED
DIODES
DIPLEX
DIPPED
DIPPER
DIRGES
DIRKED
DISHED
DISHES
DISNEY
DISPEL
DITHER
DOBBER
DOBIES
DOCKED
DOCKER
DOCKET
DODDER
DODGED
DODGER
DODGES
DODOES
DOFFED
DOFFER
DOGGED
DOGGER
DOGIES
DOLLED
DOLMEN
DONEES
DONKEY
DONNED
DOOLEE
DOOMED
DOPIER
DOREEN
DORIES
DORMER
DOSSEL
DOSSER
DOTIER
DOTTED
DOTTEL
DOTTER
DOUSED
DOUSES
DOWNED
DOWSED
DOWSER
DOWSES
DOXIES
DOYLEY
DOZIER
DRAGEE
DRAKES
DRAPED
DRAPER
DRAPES
DRAWEE
DRAWER
DRAYED
DRIVEL
DRIVEN
DRIVER
DRIVES
DRONED
DRONES
DROVED
DROVER
DROVES
DRUPES
DRUSES
DRYDEN
DUBBED
DUCKED
DUCKER
DUDEEN
DUDLEY
DUELED
DUELER
DUFFEL
DUFFER
DUIKER
DULCET
DULLED
DULLER
DUMPED
DUNCES
DUNDEE
DUNGED
DUNKED
DUNKER
DUNNED
DUODEN
DUPLEX
DUSKED
DUSTED
DUSTER
DUTIES

D••••E

DABBLE
DADDLE
DAMAGE
DANDLE
DANGLE
DANITE
DANUBE
DAPHNE
DAPPLE
DARKLE
DARTLE
DATIVE
DAWDLE
DAZZLE
DEARIE
DEBASE
DEBATE
DECADE
DECANE
DECARE
DECIDE
DECILE
DECKLE
DECODE
DECREE
DEDUCE
DEFACE
DEFAME
DEFILE
DEFINE
DEGAGE
DEGAME
DEGREE
DEKARE
DELETE
DELUDE
DELUGE
DELUXE
DEMISE
DEMODE
DEMOTE
DEMURE
DENGUE
DENISE
DENOTE
DENUDE
DEPOSE
DEPUTE
DERIDE
DERIVE
DESIRE
DEVICE
DEVISE
DEVOTE
DIBBLE
DICKIE
DIDDLE
DIEPPE
DILATE
DILUTE
DIMPLE
DINGLE
DIPLOE
DIPOLE
DISUSE
DIVIDE
DIVINE
DOABLE
DOCILE
DOGAPE
DOGGIE
DOLLIE
DONATE
DONNIE
DOODLE
DOOLEE
DOOLIE
DORMIE
DOSAGE
DOTAGE
DOTTLE

DOUBLE
DOUCHE
DOUGIE
DRAGEE
DRAWEE
DREDGE
DROWSE
DRUDGE
DUFFLE
DULCIE
DUNDEE

•DE•••
ADEEMS
ADENIS
ADEPTS
IDEALS
IDEATE
ODESSA

•D•E••
ADDEND
ADDERS
ADEEMS
ADHERE
ADIEUS
ADIEUX
ADVENT
ADVERB
ADVERT
IDLERS
IDLEST
ODDEST
UDDERS

•D••E•
ADAGES
ADDLED
ADDLES
ADOBES
ADORED
ADORER
ADORES
ADRIEN
EDDIES
EDGIER
EDILES
EDITED
EDUCED
EDUCES

•D•••E
ADDUCE
ADHERE
ADJURE
ADMIRE
ADNATE
ADVICE
ADVISE
EDIBLE
IDEATE

••DE••
ADDEND
ADDERS
AIDERS
ALDERS
ANDEAN
ARDEBS
ARDENT
BEDECK
BEDEWS
BIDETS
BODEGA
CADENT
CADETS
CIDERS
CODEIA
CODEIN
DODECA
DUDEEN
ELDERS
ELDEST
ENDEAR
FADEIN
GIDEON
HIDERS
INDEED
INDENE
INDENT
JUDEAN
MADEUP
MODELS
MODERN
MODEST
NUDELY
ODDEST
OLDEST
ORDEAL
ORDERS
REDEEM
REDEYE
RIDENT
RIDERS
RODENT
RODEOS
RUDELY
RUDEST
SEDERS
SIDERO
UDDERS
WADERS
WEDELN
WIDELY
WIDENS
WIDEST
YODELS

••D•E•
ADDLED
ADDLES
AIDMEN
ANDREA
ANDREI
ANDRES
ANDREW
AUDREY
BADGED
BADGER
BADGES
BADMEN
BEDDED
BEDDER
BIDDEN
BIDDER
BODIED
BODIES
BUDDED
BUDDER
BUDGED
BUDGES
BUDGET
CADGED
CADGER
CADGES
CADRES
CODDER
CODGER
CUDGEL
DADOES
DIDIES
DIDOES
DODDER
DODGED
DODGER
DODGES
DODOES
DUDEEN
DUDLEY
EDDIES
ELDRED
ENDUED
ENDUES
FIDGET
FODDER
FUDGED
FUDGES
GADDED
GADDER
GADGET
HEDGED
HEDGER
HEDGES
HIDDEN
HODDEN
INDEED
INDIES
INDUED
INDUES
JUDAEA
JUDAEO
JUDGED
JUDGER
JUDGES
KEDGED
KEDGES
KIDDED
KIDDER
KIDNEY
LADDER
LADIES
LADLED
LADLER
LADLES
LEDGER
LEDGES
LIDDED
LODGED
LODGER
LODGES
MADDED
MADDEN
MADDER
MADGES
MADMEN
MEDLEY
MIDDEN
MIDGES
MIDGET
MUDDED
MUDDER
NODDED
NODDER
NUDGED
NUDGES
OODLES
PADDED
PADRES
PODDED
REDDEN
REDDER
REDEEM
REDOES
RIDDED
RIDDEN
RIDGED
RIDGES
RODMEN
RODNEY
RUDDER
SADDEN
SADDER
SADIES
SEDGES
SIDLED
SIDLER
SIDLES
SIDNEY
SODDED
SODDEN
SUDDEN
SYDNEY
TEDDED
TEDDER
TIDIED
TIDIER
TIDIES
TODIES
UNDIES
UNDOER
UNDOES
UNDREW
UNDSET
WADDED
WADIES
WADSET
WEDDED
WEDGED
WEDGES

••D••E
ADDUCE
AEDILE
ALDINE
ALDOSE
AUDILE
BODICE
BUDDLE
BUDGIE
CADDIE
CODDLE
CUDDIE
CUDDLE
DADDLE
DEDUCE
DIDDLE
ENDIVE
ENDURE
FIDDLE
FUDDLE
HEDDLE
HUDDLE
HYDRAE
INDENE
INDUCE
IODATE
IODIDE
IODINE
IODIZE
KIDDIE
LADDIE
MADAME
MEDDLE
MEDIAE
MIDDLE
MODULE
MUDDLE
NADINE
NODDLE
NODOSE
NODULE
ORDURE
PADDLE
PEDATE
PEDDLE
PIDDLE
PUDDLE
RADDLE
RADOME
REDDLE
REDEYE
REDONE
REDUCE
RIDDLE
RUDDLE
SADDLE
SEDATE
SEDILE
SEDUCE
TODDLE
UNDINE
UNDONE
UPDATE
VADOSE
WADDLE
WEDGIE
WIDDIE

•••DE•
ABIDED
ABIDER
ABIDES
ABODES
ALUDEL
AMIDES
ANADEM
ANODES
ASIDES
BALDER
BANDED
BARDED
BARDES
BEADED
BEDDED
BEDDER
BENDEE
BENDER
BIDDEN
BIDDER
BINDER
BLADED
BLADES
BOLDER
BONDED
BONDER
BORDEL
BORDER
BRIDES
BUDDED
BUDDER
BURDEN
CAMDEN
CARDED
CARDER
CAUDEX
CHIDED
CHIDER
CHIDES
CINDER
CLYDES
CODDER
COLDER
CORDED
CORDER
CRUDER
CURDED
DANDER
DEADEN
DEEDED
DIADEM
DIODES
DODDER
DRYDEN
DUNDEE

DUODEN
ELIDED
ELIDES
ELUDED
ELUDES
EPODES
ERODED
ERODES
ETUDES
EVADED
EVADER
EVADES
EXUDED
EXUDES
FEEDER
FENDED
FENDER
FEUDED
FINDER
FODDER
FOLDED
FOLDER
FONDER
FORDED
FUNDED
GADDED
GADDER
GANDER
GARDEN
GELDED
GENDER
GEODES
GILDED
GILDER
GIRDED
GIRDER
GLADES
GLEDES
GLIDED
GLIDER
GLIDES
GOADED
GOLDEN
GRADED
GRADER
GRADES
GRIDED
GRIDES
GUIDED
GUIDER
GUIDES
GULDEN
HAMDEN
HANDED
HANDEL
HARDEN
HARDER
HEADED
HEADER
HEEDED
HEEDER
HERDED
HERDER
HIDDEN
HINDER
HODDEN
HOIDEN
HOLDER
HOODED
HORDED
HORDES
HOYDEN
HYADES
IBIDEM
IMIDES
IRIDES
KIDDED
KIDDER
KINDER
LADDER
LANDED
LANDER
LARDED
LARDER
LAUDED
LAUDER
LEADED
LEADEN
LEADER
LENDER
LEUDES
LEWDER
LIDDED
LIEDER
LINDEN
LOADED
LOADER
LORDED
LOUDEN
LOUDER
MADDED
MADDEN
MADDER
MAIDEN
MAUDES
MELDED
MENDED
MENDEL
MENDER
MIDDEN
MILDEN
MILDER
MILDEW
MINDED
MINDER
MOLDED
MOLDER
MUDDED
MUDDER
MURDER
NEEDED
NEEDER
NODDED
NODDER
OXIDES
PADDED
PANDER
PENDED
PODDED
POLDER
PONDER
POWDER
PRIDED
PRIDES
PRUDES
RAIDED
RAIDER
READER
REDDEN
REDDER
REEDED
RENDED
RENDER
RIDDED
RIDDEN
RONDEL
RUDDER
SADDEN
SADDER
SANDED
SANDER
SEEDED
SEEDER
SENDER
SHADED
SHADES
SLIDER
SLIDES
SODDED
SODDEN
SOLDER
SONDER
SPADED
SPADER
SPADES
SPIDER
SUBDEB
SUDDEN
SUEDES
SUNDER
SUNDEW
SWEDEN
SWEDES
SYNDET
TANDEM
TEDDED
TEDDER
TENDED
TENDER
TILDES
TINDER
TRADED
TRADER
TRADES
TSADES
VENDED
VENDEE
VENDER
VOIDED
WADDED
WANDER
WARDED
WARDEN
WARDER
WEDDED
WEEDED
WEEDER
WELDED
WELDER
WENDED
WILDER
WINDED
WINDER
WOADED
WONDER
WOODED
WOODEN
WORDED
YARDED
YONDER
ZUIDER
ZUYDER

•••D•E

BEADLE
BENDEE
BIRDIE
BOODLE
BRIDGE
BRIDIE
BRIDLE
BUDDLE
BUNDLE
BURDIE
CADDIE
CANDLE
CAUDLE
CODDLE
CRADLE
CUDDIE
CUDDLE
CURDLE
DADDLE
DANDLE
DAWDLE
DIDDLE
DOODLE
DREDGE
DRUDGE
DUNDEE
FIDDLE
FLEDGE
FONDLE
FONDUE
FRIDGE
FUDDLE
GIRDLE
GRUDGE
HANDLE
HEDDLE
HUDDLE
HURDLE
KIDDIE
KINDLE
LADDIE
MEDDLE
MIDDLE
MUDDLE
NEEDLE
NODDLE
NOODLE
PADDLE
PEDDLE
PIDDLE
PLEDGE
POODLE
PUDDLE
RADDLE
REDDLE
RIDDLE
RUDDLE
RUNDLE
SADDLE
SLEDGE
SLUDGE
SMUDGE
STODGE
SUBDUE
SUNDAE
TODDLE
TRUDGE
VENDEE
VENDUE
WADDLE
WANDLE
WIDDIE

••••DE

ABRADE
ACCEDE
ACNODE
ALLUDE
ALMUDE
ARCADE
AUBADE
BESIDE
BETIDE
BLENDE
BLONDE
BOLIDE
BORIDE
CLAUDE
DECADE
DECIDE
DECODE
DELUDE
DEMODE
DENUDE
DERIDE
DIVIDE
ENCODE
EXCIDE
FACADE
GOURDE
HALIDE
IMPEDE
INSIDE
INVADE
IODIDE
ISOLDE
OREIDE
OROIDE
PARADE
PESADE
POMADE
RECEDE
REMADE
RESIDE
SECEDE
STRIDE
STRODE
TIRADE
TRIODE
UNLADE
UNMADE
UPSIDE
UREIDE

D•F•••

DAFTLY
DEFACE
DEFAME
DEFEAT
DEFECT
DEFEND
DEFERS
DEFIED
DEFIER
DEFIES
DEFILE
DEFINE
DEFORM
DEFRAY
DEFTER
DEFTLY
DIFFER
DOFFED
DOFFER
DUFFEL
DUFFER
DUFFLE

D••F••

DAYFLY
DEAFEN
DEAFLY
DEIFIC
DIFFER
DOFFED
DOFFER
DRAFFS
DRAFFY
DRAFTS
DRAFTY
DRIFTS
DRIFTY
DUFFEL
DUFFER
DUFFLE

D•••F•

DRAFFS
DRAFFY
DWARFS

•D••F•
ADRIFT

••DF••
GADFLY
REDFIN

••D•F•
CODIFY
MODIFY
NIDIFY

D•G•••
DAGGER
DAGMAR
DAGOBA
DEGAGE
DEGAME
DEGREE
DEGUMS
DEGUST
DIGAMY
DIGEST
DIGGER
DIGITI
DIGITS
DIGLOT
DOGAPE
DOGEAR
DOGGED
DOGGER
DOGGIE
DOGIES
DOGMAS
DUGONG
DUGOUT

D••G••
DAGGER
DANGED
DANGER
DANGLE
DEIGNS
DENGUE
DIGGER
DINGED
DINGEY
DINGHY
DINGLE
DINGUS
DIRGES
DODGED
DODGER
DODGES
DOGGED
DOGGER
DOGGIE
DOUGHS
DOUGHY
DOUGIE
DRAGEE
DRAGON
DREGGY
DUNGED
DWIGHT

D•••G•
DAMAGE
DEBUGS
DEGAGE
DELUGE
DESIGN
DOINGS
DOSAGE
DOTAGE
DREDGE
DREGGY
DRONGO
DRUDGE

D••••G
DANZIG
DARING
DATING
DAZING
DEKING
DIALOG
DICING
DIKING
DINING
DIVING
DOLING
DOMING
DOPING
DORBUG
DOSING
DOTING
DOZING
DRYING
DUGONG
DUOLOG
DUPING
DURING
DYEING

•DG•••
EDGARS
EDGIER
EDGING

•D•G••
ADAGES
ADAGIO

•D•••G
ADDING
EDGING
IDLING

••DG••
BADGED
BADGER
BADGES
BUDGED
BUDGES
BUDGET
BUDGIE
CADGED
CADGER
CADGES
CODGER
CUDGEL
DODGED
DODGER
DODGES
FIDGET
FUDGED
FUDGES
GADGET
HEDGED
HEDGER
HEDGES
JUDGED
JUDGER
JUDGES
KEDGED
KEDGES
LEDGER
LEDGES
LODGED
LODGER
LODGES
MADGES
MIDGES
MIDGET
MIDGUT
NUDGED
NUDGES
PIDGIN
RIDGED
RIDGES
SEDGES
WEDGED
WEDGES
WEDGIE

••D•G•
BODEGA
INDIGO
LADOGA

••D••G
ADDING
AIDING
BEDBUG
BIDING
BODING
CEDING
CODING
ENDING
FADING
HADING
HEDWIG
HIDING
JADING
LADING
LUDWIG
NIDING
REDBUG
REDDOG
RIDING
SIDING
TIDING
WADING

•••DG•
BRIDGE
DREDGE
DRUDGE
FLEDGE
FLEDGY
FRIDGE
GRUDGE
PLEDGE
SLEDGE
SLUDGE
SLUDGY
SMUDGE
SMUDGY
STODGE
STODGY
TRUDGE

•••D•G
FOGDOG
REDDOG
SEADOG
SUNDOG

DH••••
DHARMA
DHARNA
DHOLES
DHOTIS
DHURNA

D•H•••
DAHLIA
DAHOON
DEHORN

D••H••
DACHAS
DACHAU
DAPHNE
DASHED
DASHER
DASHES
DIRHAM
DISHED
DISHES
DITHER
DURHAM

D•••H•
DEATHS
DEATHY
DELPHI
DEPTHS
DINAHS
DINGHY
DOLPHS
DOUCHE
DOUGHS
DOUGHY
DRACHM
DWIGHT

D••••H
DALETH
DANISH
DEARTH
DETACH
DOVISH
DRENCH
DROUTH
DUDISH
DULUTH

•DH•••
ADHERE

•D••H•
EDITHS

•D•••H
ADOLPH

••DH••
REDHOT
SADHUS

••D•H•
BUDDHA
JUDAHS
WIDTHS

••D••H
DUDISH
JADISH
JUDITH
KEDDAH
MODISH
OLDISH
RADISH

•••DH•
BUDDHA
GANDHI
SANDHI
SRADHA

•••D•H
HOWDAH
KEDDAH
PURDAH
WHIDAH
WHYDAH

DI••••
DIADEM
DIALED
DIALER
DIALOG
DIANAS
DIANES
DIAPER
DIATOM
DIAZIN
DIBBED
DIBBER
DIBBLE
DICAST
DICERS
DICING
DICKER
DICKEY
DICKIE
DICTUM
DIDDLE
DIDIES
DIDOES
DIEPPE
DIESEL
DIESES
DIESIS
DIETED
DIETER
DIFFER
DIGAMY
DIGEST
DIGGER
DIGITI
DIGITS
DIGLOT
DIKDIK
DIKING
DILATE
DILUTE
DIMERS
DIMITY
DIMMED
DIMMER
DIMOUT
DIMPLE
DIMPLY
DIMWIT
DINAHS
DINARS
DINERO
DINERS
DINGED
DINGEY
DINGHY
DINGLE
DINGUS
DINING
DINKEY
DINNED
DINNER
DINTED
DIOBOL
DIODES
DIPLEX
DIPLOE
DIPODY
DIPOLE
DIPPED
DIPPER
DIPSAS
DIRECT
DIRELY
DIREST
DIRGES

DIRHAM
DIRKED
DIRNDL
DISARM
DISBAR
DISCUS
DISHED
DISHES
DISMAL
DISMAY
DISNEY
DISOWN
DISPEL
DISTAL
DISTIL
DISUSE
DITHER
DITTOS
DIVANS
DIVERS
DIVERT
DIVEST
DIVIDE
DIVINE
DIVING
DIVOTS
DIWANS
DIXITS
DIZENS

D•I•••

DAIMIO
DAIMON
DAIMYO
DAINTY
DAISES
DAISYS
DEICED
DEICER
DEICES
DEIFIC
DEIGNS
DEISTS
DMITRI
DOINGS
DRIERS
DRIEST
DRIFTS
DRIFTY
DRILLS
DRINKS
DRIPPY
DRIVEL
DRIVEN
DRIVER
DRIVES
DUIKER
DWIGHT

D••I••

DANIEL
DANISH
DANITE
DARICS
DARIEN
DARING
DARIUS
DATING
DATIVE
DAVIDS
DAVIES
DAVITS
DAZING
DEBITS
DECIDE
DECILE
DEFIED
DEFIER
DEFIES
DEFILE
DEFINE
DEKING
DELIAN
DELIAS
DELICT
DELIUS
DEMIES
DEMISE
DEMITS
DENIAL
DENIED
DENIER
DENIES
DENIMS
DENISE
DEPICT
DERIDE
DERIVE
DESIGN
DESIRE
DESIST
DEVICE
DEVILS
DEVISE
DEWIER
DEWITT
DICING
DIDIES
DIGITI
DIGITS
DIKING
DIMITY
DINING
DIVIDE
DIVINE
DIVING
DIXITS
DOBIES
DOCILE
DOGIES
DOLING
DOMING
DOMINO
DOPIER
DOPING
DORIAN
DORIES
DOSING
DOTIER
DOTING
DOVISH
DOXIES
DOZIER
DOZILY
DOZING
DRAINS
DROITS
DRUIDS
DRYING
DUDISH
DUPING
DURIAN
DURING
DURION
DUTIES
DYEING

D•••I•

DACOIT
DAHLIA
DAIMIO
DAKOIT
DANAID
DANZIG
DARWIN
DEARIE
DEBRIS
DECEIT
DEIFIC
DENNIS
DENTIL
DENTIN
DERAIL
DERAIN
DERMIC
DERRIS
DESMID
DETAIL
DETAIN
DEVEIN
DEVOID
DEVOIR
DHOTIS
DIAZIN
DICKIE
DIESIS
DIKDIK
DIMWIT
DISTIL
DOBBIN
DOGGIE
DOLLIE
DOMAIN
DONNIE
DOOLIE
DORMIE
DOSSIL
DOUGIE
DUBBIN
DUBLIN
DULCIE
DUNLIN
DYADIC

D••••I

DELPHI
DENDRI
DIGITI
DMITRI

•DI•••

ADIEUS
ADIEUX
ADIPIC
EDIBLE
EDICTS
EDILES
EDISON
EDITED
EDITHS
EDITOR
IDIOCY
IDIOMS
IDIOTS
ODIOUS

•D•I••

ADDICT
ADDING
ADLIBS
ADMIRE
ADMITS
ADMIXT
ADRIAN
ADRIEN
ADRIFT
ADVICE
ADVISE
EDDIES
EDGIER
EDGING
EDWINA
EDWINS
IDLING
ODDITY

•D••I•

ADAGIO
ADENIS
ADIPIC
ADJOIN
ADONIC
ADONIS
ADROIT
EDDAIC
GDYNIA
ODYNIA

•D•••I

ADONAI

••DI••

ADDICT
ADDING
AEDILE
AIDING
ALDINE
AUDILE
AUDITS
BEDIMS
BIDING
BODICE
BODIED
BODIES
BODILY
BODING
CEDING
CODIFY
CODING
DIDIES
DUDISH
EDDIES
ENDING
ENDIVE
FADING
GODIVA
HADING
HIDING
INDIAN
INDICT
INDIES
INDIGO
INDIUM
IODIDE
IODINE
IODISM
IODIZE
JADING
JADISH
JUDITH
KODIAK
LADIES
LADING
LADINO
LYDIAS
MEDIAE
MEDIAL
MEDIAN
MEDICO
MEDICS
MEDIUM
MODIFY
MODISH
NADINE
NADIRS
NIDIFY
NIDING
NUDISM
NUDIST
NUDITY
ODDITY
OLDISH
PODIUM
RADIAL
RADIAN
RADIOS
RADISH
RADIUM
RADIUS
RIDING
SADIES
SADISM
SADIST
SEDILE
SIDING
SODIUM
TEDIUM
TIDIED
TIDIER
TIDIES
TIDILY
TIDING
TODIES
UNDIES
UNDINE
WADIES
WADING
ZODIAC

••D•I•

BEDRID
BEDUIN
BODKIN
BUDGIE
CADDIE
CADDIS
CEDRIC
CODEIA
CODEIN
CUDDIE
EDDAIC
FADEIN
GADOID
GODWIN
GODWIT
HEDWIG
HYDRIC
INDRIS
JUDAIC
KIDDIE
LADDIE
LUDWIG
MADRID
MIDAIR
MIDRIB
NUDNIK
ORDAIN
PIDGIN
REDFIN
TIDBIT
VEDAIC
WEDGIE
WIDDIE

••D••I

ANDREI
PEDATI

•••DI•

ACADIA
ACEDIA
ACIDIC
AMIDIC
AMIDIN

ANODIC
AVIDIN
BANDIT
BARDIC
BIRDIE
BRIDIE
BURDIE
CADDIE
CADDIS
CANDID
CARDIO
CREDIT
CUDDIE
DIKDIK
DYADIC
GEODIC
GRADIN
HERDIC
IRIDIC
KIDDIE
LADDIE
LEADIN
MISDID
NORDIC
OUTDID
PUNDIT
RHODIC
SORDID
SPADIX
STADIA
STUDIO
SYNDIC
VERDIN
WIDDIE

•••D•I
DENDRI
GANDHI
QUADRI
SANDHI

••••DI
SOLIDI
TULADI

D•J•••
DEJECT

D••J••
DONJON

•DJ•••
ADJOIN
ADJURE
ADJUST

D•K•••
DAKOIT
DAKOTA
DEKARE
DEKING
DIKDIK
DIKING

D••K••
DANKER
DANKLY
DARKEN
DARKER
DARKLE
DARKLY
DECKED
DECKEL
DECKER
DECKLE
DICKER
DICKEY
DICKIE
DINKEY
DIRKED
DOCKED
DOCKER
DOCKET
DONKEY
DRAKES
DUCKED
DUCKER
DUIKER
DUNKED
DUNKER
DUSKED

D•••K•
DEREKS
DRINKS
DROSKY
DRUNKS

D••••K
DAMASK
DEBARK
DEBUNK
DIKDIK
DVORAK
DYBBUK

••DK••
BODKIN
VODKAS

••D•K•
KODAKS

••D••K
BEDECK
KODIAK
NUDNIK
PODUNK

•••D•K
DIKDIK
MARDUK

D•L•••
DALETH
DALLAS
DALLES
DALTON
DELAYS
DELETE
DELIAN
DELIAS
DELICT
DELIUS
DELLAS
DELPHI
DELTAS
DELUDE
DELUGE
DELUXE
DELVED
DELVER
DELVES
DILATE
DILUTE
DOLING
DOLLAR
DOLLED
DOLLIE
DOLLOP
DOLLYS
DOLMAN
DOLMEN
DOLPHS
DULCET
DULCIE
DULLED
DULLER
DULUTH

D••L••
DAHLIA
DALLAS
DALLES
DEALER
DELLAS
DEPLOY
DEWLAP
DHOLES
DIALED
DIALER
DIALOG
DIGLOT
DIPLEX
DIPLOE
DOALLS
DOBLAS
DOBLON
DOLLAR
DOLLED
DOLLIE
DOLLOP
DOLLYS
DOOLEE
DOOLIE
DOYLEY
DRILLS
DROLLS
DROLLY
DUBLIN
DUDLEY
DUELED
DUELER
DUELLO
DULLED
DULLER
DUNLIN
DUOLOG
DUPLEX
DWELLS

D•••L•
DABBLE
DADDLE
DAFTLY
DAMPLY
DANDLE
DANGLE
DANKLY
DAPPLE
DARKLE
DARKLY
DARTLE
DAWDLE
DAYFLY
DAZZLE
DEADLY
DEAFLY
DEARLY
DECALS
DECILE
DECKLE
DEEPLY
DEFILE
DEFTLY
DESALT
DEVILS
DIBBLE
DIDDLE
DIMPLE
DIMPLY
DINGLE
DIPOLE
DIRELY
DOABLE
DOALLS
DOCILE
DONALD
DOODLE
DOTTLE
DOUBLE
DOUBLY
DOURLY
DOWELS
DOZILY
DRABLY
DRAWLS
DRAWLY
DRILLS
DROLLS
DROLLY
DROOLS
DUELLO
DUFFLE
DUMBLY
DWELLS

D••••L
DACTYL
DAEDAL
DAMSEL
DANIEL
DARNEL
DECKEL
DENIAL
DENTAL
DENTIL
DERAIL
DERMAL
DETAIL
DIESEL
DIOBOL
DIRNDL
DISMAL
DISPEL
DISTAL
DISTIL
DORSAL
DOSSAL
DOSSEL
DOSSIL
DOTTEL
DRIVEL
DUFFEL

•DL•••
ADLIBS
IDLERS
IDLEST
IDLING

•D•L••
ADDLED
ADDLES
ADOLPH
ADULTS
EDILES
IDYLLS

•D••L•
EDIBLE
IDEALS
IDYLLS

••DL••
ADDLED
ADDLES
BEDLAM
DUDLEY
LADLED
LADLER
LADLES
MEDLAR
MEDLEY
OODLES
SIDLED
SIDLER
SIDLES

••D•L•
AEDILE
AUDILE
BODILY
BUDDLE
CEDULA
CODDLE
CUDDLE
CUDDLY
DADDLE
DIDDLE
EIDOLA
ENDALL
FIDDLE
FUDDLE
GADFLY
HEDDLE
HUDDLE
INDULT
MEDALS
MEDDLE
MIDDLE
MODELS
MODULE
MUDDLE
NODDLE
NODULE
NUDELY
PADDLE
PEDALS
PEDDLE
PIDDLE
PUDDLE
PUDDLY
RADDLE
RADULA
REDDLE
RIDDLE
RUDDLE
RUDELY
SADDLE
SEDILE
TIDILY
TODDLE
UNDULY
WADDLE
WADDLY
WEDELN
WIDELY
YODELS

••D••L
CUDGEL
ENDALL
HEDRAL
MEDIAL
ORDEAL
PODSOL
PODZOL
RADIAL

•••DL•
ACIDLY
AGEDLY
ARIDLY
AVIDLY

6

BALDLY
BEADLE
BOLDLY
BOODLE
BRIDLE
BUDDLE
BUNDLE
CANDLE
CAUDLE
CODDLE
COLDLY
CRADLE
CUDDLE
CUDDLY
CURDLE
DADDLE
DANDLE
DAWDLE
DEADLY
DIDDLE
DOODLE
FIDDLE
FONDLE
FONDLY
FUDDLE
GIRDLE
GLADLY
GOODLY
HANDLE
HARDLY
HEDDLE
HUDDLE
HURDLE
KINDLE
KINDLY
LEWDLY
LORDLY
LOUDLY
MEDDLE
MIDDLE
MILDLY
MUDDLE
NEEDLE
NODDLE
NOODLE
PADDLE
PEDDLE
PIDDLE
POODLE
PUDDLE
PUDDLY
RADDLE
REDDLE
RIDDLE
RUDDLE
RUNDLE
SADDLE
TODDLE
WADDLE
WADDLY
WANDLE
WILDLY

•••D•L
ALUDEL
AMIDOL
APODAL
BORDEL
BRIDAL
CAUDAL
DAEDAL
FEUDAL
HANDEL
MENDEL
RANDAL
RONDEL
SANDAL
SENDAL
VANDAL

••••DL
DIRNDL

DM••••
DMITRI

D•M•••
DAMAGE
DAMANS
DAMASK
DAMMAR
DAMMED
DAMMER
DAMNED
DAMPED
DAMPEN
DAMPER
DAMPLY
DAMSEL
DAMSON
DEMAND
DEMEAN
DEMIES
DEMISE
DEMITS
DEMOBS
DEMODE
DEMONO
DEMONS
DEMOTE
DEMURE
DEMURS
DIMERS
DIMITY
DIMMED
DIMMER
DIMOUT
DIMPLE
DIMPLY
DIMWIT
DOMAIN
DOMING
DOMINO
DUMBLY
DUMPED

D••M••
DAEMON
DAGMAR
DAIMIO
DAIMON
DAIMYO
DAMMAR
DAMMED
DAMMER
DEEMED
DERMAL
DERMAS
DERMAT
DERMIC
DESMAN
DESMID
DIMMED
DIMMER
DISMAL
DISMAY
DOGMAS
DOLMAN
DOLMEN
DOOMED
DORMER
DORMIE
DRAMAS
DROMON

D•••M•
DECAMP
DEFAME
DEGAME
DEGUMS
DENIMS
DHARMA
DIGAMY
DREAMS
DREAMT
DREAMY
DYNAMO

D••••M
DEFORM
DIADEM
DIATOM
DICTUM
DIRHAM
DISARM
DORSUM
DRACHM
DURHAM

•DM•••
ADMIRE
ADMITS
ADMIXT
EDMOND
EDMUND

•D••M•
ADDAMS
ADEEMS
IDIOMS

•D•••M
ADYTUM

••DM••
AIDMAN
AIDMEN
BADMAN
BADMEN
CADMUS
MADMAN
MADMEN
RODMAN
RODMEN

••D•M•
ADDAMS
BEDIMS
MADAME
MADAMS
RADOME
SEDUMS
SODOMY

••D••M
BEDLAM
INDIUM
IODISM
MEDIUM
NUDISM
PODIUM
RADIUM
REDEEM
SADISM
SODIUM
TEDIUM

•••D•M
ANADEM
BELDAM
CONDOM
DIADEM
IBIDEM
RANDOM
SELDOM
TANDEM
WISDOM

D•N•••
DANAID
DANAUS
DANCED
DANCER
DANCES
DANDER
DANDLE
DANGED
DANGER
DANGLE
DANIEL
DANISH
DANITE
DANKER
DANKLY
DANNYS
DANTON
DANUBE
DANZIG
DENARY
DENDRI
DENDRO
DENGUE
DENIAL
DENIED
DENIER
DENIES
DENIMS
DENISE
DENNED
DENNIS
DENNYS
DENOTE
DENSER
DENTAL
DENTED
DENTIL
DENTIN
DENUDE
DENVER
DINAHS
DINARS
DINERO
DINERS
DINGED
DINGEY
DINGHY
DINGLE
DINGUS
DINING
DINKEY
DINNED
DINNER
DINTED
DONALD
DONATE
DONEES
DONETS
DONJON
DONKEY
DONNAS
DONNED
DONNIE
DONORS
DUNBAR
DUNCAN
DUNCES
DUNDEE
DUNGED
DUNKED
DUNKER
DUNLIN
DUNNED
DYNAMO
DYNAST

D••N••
DAINTY
DAMNED
DANNYS
DARNED
DARNEL
DAUNTS
DAWNED
DENNED
DENNIS
DENNYS
DIANAS
DIANES
DINNED
DINNER
DIRNDL
DISNEY
DOINGS
DONNAS
DONNED
DONNIE
DOWNED
DRENCH
DRINKS
DRONED
DRONES
DRONGO
DRUNKS
DUENNA
DUNNED

D•••N•
DAMANS
DAPHNE
DARING
DATING
DAZING
DEBUNK
DECANE
DECANT
DECENT
DEDANS
DEFEND
DEFINE
DEIGNS
DEKING
DEMAND
DEMONO
DEMONS
DEPEND
DETENT
DEWANS
DHARNA
DHURNA
DICING
DIKING
DINING
DIVANS
DIVINE
DIVING
DIWANS
DIZENS
DOCENT
DOESNT
DOLING
DOMING
DOMINO
DOPING

DOSING
DOTING
DOYENS
DOZENS
DOZING
DRAINS
DROWNS
DRYING
DUENNA
DUGONG
DUPING
DURING
DYEING

D••••N
DACRON
DAEMON
DAHOON
DAIMON
DALTON
DAMPEN
DAMSON
DANTON
DARDAN
DARIEN
DARKEN
DARWIN
DAWSON
DAYTON
DEACON
DEADEN
DEAFEN
DECCAN
DECERN
DEEPEN
DEEWAN
DEHORN
DELIAN
DEMEAN
DENTIN
DERAIN
DESIGN
DESMAN
DETAIN
DEVEIN
DIAZIN
DISOWN
DOBBIN
DOBLON
DOBSON
DOLMAN
DOLMEN
DOMAIN
DONJON
DOREEN
DORIAN
DRAGON
DRIVEN
DROMON
DRYDEN
DUBBIN
DUBLIN
DUDEEN
DUNCAN
DUNLIN
DUODEN
DURBAN
DURIAN
DURION

•DN•••
ADNATE
ADNOUN

•D•N••
ADENIS
ADONAI
ADONIC
ADONIS
GDYNIA
ODONTO
ODYNIA

•D••N•
ADDEND
ADDING
ADORNS
ADVENT
EDGING
EDMOND
EDMUND
EDWINA
EDWINS
IDLING

•D•••N
ADJOIN
ADNOUN
ADRIAN
ADRIEN
EDISON

••DN••
KIDNAP
KIDNEY
NUDNIK
RODNEY
SIDNEY
SYDNEY

••D•N•
ADDEND
ADDING
AIDING
ALDINE
ARDENT
BIDING
BODING
CADENT
CEDING
CODING
DEDANS
ENDING
FADING
HADING
HIDING
INDENE
INDENT
IODINE
JADING
LADING
LADINO
NADINE
NIDING
PEDANT
PODUNK
REDANS
REDONE
RIDENT
RIDING
RODENT
SEDANS
SIDING
TIDING
UNDINE
UNDONE
WADING
WIDENS

••D••N
AIDMAN
AIDMEN
ANDEAN
BADMAN
BADMEN
BEDPAN
BEDUIN
BIDDEN
BODKIN
CODEIN
DUDEEN
FADEIN
GIDEON
GODSON
GODWIN
HEDRON
HIDDEN
HODDEN
HUDSON
INDIAN
JUDEAN
KEDRON
MADDEN
MADMAN
MADMEN
MEDIAN
MIDDEN
MODERN
ORDAIN
PIDGIN
RADIAN
REDDEN
REDFIN
RIDDEN
RODMAN
RODMEN
SADDEN
SODDEN
SUDDEN
WEDELN

•••D•N
AMIDIN
AVIDIN
BIDDEN
BURDEN
CAMDEN
CORDON
DARDAN
DEADEN
DRYDEN
DUODEN
GARDEN
GOLDEN
GORDON
GRADIN
GUIDON
GULDEN
HAGDON
HAMDEN
HARDEN
HEADON
HIDDEN
HODDEN
HOIDEN
HOYDEN
JORDAN
LARDON
LEADEN
LEADIN
LINDEN
LONDON
LOUDEN
MADDEN
MAIDEN
MANDAN
MIDDEN
MILDEN
PARDON
RANDAN
REDDEN
RIDDEN
SADDEN
SODDEN
SUDDEN
SWEDEN
TENDON
VERDIN
VERDUN
WARDEN
WOODEN

DO••••
DOABLE
DOALLS
DOBBER
DOBBIN
DOBIES
DOBLAS
DOBLON
DOBRAS
DOBSON
DOCENT
DOCILE
DOCKED
DOCKER
DOCKET
DOCTOR
DODDER
DODECA
DODGED
DODGER
DODGES
DODOES
DOESNT
DOFFED
DOFFER
DOGAPE
DOGEAR
DOGGED
DOGGER
DOGGIE
DOGIES
DOGMAS
DOINGS
DOLING
DOLLAR
DOLLED
DOLLIE
DOLLOP
DOLLYS
DOLMAN
DOLMEN
DOLPHS
DOMAIN
DOMING
DOMINO
DONALD
DONATE
DONEES
DONETS
DONJON
DONKEY
DONNAS
DONNED
DONNIE
DONORS
DOODAD
DOODLE
DOOLEE
DOOLIE
DOOMED
DOPIER
DOPING
DORADO
DORBUG
DOREEN
DORIAN
DORIES
DORMER
DORMIE
DORSAD
DORSAL
DORSUM
DOSAGE
DOSERS
DOSING
DOSSAL
DOSSEL
DOSSER
DOSSIL
DOTAGE
DOTERS
DOTIER
DOTING
DOTTED
DOTTEL
DOTTER
DOTTLE
DOUBLE
DOUBLY
DOUBTS
DOUCHE
DOUGHS
DOUGHY
DOUGIE
DOURLY
DOUSED
DOUSES
DOVISH
DOWELS
DOWERS
DOWERY
DOWNED
DOWSED
DOWSER
DOWSES
DOXIES
DOYENS
DOYLEY
DOZENS
DOZIER
DOZILY
DOZING

D•O•••
DEODAR
DHOLES
DHOTIS
DIOBOL
DIODES
DOODAD
DOODLE
DOOLEE
DOOLIE
DOOMED
DROITS
DROLLS
DROLLY
DROMON
DRONED
DRONES
DRONGO
DROOLS
DROOPS
DROOPY
DROPSY
DROSKY
DROSSY
DROUTH
DROVED
DROVER
DROVES

DROWNS
DROWSE
DROWSY
DUODEN
DUOLOG
DVORAK

D••O••
DACOIT
DADOES
DAGOBA
DAHOON
DAKOIT
DAKOTA
DECOCT
DECODE
DECORS
DECOYS
DEFORM
DEHORN
DEMOBS
DEMODE
DEMONO
DEMONS
DEMOTE
DENOTE
DEPORT
DEPOSE
DEPOTS
DESOXY
DETOUR
DEVOID
DEVOIR
DEVOTE
DEVOUR
DEVOUT
DIDOES
DIMOUT
DIPODY
DIPOLE
DISOWN
DIVOTS
DODOES
DONORS
DROOLS
DROOPS
DROOPY
DUGONG
DUGOUT

D•••O•
DACRON
DAEMON
DAHOON
DAIMON
DALTON
DAMSON
DANTON
DARROW
DATTOS
DAWSON
DAYTON
DEACON
DEBTOR

DEPLOY
DESPOT
DIALOG
DIATOM
DIGLOT
DIOBOL
DIPLOE
DITTOS
DOBLON
DOBSON
DOCTOR
DOLLOP
DONJON
DRAGON
DROMON
DUOLOG
DURION

D••••O
DAIMIO
DAIMYO
DEMONO
DENDRO
DEXTRO
DINERO
DOMINO
DORADO
DRONGO
DUELLO
DYNAMO

•DO•••
ADOBES
ADOLPH
ADONAI
ADONIC
ADONIS
ADOPTS
ADORED
ADORER
ADORES
ADORNS
ODONTO

•D•O••
ADJOIN
ADNOUN
ADROIT
ADSORB
EDMOND
IDIOCY
IDIOMS
IDIOTS
ODIOUS

•D••O•
EDISON
EDITOR

•D•••O
ADAGIO
ODONTO

••DO••
ALDOSE
ALDOUS
ARDORS
DADOES
DIDOES
DODOES
EIDOLA
ENDOWS
EUDORA
FEDORA
GADOID
INDOOR
INDOWS
IODOUS
LADOGA
NODOSE
OGDOAD
PODOUS
RADOME
REDOES
REDONE
REDOWA
SODOMY
UNDOER
UNDOES
UNDONE
VADOSE
WIDOWS

••D•O•
GIDEON
GODSON
HEDRON
HUDSON
HYDROS
INDOOR
KEDRON
PEDROS
PODSOL
PODZOL
RADIOS
REDDOG
REDHOT
REDTOP
RODEOS

••D••O
INDIGO
JUDAEO
LADINO
MADURO
MEDICO
SIDERO

•••DO•
ABYDOS
AMADOU
AMIDOL
CANDOR
CONDOM
CONDOR
CORDON
CREDOS

FEODOR
FOGDOG
GORDON
GUIDON
HAGDON
HEADON
HOODOO
ISADOR
ISIDOR
KOODOO
LARDON
LONDON
MEADOW
PARDON
RANDOM
REDDOG
RONDOS
SEADOG
SELDOM
SHADOW
SUNDOG
TENDON
VENDOR
VOODOO
WALDOS
WINDOW
WISDOM

•••D•O
CARDIO
DENDRO
HOODOO
KOODOO
STUDIO
VOODOO

••••DO
ALBEDO
COMEDO
DORADO
ESCUDO
HAIRDO
LAREDO
LEPIDO
LIBIDO
MIKADO
OVERDO
PSEUDO
TEREDO
TOLEDO
TUXEDO

D•P•••
DAPHNE
DAPPED
DAPPER
DAPPLE
DEPART
DEPEND
DEPICT
DEPLOY
DEPORT
DEPOSE
DEPOTS

DEPTHS
DEPUTE
DEPUTY
DIPLEX
DIPLOE
DIPODY
DIPOLE
DIPPED
DIPPER
DIPSAS
DOPIER
DOPING
DUPERS
DUPERY
DUPING
DUPLEX

D••P••
DAMPED
DAMPEN
DAMPER
DAMPLY
DAPPED
DAPPER
DAPPLE
DEEPEN
DEEPER
DEEPLY
DELPHI
DESPOT
DIAPER
DIEPPE
DIMPLE
DIMPLY
DIPPED
DIPPER
DISPEL
DOLPHS
DRAPED
DRAPER
DRAPES
DRIPPY
DROPSY
DRUPES
DUMPED

D•••P•
DIEPPE
DOGAPE
DRIPPY
DROOPS
DROOPY

D••••P
DECAMP
DEWLAP
DOLLOP

•D•P••
ADAPTS
ADEPTS
ADIPIC
ADOPTS

•D••P•
ADOLPH

••DP••
BEDPAN

••D••P
KIDNAP
MADCAP
MADEUP
MUDCAP
REDCAP
REDTOP

•••D•P
HOLDUP

DR••••
DRABLY
DRACHM
DRAFFS
DRAFFY
DRAFTS
DRAFTY
DRAGEE
DRAGON
DRAINS
DRAKES
DRAMAS
DRAPED
DRAPER
DRAPES
DRAWEE
DRAWER
DRAWLS
DRAWLY
DRAYED
DREADS
DREAMS
DREAMT
DREAMY
DREARY
DREDGE
DREGGY
DRENCH
DRESSY
DRIERS
DRIEST
DRIFTS
DRIFTY
DRILLS
DRINKS
DRIPPY
DRIVEL
DRIVEN
DRIVER
DRIVES
DROITS
DROLLS
DROLLY
DROMON
DRONED
DRONES
DRONGO

6

DROOLS
DROOPS
DROOPY
DROPSY
DROSKY
DROSSY
DROUTH
DROVED
DROVER
DROVES
DROWNS
DROWSE
DROWSY
DRUDGE
DRUIDS
DRUNKS
DRUPES
DRUSES
DRYADS
DRYDEN
DRYERS
DRYEST
DRYING

D•R•••
DARDAN
DARERS
DARICS
DARIEN
DARING
DARIUS
DARKEN
DARKER
DARKLE
DARKLY
DARNED
DARNEL
DARROW
DARTED
DARTER
DARTLE
DARWIN
DERAIL
DERAIN
DEREKS
DERIDE
DERIVE
DERMAL
DERMAS
DERMAT
DERMIC
DERRIS
DIRECT
DIRELY
DIREST
DIRGES
DIRHAM
DIRKED
DIRNDL
DORADO
DORBUG
DOREEN
DORIAN
DORIES
DORMER
DORMIE
DORSAD
DORSAL
DORSUM
DURBAN
DURBAR
DURESS
DURHAM
DURIAN
DURING
DURION

D••R••
DACRON
DARROW
DEARER
DEARIE
DEARLY
DEARTH
DEBRIS
DECREE
DEFRAY
DEGREE
DERRIS
DHARMA
DHARNA
DHURNA
DOBRAS
DOURLY
DVORAK
DWARFS

D•••R•
DARERS
DATARY
DATERS
DATURA
DAUBRY
DEBARK
DEBARS
DECARE
DECERN
DECORS
DECURY
DEFERS
DEFORM
DEHORN
DEKARE
DEMURE
DEMURS
DENARY
DENDRI
DENDRO
DEPART
DEPORT
DESCRY
DESERT
DESIRE
DETERS
DEXTRO
DICERS
DIMERS
DINARS
DINERO
DINERS
DISARM
DIVERS
DIVERT
DMITRI
DONORS
DOSERS
DOTERS
DOWERS
DOWERY
DREARY
DRIERS
DRYERS
DUPERS
DUPERY

D••••R
DABBER
DAGGER
DAGMAR
DAMMAR
DAMMER
DAMPER
DANCER
DANDER
DANGER
DANKER
DAPPER
DARKER
DARTER
DASHER
DAUBER
DEALER
DEARER
DEBTOR
DECKER
DEEPER
DEFIER
DEFTER
DEICER
DELVER
DENIER
DENSER
DENVER
DEODAR
DETOUR
DEVOIR
DEVOUR
DEWIER
DEXTER
DIALER
DIAPER
DIBBER
DICKER
DIETER
DIFFER
DIGGER
DIMMER
DINNER
DIPPER
DISBAR
DITHER
DOBBER
DOCKER
DOCTOR
DODDER
DODGER
DOFFER
DOGEAR
DOGGER
DOLLAR
DOPIER
DORMER
DOSSER
DOTIER
DOTTER
DOWSER
DOZIER
DRAPER
DRAWER
DRIVER
DROVER
DUCKER
DUELER
DUFFER
DUIKER
DULLER
DUNBAR
DUNKER
DURBAR
DUSTER

•DR•••
ADRIAN
ADRIEN
ADRIFT
ADROIT

•D•R••
ADORED
ADORER
ADORES
ADORNS

•D••R•
ADDERS
ADHERE
ADJURE
ADMIRE
ADSORB
ADVERB
ADVERT
EDGARS
EDUARD
EDWARD
IDLERS
UDDERS

•D•••R
ADORER
EDGIER
EDITOR

••DR••
ANDREA
ANDREI
ANDRES
ANDREW
AUDREY
BEDRID
CADRES
CEDRIC
ELDRED
HEDRAL
HEDRON
HYDRAE
HYDRAS
HYDRIC
HYDROS
INDRIS
KEDRON
MADRAS
MADRID
MIDRIB
PADRES
PEDROS
UNDRAW
UNDREW

••D•R•
ADDERS
AIDERS
ALDERS
ARDORS
CEDARS
CIDERS
ELDERS
ENDURE
EUDORA
FEDORA
HIDERS
MADURA
MADURO
MODERN
NADIRS
ORDERS
ORDURE
RADARS
RIDERS
SEDERS
SIDERO
SUDARY
UDDERS
WADERS

••D••R
BADGER
BEDDER
BIDDER
BUDDER
CADGER
CODDER
CODGER
DODDER
DODGER
ENDEAR
FODDER
GADDER
HEDGER
INDOOR
JUDGER
KIDDER
LADDER
LADLER
LEDGER
LODGER
MADDER
MEDLAR
MIDAIR
MUDDER
NODDER
REDDER
RUDDER
SADDER
SIDDUR
SIDLER
TEDDER
TIDIER
UNDOER

•••DR•
AIRDRY
BAWDRY
DENDRI
DENDRO
EXEDRA
QUADRI
SANDRA
SUNDRY
TAWDRY
TUNDRA

•••D•R
ABIDER
BALDER
BEDDER
BENDER
BIDDER
BINDER
BOLDER
BONDER
BORDER
BUDDER
CANDOR
CARDER
CHIDER
CINDER
CODDER
COLDER
CONDOR
CORDER
CRUDER
DANDER
DEODAR
DODDER
EVADER
FEEDER
FENDER
FEODOR
FINDER
FODDER
FOLDER
FONDER
GADDER
GANDER

GENDER
GILDER
GIRDER
GLIDER
GRADER
GUIDER
HARDER
HEADER
HEEDER
HERDER
HINDER
HOLDER
ISADOR
ISIDOR
KIDDER
KINDER
LADDER
LANDER
LARDER
LAUDER
LEADER
LENDER
LEWDER
LIEDER
LOADER
LOUDER
MADDER
MENDER
MILDER
MINDER
MOLDER
MUDDER
MURDER
NEEDER
NODDER
PANDER
PINDAR
POLDER
PONDER
POWDER
RAIDER
READER
REDDER
RENDER
RUDDER
SADDER
SANDER
SEEDER
SENDER
SIDDUR
SIRDAR
SLIDER
SOLDER
SONDER
SPADER
SPIDER
SUNDER
TEDDER
TENDER
TINDER
TRADER
VEADAR
VENDER
VENDOR
WANDER
WARDER
WEEDER
WELDER
WILDER
WINDER
WONDER
YONDER
ZUIDER
ZUYDER

••••DR
CHONDR

D•S•••
DASHED
DASHER
DASHES
DESALT
DESCRY
DESERT
DESIGN
DESIRE
DESIST
DESMAN
DESMID
DESOXY
DESPOT
DESSAU
DISARM
DISBAR
DISCUS
DISHED
DISHES
DISMAL
DISMAY
DISNEY
DISOWN
DISPEL
DISTAL
DISTIL
DISUSE
DOSAGE
DOSERS
DOSING
DOSSAL
DOSSEL
DOSSER
DOSSIL
DUSKED
DUSTED
DUSTER

D••S••
DAISES
DAISYS
DAMSEL
DAMSON
DAWSON
DEISTS
DENSER
DESSAU
DIESEL
DIESES
DIESIS
DIPSAS
DOBSON
DOESNT
DORSAD
DORSAL
DORSUM
DOSSAL
DOSSEL
DOSSER
DOSSIL
DOUSED
DOUSES
DOWSED
DOWSER
DOWSES
DRESSY
DROSKY
DROSSY
DRUSES

D•••S•
DAMASK
DANISH
DEBASE
DEGUST
DEMISE
DENISE
DEPOSE
DESIST
DETEST
DEVEST
DEVISE
DICAST
DIGEST
DIREST
DISUSE
DIVEST
DOVISH
DRESSY
DRIEST
DROPSY
DROSSY
DROWSE
DROWSY
DRYEST
DUDISH
DURESS
DYNAST

D••••S
DACHAS
DADOES
DAISES
DAISYS
DALLAS
DALLES
DAMANS
DANAUS
DANCES
DANNYS
DARERS
DARICS
DARIUS
DASHES
DATERS
DATTOS
DAUNTS
DAVEYS
DAVIDS
DAVIES
DAVITS
DEATHS
DEBARS
DEBBYS
DEBITS
DEBRIS
DEBUGS
DEBUTS
DECALS
DECAYS
DECORS
DECOYS
DEDANS
DEFERS
DEFIES
DEGUMS
DEICES
DEIGNS
DEISTS
DELAYS
DELIAS
DELIUS
DELLAS
DELTAS
DELVES
DEMIES
DEMITS
DEMOBS
DEMONS
DEMURS
DENIES
DENIMS
DENNIS
DENNYS
DEPOTS
DEPTHS
DEREKS
DERMAS
DERRIS
DETERS
DEUCES
DEVILS
DEWANS
DHOLES
DHOTIS
DIANAS
DIANES
DICERS
DIDIES
DIDOES
DIESES
DIESIS
DIGITS
DIMERS
DINAHS
DINARS
DINERS
DINGUS
DIODES
DIPSAS
DIRGES
DISCUS
DISHES
DITTOS
DIVANS
DIVERS
DIVOTS
DIWANS
DIXITS
DIZENS
DOALLS
DOBIES
DOBLAS
DOBRAS
DODGES
DODOES
DOGIES
DOGMAS
DOINGS
DOLLYS
DOLPHS
DONEES
DONETS
DONNAS
DONORS
DORIES
DOSERS
DOTERS
DOUBTS
DOUGHS
DOUSES
DOWELS
DOWERS
DOWSES
DOXIES
DOYENS
DOZENS
DRAFFS
DRAFTS
DRAINS
DRAKES
DRAMAS
DRAPES
DRAWLS
DREADS
DREAMS
DRIERS
DRIFTS
DRILLS
DRINKS
DRIVES
DROITS
DROLLS
DRONES
DROOLS
DROOPS
DROVES
DROWNS
DRUIDS
DRUNKS
DRUPES
DRUSES
DRYADS
DRYERS
DUCATS
DUNCES
DUPERS
DURESS
DUTIES
DWARFS
DWELLS

•DS•••
ADSORB

•D•S••
EDISON
ODESSA

•D••S•
ADJUST
ADVISE
IDLEST
ODDEST
ODESSA

•D•••S
ADAGES
ADAPTS
ADDAMS
ADDERS
ADDLES
ADEEMS
ADENIS
ADEPTS
ADIEUS
ADLIBS
ADMITS
ADOBES
ADONIS
ADOPTS
ADORES
ADORNS
ADULTS
EDDIES
EDGARS
EDICTS
EDILES
EDITHS
EDUCES
EDUCTS
EDWINS
IDEALS
IDIOMS
IDIOTS
IDLERS
IDYLLS
ODIOUS
UDDERS

••DS••
GODSON
HUDSON
PODSOL
UNDSET

6

WADSET

••D•S•
ALDOSE
DUDISH
ELDEST
IODISM
JADISH
MEDUSA
MODEST
MODISH
NODOSE
NUDISM
NUDIST
ODDEST
OLDEST
OLDISH
RADISH
RUDEST
SADISM
SADIST
VADOSE
WIDEST

••D••S
ADDAMS
ADDERS
ADDLES
AIDERS
ALDERS
ALDOUS
ANDRES
ARDEBS
ARDORS
AUDADS
AUDITS
BADGES
BEDEWS
BEDIMS
BIDETS
BODIES
BUDGES
CADDIS
CADETS
CADGES
CADMUS
CADRES
CEDARS
CIDERS
DADOES
DEDANS
DIDIES
DIDOES
DODGES
DODOES
EDDIES
ELDERS
ENDOWS
ENDUES
FUDGES
HEDGES
HIDERS
HYDRAS
HYDROS
INDIES
INDOWS
INDRIS
INDUES
IODOUS
JUDAHS
JUDGES
KEDGES
KODAKS
LADIES
LADLES
LEDGES
LODGES
LYDIAS
MADAMS
MADGES
MADRAS
MEDALS
MEDICS
MIDGES
MODELS
NADIRS
NUDGES
OODLES
ORDERS
PADDYS
PADRES
PEDALS
PEDROS
PODOUS
RADARS
RADIOS
RADIUS
REDANS
REDOES
RIDERS
RIDGES
RODDYS
RODEOS
SADHUS
SADIES
SEDANS
SEDERS
SEDGES
SEDUMS
SIDLES
TEDDYS
TIDIES
TODIES
UDDERS
UNDIES
UNDOES
VODKAS
WADERS
WADIES
WEDGES
WIDENS
WIDOWS
WIDTHS
YODELS

•••DS•
AMIDST
WOODSY

•••D•S
ABIDES
ABODES
ABYDOS
AMIDES
ANODES
ASIDES
BARDES
BLADES
BRIDES
CADDIS
CHIDES
CINDYS
CLYDES
CREDOS
DIODES
ELIDES
ELUDES
EPODES
ERODES
ETUDES
EVADES
EXODUS
EXUDES
FREDAS
FUNDUS
GEODES
GILDAS
GLADES
GLADYS
GLEDES
GLIDES
GRADES
GRADUS
GRIDES
GUIDES
HILDAS
HINDUS
HORDES
HYADES
IMIDES
IRIDES
LEUDES
LINDAS
MANDYS
MAUDES
OXIDES
PADDYS
PANDAS
PINDUS
PRIDES
PRUDES
RHODAS
RODDYS
RONDOS
SANDYS
SHADES
SLIDES
SPADES
SUEDES
SWEDES
TEDDYS
THADYS
THEDAS
TILDES
TRADES
TRUDYS
TSADES
VELDTS
WALDOS
WANDAS
WENDYS

••••DS
ALMUDS
AMENDS
APHIDS
AROIDS
AUDADS
AVOIDS
AWARDS
BEARDS
BIPEDS
BIPODS
BLEEDS
BLENDS
BLINDS
BLONDS
BLOODS
BOARDS
BOUNDS
BRAIDS
BRANDS
BREADS
BREEDS
BROADS
BROODS
BUILDS
CHARDS
CHORDS
CLOUDS
CREEDS
CROWDS
CYCADS
DAVIDS
DREADS
DRUIDS
DRYADS
ELANDS
EMBEDS
EMENDS
EPHODS
FARADS
FELIDS
FIELDS
FIENDS
FIORDS
FJELDS
FJORDS
FLOODS
FLOYDS
FLUIDS
FOUNDS
FRAUDS
FRONDS
GLANDS
GONADS
GOURDS
GREEDS
GRINDS
GUARDS
GUILDS
HALIDS
HEXADS
HOARDS
HOUNDS
HYOIDS
IMBEDS
JIHADS
KNEADS
LAIRDS
LAMEDS
LIPIDS
LLOYDS
MAUNDS
MONADS
MOULDS
NAIADS
NOMADS
OCTADS
OREADS
PLAIDS
PLEADS
POINDS
POUNDS
RAPIDS
ROALDS
ROUNDS
SALADS
SCALDS
SCENDS
SCOLDS
SCRODS
SHARDS
SHERDS
SHREDS
SKALDS
SNOODS
SOLIDS
SOUNDS
SPEEDS
SPENDS
SQUADS
SQUIDS
STANDS
STEEDS
SWARDS
SWORDS
SYNODS
THIRDS
TREADS
TRENDS
TRIADS
TWEEDS
UPENDS
VIANDS
WEALDS
WIELDS
WOALDS
WORLDS
WOUNDS
YIELDS
ZOOIDS
ZOUNDS

D•T•••
DATARY
DATERS
DATING
DATIVE
DATTOS
DATURA
DETACH
DETAIL
DETAIN
DETECT
DETENT
DETERS
DETEST
DETOUR
DITHER
DITTOS
DOTAGE
DOTERS
DOTIER
DOTING
DOTTED
DOTTEL
DOTTER
DOTTLE
DUTIES

D••T••
DACTYL
DAFTLY
DALTON
DANTON
DARTED
DARTER
DARTLE
DATTOS
DAYTON
DEATHS
DEATHY
DEBTOR
DEFTER
DEFTLY
DELTAS
DENTAL
DENTED
DENTIL
DENTIN
DEPTHS
DEXTER
DEXTRO
DHOTIS
DIATOM
DICTUM
DIETED
DIETER
DINTED
DISTAL
DISTIL
DITTOS
DMITRI
DOCTOR

DOTTED
DOTTEL
DOTTER
DOTTLE
DUSTED
DUSTER

D•••T•
DAINTY
DAKOTA
DALETH
DANITE
DAUNTS
DAVITS
DEARTH
DEBATE
DEBITS
DEBUTS
DEISTS
DELETE
DEMITS
DEMOTE
DENOTE
DEPOTS
DEPUTE
DEPUTY
DEVOTE
DEWITT
DIGITI
DIGITS
DILATE
DILUTE
DIMITY
DIVOTS
DIXITS
DONATE
DONETS
DOUBTS
DRAFTS
DRAFTY
DRIFTS
DRIFTY
DROITS
DROUTH
DUCATS
DULUTH

D••••T
DACOIT
DAKOIT
DECANT
DECEIT
DECENT
DECOCT
DEDUCT
DEFEAT
DEFECT
DEGUST
DEJECT
DELICT
DEPART
DEPICT
DEPORT
DERMAT
DESALT
DESERT
DESIST
DESPOT
DETECT
DETENT
DETEST
DEVEST
DEVOUT
DEWITT
DICAST
DIGEST
DIGLOT
DIMOUT
DIMWIT
DIRECT
DIREST
DIVERT
DIVEST
DOCENT
DOCKET
DOESNT
DREAMT
DRIEST
DRYEST
DUGOUT
DULCET
DWIGHT
DYNAST

•D•T••
ADYTUM
EDITED
EDITHS
EDITOR

•D••T•
ADAPTS
ADEPTS
ADMITS
ADNATE
ADOPTS
ADULTS
EDICTS
EDUCTS
IDEATE
IDIOTS
ODDITY
ODONTO

•D•••T
ADDICT
ADDUCT
ADJUST
ADMIXT
ADRIFT
ADROIT
ADVENT
ADVERT
IDLEST
ODDEST

••DT••
REDTOP
WIDTHS

••D•T•
AUDITS
BIDETS
CADETS
IODATE
JUDITH
NUDITY
ODDITY
PEDATE
PEDATI
SEDATE
UPDATE

••D••T
ABDUCT
ADDICT
ADDUCT
ARDENT
BUDGET
CADENT
DEDUCT
ELDEST
FIDGET
GADGET
GODWIT
INDENT
INDICT
INDUCT
INDULT
MIDGET
MIDGUT
MODEST
NUDIST
ODDEST
OLDEST
PEDANT
REDACT
REDHOT
RIDENT
RODENT
RUDEST
SADIST
TIDBIT
UNDSET
WADSET
WIDEST

•••DT•
VELDTS

•••D•T
AMIDST
BANDIT
CREDIT
PUNDIT
SYNDET

DU••••
DUBBED
DUBBIN
DUBLIN
DUCATS
DUCKED
DUCKER
DUDEEN
DUDISH
DUDLEY
DUELED
DUELER
DUELLO
DUENNA
DUFFEL
DUFFER
DUFFLE
DUGONG
DUGOUT
DUIKER
DULCET
DULCIE
DULLED
DULLER
DULUTH
DUMBLY
DUMPED
DUNBAR
DUNCAN
DUNCES
DUNDEE
DUNGED
DUNKED
DUNKER
DUNLIN
DUNNED
DUODEN
DUOLOG
DUPERS
DUPERY
DUPING
DUPLEX
DURBAN
DURBAR
DURESS
DURHAM
DURIAN
DURING
DURION
DUSKED
DUSTED
DUSTER
DUTIES

D•U•••
DAUBED
DAUBER
DAUBRY
DAUNTS
DEUCED
DEUCES
DHURNA
DOUBLE
DOUBLY
DOUBTS
DOUCHE
DOUGHS
DOUGHY
DOUGIE
DOURLY
DOUSED
DOUSES
DRUDGE
DRUIDS
DRUNKS
DRUPES
DRUSES

D••U••
DANUBE
DATURA
DEBUGS
DEBUNK
DEBUTS
DECURY
DEDUCE
DEDUCT
DEGUMS
DEGUST
DELUDE
DELUGE
DELUXE
DEMURE
DEMURS
DENUDE
DEPUTE
DEPUTY
DILUTE
DISUSE
DROUTH
DULUTH

D•••U•
DANAUS
DARIUS
DELIUS
DENGUE
DETOUR
DEVOUR
DEVOUT
DICTUM
DIMOUT
DINGUS
DISCUS
DORBUG
DORSUM
DUGOUT
DYBBUK

D••••U
DACHAU
DESSAU

•DU•••
ADULTS
EDUARD
EDUCED
EDUCES
EDUCTS

•D•U••
ADDUCE
ADDUCT
ADJURE
ADJUST
EDMUND

•D••U•
ADIEUS
ADIEUX
ADNOUN
ADYTUM
ODIOUS

••DU••
ABDUCT
ADDUCE
ADDUCT
BEDUIN
CEDULA
DEDUCE
DEDUCT
ENDUED
ENDUES
ENDURE
INDUCE
INDUCT
INDUED
INDUES
INDULT
MADURA
MADURO
MEDUSA
MODULE
NODULE
ORDURE
PODUNK
RADULA
REDUCE
SEDUCE
SEDUMS
UNDULY

••D•U•
ALDOUS
BEDAUB
BEDBUG
CADMUS
INDIUM
IODOUS
MADEUP
MEDIUM
MIDGUT
PODIUM
PODOUS
RADIUM
RADIUS
REDBUD
REDBUG
SADHUS
SIDDUR
SODIUM
TEDIUM

•••DU•
EXODUS
FONDUE

6

FUNDUS
GRADUS
HINDUS
HOLDUP
MARDUK
PINDUS
SIDDUR
SUBDUE
VENDUE
VERDUN

•••D•U
AMADOU
LANDAU

DV••••
DVORAK

D•V•••
DAVEYS
DAVIDS
DAVIES
DAVITS
DEVEIN
DEVEST
DEVICE
DEVILS
DEVISE
DEVOID
DEVOIR
DEVOTE
DEVOUR
DEVOUT
DIVANS
DIVERS
DIVERT
DIVEST
DIVIDE
DIVINE
DIVING
DIVOTS
DOVISH

D••V••
DELVED
DELVER
DELVES
DENVER
DRIVEL
DRIVEN
DRIVER
DRIVES
DROVED
DROVER
DROVES

D•••V•
DATIVE
DERIVE

•DV•••
ADVENT
ADVERB
ADVERT
ADVICE
ADVISE

••D•V•
ENDIVE
GODIVA

DW••••
DWARFS
DWELLS
DWIGHT

D•W•••
DAWDLE
DAWNED
DAWSON
DEWANS
DEWIER
DEWITT
DEWLAP
DIWANS
DOWELS
DOWERS
DOWERY
DOWNED
DOWSED
DOWSER
DOWSES

D••W••
DARWIN
DEEWAN
DIMWIT
DRAWEE
DRAWER
DRAWLS
DRAWLY
DROWNS
DROWSE
DROWSY

D•••W•
DISOWN

D••••W
DARROW

•DW•••
EDWARD
EDWINA
EDWINS

••DW••
GODWIN
GODWIT
HEDWIG
LUDWIG
MIDWAY

••D•W•
BEDEWS
ENDOWS
INDOWS
REDOWA
WIDOWS

••D••W
ANDREW
UNDRAW
UNDREW

•••D•W
MEADOW
MILDEW
SHADOW
SUNDEW
WINDOW

D•X•••
DEXTER
DEXTRO
DIXITS
DOXIES

D•••X•
DELUXE
DESOXY

D••••X
DIPLEX
DUPLEX

•D••X•
ADMIXT

•D•••X
ADIEUX

•••D•X
CAUDEX
SPADIX

DY••••
DYADIC
DYBBUK
DYEING
DYNAMO
DYNAST

D•Y•••
DAYFLY
DAYTON
DOYENS
DOYLEY
DRYADS
DRYDEN
DRYERS
DRYEST
DRYING

D••Y••
DRAYED

D•••Y•
DACTYL
DAIMYO
DAISYS
DANNYS
DAVEYS
DEBBYS
DECAYS
DECOYS
DELAYS
DENNYS
DOLLYS

D••••Y
DAFTLY
DAINTY
DAMPLY
DANKLY
DARKLY
DATARY
DAUBRY
DAYFLY
DEADLY
DEAFLY
DEARLY
DEATHY
DECURY
DEEPLY
DEFRAY
DEFTLY
DENARY
DEPLOY
DEPUTY
DESCRY
DESOXY
DICKEY
DIGAMY
DIMITY
DIMPLY
DINGEY
DINGHY
DINKEY
DIPODY
DIRELY
DISMAY
DISNEY
DONKEY
DOUBLY
DOUGHY
DOURLY
DOWERY
DOYLEY
DOZILY
DRABLY
DRAFFY
DRAFTY
DRAWLY
DREAMY
DREARY
DREGGY
DRESSY
DRIFTY
DRIPPY
DROLLY
DROOPY
DROPSY
DROSKY
DROSSY
DROWSY
DUDLEY
DUMBLY
DUPERY

•DY•••
ADYTUM
GDYNIA
IDYLLS
ODYNIA

•D•••Y
IDIOCY
ODDITY

••D•Y•
PADDYS
REDEYE
RODDYS
TEDDYS

••D••Y
AUDREY
BODILY
CODIFY
CUDDLY
DUDLEY
GADFLY
KIDNEY
MEDLEY
MIDDAY
MIDWAY
MODIFY
NIDIFY
NUDELY
NUDITY
ODDITY
PUDDLY
REDBAY
RODNEY
RUDELY
SIDNEY
SODOMY
SUDARY
SYDNEY
TIDILY
UNDULY
WADDLY
WIDELY

•••DY•
CINDYS
GLADYS
MANDYS
PADDYS
RODDYS
SANDYS
TEDDYS
THADYS
TRUDYS
WENDYS

•••D•Y
ACIDLY
AGEDLY
AIRDRY
ARIDLY
AVIDLY
BALDLY
BAWDRY
BENDAY
BOLDLY
CLODDY
COLDLY
CORDAY
CUDDLY
DEADLY
FLEDGY
FONDLY
FREDDY
FRIDAY
GLADLY
GOODBY
GOODLY
HARDLY
HEYDAY
KINDLY
LAYDAY
LEWDLY
LORDLY
LOUDLY
MAYDAY
MIDDAY
MILDLY
MONDAY
PAYDAY
PUDDLY
SHODDY
SLUDGY
SMUDGY
STODGY
SUNDAY
SUNDRY
TAWDRY
THADDY
WADDLY
WILDLY
WOODSY

••••DY
BLOODY
BRANDY
BROODY
CLODDY
CLOUDY
COMEDY
CORODY
DIPODY
EMBODY
FREDDY
GREEDY
GRUNDY
IMBODY
MALADY
MAUNDY
MELODY
MILADY
MONODY
MOULDY

PARODY
REMEDY
SHINDY
SHODDY
SPEEDY
STEADY
STURDY
THADDY
TRENDY
UNTIDY
WEIRDY
WIELDY

D•Z••••
DAZING
DAZZLE
DIZENS
DOZENS
DOZIER
DOZILY
DOZING

D••Z••
DANZIG
DAZZLE
DIAZIN

••DZ••
PODZOL

••D•Z•
IODIZE

EA••••
EAGLES
EAGLET
EALING
EARFUL
EARING
EARLAP
EARLES
EARNED
EARNER
EARTHS
EARTHY
EARWAX
EARWIG
EASELS
EASIER
EASILY
EASING
EASTER
EASTON
EATERS
EATING

E•A•••
ECARTE
ELAINE
ELANDS
ELAPSE
ELATED
ELATER
ELATES
ELAYNE
ENABLE
ENACTS
ENAMEL
ENAMOR
ENATES
ENATIC
EPACTS
EPARCH
ERASED
ERASER
ERASES
ETAPES
EVADED
EVADER
EVADES
EXACTA
EXACTS
EXALTS
EXAMEN
EXARCH
EYASES

E••A••
EBOATS
ECHARD
ECLAIR
EDDAIC
EDGARS
EDUARD
EDWARD
EFFACE
EGGARS
EMBALM
EMBANK
EMBARK
EMBARS
EMBAYS
EMPALE
ENCAGE
ENCAMP
ENCASE
ENDALL
ENFACE
ENGAGE
ENLACE
ENRAGE
ENRAPT
ENTAIL
EPHAHS
EQUALS
EQUATE
ERGATE
ERRAND
ERRANT
ERRATA
ERSATZ
ESCAPE
ESCARP
ESPANA
ESSAYS
ESTATE
ETHANE
ETHANS
EXHALE
EXPAND
EXTANT

E•••A•
EARLAP
EARWAX
ELENAS
ELIJAH
ELIZAS
ENDEAR
ENEMAS
ENGRAM
ENNEAD
ENTRAP
ENWRAP
EOLIAN
EONIAN
EPICAL
ESCHAR
ESPIAL
ESTRAY
EVITAS
EXTRAS

E••••A
ECZEMA
EDWINA
EGERIA
EGESTA
EIDOLA
EJECTA
ELISHA
ELMIRA
ELVIRA
ELYTRA
EMILIA
ENCINA
ENIGMA
ENTERA
EPIZOA
ERRATA
ESPANA
EUBOEA
EUDORA
EUPNEA
EUREKA
EUROPA
EXACTA
EXEDRA

•EA•••
AEACUS
BEACHY
BEACON
BEADED
BEADLE
BEAGLE
BEAKED
BEAKER
BEAMED
BEANED
BEANIE
BEARDS
BEARED
BEARER
BEASTS
BEATEN
BEATER
BEAUTS
BEAUTY
BEAVER
CEASED
CEASES
DEACON
DEADEN
DEADLY
DEAFEN
DEAFLY
DEALER
DEARER
DEARIE
DEARLY
DEARTH
DEATHS
DEATHY
FEALTY
FEARED
FEARER
FEASED
FEASES
FEASTS
GEARED
HEADED
HEADER
HEADON
HEALED
HEALER
HEALTH
HEAPED
HEARER
HEARSE
HEARST
HEARTH
HEARTS
HEARTY
HEATED
HEATER
HEATHS
HEATHY
HEAUME
HEAVED
HEAVEN
HEAVER
HEAVES
JEANNE
LEACHY
LEADED
LEADEN
LEADER
LEADIN
LEAFED
LEAGUE
LEAKED
LEANED
LEANER
LEANLY
LEANTO
LEAPED
LEAPER
LEARNS
LEARNT
LEASED
LEASES
LEAVED
LEAVEN
LEAVER
LEAVES
MEADOW
MEAGER
MEALIE
MEANER
MEANIE
MEANLY
MEASLY
MEATUS
NEARBY
NEARED
NEARER
NEARLY
NEATER
NEATLY
PEACHY
PEAHEN
PEAKED
PEALED
PEANUT
PEARLS
PEARLY
PEASEN
PEASES
PEAVEY
REACTS
READER
REALES
REALLY
REALMS
REALTY
REAMED
REAMER
REAPED
REAPER
REARED
REARER
REARMS
REASON
REAVOW
SEABEE
SEADOG
SEALED
SEALER
SEAMAN
SEAMED
SEAMEN
SEAMER
SEAMUS
SEANCE
SEAPEN
SEARCH
SEARED
SEASON
SEATED
SEAWAN
SEAWAY
TEACUP
TEAMED
TEAPOT
TEAPOY
TEARED
TEASED
TEASEL
TEASER
TEASES
VEADAR
WEAKEN
WEAKER
WEAKLY
WEALDS
WEALTH
WEANED
WEANER
WEAPON
WEARER
WEASEL
WEAVED
WEAVER
WEAVES
YEANED
YEARLY
YEARNS
YEASTS
YEASTY
ZEALOT

•E•A••
AERATE
BECALM
BECAME
BEDAUB
BEFALL
BEHALF
BEHAVE
BELAYS
BEMATA
BERATE
BETAKE
BEWAIL
BEWARE
BEZANT
CEDARS
CERATE
CERATO
CESARE
CETANE
DEBARK
DEBARS
DEBASE
DEBATE
DECADE
DECALS
DECAMP
DECANE
DECANT
DECARE
DECAYS
DEDANS

6

DEFACE
DEFAME
DEGAGE
DEGAME
DEKARE
DELAYS
DEMAND
DENARY
DEPART
DERAIL
DERAIN
DESALT
DETACH
DETAIL
DETAIN
DEWANS
FEMALE
FEUARS
GEMARA
GERALD
GERARD
HECATE
HEMATO
HEPATO
HERALD
HEXADS
HEXANE
JEZAIL
KERALA
KERATO
LEGACY
LEGATE
LEGATO
LENAPE
LEVANT
MEDALS
MEGALO
MEGASS
MELANO
MENACE
MENAGE
METAGE
METALS
NEGATE
NEMATO
NEVADA
NEWARK
PECANS
PEDALS
PEDANT
PEDATE
PEDATI
PEKANS
PELAGE
PESACH
PESADE
PETAIN
PETALS
PETARD
REBATE
REBATO
RECALL
RECANT
RECAPS
RECAST
REDACT
REDANS
REGAIN
REGALE
REGARD
REHASH
RELATE
RELAYS
REMADE
REMAIN
REMAKE
REMAND
REMANS
REMARK
REPAID
REPAIR
REPAND
REPASS
REPAST
REPAYS
RESALE
RETAIL
RETAIN
RETAKE
RETARD
REVAMP
REWARD
SEBATS
SECANT
SEDANS
SEDATE
SEJANT
SENARY
SENATE
SEPALS
SERACS
SERAIS
SERAPE
SERAPH
SESAME
SEWAGE
SEWALL
SEWARD
TENACE
TENANT
TERAPH
TERATO
TETANY
VEDAIC
VELATE
ZENANA

•E••A•

AECIAL
AEGEAN
AENEAS
AERIAL
BEDLAM
BEDPAN
BEGGAR
BEHEAD
BELDAM
BELGAS
BELIAL
BELLAS
BEMEAN
BEMOAN
BENDAY
BENGAL
BETRAY
BEULAH
BEULAS
BEZOAR
CEIBAS
CELIAC
CELIAS
CELLAE
CELLAR
CENTAL
CEREAL
DECCAN
DEEWAN
DEFEAT
DEFRAY
DELIAN
DELIAS
DELLAS
DELTAS
DEMEAN
DENIAL
DENTAL
DEODAR
DERMAL
DERMAS
DERMAT
DESMAN
DESSAU
DEWLAP
FECIAL
FELLAH
FENIAN
FERIAL
FESTAL
FETIAL
FEUDAL
FEZZAN
GEMMAE
GENIAL
GERMAN
GEWGAW
HEDRAL
HEEHAW
HELLAS
HENNAS
HEPTAD
HERBAL
HEREAT
HERMAE
HERMAI
HERMAN
HETMAN
HEYDAY
JETSAM
KEDDAH
KEYWAY
LEEWAY
LEGMAN
LEHUAS
LEMMAS
LEONAS
LETHAL
MECCAN
MECCAS
MEDIAE
MEDIAL
MEDIAN
MEDLAR
MENIAL
MENSAL
MENTAL
MERMAN
MESCAL
MESIAL
MESIAN
NECTAR
NEURAL
PELIAS
PENIAL
PENMAN
PENNAE
PENPAL
PENTAD
RECTAL
REDBAY
REDCAP
REGNAL
REHEAR
REHEAT
RELOAD
RENTAL
REPEAT
REPLAY
RESEAT
RESEAU
REVEAL
SEAMAN
SEAWAN
SEAWAY
SECPAR
SEESAW
SEGGAR
SENDAL
SENLAC
SENNAS
SEPIAS
SEPTAL
SERDAB
SERIAL
SERVAL
SEURAT
SEXTAN
SEXUAL
TERGAL
TESTAE
TETRAD
VEADAR
VENIAL
VERBAL
VERNAL
VERNAS
VESTAL
VESTAS
WEIMAR
YEOMAN
YERBAS
ZEBRAS

•E•••A

AEOLIA
BELUGA
BEMATA
BENITA
BERTHA
CEDULA
CENTRA
CESURA
FECULA
FEDORA
FEMORA
FERULA
GEISHA
GEMARA
GENERA
GENEVA
HECUBA
HEGIRA
HEJIRA
HELENA
HERNIA
HESTIA
JEMIMA
JERBOA
KERALA
LEPSIA
MEDUSA
MERCIA
MEZUZA
NEBULA
NEVADA
PELOTA
PENNIA
PEORIA
PERSIA
PESETA
REDOWA
REGINA
REMORA
REMUDA
RESEDA
RETINA
SENECA
SENORA
SERBIA
SERENA
TELEGA
TERBIA
TERESA
VERONA
VESICA
ZENANA
ZEUGMA

••EA••

AWEARY
AYEAYE
BLEACH
BLEAKS
BLEARS
BLEARY
BLEATS
BREACH
BREADS
BREAKS
BREAMS
BREAST
BREATH
CHEATS
CLEANS
CLEARS
CLEATS
CLEAVE
CREAKS
CREAKY
CREAMS
CREAMY
CREASE
CREASY
CREATE
DREADS
DREAMS
DREAMT
DREAMY
DREARY
FLEAMS
FREAKS
FREAKY
GLEAMS
GLEAMY
GLEANS
GREASE
GREASY
GREATS
GREAVE
HBEAMS
IBEAMS
IDEALS
IDEATE
KNEADS
OCEANS
OLEATE
OREADS
PAEANS
PLEACH
PLEADS
PLEASE
PLEATS
PREACH
QUEANS
QUEASY
SHEARS
SHEATH
SHEAVE
SKEANS
SLEAVE
SLEAZY
SMEARS
SMEARY
SNEAKS
SNEAKY

SPEAKS
SPEARS
STEADY
STEAKS
STEALS
STEAMS
STEAMY
SWEARS
SWEATS
SWEATY
TREADS
TREATS
TREATY
TWEAKS
TWEAKY
UNEASY
UREASE
WHEALS
WHEATS
WREAKS
WREATH
ZBEAMS

••E•A•
ACETAL
ALEGAR
AMEBAE
AMEBAS
ARECAS
ARENAS
AXEMAN
CAESAR
CHELAE
CHELAS
CHETAH
COEVAL
CRETAN
DAEDAL
DEEWAN
ELENAS
ENEMAS
FOEMAN
FOETAL
FREDAS
GRETAS
HEEHAW
HIEMAL
HYENAS
HYETAL
ICECAP
ICEMAN
IPECAC
LEEWAY
MAENAD
OMEGAS
ONEWAY
OPERAS
PLEIAD
PREFAB
PREPAY
PRESAS
PREWAR
SEESAW
SHEBAT
STEFAN
STELAE
STELAR
STEPAN
THEBAE
THECAE
THECAL
THEDAS
THENAL
THENAR
THETAS
TOECAP
TREPAN
ULEMAS

••E••A
ACEDIA
AGENDA
ALEXIA
AMELIA
AMENRA
ANEMIA
AREOLA
AVESTA
AYESHA
BREGMA
BRENDA
CAEOMA
CREUSA
CUESTA
DUENNA
EGERIA
EGESTA
EJECTA
EXEDRA
FIESTA
HUELVA
IBERIA
LUELLA
ODESSA
OMENTA
ONEIDA
PLEGIA
PLEURA
PNEUMA
PYEMIA
SHEILA
SHERPA
SIENNA
SIERRA
SIESTA
STELLA
STERNA
TAENIA
THELMA
UREMIA
VIENNA

•••EA•
AEGEAN
AENEAS
AGLEAM
ANDEAN
ANNEAL
APNEAL
APPEAL
APPEAR
ARREAR
AUGEAN
BATEAU
BEHEAD
BEMEAN
BOREAL
BOREAS
BUREAU
CAVEAT
CEREAL
COTEAU
CUNEAL
DEFEAT
DEMEAN
DOGEAR
ENDEAR
ENNEAD
FOVEAE
FOVEAL
GALEAE
GILEAD
HEREAT
JUDEAN
JUNEAU
KOREAN
LINEAL
LINEAR
LUTEAL
MOREAU
OCREAE
ORDEAL
ORGEAT
OSTEAL
PALEAE
PINEAL
POLEAX
REHEAR
REHEAT
REPEAT
RESEAT
RESEAU
REVEAL
SABEAN
SCREAK
SCREAM
SPREAD
SQUEAK
SQUEAL
STREAK
STREAM
THREAD
THREAT
UNBEAR
UNLEAD
UNREAD
UNREAL
UNSEAL
UNSEAM
UNSEAT
UPBEAT

•••E•A
AMOEBA
ANGELA
ARBELA
ATHENA
BODEGA
CALESA
CAMERA
CATENA
CHAETA
CINEMA
CODEIA
DODECA
ECZEMA
ENTERA
EUREKA
FANEGA
FRIEDA
GALENA
GENERA
GENEVA
HELENA
HYGEIA
NOVENA
PAMELA
PESETA
RESEDA
ROWENA
SCHEMA
SCLERA
SENECA
SERENA
SISERA
TELEGA
TERESA
TOPEKA
WOMERA
ZAREBA

••••EA
ACHAEA
ALTHEA
ANDREA
ANTHEA
APNOEA
AZALEA
CHOREA
CORNEA
COWPEA
CRIMEA
EUBOEA
EUPNEA
GUINEA
JUDAEA
NAUSEA
SPIREA

EB••••
EBBING
EBOATS

E•B•••
EBBING
EGBERT
ELBERT
ELBOWS
ELBRUS
EMBALM
EMBANK
EMBARK
EMBARS
EMBAYS
EMBEDS
EMBERS
EMBLEM
EMBODY
EMBOLI
EMBOSS
EMBOWS
EMBRUE
EMBRYO
ERBIUM
EUBOEA

E••B••
EDIBLE
ENABLE
EREBUS

E•••B•
ENROBE
EPHEBI
EXURBS

E••••B
ENTOMB
ENWOMB

•EB•••
CEBOID
DEBARK
DEBARS
DEBASE
DEBATE
DEBBYS
DEBITS
DEBRIS
DEBTOR
DEBUGS
DEBUNK
DEBUTS
HEBREW
HEBRON
NEBULA
PEBBLE
PEBBLY
REBATE
REBATO
REBECS
REBELS
REBILL
REBORN
REBOZO
REBUFF
REBUKE
REBUTS
SEBATS
WEBBED
WEBERS
XEBECS
ZEBECK
ZEBECS
ZEBRAS

•E•B••
BEDBUG
BERBER
CEIBAS
DEBBYS
FEEBLE
FERBER
GERBIL
HENBIT
HERBAL
JERBOA
MEMBER
PEBBLE
PEBBLY
REDBAY
REDBUD
REDBUG
REUBEN
SEABEE
SERBIA
TERBIA
VERBAL
WEBBED
YERBAS

•E••B•
AEROBE
DEMOBS
HECUBA
HEREBY
NEARBY

•E•••B
BEDAUB
BENUMB
RESORB
SERDAB

••EB••
AMEBAE
AMEBAS
AMEBIC
BLEBBY
BYEBYE
CHEBEC
EREBUS
FEEBLE
GHEBER
GLEBES
GREBES
ICEBOX
PLEBES
PUEBLO
QUEBEC
SHEBAT
THEBAE
THEBES
TREBLE

6

••E•B•
BLEBBY
SHELBY

••E••B
CHERUB
PREFAB

•••EB•
AMOEBA
ARDEBS
CALEBS
CUBEBS
EPHEBI
GAZEBO
HEREBY
PHLEBO
PHOEBE
SAHEBS
ZAREBA

•••E•B
ADVERB
SUPERB

••••EB
COBWEB
SUBDEB

EC••••
ECARTE
ECCLES
ECESIS
ECHARD
ECHINI
ECHINO
ECHOED
ECHOER
ECHOES
ECHOIC
ECLAIR
ECOLES
ECTOMY
ECTYPE
ECZEMA

E•C•••
ECCLES
EMCEED
EMCEES
ENCAGE
ENCAMP
ENCASE
ENCINA
ENCODE
ENCORE
ENCYCL
ENCYST
EOCENE
ESCAPE
ESCARP
ESCENT
ESCHAR
ESCHEW
ESCORT
ESCROW
ESCUDO
ETCHED
ETCHER
ETCHES
EUCHRE
EUCLID
EXCEED
EXCELS
EXCEPT
EXCESS
EXCIDE
EXCISE
EXCITE
EXCUSE

E••C••
EDICTS
EDUCED
EDUCES
EDUCTS
EJECTA
EJECTS
ELECTR
ELECTS
ELICIT
ENACTS
EPACTS
EPICAL
EPOCHS
ERECTS
ERICHS
ERUCTS
EVICTS
EXACTA
EXACTS
EYECUP

E•••C•
EFFACE
EFFECT
ENCYCL
ENFACE
ENLACE
ENRICH
ENRICO
ENTICE
EPARCH
ETHICS
EUNICE
EUNUCH
EVINCE
EXARCH
EXPECT
EXSECT

E••••C
ECHOIC
EDDAIC
EMERIC
EMETIC
ENATIC
EOZOIC
EROTIC
ETHNIC
EXILIC
EXOTIC

•EC•••
AECIAL
AECIUM
BECALM
BECAME
BECKED
BECKET
BECKON
BECKYS
BECOME
CECILE
CECILS
CECILY
DECADE
DECALS
DECAMP
DECANE
DECANT
DECARE
DECAYS
DECCAN
DECEIT
DECENT
DECERN
DECIDE
DECILE
DECKED
DECKEL
DECKER
DECKLE
DECOCT
DECODE
DECORS
DECOYS
DECREE
DECURY
FECIAL
FECULA
FECUND
GECKOS
HECATE
HECKLE
HECTIC
HECTOR
HECUBA
KECKED
KECKLE
LECHER
LECTOR
MECCAN
MECCAS
NECKED
NECTAR
PECANS
PECKED
PECKER
PECTEN
PECTIC
PECTIN
RECALL
RECANT
RECAPS
RECAST
RECEDE
RECENT
RECEPT
RECESS
RECIPE
RECITE
RECKON
RECOIL
RECORD
RECOUP
RECTAL
RECTOR
RECTOS
RECTUM
RECTUS
RECURS
RECUSE
SECANT
SECEDE
SECERN
SECKEL
SECOND
SECPAR
SECRET
SECTOR
SECUND
SECURE
TECHNO
VECTOR
ZECHIN

•E•C••
AEACUS
BEACHY
BEACON
DEACON
DECCAN
DEICED
DEICER
DEICES
DESCRY
DEUCED
DEUCES
FENCED
FENCER
FENCES
FESCUE
LEACHY
MECCAN
MECCAS
MERCER
MERCIA
MESCAL
PEACHY
PENCEL
PENCIL
PERCYS
REACTS
REDCAP
REECHO
REICHS
RESCUE
SEICHE
TEACUP
TERCEL
TERCET
TETCHY
TEUCER

•E••C•
BEDECK
DECOCT
DEDUCE
DEDUCT
DEFACE
DEFECT
DEJECT
DELICT
DEPICT
DETACH
DETECT
DEVICE
FELICE
FETICH
HELICO
LEGACY
MEDICO
MEDICS
MEJICO
MENACE
MEXICO
PEIRCE
PESACH
REBECS
REDACT
REDUCE
REJECT
RELICS
RELICT
RESECT
SEANCE
SEARCH
SEDUCE
SELECT
SENECA
SERACS
TENACE
VELOCE
VENICE
VESICA
VESICO
XEBECS
ZEBECK
ZEBECS

•E•••C
AEOLIC
BELGIC
BELLOC
CEDRIC
CELIAC
CELTIC
DEIFIC
DERMIC
FENNEC
FERRIC
GEODIC
GESTIC
HECTIC
HERDIC
HEROIC
METRIC
PECTIC
PELVIC
PEPTIC
SENLAC
SEPTIC
TENREC
VEDAIC

••EC••
ALECTO
ARECAS
BRECHT
CAECUM
CHECKS
CRECHE
CZECHS
EJECTA
EJECTS
ELECTR
ELECTS
ERECTS
EYECUP
FLECHE
FLECKS
ICECAP
IPECAC
NIECES
PIECED
PIECER
PIECES
PRECIS
REECHO
SIECLE
SPECIE
SPECKS
THECAE
THECAL
TOECAP
VNECKS
WRECKS

••E•C•
AGENCY
AMERCE
APERCU
BIERCE
BLEACH
BLENCH
BREACH
BREECH
CLENCH
COERCE
DRENCH
FIERCE
FLEECE
FLEECY

FLENCH
FLETCH
FRENCH
FRESCO
GREECE
PIERCE
PLEACH
PREACH
SKETCH
SPEECH
STENCH
THENCE
TIERCE
TRENCH
ULENCE
UNESCO
WHENCE
WRENCH
WRETCH

••E••C
ACETIC
AMEBIC
ANEMIC
CHEBEC
CLERIC
CRETIC
EMERIC
EMETIC
GAELIC
IPECAC
IRENIC
LUETIC
NOETIC
POETIC
PYEMIC
QUEBEC
SCENIC
STELIC
STERIC
THETIC
URETIC

•••EC•
ABJECT
AFFECT
APIECE
ASPECT
AZTECS
BEDECK
BISECT
BREECH
DEFECT
DEJECT
DETECT
DIRECT
DODECA
EFFECT
EXPECT
EXSECT
FLEECE
FLEECY
GRAECO
GREECE
GYNECO
INFECT
INJECT
INSECT
KOPECK
LUBECK
OBJECT
OBTECT
REBECS
REJECT
RESECT
SELECT
SENECA
SPEECH
XEBECS
ZEBECK
ZEBECS

•••E•C
APNEIC

••••EC
CHEBEC
FENNEC
MYRMEC
PARSEC
QUEBEC
TANREC
TENREC
TOLTEC

ED••••
EDDAIC
EDDIES
EDGARS
EDGIER
EDGING
EDIBLE
EDICTS
EDILES
EDISON
EDITED
EDITHS
EDITOR
EDMOND
EDMUND
EDUARD
EDUCED
EDUCES
EDUCTS
EDWARD
EDWINA
EDWINS

E•D•••
EDDAIC
EDDIES
EIDOLA
ELDERS
ELDEST
ELDRED
ENDALL
ENDEAR
ENDING
ENDIVE
ENDOWS
ENDUED
ENDUES
ENDURE
EUDORA

E••D••
ELIDED
ELIDES
ELUDED
ELUDES
EPODES
ERODED
ERODES
ETUDES
EVADED
EVADER
EVADES
EXEDRA
EXODUS
EXUDED
EXUDES

E•••D•
ELANDS
EMBEDS
EMBODY
EMENDS
ENCODE
EPHODS
ESCUDO
EXCIDE

E••••D
EARNED
ECHARD
ECHOED
EDITED
EDMOND
EDMUND
EDUARD
EDUCED
EDWARD
ELATED
ELDRED
ELIDED
ELOPED
ELUDED
EMCEED
EMOTED
ENDUED
ENFOLD
ENGIRD
ENNEAD
ENSUED
ENVIED
ENWIND
ERASED
ERODED
ERRAND
ESPIED
ETCHED
EUCLID
EVADED
EVENED
EVOKED
EXCEED
EXILED
EXITED
EXPAND
EXPEND
EXTEND
EXUDED
EYELID

•ED•••
AEDILE
BEDAUB
BEDBUG
BEDDED
BEDDER
BEDECK
BEDEWS
BEDIMS
BEDLAM
BEDPAN
BEDRID
BEDUIN
CEDARS
CEDING
CEDRIC
CEDULA
DEDANS
DEDUCE
DEDUCT
FEDORA
HEDDLE
HEDGED
HEDGER
HEDGES
HEDRAL
HEDRON
HEDWIG
KEDDAH
KEDGED
KEDGES
KEDRON
LEDGER
LEDGES
MEDALS
MEDDLE
MEDIAE
MEDIAL
MEDIAN
MEDICO
MEDICS
MEDIUM
MEDLAR
MEDLEY
MEDUSA
PEDALS
PEDANT
PEDATE
PEDATI
PEDDLE
PEDROS
REDACT
REDANS
REDBAY
REDBUD
REDBUG
REDCAP
REDDEN
REDDER
REDDLE
REDDOG
REDEEM
REDEYE
REDFIN
REDHOT
REDOES
REDONE
REDOWA
REDTOP
REDUCE
SEDANS
SEDATE
SEDERS
SEDGES
SEDILE
SEDUCE
SEDUMS
TEDDED
TEDDER
TEDDYS
TEDIUM
VEDAIC
WEDDED
WEDELN
WEDGED
WEDGES
WEDGIE

•E•D••
BEADED
BEADLE
BEDDED
BEDDER
BELDAM
BENDAY
BENDEE
BENDER
DEADEN
DEADLY
DEEDED
DENDRI
DENDRO
DEODAR
FEEDER
FENDED
FENDER
FEODOR
FEUDAL
FEUDED
GELDED
GENDER
GEODES
GEODIC
HEADED
HEADER
HEADON
HEDDLE
HEEDED
HEEDER
HERDED
HERDER
HERDIC
HEYDAY
KEDDAH
LEADED
LEADEN
LEADER
LEADIN
LENDER
LEUDES
LEWDER
LEWDLY
MEADOW
MEDDLE
MELDED
MENDED
MENDEL
MENDER
NEEDED
NEEDER
NEEDLE
PEDDLE
PENDED
READER
REDDEN
REDDER
REDDLE
REDDOG
REEDED
RENDED
RENDER
SEADOG
SEEDED
SEEDER
SELDOM
SENDAL
SENDER
SERDAB
TEDDED
TEDDER
TEDDYS
TENDED
TENDER
TENDON
VEADAR
VELDTS
VENDED
VENDEE
VENDER
VENDOR
VENDUE
VERDIN
VERDUN
WEDDED
WEEDED
WEEDER
WELDED
WELDER
WENDED
WENDYS

6

•E••D•
BEARDS
BESIDE
BETIDE
DECADE
DECIDE
DECODE
DELUDE
DEMODE
DENUDE
DERIDE
FELIDS
HEXADS
LEPIDO
MELODY
NEVADA
PESADE
RECEDE
REMADE
REMEDY
REMUDA
RESEDA
RESIDE
SECEDE
TEREDO
WEALDS
WEIRDY

•E•••D
AENEID
AERIED
BEADED
BEAKED
BEAMED
BEANED
BEARED
BECKED
BEDDED
BEDRID
BEEFED
BEEPED
BEGGED
BEGIRD
BEHEAD
BEHELD
BEHIND
BEHOLD
BELIED
BELLED
BELTED
BESTED
BETTED
BEYOND
CEASED
CEBOID
CEILED
CENSED
DECKED
DEEDED
DEEMED
DEFEND
DEFIED
DEICED
DELVED
DEMAND
DENIED
DENNED
DENTED
DEPEND
DESMID
DEUCED
DEVOID
FEARED
FEASED
FECUND
FEEZED
FELLED
FENCED
FENDED
FERVID
FEUDED
GEARED
GELDED
GELLED
GEMMED
GERALD
GERARD
GERUND
HEADED
HEALED
HEAPED
HEATED
HEAVED
HEDGED
HEEDED
HEELED
HEFTED
HELPED
HEMMED
HEMOID
HEPTAD
HERALD
HERDED
HESIOD
JEERED
JELLED
JEREED
JERKED
JESSED
JESTED
JETTED
KECKED
KEDGED
KEELED
KEENED
KELOID
KENNED
KERNED
LEADED
LEAFED
LEAKED
LEANED
LEAPED
LEASED
LEAVED
LEERED
LEGEND
LEGGED
LEVIED
MELDED
MELTED
MENDED
MEOWED
MERGED
MESHED
MESSED
METHOD
MEWLED
NEARED
NECKED
NEEDED
NERVED
NESTED
NETTED
NEVOID
PEAKED
PEALED
PECKED
PEEKED
PEELED
PEENED
PEEPED
PEERED
PEEVED
PEGGED
PELTED
PENDED
PENNED
PENTAD
PEPPED
PEQUOD
PERIOD
PERKED
PETARD
PETTED
REAMED
REAPED
REARED
RECORD
REDBUD
REEDED
REEFED
REEKED
REELED
REEVED
REFUND
REGARD
REINED
RELIED
RELOAD
REMAND
REMIND
RENDED
RENTED
REPAID
REPAND
RESEND
RESOLD
RESTED
RETARD
RETOLD
RETTED
REVVED
REWARD
REWIND
REWORD
SEALED
SEAMED
SEARED
SEATED
SECOND
SECUND
SEEDED
SEEMED
SEEPED
SEINED
SEIZED
SENSED
SERVED
SEWARD
TEAMED
TEARED
TEASED
TEDDED
TEEMED
TEHEED
TENDED
TENSED
TENTED
TERMED
TESTED
TETRAD
VEERED
VEILED
VEINED
VENDED
VENTED
VERGED
VERSED
VESPID
VESTED
VETOED
VETTED
WEANED
WEAVED
WEBBED
WEDDED
WEDGED
WEEDED
WELDED
WELLED
WELTED
WENDED
WETTED
YEANED
YELLED
YELPED
YENNED
YESSED
ZEROED
ZESTED

••ED••
ACEDIA
AGEDLY
CREDIT
CREDOS
DAEDAL
DEEDED
DREDGE
EXEDRA
FEEDER
FLEDGE
FLEDGY
FREDAS
FREDDY
GLEDES
HEEDED
HEEDER
LIEDER
NEEDED
NEEDER
NEEDLE
PLEDGE
REEDED
SEEDED
SEEDER
SLEDGE
SUEDES
SWEDEN
SWEDES
THEDAS
WEEDED
WEEDER

••E•D•
AGENDA
AMENDS
BLEEDS
BLENDE
BLENDS
BREADS
BREEDS
BRENDA
CREEDS
DREADS
EMENDS
FIELDS
FIENDS
FJELDS
FREDDY
GREEDS
GREEDY
KNEADS
ONEIDA
OREADS
OREIDE
OVERDO
PLEADS
PSEUDO
SCENDS
SHERDS
SPEEDS
SPEEDY
SPENDS
STEADY
STEEDS
TREADS
TRENDS
TRENDY
TWEEDS
UPENDS
UREIDE
WIELDS
WIELDY
YIELDS

••E••D
BEEFED
BEEPED
BREWED
CHEWED
CLERID
CLEWED
CREPED
DEEDED
DEEMED
DIETED
DUELED
EVENED
EYELID
FEEZED
FLEXED
FOETID
FUELED
HEEDED
HEELED
JEERED
KEELED
KEENED
LEERED
MAENAD
NEEDED
OBEYED
OPENED
OXEYED
PEEKED
PEELED
PEENED
PEEPED
PEERED
PEEVED
PIECED
PLEIAD
PREMED
PREYED
QUEUED
REEDED
REEFED
REEKED
REELED
REEVED
SEEDED
SEEMED
SEEPED
SHEWED
SIEGED
SIEVED
SKEWED
SLEWED
SPEWED
STEWED
TEEMED
TIERED

VEERED
VIEWED
WEEDED

•••ED•
ACCEDE
ALBEDO
BIPEDS
BLEEDS
BREEDS
COMEDO
COMEDY
CREEDS
EMBEDS
FRIEDA
GREEDS
GREEDY
IMBEDS
IMPEDE
LAMEDS
LAREDO
RECEDE
REMEDY
RESEDA
SECEDE
SHREDS
SPEEDS
SPEEDY
STEEDS
TEREDO
TOLEDO
TUXEDO
TWEEDS

•••E•D
ADDEND
AENEID
AFIELD
AGREED
ANTEED
APPEND
ASCEND
ATTEND
AUGEND
AXSEED
BEHEAD
BEHELD
COOEED
DEFEND
DEPEND
EMCEED
ENNEAD
EXCEED
EXPEND
EXTEND
FRIEND
GILEAD
IMPEND
INDEED
INTEND
JEREED
LEGEND
OFFEND
PUREED
RAZEED
RESEND
SCREED
SHIELD
SHREWD
SPREAD
TEHEED
THREAD
THREED
TINEID
UNBEND
UNLEAD
UNREAD
UPHELD
VISEED

••••ED
ABASED
ABATED
ABIDED
ABUSED
ADDLED
ADORED
AERIED
AGREED
AISLED
ALATED
ALFRED
ALINED
ALIPED
ALLIED
AMAZED
AMBLED
AMUSED
ANGLED
ANTEED
ARCHED
ARCKED
ARGUED
ATONED
AUTOED
AVOWED
AWAKED
AXSEED
BABIED
BACHED
BACKED
BADGED
BAFFED
BAGGED
BAILED
BAITED
BALKED
BALLED
BANDED
BANGED
BANKED
BANNED
BARBED
BARDED
BARGED
BARKED
BARRED
BASHED
BASKED
BASTED
BATHED
BATTED
BAWLED
BEADED
BEAKED
BEAMED
BEANED
BEARED
BECKED
BEDDED
BEEFED
BEEPED
BEGGED
BELIED
BELLED
BELTED
BESTED
BETTED
BIASED
BIBBED
BIFFED
BILGED
BILKED
BILLED
BINNED
BIRLED
BIRRED
BITTED
BLADED
BLAMED
BLARED
BLAZED
BOATED
BOBBED
BODIED
BOGGED
BOILED
BOLLED
BOLTED
BOMBED
BONDED
BONGED
BOOKED
BOOMED
BOOTED
BOOZED
BOPPED
BOSSED
BOUSED
BOWLED
BOWSED
BRACED
BRAKED
BRAVED
BRAYED
BRAZED
BREWED
BRIBED
BRINED
BUCKED
BUDDED
BUDGED
BUFFED
BUGGED
BUGLED
BULGED
BULKED
BUMMED
BUMPED
BUNGED
BUNKED
BUNTED
BUOYED
BURIED
BURKED
BURLED
BURNED
BURPED
BURRED
BUSHED
BUSIED
BUSSED
BUSTED
BUTTED
BUZZED
CABLED
CACHED
CADGED
CALKED
CALLED
CALMED
CALVED
CAMPED
CANNED
CANOED
CANTED
CAPPED
CARDED
CARPED
CARTED
CARVED
CASHED
CATTED
CAUSED
CEASED
CEILED
CENSED
CHAFED
CHARED
CHASED
CHAWED
CHEWED
CHIDED
CHIMED
CHOKED
CITIED
CLAWED
CLAYED
CLEWED
CLOSED
CLOYED
COALED
COATED
COAXED
COCKED
COGGED
COIFED
COILED
COINED
COMBED
CONKED
CONNED
COOEED
COOKED
COOLED
COOPED
COPIED
COPPED
CORDED
CORKED
CORNED
COSHED
COSTED
COWLED
CRANED
CRAPED
CRATED
CRAVED
CRAZED
CREPED
CROWED
CUFFED
CULLED
CULMED
CUPPED
CURBED
CURDED
CURLED
CURSED
CURVED
CUSPED
CUSSED
CYCLED
DABBED
DAMMED
DAMNED
DAMPED
DANCED
DANGED
DAPPED
DARNED
DARTED
DASHED
DAUBED
DAWNED
DECKED
DEEDED
DEEMED
DEFIED
DEICED
DELVED
DENIED
DENNED
DENTED
DEUCED
DIALED
DIBBED
DIETED
DIMMED
DINGED
DINNED
DINTED
DIPPED
DIRKED
DISHED
DOCKED
DODGED
DOFFED
DOGGED
DOLLED
DONNED
DOOMED
DOTTED
DOUSED
DOWNED
DOWSED
DRAPED
DRAYED
DRONED
DROVED
DUBBED
DUCKED
DUELED
DULLED
DUMPED
DUNGED
DUNKED
DUNNED
DUSKED
DUSTED
EARNED
ECHOED
EDITED
EDUCED
ELATED
ELDRED
ELIDED
ELOPED
ELUDED
EMCEED
EMOTED
ENDUED
ENSUED
ENVIED
ERASED
ERODED
ESPIED
ETCHED
EVADED
EVENED
EVOKED
EXCEED
EXILED
EXITED
EXUDED
FABLED
FAGGED
FAILED
FAIRED
FANGED
FANNED
FARCED
FARMED
FASTED

6

FATTED
FAWNED
FEARED
FEASED
FEEZED
FELLED
FENCED
FENDED
FEUDED
FIBBED
FIGGED
FILLED
FILMED
FINNED
FIRMED
FISHED
FISTED
FITTED
FIZZED
FLAKED
FLAMED
FLARED
FLAWED
FLAYED
FLEXED
FLOWED
FLUKED
FLUMED
FLUTED
FLUXED
FOALED
FOAMED
FOBBED
FOGGED
FOILED
FOLDED
FOOLED
FOOTED
FORCED
FORDED
FORGED
FORKED
FORMED
FOULED
FOWLED
FRAMED
FRAYED
FUDGED
FUELED
FUGLED
FULLED
FUNDED
FUNKED
FURLED
FURRED
FUSSED
FUZZED
GABBED
GABLED
GADDED
GAFFED
GAGGED
GAINED
GAITED
GALLED
GANGED
GAPPED
GARBED
GASHED
GASPED
GASSED
GAUGED
GAWKED
GEARED
GELDED
GELLED
GEMMED
GIBBED
GIFTED
GIGGED
GILDED
GIMPED
GINNED
GIPPED
GIRDED
GIRTED
GLARED
GLAZED
GLIDED
GLOBED
GLOVED
GLOWED
GLOZED
GNAWED
GOADED
GOLFED
GOOFED
GOOSED
GORGED
GOUGED
GOWNED
GRACED
GRADED
GRATED
GRAVED
GRAYED
GRAZED
GRIDED
GRIMED
GRIPED
GROPED
GUIDED
GULFED
GULPED
GUMMED
GUNNED
GUSHED
GUTTED
GYPPED
HACKED
HAILED
HAIRED
HALTED
HALVED
HAMMED
HANDED
HANGED
HARKED
HARMED
HARPED
HASHED
HASPED
HASTED
HATRED
HATTED
HAULED
HAWKED
HEADED
HEALED
HEAPED
HEATED
HEAVED
HEDGED
HEEDED
HEELED
HEFTED
HELPED
HEMMED
HERDED
HILLED
HILTED
HINGED
HINTED
HIPPED
HISSED
HOAXED
HOCKED
HOGGED
HONIED
HONKED
HOODED
HOOFED
HOOKED
HOOPED
HOOTED
HOPPED
HORDED
HORNED
HORSED
HOSTED
HOTBED
HOUSED
HOWLED
HUFFED
HUGGED
HULKED
HULLED
HUMMED
HUMPED
HUNTED
HURLED
HUSHED
HUSKED
HUTTED
HYMNED
IMBUED
INBRED
INCHED
INDEED
INDUED
INURED
IRONED
ISSUED
ITCHED
JABBED
JACKED
JAGGED
JAILED
JAMMED
JARRED
JAZZED
JEERED
JELLED
JEREED
JERKED
JESSED
JESTED
JETTED
JIBBED
JIGGED
JILTED
JINKED
JOBBED
JOGGED
JOINED
JOLTED
JOSHED
JOTTED
JUDGED
JUGGED
JUMPED
JUNKED
JUTTED
KAYOED
KECKED
KEDGED
KEELED
KEENED
KENNED
KERNED
KICKED
KIDDED
KILLED
KILTED
KINKED
KISSED
KNIFED
LACKED
LADLED
LAGGED
LAIRED
LALLED
LAMBED
LAMMED
LAMPED
LANCED
LANDED
LAPPED
LAPSED
LARDED
LARKED
LASHED
LASTED
LATHED
LAUDED
LEADED
LEAFED
LEAKED
LEANED
LEAPED
LEASED
LEAVED
LEERED
LEGGED
LEVIED
LICKED
LIDDED
LIFTED
LILIED
LILTED
LIMBED
LIMNED
LIMPED
LINKED
LIPPED
LISPED
LISTED
LOADED
LOAFED
LOAMED
LOANED
LOBBED
LOCKED
LOCOED
LODGED
LOFTED
LOGGED
LOLLED
LONGED
LOOKED
LOOMED
LOOPED
LOOSED
LOOTED
LOPPED
LORDED
LOURED
LOUSED
LUFFED
LUGGED
LULLED
LUMPED
LUNGED
LURKED
LUSHED
LUSTED
MADDED
MAILED
MAIMED
MALLED
MALTED
MANNED
MAPPED
MARKED
MARLED
MARRED
MASHED
MASKED
MASSED
MASTED
MATTED
MAULED
MELDED
MELTED
MENDED
MEOWED
MERGED
MESHED
MESSED
MEWLED
MIFFED
MILKED
MILLED
MILTED
MINCED
MINDED
MINTED
MISSED
MISTED
MOANED
MOATED
MOBBED
MOCKED
MOILED
MOLDED
MOLTED
MONIED
MOONED
MOORED
MOOTED
MOPPED
MOUSED
MUCKED
MUDDED
MUFFED
MUGGED
MULLED
MUMMED
MUSHED
MUSSED
NABBED
NAGGED
NAILED
NAPPED
NEARED
NECKED
NEEDED
NERVED
NESTED
NETTED
NIBBED
NICHED
NICKED
NIPPED
NOCKED
NODDED
NOISED
NOOSED
NUDGED
NUMBED
NURSED
NUTTED
OBEYED
OKAYED

OPENED
OPINED
ORATED
OUSTED
OXEYED
PACKED
PADDED
PAINED
PAIRED
PALLED
PALMED
PANNED
PANTED
PARKED
PARSED
PARTED
PASSED
PASTED
PATTED
PAUSED
PAWNED
PEAKED
PEALED
PECKED
PEEKED
PEELED
PEENED
PEEPED
PEERED
PEEVED
PEGGED
PELTED
PENDED
PENNED
PEPPED
PERKED
PETTED
PHASED
PHONED
PICKED
PIECED
PIGGED
PILLED
PIMPED
PINGED
PINKED
PINNED
PIPPED
PIQUED
PISHED
PITHED
PITIED
PITTED
PLACED
PLANED
PLATED
PLAYED
PLOWED
PLUMED
PODDED
POISED
POLLED
PONIED
POOLED
POOPED
POPPED
POSTED
POTTED
POURED
POUTED
PRATED
PRAYED
PREMED
PREYED
PRICED
PRIDED
PRIMED
PRIZED
PROBED
PROSED
PROVED
PRUNED
PUFFED
PUGGED
PULLED
PULPED
PULSED
PUMPED
PUNNED
PUNTED
PUPPED
PUREED
PURGED
PURLED
PURRED
PURSED
PUSHED
PUTTED
QUAKED
QUEUED
QUIRED
QUOTED
RACKED
RAFTED
RAGGED
RAIDED
RAILED
RAINED
RAISED
RAMMED
RAMPED
RANGED
RANKED
RANTED
RAPPED
RASPED
RATTED
RAZEED
RAZZED
REAMED
REAPED
REARED
REEDED
REEFED
REEKED
REELED
REEVED
REINED
RELIED
RENDED
RENTED
RESTED
RETTED
REVVED
RHYMED
RIBBED
RICKED
RIDDED
RIDGED
RIFLED
RIFTED
RIGGED
RIMMED
RINGED
RINSED
RIOTED
RIPPED
RISKED
ROAMED
ROARED
ROBBED
ROCKED
ROGUED
ROILED
ROLLED
ROMPED
ROOFED
ROOKED
ROOMED
ROOTED
ROTTED
ROUGED
ROUSED
ROUTED
RUBBED
RUCKED
RUFFED
RUGGED
RUINED
RUSHED
RUSTED
RUTTED
SACKED
SACRED
SAGGED
SAILED
SALTED
SALVED
SANDED
SAPPED
SASHED
SASSED
SAUCED
SCALED
SCARED
SCORED
SCREED
SEALED
SEAMED
SEARED
SEATED
SEEDED
SEEMED
SEEPED
SEINED
SEIZED
SENSED
SERVED
SHADED
SHALED
SHAMED
SHAPED
SHARED
SHAVED
SHEWED
SHINED
SHOOED
SHORED
SHOVED
SHOWED
SICKED
SIDLED
SIEGED
SIEVED
SIFTED
SIGHED
SIGNED
SILOED
SILTED
SINGED
SINNED
SIPPED
SKATED
SKEWED
SKIVED
SLAKED
SLATED
SLAVED
SLEWED
SLICED
SLIMED
SLOPED
SLOWED
SMILED
SMOKED
SNAKED
SNARED
SNIPED
SNORED
SNOWED
SOAKED
SOAPED
SOARED
SOBBED
SOCKED
SOCRED
SODDED
SOILED
SOLOED
SOLVED
SOOTED
SOPPED
SORTED
SOULED
SOURED
SOUSED
SPACED
SPADED
SPARED
SPAYED
SPEWED
SPICED
SPIKED
SPILED
SPIRED
SPITED
SPOKED
SPORED
SPUMED
STAGED
STAKED
STALED
STARED
STATED
STAVED
STAYED
STEWED
STOKED
STOLED
STONED
STOPED
STORED
STOWED
STYLED
SUCKED
SUITED
SULKED
SUMMED
SUNNED
SUPPED
SURFED
SURGED
SWAGED
SWAYED
SWIPED
TABLED
TACKED
TAGGED
TAILED
TALCED
TALKED
TAMPED
TANGED
TANKED
TANNED
TAPPED
TARRED
TASKED
TASTED
TATTED
TAXIED
TEAMED
TEARED
TEASED
TEDDED
TEEMED
TEHEED
TENDED
TENSED
TENTED
TERMED
TESTED
THAWED
THREED
TICKED
TIDIED
TIERED
TIFFED
TILLED
TILTED
TINGED
TINNED
TINTED
TIPPED
TITHED
TITLED
TOGAED
TOGGED
TOILED
TOLLED
TOMBED
TONGED
TOOLED
TOOTED
TOPPED
TOSSED
TOTTED
TOURED
TOUTED
TRACED
TRADED
TRICED
TRINED
TUBBED
TUCKED
TUFTED
TUGGED
TUNNED
TUPPED
TURNED
TUSHED
TUSKED
TWINED
UNBRED
UNITED
UNTIED
UNUSED
VALUED
VALVED
VAMPED
VARIED
VATTED
VEERED
VEILED
VEINED
VENDED
VENTED
VERGED
VERSED
VESTED
VETOED
VETTED
VIALED
VIEWED

VISAED
VISEED
VOICED
VOIDED
WADDED
WAFTED
WAGGED
WAIFED
WAILED
WAITED
WAIVED
WALKED
WALLED
WANNED
WANTED
WAPPED
WARDED
WARMED
WARNED
WARPED
WARRED
WASHED
WASTED
WAULED
WAWLED
WEANED
WEAVED
WEBBED
WEDDED
WEDGED
WEEDED
WELDED
WELLED
WELTED
WENDED
WETTED
WHALED
WHILED
WHINED
WHITED
WHORED
WICKED
WIGGED
WILLED
WILTED
WINCED
WINDED
WINGED
WINKED
WISHED
WISPED
WITHED
WITTED
WOADED
WOLFED
WOMBED
WONTED
WOODED
WORDED
WORKED
WORMED
XRAYED
YAKKED
YANKED
YAPPED
YARDED
YAUPED
YAWLED
YAWNED
YAWPED
YEANED
YELLED
YELPED
YENNED
YESSED
YIPPED
YOWLED
YUKKED
ZEROED
ZESTED
ZINCED
ZINGED
ZIPPED
ZOOMED

EE••••

EERILY

E•E•••

ECESIS
EGERIA
EGESTA
EGESTS
EJECTA
EJECTS
ELECTR
ELECTS
ELEGIT
ELEMIS
ELENAS
ELEVEN
ELEVON
EMEERS
EMENDS
EMERGE
EMERIC
EMESIS
EMETIC
EMETIN
EMEUTE
ENEMAS
ENERGY
EREBUS
ERECTS
EVELYN
EVENED
EVENLY
EVENTS
EVERET
EVERTS
EXEDRA
EXEMPT
EXEQUY
EXERTS
EXETER
EXEUNT
EYECUP
EYEFUL
EYEING
EYELET
EYELID

E••E••

EASELS
EATERS
ECZEMA
EFFECT
EFFETE
EGBERT
EGGERS
EGRESS
EGRETS
EILEEN
ELBERT
ELDERS
ELDEST
ELLENS
ELMERS
ELVERS
EMBEDS
EMBERS
EMCEED
EMCEES
EMEERS
EMMETS
EMMETT
EMPERY
ENDEAR
ENGELS
ENMESH
ENNEAD
ENTERA
ENTERO
ENTERS
EOCENE
EOGENE
EPHEBI
ERNEST
ESCENT
ESKERS
ESSENE
ESTEEM
ESTERS
ETHELS
ETHERS
EUGENE
EUREKA
EXCEED
EXCELS
EXCEPT
EXCESS
EXPECT
EXPELS
EXPEND
EXPERT
EXSECT
EXSERT
EXTEND
EXTENT
EXTERN

E•••E•

EAGLES
EAGLET
EARLES
EARNED
EARNER
EASIER
EASTER
ECCLES
ECHOED
ECHOER
ECHOES
ECOLES
EDDIES
EDGIER
EDILES
EDITED
EDUCED
EDUCES
EIFFEL
EILEEN
EITHER
ELATED
ELATER
ELATES
ELDRED
ELEVEN
ELIDED
ELIDES
ELLIES
ELOPED
ELOPER
ELOPES
ELSIES
ELUDED
ELUDES
ELYSEE
EMBLEM
EMCEED
EMCEES
EMILES
EMMIES
EMOTED
EMOTES
ENAMEL
ENATES
ENDUED
ENDUES
ENSUED
ENSUES
ENTREE
ENVIED
ENVIER
ENVIES
EPODES
EPOPEE
ERASED
ERASER
ERASES
ERNIES
ERODED
ERODES
ESCHEW
ESPIED
ESPIES
ESTEEM
ESTHER
ETAPES
ETCHED
ETCHER
ETCHES
ETUDES
EUBOEA
EUPNEA
EVADED
EVADER
EVADES
EVENED
EVERET
EVOKED
EVOKES
EXAMEN
EXCEED
EXETER
EXILED
EXILES
EXITED
EXOGEN
EXUDED
EXUDES
EYASES
EYELET
EYRIES

E••••E

ECARTE
ECTYPE
EDIBLE
EFFACE
EFFETE
EFFUSE
ELAINE
ELAPSE
ELAYNE
ELOISE
ELYSEE
EMBRUE
EMERGE
EMEUTE
EMIGRE
EMILIE
EMPALE
EMPIRE
ENABLE
ENCAGE
ENCASE
ENCODE
ENCORE
ENDIVE
ENDURE
ENFACE
ENGAGE
ENGINE
ENISLE
ENLACE
ENRAGE
ENROBE
ENSILE
ENSURE
ENTICE
ENTIRE
ENTREE
ENZYME
EOCENE
EOGENE
EPOPEE
EQUATE
EQUINE
ERGATE
ERMINE
ESCAPE
ESSENE
ESTATE
ETHANE
EUCHRE
EUGENE
EUNICE
EUROPE
EVINCE
EVOLVE
EVZONE
EXCIDE
EXCISE
EXCITE
EXCUSE
EXHALE
EXHUME
EXPIRE
EXPOSE

•EE•••

AEETES
BEEFED
BEEPED
BEETLE
BEEVES
DEEDED
DEEMED
DEEPEN
DEEPER
DEEPLY
DEEWAN
FEEBLE
FEEDER
FEEING
FEELER
FEEZED
FEEZES
GEEING
GEEZER
HEEDED
HEEDER
HEEHAW
HEELED
HEELER
JEEING
JEERED
JEERER
KEELED
KEENED
KEENER
KEENLY

KEEPER
KEEVES
LEERED
LEEWAY
MEEKER
MEEKLY
MEETER
MEETLY
NEEDED
NEEDER
NEEDLE
PEEKED
PEELED
PEELER
PEENED
PEEPED
PEEPER
PEERED
PEEVED
PEEVES
PEEWEE
REECHO
REEDED
REEFED
REEFER
REEKED
REEKER
REELED
REELER
REEVED
REEVES
SEEDED
SEEDER
SEEING
SEEKER
SEEMED
SEEMER
SEEMLY
SEEPED
SEESAW
SEETHE
TEEING
TEEMED
TEEMER
TEENSY
TEETER
TEETHE
VEERED
WEEDED
WEEDER
WEEKLY
WEENIE
WEENSY
WEEPER
WEEVER
WEEVIL

•E•E••
AEGEAN
AEGEUS
AENEAS
AENEID
BEDECK
BEDEWS
BEFELL
BEGETS
BEHEAD
BEHELD
BEHEST
BEMEAN
BEREFT
BERETS
BESEEM
BESETS
BETELS
BEVELS
BEZELS
CELERY
CEMENT
CEREAL
CEREUS
DECEIT
DECENT
DECERN
DEFEAT
DEFECT
DEFEND
DEFERS
DEJECT
DELETE
DEMEAN
DEPEND
DEREKS
DESERT
DETECT
DETENT
DETERS
DETEST
DEVEIN
DEVEST
FEVERS
FEWEST
GENERA
GENETS
GENEVA
GERENT
GESELL
HELENA
HELENS
HEREAT
HEREBY
HEREIN
HEREOF
HEREON
HERESY
HERETO
HETERO
HEWERS
JEREED
JEREMY
JEWELS
JEWESS
KETENE
KEVELS
LEGEND
LEGERS
LEPERS
LEVEES
LEVELS
LEVERS
MELEES
MERELY
MEREST
METEOR
METERS
NEREIS
NEWELS
NEWEST
PELEUS
PESETA
PETERS
PEWEES
REBECS
REBELS
RECEDE
RECENT
RECEPT
RECESS
REDEEM
REDEYE
REFERS
REGENT
REHEAR
REHEAT
REJECT
RELENT
REMEDY
RENEES
RENEGE
RENEWS
REPEAT
REPELS
REPENT
RESEAT
RESEAU
RESECT
RESEDA
RESELL
RESEND
RESENT
RESETS
RETELL
RETENE
REVEAL
REVELS
REVERE
REVERT
REVEST
REVETS
SECEDE
SECERN
SEDERS
SELECT
SELENE
SELENO
SEMELE
SEMEME
SENECA
SEREIN
SERENA
SERENE
SEVENS
SEVERE
SEVERS
SEWERS
TEHEED
TEHEES
TELEGA
TENETS
TEPEES
TEPEFY
TEREDO
TERESA
TERETE
TEREUS
VENEER
VENERY
VEREIN
VEXERS
WEBERS
WEDELN
WERENT
XEBECS
YEMENI
ZEBECK
ZEBECS

•E••E•
AEETES
AERIED
AERIES
AETHER
BEADED
BEAKED
BEAKER
BEAMED
BEANED
BEARED
BEARER
BEATEN
BEATER
BEAVER
BECKED
BECKET
BEDDED
BEDDER
BEEFED
BEEPED
BEEVES
BEGGED
BEIGES
BELIED
BELIEF
BELIER
BELIES
BELLED
BELLES
BELTED
BENDEE
BENDER
BENNES
BENNET
BERBER
BERGEN
BERMES
BERNEY
BESEEM
BESTED
BETHEL
BETTED
BETTER
BETTES
BEVIES
CEASED
CEASES
CEILED
CENSED
CENSER
CENSES
CENTER
CERMET
CERTES
DEADEN
DEAFEN
DEALER
DEARER
DECKED
DECKEL
DECKER
DECREE
DEEDED
DEEMED
DEEPEN
DEEPER
DEFIED
DEFIER
DEFIES
DEFTER
DEGREE
DEICED
DEICER
DEICES
DELVED
DELVER
DELVES
DEMIES
DENIED
DENIER
DENIES
DENNED
DENSER
DENTED
DENVER
DEUCED
DEUCES
DEWIER
DEXTER
FEARED
FEARER
FEASED
FEASES
FEEDER
FEELER
FEEZED
FEEZES
FELLED
FELLER
FENCED
FENCER
FENCES
FENDED
FENDER
FENNEC
FENNEL
FERBER
FERRET
FESSES
FESTER
FETTER
FEUDED
FEZZES
GEARED
GEEZER
GEIGER
GELDED
GELLED
GEMMED
GENDER
GENIES
GENRES
GENTES
GEODES
GETTER
GEYSER
HEADED
HEADER
HEALED
HEALER
HEAPED
HEARER
HEATED
HEATER
HEAVED
HEAVEN
HEAVER
HEAVES
HEBREW
HEDGED
HEDGER
HEDGES
HEEDED
HEEDER
HEELED
HEELER
HEFTED
HEIFER
HELLEN
HELLER
HELMET
HELPED
HELPER
HELVES
HEMMED
HEMMER
HEMPEN
HENLEY
HERDED
HERDER
HERMES
HEROES
HERPES
HESTER
JEERED
JEERER

6

JELLED
JENNET
JEREED
JERKED
JERSEY
JESSED
JESSES
JESTED
JESTER
JETTED
KECKED
KEDGED
KEDGES
KEELED
KEENED
KEENER
KEEPER
KEEVES
KEGLER
KELLER
KENNED
KENNEL
KEPLER
KERMES
KERNED
KERNEL
KERSEY
KEYNES
LEADED
LEADEN
LEADER
LEAFED
LEAKED
LEANED
LEANER
LEAPED
LEAPER
LEASED
LEASES
LEAVED
LEAVEN
LEAVER
LEAVES
LECHER
LEDGER
LEDGES
LEERED
LEGGED
LEGMEN
LEGREE
LEMUEL
LENDER
LENSES
LENTEN
LESLEY
LESSEE
LESSEN
LESSER
LESTER
LETTER
LEUDES
LEVEES
LEVIED
LEVIER
LEVIES
LEWDER
MEAGER
MEANER
MEDLEY
MEEKER
MEETER
MELDED
MELEES
MELTED
MELTER
MEMBER
MENDED
MENDEL
MENDER
MENSES
MEOWED
MERCER
MERGED
MERGER
MERGES
MERLES
MERMEN
MESHED
MESHES
MESNES
MESSED
MESSES
MESTEE
METIER
MEWLED
NEARED
NEARER
NEATER
NECKED
NEEDED
NEEDER
NEPHEW
NERVED
NERVES
NESTED
NETHER
NETTED
NEUMES
NEUTER
PEAHEN
PEAKED
PEALED
PEASEN
PEASES
PEAVEY
PECKED
PECKER
PECTEN
PEEKED
PEELED
PEELER
PEENED
PEEPED
PEEPER
PEERED
PEEVED
PEEVES
PEEWEE
PEGGED
PEKOES
PELLET
PELTED
PELTER
PELVES
PENCEL
PENDED
PENMEN
PENNED
PENNER
PEPPED
PEPPER
PERKED
PESTER
PETREL
PETTED
PEWEES
PEWTER
READER
REALES
REAMED
REAMER
REAPED
REAPER
REARED
REARER
REDDEN
REDDER
REDEEM
REDOES
REEDED
REEFED
REEFER
REEKED
REEKER
REELED
REELER
REEVED
REEVES
REFLET
REFLEX
REGLET
REGRET
REINED
RELIED
RELIEF
RELIER
RELIES
RENDED
RENDER
RENEES
RENNET
RENTED
RENTER
RENTES
REOPEN
RESTED
RESTER
RETTED
REUBEN
REVIEW
REVUES
REVVED
SEABEE
SEALED
SEALER
SEAMED
SEAMEN
SEAMER
SEAPEN
SEARED
SEATED
SECKEL
SECRET
SEDGES
SEEDED
SEEDER
SEEKER
SEEMED
SEEMER
SEEPED
SEINED
SEINER
SEINES
SEIZED
SEIZER
SEIZES
SELLER
SELVES
SENDER
SENNET
SENSED
SENSES
SEPTET
SEQUEL
SERIES
SERVED
SERVER
SERVES
SESTET
SETTEE
SETTER
SEXIER
SEXTET
TEAMED
TEARED
TEASED
TEASEL
TEASER
TEASES
TEDDED
TEDDER
TEEMED
TEEMER
TEETER
TEGMEN
TEHEED
TEHEES
TELLER
TEMPER
TENDED
TENDER
TENREC
TENSED
TENSER
TENSES
TENTED
TENTER
TENUES
TEPEES
TERCEL
TERCET
TERMED
TERMER
TERRET
TERSER
TESTED
TESTER
TESTES
TETHER
TETTER
TETZEL
TEUCER
VEERED
VEILED
VEILER
VEINED
VELVET
VENDED
VENDEE
VENDER
VENEER
VENTED
VENTER
VENUES
VERGED
VERGER
VERGES
VERSED
VERSES
VERTEX
VERVET
VESPER
VESSEL
VESTED
VESTEE
VETOED
VETOER
VETOES
VETTED
WEAKEN
WEAKER
WEANED
WEANER
WEARER
WEASEL
WEAVED
WEAVER
WEAVES
WEBBED
WEDDED
WEDGED
WEDGES
WEEDED
WEEDER
WEEPER
WEEVER
WELDED
WELDER
WELLED
WELTED
WELTER
WENDED
WESLEY
WESSEX
WESTER
WETHER
WETTED
WETTER
YEANED
YELLED
YELLER
YELPED
YELPER
YENNED
YEOMEN
YESSED
YESSES
YESTER
ZENGER
ZEROED
ZEROES
ZESTED

•E•••E

AEDILE
AERATE
AEROBE
BEADLE
BEAGLE
BEANIE
BECAME
BECOME
BEETLE
BEFORE
BEHAVE
BEHOVE
BELIZE
BEMIRE
BEMUSE
BENDEE
BERATE
BERNIE
BERTHE
BERTIE
BESIDE
BESSIE
BETAKE
BETIDE
BETISE
BEWARE
CECILE
CELLAE
CERATE
CERISE
CERITE
CERUSE
CESARE
CETANE
DEARIE
DEBASE
DEBATE
DECADE
DECANE
DECARE

DECIDE
DECILE
DECKLE
DECODE
DECREE
DEDUCE
DEFACE
DEFAME
DEFILE
DEFINE
DEGAGE
DEGAME
DEGREE
DEKARE
DELETE
DELUDE
DELUGE
DELUXE
DEMISE
DEMODE
DEMOTE
DEMURE
DENGUE
DENISE
DENOTE
DENUDE
DEPOSE
DEPUTE
DERIDE
DERIVE
DESIRE
DEVICE
DEVISE
DEVOTE
FEEBLE
FELICE
FELINE
FELIPE
FELLOE
FEMALE
FERINE
FERULE
FESCUE
FETTLE
GEMMAE
GENTLE
GEORGE
GERTIE
HEARSE
HEAUME
HECATE
HECKLE
HEDDLE
HERMAE
HEXANE
HEXONE
HEXOSE
JEANNE
JEJUNE
JEROME
JESSIE
KECKLE
KENNIE
KETENE
KETONE
KETOSE
KETTLE
KEWPIE
LEAGUE
LEGATE
LEGREE
LEGUME
LENAPE
LENORE
LEONIE
LESLIE
LESSEE
LEVITE
MEALIE
MEANIE
MEDDLE
MEDIAE
MENACE
MENAGE
MESTEE
METAGE
METOPE
METTLE
NEEDLE
NEGATE
NELLIE
NESTLE
NETTIE
NETTLE
NEVILE
OEUVRE
PEBBLE
PEDATE
PEDDLE
PEEWEE
PEIRCE
PELAGE
PELITE
PENILE
PENNAE
PEOPLE
PERUKE
PERUSE
PESADE
PESTLE
PETITE
PETRIE
PEYOTE
REBATE
REBUKE
RECEDE
RECIPE
RECITE
RECUSE
REDDLE
REDEYE
REDONE
REDUCE
REFINE
REFUGE
REFUSE
REFUTE
REGALE
REGGIE
REGIME
RELATE
RELINE
RELIVE
REMADE
REMAKE
REMISE
REMOTE
REMOVE
RENEGE
REPINE
REPOSE
REPUTE
RESALE
RESCUE
RESIDE
RESILE
RESOLE
RESUME
RETAKE
RETENE
RETIRE
RETUSE
REVERE
REVILE
REVISE
REVIVE
REVOKE
SEABEE
SEANCE
SECEDE
SECURE
SEDATE
SEDILE
SEDUCE
SEETHE
SEICHE
SELENE
SEMELE
SEMEME
SEMITE
SEMPRE
SENATE
SENILE
SERAPE
SERENE
SERINE
SESAME
SETOSE
SETTEE
SETTLE
SEVERE
SEWAGE
TEETHE
TEMPLE
TENACE
TENURE
TERETE
TESSIE
TESTAE
VELATE
VELOCE
VELURE
VENDEE
VENDUE
VENICE
VENIRE
VENOSE
VENULE
VESTEE
WEDGIE
WEENIE

••EE••

ADEEMS
BLEEDS
BREECH
BREEDS
BREEZE
BREEZY
CHEEKS
CHEEKY
CHEEPS
CHEERS
CHEERY
CHEESE
CHEESY
CREEDS
CREEKS
CREELS
CREEPS
CREEPY
CREESE
EMEERS
FLEECE
FLEECY
FLEERS
FLEETS
FREELY
FREEST
FREEZE
GLEETS
GLEETY
GREECE
GREEDS
GREEDY
GREEKS
GREENS
GREETS
KNEELS
PREENS
QUEENS
QUEERS
SHEENS
SHEENY
SHEERS
SHEETS
SLEEKS
SLEEKY
SLEEPS
SLEEPY
SLEETS
SLEETY
SLEEVE
SNEERS
SNEEZE
SNEEZY
SPEECH
SPEEDS
SPEEDY
STEEDS
STEELS
STEELY
STEEPS
STEERS
STEEVE
SWEEPS
SWEEPY
SWEETS
TWEEDS
TWEETS
WHEELS
WHEEZE
WHEEZY

••E•E•

ABELES
AEETES
AKENES
APEXES
ARETES
AXEMEN
BEEFED
BEEPED
BEEVES
BREMEN
BREVES
BREVET
BREWED
BREWER
CHEBEC
CHEWED
CHEWER
CLEVER
CLEWED
CREMES
CRENEL
CREPED
CREPES
CREWEL
DEEDED
DEEMED
DEEPEN
DEEPER
DIESEL
DIESES
DIETED
DIETER
DUELED
DUELER
ELEVEN
EVENED
EVERET
EXETER
EYELET
FEEDER
FEELER
FEEZED
FEEZES
FLEXED
FLEXES
FOEMEN
FUELED
FUELER
GEEZER
GHEBER
GLEBES
GLEDES
GREBES
GRETEL
HEEDED
HEEDER
HEELED
HEELER
IBEXES
ICEMEN
ILEXES
IRENES
JAEGER
JEERED
JEERER
KEELED
KEENED
KEENER
KEEPER
KEEVES
LEERED
LIEDER
LIEGES
MEEKER
MEETER
NEEDED
NEEDER
NIECES
OBEYED
OBEYER
OMELET
OPENED
OPENER
OXEYED
OXEYES
PEEKED
PEELED
PEELER
PEENED
PEEPED
PEEPER
PEERED
PEEVED
PEEVES
PEEWEE
PIECED
PIECER
PIECES
PIETER
PLEBES
PREFER
PREMED
PRETER
PREYED
PREYER
QUEBEC
QUEUED
QUEUES
REEDED

REEFED
REEFER
REEKED
REEKER
REELED
REELER
REEVED
REEVES
SCENES
SEEDED
SEEDER
SEEKER
SEEMED
SEEMER
SEEPED
SHEKEL
SHEWED
SHEWER
SIEGED
SIEGES
SIEVED
SIEVES
SKEWED
SKEWER
SLEWED
SOEVER
SPEWED
STELES
STEREO
STERES
STEVEN
STEVES
STEWED
SUEDES
SWEDEN
SWEDES
TEEMED
TEEMER
TEETER
THEBES
THEMES
THESES
TIERED
UNEVEN
URETER
VEERED
VIEWED
VIEWER
WEEDED
WEEDER
WEEPER
WEEVER
WHEYEY
WIENER
YLEVEL

••E••E

AMEBAE
AMELIE
AMERCE
AVENGE
AVENUE
AVERSE
AYEAYE
BEETLE
BIERCE
BLENDE
BREEZE
BYEBYE
CHEESE
CHEGOE
CHELAE
CLEAVE
CLEOME
COERCE
CREASE
CREATE
CRECHE
CREESE
CREOLE
DIEPPE
DREDGE
EMERGE
EMEUTE
FAEROE
FEEBLE
FIERCE
FLECHE
FLEDGE
FLEECE
FLENSE
FREEZE
GOETHE
GREASE
GREAVE
GREECE
GREIGE
IDEATE
LIERNE
NEEDLE
OLEATE
OREIDE
PEEWEE
PIERCE
PIERRE
PLEASE
PLEDGE
PREVUE
SEETHE
SHEAVE
SHELVE
SIECLE
SLEAVE
SLEDGE
SLEEVE
SNEEZE
SPECIE
STEEVE
STELAE
STEPPE
STEVIE
SVELTE
SWERVE
TEETHE
THEBAE
THECAE
THENCE
TIERCE
TREBLE
TSETSE
TWELVE
ULENCE
UREASE
UREIDE
WEENIE
WHEEZE
WHENCE
WHERVE
WIENIE

•••EE•

AGREED
AGREES
AILEEN
ANTEED
ARLEEN
ASLEEP
AXSEED
BALEEN
BESEEM
CAREEN
CAREER
COOEED
COOEES
DONEES
DOREEN
DUDEEN
EILEEN
EMCEED
EMCEES
ESTEEM
EXCEED
FUSEES
FUZEES
INDEED
JEREED
LATEEN
LEVEES
LOREEN
LYCEES
MELEES
MOREEN
NOREEN
PAYEES
PEWEES
POTEEN
PUREED
PUREES
RANEES
RAZEED
RAZEES
REDEEM
RENEES
RUPEES
SATEEN
SCREED
SCREEN
SPLEEN
SPREES
STREET
SYCEES
TEHEED
TEHEES
TEPEES
THREED
THREES
TUREEN
UNMEET
UNREEL
UNSEEN
UPKEEP
VENEER
VISEED
YOGEES

•••E•E

ACCEDE
ACHENE
ADHERE
ALKENE
ALLEGE
ALLELE
AMPERE
APIECE
ARLENE
ATHENE
BAREGE
BIREME
BREEZE
CHEESE
COHERE
CREESE
CYBELE
CYMENE
CYRENE
DELETE
EFFETE
EOCENE
EOGENE
ESSENE
EUGENE
FLEECE
FOVEAE
FREEZE
FRIEZE
GALEAE
GAMETE
GISELE
GREECE
GRIEVE
IMPEDE
INDENE
INHERE
KETENE
LORENE
MANEGE
MYCETE
OCREAE
PALEAE
PHOEBE
PINENE
PYRENE
QUAERE
RACEME
RECEDE
REDEYE
RENEGE
RETENE
REVERE
SCHEME
SECEDE
SELENE
SEMELE
SEMEME
SERENE
SEVERE
SLEEVE
SNEEZE
SPHENE
SPHERE
STEEVE
TAXEME
TERETE
THIEVE
TUYERE
WHEEZE
XYLENE

••••EE

APOGEE
ATTLEE
BAILEE
BARGEE
BENDEE
BOOTEE
BURGEE
COFFEE
CORVEE
COULEE
DECREE
DEGREE
DOOLEE
DRAGEE
DRAWEE
DUNDEE
ELYSEE
ENTREE
EPOPEE
GOATEE
HACKEE
JAYVEE
LEGREE
LESSEE
LICHEE
LUNGEE
MALLEE
MESTEE
MUSTEE
PARSEE
PASSEE
PAWNEE
PEEWEE
POLLEE
PONGEE
PUGREE
PUTTEE
RAPPEE
SEABEE
SETTEE
SOIREE
SUTTEE
SWANEE
TOFFEE
TOUPEE
VENDEE
VESTEE
YANKEE

EF••••

EFFACE
EFFECT
EFFETE
EFFIGY
EFFLUX
EFFORT
EFFUSE

E•F•••

EFFACE
EFFECT
EFFETE
EFFIGY
EFFLUX
EFFORT
EFFUSE
EIFFEL
ELFINS
ELFISH
ENFACE
ENFOLD
ERFURT

E••F••

EARFUL
EIFFEL
EYEFUL

E••••F

ENGULF

•EF•••

BEFALL
BEFELL
BEFITS
BEFOGS
BEFOOL
BEFORE
BEFOUL
DEFACE
DEFAME
DEFEAT
DEFECT
DEFEND
DEFERS
DEFIED
DEFIER
DEFIES
DEFILE
DEFINE
DEFORM
DEFRAY
DEFTER
DEFTLY
HEFTED

REFERS
REFILL
REFINE
REFITS
REFLET
REFLEX
REFLUX
REFORM
REFUGE
REFUND
REFUSE
REFUTE
TEFLON

•E•F••
BEEFED
BELFRY
DEAFEN
DEAFLY
DEIFIC
FEOFFS
HEIFER
LEAFED
REDFIN
REEFED
REEFER

•E••F•
AERIFY
BEREFT
FEOFFS
REBUFF
SERIFS
SETOFF
TEPEFY
VERIFY

•E•••F
BEHALF
BEHOOF
BELIEF
HEREOF
REBUFF
RELIEF
SETOFF

••EF••
BEEFED
CLEFTS
EYEFUL
IREFUL
OLEFIN
PREFAB
PREFER
PREFIX
REEFED
REEFER
RUEFUL
STEFAN
THEFTS
USEFUL
WOEFUL

••E••F
SHERIF

•••EF•
BEREFT
BRIEFS
CASEFY
CHIEFS
GANEFS
GRIEFS
RAREFY
TEPEFY
TUMEFY

•••E•F
HEREOF
ITSELF
MYSELF

••••EF
BELIEF
RELIEF
UNICEF

EG••••
EGBERT
EGERIA
EGESTA
EGESTS
EGGARS
EGGERS
EGGING
EGGNOG
EGOISM
EGOIST
EGRESS
EGRETS

E•G•••
EAGLES
EAGLET
EDGARS
EDGIER
EDGING
EGGARS
EGGERS
EGGING
EGGNOG
EIGHTH
EIGHTS
EIGHTY
ENGAGE
ENGELS
ENGINE
ENGIRD
ENGIRT
ENGRAM
ENGULF
EOGENE
ERGATE
EUGENE

E••G••
ELEGIT
EMIGRE
ENIGMA
EXOGEN

E•••G•
EFFIGY
ELOIGN
EMERGE
ENCAGE
ENERGY
ENGAGE
ENOUGH
ENRAGE
ENSIGN
ERINGO
ERYNGO
EULOGY

E••••G
EALING
EARING
EARWIG
EASING
EATING
EBBING
EDGING
EGGING
EGGNOG
ENDING
EPILOG
ERRING
EYEING

•EG•••
AEGEAN
AEGEUS
BEGETS
BEGGAR
BEGGED
BEGINS
BEGIRD
BEGIRT
BEGUIN
BEGUMS
DEGAGE
DEGAME
DEGREE
DEGUMS
DEGUST
HEGIRA
KEGLER
LEGACY
LEGATE
LEGATO
LEGEND
LEGERS
LEGGED
LEGION
LEGIST
LEGMAN
LEGMEN
LEGREE
LEGUME
MEGALO
MEGASS
MEGILP
MEGRIM
NEGATE
PEGGED
PEGGYS
PEGTOP
REGAIN
REGALE
REGARD
REGENT
REGGIE
REGIME
REGINA
REGION
REGIUS
REGLET
REGNAL
REGRET
SEGGAR
TEGMEN

•E•G••
BEAGLE
BEGGAR
BEGGED
BEIGES
BELGAS
BELGIC
BENGAL
BERGEN
DEIGNS
DENGUE
FEIGNS
GEIGER
GEWGAW
HEDGED
HEDGER
HEDGES
HEIGHT
KEDGED
KEDGES
LEAGUE
LEDGER
LEDGES
LEGGED
LEIGHS
LENGTH
MEAGER
MERGED
MERGER
MERGES
NEIGHS
PEGGED
PEGGYS
PENGOS
REGGIE
REIGNS
SEDGES
SEGGAR
TERGAL
TERGUM
VERGED
VERGER
VERGES
VERGIL
WEDGED
WEDGES
WEDGIE
WEIGHS
WEIGHT
ZENGER
ZEUGMA

•E••G•
AERUGO
BEFOGS
BEINGS
BELUGA
BENIGN
DEBUGS
DEGAGE
DELUGE
DESIGN
GEORGE
GEORGI
MENAGE
METAGE
PELAGE
REFUGE
RENEGE
RESIGN
SEWAGE
TELEGA
TELUGU

•E•••G
BEDBUG
BELONG
BERING
CEDING
CERING
DEKING
FEEING
FETING
FEUING
GEEING
HEDWIG
HEWING
HEXING
JEEING
KEYING
MEKONG
METING
MEWING
PEKING
REDBUG
REDDOG
SEADOG
SEEING
SEWING
SEXING
TEEING
VEXING

••EG••
ALEGAR
BREGMA
CHEGOE
DREGGY
ELEGIT
GREGOS
JAEGER
LIEGES
OMEGAS
OREGON
PLEGIA
SIEGED
SIEGES

••E•G•
ANERGY
AVENGE
AWEIGH
CLERGY
DREDGE
DREGGY
EMERGE
ENERGY
FLEDGE
FLEDGY
GREIGE
PLEDGE
SLEDGE
SLEIGH

••E••G
AGEING
AWEING
DYEING
EYEING
FEEING
GEEING
HIEING
HOEING
JEEING
SEEING
STENOG
TEEING
TOEING

•••EG•
ALLEGE
BAREGE
BODEGA
FANEGA
FOREGO
MANEGE
NONEGO
PHLEGM
RENEGE
TELEGA
UNPEGS

••••EG
BOWLEG
MASKEG
MUSKEG
NUTMEG
PROLEG

E•H•••
ECHARD
ECHINI
ECHINO
ECHOED
ECHOER
ECHOES
ECHOIC
EPHAHS
EPHEBI
EPHODS
EPHORI
EPHORS
ETHANE
ETHANS
ETHELS
ETHERS
ETHICS
ETHNIC
ETHYLS
EXHALE
EXHORT
EXHUME

E••H••
EIGHTH
EIGHTS
EIGHTY
EITHER
ELOHIM
ESCHAR
ESCHEW
ESTHER
ETCHED
ETCHER
ETCHES
EUCHRE

E•••H•
EARTHS
EARTHY
EDITHS
ELISHA
EPHAHS
EPOCHS
ERICHS
ERYTHR

E••••H
EIGHTH
ELFISH
ELIJAH
ELVISH
ENMESH
ENOUGH
ENRICH
EOLITH
EPARCH
EUNUCH
EXARCH

•EH•••
BEHALF
BEHAVE
BEHEAD
BEHELD
BEHEST
BEHIND
BEHOLD
BEHOOF
BEHOVE
DEHORN
LEHUAS
REHASH
REHEAR
REHEAT
TEHEED
TEHEES

•E•H••
AETHER
BETHEL
HEEHAW
JETHRO
LECHER
LETHAL
MENHIR
MESHED
MESHES
METHOD
METHYL
NEPHEW
NEPHRO
NETHER
PEAHEN
REDHOT
TECHNO
TETHER
TETHYS
WETHER
ZECHIN
ZEPHYR
ZETHOS
ZETHUS

•E••H•
BEACHY
BERTHA
BERTHE
BERTHS
DEATHS
DEATHY
DELPHI
DEPTHS
GEISHA
HEATHS
HEATHY
HEIGHT
KEITHS
LEACHY
LEIGHS
NEIGHS
PEACHY
REECHO
REICHS
SEETHE
SEICHE
TEETHE
TENTHS
TETCHY
WEIGHS
WEIGHT

•E•••H
BEULAH
CERIPH
DEARTH
DETACH
FELLAH
FETICH
FETISH
HEALTH
HEARTH
JEWISH
KEDDAH
LENGTH
PERISH
PESACH
REHASH
RELISH
SEARCH
SERAPH
TERAPH
WEALTH
ZENITH

••EH••
FOEHNS
HEEHAW

••E•H•
ALEPHS
AYESHA
BRECHT
CRECHE
CZECHS
FLECHE
FLESHY
GOETHE
REECHO
SEETHE
STETHO
TEETHE
URETHR

••E••H
AWEIGH
BLEACH
BLENCH
BREACH
BREATH
BREECH
CHETAH
CLENCH
DRENCH
FLENCH
FLETCH
FRENCH
PLEACH
PREACH
SHEATH
SKETCH
SLEIGH
SLEUTH
SPEECH
STENCH
TRENCH
WREATH
WRENCH
WRETCH

•••E•H
AFRESH
BREECH
DALETH
ENMESH
IMMESH
INMESH
JOSEPH
SPEECH
THRESH
ZIBETH

••••EH
CHALEH
YAHVEH
YAHWEH

EI••••
EIDOLA
EIFFEL
EIGHTH
EIGHTS
EIGHTY
EILEEN
EITHER

E•I•••
EDIBLE
EDICTS
EDILES
EDISON
EDITED
EDITHS
EDITOR
ELICIT
ELIDED
ELIDES
ELIJAH
ELIOTS
ELISHA
ELIXIR
ELIZAS
EMIGRE
EMILES
EMILIA
EMILIE
EMILIO
EMILYS
ENIGMA
ENISLE
EPICAL
EPILOG
EPIRUS
EPIZOA
ERICHS
ERINGO
EVICTS
EVILLY
EVINCE
EVITAS
EXILED
EXILES
EXILIC
EXISTS
EXITED

E••I••
EALING
EARING
EASIER
EASILY
EASING
EATING
EBBING
ECHINI
ECHINO
EDDIES
EDGIER
EDGING
EDWINA
EDWINS
EERILY
EFFIGY
EGGING
EGOISM
EGOIST
ELAINE
ELFINS
ELFISH
ELLIES
ELLIOT
ELMIRA
ELOIGN
ELOINS
ELOISE
ELSIES
ELVIRA
ELVISH
EMMIES
EMPIRE
ENCINA
ENDING
ENDIVE
ENGINE
ENGIRD
ENGIRT
ENLIST
ENMITY
ENRICH
ENRICO
ENSIGN
ENSILE
ENTICE
ENTIRE
ENTITY
ENVIED
ENVIER
ENVIES
ENWIND
EOLIAN
EOLITH
EONIAN
EONISM
EQUINE
EQUIPS
EQUITY
ERBIUM
ERMINE
ERNIES
ERRING
ERWINS
ESKIMO
ESPIAL
ESPIED
ESPIES
ETHICS
EUNICE
EURIPI
EXCIDE
EXCISE
EXCITE
EXPIRE
EXPIRY
EYEING
EYRIES

E•••I•
EARWIG
ECESIS
ECHOIC
ECLAIR
EDDAIC
EGERIA
ELEGIT
ELEMIS
ELICIT
ELIXIR
ELOHIM
EMERIC
EMESIS
EMETIC
EMETIN
EMILIA
EMILIE
EMILIO
ENATIC
ENJOIN
ENOSIS
ENTAIL
EOZOIC
EROTIC
ESPRIT
ETHNIC
EUCLID
EXILIC
EXOTIC
EYELID

E••••I
ECHINI
EMBOLI
EPHEBI
EPHORI

EURIPI

•EI•••

BEIGES
BEINGS
BEIRUT
CEIBAS
CEILED
DEICED
DEICER
DEICES
DEIFIC
DEIGNS
DEISTS
FEIGNS
FEINTS
FEISTS
FEISTY
GEIGER
GEISHA
HEIFER
HEIGHT
HEISTS
KEITHS
LEIGHS
NEIGHS
PEIRCE
REICHS
REIGNS
REINED
SEICHE
SEINED
SEINER
SEINES
SEISIN
SEISMO
SEISMS
SEISOR
SEIZED
SEIZER
SEIZES
SEIZIN
SEIZOR
VEILED
VEILER
VEINED
WEIGHS
WEIGHT
WEIMAR
WEIRDY

•E•I••

AECIAL
AECIUM
AEDILE
AERIAL
AERIED
AERIES
AERIFY
BEDIMS
BEFITS
BEGINS
BEGIRD
BEGIRT
BEHIND
BELIAL
BELIED
BELIEF
BELIER
BELIES
BELIZE
BEMIRE
BENIGN
BENITA
BENITO
BERING
BESIDE
BETIDE
BETISE
BEVIES
CECILE
CECILS
CECILY
CEDING
CELIAC
CELIAS
CERING
CERIPH
CERISE
CERITE
CERIUM
CESIUM
DEBITS
DECIDE
DECILE
DEFIED
DEFIER
DEFIES
DEFILE
DEFINE
DEKING
DELIAN
DELIAS
DELICT
DELIUS
DEMIES
DEMISE
DEMITS
DENIAL
DENIED
DENIER
DENIES
DENIMS
DENISE
DEPICT
DERIDE
DERIVE
DESIGN
DESIRE
DESIST
DEVICE
DEVILS
DEVISE
DEWIER
DEWITT
EERILY
FECIAL
FEEING
FELICE
FELIDS
FELINE
FELIPE
FENIAN
FERIAL
FERINE
FERITY
FETIAL
FETICH
FETING
FETISH
FEUING
GEEING
GEMINI
GENIAL
GENIES
GENITO
GENIUS
HEGIRA
HEJIRA
HELICO
HELIOS
HELIUM
HERIOT
HESIOD
HEWING
HEXING
JEEING
JEMIMA
JEWISH
KEVINS
KEYING
LEGION
LEGIST
LENITY
LEPIDO
LESION
LEVIED
LEVIER
LEVIES
LEVITE
LEVITY
MEDIAE
MEDIAL
MEDIAN
MEDICO
MEDICS
MEDIUM
MEGILP
MEJICO
MENIAL
MENINX
MERINO
MERITS
MESIAL
MESIAN
METIER
METING
MEWING
MEXICO
NEVILE
NEVILL
PEKING
PELIAS
PELION
PELITE
PENIAL
PENILE
PERILS
PERIOD
PERISH
PETITE
PEWITS
REBILL
RECIPE
RECITE
REFILL
REFINE
REFITS
REGIME
REGINA
REGION
REGIUS
RELICS
RELICT
RELIED
RELIEF
RELIER
RELIES
RELINE
RELISH
RELIVE
REMIND
REMISE
REMISS
REMITS
REPINE
RESIDE
RESIGN
RESILE
RESINS
RESIST
RETINA
RETIRE
REVIEW
REVILE
REVISE
REVIVE
REWIND
SEDILE
SEEING
SEMITE
SENILE
SENIOR
SEPIAS
SERIAL
SERIES
SERIFS
SERINE
SERINS
SEWING
SEXIER
SEXING
SEXISM
SEXIST
TEDIUM
TEEING
VENIAL
VENICE
VENIRE
VERIFY
VERILY
VERISM
VERIST
VERITY
VESICA
VESICO
VEXILS
VEXING
ZENITH

•E••I•

AENEID
AEOLIA
AEOLIC
AEOLIS
BEANIE
BEDRID
BEDUIN
BEGUIN
BELGIC
BELOIT
BERLIN
BERNIE
BERTIE
BESSIE
BESTIR
BEWAIL
CEBOID
CEDRIC
CELTIC
CERVIX
DEARIE
DEBRIS
DECEIT
DEIFIC
DENNIS
DENTIL
DENTIN
DERAIL
DERAIN
DERMIC
DERRIS
DESMID
DETAIL
DETAIN
DEVEIN
DEVOID
DEVOIR
FENRIR
FERMIS
FERRIC
FERRIS
FERVID
GEODIC
GERBIL
GERTIE
GESTIC
HECTIC
HEDWIG
HEMOID
HENBIT
HENRIS
HERDIC
HEREIN
HERMIT
HERNIA
HERNIO
HEROIC
HEROIN
HESTIA
JERKIN
JERVIS
JESSIE
JESUIT
JEZAIL
KELOID
KELVIN
KENNIE
KERMIS
KEWPIE
LEADIN
LENTIL
LEONIE
LEPSIA
LESLIE
MEALIE
MEANIE
MEGRIM
MELVIN
MEMOIR
MENHIR
MERCIA
MERLIN
MERVIN
METRIC
NELLIE
NEREIS
NETTIE
NEVOID
PECTIC
PECTIN
PELVIC
PELVIS
PENCIL
PENNIA
PENNIS
PEORIA
PEPSIN
PEPTIC
PERMIT
PERSIA
PETAIN
PETRIE
RECOIL
REDFIN
REGAIN
REGGIE
REJOIN
REMAIN
RENNIN
RENOIR
REPAID
REPAIR
RETAIL

RETAIN
SEISIN
SEIZIN
SENNIT
SEPSIS
SEPTIC
SEQUIN
SERAIS
SERBIA
SEREIN
TENNIS
TENPIN
TENUIS
TERBIA
TESSIE
TESTIS
VEDAIC
VERDIN
VEREIN
VERGIL
VERMIN
VERNIX
VESPID
WEDGIE
WEENIE
WEEVIL
WELKIN
ZECHIN

•E•••I
CENTRI
DELPHI
DENDRI
GEMINI
GEORGI
HERMAI
NEROLI
NEVSKI
PEDATI
SESQUI
YEMENI

••EI••
AGEING
AWEIGH
AWEING
CHEILO
CHEIRO
CLEIST
DYEING
EYEING
FEEING
GEEING
GNEISS
GREIGE
HIEING
HOEING
JEEING
ONEIDA
ONEILL
ONEIRO
OREIDE
PLEIAD
RHEIMS
SEEING
SHEIKS
SHEILA
SKEINS
SLEIGH
SPEISS
STEINS
TEEING
THEIRS
THEISM
THEIST
TIEINS
TOEING
UREIDE

••E•I•
ACEDIA
ACETIC
ADENIS
ALEXIA
ALEXIN
ALEXIS
AMEBIC
AMELIA
AMELIE
ANEMIA
ANEMIC
BREWIS
CLERIC
CLERID
CLEVIS
CREDIT
CRETIC
CRETIN
DIESIS
ECESIS
EGERIA
ELEGIT
ELEMIS
EMERIC
EMESIS
EMETIC
EMETIN
EYELID
FOETID
GAELIC
IBERIA
IRENIC
LUETIC
MYELIN
NOESIS
NOETIC
OLEFIN
PLEGIA
POETIC
PRECIS
PREFIX
PYEMIA
PYEMIC
SCENIC
SHERIF
SPECIE
STELIC
STEPIN
STERIC
STEVIE
TAENIA
THEMIS
THESIS
THETIC
THETIS
TMESIS
UREMIA
URETIC
WEENIE
WEEVIL
WIENIE

••E••I
NIELLI
STELLI

•••EI•
AENEID
ALBEIT
APNEIC
CASEIN
CAVEIN
CODEIA
CODEIN
DECEIT
DEVEIN
FADEIN
HEREIN
HYGEIA
ISSEIS
KIBEIS
LOVEIN
NEREIS
NISEIS
ORCEIN
OSSEIN
SEREIN
TAKEIN
TINEID
UNVEIL
VEREIN

•••E•I
ASTERI
EPHEBI
KINESI
SILENI
YEMENI

••••EI
ANDREI
BRUNEI
CLYPEI
GLUTEI
SANSEI
TAIPEI

EJ••••
EJECTA
EJECTS

E•J•••
ENJOIN
ENJOYS

E••J••
ELIJAH

•EJ•••
DEJECT
HEJIRA
JEJUNE
MEJICO
REJECT
REJOIN
SEJANT

•E•J••
BENJYS
SELJUK

E•K•••
ESKERS
ESKIMO

E••K••
EVOKED
EVOKES

E•••K•
EUREKA

E••••K
EMBANK
EMBARK

•EK•••
DEKARE
DEKING
JEKYLL
MEKONG
NEKTON
PEKANS
PEKING
PEKOES

•E•K••
BEAKED
BEAKER
BECKED
BECKET
BECKON
BECKYS
DECKED
DECKEL
DECKER
DECKLE
GECKOS
HECKLE
JERKED
JERKIN
KECKED
KECKLE
LEAKED
MEEKER
MEEKLY
NECKED
PEAKED
PECKED
PECKER
PEEKED
PERKED
RECKON
REEKED
REEKER
SECKEL
SEEKER
WEAKEN
WEAKER
WEAKLY
WEEKLY
WELKIN

•E••K•
BETAKE
DEREKS
NEVSKI
PERUKE
REBUKE
REMAKE
RETAKE
REVOKE

•E•••K
BEDECK
BETOOK
DEBARK
DEBUNK
NEWARK
REMARK
RETOOK
SELJUK
ZEBECK

••EK••
MEEKER
MEEKLY
PEEKED
REEKED
REEKER
SEEKER
SHEKEL
WEEKLY

••E•K•
BLEAKS
BREAKS
CHECKS
CHEEKS
CHEEKY
CLERKS
CREAKS
CREAKY
CREEKS
FLECKS
FREAKS
FREAKY
GREEKS
SHEIKS
SLEEKS
SLEEKY
SNEAKS
SNEAKY
SPEAKS
SPECKS
STEAKS
TWEAKS
TWEAKY
VNECKS
WHELKS
WHELKY
WREAKS
WRECKS

•••EK•
CHEEKS
CHEEKY
CREEKS
DEREKS
EUREKA
GREEKS
KOPEKS
SLEEKS
SLEEKY
TOPEKA

•••E•K
BEDECK
KOPECK
LUBECK
SCREAK
SQUEAK
STREAK
ZEBECK

••••EK
SHRIEK

EL••••
ELAINE
ELANDS
ELAPSE
ELATED
ELATER
ELATES
ELAYNE
ELBERT
ELBOWS
ELBRUS
ELDERS
ELDEST
ELDRED
ELECTR
ELECTS
ELEGIT
ELEMIS
ELENAS
ELEVEN
ELEVON
ELFINS
ELFISH
ELICIT
ELIDED

ELIDES
ELIJAH
ELIOTS
ELISHA
ELIXIR
ELIZAS
ELLENS
ELLIES
ELLIOT
ELMERS
ELMIRA
ELOHIM
ELOIGN
ELOINS
ELOISE
ELOPED
ELOPER
ELOPES
ELSIES
ELUDED
ELUDES
ELVERS
ELVIRA
ELVISH
ELYSEE
ELYTRA

E•L•••

EALING
ECLAIR
EILEEN
ELLENS
ELLIES
ELLIOT
ENLACE
ENLIST
EOLIAN
EOLITH
EULOGY

E••L••

EAGLES
EAGLET
EARLAP
EARLES
ECCLES
ECOLES
EDILES
EFFLUX
EMBLEM
EMILES
EMILIA
EMILIE
EMILIO
EMILYS
EMPLOY
EPILOG
EUCLID
EVELYN
EVILLY
EVOLVE
EXALTS
EXILED
EXILES
EXILIC
EXULTS
EYELET
EYELID

E•••L•

EASELS
EASILY
EDIBLE
EERILY
EIDOLA
EMBALM
EMBOLI
EMPALE
ENABLE
ENDALL
ENFOLD
ENGELS
ENGULF
ENISLE
ENROLL
ENSILE
EQUALS
ETHELS
ETHYLS
EVENLY
EVILLY
EXCELS
EXHALE
EXPELS
EXTOLS

E••••L

EARFUL
EIFFEL
ENAMEL
ENCYCL
ENDALL
ENROLL
ENSOUL
ENTAIL
EPICAL
ESPIAL
EYEFUL

•EL•••

BELAYS
BELDAM
BELFRY
BELGAS
BELGIC
BELIAL
BELIED
BELIEF
BELIER
BELIES
BELIZE
BELLAS
BELLED
BELLES
BELLOC
BELLOW
BELOIT
BELONG
BELTED
BELUGA
CELERY
CELIAC
CELIAS
CELLAE
CELLAR
CELLOS
CELTIC
DELAYS
DELETE
DELIAN
DELIAS
DELICT
DELIUS
DELLAS
DELPHI
DELTAS
DELUDE
DELUGE
DELUXE
DELVED
DELVER
DELVES
FELICE
FELIDS
FELINE
FELIPE
FELLAH
FELLED
FELLER
FELLOE
FELLOW
FELONS
FELONY
GELDED
GELLED
HELENA
HELENS
HELICO
HELIOS
HELIUM
HELLAS
HELLEN
HELLER
HELMET
HELOTS
HELPED
HELPER
HELVES
JELLED
KELLER
KELOID
KELVIN
MELANO
MELDED
MELEES
MELLON
MELLOW
MELODY
MELONS
MELTED
MELTER
MELTON
MELVIN
NELLIE
NELLYS
NELSON
PELAGE
PELEUS
PELIAS
PELION
PELITE
PELLET
PELOPS
PELOTA
PELTED
PELTER
PELTRY
PELVES
PELVIC
PELVIS
RELATE
RELAYS
RELENT
RELICS
RELICT
RELIED
RELIEF
RELIER
RELIES
RELINE
RELISH
RELIVE
RELOAD
SELDOM
SELECT
SELENE
SELENO
SELJUK
SELLER
SELSYN
SELVES
TELEGA
TELLER
TELLUS
TELSON
TELUGU
VELATE
VELDTS
VELLUM
VELOCE
VELOUR
VELURE
VELVET
WELDED
WELDER
WELKIN
WELLED
WELTED
WELTER
YELLED
YELLER
YELLOW
YELPED
YELPER

•E•L••

AEOLIA
AEOLIC
AEOLIS
AEOLUS
BEDLAM
BELLAS
BELLED
BELLES
BELLOC
BELLOW
BERLIN
BEULAH
BEULAS
CEILED
CELLAE
CELLAR
CELLOS
CEYLON
DEALER
DELLAS
DEPLOY
DEWLAP
FEALTY
FEELER
FELLAH
FELLED
FELLER
FELLOE
FELLOW
GELLED
HEALED
HEALER
HEALTH
HEELED
HEELER
HELLAS
HELLEN
HELLER
HENLEY
JELLED
KEELED
KEGLER
KELLER
KEPLER
LESLEY
LESLIE
MEALIE
MEDLAR
MEDLEY
MELLON
MELLOW
MERLES
MERLIN
MERLON
MEWLED
NELLIE
NELLYS
PEALED
PEELED
PEELER
PELLET
PEPLOS
PEPLUM
PEPLUS
REALES
REALLY
REALMS
REALTY
REELED
REELER
REFLET
REFLEX
REFLUX
REGLET
REPLAY
SEALED
SEALER
SELLER
SENLAC
TEFLON
TELLER
TELLUS
VEILED
VEILER
VELLUM
WEALDS
WEALTH
WELLED
WESLEY
YELLED
YELLER
YELLOW
ZEALOT

•E••L•

AEDILE
BEADLE
BEAGLE
BECALM
BEETLE
BEFALL
BEFELL
BEHALF
BEHELD
BEHOLD
BERYLS
BETELS
BEVELS
BEZELS
CECILE
CECILS
CECILY
CEDULA
CEORLS
DEADLY
DEAFLY
DEARLY
DECALS
DECILE
DECKLE
DEEPLY
DEFILE
DEFTLY
DESALT
DEVILS
EERILY
FECULA

6

FEEBLE
FEMALE
FERULA
FERULE
FETTLE
GENTLE
GERALD
GESELL
HECKLE
HEDDLE
HERALD
HEXYLS
JEKYLL
JEWELS
KECKLE
KEENLY
KERALA
KETTLE
KEVELS
LEANLY
LEVELS
LEWDLY
MEANLY
MEASLY
MEDALS
MEDDLE
MEEKLY
MEETLY
MEGALO
MEGILP
MERELY
METALS
METTLE
NEARLY
NEATLY
NEBULA
NEEDLE
NEROLI
NESTLE
NETTLE
NEVILE
NEVILL
NEWELS
PEARLS
PEARLY
PEBBLE
PEBBLY
PEDALS
PEDDLE
PENILE
PENULT
PEOPLE
PERILS
PERTLY
PESTLE
PETALS
REALLY
REBELS
REBILL
RECALL
REDDLE
REFILL
REGALE
REPELS
RESALE
RESELL
RESILE
RESOLD
RESOLE
RESULT
RETELL
RETOLD
REVELS
REVILE
REVOLT
SEDILE
SEEMLY
SEMELE
SENILE
SEPALS
SETTLE
SEWALL
TEMPLE
TERMLY
VENULE
VERILY
VEXILS
WEAKLY
WEDELN
WEEKLY
YEARLY

•E•••L

AECIAL
AERIAL
BEFALL
BEFELL
BEFOOL
BEFOUL
BELIAL
BENGAL
BENZOL
BENZYL
BETHEL
BEWAIL
CENTAL
CEREAL
DECKEL
DENIAL
DENTAL
DENTIL
DERAIL
DERMAL
DETAIL
FECIAL
FENNEL
FERIAL
FESTAL
FETIAL
FEUDAL
GENIAL
GERBIL
GESELL
HEDRAL
HERBAL
JEKYLL
JEZAIL
KENNEL
KERNEL
LEMUEL
LENTIL
LETHAL
MEDIAL
MENDEL
MENIAL
MENSAL
MENTAL
MESCAL
MESIAL
METHYL
NEURAL
NEVILL
PENCEL
PENCIL
PENIAL
PENPAL
PETREL
PETROL
REBILL
RECALL
RECOIL
RECTAL
REFILL
REGNAL
RENTAL
RESELL
RETAIL
RETELL
REVEAL
SECKEL
SENDAL
SEPTAL
SEQUEL
SERIAL
SERVAL
SEWALL
SEXUAL
TEASEL
TERCEL
TERGAL
TETRYL
TETZEL
VENIAL
VERBAL
VERGIL
VERNAL
VESSEL
VESTAL
WEASEL
WEEVIL

••EL••

ABELES
AMELIA
AMELIE
CHELAE
CHELAS
COELOM
DUELED
DUELER
DUELLO
DWELLS
EVELYN
EYELET
EYELID
FEELER
FIELDS
FJELDS
FUELED
FUELER
GAELIC
HEELED
HEELER
HUELVA
KEELED
KNELLS
LUELLA
MYELIN
NIELLI
NIELLO
OBELUS
OCELOT
OMELET
PEELED
PEELER
QUELLS
REELED
REELER
SHELBY
SHELLS
SHELLY
SHELTY
SHELVE
SMELLS
SMELLY
SMELTS
SNELLS
SPELLS
STELAE
STELAR
STELES
STELIC
STELLA
STELLI
SVELTE
SWELLS
THELMA
TWELVE
WHELKS
WHELKY
WHELMS
WHELPS
WIELDS
WIELDY
YIELDS

••E•L•

AGEDLY
AREOLA
BEETLE
CHEILO
CREELS
CREOLE
DEEPLY
DUELLO
DWELLS
EVENLY
FEEBLE
FREELY
IDEALS
ISEULT
KEENLY
KNEELS
KNELLS
LUELLA
MEEKLY
MEETLY
NEEDLE
NIELLI
NIELLO
ONEILL
OPENLY
OVERLY
PUEBLO
QUELLS
SEEMLY
SHEILA
SHELLS
SHELLY
SIECLE
SMELLS
SMELLY
SNELLS
SPELLS
STEALS
STEELS
STEELY
STELLA
STELLI
SWELLS
TREBLE
WEEKLY
WHEALS
WHEELS

••E••L

ACETAL
ACETYL
CHERYL
COEVAL
CRENEL
CRESOL
CREWEL
DAEDAL
DIESEL
EYEFUL
FOETAL
GRETEL
HIEMAL
HYETAL
IREFUL
ONEILL
PHENOL
PHENYL
RUEFUL
SHEKEL
STEROL
THECAL
THENAL
USEFUL
WEEVIL
WOEFUL
YLEVEL

•••EL•

AFIELD
ALLELE
ANGELA
ANGELO
ANGELS
ANSELM
APPELS
ARBELA
ARIELS
ARTELS
BAGELS
BARELY
BASELY
BEFELL
BEHELD
BETELS
BEVELS
BEZELS
BLUELY
BOWELS
CAMELS
CAVELL
CICELY
COMELY
CREELS
CUPELS
CUTELY
CYBELE
DIRELY
DOWELS
EASELS
ENGELS
ETHELS
EXCELS
EXPELS
FINELY
FREELY
GAMELY
GAVELS
GESELL
GIMELS
GISELE
GRUELS
HAZELS
HOMELY
HOTELS
HOVELS
HUGELY
IMPELS
ITSELF
JEWELS
JURELS
KEVELS
KNEELS
LABELS
LAMELY
LAPELS
LATELY
LEVELS

LIBELS
LIKELY
LIVELY
LONELY
LOVELL
LOVELY
LOWELL
MABELS
MERELY
MICELL
MODELS
MORELS
MOTELS
MYSELF
NAMELY
NAVELS
NEWELS
NICELY
NIGELS
NOVELS
NUDELY
ORIELS
ORWELL
OUSELS
OUZELS
PALELY
PAMELA
PANELS
POMELO
POWELL
PURELY
RARELY
RATELS
RAVELS
REBELS
REPELS
RESELL
RETELL
REVELS
RIPELY
ROWELS
RUDELY
SAFELY
SAGELY
SANELY
SEMELE
SHIELD
SOLELY
SORELS
SORELY
SPIELS
STEELS
STEELY
SURELY
TIMELY
TOWELS
TUPELO
UMBELS
UNBELT
UNWELL
UPHELD
VILELY
VOWELS
WEDELN

WHEELS
WIDELY
WIFELY
WISELY
YODELS
YOKELS

•••E•L

ANNEAL
APNEAL
APPEAL
BEFELL
BOREAL
CAVELL
CEREAL
CINEOL
CUNEAL
FOVEAL
GESELL
LINEAL
LOVELL
LOWELL
LUTEAL
MICELL
ORDEAL
ORWELL
OSTEAL
PINEAL
POWELL
RESELL
RETELL
REVEAL
SQUEAL
UNREAL
UNREEL
UNSEAL
UNVEIL
UNWELL

••••EL

ALUDEL
ARABEL
AZAZEL
AZRAEL
BARBEL
BARREL
BETHEL
BORDEL
BULBEL
BUSHEL
CANCEL
CANNEL
CARCEL
CARMEL
CARPEL
CARREL
CARTEL
CARVEL
CHAPEL
CHISEL
COMPEL
CORBEL
CORNEL
CRENEL
CREWEL
CUDGEL
DAMSEL
DANIEL
DARNEL
DECKEL
DIESEL
DISPEL
DOSSEL
DOTTEL
DRIVEL
DUFFEL
EIFFEL
ENAMEL
FENNEL
FUNNEL
GOSPEL
GRAVEL
GRETEL
GRIZEL
GROVEL
GUNNEL
HALLEL
HANDEL
HANSEL
HASSEL
HOSTEL
ISABEL
ISOBEL
ISOHEL
ISRAEL
KENNEL
KERNEL
KUMMEL
LAUREL
LEMUEL
LINTEL
LIONEL
LISTEL
MANTEL
MANUEL
MARCEL
MARVEL
MENDEL
MICHEL
MIGUEL
MORSEL
MURIEL
MUSSEL
NICKEL
PARCEL
PARREL
PASTEL
PENCEL
PETREL
POMMEL
PROPEL
PUMMEL
RACHEL
RAPPEL
ROMMEL
RONDEL
RUNNEL
SAMIEL
SAMUEL
SAUREL
SECKEL
SEQUEL
SHEKEL
SHOVEL
SIMNEL
SNIVEL
SORREL
SPINEL
STIPEL
SWIVEL
TASSEL
TEASEL
TERCEL
TETZEL
TINSEL
TRAVEL
TROWEL
TUNNEL
UNREEL
VESSEL
WEASEL
YLEVEL

EM••••

EMBALM
EMBANK
EMBARK
EMBARS
EMBAYS
EMBEDS
EMBERS
EMBLEM
EMBODY
EMBOLI
EMBOSS
EMBOWS
EMBRUE
EMBRYO
EMCEED
EMCEES
EMEERS
EMENDS
EMERGE
EMERIC
EMESIS
EMETIC
EMETIN
EMEUTE
EMIGRE
EMILES
EMILIA
EMILIE
EMILIO
EMILYS
EMMETS
EMMETT
EMMIES
EMOTED
EMOTES
EMPALE
EMPERY
EMPIRE
EMPLOY

E•M•••

EDMOND
EDMUND
ELMERS
ELMIRA
EMMETS
EMMETT
EMMIES
ENMESH
ENMITY
ERMINE
EXMOOR

E••M••

ELEMIS
ENAMEL
ENAMOR
ENEMAS
ETYMON
EXAMEN
EXEMPT

E•••M•

ECTOMY
ECZEMA
ENCAMP
ENIGMA
ENTOMB
ENTOMO
ENWOMB
ENZYME
ESKIMO
EXHUME

E••••M

EGOISM
ELOHIM
EMBALM
EMBLEM
ENGRAM
EONISM
EPONYM
ERBIUM
ESTEEM

•EM•••

BEMATA
BEMEAN
BEMIRE
BEMOAN
BEMUSE
CEMENT
DEMAND
DEMEAN
DEMIES
DEMISE
DEMITS
DEMOBS
DEMODE
DEMONO
DEMONS
DEMOTE
DEMURE
DEMURS
FEMALE
FEMORA
FEMURS
GEMARA
GEMINI
GEMMAE
GEMMED
GEMOTS
HEMATO
HEMMED
HEMMER
HEMOID
HEMPEN
JEMIMA
LEMMAS
LEMNOS
LEMONS
LEMUEL
LEMURS
MEMBER
MEMOIR
MEMORY
NEMATO
REMADE
REMAIN
REMAKE
REMAND
REMANS
REMARK
REMEDY
REMIND
REMISE
REMISS
REMITS
REMORA
REMOTE
REMOVE
REMUDA
SEMELE
SEMEME
SEMITE
SEMPRE
TEMPER
TEMPLE
TEMPOS
TEMPTS
YEMENI

•E•M••

BEAMED
BERMES
CERMET
DEEMED
DERMAL
DERMAS
DERMAT
DERMIC
DESMAN
DESMID
FERMIS
GEMMAE
GEMMED

6

GERMAN
HELMET
HEMMED
HEMMER
HERMAE
HERMAI
HERMAN
HERMES
HERMIT
HETMAN
KERMES
KERMIS
LEGMAN
LEGMEN
LEMMAS
MERMAN
MERMEN
NEUMES
PENMAN
PENMEN
PERMIT
REAMED
REAMER
SEAMAN
SEAMED
SEAMEN
SEAMER
SEAMUS
SEEMED
SEEMER
SEEMLY
SERMON
TEAMED
TEEMED
TEEMER
TEGMEN
TERMED
TERMER
TERMLY
TERMOR
VERMIN
WEIMAR
YEOMAN
YEOMEN

•E••M•

BECAME
BECOME
BEDIMS
BEGUMS
BENUMB
BESOMS
DECAMP
DEFAME
DEGAME
DEGUMS
DENIMS
HEAUME
JEMIMA
JEREMY
JEROME
LEGUME
METUMP
REALMS
REARMS
REGIME
RESUME
REVAMP
SEDUMS
SEISMO
SEISMS
SEMEME
SERUMS
SESAME
VENOMS
ZEUGMA

•E•••M

AECIUM
BECALM
BEDLAM
BELDAM
BESEEM
CERIUM
CESIUM
DEFORM
FERRUM
HELIUM
JETSAM
MEDIUM
MEGRIM
PEPLUM
RECTUM
REDEEM
REFORM
SELDOM
SEPTUM
SEXISM
TEDIUM
TERGUM
VELLUM
VERISM

••EM••

ANEMIA
ANEMIC
AXEMAN
AXEMEN
BREMEN
COEMPT
CREMES
DAEMON
DEEMED
ELEMIS
ENEMAS
EXEMPT
FOEMAN
FOEMEN
HIEMAL
ICEMAN
ICEMEN
PREMED
PYEMIA
PYEMIC
SEEMED
SEEMER
SEEMLY
TEEMED
TEEMER
THEMES
THEMIS
TREMOR
ULEMAS
UREMIA

••E•M•

ADEEMS
BREAMS
BREGMA
CAEOMA
CLEOME
CREAMS
CREAMY
DREAMS
DREAMT
DREAMY
FLEAMS
GLEAMS
GLEAMY
HBEAMS
IBEAMS
PNEUMA
PNEUMO
RHEIMS
RHEUMY
SPERMO
STEAMS
STEAMY
THELMA
THERMO
THERMS
WHELMS
ZBEAMS

••E••M

ACETUM
CAECUM
COELOM
FRENUM
PLENUM
THEISM

•••EM•

ADEEMS
BIREME
CINEMA
ECZEMA
HAREMS
JEREMY
PROEMS
RACEME
SCHEMA
SCHEME
SEMEME
SOLEMN
TAXEME
TOTEMS
XYLEMS

•••E•M

AGLEAM
ANSELM
BESEEM
ESTEEM
LUTEUM
LYCEUM
MUSEUM
PHLEGM
PILEUM
REDEEM
SCREAM
STREAM
UNSEAM

••••EM

ANADEM
ANTHEM
BESEEM
DIADEM
EMBLEM
ESTEEM
HARLEM
IBIDEM
MAYHEM
MOSLEM
PHLOEM
REDEEM
SACHEM
SYSTEM
TANDEM

EN••••

ENABLE
ENACTS
ENAMEL
ENAMOR
ENATES
ENATIC
ENCAGE
ENCAMP
ENCASE
ENCINA
ENCODE
ENCORE
ENCYCL
ENCYST
ENDALL
ENDEAR
ENDING
ENDIVE
ENDOWS
ENDUED
ENDUES
ENDURE
ENEMAS
ENERGY
ENFACE
ENFOLD
ENGAGE
ENGELS
ENGINE
ENGIRD
ENGIRT
ENGRAM
ENGULF
ENIGMA
ENISLE
ENJOIN
ENJOYS
ENLACE
ENLIST
ENMESH
ENMITY
ENNEAD
ENOSIS
ENOUGH
ENRAGE
ENRAPT
ENRICH
ENRICO
ENROBE
ENROLL
ENROOT
ENSIGN
ENSILE
ENSOUL
ENSUED
ENSUES
ENSURE
ENTAIL
ENTERA
ENTERO
ENTERS
ENTICE
ENTIRE
ENTITY
ENTOMB
ENTOMO
ENTRAP
ENTREE
ENVIED
ENVIER
ENVIES
ENVOYS
ENWIND
ENWOMB
ENWRAP
ENZYME

E•N•••

ENNEAD
EONIAN
EONISM
ERNEST
ERNIES
EUNICE
EUNUCH

E••N••

EARNED
EARNER
EGGNOG
ELANDS
ELENAS
EMENDS
EPONYM
ERINGO
ERYNGO
ETHNIC
EUPNEA
EVENED
EVENLY
EVENTS
EVINCE

E•••N•

EALING
EARING
EASING
EATING
EBBING
ECHINI
ECHINO
EDGING
EDMOND
EDMUND
EDWINA
EDWINS
EGGING
ELAINE
ELAYNE
ELFINS
ELLENS
ELOINS
EMBANK
ENCINA
ENDING
ENGINE
ENWIND
EOCENE
EOGENE
EQUINE
ERMINE
ERRAND
ERRANT
ERRING
ERWINS
ESCENT
ESPANA
ESSENE
ETHANE
ETHANS
EUGENE
EVZONE
EXEUNT
EXPAND
EXPEND
EXTANT
EXTEND
EXTENT
EYEING

E••••N

EASTON
EDISON
EILEEN
ELEVEN
ELEVON
ELOIGN
EMETIN
ENJOIN
ENSIGN
EOLIAN
EONIAN

6

ETYMON
EVELYN
EXAMEN
EXOGEN
EXTERN

•EN•••

AENEAS
AENEID
BENDAY
BENDEE
BENDER
BENGAL
BENIGN
BENITA
BENITO
BENJYS
BENNES
BENNET
BENNYS
BENTON
BENUMB
BENZOL
BENZYL
CENSED
CENSER
CENSES
CENSOR
CENSUS
CENTAL
CENTER
CENTOS
CENTRA
CENTRI
CENTRO
DENARY
DENDRI
DENDRO
DENGUE
DENIAL
DENIED
DENIER
DENIES
DENIMS
DENISE
DENNED
DENNIS
DENNYS
DENOTE
DENSER
DENTAL
DENTED
DENTIL
DENTIN
DENUDE
DENVER
FENCED
FENCER
FENCES
FENDED
FENDER
FENIAN
FENNEC
FENNEL
FENRIR
GENDER
GENERA
GENETS
GENEVA
GENIAL
GENIES
GENITO
GENIUS
GENOUS
GENRES
GENROS
GENTES
GENTLE
GENTOO
GENTRY
HENBIT
HENLEY
HENNAS
HENRIS
HENRYS
JENNET
JENNYS
KENNED
KENNEL
KENNIE
KENNYS
LENAPE
LENDER
LENGTH
LENITY
LENNYS
LENORE
LENSES
LENTEN
LENTIL
LENTOS
MENACE
MENAGE
MENDED
MENDEL
MENDER
MENHIR
MENIAL
MENINX
MENSAL
MENSES
MENTAL
MENTOR
PENCEL
PENCIL
PENDED
PENGOS
PENIAL
PENILE
PENMAN
PENMEN
PENNAE
PENNED
PENNER
PENNIA
PENNIS
PENNON
PENNYS
PENPAL
PENTAD
PENTUP
PENULT
PENURY
RENDED
RENDER
RENEES
RENEGE
RENEWS
RENNET
RENNIN
RENOIR
RENOWN
RENTAL
RENTED
RENTER
RENTES
SENARY
SENATE
SENDAL
SENDER
SENECA
SENILE
SENIOR
SENLAC
SENNAS
SENNET
SENNIT
SENORA
SENSED
SENSES
SENSOR
SENTRY
TENACE
TENANT
TENDED
TENDER
TENDON
TENETS
TENNIS
TENONS
TENORS
TENPIN
TENREC
TENSED
TENSER
TENSES
TENSOR
TENTED
TENTER
TENTHS
TENUES
TENUIS
TENURE
TENUTO
VENDED
VENDEE
VENDER
VENDOR
VENDUE
VENEER
VENERY
VENIAL
VENICE
VENIRE
VENOMS
VENOSE
VENOUS
VENTED
VENTER
VENTRO
VENUES
VENULE
WENDED
WENDYS
YENNED
ZENANA
ZENGER
ZENITH

•E•N••

BEANED
BEANIE
BEINGS
BENNES
BENNET
BENNYS
BERNEY
BERNIE
DENNED
DENNIS
DENNYS
FEINTS
FENNEC
FENNEL
HENNAS
HERNIA
HERNIO
JEANNE
JENNET
JENNYS
KEENED
KEENER
KEENLY
KENNED
KENNEL
KENNIE
KENNYS
KERNED
KERNEL
KEYNES
LEANED
LEANER
LEANLY
LEANTO
LEMNOS
LENNYS
LEONAS
LEONIE
MEANER
MEANIE
MEANLY
MESNES
PEANUT
PEENED
PENNAE
PENNED
PENNER
PENNIA
PENNIS
PENNON
PENNYS
REGNAL
REINED
RENNET
RENNIN
SEANCE
SEINED
SEINER
SEINES
SENNAS
SENNET
SENNIT
TEENSY
TENNIS
VEINED
VERNAL
VERNAS
VERNIX
VERNON
WEANED
WEANER
WEENIE
WEENSY
YEANED
YENNED

•E••N•

BEGINS
BEHIND
BELONG
BERING
BETONY
BEYOND
BEZANT
CEDING
CEMENT
CERING
CETANE
DEBUNK
DECANE
DECANT
DECENT
DEDANS
DEFEND
DEFINE
DEIGNS
DEKING
DEMAND
DEMONO
DEMONS
DEPEND
DETENT
DEWANS
FECUND
FEEING
FEIGNS
FELINE
FELONS
FELONY
FERINE
FETING
FEUING
GEEING
GEMINI
GERENT
GERUND
HELENA
HELENS
HERONS
HEWING
HEXANE
HEXING
HEXONE
JEANNE
JEEING
JEJUNE
KETENE
KETONE
KEVINS
KEYING
LEARNS
LEARNT
LEGEND
LEMONS
LEVANT
MEKONG
MELANO
MELONS
MENINX
MERINO
MESONS
METING
MEWING
PECANS
PEDANT
PEKANS
PEKING
RECANT
RECENT
REDANS
REDONE
REFINE
REFUND
REGENT
REGINA
REIGNS
RELENT
RELINE
REMAND
REMANS
REMIND
REPAND
REPENT
REPINE
RERUNS
RESEND
RESENT
RESINS
RETENE
RETINA
REWIND
SECANT
SECOND
SECUND

SEDANS
SEEING
SEJANT
SELENE
SELENO
SERENA
SERENE
SERINE
SERINS
SETONS
SEVENS
SEWING
SEXING
TECHNO
TEEING
TENANT
TENONS
TETANY
TETONS
VERONA
VEXING
WERENT
YEARNS
YEMENI
ZENANA

•E•••N

AEGEAN
BEACON
BEATEN
BECKON
BEDPAN
BEDUIN
BEGUIN
BEMEAN
BEMOAN
BENIGN
BENTON
BERGEN
BERLIN
CEYLON
DEACON
DEADEN
DEAFEN
DECCAN
DECERN
DEEPEN
DEEWAN
DEHORN
DELIAN
DEMEAN
DENTIN
DERAIN
DESIGN
DESMAN
DETAIN
DEVEIN
FENIAN
FEZZAN
GERMAN
GERYON
HEADON
HEAVEN
HEBRON
HEDRON
HELLEN
HEMPEN
HEREIN
HEREON
HERMAN
HEROIN
HETMAN
JERKIN
JETTON
KEDRON
KELVIN
LEADEN
LEADIN
LEAVEN
LEGION
LEGMAN
LEGMEN
LENTEN
LEPTON
LESION
LESSEN
LESSON
MECCAN
MEDIAN
MELLON
MELTON
MELVIN
MERLIN
MERLON
MERMAN
MERMEN
MERVIN
MESIAN
NEKTON
NELSON
NEURON
NEWTON
PEAHEN
PEASEN
PECTEN
PECTIN
PELION
PENMAN
PENMEN
PENNON
PEPSIN
PERRON
PERSON
PETAIN
REASON
REBORN
RECKON
REDDEN
REDFIN
REGAIN
REGION
REJOIN
REMAIN
RENNIN
RENOWN
REOPEN
RESIGN
RETAIN
RETURN
REUBEN
SEAMAN
SEAMEN
SEAPEN
SEASON
SEAWAN
SECERN
SEISIN
SEIZIN
SELSYN
SEQUIN
SEREIN
SERMON
SEXTAN
SEXTON
TEFLON
TEGMEN
TELSON
TENDON
TENPIN
TESTON
TEUTON
VERDIN
VERDUN
VEREIN
VERMIN
VERNON
WEAKEN
WEAPON
WEDELN
WELKIN
YEOMAN
YEOMEN
ZECHIN

••EN••

ADENIS
AGENCY
AGENDA
AGENTS
AKENES
AMENDS
AMENRA
AMENTS
ARENAS
AVENGE
AVENUE
BLENCH
BLENDE
BLENDS
BLENNY
BRENDA
BRENTS
CLENCH
CRENEL
DRENCH
DUENNA
ELENAS
EMENDS
EVENED
EVENLY
EVENTS
FIENDS
FLENCH
FLENSE
FRENCH
FRENUM
FRENZY
GUENON
GWENNS
HYENAS
IRENES
IRENIC
KEENED
KEENER
KEENLY
MAENAD
OHENRY
OMENTA
OPENED
OPENER
OPENLY
PEENED
PHENOL
PHENYL
PLENTY
PLENUM
SCENDS
SCENES
SCENIC
SCENTS
SIENNA
SPENDS
STENCH
STENOG
TAENIA
TEENSY
THENAL
THENAR
THENCE
TRENCH
TRENDS
TRENDY
TWENTY
ULENCE
UPENDS
VIENNA
WEENIE
WEENSY
WHENCE
WIENER
WIENIE
WRENCH

••E•N•

AGEING
AVERNO
AWEING
BLENNY
CLEANS
DOESNT
DUENNA
DYEING
EXEUNT
EYEING
FEEING
FOEHNS
FREONS
FRESNO
GEEING
GLEANS
GREENS
GWENNS
HIEING
HOEING
JEEING
LIERNE
OCEANS
PAEANS
PAEONS
PREENS
QUEANS
QUEENS
QUERNS
SEEING
SHEENS
SHEENY
SIENNA
SKEANS
SKEINS
STEINS
STERNA
STERNO
STERNS
TEEING
TIEINS
TOEING
VIENNA

••E••N

ALEXIN
AXEMAN
AXEMEN
BREMEN
BRETON
CRETAN
CRETIN
DAEMON
DEEPEN
DEEWAN
ELEVEN
ELEVON
EMETIN
EVELYN
FOEMAN
FOEMEN
GUENON
ICEMAN
ICEMEN
MYELIN
OBERON
OLEFIN
OREGON
QUEZON
STEFAN
STEPAN
STEPIN
STEVEN
SWEDEN
TREPAN
UNEVEN

•••EN•

ABSENT
ACCENT
ACHENE
ADDEND
ADVENT
ALIENS
ALKENE
ALLENS
AMIENS
APPEND
ARDENT
ARGENT
ARLENE
ARPENS
ARPENT
ASCEND
ASCENT
ASPENS
ASSENT
ATHENA
ATHENE
ATHENS
ATTEND
AUGEND
CADENT
CATENA
CEMENT
CLIENT
COGENT
COZENS
CYMENE
CYRENE
DECENT
DEFEND
DEPEND
DETENT
DIZENS
DOCENT
DOYENS
DOZENS
ELLENS
EOCENE
EOGENE
ESCENT
ESSENE
EUGENE
EXPEND
EXTEND
EXTENT
FLUENT
FOMENT
FRIEND
GALENA
GERENT
GREENS
HAVENS
HAVENT
HELENA
HELENS
HYMENO
HYMENS
IMPEND
INDENE

INDENT
INTEND
INTENT
INVENT
KARENS
KETENE
LAMENT
LATENT
LEGEND
LIKENS
LIMENS
LINENS
LIVENS
LOMENT
LORENE
LORENZ
LUCENT
LUMENS
MOMENT
NOCENT
NOVENA
OFFEND
ORIENT
PARENS
PARENT
PATENS
PATENT
PHRENO
PINENE
PONENT
POTENT
PREENS
PYRENE
QUEENS
RAVENS
RECENT
REGENT
RELENT
REPENT
RESEND
RESENT
RETENE
RIDENT
RIPENS
RODENT
ROWENA
RUBENS
SELENE
SELENO
SERENA
SERENE
SEVENS
SHEENS
SHEENY
SILENI
SILENT
SIRENS
SOLENT
SPHENE
SPHENO
SPLENO
TALENT
TOKENS
UNBEND
UNBENT
URGENT
VIXENS
WAKENS
WERENT
WIDENS
WIZENS
XYLENE
YAMENS
YEMENI

•••E•N

AEGEAN
AILEEN
ANDEAN
ARLEEN
ASTERN
AUGEAN
BALEEN
BEMEAN
BOLEYN
CAREEN
CASEIN
CASERN
CAVEIN
CAVERN
CODEIN
COMEON
DECERN
DEMEAN
DEVEIN
DOREEN
DUDEEN
EILEEN
EXTERN
FADEIN
GIDEON
GOVERN
HEREIN
HEREON
INTERN
JUDEAN
KOREAN
LATEEN
LOREEN
LOVEIN
MODERN
MOREEN
NOREEN
ORCEIN
OSSEIN
PIGEON
POTEEN
SABEAN
SATEEN
SCREEN
SECERN
SEREIN
SIMEON
SOLEMN
SPLEEN
STREWN
TAKEIN
TAVERN
TUREEN
UNSEEN
VEREIN
WEDELN
WIGEON
WIVERN
WYVERN

••••EN

AACHEN
ACUMEN
ADRIEN
AIDMEN
AILEEN
AIRMEN
ARISEN
ARLEEN
ASHMEN
AUSTEN
AWAKEN
AXEMEN
BADMEN
BAGMEN
BALEEN
BARMEN
BARREN
BATMEN
BATTEN
BEATEN
BERGEN
BIDDEN
BIOGEN
BITTEN
BOWMEN
BRAZEN
BREMEN
BROKEN
BUNSEN
BURDEN
BUSMEN
CABMEN
CAMDEN
CAREEN
CARMEN
CARVEN
CHOSEN
CLOVEN
COWMEN
CRAVEN
DAMPEN
DARIEN
DARKEN
DEADEN
DEAFEN
DEEPEN
DOLMEN
DOREEN
DRIVEN
DRYDEN
DUDEEN
DUODEN
EILEEN
ELEVEN
EXAMEN
EXOGEN
FALLEN
FASTEN
FATTEN
FLAMEN
FLAXEN
FOEMEN
FRAUEN
FROZEN
GARDEN
GASMEN
GLUTEN
GOLDEN
GORHEN
GOSHEN
GOTTEN
GRABEN
GRAVEN
GULDEN
GUNMEN
HAMDEN
HAPPEN
HARDEN
HARKEN
HASTEN
HAUSEN
HEAVEN
HELLEN
HEMPEN
HIDDEN
HODDEN
HOIDEN
HOYDEN
HYPHEN
ICEMEN
IMOGEN
KITTEN
KRAKEN
KRONEN
KUCHEN
LATEEN
LATTEN
LAYMEN
LEADEN
LEAVEN
LEGMEN
LENTEN
LESSEN
LICHEN
LINDEN
LISTEN
LOOSEN
LOREEN
LOUDEN
LUCIEN
LUMPEN
MADDEN
MADMEN
MAIDEN
MARTEN
MERMEN
MIDDEN
MILDEN
MITTEN
MIZZEN
MOLTEN
MOREEN
MORGEN
MULLEN
NOREEN
ORIGEN
OXYGEN
PATTEN
PEAHEN
PEASEN
PECTEN
PENMEN
PIGPEN
PITMEN
PLATEN
POLLEN
POTEEN
PROVEN
RAGMEN
RATTEN
REDDEN
REOPEN
REUBEN
RIDDEN
RODMEN
ROTTEN
SADDEN
SATEEN
SCREEN
SEAMEN
SEAPEN
SHAKEN
SHAPEN
SHAVEN
SICKEN
SILKEN
SKYMEN
SLOVEN
SOCMEN
SODDEN
SOFTEN
SPLEEN
SPOKEN
STAMEN
STEVEN
STOLEN
SUDDEN
SULLEN
SUNKEN
SWEDEN
TAUTEN
TEGMEN
TUREEN
UNEVEN
UNSEEN
VANMEN
VIVIEN
WARDEN
WARREN
WEAKEN
WHITEN
WOODEN
WOOLEN
WORSEN
YEOMEN

EO••••

EOCENE
EOGENE
EOLIAN
EOLITH
EONIAN
EONISM
EOZOIC

E•O•••

EBOATS
ECOLES
EGOISM
EGOIST
ELOHIM
ELOIGN
ELOINS
ELOISE
ELOPED
ELOPER
ELOPES
EMOTED
EMOTES
ENOSIS
ENOUGH
EPOCHS
EPODES
EPONYM
EPOPEE
ERODED
ERODES
EROTIC
EVOKED
EVOKES
EVOLVE
EXODUS
EXOGEN
EXOTIC

E••O••

ECHOED
ECHOER
ECHOES
ECHOIC
ECTOMY
EDMOND
EFFORT
EIDOLA
ELBOWS
ELIOTS
EMBODY
EMBOLI
EMBOSS
EMBOWS
ENCODE
ENCORE
ENDOWS
ENFOLD
ENJOIN
ENJOYS
ENROBE

6

ENROLL
ENROOT
ENSOUL
ENTOMB
ENTOMO
ENVOYS
ENWOMB
EOZOIC
EPHODS
EPHORI
EPHORS
ERRORS
ESCORT
ESTOPS
EUBOEA
EUDORA
EULOGY
EUROPA
EUROPE
EVZONE
EXHORT
EXMOOR
EXPORT
EXPOSE
EXTOLS
EXTORT

E•••O•

EASTON
EDISON
EDITOR
EGGNOG
ELEVON
ELLIOT
EMPLOY
ENAMOR
ENROOT
EPILOG
EPIZOA
ESCROW
ETYMON
EXMOOR

E••••O

ECHINO
EMBRYO
EMILIO
ENRICO
ENTERO
ENTOMO
ERINGO
ERYNGO
ESCUDO
ESKIMO

•EO•••

AEOLIA
AEOLIC
AEOLIS
AEOLUS
CEORLS
DEODAR
FEODOR
FEOFFS
GEODES
GEODIC
GEORGE
GEORGI
LEONAS
LEONIE
MEOWED
PEOPLE
PEORIA
REOPEN
YEOMAN
YEOMEN

•E•O••

AEROBE
BECOME
BEFOGS
BEFOOL
BEFORE
BEFOUL
BEHOLD
BEHOOF
BEHOVE
BELOIT
BELONG
BEMOAN
BESOMS
BESOTS
BETONY
BETOOK
BEYOND
BEZOAR
CEBOID
CEROUS
DECOCT
DECODE
DECORS
DECOYS
DEFORM
DEHORN
DEMOBS
DEMODE
DEMONO
DEMONS
DEMOTE
DENOTE
DEPORT
DEPOSE
DEPOTS
DESOXY
DETOUR
DEVOID
DEVOIR
DEVOTE
DEVOUR
DEVOUT
FEDORA
FELONS
FELONY
FEMORA
FEROUS
FETORS
GEMOTS
GENOUS
GEROUS
HELOTS
HEMOID
HEROES
HEROIC
HEROIN
HERONS
HEXONE
HEXOSE
JEROME
KELOID
KETONE
KETOSE
LEMONS
LENORE
LEROYS
MEKONG
MELODY
MELONS
MEMOIR
MEMORY
MEROUS
MESONS
METOPE
NEROLI
NEVOID
PEKOES
PELOPS
PELOTA
PEYOTE
REBORN
REBOZO
RECOIL
RECORD
RECOUP
REDOES
REDONE
REDOWA
REFORM
REJOIN
RELOAD
REMORA
REMOTE
REMOVE
RENOIR
RENOWN
REPORT
REPOSE
RESOLD
RESOLE
RESORB
RESORT
RETOLD
RETOOK
RETORT
REVOKE
REVOLT
REWORD
SECOND
SENORA
SEPOYS
SEROUS
SEROWS
SETOFF
SETONS
SETOSE
SETOUS
TENONS
TENORS
TETONS
VELOCE
VELOUR
VENOMS
VENOSE
VENOUS
VERONA
VETOED
VETOER
VETOES
ZEROED
ZEROES

•E••O•

BEACON
BECKON
BEFOOL
BEHOOF
BELLOC
BELLOW
BENTON
BENZOL
BESTOW
BETOOK
BETTOR
CELLOS
CENSOR
CENTOS
CEYLON
DEACON
DEBTOR
DEPLOY
DESPOT
FELLOE
FELLOW
FEODOR
FERVOR
GECKOS
GENROS
GENTOO
GERYON
GESSOS
HEADON
HEBRON
HECTOR
HEDRON
HELIOS
HEREOF
HEREON
HERIOT
HESIOD
JERBOA
JETTON
KEDRON
LECTOR
LEGION
LEMNOS
LENTOS
LEPTON
LESION
LESSON
LESSOR
MEADOW
MELLON
MELLOW
MELTON
MENTOR
MERLON
METEOR
METHOD
METROS
MEZZOS
NEKTON
NELSON
NESTOR
NEURON
NEWTON
PEDROS
PEGTOP
PELION
PENGOS
PENNON
PEPLOS
PEQUOD
PEQUOT
PERIOD
PERRON
PERSON
PETROL
REASON
REAVOW
RECKON
RECTOR
RECTOS
REDDOG
REDHOT
REDTOP
REGION
RETOOK
SEADOG
SEASON
SECTOR
SEISOR
SEIZOR
SELDOM
SENIOR
SENSOR
SERMON
SERVOS
SETTOS
SEXTON
TEAPOT
TEAPOY
TEFLON
TELSON
TEMPOS
TENDON
TENSOR
TERMOR
TERROR
TESTON
TEUTON
VECTOR
VENDOR
VERNON
VERSOS
WEAPON
YELLOW
ZEALOT
ZETHOS

•E•••O

AERUGO
BENITO
CENTRO
CERATO
DEMONO
DENDRO
DEXTRO
GENITO
GENTOO
HELICO
HEMATO
HEPATO
HERETO
HERNIO
HETERO
JETHRO
KERATO
LEANTO
LEGATO
LEPIDO
MEDICO
MEGALO
MEJICO
MELANO
MERINO
MEXICO
NEMATO
NEPHRO
REBATO
REBOZO
REECHO
SEISMO
SELENO
TECHNO
TENUTO
TERATO
TEREDO
VENTRO
VESICO

••EO••

ACEOUS
AREOLA
CAEOMA
CHEOPS
CLEOME
CREOLE
FREONS
PAEONS
THEORY

••E•O•

BRETON
CHEGOE
COELOM

CREDOS
CRESOL
DAEMON
ELEVON
FAEROE
FLEXOR
FOETOR
GREGOS
GUENON
ICEBOX
OBERON
OCELOT
OREGON
PHENOL
PLEXOR
PRETOR
QUEZON
RHETOR
STENOG
STEROL
TREMOR

••E••O

ALECTO
ALEPPO
AREZZO
AVERNO
CHEILO
CHEIRO
DUELLO
FRESCO
FRESNO
GHETTO
NIELLO
ONEIRO
OVERDO
PIETRO
PLEURO
PNEUMO
PRESTO
PSEUDO
PUEBLO
REECHO
SPERMO
STEREO
STERNO
STETHO
THERMO
UNESCO

•••EO•

CAMEOS
CINEOL
COMEON
GIDEON
HEREOF
HEREON
MATEOS
METEOR
PIGEON
RODEOS
SIMEON
VIREOS
WIGEON

•••E•O

ALBEDO
ANGELO
ANTERO
ASTERO
BOLERO
CHAETO
CICERO
COMEDO
DINERO
ENTERO
FOREGO
GAMETO
GAZEBO
GRAECO
GYNECO
HERETO
HETERO
HYMENO
INFERO
KINETO
LAREDO
NONEGO
PHLEBO
PHRENO
POMELO
SCLERO
SELENO
SIDERO
SPHENO
SPLENO
TEREDO
TOLEDO
TORERO
TUPELO
TUXEDO

••••EO

ARCHEO
BORNEO
CHOREO
JUDAEO
MATTEO
PALAEO
STEREO
THYREO

EP••••

EPACTS
EPARCH
EPHAHS
EPHEBI
EPHODS
EPHORI
EPHORS
EPICAL
EPILOG
EPIRUS
EPIZOA
EPOCHS
EPODES
EPONYM
EPOPEE

E•P•••

EMPALE
EMPERY
EMPIRE
EMPLOY
ESPANA
ESPIAL
ESPIED
ESPIES
ESPRIT
EUPNEA
EXPAND
EXPECT
EXPELS
EXPEND
EXPERT
EXPIRE
EXPIRY
EXPORT
EXPOSE

E••P••

ELAPSE
ELOPED
ELOPER
ELOPES
EPOPEE
ERUPTS
ETAPES

E•••P•

ECTYPE
ENRAPT
EQUIPS
ESCAPE
ESTOPS
EURIPI
EUROPA
EUROPE
EXCEPT
EXEMPT

E••••P

EARLAP
ENCAMP
ENTRAP
ENWRAP
ESCARP
EYECUP

•EP•••

DEPART
DEPEND
DEPICT
DEPLOY
DEPORT
DEPOSE
DEPOTS
DEPTHS
DEPUTE
DEPUTY
HEPATO
HEPTAD
KEPLER
LEPERS
LEPIDO
LEPSIA
LEPTON
NEPHEW
NEPHRO
PEPLOS
PEPLUM
PEPLUS
PEPPED
PEPPER
PEPSIN
PEPTIC
REPAID
REPAIR
REPAND
REPASS
REPAST
REPAYS
REPEAT
REPELS
REPENT
REPINE
REPLAY
REPORT
REPOSE
REPUTE
SEPALS
SEPIAS
SEPOYS
SEPSIS
SEPTAL
SEPTET
SEPTIC
SEPTUM
TEPEES
TEPEFY
ZEPHYR

•E•P••

BEDPAN
BEEPED
DEEPEN
DEEPER
DEEPLY
DELPHI
DESPOT
HEAPED
HELPED
HELPER
HEMPEN
HERPES
KEEPER
KEWPIE
LEAPED
LEAPER
PEEPED
PEEPER
PENPAL
PEOPLE
PEPPED
PEPPER
REAPED
REAPER
REOPEN
SEAPEN
SECPAR
SEEPED
SEMPRE
TEAPOT
TEAPOY
TEMPER
TEMPLE
TEMPOS
TEMPTS
TENPIN
VESPER
VESPID
WEAPON
WEEPER
YELPED
YELPER

•E••P•

CERIPH
FELIPE
GETUPS
LENAPE
LETUPS
METOPE
PELOPS
RECAPS
RECEPT
RECIPE
SERAPE
SERAPH
SETUPS
TERAPH

•E•••P

DECAMP
DEWLAP
MEGILP
METUMP
PEGTOP
PENTUP
RECOUP
REDCAP
REDTOP
REVAMP
TEACUP

••EP••

ADEPTS
ALEPHS
ALEPPO
BEEPED
CREPED
CREPES
DEEPEN
DEEPER
DEEPLY
DIEPPE
KEEPER
PEEPED
PEEPER
PREPAY
SEEPED
STEPAN
STEPIN
STEPPE
STEPUP
TREPAN
WEEPER

••E•P•

ALEPPO
CHEEPS
CHEOPS
COEMPT
CREEPS
CREEPY
DIEPPE
EXEMPT
SHERPA
SLEEPS
SLEEPY
STEEPS
STEPPE
SWEEPS
SWEEPY
TIEUPS
TWERPS
WHELPS

••E••P

EYECUP
ICECAP
STEPUP
TOECAP

•••EP•

ACCEPT
BICEPS
CHEEPS
CREEPS
CREEPY
EXCEPT
INCEPT
JOSEPH
JULEPS
RECEPT
SLEEPS
SLEEPY
STEEPS
SWEEPS
SWEEPY
UNWEPT
YCLEPT

•••E•P

ASLEEP
LINEUP
MADEUP
MAKEUP
TAKEUP
TUNEUP
UPKEEP

••••EP

ASLEEP
INSTEP

6

UNSTEP
UPKEEP

EQ••••
EQUALS
EQUATE
EQUINE
EQUIPS
EQUITY

E••Q••
EXEQUY

•EQ•••
PEQUOD
PEQUOT
SEQUEL
SEQUIN

•E•Q••
SESQUI

••EQ••
EXEQUY

ER••••
ERASED
ERASER
ERASES
ERBIUM
EREBUS
ERECTS
ERFURT
ERGATE
ERICHS
ERINGO
ERMINE
ERNEST
ERNIES
ERODED
ERODES
EROTIC
ERRAND
ERRANT
ERRATA
ERRING
ERRORS
ERSATZ
ERUCTS
ERUPTS
ERWINS
ERYNGO
ERYTHR

E•R•••
EARFUL
EARING
EARLAP
EARLES
EARNED
EARNER
EARTHS
EARTHY
EARWAX
EARWIG
EERILY
EGRESS
EGRETS
ENRAGE
ENRAPT
ENRICH
ENRICO
ENROBE
ENROLL
ENROOT
ERRAND
ERRANT
ERRATA
ERRING
ERRORS
EUREKA
EURIPI
EUROPA
EUROPE
EYRIES

E••R••
ECARTE
EGERIA
ELBRUS
ELDRED
EMBRUE
EMBRYO
EMERGE
EMERIC
ENERGY
ENGRAM
ENTRAP
ENTREE
ENWRAP
EPARCH
EPIRUS
ESCROW
ESPRIT
ESTRAY
ESTRUS
EVERET
EVERTS
EXARCH
EXERTS
EXTRAS
EXURBS

E•••R•
EATERS
ECHARD
EDGARS
EDUARD
EDWARD
EFFORT
EGBERT
EGGARS
EGGERS
ELBERT
ELDERS
ELMERS
ELMIRA
ELVERS
ELVIRA
ELYTRA
EMBARK
EMBARS
EMBERS
EMEERS
EMIGRE
EMPERY
EMPIRE
ENCORE
ENDURE
ENGIRD
ENGIRT
ENSURE
ENTERA
ENTERO
ENTERS
ENTIRE
EPHORI
EPHORS
ERFURT
ERRORS
ESCARP
ESCORT
ESKERS
ESTERS
ETHERS
EUCHRE
EUDORA
EXEDRA
EXHORT
EXPERT
EXPIRE
EXPIRY
EXPORT
EXSERT
EXTERN
EXTORT

E••••R
EARNER
EASIER
EASTER
ECHOER
ECLAIR
EDGIER
EDITOR
EITHER
ELATER
ELECTR
ELIXIR
ELOPER
ENAMOR
ENDEAR
ENVIER
ERASER
ERYTHR
ESCHAR
ESTHER
ETCHER
EVADER
EXETER
EXMOOR

•ER•••
AERATE
AERIAL
AERIED
AERIES
AERIFY
AEROBE
AERUGO
BERATE
BERBER
BEREFT
BERETS
BERGEN
BERING
BERLIN
BERMES
BERNEY
BERNIE
BERTHA
BERTHE
BERTHS
BERTIE
BERYLS
CERATE
CERATO
CEREAL
CEREUS
CERING
CERIPH
CERISE
CERITE
CERIUM
CERMET
CEROUS
CERTES
CERUSE
CERVIX
DERAIL
DERAIN
DEREKS
DERIDE
DERIVE
DERMAL
DERMAS
DERMAT
DERMIC
DERRIS
EERILY
FERBER
FERIAL
FERINE
FERITY
FERMIS
FEROUS
FERRET
FERRIC
FERRIS
FERRUM
FERULA
FERULE
FERVID
FERVOR
GERALD
GERARD
GERBIL
GERENT
GERMAN
GEROUS
GERRYS
GERTIE
GERTYS
GERUND
GERYON
HERALD
HERBAL
HERDED
HERDER
HERDIC
HEREAT
HEREBY
HEREIN
HEREOF
HEREON
HERESY
HERETO
HERIOT
HERMAE
HERMAI
HERMAN
HERMES
HERMIT
HERNIA
HERNIO
HEROES
HEROIC
HEROIN
HERONS
HERPES
JERBOA
JEREED
JEREMY
JERKED
JERKIN
JEROME
JERRYS
JERSEY
JERVIS
KERALA
KERATO
KERMES
KERMIS
KERNED
KERNEL
KERSEY
LEROYS
MERCER
MERCIA
MERELY
MEREST
MERGED
MERGER
MERGES
MERINO
MERITS
MERLES
MERLIN
MERLON
MERMAN
MERMEN
MEROUS
MERVIN
NEREIS
NEROLI
NERVED
NERVES
PERCYS
PERILS
PERIOD
PERISH
PERKED
PERMIT
PERRON
PERRYS
PERSIA
PERSON
PERTLY
PERUKE
PERUSE
RERUNS
SERACS
SERAIS
SERAPE
SERAPH
SERBIA
SERDAB
SEREIN
SERENA
SERENE
SERIAL
SERIES
SERIFS
SERINE
SERINS
SERMON
SEROUS
SEROWS
SERUMS
SERVAL
SERVED
SERVER
SERVES
SERVOS
TERAPH
TERATO
TERBIA
TERCEL
TERCET
TEREDO
TERESA
TERETE
TEREUS
TERGAL
TERGUM
TERMED
TERMER
TERMLY
TERMOR
TERRET
TERROR
TERRYS
TERSER
VERBAL

6

VERDIN
VERDUN
VEREIN
VERGED
VERGER
VERGES
VERGIL
VERIFY
VERILY
VERISM
VERIST
VERITY
VERMIN
VERNAL
VERNAS
VERNIX
VERNON
VERONA
VERSED
VERSES
VERSOS
VERSTS
VERSUS
VERTEX
VERVET
WERENT
YERBAS
ZEROED
ZEROES

•E•R••

BEARDS
BEARED
BEARER
BEDRID
BEIRUT
BETRAY
CEDRIC
CEORLS
DEARER
DEARIE
DEARLY
DEARTH
DEBRIS
DECREE
DEFRAY
DEGREE
DERRIS
FEARED
FEARER
FENRIR
FERRET
FERRIC
FERRIS
FERRUM
GEARED
GENRES
GENROS
GEORGE
GEORGI
GERRYS
HEARER
HEARSE
HEARST
HEARTH
HEARTS
HEARTY
HEBREW
HEBRON
HEDRAL
HEDRON
HENRIS
HENRYS
JEERED
JEERER
JERRYS
KEDRON
LEARNS
LEARNT
LEERED
LEGREE
MEGRIM
METRIC
METROS
NEARBY
NEARED
NEARER
NEARLY
NEURAL
NEURON
PEARLS
PEARLY
PEDROS
PEERED
PEIRCE
PEORIA
PERRON
PERRYS
PETREL
PETRIE
PETROL
REARED
REARER
REARMS
REGRET
SEARCH
SEARED
SECRET
SEURAT
TEARED
TENREC
TERRET
TERROR
TERRYS
TETRAD
TETRYL
VEERED
WEARER
WEIRDY
YEARLY
YEARNS
ZEBRAS

•E••R•

BEFORE
BEGIRD
BEGIRT
BELFRY
BEMIRE
BEWARE
CEDARS
CELERY
CENTRA
CENTRI
CENTRO
CESARE
CESURA
DEBARK
DEBARS
DECARE
DECERN
DECORS
DECURY
DEFERS
DEFORM
DEHORN
DEKARE
DEMURE
DEMURS
DENARY
DENDRI
DENDRO
DEPART
DEPORT
DESCRY
DESERT
DESIRE
DETERS
DEXTRO
FEDORA
FEMORA
FEMURS
FETORS
FEUARS
FEVERS
GEMARA
GENERA
GENTRY
GERARD
HEGIRA
HEJIRA
HETERO
HEWERS
JETHRO
LEGERS
LEMURS
LENORE
LEPERS
LEVERS
MEMORY
MESSRS
METERS
NEPHRO
NEWARK
OEUVRE
PELTRY
PENURY
PETARD
PETERS
REBORN
RECORD
RECURS
REFERS
REFORM
REGARD
REMARK
REMORA
REPORT
RESORB
RESORT
RETARD
RETIRE
RETORT
RETURN
REVERE
REVERT
REWARD
REWORD
SECERN
SECURE
SEDERS
SEMPRE
SENARY
SENORA
SENTRY
SEVERE
SEVERS
SEWARD
SEWERS
TENORS
TENURE
VELURE
VENERY
VENIRE
VENTRO
VESTRY
VEXERS
WEBERS

•E•••R

AETHER
BEAKER
BEARER
BEATER
BEAVER
BEDDER
BEGGAR
BELIER
BENDER
BERBER
BESTIR
BETTER
BETTOR
BEZOAR
CELLAR
CENSER
CENSOR
CENTER
DEALER
DEARER
DEBTOR
DECKER
DEEPER
DEFIER
DEFTER
DEICER
DELVER
DENIER
DENSER
DENVER
DEODAR
DETOUR
DEVOIR
DEVOUR
DEWIER
DEXTER
FEARER
FEEDER
FEELER
FELLER
FENCER
FENDER
FENRIR
FEODOR
FERBER
FERVOR
FESTER
FETTER
GEEZER
GEIGER
GENDER
GETTER
GEYSER
HEADER
HEALER
HEARER
HEATER
HEAVER
HECTOR
HEDGER
HEEDER
HEELER
HEIFER
HELLER
HELPER
HEMMER
HERDER
HESTER
JEERER
JESTER
KEENER
KEEPER
KEGLER
KELLER
KEPLER
LEADER
LEANER
LEAPER
LEAVER
LECHER
LECTOR
LEDGER
LENDER
LESSER
LESSOR
LESTER
LETTER
LEVIER
LEWDER
MEAGER
MEANER
MEDLAR
MEEKER
MEETER
MELTER
MEMBER
MEMOIR
MENDER
MENHIR
MENTOR
MERCER
MERGER
METEOR
METIER
NEARER
NEATER
NECTAR
NEEDER
NESTOR
NETHER
NEUTER
PECKER
PEELER
PEEPER
PELTER
PENNER
PEPPER
PESTER
PEWTER
READER
REAMER
REAPER
REARER
RECTOR
REDDER
REEFER
REEKER
REELER
REHEAR
RELIER
RENDER
RENOIR
RENTER
REPAIR
RESTER
SEALER
SEAMER
SECPAR
SECTOR
SEEDER
SEEKER
SEEMER
SEGGAR
SEINER
SEISOR
SEIZER
SEIZOR
SELLER
SENDER
SENIOR
SENSOR
SERVER
SETTER
SEXIER

TEASER
TEDDER
TEEMER
TEETER
TELLER
TEMPER
TENDER
TENSER
TENSOR
TENTER
TERMER
TERMOR
TERROR
TERSER
TESTER
TETHER
TETTER
TEUCER
VEADAR
VECTOR
VEILER
VELOUR
VENDER
VENDOR
VENEER
VENTER
VERGER
VESPER
VETOER
WEAKER
WEANER
WEARER
WEAVER
WEEDER
WEEPER
WEEVER
WEIMAR
WELDER
WELTER
WESTER
WETHER
WETTER
YELLER
YELPER
YESTER
ZENGER
ZEPHYR

••ER••

ALERTS
AMERCE
ANERGY
APERCU
AVERNO
AVERSE
AVERTS
AVERYS
BIERCE
CHERRY
CHERUB
CHERYL
CLERGY
CLERIC
CLERID
CLERKS
COERCE
EGERIA
EMERGE
EMERIC
ENERGY
EVERET
EVERTS
EXERTS
FAEROE
FIERCE
IBERIA
JEERED
JEERER
LEERED
LIERNE
OBERON
OPERAS
OVERDO
OVERLY
PEERED
PIERCE
PIERRE
PIERUS
QUERNS
SHERDS
SHERIF
SHERPA
SHERRY
SIERRA
SPERMO
SPERRY
STEREO
STERES
STERIC
STERNA
STERNO
STERNS
STEROL
SWERVE
THERMO
THERMS
TIERCE
TIERED
TWERPS
UTERUS
VEERED
WHERRY
WHERVE

••E•R•

AMENRA
AWEARY
BLEARS
BLEARY
CHEERS
CHEERY
CHEIRO
CHERRY
CLEARS
DREARY
EMEERS
EXEDRA
FLEERS
FLEURY
OHENRY
ONEIRO
PIERRE
PIETRO
PLEURA
PLEURO
POETRY
QUEERS
SHEARS
SHEERS
SHERRY
SIERRA
SIEURS
SMEARS
SMEARY
SNEERS
SPEARS
SPERRY
STEERS
SWEARS
THEIRS
THEORY
WHERRY

••E••R

ALEGAR
BREWER
CAESAR
CHEWER
CLEVER
DEEPER
DIETER
DUELER
ELECTR
EXETER
FEEDER
FEELER
FLEXOR
FOETOR
FUELER
GEEZER
GHEBER
HEEDER
HEELER
JAEGER
JEERER
KEENER
KEEPER
LIEDER
MEEKER
MEETER
NEEDER
OBEYER
OPENER
PEELER
PEEPER
PIECER
PIETER
PLEXOR
PREFER
PRETER
PRETOR
PREWAR
PREYER
REEFER
REEKER
REELER
RHETOR
SEEDER
SEEKER
SEEMER
SHEWER
SKEWER
SOEVER
STELAR
TEEMER
TEETER
THENAR
TREMOR
URETER
URETHR
VIEWER
WEEDER
WEEPER
WEEVER
WIENER

•••ER•

ABNERS
ADDERS
ADHERE
ADVERB
ADVERT
AGGERS
AIDERS
ALBERT
ALDERS
ALTERS
AMBERS
AMBERY
AMPERE
ANGERS
ANTERO
ARTERY
ASKERS
ASPERS
ASSERT
ASTERI
ASTERN
ASTERO
ASTERS
AUGERS
BAKERS
BAKERY
BALERS
BITERS
BOLERO
BONERS
BORERS
BOWERS
BOWERY
BOXERS
BRIERS
BRIERY
BUYERS
CAMERA
CANERS
CAPERS
CARERS
CASERN
CATERS
CAVERN
CELERY
CHEERS
CHEERY
CICERO
CIDERS
COHERE
COMERS
COOERS
CORERS
COVERS
COVERT
COWERS
CRIERS
CURERS
DARERS
DATERS
DECERN
DEFERS
DESERT
DETERS
DICERS
DIMERS
DINERO
DINERS
DIVERS
DIVERT
DOSERS
DOTERS
DOWERS
DOWERY
DRIERS
DRYERS
DUPERS
DUPERY
EATERS
EGBERT
EGGERS
ELBERT
ELDERS
ELMERS
ELVERS
EMBERS
EMEERS
EMPERY
ENTERA
ENTERO
ENTERS
ESKERS
ESTERS
ETHERS
EXPERT
EXSERT
EXTERN
FACERS
FAKERS
FAKERY
FARERS
FEVERS
FIBERS
FIFERS
FILERS
FINERY
FIRERS
FIVERS
FIXERS
FLEERS
FLIERS
FLYERS
FOYERS
FRIERS
FRYERS
GAGERS
GAPERS
GAZERS
GENERA
GIBERS
GONERS
GOVERN
HALERS
HATERS
HAZERS
HETERO
HEWERS
HIDERS
HIKERS
HIRERS
HOMERS
HOVERS
HUBERT
IDLERS
INFERO
INFERS
INHERE
INKERS
INSERT
INTERN
INTERS
INVERT
JOKERS
LAGERS
LAKERS
LASERS
LAVERS
LAYERS
LEGERS
LEPERS
LEVERS
LIFERS
LINERS
LITERS
LIVERS
LIVERY
LONERS
LOPERS
LOSERS
LOVERS
LOWERS
LOWERY
LUGERS
LURERS
MACERS
MAKERS
MASERS

6

MAZERS
METERS
MILERS
MIMERS
MINERS
MISERS
MISERY
MITERS
MIXERS
MODERN
MOPERS
MOVERS
MOWERS
NAMERS
NAPERY
NOTERS
OBVERT
OCHERS
OCHERY
OFFERS
OGLERS
OILERS
ORDERS
ORMERS
ORNERY
ORRERY
OSBERT
OSIERS
OTHERS
OTTERS
OUTERS
OWNERS
PACERS
PAPERS
PAPERY
PARERS
PATERS
PAVERS
PAWERS
PAYERS
PETERS
PIKERS
PINERY
PIPERS
PLIERS
POKERS
POPERY
POSERS
POWERS
PRIERS
PRYERS
PULERS
QUAERE
QUEERS
RACERS
RAKERS
RATERS
RAVERS
REFERS
REVERE
REVERT
RICERS
RIDERS
RIMERS
RISERS
RIVERS
ROBERT
ROGERS
ROVERS
ROWERS
RULERS
RUPERT
SABERS
SAKERS
SAVERS
SAWERS
SAYERS
SCLERA
SCLERO
SECERN
SEDERS
SEVERE
SEVERS
SEWERS
SHEERS
SHOERS
SIDERO
SISERA
SKIERS
SNEERS
SOBERS
SOWERS
SPHERE
SPHERY
SPIERS
STEERS
SUPERB
SUPERS
TAKERS
TALERS
TAMERS
TAPERS
TAVERN
TAWERS
TAXERS
TIGERS
TILERS
TIMERS
TONERS
TOPERS
TORERO
TOTERS
TOWERS
TOWERY
TOYERS
TRIERS
TUBERS
TUNERS
TUYERE
UDDERS
ULCERS
UMBERS
UPPERS
USHERS
UTTERS
VALERY
VENERY
VEXERS
VINERY
VIPERS
VOLERY
VOMERS
VOTERS
VOWERS
WADERS
WAFERS
WAGERS
WALERS
WATERS
WATERY
WAVERS
WEBERS
WINERY
WIPERS
WIRERS
WIVERN
WIVERS
WOMERA
WOOERS
WYVERN
YAGERS

•••E•R

APPEAR
ARREAR
CAREER
DOGEAR
ENDEAR
LINEAR
METEOR
POSEUR
REHEAR
UNBEAR
VENEER
VOYEUR

••••ER

ABASER
ABATER
ABIDER
ABUSER
ADORER
AETHER
AIRIER
AMBLER
AMUSER
ANGLER
ANSWER
ANTHER
ANTLER
ARCHER
ARGUER
ASHIER
ATONER
AUSTER
AVOWER
BACKER
BADGER
BAILER
BAITER
BALDER
BANKER
BANNER
BANTER
BARBER
BARKER
BARTER
BATHER
BATTER
BAWLER
BAXTER
BEAKER
BEARER
BEATER
BEAVER
BEDDER
BELIER
BENDER
BERBER
BETTER
BIBBER
BICKER
BIDDER
BIGGER
BILKER
BINDER
BISTER
BITTER
BLAZER
BLOWER
BOBBER
BOILER
BOLDER
BOLTER
BOMBER
BONDER
BONIER
BONZER
BOOZER
BORDER
BOTHER
BOWLER
BOWYER
BRACER
BRAVER
BRAYER
BRAZER
BREWER
BRIBER
BROKER
BUCKER
BUDDER
BUFFER
BUGGER
BUGLER
BULGER
BUMMER
BUMPER
BUNKER
BURGER
BURLER
BURNER
BUSTER
BUTLER
BUTTER
BUZZER
CADGER
CAGIER
CAHIER
CALKER
CALLER
CALMER
CAMBER
CAMPER
CANCER
CANKER
CANNER
CANTER
CAPPER
CARDER
CAREER
CARPER
CARTER
CARVER
CASPER
CASTER
CATHER
CAUSER
CENSER
CENTER
CHAFER
CHASER
CHEWER
CHIDER
CHIMER
CHOKER
CHOLER
CINDER
CIPHER
CITHER
CLEVER
CLOSER
CLOVER
COALER
COAXER
COCKER
CODDER
CODGER
COFFER
COILER
COINER
COLDER
COLTER
COMBER
CONFER
CONGER
CONNER
COOKER
COOLER
COOPER
COPIER
COPPER
CORDER
CORKER
CORNER
COSHER
COTTER
COWPER
COZIER
CRATER
CRAVER
CROZER
CRUDER
CULLER
CULVER
CUMBER
CUNNER
CUPPER
CURLER
CUSTER
CUTLER
CUTTER
CYCLER
CYPHER
DABBER
DAGGER
DAMMER
DAMPER
DANCER
DANDER
DANGER
DANKER
DAPPER
DARKER
DARTER
DASHER
DAUBER
DEALER
DEARER
DECKER
DEEPER
DEFIER
DEFTER
DEICER
DELVER
DENIER
DENSER
DENVER
DEWIER
DEXTER
DIALER
DIAPER
DIBBER
DICKER
DIETER
DIFFER
DIGGER
DIMMER
DINNER
DIPPER
DITHER
DOBBER
DOCKER
DODDER
DODGER
DOFFER
DOGGER
DOPIER
DORMER
DOSSER
DOTIER
DOTTER
DOWSER
DOZIER

6

DRAPER
DRAWER
DRIVER
DROVER
DUCKER
DUELER
DUFFER
DUIKER
DULLER
DUNKER
DUSTER
EARNER
EASIER
EASTER
ECHOER
EDGIER
EITHER
ELATER
ELOPER
ENVIER
ERASER
ESTHER
ETCHER
EVADER
EXETER
FABLER
FAIRER
FALLER
FALSER
FALTER
FANNER
FARCER
FARMER
FASTER
FATHER
FATTER
FAWNER
FEARER
FEEDER
FEELER
FELLER
FENCER
FENDER
FERBER
FESTER
FETTER
FIBBER
FILLER
FILTER
FINDER
FINGER
FIRMER
FISHER
FITTER
FLAKER
FLAYER
FLOWER
FLUTER
FODDER
FOLDER
FONDER
FOOTER
FORCER
FORGER
FORMER
FOSTER
FOULER
FOWLER
FOXIER
FRAMER
FRATER
FUELER
FUHRER
FULLER
FUMIER
FUSSER
GABBER
GADDER
GAFFER
GAGGER
GAINER
GAITER
GAMIER
GAMMER
GANDER
GANGER
GAOLER
GARNER
GARTER
GASPER
GATHER
GAUGER
GEEZER
GEIGER
GENDER
GETTER
GEYSER
GHEBER
GIBBER
GILDER
GINGER
GINNER
GIRDER
GLAZER
GLIDER
GLOVER
GLOWER
GLUIER
GNAWER
GOFFER
GOITER
GOLFER
GOOBER
GOOIER
GOPHER
GORGER
GORIER
GOUGER
GRADER
GRATER
GRAVER
GRAYER
GRAZER
GRIPER
GROCER
GROPER
GROVER
GROWER
GUIDER
GULPER
GUNNER
GUSHER
GUTTER
HACKER
HAILER
HALTER
HAMMER
HAMPER
HANGER
HANKER
HARDER
HARPER
HATTER
HAULER
HAWKER
HAWSER
HAZIER
HEADER
HEALER
HEARER
HEATER
HEAVER
HEDGER
HEEDER
HEELER
HEIFER
HELLER
HELPER
HEMMER
HERDER
HESTER
HIGHER
HILLER
HINDER
HISSER
HITHER
HITLER
HITTER
HOAXER
HOLDER
HOLIER
HOLLER
HOMIER
HONKER
HOOFER
HOOKER
HOOPER
HOOVER
HOPPER
HOSIER
HOTTER
HOWLER
HUMMER
HUNGER
HUNTER
HURLER
HURTER
HUSKER
HYSTER
INKIER
INLIER
IRONER
ISOMER
ISSUER
JABBER
JAEGER
JAILER
JASPER
JAZZER
JEERER
JESTER
JIBBER
JIGGER
JILTER
JINKER
JITTER
JOBBER
JOGGER
JOINER
JOLTER
JOSHER
JUDGER
JUICER
JUMPER
JUNKER
KAISER
KEENER
KEEPER
KEGLER
KELLER
KEPLER
KHYBER
KICKER
KIDDER
KILLER
KILMER
KILTER
KINDER
KIPPER
KISSER
KNOWER
KOSHER
KRONER
LAAGER
LACIER
LADDER
LADLER
LAGGER
LAKIER
LANCER
LANDER
LANKER
LANNER
LAPPER
LAPSER
LARDER
LARGER
LARKER
LASHER
LASTER
LATHER
LATTER
LAUDER
LAWYER
LAZIER
LEADER
LEANER
LEAPER
LEAVER
LECHER
LEDGER
LENDER
LESSER
LESTER
LETTER
LEVIER
LEWDER
LIEDER
LIFTER
LIMBER
LIMIER
LIMNER
LIMPER
LINGER
LINIER
LINTER
LIPPER
LISPER
LISTER
LITHER
LITTER
LIVIER
LIVYER
LOADER
LOAFER
LOCKER
LODGER
LOFTER
LOGGER
LOGIER
LOITER
LOLLER
LONGER
LOOKER
LOOPER
LOOSER
LOOTER
LOUDER
LOUVER
LUBBER
LUGGER
LUMBER
LUNGER
LUNKER
LUSHER
LUSTER
LUTHER
MADDER
MAHLER
MAILER
MAIMER
MANGER
MANNER
MARKER
MARRER
MASHER
MASKER
MASTER
MATTER
MAULER
MAUSER
MAZIER
MEAGER
MEANER
MEEKER
MEETER
MELTER
MEMBER
MENDER
MERCER
MERGER
METIER
MILDER
MILKER
MILLER
MILTER
MINCER
MINDER
MINTER
MISTER
MOBBER
MOCKER
MOILER
MOLDER
MOLTER
MONGER
MOOTER
MOTHER
MOUSER
MUCKER
MUDDER
MUGGER
MULLER
MUMMER
MURDER
MUSHER
MUSTER
MUTTER
NAGGER
NAPIER
NAPPER
NASSER
NEARER
NEATER
NEEDER
NETHER
NEUTER
NICKER
NIGHER
NIPPER
NODDER
NOSIER
NUMBER
NURSER
NUTTER
OBEYER
OILIER
OLIVER
ONAGER
OOZIER
OPENER
OUSTER
OYSTER
PACKER

PALMER
PALTER
PAMPER
PANDER
PANZER
PARKER
PASSER
PASTER
PATTER
PAUKER
PAUPER
PAUSER
PAWNER
PECKER
PEELER
PEEPER
PELTER
PENNER
PEPPER
PESTER
PEWTER
PICKER
PIECER
PIETER
PILFER
PINIER
PINNER
PINTER
PIPIER
PLACER
PLANER
PLATER
PLAYER
PLOVER
PLOWER
POKIER
POLDER
POLLER
PONDER
POORER
POPPER
PORKER
PORTER
POSTER
POTHER
POTTER
POURER
POUTER
POWDER
POWTER
PRATER
PRAYER
PREFER
PRETER
PREYER
PRIMER
PRIZER
PROBER
PROPER
PROSER
PROVER
PRUNER
PUCKER
PUFFER
PULLER
PUMPER
PUNIER
PUNTER
PURGER
PURSER
PUSHER
PUTTER
QUAKER
QUAVER
QUIVER
QUOTER
RACIER
RACKER
RAFTER
RAIDER
RAISER
RAMMER
RANGER
RANKER
RANTER
RAPIER
RAPPER
RASHER
RASPER
RATHER
RATTER
READER
REAMER
REAPER
REARER
REDDER
REEFER
REEKER
REELER
RELIER
RENDER
RENTER
RESTER
RHYMER
RICHER
RIFLER
RIGGER
RIMMER
RINGER
RINSER
RIOTER
RIPPER
RISKER
RITTER
ROAMER
ROARER
ROBBER
ROCKER
ROLLER
ROMPER
ROOFER
ROOMER
ROOTER
ROPIER
ROSIER
ROSTER
ROTTER
ROUSER
ROUTER
RUBBER
RUDDER
RUINER
RUMMER
RUNNER
RUSHER
SACKER
SADDER
SAGGER
SAGIER
SAILER
SALTER
SALVER
SANDER
SANGER
SAPPER
SAUCER
SAUGER
SAWYER
SCALER
SCARER
SCORER
SCOTER
SEALER
SEAMER
SEEDER
SEEKER
SEEMER
SEINER
SEIZER
SELLER
SENDER
SERVER
SETTER
SEXIER
SHAKER
SHAPER
SHARER
SHAVER
SHEWER
SHINER
SHIVER
SHOVER
SHOWER
SICKER
SIDLER
SIFTER
SIGNER
SILVER
SIMMER
SIMPER
SINGER
SINKER
SINNER
SINTER
SIPPER
SISTER
SITTER
SIZIER
SKATER
SKEWER
SKIVER
SLATER
SLAVER
SLAYER
SLICER
SLIDER
SLIVER
SLOPER
SLOWER
SMILER
SMITER
SMOKER
SNARER
SNIPER
SNORER
SOAKER
SOARER
SOCCER
SOEVER
SOFTER
SOLDER
SOLVER
SOMBER
SONDER
SOONER
SOURER
SPACER
SPADER
SPARER
SPICER
SPIDER
SPRIER
SPRYER
STAGER
STALER
STARER
STATER
STAYER
STIVER
STOKER
STONER
STOVER
STYLER
SUBTER
SUCKER
SUFFER
SUMMER
SUMNER
SUNDER
SUPPER
SURFER
SURGER
SUTLER
SYPHER
TACKER
TAGGER
TALKER
TALLER
TAMPER
TANKER
TANNER
TAPPER
TARTER
TASTER
TATLER
TATTER
TAUTER
TEASER
TEDDER
TEEMER
TEETER
TELLER
TEMPER
TENDER
TENSER
TENTER
TERMER
TERSER
TESTER
TETHER
TETTER
TEUCER
THAYER
TICKER
TIDIER
TILLER
TILTER
TIMBER
TINDER
TINKER
TINNER
TIPPER
TITHER
TITTER
TOILER
TOLLER
TONIER
TOOLER
TOOTER
TOPPER
TOTHER
TOTTER
TOUTER
TRACER
TRADER
TRITER
TROVER
TUBBER
TUCKER
TURNER
TUSKER
TWINER
TWOFER
UGLIER
ULSTER
UNDOER
URETER
USURER
VAGUER
VAINER
VARIER
VASTER
VEILER
VENDER
VENEER
VENTER
VERGER
VESPER
VETOER
VIEWER
VINIER
VIZIER
WAFTER
WAGNER
WAILER
WAITER
WAIVER
WALKER
WALTER
WANDER
WANNER
WANTER
WARDER
WARIER
WARMER
WARNER
WARPER
WASHER
WASTER
WAVIER
WAXIER
WEAKER
WEANER
WEARER
WEAVER
WEEDER
WEEPER
WEEVER
WELDER
WELTER
WESTER
WETHER
WETTER
WHALER
WHINER
WHITER
WICKER
WIENER
WILBER
WILDER
WILIER
WILLER
WINCER
WINDER
WINIER
WINKER
WINNER
WINTER
WIRIER
WITHER
WOLVER
WONDER
WOOFER
WORKER
WORMER
WORSER
WOWSER
WRITER
XAVIER
XYSTER
YABBER
YAMMER
YAWNER
YAWPER

YELLER
YELPER
YESTER
YONDER
YONKER
ZAFFER
ZANIER
ZENGER
ZIPPER
ZITHER
ZOSTER
ZUIDER
ZUYDER

ES••••

ESCAPE
ESCARP
ESCENT
ESCHAR
ESCHEW
ESCORT
ESCROW
ESCUDO
ESKERS
ESKIMO
ESPANA
ESPIAL
ESPIED
ESPIES
ESPRIT
ESSAYS
ESSENE
ESTATE
ESTEEM
ESTERS
ESTHER
ESTOPS
ESTRAY
ESTRUS

E•S•••

EASELS
EASIER
EASILY
EASING
EASTER
EASTON
ELSIES
ENSIGN
ENSILE
ENSOUL
ENSUED
ENSUES
ENSURE
ERSATZ
ESSAYS
ESSENE
EXSECT
EXSERT

E••S••

ECESIS
EDISON
EGESTA
EGESTS
ELISHA
ELYSEE
EMESIS
ENISLE
ENOSIS
ERASED
ERASER
ERASES
EXISTS
EYASES

E•••S•

EFFUSE
EGOISM
EGOIST
EGRESS
ELAPSE
ELDEST
ELFISH
ELOISE
ELVISH
EMBOSS
ENCASE
ENCYST
ENLIST
ENMESH
EONISM
ERNEST
EXCESS
EXCISE
EXCUSE
EXPOSE

E••••S

EAGLES
EARLES
EARTHS
EASELS
EATERS
EBOATS
ECCLES
ECESIS
ECHOES
ECOLES
EDDIES
EDGARS
EDICTS
EDILES
EDITHS
EDUCES
EDUCTS
EDWINS
EGESTS
EGGARS
EGGERS
EGRESS
EGRETS
EIGHTS
EJECTS
ELANDS
ELATES
ELBOWS
ELBRUS
ELDERS
ELECTS
ELEMIS
ELENAS
ELFINS
ELIDES
ELIOTS
ELIZAS
ELLENS
ELLIES
ELMERS
ELOINS
ELOPES
ELSIES
ELUDES
ELVERS
EMBARS
EMBAYS
EMBEDS
EMBERS
EMBOSS
EMBOWS
EMCEES
EMEERS
EMENDS
EMESIS
EMILES
EMILYS
EMMETS
EMMIES
EMOTES
ENACTS
ENATES
ENDOWS
ENDUES
ENEMAS
ENGELS
ENJOYS
ENOSIS
ENSUES
ENTERS
ENVIES
ENVOYS
EPACTS
EPHAHS
EPHODS
EPHORS
EPIRUS
EPOCHS
EPODES
EQUALS
EQUIPS
ERASES
EREBUS
ERECTS
ERICHS
ERNIES
ERODES
ERRORS
ERUCTS
ERUPTS
ERWINS
ESKERS
ESPIES
ESSAYS
ESTERS
ESTOPS
ESTRUS
ETAPES
ETCHES
ETHANS
ETHELS
ETHERS
ETHICS
ETHYLS
ETUDES
EVADES
EVENTS
EVERTS
EVICTS
EVITAS
EVOKES
EXACTS
EXALTS
EXCELS
EXCESS
EXERTS
EXILES
EXISTS
EXODUS
EXPELS
EXTOLS
EXTRAS
EXUDES
EXULTS
EXURBS
EYASES
EYRIES

•ES•••

BESEEM
BESETS
BESIDE
BESOMS
BESOTS
BESSIE
BESSYS
BESTED
BESTIR
BESTOW
CESARE
CESIUM
CESTUS
CESURA
DESALT
DESCRY
DESERT
DESIGN
DESIRE
DESIST
DESMAN
DESMID
DESOXY
DESPOT
DESSAU
FESCUE
FESSES
FESTAL
FESTER
GESELL
GESSOS
GESTIC
HESIOD
HESTER
HESTIA
JESSED
JESSES
JESSIE
JESTED
JESTER
JESUIT
LESION
LESLEY
LESLIE
LESSEE
LESSEN
LESSER
LESSON
LESSOR
LESTER
MESCAL
MESHED
MESHES
MESIAL
MESIAN
MESNES
MESONS
MESSED
MESSES
MESSRS
MESTEE
NESSUS
NESTED
NESTLE
NESTOR
PESACH
PESADE
PESETA
PESTER
PESTLE
RESALE
RESCUE
RESEAT
RESEAU
RESECT
RESEDA
RESELL
RESEND
RESENT
RESETS
RESIDE
RESIGN
RESILE
RESINS
RESIST
RESOLD
RESOLE
RESORB
RESORT
RESTED
RESTER
RESULT
RESUME
SESAME
SESQUI
SESTET
TESSIE
TESTAE
TESTED
TESTER
TESTES
TESTIS
TESTON
VESICA
VESICO
VESPER
VESPID
VESSEL
VESTAL
VESTAS
VESTED
VESTEE
VESTRY
WESLEY
WESSEX
WESTER
YESSED
YESSES
YESTER
ZESTED

•E•S••

BEASTS
BESSIE
BESSYS
BETSYS
CEASED
CEASES
CENSED
CENSER
CENSES
CENSOR
CENSUS
DEISTS
DENSER
DESSAU
FEASED
FEASES
FEASTS
FEISTS
FEISTY
FESSES
GEISHA
GESSOS
GEYSER
HEISTS
JERSEY
JESSED
JESSES
JESSIE
JETSAM
KERSEY
LEASED
LEASES
LENSES
LEPSIA

LESSEE
LESSEN
LESSER
LESSON
LESSOR
MEASLY
MENSAL
MENSES
MESSED
MESSES
MESSRS
NELSON
NESSUS
NEVSKI
PEASEN
PEASES
PEPSIN
PERSIA
PERSON
REASON
SEASON
SEESAW
SEISIN
SEISMO
SEISMS
SEISOR
SELSYN
SENSED
SENSES
SENSOR
SEPSIS
TEASED
TEASEL
TEASER
TEASES
TELSON
TENSED
TENSER
TENSES
TENSOR
TERSER
TESSIE
VERSED
VERSES
VERSOS
VERSTS
VERSUS
VESSEL
WEASEL
WESSEX
YEASTS
YEASTY
YESSED
YESSES

•E••S•

BEHEST
BEMUSE
BETISE
CERISE
CERUSE
DEBASE
DEGUST
DEMISE
DENISE
DEPOSE
DESIST
DETEST
DEVEST
DEVISE
FETISH
FEWEST
HEARSE
HEARST
HERESY
HEXOSE
JEWESS
JEWISH
KETOSE
LEGIST
MEDUSA
MEGASS
MEREST
NEWEST
PERISH
PERUSE
RECAST
RECESS
RECUSE
REFUSE
REHASH
RELISH
REMISE
REMISS
REPASS
REPAST
REPOSE
RESIST
RETUSE
REVEST
REVISE
SETOSE
SEXISM
SEXIST
TEENSY
TERESA
VENOSE
VERISM
VERIST
WEENSY

•E•••S

AEACUS
AEETES
AEGEUS
AENEAS
AEOLIS
AEOLUS
AERIES
BEARDS
BEASTS
BEAUTS
BECKYS
BEDEWS
BEDIMS
BEEVES
BEFITS
BEFOGS
BEGETS
BEGINS
BEGUMS
BEIGES
BEINGS
BELAYS
BELGAS
BELIES
BELLAS
BELLES
BENJYS
BENNES
BENNYS
BERETS
BERMES
BERTHS
BERYLS
BESETS
BESOMS
BESOTS
BESSYS
BETELS
BETSYS
BETTES
BETTYS
BEULAS
BEVELS
BEVIES
BEZELS
CEASES
CECILS
CEDARS
CEIBAS
CELIAS
CELLOS
CENSES
CENSUS
CENTOS
CEORLS
CEREUS
CEROUS
CERTES
CESTUS
DEATHS
DEBARS
DEBBYS
DEBITS
DEBRIS
DEBUGS
DEBUTS
DECALS
DECAYS
DECORS
DECOYS
DEDANS
DEFERS
DEFIES
DEGUMS
DEICES
DEIGNS
DEISTS
DELAYS
DELIAS
DELIUS
DELLAS
DELTAS
DELVES
DEMIES
DEMITS
DEMOBS
DEMONS
DEMURS
DENIES
DENIMS
DENNIS
DENNYS
DEPOTS
DEPTHS
DEREKS
DERMAS
DERRIS
DETERS
DEUCES
DEVILS
DEWANS
FEASES
FEASTS
FEEZES
FEIGNS
FEINTS
FEISTS
FELIDS
FELONS
FEMURS
FENCES
FEOFFS
FERMIS
FEROUS
FERRIS
FESSES
FETORS
FEUARS
FEVERS
FEZZES
GECKOS
GEMOTS
GENETS
GENIES
GENIUS
GENOUS
GENRES
GENROS
GENTES
GEODES
GEROUS
GERRYS
GERTYS
GESSOS
GETUPS
HEARTS
HEATHS
HEAVES
HEDGES
HEISTS
HELENS
HELIOS
HELLAS
HELOTS
HELVES
HENNAS
HENRIS
HENRYS
HERMES
HEROES
HERONS
HERPES
HETTYS
HEWERS
HEXADS
HEXYLS
JENNYS
JERRYS
JERVIS
JESSES
JEWELS
JEWESS
KEDGES
KEEVES
KEITHS
KENNYS
KERMES
KERMIS
KEVELS
KEVINS
KEYNES
LEARNS
LEASES
LEAVES
LEDGES
LEGERS
LEHUAS
LEIGHS
LEMMAS
LEMNOS
LEMONS
LEMURS
LENNYS
LENSES
LENTOS
LEONAS
LEPERS
LEROYS
LETUPS
LEUDES
LEVEES
LEVELS
LEVERS
LEVIES
MEATUS
MECCAS
MEDALS
MEDICS
MEGASS
MELEES
MELONS
MENSES
MERGES
MERITS
MERLES
MEROUS
MESHES
MESNES
MESONS
MESSES
MESSRS
METALS
METERS
METROS
MEZZOS
NEIGHS
NELLYS
NEREIS
NERVES
NESSUS
NEUMES
NEWELS
PEARLS
PEASES
PECANS
PEDALS
PEDROS
PEEVES
PEGGYS
PEKANS
PEKOES
PELEUS
PELIAS
PELOPS
PELVES
PELVIS
PENGOS
PENNIS
PENNYS
PEPLOS
PEPLUS
PERCYS
PERILS
PERRYS
PETALS
PETERS
PEWEES
PEWITS
REACTS
REALES
REALMS
REARMS
REBECS
REBELS
REBUTS
RECAPS
RECESS
RECTOS
RECTUS
RECURS
REDANS
REDOES
REEVES
REFERS
REFITS
REGIUS
REICHS
REIGNS
RELAYS
RELICS
RELIES
REMANS

REMISS
REMITS
RENEES
RENEWS
RENTES
REPASS
REPAYS
REPELS
RERUNS
RESETS
RESINS
REVELS
REVETS
REVUES
SEAMUS
SEBATS
SEDANS
SEDERS
SEDGES
SEDUMS
SEINES
SEISMS
SEIZES
SELVES
SENNAS
SENSES
SEPALS
SEPIAS
SEPOYS
SEPSIS
SERACS
SERAIS
SERIES
SERIFS
SERINS
SEROUS
SEROWS
SERUMS
SERVES
SERVOS
SETONS
SETOUS
SETTOS
SETUPS
SEVENS
SEVERS
SEWERS
TEASES
TEDDYS
TEHEES
TELLUS
TEMPOS
TEMPTS
TENETS
TENNIS
TENONS
TENORS
TENSES
TENTHS
TENUES
TENUIS
TEPEES
TEREUS
TERRYS
TESTES
TESTIS
TETHYS
TETONS
VELDTS
VENOMS
VENOUS
VENUES
VERGES
VERNAS
VERSES
VERSOS
VERSTS
VERSUS
VESTAS
VETOES
VEXERS
VEXILS
WEALDS
WEAVES
WEBERS
WEDGES
WEIGHS
WENDYS
XEBECS
YEARNS
YEASTS
YERBAS
YESSES
ZEBECS
ZEBRAS
ZEROES
ZETHOS
ZETHUS

••ES••

AVESTA
AYESHA
CAESAR
CHESTS
CHESTY
CRESOL
CRESTS
CUESTA
DIESEL
DIESES
DIESIS
DOESNT
DRESSY
ECESIS
EGESTA
EGESTS
EMESIS
FIESTA
FLESHY
FRESCO
FRESNO
GUESTS
NOESIS
ODESSA
PRESAS
PRESTO
QUESTS
RHESUS
SEESAW
SIESTA
THESES
THESIS
TMESIS
TRESSY
UNESCO
WRESTS

••E•S•

AVERSE
BREAST
CHEESE
CHEESY
CLEIST
CREASE
CREASY
CREESE
CREUSA
DRESSY
FLENSE
FREEST
GNEISS
GREASE
GREASY
ODESSA
PLEASE
QUEASY
SPEISS
TEENSY
THEISM
THEIST
TRESSY
TSETSE
UNEASY
UREASE
WEENSY

••E••S

ABELES
ACEOUS
ADEEMS
ADENIS
ADEPTS
AEETES
AGENTS
AKENES
ALEPHS
ALERTS
ALEUTS
ALEXIS
AMEBAS
AMENDS
AMENTS
APEXES
ARECAS
ARENAS
ARETES
AVERTS
AVERYS
BEEVES
BLEAKS
BLEARS
BLEATS
BLEEDS
BLENDS
BREADS
BREAKS
BREAMS
BREEDS
BRENTS
BREVES
BREWIS
CHEATS
CHECKS
CHEEKS
CHEEPS
CHEERS
CHELAS
CHEOPS
CHESTS
CLEANS
CLEARS
CLEATS
CLEFTS
CLERKS
CLEVIS
CREAKS
CREAMS
CREDOS
CREEDS
CREEKS
CREELS
CREEPS
CREMES
CREPES
CRESTS
CZECHS
DIESES
DIESIS
DREADS
DREAMS
DWELLS
ECESIS
EGESTS
EJECTS
ELECTS
ELEMIS
ELENAS
EMEERS
EMENDS
EMESIS
ENEMAS
EREBUS
ERECTS
EVENTS
EVERTS
EXERTS
FEEZES
FIELDS
FIENDS
FJELDS
FLEAMS
FLECKS
FLEERS
FLEETS
FLEXES
FOEHNS
FOETUS
FREAKS
FREDAS
FREONS
GLEAMS
GLEANS
GLEBES
GLEDES
GLEETS
GNEISS
GREATS
GREBES
GREEDS
GREEKS
GREENS
GREETS
GREGOS
GRETAS
GUESTS
GWENNS
HBEAMS
HYENAS
IBEAMS
IBEXES
IDEALS
ILEXES
IRENES
KEEVES
KNEADS
KNEELS
KNELLS
LIEGES
NAEVUS
NIECES
NOESIS
OBELUS
OCEANS
OMEGAS
OPERAS
OREADS
OXEYES
PAEANS
PAEONS
PEEVES
PIECES
PIERUS
PLEADS
PLEATS
PLEBES
PLEXUS
PRECIS
PREENS
PRESAS
QUEANS
QUEENS
QUEERS
QUELLS
QUERNS
QUESTS
QUEUES
REEVES
RHEIMS
RHESUS
SCENDS
SCENES
SCENTS
SHEARS
SHEENS
SHEERS
SHEETS
SHEIKS
SHELLS
SHERDS
SIEGES
SIEURS
SIEVES
SKEANS
SKEINS
SLEEKS
SLEEPS
SLEETS
SMEARS
SMELLS
SMELTS
SNEAKS
SNEERS
SNELLS
SPEAKS
SPEARS
SPECKS
SPEEDS
SPEISS
SPELLS
SPENDS
STEAKS
STEALS
STEAMS
STEEDS
STEELS
STEEPS
STEERS
STEINS
STELES
STERES
STERNS
STEVES
SUEDES
SWEARS
SWEATS
SWEDES
SWEEPS
SWEETS
SWELLS
THEBES
THEDAS
THEFTS
THEIRS
THEMES
THEMIS
THERMS
THESES
THESIS
THETAS
THETIS
TIEINS
TIEUPS
TMESIS
TREADS

TREATS
TRENDS
TWEAKS
TWEEDS
TWEETS
TWERPS
ULEMAS
UPENDS
UTERUS
VNECKS
WHEALS
WHEATS
WHEELS
WHELKS
WHELMS
WHELPS
WIELDS
WREAKS
WRECKS
WRESTS
YIELDS
ZBEAMS

•••ES•

ABBESS
ABLEST
ACCESS
AFRESH
ARREST
ASSESS
ATTEST
AWLESS
BAREST
BEHEST
BLUEST
CALESA
CARESS
CHEESE
CHEESY
CREESE
CUTEST
DETEST
DEVEST
DIGEST
DIREST
DIVEST
DRIEST
DRYEST
DURESS
EGRESS
ELDEST
ENMESH
ERNEST
EXCESS
FEWEST
FINEST
FLIEST
FOREST
FREEST
FUNEST
GAYEST
HERESY
HONEST
HUGEST
ICIEST
IDLEST
IMMESH
INCEST
INFEST
INGEST
INMESH
INVEST
JEWESS
KINESI
LAMEST
LATEST
LAXEST
LOWEST
MAYEST
MEREST
MODEST
MOLEST
NEWEST
NICEST
OBSESS
OBTEST
ODDEST
OGRESS
OLDEST
PALEST
PRIEST
PUREST
RAREST
RAWEST
RECESS
REVEST
RIPEST
RUDEST
SAFEST
SAGEST
SANEST
SHIEST
SHYEST
SLIEST
SLYEST
SOREST
STRESS
SUREST
TAMEST
TERESA
THRESH
TRUEST
UNLESS
UNREST
VILEST
WIDEST
WISEST
WRIEST
WRYEST

•••E•S

ABBESS
ABBEYS
ABNERS
ACCESS
ADDERS
ADEEMS
ADIEUS
AEGEUS
AENEAS
AGGERS
AGLETS
AGREES
AIDERS
ALDERS
ALIENS
ALLENS
ALLEYS
ALTERS
AMBERS
AMIENS
ANGELS
ANGERS
APPELS
ARDEBS
ARIELS
ARMETS
ARPENS
ARTELS
ASKERS
ASPENS
ASPERS
ASSESS
ASSETS
ASTERS
ATHENS
ATREUS
AUGERS
AUREUS
AWLESS
AZTECS
BAGELS
BAKERS
BALERS
BEDEWS
BEGETS
BERETS
BESETS
BETELS
BEVELS
BEZELS
BICEPS
BIDETS
BIPEDS
BITERS
BLEEDS
BLUETS
BOGEYS
BONERS
BOREAS
BORERS
BOWELS
BOWERS
BOXERS
BREEDS
BRIEFS
BRIERS
BUYERS
CADETS
CALEBS
CAMELS
CAMEOS
CANERS
CAPERS
CARERS
CARESS
CARETS
CATERS
CEREUS
CHEEKS
CHEEPS
CHEERS
CHIEFS
CIDERS
CIVETS
COLEUS
COMERS
COMETS
CONEYS
COOEES
COOERS
COOEYS
CORERS
COVERS
COVETS
COVEYS
COWERS
COZENS
CREEDS
CREEKS
CREELS
CREEPS
CRIERS
CRUETS
CUBEBS
CULETS
CUPELS
CURERS
CUTEYS
DARERS
DATERS
DAVEYS
DEFERS
DEREKS
DETERS
DICERS
DIMERS
DINERS
DIVERS
DIZENS
DONEES
DONETS
DOSERS
DOTERS
DOWELS
DOWERS
DOYENS
DOZENS
DRIERS
DRYERS
DUPERS
DURESS
EASELS
EATERS
EGGERS
EGRESS
EGRETS
ELDERS
ELLENS
ELMERS
ELVERS
EMBEDS
EMBERS
EMCEES
EMEERS
EMMETS
ENGELS
ENTERS
ESKERS
ESTERS
ETHELS
ETHERS
EXCELS
EXCESS
EXPELS
FACERS
FACETS
FAKERS
FARERS
FEVERS
FIBERS
FIFERS
FILERS
FILETS
FIRERS
FIVERS
FIXERS
FLEERS
FLEETS
FLIERS
FLYERS
FOYERS
FRIERS
FRYERS
FUSEES
FUZEES
GAGERS
GANEFS
GAPERS
GAVELS
GAZERS
GENETS
GIBERS
GIMELS
GLEETS
GONERS
GREEDS
GREEKS
GREENS
GREETS
GRIEFS
GRUELS
HALERS
HAREMS
HATERS
HAVENS
HAZELS
HAZERS
HELENS
HEWERS
HIDERS
HIKERS
HIRERS
HOMERS
HONEYS
HOTELS
HOVELS
HOVERS
HYMENS
IDLERS
IMBEDS
IMPELS
INFERS
INKERS
INLETS
INSETS
INTERS
ISLETS
ISSEIS
JANETS
JEWELS
JEWESS
JOKERS
JULEPS
JURELS
KARENS
KEVELS
KIBEIS
KNEELS
KOPEKS
LABELS
LAGERS
LAKERS
LAMEDS
LAPELS
LASERS
LAVERS
LAYERS
LEGERS
LEPERS
LEVEES
LEVELS
LEVERS
LIBELS
LIFERS
LIKENS
LIMENS
LIMEYS
LINENS
LINERS
LITERS
LIVENS
LIVERS
LONERS
LOPERS
LOSERS
LOVERS
LOWERS
LUGERS
LUMENS
LUNETS
LURERS
LYCEES
MABELS

MACERS
MAKERS
MAMEYS
MASERS
MATEOS
MATEYS
MAZERS
MELEES
METERS
MILERS
MIMERS
MINERS
MISERS
MITERS
MIXERS
MODELS
MONEYS
MOPERS
MORELS
MOSEYS
MOTELS
MOVERS
MOWERS
NAMERS
NAVELS
NEREIS
NEWELS
NIGELS
NISEIS
NOTERS
NOVELS
OBSESS
OCHERS
OCTETS
OFFERS
OGLERS
OGRESS
OILERS
ONSETS
ORDERS
ORIELS
ORMERS
OSIERS
OTHERS
OTTERS
OUSELS
OUTERS
OUZELS
OWLETS
OWNERS
PACERS
PANELS
PAPERS
PARENS
PARERS
PAREUS
PATENS
PATERS
PAVERS
PAWERS
PAYEES
PAYERS
PELEUS
PETERS
PEWEES
PIKERS
PILEUS
PIPERS
PIPETS
PLIERS
POKERS
POSERS
POWERS
PREENS
PRIERS
PROEMS
PRYERS
PULERS
PUREES
QUEENS
QUEERS
RACERS
RAKERS
RANEES
RATELS
RATERS
RAVELS
RAVENS
RAVERS
RAZEES
REBECS
REBELS
RECESS
REFERS
RENEES
RENEWS
REPELS
RESETS
REVELS
REVETS
RICERS
RIDERS
RIMERS
RIPENS
RISERS
RIVERS
RIVETS
RODEOS
ROGERS
ROVERS
ROWELS
ROWERS
RUBENS
RULERS
RUPEES
SABERS
SAHEBS
SAKERS
SAVERS
SAWERS
SAYERS
SCREWS
SEDERS
SEVENS
SEVERS
SEWERS
SHEENS
SHEERS
SHEETS
SHOERS
SHREDS
SHREWS
SINEWS
SIRENS
SKIERS
SLEEKS
SLEEPS
SLEETS
SNEERS
SOBERS
SORELS
SOWERS
SPEEDS
SPIELS
SPIERS
SPREES
STEEDS
STEELS
STEEPS
STEERS
STRESS
STREWS
SUPERS
SWEEPS
SWEETS
SYCEES
TAKERS
TALERS
TAMERS
TAPERS
TAWERS
TAXERS
TEHEES
TENETS
TEPEES
TEREUS
THREES
TIGERS
TILERS
TIMERS
TOKENS
TONERS
TOPERS
TOTEMS
TOTERS
TOWELS
TOWERS
TOYERS
TRIERS
TUBERS
TUNERS
TWEEDS
TWEETS
UDDERS
ULCERS
UMBELS
UMBERS
UNLESS
UNMEWS
UNPEGS
UPPERS
UPSETS
URAEUS
USHERS
UTTERS
VALETS
VEXERS
VIPERS
VIREOS
VIXENS
VOMERS
VOTERS
VOWELS
VOWERS
WADERS
WAFERS
WAGERS
WAKENS
WALERS
WATERS
WAVERS
WAVEYS
WEBERS
WHEELS
WIDENS
WIPERS
WIRERS
WIVERS
WIZENS
WOOERS
XEBECS
XYLEMS
YAGERS
YAMENS
YODELS
YOGEES
YOKELS
ZEBECS
ZIBETS

••••ES

ABASES
ABATES
ABBIES
ABELES
ABIDES
ABODES
ABUSES
ADAGES
ADDLES
ADOBES
ADORES
AEETES
AERIES
AGATES
AGAVES
AGONES
AGREES
AISLES
AKENES
ALICES
ALINES
ALLIES
AMAZES
AMBLES
AMICES
AMIDES
AMOLES
AMUSES
ANDRES
ANGLES
ANISES
ANKLES
ANNIES
ANODES
ANUSES
APEXES
APICES
APPLES
ARCHES
ARETES
ARGUES
ARISES
ARMIES
ARNIES
ARTIES
ASIDES
ATONES
AWAKES
AXONES
AZINES
AZOLES
AZORES
AZURES
BABIES
BACHES
BADGES
BARDES
BARGES
BARYES
BASHES
BASSES
BASTES
BEEVES
BEIGES
BELIES
BELLES
BENNES
BERMES
BETTES
BEVIES
BIASES
BIBLES
BILGES
BINGES
BIRLES
BLADES
BLAMES
BLARES
BLAZES
BLOKES
BODIES
BOGIES
BOGLES
BOMBES
BONZES
BOOZES
BOSHES
BOSSES
BOULES
BOUSES
BOWSES
BRACES
BRAKES
BRAVES
BRAZES
BREVES
BRIBES
BRIDES
BRINES
BROMES
BRUCES
BRUGES
BRUMES
BRUTES
BUBOES
BUDGES
BUGLES
BULGES
BURIES
BURKES
BURSES
BUSHES
BUSIES
BUSSES
BUTTES
BUZZES
CABLES
CACHES
CADGES
CADRES
CALCES
CALVES
CALXES
CANNES
CANOES
CARIES
CARTES
CARVES
CASHES
CASTES
CAULES
CAUSES
CAVIES
CEASES
CENSES
CERTES
CHAFES
CHAPES
CHARES
CHASES
CHIDES
CHIMES
CHINES
CHIVES
CHLOES
CHOKES
CHORES
CHUTES
CITIES
CIVIES
CLARES
CLIMES
CLINES

CLIVES
CLONES
CLOSES
CLOVES
CLYDES
COAXES
COBLES
COLIES
CONGES
CONIES
CONTES
COOEES
COPIES
COPSES
CORSES
CORTES
CORVES
COSHES
COSSES
COUPES
COZIES
CRAKES
CRANES
CRAPES
CRATES
CRAVES
CRAZES
CREMES
CREPES
CRIMES
CRISES
CRONES
CRORES
CROZES
CRUCES
CRUSES
CRUXES
CURIES
CURSES
CURVES
CUSSES
CUTIES
CYCLES
DADOES
DAISES
DALLES
DANCES
DASHES
DAVIES
DEFIES
DEICES
DELVES
DEMIES
DENIES
DEUCES
DHOLES
DIANES
DIDIES
DIDOES
DIESES
DIODES
DIRGES
DISHES
DOBIES
DODGES
DODOES
DOGIES
DONEES
DORIES
DOUSES
DOWSES
DOXIES
DRAKES
DRAPES
DRIVES
DRONES
DROVES
DRUPES
DRUSES
DUNCES
DUTIES
EAGLES
EARLES
ECCLES
ECHOES
ECOLES
EDDIES
EDILES
EDUCES
ELATES
ELIDES
ELLIES
ELOPES
ELSIES
ELUDES
EMCEES
EMILES
EMMIES
EMOTES
ENATES
ENDUES
ENSUES
ENVIES
EPODES
ERASES
ERNIES
ERODES
ESPIES
ETAPES
ETCHES
ETUDES
EVADES
EVOKES
EXILES
EXUDES
EYASES
EYRIES
FABLES
FACIES
FARCES
FARLES
FASCES
FAUCES
FAUVES
FAWKES
FEASES
FEEZES
FENCES
FESSES
FEZZES
FICHES
FIQUES
FISHES
FIZZES
FLAKES
FLAMES
FLARES
FLAXES
FLEXES
FLUKES
FLUMES
FLUTES
FLUXES
FOGIES
FORCES
FORGES
FORTES
FOSSES
FRAMES
FRISES
FUDGES
FUGLES
FUGUES
FURIES
FURZES
FUSEES
FUSSES
FUZEES
FUZZES
GABLES
GAFFES
GANGES
GASHES
GASSES
GAUGES
GAUZES
GENIES
GENRES
GENTES
GEODES
GIGUES
GLACES
GLADES
GLARES
GLAZES
GLEBES
GLEDES
GLIDES
GLOBES
GLOVES
GLOZES
GLUMES
GNOMES
GOBIES
GOOSES
GORGES
GORSES
GOUGES
GRACES
GRADES
GRAPES
GRATES
GRAVES
GRAZES
GREBES
GRIDES
GRIMES
GRIPES
GROPES
GROVES
GRUMES
GUIDES
GUILES
GUISES
GUSHES
HALOES
HALVES
HANCES
HASHES
HASTES
HAWSES
HEAVES
HEDGES
HELVES
HERMES
HEROES
HERPES
HINGES
HISSES
HOAXES
HOBBES
HOBOES
HOLIES
HOLMES
HOOVES
HORDES
HORSES
HOUSES
HUGHES
HUSHES
HYADES
IBEXES
IBICES
IBISES
ILEXES
IMAGES
IMBUES
IMIDES
IMINES
IMMIES
INCHES
INDIES
INDUES
INGRES
INKLES
INURES
IRENES
IRIDES
IRISES
ISSUES
ITCHES
JAMIES
JAZZES
JESSES
JINXES
JORGES
JOSHES
JOSIES
JOSSES
JOULES
JOYCES
JUDGES
JUICES
JULIES
JURIES
KAASES
KATIES
KEDGES
KEEVES
KERMES
KEYNES
KISSES
KNAVES
KNIFES
KNIVES
KOINES
KOPJES
KRISES
LACHES
LADIES
LADLES
LANCES
LAPSES
LASHES
LASSES
LATHES
LEASES
LEAVES
LEDGES
LENSES
LEUDES
LEVEES
LEVIES
LIANES
LIEGES
LILIES
LIVRES
LOAVES
LODGES
LOOSES
LORIES
LOSSES
LOUPES
LOUSES
LUNGES
LUSHES
LYCEES
LYNXES
MACLES
MADGES
MAIZES
MAMIES
MANSES
MANTES
MAPLES
MARGES
MARIES
MASHES
MASSES
MATTES
MAUDES
MAUVES
MELEES
MENSES
MERGES
MERLES
MESHES
MESNES
MESSES
MIDGES
MINCES
MINXES
MISSES
MOLIES
MONIES
MONTES
MOSSES
MOUSES
MOVIES
MURRES
MUSHES
MUSSES
MYOPES
NANTES
NAOSES
NAPLES
NAPPES
NAVIES
NERVES
NEUMES
NICHES
NIECES
NIXIES
NOISES
NOOSES
NUDGES
NURSES
OGIVES
OLIVES
OLLIES
ONUSES
OODLES
OPINES
ORATES
ORGIES
ORYXES
OUNCES
OVULES
OXEYES
OXIDES
PADRES
PARIES
PARSES
PASSES
PASTES
PAUSES
PAYEES
PEASES
PEEVES
PEKOES
PELVES
PEWEES
PHASES
PHONES

PIECES
PIQUES
PISCES
PISHES
PITIES
PIXIES
PLACES
PLANES
PLATES
PLEBES
PLUMES
PLUSES
POGIES
POISES
POKIES
PONIES
PONTES
POSIES
POSSES
PRATES
PRICES
PRIDES
PRIMES
PRIZES
PROBES
PROSES
PROVES
PRUDES
PRUNES
PULSES
PUREES
PURGES
PURSES
PUSHES
PUSSES
PYXIES
QUAKES
QUEUES
QUIRES
QUOTES
RABIES
RAISES
RAMIES
RANEES
RANGES
RASHES
RAZEES
RAZZES
REALES
REDOES
REEVES
RELIES
RENEES
RENTES
REVUES
RHYMES
RICHES
RIDGES
RIFLES
RINSES
ROBLES
ROGUES
ROUGES
ROUSES
ROUTES
RUBIES
RUBLES
RUCHES
RUPEES
RUSHES
SABLES
SADIES
SALVES
SANIES
SASHES
SASSES
SAUCES
SAUTES
SCALES
SCAPES
SCARES
SCENES
SCONES
SCOPES
SCORES
SCUTES
SEDGES
SEINES
SEIZES
SELVES
SENSES
SERIES
SERVES
SHADES
SHAKES
SHALES
SHAMES
SHAPES
SHARES
SHAVES
SHINES
SHIRES
SHIVES
SHORES
SHOTES
SHOVES
SIDLES
SIEGES
SIEVES
SINGES
SIXTES
SKATES
SKIVES
SLAKES
SLATES
SLAVES
SLICES
SLIDES
SLIMES
SLOPES
SMAZES
SMILES
SMITES
SMOKES
SNAKES
SNARES
SNIPES
SNORES
SOCLES
SOLVES
SOUSES
SPACES
SPADES
SPARES
SPATES
SPICES
SPIKES
SPILES
SPINES
SPIRES
SPITES
SPOKES
SPORES
SPREES
SPRUES
SPUMES
STAGES
STAKES
STALES
STAPES
STARES
STASES
STATES
STAVES
STELES
STERES
STEVES
STILES
STIPES
STOKES
STOLES
STONES
STOPES
STORES
STOVES
STUPES
STYLES
SUCRES
SUEDES
SUITES
SURGES
SUSIES
SWAGES
SWALES
SWEDES
SWIPES
SYCEES
TABLES
TASTES
TAUPES
TBONES
TEASES
TEHEES
TENSES
TENUES
TEPEES
TESTES
THALES
THAMES
THANES
THEBES
THEMES
THESES
THOLES
THREES
THROES
THYMES
TIDIES
TILDES
TINGES
TITHES
TITLES
TOBIES
TODIES
TOGUES
TOILES
TOQUES
TORIES
TOSHES
TOSSES
TRACES
TRADES
TRAVES
TRIBES
TRICES
TRINES
TROVES
TRUCES
TSADES
TULLES
TUQUES
TUSHES
TWINES
UKASES
UMBLES
UNCLES
UNDIES
UNDOES
UNGUES
UNITES
UNTIES
UPASES
USAGES
VALUES
VALVES
VARIES
VARVES
VENUES
VERGES
VERSES
VETOES
VINCES
VOGUES
VOICES
VOILES
WADIES
WAIVES
WASHES
WASTES
WAVIES
WAYNES
WEAVES
WEDGES
WHALES
WHILES
WHINES
WHITES
WHORES
WICHES
WINCES
WINOES
WINZES
WISHES
WITHES
WOLVES
WRITES
YESSES
YOGEES
ZANIES
ZEROES

ET••••

ETAPES
ETCHED
ETCHER
ETCHES
ETHANE
ETHANS
ETHELS
ETHERS
ETHICS
ETHNIC
ETHYLS
ETUDES
ETYMON

E•T•••

EATERS
EATING
ECTOMY
ECTYPE
EITHER
ENTAIL
ENTERA
ENTERO
ENTERS
ENTICE
ENTIRE
ENTITY
ENTOMB
ENTOMO
ENTRAP
ENTREE
ESTATE
ESTEEM
ESTERS
ESTHER
ESTOPS
ESTRAY
ESTRUS
EXTANT
EXTEND
EXTENT
EXTERN
EXTOLS
EXTORT
EXTRAS

E••T••

EARTHS
EARTHY
EASTER
EASTON
EDITED
EDITHS
EDITOR
ELATED
ELATER
ELATES
ELYTRA
EMETIC
EMETIN
EMOTED
EMOTES
ENATES
ENATIC
EROTIC
ERYTHR
EVITAS
EXETER
EXITED
EXOTIC

E•••T•

EBOATS
ECARTE
EDICTS
EDUCTS
EFFETE
EGESTA
EGESTS
EGRETS
EIGHTH
EIGHTS
EIGHTY
EJECTA
EJECTS
ELECTR
ELECTS
ELIOTS
EMEUTE
EMMETS
EMMETT
ENACTS
ENMITY
ENTITY
EOLITH
EPACTS
EQUATE
EQUITY
ERECTS
ERGATE
ERRATA
ERSATZ
ERUCTS
ERUPTS
ESTATE
EVENTS
EVERTS
EVICTS
EXACTA
EXACTS
EXALTS
EXCITE

EXERTS
EXISTS
EXULTS

E••••T
EAGLET
EFFECT
EFFORT
EGBERT
EGOIST
ELBERT
ELDEST
ELEGIT
ELICIT
ELLIOT
EMMETT
ENCYST
ENGIRT
ENLIST
ENRAPT
ENROOT
ERFURT
ERNEST
ERRANT
ESCENT
ESCORT
ESPRIT
EVERET
EXCEPT
EXEMPT
EXEUNT
EXHORT
EXPECT
EXPERT
EXPORT
EXSECT
EXSERT
EXTANT
EXTENT
EXTORT
EYELET

•ET•••
AETHER
BETAKE
BETELS
BETHEL
BETIDE
BETISE
BETONY
BETOOK
BETRAY
BETSYS
BETTED
BETTER
BETTES
BETTOR
BETTYS
CETANE
DETACH
DETAIL
DETAIN
DETECT
DETENT
DETERS
DETEST
DETOUR
FETIAL
FETICH
FETING
FETISH
FETORS
FETTER
FETTLE
GETTER
GETUPS
HETERO
HETMAN
HETTYS
JETHRO
JETSAM
JETTED
JETTON
KETENE
KETONE
KETOSE
KETTLE
LETHAL
LETTER
LETUPS
METAGE
METALS
METEOR
METERS
METHOD
METHYL
METIER
METING
METOPE
METRIC
METROS
METTLE
METUMP
NETHER
NETTED
NETTIE
NETTLE
PETAIN
PETALS
PETARD
PETERS
PETITE
PETREL
PETRIE
PETROL
PETTED
RETAIL
RETAIN
RETAKE
RETARD
RETELL
RETENE
RETINA
RETIRE
RETOLD
RETOOK
RETORT
RETTED
RETURN
RETUSE
SETOFF
SETONS
SETOSE
SETOUS
SETTEE
SETTER
SETTLE
SETTOS
SETUPS
TETANY
TETCHY
TETHER
TETHYS
TETONS
TETRAD
TETRYL
TETTER
TETZEL
VETOED
VETOER
VETOES
VETTED
WETHER
WETTED
WETTER
ZETHOS
ZETHUS

•E•T••
AEETES
BEATEN
BEATER
BEETLE
BELTED
BENTON
BERTHA
BERTHE
BERTHS
BERTIE
BESTED
BESTIR
BESTOW
BETTED
BETTER
BETTES
BETTOR
BETTYS
CELTIC
CENTAL
CENTER
CENTOS
CENTRA
CENTRI
CENTRO
CERTES
CESTUS
DEATHS
DEATHY
DEBTOR
DEFTER
DEFTLY
DELTAS
DENTAL
DENTED
DENTIL
DENTIN
DEPTHS
DEXTER
DEXTRO
FESTAL
FESTER
FETTER
FETTLE
GENTES
GENTLE
GENTOO
GENTRY
GERTIE
GERTYS
GESTIC
GETTER
HEATED
HEATER
HEATHS
HEATHY
HECTIC
HECTOR
HEFTED
HEPTAD
HESTER
HESTIA
HETTYS
JESTED
JESTER
JETTED
JETTON
KEITHS
KETTLE
LECTOR
LENTEN
LENTIL
LENTOS
LEPTON
LESTER
LETTER
MEATUS
MEETER
MEETLY
MELTED
MELTER
MELTON
MENTAL
MENTOR
MESTEE
METTLE
NEATER
NEATLY
NECTAR
NEKTON
NESTED
NESTLE
NESTOR
NETTED
NETTIE
NETTLE
NEUTER
NEWTON
PECTEN
PECTIC
PECTIN
PEGTOP
PELTED
PELTER
PELTRY
PENTAD
PENTUP
PEPTIC
PERTLY
PESTER
PESTLE
PETTED
PEWTER
RECTAL
RECTOR
RECTOS
RECTUM
RECTUS
REDTOP
RENTAL
RENTED
RENTER
RENTES
RESTED
RESTER
RETTED
SEATED
SECTOR
SEETHE
SENTRY
SEPTAL
SEPTET
SEPTIC
SEPTUM
SESTET
SETTEE
SETTER
SETTLE
SETTOS
SEXTAN
SEXTET
SEXTON
TEETER
TEETHE
TENTED
TENTER
TENTHS
TESTAE
TESTED
TESTER
TESTES
TESTIS
TESTON
TETTER
TEUTON
VECTOR
VENTED
VENTER
VENTRO
VERTEX
VESTAL
VESTAS
VESTED
VESTEE
VESTRY
VETTED
WELTED
WELTER
WESTER
WETTED
WETTER
YESTER
ZESTED

•E••T•
AERATE
BEASTS
BEAUTS
BEAUTY
BEFITS
BEGETS
BEMATA
BENITA
BENITO
BERATE
BERETS
BESETS
BESOTS
CERATE
CERATO
CERITE
DEARTH
DEBATE
DEBITS
DEBUTS
DEISTS
DELETE
DEMITS
DEMOTE
DENOTE
DEPOTS
DEPUTE
DEPUTY
DEVOTE
DEWITT
FEALTY
FEASTS
FEINTS
FEISTS
FEISTY
FERITY
GEMOTS
GENETS
GENITO
HEALTH
HEARTH
HEARTS
HEARTY
HECATE
HEISTS
HELOTS
HEMATO
HEPATO
HERETO
KERATO

6

LEANTO
LEGATE
LEGATO
LENGTH
LENITY
LEVITE
LEVITY
MERITS
NEGATE
NEMATO
PEDATE
PEDATI
PELITE
PELOTA
PESETA
PETITE
PEWITS
PEYOTE
REACTS
REALTY
REBATE
REBATO
REBUTS
RECITE
REFITS
REFUTE
RELATE
REMITS
REMOTE
REPUTE
RESETS
REVETS
SEBATS
SEDATE
SEMITE
SENATE
TEMPTS
TENETS
TENUTO
TERATO
TERETE
VELATE
VELDTS
VERITY
VERSTS
WEALTH
YEASTS
YEASTY
ZENITH

•E•••T

BECKET
BEGIRT
BEHEST
BEIRUT
BELOIT
BENNET
BEREFT
BEZANT
CEMENT
CERMET
DECANT
DECEIT
DECENT
DECOCT
DEDUCT
DEFEAT
DEFECT
DEGUST
DEJECT
DELICT
DEPART
DEPICT
DEPORT
DERMAT
DESALT
DESERT
DESIST
DESPOT
DETECT
DETENT
DETEST
DEVEST
DEVOUT
DEWITT
FERRET
FEWEST
GERENT
HEARST
HEIGHT
HELMET
HENBIT
HEREAT
HERIOT
HERMIT
JENNET
JESUIT
LEARNT
LEGIST
LEVANT
MEREST
NEWEST
PEANUT
PEDANT
PELLET
PENULT
PEQUOT
PERMIT
RECANT
RECAST
RECENT
RECEPT
REDACT
REDHOT
REFLET
REGENT
REGLET
REGRET
REHEAT
REJECT
RELENT
RELICT
RENNET
REPAST
REPEAT
REPENT
REPORT
RESEAT
RESECT
RESENT
RESIST
RESORT
RESULT
RETORT
REVERT
REVEST
REVOLT
SECANT
SECRET
SEJANT
SELECT
SENNET
SENNIT
SEPTET
SESTET
SEURAT
SEXIST
SEXTET
TEAPOT
TENANT
TERCET
TERRET
VELVET
VERIST
VERVET
WEIGHT
WERENT
ZEALOT

••ET••

ACETAL
ACETIC
ACETUM
ACETYL
AEETES
ARETES
BEETLE
BRETON
CHETAH
CRETAN
CRETIC
CRETIN
DIETED
DIETER
EMETIC
EMETIN
EXETER
FLETCH
FOETAL
FOETID
FOETOR
FOETUS
FRETTY
GHETTO
GOETHE
GRETAS
GRETEL
HYETAL
LUETIC
MEETER
MEETLY
NOETIC
PIETER
PIETRO
POETIC
POETRY
PRETER
PRETOR
PRETTY
RHETOR
SEETHE
SKETCH
STETHO
TEETER
TEETHE
THETAS
THETIC
THETIS
TSETSE
URETER
URETHR
URETIC
WRETCH

••E•T•

ADEPTS
AGENTS
ALECTO
ALERTS
ALEUTS
AMENTS
AVERTS
AVESTA
BLEATS
BREATH
BRENTS
CHEATS
CHESTS
CHESTY
CLEATS
CLEFTS
CREATE
CRESTS
CUESTA
EGESTA
EGESTS
EJECTA
EJECTS
ELECTR
ELECTS
EMEUTE
ERECTS
EVENTS
EVERTS
EXERTS
FIESTA
FLEETS
FRETTY
GHETTO
GLEETS
GLEETY
GREATS
GREETS
GUESTS
IDEATE
OLEATE
OMENTA
PLEATS
PLENTY
PRESTO
PRETTY
QUESTS
SCENTS
SHEATH
SHEETS
SHELTY
SIESTA
SLEETS
SLEETY
SLEUTH
SMELTS
SVELTE
SWEATS
SWEATY
SWEETS
THEFTS
TREATS
TREATY
TWEETS
TWENTY
WHEATS
WREATH
WRESTS

••E••T

BREAST
BRECHT
BREVET
CLEIST
COEMPT
CREDIT
DOESNT
DREAMT
ELEGIT
EVERET
EXEMPT
EXEUNT
EYELET
FREEST
ISEULT
OCELOT
OMELET
SHEBAT
THEIST

•••ET•

AGLETS
ARMETS
ASSETS
BEGETS
BERETS
BESETS
BIDETS
BLUETS
CADETS
CARETS
CHAETA
CHAETO
CIVETS
COMETS
COVETS
CRUETS
CULETS
DALETH
DELETE
DONETS
EFFETE
EGRETS
EMMETS
EMMETT
FACETS
FILETS
FLEETS
GAIETY
GAMETE
GAMETO
GAYETY
GENETS
GLEETS
GLEETY
GREETS
HERETO
INLETS
INSETS
ISLETS
JANETS
KINETO
LUNETS
MOIETY
MYCETE
NICETY
NINETY
OCTETS
ONSETS
OWLETS
PESETA
PIPETS
RESETS
REVETS
RIVETS
SAFETY
SHEETS
SLEETS
SLEETY
SURETY
SWEETS
TENETS
TERETE
TWEETS
UBIETY
UPSETS
VALETS
ZIBETH
ZIBETS

•••E•T

ABJECT
ABLEST
ABSENT
ACCENT
ACCEPT
ADVENT
ADVERT
AFFECT

ALBEIT
ALBERT
ARDENT
ARGENT
ARPENT
ARREST
ASCENT
ASPECT
ASSENT
ASSERT
ATTEST
BAREST
BEHEST
BEREFT
BISECT
BLUEST
CADENT
CAVEAT
CEMENT
CLIENT
COGENT
COVERT
CUTEST
DECEIT
DECENT
DEFEAT
DEFECT
DEJECT
DESERT
DETECT
DETENT
DETEST
DEVEST
DIGEST
DIRECT
DIREST
DIVERT
DIVEST
DOCENT
DRIEST
DRYEST
EFFECT
EGBERT
ELBERT
ELDEST
EMMETT
ERNEST
ESCENT
EXCEPT
EXPECT
EXPERT
EXSECT
EXSERT
EXTENT
FEWEST
FINEST
FLIEST
FLUENT
FOMENT
FOREST
FREEST
FUNEST
GAYEST
GERENT
HAVENT
HEREAT
HONEST
HUBERT
HUGEST
ICIEST
IDLEST
INCEPT
INCEST
INDENT
INFECT
INFEST
INGEST
INJECT
INSECT
INSERT
INTENT
INVENT
INVERT
INVEST
LAMENT
LAMEST
LATENT
LATEST
LAXEST
LOMENT
LOWEST
LUCENT
MAYEST
MEREST
MODEST
MOLEST
MOMENT
NEWEST
NICEST
NOCENT
OBJECT
OBTECT
OBTEST
OBVERT
ODDEST
OLDEST
ORGEAT
ORIENT
OSBERT
PALEST
PARENT
PATENT
PONENT
POTENT
PRIEST
PUREST
RAREST
RAWEST
RECENT
RECEPT
REGENT
REHEAT
REJECT
RELENT
REPEAT
REPENT
RESEAT
RESECT
RESENT
REVERT
REVEST
RIDENT
RIPEST
ROBERT
RODENT
RUDEST
RUPERT
SAFEST
SAGEST
SANEST
SELECT
SHIEST
SHYEST
SILENT
SLIEST
SLYEST
SOLENT
SOREST
STREET
SUREST
TALENT
TAMEST
THREAT
TRUEST
UNBELT
UNBENT
UNMEET
UNREST
UNSEAT
UNVEXT
UNWEPT
UPBEAT
URGENT
URTEXT
VILEST
WERENT
WIDEST
WISEST
WRIEST
WRYEST
YCLEPT

••••ET

AIGLET
AMULET
ANKLET
ARMLET
AUKLET
AVOCET
BALLET
BARBET
BARRET
BASKET
BASSET
BECKET
BENNET
BILLET
BONNET
BOSKET
BREVET
BRUNET
BUCKET
BUDGET
BUFFET
BULLET
BURNET
CABLET
CACHET
CAMLET
CARPET
CASKET
CERMET
CHALET
CLARET
CLOSET
COLLET
COQUET
CORNET
CORSET
COSSET
CRUSET
CULLET
CURVET
CUTLET
CYGNET
DOCKET
DULCET
EAGLET
EVERET
EYELET
FANJET
FAUCET
FERRET
FIDGET
FILLET
FLORET
FORGET
GADGET
GANNET
GARGET
GARNET
GARRET
GASKET
GIBBET
GIBLET
GIGLET
GIMLET
GOBBET
GOBLET
GOGLET
GORGET
GRIVET
GULLET
GUSSET
HAMLET
HASLET
HELMET
HORNET
IMARET
JACKET
JAPHET
JENNET
JOLIET
JULIET
JUNKET
KISMET
LABRET
LANCET
LAPPET
LIMPET
LINNET
LOCKET
MAGNET
MALLET
MAMMET
MARKET
MIDGET
MILLET
MINUET
MOPPET
MULLET
MUSKET
NUGGET
NUTLET
OFFSET
OMELET
OUTLET
OUTSET
PACKET
PALLET
PARGET
PELLET
PICKET
PIQUET
PLACET
PLANET
POCKET
POPPET
POSSET
PRIVET
PROJET
PULLET
PUPPET
RABBET
RACKET
REFLET
REGLET
REGRET
RENNET
RILLET
ROCHET
ROCKET
ROQUET
RUNLET
RUSSET
SACHET
SALLET
SAMLET
SECRET
SENNET
SEPTET
SESTET
SEXTET
SIGNET
SIPPET
SOCKET
SONNET
SOVIET
SPINET
STREET
STYLET
SUBLET
SUNSET
SWIVET
SYNDET
TABLET
TAPPET
TARGET
TASSET
TERCET
TERRET
TICKET
TIPPET
TOILET
TRIVET
TURRET
UNDSET
UNMEET
VARLET
VELVET
VERVET
VIOLET
WADSET
WALLET
WICKET
WILLET

EU••••

EUBOEA
EUCHRE
EUCLID
EUDORA
EUGENE
EULOGY
EUNICE
EUNUCH
EUPNEA
EUREKA
EURIPI
EUROPA
EUROPE

E•U•••

EDUARD
EDUCED
EDUCES
EDUCTS
ELUDED
ELUDES
EQUALS
EQUATE
EQUINE
EQUIPS
EQUITY
ERUCTS
ERUPTS
ETUDES
EXUDED
EXUDES
EXULTS
EXURBS

E••U••

EDMUND

EFFUSE
EMEUTE
ENDUED
ENDUES
ENDURE
ENGULF
ENOUGH
ENSUED
ENSUES
ENSURE
ERFURT
ESCUDO
EUNUCH
EXCUSE
EXEUNT
EXHUME

E•••U•
EARFUL
EFFLUX
ELBRUS
EMBRUE
ENSOUL
EPIRUS
ERBIUM
EREBUS
ESTRUS
EXEQUY
EXODUS
EYECUP
EYEFUL

•EU•••
BEULAH
BEULAS
DEUCED
DEUCES
FEUARS
FEUDAL
FEUDED
FEUING
LEUDES
NEUMES
NEURAL
NEURON
NEUTER
OEUVRE
REUBEN
SEURAT
TEUCER
TEUTON
ZEUGMA

•E•U••
AERUGO
BEAUTS
BEAUTY
BEDUIN
BEGUIN
BEGUMS
BELUGA
BEMUSE
BENUMB
CEDULA
CERUSE
CESURA
DEBUGS
DEBUNK
DEBUTS
DECURY
DEDUCE
DEDUCT
DEGUMS
DEGUST
DELUDE
DELUGE
DELUXE
DEMURE
DEMURS
DENUDE
DEPUTE
DEPUTY
FECULA
FECUND
FEMURS
FERULA
FERULE
GERUND
GETUPS
HEAUME
HECUBA
JEJUNE
JESUIT
LEGUME
LEHUAS
LEMUEL
LEMURS
LETUPS
MEDUSA
METUMP
MEZUZA
NEBULA
PENULT
PENURY
PEQUOD
PEQUOT
PERUKE
PERUSE
REBUFF
REBUKE
REBUTS
RECURS
RECUSE
REDUCE
REFUGE
REFUND
REFUSE
REFUTE
REMUDA
REPUTE
RERUNS
RESULT
RESUME
RETURN
RETUSE
REVUES
SECUND
SECURE
SEDUCE
SEDUMS
SEQUEL
SEQUIN
SERUMS
SETUPS
SEXUAL
TELUGU
TENUES
TENUIS
TENURE
TENUTO
VELURE
VENUES
VENULE

•E••U•
AEACUS
AECIUM
AEGEUS
AEOLUS
BEDAUB
BEDBUG
BEFOUL
BEIRUT
CENSUS
CEREUS
CERIUM
CEROUS
CESIUM
CESTUS
DELIUS
DENGUE
DETOUR
DEVOUR
DEVOUT
FEROUS
FERRUM
FESCUE
GENIUS
GENOUS
GEROUS
HELIUM
LEAGUE
MEATUS
MEDIUM
MEROUS
NESSUS
PEANUT
PELEUS
PENTUP
PEPLUM
PEPLUS
RECOUP
RECTUM
RECTUS
REDBUD
REDBUG
REFLUX
REGIUS
RESCUE
SEAMUS
SELJUK
SEPTUM
SEROUS
SESQUI
SETOUS
TEACUP
TEDIUM
TELLUS
TEREUS
TERGUM
VELLUM
VELOUR
VENDUE
VENOUS
VERDUN
VERSUS
ZETHUS

•E•••U
DESSAU
RESEAU
TELUGU

••EU••
ALEUTS
CREUSA
EMEUTE
EXEUNT
FLEURY
ISEULT
PLEURA
PLEURO
PNEUMA
PNEUMO
PSEUDO
QUEUED
QUEUES
RHEUMY
SIEURS
SLEUTH
TIEUPS

••E•U•
ACEOUS
ACETUM
AVENUE
CAECUM
CHERUB
EREBUS
EXEQUY
EYECUP
EYEFUL
FOETUS
FRENUM
IREFUL
NAEVUS
OBELUS
PIERUS
PLENUM
PLEXUS
PREVUE
RHESUS
RUEFUL
STEPUP
USEFUL
UTERUS
WOEFUL

••E••U
APERCU

•••EU•
ADIEUS
ADIEUX
AEGEUS
ATREUS
AUREUS
BAYEUX
CEREUS
COLEUS
LINEUP
LUTEUM
LYCEUM
MADEUP
MAKEUP
MUSEUM
PAREUS
PELEUS
PILEUM
PILEUS
POSEUR
TAKEUP
TEREUS
TUNEUP
URAEUS
VOYEUR

•••E•U
BATEAU
BUREAU
COTEAU
JUNEAU
MOREAU
RESEAU

••••EU
MILIEU

EV••••
EVADED
EVADER
EVADES
EVELYN
EVENED
EVENLY
EVENTS
EVERET
EVERTS
EVICTS
EVILLY
EVINCE
EVITAS
EVOKED
EVOKES
EVOLVE
EVZONE

E•V•••
ELVERS
ELVIRA
ELVISH
ENVIED
ENVIER
ENVIES
ENVOYS

E••V••
ELEVEN
ELEVON

E•••V•
ENDIVE
EVOLVE

•EV•••
BEVELS
BEVIES
DEVEIN
DEVEST
DEVICE
DEVILS
DEVISE
DEVOID
DEVOIR
DEVOTE
DEVOUR
DEVOUT
FEVERS
KEVELS
KEVINS
LEVANT
LEVEES
LEVELS
LEVERS
LEVIED
LEVIER
LEVIES
LEVITE
LEVITY
NEVADA
NEVILE
NEVILL
NEVOID
NEVSKI
REVAMP
REVEAL
REVELS
REVERE
REVERT
REVEST
REVETS
REVIEW
REVILE
REVISE
REVIVE
REVOKE
REVOLT
REVUES
REVVED
SEVENS
SEVERE
SEVERS

•E•V••

BEAVER
BEEVES
CERVIX
DELVED
DELVER
DELVES
DENVER
FERVID
FERVOR
HEAVED
HEAVEN
HEAVER
HEAVES
HELVES
JERVIS
KEEVES
KELVIN
LEAVED
LEAVEN
LEAVER
LEAVES
MELVIN
MERVIN
NERVED
NERVES
OEUVRE
PEAVEY
PEEVED
PEEVES
PELVES
PELVIC
PELVIS
REAVOW
REEVED
REEVES
REVVED
SELVES
SERVAL
SERVED
SERVER
SERVES
SERVOS
VELVET
VERVET
WEAVED
WEAVER
WEAVES
WEEVER
WEEVIL

•E••V•

BEHAVE
BEHOVE
DERIVE
GENEVA
RELIVE
REMOVE
REVIVE

••EV••

BEEVES
BREVES
BREVET
CLEVER
CLEVIS
COEVAL
ELEVEN
ELEVON
KEEVES
NAEVUS
PEEVED
PEEVES
PREVUE
REEVED
REEVES
SIEVED
SIEVES
SOEVER
STEVEN
STEVES
STEVIE
UNEVEN
WEEVER
WEEVIL
YLEVEL

••E•V•

CLEAVE
GREAVE
HUELVA
SHEAVE
SHELVE
SLEAVE
SLEEVE
STEEVE
SWERVE
TWELVE
WHERVE

•••EV•

GENEVA
GRIEVE
SLEEVE
STEEVE
THIEVE

E•W•••

EDWARD
EDWINA
EDWINS
ENWIND
ENWOMB
ENWRAP
ERWINS

E••W••

EARWAX
EARWIG

E•••W•

ELBOWS
EMBOWS
ENDOWS

E••••W

ESCHEW
ESCROW

•EW•••

BEWAIL
BEWARE
DEWANS
DEWIER
DEWITT
DEWLAP
FEWEST
GEWGAW
HEWERS
HEWING
JEWELS
JEWESS
JEWISH
KEWPIE
LEWDER
LEWDLY
MEWING
MEWLED
NEWARK
NEWELS
NEWEST
NEWTON
PEWEES
PEWITS
PEWTER
REWARD
REWIND
REWORD
SEWAGE
SEWALL
SEWARD
SEWERS
SEWING

•E•W••

DEEWAN
HEDWIG
KEYWAY
LEEWAY
MEOWED
PEEWEE
SEAWAN
SEAWAY

•E••W•

BEDEWS
REDOWA
RENEWS
RENOWN
SEROWS

•E•••W

BELLOW
BESTOW
FELLOW
GEWGAW
HEBREW
HEEHAW
MEADOW
MELLOW
NEPHEW
REAVOW
REVIEW
SEESAW
YELLOW

••EW••

BREWED
BREWER
BREWIS
CHEWED
CHEWER
CLEWED
CREWEL
DEEWAN
LEEWAY
ONEWAY
PEEWEE
PREWAR
SHEWED
SHEWER
SKEWED
SKEWER
SLEWED
SPEWED
STEWED
VIEWED
VIEWER

••E••W

HEEHAW
SEESAW

•••EW•

BEDEWS
RENEWS
SCREWS
SCREWY
SHREWD
SHREWS
SINEWS
SINEWY
STREWN
STREWS
UNMEWS

••••EW

ANDREW
CASHEW
CURFEW
CURLEW
ESCHEW
HEBREW
KISLEW
MILDEW
NEPHEW
REVIEW
SUNDEW
UNDREW

EX••••

EXACTA
EXACTS
EXALTS
EXAMEN
EXARCH
EXCEED
EXCELS
EXCEPT
EXCESS
EXCIDE
EXCISE
EXCITE
EXCUSE
EXEDRA
EXEMPT
EXEQUY
EXERTS
EXETER
EXEUNT
EXHALE
EXHORT
EXHUME
EXILED
EXILES
EXILIC
EXISTS
EXITED
EXMOOR
EXODUS
EXOGEN
EXOTIC
EXPAND
EXPECT
EXPELS
EXPEND
EXPERT
EXPIRE
EXPIRY
EXPORT
EXPOSE
EXSECT
EXSERT
EXTANT
EXTEND
EXTENT
EXTERN
EXTOLS
EXTORT
EXTRAS
EXUDED
EXUDES
EXULTS
EXURBS

E••X••

ELIXIR

E••••X

EARWAX
EFFLUX

•EX•••

DEXTER
DEXTRO
HEXADS
HEXANE
HEXING
HEXONE
HEXOSE
HEXYLS
MEXICO
SEXIER
SEXING
SEXISM
SEXIST
SEXTAN
SEXTET
SEXTON
SEXUAL
VEXERS
VEXILS
VEXING

•E••X•

DELUXE
DESOXY

•E•••X

CERVIX
MENINX
REFLEX
REFLUX
VERNIX
VERTEX
WESSEX

••EX••

ALEXIA
ALEXIN
ALEXIS
APEXES
FLEXED
FLEXES
FLEXOR
IBEXES
ILEXES
PLEXOR
PLEXUS

••E••X

ICEBOX
PREFIX

•••EX•

UNVEXT
URTEXT

•••E•X

ADIEUX
BAYEUX
POLEAX

••••EX

AUSPEX
BIFLEX
CAUDEX
CONVEX
CORTEX
DIPLEX
DUPLEX
LASTEX
POLLEX
REFLEX
SCOLEX

6

UNISEX
VERTEX
VORTEX
WESSEX

EY••••
EYASES
EYECUP
EYEFUL
EYEING
EYELET
EYELID
EYRIES

E•Y•••
ELYSEE
ELYTRA
ERYNGO
ERYTHR
ETYMON

E••Y••
ECTYPE
ELAYNE
ENCYCL
ENCYST
ENZYME
ETHYLS

E•••Y•
EMBAYS
EMBRYO
EMILYS
ENJOYS
ENVOYS
EPONYM
ESSAYS
EVELYN

E••••Y
EARTHY
EASILY
ECTOMY
EERILY
EFFIGY
EIGHTY
EMBODY
EMPERY
EMPLOY
ENERGY
ENMITY
ENTITY
EQUITY
ESTRAY
EULOGY
EVENLY
EVILLY
EXEQUY
EXPIRY

•EY•••
BEYOND
CEYLON
GEYSER
HEYDAY
KEYING
KEYNES
KEYWAY
PEYOTE

•E•Y••
BERYLS
GERYON
HEXYLS
JEKYLL

•E••Y•
BECKYS
BELAYS
BENJYS
BENNYS
BENZYL
BESSYS
BETSYS
BETTYS
DEBBYS
DECAYS
DECOYS
DELAYS
DENNYS
GERRYS
GERTYS
HENRYS
HETTYS
JENNYS
JERRYS
KENNYS
LENNYS
LEROYS
METHYL
NELLYS
PEGGYS
PENNYS
PERCYS
PERRYS
REDEYE
RELAYS
REPAYS
SELSYN
SEPOYS
TEDDYS
TERRYS
TETHYS
TETRYL
WENDYS
ZEPHYR

•E•••Y
AERIFY
BEACHY
BEAUTY
BELFRY
BENDAY
BERNEY
BETONY
BETRAY
CECILY
CELERY
DEADLY
DEAFLY
DEARLY
DEATHY
DECURY
DEEPLY
DEFRAY
DEFTLY
DENARY
DEPLOY
DEPUTY
DESCRY
DESOXY
EERILY
FEALTY
FEISTY
FELONY
FERITY
GENTRY
HEARTY
HEATHY
HENLEY
HEREBY
HERESY
HEYDAY
JEREMY
JERSEY
KEENLY
KERSEY
KEYWAY
LEACHY
LEANLY
LEEWAY
LEGACY
LENITY
LESLEY
LEVITY
LEWDLY
MEANLY
MEASLY
MEDLEY
MEEKLY
MEETLY
MELODY
MEMORY
MERELY
NEARBY
NEARLY
NEATLY
PEACHY
PEARLY
PEAVEY
PEBBLY
PELTRY
PENURY
PERTLY
REALLY
REALTY
REDBAY
REMEDY
REPLAY
SEAWAY
SEEMLY
SENARY
SENTRY
TEAPOY
TEENSY
TEPEFY
TERMLY
TETANY
TETCHY
VENERY
VERIFY
VERILY
VERITY
VESTRY
WEAKLY
WEEKLY
WEENSY
WEIRDY
WESLEY
YEARLY
YEASTY

••EY••
OBEYED
OBEYER
OXEYED
OXEYES
PREYED
PREYER
WHEYEY

••E•Y•
ACETYL
AVERYS
AYEAYE
BYEBYE
CHERYL
EVELYN
PHENYL

••E••Y
AGEDLY
AGENCY
ANERGY
AWEARY
BLEARY
BLEBBY
BLENNY
BREEZY
CHEEKY
CHEERY
CHEESY
CHERRY
CHESTY
CLERGY
CREAKY
CREAMY
CREASY
CREEPY
DEEPLY
DREAMY
DREARY
DREGGY
DRESSY
ENERGY
EVENLY
EXEQUY
FLEDGY
FLEECY
FLESHY
FLEURY
FREAKY
FREDDY
FREELY
FRENZY
FRETTY
GLEAMY
GLEETY
GREASY
GREEDY
KEENLY
LEEWAY
MEEKLY
MEETLY
OHENRY
ONEWAY
OPENLY
OVERLY
PLENTY
POETRY
PREPAY
PRETTY
QUEASY
RHEUMY
SEEMLY
SHEENY
SHELBY
SHELLY
SHELTY
SHERRY
SLEAZY
SLEEKY
SLEEPY
SLEETY
SMEARY
SMELLY
SNEAKY
SNEEZY
SPEEDY
SPERRY
STEADY
STEAMY
STEELY
SWEATY
SWEEPY
TEENSY
THEORY
TREATY
TRENDY
TRESSY
TWEAKY
TWENTY
UNEASY
WEEKLY
WEENSY
WHEEZY
WHELKY
WHERRY
WHEYEY
WIELDY

•••EY•
ABBEYS
ALLEYS
BOGEYS
BOLEYN
CONEYS
COOEYS
COVEYS
CUTEYS
DAVEYS
HONEYS
LIMEYS
MAMEYS
MATEYS
MONEYS
MOSEYS
REDEYE
WAVEYS

•••E•Y
AMBERY
ARTERY
BAKERY
BARELY
BASELY
BLUELY
BOWERY
BREEZY
BRIERY
CASEFY
CELERY
CHEEKY
CHEERY
CHEESY
CICELY
COMEDY
COMELY
CREEPY
CUTELY
DIRELY
DOWERY
DUPERY
EMPERY
FAKERY
FINELY
FINERY
FLEECY
FREELY
GAIETY
GAMELY
GAYETY
GLEETY
GREEDY
HEREBY
HERESY
HOMELY
HUGELY
JEREMY
LAMELY
LATELY
LIKELY
LIVELY
LIVERY
LONELY

LOVELY
LOWERY
MERELY
MISERY
MOIETY
NAMELY
NAPERY
NICELY
NICETY
NINETY
NUDELY
OCHERY
ORNERY
ORRERY
PALELY
PAPERY
PINERY
POPERY
PURELY
RAREFY
RARELY
REMEDY
RIPELY
RUDELY
SAFELY
SAFETY
SAGELY
SANELY
SCREWY
SHEENY
SINEWY
SLEEKY
SLEEPY
SLEETY
SNEEZY
SOLELY
SORELY
SPEEDY
SPHERY
STEELY
SURELY
SURETY
SWEEPY
TEPEFY
TIMELY
TOWERY
TUMEFY
UBIETY
VALERY
VENERY
VILELY
VINERY
VOLERY
WATERY
WHEEZY
WIDELY
WIFELY
WINERY
WISELY

••••EY

ASHLEY
AUBREY
AUDREY
BAILEY
BARLEY
BARNEY
BERNEY
BURLEY
CLAYEY
CONVEY
COOKEY
COPLEY
DICKEY
DINGEY
DINKEY
DISNEY
DONKEY
DOYLEY
DUDLEY
FARLEY
FLUKEY
GALLEY
GOONEY
GOOSEY
HALLEY
HALSEY
HARLEY
HARVEY
HENLEY
HICKEY
HOCKEY
HORSEY
HUXLEY
JARVEY
JERSEY
JITNEY
JOCKEY
KERSEY
KIDNEY
KINSEY
LACKEY
LESLEY
LOWKEY
MAGUEY
MEDLEY
MICKEY
MONKEY
MOOLEY
MORLEY
MOSLEY
MOTLEY
MULLEY
MURREY
OAKLEY
OCASEY
OSPREY
PARLEY
PEAVEY
PHONEY
PHOOEY
POMPEY
PULLEY
PURVEY
PUSSEY
RICKEY
RIPLEY
RODNEY
ROMNEY
SIDNEY
STAGEY
STOGEY
STOREY
SURREY
SURVEY
SYDNEY
TACKEY
TURKEY
VALLEY
VOLLEY
WESLEY
WHEYEY
WHITEY
WINCEY
WITNEY
WOLSEY

E•Z•••

ECZEMA
ENZYME
EOZOIC
EVZONE

E••Z••

ELIZAS
EPIZOA

E••••Z

ERSATZ

•EZ•••

BEZANT
BEZELS
BEZOAR
FEZZAN
FEZZES
JEZAIL
MEZUZA
MEZZOS

•E•Z••

BENZOL
BENZYL
FEEZED
FEEZES
FEZZAN
FEZZES
GEEZER
MEZZOS
SEIZED
SEIZER
SEIZES
SEIZIN
SEIZOR
TETZEL

•E••Z•

BELIZE
MEZUZA
REBOZO

••EZ••

AREZZO
FEEZED
FEEZES
GEEZER
QUEZON

••E•Z•

AREZZO
BREEZE
BREEZY
FREEZE
FRENZY
SLEAZY
SNEEZE
SNEEZY
WHEEZE
WHEEZY

•••EZ•

BREEZE
BREEZY
FREEZE
FRIEZE
SNEEZE
SNEEZY
WHEEZE
WHEEZY

•••E•Z

LORENZ

••••EZ

CORTEZ
JUAREZ

FA••••

FABIAN
FABLED
FABLER
FABLES
FABRIC
FACADE
FACERS
FACETS
FACIAL
FACIES
FACILE
FACING
FACTOR
FACULA
FADEIN
FADING
FAEROE
FAFNIR
FAGGED
FAGGOT
FAGOTS
FAILED
FAILLE
FAINTS
FAIRED
FAIRER
FAIRLY
FAITHS
FAKERS
FAKERY
FAKING
FAKIRS
FALCON
FALLAL
FALLEN
FALLER
FALLOW
FALSER
FALTER
FAMILY
FAMINE
FAMISH
FAMOUS
FANEGA
FANGAS
FANGED
FANION
FANJET
FANNED
FANNER
FANNIE
FANNYS
FANONS
FANTAN
FANTOM
FANUMS
FARADS
FARCED
FARCER
FARCES
FARERS
FARINA
FARING
FARLES
FARLEY
FARMED
FARMER
FAROFF
FAROUT
FARROW
FASCES
FASCIA
FASTED
FASTEN
FASTER
FATHER
FATHOM
FATIMA
FATING
FATTED
FATTEN
FATTER
FAUCAL
FAUCES
FAUCET
FAULTS
FAULTY
FAUNAE
FAUNAL
FAUNAS
FAUNUS
FAUVES
FAVORS
FAWKES
FAWNED
FAWNER
FAXING
FAYING
FAZING

F•A•••

FEALTY
FEARED
FEARER
FEASED
FEASES
FEASTS
FIACRE
FIANCE
FIASCO
FLABBY
FLACKS
FLACON
FLAGGY
FLAGON
FLAILS
FLAIRS
FLAKED
FLAKER
FLAKES
FLAMBE
FLAMED
FLAMEN
FLAMES
FLANGE
FLANKS
FLARED
FLARES
FLASHY
FLASKS
FLATLY
FLATUS
FLAUNT
FLAVIA
FLAVIN
FLAVOR
FLAWED
FLAXEN
FLAXES
FLAYED
FLAYER
FOALED
FOAMED
FRACAS
FRAILS
FRAISE
FRAMED
FRAMER
FRAMES
FRANCE
FRANCK
FRANCO
FRANCS
FRANKS
FRAPPE

FRATER
FRAUDS
FRAUEN
FRAYED

F••A••
FACADE
FARADS
FEMALE
FEUARS
FINALE
FINALS
FIXATE
FLEAMS
FLOATS
FLOATY
FORAGE
FORAYS
FREAKS
FREAKY
FRIARS
FRIARY
FUSAIN

F•••A•
FABIAN
FACIAL
FALLAL
FANGAS
FANTAN
FAUCAL
FAUNAE
FAUNAL
FAUNAS
FECIAL
FELLAH
FENIAN
FERIAL
FESTAL
FETIAL
FEUDAL
FEZZAN
FIJIAN
FILIAL
FINIAL
FIRMAN
FISCAL
FLORAE
FLORAL
FLORAS
FOEMAN
FOETAL
FOLIAR
FONTAL
FORBAD
FORMAL
FORMAT
FORNAX
FOSSAE
FOVEAE
FOVEAL
FRACAS
FREDAS
FRIDAY

FRUGAL
FULMAR
FUNGAL

F••••A
FACULA
FANEGA
FARINA
FASCIA
FATIMA
FECULA
FEDORA
FEMORA
FERULA
FIBULA
FIESTA
FLAVIA
FRIEDA
FRUSTA
FULCRA

•F•A••
AFFAIR
AFLAME
AFRAID
AFRAME
EFFACE

•F••A•
AFFRAY
AFGHAN
AFLOAT

•F•••A
AFRICA
AFTOSA
SFORZA

••FA••
AFFAIR
ALFAKI
BEFALL
DEFACE
DEFAME
EFFACE
ENFACE
INFAMY
INFANT
SAFARI
UNFAIR

••F•A•
AFFRAY
CAFTAN
DEFEAT
DEFRAY
GUFFAW
SOFTAS
ZAFFAR

••F••A
RAFFIA

•••FA•
CHUFAS
CONFAB
GUFFAW
LOOFAH
PREFAB
SHOFAR
STEFAN
ZAFFAR

•••F•A
RAFFIA

F•B•••
FABIAN
FABLED
FABLER
FABLES
FABRIC
FIBBED
FIBBER
FIBERS
FIBRIL
FIBRIN
FIBULA
FOBBED

F••B••
FEEBLE
FERBER
FIBBED
FIBBER
FIMBLE
FLABBY
FLYBYS
FOBBED
FOGBOW
FOIBLE
FORBAD
FORBID
FUMBLE

F•••B•
FLABBY
FLAMBE

•••F•B
CONFAB
PREFAB

F•C•••
FACADE
FACERS
FACETS
FACIAL
FACIES
FACILE
FACING
FACTOR
FACULA
FECIAL
FECULA
FECUND
FICHES

FICHUS
FICKLE
FOCSLE
FUCOID
FUCOUS

F••C••
FALCON
FARCED
FARCER
FARCES
FASCES
FASCIA
FAUCAL
FAUCES
FAUCET
FENCED
FENCER
FENCES
FESCUE
FIACRE
FISCAL
FLACKS
FLACON
FLECHE
FLECKS
FLICKS
FLOCKS
FLOCKY
FORCED
FORCER
FORCES
FRACAS
FROCKS
FULCRA

F•••C•
FELICE
FETICH
FIANCE
FIASCO
FIERCE
FLEECE
FLEECY
FLENCH
FLETCH
FLINCH
FLITCH
FRANCE
FRANCK
FRANCO
FRANCS
FRENCH
FRESCO

F••••C
FABRIC
FENNEC
FERRIC
FINNIC
FISTIC
FORMIC
FROLIC
FUSTIC

•F•C••
AFLCIO

•F••C•
AFFECT
AFRICA
EFFACE
EFFECT
OFFICE

••F•C•
AFFECT
DEFACE
DEFECT
EFFACE
EFFECT
ENFACE
INFECT
OFFICE

•••F•C
DEIFIC
UNIFIC

F•D•••
FADEIN
FADING
FEDORA
FIDDLE
FIDGET
FODDER
FUDDLE
FUDGED
FUDGES

F••D••
FEEDER
FENDED
FENDER
FEODOR
FEUDAL
FEUDED
FIDDLE
FINDER
FLEDGE
FLEDGY
FODDER
FOGDOG
FOLDED
FOLDER
FONDER
FONDLE
FONDLY
FONDUE
FORDED
FREDAS
FREDDY
FRIDAY
FRIDGE
FUDDLE
FUNDED
FUNDUS

F•••D•
FACADE
FARADS
FELIDS
FIELDS
FIENDS
FIORDS
FJELDS
FJORDS
FLOODS
FLOYDS
FLUIDS
FOUNDS
FRAUDS
FREDDY
FRIEDA
FRONDS

F••••D
FABLED
FAGGED
FAILED
FAIRED
FANGED
FANNED
FARCED
FARMED
FASTED
FATTED
FAWNED
FEARED
FEASED
FECUND
FEEZED
FELLED
FENCED
FENDED
FERVID
FEUDED
FIBBED
FIGGED
FILLED
FILMED
FINNED
FIRMED
FISHED
FISTED
FITTED
FIZZED
FLAKED
FLAMED
FLARED
FLAWED
FLAYED
FLEXED
FLORID
FLOWED
FLUKED
FLUMED
FLUTED
FLUXED
FOALED
FOAMED
FOBBED

6

FOETID
FOGGED
FOILED
FOLDED
FOOLED
FOOTED
FORBAD
FORBID
FORCED
FORDED
FORGED
FORKED
FORMED
FOULED
FOWLED
FRAMED
FRAYED
FRIEND
FRIGID
FUCOID
FUDGED
FUELED
FUGLED
FULGID
FULLED
FUNDED
FUNKED
FURLED
FURRED
FUSSED
FUZZED

•F•••D

AFFORD
AFIELD
AFRAID
OFFEND

••F••D

AFFORD
ALFRED
BAFFED
BIFFED
BIFOLD
BUFFED
CUFFED
DEFEND
DEFIED
DOFFED
ENFOLD
GAFFED
GIFTED
HEFTED
HUFFED
INFOLD
LIFTED
LOFTED
LUFFED
MIFFED
MUFFED
OFFEND
OXFORD
PUFFED
RAFTED
REFUND
RIFLED
RIFTED
RUFFED
SIFTED
TIFFED
TUFTED
UNFOLD
WAFTED

•••F•D

BAFFED
BEEFED
BIFFED
BUFFED
CHAFED
COIFED
CUFFED
DOFFED
GAFFED
GOLFED
GOOFED
GULFED
HOOFED
HUFFED
KNIFED
LEAFED
LOAFED
LUFFED
MIFFED
MUFFED
PUFFED
REEFED
ROOFED
RUFFED
SURFED
TIFFED
TRIFID
WAIFED
WOLFED

FE••••

FEALTY
FEARED
FEARER
FEASED
FEASES
FEASTS
FECIAL
FECULA
FECUND
FEDORA
FEEBLE
FEEDER
FEEING
FEELER
FEEZED
FEEZES
FEIGNS
FEINTS
FEISTS
FEISTY
FELICE
FELIDS
FELINE
FELIPE
FELLAH
FELLED
FELLER
FELLOE
FELLOW
FELONS
FELONY
FEMALE
FEMORA
FEMURS
FENCED
FENCER
FENCES
FENDED
FENDER
FENIAN
FENNEC
FENNEL
FENRIR
FEODOR
FEOFFS
FERBER
FERIAL
FERINE
FERITY
FERMIS
FEROUS
FERRET
FERRIC
FERRIS
FERRUM
FERULA
FERULE
FERVID
FERVOR
FESCUE
FESSES
FESTAL
FESTER
FETIAL
FETICH
FETING
FETISH
FETORS
FETTER
FETTLE
FEUARS
FEUDAL
FEUDED
FEUING
FEVERS
FEWEST
FEZZAN
FEZZES

F•E•••

FAEROE
FEEBLE
FEEDER
FEEING
FEELER
FEEZED
FEEZES
FIELDS
FIENDS
FIERCE
FIESTA
FJELDS
FLEAMS
FLECHE
FLECKS
FLEDGE
FLEDGY
FLEECE
FLEECY
FLEERS
FLEETS
FLENCH
FLENSE
FLESHY
FLETCH
FLEURY
FLEXED
FLEXES
FLEXOR
FOEHNS
FOEMAN
FOEMEN
FOETAL
FOETID
FOETOR
FOETUS
FREAKS
FREAKY
FREDAS
FREDDY
FREELY
FREEST
FREEZE
FRENCH
FRENUM
FRENZY
FREONS
FRESCO
FRESNO
FRETTY
FUELED
FUELER

F••E••

FACERS
FACETS
FADEIN
FAKERS
FAKERY
FANEGA
FARERS
FEVERS
FEWEST
FIBERS
FIFERS
FILERS
FILETS
FINELY
FINERY
FINEST
FIRERS
FIVERS
FIXERS
FLEECE
FLEECY
FLEERS
FLEETS
FLIERS
FLIEST
FLUENT
FLYERS
FOMENT
FOREGO
FOREST
FOVEAE
FOVEAL
FOYERS
FREELY
FREEST
FREEZE
FRIEDA
FRIEND
FRIERS
FRIEZE
FRYERS
FUNEST
FUSEES
FUZEES

F•••E•

FABLED
FABLER
FABLES
FACIES
FAGGED
FAILED
FAIRED
FAIRER
FALLEN
FALLER
FALSER
FALTER
FANGED
FANJET
FANNED
FANNER
FARCED
FARCER
FARCES
FARLES
FARLEY
FARMED
FARMER
FASCES
FASTED
FASTEN
FASTER
FATHER
FATTED
FATTEN
FATTER
FAUCES
FAUCET
FAUVES
FAWKES
FAWNED
FAWNER
FEARED
FEARER
FEASED
FEASES
FEEDER
FEELER
FEEZED
FEEZES
FELLED
FELLER
FENCED
FENCER
FENCES
FENDED
FENDER
FENNEC
FENNEL
FERBER
FERRET
FESSES
FESTER
FETTER
FEUDED
FEZZES
FIBBED
FIBBER
FICHES
FIDGET
FIGGED
FILLED
FILLER
FILLET
FILMED
FILTER
FINDER
FINGER
FINNED
FIQUES
FIRMED
FIRMER
FISHED
FISHER
FISHES
FISTED
FITTED
FITTER
FIZZED
FIZZES
FLAKED
FLAKER
FLAKES
FLAMED
FLAMEN
FLAMES
FLARED
FLARES
FLAWED
FLAXEN
FLAXES
FLAYED
FLAYER

FLEXED
FLEXES
FLORET
FLOWED
FLOWER
FLUKED
FLUKES
FLUKEY
FLUMED
FLUMES
FLUTED
FLUTER
FLUTES
FLUXED
FLUXES
FOALED
FOAMED
FOBBED
FODDER
FOEMEN
FOGGED
FOGIES
FOILED
FOLDED
FOLDER
FONDER
FOOLED
FOOTED
FOOTER
FORCED
FORCER
FORCES
FORDED
FORGED
FORGER
FORGES
FORGET
FORKED
FORMED
FORMER
FORTES
FOSSES
FOSTER
FOULED
FOULER
FOWLED
FOWLER
FOXIER
FRAMED
FRAMER
FRAMES
FRATER
FRAUEN
FRAYED
FRISES
FROZEN
FUDGED
FUDGES
FUELED
FUELER
FUGLED
FUGLES
FUGUES
FUHRER
FULLED
FULLER
FUMIER
FUNDED
FUNKED
FUNNEL
FURIES
FURLED
FURRED
FURZES
FUSEES
FUSSED
FUSSER
FUSSES
FUZEES
FUZZED
FUZZES

F••••E
FACADE
FACILE
FAEROE
FAILLE
FAMINE
FANNIE
FAUNAE
FEEBLE
FELICE
FELINE
FELIPE
FELLOE
FEMALE
FERINE
FERULE
FESCUE
FETTLE
FIACRE
FIANCE
FICKLE
FIDDLE
FIERCE
FIGURE
FILOSE
FIMBLE
FINALE
FINITE
FIPPLE
FIXATE
FIZZLE
FLAMBE
FLANGE
FLECHE
FLEDGE
FLEECE
FLENSE
FLORAE
FOCSLE
FOIBLE
FONDLE
FONDUE
FOOTLE
FOOZLE
FORAGE
FOSSAE
FOVEAE
FRAISE
FRANCE
FRAPPE
FREEZE
FRIDGE
FRIEZE
FRINGE
FRUNZE
FUDDLE
FUMBLE
FUSILE
FUTILE
FUTURE

•F•E••
AFFECT
AFIELD
AFRESH
EFFECT
EFFETE
OFFEND
OFFERS

•F••E•
OFFSET

•F•••E
AFLAME
AFRAME
EFFACE
EFFETE
EFFUSE
OFFICE

••FE••
AFFECT
BEFELL
DEFEAT
DEFECT
DEFEND
DEFERS
EFFECT
EFFETE
FIFERS
INFECT
INFERO
INFERS
INFEST
LIFERS
OFFEND
OFFERS
REFERS
SAFELY
SAFEST
SAFETY
WAFERS
WIFELY

••F•E•
ALFRED
BAFFED
BIFFED
BIFLEX
BUFFED
BUFFER
BUFFET
COFFEE
COFFER
CUFFED
DEFIED
DEFIER
DEFIES
DEFTER
DIFFER
DOFFED
DOFFER
DUFFEL
DUFFER
EIFFEL
GAFFED
GAFFER
GAFFES
GIFTED
GOFFER
HEFTED
HUFFED
LIFTED
LIFTER
LOFTED
LOFTER
LUFFED
MIFFED
MUFFED
OFFSET
PUFFED
PUFFER
RAFTED
RAFTER
REFLET
REFLEX
RIFLED
RIFLER
RIFLES
RIFTED
RUFFED
SIFTED
SIFTER
SOFTEN
SOFTER
SUFFER
TIFFED
TOFFEE
TUFTED
WAFTED
WAFTER
ZAFFER

••F••E
BAFFLE
BEFORE
COFFEE
COFFLE
DEFACE
DEFAME
DEFILE
DEFINE
DUFFLE
EFFACE
EFFETE
EFFUSE
ENFACE
INFUSE
MUFFLE
OFFICE
PIFFLE
RAFFLE
REFINE
REFUGE
REFUSE
REFUTE
RIFFLE
RUFFLE
TOFFEE
WAFFLE
ZAFFRE

•••FE•
BAFFED
BEEFED
BIFFED
BUFFED
BUFFER
BUFFET
CHAFED
CHAFER
CHAFES
COFFEE
COFFER
COIFED
CONFER
CUFFED
CURFEW
DEAFEN
DIFFER
DOFFED
DOFFER
DUFFEL
DUFFER
EIFFEL
GAFFED
GAFFER
GAFFES
GOFFER
GOLFED
GOLFER
GOOFED
GULFED
HEIFER
HOOFED
HOOFER
HUFFED
KNIFED
KNIFES
LEAFED
LOAFED
LOAFER
LUFFED
MIFFED
MUFFED
PILFER
PREFER
PUFFED
PUFFER
REEFED
REEFER
ROOFED
ROOFER
RUFFED
SUFFER
SURFED
SURFER
TIFFED
TOFFEE
TWOFER
WAIFED
WOLFED
WOOFER
ZAFFER

•••F•E
BAFFLE
BOUFFE
COFFEE
COFFLE
DUFFLE
GRIFFE
MUFFLE
PIAFFE
PIFFLE
PURFLE
RAFFLE
RIFFLE
RUFFLE
STIFLE
TOFFEE
TRIFLE
WAFFLE
ZAFFRE

••••FE
AGRAFE
BOUFFE
CARAFE
GRIFFE
PIAFFE
STRAFE
STRIFE
UNSAFE

F•F•••
FAFNIR
FIFERS
FIFING
FIFTHS

F••F••
FEOFFS
FITFUL
FLUFFS
FLUFFY
FULFIL
FYLFOT

F•••F•
FAROFF

FEOFFS
FLUFFS
FLUFFY

F••••F
FAROFF

•FF•••
AFFAIR
AFFECT
AFFIRM
AFFLUX
AFFORD
AFFRAY
EFFACE
EFFECT
EFFETE
EFFIGY
EFFLUX
EFFORT
EFFUSE
OFFEND
OFFERS
OFFICE
OFFING
OFFISH
OFFSET

••FF••
BAFFED
BAFFIN
BAFFLE
BIFFED
BIFFIN
BUFFED
BUFFER
BUFFET
COFFEE
COFFER
COFFIN
COFFLE
CUFFED
DIFFER
DOFFED
DOFFER
DUFFEL
DUFFER
DUFFLE
EIFFEL
GAFFED
GAFFER
GAFFES
GOFFER
GUFFAW
HUFFED
KAFFIR
LUFFED
MIFFED
MUFFED
MUFFIN
MUFFLE
PIFFLE
PUFFED
PUFFER
PUFFIN
RAFFIA
RAFFLE
RIFFLE
RUFFED
RUFFLE
SOFFIT
SUFFER
SUFFIX
TIFFED
TIFFIN
TOFFEE
WAFFLE
ZAFFAR
ZAFFER
ZAFFIR
ZAFFRE

•••FF•
BLUFFS
BOUFFE
CHAFFS
CHAFFY
CLIFFS
CLIFFY
DRAFFS
DRAFFY
FEOFFS
FLUFFS
FLUFFY
GRIFFE
PIAFFE
QUAFFS
SCOFFS
SCUFFS
SKIFFS
SNIFFS
SNIFFY
SNUFFS
SNUFFY
SPIFFY
STAFFS
STUFFS
STUFFY
WHIFFS

••••FF
CUTOFF
FAROFF
LAYOFF
PAYOFF
PUTOFF
REBUFF
RIPOFF
RUNOFF
SCLAFF
SCRUFF
SETOFF
SHROFF
TARIFF
TIPOFF

F•G•••
FAGGED
FAGGOT
FAGOTS
FIGGED
FIGHTS
FIGURE
FOGBOW
FOGDOG
FOGGED
FOGIES
FUGIOS
FUGLED
FUGLES
FUGUES

F••G••
FAGGED
FAGGOT
FANGAS
FANGED
FEIGNS
FIDGET
FIGGED
FINGER
FIZGIG
FLAGGY
FLAGON
FLIGHT
FOGGED
FORGED
FORGER
FORGES
FORGET
FORGOT
FOUGHT
FRIGHT
FRIGID
FROGGY
FRUGAL
FUDGED
FUDGES
FULGID
FUNGAL
FUNGUS

F•••G•
FANEGA
FLAGGY
FLANGE
FLEDGE
FLEDGY
FLINGS
FLONGS
FORAGE
FOREGO
FRIDGE
FRINGE
FRINGY
FROGGY

F••••G
FACING
FADING
FAKING
FARING
FATING
FAXING
FAYING
FAZING
FEEING
FETING
FEUING
FIFING
FILING
FINING
FIRING
FIXING
FIZGIG
FLYING
FOGDOG
FOXING
FRYING
FUMING
FUSING
FUZING

•FG•••
AFGHAN

•F••G•
EFFIGY

•F•••G
OFFING

••F•G•
BEFOGS
EFFIGY
REFUGE

••F••G
FIFING
OFFING

F•H•••
FUHRER

F••H••
FATHER
FATHOM
FICHES
FICHUS
FIGHTS
FISHED
FISHER
FISHES
FOEHNS

F•••H•
FAITHS
FIFTHS
FILTHY
FIRTHS
FLASHY
FLECHE
FLESHY
FLIGHT
FOUGHT
FRIGHT
FRITHS
FROTHS
FROTHY

F••••H
FAMISH
FELLAH
FETICH
FETISH
FINISH
FLENCH
FLETCH
FLINCH
FLITCH
FOURTH
FRENCH

•F•H••
AFGHAN

•F•••H
AFRESH
OFFISH

••F•H•
FIFTHS

••F••H
ELFISH
OAFISH
OFFISH

•••F•H
LOOFAH

FI••••
FIACRE
FIANCE
FIASCO
FIBBED
FIBBER
FIBERS
FIBRIL
FIBRIN
FIBULA
FICHES
FICHUS
FICKLE
FIDDLE
FIDGET
FIELDS
FIENDS
FIERCE
FIESTA
FIFERS
FIFING
FIFTHS
FIGGED
FIGHTS
FIGURE
FIJIAN
FILERS
FILETS
FILIAL
FILING
FILLED
FILLER
FILLET
FILLIN
FILLIP
FILMED
FILOSE
FILTER
FILTHY
FIMBLE
FINALE
FINALS
FINDER
FINELY
FINERY
FINEST
FINGER
FINIAL
FINING
FINISH
FINITE
FINNED
FINNIC
FIORDS
FIPPLE
FIQUES
FIRERS
FIRING
FIRKIN
FIRMAN
FIRMED
FIRMER
FIRMLY
FIRSTS
FIRTHS
FISCAL
FISHED
FISHER
FISHES
FISTED
FISTIC
FITFUL
FITTED
FITTER
FIVERS
FIXATE
FIXERS
FIXING
FIXITY
FIZGIG
FIZZED
FIZZES
FIZZLE

F•I•••
FAILED
FAILLE
FAINTS
FAIRED
FAIRER
FAIRLY
FAITHS
FEIGNS

6

FEINTS
FEISTS
FEISTY
FLICKS
FLIERS
FLIEST
FLIGHT
FLIMSY
FLINCH
FLINGS
FLINTS
FLINTY
FLIRTS
FLIRTY
FLITCH
FOIBLE
FOILED
FOISTS
FRIARS
FRIARY
FRIDAY
FRIDGE
FRIEDA
FRIEND
FRIERS
FRIEZE
FRIGHT
FRIGID
FRIJOL
FRILLS
FRILLY
FRINGE
FRINGY
FRISES
FRISKS
FRISKY
FRITHS
FRIVOL
FRIZZY

F••I••
FABIAN
FACIAL
FACIES
FACILE
FACING
FADING
FAKING
FAKIRS
FAMILY
FAMINE
FAMISH
FANION
FARINA
FARING
FATIMA
FATING
FAXING
FAYING
FAZING
FECIAL
FEEING
FELICE
FELIDS
FELINE
FELIPE
FENIAN
FERIAL
FERINE
FERITY
FETIAL
FETICH
FETING
FETISH
FEUING
FIFING
FIJIAN
FILIAL
FILING
FINIAL
FINING
FINISH
FINITE
FIRING
FIXING
FIXITY
FLAILS
FLAIRS
FLUIDS
FLYING
FOGIES
FOLIAR
FOLIOS
FOLIUM
FORINT
FOXIER
FOXILY
FOXING
FRAILS
FRAISE
FRUITS
FRUITY
FRYING
FUGIOS
FUMIER
FUMING
FURIES
FUSILE
FUSILS
FUSING
FUSION
FUTILE
FUZILS
FUZING

F•••I•
FABRIC
FADEIN
FAFNIR
FANNIE
FASCIA
FENRIR
FERMIS
FERRIC
FERRIS
FERVID
FIBRIL
FIBRIN
FILLIN
FILLIP
FINNIC
FIRKIN
FISTIC
FIZGIG
FLAVIA
FLAVIN
FLORID
FLORIN
FLUVIO
FOETID
FORBID
FORMIC
FORNIX
FORTIS
FOSSIL
FRIGID
FROLIC
FUCOID
FULFIL
FULGID
FUSAIN
FUSTIC

•FI•••
AFIELD

•F•I••
AFFIRM
AFRICA
EFFIGY
OFFICE
OFFING
OFFISH

•F••I•
AFFAIR
AFLCIO
AFRAID

••FI••
AFFIRM
BEFITS
DEFIED
DEFIER
DEFIES
DEFILE
DEFINE
EFFIGY
ELFINS
ELFISH
FIFING
INFIRM
OAFISH
OFFICE
OFFING
OFFISH
REFILL
REFINE
REFITS
SUFISM

••F•I•
AFFAIR
BAFFIN
BIFFIN
COFFIN
FAFNIR
KAFFIR
MUFFIN
MUFTIS
PUFFIN
RAFFIA
SOFFIT
SUFFIX
TIFFIN
UNFAIR
ZAFFIR

••F••I
ALFAKI
SAFARI

•••FI•
BAFFIN
BIFFIN
BOWFIN
COFFIN
COMFIT
DEIFIC
FULFIL
KAFFIR
MISFIT
MUFFIN
OLEFIN
OUTFIT
PREFIX
PROFIT
PUFFIN
RAFFIA
REDFIN
SOFFIT
SUFFIX
TIFFIN
TRIFID
UNIFIC
ZAFFIR

FJ••••
FJELDS
FJORDS

F•J•••
FIJIAN

F••J••
FANJET
FRIJOL

F•K•••
FAKERS
FAKERY
FAKING
FAKIRS

F••K••
FAWKES
FICKLE
FIRKIN
FLAKED
FLAKER
FLAKES
FLUKED
FLUKES
FLUKEY
FOLKSY
FORKED
FUNKED

F•••K•
FLACKS
FLANKS
FLASKS
FLECKS
FLICKS
FLOCKS
FLOCKY
FLUNKS
FLUNKY
FRANKS
FREAKS
FREAKY
FRISKS
FRISKY
FROCKS

F••••K
FRANCK

••F•K•
ALFAKI

FL••••
FLABBY
FLACKS
FLACON
FLAGGY
FLAGON
FLAILS
FLAIRS
FLAKED
FLAKER
FLAKES
FLAMBE
FLAMED
FLAMEN
FLAMES
FLANGE
FLANKS
FLARED
FLARES
FLASHY
FLASKS
FLATLY
FLATUS
FLAUNT
FLAVIA
FLAVIN
FLAVOR
FLAWED
FLAXEN
FLAXES
FLAYED
FLAYER
FLEAMS
FLECHE
FLECKS
FLEDGE
FLEDGY
FLEECE
FLEECY
FLEERS
FLEETS
FLENCH
FLENSE
FLESHY
FLETCH
FLEURY
FLEXED
FLEXES
FLEXOR
FLICKS
FLIERS
FLIEST
FLIGHT
FLIMSY
FLINCH
FLINGS
FLINTS
FLINTY
FLIRTS
FLIRTY
FLITCH
FLOATS
FLOATY
FLOCKS
FLOCKY
FLONGS
FLOODS
FLOORS
FLOOZY
FLOPPY
FLORAE
FLORAL
FLORAS
FLORET
FLORID
FLORIN
FLOSSY
FLOURS
FLOURY
FLOUTS
FLOWED
FLOWER
FLOYDS
FLUENT
FLUFFS
FLUFFY
FLUIDS
FLUKED
FLUKES
FLUKEY
FLUMED

FLUMES
FLUMPS
FLUNKS
FLUNKY
FLUORO
FLUORS
FLURRY
FLUTED
FLUTER
FLUTES
FLUVIO
FLUXED
FLUXES
FLYBYS
FLYERS
FLYING

F•L•••

FALCON
FALLAL
FALLEN
FALLER
FALLOW
FALSER
FALTER
FELICE
FELIDS
FELINE
FELIPE
FELLAH
FELLED
FELLER
FELLOE
FELLOW
FELONS
FELONY
FILERS
FILETS
FILIAL
FILING
FILLED
FILLER
FILLET
FILLIN
FILLIP
FILMED
FILOSE
FILTER
FILTHY
FOLDED
FOLDER
FOLIAR
FOLIOS
FOLIUM
FOLKSY
FOLLOW
FULCRA
FULFIL
FULGID
FULLED
FULLER
FULMAR
FULTON
FYLFOT

F••L••

FABLED
FABLER
FABLES
FAILED
FAILLE
FALLAL
FALLEN
FALLER
FALLOW
FARLES
FARLEY
FAULTS
FAULTY
FEALTY
FEELER
FELLAH
FELLED
FELLER
FELLOE
FELLOW
FIELDS
FILLED
FILLER
FILLET
FILLIN
FILLIP
FJELDS
FOALED
FOILED
FOLLOW
FOOLED
FOULED
FOULER
FOULLY
FOWLED
FOWLER
FRILLS
FRILLY
FROLIC
FUELED
FUELER
FUGLED
FUGLES
FULLED
FULLER
FURLED

F•••L•

FACILE
FACULA
FAILLE
FAIRLY
FAMILY
FECULA
FEEBLE
FEMALE
FERULA
FERULE
FETTLE
FIBULA
FICKLE
FIDDLE
FIMBLE
FINALE
FINALS
FINELY
FIPPLE
FIRMLY
FIZZLE
FLAILS
FLATLY
FOCSLE
FOIBLE
FONDLE
FONDLY
FOOTLE
FOOZLE
FOULLY
FOXILY
FRAILS
FREELY
FRILLS
FRILLY
FUDDLE
FUMBLE
FUSILE
FUSILS
FUTILE
FUZILS

F••••L

FACIAL
FALLAL
FAUCAL
FAUNAL
FECIAL
FENNEL
FERIAL
FESTAL
FETIAL
FEUDAL
FIBRIL
FILIAL
FINIAL
FISCAL
FITFUL
FLORAL
FOETAL
FONTAL
FORMAL
FORMYL
FOSSIL
FOVEAL
FRIJOL
FRIVOL
FRUGAL
FULFIL
FUNGAL
FUNNEL

•FL•••

AFLAME
AFLCIO
AFLOAT

•F•L••

AFFLUX
EFFLUX

•F••L•

AFIELD

••FL••

AFFLUX
BIFLEX
EFFLUX
INFLOW
INFLUX
REFLET
REFLEX
REFLUX
RIFLED
RIFLER
RIFLES
TEFLON

••F•L•

BAFFLE
BEFALL
BEFELL
BIFOLD
COFFLE
DAFTLY
DEFILE
DEFTLY
DUFFLE
ENFOLD
INFOLD
MUFFLE
PIFFLE
RAFFLE
REFILL
RIFFLE
RUFFLE
SAFELY
SOFTLY
UNFOLD
WAFFLE
WIFELY

••F••L

BEFALL
BEFELL
BEFOOL
BEFOUL
DUFFEL
EIFFEL
REFILL
UNFURL

•••FL•

BAFFLE
BARFLY
BOTFLY
COFFLE
DAYFLY
DEAFLY
DUFFLE
GADFLY
MUFFLE
PIFFLE
PURFLE
RAFFLE
RIFFLE
RUFFLE
SAWFLY
STIFLE
TRIFLE
WAFFLE

•••F•L

ARMFUL
ARTFUL
CUPFUL
DUFFEL
EARFUL
EIFFEL
EYEFUL
FITFUL
FULFIL
HATFUL
IREFUL
JARFUL
JOYFUL
LAPFUL
LAWFUL
MANFUL
RUEFUL
SINFUL
USEFUL
VATFUL
WILFUL
WOEFUL

F•M•••

FAMILY
FAMINE
FAMISH
FAMOUS
FEMALE
FEMORA
FEMURS
FIMBLE
FOMENT
FUMBLE
FUMIER
FUMING

F••M••

FARMED
FARMER
FERMIS
FILMED
FIRMAN
FIRMED
FIRMER
FIRMLY
FLAMBE
FLAMED
FLAMEN
FLAMES
FLIMSY
FLUMED
FLUMES
FLUMPS
FOAMED
FOEMAN
FOEMEN
FORMAL
FORMAT
FORMED
FORMER
FORMIC
FORMYL
FRAMED
FRAMER
FRAMES
FRUMPS
FRUMPY
FULMAR

F•••M•

FANUMS
FATIMA
FLEAMS
FORUMS

F••••M

FANTOM
FATHOM
FERRUM
FOLIUM
FRENUM

•F••M•

AFLAME
AFRAME

•F•••M

AFFIRM

••F•M•

DEFAME
INFAMY

••F••M

AFFIRM
BIFORM
DEFORM
INFIRM
INFORM
REFORM
SUFISM

F•N•••

FANEGA
FANGAS
FANGED
FANION
FANJET
FANNED
FANNER
FANNIE
FANNYS
FANONS
FANTAN
FANTOM
FANUMS
FENCED

FENCER
FENCES
FENDED
FENDER
FENIAN
FENNEC
FENNEL
FENRIR
FINALE
FINALS
FINDER
FINELY
FINERY
FINEST
FINGER
FINIAL
FINING
FINISH
FINITE
FINNED
FINNIC
FONDER
FONDLE
FONDLY
FONDUE
FONTAL
FUNDED
FUNDUS
FUNEST
FUNGAL
FUNGUS
FUNKED
FUNNEL

F••N••
FAFNIR
FAINTS
FANNED
FANNER
FANNIE
FANNYS
FAUNAE
FAUNAL
FAUNAS
FAUNUS
FAWNED
FAWNER
FEINTS
FENNEC
FENNEL
FIANCE
FIENDS
FINNED
FINNIC
FLANGE
FLANKS
FLENCH
FLENSE
FLINCH
FLINGS
FLINTS
FLINTY
FLONGS
FLUNKS
FLUNKY
FORNAX
FORNIX
FOUNDS
FOUNTS
FRANCE
FRANCK
FRANCO
FRANCS
FRANKS
FRENCH
FRENUM
FRENZY
FRINGE
FRINGY
FRONDS
FRONTO
FRONTS
FRUNZE
FUNNEL

F•••N•
FACING
FADING
FAKING
FAMINE
FANONS
FARINA
FARING
FATING
FAXING
FAYING
FAZING
FECUND
FEEING
FEIGNS
FELINE
FELONS
FELONY
FERINE
FETING
FEUING
FIFING
FILING
FINING
FIRING
FIXING
FLAUNT
FLUENT
FLYING
FOEHNS
FOMENT
FORINT
FOXING
FREONS
FRESNO
FRIEND
FROWNS
FRYING
FUMING
FUSING
FUZING

F••••N
FABIAN
FADEIN
FALCON
FALLEN
FANION
FANTAN
FASTEN
FATTEN
FENIAN
FEZZAN
FIBRIN
FIJIAN
FILLIN
FIRKIN
FIRMAN
FLACON
FLAGON
FLAMEN
FLAVIN
FLAXEN
FLORIN
FOEMAN
FOEMEN
FRAUEN
FROZEN
FULTON
FUSAIN
FUSION

•F••N•
OFFEND
OFFING

•F•••N
AFGHAN

••FN••
FAFNIR

••F•N•
ALFONS
DEFEND
DEFINE
ELFINS
FIFING
INFANT
OFFEND
OFFING
REFINE
REFUND

••F••N
BAFFIN
BIFFIN
CAFTAN
COFFIN
MUFFIN
PUFFIN
SOFTEN
TEFLON
TIFFIN

•••F•N
BAFFIN
BIFFIN
BOWFIN
COFFIN
DEAFEN
MUFFIN
OLEFIN
PUFFIN
REDFIN
STEFAN
TIFFIN

FO••••
FOALED
FOAMED
FOBBED
FOCSLE
FODDER
FOEHNS
FOEMAN
FOEMEN
FOETAL
FOETID
FOETOR
FOETUS
FOGBOW
FOGDOG
FOGGED
FOGIES
FOIBLE
FOILED
FOISTS
FOLDED
FOLDER
FOLIAR
FOLIOS
FOLIUM
FOLKSY
FOLLOW
FOMENT
FONDER
FONDLE
FONDLY
FONDUE
FONTAL
FOOLED
FOOTED
FOOTER
FOOTLE
FOOZLE
FORAGE
FORAYS
FORBAD
FORBID
FORCED
FORCER
FORCES
FORDED
FOREGO
FOREST
FORGED
FORGER
FORGES
FORGET
FORGOT
FORINT
FORKED
FORMAL
FORMAT
FORMED
FORMER
FORMIC
FORMYL
FORNAX
FORNIX
FORTES
FORTIS
FORUMS
FOSSAE
FOSSES
FOSSIL
FOSTER
FOUGHT
FOULED
FOULER
FOULLY
FOUNDS
FOUNTS
FOURTH
FOVEAE
FOVEAL
FOWLED
FOWLER
FOXIER
FOXILY
FOXING
FOYERS

F•O•••
FEODOR
FEOFFS
FIORDS
FJORDS
FLOATS
FLOATY
FLOCKS
FLOCKY
FLONGS
FLOODS
FLOORS
FLOOZY
FLOPPY
FLORAE
FLORAL
FLORAS
FLORET
FLORID
FLORIN
FLOSSY
FLOURS
FLOURY
FLOUTS
FLOWED
FLOWER
FLOYDS
FOOLED
FOOTED
FOOTER
FOOTLE
FOOZLE
FROCKS
FROGGY
FROLIC
FRONDS
FRONTO
FRONTS
FROSTS
FROSTY
FROTHS
FROTHY
FROWNS
FROWZY
FROZEN

F••O••
FAGOTS
FAMOUS
FANONS
FAROFF
FAROUT
FAVORS
FEDORA
FELONS
FELONY
FEMORA
FEROUS
FETORS
FILOSE
FLOODS
FLOORS
FLOOZY
FLUORO
FLUORS
FREONS
FSTOPS
FUCOID
FUCOUS
FURORS

F•••O•
FACTOR
FAEROE
FAGGOT
FALCON
FALLOW
FANION
FANTOM
FARROW
FATHOM
FELLOE
FELLOW
FEODOR
FERVOR
FLACON
FLAGON
FLAVOR
FLEXOR
FOETOR
FOGBOW
FOGDOG
FOLIOS

6

FOLLOW
FORGOT
FRIJOL
FRIVOL
FUGIOS
FULTON
FURROW
FUSION
FYLFOT

F••••O
FIASCO
FLUORO
FLUVIO
FOREGO
FRANCO
FRESCO
FRESNO
FRONTO

•FO•••
SFORZA

•F•O••
AFFORD
AFLOAT
AFTOSA
EFFORT

•F•••O
AFLCIO

••FO••
AFFORD
ALFONS
BEFOGS
BEFOOL
BEFORE
BEFOUL
BIFOLD
BIFORM
DEFORM
EFFORT
ENFOLD
INFOLD
INFORM
OXFORD
REFORM
RUFOUS
UNFOLD

••F•O•
BEFOOL
INFLOW
TEFLON

••F••O
INFERO

•••FO•
FYLFOT
OUTFOX

F•P•••
FIPPLE

F••P••
FIPPLE
FLOPPY
FRAPPE

F•••P•
FELIPE
FLOPPY
FLUMPS
FRAPPE
FRUMPS
FRUMPY
FSTOPS

F••••P
FILLIP

F•Q•••
FIQUES

FR••••
FRACAS
FRAILS
FRAISE
FRAMED
FRAMER
FRAMES
FRANCE
FRANCK
FRANCO
FRANCS
FRANKS
FRAPPE
FRATER
FRAUDS
FRAUEN
FRAYED
FREAKS
FREAKY
FREDAS
FREDDY
FREELY
FREEST
FREEZE
FRENCH
FRENUM
FRENZY
FREONS
FRESCO
FRESNO
FRETTY
FRIARS
FRIARY
FRIDAY
FRIDGE
FRIEDA
FRIEND
FRIERS
FRIEZE
FRIGHT
FRIGID
FRIJOL
FRILLS
FRILLY
FRINGE
FRINGY
FRISES
FRISKS
FRISKY
FRITHS
FRIVOL
FRIZZY
FROCKS
FROGGY
FROLIC
FRONDS
FRONTO
FRONTS
FROSTS
FROSTY
FROTHS
FROTHY
FROWNS
FROWZY
FROZEN
FRUGAL
FRUITS
FRUITY
FRUMPS
FRUMPY
FRUNZE
FRUSTA
FRYERS
FRYING

F•R•••
FARADS
FARCED
FARCER
FARCES
FARERS
FARINA
FARING
FARLES
FARLEY
FARMED
FARMER
FAROFF
FAROUT
FARROW
FERBER
FERIAL
FERINE
FERITY
FERMIS
FEROUS
FERRET
FERRIC
FERRIS
FERRUM
FERULA
FERULE
FERVID
FERVOR
FIRERS
FIRING
FIRKIN
FIRMAN
FIRMED
FIRMER
FIRMLY
FIRSTS
FIRTHS
FORAGE
FORAYS
FORBAD
FORBID
FORCED
FORCER
FORCES
FORDED
FOREGO
FOREST
FORGED
FORGER
FORGES
FORGET
FORGOT
FORINT
FORKED
FORMAL
FORMAT
FORMED
FORMER
FORMIC
FORMYL
FORNAX
FORNIX
FORTES
FORTIS
FORUMS
FURIES
FURLED
FURORS
FURRED
FURROW
FURZES

F••R••
FABRIC
FAEROE
FAIRED
FAIRER
FAIRLY
FARROW
FEARED
FEARER
FENRIR
FERRET
FERRIC
FERRIS
FERRUM
FIBRIL
FIBRIN
FIERCE
FIORDS
FJORDS
FLARED
FLARES
FLIRTS
FLIRTY
FLORAE
FLORAL
FLORAS
FLORET
FLORID
FLORIN
FLURRY
FOURTH
FUHRER
FURRED
FURROW

F•••R•
FACERS
FAKERS
FAKERY
FAKIRS
FARERS
FAVORS
FEDORA
FEMORA
FEMURS
FETORS
FEUARS
FEVERS
FIACRE
FIBERS
FIFERS
FIGURE
FILERS
FINERY
FIRERS
FIVERS
FIXERS
FLAIRS
FLEERS
FLEURY
FLIERS
FLOORS
FLOURS
FLOURY
FLUORO
FLUORS
FLURRY
FLYERS
FOYERS
FRIARS
FRIARY
FRIERS
FRYERS
FULCRA
FURORS
FUTURE

F••••R
FABLER
FACTOR
FAFNIR
FAIRER
FALLER
FALSER
FALTER
FANNER
FARCER
FARMER
FASTER
FATHER
FATTER
FAWNER
FEARER
FEEDER
FEELER
FELLER
FENCER
FENDER
FENRIR
FEODOR
FERBER
FERVOR
FESTER
FETTER
FIBBER
FILLER
FILTER
FINDER
FINGER
FIRMER
FISHER
FITTER
FLAKER
FLAVOR
FLAYER
FLEXOR
FLOWER
FLUTER
FODDER
FOETOR
FOLDER
FOLIAR
FONDER
FOOTER
FORCER
FORGER
FORMER
FOSTER
FOULER
FOWLER
FOXIER
FRAMER
FRATER
FUELER
FUHRER
FULLER
FULMAR
FUMIER
FUSSER

•FR•••
AFRAID
AFRAME
AFRESH
AFRICA

•F•R••
AFFRAY
SFORZA

6

•F••R•
AFFIRM
AFFORD
EFFORT
OFFERS

•F•••R
AFFAIR

••FR••
AFFRAY
ALFRED
DEFRAY

••F•R•
AFFIRM
AFFORD
BEFORE
BIFORM
DEFERS
DEFORM
EFFORT
ERFURT
FIFERS
INFERO
INFERS
INFIRM
INFORM
LIFERS
OFFERS
OXFORD
REFERS
REFORM
SAFARI
UNFURL
WAFERS
ZAFFRE

••F••R
AFFAIR
BUFFER
COFFER
DEFIER
DEFTER
DIFFER
DOFFER
DUFFER
FAFNIR
GAFFER
GOFFER
KAFFIR
LIFTER
LOFTER
PUFFER
RAFTER
RIFLER
SIFTER
SOFTER
SUFFER
UNFAIR
WAFTER
ZAFFAR
ZAFFER
ZAFFIR

•••FR•
BELFRY
ZAFFRE

•••F•R
BUFFER
CHAFER
COFFER
CONFER
DIFFER
DOFFER
DUFFER
GAFFER
GOFFER
GOLFER
HEIFER
HOOFER
KAFFIR
LOAFER
PILFER
PREFER
PUFFER
REEFER
ROOFER
SHOFAR
SUFFER
SULFUR
SURFER
TWOFER
WOOFER
ZAFFAR
ZAFFER
ZAFFIR

FS••••
FSTOPS

F•S•••
FASCES
FASCIA
FASTED
FASTEN
FASTER
FESCUE
FESSES
FESTAL
FESTER
FISCAL
FISHED
FISHER
FISHES
FISTED
FISTIC
FOSSAE
FOSSES
FOSSIL
FOSTER
FUSAIN
FUSEES
FUSILE
FUSILS
FUSING
FUSION
FUSSED
FUSSER
FUSSES
FUSTIC

F••S••
FALSER
FEASED
FEASES
FEASTS
FEISTS
FEISTY
FESSES
FIASCO
FIESTA
FIRSTS
FLASHY
FLASKS
FLESHY
FLOSSY
FOCSLE
FOISTS
FOSSAE
FOSSES
FOSSIL
FRESCO
FRESNO
FRISES
FRISKS
FRISKY
FROSTS
FROSTY
FRUSTA
FUSSED
FUSSER
FUSSES

F•••S•
FAMISH
FETISH
FEWEST
FILOSE
FINEST
FINISH
FLENSE
FLIEST
FLIMSY
FLOSSY
FOLKSY
FOREST
FRAISE
FREEST
FUNEST

F••••S
FABLES
FACERS
FACETS
FACIES
FAGOTS
FAINTS
FAITHS
FAKERS
FAKIRS
FAMOUS
FANGAS
FANNYS
FANONS
FANUMS
FARADS
FARCES
FARERS
FARLES
FASCES
FAUCES
FAULTS
FAUNAS
FAUNUS
FAUVES
FAVORS
FAWKES
FEASES
FEASTS
FEEZES
FEIGNS
FEINTS
FEISTS
FELIDS
FELONS
FEMURS
FENCES
FEOFFS
FERMIS
FEROUS
FERRIS
FESSES
FETORS
FEUARS
FEVERS
FEZZES
FIBERS
FICHES
FICHUS
FIELDS
FIENDS
FIFERS
FIFTHS
FIGHTS
FILERS
FILETS
FINALS
FIORDS
FIQUES
FIRERS
FIRSTS
FIRTHS
FISHES
FIVERS
FIXERS
FIZZES
FJELDS
FJORDS
FLACKS
FLAILS
FLAIRS
FLAKES
FLAMES
FLANKS
FLARES
FLASKS
FLATUS
FLAXES
FLEAMS
FLECKS
FLEERS
FLEETS
FLEXES
FLICKS
FLIERS
FLINGS
FLINTS
FLIRTS
FLOATS
FLOCKS
FLONGS
FLOODS
FLOORS
FLORAS
FLOURS
FLOUTS
FLOYDS
FLUFFS
FLUIDS
FLUKES
FLUMES
FLUMPS
FLUNKS
FLUORS
FLUTES
FLUXES
FLYBYS
FLYERS
FOEHNS
FOETUS
FOGIES
FOISTS
FOLIOS
FORAYS
FORCES
FORGES
FORTES
FORTIS
FORUMS
FOSSES
FOUNDS
FOUNTS
FOYERS
FRACAS
FRAILS
FRAMES
FRANCS
FRANKS
FRAUDS
FREAKS
FREDAS
FREONS
FRIARS
FRIERS
FRILLS
FRISES
FRISKS
FRITHS
FROCKS
FRONDS
FRONTS
FROSTS
FROTHS
FROWNS
FRUITS
FRUMPS
FRYERS
FSTOPS
FUCOUS
FUDGES
FUGIOS
FUGLES
FUGUES
FUNDUS
FUNGUS
FURIES
FURORS
FURZES
FUSEES
FUSILS
FUSSES
FUZEES
FUZILS
FUZZES

•F•S••
OFFSET

•F••S•
AFRESH
AFTOSA
EFFUSE
OFFISH

•F•••S
OFFERS

••FS••
OFFSET

••F•S•
EFFUSE
ELFISH
INFEST
INFUSE
OAFISH
OFFISH
REFUSE
SAFEST
SUFISM

••F••S
ALFONS
BEFITS
BEFOGS
DEFERS
DEFIES
ELFINS
FIFERS
FIFTHS
GAFFES
INFERS
LIFERS

MUFTIS
OFFERS
REFERS
REFITS
RIFLES
RUFOUS
SOFTAS
WAFERS

•••F•S

BLUFFS
CHAFES
CHAFFS
CHUFAS
CLEFTS
CLIFFS
CRAFTS
CROFTS
DRAFFS
DRAFTS
DRIFTS
FEOFFS
FLUFFS
GAFFES
GRAFTS
KNIFES
QUAFFS
SCOFFS
SCUFFS
SHAFTS
SHIFTS
SKIFFS
SNAFUS
SNIFFS
SNUFFS
STAFFS
STUFFS
SWIFTS
THEFTS
WHIFFS

••••FS

BLUFFS
BRIEFS
CALIFS
CHAFFS
CHIEFS
CLIFFS
DRAFFS
DWARFS
FEOFFS
FLUFFS
GANEFS
GRIEFS
KLOOFS
MOTIFS
PILAFS
PROOFS
QUAFFS
SCARFS
SCOFFS
SCUFFS
SERIFS
SKIFFS
SNIFFS
SNUFFS
SPOOFS
STAFFS
STUFFS
WHARFS
WHIFFS

F•T•••

FATHER
FATHOM
FATIMA
FATING
FATTED
FATTEN
FATTER
FETIAL
FETICH
FETING
FETISH
FETORS
FETTER
FETTLE
FITFUL
FITTED
FITTER
FSTOPS
FUTILE
FUTURE

F••T••

FACTOR
FAITHS
FALTER
FANTAN
FANTOM
FASTED
FASTEN
FASTER
FATTED
FATTEN
FATTER
FESTAL
FESTER
FETTER
FETTLE
FIFTHS
FILTER
FILTHY
FIRTHS
FISTED
FISTIC
FITTED
FITTER
FLATLY
FLATUS
FLETCH
FLITCH
FLUTED
FLUTER
FLUTES
FOETAL
FOETID
FOETOR
FOETUS
FONTAL
FOOTED
FOOTER
FOOTLE
FORTES
FORTIS
FOSTER
FRATER
FRETTY
FRITHS
FROTHS
FROTHY
FULTON
FUSTIC

F•••T•

FACETS
FAGOTS
FAINTS
FAULTS
FAULTY
FEALTY
FEASTS
FEINTS
FEISTS
FEISTY
FERITY
FIESTA
FIGHTS
FILETS
FINITE
FIRSTS
FIXATE
FIXITY
FLEETS
FLINTS
FLINTY
FLIRTS
FLIRTY
FLOATS
FLOATY
FLOUTS
FOISTS
FOUNTS
FOURTH
FRETTY
FRONTO
FRONTS
FROSTS
FROSTY
FRUITS
FRUITY
FRUSTA

F••••T

FAGGOT
FANJET
FAROUT
FAUCET
FERRET
FEWEST
FIDGET
FILLET
FINEST
FLAUNT
FLIEST
FLIGHT
FLORET
FLUENT
FOMENT
FOREST
FORGET
FORGOT
FORINT
FORMAT
FOUGHT
FREEST
FRIGHT
FUNEST
FYLFOT

•FT•••

AFTOSA

•F••T•

EFFETE

•F•••T

AFFECT
AFLOAT
EFFECT
EFFORT
OFFSET

••FT••

CAFTAN
DAFTLY
DEFTER
DEFTLY
FIFTHS
GIFTED
HEFTED
LIFTED
LIFTER
LOFTED
LOFTER
MUFTIS
RAFTED
RAFTER
RIFTED
SIFTED
SIFTER
SOFTAS
SOFTEN
SOFTER
SOFTLY
TUFTED
WAFTED
WAFTER

••F•T•

BEFITS
EFFETE
REFITS
REFUTE
SAFETY

••F••T

AFFECT
BUFFET
DEFEAT
DEFECT
EFFECT
EFFORT
ERFURT
INFANT
INFECT
INFEST
OFFSET
REFLET
SAFEST
SOFFIT

•••FT•

CLEFTS
CRAFTS
CRAFTY
CROFTS
DRAFTS
DRAFTY
DRIFTS
DRIFTY
GRAFTS
SHAFTS
SHIFTS
SHIFTY
SWIFTS
THEFTS

•••F•T

BUFFET
COMFIT
FYLFOT
MISFIT
OUTFIT
PROFIT
SOFFIT

••••FT

ADRIFT
BEREFT
SHRIFT
THRIFT
UPLIFT

FU••••

FUCOID
FUCOUS
FUDDLE
FUDGED
FUDGES
FUELED
FUELER
FUGIOS
FUGLED
FUGLES
FUGUES
FUHRER
FULCRA
FULFIL
FULGID
FULLED
FULLER
FULMAR
FULTON
FUMBLE
FUMIER
FUMING
FUNDED
FUNDUS
FUNEST
FUNGAL
FUNGUS
FUNKED
FUNNEL
FURIES
FURLED
FURORS
FURRED
FURROW
FURZES
FUSAIN
FUSEES
FUSILE
FUSILS
FUSING
FUSION
FUSSED
FUSSER
FUSSES
FUSTIC
FUTILE
FUTURE
FUZEES
FUZILS
FUZING
FUZZED
FUZZES

F•U•••

FAUCAL
FAUCES
FAUCET
FAULTS
FAULTY
FAUNAE
FAUNAL
FAUNAS
FAUNUS
FAUVES
FEUARS
FEUDAL
FEUDED
FEUING
FLUENT
FLUFFS
FLUFFY
FLUIDS
FLUKED
FLUKES
FLUKEY
FLUMED
FLUMES
FLUMPS
FLUNKS

FLUNKY
FLUORO
FLUORS
FLURRY
FLUTED
FLUTER
FLUTES
FLUVIO
FLUXED
FLUXES
FOUGHT
FOULED
FOULER
FOULLY
FOUNDS
FOUNTS
FOURTH
FRUGAL
FRUITS
FRUITY
FRUMPS
FRUMPY
FRUNZE
FRUSTA

F••U••
FACULA
FANUMS
FECULA
FECUND
FEMURS
FERULA
FERULE
FIBULA
FIGURE
FIQUES
FLAUNT
FLEURY
FLOURS
FLOURY
FLOUTS
FORUMS
FRAUDS
FRAUEN
FUGUES
FUTURE

F•••U•
FAMOUS
FAROUT
FAUNUS
FEROUS
FERRUM
FESCUE
FICHUS
FITFUL
FLATUS
FOETUS
FOLIUM
FONDUE
FRENUM
FUCOUS
FUNDUS
FUNGUS

•F•U••
EFFUSE

•F••U•
AFFLUX
EFFLUX

••FU••
EFFUSE
ERFURT
INFUSE
REFUGE
REFUND
REFUSE
REFUTE
UNFURL

••F•U•
AFFLUX
BEFOUL
EFFLUX
INFLUX
REFLUX
RUFOUS

•••FU•
ARMFUL
ARTFUL
CUPFUL
EARFUL
EYEFUL
FITFUL
HATFUL
IREFUL
JARFUL
JOYFUL
LAPFUL
LAWFUL
MANFUL
RUEFUL
SINFUL
SNAFUS
SULFUR
USEFUL
VATFUL
WILFUL
WOEFUL

F•V•••
FAVORS
FEVERS
FIVERS
FOVEAE
FOVEAL

F••V••
FAUVES
FERVID
FERVOR
FLAVIA
FLAVIN
FLAVOR
FLUVIO
FRIVOL

F•W•••
FAWKES
FAWNED
FAWNER
FEWEST
FOWLED
FOWLER

F••W••
FLAWED
FLOWED
FLOWER
FROWNS
FROWZY

F••••W
FALLOW
FARROW
FELLOW
FOGBOW
FOLLOW
FURROW

••F••W
GUFFAW
INFLOW

•••F•W
CURFEW
GUFFAW

F•X•••
FAXING
FIXATE
FIXERS
FIXING
FIXITY
FOXIER
FOXILY
FOXING

F••X••
FLAXEN
FLAXES
FLEXED
FLEXES
FLEXOR
FLUXED
FLUXES

F••••X
FORNAX
FORNIX

•F•••X
AFFLUX
EFFLUX

••F••X
AFFLUX
BIFLEX
EFFLUX
INFLUX
REFLEX
REFLUX
SUFFIX

•••F•X
OUTFOX
PREFIX
SUFFIX

FY••••
FYLFOT

F•Y•••
FAYING
FLYBYS
FLYERS
FLYING
FOYERS
FRYERS
FRYING

F••Y••
FLAYED
FLAYER
FLOYDS
FRAYED

F•••Y•
FANNYS
FLYBYS
FORAYS
FORMYL

F••••Y
FAIRLY
FAKERY
FAMILY
FARLEY
FAULTY
FEALTY
FEISTY
FELONY
FERITY
FILTHY
FINELY
FINERY
FIRMLY
FIXITY
FLABBY
FLAGGY
FLASHY
FLATLY
FLEDGY
FLEECY
FLESHY
FLEURY
FLIMSY
FLINTY
FLIRTY
FLOATY
FLOCKY
FLOOZY
FLOPPY
FLOSSY
FLOURY
FLUFFY
FLUKEY
FLUNKY
FLURRY
FOLKSY
FONDLY
FOULLY
FOXILY
FREAKY
FREDDY
FREELY
FRENZY
FRETTY
FRIARY
FRIDAY
FRILLY
FRINGY
FRISKY
FRIZZY
FROGGY
FROSTY
FROTHY
FROWZY
FRUITY
FRUMPY

•F•••Y
AFFRAY
EFFIGY

••F••Y
AFFRAY
DAFTLY
DEFRAY
DEFTLY
EFFIGY
INFAMY
SAFELY
SAFETY
SOFTLY
WIFELY

•••F•Y
BARFLY
BELFRY
BOTFLY
CHAFFY
CLIFFY
CRAFTY
DAYFLY
DEAFLY
DRAFFY
DRAFTY
DRIFTY
FLUFFY
GADFLY
SAWFLY
SHIFTY
SNIFFY
SNUFFY
SPIFFY
STUFFY

••••FY
AERIFY
ARGUFY
BASIFY
CASEFY
CHAFFY
CLIFFY
CODIFY
DRAFFY
FLUFFY
IGNIFY
MINIFY
MODIFY
NAZIFY
NIDIFY
NOTIFY
OSSIFY
PACIFY
PURIFY
RAMIFY
RAREFY
RATIFY
SALIFY
SCURFY
SNIFFY
SNUFFY
SPIFFY
STUFFY
TEPEFY
TUMEFY
TYPIFY
UGLIFY
VERIFY
VILIFY
VIVIFY

F•Z•••
FAZING
FEZZAN
FEZZES
FIZGIG
FIZZED
FIZZES
FIZZLE
FUZEES
FUZILS
FUZING
FUZZED
FUZZES

F••Z••
FEEZED
FEEZES
FEZZAN
FEZZES
FIZZED
FIZZES
FIZZLE
FOOZLE
FRIZZY
FROZEN
FURZES
FUZZED
FUZZES

F•••Z•
FLOOZY
FREEZE
FRENZY
FRIEZE
FRIZZY
FROWZY
FRUNZE

•F••Z•
SFORZA

GA••••
GABBED
GABBER
GABBLE
GABBRO
GABION
GABLED
GABLES
GADDED
GADDER
GADFLY
GADGET
GADOID
GAELIC
GAFFED
GAFFER
GAFFES
GAGERS
GAGGED
GAGGER
GAGGLE
GAGING
GAIETY
GAINED
GAINER
GAINLY
GAITED
GAITER
GALACT
GALAXY
GALEAE
GALENA
GALIOT
GALLED
GALLEY
GALLIC
GALLON
GALLOP
GALLUP
GALLUS
GALOOT
GALOPS
GALORE
GALOSH
GALWAY
GALYAK
GAMBIA
GAMBIR
GAMBIT
GAMBLE
GAMBOL
GAMELY
GAMETE
GAMETO
GAMIER
GAMILY
GAMING
GAMINS
GAMMAS
GAMMER
GAMMON
GAMOUS
GAMUTS
GANDER
GANDHI
GANEFS
GANGED
GANGER
GANGES
GANGLI
GANGUE
GANNET
GANOID
GANTRY
GAOLER
GAPERS
GAPING
GAPPED
GARAGE
GARBED
GARBLE
GARCON
GARDEN
GARGET
GARGLE
GARISH
GARLIC
GARNER
GARNET
GARRET
GARTER
GASBAG
GASCON
GASHED
GASHES
GASKET
GASKIN
GASMAN
GASMEN
GASPAR
GASPED
GASPER
GASSED
GASSES
GASTON
GASTRO
GATHER
GATING
GAUCHE
GAUCHO
GAUGED
GAUGER
GAUGES
GAUZES
GAVELS
GAVIAL
GAVOTS
GAWAIN
GAWKED
GAYEST
GAYETY
GAZABO
GAZEBO
GAZERS
GAZING

G•A•••
GEARED
GHARRI
GHARRY
GHAUTS
GIANTS
GIAOUR
GLACES
GLACIS
GLADES
GLADLY
GLADYS
GLAIRS
GLAIRY
GLANCE
GLANDS
GLARED
GLARES
GLASSY
GLAUCO
GLAZED
GLAZER
GLAZES
GNARLS
GNARLY
GNATHO
GNAWED
GNAWER
GOADED
GOALIE
GOATEE
GRABEN
GRACED
GRACES
GRADED
GRADER
GRADES
GRADIN
GRADUS
GRAECO
GRAFTS
GRAHAM
GRAINS
GRAINY
GRANGE
GRANNY
GRANTS
GRAPES
GRAPHO
GRAPHS
GRAPHY
GRASPS
GRASSY
GRATED
GRATER
GRATES
GRATIS
GRAVED
GRAVEL
GRAVEN
GRAVER
GRAVES
GRAVID
GRAYED
GRAYER
GRAYLY
GRAZED
GRAZER
GRAZES
GUACOS
GUANIN
GUANOS
GUARDS
GUAVAS

G••A••
GALACT
GALAXY
GARAGE
GAWAIN
GAZABO
GEMARA
GERALD
GERARD
GIGANT
GITANO
GLEAMS
GLEAMY
GLEANS
GLOATS
GOCART
GOKART
GONADS
GORALS
GOTAMA
GREASE
GREASY
GREATS
GREAVE
GROANS
GROATS
GUIANA
GUYANA
GYRATE

G•••A•
GALEAE
GALWAY
GALYAK
GAMMAS
GASBAG
GASMAN
GASPAR
GAVIAL
GEMMAE
GENIAL
GERMAN
GEWGAW
GIBRAN
GILDAS
GILEAD
GINGAL
GLOBAL
GOORAL
GOTHAM
GRAHAM
GRETAS
GUAVAS
GUFFAW
GUITAR
GULLAH
GUMMAS
GUNMAN
GUNNAR
GUSTAF
GUSTAV
GUTTAE
GUTTAT

G••••A
GALENA
GAMBIA
GDYNIA
GEISHA
GEMARA
GENERA
GENEVA
GIULIA
GLIOMA
GLORIA
GODIVA
GOTAMA
GUIANA
GUINEA
GURKHA
GUYANA

•GA•••
AGAMAS
AGAMIC
AGAPAE
AGARIC
AGATES
AGATHA
AGAVES
UGANDA

•G•A••
AGHAST
AGLAIA
AGNAIL
AGNATE
AGRAFE
EGGARS
IGNACE
IGUANA

•G••A•
AGAMAS
AGAPAE
AGLEAM
AGORAE
AGORAS
OGDOAD

•G•••A
AGATHA
AGENDA
AGLAIA
EGERIA
EGESTA
IGUANA
UGANDA

••GA••
ANGARY
ARGALI
ARGALS
ASGARD
BAGASS
BIGAMY
BOGANS
CIGARS
DEGAGE
DEGAME
DIGAMY
DOGAPE
EDGARS
EGGARS
ENGAGE
ERGATE
GIGANT
HOGANS
JUGATE
LEGACY
LEGATE
LEGATO
LIGAND
LIGATE
MEGALO
MEGASS
NAGANA
NEGATE
ORGANA
ORGANO
ORGANS
ORGASM
PAGANS
REGAIN
REGALE
REGARD
RUGATE
SUGARS
SUGARY
TOGAED
UTGARD
VAGARY
WIGANS

••G•A•
AEGEAN
AFGHAN
AUGEAN
BAGDAD
BAGMAN
BEGGAR

6

COGNAC
COGWAY
DAGMAR
DOGEAR
DOGMAS
ENGRAM
JAGUAR
JIGSAW
LEGMAN
LOGJAM
MAGYAR
MUGGAR
ORGEAT
RAGLAN
RAGMAN
RAGTAG
REGNAL
SAGGAR
SEGGAR
SIGMAS
SIGNAL
UNGUAL
WIGWAG
WIGWAM
ZIGZAG

••G••A

ANGELA
ANGINA
ANGLIA
ANGOLA
ANGORA
BOGOTA
DAGOBA
HEGIRA
HYGEIA
LIGULA
LOGGIA
NAGANA
NAGOYA
ORGANA
PAGODA
REGINA
UNGULA
VAGINA
ZYGOMA

•••GA•

ALEGAR
BEGGAR
BELGAS
BENGAL
BROGAN
BULGAR
CONGAS
COUGAR
FANGAS
FRUGAL
FUNGAL
GEWGAW
GINGAL
HANGAR
JINGAL
LINGAS
LONGAN
MARGAY
MORGAN
MUGGAR
NILGAI
NOUGAT
OMEGAS
ORIGAN
PISGAH
PLAGAL
SAGGAR
SAIGAS
SANGAR
SEGGAR
SLOGAN
TAIGAS
TERGAL
VIRGAS
VULGAR

•••G•A

BORGIA
BREGMA
ENIGMA
LINGUA
LOGGIA
PHAGIA
PLEGIA
QUAGGA
STIGMA
ZEUGMA

••••GA

AURIGA
BELUGA
BODEGA
CAYUGA
FANEGA
LADOGA
MALAGA
QUAGGA
TELEGA

G•B•••

GABBED
GABBER
GABBLE
GABBRO
GABION
GABLED
GABLES
GIBBED
GIBBER
GIBBET
GIBBON
GIBERS
GIBING
GIBLET
GIBRAN
GIBSON
GOBBET
GOBBLE
GOBIES
GOBLET
GOBLIN

G••B••

GABBED
GABBER
GABBLE
GABBRO
GAMBIA
GAMBIR
GAMBIT
GAMBLE
GAMBOL
GARBED
GARBLE
GASBAG
GERBIL
GHEBER
GIBBED
GIBBER
GIBBET
GIBBON
GLEBES
GLIBLY
GLOBAL
GLOBED
GLOBES
GLOBIN
GOBBET
GOBBLE
GOOBER
GRABEN
GREBES
GRUBBY
GUMBOS

G•••B•

GAZABO
GAZEBO
GOODBY
GRUBBY

•GB•••

EGBERT

••GB••

FOGBOW
HAGBUT

••G•B•

DAGOBA

G•C•••

GECKOS
GOCART

G••C••

GARCON
GASCON
GAUCHE
GAUCHO
GLACES
GLACIS
GLYCOL
GRACED
GRACES
GROCER
GUACOS

G•••C•

GALACT
GLANCE
GLAUCO
GRAECO
GREECE
GROUCH
GYNECO

G••••C

GAELIC
GALLIC
GARLIC
GEODIC
GESTIC
GNOMIC
GOTHIC

•G••C•

AGENCY
IGNACE

•G•••C

AGAMIC
AGARIC
AGONIC

••G•C•

LEGACY

••G••C

ANGLIC
COGNAC

•••G•C

BELGIC
TRAGIC

GD••••

GDYNIA

G•D•••

GADDED
GADDER
GADFLY
GADGET
GADOID
GIDEON
GODIVA
GODSON
GODWIN
GODWIT

G••D••

GADDED
GADDER
GANDER
GANDHI
GARDEN
GELDED
GENDER
GEODES
GEODIC
GILDAS
GILDED
GILDER
GIRDED
GIRDER
GIRDLE
GLADES
GLADLY
GLADYS
GLEDES
GLIDED
GLIDER
GLIDES
GOADED
GOLDEN
GOODBY
GOODLY
GORDON
GRADED
GRADER
GRADES
GRADIN
GRADUS
GRIDED
GRIDES
GRUDGE
GUIDED
GUIDER
GUIDES
GUIDON
GULDEN

G•••D•

GLANDS
GONADS
GOURDE
GOURDS
GREEDS
GREEDY
GRINDS
GRUNDY
GUARDS
GUILDS

G••••D

GABBED
GABLED
GADDED
GADOID
GAFFED
GAGGED
GAINED
GAITED
GALLED
GANGED
GANOID
GAPPED
GARBED
GASHED
GASPED
GASSED
GAUGED
GAWKED
GEARED
GELDED
GELLED
GEMMED
GERALD
GERARD
GERUND
GIBBED
GIFTED
GIGGED
GILDED
GILEAD
GIMPED
GINNED
GIPPED
GIRDED
GIRTED
GLARED
GLAZED
GLIDED
GLOBED
GLOVED
GLOWED
GLOZED
GNAWED
GOADED
GOLFED
GOOFED
GOOSED
GORGED
GOUGED
GOWNED
GRACED
GRADED
GRATED
GRAVED
GRAVID
GRAYED
GRAZED
GRIDED
GRIMED
GRIPED
GROPED
GROUND
GUIDED
GULFED
GULPED
GUMMED
GUNNED
GUSHED
GUTTED
GYPPED

•GD•••

OGDOAD

•G•D••

AGEDLY

•G••D•

AGENDA
UGANDA

6

•G•••D
AGREED
OGDOAD

••GD••
BAGDAD
FOGDOG
HAGDON

••G•D•
PAGODA

••G••D
ALGOID
ANGLED
ARGUED
ASGARD
AUGEND
BAGDAD
BAGGED
BEGGED
BEGIRD
BOGGED
BUGGED
BUGLED
COGGED
DOGGED
ENGIRD
FAGGED
FIGGED
FOGGED
FUGLED
GAGGED
GIGGED
HOGGED
HUGGED
INGRID
JAGGED
JIGGED
JOGGED
JUGGED
LAGGED
LEGEND
LEGGED
LIGAND
LOGGED
LUGGED
MUGGED
NAGGED
PEGGED
PIGGED
PUGGED
RAGGED
REGARD
RIGGED
ROGUED
RUGGED
SAGGED
SIGHED
SIGNED
SIGRID
TAGGED
TOGAED
TOGGED
TUGGED
UNGIRD
UTGARD
WAGGED
WIGGED

•••G•D
BADGED
BAGGED
BANGED
BARGED
BEGGED
BILGED
BOGGED
BONGED
BRIGID
BUDGED
BUGGED
BULGED
BUNGED
CADGED
COGGED
DANGED
DINGED
DODGED
DOGGED
DUNGED
FAGGED
FANGED
FIGGED
FOGGED
FORGED
FRIGID
FUDGED
FULGID
GAGGED
GANGED
GAUGED
GIGGED
GORGED
GOUGED
HANGED
HEDGED
HINGED
HOGGED
HUGGED
JAGGED
JIGGED
JOGGED
JUDGED
JUGGED
KEDGED
LAGGED
LEGGED
LODGED
LOGGED
LONGED
LUGGED
LUNGED
MERGED
MUGGED
NAGGED
NUDGED
PEGGED
PIGGED
PINGED
PUGGED
PURGED
RAGGED
RANGED
RIDGED
RIGGED
RINGED
ROUGED
RUGGED
SAGGED
SIEGED
SINGED
STAGED
SURGED
SWAGED
TAGGED
TANGED
TINGED
TOGGED
TONGED
TUGGED
TURGID
VERGED
WAGGED
WEDGED
WIGGED
WINGED
ZINGED

GE••••
GEARED
GECKOS
GEEING
GEEZER
GEIGER
GEISHA
GELDED
GELLED
GEMARA
GEMINI
GEMMAE
GEMMED
GEMOTS
GENDER
GENERA
GENETS
GENEVA
GENIAL
GENIES
GENITO
GENIUS
GENOUS
GENRES
GENROS
GENTES
GENTLE
GENTOO
GENTRY
GEODES
GEODIC
GEORGE
GEORGI
GERALD
GERARD
GERBIL
GERENT
GERMAN
GEROUS
GERRYS
GERTIE
GERTYS
GERUND
GERYON
GESELL
GESSOS
GESTIC
GETTER
GETUPS
GEWGAW
GEYSER

G•E•••
GAELIC
GEEING
GEEZER
GHEBER
GHETTO
GLEAMS
GLEAMY
GLEANS
GLEBES
GLEDES
GLEETS
GLEETY
GNEISS
GOETHE
GREASE
GREASY
GREATS
GREAVE
GREBES
GREECE
GREEDS
GREEDY
GREEKS
GREENS
GREETS
GREGOS
GREIGE
GRETAS
GRETEL
GUENON
GUESTS
GWENNS

G••E••
GAGERS
GAIETY
GALEAE
GALENA
GAMELY
GAMETE
GAMETO
GANEFS
GAPERS
GAVELS
GAYEST
GAYETY
GAZEBO
GAZERS
GENERA
GENETS
GENEVA
GERENT
GESELL
GIBERS
GIDEON
GILEAD
GIMELS
GISELE
GLEETS
GLEETY
GONERS
GOVERN
GRAECO
GREECE
GREEDS
GREEDY
GREEKS
GREENS
GREETS
GRIEFS
GRIEVE
GRUELS
GYNECO

G•••E•
GABBED
GABBER
GABLED
GABLES
GADDED
GADDER
GADGET
GAFFED
GAFFER
GAFFES
GAGGED
GAGGER
GAINED
GAINER
GAITED
GAITER
GALLED
GALLEY
GAMIER
GAMMER
GANDER
GANGED
GANGER
GANGES
GANNET
GAOLER
GAPPED
GARBED
GARDEN
GARGET
GARNER
GARNET
GARRET
GARTER
GASHED
GASHES
GASKET
GASMEN
GASPED
GASPER
GASSED
GASSES
GATHER
GAUGED
GAUGER
GAUGES
GAUZES
GAWKED
GEARED
GEEZER
GEIGER
GELDED
GELLED
GEMMED
GENDER
GENIES
GENRES
GENTES
GEODES
GETTER
GEYSER
GHEBER
GIBBED
GIBBER
GIBBET
GIBLET
GIFTED
GIGGED
GIGLET
GIGUES
GILDED
GILDER
GIMLET
GIMPED
GINGER
GINNED
GINNER
GIPPED
GIRDED
GIRDER
GIRTED
GLACES
GLADES
GLARED
GLARES
GLAZED
GLAZER
GLAZES
GLEBES
GLEDES
GLIDED
GLIDER
GLIDES
GLOBED
GLOBES
GLOVED
GLOVER

6

GLOVES
GLOWED
GLOWER
GLOZED
GLOZES
GLUIER
GLUMES
GLUTEI
GLUTEN
GNAWED
GNAWER
GNOMES
GOADED
GOATEE
GOBBET
GOBIES
GOBLET
GOFFER
GOGLET
GOITER
GOLDEN
GOLFED
GOLFER
GOOBER
GOOFED
GOOIER
GOONEY
GOOSED
GOOSES
GOOSEY
GOPHER
GORGED
GORGER
GORGES
GORGET
GORHEN
GORIER
GORSES
GOSHEN
GOSPEL
GOTTEN
GOUGED
GOUGER
GOUGES
GOWNED
GRABEN
GRACED
GRACES
GRADED
GRADER
GRADES
GRAPES
GRATED
GRATER
GRATES
GRAVED
GRAVEL
GRAVEN
GRAVER
GRAVES
GRAYED
GRAYER
GRAZED
GRAZER

GRAZES
GREBES
GRETEL
GRIDED
GRIDES
GRIMED
GRIMES
GRIPED
GRIPER
GRIPES
GRIVET
GRIZEL
GROCER
GROPED
GROPER
GROPES
GROVEL
GROVER
GROVES
GROWER
GRUMES
GUIDED
GUIDER
GUIDES
GUILES
GUINEA
GUISES
GULDEN
GULFED
GULLET
GULPED
GULPER
GUMMED
GUNMEN
GUNNED
GUNNEL
GUNNER
GUSHED
GUSHER
GUSHES
GUSSET
GUTTED
GUTTER
GYPPED

G••••E

GABBLE
GAGGLE
GALEAE
GALORE
GAMBLE
GAMETE
GANGUE
GARAGE
GARBLE
GARGLE
GAUCHE
GEMMAE
GENTLE
GEORGE
GERTIE
GIGGLE
GIRDLE
GISELE
GLANCE
GOALIE
GOATEE
GOBBLE
GOETHE
GOGGLE
GOURDE
GRANGE
GREASE
GREAVE
GREECE
GREIGE
GRIEVE
GRIFFE
GRILLE
GRILSE
GRIPPE
GROOVE
GROUSE
GRUDGE
GUIMPE
GURGLE
GUSSIE
GUTTAE
GUTTLE
GUZZLE
GWYNNE
GYRATE
GYROSE

•GE•••

AGEDLY
AGEING
AGENCY
AGENDA
AGENTS
EGERIA
EGESTA
EGESTS

•G•E••

AGGERS
AGLEAM
AGLETS
AGREED
AGREES
EGBERT
EGGERS
EGRESS
EGRETS
OGLERS
OGRESS

•G••E•

AGATES
AGAVES
AGONES
AGREED
AGREES
OGIVES
UGLIER

•G•••E

AGAPAE
AGNATE
AGOGUE
AGORAE
AGRAFE
IGNACE
IGNITE
IGNORE

••GE••

AEGEAN
AEGEUS
AGGERS
ANGELA
ANGELO
ANGELS
ANGERS
ARGENT
AUGEAN
AUGEND
AUGERS
BAGELS
BEGETS
BOGEYS
COGENT
DIGEST
DOGEAR
EGGERS
ENGELS
EOGENE
EUGENE
GAGERS
HUGELY
HUGEST
HYGEIA
INGEST
LAGERS
LEGEND
LEGERS
LUGERS
NIGELS
ORGEAT
PIGEON
REGENT
ROGERS
SAGELY
SAGEST
TIGERS
URGENT
WAGERS
WIGEON
YAGERS
YOGEES

••G•E•

AIGLET
ANGLED
ANGLER
ANGLES
ARGUED
ARGUER
ARGUES
BAGGED
BAGMEN
BEGGED
BIGGER
BOGGED
BOGIES
BOGLES
BUGGED
BUGGER
BUGLED
BUGLER
BUGLES
CAGIER
COGGED
CYGNET
DAGGER
DEGREE
DIGGER
DOGGED
DOGGER
DOGIES
EAGLES
EAGLET
EDGIER
FAGGED
FIGGED
FOGGED
FOGIES
FUGLED
FUGLES
FUGUES
GAGGED
GAGGER
GIGGED
GIGLET
GIGUES
GOGLET
HIGHER
HOGGED
HUGGED
HUGHES
INGRES
JAGGED
JIGGED
JIGGER
JOGGED
JOGGER
JUGGED
KEGLER
LAGGED
LAGGER
LEGGED
LEGMEN
LEGREE
LOGGED
LOGGER
LOGIER
LUGGED
LUGGER
MAGNET
MAGUEY
MIGUEL
MUGGED
MUGGER
NAGGED
NAGGER
NIGHER
NUGGET
ORGIES
PEGGED
PIGGED
PIGPEN
POGIES
PUGGED
PUGREE
RAGGED
RAGMEN
REGLET
REGRET
RIGGED
RIGGER
ROGUED
ROGUES
RUGGED
SAGGED
SAGGER
SAGIER
SIGHED
SIGNED
SIGNER
SIGNET
TAGGED
TAGGER
TEGMEN
TOGAED
TOGGED
TOGUES
TUGGED
UNGUES
VAGUER
VOGUES
WAGGED
WAGNER
WIGGED
YOGEES

••G••E

ARGIVE
ARGYLE
AUGITE
BOGGLE
BYGONE
DEGAGE
DEGAME
DEGREE
DOGAPE
DOGGIE
ENGAGE
ENGINE
EOGENE
ERGATE
EUGENE
FIGURE
GAGGLE
GIGGLE
GOGGLE
HAGGLE
HIGGLE
HOGTIE
HUGHIE
JIGGLE

6

JOGGLE
JUGATE
JUGGLE
LAGUNE
LEGATE
LEGREE
LEGUME
LIGATE
LIGULE
LIGURE
MAGGIE
MAGPIE
MIGGLE
NEGATE
NIGGLE
PIGGIE
PUGREE
REGALE
REGGIE
REGIME
RUGATE
RUGOSE
TOGGLE
WAGGLE
WIGGLE
ZYGOTE

•••GE•

ADAGES
APOGEE
BADGED
BADGER
BADGES
BAGGED
BANGED
BARGED
BARGEE
BARGES
BEGGED
BEIGES
BERGEN
BIGGER
BILGED
BILGES
BINGES
BIOGEN
BOGGED
BONGED
BRUGES
BUDGED
BUDGES
BUDGET
BUGGED
BUGGER
BULGED
BULGER
BULGES
BUNGED
BURGEE
BURGER
CADGED
CADGER
CADGES
CODGER
COGGED
CONGER
CONGES
CUDGEL
DAGGER
DANGED
DANGER
DIGGER
DINGED
DINGEY
DIRGES
DODGED
DODGER
DODGES
DOGGED
DOGGER
DRAGEE
DUNGED
EXOGEN
FAGGED
FANGED
FIDGET
FIGGED
FINGER
FOGGED
FORGED
FORGER
FORGES
FORGET
FUDGED
FUDGES
GADGET
GAGGED
GAGGER
GANGED
GANGER
GANGES
GARGET
GAUGED
GAUGER
GAUGES
GEIGER
GIGGED
GINGER
GORGED
GORGER
GORGES
GORGET
GOUGED
GOUGER
GOUGES
HANGED
HANGER
HEDGED
HEDGER
HEDGES
HINGED
HINGES
HOGGED
HUGGED
HUNGER
IMAGES
IMOGEN
JAEGER
JAGGED
JIGGED
JIGGER
JOGGED
JOGGER
JORGES
JUDGED
JUDGER
JUDGES
JUGGED
KEDGED
KEDGES
LAAGER
LAGGED
LAGGER
LARGER
LEDGER
LEDGES
LEGGED
LIEGES
LINGER
LODGED
LODGER
LODGES
LOGGED
LOGGER
LONGED
LONGER
LUGGED
LUGGER
LUNGED
LUNGEE
LUNGER
LUNGES
MADGES
MANGER
MARGES
MEAGER
MERGED
MERGER
MERGES
MIDGES
MIDGET
MONGER
MORGEN
MUGGED
MUGGER
NAGGED
NAGGER
NUDGED
NUDGES
NUGGET
ONAGER
ORIGEN
OXYGEN
PARGET
PEGGED
PIGGED
PINGED
PONGEE
PUGGED
PURGED
PURGER
PURGES
RAGGED
RANGED
RANGER
RANGES
RIDGED
RIDGES
RIGGED
RIGGER
RINGED
RINGER
ROUGED
ROUGES
RUGGED
SAGGED
SAGGER
SANGER
SAUGER
SEDGES
SIEGED
SIEGES
SINGED
SINGER
SINGES
STAGED
STAGER
STAGES
STAGEY
STOGEY
SURGED
SURGER
SURGES
SWAGED
SWAGES
TAGGED
TAGGER
TANGED
TARGET
TINGED
TINGES
TOGGED
TONGED
TUGGED
USAGES
VERGED
VERGER
VERGES
WAGGED
WEDGED
WEDGES
WIGGED
WINGED
ZENGER
ZINGED

•••G•E

AGOGUE
APOGEE
BANGLE
BARGEE
BEAGLE
BOGGLE
BOUGIE
BROGUE
BUDGIE
BUNGLE
BURGEE
BURGLE
CANGUE
CHEGOE
CHIGOE
DANGLE
DENGUE
DINGLE
DOGGIE
DOUGIE
DRAGEE
EMIGRE
GAGGLE
GANGUE
GARGLE
GIGGLE
GOGGLE
GURGLE
HAGGLE
HIGGLE
JANGLE
JIGGLE
JINGLE
JOGGLE
JUGGLE
JUNGLE
LEAGUE
LUNGEE
MAGGIE
MAIGRE
MALGRE
MANGLE
MARGIE
MIGGLE
MINGLE
MORGUE
NIGGLE
PIGGIE
PLAGUE
PONGEE
PRAGUE
REGGIE
SINGLE
SOIGNE
TANGLE
TINGLE
TOGGLE
TONGUE
VIRGIE
WAGGLE
WANGLE
WEDGIE
WIGGLE

••••GE

ALLEGE
AMBAGE
ANLAGE
AVENGE
BAREGE
BLUNGE
BORAGE
BRIDGE
CHANGE
CHARGE
COWAGE
CRINGE
CUBAGE
DAMAGE
DEGAGE
DELUGE
DOSAGE
DOTAGE
DREDGE
DRUDGE
EMERGE
ENCAGE
ENGAGE
ENRAGE
FLANGE
FLEDGE
FORAGE
FRIDGE
FRINGE
GARAGE
GEORGE
GRANGE
GREIGE
GRUDGE
HOMAGE
INCAGE
LAVAGE
LINAGE
LOUNGE
LOVAGE
MANAGE
MANEGE
MENAGE
METAGE
MILAGE
MIRAGE
NONAGE
OBLIGE
OHMAGE
ORANGE
PELAGE
PIPAGE
PLEDGE
PLUNGE
POTAGE
RAVAGE
REFUGE
RENEGE
RRHAGE
SAVAGE
SEWAGE
SLEDGE
SLUDGE
SMUDGE
SOCAGE
SPARGE
SPONGE
SPURGE
STODGE
STOOGE
SWINGE
TOWAGE

TRUDGE
TWINGE
ULLAGE
UNCAGE
VISAGE
VOYAGE

G•F•••
GAFFED
GAFFER
GAFFES
GIFTED
GOFFER
GUFFAW

G••F••
GADFLY
GAFFED
GAFFER
GAFFES
GOFFER
GOLFED
GOLFER
GOOFED
GRAFTS
GRIFFE
GUFFAW
GULFED

G•••F•
GANEFS
GRIEFS
GRIFFE

G••••F
GUSTAF

•G••F•
AGRAFE
IGNIFY
UGLIFY

••G•F•
ARGUFY

••G••F
ENGULF
INGULF

G•G•••
GAGERS
GAGGED
GAGGER
GAGGLE
GAGING
GIGANT
GIGGED
GIGGLE
GIGGLY
GIGLET
GIGLOT
GIGOLO
GIGUES
GOGGLE
GOGLET

G••G••
GADGET
GAGGED
GAGGER
GAGGLE
GANGED
GANGER
GANGES
GANGLI
GANGUE
GARGET
GARGLE
GAUGED
GAUGER
GAUGES
GEIGER
GEWGAW
GIGGED
GIGGLE
GIGGLY
GINGAL
GINGER
GOGGLE
GOOGLY
GOOGOL
GORGED
GORGER
GORGES
GORGET
GORGON
GOUGED
GOUGER
GOUGES
GREGOS
GRIGRI
GROGGY
GRUGRU
GURGLE

G•••G•
GARAGE
GEORGE
GEORGI
GINKGO
GOINGS
GRANGE
GREIGE
GROGGY
GRUDGE

G••••G
GAGING
GAMING
GAPING
GASBAG
GATING
GAZING
GEEING
GIBING
GIVING
GLUING
GORING
GUYING

•GG•••
AGGERS
EGGARS
EGGERS
EGGING
EGGNOG

•G•G••
AGOGUE

•G•••G
AGEING
EGGING
EGGNOG
OGLING

••GG••
BAGGED
BEGGAR
BEGGED
BIGGER
BIGGIN
BOGGED
BOGGLE
BUGGED
BUGGER
COGGED
DAGGER
DIGGER
DOGGED
DOGGER
DOGGIE
FAGGED
FAGGOT
FIGGED
FOGGED
GAGGED
GAGGER
GAGGLE
GIGGED
GIGGLE
GIGGLY
GOGGLE
HAGGIS
HAGGLE
HIGGLE
HOGGED
HUGGED
JAGGED
JIGGED
JIGGER
JIGGLE
JOGGED
JOGGER
JOGGLE
JUGGED
JUGGLE
LAGGED
LAGGER
LEGGED
LOGGED
LOGGER
LOGGIA
LUGGED
LUGGER
MAGGIE
MAGGOT
MIGGLE
MUGGAR
MUGGED
MUGGER
MUGGUR
NAGGED
NAGGER
NIGGLE
NOGGIN
NUGGET
PEGGED
PEGGYS
PIGGED
PIGGIE
PIGGIN
PUGGED
PUGGRY
RAGGED
REGGIE
RIGGED
RIGGER
RUGGED
SAGGAR
SAGGED
SAGGER
SEGGAR
TAGGED
TAGGER
TOGGED
TOGGLE
TUGGED
WAGGED
WAGGLE
WAGGLY
WAGGON
WIGGED
WIGGLE
WIGGLY

••G•G•
DEGAGE
ENGAGE

••G••G
BIGWIG
CAGING
DUGONG
EDGING
EGGING
EGGNOG
FOGDOG
GAGING
PAGING
RAGING
RAGTAG
URGING
WAGING
WIGWAG
ZIGZAG

•••GG•
CLOGGY
CRAGGY
DREGGY
FLAGGY
FROGGY
GROGGY
QUAGGA
QUAGGY
SHAGGY
SLAGGY
SNAGGY
STAGGY
TWIGGY

•••G•G
FIZGIG

GH••••
GHARRI
GHARRY
GHAUTS
GHEBER
GHETTO
GHOSTS
GHOULS

G••H••
GASHED
GASHES
GATHER
GOPHER
GORHEN
GOSHEN
GOTHAM
GOTHIC
GRAHAM
GUSHED
GUSHER
GUSHES

G•••H•
GANDHI
GAUCHE
GAUCHO
GEISHA
GLYPHS
GNATHO
GOETHE
GRAPHO
GRAPHS
GRAPHY
GUNSHY
GURKHA

G••••H
GALOSH
GARISH
GROUCH
GROWTH
GULLAH

•GH•••
AGHAST

•G••H•
AGATHA

•G•••H
AGUISH
OGRISH

••GH••
AFGHAN
AUGHTS
BIGHTS
EIGHTH
EIGHTS
EIGHTY
FIGHTS
HIGHER
HIGHLY
HUGHES
HUGHIE
LIGHTS
MIGHTY
NIGHER
NIGHTS
NIGHTY
RIGHTO
RIGHTS
SIGHED
SIGHTS
TIGHTS

••G••H
EIGHTH

•••GH•
ALIGHT
ARIGHT
BLIGHT
BOUGHS
BOUGHT
BRIGHT
BURGHS
CAUGHT
COUGHS
DINGHY
DOUGHS
DOUGHY
DWIGHT
FLIGHT
FOUGHT
FRIGHT
HEIGHT
KNIGHT
LAUGHS
LEIGHS
LOUGHS
NAUGHT
NEIGHS
NOUGHT
PLIGHT
ROUGHS
SLIGHT
SORGHO
SOUGHS
SOUGHT

TAUGHT
THIGHS
TOUGHS
WEIGHS
WEIGHT
WRIGHT

•••G•H
LENGTH
PISGAH

••••GH
ARMAGH
AWEIGH
CHOUGH
CLOUGH
ENOUGH
PLOUGH
SLEIGH
SLOUGH
THOUGH
TROUGH

GI••••
GIANTS
GIAOUR
GIBBED
GIBBER
GIBBET
GIBBON
GIBERS
GIBING
GIBLET
GIBRAN
GIBSON
GIDEON
GIFTED
GIGANT
GIGGED
GIGGLE
GIGGLY
GIGLET
GIGLOT
GIGOLO
GIGUES
GILDAS
GILDED
GILDER
GILEAD
GIMELS
GIMLET
GIMPED
GINGAL
GINGER
GINKGO
GINNED
GINNER
GIOTTO
GIPONS
GIPPED
GIRDED
GIRDER
GIRDLE
GIRTED
GISELE
GISMOS
GITANO
GIULIA
GIULIO
GIVING
GIZMOS

G•I•••
GAIETY
GAINED
GAINER
GAINLY
GAITED
GAITER
GEIGER
GEISHA
GLIBLY
GLIDED
GLIDER
GLIDES
GLINTS
GLIOMA
GOINGS
GOITER
GRIDED
GRIDES
GRIEFS
GRIEVE
GRIFFE
GRIGRI
GRILLE
GRILLS
GRILSE
GRIMED
GRIMES
GRIMLY
GRINDS
GRIPED
GRIPER
GRIPES
GRIPPE
GRIPPY
GRISLY
GRITTY
GRIVET
GRIZEL
GUIANA
GUIDED
GUIDER
GUIDES
GUIDON
GUILDS
GUILES
GUILTS
GUILTY
GUIMPE
GUINEA
GUISES
GUITAR

G••I••
GABION
GAGING
GALIOT
GAMIER
GAMILY
GAMING
GAMINS
GAPING
GARISH
GATING
GAVIAL
GAZING
GEEING
GEMINI
GENIAL
GENIES
GENITO
GENIUS
GIBING
GIVING
GLAIRS
GLAIRY
GLUIER
GLUING
GNEISS
GOBIES
GODIVA
GONION
GONIUM
GOOIER
GORIER
GORILY
GORING
GRAINS
GRAINY
GREIGE
GROINS
GUYING

G•••I•
GADOID
GAELIC
GALLIC
GAMBIA
GAMBIR
GAMBIT
GANOID
GARLIC
GASKIN
GAWAIN
GDYNIA
GEODIC
GERBIL
GERTIE
GESTIC
GIULIA
GIULIO
GLACIS
GLOBIN
GLORIA
GLYNIS
GNOMIC
GNOSIS
GOALIE
GOBLIN
GODWIN
GODWIT
GOSSIP
GOTHIC
GRADIN
GRATIS
GRAVID
GUANIN
GUSSIE

G••••I
GANDHI
GANGLI
GEMINI
GEORGI
GHARRI
GLUTEI
GOMUTI
GRIGRI

•GI•••
AGISTS
OGIVES

•G•I••
AGEING
AGUISH
EGGING
EGOISM
EGOIST
IGNIFY
IGNITE
OGLING
OGRISH
UGLIER
UGLIFY
UGLILY

•G••I•
AGAMIC
AGARIC
AGLAIA
AGNAIL
AGONIC
EGERIA

•G•••I
AGOUTI

••GI••
ANGINA
ARGIVE
AUGITE
BEGINS
BEGIRD
BEGIRT
BOGIES
CAGIER
CAGILY
CAGING
DIGITI
DIGITS
DOGIES
EDGIER
EDGING
EGGING
ENGINE
ENGIRD
ENGIRT
FOGIES
FUGIOS
GAGING
HEGIRA
LEGION
LEGIST
LOGIER
LOGION
MEGILP
ORGIES
PAGING
POGIES
RAGING
REGIME
REGINA
REGION
REGIUS
SAGIER
SIGILS
UNGIRD
UNGIRT
URGING
VAGINA
VAGINO
VIGILS
WAGING
YOGINS

••G•I•
ALGOID
ANGLIA
ANGLIC
BAGNIO
BEGUIN
BIGGIN
BIGWIG
DOGGIE
HAGGIS
HOGTIE
HUGHIE
HYGEIA
INGRID
LIGNIN
LOGGIA
MAGGIE
MAGPIE
MEGRIM
NOGGIN
PIGGIE
PIGGIN
REGAIN
REGGIE
SIGRID
UNGUIS

••G••I
ARGALI
DIGITI

•••GI•
ADAGIO
BELGIC
BIGGIN
BORGIA
BOUGIE
BRIGID
BUDGIE
CORGIS
DOGGIE
DOUGIE
ELEGIT
FIZGIG
FRIGID
FULGID
HAGGIS
LOGGIA
LUNGIS
MAGGIE
MARGIE
MARGIN
NOGGIN
ORIGIN
PHAGIA
PIDGIN
PIGGIE
PIGGIN
PLAGIO
PLEGIA
REGGIE
TRAGIC
TURGID
VERGIL
VIRGIE
VIRGIL
VIRGIN
WEDGIE

•••G•I
BANGUI
GANGLI
GRIGRI
NILGAI
ONAGRI
SANGUI

••••GI
GEORGI
UBANGI

••GJ••
LOGJAM

G•K•••
GOKART

G••K••
GASKET
GASKIN
GAWKED
GECKOS
GINKGO
GURKHA

6

G•••K•
GREEKS

G••••K
GALYAK

••GK••
ANGKOR

GL••••
GLACES
GLACIS
GLADES
GLADLY
GLADYS
GLAIRS
GLAIRY
GLANCE
GLANDS
GLARED
GLARES
GLASSY
GLAUCO
GLAZED
GLAZER
GLAZES
GLEAMS
GLEAMY
GLEANS
GLEBES
GLEDES
GLEETS
GLEETY
GLIBLY
GLIDED
GLIDER
GLIDES
GLINTS
GLIOMA
GLOATS
GLOBAL
GLOBED
GLOBES
GLOBIN
GLOOMS
GLOOMY
GLORIA
GLOSSO
GLOSSY
GLOSTS
GLOTTO
GLOVED
GLOVER
GLOVES
GLOWED
GLOWER
GLOZED
GLOZES
GLUIER
GLUING
GLUMES
GLUMLY
GLUTEI
GLUTEN
GLYCOL
GLYNIS
GLYPHS
GLYPTO

G•L•••
GALACT
GALAXY
GALEAE
GALENA
GALIOT
GALLED
GALLEY
GALLIC
GALLON
GALLOP
GALLUP
GALLUS
GALOOT
GALOPS
GALORE
GALOSH
GALWAY
GALYAK
GELDED
GELLED
GILDAS
GILDED
GILDER
GILEAD
GOLDEN
GOLFED
GOLFER
GULDEN
GULFED
GULLAH
GULLET
GULPED
GULPER

G••L••
GABLED
GABLES
GAELIC
GALLED
GALLEY
GALLIC
GALLON
GALLOP
GALLUP
GALLUS
GAOLER
GARLIC
GELLED
GIBLET
GIGLET
GIGLOT
GIMLET
GIULIA
GIULIO
GOALIE
GOBLET
GOBLIN
GOGLET
GRILLE
GRILLS
GRILSE
GUILDS
GUILES
GUILTS
GUILTY
GULLAH
GULLET

G•••L•
GABBLE
GADFLY
GAGGLE
GAINLY
GAMBLE
GAMELY
GAMILY
GANGLI
GARBLE
GARGLE
GAVELS
GENTLE
GERALD
GESELL
GHOULS
GIGGLE
GIGGLY
GIGOLO
GIMELS
GIRDLE
GISELE
GLADLY
GLIBLY
GLUMLY
GNARLS
GNARLY
GOBBLE
GOGGLE
GOODLY
GOOGLY
GORALS
GORILY
GRAYLY
GRILLE
GRILLS
GRIMLY
GRISLY
GROWLS
GRUELS
GURGLE
GUTTLE
GUZZLE

G••••L
GAMBOL
GAVIAL
GENIAL
GERBIL
GESELL
GINGAL
GLOBAL
GLYCOL
GOOGOL
GOORAL
GOSPEL
GRAVEL
GRETEL
GRIZEL
GROVEL
GUNNEL

•GL•••
AGLAIA
AGLEAM
AGLETS
IGLOOS
OGLERS
OGLING
UGLIER
UGLIFY
UGLILY

•G••L•
AGEDLY
UGLILY

•G•••L
AGNAIL

••GL••
AIGLET
ANGLED
ANGLER
ANGLES
ANGLIA
ANGLIC
BOGLES
BUGLED
BUGLER
BUGLES
DIGLOT
EAGLES
EAGLET
FUGLED
FUGLES
GIGLET
GIGLOT
GOGLET
KEGLER
RAGLAN
REGLET

••G•L•
ANGELA
ANGELO
ANGELS
ANGOLA
ARGALI
ARGALS
ARGYLE
ARGYLL
BAGELS
BOGGLE
CAGILY
ENGELS
ENGULF
GAGGLE
GIGGLE
GIGGLY
GIGOLO
GOGGLE
HAGGLE
HIGGLE
HIGHLY
HUGELY
INGULF
JIGGLE
JOGGLE
JUGGLE
LIGULA
LIGULE
MEGALO
MEGILP
MIGGLE
MOGULS
NIGELS
NIGGLE
REGALE
SAGELY
SIGILS
TOGGLE
UNGULA
VIGILS
VOGULS
WAGGLE
WAGGLY
WIGGLE
WIGGLY

••G••L
ARGYLL
MIGUEL
REGNAL
SIGNAL
UNGUAL

•••GL•
BANGLE
BEAGLE
BOGGLE
BUNGLE
BURGLE
DANGLE
DINGLE
GAGGLE
GANGLI
GARGLE
GIGGLE
GIGGLY
GOGGLE
GOOGLY
GURGLE
HAGGLE
HIGGLE
JANGLE
JIGGLE
JINGLE
JOGGLE
JUGGLE
JUNGLE
JUNGLY
KINGLY
MANGLE
MIGGLE
MINGLE
NIGGLE
SINGLE
SINGLY
SMUGLY
SNUGLY
TANGLE
TANGLY
TINGLE
TINGLY
TOGGLE
TRIGLY
WAGGLE
WAGGLY
WANGLE
WIGGLE
WIGGLY

•••G•L
BENGAL
CUDGEL
FRUGAL
FUNGAL
GINGAL
GOOGOL
JINGAL
MONGOL
PLAGAL
TERGAL
VERGIL
VIRGIL

G•M•••
GAMBIA
GAMBIR
GAMBIT
GAMBLE
GAMBOL
GAMELY
GAMETE
GAMETO
GAMIER
GAMILY
GAMING
GAMINS
GAMMAS
GAMMER
GAMMON
GAMOUS
GAMUTS
GEMARA
GEMINI
GEMMAE
GEMMED
GEMOTS
GIMELS
GIMLET
GIMPED
GOMUTI
GUMBOS
GUMMAS

6

GUMMED

G••M••
GAMMAS
GAMMER
GAMMON
GASMAN
GASMEN
GEMMAE
GEMMED
GERMAN
GISMOS
GIZMOS
GLUMES
GLUMLY
GNOMES
GNOMIC
GNOMON
GRIMED
GRIMES
GRIMLY
GRUMES
GRUMPY
GUIMPE
GUMMAS
GUMMED
GUNMAN
GUNMEN

G•••M•
GLEAMS
GLEAMY
GLIOMA
GLOOMS
GLOOMY
GOTAMA
GROOMS

G••••M
GONIUM
GOTHAM
GRAHAM
GYPSUM

•G•M••
AGAMAS
AGAMIC

•G•••M
AGLEAM
EGOISM

••GM••
BAGMAN
BAGMEN
DAGMAR
DOGMAS
LEGMAN
LEGMEN
RAGMAN
RAGMEN
SIGMAS
TEGMEN

••G•M•
BEGUMS
BIGAMY
DEGAME
DEGUMS
DIGAMY
LEGUME
REGIME
ZYGOMA

••G••M
ENGRAM
LOGJAM
MAGNUM
MEGRIM
ORGASM
POGROM
WIGWAM

•••GM•
BREGMA
ENIGMA
STIGMA
ZEUGMA

•••G•M
TERGUM

••••GM
PHLEGM

GN••••
GNARLS
GNARLY
GNATHO
GNAWED
GNAWER
GNEISS
GNOMES
GNOMIC
GNOMON
GNOSIS

G•N•••
GANDER
GANDHI
GANEFS
GANGED
GANGER
GANGES
GANGLI
GANGUE
GANNET
GANOID
GANTRY
GENDER
GENERA
GENETS
GENEVA
GENIAL
GENIES
GENITO
GENIUS
GENOUS
GENRES
GENROS
GENTES
GENTLE
GENTOO
GENTRY
GINGAL
GINGER
GINKGO
GINNED
GINNER
GONADS
GONERS
GONION
GONIUM
GUNMAN
GUNMEN
GUNNAR
GUNNED
GUNNEL
GUNNER
GUNSHY
GYNECO
GYNOUS

G••N••
GAINED
GAINER
GAINLY
GANNET
GARNER
GARNET
GDYNIA
GIANTS
GINNED
GINNER
GLANCE
GLANDS
GLINTS
GLYNIS
GOINGS
GOONEY
GOWNED
GRANGE
GRANNY
GRANTS
GRINDS
GRUNDY
GRUNTS
GUANIN
GUANOS
GUENON
GUINEA
GUNNAR
GUNNED
GUNNEL
GUNNER
GWENNS
GWYNNE

G•••N•
GAGING
GALENA
GAMING
GAMINS
GAPING
GATING
GAZING
GEEING
GEMINI
GERENT
GERUND
GIBING
GIGANT
GIPONS
GITANO
GIVING
GLEANS
GLUING
GORING
GRAINS
GRAINY
GRANNY
GREENS
GROANS
GROINS
GROUND
GUIANA
GUYANA
GUYING
GWENNS
GWYNNE
GYRONS

G••••N
GABION
GALLON
GAMMON
GARCON
GARDEN
GASCON
GASKIN
GASMAN
GASMEN
GASTON
GAWAIN
GERMAN
GERYON
GIBBON
GIBRAN
GIBSON
GIDEON
GLOBIN
GLUTEN
GNOMON
GOBLIN
GODSON
GODWIN
GOLDEN
GONION
GORDON
GORGON
GORHEN
GOSHEN
GOTTEN
GOVERN
GRABEN
GRADIN
GRAVEN
GUANIN
GUENON
GUIDON
GULDEN
GUNMAN
GUNMEN

•GN•••
AGNAIL
AGNATE
IGNACE
IGNIFY
IGNITE
IGNORE

•G•N••
AGENCY
AGENDA
AGENTS
AGONES
AGONIC
EGGNOG
UGANDA

•G••N•
AGEING
EGGING
IGUANA
OGLING

••GN••
BAGNIO
COGNAC
CYGNET
CYGNUS
EGGNOG
HOGNUT
LIGNIN
MAGNET
MAGNUM
MIGNON
PIGNUS
PIGNUT
REGNAL
SIGNAL
SIGNED
SIGNER
SIGNET
SIGNOR
WAGNER

••G•N•
ANGINA
ARGENT
AUGEND
BEGINS
BOGANS
BYGONE
CAGING
COGENT
DUGONG
EDGING
EGGING
ENGINE
EOGENE
EUGENE
GAGING
GIGANT
HOGANS
LAGUNE
LEGEND
LIGAND
NAGANA
ORGANA
ORGANO
ORGANS
PAGANS
PAGING
RAGING
REGENT
REGINA
URGENT
URGING
VAGINA
VAGINO
WAGING
WAGONS
WIGANS
YOGINS

••G••N
AEGEAN
AFGHAN
AUGEAN
BAGMAN
BAGMEN
BEGUIN
BIGGIN
HAGDON
LAGOON
LEGION
LEGMAN
LEGMEN
LIGNIN
LOGION
MIGNON
NOGGIN
PIGEON
PIGGIN
PIGPEN
RAGLAN
RAGMAN
RAGMEN
REGAIN
REGION
TEGMEN
WAGGON
WIGEON

•••GN•
ALIGNS
COIGNS
DEIGNS
FEIGNS
REIGNS
SOIGNE

6

•••G•N
ARAGON
BERGEN
BIGGIN
BIOGEN
BROGAN
DRAGON
EXOGEN
FLAGON
GORGON
IMOGEN
ISOGON
JARGON
LONGAN
MARGIN
MORGAN
MORGEN
NOGGIN
OREGON
ORIGAN
ORIGEN
ORIGIN
OXYGEN
PIDGIN
PIGGIN
POPGUN
SAIGON
SARGON
SHOGUN
SLOGAN
TRIGON
TROGON
VIRGIN
WAGGON

••••GN
ASSIGN
BENIGN
COSIGN
DESIGN
ELOIGN
ENSIGN
IMPUGN
MALIGN
OPPUGN
RESIGN

GO••••
GOADED
GOALIE
GOATEE
GOBBET
GOBBLE
GOBIES
GOBLET
GOBLIN
GOCART
GODIVA
GODSON
GODWIN
GODWIT
GOETHE
GOFFER
GOGGLE
GOGLET
GOINGS
GOITER
GOKART
GOLDEN
GOLFED
GOLFER
GOMUTI
GONADS
GONERS
GONION
GONIUM
GOOBER
GOODBY
GOODLY
GOOFED
GOOGLY
GOOGOL
GOOIER
GOONEY
GOORAL
GOOSED
GOOSES
GOOSEY
GOPHER
GORALS
GORDON
GORGED
GORGER
GORGES
GORGET
GORGON
GORHEN
GORIER
GORILY
GORING
GORSES
GOSHEN
GOSPEL
GOSSIP
GOTAMA
GOTHAM
GOTHIC
GOTTEN
GOUGED
GOUGER
GOUGES
GOURDE
GOURDS
GOVERN
GOWNED

G•O•••
GAOLER
GEODES
GEODIC
GEORGE
GEORGI
GHOSTS
GHOULS
GIOTTO
GLOATS
GLOBAL
GLOBED
GLOBES
GLOBIN
GLOOMS
GLOOMY
GLORIA
GLOSSO
GLOSSY
GLOSTS
GLOTTO
GLOVED
GLOVER
GLOVES
GLOWED
GLOWER
GLOZED
GLOZES
GNOMES
GNOMIC
GNOMON
GNOSIS
GOOBER
GOODBY
GOODLY
GOOFED
GOOGLY
GOOGOL
GOOIER
GOONEY
GOORAL
GOOSED
GOOSES
GOOSEY
GROANS
GROATS
GROCER
GROGGY
GROINS
GROOMS
GROOVE
GROOVY
GROPED
GROPER
GROPES
GROSZY
GROTTO
GROUCH
GROUND
GROUPS
GROUSE
GROUTS
GROVEL
GROVER
GROVES
GROWER
GROWLS
GROWTH

G••O••
GADOID
GALOOT
GALOPS
GALORE
GALOSH
GAMOUS
GANOID
GAVOTS
GEMOTS
GENOUS
GEROUS
GIAOUR
GIGOLO
GIPONS
GLIOMA
GLOOMS
GLOOMY
GROOMS
GROOVE
GROOVY
GYNOUS
GYRONS
GYROSE

G•••O•
GABION
GALIOT
GALLON
GALLOP
GALOOT
GAMBOL
GAMMON
GARCON
GASCON
GASTON
GECKOS
GENROS
GENTOO
GERYON
GESSOS
GIBBON
GIBSON
GIDEON
GIGLOT
GISMOS
GIZMOS
GLYCOL
GNOMON
GODSON
GONION
GOOGOL
GORDON
GORGON
GREGOS
GUACOS
GUANOS
GUENON
GUIDON
GUMBOS

G••••O
GABBRO
GAMETO
GASTRO
GAUCHO
GAZABO
GAZEBO
GENITO
GENTOO
GHETTO
GIGOLO
GINKGO
GIOTTO
GITANO
GIULIO
GLAUCO
GLOSSO
GLOTTO
GLYPTO
GNATHO
GRAECO
GRAPHO
GROTTO
GYNECO

•GO•••
AGOGUE
AGONES
AGONIC
AGORAE
AGORAS
AGOUTI
AGOUTY
EGOISM
EGOIST
IGOROT

•G•O••
IGLOOS
IGNORE
OGDOAD

•G••O•
EGGNOG
IGLOOS
IGOROT

••GO••
ALGOID
ANGOLA
ANGORA
ARGOSY
ARGOTS
BIGOTS
BOGOTA
BYGONE
DAGOBA
DUGONG
DUGOUT
FAGOTS
GIGOLO
INGOTS
LAGOON
MAGOTS
NAGOYA
PAGODA
RAGOUT
RIGORS
RUGOSE
RUGOUS
VIGOUR
WAGONS
ZYGOMA
ZYGOTE

••G•O•
ANGKOR
DIGLOT
EGGNOG
FAGGOT
FOGBOW
FOGDOG
FUGIOS
GIGLOT
HAGDON
LAGOON
LEGION
LOGION
MAGGOT
MIGNON
PEGTOP
PIGEON
POGROM
REGION
SIGNOR
WAGGON
WIGEON

••G••O
ANGELO
BAGNIO
GIGOLO
LEGATO
MEGALO
ORGANO
RIGHTO
VAGINO

•••GO•
AMIGOS
ARAGON
BANGOR
BONGOS
BURGOO
BURGOS
CARGOS
CHEGOE
CHIGOE
CONGOU
DRAGON
FAGGOT
FLAGON
FORGOT
GOOGOL
GORGON
GREGOS
ISOGON
JARGON
LARGOS
MAGGOT
MANGOS
MARGOS
MARGOT
MONGOL
OREGON
PARGOS
PENGOS
PINGOS
SAIGON

6

SARGON
SORGOS
SPIGOT
TANGOS
TRIGON
TROGON
WAGGON

•••G•O
ADAGIO
BURGOO
PLAGIO
SORGHO

••••GO
AERUGO
COLUGO
DRONGO
ERINGO
ERYNGO
FOREGO
GINKGO
INDIGO
LANUGO
NONEGO
RUBIGO
TOBAGO
VIRAGO

G•P•••
GAPERS
GAPING
GAPPED
GIPONS
GIPPED
GOPHER
GYPPED
GYPSUM

G••P••
GAPPED
GASPAR
GASPED
GASPER
GIMPED
GIPPED
GLYPHS
GLYPTO
GOSPEL
GRAPES
GRAPHO
GRAPHS
GRAPHY
GRIPED
GRIPER
GRIPES
GRIPPE
GRIPPY
GROPED
GROPER
GROPES
GULPED
GULPER
GYPPED

G•••P•
GALOPS
GETUPS
GRASPS
GRIPPE
GRIPPY
GROUPS
GRUMPY
GUIMPE

G••••P
GALLOP
GALLUP
GOSSIP

•G•P••
AGAPAE

••GP••
MAGPIE
PIGPEN

••G•P•
DOGAPE

••G••P
MEGILP
PEGTOP

•••G•P
BANGUP
HANGUP

GR••••
GRABEN
GRACED
GRACES
GRADED
GRADER
GRADES
GRADIN
GRADUS
GRAECO
GRAFTS
GRAHAM
GRAINS
GRAINY
GRANGE
GRANNY
GRANTS
GRAPES
GRAPHO
GRAPHS
GRAPHY
GRASPS
GRASSY
GRATED
GRATER
GRATES
GRATIS
GRAVED
GRAVEL
GRAVEN
GRAVER
GRAVES
GRAVID
GRAYED
GRAYER
GRAYLY
GRAZED
GRAZER
GRAZES
GREASE
GREASY
GREATS
GREAVE
GREBES
GREECE
GREEDS
GREEDY
GREEKS
GREENS
GREETS
GREGOS
GREIGE
GRETAS
GRETEL
GRIDED
GRIDES
GRIEFS
GRIÉVE
GRIFFE
GRIGRI
GRILLE
GRILLS
GRILSE
GRIMED
GRIMES
GRIMLY
GRINDS
GRIPED
GRIPER
GRIPES
GRIPPE
GRIPPY
GRISLY
GRITTY
GRIVET
GRIZEL
GROANS
GROATS
GROCER
GROGGY
GROINS
GROOMS
GROOVE
GROOVY
GROPED
GROPER
GROPES
GROSZY
GROTTO
GROUCH
GROUND
GROUPS
GROUSE
GROUTS
GROVEL
GROVER
GROVES
GROWER
GROWLS
GROWTH
GRUBBY
GRUDGE
GRUELS
GRUGRU
GRUMES
GRUMPY
GRUNDY
GRUNTS

G•R•••
GARAGE
GARBED
GARBLE
GARCON
GARDEN
GARGET
GARGLE
GARISH
GARLIC
GARNER
GARNET
GARRET
GARTER
GERALD
GERARD
GERBIL
GERENT
GERMAN
GEROUS
GERRYS
GERTIE
GERTYS
GERUND
GERYON
GIRDED
GIRDER
GIRDLE
GIRTED
GORALS
GORDON
GORGED
GORGER
GORGES
GORGET
GORGON
GORHEN
GORIER
GORILY
GORING
GORSES
GURGLE
GURKHA
GYRATE
GYRONS
GYROSE

G••R••
GARRET
GEARED
GENRES
GENROS
GEORGE
GEORGI
GERRYS
GHARRI
GHARRY
GIBRAN
GLARED
GLARES
GLORIA
GNARLS
GNARLY
GOORAL
GOURDE
GOURDS
GUARDS

G•••R•
GABBRO
GAGERS
GALORE
GANTRY
GAPERS
GASTRO
GAZERS
GEMARA
GENERA
GENTRY
GERARD
GHARRI
GHARRY
GIBERS
GLAIRS
GLAIRY
GOCART
GOKART
GONERS
GOVERN
GRIGRI
GRUGRU

G••••R
GABBER
GADDER
GAFFER
GAGGER
GAINER
GAITER
GAMBIR
GAMIER
GAMMER
GANDER
GANGER
GAOLER
GARNER
GARTER
GASPAR
GASPER
GATHER
GAUGER
GEEZER
GEIGER
GENDER
GETTER
GEYSER
GHEBER
GIAOUR
GIBBER
GILDER
GINGER
GINNER
GIRDER
GLAZER
GLIDER
GLOVER
GLOWER
GLUIER
GNAWER
GOFFER
GOITER
GOLFER
GOOBER
GOOIER
GOPHER
GORGER
GORIER
GOUGER
GRADER
GRATER
GRAVER
GRAYER
GRAZER
GRIPER
GROCER
GROPER
GROVER
GROWER
GUIDER
GUITAR
GULPER
GUNNAR
GUNNER
GUSHER
GUTTER

•GR•••
AGRAFE
AGREED
AGREES
EGRESS
EGRETS
OGRESS
OGRISH

•G•R••
AGARIC
AGORAE
AGORAS
EGERIA
IGOROT

•G••R•
AGGERS
EGBERT
EGGARS
EGGERS
IGNORE

6

OGLERS

•G•••R
UGLIER

••GR••
DEGREE
ENGRAM
INGRES
INGRID
LEGREE
MEGRIM
POGROM
PUGREE
REGRET
SIGRID

••G•R•
AGGERS
ANGARY
ANGERS
ANGORA
ASGARD
AUGERS
AUGURS
AUGURY
BEGIRD
BEGIRT
CIGARS
EDGARS
EGGARS
EGGERS
ENGIRD
ENGIRT
FIGURE
GAGERS
HEGIRA
LAGERS
LEGERS
LIGURE
LUGERS
PUGGRY
REGARD
RIGORS
ROGERS
SUGARS
SUGARY
TIGERS
UNGIRD
UNGIRT
UTGARD
VAGARY
WAGERS
YAGERS
YOGURT

••G••R
ANGKOR
ANGLER
ARGUER
BEGGAR
BIGGER
BUGGER
BUGLER
CAGIER
DAGGER
DAGMAR
DIGGER
DOGEAR
DOGGER
EDGIER
GAGGER
HIGHER
JAGUAR
JIGGER
JOGGER
KEGLER
LAGGER
LOGGER
LOGIER
LUGGER
MAGYAR
MUGGAR
MUGGER
MUGGUR
NAGGER
NIGHER
RIGGER
SAGGAR
SAGGER
SAGIER
SEGGAR
SIGNER
SIGNOR
TAGGER
VAGUER
VIGOUR
WAGNER

•••GR•
EMIGRE
GRIGRI
GRUGRU
HUNGRY
MAIGRE
MALGRE
ONAGRI
PUGGRY

•••G•R
ALEGAR
BADGER
BANGOR
BEGGAR
BIGGER
BUGGER
BULGAR
BULGER
BURGER
CADGER
CODGER
CONGER
COUGAR
DAGGER
DANGER
DIGGER
DODGER
DOGGER
FINGER
FORGER
GAGGER
GANGER
GAUGER
GEIGER
GINGER
GORGER
GOUGER
HANGAR
HANGER
HEDGER
HUNGER
JAEGER
JIGGER
JOGGER
JUDGER
LAAGER
LAGGER
LANGUR
LARGER
LEDGER
LINGER
LODGER
LOGGER
LONGER
LUGGER
LUNGER
MANGER
MEAGER
MERGER
MONGER
MUGGAR
MUGGER
MUGGUR
NAGGER
ONAGER
PURGER
RANGER
RIGGER
RINGER
SAGGAR
SAGGER
SANGAR
SANGER
SAUGER
SEGGAR
SINGER
STAGER
SURGER
TAGGER
VERGER
VULGAR
ZENGER

G•S•••
GASBAG
GASCON
GASHED
GASHES
GASKET
GASKIN
GASMAN
GASMEN
GASPAR
GASPED
GASPER
GASSED
GASSES
GASTON
GASTRO
GESELL
GESSOS
GESTIC
GISELE
GISMOS
GOSHEN
GOSPEL
GOSSIP
GUSHED
GUSHER
GUSHES
GUSSET
GUSSIE
GUSTAF
GUSTAV

G••S••
GASSED
GASSES
GEISHA
GESSOS
GEYSER
GHOSTS
GIBSON
GLASSY
GLOSSO
GLOSSY
GLOSTS
GNOSIS
GODSON
GOOSED
GOOSES
GOOSEY
GORSES
GOSSIP
GRASPS
GRASSY
GRISLY
GROSZY
GUESTS
GUISES
GUNSHY
GUSSET
GUSSIE
GYPSUM

G•••S•
GALOSH
GARISH
GAYEST
GLASSY
GLOSSO
GLOSSY
GNEISS
GRASSY
GREASE
GREASY
GRILSE
GROUSE
GYROSE

G••••S
GABLES
GAFFES
GAGERS
GALLUS
GALOPS
GAMINS
GAMMAS
GAMOUS
GAMUTS
GANEFS
GANGES
GAPERS
GASHES
GASSES
GAUGES
GAUZES
GAVELS
GAVOTS
GAZERS
GECKOS
GEMOTS
GENETS
GENIES
GENIUS
GENOUS
GENRES
GENROS
GENTES
GEODES
GEROUS
GERRYS
GERTYS
GESSOS
GETUPS
GHAUTS
GHOSTS
GHOULS
GIANTS
GIBERS
GIGUES
GILDAS
GIMELS
GIPONS
GISMOS
GIZMOS
GLACES
GLACIS
GLADES
GLADYS
GLAIRS
GLANDS
GLARES
GLAZES
GLEAMS
GLEANS
GLEBES
GLEDES
GLEETS
GLIDES
GLINTS
GLOATS
GLOBES
GLOOMS
GLOSTS
GLOVES
GLOZES
GLUMES
GLYNIS
GLYPHS
GNARLS
GNEISS
GNOMES
GNOSIS
GOBIES
GOINGS
GONADS
GONERS
GOOSES
GORALS
GORGES
GORSES
GOUGES
GOURDS
GRACES
GRADES
GRADUS
GRAFTS
GRAINS
GRANTS
GRAPES
GRAPHS
GRASPS
GRATES
GRATIS
GRAVES
GRAZES
GREATS
GREBES
GREEDS
GREEKS
GREENS
GREETS
GREGOS
GRETAS
GRIDES
GRIEFS
GRILLS
GRIMES
GRINDS
GRIPES
GROANS
GROATS
GROINS
GROOMS
GROPES
GROUPS
GROUTS
GROVES
GROWLS
GRUELS
GRUMES
GRUNTS
GUACOS

GUANOS
GUARDS
GUAVAS
GUESTS
GUIDES
GUILDS
GUILES
GUILTS
GUISES
GUMBOS
GUMMAS
GUSHES
GWENNS
GYNOUS
GYRONS

•G•S••

AGISTS
EGESTA
EGESTS

•G••S•

AGHAST
AGUISH
EGOISM
EGOIST
EGRESS
OGRESS
OGRISH

•G•••S

AGAMAS
AGATES
AGAVES
AGENTS
AGGERS
AGISTS
AGLETS
AGONES
AGORAS
AGREES
EGESTS
EGGARS
EGGERS
EGRESS
EGRETS
IGLOOS
OGIVES
OGLERS
OGRESS

••GS••

JIGSAW
PIGSTY

••G•S•

ARGOSY
AUGUST
BAGASS
DEGUST
DIGEST
HUGEST
INGEST
LEGIST
MEGASS
ORGASM
RUGOSE
SAGEST

••G••S

AEGEUS
AGGERS
ANGELS
ANGERS
ANGLES
ARGALS
ARGOTS
ARGUES
AUGERS
AUGHTS
AUGURS
BAGASS
BAGELS
BEGETS
BEGINS
BEGUMS
BIGHTS
BIGOTS
BOGANS
BOGEYS
BOGIES
BOGLES
BUGLES
CIGARS
CYGNUS
DEGUMS
DIGITS
DOGIES
DOGMAS
EAGLES
EDGARS
EGGARS
EGGERS
EIGHTS
ENGELS
FAGOTS
FIGHTS
FOGIES
FUGIOS
FUGLES
FUGUES
GAGERS
GIGUES
HAGGIS
HOGANS
HUGHES
INGOTS
INGRES
LAGERS
LEGERS
LIGHTS
LUGERS
MAGOTS
MEGASS
MOGULS
NIGELS
NIGHTS
ORGANS
ORGIES
PAGANS
PEGGYS
PIGNUS
POGIES
REGIUS
RIGHTS
RIGORS
ROGERS
ROGUES
RUGOUS
SIGHTS
SIGILS
SIGMAS
SUGARS
TIGERS
TIGHTS
TOGUES
UNGUES
UNGUIS
VIGILS
VOGUES
VOGULS
WAGERS
WAGONS
WIGANS
YAGERS
YOGEES
YOGINS

•••GS•

MONGST

•••G•S

ADAGES
ALIGNS
AMIGOS
BADGES
BARGES
BEIGES
BELGAS
BILGES
BINGES
BONGOS
BOUGHS
BRUGES
BUDGES
BULGES
BURGHS
BURGOS
CADGES
CARGOS
COIGNS
CONGAS
CONGES
CORGIS
COUGHS
DEIGNS
DINGUS
DIRGES
DODGES
DOUGHS
FANGAS
FEIGNS
FORGES
FUDGES
FUNGUS
GANGES
GAUGES
GORGES
GOUGES
GREGOS
HAGGIS
HEDGES
HINGES
IMAGES
JORGES
JUDGES
KEDGES
LARGOS
LAUGHS
LEDGES
LEIGHS
LIEGES
LINGAS
LODGES
LOUGHS
LUNGES
LUNGIS
MADGES
MANGOS
MARGES
MARGOS
MERGES
MIDGES
NEIGHS
NUDGES
OMEGAS
PARGOS
PEGGYS
PENGOS
PINGOS
PURGES
RANGES
REIGNS
RIDGES
ROUGES
ROUGHS
SAIGAS
SEDGES
SIEGES
SINGES
SORGOS
SOUGHS
STAGES
SURGES
SWAGES
TAIGAS
TANGOS
THIGHS
TINGES
TOUGHS
TRAGUS
TUNGUS
USAGES
VALGUS
VERGES
VIRGAS
WEDGES
WEIGHS

••••GS

BEFOGS
BEINGS
BOURGS
BRINGS
CHANGS
CLANGS
CLINGS
CRAIGS
DEBUGS
DOINGS
FLINGS
FLONGS
GOINGS
ICINGS
ORANGS
PRONGS
SCRAGS
SHRUGS
SLINGS
SPRAGS
SPRIGS
STINGS
SWINGS
THINGS
THONGS
TWANGS
UNPEGS
UNRIGS
WHANGS
WRINGS
WRONGS

G•T•••

GATHER
GATING
GETTER
GETUPS
GITANO
GOTAMA
GOTHAM
GOTHIC
GOTTEN
GUTTAE
GUTTAT
GUTTED
GUTTER
GUTTLE

G••T••

GAITED
GAITER
GANTRY
GARTER
GASTON
GASTRO
GENTES
GENTLE
GENTOO
GENTRY
GERTIE
GERTYS
GESTIC
GETTER
GHETTO
GIFTED
GIOTTO
GIRTED
GLOTTO
GLUTEI
GLUTEN
GNATHO
GOATEE
GOETHE
GOITER
GOTTEN
GRATED
GRATER
GRATES
GRATIS
GRETAS
GRETEL
GRITTY
GROTTO
GUITAR
GUSTAF
GUSTAV
GUTTAE
GUTTAT
GUTTED
GUTTER
GUTTLE

G•••T•

GAIETY
GAMETE
GAMETO
GAMUTS
GAVOTS
GAYETY
GEMOTS
GENETS
GENITO
GHAUTS
GHETTO
GHOSTS
GIANTS
GIOTTO
GLEETS
GLEETY
GLINTS
GLOATS
GLOSTS
GLOTTO
GLYPTO
GOMUTI
GRAFTS
GRANTS
GREATS
GREETS
GRITTY
GROATS
GROTTO
GROUTS
GROWTH

GRUNTS
GUESTS
GUILTS
GUILTY
GYRATE

G••••T
GADGET
GALACT
GALIOT
GALOOT
GAMBIT
GANNET
GARGET
GARNET
GARRET
GASKET
GAYEST
GERENT
GIBBET
GIBLET
GIGANT
GIGLET
GIGLOT
GIMLET
GOBBET
GOBLET
GOCART
GODWIT
GOGLET
GOKART
GORGET
GRIVET
GULLET
GUSSET
GUTTAT

•G•T••
AGATES
AGATHA

•G••T•
AGENTS
AGISTS
AGLETS
AGNATE
AGOUTI
AGOUTY
EGESTA
EGESTS
EGRETS
IGNITE

•G•••T
AGHAST
EGBERT
EGOIST
IGOROT

••GT••
HOGTIE
PEGTOP
RAGTAG

••G•T•
ARGOTS
AUGHTS
AUGITE
BEGETS
BIGHTS
BIGOTS
BOGOTA
DIGITI
DIGITS
EIGHTH
EIGHTS
EIGHTY
ERGATE
FAGOTS
FIGHTS
INGOTS
JUGATE
LEGATE
LEGATO
LIGATE
LIGHTS
MAGOTS
MIGHTY
NEGATE
NIGHTS
NIGHTY
PIGSTY
RIGHTO
RIGHTS
RUGATE
SIGHTS
TIGHTS
ZYGOTE

••G••T
AIGLET
ARGENT
AUGUST
BEGIRT
COGENT
CYGNET
DEGUST
DIGEST
DIGLOT
DUGOUT
EAGLET
ENGIRT
FAGGOT
GIGANT
GIGLET
GIGLOT
GOGLET
HAGBUT
HOGNUT
HUGEST
INGEST
LEGIST
MAGGOT
MAGNET
NUGGET
ORGEAT
PIGNUT
RAGOUT

REGENT
REGLET
REGRET
SAGEST
SIGNET
UNGIRT
URGENT
YOGURT

•••GT•
LENGTH

•••G•T
ALIGHT
ARIGHT
BLIGHT
BOUGHT
BRIGHT
BUDGET
CATGUT
CAUGHT
DWIGHT
ELEGIT
FAGGOT
FIDGET
FLIGHT
FORGET
FORGOT
FOUGHT
FRIGHT
GADGET
GARGET
GORGET
HEIGHT
KNIGHT
MAGGOT
MARGOT
MIDGET
MIDGUT
MONGST
NAUGHT
NOUGAT
NOUGHT
NUGGET
PARGET
PLIGHT
ROTGUT
SLIGHT
SOUGHT
SPIGOT
TARGET
TAUGHT
WEIGHT
WRIGHT

GU••••
GUACOS
GUANIN
GUANOS
GUARDS
GUAVAS
GUENON
GUESTS
GUFFAW

GUIANA
GUIDED
GUIDER
GUIDES
GUIDON
GUILDS
GUILES
GUILTS
GUILTY
GUIMPE
GUINEA
GUISES
GUITAR
GULDEN
GULFED
GULLAH
GULLET
GULPED
GULPER
GUMBOS
GUMMAS
GUMMED
GUNMAN
GUNMEN
GUNNAR
GUNNED
GUNNEL
GUNNER
GUNSHY
GURGLE
GURKHA
GUSHED
GUSHER
GUSHES
GUSSET
GUSSIE
GUSTAF
GUSTAV
GUTTAE
GUTTAT
GUTTED
GUTTER
GUTTLE
GUYANA
GUYING
GUZZLE

G•U•••
GAUCHE
GAUCHO
GAUGED
GAUGER
GAUGES
GAUZES
GIULIA
GIULIO
GLUIER
GLUING
GLUMES
GLUMLY
GLUTEI
GLUTEN
GOUGED
GOUGER

GOUGES
GOURDE
GOURDS
GRUBBY
GRUDGE
GRUELS
GRUGRU
GRUMES
GRUMPY
GRUNDY
GRUNTS

G••U••
GAMUTS
GERUND
GETUPS
GHAUTS
GHOULS
GIGUES
GLAUCO
GOMUTI
GROUCH
GROUND
GROUPS
GROUSE
GROUTS

G•••U•
GALLUP
GALLUS
GAMOUS
GANGUE
GENIUS
GENOUS
GEROUS
GIAOUR
GONIUM
GRADUS
GYNOUS
GYPSUM

G••••U
GRUGRU

•GU•••
AGUISH
IGUANA

•G•U••
AGOUTI
AGOUTY

•G••U•
AGOGUE

••GU••
ARGUED
ARGUER
ARGUES
ARGUFY
AUGURS
AUGURY
AUGUST
BEGUIN

BEGUMS
DEGUMS
DEGUST
ENGULF
FIGURE
FUGUES
GIGUES
INGULF
JAGUAR
LAGUNE
LEGUME
LIGULA
LIGULE
LIGURE
MAGUEY
MIGUEL
MOGULS
ROGUED
ROGUES
TOGUES
UNGUAL
UNGUES
UNGUIS
UNGULA
VAGUER
VOGUES
VOGULS
YOGURT

••G•U•
AEGEUS
CYGNUS
DUGOUT
HAGBUT
HOGNUT
MAGNUM
MUGGUR
PIGNUS
PIGNUT
RAGOUT
REGIUS
RUGOUS
VIGOUR

•••GU•
AGOGUE
BANGUI
BANGUP
BROGUE
CANGUE
CATGUT
DENGUE
DINGUS
FUNGUS
GANGUE
HANGUP
LANGUR
LEAGUE
LINGUA
MIDGUT
MORGUE
MUGGUR
PLAGUE
PLAGUY

6

POPGUN
PRAGUE
ROTGUT
SANGUI
SHOGUN
TERGUM
TONGUE
TRAGUS
TUNGUS
VALGUS

•••G•U
CONGOU
GRUGRU

••••GU
TELUGU

G•V•••
GAVELS
GAVIAL
GAVOTS
GIVING
GOVERN

G••V••
GLOVED
GLOVER
GLOVES
GRAVED
GRAVEL
GRAVEN
GRAVER
GRAVES
GRAVID
GRIVET
GROVEL
GROVER
GROVES
GUAVAS

G•••V•
GENEVA
GODIVA
GREAVE
GRIEVE
GROOVE
GROOVY

G••••V
GUSTAV

•G•V••
AGAVES
OGIVES

••G•V•
ARGIVE

GW••••
GWENNS
GWYNNE

G•W•••
GAWAIN
GAWKED
GEWGAW
GOWNED

G••W••
GALWAY
GLOWED
GLOWER
GNAWED
GNAWER
GODWIN
GODWIT
GROWER
GROWLS
GROWTH

G••••W
GEWGAW
GUFFAW

••GW••
BIGWIG
COGWAY
WIGWAG
WIGWAM

••G••W
FOGBOW
JIGSAW

•••G•W
GEWGAW

G•••X•
GALAXY

GY••••
GYNECO
GYNOUS
GYPPED
GYPSUM
GYRATE
GYRONS
GYROSE

G•Y•••
GAYEST
GAYETY
GDYNIA
GEYSER
GLYCOL
GLYNIS
GLYPHS
GLYPTO
GUYANA
GUYING
GWYNNE

G••Y••
GALYAK
GERYON
GRAYED
GRAYER
GRAYLY

G•••Y•
GERRYS
GERTYS
GLADYS

G••••Y
GADFLY
GAIETY
GAINLY
GALAXY
GALLEY
GALWAY
GAMELY
GAMILY
GANTRY
GAYETY
GENTRY
GHARRY
GIGGLY
GLADLY
GLAIRY
GLASSY
GLEAMY
GLEETY
GLIBLY
GLOOMY
GLOSSY
GLUMLY
GNARLY
GOODBY
GOODLY
GOOGLY
GOONEY
GOOSEY
GORILY
GRAINY
GRANNY
GRAPHY
GRASSY
GRAYLY
GREASY
GREEDY
GRIMLY
GRIPPY
GRISLY
GRITTY
GROGGY
GROOVY
GROSZY
GRUBBY
GRUMPY
GRUNDY
GUILTY
GUNSHY

•G•••Y
AGEDLY
AGENCY
AGOUTY
IGNIFY
UGLIFY
UGLILY

••GY••
ARGYLE
ARGYLL
MAGYAR

••G•Y•
BOGEYS
NAGOYA
PEGGYS

••G••Y
ANGARY
ARGOSY
ARGUFY
AUGURY
BIGAMY
CAGILY
COGWAY
DIGAMY
EIGHTY
GIGGLY
HIGHLY
HUGELY
LEGACY
MAGUEY
MIGHTY
NIGHTY
PIGSTY
PUGGRY
SAGELY
SUGARY
VAGARY
WAGGLY
WIGGLY

•••GY•
PEGGYS

•••G•Y
CLOGGY
CRAGGY
DINGEY
DINGHY
DOUGHY
DREGGY
FLAGGY
FROGGY
GIGGLY
GOOGLY
GROGGY
HUNGRY
JUNGLY
KINGLY
MARGAY
PLAGUY
PUGGRY
QUAGGY
SHAGGY
SINGLY
SLAGGY
SMUGLY
SNAGGY
SNUGLY
STAGEY
STAGGY
STOGEY
TANGLY
TINGLY
TRIGLY
TWIGGY
WAGGLY
WIGGLY

••••GY
ANERGY
CLERGY
CLINGY
CLOGGY
CRAGGY
DREGGY
EFFIGY
ENERGY
EULOGY
FLAGGY
FLEDGY
FRINGY
FROGGY
GROGGY
OOLOGY
QUAGGY
RRHAGY
SHAGGY
SLAGGY
SLANGY
SLUDGY
SMUDGY
SNAGGY
SPONGY
STAGGY
STINGY
STODGY
SYZYGY
TWANGY
TWIGGY

G•Z•••
GAZABO
GAZEBO
GAZERS
GAZING
GIZMOS
GUZZLE

G••Z••
GAUZES
GEEZER
GLAZED
GLAZER
GLAZES
GLOZED
GLOZES
GRAZED
GRAZER
GRAZES
GRIZEL
GUZZLE

G•••Z•
GROSZY

••GZ••
ZIGZAG

HA••••
HABILE
HABITS
HACKED
HACKEE
HACKER
HACKIE
HACKLE
HADING
HAGBUT
HAGDON
HAGGIS
HAGGLE
HAILED
HAILER
HAIRDO
HAIRED
HAKIMS
HALERS
HALIDE
HALIDS
HALING
HALITE
HALLAH
HALLEL
HALLEY
HALLOO
HALLOW
HALLUX
HALOES
HALOID
HALSEY
HALTED
HALTER
HALUTZ
HALVED
HALVES
HAMALS
HAMAUL
HAMDEN
HAMITE
HAMLET
HAMMAL
HAMMED
HAMMER
HAMPER
HAMZAS
HANCES
HANDED
HANDEL
HANDLE
HANGAR
HANGED
HANGER
HANGUP
HANKER
HANNAH
HANNAS

6

HANSEL
HANSOM
HAPPEN
HARASS
HARBIN
HARBOR
HARDEN
HARDER
HARDLY
HAREMS
HARKED
HARKEN
HARLAN
HARLEM
HARLEY
HARLOT
HARMED
HARMIN
HAROLD
HARPED
HARPER
HARROW
HARRYS
HARTAL
HARVEY
HASHED
HASHES
HASLET
HASPED
HASSEL
HASSLE
HASTED
HASTEN
HASTES
HATBOX
HATERS
HATFUL
HATING
HATPIN
HATRED
HATTED
HATTER
HATTIE
HATTYS
HAULED
HAULER
HAULMY
HAUNCH
HAUNTS
HAUSEN
HAVANA
HAVENS
HAVENT
HAVING
HAWAII
HAWHAW
HAWING
HAWKED
HAWKER
HAWSER
HAWSES
HAYING
HAYMOW
HAZARD
HAZELS
HAZERS
HAZIER
HAZILY
HAZING
HAZZAN

H•A•••

HEADED
HEADER
HEADON
HEALED
HEALER
HEALTH
HEAPED
HEARER
HEARSE
HEARST
HEARTH
HEARTS
HEARTY
HEATED
HEATER
HEATHS
HEATHY
HEAUME
HEAVED
HEAVEN
HEAVER
HEAVES
HIATUS
HOARDS
HOARSE
HOAXED
HOAXER
HOAXES
HYADES

H••A••

HAMALS
HAMAUL
HARASS
HAVANA
HAWAII
HAZARD
HBEAMS
HECATE
HEMATO
HEPATO
HERALD
HEXADS
HEXANE
HIJACK
HILARY
HIRAMS
HOBART
HOGANS
HOLARD
HOMAGE
HORACE
HORARY
HOWARD
HUMANE
HUMANS

H•••A•

HALLAH
HAMMAL
HAMZAS
HANGAR
HANNAH
HANNAS
HARLAN
HARTAL
HAWHAW
HAZZAN
HEDRAL
HEEHAW
HELLAS
HENNAS
HEPTAD
HERBAL
HEREAT
HERMAE
HERMAI
HERMAN
HETMAN
HEYDAY
HIEMAL
HILDAS
HOOKAH
HOORAY
HOWDAH
HUBCAP
HURRAH
HURRAY
HUSSAR
HYDRAE
HYDRAS
HYENAS
HYETAL
HYMNAL
HYPHAE
HYPHAL

H••••A

HAVANA
HECUBA
HEGIRA
HEJIRA
HELENA
HERNIA
HESTIA
HOOPLA
HUELVA
HYGEIA

•HA•••

CHABUK
CHACMA
CHAETA
CHAETO
CHAFED
CHAFER
CHAFES
CHAFFS
CHAFFY
CHAINS
CHAIRS
CHAISE
CHALCO
CHALEH
CHALET
CHALKS
CHALKY
CHAMMY
CHAMPS
CHANCE
CHANCY
CHANGE
CHANGS
CHANTS
CHANTY
CHAPEL
CHAPES
CHARDS
CHARED
CHARES
CHARGE
CHARMS
CHARON
CHARRY
CHARTS
CHASED
CHASER
CHASES
CHASMS
CHASSE
CHASTE
CHATTY
CHAWED
DHARMA
DHARNA
GHARRI
GHARRY
GHAUTS
KHAKIS
PHAGIA
PHASED
PHASES
PHASIA
PHASIC
PHASIS
SHABBY
SHACKO
SHACKS
SHADED
SHADES
SHADOW
SHAFTS
SHAGGY
SHAKEN
SHAKER
SHAKES
SHAKOS
SHALED
SHALES
SHAMAN
SHAMED
SHAMES
SHAMMY
SHAMUS
SHANKS
SHANTY
SHAPED
SHAPEN
SHAPER
SHAPES
SHARDS
SHARED
SHARER
SHARES
SHARKS
SHARON
SHARPS
SHASTA
SHAVED
SHAVEN
SHAVER
SHAVES
SHAWLS
SHAWMS
THADDY
THADYS
THALES
THALIA
THAMES
THANAT
THANES
THANKS
THATCH
THAWED
THAYER
WHACKS
WHALED
WHALER
WHALES
WHAMMY
WHANGS
WHARFS
WHARVE

•H•A••

CHEATS
CHIASM
CHIAUS
IHRAMS
OHMAGE
PHIALS
PHRASE
SHEARS
SHEATH
SHEAVE
SHOALS
SHOALY
SHOATS
SHRANK
THRALL
THRASH
THWACK
THWART
WHEALS
WHEATS

•H••A•

BHUTAN
CHELAE
CHELAS
CHETAH
CHORAL
CHUFAS
OHIOAN
PHYLAE
RHINAL
RHODAS
SHAMAN
SHEBAT
SHIKAR
SHOFAR
SHORAN
THANAT
THEBAE
THECAE
THECAL
THEDAS
THENAL
THENAR
THETAS
THOMAS
THORAC
THORAX
THREAD
THREAT
THROAT
THUJAS
WHIDAH
WHYDAH

•H•••A

AHIMSA
CHACMA
CHAETA
CHOLLA
CHOREA
CHROMA
DHARMA
DHARNA
DHURNA
PHAGIA
PHASIA
PHILIA
PHOBIA
PHONIA
RHUMBA
SHASTA
SHEILA
SHERPA
THALIA
THELMA
THORIA
THULIA

••HA••

ACHAEA
ACHAIA
AGHAST
BAHAIS
BAHAMA
BEHALF
BEHAVE
BIHARI

ECHARD
EPHAHS
ETHANE
ETHANS
EXHALE
INHALE
INHAUL
ITHACA
JIHADS
JOHANN
MOHAIR
MOHAVE
MOHAWK
PSHAWS
REHASH
RRHAGE
RRHAGY
SAHARA
UNHAIR
UNHAND
UNHATS
WAHABI

••H•A•
ASHLAR
ASHMAN
BEHEAD
ISHTAR
LEHUAS
REHEAR
REHEAT
SCHWAS

••H••A
ACHAEA
ACHAIA
APHTHA
ATHENA
BAHAMA
DAHLIA
ITHACA
SAHARA
SCHEMA

•••HA•
AFGHAN
ALPHAS
BASHAW
CASHAW
CATHAY
CUSHAT
CUSHAW
DACHAS
DACHAU
DIRHAM
DURHAM
ESCHAR
GOTHAM
GRAHAM
HAWHAW
HEEHAW
HYPHAE
HYPHAL
LETHAL

MAYHAP
MISHAP
NATHAN
NUCHAE
ORPHAN
PASHAS
PATHAN
RAPHAE
SAPHAR
SASHAY
UTAHAN
WITHAL

•••H•A
ALTHEA
ANTHEA
ASTHMA
BRAHMA
ISCHIA
JOSHUA
LITHIA
LOCHIA
NASHUA
PATHIA
PYTHIA
SOPHIA

••••HA
AGATHA
APHTHA
AYESHA
BERTHA
BUDDHA
CONCHA
ELISHA
GEISHA
GURKHA
MALTHA
MARSHA
MARTHA
NYMPHA
PYRRHA
SRADHA
SULPHA

HB••••
HBEAMS
HBOMBS

H•B•••
HABILE
HABITS
HEBREW
HEBRON
HOBART
HOBBES
HOBBLE
HOBNOB
HOBOES
HUBBUB
HUBCAP
HUBERT
HUBRIS
HYBRID

HYBRIS

H••B••
HAGBUT
HARBIN
HARBOR
HATBOX
HENBIT
HERBAL
HOBBES
HOBBLE
HOMBRE
HOTBED
HOTBOX
HUBBUB
HUMBLE
HUMBLY
HUMBUG

H•••B•
HBOMBS
HECUBA
HEREBY

H••••B
HOBNOB
HUBBUB

•H•B••
CHABUK
CHEBEC
CHUBBY
GHEBER
KHYBER
PHOBIA
SHABBY
SHEBAT
THEBAE
THEBES

•H••B•
CHUBBY
PHLEBO
PHOEBE
RHOMBI
RHUMBA
RHUMBS
SHABBY
SHELBY
SHRUBS
THROBS
THUMBS

•H•••B
CHERUB

••H•B•
EPHEBI
SAHEBS
SAHIBS
WAHABI

H•C•••
HACKED

HACKEE
HACKER
HACKIE
HACKLE
HECATE
HECKLE
HECTIC
HECTOR
HECUBA
HICCUP
HICKEY
HICKOK
HOCKED
HOCKEY
HUCKLE

H••C••
HANCES
HICCUP
HOICKS
HUBCAP

H•••C•
HAUNCH
HELICO
HIJACK
HOOTCH
HORACE

H••••C
HECTIC
HERDIC
HEROIC
HOLMIC
HYDRIC
HYMNIC
HYPNIC

•H•C••
CHACMA
CHECKS
CHICHI
CHICKS
CHICLE
CHICOS
CHOCKS
CHUCKS
PHOCIS
SHACKO
SHACKS
SHOCKS
SHUCKS
THECAE
THECAL
WHACKS

•H••C•
CHALCO
CHANCE
CHANCY
CHINCH
CHOICE
CHURCH
SHTICK

THATCH
THENCE
THRICE
THWACK
WHENCE

•H•••C
CHEBEC
CHORIC
CHYMIC
PHASIC
PHONIC
PHOTIC
PHYSIC
RHODIC
THETIC
THORAC
THORIC
THYMIC

••H•C•
ETHICS
ITHACA
MOHOCK
SCHICK

••H••C
ECHOIC
ETHNIC

•••H•C
GOTHIC
LITHIC
MYTHIC
ORPHIC
PYTHIC
SOTHIC

H•D•••
HADING
HEDDLE
HEDGED
HEDGER
HEDGES
HEDRAL
HEDRON
HEDWIG
HIDDEN
HIDERS
HIDING
HODDEN
HUDDLE
HUDSON
HYDRAE
HYDRAS
HYDRIC
HYDROS

H••D••
HAGDON
HAMDEN
HANDED
HANDEL
HANDLE

HARDEN
HARDER
HARDLY
HEADED
HEADER
HEADON
HEDDLE
HEEDED
HEEDER
HERDED
HERDER
HERDIC
HEYDAY
HIDDEN
HILDAS
HINDER
HINDUS
HODDEN
HOIDEN
HOLDER
HOLDUP
HOODED
HOODOO
HORDED
HORDES
HOWDAH
HOYDEN
HUDDLE
HURDLE
HYADES

H•••D•
HAIRDO
HALIDE
HALIDS
HEXADS
HOARDS
HOUNDS
HYOIDS

H••••D
HACKED
HAILED
HAIRED
HALOID
HALTED
HALVED
HAMMED
HANDED
HANGED
HARKED
HARMED
HAROLD
HARPED
HASHED
HASPED
HASTED
HATRED
HATTED
HAULED
HAWKED
HAZARD
HEADED
HEALED

6

HEAPED
HEATED
HEAVED
HEDGED
HEEDED
HEELED
HEFTED
HELPED
HEMMED
HEMOID
HEPTAD
HERALD
HERDED
HESIOD
HILLED
HILTED
HINGED
HINTED
HIPPED
HISPID
HISSED
HOAXED
HOCKED
HOGGED
HOLARD
HONIED
HONKED
HOODED
HOOFED
HOOKED
HOOPED
HOOTED
HOPPED
HORDED
HORNED
HORRID
HORSED
HOSTED
HOTBED
HOUSED
HOWARD
HOWLED
HUFFED
HUGGED
HULKED
HULLED
HUMMED
HUMPED
HUNTED
HURLED
HUSHED
HUSKED
HUTTED
HYBRID
HYMNED

•H•D••

CHIDED
CHIDER
CHIDES
RHODAS
RHODIC
SHADED
SHADES
SHADOW
SHODDY
THADDY
THADYS
THEDAS
WHIDAH
WHYDAH

•H••D•

CHARDS
CHONDR
CHORDS
SHARDS
SHERDS
SHINDY
SHODDY
SHREDS
THADDY
THIRDS

•H•••D

CHAFED
CHARED
CHASED
CHAWED
CHEWED
CHIDED
CHIMED
CHOKED
PHASED
PHONED
RHYMED
SHADED
SHALED
SHAMED
SHAPED
SHARED
SHAVED
SHEWED
SHIELD
SHINED
SHOOED
SHORED
SHOULD
SHOVED
SHOWED
SHREWD
SHROUD
THAWED
THREAD
THREED
WHALED
WHILED
WHINED
WHITED
WHORED

••H•D•

APHIDS
EPHODS
JIHADS

••H••D

BEHEAD
BEHELD
BEHIND
BEHOLD
ECHARD
ECHOED
TEHEED
UNHAND
UPHELD
UPHOLD

•••H•D

ARCHED
BACHED
BASHED
BATHED
BUSHED
CACHED
CASHED
COSHED
DASHED
DISHED
ETCHED
FISHED
GASHED
GUSHED
HASHED
HUSHED
INCHED
ITCHED
JOSHED
LASHED
LATHED
LUSHED
MASHED
MESHED
METHOD
MUSHED
NICHED
ORCHID
PISHED
PITHED
PUSHED
RUSHED
SASHED
SIGHED
TITHED
TUSHED
WASHED
WISHED
WITHED

HE••••

HEADED
HEADER
HEADON
HEALED
HEALER
HEALTH
HEAPED
HEARER
HEARSE
HEARST
HEARTH
HEARTS
HEARTY
HEATED
HEATER
HEATHS
HEATHY
HEAUME
HEAVED
HEAVEN
HEAVER
HEAVES
HEBREW
HEBRON
HECATE
HECKLE
HECTIC
HECTOR
HECUBA
HEDDLE
HEDGED
HEDGER
HEDGES
HEDRAL
HEDRON
HEDWIG
HEEDED
HEEDER
HEEHAW
HEELED
HEELER
HEFTED
HEGIRA
HEIFER
HEIGHT
HEISTS
HEJIRA
HELENA
HELENS
HELICO
HELIOS
HELIUM
HELLAS
HELLEN
HELLER
HELMET
HELOTS
HELPED
HELPER
HELVES
HEMATO
HEMMED
HEMMER
HEMOID
HEMPEN
HENBIT
HENLEY
HENNAS
HENRIS
HENRYS
HEPATO
HEPTAD
HERALD
HERBAL
HERDED
HERDER
HERDIC
HEREAT
HEREBY
HEREIN
HEREOF
HEREON
HERESY
HERETO
HERIOT
HERMAE
HERMAI
HERMAN
HERMES
HERMIT
HERNIA
HERNIO
HEROES
HEROIC
HEROIN
HERONS
HERPES
HESIOD
HESTER
HESTIA
HETERO
HETMAN
HETTYS
HEWERS
HEWING
HEXADS
HEXANE
HEXING
HEXONE
HEXOSE
HEXYLS
HEYDAY

H•E•••

HBEAMS
HEEDED
HEEDER
HEEHAW
HEELED
HEELER
HIEING
HIEMAL
HOEING
HUELVA
HYENAS
HYETAL

H••E••

HALERS
HAREMS
HATERS
HAVENS
HAVENT
HAZELS
HAZERS
HELENA
HELENS
HEREAT
HEREBY
HEREIN
HEREOF
HEREON
HERESY
HERETO
HETERO
HEWERS
HIDERS
HIKERS
HIRERS
HOMELY
HOMERS
HONEST
HONEYS
HOTELS
HOVELS
HOVERS
HUBERT
HUGELY
HUGEST
HYGEIA
HYMENO
HYMENS

H•••E•

HACKED
HACKEE
HACKER
HAILED
HAILER
HAIRED
HALLEL
HALLEY
HALOES
HALSEY
HALTED
HALTER
HALVED
HALVES
HAMDEN
HAMLET
HAMMED
HAMMER
HAMPER
HANCES
HANDED
HANDEL
HANGED
HANGER
HANKER
HANSEL
HAPPEN
HARDEN
HARDER
HARKED
HARKEN
HARLEM
HARLEY
HARMED
HARPED
HARPER
HARVEY
HASHED
HASHES
HASLET

HASPED
HASSEL
HASTED
HASTEN
HASTES
HATRED
HATTED
HATTER
HAULED
HAULER
HAUSEN
HAWKED
HAWKER
HAWSER
HAWSES
HAZIER
HEADED
HEADER
HEALED
HEALER
HEAPED
HEARER
HEATED
HEATER
HEAVED
HEAVEN
HEAVER
HEAVES
HEBREW
HEDGED
HEDGER
HEDGES
HEEDED
HEEDER
HEELED
HEELER
HEFTED
HEIFER
HELLEN
HELLER
HELMET
HELPED
HELPER
HELVES
HEMMED
HEMMER
HEMPEN
HENLEY
HERDED
HERDER
HERMES
HEROES
HERPES
HESTER
HICKEY
HIDDEN
HIGHER
HILLED
HILLER
HILTED
HINDER
HINGED
HINGES
HINTED
HIPPED
HISSED
HISSER
HISSES
HITHER
HITLER
HITTER
HOAXED
HOAXER
HOAXES
HOBBES
HOBOES
HOCKED
HOCKEY
HODDEN
HOGGED
HOIDEN
HOLDER
HOLIER
HOLIES
HOLLER
HOLMES
HOMIER
HONIED
HONKED
HONKER
HOODED
HOOFED
HOOFER
HOOKED
HOOKER
HOOPED
HOOPER
HOOTED
HOOVER
HOOVES
HOPPED
HOPPER
HORDED
HORDES
HORNED
HORNET
HORSED
HORSES
HORSEY
HOSIER
HOSTED
HOSTEL
HOTBED
HOTTER
HOUSED
HOUSES
HOWLED
HOWLER
HOYDEN
HUFFED
HUGGED
HUGHES
HULKED
HULLED
HUMMED
HUMMER
HUMPED
HUNGER
HUNTED
HUNTER
HURLED
HURLER
HURTER
HUSHED
HUSHES
HUSKED
HUSKER
HUTTED
HUXLEY
HYADES
HYMNED
HYPHEN
HYSTER

H••••E

HABILE
HACKEE
HACKIE
HACKLE
HAGGLE
HALIDE
HALITE
HAMITE
HANDLE
HASSLE
HATTIE
HEARSE
HEAUME
HECATE
HECKLE
HEDDLE
HERMAE
HEXANE
HEXONE
HEXOSE
HIGGLE
HIPPIE
HOARSE
HOBBLE
HOGTIE
HOMAGE
HOMBRE
HONORE
HOOPOE
HOPPLE
HORACE
HORNIE
HORSTE
HUCKLE
HUDDLE
HUGHIE
HUMANE
HUMBLE
HURDLE
HURTLE
HUSTLE
HYDRAE
HYPHAE

•HE•••

CHEATS
CHEBEC
CHECKS
CHEEKS
CHEEKY
CHEEPS
CHEERS
CHEERY
CHEESE
CHEESY
CHEGOE
CHEILO
CHEIRO
CHELAE
CHELAS
CHEOPS
CHERRY
CHERUB
CHERYL
CHESTS
CHESTY
CHETAH
CHEWED
CHEWER
GHEBER
GHETTO
OHENRY
PHENOL
PHENYL
RHEIMS
RHESUS
RHETOR
RHEUMY
SHEARS
SHEATH
SHEAVE
SHEBAT
SHEENS
SHEENY
SHEERS
SHEETS
SHEIKS
SHEILA
SHEKEL
SHELBY
SHELLS
SHELLY
SHELTY
SHELVE
SHERDS
SHERIF
SHERPA
SHERRY
SHEWED
SHEWER
THEBAE
THEBES
THECAE
THECAL
THEDAS
THEFTS
THEIRS
THEISM
THEIST
THELMA
THEMES
THEMIS
THENAL
THENAR
THENCE
THEORY
THERMO
THERMS
THESES
THESIS
THETAS
THETIC
THETIS
WHEALS
WHEATS
WHEELS
WHEEZE
WHEEZY
WHELKS
WHELKY
WHELMS
WHELPS
WHENCE
WHERRY
WHERVE
WHEYEY

•H•E••

CHAETA
CHAETO
CHEEKS
CHEEKY
CHEEPS
CHEERS
CHEERY
CHEESE
CHEESY
CHIEFS
PHLEBO
PHLEGM
PHOEBE
PHRENO
SHEENS
SHEENY
SHEERS
SHEETS
SHIELD
SHIEST
SHOERS
SHREDS
SHREWD
SHREWS
SHYEST
THIEVE
THREAD
THREAT
THREED
THREES
THRESH
WHEELS
WHEEZE
WHEEZY

•H••E•

CHAFED
CHAFER
CHAFES
CHALEH
CHALET
CHAPEL
CHAPES
CHARED
CHARES
CHASED
CHASER
CHASES
CHAWED
CHEBEC
CHEWED
CHEWER
CHIDED
CHIDER
CHIDES
CHIMED
CHIMER
CHIMES
CHINES
CHISEL
CHIVES
CHLOES
CHOKED
CHOKER
CHOKES
CHOLER
CHOREA
CHOREO
CHORES
CHOSEN
CHUTES
DHOLES
GHEBER
KHYBER
PHASED
PHASES
PHLOEM
PHONED
PHONES
PHONEY
PHOOEY
RHYMED
RHYMER
RHYMES
SHADED
SHADES
SHAKEN
SHAKER
SHAKES
SHALED
SHALES
SHAMED
SHAMES
SHAPED
SHAPEN
SHAPER
SHAPES
SHARED
SHARER
SHARES
SHAVED

SHAVEN
SHAVER
SHAVES
SHEKEL
SHEWED
SHEWER
SHINED
SHINER
SHINES
SHIRES
SHIVER
SHIVES
SHOOED
SHORED
SHORES
SHOTES
SHOVED
SHOVEL
SHOVER
SHOVES
SHOWED
SHOWER
SHRIEK
THALES
THAMES
THANES
THAWED
THAYER
THEBES
THEMES
THESES
THOLES
THREED
THREES
THROES
THYMES
THYREO
WHALED
WHALER
WHALES
WHEYEY
WHILED
WHILES
WHINED
WHINER
WHINES
WHITED
WHITEN
WHITER
WHITES
WHITEY
WHORED
WHORES

•H•••E
CHAISE
CHANCE
CHANGE
CHARGE
CHASSE
CHASTE
CHEESE
CHEGOE
CHELAE
CHICLE
CHIGOE
CHOICE
CHOOSE
CHROME
OHMAGE
PHOEBE
PHRASE
PHYLAE
SHEAVE
SHELVE
SHIITE
SHOPPE
SHRIKE
SHRINE
SHRIVE
SHROVE
THEBAE
THECAE
THENCE
THIEVE
THORPE
THRICE
THRIVE
THRONE
THROVE
THYRSE
WHARVE
WHEEZE
WHENCE
WHERVE

••HE••
ACHENE
ADHERE
ATHENA
ATHENE
ATHENS
BEHEAD
BEHELD
BEHEST
COHERE
EPHEBI
ETHELS
ETHERS
INHERE
OCHERS
OCHERY
OTHERS
REHEAR
REHEAT
SAHEBS
SCHEMA
SCHEME
SPHENE
SPHENO
SPHERE
SPHERY
TEHEED
TEHEES
UPHELD
USHERS

••H•E•
ACHAEA
ASHIER
ASHLEY
ASHMEN
CAHIER
ECHOED
ECHOER
ECHOES
FUHRER
MAHLER
TEHEED
TEHEES
YAHVEH
YAHWEH

••H••E
ACHENE
ADHERE
ASHORE
ATHENE
ATHOME
AWHILE
BEHAVE
BEHOVE
COHERE
COHUNE
ETHANE
EXHALE
EXHUME
INHALE
INHERE
LAHORE
MOHAVE
MOHOLE
OPHITE
RRHAGE
SCHEME
SPHENE
SPHERE
UPHROE
WAHINE

•••HE•
AACHEN
AETHER
ALTHEA
ANTHEA
ANTHEM
ANTHER
ARCHED
ARCHEO
ARCHER
ARCHES
BACHED
BACHES
BASHED
BASHES
BATHED
BATHER
BETHEL
BOSHES
BOTHER
BUSHED
BUSHEL
BUSHES
CACHED
CACHES
CACHET
CASHED
CASHES
CASHEW
CATHER
CIPHER
CITHER
COSHED
COSHER
COSHES
CYPHER
DASHED
DASHER
DASHES
DISHED
DISHES
DITHER
EITHER
ESCHEW
ESTHER
ETCHED
ETCHER
ETCHES
FATHER
FICHES
FISHED
FISHER
FISHES
GASHED
GASHES
GATHER
GOPHER
GORHEN
GOSHEN
GUSHED
GUSHER
GUSHES
HASHED
HASHES
HIGHER
HITHER
HUGHES
HUSHED
HUSHES
HYPHEN
INCHED
INCHES
ISOHEL
ITCHED
ITCHES
JAPHET
JOSHED
JOSHER
JOSHES
KOSHER
KUCHEN
LACHES
LASHED
LASHER
LASHES
LATHED
LATHER
LATHES
LECHER
LICHEE
LICHEN
LITHER
LUSHED
LUSHER
LUSHES
LUTHER
MASHED
MASHER
MASHES
MAYHEM
MESHED
MESHES
MICHEL
MOTHER
MUSHED
MUSHER
MUSHES
NEPHEW
NETHER
NICHED
NICHES
NIGHER
PEAHEN
PISHED
PISHES
PITHED
POTHER
PUSHED
PUSHER
PUSHES
RACHEL
RASHER
RASHES
RATHER
RICHER
RICHES
ROCHET
RUCHES
RUSHED
RUSHER
RUSHES
SACHEM
SACHET
SASHED
SASHES
SIGHED
SYPHER
TETHER
TITHED
TITHER
TITHES
TOSHES
TOTHER
TUSHED
TUSHES
WASHED
WASHER
WASHES
WETHER
WICHES
WISHED
WISHES
WITHED
WITHER
WITHES
ZITHER

•••H•E
ARCHIE
DAPHNE
EUCHRE
HUGHIE
HYPHAE
KATHIE
LICHEE
MASHIE
NUCHAE
RAPHAE
RICHIE
SOPHIE

••••HE
APACHE
BERTHE
BLITHE
BUNCHE
CLICHE
CLOCHE
CLOTHE
CRECHE
DOUCHE
FLECHE
GAUCHE
GOETHE
LOATHE
MARTHE
MOISHE
PSYCHE
ROTCHE
ROUCHE
SCATHE
SCYTHE
SEETHE
SEICHE
SNATHE
SOOTHE
SPATHE
SWATHE
TEETHE
TOUCHE
TRACHE
TROCHE
WRITHE

H•F•••
HEFTED
HUFFED

H••F••
HATFUL
HEIFER
HOOFED
HOOFER

HUFFED

H••••F

HEREOF

•H•F••

CHAFED
CHAFER
CHAFES
CHAFFS
CHAFFY
CHUFAS
SHAFTS
SHIFTS
SHIFTY
SHOFAR
THEFTS
WHIFFS

•H••F•

CHAFFS
CHAFFY
CHIEFS
SHRIFT
SHROFF
THRIFT
WHARFS
WHIFFS

•H•••F

SHERIF
SHROFF

••H••F

BEHALF
BEHOOF

H•G•••

HAGBUT
HAGDON
HAGGIS
HAGGLE
HEGIRA
HIGGLE
HIGHER
HIGHLY
HOGANS
HOGGED
HOGNUT
HOGTIE
HUGELY
HUGEST
HUGGED
HUGHES
HUGHIE
HYGEIA

H••G••

HAGGIS
HAGGLE
HANGAR
HANGED
HANGER
HANGUP
HEDGED
HEDGER
HEDGES
HEIGHT
HIGGLE
HINGED
HINGES
HOGGED
HUGGED
HUNGER
HUNGRY

H•••G•

HOMAGE

H••••G

HADING
HALING
HATING
HAVING
HAWING
HAYING
HAZING
HEDWIG
HEWING
HEXING
HIDING
HIEING
HIKING
HIRING
HIVING
HOEING
HOLING
HOMING
HONING
HOPING
HOSING
HUMBUG

•H•G••

CHEGOE
CHIGOE
PHAGIA
SHAGGY
SHOGUN
THIGHS

•H••G•

CHANGE
CHANGS
CHARGE
CHOUGH
OHMAGE
PHLEGM
SHAGGY
SHRUGS
THINGS
THONGS
THOUGH
WHANGS

•H•••G

SHYING
THRONG

••H•G•

RRHAGE
RRHAGY

••H••G

ACHING

•••H•G

QUAHOG

HH••••

HHOURS

H••H••

HASHED
HASHES
HAWHAW
HEEHAW
HIGHER
HIGHLY
HITHER
HUGHES
HUGHIE
HUSHED
HUSHES
HYPHAE
HYPHAL
HYPHEN

H•••H•

HEATHS
HEATHY
HEIGHT
HONSHU

H••••H

HALLAH
HANNAH
HAUNCH
HEALTH
HEARTH
HOOKAH
HOOTCH
HOWDAH
HURRAH

•H••H•

CHICHI
RHYTHM
THIGHS

•H•••H

CHALEH
CHETAH
CHINCH
CHOUGH
CHURCH
PHOSPH
SHEATH
SHILOH
THATCH
THOUGH
THRASH
THRESH
THRUSH
WHIDAH
WHYDAH

••H•H•

APHTHA
EPHAHS
ICHTHY

••H••H

COHOSH
REHASH
YAHVEH
YAHWEH

•••H•H

EIGHTH

HI••••

HIATUS
HICCUP
HICKEY
HICKOK
HIDDEN
HIDERS
HIDING
HIEING
HIEMAL
HIGGLE
HIGHER
HIGHLY
HIJACK
HIKERS
HIKING
HILARY
HILDAS
HILLED
HILLER
HILTED
HINDER
HINDUS
HINGED
HINGES
HINTED
HIPPED
HIPPIE
HIPPOS
HIPPUS
HIRAMS
HIRERS
HIRING
HISPID
HISSED
HISSER
HISSES
HITHER
HITLER
HITTER
HIVING

H•I•••

HAILED
HAILER
HAIRDO
HAIRED
HEIFER
HEIGHT
HEISTS
HOICKS
HOIDEN
HOISTS

H••I••

HABILE
HABITS
HADING
HAKIMS
HALIDE
HALIDS
HALING
HALITE
HAMITE
HATING
HAVING
HAWING
HAYING
HAZIER
HAZILY
HAZING
HEGIRA
HEJIRA
HELICO
HELIOS
HELIUM
HERIOT
HESIOD
HEWING
HEXING
HIDING
HIEING
HIKING
HIRING
HIVING
HOEING
HOLIER
HOLIES
HOLILY
HOLING
HOLISM
HOMIER
HOMILY
HOMING
HOMINY
HONIED
HONING
HOPING
HOSIER
HOSING
HYOIDS

H•••I•

HACKIE
HAGGIS
HALOID
HARBIN
HARMIN
HATPIN
HATTIE
HAWAII
HECTIC
HEDWIG
HEMOID
HENBIT
HENRIS
HERDIC
HEREIN
HERMIT
HERNIA
HERNIO
HEROIC
HEROIN
HESTIA
HIPPIE
HISPID
HOGTIE
HOLMIC
HORNIE
HORRID
HOURIS
HUBRIS
HUGHIE
HYBRID
HYBRIS
HYDRIC
HYGEIA
HYMNIC
HYPNIC

H••••I

HAWAII
HERMAI

•HI•••

AHIMSA
CHIASM
CHIAUS
CHICHI
CHICKS
CHICLE
CHICOS
CHIDED
CHIDER
CHIDES
CHIEFS
CHIGOE
CHILLS
CHILLY
CHIMED
CHIMER
CHIMES
CHINCH
CHINES
CHINKS
CHINKY
CHINTZ
CHIPPY
CHIRMS
CHIRON
CHIRPS
CHIRRS
CHISEL
CHITIN

CHITON
CHITTY
CHIVES
OHIOAN
PHIALS
PHILIA
PHILIP
PHILOS
PHIPPS
RHINAL
RHINOS
SHIELD
SHIEST
SHIFTS
SHIFTY
SHIISM
SHIITE
SHIKAR
SHILLS
SHILOH
SHIMMY
SHINDY
SHINED
SHINER
SHINES
SHINNY
SHINTO
SHIRES
SHIRKS
SHIRRS
SHIRTS
SHIVER
SHIVES
THIEVE
THIGHS
THINGS
THINKS
THINLY
THIOLS
THIRDS
THIRST
THIRTY
WHIDAH
WHIFFS
WHILED
WHILES
WHILOM
WHILST
WHIMSY
WHINED
WHINER
WHINES
WHINNY
WHIRLS
WHISKS
WHISKY
WHITED
WHITEN
WHITER
WHITES
WHITEY

•H•I••
CHAINS
CHAIRS
CHAISE
CHEILO
CHEIRO
CHOICE
CHOIRS
CHRISM
CHRIST
RHEIMS
SHEIKS
SHEILA
SHIISM
SHIITE
SHRIEK
SHRIFT
SHRIKE
SHRILL
SHRIMP
SHRINE
SHRINK
SHRIVE
SHTICK
SHYING
THEIRS
THEISM
THEIST
THRICE
THRIFT
THRILL
THRIPS
THRIVE

•H••I•
CHITIN
CHOPIN
CHORIC
CHYMIC
DHOTIS
KHAKIS
PHAGIA
PHASIA
PHASIC
PHASIS
PHILIA
PHILIP
PHOBIA
PHOCIS
PHONIA
PHONIC
PHOTIC
PHYSIC
PHYSIO
PHYTIN
RHODIC
SHERIF
SHOJIS
SHOOIN
SHUTIN
THALIA
THEMIS
THESIS
THETIC
THETIS
THORIA
THORIC
THULIA
THYMIC

•H•••I
CHICHI
GHARRI
RHOMBI
THYRSI

••HI••
ACHING
APHIDS
ASHIER
AWHILE
AWHIRL
BEHIND
CAHIER
ECHINI
ECHINO
ETHICS
OPHITE
SAHIBS
SCHICK
SCHISM
SCHIST
SCHIZO
SPHINX
TSHIRT
UPHILL
WAHINE

••H•I•
ACHAIA
BAHAIS
DAHLIA
ECHOIC
ETHNIC
MOHAIR
SCHUIT
UNHAIR

••H••I
BIHARI
ECHINI
EPHEBI
EPHORI
WAHABI

•••HI•
ARCHIE
ARCHIL
COCHIN
ELOHIM
GOTHIC
HUGHIE
ISCHIA
KATHIE
LITHIA
LITHIC
LOCHIA
MASHIE
MENHIR
MUZHIK
MYTHIC
ORCHID
ORCHIL
ORCHIO
ORCHIS
ORPHIC
PATHIA
PYTHIA
PYTHIC
RACHIS
RAPHIS
RICHIE
SOPHIA
SOPHIE
SOTHIC
SOTHIS
SPAHIS
UNSHIP
URCHIN
WITHIN
WITHIT
ZECHIN

•••H•I
MYTHOI
TISHRI
VASHTI

••••HI
BRACHI
CANTHI
CHICHI
DELPHI
GANDHI
SANDHI
SCYPHI
TRICHI

H•J•••
HEJIRA
HIJACK

•H•J••
SHOJIS
THUJAS

H•K•••
HAKIMS
HIKERS
HIKING

H••K••
HACKED
HACKEE
HACKER
HACKIE
HACKLE
HANKER
HARKED
HARKEN
HAWKED
HAWKER
HECKLE
HICKEY
HICKOK
HOCKED
HOCKEY
HONKED
HONKER
HOOKAH
HOOKED
HOOKER
HOOKUP
HUCKLE
HULKED
HUSKED
HUSKER

H•••K•
HOICKS

H••••K
HICKOK
HIJACK

•H•K••
CHOKED
CHOKER
CHOKES
KHAKIS
SHAKEN
SHAKER
SHAKES
SHAKOS
SHEKEL
SHIKAR
ZHUKOV

•H••K•
CHALKS
CHALKY
CHECKS
CHEEKS
CHEEKY
CHICKS
CHINKS
CHINKY
CHOCKS
CHUCKS
CHUNKS
CHUNKY
SHACKO
SHACKS
SHANKS
SHARKS
SHEIKS
SHIRKS
SHOCKS
SHRIKE
SHUCKS
THANKS
THINKS
WHACKS
WHELKS
WHELKY
WHISKS
WHISKY

•H•••K
CHABUK
SHRANK
SHRIEK
SHRINK
SHRUNK
SHTICK
THWACK

••H••K
MOHAWK
MOHOCK
SCHICK
UNHOOK
UNHUSK

•••H•K
MUZHIK

H•L•••
HALERS
HALIDE
HALIDS
HALING
HALITE
HALLAH
HALLEL
HALLEY
HALLOO
HALLOW
HALLUX
HALOES
HALOID
HALSEY
HALTED
HALTER
HALUTZ
HALVED
HALVES
HELENA
HELENS
HELICO
HELIOS
HELIUM
HELLAS
HELLEN
HELLER
HELMET
HELOTS
HELPED
HELPER
HELVES
HILARY
HILDAS
HILLED
HILLER
HILTED
HOLARD
HOLDER
HOLDUP
HOLIER
HOLIES
HOLILY
HOLING

6

HOLISM
HOLLER
HOLLOW
HOLLYS
HOLMES
HOLMIC
HULKED
HULLED

H••L••

HAILED
HAILER
HALLAH
HALLEL
HALLEY
HALLOO
HALLOW
HALLUX
HAMLET
HARLAN
HARLEM
HARLEY
HARLOT
HASLET
HAULED
HAULER
HAULMY
HEALED
HEALER
HEALTH
HEELED
HEELER
HELLAS
HELLEN
HELLER
HENLEY
HILLED
HILLER
HITLER
HOLLER
HOLLOW
HOLLYS
HOWLED
HOWLER
HUELVA
HULLED
HURLED
HURLER
HUXLEY

H•••L•

HABILE
HACKLE
HAGGLE
HAMALS
HANDLE
HARDLY
HAROLD
HASSLE
HAZELS
HAZILY
HECKLE
HEDDLE
HERALD
HEXYLS
HIGGLE
HIGHLY
HOBBLE
HOLILY
HOMELY
HOMILY
HOOPLA
HOPPLE
HOTELS
HOURLY
HOVELS
HUCKLE
HUDDLE
HUGELY
HUMBLE
HUMBLY
HURDLE
HURTLE
HUSTLE

H••••L

HALLEL
HAMAUL
HAMMAL
HANDEL
HANSEL
HARTAL
HASSEL
HATFUL
HEDRAL
HERBAL
HIEMAL
HOSTEL
HYETAL
HYMNAL
HYPHAL

•HL•••

CHLOES
CHLORO
PHLEBO
PHLEGM
PHLOEM

•H•L••

CHALCO
CHALEH
CHALET
CHALKS
CHALKY
CHELAE
CHELAS
CHILLS
CHILLY
CHOLER
CHOLLA
DHOLES
PHILIA
PHILIP
PHILOS
PHYLAE
PHYLLO
PHYLUM
SHALED
SHALES
SHELBY
SHELLS
SHELLY
SHELTY
SHELVE
SHILLS
SHILOH
THALES
THALIA
THELMA
THOLES
THULIA
WHALED
WHALER
WHALES
WHELKS
WHELKY
WHELMS
WHELPS
WHILED
WHILES
WHILOM
WHILST
WHOLLY

•H••L•

CHEILO
CHICLE
CHILLS
CHILLY
CHOLLA
CHURLS
GHOULS
PHIALS
PHYLLO
SHAWLS
SHEILA
SHELLS
SHELLY
SHIELD
SHILLS
SHOALS
SHOALY
SHORLS
SHOULD
SHRILL
THINLY
THIOLS
THRALL
THRILL
WHEALS
WHEELS
WHIRLS
WHOLLY
WHORLS

•H•••L

CHAPEL
CHERYL
CHISEL
CHORAL
PHENOL
PHENYL
RHINAL
SHEKEL
SHOVEL
SHRILL
THECAL
THENAL
THRALL
THRILL
THYMOL

••HL••

ASHLAR
ASHLEY
DAHLIA
MAHLER

••H•L•

AWHILE
BEHALF
BEHELD
BEHOLD
ETHELS
ETHYLS
EXHALE
INHALE
MOHOLE
UNHOLY
UPHELD
UPHILL
UPHOLD

••H••L

AWHIRL
INHAUL
SCHOOL
SCHORL
UPHILL

•••HL•

ARCHLY
HIGHLY
RASHLY
RICHLY
TYPHLO

•••H•L

ALPHYL
ARCHIL
BETHEL
BUSHEL
HYPHAL
ISOHEL
LETHAL
METHYL
MICHEL
ORCHIL
PATHOL
RACHEL
WITHAL

H•M•••

HAMALS
HAMAUL
HAMDEN
HAMITE
HAMLET
HAMMAL
HAMMED
HAMMER
HAMPER
HAMZAS
HEMATO
HEMMED
HEMMER
HEMOID
HEMPEN
HOMAGE
HOMBRE
HOMELY
HOMERS
HOMIER
HOMILY
HOMING
HOMINY
HUMANE
HUMANS
HUMBLE
HUMBLY
HUMBUG
HUMMED
HUMMER
HUMORS
HUMPED
HYMENO
HYMENS
HYMNAL
HYMNED
HYMNIC

H••M••

HAMMAL
HAMMED
HAMMER
HARMED
HARMIN
HAYMOW
HBOMBS
HELMET
HEMMED
HEMMER
HERMAE
HERMAI
HERMAN
HERMES
HERMIT
HETMAN
HIEMAL
HOLMES
HOLMIC
HUMMED
HUMMER

H•••M•

HAKIMS
HAREMS
HAULMY
HBEAMS
HEAUME
HIRAMS

H••••M

HANSOM
HARLEM
HELIUM
HOLISM

•HM•••

OHMAGE

•H•M••

AHIMSA
CHAMMY
CHAMPS
CHIMED
CHIMER
CHIMES
CHUMMY
CHUMPS
CHYMIC
RHOMBI
RHUMBA
RHUMBS
RHYMED
RHYMER
RHYMES
SHAMAN
SHAMED
SHAMES
SHAMMY
SHAMUS
SHIMMY
THAMES
THEMES
THEMIS
THOMAS
THUMBS
THUMPS
THYMES
THYMIC
THYMOL
THYMUS
WHAMMY
WHIMSY

•H••M•

CHACMA
CHAMMY
CHARMS
CHASMS
CHIRMS
CHROMA
CHROME
CHROMO
CHUMMY
DHARMA
IHRAMS
RHEIMS
RHEUMY
SHAMMY
SHAWMS
SHIMMY

SHRIMP
THELMA
THERMO
THERMS
THRUMS
WHAMMY
WHELMS

•H•••M
CHIASM
CHRISM
PHLEGM
PHLOEM
PHYLUM
RHYTHM
SHIISM
THEISM
WHILOM

••HM••
ASHMAN
ASHMEN
SCHMOS

••H•M•
ATHOME
BAHAMA
EXHUME
NAHUMS
SCHEMA
SCHEME

••H••M
SCHISM

•••HM•
ABOHMS
ASTHMA
BRAHMA
BRAHMS

•••H•M
ANTHEM
DIRHAM
DURHAM
ELOHIM
FATHOM
GOTHAM
GRAHAM
MAYHEM
SACHEM

••••HM
DRACHM
RHYTHM

H•N•••
HANCES
HANDED
HANDEL
HANDLE
HANGAR
HANGED
HANGER
HANGUP
HANKER
HANNAH
HANNAS
HANSEL
HANSOM
HENBIT
HENLEY
HENNAS
HENRIS
HENRYS
HINDER
HINDUS
HINGED
HINGES
HINTED
HONEST
HONEYS
HONIED
HONING
HONKED
HONKER
HONORE
HONORS
HONSHU
HUNGER
HUNGRY
HUNTED
HUNTER

H••N••
HANNAH
HANNAS
HAUNCH
HAUNTS
HENNAS
HERNIA
HERNIO
HOBNOB
HOGNUT
HORNED
HORNET
HORNIE
HOUNDS
HYENAS
HYMNAL
HYMNED
HYMNIC
HYPNIC
HYPNOS

H•••N•
HADING
HALING
HATING
HAVANA
HAVENS
HAVENT
HAVING
HAWING
HAYING
HAZING
HELENA
HELENS
HERONS
HEWING
HEXANE
HEXING
HEXONE
HIDING
HIEING
HIKING
HIRING
HIVING
HOEING
HOGANS
HOLING
HOMING
HOMINY
HONING
HOPING
HOSING
HUMANE
HUMANS
HURONS
HYMENO
HYMENS

H••••N
HAGDON
HAMDEN
HAPPEN
HARBIN
HARDEN
HARKEN
HARLAN
HARMIN
HASTEN
HATPIN
HAUSEN
HAZZAN
HEADON
HEAVEN
HEBRON
HEDRON
HELLEN
HEMPEN
HEREIN
HEREON
HERMAN
HEROIN
HETMAN
HIDDEN
HODDEN
HOIDEN
HOYDEN
HUDSON
HYPHEN

•H•N••
CHANCE
CHANCY
CHANGE
CHANGS
CHANTS
CHANTY
CHINCH
CHINES
CHINKS
CHINKY
CHINTZ
CHONDR
CHUNKS
CHUNKY
OHENRY
PHENOL
PHENYL
PHONED
PHONES
PHONEY
PHONIA
PHONIC
RHINAL
RHINOS
SHANKS
SHANTY
SHINDY
SHINED
SHINER
SHINES
SHINNY
SHINTO
SHUNTS
THANAT
THANES
THANKS
THENAL
THENAR
THENCE
THINGS
THINKS
THINLY
THONGS
WHANGS
WHENCE
WHINED
WHINER
WHINES
WHINNY

•H••N•
CHAINS
CHRONO
CHURNS
DHARNA
DHURNA
PHRENO
SHEENS
SHEENY
SHINNY
SHRANK
SHRINE
SHRINK
SHRUNK
SHYING
THORNS
THORNY
THRONE
THRONG
WHINNY

•H•••N
BHUTAN
CHARON
CHIRON
CHITIN
CHITON
CHOPIN
CHOSEN
OHIOAN
PHOTON
PHYTIN
SHAKEN
SHAMAN
SHAPEN
SHARON
SHAVEN
SHOGUN
SHOOIN
SHORAN
SHUTIN
THORON
THROWN
WHITEN

••HN••
ETHNIC
JOHNNY

••H•N•
ACHENE
ACHING
ATHENA
ATHENE
ATHENS
BEHIND
COHUNE
ECHINI
ECHINO
ETHANE
ETHANS
JOHANN
JOHNNY
SPHENE
SPHENO
SPHINX
UNHAND
WAHINE

••H••N
ASHMAN
ASHMEN
DAHOON
DEHORN
JOHANN

•••HN•
DAPHNE
FOEHNS
TECHNO
VISHNU

•••H•N
AACHEN
AFGHAN
ARCHON
COCHIN
GORHEN
GOSHEN
HYPHEN
INCHON
KUCHEN
LICHEN
NATHAN
ORPHAN
PATHAN
PEAHEN
PYTHON
SIPHON
TUCHUN
TYPHON
URCHIN
UTAHAN
WITHIN
ZECHIN

HO••••
HOARDS
HOARSE
HOAXED
HOAXER
HOAXES
HOBART
HOBBES
HOBBLE
HOBNOB
HOBOES
HOCKED
HOCKEY
HODDEN
HOEING
HOGANS
HOGGED
HOGNUT
HOGTIE
HOICKS
HOIDEN
HOISTS
HOLARD
HOLDER
HOLDUP
HOLIER
HOLIES
HOLILY
HOLING
HOLISM
HOLLER
HOLLOW
HOLLYS
HOLMES
HOLMIC
HOMAGE
HOMBRE
HOMELY
HOMERS
HOMIER
HOMILY
HOMING
HOMINY

HONEST
HONEYS
HONIED
HONING
HONKED
HONKER
HONORE
HONORS
HONSHU
HOODED
HOODOO
HOOFED
HOOFER
HOOKAH
HOOKED
HOOKER
HOOKUP
HOOPED
HOOPER
HOOPLA
HOOPOE
HOORAY
HOOTCH
HOOTED
HOOVER
HOOVES
HOPING
HOPPED
HOPPER
HOPPLE
HORACE
HORARY
HORDED
HORDES
HORNED
HORNET
HORNIE
HORRID
HORROR
HORSED
HORSES
HORSEY
HORSTE
HOSIER
HOSING
HOSTED
HOSTEL
HOTBED
HOTBOX
HOTELS
HOTTER
HOUNDS
HOURIS
HOURLY
HOUSED
HOUSES
HOVELS
HOVERS
HOWARD
HOWDAH
HOWLED
HOWLER
HOYDEN

H•O•••

HBOMBS
HHOURS
HOODED
HOODOO
HOOFED
HOOFER
HOOKAH
HOOKED
HOOKER
HOOKUP
HOOPED
HOOPER
HOOPLA
HOOPOE
HOORAY
HOOTCH
HOOTED
HOOVER
HOOVES
HYOIDS

H••O••

HALOES
HALOID
HAROLD
HELOTS
HEMOID
HEROES
HEROIC
HEROIN
HERONS
HEXONE
HEXOSE
HOBOES
HONORE
HONORS
HUMORS
HURONS

H•••O•

HAGDON
HALLOO
HALLOW
HANSOM
HARBOR
HARLOT
HARROW
HATBOX
HAYMOW
HEADON
HEBRON
HECTOR
HEDRON
HELIOS
HEREOF
HEREON
HERIOT
HESIOD
HICKOK
HIPPOS
HOBNOB
HOLLOW
HOODOO
HOOPOE
HORROR
HOTBOX
HUDSON
HYDROS
HYPNOS
HYSSOP

H••••O

HAIRDO
HALLOO
HELICO
HEMATO
HEPATO
HERETO
HERNIO
HETERO
HOODOO
HYMENO

•HO•••

CHOCKS
CHOICE
CHOIRS
CHOKED
CHOKER
CHOKES
CHOLER
CHOLLA
CHONDR
CHOOSE
CHOOSY
CHOPIN
CHOPPY
CHORAL
CHORDS
CHOREA
CHOREO
CHORES
CHORIC
CHORUS
CHOSEN
CHOUGH
DHOLES
DHOTIS
GHOSTS
GHOULS
HHOURS
PHOBIA
PHOCIS
PHOEBE
PHONED
PHONES
PHONEY
PHONIA
PHONIC
PHOOEY
PHOSPH
PHOTIC
PHOTON
PHOTOS
RHODAS
RHODIC
RHOMBI
SHOALS
SHOALY
SHOATS
SHOCKS
SHODDY
SHOERS
SHOFAR
SHOGUN
SHOJIS
SHOOED
SHOOIN
SHOOTS
SHOPPE
SHORAN
SHORED
SHORES
SHORLS
SHORTS
SHOTES
SHOULD
SHOUTS
SHOVED
SHOVEL
SHOVER
SHOVES
SHOWED
SHOWER
THOLES
THOMAS
THONGS
THORAC
THORAX
THORIA
THORIC
THORNS
THORNY
THORON
THORPE
THOUGH
WHOLLY
WHOOPS
WHORED
WHORES
WHORLS
WHORTS

•H•O••

CHEOPS
CHLOES
CHLORO
CHOOSE
CHOOSY
CHROMA
CHROME
CHROMO
CHRONO
OHIOAN
PHLOEM
PHOOEY
SHOOED
SHOOIN
SHOOTS
SHROFF
SHROUD
SHROVE
THEORY
THIOLS
THROAT
THROBS
THROES
THRONE
THRONG
THROVE
THROWN
THROWS
WHOOPS

•H••O•

CHARON
CHEGOE
CHICOS
CHIGOE
CHIRON
CHITON
PHENOL
PHILOS
PHOTON
PHOTOS
RHETOR
RHINOS
SHADOW
SHAKOS
SHARON
SHILOH
THORON
THYMOL
WHILOM
ZHUKOV

•H•••O

CHAETO
CHALCO
CHEILO
CHEIRO
CHLORO
CHOREO
CHROMO
CHRONO
CHRYSO
GHETTO
PHLEBO
PHRENO
PHYLLO
PHYSIO
SHACKO
SHINTO
THERMO
THYREO

••HO••

ABHORS
ASHORE
ATHOME
BEHOLD
BEHOOF
BEHOVE
COHORT
COHOSH
DAHOON
DEHORN
ECHOED
ECHOER
ECHOES
ECHOIC
EPHODS
EPHORI
EPHORS
EXHORT
LAHORE
MAHOUT
MOHOCK
MOHOLE
SCHOOL
SCHORL
UNHOLY
UNHOOK
UPHOLD
WAHOOS
YAHOOS

••H•O•

BEHOOF
DAHOON
SCHMOS
SCHOOL
UNHOOK
UPHROE
WAHOOS
YAHOOS

••H••O

ECHINO
SCHIZO
SPHENO

•••HO•

ANCHOR
ANYHOW
ARCHON
AUTHOR
BATHOS
BISHOP
BOOHOO
CACHOU
CARHOP
CASHOO
FATHOM
INCHON
METHOD
MYTHOI
MYTHOS
NOSHOW
OOPHOR
PATHOL
PATHOS
PYTHON
QUAHOG
REDHOT
SIPHON
TYPHON
UPSHOT
YOOHOO

ZETHOS

•••H•O
ARCHEO
ARTHRO
BOOHOO
CASHOO
JETHRO
NEPHRO
ORCHIO
PASHTO
RIGHTO
TECHNO
TYPHLO
YOOHOO

••••HO
CLOTHO
GAUCHO
GNATHO
GRAPHO
LYMPHO
MORPHO
NAVAHO
NYMPHO
PONCHO
PSYCHO
RANCHO
REECHO
SAPPHO
SCYPHO
SORGHO
STETHO
SULPHO
TRICHO
TROPHO
XANTHO

H•P•••
HAPPEN
HEPATO
HEPTAD
HIPPED
HIPPIE
HIPPOS
HIPPUS
HOPING
HOPPED
HOPPER
HOPPLE
HYPHAE
HYPHAL
HYPHEN
HYPNIC
HYPNOS

H••P••
HAMPER
HAPPEN
HARPED
HARPER
HASPED
HATPIN
HEAPED
HELPED
HELPER
HEMPEN
HERPES
HIPPED
HIPPIE
HIPPOS
HIPPUS
HISPID
HOOPED
HOOPER
HOOPLA
HOOPOE
HOPPED
HOPPER
HOPPLE
HUMPED

H••••P
HANGUP
HICCUP
HOLDUP
HOOKUP
HUBCAP
HYSSOP

•H•P••
CHAPEL
CHAPES
CHIPPY
CHOPIN
CHOPPY
PHIPPS
SHAPED
SHAPEN
SHAPER
SHAPES
SHOPPE

•H••P•
CHAMPS
CHEEPS
CHEOPS
CHIPPY
CHIRPS
CHOPPY
CHUMPS
PHIPPS
PHOSPH
SHARPS
SHERPA
SHOPPE
THORPE
THRIPS
THUMPS
WHELPS
WHOOPS

•H•••P
PHILIP
SHRIMP

•••H•P
BISHOP
CARHOP
MAYHAP
MISHAP
PUSHUP
UNSHIP

H•R•••
HARASS
HARBIN
HARBOR
HARDEN
HARDER
HARDLY
HAREMS
HARKED
HARKEN
HARLAN
HARLEM
HARLEY
HARLOT
HARMED
HARMIN
HAROLD
HARPED
HARPER
HARROW
HARRYS
HARTAL
HARVEY
HERALD
HERBAL
HERDED
HERDER
HERDIC
HEREAT
HEREBY
HEREIN
HEREOF
HEREON
HERESY
HERETO
HERIOT
HERMAE
HERMAI
HERMAN
HERMES
HERMIT
HERNIA
HERNIO
HEROES
HEROIC
HEROIN
HERONS
HERPES
HIRAMS
HIRERS
HIRING
HORACE
HORARY
HORDED
HORDES
HORNED
HORNET
HORNIE
HORRID
HORROR
HORSED
HORSES
HORSEY
HORSTE
HURDLE
HURLED
HURLER
HURONS
HURRAH
HURRAY
HURTER
HURTLE

H••R••
HAIRDO
HAIRED
HARROW
HARRYS
HATRED
HEARER
HEARSE
HEARST
HEARTH
HEARTS
HEARTY
HEBREW
HEBRON
HEDRAL
HEDRON
HENRIS
HENRYS
HOARDS
HOARSE
HOORAY
HORRID
HORROR
HOURIS
HOURLY
HUBRIS
HURRAH
HURRAY
HYBRID
HYBRIS
HYDRAE
HYDRAS
HYDRIC
HYDROS

H•••R•
HALERS
HATERS
HAZARD
HAZERS
HEGIRA
HEJIRA
HETERO
HEWERS
HHOURS
HIDERS
HIKERS
HILARY
HIRERS
HOBART
HOLARD
HOMBRE
HOMERS
HONORE
HONORS
HORARY
HOVERS
HOWARD
HUBERT
HUMORS
HUNGRY

H••••R
HACKER
HAILER
HALTER
HAMMER
HAMPER
HANGAR
HANGER
HANKER
HARBOR
HARDER
HARPER
HATTER
HAULER
HAWKER
HAWSER
HAZIER
HEADER
HEALER
HEARER
HEATER
HEAVER
HECTOR
HEDGER
HEEDER
HEELER
HEIFER
HELLER
HELPER
HEMMER
HERDER
HESTER
HIGHER
HILLER
HINDER
HISSER
HITHER
HITLER
HITTER
HOAXER
HOLDER
HOLIER
HOLLER
HOMIER
HONKER
HOOFER
HOOKER
HOOPER
HOOVER
HOPPER
HORROR
HOSIER
HOTTER
HOWLER
HUMMER
HUNGER
HUNTER
HURLER
HURTER
HUSKER
HUSSAR
HYSTER

•HR•••
CHRISM
CHRIST
CHROMA
CHROME
CHROMO
CHRONO
CHRYSO
IHRAMS
PHRASE
PHRENO
SHRANK
SHREDS
SHREWD
SHREWS
SHRIEK
SHRIFT
SHRIKE
SHRILL
SHRIMP
SHRINE
SHRINK
SHRIVE
SHROFF
SHROUD
SHROVE
SHRUBS
SHRUGS
SHRUNK
THRALL
THRASH
THREAD
THREAT
THREED
THREES
THRESH
THRICE
THRIFT
THRILL
THRIPS
THRIVE
THROAT
THROBS
THROES
THRONE
THRONG
THROVE
THROWN
THROWS
THRUMS
THRUSH
THRUST

•H•R••

CHARDS
CHARED
CHARES
CHARGE
CHARMS
CHARON
CHARRY
CHARTS
CHERRY
CHERUB
CHERYL
CHIRMS
CHIRON
CHIRPS
CHIRRS
CHORAL
CHORDS
CHOREA
CHOREO
CHORES
CHORIC
CHORUS
CHURCH
CHURLS
CHURNS
CHURRS
DHARMA
DHARNA
DHURNA
GHARRI
GHARRY
SHARDS
SHARED
SHARER
SHARES
SHARKS
SHARON
SHARPS
SHERDS
SHERIF
SHERPA
SHERRY
SHIRES
SHIRKS
SHIRRS
SHIRTS
SHORAN
SHORED
SHORES
SHORLS
SHORTS
THERMO
THERMS
THIRDS
THIRST
THIRTY
THORAC
THORAX
THORIA
THORIC
THORNS
THORNY
THORON
THORPE
THYREO
THYRSE
THYRSI
WHARFS
WHARVE
WHERRY
WHERVE
WHIRLS
WHORED
WHORES
WHORLS
WHORTS

•H••R•

CHAIRS
CHARRY
CHEERS
CHEERY
CHEIRO
CHERRY
CHIRRS
CHLORO
CHOIRS
CHURRS
GHARRI
GHARRY
HHOURS
OHENRY
SHEARS
SHEERS
SHERRY
SHIRRS
SHOERS
THEIRS
THEORY
THWART
WHERRY

•H•••R

CHAFER
CHASER
CHEWER
CHIDER
CHIMER
CHOKER
CHOLER
CHONDR
GHEBER
KHYBER
RHETOR
RHYMER
SHAKER
SHAPER
SHARER
SHAVER
SHEWER
SHIKAR
SHINER
SHIVER
SHOFAR
SHOVER
SHOWER
THAYER
THENAR
WHALER
WHINER
WHITER

••HR••

FUHRER
UPHROE

••H•R•

ABHORS
ADHERE
ASHORE
AWHIRL
BIHARI
COHERE
COHORT
DEHORN
ECHARD
EPHORI
EPHORS
ETHERS
EXHORT
INHERE
LAHORE
MOHURS
OCHERS
OCHERY
OTHERS
SAHARA
SCHORL
SPHERE
SPHERY
TSHIRT
UNHURT
USHERS

••H••R

ASHIER
ASHLAR
CAHIER
ECHOER
FUHRER
ISHTAR
MAHLER
MOHAIR
REHEAR
UNHAIR

•••HR•

AMPHRS
ARTHRO
EUCHRE
JETHRO
NEPHRO
TISHRI

•••H•R

AETHER
ANCHOR
ANTHER
ARCHER
ARTHUR
AUTHOR
BATHER
BOTHER
CATHER
CIPHER
CITHER
COSHER
CYPHER
DASHER
DITHER
EITHER
ESCHAR
ESTHER
ETCHER
FATHER
FISHER
GATHER
GOPHER
GUSHER
HIGHER
HITHER
JOSHER
KOSHER
LASHER
LATHER
LECHER
LITHER
LUSHER
LUTHER
MASHER
MENHIR
MOTHER
MUSHER
NETHER
NIGHER
OOPHOR
POTHER
PUSHER
RASHER
RATHER
RICHER
RUSHER
SAPHAR
SYPHER
TETHER
TITHER
TOTHER
WASHER
WETHER
WITHER
ZEPHYR
ZITHER

••••HR

ERYTHR
URETHR

H•S•••

HASHED
HASHES
HASLET
HASPED
HASSEL
HASSLE
HASTED
HASTEN
HASTES
HESIOD
HESTER
HESTIA
HISPID
HISSED
HISSER
HISSES
HOSIER
HOSING
HOSTED
HOSTEL
HUSHED
HUSHES
HUSKED
HUSKER
HUSSAR
HUSTLE
HYSSOP
HYSTER

H••S••

HALSEY
HANSEL
HANSOM
HASSEL
HASSLE
HAUSEN
HAWSER
HAWSES
HEISTS
HISSED
HISSER
HISSES
HOISTS
HONSHU
HORSED
HORSES
HORSEY
HORSTE
HOUSED
HOUSES
HUDSON
HUSSAR
HYSSOP

H•••S•

HARASS
HEARSE
HEARST
HERESY
HEXOSE
HOARSE
HOLISM
HONEST
HUGEST

H••••S

HABITS
HAGGIS
HAKIMS
HALERS
HALIDS
HALOES
HALVES
HAMALS
HAMZAS
HANCES
HANNAS
HARASS
HAREMS
HARRYS
HASHES
HASTES
HATERS
HATTYS
HAUNTS
HAVENS
HAWSES
HAZELS
HAZERS
HBEAMS
HBOMBS
HEARTS
HEATHS
HEAVES
HEDGES
HEISTS
HELENS
HELIOS
HELLAS
HELOTS
HELVES
HENNAS
HENRIS
HENRYS
HERMES
HEROES
HERONS
HERPES
HETTYS
HEWERS
HEXADS
HEXYLS
HHOURS
HIATUS
HIDERS
HIKERS
HILDAS
HINDUS
HINGES
HIPPOS
HIPPUS
HIRAMS
HIRERS
HISSES
HOARDS
HOAXES
HOBBES
HOBOES
HOGANS
HOICKS
HOISTS
HOLIES
HOLLYS
HOLMES
HOMERS

HONEYS
HONORS
HOOVES
HORDES
HORSES
HOTELS
HOUNDS
HOURIS
HOUSES
HOVELS
HOVERS
HUBRIS
HUGHES
HUMANS
HUMORS
HURONS
HUSHES
HYADES
HYBRIS
HYDRAS
HYDROS
HYENAS
HYMENS
HYOIDS
HYPNOS

•H•S••

CHASED
CHASER
CHASES
CHASMS
CHASSE
CHASTE
CHESTS
CHESTY
CHISEL
CHOSEN
GHOSTS
PHASED
PHASES
PHASIA
PHASIC
PHASIS
PHOSPH
PHYSIC
PHYSIO
RHESUS
SHASTA
THESES
THESIS
WHISKS
WHISKY

•H••S•

AHIMSA
CHAISE
CHASSE
CHEESE
CHEESY
CHIASM
CHOOSE
CHOOSY
CHRISM
CHRIST
CHRYSO
PHRASE
SHIEST
SHIISM
SHYEST
THEISM
THEIST
THIRST
THRASH
THRESH
THRUSH
THRUST
THYRSE
THYRSI
WHILST
WHIMSY

•H•••S

CHAFES
CHAFFS
CHAINS
CHAIRS
CHALKS
CHAMPS
CHANGS
CHANTS
CHAPES
CHARDS
CHARES
CHARMS
CHARTS
CHASES
CHASMS
CHEATS
CHECKS
CHEEKS
CHEEPS
CHEERS
CHELAS
CHEOPS
CHESTS
CHIAUS
CHICKS
CHICOS
CHIDES
CHIEFS
CHILLS
CHIMES
CHINES
CHINKS
CHIRMS
CHIRPS
CHIRRS
CHIVES
CHLOES
CHOCKS
CHOIRS
CHOKES
CHORDS
CHORES
CHORUS
CHUCKS
CHUFAS
CHUMPS
CHUNKS
CHURLS
CHURNS
CHURRS
CHUTES
DHOLES
DHOTIS
GHAUTS
GHOSTS
GHOULS
HHOURS
IHRAMS
KHAKIS
PHASES
PHASIS
PHIALS
PHILOS
PHIPPS
PHOCIS
PHONES
PHOTOS
RHEIMS
RHESUS
RHINOS
RHODAS
RHUMBS
RHYMES
SHACKS
SHADES
SHAFTS
SHAKES
SHAKOS
SHALES
SHAMES
SHAMUS
SHANKS
SHAPES
SHARDS
SHARES
SHARKS
SHARPS
SHAVES
SHAWLS
SHAWMS
SHEARS
SHEENS
SHEERS
SHEETS
SHEIKS
SHELLS
SHERDS
SHIFTS
SHILLS
SHINES
SHIRES
SHIRKS
SHIRRS
SHIRTS
SHIVES
SHOALS
SHOATS
SHOCKS
SHOERS
SHOJIS
SHOOTS
SHORES
SHORLS
SHORTS
SHOTES
SHOUTS
SHOVES
SHREDS
SHREWS
SHRUBS
SHRUGS
SHUCKS
SHUNTS
THADYS
THALES
THAMES
THANES
THANKS
THEBES
THEDAS
THEFTS
THEIRS
THEMES
THEMIS
THERMS
THESES
THESIS
THETAS
THETIS
THIGHS
THINGS
THINKS
THIOLS
THIRDS
THOLES
THOMAS
THONGS
THORNS
THREES
THRIPS
THROBS
THROES
THROWS
THRUMS
THUJAS
THUMBS
THUMPS
THYMES
THYMUS
WHACKS
WHALES
WHANGS
WHARFS
WHEALS
WHEATS
WHEELS
WHELKS
WHELMS
WHELPS
WHIFFS
WHILES
WHINES
WHIRLS
WHISKS
WHITES
WHOOPS
WHORES
WHORLS
WHORTS

••H•S•

AGHAST
BEHEST
COHOSH
REHASH
SCHISM
SCHIST
SCHUSS
UNHUSK

••H••S

ABHORS
APHIDS
ATHENS
BAHAIS
ECHOES
EPHAHS
EPHODS
EPHORS
ETHANS
ETHELS
ETHERS
ETHICS
ETHYLS
JIHADS
LEHUAS
MOHURS
NAHUMS
OCHERS
OTHERS
PSHAWS
SAHEBS
SAHIBS
SCHMOS
SCHUSS
SCHWAS
TEHEES
UNHATS
USHERS
WAHOOS
YAHOOS

•••H•S

ABOHMS
ALPHAS
AMPHRS
ARCHES
ARCHYS
AUGHTS
BACHES
BASHES
BATHOS
BIGHTS
BOSHES
BRAHMS
BUSHES
CACHES
CASHES
CATHYS
COSHES
DACHAS
DASHES
DISHES
EIGHTS
ETCHES
FICHES
FICHUS
FIGHTS
FISHES
FOEHNS
GASHES
GUSHES
HASHES
HUGHES
HUSHES
INCHES
ITCHES
JOSHES
KATHYS
LACHES
LASHES
LATHES
LIGHTS
LUSHES
MASHES
MESHES
MUSHES
MYTHOS
NICHES
NIGHTS
ORCHIS
PASHAS
PATHOS
PISHES
PUSHES
RACHIS
RAPHIS
RASHES
RICHES
RIGHTS
RUCHES
RUSHES
SADHUS
SASHES
SIGHTS
SOTHIS
SPAHIS
TETHYS
TIGHTS
TITHES
TOSHES
TUSHES
TYPHUS
WASHES
WICHES
WISHES
WITHES
YACHTS
ZETHOS
ZETHUS

6

••••HS
ALEPHS
ALMAHS
BERTHS
BIRTHS
BOOTHS
BOUGHS
BROTHS
BURGHS
CLOTHS
CONCHS
COUGHS
CZECHS
DEATHS
DEPTHS
DINAHS
DOLPHS
DOUGHS
EARTHS
EDITHS
EPHAHS
EPOCHS
ERICHS
FAITHS
FIFTHS
FIRTHS
FRITHS
FROTHS
GLYPHS
GRAPHS
HEATHS
JONAHS
JUDAHS
KEITHS
LAUGHS
LEIGHS
LOTAHS
LOUGHS
MONTHS
MOUTHS
NEIGHS
NINTHS
NYMPHS
ORACHS
RAJAHS
RALPHS
RAYAHS
REICHS
ROLPHS
ROUGHS
SARAHS
SIXTHS
SLOTHS
SMITHS
SNATHS
SOUGHS
SUBAHS
SURAHS
SWATHS
SYLPHS
TENTHS
THIGHS
TILTHS
TORAHS
TOUGHS
TROTHS
TRUTHS
WEIGHS
WIDTHS
YOUTHS

H•T•••
HATBOX
HATERS
HATFUL
HATING
HATPIN
HATRED
HATTED
HATTER
HATTIE
HATTYS
HETERO
HETMAN
HETTYS
HITHER
HITLER
HITTER
HOTBED
HOTBOX
HOTELS
HOTTER
HUTTED

H••T••
HALTED
HALTER
HARTAL
HASTED
HASTEN
HASTES
HATTED
HATTER
HATTIE
HATTYS
HEATED
HEATER
HEATHS
HEATHY
HECTIC
HECTOR
HEFTED
HEPTAD
HESTER
HESTIA
HETTYS
HIATUS
HILTED
HINTED
HITTER
HOGTIE
HOOTCH
HOOTED
HOSTED
HOSTEL
HOTTER
HUNTED
HUNTER
HURTER
HURTLE
HUSTLE
HUTTED
HYETAL
HYSTER

H•••T•
HABITS
HALITE
HALUTZ
HAMITE
HAUNTS
HEALTH
HEARTH
HEARTS
HEARTY
HECATE
HEISTS
HELOTS
HEMATO
HEPATO
HERETO
HOISTS
HORSTE

H••••T
HAGBUT
HAMLET
HARLOT
HASLET
HAVENT
HEARST
HEIGHT
HELMET
HENBIT
HEREAT
HERIOT
HERMIT
HOBART
HOGNUT
HONEST
HORNET
HUBERT
HUGEST

•HT•••
SHTICK

•H•T••
BHUTAN
CHATTY
CHETAH
CHITIN
CHITON
CHITTY
CHUTES
DHOTIS
GHETTO
PHOTIC
PHOTON
PHOTOS
PHYTIN
RHETOR
RHYTHM
SHOTES
SHUTIN
THATCH
THETAS
THETIC
THETIS
WHITED
WHITEN
WHITER
WHITES
WHITEY

•H••T•
CHAETA
CHAETO
CHANTS
CHANTY
CHARTS
CHASTE
CHATTY
CHEATS
CHESTS
CHESTY
CHINTZ
CHITTY
GHAUTS
GHETTO
GHOSTS
SHAFTS
SHANTY
SHASTA
SHEATH
SHEETS
SHELTY
SHIFTS
SHIFTY
SHIITE
SHINTO
SHIRTS
SHOATS
SHOOTS
SHORTS
SHOUTS
SHUNTS
THEFTS
THIRTY
WHEATS
WHORTS

•H•••T
CHALET
CHRIST
SHEBAT
SHIEST
SHRIFT
SHYEST
THANAT
THEIST
THIRST
THREAT
THRIFT
THROAT
THRUST
THWART
WHILST

••HT••
APHTHA
ICHTHY
ISHTAR

••H•T•
OPHITE
UNHATS

••H••T
AGHAST
BEHEST
COHORT
EXHORT
MAHOUT
REHEAT
SCHIST
SCHUIT
TSHIRT
UNHURT

•••HT•
AUGHTS
BIGHTS
EIGHTH
EIGHTS
EIGHTY
FIGHTS
LIGHTS
MIGHTY
NIGHTS
NIGHTY
PASHTO
RIGHTO
RIGHTS
SIGHTS
TIGHTS
VASHTI
YACHTS

•••H•T
CACHET
CUSHAT
JAPHET
REDHOT
ROCHET
SACHET
UPSHOT
WITHIT

••••HT
ALIGHT
ARIGHT
BLIGHT
BOUGHT
BRECHT
BRIGHT
CAUGHT
DWIGHT
FLIGHT
FOUGHT
FRIGHT
HEIGHT
KNIGHT
NAUGHT
NOUGHT
PLIGHT
SLIGHT
SOUGHT
TAUGHT
WEIGHT
WRIGHT

HU••••
HUBBUB
HUBCAP
HUBERT
HUBRIS
HUCKLE
HUDDLE
HUDSON
HUELVA
HUFFED
HUGELY
HUGEST
HUGGED
HUGHES
HUGHIE
HULKED
HULLED
HUMANE
HUMANS
HUMBLE
HUMBLY
HUMBUG
HUMMED
HUMMER
HUMORS
HUMPED
HUNGER
HUNGRY
HUNTED
HUNTER
HURDLE
HURLED
HURLER
HURONS
HURRAH
HURRAY
HURTER
HURTLE
HUSHED
HUSHES
HUSKED
HUSKER
HUSSAR
HUSTLE
HUTTED
HUXLEY

H•U•••
HAULED
HAULER
HAULMY
HAUNCH

HAUNTS
HAUSEN
HOUNDS
HOURIS
HOURLY
HOUSED
HOUSES

H••U••
HALUTZ
HEAUME
HECUBA
HHOURS

H•••U•
HAGBUT
HALLUX
HAMAUL
HANGUP
HATFUL
HELIUM
HIATUS
HICCUP
HINDUS
HIPPUS
HOGNUT
HOLDUP
HOOKUP
HUBBUB
HUMBUG

H••••U
HONSHU

•HU•••
BHUTAN
CHUBBY
CHUCKS
CHUFAS
CHUMMY
CHUMPS
CHUNKS
CHUNKY
CHURCH
CHURLS
CHURNS
CHURRS
CHUTES
DHURNA
RHUMBA
RHUMBS
SHUCKS
SHUNTS
SHUTIN
THUJAS
THULIA
THUMBS
THUMPS
ZHUKOV

•H•U••
CHOUGH
GHAUTS
GHOULS

HHOURS
RHEUMY
SHOULD
SHOUTS
SHRUBS
SHRUGS
SHRUNK
THOUGH
THRUMS
THRUSH
THRUST

•H••U•
CHABUK
CHERUB
CHIAUS
CHORUS
PHYLUM
RHESUS
SHAMUS
SHOGUN
SHROUD
THYMUS

••HU••
COHUNE
EXHUME
LEHUAS
MOHURS
NAHUMS
SCHUIT
SCHUSS
UNHURT
UNHUSK

••H•U•
INHAUL
MAHOUT

•••HU•
ARTHUR
FICHUS
JOSHUA
NASHUA
PUSHUP
SADHUS
TUCHUN
TYPHUS
ZETHUS

•••H•U
CACHOU
DACHAU
VISHNU

••••HU
HONSHU
KYUSHU
MANCHU
SAMSHU

H•V•••
HAVANA
HAVENS
HAVENT
HAVING
HIVING
HOVELS
HOVERS

H••V••
HALVED
HALVES
HARVEY
HEAVED
HEAVEN
HEAVER
HEAVES
HELVES
HOOVER
HOOVES

H•••V•
HUELVA

•H•V••
CHIVES
SHAVED
SHAVEN
SHAVER
SHAVES
SHIVER
SHIVES
SHOVED
SHOVEL
SHOVER
SHOVES

•H••V•
SHEAVE
SHELVE
SHRIVE
SHROVE
THIEVE
THRIVE
THROVE
WHARVE
WHERVE

•H•••V
ZHUKOV

••HV••
YAHVEH

••H•V•
BEHAVE
BEHOVE
MOHAVE

H•W•••
HAWAII
HAWHAW
HAWING
HAWKED
HAWKER
HAWSER
HAWSES
HEWERS
HEWING
HOWARD
HOWDAH
HOWLED
HOWLER

H••W••
HEDWIG

H••••W
HALLOW
HARROW
HAWHAW
HAYMOW
HEBREW
HEEHAW
HOLLOW

•HW•••
THWACK
THWART

•H•W••
CHAWED
CHEWED
CHEWER
SHAWLS
SHAWMS
SHEWED
SHEWER
SHOWED
SHOWER
THAWED

•H••W•
SHREWD
SHREWS
THROWN
THROWS

•H•••W
SHADOW

••HW••
SCHWAS
YAHWEH

••H•W•
MOHAWK
PSHAWS

•••H•W
ANYHOW
BASHAW
CASHAW
CASHEW
CUSHAW
ESCHEW
HAWHAW
HEEHAW
NEPHEW
NOSHOW

H•X•••
HEXADS
HEXANE
HEXING
HEXONE
HEXOSE
HEXYLS
HUXLEY

H••X••
HOAXED
HOAXER
HOAXES

H••••X
HALLUX
HATBOX
HOTBOX

•H•••X
THORAX

••H••X
SPHINX

HY••••
HYADES
HYBRID
HYBRIS
HYDRAE
HYDRAS
HYDRIC
HYDROS
HYENAS
HYETAL
HYGEIA
HYMENO
HYMENS
HYMNAL
HYMNED
HYMNIC
HYOIDS
HYPHAE
HYPHAL
HYPHEN
HYPNIC
HYPNOS
HYSSOP
HYSTER

H•Y•••
HAYING
HAYMOW
HEYDAY
HOYDEN

H••Y••
HEXYLS

H•••Y•
HARRYS
HATTYS
HENRYS
HETTYS

HOLLYS
HONEYS

H••••Y
HALLEY
HALSEY
HARDLY
HARLEY
HARVEY
HAULMY
HAZILY
HEARTY
HEATHY
HENLEY
HEREBY
HERESY
HEYDAY
HICKEY
HIGHLY
HILARY
HOCKEY
HOLILY
HOMELY
HOMILY
HOMINY
HOORAY
HORARY
HORSEY
HOURLY
HUGELY
HUMBLY
HUNGRY
HURRAY
HUXLEY

•HY•••
CHYMIC
KHYBER
PHYLAE
PHYLLO
PHYLUM
PHYSIC
PHYSIO
PHYTIN
RHYMED
RHYMER
RHYMES
RHYTHM
SHYEST
SHYING
THYMES
THYMIC
THYMOL
THYMUS
THYREO
THYRSE
THYRSI
WHYDAH

•H•Y••
CHRYSO
THAYER
WHEYEY

6

•H••Y•
CHERYL
PHENYL
THADYS

•H•••Y
CHAFFY
CHALKY
CHAMMY
CHANCY
CHANTY
CHARRY
CHATTY
CHEEKY
CHEERY
CHEESY
CHERRY
CHESTY
CHILLY
CHINKY
CHIPPY
CHITTY
CHOOSY
CHOPPY
CHUBBY
CHUMMY
CHUNKY
GHARRY
OHENRY
PHONEY
PHOOEY
RHEUMY
SHABBY
SHAGGY
SHAMMY
SHANTY
SHEENY
SHELBY
SHELLY
SHELTY
SHERRY
SHIFTY
SHIMMY
SHINDY
SHINNY
SHOALY
SHODDY
THADDY
THEORY
THINLY
THIRTY
THORNY
WHAMMY
WHEEZY
WHELKY
WHERRY
WHEYEY
WHIMSY
WHINNY
WHISKY
WHITEY
WHOLLY

••HY••
ETHYLS

••H••Y
ASHLEY
ICHTHY
JOHNNY
OCHERY
RRHAGY
SPHERY
UNHOLY

•••HY•
ALPHYL
ARCHYS
CATHYS
KATHYS
METHYL
TETHYS
ZEPHYR

•••H•Y
ARCHLY
CATHAY
EIGHTY
HIGHLY
MIGHTY
NIGHTY
RASHLY
RICHLY
SASHAY

••••HY
APATHY
BEACHY
BOTCHY
BRACHY
BRASHY
BRUSHY
BUNCHY
CATCHY
CONCHY
DEATHY
DINGHY
DOUGHY
EARTHY
FILTHY
FLASHY
FLESHY
FROTHY
GRAPHY
GUNSHY
HEATHY
ICHTHY
LEACHY
MARSHY
MOUTHY
PATCHY
PEACHY
PITCHY
PLASHY
PLUSHY
POACHY
POUCHY
PUNCHY
SLOSHY
SLUSHY
SMITHY
STITHY
SYLPHY
TETCHY
TOOTHY
TOUCHY
TRACHY
TRASHY
TROPHY
WORTHY
WRATHY

H•Z•••
HAZARD
HAZELS
HAZERS
HAZIER
HAZILY
HAZING
HAZZAN

H••Z••
HAMZAS
HAZZAN

H••••Z
HALUTZ

•H••Z•
WHEEZE
WHEEZY

•H•••Z
CHINTZ

••H•Z•
SCHIZO

IA••••
IAMBIC
IAMBUS
IATRIC

I•A•••
ICALLY
ICARUS
IMAGES
IMARET
INARCH
INARMS
IRAQIS
ISAACS
ISABEL
ISADOR
ISAIAH
ITALIC

I••A••
IBEAMS
IDEALS
IDEATE
IGNACE
IGUANA
IHRAMS
IMBALM
IMBARK
IMPACT
IMPAIR
IMPALA
IMPALE
IMPARK
IMPART
IMPAWN
INCAGE
INCASE
INDABA
INFAMY
INFANT
INHALE
INHAUL
INLACE
INLAID
INLAND
INLAWS
INLAYS
INMATE
INNATE
INSANE
INTACT
INTAKE
INVADE
INWALL
INWARD
IODATE
ISAACS
ISLAND
ISRAEL
ITHACA
IZZARD

I•••A•
ICECAP
ICEMAN
INDIAN
INROAD
INSPAN
INSTAR
INWRAP
IONIAN
IPECAC
ISAIAH
ISHTAR
ISOBAR

I••••A
IBERIA
IGUANA
IMPALA
INDABA
INTIMA
ISCHIA
ITHACA

•IA•••
BIALYS
BIANCA
BIASED
BIASES
BIAXAL
DIADEM
DIALED
DIALER
DIALOG
DIANAS
DIANES
DIAPER
DIATOM
DIAZIN
FIACRE
FIANCE
FIASCO
GIANTS
GIAOUR
HIATUS
LIABLE
LIANAS
LIANES
MIASMA
MIAULS
NIACIN
PIAFFE
PIANOS
PIAZZA
RIALTO
RIATAS
SIALIC
TIARAS
VIABLE
VIALED
VIANDS
VIATIC
VIATOR

•I•A••
BICARB
BIGAMY
BIHARI
BINARY
CICADA
CICALA
CIGARS
DICAST
DIGAMY
DILATE
DINAHS
DINARS
DISARM
DIVANS
DIWANS
FINALE
FINALS
FIXATE
GIGANT
GITANO
HIJACK
HILARY
HIRAMS
JIHADS
KINASE
LIGAND
LIGATE
LILACS
LINAGE
LIPASE
LITANY
LIZARD
MIDAIR
MIKADO
MILADY
MILAGE
MIRAGE
PILAFS
PILATE
PINANG
PIPAGE
PIRACY
PIRANA
PIRATE
RIBALD
RITARD
RIVALS
RIYALS
SIMARS
SITARS
SIWASH
SIZARS
TICALS
TIRADE
TIRANA
TISANE
TITANS
VICARS
VIRAGO
VISAED
VISAGE
VISARD
VITALS
VIVACE
VIZARD
WIGANS
WIZARD

•I••A•
AIDMAN
AIRMAN
AIRWAY
BIAXAL
BILBAO
BISCAY
CILIAT
CITRAL
DIANAS
DIPSAS
DIRHAM
DISBAR
DISMAL
DISMAY
DISTAL
FIJIAN
FILIAL
FINIAL
FIRMAN
FISCAL

GIBRAN
GILDAS
GILEAD
GINGAL
HIEMAL
HILDAS
JIGSAW
JINGAL
KIBLAH
KIDNAP
LIANAS
LIBRAE
LIBRAS
LIBYAN
LILIAN
LINDAS
LINEAL
LINEAR
LINGAS
LIVIAS
MICMAC
MIDDAY
MIDWAY
MILLAY
MINOAN
MIRIAM
MISHAP
MISKAL
MISLAY
MISSAL
MITRAL
NILGAI
OILCAN
PICKAX
PILLAR
PINDAR
PINEAL
PINNAE
PINNAL
PISGAH
PITMAN
PIZZAS
RIATAS
RICTAL
RIPRAP
RIPSAW
RITUAL
SIGMAS
SIGNAL
SILVAE
SILVAN
SILVAS
SIMIAN
SINBAD
SIOUAN
SIRDAR
TIARAS
TIBIAE
TIBIAL
TIBIAS
TIMBAL
TINCAL
TITIAN
VILLAS
VIOLAS
VIRGAS
VISTAS
VISUAL
VITTAE
VIVIAN
WIGWAG
WIGWAM
WILMAS
WITHAL
ZIGZAG
ZILLAH

•I•••A

BIANCA
CICADA
CICALA
CINEMA
CITOLA
EIDOLA
FIBULA
FIESTA
GIULIA
LIGULA
LIMINA
LINGUA
LIPOMA
LISBOA
LITHIA
MIASMA
MIMOSA
PIAZZA
PIRANA
SIENNA
SIERRA
SIESTA
SILICA
SILVIA
SISERA
TIRANA
VICUNA
VIENNA
VIMINA
ZINNIA

••IA••

APIARY
ARIANS
ASIANS
AVIARY
AVIATE
BRIARS
CHIASM
CHIAUS
FRIARS
FRIARY
GUIANA
NAIADS
OPIATE
PHIALS
PLIANT
TRIADS
TRIALS
UMIAKS

••I•A•

ABIJAH
ALIDAD
ANIMAL
ANIMAS
ANITAS
APICAL
BAIKAL
BRIDAL
CAIMAN
CEIBAS
CLIMAT
CLIMAX
ELIJAH
ELIZAS
EPICAL
EVITAS
FRIDAY
GUITAR
JAINAS
MOIRAS
OHIOAN
ORIGAN
OVISAC
PLICAE
PRIMAL
PTISAN
RHINAL
SAIGAS
SAIPAN
SHIKAR
SMILAX
SPICAE
SPINAL
SPIRAL
SPITAL
TAIGAS
TAIWAN
TRIBAL
TRINAL
URINAL
WEIMAR
WHIDAH

••I••A

AHIMSA
ALICIA
ANITRA
ARISTA
AXILLA
CRIMEA
ELISHA
EMILIA
ENIGMA
EPIZOA
FRIEDA
GEISHA
GLIOMA
GUIANA
GUINEA
OJIBWA
OLIVIA
PHILIA
SPIREA
STIGMA
TRIVIA

•••IA•

ADRIAN
AECIAL
AERIAL
ANTIAR
APPIAN
ATRIAL
BANIAN
BELIAL
BURIAL
CAPIAS
CAVIAR
CELIAC
CELIAS
CILIAT
COBIAS
CURIAE
CURIAL
DELIAN
DELIAS
DENIAL
DORIAN
DURIAN
EOLIAN
EONIAN
ESPIAL
FABIAN
FACIAL
FECIAL
FENIAN
FERIAL
FETIAL
FIJIAN
FILIAL
FINIAL
FOLIAR
GAVIAL
GENIAL
INDIAN
IONIAN
ISAIAH
JOSIAH
JOSIAS
JOVIAL
JOVIAN
JULIAN
JULIAS
KALIAN
KODIAK
LABIAL
LAMIAE
LAMIAS
LARIAT
LILIAN
LIVIAS
LUCIAN
LUCIAS
LYDIAS
MANIAC
MANIAS
MARIAN
MARIAS
MEDIAE
MEDIAL
MEDIAN
MENIAL
MESIAL
MESIAN
MIRIAM
MYRIAD
NARIAL
NASIAL
NORIAS
NUBIAN
NUBIAS
OOMIAK
OSSIAN
PARIAH
PARIAN
PELIAS
PENIAL
PLEIAD
RACIAL
RADIAL
RADIAN
RUPIAH
SAMIAN
SEPIAS
SERIAL
SIMIAN
SOCIAL
SONIAS
STRIAE
SYRIAC
SYRIAN
TIBIAE
TIBIAL
TIBIAS
TITIAN
TOBIAH
TOBIAS
UNCIAL
VENIAL
VIVIAN
ZAMIAS
ZODIAC

•••I•A

AFRICA
ALMIRA
ALVINA
AMRITA
ANGINA
AQUILA
ARNICA
ATTICA
ATTILA
AURIGA
BENITA
CAMILA
CAPITA
CARINA
EDWINA
ELMIRA
ELVIRA
ENCINA
FARINA
FATIMA
GODIVA
HEGIRA
HEJIRA
INTIMA
JARINA
JEMIMA
LAMINA
LIMINA
LOLITA
LORICA
LOUISA
LUMINA
MANILA
MARINA
MONICA
MYRICA
NUMINA
ONEIDA
OPTIMA
PATINA
REGINA
RETINA
RUMINA
SABINA
SALIVA
SHEILA
SILICA
TROIKA
TUNICA
ULTIMA
VAGINA
VESICA
VIMINA
VOMICA
YAKIMA

••••IA

ABULIA
ACACIA
ACADIA
ACEDIA
ACHAIA
AEOLIA
AGLAIA
ALEXIA
ALICIA
AMELIA
ANEMIA
ANGLIA
ANOXIA
ANTLIA
APULIA
ARABIA
ATAXIA
BORGIA
CASSIA
CODEIA
CRANIA
DAHLIA
EGERIA
EMILIA

6

FASCIA
FLAVIA
GAMBIA
GDYNIA
GIULIA
GLORIA
HERNIA
HESTIA
HYGEIA
IBERIA
ISCHIA
KALMIA
LATRIA
LATVIA
LEPSIA
LITHIA
LOCHIA
LOGGIA
MARCIA
MERCIA
MYOPIA
NUTRIA
ODYNIA
OLIVIA
PATHIA
PENNIA
PEORIA
PERSIA
PHAGIA
PHASIA
PHILIA
PHOBIA
PHONIA
PLASIA
PLEGIA
PORTIA
PYEMIA
PYTHIA
PYURIA
RAFFIA
ROBBIA
RUSSIA
SALVIA
SCORIA
SCOTIA
SERBIA
SILVIA
SOPHIA
STADIA
SYLVIA
TAENIA
TERBIA
THALIA
THORIA
THULIA
TRIVIA
URANIA
UREMIA
UTOPIA
YTTRIA
ZAMBIA
ZINNIA
ZOYSIA

IB••••

IBEAMS
IBERIA
IBEXES
IBICES
IBIDEM
IBISES

I•B•••

IMBALM
IMBARK
IMBEDS
IMBIBE
IMBODY
IMBRUE
IMBUED
IMBUES
INBORN
INBRED

I••B••

IAMBIC
IAMBUS
ICEBOX
ISABEL
ISOBAR
ISOBEL

I•••B•

IMBIBE
INCUBI
INDABA

I••••B

INTOMB

•IB•••

BIBBED
BIBBER
BIBLES
BIBLIO
CIBOLS
DIBBED
DIBBER
DIBBLE
FIBBED
FIBBER
FIBERS
FIBRIL
FIBRIN
FIBULA
GIBBED
GIBBER
GIBBET
GIBBON
GIBERS
GIBING
GIBLET
GIBRAN
GIBSON
JIBBED
JIBBER
JIBING
KIBEIS
KIBITZ
KIBLAH
KIBOSH
LIBBYS
LIBELS
LIBIDO
LIBRAE
LIBRAS
LIBYAN
NIBBED
NIBBLE
RIBALD
RIBBED
RIBBON
RIBOSE
SIBYLS
TIBIAE
TIBIAL
TIBIAS
VIBRIO
ZIBETH
ZIBETS

•I•B••

BIBBED
BIBBER
BILBAO
CIMBRI
DIBBED
DIBBER
DIBBLE
DIOBOL
DISBAR
FIBBED
FIBBER
FIMBLE
GIBBED
GIBBER
GIBBET
GIBBON
JIBBED
JIBBER
LIABLE
LIBBYS
LIMBED
LIMBER
LIMBIC
LIMBUS
LISBOA
LISBON
NIBBED
NIBBLE
NIMBLE
NIMBUS
RIBBED
RIBBON
SINBAD
TIDBIT
TIMBAL
TIMBER
TIMBRE
VIABLE
WILBER
WILBUR
WIMBLE

•I•••B

BICARB
MIDRIB

••IB••

ALIBIS
ALIBLE
BRIBED
BRIBER
BRIBES
CEIBAS
EDIBLE
FOIBLE
GLIBLY
OJIBWA
ORIBIS
OVIBOS
TRIBAL
TRIBES
TWIBIL

••I•B•

AKIMBO
CLIMBS

•••IB•

ADLIBS
CARIBE
CARIBS
IMBIBE
SAHIBS
SCRIBE
SQUIBS

••••IB

MIDRIB

IC••••

ICALLY
ICARUS
ICEBOX
ICECAP
ICEMAN
ICEMEN
ICHTHY
ICICLE
ICIEST
ICINGS
ICONIC

I•C•••

INCAGE
INCASE
INCEPT
INCEST
INCHED
INCHES
INCHON
INCISE
INCITE
INCOME
INCORP
INCUBI
INCURS
INCUSE
ISCHIA
ITCHED
ITCHES

I••C••

IBICES
ICECAP
ICICLE
IOLCUS
IPECAC

I•••C•

IDIOCY
IGNACE
IMPACT
INARCH
INDICT
INDUCE
INDUCT
INFECT
INJECT
INLACE
INSECT
INTACT
ISAACS
ITHACA

I••••C

IAMBIC
IATRIC
ICONIC
IPECAC
IRENIC
IRIDIC
IRITIC
IRONIC
ITALIC

•IC•••

BICARB
BICEPS
BICKER
BICORN
CICADA
CICALA
CICELY
CICERO
DICAST
DICERS
DICING
DICKER
DICKEY
DICKIE
DICTUM
FICHES
FICHUS
FICKLE
HICCUP
HICKEY
HICKOK
KICKED
KICKER
LICHEE
LICHEN
LICKED
LICTOR
MICELL
MICHEL
MICKEY
MICKYS
MICMAC
MICRON
NICELY
NICEST
NICETY
NICHED
NICHES
NICKED
NICKEL
NICKER
NICKYS
NICOLE
PICKAX
PICKED
PICKER
PICKET
PICKLE
PICKUP
PICNIC
PICOTS
PICRIC
PICTOR
PICULS
RICERS
RICHER
RICHES
RICHIE
RICHLY
RICING
RICKED
RICKEY
RICKYS
RICTAL
RICTUS
SICILY
SICKED
SICKEN
SICKER
SICKLE
SICKLY
TICALS
TICKED
TICKER
TICKET
TICKLE
VICARS
VICKYS
VICTIM
VICTOR
VICUNA
WICHES
WICKED
WICKER
WICKET
WICOPY

6

•I•C••
BISCAY
CIRCLE
CIRCUM
CIRCUS
CISCOS
DISCUS
FIACRE
FISCAL
HICCUP
MINCED
MINCER
MINCES
MISCUE
NIACIN
NIECES
OILCAN
PIECED
PIECER
PIECES
PISCES
PITCHY
SIECLE
TINCAL
TINCTS
VINCES
VISCID
VISCUS
WINCED
WINCER
WINCES
WINCEY
ZINCED
ZINCIC
ZINCKY
ZIRCON

•I••C•
BIANCA
BIERCE
BISECT
CILICE
CIVICS
DIRECT
FIANCE
FIASCO
FIERCE
HIJACK
KIRSCH
KITSCH
LILACS
MIMICS
PIERCE
PIRACY
SILICA
SILICO
TIERCE
VIVACE

•I•••C
BIOTIC
CITRIC
FINNIC
FISTIC
LIMBIC
LITHIC
MICMAC
MIOTIC
NITRIC
PICNIC
PICRIC
SIALIC
VIATIC
VITRIC
ZINCIC

••IC••
ALICES
ALICIA
AMICES
APICAL
APICES
BRICKS
CHICHI
CHICKS
CHICLE
CHICOS
CLICHE
CLICKS
CRICKS
DEICED
DEICER
DEICES
EDICTS
ELICIT
EPICAL
ERICHS
EVICTS
FLICKS
HOICKS
IBICES
ICICLE
JUICER
JUICES
PLICAE
PRICED
PRICES
PRICKS
REICHS
SEICHE
SLICED
SLICER
SLICES
SLICKS
SNICKS
SPICAE
SPICED
SPICER
SPICES
STICKS
STICKY
TRICED
TRICES
TRICHI
TRICHO
TRICKS
TRICKY
TRICOT
UNICEF
VOICED
VOICES
YOICKS

••I•C•
APIECE
CHINCH
CLINCH
EVINCE
FLINCH
FLITCH
IDIOCY
PEIRCE
PRINCE
QUINCE
QUINCY
QUITCH
SMIRCH
SNITCH
STITCH
SWITCH
TWITCH

••I••C
ACIDIC
ADIPIC
AMIDIC
CLINIC
CRITIC
DEIFIC
EXILIC
IRIDIC
IRITIC
OVISAC
QUINIC
SAITIC
UNIFIC

•••IC•
ADDICT
ADVICE
AFRICA
ANTICS
ARNICA
ASPICS
ATTICA
ATTICS
BASICS
BODICE
CALICO
CHOICE
CILICE
CIVICS
COMICS
CONICS
CYNICS
DARICS
DELICT
DEPICT
DEVICE
ENRICH
ENRICO
ENTICE
ETHICS
EUNICE
FELICE
FETICH
HELICO
INDICT
JANICE
LORICA
LYRICS
MALICE
MEDICO
MEDICS
MEJICO
MEXICO
MIMICS
MONICA
MUNICH
MYRICA
NOTICE
NOVICE
OFFICE
OPTICS
ORRICE
PANICE
PANICS
PLAICE
POLICE
POLICY
PUMICE
RELICS
RELICT
SCHICK
SHTICK
SILICA
SILICO
SLUICE
SPLICE
STOICS
STRICK
STRICT
THRICE
TONICS
TOPICS
TUNICA
TUNICS
UNPICK
VARICO
VENICE
VESICA
VESICO
VOMICA
ZURICH

•••I•C
CELIAC
MANIAC
MANIOC
SYRIAC
ZODIAC

••••IC
ACETIC
ACIDIC
ADIPIC
ADONIC
AEOLIC
AGAMIC
AGARIC
AGONIC
ALARIC
ALCAIC
ALTAIC
AMEBIC
AMIDIC
AMYLIC
ANEMIC
ANGLIC
ANODIC
ANOMIC
ANOXIC
AORTIC
APNEIC
ARABIC
ARCTIC
ATAVIC
ATAXIC
ATOMIC
ATONIC
AZONIC
AZOTIC
BALTIC
BARDIC
BELGIC
BIOTIC
BROMIC
BUSTIC
CALCIC
CAPRIC
CARPIC
CEDRIC
CELTIC
CHORIC
CHYMIC
CITRIC
CLERIC
CLINIC
CLONIC
COPTIC
COSMIC
CRETIC
CRITIC
CUPRIC
CYANIC
CYCLIC
CYMRIC
CYSTIC
DEIFIC
DERMIC
DYADIC
ECHOIC
EDDAIC
EMERIC
EMETIC
ENATIC
EOZOIC
EROTIC
ETHNIC
EXILIC
EXOTIC
FABRIC
FERRIC
FINNIC
FISTIC
FORMIC
FROLIC
FUSTIC
GAELIC
GALLIC
GARLIC
GEODIC
GESTIC
GNOMIC
GOTHIC
HECTIC
HERDIC
HEROIC
HOLMIC
HYDRIC
HYMNIC
HYPNIC
IAMBIC
IATRIC
ICONIC
IRENIC
IRIDIC
IRITIC
IRONIC
ITALIC
JUDAIC
LACTIC
LIMBIC
LITHIC
LUETIC
MANTIC
MASTIC
METRIC
MIOTIC
MOSAIC
MYOPIC
MYSTIC
MYTHIC
NASTIC
NITRIC
NOETIC
NORDIC
ORPHIC
OXALIC
OZONIC
PECTIC
PELVIC
PEPTIC
PHASIC
PHONIC
PHOTIC
PHYSIC
PICNIC
PICRIC
POETIC
PONTIC
PUBLIC
PYEMIC
PYKNIC

6

PYTHIC
QUINIC
RHODIC
ROMAIC
RUBRIC
RUSTIC
SAITIC
SCENIC
SEPTIC
SIALIC
SLAVIC
SOTHIC
STATIC
STELIC
STERIC
SUOMIC
SYNDIC
TACTIC
TANNIC
THETIC
THORIC
THYMIC
TRAGIC
TROPIC
TURKIC
UNIFIC
URALIC
URANIC
URETIC
VEDAIC
VIATIC
VITRIC
YTTRIC
ZINCIC

ID••••

IDEALS
IDEATE
IDIOCY
IDIOMS
IDIOTS
IDLERS
IDLEST
IDLING
IDYLLS

I•D•••

INDABA
INDEED
INDENE
INDENT
INDIAN
INDICT
INDIES
INDIGO
INDIUM
INDOOR
INDOWS
INDRIS
INDUCE
INDUCT
INDUED
INDUES
INDULT
IODATE
IODIDE
IODINE
IODISM
IODIZE
IODOUS

I••D••

IBIDEM
IMIDES
IRIDES
IRIDIC
ISADOR
ISIDOR

I•••D•

IMBEDS
IMBODY
IMPEDE
INSIDE
INVADE
IODIDE
ISOLDE

I••••D

IMBUED
IMPEND
INBRED
INCHED
INDEED
INDUED
INFOLD
INGRID
INLAID
INLAND
INROAD
INTEND
INURED
INWARD
INWIND
IRONED
ISLAND
ISOPOD
ISSUED
ITCHED
IZZARD

•ID•••

AIDERS
AIDING
AIDMAN
AIDMEN
BIDDEN
BIDDER
BIDETS
BIDING
CIDERS
DIDDLE
DIDIES
DIDOES
EIDOLA
FIDDLE
FIDGET
GIDEON
HIDDEN
HIDERS
HIDING
KIDDED
KIDDER
KIDDIE
KIDNAP
KIDNEY
LIDDED
MIDAIR
MIDDAY
MIDDEN
MIDDLE
MIDGES
MIDGET
MIDGUT
MIDRIB
MIDWAY
NIDIFY
NIDING
PIDDLE
PIDGIN
RIDDED
RIDDEN
RIDDLE
RIDENT
RIDERS
RIDGED
RIDGES
RIDING
SIDDUR
SIDERO
SIDING
SIDLED
SIDLER
SIDLES
SIDNEY
TIDBIT
TIDIED
TIDIER
TIDIES
TIDILY
TIDING
WIDDIE
WIDELY
WIDENS
WIDEST
WIDOWS
WIDTHS

•I•D••

AIRDRY
BIDDEN
BIDDER
BINDER
BIRDIE
CINDER
CINDYS
DIADEM
DIDDLE
DIKDIK
DIODES
FIDDLE
FINDER
GILDAS
GILDED
GILDER
GIRDED
GIRDER
GIRDLE
HIDDEN
HILDAS
HINDER
HINDUS
KIDDED
KIDDER
KIDDIE
KINDER
KINDLE
KINDLY
LIDDED
LIEDER
LINDAS
LINDEN
MIDDAY
MIDDEN
MIDDLE
MILDEN
MILDER
MILDEW
MILDLY
MINDED
MINDER
MISDID
PIDDLE
PINDAR
PINDUS
RIDDED
RIDDEN
RIDDLE
SIDDUR
SIRDAR
TILDES
TINDER
WIDDIE
WILDER
WILDLY
WINDED
WINDER
WINDOW
WISDOM

•I••D•

BIPEDS
BIPODS
CICADA
DIPODY
DIRNDL
DIVIDE
FIELDS
FIENDS
FIORDS
JIHADS
LIBIDO
LIPIDS
MIKADO
MILADY
TIRADE
VIANDS
WIELDS
WIELDY
YIELDS

•I•••D

AISLED
BIASED
BIBBED
BIFFED
BIFOLD
BILGED
BILKED
BILLED
BINNED
BIRLED
BIRRED
BITTED
CITIED
DIALED
DIBBED
DIETED
DIMMED
DINGED
DINNED
DINTED
DIPPED
DIRKED
DISHED
FIBBED
FIGGED
FILLED
FILMED
FINNED
FIRMED
FISHED
FISTED
FITTED
FIZZED
GIBBED
GIFTED
GIGGED
GILDED
GILEAD
GIMPED
GINNED
GIPPED
GIRDED
GIRTED
HILLED
HILTED
HINGED
HINTED
HIPPED
HISPID
HISSED
JIBBED
JIGGED
JILTED
JINKED
KICKED
KIDDED
KILLED
KILTED
KINKED
KISSED
LICKED
LIDDED
LIFTED
LIGAND
LILIED
LILTED
LIMBED
LIMNED
LIMPED
LIMPID
LINKED
LIPOID
LIPPED
LIQUID
LISPED
LISTED
LIZARD
MIFFED
MILKED
MILLED
MILORD
MILTED
MINCED
MINDED
MINTED
MISDID
MISSED
MISTED
NIBBED
NICHED
NICKED
NIMROD
NIPPED
NITRID
PICKED
PIECED
PIGGED
PILLED
PIMPED
PINGED
PINKED
PINNED
PIPPED
PIQUED
PISHED
PITHED
PITIED
PITTED
RIBALD
RIBBED
RICKED
RIDDED
RIDGED
RIFLED
RIFTED
RIGGED
RIMMED
RINGED
RINSED
RIOTED
RIPPED
RISKED

RITARD
SICKED
SIDLED
SIEGED
SIEVED
SIFTED
SIGHED
SIGNED
SIGRID
SILOED
SILTED
SINBAD
SINGED
SINNED
SIPPED
TICKED
TIDIED
TIERED
TIFFED
TILLED
TILTED
TINEID
TINGED
TINNED
TINTED
TIPPED
TITHED
TITLED
VIALED
VIEWED
VISAED
VISARD
VISCID
VISEED
VIZARD
WICKED
WIGGED
WILLED
WILTED
WINCED
WINDED
WINGED
WINKED
WISHED
WISPED
WITHED
WITTED
WIZARD
YIPPED
ZINCED
ZINGED
ZIPPED

••ID••

ABIDED
ABIDER
ABIDES
ACIDIC
ACIDLY
ALIDAD
AMIDES
AMIDIC
AMIDIN
AMIDOL
AMIDST
ARIDLY
ASIDES
AVIDIN
AVIDLY
BRIDAL
BRIDES
BRIDGE
BRIDIE
BRIDLE
CHIDED
CHIDER
CHIDES
ELIDED
ELIDES
FRIDAY
FRIDGE
GLIDED
GLIDER
GLIDES
GRIDED
GRIDES
GUIDED
GUIDER
GUIDES
GUIDON
HOIDEN
IBIDEM
IMIDES
IRIDES
IRIDIC
ISIDOR
MAIDEN
OXIDES
PRIDED
PRIDES
RAIDED
RAIDER
SLIDER
SLIDES
SPIDER
VOIDED
WHIDAH
ZUIDER

••I•D•

BLINDS
BUILDS
FRIEDA
GRINDS
GUILDS
HAIRDO
LAIRDS
NAIADS
POINDS
SHINDY
THIRDS
TRIADS
TRIODE
WEIRDY

••I••D

ABIDED
AFIELD
ALIDAD
ALINED
ALIPED
BAILED
BAITED
BOILED
BRIBED
BRIGID
BRINED
CEILED
CHIDED
CHIMED
COIFED
COILED
COINED
DEICED
EDITED
ELIDED
EXILED
EXITED
FAILED
FAIRED
FOILED
FRIEND
FRIGID
GAINED
GAITED
GLIDED
GRIDED
GRIMED
GRIPED
GUIDED
HAILED
HAIRED
JAILED
JOINED
KNIFED
LAIRED
MAILED
MAIMED
MOILED
NAILED
NOISED
OPINED
PAINED
PAIRED
POISED
PRICED
PRIDED
PRIMED
PRIZED
QUIRED
RAIDED
RAILED
RAINED
RAISED
REINED
ROILED
RUINED
SAILED
SEINED
SEIZED
SHIELD
SHINED
SKIVED
SLICED
SLIMED
SMILED
SNIPED
SOILED
SPICED
SPIKED
SPILED
SPIRED
SPITED
SUITED
SWIPED
TAILED
TOILED
TRICED
TRIFID
TRINED
TRIPOD
TWINED
UNITED
VEILED
VEINED
VOICED
VOIDED
WAIFED
WAILED
WAITED
WAIVED
WHILED
WHINED
WHITED

•••ID•

APHIDS
AROIDS
AVOIDS
BESIDE
BETIDE
BOLIDE
BORIDE
BRAIDS
DAVIDS
DECIDE
DERIDE
DIVIDE
DRUIDS
EXCIDE
FELIDS
FLUIDS
HALIDE
HALIDS
HYOIDS
INSIDE
IODIDE
LEPIDO
LIBIDO
LIPIDS
ONEIDA
OREIDE
OROIDE
PLAIDS
RAPIDS
RESIDE
SOLIDI
SOLIDS
SQUIDS
STRIDE
UNTIDY
UPSIDE
UREIDE
ZOOIDS

•••I•D

AERIED
ALLIED
BABIED
BEGIRD
BEHIND
BELIED
BODIED
BURIED
BUSIED
CITIED
COPIED
DEFIED
DENIED
ENGIRD
ENVIED
ENWIND
ESPIED
HESIOD
HONIED
INWIND
LEVIED
LILIED
MONIED
MYRIAD
PERIOD
PITIED
PLEIAD
PONIED
RELIED
REMIND
REWIND
TAXIED
TIDIED
UNBIND
UNGIRD
UNKIND
UNTIED
UNWIND
VARIED

••••ID

ACARID
AENEID
AFRAID
ALGOID
ASTRID
BEDRID
BRIGID
CANDID
CEBOID
CLERID
COCCID
CONOID
CUBOID
CUSPID
CYANID
CYMOID
DANAID
DESMID
DEVOID
EUCLID
EYELID
FERVID
FLORID
FOETID
FORBID
FRIGID
FUCOID
FULGID
GADOID
GANOID
GRAVID
HALOID
HEMOID
HISPID
HORRID
HYBRID
INGRID
INLAID
KELOID
LIMPID
LIPOID
LIQUID
MADRID
MISDID
MORBID
MUCOID
NEVOID
NITRID
ORCHID
OUTBID
OUTDID
PALLID
PLACID
PUTRID
RANCID
REPAID
SALPID
SIGRID
SORDID
STOLID
STUPID
TINEID
TOROID
TORPID
TORRID
TRIFID
TURBID
TURGID
UNLAID
UNPAID
UNSAID
VESPID
VISCID
XYLOID

I•E•••

IBEAMS

6

IBERIA
IBEXES
ICEBOX
ICECAP
ICEMAN
ICEMEN
IDEALS
IDEATE
ILEXES
IPECAC
IREFUL
IRENES
IRENIC
ISEULT

I••E••

ICIEST
IDLERS
IDLEST
IMBEDS
IMMESH
IMPEDE
IMPELS
IMPEND
INCEPT
INCEST
INDEED
INDENE
INDENT
INFECT
INFERO
INFERS
INFEST
INGEST
INHERE
INJECT
INKERS
INLETS
INMESH
INSECT
INSERT
INSETS
INTEND
INTENT
INTERN
INTERS
INVENT
INVERT
INVEST
ISLETS
ISSEIS
ITSELF

I•••E•

IBEXES
IBICES
IBIDEM
IBISES
ICEMEN
ILEXES
IMAGES
IMARET
IMBUED
IMBUES
IMIDES
IMINES
IMMIES
IMOGEN
INBRED
INCHED
INCHES
INDEED
INDIES
INDUED
INDUES
INGRES
INKIER
INKLES
INLIER
INSTEP
INURED
INURES
IRENES
IRIDES
IRISES
IRONED
IRONER
ISABEL
ISOBEL
ISOHEL
ISOMER
ISRAEL
ISSUED
ISSUER
ISSUES
ITCHED
ITCHES

I••••E

ICICLE
IDEATE
IGNACE
IGNITE
IGNORE
ILLUME
ILLUSE
IMBIBE
IMBRUE
IMMUNE
IMMURE
IMPALE
IMPEDE
IMPOSE
IMPURE
IMPUTE
INCAGE
INCASE
INCISE
INCITE
INCOME
INCUSE
INDENE
INDUCE
INFUSE
INHALE
INHERE
INJURE
INLACE
INMATE
INNATE
INSANE
INSIDE
INSOLE
INSURE
INTAKE
INTONE
INVADE
INVITE
INVOKE
INWOVE
IODATE
IODIDE
IODINE
IODIZE
IOLITE
IONIZE
IONONE
ISOLDE

•IE•••

BIERCE
DIEPPE
DIESEL
DIESES
DIESIS
DIETED
DIETER
FIELDS
FIENDS
FIERCE
FIESTA
HIEING
HIEMAL
LIEDER
LIEGES
LIERNE
NIECES
NIELLI
NIELLO
PIECED
PIECER
PIECES
PIERCE
PIERRE
PIERUS
PIETER
PIETRO
SIECLE
SIEGED
SIEGES
SIENNA
SIERRA
SIESTA
SIEURS
SIEVED
SIEVES
TIEINS
TIERCE
TIERED
TIEUPS
VIENNA
VIEWED
VIEWER
WIELDS
WIELDY
WIENER
WIENIE
YIELDS

•I•E••

AIDERS
AILEEN
BICEPS
BIDETS
BIPEDS
BIREME
BISECT
BITERS
CICELY
CICERO
CIDERS
CINEMA
CINEOL
CIVETS
DICERS
DIGEST
DIMERS
DINERO
DINERS
DIRECT
DIRELY
DIREST
DIVERS
DIVERT
DIVEST
DIZENS
EILEEN
FIBERS
FIFERS
FILERS
FILETS
FINELY
FINERY
FINEST
FIRERS
FIVERS
FIXERS
GIBERS
GIDEON
GILEAD
GIMELS
GISELE
HIDERS
HIKERS
HIRERS
KIBEIS
KINESI
KINETO
LIBELS
LIFERS
LIKELY
LIKENS
LIMENS
LIMEYS
LINEAL
LINEAR
LINENS
LINERS
LINEUP
LITERS
LIVELY
LIVENS
LIVERS
LIVERY
MICELL
MILERS
MIMERS
MINERS
MISERS
MISERY
MITERS
MIXERS
NICELY
NICEST
NICETY
NIGELS
NINETY
NISEIS
OILERS
PIGEON
PIKERS
PILEUM
PILEUS
PINEAL
PINENE
PINERY
PIPERS
PIPETS
RICERS
RIDENT
RIDERS
RIMERS
RIPELY
RIPENS
RIPEST
RISERS
RIVERS
RIVETS
SIDERO
SILENI
SILENT
SIMEON
SINEWS
SINEWY
SIRENS
SISERA
TIGERS
TILERS
TIMELY
TIMERS
TINEID
VILELY
VILEST
VINERY
VIPERS
VIREOS
VISEED
VIXENS
WIDELY
WIDENS
WIDEST
WIFELY
WIGEON
WINERY
WIPERS
WIRERS
WISELY
WISEST
WIVERN
WIVERS
WIZENS
ZIBETH
ZIBETS

•I••E•

AIDMEN
AIGLET
AILEEN
AIRIER
AIRMEN
AISLED
AISLES
BIASED
BIASES
BIBBED
BIBBER
BIBLES
BICKER
BIDDEN
BIDDER
BIFFED
BIFLEX
BIGGER
BILGED
BILGES
BILKED
BILKER
BILLED
BILLET
BINDER
BINGES
BINNED
BIOGEN
BIRLED
BIRLES
BIRRED
BISTER
BITTED
BITTEN
BITTER
CINDER
CIPHER
CITHER
CITIED
CITIES
CIVIES
DIADEM
DIALED
DIALER
DIANES
DIAPER
DIBBED
DIBBER
DICKER

DICKEY
DIDIES
DIDOES
DIESEL
DIESES
DIETED
DIETER
DIFFER
DIGGER
DIMMED
DIMMER
DINGED
DINGEY
DINKEY
DINNED
DINNER
DINTED
DIODES
DIPLEX
DIPPED
DIPPER
DIRGES
DIRKED
DISHED
DISHES
DISNEY
DISPEL
DITHER
EIFFEL
EILEEN
EITHER
FIBBED
FIBBER
FICHES
FIDGET
FIGGED
FILLED
FILLER
FILLET
FILMED
FILTER
FINDER
FINGER
FINNED
FIQUES
FIRMED
FIRMER
FISHED
FISHER
FISHES
FISTED
FITTED
FITTER
FIZZED
FIZZES
GIBBED
GIBBER
GIBBET
GIBLET
GIFTED
GIGGED
GIGLET
GIGUES
GILDED

GILDER
GIMLET
GIMPED
GINGER
GINNED
GINNER
GIPPED
GIRDED
GIRDER
GIRTED
HICKEY
HIDDEN
HIGHER
HILLED
HILLER
HILTED
HINDER
HINGED
HINGES
HINTED
HIPPED
HISSED
HISSER
HISSES
HITHER
HITLER
HITTER
JIBBED
JIBBER
JIGGED
JIGGER
JILTED
JILTER
JINKED
JINKER
JINXES
JITNEY
JITTER
KICKED
KICKER
KIDDED
KIDDER
KIDNEY
KILLED
KILLER
KILMER
KILTED
KILTER
KINDER
KINKED
KINSEY
KIPPER
KISLEW
KISMET
KISSED
KISSER
KISSES
KITTEN
LIANES
LICHEE
LICHEN
LICKED
LIDDED
LIEDER

LIEGES
LIFTED
LIFTER
LILIED
LILIES
LILTED
LIMBED
LIMBER
LIMIER
LIMNED
LIMNER
LIMPED
LIMPER
LIMPET
LINDEN
LINGER
LINIER
LINKED
LINNET
LINTEL
LINTER
LIONEL
LIPPED
LIPPER
LISPED
LISPER
LISTED
LISTEL
LISTEN
LISTER
LITHER
LITTER
LIVIER
LIVRES
LIVYER
MICHEL
MICKEY
MIDDEN
MIDGES
MIDGET
MIFFED
MIGUEL
MILDEN
MILDER
MILDEW
MILIEU
MILKED
MILKER
MILLED
MILLER
MILLET
MILTED
MILTER
MINCED
MINCER
MINCES
MINDED
MINDER
MINTED
MINTER
MINUET
MINXES
MISSED
MISSES

MISTED
MISTER
MITTEN
MIZZEN
NIBBED
NICHED
NICHES
NICKED
NICKEL
NICKER
NIECES
NIGHER
NIPPED
NIPPER
NIXIES
OILIER
PICKED
PICKER
PICKET
PIECED
PIECER
PIECES
PIETER
PIGGED
PIGPEN
PILFER
PILLED
PIMPED
PINGED
PINIER
PINKED
PINNED
PINNER
PINTER
PIPIER
PIPPED
PIQUED
PIQUES
PIQUET
PISCES
PISHED
PISHES
PITHED
PITIED
PITIES
PITMEN
PITTED
PIXIES
RIBBED
RICHER
RICHES
RICKED
RICKEY
RIDDED
RIDDEN
RIDGED
RIDGES
RIFLED
RIFLER
RIFLES
RIFTED
RIGGED
RIGGER
RILLET

RIMMED
RIMMER
RINGED
RINGER
RINSED
RINSER
RINSES
RIOTED
RIOTER
RIPLEY
RIPPED
RIPPER
RISKED
RISKER
RITTER
SICKED
SICKEN
SICKER
SIDLED
SIDLER
SIDLES
SIDNEY
SIEGED
SIEGES
SIEVED
SIEVES
SIFTED
SIFTER
SIGHED
SIGNED
SIGNER
SIGNET
SILKEN
SILOED
SILTED
SILVER
SIMMER
SIMNEL
SIMPER
SINGED
SINGER
SINGES
SINKER
SINNED
SINNER
SINTER
SIPPED
SIPPER
SIPPET
SISTER
SITTER
SIXTES
SIZIER
TICKED
TICKER
TICKET
TIDIED
TIDIER
TIDIES
TIERED
TIFFED
TILDES
TILLED
TILLER

TILTED
TILTER
TIMBER
TINDER
TINGED
TINGES
TINKER
TINNED
TINNER
TINSEL
TINTED
TIPPED
TIPPER
TIPPET
TITHED
TITHER
TITHES
TITLED
TITLES
TITTER
VIALED
VIEWED
VIEWER
VINCES
VINIER
VIOLET
VISAED
VISEED
VIVIEN
VIZIER
WICHES
WICKED
WICKER
WICKET
WIENER
WIGGED
WILBER
WILDER
WILIER
WILLED
WILLER
WILLET
WILTED
WINCED
WINCER
WINCES
WINCEY
WINDED
WINDER
WINGED
WINIER
WINKED
WINKER
WINNER
WINOES
WINTER
WINZES
WIRIER
WISHED
WISHES
WISPED
WITHED
WITHER
WITHES

WITNEY
WITTED
YIPPED
ZINCED
ZINGED
ZIPPED
ZIPPER
ZITHER

•I•••E

BIERCE
BILLIE
BIRDIE
BIREME
BISQUE
CILICE
CINQUE
CIRCLE
CIRQUE
CISSIE
DIBBLE
DICKIE
DIDDLE
DIEPPE
DILATE
DILUTE
DIMPLE
DINGLE
DIPLOE
DIPOLE
DISUSE
DIVIDE
DIVINE
FIACRE
FIANCE
FICKLE
FIDDLE
FIERCE
FIGURE
FILOSE
FIMBLE
FINALE
FINITE
FIPPLE
FIXATE
FIZZLE
GIGGLE
GIRDLE
GISELE
HIGGLE
HIPPIE
JIGGLE
JIMMIE
JINGLE
KIDDIE
KILTIE
KINASE
KINDLE
LIABLE
LIBRAE
LICHEE
LIERNE
LIGATE
LIGULE
LIGURE
LINAGE
LIPASE
LITTLE
LIZZIE
MIDDLE
MIGGLE
MILAGE
MILLIE
MINGLE
MINNIE
MINUTE
MIRAGE
MISCUE
MISUSE
NIBBLE
NICOLE
NIGGLE
NIMBLE
NIPPLE
PIAFFE
PICKLE
PIDDLE
PIERCE
PIERRE
PIFFLE
PIGGIE
PILATE
PILOSE
PILULE
PIMPLE
PINENE
PINITE
PINKIE
PINNAE
PINOLE
PINTLE
PIPAGE
PIRATE
RIBOSE
RICHIE
RIDDLE
RIFFLE
RIMOSE
RIMPLE
RIPPLE
RISQUE
SICKLE
SIECLE
SILVAE
SIMILE
SIMONE
SIMPLE
SINGLE
SIZZLE
TIBIAE
TICKLE
TIERCE
TILLIE
TIMBRE
TINGLE
TINKLE
TIPPLE
TIPTOE
TIRADE
TISANE
TISSUE
TITTLE
VIABLE
VIRGIE
VIRILE
VIRTUE
VISAGE
VITTAE
VIVACE
WIDDIE
WIENIE
WIGGLE
WILLIE
WIMBLE
WIMPLE
WINKLE
WINNIE
YIPPIE
ZIZZLE

••IE••

ADIEUS
ADIEUX
AFIELD
ALIENS
AMIENS
APIECE
ARIELS
BRIEFS
BRIERS
BRIERY
CHIEFS
CLIENT
CRIERS
DRIERS
DRIEST
FLIERS
FLIEST
FRIEDA
FRIEND
FRIERS
FRIEZE
GAIETY
GRIEFS
GRIEVE
ICIEST
MOIETY
ORIELS
ORIENT
OSIERS
PLIERS
PRIERS
PRIEST
SHIELD
SHIEST
SKIERS
SLIEST
SPIELS
SPIERS
THIEVE
TRIERS
UBIETY
WRIEST

••I•E•

ABIDED
ABIDER
ABIDES
ALICES
ALINED
ALINES
ALIPED
AMICES
AMIDES
ANISES
APICES
ARISEN
ARISES
ASIDES
AZINES
BAILED
BAILEE
BAILER
BAILEY
BAITED
BAITER
BEIGES
BOILED
BOILER
BRIBED
BRIBER
BRIBES
BRIDES
BRINED
BRINES
CEILED
CHIDED
CHIDER
CHIDES
CHIMED
CHIMER
CHIMES
CHINES
CHISEL
CHIVES
CLIMES
CLINES
CLIVES
COIFED
COILED
COILER
COINED
COINER
CRIMEA
CRIMES
CRISES
DAISES
DEICED
DEICER
DEICES
DRIVEL
DRIVEN
DRIVER
DRIVES
DUIKER
EDILES
EDITED
ELIDED
ELIDES
EMILES
EXILED
EXILES
EXITED
FAILED
FAIRED
FAIRER
FOILED
FRISES
GAINED
GAINER
GAITED
GAITER
GEIGER
GLIDED
GLIDER
GLIDES
GOITER
GRIDED
GRIDES
GRIMED
GRIMES
GRIPED
GRIPER
GRIPES
GRIVET
GRIZEL
GUIDED
GUIDER
GUIDES
GUILES
GUINEA
GUISES
HAILED
HAILER
HAIRED
HEIFER
HOIDEN
IBICES
IBIDEM
IBISES
IMIDES
IMINES
IRIDES
IRISES
JAILED
JAILER
JOINED
JOINER
JUICER
JUICES
KAISER
KNIFED
KNIFES
KNIVES
KOINES
KRISES
LAIRED
LOITER
MAIDEN
MAILED
MAILER
MAIMED
MAIMER
MAIZES
MOILED
MOILER
NAILED
NOISED
NOISES
OGIVES
OLIVER
OLIVES
OPINED
OPINES
ORIGEN
OXIDES
PAINED
PAIRED
POISED
POISES
PRICED
PRICES
PRIDED
PRIDES
PRIMED
PRIMER
PRIMES
PRIVET
PRIZED
PRIZER
PRIZES
QUIRED
QUIRES
QUIVER
RAIDED
RAIDER
RAILED
RAINED
RAISED
RAISER
RAISES
REINED
ROILED
RUINED
RUINER
SAILED
SAILER
SEINED
SEINER
SEINES
SEIZED
SEIZER
SEIZES
SHINED
SHINER
SHINES
SHIRES
SHIVER
SHIVES
SKIVED
SKIVER
SKIVES
SLICED
SLICER

SLICES
SLIDER
SLIDES
SLIMED
SLIMES
SLIVER
SMILED
SMILER
SMILES
SMITER
SMITES
SNIPED
SNIPER
SNIPES
SNIVEL
SOILED
SOIREE
SPICED
SPICER
SPICES
SPIDER
SPIKED
SPIKES
SPILED
SPILES
SPINEL
SPINES
SPINET
SPIREA
SPIRED
SPIRES
SPITED
SPITES
STILES
STIPEL
STIPES
STIVER
SUITED
SUITES
SWIPED
SWIPES
SWIVEL
SWIVET
TAILED
TAIPEI
TOILED
TOILER
TOILES
TOILET
TRIBES
TRICED
TRICES
TRINED
TRINES
TRITER
TRIVET
TWINED
TWINER
TWINES
UNICEF
UNISEX
UNITED
UNITES
VAINER
VEILED
VEILER
VEINED
VOICED
VOICES
VOIDED
VOILES
WAIFED
WAILED
WAILER
WAITED
WAITER
WAIVED
WAIVER
WAIVES
WHILED
WHILES
WHINED
WHINER
WHINES
WHITED
WHITEN
WHITER
WHITES
WHITEY
WRITER
WRITES
ZUIDER

••I••E

ALIBLE
APIECE
ARIOSE
AVIATE
BAILEE
BAILIE
BLITHE
BRIDGE
BRIDIE
BRIDLE
CAIQUE
CHICLE
CHIGOE
CLICHE
CLIQUE
CRINGE
CUISSE
EDIBLE
EMIGRE
EMILIE
ENISLE
EVINCE
FAILLE
FOIBLE
FRIDGE
FRIEZE
FRINGE
GRIEVE
GRIFFE
GRILLE
GRILSE
GRIPPE
GUIMPE
ICICLE
MAIGRE
MAISIE
MAITRE
MOISHE
OPIATE
ORIOLE
OTIOSE
PAIUTE
PEIRCE
PLICAE
PRINCE
PUISNE
QUINCE
SEICHE
SHIITE
SOIGNE
SOIREE
SPICAE
STIFLE
SWINGE
SWIPLE
TAILLE
THIEVE
TRIFLE
TRIODE
TRIOSE
TRIPLE
TRISTE
TRIUNE
TRIXIE
TUILLE
TWINGE
UNIQUE
WRITHE

•••IE•

ABBIES
ADRIEN
AERIED
AERIES
AIRIER
ALLIED
ALLIES
ANNIES
ARMIES
ARNIES
ARTIES
ASHIER
BABIED
BABIES
BELIED
BELIEF
BELIER
BELIES
BEVIES
BODIED
BODIES
BOGIES
BONIER
BURIED
BURIES
BUSIED
BUSIES
CAGIER
CAHIER
CARIES
CAVIES
CITIED
CITIES
CIVIES
COLIES
CONIES
COPIED
COPIER
COPIES
COZIER
COZIES
CURIES
CUTIES
DANIEL
DARIEN
DAVIES
DEFIED
DEFIER
DEFIES
DEMIES
DENIED
DENIER
DENIES
DEWIER
DIDIES
DOBIES
DOGIES
DOPIER
DORIES
DOTIER
DOXIES
DOZIER
DUTIES
EASIER
EDDIES
EDGIER
ELLIES
ELSIES
EMMIES
ENVIED
ENVIER
ENVIES
ERNIES
ESPIED
ESPIES
EYRIES
FACIES
FOGIES
FOXIER
FUMIER
FURIES
GAMIER
GENIES
GLUIER
GOBIES
GOOIER
GORIER
HAZIER
HOLIER
HOLIES
HOMIER
HONIED
HOSIER
IMMIES
INDIES
INKIER
INLIER
JAMIES
JOLIET
JOSIES
JULIES
JULIET
JURIES
KATIES
LACIER
LADIES
LAKIER
LAZIER
LEVIED
LEVIER
LEVIES
LILIED
LILIES
LIMIER
LINIER
LIVIER
LOGIER
LORIES
LUCIEN
MAMIES
MARIES
MAZIER
METIER
MILIEU
MOLIES
MONIED
MONIES
MOVIES
MURIEL
NAPIER
NAVIES
NIXIES
NOSIER
OILIER
OLLIES
OOZIER
ORGIES
PARIES
PINIER
PIPIER
PITIED
PITIES
PIXIES
POGIES
POKIER
POKIES
PONIED
PONIES
POSIES
PUNIER
PYXIES
RABIES
RACIER
RAMIES
RAPIER
RELIED
RELIEF
RELIER
RELIES
REVIEW
ROPIER
ROSIER
RUBIES
SADIES
SAGIER
SAMIEL
SANIES
SERIES
SEXIER
SHRIEK
SIZIER
SOVIET
SPRIER
SUSIES
TAXIED
TIDIED
TIDIER
TIDIES
TOBIES
TODIES
TONIER
TORIES
UGLIER
UNDIES
UNTIED
UNTIES
VARIED
VARIER
VARIES
VINIER
VIVIEN
VIZIER
WADIES
WARIER
WAVIER
WAVIES
WAXIER
WILIER
WINIER
WIRIER
XAVIER
ZANIER
ZANIES

•••I•E

ACTIVE
ADMIRE
ADVICE
ADVISE
AEDILE
ALBITE
ALDINE
ALPINE
ALSIKE
ALVINE
APLITE
ARGIVE
ARLINE
ARRIVE
ARSINE

6

ASPIRE
ASSIZE
ATTIRE
AUDILE
AUGITE
AWHILE
AXLIKE
BABITE
BARITE
BELIZE
BEMIRE
BESIDE
BETIDE
BETISE
BODICE
BOLIDE
BORIDE
BOVINE
BRAISE
BRAIZE
BRUISE
BYLINE
CAMISE
CANINE
CARIBE
CAVITE
CECILE
CERISE
CERITE
CHAISE
CHOICE
CILICE
CLAIRE
COLINE
COSINE
CRUISE
CURIAE
DANITE
DATIVE
DECIDE
DECILE
DEFILE
DEFINE
DEMISE
DENISE
DERIDE
DERIVE
DESIRE
DEVICE
DEVISE
DIVIDE
DIVINE
DOCILE
ELAINE
ELOISE
EMPIRE
ENDIVE
ENGINE
ENSILE
ENTICE
ENTIRE
EQUINE
ERMINE
EUNICE

EXCIDE
EXCISE
EXCITE
EXPIRE
FACILE
FAMINE
FELICE
FELINE
FELIPE
FERINE
FINITE
FRAISE
FUSILE
FUTILE
GREIGE
HABILE
HALIDE
HALITE
HAMITE
IGNITE
IMBIBE
INCISE
INCITE
INSIDE
INVITE
IODIDE
IODINE
IODIZE
IOLITE
IONIZE
JANICE
LABILE
LAMIAE
LARINE
LEVITE
LOUISE
LUCILE
LUCITE
LUPINE
LYSINE
MALICE
MALINE
MARINE
MAXINE
MAXIXE
MEDIAE
MOBILE
MOLINE
MOTILE
MOTIVE
MURINE
NADINE
NARINE
NATIVE
NEVILE
NOTICE
NOVICE
NOWISE
NUBILE
OBLIGE
OFFICE
OOLITE
OPHITE
OPTIME

OREIDE
OROIDE
ORPINE
ORRICE
OSCINE
PANICE
PATINE
PAVISE
PELITE
PENILE
PETITE
PINITE
PLAICE
POLICE
POLITE
PRAISE
PUMICE
PURINE
PYRITE
RACINE
RAPINE
RATINE
RATITE
RAVINE
RECIPE
RECITE
REFINE
REGIME
RELINE
RELIVE
REMISE
REPINE
RESIDE
RESILE
RETIRE
REVILE
REVISE
REVIVE
RUSINE
RUTILE
SABINE
SALINE
SAMITE
SATIRE
SCRIBE
SCRIVE
SEDILE
SEMITE
SENILE
SERINE
SHIITE
SHRIKE
SHRINE
SHRIVE
SIMILE
SLUICE
SOMITE
SOZINE
SPLICE
SPLINE
SPRITE
SQUIRE
STRIAE
STRIDE

STRIFE
STRIKE
STRIPE
STRIVE
SUPINE
TAXITE
THRICE
THRIVE
TIBIAE
UMPIRE
UNDINE
UNLIKE
UNLIVE
UNPILE
UNRIPE
UNWISE
UPRISE
UPSIDE
UREIDE
URSINE
VALISE
VENICE
VENIRE
VIRILE
VOTIVE
WAHINE

••••IE

AMELIE
ANOMIE
ARCHIE
AUNTIE
BABBIE
BAILIE
BARBIE
BARMIE
BEANIE
BERNIE
BERTIE
BESSIE
BILLIE
BIRDIE
BOBBIE
BOCCIE
BONNIE
BOOKIE
BOOTIE
BOUGIE
BRIDIE
BUDGIE
BURDIE
CADDIE
CANNIE
CARRIE
CASSIE
CATTIE
CISSIE
COLLIE
COMMIE
CONNIE
COOKIE
COOLIE
COOTIE
COWRIE

CUDDIE
DEARIE
DICKIE
DOGGIE
DOLLIE
DONNIE
DOOLIE
DORMIE
DOUGIE
DULCIE
EMILIE
FANNIE
GERTIE
GOALIE
GUSSIE
HACKIE
HATTIE
HIPPIE
HOGTIE
HORNIE
HUGHIE
JACKIE
JESSIE
JIMMIE
JONNIE
JUNKIE
KATHIE
KENNIE
KEWPIE
KIDDIE
KILTIE
LADDIE
LAMBIE
LASSIE
LAURIE
LEONIE
LESLIE
LIZZIE
LOTTIE
MAGGIE
MAGPIE
MAISIE
MARGIE
MASHIE
MATTIE
MEALIE
MEANIE
MILLIE
MINNIE
MOLLIE
NAPPIE
NELLIE
NETTIE
PANTIE
PETRIE
PIGGIE
PINKIE
POTPIE
POTSIE
REGGIE
RICHIE
ROBBIE
RONNIE
ROOKIE

SOPHIE
SORTIE
SPECIE
STACIE
STEVIE
STYMIE
TESSIE
TILLIE
TRIXIE
VIRGIE
WALLIE
WEDGIE
WEENIE
WIDDIE
WIENIE
WILLIE
WINNIE
YIPPIE
ZOMBIE

I•F•••

INFAMY
INFANT
INFECT
INFERO
INFERS
INFEST
INFIRM
INFLOW
INFLUX
INFOLD
INFORM
INFUSE

I••F••

IREFUL

I•••F•

IGNIFY

I••••F

INGULF
ITSELF

•IF•••

BIFFED
BIFFIN
BIFLEX
BIFOLD
BIFORM
DIFFER
EIFFEL
FIFERS
FIFING
FIFTHS
GIFTED
LIFERS
LIFTED
LIFTER
MIFFED
PIFFLE
RIFFLE
RIFLED
RIFLER

RIFLES
RIFTED
SIFTED
SIFTER
TIFFED
TIFFIN
WIFELY

•I•F••

BIFFED
BIFFIN
DIFFER
EIFFEL
FITFUL
MIFFED
MISFIT
PIAFFE
PIFFLE
PILFER
RIFFLE
SINFUL
TIFFED
TIFFIN
WILFUL

•I••F•

MINIFY
NIDIFY
PIAFFE
PILAFS
RIPOFF
TIPOFF
VILIFY
VIVIFY

•I•••F

RIPOFF
TIPOFF

••IF••

CLIFFS
CLIFFY
COIFED
DEIFIC
DRIFTS
DRIFTY
GRIFFE
HEIFER
KNIFED
KNIFES
SHIFTS
SHIFTY
SKIFFS
SNIFFS
SNIFFY
SPIFFY
STIFLE
SWIFTS
TRIFID
TRIFLE
UNIFIC
WAIFED
WHIFFS

••I•F•

BRIEFS
CHIEFS
CLIFFS
CLIFFY
GRIEFS
GRIFFE
SKIFFS
SNIFFS
SNIFFY
SPIFFY
WHIFFS

••I••F

UNICEF

•••IF•

ADRIFT
AERIFY
BASIFY
CALIFS
CODIFY
IGNIFY
MINIFY
MODIFY
MOTIFS
NAZIFY
NIDIFY
NOTIFY
OSSIFY
PACIFY
PURIFY
RAMIFY
RATIFY
SALIFY
SERIFS
SHRIFT
STRIFE
TARIFF
THRIFT
TYPIFY
UGLIFY
UPLIFT
VERIFY
VILIFY
VIVIFY

•••I•F

BELIEF
RELIEF
TARIFF

••••IF

MASSIF
SHERIF

IG••••

IGLOOS
IGNACE
IGNIFY
IGNITE
IGNORE
IGOROT
IGUANA

I•G•••

INGEST
INGOTS
INGRES
INGRID
INGULF

I••G••

IMAGES
IMOGEN
ISOGON

I•••G•

ICINGS
IMPUGN
INCAGE
INDIGO

I••••G

IDLING
IMPING
INKING
INNING
IRKING
IRVING
ISLING

•IG•••

AIGLET
BIGAMY
BIGGER
BIGGIN
BIGHTS
BIGOTS
BIGWIG
CIGARS
DIGAMY
DIGEST
DIGGER
DIGITI
DIGITS
DIGLOT
EIGHTH
EIGHTS
EIGHTY
FIGGED
FIGHTS
FIGURE
GIGANT
GIGGED
GIGGLE
GIGGLY
GIGLET
GIGLOT
GIGOLO
GIGUES
HIGGLE
HIGHER
HIGHLY
JIGGED
JIGGER
JIGGLE
JIGSAW
LIGAND
LIGATE
LIGHTS
LIGNIN
LIGULA
LIGULE
LIGURE
MIGGLE
MIGHTY
MIGNON
MIGUEL
NIGELS
NIGGLE
NIGHER
NIGHTS
NIGHTY
PIGEON
PIGGED
PIGGIE
PIGGIN
PIGNUS
PIGNUT
PIGPEN
PIGSTY
RIGGED
RIGGER
RIGHTO
RIGHTS
RIGORS
SIGHED
SIGHTS
SIGILS
SIGMAS
SIGNAL
SIGNED
SIGNER
SIGNET
SIGNOR
SIGRID
TIGERS
TIGHTS
VIGILS
VIGOUR
WIGANS
WIGEON
WIGGED
WIGGLE
WIGGLY
WIGWAG
WIGWAM
ZIGZAG

•I•G••

BIGGER
BIGGIN
BILGED
BILGES
BINGES
BIOGEN
DIGGER
DINGED
DINGEY
DINGHY
DINGLE
DINGUS
DIRGES
FIDGET
FIGGED
FINGER
FIZGIG
GIGGED
GIGGLE
GIGGLY
GINGAL
GINGER
HIGGLE
HINGED
HINGES
JIGGED
JIGGER
JIGGLE
JINGAL
JINGLE
KINGLY
LIEGES
LINGAS
LINGER
LINGUA
MIDGES
MIDGET
MIDGUT
MIGGLE
MINGLE
NIGGLE
NILGAI
PIDGIN
PIGGED
PIGGIE
PIGGIN
PINGED
PINGOS
PISGAH
RIDGED
RIDGES
RIGGED
RIGGER
RINGED
RINGER
SIEGED
SIEGES
SINGED
SINGER
SINGES
SINGLE
SINGLY
TINGED
TINGES
TINGLE
TINGLY
VIRGAS
VIRGIE
VIRGIL
VIRGIN
WIGGED
WIGGLE
WIGGLY
WINGED
ZINGED

•I••G•

GINKGO
LINAGE
MILAGE
MIRAGE
PIPAGE
VIRAGO
VISAGE

•I•••G

AIDING
AILING
AIMING
AIRING
BIDING
BIGWIG
BITING
CITING
DIALOG
DICING
DIKING
DINING
DIVING
FIFING
FILING
FINING
FIRING
FIXING
FIZGIG
GIBING
GIVING
HIDING
HIEING
HIKING
HIRING
HIVING
JIBING
KITING
LIKING
LIMING
LINING
LIVING
MIMING
MINING
MIRING
MIXING
NIDING
NIXING
OILING
PIKING
PILING
PINANG
PINING
PIPING
RICING
RIDING
RILING
RIMING
RISING
RIVING
SIDING
SIRING
SIZING
TIDING

TILING
TIMING
TIRING
VIKING
VISING
WIGWAG
WILING
WINING
WIPING
WIRING
WISING
WIVING
ZIGZAG

••IG••

ALIGHT
ALIGNS
AMIGOS
ARIGHT
BEIGES
BLIGHT
BRIGHT
BRIGID
CHIGOE
COIGNS
DEIGNS
DWIGHT
EMIGRE
ENIGMA
FEIGNS
FLIGHT
FRIGHT
FRIGID
GEIGER
GRIGRI
HEIGHT
KNIGHT
LEIGHS
MAIGRE
NEIGHS
ORIGAN
ORIGEN
ORIGIN
PLIGHT
REIGNS
SAIGAS
SAIGON
SLIGHT
SOIGNE
SPIGOT
STIGMA
TAIGAS
THIGHS
TRIGLY
TRIGON
TWIGGY
WEIGHS
WEIGHT
WRIGHT

••I•G•

BEINGS
BRIDGE
BRINGS
CLINGS
CLINGY
CRINGE
DOINGS
ERINGO
FLINGS
FRIDGE
FRINGE
FRINGY
GOINGS
ICINGS
SLINGS
STINGS
STINGY
SWINGE
SWINGS
THINGS
TWIGGY
TWINGE
WRINGS

••I••G

EPILOG
SKIING

•••IG•

ASSIGN
AURIGA
AWEIGH
BENIGN
COSIGN
CRAIGS
DESIGN
EFFIGY
ELOIGN
ENSIGN
GREIGE
INDIGO
MALIGN
OBLIGE
RESIGN
RUBIGO
SLEIGH
SPRIGS
UNRIGS

•••I•G

ACHING
ACTING
ADDING
AGEING
AIDING
AILING
AIMING
AIRING
ARCING
ARMING
ASKING
AWEING
AWNING
BAAING
BAKING
BALING
BARING
BASING
BATING
BAYING
BERING
BIDING
BITING
BLUING
BODING
BONING
BOOING
BORING
BOWING
BOXING
BUSING
BUYING
CAGING
CAKING
CANING
CARING
CASING
CAVING
CAWING
CEDING
CERING
CITING
CLUING
CODING
COKING
COMING
CONING
COOING
COPING
CORING
COVING
COWING
COXING
CRYING
CUBING
CURING
DARING
DATING
DAZING
DEKING
DICING
DIKING
DINING
DIVING
DOLING
DOMING
DOPING
DOSING
DOTING
DOZING
DRYING
DUPING
DURING
DYEING
EALING
EARING
EASING
EATING
EBBING
EDGING
EGGING
ENDING
ERRING
EYEING
FACING
FADING
FAKING
FARING
FATING
FAXING
FAYING
FAZING
FEEING
FETING
FEUING
FIFING
FILING
FINING
FIRING
FIXING
FLYING
FOXING
FRYING
FUMING
FUSING
FUZING
GAGING
GAMING
GAPING
GATING
GAZING
GEEING
GIBING
GIVING
GLUING
GORING
GUYING
HADING
HALING
HATING
HAVING
HAWING
HAYING
HAZING
HEWING
HEXING
HIDING
HIEING
HIKING
HIRING
HIVING
HOEING
HOLING
HOMING
HONING
HOPING
HOSING
IDLING
IMPING
INKING
INNING
IRKING
IRVING
ISLING
JADING
JAWING
JEEING
JIBING
JOKING
JOYING
KEYING
KITING
LACING
LADING
LAKING
LAMING
LAVING
LAWING
LAYING
LAZING
LIKING
LIMING
LINING
LIVING
LOOING
LOPING
LOSING
LOVING
LOWING
LURING
LUTING
LYSING
MACING
MAKING
MATING
MAYING
MAZING
METING
MEWING
MIMING
MINING
MIRING
MIXING
MOOING
MOPING
MOVING
MOWING
MUSING
MUTING
NAMING
NIDING
NIXING
NOSING
NOTING
OARING
OFFING
OGLING
OILING
OOZING
OPTING
ORBING
OUTING
OWNING
PACING
PAGING
PALING
PARING
PAVING
PAWING
PAYING
PEKING
PIKING
PILING
PINING
PIPING
PLYING
POKING
POLING
PORING
POSING
PRYING
PUKING
PULING
RACING
RAGING
RAKING
RAPING
RARING
RATING
RAVING
RAYING
RAZING
RICING
RIDING
RILING
RIMING
RISING
RIVING
ROBING
ROPING
ROSING
ROVING
ROWING
RULING
SATING
SAVING
SAWING
SAYING
SEEING
SEWING
SEXING
SHYING
SIDING
SIRING
SIZING
SKIING
SKYING
SLUING
SOLING
SOWING
SPRING
SPYING
STRING
STYING
TAKING
TAMING
TAPING
TARING
TAWING
TAXING
TEEING
TIDING
TILING

6

TIMING
TIRING
TOEING
TONING
TOPING
TOTING
TOWING
TOYING
TRUING
TRYING
TUBING
TUNING
TYPING
UPPING
URGING
VEXING
VIKING
VISING
VOTING
VOWING
WADING
WAGING
WAKING
WALING
WANING
WAVING
WAXING
WILING
WINING
WIPING
WIRING
WISING
WIVING
WOOING
WOWING
WRYING
YAWING
YOKING
YOWING
ZONING

••••IG

BIGWIG
DANZIG
EARWIG
FIZGIG
HEDWIG
LUDWIG

IH••••

IHRAMS

I•H•••

ICHTHY
INHALE
INHAUL
INHERE
ISHTAR
ITHACA

I••H••

INCHED
INCHES
INCHON
ISCHIA
ISOHEL
ITCHED
ITCHES

I•••H•

ICHTHY

I••••H

IMMESH
IMPISH
INARCH
INMESH
INRUSH
ISAIAH

•IH•••

BIHARI
JIHADS

•I•H••

BIGHTS
BISHOP
CIPHER
CITHER
DIRHAM
DISHED
DISHES
DITHER
EIGHTH
EIGHTS
EIGHTY
EITHER
FICHES
FICHUS
FIGHTS
FISHED
FISHER
FISHES
HIGHER
HIGHLY
HITHER
LICHEE
LICHEN
LIGHTS
LITHER
LITHIA
LITHIC
MICHEL
MIGHTY
MISHAP
NICHED
NICHES
NIGHER
NIGHTS
NIGHTY
PISHED
PISHES
PITHED
RICHER
RICHES
RICHIE
RICHLY
RIGHTO
RIGHTS
SIGHED
SIGHTS
SIPHON
TIGHTS
TISHRI
TITHED
TITHER
TITHES
VISHNU
WICHES
WISHED
WISHES
WITHAL
WITHED
WITHER
WITHES
WITHIN
WITHIT
ZITHER

•I••H•

BIRTHS
DINAHS
DINGHY
FIFTHS
FILTHY
FIRTHS
NINTHS
PITCHY
SIXTHS
TILTHS
WIDTHS

•I•••H

EIGHTH
FINISH
KIBLAH
KIBOSH
KIRSCH
KITSCH
PISGAH
SIWASH
ZIBETH
ZILLAH
ZIZITH

••I•H•

ALIGHT
ARIGHT
BLIGHT
BLITHE
BRIGHT
CHICHI
CLICHE
DWIGHT
EDITHS
ELISHA
ERICHS
FAITHS
FLIGHT
FRIGHT
FRITHS
GEISHA
HEIGHT
KEITHS
KNIGHT
LEIGHS
MOISHE
NEIGHS
PLIGHT
REICHS
SEICHE
SLIGHT
SMITHS
SMITHY
STITHY
THIGHS
TRICHI
TRICHO
WEIGHS
WEIGHT
WRIGHT
WRITHE

••I••H

ABIJAH
CHINCH
CLINCH
ELIJAH
FLINCH
FLITCH
PLINTH
QUITCH
SHILOH
SMIRCH
SNITCH
SPILTH
STITCH
SWITCH
TWITCH
WHIDAH

•••I•H

AGUISH
AWEIGH
BANISH
BLUISH
BOYISH
CALIPH
CERIPH
COYISH
DANISH
DOVISH
DUDISH
ELFISH
ELVISH
ENRICH
EOLITH
FAMISH
FETICH
FETISH
FINISH
GARISH
IMPISH
ISAIAH
JADISH
JEWISH
JOSIAH
JUDITH
JUTISH
LATISH
LAVISH
MODISH
MOPISH
MULISH
MUNICH
OAFISH
OFFISH
OGRISH
OLDISH
ORNITH
OWLISH
PALISH
PARIAH
PARISH
PERISH
POLISH
POPISH
PUNISH
RADISH
RAKISH
RAVISH
RAWISH
RELISH
ROMISH
RUPIAH
SALISH
SLEIGH
SQUISH
TOBIAH
TOYISH
UNWISH
UPPISH
VANISH
WRAITH
ZENITH
ZIZITH
ZURICH

I•I•••

IBICES
IBIDEM
IBISES
ICICLE
ICIEST
ICINGS
IDIOCY
IDIOMS
IDIOTS
IMIDES
IMINES
IRIDES
IRIDIC
IRISES
IRITIC
IRITIS
ISIDOR
ITIOUS

I••I••

IDLING
IGNIFY
IGNITE
ILOILO
IMBIBE
IMMIES
IMPING
IMPISH
INCISE
INCITE
INDIAN
INDICT
INDIES
INDIGO
INDIUM
INFIRM
INKIER
INKING
INLIER
INNING
INSIDE
INSIST
INTIMA
INVITE
INWIND
IODIDE
IODINE
IODISM
IODIZE
IOLITE
IONIAN
IONIUM
IONIZE
IRKING
IRVING
IRVINS
IRWINS
ISAIAH
ISLING

I•••I•

IAMBIC
IATRIC
IBERIA
ICONIC
IMPAIR
INDRIS
INGRID
INLAID
INTUIT
INULIN
IRAQIS
IRENIC
IRIDIC
IRITIC
IRITIS
IRONIC
ISCHIA
ISSEIS
ITALIC

I••••I

INCUBI

•I•I••
AIDING
AILING
AIMING
AIRIER
AIRILY
AIRING
BIDING
BIKINI
BILITY
BINITS
BITING
CILIAT
CILICE
CILIUM
CITIED
CITIES
CITING
CIVICS
CIVIES
CIVISM
DICING
DIDIES
DIGITI
DIGITS
DIKING
DIMITY
DINING
DIVIDE
DIVINE
DIVING
DIXITS
FIFING
FIJIAN
FILIAL
FILING
FINIAL
FINING
FINISH
FINITE
FIRING
FIXING
FIXITY
GIBING
GIVING
HIDING
HIEING
HIKING
HIRING
HIVING
JIBING
KIBITZ
KININS
KITING
LIBIDO
LIKING
LILIAN
LILIED
LILIES
LIMIER
LIMINA
LIMING
LIMITS
LINIER
LINING
LIPIDS
LIVIAS
LIVIER
LIVING
MILIEU
MILIUM
MIMICS
MIMING
MINIFY
MINIMS
MINING
MINION
MINIUM
MIRIAM
MIRING
MIXING
NIDIFY
NIDING
NIMITZ
NIXIES
NIXING
OILIER
OILILY
OILING
PIKING
PILING
PINIER
PINING
PINION
PINITE
PIPIER
PIPING
PIPITS
PITIED
PITIES
PIXIES
RICING
RIDING
RILING
RIMING
RISING
RIVING
SICILY
SIDING
SIGILS
SILICA
SILICO
SIMIAN
SIMILE
SIRING
SIRIUS
SITINS
SIZIER
SIZING
TIBIAE
TIBIAL
TIBIAS
TIDIED
TIDIER
TIDIES
TIDILY
TIDING
TIEINS
TILING
TIMING
TIRING
TITIAN
VIGILS
VIKING
VILIFY
VIMINA
VINIER
VIRILE
VISING
VISION
VISITS
VIVIAN
VIVIEN
VIVIFY
VIZIER
VIZIRS
WIKIUP
WILIER
WILILY
WILING
WINIER
WINING
WIPING
WIRIER
WIRILY
WIRING
WISING
WIVING
ZIZITH

•I••I•
BIBLIO
BIFFIN
BIGGIN
BIGWIG
BILLIE
BIOSIS
BIOTIC
BIOTIN
BIRDIE
CISSIE
CITRIC
DIAZIN
DICKIE
DIESIS
DIKDIK
DIMWIT
DISTIL
FIBRIL
FIBRIN
FILLIN
FILLIP
FINNIC
FIRKIN
FISTIC
FIZGIG
GIULIA
GIULIO
HIPPIE
HISPID
JIMMIE
KIBEIS
KIDDIE
KILTIE
LIGNIN
LIMBIC
LIMPID
LIPOID
LIQUID
LITHIA
LITHIC
LIZZIE
MIDAIR
MIDRIB
MILLIE
MINNIE
MIOSIS
MIOTIC
MISDID
MISFIT
MISSIS
NIACIN
NISEIS
NITRIC
NITRID
NITWIT
PICNIC
PICRIC
PIDGIN
PIGGIE
PIGGIN
PINKIE
PINXIT
PIPKIN
PIPPIN
PISTIL
RICHIE
SIALIC
SIGRID
SIKKIM
SILVIA
SIMLIN
SISKIN
TIDBIT
TIFFIN
TILLIE
TINEID
VIATIC
VIBRIO
VICTIM
VIOLIN
VIRGIE
VIRGIL
VIRGIN
VISCID
VITRIC
WIDDIE
WIENIE
WILLIE
WILLIS
WINNIE
WITHIN
WITHIT
YIPPIE
ZINCIC
ZINNIA

•I•••I
BIHARI
BIKINI
BILOXI
CIMBRI
DIGITI
KINESI
LIMULI
NIELLI
NILGAI
SILENI
TISHRI

••II••
OBIISM
SHIISM
SHIITE
SKIING

••I•I•
ACIDIC
ADIPIC
ALIBIS
ALICIA
AMIDIC
AMIDIN
ANILIN
AVIDIN
BAILIE
BRIDIE
BRIGID
CHITIN
CLINIC
CRISIS
CRITIC
DAIMIO
DEIFIC
ELICIT
ELIXIR
EMILIA
EMILIE
EMILIO
EXILIC
FRIGID
IRIDIC
IRITIC
IRITIS
MAISIE
OLIVIA
ORIBIS
ORIGIN
OSIRIS
OTITIS
PHILIA
PHILIP
QUINIC
RAISIN
SAITIC
SCIPIO
SEISIN
SEIZIN
SPIRIT
TRIFID
TRIVIA
TRIXIE
TWIBIL
UNIFIC

••I••I
CHICHI
DMITRI
GRIGRI
TAIPEI
TRICHI

•••II•
AALIIS
TORIIS

•••I•I
ACTINI
ASSISI
BIKINI
DIGITI
ECHINI
EURIPI
GEMINI
KABIKI
LUMINI
SOLIDI
VASILI
WAKIKI
WAPITI

••••II
HAWAII

I•J•••
INJECT
INJURE
INJURY

•IJ•••
BIJOUX
FIJIAN
HIJACK

••IJ••
ABIJAH
ELIJAH
FRIJOL

I•K•••
INKERS
INKIER
INKING
INKLES
IRKING

I•••K•
INTAKE
INVOKE

I••••K
IMBARK
IMPARK

•IK•••
BIKINI
BIKOLS
DIKDIK
DIKING
HIKERS
HIKING
LIKELY
LIKENS
LIKING
MIKADO
MIKLOS
PIKERS
PIKING
SIKKIM
VIKING
WIKIUP

•I•K••
BICKER
BILKED
BILKER
DICKER
DICKEY
DICKIE
DINKEY
DIRKED
FICKLE
FIRKIN
GINKGO
HICKEY
HICKOK
JINKED
JINKER
KICKED
KICKER
KINKED
LICKED
LINKED
MICKEY
MICKYS
MILKED
MILKER
MISKAL
NICKED
NICKEL
NICKER
NICKYS
PICKAX
PICKED
PICKER
PICKET
PICKLE
PICKUP
PINKED
PINKIE
PIPKIN
RICKED
RICKEY
RICKYS
RISKED
RISKER
SICKED
SICKEN
SICKER
SICKLE
SICKLY
SIKKIM
SILKEN
SINKER
SISKIN
TICKED
TICKER
TICKET
TICKLE
TINKER
TINKLE
TINKLY
VICKYS
WICKED
WICKER
WICKET
WINKED
WINKER
WINKLE

•I••K•
KIOSKS
ZINCKY

•I•••K
DIKDIK
HICKOK
HIJACK

••IK••
BAIKAL
DUIKER
SHIKAR
SPIKED
SPIKES

••I•K•
BLINKS
BRICKS
BRINKS
BRISKS
CHICKS
CHINKS
CHINKY
CLICKS
CLINKS
CRICKS
DRINKS
FLICKS
FRISKS
FRISKY
HOICKS
PRICKS
PRINKS
QUIRKS
SHIRKS
SKINKS
SLICKS
SLINKS
SLINKY
SMIRKS
SNICKS
STICKS
STICKY
STINKS
STIRKS
THINKS
TRICKS
TRICKY
UMIAKS
WHISKS
WHISKY
YOICKS

•••IK•
ALSIKE
AXLIKE
BATIKS
KABIKI
KAMIKS
SHEIKS
SHRIKE
STRIKE
TROIKA
TUPIKS
UNLIKE
WAKIKI

•••I•K
KODIAK
OOMIAK
SCHICK
SHRIEK
SHRINK
SHTICK
STRICK
UNPICK

••••IK
BATTIK
CROJIK
DIKDIK
MUZHIK
NUDNIK
SUSLIK

IL••••
ILEXES
ILLUME
ILLUSE
ILLUST
ILOILO

I•L•••
IDLERS
IDLEST
IDLING
IGLOOS
ILLUME
ILLUSE
ILLUST
INLACE
INLAID
INLAND
INLAWS
INLAYS
INLETS
INLIER
IOLCUS
IOLITE
ISLAND
ISLETS
ISLING

I••L••
ICALLY
IDYLLS
INFLOW
INFLUX
INKLES
INULIN
ISOLDE
ITALIC

I•••L•
ICALLY
ICICLE
IDEALS
IDYLLS
ILOILO
IMBALM
IMPALA
IMPALE
IMPELS
INDULT
INFOLD
INGULF
INHALE
INSOLE
INSULT
INWALL
ISEULT
ITSELF

I••••L
INHAUL
INSOUL
INWALL
IREFUL
ISABEL
ISOBEL
ISOHEL
ISRAEL

•IL•••
AILEEN
AILING
BILBAO
BILGED
BILGES
BILITY
BILKED
BILKER
BILLED
BILLET
BILLIE
BILLON
BILLOW
BILLYS
BILOXI
CILIAT
CILICE
CILIUM
DILATE
DILUTE
EILEEN
FILERS
FILETS
FILIAL
FILING
FILLED
FILLER
FILLET
FILLIN
FILLIP
FILMED
FILOSE
FILTER
FILTHY
GILDAS
GILDED
GILDER
GILEAD
HILARY
HILDAS
HILLED
HILLER
HILTED
JILTED
JILTER
KILLED
KILLER
KILMER
KILTED
KILTER
KILTIE
LILACS
LILIAN
LILIED
LILIES
LILTED
MILADY
MILAGE
MILDEN
MILDER
MILDEW
MILDLY
MILERS
MILIEU
MILIUM
MILKED
MILKER
MILLAY
MILLED
MILLER
MILLET
MILLIE
MILLYS
MILORD
MILTED
MILTER
MILTON
NILGAI
OILCAN
OILERS
OILIER
OILILY
OILING
PILAFS
PILATE
PILEUM
PILEUS
PILFER
PILING
PILLAR
PILLED
PILLOW
PILOSE
PILOTS
PILOUS
PILULE
RILING
RILLET
SILENI
SILENT
SILICA
SILICO
SILKEN
SILOED
SILTED
SILVAE
SILVAN
SILVAS
SILVER
SILVIA
TILDES
TILERS
TILING
TILLED
TILLER
TILLIE
TILLYS
TILTED
TILTER
TILTHS
VILELY
VILEST
VILIFY
VILLAS
VILLON
VILLUS
WILBER
WILBUR
WILDER
WILDLY
WILFUL
WILIER
WILILY
WILING
WILLED
WILLER
WILLET
WILLIE
WILLIS
WILLOW
WILLYS
WILMAS
WILSON

WILTED
ZILLAH

•I•L••

AIGLET
AISLED
AISLES
BIALYS
BIBLES
BIBLIO
BIFLEX
BILLED
BILLET
BILLIE
BILLON
BILLOW
BILLYS
BIRLED
BIRLES
DIALED
DIALER
DIALOG
DIGLOT
DIPLEX
DIPLOE
FIELDS
FILLED
FILLER
FILLET
FILLIN
FILLIP
GIBLET
GIGLET
GIGLOT
GIMLET
GIULIA
GIULIO
HILLED
HILLER
HITLER
KIBLAH
KILLED
KILLER
KISLEW
MIKLOS
MILLAY
MILLED
MILLER
MILLET
MILLIE
MILLYS
MISLAY
NIELLI
NIELLO
PILLAR
PILLED
PILLOW
RIALTO
RIFLED
RIFLER
RIFLES
RILLET
RIPLEY
SIALIC
SIDLED
SIDLER
SIDLES
SIMLIN
TILLED
TILLER
TILLIE
TILLYS
TITLED
TITLES
VIALED
VILLAS
VILLON
VILLUS
VIOLAS
VIOLET
VIOLIN
WIELDS
WIELDY
WILLED
WILLER
WILLET
WILLIE
WILLIS
WILLOW
WILLYS
YIELDS
ZILLAH

•I••L•

AIRILY
BIFOLD
BIKOLS
CIBOLS
CICALA
CICELY
CIRCLE
CITOLA
DIBBLE
DIDDLE
DIMPLE
DIMPLY
DINGLE
DIPOLE
DIRELY
EIDOLA
FIBULA
FICKLE
FIDDLE
FIMBLE
FINALE
FINALS
FINELY
FIPPLE
FIRMLY
FIZZLE
GIGGLE
GIGGLY
GIGOLO
GIMELS
GIRDLE
GISELE
HIGGLE
HIGHLY
JIGGLE
JINGLE
KINDLE
KINDLY
KINGLY
LIABLE
LIBELS
LIGULA
LIGULE
LIKELY
LIMPLY
LIMULI
LITTLE
LIVELY
MIAULS
MICELL
MIDDLE
MIGGLE
MILDLY
MINGLE
NIBBLE
NICELY
NICOLE
NIELLI
NIELLO
NIGELS
NIGGLE
NIMBLE
NIPPLE
OILILY
PICKLE
PICULS
PIDDLE
PIFFLE
PILULE
PIMPLE
PIMPLY
PINOLE
PINTLE
RIBALD
RICHLY
RIDDLE
RIFFLE
RIMPLE
RIPELY
RIPPLE
RIVALS
RIYALS
SIBYLS
SICILY
SICKLE
SICKLY
SIECLE
SIGILS
SIMILE
SIMPLE
SIMPLY
SINGLE
SINGLY
SIZZLE
TICALS
TICKLE
TIDILY
TIMELY
TINGLE
TINGLY
TINKLE
TINKLY
TIPPLE
TITTLE
VIABLE
VIGILS
VILELY
VINYLS
VIRILE
VITALS
WIDELY
WIFELY
WIGGLE
WIGGLY
WILDLY
WILILY
WIMBLE
WIMPLE
WINKLE
WIRILY
WISELY
ZIZZLE

•I•••L

BIAXAL
CINEOL
CITRAL
DIESEL
DIOBOL
DIRNDL
DISMAL
DISPEL
DISTAL
DISTIL
EIFFEL
FIBRIL
FILIAL
FINIAL
FISCAL
FITFUL
GINGAL
HIEMAL
JINGAL
LINEAL
LINTEL
LIONEL
LISTEL
MICELL
MICHEL
MIGUEL
MISKAL
MISSAL
MITRAL
NICKEL
PINEAL
PINNAL
PISTIL
PISTOL
RICTAL
RITUAL
SIGNAL
SIMNEL
SINFUL
TIBIAL
TIMBAL
TINCAL
TINSEL
VIRGIL
VISUAL
WILFUL
WITHAL

••IL••

ANILIN
AXILLA
BAILED
BAILEE
BAILER
BAILEY
BAILIE
BAILOR
BOILED
BOILER
BRILLS
BUILDS
CEILED
CHILLS
CHILLY
COILED
COILER
DRILLS
EDILES
EMILES
EMILIA
EMILIE
EMILIO
EMILYS
EPILOG
EVILLY
EXILED
EXILES
EXILIC
FAILED
FAILLE
FOILED
FRILLS
FRILLY
GRILLE
GRILLS
GRILSE
GUILDS
GUILES
GUILTS
GUILTY
HAILED
HAILER
JAILED
JAILER
JAILOR
MAILED
MAILER
MOILED
MOILER
NAILED
PHILIA
PHILIP
PHILOS
POILUS
QUILLS
QUILTS
RAILED
ROILED
SAILED
SAILER
SAILOR
SHILLS
SHILOH
SKILLS
SMILAX
SMILED
SMILER
SMILES
SOILED
SPILED
SPILES
SPILLS
SPILTH
STILES
STILLS
STILLY
STILTS
SWILLS
TAILED
TAILLE
TAILOR
TOILED
TOILER
TOILES
TOILET
TRILLS
TUILLE
TWILLS
VEILED
VEILER
VOILES
WAILED
WAILER
WHILED
WHILES
WHILOM
WHILST

••I•L•

ACIDLY
AFIELD
ALIBLE
ARIDLY
ARIELS
AVIDLY
AXILLA
BRIDLE
BRILLS
CHICLE
CHILLS
CHILLY
DRILLS
EDIBLE
ENISLE
EVILLY
FAILLE

6

FAIRLY
FOIBLE
FRILLS
FRILLY
GAINLY
GLIBLY
GRILLE
GRILLS
GRIMLY
GRISLY
ICICLE
MAINLY
ORIELS
ORIOLE
PHIALS
PRIMLY
QUILLS
SHIELD
SHILLS
SKILLS
SLIMLY
SPIELS
SPILLS
STIFLE
STILLS
STILLY
SWILLS
SWIPLE
SWIRLS
SWIRLY
TAILLE
THINLY
THIOLS
TRIALS
TRIFLE
TRIGLY
TRILLS
TRIMLY
TRIPLE
TUILLE
TWILLS
TWIRLS
VAINLY
WHIRLS

••I••L
AMIDOL
ANIMAL
APICAL
BAIKAL
BRIDAL
CHISEL
DRIVEL
EPICAL
FRIJOL
FRIVOL
GRIZEL
PRIMAL
RHINAL
SNIVEL
SPINAL
SPINEL
SPIRAL
SPITAL
STIPEL
SWIVEL
TRIBAL
TRINAL
TWIBIL
URINAL

•••IL•
AEDILE
AIRILY
ANVILS
APRILS
AQUILA
ATTILA
AUDILE
AVAILS
AWHILE
BASILS
BODILY
BRAILS
BROILS
BUSILY
CAGILY
CAMILA
CAVILS
CECILE
CECILS
CECILY
CHEILO
COZILY
CYRILS
DECILE
DEFILE
DEVILS
DOCILE
DOZILY
EASILY
EERILY
ENSILE
FACILE
FAMILY
FLAILS
FOXILY
FRAILS
FUSILE
FUSILS
FUTILE
FUZILS
GAMILY
GORILY
HABILE
HAZILY
HOLILY
HOMILY
ILOILO
LABILE
LACILY
LAZILY
LUCILE
MANILA
MAZILY
MEGILP
MOBILE
MOTILE
NEVILE
NEVILL
NOSILY
NUBILE
OILILY
ONEILL
OOZILY
PENILE
PERILS
PUNILY
PUPILS
QUAILS
RACILY
REBILL
REFILL
RESILE
REVILE
ROPILY
ROSILY
RUTILE
SEDILE
SENILE
SHEILA
SHRILL
SICILY
SIGILS
SIMILE
SNAILS
SPOILS
SPOILT
SQUILL
SWAILS
SYBILS
THRILL
TIDILY
TRAILS
UGLILY
UNPILE
UPHILL
VASILI
VERILY
VEXILS
VIGILS
VIRILE
WARILY
WAVILY
WILILY
WIRILY
ZORILS

•••I•L
AECIAL
AERIAL
ATRIAL
AWHIRL
BELIAL
BURIAL
CURIAL
DANIEL
DENIAL
ESPIAL
FACIAL
FECIAL
FERIAL
FETIAL
FILIAL
FINIAL
GAVIAL
GENIAL
JOVIAL
LABIAL
MEDIAL
MENIAL
MESIAL
MURIEL
NARIAL
NASIAL
NEVILL
ONEILL
PENIAL
RACIAL
RADIAL
REBILL
REFILL
SAMIEL
SERIAL
SHRILL
SOCIAL
SQUILL
THRILL
TIBIAL
UNCIAL
UPHILL
VENIAL

••••IL
AGNAIL
ARCHIL
ASSAIL
BEWAIL
BRAZIL
BULBIL
DENTIL
DERAIL
DETAIL
DISTIL
DOSSIL
ENTAIL
FIBRIL
FOSSIL
FULFIL
GERBIL
JEZAIL
LENTIL
ORCHIL
OXTAIL
PASTIL
PENCIL
PISTIL
PONTIL
RECOIL
RETAIL
TONSIL
TWIBIL
UNCOIL
UNVEIL
VERGIL
VIRGIL
WEEVIL

IM••••
IMAGES
IMARET
IMBALM
IMBARK
IMBEDS
IMBIBE
IMBODY
IMBRUE
IMBUED
IMBUES
IMIDES
IMINES
IMMESH
IMMIES
IMMUNE
IMMUNO
IMMURE
IMOGEN
IMPACT
IMPAIR
IMPALA
IMPALE
IMPARK
IMPART
IMPAWN
IMPEDE
IMPELS
IMPEND
IMPING
IMPISH
IMPORT
IMPOSE
IMPOST
IMPUGN
IMPURE
IMPUTE

I•M•••
IAMBIC
IAMBUS
IMMESH
IMMIES
IMMUNE
IMMUNO
IMMURE
INMATE
INMESH
INMOST

I••M••
ICEMAN
ICEMEN
ISOMER

I•••M•
IBEAMS
IDIOMS
IHRAMS
ILLUME
INARMS
INCOME
INFAMY
INTIMA
INTOMB

I••••M
IBIDEM
IMBALM
INDIUM
INFIRM
INFORM
IODISM
IONIUM

•IM•••
AIMING
CIMBRI
DIMERS
DIMITY
DIMMED
DIMMER
DIMOUT
DIMPLE
DIMPLY
DIMWIT
FIMBLE
GIMELS
GIMLET
GIMPED
JIMMIE
JIMMYS
KIMONO
LIMBED
LIMBER
LIMBIC
LIMBUS
LIMENS
LIMEYS
LIMIER
LIMINA
LIMING
LIMITS
LIMNED
LIMNER
LIMPED
LIMPER
LIMPET
LIMPID
LIMPLY
LIMULI
MIMERS
MIMICS
MIMING
MIMOSA
NIMBLE
NIMBUS
NIMITZ
NIMROD
PIMPED
PIMPLE
PIMPLY
RIMERS
RIMING
RIMMED
RIMMER

RIMOSE
RIMOUS
RIMPLE
SIMARS
SIMEON
SIMIAN
SIMILE
SIMLIN
SIMMER
SIMNEL
SIMONE
SIMONS
SIMONY
SIMOOM
SIMPER
SIMPLE
SIMPLY
TIMBAL
TIMBER
TIMBRE
TIMELY
TIMERS
TIMING
TIMMYS
VIMINA
WIMBLE
WIMPLE

•I•M••

AIDMAN
AIDMEN
AIRMAN
AIRMEN
DIMMED
DIMMER
DISMAL
DISMAY
FILMED
FIRMAN
FIRMED
FIRMER
FIRMLY
GISMOS
GIZMOS
HIEMAL
JIMMIE
JIMMYS
KILMER
KISMET
LITMUS
MICMAC
PITMAN
PITMEN
RIMMED
RIMMER
SIGMAS
SIMMER
TIMMYS
WILMAS

•I••M•

BIGAMY
BIREME
CINEMA
DIGAMY
HIRAMS
LIPOMA
MIASMA
MINIMS

•I•••M

BIFORM
CILIUM
CIRCUM
CIVISM
DIADEM
DIATOM
DICTUM
DIRHAM
DISARM
MILIUM
MINIUM
MIRIAM
PILEUM
SIKKIM
SIMOOM
VICTIM
WIGWAM
WISDOM

••IM••

AHIMSA
AKIMBO
ANIMAL
ANIMAS
ANIMUS
BLIMPS
CAIMAN
CHIMED
CHIMER
CHIMES
CLIMAT
CLIMAX
CLIMBS
CLIMES
CRIMEA
CRIMES
CRIMPS
CRIMPY
DAIMIO
DAIMON
DAIMYO
FLIMSY
GRIMED
GRIMES
GRIMLY
GUIMPE
MAIMED
MAIMER
PRIMAL
PRIMED
PRIMER
PRIMES
PRIMLY
PRIMPS
SHIMMY
SKIMOS
SKIMPS
SKIMPY
SLIMED
SLIMES
SLIMLY
SLIMSY
TRIMLY
WEIMAR
WHIMSY

••I•M•

AXIOMS
CHIRMS
ENIGMA
GLIOMA
IDIOMS
PRISMS
SEISMO
SEISMS
SHIMMY
STIGMA

••I••M

CHIASM
CRINUM
IBIDEM
OBIISM
SHIISM
WHILOM

•••IM•

BEDIMS
CLAIMS
DENIMS
ESKIMO
FATIMA
HAKIMS
INTIMA
JEMIMA
MAXIMS
MINIMS
OPTIMA
OPTIME
REGIME
RHEIMS
SCRIMP
SHRIMP
ULTIMA
YAKIMA

•••I•M

ACTIUM
AECIUM
AFFIRM
ALLIUM
ATRIUM
AUTISM
BABISM
BARIUM
CERIUM
CESIUM
CHRISM
CILIUM
CIVISM
CONIUM
CORIUM
CUBISM
CURIUM
EGOISM
EONISM
ERBIUM
FOLIUM
GONIUM
HELIUM
HOLISM
INDIUM
INFIRM
IODISM
IONIUM
KALIUM
LABIUM
LYRISM
MAOISM
MEDIUM
MILIUM
MINIUM
MIRIAM
MOMISM
MONISM
MUTISM
NANISM
NAZISM
NOMISM
NUDISM
OBIISM
OSMIUM
PODIUM
PURISM
RACISM
RADIUM
SADISM
SCHISM
SEXISM
SHIISM
SODIUM
SQUIRM
SUFISM
TAOISM
TEDIUM
THEISM
TRUISM
VERISM

••••IM

ANTRIM
BAALIM
ELOHIM
MEGRIM
MUSLIM
PASSIM
SIKKIM
VICTIM

IN••••

INARCH
INARMS
INBORN
INBRED
INCAGE
INCASE
INCEPT
INCEST
INCHED
INCHES
INCHON
INCISE
INCITE
INCOME
INCORP
INCUBI
INCURS
INCUSE
INDABA
INDEED
INDENE
INDENT
INDIAN
INDICT
INDIES
INDIGO
INDIUM
INDOOR
INDOWS
INDRIS
INDUCE
INDUCT
INDUED
INDUES
INDULT
INFAMY
INFANT
INFECT
INFERO
INFERS
INFEST
INFIRM
INFLOW
INFLUX
INFOLD
INFORM
INFUSE
INGEST
INGOTS
INGRES
INGRID
INGULF
INHALE
INHAUL
INHERE
INJECT
INJURE
INJURY
INKERS
INKIER
INKING
INKLES
INLACE
INLAID
INLAND
INLAWS
INLAYS
INLETS
INLIER
INMATE
INMESH
INMOST
INNATE
INNING
INPUTS
INROAD
INRUSH
INSANE
INSECT
INSERT
INSETS
INSIDE
INSIST
INSOLE
INSOUL
INSPAN
INSTAR
INSTEP
INSULT
INSURE
INTACT
INTAKE
INTEND
INTENT
INTERN
INTERS
INTIMA
INTOMB
INTONE
INTUIT
INTURN
INULIN
INURED
INURES
INURNS
INVADE
INVENT
INVERT
INVEST
INVITE
INVOKE
INWALL
INWARD
INWIND
INWOVE
INWRAP

I•N•••

IGNACE
IGNIFY
IGNITE
IGNORE
INNATE
INNING
IONIAN
IONIUM
IONIZE
IONONE

I••N••

ICINGS
ICONIC
IMINES

IRENES
IRENIC
IRONED
IRONER
IRONIC

I•••N•

IDLING
IGUANA
IMMUNE
IMMUNO
IMPEND
IMPING
INDENE
INDENT
INFANT
INKING
INLAND
INNING
INSANE
INTEND
INTENT
INTONE
INURNS
INVENT
INWIND
IODINE
IONONE
IRKING
IRVING
IRVINS
IRWINS
ISLAND
ISLING

I••••N

ICEMAN
ICEMEN
IMOGEN
IMPAWN
IMPUGN
INBORN
INCHON
INDIAN
INSPAN
INTERN
INTURN
INULIN
IONIAN
ISOGON

•IN•••

BINARY
BINDER
BINGES
BINITS
BINNED
CINDER
CINDYS
CINEMA
CINEOL
CINQUE
DINAHS
DINARS
DINERO
DINERS
DINGED
DINGEY
DINGHY
DINGLE
DINGUS
DINING
DINKEY
DINNED
DINNER
DINTED
FINALE
FINALS
FINDER
FINELY
FINERY
FINEST
FINGER
FINIAL
FINING
FINISH
FINITE
FINNED
FINNIC
GINGAL
GINGER
GINKGO
GINNED
GINNER
HINDER
HINDUS
HINGED
HINGES
HINTED
JINGAL
JINGLE
JINKED
JINKER
JINNYS
JINXES
KINASE
KINDER
KINDLE
KINDLY
KINESI
KINETO
KINGLY
KININS
KINKED
KINSEY
LINAGE
LINDAS
LINDEN
LINEAL
LINEAR
LINENS
LINERS
LINEUP
LINGAS
LINGER
LINGUA
LINIER
LINING
LINKED
LINNET
LINTEL
LINTER
MINCED
MINCER
MINCES
MINDED
MINDER
MINERS
MINGLE
MINIFY
MINIMS
MINING
MINION
MINIUM
MINNIE
MINNOW
MINOAN
MINORS
MINTED
MINTER
MINUET
MINUTE
MINXES
NINETY
NINTHS
PINANG
PINDAR
PINDUS
PINEAL
PINENE
PINERY
PINGED
PINGOS
PINIER
PINING
PINION
PINITE
PINKED
PINKIE
PINNAE
PINNAL
PINNED
PINNER
PINOLE
PINONS
PINTER
PINTLE
PINTOS
PINUPS
PINXIT
RINGED
RINGER
RINSED
RINSER
RINSES
SINBAD
SINEWS
SINEWY
SINFUL
SINGED
SINGER
SINGES
SINGLE
SINGLY
SINKER
SINNED
SINNER
SINTER
TINCAL
TINCTS
TINDER
TINEID
TINGED
TINGES
TINGLE
TINGLY
TINKER
TINKLE
TINKLY
TINNED
TINNER
TINSEL
TINTED
VINCES
VINERY
VINIER
VINNYS
VINOUS
VINSON
VINYLS
WINCED
WINCER
WINCES
WINCEY
WINDED
WINDER
WINDOW
WINERY
WINGED
WINIER
WINING
WINKED
WINKER
WINKLE
WINNER
WINNIE
WINNOW
WINOES
WINTER
WINTRY
WINZES
ZINCED
ZINCIC
ZINCKY
ZINGED
ZINNIA

•I•N••

BIANCA
BINNED
DIANAS
DIANES
DINNED
DINNER
DIRNDL
DISNEY
FIANCE
FIENDS
FINNED
FINNIC
GIANTS
GINNED
GINNER
JINNYS
JITNEY
KIDNAP
KIDNEY
LIANAS
LIANES
LIGNIN
LIMNED
LIMNER
LINNET
LIONEL
MIGNON
MINNIE
MINNOW
PIANOS
PICNIC
PIGNUS
PIGNUT
PINNAE
PINNAL
PINNED
PINNER
SIDNEY
SIENNA
SIGNAL
SIGNED
SIGNER
SIGNET
SIGNOR
SIMNEL
SINNED
SINNER
TINNED
TINNER
VIANDS
VIENNA
VINNYS
WIENER
WIENIE
WINNER
WINNIE
WINNOW
WITNEY
ZINNIA

•I••N•

AIDING
AILING
AIMING
AIRING
BIDING
BIKINI
BITING
CITING
DICING
DIKING
DINING
DIVANS
DIVINE
DIVING
DIWANS
DIZENS
FIFING
FILING
FINING
FIRING
FIXING
GIBING
GIGANT
GIPONS
GITANO
GIVING
HIDING
HIEING
HIKING
HIRING
HIVING
JIBING
KIMONO
KININS
KITING
LIERNE
LIGAND
LIKENS
LIKING
LIMENS
LIMINA
LIMING
LINENS
LINING
LITANY
LIVENS
LIVING
MIMING
MINING
MIRING
MIXING
NIDING
NIXING
OILING
PIKING
PILING
PINANG
PINENE
PINING
PINONS
PIPING
PIRANA
PITONS
RICING
RIDENT
RIDING
RILING
RIMING
RIPENS
RISING
RIVING
SIDING
SIENNA
SILENI
SILENT

6

SIMONE
SIMONS
SIMONY
SIRENS
SIRING
SITINS
SIZING
TIDING
TIEINS
TILING
TIMING
TIRANA
TIRING
TISANE
TITANS
VICUNA
VIENNA
VIKING
VIMINA
VISHNU
VISING
VIXENS
WIDENS
WIGANS
WILING
WINING
WIPING
WIRING
WISING
WIVING
WIZENS
ZIRONS

•I•••N

AIDMAN
AIDMEN
AILEEN
AIRMAN
AIRMEN
BICORN
BIDDEN
BIFFIN
BIGGIN
BILLON
BIOGEN
BIOTIN
BITTEN
CITRON
DIAZIN
DISOWN
EILEEN
FIBRIN
FIJIAN
FILLIN
FIRKIN
FIRMAN
GIBBON
GIBRAN
GIBSON
GIDEON
HIDDEN
KITTEN
LIBYAN
LICHEN

LIGNIN
LILIAN
LINDEN
LISBON
LISTEN
MICRON
MIDDEN
MIGNON
MILDEN
MILTON
MINION
MINOAN
MITTEN
MIZZEN
NIACIN
NIPPON
OILCAN
PIDGIN
PIGEON
PIGGIN
PIGPEN
PINION
PIPKIN
PIPPIN
PISTON
PITMAN
PITMEN
RIBBON
RIDDEN
SICKEN
SILKEN
SILVAN
SIMEON
SIMIAN
SIMLIN
SIOUAN
SIPHON
SISKIN
TIFFIN
TITIAN
VILLON
VINSON
VIOLIN
VIRGIN
VISION
VIVIAN
VIVIEN
WIGEON
WILSON
WITHIN
WIVERN
ZIRCON

••IN••

ACINUS
ALINED
ALINES
AZINES
BEINGS
BLINDS
BLINKS
BLINTZ
BRINED
BRINES

BRINGS
BRINKS
CHINCH
CHINES
CHINKS
CHINKY
CHINTZ
CLINCH
CLINES
CLINGS
CLINGY
CLINIC
CLINKS
CLINTS
COINED
COINER
CRINGE
CRINUM
DAINTY
DOINGS
DRINKS
ERINGO
EVINCE
FAINTS
FEINTS
FLINCH
FLINGS
FLINTS
FLINTY
FRINGE
FRINGY
GAINED
GAINER
GAINLY
GLINTS
GOINGS
GRINDS
GUINEA
ICINGS
IMINES
JAINAS
JOINED
JOINER
JOINTS
KOINES
MAINLY
OPINED
OPINES
PAINED
PAINTS
PAINTY
PLINTH
POINDS
POINTS
POINTY
PRINCE
PRINKS
PRINTS
QUINCE
QUINCY
QUINIC
QUINSY
QUINTS
RAINED

REINED
RHINAL
RHINOS
RUINED
RUINER
SAINTS
SEINED
SEINER
SEINES
SHINDY
SHINED
SHINER
SHINES
SHINNY
SHINTO
SKINKS
SKINNY
SLINGS
SLINKS
SLINKY
SPINAL
SPINEL
SPINES
SPINET
SPINNY
STINGS
STINGY
STINKS
STINTS
SWINGE
SWINGS
TAINOS
TAINTS
THINGS
THINKS
THINLY
TRINAL
TRINED
TRINES
TWINED
TWINER
TWINES
TWINGE
URINAL
VAINER
VAINLY
VEINED
WHINED
WHINER
WHINES
WHINNY
WRINGS

••I•N•

ALIENS
ALIGNS
AMIENS
ANIONS
ARIANS
ASIANS
BAIRNS
CAIRNS
CLIENT
COIGNS

DEIGNS
FEIGNS
FRIEND
GUIANA
ONIONS
ORIENT
PLIANT
PUISNE
REIGNS
SCIONS
SHINNY
SKIING
SKINNY
SOIGNE
SPINNY
TRIUNE
UNIONS
WHINNY

••I••N

ALISON
AMIDIN
ANILIN
ARISEN
AVIDIN
BRITON
CAIMAN
CHIRON
CHITIN
CHITON
DAIMON
DRIVEN
EDISON
GUIDON
HOIDEN
MAIDEN
MAISON
OHIOAN
ORIGAN
ORIGEN
ORIGIN
POISON
PRISON
PTISAN
RAISIN
SAIGON
SAIPAN
SEISIN
SEIZIN
SLIPON
TAIWAN
TRIGON
UNISON
WHITEN

•••IN•

ACHING
ACTING
ACTINI
ACTINO
ADDING
AGEING
AIDING
AILING

AIMING
AIRING
ALBINO
ALDINE
ALPINE
ALUINO
ALUINS
ALVINA
ALVINE
ANGINA
ANOINT
ARCING
ARLINE
ARMING
ARSINE
ASKING
AUXINS
AWEING
AWNING
BAAING
BAKING
BALING
BARING
BASING
BASINS
BATING
BAYING
BEGINS
BEHIND
BERING
BIDING
BIKINI
BITING
BLAINS
BLUING
BODING
BONING
BOOING
BORING
BOVINE
BOWING
BOXING
BRAINS
BRAINY
BRUINS
BURINS
BUSING
BUYING
BYLINE
CABINS
CAGING
CAKING
CANINE
CANING
CARINA
CARING
CASING
CASINO
CAVING
CAWING
CEDING
CERING
CHAINS
CITING

6

CLUING
CODING
COKING
COLINE
COLINS
COMING
CONING
COOING
COPING
CORING
COSINE
COVING
COWING
COXING
CRYING
CUBING
CUMINS
CURING
CUTINS
DARING
DATING
DAZING
DEFINE
DEKING
DICING
DIKING
DINING
DIVINE
DIVING
DOLING
DOMING
DOMINO
DOPING
DOSING
DOTING
DOZING
DRAINS
DRYING
DUPING
DURING
DYEING
EALING
EARING
EASING
EATING
EBBING
ECHINI
ECHINO
EDGING
EDWINA
EDWINS
EGGING
ELAINE
ELFINS
ELOINS
ENCINA
ENDING
ENGINE
ENWIND
EQUINE
ERMINE
ERRING
ERWINS
EYEING
FACING
FADING
FAKING
FAMINE
FARINA
FARING
FATING
FAXING
FAYING
FAZING
FEEING
FELINE
FERINE
FETING
FEUING
FIFING
FILING
FINING
FIRING
FIXING
FLYING
FORINT
FOXING
FRYING
FUMING
FUSING
FUZING
GAGING
GAMING
GAMINS
GAPING
GATING
GAZING
GEEING
GEMINI
GIBING
GIVING
GLUING
GORING
GRAINS
GRAINY
GROINS
GUYING
HADING
HALING
HATING
HAVING
HAWING
HAYING
HAZING
HEWING
HEXING
HIDING
HIEING
HIKING
HIRING
HIVING
HOEING
HOLING
HOMING
HOMINY
HONING
HOPING
HOSING
IDLING
IMPING
INKING
INNING
INWIND
IODINE
IRKING
IRVING
IRVINS
IRWINS
ISLING
JADING
JARINA
JAWING
JEEING
JIBING
JOKING
JOYING
KEVINS
KEYING
KININS
KITING
LACING
LADING
LADINO
LAKING
LAMINA
LAMING
LAPINS
LARINE
LATINS
LAVING
LAWING
LAYING
LAZING
LIKING
LIMINA
LIMING
LINING
LIVING
LOOING
LOPING
LOSING
LOVING
LOWING
LUMINA
LUMINI
LUMINO
LUPINE
LURING
LUTING
LYSINE
LYSING
LYSINS
MACING
MAKING
MALINE
MARINA
MARINE
MATING
MATINS
MAXINE
MAYING
MAZING
MENINX
MERINO
METING
MEWING
MIMING
MINING
MIRING
MIXING
MOLINE
MOOING
MOPING
MOVING
MOWING
MURINE
MUSING
MUTING
MUTINY
NADINE
NAMING
NARINE
NIDING
NIXING
NOSING
NOTING
NUMINA
OARING
OFFING
OGLING
OILING
OOZING
OPTING
ORBING
ORPINE
ORPINS
OSCINE
OUTING
OWNING
PACING
PAGING
PALING
PARING
PATINA
PATINE
PAVING
PAWING
PAYING
PEKING
PIKING
PILING
PINING
PIPING
PLAINS
PLAINT
PLYING
POKING
POLING
PORING
POSING
PRYING
PUKING
PULING
PURINE
QUAINT
QUOINS
RACINE
RACING
RAGING
RAKING
RAPINE
RAPING
RARING
RATINE
RATING
RAVINE
RAVING
RAYING
RAZING
REFINE
REGINA
RELINE
REMIND
REPINE
RESINS
RETINA
REWIND
RICING
RIDING
RILING
RIMING
RISING
RIVING
ROBING
ROBINS
ROPING
ROSING
ROSINS
ROSINY
ROVING
ROWING
RULING
RUMINA
RUNINS
RUSINE
SABINA
SABINE
SABINS
SALINE
SASINS
SATING
SATINS
SATINY
SAVING
SAVINS
SAWING
SAYING
SEEING
SERINE
SERINS
SEWING
SEXING
SHRINE
SHRINK
SHYING
SIDING
SIRING
SITINS
SIZING
SKEINS
SKIING
SKYING
SLUING
SOLING
SOWING
SOZINE
SOZINS
SPHINX
SPLINE
SPLINT
SPRING
SPRINT
SPYING
SQUINT
STAINS
STEINS
STRING
STYING
SUPINE
SWAINS
SYRINX
TAKING
TAMING
TAPING
TARING
TAWING
TAXING
TEEING
TIDING
TIEINS
TILING
TIMING
TIRING
TOEING
TONING
TOPING
TOTING
TOWING
TOXINS
TOYING
TRAINS
TRUING
TRYING
TUBING
TUNING
TYPING
UNBIND
UNDINE
UNKIND
UNPINS
UNWIND
UPPING
URGING
URSINE
VAGINA
VAGINO
VEXING
VIKING
VIMINA
VISING
VOTING
VOWING
WADING
WAGING

WAHINE
WAKING
WALING
WANING
WAVING
WAXING
WILING
WINING
WIPING
WIRING
WISING
WIVING
WOOING
WOWING
WRYING
YAWING
YOGINS
YOKING
YOWING
ZAYINS
ZONING

•••I•N

ACTION
ADRIAN
ADRIEN
ALBION
AMNION
APPIAN
ASSIGN
BANIAN
BASION
BENIGN
BUNION
CAMION
CATION
COSIGN
DARIEN
DELIAN
DESIGN
DORIAN
DURIAN
DURION
ELOIGN
ENSIGN
EOLIAN
EONIAN
FABIAN
FANION
FENIAN
FIJIAN
FUSION
GABION
GONION
INDIAN
IONIAN
JOVIAN
JULIAN
KALIAN
KATION
LEGION
LESION
LILIAN
LOGION
LOTION
LUCIAN
LUCIEN
MALIGN
MARIAN
MARION
MEDIAN
MESIAN
MINION
MORION
MOTION
NASION
NATION
NOTION
NUBIAN
OPTION
OSSIAN
PARIAN
PELION
PINION
POTION
RADIAN
RATION
REGION
RESIGN
SAMIAN
SIMIAN
SOLION
SYRIAN
TALION
TITIAN
VISION
VIVIAN
VIVIEN
WANION

••••IN

ADJOIN
ALCUIN
ALEXIN
ALUMIN
AMIDIN
ANILIN
ATTAIN
AUSTIN
AVIDIN
BAFFIN
BEDUIN
BEGUIN
BERLIN
BIFFIN
BIGGIN
BIOTIN
BOBBIN
BODKIN
BOWFIN
BUMKIN
BUSKIN
CALVIN
CAPLIN
CASEIN
CATKIN
CATLIN
CAVEIN
CHITIN
CHOPIN
COCAIN
COCHIN
CODEIN
COFFIN
CONTIN
CORTIN
COUSIN
CRETIN
CYANIN
CYMLIN
CYPRIN
DARWIN
DENTIN
DERAIN
DETAIN
DEVEIN
DIAZIN
DOBBIN
DOMAIN
DUBBIN
DUBLIN
DUNLIN
EMETIN
ENJOIN
FADEIN
FIBRIN
FILLIN
FIRKIN
FLAVIN
FLORIN
FUSAIN
GASKIN
GAWAIN
GLOBIN
GOBLIN
GODWIN
GRADIN
GUANIN
HARBIN
HARMIN
HATPIN
HEREIN
HEROIN
INULIN
JERKIN
JOPLIN
JUSTIN
KAMSIN
KAOLIN
KELVIN
LEADIN
LIGNIN
LOOKIN
LORAIN
LOVEIN
LUBLIN
MARGIN
MARLIN
MARTIN
MARVIN
MELVIN
MERLIN
MERVIN
MOULIN
MUFFIN
MUSLIN
MYELIN
MYOSIN
NAPKIN
NIACIN
NOGGIN
NUBBIN
OBTAIN
OLEFIN
ORCEIN
ORDAIN
ORIGIN
OSSEIN
PAPAIN
PAULIN
PECTIN
PEPSIN
PETAIN
PHYTIN
PIDGIN
PIGGIN
PIPKIN
PIPPIN
POPLIN
PUFFIN
PURLIN
RAISIN
RATLIN
REDFIN
REGAIN
REJOIN
REMAIN
RENNIN
RETAIN
RUSKIN
SEISIN
SEIZIN
SEQUIN
SEREIN
SHOOIN
SHUTIN
SIMLIN
SISKIN
SPAVIN
SPRAIN
STALIN
STAMIN
STEPIN
STRAIN
TAKEIN
TANNIN
TENPIN
TIFFIN
TOCSIN
TONKIN
URCHIN
VERDIN
VEREIN
VERMIN
VIOLIN
VIRGIN
WELKIN
WITHIN
ZECHIN

IO••••

IODATE
IODIDE
IODINE
IODISM
IODIZE
IODOUS
IOLCUS
IOLITE
IONIAN
IONIUM
IONIZE
IONONE

I•O•••

ICONIC
IGOROT
ILOILO
IMOGEN
IRONED
IRONER
IRONIC
ISOBAR
ISOBEL
ISOGON
ISOHEL
ISOLDE
ISOMER
ISOPOD

I••O••

IDIOCY
IDIOMS
IDIOTS
IGLOOS
IGNORE
IMBODY
IMPORT
IMPOSE
IMPOST
INBORN
INCOME
INCORP
INDOOR
INDOWS
INFOLD
INFORM
INGOTS
INMOST
INROAD
INSOLE
INSOUL
INTOMB
INTONE
INVOKE
INWOVE
IODOUS
IONONE
ITIOUS

I•••O•

ICEBOX
IGLOOS
IGOROT
INCHON
INDOOR
INFLOW
ISADOR
ISIDOR
ISOGON
ISOPOD

I••••O

ILOILO
IMMUNO
INDIGO
INFERO

•IO•••

BIOGEN
BIOPSY
BIOSIS
BIOTIC
BIOTIN
DIOBOL
DIODES
FIORDS
GIOTTO
KIOSKS
LIONEL
MIOSIS
MIOTIC
RIOTED
RIOTER
SIOUAN
VIOLAS
VIOLET
VIOLIN

•I•O••

BICORN
BIFOLD
BIFORM
BIGOTS
BIJOUX
BIKOLS
BILOXI
BIPODS
CIBOLS
CITOLA
DIDOES
DIMOUT
DIPODY
DIPOLE
DISOWN
DIVOTS
EIDOLA
FILOSE
GIAOUR
GIGOLO
GIPONS
KIBOSH
KIMONO
LIPOID

LIPOMA
MILORD
MIMOSA
MINOAN
MINORS
NICOLE
PICOTS
PILOSE
PILOTS
PILOUS
PINOLE
PINONS
PITONS
PIVOTS
RIBOSE
RIGORS
RIMOSE
RIMOUS
RIPOFF
RIPOST
SILOED
SIMONE
SIMONS
SIMONY
SIMOOM
TIPOFF
VIGOUR
VINOUS
VISORS
VIZORS
WICOPY
WIDOWS
WINOES
ZIRONS

•I••O•
BILLON
BILLOW
BISHOP
CINEOL
CISCOS
CITRON
DIALOG
DIATOM
DIGLOT
DIOBOL
DIPLOE
DITTOS
GIBBON
GIBSON
GIDEON
GIGLOT
GISMOS
GIZMOS
HICKOK
HIPPOS
LICTOR
LIQUOR
LISBOA
LISBON
MICRON
MIGNON
MIKLOS
MILTON
MINION
MINNOW
MIRROR
NIMROD
NIPPON
PIANOS
PICTOR
PIGEON
PILLOW
PINGOS
PINION
PINTOS
PISTOL
PISTON
RIBBON
SIGNOR
SIMEON
SIMOOM
SIPHON
TIPTOE
TIPTOP
VIATOR
VICTOR
VILLON
VINSON
VIREOS
VISION
WIGEON
WILLOW
WILSON
WINDOW
WINNOW
WISDOM
ZIRCON

•I•••O
BIBLIO
BILBAO
BISTRO
CICERO
DINERO
FIASCO
GIGOLO
GINKGO
GIOTTO
GITANO
GIULIO
KIMONO
KINETO
LIBIDO
MIKADO
NIELLO
PIETRO
RIALTO
RIGHTO
SIDERO
SILICO
VIBRIO
VIRAGO

••IO••
ACIOUS
ANIONS
ARIOSE
ARIOSO
ARIOUS
AXIOMS
ELIOTS
GLIOMA
IDIOCY
IDIOMS
IDIOTS
ITIOUS
ODIOUS
OHIOAN
ONIONS
ORIOLE
OTIOSE
PRIORS
PRIORY
SCIONS
THIOLS
TRIODE
TRIOSE
UNIONS

••I•O•
ALISON
AMIDOL
AMIGOS
AVISOS
BAILOR
BRITON
CHICOS
CHIGOE
CHIRON
CHITON
DAIMON
EDISON
EDITOR
EPILOG
EPIZOA
FRIJOL
FRIVOL
GUIDON
ISIDOR
JAILOR
MAISON
OVIBOS
PHILOS
POISON
PRISON
RHINOS
SAIGON
SAILOR
SEISOR
SEIZOR
SHILOH
SKIMOS
SLIPON
SPIGOT
SUITOR
TAILOR
TAINOS
TRICOT
TRIGON
TRIPOD
TRIPOS
UNISON
WHILOM

••I••O
AKIMBO
ARIOSO
ARISTO
DAIMIO
DAIMYO
EMILIO
ERINGO
HAIRDO
SCIPIO
SEISMO
SHINTO
TRICHO

•••IO•
ACTION
ALBION
AMNION
BASION
BUNION
CAMION
CATION
CURIOS
DURION
ELLIOT
FANION
FOLIOS
FUGIOS
FUSION
GABION
GALIOT
GONION
HELIOS
HERIOT
HESIOD
JUNIOR
KATION
LEGION
LESION
LOGION
LOTION
MANIOC
MARION
MINION
MORION
MOTION
NASION
NATION
NOTION
OPTION
PATIOS
PAVIOR
PELION
PERIOD
PINION
POTION
RADIOS
RATION
RATIOS
REGION
SAVIOR
SENIOR
SOLION
TALION
VISION
WANION

•••I•O
ACTINO
ALBINO
ALUINO
BENITO
BONITO
CALICO
CASINO
CHEILO
CHEIRO
DOMINO
ECHINO
ENRICO
ESKIMO
GENITO
HELICO
ILOILO
INDIGO
LADINO
LEPIDO
LIBIDO
LUMINO
MANITO
MEDICO
MEJICO
MERINO
MEXICO
ONEIRO
RUBIGO
SCHIZO
SILICO
SUBITO
VAGINO
VARICO
VESICO
VOMITO

••••IO
ADAGIO
AFLCIO
BAGNIO
BARRIO
BIBLIO
CARDIO
CRANIO
DAIMIO
EMILIO
FLUVIO
GIULIO
HERNIO
NUNCIO
ORCHIO
PHYSIO
PLAGIO
PLUVIO
SCIPIO
STUDIO
VIBRIO

IP••••
IPECAC

I•P•••
IMPACT
IMPAIR
IMPALA
IMPALE
IMPARK
IMPART
IMPAWN
IMPEDE
IMPELS
IMPEND
IMPING
IMPISH
IMPORT
IMPOSE
IMPOST
IMPUGN
IMPURE
IMPUTE
INPUTS

I••P••
INSPAN
ISOPOD

I•••P•
INCEPT

I••••P
ICECAP
INCORP
INSTEP
INWRAP

•IP•••
BIPEDS
BIPODS
CIPHER
DIPLEX
DIPLOE
DIPODY
DIPOLE
DIPPED
DIPPER
DIPSAS
FIPPLE
GIPONS
GIPPED
HIPPED
HIPPIE
HIPPOS
HIPPUS
KIPPER
LIPASE
LIPIDS
LIPOID
LIPOMA
LIPPED
LIPPER
NIPPED
NIPPER

NIPPLE
NIPPON
PIPAGE
PIPERS
PIPETS
PIPIER
PIPING
PIPITS
PIPKIN
PIPPED
PIPPIN
RIPELY
RIPENS
RIPEST
RIPLEY
RIPOFF
RIPOST
RIPPED
RIPPER
RIPPLE
RIPRAP
RIPSAW
SIPHON
SIPPED
SIPPER
SIPPET
TIPOFF
TIPPED
TIPPER
TIPPET
TIPPLE
TIPTOE
TIPTOP
VIPERS
WIPERS
WIPING
YIPPED
YIPPIE
ZIPPED
ZIPPER

•I•P••

BIOPSY
DIAPER
DIEPPE
DIMPLE
DIMPLY
DIPPED
DIPPER
DISPEL
FIPPLE
GIMPED
GIPPED
HIPPED
HIPPIE
HIPPOS
HIPPUS
HISPID
KIPPER
LIMPED
LIMPER
LIMPET
LIMPID
LIMPLY
LIPPED
LIPPER
LISPED
LISPER
NIPPED
NIPPER
NIPPLE
NIPPON
PIGPEN
PIMPED
PIMPLE
PIMPLY
PIPPED
PIPPIN
RIMPLE
RIPPED
RIPPER
RIPPLE
SIMPER
SIMPLE
SIMPLY
SIPPED
SIPPER
SIPPET
TIPPED
TIPPER
TIPPET
TIPPLE
WIMPLE
WISPED
YIPPED
YIPPIE
ZIPPED
ZIPPER

•I••P•

BICEPS
DIEPPE
MIXUPS
PINUPS
SIRUPS
SIRUPY
TIEUPS
WICOPY

•I•••P

BISHOP
FILLIP
HICCUP
KIDNAP
LINEUP
MISHAP
PICKUP
RIPRAP
TIPTOP
TITTUP
WIKIUP

••IP••

ADIPIC
ALIPED
CHIPPY
DRIPPY
GRIPED
GRIPER
GRIPES
GRIPPE
GRIPPY
JAIPUR
PHIPPS
QUIPUS
SAIPAN
SCIPIO
SLIPON
SLIPUP
SNIPED
SNIPER
SNIPES
SNIPPY
STIPEL
STIPES
SWIPED
SWIPES
SWIPLE
TAIPEI
TRIPLE
TRIPOD
TRIPOS

••I•P•

BLIMPS
CHIPPY
CHIRPS
CRIMPS
CRIMPY
CRISPS
CRISPY
DRIPPY
GRIPPE
GRIPPY
GUIMPE
PHIPPS
PRIMPS
SKIMPS
SKIMPY
SNIPPY
STIRPS
TWIRPS

••I••P

PHILIP
SLIPUP

•••IP•

CALIPH
CERIPH
EQUIPS
EURIPI
FELIPE
OXLIPS
RECIPE
SCRIPS
SCRIPT
STRIPE
STRIPS
STRIPT
STRIPY
THRIPS
TULIPS
UNRIPE
UNRIPS

•••I•P

MEGILP
SCRIMP
SHRIMP
WIKIUP

••••IP

CATNIP
FILLIP
GOSSIP
PHILIP
TURNIP
UNSHIP

I••Q••

IRAQIS

•IQ•••

FIQUES
LIQUID
LIQUOR
PIQUED
PIQUES
PIQUET

•I•Q••

BISQUE
CINQUE
CIRQUE
RISQUE

••IQ••

CAIQUE
CLIQUE
CLIQUY
UNIQUE

IR••••

IRAQIS
IREFUL
IRENES
IRENIC
IRIDES
IRIDIC
IRISES
IRITIC
IRITIS
IRKING
IRONED
IRONER
IRONIC
IRVING
IRVINS
IRWINS

I•R•••

IHRAMS
INROAD
INRUSH
ISRAEL

I••R••

IATRIC
IBERIA
ICARUS
IGOROT
IMARET
IMBRUE
INARCH
INARMS
INBRED
INDRIS
INGRES
INGRID
INURED
INURES
INURNS
INWRAP

I•••R•

IDLERS
IGNORE
IMBARK
IMMURE
IMPARK
IMPART
IMPORT
IMPURE
INBORN
INCORP
INCURS
INFERO
INFERS
INFIRM
INFORM
INHERE
INJURE
INJURY
INKERS
INSERT
INSURE
INTERN
INTERS
INTURN
INVERT
INWARD
IZZARD

I••••R

IMPAIR
INDOOR
INKIER
INLIER
INSTAR
IRONER
ISADOR
ISHTAR
ISIDOR
ISOBAR
ISOMER
ISSUER

•IR•••

AIRDRY
AIRIER
AIRILY
AIRING
AIRMAN
AIRMEN
AIRWAY
BIRDIE
BIREME
BIRLED
BIRLES
BIRRED
BIRTHS
CIRCLE
CIRCUM
CIRCUS
CIRQUE
CIRRUS
DIRECT
DIRELY
DIREST
DIRGES
DIRHAM
DIRKED
DIRNDL
FIRERS
FIRING
FIRKIN
FIRMAN
FIRMED
FIRMER
FIRMLY
FIRSTS
FIRTHS
GIRDED
GIRDER
GIRDLE
GIRTED
HIRAMS
HIRERS
HIRING
KIRSCH
MIRAGE
MIRIAM
MIRING
MIRROR
PIRACY
PIRANA
PIRATE
SIRDAR
SIRENS
SIRING
SIRIUS
SIRUPS
SIRUPY
TIRADE
TIRANA
TIRING
VIRAGO
VIREOS
VIRGAS
VIRGIE
VIRGIL
VIRGIN
VIRILE
VIRTUE

WIRERS
WIRIER
WIRILY
WIRING
ZIRCON
ZIRONS

•I•R••

BIERCE
BIRRED
CIRRUS
CITRAL
CITRIC
CITRON
CITRUS
FIBRIL
FIBRIN
FIERCE
FIORDS
GIBRAN
LIBRAE
LIBRAS
LIERNE
LIVRES
MICRON
MIDRIB
MIRROR
MITRAL
NIMROD
NITRIC
NITRID
PICRIC
PIERCE
PIERRE
PIERUS
RIPRAP
SIERRA
SIGRID
TIARAS
TIERCE
TIERED
VIBRIO
VITRIC

•I••R•

AIDERS
AIRDRY
BICARB
BICORN
BIFORM
BIHARI
BINARY
BISTRO
BITERS
CICERO
CIDERS
CIGARS
CIMBRI
DICERS
DIMERS
DINARS
DINERO
DINERS
DISARM
DIVERS
DIVERT
FIACRE
FIBERS
FIFERS
FIGURE
FILERS
FINERY
FIRERS
FIVERS
FIXERS
GIBERS
HIDERS
HIKERS
HILARY
HIRERS
LIFERS
LIGURE
LINERS
LITERS
LIVERS
LIVERY
LIZARD
MILERS
MILORD
MIMERS
MINERS
MINORS
MISERS
MISERY
MITERS
MIXERS
OILERS
PIERRE
PIETRO
PIKERS
PINERY
PIPERS
RICERS
RIDERS
RIGORS
RIMERS
RISERS
RITARD
RIVERS
SIDERO
SIERRA
SIEURS
SIMARS
SISERA
SITARS
SIZARS
TIGERS
TILERS
TIMBRE
TIMERS
TISHRI
VICARS
VINERY
VIPERS
VISARD
VISORS
VIZARD
VIZIRS
VIZORS
WINERY
WINTRY
WIPERS
WIRERS
WIVERN
WIVERS
WIZARD

•I•••R

AIRIER
BIBBER
BICKER
BIDDER
BIGGER
BILKER
BINDER
BISTER
BITTER
CINDER
CIPHER
CITHER
DIALER
DIAPER
DIBBER
DICKER
DIETER
DIFFER
DIGGER
DIMMER
DINNER
DIPPER
DISBAR
DITHER
EITHER
FIBBER
FILLER
FILTER
FINDER
FINGER
FIRMER
FISHER
FITTER
GIAOUR
GIBBER
GILDER
GINGER
GINNER
GIRDER
HIGHER
HILLER
HINDER
HISSER
HITHER
HITLER
HITTER
JIBBER
JIGGER
JILTER
JINKER
JITTER
KICKER
KIDDER
KILLER
KILMER
KILTER
KINDER
KIPPER
KISSER
LICTOR
LIEDER
LIFTER
LIMBER
LIMIER
LIMNER
LIMPER
LINEAR
LINGER
LINIER
LINTER
LIPPER
LIQUOR
LISPER
LISTER
LITHER
LITTER
LIVIER
LIVYER
MIDAIR
MILDER
MILKER
MILLER
MILTER
MINCER
MINDER
MINTER
MIRROR
MISTER
NICKER
NIGHER
NIPPER
OILIER
PICKER
PICTOR
PIECER
PIETER
PILFER
PILLAR
PINDAR
PINIER
PINNER
PINTER
PIPIER
RICHER
RIFLER
RIGGER
RIMMER
RINGER
RINSER
RIOTER
RIPPER
RISKER
RITTER
SICKER
SIDDUR
SIDLER
SIFTER
SIGNER
SIGNOR
SILVER
SIMMER
SIMPER
SINGER
SINKER
SINNER
SINTER
SIPPER
SIRDAR
SISTER
SITTER
SIZIER
TICKER
TIDIER
TILLER
TILTER
TIMBER
TINDER
TINKER
TINNER
TIPPER
TITHER
TITTER
VIATOR
VICTOR
VIEWER
VIGOUR
VINIER
VIZIER
WICKER
WIENER
WILBER
WILBUR
WILDER
WILIER
WILLER
WINCER
WINDER
WINIER
WINKER
WINNER
WINTER
WIRIER
WITHER
ZIPPER
ZITHER

••IR••

BAIRNS
BEIRUT
CAIRNS
CHIRMS
CHIRON
CHIRPS
CHIRRS
EPIRUS
FAIRED
FAIRER
FAIRLY
FLIRTS
FLIRTY
HAIRDO
HAIRED
LAIRDS
LAIRED
MOIRAS
OSIRIS
PAIRED
PEIRCE
QUIRED
QUIRES
QUIRKS
QUIRTS
SHIRES
SHIRKS
SHIRRS
SHIRTS
SKIRRS
SKIRTS
SMIRCH
SMIRKS
SOIREE
SPIRAL
SPIREA
SPIRED
SPIRES
SPIRIT
SPIRTS
STIRKS
STIRPS
SWIRLS
SWIRLY
THIRDS
THIRST
THIRTY
TWIRLS
TWIRPS
WEIRDY
WHIRLS

••I•R•

ANITRA
APIARY
AVIARY
BRIARS
BRIERS
BRIERY
CHIRRS
CRIERS
DMITRI
DRIERS
EMIGRE
FLIERS
FRIARS
FRIARY
FRIERS
GRIGRI
MAIGRE
MAITRE
OSIERS
PLIERS
PRIERS
PRIORS
PRIORY
SHIRRS
SKIERS
SKIRRS

SPIERS
TRIERS

••I••R

ABIDER
BAILER
BAILOR
BAITER
BOILER
BRIBER
CHIDER
CHIMER
COILER
COINER
DEICER
DRIVER
DUIKER
EDITOR
ELIXIR
FAIRER
GAINER
GAITER
GEIGER
GLIDER
GOITER
GRIPER
GUIDER
GUITAR
HAILER
HEIFER
ISIDOR
JAILER
JAILOR
JAIPUR
JOINER
JUICER
KAISER
LOITER
MAILER
MAIMER
MOILER
OLIVER
PRIMER
PRIZER
QUIVER
RAIDER
RAISER
RUINER
SAILER
SAILOR
SEINER
SEISOR
SEIZER
SEIZOR
SHIKAR
SHINER
SHIVER
SKIVER
SLICER
SLIDER
SLIVER
SMILER
SMITER
SNIPER
SPICER
SPIDER
STIVER
SUITOR
TAILOR
TOILER
TRITER
TWINER
VAINER
VEILER
WAILER
WAITER
WAIVER
WEIMAR
WHINER
WHITER
WRITER
ZUIDER

•••IR•

ADMIRE
AFFIRM
ALMIRA
ASPIRE
ATTIRE
AWHIRL
BEGIRD
BEGIRT
BEMIRE
CHAIRS
CHEIRO
CHOIRS
CLAIRE
DESIRE
ELMIRA
ELVIRA
EMPIRE
ENGIRD
ENGIRT
ENTIRE
EXPIRE
EXPIRY
FAKIRS
FLAIRS
GLAIRS
GLAIRY
HEGIRA
HEJIRA
INFIRM
JABIRU
NADIRS
ONEIRO
RETIRE
SATIRE
SQUIRE
SQUIRM
SQUIRT
STAIRS
TAPIRS
THEIRS
TSHIRT
UMPIRE
UNGIRD
UNGIRT
VENIRE
VIZIRS

•••I•R

AIRIER
ANTIAR
ASHIER
BELIER
BONIER
CAGIER
CAHIER
CAVIAR
COPIER
COZIER
DEFIER
DENIER
DEWIER
DOPIER
DOTIER
DOZIER
EASIER
EDGIER
ENVIER
FOLIAR
FOXIER
FUMIER
GAMIER
GLUIER
GOOIER
GORIER
HAZIER
HOLIER
HOMIER
HOSIER
INKIER
INLIER
JUNIOR
LACIER
LAKIER
LAZIER
LEVIER
LIMIER
LINIER
LIVIER
LOGIER
MAZIER
METIER
NAPIER
NOSIER
OILIER
OOZIER
PAVIOR
PINIER
PIPIER
POKIER
PUNIER
RACIER
RAPIER
RELIER
ROPIER
ROSIER
SAGIER
SAVIOR
SENIOR
SEXIER
SIZIER
SPRIER
TIDIER
TONIER
UGLIER
VARIER
VINIER
VIZIER
WARIER
WAVIER
WAXIER
WILIER
WINIER
WIRIER
XAVIER
ZANIER

••••IR

AFFAIR
ALTAIR
BESTIR
DEVOIR
ECLAIR
ELIXIR
FAFNIR
FENRIR
GAMBIR
IMPAIR
KAFFIR
MEMOIR
MENHIR
MIDAIR
MOHAIR
NORNIR
RENOIR
REPAIR
UNFAIR
UNHAIR
ZAFFIR

IS••••

ISAACS
ISABEL
ISADOR
ISAIAH
ISCHIA
ISEULT
ISHTAR
ISIDOR
ISLAND
ISLETS
ISLING
ISOBAR
ISOBEL
ISOGON
ISOHEL
ISOLDE
ISOMER
ISOPOD
ISRAEL
ISSEIS
ISSUED
ISSUER
ISSUES

I•S•••

INSANE
INSECT
INSERT
INSETS
INSIDE
INSIST
INSOLE
INSOUL
INSPAN
INSTAR
INSTEP
INSULT
INSURE
ISSEIS
ISSUED
ISSUER
ISSUES
ITSELF

I••S••

IBISES
IRISES

I•••S•

ICIEST
IDLEST
ILLUSE
ILLUST
IMMESH
IMPISH
IMPOSE
IMPOST
INCASE
INCEST
INCISE
INCUSE
INFEST
INFUSE
INGEST
INMESH
INMOST
INRUSH
INSIST
INVEST
IODISM

I••••S

IAMBUS
IBEAMS
IBEXES
IBICES
IBISES
ICARUS
ICINGS
IDEALS
IDIOMS
IDIOTS
IDLERS
IDYLLS
IGLOOS
IHRAMS
ILEXES
IMAGES
IMBEDS
IMBUES
IMIDES
IMINES
IMMIES
IMPELS
INARMS
INCHES
INCURS
INDIES
INDOWS
INDRIS
INDUES
INFERS
INGOTS
INGRES
INKERS
INKLES
INLAWS
INLAYS
INLETS
INPUTS
INSETS
INTERS
INURES
INURNS
IODOUS
IOLCUS
IRAQIS
IRENES
IRIDES
IRISES
IRITIS
IRVINS
IRWINS
ISAACS
ISLETS
ISSEIS
ISSUES
ITCHES
ITIOUS

•IS•••

AISLED
AISLES
BISCAY
BISECT
BISHOP
BISQUE
BISTER
BISTRO
CISCOS
CISSIE
CISSYS
DISARM
DISBAR
DISCUS
DISHED
DISHES
DISMAL
DISMAY
DISNEY

DISOWN
DISPEL
DISTAL
DISTIL
DISUSE
FISCAL
FISHED
FISHER
FISHES
FISTED
FISTIC
GISELE
GISMOS
HISPID
HISSED
HISSER
HISSES
KISLEW
KISMET
KISSED
KISSER
KISSES
LISBOA
LISBON
LISPED
LISPER
LISTED
LISTEL
LISTEN
LISTER
MISCUE
MISDID
MISERS
MISERY
MISFIT
MISHAP
MISKAL
MISLAY
MISSAL
MISSED
MISSES
MISSIS
MISSUS
MISTED
MISTER
MISUSE
NISEIS
PISCES
PISGAH
PISHED
PISHES
PISTIL
PISTOL
PISTON
RISERS
RISING
RISKED
RISKER
RISQUE
SISERA
SISKIN
SISTER
TISANE
TISHRI
TISSUE
VISAED
VISAGE
VISARD
VISCID
VISCUS
VISEED
VISHNU
VISING
VISION
VISITS
VISORS
VISTAS
VISUAL
WISDOM
WISELY
WISEST
WISHED
WISHES
WISING
WISPED

•I•S••

BIASED
BIASES
BIOSIS
CISSIE
CISSYS
DIESEL
DIESES
DIESIS
DIPSAS
FIASCO
FIESTA
FIRSTS
GIBSON
HISSED
HISSER
HISSES
JIGSAW
KINSEY
KIOSKS
KIRSCH
KISSED
KISSER
KISSES
KITSCH
MIASMA
MIOSIS
MISSAL
MISSED
MISSES
MISSIS
MISSUS
PIGSTY
RINSED
RINSER
RINSES
RIPSAW
SIESTA
TINSEL
TISSUE
VINSON
WILSON

•I••S•

BIOPSY
CIVISM
DICAST
DIGEST
DIREST
DISUSE
DIVEST
FILOSE
FINEST
FINISH
KIBOSH
KINASE
KINESI
LIPASE
MIMOSA
MISUSE
NICEST
PILOSE
RIBOSE
RIMOSE
RIPEST
RIPOST
SIWASH
VILEST
WIDEST
WISEST

•I•••S

AIDERS
AISLES
BIALYS
BIASES
BIBLES
BICEPS
BIDETS
BIGHTS
BIGOTS
BIKOLS
BILGES
BILLYS
BINGES
BINITS
BIOSIS
BIPEDS
BIPODS
BIRLES
BIRTHS
BITERS
CIBOLS
CIDERS
CIGARS
CINDYS
CIRCUS
CIRRUS
CISCOS
CISSYS
CITIES
CITRUS
CIVETS
CIVICS
CIVIES
DIANAS
DIANES
DICERS
DIDIES
DIDOES
DIESES
DIESIS
DIGITS
DIMERS
DINAHS
DINARS
DINERS
DINGUS
DIODES
DIPSAS
DIRGES
DISCUS
DISHES
DITTOS
DIVANS
DIVERS
DIVOTS
DIWANS
DIXITS
DIZENS
EIGHTS
FIBERS
FICHES
FICHUS
FIELDS
FIENDS
FIFERS
FIFTHS
FIGHTS
FILERS
FILETS
FINALS
FIORDS
FIQUES
FIRERS
FIRSTS
FIRTHS
FISHES
FIVERS
FIXERS
FIZZES
GIANTS
GIBERS
GIGUES
GILDAS
GIMELS
GIPONS
GISMOS
GIZMOS
HIATUS
HIDERS
HIKERS
HILDAS
HINDUS
HINGES
HIPPOS
HIPPUS
HIRAMS
HIRERS
HISSES
JIHADS
JIMMYS
JINNYS
JINXES
KIBEIS
KININS
KIOSKS
KISSES
KITTYS
LIANAS
LIANES
LIBBYS
LIBELS
LIBRAS
LIEGES
LIFERS
LIGHTS
LIKENS
LILACS
LILIES
LIMBUS
LIMENS
LIMEYS
LIMITS
LINDAS
LINENS
LINERS
LINGAS
LIPIDS
LITERS
LITMUS
LIVENS
LIVERS
LIVIAS
LIVRES
LIZZYS
MIAULS
MICKYS
MIDGES
MIKLOS
MILERS
MILLYS
MIMERS
MIMICS
MINCES
MINERS
MINIMS
MINORS
MINXES
MIOSIS
MISERS
MISSES
MISSIS
MISSUS
MITERS
MIXERS
MIXUPS
NICHES
NICKYS
NIECES
NIGELS
NIGHTS
NIMBUS
NINTHS
NISEIS
NIXIES
OILERS
PIANOS
PICOTS
PICULS
PIECES
PIERUS
PIGNUS
PIKERS
PILAFS
PILEUS
PILOTS
PILOUS
PINDUS
PINGOS
PINONS
PINTOS
PINUPS
PIPERS
PIPETS
PIPITS
PIQUES
PISCES
PISHES
PITIES
PITONS
PIVOTS
PIXIES
PIZZAS
RIATAS
RICERS
RICHES
RICKYS
RICTUS
RIDERS
RIDGES
RIFLES
RIGHTS
RIGORS
RIMERS
RIMOUS
RINSES
RIPENS
RISERS
RIVALS
RIVERS
RIVETS
RIYALS
SIBYLS
SIDLES
SIEGES
SIEURS
SIEVES
SIGHTS
SIGILS
SIGMAS
SILVAS
SIMARS
SIMONS
SINEWS
SINGES
SIRENS
SIRIUS
SIRUPS

SITARS
SITINS
SIXTES
SIXTHS
SIZARS
TIARAS
TIBIAS
TICALS
TIDIES
TIEINS
TIEUPS
TIGERS
TIGHTS
TILDES
TILERS
TILLYS
TILTHS
TIMERS
TIMMYS
TINCTS
TINGES
TITANS
TITHES
TITLES
VIANDS
VICARS
VICKYS
VIGILS
VILLAS
VILLUS
VINCES
VINNYS
VINOUS
VINYLS
VIOLAS
VIPERS
VIREOS
VIRGAS
VISCUS
VISITS
VISORS
VISTAS
VITALS
VIXENS
VIZIRS
VIZORS
WICHES
WIDENS
WIDOWS
WIDTHS
WIELDS
WIGANS
WILLIS
WILLYS
WILMAS
WINCES
WINOES
WINZES
WIPERS
WIRERS
WISHES
WITHES
WIVERS
WIZENS
YIELDS
ZIBETS
ZIRONS

••IS••

AGISTS
ALISON
ANISES
ARISEN
ARISES
ARISTA
ARISTO
AVISOS
BRISKS
CHISEL
CRISES
CRISIS
CRISPS
CRISPY
CUISSE
DAISES
DAISYS
DEISTS
EDISON
ELISHA
ENISLE
EXISTS
FEISTS
FEISTY
FOISTS
FRISES
FRISKS
FRISKY
GEISHA
GRISLY
GUISES
HEISTS
HOISTS
IBISES
IRISES
JOISTS
KAISER
KRISES
MAISIE
MAISON
MOISHE
NOISED
NOISES
OVISAC
POISED
POISES
POISON
PRISMS
PRISON
PRISSY
PTISAN
PUISNE
RAISED
RAISER
RAISES
RAISIN
SEISIN
SEISMO
SEISMS
SEISOR
TRISTE
TWISTS
UNISEX
UNISON
WAISTS
WHISKS
WHISKY
WRISTS

••I•S•

AHIMSA
AMIDST
ARIOSE
ARIOSO
CHIASM
CUISSE
DRIEST
FLIEST
FLIMSY
GRILSE
ICIEST
OBIISM
OTIOSE
PRIEST
PRISSY
QUINSY
SHIEST
SHIISM
SLIEST
SLIMSY
THIRST
TRIOSE
WHILST
WHIMSY
WRIEST

••I••S

ABIDES
ACINUS
ACIOUS
ADIEUS
AGISTS
ALIBIS
ALICES
ALIENS
ALIGNS
ALINES
AMICES
AMIDES
AMIENS
AMIGOS
ANIMAS
ANIMUS
ANIONS
ANISES
ANITAS
APICES
ARIANS
ARIELS
ARIOUS
ARISES
ASIANS
ASIDES
AVISOS
AXIOMS
AZINES
BAIRNS
BEIGES
BEINGS
BLIMPS
BLINDS
BLINKS
BRIARS
BRIBES
BRICKS
BRIDES
BRIEFS
BRIERS
BRILLS
BRINES
BRINGS
BRINKS
BRISKS
BUILDS
CAIRNS
CEIBAS
CHIAUS
CHICKS
CHICOS
CHIDES
CHIEFS
CHILLS
CHIMES
CHINES
CHINKS
CHIRMS
CHIRPS
CHIRRS
CHIVES
CLICKS
CLIFFS
CLIMBS
CLIMES
CLINES
CLINGS
CLINKS
CLINTS
CLIVES
COIGNS
CRICKS
CRIERS
CRIMES
CRIMPS
CRISES
CRISIS
CRISPS
DAISES
DAISYS
DEICES
DEIGNS
DEISTS
DOINGS
DRIERS
DRIFTS
DRILLS
DRINKS
DRIVES
EDICTS
EDILES
EDITHS
ELIDES
ELIOTS
ELIZAS
EMILES
EMILYS
EPIRUS
ERICHS
EVICTS
EVITAS
EXILES
EXISTS
FAINTS
FAITHS
FEIGNS
FEINTS
FEISTS
FLICKS
FLIERS
FLINGS
FLINTS
FLIRTS
FOISTS
FRIARS
FRIERS
FRILLS
FRISES
FRISKS
FRITHS
GLIDES
GLINTS
GOINGS
GRIDES
GRIEFS
GRILLS
GRIMES
GRINDS
GRIPES
GUIDES
GUILDS
GUILES
GUILTS
GUISES
HEISTS
HOICKS
HOISTS
IBICES
IBISES
ICINGS
IDIOMS
IDIOTS
IMIDES
IMINES
IRIDES
IRISES
IRITIS
ITIOUS
JAINAS
JOINTS
JOISTS
JUICES
KEITHS
KNIFES
KNIVES
KOINES
KRISES
LAIRDS
LEIGHS
MAIZES
MOIRAS
NAIADS
NEIGHS
NOISES
ODIOUS
OGIVES
OLIVES
ONIONS
OPINES
ORIBIS
ORIELS
OSIERS
OSIRIS
OTITIS
OVIBOS
OXIDES
PAINTS
PHIALS
PHILOS
PHIPPS
PLIERS
POILUS
POINDS
POINTS
POISES
PRICES
PRICKS
PRIDES
PRIERS
PRIMES
PRIMPS
PRINKS
PRINTS
PRIORS
PRISMS
PRIZES
QUILLS
QUILTS
QUINTS
QUIPUS
QUIRES
QUIRKS
QUIRTS
RAISES
REICHS
REIGNS
RHINOS
SAIGAS
SAINTS
SCIONS
SEINES
SEISMS
SEIZES
SHIFTS
SHILLS
SHINES
SHIRES

6

SHIRKS
SHIRRS
SHIRTS
SHIVES
SKIERS
SKIFFS
SKILLS
SKIMOS
SKIMPS
SKINKS
SKIRRS
SKIRTS
SKIVES
SLICES
SLICKS
SLIDES
SLIMES
SLINGS
SLINKS
SMILES
SMIRKS
SMITES
SMITHS
SNICKS
SNIFFS
SNIPES
SPICES
SPIELS
SPIERS
SPIKES
SPILES
SPILLS
SPINES
SPIRES
SPIRTS
SPITES
STICKS
STILES
STILLS
STILTS
STINGS
STINKS
STINTS
STIPES
STIRKS
STIRPS
SUITES
SWIFTS
SWILLS
SWINGS
SWIPES
SWIRLS
TAIGAS
TAINOS
TAINTS
THIGHS
THINGS
THINKS
THIOLS
THIRDS
TOILES
TRIADS
TRIALS
TRIBES
TRICES
TRICKS
TRIERS
TRILLS
TRINES
TRIPOS
TRIXYS
TWILLS
TWINES
TWIRLS
TWIRPS
TWISTS
UMIAKS
UNIONS
UNITES
VOICES
VOILES
WAISTS
WAIVES
WEIGHS
WHIFFS
WHILES
WHINES
WHIRLS
WHISKS
WHITES
WRINGS
WRISTS
WRITES
YOICKS

•••IS•

ADVISE
AGUISH
AORIST
ARTIST
ASSISI
ASSIST
AURIST
AUTISM
BABISM
BABIST
BANISH
BETISE
BLUISH
BOYISH
BRAISE
BRUISE
CAMISE
CERISE
CHAISE
CHRISM
CHRIST
CIVISM
CLEIST
COYISH
CRUISE
CUBISM
CUBIST
DANISH
DEMISE
DENISE
DESIST
DEVISE
DOVISH
DUDISH
EGOISM
EGOIST
ELFISH
ELOISE
ELVISH
ENLIST
EONISM
EXCISE
FAMISH
FETISH
FINISH
FRAISE
GARISH
GNEISS
HOLISM
IMPISH
INCISE
INSIST
IODISM
JADISH
JEWISH
JURIST
JUTISH
KUMISS
LATISH
LAVISH
LEGIST
LOUISA
LOUISE
LUTIST
LYRISM
LYRIST
MAOISM
MAOIST
MARIST
MODISH
MOMISM
MONISM
MONIST
MOPISH
MULISH
MUTISM
NANISM
NAZISM
NOMISM
NOWISE
NUDISM
NUDIST
OAFISH
OBIISM
OBOIST
OFFISH
OGRISH
OLDISH
OWLISH
PALISH
PAPIST
PARISH
PAVISE
PERISH
POLISH
POPISH
PRAISE
PUNISH
PURISM
PURIST
RACISM
RACIST
RADISH
RAKISH
RAPIST
RAVISH
RAWISH
RELISH
REMISE
REMISS
RESIST
REVISE
ROMISH
SADISM
SADIST
SALISH
SCHISM
SCHIST
SEXISM
SEXIST
SHIISM
SPEISS
SQUISH
SUFISM
TANIST
TAOISM
TAOIST
THEISM
THEIST
TOYISH
TRUISM
TYPIST
UNWISE
UNWISH
UPPISH
UPRISE
VALISE
VANISH
VERISM
VERIST

•••I•S

AALIIS
ABBIES
ADLIBS
ADMITS
AERIES
ALLIES
ALUINS
AMBITS
ANNIES
ANTICS
ANVILS
APHIDS
APRILS
ARMIES
ARNIES
AROIDS
ARTIES
ASPICS
ATTICS
AUDITS
AUXINS
AVAILS
AVOIDS
AWAITS
BABIES
BASICS
BASILS
BASINS
BATIKS
BEDIMS
BEFITS
BEGINS
BELIES
BEVIES
BINITS
BLAINS
BODIES
BOGIES
BRAIDS
BRAILS
BRAINS
BROILS
BRUINS
BRUITS
BURIES
BURINS
BUSIES
CABINS
CALIFS
CAPIAS
CARIBS
CARIES
CAVIES
CAVILS
CECILS
CELIAS
CHAINS
CHAIRS
CHOIRS
CITIES
CIVICS
CIVIES
CLAIMS
COBIAS
COLIES
COLINS
COMICS
CONICS
CONIES
COPIES
COZIES
CRAIGS
CUBITS
CUMINS
CURIES
CURIOS
CUTIES
CUTINS
CYNICS
CYRILS
DARICS
DARIUS
DAVIDS
DAVIES
DAVITS
DEBITS
DEFIES
DELIAS
DELIUS
DEMIES
DEMITS
DENIES
DENIMS
DEVILS
DIDIES
DIGITS
DIXITS
DOBIES
DOGIES
DORIES
DOXIES
DRAINS
DROITS
DRUIDS
DUTIES
EDDIES
EDWINS
ELFINS
ELLIES
ELOINS
ELSIES
EMMIES
ENVIES
EQUIPS
ERNIES
ERWINS
ESPIES
ETHICS
EYRIES
FACIES
FAKIRS
FELIDS
FLAILS
FLAIRS
FLUIDS
FOGIES
FOLIOS
FRAILS
FRUITS
FUGIOS
FURIES
FUSILS
FUZILS
GAMINS
GENIES
GENIUS
GLAIRS
GNEISS
GOBIES
GRAINS
GROINS
HABITS
HAKIMS
HALIDS
HELIOS
HOLIES

HYOIDS
IMMIES
INDIES
IRVINS
IRWINS
JAMIES
JOSIAS
JOSIES
JULIAS
JULIES
JULIUS
JUNIUS
JURIES
KAMIKS
KATIES
KEVINS
KININS
KRAITS
KUMISS
LADIES
LAMIAS
LAPINS
LATINS
LEVIES
LILIES
LIMITS
LIPIDS
LIVIAS
LORIES
LUCIAS
LUCIUS
LYDIAS
LYRICS
LYSINS
MAMIES
MANIAS
MARIAS
MARIES
MATINS
MAXIMS
MEDICS
MERITS
MIMICS
MINIMS
MOBIUS
MOLIES
MONIES
MOTIFS
MOVIES
NADIRS
NAVIES
NIXIES
NORIAS
NUBIAS
OLLIES
OPTICS
ORBITS
ORGIES
ORPINS
OXLIPS
PANICS
PARIES
PATIOS
PELIAS
PERILS
PEWITS
PIPITS
PITIES
PIXIES
PLAIDS
PLAINS
PLAITS
POGIES
POKIES
PONIES
POSIES
POSITS
PUPILS
PYXIES
QUAILS
QUOINS
QUOITS
RABIES
RADIOS
RADIUS
RAMIES
RAPIDS
RATIOS
REFITS
REGIUS
RELICS
RELIES
REMISS
REMITS
RESINS
RHEIMS
ROBINS
ROSINS
RUBIES
RUNINS
SABINS
SADIES
SAHIBS
SANIES
SASINS
SATINS
SAVINS
SCRIPS
SEPIAS
SERIES
SERIFS
SERINS
SHEIKS
SIGILS
SIRIUS
SITINS
SKEINS
SNAILS
SOLIDS
SONIAS
SOZINS
SPAITS
SPEISS
SPLITS
SPOILS
SPRIGS
SPRITS
SQUIBS
SQUIDS
STAINS
STAIRS
STEINS
STOICS
STRIPS
SUSIES
SWAILS
SWAINS
SYBILS
TAPIRS
THEIRS
THRIPS
TIBIAS
TIDIES
TIEINS
TOBIAS
TOBIES
TODIES
TONICS
TOPICS
TORIES
TORIIS
TOXINS
TRAILS
TRAINS
TRAITS
TULIPS
TUNICS
TUPIKS
UNDIES
UNPINS
UNRIGS
UNRIPS
UNTIES
VARIES
VEXILS
VIGILS
VISITS
VIZIRS
VOMITS
WADIES
WAVIES
YOGINS
ZAMIAS
ZANIES
ZAYINS
ZOOIDS
ZORILS

••••IS

AALIIS
ABATIS
ADENIS
ADONIS
AEOLIS
ALEXIS
ALIBIS
ANUBIS
ARTOIS
ASSAIS
BAHAIS
BAUCIS
BIOSIS
BREWIS
CADDIS
CALAIS
CASSIS
CAULIS
CLEVIS
CLOVIS
COATIS
CORGIS
CRASIS
CRISIS
CULLIS
CURTIS
CUSPIS
DEBRIS
DENNIS
DERRIS
DHOTIS
DIESIS
ECESIS
ELEMIS
EMESIS
ENOSIS
FERMIS
FERRIS
FORTIS
GLACIS
GLYNIS
GNOSIS
GRATIS
HAGGIS
HENRIS
HOURIS
HUBRIS
HYBRIS
INDRIS
IRAQIS
IRITIS
ISSEIS
JARVIS
JERVIS
KAURIS
KERMIS
KHAKIS
KIBEIS
KRUBIS
LANAIS
LUNGIS
MANTIS
MAORIS
MAQUIS
MIOSIS
MISSIS
MORRIS
MUFTIS
MYOSIS
NAOMIS
NEREIS
NISEIS
NOESIS
NORRIS
OKAPIS
ORCHIS
ORIBIS
OSIRIS
OTITIS
OXALIS
PARSIS
PARVIS
PATOIS
PELVIS
PENNIS
PHASIS
PHOCIS
PLASIS
PRAXIS
PRECIS
PTOSIS
PYOSIS
RABBIS
RACHIS
RAPHIS
SALMIS
SEPSIS
SERAIS
SHOJIS
SOTHIS
SPAHIS
STASIS
SWAMIS
TENNIS
TENUIS
TESTIS
THEMIS
THESIS
THETIS
TMESIS
TORIIS
TURKIS
TUSSIS
TUTTIS
UNGUIS
VALOIS
WALLIS
WALVIS
WILLIS
ZOMBIS

IT••••

ITALIC
ITCHED
ITCHES
ITHACA
ITIOUS
ITSELF

I•T•••

IATRIC
INTACT
INTAKE
INTEND
INTENT
INTERN
INTERS
INTIMA
INTOMB
INTONE
INTUIT
INTURN

I••T••

ICHTHY
INSTAR
INSTEP
IRITIC
IRITIS
ISHTAR

I•••T•

IDEATE
IDIOTS
IGNITE
IMPUTE
INCITE
INGOTS
INLETS
INMATE
INNATE
INPUTS
INSETS
INVITE
IODATE
IOLITE
ISLETS

I••••T

ICIEST
IDLEST
IGOROT
ILLUST
IMARET
IMPACT
IMPART
IMPORT
IMPOST
INCEPT
INCEST
INDENT
INDICT
INDUCT
INDULT
INFANT
INFECT
INFEST
INGEST
INJECT
INMOST
INSECT
INSERT
INSIST
INSULT
INTACT
INTENT
INTUIT
INVENT
INVERT
INVEST
ISEULT

•IT•••

BITERS
BITING

BITTED
BITTEN
BITTER
CITHER
CITIED
CITIES
CITING
CITOLA
CITRAL
CITRIC
CITRON
CITRUS
DITHER
DITTOS
EITHER
FITFUL
FITTED
FITTER
GITANO
HITHER
HITLER
HITTER
JITNEY
JITTER
KITING
KITSCH
KITTEN
KITTYS
LITANY
LITERS
LITHER
LITHIA
LITHIC
LITMUS
LITTER
LITTLE
MITERS
MITRAL
MITTEN
NITRIC
NITRID
NITWIT
PITCHY
PITHED
PITIED
PITIES
PITMAN
PITMEN
PITONS
PITTED
RITARD
RITTER
RITUAL
SITARS
SITINS
SITTER
TITANS
TITHED
TITHER
TITHES
TITIAN
TITLED
TITLES
TITTER
TITTLE
TITTUP
VITALS
VITRIC
VITTAE
WITHAL
WITHED
WITHER
WITHES
WITHIN
WITHIT
WITNEY
WITTED
ZITHER

•I•T••

BIOTIC
BIOTIN
BIRTHS
BISTER
BISTRO
BITTED
BITTEN
BITTER
DIATOM
DICTUM
DIETED
DIETER
DINTED
DISTAL
DISTIL
DITTOS
FIFTHS
FILTER
FILTHY
FIRTHS
FISTED
FISTIC
FITTED
FITTER
GIFTED
GIOTTO
GIRTED
HIATUS
HILTED
HINTED
HITTER
JILTED
JILTER
JITTER
KILTED
KILTER
KILTIE
KITTEN
KITTYS
LICTOR
LIFTED
LIFTER
LILTED
LINTEL
LINTER
LISTED
LISTEL
LISTEN
LISTER
LITTER
LITTLE
MILTED
MILTER
MILTON
MINTED
MINTER
MIOTIC
MISTED
MISTER
MITTEN
NINTHS
PICTOR
PIETER
PIETRO
PINTER
PINTLE
PINTOS
PISTIL
PISTOL
PISTON
PITTED
RIATAS
RICTAL
RICTUS
RIFTED
RIOTED
RIOTER
RITTER
SIFTED
SIFTER
SILTED
SINTER
SISTER
SITTER
SIXTES
SIXTHS
TILTED
TILTER
TILTHS
TINTED
TIPTOE
TIPTOP
TITTER
TITTLE
TITTUP
VIATIC
VIATOR
VICTIM
VICTOR
VIRTUE
VISTAS
VITTAE
WIDTHS
WILTED
WINTER
WINTRY
WITTED

•I••T•

BIDETS
BIGHTS
BIGOTS
BILITY
BINITS
CIVETS
DIGITI
DIGITS
DILATE
DILUTE
DIMITY
DIVOTS
DIXITS
EIGHTH
EIGHTS
EIGHTY
FIESTA
FIGHTS
FILETS
FINITE
FIRSTS
FIXATE
FIXITY
GIANTS
GIOTTO
KIBITZ
KINETO
LIGATE
LIGHTS
LIMITS
MIGHTY
MINUTE
NICETY
NIGHTS
NIGHTY
NIMITZ
NINETY
PICOTS
PIGSTY
PILATE
PILOTS
PINITE
PIPETS
PIPITS
PIRATE
PIVOTS
RIALTO
RIGHTO
RIGHTS
RIVETS
SIESTA
SIGHTS
TIGHTS
TINCTS
VISITS
ZIBETH
ZIBETS
ZIZITH

•I•••T

AIGLET
BILLET
BISECT
CILIAT
DICAST
DIGEST
DIGLOT
DIMOUT
DIMWIT
DIRECT
DIREST
DIVERT
DIVEST
FIDGET
FILLET
FINEST
GIBBET
GIBLET
GIGANT
GIGLET
GIGLOT
GIMLET
KISMET
LIMPET
LINNET
MIDGET
MIDGUT
MILLET
MINUET
MISFIT
NICEST
NITWIT
PICKET
PIGNUT
PINXIT
PIQUET
RIDENT
RILLET
RIPEST
RIPOST
SIGNET
SILENT
SIPPET
TICKET
TIDBIT
TIPPET
VILEST
VIOLET
WICKET
WIDEST
WILLET
WISEST
WITHIT

••IT••

ANITAS
ANITRA
BAITED
BAITER
BLITHE
BRITON
CHITIN
CHITON
CHITTY
CRITIC
DMITRI
EDITED
EDITHS
EDITOR
EVITAS
EXITED
FAITHS
FLITCH
FRITHS
GAITED
GAITER
GOITER
GRITTY
GUITAR
IRITIC
IRITIS
KEITHS
LOITER
MAITRE
OTITIS
QUITCH
SAITIC
SMITER
SMITES
SMITHS
SMITHY
SNITCH
SPITAL
SPITED
SPITES
STITCH
STITHY
SUITED
SUITES
SUITOR
SWITCH
TRITER
TWITCH
UNITED
UNITES
WAITED
WAITER
WHITED
WHITEN
WHITER
WHITES
WHITEY
WRITER
WRITES
WRITHE

••I•T•

AGISTS
ARISTA
ARISTO
AVIATE
BLINTZ
CHINTZ
CHITTY
CLINTS
DAINTY
DEISTS
DRIFTS
DRIFTY
EDICTS
ELIOTS
EVICTS
EXISTS
FAINTS
FEINTS

FEISTS
FEISTY
FLINTS
FLINTY
FLIRTS
FLIRTY
FOISTS
GAIETY
GLINTS
GRITTY
GUILTS
GUILTY
HEISTS
HOISTS
IDIOTS
JOINTS
JOISTS
MOIETY
OPIATE
PAINTS
PAINTY
PAIUTE
PLINTH
POINTS
POINTY
PRINTS
QUILTS
QUINTS
QUIRTS
SAINTS
SHIFTS
SHIFTY
SHIITE
SHINTO
SHIRTS
SKIRTS
SPILTH
SPIRTS
STILTS
STINTS
SWIFTS
TAINTS
THIRTY
TRISTE
TWISTS
UBIETY
WAISTS
WRISTS

••I••T

ALIGHT
AMIDST
ARIGHT
BEIRUT
BLIGHT
BRIGHT
CLIENT
CLIMAT
DRIEST
DWIGHT
ELICIT
FLIEST
FLIGHT
FRIGHT
GRIVET
HEIGHT
ICIEST
KNIGHT
ORIENT
PLIANT
PLIGHT
PRIEST
PRIVET
SHIEST
SLIEST
SLIGHT
SPIGOT
SPINET
SPIRIT
SWIVET
THIRST
TOILET
TRICOT
TRIVET
WEIGHT
WHILST
WRIEST
WRIGHT

•••IT•

ACUITY
ADMITS
ALBITE
AMBITS
AMRITA
APLITE
AUDITS
AUGITE
AWAITS
BABITE
BARITE
BEFITS
BENITA
BENITO
BILITY
BINITS
BONITO
BRUITS
CAPITA
CAVITE
CAVITY
CERITE
COMITY
CUBITS
DANITE
DAVITS
DEBITS
DEMITS
DEWITT
DIGITI
DIGITS
DIMITY
DIXITS
DROITS
ENMITY
ENTITY
EOLITH
EQUITY
EXCITE
FERITY
FINITE
FIXITY
FRUITS
FRUITY
GENITO
HABITS
HALITE
HAMITE
IGNITE
INCITE
INVITE
IOLITE
JUDITH
KIBITZ
KRAITS
LAXITY
LENITY
LEVITE
LEVITY
LIMITS
LOLITA
LUCITE
MANITO
MANITU
MERITS
NIMITZ
NUDITY
ODDITY
OOLITE
OPHITE
ORBITS
ORNITH
PARITY
PELITE
PETITE
PEWITS
PINITE
PIPITS
PLAITS
POLITE
POLITY
POSITS
PURITY
PYRITE
QUOITS
RARITY
RATITE
RECITE
REFITS
REMITS
SAMITE
SANITY
SEMITE
SHIITE
SOMITE
SPAITS
SPLITS
SPRITE
SPRITS
SUBITO
TAXITE
TRAITS
UPPITY
VANITY
VERITY
VISITS
VOMITO
VOMITS
WAPITI
WRAITH
ZENITH
ZIZITH

•••I•T

ADDICT
ADMIXT
ADRIFT
ANOINT
AORIST
ARTIST
ASSIST
AURIST
BABIST
BEGIRT
CHRIST
CILIAT
CLEIST
CUBIST
DELICT
DEPICT
DESIST
DEWITT
EGOIST
ELLIOT
ENGIRT
ENLIST
FORINT
GALIOT
HERIOT
INDICT
INSIST
JOLIET
JULIET
JURIST
LARIAT
LEGIST
LUTIST
LYRIST
MAOIST
MARIST
MONIST
NUDIST
OBOIST
PAPIST
PLAINT
PURIST
QUAINT
RACIST
RAPIST
RELICT
RESIST
SADIST
SCHIST
SCRIPT
SEXIST
SHRIFT
SOVIET
SPLINT
SPOILT
SPRINT
SQUINT
SQUIRT
STRICT
STRIPT
TANIST
TAOIST
THEIST
THRIFT
TSHIRT
TYPIST
UNGIRT
UPLIFT
VERIST

••••IT

ACQUIT
ADROIT
ALBEIT
ARMPIT
BANDIT
BELOIT
COMFIT
COMMIT
CREDIT
DACOIT
DAKOIT
DECEIT
DIMWIT
ELEGIT
ELICIT
ESPRIT
GAMBIT
GODWIT
HENBIT
HERMIT
INTUIT
JESUIT
KUWAIT
MISFIT
MUSKIT
NITWIT
OUTFIT
OUTSIT
OUTWIT
PERMIT
PINXIT
PROFIT
PROSIT
PULPIT
PUNDIT
RABBIT
SCHUIT
SENNIT
SOFFIT
SPIRIT
STRAIT
SUBMIT
SUMMIT
SUNLIT
TIDBIT
TOMTIT
TURBIT
TWOBIT
UNKNIT
WITHIT

I•U•••

IGUANA
INULIN
INURED
INURES
INURNS

I••U••

ILLUME
ILLUSE
ILLUST
IMBUED
IMBUES
IMMUNE
IMMUNO
IMMURE
IMPUGN
IMPURE
IMPUTE
INCUBI
INCURS
INCUSE
INDUCE
INDUCT
INDUED
INDUES
INDULT
INFUSE
INGULF
INJURE
INJURY
INPUTS
INRUSH
INSULT
INSURE
INTUIT
INTURN
ISEULT
ISSUED
ISSUER
ISSUES

I•••U•

IAMBUS
ICARUS
IMBRUE
INDIUM
INFLUX
INHAUL
INSOUL
IODOUS
IOLCUS
IONIUM
IREFUL
ITIOUS

•IU•••

GIULIA

GIULIO

•I•U••
DILUTE
DISUSE
FIBULA
FIGURE
FIQUES
GIGUES
LIGULA
LIGULE
LIGURE
LIMULI
LIQUID
LIQUOR
MIAULS
MIGUEL
MINUET
MINUTE
MISUSE
MIXUPS
PICULS
PILULE
PINUPS
PIQUED
PIQUES
PIQUET
RITUAL
SIEURS
SIOUAN
SIRUPS
SIRUPY
TIEUPS
VICUNA
VISUAL

•I••U•
BIJOUX
BISQUE
CILIUM
CINQUE
CIRCUM
CIRCUS
CIRQUE
CIRRUS
CITRUS
DICTUM
DIMOUT
DINGUS
DISCUS
FICHUS
FITFUL
GIAOUR
HIATUS
HICCUP
HINDUS
HIPPUS
LIMBUS
LINEUP
LINGUA
LITMUS
MIDGUT
MILIUM
MINIUM
MISCUE
MISSUS
NIMBUS
PICKUP
PIERUS
PIGNUS
PIGNUT
PILEUM
PILEUS
PILOUS
PINDUS
RICTUS
RIMOUS
RISQUE
SIDDUR
SINFUL
SIRIUS
TISSUE
TITTUP
VIGOUR
VILLUS
VINOUS
VIRTUE
VISCUS
WIKIUP
WILBUR
WILFUL

•I•••U
MILIEU
VISHNU

••IU••
PAIUTE
TRIUNE

••I•U•
ACINUS
ACIOUS
ADIEUS
ADIEUX
ANIMUS
ARIOUS
BEIRUT
CAIQUE
CHIAUS
CLIQUE
CLIQUY
CRINUM
EPIRUS
ITIOUS
JAIPUR
ODIOUS
POILUS
QUIPUS
SLIPUP
UNIQUE

•••IU•
ACTIUM
AECIUM
ALLIUM
ATRIUM
BARIUM
CERIUM
CESIUM
CILIUM
CONIUM
CORIUM
CURIUM
DARIUS
DELIUS
ERBIUM
FOLIUM
GENIUS
GONIUM
HELIUM
INDIUM
IONIUM
JULIUS
JUNIUS
KALIUM
LABIUM
LUCIUS
MEDIUM
MILIUM
MINIUM
MOBIUS
OSMIUM
PODIUM
RADIUM
RADIUS
REGIUS
SIRIUS
SODIUM
TEDIUM
WIKIUP

•••I•U
JABIRU
MANITU
MILIEU

I•V•••
INVADE
INVENT
INVERT
INVEST
INVITE
INVOKE
IRVING
IRVINS

I•••V•
INWOVE

•IV•••
CIVETS
CIVICS
CIVIES
CIVISM
DIVANS
DIVERS
DIVERT
DIVEST
DIVIDE
DIVINE
DIVING
DIVOTS
FIVERS
GIVING
HIVING
LIVELY
LIVENS
LIVERS
LIVERY
LIVIAS
LIVIER
LIVING
LIVRES
LIVYER
PIVOTS
RIVALS
RIVERS
RIVETS
RIVING
VIVACE
VIVIAN
VIVIEN
VIVIFY
WIVERN
WIVERS
WIVING

•I•V••
SIEVED
SIEVES
SILVAE
SILVAN
SILVAS
SILVER
SILVIA

••IV••
CHIVES
CLIVES
DRIVEL
DRIVEN
DRIVER
DRIVES
FRIVOL
GRIVET
KNIVES
OGIVES
OLIVER
OLIVES
OLIVIA
PRIVET
QUIVER
SHIVER
SHIVES
SKIVED
SKIVER
SKIVES
SKIVVY
SLIVER
SNIVEL
STIVER
SWIVEL
SWIVET
TRIVET
TRIVIA
WAIVED
WAIVER
WAIVES

••I•V•
GRIEVE
SKIVVY
THIEVE

•••IV•
ACTIVE
ARGIVE
ARRIVE
DATIVE
DERIVE
ENDIVE
GODIVA
MOTIVE
NATIVE
RELIVE
REVIVE
SALIVA
SCRIVE
SHRIVE
STRIVE
THRIVE
UNLIVE
VOTIVE

I•W•••
INWALL
INWARD
INWIND
INWOVE
INWRAP
IRWINS

I•••W•
IMPAWN
INDOWS
INLAWS

I••••W
INFLOW

•IW•••
DIWANS
SIWASH

•I•W••
AIRWAY
BIGWIG
DIMWIT
MIDWAY
NITWIT
VIEWED
VIEWER
WIGWAG
WIGWAM

•I••W•
DISOWN
SINEWS
SINEWY
WIDOWS

•I•••W
BILLOW
JIGSAW
KISLEW
MILDEW
MINNOW
PILLOW
RIPSAW
WILLOW
WINDOW
WINNOW

••IW••
TAIWAN

••I•W•
OJIBWA

•••I•W
REVIEW

I••X••
IBEXES
ILEXES

I••••X
ICEBOX
INFLUX

•IX•••
DIXITS
FIXATE
FIXERS
FIXING
FIXITY
MIXERS
MIXING
MIXUPS
NIXIES
NIXING
PIXIES
SIXTES
SIXTHS
VIXENS

•I•X••
BIAXAL
JINXES
MINXES
PINXIT

•I••X•
BILOXI

•I•••X
BIFLEX
BIJOUX
DIPLEX
PICKAX

••IX••
ELIXIR

6

TRIXIE
TRIXYS

••I••X
ADIEUX
CLIMAX
SMILAX
UNISEX

•••IX•
ADMIXT
MAXIXE

•••I•X
MENINX
SPHINX
SYRINX

••••IX
BOLLIX
CERVIX
COMMIX
FORNIX
MATRIX
PREFIX
PROLIX
SPADIX
SUFFIX
VERNIX

I•Y•••
IDYLLS

I•••Y•
INLAYS

I••••Y
ICALLY
ICHTHY
IDIOCY
IGNIFY
IMBODY
INFAMY
INJURY

•IY•••
RIYALS

•I•Y••
LIBYAN
LIVYER
SIBYLS
VINYLS

•I••Y•
BIALYS
BILLYS
CINDYS
CISSYS
JIMMYS
JINNYS
KITTYS
LIBBYS
LIMEYS
LIZZYS
MICKYS
MILLYS
NICKYS
RICKYS
TILLYS
TIMMYS
VICKYS
VINNYS
WILLYS

•I•••Y
AIRDRY
AIRILY
AIRWAY
BIGAMY
BILITY
BINARY
BIOPSY
BISCAY
CICELY
DICKEY
DIGAMY
DIMITY
DIMPLY
DINGEY
DINGHY
DINKEY
DIPODY
DIRELY
DISMAY
DISNEY
EIGHTY
FILTHY
FINELY
FINERY
FIRMLY
FIXITY
GIGGLY
HICKEY
HIGHLY
HILARY
JITNEY
KIDNEY
KINDLY
KINGLY
KINSEY
LIKELY
LIMPLY
LITANY
LIVELY
LIVERY
MICKEY
MIDDAY
MIDWAY
MIGHTY
MILADY
MILDLY
MILLAY
MINIFY
MISERY
MISLAY
NICELY
NICETY
NIDIFY
NIGHTY
NINETY
OILILY
PIGSTY
PIMPLY
PINERY
PIRACY
PITCHY
RICHLY
RICKEY
RIPELY
RIPLEY
SICILY
SICKLY
SIDNEY
SIMONY
SIMPLY
SINEWY
SINGLY
SIRUPY
TIDILY
TIMELY
TINGLY
TINKLY
VILELY
VILIFY
VINERY
VIVIFY
WICOPY
WIDELY
WIELDY
WIFELY
WIGGLY
WILDLY
WILILY
WINCEY
WINERY
WINTRY
WIRILY
WISELY
WITNEY
ZINCKY

••I•Y•
DAIMYO
DAISYS
EMILYS
TRIXYS

••I••Y
ACIDLY
APIARY
ARIDLY
AVIARY
AVIDLY
BAILEY
BRIERY
CHILLY
CHINKY
CHIPPY
CHITTY
CLIFFY
CLINGY
CLIQUY
CRIMPY
CRISPY
DAINTY
DRIFTY
DRIPPY
EVILLY
FAIRLY
FEISTY
FLIMSY
FLINTY
FLIRTY
FRIARY
FRIDAY
FRILLY
FRINGY
FRISKY
FRIZZY
GAIETY
GAINLY
GLIBLY
GRIMLY
GRIPPY
GRISLY
GRITTY
GUILTY
IDIOCY
MAINLY
MOIETY
PAINTY
POINTY
PRIMLY
PRIORY
PRISSY
QUINCY
QUINSY
SHIFTY
SHIMMY
SHINDY
SHINNY
SKIMPY
SKINNY
SKIVVY
SLIMLY
SLIMSY
SLINKY
SMITHY
SNIFFY
SNIPPY
SPIFFY
SPINNY
STICKY
STILLY
STINGY
STITHY
SWIRLY
THINLY
THIRTY
TRICKY
TRIGLY
TRIMLY
TWIGGY
UBIETY
VAINLY
WEIRDY
WHIMSY
WHINNY
WHISKY
WHITEY

•••I•Y
ACUITY
AERIFY
AIRILY
BASIFY
BILITY
BODILY
BRAINY
BUSILY
CAGILY
CAVITY
CECILY
CODIFY
COMITY
COZILY
DIMITY
DOZILY
EASILY
EERILY
EFFIGY
ENMITY
ENTITY
EQUITY
EXPIRY
FAMILY
FERITY
FIXITY
FOXILY
FRUITY
GAMILY
GLAIRY
GORILY
GRAINY
HAZILY
HOLILY
HOMILY
HOMINY
IGNIFY
LACILY
LAXITY
LAZILY
LENITY
LEVITY
MAZILY
MINIFY
MODIFY
MUTINY
NAZIFY
NIDIFY
NOSILY
NOTIFY
NUDITY
ODDITY
OILILY
OOZILY
OSSIFY
PACIFY
PARITY
POLICY
POLITY
PUNILY
PURIFY
PURITY
RACILY
RAMIFY
RARITY
RATIFY
ROPILY
ROSILY
ROSINY
SALIFY
SANITY
SATINY
SICILY
STRIPY
TIDILY
TYPIFY
UGLIFY
UGLILY
UNTIDY
UPPITY
VANITY
VERIFY
VERILY
VERITY
VILIFY
VIVIFY
WARILY
WAVILY
WILILY
WIRILY

IZ••••
IZZARD

I•Z•••
IZZARD

I•••Z•
IODIZE
IONIZE

•IZ•••
DIZENS
FIZGIG
FIZZED
FIZZES
FIZZLE
GIZMOS
LIZARD
LIZZIE
LIZZYS
MIZZEN
PIZZAS
SIZARS
SIZIER
SIZING
SIZZLE
VIZARD
VIZIER
VIZIRS
VIZORS

WIZARD
WIZENS
ZIZITH
ZIZZLE

•I•Z••
DIAZIN
FIZZED
FIZZES
FIZZLE
LIZZIE
LIZZYS
MIZZEN
PIAZZA
PIZZAS
SIZZLE
WINZES
ZIGZAG
ZIZZLE

•I••Z•
PIAZZA

•I•••Z
KIBITZ
NIMITZ

••IZ••
ELIZAS
EPIZOA
FRIZZY
GRIZEL
MAIZES
PRIZED
PRIZER
PRIZES
SEIZED
SEIZER
SEIZES
SEIZIN
SEIZOR

••I•Z•
FRIEZE
FRIZZY

••I••Z
BLINTZ
CHINTZ

•••IZ•
ASSIZE
BELIZE
BRAIZE
IODIZE
IONIZE
SCHIZO

•••I•Z
KIBITZ
NIMITZ

JA••••
JABBED
JABBER
JABIRU
JABOTS
JACANA
JACKAL
JACKED
JACKET
JACKIE
JACKYS
JACOBS
JADING
JADISH
JAEGER
JAGGED
JAGUAR
JAILED
JAILER
JAILOR
JAINAS
JAIPUR
JALAPS
JALOPY
JAMIES
JAMMED
JANETS
JANGLE
JANICE
JAPANS
JAPHET
JARFUL
JARGON
JARINA
JARRED
JARVEY
JARVIS
JASONS
JASPER
JAUNTS
JAUNTY
JAWING
JAYVEE
JAZZED
JAZZER
JAZZES

J•A•••
JEANNE
JOANNA
JOANNE
JUAREZ

J••A••
JACANA
JALAPS
JAPANS
JEZAIL
JIHADS
JOHANN
JONAHS
JORAMS
JUDAEA
JUDAEO
JUDAHS
JUDAIC
JUGATE
JURANT
JURATS

J•••A•
JACKAL
JAGUAR
JAINAS
JETSAM
JIGSAW
JINGAL
JORDAN
JOSIAH
JOSIAS
JOVIAL
JOVIAN
JUBBAH
JUDEAN
JULIAN
JULIAS
JUNEAU
JUNTAS

J••••A
JACANA
JARINA
JEMIMA
JERBOA
JOANNA
JOSHUA
JUDAEA

•J••A•
AJOWAN

•J•••A
EJECTA
OJIBWA

••JA••
HIJACK
MOJAVE
PAJAMA
RAJABS
RAJAHS
SEJANT

••J•A•
FIJIAN

••J••A
HEJIRA
PAJAMA

•••JA•
ABIJAH
ELIJAH
LOGJAM
PUNJAB
SANJAK
THUJAS
TROJAN

J•B•••
JABBED
JABBER
JABIRU
JABOTS
JIBBED
JIBBER
JIBING
JOBBED
JOBBER
JUBBAH

J••B••
JABBED
JABBER
JERBOA
JIBBED
JIBBER
JOBBED
JOBBER
JUBBAH
JUMBLE

J•••B•
JACOBS
JUJUBE

•J•B••
OJIBWA

••J•B•
JUJUBE
RAJABS

•••J•B
PUNJAB

J•C•••
JACANA
JACKAL
JACKED
JACKET
JACKIE
JACKYS
JACOBS
JOCKEY
JOCKOS
JOCOSE
JOCUND

J••C••
JOYCES
JUICER
JUICES
JUNCOS

J•••C•
JANICE
JOUNCE

J••••C
JUDAIC

•J•C••
EJECTA
EJECTS

••J•C•
ABJECT
DEJECT
HIJACK
INJECT
MEJICO
OBJECT
REJECT

J•D•••
JADING
JADISH
JUDAEA
JUDAEO
JUDAHS
JUDAIC
JUDEAN
JUDGED
JUDGER
JUDGES
JUDITH

J••D••
JORDAN

J•••D•
JIHADS

J••••D
JABBED
JACKED
JAGGED
JAILED
JAMMED
JARRED
JAZZED
JEERED
JELLED
JEREED
JERKED
JESSED
JESTED
JETTED
JIBBED
JIGGED
JILTED
JINKED
JOBBED
JOCUND
JOGGED
JOINED
JOLTED
JOSHED
JOTTED
JUDGED
JUGGED
JUMPED
JUNKED
JUTTED

•J••D•
FJELDS
FJORDS

JE••••
JEANNE
JEEING
JEERED
JEERER
JEJUNE
JEKYLL
JELLED
JEMIMA
JENNET
JENNYS
JERBOA
JEREED
JEREMY
JERKED
JERKIN
JEROME
JERRYS
JERSEY
JERVIS
JESSED
JESSES
JESSIE
JESTED
JESTER
JESUIT
JETHRO
JETSAM
JETTED
JETTON
JEWELS
JEWESS
JEWISH
JEZAIL

J•E•••
JAEGER
JEEING
JEERED
JEERER

J••E••
JANETS
JEREED
JEREMY
JEWELS
JEWESS
JOKERS
JOSEPH
JUDEAN
JULEPS
JUNEAU
JURELS

J•••E•
JABBED
JABBER
JACKED
JACKET
JAEGER

6

JAGGED
JAILED
JAILER
JAMIES
JAMMED
JAPHET
JARRED
JARVEY
JASPER
JAYVEE
JAZZED
JAZZER
JAZZES
JEERED
JEERER
JELLED
JENNET
JEREED
JERKED
JERSEY
JESSED
JESSES
JESTED
JESTER
JETTED
JIBBED
JIBBER
JIGGED
JIGGER
JILTED
JILTER
JINKED
JINKER
JINXES
JITNEY
JITTER
JOBBED
JOBBER
JOCKEY
JOGGED
JOGGER
JOINED
JOINER
JOLIET
JOLTED
JOLTER
JORGES
JOSHED
JOSHER
JOSHES
JOSIES
JOSSES
JOTTED
JOULES
JOYCES
JUAREZ
JUDAEA
JUDAEO
JUDGED
JUDGER
JUDGES
JUGGED
JUICER
JUICES
JULIES
JULIET
JUMPED
JUMPER
JUNKED
JUNKER
JUNKET
JURIES
JUTTED

J••••E

JACKIE
JANGLE
JANICE
JAYVEE
JEANNE
JEJUNE
JEROME
JESSIE
JIGGLE
JIMMIE
JINGLE
JOANNE
JOCOSE
JOGGLE
JONNIE
JOSTLE
JOUNCE
JUGATE
JUGGLE
JUJUBE
JUMBLE
JUNGLE
JUNKIE

•JE•••

EJECTA
EJECTS
FJELDS

••JE••

ABJECT
DEJECT
INJECT
OBJECT
REJECT

••J••E

ABJURE
ADJURE
CAJOLE
INJURE
JEJUNE
JUJUBE
MOJAVE

•••JE•

FANJET
KOPJES
PROJET

J••F••

JARFUL
JOYFUL

J•G•••

JAGGED
JAGUAR
JIGGED
JIGGER
JIGGLE
JIGSAW
JOGGED
JOGGER
JOGGLE
JUGATE
JUGGED
JUGGLE

J••G••

JAEGER
JAGGED
JANGLE
JARGON
JIGGED
JIGGER
JIGGLE
JINGAL
JINGLE
JOGGED
JOGGER
JOGGLE
JORGES
JUDGED
JUDGER
JUDGES
JUGGED
JUGGLE
JUNGLE
JUNGLY

J••••G

JADING
JAWING
JEEING
JIBING
JOKING
JOYING

J•H•••

JIHADS
JOHANN
JOHNNY

J••H••

JAPHET
JETHRO
JOSHED
JOSHER
JOSHES
JOSHUA

J•••H•

JONAHS
JUDAHS

J••••H

JADISH
JEWISH
JOSEPH
JOSIAH
JUBBAH
JUDITH
JUTISH

••J•H•

RAJAHS

•••J•H

ABIJAH
ELIJAH

JI••••

JIBBED
JIBBER
JIBING
JIGGED
JIGGER
JIGGLE
JIGSAW
JIHADS
JILTED
JILTER
JIMMIE
JIMMYS
JINGAL
JINGLE
JINKED
JINKER
JINNYS
JINXES
JITNEY
JITTER

J•I•••

JAILED
JAILER
JAILOR
JAINAS
JAIPUR
JOINED
JOINER
JOINTS
JOISTS
JUICER
JUICES

J••I••

JABIRU
JADING
JADISH
JAMIES
JANICE
JARINA
JAWING
JEEING
JEMIMA
JEWISH
JIBING
JOKING
JOLIET
JOSIAH
JOSIAS
JOSIES
JOVIAL
JOVIAN
JOYING
JUDITH
JULIAN
JULIAS
JULIES
JULIET
JULIUS
JUNIOR
JUNIUS
JURIES
JURIST
JUTISH

J•••I•

JACKIE
JARVIS
JERKIN
JERVIS
JESSIE
JESUIT
JEZAIL
JIMMIE
JONNIE
JOPLIN
JUDAIC
JUNKIE
JUSTIN

•JI•••

OJIBWA

••JI••

FIJIAN
HEJIRA
MEJICO

••J•I•

ADJOIN
ENJOIN
REJOIN

•••JI•

CROJIK
SHOJIS

J•J•••

JEJUNE
JUJUBE

J•K•••

JEKYLL
JOKERS
JOKING

J••K••

JACKAL
JACKED
JACKET
JACKIE
JACKYS
JERKED
JERKIN
JINKED
JINKER
JOCKEY
JOCKOS
JUNKED
JUNKER
JUNKET
JUNKIE

••J••K

HIJACK

•••J•K

CROJIK
SANJAK
SELJUK

J•L•••

JALAPS
JALOPY
JELLED
JILTED
JILTER
JOLIET
JOLTED
JOLTER
JULEPS
JULIAN
JULIAS
JULIES
JULIET
JULIUS

J••L••

JAILED
JAILER
JAILOR
JELLED
JOPLIN
JOULES

J•••L•

JANGLE
JEKYLL
JEWELS
JIGGLE
JINGLE
JOGGLE
JOSTLE
JUGGLE
JUMBLE
JUNGLE
JUNGLY
JURELS
JUSTLY

J••••L

JACKAL
JARFUL
JEKYLL
JEZAIL
JINGAL
JOVIAL

JOYFUL

•J•L••
FJELDS

••J•L•
CAJOLE

•••J•L
FRIJOL

J•M•••
JAMIES
JAMMED
JEMIMA
JIMMIE
JIMMYS
JUMBLE
JUMPED
JUMPER

J••M••
JAMMED
JIMMIE
JIMMYS

J•••M•
JEMIMA
JEREMY
JEROME
JORAMS
JORUMS

J••••M
JETSAM

••J•M•
PAJAMA

•••J•M
LOGJAM

J•N•••
JANETS
JANGLE
JANICE
JENNET
JENNYS
JINGAL
JINGLE
JINKED
JINKER
JINNYS
JINXES
JONAHS
JONNIE
JONSON
JUNCOS
JUNEAU
JUNGLE
JUNGLY
JUNIOR
JUNIUS
JUNKED
JUNKER
JUNKET
JUNKIE
JUNTAS

J••N••
JAINAS
JAUNTS
JAUNTY
JEANNE
JENNET
JENNYS
JINNYS
JITNEY
JOANNA
JOANNE
JOHNNY
JOINED
JOINER
JOINTS
JONNIE
JOUNCE

J•••N•
JACANA
JADING
JAPANS
JARINA
JASONS
JAWING
JEANNE
JEEING
JEJUNE
JIBING
JOANNA
JOANNE
JOCUND
JOHANN
JOHNNY
JOKING
JOYING
JUPONS
JURANT

J••••N
JARGON
JERKIN
JETTON
JOHANN
JONSON
JOPLIN
JORDAN
JOVIAN
JUDEAN
JULIAN
JUSTIN

•J•••N
AJOWAN

••J•N•
CAJUNS
JEJUNE
SEJANT

••J••N
ADJOIN
ENJOIN
FIJIAN
REJOIN

•••J•N
DONJON
TROJAN

JO••••
JOANNA
JOANNE
JOBBED
JOBBER
JOCKEY
JOCKOS
JOCOSE
JOCUND
JOGGED
JOGGER
JOGGLE
JOHANN
JOHNNY
JOINED
JOINER
JOINTS
JOISTS
JOKERS
JOKING
JOLIET
JOLTED
JOLTER
JONAHS
JONNIE
JONSON
JOPLIN
JORAMS
JORDAN
JORGES
JORUMS
JOSEPH
JOSHED
JOSHER
JOSHES
JOSHUA
JOSIAH
JOSIAS
JOSIES
JOSSES
JOSTLE
JOTTED
JOULES
JOUNCE
JOUSTS
JOVIAL
JOVIAN
JOYCES
JOYFUL
JOYING
JOYOUS

J••O••
JABOTS
JACOBS
JALOPY
JASONS
JEROME
JOCOSE
JOYOUS
JUPONS
JURORS

J•••O•
JAILOR
JARGON
JERBOA
JETTON
JOCKOS
JONSON
JUNCOS
JUNIOR

J••••O
JETHRO
JUDAEO

•JO•••
AJOWAN
FJORDS

••JO••
ADJOIN
BIJOUX
CAJOLE
ENJOIN
ENJOYS
MAJORS
REJOIN
SAJOUS

••J••O
MEJICO

•••JO•
ACAJOU
BANJOS
DONJON
FRIJOL

••••JO
NAVAJO

J•P•••
JAPANS
JAPHET
JOPLIN
JUPONS

J••P••
JAIPUR
JASPER
JUMPED
JUMPER

J•••P•
JALAPS
JALOPY
JOSEPH
JULEPS

••JP••
RAJPUT

J•R•••
JARFUL
JARGON
JARINA
JARRED
JARVEY
JARVIS
JERBOA
JEREED
JEREMY
JERKED
JERKIN
JEROME
JERRYS
JERSEY
JERVIS
JORAMS
JORDAN
JORGES
JORUMS
JURANT
JURATS
JURELS
JURIES
JURIST
JURORS

J••R••
JARRED
JEERED
JEERER
JERRYS
JUAREZ

J•••R•
JABIRU
JETHRO
JOKERS
JURORS

J••••R
JABBER
JAEGER
JAGUAR
JAILER
JAILOR
JAIPUR
JASPER
JAZZER
JEERER
JESTER
JIBBER
JIGGER
JILTER
JINKER
JITTER
JOBBER
JOGGER
JOINER
JOLTER
JOSHER
JUDGER
JUICER
JUMPER
JUNIOR
JUNKER

•J•R••
FJORDS

••J•R•
ABJURE
ADJURE
HEJIRA
INJURE
INJURY
MAJORS

J•S•••
JASONS
JASPER
JESSED
JESSES
JESSIE
JESTED
JESTER
JESUIT
JOSEPH
JOSHED
JOSHER
JOSHES
JOSHUA
JOSIAH
JOSIAS
JOSIES
JOSSES
JOSTLE
JUSTIN
JUSTLY
JUSTUS

J••S••
JERSEY
JESSED
JESSES
JESSIE
JETSAM
JIGSAW
JOISTS
JONSON
JOSSES
JOUSTS

J•••S•
JADISH
JEWESS
JEWISH
JOCOSE
JURIST
JUTISH

J••••S
JABOTS
JACKYS
JACOBS
JAINAS
JALAPS
JAMIES
JANETS
JAPANS
JARVIS
JASONS
JAUNTS
JAZZES
JENNYS
JERRYS
JERVIS
JESSES
JEWELS
JEWESS
JIHADS
JIMMYS
JINNYS
JINXES
JOCKOS
JOINTS
JOISTS
JOKERS
JONAHS
JORAMS
JORGES
JORUMS
JOSHES
JOSIAS
JOSIES
JOSSES
JOULES
JOUSTS
JOYCES
JOYOUS
JUDAHS
JUDGES
JUICES
JULEPS
JULIAS
JULIES
JULIUS
JUNCOS
JUNIUS
JUNTAS
JUPONS
JURATS
JURELS
JURIES
JURORS
JUSTUS

•J•••S
EJECTS
FJELDS
FJORDS

••J•S•
ADJUST
UNJUST

••J••S
CAJUNS
ENJOYS
MAJORS
RAJABS
RAJAHS
SAJOUS

•••J•S
BANJOS
BENJYS
KOPJES
SHOJIS
THUJAS

J•T•••
JETHRO
JETSAM
JETTED
JETTON
JITNEY
JITTER
JOTTED
JUTISH
JUTTED

J••T••
JESTED
JESTER
JETTED
JETTON
JILTED
JILTER
JITTER
JOLTED
JOLTER
JOSTLE
JOTTED
JUNTAS
JUSTIN
JUSTLY
JUSTUS
JUTTED

J•••T•
JABOTS
JANETS
JAUNTS
JAUNTY
JOINTS
JOISTS
JOUSTS
JUDITH
JUGATE
JURATS

J••••T
JACKET
JAPHET
JENNET
JESUIT
JOLIET
JULIET
JUNKET
JURANT
JURIST

•J••T•
EJECTA
EJECTS

••J••T
ABJECT
ADJUST
DEJECT
INJECT
OBJECT
RAJPUT
REJECT
SEJANT
UNJUST

•••J•T
FANJET
PROJET

JU••••
JUAREZ
JUBBAH
JUDAEA
JUDAEO
JUDAHS
JUDAIC
JUDEAN
JUDGED
JUDGER
JUDGES
JUDITH
JUGATE
JUGGED
JUGGLE
JUICER
JUICES
JUJUBE
JULEPS
JULIAN
JULIAS
JULIES
JULIET
JULIUS
JUMBLE
JUMPED
JUMPER
JUNCOS
JUNEAU
JUNGLE
JUNGLY
JUNIOR
JUNIUS
JUNKED
JUNKER
JUNKET
JUNKIE
JUNTAS
JUPONS
JURANT
JURATS
JURELS
JURIES
JURIST
JURORS
JUSTIN
JUSTLY
JUSTUS
JUTISH
JUTTED

J•U•••
JAUNTS
JAUNTY
JOULES
JOUNCE
JOUSTS

J••U••
JAGUAR
JEJUNE
JESUIT
JOCUND
JORUMS
JUJUBE

J•••U•
JAIPUR
JARFUL
JOSHUA
JOYFUL
JOYOUS
JULIUS
JUNIUS
JUSTUS

J••••U
JABIRU
JUNEAU

••JU••
ABJURE
ADJURE
ADJUST
CAJUNS
INJURE
INJURY
JEJUNE
JUJUBE
UNJUST

••J•U•
BIJOUX
RAJPUT
SAJOUS

•••JU•
SELJUK

•••J•U
ACAJOU

J•V•••
JOVIAL
JOVIAN

J••V••
JARVEY
JARVIS
JAYVEE
JERVIS

••J•V•
MOJAVE

J•W•••
JAWING
JEWELS
JEWESS
JEWISH

J••••W
JIGSAW

•J•W••
AJOWAN

•J••W•
OJIBWA

J••X••
JINXES

••J••X
BIJOUX

J•Y•••
JAYVEE
JOYCES
JOYFUL
JOYING
JOYOUS

J••Y••
JEKYLL

J•••Y•
JACKYS
JENNYS
JERRYS
JIMMYS
JINNYS

J••••Y
JALOPY
JARVEY
JAUNTY
JEREMY
JERSEY
JITNEY
JOCKEY
JOHNNY
JUNGLY
JUSTLY

••J•Y•
ENJOYS

••J••Y
INJURY

•••JY•
BENJYS

J•Z•••
JAZZED
JAZZER
JAZZES
JEZAIL

J••Z••
JAZZED
JAZZER
JAZZES

J••••Z
JUAREZ

KA••••
KAASES
KABAKA
KABAYA
KABIKI
KABOBS
KABUKI
KAFFIR
KAISER
KAKAPO
KALIAN
KALIUM
KALMIA
KALONG
KALPAK
KAMALA
KAMIKS
KAMSIN
KANAKA
KANSAN
KANSAS
KAOLIN
KAPOKS
KAPPAS
KARATE
KARATS
KARENS
KARMAS
KARNAK
KARROO
KASPAR
KATHIE
KATHYS
KATIES
KATION
KAURIS
KAVASS
KAYAKS
KAYOED
KAZOOS

K•A•••
KAASES
KHAKIS
KLAXON
KNACKS
KNARRY

KNAVES
KOALAS
KRAALS
KRAITS
KRAKEN

K••A••
KABAKA
KABAYA
KAKAPO
KAMALA
KANAKA
KARATE
KARATS
KAVASS
KAYAKS
KERALA
KERATO
KINASE
KNEADS
KODAKS
KRAALS
KULAKS
KUWAIT

K•••A•
KALIAN
KALPAK
KANSAN
KANSAS
KAPPAS
KARMAS
KARNAK
KASPAR
KEDDAH
KEYWAY
KIBLAH
KIDNAP
KOALAS
KODIAK
KONRAD
KOREAN

K••••A
KABAKA
KABAYA
KALMIA
KAMALA
KANAKA
KERALA
KORUNA

•KA•••
OKAPIS
OKAYED
SKALDS
SKATED
SKATER
SKATES
UKASES

•K•A••
SKEANS

•K••A•
SKYCAP
SKYMAN
SKYWAY

••KA••
ACKACK
ALKALI
ALKANE
ANKARA
ASKANT
DEKARE
GOKART
KAKAPO
MIKADO
PEKANS

••K••A
ANKARA
DAKOTA
YAKIMA

•••KA•
BAIKAL
BALKAN
HOOKAH
JACKAL
MISKAL
PARKAS
PICKAX
POLKAS
PUNKAS
SHIKAR
TANKAS
VODKAS

•••K•A
BUCKRA
GURKHA
MARKKA

••••KA
ALASKA
EUREKA
KABAKA
KANAKA
MARKKA
TOPEKA
TROIKA

K•B•••
KABAKA
KABAYA
KABIKI
KABOBS
KABUKI
KIBEIS
KIBITZ
KIBLAH
KIBOSH
KOBOLD

K••B••
KHYBER
KRUBIS
KRUBUT

K•••B•
KABOBS

•K••B•
AKIMBO

K•C•••
KECKED
KECKLE
KICKED
KICKER
KUCHEN

K••C••
KNACKS
KNOCKS

K•••C•
KIRSCH
KITSCH
KOPECK

•K•C••
SKYCAP

•K••C•
SKETCH

••K•C•
ACKACK

••K••C
PYKNIC

•••K•C
TURKIC

K•D•••
KEDDAH
KEDGED
KEDGES
KEDRON
KIDDED
KIDDER
KIDDIE
KIDNAP
KIDNEY
KODAKS
KODIAK

K••D••
KEDDAH
KIDDED
KIDDER
KIDDIE
KINDER
KINDLE
KINDLY
KOODOO

K•••D•
KNEADS

K••••D
KAYOED
KECKED
KEDGED
KEELED
KEENED
KELOID
KENNED
KERNED
KICKED
KIDDED
KILLED
KILTED
KINKED
KISSED
KNIFED
KOBOLD
KONRAD

•K••D•
SKALDS

•K•••D
OKAYED
SKATED
SKEWED
SKIVED

••KD••
DIKDIK

••K•D•
MIKADO

••K••D
UNKIND
YAKKED
YUKKED

•••K•D
ARCKED
AWAKED
BACKED
BALKED
BANKED
BARKED
BASKED
BEAKED
BECKED
BILKED
BOOKED
BRAKED
BUCKED
BULKED
BUNKED
BURKED
CALKED
CHOKED
COCKED
CONKED
COOKED
CORKED
DECKED
DIRKED
DOCKED
DUCKED
DUNKED
DUSKED
EVOKED
FLAKED
FLUKED
FORKED
FUNKED
GAWKED
HACKED
HARKED
HAWKED
HOCKED
HONKED
HOOKED
HULKED
HUSKED
JACKED
JERKED
JINKED
JUNKED
KECKED
KICKED
KINKED
LACKED
LARKED
LEAKED
LICKED
LINKED
LOCKED
LOOKED
LURKED
MARKED
MASKED
MILKED
MOCKED
MUCKED
NECKED
NICKED
NOCKED
PACKED
PARKED
PEAKED
PECKED
PEEKED
PERKED
PICKED
PINKED
QUAKED
RACKED
RANKED
REEKED
RICKED
RISKED
ROCKED
ROOKED
RUCKED
SACKED
SICKED
SLAKED
SMOKED
SNAKED
SOAKED
SOCKED
SPIKED
SPOKED
STAKED
STOKED
SUCKED
SULKED
TACKED
TALKED
TANKED
TASKED
TICKED
TUCKED
TUSKED
WALKED
WICKED
WINKED
WORKED
YAKKED
YANKED
YUKKED

KE••••
KECKED
KECKLE
KEDDAH
KEDGED
KEDGES
KEDRON
KEELED
KEENED
KEENER
KEENLY
KEEPER
KEEVES
KEGLER
KEITHS
KELLER
KELOID
KELVIN
KENNED
KENNEL
KENNIE
KENNYS
KEPLER
KERALA
KERATO
KERMES
KERMIS
KERNED
KERNEL
KERSEY
KETENE
KETONE
KETOSE
KETTLE
KEVELS
KEVINS
KEWPIE
KEYING
KEYNES

KEYWAY

K•E•••

KEELED
KEENED
KEENER
KEENLY
KEEPER
KEEVES
KNEADS
KNEELS
KNELLS

K••E••

KARENS
KETENE
KEVELS
KIBEIS
KINESI
KINETO
KNEELS
KOPECK
KOPEKS
KOREAN

K•••E•

KAASES
KAISER
KATIES
KAYOED
KECKED
KEDGED
KEDGES
KEELED
KEENED
KEENER
KEEPER
KEEVES
KEGLER
KELLER
KENNED
KENNEL
KEPLER
KERMES
KERNED
KERNEL
KERSEY
KEYNES
KHYBER
KICKED
KICKER
KIDDED
KIDDER
KIDNEY
KILLED
KILLER
KILMER
KILTED
KILTER
KINDER
KINKED
KINSEY
KIPPER
KISLEW
KISMET
KISSED
KISSER
KISSES
KITTEN
KNAVES
KNIFED
KNIFES
KNIVES
KNOWER
KOINES
KOPJES
KOSHER
KRAKEN
KRISES
KRONEN
KRONER
KUCHEN
KUMMEL

K••••E

KARATE
KATHIE
KECKLE
KENNIE
KETENE
KETONE
KETOSE
KETTLE
KEWPIE
KIDDIE
KILTIE
KINASE
KINDLE

•KE•••

AKENES
SKEANS
SKEINS
SKETCH
SKEWED
SKEWER

•K•E••

SKIERS

•K••E•

AKENES
OKAYED
SKATED
SKATER
SKATES
SKEWED
SKEWER
SKIVED
SKIVER
SKIVES
SKYMEN
UKASES

••KE••

ALKENE
ASKERS
BAKERS
BAKERY
ESKERS
FAKERS
FAKERY
HIKERS
INKERS
JOKERS
LAKERS
LIKELY
LIKENS
MAKERS
MAKEUP
PIKERS
POKERS
RAKERS
SAKERS
TAKEIN
TAKERS
TAKEUP
TOKENS
UPKEEP
WAKENS
YOKELS

••K•E•

ANKLES
ANKLET
AUKLET
INKIER
INKLES
LAKIER
OAKLEY
PEKOES
POKIER
POKIES
UPKEEP
YAKKED
YUKKED

••K••E

ALKANE
ALKENE
ALKYNE
DEKARE

•••KE•

ARCKED
AWAKED
AWAKEN
AWAKES
BACKED
BACKER
BALKED
BANKED
BANKER
BARKED
BARKER
BASKED
BASKET
BEAKED
BEAKER
BECKED
BECKET
BICKER
BILKED
BILKER
BLOKES
BOOKED
BOSKET
BRAKED
BRAKES
BROKEN
BROKER
BUCKED
BUCKER
BUCKET
BULKED
BUNKED
BUNKER
BURKED
BURKES
CALKED
CALKER
CANKER
CASKET
CHOKED
CHOKER
CHOKES
COCKED
COCKER
CONKED
COOKED
COOKER
COOKEY
CORKED
CORKER
CRAKES
DANKER
DARKEN
DARKER
DECKED
DECKEL
DECKER
DICKER
DICKEY
DINKEY
DIRKED
DOCKED
DOCKER
DOCKET
DONKEY
DRAKES
DUCKED
DUCKER
DUIKER
DUNKED
DUNKER
DUSKED
EVOKED
EVOKES
FAWKES
FLAKED
FLAKER
FLAKES
FLUKED
FLUKES
FLUKEY
FORKED
FUNKED
GASKET
GAWKED
HACKED
HACKEE
HACKER
HANKER
HARKED
HARKEN
HAWKED
HAWKER
HICKEY
HOCKED
HOCKEY
HONKED
HONKER
HOOKED
HOOKER
HULKED
HUSKED
HUSKER
JACKED
JACKET
JERKED
JINKED
JINKER
JOCKEY
JUNKED
JUNKER
JUNKET
KECKED
KICKED
KICKER
KINKED
KRAKEN
LACKED
LACKEY
LANKER
LARKED
LARKER
LEAKED
LICKED
LINKED
LOCKED
LOCKER
LOCKET
LOOKED
LOOKER
LOWKEY
LUNKER
LURKED
MARKED
MARKER
MARKET
MASKED
MASKEG
MASKER
MEEKER
MICKEY
MILKED
MILKER
MOCKED
MOCKER
MONKEY
MUCKED
MUCKER
MUSKEG
MUSKET
NECKED
NICKED
NICKEL
NICKER
NOCKED
PACKED
PACKER
PACKET
PARKED
PARKER
PAUKER
PEAKED
PECKED
PECKER
PEEKED
PERKED
PICKED
PICKER
PICKET
PINKED
POCKET
PORKER
PUCKER
QUAKED
QUAKER
QUAKES
RACKED
RACKER
RACKET
RANKED
RANKER
REEKED
REEKER
RICKED
RICKEY
RISKED
RISKER
ROCKED
ROCKER
ROCKET
ROOKED
RUCKED
SACKED
SACKER
SECKEL
SEEKER
SHAKEN
SHAKER
SHAKES
SHEKEL
SICKED
SICKEN
SICKER
SILKEN
SINKER
SLAKED
SLAKES
SMOKED
SMOKER
SMOKES

SNAKED
SNAKES
SOAKED
SOAKER
SOCKED
SOCKET
SPIKED
SPIKES
SPOKED
SPOKEN
SPOKES
STAKED
STAKES
STOKED
STOKER
STOKES
SUCKED
SUCKER
SULKED
SUNKEN
TACKED
TACKER
TACKEY
TALKED
TALKER
TANKED
TANKER
TASKED
TICKED
TICKER
TICKET
TINKER
TUCKED
TUCKER
TURKEY
TUSKED
TUSKER
WALKED
WALKER
WEAKEN
WEAKER
WICKED
WICKER
WICKET
WINKED
WINKER
WORKED
WORKER
YAKKED
YANKED
YANKEE
YONKER
YUKKED

•••K•E

BOOKIE
BUCKLE
CACKLE
COCKLE
COOKIE
DARKLE
DECKLE
DICKIE
FICKLE
HACKEE
HACKIE
HACKLE
HECKLE
HUCKLE
JACKIE
JUNKIE
KECKLE
MACKLE
PICKLE
PINKIE
RANKLE
ROCKNE
ROOKIE
SICKLE
SUCKLE
TACKLE
TICKLE
TINKLE
WINKLE
YANKEE

••••KE

ALSIKE
ANANKE
AXLIKE
BETAKE
INTAKE
INVOKE
MOLTKE
MOPOKE
PERUKE
REBUKE
REMAKE
RETAKE
REVOKE
SHRIKE
SPLAKE
STRAKE
STRIKE
STROKE
UNLIKE
UNMAKE
UNYOKE
UPTAKE

K•F•••

KAFFIR

K••F••

KAFFIR
KNIFED
KNIFES

K•••F•

KLOOFS

•K•F••

SKIFFS

•K••F•

SKIFFS

K•G•••

KEGLER

K••G••

KEDGED
KEDGES
KINGLY
KNIGHT

K••••G

KALONG
KEYING
KITING

•K•••G

SKIING
SKYING

••K••G

ASKING
BAKING
CAKING
COKING
DEKING
DIKING
FAKING
HIKING
INKING
IRKING
JOKING
LAKING
LIKING
MAKING
MEKONG
PEKING
PIKING
POKING
PUKING
RAKING
TAKING
VIKING
WAKING
YOKING

•••KG•

GINKGO

•••K•G

MASKEG
MUSKEG

KH••••

KHAKIS
KHYBER

K••H••

KATHIE
KATHYS
KOSHER
KUCHEN

K•••H•

KEITHS
KNIGHT

KYUSHU

K••••H

KEDDAH
KIBLAH
KIBOSH
KIRSCH
KITSCH

•K•••H

SKETCH

••K••H

RAKISH

•••KH•

GURKHA

•••K•H

HOOKAH

KI••••

KIBEIS
KIBITZ
KIBLAH
KIBOSH
KICKED
KICKER
KIDDED
KIDDER
KIDDIE
KIDNAP
KIDNEY
KILLED
KILLER
KILMER
KILTED
KILTER
KILTIE
KIMONO
KINASE
KINDER
KINDLE
KINDLY
KINESI
KINETO
KINGLY
KININS
KINKED
KINSEY
KIOSKS
KIPPER
KIRSCH
KISLEW
KISMET
KISSED
KISSER
KISSES
KITING
KITSCH
KITTEN
KITTYS

K•I•••

KAISER
KEITHS
KNIFED
KNIFES
KNIGHT
KNIVES
KOINES
KRISES

K••I••

KABIKI
KALIAN
KALIUM
KAMIKS
KATIES
KATION
KEVINS
KEYING
KIBITZ
KININS
KITING
KODIAK
KRAITS
KUMISS

K•••I•

KAFFIR
KALMIA
KAMSIN
KAOLIN
KATHIE
KAURIS
KELOID
KELVIN
KENNIE
KERMIS
KEWPIE
KHAKIS
KIBEIS
KIDDIE
KILTIE
KRUBIS
KUWAIT

K••••I

KABIKI
KABUKI
KINESI

•KI•••

AKIMBO
SKIERS
SKIFFS
SKIING
SKILLS
SKIMOS
SKIMPS
SKIMPY
SKINKS
SKINNY
SKIRRS
SKIRTS
SKIVED
SKIVER
SKIVES
SKIVVY

•K•I••

SKEINS
SKIING
SKYING

•K••I•

OKAPIS

••KI••

ASKING
BAKING
BIKINI
CAKING
COKING
DEKING
DIKING
ESKIMO
FAKING
FAKIRS
HAKIMS
HIKING
INKIER
INKING
IRKING
JOKING
LAKIER
LAKING
LIKING
MAKING
PEKING
PIKING
POKIER
POKIES
POKING
PUKING
RAKING
RAKISH
TAKING
UNKIND
VIKING
WAKIKI
WAKING
WIKIUP
YAKIMA
YOKING

••K•I•

DAKOIT
DIKDIK
PYKNIC
SIKKIM
TAKEIN
UNKNIT

••K••I

ALKALI
BIKINI
WAKIKI

6

•••KI•
BODKIN
BOOKIE
BUMKIN
BUSKIN
CATKIN
COOKIE
DICKIE
FIRKIN
GASKIN
HACKIE
JACKIE
JERKIN
JUNKIE
KHAKIS
LOOKIN
MUSKIT
NAPKIN
PINKIE
PIPKIN
ROOKIE
RUSKIN
SIKKIM
SISKIN
TONKIN
TURKIC
TURKIS
WELKIN

••••KI
ALFAKI
KABIKI
KABUKI
NEVSKI
SALUKI
WAKIKI

K••J••
KOPJES

K•K•••
KAKAPO
KOKOMO

K••K••
KECKED
KECKLE
KHAKIS
KICKED
KICKER
KINKED
KRAKEN

K•••K•
KABAKA
KABIKI
KABUKI
KAMIKS
KANAKA
KAPOKS
KAYAKS
KIOSKS
KNACKS
KNOCKS
KODAKS
KOPEKS
KULAKS

K••••K
KALPAK
KARNAK
KODIAK
KOPECK

•K••K•
SKINKS
SKULKS
SKUNKS

••KK••
SIKKIM
YAKKED
YUKKED

••K•K•
WAKIKI

••K••K
ACKACK
DIKDIK
MUKLUK

•••KK•
MARKKA

•••K•K
HICKOK

KL••••
KLAXON
KLOOFS

K•L•••
KALIAN
KALIUM
KALMIA
KALONG
KALPAK
KELLER
KELOID
KELVIN
KILLED
KILLER
KILMER
KILTED
KILTER
KILTIE
KULAKS
KULTUR

K••L••
KAOLIN
KEELED
KEGLER
KELLER
KEPLER
KIBLAH
KILLED
KILLER
KISLEW
KNELLS
KNOLLS
KOALAS

K•••L•
KAMALA
KECKLE
KEENLY
KERALA
KETTLE
KEVELS
KINDLE
KINDLY
KINGLY
KNEELS
KNELLS
KNOLLS
KNURLS
KNURLY
KOBOLD
KRAALS

K••••L
KENNEL
KERNEL
KUMMEL

•K•L••
SKALDS
SKILLS
SKULKS
SKULLS

•K••L•
SKILLS
SKULLS

••KL••
ANKLES
ANKLET
AUKLET
INKLES
MIKLOS
MUKLUK
OAKLEY

••K•L•
ALKALI
ALKYLS
ANKYLO
BIKOLS
JEKYLL
LIKELY
YOKELS

••K••L
JEKYLL

•••KL•
BUCKLE
CACKLE
COCKLE
DANKLY
DARKLE
DARKLY
DECKLE
FICKLE
HACKLE
HECKLE
HUCKLE
KECKLE
LANKLY
MACKLE
MEEKLY
PICKLE
RANKLE
RANKLY
SICKLE
SICKLY
SUCKLE
TACKLE
TICKLE
TINKLE
TINKLY
WEAKLY
WEEKLY
WINKLE

•••K•L
BAIKAL
DECKEL
JACKAL
MISKAL
NICKEL
SECKEL
SHEKEL

K•M•••
KAMALA
KAMIKS
KAMSIN
KIMONO
KUMISS
KUMMEL

K••M••
KALMIA
KARMAS
KERMES
KERMIS
KILMER
KISMET
KUMMEL

K•••M•
KOKOMO

K••••M
KALIUM

•K•M••
AKIMBO
SKIMOS
SKIMPS
SKIMPY
SKYMAN
SKYMEN

••K•M•
ESKIMO
HAKIMS
KOKOMO
YAKIMA

••K••M
SIKKIM

•••K•M
BUNKUM
SIKKIM

KN••••
KNACKS
KNARRY
KNAVES
KNEADS
KNEELS
KNELLS
KNIFED
KNIFES
KNIGHT
KNIVES
KNOCKS
KNOLLS
KNOSPS
KNOTTY
KNOUTS
KNOWER
KNURLS
KNURLY

K•N•••
KANAKA
KANSAN
KANSAS
KENNED
KENNEL
KENNIE
KENNYS
KINASE
KINDER
KINDLE
KINDLY
KINESI
KINETO
KINGLY
KININS
KINKED
KINSEY
KONRAD

K••N••
KARNAK
KEENED
KEENER
KEENLY
KENNED
KENNEL
KENNIE
KENNYS
KERNED
KERNEL
KEYNES
KIDNAP
KIDNEY
KOINES
KRONEN
KRONER
KRONOR
KRONUR

K•••N•
KALONG
KARENS
KETENE
KETONE
KEVINS
KEYING
KIMONO
KININS
KITING
KORUNA
KORUNY

K••••N
KALIAN
KAMSIN
KANSAN
KAOLIN
KATION
KEDRON
KELVIN
KITTEN
KLAXON
KOREAN
KRAKEN
KRONEN
KUCHEN

•K•N••
AKENES
SKINKS
SKINNY
SKUNKS

•K••N•
SKEANS
SKEINS
SKIING
SKINNY
SKYING

•K•••N
SKYMAN
SKYMEN

••KN••
PYKNIC
UNKNIT

••K•N•
ALKANE
ALKENE
ALKYNE

ASKANT
ASKING
BAKING
BIKINI
CAKING
COKING
DEKING
DIKING
FAKING
HIKING
INKING
IRKING
JOKING
LAKING
LIKENS
LIKING
MAKING
MEKONG
PEKANS
PEKING
PIKING
POKING
PUKING
RAKING
TAKING
TOKENS
UNKIND
VIKING
WAKENS
WAKING
YOKING

••K••N
NEKTON
TAKEIN

•••KN•
ROCKNE

•••K•N
AWAKEN
BALKAN
BECKON
BODKIN
BROKEN
BUMKIN
BUSKIN
CATKIN
DARKEN
FIRKIN
GASKIN
HARKEN
JERKIN
KRAKEN
LOOKIN
NAPKIN
PIPKIN
RECKON
RUSKIN
SHAKEN
SICKEN
SILKEN
SISKIN
SPOKEN
SUNKEN
TONKIN
WALKON
WEAKEN
WELKIN

KO••••
KOALAS
KOBOLD
KODAKS
KODIAK
KOINES
KOKOMO
KONRAD
KOODOO
KOPECK
KOPEKS
KOPJES
KOREAN
KORUNA
KORUNY
KOSHER
KOWTOW

K•O•••
KAOLIN
KIOSKS
KLOOFS
KNOCKS
KNOLLS
KNOSPS
KNOTTY
KNOUTS
KNOWER
KOODOO
KRONEN
KRONER
KRONOR
KRONUR

K••O••
KABOBS
KALONG
KAPOKS
KAYOED
KAZOOS
KELOID
KETONE
KETOSE
KIBOSH
KIMONO
KLOOFS
KOBOLD
KOKOMO

K•••O•
KARROO
KATION
KAZOOS
KEDRON
KLAXON
KOODOO
KOWTOW
KRONOR

K••••O
KAKAPO
KARROO
KERATO
KIMONO
KINETO
KOKOMO
KOODOO

•K••O•
SKIMOS

•K•••O
AKIMBO

••KO••
BIKOLS
DAKOIT
DAKOTA
KOKOMO
MEKONG
PEKOES

••K•O•
MIKLOS
NEKTON

••K••O
ANKYLO
ESKIMO
KAKAPO
KOKOMO
MIKADO

•••KO•
ANGKOR
BECKON
CUCKOO
GECKOS
HICKOK
JOCKOS
RECKON
SHAKOS
WALKON
ZHUKOV

•••K•O
CUCKOO
GINKGO

••••KO
BAMAKO
SHACKO

K•P•••
KAPOKS
KAPPAS
KEPLER
KIPPER
KOPECK
KOPEKS
KOPJES

K••P••
KALPAK
KAPPAS
KASPAR
KEEPER
KEWPIE
KIPPER

K•••P•
KAKAPO
KNOSPS

K••••P
KIDNAP

•K•P••
OKAPIS

•K••P•
SKIMPS
SKIMPY

•K•••P
SKYCAP

••K•P•
KAKAPO

••K••P
MAKEUP
TAKEUP
UPKEEP
WIKIUP

•••K•P
COCKUP
HOOKUP
LOCKUP
MARKUP
MOCKUP
PICKUP
WALKUP

KR••••
KRAALS
KRAITS
KRAKEN
KRISES
KRONEN
KRONER
KRONOR
KRONUR
KRUBIS
KRUBUT

K•R•••
KARATE
KARATS
KARENS
KARMAS
KARNAK
KARROO
KERALA
KERATO
KERMES
KERMIS
KERNED
KERNEL
KERSEY
KIRSCH
KOREAN
KORUNA
KORUNY

K••R••
KARROO
KAURIS
KEDRON
KNARRY
KNURLS
KNURLY
KONRAD

K•••R•
KNARRY

K••••R
KAFFIR
KAISER
KASPAR
KEENER
KEEPER
KEGLER
KELLER
KEPLER
KHYBER
KICKER
KIDDER
KILLER
KILMER
KILTER
KINDER
KIPPER
KISSER
KNOWER
KOSHER
KRONER
KRONOR
KRONUR
KULTUR

•K•R••
SKIRRS
SKIRTS

•K••R•
SKIERS
SKIRRS

•K•••R
SKATER
SKEWER
SKIVER

••K•R•
ANKARA
ASKERS
BAKERS
BAKERY
DEKARE
ESKERS
FAKERS
FAKERY
FAKIRS
GOKART
HIKERS
INKERS
JOKERS
LAKERS
MAKERS
PIKERS
POKERS
RAKERS
SAKERS
TAKERS

••K••R
INKIER
LAKIER
POKIER

•••KR•
BUCKRA

•••K•R
ANGKOR
BACKER
BANKER
BARKER
BEAKER
BICKER
BILKER
BROKER
BUCKER
BUNKER
CALKER
CANKER
CHOKER
COCKER
COOKER
CORKER
DANKER
DARKER
DECKER
DICKER
DOCKER
DUCKER
DUIKER
DUNKER
FLAKER
HACKER
HANKER
HAWKER
HONKER
HOOKER
HUSKER
JINKER
JUNKER
KICKER
LANKER
LARKER
LOCKER

LOOKER
LUNKER
MARKER
MASKER
MEEKER
MILKER
MOCKER
MUCKER
NICKER
PACKER
PARKER
PAUKER
PECKER
PICKER
PORKER
PUCKER
QUAKER
RACKER
RANKER
REEKER
RISKER
ROCKER
SACKER
SEEKER
SHAKER
SHIKAR
SICKER
SINKER
SMOKER
SOAKER
STOKER
SUCKER
TACKER
TALKER
TANKER
TICKER
TINKER
TUCKER
TUSKER
VALKYR
WALKER
WEAKER
WICKER
WINKER
WORKER
YONKER

K•S•••
KASPAR
KISLEW
KISMET
KISSED
KISSER
KISSES
KOSHER

K••S••
KAASES
KAISER
KAMSIN
KANSAN
KANSAS
KERSEY
KINSEY
KIOSKS
KIRSCH
KISSED
KISSER
KISSES
KITSCH
KNOSPS
KRISES
KYUSHU

K•••S•
KAVASS
KETOSE
KIBOSH
KINASE
KINESI
KUMISS

K••••S
KAASES
KABOBS
KAMIKS
KANSAS
KAPOKS
KAPPAS
KARATS
KARENS
KARMAS
KATHYS
KATIES
KAURIS
KAVASS
KAYAKS
KAZOOS
KEDGES
KEEVES
KEITHS
KENNYS
KERMES
KERMIS
KEVELS
KEVINS
KEYNES
KHAKIS
KIBEIS
KININS
KIOSKS
KISSES
KITTYS
KLOOFS
KNACKS
KNAVES
KNEADS
KNEELS
KNELLS
KNIFES
KNIVES
KNOCKS
KNOLLS
KNOSPS
KNOUTS
KNURLS
KOALAS
KODAKS
KOINES
KOPEKS
KOPJES
KRAALS
KRAITS
KRISES
KRUBIS
KULAKS
KUMISS

•K•S••
UKASES

•K•••S
AKENES
OKAPIS
SKALDS
SKATES
SKEANS
SKEINS
SKIERS
SKIFFS
SKILLS
SKIMOS
SKIMPS
SKINKS
SKIRRS
SKIRTS
SKIVES
SKULKS
SKULLS
SKUNKS
UKASES

••K•S•
RAKISH

••K••S
ALKYLS
ANKLES
ASKERS
BAKERS
BIKOLS
ESKERS
FAKERS
FAKIRS
HAKIMS
HIKERS
INKERS
INKLES
JOKERS
LAKERS
LIKENS
MAKERS
MIKLOS
PEKANS
PEKOES
PIKERS
POKERS
POKIES
RAKERS
SAKERS
TAKERS
TOKENS
WAKENS
YOKELS

•••KS•
FOLKSY

•••K•S
AWAKES
BECKYS
BLOKES
BRAKES
BURKES
CHOKES
CRAKES
DRAKES
EVOKES
FAWKES
FLAKES
FLUKES
GECKOS
JACKYS
JOCKOS
KHAKIS
MICKYS
NICKYS
PARKAS
POLKAS
PUNKAS
QUAKES
RICKYS
RUCKUS
SHAKES
SHAKOS
SLAKES
SMOKES
SNAKES
SPIKES
SPOKES
STAKES
STOKES
TANKAS
TURKIS
VICKYS
VODKAS

••••KS
BATIKS
BLACKS
BLANKS
BLEAKS
BLINKS
BLOCKS
BREAKS
BRICKS
BRINKS
BRISKS
BROOKS
CAULKS
CHALKS
CHECKS
CHEEKS
CHICKS
CHINKS
CHOCKS
CHUCKS
CHUNKS
CLACKS
CLANKS
CLERKS
CLICKS
CLINKS
CLOAKS
CLOCKS
CLUCKS
CRACKS
CRANKS
CREAKS
CREEKS
CRICKS
CROAKS
CROCKS
CROOKS
DEREKS
DRINKS
DRUNKS
FLACKS
FLANKS
FLASKS
FLECKS
FLICKS
FLOCKS
FLUNKS
FRANKS
FREAKS
FRISKS
FROCKS
GREEKS
HOICKS
KAMIKS
KAPOKS
KAYAKS
KIOSKS
KNACKS
KNOCKS
KODAKS
KOPEKS
KULAKS
PLACKS
PLANKS
PLUCKS
PLUNKS
PRANKS
PRICKS
PRINKS
QUACKS
QUARKS
QUIRKS
SHACKS
SHANKS
SHARKS
SHEIKS
SHIRKS
SHOCKS
SHUCKS
SKINKS
SKULKS
SKUNKS
SLACKS
SLEEKS
SLICKS
SLINKS
SMACKS
SMIRKS
SMOCKS
SNACKS
SNEAKS
SNICKS
SNOOKS
SPANKS
SPARKS
SPEAKS
SPECKS
SPOOKS
STACKS
STALKS
STEAKS
STICKS
STINKS
STIRKS
STOCKS
STOOKS
STORKS
THANKS
THINKS
TORSKS
TRACKS
TRICKS
TRUCKS
TRUNKS
TUPIKS
TWEAKS
UMIAKS
VNECKS
WHACKS
WHELKS
WHISKS
WRACKS
WREAKS
WRECKS
YOICKS

K•T•••
KATHIE
KATHYS
KATIES
KATION
KETENE
KETONE
KETOSE
KETTLE
KITING
KITSCH
KITTEN
KITTYS

K••T••
KEITHS
KETTLE
KILTED
KILTER
KILTIE
KITTEN

6

KITTYS
KNOTTY
KOWTOW
KULTUR

K•••T•
KARATE
KARATS
KERATO
KIBITZ
KINETO
KNOTTY
KNOUTS
KRAITS

K••••T
KISMET
KNIGHT
KRUBUT
KUWAIT

•K•T••
SKATED
SKATER
SKATES
SKETCH

•K••T•
SKIRTS

••KT••
NEKTON

••K•T•
DAKOTA

••K••T
ANKLET
ASKANT
AUKLET
DAKOIT
GOKART
UNKNIT

•••K•T
BASKET
BECKET
BOSKET
BUCKET
CASKET
DOCKET
GASKET
JACKET
JUNKET
LOCKET
MARKET
MUSKET
MUSKIT
PACKET
PICKET
POCKET
RACKET
ROCKET
SOCKET
TICKET
WICKET

KU••••
KUCHEN
KULAKS
KULTUR
KUMISS
KUMMEL
KUWAIT

K•U•••
KAURIS
KNURLS
KNURLY
KRUBIS
KRUBUT
KYUSHU

K••U••
KABUKI
KNOUTS
KORUNA
KORUNY

K•••U•
KALIUM
KRONUR
KRUBUT
KULTUR

K••••U
KYUSHU

•KU•••
SKULKS
SKULLS
SKUNKS

••K•U•
MAKEUP
MUKLUK
TAKEUP
WIKIUP

•••KU•
BUNKUM
COCKUP
HOOKUP
LOCKUP
MARKUP
MOCKUP
PICKUP
RUCKUS
WALKUP

K•V•••
KAVASS
KEVELS
KEVINS

K••V••
KEEVES
KELVIN
KNAVES
KNIVES

•K•V••
SKIVED
SKIVER
SKIVES
SKIVVY

•K••V•
SKIVVY

•••K•V
ZHUKOV

K•W•••
KEWPIE
KOWTOW
KUWAIT

K••W••
KEYWAY
KNOWER

K••••W
KISLEW
KOWTOW

•K•W••
SKEWED
SKEWER
SKYWAY

K••X••
KLAXON

•••K•X
PICKAX

KY••••
KYUSHU

K•Y•••
KAYAKS
KAYOED
KEYING
KEYNES
KEYWAY
KHYBER

K•••Y•
KABAYA
KATHYS
KENNYS
KITTYS

K••••Y
KEENLY
KERSEY
KEYWAY
KIDNEY
KINDLY
KINGLY
KINSEY
KNARRY
KNOTTY
KNURLY
KORUNY

•KY•••
SKYCAP
SKYING
SKYMAN
SKYMEN
SKYWAY

•K•Y••
OKAYED

•K•••Y
SKIMPY
SKINNY
SKIVVY
SKYWAY

••KY••
ALKYLS
ALKYNE
ANKYLO
JEKYLL

••K••Y
BAKERY
FAKERY
LIKELY
OAKLEY

•••KY•
BECKYS
JACKYS
MICKYS
NICKYS
RICKYS
VALKYR
VICKYS

•••K•Y
COOKEY
DANKLY
DARKLY
DICKEY
DINKEY
DONKEY
FLUKEY
FOLKSY
HICKEY
HOCKEY
JOCKEY
LACKEY
LANKLY
LOWKEY
MEEKLY
MICKEY
MONKEY
RANKLY
RICKEY
SICKLY
TACKEY
TINKLY
TURKEY
WEAKLY
WEEKLY

••••KY
BLOCKY
CHALKY
CHEEKY
CHINKY
CHUNKY
CRACKY
CRANKY
CREAKY
CROAKY
DROSKY
FLOCKY
FLUNKY
FREAKY
FRISKY
PLUCKY
SLEEKY
SLINKY
SNEAKY
SPOOKY
SPUNKY
STALKY
STICKY
STOCKY
SWANKY
TRICKY
TWEAKY
WHELKY
WHISKY
ZINCKY

K•Z•••
KAZOOS

K••••Z
KIBITZ

LA••••
LAAGER
LABELS
LABIAL
LABILE
LABIUM
LABORS
LABOUR
LABRET
LABRUM
LACHES
LACIER
LACILY
LACING
LACKED
LACKEY
LACTAM
LACTIC
LACUNA
LADDER
LADDIE
LADIES
LADING
LADINO
LADLED
LADLER
LADLES
LADOGA
LAGERS
LAGGED
LAGGER
LAGOON
LAGUNE
LAHORE
LAIRDS
LAIRED
LAKERS
LAKIER
LAKING
LALLED
LAMBDA
LAMBED
LAMBIE
LAMEDS
LAMELY
LAMENT
LAMEST
LAMIAE
LAMIAS
LAMINA
LAMING
LAMMAS
LAMMED
LAMPAD
LAMPAS
LAMPED
LANAIS
LANATE
LANCED
LANCER
LANCES
LANCET
LANDAU
LANDED
LANDER
LANGUR
LANKER
LANKLY
LANNER
LANOSE
LANUGO
LAOTSE
LAPARO
LAPELS
LAPFUL
LAPINS
LAPPED
LAPPER
LAPPET
LAPSED
LAPSER
LAPSES
LAPSUS
LARDED
LARDER
LARDON

LAREDO
LARGER
LARGOS
LARIAT
LARINE
LARKED
LARKER
LARRUP
LARRYS
LARVAE
LARVAL
LARYNG
LARYNX
LASCAR
LASERS
LASHED
LASHER
LASHES
LASSES
LASSIE
LASSOS
LASTED
LASTER
LASTEX
LASTLY
LATEEN
LATELY
LATENT
LATEST
LATHED
LATHER
LATHES
LATINS
LATISH
LATRIA
LATTEN
LATTER
LATVIA
LAUDED
LAUDER
LAUGHS
LAUNCE
LAUNCH
LAURAE
LAURAS
LAUREL
LAURIE
LAVABO
LAVAGE
LAVERS
LAVING
LAVISH
LAWFUL
LAWING
LAWYER
LAXEST
LAXITY
LAYDAY
LAYERS
LAYING
LAYMAN
LAYMEN
LAYOFF
LAYOUT
LAZARS
LAZIER
LAZILY
LAZING
LAZULI

L•A•••

LAAGER
LEACHY
LEADED
LEADEN
LEADER
LEADIN
LEAFED
LEAGUE
LEAKED
LEANED
LEANER
LEANLY
LEANTO
LEAPED
LEAPER
LEARNS
LEARNT
LEASED
LEASES
LEAVED
LEAVEN
LEAVER
LEAVES
LIABLE
LIANAS
LIANES
LLAMAS
LLANOS
LOADED
LOADER
LOAFED
LOAFER
LOAMED
LOANED
LOATHE
LOAVES
LUANDA

L••A••

LANAIS
LANATE
LAPARO
LAVABO
LAVAGE
LAZARS
LEGACY
LEGATE
LEGATO
LENAPE
LEVANT
LIGAND
LIGATE
LILACS
LINAGE
LIPASE
LITANY
LIZARD
LOBATE
LOCALE
LOCALS
LOCATE
LORAIN
LOTAHS
LOVAGE
LUNACY
LUNATE
LUXATE

L•••A•

LABIAL
LACTAM
LAMIAE
LAMIAS
LAMMAS
LAMPAD
LAMPAS
LANDAU
LARIAT
LARVAE
LARVAL
LASCAR
LAURAE
LAURAS
LAYDAY
LAYMAN
LEEWAY
LEGMAN
LEHUAS
LEMMAS
LEONAS
LETHAL
LIANAS
LIBRAE
LIBRAS
LIBYAN
LILIAN
LINDAS
LINEAL
LINEAR
LINGAS
LIVIAS
LLAMAS
LOGJAM
LONGAN
LOOFAH
LOQUAT
LUCIAN
LUCIAS
LUMBAR
LUTEAL
LYDIAS
LYTTAE

L••••A

LACUNA
LADOGA
LAMBDA
LAMINA
LATRIA
LATVIA
LEPSIA
LIGULA
LIMINA
LINGUA
LIPOMA
LISBOA
LITHIA
LOCHIA
LOGGIA
LOLITA
LORICA
LOUISA
LUANDA
LUELLA
LUMINA
LUNULA

•LA•••

ALAMOS
ALARIC
ALARMS
ALARUM
ALASKA
ALATED
BLACKS
BLADED
BLADES
BLAINS
BLAMED
BLAMES
BLANCH
BLANKS
BLARED
BLARES
BLASTO
BLASTS
BLAZED
BLAZER
BLAZES
BLAZON
CLACKS
CLAIMS
CLAIRE
CLAMMY
CLAMOR
CLAMPS
CLANGS
CLANKS
CLAQUE
CLARAS
CLARES
CLARET
CLAROS
CLASPS
CLASSY
CLAUDE
CLAUSE
CLAWED
CLAYED
CLAYEY
ELAINE
ELANDS
ELAPSE
ELATED
ELATER
ELATES
ELAYNE
FLABBY
FLACKS
FLACON
FLAGGY
FLAGON
FLAILS
FLAIRS
FLAKED
FLAKER
FLAKES
FLAMBE
FLAMED
FLAMEN
FLAMES
FLANGE
FLANKS
FLARED
FLARES
FLASHY
FLASKS
FLATLY
FLATUS
FLAUNT
FLAVIA
FLAVIN
FLAVOR
FLAWED
FLAXEN
FLAXES
FLAYED
FLAYER
GLACES
GLACIS
GLADES
GLADLY
GLADYS
GLAIRS
GLAIRY
GLANCE
GLANDS
GLARED
GLARES
GLASSY
GLAUCO
GLAZED
GLAZER
GLAZES
KLAXON
LLAMAS
LLANOS
PLACED
PLACER
PLACES
PLACET
PLACID
PLACKS
PLAGAL
PLAGIO
PLAGUE
PLAGUY
PLAICE
PLAIDS
PLAINS
PLAINT
PLAITS
PLANAR
PLANCH
PLANCK
PLANED
PLANER
PLANES
PLANET
PLANKS
PLANTS
PLAQUE
PLASHY
PLASIA
PLASIS
PLASMA
PLASMO
PLASTY
PLATAN
PLATED
PLATEN
PLATER
PLATES
PLATTE
PLAYAS
PLAYED
PLAYER
PLAZAS
SLACKS
SLAGGY
SLAKED
SLAKES
SLALOM
SLANGY
SLANTS
SLATED
SLATER
SLATES
SLAVED
SLAVER
SLAVES
SLAVIC
SLAYER

•L•A••

ALBANY
ALBATA
ALCAIC
ALFAKI
ALKALI
ALKANE
ALLANS
ALLAYS
ALMAHS
ALPACA
ALSACE
ALTAIC
ALTAIR
ALTARS
ALVANS
ALWAYS
BLEACH
BLEAKS

BLEARS
BLEARY
BLEATS
BLOATS
CLEANS
CLEARS
CLEATS
CLEAVE
CLOACA
CLOAKS
FLEAMS
FLOATS
FLOATY
GLEAMS
GLEAMY
GLEANS
GLOATS
OLEATE
PLEACH
PLEADS
PLEASE
PLEATS
PLIANT
SLEAVE
SLEAZY
ULLAGE

•L••A•

ALEGAR
ALIDAD
ALPHAS
ALULAE
ALULAR
CLARAS
CLIMAT
CLIMAX
ELENAS
ELIJAH
ELIZAS
FLORAE
FLORAL
FLORAS
GLOBAL
LLAMAS
PLAGAL
PLANAR
PLATAN
PLAYAS
PLAZAS
PLEIAD
PLICAE
PLURAL
SLOGAN
SLOVAK
ULEMAS

•L•••A

ALASKA
ALBATA
ALEXIA
ALICIA
ALMIRA
ALPACA
ALTHEA
ALUMNA
ALVINA
CLOACA
ELISHA
ELMIRA
ELVIRA
ELYTRA
FLAVIA
GLIOMA
GLORIA
OLIVIA
PLASIA
PLASMA
PLEGIA
PLEURA
ULTIMA

••LA••

AALAND
ABLAUT
ABLAZE
AFLAME
AGLAIA
ALLANS
ALLAYS
ANLACE
ANLAGE
ASLANT
BALAAM
BALATA
BELAYS
BYLANE
BYLAWS
CALAIS
CALASH
DELAYS
DILATE
ECLAIR
ENLACE
GALACT
GALAXY
HILARY
HOLARD
INLACE
INLAID
INLAND
INLAWS
INLAYS
ISLAND
JALAPS
KULAKS
LILACS
MALACO
MALADY
MALAGA
MALATE
MALAWI
MALAYA
MALAYS
MELANO
MILADY
MILAGE
MOLARS
OBLAST
OBLATE
PALACE
PALAEO
PALATE
PELAGE
PILAFS
PILATE
POLAND
RELATE
RELAYS
ROLAND
SALAAM
SALADS
SALAMI
SALARY
SCLAFF
SOLACE
SOLAND
SOLANO
SOLANS
SPLAKE
SPLASH
SPLATS
SPLAYS
TULADI
ULLAGE
UMLAUT
UNLACE
UNLADE
UNLAID
UNLAYS
UPLAND
VELATE
VOLANT
XYLANS

••L•A•

AFLOAT
AGLEAM
BALAAM
BALKAN
BALLAD
BALSAM
BALSAS
BALZAC
BELDAM
BELGAS
BELIAL
BELLAS
BILBAO
BULBAR
BULGAR
BULLAE
CALCAR
CALLAO
CALLAS
CALPAC
CELIAC
CELIAS
CELLAE
CELLAR
CILIAT
COLLAR
COLZAS
CULLAY
DALLAS
DELIAN
DELIAS
DELLAS
DELTAS
DOLLAR
DOLMAN
EOLIAN
FALLAL
FELLAH
FILIAL
FOLIAR
FULMAR
GALEAE
GALWAY
GALYAK
GILDAS
GILEAD
GULLAH
HALLAH
HELLAS
HILDAS
JULIAN
JULIAS
KALIAN
KALPAK
LILIAN
MILLAY
MOLLAH
MULLAH
NILGAI
NULLAH
OILCAN
PALEAE
PALLAS
PALMAR
PELIAS
PILLAR
POLEAX
POLKAS
PULSAR
RELOAD
SALAAM
SALPAS
SILVAE
SILVAN
SILVAS
SULTAN
SYLVAE
SYLVAN
SYLVAS
UNLEAD
UNLOAD
VALVAL
VALVAR
VILLAS
VOLVAS
VULCAN
VULGAR
VULVAE
VULVAL
VULVAR
WALLAH
WALLAS
WILMAS
ZILLAH

••L••A

AGLAIA
BALATA
BALBOA
BELUGA
CALESA
FULCRA
GALENA
HELENA
KALMIA
LOLITA
MALAGA
MALAYA
MALTHA
PELOTA
SALIVA
SALVIA
SCLERA
SILICA
SILVIA
SULPHA
SYLVIA
TELEGA

•••LA•

ALULAE
ALULAR
ASHLAR
BALLAD
BEDLAM
BELLAS
BEULAH
BEULAS
BULLAE
BURLAP
BYPLAY
CALLAO
CALLAS
CARLAS
CELLAE
CELLAR
CHELAE
CHELAS
COLLAR
CULLAY
CUTLAS
DALLAS
DELLAS
DEWLAP
DOBLAS
DOLLAR
EARLAP
FALLAL
FELLAH
GULLAH
HALLAH
HARLAN
HELLAS
KIBLAH
KOALAS
MEDLAR
MILLAY
MISLAY
MOLLAH
MOOLAH
MULLAH
NULLAH
OCULAR
OUTLAW
OUTLAY
OVULAR
PALLAS
PARLAY
PAULAS
PHYLAE
PILLAR
POPLAR
RAGLAN
REPLAY
SCALAR
SENLAC
SMILAX
STALAG
STELAE
STELAR
STYLAR
UNCLAD
UVULAE
UVULAR
UVULAS
VILLAS
VIOLAS
WALLAH
WALLAS
WAYLAY
ZILLAH

•••L•A

ABOLLA
ABULIA
AEOLIA
AMELIA
ANGLIA
ANTLIA
APULIA
AXILLA
AZALEA
CHOLLA
DAHLIA
EMILIA
GIULIA
HUELVA
LUELLA
PHILIA
SCYLLA
STELLA
THALIA
THELMA
THULIA

••••LA

ABOLLA
ANGELA
ANGOLA

AQUILA
ARBELA
AREOLA
ATTILA
AXILLA
CABALA
CAMILA
CANULA
CEDULA
CHOLLA
CICALA
CITOLA
COPULA
CUPOLA
EIDOLA
FACULA
FECULA
FERULA
FIBULA
HOOPLA
IMPALA
KAMALA
KERALA
LIGULA
LUELLA
LUNULA
MACULA
MANILA
MORULA
NEBULA
PAMELA
PAPULA
PAYOLA
RADULA
ROMOLA
SCYLLA
SHEILA
STELLA
UNGULA
URSULA
ZONULA

L•B•••
LABELS
LABIAL
LABILE
LABIUM
LABORS
LABOUR
LABRET
LABRUM
LIBBYS
LIBELS
LIBIDO
LIBRAE
LIBRAS
LIBYAN
LOBATE
LOBBED
LOBULE
LUBBER
LUBECK
LUBLIN

L••B••
LAMBDA
LAMBED
LAMBIE
LIABLE
LIBBYS
LIMBED
LIMBER
LIMBIC
LIMBUS
LISBOA
LISBON
LOBBED
LOWBOY
LUBBER
LUMBAR
LUMBER

L•••B•
LAVABO

•LB•••
ALBANY
ALBATA
ALBEDO
ALBEIT
ALBERT
ALBINO
ALBION
ALBITE
ALBUMS
ELBERT
ELBOWS
ELBRUS

•L•B••
ALIBIS
ALIBLE
BLEBBY
FLABBY
FLYBYS
GLEBES
GLIBLY
GLOBAL
GLOBED
GLOBES
GLOBIN
PLEBES

•L••B•
BLEBBY
BLOWBY
BLURBS
CLIMBS
FLABBY
FLAMBE
PLUMBO
PLUMBS

••LB••
BALBOA
BILBAO
BULBAR
BULBEL
BULBIL
BULBUL
WILBER
WILBUR

••L•B•
ADLIBS
CALEBS
PHLEBO

••L••B
APLOMB

•••LB•
SHELBY

L•C•••
LACHES
LACIER
LACILY
LACING
LACKED
LACKEY
LACTAM
LACTIC
LACUNA
LECHER
LECTOR
LICHEE
LICHEN
LICKED
LICTOR
LOCALE
LOCALS
LOCATE
LOCHIA
LOCKED
LOCKER
LOCKET
LOCKUP
LOCOED
LOCUST
LUCENT
LUCIAN
LUCIAS
LUCIEN
LUCILE
LUCITE
LUCIUS
LYCEES
LYCEUM

L••C••
LANCED
LANCER
LANCES
LANCET
LASCAR
LEACHY

L•••C•
LAUNCE
LAUNCH
LEGACY
LILACS
LORICA
LUBECK
LUNACY
LYRICS

L••••C
LACTIC
LIMBIC
LITHIC
LUETIC

•LC•••
ALCAIC
ALCOTT
ALCOVE
ALCUIN
ULCERS

•L•C••
ALECTO
ALICES
ALICIA
BLACKS
BLOCKS
BLOCKY
CLACKS
CLICHE
CLICKS
CLOCHE
CLOCKS
CLUCKS
ELECTR
ELECTS
ELICIT
FLACKS
FLACON
FLECHE
FLECKS
FLICKS
FLOCKS
FLOCKY
GLACES
GLACIS
GLYCOL
PLACED
PLACER
PLACES
PLACET
PLACID
PLACKS
PLICAE
PLUCKS
PLUCKY
SLACKS
SLICED
SLICER
SLICES
SLICKS

•L••C•
ALMUCE
ALPACA
ALSACE
BLANCH
BLEACH
BLENCH
BLOTCH
CLENCH
CLINCH
CLOACA
CLUTCH
FLEECE
FLEECY
FLENCH
FLETCH
FLINCH
FLITCH
GLANCE
GLAUCO
PLAICE
PLANCH
PLANCK
PLEACH
SLOUCH
SLUICE
ULENCE

•L•••C
ALARIC
ALCAIC
ALTAIC
CLERIC
CLINIC
CLONIC
SLAVIC

••LC••
AFLCIO
CALCAR
CALCES
CALCIC
DULCET
DULCIE
FALCON
FULCRA
IOLCUS
MULCTS
OILCAN
SULCUS
TALCED
TALCUM
VULCAN

••L•C•
ANLACE
CALICO
CILICE
CULTCH
DELICT
ENLACE
FELICE
GALACT
HELICO
INLACE
LILACS
MALACO
MALICE
MOLOCH
OCLOCK
PALACE
POLICE
POLICY
RELICS
RELICT
SELECT
SILICA
SILICO
SOLACE
SPLICE
UNLACE
UNLOCK
VELOCE

••L••C
BALTIC
BALZAC
BELGIC
BELLOC
CALCIC
CALPAC
CELIAC
CELTIC
GALLIC
HOLMIC
PELVIC
TOLTEC

•••LC•
CHALCO

•••L•C
AEOLIC
AMYLIC
ANGLIC
BELLOC
CYCLIC
EXILIC
FROLIC
GAELIC
GALLIC
GARLIC
ITALIC
OXALIC
PUBLIC
SENLAC
SIALIC
STELIC
URALIC

L•D•••
LADDER
LADDIE
LADIES
LADING
LADINO
LADLED
LADLER
LADLES
LADOGA
LEDGER
LEDGES

LIDDED
LODGED
LODGER
LODGES
LUDWIG
LYDIAS

L••D••

LADDER
LADDIE
LANDAU
LANDED
LANDER
LARDED
LARDER
LARDON
LAUDED
LAUDER
LAYDAY
LEADED
LEADEN
LEADER
LEADIN
LENDER
LEUDES
LEWDER
LEWDLY
LIDDED
LIEDER
LINDAS
LINDEN
LOADED
LOADER
LONDON
LORDED
LORDLY
LOUDEN
LOUDER
LOUDLY

L•••D•

LAIRDS
LAMBDA
LAMEDS
LAREDO
LEPIDO
LIBIDO
LIPIDS
LLOYDS
LUANDA

L••••D

LACKED
LADLED
LAGGED
LAIRED
LALLED
LAMBED
LAMMED
LAMPAD
LAMPED
LANCED
LANDED
LAPPED
LAPSED
LARDED
LARKED
LASHED
LASTED
LATHED
LAUDED
LEADED
LEAFED
LEAKED
LEANED
LEAPED
LEASED
LEAVED
LEERED
LEGEND
LEGGED
LEVIED
LICKED
LIDDED
LIFTED
LIGAND
LILIED
LILTED
LIMBED
LIMNED
LIMPED
LIMPID
LINKED
LIPOID
LIPPED
LIQUID
LISPED
LISTED
LIZARD
LOADED
LOAFED
LOAMED
LOANED
LOBBED
LOCKED
LOCOED
LODGED
LOFTED
LOGGED
LOLLED
LOMOND
LONGED
LOOKED
LOOMED
LOOPED
LOOSED
LOOTED
LOPPED
LORDED
LOURED
LOUSED
LUFFED
LUGGED
LULLED
LUMPED
LUNGED
LURKED
LUSHED
LUSTED

•LD•••

ALDERS
ALDINE
ALDOSE
ALDOUS
ELDERS
ELDEST
ELDRED
OLDEST
OLDISH

•L•D••

ALIDAD
ALUDEL
BLADED
BLADES
CLODDY
CLYDES
ELIDED
ELIDES
ELUDED
ELUDES
FLEDGE
FLEDGY
GLADES
GLADLY
GLADYS
GLEDES
GLIDED
GLIDER
GLIDES
PLEDGE
SLEDGE
SLIDER
SLIDES
SLUDGE
SLUDGY

•L••D•

ALBEDO
ALLUDE
ALMUDE
ALMUDS
BLEEDS
BLENDE
BLENDS
BLINDS
BLONDE
BLONDS
BLOODS
BLOODY
CLAUDE
CLODDY
CLOUDS
CLOUDY
ELANDS
FLOODS
FLOYDS
FLUIDS
GLANDS
LLOYDS
PLAIDS
PLEADS

•L•••D

ALATED
ALFRED
ALGOID
ALIDAD
ALINED
ALIPED
ALLIED
ALMOND
BLADED
BLAMED
BLARED
BLAZED
CLAWED
CLAYED
CLERID
CLEWED
CLOSED
CLOYED
ELATED
ELDRED
ELIDED
ELOPED
ELUDED
FLAKED
FLAMED
FLARED
FLAWED
FLAYED
FLEXED
FLORID
FLOWED
FLUKED
FLUMED
FLUTED
FLUXED
GLARED
GLAZED
GLIDED
GLOBED
GLOVED
GLOWED
GLOZED
PLACED
PLACID
PLANED
PLATED
PLAYED
PLEIAD
PLOWED
PLUMED
SLAKED
SLATED
SLAVED
SLEWED
SLICED
SLIMED
SLOPED
SLOWED

••LD••

BALDER
BALDLY
BELDAM
BOLDER
BOLDLY
COLDER
COLDLY
FOLDED
FOLDER
GELDED
GILDAS
GILDED
GILDER
GOLDEN
GULDEN
HILDAS
HOLDER
HOLDUP
MELDED
MILDEN
MILDER
MILDEW
MILDLY
MOLDED
MOLDER
POLDER
SELDOM
SOLDER
TILDES
VELDTS
WALDOS
WELDED
WELDER
WILDER
WILDLY

••L•D•

ALLUDE
BOLIDE
DELUDE
FELIDS
HALIDE
HALIDS
MALADY
MELODY
MILADY
SALADS
SOLIDI
SOLIDS
TOLEDO
TULADI
UNLADE

••L••D

AALAND
ALLIED
BALKED
BALLAD
BALLED
BELIED
BELLED
BELTED
BILGED
BILKED
BILLED
BOLLED
BOLTED
BULGED
BULKED
CALKED
CALLED
CALMED
CALVED
CULLED
CULMED
DELVED
DOLLED
DULLED
FELLED
FILLED
FILMED
FOLDED
FULGID
FULLED
GALLED
GELDED
GELLED
GILDED
GILEAD
GOLFED
GULFED
GULPED
HALOID
HALTED
HALVED
HELPED
HILLED
HILTED
HOLARD
HULKED
HULLED
INLAID
INLAND
ISLAND
JELLED
JILTED
JOLTED
KELOID
KILLED
KILTED
LALLED
LILIED
LILTED
LOLLED
LULLED
MALLED
MALTED
MELDED
MELTED
MILKED
MILLED
MILORD
MILTED
MOLDED
MOLTED
MULLED
PALLED
PALLID
PALMED

PELTED
PILLED
POLAND
POLLED
PULLED
PULPED
PULSED
RELIED
RELOAD
ROLAND
ROLLED
SALPID
SALTED
SALVED
SILOED
SILTED
SOLAND
SOLOED
SOLVED
SULKED
TALCED
TALKED
TALMUD
TILLED
TILTED
TOLLED
UNLAID
UNLEAD
UNLOAD
UPLAND
VALUED
VALVED
WALKED
WALLED
WELDED
WELLED
WELTED
WILLED
WILTED
WOLFED
XYLOID
YELLED
YELPED

•••LD•
BUILDS
FIELDS
FJELDS
GUILDS
ISOLDE
MOULDS
MOULDY
ROALDS
SCALDS
SCOLDS
SKALDS
WEALDS
WIELDS
WIELDY
WOALDS
WORLDS
YIELDS

•••L•D
ADDLED
AISLED
AMBLED
ANGLED
BAILED
BALLAD
BALLED
BAWLED
BELLED
BILLED
BIRLED
BOILED
BOLLED
BOWLED
BUGLED
BURLED
CABLED
CALLED
CEILED
COALED
COILED
COOLED
COWLED
CULLED
CURLED
CYCLED
DIALED
DOLLED
DUELED
DULLED
EUCLID
EXILED
EYELID
FABLED
FAILED
FELLED
FILLED
FOALED
FOILED
FOOLED
FOULED
FOWLED
FUELED
FUGLED
FULLED
FURLED
GABLED
GALLED
GELLED
HAILED
HAULED
HEALED
HEELED
HILLED
HOWLED
HULLED
HURLED
JAILED
JELLED
KEELED
KILLED
LADLED
LALLED
LOLLED
LULLED
MAILED
MALLED
MARLED
MAULED
MEWLED
MILLED
MOILED
MULLED
NAILED
PALLED
PALLID
PEALED
PEELED
PILLED
POLLED
POOLED
PULLED
PURLED
RAILED
REELED
RIFLED
ROILED
ROLLED
SAILED
SCALED
SEALED
SHALED
SIDLED
SMILED
SOILED
SOULED
SPILED
STALED
STOLED
STOLID
STYLED
TABLED
TAILED
TILLED
TITLED
TOILED
TOLLED
TOOLED
UNCLAD
VEILED
VIALED
WAILED
WALLED
WAULED
WAWLED
WELLED
WHALED
WHILED
WILLED
YAWLED
YELLED
YOWLED

••••LD
AFIELD
ARNOLD
BEHELD
BEHOLD
BIFOLD
DONALD
ENFOLD
GERALD
HAROLD
HERALD
INFOLD
KOBOLD
OSWALD
RESOLD
RETOLD
RIBALD
RONALD
SHIELD
SHOULD
UNFOLD
UNSOLD
UNTOLD
UPHELD
UPHOLD

LE••••
LEACHY
LEADED
LEADEN
LEADER
LEADIN
LEAFED
LEAGUE
LEAKED
LEANED
LEANER
LEANLY
LEANTO
LEAPED
LEAPER
LEARNS
LEARNT
LEASED
LEASES
LEAVED
LEAVEN
LEAVER
LEAVES
LECHER
LECTOR
LEDGER
LEDGES
LEERED
LEEWAY
LEGACY
LEGATE
LEGATO
LEGEND
LEGERS
LEGGED
LEGION
LEGIST
LEGMAN
LEGMEN
LEGREE
LEGUME
LEHUAS
LEIGHS
LEMMAS
LEMNOS
LEMONS
LEMUEL
LEMURS
LENAPE
LENDER
LENGTH
LENITY
LENNYS
LENORE
LENSES
LENTEN
LENTIL
LENTOS
LEONAS
LEONIE
LEPERS
LEPIDO
LEPSIA
LEPTON
LEROYS
LESION
LESLEY
LESLIE
LESSEE
LESSEN
LESSER
LESSON
LESSOR
LESTER
LETHAL
LETTER
LETUPS
LEUDES
LEVANT
LEVEES
LEVELS
LEVERS
LEVIED
LEVIER
LEVIES
LEVITE
LEVITY
LEWDER
LEWDLY

L•E•••
LEERED
LEEWAY
LIEDER
LIEGES
LIERNE
LUELLA
LUETIC

L••E••
LABELS
LAGERS
LAKERS
LAMEDS
LAMELY
LAMENT
LAMEST
LAPELS
LAREDO
LASERS
LATEEN
LATELY
LATENT
LATEST
LAVERS
LAXEST
LAYERS
LEGEND
LEGERS
LEPERS
LEVEES
LEVELS
LEVERS
LIBELS
LIFERS
LIKELY
LIKENS
LIMENS
LIMEYS
LINEAL
LINEAR
LINENS
LINERS
LINEUP
LITERS
LIVELY
LIVENS
LIVERS
LIVERY
LOMENT
LONELY
LONERS
LOPERS
LOREEN
LORENE
LORENZ
LOSERS
LOVEIN
LOVELL
LOVELY
LOVERS
LOWELL
LOWERS
LOWERY
LOWEST
LUBECK
LUCENT
LUGERS
LUMENS
LUNETS
LURERS
LUTEAL
LUTEUM
LYCEES
LYCEUM

L•••E•
LAAGER
LABRET
LACHES

6

LACIER
LACKED
LACKEY
LADDER
LADIES
LADLED
LADLER
LADLES
LAGGED
LAGGER
LAIRED
LAKIER
LALLED
LAMBED
LAMMED
LAMPED
LANCED
LANCER
LANCES
LANCET
LANDED
LANDER
LANKER
LANNER
LAPPED
LAPPER
LAPPET
LAPSED
LAPSER
LAPSES
LARDED
LARDER
LARGER
LARKED
LARKER
LASHED
LASHER
LASHES
LASSES
LASTED
LASTER
LASTEX
LATEEN
LATHED
LATHER
LATHES
LATTEN
LATTER
LAUDED
LAUDER
LAUREL
LAWYER
LAYMEN
LAZIER
LEADED
LEADEN
LEADER
LEAFED
LEAKED
LEANED
LEANER
LEAPED
LEAPER
LEASED
LEASES
LEAVED
LEAVEN
LEAVER
LEAVES
LECHER
LEDGER
LEDGES
LEERED
LEGGED
LEGMEN
LEGREE
LEMUEL
LENDER
LENSES
LENTEN
LESLEY
LESSEE
LESSEN
LESSER
LESTER
LETTER
LEUDES
LEVEES
LEVIED
LEVIER
LEVIES
LEWDER
LIANES
LICHEE
LICHEN
LICKED
LIDDED
LIEDER
LIEGES
LIFTED
LIFTER
LILIED
LILIES
LILTED
LIMBED
LIMBER
LIMIER
LIMNED
LIMNER
LIMPED
LIMPER
LIMPET
LINDEN
LINGER
LINIER
LINKED
LINNET
LINTEL
LINTER
LIONEL
LIPPED
LIPPER
LISPED
LISPER
LISTED
LISTEL
LISTEN
LISTER
LITHER
LITTER
LIVIER
LIVRES
LIVYER
LOADED
LOADER
LOAFED
LOAFER
LOAMED
LOANED
LOAVES
LOBBED
LOCKED
LOCKER
LOCKET
LOCOED
LODGED
LODGER
LODGES
LOFTED
LOFTER
LOGGED
LOGGER
LOGIER
LOITER
LOLLED
LOLLER
LONGED
LONGER
LOOKED
LOOKER
LOOMED
LOOPED
LOOPER
LOOSED
LOOSEN
LOOSER
LOOSES
LOOTED
LOOTER
LOPPED
LORDED
LOREEN
LORIES
LOSSES
LOUDEN
LOUDER
LOUPES
LOURED
LOUSED
LOUSES
LOUVER
LOWKEY
LUBBER
LUCIEN
LUFFED
LUGGED
LUGGER
LULLED
LUMBER
LUMPED
LUMPEN
LUNGED
LUNGEE
LUNGER
LUNGES
LUNKER
LURKED
LUSHED
LUSHER
LUSHES
LUSTED
LUSTER
LUTHER
LYCEES
LYNXES

L••••E

LABILE
LADDIE
LAGUNE
LAHORE
LAMBIE
LAMIAE
LANATE
LANOSE
LAOTSE
LARINE
LARVAE
LASSIE
LAUNCE
LAURAE
LAURIE
LAVAGE
LEAGUE
LEGATE
LEGREE
LEGUME
LENAPE
LENORE
LEONIE
LESLIE
LESSEE
LEVITE
LIABLE
LIBRAE
LICHEE
LIERNE
LIGATE
LIGULE
LIGURE
LINAGE
LIPASE
LITTLE
LIZZIE
LOATHE
LOBATE
LOBULE
LOCALE
LOCATE
LORENE
LOTTIE
LOUISE
LOUNGE
LOUVRE
LOVAGE
LUCILE
LUCITE
LUNATE
LUNGEE
LUNULE
LUPINE
LUXATE
LYSINE
LYTTAE

•LE•••

ALECTO
ALEGAR
ALEPHS
ALEPPO
ALERTS
ALEUTS
ALEXIA
ALEXIN
ALEXIS
BLEACH
BLEAKS
BLEARS
BLEARY
BLEATS
BLEBBY
BLEEDS
BLENCH
BLENDE
BLENDS
BLENNY
CLEANS
CLEARS
CLEATS
CLEAVE
CLEFTS
CLEIST
CLENCH
CLEOME
CLERGY
CLERIC
CLERID
CLERKS
CLEVER
CLEVIS
CLEWED
ELECTR
ELECTS
ELEGIT
ELEMIS
ELENAS
ELEVEN
ELEVON
FLEAMS
FLECHE
FLECKS
FLEDGE
FLEDGY
FLEECE
FLEECY
FLEERS
FLEETS
FLENCH
FLENSE
FLESHY
FLETCH
FLEURY
FLEXED
FLEXES
FLEXOR
GLEAMS
GLEAMY
GLEANS
GLEBES
GLEDES
GLEETS
GLEETY
ILEXES
OLEATE
OLEFIN
PLEACH
PLEADS
PLEASE
PLEATS
PLEBES
PLEDGE
PLEGIA
PLEIAD
PLENTY
PLENUM
PLEURA
PLEURO
PLEXOR
PLEXUS
SLEAVE
SLEAZY
SLEDGE
SLEEKS
SLEEKY
SLEEPS
SLEEPY
SLEETS
SLEETY
SLEEVE
SLEIGH
SLEUTH
SLEWED
ULEMAS
ULENCE
YLEVEL

•L•E••

ALBEDO
ALBEIT
ALBERT
ALDERS
ALIENS
ALKENE
ALLEGE
ALLELE
ALLENS
ALLEYS
ALTERS
BLEEDS
BLUELY
BLUEST
BLUETS
CLIENT
ELBERT

6

ELDERS
ELDEST
ELLENS
ELMERS
ELVERS
FLEECE
FLEECY
FLEERS
FLEETS
FLIERS
FLIEST
FLUENT
FLYERS
GLEETS
GLEETY
OLDEST
PLIERS
SLEEKS
SLEEKY
SLEEPS
SLEEPY
SLEETS
SLEETY
SLEEVE
SLIEST
SLYEST
ULCERS

•L••E•

ALATED
ALFRED
ALICES
ALINED
ALINES
ALIPED
ALLIED
ALLIES
ALTHEA
ALUDEL
BLADED
BLADES
BLAMED
BLAMES
BLARED
BLARES
BLAZED
BLAZER
BLAZES
BLOKES
BLOWER
CLARES
CLARET
CLAWED
CLAYED
CLAYEY
CLEVER
CLEWED
CLIMES
CLINES
CLIVES
CLONES
CLOSED
CLOSER
CLOSES
CLOSET
CLOVEN
CLOVER
CLOVES
CLOYED
CLYDES
CLYPEI
ELATED
ELATER
ELATES
ELDRED
ELEVEN
ELIDED
ELIDES
ELLIES
ELOPED
ELOPER
ELOPES
ELSIES
ELUDED
ELUDES
ELYSEE
FLAKED
FLAKER
FLAKES
FLAMED
FLAMEN
FLAMES
FLARED
FLARES
FLAWED
FLAXEN
FLAXES
FLAYED
FLAYER
FLEXED
FLEXES
FLORET
FLOWED
FLOWER
FLUKED
FLUKES
FLUKEY
FLUMED
FLUMES
FLUTED
FLUTER
FLUTES
FLUXED
FLUXES
GLACES
GLADES
GLARED
GLARES
GLAZED
GLAZER
GLAZES
GLEBES
GLEDES
GLIDED
GLIDER
GLIDES
GLOBED
GLOBES
GLOVED
GLOVER
GLOVES
GLOWED
GLOWER
GLOZED
GLOZES
GLUIER
GLUMES
GLUTEI
GLUTEN
ILEXES
OLIVER
OLIVES
OLLIES
PLACED
PLACER
PLACES
PLACET
PLANED
PLANER
PLANES
PLANET
PLATED
PLATEN
PLATER
PLATES
PLAYED
PLAYER
PLEBES
PLOVER
PLOWED
PLOWER
PLUMED
PLUMES
PLUSES
SLAKED
SLAKES
SLATED
SLATER
SLATES
SLAVED
SLAVER
SLAVES
SLAYER
SLEWED
SLICED
SLICER
SLICES
SLIDER
SLIDES
SLIMED
SLIMES
SLIVER
SLOPED
SLOPER
SLOPES
SLOVEN
SLOWED
SLOWER
ULSTER
YLEVEL

•L•••E

ALBITE
ALCOVE
ALDINE
ALDOSE
ALIBLE
ALKANE
ALKENE
ALKYNE
ALLEGE
ALLELE
ALLUDE
ALLURE
ALMUCE
ALMUDE
ALPINE
ALSACE
ALSIKE
ALULAE
ALVINE
BLENDE
BLITHE
BLONDE
BLOUSE
BLUNGE
CLAIRE
CLAQUE
CLAUDE
CLAUSE
CLEAVE
CLEOME
CLICHE
CLIQUE
CLOCHE
CLOTHE
ELAINE
ELAPSE
ELAYNE
ELOISE
ELYSEE
FLAMBE
FLANGE
FLECHE
FLEDGE
FLEECE
FLENSE
FLORAE
GLANCE
ILLUME
ILLUSE
OLEATE
PLAGUE
PLAICE
PLAQUE
PLATTE
PLEASE
PLEDGE
PLICAE
PLUNGE
SLEAVE
SLEDGE
SLEEVE
SLUDGE
SLUICE
ULENCE
ULLAGE

••LE••

ABLEST
AGLEAM
AGLETS
AILEEN
ALLEGE
ALLELE
ALLENS
ALLEYS
ARLEEN
ARLENE
ASLEEP
AWLESS
BALEEN
BALERS
BOLERO
BOLEYN
CALEBS
CALESA
CELERY
COLEUS
CULETS
DALETH
DELETE
EILEEN
ELLENS
FILERS
FILETS
GALEAE
GALENA
GILEAD
HALERS
HELENA
HELENS
IDLERS
IDLEST
INLETS
ISLETS
JULEPS
MELEES
MILERS
MOLEST
OGLERS
OILERS
OWLETS
PALEAE
PALELY
PALEST
PELEUS
PHLEBO
PHLEGM
PILEUM
PILEUS
POLEAX
PULERS
RELENT
RULERS
SCLERA
SCLERO
SELECT
SELENE
SELENO
SILENI
SILENT
SOLELY
SOLEMN
SOLENT
SPLEEN
SPLENO
TALENT
TALERS
TELEGA
TILERS
TOLEDO
UNLEAD
UNLESS
VALERY
VALETS
VILELY
VILEST
VOLERY
WALERS
XYLEMS
XYLENE
YCLEPT

••L•E•

AILEEN
ALLIED
ALLIES
ARLEEN
ASLEEP
BALDER
BALEEN
BALKED
BALLED
BALLET
BELIED
BELIEF
BELIER
BELIES
BELLED
BELLES
BELTED
BILGED
BILGES
BILKED
BILKER
BILLED
BILLET
BOLDER
BOLLED
BOLTED
BOLTER
BULBEL
BULGED
BULGER
BULGES
BULKED
BULLET
CALCES
CALKED
CALKER
CALLED
CALLER

CALMED
CALMER
CALVED
CALVES
CALXES
CHLOES
COLDER
COLIES
COLLET
COLTER
CULLED
CULLER
CULLET
CULMED
CULVER
DALLES
DELVED
DELVER
DELVES
DOLLED
DOLMEN
DULCET
DULLED
DULLER
EILEEN
ELLIES
FALLEN
FALLER
FALSER
FALTER
FELLED
FELLER
FILLED
FILLER
FILLET
FILMED
FILTER
FOLDED
FOLDER
FULLED
FULLER
GALLED
GALLEY
GELDED
GELLED
GILDED
GILDER
GOLDEN
GOLFED
GOLFER
GULDEN
GULFED
GULLET
GULPED
GULPER
HALLEL
HALLEY
HALOES
HALSEY
HALTED
HALTER
HALVED
HALVES
HELLEN
HELLER
HELMET
HELPED
HELPER
HELVES
HILLED
HILLER
HILTED
HOLDER
HOLIER
HOLIES
HOLLER
HOLMES
HULKED
HULLED
INLIER
JELLED
JILTED
JILTER
JOLIET
JOLTED
JOLTER
JULIES
JULIET
KELLER
KILLED
KILLER
KILMER
KILTED
KILTER
LALLED
LILIED
LILIES
LILTED
LOLLED
LOLLER
LULLED
MALLED
MALLEE
MALLET
MALTED
MELDED
MELEES
MELTED
MELTER
MILDEN
MILDER
MILDEW
MILIEU
MILKED
MILKER
MILLED
MILLER
MILLET
MILTED
MILTER
MOLDED
MOLDER
MOLIES
MOLTED
MOLTEN
MOLTER
MULLED
MULLEN
MULLER
MULLET
MULLEY
OILIER
OLLIES
PALAEO
PALLED
PALLET
PALMED
PALMER
PALTER
PELLET
PELTED
PELTER
PELVES
PHLOEM
PILFER
PILLED
POLDER
POLLED
POLLEE
POLLEN
POLLER
POLLEX
PULLED
PULLER
PULLET
PULLEY
PULPED
PULSED
PULSES
RELIED
RELIEF
RELIER
RELIES
RILLET
ROLLED
ROLLER
SALLET
SALTED
SALTER
SALVED
SALVER
SALVES
SELLER
SELVES
SILKEN
SILOED
SILTED
SILVER
SOLDER
SOLOED
SOLVED
SOLVER
SOLVES
SPLEEN
SULKED
SULLEN
TALCED
TALKED
TALKER
TALLER
TELLER
TILDES
TILLED
TILLER
TILTED
TILTER
TOLLED
TOLLER
TOLTEC
TULLES
UGLIER
VALLEY
VALUED
VALUES
VALVED
VALVES
VELVET
VOLLEY
WALKED
WALKER
WALLED
WALLET
WALTER
WELDED
WELDER
WELLED
WELTED
WELTER
WILBER
WILDER
WILIER
WILLED
WILLER
WILLET
WILTED
WOLFED
WOLSEY
WOLVER
WOLVES
YELLED
YELLER
YELPED
YELPER

••L••E

ABLAZE
AFLAME
ALLEGE
ALLELE
ALLUDE
ALLURE
ANLACE
ANLAGE
APLITE
ARLENE
ARLINE
ASLOPE
AXLIKE
BELIZE
BILLIE
BOLIDE
BULLAE
BYLANE
BYLINE
CELLAE
CILICE
COLINE
COLLIE
COLURE
DELETE
DELUDE
DELUGE
DELUXE
DILATE
DILUTE
DOLLIE
DULCIE
ENLACE
FELICE
FELINE
FELIPE
FELLOE
FILOSE
GALEAE
GALORE
HALIDE
HALITE
ILLUME
ILLUSE
INLACE
IOLITE
KILTIE
MALATE
MALGRE
MALICE
MALINE
MALLEE
MILAGE
MILLIE
MOLINE
MOLLIE
MOLTKE
NELLIE
OBLATE
OBLIGE
OOLITE
PALACE
PALATE
PALEAE
PELAGE
PELITE
PILATE
PILOSE
PILULE
POLICE
POLITE
POLLEE
PULQUE
RELATE
RELINE
RELIVE
SALINE
SALOME
SALUTE
SELENE
SILVAE
SOLACE
SOLUTE
SPLAKE
SPLICE
SPLINE
SYLVAE
TILLIE
ULLAGE
UNLACE
UNLADE
UNLIKE
UNLIVE
VALISE
VELATE
VELOCE
VELURE
VOLUME
VOLUTE
VULVAE
WALLIE
WILLIE
XYLENE
XYLOSE

•••LE•

ABELES
ADDLED
ADDLES
AIGLET
AISLED
AISLES
AMBLED
AMBLER
AMBLES
AMOLES
AMULET
ANGLED
ANGLER
ANGLES
ANKLES
ANKLET
ANTLER
APPLES
ARMLET
ASHLEY
ATTLEE
AUKLET
AZALEA
AZOLES
BAILED
BAILEE
BAILER
BAILEY
BALLED
BALLET
BARLEY
BAWLED
BAWLER
BELLED
BELLES
BIBLES
BIFLEX
BILLED
BILLET
BIRLED
BIRLES
BOGLES
BOILED

BOILER
BOLLED
BOULES
BOWLED
BOWLEG
BOWLER
BUGLED
BUGLER
BUGLES
BULLET
BURLED
BURLER
BURLEY
BUTLER
CABLED
CABLES
CABLET
CALLED
CALLER
CAMLET
CAULES
CEILED
CHALEH
CHALET
CHOLER
COALED
COALER
COBLES
COILED
COILER
COLLET
COOLED
COOLER
COPLEY
COULEE
COWLED
CULLED
CULLER
CULLET
CURLED
CURLER
CURLEW
CUTLER
CUTLET
CYCLED
CYCLER
CYCLES
DALLES
DEALER
DHOLES
DIALED
DIALER
DIPLEX
DOLLED
DOOLEE
DOYLEY
DUDLEY
DUELED
DUELER
DULLED
DULLER
DUPLEX
EAGLES
EAGLET
EARLES
ECCLES
ECOLES
EDILES
EMBLEM
EMILES
EXILED
EXILES
EYELET
FABLED
FABLER
FABLES
FAILED
FALLEN
FALLER
FARLES
FARLEY
FEELER
FELLED
FELLER
FILLED
FILLER
FILLET
FOALED
FOILED
FOOLED
FOULED
FOULER
FOWLED
FOWLER
FUELED
FUELER
FUGLED
FUGLES
FULLED
FULLER
FURLED
GABLED
GABLES
GALLED
GALLEY
GAOLER
GELLED
GIBLET
GIGLET
GIMLET
GOBLET
GOGLET
GUILES
GULLET
HAILED
HAILER
HALLEL
HALLEY
HAMLET
HARLEM
HARLEY
HASLET
HAULED
HAULER
HEALED
HEALER
HEELED
HEELER
HELLEN
HELLER
HENLEY
HILLED
HILLER
HITLER
HOLLER
HOWLED
HOWLER
HULLED
HURLED
HURLER
HUXLEY
INKLES
JAILED
JAILER
JELLED
JOULES
KEELED
KEGLER
KELLER
KEPLER
KILLED
KILLER
KISLEW
LADLED
LADLER
LADLES
LALLED
LESLEY
LOLLED
LOLLER
LULLED
MACLES
MAHLER
MAILED
MAILER
MALLED
MALLEE
MALLET
MAPLES
MARLED
MAULED
MAULER
MEDLEY
MERLES
MEWLED
MILLED
MILLER
MILLET
MOILED
MOILER
MOOLEY
MORLEY
MOSLEM
MOSLEY
MOTLEY
MULLED
MULLEN
MULLER
MULLET
MULLEY
NAILED
NAPLES
NUTLET
OAKLEY
OMELET
OODLES
OUTLET
OVULES
PALLED
PALLET
PARLEY
PEALED
PEELED
PEELER
PELLET
PILLED
POLLED
POLLEE
POLLEN
POLLER
POLLEX
POOLED
PROLEG
PULLED
PULLER
PULLET
PULLEY
PURLED
RAILED
REALES
REELED
REELER
REFLET
REFLEX
REGLET
RIFLED
RIFLER
RIFLES
RILLET
RIPLEY
ROBLES
ROILED
ROLLED
ROLLER
RUBLES
RUNLET
SABLES
SAILED
SAILER
SALLET
SAMLET
SCALED
SCALER
SCALES
SCOLEX
SEALED
SEALER
SELLER
SHALED
SHALES
SIDLED
SIDLER
SIDLES
SMILED
SMILER
SMILES
SOCLES
SOILED
SOULED
SPILED
SPILES
STALED
STALER
STALES
STELES
STILES
STOLED
STOLEN
STOLES
STYLED
STYLER
STYLES
STYLET
SUBLET
SULLEN
SUTLER
SWALES
TABLED
TABLES
TABLET
TAILED
TALLER
TATLER
TELLER
THALES
THOLES
TILLED
TILLER
TITLED
TITLES
TOILED
TOILER
TOILES
TOILET
TOLLED
TOLLER
TOOLED
TOOLER
TULLES
UMBLES
UNCLES
VALLEY
VARLET
VEILED
VEILER
VIALED
VIOLET
VOILES
VOLLEY
WAILED
WAILER
WALLED
WALLET
WAULED
WAWLED
WELLED
WESLEY
WHALED
WHALER
WHALES
WHILED
WHILES
WILLED
WILLER
WILLET
WOOLEN
YAWLED
YELLED
YELLER
YOWLED

•••L•E

ALULAE
AMELIE
ATTLEE
BAILEE
BAILIE
BILLIE
BULLAE
CELLAE
CHELAE
COLLIE
COOLIE
COULEE
DIPLOE
DOLLIE
DOOLEE
DOOLIE
EMILIE
EVOLVE
FAILLE
FELLOE
GOALIE
GRILLE
GRILSE
ISOLDE
LESLIE
MALLEE
MEALIE
MILLIE
MOLLIE
NELLIE
PHYLAE
POLLEE
SHELVE
STELAE
SVELTE
TAILLE
TILLIE
TUILLE
TWELVE
UVULAE
WALLIE
WILLIE

••••LE

AEDILE
ALIBLE
ALLELE
AMPULE
ARABLE
ARGYLE
AUDILE
AWHILE

6

BABBLE
BAFFLE
BANGLE
BATTLE
BAUBLE
BEADLE
BEAGLE
BEETLE
BOBBLE
BOGGLE
BOODLE
BOTTLE
BOUCLE
BRIDLE
BUBBLE
BUCKLE
BUDDLE
BUMBLE
BUNDLE
BUNGLE
BURBLE
BURGLE
BUSTLE
CACKLE
CAJOLE
CANDLE
CANTLE
CAROLE
CASTLE
CATTLE
CAUDLE
CECILE
CHICLE
CIRCLE
COBBLE
COCKLE
CODDLE
COFFLE
COUPLE
CRADLE
CREOLE
CUDDLE
CUPULE
CURDLE
CURULE
CUTTLE
CYBELE
DABBLE
DADDLE
DANDLE
DANGLE
DAPPLE
DARKLE
DARTLE
DAWDLE
DAZZLE
DECILE
DECKLE
DEFILE
DIBBLE
DIDDLE
DIMPLE
DINGLE
DIPOLE
DOABLE
DOCILE
DOODLE
DOTTLE
DOUBLE
DUFFLE
EDIBLE
EMPALE
ENABLE
ENISLE
ENSILE
EXHALE
FACILE
FAILLE
FEEBLE
FEMALE
FERULE
FETTLE
FICKLE
FIDDLE
FIMBLE
FINALE
FIPPLE
FIZZLE
FOCSLE
FOIBLE
FONDLE
FOOTLE
FOOZLE
FUDDLE
FUMBLE
FUSILE
FUTILE
GABBLE
GAGGLE
GAMBLE
GARBLE
GARGLE
GENTLE
GIGGLE
GIRDLE
GISELE
GOBBLE
GOGGLE
GRILLE
GURGLE
GUTTLE
GUZZLE
HABILE
HACKLE
HAGGLE
HANDLE
HASSLE
HECKLE
HEDDLE
HIGGLE
HOBBLE
HOPPLE
HUCKLE
HUDDLE
HUMBLE
HURDLE
HURTLE
HUSTLE
ICICLE
IMPALE
INHALE
INSOLE
JANGLE
JIGGLE
JINGLE
JOGGLE
JOSTLE
JUGGLE
JUMBLE
JUNGLE
KECKLE
KETTLE
KINDLE
LABILE
LIABLE
LIGULE
LITTLE
LOBULE
LOCALE
LUCILE
LUNULE
MACKLE
MACULE
MANGLE
MANTLE
MARBLE
MEDDLE
METTLE
MIDDLE
MIGGLE
MINGLE
MOBILE
MODULE
MOHOLE
MORALE
MOTILE
MOTTLE
MUDDLE
MUFFLE
MUMBLE
MUSCLE
MUTULE
MUZZLE
MYRTLE
NEEDLE
NESTLE
NETTLE
NEVILE
NIBBLE
NICOLE
NIGGLE
NIMBLE
NIPPLE
NOBBLE
NODDLE
NODULE
NOODLE
NOZZLE
NUBBLE
NUBILE
NUZZLE
ORACLE
ORIOLE
OSCULE
PADDLE
PAPULE
PAROLE
PEBBLE
PEDDLE
PENILE
PEOPLE
PESTLE
PICKLE
PIDDLE
PIFFLE
PILULE
PIMPLE
PINOLE
PINTLE
POODLE
POPPLE
POTTLE
PUDDLE
PURFLE
PURPLE
PUZZLE
RABBLE
RADDLE
RAFFLE
RAMBLE
RANKLE
RATTLE
REDDLE
REGALE
RESALE
RESILE
RESOLE
REVILE
RIDDLE
RIFFLE
RIMPLE
RIPPLE
ROUBLE
RUBBLE
RUDDLE
RUFFLE
RUMBLE
RUMPLE
RUNDLE
RUSTLE
RUTILE
SADDLE
SAMPLE
SEDILE
SEMELE
SENILE
SETTLE
SICKLE
SIECLE
SIMILE
SIMPLE
SINGLE
SIZZLE
STABLE
STAPLE
STIFLE
SUABLE
SUBTLE
SUCKLE
SUPPLE
SWIPLE
TACKLE
TAILLE
TAMALE
TANGLE
TATTLE
TEMPLE
TICKLE
TINGLE
TINKLE
TIPPLE
TITTLE
TODDLE
TOGGLE
TOOTLE
TOPPLE
TOUSLE
TREBLE
TRIFLE
TRIPLE
TUBULE
TUILLE
TUMBLE
TURTLE
TUSSLE
UNABLE
UNPILE
USABLE
VENULE
VIABLE
VIRILE
WABBLE
WADDLE
WAFFLE
WAGGLE
WAMBLE
WANDLE
WANGLE
WARBLE
WATTLE
WIGGLE
WIMBLE
WIMPLE
WINKLE
WOBBLE
ZIZZLE
ZONULE

L•F•••
LIFERS
LIFTED
LIFTER
LOFTED
LOFTER
LUFFED

L••F••
LAPFUL
LAWFUL
LEAFED
LOAFED
LOAFER
LOOFAH
LUFFED

L•••F•
LAYOFF

L••••F
LAYOFF

•LF•••
ALFAKI
ALFONS
ALFRED
ELFINS
ELFISH

•L•F••
BLUFFS
CLEFTS
CLIFFS
CLIFFY
FLUFFS
FLUFFY
OLEFIN

•L••F•
BLUFFS
CLIFFS
CLIFFY
FLUFFS
FLUFFY
KLOOFS

••LF••
BELFRY
FULFIL
FYLFOT
GOLFED
GOLFER
GULFED
PILFER
SULFUR
WILFUL
WOLFED

••L•F•
CALIFS
PILAFS
SALIFY
SCLAFF
UGLIFY
UPLIFT
VILIFY

••L••F
BELIEF
RELIEF
SCLAFF

••••LF
BEHALF
ENGULF

INGULF
ITSELF
MYSELF

L•G•••

LAGERS
LAGGED
LAGGER
LAGOON
LAGUNE
LEGACY
LEGATE
LEGATO
LEGEND
LEGERS
LEGGED
LEGION
LEGIST
LEGMAN
LEGMEN
LEGREE
LEGUME
LIGAND
LIGATE
LIGHTS
LIGNIN
LIGULA
LIGULE
LIGURE
LOGGED
LOGGER
LOGGIA
LOGIER
LOGION
LOGJAM
LUGERS
LUGGED
LUGGER

L••G••

LAAGER
LAGGED
LAGGER
LANGUR
LARGER
LARGOS
LAUGHS
LEAGUE
LEDGER
LEDGES
LEGGED
LEIGHS
LENGTH
LIEGES
LINGAS
LINGER
LINGUA
LODGED
LODGER
LODGES
LOGGED
LOGGER
LOGGIA
LONGAN
LONGED
LONGER
LOUGHS
LUGGED
LUGGER
LUNGED
LUNGEE
LUNGER
LUNGES
LUNGIS

L•••G•

LADOGA
LANUGO
LAVAGE
LINAGE
LOUNGE
LOVAGE

L••••G

LACING
LADING
LAKING
LAMING
LARYNG
LAVING
LAWING
LAYING
LAZING
LIKING
LIMING
LINING
LIVING
LOOING
LOPING
LOSING
LOVING
LOWING
LUDWIG
LURING
LUTING
LYSING

•LG•••

ALGOID

•L•G••

ALEGAR
ALIGHT
ALIGNS
BLIGHT
CLOGGY
ELEGIT
FLAGGY
FLAGON
FLIGHT
PLAGAL
PLAGIO
PLAGUE
PLAGUY
PLEGIA
PLIGHT
SLAGGY
SLIGHT
SLOGAN

•L••G•

ALLEGE
BLUNGE
CLANGS
CLERGY
CLINGS
CLINGY
CLOGGY
CLOUGH
ELOIGN
FLAGGY
FLANGE
FLEDGE
FLEDGY
FLINGS
FLONGS
PLEDGE
PLOUGH
PLUNGE
SLAGGY
SLANGY
SLEDGE
SLEIGH
SLINGS
SLOUGH
SLUDGE
SLUDGY
ULLAGE

•L•••G

BLUING
CLUING
FLYING
GLUING
PLYING
SLUING

••LG••

BELGAS
BELGIC
BILGED
BILGES
BULGAR
BULGED
BULGER
BULGES
FULGID
MALGRE
NILGAI
VALGUS
VULGAR

••L•G•

ALLEGE
ANLAGE
BELUGA
COLUGO
DELUGE
EULOGY
MALAGA
MALIGN
MILAGE
OBLIGE
OOLOGY
PELAGE
PHLEGM
TELEGA
TELUGU
ULLAGE

••L••G

AILING
BALING
BELONG
DOLING
EALING
FILING
HALING
HOLING
IDLING
ISLING
KALONG
OBLONG
OGLING
OILING
OOLONG
PALING
PILING
POLING
PULING
RILING
RULING
SOLING
TILING
WALING
WILING

•••L•G

ANALOG
APOLOG
BOWLEG
DIALOG
DUOLOG
EPILOG
PROLEG
PUTLOG
STALAG

L•H•••

LAHORE
LEHUAS

L••H••

LACHES
LASHED
LASHER
LASHES
LATHED
LATHER
LATHES
LECHER
LETHAL
LICHEE
LICHEN
LIGHTS
LITHER
LITHIA
LITHIC
LOCHIA
LUSHED
LUSHER
LUSHES
LUTHER

L•••H•

LAUGHS
LEACHY
LEIGHS
LOATHE
LOTAHS
LOUGHS
LYMPHO

L••••H

LATISH
LAUNCH
LAVISH
LENGTH
LOOFAH

•L•H••

ALPHAS
ALPHYL
ALTHEA
ELOHIM

•L••H•

ALEPHS
ALIGHT
ALMAHS
BLIGHT
BLITHE
CLICHE
CLOCHE
CLOTHE
CLOTHO
CLOTHS
ELISHA
FLASHY
FLECHE
FLESHY
FLIGHT
GLYPHS
PLASHY
PLIGHT
PLUSHY
SLIGHT
SLOSHY
SLOTHS
SLUSHY

•L•••H

BLANCH
BLEACH
BLENCH
BLOTCH
BLUISH
CLENCH
CLINCH
CLOUGH
CLUTCH
ELFISH
ELIJAH
ELVISH
FLENCH
FLETCH
FLINCH
FLITCH
OLDISH
PLANCH
PLEACH
PLINTH
PLOUGH
SLEIGH
SLEUTH
SLOUCH
SLOUGH

••L•H•

DELPHI
DOLPHS
FILTHY
MALTHA
RALPHS
ROLPHS
SULPHA
SULPHO
SYLPHS
SYLPHY
TILTHS

••L••H

ABLUSH
CALASH
CALIPH
CULTCH
DALETH
DULUTH
EOLITH
FELLAH
GALOSH
GULLAH
HALLAH
MOLLAH
MOLOCH
MULISH
MULLAH
NULLAH
OWLISH
PALISH
POLISH
RELISH
SALISH
SPLASH
WALLAH
ZILLAH

•••L•H

ADOLPH
BEULAH
CHALEH
FELLAH
GULLAH
HALLAH

HEALTH
KIBLAH
MOLLAH
MOOLAH
MULLAH
NULLAH
SHILOH
SPILTH
WALLAH
WEALTH
ZILLAH

LI••••

LIABLE
LIANAS
LIANES
LIBBYS
LIBELS
LIBIDO
LIBRAE
LIBRAS
LIBYAN
LICHEE
LICHEN
LICKED
LICTOR
LIDDED
LIEDER
LIEGES
LIERNE
LIFERS
LIFTED
LIFTER
LIGAND
LIGATE
LIGHTS
LIGNIN
LIGULA
LIGULE
LIGURE
LIKELY
LIKENS
LIKING
LILACS
LILIAN
LILIED
LILIES
LILTED
LIMBED
LIMBER
LIMBIC
LIMBUS
LIMENS
LIMEYS
LIMIER
LIMINA
LIMING
LIMITS
LIMNED
LIMNER
LIMPED
LIMPER
LIMPET
LIMPID
LIMPLY
LIMULI
LINAGE
LINDAS
LINDEN
LINEAL
LINEAR
LINENS
LINERS
LINEUP
LINGAS
LINGER
LINGUA
LINIER
LINING
LINKED
LINNET
LINTEL
LINTER
LIONEL
LIPASE
LIPIDS
LIPOID
LIPOMA
LIPPED
LIPPER
LIQUID
LIQUOR
LISBOA
LISBON
LISPED
LISPER
LISTED
LISTEL
LISTEN
LISTER
LITANY
LITERS
LITHER
LITHIA
LITHIC
LITMUS
LITTER
LITTLE
LIVELY
LIVENS
LIVERS
LIVERY
LIVIAS
LIVIER
LIVING
LIVRES
LIVYER
LIZARD
LIZZIE
LIZZYS

L•I•••

LAIRDS
LAIRED
LEIGHS
LOITER

L••I••

LABIAL
LABILE
LABIUM
LACIER
LACILY
LACING
LADIES
LADING
LADINO
LAKIER
LAKING
LAMIAE
LAMIAS
LAMINA
LAMING
LAPINS
LARIAT
LARINE
LATINS
LATISH
LAVING
LAVISH
LAWING
LAXITY
LAYING
LAZIER
LAZILY
LAZING
LEGION
LEGIST
LENITY
LEPIDO
LESION
LEVIED
LEVIER
LEVIES
LEVITE
LEVITY
LIBIDO
LIKING
LILIAN
LILIED
LILIES
LIMIER
LIMINA
LIMING
LIMITS
LINIER
LINING
LIPIDS
LIVIAS
LIVIER
LIVING
LOGIER
LOGION
LOLITA
LOOING
LOPING
LORICA
LORIES
LOSING
LOTION
LOUISA
LOUISE
LOVING
LOWING
LUCIAN
LUCIAS
LUCIEN
LUCILE
LUCITE
LUCIUS
LUMINA
LUMINI
LUMINO
LUPINE
LURING
LUTING
LUTIST
LYDIAS
LYRICS
LYRISM
LYRIST
LYSINE
LYSING
LYSINS

L•••I•

LACTIC
LADDIE
LAMBIE
LANAIS
LASSIE
LATRIA
LATVIA
LAURIE
LEADIN
LENTIL
LEONIE
LEPSIA
LESLIE
LIGNIN
LIMBIC
LIMPID
LIPOID
LIQUID
LITHIA
LITHIC
LIZZIE
LOCHIA
LOGGIA
LOOKIN
LORAIN
LOTTIE
LOVEIN
LUBLIN
LUDWIG
LUETIC
LUNGIS

L••••I

LAZULI
LIMULI
LUMINI

•LI•••

ALIBIS
ALIBLE
ALICES
ALICIA
ALIDAD
ALIENS
ALIGHT
ALIGNS
ALINED
ALINES
ALIPED
ALISON
BLIGHT
BLIMPS
BLINDS
BLINKS
BLINTZ
BLITHE
CLICHE
CLICKS
CLIENT
CLIFFS
CLIFFY
CLIMAT
CLIMAX
CLIMBS
CLIMES
CLINCH
CLINES
CLINGS
CLINGY
CLINIC
CLINKS
CLINTS
CLIQUE
CLIQUY
CLIVES
ELICIT
ELIDED
ELIDES
ELIJAH
ELIOTS
ELISHA
ELIXIR
ELIZAS
FLICKS
FLIERS
FLIEST
FLIGHT
FLIMSY
FLINCH
FLINGS
FLINTS
FLINTY
FLIRTS
FLIRTY
FLITCH
GLIBLY
GLIDED
GLIDER
GLIDES
GLINTS
GLIOMA
OLIVER
OLIVES
OLIVIA
PLIANT
PLICAE
PLIERS
PLIGHT
PLINTH
SLICED
SLICER
SLICES
SLICKS
SLIDER
SLIDES
SLIEST
SLIGHT
SLIMED
SLIMES
SLIMLY
SLIMSY
SLINGS
SLINKS
SLINKY
SLIPON
SLIPUP
SLIVER

•L•I••

ALBINO
ALBION
ALBITE
ALDINE
ALLIED
ALLIES
ALLIUM
ALMIRA
ALPINE
ALSIKE
ALUINO
ALUINS
ALVINA
ALVINE
BLAINS
BLUING
BLUISH
CLAIMS
CLAIRE
CLEIST
CLUING
ELAINE
ELFINS
ELFISH
ELLIES
ELLIOT
ELMIRA
ELOIGN
ELOINS
ELOISE
ELSIES
ELVIRA
ELVISH
FLAILS
FLAIRS
FLUIDS
FLYING
GLAIRS

GLAIRY
GLUIER
GLUING
ILOILO
OLDISH
OLLIES
PLAICE
PLAIDS
PLAINS
PLAINT
PLAITS
PLEIAD
PLYING
SLEIGH
SLUICE
SLUING
ULTIMA

•L••I•

ALARIC
ALBEIT
ALCAIC
ALCUIN
ALEXIA
ALEXIN
ALEXIS
ALGOID
ALIBIS
ALICIA
ALTAIC
ALTAIR
ALUMIN
CLERIC
CLERID
CLEVIS
CLINIC
CLONIC
CLOVIS
ELEGIT
ELEMIS
ELICIT
ELIXIR
ELOHIM
FLAVIA
FLAVIN
FLORID
FLORIN
FLUVIO
GLACIS
GLOBIN
GLORIA
GLYNIS
OLEFIN
OLIVIA
PLACID
PLAGIO
PLASIA
PLASIS
PLEGIA
PLUVIO
SLAVIC

•L•••I

ALFAKI
ALKALI
ALUMNI
CLYPEI
GLUTEI

••LI••

AALIIS
ADLIBS
AILING
ALLIED
ALLIES
ALLIUM
APLITE
ARLINE
AXLIKE
BALING
BELIAL
BELIED
BELIEF
BELIER
BELIES
BELIZE
BILITY
BOLIDE
BYLINE
CALICO
CALIFS
CALIPH
CELIAC
CELIAS
CILIAT
CILICE
CILIUM
COLIES
COLINE
COLINS
DELIAN
DELIAS
DELICT
DELIUS
DOLING
EALING
ELLIES
ELLIOT
ENLIST
EOLIAN
EOLITH
FELICE
FELIDS
FELINE
FELIPE
FILIAL
FILING
FOLIAR
FOLIOS
FOLIUM
GALIOT
HALIDE
HALIDS
HALING
HALITE
HELICO
HELIOS
HELIUM
HOLIER
HOLIES
HOLILY
HOLING
HOLISM
IDLING
INLIER
IOLITE
ISLING
JOLIET
JULIAN
JULIAS
JULIES
JULIET
JULIUS
KALIAN
KALIUM
LILIAN
LILIED
LILIES
LOLITA
MALICE
MALIGN
MALINE
MILIEU
MILIUM
MOLIES
MOLINE
MULISH
OBLIGE
OGLING
OILIER
OILILY
OILING
OLLIES
OOLITE
OWLISH
OXLIPS
PALING
PALISH
PELIAS
PELION
PELITE
PILING
POLICE
POLICY
POLING
POLISH
POLITE
POLITY
PULING
RELICS
RELICT
RELIED
RELIEF
RELIER
RELIES
RELINE
RELISH
RELIVE
RILING
RULING
SALIFY
SALINE
SALISH
SALIVA
SILICA
SILICO
SOLIDI
SOLIDS
SOLING
SOLION
SPLICE
SPLINE
SPLINT
SPLITS
TALION
TILING
TULIPS
UGLIER
UGLIFY
UGLILY
UNLIKE
UNLIVE
UPLIFT
VALISE
VILIFY
WALING
WILIER
WILILY
WILING

••L•I•

AALIIS
AFLCIO
AGLAIA
BALTIC
BELGIC
BELOIT
BILLIE
BOLLIX
BULBIL
CALAIS
CALCIC
CALVIN
CELTIC
COLLIE
CULLIS
DOLLIE
DULCIE
ECLAIR
FILLIN
FILLIP
FULFIL
FULGID
GALLIC
HALOID
HOLMIC
INLAID
KALMIA
KELOID
KELVIN
KILTIE
MELVIN
MILLIE
MOLLIE
NELLIE
PALLID
PELVIC
PELVIS
PULPIT
SALMIS
SALPID
SALVIA
SILVIA
SYLVIA
TILLIE
UNLAID
VALOIS
WALLIE
WALLIS
WALVIS
WELKIN
WILLIE
WILLIS
XYLOID

••L••I

BILOXI
DELPHI
MALAWI
NILGAI
SALAMI
SALUKI
SILENI
SOLIDI
TULADI

•••LI•

ABULIA
AEOLIA
AEOLIC
AEOLIS
AMELIA
AMELIE
AMYLIC
ANGLIA
ANGLIC
ANILIN
ANTLIA
APULIA
BAALIM
BAILIE
BERLIN
BIBLIO
BILLIE
BOLLIX
CAPLIN
CATLIN
CAULIS
COLLIE
COOLIE
CULLIS
CYCLIC
CYMLIN
DAHLIA
DOLLIE
DOOLIE
DUBLIN
DUNLIN
EMILIA
EMILIE
EMILIO
EUCLID
EXILIC
EYELID
FILLIN
FILLIP
FROLIC
GAELIC
GALLIC
GARLIC
GIULIA
GIULIO
GOALIE
GOBLIN
INULIN
ITALIC
JOPLIN
KAOLIN
LESLIE
LUBLIN
MARLIN
MEALIE
MERLIN
MILLIE
MOLLIE
MOULIN
MUSLIM
MUSLIN
MYELIN
NELLIE
OXALIC
OXALIS
PALLID
PAULIN
PHILIA
PHILIP
POPLIN
PROLIX
PUBLIC
PURLIN
RATLIN
SIALIC
SIMLIN
STALIN
STELIC
STOLID
SUNLIT
SUSLIK
THALIA
THULIA
TILLIE
URALIC
VIOLIN
WALLIE
WALLIS
WILLIE
WILLIS

•••L•I

NIELLI
SMALTI
STELLI

••••LI
ALKALI
ARGALI
EMBOLI
GANGLI
LAZULI
LIMULI
NEROLI
NIELLI
STELLI
VASILI

L••J••
LOGJAM

•L•J••
ELIJAH

••LJ••
SELJUK

L•K•••
LAKERS
LAKIER
LAKING
LIKELY
LIKENS
LIKING

L••K••
LACKED
LACKEY
LANKER
LANKLY
LARKED
LARKER
LEAKED
LICKED
LINKED
LOCKED
LOCKER
LOCKET
LOCKUP
LOOKED
LOOKER
LOOKIN
LOWKEY
LUNKER
LURKED

L••••K
LUBECK

•LK•••
ALKALI
ALKANE
ALKENE
ALKYLS
ALKYNE

•L•K••
BLOKES
FLAKED
FLAKER
FLAKES
FLUKED
FLUKES
FLUKEY
SLAKED
SLAKES

•L••K•
ALASKA
ALFAKI
ALSIKE
BLACKS
BLANKS
BLEAKS
BLINKS
BLOCKS
BLOCKY
CLACKS
CLANKS
CLERKS
CLICKS
CLINKS
CLOAKS
CLOCKS
CLUCKS
FLACKS
FLANKS
FLASKS
FLECKS
FLICKS
FLOCKS
FLOCKY
FLUNKS
FLUNKY
PLACKS
PLANKS
PLUCKS
PLUCKY
PLUNKS
SLACKS
SLEEKS
SLEEKY
SLICKS
SLINKS
SLINKY

•L•••K
PLANCK
SLOVAK

••LK••
BALKAN
BALKED
BILKED
BILKER
BULKED
CALKED
CALKER
FOLKSY
HULKED
MILKED
MILKER
POLKAS
SILKEN
SULKED
TALKED
TALKER
VALKYR
WALKED
WALKER
WALKON
WALKUP
WELKIN

••L•K•
AXLIKE
KULAKS
MOLTKE
SALUKI
SPLAKE
UNLIKE

••L••K
GALYAK
KALPAK
OCLOCK
SELJUK
UNLOCK

•••LK•
CAULKS
CHALKS
CHALKY
SKULKS
STALKS
STALKY
WHELKS
WHELKY

•••L•K
MUKLUK
SUSLIK

••••LK
BYTALK

LL••••
LLAMAS
LLANOS
LLOYDS

L•L•••
LALLED
LILACS
LILIAN
LILIED
LILIES
LILTED
LOLITA
LOLLED
LOLLER
LULLED

L••L••
LADLED
LADLER
LADLES
LALLED
LESLEY
LESLIE
LOLLED
LOLLER
LUBLIN
LUELLA
LULLED

L•••L•
LABELS
LABILE
LACILY
LAMELY
LANKLY
LAPELS
LASTLY
LATELY
LAZILY
LAZULI
LEANLY
LEVELS
LEWDLY
LIABLE
LIBELS
LIGULA
LIGULE
LIKELY
LIMPLY
LIMULI
LITTLE
LIVELY
LOBULE
LOCALE
LOCALS
LONELY
LORDLY
LOUDLY
LOVELL
LOVELY
LOWELL
LUCILE
LUELLA
LUNULA
LUNULE

L••••L
LABIAL
LAPFUL
LARVAL
LAUREL
LAWFUL
LEMUEL
LENTIL
LETHAL
LINEAL
LINTEL
LIONEL
LISTEL
LOVELL
LOWELL
LUTEAL

•LL•••
ALLANS
ALLAYS
ALLEGE
ALLELE
ALLENS
ALLEYS
ALLIED
ALLIES
ALLIUM
ALLOTS
ALLOUT
ALLOWS
ALLOYS
ALLUDE
ALLURE
ALLYLS
ELLENS
ELLIES
ELLIOT
ILLUME
ILLUSE
ILLUST
OLLIES
ULLAGE

•L•L••
ALULAE
ALULAR
SLALOM

•L••L•
ALIBLE
ALKALI
ALKYLS
ALLELE
ALLYLS
BLUELY
FLAILS
FLATLY
GLADLY
GLIBLY
GLUMLY
ILOILO
SLIMLY
SLOWLY

•L•••L
ALPHYL
ALUDEL
FLORAL
GLOBAL
GLYCOL
PLAGAL
PLURAL
YLEVEL

••LL••
BALLAD
BALLED
BALLET
BALLOT
BELLAS
BELLED
BELLES
BELLOC
BELLOW
BILLED
BILLET
BILLIE
BILLON
BILLOW
BILLYS
BOLLED
BOLLIX
BULLAE
BULLET
CALLAO
CALLAS
CALLED
CALLER
CALLOW
CALLUS
CELLAE
CELLAR
CELLOS
COLLAR
COLLET
COLLIE
COLLOP
CULLAY
CULLED
CULLER
CULLET
CULLIS
DALLAS
DALLES
DELLAS
DOLLAR
DOLLED
DOLLIE
DOLLOP
DOLLYS
DULLED
DULLER
FALLAL
FALLEN
FALLER
FALLOW
FELLAH
FELLED
FELLER
FELLOE
FELLOW
FILLED
FILLER
FILLET
FILLIN
FILLIP
FOLLOW
FULLED
FULLER
GALLED
GALLEY
GALLIC
GALLON
GALLOP
GALLUP
GALLUS
GELLED

6

GULLAH
GULLET
HALLAH
HALLEL
HALLEY
HALLOO
HALLOW
HALLUX
HELLAS
HELLEN
HELLER
HILLED
HILLER
HOLLER
HOLLOW
HOLLYS
HULLED
JELLED
KELLER
KILLED
KILLER
LALLED
LOLLED
LOLLER
LULLED
MALLED
MALLEE
MALLET
MALLOW
MELLON
MELLOW
MILLAY
MILLED
MILLER
MILLET
MILLIE
MILLYS
MOLLAH
MOLLIE
MOLLYS
MULLAH
MULLED
MULLEN
MULLER
MULLET
MULLEY
NELLIE
NELLYS
NULLAH
PALLAS
PALLED
PALLET
PALLID
PALLOR
PELLET
PILLAR
PILLED
PILLOW
POLLED
POLLEE
POLLEN
POLLER
POLLEX
POLLUX
POLLYS
PULLED
PULLER
PULLET
PULLEY
RILLET
ROLLED
ROLLER
SALLET
SALLOW
SALLYS
SELLER
SULLEN
TALLER
TALLOW
TELLER
TELLUS
TILLED
TILLER
TILLIE
TILLYS
TOLLED
TOLLER
TULLES
VALLEY
VELLUM
VILLAS
VILLON
VILLUS
VOLLEY
WALLAH
WALLAS
WALLED
WALLET
WALLIE
WALLIS
WALLOP
WALLOW
WALLYS
WELLED
WILLED
WILLER
WILLET
WILLIE
WILLIS
WILLOW
WILLYS
YELLED
YELLER
YELLOW
ZILLAH

••L•L•
ALLELE
ALLYLS
BALDLY
BOLDLY
CALMLY
COLDLY
HOLILY
MILDLY
OILILY
PALELY
PILULE
SOLELY
UGLILY
VILELY
WILDLY
WILILY
XYLOLS

••L••L
BELIAL
BULBEL
BULBIL
BULBUL
FALLAL
FILIAL
FULFIL
HALLEL
TOLUOL
TOLUYL
VALVAL
VULVAL
WILFUL

•••LL•
ABOLLA
APOLLO
ATOLLS
AXILLA
BRILLS
CHILLS
CHILLY
CHOLLA
COOLLY
DOALLS
DRILLS
DROLLS
DROLLY
DUELLO
DWELLS
EVILLY
FAILLE
FOULLY
FRILLS
FRILLY
GRILLE
GRILLS
ICALLY
IDYLLS
KNELLS
KNOLLS
LUELLA
NIELLI
NIELLO
ORALLY
OVALLY
PHYLLO
QUELLS
QUILLS
REALLY
SCULLS
SCYLLA
SHELLS
SHELLY
SHILLS
SKILLS
SKULLS
SMALLS
SMELLS
SMELLY
SNELLS
SPALLS
SPELLS
SPILLS
STALLS
STELLA
STELLI
STILLS
STILLY
STULLS
SWELLS
SWILLS
TAILLE
TRILLS
TROLLS
TUILLE
TWILLS
WHOLLY
WOOLLY

•••L•L
FALLAL
HALLEL

••••LL
APPALL
ARGYLL
BEFALL
BEFELL
CAVELL
ENDALL
ENROLL
GESELL
INWALL
JEKYLL
LOVELL
LOWELL
MICELL
NEVILL
NOBALL
ONEILL
ORWELL
POWELL
REBILL
RECALL
REFILL
RESELL
RETELL
SCROLL
SEWALL
SHRILL
SQUALL
SQUILL
STROLL
THRALL
THRILL
UNROLL
UNWELL
UPHILL

L•M•••
LAMBDA
LAMBED
LAMBIE
LAMEDS
LAMELY
LAMENT
LAMEST
LAMIAE
LAMIAS
LAMINA
LAMING
LAMMAS
LAMMED
LAMPAD
LAMPAS
LAMPED
LEMMAS
LEMNOS
LEMONS
LEMUEL
LEMURS
LIMBED
LIMBER
LIMBIC
LIMBUS
LIMENS
LIMEYS
LIMIER
LIMINA
LIMING
LIMITS
LIMNED
LIMNER
LIMPED
LIMPER
LIMPET
LIMPID
LIMPLY
LIMULI
LOMENT
LOMOND
LUMBAR
LUMBER
LUMENS
LUMINA
LUMINI
LUMINO
LUMMOX
LUMPED
LUMPEN
LYMPHO

L••M••
LAMMAS
LAMMED
LAYMAN
LAYMEN
LEGMAN
LEGMEN
LEMMAS
LITMUS
LLAMAS
LOAMED
LOOMED
LUMMOX

L•••M•
LEGUME
LIPOMA

L••••M
LABIUM
LABRUM
LACTAM
LOGJAM
LUTEUM
LYCEUM
LYRISM

•LM•••
ALMAHS
ALMIRA
ALMOND
ALMOST
ALMUCE
ALMUDE
ALMUDS
ELMERS
ELMIRA

•L•M••
ALAMOS
ALUMIN
ALUMNA
ALUMNI
BLAMED
BLAMES
BLIMPS
CLAMMY
CLAMOR
CLAMPS
CLIMAT
CLIMAX
CLIMBS
CLIMES
CLUMPS
CLUMPY
CLUMSY
ELEMIS
FLAMBE
FLAMED
FLAMEN
FLAMES
FLIMSY
FLUMED
FLUMES
FLUMPS
GLUMES
GLUMLY
LLAMAS
PLUMBO
PLUMBS
PLUMED
PLUMES
PLUMMY
PLUMPS
SLIMED

SLIMES
SLIMLY
SLIMSY
SLUMMY
SLUMPS
ULEMAS

•L••M•
ALARMS
ALBUMS
BLOOMS
BLOOMY
CLAIMS
CLAMMY
CLEOME
FLEAMS
GLEAMS
GLEAMY
GLIOMA
GLOOMS
GLOOMY
ILLUME
PLASMA
PLASMO
PLUMMY
SLUMMY
ULTIMA

•L•••M
ALARUM
ALLIUM
ELOHIM
PLENUM
SLALOM

••LM••
CALMED
CALMER
CALMLY
CULMED
DOLMAN
DOLMEN
FILMED
FULMAR
HELMET
HOLMES
HOLMIC
KALMIA
KILMER
PALMAR
PALMED
PALMER
SALMIS
SALMON
TALMUD
WILMAS

••L•M•
AFLAME
APLOMB
COLUMN
ILLUME
SALAMI
SALOME

SOLEMN
VOLUME
XYLEMS

••L••M
ABLOOM
AGLEAM
ALLIUM
BALAAM
BALSAM
BELDAM
CILIUM
FOLIUM
HELIUM
HOLISM
KALIUM
MILIUM
PHLEGM
PHLOEM
PILEUM
SALAAM
SELDOM
TALCUM
VELLUM

•••LM•
HAULMY
PSALMS
QUALMS
QUALMY
REALMS
THELMA
WHELMS

•••L•M
AMYLUM
ASYLUM
BAALIM
BEDLAM
COELOM
EMBLEM
HARLEM
MOSLEM
MUSLIM
PEPLUM
PHYLUM
SLALOM
VELLUM
WHILOM

••••LM
ANSELM
BECALM
COPALM
EMBALM
IMBALM
NAPALM

L•N•••
LANAIS
LANATE
LANCED
LANCER
LANCES
LANCET
LANDAU
LANDED
LANDER
LANGUR
LANKER
LANKLY
LANNER
LANOSE
LANUGO
LENAPE
LENDER
LENGTH
LENITY
LENNYS
LENORE
LENSES
LENTEN
LENTIL
LENTOS
LINAGE
LINDAS
LINDEN
LINEAL
LINEAR
LINENS
LINERS
LINEUP
LINGAS
LINGER
LINGUA
LINIER
LINING
LINKED
LINNET
LINTEL
LINTER
LONDON
LONELY
LONERS
LONGAN
LONGED
LONGER
LUNACY
LUNATE
LUNETS
LUNGED
LUNGEE
LUNGER
LUNGES
LUNGIS
LUNKER
LUNULA
LUNULE
LYNXES

L••N••
LANNER
LAUNCE
LAUNCH
LEANED
LEANER
LEANLY
LEANTO
LEMNOS
LENNYS
LEONAS
LEONIE
LIANAS
LIANES
LIGNIN
LIMNED
LIMNER
LINNET
LIONEL
LLANOS
LOANED
LOUNGE
LUANDA

L•••N•
LACING
LACUNA
LADING
LADINO
LAGUNE
LAKING
LAMENT
LAMINA
LAMING
LAPINS
LARINE
LARYNG
LARYNX
LATENT
LATINS
LAVING
LAWING
LAYING
LAZING
LEARNS
LEARNT
LEGEND
LEMONS
LEVANT
LIERNE
LIGAND
LIKENS
LIKING
LIMENS
LIMINA
LIMING
LINENS
LINING
LITANY
LIVENS
LIVING
LOMENT
LOMOND
LOOING
LOPING
LORENE
LORENZ
LOSING
LOVING
LOWING
LUCENT
LUMENS
LUMINA
LUMINI
LUMINO
LUPINE
LURING
LUTING
LYSINE
LYSING
LYSINS

L••••N
LAGOON
LARDON
LATEEN
LATTEN
LAYMAN
LAYMEN
LEADEN
LEADIN
LEAVEN
LEGION
LEGMAN
LEGMEN
LENTEN
LEPTON
LESION
LESSEN
LESSON
LIBYAN
LICHEN
LIGNIN
LILIAN
LINDEN
LISBON
LISTEN
LOGION
LONDON
LONGAN
LOOKIN
LOOSEN
LORAIN
LOREEN
LOTION
LOUDEN
LOVEIN
LUBLIN
LUCIAN
LUCIEN
LUMPEN

•L•N••
ALINED
ALINES
ALONSO
ALONZO
BLANCH
BLANKS
BLENCH
BLENDE
BLENDS
BLENNY
BLINDS
BLINKS
BLINTZ
BLONDE
BLONDS
BLUNGE
BLUNTS
CLANGS
CLANKS
CLENCH
CLINCH
CLINES
CLINGS
CLINGY
CLINIC
CLINKS
CLINTS
CLONES
CLONIC
CLONUS
ELANDS
ELENAS
FLANGE
FLANKS
FLENCH
FLENSE
FLINCH
FLINGS
FLINTS
FLINTY
FLONGS
FLUNKS
FLUNKY
GLANCE
GLANDS
GLINTS
GLYNIS
LLANOS
PLANAR
PLANCH
PLANCK
PLANED
PLANER
PLANES
PLANET
PLANKS
PLANTS
PLENTY
PLENUM
PLINTH
PLUNGE
PLUNKS
SLANGY
SLANTS
SLINGS
SLINKS
SLINKY
ULENCE

•L••N•
ALBANY
ALBINO
ALDINE
ALFONS
ALIENS
ALIGNS
ALKANE

6

ALKENE
ALKYNE
ALLANS
ALLENS
ALMOND
ALPINE
ALUINO
ALUINS
ALUMNA
ALUMNI
ALVANS
ALVINA
ALVINE
BLAINS
BLENNY
BLUING
CLEANS
CLIENT
CLOWNS
CLUING
ELAINE
ELAYNE
ELFINS
ELLENS
ELOINS
FLAUNT
FLUENT
FLYING
GLEANS
GLUING
PLAINS
PLAINT
PLIANT
PLYING
SLUING

•L•••N

ALBION
ALCUIN
ALEXIN
ALISON
ALUMIN
BLAZON
CLOVEN
ELEVEN
ELEVON
ELOIGN
FLACON
FLAGON
FLAMEN
FLAVIN
FLAXEN
FLORIN
GLOBIN
GLUTEN
KLAXON
OLEFIN
PLATAN
PLATEN
SLIPON
SLOGAN
SLOVEN

••LN••

WALNUT

••L•N•

AALAND
AILING
ALLANS
ALLENS
ARLENE
ARLINE
ASLANT
BALING
BELONG
BYLANE
BYLINE
COLINE
COLINS
COLONS
COLONY
DOLING
EALING
ELLENS
FELINE
FELONS
FELONY
FILING
GALENA
HALING
HELENA
HELENS
HOLING
IDLING
INLAND
ISLAND
ISLING
KALONG
MALINE
MELANO
MELONS
MOLINE
NYLONS
OBLONG
OGLING
OILING
OOLONG
PALING
PILING
POLAND
POLING
PULING
PYLONS
RELENT
RELINE
RILING
ROLAND
RULING
SALINE
SALONS
SELENE
SELENO
SILENI
SILENT
SOLAND
SOLANO
SOLANS
SOLENT
SOLING
SPLENO
SPLINE
SPLINT
TALENT
TALONS
TILING
UPLAND
VOLANT
WALING
WILING
XYLANS
XYLENE

••L••N

AILEEN
ARLEEN
BALEEN
BALKAN
BILLON
BOLEYN
BOLSON
CALVIN
COLUMN
DALTON
DELIAN
DOLMAN
DOLMEN
EILEEN
EOLIAN
FALCON
FALLEN
FILLIN
FULTON
GALLON
GOLDEN
GULDEN
HELLEN
JULIAN
KALIAN
KELVIN
LILIAN
MALIGN
MELLON
MELTON
MELVIN
MILDEN
MILTON
MOLTEN
MULLEN
NELSON
OILCAN
PELION
POLLEN
SALMON
SALOON
SELSYN
SILKEN
SILVAN
SOLEMN
SOLION
SPLEEN
SULLEN
SULTAN
SYLVAN
TALION
TELSON
VILLON
VULCAN
WALKON
WALTON
WELKIN
WILSON

•••L•N

ANILIN
AVALON
BERLIN
BILLON
CAPLIN
CATLIN
CEYLON
CYMLIN
DOBLON
DUBLIN
DUNLIN
EVELYN
FALLEN
FILLIN
GALLON
GOBLIN
HARLAN
HELLEN
INULIN
JOPLIN
KAOLIN
LUBLIN
MARLIN
MELLON
MERLIN
MERLON
MOULIN
MULLEN
MUSLIN
MYELIN
PAULIN
POLLEN
POPLIN
PURLIN
RAGLAN
RATLIN
SIMLIN
STALIN
STOLEN
STOLON
SULLEN
TEFLON
TOULON
VILLON
VIOLIN
WOOLEN

••••LN

WEDELN

LO••••

LOADED
LOADER
LOAFED
LOAFER
LOAMED
LOANED
LOATHE
LOAVES
LOBATE
LOBBED
LOBULE
LOCALE
LOCALS
LOCATE
LOCHIA
LOCKED
LOCKER
LOCKET
LOCKUP
LOCOED
LOCUST
LODGED
LODGER
LODGES
LOFTED
LOFTER
LOGGED
LOGGER
LOGGIA
LOGIER
LOGION
LOGJAM
LOITER
LOLITA
LOLLED
LOLLER
LOMENT
LOMOND
LONDON
LONELY
LONERS
LONGAN
LONGED
LONGER
LOOFAH
LOOING
LOOKED
LOOKER
LOOKIN
LOOMED
LOOPED
LOOPER
LOOSED
LOOSEN
LOOSER
LOOSES
LOOTED
LOOTER
LOPERS
LOPING
LOPPED
LOQUAT
LORAIN
LORDED
LORDLY
LOREEN
LORENE
LORENZ
LORICA
LORIES
LOSERS
LOSING
LOSSES
LOTAHS
LOTION
LOTTIE
LOUDEN
LOUDER
LOUDLY
LOUGHS
LOUISA
LOUISE
LOUNGE
LOUPES
LOURED
LOUSED
LOUSES
LOUVER
LOUVRE
LOVAGE
LOVEIN
LOVELL
LOVELY
LOVERS
LOVING
LOWBOY
LOWELL
LOWERS
LOWERY
LOWEST
LOWING
LOWKEY

L•O•••

LAOTSE
LEONAS
LEONIE
LIONEL
LLOYDS
LOOFAH
LOOING
LOOKED
LOOKER
LOOKIN
LOOMED
LOOPED
LOOPER
LOOSED
LOOSEN
LOOSER
LOOSES
LOOTED
LOOTER

L••O••

LABORS
LABOUR

LADOGA
LAGOON
LAHORE
LANOSE
LAYOFF
LAYOUT
LEMONS
LENORE
LEROYS
LIPOID
LIPOMA
LOCOED
LOMOND

L•••O•
LAGOON
LARDON
LARGOS
LASSOS
LECTOR
LEGION
LEMNOS
LENTOS
LEPTON
LESION
LESSON
LESSOR
LICTOR
LIQUOR
LISBOA
LISBON
LLANOS
LOGION
LONDON
LOTION
LOWBOY
LUMMOX

L••••O
LADINO
LANUGO
LAPARO
LAREDO
LAVABO
LEANTO
LEGATO
LEPIDO
LIBIDO
LUMINO
LYMPHO

•LO•••
ALONSO
ALONZO
BLOATS
BLOCKS
BLOCKY
BLOKES
BLONDE
BLONDS
BLOODS
BLOODY
BLOOMS
BLOOMY
BLOTCH
BLOUSE
BLOWBY
BLOWER
BLOWUP
BLOWZY
CLOACA
CLOAKS
CLOCHE
CLOCKS
CLODDY
CLOGGY
CLONES
CLONIC
CLONUS
CLOSED
CLOSER
CLOSES
CLOSET
CLOTHE
CLOTHO
CLOTHS
CLOTTY
CLOUDS
CLOUDY
CLOUGH
CLOUTS
CLOVEN
CLOVER
CLOVES
CLOVIS
CLOWNS
CLOYED
ELOHIM
ELOIGN
ELOINS
ELOISE
ELOPED
ELOPER
ELOPES
FLOATS
FLOATY
FLOCKS
FLOCKY
FLONGS
FLOODS
FLOORS
FLOOZY
FLOPPY
FLORAE
FLORAL
FLORAS
FLORET
FLORID
FLORIN
FLOSSY
FLOURS
FLOURY
FLOUTS
FLOWED
FLOWER
FLOYDS
GLOATS
GLOBAL
GLOBED
GLOBES
GLOBIN
GLOOMS
GLOOMY
GLORIA
GLOSSO
GLOSSY
GLOSTS
GLOTTO
GLOVED
GLOVER
GLOVES
GLOWED
GLOWER
GLOZED
GLOZES
ILOILO
KLOOFS
LLOYDS
PLOUGH
PLOVER
PLOWED
PLOWER
SLOGAN
SLOOPS
SLOPED
SLOPER
SLOPES
SLOPPY
SLOSHY
SLOTHS
SLOUCH
SLOUGH
SLOVAK
SLOVEN
SLOWED
SLOWER
SLOWLY
ZLOTYS

•L•O••
ALCOTT
ALCOVE
ALDOSE
ALDOUS
ALFONS
ALGOID
ALLOTS
ALLOUT
ALLOWS
ALLOYS
ALMOND
ALMOST
BLOODS
BLOODY
BLOOMS
BLOOMY
CLEOME
ELBOWS
ELIOTS
FLOODS
FLOORS
FLOOZY
FLUORO
FLUORS
GLIOMA
GLOOMS
GLOOMY
KLOOFS
SLOOPS

•L••O•
ALAMOS
ALBION
ALISON
BLAZON
CLAMOR
CLAROS
ELEVON
ELLIOT
FLACON
FLAGON
FLAVOR
FLEXOR
GLYCOL
KLAXON
LLANOS
PLEXOR
SLALOM
SLIPON

•L•••O
ALBEDO
ALBINO
ALECTO
ALEPPO
ALONSO
ALONZO
ALUINO
BLASTO
CLOTHO
FLUORO
FLUVIO
GLAUCO
GLOSSO
GLOTTO
GLYPTO
ILOILO
PLAGIO
PLASMO
PLEURO
PLUMBO
PLUVIO

••LO••
ABLOOM
AFLOAT
ALLOTS
ALLOUT
ALLOWS
ALLOYS
APLOMB
ASLOPE
BELOIT
BELONG
BILOXI
CALORY
CHLOES
CHLORO
COLONS
COLONY
COLORS
COLOUS
EULOGY
FELONS
FELONY
FILOSE
GALOOT
GALOPS
GALORE
GALOSH
HALOES
HALOID
HELOTS
IGLOOS
JALOPY
KALONG
KELOID
MALORY
MELODY
MELONS
MILORD
MOLOCH
NYLONS
OBLONG
OCLOCK
OOLOGY
OOLONG
ORLOPS
PELOPS
PELOTA
PHLOEM
PILOSE
PILOTS
PILOUS
PYLONS
RELOAD
SALOME
SALONS
SALOON
SALOOP
SILOED
SOLOED
TALONS
UNLOAD
UNLOCK
VALOIS
VELOCE
VELOUR
VOLOST
XYLOID
XYLOLS
XYLOSE

••L•O•
ABLOOM
BALBOA
BALLOT
BELLOC
BELLOW
BILLON
BILLOW
BOLSON
CALLOW
CELLOS
COLLOP
DALTON
DOLLOP
ELLIOT
FALCON
FALLOW
FELLOE
FELLOW
FOLIOS
FOLLOW
FULTON
FYLFOT
GALIOT
GALLON
GALLOP
GALOOT
HALLOO
HALLOW
HELIOS
HOLLOW
IGLOOS
MALLOW
MELLON
MELLOW
MELTON
MILTON
NELSON
PALLOR
PELION
PILLOW
SALLOW
SALMON
SALOON
SALOOP
SALVOR
SALVOS
SELDOM
SOLION
TALION
TALLOW
TELSON
TOLUOL
VILLON
VOLVOX
WALDOS
WALKON
WALLOP
WALLOW
WALTON
WILLOW
WILSON
YELLOW

••L••O
AFLCIO
BILBAO
BOLERO
CALICO
CALLAO
CHLORO

6

COLUGO
HALLOO
HELICO
MALACO
MELANO
PALAEO
PHLEBO
SCLERO
SELENO
SILICO
SOLANO
SPLENO
SULPHO
TOLEDO

•••LO•

ANALOG
APOLOG
AVALON
BAILOR
BALLOT
BELLOC
BELLOW
BILLON
BILLOW
BRULOT
BYBLOW
CALLOW
CARLOS
CELLOS
CEYLON
COELOM
COLLOP
DEPLOY
DIALOG
DIGLOT
DIPLOE
DOBLON
DOLLOP
DUOLOG
EMPLOY
EPILOG
FALLOW
FELLOE
FELLOW
FOLLOW
GALLON
GALLOP
GIGLOT
HALLOO
HALLOW
HARLOT
HOLLOW
INFLOW
JAILOR
MALLOW
MELLON
MELLOW
MERLON
MIKLOS
OCELOT
PALLOR
PARLOR
PAVLOV
PEPLOS
PHILOS
PILLOW
PUTLOG
SAILOR
SALLOW
SHILOH
SLALOM
STOLON
TAILOR
TALLOW
TAYLOR
TEFLON
TOULON
VILLON
WALLOP
WALLOW
WHILOM
WILLOW
YELLOW
ZEALOT

•••L•O

APOLLO
BIBLIO
CALLAO
CHALCO
DUELLO
EMILIO
GIULIO
HALLOO
NIELLO
PHYLLO
RIALTO
SMALTO

••••LO

ANGELO
ANKYLO
APOLLO
CATALO
CHEILO
DUELLO
GIGOLO
ILOILO
MEGALO
NIELLO
PHYLLO
POMELO
PUEBLO
ROBALO
ROMULO
TAPALO
TUPELO
TYPHLO

L•P•••

LAPARO
LAPELS
LAPFUL
LAPINS
LAPPED
LAPPER
LAPPET
LAPSED
LAPSER
LAPSES
LAPSUS
LEPERS
LEPIDO
LEPSIA
LEPTON
LIPASE
LIPIDS
LIPOID
LIPOMA
LIPPED
LIPPER
LOPERS
LOPING
LOPPED
LUPINE

L••P••

LAMPAD
LAMPAS
LAMPED
LAPPED
LAPPER
LAPPET
LEAPED
LEAPER
LIMPED
LIMPER
LIMPET
LIMPID
LIMPLY
LIPPED
LIPPER
LISPED
LISPER
LOOPED
LOOPER
LOPPED
LOUPES
LUMPED
LUMPEN
LYMPHO

L•••P•

LENAPE
LETUPS

L••••P

LARRUP
LINEUP
LOCKUP

•LP•••

ALPACA
ALPHAS
ALPHYL
ALPINE

•L•P••

ALEPHS
ALEPPO
ALIPED
CLYPEI
ELAPSE
ELOPED
ELOPER
ELOPES
FLOPPY
GLYPHS
GLYPTO
SLIPON
SLIPUP
SLOPED
SLOPER
SLOPES
SLOPPY

•L••P•

ALEPPO
BLIMPS
CLAMPS
CLASPS
CLUMPS
CLUMPY
FLOPPY
FLUMPS
PLUMPS
SLEEPS
SLEEPY
SLOOPS
SLOPPY
SLUMPS
SLURPS

•L•••P

BLOWUP
SLIPUP

••LP••

CALPAC
DELPHI
DOLPHS
GULPED
GULPER
HELPED
HELPER
KALPAK
PALPUS
PULPED
PULPIT
RALPHS
ROLPHS
SALPAS
SALPID
SULPHA
SULPHO
SYLPHS
SYLPHY
YELPED
YELPER

••L•P•

ASLOPE
CALIPH
FELIPE
GALOPS
JALAPS
JALOPY
JULEPS
ORLOPS
OXLIPS
PELOPS
POLYPS
TULIPS
YCLEPT

••L••P

ASLEEP
COLLOP
DOLLOP
FILLIP
GALLOP
GALLUP
HOLDUP
SALOOP
WALKUP
WALLOP

•••LP•

ADOLPH
SCALPS
SCULPT
WHELPS

•••L•P

BURLAP
COLLOP
DEWLAP
DOLLOP
EARLAP
FILLIP
GALLOP
GALLUP
PHILIP
WALLOP

••••LP

MEGILP

L•Q•••

LIQUID
LIQUOR
LOQUAT

•L•Q••

CLAQUE
CLIQUE
CLIQUY
PLAQUE

••LQ••

PULQUE

L•R•••

LARDED
LARDER
LARDON
LAREDO
LARGER
LARGOS
LARIAT
LARINE
LARKED
LARKER
LARRUP
LARRYS
LARVAE
LARVAL
LARYNG
LARYNX
LEROYS
LORAIN
LORDED
LORDLY
LOREEN
LORENE
LORENZ
LORICA
LORIES
LURERS
LURING
LURKED
LYRICS
LYRISM
LYRIST

L••R••

LABRET
LABRUM
LAIRDS
LAIRED
LARRUP
LARRYS
LATRIA
LAURAE
LAURAS
LAUREL
LAURIE
LEARNS
LEARNT
LEERED
LEGREE
LIBRAE
LIBRAS
LIERNE
LIVRES
LOURED

L•••R•

LABORS
LAGERS
LAHORE
LAKERS
LAPARO
LASERS
LAVERS
LAYERS
LAZARS
LEGERS
LEMURS
LENORE
LEPERS
LEVERS
LIFERS

LIGURE
LINERS
LITERS
LIVERS
LIVERY
LIZARD
LONERS
LOPERS
LOSERS
LOUVRE
LOVERS
LOWERS
LOWERY
LUGERS
LURERS
LUXURY

L••••R

LAAGER
LABOUR
LACIER
LADDER
LADLER
LAGGER
LAKIER
LANCER
LANDER
LANGUR
LANKER
LANNER
LAPPER
LAPSER
LARDER
LARGER
LARKER
LASCAR
LASHER
LASTER
LATHER
LATTER
LAUDER
LAWYER
LAZIER
LEADER
LEANER
LEAPER
LEAVER
LECHER
LECTOR
LEDGER
LENDER
LESSER
LESSOR
LESTER
LETTER
LEVIER
LEWDER
LICTOR
LIEDER
LIFTER
LIMBER
LIMIER
LIMNER
LIMPER
LINEAR
LINGER
LINIER
LINTER
LIPPER
LIQUOR
LISPER
LISTER
LITHER
LITTER
LIVIER
LIVYER
LOADER
LOAFER
LOCKER
LODGER
LOFTER
LOGGER
LOGIER
LOITER
LOLLER
LONGER
LOOKER
LOOPER
LOOSER
LOOTER
LOUDER
LOUVER
LUBBER
LUGGER
LUMBAR
LUMBER
LUNGER
LUNKER
LUSHER
LUSTER
LUTHER

•L•R••

ALARIC
ALARMS
ALARUM
ALERTS
ALFRED
BLARED
BLARES
BLURBS
BLURRY
BLURTS
CLARAS
CLARES
CLARET
CLAROS
CLERGY
CLERIC
CLERID
CLERKS
ELBRUS
ELDRED
FLARED
FLARES
FLIRTS
FLIRTY
FLORAE
FLORAL
FLORAS
FLORET
FLORID
FLORIN
FLURRY
GLARED
GLARES
GLORIA
PLURAL
SLURPS
SLURRY

•L••R•

ALBERT
ALDERS
ALLURE
ALMIRA
ALTARS
ALTERS
BLEARS
BLEARY
BLURRY
CLAIRE
CLEARS
ELBERT
ELDERS
ELMERS
ELMIRA
ELVERS
ELVIRA
ELYTRA
FLAIRS
FLEERS
FLEURY
FLIERS
FLOORS
FLOURS
FLOURY
FLUORO
FLUORS
FLURRY
FLYERS
GLAIRS
GLAIRY
PLEURA
PLEURO
PLIERS
SLURRY
ULCERS

•L•••R

ALEGAR
ALTAIR
ALULAR
BLAZER
BLOWER
CLAMOR
CLEVER
CLOSER
CLOVER
ELATER
ELECTR
ELIXIR
ELOPER
FLAKER
FLAVOR
FLAYER
FLEXOR
FLOWER
FLUTER
GLAZER
GLIDER
GLOVER
GLOWER
GLUIER
OLIVER
PLACER
PLANAR
PLANER
PLATER
PLAYER
PLEXOR
PLOVER
PLOWER
SLATER
SLAVER
SLAYER
SLICER
SLIDER
SLIVER
SLOPER
SLOWER
ULSTER

••LR••

WALRUS

••L•R•

ALLURE
BALERS
BELFRY
BOLERO
CALORY
CELERY
CHLORO
COLORS
COLURE
FILERS
FULCRA
GALORE
HALERS
HILARY
HOLARD
IDLERS
MALGRE
MALORY
MILERS
MILORD
MOLARS
OGLERS
OILERS
PALTRY
PELTRY
PULERS
RULERS
SALARY
SCLERA
SCLERO
SULTRY
TALERS
TILERS
VALERY
VELURE
VOLERY
WALERS

••L••R

BALDER
BELIER
BILKER
BOLDER
BOLTER
BULBAR
BULGAR
BULGER
CALCAR
CALKER
CALLER
CALMER
CELLAR
COLDER
COLLAR
COLTER
CULLER
CULVER
DELVER
DOLLAR
DULLER
ECLAIR
FALLER
FALSER
FALTER
FELLER
FILLER
FILTER
FOLDER
FOLIAR
FULLER
FULMAR
GILDER
GOLFER
GULPER
HALTER
HELLER
HELPER
HILLER
HOLDER
HOLIER
HOLLER
INLIER
JILTER
JOLTER
KELLER
KILLER
KILMER
KILTER
KULTUR
LOLLER
MELTER
MILDER
MILKER
MILLER
MILTER
MOLDER
MOLTER
MULLER
OILIER
PALLOR
PALMAR
PALMER
PALTER
PELTER
PILFER
PILLAR
POLDER
POLLER
PULLER
PULSAR
RELIER
ROLLER
SALTER
SALVER
SALVOR
SELLER
SILVER
SOLDER
SOLVER
SULFUR
TALKER
TALLER
TELLER
TILLER
TILTER
TOLLER
UGLIER
VALKYR
VALVAR
VELOUR
VULGAR
VULVAR
WALKER
WALTER
WELDER
WELTER
WILBER
WILBUR
WILDER
WILIER
WILLER
WOLVER
YELLER
YELPER

•••L•R

ALULAR
AMBLER
ANGLER
ANTLER
ASHLAR
BAILER
BAILOR
BAWLER
BOILER
BOWLER
BUGLER

6

BURLER
BUTLER
CALLER
CELLAR
CHOLER
COALER
COILER
COLLAR
COOLER
CULLER
CURLER
CUTLER
CYCLER
DEALER
DIALER
DOLLAR
DUELER
DULLER
FABLER
FALLER
FEELER
FELLER
FILLER
FOULER
FOWLER
FUELER
FULLER
GAOLER
HAILER
HAULER
HEALER
HEELER
HELLER
HILLER
HITLER
HOLLER
HOWLER
HURLER
JAILER
JAILOR
KEGLER
KELLER
KEPLER
KILLER
LADLER
LOLLER
MAHLER
MAILER
MAULER
MEDLAR
MILLER
MOILER
MULLER
OCULAR
OVULAR
PALLOR
PARLOR
PEELER
PILLAR
POLLER
POPLAR
PULLER
REELER
RIFLER
ROLLER
SAILER
SAILOR
SCALAR
SCALER
SEALER
SELLER
SIDLER
SMILER
STALER
STELAR
STYLAR
STYLER
SUTLER
TAILOR
TALLER
TATLER
TAYLOR
TELLER
TILLER
TOILER
TOLLER
TOOLER
UVULAR
VEILER
WAILER
WHALER
WILLER
YELLER

L•S•••

LASCAR
LASERS
LASHED
LASHER
LASHES
LASSES
LASSIE
LASSOS
LASTED
LASTER
LASTEX
LASTLY
LESION
LESLEY
LESLIE
LESSEE
LESSEN
LESSER
LESSON
LESSOR
LESTER
LISBOA
LISBON
LISPED
LISPER
LISTED
LISTEL
LISTEN
LISTER
LOSERS
LOSING
LOSSES
LUSHED
LUSHER
LUSHES
LUSTED
LUSTER
LYSINE
LYSING
LYSINS

L••S••

LAPSED
LAPSER
LAPSES
LAPSUS
LASSES
LASSIE
LASSOS
LEASED
LEASES
LENSES
LEPSIA
LESSEE
LESSEN
LESSER
LESSON
LESSOR
LOOSED
LOOSEN
LOOSER
LOOSES
LOSSES
LOUSED
LOUSES

L•••S•

LAMEST
LANOSE
LAOTSE
LATEST
LATISH
LAVISH
LAXEST
LEGIST
LIPASE
LOCUST
LOUISA
LOUISE
LOWEST
LUTIST
LYRISM
LYRIST

L••••S

LABELS
LABORS
LACHES
LADIES
LADLES
LAGERS
LAIRDS
LAKERS
LAMEDS
LAMIAS
LAMMAS
LAMPAS
LANAIS
LANCES
LAPELS
LAPINS
LAPSES
LAPSUS
LARGOS
LARRYS
LASERS
LASHES
LASSES
LASSOS
LATHES
LATINS
LAUGHS
LAURAS
LAVERS
LAYERS
LAZARS
LEARNS
LEASES
LEAVES
LEDGES
LEGERS
LEHUAS
LEIGHS
LEMMAS
LEMNOS
LEMONS
LEMURS
LENNYS
LENSES
LENTOS
LEONAS
LEPERS
LEROYS
LETUPS
LEUDES
LEVEES
LEVELS
LEVERS
LEVIES
LIANAS
LIANES
LIBBYS
LIBELS
LIBRAS
LIEGES
LIFERS
LIGHTS
LIKENS
LILACS
LILIES
LIMBUS
LIMENS
LIMEYS
LIMITS
LINDAS
LINENS
LINERS
LINGAS
LIPIDS
LITERS
LITMUS
LIVENS
LIVERS
LIVIAS
LIVRES
LIZZYS
LLAMAS
LLANOS
LLOYDS
LOAVES
LOCALS
LODGES
LONERS
LOOSES
LOPERS
LORIES
LOSERS
LOSSES
LOTAHS
LOUGHS
LOUPES
LOUSES
LOVERS
LOWERS
LUCIAS
LUCIUS
LUGERS
LUMENS
LUNETS
LUNGES
LUNGIS
LURERS
LUSHES
LYCEES
LYDIAS
LYNXES
LYRICS
LYSINS

•LS•••

ALSACE
ALSIKE
ELSIES
ULSTER

•L•S••

ALASKA
ALISON
BLASTO
BLASTS
CLASPS
CLASSY
CLOSED
CLOSER
CLOSES
CLOSET
ELISHA
ELYSEE
FLASHY
FLASKS
FLESHY
FLOSSY
GLASSY
GLOSSO
GLOSSY
GLOSTS
PLASHY
PLASIA
PLASIS
PLASMA
PLASMO
PLASTY
PLUSES
PLUSHY
SLOSHY
SLUSHY

•L••S•

ALDOSE
ALMOST
ALONSO
BLOUSE
BLUEST
BLUISH
CLASSY
CLAUSE
CLEIST
CLUMSY
ELAPSE
ELDEST
ELFISH
ELOISE
ELVISH
FLENSE
FLIEST
FLIMSY
FLOSSY
GLASSY
GLOSSO
GLOSSY
ILLUSE
ILLUST
OLDEST
OLDISH
PLEASE
SLIEST
SLIMSY
SLYEST

•L•••S

ALAMOS
ALARMS
ALBUMS
ALDERS
ALDOUS
ALEPHS
ALERTS
ALEUTS
ALEXIS
ALFONS
ALIBIS
ALICES
ALIENS
ALIGNS
ALINES
ALKYLS
ALLANS
ALLAYS
ALLENS

6

ALLEYS
ALLIES
ALLOTS
ALLOWS
ALLOYS
ALLYLS
ALMAHS
ALMUDS
ALPHAS
ALTARS
ALTERS
ALUINS
ALVANS
ALWAYS
BLACKS
BLADES
BLAINS
BLAMES
BLANKS
BLARES
BLASTS
BLAZES
BLEAKS
BLEARS
BLEATS
BLEEDS
BLENDS
BLIMPS
BLINDS
BLINKS
BLOATS
BLOCKS
BLOKES
BLONDS
BLOODS
BLOOMS
BLUETS
BLUFFS
BLUNTS
BLURBS
BLURTS
CLACKS
CLAIMS
CLAMPS
CLANGS
CLANKS
CLARAS
CLARES
CLAROS
CLASPS
CLEANS
CLEARS
CLEATS
CLEFTS
CLERKS
CLEVIS
CLICKS
CLIFFS
CLIMBS
CLIMES
CLINES
CLINGS
CLINKS
CLINTS

CLIVES
CLOAKS
CLOCKS
CLONES
CLONUS
CLOSES
CLOTHS
CLOUDS
CLOUTS
CLOVES
CLOVIS
CLOWNS
CLUCKS
CLUMPS
CLYDES
ELANDS
ELATES
ELBOWS
ELBRUS
ELDERS
ELECTS
ELEMIS
ELENAS
ELFINS
ELIDES
ELIOTS
ELIZAS
ELLENS
ELLIES
ELMERS
ELOINS
ELOPES
ELSIES
ELUDES
ELVERS
FLACKS
FLAILS
FLAIRS
FLAKES
FLAMES
FLANKS
FLARES
FLASKS
FLATUS
FLAXES
FLEAMS
FLECKS
FLEERS
FLEETS
FLEXES
FLICKS
FLIERS
FLINGS
FLINTS
FLIRTS
FLOATS
FLOCKS
FLONGS
FLOODS
FLOORS
FLORAS
FLOURS
FLOUTS
FLOYDS

FLUFFS
FLUIDS
FLUKES
FLUMES
FLUMPS
FLUNKS
FLUORS
FLUTES
FLUXES
FLYBYS
FLYERS
GLACES
GLACIS
GLADES
GLADYS
GLAIRS
GLANDS
GLARES
GLAZES
GLEAMS
GLEANS
GLEBES
GLEDES
GLEETS
GLIDES
GLINTS
GLOATS
GLOBES
GLOOMS
GLOSTS
GLOVES
GLOZES
GLUMES
GLYNIS
GLYPHS
ILEXES
KLOOFS
LLAMAS
LLANOS
LLOYDS
OLIVES
OLLIES
PLACES
PLACKS
PLAIDS
PLAINS
PLAITS
PLANES
PLANKS
PLANTS
PLASIS
PLATES
PLAYAS
PLAZAS
PLEADS
PLEATS
PLEBES
PLEXUS
PLIERS
PLUCKS
PLUMBS
PLUMES
PLUMPS
PLUNKS

PLUSES
PLUTUS
SLACKS
SLAKES
SLANTS
SLATES
SLAVES
SLEEKS
SLEEPS
SLEETS
SLICES
SLICKS
SLIDES
SLIMES
SLINGS
SLINKS
SLOOPS
SLOPES
SLOTHS
SLUMPS
SLURPS
ULCERS
ULEMAS
ZLOTYS

••LS••

BALSAM
BALSAS
BOLSON
FALSER
HALSEY
NELSON
PULSAR
PULSED
PULSES
SELSYN
TELSON
WILSON
WOLSEY

••L•S•

ABLEST
ABLUSH
AWLESS
CALASH
CALESA
ENLIST
FILOSE
FOLKSY
GALOSH
HOLISM
IDLEST
ILLUSE
ILLUST
MOLEST
MULISH
OBLAST
OWLISH
PALEST
PALISH
PILOSE
POLISH
RELISH
SALISH

SPLASH
UNLESS
VALISE
VILEST
VOLOST
XYLOSE

••L••S

AALIIS
ADLIBS
AGLETS
ALLANS
ALLAYS
ALLENS
ALLEYS
ALLIES
ALLOTS
ALLOWS
ALLOYS
ALLYLS
AWLESS
BALERS
BALSAS
BELAYS
BELGAS
BELIES
BELLAS
BELLES
BILGES
BILLYS
BULGES
BYLAWS
CALAIS
CALCES
CALEBS
CALIFS
CALLAS
CALLUS
CALVES
CALXES
CELIAS
CELLOS
CHLOES
COLEUS
COLIES
COLINS
COLONS
COLORS
COLOUS
COLZAS
CULETS
CULLIS
CULTUS
DALLAS
DALLES
DELAYS
DELIAS
DELIUS
DELLAS
DELTAS
DELVES
DOLLYS
DOLPHS
ELLENS

ELLIES
FELIDS
FELONS
FILERS
FILETS
FOLIOS
GALLUS
GALOPS
GILDAS
HALERS
HALIDS
HALOES
HALVES
HELENS
HELIOS
HELLAS
HELOTS
HELVES
HILDAS
HOLIES
HOLLYS
HOLMES
IDLERS
IGLOOS
INLAWS
INLAYS
INLETS
IOLCUS
ISLETS
JALAPS
JULEPS
JULIAS
JULIES
JULIUS
KULAKS
LILACS
LILIES
MALAYS
MELEES
MELONS
MILERS
MILLYS
MOLARS
MOLIES
MOLLYS
MULCTS
NELLYS
NYLONS
OGLERS
OILERS
OLLIES
ORLOPS
OWLETS
OXLIPS
PALLAS
PALPUS
PELEUS
PELIAS
PELOPS
PELVES
PELVIS
PILAFS
PILEUS
PILOTS

PILOUS
POLKAS
POLLYS
POLYPS
PULERS
PULSES
PYLONS
RALPHS
RELAYS
RELICS
RELIES
ROLPHS
RULERS
SALADS
SALLYS
SALMIS
SALONS
SALPAS
SALVES
SALVOS
SELVES
SILVAS
SOLANS
SOLIDS
SOLVES
SPLATS
SPLAYS
SPLITS
SULCUS
SYLPHS
SYLVAS
TALERS
TALONS
TELLUS
TILDES
TILERS
TILLYS
TILTHS
TULIPS
TULLES
UNLAYS
UNLESS
VALETS
VALGUS
VALOIS
VALUES
VALVES
VELDTS
VILLAS
VILLUS
VOLVAS
WALDOS
WALERS
WALLAS
WALLIS
WALLYS
WALRUS
WALVIS
WILLIS
WILLYS
WILMAS
WOLVES
XYLANS
XYLEMS
XYLOLS

•••LS•

GRILSE
WHILST

•••L•S

ABELES
ADDLES
ADULTS
AEOLIS
AEOLUS
AISLES
AMBLES
AMOLES
ANGLES
ANKLES
APPLES
ATOLLS
AZOLES
BELLAS
BELLES
BEULAS
BIALYS
BIBLES
BILLYS
BIRLES
BOGLES
BOULES
BRILLS
BUGLES
BUILDS
CABLES
CALLAS
CALLUS
CARLAS
CARLOS
CAULES
CAULIS
CAULKS
CELLOS
CHALKS
CHELAS
CHILLS
COBLES
CULLIS
CUTLAS
CYCLES
DALLAS
DALLES
DELLAS
DHOLES
DOALLS
DOBLAS
DOLLYS
DRILLS
DROLLS
DWELLS
EAGLES
EARLES
ECCLES
ECOLES
EDILES
EMILES
EMILYS
EXALTS
EXILES
EXULTS
FABLES
FARLES
FAULTS
FIELDS
FJELDS
FRILLS
FUGLES
GABLES
GALLUS
GRILLS
GUILDS
GUILES
GUILTS
HELLAS
HOLLYS
IDYLLS
INKLES
JOULES
KNELLS
KNOLLS
KOALAS
LADLES
MACLES
MAPLES
MERLES
MIKLOS
MILLYS
MOLLYS
MOULDS
MOULTS
NAPLES
NELLYS
OBELUS
OBOLUS
OODLES
OVULES
OXALIS
PALLAS
PAULAS
PAULUS
PEPLOS
PEPLUS
PHILOS
POILUS
POLLYS
POULTS
PSALMS
QUALMS
QUELLS
QUILLS
QUILTS
REALES
REALMS
RIFLES
ROALDS
ROBLES
RUBLES
SABLES
SALLYS
SAULTS
SCALDS
SCALES
SCALPS
SCOLDS
SCULLS
SHALES
SHELLS
SHILLS
SIDLES
SKALDS
SKILLS
SKULKS
SKULLS
SMALLS
SMELLS
SMELTS
SMILES
SMOLTS
SNELLS
SOCLES
SPALLS
SPELLS
SPILES
SPILLS
STALES
STALKS
STALLS
STELES
STILES
STILLS
STILTS
STOLES
STULLS
STYLES
STYLUS
SWALES
SWELLS
SWILLS
TABLES
TELLUS
THALES
THOLES
TILLYS
TITLES
TOILES
TRILLS
TROLLS
TULLES
TWILLS
UBOLTS
UMBLES
UNCLES
UVULAS
VAULTS
VILLAS
VILLUS
VIOLAS
VOILES
WALLAS
WALLIS
WALLYS
WEALDS
WHALES
WHELKS
WHELMS
WHELPS
WHILES
WIELDS
WILLIS
WILLYS
WOALDS
WORLDS
YIELDS

••••LS

ALKYLS
ALLYLS
AMPULS
ANGELS
ANNALS
ANNULS
ANVILS
APPALS
APPELS
APRILS
ARGALS
ARIELS
ARTELS
ATOLLS
AVAILS
BABULS
BAGELS
BASILS
BERYLS
BETELS
BEVELS
BEZELS
BIKOLS
BOWELS
BRAILS
BRAWLS
BRILLS
BROILS
BUBALS
CABALS
CAMELS
CANALS
CAROLS
CASALS
CAVILS
CECILS
CEORLS
CHILLS
CHURLS
CIBOLS
CORALS
CRAALS
CRAWLS
CREELS
CUPELS
CYRILS
DECALS
DEVILS
DOALLS
DOWELS
DRAWLS
DRILLS
DROLLS
DROOLS
DWELLS
EASELS
ENGELS
EQUALS
ETHELS
ETHYLS
EXCELS
EXPELS
EXTOLS
FINALS
FLAILS
FRAILS
FRILLS
FUSILS
FUZILS
GAVELS
GHOULS
GIMELS
GNARLS
GORALS
GRILLS
GROWLS
GRUELS
HAMALS
HAZELS
HEXYLS
HOTELS
HOVELS
IDEALS
IDYLLS
IMPELS
JEWELS
JURELS
KEVELS
KNEELS
KNELLS
KNOLLS
KNURLS
KRAALS
LABELS
LAPELS
LEVELS
LIBELS
LOCALS
MABELS
MEDALS
METALS
MIAULS
MODELS
MOGULS
MORALS
MORELS
MOTELS
MURALS
NASALS
NAVELS
NEWELS
NIGELS
NOPALS
NOVELS
ORIELS
OUSELS
OUZELS

PANELS
PEARLS
PEDALS
PERILS
PETALS
PHIALS
PICULS
PROWLS
PUPILS
QUAILS
QUELLS
QUILLS
RAOULS
RATALS
RATELS
RAVELS
REBELS
REPELS
REVELS
RIVALS
RIYALS
ROWELS
ROYALS
SCOWLS
SCULLS
SEPALS
SHAWLS
SHELLS
SHILLS
SHOALS
SHORLS
SIBYLS
SIGILS
SKILLS
SKULLS
SMALLS
SMELLS
SNAILS
SNARLS
SNELLS
SORELS
SOTOLS
SPALLS
SPELLS
SPIELS
SPILLS
SPOILS
SPOOLS
STALLS
STEALS
STEELS
STILLS
STOOLS
STULLS
SWAILS
SWELLS
SWILLS
SWIRLS
SYBILS
THIOLS
TICALS
TOTALS
TOWELS
TRAILS
TRAWLS
TRIALS
TRILLS
TROLLS
TWILLS
TWIRLS
UMBELS
VEXILS
VIGILS
VINYLS
VITALS
VOCALS
VOGULS
VOWELS
WHEALS
WHEELS
WHIRLS
WHORLS
XYLOLS
YODELS
YOKELS
ZORILS

L•T•••

LATEEN
LATELY
LATENT
LATEST
LATHED
LATHER
LATHES
LATINS
LATISH
LATRIA
LATTEN
LATTER
LATVIA
LETHAL
LETTER
LETUPS
LITANY
LITERS
LITHER
LITHIA
LITHIC
LITMUS
LITTER
LITTLE
LOTAHS
LOTION
LOTTIE
LUTEAL
LUTEUM
LUTHER
LUTING
LUTIST
LYTTAE

L••T••

LACTAM
LACTIC
LAOTSE
LASTED
LASTER
LASTEX
LASTLY
LATTEN
LATTER
LECTOR
LENTEN
LENTIL
LENTOS
LEPTON
LESTER
LETTER
LICTOR
LIFTED
LIFTER
LILTED
LINTEL
LINTER
LISTED
LISTEL
LISTEN
LISTER
LITTER
LITTLE
LOATHE
LOFTED
LOFTER
LOITER
LOOTED
LOOTER
LOTTIE
LUETIC
LUSTED
LUSTER
LYTTAE

L•••T•

LANATE
LAXITY
LEANTO
LEGATE
LEGATO
LENGTH
LENITY
LEVITE
LEVITY
LIGATE
LIGHTS
LIMITS
LOBATE
LOCATE
LOLITA
LUCITE
LUNATE
LUNETS
LUXATE

L••••T

LABRET
LAMENT
LAMEST
LANCET
LAPPET
LARIAT
LATENT
LATEST
LAXEST
LAYOUT
LEARNT
LEGIST
LEVANT
LIMPET
LINNET
LOCKET
LOCUST
LOMENT
LOQUAT
LOWEST
LUCENT
LUTIST
LYRIST

•LT•••

ALTAIC
ALTAIR
ALTARS
ALTERS
ALTHEA
ULTIMA

•L•T••

ALATED
BLITHE
BLOTCH
CLOTHE
CLOTHO
CLOTHS
CLOTTY
CLUTCH
ELATED
ELATER
ELATES
ELYTRA
FLATLY
FLATUS
FLETCH
FLITCH
FLUTED
FLUTER
FLUTES
GLOTTO
GLUTEI
GLUTEN
PLATAN
PLATED
PLATEN
PLATER
PLATES
PLATTE
PLUTUS
SLATED
SLATER
SLATES
SLOTHS
ULSTER
ZLOTYS

•L••T•

ALBATA
ALBITE
ALCOTT
ALECTO
ALERTS
ALEUTS
ALLOTS
BLASTO
BLASTS
BLEATS
BLINTZ
BLOATS
BLUETS
BLUNTS
BLURTS
CLEATS
CLEFTS
CLINTS
CLOTTY
CLOUTS
ELECTR
ELECTS
ELIOTS
FLEETS
FLINTS
FLINTY
FLIRTS
FLIRTY
FLOATS
FLOATY
FLOUTS
GLEETS
GLEETY
GLINTS
GLOATS
GLOSTS
GLOTTO
GLYPTO
OLEATE
PLAITS
PLANTS
PLASTY
PLATTE
PLEATS
PLENTY
PLINTH
SLANTS
SLEETS
SLEETY
SLEUTH

•L•••T

ALBEIT
ALBERT
ALCOTT
ALIGHT
ALLOUT
ALMOST
BLIGHT
BLUEST
CLARET
CLEIST
CLIENT
CLIMAT
CLOSET
ELBERT
ELDEST
ELEGIT
ELICIT
ELLIOT
FLAUNT
FLIEST
FLIGHT
FLORET
FLUENT
ILLUST
OLDEST
PLACET
PLAINT
PLANET
PLIANT
PLIGHT
SLIEST
SLIGHT
SLYEST

••LT••

BALTIC
BELTED
BOLTED
BOLTER
CELTIC
COLTER
CULTCH
CULTUS
DALTON
DELTAS
FALTER
FILTER
FILTHY
FULTON
HALTED
HALTER
HILTED
JILTED
JILTER
JOLTED
JOLTER
KILTED
KILTER
KILTIE
KULTUR
LILTED
MALTED
MALTHA
MELTED
MELTER
MELTON
MILTED
MILTER
MILTON
MOLTED
MOLTEN
MOLTER
MOLTKE
PALTER
PALTRY
PELTED
PELTER

PELTRY
SALTED
SALTER
SILTED
SULTAN
SULTRY
TILTED
TILTER
TILTHS
TOLTEC
WALTER
WALTON
WELTED
WELTER
WILTED

••L•T•

AGLETS
ALLOTS
APLITE
BALATA
BILITY
CULETS
DALETH
DELETE
DILATE
DILUTE
DULUTH
EOLITH
FILETS
HALITE
HALUTZ
HELOTS
INLETS
IOLITE
ISLETS
LOLITA
MALATE
MULCTS
OBLATE
OOLITE
OWLETS
PALATE
PELITE
PELOTA
PILATE
PILOTS
POLITE
POLITY
RELATE
SALUTE
SOLUTE
SPLATS
SPLITS
VALETS
VELATE
VELDTS
VOLUTE

••L••T

ABLAUT
ABLEST
AFLOAT
ALLOUT
ASLANT
BALLET
BALLOT
BELOIT
BILLET
BULLET
CILIAT
COLLET
CULLET
DELICT
DULCET
ELLIOT
ENLIST
FILLET
FYLFOT
GALACT
GALIOT
GALOOT
GULLET
HELMET
IDLEST
ILLUST
JOLIET
JULIET
MALLET
MILLET
MOLEST
MULLET
OBLAST
PALEST
PALLET
PELLET
PULLET
PULPIT
RELENT
RELICT
RILLET
SALLET
SELECT
SILENT
SOLENT
SPLINT
TALENT
UMLAUT
UPLIFT
VELVET
VILEST
VOLANT
VOLOST
WALLET
WALNUT
WILLET
YCLEPT

•••LT•

ADULTS
EXALTS
EXULTS
FAULTS
FAULTY
FEALTY
GUILTS
GUILTY
HEALTH
MOULTS
POULTS
QUILTS
REALTY
RIALTO
SAULTS
SHELTY
SMALTI
SMALTO
SMELTS
SMOLTS
SPILTH
STILTS
SVELTE
UBOLTS
VAULTS
WEALTH

•••L•T

AIGLET
AMULET
ANKLET
ARMLET
AUKLET
BALLET
BALLOT
BILLET
BRULOT
BULLET
CABLET
CAMLET
CHALET
COLLET
CULLET
CUTLET
DIGLOT
EAGLET
EYELET
FILLET
GIBLET
GIGLET
GIGLOT
GIMLET
GOBLET
GOGLET
GULLET
HAMLET
HARLOT
HASLET
MALLET
MILLET
MULLET
NUTLET
OCELOT
OMELET
OUTLET
PALLET
PELLET
PULLET
REFLET
REGLET
RILLET
RUNLET
SALLET
SAMLET
SCULPT
STYLET
SUBLET
SUNLIT
TABLET
TOILET
VARLET
VIOLET
WALLET
WHILST
WILLET
ZEALOT

••••LT

ABVOLT
BASALT
COBALT
DESALT
INDULT
INSULT
ISEULT
OCCULT
PENULT
RESULT
REVOLT
SPOILT
TUMULT
TYBALT
UNBELT
UNBOLT

LU••••

LUANDA
LUBBER
LUBECK
LUBLIN
LUCENT
LUCIAN
LUCIAS
LUCIEN
LUCILE
LUCITE
LUCIUS
LUDWIG
LUELLA
LUETIC
LUFFED
LUGERS
LUGGED
LUGGER
LULLED
LUMBAR
LUMBER
LUMENS
LUMINA
LUMINI
LUMINO
LUMMOX
LUMPED
LUMPEN
LUNACY
LUNATE
LUNETS
LUNGED
LUNGEE
LUNGER
LUNGES
LUNGIS
LUNKER
LUNULA
LUNULE
LUPINE
LURERS
LURING
LURKED
LUSHED
LUSHER
LUSHES
LUSTED
LUSTER
LUTEAL
LUTEUM
LUTHER
LUTING
LUTIST
LUXATE
LUXURY

L•U•••

LAUDED
LAUDER
LAUGHS
LAUNCE
LAUNCH
LAURAE
LAURAS
LAUREL
LAURIE
LEUDES
LOUDEN
LOUDER
LOUDLY
LOUGHS
LOUISA
LOUISE
LOUNGE
LOUPES
LOURED
LOUSED
LOUSES
LOUVER
LOUVRE

L••U••

LACUNA
LAGUNE
LANUGO
LAZULI
LEGUME
LEHUAS
LEMUEL
LEMURS
LETUPS
LIGULA
LIGULE
LIGURE
LIMULI
LIQUID
LIQUOR
LOBULE
LOCUST
LOQUAT
LUNULA
LUNULE
LUXURY

L•••U•

LABIUM
LABOUR
LABRUM
LANGUR
LAPFUL
LAPSUS
LARRUP
LAWFUL
LAYOUT
LEAGUE
LIMBUS
LINEUP
LINGUA
LITMUS
LOCKUP
LUCIUS
LUTEUM
LYCEUM

L••••U

LANDAU

•LU•••

ALUDEL
ALUINO
ALUINS
ALULAE
ALULAR
ALUMIN
ALUMNA
ALUMNI
BLUELY
BLUEST
BLUETS
BLUFFS
BLUING
BLUISH
BLUNGE
BLUNTS
BLURBS
BLURRY
BLURTS
CLUCKS
CLUING
CLUMPS
CLUMPY
CLUMSY
CLUTCH
ELUDED
ELUDES
FLUENT
FLUFFS
FLUFFY
FLUIDS

FLUKED
FLUKES
FLUKEY
FLUMED
FLUMES
FLUMPS
FLUNKS
FLUNKY
FLUORO
FLUORS
FLURRY
FLUTED
FLUTER
FLUTES
FLUVIO
FLUXED
FLUXES
GLUIER
GLUING
GLUMES
GLUMLY
GLUTEI
GLUTEN
PLUCKS
PLUCKY
PLUMBO
PLUMBS
PLUMED
PLUMES
PLUMMY
PLUMPS
PLUNGE
PLUNKS
PLURAL
PLUSES
PLUSHY
PLUTUS
PLUVIO
SLUDGE
SLUDGY
SLUICE
SLUING
SLUMMY
SLUMPS
SLURPS
SLURRY
SLUSHY

•L•U••

ALBUMS
ALCUIN
ALEUTS
ALLUDE
ALLURE
ALMUCE
ALMUDE
ALMUDS
BLOUSE
CLAUDE
CLAUSE
CLOUDS
CLOUDY
CLOUGH
CLOUTS
FLAUNT
FLEURY
FLOURS
FLOURY
FLOUTS
GLAUCO
ILLUME
ILLUSE
ILLUST
PLEURA
PLEURO
PLOUGH
SLEUTH
SLOUCH
SLOUGH

•L••U•

ALARUM
ALDOUS
ALLIUM
ALLOUT
BLOWUP
CLAQUE
CLIQUE
CLIQUY
CLONUS
ELBRUS
FLATUS
PLAGUE
PLAGUY
PLAQUE
PLENUM
PLEXUS
PLUTUS
SLIPUP

••LU••

ABLUSH
ALLUDE
ALLURE
BELUGA
COLUGO
COLUMN
COLURE
DELUDE
DELUGE
DELUXE
DILUTE
DULUTH
HALUTZ
ILLUME
ILLUSE
ILLUST
PILULE
SALUKI
SALUTE
SOLUTE
TELUGU
TOLUOL
TOLUYL
VALUED
VALUES
VELURE
VOLUME
VOLUTE

••L•U•

ABLAUT
ALLIUM
ALLOUT
BULBUL
CALLUS
CILIUM
COLEUS
COLOUS
CULTUS
DELIUS
FOLIUM
GALLUP
GALLUS
HALLUX
HELIUM
HOLDUP
IOLCUS
JULIUS
KALIUM
KULTUR
MILIUM
PALPUS
PELEUS
PILEUM
PILEUS
PILOUS
POLLUX
PULQUE
SELJUK
SULCUS
SULFUR
TALCUM
TALMUD
TELLUS
UMLAUT
VALGUS
VELLUM
VELOUR
VILLUS
WALKUP
WALNUT
WALRUS
WILBUR
WILFUL

••L••U

MILIEU
TELUGU

•••LU•

AEOLUS
AFFLUX
AMYLUM
ASYLUM
CALLUS
EFFLUX
GALLUP
GALLUS
HALLUX
INFLUX
MUKLUK
OBELUS
OBOLUS
PAULUS
PEPLUM
PEPLUS
PHYLUM
POILUS
POLLUX
REFLUX
STYLUS
TELLUS
VELLUM
VILLUS

••••LU

ORMOLU

L•V•••

LAVABO
LAVAGE
LAVERS
LAVING
LAVISH
LEVANT
LEVEES
LEVELS
LEVERS
LEVIED
LEVIER
LEVIES
LEVITE
LEVITY
LIVELY
LIVENS
LIVERS
LIVERY
LIVIAS
LIVIER
LIVING
LIVRES
LIVYER
LOVAGE
LOVEIN
LOVELL
LOVELY
LOVERS
LOVING

L••V••

LARVAE
LARVAL
LATVIA
LEAVED
LEAVEN
LEAVER
LEAVES
LOAVES
LOUVER
LOUVRE

•LV•••

ALVANS
ALVINA
ALVINE
ELVERS
ELVIRA
ELVISH

•L•V••

CLEVER
CLEVIS
CLIVES
CLOVEN
CLOVER
CLOVES
CLOVIS
ELEVEN
ELEVON
FLAVIA
FLAVIN
FLAVOR
FLUVIO
GLOVED
GLOVER
GLOVES
OLIVER
OLIVES
OLIVIA
PLOVER
PLUVIO
SLAVED
SLAVER
SLAVES
SLAVIC
SLIVER
SLOVAK
SLOVEN
YLEVEL

•L••V•

ALCOVE
CLEAVE
SLEAVE
SLEEVE

••LV••

CALVED
CALVES
CALVIN
CULVER
DELVED
DELVER
DELVES
HALVED
HALVES
HELVES
KELVIN
MELVIN
PELVES
PELVIC
PELVIS
SALVED
SALVER
SALVES
SALVIA
SALVOR
SALVOS
SELVES
SILVAE
SILVAN
SILVAS
SILVER
SILVIA
SOLVED
SOLVER
SOLVES
SYLVAE
SYLVAN
SYLVAS
SYLVIA
VALVAL
VALVAR
VALVED
VALVES
VELVET
VOLVAS
VOLVOX
VULVAE
VULVAL
VULVAR
WALVIS
WOLVER
WOLVES

••L•V•

RELIVE
SALIVA
UNLIVE

•••LV•

EVOLVE
HUELVA
SHELVE
TWELVE

•••L•V

PAVLOV

L•W•••

LAWFUL
LAWING
LAWYER
LEWDER
LEWDLY
LOWBOY
LOWELL
LOWERS
LOWERY
LOWEST
LOWING
LOWKEY

L••W••

LEEWAY
LUDWIG

•LW•••

ALWAYS

•L•W••

BLOWBY
BLOWER

6

BLOWUP
BLOWZY
CLAWED
CLEWED
CLOWNS
FLAWED
FLOWED
FLOWER
GLOWED
GLOWER
PLOWED
PLOWER
SLEWED
SLOWED
SLOWER
SLOWLY

•L••W•
ALLOWS
ELBOWS

••LW••
GALWAY

••L•W•
ALLOWS
BYLAWS
INLAWS
MALAWI

••L••W
BELLOW
BILLOW
CALLOW
FALLOW
FELLOW
FOLLOW
HALLOW
HOLLOW
MALLOW
MELLOW
MILDEW
PILLOW
SALLOW
TALLOW
WALLOW
WILLOW
YELLOW

•••L•W
BELLOW
BILLOW
BYBLOW
CALLOW
CURLEW
FALLOW
FELLOW
FOLLOW
HALLOW
HOLLOW
INFLOW
KISLEW
MALLOW
MELLOW
OUTLAW
PILLOW
SALLOW
TALLOW
WALLOW
WILLOW
YELLOW

L•X•••
LAXEST
LAXITY
LUXATE
LUXURY

L••X••
LYNXES

L••••X
LARYNX
LASTEX
LUMMOX

•L•X••
ALEXIA
ALEXIN
ALEXIS
ELIXIR
FLAXEN
FLAXES
FLEXED
FLEXES
FLEXOR
FLUXED
FLUXES
ILEXES
KLAXON
PLEXOR
PLEXUS

•L•••X
CLIMAX

••LX••
CALXES

••L•X•
BILOXI
DELUXE
GALAXY

••L••X
BOLLIX
HALLUX
POLEAX
POLLEX
POLLUX
VOLVOX

•••L•X
AFFLUX
BIFLEX
BOLLIX
DIPLEX
DUPLEX
EFFLUX
HALLUX
INFLUX
POLLEX
POLLUX
PROLIX
REFLEX
REFLUX
SCOLEX
SMILAX

LY••••
LYCEES
LYCEUM
LYDIAS
LYMPHO
LYNXES
LYRICS
LYRISM
LYRIST
LYSINE
LYSING
LYSINS
LYTTAE

L•Y•••
LAYDAY
LAYERS
LAYING
LAYMAN
LAYMEN
LAYOFF
LAYOUT

L••Y••
LARYNG
LARYNX
LAWYER
LIBYAN
LIVYER
LLOYDS

L•••Y•
LARRYS
LENNYS
LEROYS
LIBBYS
LIMEYS
LIZZYS

L••••Y
LACILY
LACKEY
LAMELY
LANKLY
LASTLY
LATELY
LAXITY
LAYDAY
LAZILY
LEACHY
LEANLY
LEEWAY
LEGACY
LENITY
LESLEY
LEVITY
LEWDLY
LIKELY
LIMPLY
LITANY
LIVELY
LIVERY
LONELY
LORDLY
LOUDLY
LOVELY
LOWBOY
LOWERY
LOWKEY
LUNACY
LUXURY

•LY•••
CLYDES
CLYPEI
ELYSEE
ELYTRA
FLYBYS
FLYERS
FLYING
GLYCOL
GLYNIS
GLYPHS
GLYPTO
PLYING
SLYEST

•L•Y••
ALKYLS
ALKYNE
ALLYLS
CLAYED
CLAYEY
CLOYED
ELAYNE
FLAYED
FLAYER
FLOYDS
LLOYDS
PLAYAS
PLAYED
PLAYER
SLAYER

•L••Y•
ALLAYS
ALLEYS
ALLOYS
ALPHYL
ALWAYS
FLYBYS
GLADYS
ZLOTYS

•L•••Y
ALBANY
BLEARY
BLEBBY
BLENNY
BLOCKY
BLOODY
BLOOMY
BLOWBY
BLOWZY
BLUELY
BLURRY
CLAMMY
CLASSY
CLAYEY
CLERGY
CLIFFY
CLINGY
CLIQUY
CLODDY
CLOGGY
CLOTTY
CLOUDY
CLUMPY
CLUMSY
FLABBY
FLAGGY
FLASHY
FLATLY
FLEDGY
FLEECY
FLESHY
FLEURY
FLIMSY
FLINTY
FLIRTY
FLOATY
FLOCKY
FLOOZY
FLOPPY
FLOSSY
FLOURY
FLUFFY
FLUKEY
FLUNKY
FLURRY
GLADLY
GLAIRY
GLASSY
GLEAMY
GLEETY
GLIBLY
GLOOMY
GLOSSY
GLUMLY
PLAGUY
PLASHY
PLASTY
PLENTY
PLUCKY
PLUMMY
PLUSHY
SLAGGY
SLANGY
SLEAZY
SLEEKY
SLEEPY
SLEETY
SLIMLY
SLIMSY
SLINKY
SLOPPY
SLOSHY
SLOWLY
SLUDGY
SLUMMY
SLURRY
SLUSHY

••LY••
ALLYLS
GALYAK
POLYPS

••L•Y•
ALLAYS
ALLEYS
ALLOYS
BELAYS
BILLYS
BOLEYN
DELAYS
DOLLYS
HOLLYS
INLAYS
MALAYA
MALAYS
MILLYS
MOLLYS
NELLYS
POLLYS
RELAYS
SALLYS
SELSYN
SPLAYS
TILLYS
TOLUYL
UNLAYS
VALKYR
WALLYS
WILLYS

••L••Y
BALDLY
BELFRY
BILITY
BOLDLY
CALMLY
CALORY
CELERY
COLDLY
COLONY
CULLAY
EULOGY
FELONY
FILTHY
FOLKSY
GALAXY
GALLEY
GALWAY
HALLEY

6

HALSEY
HILARY
HOLILY
JALOPY
MALADY
MALORY
MELODY
MILADY
MILDLY
MILLAY
MULLEY
OILILY
OOLOGY
PALELY
PALTRY
PELTRY
POLICY
POLITY
PULLEY
SALARY
SALIFY
SOLELY
SULTRY
SYLPHY
UGLIFY
UGLILY
VALERY
VALLEY
VILELY
VILIFY
VOLERY
VOLLEY
WILDLY
WILILY
WOLSEY

•••LY•
BIALYS
BILLYS
DOLLYS
EMILYS
EVELYN
HOLLYS
MILLYS
MOLLYS
NELLYS
POLLYS
SALLYS
TILLYS
WALLYS
WILLYS

•••L•Y
ASHLEY
BAILEY
BARLEY
BURLEY
BYPLAY
CHALKY
CHILLY
COOLLY
COPLEY
CULLAY
DEPLOY
DOYLEY
DROLLY
DUDLEY
EMPLOY
EVILLY
FARLEY
FAULTY
FEALTY
FOULLY
FRILLY
GALLEY
GUILTY
HALLEY
HARLEY
HAULMY
HENLEY
HUXLEY
ICALLY
LESLEY
MEDLEY
MILLAY
MISLAY
MOOLEY
MORLEY
MOSLEY
MOTLEY
MOULDY
MULLEY
OAKLEY
ORALLY
OUTLAY
OVALLY
PARLAY
PARLEY
PULLEY
QUALMY
REALLY
REALTY
REPLAY
RIPLEY
SHELBY
SHELLY
SHELTY
SMELLY
STALKY
STILLY
VALLEY
VOLLEY
WAYLAY
WESLEY
WHELKY
WHOLLY
WIELDY
WOOLLY

••••LY
ACIDLY
AGEDLY
AIRILY
ARCHLY
ARIDLY
AVIDLY
BALDLY
BARELY
BARFLY
BASELY
BLUELY
BODILY
BOLDLY
BOTFLY
BUBBLY
BUSILY
CAGILY
CALMLY
CECILY
CHILLY
CICELY
COLDLY
COMELY
COMPLY
COOLLY
COSTLY
COZILY
CRAWLY
CUDDLY
CURTLY
CUTELY
DAFTLY
DAMPLY
DANKLY
DARKLY
DAYFLY
DEADLY
DEAFLY
DEARLY
DEEPLY
DEFTLY
DIMPLY
DIRELY
DOUBLY
DOURLY
DOZILY
DRABLY
DRAWLY
DROLLY
DUMBLY
EASILY
EERILY
EVENLY
EVILLY
FAIRLY
FAMILY
FINELY
FIRMLY
FLATLY
FONDLY
FOULLY
FOXILY
FREELY
FRILLY
GADFLY
GAINLY
GAMELY
GAMILY
GIGGLY
GLADLY
GLIBLY
GLUMLY
GNARLY
GOODLY
GOOGLY
GORILY
GRAYLY
GRIMLY
GRISLY
HARDLY
HAZILY
HIGHLY
HOLILY
HOMELY
HOMILY
HOURLY
HUGELY
HUMBLY
ICALLY
JUNGLY
JUSTLY
KEENLY
KINDLY
KINGLY
KNURLY
LACILY
LAMELY
LANKLY
LASTLY
LATELY
LAZILY
LEANLY
LEWDLY
LIKELY
LIMPLY
LIVELY
LONELY
LORDLY
LOUDLY
LOVELY
MAINLY
MAZILY
MEANLY
MEASLY
MEEKLY
MEETLY
MERELY
MILDLY
MOSTLY
NAMELY
NEARLY
NEATLY
NICELY
NOSILY
NUBBLY
NUDELY
NUMBLY
OILILY
OOZILY
OPENLY
ORALLY
OVALLY
OVERLY
PALELY
PARTLY
PEARLY
PEBBLY
PERTLY
PIMPLY
POORLY
PORTLY
PRIMLY
PUDDLY
PUNILY
PURELY
PUSSLY
RACILY
RANKLY
RARELY
RASHLY
RATTLY
REALLY
RICHLY
RIPELY
ROPILY
ROSILY
RUDELY
SAFELY
SAGELY
SANELY
SAWFLY
SEEMLY
SHELLY
SHOALY
SICILY
SICKLY
SIMPLY
SINGLY
SLIMLY
SLOWLY
SMELLY
SMUGLY
SNARLY
SNUGLY
SOFTLY
SOLELY
SORELY
SOURLY
SPRYLY
STEELY
STILLY
SUBTLY
SUPPLY
SURELY
SWIRLY
TANGLY
TARTLY
TAUTLY
TERMLY
THINLY
TIDILY
TIMELY
TINGLY
TINKLY
TRIGLY
TRIMLY
TWOPLY
UGLILY
UNDULY
UNHOLY
UNRULY
USABLY
VAINLY
VASTLY
VERILY
VILELY
WABBLY
WADDLY
WAGGLY
WAMBLY
WARILY
WARMLY
WAVILY
WEAKLY
WEEKLY
WHOLLY
WIDELY
WIFELY
WIGGLY
WILDLY
WILILY
WIRILY
WISELY
WOBBLY
WOOLLY
YEARLY

L•Z•••
LAZARS
LAZIER
LAZILY
LAZING
LAZULI
LIZARD
LIZZIE
LIZZYS

L••Z••
LIZZIE
LIZZYS

L••••Z
LORENZ

•L•Z••
BLAZED
BLAZER
BLAZES
BLAZON
ELIZAS
GLAZED
GLAZER
GLAZES
GLOZED
GLOZES
PLAZAS

•L••Z•
ALONZO
BLOWZY
FLOOZY
SLEAZY

•L•••Z
BLINTZ

••LZ••
BALZAC
COLZAS

••L•Z•
ABLAZE
BELIZE

••L••Z
HALUTZ

MA••••
MABELS
MACACO
MACAWS
MACERS
MACING
MACKLE
MACLES
MACRON
MACULA
MACULE
MADAME
MADAMS
MADCAP
MADDED
MADDEN
MADDER
MADEUP
MADGES
MADMAN
MADMEN
MADRAS
MADRID
MADURA
MADURO
MAENAD
MAGGIE
MAGGOT
MAGNET
MAGNUM
MAGOTS
MAGPIE
MAGUEY
MAGYAR
MAHLER
MAHOUT
MAIDEN
MAIGRE
MAILED
MAILER
MAIMED
MAIMER
MAINLY
MAISIE
MAISON
MAITRE
MAIZES
MAJORS
MAKERS
MAKEUP
MAKING
MALACO
MALADY
MALAGA
MALATE
MALAWI
MALAYA
MALAYS
MALGRE
MALICE
MALIGN
MALINE
MALLED
MALLEE
MALLET
MALLOW
MALORY
MALTED
MALTHA
MAMBAS
MAMBOS
MAMEYS
MAMIES
MAMMAE
MAMMAL
MAMMAS
MAMMET
MAMMON
MANAGE
MANANA
MANCHU
MANDAN
MANDYS
MANEGE
MANFUL
MANGER
MANGLE
MANGOS
MANIAC
MANIAS
MANILA
MANIOC
MANITO
MANITU
MANNED
MANNER
MANORS
MANQUE
MANSES
MANTAS
MANTEL
MANTES
MANTIC
MANTIS
MANTLE
MANTUA
MANUAL
MANUEL
MANURE
MAOISM
MAOIST
MAORIS
MAPLES
MAPPED
MAQUIS
MARACA
MARAUD
MARBLE
MARCEL
MARCIA
MARCOS
MARCUS
MARDUK
MARGAY
MARGES
MARGIE
MARGIN
MARGOS
MARGOT
MARIAN
MARIAS
MARIES
MARINA
MARINE
MARION
MARIST
MARKED
MARKER
MARKET
MARKKA
MARKUP
MARLED
MARLIN
MARMOT
MAROON
MARQUE
MARRED
MARRER
MARROW
MARSHA
MARSHY
MARTAS
MARTEN
MARTHA
MARTHE
MARTIN
MARTYR
MARTYS
MARVEL
MARVIN
MASCON
MASCOT
MASERS
MASHED
MASHER
MASHES
MASHIE
MASKED
MASKEG
MASKER
MASONS
MASORA
MASQUE
MASSED
MASSES
MASSIF
MASTED
MASTER
MASTIC
MATEOS
MATEYS
MATING
MATINS
MATRIX
MATRON
MATTED
MATTEO
MATTER
MATTES
MATTIE
MATURE
MATZOS
MATZOT
MAUDES
MAULED
MAULER
MAUMAU
MAUNDS
MAUNDY
MAUSER
MAUVES
MAXIMS
MAXINE
MAXIXE
MAYDAY
MAYEST
MAYHAP
MAYHEM
MAYING
MAYORS
MAYPOP
MAZERS
MAZIER
MAZILY
MAZING
MAZUMA

M•A•••
MEADOW
MEAGER
MEALIE
MEANER
MEANIE
MEANLY
MEASLY
MEATUS
MIASMA
MIAULS
MOANED
MOATED

M••A••
MACACO
MACAWS
MADAME
MADAMS
MALACO
MALADY
MALAGA
MALATE
MALAWI
MALAYA
MALAYS
MANAGE
MANANA
MARACA
MARAUD
MEDALS
MEGALO
MEGASS
MELANO
MENACE
MENAGE
METAGE
METALS
MIDAIR
MIKADO
MILADY
MILAGE
MIRAGE
MOHAIR
MOHAVE
MOHAWK
MOJAVE
MOLARS
MONADS
MORALE
MORALS
MORASS
MORAYS
MOSAIC
MOZART
MURALS
MUTANT
MUTATE

M•••A•
MADCAP
MADMAN
MADRAS
MAENAD
MAGYAR
MAMBAS
MAMMAE
MAMMAL
MAMMAS
MANDAN
MANIAC
MANIAS
MANTAS
MANUAL
MARGAY
MARIAN
MARIAS
MARTAS
MAUMAU
MAYDAY
MAYHAP
MECCAN
MECCAS
MEDIAE
MEDIAL
MEDIAN
MEDLAR
MENIAL
MENSAL
MENTAL
MERMAN
MESCAL
MESIAL
MESIAN
MICMAC
MIDDAY
MIDWAY
MILLAY
MINOAN
MIRIAM
MISHAP
MISKAL
MISLAY
MISSAL
MITRAL
MOBCAP
MOIRAS
MOLLAH
MONDAY
MOOLAH
MOREAU
MORGAN
MORTAL
MORTAR
MUDCAP
MUGGAR
MULLAH
MURRAY
MUSCAE
MUSCAT
MUTUAL
MYRIAD
MYRNAS

M••••A
MACULA
MADURA
MALAGA
MALAYA
MALTHA
MANANA
MANILA
MANTUA
MARACA
MARCIA
MARINA
MARKKA
MARSHA
MARTHA
MASORA
MAZUMA
MEDUSA
MERCIA
MEZUZA
MIASMA
MIMOSA
MONICA
MORULA
MUCOSA
MYOPIA
MYRICA
MYXOMA

•MA•••
AMADOU
AMANDA
AMATOL
AMAZED
AMAZES
AMAZON
IMAGES
IMARET
OMASUM
SMACKS
SMALLS
SMALTI
SMALTO
SMARMY
SMARTS
SMAZES

•M•A••
AMBAGE
AMBARI
AMBARY
EMBALM
EMBANK
EMBARK
EMBARS
EMBAYS
EMPALE
IMBALM
IMBARK
IMPACT
IMPAIR
IMPALA
IMPALE
IMPARK
IMPART
IMPAWN
SMEARS
SMEARY
UMIAKS
UMLAUT

•M••A•
AMEBAE
AMEBAS
AMORAL
AMYTAL
OMEGAS
SMILAX
UMBRAE
UMBRAS

•M•••A
AMANDA
AMELIA
AMENRA
AMOEBA
AMRITA
EMILIA
IMPALA
OMENTA

••MA••
ALMAHS
ARMADA
ARMAGH
ARMAND
AYMARA
BAMAKO
BEMATA
CAMASS
COMATE
CYMARS
DAMAGE
DAMANS
DAMASK
DEMAND
DOMAIN
FEMALE
GEMARA
HAMALS
HAMAUL
HEMATO
HOMAGE
HUMANE
HUMANS
INMATE
KAMALA
NEMATO
NOMADS
OHMAGE
POMACE
POMADE
REMADE
REMAIN
REMAKE
REMAND
REMANS
REMARK
ROMAIC
ROMANS
ROMANY
SAMARA
SIMARS
SOMATA
SOMATO
SUMACS
TAMALE
TOMANS
TOMATO
UNMADE
UNMAKE
UNMANS
UNMASK
ZYMASE

••M•A•
BEMEAN
BEMOAN
BOMBAY
COMBAT
COMMAS
CYMBAL
DAMMAR
DEMEAN
GAMMAS
GEMMAE
GUMMAS
HAMMAL
HAMZAS
HYMNAL
LAMIAE
LAMIAS
LAMMAS
LAMPAD
LAMPAS
LEMMAS
LUMBAR
MAMBAS
MAMMAE
MAMMAL
MAMMAS
OOMIAK
PAMPAS
RUMBAS
SAMBAS
SAMIAN
SAMOAN
SAMPAN
SIMIAN
TAMBAC
TAMPAN
TAMTAM
TIMBAL
TOMBAC
TOMCAT
TYMPAN
WOMBAT
ZAMIAS

••M••A
ALMIRA
ARMADA
AYMARA
BEMATA
CAMERA
CAMILA
ELMIRA
FEMORA
GAMBIA
GEMARA
JEMIMA
KAMALA
LAMBDA
LAMINA
LIMINA
LUMINA
MIMOSA
NOMURA
NUMINA
NYMPHA
PAMELA
POMONA
RAMONA
REMORA
REMUDA
ROMOLA
RUMINA
SAMARA
SOMATA
VIMINA
VOMICA
WOMERA
ZAMBIA

•••MA•
ABOMAS
AGAMAS
AIDMAN
AIRMAN
ANIMAL
ANIMAS
AROMAS
ASHMAN
ATAMAN
AXEMAN
BADMAN
BAGMAN
BARMAN
BATMAN
BOWMAN
BROMAL
BRUMAL
BUSMAN
CABMAN
CAIMAN
CARMAN
CAYMAN
CLIMAT
CLIMAX
COMMAS
COWMAN
DAGMAR
DAMMAR
DERMAL
DERMAS
DERMAT
DESMAN
DISMAL
DISMAY
DOGMAS
DOLMAN
DRAMAS
ENEMAS
FIRMAN
FOEMAN
FORMAL
FORMAT
FULMAR
GAMMAS
GASMAN
GEMMAE
GERMAN
GUMMAS
GUNMAN
HAMMAL
HERMAE
HERMAI
HERMAN
HETMAN
HIEMAL
ICEMAN
KARMAS
LAMMAS
LAYMAN
LEGMAN
LEMMAS
LLAMAS
MADMAN
MAMMAE
MAMMAL
MAMMAS
MAUMAU
MERMAN
MICMAC
NORMAL
NORMAN
NORMAS
OUTMAN
PALMAR
PENMAN
PITMAN
PRIMAL
RAGMAN
RODMAN
SEAMAN
SHAMAN
SIGMAS
SKYMAN
SOCMAN
STOMAT
TARMAC
TASMAN
THOMAS
TRUMAN
ULEMAS
VANMAN
WEIMAR
WILMAS
YASMAK
YEOMAN

•••M•A
AHIMSA
ALUMNA
ANEMIA
CRIMEA
KALMIA
PYEMIA
RHUMBA
UREMIA

••••MA
ASTHMA
BAHAMA
BRAHMA
BREGMA
CAEOMA
CHACMA
CHROMA
CINEMA
DHARMA
ECZEMA
ENIGMA
FATIMA
GLIOMA
GOTAMA
INTIMA
JEMIMA
LIPOMA
MAZUMA
MIASMA
MYXOMA
OPTIMA
PAJAMA
PANAMA
PLASMA
PNEUMA
SCHEMA
SQUAMA
STIGMA
STROMA
STRUMA
TACOMA
THELMA
TRAUMA
ULTIMA
YAKIMA
ZEUGMA
ZYGOMA

M•B•••
MABELS
MOBBED
MOBBER
MOBCAP
MOBILE
MOBIUS

M••B••
MAMBAS
MAMBOS
MARBLE
MEMBER
MOBBED
MOBBER
MORBID
MUMBLE

M••••B
MIDRIB

•MB•••
AMBAGE
AMBARI
AMBARY
AMBERS
AMBERY
AMBITS
AMBLED
AMBLER
AMBLES
AMBUSH
EMBALM
EMBANK
EMBARK
EMBARS
EMBAYS
EMBEDS
EMBERS
EMBLEM
EMBODY
EMBOLI
EMBOSS

EMBOWS
EMBRUE
EMBRYO
IMBALM
IMBARK
IMBEDS
IMBIBE
IMBODY
IMBRUE
IMBUED
IMBUES
UMBELS
UMBERS
UMBLES
UMBRAE
UMBRAS

•M•B••
AMEBAE
AMEBAS
AMEBIC

•M••B•
AMOEBA
IMBIBE

••MB••
BAMBOO
BOMBAY
BOMBED
BOMBER
BOMBES
BUMBLE
CAMBER
CIMBRI
COMBAT
COMBED
COMBER
COMBOS
CUMBER
CYMBAL
DUMBLY
FIMBLE
FUMBLE
GAMBIA
GAMBIR
GAMBIT
GAMBLE
GAMBOL
GUMBOS
HOMBRE
HUMBLE
HUMBLY
HUMBUG
IAMBIC
IAMBUS
JUMBLE
LAMBDA
LAMBED
LAMBIE
LIMBED
LIMBER
LIMBIC
LIMBUS
LUMBAR
LUMBER
MAMBAS
MAMBOS
MEMBER
MUMBLE
NIMBLE
NIMBUS
NUMBED
NUMBER
NUMBLY
RAMBLE
RUMBAS
RUMBLE
SAMBAS
SAMBOS
SAMBUR
SOMBER
SYMBOL
TAMBAC
TIMBAL
TIMBER
TIMBRE
TOMBAC
TOMBED
TOMBOY
TUMBLE
WAMBLE
WAMBLY
WIMBLE
WOMBAT
WOMBED
ZAMBIA
ZOMBIE
ZOMBIS

••M•B•
DEMOBS

•••MB•
ABOMBS
AKIMBO
CLIMBS
COOMBS
CRAMBO
CRUMBS
CRUMBY
FLAMBE
HBOMBS
PLUMBO
PLUMBS
RHOMBI
RHUMBA
RHUMBS
THUMBS

••••MB
APLOMB
BENUMB
CORYMB
ENTOMB
ENWOMB
INTOMB

M•C•••
MACACO
MACAWS
MACERS
MACING
MACKLE
MACLES
MACRON
MACULA
MACULE
MECCAN
MECCAS
MICELL
MICHEL
MICKEY
MICKYS
MICMAC
MICRON
MOCKED
MOCKER
MOCKUP
MUCKED
MUCKER
MUCOID
MUCOSA
MUCOSE
MUCOUS
MYCETE

M••C••
MADCAP
MANCHU
MARCEL
MARCIA
MARCOS
MARCUS
MASCON
MASCOT
MECCAN
MECCAS
MERCER
MERCIA
MESCAL
MINCED
MINCER
MINCES
MISCUE
MOBCAP
MOSCOW
MUDCAP
MULCTS
MUSCAE
MUSCAT
MUSCLE

M•••C•
MACACO
MALACO
MALICE
MARACA
MEDICO
MEDICS
MEJICO
MENACE
MEXICO
MIMICS
MOHOCK
MOLOCH
MONICA
MUNICH
MYRICA

M••••C
MANIAC
MANIOC
MANTIC
MASTIC
METRIC
MICMAC
MIOTIC
MOSAIC
MYOPIC
MYRMEC
MYSTIC
MYTHIC

•MC•••
EMCEED
EMCEES

•M•C••
AMICES
SMACKS
SMOCKS

•M••C•
AMERCE
IMPACT
SMIRCH
SMOOCH
SMUTCH

•M•••C
AMEBIC
AMIDIC
AMYLIC
EMERIC
EMETIC

••MC••
TOMCAT
TOMCOD

••M•C•
ALMUCE
COMICS
MIMICS
POMACE
PUMICE
SUMACS
VOMICA

••M••C
CYMRIC
HYMNIC
IAMBIC
LIMBIC
ROMAIC
TAMBAC
TOMBAC

•••M•C
AGAMIC
ANEMIC
ANOMIC
ATOMIC
BROMIC
CHYMIC
COSMIC
DERMIC
FORMIC
GNOMIC
HOLMIC
MICMAC
MYRMEC
PYEMIC
SUOMIC
TARMAC
THYMIC

M•D•••
MADAME
MADAMS
MADCAP
MADDED
MADDEN
MADDER
MADEUP
MADGES
MADMAN
MADMEN
MADRAS
MADRID
MADURA
MADURO
MEDALS
MEDDLE
MEDIAE
MEDIAL
MEDIAN
MEDICO
MEDICS
MEDIUM
MEDLAR
MEDLEY
MEDUSA
MIDAIR
MIDDAY
MIDDEN
MIDDLE
MIDGES
MIDGET
MIDGUT
MIDRIB
MIDWAY
MODELS
MODERN
MODEST
MODIFY
MODISH
MODULE
MUDCAP
MUDDED
MUDDER
MUDDLE

M••D••
MADDED
MADDEN
MADDER
MAIDEN
MANDAN
MANDYS
MARDUK
MAUDES
MAYDAY
MEADOW
MEDDLE
MELDED
MENDED
MENDEL
MENDER
MIDDAY
MIDDEN
MIDDLE
MILDEN
MILDER
MILDEW
MILDLY
MINDED
MINDER
MISDID
MOLDED
MOLDER
MONDAY
MUDDED
MUDDER
MUDDLE
MURDER

M•••D•
MALADY
MAUNDS
MAUNDY
MELODY
MIKADO
MILADY
MONADS
MONODY
MOULDS
MOULDY

M••••D
MADDED
MADRID
MAENAD
MAILED
MAIMED
MALLED
MALTED
MANNED
MAPPED
MARAUD
MARKED
MARLED
MARRED

6

MASHED
MASKED
MASSED
MASTED
MATTED
MAULED
MELDED
MELTED
MENDED
MEOWED
MERGED
MESHED
MESSED
METHOD
MEWLED
MIFFED
MILKED
MILLED
MILORD
MILTED
MINCED
MINDED
MINTED
MISDID
MISSED
MISTED
MOANED
MOATED
MOBBED
MOCKED
MOILED
MOLDED
MOLTED
MONIED
MOONED
MOORED
MOOTED
MOPPED
MORBID
MOUSED
MUCKED
MUCOID
MUDDED
MUFFED
MUGGED
MULLED
MUMMED
MUSHED
MUSSED
MYRIAD

•M•D••
AMADOU
AMIDES
AMIDIC
AMIDIN
AMIDOL
AMIDST
IMIDES
SMUDGE
SMUDGY

•M••D•
AMANDA
AMENDS
EMBEDS
EMBODY
EMENDS
IMBEDS
IMBODY
IMPEDE

•M•••D
AMAZED
AMBLED
AMUSED
EMCEED
EMOTED
IMBUED
IMPEND
SMILED
SMOKED

••MD••
CAMDEN
HAMDEN

••M•D•
ALMUDE
ALMUDS
ARMADA
COMEDO
COMEDY
DEMODE
LAMBDA
LAMEDS
NOMADS
POMADE
REMADE
REMEDY
REMUDA
UNMADE

••M••D
ALMOND
ARMAND
BOMBED
BUMMED
BUMPED
CAMPED
COMBED
CYMOID
DAMMED
DAMNED
DAMPED
DEMAND
DIMMED
DUMPED
EDMOND
EDMUND
GEMMED
GIMPED
GUMMED
HAMMED
HEMMED
HEMOID
HUMMED
HUMPED
HYMNED
JAMMED
JUMPED
LAMBED
LAMMED
LAMPAD
LAMPED
LIMBED
LIMNED
LIMPED
LIMPID
LOMOND
LUMPED
MUMMED
NIMROD
NUMBED
ORMUZD
OSMOND
OSMUND
PIMPED
PUMPED
RAMMED
RAMPED
RAMROD
REMAND
REMIND
RIMMED
ROMPED
SUMMED
TAMPED
TOMBED
TOMCOD
VAMPED
WOMBED

•••M•D
BEAMED
BLAMED
BOOMED
BUMMED
CALMED
CHIMED
CULMED
DAMMED
DEEMED
DESMID
DIMMED
DOOMED
FARMED
FILMED
FIRMED
FLAMED
FLUMED
FOAMED
FORMED
FRAMED
GEMMED
GRIMED
GUMMED
HAMMED
HARMED
HEMMED
HUMMED
JAMMED
LAMMED
LOAMED
LOOMED
MAIMED
MUMMED
PALMED
PLUMED
PREMED
PRIMED
RAMMED
REAMED
RHYMED
RIMMED
ROAMED
ROOMED
SEAMED
SEEMED
SHAMED
SLIMED
SPUMED
SUMMED
TALMUD
TEAMED
TEEMED
TERMED
WARMED
WORMED
ZOOMED

ME••••
MEADOW
MEAGER
MEALIE
MEANER
MEANIE
MEANLY
MEASLY
MEATUS
MECCAN
MECCAS
MEDALS
MEDDLE
MEDIAE
MEDIAL
MEDIAN
MEDICO
MEDICS
MEDIUM
MEDLAR
MEDLEY
MEDUSA
MEEKER
MEEKLY
MEETER
MEETLY
MEGALO
MEGASS
MEGILP
MEGRIM
MEJICO
MEKONG
MELANO
MELDED
MELEES
MELLON
MELLOW
MELODY
MELONS
MELTED
MELTER
MELTON
MELVIN
MEMBER
MEMOIR
MEMORY
MENACE
MENAGE
MENDED
MENDEL
MENDER
MENHIR
MENIAL
MENINX
MENSAL
MENSES
MENTAL
MENTOR
MEOWED
MERCER
MERCIA
MERELY
MEREST
MERGED
MERGER
MERGES
MERINO
MERITS
MERLES
MERLIN
MERLON
MERMAN
MERMEN
MEROUS
MERVIN
MESCAL
MESHED
MESHES
MESIAL
MESIAN
MESNES
MESONS
MESSED
MESSES
MESSRS
MESTEE
METAGE
METALS
METEOR
METERS
METHOD
METHYL
METIER
METING
METOPE
METRIC
METROS
METTLE
METUMP
MEWING
MEWLED
MEXICO
MEZUZA
MEZZOS

M•E•••
MAENAD
MEEKER
MEEKLY
MEETER
MEETLY
MYELIN

M••E••
MABELS
MACERS
MADEUP
MAKERS
MAKEUP
MAMEYS
MANEGE
MASERS
MATEOS
MATEYS
MAYEST
MAZERS
MELEES
MERELY
MEREST
METEOR
METERS
MICELL
MILERS
MIMERS
MINERS
MISERS
MISERY
MITERS
MIXERS
MODELS
MODERN
MODEST
MOIETY
MOLEST
MOMENT
MONEYS
MOPERS
MOREAU
MOREEN
MORELS
MOSEYS
MOTELS
MOVERS
MOWERS
MUSEUM
MYCETE
MYSELF

M•••E•
MACLES
MADDED
MADDEN
MADDER

6

MADGES
MADMEN
MAGNET
MAGUEY
MAHLER
MAIDEN
MAILED
MAILER
MAIMED
MAIMER
MAIZES
MALLED
MALLEE
MALLET
MALTED
MAMIES
MAMMET
MANGER
MANNED
MANNER
MANSES
MANTEL
MANTES
MANUEL
MAPLES
MAPPED
MARCEL
MARGES
MARIES
MARKED
MARKER
MARKET
MARLED
MARRED
MARRER
MARTEN
MARVEL
MASHED
MASHER
MASHES
MASKED
MASKEG
MASKER
MASSED
MASSES
MASTED
MASTER
MATTED
MATTEO
MATTER
MATTES
MAUDES
MAULED
MAULER
MAUSER
MAUVES
MAYHEM
MAZIER
MEAGER
MEANER
MEDLEY
MEEKER
MEETER
MELDED
MELEES
MELTED
MELTER
MEMBER
MENDED
MENDEL
MENDER
MENSES
MEOWED
MERCER
MERGED
MERGER
MERGES
MERLES
MERMEN
MESHED
MESHES
MESNES
MESSED
MESSES
MESTEE
METIER
MEWLED
MICHEL
MICKEY
MIDDEN
MIDGES
MIDGET
MIFFED
MIGUEL
MILDEN
MILDER
MILDEW
MILIEU
MILKED
MILKER
MILLED
MILLER
MILLET
MILTED
MILTER
MINCED
MINCER
MINCES
MINDED
MINDER
MINTED
MINTER
MINUET
MINXES
MISSED
MISSES
MISTED
MISTER
MITTEN
MIZZEN
MOANED
MOATED
MOBBED
MOBBER
MOCKED
MOCKER
MOILED
MOILER
MOLDED
MOLDER
MOLIES
MOLTED
MOLTEN
MOLTER
MONGER
MONIED
MONIES
MONKEY
MONTES
MOOLEY
MOONED
MOORED
MOOTED
MOOTER
MOPPED
MOPPET
MOREEN
MORGEN
MORLEY
MORSEL
MOSLEM
MOSLEY
MOSSES
MOTHER
MOTLEY
MOUSED
MOUSER
MOUSES
MOVIES
MUCKED
MUCKER
MUDDED
MUDDER
MUFFED
MUGGED
MUGGER
MULLED
MULLEN
MULLER
MULLET
MULLEY
MUMMED
MUMMER
MURDER
MURIEL
MURRES
MURREY
MUSHED
MUSHER
MUSHES
MUSKEG
MUSKET
MUSSED
MUSSEL
MUSSES
MUSTEE
MUSTER
MUTTER
MYOPES
MYRMEC

M••••E

MACKLE
MACULE
MADAME
MAGGIE
MAGPIE
MAIGRE
MAISIE
MAITRE
MALATE
MALGRE
MALICE
MALINE
MALLEE
MAMMAE
MANAGE
MANEGE
MANGLE
MANQUE
MANTLE
MANURE
MARBLE
MARGIE
MARINE
MARQUE
MARTHE
MASHIE
MASQUE
MATTIE
MATURE
MAXINE
MAXIXE
MEALIE
MEANIE
MEDDLE
MEDIAE
MENACE
MENAGE
MESTEE
METAGE
METOPE
METTLE
MIDDLE
MIGGLE
MILAGE
MILLIE
MINGLE
MINNIE
MINUTE
MIRAGE
MISCUE
MISUSE
MOBILE
MODULE
MOHAVE
MOHOLE
MOISHE
MOJAVE
MOLINE
MOLLIE
MOLTKE
MONROE
MOPOKE
MORALE
MORGUE
MOROSE
MOSQUE
MOTILE
MOTIVE
MOTTLE
MOUSSE
MUCOSE
MUDDLE
MUFFLE
MUMBLE
MURINE
MUSCAE
MUSCLE
MUSTEE
MUTATE
MUTULE
MUZZLE
MYCETE
MYRTLE

•ME•••

AMEBAE
AMEBAS
AMEBIC
AMELIA
AMELIE
AMENDS
AMENRA
AMENTS
AMERCE
EMEERS
EMENDS
EMERGE
EMERIC
EMESIS
EMETIC
EMETIN
EMEUTE
OMEGAS
OMELET
OMENTA
SMEARS
SMEARY
SMELLS
SMELLY
SMELTS
TMESIS

•M•E••

AMBERS
AMBERY
AMIENS
AMOEBA
AMPERE
EMBEDS
EMBERS
EMCEED
EMCEES
EMEERS
EMMETS
EMMETT
EMPERY
IMBEDS
IMMESH
IMPEDE
IMPELS
IMPEND
UMBELS
UMBERS

•M••E•

AMAZED
AMAZES
AMBLED
AMBLER
AMBLES
AMICES
AMIDES
AMOLES
AMULET
AMUSED
AMUSER
AMUSES
EMBLEM
EMCEED
EMCEES
EMILES
EMMIES
EMOTED
EMOTES
IMAGES
IMARET
IMBUED
IMBUES
IMIDES
IMINES
IMMIES
IMOGEN
OMELET
SMAZES
SMILED
SMILER
SMILES
SMITER
SMITES
SMOKED
SMOKER
SMOKES
UMBLES

•M•••E

AMBAGE
AMEBAE
AMELIE
AMERCE
AMPERE
AMPULE
EMBRUE
EMERGE
EMEUTE
EMIGRE
EMILIE
EMPALE
EMPIRE
IMBIBE
IMBRUE
IMMUNE

6

IMMURE
IMPALE
IMPEDE
IMPOSE
IMPURE
IMPUTE
SMUDGE
UMBRAE
UMPIRE

••ME••

ARMETS
BEMEAN
CAMELS
CAMEOS
CAMERA
CEMENT
COMEDO
COMEDY
COMELY
COMEON
COMERS
COMETS
CYMENE
DEMEAN
DIMERS
ELMERS
EMMETS
EMMETT
ENMESH
FOMENT
GAMELY
GAMETE
GAMETO
GIMELS
HOMELY
HOMERS
HYMENO
HYMENS
IMMESH
INMESH
LAMEDS
LAMELY
LAMENT
LAMEST
LIMENS
LIMEYS
LOMENT
LUMENS
MAMEYS
MIMERS
MOMENT
NAMELY
NAMERS
ORMERS
PAMELA
POMELO
REMEDY
RIMERS
SEMELE
SEMEME
SIMEON
TAMERS
TAMEST
TIMELY
TIMERS
TUMEFY
UNMEET
UNMEWS
VOMERS
WOMERA
YAMENS
YEMENI

••M•E•

ARMIES
ARMLET
BOMBED
BOMBER
BOMBES
BUMMED
BUMMER
BUMPED
BUMPER
CAMBER
CAMDEN
CAMLET
CAMPED
CAMPER
COMBED
COMBER
COMPEL
CUMBER
DAMMED
DAMMER
DAMNED
DAMPED
DAMPEN
DAMPER
DAMSEL
DEMIES
DIMMED
DIMMER
DUMPED
EMMIES
FUMIER
GAMIER
GAMMER
GEMMED
GIMLET
GIMPED
GUMMED
HAMDEN
HAMLET
HAMMED
HAMMER
HAMPER
HEMMED
HEMMER
HEMPEN
HOMIER
HUMMED
HUMMER
HUMPED
HYMNED
IMMIES
JAMIES
JAMMED
JUMPED
JUMPER
KUMMEL
LAMBED
LAMMED
LAMPED
LEMUEL
LIMBED
LIMBER
LIMIER
LIMNED
LIMNER
LIMPED
LIMPER
LIMPET
LUMBER
LUMPED
LUMPEN
MAMIES
MAMMET
MEMBER
MUMMED
MUMMER
NUMBED
NUMBER
PAMPER
PIMPED
POMMEL
POMPEY
PUMMEL
PUMPED
PUMPER
RAMIES
RAMMED
RAMMER
RAMPED
RIMMED
RIMMER
ROMMEL
ROMNEY
ROMPED
ROMPER
RUMMER
SAMIEL
SAMLET
SAMUEL
SIMMER
SIMNEL
SIMPER
SOMBER
SUMMED
SUMMER
SUMNER
TAMPED
TAMPER
TEMPER
TIMBER
TOMBED
UNMEET
VAMPED
WOMBED
YAMMER

••M••E

ADMIRE
ALMUCE
ALMUDE
ARMURE
BEMIRE
BEMUSE
BUMBLE
CAMISE
COMATE
COMMIE
COMOSE
CYMENE
CYMOSE
DAMAGE
DEMISE
DEMODE
DEMOTE
DEMURE
DIMPLE
ERMINE
FAMINE
FEMALE
FIMBLE
FUMBLE
GAMBLE
GAMETE
GEMMAE
HAMITE
HOMAGE
HOMBRE
HUMANE
HUMBLE
IMMUNE
IMMURE
INMATE
JIMMIE
JUMBLE
LAMBIE
LAMIAE
MAMMAE
MUMBLE
NIMBLE
OHMAGE
OSMOSE
PIMPLE
POMACE
POMADE
PUMICE
RAMBLE
RAMOSE
REMADE
REMAKE
REMISE
REMOTE
REMOVE
RIMOSE
RIMPLE
RUMBLE
RUMPLE
SAMITE
SAMPLE
SEMELE
SEMEME
SEMITE
SEMPRE
SIMILE
SIMONE
SIMPLE
SOMITE
TAMALE
TEMPLE
TIMBRE
TUMBLE
UNMADE
UNMAKE
WAMBLE
WIMBLE
WIMPLE
ZOMBIE
ZYMASE

•••ME•

ACUMEN
AIDMEN
AIRMEN
ASHMEN
AXEMEN
BADMEN
BAGMEN
BARMEN
BATMEN
BEAMED
BERMES
BLAMED
BLAMES
BOOMED
BOWMEN
BREMEN
BROMES
BRUMES
BUMMED
BUMMER
BUSMEN
CABMEN
CALMED
CALMER
CARMEL
CARMEN
CERMET
CHIMED
CHIMER
CHIMES
CLIMES
COWMEN
CREMES
CRIMEA
CRIMES
CULMED
DAMMED
DAMMER
DEEMED
DIMMED
DIMMER
DOLMEN
DOOMED
DORMER
ENAMEL
EXAMEN
FARMED
FARMER
FILMED
FIRMED
FIRMER
FLAMED
FLAMEN
FLAMES
FLUMED
FLUMES
FOAMED
FOEMEN
FORMED
FORMER
FRAMED
FRAMER
FRAMES
GAMMER
GASMEN
GEMMED
GLUMES
GNOMES
GRIMED
GRIMES
GRUMES
GUMMED
GUNMEN
HAMMED
HAMMER
HARMED
HELMET
HEMMED
HEMMER
HERMES
HOLMES
HUMMED
HUMMER
ICEMEN
ISOMER
JAMMED
KERMES
KILMER
KISMET
KUMMEL
LAMMED
LAYMEN
LEGMEN
LOAMED
LOOMED
MADMEN
MAIMED
MAIMER
MAMMET
MERMEN
MUMMED
MUMMER
MYRMEC
NEUMES
NUTMEG
PALMED
PALMER
PENMEN
PITMEN

PLUMED
PLUMES
POMMEL
PREMED
PRIMED
PRIMER
PRIMES
PUMMEL
RAGMEN
RAMMED
RAMMER
REAMED
REAMER
RHYMED
RHYMER
RHYMES
RIMMED
RIMMER
ROAMED
ROAMER
RODMEN
ROMMEL
ROOMED
ROOMER
RUMMER
SEAMED
SEAMEN
SEAMER
SEEMED
SEEMER
SHAMED
SHAMES
SIMMER
SKYMEN
SLIMED
SLIMES
SOCMEN
SPUMED
SPUMES
STAMEN
SUMMED
SUMMER
TEAMED
TEEMED
TEEMER
TEGMEN
TERMED
TERMER
THAMES
THEMES
THYMES
VANMEN
WARMED
WARMER
WORMED
WORMER
YAMMER
YEOMEN
ZOOMED

•••M•E
ANOMIE
BARMIE
COMMIE
DORMIE
FLAMBE
GEMMAE
GUIMPE
HERMAE
JIMMIE
MAMMAE
STYMIE

••••ME
AFLAME
AFRAME
ASSUME
ATHOME
BECAME
BECOME
BIREME
BYNAME
CHROME
CLEOME
DEFAME
DEGAME
ENZYME
EXHUME
HEAUME
ILLUME
INCOME
JEROME
LEGUME
MADAME
OPTIME
RACEME
RADOME
REGIME
RESUME
SALOME
SCHEME
SEMEME
SESAME
TAXEME
VOLUME

M•F•••
MIFFED
MUFFED
MUFFIN
MUFFLE
MUFTIS

M••F••
MANFUL
MIFFED
MISFIT
MUFFED
MUFFIN
MUFFLE

M•••F•
MINIFY
MODIFY
MOTIFS

M••••F
MASSIF
MYSELF

••MF••
ARMFUL
COMFIT

••M•F•
RAMIFY
TUMEFY

M•G•••
MAGGIE
MAGGOT
MAGNET
MAGNUM
MAGOTS
MAGPIE
MAGUEY
MAGYAR
MEGALO
MEGASS
MEGILP
MEGRIM
MIGGLE
MIGHTY
MIGNON
MIGUEL
MOGULS
MUGGAR
MUGGED
MUGGER
MUGGUR

M••G••
MADGES
MAGGIE
MAGGOT
MAIGRE
MALGRE
MANGER
MANGLE
MANGOS
MARGAY
MARGES
MARGIE
MARGIN
MARGOS
MARGOT
MEAGER
MERGED
MERGER
MERGES
MIDGES
MIDGET
MIDGUT
MIGGLE
MINGLE
MONGER
MONGOL
MONGST
MORGAN
MORGEN
MORGUE
MUGGAR
MUGGED
MUGGER
MUGGUR

M•••G•
MALAGA
MALIGN
MANAGE
MANEGE
MENAGE
METAGE
MILAGE
MIRAGE

M••••G
MACING
MAKING
MASKEG
MATING
MAYING
MAZING
MEKONG
METING
MEWING
MIMING
MINING
MIRING
MIXING
MOOING
MOPING
MOVING
MOWING
MUSING
MUSKEG
MUTING

•M•G••
AMIGOS
EMIGRE
IMAGES
IMOGEN
OMEGAS
SMUGLY

•M••G•
AMBAGE
EMERGE
IMPUGN
SMUDGE
SMUDGY

•M•••G
IMPING

••M•G•
ARMAGH
DAMAGE
HOMAGE
OHMAGE

••M••G
AIMING
ARMING
COMING
DOMING
FUMING
GAMING
HOMING
HUMBUG
LAMING
LIMING
MIMING
NAMING
RIMING
TAMING
TIMING

•••M•G
NUTMEG

M•H•••
MAHLER
MAHOUT
MOHAIR
MOHAVE
MOHAWK
MOHOCK
MOHOLE
MOHURS

M••H••
MASHED
MASHER
MASHES
MASHIE
MAYHAP
MAYHEM
MENHIR
MESHED
MESHES
METHOD
METHYL
MICHEL
MIGHTY
MISHAP
MOTHER
MUSHED
MUSHER
MUSHES
MUZHIK
MYTHIC
MYTHOI
MYTHOS

M•••H•
MALTHA
MANCHU
MARSHA
MARSHY
MARTHA
MARTHE
MOISHE
MONTHS
MORPHO
MOUTHS
MOUTHY

M••••H
MODISH
MOLLAH
MOLOCH
MOOLAH
MOPISH
MULISH
MULLAH
MUNICH

•M•H••
AMPHRS

•M••H•
SMITHS
SMITHY

•M•••H
AMBUSH
IMMESH
IMPISH
SMIRCH
SMOOCH
SMOOTH
SMUTCH

••M•H•
ALMAHS
LYMPHO
NYMPHA
NYMPHO
NYMPHS
SAMSHU

••M••H
ARMAGH
ENMESH
FAMISH
IMMESH
INMESH
ROMISH

•••M•H
WARMTH

MI••••
MIASMA
MIAULS
MICELL
MICHEL
MICKEY
MICKYS
MICMAC
MICRON
MIDAIR
MIDDAY
MIDDEN
MIDDLE
MIDGES
MIDGET
MIDGUT
MIDRIB
MIDWAY
MIFFED

6

MIGGLE
MIGHTY
MIGNON
MIGUEL
MIKADO
MIKLOS
MILADY
MILAGE
MILDEN
MILDER
MILDEW
MILDLY
MILERS
MILIEU
MILIUM
MILKED
MILKER
MILLAY
MILLED
MILLER
MILLET
MILLIE
MILLYS
MILORD
MILTED
MILTER
MILTON
MIMERS
MIMICS
MIMING
MIMOSA
MINCED
MINCER
MINCES
MINDED
MINDER
MINERS
MINGLE
MINIFY
MINIMS
MINING
MINION
MINIUM
MINNIE
MINNOW
MINOAN
MINORS
MINTED
MINTER
MINUET
MINUTE
MINXES
MIOSIS
MIOTIC
MIRAGE
MIRIAM
MIRING
MIRROR
MISCUE
MISDID
MISERS
MISERY
MISFIT
MISHAP

MISKAL
MISLAY
MISSAL
MISSED
MISSES
MISSIS
MISSUS
MISTED
MISTER
MISUSE
MITERS
MITRAL
MITTEN
MIXERS
MIXING
MIXUPS
MIZZEN

M•I•••

MAIDEN
MAIGRE
MAILED
MAILER
MAIMED
MAIMER
MAINLY
MAISIE
MAISON
MAITRE
MAIZES
MOIETY
MOILED
MOILER
MOIRAS
MOISHE

M••I••

MACING
MAKING
MALICE
MALIGN
MALINE
MAMIES
MANIAC
MANIAS
MANILA
MANIOC
MANITO
MANITU
MAOISM
MAOIST
MARIAN
MARIAS
MARIES
MARINA
MARINE
MARION
MARIST
MATING
MATINS
MAXIMS
MAXINE
MAXIXE
MAYING

MAZIER
MAZILY
MAZING
MEDIAE
MEDIAL
MEDIAN
MEDICO
MEDICS
MEDIUM
MEGILP
MEJICO
MENIAL
MENINX
MERINO
MERITS
MESIAL
MESIAN
METIER
METING
MEWING
MEXICO
MILIEU
MILIUM
MIMICS
MIMING
MINIFY
MINIMS
MINING
MINION
MINIUM
MIRIAM
MIRING
MIXING
MOBILE
MOBIUS
MODIFY
MODISH
MOLIES
MOLINE
MOMISM
MONICA
MONIED
MONIES
MONISM
MONIST
MOOING
MOPING
MOPISH
MORION
MOTIFS
MOTILE
MOTION
MOTIVE
MOVIES
MOVING
MOWING
MULISH
MUNICH
MURIEL
MURINE
MUSING
MUTING
MUTINY
MUTISM

MYRIAD
MYRICA

M•••I•

MADRID
MAGGIE
MAGPIE
MAISIE
MANTIC
MANTIS
MAORIS
MAQUIS
MARCIA
MARGIE
MARGIN
MARLIN
MARTIN
MARVIN
MASHIE
MASSIF
MASTIC
MATRIX
MATTIE
MEALIE
MEANIE
MEGRIM
MELVIN
MEMOIR
MENHIR
MERCIA
MERLIN
MERVIN
METRIC
MIDAIR
MIDRIB
MILLIE
MINNIE
MIOSIS
MIOTIC
MISDID
MISFIT
MISSIS
MOHAIR
MOLLIE
MORBID
MORRIS
MOSAIC
MOULIN
MUCOID
MUFFIN
MUFTIS
MUSKIT
MUSLIM
MUSLIN
MUZHIK
MYELIN
MYOPIA
MYOPIC
MYOSIN
MYOSIS
MYSTIC
MYTHIC

M••••I

MALAWI
MYTHOI

•MI•••

AMICES
AMIDES
AMIDIC
AMIDIN
AMIDOL
AMIDST
AMIENS
AMIGOS
DMITRI
EMIGRE
EMILES
EMILIA
EMILIE
EMILIO
EMILYS
IMIDES
IMINES
SMILAX
SMILED
SMILER
SMILES
SMIRCH
SMIRKS
SMITER
SMITES
SMITHS
SMITHY
UMIAKS

•M•I••

AMBITS
AMNION
AMRITA
EMMIES
EMPIRE
IMBIBE
IMMIES
IMPING
IMPISH
UMPIRE

•M••I•

AMEBIC
AMELIA
AMELIE
AMIDIC
AMIDIN
AMYLIC
EMERIC
EMESIS
EMETIC
EMETIN
EMILIA
EMILIE
EMILIO
IMPAIR
TMESIS

•M•••I

AMBARI
DMITRI
EMBOLI
SMALTI

••MI••

ADMIRE
ADMITS
ADMIXT
AIMING
ALMIRA
ARMIES
ARMING
BEMIRE
CAMILA
CAMION
CAMISE
COMICS
COMING
COMITY
CUMINS
DEMIES
DEMISE
DEMITS
DIMITY
DOMING
DOMINO
ELMIRA
EMMIES
ENMITY
ERMINE
FAMILY
FAMINE
FAMISH
FUMIER
FUMING
GAMIER
GAMILY
GAMING
GAMINS
GEMINI
HAMITE
HOMIER
HOMILY
HOMING
HOMINY
IMMIES
JAMIES
JEMIMA
KAMIKS
KUMISS
LAMIAE
LAMIAS
LAMINA
LAMING
LIMIER
LIMINA
LIMING
LIMITS
LUMINA
LUMINI
LUMINO
MAMIES

MIMICS
MIMING
MOMISM
NAMING
NIMITZ
NOMISM
NUMINA
OOMIAK
OSMIUM
PUMICE
RAMIES
RAMIFY
REMIND
REMISE
REMISS
REMITS
RIMING
ROMISH
RUMINA
SAMIAN
SAMIEL
SAMITE
SEMITE
SIMIAN
SIMILE
SOMITE
TAMING
TIMING
VIMINA
VOMICA
VOMITO
VOMITS
ZAMIAS

••M•I•

ARMPIT
BUMKIN
COMFIT
COMMIE
COMMIT
COMMIX
CYMLIN
CYMOID
CYMRIC
DIMWIT
DOMAIN
GAMBIA
GAMBIR
GAMBIT
HEMOID
HYMNIC
IAMBIC
JIMMIE
KAMSIN
LAMBIE
LIMBIC
LIMPID
MEMOIR
REMAIN
ROMAIC
SIMLIN
SUMMIT
TOMTIT
ZAMBIA
ZOMBIE
ZOMBIS

••M••I

CIMBRI
GEMINI
GOMUTI
LIMULI
LUMINI
YEMENI

•••MI•

AGAMIC
ALUMIN
ANEMIA
ANEMIC
ANOMIC
ANOMIE
ATOMIC
BARMIE
BROMIC
CHYMIC
COMMIE
COMMIT
COMMIX
COSMIC
DAIMIO
DERMIC
DESMID
DORMIE
ELEMIS
FERMIS
FORMIC
GNOMIC
HARMIN
HERMIT
HOLMIC
JIMMIE
KALMIA
KERMIS
NAOMIS
PERMIT
PYEMIA
PYEMIC
SALMIS
STAMIN
STYMIE
SUBMIT
SUMMIT
SUOMIC
SWAMIS
THEMIS
THYMIC
UREMIA
VERMIN

•••M•I

ALUMNI
HERMAI
RHOMBI
SCAMPI

••••MI

SALAMI

M•J•••

MAJORS
MEJICO
MOJAVE

M•K•••

MAKERS
MAKEUP
MAKING
MEKONG
MIKADO
MIKLOS
MUKLUK

M••K••

MACKLE
MARKED
MARKER
MARKET
MARKKA
MARKUP
MASKED
MASKEG
MASKER
MEEKER
MEEKLY
MICKEY
MICKYS
MILKED
MILKER
MISKAL
MOCKED
MOCKER
MOCKUP
MONKEY
MUCKED
MUCKER
MUSKEG
MUSKET
MUSKIT

M•••K•

MARKKA
MOLTKE
MOPOKE

M••••K

MARDUK
MOHAWK
MOHOCK
MUKLUK
MUZHIK

•M•K••

SMOKED
SMOKER
SMOKES

•M••K•

SMACKS
SMIRKS
SMOCKS
UMIAKS

•M•••K

EMBANK
EMBARK
IMBARK
IMPARK

••MK••

BUMKIN

••M•K•

BAMAKO
KAMIKS
REMAKE
UNMAKE

••M••K

DAMASK
OOMIAK
REMARK
UNMASK

•••M•K

YASMAK

M•L•••

MALACO
MALADY
MALAGA
MALATE
MALAWI
MALAYA
MALAYS
MALGRE
MALICE
MALIGN
MALINE
MALLED
MALLEE
MALLET
MALLOW
MALORY
MALTED
MALTHA
MELANO
MELDED
MELEES
MELLON
MELLOW
MELODY
MELONS
MELTED
MELTER
MELTON
MELVIN
MILADY
MILAGE
MILDEN
MILDER
MILDEW
MILDLY
MILERS
MILIEU
MILIUM
MILKED
MILKER
MILLAY
MILLED
MILLER
MILLET
MILLIE
MILLYS
MILORD
MILTED
MILTER
MILTON
MOLARS
MOLDED
MOLDER
MOLEST
MOLIES
MOLINE
MOLLAH
MOLLIE
MOLLYS
MOLOCH
MOLTED
MOLTEN
MOLTER
MOLTKE
MULCTS
MULISH
MULLAH
MULLED
MULLEN
MULLER
MULLET
MULLEY

M••L••

MACLES
MAHLER
MAILED
MAILER
MALLED
MALLEE
MALLET
MALLOW
MAPLES
MARLED
MARLIN
MAULED
MAULER
MEALIE
MEDLAR
MEDLEY
MELLON
MELLOW
MERLES
MERLIN
MERLON
MEWLED
MIKLOS
MILLAY
MILLED
MILLER
MILLET
MILLIE
MILLYS
MISLAY
MOILED
MOILER
MOLLAH
MOLLIE
MOLLYS
MOOLAH
MOOLEY
MORLEY
MOSLEM
MOSLEY
MOTLEY
MOULDS
MOULDY
MOULIN
MOULTS
MUKLUK
MULLAH
MULLED
MULLEN
MULLER
MULLET
MULLEY
MUSLIM
MUSLIN
MYELIN

M•••L•

MABELS
MACKLE
MACULA
MACULE
MAINLY
MANGLE
MANILA
MANTLE
MARBLE
MAZILY
MEANLY
MEASLY
MEDALS
MEDDLE
MEEKLY
MEETLY
MEGALO
MEGILP
MERELY
METALS
METTLE
MIAULS
MICELL
MIDDLE
MIGGLE
MILDLY
MINGLE
MOBILE
MODELS
MODULE
MOGULS
MOHOLE
MORALE
MORALS
MORELS
MORULA

MOSTLY
MOTELS
MOTILE
MOTTLE
MUDDLE
MUFFLE
MUMBLE
MURALS
MUSCLE
MUTULE
MUZZLE
MYRTLE
MYSELF

M••••L
MAMMAL
MANFUL
MANTEL
MANUAL
MANUEL
MARCEL
MARVEL
MEDIAL
MENDEL
MENIAL
MENSAL
MENTAL
MESCAL
MESIAL
METHYL
MICELL
MICHEL
MIGUEL
MISKAL
MISSAL
MITRAL
MONGOL
MORSEL
MORTAL
MURIEL
MUSSEL
MUTUAL

•ML•••
UMLAUT

•M•L••
AMBLED
AMBLER
AMBLES
AMELIA
AMELIE
AMOLES
AMULET
AMYLIC
AMYLUM
EMBLEM
EMILES
EMILIA
EMILIE
EMILIO
EMILYS
EMPLOY
OMELET

SMALLS
SMALTI
SMALTO
SMELLS
SMELLY
SMELTS
SMILAX
SMILED
SMILER
SMILES
SMOLTS
UMBLES

•M••L•
AMPULE
AMPULS
EMBALM
EMBOLI
EMPALE
IMBALM
IMPALA
IMPALE
IMPELS
SMALLS
SMELLS
SMELLY
SMUGLY
UMBELS

•M•••L
AMATOL
AMIDOL
AMORAL
AMYTAL

••ML••
ARMLET
CAMLET
CYMLIN
GIMLET
HAMLET
SAMLET
SIMLIN

••M•L•
BUMBLE
CAMELS
CAMILA
COMELY
COMPLY
DAMPLY
DIMPLE
DIMPLY
DUMBLY
FAMILY
FEMALE
FIMBLE
FUMBLE
GAMBLE
GAMELY
GAMILY
GIMELS
HAMALS
HOMELY

HOMILY
HUMBLE
HUMBLY
JUMBLE
KAMALA
LAMELY
LIMPLY
LIMULI
MUMBLE
NAMELY
NIMBLE
NUMBLY
ORMOLU
PAMELA
PIMPLE
PIMPLY
POMELO
RAMBLE
RIMPLE
ROMOLA
ROMULO
RUMBLE
RUMPLE
SAMPLE
SEMELE
SIMILE
SIMPLE
SIMPLY
TAMALE
TEMPLE
TIMELY
TUMBLE
TUMULT
WAMBLE
WAMBLY
WIMBLE
WIMPLE

••M••L
ARMFUL
COMPEL
CYMBAL
DAMSEL
GAMBOL
HAMAUL
HAMMAL
HYMNAL
KUMMEL
LEMUEL
MAMMAL
POMMEL
PUMMEL
ROMMEL
SAMIEL
SAMUEL
SIMNEL
SYMBOL
TIMBAL

•••ML•
CALMLY
FIRMLY
GLUMLY
GRIMLY

PRIMLY
SEEMLY
SLIMLY
TERMLY
TRIMLY
WARMLY

•••M•L
ANIMAL
BROMAL
BRUMAL
CARMEL
DERMAL
DISMAL
ENAMEL
FORMAL
FORMYL
HAMMAL
HIEMAL
KUMMEL
MAMMAL
NORMAL
POMMEL
PRIMAL
PUMMEL
ROMMEL
THYMOL

M•M•••
MAMBAS
MAMBOS
MAMEYS
MAMIES
MAMMAE
MAMMAL
MAMMAS
MAMMET
MAMMON
MEMBER
MEMOIR
MEMORY
MIMERS
MIMICS
MIMING
MIMOSA
MOMENT
MOMISM
MUMBLE
MUMMED
MUMMER

M••M••
MADMAN
MADMEN
MAIMED
MAIMER
MAMMAE
MAMMAL
MAMMAS
MAMMET
MAMMON
MARMOT
MAUMAU
MERMAN

MERMEN
MICMAC
MORMON
MOTMOT
MUMMED
MUMMER
MURMUR
MUUMUU
MYRMEC

M•••M•
MADAME
MADAMS
MAXIMS
MAZUMA
METUMP
MIASMA
MINIMS
MYXOMA

M••••M
MAGNUM
MAOISM
MAYHEM
MEDIUM
MEGRIM
MILIUM
MINIUM
MIRIAM
MOMISM
MONISM
MOSLEM
MUSEUM
MUSLIM
MUTISM

•MM•••
EMMETS
EMMETT
EMMIES
IMMESH
IMMIES
IMMUNE
IMMUNO
IMMURE

•M••M•
SMARMY

•M•••M
AMYLUM
EMBALM
EMBLEM
IMBALM
OMASUM

••MM••
BUMMED
BUMMER
COMMAS
COMMIE
COMMIT
COMMIX
COMMON

DAMMAR
DAMMED
DAMMER
DIMMED
DIMMER
GAMMAS
GAMMER
GAMMON
GEMMAE
GEMMED
GUMMAS
GUMMED
HAMMAL
HAMMED
HAMMER
HEMMED
HEMMER
HUMMED
HUMMER
JAMMED
JIMMIE
JIMMYS
KUMMEL
LAMMAS
LAMMED
LEMMAS
LUMMOX
MAMMAE
MAMMAL
MAMMAS
MAMMET
MAMMON
MUMMED
MUMMER
POMMEL
PUMMEL
RAMMED
RAMMER
RIMMED
RIMMER
ROMMEL
RUMMER
SAMMYS
SIMMER
SUMMED
SUMMER
SUMMIT
SUMMON
TIMMYS
TOMMYS
WAMMUS
YAMMER

••M•M•
JEMIMA
SEMEME

••M••M
MOMISM
NOMISM
OSMIUM
POMPOM
SIMOOM
TAMTAM

6

TOMTOM
WAMPUM

•••MM•

CHAMMY
CHUMMY
CLAMMY
CRUMMY
PLUMMY
SCUMMY
SHAMMY
SHIMMY
SLUMMY
WHAMMY

M•N•••

MANAGE
MANANA
MANCHU
MANDAN
MANDYS
MANEGE
MANFUL
MANGER
MANGLE
MANGOS
MANIAC
MANIAS
MANILA
MANIOC
MANITO
MANITU
MANNED
MANNER
MANORS
MANQUE
MANSES
MANTAS
MANTEL
MANTES
MANTIC
MANTIS
MANTLE
MANTUA
MANUAL
MANUEL
MANURE
MENACE
MENAGE
MENDED
MENDEL
MENDER
MENHIR
MENIAL
MENINX
MENSAL
MENSES
MENTAL
MENTOR
MINCED
MINCER
MINCES
MINDED
MINDER
MINERS
MINGLE
MINIFY
MINIMS
MINING
MINION
MINIUM
MINNIE
MINNOW
MINOAN
MINORS
MINTED
MINTER
MINUET
MINUTE
MINXES
MONADS
MONDAY
MONEYS
MONGER
MONGOL
MONGST
MONICA
MONIED
MONIES
MONISM
MONIST
MONKEY
MONODY
MONROE
MONTES
MONTHS
MONTYS
MUNICH

M••N••

MAENAD
MAGNET
MAGNUM
MAINLY
MANNED
MANNER
MAUNDS
MAUNDY
MEANER
MEANIE
MEANLY
MESNES
MIGNON
MINNIE
MINNOW
MOANED
MOONED
MOUNTS
MOUNTY
MYRNAS

M•••N•

MACING
MAKING
MALINE
MANANA
MARINA
MARINE
MASONS
MATING
MATINS
MAXINE
MAYING
MAZING
MEKONG
MELANO
MELONS
MENINX
MERINO
MESONS
METING
MEWING
MIMING
MINING
MIRING
MIXING
MOLINE
MOMENT
MOOING
MOPING
MORONS
MOURNS
MOVING
MOWING
MURINE
MUSING
MUTANT
MUTING
MUTINY

M••••N

MACRON
MADDEN
MADMAN
MADMEN
MAIDEN
MAISON
MALIGN
MAMMON
MANDAN
MARGIN
MARIAN
MARION
MARLIN
MAROON
MARTEN
MARTIN
MARVIN
MASCON
MATRON
MECCAN
MEDIAN
MELLON
MELTON
MELVIN
MERLIN
MERLON
MERMAN
MERMEN
MERVIN
MESIAN
MICRON
MIDDEN
MIGNON
MILDEN
MILTON
MINION
MINOAN
MITTEN
MIZZEN
MODERN
MOLTEN
MOREEN
MORGAN
MORGEN
MORION
MORMON
MORTON
MOTION
MOULIN
MOUTON
MUFFIN
MULLEN
MUSLIN
MUTTON
MYELIN
MYOSIN

•MN•••

AMNION

•M•N••

AMANDA
AMENDS
AMENRA
AMENTS
EMENDS
IMINES
OMENTA

•M••N•

AMIENS
AMOUNT
EMBANK
IMMUNE
IMMUNO
IMPEND
IMPING

•M•••N

AMAZON
AMIDIN
AMNION
EMETIN
IMOGEN
IMPAWN
IMPUGN

••MN••

DAMNED
HYMNAL
HYMNED
HYMNIC
LEMNOS
LIMNED
LIMNER
ROMNEY
SIMNEL
SUMNER

••M•N•

AIMING
ALMOND
ARMAND
ARMING
CEMENT
COMING
CUMINS
CYMENE
DAMANS
DEMAND
DEMONO
DEMONS
DOMING
DOMINO
EDMOND
EDMUND
ERMINE
FAMINE
FOMENT
FUMING
GAMING
GAMINS
GEMINI
HOMING
HOMINY
HUMANE
HUMANS
HYMENO
HYMENS
IMMUNE
IMMUNO
KIMONO
LAMENT
LAMINA
LAMING
LEMONS
LIMENS
LIMINA
LIMING
LOMENT
LOMOND
LUMENS
LUMINA
LUMINI
LUMINO
MIMING
MOMENT
NAMING
NUMINA
OSMOND
OSMUND
POMONA
RAMONA
REMAND
REMANS
REMIND
RIMING
ROMANS
ROMANY
RUMINA
SIMONE
SIMONS
SIMONY
TAMING
TIMING
TOMANS
UNMANS
VIMINA
YAMENS
YAMUNS
YEMENI

••M••N

BEMEAN
BEMOAN
BUMKIN
CAMDEN
CAMION
COMEON
COMMON
CYMLIN
DAMPEN
DAMSON
DEMEAN
DOMAIN
GAMMON
HAMDEN
HEMPEN
KAMSIN
LUMPEN
MAMMON
POMPON
RAMSON
REMAIN
SAMIAN
SAMOAN
SAMPAN
SAMSON
SIMEON
SIMIAN
SIMLIN
SUMMON
TAMPAN
TAMPON
TYMPAN

•••MN•

ALUMNA
ALUMNI

•••M•N

ACUMEN
AIDMAN
AIDMEN
AIRMAN
AIRMEN
ALUMIN
ASHMAN
ASHMEN
ATAMAN
AXEMAN
AXEMEN
BADMAN

BADMEN
BAGMAN
BAGMEN
BARMAN
BARMEN
BATMAN
BATMEN
BOWMAN
BOWMEN
BREMEN
BUSMAN
BUSMEN
CABMAN
CABMEN
CAIMAN
CARMAN
CARMEN
CAYMAN
COMMON
COWMAN
COWMEN
DAEMON
DAIMON
DESMAN
DOLMAN
DOLMEN
DROMON
ETYMON
EXAMEN
FIRMAN
FLAMEN
FOEMAN
FOEMEN
GAMMON
GASMAN
GASMEN
GERMAN
GNOMON
GUNMAN
GUNMEN
HARMIN
HERMAN
HETMAN
ICEMAN
ICEMEN
LAYMAN
LAYMEN
LEGMAN
LEGMEN
MADMAN
MADMEN
MAMMON
MERMAN
MERMEN
MORMON
NORMAN
OUTMAN
PENMAN
PENMEN
PITMAN
PITMEN
RAGMAN
RAGMEN
RODMAN
RODMEN
SALMON
SEAMAN
SEAMEN
SERMON
SHAMAN
SKYMAN
SKYMEN
SOCMAN
SOCMEN
STAMEN
STAMIN
SUMMON
TASMAN
TEGMEN
TRUMAN
VANMAN
VANMEN
VERMIN
YEOMAN
YEOMEN

••••MN

AUTUMN
COLUMN
SOLEMN

MO••••

MOANED
MOATED
MOBBED
MOBBER
MOBCAP
MOBILE
MOBIUS
MOCKED
MOCKER
MOCKUP
MODELS
MODERN
MODEST
MODIFY
MODISH
MODULE
MOGULS
MOHAIR
MOHAVE
MOHAWK
MOHOCK
MOHOLE
MOHURS
MOIETY
MOILED
MOILER
MOIRAS
MOISHE
MOJAVE
MOLARS
MOLDED
MOLDER
MOLEST
MOLIES
MOLINE
MOLLAH
MOLLIE
MOLLYS
MOLOCH
MOLTED
MOLTEN
MOLTER
MOLTKE
MOMENT
MOMISM
MONADS
MONDAY
MONEYS
MONGER
MONGOL
MONGST
MONICA
MONIED
MONIES
MONISM
MONIST
MONKEY
MONODY
MONROE
MONTES
MONTHS
MONTYS
MOOING
MOOLAH
MOOLEY
MOONED
MOORED
MOOTED
MOOTER
MOPERS
MOPING
MOPISH
MOPOKE
MOPPED
MOPPET
MORALE
MORALS
MORASS
MORAYS
MORBID
MOREAU
MOREEN
MORELS
MORGAN
MORGEN
MORGUE
MORION
MORLEY
MORMON
MORONS
MOROSE
MORPHO
MORRIS
MORROS
MORROW
MORSEL
MORTAL
MORTAR
MORTON
MORTYS
MORULA
MOSAIC
MOSCOW
MOSEYS
MOSLEM
MOSLEY
MOSQUE
MOSSES
MOSTLY
MOTELS
MOTHER
MOTIFS
MOTILE
MOTION
MOTIVE
MOTLEY
MOTMOT
MOTORS
MOTTLE
MOTTOS
MOULDS
MOULDY
MOULIN
MOULTS
MOUNTS
MOUNTY
MOURNS
MOUSED
MOUSER
MOUSES
MOUSSE
MOUTHS
MOUTHY
MOUTON
MOVERS
MOVIES
MOVING
MOWERS
MOWING
MOZART

M•O•••

MAOISM
MAOIST
MAORIS
MEOWED
MIOSIS
MIOTIC
MOOING
MOOLAH
MOOLEY
MOONED
MOORED
MOOTED
MOOTER
MYOPES
MYOPIA
MYOPIC
MYOSIN
MYOSIS

M••O••

MAGOTS
MAHOUT
MAJORS
MALORY
MANORS
MAROON
MASONS
MASORA
MAYORS
MEKONG
MELODY
MELONS
MEMOIR
MEMORY
MEROUS
MESONS
METOPE
MILORD
MIMOSA
MINOAN
MINORS
MOHOCK
MOHOLE
MOLOCH
MONODY
MOPOKE
MORONS
MOROSE
MOTORS
MUCOID
MUCOSA
MUCOSE
MUCOUS
MYXOMA

M•••O•

MACRON
MAGGOT
MAISON
MALLOW
MAMBOS
MAMMON
MANGOS
MANIOC
MARCOS
MARGOS
MARGOT
MARION
MARMOT
MAROON
MARROW
MASCON
MASCOT
MATEOS
MATRON
MATZOS
MATZOT
MAYPOP
MEADOW
MELLON
MELLOW
MELTON
MENTOR
MERLON
METEOR
METHOD
METROS
MEZZOS
MICRON
MIGNON
MIKLOS
MILTON
MINION
MINNOW
MIRROR
MONGOL
MONROE
MORION
MORMON
MORROS
MORROW
MORTON
MOSCOW
MOTION
MOTMOT
MOTTOS
MOUTON
MUTTON
MYTHOI
MYTHOS

M••••O

MACACO
MADURO
MALACO
MANITO
MATTEO
MEDICO
MEGALO
MEJICO
MELANO
MERINO
MEXICO
MIKADO
MORPHO

•MO•••

AMOEBA
AMOLES
AMORAL
AMOUNT
AMOURS
EMOTED
EMOTES
IMOGEN
SMOCKS
SMOKED
SMOKER
SMOKES
SMOLTS
SMOOCH
SMOOTH

•M•O••

EMBODY
EMBOLI
EMBOSS
EMBOWS
IMBODY
IMPORT

IMPOSE
IMPOST
SMOOCH
SMOOTH

•M••O•
AMADOU
AMATOL
AMAZON
AMIDOL
AMIGOS
AMNION
EMPLOY

•M•••O
EMBRYO
EMILIO
IMMUNO
SMALTO

••MO••
ALMOND
ALMOST
ARMORS
ARMORY
BEMOAN
COMOSE
COMOUS
CYMOID
CYMOSE
CYMOUS
DEMOBS
DEMODE
DEMONO
DEMONS
DEMOTE
DIMOUT
EDMOND
EXMOOR
FAMOUS
FEMORA
GAMOUS
GEMOTS
HEMOID
HUMORS
INMOST
KIMONO
LEMONS
LOMOND
MEMOIR
MEMORY
MIMOSA
ORMOLU
OSMOND
OSMOSE
POMONA
RAMONA
RAMOSE
RAMOUS
REMORA
REMOTE
REMOVE
RIMOSE
RIMOUS

ROMOLA
RUMORS
SAMOAN
SIMONE
SIMONS
SIMONY
SIMOOM
TUMORS
UNMOOR
UPMOST
UTMOST

••M•O•
BAMBOO
CAMEOS
CAMION
CAMPOS
COMBOS
COMEON
COMMON
COMPOS
DAMSON
EXMOOR
GAMBOL
GAMMON
GUMBOS
LEMNOS
LUMMOX
MAMBOS
MAMMON
NIMROD
POMPOM
POMPON
RAMROD
RAMSON
SAMBOS
SAMSON
SIMEON
SIMOOM
SUMMON
SYMBOL
TAMPON
TEMPOS
TOMBOY
TOMCOD
TOMTOM
UNMOOR

••M••O
BAMAKO
BAMBOO
COMEDO
DEMONO
DOMINO
GAMETO
HEMATO
HYMENO
IMMUNO
KIMONO
LUMINO
LYMPHO
NEMATO
NYMPHO
POMELO

ROMULO
SOMATO
TOMATO
VOMITO

•••MO•
ALAMOS
CLAMOR
COMMON
COSMOS
DAEMON
DAIMON
DROMON
ENAMOR
ETYMON
GAMMON
GISMOS
GIZMOS
GNOMON
HAYMOW
LUMMOX
MAMMON
MARMOT
MORMON
MOTMOT
SALMON
SCHMOS
SERMON
SKIMOS
SUMMON
TERMOR
THYMOL
TREMOR

•••M•O
AKIMBO
CRAMBO
DAIMIO
DAIMYO
PLUMBO

••••MO
CHROMO
DYNAMO
ENTOMO
ESKIMO
KOKOMO
PLASMO
PNEUMO
SEISMO
SPERMO
THERMO

M•P•••
MAPLES
MAPPED
MOPERS
MOPING
MOPISH
MOPOKE
MOPPED
MOPPET

M••P••
MAGPIE
MAPPED
MAYPOP
MOPPED
MOPPET
MORPHO
MYOPES
MYOPIA
MYOPIC

M•••P•
METOPE
MIXUPS

M••••P
MADCAP
MADEUP
MAKEUP
MARKUP
MAYHAP
MAYPOP
MEGILP
METUMP
MISHAP
MOBCAP
MOCKUP
MUDCAP

•MP•••
AMPERE
AMPHRS
AMPULE
AMPULS
EMPALE
EMPERY
EMPIRE
EMPLOY
IMPACT
IMPAIR
IMPALA
IMPALE
IMPARK
IMPART
IMPAWN
IMPEDE
IMPELS
IMPEND
IMPING
IMPISH
IMPORT
IMPOSE
IMPOST
IMPUGN
IMPURE
IMPUTE
UMPIRE

••MP••
ARMPIT
BUMPED
BUMPER
CAMPED
CAMPER

CAMPOS
CAMPUS
COMPEL
COMPLY
COMPOS
DAMPED
DAMPEN
DAMPER
DAMPLY
DIMPLE
DIMPLY
DUMPED
GIMPED
HAMPER
HEMPEN
HUMPED
JUMPED
JUMPER
LAMPAD
LAMPAS
LAMPED
LIMPED
LIMPER
LIMPET
LIMPID
LIMPLY
LUMPED
LUMPEN
LYMPHO
NYMPHA
NYMPHO
NYMPHS
PAMPAS
PAMPER
PIMPED
PIMPLE
PIMPLY
POMPEY
POMPOM
POMPON
PUMPED
PUMPER
RAMPED
RIMPLE
ROMPED
ROMPER
RUMPLE
RUMPUS
SAMPAN
SAMPLE
SEMPRE
SIMPER
SIMPLE
SIMPLY
TAMPAN
TAMPED
TAMPER
TAMPON
TEMPER
TEMPLE
TEMPOS
TEMPTS
TYMPAN
VAMPED

WAMPUM
WAMPUS
WIMPLE

•••MP•
BLIMPS
CHAMPS
CHUMPS
CLAMPS
CLUMPS
CLUMPY
COEMPT
CRAMPS
CRIMPS
CRIMPY
CRUMPS
EXEMPT
FLUMPS
FRUMPS
FRUMPY
GRUMPY
GUIMPE
PLUMPS
PRIMPS
PROMPT
SCAMPI
SCAMPS
SKIMPS
SKIMPY
SLUMPS
STAMPS
STOMPS
STUMPS
STUMPY
SWAMPS
SWAMPY
THUMPS
TRAMPS
TRUMPS

•••M•P
WARMUP

••••MP
DECAMP
ENCAMP
METUMP
REVAMP
SCRIMP
SHRIMP

M•Q•••
MAQUIS

M••Q••
MANQUE
MARQUE
MASQUE
MOSQUE

M•R•••
MARACA
MARAUD
MARBLE

6

MARCEL
MARCIA
MARCOS
MARCUS
MARDUK
MARGAY
MARGES
MARGIE
MARGIN
MARGOS
MARGOT
MARIAN
MARIAS
MARIES
MARINA
MARINE
MARION
MARIST
MARKED
MARKER
MARKET
MARKKA
MARKUP
MARLED
MARLIN
MARMOT
MAROON
MARQUE
MARRED
MARRER
MARROW
MARSHA
MARSHY
MARTAS
MARTEN
MARTHA
MARTHE
MARTIN
MARTYR
MARTYS
MARVEL
MARVIN
MERCER
MERCIA
MERELY
MEREST
MERGED
MERGER
MERGES
MERINO
MERITS
MERLES
MERLIN
MERLON
MERMAN
MERMEN
MEROUS
MERVIN
MIRAGE
MIRIAM
MIRING
MIRROR
MORALE
MORALS
MORASS
MORAYS
MORBID
MOREAU
MOREEN
MORELS
MORGAN
MORGEN
MORGUE
MORION
MORLEY
MORMON
MORONS
MOROSE
MORPHO
MORRIS
MORROS
MORROW
MORSEL
MORTAL
MORTAR
MORTON
MORTYS
MORULA
MURALS
MURDER
MURIEL
MURINE
MURMUR
MURRAY
MURRES
MURREY
MYRIAD
MYRICA
MYRMEC
MYRNAS
MYRTLE

M••R••

MACRON
MADRAS
MADRID
MAORIS
MARRED
MARRER
MARROW
MATRIX
MATRON
MEGRIM
METRIC
METROS
MICRON
MIDRIB
MIRROR
MITRAL
MOIRAS
MONROE
MOORED
MORRIS
MORROS
MORROW
MOURNS
MURRAY
MURRES
MURREY

M•••R•

MACERS
MADURA
MADURO
MAIGRE
MAITRE
MAJORS
MAKERS
MALGRE
MALORY
MANORS
MANURE
MASERS
MASORA
MATURE
MAYORS
MAZERS
MEMORY
MESSRS
METERS
MILERS
MILORD
MIMERS
MINERS
MINORS
MISERS
MISERY
MITERS
MIXERS
MODERN
MOHURS
MOLARS
MOPERS
MOTORS
MOVERS
MOWERS
MOZART

M••••R

MADDER
MAGYAR
MAHLER
MAILER
MAIMER
MANGER
MANNER
MARKER
MARRER
MARTYR
MASHER
MASKER
MASTER
MATTER
MAULER
MAUSER
MAZIER
MEAGER
MEANER
MEDLAR
MEEKER
MEETER
MELTER
MEMBER
MEMOIR
MENDER
MENHIR
MENTOR
MERCER
MERGER
METEOR
METIER
MIDAIR
MILDER
MILKER
MILLER
MILTER
MINCER
MINDER
MINTER
MIRROR
MISTER
MOBBER
MOCKER
MOHAIR
MOILER
MOLDER
MOLTER
MONGER
MOOTER
MORTAR
MOTHER
MOUSER
MUCKER
MUDDER
MUGGAR
MUGGER
MUGGUR
MULLER
MUMMER
MURDER
MURMUR
MUSHER
MUSTER
MUTTER

•MR•••

AMRITA

•M•R••

AMERCE
AMORAL
EMBRUE
EMBRYO
EMERGE
EMERIC
IMARET
IMBRUE
SMARMY
SMARTS
SMIRCH
SMIRKS
UMBRAE
UMBRAS

•M••R•

AMBARI
AMBARY
AMBERS
AMBERY
AMENRA
AMOURS
AMPERE
AMPHRS
DMITRI
EMBARK
EMBARS
EMBERS
EMEERS
EMIGRE
EMPERY
EMPIRE
IMBARK
IMMURE
IMPARK
IMPART
IMPORT
IMPURE
SMEARS
SMEARY
UMBERS
UMPIRE

•M•••R

AMBLER
AMUSER
IMPAIR
SMILER
SMITER
SMOKER

••MR••

CYMRIC
NIMROD
RAMROD

••M•R•

ADMIRE
ALMIRA
ARMORS
ARMORY
ARMURE
AYMARA
BEMIRE
CAMERA
CIMBRI
COMERS
CYMARS
DEMURE
DEMURS
DIMERS
ELMERS
ELMIRA
FEMORA
FEMURS
GEMARA
HOMBRE
HOMERS
HUMORS
IMMURE
LEMURS
MEMORY
MIMERS
NAMERS
NOMURA
ORMERS
REMARK
REMORA
RIMERS
RUMORS
SAMARA
SEMPRE
SIMARS
TAMERS
TIMBRE
TIMERS
TUMORS
VOMERS
WOMERA

••M••R

BOMBER
BUMMER
BUMPER
CAMBER
CAMPER
COMBER
CUMBER
DAMMAR
DAMMER
DAMPER
DIMMER
EXMOOR
FUMIER
GAMBIR
GAMIER
GAMMER
HAMMER
HAMPER
HEMMER
HOMIER
HUMMER
JUMPER
LIMBER
LIMIER
LIMNER
LIMPER
LUMBAR
LUMBER
MEMBER
MEMOIR
MUMMER
NUMBER
PAMPER
PUMPER
RAMMER
RIMMER
ROMPER
RUMMER
SAMBUR
SIMMER
SIMPER
SOMBER
SUMMER
SUMNER

6

TAMPER
TEMPER
TIMBER
UNMOOR
YAMMER

•••M•R
BUMMER
CALMER
CHIMER
CLAMOR
DAGMAR
DAMMAR
DAMMER
DIMMER
DORMER
ENAMOR
FARMER
FIRMER
FORMER
FRAMER
FULMAR
GAMMER
HAMMER
HEMMER
HUMMER
ISOMER
KILMER
MAIMER
MUMMER
MURMUR
PALMAR
PALMER
PRIMER
RAMMER
REAMER
RHYMER
RIMMER
ROAMER
ROOMER
RUMMER
SEAMER
SEEMER
SIMMER
SUMMER
TEEMER
TERMER
TERMOR
TREMOR
WARMER
WEIMAR
WORMER
YAMMER

M•S•••
MASCON
MASCOT
MASERS
MASHED
MASHER
MASHES
MASHIE
MASKED
MASKEG
MASKER
MASONS
MASORA
MASQUE
MASSED
MASSES
MASSIF
MASTED
MASTER
MASTIC
MESCAL
MESHED
MESHES
MESIAL
MESIAN
MESNES
MESONS
MESSED
MESSES
MESSRS
MESTEE
MISCUE
MISDID
MISERS
MISERY
MISFIT
MISHAP
MISKAL
MISLAY
MISSAL
MISSED
MISSES
MISSIS
MISSUS
MISTED
MISTER
MISUSE
MOSAIC
MOSCOW
MOSEYS
MOSLEM
MOSLEY
MOSQUE
MOSSES
MOSTLY
MUSCAE
MUSCAT
MUSCLE
MUSEUM
MUSHED
MUSHER
MUSHES
MUSING
MUSKEG
MUSKET
MUSKIT
MUSLIM
MUSLIN
MUSSED
MUSSEL
MUSSES
MUSTEE
MUSTER
MYSELF
MYSTIC

M••S••
MAISIE
MAISON
MANSES
MARSHA
MARSHY
MASSED
MASSES
MASSIF
MAUSER
MEASLY
MENSAL
MENSES
MESSED
MESSES
MESSRS
MIASMA
MIOSIS
MISSAL
MISSED
MISSES
MISSIS
MISSUS
MOISHE
MORSEL
MOSSES
MOUSED
MOUSER
MOUSES
MOUSSE
MUSSED
MUSSEL
MUSSES
MYOSIN
MYOSIS

M•••S•
MAOISM
MAOIST
MARIST
MAYEST
MEDUSA
MEGASS
MEREST
MIMOSA
MISUSE
MODEST
MODISH
MOLEST
MOMISM
MONGST
MONISM
MONIST
MOPISH
MORASS
MOROSE
MOUSSE
MUCOSA
MUCOSE
MULISH
MUTISM

M••••S
MABELS
MACAWS
MACERS
MACLES
MADAMS
MADGES
MADRAS
MAGOTS
MAIZES
MAJORS
MAKERS
MALAYS
MAMBAS
MAMBOS
MAMEYS
MAMIES
MAMMAS
MANDYS
MANGOS
MANIAS
MANORS
MANSES
MANTAS
MANTES
MANTIS
MAORIS
MAPLES
MAQUIS
MARCOS
MARCUS
MARGES
MARGOS
MARIAS
MARIES
MARTAS
MARTYS
MASERS
MASHES
MASONS
MASSES
MATEOS
MATEYS
MATINS
MATTES
MATZOS
MAUDES
MAUNDS
MAUVES
MAXIMS
MAYORS
MAZERS
MEATUS
MECCAS
MEDALS
MEDICS
MEGASS
MELEES
MELONS
MENSES
MERGES
MERITS
MERLES
MEROUS
MESHES
MESNES
MESONS
MESSES
MESSRS
METALS
METERS
METROS
MEZZOS
MIAULS
MICKYS
MIDGES
MIKLOS
MILERS
MILLYS
MIMERS
MIMICS
MINCES
MINERS
MINIMS
MINORS
MINXES
MIOSIS
MISERS
MISSES
MISSIS
MISSUS
MITERS
MIXERS
MIXUPS
MOBIUS
MODELS
MOGULS
MOHURS
MOIRAS
MOLARS
MOLIES
MOLLYS
MONADS
MONEYS
MONIES
MONTES
MONTHS
MONTYS
MOPERS
MORALS
MORASS
MORAYS
MORELS
MORONS
MORRIS
MORROS
MORTYS
MOSEYS
MOSSES
MOTELS
MOTIFS
MOTORS
MOTTOS
MOULDS
MOULTS
MOUNTS
MOURNS
MOUSES
MOUTHS
MOVERS
MOVIES
MOWERS
MUCOUS
MUFTIS
MULCTS
MURALS
MURRES
MUSHES
MUSSES
MYOPES
MYOSIS
MYRNAS
MYTHOS

•M•S••
AMUSED
AMUSER
AMUSES
EMESIS
OMASUM
TMESIS

•M••S•
AMBUSH
AMIDST
EMBOSS
IMMESH
IMPISH
IMPOSE
IMPOST

•M•••S
AMAZES
AMBERS
AMBITS
AMBLES
AMEBAS
AMENDS
AMENTS
AMICES
AMIDES
AMIENS
AMIGOS
AMOLES
AMOURS
AMPHRS
AMPULS
AMUSES
EMBARS
EMBAYS
EMBEDS
EMBERS
EMBOSS
EMBOWS
EMCEES
EMEERS
EMENDS
EMESIS
EMILES
EMILYS
EMMETS
EMMIES

EMOTES
IMAGES
IMBEDS
IMBUES
IMIDES
IMINES
IMMIES
IMPELS
OMEGAS
SMACKS
SMALLS
SMARTS
SMAZES
SMEARS
SMELLS
SMELTS
SMILES
SMIRKS
SMITES
SMITHS
SMOCKS
SMOKES
SMOLTS
TMESIS
UMBELS
UMBERS
UMBLES
UMBRAS
UMIAKS

••MS••
DAMSEL
DAMSON
KAMSIN
RAMSON
SAMSHU
SAMSON

••M•S•
ALMOST
BEMUSE
CAMASS
CAMISE
COMOSE
CYMOSE
DAMASK
DEMISE
ENMESH
FAMISH
IMMESH
INMESH
INMOST
KUMISS
LAMEST
MIMOSA
MOMISM
NOMISM
OSMOSE
RAMOSE
REMISE
REMISS
RIMOSE
ROMISH
TAMEST
UNMASK
UPMOST
UTMOST
ZYMASE

••M••S
ADMITS
ALMAHS
ALMUDS
ARMETS
ARMIES
ARMORS
BOMBES
CAMASS
CAMELS
CAMEOS
CAMPOS
CAMPUS
COMBOS
COMERS
COMETS
COMICS
COMMAS
COMOUS
COMPOS
CUMINS
CYMARS
CYMOUS
DAMANS
DEMIES
DEMITS
DEMOBS
DEMONS
DEMURS
DIMERS
ELMERS
EMMETS
EMMIES
FAMOUS
FEMURS
GAMINS
GAMMAS
GAMOUS
GAMUTS
GEMOTS
GIMELS
GUMBOS
GUMMAS
HAMALS
HAMZAS
HOMERS
HUMANS
HUMORS
HYMENS
IAMBUS
IMMIES
JAMIES
JIMMYS
KAMIKS
KUMISS
LAMEDS
LAMIAS
LAMMAS
LAMPAS
LEMMAS
LEMNOS
LEMONS
LEMURS
LIMBUS
LIMENS
LIMEYS
LIMITS
LUMENS
MAMBAS
MAMBOS
MAMEYS
MAMIES
MAMMAS
MIMERS
MIMICS
NAMERS
NIMBUS
NOMADS
NYMPHS
ORMERS
PAMPAS
RAMIES
RAMOUS
REMANS
REMISS
REMITS
RIMERS
RIMOUS
ROMANS
RUMBAS
RUMORS
RUMPUS
SAMBAS
SAMBOS
SAMMYS
SIMARS
SIMONS
SUMACS
TAMERS
TEMPOS
TEMPTS
TIMERS
TIMMYS
TOMANS
TOMMYS
TUMORS
UNMANS
UNMEWS
VOMERS
VOMITS
WAMMUS
WAMPUS
YAMENS
YAMUNS
ZAMIAS
ZOMBIS

•••MS•
AHIMSA
CLUMSY
FLIMSY
SLIMSY
WHIMSY

•••M•S
ABOMAS
ABOMBS
AGAMAS
ALAMOS
ANIMAS
ANIMUS
AROMAS
BERMES
BLAMES
BLIMPS
BROMES
BRUMES
CADMUS
CHAMPS
CHIMES
CHUMPS
CLAMPS
CLIMBS
CLIMES
CLUMPS
COMMAS
COOMBS
COSMOS
CRAMPS
CREMES
CRIMES
CRIMPS
CRUMBS
CRUMPS
DERMAS
DOGMAS
DRAMAS
ELEMIS
ENEMAS
FERMIS
FLAMES
FLUMES
FLUMPS
FRAMES
FRUMPS
GAMMAS
GISMOS
GIZMOS
GLUMES
GNOMES
GRIMES
GRUMES
GUMMAS
HBOMBS
HERMES
HOLMES
JIMMYS
KARMAS
KERMES
KERMIS
LAMMAS
LEMMAS
LITMUS
LLAMAS
MAMMAS
NAOMIS
NEUMES
NORMAS
PLUMBS
PLUMES
PLUMPS
PRIMES
PRIMPS
RHUMBS
RHYMES
SALMIS
SAMMYS
SCAMPS
SCHMOS
SEAMUS
SHAMES
SHAMUS
SIGMAS
SKIMOS
SKIMPS
SLIMES
SLUMPS
SPUMES
STAMPS
STOMPS
STUMPS
SWAMIS
SWAMPS
THAMES
THEMES
THEMIS
THOMAS
THUMBS
THUMPS
THYMES
THYMUS
TIMMYS
TOMMYS
TRAMPS
TRUMPS
ULEMAS
WAMMUS
WILMAS

••••MS
ABOHMS
ABRAMS
ABYSMS
ADDAMS
ADEEMS
ALARMS
ALBUMS
AXIOMS
BEDIMS
BEGUMS
BESOMS
BLOOMS
BOSOMS
BRAHMS
BREAMS
BROOMS
CAROMS
CHARMS
CHASMS
CHIRMS
CLAIMS
CREAMS
DEGUMS
DENIMS
DREAMS
FANUMS
FLEAMS
FORUMS
GLEAMS
GLOOMS
GROOMS
HAKIMS
HAREMS
HBEAMS
HIRAMS
IBEAMS
IDIOMS
IHRAMS
INARMS
JORAMS
JORUMS
MADAMS
MAXIMS
MINIMS
NAHUMS
PRISMS
PROEMS
PSALMS
QUALMS
REALMS
REARMS
RHEIMS
SCRAMS
SCRUMS
SEDUMS
SEISMS
SERUMS
SHAWMS
SPASMS
STEAMS
STORMS
STRUMS
SWARMS
THERMS
THRUMS
TOTEMS
VENOMS
WHELMS
XYLEMS
ZBEAMS

M•T•••
MATEOS
MATEYS
MATING
MATINS
MATRIX
MATRON
MATTED
MATTEO
MATTER
MATTES
MATTIE
MATURE
MATZOS
MATZOT

METAGE
METALS
METEOR
METERS
METHOD
METHYL
METIER
METING
METOPE
METRIC
METROS
METTLE
METUMP
MITERS
MITRAL
MITTEN
MOTELS
MOTHER
MOTIFS
MOTILE
MOTION
MOTIVE
MOTLEY
MOTMOT
MOTORS
MOTTLE
MOTTOS
MUTANT
MUTATE
MUTING
MUTINY
MUTISM
MUTTER
MUTTON
MUTUAL
MUTULE
MYTHIC
MYTHOI
MYTHOS

M••T••
MAITRE
MALTED
MALTHA
MANTAS
MANTEL
MANTES
MANTIC
MANTIS
MANTLE
MANTUA
MARTAS
MARTEN
MARTHA
MARTHE
MARTIN
MARTYR
MARTYS
MASTED
MASTER
MASTIC
MATTED
MATTEO
MATTER
MATTES
MATTIE
MEATUS
MEETER
MEETLY
MELTED
MELTER
MELTON
MENTAL
MENTOR
MESTEE
METTLE
MILTED
MILTER
MILTON
MINTED
MINTER
MIOTIC
MISTED
MISTER
MITTEN
MOATED
MOLTED
MOLTEN
MOLTER
MOLTKE
MONTES
MONTHS
MONTYS
MOOTED
MOOTER
MORTAL
MORTAR
MORTON
MORTYS
MOSTLY
MOTTLE
MOTTOS
MOUTHS
MOUTHY
MOUTON
MUFTIS
MUSTEE
MUSTER
MUTTER
MUTTON
MYRTLE
MYSTIC

M•••T•
MAGOTS
MALATE
MANITO
MANITU
MERITS
MIGHTY
MINUTE
MOIETY
MOULTS
MOUNTS
MOUNTY
MULCTS
MUTATE
MYCETE

M••••T
MAGGOT
MAGNET
MAHOUT
MALLET
MAMMET
MAOIST
MARGOT
MARIST
MARKET
MARMOT
MASCOT
MATZOT
MAYEST
MEREST
MIDGET
MIDGUT
MILLET
MINUET
MISFIT
MODEST
MOLEST
MOMENT
MONGST
MONIST
MOPPET
MOTMOT
MOZART
MULLET
MUSCAT
MUSKET
MUSKIT
MUTANT

•M•T••
AMATOL
AMYTAL
DMITRI
EMETIC
EMETIN
EMOTED
EMOTES
SMITER
SMITES
SMITHS
SMITHY
SMUTCH
SMUTTY

•M••T•
AMBITS
AMENTS
AMRITA
EMEUTE
EMMETS
EMMETT
IMPUTE
OMENTA
SMALTI
SMALTO
SMARTS
SMELTS
SMOLTS
SMOOTH
SMUTTY

•M•••T
AMIDST
AMOUNT
AMULET
EMMETT
IMARET
IMPACT
IMPART
IMPORT
IMPOST
OMELET
UMLAUT

••MT••
TAMTAM
TOMTIT
TOMTOM

••M•T•
ADMITS
ARMETS
BEMATA
COMATE
COMETS
COMITY
DEMITS
DEMOTE
DIMITY
EMMETS
EMMETT
ENMITY
GAMETE
GAMETO
GAMUTS
GEMOTS
GOMUTI
HAMITE
HEMATO
INMATE
LIMITS
NEMATO
NIMITZ
REMITS
REMOTE
SAMITE
SEMITE
SOMATA
SOMATO
SOMITE
TEMPTS
TOMATO
VOMITO
VOMITS

••M••T
ADMIXT
ALMOST
ARMLET
ARMPIT
CAMLET
CEMENT
COMBAT
COMFIT
COMMIT
DIMOUT
DIMWIT
EMMETT
FOMENT
GAMBIT
GIMLET
HAMLET
INMOST
LAMENT
LAMEST
LIMPET
LOMENT
MAMMET
MOMENT
SAMLET
SUMMIT
TAMEST
TOMCAT
TOMTIT
TUMULT
UNMEET
UPMOST
UTMOST
WOMBAT

•••MT•
WARMTH

•••M•T
CERMET
CLIMAT
COEMPT
COMMIT
DERMAT
EXEMPT
FORMAT
HELMET
HERMIT
KISMET
MAMMET
MARMOT
MOTMOT
PERMIT
PROMPT
STOMAT
SUBMIT
SUMMIT

••••MT
DREAMT

MU••••
MUCKED
MUCKER
MUCOID
MUCOSA
MUCOSE
MUCOUS
MUDCAP
MUDDED
MUDDER
MUDDLE
MUFFED
MUFFIN
MUFFLE
MUFTIS
MUGGAR
MUGGED
MUGGER
MUGGUR
MUKLUK
MULCTS
MULISH
MULLAH
MULLED
MULLEN
MULLER
MULLET
MULLEY
MUMBLE
MUMMED
MUMMER
MUNICH
MURALS
MURDER
MURIEL
MURINE
MURMUR
MURRAY
MURRES
MURREY
MUSCAE
MUSCAT
MUSCLE
MUSEUM
MUSHED
MUSHER
MUSHES
MUSING
MUSKEG
MUSKET
MUSKIT
MUSLIM
MUSLIN
MUSSED
MUSSEL
MUSSES
MUSTEE
MUSTER
MUTANT
MUTATE
MUTING
MUTINY
MUTISM
MUTTER
MUTTON
MUTUAL
MUTULE
MUUMUU
MUZHIK
MUZZLE

M•U•••
MAUDES
MAULED
MAULER

6

MAUMAU
MAUNDS
MAUNDY
MAUSER
MAUVES
MOULDS
MOULDY
MOULIN
MOULTS
MOUNTS
MOUNTY
MOURNS
MOUSED
MOUSER
MOUSES
MOUSSE
MOUTHS
MOUTHY
MOUTON
MUUMUU

M••U••
MACULA
MACULE
MADURA
MADURO
MAGUEY
MANUAL
MANUEL
MANURE
MAQUIS
MATURE
MAZUMA
MEDUSA
METUMP
MEZUZA
MIAULS
MIGUEL
MINUET
MINUTE
MISUSE
MIXUPS
MODULE
MOGULS
MOHURS
MORULA
MUTUAL
MUTULE

M•••U•
MADEUP
MAGNUM
MAHOUT
MAKEUP
MANFUL
MANQUE
MANTUA
MARAUD
MARCUS
MARDUK
MARKUP
MARQUE
MASQUE
MEATUS
MEDIUM
MEROUS
MIDGUT
MILIUM
MINIUM
MISCUE
MISSUS
MOBIUS
MOCKUP
MORGUE
MOSQUE
MUCOUS
MUGGUR
MUKLUK
MURMUR
MUSEUM
MUUMUU

M••••U
MANCHU
MANITU
MAUMAU
MILIEU
MOREAU
MUUMUU

•MU•••
AMULET
AMUSED
AMUSER
AMUSES
SMUDGE
SMUDGY
SMUGLY
SMUTCH
SMUTTY

•M•U••
AMBUSH
AMOUNT
AMOURS
AMPULE
AMPULS
EMEUTE
IMBUED
IMBUES
IMMUNE
IMMUNO
IMMURE
IMPUGN
IMPURE
IMPUTE

•M••U•
AMYLUM
EMBRUE
IMBRUE
OMASUM
UMLAUT

•M•••U
AMADOU

••MU••
ALMUCE
ALMUDE
ALMUDS
ARMURE
BEMUSE
DEMURE
DEMURS
EDMUND
FEMURS
GAMUTS
GOMUTI
IMMUNE
IMMUNO
IMMURE
LEMUEL
LEMURS
LIMULI
NOMURA
ORMUZD
OSMUND
REMUDA
ROMULO
SAMUEL
TUMULT
YAMUNS

••M•U•
ARMFUL
CAMPUS
COMOUS
CYMOUS
DIMOUT
FAMOUS
GAMOUS
HAMAUL
HUMBUG
IAMBUS
LIMBUS
NIMBUS
OSMIUM
RAMOUS
RIMOUS
RUMPUS
SAMBUR
WAMMUS
WAMPUM
WAMPUS

••M••U
ORMOLU
SAMSHU

•••MU•
ANIMUS
CADMUS
LITMUS
MURMUR
MUUMUU
SEAMUS
SHAMUS
TALMUD
THYMUS
WAMMUS
WARMUP

•••M•U
MAUMAU
MUUMUU

M•V•••
MOVERS
MOVIES
MOVING

M••V••
MARVEL
MARVIN
MAUVES
MELVIN
MERVIN

M•••V•
MOHAVE
MOJAVE
MOTIVE

••M•V•
REMOVE

M•W•••
MEWING
MEWLED
MOWERS
MOWING

M••W••
MEOWED
MIDWAY

M•••W•
MACAWS
MALAWI
MOHAWK

M••••W
MALLOW
MARROW
MEADOW
MELLOW
MILDEW
MINNOW
MORROW
MOSCOW

•M••W•
EMBOWS
IMPAWN

••MW••
DIMWIT

••M•W•
UNMEWS

•••M•W
HAYMOW

M•X•••
MAXIMS
MAXINE
MAXIXE
MEXICO
MIXERS
MIXING
MIXUPS
MYXOMA

M••X••
MINXES

M•••X•
MAXIXE

M••••X
MATRIX
MENINX

•M•••X
SMILAX

••M•X•
ADMIXT

••M••X
COMMIX
LUMMOX

•••M•X
CLIMAX
COMMIX
LUMMOX

MY••••
MYCETE
MYELIN
MYOPES
MYOPIA
MYOPIC
MYOSIN
MYOSIS
MYRIAD
MYRICA
MYRMEC
MYRNAS
MYRTLE
MYSELF
MYSTIC
MYTHIC
MYTHOI
MYTHOS
MYXOMA

M•Y•••
MAYDAY
MAYEST
MAYHAP
MAYHEM
MAYING
MAYORS
MAYPOP

M••Y••
MAGYAR

M•••Y•
MALAYA
MALAYS
MAMEYS
MANDYS
MARTYR
MARTYS
MATEYS
METHYL
MICKYS
MILLYS
MOLLYS
MONEYS
MONTYS
MORAYS
MORTYS
MOSEYS

M••••Y
MAGUEY
MAINLY
MALADY
MALORY
MARGAY
MARSHY
MAUNDY
MAYDAY
MAZILY
MEANLY
MEASLY
MEDLEY
MEEKLY
MEETLY
MELODY
MEMORY
MERELY
MICKEY
MIDDAY
MIDWAY
MIGHTY
MILADY
MILDLY
MILLAY
MINIFY
MISERY
MISLAY
MODIFY
MOIETY
MONDAY
MONKEY
MONODY
MOOLEY
MORLEY
MOSLEY
MOSTLY
MOTLEY
MOULDY
MOUNTY
MOUTHY
MULLEY
MURRAY

MURREY
MUTINY

•MY•••
AMYLIC
AMYLUM
AMYTAL

•M••Y•
EMBAYS
EMBRYO
EMILYS

•M•••Y
AMBARY
AMBERY
EMBODY
EMPERY
EMPLOY
IMBODY
SMARMY
SMEARY
SMELLY
SMITHY
SMUDGY
SMUGLY
SMUTTY

••M•Y•
JIMMYS
LIMEYS
MAMEYS
SAMMYS
TIMMYS
TOMMYS

••M••Y
ARMORY
BOMBAY
COMEDY
COMELY
COMITY
COMPLY
DAMPLY
DIMITY
DIMPLY
DUMBLY
ENMITY
FAMILY
GAMELY
GAMILY
HOMELY
HOMILY
HOMINY
HUMBLY
LAMELY
LIMPLY
MEMORY
NAMELY
NUMBLY
PIMPLY
POMPEY
RAMIFY
REMEDY
ROMANY
ROMNEY
SIMONY
SIMPLY
TIMELY
TOMBOY
TUMEFY
WAMBLY

•••MY•
DAIMYO
FORMYL
JIMMYS
SAMMYS
TIMMYS
TOMMYS

•••M•Y
CALMLY
CHAMMY
CHUMMY
CLAMMY
CLUMPY
CLUMSY
CRIMPY
CRUMBY
CRUMMY
DISMAY
FIRMLY
FLIMSY
FRUMPY
GLUMLY
GRIMLY
GRUMPY
PLUMMY
PRIMLY
SCUMMY
SEEMLY
SHAMMY
SHIMMY
SKIMPY
SLIMLY
SLIMSY
SLUMMY
STUMPY
SWAMPY
TERMLY
TRIMLY
WARMLY
WHAMMY
WHIMSY

••••MY
BIGAMY
BLOOMY
BROOMY
CHAMMY
CHUMMY
CLAMMY
CREAMY
CRUMMY
DIGAMY
DREAMY
ECTOMY
GLEAMY
GLOOMY
HAULMY
INFAMY
JEREMY
PLUMMY
QUALMY
RHEUMY
SCUMMY
SHAMMY
SHIMMY
SLUMMY
SMARMY
SODOMY
STEAMY
STORMY
WHAMMY

M•Z•••
MAZERS
MAZIER
MAZILY
MAZING
MAZUMA
MEZUZA
MEZZOS
MIZZEN
MOZART
MUZHIK
MUZZLE

M••Z••
MAIZES
MATZOS
MATZOT
MEZZOS
MIZZEN
MUZZLE

M•••Z•
MEZUZA

•M•Z••
AMAZED
AMAZES
AMAZON
SMAZES

••MZ••
HAMZAS

••M•Z•
ORMUZD

••M••Z
NIMITZ

NA••••
NABBED
NABOBS
NADINE
NADIRS
NAEVUS
NAGANA
NAGGED
NAGGER
NAGOYA
NAHUMS
NAIADS
NAILED
NAMELY
NAMERS
NAMING
NANCYS
NANISM
NANTES
NAOMIS
NAOSES
NAPALM
NAPERY
NAPIER
NAPKIN
NAPLES
NAPPED
NAPPER
NAPPES
NAPPIE
NARIAL
NARINE
NARROW
NARWAL
NASALS
NASHUA
NASIAL
NASION
NASSAU
NASSER
NASTIC
NATANT
NATHAN
NATION
NATIVE
NATRON
NATURE
NAUGHT
NAUSEA
NAUTCH
NAVAHO
NAVAJO
NAVELS
NAVIES
NAWABS
NAZIFY
NAZISM

N•A•••
NEARBY
NEARED
NEARER
NEARLY
NEATER
NEATLY
NIACIN
NUANCE

N••A••
NAGANA
NAIADS
NAPALM
NASALS
NATANT
NAVAHO
NAVAJO
NAWABS
NEGATE
NEMATO
NEVADA
NEWARK
NOBALL
NOMADS
NONAGE
NOPALS
NOTARY
NOWAYS

N•••A•
NARIAL
NARWAL
NASIAL
NASSAU
NATHAN
NECTAR
NEURAL
NILGAI
NORIAS
NORMAL
NORMAN
NORMAS
NORWAY
NOUGAT
NOUNAL
NUBIAN
NUBIAS
NUCHAE
NULLAH

N••••A
NAGANA
NAGOYA
NASHUA
NAUSEA
NEBULA
NEVADA
NOMURA
NOVENA
NUMINA
NUTRIA
NYMPHA

•NA•••
ANABAS
ANADEM
ANALOG
ANANKE
ANATTO
ENABLE
ENACTS
ENAMEL
ENAMOR
ENATES
ENATIC
GNARLS
GNARLY
GNATHO
GNAWED
GNAWER
INARCH
INARMS
KNACKS
KNARRY
KNAVES
ONAGER
ONAGRI
SNACKS
SNAFUS
SNAGGY
SNAILS
SNAKED
SNAKES
SNAPPY
SNARED
SNARER
SNARES
SNARLS
SNARLY
SNATCH
SNATHE
SNATHS
UNABLE

•N•A••
ANGARY
ANKARA
ANLACE
ANLAGE
ANNALS
ANSATE
ENCAGE
ENCAMP
ENCASE
ENDALL
ENFACE
ENGAGE
ENLACE
ENRAGE
ENRAPT
ENTAIL
INCAGE
INCASE
INDABA
INFAMY
INFANT
INHALE
INHAUL
INLACE
INLAID
INLAND
INLAWS
INLAYS
INMATE
INNATE
INSANE
INTACT
INTAKE
INVADE
INWALL

INWARD
KNEADS
ONWARD
SNEAKS
SNEAKY
UNBARS
UNCAGE
UNCAPS
UNEASY
UNFAIR
UNHAIR
UNHAND
UNHATS
UNLACE
UNLADE
UNLAID
UNLAYS
UNMADE
UNMAKE
UNMANS
UNMASK
UNPACK
UNPAID
UNSAFE
UNSAID
UNSAYS
UNWARY

•N••A•

ANABAS
ANDEAN
ANIMAL
ANIMAS
ANITAS
ANNEAL
ANNUAL
ANORAK
ANTIAR
ANURAN
ANYWAY
ENDEAR
ENEMAS
ENGRAM
ENNEAD
ENTRAP
ENWRAP
INDIAN
INROAD
INSPAN
INSTAR
INWRAP
ONEWAY
SNOCAT
UNBEAR
UNCIAL
UNCLAD
UNDRAW
UNGUAL
UNLEAD
UNLOAD
UNREAD
UNREAL
UNSEAL
UNSEAM
UNSEAT
UNSNAP
UNWRAP

•N•••A

ANCONA
ANDREA
ANEMIA
ANGELA
ANGINA
ANGLIA
ANGOLA
ANGORA
ANITRA
ANKARA
ANOXIA
ANTHEA
ANTLIA
ENCINA
ENIGMA
ENTERA
INDABA
INTIMA
ONEIDA
PNEUMA
UNGULA

••NA••

ADNATE
AGNAIL
AGNATE
ANNALS
ARNAUD
BANANA
BINARY
BONACI
BYNAME
CANAAN
CANADA
CANALS
CANAPE
CANARD
CANARY
DANAID
DANAUS
DENARY
DINAHS
DINARS
DONALD
DONATE
DYNAMO
DYNAST
FINALE
FINALS
GONADS
IGNACE
INNATE
JONAHS
KANAKA
KINASE
LANAIS
LANATE
LENAPE
LINAGE
LUNACY
LUNATE
MANAGE
MANANA
MENACE
MENAGE
MONADS
NONAGE
ORNATE
PANADA
PANAMA
PINANG
RONALD
SENARY
SENATE
SONANT
SONARS
SONATA
TENACE
TENANT
ZANANA
ZENANA
ZONARY
ZONATE

••N•A•

AENEAS
ANNEAL
ANNUAL
APNEAL
BANIAN
BANTAM
BANYAN
BANZAI
BENDAY
BENGAL
BONSAI
BUNYAN
CANAAN
CANCAN
CANNAE
CANNAS
CANVAS
CENTAL
CONFAB
CONGAS
CONRAD
CUNEAL
DENIAL
DENTAL
DONNAS
DUNBAR
DUNCAN
ENNEAD
EONIAN
FANGAS
FANTAN
FENIAN
FINIAL
FONTAL
FUNGAL
GENIAL
GINGAL
GUNMAN
GUNNAR
HANGAR
HANNAH
HANNAS
HENNAS
IONIAN
JINGAL
JUNEAU
JUNTAS
KANSAN
KANSAS
KONRAD
LANDAU
LINDAS
LINEAL
LINEAR
LINGAS
LONGAN
MANDAN
MANIAC
MANIAS
MANTAS
MANUAL
MENIAL
MENSAL
MENTAL
MINOAN
MONDAY
PANDAS
PENIAL
PENMAN
PENNAE
PENPAL
PENTAD
PINDAR
PINEAL
PINNAE
PINNAL
PUNJAB
PUNKAS
RANDAL
RANDAN
RENTAL
RUNWAY
SANDAL
SANGAR
SANJAK
SANSAR
SENDAL
SENLAC
SENNAS
SINBAD
SONIAS
SONYAS
SUNDAE
SUNDAY
SUNNAH
SYNTAX
TANKAS
TINCAL
VANDAL
VANMAN
VENIAL
WANDAS

••N••A

APNOEA
ARNICA
BANANA
BENITA
CANADA
CANULA
CENTRA
CINEMA
CONCHA
CONTRA
FANEGA
GENERA
GENEVA
KANAKA
LINGUA
LUNULA
MANANA
MANILA
MANTUA
MONICA
PANADA
PANAMA
PENNIA
SANDRA
SENECA
SENORA
SONATA
SYNURA
TUNDRA
TUNICA
ZANANA
ZENANA
ZINNIA
ZONULA

•••NA•

ADONAI
ARENAS
ATONAL
BWANAS
CANNAE
CANNAS
CARNAL
COGNAC
DIANAS
DONNAS
ELENAS
FAUNAE
FAUNAL
FAUNAS
FORNAX
GUNNAR
HANNAH
HANNAS
HENNAS
HYENAS
HYMNAL
JAINAS
KARNAK
KIDNAP
LEONAS
LIANAS
MAENAD
MYRNAS
NOUNAL
PENNAE
PINNAE
PINNAL
PLANAR
PUTNAM
REGNAL
RHINAL
SAUNAS
SENNAS
SIGNAL
SPINAL
SUNNAH
TARNAL
THANAT
THENAL
THENAR
TRINAL
UNSNAP
URINAL
VERNAL
VERNAS
ZOONAL

•••N•A

AGENDA
AMANDA
AMENRA
ARANTA
ARUNTA
BIANCA
BRENDA
CORNEA
CORNUA
CRANIA
DUENNA
EUPNEA
GDYNIA
GUINEA
HERNIA
JOANNA
LUANDA
ODYNIA
OMENTA
PENNIA
PHONIA
QUANTA
RWANDA
SIENNA
STANZA
TAENIA
UGANDA
URANIA
VIENNA
ZINNIA

••••NA

ALUMNA
ALVINA
ANCONA
ANGINA
ATHENA
BANANA

CABANA
CARINA
CATENA
CORONA
DHARNA
DHURNA
DUENNA
EDWINA
ENCINA
ESPANA
FARINA
GALENA
GUIANA
GUYANA
HAVANA
HELENA
IGUANA
JACANA
JARINA
JOANNA
KORUNA
LACUNA
LAMINA
LIMINA
LUMINA
MANANA
MARINA
NAGANA
NOVENA
NUMINA
ORGANA
PATINA
PIRANA
POMONA
PURANA
RAMONA
REGINA
RETINA
ROWENA
ROXANA
RUMINA
SABINA
SERENA
SIENNA
STERNA
TIRANA
VAGINA
VARUNA
VERONA
VICUNA
VIENNA
VIMINA
ZANANA
ZENANA

N•B•••
NABBED
NABOBS
NEBULA
NIBBED
NIBBLE
NOBALL
NOBBLE
NUBBIN
NUBBLE
NUBBLY
NUBIAN
NUBIAS
NUBILE

N••B••
NABBED
NIBBED
NIBBLE
NIMBLE
NIMBUS
NOBBLE
NUBBIN
NUBBLE
NUBBLY
NUMBED
NUMBER
NUMBLY

N•••B•
NABOBS
NAWABS
NEARBY

•NB•••
INBORN
INBRED
UNBARS
UNBEAR
UNBELT
UNBEND
UNBENT
UNBIND
UNBOLT
UNBORN
UNBRED

•N•B••
ANABAS
ANUBIS
ENABLE
UNABLE

•N••B•
ENROBE
INCUBI
INDABA

•N•••B
ENTOMB
ENWOMB
INTOMB

••NB••
BONBON
DUNBAR
HENBIT
SINBAD
SUNBOW

••N•B•
DANUBE

••N••B
BENUMB
CONFAB
PUNJAB

•••N•B
HOBNOB

N•C•••
NECKED
NECTAR
NICELY
NICEST
NICETY
NICHED
NICHES
NICKED
NICKEL
NICKER
NICKYS
NICOLE
NOCENT
NOCKED
NUCHAE

N••C••
NANCYS
NIACIN
NIECES
NONCOM
NUNCIO

N•••C•
NAUTCH
NOTICE
NOVICE
NUANCE

N••••C
NASTIC
NITRIC
NOETIC
NORDIC
NOSTOC

•NC•••
ANCHOR
ANCONA
ANCONE
ENCAGE
ENCAMP
ENCASE
ENCINA
ENCODE
ENCORE
ENCYCL
ENCYST
INCAGE
INCASE
INCEPT
INCEST
INCHED
INCHES
INCHON
INCISE
INCITE
INCOME
INCORP
INCUBI
INCURS
INCUSE
UNCAGE
UNCAPS
UNCIAL
UNCLAD
UNCLES
UNCOCK
UNCOIL
UNCORK
UNCURL

•N•C••
ENACTS
KNACKS
KNOCKS
SNACKS
SNICKS
SNOCAT
UNICEF
VNECKS

•N••C•
ANLACE
ANTICS
ENCYCL
ENFACE
ENLACE
ENRICH
ENRICO
ENTICE
INARCH
INDICT
INDUCE
INDUCT
INFECT
INJECT
INLACE
INSECT
INTACT
SNATCH
SNITCH
UNCOCK
UNESCO
UNLACE
UNLOCK
UNPACK
UNPICK

•N•••C
ANEMIC
ANGLIC
ANODIC
ANOMIC
ANOXIC
ENATIC
GNOMIC
UNIFIC

••NC••
BUNCHE
BUNCHY
BUNCOS
CANCAN
CANCEL
CANCER
CONCHA
CONCHS
CONCHY
CONCUR
DANCED
DANCER
DANCES
DUNCAN
DUNCES
FENCED
FENCER
FENCES
HANCES
JUNCOS
LANCED
LANCER
LANCES
LANCET
MANCHU
MINCED
MINCER
MINCES
NANCYS
NONCOM
NUNCIO
OUNCES
PENCEL
PENCIL
PONCHO
PUNCHY
RANCHO
RANCID
RANCOR
TINCAL
TINCTS
VINCES
WINCED
WINCER
WINCES
WINCEY
ZINCED
ZINCIC
ZINCKY

••N•C•
ARNICA
BONACI
CANUCK
CONICS
CYNICS
EUNICE
EUNUCH
GYNECO
IGNACE
JANICE
LUNACY
MENACE
MONICA
MUNICH
PANICE
PANICS
SENECA
TENACE
TONICS
TUNICA
TUNICS
VENICE

••N••C
APNEIC
FENNEC
FINNIC
MANIAC
MANIOC
MANTIC
PONTIC
SENLAC
SYNDIC
TANNIC
TANREC
TENREC
ZINCIC

•••NC•
AGENCY
BIANCA
BLANCH
BLENCH
BOUNCE
BOUNCY
BRANCH
BRONCO
BRONCS
BRUNCH
CHANCE
CHANCY
CHINCH
CLENCH
CLINCH
CRUNCH
DRENCH
EVINCE
FIANCE
FLENCH
FLINCH
FRANCE
FRANCK
FRANCO
FRANCS
FRENCH
GLANCE
HAUNCH
JOUNCE
LAUNCE
LAUNCH
NUANCE
PAUNCH
PLANCH
PLANCK
POUNCE
PRANCE

PRINCE
QUINCE
QUINCY
SCONCE
SEANCE
STANCE
STANCH
STENCH
THENCE
TRANCE
TRENCH
ULENCE
USANCE
WHENCE
WRENCH

•••N•C

ADONIC
AGONIC
ATONIC
AZONIC
CLINIC
CLONIC
COGNAC
CYANIC
ETHNIC
FENNEC
FINNIC
HYMNIC
HYPNIC
ICONIC
IRENIC
IRONIC
OZONIC
PHONIC
PICNIC
PYKNIC
QUINIC
SCENIC
TANNIC
URANIC

N•D•••

NADINE
NADIRS
NIDIFY
NIDING
NODDED
NODDER
NODDLE
NODOSE
NODULE
NUDELY
NUDGED
NUDGES
NUDISM
NUDIST
NUDITY
NUDNIK

N••D••

NEEDED
NEEDER
NEEDLE
NODDED
NODDER
NODDLE
NOODLE
NORDIC

N•••D•

NAIADS
NEVADA
NOMADS

N••••D

NABBED
NAGGED
NAILED
NAPPED
NEARED
NECKED
NEEDED
NERVED
NESTED
NETTED
NEVOID
NIBBED
NICHED
NICKED
NIMROD
NIPPED
NITRID
NOCKED
NODDED
NOISED
NOOSED
NUDGED
NUMBED
NURSED
NUTTED

•ND•••

ANDEAN
ANDREA
ANDREI
ANDRES
ANDREW
ENDALL
ENDEAR
ENDING
ENDIVE
ENDOWS
ENDUED
ENDUES
ENDURE
INDABA
INDEED
INDENE
INDENT
INDIAN
INDICT
INDIES
INDIGO
INDIUM
INDOOR
INDOWS
INDRIS
INDUCE
INDUCT
INDUED
INDUES
INDULT
UNDIES
UNDINE
UNDOER
UNDOES
UNDONE
UNDRAW
UNDREW
UNDSET
UNDULY

•N•D••

ANADEM
ANODES
ANODIC

•N••D•

ENCODE
INSIDE
INVADE
KNEADS
ONEIDA
SNOODS
UNLADE
UNMADE
UNTIDY

•N•••D

ANGLED
ANTEED
ENDUED
ENFOLD
ENGIRD
ENNEAD
ENSUED
ENVIED
ENWIND
GNAWED
INBRED
INCHED
INDEED
INDUED
INFOLD
INGRID
INLAID
INLAND
INROAD
INTEND
INURED
INWARD
INWIND
KNIFED
ONWARD
SNAKED
SNARED
SNIPED
SNORED
SNOWED
UNBEND
UNBIND
UNBRED
UNCLAD
UNFOLD
UNGIRD
UNHAND
UNITED
UNKIND
UNLAID
UNLEAD
UNLOAD
UNPAID
UNREAD
UNSAID
UNSOLD
UNTIED
UNTOLD
UNTROD
UNUSED
UNWIND

••ND••

BANDED
BANDIT
BENDAY
BENDEE
BENDER
BINDER
BONDED
BONDER
BUNDLE
CANDID
CANDLE
CANDOR
CINDER
CINDYS
CONDOM
CONDOR
DANDER
DANDLE
DENDRI
DENDRO
DUNDEE
FENDED
FENDER
FINDER
FONDER
FONDLE
FONDLY
FONDUE
FUNDED
FUNDUS
GANDER
GANDHI
GENDER
HANDED
HANDEL
HANDLE
HINDER
HINDUS
KINDER
KINDLE
KINDLY
LANDAU
LANDED
LANDER
LENDER
LINDAS
LINDEN
LONDON
MANDAN
MANDYS
MENDED
MENDEL
MENDER
MINDED
MINDER
MONDAY
PANDAS
PANDER
PENDED
PINDAR
PINDUS
PONDER
PUNDIT
RANDAL
RANDAN
RANDOM
RENDED
RENDER
RONDEL
RONDOS
RUNDLE
SANDAL
SANDED
SANDER
SANDHI
SANDRA
SANDYS
SENDAL
SENDER
SONDER
SUNDAE
SUNDAY
SUNDER
SUNDEW
SUNDOG
SUNDRY
SYNDET
SYNDIC
TANDEM
TENDED
TENDER
TENDON
TINDER
TUNDRA
VANDAL
VENDED
VENDEE
VENDER
VENDOR
VENDUE
WANDAS
WANDER
WANDLE
WENDED
WENDYS
WINDED
WINDER
WINDOW
WONDER
YONDER

••N•D•

ACNODE
CANADA
DENUDE
GONADS
MONADS
MONODY
PANADA
SYNODS

••N••D

AENEID
ARNAUD
ARNOLD
BANDED
BANGED
BANKED
BANNED
BINNED
BONDED
BONGED
BUNGED
BUNKED
BUNTED
CANARD
CANDID
CANNED
CANOED
CANTED
CENSED
CONKED
CONNED
CONOID
CONRAD
DANAID
DANCED
DANGED
DENIED
DENNED
DENTED
DINGED
DINNED
DINTED
DONALD
DONNED
DUNGED
DUNKED
DUNNED
ENNEAD
FANGED
FANNED
FENCED
FENDED
FINNED
FUNDED
FUNKED
GANGED
GANOID
GINNED
GUNNED

6

HANDED
HANGED
HINGED
HINTED
HONIED
HONKED
HUNTED
JINKED
JUNKED
KENNED
KINKED
KONRAD
LANCED
LANDED
LINKED
LONGED
LUNGED
MANNED
MENDED
MINCED
MINDED
MINTED
MONIED
PANNED
PANTED
PENDED
PENNED
PENTAD
PINGED
PINKED
PINNED
PONIED
PUNNED
PUNTED
RANCID
RANGED
RANKED
RANTED
RENDED
RENTED
RINGED
RINSED
RONALD
SANDED
SENSED
SINBAD
SINGED
SINNED
SUNNED
TANGED
TANKED
TANNED
TENDED
TENSED
TENTED
TINEID
TINGED
TINNED
TINTED
TONGED
TUNNED
VENDED
VENTED
WANNED
WANTED
WENDED
WINCED
WINDED
WINGED
WINKED
WONTED
YANKED
YENNED
ZINCED
ZINGED

•••ND•

AGENDA
AMANDA
AMENDS
BLENDE
BLENDS
BLINDS
BLONDE
BLONDS
BOUNDS
BRANDS
BRANDY
BRENDA
CHONDR
DIRNDL
ELANDS
EMENDS
FIENDS
FOUNDS
FRONDS
GLANDS
GRINDS
GRUNDY
HOUNDS
LUANDA
MAUNDS
MAUNDY
POINDS
POUNDS
ROUNDS
RWANDA
SCENDS
SHINDY
SOUNDS
SPENDS
STANDS
TRENDS
TRENDY
UGANDA
UPENDS
VIANDS
WOUNDS
ZOUNDS

•••N•D

ALINED
ATONED
BANNED
BEANED
BINNED
BRINED
BURNED
CANNED
COINED
CONNED
CORNED
CRANED
CYANID
DAMNED
DARNED
DAWNED
DENNED
DINNED
DONNED
DOWNED
DRONED
DUNNED
EARNED
EVENED
FANNED
FAWNED
FINNED
GAINED
GINNED
GOWNED
GUNNED
HORNED
HYMNED
IRONED
JOINED
KEENED
KENNED
KERNED
LEANED
LIMNED
LOANED
MAENAD
MANNED
MOANED
MOONED
OPENED
OPINED
PAINED
PANNED
PAWNED
PEENED
PENNED
PHONED
PINNED
PLANED
PRUNED
PUNNED
RAINED
REINED
RUINED
SEINED
SHINED
SIGNED
SINNED
STONED
SUNNED
TANNED
TINNED
TRINED
TUNNED
TURNED
TWINED
VEINED
WANNED
WARNED
WEANED
WHINED
YAWNED
YEANED
YENNED

••••ND

AALAND
ABOUND
ADDEND
ALMOND
APPEND
ARMAND
AROUND
ASCEND
ATTEND
AUGEND
BEHIND
BEYOND
DEFEND
DEMAND
DEPEND
EDMOND
EDMUND
ENWIND
ERRAND
EXPAND
EXPEND
EXTEND
FECUND
FRIEND
GERUND
GROUND
IMPEND
INLAND
INTEND
INWIND
ISLAND
JOCUND
LEGEND
LIGAND
LOMOND
OBTUND
OFFEND
OSMOND
OSMUND
POLAND
REFUND
REMAND
REMIND
REPAND
RESEND
REWIND
ROBAND
ROLAND
ROTUND
SECOND
SECUND
SOLAND
STRAND
UNBEND
UNBIND
UNHAND
UNKIND
UNWIND
UPLAND

NE••••

NEARBY
NEARED
NEARER
NEARLY
NEATER
NEATLY
NEBULA
NECKED
NECTAR
NEEDED
NEEDER
NEEDLE
NEGATE
NEIGHS
NEKTON
NELLIE
NELLYS
NELSON
NEMATO
NEPHEW
NEPHRO
NEREIS
NEROLI
NERVED
NERVES
NESSUS
NESTED
NESTLE
NESTOR
NETHER
NETTED
NETTIE
NETTLE
NEUMES
NEURAL
NEURON
NEUTER
NEVADA
NEVILE
NEVILL
NEVOID
NEVSKI
NEWARK
NEWELS
NEWEST
NEWTON

N•E•••

NAEVUS
NEEDED
NEEDER
NEEDLE
NIECES
NIELLI
NIELLO
NOESIS
NOETIC

N••E••

NAMELY
NAMERS
NAPERY
NAVELS
NEREIS
NEWELS
NEWEST
NICELY
NICEST
NICETY
NIGELS
NINETY
NISEIS
NOCENT
NONEGO
NOREEN
NOTERS
NOVELS
NOVENA
NUDELY

N•••E•

NABBED
NAGGED
NAGGER
NAILED
NANTES
NAOSES
NAPIER
NAPLES
NAPPED
NAPPER
NAPPES
NASSER
NAUSEA
NAVIES
NEARED
NEARER
NEATER
NECKED
NEEDED
NEEDER
NEPHEW
NERVED
NERVES
NESTED
NETHER
NETTED
NEUMES
NEUTER
NIBBED
NICHED
NICHES
NICKED
NICKEL
NICKER
NIECES
NIGHER
NIPPED
NIPPER
NIXIES

NOCKED
NODDED
NODDER
NOISED
NOISES
NOOSED
NOOSES
NOREEN
NOSIER
NUDGED
NUDGES
NUGGET
NUMBED
NUMBER
NURSED
NURSER
NURSES
NUTLET
NUTMEG
NUTTED
NUTTER

N••••E

NADINE
NAPPIE
NARINE
NATIVE
NATURE
NEEDLE
NEGATE
NELLIE
NESTLE
NETTIE
NETTLE
NEVILE
NIBBLE
NICOLE
NIGGLE
NIMBLE
NIPPLE
NOBBLE
NODDLE
NODOSE
NODULE
NONAGE
NOODLE
NOTICE
NOVICE
NOWISE
NOZZLE
NUANCE
NUBBLE
NUBILE
NUCHAE
NUZZLE

•NE•••

ANEMIA
ANEMIC
ANERGY
ENEMAS
ENERGY
GNEISS
KNEADS
KNEELS
KNELLS
ONEIDA
ONEILL
ONEIRO
ONEWAY
PNEUMA
PNEUMO
SNEAKS
SNEAKY
SNEERS
SNEEZE
SNEEZY
SNELLS
UNEASY
UNESCO
UNEVEN
VNECKS

•N•E••

ANDEAN
ANGELA
ANGELO
ANGELS
ANGERS
ANNEAL
ANSELM
ANTEED
ANTERO
ENDEAR
ENGELS
ENMESH
ENNEAD
ENTERA
ENTERO
ENTERS
INCEPT
INCEST
INDEED
INDENE
INDENT
INFECT
INFERO
INFERS
INFEST
INGEST
INHERE
INJECT
INKERS
INLETS
INMESH
INSECT
INSERT
INSETS
INTEND
INTENT
INTERN
INTERS
INVENT
INVERT
INVEST
KNEELS
ONSETS
SNEERS
SNEEZE
SNEEZY
UNBEAR
UNBELT
UNBEND
UNBENT
UNLEAD
UNLESS
UNMEET
UNMEWS
UNPEGS
UNREAD
UNREAL
UNREEL
UNREST
UNSEAL
UNSEAM
UNSEAT
UNSEEN
UNVEIL
UNVEXT
UNWELL
UNWEPT

•N••E•

ANADEM
ANDREA
ANDREI
ANDRES
ANDREW
ANGLED
ANGLER
ANGLES
ANISES
ANKLES
ANKLET
ANNIES
ANODES
ANSWER
ANTEED
ANTHEA
ANTHEM
ANTHER
ANTLER
ANUSES
ENAMEL
ENATES
ENDUED
ENDUES
ENSUED
ENSUES
ENTREE
ENVIED
ENVIER
ENVIES
GNAWED
GNAWER
GNOMES
INBRED
INCHED
INCHES
INDEED
INDIES
INDUED
INDUES
INGRES
INKIER
INKLES
INLIER
INSTEP
INURED
INURES
KNAVES
KNIFED
KNIFES
KNIVES
KNOWER
ONAGER
ONUSES
SNAKED
SNAKES
SNARED
SNARER
SNARES
SNIPED
SNIPER
SNIPES
SNIVEL
SNORED
SNORER
SNORES
SNOWED
UNBRED
UNCLES
UNDIES
UNDOER
UNDOES
UNDREW
UNDSET
UNEVEN
UNGUES
UNICEF
UNISEX
UNITED
UNITES
UNMEET
UNREEL
UNSEEN
UNSTEP
UNTIED
UNTIES
UNUSED

•N•••E

ANANKE
ANCONE
ANLACE
ANLAGE
ANOMIE
ANSATE
ANYONE
ENABLE
ENCAGE
ENCASE
ENCODE
ENCORE
ENDIVE
ENDURE
ENFACE
ENGAGE
ENGINE
ENISLE
ENLACE
ENRAGE
ENROBE
ENSILE
ENSURE
ENTICE
ENTIRE
ENTREE
ENZYME
INCAGE
INCASE
INCISE
INCITE
INCOME
INCUSE
INDENE
INDUCE
INFUSE
INHALE
INHERE
INJURE
INLACE
INMATE
INNATE
INSANE
INSIDE
INSOLE
INSURE
INTAKE
INTONE
INVADE
INVITE
INVOKE
INWOVE
SNATHE
SNEEZE
SNOOZE
UNABLE
UNCAGE
UNDINE
UNDONE
UNIQUE
UNLACE
UNLADE
UNLIKE
UNLIVE
UNMADE
UNMAKE
UNPILE
UNRIPE
UNSAFE
UNSURE
UNTRUE
UNWISE
UNYOKE

••NE••

ABNERS
AENEAS
AENEID
ANNEAL
APNEAL
APNEIC
BONERS
CANERS
CINEMA
CINEOL
CONEYS
CUNEAL
DINERO
DINERS
DONEES
DONETS
ENNEAD
ERNEST
FANEGA
FINELY
FINERY
FINEST
FUNEST
GANEFS
GENERA
GENETS
GENEVA
GONERS
GYNECO
HONEST
HONEYS
JANETS
JUNEAU
KINESI
KINETO
LINEAL
LINEAR
LINENS
LINERS
LINEUP
LONELY
LONERS
LUNETS
MANEGE
MINERS
MONEYS
NINETY
NONEGO
ORNERY
OWNERS
PANELS
PINEAL
PINENE
PINERY
PONENT
RANEES
RENEES
RENEGE
RENEWS
SANELY
SANEST
SENECA
SINEWS
SINEWY
TENETS
TINEID
TONERS

TUNERS
TUNEUP
VENEER
VENERY
VINERY
WINERY

••N•E•

ANNIES
APNOEA
ARNIES
BANDED
BANGED
BANKED
BANKER
BANNED
BANNER
BANTER
BENDEE
BENDER
BENNES
BENNET
BINDER
BINGES
BINNED
BONDED
BONDER
BONGED
BONIER
BONNET
BONZER
BONZES
BUNGED
BUNKED
BUNKER
BUNSEN
BUNTED
CANCEL
CANCER
CANKER
CANNED
CANNEL
CANNER
CANNES
CANOED
CANOES
CANTED
CANTER
CENSED
CENSER
CENSES
CENTER
CINDER
CONFER
CONGER
CONGES
CONIES
CONKED
CONNED
CONNER
CONTES
CONVEX
CONVEY
CUNNER
DANCED
DANCER
DANCES
DANDER
DANGED
DANGER
DANIEL
DANKER
DENIED
DENIER
DENIES
DENNED
DENSER
DENTED
DENVER
DINGED
DINGEY
DINKEY
DINNED
DINNER
DINTED
DONEES
DONKEY
DONNED
DUNCES
DUNDEE
DUNGED
DUNKED
DUNKER
DUNNED
ERNIES
FANGED
FANJET
FANNED
FANNER
FENCED
FENCER
FENCES
FENDED
FENDER
FENNEC
FENNEL
FINDER
FINGER
FINNED
FONDER
FUNDED
FUNKED
FUNNEL
GANDER
GANGED
GANGER
GANGES
GANNET
GENDER
GENIES
GENRES
GENTES
GINGER
GINNED
GINNER
GUNMEN
GUNNED
GUNNEL
GUNNER
HANCES
HANDED
HANDEL
HANGED
HANGER
HANKER
HANSEL
HENLEY
HINDER
HINGED
HINGES
HINTED
HONIED
HONKED
HONKER
HUNGER
HUNTED
HUNTER
JENNET
JINKED
JINKER
JINXES
JUNKED
JUNKER
JUNKET
KENNED
KENNEL
KINDER
KINKED
KINSEY
LANCED
LANCER
LANCES
LANCET
LANDED
LANDER
LANKER
LANNER
LENDER
LENSES
LENTEN
LINDEN
LINGER
LINIER
LINKED
LINNET
LINTEL
LINTER
LONGED
LONGER
LUNGED
LUNGEE
LUNGER
LUNGES
LUNKER
LYNXES
MANGER
MANNED
MANNER
MANSES
MANTEL
MANTES
MANUEL
MENDED
MENDEL
MENDER
MENSES
MINCED
MINCER
MINCES
MINDED
MINDER
MINTED
MINTER
MINUET
MINXES
MONGER
MONIED
MONIES
MONKEY
MONTES
NANTES
OUNCES
PANDER
PANNED
PANTED
PANZER
PENCEL
PENDED
PENMEN
PENNED
PENNER
PINGED
PINIER
PINKED
PINNED
PINNER
PINTER
PONDER
PONGEE
PONIED
PONIES
PONTES
PUNIER
PUNNED
PUNTED
PUNTER
RANEES
RANGED
RANGER
RANGES
RANKED
RANKER
RANTED
RANTER
RENDED
RENDER
RENEES
RENNET
RENTED
RENTER
RENTES
RINGED
RINGER
RINSED
RINSER
RINSES
RONDEL
RUNLET
RUNNEL
RUNNER
SANDED
SANDER
SANGER
SANIES
SANSEI
SENDER
SENNET
SENSED
SENSES
SINGED
SINGER
SINGES
SINKER
SINNED
SINNER
SINTER
SONDER
SONNET
SUNDER
SUNDEW
SUNKEN
SUNNED
SUNSET
SYNDET
TANDEM
TANGED
TANKED
TANKER
TANNED
TANNER
TANREC
TENDED
TENDER
TENREC
TENSED
TENSER
TENSES
TENTED
TENTER
TENUES
TINDER
TINGED
TINGES
TINKER
TINNED
TINNER
TINSEL
TINTED
TONGED
TONIER
TUNNED
TUNNEL
VANMEN
VENDED
VENDEE
VENDER
VENEER
VENTED
VENTER
VENUES
VINCES
VINIER
WANDER
WANNED
WANNER
WANTED
WANTER
WENDED
WINCED
WINCER
WINCES
WINCEY
WINDED
WINDER
WINGED
WINIER
WINKED
WINKER
WINNER
WINOES
WINTER
WINZES
WONDER
WONTED
YANKED
YANKEE
YENNED
YONDER
YONKER
ZANIER
ZANIES
ZENGER
ZINCED
ZINGED

••N••E

ACNODE
ADNATE
AGNATE
AUNTIE
BANGLE
BENDEE
BONNIE
BUNCHE
BUNDLE
BUNGLE
BYNAME
CANAPE
CANDLE
CANGUE
CANINE
CANNAE
CANNIE
CANTLE
CANUTE
CINQUE
CONNIE
CONTRE
DANDLE
DANGLE
DANITE
DANUBE
DENGUE
DENISE

6

DENOTE
DENUDE
DINGLE
DONATE
DONNIE
DUNDEE
EUNICE
FANNIE
FINALE
FINITE
FONDLE
FONDUE
GANGUE
GENTLE
HANDLE
HONORE
IGNACE
IGNITE
IGNORE
INNATE
IONIZE
IONONE
JANGLE
JANICE
JINGLE
JONNIE
JUNGLE
JUNKIE
KENNIE
KINASE
KINDLE
LANATE
LANOSE
LENAPE
LENORE
LINAGE
LUNATE
LUNGEE
LUNULE
MANAGE
MANEGE
MANGLE
MANQUE
MANTLE
MANURE
MENACE
MENAGE
MINGLE
MINNIE
MINUTE
MONROE
NONAGE
ORNATE
PANICE
PANTIE
PENILE
PENNAE
PINENE
PINITE
PINKIE
PINNAE
PINOLE
PINTLE
PONGEE
RANKLE
RENEGE
RONNIE
RUNDLE
SENATE
SENILE
SINGLE
SUNDAE
TANGLE
TENACE
TENURE
TINGLE
TINKLE
TONGUE
VENDEE
VENDUE
VENICE
VENIRE
VENOSE
VENULE
WANDLE
WANGLE
WINKLE
WINNIE
YANKEE
ZONATE
ZONULE

•••NE•

AGONES
AKENES
ALINED
ALINES
ATONED
ATONER
ATONES
AXONES
AZINES
BANNED
BANNER
BARNEY
BEANED
BENNES
BENNET
BERNEY
BINNED
BONNET
BORNEO
BRINED
BRINES
BRUNEI
BRUNET
BURNED
BURNER
BURNET
CANNED
CANNEL
CANNER
CANNES
CHINES
CLINES
CLONES
COINED
COINER
CONNED
CONNER
CORNEA
CORNED
CORNEL
CORNER
CORNET
CRANED
CRANES
CRENEL
CRONES
CUNNER
CYGNET
DAMNED
DARNED
DARNEL
DAWNED
DENNED
DIANES
DINNED
DINNER
DISNEY
DONNED
DOWNED
DRONED
DRONES
DUNNED
EARNED
EARNER
EUPNEA
EVENED
FANNED
FANNER
FAWNED
FAWNER
FENNEC
FENNEL
FINNED
FUNNEL
GAINED
GAINER
GANNET
GARNER
GARNET
GINNED
GINNER
GOONEY
GOWNED
GUINEA
GUNNED
GUNNEL
GUNNER
HORNED
HORNET
HYMNED
IMINES
IRENES
IRONED
IRONER
JENNET
JITNEY
JOINED
JOINER
KEENED
KEENER
KENNED
KENNEL
KERNED
KERNEL
KEYNES
KIDNEY
KOINES
KRONEN
KRONER
LANNER
LEANED
LEANER
LIANES
LIMNED
LIMNER
LINNET
LIONEL
LOANED
MAGNET
MANNED
MANNER
MEANER
MESNES
MOANED
MOONED
OPENED
OPENER
OPINED
OPINES
PAINED
PANNED
PAWNED
PAWNEE
PAWNER
PEENED
PENNED
PENNER
PHONED
PHONES
PHONEY
PINNED
PINNER
PLANED
PLANER
PLANES
PLANET
PRUNED
PRUNER
PRUNES
PUNNED
RAINED
REINED
RENNET
RODNEY
ROMNEY
RUINED
RUINER
RUNNEL
RUNNER
SCENES
SCONES
SEINED
SEINER
SEINES
SENNET
SHINED
SHINER
SHINES
SIDNEY
SIGNED
SIGNER
SIGNET
SIMNEL
SINNED
SINNER
SONNET
SOONER
SPINEL
SPINES
SPINET
STONED
STONER
STONES
SUMNER
SUNNED
SWANEE
SYDNEY
TANNED
TANNER
TBONES
THANES
TINNED
TINNER
TRINED
TRINES
TUNNED
TUNNEL
TURNED
TURNER
TWINED
TWINER
TWINES
VAINER
VEINED
WAGNER
WANNED
WANNER
WARNED
WARNER
WAYNES
WEANED
WEANER
WHINED
WHINER
WHINES
WIENER
WINNER
WITNEY
YAWNED
YAWNER
YEANED
YENNED

•••N•E

ANANKE
AVENGE
AVENUE
BEANIE
BERNIE
BLENDE
BLONDE
BLUNGE
BONNIE
BOUNCE
BRONTE
BRONZE
CANNAE
CANNIE
CHANCE
CHANGE
CONNIE
CRINGE
DONNIE
EVINCE
FANNIE
FAUNAE
FIANCE
FLANGE
FLENSE
FRANCE
FRINGE
FRUNZE
GLANCE
GRANGE
GWYNNE
HORNIE
JEANNE
JOANNE
JONNIE
JOUNCE
KENNIE
LAUNCE
LEONIE
LOUNGE
MEANIE
MINNIE
NUANCE
ORANGE
PAWNEE
PENNAE
PINNAE
PLUNGE
POUNCE
PRANCE
PRINCE
QUINCE
RONNIE
SCONCE
SEANCE
SPONGE
STANCE
SWANEE
SWINGE
THENCE
TRANCE
TWINGE
ULENCE
USANCE
WEENIE
WHENCE
WIENIE

WINNIE
YVONNE

••••NE

ACHENE
ALDINE
ALKANE
ALKENE
ALKYNE
ALPINE
ALVINE
ANCONE
ANYONE
ARCANE
ARLENE
ARLINE
ARSINE
ATHENE
ATTUNE
BORANE
BOURNE
BOVINE
BUTANE
BYGONE
BYLANE
BYLINE
CANINE
CETANE
COHUNE
COLINE
COSINE
CYMENE
CYRENE
DAPHNE
DECANE
DEFINE
DIVINE
ELAINE
ELAYNE
ENGINE
EOCENE
EOGENE
EQUINE
ERMINE
ESSENE
ETHANE
EUGENE
EVZONE
FAMINE
FELINE
FERINE
GWYNNE
HEXANE
HEXONE
HUMANE
IMMUNE
INDENE
INSANE
INTONE
IODINE
IONONE
JEANNE
JEJUNE
JOANNE
KETENE
KETONE
LAGUNE
LARINE
LIERNE
LORENE
LUPINE
LYSINE
MALINE
MARINE
MAXINE
MOLINE
MURINE
NADINE
NARINE
OCTANE
ORPINE
OSCINE
PATINE
PINENE
PROCNE
PUISNE
PURINE
PYRENE
PYRONE
RACINE
RAPINE
RATINE
RAVINE
REDONE
REFINE
RELINE
REPINE
RETENE
ROCKNE
ROXANE
RUSINE
SABINE
SALINE
SELENE
SERENE
SERINE
SHRINE
SIMONE
SOIGNE
SOZINE
SPHENE
SPLINE
SUPINE
THRONE
TISANE
TRIUNE
TYRONE
UNDINE
UNDONE
URBANE
URSINE
WAHINE
XYLENE
YVONNE

N•••F•

NAZIFY
NIDIFY
NOTIFY

•NF•••

ENFACE
ENFOLD
INFAMY
INFANT
INFECT
INFERO
INFERS
INFEST
INFIRM
INFLOW
INFLUX
INFOLD
INFORM
INFUSE
UNFAIR
UNFOLD
UNFURL

•N•F••

KNIFED
KNIFES
SNAFUS
SNIFFS
SNIFFY
SNUFFS
SNUFFY
UNIFIC

•N••F•

SNIFFS
SNIFFY
SNUFFS
SNUFFY
UNSAFE

•N•••F

ENGULF
INGULF
UNICEF

••NF••

CONFAB
CONFER
MANFUL
SINFUL

••N•F•

GANEFS
IGNIFY
MINIFY
RUNOFF

••N••F

RUNOFF

N•G•••

NAGANA
NAGGED
NAGGER
NAGOYA
NEGATE
NIGELS
NIGGLE
NIGHER
NIGHTS
NIGHTY
NOGGIN
NUGGET

N••G••

NAGGED
NAGGER
NAUGHT
NEIGHS
NIGGLE
NILGAI
NOGGIN
NOUGAT
NOUGHT
NUDGED
NUDGES
NUGGET

N•••G•

NONAGE
NONEGO

N••••G

NAMING
NIDING
NIXING
NOSING
NOTING
NUTMEG

•NG•••

ANGARY
ANGELA
ANGELO
ANGELS
ANGERS
ANGINA
ANGKOR
ANGLED
ANGLER
ANGLES
ANGLIA
ANGLIC
ANGOLA
ANGORA
ENGAGE
ENGELS
ENGINE
ENGIRD
ENGIRT
ENGRAM
ENGULF
INGEST
INGOTS
INGRES
INGRID
INGULF
UNGIRD
UNGIRT
UNGUAL
UNGUES
UNGUIS
UNGULA

•N•G••

ENIGMA
KNIGHT
ONAGER
ONAGRI
SNAGGY
SNUGLY

•N••G•

ANERGY
ANLAGE
ENCAGE
ENERGY
ENGAGE
ENOUGH
ENRAGE
ENSIGN
INCAGE
INDIGO
SNAGGY
UNCAGE
UNPEGS
UNRIGS

•N•••G

ANALOG
ENDING
INKING
INNING
UNSUNG

••NG••

BANGED
BANGLE
BANGOR
BANGUI
BANGUP
BENGAL
BINGES
BONGED
BONGOS
BUNGED
BUNGLE
CANGUE
CONGAS
CONGER
CONGES
CONGOU
DANGED
DANGER
DANGLE
DENGUE
DINGED
DINGEY
DINGHY
DINGLE
DINGUS
DUNGED
FANGAS
FANGED
FINGER
FUNGAL
FUNGUS
GANGED
GANGER
GANGES
GANGLI
GANGUE
GINGAL
GINGER
HANGAR
HANGED
HANGER
HANGUP
HINGED
HINGES
HUNGER
HUNGRY
JANGLE
JINGAL
JINGLE
JUNGLE
JUNGLY
KINGLY
LANGUR
LENGTH
LINGAS
LINGER
LINGUA
LONGAN
LONGED
LONGER
LUNGED
LUNGEE
LUNGER
LUNGES
LUNGIS
MANGER
MANGLE
MANGOS
MINGLE
MONGER
MONGOL
MONGST
PENGOS
PINGED
PINGOS
PONGEE
RANGED
RANGER
RANGES
RINGED
RINGER
SANGAR
SANGER
SANGUI
SINGED
SINGER
SINGES
SINGLE
SINGLY
TANGED
TANGLE
TANGLY

6

TANGOS
TINGED
TINGES
TINGLE
TINGLY
TONGED
TONGUE
TUNGUS
WANGLE
WINGED
ZENGER
ZINGED

••N•G•

BENIGN
FANEGA
GINKGO
LANUGO
LINAGE
MANAGE
MANEGE
MENAGE
NONAGE
NONEGO
RENEGE

••N••G

AWNING
BONING
CANING
CONING
DANZIG
DINING
FINING
HONING
INNING
LINING
MINING
OWNING
PINANG
PINING
SUNDOG
TONING
TUNING
WANING
WINING
ZONING

•••NG•

AVENGE
BEINGS
BLUNGE
BRINGS
CHANGE
CHANGS
CLANGS
CLINGS
CLINGY
CRINGE
DOINGS
DRONGO
ERINGO
ERYNGO
FLANGE
FLINGS
FLONGS
FRINGE
FRINGY
GOINGS
GRANGE
ICINGS
LOUNGE
ORANGE
ORANGS
PLUNGE
PRONGS
SLANGY
SLINGS
SPONGE
SPONGY
STINGS
STINGY
SWINGE
SWINGS
THINGS
THONGS
TWANGS
TWANGY
TWINGE
UBANGI
WHANGS
WRINGS
WRONGS

•••N•G

EGGNOG
STENOG

••••NG

ACHING
ACTING
ADDING
AGEING
AIDING
AILING
AIMING
AIRING
ARCING
ARMING
ASKING
AWEING
AWNING
BAAING
BAKING
BALING
BARING
BARONG
BASING
BATING
BAYING
BELONG
BERING
BIDING
BITING
BLUING
BODING
BONING
BOOING
BORING
BOWING
BOXING
BUSING
BUYING
CAGING
CAKING
CANING
CARING
CASING
CAVING
CAWING
CEDING
CERING
CITING
CLUING
CODING
COKING
COMING
CONING
COOING
COPING
CORING
COVING
COWING
COXING
CRYING
CUBING
CURING
DARING
DATING
DAZING
DEKING
DICING
DIKING
DINING
DIVING
DOLING
DOMING
DOPING
DOSING
DOTING
DOZING
DRYING
DUGONG
DUPING
DURING
DYEING
EALING
EARING
EASING
EATING
EBBING
EDGING
EGGING
ENDING
ERRING
EYEING
FACING
FADING
FAKING
FARING
FATING
FAXING
FAYING
FAZING
FEEING
FETING
FEUING
FIFING
FILING
FINING
FIRING
FIXING
FLYING
FOXING
FRYING
FUMING
FUSING
FUZING
GAGING
GAMING
GAPING
GATING
GAZING
GEEING
GIBING
GIVING
GLUING
GORING
GUYING
HADING
HALING
HATING
HAVING
HAWING
HAYING
HAZING
HEWING
HEXING
HIDING
HIEING
HIKING
HIRING
HIVING
HOEING
HOLING
HOMING
HONING
HOPING
HOSING
IDLING
IMPING
INKING
INNING
IRKING
IRVING
ISLING
JADING
JAWING
JEEING
JIBING
JOKING
JOYING
KALONG
KEYING
KITING
LACING
LADING
LAKING
LAMING
LARYNG
LAVING
LAWING
LAYING
LAZING
LIKING
LIMING
LINING
LIVING
LOOING
LOPING
LOSING
LOVING
LOWING
LURING
LUTING
LYSING
MACING
MAKING
MATING
MAYING
MAZING
MEKONG
METING
MEWING
MIMING
MINING
MIRING
MIXING
MOOING
MOPING
MOVING
MOWING
MUSING
MUTING
NAMING
NIDING
NIXING
NOSING
NOTING
OARING
OBLONG
OFFING
OGLING
OILING
OOLONG
OOZING
OPTING
ORBING
OUTING
OWNING
PACING
PAGING
PALING
PARANG
PARING
PAVING
PAWING
PAYING
PEKING
PIKING
PILING
PINANG
PINING
PIPING
PLYING
POKING
POLING
PORING
POSING
PRYING
PUKING
PULING
RACING
RAGING
RAKING
RAPING
RARING
RATING
RAVING
RAYING
RAZING
RICING
RIDING
RILING
RIMING
RISING
RIVING
ROBING
ROPING
ROSING
ROVING
ROWING
RULING
SARONG
SATANG
SATING
SAVING
SAWING
SAYING
SEEING
SEWING
SEXING
SHYING
SIDING
SIRING
SIZING
SKIING
SKYING
SLUING
SOLING
SOWING
SPRANG
SPRING
SPRUNG
SPYING
STRING
STRONG
STYING
TAKING
TAMING
TAPING
TARING
TAWING
TAXING

6

TEEING
THRONG
TIDING
TILING
TIMING
TIRING
TOEING
TONING
TOPING
TOTING
TOWING
TOYING
TRUING
TRYING
TUBING
TUNING
TYPING
UNSUNG
UPPING
URGING
VEXING
VIKING
VISING
VOTING
VOWING
WADING
WAGING
WAKING
WALING
WANING
WAVING
WAXING
WILING
WINING
WIPING
WIRING
WISING
WIVING
WOOING
WOWING
WRYING
YAWING
YOKING
YOWING
ZONING

N•H•••
NAHUMS

N••H••
NASHUA
NATHAN
NEPHEW
NEPHRO
NETHER
NICHED
NICHES
NIGHER
NIGHTS
NIGHTY
NOSHOW
NUCHAE

N•••H•
NAUGHT
NAVAHO
NEIGHS
NINTHS
NOUGHT
NYMPHA
NYMPHO
NYMPHS

N••••H
NAUTCH
NULLAH

•NH•••
INHALE
INHAUL
INHERE
UNHAIR
UNHAND
UNHATS
UNHOLY
UNHOOK
UNHURT
UNHUSK

•N•H••
ANCHOR
ANTHEA
ANTHEM
ANTHER
ANYHOW
INCHED
INCHES
INCHON
UNSHIP

•N••H•
GNATHO
KNIGHT
SNATHE
SNATHS

•N•••H
ENMESH
ENOUGH
ENRICH
INARCH
INMESH
INRUSH
ONRUSH
SNATCH
SNITCH
UNWISH

••NH••
MENHIR

••N•H•
BUNCHE
BUNCHY
CANTHI
CONCHA
CONCHS
CONCHY
DINAHS
DINGHY
GANDHI
GUNSHY
HONSHU
JONAHS
MANCHU
MONTHS
NINTHS
PONCHO
PUNCHY
RANCHO
SANDHI
TENTHS
XANTHO

••N••H
BANISH
DANISH
EUNUCH
FINISH
HANNAH
LENGTH
MUNICH
ORNITH
PUNISH
SUNNAH
VANISH
ZENITH

•••N•H
BLANCH
BLENCH
BRANCH
BRUNCH
CHINCH
CLENCH
CLINCH
CRUNCH
DRENCH
FLENCH
FLINCH
FRENCH
HANNAH
HAUNCH
LAUNCH
PAUNCH
PLANCH
PLINTH
STANCH
STENCH
SUNNAH
TRENCH
WRENCH

NI••••
NIACIN
NIBBED
NIBBLE
NICELY
NICEST
NICETY
NICHED
NICHES
NICKED
NICKEL
NICKER
NICKYS
NICOLE
NIDIFY
NIDING
NIECES
NIELLI
NIELLO
NIGELS
NIGGLE
NIGHER
NIGHTS
NIGHTY
NILGAI
NIMBLE
NIMBUS
NIMITZ
NIMROD
NINETY
NINTHS
NIPPED
NIPPER
NIPPLE
NIPPON
NISEIS
NITRIC
NITRID
NITWIT
NIXIES
NIXING

N•I•••
NAIADS
NAILED
NEIGHS
NOISED
NOISES

N••I••
NADINE
NADIRS
NAMING
NANISM
NAPIER
NARIAL
NARINE
NASIAL
NASION
NATION
NATIVE
NAVIES
NAZIFY
NAZISM
NEVILE
NEVILL
NIDIFY
NIDING
NIMITZ
NIXIES
NIXING
NOMISM
NORIAS
NOSIER
NOSILY
NOSING
NOTICE
NOTIFY
NOTING
NOTION
NOVICE
NOWISE
NUBIAN
NUBIAS
NUBILE
NUDISM
NUDIST
NUDITY
NUMINA

N•••I•
NAOMIS
NAPKIN
NAPPIE
NASTIC
NELLIE
NEREIS
NETTIE
NEVOID
NIACIN
NISEIS
NITRIC
NITRID
NITWIT
NOESIS
NOETIC
NOGGIN
NORDIC
NORNIR
NORRIS
NUBBIN
NUDNIK
NUNCIO
NUTRIA

N••••I
NEROLI
NEVSKI
NIELLI
NILGAI

•NI•••
ANILIN
ANIMAL
ANIMAS
ANIMUS
ANIONS
ANISES
ANITAS
ANITRA
ENIGMA
ENISLE
KNIFED
KNIFES
KNIGHT
KNIVES
ONIONS
SNICKS
SNIFFS
SNIFFY
SNIPED
SNIPER
SNIPES
SNIPPY
SNITCH
SNIVEL
UNICEF
UNIFIC
UNIONS
UNIQUE
UNISEX
UNISON
UNITED
UNITES

•N•I••
ANGINA
ANNIES
ANOINT
ANTIAR
ANTICS
ANVILS
ENCINA
ENDING
ENDIVE
ENGINE
ENGIRD
ENGIRT
ENLIST
ENMITY
ENRICH
ENRICO
ENSIGN
ENSILE
ENTICE
ENTIRE
ENTITY
ENVIED
ENVIER
ENVIES
ENWIND
GNEISS
INCISE
INCITE
INDIAN
INDICT
INDIES
INDIGO
INDIUM
INFIRM
INKIER
INKING
INLIER
INNING
INSIDE
INSIST
INTIMA
INVITE
INWIND
ONEIDA

6

ONEILL
ONEIRO
SNAILS
UNBIND
UNCIAL
UNDIES
UNDINE
UNGIRD
UNGIRT
UNKIND
UNLIKE
UNLIVE
UNPICK
UNPILE
UNPINS
UNRIGS
UNRIPE
UNRIPS
UNTIDY
UNTIED
UNTIES
UNWIND
UNWISE
UNWISH

•N••I•

ANEMIA
ANEMIC
ANGLIA
ANGLIC
ANILIN
ANODIC
ANOMIC
ANOMIE
ANOXIA
ANOXIC
ANTLIA
ANTRIM
ANUBIS
ENATIC
ENJOIN
ENOSIS
ENTAIL
GNOMIC
GNOSIS
INDRIS
INGRID
INLAID
INTUIT
INULIN
UNCOIL
UNFAIR
UNGUIS
UNHAIR
UNIFIC
UNKNIT
UNLAID
UNPAID
UNSAID
UNSHIP
UNVEIL

•N•••I

ANDREI
INCUBI
ONAGRI

••NI••

AMNION
ANNIES
ARNICA
ARNIES
AWNING
BANIAN
BANISH
BENIGN
BENITA
BENITO
BINITS
BONIER
BONING
BONITO
BUNION
CANINE
CANING
CONICS
CONIES
CONING
CONIUM
CYNICS
DANIEL
DANISH
DANITE
DENIAL
DENIED
DENIER
DENIES
DENIMS
DENISE
DINING
EONIAN
EONISM
ERNIES
EUNICE
FANION
FENIAN
FINIAL
FINING
FINISH
FINITE
GENIAL
GENIES
GENITO
GENIUS
GONION
GONIUM
HONIED
HONING
IGNIFY
IGNITE
INNING
IONIAN
IONIUM
IONIZE
JANICE
JUNIOR
JUNIUS
KININS
LENITY
LINIER
LINING
MANIAC
MANIAS
MANILA
MANIOC
MANITO
MANITU
MENIAL
MENINX
MINIFY
MINIMS
MINING
MINION
MINIUM
MONICA
MONIED
MONIES
MONISM
MONIST
MUNICH
NANISM
ORNITH
OWNING
PANICE
PANICS
PENIAL
PENILE
PINIER
PINING
PINION
PINITE
PONIED
PONIES
PUNIER
PUNILY
PUNISH
RUNINS
SANIES
SANITY
SENILE
SENIOR
SONIAS
TANIST
TONICS
TONIER
TONING
TUNICA
TUNICS
TUNING
VANISH
VANITY
VENIAL
VENICE
VENIRE
VINIER
WANING
WANION
WINIER
WINING
ZANIER
ZANIES
ZENITH
ZONING

••N•I•

AENEID
AGNAIL
APNEIC
AUNTIE
BANDIT
BONNIE
CANDID
CANNIE
CONNIE
CONOID
CONTIN
DANAID
DANZIG
DENNIS
DENTIL
DENTIN
DONNIE
DUNLIN
FANNIE
FENRIR
FINNIC
GANOID
HENBIT
HENRIS
JONNIE
JUNKIE
KENNIE
LANAIS
LENTIL
LUNGIS
MANTIC
MANTIS
MENHIR
MINNIE
NUNCIO
PANTIE
PENCIL
PENNIA
PENNIS
PINKIE
PINXIT
PONTIC
PONTIL
PUNDIT
RANCID
RENNIN
RENOIR
RONNIE
SENNIT
SUNLIT
SYNDIC
TANNIC
TANNIN
TENNIS
TENPIN
TENUIS
TINEID
TONKIN
TONSIL
WINNIE
ZINCIC
ZINNIA

••N••I

BANGUI
BANZAI
BONACI
BONSAI
CANTHI
CENTRI
DENDRI
GANDHI
GANGLI
KINESI
SANDHI
SANGUI
SANSEI

•••NI•

ADENIS
ADONIC
ADONIS
AGONIC
ATONIC
AZONIC
BAGNIO
BEANIE
BERNIE
BONNIE
CANNIE
CATNIP
CLINIC
CLONIC
CONNIE
CRANIA
CRANIO
CYANIC
CYANID
CYANIN
DENNIS
DONNIE
ETHNIC
FAFNIR
FANNIE
FINNIC
FORNIX
GDYNIA
GLYNIS
GUANIN
HERNIA
HERNIO
HORNIE
HYMNIC
HYPNIC
ICONIC
IRENIC
IRONIC
JONNIE
KENNIE
LEONIE
LIGNIN
MEANIE
MINNIE
NORNIR
NUDNIK
ODYNIA
OZONIC
PENNIA
PENNIS
PHONIA
PHONIC
PICNIC
PYKNIC
QUINIC
RENNIN
RONNIE
SCENIC
SENNIT
TAENIA
TANNIC
TANNIN
TENNIS
TURNIP
UNKNIT
URANIA
URANIC
VERNIX
WEENIE
WIENIE
WINNIE
ZINNIA

•••N•I

ADONAI
BRUNEI
UBANGI

••••NI

ACTINI
ALUMNI
BIKINI
ECHINI
GEMINI
LUMINI
SILENI
YEMENI

N•••J•

NAVAJO

•NJ•••

ENJOIN
ENJOYS
INJECT
INJURE
INJURY
UNJUST

••NJ••

BANJOS
BENJYS
DONJON
FANJET
PUNJAB
SANJAK

N•K•••

NEKTON

6

N••K••
NAPKIN
NECKED
NICKED
NICKEL
NICKER
NICKYS
NOCKED

N•••K•
NEVSKI

N••••K
NEWARK
NUDNIK

•NK•••
ANKARA
ANKLES
ANKLET
ANKYLO
INKERS
INKIER
INKING
INKLES
UNKIND
UNKNIT

•N•K••
ANGKOR
SNAKED
SNAKES

•N••K•
ANANKE
INTAKE
INVOKE
KNACKS
KNOCKS
SNACKS
SNEAKS
SNEAKY
SNICKS
SNOOKS
UNLIKE
UNMAKE
UNYOKE
VNECKS

•N•••K
ANORAK
UNCOCK
UNCORK
UNHOOK
UNHUSK
UNLOCK
UNMASK
UNPACK
UNPICK

••NK••
BANKED
BANKER
BUNKED
BUNKER
BUNKUM
CANKER
CONKED
DANKER
DANKLY
DINKEY
DONKEY
DUNKED
DUNKER
FUNKED
GINKGO
HANKER
HONKED
HONKER
JINKED
JINKER
JUNKED
JUNKER
JUNKET
JUNKIE
KINKED
LANKER
LANKLY
LINKED
LUNKER
MONKEY
PINKED
PINKIE
PUNKAS
RANKED
RANKER
RANKLE
RANKLY
SINKER
SUNKEN
TANKAS
TANKED
TANKER
TINKER
TINKLE
TINKLY
TONKIN
WINKED
WINKER
WINKLE
YANKED
YANKEE
YONKER

••N•K•
KANAKA
ZINCKY

••N••K
CANUCK
SANJAK

•••NK•
ANANKE
BLANKS
BLINKS
BRINKS
CHINKS
CHINKY
CHUNKS
CHUNKY
CLANKS
CLINKS
CRANKS
CRANKY
DRINKS
DRUNKS
FLANKS
FLUNKS
FLUNKY
FRANKS
PLANKS
PLUNKS
PRANKS
PRINKS
SHANKS
SKINKS
SKUNKS
SLINKS
SLINKY
SPANKS
SPUNKY
STINKS
SWANKY
THANKS
THINKS
TRUNKS

•••N•K
FRANCK
KARNAK
NUDNIK
PLANCK

••••NK
DEBUNK
EMBANK
PODUNK
SHRANK
SHRINK
SHRUNK

N•L•••
NELLIE
NELLYS
NELSON
NILGAI
NULLAH
NYLONS

N••L••
NAILED
NAPLES
NELLIE
NELLYS
NIELLI
NIELLO
NULLAH
NUTLET

N•••L•
NAMELY
NAPALM
NASALS
NAVELS
NEARLY
NEATLY
NEBULA
NEEDLE
NEROLI
NESTLE
NETTLE
NEVILE
NEVILL
NEWELS
NIBBLE
NICELY
NICOLE
NIELLI
NIELLO
NIGELS
NIGGLE
NIMBLE
NIPPLE
NOBALL
NOBBLE
NODDLE
NODULE
NOODLE
NOPALS
NOSILY
NOVELS
NOZZLE
NUBBLE
NUBBLY
NUBILE
NUDELY
NUMBLY
NUZZLE

N••••L
NARIAL
NARWAL
NASIAL
NEURAL
NEVILL
NICKEL
NOBALL
NORMAL
NOUNAL

•NL•••
ANLACE
ANLAGE
ENLACE
ENLIŞT
INLACE
INLAID
INLAND
INLAWS
INLAYS
INLETS
INLIER
UNLACE
UNLADE
UNLAID
UNLAYS
UNLEAD
UNLESS
UNLIKE
UNLIVE
UNLOAD
UNLOCK

•N•L••
ANALOG
ANGLED
ANGLER
ANGLES
ANGLIA
ANGLIC
ANILIN
ANKLES
ANKLET
ANTLER
ANTLIA
INFLOW
INFLUX
INKLES
INULIN
KNELLS
KNOLLS
SNELLS
UNCLAD
UNCLES

•N••L•
ANGELA
ANGELO
ANGELS
ANGOLA
ANKYLO
ANNALS
ANNULS
ANSELM
ANVILS
ENABLE
ENDALL
ENFOLD
ENGELS
ENGULF
ENISLE
ENROLL
ENSILE
GNARLS
GNARLY
INDULT
INFOLD
INGULF
INHALE
INSOLE
INSULT
INWALL
KNEELS
KNELLS
KNOLLS
KNURLS
KNURLY
ONEILL
SNAILS
SNARLS
SNARLY
SNELLS
SNUGLY
UNABLE
UNBELT
UNBOLT
UNDULY
UNFOLD
UNGULA
UNHOLY
UNPILE
UNROLL
UNRULY
UNSOLD
UNTOLD
UNWELL

•N•••L
ANIMAL
ANNEAL
ANNUAL
ENAMEL
ENCYCL
ENDALL
ENROLL
ENSOUL
ENTAIL
INHAUL
INSOUL
INWALL
ONEILL
SNIVEL
UNCIAL
UNCOIL
UNCURL
UNFURL
UNGUAL
UNREAL
UNREEL
UNROLL
UNSEAL
UNVEIL
UNWELL

••NL••
DUNLIN
HENLEY
RUNLET
SENLAC
SUNLIT

••N•L•
ANNALS
ANNULS
ARNOLD
BANGLE
BUNDLE
BUNGLE
CANALS
CANDLE
CANTLE
CANULA
DANDLE

DANGLE
DANKLY
DINGLE
DONALD
FINALE
FINALS
FINELY
FONDLE
FONDLY
GANGLI
GENTLE
HANDLE
JANGLE
JINGLE
JUNGLE
JUNGLY
KINDLE
KINDLY
KINGLY
LANKLY
LONELY
LUNULA
LUNULE
MANGLE
MANILA
MANTLE
MINGLE
PANELS
PENILE
PENULT
PINOLE
PINTLE
PUNILY
RANKLE
RANKLY
RONALD
RUNDLE
SANELY
SENILE
SINGLE
SINGLY
TANGLE
TANGLY
TINGLE
TINGLY
TINKLE
TINKLY
VENULE
VINYLS
WANDLE
WANGLE
WINKLE
ZONULA
ZONULE

••N••L
AGNAIL
ANNEAL
ANNUAL
APNEAL
BENGAL
BENZOL
BENZYL
CANCEL
CANNEL
CENTAL
CINEOL
CONSUL
CUNEAL
DANIEL
DENIAL
DENTAL
DENTIL
FENNEL
FINIAL
FONTAL
FUNGAL
FUNNEL
GENIAL
GINGAL
GUNNEL
HANDEL
HANSEL
JINGAL
KENNEL
LENTIL
LINEAL
LINTEL
MANFUL
MANTEL
MANUAL
MANUEL
MENDEL
MENIAL
MENSAL
MENTAL
MONGOL
PENCEL
PENCIL
PENIAL
PENPAL
PINEAL
PINNAL
PONTIL
RANDAL
RENTAL
RONDEL
RUNNEL
SANDAL
SANTOL
SENDAL
SINFUL
TINCAL
TINSEL
TONSIL
TUNNEL
VANDAL
VENIAL

•••NL•
EVENLY
GAINLY
KEENLY
LEANLY
MAINLY
MEANLY
OPENLY
THINLY
VAINLY

•••N•L
ATONAL
CANNEL
CARNAL
CORNEL
CRENEL
DARNEL
DIRNDL
FAUNAL
FENNEL
FUNNEL
GUNNEL
HYMNAL
KENNEL
KERNEL
LIONEL
NOUNAL
PHENOL
PHENYL
PINNAL
REGNAL
RHINAL
RUNNEL
SIGNAL
SIMNEL
SPINAL
SPINEL
TARNAL
THENAL
TRINAL
TUNNEL
URANYL
URINAL
VERNAL
ZOONAL

N•M•••
NAMELY
NAMERS
NAMING
NEMATO
NIMBLE
NIMBUS
NIMITZ
NIMROD
NOMADS
NOMISM
NOMURA
NUMBED
NUMBER
NUMBLY
NUMINA
NYMPHA
NYMPHO
NYMPHS

N••M••
NAOMIS
NEUMES
NORMAL
NORMAN
NORMAS
NUTMEG

N•••M•
NAHUMS

N••••M
NANISM
NAPALM
NAZISM
NOMISM
NONCOM
NUDISM

•NM•••
ENMESH
ENMITY
INMATE
INMESH
INMOST
UNMADE
UNMAKE
UNMANS
UNMASK
UNMEET
UNMEWS
UNMOOR

•N•M••
ANEMIA
ANEMIC
ANIMAL
ANIMAS
ANIMUS
ANOMIC
ANOMIE
ENAMEL
ENAMOR
ENEMAS
GNOMES
GNOMIC
GNOMON

•N••M•
ENCAMP
ENIGMA
ENTOMB
ENTOMO
ENWOMB
ENZYME
INARMS
INCOME
INFAMY
INTIMA
INTOMB
PNEUMA
PNEUMO

•N•••M
ANADEM
ANONYM
ANSELM
ANTHEM
ANTRIM
ANTRUM
ENGRAM
INDIUM
INFIRM
INFORM
UNSEAM

••NM••
GUNMAN
GUNMEN
PENMAN
PENMEN
VANMAN
VANMEN

••N•M•
BENUMB
BYNAME
CINEMA
DENIMS
DYNAMO
FANUMS
MINIMS
PANAMA
VENOMS

••N••M
BANTAM
BUNKUM
CONDOM
CONIUM
EONISM
FANTOM
GONIUM
HANSOM
IONIUM
MINIUM
MONISM
NANISM
NONCOM
RANDOM
RANSOM
TANDEM

•••N•M
ANONYM
BARNUM
CRINUM
EPONYM
FRENUM
MAGNUM
PLENUM
PUTNAM

N•N•••
NANCYS
NANISM
NANTES
NINETY
NINTHS
NONAGE
NONCOM
NONEGO
NUNCIO

N••N••
NORNIR
NOUNAL
NUANCE
NUDNIK

N•••N•
NADINE
NAGANA
NAMING
NARINE
NATANT
NIDING
NIXING
NOCENT
NOSING
NOTING
NOVENA
NUMINA
NYLONS

N••••N
NAPKIN
NASION
NATHAN
NATION
NATRON
NEKTON
NELSON
NEURON
NEWTON
NIACIN
NIPPON
NOGGIN
NOREEN
NORMAN
NOTION
NUBBIN
NUBIAN

•NN•••
ANNALS
ANNEAL
ANNIES
ANNOYS
ANNUAL
ANNULS
ENNEAD
INNATE
INNING

•N•N••
ANANKE
ANONYM
UNKNIT
UNSNAP

•N••N•
ANCONA
ANCONE
ANGINA
ANIONS
ANOINT
ANTONS

6

ANTONY
ANYONE
ENCINA
ENDING
ENGINE
ENWIND
INDENE
INDENT
INFANT
INKING
INLAND
INNING
INSANE
INTEND
INTENT
INTONE
INURNS
INVENT
INWIND
ONIONS
UNBEND
UNBENT
UNBIND
UNDINE
UNDONE
UNHAND
UNIONS
UNKIND
UNMANS
UNPINS
UNSUNG
UNWIND

•N•••N

ANDEAN
ANILIN
ANURAN
ENJOIN
ENSIGN
GNOMON
INBORN
INCHON
INDIAN
INSPAN
INTERN
INTURN
INULIN
UNBORN
UNEVEN
UNISON
UNSEEN

••NN••

BANNED
BANNER
BENNES
BENNET
BENNYS
BINNED
BONNET
BONNIE
BONNYS
CANNAE
CANNAS
CANNED
CANNEL
CANNER
CANNES
CANNIE
CANNON
CANNOT
CONNED
CONNER
CONNIE
CUNNER
DANNYS
DENNED
DENNIS
DENNYS
DINNED
DINNER
DONNAS
DONNED
DONNIE
DUNNED
FANNED
FANNER
FANNIE
FANNYS
FENNEC
FENNEL
FINNED
FINNIC
FUNNEL
GANNET
GINNED
GINNER
GUNNAR
GUNNED
GUNNEL
GUNNER
HANNAH
HANNAS
HENNAS
JENNET
JENNYS
JINNYS
JONNIE
KENNED
KENNEL
KENNIE
KENNYS
LANNER
LENNYS
LINNET
MANNED
MANNER
MINNIE
MINNOW
PANNED
PENNAE
PENNED
PENNER
PENNIA
PENNIS
PENNON
PENNYS
PINNAE
PINNAL
PINNED
PINNER
PUNNED
RENNET
RENNIN
RONNIE
RUNNEL
RUNNER
SANNUP
SENNAS
SENNET
SENNIT
SINNED
SINNER
SONNET
SUNNAH
SUNNED
TANNED
TANNER
TANNIC
TANNIN
TENNIS
TINNED
TINNER
TUNNED
TUNNEL
VINNYS
WANNED
WANNER
WINNER
WINNIE
WINNOW
YENNED
ZINNIA

••N•N•

AWNING
BANANA
BONING
CANINE
CANING
CANONS
CONING
DINING
FANONS
FINING
HONING
INNING
IONONE
KININS
LINENS
LINING
MANANA
MENINX
MINING
OWNING
PINANG
PINENE
PINING
PINONS
PONENT
RUNINS
RUNONS
SONANT
TENANT
TENONS
TONING
TUNING
WANING
WINING
ZANANA
ZENANA
ZONING

••N••N

ADNOUN
AMNION
BANIAN
BANYAN
BENIGN
BENTON
BONBON
BUNION
BUNSEN
BUNYAN
CANAAN
CANCAN
CANNON
CANTON
CANYON
CONTIN
DANTON
DENTIN
DONJON
DUNCAN
DUNLIN
EONIAN
FANION
FANTAN
FENIAN
GONION
GUNMAN
GUNMEN
IONIAN
JONSON
KANSAN
LENTEN
LINDEN
LONDON
LONGAN
MANDAN
MINION
MINOAN
PENMAN
PENMEN
PENNON
PINION
PONTON
RANDAN
RENNIN
RENOWN
RUNYON
SUNKEN
TANNIN
TENDON
TENPIN
TONKIN
VANMAN
VANMEN
VINSON
WANION
WANTON

•••NN•

BLENNY
BRANNY
CRANNY
DUENNA
GRANNY
GWENNS
GWYNNE
JEANNE
JOANNA
JOANNE
JOHNNY
SHINNY
SIENNA
SKINNY
SPINNY
VIENNA
WHINNY
YVONNE

•••N•N

CANNON
CYANIN
GUANIN
GUENON
KRONEN
LIGNIN
MIGNON
PENNON
RENNIN
TANNIN
VERNON

••••NN

JOHANN

NO••••

NOBALL
NOBBLE
NOCENT
NOCKED
NODDED
NODDER
NODDLE
NODOSE
NODULE
NOESIS
NOETIC
NOGGIN
NOISED
NOISES
NOMADS
NOMISM
NOMURA
NONAGE
NONCOM
NONEGO
NOODLE
NOOSED
NOOSES
NOPALS
NORDIC
NOREEN
NORIAS
NORMAL
NORMAN
NORMAS
NORNIR
NORRIS
NORWAY
NOSHOW
NOSIER
NOSILY
NOSING
NOSTOC
NOTARY
NOTERS
NOTICE
NOTIFY
NOTING
NOTION
NOUGAT
NOUGHT
NOUNAL
NOVELS
NOVENA
NOVICE
NOWAYS
NOWISE
NOZZLE

N•O•••

NAOMIS
NAOSES
NOODLE
NOOSED
NOOSES

N••O••

NABOBS
NAGOYA
NEROLI
NEVOID
NICOLE
NODOSE
NYLONS

N•••O•

NARROW
NASION
NATION
NATRON
NEKTON
NELSON
NESTOR
NEURON
NEWTON
NIMROD
NIPPON
NONCOM
NOSHOW
NOSTOC

NOTION

N••••O
NAVAHO
NAVAJO
NEMATO
NEPHRO
NIELLO
NONEGO
NUNCIO
NYMPHO

•NO•••
ANODES
ANODIC
ANOINT
ANOMIC
ANOMIE
ANONYM
ANORAK
ANOXIA
ANOXIC
ENOSIS
ENOUGH
GNOMES
GNOMIC
GNOMON
GNOSIS
KNOCKS
KNOLLS
KNOSPS
KNOTTY
KNOUTS
KNOWER
SNOCAT
SNOODS
SNOOKS
SNOOPS
SNOOPY
SNOOTS
SNOOTY
SNOOZE
SNORED
SNORER
SNORES
SNORTS
SNOTTY
SNOUTS
SNOWED

•N•O••
ANCONA
ANCONE
ANGOLA
ANGORA
ANIONS
ANNOYS
ANTONS
ANTONY
ANYONE
ENCODE
ENCORE
ENDOWS
ENFOLD
ENJOIN
ENJOYS
ENROBE
ENROLL
ENROOT
ENSOUL
ENTOMB
ENTOMO
ENVOYS
ENWOMB
INBORN
INCOME
INCORP
INDOOR
INDOWS
INFOLD
INFORM
INGOTS
INMOST
INROAD
INSOLE
INSOUL
INTOMB
INTONE
INVOKE
INWOVE
ONIONS
SNOODS
SNOOKS
SNOOPS
SNOOPY
SNOOTS
SNOOTY
SNOOZE
UNBOLT
UNBORN
UNCOCK
UNCOIL
UNCORK
UNDOER
UNDOES
UNDONE
UNFOLD
UNHOLY
UNHOOK
UNIONS
UNLOAD
UNLOCK
UNMOOR
UNROLL
UNROOT
UNSOLD
UNTOLD
UNYOKE

•N••O•
ANALOG
ANCHOR
ANGKOR
ANYHOW
ENAMOR
ENROOT
GNOMON
INCHON
INDOOR
INFLOW
UNHOOK
UNISON
UNMOOR
UNROOT
UNSTOP
UNTROD

•N•••O
ANATTO
ANGELO
ANKYLO
ANTERO
ENRICO
ENTERO
ENTOMO
GNATHO
INDIGO
INFERO
ONEIRO
PNEUMO
UNESCO

••NO••
ACNODE
ADNOUN
ANNOYS
APNOEA
ARNOLD
CANOED
CANOES
CANONS
CANOPY
CONOID
DENOTE
DONORS
FANONS
GANOID
GENOUS
GYNOUS
HONORE
HONORS
IGNORE
IONONE
LANOSE
LENORE
MANORS
MINOAN
MINORS
MONODY
PINOLE
PINONS
RENOIR
RENOWN
RUNOFF
RUNONS
RUNOUT
SENORA
SYNODS
TENONS
TENORS
VENOMS
VENOSE
VENOUS
VINOUS
WINOES

••N•O•
AMNION
BANGOR
BANJOS
BENTON
BENZOL
BONBON
BONGOS
BUNCOS
BUNION
CANDOR
CANNON
CANNOT
CANSOS
CANTON
CANTOR
CANTOS
CANYON
CENSOR
CENTOS
CINEOL
CONDOM
CONDOR
CONGOU
CONTOS
CONVOY
DANTON
DONJON
FANION
FANTOM
GENROS
GENTOO
GONION
HANSOM
JONSON
JUNCOS
JUNIOR
LENTOS
LONDON
MANGOS
MANIOC
MENTOR
MINION
MINNOW
MONGOL
MONROE
NONCOM
PENGOS
PENNON
PINGOS
PINION
PINTOS
PONTON
PUNTOS
RANCOR
RANDOM
RANSOM
RONDOS
RUNYON
SANTOL
SENIOR
SENSOR
SUNBOW
SUNDOG
TANGOS
TENDON
TENSOR
VENDOR
VINSON
WANION
WANTON
WINDOW
WINNOW

••N••O
BENITO
BONITO
CENTRO
DENDRO
DINERO
DYNAMO
GENITO
GENTOO
GINKGO
GYNECO
KINETO
LANUGO
MANITO
NONEGO
NUNCIO
PONCHO
RANCHO
TENUTO
VENTRO
XANTHO

•••NO•
BRUNOS
CANNON
CANNOT
EGGNOG
GUANOS
GUENON
HOBNOB
HYPNOS
KRONOR
LEMNOS
LLANOS
MIGNON
MINNOW
PENNON
PHENOL
PIANOS
RHINOS
SIGNOR
STENOG
TAINOS
VERNON
WINNOW

•••N•O
ALONSO
ALONZO
BAGNIO
BORNEO
BRONCO
CRANIO
DRONGO
ERINGO
ERYNGO
FRANCO
FRONTO
HERNIO
LEANTO
ODONTO
PRONTO
SHINTO

••••NO
ACTINO
ALBINO
ALUINO
AVERNO
CASINO
CHRONO
CYRANO
DEMONO
DOMINO
ECHINO
FRESNO
GITANO
HYMENO
IMMUNO
KIMONO
LADINO
LUMINO
MELANO
MERINO
ORGANO
PHRENO
SELENO
SOLANO
SPHENO
SPLENO
STERNO
TECHNO
VAGINO

N•P•••
NAPALM
NAPERY
NAPIER
NAPKIN
NAPLES
NAPPED
NAPPER
NAPPES
NAPPIE
NEPHEW
NEPHRO
NIPPED
NIPPER
NIPPLE
NIPPON
NOPALS

N••P••
NAPPED

6

NAPPER
NAPPES
NAPPIE
NIPPED
NIPPER
NIPPLE
NIPPON
NYMPHA
NYMPHO
NYMPHS

•NP•••
INPUTS
UNPACK
UNPAID
UNPEGS
UNPICK
UNPILE
UNPINS

•N•P••
INSPAN
SNAPPY
SNIPED
SNIPER
SNIPES
SNIPPY

•N••P•
ENRAPT
INCEPT
KNOSPS
SNAPPY
SNIPPY
SNOOPS
SNOOPY
UNCAPS
UNRIPE
UNRIPS
UNWEPT

•N•••P
ENCAMP
ENTRAP
ENWRAP
INCORP
INSTEP
INWRAP
UNSHIP
UNSNAP
UNSTEP
UNSTOP
UNWRAP

••NP••
PENPAL
TENPIN

••N•P•
CANAPE
CANOPY
LENAPE
PINUPS
SUNUPS

••N••P
BANGUP
HANGUP
LINEUP
PENTUP
SANNUP
TUNEUP

•••N•P
CATNIP
KIDNAP
SANNUP
TRANSP
TURNIP
UNSNAP

•N•Q••
UNIQUE

••NQ••
CINQUE
MANQUE

N•R•••
NARIAL
NARINE
NARROW
NARWAL
NEREIS
NEROLI
NERVED
NERVES
NORDIC
NOREEN
NORIAS
NORMAL
NORMAN
NORMAS
NORNIR
NORRIS
NORWAY
NURSED
NURSER
NURSES

N••R••
NARROW
NATRON
NEARBY
NEARED
NEARER
NEARLY
NEURAL
NEURON
NIMROD
NITRIC
NITRID
NORRIS
NUTRIA

N•••R•
NADIRS
NAMERS
NAPERY
NATURE
NEPHRO
NEWARK
NOMURA
NOTARY
NOTERS

N••••R
NAGGER
NAPIER
NAPPER
NASSER
NEARER
NEATER
NECTAR
NEEDER
NESTOR
NETHER
NEUTER
NICKER
NIGHER
NIPPER
NODDER
NORNIR
NOSIER
NUMBER
NURSER
NUTTER

•NR•••
ENRAGE
ENRAPT
ENRICH
ENRICO
ENROBE
ENROLL
ENROOT
INROAD
INRUSH
ONRUSH
UNREAD
UNREAL
UNREEL
UNREST
UNRIGS
UNRIPE
UNRIPS
UNROLL
UNROOT
UNRULY

•N•R••
ANDREA
ANDREI
ANDRES
ANDREW
ANERGY
ANORAK
ANTRIM
ANTRUM
ANURAN
ENERGY
ENGRAM
ENTRAP
ENTREE
ENWRAP
GNARLS
GNARLY
INARCH
INARMS
INBRED
INDRIS
INGRES
INGRID
INURED
INURES
INURNS
INWRAP
KNARRY
KNURLS
KNURLY
SNARED
SNARER
SNARES
SNARLS
SNARLY
SNORED
SNORER
SNORES
SNORTS
UNBRED
UNDRAW
UNDREW
UNTROD
UNTRUE
UNWRAP

•N••R•
ANGARY
ANGERS
ANGORA
ANITRA
ANKARA
ANTERO
ENCORE
ENDURE
ENGIRD
ENGIRT
ENSURE
ENTERA
ENTERO
ENTERS
ENTIRE
INBORN
INCORP
INCURS
INFERO
INFERS
INFIRM
INFORM
INHERE
INJURE
INJURY
INKERS
INSERT
INSURE
INTERN
INTERS
INTURN
INVERT
INWARD
KNARRY
ONAGRI
ONEIRO
ONWARD
SNEERS
UNBARS
UNBORN
UNCORK
UNCURL
UNFURL
UNGIRD
UNGIRT
UNHURT
UNSURE
UNWARY

•N•••R
ANCHOR
ANGKOR
ANGLER
ANSWER
ANTHER
ANTIAR
ANTLER
ENAMOR
ENDEAR
ENVIER
GNAWER
INDOOR
INKIER
INLIER
INSTAR
KNOWER
ONAGER
SNARER
SNIPER
SNORER
UNBEAR
UNDOER
UNFAIR
UNHAIR
UNMOOR

••NR••
CONRAD
FENRIR
GENRES
GENROS
HENRIS
HENRYS
KONRAD
MONROE
TANREC
TENREC

••N•R•
ABNERS
BINARY
BONERS
CANARD
CANARY
CANERS
CENTRA
CENTRI
CENTRO
CONTRA
CONTRE
DENARY
DENDRI
DENDRO
DINARS
DINERO
DINERS
DONORS
FINERY
GANTRY
GENERA
GENTRY
GONERS
HONORE
HONORS
HUNGRY
IGNORE
LENORE
LINERS
LONERS
MANORS
MANURE
MINERS
MINORS
ORNERY
OWNERS
PANTRY
PENURY
PINERY
SANDRA
SENARY
SENORA
SENTRY
SONARS
SUNDRY
SYNURA
TENORS
TENURE
TONERS
TUNDRA
TUNERS
VENERY
VENIRE
VENTRO
VINERY
WINERY
WINTRY
ZONARY

••N••R
BANGOR
BANKER
BANNER
BANTER
BENDER
BINDER
BONDER
BONIER
BONZER

6

BUNKER
CANCER
CANDOR
CANKER
CANNER
CANTER
CANTOR
CENSER
CENSOR
CENTER
CINDER
CONCUR
CONDOR
CONFER
CONGER
CONNER
CUNNER
DANCER
DANDER
DANGER
DANKER
DENIER
DENSER
DENVER
DINNER
DUNBAR
DUNKER
FANNER
FENCER
FENDER
FENRIR
FINDER
FINGER
FONDER
GANDER
GANGER
GENDER
GINGER
GINNER
GUNNAR
GUNNER
HANGAR
HANGER
HANKER
HINDER
HONKER
HUNGER
HUNTER
JINKER
JUNIOR
JUNKER
KINDER
LANCER
LANDER
LANGUR
LANKER
LANNER
LENDER
LINEAR
LINGER
LINIER
LINTER
LONGER
LUNGER
LUNKER
MANGER
MANNER
MENDER
MENHIR
MENTOR
MINCER
MINDER
MINTER
MONGER
PANDER
PANZER
PENNER
PINDAR
PINIER
PINNER
PINTER
PONDER
PUNIER
PUNTER
RANCOR
RANGER
RANKER
RANTER
RENDER
RENOIR
RENTER
RINGER
RINSER
RUNNER
SANDER
SANGAR
SANGER
SANSAR
SENDER
SENIOR
SENSOR
SINGER
SINKER
SINNER
SINTER
SONDER
SUNDER
TANKER
TANNER
TENDER
TENSER
TENSOR
TENTER
TINDER
TINKER
TINNER
TONIER
VENDER
VENDOR
VENEER
VENTER
VINIER
WANDER
WANNER
WANTER
WINCER
WINDER
WINIER
WINKER
WINNER
WINTER
WONDER
YONDER
YONKER
ZANIER
ZENGER

•••NR•

AMENRA
OHENRY

•••N•R

ATONER
BANNER
BURNER
CANNER
CHONDR
COINER
CONNER
CORNER
CUNNER
DINNER
EARNER
FAFNIR
FANNER
FAWNER
GAINER
GARNER
GINNER
GUNNAR
GUNNER
IRONER
JOINER
KEENER
KRONER
KRONOR
KRONUR
LANNER
LEANER
LIMNER
MANNER
MEANER
NORNIR
OPENER
PAWNER
PENNER
PINNER
PLANAR
PLANER
PRUNER
RUINER
RUNNER
SEINER
SHINER
SIGNER
SIGNOR
SINNER
SOONER
STONER
SUMNER
TANNER
THENAR
TINNER
TURNER
TWINER
VAINER
WAGNER
WANNER
WARNER
WEANER
WHINER
WIENER
WINNER
YAWNER

N•S•••

NASALS
NASHUA
NASIAL
NASION
NASSAU
NASSER
NASTIC
NESSUS
NESTED
NESTLE
NESTOR
NISEIS
NOSHOW
NOSIER
NOSILY
NOSING
NOSTOC

N••S••

NAOSES
NASSAU
NASSER
NAUSEA
NELSON
NESSUS
NEVSKI
NOESIS
NOISED
NOISES
NOOSED
NOOSES
NURSED
NURSER
NURSES

N•••S•

NANISM
NAZISM
NEWEST
NICEST
NODOSE
NOMISM
NOWISE
NUDISM
NUDIST

N••••S

NABOBS
NADIRS
NAEVUS
NAHUMS
NAIADS
NAMERS
NANCYS
NANTES
NAOMIS
NAOSES
NAPLES
NAPPES
NASALS
NAVELS
NAVIES
NAWABS
NEIGHS
NELLYS
NEREIS
NERVES
NESSUS
NEUMES
NEWELS
NICHES
NICKYS
NIECES
NIGELS
NIGHTS
NIMBUS
NINTHS
NISEIS
NIXIES
NOESIS
NOISES
NOMADS
NOOSES
NOPALS
NORIAS
NORMAS
NORRIS
NOTERS
NOVELS
NOWAYS
NUBIAS
NUDGES
NURSES
NYLONS
NYMPHS

•NS•••

ANSATE
ANSELM
ANSWER
ENSIGN
ENSILE
ENSOUL
ENSUED
ENSUES
ENSURE
INSANE
INSECT
INSERT
INSETS
INSIDE
INSIST
INSOLE
INSOUL
INSPAN
INSTAR
INSTEP
INSULT
INSURE
ONSETS
UNSAFE
UNSAID
UNSAYS
UNSEAL
UNSEAM
UNSEAT
UNSEEN
UNSHIP
UNSNAP
UNSOLD
UNSTEP
UNSTOP
UNSUNG
UNSURE

•N•S••

ANISES
ANUSES
ENISLE
ENOSIS
GNOSIS
KNOSPS
ONUSES
UNDSET
UNESCO
UNISEX
UNISON
UNUSED

•N••S•

ENCASE
ENCYST
ENLIST
ENMESH
GNEISS
INCASE
INCEST
INCISE
INCUSE
INFEST
INFUSE
INGEST
INMESH
INMOST
INRUSH
INSIST
INVEST
ONRUSH
UNEASY
UNHUSK
UNJUST
UNLESS
UNMASK
UNREST
UNWISE
UNWISH

6

•N•••S
ANABAS
ANDRES
ANGELS
ANGERS
ANGLES
ANIMAS
ANIMUS
ANIONS
ANISES
ANITAS
ANKLES
ANNALS
ANNIES
ANNOYS
ANNULS
ANODES
ANTICS
ANTONS
ANUBIS
ANUSES
ANVILS
ENACTS
ENATES
ENDOWS
ENDUES
ENEMAS
ENGELS
ENJOYS
ENOSIS
ENSUES
ENTERS
ENVIES
ENVOYS
GNARLS
GNEISS
GNOMES
GNOSIS
INARMS
INCHES
INCURS
INDIES
INDOWS
INDRIS
INDUES
INFERS
INGOTS
INGRES
INKERS
INKLES
INLAWS
INLAYS
INLETS
INPUTS
INSETS
INTERS
INURES
INURNS
KNACKS
KNAVES
KNEADS
KNEELS
KNELLS
KNIFES
KNIVES
KNOCKS
KNOLLS
KNOSPS
KNOUTS
KNURLS
ONIONS
ONSETS
ONUSES
SNACKS
SNAFUS
SNAILS
SNAKES
SNARES
SNARLS
SNATHS
SNEAKS
SNEERS
SNELLS
SNICKS
SNIFFS
SNIPES
SNOODS
SNOOKS
SNOOPS
SNOOTS
SNORES
SNORTS
SNOUTS
SNUFFS
UNBARS
UNCAPS
UNCLES
UNDIES
UNDOES
UNGUES
UNGUIS
UNHATS
UNIONS
UNITES
UNLAYS
UNLESS
UNMANS
UNMEWS
UNPEGS
UNPINS
UNRIGS
UNRIPS
UNSAYS
UNTIES
VNECKS

••NS••
BONSAI
BUNSEN
CANSOS
CENSED
CENSER
CENSES
CENSOR
CENSUS
CONSUL
DENSER
GUNSHY
HANSEL
HANSOM
HONSHU
JONSON
KANSAN
KANSAS
KINSEY
LENSES
MANSES
MENSAL
MENSES
PANSYS
RANSOM
RINSED
RINSER
RINSES
SANSAR
SANSEI
SENSED
SENSES
SENSOR
SUNSET
TENSED
TENSER
TENSES
TENSOR
TINSEL
TONSIL
VINSON

••N•S•
BANISH
DANISH
DENISE
DYNAST
EONISM
ERNEST
FINEST
FINISH
FUNEST
HONEST
KINASE
KINESI
LANOSE
MONGST
MONISM
MONIST
NANISM
PUNISH
SANEST
TANIST
VANISH
VENOSE

••N••S
ABNERS
AENEAS
ANNALS
ANNIES
ANNOYS
ANNULS
ARNIES
BANJOS
BANTUS
BENJYS
BENNES
BENNYS
BINGES
BINITS
BONERS
BONGOS
BONNYS
BONZES
BUNCOS
CANALS
CANERS
CANNAS
CANNES
CANOES
CANONS
CANSOS
CANTOS
CANTUS
CANVAS
CENSES
CENSUS
CENTOS
CINDYS
CONCHS
CONEYS
CONGAS
CONGES
CONICS
CONIES
CONTES
CONTOS
CYNICS
DANAUS
DANCES
DANNYS
DENIES
DENIMS
DENNIS
DENNYS
DINAHS
DINARS
DINERS
DINGUS
DONEES
DONETS
DONNAS
DONORS
DUNCES
ERNIES
FANGAS
FANNYS
FANONS
FANUMS
FENCES
FINALS
FUNDUS
FUNGUS
GANEFS
GANGES
GENETS
GENIES
GENIUS
GENOUS
GENRES
GENROS
GENTES
GONADS
GONERS
GYNOUS
HANCES
HANNAS
HENNAS
HENRIS
HENRYS
HINDUS
HINGES
HONEYS
HONORS
JANETS
JENNYS
JINNYS
JINXES
JONAHS
JUNCOS
JUNIUS
JUNTAS
KANSAS
KENNYS
KININS
LANAIS
LANCES
LENNYS
LENSES
LENTOS
LINDAS
LINENS
LINERS
LINGAS
LONERS
LUNETS
LUNGES
LUNGIS
LYNXES
MANDYS
MANGOS
MANIAS
MANORS
MANSES
MANTAS
MANTES
MANTIS
MENSES
MINCES
MINERS
MINIMS
MINORS
MINXES
MONADS
MONEYS
MONIES
MONTES
MONTHS
MONTYS
NANCYS
NANTES
NINTHS
OUNCES
OWNERS
PANDAS
PANELS
PANICS
PANSYS
PENGOS
PENNIS
PENNYS
PINDUS
PINGOS
PINONS
PINTOS
PINUPS
PONIES
PONTES
PUNKAS
PUNTOS
RANEES
RANGES
RENEES
RENEWS
RENTES
RINSES
RONDOS
RUNINS
RUNONS
SANDYS
SANIES
SENNAS
SENSES
SINEWS
SINGES
SONARS
SONIAS
SONYAS
SUNUPS
SYNODS
TANGOS
TANKAS
TENETS
TENNIS
TENONS
TENORS
TENSES
TENTHS
TENUES
TENUIS
TINCTS
TINGES
TONERS
TONICS
TUNERS
TUNGUS
TUNICS
VENOMS
VENOUS
VENUES
VINCES
VINNYS
VINOUS
VINYLS
WANDAS
WENDYS
WINCES

6

WINOES
WINZES
ZANIES

•••NS•

ALONSO
FLENSE
QUINSY
TEENSY
TRANSP
WEENSY

•••N•S

ACINUS
ADENIS
ADONIS
AGENTS
AGONES
AKENES
ALINES
AMENDS
AMENTS
ARENAS
ATONES
AXONES
AZINES
BEINGS
BENNES
BENNYS
BLANKS
BLENDS
BLINDS
BLINKS
BLONDS
BLUNTS
BONNYS
BOUNDS
BRANDS
BRANTS
BRENTS
BRINES
BRINGS
BRINKS
BRONCS
BRUNOS
BWANAS
CANNAS
CANNES
CHANGS
CHANTS
CHINES
CHINKS
CHUNKS
CLANGS
CLANKS
CLINES
CLINGS
CLINKS
CLINTS
CLONES
CLONUS
CORNUS
COUNTS
CRANES
CRANKS
CRONES
CRONUS
CYGNUS
DANNYS
DAUNTS
DENNIS
DENNYS
DIANAS
DIANES
DOINGS
DONNAS
DRINKS
DRONES
DRUNKS
ELANDS
ELENAS
EMENDS
EVENTS
FAINTS
FANNYS
FAUNAS
FAUNUS
FEINTS
FIENDS
FLANKS
FLINGS
FLINTS
FLONGS
FLUNKS
FOUNDS
FOUNTS
FRANCS
FRANKS
FRONDS
FRONTS
GIANTS
GLANDS
GLINTS
GLYNIS
GOINGS
GRANTS
GRINDS
GRUNTS
GUANOS
GWENNS
HANNAS
HAUNTS
HENNAS
HOUNDS
HYENAS
HYPNOS
ICINGS
IMINES
IRENES
JAINAS
JAUNTS
JENNYS
JINNYS
JOINTS
KENNYS
KEYNES
KOINES
LEMNOS
LENNYS
LEONAS
LIANAS
LIANES
LLANOS
MAUNDS
MESNES
MOUNTS
MYRNAS
OPINES
ORANGS
PAINTS
PENNIS
PENNYS
PHONES
PIANOS
PIGNUS
PLANES
PLANKS
PLANTS
PLUNKS
POINDS
POINTS
POUNDS
PRANKS
PRINKS
PRINTS
PRONGS
PRUNES
QUANTS
QUINTS
RHINOS
ROUNDS
SAINTS
SAUNAS
SCENDS
SCENES
SCENTS
SCONES
SEINES
SENNAS
SHANKS
SHINES
SHUNTS
SKINKS
SKUNKS
SLANTS
SLINGS
SLINKS
SOUNDS
SPANKS
SPENDS
SPINES
STANDS
STINGS
STINKS
STINTS
STONES
STUNTS
SWINGS
TAINOS
TAINTS
TAUNTS
TBONES
TENNIS
THANES
THANKS
THINGS
THINKS
THONGS
TRENDS
TRINES
TRUNKS
TWANGS
TWINES
UPENDS
URANUS
VAUNTS
VERNAS
VIANDS
VINNYS
WAYNES
WHANGS
WHINES
WOUNDS
WRINGS
WRONGS
ZOUNDS

••••NS

AARONS
ACORNS
ADORNS
ALFONS
ALIENS
ALIGNS
ALLANS
ALLENS
ALUINS
ALVANS
AMIENS
ANIONS
ANTONS
APRONS
ARIANS
ARPENS
ARYANS
ASIANS
ASPENS
ATHENS
AUXINS
BAIRNS
BARONS
BASINS
BATONS
BEGINS
BLAINS
BOGANS
BOURNS
BRAINS
BROWNS
BRUINS
BURANS
BURINS
CABINS
CAIRNS
CAJUNS
CANONS
CAPONS
CHAINS
CHURNS
CLEANS
CLOWNS
COIGNS
COLINS
COLONS
COZENS
CROONS
CROWNS
CUBANS
CUMINS
CUTINS
DAMANS
DEDANS
DEIGNS
DEMONS
DEWANS
DIVANS
DIWANS
DIZENS
DOYENS
DOZENS
DRAINS
DROWNS
EDWINS
ELFINS
ELLENS
ELOINS
ERWINS
ETHANS
FANONS
FEIGNS
FELONS
FOEHNS
FREONS
FROWNS
GAMINS
GIPONS
GLEANS
GRAINS
GREENS
GROANS
GROINS
GWENNS
GYRONS
HAVENS
HELENS
HERONS
HOGANS
HUMANS
HURONS
HYMENS
INURNS
IRVINS
IRWINS
JAPANS
JASONS
JUPONS
KARENS
KEVINS
KININS
LAPINS
LATINS
LEARNS
LEMONS
LIKENS
LIMENS
LINENS
LIVENS
LUMENS
LYSINS
MASONS
MATINS
MELONS
MESONS
MORONS
MOURNS
NYLONS
OCEANS
ONIONS
ORGANS
ORPINS
OSCANS
PAEANS
PAEONS
PAGANS
PARENS
PATENS
PAVANS
PECANS
PEKANS
PINONS
PITONS
PLAINS
PRAWNS
PREENS
PUTONS
PYLONS
PYRANS
QUEANS
QUEENS
QUERNS
QUOINS
RAVENS
RAYONS
REDANS
REIGNS
REMANS
RERUNS
RESINS
RIPENS
ROBINS
ROMANS
ROSINS
ROWANS
RUBENS
RUNINS
RUNONS
SABINS
SALONS
SASINS
SATINS
SAVINS
SAXONS
SCIONS
SCORNS

SEDANS
SERINS
SETONS
SEVENS
SHEENS
SIMONS
SIRENS
SITINS
SKEANS
SKEINS
SOLANS
SOZINS
SPAWNS
SPOONS
SPURNS
STAINS
STEINS
STERNS
SUSANS
SWAINS
SWOONS
TALONS
TENONS
TETONS
THORNS
TIEINS
TITANS
TOKENS
TOMANS
TOXINS
TOYONS
TRAINS
UNIONS
UNMANS
UNPINS
UTURNS
VIXENS
WAGONS
WAKENS
WIDENS
WIGANS
WIZENS
XYLANS
YAMENS
YAMUNS
YAPONS
YEARNS
YOGINS
YUPONS
ZAYINS
ZIRONS

N•T•••

NATANT
NATHAN
NATION
NATIVE
NATRON
NATURE
NETHER
NETTED
NETTIE
NETTLE
NITRIC
NITRID
NITWIT
NOTARY
NOTERS
NOTICE
NOTIFY
NOTING
NOTION
NUTLET
NUTMEG
NUTRIA
NUTTED
NUTTER

N••T••

NANTES
NASTIC
NAUTCH
NEATER
NEATLY
NECTAR
NEKTON
NESTED
NESTLE
NESTOR
NETTED
NETTIE
NETTLE
NEUTER
NEWTON
NINTHS
NOETIC
NOSTOC
NUTTED
NUTTER

N•••T•

NEGATE
NEMATO
NICETY
NIGHTS
NIGHTY
NIMITZ
NINETY
NUDITY

N••••T

NATANT
NAUGHT
NEWEST
NICEST
NITWIT
NOCENT
NOUGAT
NOUGHT
NUDIST
NUGGET
NUTLET

•NT•••

ANTEED
ANTERO
ANTHEA
ANTHEM
ANTHER
ANTIAR
ANTICS
ANTLER
ANTLIA
ANTONS
ANTONY
ANTRIM
ANTRUM
ENTAIL
ENTERA
ENTERO
ENTERS
ENTICE
ENTIRE
ENTITY
ENTOMB
ENTOMO
ENTRAP
ENTREE
INTACT
INTAKE
INTEND
INTENT
INTERN
INTERS
INTIMA
INTOMB
INTONE
INTUIT
INTURN
UNTIDY
UNTIED
UNTIES
UNTOLD
UNTROD
UNTRUE

•N•T••

ANATTO
ANITAS
ANITRA
ENATES
ENATIC
GNATHO
INSTAR
INSTEP
KNOTTY
SNATCH
SNATHE
SNATHS
SNITCH
SNOTTY
UNITED
UNITES
UNSTEP
UNSTOP

•N••T•

ANATTO
ANSATE
ENACTS
ENMITY
ENTITY
INCITE
INGOTS
INLETS
INMATE
INNATE
INPUTS
INSETS
INVITE
KNOTTY
KNOUTS
ONSETS
SNOOTS
SNOOTY
SNORTS
SNOTTY
SNOUTS
UNHATS

•N•••T

ANKLET
ANOINT
ENCYST
ENGIRT
ENLIST
ENRAPT
ENROOT
INCEPT
INCEST
INDENT
INDICT
INDUCT
INDULT
INFANT
INFECT
INFEST
INGEST
INJECT
INMOST
INSECT
INSERT
INSIST
INSULT
INTACT
INTENT
INTUIT
INVENT
INVERT
INVEST
KNIGHT
SNOCAT
UNBELT
UNBENT
UNBOLT
UNDSET
UNGIRT
UNHURT
UNJUST
UNKNIT
UNMEET
UNREST
UNROOT
UNSEAT
UNVEXT
UNWEPT

••NT••

AUNTIE
BANTAM
BANTER
BANTUS
BENTON
BUNTED
CANTED
CANTER
CANTHI
CANTLE
CANTON
CANTOR
CANTOS
CANTUS
CENTAL
CENTER
CENTOS
CENTRA
CENTRI
CENTRO
CONTES
CONTIN
CONTOS
CONTRA
CONTRE
DANTON
DENTAL
DENTED
DENTIL
DENTIN
DINTED
FANTAN
FANTOM
FONTAL
GANTRY
GENTES
GENTLE
GENTOO
GENTRY
HINTED
HUNTED
HUNTER
JUNTAS
LENTEN
LENTIL
LENTOS
LINTEL
LINTER
MANTAS
MANTEL
MANTES
MANTIC
MANTIS
MANTLE
MANTUA
MENTAL
MENTOR
MINTED
MINTER
MONTES
MONTHS
MONTYS
NANTES
NINTHS
PANTED
PANTIE
PANTRY
PENTAD
PENTUP
PINTER
PINTLE
PINTOS
PONTES
PONTIC
PONTIL
PONTON
PUNTED
PUNTER
PUNTOS
RANTED
RANTER
RENTAL
RENTED
RENTER
RENTES
SANTOL
SENTRY
SINTER
SYNTAX
TENTED
TENTER
TENTHS
TINTED
VENTED
VENTER
VENTRO
WANTED
WANTER
WANTON
WINTER
WINTRY
WONTED
XANTHO

••N•T•

ADNATE
AGNATE
BENITA
BENITO
BINITS
BONITO
CANUTE
DANITE
DENOTE
DONATE
DONETS
FINITE
GENETS
GENITO
IGNITE
INNATE
JANETS
KINETO
LANATE
LENGTH
LENITY
LUNATE

LUNETS
MANITO
MANITU
MINUTE
NINETY
ORNATE
ORNITH
PINITE
SANITY
SENATE
SONATA
TENETS
TENUTO
TINCTS
VANITY
ZENITH
ZONATE

••N••T

BANDIT
BENNET
BONNET
CANNOT
DYNAST
ERNEST
FANJET
FINEST
FUNEST
GANNET
HENBIT
HONEST
JENNET
JUNKET
LANCET
LINNET
MINUET
MONGST
MONIST
PENULT
PINXIT
PONENT
PUNDIT
RENNET
RUNLET
RUNOUT
SANEST
SENNET
SENNIT
SONANT
SONNET
SUNLIT
SUNSET
SYNDET
TANIST
TENANT

•••NT•

AGENTS
AMENTS
ARANTA
ARUNTA
BLINTZ
BLUNTS
BOUNTY
BRANTS
BRENTS
BRONTE
CHANTS
CHANTY
CHINTZ
CLINTS
COUNTS
COUNTY
DAINTY
DAUNTS
EVENTS
FAINTS
FEINTS
FLINTS
FLINTY
FOUNTS
FRONTO
FRONTS
GIANTS
GLINTS
GRANTS
GRUNTS
HAUNTS
JAUNTS
JAUNTY
JOINTS
LEANTO
MOUNTS
MOUNTY
ODONTO
OMENTA
PAINTS
PAINTY
PLANTS
PLENTY
PLINTH
POINTS
POINTY
PRINTS
PRONTO
QUANTA
QUANTS
QUINTS
SAINTS
SCANTY
SCENTS
SHANTY
SHINTO
SHUNTS
SLANTS
STINTS
STUNTS
TAINTS
TAUNTS
TWENTY
VAUNTS

•••N•T

BENNET
BONNET
BRUNET
BURNET
CANNOT
COBNUT
CORNET
CYGNET
GANNET
GARNET
HOGNUT
HORNET
JENNET
LINNET
MAGNET
PEANUT
PIGNUT
PLANET
RENNET
SENNET
SENNIT
SIGNET
SONNET
SPINET
THANAT
UNKNIT
WALNUT

••••NT

ABSENT
ACCENT
ADVENT
AMOUNT
ANOINT
ARDENT
ARGENT
ARPENT
ARRANT
ASCENT
ASKANT
ASLANT
ASSENT
BEZANT
BRYANT
CADENT
CEMENT
CLIENT
COGENT
DECANT
DECENT
DETENT
DOCENT
DOESNT
ERRANT
ESCENT
EXEUNT
EXTANT
EXTENT
FLAUNT
FLUENT
FOMENT
FORINT
GERENT
GIGANT
HAVENT
INDENT
INFANT
INTENT
INVENT
JURANT
LAMENT
LATENT
LEARNT
LEVANT
LOMENT
LUCENT
MOMENT
MUTANT
NATANT
NOCENT
OCTANT
ORIENT
PARENT
PATENT
PEDANT
PLAINT
PLIANT
PONENT
POTENT
QUAINT
RECANT
RECENT
REGENT
RELENT
REPENT
RESENT
RIDENT
RODENT
SAVANT
SECANT
SEJANT
SILENT
SOLENT
SONANT
SPLINT
SPRINT
SQUINT
TALENT
TENANT
TRUANT
TYRANT
UNBENT
URGENT
VACANT
VOLANT
WERENT

NU••••

NUANCE
NUBBIN
NUBBLE
NUBBLY
NUBIAN
NUBIAS
NUBILE
NUCHAE
NUDELY
NUDGED
NUDGES
NUDISM
NUDIST
NUDITY
NUDNIK
NUGGET
NULLAH
NUMBED
NUMBER
NUMBLY
NUMINA
NUNCIO
NURSED
NURSER
NURSES
NUTLET
NUTMEG
NUTRIA
NUTTED
NUTTER
NUZZLE

N•U•••

NAUGHT
NAUSEA
NAUTCH
NEUMES
NEURAL
NEURON
NEUTER
NOUGAT
NOUGHT
NOUNAL

N••U••

NAHUMS
NATURE
NEBULA
NODULE
NOMURA

N•••U•

NAEVUS
NASHUA
NESSUS
NIMBUS

N••••U

NASSAU

•NU•••

ANUBIS
ANURAN
ANUSES
INULIN
INURED
INURES
INURNS
KNURLS
KNURLY
ONUSES
SNUFFS
SNUFFY
SNUGLY
UNUSED

•N•U••

ANNUAL
ANNULS
ENDUED
ENDUES
ENDURE
ENGULF
ENOUGH
ENSUED
ENSUES
ENSURE
INCUBI
INCURS
INCUSE
INDUCE
INDUCT
INDUED
INDUES
INDULT
INFUSE
INGULF
INJURE
INJURY
INPUTS
INRUSH
INSULT
INSURE
INTUIT
INTURN
KNOUTS
ONRUSH
PNEUMA
PNEUMO
SNOUTS
UNCURL
UNDULY
UNFURL
UNGUAL
UNGUES
UNGUIS
UNGULA
UNHURT
UNHUSK
UNJUST
UNRULY
UNSUNG
UNSURE

•N••U•

ANIMUS
ANTRUM
ENSOUL
INDIUM
INFLUX
INHAUL
INSOUL
SNAFUS
UNIQUE
UNTRUE

••NU••

ANNUAL
ANNULS
BENUMB
CANUCK
CANULA
CANUTE

6

DANUBE
DENUDE
EUNUCH
FANUMS
LANUGO
LUNULA
LUNULE
MANUAL
MANUEL
MANURE
MINUET
MINUTE
PENULT
PENURY
PINUPS
SUNUPS
SYNURA
TENUES
TENUIS
TENURE
TENUTO
VENUES
VENULE
ZONULA
ZONULE

••N•U•
ADNOUN
ARNAUD
BANGUI
BANGUP
BANTUS
BUNKUM
CANGUE
CANTUS
CENSUS
CINQUE
CONCUR
CONIUM
CONSUL
DANAUS
DENGUE
DINGUS
FONDUE
FUNDUS
FUNGUS
GANGUE
GENIUS
GENOUS
GONIUM
GYNOUS
HANGUP
HINDUS
IONIUM
JUNIUS
LANGUR
LINEUP
LINGUA
MANFUL
MANQUE
MANTUA
MINIUM
PENTUP
PINDUS
RUNOUT
SANGUI
SANNUP
SINFUL
TONGUE
TUNEUP
TUNGUS
VENDUE
VENOUS
VINOUS

••N••U
CONGOU
HONSHU
JUNEAU
LANDAU
MANCHU
MANITU

•••NU•
ACINUS
AVENUE
BARNUM
CLONUS
COBNUT
CORNUA
CORNUS
CRINUM
CRONUS
CYGNUS
FAUNUS
FRENUM
HOGNUT
KRONUR
MAGNUM
PEANUT
PIGNUS
PIGNUT
PLENUM
SANNUP
URANUS
WALNUT

••••NU
VISHNU

N•V•••
NAVAHO
NAVAJO
NAVELS
NAVIES
NEVADA
NEVILE
NEVILL
NEVOID
NEVSKI
NOVELS
NOVENA
NOVICE

N••V••
NAEVUS
NERVED
NERVES

N•••V•
NATIVE

•NV•••
ANVILS
ENVIED
ENVIER
ENVIES
ENVOYS
INVADE
INVENT
INVERT
INVEST
INVITE
INVOKE
UNVEIL
UNVEXT

•N•V••
KNAVES
KNIVES
SNIVEL
UNEVEN

•N••V•
ENDIVE
INWOVE
UNLIVE

••NV••
CANVAS
CONVEX
CONVEY
CONVOY
DENVER

••N•V•
GENEVA

N•W•••
NAWABS
NEWARK
NEWELS
NEWEST
NEWTON
NOWAYS
NOWISE

N••W••
NARWAL
NITWIT
NORWAY

N••••W
NARROW
NEPHEW
NOSHOW

•NW•••
ENWIND
ENWOMB
ENWRAP
INWALL
INWARD
INWIND
INWOVE
INWRAP
ONWARD
UNWARY
UNWELL
UNWEPT
UNWIND
UNWISE
UNWISH
UNWRAP

•N•W••
ANSWER
ANYWAY
GNAWED
GNAWER
KNOWER
ONEWAY
SNOWED

•N••W•
ENDOWS
INDOWS
INLAWS
UNMEWS

•N•••W
ANDREW
ANYHOW
INFLOW
UNDRAW
UNDREW

••NW••
RUNWAY

••N•W•
RENEWS
RENOWN
SINEWS
SINEWY

••N••W
MINNOW
SUNBOW
SUNDEW
WINDOW
WINNOW

•••N•W
MINNOW
WINNOW

N•X•••
NIXIES
NIXING

•N•X••
ANOXIA
ANOXIC

•N••X•
UNVEXT

•N•••X
INFLUX
UNISEX

••NX••
JINXES
LYNXES
MINXES
PINXIT

••N••X
CONVEX
MENINX
SYNTAX

•••N•X
FORNAX
FORNIX
VERNIX

••••NX
LARYNX
MENINX
SPHINX
SYRINX

NY••••
NYLONS
NYMPHA
NYMPHO
NYMPHS

N•••Y•
NAGOYA
NANCYS
NELLYS
NICKYS
NOWAYS

N••••Y
NAMELY
NAPERY
NAZIFY
NEARBY
NEARLY
NEATLY
NICELY
NICETY
NIDIFY
NIGHTY
NINETY
NORWAY
NOSILY
NOTARY
NOTIFY
NUBBLY
NUDELY
NUDITY
NUMBLY

•NY•••
ANYHOW
ANYONE
ANYWAY
UNYOKE

•N•Y••
ANKYLO
ENCYCL
ENCYST
ENZYME

•N••Y•
ANNOYS
ANONYM
ENJOYS
ENVOYS
INLAYS
UNLAYS
UNSAYS

•N•••Y
ANERGY
ANGARY
ANTONY
ANYWAY
ENERGY
ENMITY
ENTITY
GNARLY
INFAMY
INJURY
KNARRY
KNOTTY
KNURLY
ONEWAY
SNAGGY
SNAPPY
SNARLY
SNEAKY
SNEEZY
SNIFFY
SNIPPY
SNOOPY
SNOOTY
SNOTTY
SNUFFY
SNUGLY
UNDULY
UNEASY
UNHOLY
UNRULY
UNTIDY
UNWARY

••NY••
BANYAN
BUNYAN
CANYON
RUNYON
SONYAS
VINYLS

••N•Y•
ANNOYS
BENJYS
BENNYS
BENZYL

BONNYS
CINDYS
CONEYS
DANNYS
DENNYS
FANNYS
HENRYS
HONEYS
JENNYS
JINNYS
KENNYS
LENNYS
MANDYS
MONEYS
MONTYS
NANCYS
PANSYS
PENNYS
SANDYS
VINNYS
WENDYS

••N••Y
BENDAY
BINARY
BUNCHY
CANARY
CANOPY
CONCHY
CONVEY
CONVOY
DANKLY
DENARY
DINGEY
DINGHY
DINKEY
DONKEY
FINELY
FINERY
FONDLY
GANTRY
GENTRY
GUNSHY
HENLEY
HUNGRY
IGNIFY
JUNGLY
KINDLY
KINGLY
KINSEY
LANKLY
LENITY
LONELY
LUNACY
MINIFY
MONDAY
MONKEY
MONODY
NINETY
ORNERY
PANTRY
PENURY
PINERY
PUNCHY
PUNILY
RANKLY
RUNWAY
SANELY
SANITY
SENARY
SENTRY
SINEWY
SINGLY
SUNDAY
SUNDRY
TANGLY
TINGLY
TINKLY
VANITY
VENERY
VINERY
WINCEY
WINERY
WINTRY
ZINCKY
ZONARY

•••NY•
ANONYM
BENNYS
BONNYS
DANNYS
DENNYS
EPONYM
FANNYS
JENNYS
JINNYS
KENNYS
LENNYS
PENNYS
PHENYL
URANYL
VINNYS

•••N•Y
AGENCY
BARNEY
BERNEY
BLENNY
BOUNCY
BOUNTY
BRANDY
BRANNY
BRONZY
CHANCY
CHANTY
CHINKY
CHUNKY
CLINGY
COUNTY
CRANKY
CRANNY
DAINTY
DISNEY
EVENLY
FLINTY
FLUNKY
FRENZY
FRINGY
GAINLY
GOONEY
GRANNY
GRUNDY
JAUNTY
JITNEY
JOHNNY
KEENLY
KIDNEY
LEANLY
MAINLY
MAUNDY
MEANLY
MOUNTY
OHENRY
OPENLY
PAINTY
PHONEY
PLENTY
POINTY
QUINCY
QUINSY
RODNEY
ROMNEY
SCANTY
SHANTY
SHINDY
SHINNY
SIDNEY
SKINNY
SLANGY
SLINKY
SPINNY
SPONGY
SPUNKY
STINGY
SWANKY
SYDNEY
TEENSY
THINLY
TRENDY
TWANGY
TWENTY
VAINLY
WEENSY
WHINNY
WITNEY

••••NY
ALBANY
ANTONY
BARONY
BETONY
BLENNY
BOTANY
BRAINY
BRANNY
BRAWNY
BRYONY
COLONY
CRANNY
FELONY
GRAINY
GRANNY
HOMINY
JOHNNY
KORUNY
LITANY
MUTINY
ROMANY
ROSINY
SATINY
SAXONY
SHEENY
SHINNY
SIMONY
SKINNY
SPINNY
SPOONY
TETANY
THORNY
WHINNY

N•Z•••
NAZIFY
NAZISM
NOZZLE
NUZZLE

N••Z••
NOZZLE
NUZZLE

N••••Z
NIMITZ

•NZ•••
ENZYME

•N••Z•
SNEEZE
SNEEZY
SNOOZE

••NZ••
BANZAI
BENZOL
BENZYL
BONZER
BONZES
DANZIG
PANZER
WINZES

••N•Z•
IONIZE

•••NZ•
ALONZO
BRONZE
BRONZY
FRENZY
FRUNZE
STANZA

•••N•Z
BLINTZ
CHINTZ

••••NZ
LORENZ

OA••••
OAFISH
OAKLEY
OARING

O•A•••
OCASEY
OKAPIS
OKAYED
OMASUM
ONAGER
ONAGRI
OPAQUE
ORACHS
ORACLE
ORALLY
ORANGE
ORANGS
ORATED
ORATES
ORATOR
OVALLY
OXALIC
OXALIS

O••A••
OBLAST
OBLATE
OBTAIN
OCEANS
OCTADS
OCTANE
OCTANT
OCTAVE
OCTAVO
OHMAGE
OLEATE
ONWARD
OPIATE
ORDAIN
OREADS
ORGANA
ORGANO
ORGANS
ORGASM
ORNATE
OSCANS
OSCARS
OSWALD
OTTAVA
OTTAWA
OXTAIL

O•••A•
OCREAE
OCULAR
OGDOAD
OHIOAN
OILCAN
OMEGAS
ONEWAY
OOMIAK
OPERAS
ORDEAL
ORGEAT
ORIGAN
ORPHAN
OSSIAN
OSTEAL
OUTLAW
OUTLAY
OUTMAN
OUTRAN
OUTSAT
OVISAC
OVULAR

O••••A
ODESSA
ODYNIA
OJIBWA
OLIVIA
OMENTA
ONEIDA
OPTIMA
ORGANA
OTTAVA
OTTAWA

•OA•••
BOARDS
BOASTS
BOATED
COALED
COALER
COARSE
COASTS
COATED
COATIS
COAXAL
COAXED
COAXER
COAXES
DOABLE
DOALLS
FOALED
FOAMED
GOADED
GOALIE
GOATEE
HOARDS
HOARSE
HOAXED
HOAXER
HOAXES
JOANNA
JOANNE
KOALAS
LOADED
LOADER
LOAFED
LOAFER
LOAMED

LOANED
LOATHE
LOAVES
MOANED
MOATED
POACHY
ROALDS
ROAMED
ROAMER
ROARED
ROARER
ROASTS
SOAKED
SOAKER
SOAPED
SOARED
SOARER
TOASTS
WOADED
WOALDS

•O•A••

BOGANS
BONACI
BORAGE
BORANE
BORATE
BOTANY
BOYARD
BOYARS
COBALT
COCAIN
COMATE
COPALM
CORALS
COWAGE
COWARD
DOGAPE
DOMAIN
DONALD
DONATE
DORADO
DOSAGE
DOTAGE
FORAGE
FORAYS
GOCART
GOKART
GONADS
GORALS
GOTAMA
HOBART
HOGANS
HOLARD
HOMAGE
HORACE
HORARY
HOWARD
IODATE
JOHANN
JONAHS
JORAMS
KODAKS
LOBATE
LOCALE
LOCALS
LOCATE
LORAIN
LOTAHS
LOVAGE
MOHAIR
MOHAVE
MOHAWK
MOJAVE
MOLARS
MONADS
MORALE
MORALS
MORASS
MORAYS
MOSAIC
MOZART
NOBALL
NOMADS
NONAGE
NOPALS
NOTARY
NOWAYS
POLAND
POMACE
POMADE
POSADA
POTAGE
POTASH
POTATO
ROBALO
ROBAND
ROLAND
ROMAIC
ROMANS
ROMANY
RONALD
ROSARY
ROTARY
ROTATE
ROWANS
ROXANA
ROXANE
ROYALS
SOCAGE
SOLACE
SOLAND
SOLANO
SOLANS
SOMATA
SOMATO
SONANT
SONARS
SONATA
SOUARI
SOWARS
TOBAGO
TOGAED
TOMANS
TOMATO
TORAHS
TOTALS
TOWAGE
TOWARD
VOCALS
VOLANT
VOTARY
VOYAGE
ZONARY
ZONATE
ZOUAVE

•O••A•

AORTAE
AORTAL
AORTAS
AOUDAD
BOBCAT
BOMBAY
BONSAI
BOREAL
BOREAS
BOWMAN
BOXCAR
COAXAL
COBIAS
COBRAS
COCCAL
COCOAS
COEVAL
COGNAC
COGWAY
COLLAR
COLZAS
COMBAT
COMMAS
CONFAB
CONGAS
CONRAD
COPRAH
CORBAN
CORDAY
CORRAL
CORSAC
COSTAE
COSTAL
COSTAR
COTEAU
COTTAE
COTTAR
COTTAS
COUGAR
COWMAN
DOBLAS
DOBRAS
DOGEAR
DOGMAS
DOLLAR
DOLMAN
DONNAS
DOODAD
DORIAN
DORSAD
DORSAL
DOSSAL
EOLIAN
EONIAN
FOEMAN
FOETAL
FOLIAR
FONTAL
FORBAD
FORMAL
FORMAT
FORNAX
FOSSAE
FOVEAE
FOVEAL
GOORAL
GOTHAM
HOOKAH
HOORAY
HOWDAH
IONIAN
JORDAN
JOSIAH
JOSIAS
JOVIAL
JOVIAN
KOALAS
KODIAK
KONRAD
KOREAN
LOGJAM
LONGAN
LOOFAH
LOQUAT
MOBCAP
MOIRAS
MOLLAH
MONDAY
MOOLAH
MOREAU
MORGAN
MORTAL
MORTAR
NORIAS
NORMAL
NORMAN
NORMAS
NORWAY
NOUGAT
NOUNAL
OOMIAK
POLEAX
POLKAS
POPLAR
PORTAL
POSTAL
RODMAN
SOCIAL
SOCMAN
SOFTAS
SONIAS
SONYAS
TOBIAH
TOBIAS
TOECAP
TOMBAC
TOMCAT
VODKAS
VOLVAS
WOMBAT
ZODIAC
ZOONAL

•O•••A

BODEGA
BOGOTA
BORGIA
CODEIA
CONCHA
CONTRA
COPPRA
COPULA
CORNEA
CORNUA
CORONA
CORYZA
COWPEA
DODECA
GODIVA
GOTAMA
HOOPLA
JOANNA
JOSHUA
KORUNA
LOCHIA
LOGGIA
LOLITA
LORICA
LOUISA
MONICA
MORULA
NOMURA
NOVENA
POMONA
PORTIA
POSADA
ROBBIA
ROMOLA
ROSTRA
ROWENA
ROXANA
SOMATA
SONATA
SOPHIA
TOPEKA
VOMICA
WOMERA
YORUBA
ZONULA
ZOYSIA

••OA••

ABOARD
BLOATS
BROACH
BROADS
CLOACA
CLOAKS
CROAKS
CROAKY
CROATS
EBOATS
FLOATS
FLOATY
GLOATS
GROANS
GROATS
SHOALS
SHOALY
SHOATS
STOATS
UBOATS

••O•A•

ABOMAS
ABORAL
ADONAI
AGORAE
AGORAS
AJOWAN
AMORAL
ANORAK
APODAL
AROMAS
ATONAL
AVOWAL
BAOBAB
BROGAN
BROMAL
CHORAL
DEODAR
DOODAD
DVORAK
FLORAE
FLORAL
FLORAS
GLOBAL
GOORAL
HOOKAH
HOORAY
ISOBAR
LEONAS
LOOFAH
MOOLAH
QUOTAS
RHODAS
SHOFAR
SHORAN
SIOUAN
SLOGAN
SLOVAK
SNOCAT
STOMAT
STORAX
THOMAS
THORAC
THORAX
TROCAR
TROJAN
TROPAL
TWOWAY
VIOLAS
YEOMAN
ZOONAL

••O••A
ABOLLA
AEOLIA
AMOEBA
ANOXIA
CHOLLA
CHOREA
CLOACA
GLORIA
HOOPLA
MYOPIA
PEORIA
PHOBIA
PHONIA
SCORIA
SCOTIA
SFORZA
THORIA
TROIKA
UTOPIA

•••OA•
ABROAD
AFLOAT
BEMOAN
BEZOAR
BYROAD
COCOAS
INROAD
MINOAN
OGDOAD
OHIOAN
RELOAD
SAMOAN
THROAT
UNLOAD
UPROAR

•••O•A
AFTOSA
ANCONA
ANGOLA
ANGORA
APNOEA
AREOLA
ARROBA
AURORA
BOGOTA
CAEOMA
CHROMA
CITOLA
CORONA
CUPOLA
DAGOBA
DAKOTA
EIDOLA
EUBOEA
EUDORA
EUROPA
FEDORA
FEMORA
GLIOMA
LADOGA
LIPOMA
MASORA
MIMOSA
MUCOSA
MYXOMA
NAGOYA
PAGODA
PAYOLA
PELOTA
POMONA
RAMONA
REDOWA
REMORA
ROMOLA
SENORA
STROMA
TACOMA
VERONA
ZYGOMA

••••OA
BALBOA
EPIZOA
JERBOA
LISBOA

OB••••
OBELUS
OBERON
OBEYED
OBEYER
OBIISM
OBJECT
OBLAST
OBLATE
OBLIGE
OBLONG
OBOIST
OBOLUS
OBSESS
OBTAIN
OBTECT
OBTEST
OBTUND
OBTUSE
OBVERT

O•B•••
ORBING
ORBITS
OSBERT
OSBORN
OXBOWS

O••B••
OJIBWA
ORIBIS
OUTBID
OVIBOS

•OB•••
BOBBED
BOBBER
BOBBIE
BOBBIN
BOBBLE
BOBBYS
BOBCAT
COBALT
COBBLE
COBIAS
COBLES
COBNUT
COBRAS
COBWEB
DOBBER
DOBBIN
DOBIES
DOBLAS
DOBLON
DOBRAS
DOBSON
FOBBED
GOBBET
GOBBLE
GOBIES
GOBLET
GOBLIN
HOBART
HOBBES
HOBBLE
HOBNOB
HOBOES
JOBBED
JOBBER
KOBOLD
LOBATE
LOBBED
LOBULE
MOBBED
MOBBER
MOBCAP
MOBILE
MOBIUS
NOBALL
NOBBLE
ROBALO
ROBAND
ROBBED
ROBBER
ROBBIA
ROBBIE
ROBERT
ROBING
ROBINS
ROBLES
ROBOTS
ROBSON
ROBUST
SOBBED
SOBERS
TOBAGO
TOBIAH
TOBIAS
TOBIES
WOBBLE
WOBBLY

•O•B••
BOBBED
BOBBER
BOBBIE
BOBBIN
BOBBLE
BOBBYS
BOMBAY
BOMBED
BOMBER
BOMBES
BONBON
BOOBOO
COBBLE
COMBAT
COMBED
COMBER
COMBOS
CORBAN
CORBEL
COWBOY
DOABLE
DOBBER
DOBBIN
DORBUG
DOUBLE
DOUBLY
DOUBTS
FOBBED
FOGBOW
FOIBLE
FORBAD
FORBID
GOBBET
GOBBLE
GOOBER
HOBBES
HOBBLE
HOMBRE
HOTBED
HOTBOX
JOBBED
JOBBER
LOBBED
LOWBOY
MOBBED
MOBBER
MORBID
NOBBLE
POTBOY
ROBBED
ROBBER
ROBBIA
ROBBIE
ROUBLE
SOBBED
SOMBER
TOMBAC
TOMBED
TOMBOY
WOBBLE
WOBBLY
WOMBAT
WOMBED
ZOMBIE
ZOMBIS

•O••B•
COOMBS
GOODBY
YORUBA

•O•••B
COBWEB
CONFAB
CORYMB
HOBNOB

••OB••
ADOBES
BAOBAB
BOOBOO
DIOBOL
GLOBAL
GLOBED
GLOBES
GLOBIN
GOOBER
ISOBAR
ISOBEL
PHOBIA
PROBED
PROBER
PROBES
TWOBIT

••O•B•
ABOMBS
AMOEBA
BLOWBY
COOMBS
GOODBY
HBOMBS
PHOEBE
RHOMBI

••O••B
BAOBAB

•••OB•
AEROBE
ARROBA
CABOBS
CAROBS
DAGOBA
DEMOBS
ENROBE
JACOBS
KABOBS
NABOBS
THROBS

•••O•B
ABSORB
ADSORB
APLOMB
ENTOMB
ENWOMB
INTOMB
RESORB

••••OB
HOBNOB

OC••••
OCASEY
OCCULT
OCCUPY
OCCURS
OCEANS
OCELOT
OCHERS
OCHERY
OCLOCK
OCREAE
OCTADS
OCTANE
OCTANT
OCTAVE
OCTAVO
OCTETS
OCTOPI
OCTROI
OCULAR

O•C•••
OCCULT
OCCUPY
OCCURS
OOCYTE
ORCEIN
ORCHID
ORCHIL
ORCHIO
ORCHIS
OSCANS
OSCARS
OSCINE
OSCULE

O••C••
OILCAN
ORACHS
ORACLE
OUNCES
OUTCRY

O•••C•
OBJECT
OBTECT
OCLOCK
OFFICE
OPTICS
ORRICE

O••••C
ORPHIC
OVISAC
OXALIC
OZONIC

•OC•••

BOCCIE
COCAIN
COCCAL
COCCID
COCCUS
COCCYX
COCHIN
COCKED
COCKER
COCKLE
COCKUP
COCOAS
COCOON
DOCENT
DOCILE
DOCKED
DOCKER
DOCKET
DOCTOR
EOCENE
FOCSLE
GOCART
HOCKED
HOCKEY
JOCKEY
JOCKOS
JOCOSE
JOCUND
LOCALE
LOCALS
LOCATE
LOCHIA
LOCKED
LOCKER
LOCKET
LOCKUP
LOCOED
LOCUST
MOCKED
MOCKER
MOCKUP
NOCENT
NOCKED
OOCYTE
POCKET
ROCHET
ROCKED
ROCKER
ROCKET
ROCKNE
ROCOCO
SOCAGE
SOCCER
SOCIAL
SOCKED
SOCKET
SOCLES
SOCMAN
SOCMEN
SOCRED
TOCSIN
VOCALS

•O•C••

BOBCAT
BOCCIE
BOTCHY
BOUCLE
BOXCAR
COCCAL
COCCID
COCCUS
COCCYX
CONCHA
CONCHS
CONCHY
CONCUR
DOUCHE
FORCED
FORCER
FORCES
HOICKS
IOLCUS
JOYCES
MOBCAP
MOSCOW
NONCOM
POACHY
PONCHO
POUCHY
ROSCOE
ROTCHE
ROUCHE
SOCCER
TOECAP
TOMCAT
TOMCOD
TOUCHE
TOUCHY
VOICED
VOICES
YOICKS

•O••C•

BODICE
BONACI
BORSCH
BOUNCE
BOUNCY
COERCE
COMICS
CONICS
DODECA
HOOTCH
HORACE
JOUNCE
KOPECK
LORICA
MOHOCK
MOLOCH
MONICA
NOTICE
NOVICE
POLICE
POLICY
POMACE
POUNCE
ROCOCO
SOLACE
SOURCE
TONICS
TOPICS
VOMICA

•O•••C

AORTIC
COGNAC
COPTIC
CORSAC
COSMIC
EOZOIC
FORMIC
GOTHIC
HOLMIC
MOSAIC
NOETIC
NORDIC
NOSTOC
POETIC
PONTIC
ROMAIC
SOTHIC
TOLTEC
TOMBAC
ZODIAC

••OC••

AVOCET
BLOCKS
BLOCKY
CHOCKS
CLOCHE
CLOCKS
CROCKS
CROCUS
EPOCHS
FLOCKS
FLOCKY
FROCKS
GROCER
KNOCKS
PHOCIS
PROCNE
PROCTO
SHOCKS
SMOCKS
SNOCAT
STOCKS
STOCKY
TROCAR
TROCHE

••O•C•

AVOUCH
BLOTCH
BROACH
BRONCO
BRONCS
BROOCH
CHOICE
CLOACA
CROTCH
CROUCH
GROUCH
HOOTCH
SCONCE
SCORCH
SCOTCH
SLOUCH
SMOOCH
STOICS

••O••C

ADONIC
AEOLIC
AGONIC
ANODIC
ANOMIC
ANOXIC
ATOMIC
ATONIC
AZONIC
AZOTIC
BIOTIC
BROMIC
CHORIC
CLONIC
EROTIC
EXOTIC
FROLIC
GEODIC
GNOMIC
ICONIC
IRONIC
MIOTIC
MYOPIC
OZONIC
PHONIC
PHOTIC
RHODIC
SUOMIC
THORAC
THORIC
TROPIC

•••OC•

BROOCH
DECOCT
IDIOCY
MOHOCK
MOLOCH
OCLOCK
ROCOCO
SMOOCH
UNCOCK
UNLOCK
VELOCE

•••O•C

ECHOIC
EOZOIC
HEROIC

••••OC

BELLOC
MANIOC
NOSTOC

OD••••

ODDEST
ODDITY
ODESSA
ODIOUS
ODONTO
ODYNIA

O•D•••

ODDEST
ODDITY
OGDOAD
OLDEST
OLDISH
OODLES
ORDAIN
ORDEAL
ORDERS
ORDURE

O••D••

OUTDID
OXIDES

O•••D•

OCTADS
ONEIDA
OREADS
OREIDE
OROIDE
OVERDO

O••••D

OBEYED
OBTUND
OFFEND
OGDOAD
OKAYED
ONWARD
OPENED
OPINED
ORATED
ORCHID
ORMUZD
OSMOND
OSMUND
OSWALD
OUSTED
OUTBID
OUTDID
OXEYED
OXFORD

•OD•••

BODEGA
BODICE
BODIED
BODIES
BODILY
BODING
BODKIN
CODDER
CODDLE
CODEIA
CODEIN
CODGER
CODIFY
CODING
DODDER
DODECA
DODGED
DODGER
DODGES
DODOES
FODDER
GODIVA
GODSON
GODWIN
GODWIT
HODDEN
IODATE
IODIDE
IODINE
IODISM
IODIZE
IODOUS
KODAKS
KODIAK
LODGED
LODGER
LODGES
MODELS
MODERN
MODEST
MODIFY
MODISH
MODULE
NODDED
NODDER
NODDLE
NODOSE
NODULE
OODLES
PODDED
PODIUM
PODOUS
PODSOL
PODUNK
PODZOL
RODDYS
RODENT
RODEOS
RODMAN
RODMEN
RODNEY
SODDED
SODDEN
SODIUM
SODOMY
TODDLE
TODIES
VODKAS
YODELS
ZODIAC

•O•D••
AOUDAD
BOLDER
BOLDLY
BONDED
BONDER
BOODLE
BORDEL
BORDER
CODDER
CODDLE
COLDER
COLDLY
CONDOM
CONDOR
CORDAY
CORDED
CORDER
CORDON
DODDER
DOODAD
DOODLE
FODDER
FOGDOG
FOLDED
FOLDER
FONDER
FONDLE
FONDLY
FONDUE
FORDED
GOADED
GOLDEN
GOODBY
GOODLY
GORDON
HODDEN
HOIDEN
HOLDER
HOLDUP
HOODED
HOODOO
HORDED
HORDES
HOWDAH
HOYDEN
JORDAN
KOODOO
LOADED
LOADER
LONDON
LORDED
LORDLY
LOUDEN
LOUDER
LOUDLY
MOLDED
MOLDER
MONDAY
NODDED
NODDER
NODDLE
NOODLE
NORDIC
PODDED
POLDER
PONDER
POODLE
POWDER
RODDYS
RONDEL
RONDOS
SODDED
SODDEN
SOLDER
SONDER
SORDID
TODDLE
VOIDED
VOODOO
WOADED
WONDER
WOODED
WOODEN
WOODSY
WORDED
YONDER

•O••D•
BOARDS
BOLIDE
BORIDE
BOUNDS
COMEDO
COMEDY
CORODY
DORADO
FOUNDS
GONADS
GOURDE
GOURDS
HOARDS
HOUNDS
IODIDE
MONADS
MONODY
MOULDS
MOULDY
NOMADS
POINDS
POMADE
POSADA
POUNDS
ROALDS
ROUNDS
SOLIDI
SOLIDS
SOUNDS
TOLEDO
WOALDS
WORLDS
WOUNDS
ZOOIDS
ZOUNDS

•O•••D
AOUDAD
BOATED
BOBBED
BODIED
BOGGED
BOILED
BOLLED
BOLTED
BOMBED
BONDED
BONGED
BOOKED
BOOMED
BOOTED
BOOZED
BOPPED
BOSSED
BOUSED
BOWLED
BOWSED
BOYARD
COALED
COATED
COAXED
COCCID
COCKED
COGGED
COIFED
COILED
COINED
COMBED
CONKED
CONNED
CONOID
CONRAD
COOEED
COOKED
COOLED
COOPED
COPIED
COPPED
CORDED
CORKED
CORNED
COSHED
COSTED
COWARD
COWLED
DOCKED
DODGED
DOFFED
DOGGED
DOLLED
DONALD
DONNED
DOODAD
DOOMED
DORSAD
DOTTED
DOUSED
DOWNED
DOWSED
FOALED
FOAMED
FOBBED
FOETID
FOGGED
FOILED
FOLDED
FOOLED
FOOTED
FORBAD
FORBID
FORCED
FORDED
FORGED
FORKED
FORMED
FOULED
FOWLED
GOADED
GOLFED
GOOFED
GOOSED
GORGED
GOUGED
GOWNED
HOAXED
HOCKED
HOGGED
HOLARD
HONIED
HONKED
HOODED
HOOFED
HOOKED
HOOPED
HOOTED
HOPPED
HORDED
HORNED
HORRID
HORSED
HOSTED
HOTBED
HOUSED
HOWARD
HOWLED
JOBBED
JOCUND
JOGGED
JOINED
JOLTED
JOSHED
JOTTED
KOBOLD
KONRAD
LOADED
LOAFED
LOAMED
LOANED
LOBBED
LOCKED
LOCOED
LODGED
LOFTED
LOGGED
LOLLED
LOMOND
LONGED
LOOKED
LOOMED
LOOPED
LOOSED
LOOTED
LOPPED
LORDED
LOURED
LOUSED
MOANED
MOATED
MOBBED
MOCKED
MOILED
MOLDED
MOLTED
MONIED
MOONED
MOORED
MOOTED
MOPPED
MORBID
MOUSED
NOCKED
NODDED
NOISED
NOOSED
PODDED
POISED
POLAND
POLLED
PONIED
POOLED
POOPED
POPPED
POSTED
POTTED
POURED
POUTED
ROAMED
ROARED
ROBAND
ROBBED
ROCKED
ROGUED
ROILED
ROLAND
ROLLED
ROMPED
RONALD
ROOFED
ROOKED
ROOMED
ROOTED
ROTTED
ROTUND
ROUGED
ROUSED
ROUTED
SOAKED
SOAPED
SOARED
SOBBED
SOCKED
SOCRED
SODDED
SOILED
SOLAND
SOLOED
SOLVED
SOOTED
SOPPED
SORDID
SORTED
SOULED
SOURED
SOUSED
TOGAED
TOGGED
TOILED
TOLLED
TOMBED
TOMCOD
TONGED
TOOLED
TOOTED
TOPPED
TOROID
TORPID
TORRID
TOSSED
TOTTED
TOURED
TOUTED
TOWARD
VOICED
VOIDED
WOADED
WOLFED
WOMBED
WONTED
WOODED
WORDED
WORKED
WORMED
YOWLED
ZOOMED

••OD••
ABODES
ANODES
ANODIC
APODAL
BOODLE
CLODDY
DEODAR
DIODES
DOODAD
DOODLE
DUODEN
EPODES
ERODED
ERODES
EXODUS
FEODOR
GEODES
GEODIC
GOODBY

6

GOODLY
HOODED
HOODOO
KOODOO
NOODLE
POODLE
RHODAS
RHODIC
SHODDY
STODGE
STODGY
VOODOO
WOODED
WOODEN
WOODSY

••O•D•
AROIDS
AVOIDS
BLONDE
BLONDS
BLOODS
BLOODY
BROADS
BROODS
BROODY
CHONDR
CHORDS
CLODDY
CLOUDS
CLOUDY
CROWDS
FIORDS
FJORDS
FLOODS
FLOYDS
FRONDS
HYOIDS
ISOLDE
LLOYDS
OROIDE
SCOLDS
SHODDY
SNOODS
SWORDS
ZOOIDS

••O••D
ABOARD
ABOUND
ADORED
AROUND
ATONED
AVOWED
BOOKED
BOOMED
BOOTED
BOOZED
BUOYED
CHOKED
CLOSED
CLOYED
COOEED
COOKED
COOLED
COOPED
CROWED
DOODAD
DOOMED
DRONED
DROVED
ELOPED
EMOTED
ERODED
EVOKED
FLORID
FLOWED
FOOLED
FOOTED
GLOBED
GLOVED
GLOWED
GLOZED
GOOFED
GOOSED
GROPED
GROUND
HOODED
HOOFED
HOOKED
HOOPED
HOOTED
IRONED
ISOPOD
LOOKED
LOOMED
LOOPED
LOOSED
LOOTED
MEOWED
MOONED
MOORED
MOOTED
NOOSED
PHONED
PLOWED
POOLED
POOPED
PROBED
PROSED
PROVED
QUOTED
RIOTED
ROOFED
ROOKED
ROOMED
ROOTED
SCORED
SHOOED
SHORED
SHOULD
SHOVED
SHOWED
SLOPED
SLOWED
SMOKED
SNORED
SNOWED
SOOTED
SPOKED
SPORED
STOKED
STOLED
STOLID
STONED
STOPED
STORED
STOWED
TOOLED
TOOTED
UROPOD
WHORED
WOODED
ZOOMED

•••OD•
ACNODE
BIPODS
BLOODS
BLOODY
BROODS
BROODY
CORODY
DECODE
DEMODE
DIPODY
EMBODY
ENCODE
EPHODS
FLOODS
IMBODY
MELODY
MONODY
PAGODA
PARODY
SCRODS
SNOODS
STRODE
SYNODS
TRIODE

•••O•D
ABROAD
ACCORD
AFFORD
ALGOID
ALMOND
ARNOLD
AUTOED
BEHOLD
BEYOND
BIFOLD
BYROAD
BYWORD
CANOED
CEBOID
CONOID
CUBOID
CYMOID
DEVOID
ECHOED
EDMOND
ENFOLD
FUCOID
GADOID
GANOID
HALOID
HAROLD
HEMOID
INFOLD
INROAD
KAYOED
KELOID
KOBOLD
LIPOID
LOCOED
LOMOND
MILORD
MUCOID
NEVOID
OGDOAD
OSMOND
OXFORD
RECORD
RELOAD
RESOLD
RETOLD
REWORD
SECOND
SHOOED
SHROUD
SILOED
SOLOED
STROUD
TOROID
UNFOLD
UNLOAD
UNSOLD
UNTOLD
UPHOLD
VETOED
XYLOID
ZEROED

••••OD
HESIOD
ISOPOD
METHOD
NIMROD
PEQUOD
PERIOD
RAMROD
TOMCOD
TRIPOD
UNTROD
UROPOD

OE••••
OEUVRE

O•E•••
OBELUS
OBERON
OBEYED
OBEYER
OCEANS
OCELOT
ODESSA
OHENRY
OLEATE
OLEFIN
OMEGAS
OMELET
OMENTA
ONEIDA
ONEILL
ONEIRO
ONEWAY
OPENED
OPENER
OPENLY
OPERAS
OREADS
OREGON
OREIDE
OVERDO
OVERLY
OXEYED
OXEYES

O••E••
OBJECT
OBSESS
OBTECT
OBTEST
OBVERT
OCHERS
OCHERY
OCREAE
OCTETS
ODDEST
OFFEND
OFFERS
OGLERS
OGRESS
OILERS
OLDEST
ONSETS
ORCEIN
ORDEAL
ORDERS
ORGEAT
ORIELS
ORIENT
ORMERS
ORNERY
ORRERY
ORWELL
OSBERT
OSIERS
OSSEIN
OSTEAL
OTHERS
OTTERS
OUSELS
OUTERS
OUZELS
OWLETS
OWNERS

O•••E•
OAKLEY
OBEYED
OBEYER
OCASEY
OFFSET
OGIVES
OILIER
OKAYED
OLIVER
OLIVES
OLLIES
OMELET
ONAGER
ONUSES
OODLES
OOZIER
OPENED
OPENER
OPINED
OPINES
ORATED
ORATES
ORGIES
ORIGEN
ORYXES
OSPREY
OUNCES
OUSTED
OUSTER
OUTLET
OUTSET
OVULES
OXEYED
OXEYES
OXIDES
OXYGEN
OYSTER

O••••E
OBLATE
OBLIGE
OBTUSE
OCREAE
OCTANE
OCTAVE
OEUVRE
OFFICE
OHMAGE
OLEATE
OOCYTE
OOLITE
OPAQUE
OPHITE
OPIATE
OPPOSE
OPTIME
ORACLE
ORANGE
ORDURE
OREIDE
ORIOLE
ORNATE
OROIDE

6

ORPINE
ORRICE
OSCINE
OSCULE
OSMOSE
OTIOSE

•OE•••
COELOM
COEMPT
COERCE
COEVAL
DOESNT
FOEHNS
FOEMAN
FOEMEN
FOETAL
FOETID
FOETOR
FOETUS
GOETHE
HOEING
NOESIS
NOETIC
POETIC
POETRY
SOEVER
TOECAP
TOEING
WOEFUL

•O•E••
BODEGA
BOGEYS
BOLERO
BOLEYN
BONERS
BOREAL
BOREAS
BORERS
BOWELS
BOWERS
BOWERY
BOXERS
CODEIA
CODEIN
COGENT
COHERE
COLEUS
COMEDO
COMEDY
COMELY
COMEON
COMERS
COMETS
CONEYS
COOEED
COOEES
COOERS
COOEYS
CORERS
COTEAU
COVERS
COVERT
COVETS
COVEYS
COWERS
COZENS
DOCENT
DODECA
DOGEAR
DONEES
DONETS
DOREEN
DOSERS
DOTERS
DOWELS
DOWERS
DOWERY
DOYENS
DOZENS
EOCENE
EOGENE
FOMENT
FOREGO
FOREST
FOVEAE
FOVEAL
FOYERS
GONERS
GOVERN
HOMELY
HOMERS
HONEST
HONEYS
HOTELS
HOVELS
HOVERS
JOKERS
JOSEPH
KOPECK
KOPEKS
KOREAN
LOMENT
LONELY
LONERS
LOPERS
LOREEN
LORENE
LORENZ
LOSERS
LOVEIN
LOVELL
LOVELY
LOVERS
LOWELL
LOWERS
LOWERY
LOWEST
MODELS
MODERN
MODEST
MOIETY
MOLEST
MOMENT
MONEYS
MOPERS
MOREAU
MOREEN
MORELS
MOSEYS
MOTELS
MOVERS
MOWERS
NOCENT
NONEGO
NOREEN
NOTERS
NOVELS
NOVENA
POKERS
POLEAX
POMELO
PONENT
POPERY
POSERS
POSEUR
POTEEN
POTENT
POWELL
POWERS
ROBERT
RODENT
RODEOS
ROGERS
ROVERS
ROWELS
ROWENA
ROWERS
SOBERS
SOLELY
SOLEMN
SOLENT
SORELS
SORELY
SOREST
SOWERS
TOKENS
TOLEDO
TONERS
TOPEKA
TOPERS
TORERO
TOTEMS
TOTERS
TOWELS
TOWERS
TOWERY
TOYERS
VOLERY
VOMERS
VOTERS
VOWELS
VOWERS
VOYEUR
WOMERA
WOOERS
YODELS
YOGEES
YOKELS

•O••E•
BOATED
BOBBED
BOBBER
BODIED
BODIES
BOGGED
BOGIES
BOGLES
BOILED
BOILER
BOLDER
BOLLED
BOLTED
BOLTER
BOMBED
BOMBER
BOMBES
BONDED
BONDER
BONGED
BONIER
BONNET
BONZER
BONZES
BOOKED
BOOMED
BOOTED
BOOTEE
BOOZED
BOOZER
BOOZES
BOPPED
BORDEL
BORDER
BORNEO
BOSHES
BOSKET
BOSSED
BOSSES
BOTHER
BOULES
BOUSED
BOUSES
BOWLED
BOWLEG
BOWLER
BOWMEN
BOWSED
BOWSES
BOWYER
COALED
COALER
COATED
COAXED
COAXER
COAXES
COBLES
COBWEB
COCKED
COCKER
CODDER
CODGER
COFFEE
COFFER
COGGED
COIFED
COILED
COILER
COINED
COINER
COLDER
COLIES
COLLET
COLTER
COMBED
COMBER
COMPEL
CONFER
CONGER
CONGES
CONIES
CONKED
CONNED
CONNER
CONTES
CONVEX
CONVEY
COOEED
COOEES
COOKED
COOKER
COOKEY
COOLED
COOLER
COOPED
COOPER
COPIED
COPIER
COPIES
COPLEY
COPPED
COPPER
COPSES
COQUET
CORBEL
CORDED
CORDER
CORKED
CORKER
CORNEA
CORNED
CORNEL
CORNER
CORNET
CORSES
CORSET
CORTES
CORTEX
CORTEZ
CORVEE
CORVES
COSHED
COSHER
COSHES
COSSES
COSSET
COSTED
COTTER
COULEE
COUPES
COWLED
COWMEN
COWPEA
COWPER
COZIER
COZIES
DOBBER
DOBIES
DOCKED
DOCKER
DOCKET
DODDER
DODGED
DODGER
DODGES
DODOES
DOFFED
DOFFER
DOGGED
DOGGER
DOGIES
DOLLED
DOLMEN
DONEES
DONKEY
DONNED
DOOLEE
DOOMED
DOPIER
DOREEN
DORIES
DORMER
DOSSEL
DOSSER
DOTIER
DOTTED
DOTTEL
DOTTER
DOUSED
DOUSES
DOWNED
DOWSED
DOWSER
DOWSES
DOXIES
DOYLEY
DOZIER
FOALED
FOAMED
FOBBED
FODDER
FOEMEN
FOGGED
FOGIES
FOILED
FOLDED
FOLDER
FONDER
FOOLED
FOOTED
FOOTER

6

FORCED
FORCER
FORCES
FORDED
FORGED
FORGER
FORGES
FORGET
FORKED
FORMED
FORMER
FORTES
FOSSES
FOSTER
FOULED
FOULER
FOWLED
FOWLER
FOXIER
GOADED
GOATEE
GOBBET
GOBIES
GOBLET
GOFFER
GOGLET
GOITER
GOLDEN
GOLFED
GOLFER
GOOBER
GOOFED
GOOIER
GOONEY
GOOSED
GOOSES
GOOSEY
GOPHER
GORGED
GORGER
GORGES
GORGET
GORHEN
GORIER
GORSES
GOSHEN
GOSPEL
GOTTEN
GOUGED
GOUGER
GOUGES
GOWNED
HOAXED
HOAXER
HOAXES
HOBBES
HOBOES
HOCKED
HOCKEY
HODDEN
HOGGED
HOIDEN
HOLDER
HOLIER

HOLIES
HOLLER
HOLMES
HOMIER
HONIED
HONKED
HONKER
HOODED
HOOFED
HOOFER
HOOKED
HOOKER
HOOPED
HOOPER
HOOTED
HOOVER
HOOVES
HOPPED
HOPPER
HORDED
HORDES
HORNED
HORNET
HORSED
HORSES
HORSEY
HOSIER
HOSTED
HOSTEL
HOTBED
HOTTER
HOUSED
HOUSES
HOWLED
HOWLER
HOYDEN
JOBBED
JOBBER
JOCKEY
JOGGED
JOGGER
JOINED
JOINER
JOLIET
JOLTED
JOLTER
JORGES
JOSHED
JOSHER
JOSHES
JOSIES
JOSSES
JOTTED
JOULES
JOYCES
KOINES
KOPJES
KOSHER
LOADED
LOADER
LOAFED
LOAFER
LOAMED
LOANED

LOAVES
LOBBED
LOCKED
LOCKER
LOCKET
LOCOED
LODGED
LODGER
LODGES
LOFTED
LOFTER
LOGGED
LOGGER
LOGIER
LOITER
LOLLED
LOLLER
LONGED
LONGER
LOOKED
LOOKER
LOOMED
LOOPED
LOOPER
LOOSED
LOOSEN
LOOSER
LOOSES
LOOTED
LOOTER
LOPPED
LORDED
LOREEN
LORIES
LOSSES
LOUDEN
LOUDER
LOUPES
LOURED
LOUSED
LOUSES
LOUVER
LOWKEY
MOANED
MOATED
MOBBED
MOBBER
MOCKED
MOCKER
MOILED
MOILER
MOLDED
MOLDER
MOLIES
MOLTED
MOLTEN
MOLTER
MONGER
MONIED
MONIES
MONKEY
MONTES
MOOLEY
MOONED

MOORED
MOOTED
MOOTER
MOPPED
MOPPET
MOREEN
MORGEN
MORLEY
MORSEL
MOSLEM
MOSLEY
MOSSES
MOTHER
MOTLEY
MOUSED
MOUSER
MOUSES
MOVIES
NOCKED
NODDED
NODDER
NOISED
NOISES
NOOSED
NOOSES
NOREEN
NOSIER
OODLES
OOZIER
POCKET
PODDED
POGIES
POISED
POISES
POKIER
POKIES
POLDER
POLLED
POLLEE
POLLEN
POLLER
POLLEX
POMMEL
POMPEY
PONDER
PONGEE
PONIED
PONIES
PONTES
POOLED
POOPED
POORER
POPPED
POPPER
POPPET
PORKER
PORTER
POSIES
POSSES
POSSET
POSTED
POSTER
POTEEN
POTHER

POTTED
POTTER
POURED
POURER
POUTED
POUTER
POWDER
POWTER
ROAMED
ROAMER
ROARED
ROARER
ROBBED
ROBBER
ROBLES
ROCHET
ROCKED
ROCKER
ROCKET
RODMEN
RODNEY
ROGUED
ROGUES
ROILED
ROLLED
ROLLER
ROMMEL
ROMNEY
ROMPED
ROMPER
RONDEL
ROOFED
ROOFER
ROOKED
ROOMED
ROOMER
ROOTED
ROOTER
ROPIER
ROQUET
ROSIER
ROSTER
ROTTED
ROTTEN
ROTTER
ROUGED
ROUGES
ROUSED
ROUSER
ROUSES
ROUTED
ROUTER
ROUTES
SOAKED
SOAKER
SOAPED
SOARED
SOARER
SOBBED
SOCCER
SOCKED
SOCKET
SOCLES
SOCMEN

SOCRED
SODDED
SODDEN
SOEVER
SOFTEN
SOFTER
SOILED
SOIREE
SOLDER
SOLOED
SOLVED
SOLVER
SOLVES
SOMBER
SONDER
SONNET
SOONER
SOOTED
SOPPED
SORREL
SORTED
SOULED
SOURED
SOURER
SOUSED
SOUSES
SOVIET
TOBIES
TODIES
TOFFEE
TOGAED
TOGGED
TOGUES
TOILED
TOILER
TOILES
TOILET
TOLLED
TOLLER
TOLTEC
TOMBED
TONGED
TONIER
TOOLED
TOOLER
TOOTED
TOOTER
TOPPED
TOPPER
TOQUES
TORIES
TOSHES
TOSSED
TOSSES
TOTHER
TOTTED
TOTTER
TOUPEE
TOURED
TOUTED
TOUTER
VOGUES
VOICED
VOICES

VOIDED
VOILES
VOLLEY
VORTEX
WOADED
WOLFED
WOLSEY
WOLVER
WOLVES
WOMBED
WONDER
WONTED
WOODED
WOODEN
WOOFER
WOOLEN
WORDED
WORKED
WORKER
WORMED
WORMER
WORSEN
WORSER
WOWSER
YOGEES
YONDER
YONKER
YOWLED
ZOOMED
ZOSTER

•O•••E

AORTAE
BOBBIE
BOBBLE
BOCCIE
BODICE
BOGGLE
BOLIDE
BONNIE
BOODLE
BOOKIE
BOOTEE
BOOTIE
BORAGE
BORANE
BORATE
BORIDE
BOTTLE
BOUCLE
BOUFFE
BOUGIE
BOUNCE
BOURNE
BOURSE
BOVINE
COARSE
COBBLE
COCKLE
CODDLE
COERCE
COFFEE
COFFLE
COHERE
COHUNE
COLINE
COLLIE
COLURE
COMATE
COMMIE
COMOSE
CONNIE
CONTRE
COOKIE
COOLIE
COOTIE
CORPSE
CORVEE
COSINE
COSTAE
COTTAE
COULEE
COUPLE
COURSE
COWAGE
COWRIE
COYOTE
DOABLE
DOCILE
DOGAPE
DOGGIE
DOLLIE
DONATE
DONNIE
DOODLE
DOOLEE
DOOLIE
DORMIE
DOSAGE
DOTAGE
DOTTLE
DOUBLE
DOUCHE
DOUGIE
EOCENE
EOGENE
FOCSLE
FOIBLE
FONDLE
FONDUE
FOOTLE
FOOZLE
FORAGE
FOSSAE
FOVEAE
GOALIE
GOATEE
GOBBLE
GOETHE
GOGGLE
GOURDE
HOARSE
HOBBLE
HOGTIE
HOMAGE
HOMBRE
HONORE
HOOPOE
HOPPLE
HORACE
HORNIE
HORSTE
IODATE
IODIDE
IODINE
IODIZE
IOLITE
IONIZE
IONONE
JOANNE
JOCOSE
JOGGLE
JONNIE
JOSTLE
JOUNCE
LOATHE
LOBATE
LOBULE
LOCALE
LOCATE
LORENE
LOTTIE
LOUISE
LOUNGE
LOUVRE
LOVAGE
MOBILE
MODULE
MOHAVE
MOHOLE
MOISHE
MOJAVE
MOLINE
MOLLIE
MOLTKE
MONROE
MOPOKE
MORALE
MORGUE
MOROSE
MOSQUE
MOTILE
MOTIVE
MOTTLE
MOUSSE
NOBBLE
NODDLE
NODOSE
NODULE
NONAGE
NOODLE
NOTICE
NOVICE
NOWISE
NOZZLE
OOCYTE
OOLITE
POLICE
POLITE
POLLEE
POMACE
POMADE
PONGEE
POODLE
POPPLE
POTAGE
POTPIE
POTSIE
POTTLE
POUNCE
ROBBIE
ROCKNE
RONNIE
ROOKIE
ROSCOE
ROTATE
ROTCHE
ROUBLE
ROUCHE
ROXANE
SOCAGE
SOIGNE
SOIREE
SOLACE
SOLUTE
SOMITE
SOOTHE
SOPHIE
SORTIE
SOURCE
SOZINE
TODDLE
TOFFEE
TOGGLE
TONGUE
TOOTLE
TOPPLE
TOROSE
TORQUE
TOUCHE
TOUPEE
TOUSLE
TOWAGE
VOLUME
VOLUTE
VOTIVE
VOYAGE
WOBBLE
ZOMBIE
ZONATE
ZONULE
ZOUAVE

••OE••

AMOEBA
COOEED
COOEES
COOERS
COOEYS
PHOEBE
PROEMS
SHOERS
WOOERS

••O•E•

ABODES
ADOBES
ADORED
ADORER
ADORES
AGONES
AMOLES
ANODES
APOGEE
ATONED
ATONER
ATONES
AVOCET
AVOWED
AVOWER
AXONES
AZOLES
AZORES
BIOGEN
BLOKES
BLOWER
BOOKED
BOOMED
BOOTED
BOOTEE
BOOZED
BOOZER
BOOZES
BROKEN
BROKER
BROMES
BUOYED
CHOKED
CHOKER
CHOKES
CHOLER
CHOREA
CHOREO
CHORES
CHOSEN
CLONES
CLOSED
CLOSER
CLOSES
CLOSET
CLOVEN
CLOVER
CLOVES
CLOYED
COOEED
COOEES
COOKED
COOKER
COOKEY
COOLED
COOLER
COOPED
COOPER
CRONES
CRORES
CROWED
CROZER
CROZES
DHOLES
DIODES
DOOLEE
DOOMED
DRONED
DRONES
DROVED
DROVER
DROVES
DUODEN
ECOLES
ELOPED
ELOPER
ELOPES
EMOTED
EMOTES
EPODES
EPOPEE
ERODED
ERODES
EVOKED
EVOKES
EXOGEN
FLORET
FLOWED
FLOWER
FOOLED
FOOTED
FOOTER
FROZEN
GAOLER
GEODES
GLOBED
GLOBES
GLOVED
GLOVER
GLOVES
GLOWED
GLOWER
GLOZED
GLOZES
GNOMES
GOOBER
GOOFED
GOOIER
GOONEY
GOOSED
GOOSES
GOOSEY
GROCER
GROPED
GROPER
GROPES
GROVEL
GROVER
GROVES
GROWER
HOODED
HOOFED
HOOFER
HOOKED
HOOKER
HOOPED
HOOPER
HOOTED
HOOVER

HOOVES
IMOGEN
IRONED
IRONER
ISOBEL
ISOHEL
ISOMER
KNOWER
KRONEN
KRONER
LIONEL
LOOKED
LOOKER
LOOMED
LOOPED
LOOPER
LOOSED
LOOSEN
LOOSER
LOOSES
LOOTED
LOOTER
MEOWED
MOOLEY
MOONED
MOORED
MOOTED
MOOTER
MYOPES
NAOSES
NOOSED
NOOSES
PHONED
PHONES
PHONEY
PHOOEY
PLOVER
PLOWED
PLOWER
POOLED
POOPED
POORER
PROBED
PROBER
PROBES
PROJET
PROLEG
PROPEL
PROPER
PROSED
PROSER
PROSES
PROVED
PROVEN
PROVER
PROVES
QUOTED
QUOTER
QUOTES
REOPEN
RIOTED
RIOTER
ROOFED
ROOFER
ROOKED
ROOMED
ROOMER
ROOTED
ROOTER
SCOLEX
SCONES
SCOPES
SCORED
SCORER
SCORES
SCOTER
SHOOED
SHORED
SHORES
SHOTES
SHOVED
SHOVEL
SHOVER
SHOVES
SHOWED
SHOWER
SLOPED
SLOPER
SLOPES
SLOVEN
SLOWED
SLOWER
SMOKED
SMOKER
SMOKES
SNORED
SNORER
SNORES
SNOWED
SOONER
SOOTED
SPOKED
SPOKEN
SPOKES
SPORED
SPORES
STOGEY
STOKED
STOKER
STOKES
STOLED
STOLEN
STOLES
STONED
STONER
STONES
STOPED
STOPES
STORED
STORES
STOREY
STOVER
STOVES
STOWED
TBONES
THOLES
TOOLED
TOOLER
TOOTED
TOOTER
TROVER
TROVES
TROWEL
TWOFER
VIOLET
WHORED
WHORES
WOODED
WOODEN
WOOFER
WOOLEN
YEOMEN
ZOOMED

••O••E

AGOGUE
AGORAE
ANOMIE
APOGEE
AROUSE
BLONDE
BLOUSE
BOODLE
BOOKIE
BOOTEE
BOOTIE
BROGUE
BRONTE
BRONZE
BROWSE
CHOICE
CHOOSE
CLOCHE
CLOTHE
COOKIE
COOLIE
COOTIE
CROSSE
CROUPE
DOODLE
DOOLEE
DOOLIE
DROWSE
ELOISE
EPOPEE
EVOLVE
FLORAE
FOOTLE
FOOZLE
GEORGE
GROOVE
GROUSE
HOOPOE
ISOLDE
LAOTSE
LEONIE
NOODLE
OROIDE
PEOPLE
PHOEBE
POODLE
PROCNE
ROOKIE
SCONCE
SHOPPE
SNOOZE
SOOTHE
SPONGE
SPOUSE
STODGE
STOOGE
THORPE
TOOTLE
TROCHE
TROUPE
YVONNE

•••OE•

APNOEA
AUTOED
BUBOES
CANOED
CANOES
CHLOES
DADOES
DIDOES
DODOES
ECHOED
ECHOER
ECHOES
EUBOEA
HALOES
HEROES
HOBOES
KAYOED
LOCOED
PEKOES
PHLOEM
PHOOEY
REDOES
SHOOED
SILOED
SOLOED
THROES
UNDOER
UNDOES
VETOED
VETOER
VETOES
WINOES
ZEROED
ZEROES

•••O•E

ACNODE
AEROBE
ALCOVE
ALDOSE
ANCONE
ANYONE
APPOSE
ARIOSE
ASHORE
ASLOPE
ATHOME
BECOME
BEFORE
BEHOVE
BYGONE
CAJOLE
CAPOTE
CAROLE
CHOOSE
CHROME
CLEOME
COMOSE
COYOTE
CREOLE
CYMOSE
DECODE
DEMODE
DEMOTE
DENOTE
DEPOSE
DEVOTE
DIPOLE
ENCODE
ENCORE
ENROBE
EUROPE
EVZONE
EXPOSE
FILOSE
GALORE
GROOVE
GYROSE
HEXONE
HEXOSE
HONORE
IGNORE
IMPOSE
INCOME
INSOLE
INTONE
INVOKE
INWOVE
IONONE
JEROME
JOCOSE
KETONE
KETOSE
LAHORE
LANOSE
LENORE
METOPE
MOHOLE
MOPOKE
MOROSE
MUCOSE
NICOLE
NODOSE
OPPOSE
ORIOLE
OSMOSE
OTIOSE
PAROLE
PEYOTE
PILOSE
PINOLE
PYRONE
PYROPE
RADOME
RAMOSE
REDONE
REMOTE
REMOVE
REPOSE
RESOLE
REVOKE
RIBOSE
RIMOSE
RUGOSE
SALOME
SETOSE
SHROVE
SIMONE
SNOOZE
STOOGE
STRODE
STROKE
STROVE
THRONE
THROVE
TOROSE
TRIODE
TRIOSE
TYRONE
UNDONE
UNYOKE
UPROSE
VADOSE
VELOCE
VENOSE
XYLOSE
ZYGOTE

••••OE

CHEGOE
CHIGOE
CRUSOE
DIPLOE
FAEROE
FELLOE
HOOPOE
MONROE
ROSCOE
TIPTOE
UPHROE

OF••••

OFFEND
OFFERS
OFFICE
OFFING
OFFISH
OFFSET

O•F•••

OAFISH
OFFEND
OFFERS
OFFICE
OFFING
OFFISH

6

OFFSET
OXFORD

O••F••
OLEFIN
OUTFIT
OUTFOX

O•••F•
OSSIFY

•OF•••
COFFEE
COFFER
COFFIN
COFFLE
DOFFED
DOFFER
GOFFER
LOFTED
LOFTER
SOFFIT
SOFTAS
SOFTEN
SOFTER
SOFTLY
TOFFEE

•O•F••
BOTFLY
BOUFFE
BOWFIN
COFFEE
COFFER
COFFIN
COFFLE
COIFED
COMFIT
CONFAB
CONFER
DOFFED
DOFFER
GOFFER
GOLFED
GOLFER
GOOFED
HOOFED
HOOFER
JOYFUL
LOAFED
LOAFER
LOOFAH
ROOFED
ROOFER
SOFFIT
TOFFEE
WOEFUL
WOLFED
WOOFER

•O••F•
BOUFFE
CODIFY
MODIFY
MOTIFS
NOTIFY

••OF••
CROFTS
FEOFFS
GOOFED
HOOFED
HOOFER
LOOFAH
PROFIT
ROOFED
ROOFER
SCOFFS
SHOFAR
TWOFER
WOOFER

••O•F•
FEOFFS
KLOOFS
PROOFS
SCOFFS
SPOOFS

•••OF•
CUTOFF
FAROFF
KLOOFS
LAYOFF
PAYOFF
PROOFS
PUTOFF
RIPOFF
RUNOFF
SETOFF
SHROFF
SPOOFS
TIPOFF

•••O•F
BEHOOF
CUTOFF
FAROFF
LAYOFF
PAYOFF
PUTOFF
RIPOFF
RUNOFF
SETOFF
SHROFF
TIPOFF

••••OF
BEHOOF
HEREOF

OG••••
OGDOAD
OGIVES
OGLERS
OGLING
OGRESS
OGRISH

O•G•••
ORGANA
ORGANO
ORGANS
ORGASM
ORGEAT
ORGIES

O••G••
OMEGAS
ONAGER
ONAGRI
OREGON
ORIGAN
ORIGEN
ORIGIN
OXYGEN

O•••G•
OBLIGE
OHMAGE
OOLOGY
OPPUGN
ORANGE
ORANGS

O••••G
OARING
OBLONG
OFFING
OGLING
OILING
OOLONG
OOZING
OPTING
ORBING
OUTING
OWNING

•OG•••
BOGANS
BOGEYS
BOGGED
BOGGLE
BOGIES
BOGLES
BOGOTA
COGENT
COGGED
COGNAC
COGWAY
DOGAPE
DOGEAR
DOGGED
DOGGER
DOGGIE
DOGIES
DOGMAS
EOGENE
FOGBOW
FOGDOG
FOGGED
FOGIES
GOGGLE
GOGLET
HOGANS
HOGGED
HOGNUT
HOGTIE
JOGGED
JOGGER
JOGGLE
LOGGED
LOGGER
LOGGIA
LOGIER
LOGION
LOGJAM
MOGULS
NOGGIN
POGIES
POGROM
ROGERS
ROGUED
ROGUES
TOGAED
TOGGED
TOGGLE
TOGUES
VOGUES
VOGULS
YOGEES
YOGINS
YOGURT

•O•G••
BOGGED
BOGGLE
BONGED
BONGOS
BORGIA
BOUGHS
BOUGHT
BOUGIE
CODGER
COGGED
COIGNS
CONGAS
CONGER
CONGES
CONGOU
CORGIS
COUGAR
COUGHS
DODGED
DODGER
DODGES
DOGGED
DOGGER
DOGGIE
DOUGHS
DOUGHY
DOUGIE
FOGGED
FORGED
FORGER
FORGES
FORGET
FORGOT
FOUGHT
GOGGLE
GOOGLY
GOOGOL
GORGED
GORGER
GORGES
GORGET
GORGON
GOUGED
GOUGER
GOUGES
HOGGED
JOGGED
JOGGER
JOGGLE
JORGES
LODGED
LODGER
LODGES
LOGGED
LOGGER
LOGGIA
LONGAN
LONGED
LONGER
LOUGHS
MONGER
MONGOL
MONGST
MORGAN
MORGEN
MORGUE
NOGGIN
NOUGAT
NOUGHT
PONGEE
POPGUN
ROTGUT
ROUGED
ROUGES
ROUGHS
SOIGNE
SORGHO
SORGOS
SOUGHS
SOUGHT
TOGGED
TOGGLE
TONGED
TONGUE
TOUGHS

•O••G•
BODEGA
BORAGE
BOURGS
COLUGO
COSIGN
COWAGE
DOINGS
DOSAGE
DOTAGE
FORAGE
FOREGO
GOINGS
HOMAGE
LOUNGE
LOVAGE
NONAGE
NONEGO
OOLOGY
POTAGE
SOCAGE
TOBAGO
TOWAGE
VOYAGE

•O•••G
BODING
BONING
BOOING
BORING
BOWING
BOWLEG
BOXING
CODING
COKING
COMING
CONING
COOING
COPING
CORING
COVING
COWING
COXING
DOLING
DOMING
DOPING
DORBUG
DOSING
DOTING
DOZING
FOGDOG
FOXING
GORING
HOEING
HOLING
HOMING
HONING
HOPING
HOSING
JOKING
JOYING
LOOING
LOPING
LOSING
LOVING
LOWING
MOOING
MOPING
MOVING
MOWING
NOSING
NOTING
OOLONG
OOZING

POKING
POLING
PORING
POSING
ROBING
ROPING
ROSING
ROVING
ROWING
SOLING
SOWING
TOEING
TONING
TOPING
TOTING
TOWING
TOYING
VOTING
VOWING
WOOING
WOWING
YOKING
YOWING
ZONING

••OG••
AGOGUE
APOGEE
BIOGEN
BROGAN
BROGUE
CLOGGY
EXOGEN
FROGGY
GOOGLY
GOOGOL
GROGGY
IMOGEN
ISOGON
SHOGUN
SLOGAN
STOGEY
TROGON

••O•G•
CHOUGH
CLOGGY
CLOUGH
DRONGO
ELOIGN
ENOUGH
FLONGS
FROGGY
GEORGE
GEORGI
GROGGY
PLOUGH
PRONGS
SLOUGH
SPONGE
SPONGY
STODGE
STODGY
STOOGE
THONGS
THOUGH
TROUGH
WRONGS

••O••G
APOLOG
BOOING
COOING
DUOLOG
LOOING
MOOING
PROLEG
WOOING

•••OG•
BEFOGS
EULOGY
LADOGA
OOLOGY
STOOGE

•••O•G
BARONG
BELONG
DUGONG
KALONG
MEKONG
OBLONG
OOLONG
SARONG
STRONG
THRONG

••••OG
ANALOG
APOLOG
DIALOG
DUOLOG
EGGNOG
EPILOG
FOGDOG
PUTLOG
QUAHOG
REDDOG
SEADOG
STENOG
SUNDOG

OH••••
OHENRY
OHIOAN
OHMAGE

O•H•••
OCHERS
OCHERY
OPHITE
OTHERS

O••H••
OOPHOR
ORCHID
ORCHIL
ORCHIO
ORCHIS
ORPHAN
ORPHIC

O•••H•
ORACHS

O••••H
OAFISH
OFFISH
OGRISH
OLDISH
ONRUSH
ORNITH
OWLISH

•OH•••
COHERE
COHORT
COHOSH
COHUNE
JOHANN
JOHNNY
MOHAIR
MOHAVE
MOHAWK
MOHOCK
MOHOLE
MOHURS

•O•H••
BOOHOO
BOSHES
BOTHER
COCHIN
COSHED
COSHER
COSHES
FOEHNS
GOPHER
GORHEN
GOSHEN
GOTHAM
GOTHIC
JOSHED
JOSHER
JOSHES
JOSHUA
KOSHER
LOCHIA
MOTHER
NOSHOW
OOPHOR
POTHER
ROCHET
SOPHIA
SOPHIE
SOTHIC
SOTHIS
TOSHES
TOTHER
YOOHOO

•O••H•
BOOTHS
BOTCHY
BOUGHS
BOUGHT
CONCHA
CONCHS
CONCHY
COUGHS
DOLPHS
DOUCHE
DOUGHS
DOUGHY
FOUGHT
GOETHE
HONSHU
JONAHS
LOATHE
LOTAHS
LOUGHS
MOISHE
MONTHS
MORPHO
MOUTHS
MOUTHY
NOUGHT
POACHY
PONCHO
POUCHY
ROLPHS
ROTCHE
ROUCHE
ROUGHS
SOOTHE
SORGHO
SOUGHS
SOUGHT
TOOTHY
TORAHS
TOUCHE
TOUCHY
TOUGHS
WORTHY
YOUTHS

•O•••H
BORSCH
BOYISH
COHOSH
COPRAH
COYISH
DOVISH
EOLITH
FOURTH
HOOKAH
HOOTCH
HOWDAH
JOSEPH
JOSIAH
LOOFAH
MODISH
MOLLAH
MOLOCH
MOOLAH
MOPISH
POLISH
POPISH
POTASH
ROMISH
TOBIAH
TOYISH

••OH••
ABOHMS
BOOHOO
ELOHIM
ISOHEL
YOOHOO

••O•H•
BOOTHS
BROTHS
CLOCHE
CLOTHE
CLOTHO
CLOTHS
EPOCHS
FROTHS
FROTHY
SLOSHY
SLOTHS
SOOTHE
TOOTHY
TROCHE
TROPHO
TROPHY
TROTHS

••O••H
ADOLPH
AVOUCH
BLOTCH
BROACH
BROOCH
CHOUGH
CLOUGH
CROTCH
CROUCH
DROUTH
ENOUGH
GROUCH
GROWTH
HOOKAH
HOOTCH
LOOFAH
MOOLAH
PHOSPH
PLOUGH
SCORCH
SCOTCH
SLOUCH
SLOUGH
SMOOCH
SMOOTH
THOUGH
TROUGH

•••O•H
BROOCH
COHOSH
GALOSH
KIBOSH
MOLOCH
SMOOCH
SMOOTH

••••OH
SHILOH

OI••••
OILCAN
OILERS
OILIER
OILILY
OILING

O•I•••
OBIISM
ODIOUS
OGIVES
OHIOAN
OJIBWA
OLIVER
OLIVES
OLIVIA
ONIONS
OPIATE
OPINED
OPINES
ORIBIS
ORIELS
ORIENT
ORIGAN
ORIGEN
ORIGIN
ORIOLE
OSIERS
OSIRIS
OTIOSE
OTITIS
OVIBOS
OVISAC
OXIDES

O••I••
OAFISH
OARING
OBIISM
OBLIGE
OBOIST
ODDITY
OFFICE
OFFING
OFFISH
OGLING
OGRISH
OILIER
OILILY
OILING
OLDISH
OLLIES

ONEIDA
ONEILL
ONEIRO
OOLITE
OOMIAK
OOZIER
OOZILY
OOZING
OPHITE
OPTICS
OPTIMA
OPTIME
OPTING
OPTION
ORBING
ORBITS
OREIDE
ORGIES
ORNITH
OROIDE
ORPINE
ORPINS
ORRICE
OSCINE
OSMIUM
OSSIAN
OSSIFY
OUTING
OWLISH
OWNING
OXLIPS

O•••I•

OBTAIN
ODYNIA
OKAPIS
OLEFIN
OLIVIA
ORCEIN
ORCHID
ORCHIL
ORCHIO
ORCHIS
ORDAIN
ORIBIS
ORIGIN
ORPHIC
OSIRIS
OSSEIN
OTITIS
OUTBID
OUTDID
OUTFIT
OUTSIT
OUTWIT
OXALIC
OXALIS
OXTAIL
OZONIC

O••••I

OCTOPI
OCTROI
ONAGRI

•OI•••

BOILED
BOILER
COIFED
COIGNS
COILED
COILER
COINED
COINER
DOINGS
FOIBLE
FOILED
FOISTS
GOINGS
GOITER
HOICKS
HOIDEN
HOISTS
JOINED
JOINER
JOINTS
JOISTS
KOINES
LOITER
MOIETY
MOILED
MOILER
MOIRAS
MOISHE
NOISED
NOISES
POILUS
POINDS
POINTS
POINTY
POISED
POISES
POISON
ROILED
SOIGNE
SOILED
SOIREE
TOILED
TOILER
TOILES
TOILET
VOICED
VOICES
VOIDED
VOILES
YOICKS

•O•I••

AORIST
BODICE
BODIED
BODIES
BODILY
BODING
BOGIES
BOLIDE
BONIER
BONING
BONITO
BOOING
BORIDE
BORING
BOVINE
BOWING
BOXING
BOYISH
COBIAS
CODIFY
CODING
COKING
COLIES
COLINE
COLINS
COMICS
COMING
COMITY
CONICS
CONIES
CONING
CONIUM
COOING
COPIED
COPIER
COPIES
COPING
CORING
CORIUM
COSIGN
COSINE
COVING
COWING
COXING
COYISH
COZIER
COZIES
COZILY
DOBIES
DOCILE
DOGIES
DOLING
DOMING
DOMINO
DOPIER
DOPING
DORIAN
DORIES
DOSING
DOTIER
DOTING
DOVISH
DOXIES
DOZIER
DOZILY
DOZING
EOLIAN
EOLITH
EONIAN
EONISM
FOGIES
FOLIAR
FOLIOS
FOLIUM
FORINT
FOXIER
FOXILY
FOXING
GOBIES
GODIVA
GONION
GONIUM
GOOIER
GORIER
GORILY
GORING
HOEING
HOLIER
HOLIES
HOLILY
HOLING
HOLISM
HOMIER
HOMILY
HOMING
HOMINY
HONIED
HONING
HOPING
HOSIER
HOSING
IODIDE
IODINE
IODISM
IODIZE
IOLITE
IONIAN
IONIUM
IONIZE
JOKING
JOLIET
JOSIAH
JOSIAS
JOSIES
JOVIAL
JOVIAN
JOYING
KODIAK
LOGIER
LOGION
LOLITA
LOOING
LOPING
LORICA
LORIES
LOSING
LOTION
LOUISA
LOUISE
LOVING
LOWING
MOBILE
MOBIUS
MODIFY
MODISH
MOLIES
MOLINE
MOMISM
MONICA
MONIED
MONIES
MONISM
MONIST
MOOING
MOPING
MOPISH
MORION
MOTIFS
MOTILE
MOTION
MOTIVE
MOVIES
MOVING
MOWING
NOMISM
NORIAS
NOSIER
NOSILY
NOSING
NOTICE
NOTIFY
NOTING
NOTION
NOVICE
NOWISE
OOLITE
OOMIAK
OOZIER
OOZILY
OOZING
PODIUM
POGIES
POKIER
POKIES
POKING
POLICE
POLICY
POLING
POLISH
POLITE
POLITY
PONIED
PONIES
POPISH
PORING
POSIES
POSING
POSITS
POTION
ROBING
ROBINS
ROMISH
ROPIER
ROPILY
ROPING
ROSIER
ROSILY
ROSING
ROSINS
ROSINY
ROVING
ROWING
SOCIAL
SODIUM
SOLIDI
SOLIDS
SOLING
SOLION
SOMITE
SONIAS
SOVIET
SOWING
SOZINE
SOZINS
TOBIAH
TOBIAS
TOBIES
TODIES
TOEING
TONICS
TONIER
TONING
TOPICS
TOPING
TORIES
TORIIS
TOTING
TOWING
TOXINS
TOYING
TOYISH
VOMICA
VOMITO
VOMITS
VOTING
VOTIVE
VOWING
WOOING
WOWING
YOGINS
YOKING
YOWING
ZODIAC
ZONING
ZOOIDS
ZORILS

•O••I•

AORTIC
BOBBIE
BOBBIN
BOCCIE
BODKIN
BOLLIX
BONNIE
BOOKIE
BOOTIE
BORGIA
BOUGIE
BOWFIN
COATIS
COCAIN
COCCID
COCHIN
CODEIA
CODEIN
COFFIN

COLLIE
COMFIT
COMMIE
COMMIT
COMMIX
CONNIE
CONOID
CONTIN
COOKIE
COOLIE
COOTIE
COPTIC
CORGIS
CORTIN
COSMIC
COUSIN
COWRIE
DOBBIN
DOGGIE
DOLLIE
DOMAIN
DONNIE
DOOLIE
DORMIE
DOSSIL
DOUGIE
EOZOIC
FOETID
FORBID
FORMIC
FORNIX
FORTIS
FOSSIL
GOALIE
GOBLIN
GODWIN
GODWIT
GOSSIP
GOTHIC
HOGTIE
HOLMIC
HORNIE
HORRID
HOURIS
JONNIE
JOPLIN
LOCHIA
LOGGIA
LOOKIN
LORAIN
LOTTIE
LOVEIN
MOHAIR
MOLLIE
MORBID
MORRIS
MOSAIC
MOULIN
NOESIS
NOETIC
NOGGIN
NORDIC
NORNIR
NORRIS

POETIC
PONTIC
PONTIL
POPLIN
PORTIA
POTPIE
POTSIE
ROBBIA
ROBBIE
ROMAIC
RONNIE
ROOKIE
SOFFIT
SOPHIA
SOPHIE
SORDID
SORTIE
SOTHIC
SOTHIS
TOCSIN
TOMTIT
TONKIN
TONSIL
TORIIS
TOROID
TORPID
TORRID
ZOMBIE
ZOMBIS
ZOYSIA

•O•••I

BONACI
BONSAI
BORZOI
GOMUTI
SOLIDI
SOUARI

••OI••

ANOINT
AROIDS
AVOIDS
BOOING
BROILS
CHOICE
CHOIRS
COOING
DROITS
EGOISM
EGOIST
ELOIGN
ELOINS
ELOISE
GOOIER
GROINS
HYOIDS
ILOILO
LOOING
MAOISM
MAOIST
MOOING
OBOIST
OROIDE

QUOINS
QUOITS
SPOILS
SPOILT
STOICS
TAOISM
TAOIST
TROIKA
WOOING
ZOOIDS

••O•I•

ADONIC
ADONIS
AEOLIA
AEOLIC
AEOLIS
AGONIC
ANODIC
ANOMIC
ANOMIE
ANOXIA
ANOXIC
ATOMIC
ATONIC
AZONIC
AZOTIC
BIOSIS
BIOTIC
BIOTIN
BOOKIE
BOOTIE
BROMIC
CHOPIN
CHORIC
CLONIC
CLOVIS
COOKIE
COOLIE
COOTIE
CROJIK
DHOTIS
DOOLIE
ELOHIM
ENOSIS
EROTIC
EXOTIC
FLORID
FLORIN
FROLIC
GEODIC
GLOBIN
GLORIA
GNOMIC
GNOSIS
ICONIC
IRONIC
KAOLIN
LEONIE
LOOKIN
MAORIS
MIOSIS
MIOTIC
MYOPIA

MYOPIC
MYOSIN
MYOSIS
NAOMIS
OZONIC
PEORIA
PHOBIA
PHOCIS
PHONIA
PHONIC
PHOTIC
PROFIT
PROLIX
PROSIT
PTOSIS
PYOSIS
RHODIC
ROOKIE
SCORIA
SCOTIA
SHOJIS
SHOOIN
STOLID
SUOMIC
THORIA
THORIC
TROPIC
TWOBIT
UTOPIA
VIOLIN

••O••I

ADONAI
AGOUTI
GEORGI
RHOMBI

•••OI•

ADJOIN
ADROIT
ALGOID
ARTOIS
BELOIT
CEBOID
CONOID
CUBOID
CYMOID
DACOIT
DAKOIT
DEVOID
DEVOIR
ECHOIC
ENJOIN
EOZOIC
FUCOID
GADOID
GANOID
HALOID
HEMOID
HEROIC
HEROIN
KELOID
LIPOID
MEMOIR

MUCOID
NEVOID
PATOIS
RECOIL
REJOIN
RENOIR
SHOOIN
TOROID
UNCOIL
VALOIS
XYLOID

•••O•I

ARBORI
BILOXI
EMBOLI
EPHORI
NEROLI
OCTOPI
SATORI
VAPORI

••••OI

BORZOI
MYTHOI
OCTROI

OJ••••

OJIBWA

O•J•••

OBJECT

•OJ•••

MOJAVE

•O•J••

DONJON
KOPJES
LOGJAM

••OJ••

CROJIK
PROJET
SHOJIS
TROJAN

OK••••

OKAPIS
OKAYED

O•K•••

OAKLEY

O••••K

OCLOCK
OOMIAK

•OK•••

COKING
GOKART
JOKERS
JOKING
KOKOMO

POKERS
POKIER
POKIES
POKING
TOKENS
YOKELS
YOKING

•O•K••

BODKIN
BOOKED
BOOKIE
BOSKET
COCKED
COCKER
COCKLE
COCKUP
CONKED
COOKED
COOKER
COOKEY
COOKIE
CORKED
CORKER
DOCKED
DOCKER
DOCKET
DONKEY
FOLKSY
FORKED
HOCKED
HOCKEY
HONKED
HONKER
HOOKAH
HOOKED
HOOKER
HOOKUP
JOCKEY
JOCKOS
LOCKED
LOCKER
LOCKET
LOCKUP
LOOKED
LOOKER
LOOKIN
LOWKEY
MOCKED
MOCKER
MOCKUP
MONKEY
NOCKED
POCKET
POLKAS
PORKER
ROCKED
ROCKER
ROCKET
ROCKNE
ROOKED
ROOKIE
SOAKED
SOAKER

6

SOCKED
SOCKET
TONKIN
VODKAS
WORKED
WORKER
YONKER

•O••K•

HOICKS
KODAKS
KOPEKS
MOLTKE
MOPOKE
TOPEKA
TORSKS
YOICKS

•O•••K

KODIAK
KOPECK
MOHAWK
MOHOCK
OOMIAK
PODUNK

••OK••

BLOKES
BOOKED
BOOKIE
BROKEN
BROKER
CHOKED
CHOKER
CHOKES
COOKED
COOKER
COOKEY
COOKIE
EVOKED
EVOKES
HOOKAH
HOOKED
HOOKER
HOOKUP
LOOKED
LOOKER
LOOKIN
ROOKED
ROOKIE
SMOKED
SMOKER
SMOKES
SPOKED
SPOKEN
SPOKES
STOKED
STOKER
STOKES

••O•K•

BLOCKS
BLOCKY
BROOKS
CHOCKS
CLOAKS
CLOCKS
CROAKS
CROAKY
CROCKS
CROOKS
DROSKY
FLOCKS
FLOCKY
FROCKS
KIOSKS
KNOCKS
SHOCKS
SMOCKS
SNOOKS
SPOOKS
SPOOKY
STOCKS
STOCKY
STOOKS
STORKS
TROIKA

••O••K

ANORAK
CROJIK
DVORAK
SLOVAK

•••OK•

BROOKS
CROOKS
INVOKE
KAPOKS
MOPOKE
REVOKE
SNOOKS
SPOOKS
SPOOKY
STOOKS
STROKE
UNYOKE

•••O•K

BETOOK
BYWORK
MOHOCK
OCLOCK
RETOOK
UNCOCK
UNCORK
UNHOOK
UNLOCK

••••OK

BARTOK
BETOOK
HICKOK
RETOOK
UNHOOK

OL••••

OLDEST
OLDISH
OLEATE
OLEFIN
OLIVER
OLIVES
OLIVIA
OLLIES

O•L•••

OBLAST
OBLATE
OBLIGE
OBLONG
OCLOCK
OGLERS
OGLING
OILCAN
OILERS
OILIER
OILILY
OILING
OLLIES
OOLITE
OOLOGY
OOLONG
ORLOPS
OWLETS
OWLISH
OXLIPS

O••L••

OAKLEY
OBELUS
OBOLUS
OCELOT
OCULAR
OMELET
OODLES
ORALLY
OUTLAW
OUTLAY
OUTLET
OVALLY
OVULAR
OVULES
OXALIC
OXALIS

O•••L•

OCCULT
OILILY
ONEILL
OOZILY
OPENLY
ORACLE
ORALLY
ORIELS
ORIOLE
ORMOLU
ORWELL
OSCULE
OSWALD
OUSELS
OUZELS
OVALLY
OVERLY

O••••L

ONEILL
ORCHIL
ORDEAL
ORWELL
OSTEAL
OXTAIL

•OL•••

BOLDER
BOLDLY
BOLERO
BOLEYN
BOLIDE
BOLLED
BOLLIX
BOLSON
BOLTED
BOLTER
COLDER
COLDLY
COLEUS
COLIES
COLINE
COLINS
COLLAR
COLLET
COLLIE
COLLOP
COLONS
COLONY
COLORS
COLOUS
COLTER
COLUGO
COLUMN
COLURE
COLZAS
DOLING
DOLLAR
DOLLED
DOLLIE
DOLLOP
DOLLYS
DOLMAN
DOLMEN
DOLPHS
EOLIAN
EOLITH
FOLDED
FOLDER
FOLIAR
FOLIOS
FOLIUM
FOLKSY
FOLLOW
GOLDEN
GOLFED
GOLFER
HOLARD
HOLDER
HOLDUP
HOLIER
HOLIES
HOLILY
HOLING
HOLISM
HOLLER
HOLLOW
HOLLYS
HOLMES
HOLMIC
IOLCUS
IOLITE
JOLIET
JOLTED
JOLTER
LOLITA
LOLLED
LOLLER
MOLARS
MOLDED
MOLDER
MOLEST
MOLIES
MOLINE
MOLLAH
MOLLIE
MOLLYS
MOLOCH
MOLTED
MOLTEN
MOLTER
MOLTKE
OOLITE
OOLOGY
OOLONG
POLAND
POLDER
POLEAX
POLICE
POLICY
POLING
POLISH
POLITE
POLITY
POLKAS
POLLED
POLLEE
POLLEN
POLLER
POLLEX
POLLUX
POLLYS
POLYPS
ROLAND
ROLLED
ROLLER
ROLPHS
SOLACE
SOLAND
SOLANO
SOLANS
SOLDER
SOLELY
SOLEMN
SOLENT
SOLIDI
SOLIDS
SOLING
SOLION
SOLOED
SOLUTE
SOLVED
SOLVER
SOLVES
TOLEDO
TOLLED
TOLLER
TOLTEC
TOLUOL
TOLUYL
VOLANT
VOLERY
VOLLEY
VOLOST
VOLUME
VOLUTE
VOLVAS
VOLVOX
WOLFED
WOLSEY
WOLVER
WOLVES

•O•L••

BOGLES
BOILED
BOILER
BOLLED
BOLLIX
BOULES
BOWLED
BOWLEG
BOWLER
COALED
COALER
COBLES
COELOM
COILED
COILER
COLLAR
COLLET
COLLIE
COLLOP
COOLED
COOLER
COOLIE
COOLLY
COPLEY
COULEE
COWLED
DOALLS
DOBLAS
DOBLON
DOLLAR
DOLLED
DOLLIE
DOLLOP

DOLLYS
DOOLEE
DOOLIE
DOYLEY
FOALED
FOILED
FOLLOW
FOOLED
FOULED
FOULER
FOULLY
FOWLED
FOWLER
GOALIE
GOBLET
GOBLIN
GOGLET
HOLLER
HOLLOW
HOLLYS
HOWLED
HOWLER
JOPLIN
JOULES
KOALAS
LOLLED
LOLLER
MOILED
MOILER
MOLLAH
MOLLIE
MOLLYS
MOOLAH
MOOLEY
MORLEY
MOSLEM
MOSLEY
MOTLEY
MOULDS
MOULDY
MOULIN
MOULTS
OODLES
POILUS
POLLED
POLLEE
POLLEN
POLLER
POLLEX
POLLUX
POLLYS
POOLED
POPLAR
POPLIN
POULTS
ROALDS
ROBLES
ROILED
ROLLED
ROLLER
SOCLES
SOILED
SOULED
TOILED
TOILER
TOILES
TOILET
TOLLED
TOLLER
TOOLED
TOOLER
TOULON
VOILES
VOLLEY
WOALDS
WOOLEN
WOOLLY
WORLDS
YOWLED

•O••L•

BOBBLE
BODILY
BOGGLE
BOLDLY
BOODLE
BOTFLY
BOTTLE
BOUCLE
BOWELS
COBALT
COBBLE
COCKLE
CODDLE
COFFLE
COLDLY
COMELY
COMPLY
COOLLY
COPALM
COPULA
CORALS
COSTLY
COUPLE
COZILY
DOABLE
DOALLS
DOCILE
DONALD
DOODLE
DOTTLE
DOUBLE
DOUBLY
DOURLY
DOWELS
DOZILY
FOCSLE
FOIBLE
FONDLE
FONDLY
FOOTLE
FOOZLE
FOULLY
FOXILY
GOBBLE
GOGGLE
GOODLY
GOOGLY
GORALS
GORILY
HOBBLE
HOLILY
HOMELY
HOMILY
HOOPLA
HOPPLE
HOTELS
HOURLY
HOVELS
JOGGLE
JOSTLE
KOBOLD
LOBULE
LOCALE
LOCALS
LONELY
LORDLY
LOUDLY
LOVELL
LOVELY
LOWELL
MOBILE
MODELS
MODULE
MOGULS
MOHOLE
MORALE
MORALS
MORELS
MORULA
MOSTLY
MOTELS
MOTILE
MOTTLE
NOBALL
NOBBLE
NODDLE
NODULE
NOODLE
NOPALS
NOSILY
NOVELS
NOZZLE
OOZILY
POMELO
POODLE
POORLY
POPPLE
PORTLY
POTTLE
POWELL
ROBALO
ROMOLA
ROMULO
RONALD
ROPILY
ROSILY
ROUBLE
ROWELS
ROYALS
SOFTLY
SOLELY
SORELS
SORELY
SOTOLS
SOURLY
TODDLE
TOGGLE
TOOTLE
TOPPLE
TOTALS
TOUSLE
TOWELS
VOCALS
VOGULS
VOWELS
WOBBLE
WOBBLY
WOOLLY
YODELS
YOKELS
ZONULA
ZONULE
ZORILS

•O•••L

AORTAL
BORDEL
BOREAL
COAXAL
COCCAL
COEVAL
COMPEL
CONSUL
CORBEL
CORNEL
CORRAL
COSTAL
DORSAL
DOSSAL
DOSSEL
DOSSIL
DOTTEL
FOETAL
FONTAL
FORMAL
FORMYL
FOSSIL
FOVEAL
GOOGOL
GOORAL
GOSPEL
HOSTEL
JOVIAL
JOYFUL
LOVELL
LOWELL
MONGOL
MORSEL
MORTAL
NOBALL
NORMAL
NOUNAL
PODSOL
PODZOL
POMMEL
PONTIL
PORTAL
POSTAL
POWELL
ROMMEL
RONDEL
SOCIAL
SORREL
TOLUOL
TOLUYL
TONSIL
WOEFUL
ZOONAL

••OL••

ABOLLA
ADOLPH
AEOLIA
AEOLIC
AEOLIS
AEOLUS
AMOLES
APOLLO
APOLOG
ATOLLS
AZOLES
CHOLER
CHOLLA
COOLED
COOLER
COOLIE
COOLLY
DHOLES
DOOLEE
DOOLIE
DROLLS
DROLLY
DUOLOG
ECOLES
EVOLVE
FOOLED
FROLIC
GAOLER
ISOLDE
KAOLIN
KNOLLS
MOOLAH
MOOLEY
OBOLUS
POOLED
PROLEG
PROLIX
SCOLDS
SCOLEX
SMOLTS
STOLED
STOLEN
STOLES
STOLID
STOLON
THOLES
TOOLED
TOOLER
TROLLS
UBOLTS
VIOLAS
VIOLET
VIOLIN
WHOLLY
WOOLEN
WOOLLY

••O•L•

ABOLLA
APOLLO
ATOLLS
BOODLE
BROILS
CEORLS
CHOLLA
COOLLY
DOODLE
DROLLS
DROLLY
DROOLS
FOOTLE
FOOZLE
GHOULS
GOODLY
GOOGLY
GROWLS
HOOPLA
ILOILO
KNOLLS
NOODLE
PEOPLE
POODLE
POORLY
PROWLS
RAOULS
SCOWLS
SHOALS
SHOALY
SHORLS
SHOULD
SLOWLY
SPOILS
SPOILT
SPOOLS
STOOLS
TOOTLE
TROLLS
TWOPLY
WHOLLY
WHORLS
WOOLLY

••O••L

ABORAL
AMORAL
APODAL
ATONAL
AVOWAL
BROMAL
CHORAL
DIOBOL
FLORAL
GLOBAL

GOOGOL
GOORAL
GROVEL
ISOBEL
ISOHEL
LIONEL
PROPEL
PROPYL
SHOVEL
TROPAL
TROTYL
TROWEL
ZOONAL

•••OL•
ABVOLT
ANGOLA
AREOLA
ARNOLD
BEHOLD
BIFOLD
BIKOLS
CAJOLE
CAROLE
CAROLS
CIBOLS
CITOLA
CREOLE
CUPOLA
DIPOLE
DROOLS
EIDOLA
EMBOLI
ENFOLD
ENROLL
EXTOLS
GIGOLO
HAROLD
INFOLD
INSOLE
KOBOLD
MOHOLE
NEROLI
NICOLE
ORIOLE
ORMOLU
PAROLE
PAYOLA
PINOLE
RESOLD
RESOLE
RETOLD
REVOLT
ROMOLA
SCROLL
SOTOLS
SPOOLS
STOOLS
STROLL
THIOLS
UNBOLT
UNFOLD
UNHOLY
UNROLL
UNSOLD
UNTOLD
UPHOLD
XYLOLS

•••O•L
BEFOOL
BEFOUL
ENROLL
ENSOUL
INSOUL
RECOIL
SCHOOL
SCHORL
SCROLL
STROLL
UNCOIL
UNROLL

••••OL
AMATOL
AMIDOL
BEFOOL
BENZOL
CINEOL
CRESOL
DIOBOL
FRIJOL
FRIVOL
GAMBOL
GLYCOL
GOOGOL
MONGOL
PATHOL
PATROL
PETROL
PHENOL
PISTOL
PODSOL
PODZOL
SANTOL
SCHOOL
STEROL
SYMBOL
THYMOL
TOLUOL

OM••••
OMASUM
OMEGAS
OMELET
OMENTA

O•M•••
OHMAGE
OOMIAK
ORMERS
ORMOLU
ORMUZD
OSMIUM
OSMOND
OSMOSE
OSMUND

O••M••
OUTMAN

O•••M•
OPTIMA
OPTIME

O••••M
OBIISM
OMASUM
ORGASM
OSMIUM

•OM•••
BOMBAY
BOMBED
BOMBER
BOMBES
COMATE
COMBAT
COMBED
COMBER
COMBOS
COMEDO
COMEDY
COMELY
COMEON
COMERS
COMETS
COMFIT
COMICS
COMING
COMITY
COMMAS
COMMIE
COMMIT
COMMIX
COMMON
COMOSE
COMOUS
COMPEL
COMPLY
COMPOS
DOMAIN
DOMING
DOMINO
FOMENT
GOMUTI
HOMAGE
HOMBRE
HOMELY
HOMERS
HOMIER
HOMILY
HOMING
HOMINY
LOMENT
LOMOND
MOMENT
MOMISM
NOMADS
NOMISM
NOMURA
OOMIAK
POMACE
POMADE
POMELO
POMMEL
POMONA
POMPEY
POMPOM
POMPON
ROMAIC
ROMANS
ROMANY
ROMISH
ROMMEL
ROMNEY
ROMOLA
ROMPED
ROMPER
ROMULO
SOMATA
SOMATO
SOMBER
SOMITE
TOMANS
TOMATO
TOMBAC
TOMBED
TOMBOY
TOMCAT
TOMCOD
TOMMYS
TOMTIT
TOMTOM
VOMERS
VOMICA
VOMITO
VOMITS
WOMBAT
WOMBED
WOMERA
ZOMBIE
ZOMBIS

•O•M••
BOOMED
BOWMAN
BOWMEN
COEMPT
COMMAS
COMMIE
COMMIT
COMMIX
COMMON
COOMBS
COSMIC
COSMOS
COWMAN
COWMEN
DOGMAS
DOLMAN
DOLMEN
DOOMED
DORMER
DORMIE
FOAMED
FOEMAN
FOEMEN
FORMAL
FORMAT
FORMED
FORMER
FORMIC
FORMYL
HOLMES
HOLMIC
LOAMED
LOOMED
MORMON
MOTMOT
NORMAL
NORMAN
NORMAS
POMMEL
ROAMED
ROAMER
RODMAN
RODMEN
ROMMEL
ROOMED
ROOMER
SOCMAN
SOCMEN
TOMMYS
WORMED
WORMER
ZOOMED

•O••M•
BOSOMS
COLUMN
CORYMB
FORUMS
GOTAMA
JORAMS
JORUMS
KOKOMO
SODOMY
SOLEMN
TOTEMS
VOLUME

•O•••M
BOTTOM
COELOM
CONDOM
CONIUM
COPALM
CORIUM
DORSUM
EONISM
FOLIUM
GONIUM
GOTHAM
HOLISM
IODISM
IONIUM
LOGJAM
MOMISM
MONISM
MOSLEM
NOMISM
NONCOM
PODIUM
POGROM
POMPOM
POSSUM
SODIUM
TOMTOM

••OM••
ABOMAS
ABOMBS
ANOMIC
ANOMIE
AROMAS
ATOMIC
BOOMED
BROMAL
BROMES
BROMIC
COOMBS
DOOMED
DROMON
GNOMES
GNOMIC
GNOMON
HBOMBS
ISOMER
LOOMED
NAOMIS
PROMPT
RHOMBI
ROOMED
ROOMER
STOMAT
STOMPS
SUOMIC
THOMAS
YEOMAN
YEOMEN
ZOOMED

••O•M•
ABOHMS
BLOOMS
BLOOMY
BROOMS
BROOMY
GLOOMS
GLOOMY
GROOMS
PROEMS
STORMS
STORMY

••O••M
ANONYM
EGOISM
ELOHIM
EPONYM
MAOISM
QUORUM
TAOISM

•••OM•
APLOMB
ATHOME
AXIOMS
BECOME
BESOMS
BLOOMS
BLOOMY
BOSOMS
BROOMS
BROOMY
CAEOMA
CAROMS
CHROMA
CHROME
CHROMO
CLEOME
ECTOMY
ENTOMB
ENTOMO
ENWOMB
GLIOMA
GLOOMS
GLOOMY
GROOMS
IDIOMS
INCOME
INTOMB
JEROME
KOKOMO
LIPOMA
MYXOMA
RADOME
SALOME
SODOMY
STROMA
TACOMA
VENOMS
ZYGOMA

•••O•M
ABLOOM
BIFORM
DEFORM
INFORM
PHLOEM
REFORM
SIMOOM

••••OM
ABLOOM
BOTTOM
COELOM
CONDOM
CUSTOM
DIATOM
FANTOM
FATHOM
HANSOM
NONCOM
POGROM
POMPOM
RANDOM
RANSOM
SELDOM
SIMOOM
SLALOM
TOMTOM
WHILOM
WISDOM

ON••••
ONAGER
ONAGRI
ONEIDA
ONEILL
ONEIRO
ONEWAY
ONIONS
ONRUSH
ONSETS
ONUSES
ONWARD

O•N•••
ORNATE
ORNERY
ORNITH
OUNCES
OWNERS
OWNING

O••N••
ODONTO
ODYNIA
OHENRY
OMENTA
OPENED
OPENER
OPENLY
OPINED
OPINES
ORANGE
ORANGS
OZONIC

O•••N•
OARING
OBLONG
OBTUND
OCEANS
OCTANE
OCTANT
OFFEND
OFFING
OGLING
OILING
ONIONS
OOLONG
OOZING
OPTING
ORBING
ORGANA
ORGANO
ORGANS
ORIENT
ORPINE
ORPINS
OSCANS
OSCINE
OSMOND
OSMUND
OUTING
OWNING

O••••N
OBERON
OBTAIN
OHIOAN
OILCAN
OLEFIN
OPPUGN
OPTION
ORCEIN
ORDAIN
OREGON
ORIGAN
ORIGEN
ORIGIN
ORPHAN
OSBORN
OSSEIN
OSSIAN
OUTMAN
OUTRAN
OUTRUN
OXYGEN

•ON•••
BONACI
BONBON
BONDED
BONDER
BONERS
BONGED
BONGOS
BONIER
BONING
BONITO
BONNET
BONNIE
BONNYS
BONSAI
BONZER
BONZES
CONCHA
CONCHS
CONCHY
CONCUR
CONDOM
CONDOR
CONEYS
CONFAB
CONFER
CONGAS
CONGER
CONGES
CONGOU
CONICS
CONIES
CONING
CONIUM
CONKED
CONNED
CONNER
CONNIE
CONOID
CONRAD
CONSUL
CONTES
CONTIN
CONTOS
CONTRA
CONTRE
CONVEX
CONVEY
CONVOY
DONALD
DONATE
DONEES
DONETS
DONJON
DONKEY
DONNAS
DONNED
DONNIE
DONORS
EONIAN
EONISM
FONDER
FONDLE
FONDLY
FONDUE
FONTAL
GONADS
GONERS
GONION
GONIUM
HONEST
HONEYS
HONIED
HONING
HONKED
HONKER
HONORE
HONORS
HONSHU
IONIAN
IONIUM
IONIZE
IONONE
JONAHS
JONNIE
JONSON
KONRAD
LONDON
LONELY
LONERS
LONGAN
LONGED
LONGER
MONADS
MONDAY
MONEYS
MONGER
MONGOL
MONGST
MONICA
MONIED
MONIES
MONISM
MONIST
MONKEY
MONODY
MONROE
MONTES
MONTHS
MONTYS
NONAGE
NONCOM
NONEGO
PONCHO
PONDER
PONENT
PONGEE
PONIED
PONIES
PONTES
PONTIC
PONTIL
PONTON
RONALD
RONDEL
RONDOS
RONNIE
SONANT
SONARS
SONATA
SONDER
SONIAS
SONNET
SONYAS
TONERS
TONGED
TONGUE
TONICS
TONIER
TONING
TONKIN
TONSIL
WONDER
WONTED
YONDER
YONKER
ZONARY
ZONATE
ZONING
ZONULA
ZONULE

•O•N••
BONNET
BONNIE
BONNYS
BORNEO
BOUNCE
BOUNCY
BOUNDS
BOUNTY
COBNUT
COGNAC
COINED
COINER
CONNED
CONNER
CONNIE
CORNEA
CORNED
CORNEL
CORNER
CORNET
CORNUA
CORNUS
COUNTS
COUNTY
DOINGS
DONNAS
DONNED
DONNIE
DOWNED
FORNAX
FORNIX
FOUNDS
FOUNTS
GOINGS
GOONEY
GOWNED
HOBNOB
HOGNUT
HORNED
HORNET
HORNIE
HOUNDS
JOANNA
JOANNE
JOHNNY
JOINED
JOINER
JOINTS
JONNIE
JOUNCE
KOINES
LOANED
LOUNGE
MOANED
MOONED
MOUNTS
MOUNTY
NORNIR
NOUNAL
POINDS
POINTS
POINTY
POUNCE
POUNDS
RODNEY
ROMNEY
RONNIE
ROUNDS
SONNET
SOONER
SOUNDS
WOUNDS
ZOONAL

6

ZOUNDS

•O••N•

BODING
BOGANS
BONING
BOOING
BORANE
BORING
BOTANY
BOURNE
BOURNS
BOVINE
BOWING
BOXING
CODING
COGENT
COHUNE
COIGNS
COKING
COLINE
COLINS
COLONS
COLONY
COMING
CONING
COOING
COPING
CORING
CORONA
COSINE
COVING
COWING
COXING
COZENS
DOCENT
DOESNT
DOLING
DOMING
DOMINO
DOPING
DOSING
DOTING
DOYENS
DOZENS
DOZING
EOCENE
EOGENE
FOEHNS
FOMENT
FORINT
FOXING
GORING
HOEING
HOGANS
HOLING
HOMING
HOMINY
HONING
HOPING
HOSING
IODINE
IONONE
JOANNA
JOANNE
JOCUND
JOHANN
JOHNNY
JOKING
JOYING
KORUNA
KORUNY
LOMENT
LOMOND
LOOING
LOPING
LORENE
LORENZ
LOSING
LOVING
LOWING
MOLINE
MOMENT
MOOING
MOPING
MORONS
MOURNS
MOVING
MOWING
NOCENT
NOSING
NOTING
NOVENA
OOLONG
OOZING
PODUNK
POKING
POLAND
POLING
POMONA
PONENT
PORING
POSING
POTENT
ROBAND
ROBING
ROBINS
ROCKNE
RODENT
ROLAND
ROMANS
ROMANY
ROPING
ROSING
ROSINS
ROSINY
ROTUND
ROVING
ROWANS
ROWENA
ROWING
ROXANA
ROXANE
SOIGNE
SOLAND
SOLANO
SOLANS
SOLENT
SOLING
SONANT
SOWING
SOZINE
SOZINS
TOEING
TOKENS
TOMANS
TONING
TOPING
TOTING
TOWING
TOXINS
TOYING
TOYONS
VOLANT
VOTING
VOWING
WOOING
WOWING
YOGINS
YOKING
YOWING
ZONING

•O•••N

BOBBIN
BODKIN
BOLEYN
BOLSON
BONBON
BOSTON
BOWFIN
BOWMAN
BOWMEN
COCAIN
COCHIN
COCOON
CODEIN
COFFIN
COLUMN
COMEON
COMMON
CONTIN
CORBAN
CORDON
CORTIN
COSIGN
COTTON
COUPON
COUSIN
COWMAN
COWMEN
DOBBIN
DOBLON
DOBSON
DOLMAN
DOLMEN
DOMAIN
DONJON
DOREEN
DORIAN
EOLIAN
EONIAN
FOEMAN
FOEMEN
GOBLIN
GODSON
GODWIN
GOLDEN
GONION
GORDON
GORGON
GORHEN
GOSHEN
GOTTEN
GOVERN
HODDEN
HOIDEN
HOYDEN
IONIAN
JOHANN
JONSON
JOPLIN
JORDAN
JOVIAN
KOREAN
LOGION
LONDON
LONGAN
LOOKIN
LOOSEN
LORAIN
LOREEN
LOTION
LOUDEN
LOVEIN
MODERN
MOLTEN
MOREEN
MORGAN
MORGEN
MORION
MORMON
MORTON
MOTION
MOULIN
MOUTON
NOGGIN
NOREEN
NORMAN
NOTION
POISON
POLLEN
POMPON
PONTON
POPGUN
POPLIN
POTEEN
POTION
ROBSON
RODMAN
RODMEN
ROTTEN
SOCMAN
SOCMEN
SODDEN
SOFTEN
SOLEMN
SOLION
TOCSIN
TONKIN
TOULON
WOODEN
WOOLEN
WORSEN
YOUPON

••ON••

ADONAI
ADONIC
ADONIS
AGONES
AGONIC
ALONSO
ALONZO
ANONYM
ATONAL
ATONED
ATONER
ATONES
ATONIC
AXONES
AZONIC
BLONDE
BLONDS
BRONCO
BRONCS
BRONTE
BRONZE
BRONZY
CHONDR
CLONES
CLONIC
CLONUS
CRONES
CRONUS
DRONED
DRONES
DRONGO
EPONYM
FLONGS
FRONDS
FRONTO
FRONTS
GOONEY
ICONIC
IRONED
IRONER
IRONIC
KRONEN
KRONER
KRONOR
KRONUR
LEONAS
LEONIE
LIONEL
MOONED
ODONTO
OZONIC
PHONED
PHONES
PHONEY
PHONIA
PHONIC
PRONGS
PRONTO
SCONCE
SCONES
SOONER
SPONGE
SPONGY
STONED
STONER
STONES
TBONES
THONGS
WRONGS
YVONNE
ZOONAL

••O•N•

ABOUND
ACORNS
ADORNS
AMOUNT
ANOINT
AROUND
BOOING
BROWNS
CLOWNS
COOING
CROONS
CROWNS
DROWNS
ELOINS
FROWNS
GROANS
GROINS
GROUND
LOOING
MOOING
PROCNE
QUOINS
SCORNS
SPOONS
SPOONY
SWOONS
THORNS
THORNY
WOOING
YVONNE

••O••N

AJOWAN
BIOGEN
BIOTIN
BROGAN
BROKEN
CHOPIN
CHOSEN
CLOVEN
CROTON
DROMON
DUODEN
ELOIGN

EXOGEN
FLORIN
FROZEN
GLOBIN
GNOMON
IMOGEN
ISOGON
KAOLIN
KRONEN
LOOKIN
LOOSEN
MYOSIN
PHOTON
PROTON
PROVEN
REOPEN
SHOGUN
SHOOIN
SHORAN
SIOUAN
SLOGAN
SLOVEN
SPOKEN
STOLEN
STOLON
THORON
TROGON
TROJAN
VIOLIN
WOODEN
WOOLEN
YEOMAN
YEOMEN

•••ON•

AARONS
ALFONS
ALMOND
ANCONA
ANCONE
ANIONS
ANTONS
ANTONY
ANYONE
APRONS
BARONG
BARONS
BARONY
BATONS
BELONG
BETONY
BEYOND
BRYONY
BYGONE
CANONS
CAPONS
CHRONO
COLONS
COLONY
CORONA
CROONS
DEMONO
DEMONS
DUGONG
EDMOND
EVZONE
FANONS
FELONS
FELONY
FREONS
GIPONS
GYRONS
HERONS
HEXONE
HURONS
INTONE
IONONE
JASONS
JUPONS
KALONG
KETONE
KIMONO
LEMONS
LOMOND
MASONS
MEKONG
MELONS
MESONS
MORONS
NYLONS
OBLONG
ONIONS
OOLONG
OSMOND
PAEONS
PINONS
PITONS
POMONA
PUTONS
PYLONS
PYRONE
RAMONA
RAYONS
REDONE
RUNONS
SALONS
SARONG
SAXONS
SAXONY
SCIONS
SECOND
SETONS
SIMONE
SIMONS
SIMONY
SPOONS
SPOONY
STRONG
SWOONS
TALONS
TENONS
TETONS
THRONE
THRONG
TOYONS
TYRONE
UNDONE
UNIONS
VERONA
WAGONS
YAPONS
YUPONS
ZIRONS

•••O•N

ADJOIN
ADNOUN
ATTORN
BABOON
BEMOAN
BICORN
COCOON
DAHOON
DEHORN
DISOWN
ENJOIN
HEROIN
INBORN
LAGOON
MAROON
MINOAN
OHIOAN
OSBORN
RACOON
RATOON
REBORN
REJOIN
RENOWN
SALOON
SAMOAN
SHOOIN
SUBORN
THROWN
TYCOON
UNBORN
UPTOWN

••••ON

ACTION
ALBION
ALISON
AMAZON
AMNION
ARAGON
ARCHON
AVALON
BABOON
BARTON
BARYON
BASION
BEACON
BECKON
BENTON
BILLON
BLAZON
BOLSON
BONBON
BOSTON
BRETON
BRITON
BUNION
BUTTON
CAMION
CANNON
CANTON
CANYON
CARBON
CARSON
CARTON
CATION
CEYLON
CHARON
CHIRON
CHITON
CITRON
COCOON
COMEON
COMMON
CORDON
COTTON
COUPON
CRAYON
CROTON
DACRON
DAEMON
DAHOON
DAIMON
DALTON
DAMSON
DANTON
DAWSON
DAYTON
DEACON
DOBLON
DOBSON
DONJON
DRAGON
DROMON
DURION
EASTON
EDISON
ELEVON
ETYMON
FALCON
FANION
FLACON
FLAGON
FULTON
FUSION
GABION
GALLON
GAMMON
GARCON
GASCON
GASTON
GERYON
GIBBON
GIBSON
GIDEON
GNOMON
GODSON
GONION
GORDON
GORGON
GUENON
GUIDON
HAGDON
HEADON
HEBRON
HEDRON
HEREON
HUDSON
INCHON
ISOGON
JARGON
JETTON
JONSON
KATION
KEDRON
KLAXON
LAGOON
LARDON
LEGION
LEPTON
LESION
LESSON
LISBON
LOGION
LONDON
LOTION
MACRON
MAISON
MAMMON
MARION
MAROON
MASCON
MATRON
MELLON
MELTON
MERLON
MICRON
MIGNON
MILTON
MINION
MORION
MORMON
MORTON
MOTION
MOUTON
MUTTON
NASION
NATION
NATRON
NEKTON
NELSON
NEURON
NEWTON
NIPPON
NOTION
OBERON
OPTION
OREGON
PARDON
PARSON
PATRON
PATTON
PELION
PENNON
PERRON
PERSON
PHOTON
PIGEON
PINION
PISTON
POISON
POMPON
PONTON
POTION
PRISON
PROTON
PYTHON
QUEZON
RACOON
RAMSON
RATION
RATOON
REASON
RECKON
REGION
RIBBON
ROBSON
RUNYON
SAIGON
SALMON
SALOON
SAMSON
SARGON
SEASON
SERMON
SEXTON
SHARON
SIMEON
SIPHON
SLIPON
SOLION
STOLON
SUMMON
TALION
TAMPON
TARPON
TEFLON
TELSON
TENDON
TESTON
TEUTON
THORON
TOULON
TRIGON
TROGON
TUCSON
TYCOON
TYPHON
UNISON
VERNON
VILLON
VINSON
VISION
WAGGON
WALKON
WALTON
WANION
WANTON
WATSON
WEAPON

WIGEON
WILSON
YAUPON
YOUPON
ZIRCON

OO••••
OOCYTE
OODLES
OOLITE
OOLOGY
OOLONG
OOMIAK
OOPHOR
OOZIER
OOZILY
OOZING

O•O•••
OBOIST
OBOLUS
ODONTO
OROIDE
OZONIC

O••O••
OBLONG
OCLOCK
OCTOPI
ODIOUS
OGDOAD
OHIOAN
ONIONS
OOLOGY
OOLONG
OPPOSE
ORIOLE
ORLOPS
ORMOLU
OSBORN
OSMOND
OSMOSE
OTIOSE
OXBOWS
OXFORD

O•••O•
OBERON
OCELOT
OCTROI
OOPHOR
OPTION
ORATOR
OREGON
OUTFOX
OVIBOS

O••••O
OCTAVO
ODONTO
ONEIRO
ORCHIO
ORGANO
OVERDO

•OO•••
BOOBOO
BOODLE
BOOHOO
BOOING
BOOKED
BOOKIE
BOOMED
BOOSTS
BOOTED
BOOTEE
BOOTHS
BOOTIE
BOOZED
BOOZER
BOOZES
COOEED
COOEES
COOERS
COOEYS
COOING
COOKED
COOKER
COOKEY
COOKIE
COOLED
COOLER
COOLIE
COOLLY
COOMBS
COOPED
COOPER
COOPTS
COOTIE
DOODAD
DOODLE
DOOLEE
DOOLIE
DOOMED
FOOLED
FOOTED
FOOTER
FOOTLE
FOOZLE
GOOBER
GOODBY
GOODLY
GOOFED
GOOGLY
GOOGOL
GOOIER
GOONEY
GOORAL
GOOSED
GOOSES
GOOSEY
HOODED
HOODOO
HOOFED
HOOFER
HOOKAH
HOOKED
HOOKER
HOOKUP

HOOPED
HOOPER
HOOPLA
HOOPOE
HOORAY
HOOTCH
HOOTED
HOOVER
HOOVES
KOODOO
LOOFAH
LOOING
LOOKED
LOOKER
LOOKIN
LOOMED
LOOPED
LOOPER
LOOSED
LOOSEN
LOOSER
LOOSES
LOOTED
LOOTER
MOOING
MOOLAH
MOOLEY
MOONED
MOORED
MOOTED
MOOTER
NOODLE
NOOSED
NOOSES
POODLE
POOLED
POOPED
POORER
POORLY
ROOFED
ROOFER
ROOKED
ROOKIE
ROOMED
ROOMER
ROOSTS
ROOTED
ROOTER
SOONER
SOOTED
SOOTHE
TOOLED
TOOLER
TOOTED
TOOTER
TOOTHY
TOOTLE
TOOTSY
VOODOO
WOODED
WOODEN
WOODSY
WOOERS
WOOFER

WOOING
WOOLEN
WOOLLY
YOOHOO
ZOOIDS
ZOOMED
ZOONAL

•O•O••
BOGOTA
BOSOMS
COCOAS
COCOON
COHORT
COHOSH
COLONS
COLONY
COLORS
COLOUS
COMOSE
COMOUS
CONOID
COPOUT
CORODY
CORONA
COYOTE
DODOES
DONORS
EOZOIC
HOBOES
HONORE
HONORS
IODOUS
IONONE
JOCOSE
JOYOUS
KOBOLD
KOKOMO
LOCOED
LOMOND
MOHOCK
MOHOLE
MOLOCH
MONODY
MOPOKE
MORONS
MOROSE
MOTORS
NODOSE
OOLOGY
OOLONG
PODOUS
POMONA
POROUS
POYOUS
ROBOTS
ROCOCO
ROMOLA
ROTORS
SODOMY
SOLOED
SOTOLS
TOROID
TOROSE

TOROUS
TOYONS
VOLOST
VOROUS

•O••O•
BOLSON
BONBON
BONGOS
BOOBOO
BOOHOO
BORROW
BORZOI
BOSTON
BOTTOM
BOWWOW
COCOON
COELOM
COLLOP
COMBOS
COMEON
COMMON
COMPOS
CONDOM
CONDOR
CONGOU
CONTOS
CONVOY
CORDON
COSMOS
COTTON
COUPON
COWBOY
COWPOX
DOBLON
DOBSON
DOCTOR
DOLLOP
DONJON
FOETOR
FOGBOW
FOGDOG
FOLIOS
FOLLOW
FORGOT
GODSON
GONION
GOOGOL
GORDON
GORGON
HOBNOB
HOLLOW
HOODOO
HOOPOE
HORROR
HOTBOX
JOCKOS
JONSON
KOODOO
KOWTOW
LOGION
LONDON
LOTION
LOWBOY

MONGOL
MONROE
MORION
MORMON
MORROS
MORROW
MORTON
MOSCOW
MOTION
MOTMOT
MOTTOS
MOUTON
NONCOM
NOSHOW
NOSTOC
NOTION
OOPHOR
PODSOL
PODZOL
POGROM
POISON
POMPOM
POMPON
PONTON
POTBOY
POTION
POTTOS
POWWOW
ROBSON
RODEOS
RONDOS
ROSCOE
SOLION
SORGOS
SORROW
TOLUOL
TOMBOY
TOMCOD
TOMTOM
TORPOR
TORSOS
TOULON
VOLVOX
VOODOO
YOOHOO
YOUPON

•O•••O
BOLERO
BONITO
BOOBOO
BOOHOO
BORNEO
COLUGO
COMEDO
DOMINO
DORADO
FOREGO
HOODOO
KOKOMO
KOODOO
MORPHO
NONEGO
POMELO

6

PONCHO
POTATO
POUSTO
ROBALO
ROCOCO
ROMULO
SOLANO
SOMATO
SORGHO
TOBAGO
TOLEDO
TOMATO
TORERO
VOMITO
VOODOO
YOOHOO

••OO••
BLOODS
BLOODY
BLOOMS
BLOOMY
BROOCH
BROODS
BROODY
BROOKS
BROOMS
BROOMY
CHOOSE
CHOOSY
CROOKS
CROONS
DROOLS
DROOPS
DROOPY
FLOODS
FLOORS
FLOOZY
GLOOMS
GLOOMY
GROOMS
GROOVE
GROOVY
KLOOFS
PHOOEY
PROOFS
SCOOPS
SCOOTS
SHOOED
SHOOIN
SHOOTS
SLOOPS
SMOOCH
SMOOTH
SNOODS
SNOOKS
SNOOPS
SNOOPY
SNOOTS
SNOOTY
SNOOZE
SPOOFS
SPOOKS
SPOOKY
SPOOLS
SPOONS
SPOONY
SPOORS
STOOGE
STOOKS
STOOLS
STOOPS
SWOONS
SWOOPS
TROOPS
WHOOPS

••O•O•
APOLOG
BOOBOO
BOOHOO
CROTON
DIOBOL
DROMON
DUOLOG
FEODOR
GNOMON
GOOGOL
HOODOO
HOOPOE
IGOROT
ISOGON
ISOPOD
KOODOO
KRONOR
PHOTON
PHOTOS
PROTON
STOLON
THORON
TROGON
UROPOD
VOODOO
YOOHOO

••O••O
ALONSO
ALONZO
APOLLO
BOOBOO
BOOHOO
BRONCO
CHOREO
CLOTHO
DRONGO
FRONTO
GIOTTO
GLOSSO
GLOTTO
GROTTO
HOODOO
ILOILO
KOODOO
ODONTO
PROCTO
PRONTO
TROPHO
VOODOO
YOOHOO

•••OO•
ABLOOM
BABOON
BABOOS
BEFOOL
BEHOOF
BETOOK
COCOON
DAHOON
ENROOT
EXMOOR
GALOOT
IGLOOS
INDOOR
KAZOOS
LAGOON
MAROON
RACOON
RATOON
RETOOK
SALOON
SALOOP
SCHOOL
SCROOP
SIMOOM
TABOOS
TYCOON
UNHOOK
UNMOOR
UNROOT
UPROOT
WAHOOS
YAHOOS

•••O•O
ARIOSO
ARROYO
CHLORO
CHROMO
CHRONO
DEMONO
ENTOMO
FLUORO
GIGOLO
KIMONO
KOKOMO
REBOZO
ROCOCO

••••OO
BAMBOO
BOOBOO
BOOHOO
BURGOO
CASHOO
CUCKOO
GENTOO
HALLOO
HOODOO
KARROO
KOODOO
TATTOO
VOODOO
YOOHOO

OP••••
OPAQUE
OPENED
OPENER
OPENLY
OPERAS
OPHITE
OPIATE
OPINED
OPINES
OPPOSE
OPPUGN
OPTICS
OPTIMA
OPTIME
OPTING
OPTION

O•P•••
OOPHOR
OPPOSE
OPPUGN
ORPHAN
ORPHIC
ORPINE
ORPINS
OSPREY

O••P••
OKAPIS
OUTPUT

O•••P•
OCCUPY
OCTOPI
ORLOPS
OXLIPS

•OP•••
BOPPED
COPALM
COPIED
COPIER
COPIES
COPING
COPLEY
COPOUT
COPPED
COPPER
COPPRA
COPRAH
COPSES
COPTIC
COPULA
DOPIER
DOPING
GOPHER
HOPING
HOPPED
HOPPER
HOPPLE
JOPLIN
KOPECK
KOPEKS
KOPJES
LOPERS
LOPING
LOPPED
MOPERS
MOPING
MOPISH
MOPOKE
MOPPED
MOPPET
NOPALS
OOPHOR
POPERY
POPGUN
POPISH
POPLAR
POPLIN
POPPED
POPPER
POPPET
POPPLE
POPPYS
ROPIER
ROPILY
ROPING
SOPHIA
SOPHIE
SOPPED
TOPEKA
TOPERS
TOPICS
TOPING
TOPPED
TOPPER
TOPPLE

•O•P••
BOPPED
COMPEL
COMPLY
COMPOS
COOPED
COOPER
COOPTS
COPPED
COPPER
COPPRA
CORPSE
CORPUS
COUPES
COUPLE
COUPON
COWPEA
COWPER
COWPOX
COYPUS
DOLPHS
GOSPEL
HOOPED
HOOPER
HOOPLA
HOOPOE
HOPPED
HOPPER
HOPPLE
LOOPED
LOOPER
LOPPED
LOUPES
MOPPED
MOPPET
MORPHO
POMPEY
POMPOM
POMPON
POOPED
POPPED
POPPER
POPPET
POPPLE
POPPYS
POTPIE
ROLPHS
ROMPED
ROMPER
SOAPED
SOPPED
TOPPED
TOPPER
TOPPLE
TORPID
TORPOR
TOUPEE
YOUPON

•O••P•
COEMPT
DOGAPE
JOSEPH
POLYPS

•O•••P
COCKUP
COLLOP
DOLLOP
GOSSIP
HOLDUP
HOOKUP
LOCKUP
MOBCAP
MOCKUP
TOECAP
TOSSUP

••OP••
ADOPTS
BIOPSY
CHOPIN
CHOPPY
COOPED
COOPER
COOPTS
DROPSY
ELOPED
ELOPER

6

ELOPES
EPOPEE
FLOPPY
GROPED
GROPER
GROPES
HOOPED
HOOPER
HOOPLA
HOOPOE
ISOPOD
LOOPED
LOOPER
MYOPES
MYOPIA
MYOPIC
PEOPLE
POOPED
PROPEL
PROPER
PROPYL
REOPEN
SCOPES
SCOPUS
SHOPPE
SLOPED
SLOPER
SLOPES
SLOPPY
STOPED
STOPES
TROPAL
TROPHO
TROPHY
TROPIC
TWOPLY
UROPOD
UTOPIA

••O•P•

ADOLPH
CHOPPY
CROUPE
CROUPS
CROUPY
DROOPS
DROOPY
FLOPPY
GROUPS
KNOSPS
PHOSPH
PROMPT
SCOOPS
SHOPPE
SLOOPS
SLOPPY
SNOOPS
SNOOPY
STOMPS
STOOPS
STOUPS
SWOOPS
THORPE
TROOPS
TROUPE
WHOOPS

••O••P

BLOWUP
HOOKUP

•••OP•

ASLOPE
CANOPY
CHEOPS
DROOPS
DROOPY
ESTOPS
EUROPA
EUROPE
FSTOPS
GALOPS
JALOPY
METOPE
OCTOPI
ORLOPS
PELOPS
PYROPE
SCOOPS
SLOOPS
SNOOPS
SNOOPY
STOOPS
STROPS
SWOOPS
TROOPS
WHOOPS
WICOPY

•••O•P

INCORP
RECOUP
SALOOP
SCROOP

••••OP

BISHOP
CARHOP
COLLOP
DOLLOP
GALLOP
HYSSOP
MAYPOP
PEGTOP
REDTOP
SALOOP
SCROOP
TIPTOP
UNSTOP
WALLOP

O••Q••

OPAQUE

•OQ•••

COQUET
LOQUAT
ROQUET
TOQUES

•O•Q••

MOSQUE
TORQUE

OR••••

ORACHS
ORACLE
ORALLY
ORANGE
ORANGS
ORATED
ORATES
ORATOR
ORBING
ORBITS
ORCEIN
ORCHID
ORCHIL
ORCHIO
ORCHIS
ORDAIN
ORDEAL
ORDERS
ORDURE
OREADS
OREGON
OREIDE
ORGANA
ORGANO
ORGANS
ORGASM
ORGEAT
ORGIES
ORIBIS
ORIELS
ORIENT
ORIGAN
ORIGEN
ORIGIN
ORIOLE
ORLOPS
ORMERS
ORMOLU
ORMUZD
ORNATE
ORNERY
ORNITH
OROIDE
ORPHAN
ORPHIC
ORPINE
ORPINS
ORRERY
ORRICE
ORWELL
ORYXES

O•R•••

OARING
OCREAE
OGRESS
OGRISH
ONRUSH
ORRERY
ORRICE

O••R••

OBERON
OCTROI
OPERAS
OSIRIS
OSPREY
OUTRAN
OUTRUN
OVERDO
OVERLY

O•••R•

OBVERT
OCCURS
OCHERS
OCHERY
OEUVRE
OFFERS
OGLERS
OHENRY
OILERS
ONAGRI
ONEIRO
ONWARD
ORDERS
ORDURE
ORMERS
ORNERY
ORRERY
OSBERT
OSBORN
OSCARS
OSIERS
OTHERS
OTTERS
OUTCRY
OUTERS
OWNERS
OXFORD

O••••R

OBEYER
OCULAR
OILIER
OLIVER
ONAGER
OOPHOR
OOZIER
OPENER
ORATOR
OUSTER
OVULAR
OYSTER

•OR•••

AORIST
AORTAE
AORTAL
AORTAS
AORTIC
BORAGE
BORANE
BORATE
BORDEL
BORDER
BOREAL
BOREAS
BORERS
BORGIA
BORIDE
BORING
BORNEO
BORROW
BORSCH
BORZOI
CORALS
CORBAN
CORBEL
CORDAY
CORDED
CORDER
CORDON
CORERS
CORGIS
CORING
CORIUM
CORKED
CORKER
CORNEA
CORNED
CORNEL
CORNER
CORNET
CORNUA
CORNUS
CORODY
CORONA
CORPSE
CORPUS
CORRAL
CORSAC
CORSES
CORSET
CORTES
CORTEX
CORTEZ
CORTIN
CORVEE
CORVES
CORVUS
CORYMB
CORYZA
DORADO
DORBUG
DOREEN
DORIAN
DORIES
DORMER
DORMIE
DORSAD
DORSAL
DORSUM
FORAGE
FORAYS
FORBAD
FORBID
FORCED
FORCER
FORCES
FORDED
FOREGO
FOREST
FORGED
FORGER
FORGES
FORGET
FORGOT
FORINT
FORKED
FORMAL
FORMAT
FORMED
FORMER
FORMIC
FORMYL
FORNAX
FORNIX
FORTES
FORTIS
FORUMS
GORALS
GORDON
GORGED
GORGER
GORGES
GORGET
GORGON
GORHEN
GORIER
GORILY
GORING
GORSES
HORACE
HORARY
HORDED
HORDES
HORNED
HORNET
HORNIE
HORRID
HORROR
HORSED
HORSES
HORSEY
HORSTE
JORAMS
JORDAN
JORGES
JORUMS
KOREAN
KORUNA
KORUNY
LORAIN
LORDED
LORDLY
LOREEN
LORENE
LORENZ

LORICA
LORIES
MORALE
MORALS
MORASS
MORAYS
MORBID
MOREAU
MOREEN
MORELS
MORGAN
MORGEN
MORGUE
MORION
MORLEY
MORMON
MORONS
MOROSE
MORPHO
MORRIS
MORROS
MORROW
MORSEL
MORTAL
MORTAR
MORTON
MORTYS
MORULA
NORDIC
NOREEN
NORIAS
NORMAL
NORMAN
NORMAS
NORNIR
NORRIS
NORWAY
PORING
PORKER
POROUS
PORTAL
PORTER
PORTIA
PORTLY
SORDID
SORELS
SORELY
SOREST
SORGHO
SORGOS
SORREL
SORROW
SORTED
SORTIE
TORAHS
TORERO
TORIES
TORIIS
TOROID
TOROSE
TOROUS
TORPID
TORPOR
TORQUE
TORRID
TORSKS
TORSOS
VOROUS
VORTEX
WORDED
WORKED
WORKER
WORLDS
WORMED
WORMER
WORSEN
WORSER
WORSTS
WORTHY
YORUBA
ZORILS

•O•R••

BOARDS
BORROW
BOURGS
BOURNE
BOURNS
BOURSE
COARSE
COBRAS
COERCE
CONRAD
COPRAH
CORRAL
COURSE
COURTS
COWRIE
DOBRAS
DOURLY
FOURTH
GOORAL
GOURDE
GOURDS
HOARDS
HOARSE
HOORAY
HORRID
HORROR
HOURIS
HOURLY
KONRAD
LOURED
MOIRAS
MONROE
MOORED
MORRIS
MORROS
MORROW
MOURNS
NORRIS
POGROM
POORER
POORLY
POURED
POURER
ROARED
ROARER
SOARED
SOARER
SOCRED
SOIREE
SORREL
SORROW
SOURCE
SOURED
SOURER
SOURLY
TORRID
TOURED

•O••R•

BOLERO
BONERS
BORERS
BOWERS
BOWERY
BOXERS
BOYARD
BOYARS
COHERE
COHORT
COLORS
COLURE
COMERS
CONTRA
CONTRE
COOERS
COPPRA
CORERS
COVERS
COVERT
COWARD
COWERS
DONORS
DOSERS
DOTERS
DOWERS
DOWERY
FOYERS
GOCART
GOKART
GONERS
GOVERN
HOBART
HOLARD
HOMBRE
HOMERS
HONORE
HONORS
HORARY
HOVERS
HOWARD
JOKERS
LONERS
LOPERS
LOSERS
LOUVRE
LOVERS
LOWERS
LOWERY
MODERN
MOHURS
MOLARS
MOPERS
MOTORS
MOVERS
MOWERS
MOZART
NOMURA
NOTARY
NOTERS
POETRY
POKERS
POPERY
POSERS
POWERS
ROBERT
ROGERS
ROSARY
ROSTRA
ROTARY
ROTORS
ROVERS
ROWERS
SOBERS
SONARS
SOUARI
SOWARS
SOWERS
TONERS
TOPERS
TORERO
TOTERS
TOWARD
TOWERS
TOWERY
TOYERS
VOLERY
VOMERS
VOTARY
VOTERS
VOWERS
WOMERA
WOOERS
YOGURT
ZONARY

•O•••R

BOBBER
BOILER
BOLDER
BOLTER
BOMBER
BONDER
BONIER
BONZER
BOOZER
BORDER
BOTHER
BOWLER
BOWYER
BOXCAR
COALER
COAXER
COCKER
CODDER
CODGER
COFFER
COILER
COINER
COLDER
COLLAR
COLTER
COMBER
CONCUR
CONDOR
CONFER
CONGER
CONNER
COOKER
COOLER
COOPER
COPIER
COPPER
CORDER
CORKER
CORNER
COSHER
COSTAR
COTTAR
COTTER
COUGAR
COWPER
COZIER
DOBBER
DOCKER
DOCTOR
DODDER
DODGER
DOFFER
DOGEAR
DOGGER
DOLLAR
DOPIER
DORMER
DOSSER
DOTIER
DOTTER
DOWSER
DOZIER
FODDER
FOETOR
FOLDER
FOLIAR
FONDER
FOOTER
FORCER
FORGER
FORMER
FOSTER
FOULER
FOWLER
FOXIER
GOFFER
GOITER
GOLFER
GOOBER
GOOIER
GOPHER
GORGER
GORIER
GOUGER
HOAXER
HOLDER
HOLIER
HOLLER
HOMIER
HONKER
HOOFER
HOOKER
HOOPER
HOOVER
HOPPER
HORROR
HOSIER
HOTTER
HOWLER
JOBBER
JOGGER
JOINER
JOLTER
JOSHER
KOSHER
LOADER
LOAFER
LOCKER
LODGER
LOFTER
LOGGER
LOGIER
LOITER
LOLLER
LONGER
LOOKER
LOOPER
LOOSER
LOOTER
LOUDER
LOUVER
MOBBER
MOCKER
MOHAIR
MOILER
MOLDER
MOLTER
MONGER
MOOTER
MORTAR
MOTHER
MOUSER
NODDER
NORNIR
NOSIER
OOPHOR
OOZIER
POKIER
POLDER
POLLER
PONDER
POORER
POPLAR
POPPER
PORKER

6

PORTER
POSEUR
POSTER
POTHER
POTTER
POURER
POUTER
POWDER
POWTER
ROAMER
ROARER
ROBBER
ROCKER
ROLLER
ROMPER
ROOFER
ROOMER
ROOTER
ROPIER
ROSIER
ROSTER
ROTTER
ROUSER
ROUTER
SOAKER
SOARER
SOCCER
SOEVER
SOFTER
SOLDER
SOLVER
SOMBER
SONDER
SOONER
SOURER
TOILER
TOLLER
TONIER
TOOLER
TOOTER
TOPPER
TORPOR
TOTHER
TOTTER
TOUTER
VOYEUR
WOLVER
WONDER
WOOFER
WORKER
WORMER
WORSER
WOWSER
YONDER
YONKER
ZOSTER

••OR••

ABORAL
ABORTS
ACORNS
ADORED
ADORER
ADORES
ADORNS
AGORAE
AGORAS
AMORAL
ANORAK
AZORES
CEORLS
CHORAL
CHORDS
CHOREA
CHOREO
CHORES
CHORIC
CHORUS
CRORES
DVORAK
FIORDS
FJORDS
FLORAE
FLORAL
FLORAS
FLORET
FLORID
FLORIN
GEORGE
GEORGI
GLORIA
GOORAL
HOORAY
IGOROT
MAORIS
MOORED
PEORIA
POORER
POORLY
QUORUM
SCORCH
SCORED
SCORER
SCORES
SCORIA
SCORNS
SFORZA
SHORAN
SHORED
SHORES
SHORLS
SHORTS
SNORED
SNORER
SNORES
SNORTS
SPORED
SPORES
SPORTS
SPORTY
STORAX
STORED
STORES
STOREY
STORKS
STORMS
STORMY
SWORDS
THORAC
THORAX
THORIA
THORIC
THORNS
THORNY
THORON
THORPE
WHORED
WHORES
WHORLS
WHORTS

••O•R•

ABOARD
AMOURS
CHOIRS
COOERS
FLOORS
FLOURS
FLOURY
HHOURS
SCOURS
SHOERS
SPOORS
WOOERS

••O••R

ADORER
ATONER
AVOWER
BLOWER
BOOZER
BROKER
CHOKER
CHOLER
CHONDR
CLOSER
CLOVER
COOKER
COOLER
COOPER
CROZER
DEODAR
DROVER
ELOPER
FEODOR
FLOWER
FOOTER
GAOLER
GLOVER
GLOWER
GOOBER
GOOIER
GROCER
GROPER
GROVER
GROWER
HOOFER
HOOKER
HOOPER
HOOVER
IRONER
ISOBAR
ISOMER
KNOWER
KRONER
KRONOR
KRONUR
LOOKER
LOOPER
LOOSER
LOOTER
MOOTER
PLOVER
PLOWER
POORER
PROBER
PROPER
PROSER
PROVER
QUOTER
RIOTER
ROOFER
ROOMER
ROOTER
SCORER
SCOTER
SHOFAR
SHOVER
SHOWER
SLOPER
SLOWER
SMOKER
SNORER
SOONER
STOKER
STONER
STOVER
TOOLER
TOOTER
TROCAR
TROVER
TWOFER
WOOFER

•••OR•

ABHORS
ABSORB
ACCORD
ACTORS
ADSORB
AFFORD
ANGORA
ARBORI
ARBORS
ARDORS
ARMORS
ARMORY
ASHORE
ASSORT
ATTORN
AURORA
BEFORE
BICORN
BIFORM
BYWORD
BYWORK
CALORY
CAVORT
CHLORO
COHORT
COLORS
DECORS
DEFORM
DEHORN
DEPORT
DONORS
EFFORT
ENCORE
EPHORI
EPHORS
ERRORS
ESCORT
EUDORA
EXHORT
EXPORT
EXTORT
FAVORS
FEDORA
FEMORA
FETORS
FLOORS
FLUORO
FLUORS
FURORS
GALORE
HONORE
HONORS
HUMORS
IGNORE
IMPORT
INBORN
INCORP
INFORM
JURORS
LABORS
LAHORE
LENORE
MAJORS
MALORY
MANORS
MASORA
MAYORS
MEMORY
MILORD
MINORS
MOTORS
OSBORN
OXFORD
PRIORS
PRIORY
RAZORS
REBORN
RECORD
REFORM
REMORA
REPORT
RESORB
RESORT
RETORT
REWORD
RIGORS
ROTORS
RUMORS
SATORI
SAVORS
SAVORY
SCHORL
SENORA
SPOORS
SUBORN
TABORS
TENORS
THEORY
TUMORS
TUTORS
UNBORN
UNCORK
VAPORI
VAPORS
VISORS
VIZORS

•••O•R

BEZOAR
DETOUR
DEVOIR
DEVOUR
ECHOER
EXMOOR
GIAOUR
INDOOR
LABOUR
MEMOIR
RENOIR
UNDOER
UNMOOR
UPROAR
VELOUR
VETOER
VIGOUR

••••OR

ABATOR
ANCHOR
ANGKOR
AUTHOR
BAILOR
BANGOR
BETTOR
CANDOR
CANTOR
CAPTOR
CASTOR
CENSOR
CLAMOR
CONDOR
DEBTOR
DOCTOR
EDITOR
ENAMOR
EXMOOR
FACTOR
FEODOR
FERVOR

FLAVOR
FLEXOR
FOETOR
HARBOR
HECTOR
HORROR
INDOOR
ISADOR
ISIDOR
JAILOR
JUNIOR
KRONOR
LECTOR
LESSOR
LICTOR
LIQUOR
MENTOR
METEOR
MIRROR
NESTOR
OOPHOR
ORATOR
PALLOR
PARLOR
PASTOR
PAVIOR
PICTOR
PLEXOR
PRETOR
RANCOR
RECTOR
RHETOR
SAILOR
SALVOR
SARTOR
SAVIOR
SECTOR
SEISOR
SEIZOR
SENIOR
SENSOR
SIGNOR
STATOR
STUPOR
SUCCOR
SUITOR
TAILOR
TAYLOR
TENSOR
TERMOR
TERROR
TORPOR
TREMOR
UNMOOR
VECTOR
VENDOR
VIATOR
VICTOR

OS••••

OSBERT
OSBORN
OSCANS
OSCARS
OSCINE
OSCULE
OSIERS
OSIRIS
OSMIUM
OSMOND
OSMOSE
OSMUND
OSPREY
OSSEIN
OSSIAN
OSSIFY
OSTEAL
OSWALD

O•S•••

OBSESS
ONSETS
OSSEIN
OSSIAN
OSSIFY
OUSELS
OUSTED
OUSTER
OYSTER

O••S••

OCASEY
ODESSA
OFFSET
OMASUM
ONUSES
OUTSAT
OUTSET
OUTSIT
OVISAC

O•••S•

OAFISH
OBIISM
OBLAST
OBOIST
OBSESS
OBTEST
OBTUSE
ODDEST
ODESSA
OFFISH
OGRESS
OGRISH
OLDEST
OLDISH
ONRUSH
OPPOSE
ORGASM
OSMOSE
OTIOSE
OWLISH

O••••S

OBELUS
OBOLUS
OBSESS
OCCURS
OCEANS
OCHERS
OCTADS
OCTETS
ODIOUS
OFFERS
OGIVES
OGLERS
OGRESS
OILERS
OKAPIS
OLIVES
OLLIES
OMEGAS
ONIONS
ONSETS
ONUSES
OODLES
OPERAS
OPINES
OPTICS
ORACHS
ORANGS
ORATES
ORBITS
ORCHIS
ORDERS
OREADS
ORGANS
ORGIES
ORIBIS
ORIELS
ORLOPS
ORMERS
ORPINS
ORYXES
OSCANS
OSCARS
OSIERS
OSIRIS
OTHERS
OTITIS
OTTERS
OUNCES
OUSELS
OUTERS
OUZELS
OVIBOS
OVULES
OWLETS
OWNERS
OXALIS
OXBOWS
OXEYES
OXIDES
OXLIPS

•OS•••

BOSHES
BOSKET
BOSOMS
BOSSED
BOSSES
BOSTON
COSHED
COSHER
COSHES
COSIGN
COSINE
COSMIC
COSMOS
COSSES
COSSET
COSTAE
COSTAL
COSTAR
COSTED
COSTLY
DOSAGE
DOSERS
DOSING
DOSSAL
DOSSEL
DOSSER
DOSSIL
FOSSAE
FOSSES
FOSSIL
FOSTER
GOSHEN
GOSPEL
GOSSIP
HOSIER
HOSING
HOSTED
HOSTEL
JOSEPH
JOSHED
JOSHER
JOSHES
JOSHUA
JOSIAH
JOSIAS
JOSIES
JOSSES
JOSTLE
KOSHER
LOSERS
LOSING
LOSSES
MOSAIC
MOSCOW
MOSEYS
MOSLEM
MOSLEY
MOSQUE
MOSSES
MOSTLY
NOSHOW
NOSIER
NOSILY
NOSING
NOSTOC
POSADA
POSERS
POSEUR
POSIES
POSING
POSITS
POSSES
POSSET
POSSUM
POSTAL
POSTED
POSTER
ROSARY
ROSCOE
ROSIER
ROSILY
ROSING
ROSINS
ROSINY
ROSTER
ROSTRA
TOSHES
TOSSED
TOSSES
TOSSUP
ZOSTER

•O•S••

BOASTS
BOLSON
BONSAI
BOOSTS
BORSCH
BOSSED
BOSSES
BOUSED
BOUSES
BOWSED
BOWSES
COASTS
CONSUL
COPSES
CORSAC
CORSES
CORSET
COSSES
COSSET
COUSIN
DOBSON
DOESNT
DORSAD
DORSAL
DORSUM
DOSSAL
DOSSEL
DOSSER
DOSSIL
DOUSED
DOUSES
DOWSED
DOWSER
DOWSES
FOCSLE
FOISTS
FOSSAE
FOSSES
FOSSIL
GODSON
GOOSED
GOOSES
GOOSEY
GORSES
GOSSIP
HOISTS
HONSHU
HORSED
HORSES
HORSEY
HORSTE
HOUSED
HOUSES
JOISTS
JONSON
JOSSES
JOUSTS
LOOSED
LOOSEN
LOOSER
LOOSES
LOSSES
LOUSED
LOUSES
MOISHE
MORSEL
MOSSES
MOUSED
MOUSER
MOUSES
MOUSSE
NOESIS
NOISED
NOISES
NOOSED
NOOSES
PODSOL
POISED
POISES
POISON
POSSES
POSSET
POSSUM
POTSIE
POUSTO
ROASTS
ROBSON
ROOSTS
ROUSED
ROUSER
ROUSES
ROUSTS
SOUSED
SOUSES
TOASTS
TOCSIN
TONSIL
TORSKS
TORSOS
TOSSED
TOSSES
TOSSUP
TOUSLE
WOLSEY
WORSEN

WORSER
WORSTS
WOWSER
ZOYSIA

•O••S•

AORIST
BOURSE
BOYISH
COARSE
COHOSH
COMOSE
CORPSE
COURSE
COYISH
DOVISH
EONISM
FOLKSY
FOREST
HOARSE
HOLISM
HONEST
IODISM
JOCOSE
LOCUST
LOUISA
LOUISE
LOWEST
MODEST
MODISH
MOLEST
MOMISM
MONGST
MONISM
MONIST
MOPISH
MORASS
MOROSE
MOUSSE
NODOSE
NOMISM
NOWISE
POLISH
POPISH
POTASH
ROBUST
ROMISH
SOREST
TOOTSY
TOROSE
TOYISH
VOLOST
WOODSY

•O•••S

AORTAS
BOARDS
BOASTS
BOBBYS
BODIES
BOGANS
BOGEYS
BOGIES
BOGLES
BOMBES
BONERS
BONGOS
BONNYS
BONZES
BOOSTS
BOOTHS
BOOZES
BOREAS
BORERS
BOSHES
BOSOMS
BOSSES
BOUGHS
BOULES
BOUNDS
BOURGS
BOURNS
BOUSES
BOWELS
BOWERS
BOWSES
BOXERS
BOYARS
COASTS
COATIS
COAXES
COBIAS
COBLES
COBRAS
COCCUS
COCOAS
COIGNS
COLEUS
COLIES
COLINS
COLONS
COLORS
COLOUS
COLZAS
COMBOS
COMERS
COMETS
COMICS
COMMAS
COMOUS
COMPOS
CONCHS
CONEYS
CONGAS
CONGES
CONICS
CONIES
CONTES
CONTOS
COOEES
COOERS
COOEYS
COOMBS
COOPTS
COPIES
COPSES
CORALS
CORERS
CORGIS
CORNUS
CORPUS
CORSES
CORTES
CORVES
CORVUS
COSHES
COSMOS
COSSES
COTTAS
COUGHS
COUNTS
COUPES
COURTS
COVERS
COVETS
COVEYS
COWERS
COYPUS
COZENS
COZIES
DOALLS
DOBIES
DOBLAS
DOBRAS
DODGES
DODOES
DOGIES
DOGMAS
DOINGS
DOLLYS
DOLPHS
DONEES
DONETS
DONNAS
DONORS
DORIES
DOSERS
DOTERS
DOUBTS
DOUGHS
DOUSES
DOWELS
DOWERS
DOWSES
DOXIES
DOYENS
DOZENS
FOEHNS
FOETUS
FOGIES
FOISTS
FOLIOS
FORAYS
FORCES
FORGES
FORTES
FORTIS
FORUMS
FOSSES
FOUNDS
FOUNTS
FOYERS
GOBIES
GOINGS
GONADS
GONERS
GOOSES
GORALS
GORGES
GORSES
GOUGES
GOURDS
HOARDS
HOAXES
HOBBES
HOBOES
HOGANS
HOICKS
HOISTS
HOLIES
HOLLYS
HOLMES
HOMERS
HONEYS
HONORS
HOOVES
HORDES
HORSES
HOTELS
HOUNDS
HOURIS
HOUSES
HOVELS
HOVERS
IODOUS
IOLCUS
JOCKOS
JOINTS
JOISTS
JOKERS
JONAHS
JORAMS
JORGES
JORUMS
JOSHES
JOSIAS
JOSIES
JOSSES
JOULES
JOUSTS
JOYCES
JOYOUS
KOALAS
KODAKS
KOINES
KOPEKS
KOPJES
LOAVES
LOCALS
LODGES
LONERS
LOOSES
LOPERS
LORIES
LOSERS
LOSSES
LOTAHS
LOUGHS
LOUPES
LOUSES
LOVERS
LOWERS
MOBIUS
MODELS
MOGULS
MOHURS
MOIRAS
MOLARS
MOLIES
MOLLYS
MONADS
MONEYS
MONIES
MONTES
MONTHS
MONTYS
MOPERS
MORALS
MORASS
MORAYS
MORELS
MORONS
MORRIS
MORROS
MORTYS
MOSEYS
MOSSES
MOTELS
MOTIFS
MOTORS
MOTTOS
MOULDS
MOULTS
MOUNTS
MOURNS
MOUSES
MOUTHS
MOVERS
MOVIES
MOWERS
NOESIS
NOISES
NOMADS
NOOSES
NOPALS
NORIAS
NORMAS
NORRIS
NOTERS
NOVELS
NOWAYS
OODLES
PODOUS
POGIES
POILUS
POINDS
POINTS
POISES
POKERS
POKIES
POLKAS
POLLYS
POLYPS
PONIES
PONTES
POPPYS
POROUS
POSERS
POSIES
POSITS
POSSES
POTTOS
POULTS
POUNDS
POWERS
POYOUS
ROALDS
ROASTS
ROBINS
ROBLES
ROBOTS
RODDYS
RODEOS
ROGERS
ROGUES
ROLPHS
ROMANS
RONDOS
ROOSTS
ROSINS
ROTORS
ROUGES
ROUGHS
ROUNDS
ROUSES
ROUSTS
ROUTES
ROVERS
ROWANS
ROWELS
ROWERS
ROYALS
SOBERS
SOCLES
SOFTAS
SOLANS
SOLIDS
SOLVES
SONARS
SONIAS
SONYAS
SORELS
SORGOS
SOTHIS
SOTOLS
SOUGHS
SOUNDS
SOUSES
SOWARS
SOWERS
SOZINS
TOASTS
TOBIAS
TOBIES

TODIES
TOGUES
TOILES
TOKENS
TOMANS
TOMMYS
TONERS
TONICS
TOPERS
TOPICS
TOQUES
TORAHS
TORIES
TORIIS
TOROUS
TORSKS
TORSOS
TOSHES
TOSSES
TOTALS
TOTEMS
TOTERS
TOUGHS
TOWELS
TOWERS
TOXINS
TOYERS
TOYONS
VOCALS
VODKAS
VOGUES
VOGULS
VOICES
VOILES
VOLVAS
VOMERS
VOMITS
VOROUS
VOTERS
VOWELS
VOWERS
WOALDS
WOLVES
WOOERS
WORLDS
WORSTS
WOUNDS
YODELS
YOGEES
YOGINS
YOICKS
YOKELS
YOUTHS
ZOMBIS
ZOOIDS
ZORILS
ZOUNDS

••OS••

BIOSIS
BOOSTS
CHOSEN
CLOSED
CLOSER
CLOSES
CLOSET
CROSSE
DROSKY
DROSSY
ENOSIS
FLOSSY
FROSTS
FROSTY
GHOSTS
GLOSSO
GLOSSY
GLOSTS
GNOSIS
GOOSED
GOOSES
GOOSEY
GROSZY
KIOSKS
KNOSPS
LOOSED
LOOSEN
LOOSER
LOOSES
MIOSIS
MYOSIN
MYOSIS
NAOSES
NOOSED
NOOSES
PHOSPH
PROSED
PROSER
PROSES
PROSIT
PTOSIS
PYOSIS
ROOSTS
SLOSHY

••O•S•

ALONSO
AROUSE
BIOPSY
BLOUSE
BROWSE
CHOOSE
CHOOSY
CROSSE
DROPSY
DROSSY
DROWSE
DROWSY
EGOISM
EGOIST
ELOISE
FLOSSY
GLOSSO
GLOSSY
GROUSE
LAOTSE
MAOISM
MAOIST
OBOIST
PROUST
SPOUSE
TAOISM
TAOIST
TOOTSY
WOODSY

••O••S

ABODES
ABOHMS
ABOMAS
ABOMBS
ABORTS
ACORNS
ADOBES
ADONIS
ADOPTS
ADORES
ADORNS
AEOLIS
AEOLUS
AGONES
AGORAS
AMOLES
AMOURS
ANODES
AROIDS
AROMAS
ATOLLS
ATONES
AVOIDS
AXONES
AZOLES
AZORES
BIOSIS
BLOATS
BLOCKS
BLOKES
BLONDS
BLOODS
BLOOMS
BOOSTS
BOOTHS
BOOZES
BROADS
BROILS
BROMES
BRONCS
BROODS
BROOKS
BROOMS
BROTHS
BROWNS
CEORLS
CHOCKS
CHOIRS
CHOKES
CHORDS
CHORES
CHORUS
CLOAKS
CLOCKS
CLONES
CLONUS
CLOSES
CLOTHS
CLOUDS
CLOUTS
CLOVES
CLOVIS
CLOWNS
COOEES
COOERS
COOEYS
COOMBS
COOPTS
CROAKS
CROATS
CROCKS
CROCUS
CROFTS
CRONES
CRONUS
CROOKS
CROONS
CRORES
CROUPS
CROWDS
CROWNS
CROZES
DHOLES
DHOTIS
DIODES
DROITS
DROLLS
DRONES
DROOLS
DROOPS
DROVES
DROWNS
EBOATS
ECOLES
ELOINS
ELOPES
EMOTES
ENOSIS
EPOCHS
EPODES
ERODES
EVOKES
EXODUS
FEOFFS
FIORDS
FJORDS
FLOATS
FLOCKS
FLONGS
FLOODS
FLOORS
FLORAS
FLOURS
FLOUTS
FLOYDS
FROCKS
FRONDS
FRONTS
FROSTS
FROTHS
FROWNS
GEODES
GHOSTS
GHOULS
GLOATS
GLOBES
GLOOMS
GLOSTS
GLOVES
GLOZES
GNOMES
GNOSIS
GOOSES
GROANS
GROATS
GROINS
GROOMS
GROPES
GROUPS
GROUTS
GROVES
GROWLS
HBOMBS
HHOURS
HOOVES
HYOIDS
KIOSKS
KLOOFS
KNOCKS
KNOLLS
KNOSPS
KNOUTS
LEONAS
LLOYDS
LOOSES
MAORIS
MIOSIS
MYOPES
MYOSIS
NAOMIS
NAOSES
NOOSES
OBOLUS
PHOCIS
PHONES
PHOTOS
PROBES
PROEMS
PRONGS
PROOFS
PROSES
PROVES
PROWLS
PTOSIS
PYOSIS
QUOINS
QUOITS
QUOTAS
QUOTES
RAOULS
RHODAS
ROOSTS
SCOFFS
SCOLDS
SCONES
SCOOPS
SCOOTS
SCOPES
SCOPUS
SCORES
SCORNS
SCOTTS
SCOURS
SCOUTS
SCOWLS
SHOALS
SHOATS
SHOCKS
SHOERS
SHOJIS
SHOOTS
SHORES
SHORLS
SHORTS
SHOTES
SHOUTS
SHOVES
SLOOPS
SLOPES
SLOTHS
SMOCKS
SMOKES
SMOLTS
SNOODS
SNOOKS
SNOOPS
SNOOTS
SNORES
SNORTS
SNOUTS
SPOILS
SPOKES
SPOOFS
SPOOKS
SPOOLS
SPOONS
SPOORS
SPORES
SPORTS
SPOUTS
STOATS
STOCKS
STOICS
STOKES
STOLES
STOMPS
STONES
STOOKS
STOOLS
STOOPS
STOPES
STORES
STORKS
STORMS
STOUPS
STOUTS
STOVES
SWOONS

SWOOPS
SWORDS
TBONES
THOLES
THOMAS
THONGS
THORNS
TROLLS
TROOPS
TROTHS
TROUTS
TROVES
UBOATS
UBOLTS
VIOLAS
WHOOPS
WHORES
WHORLS
WHORTS
WOOERS
WRONGS
ZLOTYS
ZOOIDS

•••OS•

ACCOST
ACROSS
AFTOSA
ALDOSE
ALMOST
APPOSE
ARGOSY
ARIOSE
ARIOSO
CHOOSE
CHOOSY
COHOSH
COMOSE
CYMOSE
DEPOSE
EMBOSS
EXPOSE
FILOSE
GALOSH
GYROSE
HEXOSE
IMPOSE
IMPOST
INMOST
JOCOSE
KETOSE
KIBOSH
LANOSE
MIMOSA
MOROSE
MUCOSA
MUCOSE
NODOSE
OPPOSE
OSMOSE
OTIOSE
PILOSE
RAMOSE
REPOSE
RIBOSE
RIMOSE
RIPOST
RUGOSE
SETOSE
TOROSE
TRIOSE
UPMOST
UPROSE
UTMOST
VADOSE
VENOSE
VOLOST
XYLOSE

•••O•S

AARONS
ABBOTS
ABHORS
ACEOUS
ACIOUS
ACROSS
ACTORS
ALDOUS
ALFONS
ALLOTS
ALLOWS
ALLOYS
ANIONS
ANNOYS
ANTONS
APRONS
ARBORS
ARDORS
ARGOTS
ARIOUS
ARMORS
ARROWS
ARTOIS
ASCOTS
AUROUS
AXIOMS
BABOOS
BARONS
BATONS
BAYOUS
BEFOGS
BESOMS
BESOTS
BIGOTS
BIKOLS
BIPODS
BLOODS
BLOOMS
BOSOMS
BROODS
BROOKS
BROOMS
BUBOES
CABOBS
CANOES
CANONS
CAPONS
CAROBS
CAROLS
CAROMS
CEROUS
CHEOPS
CHLOES
CIBOLS
COCOAS
COLONS
COLORS
COLOUS
COMOUS
CROOKS
CROONS
CYMOUS
DADOES
DECORS
DECOYS
DEMOBS
DEMONS
DEPOTS
DIDOES
DIVOTS
DODOES
DONORS
DROOLS
DROOPS
ECHOES
ELBOWS
ELIOTS
EMBOSS
EMBOWS
ENDOWS
ENJOYS
ENVOYS
EPHODS
EPHORS
ERRORS
ESTOPS
EXTOLS
FAGOTS
FAMOUS
FANONS
FAVORS
FELONS
FEROUS
FETORS
FLOODS
FLOORS
FLUORS
FREONS
FSTOPS
FUCOUS
FURORS
GALOPS
GAMOUS
GAVOTS
GEMOTS
GENOUS
GEROUS
GIPONS
GLOOMS
GROOMS
GYNOUS
GYRONS
HALOES
HELOTS
HEROES
HERONS
HOBOES
HONORS
HUMORS
HURONS
IDIOMS
IDIOTS
IGLOOS
INDOWS
INGOTS
IODOUS
ITIOUS
JABOTS
JACOBS
JASONS
JOYOUS
JUPONS
JURORS
KABOBS
KAPOKS
KAZOOS
KLOOFS
LABORS
LEMONS
LEROYS
MAGOTS
MAJORS
MANORS
MASONS
MAYORS
MELONS
MEROUS
MESONS
MINORS
MORONS
MOTORS
MUCOUS
NABOBS
NYLONS
ODIOUS
ONIONS
ORLOPS
OXBOWS
PAEONS
PATOIS
PEKOES
PELOPS
PICOTS
PILOTS
PILOUS
PINONS
PITONS
PIVOTS
PODOUS
POROUS
POYOUS
PRIORS
PROOFS
PUTONS
PYLONS
RAMOUS
RAYONS
RAZORS
REDOES
RIGORS
RIMOUS
ROBOTS
ROTORS
RUFOUS
RUGOUS
RUMORS
RUNONS
SABOTS
SAJOUS
SALONS
SAVORS
SAXONS
SCIONS
SCOOPS
SCOOTS
SCRODS
SEPOYS
SEROUS
SEROWS
SETONS
SETOUS
SHOOTS
SIMONS
SLOOPS
SNOODS
SNOOKS
SNOOPS
SNOOTS
SOTOLS
SPOOFS
SPOOKS
SPOOLS
SPOONS
SPOORS
STOOKS
STOOLS
STOOPS
STROPS
SWOONS
SWOOPS
SYNODS
TABOOS
TABORS
TALONS
TAROTS
TENONS
TENORS
TETONS
THIOLS
THROBS
THROES
THROWS
TOROUS
TOYONS
TROOPS
TUMORS
TUTORS
UNDOES
UNIONS
UPBOWS
VALOIS
VAPORS
VENOMS
VENOUS
VETOES
VINOUS
VISORS
VIZORS
VOROUS
WAGONS
WAHOOS
WHOOPS
WIDOWS
WINOES
XYLOLS
YAHOOS
YAPONS
YUPONS
ZEROES
ZIRONS

••••OS

ABYDOS
ALAMOS
AMIGOS
AVISOS
BABOOS
BANJOS
BASSOS
BATHOS
BONGOS
BRAVOS
BRAZOS
BRUNOS
BUNCOS
BURGOS
BURROS
CACAOS
CAMEOS
CAMPOS
CANSOS
CANTOS
CARGOS
CARLOS
CELLOS
CENTOS
CHICOS
CISCOS
CLAROS
COMBOS
COMPOS
CONTOS
COSMOS
CREDOS
CURIOS
CUSSOS
CUSTOS
DATTOS
DITTOS
FOLIOS
FUGIOS
GECKOS
GENROS
GESSOS

GISMOS
GIZMOS
GREGOS
GUACOS
GUANOS
GUMBOS
HELIOS
HIPPOS
HYDROS
HYPNOS
IGLOOS
JOCKOS
JUNCOS
KAZOOS
LARGOS
LASSOS
LEMNOS
LENTOS
LLANOS
MAMBOS
MANGOS
MARCOS
MARGOS
MATEOS
MATZOS
METROS
MEZZOS
MIKLOS
MORROS
MOTTOS
MYTHOS
OVIBOS
PARGOS
PATHOS
PATIOS
PEDROS
PENGOS
PEPLOS
PHILOS
PHOTOS
PIANOS
PINGOS
PINTOS
POTTOS
PUNTOS
RADIOS
RATIOS
RECTOS
RHINOS
RODEOS
RONDOS
SALVOS
SAMBOS
SCHMOS
SERVOS
SETTOS
SHAKOS
SKIMOS
SORGOS
TABOOS
TAINOS
TANGOS
TEMPOS
TORSOS
TRIPOS
TURCOS
VERSOS
VIREOS
WAHOOS
WALDOS
XYSTOS
YAHOOS
ZETHOS

OT••••

OTHERS
OTIOSE
OTITIS
OTTAVA
OTTAWA
OTTERS

O•T•••

OBTAIN
OBTECT
OBTEST
OBTUND
OBTUSE
OCTADS
OCTANE
OCTANT
OCTAVE
OCTAVO
OCTETS
OCTOPI
OCTROI
OPTICS
OPTIMA
OPTIME
OPTING
OPTION
OSTEAL
OTTAVA
OTTAWA
OTTERS
OUTBID
OUTCRY
OUTDID
OUTERS
OUTFIT
OUTFOX
OUTING
OUTLAW
OUTLAY
OUTLET
OUTMAN
OUTPUT
OUTRAN
OUTRUN
OUTSAT
OUTSET
OUTSIT
OUTWIT
OXTAIL

O••T••

ORATED
ORATES
ORATOR
OTITIS
OUSTED
OUSTER
OYSTER

O•••T•

OBLATE
OCTETS
ODDITY
ODONTO
OLEATE
OMENTA
ONSETS
OOCYTE
OOLITE
OPHITE
OPIATE
ORBITS
ORNATE
ORNITH
OWLETS

O••••T

OBJECT
OBLAST
OBOIST
OBTECT
OBTEST
OBVERT
OCCULT
OCELOT
OCTANT
ODDEST
OFFSET
OLDEST
OMELET
ORGEAT
ORIENT
OSBERT
OUTFIT
OUTLET
OUTPUT
OUTSAT
OUTSET
OUTSIT
OUTWIT

•OT•••

BOTANY
BOTCHY
BOTFLY
BOTHER
BOTTLE
BOTTOM
COTEAU
COTTAE
COTTAR
COTTAS
COTTER
COTTON
DOTAGE
DOTERS
DOTIER
DOTING
DOTTED
DOTTEL
DOTTER
DOTTLE
GOTAMA
GOTHAM
GOTHIC
GOTTEN
HOTBED
HOTBOX
HOTELS
HOTTER
JOTTED
LOTAHS
LOTION
LOTTIE
MOTELS
MOTHER
MOTIFS
MOTILE
MOTION
MOTIVE
MOTLEY
MOTMOT
MOTORS
MOTTLE
MOTTOS
NOTARY
NOTERS
NOTICE
NOTIFY
NOTING
NOTION
POTAGE
POTASH
POTATO
POTBOY
POTEEN
POTENT
POTHER
POTION
POTPIE
POTSIE
POTTED
POTTER
POTTLE
POTTOS
ROTARY
ROTATE
ROTCHE
ROTGUT
ROTORS
ROTTED
ROTTEN
ROTTER
ROTUND
SOTHIC
SOTHIS
SOTOLS
TOTALS
TOTEMS
TOTERS
TOTHER
TOTING
TOTTED
TOTTER
VOTARY
VOTERS
VOTING
VOTIVE

•O•T••

AORTAE
AORTAL
AORTAS
AORTIC
BOATED
BOLTED
BOLTER
BOOTED
BOOTEE
BOOTHS
BOOTIE
BOSTON
BOTTLE
BOTTOM
COATED
COATIS
COLTER
CONTES
CONTIN
CONTOS
CONTRA
CONTRE
COOTIE
COPTIC
CORTES
CORTEX
CORTEZ
CORTIN
COSTAE
COSTAL
COSTAR
COSTED
COSTLY
COTTAE
COTTAR
COTTAS
COTTER
COTTON
DOCTOR
DOTTED
DOTTEL
DOTTER
DOTTLE
FOETAL
FOETID
FOETOR
FOETUS
FONTAL
FOOTED
FOOTER
FOOTLE
FORTES
FORTIS
FOSTER
GOATEE
GOETHE
GOITER
GOTTEN
HOGTIE
HOOTCH
HOOTED
HOSTED
HOSTEL
HOTTER
JOLTED
JOLTER
JOSTLE
JOTTED
KOWTOW
LOATHE
LOFTED
LOFTER
LOITER
LOOTED
LOOTER
LOTTIE
MOATED
MOLTED
MOLTEN
MOLTER
MOLTKE
MONTES
MONTHS
MONTYS
MOOTED
MOOTER
MORTAL
MORTAR
MORTON
MORTYS
MOSTLY
MOTTLE
MOTTOS
MOUTHS
MOUTHY
MOUTON
NOETIC
NOSTOC
POETIC
POETRY
PONTES
PONTIC
PONTIL
PONTON
PORTAL
PORTER
PORTIA
PORTLY
POSTAL
POSTED
POSTER
POTTED
POTTER
POTTLE
POTTOS
POUTED
POUTER
POWTER
ROOTED

ROOTER
ROSTER
ROSTRA
ROTTED
ROTTEN
ROTTER
ROUTED
ROUTER
ROUTES
SOFTAS
SOFTEN
SOFTER
SOFTLY
SOOTED
SOOTHE
SORTED
SORTIE
TOLTEC
TOMTIT
TOMTOM
TOOTED
TOOTER
TOOTHY
TOOTLE
TOOTSY
TOTTED
TOTTER
TOUTED
TOUTER
VORTEX
WONTED
WORTHY
YOUTHS
ZOSTER

•O••T•
BOASTS
BOGOTA
BONITO
BOOSTS
BORATE
BOUNTY
COASTS
COMATE
COMETS
COMITY
COOPTS
COUNTS
COUNTY
COURTS
COVETS
COYOTE
DONATE
DONETS
DOUBTS
EOLITH
FOISTS
FOUNTS
FOURTH
GOMUTI
HOISTS
HORSTE
IODATE
IOLITE
JOINTS
JOISTS
JOUSTS
LOBATE
LOCATE
LOLITA
MOIETY
MOULTS
MOUNTS
MOUNTY
OOCYTE
OOLITE
POINTS
POINTY
POLITE
POLITY
POSITS
POTATO
POULTS
POUSTO
ROASTS
ROBOTS
ROOSTS
ROTATE
ROUSTS
SOLUTE
SOMATA
SOMATO
SOMITE
SONATA
TOASTS
TOMATO
VOLUTE
VOMITO
VOMITS
WORSTS
ZONATE

•O•••T
AORIST
BOBCAT
BONNET
BOSKET
BOUGHT
COBALT
COBNUT
COEMPT
COGENT
COHORT
COLLET
COMBAT
COMFIT
COMMIT
COPOUT
COQUET
CORNET
CORSET
COSSET
COVERT
DOCENT
DOCKET
DOESNT
FOMENT
FOREST
FORGET
FORGOT
FORINT
FORMAT
FOUGHT
GOBBET
GOBLET
GOCART
GODWIT
GOGLET
GOKART
GORGET
HOBART
HOGNUT
HONEST
HORNET
JOLIET
LOCKET
LOCUST
LOMENT
LOQUAT
LOWEST
MODEST
MOLEST
MOMENT
MONGST
MONIST
MOPPET
MOTMOT
MOZART
NOCENT
NOUGAT
NOUGHT
POCKET
PONENT
POPPET
POSSET
POTENT
ROBERT
ROBUST
ROCHET
ROCKET
RODENT
ROQUET
ROTGUT
SOCKET
SOFFIT
SOLENT
SONANT
SONNET
SOREST
SOUGHT
SOVIET
TOILET
TOMCAT
TOMTIT
VOLANT
VOLOST
WOMBAT
YOGURT

••OT••
AZOTIC
BIOTIC
BIOTIN
BLOTCH
BOOTED
BOOTEE
BOOTHS
BOOTIE
BROTHS
CLOTHE
CLOTHO
CLOTHS
CLOTTY
COOTIE
CROTCH
CROTON
DHOTIS
EMOTED
EMOTES
EROTIC
EXOTIC
FOOTED
FOOTER
FOOTLE
FROTHS
FROTHY
GIOTTO
GLOTTO
GROTTO
HOOTCH
HOOTED
KNOTTY
LAOTSE
LOOTED
LOOTER
MIOTIC
MOOTED
MOOTER
PHOTIC
PHOTON
PHOTOS
PROTON
QUOTAS
QUOTED
QUOTER
QUOTES
RIOTED
RIOTER
ROOTED
ROOTER
SCOTCH
SCOTER
SCOTIA
SCOTTS
SHOTES
SLOTHS
SNOTTY
SOOTED
SOOTHE
SPOTTY
TOOTED
TOOTER
TOOTHY
TOOTLE
TOOTSY
TROTHS
TROTYL
ZLOTYS

••O•T•
ABORTS
ADOPTS
AGOUTI
AGOUTY
BLOATS
BOOSTS
BRONTE
CLOTTY
CLOUTS
COOPTS
CROATS
CROFTS
DROITS
DROUTH
EBOATS
FLOATS
FLOATY
FLOUTS
FRONTO
FRONTS
FROSTS
FROSTY
GHOSTS
GIOTTO
GLOATS
GLOSTS
GLOTTO
GROATS
GROTTO
GROUTS
GROWTH
KNOTTY
KNOUTS
ODONTO
PROCTO
PRONTO
QUOITS
ROOSTS
SCOOTS
SCOTTS
SCOUTS
SHOATS
SHOOTS
SHORTS
SHOUTS
SMOLTS
SMOOTH
SNOOTS
SNOOTY
SNORTS
SNOTTY
SNOUTS
SPORTS
SPORTY
SPOTTY
SPOUTS
STOATS
STOUTS
TROUTS
UBOATS
UBOLTS
WHORTS

••O••T
AMOUNT
ANOINT
AVOCET
CLOSET
EGOIST
FLORET
IGOROT
MAOIST
OBOIST
PROFIT
PROJET
PROMPT
PROSIT
PROUST
SNOCAT
SPOILT
STOMAT
TAOIST
TWOBIT
VIOLET

•••OT•
ABBOTS
ALCOTT
ALLOTS
ARGOTS
ASCOTS
BESOTS
BIGOTS
BOGOTA
CAPOTE
COYOTE
DAKOTA
DEMOTE
DENOTE
DEPOTS
DEVOTE
DIVOTS
ELIOTS
FAGOTS
GAVOTS
GEMOTS
HELOTS
IDIOTS
INGOTS
JABOTS
MAGOTS
PELOTA
PEYOTE
PICOTS
PILOTS
PIVOTS
REMOTE
ROBOTS
SABOTS
SCOOTS
SHOOTS
SMOOTH
SNOOTS
SNOOTY

6

TAROTS
ZYGOTE

•••O•T

ABVOLT
ACCOST
ADROIT
AFLOAT
ALCOTT
ALLOUT
ALMOST
ASSORT
BELOIT
CAVORT
COHORT
COPOUT
CUTOUT
DACOIT
DAKOIT
DECOCT
DEPORT
DEVOUT
DIMOUT
DUGOUT
EFFORT
ENROOT
ESCORT
EXHORT
EXPORT
EXTORT
FAROUT
GALOOT
IMPORT
IMPOST
INMOST
LAYOUT
MAHOUT
PUTOUT
RAGOUT
REPORT
RESORT
RETORT
REVOLT
RIPOST
RUNOUT
SPROUT
THROAT
TRYOUT
UNBOLT
UNROOT
UPMOST
UPROOT
UTMOST
VOLOST
WAYOUT

••••OT

BALLOT
BRULOT
BURBOT
CANNOT
CARROT
DESPOT
DIGLOT
ELLIOT
ENROOT
FAGGOT
FORGOT
FYLFOT
GALIOT
GALOOT
GIGLOT
HARLOT
HERIOT
IGOROT
MAGGOT
MARGOT
MARMOT
MASCOT
MATZOT
MOTMOT
OCELOT
PARROT
PEQUOT
REDHOT
SPIGOT
TEAPOT
TRICOT
TURBOT
UNROOT
UPROOT
UPSHOT
ZEALOT

OU••••

OUNCES
OUSELS
OUSTED
OUSTER
OUTBID
OUTCRY
OUTDID
OUTERS
OUTFIT
OUTFOX
OUTING
OUTLAW
OUTLAY
OUTLET
OUTMAN
OUTPUT
OUTRAN
OUTRUN
OUTSAT
OUTSET
OUTSIT
OUTWIT
OUZELS

O•U•••

OCULAR
OEUVRE
ONUSES
OVULAR
OVULES

O••U••

OBTUND
OBTUSE
OCCULT
OCCUPY
OCCURS
ONRUSH
OPPUGN
ORDURE
ORMUZD
OSCULE
OSMUND

O•••U•

OBELUS
OBOLUS
ODIOUS
OMASUM
OPAQUE
OSMIUM
OUTPUT
OUTRUN

O••••U

ORMOLU

•OU•••

AOUDAD
BOUCLE
BOUFFE
BOUGHS
BOUGHT
BOUGIE
BOULES
BOUNCE
BOUNCY
BOUNDS
BOUNTY
BOURGS
BOURNE
BOURNS
BOURSE
BOUSED
BOUSES
COUGAR
COUGHS
COULEE
COUNTS
COUNTY
COUPES
COUPLE
COUPON
COURSE
COURTS
COUSIN
DOUBLE
DOUBLY
DOUBTS
DOUCHE
DOUGHS
DOUGHY
DOUGIE
DOURLY
DOUSED
DOUSES
FOUGHT
FOULED
FOULER
FOULLY
FOUNDS
FOUNTS
FOURTH
GOUGED
GOUGER
GOUGES
GOURDE
GOURDS
HOUNDS
HOURIS
HOURLY
HOUSED
HOUSES
JOULES
JOUNCE
JOUSTS
LOUDEN
LOUDER
LOUDLY
LOUGHS
LOUISA
LOUISE
LOUNGE
LOUPES
LOURED
LOUSED
LOUSES
LOUVER
LOUVRE
MOULDS
MOULDY
MOULIN
MOULTS
MOUNTS
MOUNTY
MOURNS
MOUSED
MOUSER
MOUSES
MOUSSE
MOUTHS
MOUTHY
MOUTON
NOUGAT
NOUGHT
NOUNAL
POUCHY
POULTS
POUNCE
POUNDS
POURED
POURER
POUSTO
POUTED
POUTER
ROUBLE
ROUCHE
ROUGED
ROUGES
ROUGHS
ROUNDS
ROUSED
ROUSER
ROUSES
ROUSTS
ROUTED
ROUTER
ROUTES
SOUARI
SOUGHS
SOUGHT
SOULED
SOUNDS
SOURCE
SOURED
SOURER
SOURLY
SOUSED
SOUSES
TOUCHE
TOUCHY
TOUGHS
TOULON
TOUPEE
TOURED
TOUSLE
TOUTED
TOUTER
WOUNDS
YOUPON
YOUTHS
ZOUAVE
ZOUNDS

•O•U••

COHUNE
COLUGO
COLUMN
COLURE
COPULA
COQUET
FORUMS
GOMUTI
JOCUND
JORUMS
KORUNA
KORUNY
LOBULE
LOCUST
LOQUAT
MODULE
MOGULS
MOHURS
MORULA
NODULE
NOMURA
PODUNK
ROBUST
ROGUED
ROGUES
ROMULO
ROQUET
ROTUND
SOLUTE
TOGUES
TOLUOL
TOLUYL
TOQUES
VOGUES
VOGULS
VOLUME
VOLUTE
YOGURT
YORUBA
ZONULA
ZONULE

•O••U•

COBNUT
COCCUS
COCKUP
COLEUS
COLOUS
COMOUS
CONCUR
CONIUM
CONSUL
COPOUT
CORIUM
CORNUA
CORNUS
CORPUS
CORVUS
COYPUS
DORBUG
DORSUM
FOETUS
FOLIUM
FONDUE
GONIUM
HOGNUT
HOLDUP
HOOKUP
IODOUS
IOLCUS
IONIUM
JOSHUA
JOYFUL
JOYOUS
LOCKUP
MOBIUS
MOCKUP
MORGUE
MOSQUE
PODIUM
PODOUS
POILUS
POLLUX
POPGUN
POROUS
POSEUR
POSSUM
POYOUS
ROTGUT
SODIUM
TONGUE
TOROUS
TORQUE
TOSSUP

VOROUS
VOYEUR
WOEFUL

•O•••U
CONGOU
COTEAU
HONSHU
MOREAU

••OU••
ABOUND
AGOUTI
AGOUTY
AMOUNT
AMOURS
AROUND
AROUSE
AVOUCH
BLOUSE
CHOUGH
CLOUDS
CLOUDY
CLOUGH
CLOUTS
CROUCH
CROUPE
CROUPS
CROUPY
DROUTH
ENOUGH
FLOURS
FLOURY
FLOUTS
GHOULS
GROUCH
GROUND
GROUPS
GROUSE
GROUTS
HHOURS
KNOUTS
PLOUGH
PROUST
RAOULS
SCOURS
SCOUTS
SHOULD
SHOUTS
SIOUAN
SLOUCH
SLOUGH
SNOUTS
SPOUSE
SPOUTS
STOUPS
STOUTS
THOUGH
TROUGH
TROUPE
TROUTS

••O•U•
AEOLUS
AGOGUE
BLOWUP
BROGUE
CHORUS
CLONUS
CROCUS
CRONUS
EXODUS
HOOKUP
KRONUR
OBOLUS
QUORUM
SCOPUS
SHOGUN

•••OU•
ACEOUS
ACIOUS
ADNOUN
ALDOUS
ALLOUT
ARIOUS
AUROUS
BAYOUS
BEFOUL
BIJOUX
CEROUS
COLOUS
COMOUS
COPOUT
CUTOUT
CYMOUS
DETOUR
DEVOUR
DEVOUT
DIMOUT
DUGOUT
ENSOUL
FAMOUS
FAROUT
FEROUS
FUCOUS
GAMOUS
GENOUS
GEROUS
GIAOUR
GYNOUS
INSOUL
IODOUS
ITIOUS
JOYOUS
LABOUR
LAYOUT
MAHOUT
MEROUS
MUCOUS
ODIOUS
PILOUS
PODOUS
POROUS
POYOUS
PUTOUT
RAGOUT
RAMOUS
RECOUP
RIMOUS
RUFOUS
RUGOUS
RUNOUT
SAJOUS
SEROUS
SETOUS
SHROUD
SPROUT
STROUD
TOROUS
TRYOUT
VELOUR
VENOUS
VIGOUR
VINOUS
VOROUS
WAYOUT

•••O•U
ORMOLU

••••OU
ACAJOU
AMADOU
CACHOU
CONGOU

OV••••
OVALLY
OVERDO
OVERLY
OVIBOS
OVISAC
OVULAR
OVULES

O•V•••
OBVERT

O••V••
OEUVRE
OGIVES
OLIVER
OLIVES
OLIVIA

O•••V•
OCTAVE
OCTAVO
OTTAVA

•OV•••
BOVINE
COVERS
COVERT
COVETS
COVEYS
COVING
DOVISH
FOVEAE
FOVEAL
GOVERN
HOVELS
HOVERS
JOVIAL
JOVIAN
LOVAGE
LOVEIN
LOVELL
LOVELY
LOVERS
LOVING
MOVERS
MOVIES
MOVING
NOVELS
NOVENA
NOVICE
ROVERS
ROVING
SOVIET

•O•V••
COEVAL
CONVEX
CONVEY
CONVOY
CORVEE
CORVES
CORVUS
HOOVER
HOOVES
LOAVES
LOUVER
LOUVRE
SOEVER
SOLVED
SOLVER
SOLVES
VOLVAS
VOLVOX
WOLVER
WOLVES

•O••V•
GODIVA
MOHAVE
MOJAVE
MOTIVE
VOTIVE
ZOUAVE

••OV••
CLOVEN
CLOVER
CLOVES
CLOVIS
DROVED
DROVER
DROVES
GLOVED
GLOVER
GLOVES
GROVEL
GROVER
GROVES
HOOVER
HOOVES
PLOVER
PROVED
PROVEN
PROVER
PROVES
SHOVED
SHOVEL
SHOVER
SHOVES
SLOVAK
SLOVEN
STOVER
STOVES
TROVER
TROVES

••O•V•
EVOLVE
GROOVE
GROOVY

•••OV•
ALCOVE
BEHOVE
GROOVE
GROOVY
INWOVE
REMOVE
SHROVE
STROVE
THROVE

••••OV
PAVLOV
ZHUKOV

OW••••
OWLETS
OWLISH
OWNERS
OWNING

O•W•••
ONWARD
ORWELL
OSWALD

O••W••
ONEWAY
OUTWIT

O•••W•
OJIBWA
OTTAWA
OXBOWS

O••••W
OUTLAW

•OW•••
BOWELS
BOWERS
BOWERY
BOWFIN
BOWING
BOWLED
BOWLEG
BOWLER
BOWMAN
BOWMEN
BOWSED
BOWSES
BOWWOW
BOWYER
COWAGE
COWARD
COWBOY
COWERS
COWING
COWLED
COWMAN
COWMEN
COWPEA
COWPER
COWPOX
COWRIE
DOWELS
DOWERS
DOWERY
DOWNED
DOWSED
DOWSER
DOWSES
FOWLED
FOWLER
GOWNED
HOWARD
HOWDAH
HOWLED
HOWLER
KOWTOW
LOWBOY
LOWELL
LOWERS
LOWERY
LOWEST
LOWING
LOWKEY
MOWERS
MOWING
NOWAYS
NOWISE
POWDER
POWELL
POWERS
POWTER
POWWOW
ROWANS
ROWELS
ROWENA
ROWERS
ROWING
SOWARS
SOWERS
SOWING
TOWAGE

TOWARD
TOWELS
TOWERS
TOWERY
TOWING
VOWELS
VOWERS
VOWING
WOWING
WOWSER
YOWING
YOWLED

•O•W••
BOWWOW
COBWEB
COGWAY
GODWIN
GODWIT
NORWAY
POWWOW

•O••W•
MOHAWK

•O•••W
BORROW
BOWWOW
FOGBOW
FOLLOW
HOLLOW
KOWTOW
MORROW
MOSCOW
NOSHOW
POWWOW
SORROW

••OW••
AJOWAN
AVOWAL
AVOWED
AVOWER
BLOWBY
BLOWER
BLOWUP
BLOWZY
BROWNS
BROWSE
CLOWNS
CROWDS
CROWED
CROWNS
DROWNS
DROWSE
DROWSY
FLOWED
FLOWER
FROWNS
FROWZY
GLOWED
GLOWER
GROWER
GROWLS
GROWTH
KNOWER
MEOWED
PLOWED
PLOWER
PROWLS
SCOWLS
SHOWED
SHOWER
SLOWED
SLOWER
SLOWLY
SNOWED
STOWED
TROWEL
TWOWAY

•••OW•
ALLOWS
ARROWS
DISOWN
ELBOWS
EMBOWS
ENDOWS
INDOWS
OXBOWS
REDOWA
RENOWN
SEROWS
THROWN
THROWS
UPBOWS
UPTOWN
WIDOWS

••••OW
ANYHOW
BARROW
BELLOW
BESTOW
BILLOW
BORROW
BOWWOW
BURROW
BYBLOW
CALLOW
CRACOW
DARROW
ESCROW
FALLOW
FARROW
FELLOW
FOGBOW
FOLLOW
FURROW
HALLOW
HARROW
HAYMOW
HOLLOW
INFLOW
KOWTOW
MALLOW
MARROW
MEADOW
MELLOW
MINNOW
MORROW
MOSCOW
NARROW
NOSHOW
PILLOW
POWWOW
REAVOW
SALLOW
SHADOW
SORROW
SUNBOW
TALLOW
WALLOW
WILLOW
WINDOW
WINNOW
YARROW
YELLOW

OX••••
OXALIC
OXALIS
OXBOWS
OXEYED
OXEYES
OXFORD
OXIDES
OXLIPS
OXTAIL
OXYGEN

O••X••
ORYXES

O••••X
OUTFOX

•OX•••
BOXCAR
BOXERS
BOXING
COXING
DOXIES
FOXIER
FOXILY
FOXING
ROXANA
ROXANE
TOXINS

•O•X••
COAXAL
COAXED
COAXER
COAXES
HOAXED
HOAXER
HOAXES

•O•••X
BOLLIX
COCCYX
COMMIX
CONVEX
CORTEX
COWPOX
FORNAX
FORNIX
HOTBOX
POLEAX
POLLEX
POLLUX
VOLVOX
VORTEX

••OX••
ANOXIA
ANOXIC

••O••X
PROLIX
SCOLEX
STORAX
THORAX

•••OX•
BILOXI
DESOXY

•••O•X
BIJOUX

••••OX
COWPOX
HATBOX
HOTBOX
ICEBOX
LUMMOX
OUTFOX
VOLVOX

OY••••
OYSTER

O•Y•••
ODYNIA
ORYXES
OXYGEN

O••Y••
OBEYED
OBEYER
OKAYED
OOCYTE
OXEYED
OXEYES

O••••Y
OAKLEY
OCASEY
OCCUPY
OCHERY
ODDITY
OHENRY
OILILY
ONEWAY
OOLOGY
OOZILY
OPENLY
ORALLY
ORNERY
ORRERY
OSPREY
OSSIFY
OUTCRY
OUTLAY
OVALLY
OVERLY

•OY•••
BOYARD
BOYARS
BOYISH
COYISH
COYOTE
COYPUS
DOYENS
DOYLEY
FOYERS
HOYDEN
JOYCES
JOYFUL
JOYING
JOYOUS
POYOUS
ROYALS
TOYERS
TOYING
TOYISH
TOYONS
VOYAGE
VOYEUR
ZOYSIA

•O•Y••
BOWYER
CORYMB
CORYZA
OOCYTE
POLYPS
SONYAS

•O••Y•
BOBBYS
BOGEYS
BOLEYN
BONNYS
COCCYX
CONEYS
COOEYS
COVEYS
DOLLYS
FORAYS
FORMYL
HOLLYS
HONEYS
MOLLYS
MONEYS
MONTYS
MORAYS
MORTYS
MOSEYS
NOWAYS
POLLYS
POPPYS
RODDYS
TOLUYL
TOMMYS

•O•••Y
BODILY
BOLDLY
BOMBAY
BOTANY
BOTCHY
BOTFLY
BOUNCY
BOUNTY
BOWERY
CODIFY
COGWAY
COLDLY
COLONY
COMEDY
COMELY
COMITY
COMPLY
CONCHY
CONVEY
CONVOY
COOKEY
COOLLY
COPLEY
CORDAY
CORODY
COSTLY
COUNTY
COWBOY
COZILY
DONKEY
DOUBLY
DOUGHY
DOURLY
DOWERY
DOYLEY
DOZILY
FOLKSY
FONDLY
FOULLY
FOXILY
GOODBY
GOODLY
GOOGLY
GOONEY
GOOSEY
GORILY
HOCKEY
HOLILY
HOMELY
HOMILY
HOMINY
HOORAY
HORARY
HORSEY

HOURLY
JOCKEY
JOHNNY
KORUNY
LONELY
LORDLY
LOUDLY
LOVELY
LOWBOY
LOWERY
LOWKEY
MODIFY
MOIETY
MONDAY
MONKEY
MONODY
MOOLEY
MORLEY
MOSLEY
MOSTLY
MOTLEY
MOULDY
MOUNTY
MOUTHY
NORWAY
NOSILY
NOTARY
NOTIFY
OOLOGY
OOZILY
POACHY
POETRY
POINTY
POLICY
POLITY
POMPEY
POORLY
POPERY
PORTLY
POTBOY
POUCHY
RODNEY
ROMANY
ROMNEY
ROPILY
ROSARY
ROSILY
ROSINY
ROTARY
SODOMY
SOFTLY
SOLELY
SORELY
SOURLY
TOMBOY
TOOTHY
TOOTSY
TOUCHY
TOWERY
VOLERY
VOLLEY
VOTARY
WOBBLY
WOLSEY
WOODSY
WOOLLY
WORTHY
ZONARY

••OY••
BUOYED
CLOYED
FLOYDS
LLOYDS

••O•Y•
ANONYM
COOEYS
EPONYM
PROPYL
TROTYL
ZLOTYS

••O••Y
AGOUTY
BIOPSY
BLOCKY
BLOODY
BLOOMY
BLOWBY
BLOWZY
BRONZY
BROODY
BROOMY
CHOOSY
CHOPPY
CLODDY
CLOGGY
CLOTTY
CLOUDY
COOKEY
COOLLY
CROAKY
CROUPY
DROLLY
DROOPY
DROPSY
DROSKY
DROSSY
DROWSY
FLOATY
FLOCKY
FLOOZY
FLOPPY
FLOSSY
FLOURY
FROGGY
FROSTY
FROTHY
FROWZY
GLOOMY
GLOSSY
GOODBY
GOODLY
GOOGLY
GOONEY
GOOSEY
GROGGY
GROOVY
GROSZY
HOORAY
KNOTTY
MOOLEY
PHONEY
PHOOEY
POORLY
SHOALY
SHODDY
SLOPPY
SLOSHY
SLOWLY
SNOOPY
SNOOTY
SNOTTY
SPONGY
SPOOKY
SPOONY
SPORTY
SPOTTY
STOCKY
STODGY
STOGEY
STOREY
STORMY
THORNY
TOOTHY
TOOTSY
TROPHY
TWOPLY
TWOWAY
WHOLLY
WOODSY
WOOLLY

•••OY•
ALLOYS
ANNOYS
ARROYO
DECOYS
ENJOYS
ENVOYS
LEROYS
NAGOYA
SEPOYS

•••O•Y
ANTONY
ARGOSY
ARMORY
BARONY
BETONY
BLOODY
BLOOMY
BROODY
BROOMY
BRYONY
CALORY
CANOPY
CHOOSY
COLONY
CORODY
DESOXY
DIPODY
DROOPY
ECTOMY
EMBODY
EULOGY
FELONY
FLOOZY
GLOOMY
GROOVY
IDIOCY
IMBODY
JALOPY
MALORY
MELODY
MEMORY
MONODY
OOLOGY
PARODY
PHOOEY
PRIORY
SAVORY
SAXONY
SIMONY
SNOOPY
SNOOTY
SODOMY
SPOOKY
SPOONY
THEORY
UNHOLY
WICOPY

••••OY
CARBOY
CONVOY
COWBOY
DEPLOY
EMPLOY
LOWBOY
POTBOY
TEAPOY
TOMBOY

OZ••••
OZONIC

O•Z•••
OOZIER
OOZILY
OOZING
OUZELS

O•••Z•
ORMUZD

•OZ•••
COZENS
COZIER
COZIES
COZILY
DOZENS
DOZIER
DOZILY
DOZING
EOZOIC
MOZART
NOZZLE
OOZIER
OOZILY
OOZING
SOZINE
SOZINS

•O•Z••
BONZER
BONZES
BOOZED
BOOZER
BOOZES
BORZOI
COLZAS
FOOZLE
NOZZLE
PODZOL

•O••Z•
CORYZA
IODIZE
IONIZE

•O•••Z
CORTEZ
LORENZ

••OZ••
BOOZED
BOOZER
BOOZES
CROZER
CROZES
FOOZLE
FROZEN
GLOZED
GLOZES

••O•Z•
ALONZO
BLOWZY
BRONZE
BRONZY
FLOOZY
FROWZY
GROSZY
SFORZA
SNOOZE

•••OZ•
FLOOZY
REBOZO
SNOOZE

PA••••
PACERS
PACIFY
PACING
PACKED
PACKER
PACKET
PADDED
PADDLE
PADDYS
PADRES
PAEANS
PAEONS
PAGANS
PAGING
PAGODA
PAINED
PAINTS
PAINTY
PAIRED
PAIUTE
PAJAMA
PALACE
PALAEO
PALATE
PALEAE
PALELY
PALEST
PALING
PALISH
PALLAS
PALLED
PALLET
PALLID
PALLOR
PALMAR
PALMED
PALMER
PALPUS
PALTER
PALTRY
PAMELA
PAMPAS
PAMPER
PANADA
PANAMA
PANDAS
PANDER
PANELS
PANICE
PANICS
PANNED
PANSYS
PANTED
PANTIE
PANTRY
PANZER
PAPACY
PAPAIN
PAPAWS
PAPAYA
PAPERS
PAPERY
PAPIST
PAPPUS
PAPUAN
PAPULA
PAPULE
PARADE
PARANG
PARAPH

6

PARCAE
PARCEL
PARDON
PARENS
PARENT
PARERS
PAREUS
PARGET
PARGOS
PARIAH
PARIAN
PARIES
PARING
PARISH
PARITY
PARKAS
PARKED
PARKER
PARLAY
PARLEY
PARLOR
PARODY
PAROLE
PARRAL
PARREL
PARROT
PARSEC
PARSED
PARSEE
PARSES
PARSIS
PARSON
PARTED
PARTLY
PARURE
PARVIS
PASCAL
PASHAS
PASHTO
PASSED
PASSEE
PASSER
PASSES
PASSIM
PASSUS
PASTAS
PASTED
PASTEL
PASTER
PASTES
PASTIL
PASTOR
PASTRY
PATCHY
PATENS
PATENT
PATERS
PATHAN
PATHIA
PATHOL
PATHOS
PATINA
PATINE
PATIOS
PATOIS
PATROL
PATRON
PATSYS
PATTED
PATTEN
PATTER
PATTON
PAUKER
PAULAS
PAULIN
PAULUS
PAUNCH
PAUPER
PAUSED
PAUSER
PAUSES
PAVANS
PAVERS
PAVING
PAVIOR
PAVISE
PAVLOV
PAWERS
PAWING
PAWNED
PAWNEE
PAWNER
PAWPAW
PAXWAX
PAYDAY
PAYEES
PAYERS
PAYING
PAYOFF
PAYOLA

P•A•••

PEACHY
PEAHEN
PEAKED
PEALED
PEANUT
PEARLS
PEARLY
PEASEN
PEASES
PEAVEY
PHAGIA
PHASED
PHASES
PHASIA
PHASIC
PHASIS
PIAFFE
PIANOS
PIAZZA
PLACED
PLACER
PLACES
PLACET
PLACID
PLACKS
PLAGAL
PLAGIO
PLAGUE
PLAGUY
PLAICE
PLAIDS
PLAINS
PLAINT
PLAITS
PLANAR
PLANCH
PLANCK
PLANED
PLANER
PLANES
PLANET
PLANKS
PLANTS
PLAQUE
PLASHY
PLASIA
PLASIS
PLASMA
PLASMO
PLASTY
PLATAN
PLATED
PLATEN
PLATER
PLATES
PLATTE
PLAYAS
PLAYED
PLAYER
PLAZAS
POACHY
PRAGUE
PRAISE
PRANCE
PRANKS
PRATED
PRATER
PRATES
PRAVDA
PRAWNS
PRAXIS
PRAYED
PRAYER
PSALMS

P••A••

PAEANS
PAGANS
PAJAMA
PALACE
PALAEO
PALATE
PANADA
PANAMA
PAPACY
PAPAIN
PAPAWS
PAPAYA
PARADE
PARANG
PARAPH
PAVANS
PECANS
PEDALS
PEDANT
PEDATE
PEDATI
PEKANS
PELAGE
PESACH
PESADE
PETAIN
PETALS
PETARD
PHIALS
PHRASE
PILAFS
PILATE
PINANG
PIPAGE
PIRACY
PIRANA
PIRATE
PLEACH
PLEADS
PLEASE
PLEATS
PLIANT
POLAND
POMACE
POMADE
POSADA
POTAGE
POTASH
POTATO
PREACH
PSHAWS
PUPATE
PURANA
PYRANS

P•••A•

PALEAE
PALLAS
PALMAR
PAMPAS
PANDAS
PAPUAN
PARCAE
PARIAH
PARIAN
PARKAS
PARLAY
PARRAL
PASCAL
PASHAS
PASTAS
PATHAN
PAULAS
PAWPAW
PAXWAX
PAYDAY
PELIAS
PENIAL
PENMAN
PENNAE
PENPAL
PENTAD
PHYLAE
PICKAX
PILLAR
PINDAR
PINEAL
PINNAE
PINNAL
PISGAH
PITMAN
PIZZAS
PLAGAL
PLANAR
PLATAN
PLAYAS
PLAZAS
PLEIAD
PLICAE
PLURAL
POLEAX
POLKAS
POPLAR
PORTAL
POSTAL
PREFAB
PREPAY
PRESAS
PREWAR
PRIMAL
PTISAN
PULSAR
PUNJAB
PUNKAS
PURDAH
PUTNAM

P••••A

PAGODA
PAJAMA
PAMELA
PANADA
PANAMA
PAPAYA
PAPULA
PATHIA
PATINA
PAYOLA
PELOTA
PENNIA
PEORIA
PERSIA
PESETA
PHAGIA
PHASIA
PHILIA
PHOBIA
PHONIA
PIAZZA
PIRANA
PLASIA
PLASMA
PLEGIA
PLEURA
PNEUMA
POMONA
PORTIA
POSADA
PRAVDA
PURANA
PYEMIA
PYRRHA
PYTHIA
PYURIA

•PA•••

APACHE
APATHY
EPACTS
EPARCH
OPAQUE
SPACED
SPACER
SPACES
SPADED
SPADER
SPADES
SPADIX
SPAHIS
SPAITS
SPALLS
SPANKS
SPARED
SPARER
SPARES
SPARGE
SPARKS
SPARRY
SPARSE
SPARTA
SPASMS
SPATES
SPATHE
SPAVIN
SPAWNS
SPAYED
UPASES

•P•A••

APIARY
APPALL
APPALS
EPHAHS
OPIATE
SPEAKS
SPEARS
SPLAKE
SPLASH
SPLATS
SPLAYS
SPRAGS
SPRAIN
SPRANG
SPRATS
SPRAWL
SPRAYS

UPCAST
UPDATE
UPLAND
UPTAKE
UPWARD

•P••A•
APICAL
APNEAL
APODAL
APPEAL
APPEAR
APPIAN
EPICAL
IPECAC
OPERAS
SPICAE
SPINAL
SPIRAL
SPITAL
SPREAD
UPBEAT
UPROAR

•P•••A
APHTHA
APNOEA
APULIA
EPIZOA
OPTIMA
SPARTA
SPIREA

••PA••
ALPACA
APPALL
APPALS
BYPASS
BYPAST
BYPATH
COPALM
DEPART
EMPALE
ESPANA
EXPAND
HEPATO
IMPACT
IMPAIR
IMPALA
IMPALE
IMPARK
IMPART
IMPAWN
JAPANS
LAPARO
LIPASE
NAPALM
NOPALS
PAPACY
PAPAIN
PAPAWS
PAPAYA
PIPAGE
PUPATE

REPAID
REPAIR
REPAND
REPASS
REPAST
REPAYS
SEPALS
TAPALO
UNPACK
UNPAID

••P•A•
ALPHAS
APPEAL
APPEAR
APPIAN
BYPLAY
CAPIAS
COPRAH
DIPSAS
ESPIAL
HEPTAD
HYPHAE
HYPHAL
KAPPAS
ORPHAN
PAPUAN
POPLAR
RAPHAE
REPEAT
REPLAY
RIPRAP
RIPSAW
RUPIAH
SAPHAR
SEPIAS
SEPTAL

••P••A
ALPACA
CAPITA
COPPRA
COPULA
CUPOLA
ESPANA
EUPNEA
IMPALA
LEPSIA
LIPOMA
PAPAYA
PAPULA
SOPHIA
TOPEKA

•••PA•
AGAPAE
BEDPAN
CALPAC
CARPAL
CASPAR
GASPAR
INSPAN
KALPAK
KAPPAS

KASPAR
LAMPAD
LAMPAS
PAMPAS
PAWPAW
PENPAL
PREPAY
QUAPAW
SAIPAN
SALPAS
SAMPAN
SECPAR
STEPAN
STUPAS
TAMPAN
TREPAN
TROPAL
TYMPAN

•••P•A
COPPRA
COWPEA
HOOPLA
MYOPIA
NYMPHA
SULPHA
UTOPIA

••••PA
EUROPA
SHERPA

P•B•••
PEBBLE
PEBBLY
PUBLIC

P••B••
PEBBLE
PEBBLY
PHOBIA
PLEBES
POTBOY
PROBED
PROBER
PROBES
PUEBLO

P•••B•
PHLEBO
PHOEBE
PLUMBO
PLUMBS

P••••B
PREFAB
PUNJAB

•PB•••
UPBEAT
UPBOWS

•P••B•
EPHEBI

•P•••B
APLOMB

••P••B
SUPERB

P•C•••
PACERS
PACIFY
PACING
PACKED
PACKER
PACKET
PECANS
PECKED
PECKER
PECTEN
PECTIC
PECTIN
PICKAX
PICKED
PICKER
PICKET
PICKLE
PICKUP
PICNIC
PICOTS
PICRIC
PICTOR
PICULS
POCKET
PUCKER

P••C••
PARCAE
PARCEL
PASCAL
PATCHY
PEACHY
PENCEL
PENCIL
PERCYS
PHOCIS
PIECED
PIECER
PIECES
PISCES
PITCHY
PLACED
PLACER
PLACES
PLACET
PLACID
PLACKS
PLICAE
PLUCKS
PLUCKY
POACHY
PONCHO
POUCHY
PRECIS
PRICED
PRICES
PRICKS

PROCNE
PROCTO
PSYCHE
PSYCHO
PUNCHY

P•••C•
PALACE
PANICE
PANICS
PAPACY
PAUNCH
PEIRCE
PESACH
PIERCE
PIRACY
PLAICE
PLANCH
PLANCK
PLEACH
POLICE
POLICY
POMACE
POUNCE
PRANCE
PREACH
PRINCE
PUMICE
PUTSCH

P••••C
PARSEC
PECTIC
PELVIC
PEPTIC
PHASIC
PHONIC
PHOTIC
PHYSIC
PICNIC
PICRIC
POETIC
PONTIC
PUBLIC
PYEMIC
PYKNIC
PYTHIC

•PC•••
UPCAST

•P•C••
APACHE
APICAL
APICES
EPACTS
EPICAL
EPOCHS
IPECAC
SPACED
SPACER
SPACES
SPECIE
SPECKS

SPICAE
SPICED
SPICER
SPICES

•P••C•
APERCU
APIECE
EPARCH
OPTICS
SPEECH
SPLICE
SPRUCE

•P•••C
APNEIC
IPECAC

••P•C•
ALPACA
ASPECT
ASPICS
DEPICT
EXPECT
IMPACT
KOPECK
PAPACY
TOPICS
UNPACK
UNPICK

••P••C
CAPRIC
COPTIC
CUPRIC
HYPNIC
ORPHIC
PEPTIC
SEPTIC

•••P•C
ADIPIC
CALPAC
CARPIC
MYOPIC
TROPIC

P•D•••
PADDED
PADDLE
PADDYS
PADRES
PEDALS
PEDANT
PEDATE
PEDATI
PEDDLE
PEDROS
PIDDLE
PIDGIN
PODDED
PODIUM
PODOUS
PODSOL

6

PODUNK
PODZOL
PUDDLE
PUDDLY

P••D••
PADDED
PADDLE
PADDYS
PANDAS
PANDER
PARDON
PAYDAY
PEDDLE
PENDED
PIDDLE
PINDAR
PINDUS
PLEDGE
PODDED
POLDER
PONDER
POODLE
POWDER
PRIDED
PRIDES
PRUDES
PUDDLE
PUDDLY
PUNDIT
PURDAH

P•••D•
PAGODA
PANADA
PARADE
PARODY
PESADE
PLAIDS
PLEADS
POINDS
POMADE
POSADA
POUNDS
PRAVDA
PSEUDO

P••••D
PACKED
PADDED
PAINED
PAIRED
PALLED
PALLID
PALMED
PANNED
PANTED
PARKED
PARSED
PARTED
PASSED
PASTED
PATTED
PAUSED
PAWNED
PEAKED
PEALED
PECKED
PEEKED
PEELED
PEENED
PEEPED
PEERED
PEEVED
PEGGED
PELTED
PENDED
PENNED
PENTAD
PEPPED
PEQUOD
PERIOD
PERKED
PETARD
PETTED
PHASED
PHONED
PICKED
PIECED
PIGGED
PILLED
PIMPED
PINGED
PINKED
PINNED
PIPPED
PIQUED
PISHED
PITHED
PITIED
PITTED
PLACED
PLACID
PLANED
PLATED
PLAYED
PLEIAD
PLOWED
PLUMED
PODDED
POISED
POLAND
POLLED
PONIED
POOLED
POOPED
POPPED
POSTED
POTTED
POURED
POUTED
PRATED
PRAYED
PREMED
PREYED
PRICED
PRIDED
PRIMED
PRIZED
PROBED
PROSED
PROVED
PRUNED
PUFFED
PUGGED
PULLED
PULPED
PULSED
PUMPED
PUNNED
PUNTED
PUPPED
PUREED
PURGED
PURLED
PURRED
PURSED
PUSHED
PUTRID
PUTTED

•PD•••
UPDATE

•P•D••
APODAL
EPODES
SPADED
SPADER
SPADES
SPADIX
SPIDER

•P••D•
APHIDS
EPHODS
SPEEDS
SPEEDY
SPENDS
UPENDS
UPSIDE

•P•••D
APPEND
OPENED
OPINED
SPACED
SPADED
SPARED
SPAYED
SPEWED
SPICED
SPIKED
SPILED
SPIRED
SPITED
SPOKED
SPORED
SPREAD
SPUMED
UPHELD
UPHOLD
UPLAND
UPWARD

••P•D•
BIPEDS
BIPODS
DIPODY
IMPEDE
LEPIDO
LIPIDS
RAPIDS

••P••D
APPEND
BOPPED
CAPPED
COPIED
COPPED
CUPPED
DAPPED
DEPEND
DIPPED
ESPIED
EXPAND
EXPEND
GAPPED
GIPPED
GYPPED
HEPTAD
HIPPED
HOPPED
IMPEND
LAPPED
LAPSED
LIPOID
LIPPED
LOPPED
MAPPED
MOPPED
NAPPED
NIPPED
PEPPED
PIPPED
POPPED
PUPPED
RAPPED
REPAID
REPAND
RIPPED
SAPPED
SIPPED
SOPPED
SUPPED
TAPPED
TIPPED
TOPPED
TUPPED
UNPAID
WAPPED
YAPPED
YIPPED
ZIPPED

•••P•D
ALIPED
BEEPED
BOPPED
BUMPED
BURPED
CAMPED
CAPPED
CARPED
COOPED
COPPED
CRAPED
CREPED
CUPPED
CUSPED
CUSPID
DAMPED
DAPPED
DIPPED
DRAPED
DUMPED
ELOPED
GAPPED
GASPED
GIMPED
GIPPED
GRIPED
GROPED
GULPED
GYPPED
HARPED
HASPED
HEAPED
HELPED
HIPPED
HISPID
HOOPED
HOPPED
HUMPED
ISOPOD
JUMPED
LAMPAD
LAMPED
LAPPED
LEAPED
LIMPED
LIMPID
LIPPED
LISPED
LOOPED
LOPPED
LUMPED
MAPPED
MOPPED
NAPPED
NIPPED
PEEPED
PEPPED
PIMPED
PIPPED
POOPED
POPPED
PULPED
PUMPED
PUPPED
RAMPED
RAPPED
RASPED
REAPED
RIPPED
ROMPED
SALPID
SAPPED
SEEPED
SHAPED
SIPPED
SLOPED
SNIPED
SOAPED
SOPPED
STOPED
STUPID
SUPPED
SWIPED
TAMPED
TAPPED
TIPPED
TOPPED
TORPID
TRIPOD
TUPPED
UROPOD
VAMPED
VESPID
WAPPED
WARPED
WISPED
YAPPED
YAUPED
YAWPED
YELPED
YIPPED
ZIPPED

PE••••
PEACHY
PEAHEN
PEAKED
PEALED
PEANUT
PEARLS
PEARLY
PEASEN
PEASES
PEAVEY
PEBBLE
PEBBLY
PECANS
PECKED
PECKER
PECTEN
PECTIC
PECTIN
PEDALS
PEDANT
PEDATE
PEDATI
PEDDLE

PEDROS
PEEKED
PEELED
PEELER
PEENED
PEEPED
PEEPER
PEERED
PEEVED
PEEVES
PEEWEE
PEGGED
PEGGYS
PEGTOP
PEIRCE
PEKANS
PEKING
PEKOES
PELAGE
PELEUS
PELIAS
PELION
PELITE
PELLET
PELOPS
PELOTA
PELTED
PELTER
PELTRY
PELVES
PELVIC
PELVIS
PENCEL
PENCIL
PENDED
PENGOS
PENIAL
PENILE
PENMAN
PENMEN
PENNAE
PENNED
PENNER
PENNIA
PENNIS
PENNON
PENNYS
PENPAL
PENTAD
PENTUP
PENULT
PENURY
PEOPLE
PEORIA
PEPLOS
PEPLUM
PEPLUS
PEPPED
PEPPER
PEPSIN
PEPTIC
PEQUOD
PEQUOT
PERCYS
PERILS
PERIOD
PERISH
PERKED
PERMIT
PERRON
PERRYS
PERSIA
PERSON
PERTLY
PERUKE
PERUSE
PESACH
PESADE
PESETA
PESTER
PESTLE
PETAIN
PETALS
PETARD
PETERS
PETITE
PETREL
PETRIE
PETROL
PETTED
PEWEES
PEWITS
PEWTER
PEYOTE

P•E•••

PAEANS
PAEONS
PEEKED
PEELED
PEELER
PEENED
PEEPED
PEEPER
PEERED
PEEVED
PEEVES
PEEWEE
PHENOL
PHENYL
PIECED
PIECER
PIECES
PIERCE
PIERRE
PIERUS
PIETER
PIETRO
PLEACH
PLEADS
PLEASE
PLEATS
PLEBES
PLEDGE
PLEGIA
PLEIAD
PLENTY
PLENUM
PLEURA
PLEURO
PLEXOR
PLEXUS
PNEUMA
PNEUMO
POETIC
POETRY
PREACH
PRECIS
PREENS
PREFAB
PREFER
PREFIX
PREMED
PREPAY
PRESAS
PRESTO
PRETER
PRETOR
PRETTY
PREVUE
PREWAR
PREYED
PREYER
PSEUDO
PUEBLO
PYEMIA
PYEMIC

P••E••

PACERS
PALEAE
PALELY
PALEST
PAMELA
PANELS
PAPERS
PAPERY
PARENS
PARENT
PARERS
PAREUS
PATENS
PATENT
PATERS
PAVERS
PAWERS
PAYEES
PAYERS
PELEUS
PESETA
PETERS
PEWEES
PHLEBO
PHLEGM
PHOEBE
PHRENO
PIGEON
PIKERS
PILEUM
PILEUS
PINEAL
PINENE
PINERY
PIPERS
PIPETS
PLIERS
POKERS
POLEAX
POMELO
PONENT
POPERY
POSERS
POSEUR
POTEEN
POTENT
POWELL
POWERS
PREENS
PRIERS
PRIEST
PROEMS
PRYERS
PULERS
PUREED
PUREES
PURELY
PUREST
PYRENE

P•••E•

PACKED
PACKER
PACKET
PADDED
PADRES
PAINED
PAIRED
PALAEO
PALLED
PALLET
PALMED
PALMER
PALTER
PAMPER
PANDER
PANNED
PANTED
PANZER
PARCEL
PARGET
PARIES
PARKED
PARKER
PARLEY
PARREL
PARSEC
PARSED
PARSEE
PARSES
PARTED
PASSED
PASSEE
PASSER
PASSES
PASTED
PASTEL
PASTER
PASTES
PATTED
PATTEN
PATTER
PAUKER
PAUPER
PAUSED
PAUSER
PAUSES
PAWNED
PAWNEE
PAWNER
PAYEES
PEAHEN
PEAKED
PEALED
PEASEN
PEASES
PEAVEY
PECKED
PECKER
PECTEN
PEEKED
PEELED
PEELER
PEENED
PEEPED
PEEPER
PEERED
PEEVED
PEEVES
PEEWEE
PEGGED
PEKOES
PELLET
PELTED
PELTER
PELVES
PENCEL
PENDED
PENMEN
PENNED
PENNER
PEPPED
PEPPER
PERKED
PESTER
PETREL
PETTED
PEWEES
PEWTER
PHASED
PHASES
PHLOEM
PHONED
PHONES
PHONEY
PHOOEY
PICKED
PICKER
PICKET
PIECED
PIECER
PIECES
PIETER
PIGGED
PIGPEN
PILFER
PILLED
PIMPED
PINGED
PINIER
PINKED
PINNED
PINNER
PINTER
PIPIER
PIPPED
PIQUED
PIQUES
PIQUET
PISCES
PISHED
PISHES
PITHED
PITIED
PITIES
PITMEN
PITTED
PIXIES
PLACED
PLACER
PLACES
PLACET
PLANED
PLANER
PLANES
PLANET
PLATED
PLATEN
PLATER
PLATES
PLAYED
PLAYER
PLEBES
PLOVER
PLOWED
PLOWER
PLUMED
PLUMES
PLUSES
POCKET
PODDED
POGIES
POISED
POISES
POKIER
POKIES
POLDER
POLLED
POLLEE
POLLEN
POLLER
POLLEX
POMMEL
POMPEY
PONDER

PONGEE
PONIED
PONIES
PONTES
POOLED
POOPED
POORER
POPPED
POPPER
POPPET
PORKER
PORTER
POSIES
POSSES
POSSET
POSTED
POSTER
POTEEN
POTHER
POTTED
POTTER
POURED
POURER
POUTED
POUTER
POWDER
POWTER
PRATED
PRATER
PRATES
PRAYED
PRAYER
PREFER
PREMED
PRETER
PREYED
PREYER
PRICED
PRICES
PRIDED
PRIDES
PRIMED
PRIMER
PRIMES
PRIVET
PRIZED
PRIZER
PRIZES
PROBED
PROBER
PROBES
PROJET
PROLEG
PROPEL
PROPER
PROSED
PROSER
PROSES
PROVED
PROVEN
PROVER
PROVES
PRUDES
PRUNED
PRUNER
PRUNES
PUCKER
PUFFED
PUFFER
PUGGED
PUGREE
PULLED
PULLER
PULLET
PULLEY
PULPED
PULSED
PULSES
PUMMEL
PUMPED
PUMPER
PUNIER
PUNNED
PUNTED
PUNTER
PUPPED
PUPPET
PUREED
PUREES
PURGED
PURGER
PURGES
PURLED
PURRED
PURSED
PURSER
PURSES
PURVEY
PUSHED
PUSHER
PUSHES
PUSSES
PUSSEY
PUTTED
PUTTEE
PUTTER
PYXIES

P••••E

PADDLE
PAIUTE
PALACE
PALATE
PALEAE
PANICE
PANTIE
PAPULE
PARADE
PARCAE
PAROLE
PARSEE
PARURE
PASSEE
PATINE
PAVISE
PAWNEE
PEBBLE
PEDATE
PEDDLE
PEEWEE
PEIRCE
PELAGE
PELITE
PENILE
PENNAE
PEOPLE
PERUKE
PERUSE
PESADE
PESTLE
PETITE
PETRIE
PEYOTE
PHOEBE
PHRASE
PHYLAE
PIAFFE
PICKLE
PIDDLE
PIERCE
PIERRE
PIFFLE
PIGGIE
PILATE
PILOSE
PILULE
PIMPLE
PINENE
PINITE
PINKIE
PINNAE
PINOLE
PINTLE
PIPAGE
PIRATE
PLAGUE
PLAICE
PLAQUE
PLATTE
PLEASE
PLEDGE
PLICAE
PLUNGE
POLICE
POLITE
POLLEE
POMACE
POMADE
PONGEE
POODLE
POPPLE
POTAGE
POTPIE
POTSIE
POTTLE
POUNCE
PRAGUE
PRAISE
PRANCE
PREVUE
PRINCE
PROCNE
PSYCHE
PUDDLE
PUGREE
PUISNE
PULQUE
PUMICE
PUPATE
PURFLE
PURINE
PURPLE
PURSUE
PUTTEE
PUZZLE
PYRENE
PYRITE
PYRONE
PYROPE

•PE•••

APERCU
APEXES
IPECAC
OPENED
OPENER
OPENLY
OPERAS
SPEAKS
SPEARS
SPECIE
SPECKS
SPEECH
SPEEDS
SPEEDY
SPEISS
SPELLS
SPENDS
SPERMO
SPERRY
SPEWED
UPENDS

•P•E••

APIECE
APNEAL
APNEIC
APPEAL
APPEAR
APPELS
APPEND
EPHEBI
SPEECH
SPEEDS
SPEEDY
SPHENE
SPHENO
SPHERE
SPHERY
SPIELS
SPIERS
SPLEEN
SPLENO
SPREAD
SPREES
UPBEAT
UPHELD
UPKEEP
UPPERS
UPSETS

•P••E•

APEXES
APICES
APNOEA
APOGEE
APPLES
EPODES
EPOPEE
OPENED
OPENER
OPINED
OPINES
SPACED
SPACER
SPACES
SPADED
SPADER
SPADES
SPARED
SPARER
SPARES
SPATES
SPAYED
SPEWED
SPICED
SPICER
SPICES
SPIDER
SPIKED
SPIKES
SPILED
SPILES
SPINEL
SPINES
SPINET
SPIREA
SPIRED
SPIRES
SPITED
SPITES
SPLEEN
SPOKED
SPOKEN
SPOKES
SPORED
SPORES
SPREES
SPRIER
SPRUES
SPRYER
SPUMED
SPUMES
UPASES
UPKEEP

•P•••E

APACHE
APIECE
APLITE
APOGEE
APPOSE
EPOPEE
OPAQUE
OPHITE
OPIATE
OPPOSE
OPTIME
SPARGE
SPARSE
SPATHE
SPECIE
SPHENE
SPHERE
SPICAE
SPLAKE
SPLICE
SPLINE
SPONGE
SPOUSE
SPRITE
SPRUCE
SPURGE
UPDATE
UPHROE
UPRISE
UPROSE
UPSIDE
UPTAKE

••PE••

AMPERE
APPEAL
APPEAR
APPELS
APPEND
ARPENS
ARPENT
ASPECT
ASPENS
ASPERS
BIPEDS
CAPERS
CUPELS
DEPEND
DUPERS
DUPERY
EMPERY
EXPECT
EXPELS
EXPEND
EXPERT
GAPERS
IMPEDE
IMPELS
IMPEND
KOPECK
KOPEKS
LAPELS
LEPERS
LOPERS
MOPERS
NAPERY
PAPERS

PAPERY
PIPERS
PIPETS
POPERY
REPEAT
REPELS
REPENT
RIPELY
RIPENS
RIPEST
RUPEES
RUPERT
SUPERB
SUPERS
TAPERS
TEPEES
TEPEFY
TOPEKA
TOPERS
TUPELO
UNPEGS
UPPERS
VIPERS
WIPERS

••P•E•
APPLES
BOPPED
CAPPED
CAPPER
CIPHER
COPIED
COPIER
COPIES
COPLEY
COPPED
COPPER
COPSES
CUPPED
CUPPER
CYPHER
DAPPED
DAPPER
DIPLEX
DIPPED
DIPPER
DOPIER
DUPLEX
ESPIED
ESPIES
EUPNEA
GAPPED
GIPPED
GOPHER
GYPPED
HAPPEN
HIPPED
HOPPED
HOPPER
HYPHEN
JAPHET
KEPLER
KIPPER
KOPJES
LAPPED
LAPPER
LAPPET
LAPSED
LAPSER
LAPSES
LIPPED
LIPPER
LOPPED
MAPLES
MAPPED
MOPPED
MOPPET
NAPIER
NAPLES
NAPPED
NAPPER
NAPPES
NEPHEW
NIPPED
NIPPER
OSPREY
PEPPED
PEPPER
PIPIER
PIPPED
POPPED
POPPER
POPPET
PUPPED
PUPPET
RAPIER
RAPPED
RAPPEE
RAPPEL
RAPPER
RIPLEY
RIPPED
RIPPER
ROPIER
RUPEES
SAPPED
SAPPER
SEPTET
SIPPED
SIPPER
SIPPET
SOPPED
SUPPED
SUPPER
SYPHER
TAPPED
TAPPER
TAPPET
TEPEES
TIPPED
TIPPER
TIPPET
TOPPED
TOPPER
TUPPED
WAPPED
YAPPED
YIPPED
ZIPPED
ZIPPER

••P••E
ALPINE
AMPERE
AMPULE
APPOSE
ASPIRE
CAPOTE
CUPULE
DAPHNE
DAPPLE
DEPOSE
DEPUTE
DIPLOE
DIPOLE
EMPALE
EMPIRE
EXPIRE
EXPOSE
FIPPLE
HIPPIE
HOPPLE
HYPHAE
IMPALE
IMPEDE
IMPOSE
IMPURE
IMPUTE
LIPASE
LUPINE
MOPOKE
NAPPIE
NIPPLE
OPPOSE
ORPINE
PAPULE
PIPAGE
POPPLE
PUPATE
RAPHAE
RAPINE
RAPPEE
REPINE
REPOSE
REPUTE
RIPPLE
SOPHIE
SUPINE
SUPPLE
TIPPLE
TIPTOE
TOPPLE
UMPIRE
UNPILE
YIPPIE

•••PE•
ALIPED
AUSPEX
BEEPED
BOPPED
BUMPED
BUMPER
BURPED
CAMPED
CAMPER
CAPPED
CAPPER
CARPED
CARPEL
CARPER
CARPET
CASPER
CHAPEL
CHAPES
CLYPEI
COMPEL
COOPED
COOPER
COPPED
COPPER
COUPES
COWPEA
COWPER
CRAPED
CRAPES
CREPED
CREPES
CUPPED
CUPPER
CUSPED
DAMPED
DAMPEN
DAMPER
DAPPED
DAPPER
DEEPEN
DEEPER
DIAPER
DIPPED
DIPPER
DISPEL
DRAPED
DRAPER
DRAPES
DRUPES
DUMPED
ELOPED
ELOPER
ELOPES
EPOPEE
ETAPES
GAPPED
GASPED
GASPER
GIMPED
GIPPED
GOSPEL
GRAPES
GRIPED
GRIPER
GRIPES
GROPED
GROPER
GROPES
GULPED
GULPER
GYPPED
HAMPER
HAPPEN
HARPED
HARPER
HASPED
HEAPED
HELPED
HELPER
HEMPEN
HERPES
HIPPED
HOOPED
HOOPER
HOPPED
HOPPER
HUMPED
JASPER
JUMPED
JUMPER
KEEPER
KIPPER
LAMPED
LAPPED
LAPPER
LAPPET
LEAPED
LEAPER
LIMPED
LIMPER
LIMPET
LIPPED
LIPPER
LISPED
LISPER
LOOPED
LOOPER
LOPPED
LOUPES
LUMPED
LUMPEN
MAPPED
MOPPED
MOPPET
MYOPES
NAPPED
NAPPER
NAPPES
NIPPED
NIPPER
PAMPER
PAUPER
PEEPED
PEEPER
PEPPED
PEPPER
PIGPEN
PIMPED
PIPPED
POMPEY
POOPED
POPPED
POPPER
POPPET
PROPEL
PROPER
PULPED
PUMPED
PUMPER
PUPPED
PUPPET
RAMPED
RAPPED
RAPPEE
RAPPEL
RAPPER
RASPED
RASPER
REAPED
REAPER
REOPEN
RIPPED
RIPPER
ROMPED
ROMPER
SAPPED
SAPPER
SCAPES
SCOPES
SEAPEN
SEEPED
SHAPED
SHAPEN
SHAPER
SHAPES
SIMPER
SIPPED
SIPPER
SIPPET
SLOPED
SLOPER
SLOPES
SNIPED
SNIPER
SNIPES
SOAPED
SOPPED
STAPES
STIPEL
STIPES
STOPED
STOPES
STUPES
SUPPED
SUPPER
SWIPED
SWIPES
TAIPEI
TAMPED
TAMPER
TAPPED
TAPPER
TAPPET
TAUPES
TEMPER
TIPPED
TIPPER

TIPPET
TOPPED
TOPPER
TOUPEE
TUPPED
VAMPED
VESPER
WAPPED
WARPED
WARPER
WEEPER
WISPED
YAPPED
YAUPED
YAWPED
YAWPER
YELPED
YELPER
YIPPED
ZIPPED
ZIPPER

•••P•E
AGAPAE
CORPSE
COUPLE
DAPPLE
DIEPPE
DIMPLE
ELAPSE
EPOPEE
FIPPLE
FRAPPE
GRIPPE
HIPPIE
HOOPOE
HOPPLE
KEWPIE
MAGPIE
NAPPIE
NIPPLE
PEOPLE
PIMPLE
POPPLE
POTPIE
PURPLE
RAPPEE
RIMPLE
RIPPLE
RUMPLE
SAMPLE
SEMPRE
SHOPPE
SIMPLE
STAPLE
STEPPE
SUPPLE
SWIPLE
TEMPLE
TIPPLE
TOPPLE
TOUPEE
TRIPLE
WIMPLE
YIPPIE

••••PE
ASLOPE
CANAPE
CROUPE
DIEPPE
DOGAPE
ECTYPE
ESCAPE
EUROPE
FELIPE
FRAPPE
GRIPPE
GUIMPE
LENAPE
METOPE
PYROPE
RECIPE
SARAPE
SCRAPE
SERAPE
SHOPPE
STEPPE
STRIPE
THORPE
TROUPE
UNRIPE
WATAPE

P•F•••
PIFFLE
PUFFED
PUFFER
PUFFIN

P••F••
PIAFFE
PIFFLE
PILFER
PREFAB
PREFER
PREFIX
PROFIT
PUFFED
PUFFER
PUFFIN
PURFLE

P•••F•
PACIFY
PAYOFF
PIAFFE
PILAFS
PROOFS
PURIFY
PUTOFF

P••••F
PAYOFF
PUTOFF

•P•F••
SPIFFY

•P••F•
SPIFFY
SPOOFS
UPLIFT

••PF••
CUPFUL
LAPFUL

••P•F•
RIPOFF
TEPEFY
TIPOFF
TYPIFY

••P••F
RIPOFF
TIPOFF

P•G•••
PAGANS
PAGING
PAGODA
PEGGED
PEGGYS
PEGTOP
PIGEON
PIGGED
PIGGIE
PIGGIN
PIGNUS
PIGNUT
PIGPEN
PIGSTY
POGIES
POGROM
PUGGED
PUGGRY
PUGREE

P••G••
PARGET
PARGOS
PEGGED
PEGGYS
PENGOS
PHAGIA
PIDGIN
PIGGED
PIGGIE
PIGGIN
PINGED
PINGOS
PISGAH
PLAGAL
PLAGIO
PLAGUE
PLAGUY
PLEGIA
PLIGHT
PONGEE
POPGUN
PRAGUE
PUGGED
PUGGRY
PURGED
PURGER
PURGES

P•••G•
PELAGE
PHLEGM
PIPAGE
PLEDGE
PLOUGH
PLUNGE
POTAGE
PRONGS

P••••G
PACING
PAGING
PALING
PARANG
PARING
PAVING
PAWING
PAYING
PEKING
PIKING
PILING
PINANG
PINING
PIPING
PLYING
POKING
POLING
PORING
POSING
PROLEG
PRYING
PUKING
PULING
PUTLOG

•P•G••
APOGEE
SPIGOT

•P••G•
OPPUGN
SPARGE
SPONGE
SPONGY
SPRAGS
SPRIGS
SPURGE

•P•••G
APOLOG
EPILOG
OPTING
SPRANG
SPRING
SPRUNG
SPYING
UPPING

••PG••
POPGUN

••P•G•
IMPUGN
OPPUGN
PIPAGE
UNPEGS

••P••G
COPING
DOPING
DUPING
GAPING
HOPING
IMPING
LOPING
MOPING
PIPING
RAPING
ROPING
TAPING
TOPING
TYPING
UPPING
WIPING

PH••••
PHAGIA
PHASED
PHASES
PHASIA
PHASIC
PHASIS
PHENOL
PHENYL
PHIALS
PHILIA
PHILIP
PHILOS
PHIPPS
PHLEBO
PHLEGM
PHLOEM
PHOBIA
PHOCIS
PHOEBE
PHONED
PHONES
PHONEY
PHONIA
PHONIC
PHOOEY
PHOSPH
PHOTIC
PHOTON
PHOTOS
PHRASE
PHRENO
PHYLAE
PHYLLO
PHYLUM
PHYSIC
PHYSIO
PHYTIN

P•H•••
PSHAWS

P••H••
PASHAS
PASHTO
PATHAN
PATHIA
PATHOL
PATHOS
PEAHEN
PISHED
PISHES
PITHED
POTHER
PUSHED
PUSHER
PUSHES
PUSHUP
PYTHIA
PYTHIC
PYTHON

P•••H•
PATCHY
PEACHY
PITCHY
PLASHY
PLIGHT
PLUSHY
POACHY
PONCHO
POUCHY
PSYCHE
PSYCHO
PUNCHY
PYRRHA

P••••H
PALISH
PARAPH
PARIAH
PARISH
PAUNCH
PERISH
PESACH
PHOSPH
PISGAH
PLANCH
PLEACH
PLINTH
PLOUGH
POLISH
POPISH
POTASH
PREACH
PUNISH
PURDAH
PUTSCH

•PH•••
APHIDS

APHTHA
EPHAHS
EPHEBI
EPHODS
EPHORI
EPHORS
OPHITE
SPHENE
SPHENO
SPHERE
SPHERY
SPHINX
UPHELD
UPHILL
UPHOLD
UPHROE

•P•H••
SPAHIS
UPSHOT

•P••H•
APACHE
APATHY
APHTHA
EPHAHS
EPOCHS
SPATHE

•P•••H
EPARCH
SPEECH
SPILTH
SPLASH
UPPISH

••PH••
ALPHAS
ALPHYL
AMPHRS
CIPHER
CYPHER
DAPHNE
GOPHER
HYPHAE
HYPHAL
HYPHEN
JAPHET
NEPHEW
NEPHRO
OOPHOR
ORPHAN
ORPHIC
RAPHAE
RAPHIS
SAPHAR
SIPHON
SOPHIA
SOPHIE
SYPHER
TYPHLO
TYPHON
TYPHUS
ZEPHYR

••P•H•
DEPTHS
SAPPHO

••P••H
BYPATH
COPRAH
IMPISH
MOPISH
POPISH
RUPIAH
UPPISH

•••PH•
ALEPHS
DELPHI
DOLPHS
GLYPHS
GRAPHO
GRAPHS
GRAPHY
LYMPHO
MORPHO
NYMPHA
NYMPHO
NYMPHS
RALPHS
ROLPHS
SAPPHO
SCYPHI
SCYPHO
SULPHA
SULPHO
SYLPHS
SYLPHY
TROPHO
TROPHY

••••PH
ADOLPH
CALIPH
CERIPH
JOSEPH
PARAPH
PHOSPH
SERAPH
TERAPH

PI••••
PIAFFE
PIANOS
PIAZZA
PICKAX
PICKED
PICKER
PICKET
PICKLE
PICKUP
PICNIC
PICOTS
PICRIC
PICTOR
PICULS
PIDDLE
PIDGIN
PIECED
PIECER
PIECES
PIERCE
PIERRE
PIERUS
PIETER
PIETRO
PIFFLE
PIGEON
PIGGED
PIGGIE
PIGGIN
PIGNUS
PIGNUT
PIGPEN
PIGSTY
PIKERS
PIKING
PILAFS
PILATE
PILEUM
PILEUS
PILFER
PILING
PILLAR
PILLED
PILLOW
PILOSE
PILOTS
PILOUS
PILULE
PIMPED
PIMPLE
PIMPLY
PINANG
PINDAR
PINDUS
PINEAL
PINENE
PINERY
PINGED
PINGOS
PINIER
PINING
PINION
PINITE
PINKED
PINKIE
PINNAE
PINNAL
PINNED
PINNER
PINOLE
PINONS
PINTER
PINTLE
PINTOS
PINUPS
PINXIT
PIPAGE
PIPERS
PIPETS
PIPIER
PIPING
PIPITS
PIPKIN
PIPPED
PIPPIN
PIQUED
PIQUES
PIQUET
PIRACY
PIRANA
PIRATE
PISCES
PISGAH
PISHED
PISHES
PISTIL
PISTOL
PISTON
PITCHY
PITHED
PITIED
PITIES
PITMAN
PITMEN
PITONS
PITTED
PIVOTS
PIXIES
PIZZAS

P•I•••
PAINED
PAINTS
PAINTY
PAIRED
PAIUTE
PEIRCE
PHIALS
PHILIA
PHILIP
PHILOS
PHIPPS
PLIANT
PLICAE
PLIERS
PLIGHT
PLINTH
POILUS
POINDS
POINTS
POINTY
POISED
POISES
POISON
PRICED
PRICES
PRICKS
PRIDED
PRIDES
PRIERS
PRIEST
PRIMAL
PRIMED
PRIMER
PRIMES
PRIMLY
PRIMPS
PRINCE
PRINKS
PRINTS
PRIORS
PRIORY
PRISMS
PRISON
PRISSY
PRIVET
PRIZED
PRIZER
PRIZES
PTISAN
PUISNE

P••I••
PACIFY
PACING
PAGING
PALING
PALISH
PANICE
PANICS
PAPIST
PARIAH
PARIAN
PARIES
PARING
PARISH
PARITY
PATINA
PATINE
PATIOS
PAVING
PAVIOR
PAVISE
PAWING
PAYING
PEKING
PELIAS
PELION
PELITE
PENIAL
PENILE
PERILS
PERIOD
PERISH
PETITE
PEWITS
PIKING
PILING
PINIER
PINING
PINION
PINITE
PIPIER
PIPING
PIPITS
PITIED
PITIES
PIXIES
PLAICE
PLAIDS
PLAINS
PLAINT
PLAITS
PLEIAD
PLYING
PODIUM
POGIES
POKIER
POKIES
POKING
POLICE
POLICY
POLING
POLISH
POLITE
POLITY
PONIED
PONIES
POPISH
PORING
POSIES
POSING
POSITS
POTION
PRAISE
PRYING
PUKING
PULING
PUMICE
PUNIER
PUNILY
PUNISH
PUPILS
PURIFY
PURINE
PURISM
PURIST
PURITY
PYRITE
PYXIES

P•••I•
PALLID
PANTIE
PAPAIN
PARSIS
PARVIS
PASSIM
PASTIL
PATHIA
PATOIS
PAULIN
PECTIC
PECTIN
PELVIC
PELVIS
PENCIL
PENNIA
PENNIS
PEORIA
PEPSIN

PEPTIC
PERMIT
PERSIA
PETAIN
PETRIE
PHAGIA
PHASIA
PHASIC
PHASIS
PHILIA
PHILIP
PHOBIA
PHOCIS
PHONIA
PHONIC
PHOTIC
PHYSIC
PHYSIO
PHYTIN
PICNIC
PICRIC
PIDGIN
PIGGIE
PIGGIN
PINKIE
PINXIT
PIPKIN
PIPPIN
PISTIL
PLACID
PLAGIO
PLASIA
PLASIS
PLEGIA
PLUVIO
POETIC
PONTIC
PONTIL
POPLIN
PORTIA
POTPIE
POTSIE
PRAXIS
PRECIS
PREFIX
PROFIT
PROLIX
PROSIT
PTOSIS
PUBLIC
PUFFIN
PULPIT
PUNDIT
PURLIN
PUTRID
PYEMIA
PYEMIC
PYKNIC
PYOSIS
PYTHIA
PYTHIC
PYURIA

P••••I
PEDATI

•PI•••
APIARY
APICAL
APICES
APIECE
EPICAL
EPILOG
EPIRUS
EPIZOA
OPIATE
OPINED
OPINES
SPICAE
SPICED
SPICER
SPICES
SPIDER
SPIELS
SPIERS
SPIFFY
SPIGOT
SPIKED
SPIKES
SPILED
SPILES
SPILLS
SPILTH
SPINAL
SPINEL
SPINES
SPINET
SPINNY
SPIRAL
SPIREA
SPIRED
SPIRES
SPIRIT
SPIRTS
SPITAL
SPITED
SPITES

•P•I••
APHIDS
APLITE
APPIAN
APRILS
OPHITE
OPTICS
OPTIMA
OPTIME
OPTING
OPTION
SPAITS
SPEISS
SPHINX
SPLICE
SPLINE
SPLINT
SPLITS
SPOILS
SPOILT
SPRIER
SPRIGS
SPRING
SPRINT
SPRITE
SPRITS
SPYING
UPHILL
UPLIFT
UPPING
UPPISH
UPPITY
UPRISE
UPSIDE

•P••I•
APNEIC
APULIA
SPADIX
SPAHIS
SPAVIN
SPECIE
SPIRIT
SPRAIN

•P•••I
EPHEBI
EPHORI

••PI••
ALPINE
APPIAN
ASPICS
ASPIRE
CAPIAS
CAPITA
COPIED
COPIER
COPIES
COPING
DEPICT
DOPIER
DOPING
DUPING
EMPIRE
ESPIAL
ESPIED
ESPIES
EXPIRE
EXPIRY
GAPING
HOPING
IMPING
IMPISH
LAPINS
LEPIDO
LIPIDS
LOPING
LUPINE
MOPING
MOPISH
NAPIER
ORPINE
ORPINS
PAPIST
PIPIER
PIPING
PIPITS
POPISH
PUPILS
RAPIDS
RAPIER
RAPINE
RAPING
RAPIST
REPINE
ROPIER
ROPILY
ROPING
RUPIAH
SEPIAS
SUPINE
TAPING
TAPIRS
TOPICS
TOPING
TUPIKS
TYPIFY
TYPING
TYPIST
UMPIRE
UNPICK
UNPILE
UNPINS
UPPING
UPPISH
UPPITY
WAPITI
WIPING

••P•I•
CAPLIN
CAPRIC
COPTIC
CUPRIC
CYPRIN
ESPRIT
HIPPIE
HYPNIC
IMPAIR
JOPLIN
LEPSIA
LIPOID
NAPKIN
NAPPIE
ORPHIC
PAPAIN
PEPSIN
PEPTIC
PIPKIN
PIPPIN
POPLIN
RAPHIS
REPAID
REPAIR
SEPSIS
SEPTIC
SOPHIA
SOPHIE
UNPAID
YIPPIE

••P••I
VAPORI
WAPITI

•••PI•
ADIPIC
ARMPIT
CARPIC
CHOPIN
CUSPID
CUSPIS
HATPIN
HIPPIE
HISPID
KEWPIE
LIMPID
MAGPIE
MYOPIA
MYOPIC
NAPPIE
OKAPIS
PIPPIN
POTPIE
PULPIT
SALPID
SCIPIO
STEPIN
STUPID
TENPIN
TORPID
TROPIC
UTOPIA
VESPID
YIPPIE

•••P•I
CLYPEI
DELPHI
SCYPHI
TAIPEI

••••PI
EURIPI
OCTOPI
SCAMPI

P•J•••
PAJAMA

P••J••
PROJET
PUNJAB

••PJ••
KOPJES

P•K•••
PEKANS
PEKING
PEKOES
PIKERS
PIKING
POKERS
POKIER
POKIES
POKING
PUKING
PYKNIC

P••K••
PACKED
PACKER
PACKET
PARKAS
PARKED
PARKER
PAUKER
PEAKED
PECKED
PECKER
PEEKED
PERKED
PICKAX
PICKED
PICKER
PICKET
PICKLE
PICKUP
PINKED
PINKIE
PIPKIN
POCKET
POLKAS
PORKER
PUCKER
PUNKAS

P•••K•
PERUKE
PLACKS
PLANKS
PLUCKS
PLUCKY
PLUNKS
PRANKS
PRICKS
PRINKS

P••••K
PLANCK
PODUNK

•PK•••
UPKEEP

•P•K••
SPIKED
SPIKES
SPOKED
SPOKEN
SPOKES

6

•P••K•
SPANKS
SPARKS
SPEAKS
SPECKS
SPLAKE
SPOOKS
SPOOKY
SPUNKY
UPTAKE

••PK••
NAPKIN
PIPKIN

••P•K•
KAPOKS
KOPEKS
MOPOKE
TOPEKA
TUPIKS

••P••K
IMPARK
KOPECK
UNPACK
UNPICK

•••P•K
KALPAK

PL••••
PLACED
PLACER
PLACES
PLACET
PLACID
PLACKS
PLAGAL
PLAGIO
PLAGUE
PLAGUY
PLAICE
PLAIDS
PLAINS
PLAINT
PLAITS
PLANAR
PLANCH
PLANCK
PLANED
PLANER
PLANES
PLANET
PLANKS
PLANTS
PLAQUE
PLASHY
PLASIA
PLASIS
PLASMA
PLASMO
PLASTY
PLATAN
PLATED
PLATEN
PLATER
PLATES
PLATTE
PLAYAS
PLAYED
PLAYER
PLAZAS
PLEACH
PLEADS
PLEASE
PLEATS
PLEBES
PLEDGE
PLEGIA
PLEIAD
PLENTY
PLENUM
PLEURA
PLEURO
PLEXOR
PLEXUS
PLIANT
PLICAE
PLIERS
PLIGHT
PLINTH
PLOUGH
PLOVER
PLOWED
PLOWER
PLUCKS
PLUCKY
PLUMBO
PLUMBS
PLUMED
PLUMES
PLUMMY
PLUMPS
PLUNGE
PLUNKS
PLURAL
PLUSES
PLUSHY
PLUTUS
PLUVIO
PLYING

P•L•••
PALACE
PALAEO
PALATE
PALEAE
PALELY
PALEST
PALING
PALISH
PALLAS
PALLED
PALLET
PALLID
PALLOR
PALMAR
PALMED
PALMER
PALPUS
PALTER
PALTRY
PELAGE
PELEUS
PELIAS
PELION
PELITE
PELLET
PELOPS
PELOTA
PELTED
PELTER
PELTRY
PELVES
PELVIC
PELVIS
PHLEBO
PHLEGM
PHLOEM
PILAFS
PILATE
PILEUM
PILEUS
PILFER
PILING
PILLAR
PILLED
PILLOW
PILOSE
PILOTS
PILOUS
PILULE
POLAND
POLDER
POLEAX
POLICE
POLICY
POLING
POLISH
POLITE
POLITY
POLKAS
POLLED
POLLEE
POLLEN
POLLER
POLLEX
POLLUX
POLLYS
POLYPS
PULERS
PULING
PULLED
PULLER
PULLET
PULLEY
PULPED
PULPIT
PULQUE
PULSAR
PULSED
PULSES
PYLONS

P••L••
PALLAS
PALLED
PALLET
PALLID
PALLOR
PARLAY
PARLEY
PARLOR
PAULAS
PAULIN
PAULUS
PAVLOV
PEALED
PEELED
PEELER
PELLET
PEPLOS
PEPLUM
PEPLUS
PHILIA
PHILIP
PHILOS
PHYLAE
PHYLLO
PHYLUM
PILLAR
PILLED
PILLOW
POILUS
POLLED
POLLEE
POLLEN
POLLER
POLLEX
POLLUX
POLLYS
POOLED
POPLAR
POPLIN
POULTS
PROLEG
PROLIX
PSALMS
PUBLIC
PULLED
PULLER
PULLET
PULLEY
PURLED
PURLIN
PUTLOG

P•••L•
PADDLE
PALELY
PAMELA
PANELS
PAPULA
PAPULE
PAROLE
PARTLY
PAYOLA
PEARLS
PEARLY
PEBBLE
PEBBLY
PEDALS
PEDDLE
PENILE
PENULT
PEOPLE
PERILS
PERTLY
PESTLE
PETALS
PHIALS
PHYLLO
PICKLE
PICULS
PIDDLE
PIFFLE
PILULE
PIMPLE
PIMPLY
PINOLE
PINTLE
POMELO
POODLE
POORLY
POPPLE
PORTLY
POTTLE
POWELL
PRIMLY
PROWLS
PUDDLE
PUDDLY
PUEBLO
PUNILY
PUPILS
PURELY
PURFLE
PURPLE
PUSSLY
PUZZLE

P••••L
PARCEL
PARRAL
PARREL
PASCAL
PASTEL
PASTIL
PATHOL
PATROL
PENCEL
PENCIL
PENIAL
PENPAL
PETREL
PETROL
PHENOL
PHENYL
PINEAL
PINNAL
PISTIL
PISTOL
PLAGAL
PLURAL
PODSOL
PODZOL
POMMEL
PONTIL
PORTAL
POSTAL
POWELL
PRIMAL
PROPEL
PROPYL
PUMMEL

•PL•••
APLITE
APLOMB
SPLAKE
SPLASH
SPLATS
SPLAYS
SPLEEN
SPLENO
SPLICE
SPLINE
SPLINT
SPLITS
UPLAND
UPLIFT

•P•L••
APOLLO
APOLOG
APPLES
APULIA
EPILOG
SPALLS
SPELLS
SPILED
SPILES
SPILLS
SPILTH

•P••L•
APOLLO
APPALL
APPALS
APPELS
APRILS
OPENLY
SPALLS
SPELLS
SPIELS
SPILLS
SPOILS
SPOILT
SPOOLS
SPRYLY
UPHELD
UPHILL
UPHOLD

6

•P•••L
APICAL
APNEAL
APODAL
APPALL
APPEAL
EPICAL
SPINAL
SPINEL
SPIRAL
SPITAL
SPRAWL
UPHILL

••PL••
APPLES
BYPLAY
CAPLIN
COPLEY
DEPLOY
DIPLEX
DIPLOE
DUPLEX
EMPLOY
JOPLIN
KEPLER
MAPLES
NAPLES
PEPLOS
PEPLUM
PEPLUS
POPLAR
POPLIN
REPLAY
RIPLEY

••P•L•
AMPULE
AMPULS
APPALL
APPALS
APPELS
COPALM
COPULA
CUPELS
CUPOLA
CUPULE
DAPPLE
DIPOLE
EMPALE
EXPELS
FIPPLE
HOPPLE
IMPALA
IMPALE
IMPELS
LAPELS
NAPALM
NIPPLE
NOPALS
PAPULA
PAPULE
POPPLE
PUPILS
REPELS
RIPELY
RIPPLE
ROPILY
SEPALS
SUPPLE
SUPPLY
TAPALO
TIPPLE
TOPPLE
TUPELO
TYPHLO
UNPILE

••P••L
ALPHYL
APPALL
APPEAL
CUPFUL
ESPIAL
HYPHAL
LAPFUL
RAPPEL
SEPTAL

•••PL•
COMPLY
COUPLE
DAMPLY
DAPPLE
DEEPLY
DIMPLE
DIMPLY
FIPPLE
HOOPLA
HOPPLE
LIMPLY
NIPPLE
PEOPLE
PIMPLE
PIMPLY
POPPLE
PURPLE
RIMPLE
RIPPLE
RUMPLE
SAMPLE
SIMPLE
SIMPLY
STAPLE
SUPPLE
SUPPLY
SWIPLE
TEMPLE
TIPPLE
TOPPLE
TRIPLE
TWOPLY
WIMPLE

•••P•L
CARPAL
CARPEL
CHAPEL
COMPEL
DISPEL
GOSPEL
PENPAL
PROPEL
PROPYL
RAPPEL
STIPEL
TROPAL

P•M•••
PAMELA
PAMPAS
PAMPER
PIMPED
PIMPLE
PIMPLY
POMACE
POMADE
POMELO
POMMEL
POMONA
POMPEY
POMPOM
POMPON
PUMICE
PUMMEL
PUMPED
PUMPER

P••M••
PALMAR
PALMED
PALMER
PENMAN
PENMEN
PERMIT
PITMAN
PITMEN
PLUMBO
PLUMBS
PLUMED
PLUMES
PLUMMY
PLUMPS
POMMEL
PREMED
PRIMAL
PRIMED
PRIMER
PRIMES
PRIMLY
PRIMPS
PROMPT
PUMMEL
PYEMIA
PYEMIC

P•••M•
PAJAMA
PANAMA
PLASMA
PLASMO
PLUMMY
PNEUMA
PNEUMO
PRISMS
PROEMS
PSALMS

P••••M
PASSIM
PEPLUM
PHLEGM
PHLOEM
PHYLUM
PILEUM
PLENUM
PODIUM
POGROM
POMPOM
POSSUM
PURISM
PUTNAM

•PM•••
UPMOST

•P•M••
SPUMED
SPUMES

•P••M•
APLOMB
OPTIMA
OPTIME
SPASMS
SPERMO

•P•••M
EPONYM
SPUTUM

••P•M•
LIPOMA

••P••M
COPALM
CUPRUM
GYPSUM
NAPALM
PEPLUM
SEPTUM

•••P•M
POMPOM
WAMPUM

PN••••
PNEUMA
PNEUMO

P•N•••
PANADA
PANAMA
PANDAS
PANDER
PANELS
PANICE
PANICS
PANNED
PANSYS
PANTED
PANTIE
PANTRY
PANZER
PENCEL
PENCIL
PENDED
PENGOS
PENIAL
PENILE
PENMAN
PENMEN
PENNAE
PENNED
PENNER
PENNIA
PENNIS
PENNON
PENNYS
PENPAL
PENTAD
PENTUP
PENULT
PENURY
PINANG
PINDAR
PINDUS
PINEAL
PINENE
PINERY
PINGED
PINGOS
PINIER
PINING
PINION
PINITE
PINKED
PINKIE
PINNAE
PINNAL
PINNED
PINNER
PINOLE
PINONS
PINTER
PINTLE
PINTOS
PINUPS
PINXIT
PONCHO
PONDER
PONENT
PONGEE
PONIED
PONIES
PONTES
PONTIC
PONTIL
PONTON
PUNCHY
PUNDIT
PUNIER
PUNILY
PUNISH
PUNJAB
PUNKAS
PUNNED
PUNTED
PUNTER
PUNTOS

P••N••
PAINED
PAINTS
PAINTY
PANNED
PAUNCH
PAWNED
PAWNEE
PAWNER
PEANUT
PEENED
PENNAE
PENNED
PENNER
PENNIA
PENNIS
PENNON
PENNYS
PHENOL
PHENYL
PHONED
PHONES
PHONEY
PHONIA
PHONIC
PIANOS
PICNIC
PIGNUS
PIGNUT
PINNAE
PINNAL
PINNED
PINNER
PLANAR
PLANCH
PLANCK
PLANED
PLANER
PLANES
PLANET
PLANKS
PLANTS
PLENTY
PLENUM
PLINTH
PLUNGE
PLUNKS
POINDS
POINTS
POINTY
POUNCE
POUNDS
PRANCE

6

PRANKS
PRINCE
PRINKS
PRINTS
PRONGS
PRONTO
PRUNED
PRUNER
PRUNES
PUNNED
PUTNAM
PYKNIC

P•••N•

PACING
PAEANS
PAEONS
PAGANS
PAGING
PALING
PARANG
PARENS
PARENT
PARING
PATENS
PATENT
PATINA
PATINE
PAVANS
PAVING
PAWING
PAYING
PECANS
PEDANT
PEKANS
PEKING
PHRENO
PIKING
PILING
PINANG
PINENE
PINING
PINONS
PIPING
PIRANA
PITONS
PLAINS
PLAINT
PLIANT
PLYING
PODUNK
POKING
POLAND
POLING
POMONA
PONENT
PORING
POSING
POTENT
PRAWNS
PREENS
PROCNE
PRYING
PUISNE
PUKING
PULING
PURANA
PURINE
PUTONS
PYLONS
PYRANS
PYRENE
PYRONE

P••••N

PAPAIN
PAPUAN
PARDON
PARIAN
PARSON
PATHAN
PATRON
PATTEN
PATTON
PAULIN
PEAHEN
PEASEN
PECTEN
PECTIN
PELION
PENMAN
PENMEN
PENNON
PEPSIN
PERRON
PERSON
PETAIN
PHOTON
PHYTIN
PIDGIN
PIGEON
PIGGIN
PIGPEN
PINION
PIPKIN
PIPPIN
PISTON
PITMAN
PITMEN
PLATAN
PLATEN
POISON
POLLEN
POMPON
PONTON
POPGUN
POPLIN
POTEEN
POTION
PRISON
PROTON
PROVEN
PTISAN
PUFFIN
PURLIN
PYTHON

•PN•••

APNEAL
APNEIC
APNOEA

•P•N••

EPONYM
OPENED
OPENER
OPENLY
OPINED
OPINES
SPANKS
SPENDS
SPINAL
SPINEL
SPINES
SPINET
SPINNY
SPONGE
SPONGY
SPUNKY
UPENDS

•P••N•

APPEND
APRONS
OPTING
SPAWNS
SPHENE
SPHENO
SPHINX
SPINNY
SPLENO
SPLINE
SPLINT
SPOONS
SPOONY
SPRANG
SPRING
SPRINT
SPRUNG
SPURNS
SPYING
UPLAND
UPPING

•P•••N

APPIAN
OPPUGN
OPTION
SPAVIN
SPLEEN
SPOKEN
SPRAIN
UPTOWN
UPTURN

••PN••

EUPNEA
HYPNIC
HYPNOS

••P•N•

ALPINE
APPEND
ARPENS
ARPENT
ASPENS
CAPONS
COPING
DAPHNE
DEPEND
DOPING
DUPING
ESPANA
EXPAND
EXPEND
GAPING
GIPONS
HOPING
IMPEND
IMPING
JAPANS
JUPONS
LAPINS
LOPING
LUPINE
MOPING
ORPINE
ORPINS
PIPING
RAPINE
RAPING
REPAND
REPENT
REPINE
RIPENS
ROPING
SUPINE
TAPING
TOPING
TYPING
UNPINS
UPPING
WIPING
YAPONS
YUPONS

••P••N

APPIAN
CAPLIN
CYPRIN
HAPPEN
HYPHEN
IMPAWN
IMPUGN
JOPLIN
LEPTON
NAPKIN
NIPPON
OPPUGN
ORPHAN
PAPAIN
PAPUAN
PEPSIN
PIPKIN
PIPPIN
POPGUN
POPLIN
SIPHON
TYPHON

•••P•N

BEDPAN
CHOPIN
COUPON
DAMPEN
DEEPEN
HAPPEN
HATPIN
HEMPEN
INSPAN
LUMPEN
NIPPON
PIGPEN
PIPPIN
POMPON
REOPEN
SAIPAN
SAMPAN
SEAPEN
SHAPEN
SLIPON
STEPAN
STEPIN
TAMPAN
TAMPON
TARPON
TENPIN
TREPAN
TYMPAN
WEAPON
YAUPON
YOUPON

PO••••

POACHY
POCKET
PODDED
PODIUM
PODOUS
PODSOL
PODUNK
PODZOL
POETIC
POETRY
POGIES
POGROM
POILUS
POINDS
POINTS
POINTY
POISED
POISES
POISON
POKERS
POKIER
POKIES
POKING
POLAND
POLDER
POLEAX
POLICE
POLICY
POLING
POLISH
POLITE
POLITY
POLKAS
POLLED
POLLEE
POLLEN
POLLER
POLLEX
POLLUX
POLLYS
POLYPS
POMACE
POMADE
POMELO
POMMEL
POMONA
POMPEY
POMPOM
POMPON
PONCHO
PONDER
PONENT
PONGEE
PONIED
PONIES
PONTES
PONTIC
PONTIL
PONTON
POODLE
POOLED
POOPED
POORER
POORLY
POPERY
POPGUN
POPISH
POPLAR
POPLIN
POPPED
POPPER
POPPET
POPPLE
POPPYS
PORING
PORKER
POROUS
PORTAL
PORTER
PORTIA
PORTLY
POSADA
POSERS
POSEUR
POSIES
POSING
POSITS
POSSES

POSSET
POSSUM
POSTAL
POSTED
POSTER
POTAGE
POTASH
POTATO
POTBOY
POTEEN
POTENT
POTHER
POTION
POTPIE
POTSIE
POTTED
POTTER
POTTLE
POTTOS
POUCHY
POULTS
POUNCE
POUNDS
POURED
POURER
POUSTO
POUTED
POUTER
POWDER
POWELL
POWERS
POWTER
POWWOW
POYOUS

P•O•••

PEOPLE
PEORIA
PHOBIA
PHOCIS
PHOEBE
PHONED
PHONES
PHONEY
PHONIA
PHONIC
PHOOEY
PHOSPH
PHOTIC
PHOTON
PHOTOS
PLOUGH
PLOVER
PLOWED
PLOWER
POODLE
POOLED
POOPED
POORER
POORLY
PROBED
PROBER
PROBES
PROCNE
PROCTO
PROEMS
PROFIT
PROJET
PROLEG
PROLIX
PROMPT
PRONGS
PRONTO
PROOFS
PROPEL
PROPER
PROPYL
PROSED
PROSER
PROSES
PROSIT
PROTON
PROUST
PROVED
PROVEN
PROVER
PROVES
PROWLS
PTOSIS
PYOSIS

P••O••

PAEONS
PAGODA
PARODY
PAROLE
PATOIS
PAYOFF
PAYOLA
PEKOES
PELOPS
PELOTA
PEYOTE
PHLOEM
PHOOEY
PICOTS
PILOSE
PILOTS
PILOUS
PINOLE
PINONS
PITONS
PIVOTS
PODOUS
POMONA
POROUS
POYOUS
PRIORS
PRIORY
PROOFS
PUTOFF
PUTONS
PUTOUT
PYLONS
PYRONE
PYROPE

P•••O•

PALLOR
PARDON
PARGOS
PARLOR
PARROT
PARSON
PASTOR
PATHOL
PATHOS
PATIOS
PATROL
PATRON
PATTON
PAVIOR
PAVLOV
PEDROS
PEGTOP
PELION
PENGOS
PENNON
PEPLOS
PEQUOD
PEQUOT
PERIOD
PERRON
PERSON
PETROL
PHENOL
PHILOS
PHOTON
PHOTOS
PIANOS
PICTOR
PIGEON
PILLOW
PINGOS
PINION
PINTOS
PISTOL
PISTON
PLEXOR
PODSOL
PODZOL
POGROM
POISON
POMPOM
POMPON
PONTON
POTBOY
POTION
POTTOS
POWWOW
PRETOR
PRISON
PROTON
PUNTOS
PUTLOG
PYTHON

P••••O

PALAEO
PASHTO
PHLEBO
PHRENO
PHYLLO
PHYSIO
PIETRO
PLAGIO
PLASMO
PLEURO
PLUMBO
PLUVIO
PNEUMO
POMELO
PONCHO
POTATO
POUSTO
PRESTO
PROCTO
PRONTO
PSEUDO
PSYCHO
PUEBLO

•PO•••

APODAL
APOGEE
APOLLO
APOLOG
EPOCHS
EPODES
EPONYM
EPOPEE
SPOILS
SPOILT
SPOKED
SPOKEN
SPOKES
SPONGE
SPONGY
SPOOFS
SPOOKS
SPOOKY
SPOOLS
SPOONS
SPOONY
SPOORS
SPORED
SPORES
SPORTS
SPORTY
SPOTTY
SPOUSE
SPOUTS

•P•O••

APLOMB
APNOEA
APPOSE
APRONS
EPHODS
EPHORI
EPHORS
OPPOSE
SPOOFS
SPOOKS
SPOOKY
SPOOLS
SPOONS
SPOONY
SPOORS
SPROUT
UPBOWS
UPHOLD
UPMOST
UPROAR
UPROOT
UPROSE
UPTOWN

•P••O•

APOLOG
EPILOG
EPIZOA
OPTION
SPIGOT
UPHROE
UPROOT
UPSHOT

•P•••O

APOLLO
SPERMO
SPHENO
SPLENO

••PO••

APPOSE
BIPODS
CAPONS
CAPOTE
COPOUT
CUPOLA
DEPORT
DEPOSE
DEPOTS
DIPODY
DIPOLE
EXPORT
EXPOSE
GIPONS
IMPORT
IMPOSE
IMPOST
JUPONS
KAPOKS
LIPOID
LIPOMA
MOPOKE
OPPOSE
REPORT
REPOSE
RIPOFF
RIPOST
SEPOYS
TIPOFF
VAPORI
VAPORS
YAPONS
YUPONS

••P•O•

CAPTOR
DEPLOY
DIPLOE
EMPLOY
HIPPOS
HYPNOS
LEPTON
NIPPON
OOPHOR
PEPLOS
SIPHON
TIPTOE
TIPTOP
TYPHON

••P••O

HEPATO
LAPARO
LEPIDO
NEPHRO
SAPPHO
TAPALO
TUPELO
TYPHLO

•••PO•

CAMPOS
COMPOS
COUPON
COWPOX
DESPOT
HIPPOS
HOOPOE
ISOPOD
MAYPOP
NIPPON
POMPOM
POMPON
SLIPON
STUPOR
TAMPON
TARPON
TEAPOT
TEAPOY
TEMPOS
TORPOR
TRIPOD
TRIPOS
UROPOD
WEAPON
YAUPON
YOUPON

•••P•O

ALEPPO
CRYPTO
GLYPTO
GRAPHO
LYMPHO
MORPHO
NYMPHO
SAPPHO
SCIPIO

SCYPHO
SULPHO
TROPHO

••••PO
ALEPPO
KAKAPO

P•P•••
PAPACY
PAPAIN
PAPAWS
PAPAYA
PAPERS
PAPERY
PAPIST
PAPPUS
PAPUAN
PAPULA
PAPULE
PEPLOS
PEPLUM
PEPLUS
PEPPED
PEPPER
PEPSIN
PEPTIC
PIPAGE
PIPERS
PIPETS
PIPIER
PIPING
PIPITS
PIPKIN
PIPPED
PIPPIN
POPERY
POPGUN
POPISH
POPLAR
POPLIN
POPPED
POPPER
POPPET
POPPLE
POPPYS
PUPATE
PUPILS
PUPPED
PUPPET

P••P••
PALPUS
PAMPAS
PAMPER
PAPPUS
PAUPER
PAWPAW
PEEPED
PEEPER
PENPAL
PEOPLE
PEPPED
PEPPER
PHIPPS
PIGPEN
PIMPED
PIMPLE
PIMPLY
PIPPED
PIPPIN
POMPEY
POMPOM
POMPON
POOPED
POPPED
POPPER
POPPET
POPPLE
POPPYS
POTPIE
PREPAY
PROPEL
PROPER
PROPYL
PULPED
PULPIT
PUMPED
PUMPER
PUPPED
PUPPET
PURPLE
PUTPUT

P•••P•
PARAPH
PELOPS
PHIPPS
PHOSPH
PINUPS
PLUMPS
POLYPS
PRIMPS
PROMPT
PYROPE

P••••P
PEGTOP
PENTUP
PHILIP
PICKUP
PUSHUP

•PP•••
APPALL
APPALS
APPEAL
APPEAR
APPELS
APPEND
APPIAN
APPLES
APPOSE
OPPOSE
OPPUGN
UPPERS
UPPING
UPPISH
UPPITY

•P•P••
EPOPEE

•P•••P
UPKEEP

••PP••
BOPPED
CAPPED
CAPPER
COPPED
COPPER
COPPRA
CUPPED
CUPPER
DAPPED
DAPPER
DAPPLE
DIPPED
DIPPER
FIPPLE
GAPPED
GIPPED
GYPPED
HAPPEN
HIPPED
HIPPIE
HIPPOS
HIPPUS
HOPPED
HOPPER
HOPPLE
KAPPAS
KIPPER
LAPPED
LAPPER
LAPPET
LIPPED
LIPPER
LOPPED
MAPPED
MOPPED
MOPPET
NAPPED
NAPPER
NAPPES
NAPPIE
NIPPED
NIPPER
NIPPLE
NIPPON
PAPPUS
PEPPED
PEPPER
PIPPED
PIPPIN
POPPED
POPPER
POPPET
POPPLE
POPPYS
PUPPED
PUPPET
RAPPED
RAPPEE
RAPPEL
RAPPER
RIPPED
RIPPER
RIPPLE
SAPPED
SAPPER
SAPPHO
SIPPED
SIPPER
SIPPET
SOPPED
SUPPED
SUPPER
SUPPLE
SUPPLY
TAPPED
TAPPER
TAPPET
TIPPED
TIPPER
TIPPET
TIPPLE
TOPPED
TOPPER
TOPPLE
TUPPED
WAPPED
YAPPED
YIPPED
YIPPIE
ZIPPED
ZIPPER

••P••P
RIPRAP
TIPTOP

•••PP•
ALEPPO
CHIPPY
CHOPPY
DIEPPE
DRIPPY
FLOPPY
FRAPPE
GRIPPE
GRIPPY
PHIPPS
SHOPPE
SLOPPY
SNAPPY
SNIPPY
STEPPE

•••P•P
MAYPOP
SLIPUP
STEPUP
WRAPUP

P•Q•••
PEQUOD
PEQUOT
PIQUED
PIQUES
PIQUET

P••Q••
PLAQUE
PULQUE

•P•Q••
OPAQUE

PR••••
PRAGUE
PRAISE
PRANCE
PRANKS
PRATED
PRATER
PRATES
PRAVDA
PRAWNS
PRAXIS
PRAYED
PRAYER
PREACH
PRECIS
PREENS
PREFAB
PREFER
PREFIX
PREMED
PREPAY
PRESAS
PRESTO
PRETER
PRETOR
PRETTY
PREVUE
PREWAR
PREYED
PREYER
PRICED
PRICES
PRICKS
PRIDED
PRIDES
PRIERS
PRIEST
PRIMAL
PRIMED
PRIMER
PRIMES
PRIMLY
PRIMPS
PRINCE
PRINKS
PRINTS
PRIORS
PRIORY
PRISMS
PRISON
PRISSY
PRIVET
PRIZED
PRIZER
PRIZES
PROBED
PROBER
PROBES
PROCNE
PROCTO
PROEMS
PROFIT
PROJET
PROLEG
PROLIX
PROMPT
PRONGS
PRONTO
PROOFS
PROPEL
PROPER
PROPYL
PROSED
PROSER
PROSES
PROSIT
PROTON
PROUST
PROVED
PROVEN
PROVER
PROVES
PROWLS
PRUDES
PRUNED
PRUNER
PRUNES
PRYERS
PRYING

P•R•••
PARADE
PARANG
PARAPH
PARCAE
PARCEL
PARDON
PARENS
PARENT
PARERS
PAREUS
PARGET
PARGOS
PARIAH
PARIAN
PARIES
PARING
PARISH
PARITY
PARKAS
PARKED
PARKER
PARLAY
PARLEY

PARLOR
PARODY
PAROLE
PARRAL
PARREL
PARROT
PARSEC
PARSED
PARSEE
PARSES
PARSIS
PARSON
PARTED
PARTLY
PARURE
PARVIS
PERCYS
PERILS
PERIOD
PERISH
PERKED
PERMIT
PERRON
PERRYS
PERSIA
PERSON
PERTLY
PERUKE
PERUSE
PHRASE
PHRENO
PIRACY
PIRANA
PIRATE
PORING
PORKER
POROUS
PORTAL
PORTER
PORTIA
PORTLY
PURANA
PURDAH
PUREED
PUREES
PURELY
PUREST
PURFLE
PURGED
PURGER
PURGES
PURIFY
PURINE
PURISM
PURIST
PURITY
PURLED
PURLIN
PURPLE
PURRED
PURSED
PURSER
PURSES
PURSUE
PURVEY
PYRANS
PYRENE
PYRITE
PYRONE
PYROPE
PYRRHA

P••R••

PADRES
PAIRED
PARRAL
PARREL
PARROT
PATROL
PATRON
PEARLS
PEARLY
PEDROS
PEERED
PEIRCE
PEORIA
PERRON
PERRYS
PETREL
PETRIE
PETROL
PICRIC
PIERCE
PIERRE
PIERUS
PLURAL
POGROM
POORER
POORLY
POURED
POURER
PUGREE
PURRED
PUTRID
PYRRHA
PYURIA

P•••R•

PACERS
PALTRY
PANTRY
PAPERS
PAPERY
PARERS
PARURE
PASTRY
PATERS
PAVERS
PAWERS
PAYERS
PELTRY
PENURY
PETARD
PETERS
PIERRE
PIETRO
PIKERS
PINERY
PIPERS
PLEURA
PLEURO
PLIERS
POETRY
POKERS
POPERY
POSERS
POWERS
PRIERS
PRIORS
PRIORY
PRYERS
PUGGRY
PULERS

P••••R

PACKER
PALLOR
PALMAR
PALMER
PALTER
PAMPER
PANDER
PANZER
PARKER
PARLOR
PASSER
PASTER
PASTOR
PATTER
PAUKER
PAUPER
PAUSER
PAVIOR
PAWNER
PECKER
PEELER
PEEPER
PELTER
PENNER
PEPPER
PESTER
PEWTER
PICKER
PICTOR
PIECER
PIETER
PILFER
PILLAR
PINDAR
PINIER
PINNER
PINTER
PIPIER
PLACER
PLANAR
PLANER
PLATER
PLAYER
PLEXOR
PLOVER
PLOWER
POKIER
POLDER
POLLER
PONDER
POORER
POPLAR
POPPER
PORKER
PORTER
POSEUR
POSTER
POTHER
POTTER
POURER
POUTER
POWDER
POWTER
PRATER
PRAYER
PREFER
PRETER
PRETOR
PREWAR
PREYER
PRIMER
PRIZER
PROBER
PROPER
PROSER
PROVER
PRUNER
PUCKER
PUFFER
PULLER
PULSAR
PUMPER
PUNIER
PUNTER
PURGER
PURSER
PUSHER
PUTTER

•PR•••

APRILS
APRONS
SPRAGS
SPRAIN
SPRANG
SPRATS
SPRAWL
SPRAYS
SPREAD
SPREES
SPRIER
SPRIGS
SPRING
SPRINT
SPRITE
SPRITS
SPROUT
SPRUCE
SPRUES
SPRUNG
SPRYER
SPRYLY
UPRISE
UPROAR
UPROOT
UPROSE

•P•R••

APERCU
EPARCH
EPIRUS
OPERAS
SPARED
SPARER
SPARES
SPARGE
SPARKS
SPARRY
SPARSE
SPARTA
SPERMO
SPERRY
SPIRAL
SPIREA
SPIRED
SPIRES
SPIRIT
SPIRTS
SPORED
SPORES
SPORTS
SPORTY
SPURGE
SPURNS
SPURRY
SPURTS
UPHROE

•P••R•

APIARY
EPHORI
EPHORS
SPARRY
SPEARS
SPERRY
SPHERE
SPHERY
SPIERS
SPOORS
SPURRY
UPPERS
UPTURN
UPWARD

•P•••R

APPEAR
OPENER
SPACER
SPADER
SPARER
SPICER
SPIDER
SPRIER
SPRYER
UPROAR

••PR••

CAPRIC
COPRAH
CUPRIC
CUPRUM
CYPRIN
CYPRUS
ESPRIT
OSPREY
RIPRAP

••P•R•

AMPERE
AMPHRS
ASPERS
ASPIRE
CAPERS
COPPRA
DEPART
DEPORT
DUPERS
DUPERY
EMPERY
EMPIRE
EXPERT
EXPIRE
EXPIRY
EXPORT
GAPERS
IMPARK
IMPART
IMPORT
IMPURE
LAPARO
LEPERS
LOPERS
MOPERS
NAPERY
NEPHRO
PAPERS
PAPERY
PIPERS
POPERY
REPORT
RUPERT
SUPERB
SUPERS
TAPERS
TAPIRS
TOPERS
UMPIRE
UPPERS
VAPORI
VAPORS
VIPERS
WIPERS

••P••R

APPEAR
CAPPER
CAPTOR
CIPHER
COPIER
COPPER

CUPPER
CYPHER
DAPPER
DIPPER
DOPIER
GOPHER
HOPPER
IMPAIR
KEPLER
KIPPER
LAPPER
LAPSER
LIPPER
NAPIER
NAPPER
NIPPER
OOPHOR
PEPPER
PIPIER
POPLAR
POPPER
RAPIER
RAPPER
REPAIR
RIPPER
ROPIER
SAPHAR
SAPPER
SIPPER
SUPPER
SYPHER
TAPPER
TIPPER
TOPPER
ZEPHYR
ZIPPER

•••PR•

COPPRA
SEMPRE

•••P•R

BUMPER
CAMPER
CAPPER
CARPER
CASPAR
CASPER
COOPER
COPPER
COWPER
CUPPER
DAMPER
DAPPER
DEEPER
DIAPER
DIPPER
DRAPER
ELOPER
GASPAR
GASPER
GRIPER
GROPER
GULPER
HAMPER
HARPER
HELPER
HOOPER
HOPPER
JAIPUR
JASPER
JUMPER
KASPAR
KEEPER
KIPPER
LAPPER
LEAPER
LIMPER
LIPPER
LISPER
LOOPER
NAPPER
NIPPER
PAMPER
PAUPER
PEEPER
PEPPER
POPPER
PROPER
PUMPER
RAPPER
RASPER
REAPER
RIPPER
ROMPER
SAPPER
SECPAR
SHAPER
SIMPER
SIPPER
SLOPER
SNIPER
STUPOR
SUPPER
TAMPER
TAPPER
TEMPER
TIPPER
TOPPER
TORPOR
VESPER
WARPER
WEEPER
YAWPER
YELPER
ZIPPER

PS••••

PSALMS
PSEUDO
PSHAWS
PSYCHE
PSYCHO

P•S•••

PASCAL
PASHAS
PASHTO
PASSED
PASSEE
PASSER
PASSES
PASSIM
PASSUS
PASTAS
PASTED
PASTEL
PASTER
PASTES
PASTIL
PASTOR
PASTRY
PESACH
PESADE
PESETA
PESTER
PESTLE
PISCES
PISGAH
PISHED
PISHES
PISTIL
PISTOL
PISTON
POSADA
POSERS
POSEUR
POSIES
POSING
POSITS
POSSES
POSSET
POSSUM
POSTAL
POSTED
POSTER
PUSHED
PUSHER
PUSHES
PUSHUP
PUSSES
PUSSEY
PUSSLY

P••S••

PANSYS
PARSEC
PARSED
PARSEE
PARSES
PARSIS
PARSON
PASSED
PASSEE
PASSER
PASSES
PASSIM
PASSUS
PATSYS
PAUSED
PAUSER
PAUSES
PEASEN
PEASES
PEPSIN
PERSIA
PERSON
PHASED
PHASES
PHASIA
PHASIC
PHASIS
PHOSPH
PHYSIC
PHYSIO
PIGSTY
PLASHY
PLASIA
PLASIS
PLASMA
PLASMO
PLASTY
PLUSES
PLUSHY
PODSOL
POISED
POISES
POISON
POSSES
POSSET
POSSUM
POTSIE
POUSTO
PRESAS
PRESTO
PRISMS
PRISON
PRISSY
PROSED
PROSER
PROSES
PROSIT
PTISAN
PTOSIS
PUISNE
PULSAR
PULSED
PULSES
PURSED
PURSER
PURSES
PURSUE
PUSSES
PUSSEY
PUSSLY
PUTSCH
PYOSIS

P•••S•

PALEST
PALISH
PAPIST
PARISH
PAVISE
PERISH
PERUSE
PHRASE
PILOSE
PLEASE
POLISH
POPISH
POTASH
PRAISE
PRIEST
PRISSY
PROUST
PUNISH
PUREST
PURISM
PURIST

P••••S

PACERS
PADDYS
PADRES
PAEANS
PAEONS
PAGANS
PAINTS
PALLAS
PALPUS
PAMPAS
PANDAS
PANELS
PANICS
PANSYS
PAPAWS
PAPERS
PAPPUS
PARENS
PARERS
PAREUS
PARGOS
PARIES
PARKAS
PARSES
PARSIS
PARVIS
PASHAS
PASSES
PASSUS
PASTAS
PASTES
PATENS
PATERS
PATHOS
PATIOS
PATOIS
PATSYS
PAULAS
PAULUS
PAUSES
PAVANS
PAVERS
PAWERS
PAYEES
PAYERS
PEARLS
PEASES
PECANS
PEDALS
PEDROS
PEEVES
PEGGYS
PEKANS
PEKOES
PELEUS
PELIAS
PELOPS
PELVES
PELVIS
PENGOS
PENNIS
PENNYS
PEPLOS
PEPLUS
PERCYS
PERILS
PERRYS
PETALS
PETERS
PEWEES
PEWITS
PHASES
PHASIS
PHIALS
PHILOS
PHIPPS
PHOCIS
PHONES
PHOTOS
PIANOS
PICOTS
PICULS
PIECES
PIERUS
PIGNUS
PIKERS
PILAFS
PILEUS
PILOTS
PILOUS
PINDUS
PINGOS
PINONS
PINTOS
PINUPS
PIPERS
PIPETS
PIPITS
PIQUES
PISCES
PISHES
PITIES
PITONS
PIVOTS
PIXIES
PIZZAS
PLACES
PLACKS
PLAIDS
PLAINS
PLAITS
PLANES

PLANKS
PLANTS
PLASIS
PLATES
PLAYAS
PLAZAS
PLEADS
PLEATS
PLEBES
PLEXUS
PLIERS
PLUCKS
PLUMBS
PLUMES
PLUMPS
PLUNKS
PLUSES
PLUTUS
PODOUS
POGIES
POILUS
POINDS
POINTS
POISES
POKERS
POKIES
POLKAS
POLLYS
POLYPS
PONIES
PONTES
POPPYS
POROUS
POSERS
POSIES
POSITS
POSSES
POTTOS
POULTS
POUNDS
POWERS
POYOUS
PRANKS
PRATES
PRAWNS
PRAXIS
PRECIS
PREENS
PRESAS
PRICES
PRICKS
PRIDES
PRIERS
PRIMES
PRIMPS
PRINKS
PRINTS
PRIORS
PRISMS
PRIZES
PROBES
PROEMS
PRONGS
PROOFS
PROSES
PROVES
PROWLS
PRUDES
PRUNES
PRYERS
PSALMS
PSHAWS
PTOSIS
PULERS
PULSES
PUNKAS
PUNTOS
PUPILS
PUREES
PURGES
PURSES
PUSHES
PUSSES
PUTONS
PYLONS
PYOSIS
PYRANS
PYXIES

•PS•••

UPSETS
UPSHOT
UPSIDE

•P•S••

SPASMS
UPASES

•P••S•

APPOSE
OPPOSE
SPARSE
SPEISS
SPLASH
SPOUSE
UPCAST
UPMOST
UPPISH
UPRISE
UPROSE

•P•••S

APEXES
APHIDS
APICES
APPALS
APPELS
APPLES
APRILS
APRONS
EPACTS
EPHAHS
EPHODS
EPHORS
EPIRUS
EPOCHS
EPODES
OPERAS
OPINES
OPTICS
SPACES
SPADES
SPAHIS
SPAITS
SPALLS
SPANKS
SPARES
SPARKS
SPASMS
SPATES
SPAWNS
SPEAKS
SPEARS
SPECKS
SPEEDS
SPEISS
SPELLS
SPENDS
SPICES
SPIELS
SPIERS
SPIKES
SPILES
SPILLS
SPINES
SPIRES
SPIRTS
SPITES
SPLATS
SPLAYS
SPLITS
SPOILS
SPOKES
SPOOFS
SPOOKS
SPOOLS
SPOONS
SPOORS
SPORES
SPORTS
SPOUTS
SPRAGS
SPRATS
SPRAYS
SPREES
SPRIGS
SPRITS
SPRUES
SPUMES
SPURNS
SPURTS
UPASES
UPBOWS
UPENDS
UPPERS
UPSETS

••PS••

COPSES
DIPSAS
GYPSUM
LAPSED
LAPSER
LAPSES
LAPSUS
LEPSIA
PEPSIN
RIPSAW
SEPSIS

••P•S•

APPOSE
BYPASS
BYPAST
DEPOSE
EXPOSE
IMPISH
IMPOSE
IMPOST
LIPASE
MOPISH
OPPOSE
PAPIST
POPISH
RAPIST
REPASS
REPAST
REPOSE
RIPEST
RIPOST
TYPIST
UPPISH

••P••S

ALPHAS
AMPHRS
AMPULS
APPALS
APPELS
APPLES
ARPENS
ASPENS
ASPERS
ASPICS
BIPEDS
BIPODS
BYPASS
CAPERS
CAPIAS
CAPONS
COPIES
COPSES
CUPELS
CYPRUS
DEPOTS
DEPTHS
DIPSAS
DUPERS
ESPIES
EXPELS
GAPERS
GIPONS
HIPPOS
HIPPUS
HYPNOS
IMPELS
INPUTS
JAPANS
JUPONS
KAPOKS
KAPPAS
KOPEKS
KOPJES
LAPELS
LAPINS
LAPSES
LAPSUS
LEPERS
LIPIDS
LOPERS
MAPLES
MOPERS
NAPLES
NAPPES
NOPALS
ORPINS
PAPAWS
PAPERS
PAPPUS
PEPLOS
PEPLUS
PIPERS
PIPETS
PIPITS
POPPYS
PUPILS
RAPHIS
RAPIDS
REPASS
REPAYS
REPELS
RIPENS
RUPEES
SEPALS
SEPIAS
SEPOYS
SEPSIS
SUPERS
TAPERS
TAPIRS
TEPEES
TOPERS
TOPICS
TUPIKS
TYPHUS
UNPEGS
UNPINS
UPPERS
VAPORS
VIPERS
WIPERS
YAPONS
YUPONS

•••PS•

BIOPSY
CORPSE
DROPSY
ELAPSE

•••P•S

ADAPTS
ADEPTS
ADOPTS
ALEPHS
CAMPOS
CAMPUS
CARPUS
CHAPES
COMPOS
COOPTS
CORPUS
COUPES
COYPUS
CRAPES
CREPES
CRYPTS
CUSPIS
DOLPHS
DRAPES
DRUPES
ELOPES
ERUPTS
ETAPES
GLYPHS
GRAPES
GRAPHS
GRIPES
GROPES
HERPES
HIPPOS
HIPPUS
KAPPAS
LAMPAS
LOUPES
MYOPES
NAPPES
NYMPHS
OKAPIS
PALPUS
PAMPAS
PAPPUS
PHIPPS
POPPYS
QUIPUS
RALPHS
ROLPHS
RUMPUS
SALPAS
SCAPES
SCOPES
SCOPUS
SHAPES
SLOPES
SNIPES
STAPES
STIPES
STOPES
STUPAS
STUPES
SWIPES
SYLPHS
TAUPES
TEMPOS

TEMPTS
TRIPOS
WAMPUS

••••PS
BICEPS
BLIMPS
CHAMPS
CHEEPS
CHEOPS
CHIRPS
CHUMPS
CLAMPS
CLASPS
CLUMPS
CRAMPS
CREEPS
CRIMPS
CRISPS
CROUPS
CRUMPS
CUTUPS
DROOPS
EQUIPS
ESTOPS
FLUMPS
FRUMPS
FSTOPS
GALOPS
GETUPS
GRASPS
GROUPS
JALAPS
JULEPS
KNOSPS
LETUPS
MIXUPS
ORLOPS
OXLIPS
PELOPS
PHIPPS
PINUPS
PLUMPS
POLYPS
PRIMPS
RECAPS
SCALPS
SCAMPS
SCARPS
SCAUPS
SCOOPS
SCRAPS
SCRIPS
SETUPS
SHARPS
SIRUPS
SKIMPS
SLEEPS
SLOOPS
SLUMPS
SLURPS
SNOOPS
STAMPS
STEEPS
STIRPS
STOMPS
STOOPS
STOUPS
STRAPS
STRIPS
STROPS
STUMPS
SUNUPS
SWAMPS
SWEEPS
SWOOPS
SYRUPS
THRIPS
THUMPS
TIEUPS
TRAMPS
TROOPS
TRUMPS
TULIPS
TWERPS
TWIRPS
UNCAPS
UNRIPS
USURPS
WATAPS
WHELPS
WHOOPS

PT••••
PTISAN
PTOSIS

P•T•••
PATCHY
PATENS
PATENT
PATERS
PATHAN
PATHIA
PATHOL
PATHOS
PATINA
PATINE
PATIOS
PATOIS
PATROL
PATRON
PATSYS
PATTED
PATTEN
PATTER
PATTON
PETAIN
PETALS
PETARD
PETERS
PETITE
PETREL
PETRIE
PETROL
PETTED
PITCHY
PITHED
PITIED
PITIES
PITMAN
PITMEN
PITONS
PITTED
POTAGE
POTASH
POTATO
POTBOY
POTEEN
POTENT
POTHER
POTION
POTPIE
POTSIE
POTTED
POTTER
POTTLE
POTTOS
PUTLOG
PUTNAM
PUTOFF
PUTONS
PUTOUT
PUTPUT
PUTRID
PUTSCH
PUTTED
PUTTEE
PUTTER
PYTHIA
PYTHIC
PYTHON

P••T••
PALTER
PALTRY
PANTED
PANTIE
PANTRY
PARTED
PARTLY
PASTAS
PASTED
PASTEL
PASTER
PASTES
PASTIL
PASTOR
PASTRY
PATTED
PATTEN
PATTER
PATTON
PECTEN
PECTIC
PECTIN
PEGTOP
PELTED
PELTER
PELTRY
PENTAD
PENTUP
PEPTIC
PERTLY
PESTER
PESTLE
PETTED
PEWTER
PHOTIC
PHOTON
PHOTOS
PHYTIN
PICTOR
PIETER
PIETRO
PINTER
PINTLE
PINTOS
PISTIL
PISTOL
PISTON
PITTED
PLATAN
PLATED
PLATEN
PLATER
PLATES
PLATTE
PLUTUS
POETIC
POETRY
PONTES
PONTIC
PONTIL
PONTON
PORTAL
PORTER
PORTIA
PORTLY
POSTAL
POSTED
POSTER
POTTED
POTTER
POTTLE
POTTOS
POUTED
POUTER
POWTER
PRATED
PRATER
PRATES
PRETER
PRETOR
PRETTY
PROTON
PUNTED
PUNTER
PUNTOS
PUTTED
PUTTEE
PUTTER

P•••T•
PAINTS
PAINTY
PAIUTE
PALATE
PARITY
PASHTO
PEDATE
PEDATI
PELITE
PELOTA
PESETA
PETITE
PEWITS
PEYOTE
PICOTS
PIGSTY
PILATE
PILOTS
PINITE
PIPETS
PIPITS
PIRATE
PIVOTS
PLAITS
PLANTS
PLASTY
PLATTE
PLEATS
PLENTY
PLINTH
POINTS
POINTY
POLITE
POLITY
POSITS
POTATO
POULTS
POUSTO
PRESTO
PRETTY
PRINTS
PROCTO
PRONTO
PUPATE
PURITY
PYRITE

P••••T
PACKET
PALEST
PALLET
PAPIST
PARENT
PARGET
PARROT
PATENT
PEANUT
PEDANT
PELLET
PENULT
PEQUOT
PERMIT
PICKET
PIGNUT
PINXIT
PIQUET
PLACET
PLAINT
PLANET
PLIANT
PLIGHT
POCKET
PONENT
POPPET
POSSET
POTENT
PRIEST
PRIVET
PROFIT
PROJET
PROMPT
PROSIT
PROUST
PULLET
PULPIT
PUNDIT
PUPPET
PUREST
PURIST
PUTOUT
PUTPUT

•PT•••
OPTICS
OPTIMA
OPTIME
OPTING
OPTION
UPTAKE
UPTOWN
UPTURN

•P•T••
APATHY
APHTHA
SPATES
SPATHE
SPITAL
SPITED
SPITES
SPOTTY
SPUTUM

•P••T•
APLITE
EPACTS
OPHITE
OPIATE
SPAITS
SPARTA
SPILTH
SPIRTS
SPLATS
SPLITS
SPORTS
SPORTY
SPOTTY
SPOUTS
SPRATS
SPRITE

SPRITS
SPURTS
UPDATE
UPPITY
UPSETS

•P•••T

SPIGOT
SPINET
SPIRIT
SPLINT
SPOILT
SPRINT
SPROUT
UPBEAT
UPCAST
UPLIFT
UPMOST
UPROOT
UPSHOT

••PT••

CAPTOR
COPTIC
DEPTHS
HEPTAD
LEPTON
PEPTIC
SEPTAL
SEPTET
SEPTIC
SEPTUM
TIPTOE
TIPTOP

••P•T•

BYPATH
CAPITA
CAPOTE
DEPOTS
DEPUTE
DEPUTY
HEPATO
IMPUTE
INPUTS
PIPETS
PIPITS
PUPATE
REPUTE
UPPITY
WAPITI

••P••T

ARPENT
ASPECT
BYPAST
COPOUT
DEPART
DEPICT
DEPORT
ESPRIT
EXPECT
EXPERT
EXPORT
IMPACT
IMPART
IMPORT
IMPOST
JAPHET
LAPPET
MOPPET
PAPIST
POPPET
PUPPET
RAPIST
REPAST
REPEAT
REPENT
REPORT
RIPEST
RIPOST
RUPERT
SEPTET
SIPPET
TAPPET
TIPPET
TYPIST

•••PT•

ADAPTS
ADEPTS
ADOPTS
COOPTS
CRYPTO
CRYPTS
ERUPTS
GLYPTO
TEMPTS

•••P•T

ARMPIT
CARPET
DESPOT
LAPPET
LIMPET
MOPPET
OUTPUT
POPPET
PULPIT
PUPPET
PUTPUT
RAJPUT
SIPPET
TAPPET
TEAPOT
TIPPET

••••PT

ABRUPT
ACCEPT
COEMPT
ENRAPT
EXCEPT
EXEMPT
INCEPT
PROMPT
RECEPT
SCRIPT
SCULPT
STRIPT
UNWEPT
YCLEPT

PU••••

PUBLIC
PUCKER
PUDDLE
PUDDLY
PUEBLO
PUFFED
PUFFER
PUFFIN
PUGGED
PUGGRY
PUGREE
PUISNE
PUKING
PULERS
PULING
PULLED
PULLER
PULLET
PULLEY
PULPED
PULPIT
PULQUE
PULSAR
PULSED
PULSES
PUMICE
PUMMEL
PUMPED
PUMPER
PUNCHY
PUNDIT
PUNIER
PUNILY
PUNISH
PUNJAB
PUNKAS
PUNNED
PUNTED
PUNTER
PUNTOS
PUPATE
PUPILS
PUPPED
PUPPET
PURANA
PURDAH
PUREED
PUREES
PURELY
PUREST
PURFLE
PURGED
PURGER
PURGES
PURIFY
PURINE
PURISM
PURIST
PURITY
PURLED
PURLIN
PURPLE
PURRED
PURSED
PURSER
PURSES
PURSUE
PURVEY
PUSHED
PUSHER
PUSHES
PUSHUP
PUSSES
PUSSEY
PUSSLY
PUTLOG
PUTNAM
PUTOFF
PUTONS
PUTOUT
PUTPUT
PUTRID
PUTSCH
PUTTED
PUTTEE
PUTTER
PUZZLE

P•U•••

PAUKER
PAULAS
PAULIN
PAULUS
PAUNCH
PAUPER
PAUSED
PAUSER
PAUSES
PLUCKS
PLUCKY
PLUMBO
PLUMBS
PLUMED
PLUMES
PLUMMY
PLUMPS
PLUNGE
PLUNKS
PLURAL
PLUSES
PLUSHY
PLUTUS
PLUVIO
POUCHY
POULTS
POUNCE
POUNDS
POURED
POURER
POUSTO
POUTED
POUTER
PRUDES
PRUNED
PRUNER
PRUNES
PYURIA

P••U••

PAIUTE
PAPUAN
PAPULA
PAPULE
PARURE
PENULT
PENURY
PEQUOD
PEQUOT
PERUKE
PERUSE
PICULS
PILULE
PINUPS
PIQUED
PIQUES
PIQUET
PLEURA
PLEURO
PLOUGH
PNEUMA
PNEUMO
PODUNK
PROUST
PSEUDO

P•••U•

PALPUS
PAPPUS
PAREUS
PASSUS
PAULUS
PEANUT
PELEUS
PENTUP
PEPLUM
PEPLUS
PHYLUM
PICKUP
PIERUS
PIGNUS
PIGNUT
PILEUM
PILEUS
PILOUS
PINDUS
PLAGUE
PLAGUY
PLAQUE
PLENUM
PLEXUS
PLUTUS
PODIUM
PODOUS
POILUS
POLLUX
POPGUN
POROUS
POSEUR
POSSUM
POYOUS
PRAGUE
PREVUE
PULQUE
PURSUE
PUSHUP
PUTOUT
PUTPUT

•PU•••

APULIA
SPUMED
SPUMES
SPUNKY
SPURGE
SPURNS
SPURRY
SPURTS
SPUTUM

•P•U••

OPPUGN
SPOUSE
SPOUTS
SPRUCE
SPRUES
SPRUNG
UPTURN

•P••U•

EPIRUS
OPAQUE
SPROUT
SPUTUM

•P•••U

APERCU

••PU••

AMPULE
AMPULS
COPULA
CUPULE
DEPUTE
DEPUTY
IMPUGN
IMPURE
IMPUTE
INPUTS
OPPUGN
PAPUAN
PAPULA
PAPULE
REPUTE

••P•U•

COPOUT
CUPFUL
CUPRUM
CYPRUS
GYPSUM

HIPPUS
LAPFUL
LAPSUS
PAPPUS
PEPLUM
PEPLUS
POPGUN
SEPTUM
TYPHUS

•••PU•
CAMPUS
CARPUS
CORPUS
COYPUS
HIPPUS
JAIPUR
OUTPUT
PALPUS
PAPPUS
PUTPUT
QUIPUS
RAJPUT
RUMPUS
SCOPUS
SLIPUP
STEPUP
WAMPUM
WAMPUS
WRAPUP

P•V•••
PAVANS
PAVERS
PAVING
PAVIOR
PAVISE
PAVLOV
PIVOTS

P••V••
PARVIS
PEAVEY
PEEVED
PEEVES
PELVES
PELVIC
PELVIS
PLOVER
PLUVIO
PRAVDA
PREVUE
PRIVET
PROVED
PROVEN
PROVER
PROVES
PURVEY

P••••V
PAVLOV

•P•V••
SPAVIN

P•W•••
PAWERS
PAWING
PAWNED
PAWNEE
PAWNER
PAWPAW
PEWEES
PEWITS
PEWTER
POWDER
POWELL
POWERS
POWTER
POWWOW

P••W••
PAXWAX
PEEWEE
PLOWED
PLOWER
POWWOW
PRAWNS
PREWAR
PROWLS

P•••W•
PAPAWS
PSHAWS

P••••W
PAWPAW
PILLOW
POWWOW

•PW•••
UPWARD

•P•W••
SPAWNS
SPEWED

•P••W•
SPRAWL
UPBOWS
UPTOWN

••P•W•
IMPAWN
PAPAWS

••P••W
NEPHEW
RIPSAW

•••P•W
PAWPAW
QUAPAW

P•X•••
PAXWAX
PIXIES
PYXIES

P••X••
PINXIT
PLEXOR
PLEXUS
PRAXIS

P••••X
PAXWAX
PICKAX
POLEAX
POLLEX
POLLUX
PREFIX
PROLIX

•P•X••
APEXES

•P•••X
SPADIX
SPHINX

••P••X
DIPLEX
DUPLEX

•••P•X
AUSPEX
COWPOX

PY••••
PYEMIA
PYEMIC
PYKNIC
PYLONS
PYOSIS
PYRANS
PYRENE
PYRITE
PYRONE
PYROPE
PYRRHA
PYTHIA
PYTHIC
PYTHON
PYURIA
PYXIES

P•Y•••
PAYDAY
PAYEES
PAYERS
PAYING
PAYOFF
PAYOLA
PEYOTE
PHYLAE
PHYLLO
PHYLUM
PHYSIC
PHYSIO
PHYTIN
PLYING
POYOUS
PRYERS
PRYING
PSYCHE
PSYCHO

P••Y••
PLAYAS
PLAYED
PLAYER
POLYPS
PRAYED
PRAYER
PREYED
PREYER

P•••Y•
PADDYS
PANSYS
PAPAYA
PATSYS
PEGGYS
PENNYS
PERCYS
PERRYS
PHENYL
POLLYS
POPPYS
PROPYL

P••••Y
PACIFY
PAINTY
PALELY
PALTRY
PANTRY
PAPACY
PAPERY
PARITY
PARLAY
PARLEY
PARODY
PARTLY
PASTRY
PATCHY
PAYDAY
PEACHY
PEARLY
PEAVEY
PEBBLY
PELTRY
PENURY
PERTLY
PHONEY
PHOOEY
PIGSTY
PIMPLY
PINERY
PIRACY
PITCHY
PLAGUY
PLASHY
PLASTY
PLENTY
PLUCKY
PLUMMY
PLUSHY
POACHY
POETRY
POINTY
POLICY
POLITY
POMPEY
POORLY
POPERY
PORTLY
POTBOY
POUCHY
PREPAY
PRETTY
PRIMLY
PRIORY
PRISSY
PUDDLY
PUGGRY
PULLEY
PUNCHY
PUNILY
PURELY
PURIFY
PURITY
PURVEY
PUSSEY
PUSSLY

•PY•••
SPYING

•P•Y••
SPAYED
SPRYER
SPRYLY

•P••Y•
EPONYM
SPLAYS
SPRAYS

•P•••Y
APATHY
APIARY
OPENLY
SPARRY
SPEEDY
SPERRY
SPHERY
SPIFFY
SPINNY
SPONGY
SPOOKY
SPOONY
SPORTY
SPOTTY
SPRYLY
SPUNKY
SPURRY
UPPITY

••P•Y•
ALPHYL
PAPAYA
POPPYS
REPAYS
SEPOYS
ZEPHYR

••P••Y
BYPLAY
COPLEY
DEPLOY
DEPUTY
DIPODY
DUPERY
EMPERY
EMPLOY
EXPIRY
NAPERY
OSPREY
PAPACY
PAPERY
POPERY
REPLAY
RIPELY
RIPLEY
ROPILY
SUPPLY
TEPEFY
TYPIFY
UPPITY

•••PY•
POPPYS
PROPYL

•••P•Y
BIOPSY
CHIPPY
CHOPPY
COMPLY
DAMPLY
DEEPLY
DIMPLY
DRIPPY
DROPSY
FLOPPY
GRAPHY
GRIPPY
LIMPLY
PIMPLY
POMPEY
PREPAY
SIMPLY
SLOPPY
SNAPPY
SNIPPY
SUPPLY
SYLPHY
TEAPOY
TROPHY
TWOPLY

••••PY
CANOPY
CHIPPY
CHOPPY
CLUMPY
CREEPY
CRIMPY
CRISPY
CROUPY
DRIPPY
DROOPY
FLOPPY
FRUMPY
GRIPPY
GRUMPY
JALOPY
OCCUPY
SIRUPY
SKIMPY
SLEEPY
SLOPPY
SNAPPY
SNIPPY
SNOOPY
STRIPY
STUMPY
SWAMPY
SWEEPY
SYRUPY
WICOPY

P•Z•••
PIZZAS
PUZZLE

P••Z••
PANZER
PIAZZA
PIZZAS
PLAZAS
PODZOL
PRIZED
PRIZER
PRIZES
PUZZLE

P•••Z•
PIAZZA

•P•Z••
EPIZOA

Q•A•••
QUACKS
QUADRI
QUAERE
QUAFFS
QUAGGA
QUAGGY
QUAHOG
QUAILS
QUAINT
QUAKED
QUAKER
QUAKES
QUALMS
QUALMY
QUANTA
QUANTS
QUAPAW
QUARKS
QUARRY
QUARTE
QUARTO
QUARTS
QUARTZ
QUASAR
QUATRE
QUAVER

Q••A••
QUEANS
QUEASY

Q•••A•
QUAPAW
QUASAR
QUOTAS

Q••••A
QUAGGA
QUANTA

•Q•A••
EQUALS
EQUATE
SQUABS
SQUADS
SQUALL
SQUAMA
SQUARE
SQUASH
SQUATS
SQUAWK
SQUAWS

•Q••A•
SQUEAK
SQUEAL

•Q•••A
AQUILA
SQUAMA

••Q•A•
LOQUAT

Q••B••
QUEBEC

•Q••B•
SQUABS
SQUIBS

Q••C••
QUACKS

Q•••C•
QUINCE
QUINCY
QUITCH

Q••••C
QUEBEC
QUINIC

Q••D••
QUADRI

Q••••D
QUAKED
QUEUED
QUIRED
QUOTED

•Q••D•
SQUADS
SQUIDS

••Q••D
LIQUID
PEQUOD
PIQUED

Q•E•••
QUEANS
QUEASY
QUEBEC
QUEENS
QUEERS
QUELLS
QUERNS
QUESTS
QUEUED
QUEUES
QUEZON

Q••E••
QUAERE
QUEENS
QUEERS

Q•••E•
QUAKED
QUAKER
QUAKES
QUAVER
QUEBEC
QUEUED
QUEUES
QUIRED
QUIRES
QUIVER
QUOTED
QUOTER
QUOTES

Q••••E
QUAERE
QUARTE
QUATRE
QUINCE

•Q•E••
SQUEAK
SQUEAL

•Q•••E
EQUATE
EQUINE
SQUARE
SQUIRE

••Q•E•
COQUET
FIQUES
PIQUED
PIQUES
PIQUET
ROQUET
SEQUEL
TOQUES
TUQUES

•••Q•E
BARQUE
BASQUE
BISQUE
BRAQUE
CAIQUE
CASQUE
CINQUE
CIRQUE
CLAQUE
CLIQUE
MANQUE
MARQUE
MASQUE
MOSQUE
OPAQUE
PLAQUE
PULQUE
RISQUE
TORQUE
UNIQUE

Q••F••
QUAFFS

Q•••F•
QUAFFS

Q••G••
QUAGGA
QUAGGY

Q•••G•
QUAGGA
QUAGGY

Q••••G
QUAHOG

Q••H••
QUAHOG

Q••••H
QUITCH

•Q•••H
SQUASH
SQUISH

Q•I•••
QUILLS
QUILTS
QUINCE
QUINCY
QUINIC
QUINSY
QUINTS
QUIPUS
QUIRED
QUIRES
QUIRKS
QUIRTS
QUITCH
QUIVER

Q••I••
QUAILS
QUAINT
QUOINS
QUOITS

Q•••I•
QUINIC

Q••••I
QUADRI

•Q•I••
AQUILA
EQUINE
EQUIPS
EQUITY
SQUIBS
SQUIDS
SQUILL
SQUINT
SQUIRE
SQUIRM
SQUIRT
SQUISH

••Q•I•
ACQUIT
LIQUID
MAQUIS
SEQUIN

•••QI•
IRAQIS

•••Q•I
SESQUI

Q••K••
QUAKED
QUAKER
QUAKES

Q•••K•
QUACKS
QUARKS
QUIRKS

•Q•••K
SQUAWK
SQUEAK

Q••L••
QUALMS
QUALMY
QUELLS
QUILLS
QUILTS

Q•••L•
QUAILS
QUELLS
QUILLS

•Q••L•
AQUILA
EQUALS
SQUALL
SQUILL

•Q•••L
SQUALL
SQUEAL
SQUILL

••Q••L
SEQUEL

Q•••M•
QUALMS
QUALMY

Q••••M
QUORUM

•Q••M•
SQUAMA

•Q•••M
SQUIRM

Q••N••
QUANTA
QUANTS
QUINCE
QUINCY
QUINIC
QUINSY
QUINTS

Q•••N•
QUAINT
QUEANS
QUEENS
QUERNS

QUOINS

Q••••N
QUEZON

•Q••N•
EQUINE
SQUINT

••Q••N
SEQUIN

Q•O•••
QUOINS
QUOITS
QUORUM
QUOTAS
QUOTED
QUOTER
QUOTES

Q•••O•
QUAHOG
QUEZON

Q••••O
QUARTO

••Q•O•
LIQUOR
PEQUOD
PEQUOT

Q••P••
QUAPAW
QUIPUS

•Q••P•
EQUIPS

Q••R••
QUARKS
QUARRY
QUARTE
QUARTO
QUARTS
QUARTZ
QUERNS
QUIRED
QUIRES
QUIRKS
QUIRTS
QUORUM

Q•••R•
QUADRI
QUAERE
QUARRY
QUATRE
QUEERS

Q••••R
QUAKER
QUASAR
QUAVER
QUIVER
QUOTER

•Q••R•
SQUARE
SQUIRE
SQUIRM
SQUIRT

••Q••R
LIQUOR

Q••S••
QUASAR
QUESTS

Q•••S•
QUEASY
QUINSY

Q••••S
QUACKS
QUAFFS
QUAILS
QUAKES
QUALMS
QUANTS
QUARKS
QUARTS
QUEANS
QUEENS
QUEERS
QUELLS
QUERNS
QUESTS
QUEUES
QUILLS
QUILTS
QUINTS
QUIPUS
QUIRES
QUIRKS
QUIRTS
QUOINS
QUOITS
QUOTAS
QUOTES

•Q••S•
SQUASH
SQUISH

•Q•••S
EQUALS
EQUIPS
SQUABS
SQUADS
SQUATS
SQUAWS
SQUIBS
SQUIDS

••Q••S
FIQUES
MAQUIS
PIQUES
TOQUES
TUQUES

•••Q•S
IRAQIS

Q••T••
QUATRE
QUITCH
QUOTAS
QUOTED
QUOTER
QUOTES

Q•••T•
QUANTA
QUANTS
QUARTE
QUARTO
QUARTS
QUARTZ
QUESTS
QUILTS
QUINTS
QUIRTS
QUOITS

Q••••T
QUAINT

•Q••T•
EQUATE
EQUITY
SQUATS

•Q•••T
SQUINT
SQUIRT

••Q••T
ACQUIT
COQUET
LOQUAT
PEQUOT
PIQUET
ROQUET

QU••••
QUACKS
QUADRI
QUAERE
QUAFFS
QUAGGA
QUAGGY
QUAHOG
QUAILS
QUAINT
QUAKED
QUAKER
QUAKES
QUALMS
QUALMY
QUANTA
QUANTS
QUAPAW
QUARKS
QUARRY
QUARTE
QUARTO
QUARTS
QUARTZ
QUASAR
QUATRE
QUAVER
QUEANS
QUEASY
QUEBEC
QUEENS
QUEERS
QUELLS
QUERNS
QUESTS
QUEUED
QUEUES
QUEZON
QUILLS
QUILTS
QUINCE
QUINCY
QUINIC
QUINSY
QUINTS
QUIPUS
QUIRED
QUIRES
QUIRKS
QUIRTS
QUITCH
QUIVER
QUOINS
QUOITS
QUORUM
QUOTAS
QUOTED
QUOTER
QUOTES

Q••U••
QUEUED
QUEUES

Q•••U•
QUIPUS
QUORUM

•QU•••
AQUILA
EQUALS
EQUATE
EQUINE
EQUIPS
EQUITY
SQUABS
SQUADS
SQUALL
SQUAMA
SQUARE
SQUASH
SQUATS
SQUAWK
SQUAWS
SQUEAK
SQUEAL
SQUIBS
SQUIDS
SQUILL
SQUINT
SQUIRE
SQUIRM
SQUIRT
SQUISH

••QU••
ACQUIT
COQUET
FIQUES
LIQUID
LIQUOR
LOQUAT
MAQUIS
PEQUOD
PEQUOT
PIQUED
PIQUES
PIQUET
ROQUET
SEQUEL
SEQUIN
TOQUES
TUQUES

•••QU•
BARQUE
BASQUE
BISQUE
BRAQUE
CAIQUE
CASQUE
CINQUE
CIRQUE
CLAQUE
CLIQUE
CLIQUY
EXEQUY
MANQUE
MARQUE
MASQUE
MOSQUE
OPAQUE
PLAQUE
PULQUE
RISQUE
SESQUI
TORQUE
UNIQUE

Q••V••
QUAVER
QUIVER

Q••••W
QUAPAW

•Q••W•
SQUAWK
SQUAWS

Q••••Y
QUAGGY
QUALMY
QUARRY
QUEASY
QUINCY
QUINSY

•Q•••Y
EQUITY

•••Q•Y
CLIQUY
EXEQUY

Q••Z••
QUEZON

Q••••Z
QUARTZ

RA••••
RABBET
RABBIS
RABBIT
RABBLE
RABIES
RACEME
RACERS
RACHEL
RACHIS
RACIAL
RACIER
RACILY
RACINE
RACING
RACISM
RACIST
RACKED
RACKER
RACKET
RACOON
RADARS
RADDLE
RADIAL
RADIAN
RADIOS
RADISH
RADIUM
RADIUS
RADOME
RADULA
RAFFIA
RAFFLE
RAFTED

6

RAFTER
RAGGED
RAGING
RAGLAN
RAGMAN
RAGMEN
RAGOUT
RAGTAG
RAIDED
RAIDER
RAILED
RAINED
RAISED
RAISER
RAISES
RAISIN
RAJABS
RAJAHS
RAJPUT
RAKERS
RAKING
RAKISH
RALPHS
RAMBLE
RAMIES
RAMIFY
RAMMED
RAMMER
RAMONA
RAMOSE
RAMOUS
RAMPED
RAMROD
RAMSON
RANCHO
RANCID
RANCOR
RANDAL
RANDAN
RANDOM
RANEES
RANGED
RANGER
RANGES
RANKED
RANKER
RANKLE
RANKLY
RANSOM
RANTED
RANTER
RAOULS
RAPHAE
RAPHIS
RAPIDS
RAPIER
RAPINE
RAPING
RAPIST
RAPPED
RAPPEE
RAPPEL
RAPPER
RAREFY
RARELY
RAREST
RARING
RARITY
RASCAL
RASHER
RASHES
RASHLY
RASPED
RASPER
RATALS
RATELS
RATERS
RATHER
RATIFY
RATINE
RATING
RATION
RATIOS
RATITE
RATLIN
RATOON
RATTAN
RATTED
RATTEN
RATTER
RATTLE
RATTLY
RAVAGE
RAVELS
RAVENS
RAVERS
RAVINE
RAVING
RAVISH
RAWEST
RAWISH
RAYAHS
RAYING
RAYONS
RAZEED
RAZEES
RAZING
RAZORS
RAZZED
RAZZES

R•A•••

REACTS
READER
REALES
REALLY
REALMS
REALTY
REAMED
REAMER
REAPED
REAPER
REARED
REARER
REARMS
REASON
REAVOW
RIALTO
RIATAS
ROALDS
ROAMED
ROAMER
ROARED
ROARER
ROASTS
RWANDA

R••A••

RADARS
RAJABS
RAJAHS
RATALS
RAVAGE
RAYAHS
REBATE
REBATO
RECALL
RECANT
RECAPS
RECAST
REDACT
REDANS
REGAIN
REGALE
REGARD
REHASH
RELATE
RELAYS
REMADE
REMAIN
REMAKE
REMAND
REMANS
REMARK
REPAID
REPAIR
REPAND
REPASS
REPAST
REPAYS
RESALE
RETAIL
RETAIN
RETAKE
RETARD
REVAMP
REWARD
RIBALD
RITARD
RIVALS
RIYALS
ROBALO
ROBAND
ROLAND
ROMAIC
ROMANS
ROMANY
RONALD
ROSARY
ROTARY
ROTATE
ROWANS
ROXANA
ROXANE
ROYALS
RRHAGE
RRHAGY
RUBACE
RUBATO
RUGATE

R•••A•

RACIAL
RADIAL
RADIAN
RAGLAN
RAGMAN
RAGTAG
RANDAL
RANDAN
RAPHAE
RASCAL
RATTAN
RECTAL
REDBAY
REDCAP
REGNAL
REHEAR
REHEAT
RELOAD
RENTAL
REPEAT
REPLAY
RESEAT
RESEAU
REVEAL
RHINAL
RHODAS
RIATAS
RICTAL
RIPRAP
RIPSAW
RITUAL
RODMAN
RUMBAS
RUNWAY
RUPIAH

R••••A

RADULA
RAFFIA
RAMONA
REDOWA
REGINA
REMORA
REMUDA
RESEDA
RETINA
RHUMBA
ROBBIA
ROMOLA
ROSTRA
ROWENA
ROXANA
RUMINA
RUSSIA
RWANDA

•RA•••

ARABEL
ARABIA
ARABIC
ARABLE
ARAGON
ARANTA
ARARAT
ARAWAK
BRACED
BRACER
BRACES
BRACHI
BRACHY
BRACTS
BRAHMA
BRAHMS
BRAIDS
BRAILS
BRAINS
BRAINY
BRAISE
BRAIZE
BRAKED
BRAKES
BRANCH
BRANDS
BRANDY
BRANNY
BRANTS
BRAQUE
BRASHY
BRASSY
BRAVED
BRAVER
BRAVES
BRAVOS
BRAWLS
BRAWNY
BRAYED
BRAYER
BRAZAS
BRAZED
BRAZEN
BRAZER
BRAZES
BRAZIL
BRAZOS
CRAALS
CRABBY
CRACKS
CRACKY
CRACOW
CRADLE
CRAFTS
CRAFTY
CRAGGY
CRAIGS
CRAKES
CRAMBO
CRAMPS
CRANED
CRANES
CRANIA
CRANIO
CRANKS
CRANKY
CRANNY
CRAPED
CRAPES
CRASIS
CRATCH
CRATED
CRATER
CRATES
CRAVAT
CRAVED
CRAVEN
CRAVER
CRAVES
CRAWLS
CRAWLY
CRAYON
CRAZED
CRAZES
DRABLY
DRACHM
DRAFFS
DRAFFY
DRAFTS
DRAFTY
DRAGEE
DRAGON
DRAINS
DRAKES
DRAMAS
DRAPED
DRAPER
DRAPES
DRAWEE
DRAWER
DRAWLS
DRAWLY
DRAYED
ERASED
ERASER
ERASES
FRACAS
FRAILS
FRAISE
FRAMED
FRAMER
FRAMES
FRANCE
FRANCK
FRANCO
FRANCS
FRANKS
FRAPPE
FRATER
FRAUDS
FRAUEN
FRAYED
GRABEN
GRACED
GRACES

GRADED
GRADER
GRADES
GRADIN
GRADUS
GRAECO
GRAFTS
GRAHAM
GRAINS
GRAINY
GRANGE
GRANNY
GRANTS
GRAPES
GRAPHO
GRAPHS
GRAPHY
GRASPS
GRASSY
GRATED
GRATER
GRATES
GRATIS
GRAVED
GRAVEL
GRAVEN
GRAVER
GRAVES
GRAVID
GRAYED
GRAYER
GRAYLY
GRAZED
GRAZER
GRAZES
IRAQIS
KRAALS
KRAITS
KRAKEN
ORACHS
ORACLE
ORALLY
ORANGE
ORANGS
ORATED
ORATES
ORATOR
PRAGUE
PRAISE
PRANCE
PRANKS
PRATED
PRATER
PRATES
PRAVDA
PRAWNS
PRAXIS
PRAYED
PRAYER
SRADHA
TRACED
TRACER
TRACES
TRACHE
TRACHY
TRACKS
TRACTS
TRADED
TRADER
TRADES
TRAGIC
TRAGUS
TRAILS
TRAINS
TRAITS
TRAMPS
TRANCE
TRANSP
TRASHY
TRAUMA
TRAVEL
TRAVES
TRAWLS
URAEUS
URALIC
URANIA
URANIC
URANUS
URANYL
WRACKS
WRAITH
WRAPUP
WRASSE
WRATHY
XRAYED

•R•A••

ARCADE
ARCANE
ARGALI
ARGALS
ARIANS
ARMADA
ARMAGH
ARMAND
ARNAUD
ARRACK
ARRANT
ARRAYS
ARYANS
BREACH
BREADS
BREAKS
BREAMS
BREAST
BREATH
BRIARS
BROACH
BROADS
BRYANT
CRAALS
CREAKS
CREAKY
CREAMS
CREAMY
CREASE
CREASY
CREATE
CROAKS
CROAKY
CROATS
DREADS
DREAMS
DREAMT
DREAMY
DREARY
DRYADS
ERGATE
ERRAND
ERRANT
ERRATA
ERSATZ
FREAKS
FREAKY
FRIARS
FRIARY
GREASE
GREASY
GREATS
GREAVE
GROANS
GROATS
KRAALS
ORDAIN
OREADS
ORGANA
ORGANO
ORGANS
ORGASM
ORNATE
PREACH
RRHAGE
RRHAGY
TREADS
TREATS
TREATY
TRIADS
TRIALS
TRUANT
URBANE
UREASE
WREAKS
WREATH

•R••A•

ARARAT
ARAWAK
ARECAS
ARENAS
AROMAS
ARREAR
BRAZAS
BRIDAL
BROGAN
BROMAL
BRUMAL
BRUTAL
CRAVAT
CRETAN
CRURAL
DRAMAS
FRACAS
FREDAS
FRIDAY
FRUGAL
GRAHAM
GRETAS
ORDEAL
ORGEAT
ORIGAN
ORPHAN
PREFAB
PREPAY
PRESAS
PREWAR
PRIMAL
TREPAN
TRIBAL
TRINAL
TROCAR
TROJAN
TROPAL
TRUMAN
URINAL

•R•••A

ARABIA
ARANTA
ARBELA
AREOLA
ARISTA
ARMADA
ARNICA
ARROBA
ARUNTA
BRAHMA
BREGMA
BRENDA
CRANIA
CREUSA
CRIMEA
ERRATA
FRIEDA
FRUSTA
ORGANA
PRAVDA
SRADHA
TRAUMA
TRIVIA
TROIKA
URANIA
UREMIA
URSULA

••RA••

ABRADE
ABRAMS
AERATE
AFRAID
AFRAME
AGRAFE
ARRACK
ARRANT
ARRAYS
AURATE
AZRAEL
BERATE
BORAGE
BORANE
BORATE
BURANS
CARACK
CARAFE
CARATE
CARATS
CERATE
CERATO
CORALS
CURACY
CURARE
CURATE
CYRANO
DERAIL
DERAIN
DORADO
ENRAGE
ENRAPT
ERRAND
ERRANT
ERRATA
FARADS
FORAGE
FORAYS
GARAGE
GERALD
GERARD
GORALS
GYRATE
HARASS
HERALD
HIRAMS
HORACE
HORARY
IHRAMS
ISRAEL
JORAMS
JURANT
JURATS
KARATE
KARATS
KERALA
KERATO
LORAIN
MARACA
MARAUD
MIRAGE
MORALE
MORALS
MORASS
MORAYS
MURALS
PARADE
PARANG
PARAPH
PHRASE
PIRACY
PIRANA
PIRATE
PURANA
PYRANS
SARAHS
SARAPE
SCRAGS
SCRAMS
SCRAPE
SCRAPS
SCRAWL
SERACS
SERAIS
SERAPE
SERAPH
SHRANK
SPRAGS
SPRAIN
SPRANG
SPRATS
SPRAWL
SPRAYS
STRAFE
STRAIN
STRAIT
STRAKE
STRAND
STRAPS
STRASS
STRATA
STRATI
STRAWS
STRAWY
STRAYS
SURAHS
TERAPH
TERATO
THRALL
THRASH
TIRADE
TIRANA
TORAHS
TYRANT
VIRAGO

••R•A•

ABROAD
ADRIAN
AERIAL
AIRMAN
AIRWAY
AORTAE
AORTAL
AORTAS
ARREAR
ATRIAL
BARMAN
BOREAL
BOREAS
BUREAU
BURIAL
BURLAP
BURSAE
BURSAL
BURSAR
BURSAS
BYROAD
CARLAS

6

CARMAN
CARNAL
CARPAL
CEREAL
CORBAN
CORDAY
CORRAL
CORSAC
CURIAE
CURIAL
DARDAN
DERMAL
DERMAS
DERMAT
DIRHAM
DORIAN
DORSAD
DORSAL
DURBAN
DURBAR
DURHAM
DURIAN
EARLAP
EARWAX
FERIAL
FIRMAN
FORBAD
FORMAL
FORMAT
FORNAX
GERMAN
HARLAN
HARTAL
HERBAL
HEREAT
HERMAE
HERMAI
HERMAN
HURRAH
HURRAY
INROAD
JORDAN
KARMAS
KARNAK
KOREAN
LARIAT
LARVAE
LARVAL
MARGAY
MARIAN
MARIAS
MARTAS
MERMAN
MIRIAM
MOREAU
MORGAN
MORTAL
MORTAR
MURRAY
MYRIAD
MYRNAS
NARIAL
NARWAL
NORIAS
NORMAL
NORMAN
NORMAS
NORWAY
OCREAE
PARCAE
PARIAH
PARIAN
PARKAS
PARLAY
PARRAL
PORTAL
PURDAH
SARSAR
SCREAK
SCREAM
SERDAB
SERIAL
SERVAL
SIRDAR
SPREAD
STREAK
STREAM
STRIAE
SURTAX
SYRIAC
SYRIAN
TARMAC
TARNAL
TARSAL
TARTAN
TARTAR
TARZAN
TERGAL
THREAD
THREAT
THROAT
TURBAN
UNREAD
UNREAL
UPROAR
VERBAL
VERNAL
VERNAS
VIRGAS
WARSAW
YERBAS

••R••A

AFRICA
AMRITA
ARROBA
AURIGA
AURORA
BARYTA
BERTHA
BORGIA
CARINA
CHROMA
CORNEA
CORNUA
CORONA
CORYZA
ERRATA
EUREKA
EUROPA
FARINA
FERULA
GURKHA
HERNIA
JARINA
JERBOA
KERALA
KORUNA
LORICA
MARACA
MARCIA
MARINA
MARKKA
MARSHA
MARTHA
MERCIA
MORULA
MYRICA
PERSIA
PIRANA
PORTIA
PURANA
PYRRHA
SERBIA
SERENA
STRATA
STROMA
STRUMA
TERBIA
TERESA
TIRANA
VARUNA
VERONA
YORUBA
ZAREBA

•••RA•

ABORAL
AFFRAY
AGORAE
AGORAS
AMORAL
ANORAK
ANURAN
ARARAT
ASTRAL
ASTRAY
BASRAH
BETRAY
CHORAL
CITRAL
CLARAS
COBRAS
CONRAD
COPRAH
CORRAL
CRURAL
DEFRAY
DOBRAS
DVORAK
ENGRAM
ENTRAP
ENWRAP
ESTRAY
EXTRAS
FLORAE
FLORAL
FLORAS
GIBRAN
GOORAL
HEDRAL
HOORAY
HURRAH
HURRAY
HYDRAE
HYDRAS
INWRAP
KONRAD
LAURAE
LAURAS
LIBRAE
LIBRAS
MADRAS
MITRAL
MOIRAS
MURRAY
NEURAL
OPERAS
OUTRAN
PARRAL
PLURAL
RIPRAP
SABRAS
SACRAL
SATRAP
SCARAB
SEURAT
SHORAN
SPIRAL
STORAX
SUTRAS
SWARAJ
TETRAD
THORAC
THORAX
TIARAS
UMBRAE
UMBRAS
UNDRAW
UNWRAP
ZEBRAS

•••R•A

ANDREA
CHOREA
DHARMA
DHARNA
DHURNA
EGERIA
GLORIA
IBERIA
LATRIA
NUTRIA
PEORIA
PYRRHA
PYURIA
SCORIA
SFORZA
SHERPA
SIERRA
SPARTA
SPIREA
STERNA
THORIA
YTTRIA

••••RA

ALMIRA
AMENRA
ANGORA
ANITRA
ANKARA
AURORA
AYMARA
BUCKRA
CAMERA
CENTRA
CESURA
CONTRA
COPPRA
DATURA
ELMIRA
ELVIRA
ELYTRA
ENTERA
EUDORA
EXEDRA
FEDORA
FEMORA
FULCRA
GEMARA
GENERA
HEGIRA
HEJIRA
MADURA
MASORA
NOMURA
PLEURA
REMORA
ROSTRA
SAHARA
SAMARA
SANDRA
SATARA
SCLERA
SENORA
SIERRA
SISERA
SYNURA
TUNDRA
WOMERA

R•B•••

RABBET
RABBIS
RABBIT
RABBLE
RABIES
REBATE
REBATO
REBECS
REBELS
REBILL
REBORN
REBOZO
REBUFF
REBUKE
REBUTS
RIBALD
RIBBED
RIBBON
RIBOSE
ROBALO
ROBAND
ROBBED
ROBBER
ROBBIA
ROBBIE
ROBERT
ROBING
ROBINS
ROBLES
ROBOTS
ROBSON
ROBUST
RUBACE
RUBATO
RUBBED
RUBBER
RUBBLE
RUBENS
RUBIES
RUBIGO
RUBLES
RUBRIC

R••B••

RABBET
RABBIS
RABBIT
RABBLE
RAMBLE
REDBAY
REDBUD
REDBUG
REUBEN
RIBBED
RIBBON
ROBBED
ROBBER
ROBBIA
ROBBIE
ROUBLE
RUBBED
RUBBER
RUBBLE
RUMBAS
RUMBLE

R•••B•

RAJABS
RHOMBI
RHUMBA
RHUMBS

R••••B
RESORB

•RB•••
ARBELA
ARBORI
ARBORS
ARBUTE
ERBIUM
ORBING
ORBITS
URBANE

•R•B••
ARABEL
ARABIA
ARABIC
ARABLE
BRIBED
BRIBER
BRIBES
CRABBY
DRABLY
EREBUS
GRABEN
GREBES
GRUBBY
KRUBIS
KRUBUT
ORIBIS
PROBED
PROBER
PROBES
TREBLE
TRIBAL
TRIBES

•R••B•
ARDEBS
ARROBA
CRABBY
CRAMBO
CRUMBS
CRUMBY
GRUBBY

•R•••B
PREFAB

••RB••
BARBED
BARBEL
BARBER
BARBET
BARBIE
BERBER
BURBLE
BURBOT
CARBON
CARBOY
CORBAN
CORBEL
CURBED
DORBUG
DURBAN
DURBAR
FERBER
FORBAD
FORBID
GARBED
GARBLE
GERBIL
HARBIN
HARBOR
HERBAL
JERBOA
MARBLE
MORBID
SERBIA
TERBIA
TURBAN
TURBID
TURBIT
TURBOT
VERBAL
WARBLE
YERBAS

••R•B•
AEROBE
ARROBA
CARIBE
CARIBS
CAROBS
ENROBE
HEREBY
SCRIBE
SCRUBS
SHRUBS
THROBS
YORUBA
ZAREBA

••R••B
CORYMB
SERDAB

•••RB•
BLURBS
EXURBS
NEARBY

•••R•B
CHERUB
MIDRIB
SCARAB

••••RB
ABSORB
ADSORB
ADVERB
BICARB
RESORB
SUBURB
SUPERB

R•C•••
RACEME
RACERS
RACHEL
RACHIS
RACIAL
RACIER
RACILY
RACINE
RACING
RACISM
RACIST
RACKED
RACKER
RACKET
RACOON
RECALL
RECANT
RECAPS
RECAST
RECEDE
RECENT
RECEPT
RECESS
RECIPE
RECITE
RECKON
RECOIL
RECORD
RECOUP
RECTAL
RECTOR
RECTOS
RECTUM
RECTUS
RECURS
RECUSE
RICERS
RICHER
RICHES
RICHIE
RICHLY
RICING
RICKED
RICKEY
RICKYS
RICTAL
RICTUS
ROCHET
ROCKED
ROCKER
ROCKET
ROCKNE
ROCOCO
RUCHES
RUCKED
RUCKUS

R••C••
RANCHO
RANCID
RANCOR
RASCAL
REACTS
REDCAP
REECHO
REICHS
RESCUE
ROSCOE
ROTCHE
ROUCHE

R•••C•
REBECS
REDACT
REDUCE
REJECT
RELICS
RELICT
RESECT
ROCOCO
RUBACE

R••••C
RHODIC
ROMAIC
RUBRIC
RUSTIC

•RC•••
ARCADE
ARCANE
ARCHED
ARCHEO
ARCHER
ARCHES
ARCHIE
ARCHIL
ARCHLY
ARCHON
ARCHYS
ARCING
ARCKED
ARCTIC
ORCEIN
ORCHID
ORCHIL
ORCHIO
ORCHIS
URCHIN

•R•C••
ARECAS
BRACED
BRACER
BRACES
BRACHI
BRACHY
BRACTS
BRECHT
BRICKS
BRUCES
CRACKS
CRACKY
CRACOW
CRECHE
CRICKS
CROCKS
CROCUS
CRUCES
DRACHM
ERECTS
ERICHS
ERUCTS
FRACAS
FROCKS
GRACED
GRACES
GROCER
ORACHS
ORACLE
PRECIS
PRICED
PRICES
PRICKS
PROCNE
PROCTO
TRACED
TRACER
TRACES
TRACHE
TRACHY
TRACKS
TRACTS
TRICED
TRICES
TRICHI
TRICHO
TRICKS
TRICKY
TRICOT
TROCAR
TROCHE
TRUCES
TRUCKS
WRACKS
WRECKS

•R••C•
ARNICA
ARRACK
BRANCH
BREACH
BREECH
BROACH
BRONCO
BRONCS
BROOCH
BRUNCH
CRATCH
CROTCH
CROUCH
CRUNCH
CRUTCH
DRENCH
FRANCE
FRANCK
FRANCO
FRANCS
FRENCH
FRESCO
GRAECO
GREECE
GROUCH
ORRICE
PRANCE
PREACH
PRINCE
TRANCE
TRENCH
WRENCH
WRETCH

•R•••C
ARABIC
ARCTIC
BROMIC
CRETIC
CRITIC
EROTIC
FROLIC
IRENIC
IRIDIC
IRITIC
IRONIC
ORPHIC
TRAGIC
TROPIC
URALIC
URANIC
URETIC

••RC••
CARCEL
CIRCLE
CIRCUM
CIRCUS
FARCED
FARCER
FARCES
FORCED
FORCER
FORCES
GARCON
MARCEL
MARCIA
MARCOS
MARCUS
MERCER
MERCIA
PARCAE
PARCEL
PERCYS
TERCEL
TERCET
TURCOS
ZIRCON

••R•C•
AFRICA
ARRACK
BARUCH
BORSCH
CARACK
CURACY
DARICS
DIRECT
ENRICH

6

ENRICO
HORACE
KIRSCH
LORICA
LYRICS
MARACA
MYRICA
ORRICE
PIRACY
SERACS
SPRUCE
STRICK
STRICT
STRUCK
THRICE
VARICO
ZURICH

••R••C
AORTIC
BARDIC
CARPIC
CORSAC
DERMIC
FERRIC
FORMIC
GARLIC
HERDIC
HEROIC
MYRMEC
NORDIC
PARSEC
SYRIAC
TARMAC
TURKIC

•••RC•
AMERCE
APERCU
BIERCE
CHURCH
COERCE
EPARCH
EXARCH
FIERCE
INARCH
PEIRCE
PIERCE
SCARCE
SCORCH
SEARCH
SMIRCH
SOURCE
STARCH
TIERCE

•••R•C
AGARIC
ALARIC
CAPRIC
CEDRIC
CHORIC
CITRIC
CLERIC
CUPRIC
CYMRIC
EMERIC
FABRIC
FERRIC
HYDRIC
IATRIC
METRIC
NITRIC
PICRIC
RUBRIC
STERIC
TANREC
TENREC
THORAC
THORIC
VITRIC
YTTRIC

R•D•••
RADARS
RADDLE
RADIAL
RADIAN
RADIOS
RADISH
RADIUM
RADIUS
RADOME
RADULA
REDACT
REDANS
REDBAY
REDBUD
REDBUG
REDCAP
REDDEN
REDDER
REDDLE
REDDOG
REDEEM
REDEYE
REDFIN
REDHOT
REDOES
REDONE
REDOWA
REDTOP
REDUCE
RIDDED
RIDDEN
RIDDLE
RIDENT
RIDERS
RIDGED
RIDGES
RIDING
RODDYS
RODENT
RODEOS
RODMAN
RODMEN
RODNEY
RUDDER
RUDDLE
RUDELY
RUDEST

R••D••
RADDLE
RAIDED
RAIDER
RANDAL
RANDAN
RANDOM
READER
REDDEN
REDDER
REDDLE
REDDOG
REEDED
RENDED
RENDER
RHODAS
RHODIC
RIDDED
RIDDEN
RIDDLE
RODDYS
RONDEL
RONDOS
RUDDER
RUDDLE
RUNDLE

R•••D•
RAPIDS
RECEDE
REMADE
REMEDY
REMUDA
RESEDA
RESIDE
ROALDS
ROUNDS
RWANDA

R••••D
RACKED
RAFTED
RAGGED
RAIDED
RAILED
RAINED
RAISED
RAMMED
RAMPED
RAMROD
RANCID
RANGED
RANKED
RANTED
RAPPED
RASPED
RATTED
RAZEED
RAZZED
REAMED
REAPED
REARED
RECORD
REDBUD
REEDED
REEFED
REEKED
REELED
REEVED
REFUND
REGARD
REINED
RELIED
RELOAD
REMAND
REMIND
RENDED
RENTED
REPAID
REPAND
RESEND
RESOLD
RESTED
RETARD
RETOLD
RETTED
REVVED
REWARD
REWIND
REWORD
RHYMED
RIBALD
RIBBED
RICKED
RIDDED
RIDGED
RIFLED
RIFTED
RIGGED
RIMMED
RINGED
RINSED
RIOTED
RIPPED
RISKED
RITARD
ROAMED
ROARED
ROBAND
ROBBED
ROCKED
ROGUED
ROILED
ROLAND
ROLLED
ROMPED
RONALD
ROOFED
ROOKED
ROOMED
ROOTED
ROTTED
ROTUND
ROUGED
ROUSED
ROUTED
RUBBED
RUCKED
RUFFED
RUGGED
RUINED
RUSHED
RUSTED
RUTTED

•RD•••
ARDEBS
ARDENT
ARDORS
ORDAIN
ORDEAL
ORDERS
ORDURE

•R•D••
ARIDLY
BRIDAL
BRIDES
BRIDGE
BRIDIE
BRIDLE
CRADLE
CREDIT
CREDOS
CRUDER
DREDGE
DRUDGE
DRYDEN
ERODED
ERODES
FREDAS
FREDDY
FRIDAY
FRIDGE
GRADED
GRADER
GRADES
GRADIN
GRADUS
GRIDED
GRIDES
GRUDGE
IRIDES
IRIDIC
PRIDED
PRIDES
PRUDES
SRADHA
TRADED
TRADER
TRADES
TRUDGE
TRUDYS

•R••D•
ARCADE
ARMADA
AROIDS
BRAIDS
BRANDS
BRANDY
BREADS
BREEDS
BRENDA
BROADS
BROODS
BROODY
CREEDS
CROWDS
DREADS
DRUIDS
DRYADS
FRAUDS
FREDDY
FRIEDA
FRONDS
GREEDS
GREEDY
GRINDS
GRUNDY
OREADS
OREIDE
OROIDE
PRAVDA
TREADS
TRENDS
TRENDY
TRIADS
TRIODE
UREIDE

•R•••D
ARCHED
ARCKED
ARGUED
ARMAND
ARNAUD
ARNOLD
AROUND
BRACED
BRAKED
BRAVED
BRAYED
BRAZED
BREWED
BRIBED
BRIGID
BRINED
CRANED
CRAPED
CRATED
CRAVED
CRAZED
CREPED
CROWED
DRAPED
DRAYED
DRONED
DROVED
ERASED
ERODED
ERRAND

6

FRAMED
FRAYED
FRIEND
FRIGID
GRACED
GRADED
GRATED
GRAVED
GRAVID
GRAYED
GRAZED
GRIDED
GRIMED
GRIPED
GROPED
GROUND
IRONED
ORATED
ORCHID
ORMUZD
PRATED
PRAYED
PREMED
PREYED
PRICED
PRIDED
PRIMED
PRIZED
PROBED
PROSED
PROVED
PRUNED
TRACED
TRADED
TRICED
TRIFID
TRINED
TRIPOD
UROPOD
XRAYED

••RD••

AIRDRY
BARDED
BARDES
BARDIC
BIRDIE
BORDEL
BORDER
BURDEN
BURDIE
CARDED
CARDER
CARDIO
CORDAY
CORDED
CORDER
CORDON
CURDED
CURDLE
DARDAN
FORDED
GARDEN
GIRDED
GIRDER
GIRDLE
GORDON
HARDEN
HARDER
HARDLY
HERDED
HERDER
HERDIC
HORDED
HORDES
HURDLE
JORDAN
LARDED
LARDER
LARDON
LORDED
LORDLY
MARDUK
MURDER
NORDIC
PARDON
PURDAH
SERDAB
SIRDAR
SORDID
VERDIN
VERDUN
WARDED
WARDEN
WARDER
WORDED
YARDED

••R•D•

ABRADE
BORIDE
CORODY
DERIDE
DIRNDL
DORADO
FARADS
LAREDO
PARADE
PARODY
SCRODS
SHREDS
STRIDE
STRODE
TEREDO
TIRADE
WORLDS

••R••D

ABROAD
AERIED
AFRAID
AGREED
BARBED
BARDED
BARGED
BARKED
BARRED
BIRLED
BIRRED
BURIED
BURKED
BURLED
BURNED
BURPED
BURRED
BYROAD
CARDED
CARPED
CARTED
CARVED
CORDED
CORKED
CORNED
CURBED
CURDED
CURLED
CURSED
CURVED
DARNED
DARTED
DIRKED
DORSAD
EARNED
ERRAND
FARCED
FARMED
FERVID
FIRMED
FORBAD
FORBID
FORCED
FORDED
FORGED
FORKED
FORMED
FURLED
FURRED
GARBED
GERALD
GERARD
GERUND
GIRDED
GIRTED
GORGED
HARKED
HARMED
HAROLD
HARPED
HERALD
HERDED
HORDED
HORNED
HORRID
HORSED
HURLED
INROAD
JARRED
JEREED
JERKED
KERNED
LARDED
LARKED
LORDED
LURKED
MARAUD
MARKED
MARLED
MARRED
MERGED
MORBID
MYRIAD
NERVED
NURSED
PARKED
PARSED
PARTED
PERIOD
PERKED
PUREED
PURGED
PURLED
PURRED
PURSED
SCREED
SERVED
SHREWD
SHROUD
SORDID
SORTED
SPREAD
STRAND
STROUD
SURFED
SURGED
TARRED
TERMED
THREAD
THREED
TOROID
TORPID
TORRID
TURBID
TURGID
TURNED
UNREAD
VARIED
VERGED
VERSED
WARDED
WARMED
WARNED
WARPED
WARRED
WORDED
WORKED
WORMED
YARDED
ZEROED

•••RD•

AWARDS
BEARDS
BOARDS
CHARDS
CHORDS
FIORDS
FJORDS
GOURDE
GOURDS
GUARDS
HAIRDO
HOARDS
LAIRDS
OVERDO
SHARDS
SHERDS
STURDY
SWARDS
SWORDS
THIRDS
WEIRDY

•••R•D

ACARID
ADORED
ALFRED
ASTRID
BARRED
BEARED
BEDRID
BIRRED
BLARED
BURRED
CHARED
CLERID
CONRAD
ELDRED
FAIRED
FEARED
FLARED
FLORID
FURRED
GEARED
GLARED
HAIRED
HATRED
HORRID
HYBRID
INBRED
INGRID
INURED
JARRED
JEERED
KONRAD
LAIRED
LEERED
LOURED
MADRID
MARRED
MOORED
NEARED
NIMROD
NITRID
PAIRED
PEERED
POURED
PURRED
PUTRID
QUIRED
RAMROD
REARED
ROARED
SACRED
SCARED
SCORED
SEARED
SHARED
SHORED
SIGRID
SNARED
SNORED
SOARED
SOCRED
SOURED
SPARED
SPIRED
SPORED
STARED
STORED
TARRED
TEARED
TETRAD
TIERED
TORRID
TOURED
UNBRED
UNTROD
VEERED
WARRED
WHORED

••••RD

ABOARD
ABSURD
ACCORD
AFFORD
ASGARD
BAYARD
BEGIRD
BOYARD
BYWORD
CANARD
COWARD
ECHARD
EDUARD
EDWARD
ENGIRD
GERARD
HAZARD
HOLARD
HOWARD
INWARD
IZZARD
LIZARD
MILORD
ONWARD
OXFORD
PETARD
RECORD
REGARD
RETARD
REWARD
REWORD
RITARD

SEWARD
TABARD
TOWARD
UNGIRD
UPWARD
UTGARD
VISARD
VIZARD
WIZARD

RE••••

REACTS
READER
REALES
REALLY
REALMS
REALTY
REAMED
REAMER
REAPED
REAPER
REARED
REARER
REARMS
REASON
REAVOW
REBATE
REBATO
REBECS
REBELS
REBILL
REBORN
REBOZO
REBUFF
REBUKE
REBUTS
RECALL
RECANT
RECAPS
RECAST
RECEDE
RECENT
RECEPT
RECESS
RECIPE
RECITE
RECKON
RECOIL
RECORD
RECOUP
RECTAL
RECTOR
RECTOS
RECTUM
RECTUS
RECURS
RECUSE
REDACT
REDANS
REDBAY
REDBUD
REDBUG
REDCAP
REDDEN
REDDER
REDDLE
REDDOG
REDEEM
REDEYE
REDFIN
REDHOT
REDOES
REDONE
REDOWA
REDTOP
REDUCE
REECHO
REEDED
REEFED
REEFER
REEKED
REEKER
REELED
REELER
REEVED
REEVES
REFERS
REFILL
REFINE
REFITS
REFLET
REFLEX
REFLUX
REFORM
REFUGE
REFUND
REFUSE
REFUTE
REGAIN
REGALE
REGARD
REGENT
REGGIE
REGIME
REGINA
REGION
REGIUS
REGLET
REGNAL
REGRET
REHASH
REHEAR
REHEAT
REICHS
REIGNS
REINED
REJECT
REJOIN
RELATE
RELAYS
RELENT
RELICS
RELICT
RELIED
RELIEF
RELIER
RELIES
RELINE
RELISH
RELIVE
RELOAD
REMADE
REMAIN
REMAKE
REMAND
REMANS
REMARK
REMEDY
REMIND
REMISE
REMISS
REMITS
REMORA
REMOTE
REMOVE
REMUDA
RENDED
RENDER
RENEES
RENEGE
RENEWS
RENNET
RENNIN
RENOIR
RENOWN
RENTAL
RENTED
RENTER
RENTES
REOPEN
REPAID
REPAIR
REPAND
REPASS
REPAST
REPAYS
REPEAT
REPELS
REPENT
REPINE
REPLAY
REPORT
REPOSE
REPUTE
RERUNS
RESALE
RESCUE
RESEAT
RESEAU
RESECT
RESEDA
RESELL
RESEND
RESENT
RESETS
RESIDE
RESIGN
RESILE
RESINS
RESIST
RESOLD
RESOLE
RESORB
RESORT
RESTED
RESTER
RESULT
RESUME
RETAIL
RETAIN
RETAKE
RETARD
RETELL
RETENE
RETINA
RETIRE
RETOLD
RETOOK
RETORT
RETTED
RETURN
RETUSE
REUBEN
REVAMP
REVEAL
REVELS
REVERE
REVERT
REVEST
REVETS
REVIEW
REVILE
REVISE
REVIVE
REVOKE
REVOLT
REVUES
REVVED
REWARD
REWIND
REWORD

R•E•••

REECHO
REEDED
REEFED
REEFER
REEKED
REEKER
REELED
REELER
REEVED
REEVES
RHEIMS
RHESUS
RHETOR
RHEUMY
RUEFUL

R••E••

RACEME
RACERS
RAKERS
RANEES
RAREFY
RARELY
RAREST
RATELS
RATERS
RAVELS
RAVENS
RAVERS
RAWEST
RAZEED
RAZEES
REBECS
REBELS
RECEDE
RECENT
RECEPT
RECESS
REDEEM
REDEYE
REFERS
REGENT
REHEAR
REHEAT
REJECT
RELENT
REMEDY
RENEES
RENEGE
RENEWS
REPEAT
REPELS
REPENT
RESEAT
RESEAU
RESECT
RESEDA
RESELL
RESEND
RESENT
RESETS
RETELL
RETENE
REVEAL
REVELS
REVERE
REVERT
REVEST
REVETS
RICERS
RIDENT
RIDERS
RIMERS
RIPELY
RIPENS
RIPEST
RISERS
RIVERS
RIVETS
ROBERT
RODENT
RODEOS
ROGERS
ROVERS
ROWELS
ROWENA
ROWERS
RUBENS
RUDELY
RUDEST
RULERS
RUPEES
RUPERT

R•••E•

RABBET
RABIES
RACHEL
RACIER
RACKED
RACKER
RACKET
RAFTED
RAFTER
RAGGED
RAGMEN
RAIDED
RAIDER
RAILED
RAINED
RAISED
RAISER
RAISES
RAMIES
RAMMED
RAMMER
RAMPED
RANEES
RANGED
RANGER
RANGES
RANKED
RANKER
RANTED
RANTER
RAPIER
RAPPED
RAPPEE
RAPPEL
RAPPER
RASHER
RASHES
RASPED
RASPER
RATHER
RATTED
RATTEN
RATTER
RAZEED
RAZEES
RAZZED
RAZZES
READER
REALES
REAMED
REAMER
REAPED
REAPER
REARED
REARER
REDDEN

6

REDDER
REDEEM
REDOES
REEDED
REEFED
REEFER
REEKED
REEKER
REELED
REELER
REEVED
REEVES
REFLET
REFLEX
REGLET
REGRET
REINED
RELIED
RELIEF
RELIER
RELIES
RENDED
RENDER
RENEES
RENNET
RENTED
RENTER
RENTES
REOPEN
RESTED
RESTER
RETTED
REUBEN
REVIEW
REVUES
REVVED
RHYMED
RHYMER
RHYMES
RIBBED
RICHER
RICHES
RICKED
RICKEY
RIDDED
RIDDEN
RIDGED
RIDGES
RIFLED
RIFLER
RIFLES
RIFTED
RIGGED
RIGGER
RILLET
RIMMED
RIMMER
RINGED
RINGER
RINSED
RINSER
RINSES
RIOTED
RIOTER
RIPLEY
RIPPED
RIPPER
RISKED
RISKER
RITTER
ROAMED
ROAMER
ROARED
ROARER
ROBBED
ROBBER
ROBLES
ROCHET
ROCKED
ROCKER
ROCKET
RODMEN
RODNEY
ROGUED
ROGUES
ROILED
ROLLED
ROLLER
ROMMEL
ROMNEY
ROMPED
ROMPER
RONDEL
ROOFED
ROOFER
ROOKED
ROOMED
ROOMER
ROOTED
ROOTER
ROPIER
ROQUET
ROSIER
ROSTER
ROTTED
ROTTEN
ROTTER
ROUGED
ROUGES
ROUSED
ROUSER
ROUSES
ROUTED
ROUTER
ROUTES
RUBBED
RUBBER
RUBIES
RUBLES
RUCHES
RUCKED
RUDDER
RUFFED
RUGGED
RUINED
RUINER
RUMMER
RUNLET
RUNNEL
RUNNER
RUPEES
RUSHED
RUSHER
RUSHES
RUSSET
RUSTED
RUTTED

R••••E

RABBLE
RACEME
RACINE
RADDLE
RADOME
RAFFLE
RAMBLE
RAMOSE
RANKLE
RAPHAE
RAPINE
RAPPEE
RATINE
RATITE
RATTLE
RAVAGE
RAVINE
REBATE
REBUKE
RECEDE
RECIPE
RECITE
RECUSE
REDDLE
REDEYE
REDONE
REDUCE
REFINE
REFUGE
REFUSE
REFUTE
REGALE
REGGIE
REGIME
RELATE
RELINE
RELIVE
REMADE
REMAKE
REMISE
REMOTE
REMOVE
RENEGE
REPINE
REPOSE
REPUTE
RESALE
RESCUE
RESIDE
RESILE
RESOLE
RESUME
RETAKE
RETENE
RETIRE
RETUSE
REVERE
REVILE
REVISE
REVIVE
REVOKE
RIBOSE
RICHIE
RIDDLE
RIFFLE
RIMOSE
RIMPLE
RIPPLE
RISQUE
ROBBIE
ROCKNE
RONNIE
ROOKIE
ROSCOE
ROTATE
ROTCHE
ROUBLE
ROUCHE
ROXANE
RRHAGE
RUBACE
RUBBLE
RUDDLE
RUFFLE
RUGATE
RUGOSE
RUMBLE
RUMPLE
RUNDLE
RUSINE
RUSTLE
RUTILE

•RE•••

ARECAS
ARENAS
AREOLA
ARETES
AREZZO
BREACH
BREADS
BREAKS
BREAMS
BREAST
BREATH
BRECHT
BREECH
BREEDS
BREEZE
BREEZY
BREGMA
BREMEN
BRENDA
BRENTS
BRETON
BREVES
BREVET
BREWED
BREWER
BREWIS
CREAKS
CREAKY
CREAMS
CREAMY
CREASE
CREASY
CREATE
CRECHE
CREDIT
CREDOS
CREEDS
CREEKS
CREELS
CREEPS
CREEPY
CREESE
CREMES
CRENEL
CREOLE
CREPED
CREPES
CRESOL
CRESTS
CRETAN
CRETIC
CRETIN
CREUSA
CREWEL
DREADS
DREAMS
DREAMT
DREAMY
DREARY
DREDGE
DREGGY
DRENCH
DRESSY
EREBUS
ERECTS
FREAKS
FREAKY
FREDAS
FREDDY
FREELY
FREEST
FREEZE
FRENCH
FRENUM
FRENZY
FREONS
FRESCO
FRESNO
FRETTY
GREASE
GREASY
GREATS
GREAVE
GREBES
GREECE
GREEDS
GREEDY
GREEKS
GREENS
GREETS
GREGOS
GREIGE
GRETAS
GRETEL
IREFUL
IRENES
IRENIC
OREADS
OREGON
OREIDE
PREACH
PRECIS
PREENS
PREFAB
PREFER
PREFIX
PREMED
PREPAY
PRESAS
PRESTO
PRETER
PRETOR
PRETTY
PREVUE
PREWAR
PREYED
PREYER
TREADS
TREATS
TREATY
TREBLE
TREMOR
TRENCH
TRENDS
TRENDY
TREPAN
TRESSY
UREASE
UREIDE
UREMIA
URETER
URETHR
URETIC
WREAKS
WREATH
WRECKS
WRENCH
WRESTS
WRETCH

•R•E••

ARBELA
ARDEBS
ARDENT
ARGENT
ARIELS
ARLEEN
ARLENE
ARMETS
ARPENS
ARPENT

6

ARREAR
ARREST
ARTELS
ARTERY
BREECH
BREEDS
BREEZE
BREEZY
BRIEFS
BRIERS
BRIERY
CREEDS
CREEKS
CREELS
CREEPS
CREEPY
CREESE
CRIERS
CRUETS
DRIERS
DRIEST
DRYERS
DRYEST
ERNEST
FREELY
FREEST
FREEZE
FRIEDA
FRIEND
FRIERS
FRIEZE
FRYERS
GRAECO
GREECE
GREEDS
GREEDY
GREEKS
GREENS
GREETS
GRIEFS
GRIEVE
GRUELS
ORCEIN
ORDEAL
ORDERS
ORGEAT
ORIELS
ORIENT
ORMERS
ORNERY
ORRERY
ORWELL
PREENS
PRIERS
PRIEST
PROEMS
PRYERS
TRIERS
TRUEST
URAEUS
URGENT
URTEXT
WRIEST
WRYEST

•R••E•

ARABEL
ARCHED
ARCHEO
ARCHER
ARCHES
ARCKED
ARETES
ARGUED
ARGUER
ARGUES
ARISEN
ARISES
ARLEEN
ARMIES
ARMLET
ARNIES
ARTIES
BRACED
BRACER
BRACES
BRAKED
BRAKES
BRAVED
BRAVER
BRAVES
BRAYED
BRAYER
BRAZED
BRAZEN
BRAZER
BRAZES
BREMEN
BREVES
BREVET
BREWED
BREWER
BRIBED
BRIBER
BRIBES
BRIDES
BRINED
BRINES
BROKEN
BROKER
BROMES
BRUCES
BRUGES
BRUMES
BRUNEI
BRUNET
BRUTES
CRAKES
CRANED
CRANES
CRAPED
CRAPES
CRATED
CRATER
CRATES
CRAVED
CRAVEN
CRAVER
CRAVES
CRAZED
CRAZES
CREMES
CRENEL
CREPED
CREPES
CREWEL
CRIMEA
CRIMES
CRISES
CRONES
CRORES
CROWED
CROZER
CROZES
CRUCES
CRUDER
CRUSES
CRUSET
CRUXES
DRAGEE
DRAKES
DRAPED
DRAPER
DRAPES
DRAWEE
DRAWER
DRAYED
DRIVEL
DRIVEN
DRIVER
DRIVES
DRONED
DRONES
DROVED
DROVER
DROVES
DRUPES
DRUSES
DRYDEN
ERASED
ERASER
ERASES
ERNIES
ERODED
ERODES
FRAMED
FRAMER
FRAMES
FRATER
FRAUEN
FRAYED
FRISES
FROZEN
GRABEN
GRACED
GRACES
GRADED
GRADER
GRADES
GRAPES
GRATED
GRATER
GRATES
GRAVED
GRAVEL
GRAVEN
GRAVER
GRAVES
GRAYED
GRAYER
GRAZED
GRAZER
GRAZES
GREBES
GRETEL
GRIDED
GRIDES
GRIMED
GRIMES
GRIPED
GRIPER
GRIPES
GRIVET
GRIZEL
GROCER
GROPED
GROPER
GROPES
GROVEL
GROVER
GROVES
GROWER
GRUMES
IRENES
IRIDES
IRISES
IRONED
IRONER
KRAKEN
KRISES
KRONEN
KRONER
ORATED
ORATES
ORGIES
ORIGEN
ORYXES
PRATED
PRATER
PRATES
PRAYED
PRAYER
PREFER
PREMED
PRETER
PREYED
PREYER
PRICED
PRICES
PRIDED
PRIDES
PRIMED
PRIMER
PRIMES
PRIVET
PRIZED
PRIZER
PRIZES
PROBED
PROBER
PROBES
PROJET
PROLEG
PROPEL
PROPER
PROSED
PROSER
PROSES
PROVED
PROVEN
PROVER
PROVES
PRUDES
PRUNED
PRUNER
PRUNES
TRACED
TRACER
TRACES
TRADED
TRADER
TRADES
TRAVEL
TRAVES
TRIBES
TRICED
TRICES
TRINED
TRINES
TRITER
TRIVET
TROVER
TROVES
TROWEL
TRUCES
URETER
WRITER
WRITES
XRAYED

•R•••E

ARABLE
ARBUTE
ARCADE
ARCANE
ARCHIE
ARGIVE
ARGYLE
ARIOSE
ARLENE
ARLINE
ARMURE
AROUSE
ARRIVE
ARSINE
BRAISE
BRAIZE
BRAQUE
BREEZE
BRIDGE
BRIDIE
BRIDLE
BROGUE
BRONTE
BRONZE
BROWSE
BRUISE
CRADLE
CREASE
CREATE
CRECHE
CREESE
CREOLE
CRINGE
CROSSE
CROUPE
CRUISE
CRUSOE
DRAGEE
DRAWEE
DREDGE
DROWSE
DRUDGE
ERGATE
ERMINE
FRAISE
FRANCE
FRAPPE
FREEZE
FRIDGE
FRIEZE
FRINGE
FRUNZE
GRANGE
GREASE
GREAVE
GREECE
GREIGE
GRIEVE
GRIFFE
GRILLE
GRILSE
GRIPPE
GROOVE
GROUSE
GRUDGE
ORACLE
ORANGE
ORDURE
OREIDE
ORIOLE
ORNATE
OROIDE
ORPINE
ORRICE
PRAGUE
PRAISE
PRANCE
PREVUE
PRINCE
PROCNE
RRHAGE
TRACHE
TRANCE
TREBLE

6

TRIFLE
TRIODE
TRIOSE
TRIPLE
TRISTE
TRIUNE
TRIXIE
TROCHE
TROUPE
TRUDGE
URBANE
UREASE
UREIDE
URSINE
WRASSE
WRITHE

••RE••

AFRESH
AGREED
AGREES
ARREAR
ARREST
ATREUS
AUREUS
BAREGE
BARELY
BAREST
BEREFT
BERETS
BIREME
BOREAL
BOREAS
BORERS
BUREAU
CAREEN
CAREER
CARERS
CARESS
CARETS
CEREAL
CEREUS
CORERS
CURERS
CYRENE
DARERS
DEREKS
DIRECT
DIRELY
DIREST
DOREEN
DURESS
EGRESS
EGRETS
EUREKA
FARERS
FIRERS
FOREGO
FOREST
GERENT
HAREMS
HEREAT
HEREBY
HEREIN
HEREOF
HEREON
HERESY
HERETO
HIRERS
JEREED
JEREMY
JURELS
KARENS
KOREAN
LAREDO
LOREEN
LORENE
LORENZ
LURERS
MERELY
MEREST
MOREAU
MOREEN
MORELS
NEREIS
NOREEN
OCREAE
OGRESS
ORRERY
PARENS
PARENT
PARERS
PAREUS
PHRENO
PUREED
PUREES
PURELY
PUREST
PYRENE
RAREFY
RARELY
RAREST
SCREAK
SCREAM
SCREED
SCREEN
SCREWS
SCREWY
SEREIN
SERENA
SERENE
SHREDS
SHREWD
SHREWS
SIRENS
SORELS
SORELY
SOREST
SPREAD
SPREES
STREAK
STREAM
STREET
STRESS
STREWN
STREWS
SURELY
SUREST
SURETY
TEREDO
TERESA
TERETE
TEREUS
THREAD
THREAT
THREED
THREES
THRESH
TORERO
TUREEN
UNREAD
UNREAL
UNREEL
UNREST
VEREIN
VIREOS
WERENT
WIRERS
ZAREBA

••R•E•

ADRIEN
AERIED
AERIES
AGREED
AGREES
AIRIER
AIRMEN
AZRAEL
BARBED
BARBEL
BARBER
BARBET
BARDED
BARDES
BARGED
BARGEE
BARGES
BARKED
BARKER
BARLEY
BARMEN
BARNEY
BARRED
BARREL
BARREN
BARRET
BARTER
BARYES
BERBER
BERGEN
BERMES
BERNEY
BIRLED
BIRLES
BIRRED
BORDEL
BORDER
BORNEO
BURDEN
BURGEE
BURGER
BURIED
BURIES
BURKED
BURKES
BURLED
BURLER
BURLEY
BURNED
BURNER
BURNET
BURPED
BURRED
BURSES
CARCEL
CARDED
CARDER
CAREEN
CAREER
CARIES
CARMEL
CARMEN
CARPED
CARPEL
CARPER
CARPET
CARREL
CARTED
CARTEL
CARTER
CARTES
CARVED
CARVEL
CARVEN
CARVER
CARVES
CERMET
CERTES
CORBEL
CORDED
CORDER
CORKED
CORKER
CORNEA
CORNED
CORNEL
CORNER
CORNET
CORSES
CORSET
CORTES
CORTEX
CORTEZ
CORVEE
CORVES
CURBED
CURDED
CURFEW
CURIES
CURLED
CURLER
CURLEW
CURSED
CURSES
CURVED
CURVES
CURVET
DARIEN
DARKEN
DARKER
DARNED
DARNEL
DARTED
DARTER
DIRGES
DIRKED
DOREEN
DORIES
DORMER
EARLES
EARNED
EARNER
EYRIES
FARCED
FARCER
FARCES
FARLES
FARLEY
FARMED
FARMER
FERBER
FERRET
FIRMED
FIRMER
FORCED
FORCER
FORCES
FORDED
FORGED
FORGER
FORGES
FORGET
FORKED
FORMED
FORMER
FORTES
FURIES
FURLED
FURRED
FURZES
GARBED
GARDEN
GARGET
GARNER
GARNET
GARRET
GARTER
GIRDED
GIRDER
GIRTED
GORGED
GORGER
GORGES
GORGET
GORHEN
GORIER
GORSES
HARDEN
HARDER
HARKED
HARKEN
HARLEM
HARLEY
HARMED
HARPED
HARPER
HARVEY
HERDED
HERDER
HERMES
HEROES
HERPES
HORDED
HORDES
HORNED
HORNET
HORSED
HORSES
HORSEY
HURLED
HURLER
HURTER
ISRAEL
JARRED
JARVEY
JEREED
JERKED
JERSEY
JORGES
JURIES
KERMES
KERNED
KERNEL
KERSEY
LARDED
LARDER
LARGER
LARKED
LARKER
LORDED
LOREEN
LORIES
LURKED
MARCEL
MARGES
MARIES
MARKED
MARKER
MARKET
MARLED
MARRED
MARRER
MARTEN
MARVEL
MERCER
MERGED
MERGER
MERGES
MERLES
MERMEN
MOREEN
MORGEN
MORLEY

6

MORSEL
MURDER
MURIEL
MURRES
MURREY
MYRMEC
NERVED
NERVES
NOREEN
NURSED
NURSER
NURSES
PARCEL
PARGET
PARIES
PARKED
PARKER
PARLEY
PARREL
PARSEC
PARSED
PARSEE
PARSES
PARTED
PERKED
PORKER
PORTER
PUREED
PUREES
PURGED
PURGER
PURGES
PURLED
PURRED
PURSED
PURSER
PURSES
PURVEY
SCREED
SCREEN
SERIES
SERVED
SERVER
SERVES
SHRIEK
SORREL
SORTED
SPREES
SPRIER
SPRUES
SPRYER
STREET
SURFED
SURFER
SURGED
SURGER
SURGES
SURREY
SURVEY
TARGET
TARRED
TARTER
TERCEL
TERCET
TERMED
TERMER
TERRET
TERSER
THREED
THREES
THROES
TORIES
TUREEN
TURKEY
TURNED
TURNER
TURRET
UNREEL
VARIED
VARIER
VARIES
VARLET
VARVES
VERGED
VERGER
VERGES
VERSED
VERSES
VERTEX
VERVET
VORTEX
WARDED
WARDEN
WARDER
WARIER
WARMED
WARMER
WARNED
WARNER
WARPED
WARPER
WARRED
WARREN
WIRIER
WORDED
WORKED
WORKER
WORMED
WORMER
WORSEN
WORSER
YARDED
ZEROED
ZEROES

••R••E

ABRADE
AERATE
AEROBE
AFRAME
AGRAFE
AORTAE
ARRIVE
AURATE
BARBIE
BAREGE
BARGEE
BARITE
BARMIE
BARQUE
BERATE
BERNIE
BERTHE
BERTIE
BIRDIE
BIREME
BORAGE
BORANE
BORATE
BORIDE
BURBLE
BURDIE
BURGEE
BURGLE
BURSAE
CARAFE
CARATE
CARIBE
CAROLE
CARRIE
CERATE
CERISE
CERITE
CERUSE
CHROME
CIRCLE
CIRQUE
CORPSE
CORVEE
CURARE
CURATE
CURDLE
CURIAE
CURULE
CYRENE
DARKLE
DARTLE
DERIDE
DERIVE
DORMIE
ENRAGE
ENROBE
EUROPE
FERINE
FERULE
FORAGE
GARAGE
GARBLE
GARGLE
GERTIE
GIRDLE
GURGLE
GYRATE
GYROSE
HERMAE
HORACE
HORNIE
HORSTE
HURDLE
HURTLE
JEROME
KARATE
LARINE
LARVAE
LORENE
MARBLE
MARGIE
MARINE
MARQUE
MARTHE
MIRAGE
MORALE
MORGUE
MOROSE
MURINE
MYRTLE
NARINE
OCREAE
ORRICE
PARADE
PARCAE
PAROLE
PARSEE
PARURE
PERUKE
PERUSE
PHRASE
PIRATE
PURFLE
PURINE
PURPLE
PURSUE
PYRENE
PYRITE
PYRONE
PYROPE
SARAPE
SARTRE
SCRAPE
SCRIBE
SCRIVE
SERAPE
SERENE
SERINE
SHRIKE
SHRINE
SHRIVE
SHROVE
SORTIE
SPRITE
SPRUCE
STRAFE
STRAKE
STRIAE
STRIDE
STRIFE
STRIKE
STRIPE
STRIVE
STRODE
STROKE
STROVE
TERETE
THRICE
THRIVE
THRONE
THROVE
TIRADE
TOROSE
TORQUE
TURTLE
TYRONE
UNRIPE
UPRISE
UPROSE
VIRGIE
VIRILE
VIRTUE
WARBLE

•••RE•

ADORED
ADORER
ADORES
ALFRED
ANDREA
ANDREI
ANDRES
ANDREW
AUBREY
AUDREY
AZORES
AZURES
BARRED
BARREL
BARREN
BARRET
BEARED
BEARER
BIRRED
BLARED
BLARES
BURRED
CADRES
CARREL
CHARED
CHARES
CHOREA
CHOREO
CHORES
CLARES
CLARET
CRORES
DEARER
DECREE
DEGREE
ELDRED
ENTREE
EVERET
FAIRED
FAIRER
FEARED
FEARER
FERRET
FLARED
FLARES
FLORET
FUHRER
FURRED
GARRET
GEARED
GENRES
GLARED
GLARES
HAIRED
HATRED
HEARER
HEBREW
IMARET
INBRED
INGRES
INURED
INURES
JARRED
JEERED
JEERER
JUAREZ
LABRET
LAIRED
LAUREL
LEERED
LEGREE
LIVRES
LOURED
MARRED
MARRER
MOORED
MURRES
MURREY
NEARED
NEARER
OSPREY
PADRES
PAIRED
PARREL
PEERED
PETREL
POORER
POURED
POURER
PUGREE
PURRED
QUIRED
QUIRES
REARED
REARER
REGRET
ROARED
ROARER
SACRED
SAUREL
SCARED
SCARER
SCARES
SCORED
SCORER
SCORES
SEARED
SECRET
SHARED
SHARER
SHARES
SHIRES
SHORED

SHORES
SNARED
SNARER
SNARES
SNORED
SNORER
SNORES
SOARED
SOARER
SOCRED
SOIREE
SORREL
SOURED
SOURER
SPARED
SPARER
SPARES
SPIREA
SPIRED
SPIRES
SPORED
SPORES
STARED
STARER
STARES
STEREO
STERES
STORED
STORES
STOREY
SUCRES
SURREY
TANREC
TARRED
TEARED
TENREC
TERRET
THYREO
TIERED
TOURED
TURRET
UNBRED
UNDREW
USURER
VEERED
WARRED
WARREN
WEARER
WHORED
WHORES

•••R•E
ACCRUE
AGORAE
AMERCE
AVERSE
BIERCE
BOURNE
BOURSE
CARRIE
CHARGE
COARSE
COERCE
COURSE
COWRIE
DEARIE
DECREE
DEGREE
ECARTE
EMBRUE
EMERGE
ENTREE
FAEROE
FIERCE
FLORAE
GEORGE
GOURDE
HEARSE
HOARSE
HYDRAE
IMBRUE
LAURAE
LAURIE
LEGREE
LIBRAE
LIERNE
MONROE
PEIRCE
PETRIE
PIERCE
PIERRE
PUGREE
QUARTE
SCARCE
SCURVE
SOIREE
SOURCE
SPARGE
SPARSE
SPURGE
STARVE
SWERVE
THORPE
THYRSE
TIERCE
UMBRAE
UNTRUE
UPHROE
WHARVE
WHERVE

••••RE
ABJURE
ADHERE
ADJURE
ADMIRE
ALLURE
AMPERE
ARMURE
ASHORE
ASPIRE
ASSURE
ATTIRE
BEFORE
BEMIRE
BEWARE
CESARE
CLAIRE
COHERE
COLURE
CONTRE
CURARE
DECARE
DEKARE
DEMURE
DESIRE
EMIGRE
EMPIRE
ENCORE
ENDURE
ENSURE
ENTIRE
EUCHRE
EXPIRE
FIACRE
FIGURE
FUTURE
GALORE
HOMBRE
HONORE
IGNORE
IMMURE
IMPURE
INHERE
INJURE
INSURE
LAHORE
LENORE
LIGURE
LOUVRE
MAIGRE
MAITRE
MALGRE
MANURE
MATURE
NATURE
OEUVRE
ORDURE
PARURE
PIERRE
QUAERE
QUATRE
RETIRE
REVERE
SARTRE
SATIRE
SECURE
SEMPRE
SEVERE
SPHERE
SQUARE
SQUIRE
SUTURE
TENURE
TIMBRE
TUYERE
UMPIRE
UNSURE
VELURE
VENIRE
ZAFFRE

R•F•••
RAFFIA
RAFFLE
RAFTED
RAFTER
REFERS
REFILL
REFINE
REFITS
REFLET
REFLEX
REFLUX
REFORM
REFUGE
REFUND
REFUSE
REFUTE
RIFFLE
RIFLED
RIFLER
RIFLES
RIFTED
RUFFED
RUFFLE
RUFOUS

R••F••
RAFFIA
RAFFLE
REDFIN
REEFED
REEFER
RIFFLE
ROOFED
ROOFER
RUEFUL
RUFFED
RUFFLE

R•••F•
RAMIFY
RAREFY
RATIFY
REBUFF
RIPOFF
RUNOFF

R••••F
REBUFF
RELIEF
RIPOFF
RUNOFF

•RF•••
ERFURT

•R•F••
ARMFUL
ARTFUL
CRAFTS
CRAFTY
CROFTS
DRAFFS
DRAFFY
DRAFTS
DRAFTY
DRIFTS
DRIFTY
GRAFTS
GRIFFE
IREFUL
PREFAB
PREFER
PREFIX
PROFIT
TRIFID
TRIFLE

•R••F•
ARGUFY
BRIEFS
DRAFFS
DRAFFY
GRIEFS
GRIFFE
PROOFS

••RF••
BARFLY
CURFEW
EARFUL
JARFUL
PURFLE
SURFED
SURFER

••R•F•
ADRIFT
AERIFY
AGRAFE
BEREFT
CARAFE
FAROFF
PURIFY
RAREFY
SCRUFF
SERIFS
SHRIFT
SHROFF
STRAFE
STRIFE
TARIFF
THRIFT
VERIFY

••R••F
FAROFF
HEREOF
SCRUFF
SHROFF
TARIFF

•••RF•
DWARFS
SCARFS
SCURFY
WHARFS

•••R•F
SHERIF

R•G•••
RAGGED
RAGING
RAGLAN
RAGMAN
RAGMEN
RAGOUT
RAGTAG
REGAIN
REGALE
REGARD
REGENT
REGGIE
REGIME
REGINA
REGION
REGIUS
REGLET
REGNAL
REGRET
RIGGED
RIGGER
RIGHTO
RIGHTS
RIGORS
ROGERS
ROGUED
ROGUES
RUGATE
RUGGED
RUGOSE
RUGOUS

R••G••
RAGGED
RANGED
RANGER
RANGES
REGGIE
REIGNS
RIDGED
RIDGES
RIGGED
RIGGER
RINGED
RINGER
ROTGUT
ROUGED
ROUGES
ROUGHS
RUGGED

R•••G•
RAVAGE
REFUGE
RENEGE
RESIGN
RRHAGE
RRHAGY
RUBIGO

6

R••••G
RACING
RAGING
RAGTAG
RAKING
RAPING
RARING
RATING
RAVING
RAYING
RAZING
REDBUG
REDDOG
RICING
RIDING
RILING
RIMING
RISING
RIVING
ROBING
ROPING
ROSING
ROVING
ROWING
RULING

•RG•••
ARGALI
ARGALS
ARGENT
ARGIVE
ARGOSY
ARGOTS
ARGUED
ARGUER
ARGUES
ARGUFY
ARGYLE
ARGYLL
ERGATE
ORGANA
ORGANO
ORGANS
ORGASM
ORGEAT
ORGIES
URGENT
URGING

•R•G••
ARAGON
ARIGHT
BREGMA
BRIGHT
BRIGID
BROGAN
BROGUE
BRUGES
CRAGGY
DRAGEE
DRAGON
DREGGY
FRIGHT
FRIGID
FROGGY
FRUGAL
GREGOS
GRIGRI
GROGGY
GRUGRU
OREGON
ORIGAN
ORIGEN
ORIGIN
PRAGUE
TRAGIC
TRAGUS
TRIGLY
TRIGON
TROGON
WRIGHT

•R••G•
ARMAGH
BRIDGE
BRINGS
CRAGGY
CRAIGS
CRINGE
DREDGE
DREGGY
DRONGO
DRUDGE
ERINGO
ERYNGO
FRIDGE
FRINGE
FRINGY
FROGGY
GRANGE
GREIGE
GROGGY
GRUDGE
ORANGE
ORANGS
PRONGS
RRHAGE
RRHAGY
TROUGH
TRUDGE
WRINGS
WRONGS

•R•••G
ARCING
ARMING
CRYING
DRYING
ERRING
FRYING
IRKING
IRVING
ORBING
PROLEG
PRYING
TRUING
TRYING
URGING
WRYING

••RG••
BARGED
BARGEE
BARGES
BERGEN
BORGIA
BURGEE
BURGER
BURGHS
BURGLE
BURGOO
BURGOS
CARGOS
CORGIS
DIRGES
FORGED
FORGER
FORGES
FORGET
FORGOT
GARGET
GARGLE
GORGED
GORGER
GORGES
GORGET
GORGON
GURGLE
JARGON
JORGES
LARGER
LARGOS
MARGAY
MARGES
MARGIE
MARGIN
MARGOS
MARGOT
MERGED
MERGER
MERGES
MORGAN
MORGEN
MORGUE
PARGET
PARGOS
PURGED
PURGER
PURGES
SARGON
SORGHO
SORGOS
SURGED
SURGER
SURGES
TARGET
TERGAL
TERGUM
TURGID
VERGED
VERGER
VERGES
VERGIL
VIRGAS
VIRGIE
VIRGIL
VIRGIN

••R•G•
AERUGO
AURIGA
BAREGE
BORAGE
ENRAGE
FORAGE
FOREGO
GARAGE
MIRAGE
SCRAGS
SHRUGS
SPRAGS
SPRIGS
UNRIGS
VIRAGO

••R••G
AIRING
BARING
BARONG
BERING
BORING
CARING
CERING
CORING
CURING
DARING
DORBUG
DURING
EARING
EARWIG
ERRING
FARING
FIRING
GORING
HIRING
LARYNG
LURING
MIRING
OARING
PARANG
PARING
PORING
RARING
SARONG
SIRING
SPRANG
SPRING
SPRUNG
STRING
STRONG
TARING
THRONG
TIRING
WIRING

•••RG•
ANERGY
BOURGS
CHARGE
CLERGY
EMERGE
ENERGY
GEORGE
GEORGI
SPARGE
SPURGE

RH••••
RHEIMS
RHESUS
RHETOR
RHEUMY
RHINAL
RHINOS
RHODAS
RHODIC
RHOMBI
RHUMBA
RHUMBS
RHYMED
RHYMER
RHYMES
RHYTHM

R•H•••
REHASH
REHEAR
REHEAT
RRHAGE
RRHAGY

R••H••
RACHEL
RACHIS
RAPHAE
RAPHIS
RASHER
RASHES
RASHLY
RATHER
REDHOT
RICHER
RICHES
RICHIE
RICHLY
RIGHTO
RIGHTS
ROCHET
RUCHES
RUSHED
RUSHER
RUSHES

R•••H•
RAJAHS
RALPHS
RANCHO
RAYAHS
REECHO
REICHS
RHYTHM
ROLPHS
ROTCHE
ROUCHE
ROUGHS

R••••H
RADISH
RAKISH
RAVISH
RAWISH
REHASH
RELISH
ROMISH
RUPIAH

•RH•••
RRHAGE
RRHAGY

•R•H••
ARCHED
ARCHEO
ARCHER
ARCHES
ARCHIE
ARCHIL
ARCHLY
ARCHON
ARCHYS
ARTHRO
ARTHUR
BRAHMA
BRAHMS
GRAHAM
ORCHID
ORCHIL
ORCHIO
ORCHIS
ORPHAN
ORPHIC
URCHIN

•R••H•
ARIGHT
BRACHI
BRACHY
BRASHY
BRECHT
BRIGHT
BROTHS
BRUSHY
CRECHE
DRACHM
ERICHS
ERYTHR
FRIGHT
FRITHS
FROTHS
FROTHY
GRAPHO
GRAPHS
GRAPHY

ORACHS
SRADHA
TRACHE
TRACHY
TRASHY
TRICHI
TRICHO
TROCHE
TROPHO
TROPHY
TROTHS
TRUTHS
URETHR
WRATHY
WRIGHT
WRITHE

•R•••H
ARMAGH
BRANCH
BREACH
BREATH
BREECH
BROACH
BROOCH
BRUNCH
CRATCH
CROTCH
CROUCH
CRUNCH
CRUTCH
DRENCH
DROUTH
FRENCH
GROUCH
GROWTH
ORNITH
PREACH
TRENCH
TROUGH
WRAITH
WREATH
WRENCH
WRETCH

••RH••
CARHOP
DIRHAM
DURHAM
GORHEN

••R•H•
BERTHA
BERTHE
BERTHS
BIRTHS
BURGHS
EARTHS
EARTHY
FIRTHS
GURKHA
MARSHA
MARSHY
MARTHA
MARTHE
MORPHO
PYRRHA
SARAHS
SORGHO
SURAHS
TORAHS
WORTHY

••R••H
AFRESH
BARUCH
BORSCH
CERIPH
ENRICH
GARISH
HURRAH
INRUSH
KIRSCH
OGRISH
ONRUSH
PARAPH
PARIAH
PARISH
PERISH
PURDAH
SERAPH
TERAPH
THRASH
THRESH
THRUSH
WARMTH
ZURICH

•••RH•
PYRRHA

•••R•H
BASRAH
CHURCH
COPRAH
DEARTH
EPARCH
EXARCH
FOURTH
HEARTH
HURRAH
INARCH
SCORCH
SEARCH
SMIRCH
STARCH
SWARTH

RI••••
RIALTO
RIATAS
RIBALD
RIBBED
RIBBON
RIBOSE
RICERS
RICHER
RICHES
RICHIE
RICHLY
RICING
RICKED
RICKEY
RICKYS
RICTAL
RICTUS
RIDDED
RIDDEN
RIDDLE
RIDENT
RIDERS
RIDGED
RIDGES
RIDING
RIFFLE
RIFLED
RIFLER
RIFLES
RIFTED
RIGGED
RIGGER
RIGHTO
RIGHTS
RIGORS
RILING
RILLET
RIMERS
RIMING
RIMMED
RIMMER
RIMOSE
RIMOUS
RIMPLE
RINGED
RINGER
RINSED
RINSER
RINSES
RIOTED
RIOTER
RIPELY
RIPENS
RIPEST
RIPLEY
RIPOFF
RIPOST
RIPPED
RIPPER
RIPPLE
RIPRAP
RIPSAW
RISERS
RISING
RISKED
RISKER
RISQUE
RITARD
RITTER
RITUAL
RIVALS
RIVERS
RIVETS
RIVING
RIYALS

R•I•••
RAIDED
RAIDER
RAILED
RAINED
RAISED
RAISER
RAISES
RAISIN
REICHS
REIGNS
REINED
RHINAL
RHINOS
ROILED
RUINED
RUINER

R••I••
RABIES
RACIAL
RACIER
RACILY
RACINE
RACING
RACISM
RACIST
RADIAL
RADIAN
RADIOS
RADISH
RADIUM
RADIUS
RAGING
RAKING
RAKISH
RAMIES
RAMIFY
RAPIDS
RAPIER
RAPINE
RAPING
RAPIST
RARING
RARITY
RATIFY
RATINE
RATING
RATION
RATIOS
RATITE
RAVINE
RAVING
RAVISH
RAWISH
RAYING
RAZING
REBILL
RECIPE
RECITE
REFILL
REFINE
REFITS
REGIME
REGINA
REGION
REGIUS
RELICS
RELICT
RELIED
RELIEF
RELIER
RELIES
RELINE
RELISH
RELIVE
REMIND
REMISE
REMISS
REMITS
REPINE
RESIDE
RESIGN
RESILE
RESINS
RESIST
RETINA
RETIRE
REVIEW
REVILE
REVISE
REVIVE
REWIND
RHEIMS
RICING
RIDING
RILING
RIMING
RISING
RIVING
ROBING
ROBINS
ROMISH
ROPIER
ROPILY
ROPING
ROSIER
ROSILY
ROSING
ROSINS
ROSINY
ROVING
ROWING
RUBIES
RUBIGO
RULING
RUMINA
RUNINS
RUPIAH
RUSINE
RUTILE

R•••I•
RABBIS
RABBIT
RACHIS
RAFFIA
RAISIN
RANCID
RAPHIS
RATLIN
RECOIL
REDFIN
REGAIN
REGGIE
REJOIN
REMAIN
RENNIN
RENOIR
REPAID
REPAIR
RETAIL
RETAIN
RHODIC
RICHIE
ROBBIA
ROBBIE
ROMAIC
RONNIE
ROOKIE
RUBRIC
RUSKIN
RUSSIA
RUSTIC

R••••I
RHOMBI

•RI•••
ARIANS
ARIDLY
ARIELS
ARIGHT
ARIOSE
ARIOSO
ARIOUS
ARISEN
ARISES
ARISTA
ARISTO
BRIARS
BRIBED
BRIBER
BRIBES
BRICKS
BRIDAL
BRIDES
BRIDGE
BRIDIE
BRIDLE
BRIEFS
BRIERS
BRIERY
BRIGHT
BRIGID
BRILLS
BRINED
BRINES
BRINGS

6

BRINKS
BRISKS
BRITON
CRICKS
CRIERS
CRIMEA
CRIMES
CRIMPS
CRIMPY
CRINGE
CRINUM
CRISES
CRISIS
CRISPS
CRISPY
CRITIC
DRIERS
DRIEST
DRIFTS
DRIFTY
DRILLS
DRINKS
DRIPPY
DRIVEL
DRIVEN
DRIVER
DRIVES
ERICHS
ERINGO
FRIARS
FRIARY
FRIDAY
FRIDGE
FRIEDA
FRIEND
FRIERS
FRIEZE
FRIGHT
FRIGID
FRIJOL
FRILLS
FRILLY
FRINGE
FRINGY
FRISES
FRISKS
FRISKY
FRITHS
FRIVOL
FRIZZY
GRIDED
GRIDES
GRIEFS
GRIEVE
GRIFFE
GRIGRI
GRILLE
GRILLS
GRILSE
GRIMED
GRIMES
GRIMLY
GRINDS
GRIPED
GRIPER
GRIPES
GRIPPE
GRIPPY
GRISLY
GRITTY
GRIVET
GRIZEL
IRIDES
IRIDIC
IRISES
IRITIC
IRITIS
KRISES
ORIBIS
ORIELS
ORIENT
ORIGAN
ORIGEN
ORIGIN
ORIOLE
PRICED
PRICES
PRICKS
PRIDED
PRIDES
PRIERS
PRIEST
PRIMAL
PRIMED
PRIMER
PRIMES
PRIMLY
PRIMPS
PRINCE
PRINKS
PRINTS
PRIORS
PRIORY
PRISMS
PRISON
PRISSY
PRIVET
PRIZED
PRIZER
PRIZES
TRIADS
TRIALS
TRIBAL
TRIBES
TRICED
TRICES
TRICHI
TRICHO
TRICKS
TRICKY
TRICOT
TRIERS
TRIFID
TRIFLE
TRIGLY
TRIGON
TRILLS
TRIMLY
TRINAL
TRINED
TRINES
TRIODE
TRIOSE
TRIPLE
TRIPOD
TRIPOS
TRISTE
TRITER
TRIUNE
TRIVET
TRIVIA
TRIXIE
TRIXYS
URINAL
WRIEST
WRIGHT
WRINGS
WRISTS
WRITER
WRITES
WRITHE

•R•I••

ARCING
ARGIVE
ARLINE
ARMIES
ARMING
ARNICA
ARNIES
AROIDS
ARRIVE
ARSINE
ARTIES
ARTIST
BRAIDS
BRAILS
BRAINS
BRAINY
BRAISE
BRAIZE
BROILS
BRUINS
BRUISE
BRUITS
CRAIGS
CRUISE
CRYING
DRAINS
DROITS
DRUIDS
DRYING
ERBIUM
ERMINE
ERNIES
ERRING
ERWINS
FRAILS
FRAISE
FRUITS
FRUITY
FRYING
GRAINS
GRAINY
GREIGE
GROINS
IRKING
IRVING
IRVINS
IRWINS
KRAITS
ORBING
ORBITS
OREIDE
ORGIES
ORNITH
OROIDE
ORPINE
ORPINS
ORRICE
PRAISE
PRYING
TRAILS
TRAINS
TRAITS
TROIKA
TRUING
TRUISM
TRYING
UREIDE
URGING
URSINE
WRAITH
WRYING

•R••I•

ARABIA
ARABIC
ARCHIE
ARCHIL
ARCTIC
ARMPIT
ARTOIS
BRAZIL
BREWIS
BRIDIE
BRIGID
BROMIC
CRANIA
CRANIO
CRASIS
CREDIT
CRETIC
CRETIN
CRISIS
CRITIC
CROJIK
EROTIC
FRIGID
FROLIC
GRADIN
GRATIS
GRAVID
IRAQIS
IRENIC
IRIDIC
IRITIC
IRITIS
IRONIC
KRUBIS
ORCEIN
ORCHID
ORCHIL
ORCHIO
ORCHIS
ORDAIN
ORIBIS
ORIGIN
ORPHIC
PRAXIS
PRECIS
PREFIX
PROFIT
PROLIX
PROSIT
TRAGIC
TRIFID
TRIVIA
TRIXIE
TROPIC
URALIC
URANIA
URANIC
URCHIN
UREMIA
URETIC

•R•••I

ARBORI
ARGALI
BRACHI
BRUNEI
GRIGRI
TRICHI

••RI••

ADRIAN
ADRIEN
ADRIFT
AERIAL
AERIED
AERIES
AERIFY
AFRICA
AIRIER
AIRILY
AIRING
AMRITA
AORIST
APRILS
ARRIVE
ATRIAL
ATRIUM
AURIGA
AURIST
BARING
BARITE
BARIUM
BERING
BORIDE
BORING
BURIAL
BURIED
BURIES
BURINS
CARIBE
CARIBS
CARIES
CARINA
CARING
CERING
CERIPH
CERISE
CERITE
CERIUM
CHRISM
CHRIST
CORING
CORIUM
CURIAE
CURIAL
CURIES
CURING
CURIOS
CURIUM
CYRILS
DARICS
DARIEN
DARING
DARIUS
DERIDE
DERIVE
DORIAN
DORIES
DURIAN
DURING
DURION
EARING
EERILY
ENRICH
ENRICO
ERRING
EURIPI
EYRIES
FARINA
FARING
FERIAL
FERINE
FERITY
FIRING
FORINT
FURIES
GARISH
GORIER
GORILY
GORING
HERIOT
HIRING
JARINA
JURIES
JURIST
LARIAT
LARINE
LORICA

LORIES
LURING
LYRICS
LYRISM
LYRIST
MARIAN
MARIAS
MARIES
MARINA
MARINE
MARION
MARIST
MERINO
MERITS
MIRIAM
MIRING
MORION
MURIEL
MURINE
MYRIAD
MYRICA
NARIAL
NARINE
NORIAS
OARING
OGRISH
ORRICE
PARIAH
PARIAN
PARIES
PARING
PARISH
PARITY
PERILS
PERIOD
PERISH
PORING
PURIFY
PURINE
PURISM
PURIST
PURITY
PYRITE
RARING
RARITY
SCRIBE
SCRIMP
SCRIPS
SCRIPT
SCRIVE
SERIAL
SERIES
SERIFS
SERINE
SERINS
SHRIEK
SHRIFT
SHRIKE
SHRILL
SHRIMP
SHRINE
SHRINK
SHRIVE
SIRING
SIRIUS
SPRIER
SPRIGS
SPRING
SPRINT
SPRITE
SPRITS
STRIAE
STRICK
STRICT
STRIDE
STRIFE
STRIKE
STRING
STRIPE
STRIPS
STRIPT
STRIPY
STRIVE
SYRIAC
SYRIAN
SYRINX
TARIFF
TARING
THRICE
THRIFT
THRILL
THRIPS
THRIVE
TIRING
TORIES
TORIIS
UNRIGS
UNRIPE
UNRIPS
UPRISE
VARICO
VARIED
VARIER
VARIES
VERIFY
VERILY
VERISM
VERIST
VERITY
VIRILE
WARIER
WARILY
WIRIER
WIRILY
WIRING
ZORILS
ZURICH

••R•I•

ADROIT
AFRAID
AORTIC
BARBIE
BARDIC
BARMIE
BARRIO
BERLIN
BERNIE
BERTIE
BIRDIE
BORGIA
BURDIE
CARDIO
CARPIC
CARRIE
CERVIX
CORGIS
CORTIN
CURTIS
DARWIN
DERAIL
DERAIN
DERMIC
DERRIS
DORMIE
EARWIG
FERMIS
FERRIC
FERRIS
FERVID
FIRKIN
FORBID
FORMIC
FORNIX
FORTIS
GARLIC
GERBIL
GERTIE
HARBIN
HARMIN
HERDIC
HEREIN
HERMIT
HERNIA
HERNIO
HEROIC
HEROIN
HORNIE
HORRID
JARVIS
JERKIN
JERVIS
KERMIS
LORAIN
MARCIA
MARGIE
MARGIN
MARLIN
MARTIN
MARVIN
MERCIA
MERLIN
MERVIN
MORBID
MORRIS
NEREIS
NORDIC
NORNIR
NORRIS
PARSIS
PARVIS
PERMIT
PERSIA
PORTIA
PURLIN
SERAIS
SERBIA
SEREIN
SORDID
SORTIE
SPRAIN
STRAIN
STRAIT
TERBIA
TORIIS
TOROID
TORPID
TORRID
TURBID
TURBIT
TURGID
TURKIC
TURKIS
TURNIP
VERDIN
VEREIN
VERGIL
VERMIN
VERNIX
VIRGIE
VIRGIL
VIRGIN

••R••I

BORZOI
EURIPI
HERMAI
NEROLI
STRATI

•••RI•

ACARID
AGARIC
ALARIC
ANTRIM
ASTRID
BARRIO
BEDRID
CAPRIC
CARRIE
CEDRIC
CHORIC
CITRIC
CLERIC
CLERID
COWRIE
CUPRIC
CYMRIC
CYPRIN
DEARIE
DEBRIS
DERRIS
EGERIA
EMERIC
ESPRIT
FABRIC
FENRIR
FERRIC
FERRIS
FIBRIL
FIBRIN
FLORID
FLORIN
GLORIA
HENRIS
HORRID
HOURIS
HUBRIS
HYBRID
HYBRIS
HYDRIC
IATRIC
IBERIA
INDRIS
INGRID
KAURIS
LATRIA
LAURIE
MADRID
MAORIS
MATRIX
MEGRIM
METRIC
MIDRIB
MORRIS
NITRIC
NITRID
NORRIS
NUTRIA
OSIRIS
PEORIA
PETRIE
PICRIC
PUTRID
PYURIA
RUBRIC
SCORIA
SHERIF
SIGRID
SPIRIT
STERIC
THORIA
THORIC
TORRID
VIBRIO
VITRIC
YTTRIA
YTTRIC

•••R•I

ANDREI
GEORGI
GHARRI
OCTROI
THYRSI

••••RI

AMBARI
ARBORI
ASTERI
BIHARI
CENTRI
CIMBRI
DENDRI
DMITRI
EPHORI
GHARRI
GRIGRI
ONAGRI
QUADRI
SAFARI
SATORI
SOUARI
TISHRI
VAPORI
VASARI

R•J•••

RAJABS
RAJAHS
RAJPUT
REJECT
REJOIN

•R•J••

CROJIK
FRIJOL
PROJET
TROJAN

•••R•J

SWARAJ

R•K•••

RAKERS
RAKING
RAKISH

R••K••

RACKED
RACKER
RACKET
RANKED
RANKER
RANKLE
RANKLY
RECKON
REEKED
REEKER
RICKED
RICKEY
RICKYS
RISKED
RISKER
ROCKED
ROCKER
ROCKET
ROCKNE
ROOKED
ROOKIE
RUCKED
RUCKUS
RUSKIN

R•••K•
REBUKE
REMAKE
RETAKE
REVOKE

R••••K
REMARK
RETOOK

•RK•••
IRKING

•R•K••
ARCKED
BRAKED
BRAKES
BROKEN
BROKER
CRAKES
DRAKES
KRAKEN

•R••K•
BREAKS
BRICKS
BRINKS
BRISKS
BROOKS
CRACKS
CRACKY
CRANKS
CRANKY
CREAKS
CREAKY
CREEKS
CRICKS
CROAKS
CROAKY
CROCKS
CROOKS
DRINKS
DROSKY
DRUNKS
FRANKS
FREAKS
FREAKY
FRISKS
FRISKY
FROCKS
GREEKS
PRANKS
PRICKS
PRINKS
TRACKS
TRICKS
TRICKY
TROIKA
TRUCKS
TRUNKS
WRACKS
WREAKS
WRECKS

•R•••K
ARAWAK
ARRACK
CROJIK
FRANCK

••RK••
BARKED
BARKER
BURKED
BURKES
CORKED
CORKER
DARKEN
DARKER
DARKLE
DARKLY
DIRKED
FIRKIN
FORKED
GURKHA
HARKED
HARKEN
JERKED
JERKIN
LARKED
LARKER
LURKED
MARKED
MARKER
MARKET
MARKKA
MARKUP
PARKAS
PARKED
PARKER
PERKED
PORKER
TURKEY
TURKIC
TURKIS
WORKED
WORKER

••R•K•
DEREKS
EUREKA
MARKKA
PERUKE
SHRIKE
STRAKE
STRIKE
STROKE
TORSKS

••R••K
ARRACK
BARTOK
CARACK
KARNAK
MARDUK
SCREAK
SHRANK
SHRIEK
SHRINK
SHRUNK
STREAK
STRICK
STRUCK

•••RK•
CLERKS
QUARKS
QUIRKS
SHARKS
SHIRKS
SMIRKS
SPARKS
STIRKS
STORKS

•••R•K
ANORAK
DVORAK

••••RK
BYWORK
DEBARK
EMBARK
IMBARK
IMPARK
NEWARK
REMARK
UNCORK

R•L•••
RALPHS
RELATE
RELAYS
RELENT
RELICS
RELICT
RELIED
RELIEF
RELIER
RELIES
RELINE
RELISH
RELIVE
RELOAD
RILING
RILLET
ROLAND
ROLLED
ROLLER
ROLPHS
RULERS
RULING

R••L••
RAGLAN
RAILED
RATLIN
REALES
REALLY
REALMS
REALTY
REELED
REELER
REFLET
REFLEX
REFLUX
REGLET
REPLAY
RIALTO
RIFLED
RIFLER
RIFLES
RILLET
RIPLEY
ROALDS
ROBLES
ROILED
ROLLED
ROLLER
RUBLES
RUNLET

R•••L•
RABBLE
RACILY
RADDLE
RADULA
RAFFLE
RAMBLE
RANKLE
RANKLY
RAOULS
RARELY
RASHLY
RATALS
RATELS
RATTLE
RATTLY
RAVELS
REALLY
REBELS
REBILL
RECALL
REDDLE
REFILL
REGALE
REPELS
RESALE
RESELL
RESILE
RESOLD
RESOLE
RESULT
RETELL
RETOLD
REVELS
REVILE
REVOLT
RIBALD
RICHLY
RIDDLE
RIFFLE
RIMPLE
RIPELY
RIPPLE
RIVALS
RIYALS
ROBALO
ROMOLA
ROMULO
RONALD
ROPILY
ROSILY
ROUBLE
ROWELS
ROYALS
RUBBLE
RUDDLE
RUDELY
RUFFLE
RUMBLE
RUMPLE
RUNDLE
RUSTLE
RUTILE

R••••L
RACHEL
RACIAL
RADIAL
RANDAL
RAPPEL
RASCAL
REBILL
RECALL
RECOIL
RECTAL
REFILL
REGNAL
RENTAL
RESELL
RETAIL
RETELL
REVEAL
RHINAL
RICTAL
RITUAL
ROMMEL
RONDEL
RUEFUL
RUNNEL

•RL•••
ARLEEN
ARLENE
ARLINE
ORLOPS

•R•L••
ARMLET
BRILLS
BRULOT
DRILLS
DROLLS
DROLLY
FRILLS
FRILLY
FROLIC
GRILLE
GRILLS
GRILSE
ORALLY
PROLEG
PROLIX
TRILLS
TROLLS
URALIC

•R••L•
ARABLE
ARBELA
ARCHLY
AREOLA
ARGALI
ARGALS
ARGYLE
ARGYLL
ARIDLY
ARIELS
ARNOLD
ARTELS
BRAILS
BRAWLS
BRIDLE
BRILLS
BROILS
CRAALS
CRADLE
CRAWLS
CRAWLY
CREELS
CREOLE
DRABLY
DRAWLS
DRAWLY
DRILLS
DROLLS
DROLLY
DROOLS
FRAILS
FREELY
FRILLS
FRILLY
GRAYLY
GRILLE
GRILLS
GRIMLY
GRISLY
GROWLS
GRUELS
KRAALS
ORACLE
ORALLY
ORIELS
ORIOLE
ORMOLU
ORWELL
PRIMLY
PROWLS
TRAILS
TRAWLS
TREBLE
TRIALS
TRIFLE

TRIGLY
TRILLS
TRIMLY
TRIPLE
TROLLS
URSULA

•R•••L

ARABEL
ARCHIL
ARGYLL
ARMFUL
ARTFUL
BRAZIL
BRIDAL
BROMAL
BRUMAL
BRUTAL
CRENEL
CRESOL
CREWEL
CRURAL
DRIVEL
FRIJOL
FRIVOL
FRUGAL
GRAVEL
GRETEL
GRIZEL
GROVEL
IREFUL
ORCHIL
ORDEAL
ORWELL
PRIMAL
PROPEL
PROPYL
TRAVEL
TRIBAL
TRINAL
TROPAL
TROTYL
TROWEL
URANYL
URINAL

••RL••

BARLEY
BERLIN
BIRLED
BIRLES
BURLAP
BURLED
BURLER
BURLEY
CARLAS
CARLOS
CURLED
CURLER
CURLEW
EARLAP
EARLES
FARLES
FARLEY
FURLED
GARLIC
HARLAN
HARLEM
HARLEY
HARLOT
HURLED
HURLER
MARLED
MARLIN
MERLES
MERLIN
MERLON
MORLEY
PARLAY
PARLEY
PARLOR
PURLED
PURLIN
VARLET
WORLDS

••R•L•

AIRILY
APRILS
BARELY
BARFLY
BERYLS
BURBLE
BURGLE
CAROLE
CAROLS
CIRCLE
CORALS
CURDLE
CURTLY
CURULE
CYRILS
DARKLE
DARKLY
DARTLE
DIRELY
EERILY
ENROLL
FERULA
FERULE
FIRMLY
GARBLE
GARGLE
GERALD
GIRDLE
GORALS
GORILY
GURGLE
HARDLY
HAROLD
HERALD
HURDLE
HURTLE
JURELS
KERALA
LORDLY
MARBLE
MERELY
MORALE
MORALS
MORELS
MORULA
MURALS
MYRTLE
NEROLI
PAROLE
PARTLY
PERILS
PERTLY
PORTLY
PURELY
PURFLE
PURPLE
RARELY
SCROLL
SHRILL
SORELS
SORELY
SPRYLY
STROLL
SURELY
TARTLY
TERMLY
THRALL
THRILL
TURTLE
UNROLL
UNRULY
VERILY
VIRILE
WARBLE
WARILY
WARMLY
WIRILY
ZORILS

••R••L

AERIAL
AORTAL
ATRIAL
AZRAEL
BARBEL
BARREL
BORDEL
BOREAL
BURIAL
BURSAL
CARCEL
CARMEL
CARNAL
CARPAL
CARPEL
CARREL
CARTEL
CARVEL
CEREAL
CORBEL
CORNEL
CORRAL
CURIAL
DARNEL
DERAIL
DERMAL
DIRNDL
DORSAL
EARFUL
ENROLL
FERIAL
FORMAL
FORMYL
GERBIL
HARTAL
HERBAL
ISRAEL
JARFUL
KERNEL
LARVAL
MARCEL
MARVEL
MORSEL
MORTAL
MURIEL
NARIAL
NARWAL
NORMAL
PARCEL
PARRAL
PARREL
PORTAL
SCRAWL
SCROLL
SERIAL
SERVAL
SHRILL
SORREL
SPRAWL
STROLL
TARNAL
TARSAL
TERCEL
TERGAL
THRALL
THRILL
UNREAL
UNREEL
UNROLL
VERBAL
VERGIL
VERNAL
VIRGIL

•••RL•

CEORLS
CHURLS
DEARLY
DOURLY
FAIRLY
GNARLS
GNARLY
HOURLY
KNURLS
KNURLY
NEARLY
OVERLY
PEARLS
PEARLY
POORLY
SHORLS
SNARLS
SNARLY
SOURLY
SWIRLS
SWIRLY
TWIRLS
WHIRLS
WHORLS
YEARLY

•••R•L

ABORAL
AMORAL
ASTRAL
BARREL
CARREL
CHERYL
CHORAL
CITRAL
CORRAL
CRURAL
FIBRIL
FLORAL
GOORAL
HEDRAL
LAUREL
MITRAL
NEURAL
PARRAL
PARREL
PATROL
PETREL
PETROL
PLURAL
SACRAL
SAUREL
SORREL
SPIRAL
STEROL
TETRYL

••••RL

AWHIRL
SCHORL
UNCURL
UNFURL

R•M•••

RAMBLE
RAMIES
RAMIFY
RAMMED
RAMMER
RAMONA
RAMOSE
RAMOUS
RAMPED
RAMROD
RAMSON
REMADE
REMAIN
REMAKE
REMAND
REMANS
REMARK
REMEDY
REMIND
REMISE
REMISS
REMITS
REMORA
REMOTE
REMOVE
REMUDA
RIMERS
RIMING
RIMMED
RIMMER
RIMOSE
RIMOUS
RIMPLE
ROMAIC
ROMANS
ROMANY
ROMISH
ROMMEL
ROMNEY
ROMOLA
ROMPED
ROMPER
ROMULO
RUMBAS
RUMBLE
RUMINA
RUMMER
RUMORS
RUMPLE
RUMPUS

R••M••

RAGMAN
RAGMEN
RAMMED
RAMMER
REAMED
REAMER
RHOMBI
RHUMBA
RHUMBS
RHYMED
RHYMER
RHYMES
RIMMED
RIMMER
ROAMED
ROAMER
RODMAN
RODMEN
ROMMEL
ROOMED
ROOMER
RUMMER

R•••M•

RACEME
RADOME

REALMS
REARMS
REGIME
RESUME
REVAMP
RHEIMS
RHEUMY

R••••M
RACISM
RADIUM
RANDOM
RANSOM
RECTUM
REDEEM
REFORM
RHYTHM

•RM•••
ARMADA
ARMAGH
ARMAND
ARMETS
ARMFUL
ARMIES
ARMING
ARMLET
ARMORS
ARMORY
ARMPIT
ARMURE
ERMINE
ORMERS
ORMOLU
ORMUZD

•R•M••
AROMAS
BREMEN
BROMAL
BROMES
BROMIC
BRUMAL
BRUMES
CRAMBO
CRAMPS
CREMES
CRIMEA
CRIMES
CRIMPS
CRIMPY
CRUMBS
CRUMBY
CRUMMY
CRUMPS
DRAMAS
DROMON
FRAMED
FRAMER
FRAMES
FRUMPS
FRUMPY
GRIMED
GRIMES

GRIMLY
GRUMES
GRUMPY
PREMED
PRIMAL
PRIMED
PRIMER
PRIMES
PRIMLY
PRIMPS
PROMPT
TRAMPS
TREMOR
TRIMLY
TRUMAN
TRUMPS
UREMIA

•R••M•
BRAHMA
BRAHMS
BREAMS
BREGMA
BROOMS
BROOMY
CREAMS
CREAMY
CRUMMY
DREAMS
DREAMT
DREAMY
GROOMS
PRISMS
PROEMS
TRAUMA

•R•••M
CRINUM
DRACHM
ERBIUM
FRENUM
GRAHAM
ORGASM
TRUISM

••RM••
AIRMAN
AIRMEN
BARMAN
BARMEN
BARMIE
BERMES
CARMAN
CARMEL
CARMEN
CERMET
DERMAL
DERMAS
DERMAT
DERMIC
DORMER
DORMIE
FARMED
FARMER

FERMIS
FIRMAN
FIRMED
FIRMER
FIRMLY
FORMAL
FORMAT
FORMED
FORMER
FORMIC
FORMYL
GERMAN
HARMED
HARMIN
HERMAE
HERMAI
HERMAN
HERMES
HERMIT
KARMAS
KERMES
KERMIS
MARMOT
MERMAN
MERMEN
MORMON
MURMUR
MYRMEC
NORMAL
NORMAN
NORMAS
PERMIT
SERMON
TARMAC
TERMED
TERMER
TERMLY
TERMOR
VERMIN
WARMED
WARMER
WARMLY
WARMTH
WARMUP
WORMED
WORMER

••R•M•
ABRAMS
AFRAME
BIREME
CAROMS
CHROMA
CHROME
CHROMO
CORYMB
FORUMS
HAREMS
HIRAMS
IHRAMS
JEREMY
JEROME
JORAMS
JORUMS

SCRAMS
SCRIMP
SCRUMS
SERUMS
SHRIMP
STROMA
STRUMA
STRUMS
THRUMS

••R••M
ATRIUM
BARIUM
BARNUM
CERIUM
CHRISM
CIRCUM
CORIUM
CURIUM
DIRHAM
DORSUM
DURHAM
FERRUM
HARLEM
LYRISM
MIRIAM
PURISM
SCREAM
STREAM
TERGUM
VERISM

•••RM•
ALARMS
CHARMS
CHIRMS
DHARMA
INARMS
REARMS
SMARMY
SPERMO
STORMS
STORMY
SWARMS
THERMO
THERMS

•••R•M
ALARUM
ANTRIM
ANTRUM
ASARUM
CUPRUM
ENGRAM
FERRUM
LABRUM
MEGRIM
POGROM
QUORUM
SACRUM

••••RM
AFFIRM
BIFORM

DEFORM
DISARM
INFIRM
INFORM
REFORM
SQUIRM

R•N•••
RANCHO
RANCID
RANCOR
RANDAL
RANDAN
RANDOM
RANEES
RANGED
RANGER
RANGES
RANKED
RANKER
RANKLE
RANKLY
RANSOM
RANTED
RANTER
RENDED
RENDER
RENEES
RENEGE
RENEWS
RENNET
RENNIN
RENOIR
RENOWN
RENTAL
RENTED
RENTER
RENTES
RINGED
RINGER
RINSED
RINSER
RINSES
RONALD
RONDEL
RONDOS
RONNIE
RUNDLE
RUNINS
RUNLET
RUNNEL
RUNNER
RUNOFF
RUNONS
RUNOUT
RUNWAY
RUNYON

R••N••
RAINED
REGNAL
REINED
RENNET
RENNIN

RHINAL
RHINOS
RODNEY
ROMNEY
RONNIE
ROUNDS
RUINED
RUINER
RUNNEL
RUNNER
RWANDA

R•••N•
RACINE
RACING
RAGING
RAKING
RAMONA
RAPINE
RAPING
RARING
RATINE
RATING
RAVENS
RAVINE
RAVING
RAYING
RAYONS
RAZING
RECANT
RECENT
REDANS
REDONE
REFINE
REFUND
REGENT
REGINA
REIGNS
RELENT
RELINE
REMAND
REMANS
REMIND
REPAND
REPENT
REPINE
RERUNS
RESEND
RESENT
RESINS
RETENE
RETINA
REWIND
RICING
RIDENT
RIDING
RILING
RIMING
RIPENS
RISING
RIVING
ROBAND
ROBING
ROBINS

ROCKNE
RODENT
ROLAND
ROMANS
ROMANY
ROPING
ROSING
ROSINS
ROSINY
ROTUND
ROVING
ROWANS
ROWENA
ROWING
ROXANA
ROXANE
RUBENS
RULING
RUMINA
RUNINS
RUNONS
RUSINE

R••••N
RACOON
RADIAN
RAGLAN
RAGMAN
RAGMEN
RAISIN
RAMSON
RANDAN
RATION
RATLIN
RATOON
RATTAN
RATTEN
REASON
REBORN
RECKON
REDDEN
REDFIN
REGAIN
REGION
REJOIN
REMAIN
RENNIN
RENOWN
REOPEN
RESIGN
RETAIN
RETURN
REUBEN
RIBBON
RIDDEN
ROBSON
RODMAN
RODMEN
ROTTEN
RUNYON
RUSKIN

•RN•••
ARNAUD
ARNICA
ARNIES
ARNOLD
ERNEST
ERNIES
ORNATE
ORNERY
ORNITH

•R•N••
ARANTA
ARENAS
ARUNTA
BRANCH
BRANDS
BRANDY
BRANNY
BRANTS
BRENDA
BRENTS
BRINED
BRINES
BRINGS
BRINKS
BRONCO
BRONCS
BRONTE
BRONZE
BRONZY
BRUNCH
BRUNEI
BRUNET
BRUNOS
CRANED
CRANES
CRANIA
CRANIO
CRANKS
CRANKY
CRANNY
CRENEL
CRINGE
CRINUM
CRONES
CRONUS
CRUNCH
DRENCH
DRINKS
DRONED
DRONES
DRONGO
DRUNKS
ERINGO
ERYNGO
FRANCE
FRANCK
FRANCO
FRANCS
FRANKS
FRENCH
FRENUM
FRENZY
FRINGE
FRINGY
FRONDS
FRONTO
FRONTS
FRUNZE
GRANGE
GRANNY
GRANTS
GRINDS
GRUNDY
GRUNTS
IRENES
IRENIC
IRONED
IRONER
IRONIC
KRONEN
KRONER
KRONOR
KRONUR
ORANGE
ORANGS
PRANCE
PRANKS
PRINCE
PRINKS
PRINTS
PRONGS
PRONTO
PRUNED
PRUNER
PRUNES
TRANCE
TRANSP
TRENCH
TRENDS
TRENDY
TRINAL
TRINED
TRINES
TRUNKS
URANIA
URANIC
URANUS
URANYL
URINAL
WRENCH
WRINGS
WRONGS

•R••N•
ARCANE
ARCING
ARDENT
ARGENT
ARIANS
ARLENE
ARLINE
ARMAND
ARMING
AROUND
ARPENS
ARPENT
ARRANT
ARSINE
ARYANS
BRAINS
BRAINY
BRANNY
BRAWNY
BROWNS
BRUINS
BRYANT
BRYONY
CRANNY
CROONS
CROWNS
CRYING
DRAINS
DROWNS
DRYING
ERMINE
ERRAND
ERRANT
ERRING
ERWINS
FREONS
FRESNO
FRIEND
FROWNS
FRYING
GRAINS
GRAINY
GRANNY
GREENS
GROANS
GROINS
GROUND
IRKING
IRVING
IRVINS
IRWINS
ORBING
ORGANA
ORGANO
ORGANS
ORIENT
ORPINE
ORPINS
PRAWNS
PREENS
PROCNE
PRYING
TRAINS
TRIUNE
TRUANT
TRUING
TRYING
URBANE
URGENT
URGING
URSINE
WRYING

•R•••N
ARAGON
ARCHON
ARISEN
ARLEEN
BRAZEN
BREMEN
BRETON
BRITON
BROGAN
BROKEN
CRAVEN
CRAYON
CRETAN
CRETIN
CROTON
DRAGON
DRIVEN
DROMON
DRYDEN
FRAUEN
FROZEN
GRABEN
GRADIN
GRAVEN
KRAKEN
KRONEN
ORCEIN
ORDAIN
OREGON
ORIGAN
ORIGEN
ORIGIN
ORPHAN
PRISON
PROTON
PROVEN
TREPAN
TRIGON
TROGON
TROJAN
TRUMAN
URCHIN

••RN••
BARNEY
BARNUM
BERNEY
BERNIE
BORNEO
BURNED
BURNER
BURNET
CARNAL
CORNEA
CORNED
CORNEL
CORNER
CORNET
CORNUA
CORNUS
DARNED
DARNEL
DIRNDL
EARNED
EARNER
FORNAX
FORNIX
GARNER
GARNET
HERNIA
HERNIO
HORNED
HORNET
HORNIE
KARNAK
KERNED
KERNEL
MYRNAS
NORNIR
TARNAL
TURNED
TURNER
TURNIP
VERNAL
VERNAS
VERNIX
VERNON
WARNED
WARNER

••R•N•
AARONS
AIRING
APRONS
ARRANT
BARING
BARONG
BARONS
BARONY
BERING
BORANE
BORING
BURANS
BURINS
CARINA
CARING
CERING
CHRONO
CORING
CORONA
CURING
CYRANO
CYRENE
DARING
DURING
EARING
ERRAND
ERRANT
ERRING
FARINA
FARING
FERINE
FIRING
FORINT
GERENT
GERUND
GORING
GYRONS
HERONS
HIRING
HURONS
JARINA

6

JURANT
KARENS
KORUNA
KORUNY
LARINE
LARYNG
LARYNX
LORENE
LORENZ
LURING
MARINA
MARINE
MERINO
MIRING
MORONS
MURINE
NARINE
OARING
PARANG
PARENS
PARENT
PARING
PHRENO
PIRANA
PORING
PURANA
PURINE
PYRANS
PYRENE
PYRONE
RARING
RERUNS
SARONG
SERENA
SERENE
SERINE
SERINS
SHRANK
SHRINE
SHRINK
SHRUNK
SIRENS
SIRING
SPRANG
SPRING
SPRINT
SPRUNG
STRAND
STRING
STRONG
SYRINX
TARING
THRONE
THRONG
TIRANA
TIRING
TYRANT
TYRONE
VARUNA
VERONA
WERENT
WIRING
ZIRONS

••R••N

ADRIAN
ADRIEN
AIRMAN
AIRMEN
BARMAN
BARMEN
BARREN
BARTON
BARYON
BERGEN
BERLIN
BURDEN
CARBON
CAREEN
CARMAN
CARMEN
CARSON
CARTON
CARVEN
CORBAN
CORDON
CORTIN
DARDAN
DARIEN
DARKEN
DARWIN
DERAIN
DOREEN
DORIAN
DURBAN
DURIAN
DURION
FIRKIN
FIRMAN
GARCON
GARDEN
GERMAN
GERYON
GORDON
GORGON
GORHEN
HARBIN
HARDEN
HARKEN
HARLAN
HARMIN
HEREIN
HEREON
HERMAN
HEROIN
JARGON
JERKIN
JORDAN
KOREAN
LARDON
LORAIN
LOREEN
MARGIN
MARIAN
MARION
MARLIN
MAROON
MARTEN
MARTIN
MARVIN
MERLIN
MERLON
MERMAN
MERMEN
MERVIN
MOREEN
MORGAN
MORGEN
MORION
MORMON
MORTON
NOREEN
NORMAN
PARDON
PARIAN
PARSON
PERRON
PERSON
PURLIN
SARGON
SCREEN
SEREIN
SERMON
SPRAIN
STRAIN
STREWN
SYRIAN
TARPON
TARTAN
TARZAN
THROWN
TURBAN
TUREEN
VERDIN
VERDUN
VEREIN
VERMIN
VERNON
VIRGIN
WARDEN
WARREN
WORSEN
ZIRCON

•••RN•

ACORNS
ADORNS
AVERNO
BAIRNS
BOURNE
BOURNS
CAIRNS
CHURNS
DHARNA
DHURNA
INURNS
LEARNS
LEARNT
LIERNE
MOURNS
QUERNS
SCORNS
SPURNS
STERNA
STERNO
STERNS
THORNS
THORNY
UTURNS
YEARNS

•••R•N

ANURAN
BARREN
CHARON
CHIRON
CITRON
CYPRIN
DACRON
FIBRIN
FLORIN
GIBRAN
HEBRON
HEDRON
KEDRON
MACRON
MATRON
MICRON
NATRON
NEURON
OBERON
OUTRAN
OUTRUN
PATRON
PERRON
SHARON
SHORAN
THORON
WARREN

••••RN

ASTERN
ATTORN
AUBURN
BICORN
CASERN
CAVERN
DECERN
DEHORN
EXTERN
GOVERN
INBORN
INTERN
INTURN
MODERN
OSBORN
REBORN
RETURN
SATURN
SECERN
SUBORN
TAVERN
UNBORN
UPTURN
WIVERN
WYVERN

RO••••

ROALDS
ROAMED
ROAMER
ROARED
ROARER
ROASTS
ROBALO
ROBAND
ROBBED
ROBBER
ROBBIA
ROBBIE
ROBERT
ROBING
ROBINS
ROBLES
ROBOTS
ROBSON
ROBUST
ROCHET
ROCKED
ROCKER
ROCKET
ROCKNE
ROCOCO
RODDYS
RODENT
RODEOS
RODMAN
RODMEN
RODNEY
ROGERS
ROGUED
ROGUES
ROILED
ROLAND
ROLLED
ROLLER
ROLPHS
ROMAIC
ROMANS
ROMANY
ROMISH
ROMMEL
ROMNEY
ROMOLA
ROMPED
ROMPER
ROMULO
RONALD
RONDEL
RONDOS
RONNIE
ROOFED
ROOFER
ROOKED
ROOKIE
ROOMED
ROOMER
ROOSTS
ROOTED
ROOTER
ROPIER
ROPILY
ROPING
ROQUET
ROSARY
ROSCOE
ROSIER
ROSILY
ROSING
ROSINS
ROSINY
ROSTER
ROSTRA
ROTARY
ROTATE
ROTCHE
ROTGUT
ROTORS
ROTTED
ROTTEN
ROTTER
ROTUND
ROUBLE
ROUCHE
ROUGED
ROUGES
ROUGHS
ROUNDS
ROUSED
ROUSER
ROUSES
ROUSTS
ROUTED
ROUTER
ROUTES
ROVERS
ROVING
ROWANS
ROWELS
ROWENA
ROWERS
ROWING
ROXANA
ROXANE
ROYALS

R•O•••

RAOULS
REOPEN
RHODAS
RHODIC
RHOMBI
RIOTED
RIOTER
ROOFED
ROOFER
ROOKED
ROOKIE
ROOMED
ROOMER
ROOSTS
ROOTED
ROOTER

R••O••
RACOON
RADOME
RAGOUT
RAMONA
RAMOSE
RAMOUS
RATOON
RAYONS
RAZORS
REBORN
REBOZO
RECOIL
RECORD
RECOUP
REDOES
REDONE
REDOWA
REFORM
REJOIN
RELOAD
REMORA
REMOTE
REMOVE
RENOIR
RENOWN
REPORT
REPOSE
RESOLD
RESOLE
RESORB
RESORT
RETOLD
RETOOK
RETORT
REVOKE
REVOLT
REWORD
RIBOSE
RIGORS
RIMOSE
RIMOUS
RIPOFF
RIPOST
ROBOTS
ROCOCO
ROMOLA
ROTORS
RUFOUS
RUGOSE
RUGOUS
RUMORS
RUNOFF
RUNONS
RUNOUT

R•••O•
RACOON
RADIOS
RAMROD
RAMSON
RANCOR
RANDOM
RANSOM
RATION
RATIOS
RATOON
REASON
REAVOW
RECKON
RECTOR
RECTOS
REDDOG
REDHOT
REDTOP
REGION
RETOOK
RHETOR
RHINOS
RIBBON
ROBSON
RODEOS
RONDOS
ROSCOE
RUNYON

R••••O
RANCHO
REBATO
REBOZO
REECHO
RIALTO
RIGHTO
ROBALO
ROCOCO
ROMULO
RUBATO
RUBIGO

•RO•••
AROIDS
AROMAS
AROUND
AROUSE
BROACH
BROADS
BROGAN
BROGUE
BROILS
BROKEN
BROKER
BROMAL
BROMES
BROMIC
BRONCO
BRONCS
BRONTE
BRONZE
BRONZY
BROOCH
BROODS
BROODY
BROOKS
BROOMS
BROOMY
BROTHS
BROWNS
BROWSE
CROAKS
CROAKY
CROATS
CROCKS
CROCUS
CROFTS
CROJIK
CRONES
CRONUS
CROOKS
CROONS
CRORES
CROSSE
CROTCH
CROTON
CROUCH
CROUPE
CROUPS
CROUPY
CROWDS
CROWED
CROWNS
CROZER
CROZES
DROITS
DROLLS
DROLLY
DROMON
DRONED
DRONES
DRONGO
DROOLS
DROOPS
DROOPY
DROPSY
DROSKY
DROSSY
DROUTH
DROVED
DROVER
DROVES
DROWNS
DROWSE
DROWSY
ERODED
ERODES
EROTIC
FROCKS
FROGGY
FROLIC
FRONDS
FRONTO
FRONTS
FROSTS
FROSTY
FROTHS
FROTHY
FROWNS
FROWZY
FROZEN
GROANS
GROATS
GROCER
GROGGY
GROINS
GROOMS
GROOVE
GROOVY
GROPED
GROPER
GROPES
GROSZY
GROTTO
GROUCH
GROUND
GROUPS
GROUSE
GROUTS
GROVEL
GROVER
GROVES
GROWER
GROWLS
GROWTH
IRONED
IRONER
IRONIC
KRONEN
KRONER
KRONOR
KRONUR
OROIDE
PROBED
PROBER
PROBES
PROCNE
PROCTO
PROEMS
PROFIT
PROJET
PROLEG
PROLIX
PROMPT
PRONGS
PRONTO
PROOFS
PROPEL
PROPER
PROPYL
PROSED
PROSER
PROSES
PROSIT
PROTON
PROUST
PROVED
PROVEN
PROVER
PROVES
PROWLS
TROCAR
TROCHE
TROGON
TROIKA
TROJAN
TROLLS
TROOPS
TROPAL
TROPHO
TROPHY
TROPIC
TROTHS
TROTYL
TROUGH
TROUPE
TROUTS
TROVER
TROVES
TROWEL
UROPOD
WRONGS

•R•O••
ARBORI
ARBORS
ARDORS
AREOLA
ARGOSY
ARGOTS
ARIOSE
ARIOSO
ARIOUS
ARMORS
ARMORY
ARNOLD
ARROBA
ARROWS
ARROYO
ARTOIS
BROOCH
BROODS
BROODY
BROOKS
BROOMS
BROOMY
BRYONY
CREOLE
CROOKS
CROONS
DROOLS
DROOPS
DROOPY
ERRORS
FREONS
GROOMS
GROOVE
GROOVY
ORIOLE
ORLOPS
ORMOLU
PRIORS
PRIORY
PROOFS
TRIODE
TRIOSE
TROOPS
TRYOUT

•R••O•
ARAGON
ARCHON
BRAVOS
BRAZOS
BRETON
BRITON
BRULOT
BRUNOS
CRACOW
CRAYON
CREDOS
CRESOL
CROTON
CRUSOE
DRAGON
DROMON
FRIJOL
FRIVOL
GREGOS
KRONOR
ORATOR
OREGON
PRETOR
PRISON
PROTON
TREMOR
TRICOT
TRIGON
TRIPOD
TRIPOS
TROGON
UROPOD

•R•••O
ARCHEO
AREZZO
ARIOSO
ARISTO
ARROYO
ARTHRO
ARTURO
BRONCO
CRAMBO
CRANIO
CRYPTO
DRONGO
ERINGO
ERYNGO
FRANCO
FRESCO
FRESNO
FRONTO
GRAECO
GRAPHO
GROTTO
ORCHIO
ORGANO
PRESTO
PROCTO
PRONTO
TRICHO
TROPHO

••RO••
AARONS
ABROAD
ACROSS

6

ADROIT
AEROBE
APRONS
ARROBA
ARROWS
ARROYO
AURORA
AUROUS
BARONG
BARONS
BARONY
BYROAD
CAROBS
CAROLE
CAROLS
CAROMS
CEROUS
CHROMA
CHROME
CHROMO
CHRONO
CORODY
CORONA
ENROBE
ENROLL
ENROOT
ERRORS
EUROPA
EUROPE
FAROFF
FAROUT
FEROUS
FURORS
GEROUS
GYRONS
GYROSE
HAROLD
HEROES
HEROIC
HEROIN
HERONS
HURONS
INROAD
JEROME
JURORS
LEROYS
MAROON
MEROUS
MORONS
MOROSE
NEROLI
PARODY
PAROLE
POROUS
PYRONE
PYROPE
SARONG
SCRODS
SCROLL
SCROOP
SEROUS
SEROWS
SHROFF
SHROUD
SHROVE
SPROUT
STRODE
STROKE
STROLL
STROMA
STRONG
STROPS
STROUD
STROVE
TAROTS
THROAT
THROBS
THROES
THRONE
THRONG
THROVE
THROWN
THROWS
TOROID
TOROSE
TOROUS
TYRONE
UNROLL
UNROOT
UPROAR
UPROOT
UPROSE
VERONA
VOROUS
ZEROED
ZEROES
ZIRONS

••R•O•

BARROW
BARTOK
BARTON
BARYON
BORROW
BORZOI
BURBOT
BURGOO
BURGOS
BURROS
BURROW
CARBON
CARBOY
CARGOS
CARHOP
CARLOS
CARROT
CARSON
CARTON
CORDON
CURIOS
DARROW
DURION
ENROOT
FARROW
FERVOR
FORGOT
FURROW
GARCON
GERYON
GORDON
GORGON
HARBOR
HARLOT
HARROW
HEREOF
HEREON
HERIOT
HORROR
JARGON
JERBOA
KARROO
LARDON
LARGOS
MARCOS
MARGOS
MARGOT
MARION
MARMOT
MAROON
MARROW
MERLON
MIRROR
MORION
MORMON
MORROS
MORROW
MORTON
NARROW
PARDON
PARGOS
PARLOR
PARROT
PARSON
PERIOD
PERRON
PERSON
SARGON
SARTOR
SCROOP
SERMON
SERVOS
SORGOS
SORROW
TARPON
TERMOR
TERROR
TORPOR
TORSOS
TURBOT
TURCOS
UNROOT
UPROOT
VERNON
VERSOS
VIREOS
YARROW
ZIRCON

••R••O

AERUGO
ARROYO
BARRIO
BORNEO
BURGOO
CARDIO
CARUSO
CERATO
CHROMO
CHRONO
CHRYSO
CYRANO
DORADO
ENRICO
FOREGO
HERETO
HERNIO
KARROO
KERATO
LAREDO
MERINO
MORPHO
PHRENO
SORGHO
TERATO
TEREDO
TORERO
VARICO
VIRAGO

•••RO•

BARROW
BORROW
BURROS
BURROW
CARROT
CHARON
CHIRON
CITRON
CLAROS
DACRON
DARROW
ESCROW
FAEROE
FARROW
FURROW
GENROS
HARROW
HEBRON
HEDRON
HORROR
HYDROS
IGOROT
KARROO
KEDRON
MACRON
MARROW
MATRON
METROS
MICRON
MIRROR
MONROE
MORROS
MORROW
NARROW
NATRON
NEURON
NIMROD
OBERON
OCTROI
PARROT
PATROL
PATRON
PEDROS
PERRON
PETROL
POGROM
RAMROD
SHARON
SORROW
STEROL
TERROR
THORON
UNTROD
UPHROE
YARROW

•••R•O

AVERNO
BARRIO
CHOREO
EMBRYO
HAIRDO
KARROO
OVERDO
QUARTO
SPERMO
STEREO
STERNO
THERMO
THYREO
VIBRIO

••••RO

ANTERO
ARTHRO
ARTURO
ASTERO
AUSTRO
BISTRO
BOLERO
CASTRO
CENTRO
CHEIRO
CHLORO
CICERO
DENDRO
DEXTRO
DINERO
ENTERO
FLUORO
GABBRO
GASTRO
HETERO
INFERO
JETHRO
LAPARO
MADURO
NEPHRO
ONEIRO
PIETRO
PLEURO
SCLERO
SIDERO
STAURO
TORERO
VENTRO

R•P•••

RAPHAE
RAPHIS
RAPIDS
RAPIER
RAPINE
RAPING
RAPIST
RAPPED
RAPPEE
RAPPEL
RAPPER
REPAID
REPAIR
REPAND
REPASS
REPAST
REPAYS
REPEAT
REPELS
REPENT
REPINE
REPLAY
REPORT
REPOSE
REPUTE
RIPELY
RIPENS
RIPEST
RIPLEY
RIPOFF
RIPOST
RIPPED
RIPPER
RIPPLE
RIPRAP
RIPSAW
ROPIER
ROPILY
ROPING
RUPEES
RUPERT
RUPIAH

R••P••

RAJPUT
RALPHS
RAMPED
RAPPED
RAPPEE
RAPPEL
RAPPER
RASPED
RASPER
REAPED
REAPER
REOPEN

RIMPLE
RIPPED
RIPPER
RIPPLE
ROLPHS
ROMPED
ROMPER
RUMPLE
RUMPUS

R•••P•
RECAPS
RECEPT
RECIPE

R••••P
RECOUP
REDCAP
REDTOP
REVAMP
RIPRAP

•RP•••
ARPENS
ARPENT
ORPHAN
ORPHIC
ORPINE
ORPINS

•R•P••
ARMPIT
CRAPED
CRAPES
CREPED
CREPES
CRYPTO
CRYPTS
DRAPED
DRAPER
DRAPES
DRIPPY
DROPSY
DRUPES
ERUPTS
FRAPPE
GRAPES
GRAPHO
GRAPHS
GRAPHY
GRIPED
GRIPER
GRIPES
GRIPPE
GRIPPY
GROPED
GROPER
GROPES
PREPAY
PROPEL
PROPER
PROPYL
TREPAN
TRIPLE
TRIPOD
TRIPOS
TROPAL
TROPHO
TROPHY
TROPIC
UROPOD
WRAPUP

•R••P•
CRAMPS
CREEPS
CREEPY
CRIMPS
CRIMPY
CRISPS
CRISPY
CROUPE
CROUPS
CROUPY
CRUMPS
DRIPPY
DROOPS
DROOPY
FRAPPE
FRUMPS
FRUMPY
GRASPS
GRIPPE
GRIPPY
GROUPS
GRUMPY
ORLOPS
PRIMPS
PROMPT
TRAMPS
TROOPS
TROUPE
TRUMPS

•R•••P
TRANSP
WRAPUP

••RP••
BURPED
CARPAL
CARPED
CARPEL
CARPER
CARPET
CARPIC
CARPUS
CORPSE
CORPUS
HARPED
HARPER
HERPES
MORPHO
PURPLE
TARPON
TORPID
TORPOR
WARPED
WARPER

••R•P•
ABRUPT
CERIPH
ENRAPT
EURIPI
EUROPA
EUROPE
PARAPH
PYROPE
SARAPE
SCRAPE
SCRAPS
SCRIPS
SCRIPT
SERAPE
SERAPH
SIRUPS
SIRUPY
STRAPS
STRIPE
STRIPS
STRIPT
STRIPY
STROPS
SYRUPS
SYRUPY
TERAPH
THRIPS
UNRIPE
UNRIPS

••R••P
BURLAP
CARHOP
EARLAP
LARRUP
MARKUP
SCRIMP
SCROOP
SHRIMP
TURNIP
WARMUP

•••RP•
CHIRPS
SCARPS
SHARPS
SHERPA
SLURPS
STIRPS
THORPE
TWERPS
TWIRPS
USURPS

•••R•P
ENTRAP
ENWRAP
INWRAP
LARRUP
RIPRAP
SATRAP
UNWRAP

••••RP
ESCARP
INCORP

R•Q•••
ROQUET

R••Q••
RISQUE

•R•Q••
BRAQUE
IRAQIS

••RQ••
BARQUE
CIRQUE
MARQUE
TORQUE

RR••••
RRHAGE
RRHAGY

R•R•••
RAREFY
RARELY
RAREST
RARING
RARITY
RERUNS

R••R••
RAMROD
REARED
REARER
REARMS
REGRET
RIPRAP
ROARED
ROARER
RUBRIC

R•••R•
RACERS
RADARS
RAKERS
RATERS
RAVERS
RAZORS
REBORN
RECORD
RECURS
REFERS
REFORM
REGARD
REMARK
REMORA
REPORT
RESORB
RESORT
RETARD
RETIRE
RETORT
RETURN
REVERE
REVERT
REWARD
REWORD
RICERS
RIDERS
RIGORS
RIMERS
RISERS
RITARD
RIVERS
ROBERT
ROGERS
ROSARY
ROSTRA
ROTARY
ROTORS
ROVERS
ROWERS
RULERS
RUMORS
RUPERT

R••••R
RACIER
RACKER
RAFTER
RAIDER
RAISER
RAMMER
RANCOR
RANGER
RANKER
RANTER
RAPIER
RAPPER
RASHER
RASPER
RATHER
RATTER
READER
REAMER
REAPER
REARER
RECTOR
REDDER
REEFER
REEKER
REELER
REHEAR
RELIER
RENDER
RENOIR
RENTER
REPAIR
RESTER
RHETOR
RHYMER
RICHER
RIFLER
RIGGER
RIMMER
RINGER
RINSER
RIOTER
RIPPER
RISKER
RITTER
ROAMER
ROARER
ROBBER
ROCKER
ROLLER
ROMPER
ROOFER
ROOMER
ROOTER
ROPIER
ROSIER
ROSTER
ROTTER
ROUSER
ROUTER
RUBBER
RUDDER
RUINER
RUMMER
RUNNER
RUSHER

•RR•••
ARRACK
ARRANT
ARRAYS
ARREAR
ARREST
ARRIVE
ARROBA
ARROWS
ARROYO
ERRAND
ERRANT
ERRATA
ERRING
ERRORS
ORRERY
ORRICE

•R•R••
ARARAT
CRORES
CRURAL

•R••R•
ARBORI
ARBORS
ARDORS
ARMORS
ARMORY
ARMURE
ARTERY
ARTHRO
ARTURO
BRIARS
BRIERS

BRIERY
CRIERS
DREARY
DRIERS
DRYERS
ERFURT
ERRORS
FRIARS
FRIARY
FRIERS
FRYERS
GRIGRI
GRUGRU
ORDERS
ORDURE
ORMERS
ORNERY
ORRERY
PRIERS
PRIORS
PRIORY
PRYERS
TRIERS

•R•••R

ARCHER
ARGUER
ARREAR
ARTHUR
BRACER
BRAVER
BRAYER
BRAZER
BREWER
BRIBER
BROKER
CRATER
CRAVER
CROZER
CRUDER
DRAPER
DRAWER
DRIVER
DROVER
ERASER
ERYTHR
FRAMER
FRATER
GRADER
GRATER
GRAVER
GRAYER
GRAZER
GRIPER
GROCER
GROPER
GROVER
GROWER
IRONER
KRONER
KRONOR
KRONUR
ORATOR
PRATER
PRAYER
PREFER
PRETER
PRETOR
PREWAR
PREYER
PRIMER
PRIZER
PROBER
PROPER
PROSER
PROVER
PRUNER
TRACER
TRADER
TREMOR
TRITER
TROCAR
TROVER
URETER
URETHR
WRITER

••RR••

BARRED
BARREL
BARREN
BARRET
BARRIO
BARROW
BARRYS
BIRRED
BORROW
BURRED
BURROS
BURROW
CARREL
CARRIE
CARROT
CIRRUS
CORRAL
DARROW
DERRIS
FARROW
FERRET
FERRIC
FERRIS
FERRUM
FURRED
FURROW
GARRET
GERRYS
HARROW
HARRYS
HORRID
HORROR
HURRAH
HURRAY
JARRED
JERRYS
KARROO
LARRUP
LARRYS
MARRED
MARRER
MARROW
MIRROR
MORRIS
MORROS
MORROW
MURRAY
MURRES
MURREY
NARROW
NORRIS
PARRAL
PARREL
PARROT
PERRON
PERRYS
PURRED
PYRRHA
SORREL
SORROW
SURREY
TARRED
TERRET
TERROR
TERRYS
TORRID
TURRET
WARRED
WARREN
YARROW

••R•R•

AIRDRY
AURORA
BORERS
CARERS
CORERS
CURARE
CURERS
DARERS
ERRORS
FARERS
FIRERS
FURORS
GERARD
HIRERS
HORARY
JURORS
LURERS
ORRERY
PARERS
PARURE
SARTRE
TORERO
WIRERS

••R••R

AIRIER
ARREAR
BARBER
BARKER
BARTER
BERBER
BORDER
BURGER
BURLER
BURNER
BURSAR
CARDER
CAREER
CARPER
CARTER
CARVER
CORDER
CORKER
CORNER
CURLER
DARKER
DARTER
DORMER
DURBAR
EARNER
FARCER
FARMER
FERBER
FERVOR
FIRMER
FORCER
FORGER
FORMER
GARNER
GARTER
GIRDER
GORGER
GORIER
HARBOR
HARDER
HARPER
HERDER
HORROR
HURLER
HURTER
LARDER
LARGER
LARKER
MARKER
MARRER
MARTYR
MERCER
MERGER
MIRROR
MORTAR
MURDER
MURMUR
NORNIR
NURSER
PARKER
PARLOR
PORKER
PORTER
PURGER
PURSER
SARSAR
SARTOR
SERVER
SIRDAR
SPRIER
SPRYER
SURFER
SURGER
TARTAR
TARTER
TERMER
TERMOR
TERROR
TERSER
TORPOR
TURNER
UPROAR
VARIER
VERGER
WARDER
WARIER
WARMER
WARNER
WARPER
WIRIER
WORKER
WORMER
WORSER

•••RR•

BLURRY
CHARRY
CHERRY
CHIRRS
CHURRS
FLURRY
GHARRI
GHARRY
KNARRY
PIERRE
QUARRY
SCURRY
SHERRY
SHIRRS
SIERRA
SKIRRS
SLURRY
SPARRY
SPERRY
SPURRY
STARRY
WHERRY

•••R•R

ADORER
BEARER
DEARER
FAIRER
FEARER
FENRIR
FUHRER
HEARER
HORROR
JEERER
MARRER
MIRROR
NEARER
POORER
POURER
REARER
ROARER
SCARER
SCORER
SHARER
SNARER
SNORER
SOARER
SOURER
SPARER
STARER
TERROR
USURER
WEARER

R•S•••

RASCAL
RASHER
RASHES
RASHLY
RASPED
RASPER
RESALE
RESCUE
RESEAT
RESEAU
RESECT
RESEDA
RESELL
RESEND
RESENT
RESETS
RESIDE
RESIGN
RESILE
RESINS
RESIST
RESOLD
RESOLE
RESORB
RESORT
RESTED
RESTER
RESULT
RESUME
RISERS
RISING
RISKED
RISKER
RISQUE
ROSARY
ROSCOE
ROSIER
ROSILY
ROSING
ROSINS
ROSINY
ROSTER
ROSTRA
RUSHED
RUSHER
RUSHES
RUSINE
RUSKIN
RUSSET

6

RUSSIA
RUSTED
RUSTIC
RUSTLE

R••S••

RAISED
RAISER
RAISES
RAISIN
RAMSON
RANSOM
REASON
RHESUS
RINSED
RINSER
RINSES
RIPSAW
ROASTS
ROBSON
ROOSTS
ROUSED
ROUSER
ROUSES
ROUSTS
RUSSET
RUSSIA

R•••S•

RACISM
RACIST
RADISH
RAKISH
RAMOSE
RAPIST
RAREST
RAVISH
RAWEST
RAWISH
RECAST
RECESS
RECUSE
REFUSE
REHASH
RELISH
REMISE
REMISS
REPASS
REPAST
REPOSE
RESIST
RETUSE
REVEST
REVISE
RIBOSE
RIMOSE
RIPEST
RIPOST
ROBUST
ROMISH
RUDEST
RUGOSE

R••••S

RABBIS
RABIES
RACERS
RACHIS
RADARS
RADIOS
RADIUS
RAISES
RAJABS
RAJAHS
RAKERS
RALPHS
RAMIES
RAMOUS
RANEES
RANGES
RAOULS
RAPHIS
RAPIDS
RASHES
RATALS
RATELS
RATERS
RATIOS
RAVELS
RAVENS
RAVERS
RAYAHS
RAYONS
RAZEES
RAZORS
RAZZES
REACTS
REALES
REALMS
REARMS
REBECS
REBELS
REBUTS
RECAPS
RECESS
RECTOS
RECTUS
RECURS
REDANS
REDOES
REEVES
REFERS
REFITS
REGIUS
REICHS
REIGNS
RELAYS
RELICS
RELIES
REMANS
REMISS
REMITS
RENEES
RENEWS
RENTES
REPASS
REPAYS
REPELS
RERUNS
RESETS
RESINS
REVELS
REVETS
REVUES
RHEIMS
RHESUS
RHINOS
RHODAS
RHUMBS
RHYMES
RIATAS
RICERS
RICHES
RICKYS
RICTUS
RIDERS
RIDGES
RIFLES
RIGHTS
RIGORS
RIMERS
RIMOUS
RINSES
RIPENS
RISERS
RIVALS
RIVERS
RIVETS
RIYALS
ROALDS
ROASTS
ROBINS
ROBLES
ROBOTS
RODDYS
RODEOS
ROGERS
ROGUES
ROLPHS
ROMANS
RONDOS
ROOSTS
ROSINS
ROTORS
ROUGES
ROUGHS
ROUNDS
ROUSES
ROUSTS
ROUTES
ROVERS
ROWANS
ROWELS
ROWERS
ROYALS
RUBENS
RUBIES
RUBLES
RUCHES
RUCKUS
RUFOUS
RUGOUS
RULERS
RUMBAS
RUMORS
RUMPUS
RUNINS
RUNONS
RUPEES
RUSHES

•RS•••

ARSINE
ERSATZ
URSINE
URSULA

•R•S••

ARISEN
ARISES
ARISTA
ARISTO
BRASHY
BRASSY
BRISKS
BRUSHY
CRASIS
CRESOL
CRESTS
CRISES
CRISIS
CRISPS
CRISPY
CROSSE
CRUSES
CRUSET
CRUSOE
CRUSTS
CRUSTY
DRESSY
DROSKY
DROSSY
DRUSES
ERASED
ERASER
ERASES
FRESCO
FRESNO
FRISES
FRISKS
FRISKY
FROSTS
FROSTY
FRUSTA
GRASPS
GRASSY
GRISLY
GROSZY
IRISES
KRISES
PRESAS
PRESTO
PRISMS
PRISON
PRISSY
PROSED
PROSER
PROSES
PROSIT
TRASHY
TRESSY
TRISTE
TRUSTS
TRUSTY
TRYSTS
WRASSE
WRESTS
WRISTS

•R••S•

ARGOSY
ARIOSE
ARIOSO
AROUSE
ARREST
ARTIST
BRAISE
BRASSY
BREAST
BROWSE
BRUISE
CREASE
CREASY
CREESE
CREUSA
CROSSE
CRUISE
DRESSY
DRIEST
DROPSY
DROSSY
DROWSE
DROWSY
DRYEST
ERNEST
FRAISE
FREEST
GRASSY
GREASE
GREASY
GRILSE
GROUSE
ORGASM
PRAISE
PRIEST
PRISSY
PROUST
TRANSP
TRESSY
TRIOSE
TRUEST
TRUISM
UREASE
WRASSE
WRIEST
WRYEST

•R•••S

ARBORS
ARCHES
ARCHYS
ARDEBS
ARDORS
ARECAS
ARENAS
ARETES
ARGALS
ARGOTS
ARGUES
ARIANS
ARIELS
ARIOUS
ARISES
ARMETS
ARMIES
ARMORS
ARNIES
AROIDS
AROMAS
ARPENS
ARRAYS
ARROWS
ARTELS
ARTIES
ARTOIS
ARYANS
BRACES
BRACTS
BRAHMS
BRAIDS
BRAILS
BRAINS
BRAKES
BRANDS
BRANTS
BRAVES
BRAVOS
BRAWLS
BRAZAS
BRAZES
BRAZOS
BREADS
BREAKS
BREAMS
BREEDS
BRENTS
BREVES
BREWIS
BRIARS
BRIBES
BRICKS
BRIDES
BRIEFS
BRIERS
BRILLS
BRINES
BRINGS
BRINKS
BRISKS
BROADS
BROILS
BROMES
BRONCS

BROODS
BROOKS
BROOMS
BROTHS
BROWNS
BRUCES
BRUGES
BRUINS
BRUITS
BRUMES
BRUNOS
BRUTES
BRUTUS
CRAALS
CRACKS
CRAFTS
CRAIGS
CRAKES
CRAMPS
CRANES
CRANKS
CRAPES
CRASIS
CRATES
CRAVES
CRAWLS
CRAZES
CREAKS
CREAMS
CREDOS
CREEDS
CREEKS
CREELS
CREEPS
CREMES
CREPES
CRESTS
CRICKS
CRIERS
CRIMES
CRIMPS
CRISES
CRISIS
CRISPS
CROAKS
CROATS
CROCKS
CROCUS
CROFTS
CRONES
CRONUS
CROOKS
CROONS
CRORES
CROUPS
CROWDS
CROWNS
CROZES
CRUCES
CRUETS
CRUMBS
CRUMPS
CRUSES
CRUSTS
CRUXES
CRYPTS
DRAFFS
DRAFTS
DRAINS
DRAKES
DRAMAS
DRAPES
DRAWLS
DREADS
DREAMS
DRIERS
DRIFTS
DRILLS
DRINKS
DRIVES
DROITS
DROLLS
DRONES
DROOLS
DROOPS
DROVES
DROWNS
DRUIDS
DRUNKS
DRUPES
DRUSES
DRYADS
DRYERS
ERASES
EREBUS
ERECTS
ERICHS
ERNIES
ERODES
ERRORS
ERUCTS
ERUPTS
ERWINS
FRACAS
FRAILS
FRAMES
FRANCS
FRANKS
FRAUDS
FREAKS
FREDAS
FREONS
FRIARS
FRIERS
FRILLS
FRISES
FRISKS
FRITHS
FROCKS
FRONDS
FRONTS
FROSTS
FROTHS
FROWNS
FRUITS
FRUMPS
FRYERS
GRACES
GRADES
GRADUS
GRAFTS
GRAINS
GRANTS
GRAPES
GRAPHS
GRASPS
GRATES
GRATIS
GRAVES
GRAZES
GREATS
GREBES
GREEDS
GREEKS
GREENS
GREETS
GREGOS
GRETAS
GRIDES
GRIEFS
GRILLS
GRIMES
GRINDS
GRIPES
GROANS
GROATS
GROINS
GROOMS
GROPES
GROUPS
GROUTS
GROVES
GROWLS
GRUELS
GRUMES
GRUNTS
IRAQIS
IRENES
IRIDES
IRISES
IRITIS
IRVINS
IRWINS
KRAALS
KRAITS
KRISES
KRUBIS
ORACHS
ORANGS
ORATES
ORBITS
ORCHIS
ORDERS
OREADS
ORGANS
ORGIES
ORIBIS
ORIELS
ORLOPS
ORMERS
ORPINS
ORYXES
PRANKS
PRATES
PRAWNS
PRAXIS
PRECIS
PREENS
PRESAS
PRICES
PRICKS
PRIDES
PRIERS
PRIMES
PRIMPS
PRINKS
PRINTS
PRIORS
PRISMS
PRIZES
PROBES
PROEMS
PRONGS
PROOFS
PROSES
PROVES
PROWLS
PRUDES
PRUNES
PRYERS
TRACES
TRACKS
TRACTS
TRADES
TRAGUS
TRAILS
TRAINS
TRAITS
TRAMPS
TRAVES
TRAWLS
TREADS
TREATS
TRENDS
TRIADS
TRIALS
TRIBES
TRICES
TRICKS
TRIERS
TRILLS
TRINES
TRIPOS
TRIXYS
TROLLS
TROOPS
TROTHS
TROUTS
TROVES
TRUCES
TRUCKS
TRUDYS
TRUMPS
TRUNKS
TRUSTS
TRUTHS
TRYSTS
URAEUS
URANUS
WRACKS
WREAKS
WRECKS
WRESTS
WRINGS
WRISTS
WRITES
WRONGS

••RS••

BORSCH
BURSAE
BURSAL
BURSAR
BURSAS
BURSES
BURSTS
CARSON
CORSAC
CORSES
CORSET
CURSED
CURSES
DORSAD
DORSAL
DORSUM
FIRSTS
GORSES
HORSED
HORSES
HORSEY
HORSTE
JERSEY
KERSEY
KIRSCH
MARSHA
MARSHY
MORSEL
NURSED
NURSER
NURSES
PARSEC
PARSED
PARSEE
PARSES
PARSIS
PARSON
PERSIA
PERSON
PURSED
PURSER
PURSES
PURSUE
SARSAR
TARSAL
TARSUS
TERSER
TORSKS
TORSOS
VERSED
VERSES
VERSOS
VERSTS
VERSUS
WARSAW
WORSEN
WORSER
WORSTS

••R•S•

ACROSS
AFRESH
AORIST
ARREST
AURIST
BAREST
CARESS
CARUSO
CERISE
CERUSE
CHRISM
CHRIST
CHRYSO
CORPSE
CURTSY
DIREST
DURESS
EGRESS
FOREST
GARISH
GYROSE
HARASS
HERESY
INRUSH
JURIST
LYRISM
LYRIST
MARIST
MEREST
MORASS
MOROSE
OGRESS
OGRISH
ONRUSH
PARISH
PERISH
PERUSE
PHRASE
PUREST
PURISM
PURIST
RAREST
SOREST
STRASS
STRESS
SUREST
TERESA
THRASH
THRESH
THRUSH
THRUST
TOROSE
UNREST
UPRISE
UPROSE

VERISM
VERIST

••R••S

AARONS
ABRAMS
ACROSS
AERIES
AGREES
AORTAS
APRILS
APRONS
ARRAYS
ARROWS
ATREUS
AUREUS
AUROUS
BARDES
BARGES
BARONS
BARRYS
BARYES
BERETS
BERMES
BERTHS
BERYLS
BIRLES
BIRTHS
BOREAS
BORERS
BURANS
BURGHS
BURGOS
BURIES
BURINS
BURKES
BURROS
BURSAS
BURSES
BURSTS
CARATS
CARERS
CARESS
CARETS
CARGOS
CARIBS
CARIES
CARLAS
CARLOS
CAROBS
CAROLS
CAROMS
CARPUS
CARTES
CARVES
CEREUS
CEROUS
CERTES
CIRCUS
CIRRUS
CORALS
CORERS
CORGIS
CORNUS
CORPUS
CORSES
CORTES
CORVES
CORVUS
CURERS
CURIES
CURIOS
CURSES
CURTIS
CURVES
CYRILS
DARERS
DARICS
DARIUS
DEREKS
DERMAS
DERRIS
DIRGES
DORIES
DURESS
EARLES
EARTHS
EGRESS
EGRETS
ERRORS
EYRIES
FARADS
FARCES
FARERS
FARLES
FERMIS
FEROUS
FERRIS
FIRERS
FIRSTS
FIRTHS
FORAYS
FORCES
FORGES
FORTES
FORTIS
FORUMS
FURIES
FURORS
FURZES
GEROUS
GERRYS
GERTYS
GORALS
GORGES
GORSES
GYRONS
HARASS
HAREMS
HARRYS
HERMES
HEROES
HERONS
HERPES
HIRAMS
HIRERS
HORDES
HORSES
HURONS
IHRAMS
JARVIS
JERRYS
JERVIS
JORAMS
JORGES
JORUMS
JURATS
JURELS
JURIES
JURORS
KARATS
KARENS
KARMAS
KERMES
KERMIS
LARGOS
LARRYS
LEROYS
LORIES
LURERS
LYRICS
MARCOS
MARCUS
MARGES
MARGOS
MARIAS
MARIES
MARTAS
MARTYS
MERGES
MERITS
MERLES
MEROUS
MORALS
MORASS
MORAYS
MORELS
MORONS
MORRIS
MORROS
MORTYS
MURALS
MURRES
MYRNAS
NEREIS
NERVES
NORIAS
NORMAS
NORRIS
NURSES
OGRESS
PARENS
PARERS
PAREUS
PARGOS
PARIES
PARKAS
PARSES
PARSIS
PARVIS
PERCYS
PERILS
PERRYS
POROUS
PUREES
PURGES
PURSES
PYRANS
RERUNS
SARAHS
SCRAGS
SCRAMS
SCRAPS
SCREWS
SCRIPS
SCRODS
SCRUBS
SCRUMS
SERACS
SERAIS
SERIES
SERIFS
SERINS
SEROUS
SEROWS
SERUMS
SERVES
SERVOS
SHREDS
SHREWS
SHRUBS
SHRUGS
SIRENS
SIRIUS
SIRUPS
SORELS
SORGOS
SPRAGS
SPRATS
SPRAYS
SPREES
SPRIGS
SPRITS
SPRUES
STRAPS
STRASS
STRAWS
STRAYS
STRESS
STREWS
STRIPS
STROPS
STRUMS
STRUTS
SURAHS
SURGES
SYRUPS
TAROTS
TARSUS
TEREUS
TERRYS
THREES
THRIPS
THROBS
THROES
THROWS
THRUMS
TORAHS
TORIES
TORIIS
TOROUS
TORSKS
TORSOS
TURCOS
TURKIS
UNRIGS
UNRIPS
VARIES
VARVES
VERGES
VERNAS
VERSES
VERSOS
VERSTS
VERSUS
VIREOS
VIRGAS
VOROUS
WIRERS
WORLDS
WORSTS
YERBAS
ZEROES
ZIRONS
ZORILS

•••RS•

AVERSE
BOURSE
COARSE
COURSE
HEARSE
HEARST
HOARSE
SPARSE
THIRST
THYRSE
THYRSI

•••R•S

ABORTS
ACORNS
ADORES
ADORNS
AGORAS
ALARMS
ALERTS
ANDRES
AVERTS
AVERYS
AWARDS
AZORES
AZURES
BAIRNS
BARRYS
BEARDS
BLARES
BLURBS
BLURTS
BOARDS
BOURGS
BOURNS
BURROS
CADRES
CAIRNS
CEORLS
CHARDS
CHARES
CHARMS
CHARTS
CHIRMS
CHIRPS
CHIRRS
CHORDS
CHORES
CHORUS
CHURLS
CHURNS
CHURRS
CIRRUS
CITRUS
CLARAS
CLARES
CLAROS
CLERKS
COBRAS
COURTS
CRORES
CYPRUS
DEBRIS
DERRIS
DOBRAS
DWARFS
ELBRUS
EPIRUS
ESTRUS
EVERTS
EXERTS
EXTRAS
EXURBS
FERRIS
FIORDS
FJORDS
FLARES
FLIRTS
FLORAS
GENRES
GENROS
GERRYS
GLARES
GNARLS
GOURDS
GUARDS
HARRYS
HEARTS
HENRIS
HENRYS
HOARDS
HOURIS
HUBRIS
HYBRIS
HYDRAS
HYDROS
ICARUS

INARMS
INDRIS
INGRES
INURES
INURNS
JERRYS
KAURIS
KNURLS
LAIRDS
LARRYS
LAURAS
LEARNS
LIBRAS
LIVRES
MADRAS
MAORIS
METROS
MOIRAS
MORRIS
MORROS
MOURNS
MURRES
NORRIS
OPERAS
OSIRIS
PADRES
PEARLS
PEDROS
PERRYS
PIERUS
QUARKS
QUARTS
QUERNS
QUIRES
QUIRKS
QUIRTS
REARMS
SABRAS
SAURUS
SCARES
SCARFS
SCARPS
SCORES
SCORNS
SHARDS
SHARES
SHARKS
SHARPS
SHERDS
SHIRES
SHIRKS
SHIRRS
SHIRTS
SHORES
SHORLS
SHORTS
SKIRRS
SKIRTS
SLURPS
SMARTS
SMIRKS
SNARES
SNARLS
SNORES
SNORTS
SPARES
SPARKS
SPIRES
SPIRTS
SPORES
SPORTS
SPURNS
SPURTS
STARES
STARTS
STERES
STERNS
STIRKS
STIRPS
STORES
STORKS
STORMS
SUCRES
SUTRAS
SWARDS
SWARMS
SWIRLS
SWORDS
TAURUS
TERRYS
THERMS
THIRDS
THORNS
TIARAS
TWERPS
TWIRLS
TWIRPS
UMBRAS
USURPS
UTERUS
UTURNS
WALRUS
WHARFS
WHIRLS
WHORES
WHORLS
WHORTS
YEARNS
ZEBRAS

••••RS

ABHORS
ABNERS
ACTORS
ADDERS
AGGERS
AIDERS
ALDERS
ALTARS
ALTERS
AMBERS
AMOURS
AMPHRS
ANGERS
ARBORS
ARDORS
ARMORS
ASKERS
ASPERS
ASTERS
ATTARS
AUGERS
AUGURS
BAKERS
BALERS
BITERS
BLEARS
BONERS
BORERS
BOWERS
BOXERS
BOYARS
BRIARS
BRIERS
BUYERS
CANERS
CAPERS
CARERS
CATERS
CEDARS
CHAIRS
CHEERS
CHIRRS
CHOIRS
CHURRS
CIDERS
CIGARS
CLEARS
COLORS
COMERS
COOERS
CORERS
COVERS
COWERS
CRIERS
CURERS
CYMARS
DARERS
DATERS
DEBARS
DECORS
DEFERS
DEMURS
DETERS
DICERS
DIMERS
DINARS
DINERS
DIVERS
DONORS
DOSERS
DOTERS
DOWERS
DRIERS
DRYERS
DUPERS
EATERS
EDGARS
EGGARS
EGGERS
ELDERS
ELMERS
ELVERS
EMBARS
EMBERS
EMEERS
ENTERS
EPHORS
ERRORS
ESKERS
ESTERS
ETHERS
FACERS
FAKERS
FAKIRS
FARERS
FAVORS
FEMURS
FETORS
FEUARS
FEVERS
FIBERS
FIFERS
FILERS
FIRERS
FIVERS
FIXERS
FLAIRS
FLEERS
FLIERS
FLOORS
FLOURS
FLUORS
FLYERS
FOYERS
FRIARS
FRIERS
FRYERS
FURORS
GAGERS
GAPERS
GAZERS
GIBERS
GLAIRS
GONERS
HALERS
HATERS
HAZERS
HEWERS
HHOURS
HIDERS
HIKERS
HIRERS
HOMERS
HONORS
HOVERS
HUMORS
IDLERS
INCURS
INFERS
INKERS
INTERS
JOKERS
JURORS
LABORS
LAGERS
LAKERS
LASERS
LAVERS
LAYERS
LAZARS
LEGERS
LEMURS
LEPERS
LEVERS
LIFERS
LINERS
LITERS
LIVERS
LONERS
LOPERS
LOSERS
LOVERS
LOWERS
LUGERS
LURERS
MACERS
MAJORS
MAKERS
MANORS
MASERS
MAYORS
MAZERS
MESSRS
METERS
MILERS
MIMERS
MINERS
MINORS
MISERS
MITERS
MIXERS
MOHURS
MOLARS
MOPERS
MOTORS
MOVERS
MOWERS
NADIRS
NAMERS
NOTERS
OCCURS
OCHERS
OFFERS
OGLERS
OILERS
ORDERS
ORMERS
OSCARS
OSIERS
OTHERS
OTTERS
OUTERS
OWNERS
PACERS
PAPERS
PARERS
PATERS
PAVERS
PAWERS
PAYERS
PETERS
PIKERS
PIPERS
PLIERS
POKERS
POSERS
POWERS
PRIERS
PRIORS
PRYERS
PULERS
QUEERS
RACERS
RADARS
RAKERS
RATERS
RAVERS
RAZORS
RECURS
REFERS
RICERS
RIDERS
RIGORS
RIMERS
RISERS
RIVERS
ROGERS
ROTORS
ROVERS
ROWERS
RULERS
RUMORS
SABERS
SAKERS
SATYRS
SAVERS
SAVORS
SAWERS
SAYERS
SCOURS
SEDERS
SEVERS
SEWERS
SHEARS
SHEERS
SHIRRS
SHOERS
SIEURS
SIMARS
SITARS
SIZARS
SKIERS
SKIRRS
SMEARS
SNEERS
SOBERS
SONARS
SOWARS
SOWERS
SPEARS
SPIERS
SPOORS
STAIRS

STEERS
SUGARS
SUPERS
SWEARS
TABORS
TAKERS
TALERS
TAMERS
TAPERS
TAPIRS
TATARS
TAWERS
TAXERS
TENORS
THEIRS
TIGERS
TILERS
TIMERS
TONERS
TOPERS
TOTERS
TOWERS
TOYERS
TRIERS
TUBERS
TUMORS
TUNERS
TUTORS
UDDERS
ULCERS
UMBERS
UNBARS
UPPERS
USHERS
UTTERS
VAPORS
VEXERS
VICARS
VIPERS
VISORS
VIZIRS
VIZORS
VOMERS
VOTERS
VOWERS
WADERS
WAFERS
WAGERS
WALERS
WATERS
WAVERS
WEBERS
WIPERS
WIRERS
WIVERS
WOOERS
YAGERS

R•T•••

RATALS
RATELS
RATERS
RATHER
RATIFY
RATINE
RATING
RATION
RATIOS
RATITE
RATLIN
RATOON
RATTAN
RATTED
RATTEN
RATTER
RATTLE
RATTLY
RETAIL
RETAIN
RETAKE
RETARD
RETELL
RETENE
RETINA
RETIRE
RETOLD
RETOOK
RETORT
RETTED
RETURN
RETUSE
RITARD
RITTER
RITUAL
ROTARY
ROTATE
ROTCHE
ROTGUT
ROTORS
ROTTED
ROTTEN
ROTTER
ROTUND
RUTILE
RUTTED

R••T••

RAFTED
RAFTER
RAGTAG
RANTED
RANTER
RATTAN
RATTED
RATTEN
RATTER
RATTLE
RATTLY
RECTAL
RECTOR
RECTOS
RECTUM
RECTUS
REDTOP
RENTAL
RENTED
RENTER
RENTES
RESTED
RESTER
RETTED
RHETOR
RHYTHM
RIATAS
RICTAL
RICTUS
RIFTED
RIOTED
RIOTER
RITTER
ROOTED
ROOTER
ROSTER
ROSTRA
ROTTED
ROTTEN
ROTTER
ROUTED
ROUTER
ROUTES
RUSTED
RUSTIC
RUSTLE
RUTTED

R•••T•

RARITY
RATITE
REACTS
REALTY
REBATE
REBATO
REBUTS
RECITE
REFITS
REFUTE
RELATE
REMITS
REMOTE
REPUTE
RESETS
REVETS
RIALTO
RIGHTO
RIGHTS
RIVETS
ROASTS
ROBOTS
ROOSTS
ROTATE
ROUSTS
RUBATO
RUGATE

R••••T

RABBET
RABBIT
RACIST
RACKET
RAGOUT
RAJPUT
RAPIST
RAREST
RAWEST
RECANT
RECAST
RECENT
RECEPT
REDACT
REDHOT
REFLET
REGENT
REGLET
REGRET
REHEAT
REJECT
RELENT
RELICT
RENNET
REPAST
REPEAT
REPENT
REPORT
RESEAT
RESECT
RESENT
RESIST
RESORT
RESULT
RETORT
REVERT
REVEST
REVOLT
RIDENT
RILLET
RIPEST
RIPOST
ROBERT
ROBUST
ROCHET
ROCKET
RODENT
ROQUET
ROTGUT
RUDEST
RUNLET
RUNOUT
RUPERT
RUSSET

•RT•••

ARTELS
ARTERY
ARTFUL
ARTHRO
ARTHUR
ARTIES
ARTIST
ARTOIS
ARTURO
URTEXT

•R•T••

ARCTIC
ARETES
BRETON
BRITON
BROTHS
BRUTAL
BRUTES
BRUTUS
CRATCH
CRATED
CRATER
CRATES
CRETAN
CRETIC
CRETIN
CRITIC
CROTCH
CROTON
CRUTCH
EROTIC
ERYTHR
FRATER
FRETTY
FRITHS
FROTHS
FROTHY
GRATED
GRATER
GRATES
GRATIS
GRETAS
GRETEL
GRITTY
GROTTO
IRITIC
IRITIS
ORATED
ORATES
ORATOR
PRATED
PRATER
PRATES
PRETER
PRETOR
PRETTY
PROTON
TRITER
TROTHS
TROTYL
TRUTHS
URETER
URETHR
URETIC
WRATHY
WRETCH
WRITER
WRITES
WRITHE

•R••T•

ARANTA
ARBUTE
ARGOTS
ARISTA
ARISTO
ARMETS
ARUNTA
BRACTS
BRANTS
BREATH
BRENTS
BRONTE
BRUITS
CRAFTS
CRAFTY
CREATE
CRESTS
CROATS
CROFTS
CRUETS
CRUSTS
CRUSTY
CRYPTO
CRYPTS
DRAFTS
DRAFTY
DRIFTS
DRIFTY
DROITS
DROUTH
ERECTS
ERGATE
ERRATA
ERSATZ
ERUCTS
ERUPTS
FRETTY
FRONTO
FRONTS
FROSTS
FROSTY
FRUITS
FRUITY
FRUSTA
GRAFTS
GRANTS
GREATS
GREETS
GRITTY
GROATS
GROTTO
GROUTS
GROWTH
GRUNTS
KRAITS
ORBITS
ORNATE
ORNITH
PRESTO
PRETTY
PRINTS
PROCTO
PRONTO
TRACTS
TRAITS
TREATS
TREATY
TRISTE
TROUTS
TRUSTS
TRUSTY

TRYSTS
WRAITH
WREATH
WRESTS
WRISTS

•R•••T

ARARAT
ARDENT
ARGENT
ARIGHT
ARMLET
ARMPIT
ARPENT
ARRANT
ARREST
ARTIST
BREAST
BRECHT
BREVET
BRIGHT
BRULOT
BRUNET
BRYANT
CRAVAT
CREDIT
CRUSET
DREAMT
DRIEST
DRYEST
ERFURT
ERNEST
ERRANT
FREEST
FRIGHT
GRIVET
KRUBUT
ORGEAT
ORIENT
PRIEST
PRIVET
PROFIT
PROJET
PROMPT
PROSIT
PROUST
TRICOT
TRIVET
TRUANT
TRUEST
TRYOUT
URGENT
URTEXT
WRIEST
WRIGHT
WRYEST

••RT••

AORTAE
AORTAL
AORTAS
AORTIC
BARTER
BARTOK
BARTON
BERTHA
BERTHE
BERTHS
BERTIE
BIRTHS
CARTED
CARTEL
CARTER
CARTES
CARTON
CERTES
CORTES
CORTEX
CORTEZ
CORTIN
CURTIS
CURTLY
CURTSY
DARTED
DARTER
DARTLE
EARTHS
EARTHY
FIRTHS
FORTES
FORTIS
GARTER
GERTIE
GERTYS
GIRTED
HARTAL
HURTER
HURTLE
MARTAS
MARTEN
MARTHA
MARTHE
MARTIN
MARTYR
MARTYS
MORTAL
MORTAR
MORTON
MORTYS
MYRTLE
PARTED
PARTLY
PERTLY
PORTAL
PORTER
PORTIA
PORTLY
SARTOR
SARTRE
SORTED
SORTIE
SURTAX
TARTAN
TARTAR
TARTER
TARTLY
TURTLE
VERTEX
VIRTUE
VORTEX
WORTHY

••R•T•

AERATE
AMRITA
AURATE
BARITE
BARYTA
BERATE
BERETS
BORATE
BURSTS
CARATE
CARATS
CARETS
CERATE
CERATO
CERITE
CURATE
EGRETS
ERRATA
FERITY
FIRSTS
GYRATE
HERETO
HORSTE
JURATS
KARATE
KARATS
KERATO
MERITS
PARITY
PIRATE
PURITY
PYRITE
RARITY
SPRATS
SPRITE
SPRITS
STRATA
STRATI
STRUTS
SURETY
TAROTS
TERATO
TERETE
VERITY
VERSTS
WARMTH
WORSTS

••R••T

ABRUPT
ADRIFT
ADROIT
AORIST
ARRANT
ARREST
AURIST
BARBET
BAREST
BARRET
BEREFT
BURBOT
BURNET
CARPET
CARROT
CERMET
CHRIST
CORNET
CORSET
CURVET
DERMAT
DIRECT
DIREST
ENRAPT
ENROOT
ERRANT
FAROUT
FERRET
FOREST
FORGET
FORGOT
FORINT
FORMAT
GARGET
GARNET
GARRET
GERENT
GORGET
HARLOT
HEREAT
HERIOT
HERMIT
HORNET
JURANT
JURIST
LARIAT
LYRIST
MARGOT
MARIST
MARKET
MARMOT
MEREST
PARENT
PARGET
PARROT
PERMIT
PUREST
PURIST
RAREST
SCRIPT
SHRIFT
SOREST
SPRINT
SPROUT
STRAIT
STREET
STRICT
STRIPT
SUREST
TARGET
TERCET
TERRET
THREAT
THRIFT
THROAT
THRUST
TURBIT
TURBOT
TURRET
TYRANT
UNREST
UNROOT
UPROOT
VARLET
VERIST
VERVET
WERENT

•••RT•

ABORTS
ALERTS
AVERTS
BLURTS
CHARTS
COURTS
DEARTH
ECARTE
EVERTS
EXERTS
FLIRTS
FLIRTY
FOURTH
HEARTH
HEARTS
HEARTY
QUARTE
QUARTO
QUARTS
QUARTZ
QUIRTS
SHIRTS
SHORTS
SKIRTS
SMARTS
SNORTS
SPARTA
SPIRTS
SPORTS
SPORTY
SPURTS
STARTS
SWARTH
SWARTY
THIRTY
WHORTS

•••R•T

ARARAT
BARRET
BEIRUT
CARROT
CLARET
ESPRIT
EVERET
FERRET
FLORET
GARRET
HEARST
IGOROT
IMARET
LABRET
LEARNT
PARROT
REGRET
SECRET
SEURAT
SPIRIT
TERRET
THIRST
TURRET

••••RT

ADVERT
ALBERT
ASSERT
ASSORT
BEGIRT
CAVORT
COHORT
COVERT
DEPART
DEPORT
DESERT
DIVERT
EFFORT
EGBERT
ELBERT
ENGIRT
ERFURT
ESCORT
EXHORT
EXPERT
EXPORT
EXSERT
EXTORT
GOCART
GOKART
HOBART
HUBERT
IMPART
IMPORT
INSERT
INVERT
MOZART
OBVERT
OSBERT
REPORT
RESORT
RETORT
REVERT
ROBERT
RUPERT
SQUIRT
STUART
THWART
TSHIRT
UNGIRT
UNHURT
YOGURT

RU••••

RUBACE

RUBATO
RUBBED
RUBBER
RUBBLE
RUBENS
RUBIES
RUBIGO
RUBLES
RUBRIC
RUCHES
RUCKED
RUCKUS
RUDDER
RUDDLE
RUDELY
RUDEST
RUEFUL
RUFFED
RUFFLE
RUFOUS
RUGATE
RUGGED
RUGOSE
RUGOUS
RUINED
RUINER
RULERS
RULING
RUMBAS
RUMBLE
RUMINA
RUMMER
RUMORS
RUMPLE
RUMPUS
RUNDLE
RUNINS
RUNLET
RUNNEL
RUNNER
RUNOFF
RUNONS
RUNOUT
RUNWAY
RUNYON
RUPEES
RUPERT
RUPIAH
RUSHED
RUSHER
RUSHES
RUSINE
RUSKIN
RUSSET
RUSSIA
RUSTED
RUSTIC
RUSTLE
RUTILE
RUTTED

R•U•••
REUBEN
RHUMBA
RHUMBS
ROUBLE
ROUCHE
ROUGED
ROUGES
ROUGHS
ROUNDS
ROUSED
ROUSER
ROUSES
ROUSTS
ROUTED
ROUTER
ROUTES

R••U••
RADULA
RAOULS
REBUFF
REBUKE
REBUTS
RECURS
RECUSE
REDUCE
REFUGE
REFUND
REFUSE
REFUTE
REMUDA
REPUTE
RERUNS
RESULT
RESUME
RETURN
RETUSE
REVUES
RHEUMY
RITUAL
ROBUST
ROGUED
ROGUES
ROMULO
ROQUET
ROTUND

R•••U•
RADIUM
RADIUS
RAGOUT
RAJPUT
RAMOUS
RECOUP
RECTUM
RECTUS
REDBUD
REDBUG
REFLUX
REGIUS
RESCUE
RHESUS
RICTUS
RIMOUS
RISQUE
ROTGUT
RUCKUS
RUEFUL
RUFOUS
RUGOUS
RUMPUS
RUNOUT

R••••U
RESEAU

•RU•••
ARUNTA
BRUCES
BRUGES
BRUINS
BRUISE
BRUITS
BRULOT
BRUMAL
BRUMES
BRUNCH
BRUNEI
BRUNET
BRUNOS
BRUSHY
BRUTAL
BRUTES
BRUTUS
CRUCES
CRUDER
CRUETS
CRUISE
CRUMBS
CRUMBY
CRUMMY
CRUMPS
CRUNCH
CRURAL
CRUSES
CRUSET
CRUSOE
CRUSTS
CRUSTY
CRUTCH
CRUXES
DRUDGE
DRUIDS
DRUNKS
DRUPES
DRUSES
ERUCTS
ERUPTS
FRUGAL
FRUITS
FRUITY
FRUMPS
FRUMPY
FRUNZE
FRUSTA
GRUBBY
GRUDGE
GRUELS
GRUGRU
GRUMES
GRUMPY
GRUNDY
GRUNTS
KRUBIS
KRUBUT
PRUDES
PRUNED
PRUNER
PRUNES
TRUANT
TRUCES
TRUCKS
TRUDGE
TRUDYS
TRUEST
TRUING
TRUISM
TRUMAN
TRUMPS
TRUNKS
TRUSTS
TRUSTY
TRUTHS

•R•U••
ARBUTE
ARGUED
ARGUER
ARGUES
ARGUFY
ARMURE
AROUND
AROUSE
ARTURO
CREUSA
CROUCH
CROUPE
CROUPS
CROUPY
DROUTH
ERFURT
FRAUDS
FRAUEN
GROUCH
GROUND
GROUPS
GROUSE
GROUTS
ORDURE
ORMUZD
PROUST
TRAUMA
TRIUNE
TROUGH
TROUPE
TROUTS
URSULA

•R••U•
ARIOUS
ARMFUL
ARNAUD
ARTFUL
ARTHUR
BRAQUE
BROGUE
BRUTUS
CRINUM
CROCUS
CRONUS
ERBIUM
EREBUS
FRENUM
GRADUS
IREFUL
KRONUR
KRUBUT
PRAGUE
PREVUE
TRAGUS
TRYOUT
URAEUS
URANUS
WRAPUP

•R•••U
GRUGRU
ORMOLU

••RU••
ABRUPT
AERUGO
BARUCH
CARUSO
CERUSE
CURULE
FERULA
FERULE
FORUMS
GERUND
INRUSH
JORUMS
KORUNA
KORUNY
MORULA
ONRUSH
PARURE
PERUKE
PERUSE
RERUNS
SCRUBS
SCRUFF
SCRUMS
SERUMS
SHRUBS
SHRUGS
SHRUNK
SIRUPS
SIRUPY
SPRUCE
SPRUES
SPRUNG
STRUCK
STRUMA
STRUMS
STRUTS
SYRUPS
SYRUPY
THRUMS
THRUSH
THRUST
UNRULY
VARUNA
YORUBA

••R•U•
ATREUS
ATRIUM
AUREUS
AUROUS
BARIUM
BARNUM
BARQUE
CARPUS
CEREUS
CERIUM
CEROUS
CIRCUM
CIRCUS
CIRQUE
CIRRUS
CORIUM
CORNUA
CORNUS
CORPUS
CORVUS
CURIUM
DARIUS
DORBUG
DORSUM
EARFUL
FAROUT
FEROUS
FERRUM
GEROUS
JARFUL
LARRUP
MARAUD
MARCUS
MARDUK
MARKUP
MARQUE
MEROUS
MORGUE
MURMUR
PAREUS
POROUS
PURSUE
SEROUS
SHROUD
SIRIUS
SPROUT
STROUD
TARSUS
TEREUS
TERGUM
TOROUS
TORQUE
VERDUN
VERSUS
VIRTUE
VOROUS

WARMUP

••R••U
BUREAU
MOREAU

•••RU•
ACCRUE
ALARUM
ANTRUM
ASARUM
BEIRUT
CHERUB
CHORUS
CIRRUS
CITRUS
CUPRUM
CYPRUS
ELBRUS
EMBRUE
EPIRUS
ESTRUS
FERRUM
ICARUS
IMBRUE
LABRUM
LARRUP
OUTRUN
PIERUS
QUORUM
SACRUM
SAURUS
TAURUS
UNTRUE
UTERUS
WALRUS

•••R•U
APERCU

••••RU
GRUGRU
JABIRU

R•V•••
RAVAGE
RAVELS
RAVENS
RAVERS
RAVINE
RAVING
RAVISH
REVAMP
REVEAL
REVELS
REVERE
REVERT
REVEST
REVETS
REVIEW
REVILE
REVISE
REVIVE
REVOKE
REVOLT
REVUES
REVVED
RIVALS
RIVERS
RIVETS
RIVING
ROVERS
ROVING

R••V••
REAVOW
REEVED
REEVES
REVVED

R•••V•
RELIVE
REMOVE
REVIVE

•RV•••
IRVING
IRVINS

•R•V••
BRAVED
BRAVER
BRAVES
BRAVOS
BREVES
BREVET
CRAVAT
CRAVED
CRAVEN
CRAVER
CRAVES
DRIVEL
DRIVEN
DRIVER
DRIVES
DROVED
DROVER
DROVES
FRIVOL
GRAVED
GRAVEL
GRAVEN
GRAVER
GRAVES
GRAVID
GRIVET
GROVEL
GROVER
GROVES
PRAVDA
PREVUE
PRIVET
PROVED
PROVEN
PROVER
PROVES
TRAVEL
TRAVES
TRIVET
TRIVIA
TROVER
TROVES

•R••V•
ARGIVE
ARRIVE
GREAVE
GRIEVE
GROOVE
GROOVY

••RV••
CARVED
CARVEL
CARVEN
CARVER
CARVES
CERVIX
CORVEE
CORVES
CORVUS
CURVED
CURVES
CURVET
FERVID
FERVOR
HARVEY
JARVEY
JARVIS
JERVIS
LARVAE
LARVAL
MARVEL
MARVIN
MERVIN
NERVED
NERVES
PARVIS
PURVEY
SERVAL
SERVED
SERVER
SERVES
SERVOS
SURVEY
VARVES
VERVET

••R•V•
ARRIVE
DERIVE
SCRIVE
SHRIVE
SHROVE
STRIVE
STROVE
THRIVE
THROVE

•••RV•
SCURVE
SCURVY
STARVE
SWERVE
WHARVE
WHERVE

RW••••
RWANDA

R•W•••
RAWEST
RAWISH
REWARD
REWIND
REWORD
ROWANS
ROWELS
ROWENA
ROWERS
ROWING

R••W••
RUNWAY

R•••W•
REDOWA
RENEWS
RENOWN

R••••W
REAVOW
REVIEW
RIPSAW

•RW•••
ERWINS
IRWINS
ORWELL

•R•W••
ARAWAK
BRAWLS
BRAWNY
BREWED
BREWER
BREWIS
BROWNS
BROWSE
CRAWLS
CRAWLY
CREWEL
CROWDS
CROWED
CROWNS
DRAWEE
DRAWER
DRAWLS
DRAWLY
DROWNS
DROWSE
DROWSY
FROWNS
FROWZY
GROWER
GROWLS
GROWTH
PRAWNS
PREWAR
PROWLS
TRAWLS
TROWEL

•R••W•
ARROWS

•R•••W
CRACOW

••RW••
AIRWAY
DARWIN
EARWAX
EARWIG
NARWAL
NORWAY

••R•W•
ARROWS
SCRAWL
SCREWS
SCREWY
SEROWS
SHREWD
SHREWS
SPRAWL
STRAWS
STRAWY
STREWN
STREWS
THROWN
THROWS

••R••W
BARROW
BORROW
BURROW
CURFEW
CURLEW
DARROW
FARROW
FURROW
HARROW
MARROW
MORROW
NARROW
SORROW
WARSAW
YARROW

•••R•W
ANDREW
BARROW
BORROW
BURROW
DARROW
ESCROW
FARROW
FURROW
HARROW
HEBREW
MARROW
MORROW
NARROW
SORROW
UNDRAW
UNDREW
YARROW

R•X•••
ROXANA
ROXANE

R••••X
REFLEX
REFLUX

•R•X••
CRUXES
ORYXES
PRAXIS
TRIXIE
TRIXYS

•R••X•
URTEXT

•R•••X
PREFIX
PROLIX

••R••X
CERVIX
CORTEX
EARWAX
FORNAX
FORNIX
LARYNX
SURTAX
SYRINX
VERNIX
VERTEX
VORTEX

•••R•X
MATRIX
STORAX
THORAX

R•Y•••
RAYAHS
RAYING
RAYONS
RHYMED
RHYMER
RHYMES
RHYTHM
RIYALS
ROYALS

R••Y••
RUNYON

6

R•••Y•
REDEYE
RELAYS
REPAYS
RICKYS
RODDYS

R••••Y
RACILY
RAMIFY
RANKLY
RAREFY
RARELY
RARITY
RASHLY
RATIFY
RATTLY
REALLY
REALTY
REDBAY
REMEDY
REPLAY
RHEUMY
RICHLY
RICKEY
RIPELY
RIPLEY
RODNEY
ROMANY
ROMNEY
ROPILY
ROSARY
ROSILY
ROSINY
ROTARY
RRHAGY
RUDELY
RUNWAY

•RY•••
ARYANS
BRYANT
BRYONY
CRYING
CRYPTO
CRYPTS
DRYADS
DRYDEN
DRYERS
DRYEST
DRYING
ERYNGO
ERYTHR
FRYERS
FRYING
ORYXES
PRYERS
PRYING
TRYING
TRYOUT
TRYSTS
WRYEST
WRYING

•R•Y••
ARGYLE
ARGYLL
BRAYED
BRAYER
CRAYON
DRAYED
FRAYED
GRAYED
GRAYER
GRAYLY
PRAYED
PRAYER
PREYED
PREYER
XRAYED

•R••Y•
ARCHYS
ARRAYS
ARROYO
PROPYL
TRIXYS
TROTYL
TRUDYS
URANYL

•R•••Y
ARCHLY
ARGOSY
ARGUFY
ARIDLY
ARMORY
ARTERY
BRACHY
BRAINY
BRANDY
BRANNY
BRASHY
BRASSY
BRAWNY
BREEZY
BRIERY
BRONZY
BROODY
BROOMY
BRUSHY
BRYONY
CRABBY
CRACKY
CRAFTY
CRAGGY
CRANKY
CRANNY
CRAWLY
CREAKY
CREAMY
CREASY
CREEPY
CRIMPY
CRISPY
CROAKY
CROUPY
CRUMBY
CRUMMY
CRUSTY
DRABLY
DRAFFY
DRAFTY
DRAWLY
DREAMY
DREARY
DREGGY
DRESSY
DRIFTY
DRIPPY
DROLLY
DROOPY
DROPSY
DROSKY
DROSSY
DROWSY
FREAKY
FREDDY
FREELY
FRENZY
FRETTY
FRIARY
FRIDAY
FRILLY
FRINGY
FRISKY
FRIZZY
FROGGY
FROSTY
FROTHY
FROWZY
FRUITY
FRUMPY
GRAINY
GRANNY
GRAPHY
GRASSY
GRAYLY
GREASY
GREEDY
GRIMLY
GRIPPY
GRISLY
GRITTY
GROGGY
GROOVY
GROSZY
GRUBBY
GRUMPY
GRUNDY
ORALLY
ORNERY
ORRERY
PREPAY
PRETTY
PRIMLY
PRIORY
PRISSY
RRHAGY
TRACHY
TRASHY
TREATY
TRENDY
TRESSY
TRICKY
TRIGLY
TRIMLY
TROPHY
TRUSTY
WRATHY

••RY••
BARYES
BARYON
BARYTA
BERYLS
CHRYSO
CORYMB
CORYZA
GERYON
LARYNG
LARYNX
SPRYER
SPRYLY

••R•Y•
ARRAYS
ARROYO
BARRYS
FORAYS
FORMYL
GERRYS
GERTYS
HARRYS
JERRYS
LARRYS
LEROYS
MARTYR
MARTYS
MORAYS
MORTYS
PERCYS
PERRYS
SPRAYS
STRAYS
TERRYS

••R••Y
AERIFY
AIRDRY
AIRILY
AIRWAY
BARELY
BARFLY
BARLEY
BARNEY
BARONY
BERNEY
BURLEY
CARBOY
CORDAY
CORODY
CURACY
CURTLY
CURTSY
DARKLY
DIRELY
EARTHY
EERILY
FARLEY
FERITY
FIRMLY
GORILY
HARDLY
HARLEY
HARVEY
HEREBY
HERESY
HORARY
HORSEY
HURRAY
JARVEY
JEREMY
JERSEY
KERSEY
KORUNY
LORDLY
MARGAY
MARSHY
MERELY
MORLEY
MURRAY
MURREY
NORWAY
ORRERY
PARITY
PARLAY
PARLEY
PARODY
PARTLY
PERTLY
PIRACY
PORTLY
PURELY
PURIFY
PURITY
PURVEY
RAREFY
RARELY
RARITY
SCREWY
SIRUPY
SORELY
SPRYLY
STRAWY
STRIPY
SURELY
SURETY
SURREY
SURVEY
SYRUPY
TARTLY
TERMLY
TURKEY
UNRULY
VERIFY
VERILY
VERITY
WARILY
WARMLY
WIRILY
WORTHY

•••RY•
AVERYS
BARRYS
CHERYL
EMBRYO
GERRYS
HARRYS
HENRYS
JERRYS
LARRYS
PERRYS
TERRYS
TETRYL

•••R•Y
AFFRAY
ANERGY
ASTRAY
AUBREY
AUDREY
BETRAY
BLURRY
CHARRY
CHERRY
CLERGY
DEARLY
DEFRAY
DOURLY
ENERGY
ESTRAY
FAIRLY
FLIRTY
FLURRY
GHARRY
GNARLY
HEARTY
HOORAY
HOURLY
HURRAY
KNARRY
KNURLY
MURRAY
MURREY
NEARBY
NEARLY
OSPREY
OVERLY
PEARLY
POORLY
QUARRY
SCURFY
SCURRY
SCURVY
SHERRY
SLURRY
SMARMY
SNARLY
SOURLY
SPARRY
SPERRY
SPORTY

6

SPURRY
STARRY
STOREY
STORMY
STURDY
SURREY
SWARTY
SWIRLY
THIRTY
THORNY
WEIRDY
WHERRY
YEARLY

••••RY
AIRDRY
AMBARY
AMBERY
ANGARY
APIARY
ARMORY
ARTERY
ASBURY
AUGURY
AVIARY
AWEARY
BAKERY
BAWDRY
BELFRY
BINARY
BLEARY
BLURRY
BOWERY
BRIERY
CALORY
CANARY
CELERY
CHARRY
CHEERY
CHERRY
DATARY
DAUBRY
DECURY
DENARY
DESCRY
DOWERY
DREARY
DUPERY
EMPERY
EXPIRY
FAKERY
FINERY
FLEURY
FLOURY
FLURRY
FRIARY
GANTRY
GENTRY
GHARRY
GLAIRY
HILARY
HORARY
HUNGRY
INJURY
KNARRY
LIVERY
LOWERY
LUXURY
MALORY
MEMORY
MISERY
NAPERY
NOTARY
OCHERY
OHENRY
ORNERY
ORRERY
OUTCRY
PALTRY
PANTRY
PAPERY
PASTRY
NELTRY
PENURY
PINERY
POETRY
POPERY
PRIORY
PUGGRY
QUARRY
ROSARY
ROTARY
SALARY
SAVORY
SCURRY
SENARY
SENTRY
SHERRY
SLURRY
SMEARY
SPARRY
SPERRY
SPHERY
SPURRY
STARRY
SUDARY
SUGARY
SULTRY
SUNDRY
TAWDRY
THEORY
TOWERY
UNWARY
VAGARY
VALERY
VENERY
VESTRY
VINERY
VOLERY
VOTARY
WATERY
WHERRY
WINERY
WINTRY
ZONARY

R•Z•••
RAZEED
RAZEES
RAZING
RAZORS
RAZZED
RAZZES

R••Z••
RAZZED
RAZZES

R•••Z•
REBOZO

•R•Z••
AREZZO
BRAZAS
BRAZED
BRAZEN
BRAZER
BRAZES
BRAZIL
BRAZOS
CRAZED
CRAZES
CROZER
CROZES
FRIZZY
FROZEN
GRAZED
GRAZER
GRAZES
GRIZEL
PRIZED
PRIZER
PRIZES

•R••Z•
AREZZO
BRAIZE
BREEZE
BREEZY
BRONZE
BRONZY
FREEZE
FRENZY
FRIEZE
FRIZZY
FROWZY
FRUNZE
GROSZY
ORMUZD

•R•••Z
ERSATZ

••RZ••
BORZOI
FURZES
TARZAN

••R•Z•
CORYZA

••R••Z
CORTEZ
LORENZ

•••RZ•
SFORZA

•••R•Z
JUAREZ
QUARTZ

SA••••
SABBAT
SABEAN
SABERS
SABINA
SABINE
SABINS
SABLES
SABOTS
SABRAS
SACHEM
SACHET
SACKED
SACKER
SACRAL
SACRED
SACRUM
SADDEN
SADDER
SADDLE
SADHUS
SADIES
SADISM
SADIST
SAFARI
SAFELY
SAFEST
SAFETY
SAGELY
SAGEST
SAGGAR
SAGGED
SAGGER
SAGIER
SAHARA
SAHEBS
SAHIBS
SAIGAS
SAIGON
SAILED
SAILER
SAILOR
SAINTS
SAIPAN
SAITIC
SAJOUS
SAKERS
SALAAM
SALADS
SALAMI
SALARY
SALIFY
SALINE
SALISH
SALIVA
SALLET
SALLOW
SALLYS
SALMIS
SALMON
SALOME
SALONS
SALOON
SALOOP
SALPAS
SALPID
SALTED
SALTER
SALUKI
SALUTE
SALVED
SALVER
SALVES
SALVIA
SALVOR
SALVOS
SAMARA
SAMBAS
SAMBOS
SAMBUR
SAMIAN
SAMIEL
SAMITE
SAMLET
SAMMYS
SAMOAN
SAMPAN
SAMPLE
SAMSHU
SAMSON
SAMUEL
SANDAL
SANDED
SANDER
SANDHI
SANDRA
SANDYS
SANELY
SANEST
SANGAR
SANGER
SANGUI
SANIES
SANITY
SANJAK
SANNUP
SANSAR
SANSEI
SANTOL
SAPHAR
SAPPED
SAPPER
SAPPHO
SARAHS
SARAPE
SARGON
SARONG
SARSAR
SARTOR
SARTRE
SASHAY
SASHED
SASHES
SASINS
SASSED
SASSES
SATANG
SATARA
SATEEN
SATING
SATINS
SATINY
SATIRE
SATORI
SATRAP
SATURN
SATYRS
SAUCED
SAUCER
SAUCES
SAUGER
SAULTS
SAUNAS
SAUREL
SAURUS
SAUTES
SAVAGE
SAVANT
SAVERS
SAVING
SAVINS
SAVIOR
SAVORS
SAVORY
SAWERS
SAWFLY
SAWING
SAWYER
SAXONS
SAXONY
SAYERS
SAYING

S•A•••
SCABBY
SCALAR
SCALDS
SCALED
SCALER
SCALES
SCALPS
SCAMPI
SCAMPS
SCANTY
SCAPES
SCARAB
SCARCE
SCARED
SCARER
SCARES
SCARFS

6

SCARPS
SCATHE
SCAUPS
SEABEE
SEADOG
SEALED
SEALER
SEAMAN
SEAMED
SEAMEN
SEAMER
SEAMUS
SEANCE
SEAPEN
SEARCH
SEARED
SEASON
SEATED
SEAWAN
SEAWAY
SHABBY
SHACKO
SHACKS
SHADED
SHADES
SHADOW
SHAFTS
SHAGGY
SHAKEN
SHAKER
SHAKES
SHAKOS
SHALED
SHALES
SHAMAN
SHAMED
SHAMES
SHAMMY
SHAMUS
SHANKS
SHANTY
SHAPED
SHAPEN
SHAPER
SHAPES
SHARDS
SHARED
SHARER
SHARES
SHARKS
SHARON
SHARPS
SHASTA
SHAVED
SHAVEN
SHAVER
SHAVES
SHAWLS
SHAWMS
SIALIC
SKALDS
SKATED
SKATER
SKATES

SLACKS
SLAGGY
SLAKED
SLAKES
SLALOM
SLANGY
SLANTS
SLATED
SLATER
SLATES
SLAVED
SLAVER
SLAVES
SLAVIC
SLAYER
SMACKS
SMALLS
SMALTI
SMALTO
SMARMY
SMARTS
SMAZES
SNACKS
SNAFUS
SNAGGY
SNAILS
SNAKED
SNAKES
SNAPPY
SNARED
SNARER
SNARES
SNARLS
SNARLY
SNATCH
SNATHE
SNATHS
SOAKED
SOAKER
SOAPED
SOARED
SOARER
SPACED
SPACER
SPACES
SPADED
SPADER
SPADES
SPADIX
SPAHIS
SPAITS
SPALLS
SPANKS
SPARED
SPARER
SPARES
SPARGE
SPARKS
SPARRY
SPARSE
SPARTA
SPASMS
SPATES
SPATHE

SPAVIN
SPAWNS
SPAYED
SRADHA
STABLE
STACIE
STACKS
STACTE
STACYS
STADIA
STAFFS
STAGED
STAGER
STAGES
STAGEY
STAGGY
STAINS
STAIRS
STAKED
STAKES
STALAG
STALED
STALER
STALES
STALIN
STALKS
STALKY
STALLS
STAMEN
STAMIN
STAMPS
STANCE
STANCH
STANDS
STANZA
STAPES
STAPLE
STARCH
STARED
STARER
STARES
STARRY
STARTS
STARVE
STASES
STASIS
STATAL
STATED
STATER
STATES
STATIC
STATOR
STATUE
STATUS
STAURO
STAVED
STAVES
STAYED
STAYER
SUABLE
SWAGED
SWAGES
SWAILS
SWAINS

SWALES
SWAMIS
SWAMPS
SWAMPY
SWANEE
SWANKY
SWARAJ
SWARDS
SWARMS
SWARTH
SWARTY
SWATCH
SWATHE
SWATHS
SWAYED

S••A••

SAFARI
SAHARA
SALAAM
SALADS
SALAMI
SALARY
SAMARA
SARAHS
SARAPE
SATANG
SATARA
SAVAGE
SAVANT
SCLAFF
SCRAGS
SCRAMS
SCRAPE
SCRAPS
SCRAWL
SEBATS
SECANT
SEDANS
SEDATE
SEJANT
SENARY
SENATE
SEPALS
SERACS
SERAIS
SERAPE
SERAPH
SESAME
SEWAGE
SEWALL
SEWARD
SHEARS
SHEATH
SHEAVE
SHOALS
SHOALY
SHOATS
SHRANK
SIMARS
SITARS
SIWASH
SIZARS
SKEANS

SLEAVE
SLEAZY
SMEARS
SMEARY
SNEAKS
SNEAKY
SOCAGE
SOLACE
SOLAND
SOLANO
SOLANS
SOMATA
SOMATO
SONANT
SONARS
SONATA
SOUARI
SOWARS
SPEAKS
SPEARS
SPLAKE
SPLASH
SPLATS
SPLAYS
SPRAGS
SPRAIN
SPRANG
SPRATS
SPRAWL
SPRAYS
SQUABS
SQUADS
SQUALL
SQUAMA
SQUARE
SQUASH
SQUATS
SQUAWK
SQUAWS
STEADY
STEAKS
STEALS
STEAMS
STEAMY
STOATS
STRAFE
STRAIN
STRAIT
STRAKE
STRAND
STRAPS
STRASS
STRATA
STRATI
STRAWS
STRAWY
STRAYS
STUART
SUBAHS
SUDARY
SUGARS
SUGARY
SUMACS
SURAHS

SUSANS
SWEARS
SWEATS
SWEATY

S•••A•

SABBAT
SABEAN
SABRAS
SACRAL
SAGGAR
SAIGAS
SAIPAN
SALAAM
SALPAS
SAMBAS
SAMIAN
SAMOAN
SAMPAN
SANDAL
SANGAR
SANJAK
SANSAR
SAPHAR
SARSAR
SASHAY
SATRAP
SAUNAS
SCALAR
SCARAB
SCHWAS
SCREAK
SCREAM
SCUBAS
SEAMAN
SEAWAN
SEAWAY
SECPAR
SEESAW
SEGGAR
SENDAL
SENLAC
SENNAS
SEPIAS
SEPTAL
SERDAB
SERIAL
SERVAL
SEURAT
SEXTAN
SEXUAL
SHAMAN
SHEBAT
SHIKAR
SHOFAR
SHORAN
SIGMAS
SIGNAL
SILVAE
SILVAN
SILVAS
SIMIAN
SINBAD
SIOUAN

SIRDAR
SKYCAP
SKYMAN
SKYWAY
SLOGAN
SLOVAK
SMILAX
SNOCAT
SOCIAL
SOCMAN
SOFTAS
SONIAS
SONYAS
SPICAE
SPINAL
SPIRAL
SPITAL
SPREAD
SQUEAK
SQUEAL
STALAG
STATAL
STEFAN
STELAE
STELAR
STEPAN
STOMAT
STORAX
STREAK
STREAM
STRIAE
STUPAS
STYLAR
SUBWAY
SULTAN
SUNDAE
SUNDAY
SUNNAH
SURTAX
SUTRAS
SWARAJ
SYLVAE
SYLVAN
SYLVAS
SYNTAX
SYRIAC
SYRIAN

S••••A

SABINA
SAHARA
SALIVA
SALVIA
SAMARA
SANDRA
SATARA
SCHEMA
SCLERA
SCORIA
SCOTIA
SCYLLA
SENECA
SENORA
SERBIA
SERENA
SFORZA
SHASTA
SHEILA
SHERPA
SIENNA
SIERRA
SIESTA
SILICA
SILVIA
SISERA
SOMATA
SONATA
SOPHIA
SPARTA
SPIREA
SQUAMA
SRADHA
STADIA
STANZA
STELLA
STERNA
STIGMA
STRATA
STROMA
STRUMA
SULPHA
SYLVIA
SYNURA

•SA•••

ASARUM
ISAACS
ISABEL
ISADOR
ISAIAH
PSALMS
TSADES
USABLE
USABLY
USAGES
USANCE

•S•A••

ASGARD
ASIANS
ASKANT
ASLANT
ASSAIL
ASSAIS
ASSAYS
ESCAPE
ESCARP
ESPANA
ESSAYS
ESTATE
ISAACS
ISLAND
ISRAEL
OSCANS
OSCARS
OSWALD
PSHAWS

•S••A•

ASHLAR
ASHMAN
ASTRAL
ASTRAY
ESCHAR
ESPIAL
ESTRAY
ISAIAH
ISHTAR
ISOBAR
OSSIAN
OSTEAL

•S•••A

ASTHMA
ESPANA
ISCHIA

••SA••

ALSACE
ANSATE
ASSAIL
ASSAIS
ASSAYS
BASALT
CASABA
CASALS
CASAVA
CESARE
DESALT
DISARM
DOSAGE
ERSATZ
ESSAYS
FUSAIN
INSANE
MOSAIC
NASALS
PESACH
PESADE
POSADA
RESALE
ROSARY
SESAME
SUSANS
TISANE
UNSAFE
UNSAID
UNSAYS
VASARI
VISAED
VISAGE
VISARD

••S•A•

BASHAW
BASRAH
BISCAY
BUSMAN
CASBAH
CASHAW
CASPAR
CASUAL
COSTAE
COSTAL
COSTAR
CUSHAT
CUSHAW
DESMAN
DESSAU
DISBAR
DISMAL
DISMAY
DISTAL
DOSSAL
FESTAL
FISCAL
FOSSAE
GASBAG
GASMAN
GASPAR
GUSTAF
GUSTAV
HUSSAR
INSPAN
INSTAR
JOSIAH
JOSIAS
KASPAR
LASCAR
MESCAL
MESIAL
MESIAN
MISHAP
MISKAL
MISLAY
MISSAL
MUSCAE
MUSCAT
NASIAL
NASSAU
OSSIAN
PASCAL
PASHAS
PASTAS
PISGAH
POSTAL
RASCAL
RESEAT
RESEAU
SASHAY
TASMAN
TESTAE
TUSCAN
TUSSAH
TUSSAL
TUSSAR
UNSEAL
UNSEAM
UNSEAT
UNSNAP
VASSAL
VESTAL
VESTAS
VISTAS
VISUAL
WYSTAN
YASMAK

••S••A

CASABA
CASAVA
CASSIA
CESURA
FASCIA
HESTIA
JOSHUA
LISBOA
MASORA
NASHUA
PESETA
POSADA
RESEDA
ROSTRA
RUSSIA
SISERA
URSULA
VESICA

•••SA•

BALSAM
BALSAS
BONSAI
BURSAE
BURSAL
BURSAR
BURSAS
CAESAR
CAUSAL
CORSAC
DESSAU
DIPSAS
DORSAD
DORSAL
DOSSAL
FOSSAE
HUSSAR
JETSAM
JIGSAW
KANSAN
KANSAS
MENSAL
MISSAL
NASSAU
OUTSAT
OVISAC
PRESAS
PTISAN
PULSAR
QUASAR
RIPSAW
SANSAR
SARSAR
SEESAW
TARSAL
TUSSAH
TUSSAL
TUSSAR
VASSAL
WARSAW

•••S•A

ALASKA
ARISTA
AVESTA
AYESHA
CASSIA
CUESTA
EGESTA
ELISHA
FIESTA
FRUSTA
GEISHA
LEPSIA
MARSHA
MIASMA
NAUSEA
ODESSA
PERSIA
PHASIA
PLASIA
PLASMA
RUSSIA
SHASTA
SIESTA
ZOYSIA

••••SA

AFTOSA
AHIMSA
CALESA
CREUSA
LOUISA
MEDUSA
MIMOSA
MUCOSA
ODESSA
TERESA

S•B•••

SABBAT
SABEAN
SABERS
SABINA
SABINE
SABINS
SABLES
SABOTS
SABRAS
SEBATS
SIBYLS
SOBBED
SOBERS
SUBAHS
SUBDEB
SUBDUE
SUBITO
SUBLET
SUBMIT
SUBORN
SUBTER
SUBTLE
SUBTLY
SUBURB
SUBWAY

6

SYBILS

S••B••
SABBAT
SAMBAS
SAMBOS
SAMBUR
SCABBY
SCUBAS
SEABEE
SERBIA
SHABBY
SHEBAT
SINBAD
SOBBED
SOMBER
STABLE
STUBBY
SUABLE
SUNBOW
SYMBOL

S•••B•
SAHEBS
SAHIBS
SCABBY
SCRIBE
SCRUBS
SHABBY
SHELBY
SHRUBS
SQUABS
SQUIBS
STUBBY

S••••B
SCARAB
SERDAB
SUBDEB
SUBURB
SUPERB

•SB•••
ASBURY
OSBERT
OSBORN

•S•B••
ISABEL
ISOBAR
ISOBEL
USABLE
USABLY

••SB••
CASBAH
DISBAR
GASBAG
LISBOA
LISBON

••S•B•
CASABA

••S••B
ABSORB
ADSORB
RESORB

SC••••
SCABBY
SCALAR
SCALDS
SCALED
SCALER
SCALES
SCALPS
SCAMPI
SCAMPS
SCANTY
SCAPES
SCARAB
SCARCE
SCARED
SCARER
SCARES
SCARFS
SCARPS
SCATHE
SCAUPS
SCENDS
SCENES
SCENIC
SCENTS
SCHEMA
SCHEME
SCHICK
SCHISM
SCHIST
SCHIZO
SCHMOS
SCHOOL
SCHORL
SCHUIT
SCHUSS
SCHWAS
SCIONS
SCIPIO
SCLAFF
SCLERA
SCLERO
SCOFFS
SCOLDS
SCOLEX
SCONCE
SCONES
SCOOPS
SCOOTS
SCOPES
SCOPUS
SCORCH
SCORED
SCORER
SCORES
SCORIA
SCORNS
SCOTCH
SCOTER
SCOTIA
SCOTTS
SCOURS
SCOUTS
SCOWLS
SCRAGS
SCRAMS
SCRAPE
SCRAPS
SCRAWL
SCREAK
SCREAM
SCREED
SCREEN
SCREWS
SCREWY
SCRIBE
SCRIMP
SCRIPS
SCRIPT
SCRIVE
SCRODS
SCROLL
SCROOP
SCRUBS
SCRUFF
SCRUMS
SCUBAS
SCUFFS
SCULLS
SCULPT
SCUMMY
SCURFY
SCURRY
SCURVE
SCURVY
SCUTCH
SCUTES
SCUTUM
SCYLLA
SCYPHI
SCYPHO
SCYTHE

S•C•••
SACHEM
SACHET
SACKED
SACKER
SACRAL
SACRED
SACRUM
SECANT
SECEDE
SECERN
SECKEL
SECOND
SECPAR
SECRET
SECTOR
SECUND
SECURE
SICILY
SICKED
SICKEN
SICKER
SICKLE
SICKLY
SOCAGE
SOCCER
SOCIAL
SOCKED
SOCKET
SOCLES
SOCMAN
SOCMEN
SOCRED
SUCCOR
SUCKED
SUCKER
SUCKLE
SUCRES
SYCEES

S••C••
SAUCED
SAUCER
SAUCES
SEICHE
SHACKO
SHACKS
SHOCKS
SHUCKS
SIECLE
SKYCAP
SLACKS
SLICED
SLICER
SLICES
SLICKS
SMACKS
SMOCKS
SNACKS
SNICKS
SNOCAT
SOCCER
SPACED
SPACER
SPACES
SPECIE
SPECKS
SPICAE
SPICED
SPICER
SPICES
STACIE
STACKS
STACTE
STACYS
STICKS
STICKY
STOCKS
STOCKY
STUCCO
SUCCOR
SULCUS

S•••C•
SCARCE
SCHICK
SCONCE
SCORCH
SCOTCH
SCUTCH
SEANCE
SEARCH
SEDUCE
SELECT
SENECA
SERACS
SHTICK
SILICA
SILICO
SKETCH
SLOUCH
SLUICE
SMIRCH
SMOOCH
SMUTCH
SNATCH
SNITCH
SOLACE
SOURCE
SPEECH
SPLICE
SPRUCE
STANCE
STANCH
STARCH
STENCH
STITCH
STOICS
STRICK
STRICT
STRUCK
STUCCO
SUMACS
SWATCH
SWITCH

S••••C
SAITIC
SCENIC
SENLAC
SEPTIC
SIALIC
SLAVIC
SOTHIC
STATIC
STELIC
STERIC
SUOMIC
SYNDIC
SYRIAC

•SC•••
ASCEND
ASCENT
ASCOTS
ESCAPE
ESCARP
ESCENT
ESCHAR
ESCHEW
ESCORT
ESCROW
ESCUDO
ISCHIA
OSCANS
OSCARS
OSCINE
OSCULE

•S•C••
PSYCHE
PSYCHO

•S••C•
ASPECT
ASPICS
ISAACS
USANCE

••SC••
BISCAY
CISCOS
DESCRY
DISCUS
FASCES
FASCIA
FESCUE
FISCAL
GASCON
LASCAR
MASCON
MASCOT
MESCAL
MISCUE
MOSCOW
MUSCAE
MUSCAT
MUSCLE
PASCAL
PISCES
RASCAL
RESCUE
ROSCOE
TUSCAN
VISCID
VISCUS

••S•C•
ALSACE
BASICS
BISECT
EXSECT
INSECT
PESACH
RESECT
VESICA
VESICO

••S••C
BUSTIC
COSMIC

6

CYSTIC
FISTIC
FUSTIC
GESTIC
MASTIC
MOSAIC
MYSTIC
NASTIC
NOSTOC
RUSTIC

•••SC•
BORSCH
FIASCO
FRESCO
KIRSCH
KITSCH
PUTSCH
UNESCO

•••S•C
CORSAC
OVISAC
PARSEC
PHASIC
PHYSIC

S•D•••
SADDEN
SADDER
SADDLE
SADHUS
SADIES
SADISM
SADIST
SEDANS
SEDATE
SEDERS
SEDGES
SEDILE
SEDUCE
SEDUMS
SIDDUR
SIDERO
SIDING
SIDLED
SIDLER
SIDLES
SIDNEY
SODDED
SODDEN
SODIUM
SODOMY
SUDARY
SUDDEN
SYDNEY

S••D••
SADDEN
SADDER
SADDLE
SANDAL
SANDED
SANDER
SANDHI
SANDRA
SANDYS
SEADOG
SEEDED
SEEDER
SELDOM
SENDAL
SENDER
SERDAB
SHADED
SHADES
SHADOW
SHODDY
SIDDUR
SIRDAR
SLEDGE
SLIDER
SLIDES
SLUDGE
SLUDGY
SMUDGE
SMUDGY
SODDED
SODDEN
SOLDER
SONDER
SORDID
SPADED
SPADER
SPADES
SPADIX
SPIDER
SRADHA
STADIA
STODGE
STODGY
STUDIO
SUBDEB
SUBDUE
SUDDEN
SUEDES
SUNDAE
SUNDAY
SUNDER
SUNDEW
SUNDOG
SUNDRY
SWEDEN
SWEDES
SYNDET
SYNDIC

S•••D•
SALADS
SCALDS
SCENDS
SCOLDS
SCRODS
SECEDE
SHARDS
SHERDS
SHINDY
SHODDY
SHREDS
SKALDS
SNOODS
SOLIDI
SOLIDS
SOUNDS
SPEEDS
SPEEDY
SPENDS
SQUADS
SQUIDS
STANDS
STEADY
STEEDS
STRIDE
STRODE
STURDY
SWARDS
SWORDS
SYNODS

S••••D
SACKED
SACRED
SAGGED
SAILED
SALPID
SALTED
SALVED
SANDED
SAPPED
SASHED
SASSED
SAUCED
SCALED
SCARED
SCORED
SCREED
SEALED
SEAMED
SEARED
SEATED
SECOND
SECUND
SEEDED
SEEMED
SEEPED
SEINED
SEIZED
SENSED
SERVED
SEWARD
SHADED
SHALED
SHAMED
SHAPED
SHARED
SHAVED
SHEWED
SHIELD
SHINED
SHOOED
SHORED
SHOULD
SHOVED
SHOWED
SHREWD
SHROUD
SICKED
SIDLED
SIEGED
SIEVED
SIFTED
SIGHED
SIGNED
SIGRID
SILOED
SILTED
SINBAD
SINGED
SINNED
SIPPED
SKATED
SKEWED
SKIVED
SLAKED
SLATED
SLAVED
SLEWED
SLICED
SLIMED
SLOPED
SLOWED
SMILED
SMOKED
SNAKED
SNARED
SNIPED
SNORED
SNOWED
SOAKED
SOAPED
SOARED
SOBBED
SOCKED
SOCRED
SODDED
SOILED
SOLAND
SOLOED
SOLVED
SOOTED
SOPPED
SORDID
SORTED
SOULED
SOURED
SOUSED
SPACED
SPADED
SPARED
SPAYED
SPEWED
SPICED
SPIKED
SPILED
SPIRED
SPITED
SPOKED
SPORED
SPREAD
SPUMED
STAGED
STAKED
STALED
STARED
STATED
STAVED
STAYED
STEWED
STOKED
STOLED
STOLID
STONED
STOPED
STORED
STOWED
STRAND
STROUD
STUPID
STYLED
SUCKED
SUITED
SULKED
SUMMED
SUNNED
SUPPED
SURFED
SURGED
SWAGED
SWAYED
SWIPED

•S•D••
ASIDES
ISADOR
ISIDOR
TSADES

•S••D•
ESCUDO
ISOLDE
PSEUDO

•S•••D
ASCEND
ASGARD
ASTRID
ESPIED
ISLAND
ISOPOD
ISSUED
OSMOND
OSMUND
OSWALD

••SD••
MISDID
WISDOM

••S•D•
BESIDE
INSIDE
PESADE
POSADA
RESEDA
RESIDE
UPSIDE

••S••D
ABSURD
AISLED
AXSEED
BASHED
BASKED
BASTED
BESTED
BOSSED
BUSHED
BUSIED
BUSSED
BUSTED
CASHED
COSHED
COSTED
CUSPED
CUSPID
CUSSED
DASHED
DESMID
DISHED
DUSKED
DUSTED
ENSUED
FASTED
FISHED
FISTED
FUSSED
GASHED
GASPED
GASSED
GUSHED
HASHED
HASPED
HASTED
HESIOD
HISPID
HISSED
HOSTED
HUSHED
HUSKED
ISSUED
JESSED
JESTED
JOSHED
KISSED
LASHED
LASTED
LISPED
LISTED
LUSHED
LUSTED
MASHED
MASKED
MASSED
MASTED

MESHED
MESSED
MISDID
MISSED
MISTED
MUSHED
MUSSED
NESTED
OUSTED
PASSED
PASTED
PISHED
POSTED
PUSHED
RASPED
RESEND
RESOLD
RESTED
RISKED
RUSHED
RUSTED
SASHED
SASSED
TASKED
TASTED
TESTED
TOSSED
TUSHED
TUSKED
UNSAID
UNSOLD
VESPID
VESTED
VISAED
VISARD
VISCID
VISEED
WASHED
WASTED
WISHED
WISPED
YESSED
ZESTED

•••S•D

ABASED
ABUSED
AMUSED
BIASED
BOSSED
BOUSED
BOWSED
BUSSED
CAUSED
CEASED
CENSED
CHASED
CLOSED
CURSED
CUSSED
DORSAD
DOUSED
DOWSED
ERASED
FEASED
FUSSED
GASSED
GOOSED
HISSED
HORSED
HOUSED
JESSED
KISSED
LAPSED
LEASED
LOOSED
LOUSED
MASSED
MESSED
MISSED
MOUSED
MUSSED
NOISED
NOOSED
NURSED
PARSED
PASSED
PAUSED
PHASED
POISED
PROSED
PULSED
PURSED
RAISED
RINSED
ROUSED
SASSED
SENSED
SOUSED
TEASED
TENSED
TOSSED
UNUSED
VERSED
YESSED

SE••••

SEABEE
SEADOG
SEALED
SEALER
SEAMAN
SEAMED
SEAMEN
SEAMER
SEAMUS
SEANCE
SEAPEN
SEARCH
SEARED
SEASON
SEATED
SEAWAN
SEAWAY
SEBATS
SECANT
SECEDE
SECERN
SECKEL
SECOND
SECPAR
SECRET
SECTOR
SECUND
SECURE
SEDANS
SEDATE
SEDERS
SEDGES
SEDILE
SEDUCE
SEDUMS
SEEDED
SEEDER
SEEING
SEEKER
SEEMED
SEEMER
SEEMLY
SEEPED
SEESAW
SEETHE
SEGGAR
SEICHE
SEINED
SEINER
SEINES
SEISIN
SEISMO
SEISMS
SEISOR
SEIZED
SEIZER
SEIZES
SEIZIN
SEIZOR
SEJANT
SELDOM
SELECT
SELENE
SELENO
SELJUK
SELLER
SELSYN
SELVES
SEMELE
SEMEME
SEMITE
SEMPRE
SENARY
SENATE
SENDAL
SENDER
SENECA
SENILE
SENIOR
SENLAC
SENNAS
SENNET
SENNIT
SENORA
SENSED
SENSES
SENSOR
SENTRY
SEPALS
SEPIAS
SEPOYS
SEPSIS
SEPTAL
SEPTET
SEPTIC
SEPTUM
SEQUEL
SEQUIN
SERACS
SERAIS
SERAPE
SERAPH
SERBIA
SERDAB
SEREIN
SERENA
SERENE
SERIAL
SERIES
SERIFS
SERINE
SERINS
SERMON
SEROUS
SEROWS
SERUMS
SERVAL
SERVED
SERVER
SERVES
SERVOS
SESAME
SESQUI
SESTET
SETOFF
SETONS
SETOSE
SETOUS
SETTEE
SETTER
SETTLE
SETTOS
SETUPS
SEURAT
SEVENS
SEVERE
SEVERS
SEWAGE
SEWALL
SEWARD
SEWERS
SEWING
SEXIER
SEXING
SEXISM
SEXIST
SEXTAN
SEXTET
SEXTON
SEXUAL

S•E•••

SCENDS
SCENES
SCENIC
SCENTS
SEEDED
SEEDER
SEEING
SEEKER
SEEMED
SEEMER
SEEMLY
SEEPED
SEESAW
SEETHE
SHEARS
SHEATH
SHEAVE
SHEBAT
SHEENS
SHEENY
SHEERS
SHEETS
SHEIKS
SHEILA
SHEKEL
SHELBY
SHELLS
SHELLY
SHELTY
SHELVE
SHERDS
SHERIF
SHERPA
SHERRY
SHEWED
SHEWER
SIECLE
SIEGED
SIEGES
SIENNA
SIERRA
SIESTA
SIEURS
SIEVED
SIEVES
SKEANS
SKEINS
SKETCH
SKEWED
SKEWER
SLEAVE
SLEAZY
SLEDGE
SLEEKS
SLEEKY
SLEEPS
SLEEPY
SLEETS
SLEETY
SLEEVE
SLEIGH
SLEUTH
SLEWED
SMEARS
SMEARY
SMELLS
SMELLY
SMELTS
SNEAKS
SNEAKY
SNEERS
SNEEZE
SNEEZY
SNELLS
SOEVER
SPEAKS
SPEARS
SPECIE
SPECKS
SPEECH
SPEEDS
SPEEDY
SPEISS
SPELLS
SPENDS
SPERMO
SPERRY
SPEWED
STEADY
STEAKS
STEALS
STEAMS
STEAMY
STEEDS
STEELS
STEELY
STEEPS
STEERS
STEEVE
STEFAN
STEINS
STELAE
STELAR
STELES
STELIC
STELLA
STELLI
STENCH
STENOG
STEPAN
STEPIN
STEPPE
STEPUP
STEREO
STERES
STERIC
STERNA
STERNO
STERNS
STEROL
STETHO
STEVEN
STEVES
STEVIE
STEWED

SUEDES
SVELTE
SWEARS
SWEATS
SWEATY
SWEDEN
SWEDES
SWEEPS
SWEEPY
SWEETS
SWELLS
SWERVE

S••E••

SABEAN
SABERS
SAFELY
SAFEST
SAFETY
SAGELY
SAGEST
SAHEBS
SAKERS
SANELY
SANEST
SATEEN
SAVERS
SAWERS
SAYERS
SCHEMA
SCHEME
SCLERA
SCLERO
SCREAK
SCREAM
SCREED
SCREEN
SCREWS
SCREWY
SECEDE
SECERN
SEDERS
SELECT
SELENE
SELENO
SEMELE
SEMEME
SENECA
SEREIN
SERENA
SERENE
SEVENS
SEVERE
SEVERS
SEWERS
SHEENS
SHEENY
SHEERS
SHEETS
SHIELD
SHIEST
SHOERS
SHREDS
SHREWD
SHREWS
SHYEST
SIDERO
SILENI
SILENT
SIMEON
SINEWS
SINEWY
SIRENS
SISERA
SKIERS
SLEEKS
SLEEKY
SLEEPS
SLEEPY
SLEETS
SLEETY
SLEEVE
SLIEST
SLYEST
SNEERS
SNEEZE
SNEEZY
SOBERS
SOLELY
SOLEMN
SOLENT
SORELS
SORELY
SOREST
SOWERS
SPEECH
SPEEDS
SPEEDY
SPHENE
SPHENO
SPHERE
SPHERY
SPIELS
SPIERS
SPLEEN
SPLENO
SPREAD
SPREES
SQUEAK
SQUEAL
STEEDS
STEELS
STEELY
STEEPS
STEERS
STEEVE
STREAK
STREAM
STREET
STRESS
STREWN
STREWS
SUPERB
SUPERS
SURELY
SUREST
SURETY
SWEEPS
SWEEPY
SWEETS
SYCEES

S•••E•

SABLES
SACHEM
SACHET
SACKED
SACKER
SACRED
SADDEN
SADDER
SADIES
SAGGED
SAGGER
SAGIER
SAILED
SAILER
SALLET
SALTED
SALTER
SALVED
SALVER
SALVES
SAMIEL
SAMLET
SAMUEL
SANDED
SANDER
SANGER
SANIES
SANSEI
SAPPED
SAPPER
SASHED
SASHES
SASSED
SASSES
SATEEN
SAUCED
SAUCER
SAUCES
SAUGER
SAUREL
SAUTES
SAWYER
SCALED
SCALER
SCALES
SCAPES
SCARED
SCARER
SCARES
SCENES
SCOLEX
SCONES
SCOPES
SCORED
SCORER
SCORES
SCOTER
SCREED
SCREEN
SCUTES
SEABEE
SEALED
SEALER
SEAMED
SEAMEN
SEAMER
SEAPEN
SEARED
SEATED
SECKEL
SECRET
SEDGES
SEEDED
SEEDER
SEEKER
SEEMED
SEEMER
SEEPED
SEINED
SEINER
SEINES
SEIZED
SEIZER
SEIZES
SELLER
SELVES
SENDER
SENNET
SENSED
SENSES
SEPTET
SEQUEL
SERIES
SERVED
SERVER
SERVES
SESTET
SETTEE
SETTER
SEXIER
SEXTET
SHADED
SHADES
SHAKEN
SHAKER
SHAKES
SHALED
SHALES
SHAMED
SHAMES
SHAPED
SHAPEN
SHAPER
SHAPES
SHARED
SHARER
SHARES
SHAVED
SHAVEN
SHAVER
SHAVES
SHEKEL
SHEWED
SHEWER
SHINED
SHINER
SHINES
SHIRES
SHIVER
SHIVES
SHOOED
SHORED
SHORES
SHOTES
SHOVED
SHOVEL
SHOVER
SHOVES
SHOWED
SHOWER
SHRIEK
SICKED
SICKEN
SICKER
SIDLED
SIDLER
SIDLES
SIDNEY
SIEGED
SIEGES
SIEVED
SIEVES
SIFTED
SIFTER
SIGHED
SIGNED
SIGNER
SIGNET
SILKEN
SILOED
SILTED
SILVER
SIMMER
SIMNEL
SIMPER
SINGED
SINGER
SINGES
SINKER
SINNED
SINNER
SINTER
SIPPED
SIPPER
SIPPET
SISTER
SITTER
SIXTES
SIZIER
SKATED
SKATER
SKATES
SKEWED
SKEWER
SKIVED
SKIVER
SKIVES
SKYMEN
SLAKED
SLAKES
SLATED
SLATER
SLATES
SLAVED
SLAVER
SLAVES
SLAYER
SLEWED
SLICED
SLICER
SLICES
SLIDER
SLIDES
SLIMED
SLIMES
SLIVER
SLOPED
SLOPER
SLOPES
SLOVEN
SLOWED
SLOWER
SMAZES
SMILED
SMILER
SMILES
SMITER
SMITES
SMOKED
SMOKER
SMOKES
SNAKED
SNAKES
SNARED
SNARER
SNARES
SNIPED
SNIPER
SNIPES
SNIVEL
SNORED
SNORER
SNORES
SNOWED
SOAKED
SOAKER
SOAPED
SOARED
SOARER
SOBBED
SOCCER
SOCKED
SOCKET
SOCLES
SOCMEN
SOCRED
SODDED
SODDEN
SOEVER
SOFTEN
SOFTER

6

SOILED
SOIREE
SOLDER
SOLOED
SOLVED
SOLVER
SOLVES
SOMBER
SONDER
SONNET
SOONER
SOOTED
SOPPED
SORREL
SORTED
SOULED
SOURED
SOURER
SOUSED
SOUSES
SOVIET
SPACED
SPACER
SPACES
SPADED
SPADER
SPADES
SPARED
SPARER
SPARES
SPATES
SPAYED
SPEWED
SPICED
SPICER
SPICES
SPIDER
SPIKED
SPIKES
SPILED
SPILES
SPINEL
SPINES
SPINET
SPIREA
SPIRED
SPIRES
SPITED
SPITES
SPLEEN
SPOKED
SPOKEN
SPOKES
SPORED
SPORES
SPREES
SPRIER
SPRUES
SPRYER
SPUMED
SPUMES
STAGED
STAGER
STAGES
STAGEY
STAKED
STAKES
STALED
STALER
STALES
STAMEN
STAPES
STARED
STARER
STARES
STASES
STATED
STATER
STATES
STAVED
STAVES
STAYED
STAYER
STELES
STEREO
STERES
STEVEN
STEVES
STEWED
STILES
STIPEL
STIPES
STIVER
STOGEY
STOKED
STOKER
STOKES
STOLED
STOLEN
STOLES
STONED
STONER
STONES
STOPED
STOPES
STORED
STORES
STOREY
STOVER
STOVES
STOWED
STREET
STUPES
STYLED
STYLER
STYLES
STYLET
SUBDEB
SUBLET
SUBTER
SUCKED
SUCKER
SUCRES
SUDDEN
SUEDES
SUFFER
SUITED
SUITES
SULKED
SULLEN
SUMMED
SUMMER
SUMNER
SUNDER
SUNDEW
SUNKEN
SUNNED
SUNSET
SUPPED
SUPPER
SURFED
SURFER
SURGED
SURGER
SURGES
SURREY
SURVEY
SUSIES
SUTLER
SUTTEE
SWAGED
SWAGES
SWALES
SWANEE
SWAYED
SWEDEN
SWEDES
SWIPED
SWIPES
SWIVEL
SWIVET
SYCEES
SYDNEY
SYNDET
SYPHER
SYSTEM

S••••E

SABINE
SADDLE
SALINE
SALOME
SALUTE
SAMITE
SAMPLE
SARAPE
SARTRE
SATIRE
SAVAGE
SCARCE
SCATHE
SCHEME
SCONCE
SCRAPE
SCRIBE
SCRIVE
SCURVE
SCYTHE
SEABEE
SEANCE
SECEDE
SECURE
SEDATE
SEDILE
SEDUCE
SEETHE
SEICHE
SELENE
SEMELE
SEMEME
SEMITE
SEMPRE
SENATE
SENILE
SERAPE
SERENE
SERINE
SESAME
SETOSE
SETTEE
SETTLE
SEVERE
SEWAGE
SHEAVE
SHELVE
SHIITE
SHOPPE
SHRIKE
SHRINE
SHRIVE
SHROVE
SICKLE
SIECLE
SILVAE
SIMILE
SIMONE
SIMPLE
SINGLE
SIZZLE
SLEAVE
SLEDGE
SLEEVE
SLUDGE
SLUICE
SMUDGE
SNATHE
SNEEZE
SNOOZE
SOCAGE
SOIGNE
SOIREE
SOLACE
SOLUTE
SOMITE
SOOTHE
SOPHIE
SORTIE
SOURCE
SOZINE
SPARGE
SPARSE
SPATHE
SPECIE
SPHENE
SPHERE
SPICAE
SPLAKE
SPLICE
SPLINE
SPONGE
SPOUSE
SPRITE
SPRUCE
SPURGE
SQUARE
SQUIRE
STABLE
STACIE
STACTE
STANCE
STAPLE
STARVE
STATUE
STEEVE
STELAE
STEPPE
STEVIE
STIFLE
STODGE
STOOGE
STRAFE
STRAKE
STRIAE
STRIDE
STRIFE
STRIKE
STRIPE
STRIVE
STRODE
STROKE
STROVE
STYMIE
SUABLE
SUBDUE
SUBTLE
SUCKLE
SUNDAE
SUPINE
SUPPLE
SUTTEE
SUTURE
SVELTE
SWANEE
SWATHE
SWERVE
SWINGE
SWIPLE
SYLVAE

•SE•••

ISEULT
PSEUDO
TSETSE
USEFUL

•S•E••

ASCEND
ASCENT
ASKERS
ASLEEP
ASPECT
ASPENS
ASPERS
ASSENT
ASSERT
ASSESS
ASSETS
ASTERI
ASTERN
ASTERO
ASTERS
ESCENT
ESKERS
ESSENE
ESTEEM
ESTERS
ISLETS
ISSEIS
OSBERT
OSIERS
OSSEIN
OSTEAL
USHERS

•S••E•

ASHIER
ASHLEY
ASHMEN
ASIDES
ASLEEP
ESCHEW
ESPIED
ESPIES
ESTEEM
ESTHER
ISABEL
ISOBEL
ISOHEL
ISOMER
ISRAEL
ISSUED
ISSUER
ISSUES
OSPREY
TSADES
USAGES
USURER

•S•••E

ASHORE
ASLOPE
ASPIRE
ASSIZE
ASSUME
ASSURE
ASTUTE
ESCAPE
ESSENE
ESTATE
ISOLDE
OSCINE
OSCULE
OSMOSE
PSYCHE

TSETSE
USABLE
USANCE

••SE••

ABSENT
ANSELM
ASSENT
ASSERT
ASSESS
ASSETS
AXSEED
BASELY
BESEEM
BESETS
BISECT
CASEFY
CASEIN
CASERN
DESERT
DOSERS
EASELS
ESSENE
EXSECT
EXSERT
FUSEES
GESELL
GISELE
INSECT
INSERT
INSETS
ISSEIS
ITSELF
JOSEPH
LASERS
LOSERS
MASERS
MISERS
MISERY
MOSEYS
MUSEUM
MYSELF
NISEIS
OBSESS
ONSETS
OSSEIN
OUSELS
PESETA
POSERS
POSEUR
RESEAT
RESEAU
RESECT
RESEDA
RESELL
RESEND
RESENT
RESETS
RISERS
SISERA
UNSEAL
UNSEAM
UNSEAT
UNSEEN
UPSETS
VISEED
WISELY
WISEST

••S•E•

AISLED
AISLES
ANSWER
AUSPEX
AUSTEN
AUSTER
AXSEED
BASHED
BASHES
BASKED
BASKET
BASSES
BASSET
BASTED
BASTES
BESEEM
BESTED
BISTER
BOSHES
BOSKET
BOSSED
BOSSES
BUSHED
BUSHEL
BUSHES
BUSIED
BUSIES
BUSMEN
BUSSED
BUSSES
BUSTED
BUSTER
CASHED
CASHES
CASHEW
CASKET
CASPER
CASTER
CASTES
COSHED
COSHER
COSHES
COSSES
COSSET
COSTED
CUSPED
CUSSED
CUSSES
CUSTER
DASHED
DASHER
DASHES
DISHED
DISHES
DISNEY
DISPEL
DOSSEL
DOSSER
DUSKED
DUSTED
DUSTER
EASIER
EASTER
ELSIES
ENSUED
ENSUES
FASCES
FASTED
FASTEN
FASTER
FESSES
FESTER
FISHED
FISHER
FISHES
FISTED
FOSSES
FOSTER
FUSEES
FUSSED
FUSSER
FUSSES
GASHED
GASHES
GASKET
GASMEN
GASPED
GASPER
GASSED
GASSES
GOSHEN
GOSPEL
GUSHED
GUSHER
GUSHES
GUSSET
HASHED
HASHES
HASLET
HASPED
HASSEL
HASTED
HASTEN
HASTES
HESTER
HISSED
HISSER
HISSES
HOSIER
HOSTED
HOSTEL
HUSHED
HUSHES
HUSKED
HUSKER
HYSTER
INSTEP
ISSUED
ISSUER
ISSUES
JASPER
JESSED
JESSES
JESTED
JESTER
JOSHED
JOSHER
JOSHES
JOSIES
JOSSES
KISLEW
KISMET
KISSED
KISSER
KISSES
KOSHER
LASHED
LASHER
LASHES
LASSES
LASTED
LASTER
LASTEX
LESLEY
LESSEE
LESSEN
LESSER
LESTER
LISPED
LISPER
LISTED
LISTEL
LISTEN
LISTER
LOSSES
LUSHED
LUSHER
LUSHES
LUSTED
LUSTER
MASHED
MASHER
MASHES
MASKED
MASKEG
MASKER
MASSED
MASSES
MASTED
MASTER
MESHED
MESHES
MESNES
MESSED
MESSES
MESTEE
MISSED
MISSES
MISTED
MISTER
MOSLEM
MOSLEY
MOSSES
MUSHED
MUSHER
MUSHES
MUSKEG
MUSKET
MUSSED
MUSSEL
MUSSES
MUSTEE
MUSTER
NASSER
NESTED
NOSIER
OUSTED
OUSTER
OYSTER
PASSED
PASSEE
PASSER
PASSES
PASTED
PASTEL
PASTER
PASTES
PESTER
PISCES
PISHED
PISHES
POSIES
POSSES
POSSET
POSTED
POSTER
PUSHED
PUSHER
PUSHES
PUSSES
PUSSEY
RASHER
RASHES
RASPED
RASPER
RESTED
RESTER
RISKED
RISKER
ROSIER
ROSTER
RUSHED
RUSHER
RUSHES
RUSSET
RUSTED
SASHED
SASHES
SASSED
SASSES
SESTET
SISTER
SUSIES
SYSTEM
TASKED
TASSEL
TASSET
TASTED
TASTER
TASTES
TESTED
TESTER
TESTES
TOSHES
TOSSED
TOSSES
TUSHED
TUSHES
TUSKED
TUSKER
ULSTER
UNSEEN
UNSTEP
VASTER
VESPER
VESSEL
VESTED
VESTEE
VISAED
VISEED
WASHED
WASHER
WASHES
WASTED
WASTER
WASTES
WESLEY
WESSEX
WESTER
WISHED
WISHES
WISPED
XYSTER
YESSED
YESSES
YESTER
ZESTED
ZOSTER

••S••E

ALSACE
ALSIKE
ANSATE
ARSINE
ASSIZE
ASSUME
ASSURE
BASQUE
BESIDE
BESSIE
BISQUE
BUSTLE
CASQUE
CASSIE
CASTLE
CESARE
CISSIE
COSINE
COSTAE
DESIRE
DISUSE
DOSAGE
ENSILE
ENSURE

ESSENE
FESCUE
FOSSAE
FUSILE
GISELE
GUSSIE
HASSLE
HUSTLE
INSANE
INSIDE
INSOLE
INSURE
JESSIE
JOSTLE
LASSIE
LESLIE
LESSEE
LYSINE
MASHIE
MASQUE
MESTEE
MISCUE
MISUSE
MOSQUE
MUSCAE
MUSCLE
MUSTEE
NESTLE
PASSEE
PESADE
PESTLE
RESALE
RESCUE
RESIDE
RESILE
RESOLE
RESUME
RISQUE
ROSCOE
RUSINE
RUSTLE
SESAME
TESSIE
TESTAE
TISANE
TISSUE
TUSSLE
UNSAFE
UNSURE
UPSIDE
URSINE
VESTEE
VISAGE

•••SE•

ABASED
ABASER
ABASES
ABUSED
ABUSER
ABUSES
AMUSED
AMUSER
AMUSES
ANISES
ANUSES
ARISEN
ARISES
BASSES
BASSET
BIASED
BIASES
BOSSED
BOSSES
BOUSED
BOUSES
BOWSED
BOWSES
BUNSEN
BURSES
BUSSED
BUSSES
CAUSED
CAUSER
CAUSES
CEASED
CEASES
CENSED
CENSER
CENSES
CHASED
CHASER
CHASES
CHISEL
CHOSEN
CLOSED
CLOSER
CLOSES
CLOSET
COPSES
CORSES
CORSET
COSSES
COSSET
CRISES
CRUSES
CRUSET
CURSED
CURSES
CUSSED
CUSSES
DAISES
DAMSEL
DENSER
DIESEL
DIESES
DOSSEL
DOSSER
DOUSED
DOUSES
DOWSED
DOWSER
DOWSES
DRUSES
ELYSEE
ERASED
ERASER
ERASES
EYASES
FALSER
FEASED
FEASES
FESSES
FOSSES
FRISES
FUSSED
FUSSER
FUSSES
GASSED
GASSES
GEYSER
GOOSED
GOOSES
GOOSEY
GORSES
GUISES
GUSSET
HALSEY
HANSEL
HASSEL
HAUSEN
HAWSER
HAWSES
HISSED
HISSER
HISSES
HORSED
HORSES
HORSEY
HOUSED
HOUSES
IBISES
IRISES
JERSEY
JESSED
JESSES
JOSSES
KAASES
KAISER
KERSEY
KINSEY
KISSED
KISSER
KISSES
KRISES
LAPSED
LAPSER
LAPSES
LASSES
LEASED
LEASES
LENSES
LESSEE
LESSEN
LESSER
LOOSED
LOOSEN
LOOSER
LOOSES
LOSSES
LOUSED
LOUSES
MANSES
MASSED
MASSES
MAUSER
MENSES
MESSED
MESSES
MISSED
MISSES
MORSEL
MOSSES
MOUSED
MOUSER
MOUSES
MUSSED
MUSSEL
MUSSES
NAOSES
NASSER
NAUSEA
NOISED
NOISES
NOOSED
NOOSES
NURSED
NURSER
NURSES
OCASEY
OFFSET
ONUSES
OUTSET
PARSEC
PARSED
PARSEE
PARSES
PASSED
PASSEE
PASSER
PASSES
PAUSED
PAUSER
PAUSES
PEASEN
PEASES
PHASED
PHASES
PLUSES
POISED
POISES
POSSES
POSSET
PROSED
PROSER
PROSES
PULSED
PULSES
PURSED
PURSER
PURSES
PUSSES
PUSSEY
RAISED
RAISER
RAISES
RINSED
RINSER
RINSES
ROUSED
ROUSER
ROUSES
RUSSET
SANSEI
SASSED
SASSES
SENSED
SENSES
SOUSED
SOUSES
STASES
SUNSET
TASSEL
TASSET
TEASED
TEASEL
TEASER
TEASES
TENSED
TENSER
TENSES
TERSER
THESES
TINSEL
TOSSED
TOSSES
UKASES
UNDSET
UNISEX
UNUSED
UPASES
VERSED
VERSES
VESSEL
WADSET
WEASEL
WESSEX
WOLSEY
WORSEN
WORSER
WOWSER
YESSED
YESSES

•••S•E

BESSIE
BURSAE
CASSIE
CHASSE
CHASTE
CISSIE
CROSSE
CRUSOE
CUISSE
ELYSEE
ENISLE
FOCSLE
FOSSAE
GUSSIE
HASSLE
HORSTE
JESSIE
LASSIE
LESSEE
MAISIE
MOISHE
MOUSSE
PARSEE
PASSEE
POTSIE
PUISNE
PURSUE
TESSIE
TISSUE
TOUSLE
TRISTE
TUSSLE
WRASSE

••••SE

ACCUSE
ADVISE
ALDOSE
APPOSE
ARIOSE
AROUSE
AVERSE
BEMUSE
BETISE
BLOUSE
BOURSE
BRAISE
BROWSE
BRUISE
CAMISE
CAYUSE
CERISE
CERUSE
CHAISE
CHASSE
CHEESE
CHOOSE
CLAUSE
COARSE
COMOSE
CORPSE
COURSE
CREASE
CREESE
CROSSE
CRUISE
CUISSE
CYMOSE
DEBASE
DEMISE
DENISE
DEPOSE
DEVISE
DISUSE
DROWSE
EFFUSE
ELAPSE
ELOISE
ENCASE

EXCISE
EXCUSE
EXPOSE
FILOSE
FLENSE
FRAISE
GREASE
GRILSE
GROUSE
GYROSE
HEARSE
HEXOSE
HOARSE
ILLUSE
IMPOSE
INCASE
INCISE
INCUSE
INFUSE
JOCOSE
KETOSE
KINASE
LANOSE
LAOTSE
LIPASE
LOUISE
MISUSE
MOROSE
MOUSSE
MUCOSE
NODOSE
NOWISE
OBTUSE
OPPOSE
OSMOSE
OTIOSE
PAVISE
PERUSE
PHRASE
PILOSE
PLEASE
PRAISE
RAMOSE
RECUSE
REFUSE
REMISE
REPOSE
RETUSE
REVISE
RIBOSE
RIMOSE
RUGOSE
SETOSE
SPARSE
SPOUSE
THYRSE
TOROSE
TRIOSE
TSETSE
UNWISE
UPRISE
UPROSE
UREASE
VADOSE
VALISE
VENOSE
WRASSE
XYLOSE
ZYMASE

SF••••
SFORZA

S•F•••
SAFARI
SAFELY
SAFEST
SAFETY
SIFTED
SIFTER
SOFFIT
SOFTAS
SOFTEN
SOFTER
SOFTLY
SUFFER
SUFFIX
SUFISM

S••F••
SAWFLY
SCOFFS
SCUFFS
SHAFTS
SHIFTS
SHIFTY
SHOFAR
SINFUL
SKIFFS
SNAFUS
SNIFFS
SNIFFY
SNUFFS
SNUFFY
SOFFIT
SPIFFY
STAFFS
STEFAN
STIFLE
STUFFS
STUFFY
SUFFER
SUFFIX
SULFUR
SURFED
SURFER
SWIFTS

S•••F•
SALIFY
SCARFS
SCLAFF
SCOFFS
SCRUFF
SCUFFS
SCURFY
SERIFS
SETOFF
SHRIFT
SHROFF
SKIFFS
SNIFFS
SNIFFY
SNUFFS
SNUFFY
SPIFFY
SPOOFS
STAFFS
STRAFE
STRIFE
STUFFS
STUFFY

S••••F
SCLAFF
SCRUFF
SETOFF
SHERIF
SHROFF

•S•F••
USEFUL

•S••F•
OSSIFY

••SF••
MISFIT

••S•F•
BASIFY
CASEFY
OSSIFY
UNSAFE

••S••F
GUSTAF
ITSELF
MASSIF
MYSELF

•••S•F
MASSIF

S•G•••
SAGELY
SAGEST
SAGGAR
SAGGED
SAGGER
SAGIER
SEGGAR
SIGHED
SIGHTS
SIGILS
SIGMAS
SIGNAL
SIGNED
SIGNER
SIGNET
SIGNOR
SIGRID
SUGARS
SUGARY

S••G••
SAGGAR
SAGGED
SAGGER
SAIGAS
SAIGON
SANGAR
SANGER
SANGUI
SARGON
SAUGER
SEDGES
SEGGAR
SHAGGY
SHOGUN
SIEGED
SIEGES
SINGED
SINGER
SINGES
SINGLE
SINGLY
SLAGGY
SLIGHT
SLOGAN
SMUGLY
SNAGGY
SNUGLY
SOIGNE
SORGHO
SORGOS
SOUGHS
SOUGHT
SPIGOT
STAGED
STAGER
STAGES
STAGEY
STAGGY
STIGMA
STOGEY
SURGED
SURGER
SURGES
SWAGED
SWAGES

S•••G•
SAVAGE
SCRAGS
SEWAGE
SHAGGY
SHRUGS
SLAGGY
SLANGY
SLEDGE
SLEIGH
SLINGS
SLOUGH
SLUDGE
SLUDGY
SMUDGE
SMUDGY
SNAGGY
SOCAGE
SPARGE
SPONGE
SPONGY
SPRAGS
SPRIGS
SPURGE
STAGGY
STINGS
STINGY
STODGE
STODGY
STOOGE
SWINGE
SWINGS
SYZYGY

S••••G
SARONG
SATANG
SATING
SAVING
SAWING
SAYING
SEADOG
SEEING
SEWING
SEXING
SHYING
SIDING
SIRING
SIZING
SKIING
SKYING
SLUING
SOLING
SOWING
SPRANG
SPRING
SPRUNG
SPYING
STALAG
STENOG
STRING
STRONG
STYING
SUNDOG

•SG•••
ASGARD

•S•G••
ISOGON
USAGES

•S••G•
ASSIGN

•S•••G
ASKING
ISLING

••SG••
PISGAH

••S•G•
ASSIGN
COSIGN
DESIGN
DOSAGE
ENSIGN
RESIGN
VISAGE

••S••G
BASING
BUSING
CASING
DOSING
EASING
FUSING
GASBAG
HOSING
LOSING
LYSING
MASKEG
MUSING
MUSKEG
NOSING
POSING
RISING
ROSING
UNSUNG
VISING
WISING

SH••••
SHABBY
SHACKO
SHACKS
SHADED
SHADES
SHADOW
SHAFTS
SHAGGY
SHAKEN
SHAKER
SHAKES
SHAKOS
SHALED
SHALES
SHAMAN
SHAMED
SHAMES
SHAMMY
SHAMUS
SHANKS
SHANTY
SHAPED
SHAPEN
SHAPER
SHAPES
SHARDS
SHARED
SHARER
SHARES

SHARKS
SHARON
SHARPS
SHASTA
SHAVED
SHAVEN
SHAVER
SHAVES
SHAWLS
SHAWMS
SHEARS
SHEATH
SHEAVE
SHEBAT
SHEENS
SHEENY
SHEERS
SHEETS
SHEIKS
SHEILA
SHEKEL
SHELBY
SHELLS
SHELLY
SHELTY
SHELVE
SHERDS
SHERIF
SHERPA
SHERRY
SHEWED
SHEWER
SHIELD
SHIEST
SHIFTS
SHIFTY
SHIISM
SHIITE
SHIKAR
SHILLS
SHILOH
SHIMMY
SHINDY
SHINED
SHINER
SHINES
SHINNY
SHINTO
SHIRES
SHIRKS
SHIRRS
SHIRTS
SHIVER
SHIVES
SHOALS
SHOALY
SHOATS
SHOCKS
SHODDY
SHOERS
SHOFAR
SHOGUN
SHOJIS
SHOOED
SHOOIN
SHOOTS
SHOPPE
SHORAN
SHORED
SHORES
SHORLS
SHORTS
SHOTES
SHOULD
SHOUTS
SHOVED
SHOVEL
SHOVER
SHOVES
SHOWED
SHOWER
SHRANK
SHREDS
SHREWD
SHREWS
SHRIEK
SHRIFT
SHRIKE
SHRILL
SHRIMP
SHRINE
SHRINK
SHRIVE
SHROFF
SHROUD
SHROVE
SHRUBS
SHRUGS
SHRUNK
SHTICK
SHUCKS
SHUNTS
SHUTIN
SHYEST
SHYING

S•H•••

SAHARA
SAHEBS
SAHIBS
SCHEMA
SCHEME
SCHICK
SCHISM
SCHIST
SCHIZO
SCHMOS
SCHOOL
SCHORL
SCHUIT
SCHUSS
SCHWAS
SPHENE
SPHENO
SPHERE
SPHERY
SPHINX

S••H••

SACHEM
SACHET
SADHUS
SAPHAR
SASHAY
SASHED
SASHES
SIGHED
SIGHTS
SIPHON
SOPHIA
SOPHIE
SOTHIC
SOTHIS
SPAHIS
SYPHER

S•••H•

SAMSHU
SANDHI
SAPPHO
SARAHS
SCATHE
SCYPHI
SCYPHO
SCYTHE
SEETHE
SEICHE
SIXTHS
SLIGHT
SLOSHY
SLOTHS
SLUSHY
SMITHS
SMITHY
SNATHE
SNATHS
SOOTHE
SORGHO
SOUGHS
SOUGHT
SPATHE
SRADHA
STETHO
STITHY
SUBAHS
SULPHA
SULPHO
SURAHS
SWATHE
SWATHS
SYLPHS
SYLPHY

S••••H

SALISH
SCORCH
SCOTCH
SCUTCH
SEARCH
SERAPH
SHEATH
SHILOH
SIWASH
SKETCH
SLEIGH
SLEUTH
SLOUCH
SLOUGH
SMIRCH
SMOOCH
SMOOTH
SMUTCH
SNATCH
SNITCH
SPEECH
SPILTH
SPLASH
SQUASH
SQUISH
STANCH
STARCH
STENCH
STITCH
SUNNAH
SWARTH
SWATCH
SWITCH

•SH•••

ASHIER
ASHLAR
ASHLEY
ASHMAN
ASHMEN
ASHORE
ISHTAR
PSHAWS
TSHIRT
USHERS

•S•H••

ASTHMA
ESCHAR
ESCHEW
ESTHER
ISCHIA
ISOHEL

•S••H•

PSYCHE
PSYCHO

•S•••H

ISAIAH

••SH••

BASHAW
BASHED
BASHES
BISHOP
BOSHES
BUSHED
BUSHEL
BUSHES
CASHAW
CASHED
CASHES
CASHEW
CASHOO
COSHED
COSHER
COSHES
CUSHAT
CUSHAW
DASHED
DASHER
DASHES
DISHED
DISHES
FISHED
FISHER
FISHES
GASHED
GASHES
GOSHEN
GUSHED
GUSHER
GUSHES
HASHED
HASHES
HUSHED
HUSHES
JOSHED
JOSHER
JOSHES
JOSHUA
KOSHER
LASHED
LASHER
LASHES
LUSHED
LUSHER
LUSHES
MASHED
MASHER
MASHES
MASHIE
MESHED
MESHES
MISHAP
MUSHED
MUSHER
MUSHES
NASHUA
NOSHOW
PASHAS
PASHTO
PISHED
PISHES
PUSHED
PUSHER
PUSHES
PUSHUP
RASHER
RASHES
RASHLY
RUSHED
RUSHER
RUSHES
SASHAY
SASHED
SASHES
TISHRI
TOSHES
TUSHED
TUSHES
UNSHIP
UPSHOT
VASHTI
VISHNU
WASHED
WASHER
WASHES
WISHED
WISHES

••S••H

BASRAH
CASBAH
JOSEPH
JOSIAH
PESACH
PISGAH
TUSSAH

•••SH•

AYESHA
BRASHY
BRUSHY
ELISHA
FLASHY
FLESHY
GEISHA
GUNSHY
HONSHU
KYUSHU
MARSHA
MARSHY
MOISHE
PLASHY
PLUSHY
SAMSHU
SLOSHY
SLUSHY
TRASHY

•••S•H

BORSCH
KIRSCH
KITSCH
PHOSPH
PUTSCH
TUSSAH

••••SH

ABLUSH
AFRESH
AGUISH
AMBUSH
BANISH
BLUISH
BOYISH
CALASH
COHOSH

COYISH
DANISH
DOVISH
DUDISH
ELFISH
ELVISH
ENMESH
FAMISH
FETISH
FINISH
GALOSH
GARISH
IMMESH
IMPISH
INMESH
INRUSH
JADISH
JEWISH
JUTISH
KIBOSH
LATISH
LAVISH
MODISH
MOPISH
MULISH
OAFISH
OFFISH
OGRISH
OLDISH
ONRUSH
OWLISH
PALISH
PARISH
PERISH
POLISH
POPISH
POTASH
PUNISH
RADISH
RAKISH
RAVISH
RAWISH
REHASH
RELISH
ROMISH
SALISH
SIWASH
SPLASH
SQUASH
SQUISH
THRASH
THRESH
THRUSH
TOYISH
UNWISH
UPPISH
VANISH
WABASH

SI••••

SIALIC
SIBYLS
SICILY
SICKED
SICKEN
SICKER
SICKLE
SICKLY
SIDDUR
SIDERO
SIDING
SIDLED
SIDLER
SIDLES
SIDNEY
SIECLE
SIEGED
SIEGES
SIENNA
SIERRA
SIESTA
SIEURS
SIEVED
SIEVES
SIFTED
SIFTER
SIGHED
SIGHTS
SIGILS
SIGMAS
SIGNAL
SIGNED
SIGNER
SIGNET
SIGNOR
SIGRID
SIKKIM
SILENI
SILENT
SILICA
SILICO
SILKEN
SILOED
SILTED
SILVAE
SILVAN
SILVAS
SILVER
SILVIA
SIMARS
SIMEON
SIMIAN
SIMILE
SIMLIN
SIMMER
SIMNEL
SIMONE
SIMONS
SIMONY
SIMOOM
SIMPER
SIMPLE
SIMPLY
SINBAD
SINEWS
SINEWY
SINFUL
SINGED
SINGER
SINGES
SINGLE
SINGLY
SINKER
SINNED
SINNER
SINTER
SIOUAN
SIPHON
SIPPED
SIPPER
SIPPET
SIRDAR
SIRENS
SIRING
SIRIUS
SIRUPS
SIRUPY
SISERA
SISKIN
SISTER
SITARS
SITINS
SITTER
SIWASH
SIXTES
SIXTHS
SIZARS
SIZIER
SIZING
SIZZLE

S•I•••

SAIGAS
SAIGON
SAILED
SAILER
SAILOR
SAINTS
SAIPAN
SAITIC
SCIONS
SCIPIO
SEICHE
SEINED
SEINER
SEINES
SEISIN
SEISMO
SEISMS
SEISOR
SEIZED
SEIZER
SEIZES
SEIZIN
SEIZOR
SHIELD
SHIEST
SHIFTS
SHIFTY
SHIISM
SHIITE
SHIKAR
SHILLS
SHILOH
SHIMMY
SHINDY
SHINED
SHINER
SHINES
SHINNY
SHINTO
SHIRES
SHIRKS
SHIRRS
SHIRTS
SHIVER
SHIVES
SKIERS
SKIFFS
SKIING
SKILLS
SKIMOS
SKIMPS
SKIMPY
SKINKS
SKINNY
SKIRRS
SKIRTS
SKIVED
SKIVER
SKIVES
SKIVVY
SLICED
SLICER
SLICES
SLICKS
SLIDER
SLIDES
SLIEST
SLIGHT
SLIMED
SLIMES
SLIMLY
SLIMSY
SLINGS
SLINKS
SLINKY
SLIPON
SLIPUP
SLIVER
SMILAX
SMILED
SMILER
SMILES
SMIRCH
SMIRKS
SMITER
SMITES
SMITHS
SMITHY
SNICKS
SNIFFS
SNIFFY
SNIPED
SNIPER
SNIPES
SNIPPY
SNITCH
SNIVEL
SOIGNE
SOILED
SOIREE
SPICAE
SPICED
SPICER
SPICES
SPIDER
SPIELS
SPIERS
SPIFFY
SPIGOT
SPIKED
SPIKES
SPILED
SPILES
SPILLS
SPILTH
SPINAL
SPINEL
SPINES
SPINET
SPINNY
SPIRAL
SPIREA
SPIRED
SPIRES
SPIRIT
SPIRTS
SPITAL
SPITED
SPITES
STICKS
STICKY
STIFLE
STIGMA
STILES
STILLS
STILLY
STILTS
STINGS
STINGY
STINKS
STINTS
STIPEL
STIPES
STIRKS
STIRPS
STITCH
STITHY
STIVER
SUITED
SUITES
SUITOR
SWIFTS
SWILLS
SWINGE
SWINGS
SWIPED
SWIPES
SWIPLE
SWIRLS
SWIRLY
SWITCH
SWIVEL
SWIVET

S••I••

SABINA
SABINE
SABINS
SADIES
SADISM
SADIST
SAGIER
SAHIBS
SALIFY
SALINE
SALISH
SALIVA
SAMIAN
SAMIEL
SAMITE
SANIES
SANITY
SASINS
SATING
SATINS
SATINY
SATIRE
SAVING
SAVINS
SAVIOR
SAWING
SAYING
SCHICK
SCHISM
SCHIST
SCHIZO
SCRIBE
SCRIMP
SCRIPS
SCRIPT
SCRIVE
SEDILE
SEEING
SEMITE
SENILE
SENIOR
SEPIAS
SERIAL
SERIES
SERIFS
SERINE
SERINS
SEWING
SEXIER
SEXING
SEXISM
SEXIST
SHEIKS
SHEILA
SHIISM
SHIITE
SHRIEK

SHRIFT
SHRIKE
SHRILL
SHRIMP
SHRINE
SHRINK
SHRIVE
SHTICK
SHYING
SICILY
SIDING
SIGILS
SILICA
SILICO
SIMIAN
SIMILE
SIRING
SIRIUS
SITINS
SIZIER
SIZING
SKEINS
SKIING
SKYING
SLEIGH
SLUICE
SLUING
SNAILS
SOCIAL
SODIUM
SOLIDI
SOLIDS
SOLING
SOLION
SOMITE
SONIAS
SOVIET
SOWING
SOZINE
SOZINS
SPAITS
SPEISS
SPHINX
SPLICE
SPLINE
SPLINT
SPLITS
SPOILS
SPOILT
SPRIER
SPRIGS
SPRING
SPRINT
SPRITE
SPRITS
SPYING
SQUIBS
SQUIDS
SQUILL
SQUINT
SQUIRE
SQUIRM
SQUIRT
SQUISH
STAINS
STAIRS
STEINS
STOICS
STRIAE
STRICK
STRICT
STRIDE
STRIFE
STRIKE
STRING
STRIPE
STRIPS
STRIPT
STRIPY
STRIVE
STYING
SUBITO
SUFISM
SUPINE
SUSIES
SWAILS
SWAINS
SYBILS
SYRIAC
SYRIAN
SYRINX

S•••I•

SAITIC
SALMIS
SALPID
SALVIA
SCENIC
SCHUIT
SCIPIO
SCORIA
SCOTIA
SEISIN
SEIZIN
SENNIT
SEPSIS
SEPTIC
SEQUIN
SERAIS
SERBIA
SEREIN
SHERIF
SHOJIS
SHOOIN
SHUTIN
SIALIC
SIGRID
SIKKIM
SILVIA
SIMLIN
SISKIN
SLAVIC
SOFFIT
SOPHIA
SOPHIE
SORDID
SORTIE
SOTHIC
SOTHIS
SPADIX
SPAHIS
SPAVIN
SPECIE
SPIRIT
SPRAIN
STACIE
STADIA
STALIN
STAMIN
STASIS
STATIC
STELIC
STEPIN
STERIC
STEVIE
STOLID
STRAIN
STRAIT
STUDIO
STUPID
STYMIE
SUBMIT
SUFFIX
SUMMIT
SUNLIT
SUOMIC
SUSLIK
SWAMIS
SYLVIA
SYNDIC

S••••I

SAFARI
SALAMI
SALUKI
SANDHI
SANGUI
SANSEI
SATORI
SCAMPI
SCYPHI
SESQUI
SILENI
SMALTI
SOLIDI
SOUARI
STELLI
STRATI

•SI•••

ASIANS
ASIDES
ISIDOR
OSIERS
OSIRIS

•S•I••

ASHIER
ASKING
ASPICS
ASPIRE
ASSIGN
ASSISI
ASSIST
ASSIZE
ESKIMO
ESPIAL
ESPIED
ESPIES
ISAIAH
ISLING
OSCINE
OSMIUM
OSSIAN
OSSIFY
TSHIRT

•S••I•

ASSAIL
ASSAIS
ASTRID
ESPRIT
ISCHIA
ISSEIS
OSIRIS
OSSEIN

•S•••I

ASSISI
ASTERI

••SI••

ALSIKE
ARSINE
ASSIGN
ASSISI
ASSIST
ASSIZE
BASICS
BASIFY
BASILS
BASING
BASINS
BASION
BESIDE
BUSIED
BUSIES
BUSILY
BUSING
CASING
CASINO
CESIUM
COSIGN
COSINE
DESIGN
DESIRE
DESIST
DOSING
EASIER
EASILY
EASING
ELSIES
ENSIGN
ENSILE
FUSILE
FUSILS
FUSING
FUSION
HESIOD
HOSIER
HOSING
INSIDE
INSIST
JOSIAH
JOSIAS
JOSIES
LESION
LOSING
LYSINE
LYSING
LYSINS
MESIAL
MESIAN
MUSING
NASIAL
NASION
NOSIER
NOSILY
NOSING
OSSIAN
OSSIFY
POSIES
POSING
POSITS
RESIDE
RESIGN
RESILE
RESINS
RESIST
RISING
ROSIER
ROSILY
ROSING
ROSINS
ROSINY
RUSINE
SASINS
SUSIES
UPSIDE
URSINE
VASILI
VESICA
VESICO
VISING
VISION
VISITS
WISING

••S•I•

ASSAIL
ASSAIS
AUSTIN
BESSIE
BESTIR
BUSKIN
BUSTIC
CASEIN
CASSIA
CASSIE
CASSIS
CISSIE
COSMIC
CUSPID
CUSPIS
CYSTIC
DESMID
DISTIL
DOSSIL
FASCIA
FISTIC
FOSSIL
FUSAIN
FUSTIC
GASKIN
GESTIC
GOSSIP
GUSSIE
HESTIA
HISPID
ISSEIS
JESSIE
JESUIT
JUSTIN
LASSIE
LESLIE
MASHIE
MASSIF
MASTIC
MISDID
MISFIT
MISSIS
MOSAIC
MUSKIT
MUSLIM
MUSLIN
MYSTIC
NASTIC
NISEIS
OSSEIN
PASSIM
PASTIL
PISTIL
RUSKIN
RUSSIA
RUSTIC
SISKIN
SUSLIK
TESSIE
TESTIS
TUSSIS
UNSAID
UNSHIP
VESPID
VISCID

••S••I

ASSISI
SESQUI
TISHRI
VASARI
VASHTI
VASILI

•••SI•
BESSIE
BIOSIS
CASSIA
CASSIE
CASSIS
CISSIE
COUSIN
CRASIS
CRISIS
DIESIS
DOSSIL
ECESIS
EMESIS
ENOSIS
FOSSIL
GNOSIS
GOSSIP
GUSSIE
JESSIE
KAMSIN
LASSIE
LEPSIA
MAISIE
MASSIF
MIOSIS
MISSIS
MYOSIN
MYOSIS
NOESIS
OUTSIT
PARSIS
PASSIM
PEPSIN
PERSIA
PHASIA
PHASIC
PHASIS
PHYSIC
PHYSIO
PLASIA
PLASIS
POTSIE
PROSIT
PTOSIS
PYOSIS
RAISIN
RUSSIA
SEISIN
SEPSIS
STASIS
TESSIE
THESIS
TMESIS
TOCSIN
TONSIL
TUSSIS
ZOYSIA

•••S•I
BONSAI
NEVSKI
SANSEI

••••SI
ASSISI
KINESI
THYRSI
WATUSI

S•J•••
SAJOUS
SEJANT

S••J••
SANJAK
SELJUK
SHOJIS

S••••J
SWARAJ

SK••••
SKALDS
SKATED
SKATER
SKATES
SKEANS
SKEINS
SKETCH
SKEWED
SKEWER
SKIERS
SKIFFS
SKIING
SKILLS
SKIMOS
SKIMPS
SKIMPY
SKINKS
SKINNY
SKIRRS
SKIRTS
SKIVED
SKIVER
SKIVES
SKIVVY
SKULKS
SKULLS
SKUNKS
SKYCAP
SKYING
SKYMAN
SKYMEN
SKYWAY

S•K•••
SAKERS
SIKKIM

S••K••
SACKED
SACKER
SECKEL
SEEKER
SHAKEN
SHAKER
SHAKES
SHAKOS
SHEKEL
SHIKAR
SICKED
SICKEN
SICKER
SICKLE
SICKLY
SIKKIM
SILKEN
SINKER
SISKIN
SLAKED
SLAKES
SMOKED
SMOKER
SMOKES
SNAKED
SNAKES
SOAKED
SOAKER
SOCKED
SOCKET
SPIKED
SPIKES
SPOKED
SPOKEN
SPOKES
STAKED
STAKES
STOKED
STOKER
STOKES
SUCKED
SUCKER
SUCKLE
SULKED
SUNKEN

S•••K•
SALUKI
SHACKO
SHACKS
SHANKS
SHARKS
SHEIKS
SHIRKS
SHOCKS
SHRIKE
SHUCKS
SKINKS
SKULKS
SKUNKS
SLACKS
SLEEKS
SLEEKY
SLICKS
SLINKS
SLINKY
SMACKS
SMIRKS
SMOCKS
SNACKS
SNEAKS
SNEAKY
SNICKS
SNOOKS
SPANKS
SPARKS
SPEAKS
SPECKS
SPLAKE
SPOOKS
SPOOKY
SPUNKY
STACKS
STALKS
STALKY
STEAKS
STICKS
STICKY
STINKS
STIRKS
STOCKS
STOCKY
STOOKS
STORKS
STRAKE
STRIKE
STROKE
SWANKY

S••••K
SANJAK
SCHICK
SCREAK
SELJUK
SHRANK
SHRIEK
SHRINK
SHRUNK
SHTICK
SLOVAK
SQUAWK
SQUEAK
STREAK
STRICK
STRUCK
SUSLIK

•SK•••
ASKANT
ASKERS
ASKING
ESKERS
ESKIMO

••SK••
BASKED
BASKET
BOSKET
BUSKIN
CASKET
DUSKED
GASKET
GASKIN
HUSKED
HUSKER
MASKED
MASKEG
MASKER
MISKAL
MUSKEG
MUSKET
MUSKIT
RISKED
RISKER
RUSKIN
SISKIN
TASKED
TUSKED
TUSKER

••S•K•
ALSIKE

••S••K
SUSLIK
YASMAK

•••SK•
ALASKA
BRISKS
DROSKY
FLASKS
FRISKS
FRISKY
KIOSKS
NEVSKI
TORSKS
WHISKS
WHISKY

••••SK
DAMASK
UNHUSK
UNMASK

SL••••
SLACKS
SLAGGY
SLAKED
SLAKES
SLALOM
SLANGY
SLANTS
SLATED
SLATER
SLATES
SLAVED
SLAVER
SLAVES
SLAVIC
SLAYER
SLEAVE
SLEAZY
SLEDGE
SLEEKS
SLEEKY
SLEEPS
SLEEPY
SLEETS
SLEETY
SLEEVE
SLEIGH
SLEUTH
SLEWED
SLICED
SLICER
SLICES
SLICKS
SLIDER
SLIDES
SLIEST
SLIGHT
SLIMED
SLIMES
SLIMLY
SLIMSY
SLINGS
SLINKS
SLINKY
SLIPON
SLIPUP
SLIVER
SLOGAN
SLOOPS
SLOPED
SLOPER
SLOPES
SLOPPY
SLOSHY
SLOTHS
SLOUCH
SLOUGH
SLOVAK
SLOVEN
SLOWED
SLOWER
SLOWLY
SLUDGE
SLUDGY
SLUICE
SLUING
SLUMMY
SLUMPS
SLURPS
SLURRY
SLUSHY
SLYEST

S•L•••
SALAAM
SALADS
SALAMI
SALARY
SALIFY
SALINE
SALISH
SALIVA
SALLET
SALLOW
SALLYS
SALMIS
SALMON
SALOME

6

SALONS
SALOON
SALOOP
SALPAS
SALPID
SALTED
SALTER
SALUKI
SALUTE
SALVED
SALVER
SALVES
SALVIA
SALVOR
SALVOS
SCLAFF
SCLERA
SCLERO
SELDOM
SELECT
SELENE
SELENO
SELJUK
SELLER
SELSYN
SELVES
SILENI
SILENT
SILICA
SILICO
SILKEN
SILOED
SILTED
SILVAE
SILVAN
SILVAS
SILVER
SILVIA
SOLACE
SOLAND
SOLANO
SOLANS
SOLDER
SOLELY
SOLEMN
SOLENT
SOLIDI
SOLIDS
SOLING
SOLION
SOLOED
SOLUTE
SOLVED
SOLVER
SOLVES
SPLAKE
SPLASH
SPLATS
SPLAYS
SPLEEN
SPLENO
SPLICE
SPLINE
SPLINT
SPLITS
SULCUS
SULFUR
SULKED
SULLEN
SULPHA
SULPHO
SULTAN
SULTRY
SYLPHS
SYLPHY
SYLVAE
SYLVAN
SYLVAS
SYLVIA

S••L••

SABLES
SAILED
SAILER
SAILOR
SALLET
SALLOW
SALLYS
SAMLET
SAULTS
SCALAR
SCALDS
SCALED
SCALER
SCALES
SCALPS
SCOLDS
SCOLEX
SCULLS
SCULPT
SCYLLA
SEALED
SEALER
SELLER
SENLAC
SHALED
SHALES
SHELBY
SHELLS
SHELLY
SHELTY
SHELVE
SHILLS
SHILOH
SIALIC
SIDLED
SIDLER
SIDLES
SIMLIN
SKALDS
SKILLS
SKULKS
SKULLS
SLALOM
SMALLS
SMALTI
SMALTO
SMELLS
SMELLY
SMELTS
SMILAX
SMILED
SMILER
SMILES
SMOLTS
SNELLS
SOCLES
SOILED
SOULED
SPALLS
SPELLS
SPILED
SPILES
SPILLS
SPILTH
STALAG
STALED
STALER
STALES
STALIN
STALKS
STALKY
STALLS
STELAE
STELAR
STELES
STELIC
STELLA
STELLI
STILES
STILLS
STILLY
STILTS
STOLED
STOLEN
STOLES
STOLID
STOLON
STULLS
STYLAR
STYLED
STYLER
STYLES
STYLET
STYLUS
SUBLET
SULLEN
SUNLIT
SUSLIK
SUTLER
SVELTE
SWALES
SWELLS
SWILLS

S•••L•

SADDLE
SAFELY
SAGELY
SAMPLE
SANELY
SAWFLY
SCOWLS
SCROLL
SCULLS
SCYLLA
SEDILE
SEEMLY
SEMELE
SENILE
SEPALS
SETTLE
SEWALL
SHAWLS
SHEILA
SHELLS
SHELLY
SHIELD
SHILLS
SHOALS
SHOALY
SHORLS
SHOULD
SHRILL
SIBYLS
SICILY
SICKLE
SICKLY
SIECLE
SIGILS
SIMILE
SIMPLE
SIMPLY
SINGLE
SINGLY
SIZZLE
SKILLS
SKULLS
SLIMLY
SLOWLY
SMALLS
SMELLS
SMELLY
SMUGLY
SNAILS
SNARLS
SNARLY
SNELLS
SNUGLY
SOFTLY
SOLELY
SORELS
SORELY
SOTOLS
SOURLY
SPALLS
SPELLS
SPIELS
SPILLS
SPOILS
SPOILT
SPOOLS
SPRYLY
SQUALL
SQUILL
STABLE
STALLS
STAPLE
STEALS
STEELS
STEELY
STELLA
STELLI
STIFLE
STILLS
STILLY
STOOLS
STROLL
STULLS
SUABLE
SUBTLE
SUBTLY
SUCKLE
SUPPLE
SUPPLY
SURELY
SWAILS
SWELLS
SWILLS
SWIPLE
SWIRLS
SWIRLY
SYBILS

S••••L

SACRAL
SAMIEL
SAMUEL
SANDAL
SANTOL
SAUREL
SCHOOL
SCHORL
SCRAWL
SCROLL
SECKEL
SENDAL
SEPTAL
SEQUEL
SERIAL
SERVAL
SEWALL
SEXUAL
SHEKEL
SHOVEL
SHRILL
SIGNAL
SIMNEL
SINFUL
SNIVEL
SOCIAL
SORREL
SPINAL
SPINEL
SPIRAL
SPITAL
SPRAWL
SQUALL
SQUEAL
SQUILL
STATAL
STEROL
STIPEL
STROLL
SWIVEL
SYMBOL

•SL•••

ASLANT
ASLEEP
ASLOPE
ISLAND
ISLETS
ISLING

•S•L••

ASHLAR
ASHLEY
ASYLUM
ISOLDE
PSALMS

•S••L•

ISEULT
OSCULE
OSWALD
USABLE
USABLY

•S•••L

ASSAIL
ASTRAL
ESPIAL
ISABEL
ISOBEL
ISOHEL
ISRAEL
OSTEAL
USEFUL

••SL••

AISLED
AISLES
HASLET
KISLEW
LESLEY
LESLIE
MISLAY
MOSLEM
MOSLEY
MUSLIM
MUSLIN
SUSLIK
WESLEY

••S•L•

ANSELM
BASALT
BASELY
BASILS
BUSILY
BUSTLE
CASALS
CASTLE

6

COSTLY
DESALT
EASELS
EASILY
ENSILE
FUSILE
FUSILS
GESELL
GISELE
HASSLE
HUSTLE
INSOLE
INSULT
ITSELF
JOSTLE
JUSTLY
LASTLY
MOSTLY
MUSCLE
MYSELF
NASALS
NESTLE
NOSILY
OUSELS
PESTLE
PUSSLY
RASHLY
RESALE
RESELL
RESILE
RESOLD
RESOLE
RESULT
ROSILY
RUSTLE
TUSSLE
UNSOLD
URSULA
VASILI
VASTLY
WISELY

••S••L
ASSAIL
BUSHEL
CASUAL
COSTAL
DISMAL
DISPEL
DISTAL
DISTIL
DOSSAL
DOSSEL
DOSSIL
ENSOUL
FESTAL
FISCAL
FOSSIL
GESELL
GOSPEL
HASSEL
HOSTEL
INSOUL
LISTEL
MESCAL
MESIAL
MISKAL
MISSAL
MUSSEL
NASIAL
PASCAL
PASTEL
PASTIL
PISTIL
PISTOL
POSTAL
RASCAL
RESELL
TASSEL
TUSSAL
UNSEAL
VASSAL
VESSEL
VESTAL
VISUAL

•••SL•
ENISLE
FOCSLE
GRISLY
HASSLE
MEASLY
PUSSLY
TOUSLE
TUSSLE

•••S•L
BURSAL
CAUSAL
CHISEL
CONSUL
CRESOL
DAMSEL
DIESEL
DORSAL
DOSSAL
DOSSEL
DOSSIL
FOSSIL
HANSEL
HASSEL
MENSAL
MISSAL
MORSEL
MUSSEL
PODSOL
TARSAL
TASSEL
TEASEL
TINSEL
TONSIL
TUSSAL
VASSAL
VESSEL
WEASEL

SM••••
SMACKS
SMALLS
SMALTI
SMALTO
SMARMY
SMARTS
SMAZES
SMEARS
SMEARY
SMELLS
SMELLY
SMELTS
SMILAX
SMILED
SMILER
SMILES
SMIRCH
SMIRKS
SMITER
SMITES
SMITHS
SMITHY
SMOCKS
SMOKED
SMOKER
SMOKES
SMOLTS
SMOOCH
SMOOTH
SMUDGE
SMUDGY
SMUGLY
SMUTCH
SMUTTY

S•M•••
SAMARA
SAMBAS
SAMBOS
SAMBUR
SAMIAN
SAMIEL
SAMITE
SAMLET
SAMMYS
SAMOAN
SAMPAN
SAMPLE
SAMSHU
SAMSON
SAMUEL
SEMELE
SEMEME
SEMITE
SEMPRE
SIMARS
SIMEON
SIMIAN
SIMILE
SIMLIN
SIMMER
SIMNEL
SIMONE
SIMONS
SIMONY
SIMOOM
SIMPER
SIMPLE
SIMPLY
SOMATA
SOMATO
SOMBER
SOMITE
SUMACS
SUMMED
SUMMER
SUMMIT
SUMMON
SUMNER
SYMBOL

S••M••
SALMIS
SALMON
SAMMYS
SCAMPI
SCAMPS
SCHMOS
SCUMMY
SEAMAN
SEAMED
SEAMEN
SEAMER
SEAMUS
SEEMED
SEEMER
SEEMLY
SERMON
SHAMAN
SHAMED
SHAMES
SHAMMY
SHAMUS
SHIMMY
SIGMAS
SIMMER
SKIMOS
SKIMPS
SKIMPY
SKYMAN
SKYMEN
SLIMED
SLIMES
SLIMLY
SLIMSY
SLUMMY
SLUMPS
SOCMAN
SOCMEN
SPUMED
SPUMES
STAMEN
STAMIN
STAMPS
STOMAT
STOMPS
STUMPS
STUMPY
STYMIE
SUBMIT
SUMMED
SUMMER
SUMMIT
SUMMON
SUOMIC
SWAMIS
SWAMPS
SWAMPY

S•••M•
SALAMI
SALOME
SCHEMA
SCHEME
SCRAMS
SCRIMP
SCRUMS
SCUMMY
SEDUMS
SEISMO
SEISMS
SEMEME
SERUMS
SESAME
SHAMMY
SHAWMS
SHIMMY
SHRIMP
SLUMMY
SMARMY
SODOMY
SOLEMN
SPASMS
SPERMO
SQUAMA
STEAMS
STEAMY
STIGMA
STORMS
STORMY
STROMA
STRUMA
STRUMS
SWARMS

S••••M
SACHEM
SACRUM
SADISM
SALAAM
SCHISM
SCREAM
SCUTUM
SELDOM
SEPTUM
SEXISM
SHIISM
SIKKIM
SIMOOM
SLALOM
SODIUM
SPUTUM
SQUIRM
STREAM
SUFISM
SYSTEM

•SM•••
OSMIUM
OSMOND
OSMOSE
OSMUND

•S•M••
ASHMAN
ASHMEN
ISOMER

•S••M•
ASSUME
ASTHMA
ESKIMO
PSALMS

•S•••M
ASARUM
ASYLUM
ESTEEM
OSMIUM

••SM••
BUSMAN
BUSMEN
COSMIC
COSMOS
DESMAN
DESMID
DISMAL
DISMAY
GASMAN
GASMEN
GISMOS
KISMET
TASMAN
YASMAK

••S•M•
ASSUME
BESOMS
BOSOMS
RESUME
SESAME

••S••M
ANSELM
BESEEM
CESIUM
CUSTOM
DISARM
MOSLEM
MUSEUM
MUSLIM
PASSIM
POSSUM
SYSTEM
UNSEAM
WISDOM

•••SM•
ABYSMS
CHASMS
MIASMA
PLASMA
PLASMO
PRISMS
SEISMO
SEISMS
SPASMS

•••S•M
BALSAM
DORSUM
GYPSUM
HANSOM
JETSAM
OMASUM
PASSIM
POSSUM
RANSOM

••••SM
AUTISM
BABISM
CHIASM
CHRISM
CIVISM
CUBISM
EGOISM
EONISM
HOLISM
IODISM
LYRISM
MAOISM
MOMISM
MONISM
MUTISM
NANISM
NAZISM
NOMISM
NUDISM
OBIISM
ORGASM
PURISM
RACISM
SADISM
SCHISM
SEXISM
SHIISM
SUFISM
TAOISM
THEISM
TRUISM
VERISM

SN••••
SNACKS
SNAFUS
SNAGGY
SNAILS
SNAKED
SNAKES
SNAPPY
SNARED
SNARER
SNARES
SNARLS
SNARLY
SNATCH
SNATHE
SNATHS
SNEAKS
SNEAKY
SNEERS
SNEEZE
SNEEZY
SNELLS
SNICKS
SNIFFS
SNIFFY
SNIPED
SNIPER
SNIPES
SNIPPY
SNITCH
SNIVEL
SNOCAT
SNOODS
SNOOKS
SNOOPS
SNOOPY
SNOOTS
SNOOTY
SNOOZE
SNORED
SNORER
SNORES
SNORTS
SNOTTY
SNOUTS
SNOWED
SNUFFS
SNUFFY
SNUGLY

S•N•••
SANDAL
SANDED
SANDER
SANDHI
SANDRA
SANDYS
SANELY
SANEST
SANGAR
SANGER
SANGUI
SANIES
SANITY
SANJAK
SANNUP
SANSAR
SANSEI
SANTOL
SENARY
SENATE
SENDAL
SENDER
SENECA
SENILE
SENIOR
SENLAC
SENNAS
SENNET
SENNIT
SENORA
SENSED
SENSES
SENSOR
SENTRY
SINBAD
SINEWS
SINEWY
SINFUL
SINGED
SINGER
SINGES
SINGLE
SINGLY
SINKER
SINNED
SINNER
SINTER
SONANT
SONARS
SONATA
SONDER
SONIAS
SONNET
SONYAS
SUNBOW
SUNDAE
SUNDAY
SUNDER
SUNDEW
SUNDOG
SUNDRY
SUNKEN
SUNLIT
SUNNAH
SUNNED
SUNSET
SUNUPS
SYNDET
SYNDIC
SYNODS
SYNTAX
SYNURA

S••N••
SAINTS
SANNUP
SAUNAS
SCANTY
SCENDS
SCENES
SCENIC
SCENTS
SCONCE
SCONES
SEANCE
SEINED
SEINER
SEINES
SENNAS
SENNET
SENNIT
SHANKS
SHANTY
SHINDY
SHINED
SHINER
SHINES
SHINNY
SHINTO
SHUNTS
SIDNEY
SIENNA
SIGNAL
SIGNED
SIGNER
SIGNET
SIGNOR
SIMNEL
SINNED
SINNER
SKINKS
SKINNY
SKUNKS
SLANGY
SLANTS
SLINGS
SLINKS
SLINKY
SONNET
SOONER
SOUNDS
SPANKS
SPENDS
SPINAL
SPINEL
SPINES
SPINET
SPINNY
SPONGE
SPONGY
SPUNKY
STANCE
STANCH
STANDS
STANZA
STENCH
STENOG
STINGS
STINGY
STINKS
STINTS
STONED
STONER
STONES
STUNTS
SUMNER
SUNNAH
SUNNED
SWANEE
SWANKY
SWINGE
SWINGS
SYDNEY

S•••N•
SABINA
SABINE
SABINS
SALINE
SALONS
SARONG
SASINS
SATANG
SATING
SATINS
SATINY
SAVANT
SAVING
SAVINS
SAWING
SAXONS
SAXONY
SAYING
SCIONS
SCORNS
SECANT
SECOND
SECUND
SEDANS
SEEING
SEJANT
SELENE
SELENO
SERENA
SERENE
SERINE
SERINS
SETONS
SEVENS
SEWING
SEXING
SHEENS
SHEENY
SHINNY
SHRANK
SHRINE
SHRINK
SHRUNK
SHYING
SIDING
SIENNA
SILENI
SILENT
SIMONE
SIMONS
SIMONY
SIRENS
SIRING
SITINS
SIZING
SKEANS
SKEINS
SKIING
SKINNY
SKYING
SLUING
SOIGNE
SOLAND
SOLANO
SOLANS
SOLENT
SOLING
SONANT
SOWING
SOZINE
SOZINS
SPAWNS
SPHENE
SPHENO
SPHINX
SPINNY
SPLENO
SPLINE
SPLINT
SPOONS
SPOONY
SPRANG
SPRING
SPRINT
SPRUNG
SPURNS
SPYING
SQUINT
STAINS
STEINS
STERNA
STERNO
STERNS
STRAND
STRING
STRONG
STYING
SUPINE
SUSANS
SWAINS
SWOONS
SYRINX

S••••N
SABEAN
SADDEN
SAIGON
SAIPAN
SALMON
SALOON
SAMIAN
SAMOAN
SAMPAN
SAMSON
SARGON
SATEEN
SATURN
SCREEN
SEAMAN
SEAMEN
SEAPEN
SEASON

6

SEAWAN
SECERN
SEISIN
SEIZIN
SELSYN
SEQUIN
SEREIN
SERMON
SEXTAN
SEXTON
SHAKEN
SHAMAN
SHAPEN
SHARON
SHAVEN
SHOGUN
SHOOIN
SHORAN
SHUTIN
SICKEN
SILKEN
SILVAN
SIMEON
SIMIAN
SIMLIN
SIOUAN
SIPHON
SISKIN
SKYMAN
SKYMEN
SLIPON
SLOGAN
SLOVEN
SOCMAN
SOCMEN
SODDEN
SOFTEN
SOLEMN
SOLION
SPAVIN
SPLEEN
SPOKEN
SPRAIN
STALIN
STAMEN
STAMIN
STEFAN
STEPAN
STEPIN
STEVEN
STOLEN
STOLON
STRAIN
STREWN
SUBORN
SUDDEN
SULLEN
SULTAN
SUMMON
SUNKEN
SWEDEN
SYLVAN
SYRIAN

•S•N••

USANCE

•S••N•

ASCEND
ASCENT
ASIANS
ASKANT
ASKING
ASLANT
ASPENS
ASSENT
ESCENT
ESPANA
ESSENE
ISLAND
ISLING
OSCANS
OSCINE
OSMOND
OSMUND

•S•••N

ASHMAN
ASHMEN
ASSIGN
ASTERN
ISOGON
OSBORN
OSSEIN
OSSIAN

••SN••

DISNEY
MESNES
UNSNAP

••S•N•

ABSENT
ARSINE
ASSENT
BASING
BASINS
BUSING
CASING
CASINO
COSINE
DOSING
EASING
ESSENE
FUSING
HOSING
INSANE
JASONS
LOSING
LYSINE
LYSING
LYSINS
MASONS
MESONS
MUSING
NOSING
POSING
RESEND
RESENT
RESINS
RISING
ROSING
ROSINS
ROSINY
RUSINE
SASINS
SUSANS
TISANE
UNSUNG
URSINE
VISHNU
VISING
WISING

••S••N

ASSIGN
AUSTEN
AUSTIN
BASION
BOSTON
BUSKIN
BUSMAN
BUSMEN
CASEIN
CASERN
COSIGN
DESIGN
DESMAN
DISOWN
EASTON
ENSIGN
FASTEN
FUSAIN
FUSION
GASCON
GASKIN
GASMAN
GASMEN
GASTON
GOSHEN
HASTEN
INSPAN
JUSTIN
LESION
LESSEN
LESSON
LISBON
LISTEN
MASCON
MESIAN
MUSLIN
NASION
OSSEIN
OSSIAN
PISTON
RESIGN
RUSKIN
SISKIN
TASMAN
TESTON
TUSCAN
UNSEEN
VISION
WYSTAN

•••SN•

DOESNT
FRESNO
PUISNE

•••S•N

ALISON
ARISEN
BOLSON
BUNSEN
CARSON
CHOSEN
COUSIN
DAMSON
DAWSON
DOBSON
EDISON
GIBSON
GODSON
HAUSEN
HUDSON
JONSON
KAMSIN
KANSAN
LESSEN
LESSON
LOOSEN
MAISON
MYOSIN
NELSON
PARSON
PEASEN
PEPSIN
PERSON
POISON
PRISON
PTISAN
RAISIN
RAMSON
REASON
ROBSON
SAMSON
SEASON
SEISIN
SELSYN
TELSON
TOCSIN
TUCSON
UNISON
VINSON
WATSON
WILSON
WORSEN

SO••••

SOAKED
SOAKER
SOAPED
SOARED
SOARER
SOBBED
SOBERS
SOCAGE
SOCCER
SOCIAL
SOCKED
SOCKET
SOCLES
SOCMAN
SOCMEN
SOCRED
SODDED
SODDEN
SODIUM
SODOMY
SOEVER
SOFFIT
SOFTAS
SOFTEN
SOFTER
SOFTLY
SOIGNE
SOILED
SOIREE
SOLACE
SOLAND
SOLANO
SOLANS
SOLDER
SOLELY
SOLEMN
SOLENT
SOLIDI
SOLIDS
SOLING
SOLION
SOLOED
SOLUTE
SOLVED
SOLVER
SOLVES
SOMATA
SOMATO
SOMBER
SOMITE
SONANT
SONARS
SONATA
SONDER
SONIAS
SONNET
SONYAS
SOONER
SOOTED
SOOTHE
SOPHIA
SOPHIE
SOPPED
SORDID
SORELS
SORELY
SOREST
SORGHO
SORGOS
SORREL
SORROW
SORTED
SORTIE
SOTHIC
SOTHIS
SOTOLS
SOUARI
SOUGHS
SOUGHT
SOULED
SOUNDS
SOURCE
SOURED
SOURER
SOURLY
SOUSED
SOUSES
SOVIET
SOWARS
SOWERS
SOWING
SOZINE
SOZINS

S•O•••

SCOFFS
SCOLDS
SCOLEX
SCONCE
SCONES
SCOOPS
SCOOTS
SCOPES
SCOPUS
SCORCH
SCORED
SCORER
SCORES
SCORIA
SCORNS
SCOTCH
SCOTER
SCOTIA
SCOTTS
SCOURS
SCOUTS
SCOWLS
SFORZA
SHOALS
SHOALY
SHOATS
SHOCKS
SHODDY
SHOERS
SHOFAR
SHOGUN
SHOJIS
SHOOED
SHOOIN
SHOOTS
SHOPPE
SHORAN
SHORED
SHORES

SHORLS
SHORTS
SHOTES
SHOULD
SHOUTS
SHOVED
SHOVEL
SHOVER
SHOVES
SHOWED
SHOWER
SIOUAN
SLOGAN
SLOOPS
SLOPED
SLOPER
SLOPES
SLOPPY
SLOSHY
SLOTHS
SLOUCH
SLOUGH
SLOVAK
SLOVEN
SLOWED
SLOWER
SLOWLY
SMOCKS
SMOKED
SMOKER
SMOKES
SMOLTS
SMOOCH
SMOOTH
SNOCAT
SNOODS
SNOOKS
SNOOPS
SNOOPY
SNOOTS
SNOOTY
SNOOZE
SNORED
SNORER
SNORES
SNORTS
SNOTTY
SNOUTS
SNOWED
SOONER
SOOTED
SOOTHE
SPOILS
SPOILT
SPOKED
SPOKEN
SPOKES
SPONGE
SPONGY
SPOOFS
SPOOKS
SPOOKY
SPOOLS
SPOONS
SPOONY
SPOORS
SPORED
SPORES
SPORTS
SPORTY
SPOTTY
SPOUSE
SPOUTS
STOATS
STOCKS
STOCKY
STODGE
STODGY
STOGEY
STOICS
STOKED
STOKER
STOKES
STOLED
STOLEN
STOLES
STOLID
STOLON
STOMAT
STOMPS
STONED
STONER
STONES
STOOGE
STOOKS
STOOLS
STOOPS
STOPED
STOPES
STORAX
STORED
STORES
STOREY
STORKS
STORMS
STORMY
STOUPS
STOUTS
STOVER
STOVES
STOWED
SUOMIC
SWOONS
SWOOPS
SWORDS

S••O••

SABOTS
SAJOUS
SALOME
SALONS
SALOON
SALOOP
SAMOAN
SARONG
SATORI
SAVORS
SAVORY
SAXONS
SAXONY
SCHOOL
SCHORL
SCIONS
SCOOPS
SCOOTS
SCRODS
SCROLL
SCROOP
SECOND
SENORA
SEPOYS
SEROUS
SEROWS
SETOFF
SETONS
SETOSE
SETOUS
SHOOED
SHOOIN
SHOOTS
SHROFF
SHROUD
SHROVE
SILOED
SIMONE
SIMONS
SIMONY
SIMOOM
SLOOPS
SMOOCH
SMOOTH
SNOODS
SNOOKS
SNOOPS
SNOOPY
SNOOTS
SNOOTY
SNOOZE
SODOMY
SOLOED
SOTOLS
SPOOFS
SPOOKS
SPOOKY
SPOOLS
SPOONS
SPOONY
SPOORS
SPROUT
STOOGE
STOOKS
STOOLS
STOOPS
STRODE
STROKE
STROLL
STROMA
STRONG
STROPS
STROUD
STROVE
SUBORN
SWOONS
SWOOPS
SYNODS

S•••O•

SAIGON
SAILOR
SALLOW
SALMON
SALOON
SALOOP
SALVOR
SALVOS
SAMBOS
SAMSON
SANTOL
SARGON
SARTOR
SAVIOR
SCHMOS
SCHOOL
SCROOP
SEADOG
SEASON
SECTOR
SEISOR
SEIZOR
SELDOM
SENIOR
SENSOR
SERMON
SERVOS
SETTOS
SEXTON
SHADOW
SHAKOS
SHARON
SHILOH
SIGNOR
SIMEON
SIMOOM
SIPHON
SKIMOS
SLALOM
SLIPON
SOLION
SORGOS
SORROW
SPIGOT
STATOR
STENOG
STEROL
STOLON
STUPOR
SUCCOR
SUITOR
SUMMON
SUNBOW
SUNDOG
SYMBOL

S••••O

SAPPHO
SCHIZO
SCIPIO
SCLERO
SCYPHO
SEISMO
SELENO
SHACKO
SHINTO
SIDERO
SILICO
SMALTO
SOLANO
SOMATO
SORGHO
SPERMO
SPHENO
SPLENO
STAURO
STEREO
STERNO
STETHO
STUCCO
STUDIO
SUBITO
SULPHO

•SO•••

ISOBAR
ISOBEL
ISOGON
ISOHEL
ISOLDE
ISOMER
ISOPOD

•S•O••

ASCOTS
ASHORE
ASLOPE
ASSORT
ESCORT
ESTOPS
FSTOPS
OSBORN
OSMOND
OSMOSE

•S••O•

ESCROW
ISADOR
ISIDOR
ISOGON
ISOPOD

•S•••O

ASTERO
ESCUDO
ESKIMO
PSEUDO
PSYCHO

••SO••

ABSORB
ADSORB
ASSORT
BESOMS
BESOTS
BOSOMS
DESOXY
DISOWN
ENSOUL
INSOLE
INSOUL
JASONS
MASONS
MASORA
MESONS
RESOLD
RESOLE
RESORB
RESORT
UNSOLD
VISORS

••S•O•

BASION
BASSOS
BESTOW
BISHOP
BOSTON
CASHOO
CASTOR
CISCOS
COSMOS
CUSSOS
CUSTOM
CUSTOS
DESPOT
EASTON
FUSION
GASCON
GASTON
GESSOS
GISMOS
HESIOD
HYSSOP
LASSOS
LESION
LESSON
LESSOR
LISBOA
LISBON
MASCON
MASCOT
MOSCOW
NASION
NESTOR
NOSHOW
NOSTOC
PASTOR
PISTOL
PISTON
ROSCOE
TESTON
UNSTOP
UPSHOT
VISION
WISDOM
XYSTOS

••S••O
AUSTRO
BASUTO
BISTRO
CASHOO
CASINO
CASTRO
GASTRO
PASHTO
VESICO

•••SO•
ALISON
AVISOS
BASSOS
BOLSON
CANSOS
CARSON
CENSOR
CRESOL
CRUSOE
CUSSOS
DAMSON
DAWSON
DOBSON
EDISON
GESSOS
GIBSON
GODSON
HANSOM
HUDSON
HYSSOP
JONSON
LASSOS
LESSON
LESSOR
MAISON
NELSON
PARSON
PERSON
PODSOL
POISON
PRISON
RAMSON
RANSOM
REASON
ROBSON
SAMSON
SEASON
SEISOR
SENSOR
TELSON
TENSOR
TORSOS
TUCSON
UNISON
VERSOS
VINSON
WATSON
WILSON

•••S•O
ARISTO
BLASTO
FIASCO
FRESCO
FRESNO
GLOSSO
PHYSIO
PLASMO
POUSTO
PRESTO
SEISMO
UNESCO

••••SO
ALONSO
ARIOSO
CARUSO
CHRYSO
GLOSSO

SP••••
SPACED
SPACER
SPACES
SPADED
SPADER
SPADES
SPADIX
SPAHIS
SPAITS
SPALLS
SPANKS
SPARED
SPARER
SPARES
SPARGE
SPARKS
SPARRY
SPARSE
SPARTA
SPASMS
SPATES
SPATHE
SPAVIN
SPAWNS
SPAYED
SPEAKS
SPEARS
SPECIE
SPECKS
SPEECH
SPEEDS
SPEEDY
SPEISS
SPELLS
SPENDS
SPERMO
SPERRY
SPEWED
SPHENE
SPHENO
SPHERE
SPHERY
SPHINX
SPICAE
SPICED
SPICER
SPICES
SPIDER
SPIELS
SPIERS
SPIFFY
SPIGOT
SPIKED
SPIKES
SPILED
SPILES
SPILLS
SPILTH
SPINAL
SPINEL
SPINES
SPINET
SPINNY
SPIRAL
SPIREA
SPIRED
SPIRES
SPIRIT
SPIRTS
SPITAL
SPITED
SPITES
SPLAKE
SPLASH
SPLATS
SPLAYS
SPLEEN
SPLENO
SPLICE
SPLINE
SPLINT
SPLITS
SPOILS
SPOILT
SPOKED
SPOKEN
SPOKES
SPONGE
SPONGY
SPOOFS
SPOOKS
SPOOKY
SPOOLS
SPOONS
SPOONY
SPOORS
SPORED
SPORES
SPORTS
SPORTY
SPOTTY
SPOUSE
SPOUTS
SPRAGS
SPRAIN
SPRANG
SPRATS
SPRAWL
SPRAYS
SPREAD
SPREES
SPRIER
SPRIGS
SPRING
SPRINT
SPRITE
SPRITS
SPROUT
SPRUCE
SPRUES
SPRUNG
SPRYER
SPRYLY
SPUMED
SPUMES
SPUNKY
SPURGE
SPURNS
SPURRY
SPURTS
SPUTUM
SPYING

S•P•••
SAPHAR
SAPPED
SAPPER
SAPPHO
SEPALS
SEPIAS
SEPOYS
SEPSIS
SEPTAL
SEPTET
SEPTIC
SEPTUM
SIPHON
SIPPED
SIPPER
SIPPET
SOPHIA
SOPHIE
SOPPED
SUPERB
SUPERS
SUPINE
SUPPED
SUPPER
SUPPLE
SUPPLY
SYPHER

S••P••
SAIPAN
SALPAS
SALPID
SAMPAN
SAMPLE
SAPPED
SAPPER
SAPPHO
SCAPES
SCIPIO
SCOPES
SCOPUS
SCYPHI
SCYPHO
SEAPEN
SECPAR
SEEPED
SEMPRE
SHAPED
SHAPEN
SHAPER
SHAPES
SHOPPE
SIMPER
SIMPLE
SIMPLY
SIPPED
SIPPER
SIPPET
SLIPON
SLIPUP
SLOPED
SLOPER
SLOPES
SLOPPY
SNAPPY
SNIPED
SNIPER
SNIPES
SNIPPY
SOAPED
SOPPED
STAPES
STAPLE
STEPAN
STEPIN
STEPPE
STEPUP
STIPEL
STIPES
STOPED
STOPES
STUPAS
STUPES
STUPID
STUPOR
SULPHA
SULPHO
SUPPED
SUPPER
SUPPLE
SUPPLY
SWIPED
SWIPES
SWIPLE
SYLPHS
SYLPHY

S•••P•
SARAPE
SCALPS
SCAMPI
SCAMPS
SCARPS
SCAUPS
SCOOPS
SCRAPE
SCRAPS
SCRIPS
SCRIPT
SCULPT
SERAPE
SERAPH
SETUPS
SHARPS
SHERPA
SHOPPE
SIRUPS
SIRUPY
SKIMPS
SKIMPY
SLEEPS
SLEEPY
SLOOPS
SLOPPY
SLUMPS
SLURPS
SNAPPY
SNIPPY
SNOOPS
SNOOPY
STAMPS
STEEPS
STEPPE
STIRPS
STOMPS
STOOPS
STOUPS
STRAPS
STRIPE
STRIPS
STRIPT
STRIPY
STROPS
STUMPS
STUMPY
SUNUPS
SWAMPS
SWAMPY
SWEEPS
SWEEPY
SWOOPS
SYRUPS
SYRUPY

S••••P
SALOOP
SANNUP
SATRAP
SCRIMP
SCROOP
SHRIMP
SKYCAP
SLIPUP
STEPUP

•SP•••
ASPECT

6

ASPENS
ASPERS
ASPICS
ASPIRE
ESPANA
ESPIAL
ESPIED
ESPIES
ESPRIT
OSPREY

•S•P••

ISOPOD

•S••P•

ASLOPE
ESCAPE
ESTOPS
FSTOPS
USURPS

•S•••P

ASLEEP
ESCARP

••SP••

AUSPEX
CASPAR
CASPER
CUSPED
CUSPID
CUSPIS
DESPOT
DISPEL
GASPAR
GASPED
GASPER
GOSPEL
HASPED
HISPID
INSPAN
JASPER
KASPAR
LISPED
LISPER
RASPED
RASPER
VESPER
VESPID
WISPED

••S•P•

JOSEPH

••S••P

BISHOP
GOSSIP
HYSSOP
INSTEP
MISHAP
PUSHUP
TOSSUP
UNSHIP
UNSNAP
UNSTEP
UNSTOP

•••SP•

CLASPS
CRISPS
CRISPY
GRASPS
KNOSPS
PHOSPH

•••S•P

CATSUP
GOSSIP
HYSSOP
TOSSUP

••••SP

TRANSP

SQ••••

SQUABS
SQUADS
SQUALL
SQUAMA
SQUARE
SQUASH
SQUATS
SQUAWK
SQUAWS
SQUEAK
SQUEAL
SQUIBS
SQUIDS
SQUILL
SQUINT
SQUIRE
SQUIRM
SQUIRT
SQUISH

S•Q•••

SEQUEL
SEQUIN

S••Q••

SESQUI

••SQ••

BASQUE
BISQUE
CASQUE
MASQUE
MOSQUE
RISQUE
SESQUI

SR••••

SRADHA

S•R•••

SARAHS
SARAPE
SARGON
SARONG
SARSAR
SARTOR
SARTRE
SCRAGS
SCRAMS
SCRAPE
SCRAPS
SCRAWL
SCREAK
SCREAM
SCREED
SCREEN
SCREWS
SCREWY
SCRIBE
SCRIMP
SCRIPS
SCRIPT
SCRIVE
SCRODS
SCROLL
SCROOP
SCRUBS
SCRUFF
SCRUMS
SERACS
SERAIS
SERAPE
SERAPH
SERBIA
SERDAB
SEREIN
SERENA
SERENE
SERIAL
SERIES
SERIFS
SERINE
SERINS
SERMON
SEROUS
SEROWS
SERUMS
SERVAL
SERVED
SERVER
SERVES
SERVOS
SHRANK
SHREDS
SHREWD
SHREWS
SHRIEK
SHRIFT
SHRIKE
SHRILL
SHRIMP
SHRINE
SHRINK
SHRIVE
SHROFF
SHROUD
SHROVE
SHRUBS
SHRUGS
SHRUNK
SIRDAR
SIRENS
SIRING
SIRIUS
SIRUPS
SIRUPY
SORDID
SORELS
SORELY
SOREST
SORGHO
SORGOS
SORREL
SORROW
SORTED
SORTIE
SPRAGS
SPRAIN
SPRANG
SPRATS
SPRAWL
SPRAYS
SPREAD
SPREES
SPRIER
SPRIGS
SPRING
SPRINT
SPRITE
SPRITS
SPROUT
SPRUCE
SPRUES
SPRUNG
SPRYER
SPRYLY
STRAFE
STRAIN
STRAIT
STRAKE
STRAND
STRAPS
STRASS
STRATA
STRATI
STRAWS
STRAWY
STRAYS
STREAK
STREAM
STREET
STRESS
STREWN
STREWS
STRIAE
STRICK
STRICT
STRIDE
STRIFE
STRIKE
STRING
STRIPE
STRIPS
STRIPT
STRIPY
STRIVE
STRODE
STROKE
STROLL
STROMA
STRONG
STROPS
STROUD
STROVE
STRUCK
STRUMA
STRUMS
STRUTS
SURAHS
SURELY
SUREST
SURETY
SURFED
SURFER
SURGED
SURGER
SURGES
SURREY
SURTAX
SURVEY
SYRIAC
SYRIAN
SYRINX
SYRUPS
SYRUPY

S••R••

SABRAS
SACRAL
SACRED
SACRUM
SATRAP
SAUREL
SAURUS
SCARAB
SCARCE
SCARED
SCARER
SCARES
SCARFS
SCARPS
SCORCH
SCORED
SCORER
SCORES
SCORIA
SCORNS
SCURFY
SCURRY
SCURVE
SCURVY
SEARCH
SEARED
SECRET
SEURAT
SFORZA
SHARDS
SHARED
SHARER
SHARES
SHARKS
SHARON
SHARPS
SHERDS
SHERIF
SHERPA
SHERRY
SHIRES
SHIRKS
SHIRRS
SHIRTS
SHORAN
SHORED
SHORES
SHORLS
SHORTS
SIERRA
SIGRID
SKIRRS
SKIRTS
SLURPS
SLURRY
SMARMY
SMARTS
SMIRCH
SMIRKS
SNARED
SNARER
SNARES
SNARLS
SNARLY
SNORED
SNORER
SNORES
SNORTS
SOARED
SOARER
SOCRED
SOIREE
SORREL
SORROW
SOURCE
SOURED
SOURER
SOURLY
SPARED
SPARER
SPARES
SPARGE
SPARKS
SPARRY
SPARSE
SPARTA
SPERMO
SPERRY
SPIRAL
SPIREA
SPIRED
SPIRES

SPIRIT
SPIRTS
SPORED
SPORES
SPORTS
SPORTY
SPURGE
SPURNS
SPURRY
SPURTS
STARCH
STARED
STARER
STARES
STARRY
STARTS
STARVE
STEREO
STERES
STERIC
STERNA
STERNO
STERNS
STEROL
STIRKS
STIRPS
STORAX
STORED
STORES
STOREY
STORKS
STORMS
STORMY
STURDY
SUCRES
SURREY
SUTRAS
SWARAJ
SWARDS
SWARMS
SWARTH
SWARTY
SWERVE
SWIRLS
SWIRLY
SWORDS

S•••R•

SABERS
SAFARI
SAHARA
SAKERS
SALARY
SAMARA
SANDRA
SARTRE
SATARA
SATIRE
SATORI
SATURN
SATYRS
SAVERS
SAVORS
SAVORY
SAWERS
SAYERS
SCHORL
SCLERA
SCLERO
SCOURS
SCURRY
SECERN
SECURE
SEDERS
SEMPRE
SENARY
SENORA
SENTRY
SEVERE
SEVERS
SEWARD
SEWERS
SHEARS
SHEERS
SHERRY
SHIRRS
SHOERS
SIDERO
SIERRA
SIEURS
SIMARS
SISERA
SITARS
SIZARS
SKIERS
SKIRRS
SLURRY
SMEARS
SMEARY
SNEERS
SOBERS
SONARS
SOUARI
SOWARS
SOWERS
SPARRY
SPEARS
SPERRY
SPHERE
SPHERY
SPIERS
SPOORS
SPURRY
SQUARE
SQUIRE
SQUIRM
SQUIRT
STAIRS
STARRY
STAURO
STEERS
STUART
SUBORN
SUBURB
SUDARY
SUGARS
SUGARY
SULTRY
SUNDRY
SUPERB
SUPERS
SUTURE
SWEARS
SYNURA

S••••R

SACKER
SADDER
SAGGAR
SAGGER
SAGIER
SAILER
SAILOR
SALTER
SALVER
SALVOR
SAMBUR
SANDER
SANGAR
SANGER
SANSAR
SAPHAR
SAPPER
SARSAR
SARTOR
SAUCER
SAUGER
SAVIOR
SAWYER
SCALAR
SCALER
SCARER
SCORER
SCOTER
SEALER
SEAMER
SECPAR
SECTOR
SEEDER
SEEKER
SEEMER
SEGGAR
SEINER
SEISOR
SEIZER
SEIZOR
SELLER
SENDER
SENIOR
SENSOR
SERVER
SETTER
SEXIER
SHAKER
SHAPER
SHARER
SHAVER
SHEWER
SHIKAR
SHINER
SHIVER
SHOFAR
SHOVER
SHOWER
SICKER
SIDDUR
SIDLER
SIFTER
SIGNER
SIGNOR
SILVER
SIMMER
SIMPER
SINGER
SINKER
SINNER
SINTER
SIPPER
SIRDAR
SISTER
SITTER
SIZIER
SKATER
SKEWER
SKIVER
SLATER
SLAVER
SLAYER
SLICER
SLIDER
SLIVER
SLOPER
SLOWER
SMILER
SMITER
SMOKER
SNARER
SNIPER
SNORER
SOAKER
SOARER
SOCCER
SOEVER
SOFTER
SOLDER
SOLVER
SOMBER
SONDER
SOONER
SOURER
SPACER
SPADER
SPARER
SPICER
SPIDER
SPRIER
SPRYER
STAGER
STALER
STARER
STATER
STATOR
STAYER
STELAR
STIVER
STOKER
STONER
STOVER
STUPOR
STYLAR
STYLER
SUBTER
SUCCOR
SUCKER
SUFFER
SUITOR
SULFUR
SUMMER
SUMNER
SUNDER
SUPPER
SURFER
SURGER
SUTLER
SYPHER

•SR•••

ISRAEL

•S•R••

ASARUM
ASTRAL
ASTRAY
ASTRID
ESCROW
ESPRIT
ESTRAY
ESTRUS
OSIRIS
OSPREY
USURER
USURPS

•S••R•

ASBURY
ASGARD
ASHORE
ASKERS
ASPERS
ASPIRE
ASSERT
ASSORT
ASSURE
ASTERI
ASTERN
ASTERO
ASTERS
ESCARP
ESCORT
ESKERS
ESTERS
OSBERT
OSBORN
OSCARS
OSIERS
TSHIRT
USHERS

•S•••R

ASHIER
ASHLAR
ESCHAR
ESTHER
ISADOR
ISHTAR
ISIDOR
ISOBAR
ISOMER
ISSUER
USURER

••SR••

BASRAH

••S•R•

ABSORB
ABSURD
ADSORB
ASSERT
ASSORT
ASSURE
AUSTRO
BISTRO
CASERN
CASTRO
CESARE
CESURA
DESCRY
DESERT
DESIRE
DISARM
DOSERS
ENSURE
EXSERT
GASTRO
INSERT
INSURE
LASERS
LOSERS
MASERS
MASORA
MESSRS
MISERS
MISERY
PASTRY
POSERS
RESORB
RESORT
RISERS
ROSARY
ROSTRA
SISERA
TISHRI
UNSURE
VASARI
VESTRY
VISARD
VISORS

••S••R

ANSWER
AUSTER
BESTIR
BISTER

BUSTER
CASPAR
CASPER
CASTER
CASTOR
COSHER
COSTAR
CUSTER
DASHER
DISBAR
DOSSER
DUSTER
EASIER
EASTER
FASTER
FESTER
FISHER
FOSTER
FUSSER
GASPAR
GASPER
GUSHER
HESTER
HISSER
HOSIER
HUSKER
HUSSAR
HYSTER
INSTAR
ISSUER
JASPER
JESTER
JOSHER
KASPAR
KISSER
KOSHER
LASCAR
LASHER
LASTER
LESSER
LESSOR
LESTER
LISPER
LISTER
LUSHER
LUSTER
MASHER
MASKER
MASTER
MISTER
MUSHER
MUSTER
NASSER
NESTOR
NOSIER
OUSTER
OYSTER
PASSER
PASTER
PASTOR
PESTER
POSEUR
POSTER
PUSHER
RASHER
RASPER
RESTER
RISKER
ROSIER
ROSTER
RUSHER
SISTER
TASTER
TESTER
TUSKER
TUSSAR
ULSTER
VASTER
VESPER
WASHER
WASTER
WESTER
XYSTER
YESTER
ZOSTER

•••SR•

MESSRS

•••S•R

ABASER
ABUSER
AMUSER
BURSAR
CAESAR
CAUSER
CENSER
CENSOR
CHASER
CLOSER
DENSER
DOSSER
DOWSER
ERASER
FALSER
FUSSER
GEYSER
HAWSER
HISSER
HUSSAR
KAISER
KISSER
LAPSER
LESSER
LESSOR
LOOSER
MAUSER
MOUSER
NASSER
NURSER
PASSER
PAUSER
PROSER
PULSAR
PURSER
QUASAR
RAISER
RINSER
ROUSER
SANSAR
SARSAR
SEISOR
SENSOR
TEASER
TENSER
TENSOR
TERSER
TUSSAR
WORSER
WOWSER

S•S•••

SASHAY
SASHED
SASHES
SASINS
SASSED
SASSES
SESAME
SESQUI
SESTET
SISERA
SISKIN
SISTER
SUSANS
SUSIES
SUSLIK
SYSTEM

S••S••

SAMSHU
SAMSON
SANSAR
SANSEI
SARSAR
SASSED
SASSES
SEASON
SEESAW
SEISIN
SEISMO
SEISMS
SEISOR
SELSYN
SENSED
SENSES
SENSOR
SEPSIS
SHASTA
SIESTA
SLOSHY
SLUSHY
SOUSED
SOUSES
SPASMS
STASES
STASIS
SUNSET

S•••S•

SADISM
SADIST
SAFEST
SAGEST
SALISH
SANEST
SCHISM
SCHIST
SCHUSS
SETOSE
SEXISM
SEXIST
SHIEST
SHIISM
SHYEST
SIWASH
SLIEST
SLIMSY
SLYEST
SOREST
SPARSE
SPEISS
SPLASH
SPOUSE
SQUASH
SQUISH
STRASS
STRESS
SUFISM
SUREST

S••••S

SABERS
SABINS
SABLES
SABOTS
SABRAS
SADHUS
SADIES
SAHEBS
SAHIBS
SAIGAS
SAINTS
SAJOUS
SAKERS
SALADS
SALLYS
SALMIS
SALONS
SALPAS
SALVES
SALVOS
SAMBAS
SAMBOS
SAMMYS
SANDYS
SANIES
SARAHS
SASHES
SASINS
SASSES
SATINS
SATYRS
SAUCES
SAULTS
SAUNAS
SAURUS
SAUTES
SAVERS
SAVINS
SAVORS
SAWERS
SAXONS
SAYERS
SCALDS
SCALES
SCALPS
SCAMPS
SCAPES
SCARES
SCARFS
SCARPS
SCAUPS
SCENDS
SCENES
SCENTS
SCHMOS
SCHUSS
SCHWAS
SCIONS
SCOFFS
SCOLDS
SCONES
SCOOPS
SCOOTS
SCOPES
SCOPUS
SCORES
SCORNS
SCOTTS
SCOURS
SCOUTS
SCOWLS
SCRAGS
SCRAMS
SCRAPS
SCREWS
SCRIPS
SCRODS
SCRUBS
SCRUMS
SCUBAS
SCUFFS
SCULLS
SCUTES
SEAMUS
SEBATS
SEDANS
SEDERS
SEDGES
SEDUMS
SEINES
SEISMS
SEIZES
SELVES
SENNAS
SENSES
SEPALS
SEPIAS
SEPOYS
SEPSIS
SERACS
SERAIS
SERIES
SERIFS
SERINS
SEROUS
SEROWS
SERUMS
SERVES
SERVOS
SETONS
SETOUS
SETTOS
SETUPS
SEVENS
SEVERS
SEWERS
SHACKS
SHADES
SHAFTS
SHAKES
SHAKOS
SHALES
SHAMES
SHAMUS
SHANKS
SHAPES
SHARDS
SHARES
SHARKS
SHARPS
SHAVES
SHAWLS
SHAWMS
SHEARS
SHEENS
SHEERS
SHEETS
SHEIKS
SHELLS
SHERDS
SHIFTS
SHILLS
SHINES
SHIRES
SHIRKS
SHIRRS
SHIRTS
SHIVES
SHOALS
SHOATS
SHOCKS
SHOERS
SHOJIS
SHOOTS
SHORES
SHORLS
SHORTS
SHOTES
SHOUTS
SHOVES
SHREDS
SHREWS

SHRUBS
SHRUGS
SHUCKS
SHUNTS
SIBYLS
SIDLES
SIEGES
SIEURS
SIEVES
SIGHTS
SIGILS
SIGMAS
SILVAS
SIMARS
SIMONS
SINEWS
SINGES
SIRENS
SIRIUS
SIRUPS
SITARS
SITINS
SIXTES
SIXTHS
SIZARS
SKALDS
SKATES
SKEANS
SKEINS
SKIERS
SKIFFS
SKILLS
SKIMOS
SKIMPS
SKINKS
SKIRRS
SKIRTS
SKIVES
SKULKS
SKULLS
SKUNKS
SLACKS
SLAKES
SLANTS
SLATES
SLAVES
SLEEKS
SLEEPS
SLEETS
SLICES
SLICKS
SLIDES
SLIMES
SLINGS
SLINKS
SLOOPS
SLOPES
SLOTHS
SLUMPS
SLURPS
SMACKS
SMALLS
SMARTS
SMAZES

SMEARS
SMELLS
SMELTS
SMILES
SMIRKS
SMITES
SMITHS
SMOCKS
SMOKES
SMOLTS
SNACKS
SNAFUS
SNAILS
SNAKES
SNARES
SNARLS
SNATHS
SNEAKS
SNEERS
SNELLS
SNICKS
SNIFFS
SNIPES
SNOODS
SNOOKS
SNOOPS
SNOOTS
SNORES
SNORTS
SNOUTS
SNUFFS
SOBERS
SOCLES
SOFTAS
SOLANS
SOLIDS
SOLVES
SONARS
SONIAS
SONYAS
SORELS
SORGOS
SOTHIS
SOTOLS
SOUGHS
SOUNDS
SOUSES
SOWARS
SOWERS
SOZINS
SPACES
SPADES
SPAHIS
SPAITS
SPALLS
SPANKS
SPARES
SPARKS
SPASMS
SPATES
SPAWNS
SPEAKS
SPEARS
SPECKS

SPEEDS
SPEISS
SPELLS
SPENDS
SPICES
SPIELS
SPIERS
SPIKES
SPILES
SPILLS
SPINES
SPIRES
SPIRTS
SPITES
SPLATS
SPLAYS
SPLITS
SPOILS
SPOKES
SPOOFS
SPOOKS
SPOOLS
SPOONS
SPOORS
SPORES
SPORTS
SPOUTS
SPRAGS
SPRATS
SPRAYS
SPREES
SPRIGS
SPRITS
SPRUES
SPUMES
SPURNS
SPURTS
SQUABS
SQUADS
SQUATS
SQUAWS
SQUIBS
SQUIDS
STACKS
STACYS
STAFFS
STAGES
STAINS
STAIRS
STAKES
STALES
STALKS
STALLS
STAMPS
STANDS
STAPES
STARES
STARTS
STASES
STASIS
STATES
STATUS
STAVES
STEAKS

STEALS
STEAMS
STEEDS
STEELS
STEEPS
STEERS
STEINS
STELES
STERES
STERNS
STEVES
STICKS
STILES
STILLS
STILTS
STINGS
STINKS
STINTS
STIPES
STIRKS
STIRPS
STOATS
STOCKS
STOICS
STOKES
STOLES
STOMPS
STONES
STOOKS
STOOLS
STOOPS
STOPES
STORES
STORKS
STORMS
STOUPS
STOUTS
STOVES
STRAPS
STRASS
STRAWS
STRAYS
STRESS
STREWS
STRIPS
STROPS
STRUMS
STRUTS
STUFFS
STULLS
STUMPS
STUNTS
STUPAS
STUPES
STYLES
STYLUS
SUBAHS
SUCRES
SUEDES
SUGARS
SUITES
SULCUS
SUMACS
SUNUPS

SUPERS
SURAHS
SURGES
SUSANS
SUSIES
SUTRAS
SWAGES
SWAILS
SWAINS
SWALES
SWAMIS
SWAMPS
SWARDS
SWARMS
SWATHS
SWEARS
SWEATS
SWEDES
SWEEPS
SWEETS
SWELLS
SWIFTS
SWILLS
SWINGS
SWIPES
SWIRLS
SWOONS
SWOOPS
SWORDS
SYBILS
SYCEES
SYLPHS
SYLVAS
SYNODS
SYRUPS

•SS•••

ASSAIL
ASSAIS
ASSAYS
ASSENT
ASSERT
ASSESS
ASSETS
ASSIGN
ASSISI
ASSIST
ASSIZE
ASSORT
ASSUME
ASSURE
ESSAYS
ESSENE
ISSEIS
ISSUED
ISSUER
ISSUES
OSSEIN
OSSIAN
OSSIFY

•S••S•

ASSESS
ASSISI

ASSIST
OSMOSE
TSETSE

•S•••S

ASCOTS
ASIANS
ASIDES
ASKERS
ASPENS
ASPERS
ASPICS
ASSAIS
ASSAYS
ASSESS
ASSETS
ASTERS
ESKERS
ESPIES
ESSAYS
ESTERS
ESTOPS
ESTRUS
FSTOPS
ISAACS
ISLETS
ISSEIS
ISSUES
OSCANS
OSCARS
OSIERS
OSIRIS
PSALMS
PSHAWS
TSADES
USAGES
USHERS
USURPS

••SS••

BASSES
BASSET
BASSOS
BESSIE
BESSYS
BOSSED
BOSSES
BUSSED
BUSSES
BYSSUS
CASSIA
CASSIE
CASSIS
CISSIE
CISSYS
COSSES
COSSET
CUSSED
CUSSES
CUSSOS
DESSAU
DOSSAL
DOSSEL
DOSSER

DOSSIL
FESSES
FOSSAE
FOSSES
FOSSIL
FUSSED
FUSSER
FUSSES
GASSED
GASSES
GESSOS
GOSSIP
GUSSET
GUSSIE
HASSEL
HASSLE
HISSED
HISSER
HISSES
HUSSAR
HYSSOP
JESSED
JESSES
JESSIE
JOSSES
KISSED
KISSER
KISSES
LASSES
LASSIE
LASSOS
LESSEE
LESSEN
LESSER
LESSON
LESSOR
LOSSES
MASSED
MASSES
MASSIF
MESSED
MESSES
MESSRS
MISSAL
MISSED
MISSES
MISSIS
MISSUS
MOSSES
MUSSED
MUSSEL
MUSSES
NASSAU
NASSER
NESSUS
PASSED
PASSEE
PASSER
PASSES
PASSIM
PASSUS
POSSES
POSSET
POSSUM
PUSSES
PUSSEY
PUSSLY
RUSSET
RUSSIA
SASSED
SASSES
TASSEL
TASSET
TESSIE
TISSUE
TOSSED
TOSSES
TOSSUP
TUSSAH
TUSSAL
TUSSAR
TUSSIS
TUSSLE
VASSAL
VESSEL
WESSEX
YESSED
YESSES

••S•S•

ASSESS
ASSISI
ASSIST
DESIST
DISUSE
INSIST
MISUSE
OBSESS
RESIST
WISEST

••S••S

AISLES
ASSAIS
ASSAYS
ASSESS
ASSETS
BASHES
BASICS
BASILS
BASINS
BASSES
BASSOS
BASTES
BESETS
BESOMS
BESOTS
BESSYS
BOSHES
BOSOMS
BOSSES
BUSHES
BUSIES
BUSSES
BYSSUS
CASALS
CASHES
CASSIS
CASTES
CESTUS
CISCOS
CISSYS
COSHES
COSMOS
COSSES
CUSPIS
CUSSES
CUSSOS
CUSTOS
DASHES
DISCUS
DISHES
DOSERS
EASELS
ELSIES
ENSUES
ESSAYS
FASCES
FESSES
FISHES
FOSSES
FUSEES
FUSILS
FUSSES
GASHES
GASSES
GESSOS
GISMOS
GUSHES
HASHES
HASTES
HISSES
HUSHES
INSETS
ISSEIS
ISSUES
JASONS
JESSES
JOSHES
JOSIAS
JOSIES
JOSSES
JUSTUS
KISSES
LASERS
LASHES
LASSES
LASSOS
LOSERS
LOSSES
LUSHES
LYSINS
MASERS
MASHES
MASONS
MASSES
MESHES
MESNES
MESONS
MESSES
MESSRS
MISERS
MISSES
MISSIS
MISSUS
MOSEYS
MOSSES
MUSHES
MUSSES
NASALS
NESSUS
NISEIS
OBSESS
ONSETS
OUSELS
PASHAS
PASSES
PASSUS
PASTAS
PASTES
PISCES
PISHES
POSERS
POSIES
POSITS
POSSES
PUSHES
PUSSES
RASHES
RESETS
RESINS
RISERS
ROSINS
RUSHES
SASHES
SASINS
SASSES
SUSANS
SUSIES
TASTES
TESTES
TESTIS
TOSHES
TOSSES
TUSHES
TUSSIS
UNSAYS
UPSETS
VESTAS
VISCUS
VISITS
VISORS
VISTAS
WASHES
WASTES
WISHES
XYSTOS
XYSTUS
YESSES

•••SS•

BRASSY
CHASSE
CLASSY
CROSSE
CUISSE
DRESSY
DROSSY
FLOSSY
GLASSY
GLOSSO
GLOSSY
GRASSY
MOUSSE
ODESSA
PRISSY
TRESSY
WRASSE

•••S•S

ABASES
ABUSES
ABYSMS
AGISTS
AMUSES
ANISES
ANUSES
ARISES
AVISOS
BALSAS
BASSES
BASSOS
BEASTS
BESSYS
BETSYS
BIASES
BIOSIS
BLASTS
BOASTS
BOOSTS
BOSSES
BOUSES
BOWSES
BRISKS
BURSAS
BURSES
BURSTS
BUSSES
BYSSUS
CANSOS
CASSIS
CAUSES
CEASES
CENSES
CENSUS
CHASES
CHASMS
CHESTS
CISSYS
CLASPS
CLOSES
COASTS
COPSES
CORSES
COSSES
CRASIS
CRESTS
CRISES
CRISIS
CRISPS
CRUSES
CRUSTS
CURSES
CUSSES
CUSSOS
DAISES
DAISYS
DEISTS
DIESES
DIESIS
DIPSAS
DOUSES
DOWSES
DRUSES
ECESIS
EGESTS
EMESIS
ENOSIS
ERASES
EXISTS
EYASES
FEASES
FEASTS
FEISTS
FESSES
FIRSTS
FLASKS
FOISTS
FOSSES
FRISES
FRISKS
FROSTS
FUSSES
GASSES
GESSOS
GHOSTS
GLOSTS
GNOSIS
GOOSES
GORSES
GRASPS
GUESTS
GUISES
HAWSES
HEISTS
HISSES
HOISTS
HORSES
HOUSES
IBISES
IRISES
JESSES
JOISTS
JOSSES
JOUSTS
KAASES
KANSAS
KIOSKS
KISSES
KNOSPS
KRISES
LAPSES
LAPSUS
LASSES

6

LASSOS
LEASES
LENSES
LOOSES
LOSSES
LOUSES
MANSES
MASSES
MENSES
MESSES
MESSRS
MIOSIS
MISSES
MISSIS
MISSUS
MOSSES
MOUSES
MUSSES
MYOSIS
NAOSES
NESSUS
NOESIS
NOISES
NOOSES
NURSES
ONUSES
PANSYS
PARSES
PARSIS
PASSES
PASSUS
PATSYS
PAUSES
PEASES
PHASES
PHASIS
PLASIS
PLUSES
POISES
POSSES
PRESAS
PRISMS
PROSES
PTOSIS
PULSES
PURSES
PUSSES
PYOSIS
QUESTS
RAISES
RHESUS
RINSES
ROASTS
ROOSTS
ROUSES
ROUSTS
SASSES
SEISMS
SENSES
SEPSIS
SOUSES
SPASMS
STASES
STASIS
TARSUS
TEASES
TENSES
THESES
THESIS
TMESIS
TOASTS
TORSKS
TORSOS
TOSSES
TRUSTS
TRYSTS
TUSSIS
TWISTS
UKASES
UPASES
VERSES
VERSOS
VERSTS
VERSUS
WAISTS
WHISKS
WORSTS
WRESTS
WRISTS
YEASTS
YESSES

••••SS

ABBESS
ACCESS
ACROSS
ASSESS
AWLESS
BAGASS
BYPASS
CAMASS
CARESS
DURESS
EGRESS
EMBOSS
EXCESS
GNEISS
HARASS
JEWESS
KAVASS
KUMISS
MEGASS
MORASS
OBSESS
OGRESS
RECESS
REMISS
REPASS
SCHUSS
SPEISS
STRASS
STRESS
UNLESS

ST••••

STABLE
STACIE
STACKS
STACTE
STACYS
STADIA
STAFFS
STAGED
STAGER
STAGES
STAGEY
STAGGY
STAINS
STAIRS
STAKED
STAKES
STALAG
STALED
STALER
STALES
STALIN
STALKS
STALKY
STALLS
STAMEN
STAMIN
STAMPS
STANCE
STANCH
STANDS
STANZA
STAPES
STAPLE
STARCH
STARED
STARER
STARES
STARRY
STARTS
STARVE
STASES
STASIS
STATAL
STATED
STATER
STATES
STATIC
STATOR
STATUE
STATUS
STAURO
STAVED
STAVES
STAYED
STAYER
STEADY
STEAKS
STEALS
STEAMS
STEAMY
STEEDS
STEELS
STEELY
STEEPS
STEERS
STEEVE
STEFAN
STEINS
STELAE
STELAR
STELES
STELIC
STELLA
STELLI
STENCH
STENOG
STEPAN
STEPIN
STEPPE
STEPUP
STEREO
STERES
STERIC
STERNA
STERNO
STERNS
STEROL
STETHO
STEVEN
STEVES
STEVIE
STEWED
STICKS
STICKY
STIFLE
STIGMA
STILES
STILLS
STILLY
STILTS
STINGS
STINGY
STINKS
STINTS
STIPEL
STIPES
STIRKS
STIRPS
STITCH
STITHY
STIVER
STOATS
STOCKS
STOCKY
STODGE
STODGY
STOGEY
STOICS
STOKED
STOKER
STOKES
STOLED
STOLEN
STOLES
STOLID
STOLON
STOMAT
STOMPS
STONED
STONER
STONES
STOOGE
STOOKS
STOOLS
STOOPS
STOPED
STOPES
STORAX
STORED
STORES
STOREY
STORKS
STORMS
STORMY
STOUPS
STOUTS
STOVER
STOVES
STOWED
STRAFE
STRAIN
STRAIT
STRAKE
STRAND
STRAPS
STRASS
STRATA
STRATI
STRAWS
STRAWY
STRAYS
STREAK
STREAM
STREET
STRESS
STREWN
STREWS
STRIAE
STRICK
STRICT
STRIDE
STRIFE
STRIKE
STRING
STRIPE
STRIPS
STRIPT
STRIPY
STRIVE
STRODE
STROKE
STROLL
STROMA
STRONG
STROPS
STROUD
STROVE
STRUCK
STRUMA
STRUMS
STRUTS
STUART
STUBBY
STUCCO
STUDIO
STUFFS
STUFFY
STULLS
STUMPS
STUMPY
STUNTS
STUPAS
STUPES
STUPID
STUPOR
STURDY
STYING
STYLAR
STYLED
STYLER
STYLES
STYLET
STYLUS
STYMIE

S•T•••

SATANG
SATARA
SATEEN
SATING
SATINS
SATINY
SATIRE
SATORI
SATRAP
SATURN
SATYRS
SETOFF
SETONS
SETOSE
SETOUS
SETTEE
SETTER
SETTLE
SETTOS
SETUPS
SHTICK
SITARS
SITINS
SITTER
SOTHIC
SOTHIS
SOTOLS
SUTLER
SUTRAS
SUTTEE
SUTURE

S••T••

SAITIC
SALTED
SALTER
SANTOL
SARTOR
SARTRE
SAUTES
SCATHE
SCOTCH
SCOTER

SCOTIA
SCOTTS
SCUTCH
SCUTES
SCUTUM
SCYTHE
SEATED
SECTOR
SEETHE
SENTRY
SEPTAL
SEPTET
SEPTIC
SEPTUM
SESTET
SETTEE
SETTER
SETTLE
SETTOS
SEXTAN
SEXTET
SEXTON
SHOTES
SHUTIN
SIFTED
SIFTER
SILTED
SINTER
SISTER
SITTER
SIXTES
SIXTHS
SKATED
SKATER
SKATES
SKETCH
SLATED
SLATER
SLATES
SLOTHS
SMITER
SMITES
SMITHS
SMITHY
SMUTCH
SMUTTY
SNATCH
SNATHE
SNATHS
SNITCH
SNOTTY
SOFTAS
SOFTEN
SOFTER
SOFTLY
SOOTED
SOOTHE
SORTED
SORTIE
SPATES
SPATHE
SPITAL
SPITED
SPITES
SPOTTY
SPUTUM
STATAL
STATED
STATER
STATES
STATIC
STATOR
STATUE
STATUS
STETHO
STITCH
STITHY
SUBTER
SUBTLE
SUBTLY
SUITED
SUITES
SUITOR
SULTAN
SULTRY
SURTAX
SUTTEE
SWATCH
SWATHE
SWATHS
SWITCH
SYNTAX
SYSTEM

S•••T•

SABOTS
SAFETY
SAINTS
SALUTE
SAMITE
SANITY
SAULTS
SCANTY
SCENTS
SCOOTS
SCOTTS
SCOUTS
SEBATS
SEDATE
SEMITE
SENATE
SHAFTS
SHANTY
SHASTA
SHEATH
SHEETS
SHELTY
SHIFTS
SHIFTY
SHIITE
SHINTO
SHIRTS
SHOATS
SHOOTS
SHORTS
SHOUTS
SHUNTS
SIESTA
SIGHTS
SKIRTS
SLANTS
SLEETS
SLEETY
SLEUTH
SMALTI
SMALTO
SMARTS
SMELTS
SMOLTS
SMOOTH
SMUTTY
SNOOTS
SNOOTY
SNORTS
SNOTTY
SNOUTS
SOLUTE
SOMATA
SOMATO
SOMITE
SONATA
SPAITS
SPARTA
SPILTH
SPIRTS
SPLATS
SPLITS
SPORTS
SPORTY
SPOTTY
SPOUTS
SPRATS
SPRITE
SPRITS
SPURTS
SQUATS
STACTE
STARTS
STILTS
STINTS
STOATS
STOUTS
STRATA
STRATI
STRUTS
STUNTS
SUBITO
SURETY
SVELTE
SWARTH
SWARTY
SWEATS
SWEATY
SWEETS
SWIFTS

S••••T

SABBAT
SACHET
SADIST
SAFEST
SAGEST
SALLET
SAMLET
SANEST
SAVANT
SCHIST
SCHUIT
SCRIPT
SCULPT
SECANT
SECRET
SEJANT
SELECT
SENNET
SENNIT
SEPTET
SESTET
SEURAT
SEXIST
SEXTET
SHEBAT
SHIEST
SHRIFT
SHYEST
SIGNET
SILENT
SIPPET
SLIEST
SLIGHT
SLYEST
SNOCAT
SOCKET
SOFFIT
SOLENT
SONANT
SONNET
SOREST
SOUGHT
SOVIET
SPIGOT
SPINET
SPIRIT
SPLINT
SPOILT
SPRINT
SPROUT
SQUINT
SQUIRT
STOMAT
STRAIT
STREET
STRICT
STRIPT
STUART
STYLET
SUBLET
SUBMIT
SUMMIT
SUNLIT
SUNSET
SUREST
SWIVET
SYNDET

•ST•••

ASTERI
ASTERN
ASTERO
ASTERS
ASTHMA
ASTRAL
ASTRAY
ASTRID
ASTUTE
ESTATE
ESTEEM
ESTERS
ESTHER
ESTOPS
ESTRAY
ESTRUS
FSTOPS
OSTEAL

•S•T••

ISHTAR
TSETSE

•S••T•

ASCOTS
ASSETS
ASTUTE
ESTATE
ISLETS

•S•••T

ASCENT
ASKANT
ASLANT
ASPECT
ASSENT
ASSERT
ASSIST
ASSORT
ESCENT
ESCORT
ESPRIT
ISEULT
OSBERT
TSHIRT

••ST••

AUSTEN
AUSTER
AUSTIN
AUSTRO
BASTED
BASTES
BESTED
BESTIR
BESTOW
BISTER
BISTRO
BOSTON
BUSTED
BUSTER
BUSTIC
BUSTLE
CASTER
CASTES
CASTLE
CASTOR
CASTRO
CESTUS
COSTAE
COSTAL
COSTAR
COSTED
COSTLY
CUSTER
CUSTOM
CUSTOS
CYSTIC
DISTAL
DISTIL
DUSTED
DUSTER
EASTER
EASTON
FASTED
FASTEN
FASTER
FESTAL
FESTER
FISTED
FISTIC
FOSTER
FUSTIC
GASTON
GASTRO
GESTIC
GUSTAF
GUSTAV
HASTED
HASTEN
HASTES
HESTER
HESTIA
HOSTED
HOSTEL
HUSTLE
HYSTER
INSTAR
INSTEP
JESTED
JESTER
JOSTLE
JUSTIN
JUSTLY
JUSTUS
LASTED
LASTER
LASTEX
LASTLY
LESTER
LISTED
LISTEL
LISTEN
LISTER
LUSTED
LUSTER
MASTED

MASTER
MASTIC
MESTEE
MISTED
MISTER
MOSTLY
MUSTEE
MUSTER
MYSTIC
NASTIC
NESTED
NESTLE
NESTOR
NOSTOC
OUSTED
OUSTER
OYSTER
PASTAS
PASTED
PASTEL
PASTER
PASTES
PASTIL
PASTOR
PASTRY
PESTER
PESTLE
PISTIL
PISTOL
PISTON
POSTAL
POSTED
POSTER
RESTED
RESTER
ROSTER
ROSTRA
RUSTED
RUSTIC
RUSTLE
SESTET
SISTER
SYSTEM
TASTED
TASTER
TASTES
TESTAE
TESTED
TESTER
TESTES
TESTIS
TESTON
ULSTER
UNSTEP
UNSTOP
VASTER
VASTLY
VESTAL
VESTAS
VESTED
VESTEE
VESTRY
VISTAS
WASTED
WASTER
WASTES
WESTER
WYSTAN
XYSTER
XYSTOS
XYSTUS
YESTER
ZESTED
ZOSTER

••S•T•

ANSATE
ASSETS
BASUTO
BESETS
BESOTS
ERSATZ
INSETS
ONSETS
PASHTO
PESETA
POSITS
RESETS
UPSETS
VASHTI
VISITS

••S••T

ABSENT
ASSENT
ASSERT
ASSIST
ASSORT
BASALT
BASKET
BASSET
BISECT
BOSKET
CASKET
COSSET
CUSHAT
DESALT
DESERT
DESIST
DESPOT
EXSECT
EXSERT
GASKET
GUSSET
HASLET
INSECT
INSERT
INSIST
INSULT
JESUIT
KISMET
MASCOT
MISFIT
MUSCAT
MUSKET
MUSKIT
POSSET
RESEAT
RESECT
RESENT
RESIST
RESORT
RESULT
RUSSET
SESTET
TASSET
UNSEAT
UPSHOT
WISEST

•••ST•

AGISTS
ARISTA
ARISTO
AVESTA
BEASTS
BLASTO
BLASTS
BOASTS
BOOSTS
BURSTS
CHASTE
CHESTS
CHESTY
COASTS
CRESTS
CRUSTS
CRUSTY
CUESTA
DEISTS
EGESTA
EGESTS
EXISTS
FEASTS
FEISTS
FEISTY
FIESTA
FIRSTS
FOISTS
FROSTS
FROSTY
FRUSTA
GHOSTS
GLOSTS
GUESTS
HEISTS
HOISTS
HORSTE
JOISTS
JOUSTS
PIGSTY
PLASTY
POUSTO
PRESTO
QUESTS
ROASTS
ROOSTS
ROUSTS
SHASTA
SIESTA
TOASTS
TRISTE
TRUSTS
TRUSTY
TRYSTS
TWISTS
VERSTS
WAISTS
WORSTS
WRESTS
WRISTS
YEASTS
YEASTY

•••S•T

BASSET
CLOSET
CORSET
COSSET
CRUSET
DOESNT
GUSSET
OFFSET
OUTSAT
OUTSET
OUTSIT
POSSET
PROSIT
RUSSET
SUNSET
TASSET
UNDSET
WADSET

••••ST

ABLEST
ACCOST
ADJUST
AGHAST
ALMOST
AMIDST
AORIST
ARREST
ARTIST
ASSIST
ATTEST
AUGUST
AURIST
BABIST
BAREST
BEHEST
BLUEST
BREAST
BYPAST
CHRIST
CLEIST
CUBIST
CUTEST
DEGUST
DESIST
DETEST
DEVEST
DICAST
DIGEST
DIREST
DIVEST
DRIEST
DRYEST
DYNAST
EGOIST
ELDEST
ENCYST
ENLIST
ERNEST
FEWEST
FINEST
FLIEST
FOREST
FREEST
FUNEST
GAYEST
HEARST
HONEST
HUGEST
ICIEST
IDLEST
ILLUST
IMPOST
INCEST
INFEST
INGEST
INMOST
INSIST
INVEST
JURIST
LAMEST
LATEST
LAXEST
LEGIST
LOCUST
LOWEST
LUTIST
LYRIST
MAOIST
MARIST
MAYEST
MEREST
MODEST
MOLEST
MONGST
MONIST
NEWEST
NICEST
NUDIST
OBLAST
OBOIST
OBTEST
ODDEST
OLDEST
PALEST
PAPIST
PRIEST
PROUST
PUREST
PURIST
RACIST
RAPIST
RAREST
RAWEST
RECAST
REPAST
RESIST
REVEST
RIPEST
RIPOST
ROBUST
RUDEST
SADIST
SAFEST
SAGEST
SANEST
SCHIST
SEXIST
SHIEST
SHYEST
SLIEST
SLYEST
SOREST
SUREST
TAMEST
TANIST
TAOIST
THEIST
THIRST
THRUST
TRUEST
TYPIST
UNJUST
UNREST
UPCAST
UPMOST
UTMOST
VERIST
VILEST
VOLOST
WHILST
WIDEST
WISEST
WRIEST
WRYEST

SU••••

SUABLE
SUBAHS
SUBDEB
SUBDUE
SUBITO
SUBLET
SUBMIT
SUBORN
SUBTER
SUBTLE
SUBTLY
SUBURB
SUBWAY
SUCCOR
SUCKED
SUCKER
SUCKLE
SUCRES
SUDARY
SUDDEN
SUEDES
SUFFER

SUFFIX
SUFISM
SUGARS
SUGARY
SUITED
SUITES
SUITOR
SULCUS
SULFUR
SULKED
SULLEN
SULPHA
SULPHO
SULTAN
SULTRY
SUMACS
SUMMED
SUMMER
SUMMIT
SUMMON
SUMNER
SUNBOW
SUNDAE
SUNDAY
SUNDER
SUNDEW
SUNDOG
SUNDRY
SUNKEN
SUNLIT
SUNNAH
SUNNED
SUNSET
SUNUPS
SUOMIC
SUPERB
SUPERS
SUPINE
SUPPED
SUPPER
SUPPLE
SUPPLY
SURAHS
SURELY
SUREST
SURETY
SURFED
SURFER
SURGED
SURGER
SURGES
SURREY
SURTAX
SURVEY
SUSANS
SUSIES
SUSLIK
SUTLER
SUTRAS
SUTTEE
SUTURE

S•U•••
SAUCED
SAUCER
SAUCES
SAUGER
SAULTS
SAUNAS
SAUREL
SAURUS
SAUTES
SCUBAS
SCUFFS
SCULLS
SCULPT
SCUMMY
SCURFY
SCURRY
SCURVE
SCURVY
SCUTCH
SCUTES
SCUTUM
SEURAT
SHUCKS
SHUNTS
SHUTIN
SKULKS
SKULLS
SKUNKS
SLUDGE
SLUDGY
SLUICE
SLUING
SLUMMY
SLUMPS
SLURPS
SLURRY
SLUSHY
SMUDGE
SMUDGY
SMUGLY
SMUTCH
SMUTTY
SNUFFS
SNUFFY
SNUGLY
SOUARI
SOUGHS
SOUGHT
SOULED
SOUNDS
SOURCE
SOURED
SOURER
SOURLY
SOUSED
SOUSES
SPUMED
SPUMES
SPUNKY
SPURGE
SPURNS
SPURRY
SPURTS
SPUTUM
SQUABS
SQUADS
SQUALL
SQUAMA
SQUARE
SQUASH
SQUATS
SQUAWK
SQUAWS
SQUEAK
SQUEAL
SQUIBS
SQUIDS
SQUILL
SQUINT
SQUIRE
SQUIRM
SQUIRT
SQUISH
STUART
STUBBY
STUCCO
STUDIO
STUFFS
STUFFY
STULLS
STUMPS
STUMPY
STUNTS
STUPAS
STUPES
STUPID
STUPOR
STURDY

S••U••
SALUKI
SALUTE
SAMUEL
SATURN
SCAUPS
SCHUIT
SCHUSS
SCOURS
SCOUTS
SCRUBS
SCRUFF
SCRUMS
SECUND
SECURE
SEDUCE
SEDUMS
SEQUEL
SEQUIN
SERUMS
SETUPS
SEXUAL
SHOULD
SHOUTS
SHRUBS
SHRUGS
SHRUNK
SIEURS
SIOUAN
SIRUPS
SIRUPY
SLEUTH
SLOUCH
SLOUGH
SNOUTS
SOLUTE
SPOUSE
SPOUTS
SPRUCE
SPRUES
SPRUNG
STAURO
STOUPS
STOUTS
STRUCK
STRUMA
STRUMS
STRUTS
SUBURB
SUNUPS
SUTURE
SYNURA
SYRUPS
SYRUPY

S•••U•
SACRUM
SADHUS
SAJOUS
SAMBUR
SANGUI
SANNUP
SAURUS
SCOPUS
SCUTUM
SEAMUS
SELJUK
SEPTUM
SEROUS
SESQUI
SETOUS
SHAMUS
SHOGUN
SHROUD
SIDDUR
SINFUL
SIRIUS
SLIPUP
SNAFUS
SODIUM
SPROUT
SPUTUM
STATUE
STATUS
STEPUP
STROUD
STYLUS
SUBDUE
SULCUS
SULFUR

S••••U
SAMSHU

•SU•••
USURER
USURPS

•S•U••
ASBURY
ASSUME
ASSURE
ASTUTE
ESCUDO
ISEULT
ISSUED
ISSUER
ISSUES
OSCULE
OSMUND
PSEUDO

•S••U•
ASARUM
ASYLUM
ESTRUS
OSMIUM
USEFUL

••SU••
ABSURD
ASSUME
ASSURE
BASUTO
CASUAL
CESURA
DISUSE
ENSUED
ENSUES
ENSURE
INSULT
INSURE
ISSUED
ISSUER
ISSUES
JESUIT
MISUSE
RESULT
RESUME
UNSUNG
UNSURE
URSULA
VISUAL

••S•U•
BASQUE
BISQUE
BYSSUS
CASQUE
CESIUM
CESTUS
DISCUS
ENSOUL
FESCUE
INSOUL
JOSHUA
JUSTUS
MASQUE
MISCUE
MISSUS
MOSQUE
MUSEUM
NASHUA
NESSUS
PASSUS
POSEUR
POSSUM
PUSHUP
RESCUE
RISQUE
SESQUI
TISSUE
TOSSUP
VISCUS
XYSTUS

••S••U
DESSAU
NASSAU
RESEAU
VISHNU

•••SU•
BYSSUS
CATSUP
CENSUS
CONSUL
DORSUM
GYPSUM
LAPSUS
MISSUS
NESSUS
OMASUM
PASSUS
POSSUM
PURSUE
RHESUS
TARSUS
TISSUE
TOSSUP
VERSUS

•••S•U
DESSAU
HONSHU
KYUSHU
NASSAU
SAMSHU

SV••••
SVELTE

S•V•••
SAVAGE
SAVANT
SAVERS
SAVING
SAVINS
SAVIOR
SAVORS
SAVORY
SEVENS

SEVERE
SEVERS
SOVIET

S••V••
SALVED
SALVER
SALVES
SALVIA
SALVOR
SALVOS
SELVES
SERVAL
SERVED
SERVER
SERVES
SERVOS
SHAVED
SHAVEN
SHAVER
SHAVES
SHIVER
SHIVES
SHOVED
SHOVEL
SHOVER
SHOVES
SIEVED
SIEVES
SILVAE
SILVAN
SILVAS
SILVER
SILVIA
SKIVED
SKIVER
SKIVES
SKIVVY
SLAVED
SLAVER
SLAVES
SLAVIC
SLIVER
SLOVAK
SLOVEN
SNIVEL
SOEVER
SOLVED
SOLVER
SOLVES
SPAVIN
STAVED
STAVES
STEVEN
STEVES
STEVIE
STIVER
STOVER
STOVES
SURVEY
SWIVEL
SWIVET
SYLVAE
SYLVAN
SYLVAS
SYLVIA

S•••V•
SALIVA
SCRIVE
SCURVE
SCURVY
SHEAVE
SHELVE
SHRIVE
SHROVE
SKIVVY
SLEAVE
SLEEVE
STARVE
STEEVE
STRIVE
STROVE
SWERVE

••S•V•
CASAVA

••S••V
GUSTAV

SW••••
SWAGED
SWAGES
SWAILS
SWAINS
SWALES
SWAMIS
SWAMPS
SWAMPY
SWANEE
SWANKY
SWARAJ
SWARDS
SWARMS
SWARTH
SWARTY
SWATCH
SWATHE
SWATHS
SWAYED
SWEARS
SWEATS
SWEATY
SWEDEN
SWEDES
SWEEPS
SWEEPY
SWEETS
SWELLS
SWERVE
SWIFTS
SWILLS
SWINGE
SWINGS
SWIPED
SWIPES
SWIPLE
SWIRLS
SWIRLY
SWITCH
SWIVEL
SWIVET
SWOONS
SWOOPS
SWORDS

S•W•••
SAWERS
SAWFLY
SAWING
SAWYER
SEWAGE
SEWALL
SEWARD
SEWERS
SEWING
SIWASH
SOWARS
SOWERS
SOWING

S••W••
SCHWAS
SCOWLS
SEAWAN
SEAWAY
SHAWLS
SHAWMS
SHEWED
SHEWER
SHOWED
SHOWER
SKEWED
SKEWER
SKYWAY
SLEWED
SLOWED
SLOWER
SLOWLY
SNOWED
SPAWNS
SPEWED
STEWED
STOWED
SUBWAY

S•••W•
SCRAWL
SCREWS
SCREWY
SEROWS
SHREWD
SHREWS
SINEWS
SINEWY
SPRAWL
SQUAWK
SQUAWS
STRAWS
STRAWY
STREWN
STREWS

S••••W
SALLOW
SEESAW
SHADOW
SORROW
SUNBOW
SUNDEW

•SW•••
OSWALD

•S••W•
PSHAWS

•S•••W
ESCHEW
ESCROW

••SW••
ANSWER

••S•W•
DISOWN

••S••W
BASHAW
BESTOW
CASHAW
CASHEW
CUSHAW
KISLEW
MOSCOW
NOSHOW

•••S•W
JIGSAW
RIPSAW
SEESAW
WARSAW

S•X•••
SAXONS
SAXONY
SEXIER
SEXING
SEXISM
SEXIST
SEXTAN
SEXTET
SEXTON
SEXUAL
SIXTES
SIXTHS

S••••X
SCOLEX
SMILAX
SPADIX
SPHINX
STORAX
SUFFIX
SURTAX
SYNTAX
SYRINX

••S•X•
DESOXY

••S••X
AUSPEX
LASTEX
WESSEX

•••S•X
UNISEX
WESSEX

SY••••
SYBILS
SYCEES
SYDNEY
SYLPHS
SYLPHY
SYLVAE
SYLVAN
SYLVAS
SYLVIA
SYMBOL
SYNDET
SYNDIC
SYNODS
SYNTAX
SYNURA
SYPHER
SYRIAC
SYRIAN
SYRINX
SYRUPS
SYRUPY
SYSTEM
SYZYGY

S•Y•••
SAYERS
SAYING
SCYLLA
SCYPHI
SCYPHO
SCYTHE
SHYEST
SHYING
SKYCAP
SKYING
SKYMAN
SKYMEN
SKYWAY
SLYEST
SPYING
STYING
STYLAR
STYLED
STYLER
STYLES
STYLET
STYLUS
STYMIE

S••Y••
SATYRS
SAWYER
SIBYLS
SLAYER
SONYAS
SPAYED
SPRYER
SPRYLY
STAYED
STAYER
SWAYED
SYZYGY

S•••Y•
SALLYS
SAMMYS
SANDYS
SELSYN
SEPOYS
SPLAYS
SPRAYS
STACYS
STRAYS

S••••Y
SAFELY
SAFETY
SAGELY
SALARY
SALIFY
SANELY
SANITY
SASHAY
SATINY
SAVORY
SAWFLY
SAXONY
SCABBY
SCANTY
SCREWY
SCUMMY
SCURFY
SCURRY
SCURVY
SEAWAY
SEEMLY
SENARY
SENTRY
SHABBY
SHAGGY
SHAMMY
SHANTY
SHEENY
SHELBY
SHELLY
SHELTY
SHERRY
SHIFTY
SHIMMY
SHINDY
SHINNY
SHOALY
SHODDY

6

SICILY
SICKLY
SIDNEY
SIMONY
SIMPLY
SINEWY
SINGLY
SIRUPY
SKIMPY
SKINNY
SKIVVY
SKYWAY
SLAGGY
SLANGY
SLEAZY
SLEEKY
SLEEPY
SLEETY
SLIMLY
SLIMSY
SLINKY
SLOPPY
SLOSHY
SLOWLY
SLUDGY
SLUMMY
SLURRY
SLUSHY
SMARMY
SMEARY
SMELLY
SMITHY
SMUDGY
SMUGLY
SMUTTY
SNAGGY
SNAPPY
SNARLY
SNEAKY
SNEEZY
SNIFFY
SNIPPY
SNOOPY
SNOOTY
SNOTTY
SNUFFY
SNUGLY
SODOMY
SOFTLY
SOLELY
SORELY
SOURLY
SPARRY
SPEEDY
SPERRY
SPHERY
SPIFFY
SPINNY
SPONGY
SPOOKY
SPOONY
SPORTY
SPOTTY
SPRYLY

SPUNKY
SPURRY
STAGEY
STAGGY
STALKY
STARRY
STEADY
STEAMY
STEELY
STICKY
STILLY
STINGY
STITHY
STOCKY
STODGY
STOGEY
STOREY
STORMY
STRAWY
STRIPY
STUBBY
STUFFY
STUMPY
STURDY
SUBTLY
SUBWAY
SUDARY
SUGARY
SULTRY
SUNDAY
SUNDRY
SUPPLY
SURELY
SURETY
SURREY
SURVEY
SWAMPY
SWANKY
SWARTY
SWEATY
SWEEPY
SWIRLY
SYDNEY
SYLPHY
SYRUPY
SYZYGY

•SY•••
ASYLUM
PSYCHE
PSYCHO

•S••Y•
ASSAYS
ESSAYS

•S•••Y
ASBURY
ASHLEY
ASTRAY
ESTRAY
OSPREY
OSSIFY
USABLY

••S•Y•
ASSAYS
BESSYS
CISSYS
ESSAYS
MOSEYS
UNSAYS

••S••Y
BASELY
BASIFY
BISCAY
BUSILY
CASEFY
COSTLY
DESCRY
DESOXY
DISMAY
DISNEY
EASILY
JUSTLY
LASTLY
LESLEY
MISERY
MISLAY
MOSLEY
MOSTLY
NOSILY
OSSIFY
PASTRY
PUSSEY
PUSSLY
RASHLY
ROSARY
ROSILY
ROSINY
SASHAY
VASTLY
VESTRY
WESLEY
WISELY

•••SY•
BESSYS
BETSYS
CISSYS
DAISYS
PANSYS
PATSYS
SELSYN

•••S•Y
BRASHY
BRASSY
BRUSHY
CHESTY
CLASSY
CRISPY
CRUSTY
DRESSY
DROSKY
DROSSY
FEISTY
FLASHY
FLESHY
FLOSSY
FRISKY
FROSTY
GLASSY
GLOSSY
GOOSEY
GRASSY
GRISLY
GROSZY
GUNSHY
HALSEY
HORSEY
JERSEY
KERSEY
KINSEY
MARSHY
MEASLY
OCASEY
PIGSTY
PLASHY
PLASTY
PLUSHY
PRISSY
PUSSEY
PUSSLY
SLOSHY
SLUSHY
TRASHY
TRESSY
TRUSTY
WHISKY
WOLSEY
YEASTY

••••SY
ARGOSY
BIOPSY
BRASSY
CHEESY
CHOOSY
CLASSY
CLUMSY
CREASY
CURTSY
DRESSY
DROPSY
DROSSY
DROWSY
FLIMSY
FLOSSY
FOLKSY
GLASSY
GLOSSY
GRASSY
GREASY
HERESY
PRISSY
QUEASY
QUINSY
SLIMSY
TEENSY
TOOTSY
TRESSY
UNEASY
WEENSY
WHIMSY
WOODSY

S•Z•••
SIZARS
SIZIER
SIZING
SIZZLE
SOZINE
SOZINS
SYZYGY

S••Z••
SEIZED
SEIZER
SEIZES
SEIZIN
SEIZOR
SIZZLE
SMAZES

S•••Z•
SCHIZO
SFORZA
SLEAZY
SNEEZE
SNEEZY
SNOOZE
STANZA

•S••Z•
ASSIZE

••S•Z•
ASSIZE

••S••Z
ERSATZ

•••SZ•
GROSZY

TA••••
TABARD
TABLED
TABLES
TABLET
TABOOS
TABORS
TACKED
TACKER
TACKEY
TACKLE
TACOMA
TACTIC
TAENIA
TAGGED
TAGGER
TAIGAS
TAILED
TAILLE
TAILOR
TAINOS
TAINTS
TAIPEI
TAIWAN
TAKEIN
TAKERS
TAKEUP
TAKING
TALCED
TALCUM
TALENT
TALERS
TALION
TALKED
TALKER
TALLER
TALLOW
TALMUD
TALONS
TAMALE
TAMBAC
TAMERS
TAMEST
TAMING
TAMPAN
TAMPED
TAMPER
TAMPON
TAMTAM
TANDEM
TANGED
TANGLE
TANGLY
TANGOS
TANIST
TANKAS
TANKED
TANKER
TANNED
TANNER
TANNIC
TANNIN
TANREC
TAOISM
TAOIST
TAPALO
TAPERS
TAPING
TAPIRS
TAPPED
TAPPER
TAPPET
TARGET
TARIFF
TARING
TARMAC
TARNAL
TAROTS
TARPON
TARRED
TARSAL
TARSUS
TARTAN
TARTAR

TARTER
TARTLY
TARZAN
TASKED
TASMAN
TASSEL
TASSET
TASTED
TASTER
TASTES
TATARS
TATLER
TATTED
TATTER
TATTLE
TATTOO
TAUGHT
TAUNTS
TAUPES
TAURUS
TAUTEN
TAUTER
TAUTLY
TAVERN
TAWDRY
TAWERS
TAWING
TAXEME
TAXERS
TAXIED
TAXING
TAXITE
TAYLOR
TAZZAS

T•A•••

TEACUP
TEAMED
TEAPOT
TEAPOY
TEARED
TEASED
TEASEL
TEASER
TEASES
THADDY
THADYS
THALES
THALIA
THAMES
THANAT
THANES
THANKS
THATCH
THAWED
THAYER
TIARAS
TOASTS
TRACED
TRACER
TRACES
TRACHE
TRACHY
TRACKS
TRACTS
TRADED
TRADER
TRADES
TRAGIC
TRAGUS
TRAILS
TRAINS
TRAITS
TRAMPS
TRANCE
TRANSP
TRASHY
TRAUMA
TRAVEL
TRAVES
TRAWLS
TSADES
TWANGS
TWANGY

T••A••

TABARD
TAMALE
TAPALO
TATARS
TENACE
TENANT
TERAPH
TERATO
TETANY
THRALL
THRASH
THWACK
THWART
TICALS
TIRADE
TIRANA
TISANE
TITANS
TOBAGO
TOGAED
TOMANS
TOMATO
TORAHS
TOTALS
TOWAGE
TOWARD
TREADS
TREATS
TREATY
TRIADS
TRIALS
TRUANT
TUBATE
TULADI
TWEAKS
TWEAKY
TYBALT
TYRANT

T•••A•

TAIGAS
TAIWAN
TAMBAC
TAMPAN
TAMTAM
TANKAS
TARMAC
TARNAL
TARSAL
TARTAN
TARTAR
TARZAN
TASMAN
TAZZAS
TERGAL
TESTAE
TETRAD
THANAT
THEBAE
THECAE
THECAL
THEDAS
THENAL
THENAR
THETAS
THOMAS
THORAC
THORAX
THREAD
THREAT
THROAT
THUJAS
TIARAS
TIBIAE
TIBIAL
TIBIAS
TIMBAL
TINCAL
TITIAN
TOBIAH
TOBIAS
TOECAP
TOMBAC
TOMCAT
TREPAN
TRIBAL
TRINAL
TROCAR
TROJAN
TROPAL
TRUMAN
TURBAN
TUSCAN
TUSSAH
TUSSAL
TUSSAR
TWOWAY
TYMPAN

T••••A

TACOMA
TAENIA
TELEGA
TERBIA
TERESA
THALIA
THELMA
THORIA
THULIA
TIRANA
TOPEKA
TRAUMA
TRIVIA
TROIKA
TUNDRA
TUNICA

•TA•••

ATABAL
ATAMAN
ATAVIC
ATAXIA
ATAXIC
ETAPES
ITALIC
STABLE
STACIE
STACKS
STACTE
STACYS
STADIA
STAFFS
STAGED
STAGER
STAGES
STAGEY
STAGGY
STAINS
STAIRS
STAKED
STAKES
STALAG
STALED
STALER
STALES
STALIN
STALKS
STALKY
STALLS
STAMEN
STAMIN
STAMPS
STANCE
STANCH
STANDS
STANZA
STAPES
STAPLE
STARCH
STARED
STARER
STARES
STARRY
STARTS
STARVE
STASES
STASIS
STATAL
STATED
STATER
STATES
STATIC
STATOR
STATUE
STATUS
STAURO
STAVED
STAVES
STAYED
STAYER
UTAHAN

•T•A••

ATTACH
ATTACK
ATTAIN
ATTARS
ETHANE
ETHANS
ITHACA
OTTAVA
OTTAWA
STEADY
STEAKS
STEALS
STEAMS
STEAMY
STOATS
STRAFE
STRAIN
STRAIT
STRAKE
STRAND
STRAPS
STRASS
STRATA
STRATI
STRAWS
STRAWY
STRAYS
STUART
UTGARD

•T••A•

ATABAL
ATAMAN
ATONAL
ATRIAL
PTISAN
STALAG
STATAL
STEFAN
STELAE
STELAR
STEPAN
STOMAT
STORAX
STREAK
STREAM
STRIAE
STUPAS
STYLAR
UTAHAN

•T•••A

ATAXIA
ATHENA
ATTICA
ATTILA
ITHACA
OTTAVA
OTTAWA
STADIA
STANZA
STELLA
STERNA
STIGMA
STRATA
STROMA
STRUMA
UTOPIA
YTTRIA

••TA••

ALTAIC
ALTAIR
ALTARS
ATTACH
ATTACK
ATTAIN
ATTARS
BATAAN
BETAKE
BOTANY
BUTANE
BYTALK
CATALO
CETANE
DATARY
DETACH
DETAIL
DETAIN
DOTAGE
ENTAIL
ESTATE
EXTANT
GITANO
GOTAMA
INTACT
INTAKE
LITANY
LOTAHS
METAGE
METALS
MUTANT
MUTATE
NATANT
NOTARY
OBTAIN
OCTADS
OCTANE
OCTANT
OCTAVE
OCTAVO
OTTAVA
OTTAWA
OXTAIL
PETAIN

PETALS
PETARD
POTAGE
POTASH
POTATO
RATALS
RETAIL
RETAIN
RETAKE
RETARD
RITARD
ROTARY
ROTATE
SATANG
SATARA
SITARS
TATARS
TETANY
TITANS
TOTALS
UPTAKE
VITALS
VOTARY
WATAPE
WATAPS

••T•A•
ACTUAL
ANTIAR
ASTRAL
ASTRAY
BATAAN
BATEAU
BATMAN
BETRAY
CATHAY
CITRAL
COTEAU
COTTAE
COTTAR
COTTAS
CUTLAS
ENTRAP
ESTRAY
EXTRAS
FETIAL
GOTHAM
GUTTAE
GUTTAT
HETMAN
JETSAM
LETHAL
LUTEAL
LYTTAE
MITRAL
MUTUAL
NATHAN
OSTEAL
OUTLAW
OUTLAY
OUTMAN
OUTRAN
OUTSAT
PATHAN
PITMAN
PUTNAM
RATTAN
RITUAL
SATRAP
SUTRAS
TETRAD
TITIAN
VITTAE
WITHAL

••T••A
AFTOSA
ALTHEA
ANTHEA
ANTLIA
ASTHMA
ATTICA
ATTILA
CATENA
CITOLA
DATURA
ENTERA
FATIMA
GOTAMA
INTIMA
LATRIA
LATVIA
LITHIA
NUTRIA
OPTIMA
OTTAVA
OTTAWA
PATHIA
PATINA
PYTHIA
RETINA
SATARA
ULTIMA
YTTRIA

•••TA•
ACETAL
AMYTAL
ANITAS
AORTAE
AORTAL
AORTAS
AVATAR
BANTAM
BHUTAN
BRUTAL
CAFTAN
CENTAL
CHETAH
COSTAE
COSTAL
COSTAR
COTTAE
COTTAR
COTTAS
CRETAN
DELTAS
DENTAL
DISTAL
EVITAS
FANTAN
FESTAL
FOETAL
FONTAL
GRETAS
GUITAR
GUSTAF
GUSTAV
GUTTAE
GUTTAT
HARTAL
HEPTAD
HYETAL
INSTAR
ISHTAR
JUNTAS
LACTAM
LYTTAE
MANTAS
MARTAS
MENTAL
MORTAL
MORTAR
NECTAR
PASTAS
PENTAD
PLATAN
PORTAL
POSTAL
QUOTAS
RAGTAG
RATTAN
RECTAL
RENTAL
RIATAS
RICTAL
SEPTAL
SEXTAN
SOFTAS
SPITAL
STATAL
SULTAN
SURTAX
SYNTAX
TAMTAM
TARTAN
TARTAR
TESTAE
THETAS
VESTAL
VESTAS
VISTAS
VITTAE
WYSTAN

•••T•A
AGATHA
ANITRA
APHTHA
BERTHA
CENTRA
CONTRA
ELYTRA
HESTIA
MALTHA
MANTUA
MARTHA
PORTIA
ROSTRA
SCOTIA

••••TA
ALBATA
AMRITA
ARANTA
ARISTA
ARUNTA
AVESTA
BALATA
BARYTA
BEMATA
BENITA
BOGOTA
CAPITA
CHAETA
CUESTA
DAKOTA
EGESTA
EJECTA
ERRATA
EXACTA
FIESTA
FRUSTA
LOLITA
OMENTA
PELOTA
PESETA
QUANTA
SHASTA
SIESTA
SOMATA
SONATA
SPARTA
STRATA

TB••••
TBONES

T•B•••
TABARD
TABLED
TABLES
TABLET
TABOOS
TABORS
TIBIAE
TIBIAL
TIBIAS
TOBAGO
TOBIAH
TOBIAS
TOBIES
TUBATE
TUBBED
TUBBER
TUBERS
TUBING
TUBULE
TYBALT

T••B••
TAMBAC
TERBIA
THEBAE
THEBES
TIDBIT
TIMBAL
TIMBER
TIMBRE
TOMBAC
TOMBED
TOMBOY
TREBLE
TRIBAL
TRIBES
TUBBED
TUBBER
TUMBLE
TURBAN
TURBID
TURBIT
TURBOT
TWIBIL
TWOBIT

T•••B•
THROBS
THUMBS

•T•B••
ATABAL
STABLE
STUBBY

•T••B•
STUBBY

••TB••
HATBOX
HOTBED
HOTBOX
OUTBID
POTBOY

••T••B
ENTOMB
INTOMB

T•C•••
TACKED
TACKER
TACKEY
TACKLE
TACOMA
TACTIC
TECHNO
TICALS
TICKED
TICKER
TICKET
TICKLE
TOCSIN
TUCHUN
TUCKED
TUCKER
TUCSON
TYCOON

T••C••
TALCED
TALCUM
TEACUP
TERCEL
TERCET
TETCHY
TEUCER
THECAE
THECAL
TINCAL
TINCTS
TOECAP
TOMCAT
TOMCOD
TOUCHE
TOUCHY
TRACED
TRACER
TRACES
TRACHE
TRACHY
TRACKS
TRACTS
TRICED
TRICES
TRICHI
TRICHO
TRICKS
TRICKY
TRICOT
TROCAR
TROCHE
TRUCES
TRUCKS
TURCOS
TUSCAN

T•••C•
TENACE
THATCH
THENCE
THRICE
THWACK
TIERCE
TONICS
TOPICS
TRANCE
TRENCH
TUNICA
TUNICS
TWITCH

T••••C
TACTIC
TAMBAC

6

TANNIC
TANREC
TARMAC
TENREC
THETIC
THORAC
THORIC
THYMIC
TOLTEC
TOMBAC
TRAGIC
TROPIC
TURKIC

•TC•••
ETCHED
ETCHER
ETCHES
ITCHED
ITCHES

•T•C••
STACIE
STACKS
STACTE
STACYS
STICKS
STICKY
STOCKS
STOCKY
STUCCO

•T••C•
ATTACH
ATTACK
ATTICA
ATTICS
ETHICS
ITHACA
STANCE
STANCH
STARCH
STENCH
STITCH
STOICS
STRICK
STRICT
STRUCK
STUCCO

•T•••C
ATAVIC
ATAXIC
ATOMIC
ATONIC
ETHNIC
ITALIC
STATIC
STELIC
STERIC
YTTRIC

••TC••
BOTCHY
CATCHY
OUTCRY
PATCHY
PITCHY
ROTCHE
TETCHY

••T•C•
ANTICS
ATTACH
ATTACK
ATTICA
ATTICS
AZTECS
DETACH
DETECT
ENTICE
FETICH
INTACT
KITSCH
NOTICE
OBTECT
OPTICS
PUTSCH
SHTICK

••T••C
ALTAIC
CITRIC
GOTHIC
IATRIC
LITHIC
METRIC
MYTHIC
NITRIC
PYTHIC
SOTHIC
VITRIC
YTTRIC

•••TC•
BLOTCH
CLUTCH
CRATCH
CROTCH
CRUTCH
CULTCH
FLETCH
FLITCH
HOOTCH
NAUTCH
QUITCH
SCOTCH
SCUTCH
SKETCH
SMUTCH
SNATCH
SNITCH
STITCH
SWATCH
SWITCH
THATCH
TWITCH
WRETCH

•••T•C
ACETIC
AORTIC
ARCTIC
AZOTIC
BALTIC
BIOTIC
BUSTIC
CELTIC
COPTIC
CRETIC
CRITIC
CYSTIC
EMETIC
ENATIC
EROTIC
EXOTIC
FISTIC
FUSTIC
GESTIC
HECTIC
IRITIC
LACTIC
LUETIC
MANTIC
MASTIC
MIOTIC
MYSTIC
NASTIC
NOETIC
NOSTOC
PECTIC
PEPTIC
PHOTIC
POETIC
PONTIC
RUSTIC
SAITIC
SEPTIC
STATIC
TACTIC
THETIC
TOLTEC
URETIC
VIATIC

T•D•••
TEDDED
TEDDER
TEDDYS
TEDIUM
TIDBIT
TIDIED
TIDIER
TIDIES
TIDILY
TIDING
TODDLE
TODIES

T••D••
TANDEM
TAWDRY
TEDDED
TEDDER
TEDDYS
TENDED
TENDER
TENDON
THADDY
THADYS
THEDAS
TILDES
TINDER
TODDLE
TRADED
TRADER
TRADES
TRUDGE
TRUDYS
TSADES
TUNDRA

T•••D•
TEREDO
THADDY
THIRDS
TIRADE
TOLEDO
TREADS
TRENDS
TRENDY
TRIADS
TRIODE
TULADI
TUXEDO
TWEEDS

T••••D
TABARD
TABLED
TACKED
TAGGED
TAILED
TALCED
TALKED
TALMUD
TAMPED
TANGED
TANKED
TANNED
TAPPED
TARRED
TASKED
TASTED
TATTED
TAXIED
TEAMED
TEARED
TEASED
TEDDED
TEEMED
TEHEED
TENDED
TENSED
TENTED
TERMED
TESTED
TETRAD
THAWED
THREAD
THREED
TICKED
TIDIED
TIERED
TIFFED
TILLED
TILTED
TINEID
TINGED
TINNED
TINTED
TIPPED
TITHED
TITLED
TOGAED
TOGGED
TOILED
TOLLED
TOMBED
TOMCOD
TONGED
TOOLED
TOOTED
TOPPED
TOROID
TORPID
TORRID
TOSSED
TOTTED
TOURED
TOUTED
TOWARD
TRACED
TRADED
TRICED
TRIFID
TRINED
TRIPOD
TUBBED
TUCKED
TUFTED
TUGGED
TUNNED
TUPPED
TURBID
TURGID
TURNED
TUSHED
TUSKED
TWINED

•T•D••
ETUDES
STADIA
STODGE
STODGY
STUDIO

•T••D•
STANDS
STEADY
STEEDS
STRIDE
STRODE
STURDY

•T•••D
ATONED
ATTEND
ETCHED
ITCHED
STAGED
STAKED
STALED
STARED
STATED
STAVED
STAYED
STEWED
STOKED
STOLED
STOLID
STONED
STOPED
STORED
STOWED
STRAND
STROUD
STUPID
STYLED
UTGARD

••TD••
OUTDID

••T•D•
BETIDE
OCTADS
UNTIDY

••T••D
ANTEED
ASTRID
ATTEND
AUTOED
BATHED
BATTED
BETTED
BITTED
BUTTED
CATTED
CITIED
DOTTED
EXTEND
FATTED
FITTED
GUTTED
HATRED
HATTED
HOTBED
HUTTED
INTEND
JETTED
JOTTED
JUTTED

6

LATHED
MATTED
METHOD
NETTED
NITRID
NUTTED
OBTUND
OUTBID
OUTDID
PATTED
PETARD
PETTED
PITHED
PITIED
PITTED
POTTED
PUTRID
PUTTED
RATTED
RETARD
RETOLD
RETTED
RITARD
ROTTED
ROTUND
RUTTED
TATTED
TETRAD
TITHED
TITLED
TOTTED
UNTIED
UNTOLD
UNTROD
VATTED
VETOED
VETTED
WETTED
WITHED
WITTED

•••T•D

ABATED
ALATED
BAITED
BASTED
BATTED
BELTED
BESTED
BETTED
BITTED
BOATED
BOLTED
BOOTED
BUNTED
BUSTED
BUTTED
CANTED
CARTED
CATTED
COATED
COSTED
CRATED
DARTED
DENTED
DIETED
DINTED
DOTTED
DUSTED
EDITED
ELATED
EMOTED
EXITED
FASTED
FATTED
FISTED
FITTED
FLUTED
FOETID
FOOTED
GAITED
GIFTED
GIRTED
GRATED
GUTTED
HALTED
HASTED
HATTED
HEATED
HEFTED
HEPTAD
HILTED
HINTED
HOOTED
HOSTED
HUNTED
HUTTED
JESTED
JETTED
JILTED
JOLTED
JOTTED
JUTTED
KILTED
LASTED
LIFTED
LILTED
LISTED
LOFTED
LOOTED
LUSTED
MALTED
MASTED
MATTED
MELTED
MILTED
MINTED
MISTED
MOATED
MOLTED
MOOTED
NESTED
NETTED
NUTTED
ORATED
OUSTED
PANTED
PARTED
PASTED
PATTED
PELTED
PENTAD
PETTED
PITTED
PLATED
POSTED
POTTED
POUTED
PRATED
PUNTED
PUTTED
QUOTED
RAFTED
RANTED
RATTED
RENTED
RESTED
RETTED
RIFTED
RIOTED
ROOTED
ROTTED
ROUTED
RUSTED
RUTTED
SALTED
SEATED
SIFTED
SILTED
SKATED
SLATED
SOOTED
SORTED
SPITED
STATED
SUITED
TASTED
TATTED
TENTED
TESTED
TILTED
TINTED
TOOTED
TOTTED
TOUTED
TUFTED
UNITED
VATTED
VENTED
VESTED
VETTED
WAFTED
WAITED
WANTED
WASTED
WELTED
WETTED
WHITED
WILTED
WITTED
WONTED
ZESTED

TE••••

TEACUP
TEAMED
TEAPOT
TEAPOY
TEARED
TEASED
TEASEL
TEASER
TEASES
TECHNO
TEDDED
TEDDER
TEDDYS
TEDIUM
TEEING
TEEMED
TEEMER
TEENSY
TEETER
TEETHE
TEFLON
TEGMEN
TEHEED
TEHEES
TELEGA
TELLER
TELLUS
TELSON
TELUGU
TEMPER
TEMPLE
TEMPOS
TEMPTS
TENACE
TENANT
TENDED
TENDER
TENDON
TENETS
TENNIS
TENONS
TENORS
TENPIN
TENREC
TENSED
TENSER
TENSES
TENSOR
TENTED
TENTER
TENTHS
TENUES
TENUIS
TENURE
TENUTO
TEPEES
TEPEFY
TERAPH
TERATO
TERBIA
TERCEL
TERCET
TEREDO
TERESA
TERETE
TEREUS
TERGAL
TERGUM
TERMED
TERMER
TERMLY
TERMOR
TERRET
TERROR
TERRYS
TERSER
TESSIE
TESTAE
TESTED
TESTER
TESTES
TESTIS
TESTON
TETANY
TETCHY
TETHER
TETHYS
TETONS
TETRAD
TETRYL
TETTER
TETZEL
TEUCER
TEUTON

T•E•••

TAENIA
TEEING
TEEMED
TEEMER
TEENSY
TEETER
TEETHE
THEBAE
THEBES
THECAE
THECAL
THEDAS
THEFTS
THEIRS
THEISM
THEIST
THELMA
THEMES
THEMIS
THENAL
THENAR
THENCE
THEORY
THERMO
THERMS
THESES
THESIS
THETAS
THETIC
THETIS
TIEINS
TIERCE
TIERED
TIEUPS
TMESIS
TOECAP
TOEING
TREADS
TREATS
TREATY
TREBLE
TREMOR
TRENCH
TRENDS
TRENDY
TREPAN
TRESSY
TSETSE
TWEAKS
TWEAKY
TWEEDS
TWEETS
TWELVE
TWENTY
TWERPS

T••E••

TAKEIN
TAKERS
TAKEUP
TALENT
TALERS
TAMERS
TAMEST
TAPERS
TAVERN
TAWERS
TAXEME
TAXERS
TEHEED
TEHEES
TELEGA
TENETS
TEPEES
TEPEFY
TEREDO
TERESA
TERETE
TEREUS
THIEVE
THREAD
THREAT
THREED
THREES
THRESH
TIGERS
TILERS
TIMELY
TIMERS
TINEID
TOKENS
TOLEDO
TONERS
TOPEKA
TOPERS

TORERO
TOTEMS
TOTERS
TOWELS
TOWERS
TOWERY
TOYERS
TRIERS
TRUEST
TUBERS
TUMEFY
TUNERS
TUNEUP
TUPELO
TUREEN
TUXEDO
TUYERE
TWEEDS
TWEETS

T•••E•

TABLED
TABLES
TABLET
TACKED
TACKER
TACKEY
TAGGED
TAGGER
TAILED
TAIPEI
TALCED
TALKED
TALKER
TALLER
TAMPED
TAMPER
TANDEM
TANGED
TANKED
TANKER
TANNED
TANNER
TANREC
TAPPED
TAPPER
TAPPET
TARGET
TARRED
TARTER
TASKED
TASSEL
TASSET
TASTED
TASTER
TASTES
TATLER
TATTED
TATTER
TAUPES
TAUTEN
TAUTER
TAXIED
TBONES
TEAMED
TEARED
TEASED
TEASEL
TEASER
TEASES
TEDDED
TEDDER
TEEMED
TEEMER
TEETER
TEGMEN
TEHEED
TEHEES
TELLER
TEMPER
TENDED
TENDER
TENREC
TENSED
TENSER
TENSES
TENTED
TENTER
TENUES
TEPEES
TERCEL
TERCET
TERMED
TERMER
TERRET
TERSER
TESTED
TESTER
TESTES
TETHER
TETTER
TETZEL
TEUCER
THALES
THAMES
THANES
THAWED
THAYER
THEBES
THEMES
THESES
THOLES
THREED
THREES
THROES
THYMES
THYREO
TICKED
TICKER
TICKET
TIDIED
TIDIER
TIDIES
TIERED
TIFFED
TILDES
TILLED
TILLER
TILTED
TILTER
TIMBER
TINDER
TINGED
TINGES
TINKER
TINNED
TINNER
TINSEL
TINTED
TIPPED
TIPPER
TIPPET
TITHED
TITHER
TITHES
TITLED
TITLES
TITTER
TOBIES
TODIES
TOFFEE
TOGAED
TOGGED
TOGUES
TOILED
TOILER
TOILES
TOILET
TOLLED
TOLLER
TOLTEC
TOMBED
TONGED
TONIER
TOOLED
TOOLER
TOOTED
TOOTER
TOPPED
TOPPER
TOQUES
TORIES
TOSHES
TOSSED
TOSSES
TOTHER
TOTTED
TOTTER
TOUPEE
TOURED
TOUTED
TOUTER
TRACED
TRACER
TRACES
TRADED
TRADER
TRADES
TRAVEL
TRAVES
TRIBES
TRICED
TRICES
TRINED
TRINES
TRITER
TRIVET
TROVER
TROVES
TROWEL
TRUCES
TSADES
TUBBED
TUBBER
TUCKED
TUCKER
TUFTED
TUGGED
TULLES
TUNNED
TUNNEL
TUPPED
TUQUES
TUREEN
TURKEY
TURNED
TURNER
TURRET
TUSHED
TUSHES
TUSKED
TUSKER
TWINED
TWINER
TWINES
TWOFER

T••••E

TACKLE
TAILLE
TAMALE
TANGLE
TATTLE
TAXEME
TAXITE
TEETHE
TEMPLE
TENACE
TENURE
TERETE
TESSIE
TESTAE
THEBAE
THECAE
THENCE
THIEVE
THORPE
THRICE
THRIVE
THRONE
THROVE
THYRSE
TIBIAE
TICKLE
TIERCE
TILLIE
TIMBRE
TINGLE
TINKLE
TIPPLE
TIPTOE
TIRADE
TISANE
TISSUE
TITTLE
TODDLE
TOFFEE
TOGGLE
TONGUE
TOOTLE
TOPPLE
TOROSE
TORQUE
TOUCHE
TOUPEE
TOUSLE
TOWAGE
TRACHE
TRANCE
TREBLE
TRIFLE
TRIODE
TRIOSE
TRIPLE
TRISTE
TRIUNE
TRIXIE
TROCHE
TROUPE
TRUDGE
TSETSE
TUBATE
TUBULE
TUILLE
TUMBLE
TURTLE
TUSSLE
TUYERE
TWELVE
TWINGE
TYRONE

•TE•••

STEADY
STEAKS
STEALS
STEAMS
STEAMY
STEEDS
STEELS
STEELY
STEEPS
STEERS
STEEVE
STEFAN
STEINS
STELAE
STELAR
STELES
STELIC
STELLA
STELLI
STENCH
STENOG
STEPAN
STEPIN
STEPPE
STEPUP
STEREO
STERES
STERIC
STERNA
STERNO
STERNS
STEROL
STETHO
STEVEN
STEVES
STEVIE
STEWED
UTERUS

•T•E••

ATHENA
ATHENE
ATHENS
ATREUS
ATTEND
ATTEST
ETHELS
ETHERS
ITSELF
OTHERS
OTTERS
STEEDS
STEELS
STEELY
STEEPS
STEERS
STEEVE
STREAK
STREAM
STREET
STRESS
STREWN
STREWS
UTTERS

•T••E•

ATONED
ATONER
ATONES
ATTLEE
ETAPES
ETCHED
ETCHER
ETCHES
ETUDES
ITCHED
ITCHES
STAGED
STAGER
STAGES
STAGEY

6

STAKED
STAKES
STALED
STALER
STALES
STAMEN
STAPES
STARED
STARER
STARES
STASES
STATED
STATER
STATES
STAVED
STAVES
STAYED
STAYER
STELES
STEREO
STERES
STEVEN
STEVES
STEWED
STILES
STIPEL
STIPES
STIVER
STOGEY
STOKED
STOKER
STOKES
STOLED
STOLEN
STOLES
STONED
STONER
STONES
STOPED
STOPES
STORED
STORES
STOREY
STOVER
STOVES
STOWED
STREET
STUPES
STYLED
STYLER
STYLES
STYLET

•T•••E

ATHENE
ATHOME
ATTIRE
ATTLEE
ATTUNE
ETHANE
OTIOSE
STABLE
STACIE
STACTE
STANCE
STAPLE
STARVE
STATUE
STEEVE
STELAE
STEPPE
STEVIE
STIFLE
STODGE
STOOGE
STRAFE
STRAKE
STRIAE
STRIDE
STRIFE
STRIKE
STRIPE
STRIVE
STRODE
STROKE
STROVE
STYMIE

••TE••

ALTERS
ANTEED
ANTERO
ARTELS
ARTERY
ASTERI
ASTERN
ASTERO
ASTERS
ATTEND
ATTEST
AZTECS
BATEAU
BETELS
BITERS
CATENA
CATERS
COTEAU
CUTELY
CUTEST
CUTEYS
DATERS
DETECT
DETENT
DETERS
DETEST
DOTERS
EATERS
ENTERA
ENTERO
ENTERS
ESTEEM
ESTERS
EXTEND
EXTENT
EXTERN
HATERS
HETERO
HOTELS
INTEND
INTENT
INTERN
INTERS
KETENE
LATEEN
LATELY
LATENT
LATEST
LITERS
LUTEAL
LUTEUM
MATEOS
MATEYS
METEOR
METERS
MITERS
MOTELS
NOTERS
OBTECT
OBTEST
OCTETS
OSTEAL
OTTERS
OUTERS
PATENS
PATENT
PATERS
PETERS
POTEEN
POTENT
RATELS
RATERS
RETELL
RETENE
SATEEN
TOTEMS
TOTERS
URTEXT
UTTERS
VOTERS
WATERS
WATERY

••T•E•

AETHER
ALTHEA
ANTEED
ANTHEA
ANTHEM
ANTHER
ANTLER
ARTIES
ATTLEE
AUTOED
BATHED
BATHER
BATMEN
BATTED
BATTEN
BATTER
BETHEL
BETTED
BETTER
BETTES
BITTED
BITTEN
BITTER
BOTHER
BUTLER
BUTTED
BUTTER
BUTTES
CATHER
CATTED
CITHER
CITIED
CITIES
COTTER
CUTIES
CUTLER
CUTLET
CUTTER
DITHER
DOTIER
DOTTED
DOTTEL
DOTTER
DUTIES
EITHER
ENTREE
ESTEEM
ESTHER
FATHER
FATTED
FATTEN
FATTER
FETTER
FITTED
FITTER
GATHER
GETTER
GOTTEN
GUTTED
GUTTER
HATRED
HATTED
HATTER
HITHER
HITLER
HITTER
HOTBED
HOTTER
HUTTED
JETTED
JITNEY
JITTER
JOTTED
JUTTED
KATIES
KITTEN
LATEEN
LATHED
LATHER
LATHES
LATTEN
LATTER
LETTER
LITHER
LITTER
LUTHER
MATTED
MATTEO
MATTER
MATTES
METIER
MITTEN
MOTHER
MOTLEY
MUTTER
NETHER
NETTED
NUTLET
NUTMEG
NUTTED
NUTTER
OUTLET
OUTSET
PATTED
PATTEN
PATTER
PETREL
PETTED
PITHED
PITIED
PITIES
PITMEN
PITTED
POTEEN
POTHER
POTTED
POTTER
PUTTED
PUTTEE
PUTTER
RATHER
RATTED
RATTEN
RATTER
RETTED
RITTER
ROTTED
ROTTEN
ROTTER
RUTTED
SATEEN
SETTEE
SETTER
SITTER
SUTLER
SUTTEE
TATLER
TATTED
TATTER
TETHER
TETTER
TETZEL
TITHED
TITHER
TITHES
TITLED
TITLES
TITTER
TOTHER
TOTTED
TOTTER
UNTIED
UNTIES
VATTED
VETOED
VETOER
VETOES
VETTED
WETHER
WETTED
WETTER
WITHED
WITHER
WITHES
WITNEY
WITTED
ZITHER

••T••E

ACTIVE
ASTUTE
ATTIRE
ATTLEE
ATTUNE
BATTLE
BATTUE
BETAKE
BETIDE
BETISE
BOTTLE
BUTANE
CATTIE
CATTLE
CETANE
COTTAE
CUTTLE
DATIVE
DOTAGE
DOTTLE
ECTYPE
ENTICE
ENTIRE
ENTREE
ESTATE
FETTLE
FUTILE
FUTURE
GUTTAE
GUTTLE
HATTIE
INTAKE
INTONE
KATHIE
KETENE
KETONE
KETOSE
KETTLE
LITTLE
LOTTIE
LYTTAE
MATTIE

6

MATURE
METAGE
METOPE
METTLE
MOTILE
MOTIVE
MOTTLE
MUTATE
MUTULE
NATIVE
NATURE
NETTIE
NETTLE
NOTICE
OBTUSE
OCTANE
OCTAVE
OPTIME
PATINE
PETITE
PETRIE
POTAGE
POTPIE
POTSIE
POTTLE
PUTTEE
RATINE
RATITE
RATTLE
RETAKE
RETENE
RETIRE
RETUSE
ROTATE
ROTCHE
RUTILE
SATIRE
SETOSE
SETTEE
SETTLE
SUTTEE
SUTURE
TATTLE
TITTLE
UNTRUE
UPTAKE
VITTAE
VOTIVE
WATAPE
WATTLE

•••TE•

ABATED
ABATER
ABATES
AEETES
AGATES
ALATED
ARETES
AUSTEN
AUSTER
BAITED
BAITER
BANTER
BARTER
BASTED
BASTES
BATTED
BATTEN
BATTER
BAXTER
BEATEN
BEATER
BELTED
BESTED
BETTED
BETTER
BETTES
BISTER
BITTED
BITTEN
BITTER
BOATED
BOLTED
BOLTER
BOOTED
BOOTEE
BRUTES
BUNTED
BUSTED
BUSTER
BUTTED
BUTTER
BUTTES
CANTED
CANTER
CARTED
CARTEL
CARTER
CARTES
CASTER
CASTES
CATTED
CENTER
CERTES
CHUTES
COATED
COLTER
CONTES
CORTES
CORTEX
CORTEZ
COSTED
COTTER
CRATED
CRATER
CRATES
CUSTER
CUTTER
DARTED
DARTER
DEFTER
DENTED
DEXTER
DIETED
DIETER
DINTED
DOTTED
DOTTEL
DOTTER
DUSTED
DUSTER
EASTER
EDITED
ELATED
ELATER
ELATES
EMOTED
EMOTES
ENATES
EXETER
EXITED
FALTER
FASTED
FASTEN
FASTER
FATTED
FATTEN
FATTER
FESTER
FETTER
FILTER
FISTED
FITTED
FITTER
FLUTED
FLUTER
FLUTES
FOOTED
FOOTER
FORTES
FOSTER
FRATER
GAITED
GAITER
GARTER
GENTES
GETTER
GIFTED
GIRTED
GLUTEI
GLUTEN
GOATEE
GOITER
GOTTEN
GRATED
GRATER
GRATES
GRETEL
GUTTED
GUTTER
HALTED
HALTER
HASTED
HASTEN
HASTES
HATTED
HATTER
HEATED
HEATER
HEFTED
HESTER
HILTED
HINTED
HITTER
HOOTED
HOSTED
HOSTEL
HOTTER
HUNTED
HUNTER
HURTER
HUTTED
HYSTER
INSTEP
JESTED
JESTER
JETTED
JILTED
JILTER
JITTER
JOLTED
JOLTER
JOTTED
JUTTED
KILTED
KILTER
KITTEN
LASTED
LASTER
LASTEX
LATTEN
LATTER
LENTEN
LESTER
LETTER
LIFTED
LIFTER
LILTED
LINTEL
LINTER
LISTED
LISTEL
LISTEN
LISTER
LITTER
LOFTED
LOFTER
LOITER
LOOTED
LOOTER
LUSTED
LUSTER
MALTED
MANTEL
MANTES
MARTEN
MASTED
MASTER
MATTED
MATTEO
MATTER
MATTES
MEETER
MELTED
MELTER
MESTEE
MILTED
MILTER
MINTED
MINTER
MISTED
MISTER
MITTEN
MOATED
MOLTED
MOLTEN
MOLTER
MONTES
MOOTED
MOOTER
MUSTEE
MUSTER
MUTTER
NANTES
NEATER
NESTED
NETTED
NEUTER
NUTTED
NUTTER
ORATED
ORATES
OUSTED
OUSTER
OYSTER
PALTER
PANTED
PARTED
PASTED
PASTEL
PASTER
PASTES
PATTED
PATTEN
PATTER
PECTEN
PELTED
PELTER
PESTER
PETTED
PEWTER
PIETER
PINTER
PITTED
PLATED
PLATEN
PLATER
PLATES
PONTES
PORTER
POSTED
POSTER
POTTED
POTTER
POUTED
POUTER
POWTER
PRATED
PRATER
PRATES
PRETER
PUNTED
PUNTER
PUTTED
PUTTEE
PUTTER
QUOTED
QUOTER
QUOTES
RAFTED
RAFTER
RANTED
RANTER
RATTED
RATTEN
RATTER
RENTED
RENTER
RENTES
RESTED
RESTER
RETTED
RIFTED
RIOTED
RIOTER
RITTER
ROOTED
ROOTER
ROSTER
ROTTED
ROTTEN
ROTTER
ROUTED
ROUTER
ROUTES
RUSTED
RUTTED
SALTED
SALTER
SAUTES
SCOTER
SCUTES
SEATED
SEPTET
SESTET
SETTEE
SETTER
SEXTET
SHOTES
SIFTED
SIFTER
SILTED
SINTER
SISTER
SITTER
SIXTES
SKATED
SKATER
SKATES
SLATED
SLATER
SLATES
SMITER

SMITES
SOFTEN
SOFTER
SOOTED
SORTED
SPATES
SPITED
SPITES
STATED
STATER
STATES
SUBTER
SUITED
SUITES
SUTTEE
SYSTEM
TARTER
TASTED
TASTER
TASTES
TATTED
TATTER
TAUTEN
TAUTER
TEETER
TENTED
TENTER
TESTED
TESTER
TESTES
TETTER
TILTED
TILTER
TINTED
TITTER
TOLTEC
TOOTED
TOOTER
TOTTED
TOTTER
TOUTED
TOUTER
TRITER
TUFTED
ULSTER
UNITED
UNITES
UNSTEP
URETER
VASTER
VATTED
VENTED
VENTER
VERTEX
VESTED
VESTEE
VETTED
VORTEX
WAFTED
WAFTER
WAITED
WAITER
WALTER
WANTED
WANTER
WASTED
WASTER
WASTES
WELTED
WELTER
WESTER
WETTED
WETTER
WHITED
WHITEN
WHITER
WHITES
WHITEY
WILTED
WINTER
WITTED
WONTED
WRITER
WRITES
XYSTER
YESTER
ZESTED
ZOSTER

•••T•E

AORTAE
AUNTIE
BATTLE
BATTUE
BEETLE
BERTHE
BERTIE
BLITHE
BOOTEE
BOOTIE
BOTTLE
BUSTLE
CANTLE
CASTLE
CATTIE
CATTLE
CLOTHE
CONTRE
COOTIE
COSTAE
COTTAE
CUTTLE
DARTLE
DOTTLE
FETTLE
FOOTLE
GENTLE
GERTIE
GOATEE
GOETHE
GUTTAE
GUTTLE
HATTIE
HOGTIE
HURTLE
HUSTLE
JOSTLE
KETTLE
KILTIE
LAOTSE
LITTLE
LOATHE
LOTTIE
LYTTAE
MAITRE
MANTLE
MARTHE
MATTIE
MESTEE
METTLE
MOLTKE
MOTTLE
MUSTEE
MYRTLE
NESTLE
NETTIE
NETTLE
PANTIE
PESTLE
PINTLE
PLATTE
POTTLE
PUTTEE
QUATRE
RATTLE
RUSTLE
SARTRE
SCATHE
SCYTHE
SEETHE
SETTEE
SETTLE
SNATHE
SOOTHE
SORTIE
SPATHE
STATUE
SUBTLE
SUTTEE
SWATHE
TATTLE
TEETHE
TESTAE
TIPTOE
TITTLE
TOOTLE
TSETSE
TURTLE
VESTEE
VIRTUE
VITTAE
WATTLE
WRITHE

••••TE

ACUATE
ADNATE
AERATE
AGNATE
ALBITE
ANSATE
APLITE
ARBUTE
ASTUTE
AUGITE
AURATE
AVIATE
BABITE
BARITE
BERATE
BORATE
BRONTE
CANUTE
CAPOTE
CARATE
CAVITE
CERATE
CERITE
CHASTE
COMATE
COYOTE
CREATE
CURATE
DANITE
DEBATE
DELETE
DEMOTE
DENOTE
DEPUTE
DEVOTE
DILATE
DILUTE
DONATE
ECARTE
EFFETE
EMEUTE
EQUATE
ERGATE
ESTATE
EXCITE
FINITE
FIXATE
GAMETE
GYRATE
HALITE
HAMITE
HECATE
HORSTE
IDEATE
IGNITE
IMPUTE
INCITE
INMATE
INNATE
INVITE
IODATE
IOLITE
JUGATE
KARATE
LANATE
LEGATE
LEVITE
LIGATE
LOBATE
LOCATE
LUCITE
LUNATE
LUXATE
MALATE
MINUTE
MUTATE
MYCETE
NEGATE
OBLATE
OLEATE
OOCYTE
OOLITE
OPHITE
OPIATE
ORNATE
PAIUTE
PALATE
PEDATE
PELITE
PETITE
PEYOTE
PILATE
PINITE
PIRATE
PLATTE
POLITE
PUPATE
PYRITE
QUARTE
RATITE
REBATE
RECITE
REFUTE
RELATE
REMOTE
REPUTE
ROTATE
RUGATE
SALUTE
SAMITE
SEDATE
SEMITE
SENATE
SHIITE
SOLUTE
SOMITE
SPRITE
STACTE
SVELTE
TAXITE
TERETE
TRISTE
TUBATE
UPDATE
VACATE
VELATE
VOLUTE
ZONATE
ZYGOTE

T•F•••

TEFLON
TIFFED
TIFFIN
TOFFEE
TUFTED

T••F••

THEFTS
TIFFED
TIFFIN
TOFFEE
TRIFID
TRIFLE
TWOFER

T•••F•

TARIFF
TEPEFY
THRIFT
TIPOFF
TUMEFY
TYPIFY

T••••F

TARIFF
TIPOFF

•T•F••

STAFFS
STEFAN
STIFLE
STUFFS
STUFFY

•T••F•

STAFFS
STRAFE
STRIFE
STUFFS
STUFFY

•T•••F

ITSELF

••TF••

ARTFUL
BOTFLY
FITFUL
HATFUL
OUTFIT
OUTFOX
VATFUL

••T•F•

CUTOFF
MOTIFS
NOTIFY
PUTOFF
RATIFY
SETOFF

••T••F

CUTOFF
PUTOFF
SETOFF

•••T•F

GUSTAF

6

T•G•••
TAGGED
TAGGER
TEGMEN
TIGERS
TIGHTS
TOGAED
TOGGED
TOGGLE
TOGUES
TUGGED

T••G••
TAGGED
TAGGER
TAIGAS
TANGED
TANGLE
TANGLY
TANGOS
TARGET
TAUGHT
TERGAL
TERGUM
THIGHS
TINGED
TINGES
TINGLE
TINGLY
TOGGED
TOGGLE
TONGED
TONGUE
TOUGHS
TRAGIC
TRAGUS
TRIGLY
TRIGON
TROGON
TUGGED
TUNGUS
TURGID
TWIGGY

T•••G•
TELEGA
TELUGU
THINGS
THONGS
THOUGH
TOBAGO
TOWAGE
TROUGH
TRUDGE
TWANGS
TWANGY
TWIGGY
TWINGE

T••••G
TAKING
TAMING
TAPING
TARING
TAWING
TAXING
TEEING
THRONG
TIDING
TILING
TIMING
TIRING
TOEING
TONING
TOPING
TOTING
TOWING
TOYING
TRUING
TRYING
TUBING
TUNING
TYPING

•TG•••
UTGARD

•T•G••
STAGED
STAGER
STAGES
STAGEY
STAGGY
STIGMA
STOGEY

•T••G•
STAGGY
STINGS
STINGY
STODGE
STODGY
STOOGE

•T•••G
STALAG
STENOG
STRING
STRONG
STYING

••TG••
CATGUT
ROTGUT

••T•G•
DOTAGE
METAGE
POTAGE

••T••G
ACTING
BATING
BITING
CITING
DATING
DOTING
EATING
FATING
FETING
GATING
HATING
KITING
LUTING
MATING
METING
MUTING
NOTING
NUTMEG
OPTING
OUTING
PUTLOG
RATING
SATANG
SATING
TOTING
VOTING

•••T•G
RAGTAG

TH••••
THADDY
THADYS
THALES
THALIA
THAMES
THANAT
THANES
THANKS
THATCH
THAWED
THAYER
THEBAE
THEBES
THECAE
THECAL
THEDAS
THEFTS
THEIRS
THEISM
THEIST
THELMA
THEMES
THEMIS
THENAL
THENAR
THENCE
THEORY
THERMO
THERMS
THESES
THESIS
THETAS
THETIC
THETIS
THIEVE
THIGHS
THINGS
THINKS
THINLY
THIOLS
THIRDS
THIRST
THIRTY
THOLES
THOMAS
THONGS
THORAC
THORAX
THORIA
THORIC
THORNS
THORNY
THORON
THORPE
THOUGH
THRALL
THRASH
THREAD
THREAT
THREED
THREES
THRESH
THRICE
THRIFT
THRILL
THRIPS
THRIVE
THROAT
THROBS
THROES
THRONE
THRONG
THROVE
THROWN
THROWS
THRUMS
THRUSH
THRUST
THUJAS
THULIA
THUMBS
THUMPS
THWACK
THWART
THYMES
THYMIC
THYMOL
THYMUS
THYREO
THYRSE
THYRSI

T•H•••
TEHEED
TEHEES
TSHIRT

T••H••
TECHNO
TETHER
TETHYS
TIGHTS
TISHRI
TITHED
TITHER
TITHES
TOSHES
TOTHER
TUCHUN
TUSHED
TUSHES
TYPHLO
TYPHON
TYPHUS

T•••H•
TAUGHT
TEETHE
TENTHS
TETCHY
THIGHS
TILTHS
TOOTHY
TORAHS
TOUCHE
TOUCHY
TOUGHS
TRACHE
TRACHY
TRASHY
TRICHI
TRICHO
TROCHE
TROPHO
TROPHY
TROTHS
TRUTHS

T••••H
TERAPH
THATCH
THOUGH
THRASH
THRESH
THRUSH
TOBIAH
TOYISH
TRENCH
TROUGH
TUSSAH
TWITCH

•TH•••
ATHENA
ATHENE
ATHENS
ATHOME
ETHANE
ETHANS
ETHELS
ETHERS
ETHICS
ETHNIC
ETHYLS
ITHACA
OTHERS

•T•H••
ETCHED
ETCHER
ETCHES
ITCHED
ITCHES
UTAHAN

•T••H•
STETHO
STITHY

•T•••H
ATTACH
STANCH
STARCH
STENCH
STITCH

••TH••
AETHER
ALTHEA
ANTHEA
ANTHEM
ANTHER
ARTHRO
ARTHUR
ASTHMA
AUTHOR
BATHED
BATHER
BATHOS
BETHEL
BOTHER
CATHAY
CATHER
CATHYS
CITHER
DITHER
EITHER
ESTHER
FATHER
FATHOM
GATHER
GOTHAM
GOTHIC
HITHER
JETHRO
KATHIE
KATHYS
LATHED
LATHER
LATHES
LETHAL
LITHER
LITHIA
LITHIC
LUTHER
METHOD
METHYL
MOTHER
MYTHIC
MYTHOI
MYTHOS

NATHAN
NETHER
PATHAN
PATHIA
PATHOL
PATHOS
PITHED
POTHER
PYTHIA
PYTHIC
PYTHON
RATHER
SOTHIC
SOTHIS
TETHER
TETHYS
TITHED
TITHER
TITHES
TOTHER
WETHER
WITHAL
WITHED
WITHER
WITHES
WITHIN
WITHIT
ZETHOS
ZETHUS
ZITHER

••T•H•

BOTCHY
CATCHY
LOTAHS
PATCHY
PITCHY
ROTCHE
TETCHY

••T••H

ATTACH
DETACH
FETICH
FETISH
JUTISH
KITSCH
LATISH
POTASH
PUTSCH

•••TH•

AGATHA
APATHY
APHTHA
BERTHA
BERTHE
BERTHS
BIRTHS
BLITHE
BOOTHS
BROTHS
CANTHI
CLOTHE
CLOTHO
CLOTHS
DEATHS
DEATHY
DEPTHS
EARTHS
EARTHY
EDITHS
ERYTHR
FAITHS
FIFTHS
FILTHY
FIRTHS
FRITHS
FROTHS
FROTHY
GNATHO
GOETHE
HEATHS
HEATHY
ICHTHY
KEITHS
LOATHE
MALTHA
MARTHA
MARTHE
MONTHS
MOUTHS
MOUTHY
NINTHS
RHYTHM
SCATHE
SCYTHE
SEETHE
SIXTHS
SLOTHS
SMITHS
SMITHY
SNATHE
SNATHS
SOOTHE
SPATHE
STETHO
STITHY
SWATHE
SWATHS
TEETHE
TENTHS
TILTHS
TOOTHY
TROTHS
TRUTHS
URETHR
WIDTHS
WORTHY
WRATHY
WRITHE
XANTHO
YOUTHS

•••T•H

BLOTCH
CHETAH
CLUTCH
CRATCH
CROTCH
CRUTCH
CULTCH
FLETCH
FLITCH
HOOTCH
NAUTCH
QUITCH
SCOTCH
SCUTCH
SKETCH
SMUTCH
SNATCH
SNITCH
STITCH
SWATCH
SWITCH
THATCH
TWITCH
WRETCH

••••TH

BREATH
BYPATH
DALETH
DEARTH
DROUTH
DULUTH
EIGHTH
EOLITH
FOURTH
GROWTH
HEALTH
HEARTH
JUDITH
LENGTH
ORNITH
PLINTH
SHEATH
SLEUTH
SMOOTH
SPILTH
SWARTH
WARMTH
WEALTH
WRAITH
WREATH
ZENITH
ZIBETH
ZIZITH

TI••••

TIARAS
TIBIAE
TIBIAL
TIBIAS
TICALS
TICKED
TICKER
TICKET
TICKLE
TIDBIT
TIDIED
TIDIER
TIDIES
TIDILY
TIDING
TIEINS
TIERCE
TIERED
TIEUPS
TIFFED
TIFFIN
TIGERS
TIGHTS
TILDES
TILERS
TILING
TILLED
TILLER
TILLIE
TILLYS
TILTED
TILTER
TILTHS
TIMBAL
TIMBER
TIMBRE
TIMELY
TIMERS
TIMING
TIMMYS
TINCAL
TINCTS
TINDER
TINEID
TINGED
TINGES
TINGLE
TINGLY
TINKER
TINKLE
TINKLY
TINNED
TINNER
TINSEL
TINTED
TIPOFF
TIPPED
TIPPER
TIPPET
TIPPLE
TIPTOE
TIPTOP
TIRADE
TIRANA
TIRING
TISANE
TISHRI
TISSUE
TITANS
TITHED
TITHER
TITHES
TITIAN
TITLED
TITLES
TITTER
TITTLE
TITTUP

T•I•••

TAIGAS
TAILED
TAILLE
TAILOR
TAINOS
TAINTS
TAIPEI
TAIWAN
THIEVE
THIGHS
THINGS
THINKS
THINLY
THIOLS
THIRDS
THIRST
THIRTY
TOILED
TOILER
TOILES
TOILET
TRIADS
TRIALS
TRIBAL
TRIBES
TRICED
TRICES
TRICHI
TRICHO
TRICKS
TRICKY
TRICOT
TRIERS
TRIFID
TRIFLE
TRIGLY
TRIGON
TRILLS
TRIMLY
TRINAL
TRINED
TRINES
TRIODE
TRIOSE
TRIPLE
TRIPOD
TRIPOS
TRISTE
TRITER
TRIUNE
TRIVET
TRIVIA
TRIXIE
TRIXYS
TUILLE
TWIBIL
TWIGGY
TWILLS
TWINED
TWINER
TWINES
TWINGE
TWIRLS
TWIRPS
TWISTS
TWITCH

T••I••

TAKING
TALION
TAMING
TANIST
TAOISM
TAOIST
TAPING
TAPIRS
TARIFF
TARING
TAWING
TAXIED
TAXING
TAXITE
TEDIUM
TEEING
THEIRS
THEISM
THEIST
THRICE
THRIFT
THRILL
THRIPS
THRIVE
TIBIAE
TIBIAL
TIBIAS
TIDIED
TIDIER
TIDIES
TIDILY
TIDING
TIEINS
TILING
TIMING
TIRING
TITIAN
TOBIAH
TOBIAS
TOBIES
TODIES
TOEING
TONICS
TONIER
TONING
TOPICS
TOPING
TORIES
TORIIS
TOTING
TOWING
TOXINS
TOYING
TOYISH
TRAILS

TRAINS
TRAITS
TROIKA
TRUING
TRUISM
TRYING
TSHIRT
TUBING
TULIPS
TUNICA
TUNICS
TUNING
TUPIKS
TYPIFY
TYPING
TYPIST

T•••I•

TACTIC
TAENIA
TAKEIN
TANNIC
TANNIN
TENNIS
TENPIN
TENUIS
TERBIA
TESSIE
TESTIS
THALIA
THEMIS
THESIS
THETIC
THETIS
THORIA
THORIC
THULIA
THYMIC
TIDBIT
TIFFIN
TILLIE
TINEID
TMESIS
TOCSIN
TOMTIT
TONKIN
TONSIL
TORIIS
TOROID
TORPID
TORRID
TRAGIC
TRIFID
TRIVIA
TRIXIE
TROPIC
TURBID
TURBIT
TURGID
TURKIC
TURKIS
TURNIP
TUSSIS
TUTTIS
TWIBIL
TWOBIT

T••••I

TAIPEI
THYRSI
TISHRI
TRICHI
TULADI

•TI•••

ITIOUS
OTIOSE
OTITIS
PTISAN
STICKS
STICKY
STIFLE
STIGMA
STILES
STILLS
STILLY
STILTS
STINGS
STINGY
STINKS
STINTS
STIPEL
STIPES
STIRKS
STIRPS
STITCH
STITHY
STIVER

•T•I••

ATRIAL
ATRIUM
ATTICA
ATTICS
ATTILA
ATTIRE
ETHICS
STAINS
STAIRS
STEINS
STOICS
STRIAE
STRICK
STRICT
STRIDE
STRIFE
STRIKE
STRING
STRIPE
STRIPS
STRIPT
STRIPY
STRIVE
STYING

•T••I•

ATAVIC
ATAXIA
ATAXIC
ATOMIC
ATONIC
ATTAIN
ETHNIC
ITALIC
OTITIS
PTOSIS
STACIE
STADIA
STALIN
STAMIN
STASIS
STATIC
STELIC
STEPIN
STERIC
STEVIE
STOLID
STRAIN
STRAIT
STUDIO
STUPID
STYMIE
UTOPIA
YTTRIA
YTTRIC

•T•••I

STELLI
STRATI

••TI••

ACTING
ACTINI
ACTINO
ACTION
ACTIUM
ACTIVE
ANTIAR
ANTICS
ARTIES
ARTIST
ATTICA
ATTICS
ATTILA
ATTIRE
AUTISM
BATIKS
BATING
BETIDE
BETISE
BITING
CATION
CITIED
CITIES
CITING
CUTIES
CUTINS
DATING
DATIVE
DOTIER
DOTING
DUTIES
EATING
ENTICE
ENTIRE
ENTITY
FATIMA
FATING
FETIAL
FETICH
FETING
FETISH
FUTILE
GATING
HATING
INTIMA
JUTISH
KATIES
KATION
KITING
LATINS
LATISH
LOTION
LUTING
LUTIST
MATING
MATINS
METIER
METING
MOTIFS
MOTILE
MOTION
MOTIVE
MUTING
MUTINY
MUTISM
NATION
NATIVE
NOTICE
NOTIFY
NOTING
NOTION
OPTICS
OPTIMA
OPTIME
OPTING
OPTION
OUTING
PATINA
PATINE
PATIOS
PETITE
PITIED
PITIES
POTION
RATIFY
RATINE
RATING
RATION
RATIOS
RATITE
RETINA
RETIRE
RUTILE
SATING
SATINS
SATINY
SATIRE
SHTICK
SITINS
TITIAN
TOTING
ULTIMA
UNTIDY
UNTIED
UNTIES
VOTING
VOTIVE

••T•I•

ALTAIC
ALTAIR
ANTLIA
ANTRIM
ARTOIS
ASTRID
ATTAIN
BATTIK
CATKIN
CATLIN
CATNIP
CATTIE
CITRIC
DETAIL
DETAIN
ENTAIL
GOTHIC
HATPIN
HATTIE
IATRIC
INTUIT
KATHIE
LATRIA
LATVIA
LITHIA
LITHIC
LOTTIE
MATRIX
MATTIE
METRIC
MYTHIC
NETTIE
NITRIC
NITRID
NITWIT
NUTRIA
OBTAIN
OUTBID
OUTDID
OUTFIT
OUTSIT
OUTWIT
OXTAIL
PATHIA
PATOIS
PETAIN
PETRIE
POTPIE
POTSIE
PUTRID
PYTHIA
PYTHIC
RATLIN
RETAIL
RETAIN
SOTHIC
SOTHIS
TUTTIS
VITRIC
WITHIN
WITHIT
YTTRIA
YTTRIC

••T••I

ACTINI
ASTERI
MYTHOI
OCTOPI
OCTROI
SATORI
WATUSI

•••TI•

ABATIS
ACETIC
AORTIC
ARCTIC
AUNTIE
AUSTIN
AZOTIC
BALTIC
BATTIK
BERTIE
BESTIR
BIOTIC
BIOTIN
BOOTIE
BUSTIC
CATTIE
CELTIC
CHITIN
COATIS
CONTIN
COOTIE
COPTIC
CORTIN
CRETIC
CRETIN
CRITIC
CURTIS
CYSTIC
DENTIL
DENTIN
DHOTIS
DISTIL
EMETIC
EMETIN
ENATIC
EROTIC
EXOTIC
FISTIC
FOETID
FORTIS

FUSTIC
GERTIE
GESTIC
GRATIS
HATTIE
HECTIC
HESTIA
HOGTIE
IRITIC
IRITIS
JUSTIN
KILTIE
LACTIC
LENTIL
LOTTIE
LUETIC
MANTIC
MANTIS
MARTIN
MASTIC
MATTIE
MIOTIC
MUFTIS
MYSTIC
NASTIC
NETTIE
NOETIC
OTITIS
PANTIE
PASTIL
PECTIC
PECTIN
PEPTIC
PHOTIC
PHYTIN
PISTIL
POETIC
PONTIC
PONTIL
PORTIA
RUSTIC
SAITIC
SCOTIA
SEPTIC
SHUTIN
SORTIE
STATIC
TACTIC
TESTIS
THETIC
THETIS
TOMTIT
TUTTIS
URETIC
VIATIC
VICTIM

•••T•I
CANTHI
CENTRI
DMITRI
GLUTEI

••••TI
AGOUTI
DIGITI
GOMUTI
PEDATI
SMALTI
STRATI
VASHTI
WAPITI

T••J••
THUJAS
TROJAN

T•K•••
TAKEIN
TAKERS
TAKEUP
TAKING
TOKENS

T••K••
TACKED
TACKER
TACKEY
TACKLE
TALKED
TALKER
TANKAS
TANKED
TANKER
TASKED
TICKED
TICKER
TICKET
TICKLE
TINKER
TINKLE
TINKLY
TONKIN
TUCKED
TUCKER
TURKEY
TURKIC
TURKIS
TUSKED
TUSKER

T•••K•
THANKS
THINKS
TOPEKA
TORSKS
TRACKS
TRICKS
TRICKY
TROIKA
TRUCKS
TRUNKS
TUPIKS
TWEAKS
TWEAKY

T••••K
THWACK

•T•K••
STAKED
STAKES
STOKED
STOKER
STOKES

•T••K•
STACKS
STALKS
STALKY
STEAKS
STICKS
STICKY
STINKS
STIRKS
STOCKS
STOCKY
STOOKS
STORKS
STRAKE
STRIKE
STROKE

•T•••K
ATTACK
STREAK
STRICK
STRUCK

••TK••
CATKIN

••T•K•
BATIKS
BETAKE
INTAKE
RETAKE
UPTAKE

••T••K
ATTACK
BATTIK
BETOOK
BYTALK
RETOOK
SHTICK

•••TK•
MOLTKE

•••T•K
BARTOK
BATTIK

T•L•••
TALCED
TALCUM
TALENT
TALERS
TALION
TALKED
TALKER
TALLER
TALLOW
TALMUD
TALONS
TELEGA
TELLER
TELLUS
TELSON
TELUGU
TILDES
TILERS
TILING
TILLED
TILLER
TILLIE
TILLYS
TILTED
TILTER
TILTHS
TOLEDO
TOLLED
TOLLER
TOLTEC
TOLUOL
TOLUYL
TULADI
TULIPS
TULLES

T••L••
TABLED
TABLES
TABLET
TAILED
TAILLE
TAILOR
TALLER
TALLOW
TATLER
TAYLOR
TEFLON
TELLER
TELLUS
THALES
THALIA
THELMA
THOLES
THULIA
TILLED
TILLER
TILLIE
TILLYS
TITLED
TITLES
TOILED
TOILER
TOILES
TOILET
TOLLED
TOLLER
TOOLED
TOOLER
TOULON
TRILLS
TROLLS
TUILLE
TULLES
TWELVE
TWILLS

T•••L•
TACKLE
TAILLE
TAMALE
TANGLE
TANGLY
TAPALO
TARTLY
TATTLE
TAUTLY
TEMPLE
TERMLY
THINLY
THIOLS
THRALL
THRILL
TICALS
TICKLE
TIDILY
TIMELY
TINGLE
TINGLY
TINKLE
TINKLY
TIPPLE
TITTLE
TODDLE
TOGGLE
TOOTLE
TOPPLE
TOTALS
TOUSLE
TOWELS
TRAILS
TRAWLS
TREBLE
TRIALS
TRIFLE
TRIGLY
TRILLS
TRIMLY
TRIPLE
TROLLS
TUBULE
TUILLE
TUMBLE
TUMULT
TUPELO
TURTLE
TUSSLE
TWILLS
TWIRLS
TWOPLY
TYBALT
TYPHLO

T••••L
TARNAL
TARSAL
TASSEL
TEASEL
TERCEL
TERGAL
TETRYL
TETZEL
THECAL
THENAL
THRALL
THRILL
THYMOL
TIBIAL
TIMBAL
TINCAL
TINSEL
TOLUOL
TOLUYL
TONSIL
TRAVEL
TRIBAL
TRINAL
TROPAL
TROTYL
TROWEL
TUNNEL
TUSSAL
TWIBIL

•T•L••
ATOLLS
ATTLEE
ITALIC
STALAG
STALED
STALER
STALES
STALIN
STALKS
STALKY
STALLS
STELAE
STELAR
STELES
STELIC
STELLA
STELLI
STILES
STILLS
STILLY
STILTS
STOLED
STOLEN
STOLES
STOLID
STOLON
STULLS
STYLAR
STYLED
STYLER
STYLES
STYLET

6

STYLUS

•T••L•

ATOLLS
ATTILA
ETHELS
ETHYLS
ITSELF
STABLE
STALLS
STAPLE
STEALS
STEELS
STEELY
STELLA
STELLI
STIFLE
STILLS
STILLY
STOOLS
STROLL
STULLS

•T•••L

ATABAL
ATONAL
ATRIAL
STATAL
STEROL
STIPEL
STROLL

••TL••

ANTLER
ANTLIA
ATTLEE
BUTLER
CATLIN
CUTLAS
CUTLER
CUTLET
HITLER
MOTLEY
NUTLET
OUTLAW
OUTLAY
OUTLET
PUTLOG
RATLIN
SUTLER
TATLER
TITLED
TITLES

••T•L•

ARTELS
ATTILA
BATTLE
BETELS
BOTFLY
BOTTLE
BYTALK
CATALO
CATTLE
CITOLA
CUTELY
CUTTLE
DOTTLE
EXTOLS
FETTLE
FUTILE
GUTTLE
HOTELS
KETTLE
LATELY
LITTLE
METALS
METTLE
MOTELS
MOTILE
MOTTLE
MUTULE
NETTLE
PETALS
POTTLE
RATALS
RATELS
RATTLE
RATTLY
RETELL
RETOLD
RUTILE
SETTLE
SOTOLS
TATTLE
TITTLE
TOTALS
UNTOLD
VITALS
WATTLE

••T••L

ACTUAL
ARTFUL
ASTRAL
BETHEL
CITRAL
DETAIL
DOTTEL
ENTAIL
FETIAL
FITFUL
HATFUL
LETHAL
LUTEAL
METHYL
MITRAL
MUTUAL
OSTEAL
OXTAIL
PATHOL
PATROL
PETREL
PETROL
RETAIL
RETELL
RITUAL
TETRYL
TETZEL
VATFUL
WITHAL

•••TL•

BATTLE
BEETLE
BOTTLE
BUSTLE
CANTLE
CASTLE
CATTLE
COSTLY
CURTLY
CUTTLE
DAFTLY
DARTLE
DEFTLY
DOTTLE
FETTLE
FLATLY
FOOTLE
GENTLE
GUTTLE
HURTLE
HUSTLE
JOSTLE
JUSTLY
KETTLE
LASTLY
LITTLE
MANTLE
MEETLY
METTLE
MOSTLY
MOTTLE
MYRTLE
NEATLY
NESTLE
NETTLE
PARTLY
PERTLY
PESTLE
PINTLE
PORTLY
POTTLE
RATTLE
RATTLY
RUSTLE
SETTLE
SOFTLY
SUBTLE
SUBTLY
TARTLY
TATTLE
TAUTLY
TITTLE
TOOTLE
TURTLE
VASTLY
WATTLE

•••T•L

ACETAL
ACETYL
AMATOL
AMYTAL
AORTAL
BRUTAL
CARTEL
CENTAL
COSTAL
DACTYL
DENTAL
DENTIL
DISTAL
DISTIL
DOTTEL
FESTAL
FOETAL
FONTAL
GRETEL
HARTAL
HOSTEL
HYETAL
LENTIL
LINTEL
LISTEL
MANTEL
MENTAL
MORTAL
PASTEL
PASTIL
PISTIL
PISTOL
PONTIL
PORTAL
POSTAL
RECTAL
RENTAL
RICTAL
SANTOL
SEPTAL
SPITAL
STATAL
TROTYL
VESTAL

TM••••

TMESIS

T•M•••

TAMALE
TAMBAC
TAMERS
TAMEST
TAMING
TAMPAN
TAMPED
TAMPER
TAMPON
TAMTAM
TEMPER
TEMPLE
TEMPOS
TEMPTS
TIMBAL
TIMBER
TIMBRE
TIMELY
TIMERS
TIMING
TIMMYS
TOMANS
TOMATO
TOMBAC
TOMBED
TOMBOY
TOMCAT
TOMCOD
TOMMYS
TOMTIT
TOMTOM
TUMBLE
TUMEFY
TUMORS
TUMULT
TYMPAN

T••M••

TALMUD
TARMAC
TASMAN
TEAMED
TEEMED
TEEMER
TEGMEN
TERMED
TERMER
TERMLY
TERMOR
THAMES
THEMES
THEMIS
THOMAS
THUMBS
THUMPS
THYMES
THYMIC
THYMOL
THYMUS
TIMMYS
TOMMYS
TRAMPS
TREMOR
TRIMLY
TRUMAN
TRUMPS

T•••M•

TACOMA
TAXEME
THELMA
THERMO
THERMS
THRUMS
TOTEMS
TRAUMA

T••••M

TALCUM
TAMTAM
TANDEM
TAOISM
TEDIUM
TERGUM
THEISM
TOMTOM
TRUISM

•TM•••

UTMOST

•T•M••

ATAMAN
ATOMIC
ETYMON
STAMEN
STAMIN
STAMPS
STOMAT
STOMPS
STUMPS
STUMPY
STYMIE

•T••M•

ATHOME
STEAMS
STEAMY
STIGMA
STORMS
STORMY
STROMA
STRUMA
STRUMS

•T•••M

ATRIUM
STREAM

••TM••

BATMAN
BATMEN
HETMAN
LITMUS
MOTMOT
NUTMEG
OUTMAN
PITMAN
PITMEN

••T•M•

ASTHMA
AUTUMN
ECTOMY
ENTOMB
ENTOMO
FATIMA
GOTAMA
INTIMA
INTOMB
METUMP
OPTIMA
OPTIME
TOTEMS

ULTIMA

••T••M

ACTIUM
ANTHEM
ANTRIM
ANTRUM
AUTISM
BOTTOM
ESTEEM
FATHOM
GOTHAM
JETSAM
LUTEUM
MUTISM
PUTNAM

•••T•M

ACETUM
ADYTUM
BANTAM
BOTTOM
CUSTOM
DIATOM
DICTUM
FANTOM
LACTAM
RECTUM
RHYTHM
SCUTUM
SEPTUM
SPUTUM
SYSTEM
TAMTAM
TOMTOM
VICTIM

T•N•••

TANDEM
TANGED
TANGLE
TANGLY
TANGOS
TANIST
TANKAS
TANKED
TANKER
TANNED
TANNER
TANNIC
TANNIN
TANREC
TENACE
TENANT
TENDED
TENDER
TENDON
TENETS
TENNIS
TENONS
TENORS
TENPIN
TENREC
TENSED
TENSER
TENSES
TENSOR
TENTED
TENTER
TENTHS
TENUES
TENUIS
TENURE
TENUTO
TINCAL
TINCTS
TINDER
TINEID
TINGED
TINGES
TINGLE
TINGLY
TINKER
TINKLE
TINKLY
TINNED
TINNER
TINSEL
TINTED
TONERS
TONGED
TONGUE
TONICS
TONIER
TONING
TONKIN
TONSIL
TUNDRA
TUNERS
TUNEUP
TUNGUS
TUNICA
TUNICS
TUNING
TUNNED
TUNNEL

T••N••

TAENIA
TAINOS
TAINTS
TANNED
TANNER
TANNIC
TANNIN
TARNAL
TAUNTS
TBONES
TEENSY
TENNIS
THANAT
THANES
THANKS
THENAL
THENAR
THENCE
THINGS
THINKS
THINLY
THONGS
TINNED
TINNER
TRANCE
TRANSP
TRENCH
TRENDS
TRENDY
TRINAL
TRINED
TRINES
TRUNKS
TUNNED
TUNNEL
TURNED
TURNER
TURNIP
TWANGS
TWANGY
TWENTY
TWINED
TWINER
TWINES
TWINGE

T•••N•

TAKING
TALENT
TALONS
TAMING
TAPING
TARING
TAWING
TAXING
TECHNO
TEEING
TENANT
TENONS
TETANY
TETONS
THORNS
THORNY
THRONE
THRONG
TIDING
TIEINS
TILING
TIMING
TIRANA
TIRING
TISANE
TITANS
TOEING
TOKENS
TOMANS
TONING
TOPING
TOTING
TOWING
TOXINS
TOYING
TOYONS
TRAINS
TRIUNE
TRUANT
TRUING
TRYING
TUBING
TUNING
TYPING
TYRANT
TYRONE

T••••N

TAIWAN
TAKEIN
TALION
TAMPAN
TAMPON
TANNIN
TARPON
TARTAN
TARZAN
TASMAN
TAUTEN
TAVERN
TEFLON
TEGMEN
TELSON
TENDON
TENPIN
TESTON
TEUTON
THORON
THROWN
TIFFIN
TITIAN
TOCSIN
TONKIN
TOULON
TREPAN
TRIGON
TROGON
TROJAN
TRUMAN
TUCHUN
TUCSON
TURBAN
TUREEN
TUSCAN
TYCOON
TYMPAN
TYPHON

•T•N••

ATONAL
ATONED
ATONER
ATONES
ATONIC
ETHNIC
STANCE
STANCH
STANDS
STANZA
STENCH
STENOG
STINGS
STINGY
STINKS
STINTS
STONED
STONER
STONES
STUNTS

•T••N•

ATHENA
ATHENE
ATHENS
ATTEND
ATTUNE
ETHANE
ETHANS
STAINS
STEINS
STERNA
STERNO
STERNS
STRAND
STRING
STRONG
STYING
UTURNS

•T•••N

ATAMAN
ATTAIN
ATTORN
ETYMON
PTISAN
STALIN
STAMEN
STAMIN
STEFAN
STEPAN
STEPIN
STEVEN
STOLEN
STOLON
STRAIN
STREWN
UTAHAN

••TN••

CATNIP
JITNEY
PUTNAM
WITNEY

••T•N•

ACTING
ACTINI
ACTINO
ANTONS
ANTONY
ATTEND
ATTUNE
BATING
BATONS
BETONY
BITING
BOTANY
BUTANE
CATENA
CETANE
CITING
CUTINS
DATING
DETENT
DOTING
EATING
EXTANT
EXTEND
EXTENT
FATING
FETING
GATING
GITANO
HATING
INTEND
INTENT
INTONE
KETENE
KETONE
KITING
LATENT
LATINS
LITANY
LUTING
MATING
MATINS
METING
MUTANT
MUTING
MUTINY
NATANT
NOTING
OBTUND
OCTANE
OCTANT
OPTING
OUTING
PATENS
PATENT
PATINA
PATINE
PITONS
POTENT
PUTONS
RATINE
RATING
RETENE
RETINA
ROTUND
SATANG
SATING
SATINS
SATINY
SETONS
SITINS
TETANY
TETONS
TITANS
TOTING

VOTING

••T••N

ACTION
ASTERN
ATTAIN
ATTORN
AUTUMN
BATAAN
BATMAN
BATMEN
BATTEN
BITTEN
BUTTON
CATION
CATKIN
CATLIN
CITRON
COTTON
DETAIN
EXTERN
FATTEN
GOTTEN
HATPIN
HETMAN
INTERN
INTURN
JETTON
KATION
KITTEN
LATEEN
LATTEN
LOTION
MATRON
MITTEN
MOTION
MUTTON
NATHAN
NATION
NATRON
NOTION
OBTAIN
OPTION
OUTMAN
OUTRAN
OUTRUN
PATHAN
PATRON
PATTEN
PATTON
PETAIN
PITMAN
PITMEN
POTEEN
POTION
PYTHON
RATION
RATLIN
RATOON
RATTAN
RATTEN
RETAIN
RETURN
ROTTEN
SATEEN
SATURN
TITIAN
UPTOWN
UPTURN
WATSON
WITHIN

•••T•N

AUSTEN
AUSTIN
BARTON
BATTEN
BEATEN
BENTON
BHUTAN
BIOTIN
BITTEN
BOSTON
BRETON
BRITON
BUTTON
CAFTAN
CANTON
CARTON
CHITIN
CHITON
CONTIN
CORTIN
COTTON
CRETAN
CRETIN
CROTON
DALTON
DANTON
DAYTON
DENTIN
EASTON
EMETIN
FANTAN
FASTEN
FATTEN
FULTON
GASTON
GLUTEN
GOTTEN
HASTEN
JETTON
JUSTIN
KITTEN
LATTEN
LENTEN
LEPTON
LISTEN
MARTEN
MARTIN
MELTON
MILTON
MITTEN
MOLTEN
MORTON
MOUTON
MUTTON
NEKTON
NEWTON
PATTEN
PATTON
PECTEN
PECTIN
PHOTON
PHYTIN
PISTON
PLATAN
PLATEN
PONTON
PROTON
RATTAN
RATTEN
ROTTEN
SEXTAN
SEXTON
SHUTIN
SOFTEN
SULTAN
TARTAN
TAUTEN
TESTON
TEUTON
WALTON
WANTON
WHITEN
WYSTAN

TO••••

TOASTS
TOBAGO
TOBIAH
TOBIAS
TOBIES
TOCSIN
TODDLE
TODIES
TOECAP
TOEING
TOFFEE
TOGAED
TOGGED
TOGGLE
TOGUES
TOILED
TOILER
TOILES
TOILET
TOKENS
TOLEDO
TOLLED
TOLLER
TOLTEC
TOLUOL
TOLUYL
TOMANS
TOMATO
TOMBAC
TOMBED
TOMBOY
TOMCAT
TOMCOD
TOMMYS
TOMTIT
TOMTOM
TONERS
TONGED
TONGUE
TONICS
TONIER
TONING
TONKIN
TONSIL
TOOLED
TOOLER
TOOTED
TOOTER
TOOTHY
TOOTLE
TOOTSY
TOPEKA
TOPERS
TOPICS
TOPING
TOPPED
TOPPER
TOPPLE
TOQUES
TORAHS
TORERO
TORIES
TORIIS
TOROID
TOROSE
TOROUS
TORPID
TORPOR
TORQUE
TORRID
TORSKS
TORSOS
TOSHES
TOSSED
TOSSES
TOSSUP
TOTALS
TOTEMS
TOTERS
TOTHER
TOTING
TOTTED
TOTTER
TOUCHE
TOUCHY
TOUGHS
TOULON
TOUPEE
TOURED
TOUSLE
TOUTED
TOUTER
TOWAGE
TOWARD
TOWELS
TOWERS
TOWERY
TOWING
TOXINS
TOYERS
TOYING
TOYISH
TOYONS

T•O•••

TAOISM
TAOIST
TBONES
THOLES
THOMAS
THONGS
THORAC
THORAX
THORIA
THORIC
THORNS
THORNY
THORON
THORPE
THOUGH
TOOLED
TOOLER
TOOTED
TOOTER
TOOTHY
TOOTLE
TOOTSY
TROCAR
TROCHE
TROGON
TROIKA
TROJAN
TROLLS
TROOPS
TROPAL
TROPHO
TROPHY
TROPIC
TROTHS
TROTYL
TROUGH
TROUPE
TROUTS
TROVER
TROVES
TROWEL
TWOBIT
TWOFER
TWOPLY
TWOWAY

T••O••

TABOOS
TABORS
TACOMA
TALONS
TAROTS
TENONS
TENORS
TETONS
THEORY
THIOLS
THROAT
THROBS
THROES
THRONE
THRONG
THROVE
THROWN
THROWS
TIPOFF
TOROID
TOROSE
TOROUS
TOYONS
TRIODE
TRIOSE
TROOPS
TRYOUT
TUMORS
TUTORS
TYCOON
TYRONE

T•••O•

TABOOS
TAILOR
TAINOS
TALION
TALLOW
TAMPON
TANGOS
TARPON
TATTOO
TAYLOR
TEAPOT
TEAPOY
TEFLON
TELSON
TEMPOS
TENDON
TENSOR
TERMOR
TERROR
TESTON
TEUTON
THORON
THYMOL
TIPTOE
TIPTOP
TOLUOL
TOMBOY
TOMCOD
TOMTOM
TORPOR
TORSOS
TOULON
TREMOR
TRICOT
TRIGON
TRIPOD
TRIPOS
TROGON
TUCSON
TURBOT
TURCOS

TYCOON
TYPHON

T••••O
TAPALO
TATTOO
TECHNO
TENUTO
TERATO
TEREDO
THERMO
THYREO
TOBAGO
TOLEDO
TOMATO
TORERO
TRICHO
TROPHO
TUPELO
TUXEDO
TYPHLO

•TO•••
ATOLLS
ATOMIC
ATONAL
ATONED
ATONER
ATONES
ATONIC
PTOSIS
STOATS
STOCKS
STOCKY
STODGE
STODGY
STOGEY
STOICS
STOKED
STOKER
STOKES
STOLED
STOLEN
STOLES
STOLID
STOLON
STOMAT
STOMPS
STONED
STONER
STONES
STOOGE
STOOKS
STOOLS
STOOPS
STOPED
STOPES
STORAX
STORED
STORES
STOREY
STORKS
STORMS
STORMY
STOUPS
STOUTS
STOVER
STOVES
STOWED
UTOPIA

•T•O••
ATHOME
ATTORN
ITIOUS
OTIOSE
STOOGE
STOOKS
STOOLS
STOOPS
STRODE
STROKE
STROLL
STROMA
STRONG
STROPS
STROUD
STROVE
UTMOST

•T••O•
ETYMON
STATOR
STENOG
STEROL
STOLON
STUPOR

•T•••O
STAURO
STEREO
STERNO
STETHO
STUCCO
STUDIO

••TO••
ACTORS
AFTOSA
ANTONS
ANTONY
ARTOIS
ATTORN
AUTOED
BATONS
BETONY
BETOOK
CITOLA
CUTOFF
CUTOUT
DETOUR
ECTOMY
ENTOMB
ENTOMO
ESTOPS
EXTOLS
EXTORT
FETORS
FSTOPS
INTOMB
INTONE
KETONE
KETOSE
METOPE
MOTORS
OCTOPI
PATOIS
PITONS
PUTOFF
PUTONS
PUTOUT
RATOON
RETOLD
RETOOK
RETORT
ROTORS
SATORI
SETOFF
SETONS
SETOSE
SETOUS
SOTOLS
TETONS
TUTORS
UNTOLD
UPTOWN
VETOED
VETOER
VETOES

••T•O•
ACTION
AUTHOR
BATHOS
BETOOK
BETTOR
BOTTOM
BUTTON
CATION
CITRON
COTTON
DATTOS
DITTOS
FATHOM
HATBOX
HOTBOX
JETTON
KATION
LOTION
MATEOS
MATRON
MATZOS
MATZOT
METEOR
METHOD
METROS
MOTION
MOTMOT
MOTTOS
MUTTON
MYTHOI
MYTHOS
NATION
NATRON
NOTION
OCTROI
OPTION
OUTFOX
PATHOL
PATHOS
PATIOS
PATROL
PATRON
PATTON
PETROL
POTBOY
POTION
POTTOS
PUTLOG
PYTHON
RATION
RATIOS
RATOON
RETOOK
SETTOS
TATTOO
UNTROD
WATSON
ZETHOS

••T••O
ACTINO
ANTERO
ARTHRO
ARTURO
ASTERO
CATALO
ENTERO
ENTOMO
GITANO
HETERO
JETHRO
MATTEO
OCTAVO
POTATO
TATTOO

•••TO•
ABATOR
AMATOL
BARTOK
BARTON
BENTON
BESTOW
BETTOR
BOSTON
BOTTOM
BRETON
BRITON
BUTTON
CANTON
CANTOR
CANTOS
CAPTOR
CARTON
CASTOR
CENTOS
CHITON
CONTOS
COTTON
CROTON
CUSTOM
CUSTOS
DALTON
DANTON
DATTOS
DAYTON
DEBTOR
DIATOM
DITTOS
DOCTOR
EASTON
EDITOR
FACTOR
FANTOM
FOETOR
FULTON
GASTON
GENTOO
HECTOR
JETTON
KOWTOW
LECTOR
LENTOS
LEPTON
LICTOR
MELTON
MENTOR
MILTON
MORTON
MOTTOS
MOUTON
MUTTON
NEKTON
NESTOR
NEWTON
NOSTOC
ORATOR
PASTOR
PATTON
PEGTOP
PHOTON
PHOTOS
PICTOR
PINTOS
PISTOL
PISTON
PONTON
POTTOS
PRETOR
PROTON
PUNTOS
RECTOR
RECTOS
REDTOP
RHETOR
SANTOL
SARTOR
SECTOR
SETTOS
SEXTON
STATOR
SUITOR
TATTOO
TESTON
TEUTON
TIPTOE
TIPTOP
TOMTOM
UNSTOP
VECTOR
VIATOR
VICTOR
WALTON
WANTON
XYSTOS

•••T•O
ANATTO
AUSTRO
BISTRO
CASTRO
CENTRO
CLOTHO
DEXTRO
GASTRO
GENTOO
GHETTO
GIOTTO
GLOTTO
GNATHO
GROTTO
MATTEO
PIETRO
STETHO
TATTOO
VENTRO
XANTHO

••••TO
ALECTO
ANATTO
ARISTO
BASUTO
BENITO
BLASTO
BONITO
CERATO
CHAETO
CRYPTO
FRONTO
GAMETO
GENITO
GHETTO
GIOTTO
GLOTTO
GLYPTO
GROTTO
HEMATO
HEPATO
HERETO
KERATO
KINETO
LEANTO

LEGATO
MANITO
NEMATO
ODONTO
PASHTO
POTATO
POUSTO
PRESTO
PROCTO
PRONTO
QUARTO
REBATO
RIALTO
RIGHTO
RUBATO
SHINTO
SMALTO
SOMATO
SUBITO
TENUTO
TERATO
TOMATO
VOMITO

T•P•••
TAPALO
TAPERS
TAPING
TAPIRS
TAPPED
TAPPER
TAPPET
TEPEES
TEPEFY
TIPOFF
TIPPED
TIPPER
TIPPET
TIPPLE
TIPTOE
TIPTOP
TOPEKA
TOPERS
TOPICS
TOPING
TOPPED
TOPPER
TOPPLE
TUPELO
TUPIKS
TUPPED
TYPHLO
TYPHON
TYPHUS
TYPIFY
TYPING
TYPIST

T••P••
TAIPEI
TAMPAN
TAMPED
TAMPER
TAMPON
TAPPED
TAPPER
TAPPET
TARPON
TAUPES
TEAPOT
TEAPOY
TEMPER
TEMPLE
TEMPOS
TEMPTS
TENPIN
TIPPED
TIPPER
TIPPET
TIPPLE
TOPPED
TOPPER
TOPPLE
TORPID
TORPOR
TOUPEE
TREPAN
TRIPLE
TRIPOD
TRIPOS
TROPAL
TROPHO
TROPHY
TROPIC
TUPPED
TWOPLY
TYMPAN

T•••P•
TERAPH
THORPE
THRIPS
THUMPS
TIEUPS
TRAMPS
TROOPS
TROUPE
TRUMPS
TULIPS
TWERPS
TWIRPS

T••••P
TAKEUP
TEACUP
TIPTOP
TITTUP
TOECAP
TOSSUP
TRANSP
TUNEUP
TURNIP

•T•P••
ETAPES
STAPES
STAPLE
STEPAN
STEPIN
STEPPE
STEPUP
STIPEL
STIPES
STOPED
STOPES
STUPAS
STUPES
STUPID
STUPOR
UTOPIA

•T••P•
STAMPS
STEEPS
STEPPE
STIRPS
STOMPS
STOOPS
STOUPS
STRAPS
STRIPE
STRIPS
STRIPT
STRIPY
STROPS
STUMPS
STUMPY

•T•••P
STEPUP

••TP••
HATPIN
OUTPUT
POTPIE
PUTPUT

••T•P•
CUTUPS
ECTYPE
ESTOPS
FSTOPS
GETUPS
LETUPS
METOPE
OCTOPI
SETUPS
WATAPE
WATAPS

••T••P
CATNIP
CATSUP
ENTRAP
METUMP
SATRAP
TITTUP

•••T•P
INSTEP
PEGTOP
PENTUP
REDTOP
TIPTOP
TITTUP
UNSTEP
UNSTOP

T•Q•••
TOQUES
TUQUES

T••Q••
TORQUE

TR••••
TRACED
TRACER
TRACES
TRACHE
TRACHY
TRACKS
TRACTS
TRADED
TRADER
TRADES
TRAGIC
TRAGUS
TRAILS
TRAINS
TRAITS
TRAMPS
TRANCE
TRANSP
TRASHY
TRAUMA
TRAVEL
TRAVES
TRAWLS
TREADS
TREATS
TREATY
TREBLE
TREMOR
TRENCH
TRENDS
TRENDY
TREPAN
TRESSY
TRIADS
TRIALS
TRIBAL
TRIBES
TRICED
TRICES
TRICHI
TRICHO
TRICKS
TRICKY
TRICOT
TRIERS
TRIFID
TRIFLE
TRIGLY
TRIGON
TRILLS
TRIMLY
TRINAL
TRINED
TRINES
TRIODE
TRIOSE
TRIPLE
TRIPOD
TRIPOS
TRISTE
TRITER
TRIUNE
TRIVET
TRIVIA
TRIXIE
TRIXYS
TROCAR
TROCHE
TROGON
TROIKA
TROJAN
TROLLS
TROOPS
TROPAL
TROPHO
TROPHY
TROPIC
TROTHS
TROTYL
TROUGH
TROUPE
TROUTS
TROVER
TROVES
TROWEL
TRUANT
TRUCES
TRUCKS
TRUDGE
TRUDYS
TRUEST
TRUING
TRUISM
TRUMAN
TRUMPS
TRUNKS
TRUSTS
TRUSTY
TRUTHS
TRYING
TRYOUT
TRYSTS

T•R•••
TARGET
TARIFF
TARING
TARMAC
TARNAL
TAROTS
TARPON
TARRED
TARSAL
TARSUS
TARTAN
TARTAR
TARTER
TARTLY
TARZAN
TERAPH
TERATO
TERBIA
TERCEL
TERCET
TEREDO
TERESA
TERETE
TEREUS
TERGAL
TERGUM
TERMED
TERMER
TERMLY
TERMOR
TERRET
TERROR
TERRYS
TERSER
THRALL
THRASH
THREAD
THREAT
THREED
THREES
THRESH
THRICE
THRIFT
THRILL
THRIPS
THRIVE
THROAT
THROBS
THROES
THRONE
THRONG
THROVE
THROWN
THROWS
THRUMS
THRUSH
THRUST
TIRADE
TIRANA
TIRING
TORAHS
TORERO
TORIES
TORIIS
TOROID
TOROSE
TOROUS
TORPID
TORPOR
TORQUE
TORRID
TORSKS
TORSOS
TURBAN

TURBID
TURBIT
TURBOT
TURCOS
TUREEN
TURGID
TURKEY
TURKIC
TURKIS
TURNED
TURNER
TURNIP
TURRET
TURTLE
TYRANT
TYRONE

T••R••
TANREC
TARRED
TAURUS
TEARED
TENREC
TERRET
TERROR
TERRYS
TETRAD
TETRYL
THERMO
THERMS
THIRDS
THIRST
THIRTY
THORAC
THORAX
THORIA
THORIC
THORNS
THORNY
THORON
THORPE
THYREO
THYRSE
THYRSI
TIARAS
TIERCE
TIERED
TORRID
TOURED
TURRET
TWERPS
TWIRLS
TWIRPS

T•••R•
TABARD
TABORS
TAKERS
TALERS
TAMERS
TAPERS
TAPIRS
TATARS
TAVERN
TAWDRY
TAWERS
TAXERS
TENORS
TENURE
THEIRS
THEORY
THWART
TIGERS
TILERS
TIMBRE
TIMERS
TISHRI
TONERS
TOPERS
TORERO
TOTERS
TOWARD
TOWERS
TOWERY
TOYERS
TRIERS
TSHIRT
TUBERS
TUMORS
TUNDRA
TUNERS
TUTORS
TUYERE

T••••R
TACKER
TAGGER
TAILOR
TALKER
TALLER
TAMPER
TANKER
TANNER
TAPPER
TARTAR
TARTER
TASTER
TATLER
TATTER
TAUTER
TAYLOR
TEASER
TEDDER
TEEMER
TEETER
TELLER
TEMPER
TENDER
TENSER
TENSOR
TENTER
TERMER
TERMOR
TERROR
TERSER
TESTER
TETHER
TETTER
TEUCER
THAYER
THENAR
TICKER
TIDIER
TILLER
TILTER
TIMBER
TINDER
TINKER
TINNER
TIPPER
TITHER
TITTER
TOILER
TOLLER
TONIER
TOOLER
TOOTER
TOPPER
TORPOR
TOTHER
TOTTER
TOUTER
TRACER
TRADER
TREMOR
TRITER
TROCAR
TROVER
TUBBER
TUCKER
TURNER
TUSKER
TUSSAR
TWINER
TWOFER

•TR•••
ATREUS
ATRIAL
ATRIUM
STRAFE
STRAIN
STRAIT
STRAKE
STRAND
STRAPS
STRASS
STRATA
STRATI
STRAWS
STRAWY
STRAYS
STREAK
STREAM
STREET
STRESS
STREWN
STREWS
STRIAE
STRICK
STRICT
STRIDE
STRIFE
STRIKE
STRING
STRIPE
STRIPS
STRIPT
STRIPY
STRIVE
STRODE
STROKE
STROLL
STROMA
STRONG
STROPS
STROUD
STROVE
STRUCK
STRUMA
STRUMS
STRUTS

•T•R••
STARCH
STARED
STARER
STARES
STARRY
STARTS
STARVE
STEREO
STERES
STERIC
STERNA
STERNO
STERNS
STEROL
STIRKS
STIRPS
STORAX
STORED
STORES
STOREY
STORKS
STORMS
STORMY
STURDY
UTERUS
UTURNS
YTTRIA
YTTRIC

•T••R•
ATTARS
ATTIRE
ATTORN
ETHERS
OTHERS
OTTERS
STAIRS
STARRY
STAURO
STEERS
STUART
UTGARD
UTTERS

•T•••R
ATONER
ETCHER
STAGER
STALER
STARER
STATER
STATOR
STAYER
STELAR
STIVER
STOKER
STONER
STOVER
STUPOR
STYLAR
STYLER

••TR••
ANTRIM
ANTRUM
ASTRAL
ASTRAY
ASTRID
BETRAY
CITRAL
CITRIC
CITRON
CITRUS
ENTRAP
ENTREE
ESTRAY
ESTRUS
EXTRAS
HATRED
IATRIC
LATRIA
MATRIX
MATRON
METRIC
METROS
MITRAL
NATRON
NITRIC
NITRID
NUTRIA
OCTROI
OUTRAN
OUTRUN
PATROL
PATRON
PETREL
PETRIE
PETROL
PUTRID
SATRAP
SUTRAS
TETRAD
TETRYL
UNTROD
UNTRUE
VITRIC
YTTRIA
YTTRIC

••T•R•
ACTORS
ALTARS
ALTERS
ANTERO
ARTERY
ARTHRO
ARTURO
ASTERI
ASTERN
ASTERO
ASTERS
ATTARS
ATTIRE
ATTORN
BITERS
CATERS
DATARY
DATERS
DATURA
DETERS
DOTERS
EATERS
ENTERA
ENTERO
ENTERS
ENTIRE
ESTERS
EXTERN
EXTORT
FETORS
FUTURE
HATERS
HETERO
INTERN
INTERS
INTURN
JETHRO
LITERS
MATURE
METERS
MITERS
MOTORS
NATURE
NOTARY
NOTERS
OTTERS
OUTCRY
OUTERS
PATERS
PETARD
PETERS
RATERS
RETARD
RETIRE
RETORT
RETURN
RITARD
ROTARY
ROTORS
SATARA

SATIRE
SATORI
SATURN
SATYRS
SITARS
SUTURE
TATARS
TOTERS
TUTORS
UPTURN
UTTERS
VOTARY
VOTERS
WATERS
WATERY

••T••R
AETHER
ALTAIR
ANTHER
ANTIAR
ANTLER
ARTHUR
AUTHOR
BATHER
BATTER
BETTER
BETTOR
BITTER
BOTHER
BUTLER
BUTTER
CATHER
CITHER
COTTAR
COTTER
CUTLER
CUTTER
DETOUR
DITHER
DOTIER
DOTTER
EITHER
ESTHER
FATHER
FATTER
FETTER
FITTER
GATHER
GETTER
GUTTER
HATTER
HITHER
HITLER
HITTER
HOTTER
JITTER
LATHER
LATTER
LETTER
LITHER
LITTER
LUTHER
MATTER
METEOR
METIER
MOTHER
MUTTER
NETHER
NUTTER
PATTER
POTHER
POTTER
PUTTER
RATHER
RATTER
RITTER
ROTTER
SETTER
SITTER
SUTLER
TATLER
TATTER
TETHER
TETTER
TITHER
TITTER
TOTHER
TOTTER
VETOER
WETHER
WETTER
WITHER
ZITHER

•••TR•
ANITRA
AUSTRO
BISTRO
CASTRO
CENTRA
CENTRI
CENTRO
CONTRA
CONTRE
DEXTRO
DMITRI
ELYTRA
GANTRY
GASTRO
GENTRY
MAITRE
PALTRY
PANTRY
PASTRY
PELTRY
PIETRO
POETRY
QUATRE
ROSTRA
SARTRE
SENTRY
SULTRY
VENTRO
VESTRY
WINTRY

•••T•R
ABATER
ABATOR
AUSTER
AVATAR
BAITER
BANTER
BARTER
BATTER
BAXTER
BEATER
BESTIR
BETTER
BETTOR
BISTER
BITTER
BOLTER
BUSTER
BUTTER
CANTER
CANTOR
CAPTOR
CARTER
CASTER
CASTOR
CENTER
COLTER
COSTAR
COTTAR
COTTER
CRATER
CUSTER
CUTTER
DARTER
DEBTOR
DEFTER
DEXTER
DIETER
DOCTOR
DOTTER
DUSTER
EASTER
EDITOR
ELATER
ERYTHR
EXETER
FACTOR
FALTER
FASTER
FATTER
FESTER
FETTER
FILTER
FITTER
FLUTER
FOETOR
FOOTER
FOSTER
FRATER
GAITER
GARTER
GETTER
GOITER
GRATER
GUITAR
GUTTER
HALTER
HATTER
HEATER
HECTOR
HESTER
HITTER
HOTTER
HUNTER
HURTER
HYSTER
INSTAR
ISHTAR
JESTER
JILTER
JITTER
JOLTER
KILTER
KULTUR
LASTER
LATTER
LECTOR
LESTER
LETTER
LICTOR
LIFTER
LINTER
LISTER
LITTER
LOFTER
LOITER
LOOTER
LUSTER
MARTYR
MASTER
MATTER
MEETER
MELTER
MENTOR
MILTER
MINTER
MISTER
MOLTER
MOOTER
MORTAR
MUSTER
MUTTER
NEATER
NECTAR
NESTOR
NEUTER
NUTTER
ORATOR
OUSTER
OYSTER
PALTER
PASTER
PASTOR
PATTER
PELTER
PESTER
PEWTER
PICTOR
PIETER
PINTER
PLATER
PORTER
POSTER
POTTER
POUTER
POWTER
PRATER
PRETER
PRETOR
PUNTER
PUTTER
QUOTER
RAFTER
RANTER
RATTER
RECTOR
RENTER
RESTER
RHETOR
RIOTER
RITTER
ROOTER
ROSTER
ROTTER
ROUTER
SALTER
SARTOR
SCOTER
SECTOR
SETTER
SIFTER
SINTER
SISTER
SITTER
SKATER
SLATER
SMITER
SOFTER
STATER
STATOR
SUBTER
SUITOR
TARTAR
TARTER
TASTER
TATTER
TAUTER
TEETER
TENTER
TESTER
TETTER
TILTER
TITTER
TOOTER
TOTTER
TOUTER
TRITER
ULSTER
URETER
URETHR
VASTER
VECTOR
VENTER
VIATOR
VICTOR
WAFTER
WAITER
WALTER
WANTER
WASTER
WELTER
WESTER
WETTER
WHITER
WINTER
WRITER
XYSTER
YESTER
ZOSTER

••••TR
ELECTR

TS••••
TSADES
TSETSE
TSHIRT

T•S•••
TASKED
TASMAN
TASSEL
TASSET
TASTED
TASTER
TASTES
TESSIE
TESTAE
TESTED
TESTER
TESTES
TESTIS
TESTON
TISANE
TISHRI
TISSUE
TOSHES
TOSSED
TOSSES
TOSSUP
TUSCAN
TUSHED
TUSHES
TUSKED
TUSKER
TUSSAH
TUSSAL
TUSSAR
TUSSIS
TUSSLE

T••S••
TARSAL
TARSUS
TASSEL
TASSET

6

TEASED
TEASEL
TEASER
TEASES
TELSON
TENSED
TENSER
TENSES
TENSOR
TERSER
TESSIE
THESES
THESIS
TINSEL
TISSUE
TMESIS
TOASTS
TOCSIN
TONSIL
TORSKS
TORSOS
TOSSED
TOSSES
TOSSUP
TOUSLE
TRASHY
TRESSY
TRISTE
TRUSTS
TRUSTY
TRYSTS
TUCSON
TUSSAH
TUSSAL
TUSSAR
TUSSIS
TUSSLE
TWISTS

T•••S•

TAMEST
TANIST
TAOISM
TAOIST
TEENSY
TERESA
THEISM
THEIST
THIRST
THRASH
THRESH
THRUSH
THRUST
THYRSE
THYRSI
TOOTSY
TOROSE
TOYISH
TRANSP
TRESSY
TRIOSE
TRUEST
TRUISM
TSETSE
TYPIST

T••••S

TABLES
TABOOS
TABORS
TAIGAS
TAINOS
TAINTS
TAKERS
TALERS
TALONS
TAMERS
TANGOS
TANKAS
TAPERS
TAPIRS
TAROTS
TARSUS
TASTES
TATARS
TAUNTS
TAUPES
TAURUS
TAWERS
TAXERS
TAZZAS
TBONES
TEASES
TEDDYS
TEHEES
TELLUS
TEMPOS
TEMPTS
TENETS
TENNIS
TENONS
TENORS
TENSES
TENTHS
TENUES
TENUIS
TEPEES
TEREUS
TERRYS
TESTES
TESTIS
TETHYS
TETONS
THADYS
THALES
THAMES
THANES
THANKS
THEBES
THEDAS
THEFTS
THEIRS
THEMES
THEMIS
THERMS
THESES
THESIS
THETAS
THETIS
THIGHS
THINGS
THINKS
THIOLS
THIRDS
THOLES
THOMAS
THONGS
THORNS
THREES
THRIPS
THROBS
THROES
THROWS
THRUMS
THUJAS
THUMBS
THUMPS
THYMES
THYMUS
TIARAS
TIBIAS
TICALS
TIDIES
TIEINS
TIEUPS
TIGERS
TIGHTS
TILDES
TILERS
TILLYS
TILTHS
TIMERS
TIMMYS
TINCTS
TINGES
TITANS
TITHES
TITLES
TMESIS
TOASTS
TOBIAS
TOBIES
TODIES
TOGUES
TOILES
TOKENS
TOMANS
TOMMYS
TONERS
TONICS
TOPERS
TOPICS
TOQUES
TORAHS
TORIES
TORIIS
TOROUS
TORSKS
TORSOS
TOSHES
TOSSES
TOTALS
TOTEMS
TOTERS
TOUGHS
TOWELS
TOWERS
TOXINS
TOYERS
TOYONS
TRACES
TRACKS
TRACTS
TRADES
TRAGUS
TRAILS
TRAINS
TRAITS
TRAMPS
TRAVES
TRAWLS
TREADS
TREATS
TRENDS
TRIADS
TRIALS
TRIBES
TRICES
TRICKS
TRIERS
TRILLS
TRINES
TRIPOS
TRIXYS
TROLLS
TROOPS
TROTHS
TROUTS
TROVES
TRUCES
TRUCKS
TRUDYS
TRUMPS
TRUNKS
TRUSTS
TRUTHS
TRYSTS
TSADES
TUBERS
TULIPS
TULLES
TUMORS
TUNERS
TUNGUS
TUNICS
TUPIKS
TUQUES
TURCOS
TURKIS
TUSHES
TUSSIS
TUTORS
TUTTIS
TWANGS
TWEAKS
TWEEDS
TWEETS
TWERPS
TWILLS
TWINES
TWIRLS
TWIRPS
TWISTS
TYPHUS

•TS•••

ITSELF

•T•S••

PTISAN
PTOSIS
STASES
STASIS

•T••S•

ATTEST
OTIOSE
STRASS
STRESS
UTMOST

•T•••S

ATHENS
ATOLLS
ATONES
ATREUS
ATTARS
ATTICS
ETAPES
ETCHES
ETHANS
ETHELS
ETHERS
ETHICS
ETHYLS
ETUDES
ITCHES
ITIOUS
OTHERS
OTITIS
OTTERS
PTOSIS
STACKS
STACYS
STAFFS
STAGES
STAINS
STAIRS
STAKES
STALES
STALKS
STALLS
STAMPS
STANDS
STAPES
STARES
STARTS
STASES
STASIS
STATES
STATUS
STAVES
STEAKS
STEALS
STEAMS
STEEDS
STEELS
STEEPS
STEERS
STEINS
STELES
STERES
STERNS
STEVES
STICKS
STILES
STILLS
STILTS
STINGS
STINKS
STINTS
STIPES
STIRKS
STIRPS
STOATS
STOCKS
STOICS
STOKES
STOLES
STOMPS
STONES
STOOKS
STOOLS
STOOPS
STOPES
STORES
STORKS
STORMS
STOUPS
STOUTS
STOVES
STRAPS
STRASS
STRAWS
STRAYS
STRESS
STREWS
STRIPS
STROPS
STRUMS
STRUTS
STUFFS
STULLS
STUMPS
STUNTS
STUPAS
STUPES
STYLES
STYLUS
UTERUS
UTTERS
UTURNS

••TS••

BETSYS
CATSUP
JETSAM
KITSCH
OUTSAT
OUTSET
OUTSIT
PATSYS
POTSIE
PUTSCH
WATSON

••T•S•

AFTOSA
ARTIST
ATTEST
AUTISM
BETISE
CUTEST
DETEST
FETISH
JUTISH
KETOSE
LATEST
LATISH
LUTIST
MUTISM
OBTEST
OBTUSE
POTASH
RETUSE
SETOSE
WATUSI

••T••S

ACTORS
ALTARS
ALTERS
ANTICS
ANTONS
ARTELS
ARTIES
ARTOIS
ASTERS
ATTARS
ATTICS
AZTECS
BATHOS
BATIKS
BATONS
BETELS
BETSYS
BETTES
BETTYS
BITERS
BUTTES
CATERS
CATHYS
CITIES
CITRUS
COTTAS
CUTEYS
CUTIES
CUTINS
CUTLAS
CUTUPS
DATERS
DATTOS
DETERS
DITTOS
DOTERS
DUTIES
EATERS
ENTERS
ESTERS
ESTOPS
ESTRUS
EXTOLS
EXTRAS
FETORS
FSTOPS
GETUPS
HATERS
HATTYS
HETTYS
HOTELS
INTERS
KATHYS
KATIES
KITTYS
LATHES
LATINS
LETUPS
LITERS
LITMUS
LOTAHS
MATEOS
MATEYS
MATINS
MATTES
MATZOS
METALS
METERS
METROS
MITERS
MOTELS
MOTIFS
MOTORS
MOTTOS
MYTHOS
NOTERS
OCTADS
OCTETS
OPTICS
OTTERS
OUTERS
PATENS
PATERS
PATHOS
PATIOS
PATOIS
PATSYS
PETALS
PETERS
PITIES
PITONS
POTTOS
PUTONS
RATALS
RATELS
RATERS
RATIOS
ROTORS
SATINS
SATYRS
SETONS
SETOUS
SETTOS
SETUPS
SITARS
SITINS
SOTHIS
SOTOLS
SUTRAS
TATARS
TETHYS
TETONS
TITANS
TITHES
TITLES
TOTALS
TOTEMS
TOTERS
TUTORS
TUTTIS
UNTIES
UTTERS
VETOES
VITALS
VOTERS
WATAPS
WATERS
WITHES
ZETHOS
ZETHUS

•••TS•

CURTSY
LAOTSE
TOOTSY
TSETSE

•••T•S

ABATES
ABATIS
AEETES
AGATES
ANITAS
AORTAS
ARETES
BANTUS
BASTES
BERTHS
BETTES
BETTYS
BIRTHS
BOOTHS
BROTHS
BRUTES
BRUTUS
BUTTES
CACTUS
CANTOS
CANTUS
CARTES
CASTES
CENTOS
CERTES
CESTUS
CHUTES
CLOTHS
COATIS
CONTES
CONTOS
CORTES
COTTAS
CRATES
CULTUS
CURTIS
CUSTOS
DATTOS
DEATHS
DELTAS
DEPTHS
DHOTIS
DITTOS
EARTHS
EDITHS
ELATES
EMOTES
ENATES
EVITAS
FAITHS
FIFTHS
FIRTHS
FLATUS
FLUTES
FOETUS
FORTES
FORTIS
FRITHS
FROTHS
GENTES
GERTYS
GRATES
GRATIS
GRETAS
HASTES
HATTYS
HEATHS
HETTYS
HIATUS
IRITIS
JUNTAS
JUSTUS
KEITHS
KITTYS
LENTOS
MANTAS
MANTES
MANTIS
MARTAS
MARTYS
MATTES
MEATUS
MONTES
MONTHS
MONTYS
MORTYS
MOTTOS
MOUTHS
MUFTIS
NANTES
NINTHS
ORATES
OTITIS
PASTAS
PASTES
PHOTOS
PINTOS
PLATES
PLUTUS
PONTES
POTTOS
PRATES
PUNTOS
QUOTAS
QUOTES
RECTOS
RECTUS
RENTES
RIATAS
RICTUS
ROUTES
SAUTES
SCOTTS
SCUTES
SETTOS
SHOTES
SIXTES
SIXTHS
SKATES
SLATES
SLOTHS
SMITES
SMITHS
SNATHS
SOFTAS
SPATES
SPITES
STATES
STATUS
SUITES
SWATHS
TASTES
TENTHS
TESTES
TESTIS
THETAS
THETIS
TILTHS
TROTHS
TRUTHS
TUTTIS
UNITES
VESTAS
VISTAS
WASTES
WHITES
WIDTHS
WRITES
XYSTOS
XYSTUS
YOUTHS
ZLOTYS

••••TS

ABBOTS
ABORTS
ADAPTS
ADEPTS
ADMITS
ADOPTS
ADULTS
AGENTS
AGISTS
AGLETS
ALERTS
ALEUTS
ALLOTS
AMBITS
AMENTS
ARGOTS
ARMETS
ASCOTS
ASSETS
AUDITS
AUGHTS
AVERTS
AWAITS
BEASTS
BEAUTS
BEFITS
BEGETS
BERETS
BESETS
BESOTS
BIDETS
BIGHTS
BIGOTS
BINITS
BLASTS
BLEATS
BLOATS
BLUETS
BLUNTS
BLURTS
BOASTS
BOOSTS
BRACTS
BRANTS
BRENTS
BRUITS
BURSTS
CADETS
CARATS
CARETS
CHANTS
CHARTS
CHEATS
CHESTS
CIVETS
CLEATS

CLEFTS
CLINTS
CLOUTS
COASTS
COMETS
COOPTS
COUNTS
COURTS
COVETS
CRAFTS
CRESTS
CROATS
CROFTS
CRUETS
CRUSTS
CRYPTS
CUBITS
CULETS
DAUNTS
DAVITS
DEBITS
DEBUTS
DEISTS
DEMITS
DEPOTS
DIGITS
DIVOTS
DIXITS
DONETS
DOUBTS
DRAFTS
DRIFTS
DROITS
DUCATS
EBOATS
EDICTS
EDUCTS
EGESTS
EGRETS
EIGHTS
EJECTS
ELECTS
ELIOTS
EMMETS
ENACTS
EPACTS
ERECTS
ERUCTS
ERUPTS
EVENTS
EVERTS
EVICTS
EXACTS
EXALTS
EXERTS
EXISTS
EXULTS
FACETS
FAGOTS
FAINTS
FAULTS
FEASTS
FEINTS
FEISTS

FIGHTS
FILETS
FIRSTS
FLEETS
FLINTS
FLIRTS
FLOATS
FLOUTS
FOISTS
FOUNTS
FRONTS
FROSTS
FRUITS
GAMUTS
GAVOTS
GEMOTS
GENETS
GHAUTS
GHOSTS
GIANTS
GLEETS
GLINTS
GLOATS
GLOSTS
GRAFTS
GRANTS
GREATS
GREETS
GROATS
GROUTS
GRUNTS
GUESTS
GUILTS
HABITS
HAUNTS
HEARTS
HEISTS
HELOTS
HOISTS
IDIOTS
INGOTS
INLETS
INPUTS
INSETS
ISLETS
JABOTS
JANETS
JAUNTS
JOINTS
JOISTS
JOUSTS
JURATS
KARATS
KNOUTS
KRAITS
LIGHTS
LIMITS
LUNETS
MAGOTS
MERITS
MOULTS
MOUNTS
MULCTS
NIGHTS

OCTETS
ONSETS
ORBITS
OWLETS
PAINTS
PEWITS
PICOTS
PILOTS
PIPETS
PIPITS
PIVOTS
PLAITS
PLANTS
PLEATS
POINTS
POSITS
POULTS
PRINTS
QUANTS
QUARTS
QUESTS
QUILTS
QUINTS
QUIRTS
QUOITS
REACTS
REBUTS
REFITS
REMITS
RESETS
REVETS
RIGHTS
RIVETS
ROASTS
ROBOTS
ROOSTS
ROUSTS
SABOTS
SAINTS
SAULTS
SCENTS
SCOOTS
SCOTTS
SCOUTS
SEBATS
SHAFTS
SHEETS
SHIFTS
SHIRTS
SHOATS
SHOOTS
SHORTS
SHOUTS
SHUNTS
SIGHTS
SKIRTS
SLANTS
SLEETS
SMARTS
SMELTS
SMOLTS
SNOOTS
SNORTS
SNOUTS

SPAITS
SPIRTS
SPLATS
SPLITS
SPORTS
SPOUTS
SPRATS
SPRITS
SPURTS
SQUATS
STARTS
STILTS
STINTS
STOATS
STOUTS
STRUTS
STUNTS
SWEATS
SWEETS
SWIFTS
TAINTS
TAROTS
TAUNTS
TEMPTS
TENETS
THEFTS
TIGHTS
TINCTS
TOASTS
TRACTS
TRAITS
TREATS
TROUTS
TRUSTS
TRYSTS
TWEETS
TWISTS
UBOATS
UBOLTS
UNHATS
UPSETS
VALETS
VAULTS
VAUNTS
VELDTS
VERSTS
VISITS
VOMITS
WAISTS
WHEATS
WHORTS
WORSTS
WRESTS
WRISTS
YACHTS
YEASTS
ZIBETS

T•T•••

TATARS
TATLER
TATTED
TATTER
TATTLE

TATTOO
TETANY
TETCHY
TETHER
TETHYS
TETONS
TETRAD
TETRYL
TETTER
TETZEL
TITANS
TITHED
TITHER
TITHES
TITIAN
TITLED
TITLES
TITTER
TITTLE
TITTUP
TOTALS
TOTEMS
TOTERS
TOTHER
TOTING
TOTTED
TOTTER
TUTORS
TUTTIS

T••T••

TACTIC
TAMTAM
TARTAN
TARTAR
TARTER
TARTLY
TASTED
TASTER
TASTES
TATTED
TATTER
TATTLE
TATTOO
TAUTEN
TAUTER
TAUTLY
TEETER
TEETHE
TENTED
TENTER
TENTHS
TESTAE
TESTED
TESTER
TESTES
TESTIS
TESTON
TETTER
TEUTON
THATCH
THETAS
THETIC
THETIS

TILTED
TILTER
TILTHS
TINTED
TIPTOE
TIPTOP
TITTER
TITTLE
TITTUP
TOLTEC
TOMTIT
TOMTOM
TOOTED
TOOTER
TOOTHY
TOOTLE
TOOTSY
TOTTED
TOTTER
TOUTED
TOUTER
TRITER
TROTHS
TROTYL
TRUTHS
TSETSE
TUFTED
TURTLE
TUTTIS
TWITCH

T•••T•

TAINTS
TAROTS
TAUNTS
TAXITE
TEMPTS
TENETS
TENUTO
TERATO
TERETE
THEFTS
THIRTY
TIGHTS
TINCTS
TOASTS
TOMATO
TRACTS
TRAITS
TREATS
TREATY
TRISTE
TROUTS
TRUSTS
TRUSTY
TRYSTS
TUBATE
TWEETS
TWENTY
TWISTS

T••••T

TABLET
TALENT

TAMEST
TANIST
TAOIST
TAPPET
TARGET
TASSET
TAUGHT
TEAPOT
TENANT
TERCET
TERRET
THANAT
THEIST
THIRST
THREAT
THRIFT
THROAT
THRUST
THWART
TICKET
TIDBIT
TIPPET
TOILET
TOMCAT
TOMTIT
TRICOT
TRIVET
TRUANT
TRUEST
TRYOUT
TSHIRT
TUMULT
TURBIT
TURBOT
TURRET
TWOBIT
TYBALT
TYPIST
TYRANT

•TT•••
ATTACH
ATTACK
ATTAIN
ATTARS
ATTEND
ATTEST
ATTICA
ATTICS
ATTILA
ATTIRE
ATTLEE
ATTORN
ATTUNE
OTTAVA
OTTAWA
OTTERS
UTTERS
YTTRIA
YTTRIC

•T•T••
OTITIS
STATAL

STATED
STATER
STATES
STATIC
STATOR
STATUE
STATUS
STETHO
STITCH
STITHY

•T••T•
STACTE
STARTS
STILTS
STINTS
STOATS
STOUTS
STRATA
STRATI
STRUTS
STUNTS

•T•••T
ATTEST
STOMAT
STRAIT
STREET
STRICT
STRIPT
STUART
STYLET
UTMOST

••TT••
BATTED
BATTEN
BATTER
BATTIK
BATTLE
BATTUE
BETTED
BETTER
BETTES
BETTOR
BETTYS
BITTED
BITTEN
BITTER
BOTTLE
BOTTOM
BUTTED
BUTTER
BUTTES
BUTTON
CATTED
CATTIE
CATTLE
COTTAE
COTTAR
COTTAS
COTTER
COTTON
CUTTER

CUTTLE
DATTOS
DITTOS
DOTTED
DOTTEL
DOTTER
DOTTLE
FATTED
FATTEN
FATTER
FETTER
FETTLE
FITTED
FITTER
GETTER
GOTTEN
GUTTAE
GUTTAT
GUTTED
GUTTER
GUTTLE
HATTED
HATTER
HATTIE
HATTYS
HETTYS
HITTER
HOTTER
HUTTED
JETTED
JETTON
JITTER
JOTTED
JUTTED
KETTLE
KITTEN
KITTYS
LATTEN
LATTER
LETTER
LITTER
LITTLE
LOTTIE
LYTTAE
MATTED
MATTEO
MATTER
MATTES
MATTIE
METTLE
MITTEN
MOTTLE
MOTTOS
MUTTER
MUTTON
NETTED
NETTIE
NETTLE
NUTTED
NUTTER
PATTED
PATTEN
PATTER
PATTON

PETTED
PITTED
POTTED
POTTER
POTTLE
POTTOS
PUTTED
PUTTEE
PUTTER
RATTAN
RATTED
RATTEN
RATTER
RATTLE
RATTLY
RETTED
RITTER
ROTTED
ROTTEN
ROTTER
RUTTED
SETTEE
SETTER
SETTLE
SETTOS
SITTER
SUTTEE
TATTED
TATTER
TATTLE
TATTOO
TETTER
TITTER
TITTLE
TITTUP
TOTTED
TOTTER
TUTTIS
VATTED
VETTED
VITTAE
WATTLE
WETTED
WETTER
WITTED

••T•T•
ASTUTE
ENTITY
ESTATE
MUTATE
OCTETS
PETITE
POTATO
RATITE
ROTATE

••T••T
ARTIST
ATTEST
CATGUT
CUTEST
CUTLET
CUTOUT

DETECT
DETENT
DETEST
EXTANT
EXTENT
EXTORT
GUTTAT
INTACT
INTENT
INTUIT
LATENT
LATEST
LUTIST
MATZOT
MOTMOT
MUTANT
NATANT
NITWIT
NUTLET
OBTECT
OBTEST
OCTANT
OUTFIT
OUTLET
OUTPUT
OUTSAT
OUTSET
OUTSIT
OUTWIT
PATENT
POTENT
PUTOUT
PUTPUT
RETORT
ROTGUT
URTEXT
WITHIT

•••TT•
ANATTO
CHATTY
CHITTY
CLOTTY
FRETTY
GHETTO
GIOTTO
GLOTTO
GRITTY
GROTTO
KNOTTY
PLATTE
PRETTY
SCOTTS
SMUTTY
SNOTTY
SPOTTY

•••T•T
GUTTAT
SEPTET
SESTET
SEXTET
TOMTIT

••••TT
ABWATT
ALCOTT
DEWITT
EMMETT

TU••••
TUBATE
TUBBED
TUBBER
TUBERS
TUBING
TUBULE
TUCHUN
TUCKED
TUCKER
TUCSON
TUFTED
TUGGED
TUILLE
TULADI
TULIPS
TULLES
TUMBLE
TUMEFY
TUMORS
TUMULT
TUNDRA
TUNERS
TUNEUP
TUNGUS
TUNICA
TUNICS
TUNING
TUNNED
TUNNEL
TUPELO
TUPIKS
TUPPED
TUQUES
TURBAN
TURBID
TURBIT
TURBOT
TURCOS
TUREEN
TURGID
TURKEY
TURKIC
TURKIS
TURNED
TURNER
TURNIP
TURRET
TURTLE
TUSCAN
TUSHED
TUSHES
TUSKED
TUSKER
TUSSAH
TUSSAL
TUSSAR
TUSSIS

TUSSLE
TUTORS
TUTTIS
TUXEDO
TUYERE

T•U•••

TAUGHT
TAUNTS
TAUPES
TAURUS
TAUTEN
TAUTER
TAUTLY
TEUCER
TEUTON
THUJAS
THULIA
THUMBS
THUMPS
TOUCHE
TOUCHY
TOUGHS
TOULON
TOUPEE
TOURED
TOUSLE
TOUTED
TOUTER
TRUANT
TRUCES
TRUCKS
TRUDGE
TRUDYS
TRUEST
TRUING
TRUISM
TRUMAN
TRUMPS
TRUNKS
TRUSTS
TRUSTY
TRUTHS

T••U••

TELUGU
TENUES
TENUIS
TENURE
TENUTO
THOUGH
THRUMS
THRUSH
THRUST
TIEUPS
TOGUES
TOLUOL
TOLUYL
TOQUES
TRAUMA
TRIUNE
TROUGH
TROUPE
TROUTS
TUBULE
TUMULT
TUQUES

T•••U•

TAKEUP
TALCUM
TALMUD
TARSUS
TAURUS
TEACUP
TEDIUM
TELLUS
TEREUS
TERGUM
THYMUS
TISSUE
TITTUP
TONGUE
TOROUS
TORQUE
TOSSUP
TRAGUS
TRYOUT
TUCHUN
TUNEUP
TUNGUS
TYPHUS

T••••U

TELUGU

•TU•••

ETUDES
STUART
STUBBY
STUCCO
STUDIO
STUFFS
STUFFY
STULLS
STUMPS
STUMPY
STUNTS
STUPAS
STUPES
STUPID
STUPOR
STURDY
UTURNS

•T•U••

ATTUNE
STAURO
STOUPS
STOUTS
STRUCK
STRUMA
STRUMS
STRUTS

•T••U•

ATREUS
ATRIUM
ITIOUS
STATUE
STATUS
STEPUP
STROUD
STYLUS
UTERUS

••TU••

ACTUAL
ARTURO
ASTUTE
ATTUNE
AUTUMN
CUTUPS
DATURA
FUTURE
GETUPS
INTUIT
INTURN
LETUPS
MATURE
METUMP
MUTUAL
MUTULE
NATURE
OBTUND
OBTUSE
RETURN
RETUSE
RITUAL
ROTUND
SATURN
SETUPS
SUTURE
UPTURN
WATUSI

••T•U•

ACTIUM
ANTRUM
ARTFUL
ARTHUR
BATTUE
CATGUT
CATSUP
CITRUS
CUTOUT
DETOUR
ESTRUS
FITFUL
HATFUL
LITMUS
LUTEUM
OUTPUT
OUTRUN
PUTOUT
PUTPUT
ROTGUT
SETOUS
TITTUP
UNTRUE
VATFUL
ZETHUS

••T••U

BATEAU
COTEAU

•••TU•

ACETUM
ADYTUM
BANTUS
BATTUE
BRUTUS
CACTUS
CANTUS
CESTUS
CULTUS
DICTUM
FLATUS
FOETUS
HIATUS
JUSTUS
KULTUR
MANTUA
MEATUS
PENTUP
PLUTUS
RECTUM
RECTUS
RICTUS
SCUTUM
SEPTUM
SPUTUM
STATUE
STATUS
TITTUP
VIRTUE
XYSTUS

••••TU

MANITU

T•V•••

TAVERN

T••V••

TRAVEL
TRAVES
TRIVET
TRIVIA
TROVER
TROVES

T•••V•

THIEVE
THRIVE
THROVE
TWELVE

•T•V••

ATAVIC
STAVED
STAVES
STEVEN
STEVES
STEVIE
STIVER
STOVER
STOVES

•T••V•

OTTAVA
STARVE
STEEVE
STRIVE
STROVE

••TV••

LATVIA

••T•V•

ACTIVE
DATIVE
MOTIVE
NATIVE
OCTAVE
OCTAVO
OTTAVA
VOTIVE

•••T•V

GUSTAV

TW••••

TWANGS
TWANGY
TWEAKS
TWEAKY
TWEEDS
TWEETS
TWELVE
TWENTY
TWERPS
TWIBIL
TWIGGY
TWILLS
TWINED
TWINER
TWINES
TWINGE
TWIRLS
TWIRPS
TWISTS
TWITCH
TWOBIT
TWOFER
TWOPLY
TWOWAY

T•W•••

TAWDRY
TAWERS
TAWING
THWACK
THWART
TOWAGE
TOWARD
TOWELS
TOWERS
TOWERY
TOWING

T••W••

TAIWAN
THAWED
TRAWLS
TROWEL
TWOWAY

T•••W•

THROWN
THROWS

T••••W

TALLOW

•T•W••

STEWED
STOWED

•T••W•

OTTAWA
STRAWS
STRAWY
STREWN
STREWS

••TW••

NITWIT
OUTWIT

••T•W•

OTTAWA
UPTOWN

••T••W

OUTLAW

•••T•W

BESTOW
KOWTOW

T•X•••

TAXEME
TAXERS
TAXIED
TAXING
TAXITE
TOXINS
TUXEDO

T••X••

TRIXIE
TRIXYS

T••••X

THORAX

•T•X••

ATAXIA
ATAXIC

•T•••X

STORAX

••T•X•
URTEXT

••T••X
HATBOX
HOTBOX
MATRIX
OUTFOX

•••T•X
CORTEX
LASTEX
SURTAX
SYNTAX
VERTEX
VORTEX

TY••••
TYBALT
TYCOON
TYMPAN
TYPHLO
TYPHON
TYPHUS
TYPIFY
TYPING
TYPIST
TYRANT
TYRONE

T•Y•••
TAYLOR
THYMES
THYMIC
THYMOL
THYMUS
THYREO
THYRSE
THYRSI
TOYERS
TOYING
TOYISH
TOYONS
TRYING
TRYOUT
TRYSTS
TUYERE

T••Y••
THAYER

T•••Y•
TEDDYS
TERRYS
TETHYS
TETRYL
THADYS
TILLYS
TIMMYS
TOLUYL
TOMMYS
TRIXYS
TROTYL
TRUDYS

T••••Y
TACKEY
TANGLY
TARTLY
TAUTLY
TAWDRY
TEAPOY
TEENSY
TEPEFY
TERMLY
TETANY
TETCHY
THADDY
THEORY
THINLY
THIRTY
THORNY
TIDILY
TIMELY
TINGLY
TINKLY
TOMBOY
TOOTHY
TOOTSY
TOUCHY
TOWERY
TRACHY
TRASHY
TREATY
TRENDY
TRESSY
TRICKY
TRIGLY
TRIMLY
TROPHY
TRUSTY
TUMEFY
TURKEY
TWANGY
TWEAKY
TWENTY
TWIGGY
TWOPLY
TWOWAY
TYPIFY

•TY•••
ETYMON
STYING
STYLAR
STYLED
STYLER
STYLES
STYLET
STYLUS
STYMIE

•T•Y••
ETHYLS
STAYED
STAYER

•T••Y•
STACYS
STRAYS

•T•••Y
STAGEY
STAGGY
STALKY
STARRY
STEADY
STEAMY
STEELY
STICKY
STILLY
STINGY
STITHY
STOCKY
STODGY
STOGEY
STOREY
STORMY
STRAWY
STRIPY
STUBBY
STUFFY
STUMPY
STURDY

••TY••
ECTYPE
SATYRS

••T•Y•
BETSYS
BETTYS
CATHYS
CUTEYS
HATTYS
HETTYS
KATHYS
KITTYS
MATEYS
METHYL
PATSYS
TETHYS
TETRYL

••T••Y
ANTONY
ARTERY
ASTRAY
BETONY
BETRAY
BOTANY
BOTCHY
BOTFLY
CATCHY
CATHAY
CUTELY
DATARY
ECTOMY
ENTITY
ESTRAY
JITNEY
LATELY
LITANY
MOTLEY
MUTINY
NOTARY
NOTIFY
OUTCRY
OUTLAY
PATCHY
PITCHY
POTBOY
RATIFY
RATTLY
ROTARY
SATINY
TETANY
TETCHY
UNTIDY
VOTARY
WATERY
WITNEY

•••TY•
ACETYL
BETTYS
DACTYL
GERTYS
HATTYS
HETTYS
KITTYS
MARTYR
MARTYS
MONTYS
MORTYS
TROTYL
ZLOTYS

•••T•Y
APATHY
CHATTY
CHITTY
CLOTTY
COSTLY
CURTLY
CURTSY
DAFTLY
DEATHY
DEFTLY
EARTHY
FILTHY
FLATLY
FRETTY
FROTHY
GANTRY
GENTRY
GRITTY
HEATHY
ICHTHY
JUSTLY
KNOTTY
LASTLY
MEETLY
MOSTLY
MOUTHY
NEATLY
PALTRY
PANTRY
PARTLY
PASTRY
PELTRY
PERTLY
POETRY
PORTLY
PRETTY
RATTLY
SENTRY
SMITHY
SMUTTY
SNOTTY
SOFTLY
SPOTTY
STITHY
SUBTLY
SULTRY
TARTLY
TAUTLY
TOOTHY
TOOTSY
VASTLY
VESTRY
WHITEY
WINTRY
WORTHY
WRATHY

••••TY
ACUITY
AGOUTY
BEAUTY
BILITY
BOUNTY
CAVITY
CHANTY
CHATTY
CHESTY
CHITTY
CLOTTY
COMITY
COUNTY
CRAFTY
CRUSTY
DAINTY
DEPUTY
DIMITY
DRAFTY
DRIFTY
EIGHTY
ENMITY
ENTITY
EQUITY
FAULTY
FEALTY
FEISTY
FERITY
FIXITY
FLINTY
FLIRTY
FLOATY
FRETTY
FROSTY
FRUITY
GAIETY
GAYETY
GLEETY
GRITTY
GUILTY
HEARTY
JAUNTY
KNOTTY
LAXITY
LENITY
LEVITY
MIGHTY
MOIETY
MOUNTY
NICETY
NIGHTY
NINETY
NUDITY
ODDITY
PAINTY
PARITY
PIGSTY
PLASTY
PLENTY
POINTY
POLITY
PRETTY
PURITY
RARITY
REALTY
SAFETY
SANITY
SCANTY
SHANTY
SHELTY
SHIFTY
SLEETY
SMUTTY
SNOOTY
SNOTTY
SPORTY
SPOTTY
SURETY
SWARTY
SWEATY
THIRTY
TREATY
TRUSTY
TWENTY
UBIETY
UPPITY
VANITY
VERITY
YEASTY

T•Z•••
TAZZAS

T••Z••
TARZAN
TAZZAS
TETZEL

•T••Z•
STANZA

••TZ••
MATZOS
MATZOT
TETZEL

•••T•Z
CORTEZ

••••TZ
BLINTZ
CHINTZ
ERSATZ
HALUTZ
KIBITZ
NIMITZ
QUARTZ

U•A•••
UBANGI
UGANDA
UKASES
UNABLE
UPASES
URAEUS
URALIC
URANIA
URANIC
URANUS
URANYL
USABLE
USABLY
USAGES
USANCE
UTAHAN

U••A••
UBOATS
ULLAGE
UMIAKS
UMLAUT
UNBARS
UNCAGE
UNCAPS
UNEASY
UNFAIR
UNHAIR
UNHAND
UNHATS
UNLACE
UNLADE
UNLAID
UNLAYS
UNMADE
UNMAKE
UNMANS
UNMASK
UNPACK
UNPAID
UNSAFE
UNSAID
UNSAYS
UNWARY
UPCAST
UPDATE
UPLAND
UPTAKE
UPWARD
URBANE
UREASE
UTGARD

U•••A•
ULEMAS
UMBRAE
UMBRAS
UNBEAR
UNCIAL
UNCLAD
UNDRAW
UNGUAL
UNLEAD
UNLOAD
UNREAD
UNREAL
UNSEAL
UNSEAM
UNSEAT
UNSNAP
UNWRAP
UPBEAT
UPROAR
URINAL
UTAHAN
UVULAE
UVULAR
UVULAS

U••••A
UGANDA
ULTIMA
UNGULA
URANIA
UREMIA
URSULA
UTOPIA

•UA•••
GUACOS
GUANIN
GUANOS
GUARDS
GUAVAS
JUAREZ
LUANDA
NUANCE
QUACKS
QUADRI
QUAERE
QUAFFS
QUAGGA
QUAGGY
QUAHOG
QUAILS
QUAINT
QUAKED
QUAKER
QUAKES
QUALMS
QUALMY
QUANTA
QUANTS
QUAPAW
QUARKS
QUARRY
QUARTE
QUARTO
QUARTS
QUARTZ
QUASAR
QUATRE
QUAVER
SUABLE

•U•A••
AUBADE
AUDADS
AURATE
BUBALS
BURANS
BUTANE
CUBAGE
CUBANS
CURACY
CURARE
CURATE
DUCATS
FUSAIN
GUIANA
GUYANA
HUMANE
HUMANS
JUDAEA
JUDAEO
JUDAHS
JUDAIC
JUGATE
JURANT
JURATS
KULAKS
KUWAIT
LUNACY
LUNATE
LUXATE
MURALS
MUTANT
MUTATE
PUPATE
PURANA
QUEANS
QUEASY
RUBACE
RUBATO
RUGATE
SUBAHS
SUDARY
SUGARS
SUGARY
SUMACS
SURAHS
SUSANS
TUBATE
TULADI

•U••A•
AUGEAN
BUCCAL
BULBAR
BULGAR
BULLAE
BUNYAN
BUREAU
BURIAL
BURLAP
BURSAE
BURSAL
BURSAR
BURSAS
BUSMAN
CULLAY
CUNEAL
CURIAE
CURIAL
CUSHAT
CUSHAW
CUTLAS
DUNBAR
DUNCAN
DURBAN
DURBAR
DURHAM
DURIAN
FULMAR
FUNGAL
GUAVAS
GUFFAW
GUITAR
GULLAH
GUMMAS
GUNMAN
GUNNAR
GUSTAF
GUSTAV
GUTTAE
GUTTAT
HUBCAP
HURRAH
HURRAY
HUSSAR
JUBBAH
JUDEAN
JULIAN
JULIAS
JUNEAU
JUNTAS
LUCIAN
LUCIAS
LUMBAR
LUTEAL
MUDCAP
MUGGAR
MULLAH
MURRAY
MUSCAE
MUSCAT
MUTUAL
NUBIAN
NUBIAS
NUCHAE
NULLAH
OUTLAW
OUTLAY
OUTMAN
OUTRAN
OUTSAT
PULSAR
PUNJAB
PUNKAS
PURDAH
PUTNAM
QUAPAW
QUASAR
QUOTAS
RUMBAS
RUNWAY
RUPIAH
SUBWAY
SULTAN
SUNDAE
SUNDAY
SUNNAH
SURTAX
SUTRAS
TURBAN
TUSCAN
TUSSAH
TUSSAL
TUSSAR
VULCAN
VULGAR
VULVAE
VULVAL
VULVAR
YUCCAS

•U•••A
AURIGA
AURORA
BUCKRA
BUDDHA
CUESTA
CUPOLA
DUENNA
EUBOEA
EUDORA
EUPNEA
EUREKA
EUROPA
FULCRA
GUIANA
GUINEA
GURKHA
GUYANA
HUELVA
JUDAEA
LUANDA
LUELLA
LUMINA
LUNULA
MUCOSA
NUMINA
NUTRIA
PURANA
QUAGGA
QUANTA
RUMINA
RUSSIA
SULPHA
TUNDRA
TUNICA

••UA••
ACUATE
EDUARD
EQUALS
EQUATE
FEUARS
IGUANA
SOUARI
SQUABS
SQUADS
SQUALL
SQUAMA
SQUARE
SQUASH
SQUATS
SQUAWK
SQUAWS
STUART
TRUANT
ZOUAVE

••U•A•
ALULAE
ALULAR
ANURAN
AOUDAD
BEULAH
BEULAS
BHUTAN
BRUMAL
BRUTAL
CAUDAD
CAUDAL
CAUSAL
CHUFAS
COUGAR
CRURAL
FAUCAL
FAUNAE
FAUNAL
FAUNAS
FEUDAL
FRUGAL
LAURAE
LAURAS
MAUMAU
NEURAL
NOUGAT
NOUNAL
OCULAR
OVULAR

PAULAS
PLURAL
SAUNAS
SCUBAS
SEURAT
SQUEAK
SQUEAL
STUPAS
THUJAS
TRUMAN
UVULAE
UVULAR
UVULAS

••U••A
ABULIA
ALUMNA
APULIA
AQUILA
ARUNTA
DHURNA
FRUSTA
GIULIA
IGUANA
LOUISA
NAUSEA
PYURIA
RHUMBA
SQUAMA
THULIA
ZEUGMA

•••UA•
ACTUAL
ANNUAL
CASUAL
JAGUAR
LEHUAS
LOQUAT
MANUAL
MUTUAL
PAPUAN
RITUAL
SEXUAL
SIOUAN
UNGUAL
VISUAL

•••U•A
BELUGA
CANULA
CAYUGA
CEDULA
CESURA
COPULA
CREUSA
DATURA
FACULA
FECULA
FERULA
FIBULA
HECUBA
KORUNA
LACUNA
LIGULA
LUNULA
MACULA
MADURA
MAZUMA
MEDUSA
MEZUZA
MORULA
NEBULA
NOMURA
PAPULA
PLEURA
PNEUMA
RADULA
REMUDA
STRUMA
SYNURA
TRAUMA
UNGULA
URSULA
VARUNA
VICUNA
YORUBA
ZONULA

••••UA
CORNUA
JOSHUA
LINGUA
MANTUA
NASHUA

UB••••
UBANGI
UBIETY
UBOATS
UBOLTS

U•B•••
UMBELS
UMBERS
UMBLES
UMBRAE
UMBRAS
UNBARS
UNBEAR
UNBELT
UNBEND
UNBENT
UNBIND
UNBOLT
UNBORN
UNBRED
UPBEAT
UPBOWS
URBANE

U••B••
UNABLE
USABLE
USABLY

•UB•••
AUBADE
AUBREY
AUBURN
BUBALS
BUBBLE
BUBBLY
BUBOES
CUBAGE
CUBANS
CUBEBS
CUBING
CUBISM
CUBIST
CUBITS
CUBOID
DUBBED
DUBBIN
DUBLIN
EUBOEA
HUBBUB
HUBCAP
HUBERT
HUBRIS
JUBBAH
LUBBER
LUBECK
LUBLIN
NUBBIN
NUBBLE
NUBBLY
NUBIAN
NUBIAS
NUBILE
PUBLIC
RUBACE
RUBATO
RUBBED
RUBBER
RUBBLE
RUBENS
RUBIES
RUBIGO
RUBLES
RUBRIC
SUBAHS
SUBDEB
SUBDUE
SUBITO
SUBLET
SUBMIT
SUBORN
SUBTER
SUBTLE
SUBTLY
SUBURB
SUBWAY
TUBATE
TUBBED
TUBBER
TUBERS
TUBING
TUBULE

•U•B••
BUBBLE
BUBBLY
BULBAR
BULBEL
BULBIL
BULBUL
BUMBLE
BURBLE
BURBOT
CUMBER
CURBED
DUBBED
DUBBIN
DUMBLY
DUNBAR
DURBAN
DURBAR
FUMBLE
GUMBOS
HUBBUB
HUMBLE
HUMBLY
HUMBUG
JUBBAH
JUMBLE
LUBBER
LUMBAR
LUMBER
MUMBLE
NUBBIN
NUBBLE
NUBBLY
NUMBED
NUMBER
NUMBLY
OUTBID
PUEBLO
QUEBEC
RUBBED
RUBBER
RUBBLE
RUMBAS
RUMBLE
SUABLE
SUNBOW
TUBBED
TUBBER
TUMBLE
TURBAN
TURBID
TURBIT
TURBOT

•U••B•
CUBEBS
JUJUBE

•U•••B
HUBBUB
PUNJAB
SUBDEB
SUBURB
SUPERB

••UB••
ANUBIS
BAUBLE
CHUBBY
DAUBED
DAUBER
DAUBRY
DOUBLE
DOUBLY
DOUBTS
GRUBBY
KRUBIS
KRUBUT
REUBEN
ROUBLE
SCUBAS
STUBBY

••U•B•
BLURBS
CHUBBY
CRUMBS
CRUMBY
EXURBS
GRUBBY
PLUMBO
PLUMBS
RHUMBA
RHUMBS
SQUABS
SQUIBS
STUBBY
THUMBS

•••UB•
DANUBE
HECUBA
INCUBI
JUJUBE
SCRUBS
SHRUBS
YORUBA

•••U•B
BENUMB
SUBURB

••••UB
BEDAUB
CHERUB
HUBBUB

U•C•••
ULCERS
UNCAGE
UNCAPS
UNCIAL
UNCLAD
UNCLES
UNCOCK
UNCOIL
UNCORK
UNCURL
UPCAST
URCHIN

U••C••
UNICEF

U•••C•
ULENCE
UNCOCK
UNESCO
UNLACE
UNLOCK
UNPACK
UNPICK
USANCE

U••••C
UNIFIC
URALIC
URANIC
URETIC

•UC•••
BUCCAL
BUCKED
BUCKER
BUCKET
BUCKLE
BUCKRA
CUCKOO
DUCATS
DUCKED
DUCKER
EUCHRE
EUCLID
FUCOID
FUCOUS
HUCKLE
KUCHEN
LUCENT
LUCIAN
LUCIAS
LUCIEN
LUCILE
LUCITE
LUCIUS
MUCKED
MUCKER
MUCOID
MUCOSA
MUCOSE
MUCOUS
NUCHAE
PUCKER
RUCHES
RUCKED
RUCKUS
SUCCOR
SUCKED
SUCKER
SUCKLE
SUCRES
TUCHUN
TUCKED
TUCKER

TUCSON
YUCCAS

•U•C••

BUCCAL
BUNCHE
BUNCHY
BUNCOS
DULCET
DULCIE
DUNCAN
DUNCES
FULCRA
GUACOS
HUBCAP
JUICER
JUICES
JUNCOS
MUDCAP
MULCTS
MUSCAE
MUSCAT
MUSCLE
NUNCIO
OUNCES
OUTCRY
PUNCHY
QUACKS
SUCCOR
SULCUS
TURCOS
TUSCAN
VULCAN
YUCCAS

•U••C•

CULTCH
CURACY
EUNICE
EUNUCH
LUBECK
LUNACY
MUNICH
NUANCE
PUMICE
PUTSCH
QUINCE
QUINCY
QUITCH
RUBACE
SUMACS
TUNICA
TUNICS
ZURICH

•U•••C

BUSTIC
CUPRIC
FUSTIC
JUDAIC
LUETIC
PUBLIC
QUEBEC
QUINIC
RUBRIC
RUSTIC
SUOMIC
TURKIC

••UC••

BAUCIS
BOUCLE
BRUCES
CAUCUS
CHUCKS
CLUCKS
CRUCES
DEUCED
DEUCES
DOUCHE
EDUCED
EDUCES
EDUCTS
ERUCTS
FAUCAL
FAUCES
FAUCET
GAUCHE
GAUCHO
PLUCKS
PLUCKY
POUCHY
ROUCHE
SAUCED
SAUCER
SAUCES
SHUCKS
STUCCO
TEUCER
TOUCHE
TOUCHY
TRUCES
TRUCKS

••U•C•

BOUNCE
BOUNCY
BRUNCH
CHURCH
CLUTCH
CRUNCH
CRUTCH
HAUNCH
JOUNCE
LAUNCE
LAUNCH
NAUTCH
PAUNCH
POUNCE
SCUTCH
SLUICE
SMUTCH
SOURCE
STUCCO

•••UC•

ABDUCT
ADDUCE
ADDUCT
ALMUCE
AVOUCH
BARUCH
CANUCK
CROUCH
DEDUCE
DEDUCT
EUNUCH
GLAUCO
GROUCH
INDUCE
INDUCT
REDUCE
SEDUCE
SLOUCH
SPRUCE
STRUCK

UD••••

UDDERS

U•D•••

UDDERS
UNDIES
UNDINE
UNDOER
UNDOES
UNDONE
UNDRAW
UNDREW
UNDSET
UNDULY
UPDATE

U•••D•

UGANDA
UNLADE
UNMADE
UNTIDY
UPENDS
UPSIDE
UREIDE

U••••D

UNBEND
UNBIND
UNBRED
UNCLAD
UNFOLD
UNGIRD
UNHAND
UNITED
UNKIND
UNLAID
UNLEAD
UNLOAD
UNPAID
UNREAD
UNSAID
UNSOLD
UNTIED
UNTOLD
UNTROD
UNUSED
UNWIND
UPHELD
UPHOLD
UPLAND
UPWARD
UROPOD
UTGARD

•UD•••

AUDADS
AUDILE
AUDITS
AUDREY
BUDDED
BUDDER
BUDDHA
BUDDLE
BUDGED
BUDGES
BUDGET
BUDGIE
CUDDIE
CUDDLE
CUDDLY
CUDGEL
DUDEEN
DUDISH
DUDLEY
EUDORA
FUDDLE
FUDGED
FUDGES
HUDDLE
HUDSON
JUDAEA
JUDAEO
JUDAHS
JUDAIC
JUDEAN
JUDGED
JUDGER
JUDGES
JUDITH
LUDWIG
MUDCAP
MUDDED
MUDDER
MUDDLE
NUDELY
NUDGED
NUDGES
NUDISM
NUDIST
NUDITY
NUDNIK
PUDDLE
PUDDLY
RUDDER
RUDDLE
RUDELY
RUDEST
SUDARY
SUDDEN

•U•D••

BUDDED
BUDDER
BUDDHA
BUDDLE
BUNDLE
BURDEN
BURDIE
CUDDIE
CUDDLE
CUDDLY
CURDED
CURDLE
DUNDEE
DUODEN
FUDDLE
FUNDED
FUNDUS
GUIDED
GUIDER
GUIDES
GUIDON
GULDEN
HUDDLE
HURDLE
MUDDED
MUDDER
MUDDLE
MURDER
OUTDID
PUDDLE
PUDDLY
PUNDIT
PURDAH
QUADRI
RUDDER
RUDDLE
RUNDLE
SUBDEB
SUBDUE
SUDDEN
SUEDES
SUNDAE
SUNDAY
SUNDER
SUNDEW
SUNDOG
SUNDRY
TUNDRA
ZUIDER
ZUYDER

•U••D•

AUBADE
AUDADS
BUILDS
GUARDS
GUILDS
LUANDA
TULADI
TUXEDO

•U•••D

AUGEND
AUTOED
BUCKED
BUDDED
BUDGED
BUFFED
BUGGED
BUGLED
BULGED
BULKED
BUMMED
BUMPED
BUNGED
BUNKED
BUNTED
BUOYED
BURIED
BURKED
BURLED
BURNED
BURPED
BURRED
BUSHED
BUSIED
BUSSED
BUSTED
BUTTED
BUZZED
CUBOID
CUFFED
CULLED
CULMED
CUPPED
CURBED
CURDED
CURLED
CURSED
CURVED
CUSPED
CUSPID
CUSSED
DUBBED
DUCKED
DUELED
DULLED
DUMPED
DUNGED
DUNKED
DUNNED
DUSKED
DUSTED
EUCLID
FUCOID
FUDGED
FUELED
FUGLED
FULGID
FULLED
FUNDED
FUNKED
FURLED
FURRED
FUSSED
FUZZED
GUIDED

GULFED
GULPED
GUMMED
GUNNED
GUSHED
GUTTED
HUFFED
HUGGED
HULKED
HULLED
HUMMED
HUMPED
HUNTED
HURLED
HUSHED
HUSKED
HUTTED
JUDGED
JUGGED
JUMPED
JUNKED
JUTTED
LUFFED
LUGGED
LULLED
LUMPED
LUNGED
LURKED
LUSHED
LUSTED
MUCKED
MUCOID
MUDDED
MUFFED
MUGGED
MULLED
MUMMED
MUSHED
MUSSED
NUDGED
NUMBED
NURSED
NUTTED
OUSTED
OUTBID
OUTDID
PUFFED
PUGGED
PULLED
PULPED
PULSED
PUMPED
PUNNED
PUNTED
PUPPED
PUREED
PURGED
PURLED
PURRED
PURSED
PUSHED
PUTRID
PUTTED
QUAKED
QUEUED
QUIRED
QUOTED
RUBBED
RUCKED
RUFFED
RUGGED
RUINED
RUSHED
RUSTED
RUTTED
SUCKED
SUITED
SULKED
SUMMED
SUNNED
SUPPED
SURFED
SURGED
TUBBED
TUCKED
TUFTED
TUGGED
TUNNED
TUPPED
TURBID
TURGID
TURNED
TUSHED
TUSKED
YUKKED

••UD••

ALUDEL
AOUDAD
CAUDAD
CAUDAL
CAUDEX
CAUDLE
CRUDER
DRUDGE
ELUDED
ELUDES
ETUDES
EXUDED
EXUDES
FEUDAL
FEUDED
GRUDGE
LAUDED
LAUDER
LEUDES
LOUDEN
LOUDER
LOUDLY
MAUDES
PRUDES
SLUDGE
SLUDGY
SMUDGE
SMUDGY
STUDIO
TRUDGE
TRUDYS

••U•D•

BOUNDS
DRUIDS
FLUIDS
FOUNDS
GOURDE
GOURDS
GRUNDY
HOUNDS
MAUNDS
MAUNDY
MOULDS
MOULDY
POUNDS
ROUNDS
SOUNDS
SQUADS
SQUIDS
STURDY
WOUNDS
ZOUNDS

••U••D

ABUSED
AMUSED
AOUDAD
BOUSED
CAUDAD
CAUSED
DAUBED
DEUCED
DOUSED
EDUARD
EDUCED
ELUDED
EXUDED
FEUDED
FLUKED
FLUMED
FLUTED
FLUXED
FOULED
GAUGED
GOUGED
HAULED
HOUSED
INURED
LAUDED
LOURED
LOUSED
MAULED
MOUSED
PAUSED
PLUMED
POURED
POUTED
PRUNED
ROUGED
ROUSED
ROUTED
SAUCED
SOULED
SOURED
SOUSED
SPUMED
STUPID
TOURED
TOUTED
UNUSED
WAULED
YAUPED

•••UD•

ALLUDE
ALMUDE
ALMUDS
CLAUDE
CLOUDS
CLOUDY
DELUDE
DENUDE
ESCUDO
FRAUDS
PSEUDO
REMUDA

•••U•D

ABOUND
ABSURD
ARGUED
AROUND
EDMUND
ENDUED
ENSUED
FECUND
GERUND
GROUND
IMBUED
INDUED
ISSUED
JOCUND
LIQUID
OBTUND
ORMUZD
OSMUND
PEQUOD
PIQUED
QUEUED
REFUND
ROGUED
ROTUND
SECUND
SHOULD
VALUED

••••UD

ARNAUD
MARAUD
REDBUD
SHROUD
STROUD
TALMUD

U•E•••

ULEMAS
ULENCE
UNEASY
UNESCO
UNEVEN
UPENDS
UREASE
UREIDE
UREMIA
URETER
URETHR
URETIC
USEFUL
UTERUS

U••E••

UBIETY
UDDERS
ULCERS
UMBELS
UMBERS
UNBEAR
UNBELT
UNBEND
UNBENT
UNLEAD
UNLESS
UNMEET
UNMEWS
UNPEGS
UNREAD
UNREAL
UNREEL
UNREST
UNSEAL
UNSEAM
UNSEAT
UNSEEN
UNVEIL
UNVEXT
UNWELL
UNWEPT
UPBEAT
UPHELD
UPKEEP
UPPERS
UPSETS
URAEUS
URGENT
URTEXT
USHERS
UTTERS

U•••E•

UGLIER
UKASES
ULSTER
UMBLES
UNBRED
UNCLES
UNDIES
UNDOER
UNDOES
UNDREW
UNDSET
UNEVEN
UNGUES
UNICEF
UNISEX
UNITED
UNITES
UNMEET
UNREEL
UNSEEN
UNSTEP
UNTIED
UNTIES
UNUSED
UPASES
UPKEEP
URETER
USAGES
USURER

U••••E

ULENCE
ULLAGE
UMBRAE
UMPIRE
UNABLE
UNCAGE
UNDINE
UNDONE
UNIQUE
UNLACE
UNLADE
UNLIKE
UNLIVE
UNMADE
UNMAKE
UNPILE
UNRIPE
UNSAFE
UNSURE
UNTRUE
UNWISE
UNYOKE
UPDATE
UPHROE
UPRISE
UPROSE
UPSIDE
UPTAKE
URBANE
UREASE
UREIDE
URSINE
USABLE
USANCE
UVULAE

•UE•••

CUESTA
DUELED
DUELER
DUELLO
DUENNA
FUELED
FUELER
GUENON
GUESTS
HUELVA

LUELLA
LUETIC
PUEBLO
QUEANS
QUEASY
QUEBEC
QUEENS
QUEERS
QUELLS
QUERNS
QUESTS
QUEUED
QUEUES
QUEZON
RUEFUL
SUEDES

•U•E••

AUGEAN
AUGEND
AUGERS
AUREUS
BUREAU
BUYERS
CUBEBS
CULETS
CUNEAL
CUPELS
CURERS
CUTELY
CUTEST
CUTEYS
DUDEEN
DUPERS
DUPERY
DURESS
EUGENE
EUREKA
FUNEST
FUSEES
FUZEES
HUBERT
HUGELY
HUGEST
JUDEAN
JULEPS
JUNEAU
JURELS
LUBECK
LUCENT
LUGERS
LUMENS
LUNETS
LURERS
LUTEAL
LUTEUM
MUSEUM
NUDELY
OUSELS
OUTERS
OUZELS
PULERS
PUREED
PUREES
PURELY
PUREST
QUAERE
QUEENS
QUEERS
RUBENS
RUDELY
RUDEST
RULERS
RUPEES
RUPERT
SUPERB
SUPERS
SURELY
SUREST
SURETY
TUBERS
TUMEFY
TUNERS
TUNEUP
TUPELO
TUREEN
TUXEDO
TUYERE

•U••E•

AUBREY
AUDREY
AUKLET
AUSPEX
AUSTEN
AUSTER
AUTOED
BUBOES
BUCKED
BUCKER
BUCKET
BUDDED
BUDDER
BUDGED
BUDGES
BUDGET
BUFFED
BUFFER
BUFFET
BUGGED
BUGGER
BUGLED
BUGLER
BUGLES
BULBEL
BULGED
BULGER
BULGES
BULKED
BULLET
BUMMED
BUMMER
BUMPED
BUMPER
BUNGED
BUNKED
BUNKER
BUNSEN
BUNTED
BUOYED
BURDEN
BURGEE
BURGER
BURIED
BURIES
BURKED
BURKES
BURLED
BURLER
BURLEY
BURNED
BURNER
BURNET
BURPED
BURRED
BURSES
BUSHED
BUSHEL
BUSHES
BUSIED
BUSIES
BUSMEN
BUSSED
BUSSES
BUSTED
BUSTER
BUTLER
BUTTED
BUTTER
BUTTES
BUZZED
BUZZER
BUZZES
CUDGEL
CUFFED
CULLED
CULLER
CULLET
CULMED
CULVER
CUMBER
CUNNER
CUPPED
CUPPER
CURBED
CURDED
CURFEW
CURIES
CURLED
CURLER
CURLEW
CURSED
CURSES
CURVED
CURVES
CURVET
CUSPED
CUSSED
CUSSES
CUSTER
CUTIES
CUTLER
CUTLET
CUTTER
DUBBED
DUCKED
DUCKER
DUDEEN
DUDLEY
DUELED
DUELER
DUFFEL
DUFFER
DUIKER
DULCET
DULLED
DULLER
DUMPED
DUNCES
DUNDEE
DUNGED
DUNKED
DUNKER
DUNNED
DUODEN
DUPLEX
DUSKED
DUSTED
DUSTER
DUTIES
EUBOEA
EUPNEA
FUDGED
FUDGES
FUELED
FUELER
FUGLED
FUGLES
FUGUES
FUHRER
FULLED
FULLER
FUMIER
FUNDED
FUNKED
FUNNEL
FURIES
FURLED
FURRED
FURZES
FUSEES
FUSSED
FUSSER
FUSSES
FUZEES
FUZZED
FUZZES
GUIDED
GUIDER
GUIDES
GUILES
GUINEA
GUISES
GULDEN
GULFED
GULLET
GULPED
GULPER
GUMMED
GUNMEN
GUNNED
GUNNEL
GUNNER
GUSHED
GUSHER
GUSHES
GUSSET
GUTTED
GUTTER
HUFFED
HUGGED
HUGHES
HULKED
HULLED
HUMMED
HUMMER
HUMPED
HUNGER
HUNTED
HUNTER
HURLED
HURLER
HURTER
HUSHED
HUSHES
HUSKED
HUSKER
HUTTED
HUXLEY
JUAREZ
JUDAEA
JUDAEO
JUDGED
JUDGER
JUDGES
JUGGED
JUICER
JUICES
JULIES
JULIET
JUMPED
JUMPER
JUNKED
JUNKER
JUNKET
JURIES
JUTTED
KUCHEN
KUMMEL
LUBBER
LUCIEN
LUFFED
LUGGED
LUGGER
LULLED
LUMBER
LUMPED
LUMPEN
LUNGED
LUNGEE
LUNGER
LUNGES
LUNKER
LURKED
LUSHED
LUSHER
LUSHES
LUSTED
LUSTER
LUTHER
MUCKED
MUCKER
MUDDED
MUDDER
MUFFED
MUGGED
MUGGER
MULLED
MULLEN
MULLER
MULLET
MULLEY
MUMMED
MUMMER
MURDER
MURIEL
MURRES
MURREY
MUSHED
MUSHER
MUSHES
MUSKEG
MUSKET
MUSSED
MUSSEL
MUSSES
MUSTEE
MUSTER
MUTTER
NUDGED
NUDGES
NUGGET
NUMBED
NUMBER
NURSED
NURSER
NURSES
NUTLET
NUTMEG
NUTTED
NUTTER
OUNCES
OUSTED
OUSTER
OUTLET
OUTSET
PUCKER
PUFFED
PUFFER
PUGGED
PUGREE
PULLED
PULLER
PULLET

PULLEY
PULPED
PULSED
PULSES
PUMMEL
PUMPED
PUMPER
PUNIER
PUNNED
PUNTED
PUNTER
PUPPED
PUPPET
PUREED
PUREES
PURGED
PURGER
PURGES
PURLED
PURRED
PURSED
PURSER
PURSES
PURVEY
PUSHED
PUSHER
PUSHES
PUSSES
PUSSEY
PUTTED
PUTTEE
PUTTER
QUAKED
QUAKER
QUAKES
QUAVER
QUEBEC
QUEUED
QUEUES
QUIRED
QUIRES
QUIVER
QUOTED
QUOTER
QUOTES
RUBBED
RUBBER
RUBIES
RUBLES
RUCHES
RUCKED
RUDDER
RUFFED
RUGGED
RUINED
RUINER
RUMMER
RUNLET
RUNNEL
RUNNER
RUPEES
RUSHED
RUSHER
RUSHES
RUSSET
RUSTED
RUTTED
SUBDEB
SUBLET
SUBTER
SUCKED
SUCKER
SUCRES
SUDDEN
SUEDES
SUFFER
SUITED
SUITES
SULKED
SULLEN
SUMMED
SUMMER
SUMNER
SUNDER
SUNDEW
SUNKEN
SUNNED
SUNSET
SUPPED
SUPPER
SURFED
SURFER
SURGED
SURGER
SURGES
SURREY
SURVEY
SUSIES
SUTLER
SUTTEE
TUBBED
TUBBER
TUCKED
TUCKER
TUFTED
TUGGED
TULLES
TUNNED
TUNNEL
TUPPED
TUQUES
TUREEN
TURKEY
TURNED
TURNER
TURRET
TUSHED
TUSHES
TUSKED
TUSKER
YUKKED
ZUIDER
ZUYDER

•U•••E

AUBADE
AUDILE
AUGITE
AUNTIE
AURATE
BUBBLE
BUCKLE
BUDDLE
BUDGIE
BULLAE
BUMBLE
BUNCHE
BUNDLE
BUNGLE
BURBLE
BURDIE
BURGEE
BURGLE
BURSAE
BUSTLE
BUTANE
CUBAGE
CUDDIE
CUDDLE
CUISSE
CUPULE
CURARE
CURATE
CURDLE
CURIAE
CURULE
CUTTLE
DUFFLE
DULCIE
DUNDEE
EUCHRE
EUGENE
EUNICE
EUROPE
FUDDLE
FUMBLE
FUSILE
FUTILE
FUTURE
GUIMPE
GURGLE
GUSSIE
GUTTAE
GUTTLE
GUZZLE
HUCKLE
HUDDLE
HUGHIE
HUMANE
HUMBLE
HURDLE
HURTLE
HUSTLE
JUGATE
JUGGLE
JUJUBE
JUMBLE
JUNGLE
JUNKIE
LUCILE
LUCITE
LUNATE
LUNGEE
LUNULE
LUPINE
LUXATE
MUCOSE
MUDDLE
MUFFLE
MUMBLE
MURINE
MUSCAE
MUSCLE
MUSTEE
MUTATE
MUTULE
MUZZLE
NUANCE
NUBBLE
NUBILE
NUCHAE
NUZZLE
PUDDLE
PUGREE
PUISNE
PULQUE
PUMICE
PUPATE
PURFLE
PURINE
PURPLE
PURSUE
PUTTEE
PUZZLE
QUAERE
QUARTE
QUATRE
QUINCE
RUBACE
RUBBLE
RUDDLE
RUFFLE
RUGATE
RUGOSE
RUMBLE
RUMPLE
RUNDLE
RUSINE
RUSTLE
RUTILE
SUABLE
SUBDUE
SUBTLE
SUCKLE
SUNDAE
SUPINE
SUPPLE
SUTTEE
SUTURE
TUBATE
TUBULE
TUILLE
TUMBLE
TURTLE
TUSSLE
TUYERE
VULVAE

••UE••

BLUELY
BLUEST
BLUETS
CRUETS
FLUENT
GRUELS
SQUEAK
SQUEAL
TRUEST

••U•E•

ABUSED
ABUSER
ABUSES
ACUMEN
ALUDEL
AMULET
AMUSED
AMUSER
AMUSES
ANUSES
AZURES
BOULES
BOUSED
BOUSES
BRUCES
BRUGES
BRUMES
BRUNEI
BRUNET
BRUTES
CAUDEX
CAULES
CAUSED
CAUSER
CAUSES
CHUTES
COULEE
COUPES
CRUCES
CRUDER
CRUSES
CRUSET
CRUXES
DAUBED
DAUBER
DEUCED
DEUCES
DOUSED
DOUSES
DRUPES
DRUSES
EDUCED
EDUCES
ELUDED
ELUDES
ETUDES
EXUDED
EXUDES
FAUCES
FAUCET
FAUVES
FEUDED
FLUKED
FLUKES
FLUKEY
FLUMED
FLUMES
FLUTED
FLUTER
FLUTES
FLUXED
FLUXES
FOULED
FOULER
GAUGED
GAUGER
GAUGES
GAUZES
GLUIER
GLUMES
GLUTEI
GLUTEN
GOUGED
GOUGER
GOUGES
GRUMES
HAULED
HAULER
HAUSEN
HOUSED
HOUSES
INURED
INURES
JOULES
LAUDED
LAUDER
LAUREL
LEUDES
LOUDEN
LOUDER
LOUPES
LOURED
LOUSED
LOUSES
LOUVER
MAUDES
MAULED
MAULER
MAUSER
MAUVES
MOUSED
MOUSER
MOUSES
NAUSEA
NEUMES
NEUTER
ONUSES
OVULES
PAUKER
PAUPER
PAUSED
PAUSER
PAUSES
PLUMED

6

PLUMES
PLUSES
POURED
POURER
POUTED
POUTER
PRUDES
PRUNED
PRUNER
PRUNES
REUBEN
ROUGED
ROUGES
ROUSED
ROUSER
ROUSES
ROUTED
ROUTER
ROUTES
SAUCED
SAUCER
SAUCES
SAUGER
SAUREL
SAUTES
SCUTES
SOULED
SOURED
SOURER
SOUSED
SOUSES
SPUMED
SPUMES
STUPES
TAUPES
TAUTEN
TAUTER
TEUCER
TOUPEE
TOURED
TOUTED
TOUTER
TRUCES
UNUSED
USURER
WAULED
YAUPED

••U••E

ACUATE
ALULAE
BAUBLE
BLUNGE
BOUCLE
BOUFFE
BOUGIE
BOUNCE
BOURNE
BOURSE
BRUISE
CAUDLE
COULEE
COUPLE
COURSE
CRUISE
CRUSOE
DOUBLE
DOUCHE
DOUGIE
DRUDGE
EQUATE
EQUINE
FAUNAE
FRUNZE
GAUCHE
GOURDE
GRUDGE
JOUNCE
LAUNCE
LAURAE
LAURIE
LOUISE
LOUNGE
LOUVRE
MOUSSE
OEUVRE
PLUNGE
POUNCE
ROUBLE
ROUCHE
SCURVE
SLUDGE
SLUICE
SMUDGE
SOURCE
SPURGE
SQUARE
SQUIRE
TOUCHE
TOUPEE
TOUSLE
TRUDGE
UVULAE
ZOUAVE

•••UE•

ARGUED
ARGUER
ARGUES
COQUET
ENDUED
ENDUES
ENSUED
ENSUES
FIQUES
FRAUEN
FUGUES
GIGUES
IMBUED
IMBUES
INDUED
INDUES
ISSUED
ISSUER
ISSUES
LEMUEL
MAGUEY
MANUEL
MIGUEL
MINUET
PIQUED
PIQUES
PIQUET
QUEUED
QUEUES
REVUES
ROGUED
ROGUES
ROQUET
SAMUEL
SEQUEL
SPRUES
TENUES
TOGUES
TOQUES
TUQUES
UNGUES
VAGUER
VALUED
VALUES
VENUES
VOGUES

•••U•E

ABJURE
ACCUSE
ADDUCE
ADJURE
ALLUDE
ALLURE
ALMUCE
ALMUDE
AMPULE
ARBUTE
ARMURE
AROUSE
ASSUME
ASSURE
ASTUTE
ATTUNE
BEMUSE
BLOUSE
CANUTE
CAYUSE
CERUSE
CLAUDE
CLAUSE
COHUNE
COLURE
CROUPE
CUPULE
CURULE
DANUBE
DEDUCE
DELUDE
DELUGE
DELUXE
DEMURE
DENUDE
DEPUTE
DILUTE
DISUSE
EFFUSE
EMEUTE
ENDURE
ENSURE
EXCUSE
EXHUME
FERULE
FIGURE
FUTURE
GROUSE
HEAUME
ILLUME
ILLUSE
IMMUNE
IMMURE
IMPURE
IMPUTE
INCUSE
INDUCE
INFUSE
INJURE
INSURE
JEJUNE
JUJUBE
LAGUNE
LEGUME
LIGULE
LIGURE
LOBULE
LUNULE
MACULE
MANURE
MATURE
MINUTE
MISUSE
MODULE
MUTULE
NATURE
NODULE
OBTUSE
ORDURE
OSCULE
PAIUTE
PAPULE
PARURE
PERUKE
PERUSE
PILULE
REBUKE
RECUSE
REDUCE
REFUGE
REFUSE
REFUTE
REPUTE
RESUME
RETUSE
SALUTE
SECURE
SEDUCE
SOLUTE
SPOUSE
SPRUCE
SUTURE
TENURE
TRIUNE
TROUPE
TUBULE
UNSURE
VELURE
VENULE
VOLUME
VOLUTE
ZONULE

••••UE

ACCRUE
AGOGUE
AVENUE
BARQUE
BASQUE
BATTUE
BISQUE
BRAQUE
BROGUE
CAIQUE
CANGUE
CASQUE
CINQUE
CIRQUE
CLAQUE
CLIQUE
DENGUE
EMBRUE
FESCUE
FONDUE
GANGUE
IMBRUE
LEAGUE
MANQUE
MARQUE
MASQUE
MISCUE
MORGUE
MOSQUE
OPAQUE
PLAGUE
PLAQUE
PRAGUE
PREVUE
PULQUE
PURSUE
RESCUE
RISQUE
STATUE
SUBDUE
TISSUE
TONGUE
TORQUE
UNIQUE
UNTRUE
VENDUE
VIRTUE

U•F•••

UNFAIR
UNFOLD
UNFURL

U••F••

UNIFIC
USEFUL

U•••F•

UGLIFY
UNSAFE
UPLIFT

U••••F

UNICEF

•UF•••

BUFFED
BUFFER
BUFFET
CUFFED
DUFFEL
DUFFER
DUFFLE
GUFFAW
HUFFED
LUFFED
MUFFED
MUFFIN
MUFFLE
MUFTIS
PUFFED
PUFFER
PUFFIN
RUFFED
RUFFLE
RUFOUS
SUFFER
SUFFIX
SUFISM
TUFTED

•U•F••

BUFFED
BUFFER
BUFFET
CUFFED
CUPFUL
CURFEW
DUFFEL
DUFFER
DUFFLE
FULFIL
GUFFAW
GULFED
HUFFED
LUFFED
MUFFED
MUFFIN
MUFFLE
OUTFIT
OUTFOX
PUFFED
PUFFER
PUFFIN
PURFLE
QUAFFS
RUEFUL

RUFFED
RUFFLE
SUFFER
SUFFIX
SULFUR
SURFED
SURFER

•U••F•
CUTOFF
PURIFY
PUTOFF
QUAFFS
RUNOFF
TUMEFY

•U•••F
CUTOFF
GUSTAF
PUTOFF
RUNOFF

••UF••
BLUFFS
BOUFFE
CHUFAS
FLUFFS
FLUFFY
SCUFFS
SNUFFS
SNUFFY
STUFFS
STUFFY

••U•F•
BLUFFS
BOUFFE
FLUFFS
FLUFFY
SCUFFS
SCURFY
SNUFFS
SNUFFY
STUFFS
STUFFY

•••UF•
ARGUFY
REBUFF
SCRUFF

•••U•F
ENGULF
INGULF
REBUFF
SCRUFF

UG••••
UGANDA
UGLIER
UGLIFY
UGLILY

U•G•••
UNGIRD
UNGIRT
UNGUAL
UNGUES
UNGUIS
UNGULA
URGENT
URGING
UTGARD

U••G••
USAGES

U•••G•
UBANGI
ULLAGE
UNCAGE
UNPEGS
UNRIGS

U••••G
UNSUNG
UPPING
URGING

•UG•••
AUGEAN
AUGEND
AUGERS
AUGHTS
AUGITE
AUGURS
AUGURY
AUGUST
BUGGED
BUGGER
BUGLED
BUGLER
BUGLES
DUGONG
DUGOUT
EUGENE
FUGIOS
FUGLED
FUGLES
FUGUES
HUGELY
HUGEST
HUGGED
HUGHES
HUGHIE
JUGATE
JUGGED
JUGGLE
LUGERS
LUGGED
LUGGER
MUGGAR
MUGGED
MUGGER
MUGGUR
NUGGET
PUGGED
PUGGRY
PUGREE
RUGATE
RUGGED
RUGOSE
RUGOUS
SUGARS
SUGARY
TUGGED

•U•G••
BUDGED
BUDGES
BUDGET
BUDGIE
BUGGED
BUGGER
BULGAR
BULGED
BULGER
BULGES
BUNGED
BUNGLE
BURGEE
BURGER
BURGHS
BURGLE
BURGOO
BURGOS
CUDGEL
DUNGED
FUDGED
FUDGES
FULGID
FUNGAL
FUNGUS
GURGLE
HUGGED
HUNGER
HUNGRY
JUDGED
JUDGER
JUDGES
JUGGED
JUGGLE
JUNGLE
JUNGLY
LUGGED
LUGGER
LUNGED
LUNGEE
LUNGER
LUNGES
LUNGIS
MUGGAR
MUGGED
MUGGER
MUGGUR
NUDGED
NUDGES
NUGGET
PUGGED
PUGGRY
PURGED
PURGER
PURGES
QUAGGA
QUAGGY
RUGGED
SURGED
SURGER
SURGES
TUGGED
TUNGUS
TURGID
VULGAR

•U••G•
AURIGA
CUBAGE
EULOGY
QUAGGA
QUAGGY
RUBIGO

•U•••G
BUSING
BUYING
CUBING
CURING
DUGONG
DUOLOG
DUPING
DURING
FUMING
FUSING
FUZING
GUYING
HUMBUG
LUDWIG
LURING
LUTING
MUSING
MUSKEG
MUTING
NUTMEG
OUTING
PUKING
PULING
PUTLOG
QUAHOG
RULING
SUNDOG
TUBING
TUNING

••UG••
BOUGHS
BOUGHT
BOUGIE
BRUGES
CAUGHT
COUGAR
COUGHS
DOUGHS
DOUGHY
DOUGIE
FOUGHT
FRUGAL
GAUGED
GAUGER
GAUGES
GOUGED
GOUGER
GOUGES
GRUGRU
LAUGHS
LOUGHS
NAUGHT
NOUGAT
NOUGHT
ROUGED
ROUGES
ROUGHS
SAUGER
SMUGLY
SNUGLY
SOUGHS
SOUGHT
TAUGHT
TOUGHS
ZEUGMA

••U•G•
BLUNGE
BOURGS
DRUDGE
GRUDGE
LOUNGE
PLUNGE
SLUDGE
SLUDGY
SMUDGE
SMUDGY
SPURGE
TRUDGE

••U••G
BLUING
CLUING
FEUING
GLUING
SLUING
TRUING

•••UG•
AERUGO
BELUGA
CAYUGA
CHOUGH
CLOUGH
COLUGO
DEBUGS
DELUGE
ENOUGH
IMPUGN
LANUGO
OPPUGN
PLOUGH
REFUGE
SHRUGS
SLOUGH
TELUGU
THOUGH
TROUGH

•••U•G
SPRUNG
UNSUNG

••••UG
BEDBUG
DORBUG
HUMBUG
REDBUG

U•H•••
UNHAIR
UNHAND
UNHATS
UNHOLY
UNHOOK
UNHURT
UNHUSK
UPHELD
UPHILL
UPHOLD
UPHROE
USHERS

U••H••
UNSHIP
UPSHOT
URCHIN
UTAHAN

U•••H•
URETHR

U••••H
UNWISH
UPPISH

•UH•••
FUHRER

•U•H••
AUGHTS
AUTHOR
BUSHED
BUSHEL
BUSHES
CUSHAT
CUSHAW
DURHAM
EUCHRE
GUSHED
GUSHER
GUSHES
HUGHES
HUGHIE
HUSHED
HUSHES
KUCHEN
LUSHED
LUSHER

LUSHES
LUTHER
MUSHED
MUSHER
MUSHES
MUZHIK
NUCHAE
PUSHED
PUSHER
PUSHES
PUSHUP
QUAHOG
RUCHES
RUSHED
RUSHER
RUSHES
TUCHUN
TUSHED
TUSHES

•U••H•
BUDDHA
BUNCHE
BUNCHY
BURGHS
GUNSHY
GURKHA
JUDAHS
PUNCHY
SUBAHS
SULPHA
SULPHO
SURAHS

•U•••H
CULTCH
DUDISH
DULUTH
EUNUCH
GULLAH
HURRAH
JUBBAH
JUDITH
JUTISH
MULISH
MULLAH
MUNICH
NULLAH
PUNISH
PURDAH
PUTSCH
QUITCH
RUPIAH
SUNNAH
TUSSAH
ZURICH

••U•H•
BOUGHS
BOUGHT
BRUSHY
CAUGHT
COUGHS
DOUCHE
DOUGHS
DOUGHY
FOUGHT
GAUCHE
GAUCHO
KYUSHU
LAUGHS
LOUGHS
MOUTHS
MOUTHY
NAUGHT
NOUGHT
PLUSHY
POUCHY
ROUCHE
ROUGHS
SLUSHY
SOUGHS
SOUGHT
TAUGHT
TOUCHE
TOUCHY
TOUGHS
TRUTHS
YOUTHS

••U••H
AGUISH
BEULAH
BLUISH
BRUNCH
CHURCH
CLUTCH
CRUNCH
CRUTCH
FOURTH
HAUNCH
LAUNCH
NAUTCH
PAUNCH
SCUTCH
SMUTCH
SQUASH
SQUISH

•••U•H
ABLUSH
AMBUSH
AVOUCH
BARUCH
CHOUGH
CLOUGH
CROUCH
DROUTH
DULUTH
ENOUGH
EUNUCH
GROUCH
INRUSH
ONRUSH
PLOUGH
SLEUTH
SLOUCH
SLOUGH
THOUGH
THRUSH
TROUGH

U•I•••
UBIETY
UMIAKS
UNICEF
UNIFIC
UNIONS
UNIQUE
UNISEX
UNISON
UNITED
UNITES
URINAL

U••I••
UGLIER
UGLIFY
UGLILY
ULTIMA
UMPIRE
UNBIND
UNCIAL
UNDIES
UNDINE
UNGIRD
UNGIRT
UNKIND
UNLIKE
UNLIVE
UNPICK
UNPILE
UNPINS
UNRIGS
UNRIPE
UNRIPS
UNTIDY
UNTIED
UNTIES
UNWIND
UNWISE
UNWISH
UPHILL
UPLIFT
UPPING
UPPISH
UPPITY
UPRISE
UPSIDE
UREIDE
URGING
URSINE

U•••I•
UNCOIL
UNFAIR
UNGUIS
UNHAIR
UNIFIC
UNKNIT
UNLAID
UNPAID
UNSAID
UNSHIP
UNVEIL
URALIC
URANIA
URANIC
URCHIN
UREMIA
URETIC
UTOPIA

U••••I
UBANGI

•UI•••
BUILDS
CUISSE
DUIKER
GUIANA
GUIDED
GUIDER
GUIDES
GUIDON
GUILDS
GUILES
GUILTS
GUILTY
GUIMPE
GUINEA
GUISES
GUITAR
JUICER
JUICES
PUISNE
QUILLS
QUILTS
QUINCE
QUINCY
QUINIC
QUINSY
QUINTS
QUIPUS
QUIRED
QUIRES
QUIRKS
QUIRTS
QUITCH
QUIVER
RUINED
RUINER
SUITED
SUITES
SUITOR
TUILLE
ZUIDER

•U•I••
AUDILE
AUDITS
AUGITE
AURIGA
AURIST
AUTISM
AUXINS
BUNION
BURIAL
BURIED
BURIES
BURINS
BUSIED
BUSIES
BUSILY
BUSING
BUYING
CUBING
CUBISM
CUBIST
CUBITS
CUMINS
CURIAE
CURIAL
CURIES
CURING
CURIOS
CURIUM
CUTIES
CUTINS
DUDISH
DUPING
DURIAN
DURING
DURION
DUTIES
EUNICE
EURIPI
FUGIOS
FUMIER
FUMING
FURIES
FUSILE
FUSILS
FUSING
FUSION
FUTILE
FUZILS
FUZING
GUYING
JUDITH
JULIAN
JULIAS
JULIES
JULIET
JULIUS
JUNIOR
JUNIUS
JURIES
JURIST
JUTISH
KUMISS
LUCIAN
LUCIAS
LUCIEN
LUCILE
LUCITE
LUCIUS
LUMINA
LUMINI
LUMINO
LUPINE
LURING
LUTING
LUTIST
MULISH
MUNICH
MURIEL
MURINE
MUSING
MUTING
MUTINY
MUTISM
NUBIAN
NUBIAS
NUBILE
NUDISM
NUDIST
NUDITY
NUMINA
OUTING
PUKING
PULING
PUMICE
PUNIER
PUNILY
PUNISH
PUPILS
PURIFY
PURINE
PURISM
PURIST
PURITY
QUAILS
QUAINT
QUOINS
QUOITS
RUBIES
RUBIGO
RULING
RUMINA
RUNINS
RUPIAH
RUSINE
RUTILE
SUBITO
SUFISM
SUPINE
SUSIES
TUBING
TULIPS
TUNICA
TUNICS
TUNING
TUPIKS
ZURICH

•U••I•
AUNTIE
AUSTIN
BUDGIE
BULBIL
BUMKIN
BURDIE
BUSKIN

BUSTIC
CUBOID
CUDDIE
CULLIS
CUPRIC
CURTIS
CUSPID
CUSPIS
DUBBIN
DUBLIN
DULCIE
DUNLIN
EUCLID
FUCOID
FULFIL
FULGID
FUSAIN
FUSTIC
GUANIN
GUSSIE
HUBRIS
HUGHIE
JUDAIC
JUNKIE
JUSTIN
KUWAIT
LUBLIN
LUDWIG
LUETIC
LUNGIS
MUCOID
MUFFIN
MUFTIS
MUSKIT
MUSLIM
MUSLIN
MUZHIK
NUBBIN
NUDNIK
NUNCIO
NUTRIA
OUTBID
OUTDID
OUTFIT
OUTSIT
OUTWIT
PUBLIC
PUFFIN
PULPIT
PUNDIT
PURLIN
PUTRID
QUINIC
RUBRIC
RUSKIN
RUSSIA
RUSTIC
SUBMIT
SUFFIX
SUMMIT
SUNLIT
SUOMIC
SUSLIK
TURBID
TURBIT
TURGID
TURKIC
TURKIS
TURNIP
TUSSIS
TUTTIS

•U•••I
EURIPI
LUMINI
QUADRI
TULADI

••UI••
ACUITY
AGUISH
ALUINO
ALUINS
AQUILA
BLUING
BLUISH
BRUINS
BRUISE
BRUITS
CLUING
CRUISE
DRUIDS
EQUINE
EQUIPS
EQUITY
FEUING
FLUIDS
FRUITS
FRUITY
GLUIER
GLUING
LOUISA
LOUISE
SLUICE
SLUING
SQUIBS
SQUIDS
SQUILL
SQUINT
SQUIRE
SQUIRM
SQUIRT
SQUISH
TRUING
TRUISM

••U•I•
ABULIA
ALUMIN
ANUBIS
APULIA
BAUCIS
BOUGIE
CAULIS
COUSIN
DOUGIE
FLUVIO
GIULIA
GIULIO
HOURIS
INULIN
KAURIS
KRUBIS
LAURIE
MOULIN
PAULIN
PLUVIO
PYURIA
SHUTIN
STUDIO
STUPID
THULIA

••U••I
ALUMNI
BRUNEI
GLUTEI
SOUARI

•••UI•
ACQUIT
ALCUIN
BEDUIN
BEGUIN
INTUIT
JESUIT
LIQUID
MAQUIS
SCHUIT
SEQUIN
TENUIS
UNGUIS

•••U•I
AGOUTI
GOMUTI
INCUBI
KABUKI
LAZULI
LIMULI
SALUKI
WATUSI

••••UI
BANGUI
SANGUI
SESQUI

U•J•••
UNJUST

•UJ•••
JUJUBE

•U•J••
PUNJAB

••UJ••
THUJAS

UK••••
UKASES

U•K•••
UNKIND
UNKNIT
UPKEEP

U•••K•
UMIAKS
UNLIKE
UNMAKE
UNYOKE
UPTAKE

U••••K
UNCOCK
UNCORK
UNHOOK
UNHUSK
UNLOCK
UNMASK
UNPACK
UNPICK

•UK•••
AUKLET
MUKLUK
PUKING
YUKKED

•U•K••
BUCKED
BUCKER
BUCKET
BUCKLE
BUCKRA
BULKED
BUMKIN
BUNKED
BUNKER
BUNKUM
BURKED
BURKES
BUSKIN
CUCKOO
DUCKED
DUCKER
DUIKER
DUNKED
DUNKER
DUSKED
FUNKED
GURKHA
HUCKLE
HULKED
HUSKED
HUSKER
JUNKED
JUNKER
JUNKET
JUNKIE
LUNKER
LURKED
MUCKED
MUCKER
MUSKEG
MUSKET
MUSKIT
PUCKER
PUNKAS
QUAKED
QUAKER
QUAKES
RUCKED
RUCKUS
RUSKIN
SUCKED
SUCKER
SUCKLE
SULKED
SUNKEN
TUCKED
TUCKER
TURKEY
TURKIC
TURKIS
TUSKED
TUSKER
YUKKED

•U••K•
EUREKA
KULAKS
QUACKS
QUARKS
QUIRKS
TUPIKS

•U•••K
LUBECK
MUKLUK
MUZHIK
NUDNIK
SUSLIK

••UK••
FLUKED
FLUKES
FLUKEY
PAUKER
ZHUKOV

••U•K•
CAULKS
CHUCKS
CHUNKS
CHUNKY
CLUCKS
DRUNKS
FLUNKS
FLUNKY
PLUCKS
PLUCKY
PLUNKS
SHUCKS
SKULKS
SKUNKS
SPUNKY
TRUCKS
TRUNKS

••U••K
SQUAWK
SQUEAK

•••UK•
KABUKI
PERUKE
REBUKE
SALUKI

•••U•K
CANUCK
DEBUNK
PODUNK
SHRUNK
STRUCK
UNHUSK

••••UK
CHABUK
DYBBUK
MARDUK
MUKLUK
SELJUK

UL••••
ULCERS
ULEMAS
ULENCE
ULLAGE
ULSTER
ULTIMA

U•L•••
UGLIER
UGLIFY
UGLILY
ULLAGE
UMLAUT
UNLACE
UNLADE
UNLAID
UNLAYS
UNLEAD
UNLESS
UNLIKE
UNLIVE
UNLOAD
UNLOCK
UPLAND
UPLIFT

U••L••
UBOLTS
UMBLES
UNCLAD
UNCLES
URALIC
UVULAE
UVULAR
UVULAS

U•••L•
UGLILY

6

UMBELS
UNABLE
UNBELT
UNBOLT
UNDULY
UNFOLD
UNGULA
UNHOLY
UNPILE
UNROLL
UNRULY
UNSOLD
UNTOLD
UNWELL
UPHELD
UPHILL
UPHOLD
URSULA
USABLE
USABLY

U••••L
UNCIAL
UNCOIL
UNCURL
UNFURL
UNGUAL
UNREAL
UNREEL
UNROLL
UNSEAL
UNVEIL
UNWELL
UPHILL
URANYL
URINAL
USEFUL

•UL•••
BULBAR
BULBEL
BULBIL
BULBUL
BULGAR
BULGED
BULGER
BULGES
BULKED
BULLAE
BULLET
CULETS
CULLAY
CULLED
CULLER
CULLET
CULLIS
CULMED
CULTCH
CULTUS
CULVER
DULCET
DULCIE
DULLED
DULLER
DULUTH
EULOGY
FULCRA
FULFIL
FULGID
FULLED
FULLER
FULMAR
FULTON
GULDEN
GULFED
GULLAH
GULLET
GULPED
GULPER
HULKED
HULLED
JULEPS
JULIAN
JULIAS
JULIES
JULIET
JULIUS
KULAKS
KULTUR
LULLED
MULCTS
MULISH
MULLAH
MULLED
MULLEN
MULLER
MULLET
MULLEY
NULLAH
PULERS
PULING
PULLED
PULLER
PULLET
PULLEY
PULPED
PULPIT
PULQUE
PULSAR
PULSED
PULSES
RULERS
RULING
SULCUS
SULFUR
SULKED
SULLEN
SULPHA
SULPHO
SULTAN
SULTRY
TULADI
TULIPS
TULLES
VULCAN
VULGAR
VULVAE
VULVAL
VULVAR

•U•L••
AUKLET
BUGLED
BUGLER
BUGLES
BUILDS
BULLAE
BULLET
BURLAP
BURLED
BURLER
BURLEY
BUTLER
CULLAY
CULLED
CULLER
CULLET
CULLIS
CURLED
CURLER
CURLEW
CUTLAS
CUTLER
CUTLET
DUBLIN
DUDLEY
DUELED
DUELER
DUELLO
DULLED
DULLER
DUNLIN
DUOLOG
DUPLEX
EUCLID
FUELED
FUELER
FUGLED
FUGLES
FULLED
FULLER
FURLED
GUILDS
GUILES
GUILTS
GUILTY
GULLAH
GULLET
HUELVA
HULLED
HURLED
HURLER
HUXLEY
LUBLIN
LUELLA
LULLED
MUKLUK
MULLAH
MULLED
MULLEN
MULLER
MULLET
MULLEY
MUSLIM
MUSLIN
NULLAH
NUTLET
OUTLAW
OUTLAY
OUTLET
PUBLIC
PULLED
PULLER
PULLET
PULLEY
PURLED
PURLIN
PUTLOG
QUALMS
QUALMY
QUELLS
QUILLS
QUILTS
RUBLES
RUNLET
SUBLET
SULLEN
SUNLIT
SUSLIK
SUTLER
TUILLE
TULLES

•U••L•
AUDILE
BUBALS
BUBBLE
BUBBLY
BUCKLE
BUDDLE
BUMBLE
BUNDLE
BUNGLE
BURBLE
BURGLE
BUSILY
BUSTLE
CUDDLE
CUDDLY
CUPELS
CUPOLA
CUPULE
CURDLE
CURTLY
CURULE
CUTELY
CUTTLE
DUELLO
DUFFLE
DUMBLY
FUDDLE
FUMBLE
FUSILE
FUSILS
FUTILE
FUZILS
GURGLE
GUTTLE
GUZZLE
HUCKLE
HUDDLE
HUGELY
HUMBLE
HUMBLY
HURDLE
HURTLE
HUSTLE
JUGGLE
JUMBLE
JUNGLE
JUNGLY
JURELS
JUSTLY
LUCILE
LUELLA
LUNULA
LUNULE
MUDDLE
MUFFLE
MUMBLE
MURALS
MUSCLE
MUTULE
MUZZLE
NUBBLE
NUBBLY
NUBILE
NUDELY
NUMBLY
NUZZLE
OUSELS
OUZELS
PUDDLE
PUDDLY
PUEBLO
PUNILY
PUPILS
PURELY
PURFLE
PURPLE
PUSSLY
PUZZLE
QUAILS
QUELLS
QUILLS
RUBBLE
RUDDLE
RUDELY
RUFFLE
RUMBLE
RUMPLE
RUNDLE
RUSTLE
RUTILE
SUABLE
SUBTLE
SUBTLY
SUCKLE
SUPPLE
SUPPLY
SURELY
TUBULE
TUILLE
TUMBLE
TUMULT
TUPELO
TURTLE
TUSSLE

•U•••L
BUCCAL
BULBEL
BULBIL
BULBUL
BURIAL
BURSAL
BUSHEL
CUDGEL
CUNEAL
CUPFUL
CURIAL
DUFFEL
FULFIL
FUNGAL
FUNNEL
GUNNEL
KUMMEL
LUTEAL
MURIEL
MUSSEL
MUTUAL
PUMMEL
RUEFUL
RUNNEL
TUNNEL
TUSSAL
VULVAL

••UL••
ABULIA
ADULTS
ALULAE
ALULAR
AMULET
APULIA
BEULAH
BEULAS
BOULES
BRULOT
CAULES
CAULIS
CAULKS
COULEE
EXULTS
FAULTS
FAULTY
FOULED
FOULER
FOULLY
GIULIA
GIULIO
HAULED
HAULER
HAULMY

INULIN
JOULES
MAULED
MAULER
MOULDS
MOULDY
MOULIN
MOULTS
OCULAR
OVULAR
OVULES
PAULAS
PAULIN
PAULUS
POULTS
SAULTS
SCULLS
SCULPT
SKULKS
SKULLS
SOULED
STULLS
THULIA
TOULON
UVULAE
UVULAR
UVULAS
VAULTS
WAULED

••U•L•

AQUILA
BAUBLE
BLUELY
BOUCLE
CAUDLE
CHURLS
COUPLE
DOUBLE
DOUBLY
DOURLY
EQUALS
FOULLY
GLUMLY
GRUELS
HOURLY
KNURLS
KNURLY
LOUDLY
ROUBLE
SCULLS
SKULLS
SMUGLY
SNUGLY
SOURLY
SQUALL
SQUILL
STULLS
TAUTLY
TOUSLE

••U••L

ALUDEL
BRUMAL
BRUTAL
CAUDAL
CAUSAL
CRURAL
FAUCAL
FAUNAL
FEUDAL
FRUGAL
LAUREL
NEURAL
NOUNAL
PLURAL
SAUREL
SQUALL
SQUEAL
SQUILL

•••UL•

AMPULE
AMPULS
ANNULS
BABULS
CANULA
CEDULA
COPULA
CUPULE
CURULE
ENGULF
FACULA
FECULA
FERULA
FERULE
FIBULA
GHOULS
INDULT
INGULF
INSULT
ISEULT
LAZULI
LIGULA
LIGULE
LIMULI
LOBULE
LUNULA
LUNULE
MACULA
MACULE
MIAULS
MODULE
MOGULS
MORULA
MUTULE
NEBULA
NODULE
OCCULT
OSCULE
PAPULA
PAPULE
PENULT
PICULS
PILULE
RADULA
RAOULS
RESULT
ROMULO
SHOULD
TUBULE
TUMULT
UNDULY
UNGULA
UNRULY
URSULA
VENULE
VOGULS
ZONULA
ZONULE

•••U•L

ACTUAL
ANNUAL
CASUAL
LEMUEL
MANUAL
MANUEL
MIGUEL
MUTUAL
RITUAL
SAMUEL
SEQUEL
SEXUAL
TOLUOL
TOLUYL
UNCURL
UNFURL
UNGUAL
VISUAL

••••UL

ARMFUL
ARTFUL
BEFOUL
BULBUL
CONSUL
CUPFUL
EARFUL
ENSOUL
EYEFUL
FITFUL
HAMAUL
HATFUL
INHAUL
INSOUL
IREFUL
JARFUL
JOYFUL
LAPFUL
LAWFUL
MANFUL
RUEFUL
SINFUL
USEFUL
VATFUL
WILFUL
WOEFUL

UM••••

UMBELS
UMBERS
UMBLES
UMBRAE
UMBRAS
UMIAKS
UMLAUT
UMPIRE

U•M•••

UNMADE
UNMAKE
UNMANS
UNMASK
UNMEET
UNMEWS
UNMOOR
UPMOST
UTMOST

U••M••

ULEMAS
UREMIA

U•••M•

ULTIMA

U••••M

UNSEAM

•UM•••

BUMBLE
BUMKIN
BUMMED
BUMMER
BUMPED
BUMPER
CUMBER
CUMINS
DUMBLY
DUMPED
FUMBLE
FUMIER
FUMING
GUMBOS
GUMMAS
GUMMED
HUMANE
HUMANS
HUMBLE
HUMBLY
HUMBUG
HUMMED
HUMMER
HUMORS
HUMPED
JUMBLE
JUMPED
JUMPER
KUMISS
KUMMEL
LUMBAR
LUMBER
LUMENS
LUMINA
LUMINI
LUMINO
LUMMOX
LUMPED
LUMPEN
MUMBLE
MUMMED
MUMMER
NUMBED
NUMBER
NUMBLY
NUMINA
PUMICE
PUMMEL
PUMPED
PUMPER
RUMBAS
RUMBLE
RUMINA
RUMMER
RUMORS
RUMPLE
RUMPUS
SUMACS
SUMMED
SUMMER
SUMMIT
SUMMON
SUMNER
TUMBLE
TUMEFY
TUMORS
TUMULT

•U•M••

BUMMED
BUMMER
BUSMAN
BUSMEN
CULMED
FULMAR
GUIMPE
GUMMAS
GUMMED
GUNMAN
GUNMEN
HUMMED
HUMMER
KUMMEL
LUMMOX
MUMMED
MUMMER
MURMUR
MUUMUU
NUTMEG
OUTMAN
PUMMEL
RUMMER
SUBMIT
SUMMED
SUMMER
SUMMIT
SUMMON
SUOMIC

•U••M•

AUTUMN
QUALMS
QUALMY

•U•••M

AUTISM
BUNKUM
CUBISM
CUPRUM
CURIUM
CUSTOM
DURHAM
LUTEUM
MUSEUM
MUSLIM
MUTISM
NUDISM
PURISM
PUTNAM
QUORUM
SUFISM

••UM••

ACUMEN
ALUMIN
ALUMNA
ALUMNI
BRUMAL
BRUMES
CHUMMY
CHUMPS
CLUMPS
CLUMPY
CLUMSY
CRUMBS
CRUMBY
CRUMMY
CRUMPS
FLUMED
FLUMES
FLUMPS
FRUMPS
FRUMPY
GLUMES
GLUMLY
GRUMES
GRUMPY
MAUMAU
MUUMUU
NEUMES
PLUMBO
PLUMBS
PLUMED
PLUMES
PLUMMY
PLUMPS
RHUMBA
RHUMBS
SCUMMY
SLUMMY
SLUMPS
SPUMED
SPUMES

6

STUMPS
STUMPY
THUMBS
THUMPS
TRUMAN
TRUMPS

••U•M•
CHUMMY
CRUMMY
HAULMY
PLUMMY
SCUMMY
SLUMMY
SQUAMA
ZEUGMA

••U••M
SCUTUM
SPUTUM
SQUIRM
TRUISM

•••UM•
ALBUMS
ASSUME
AUTUMN
BEGUMS
BENUMB
COLUMN
DEGUMS
EXHUME
FANUMS
FORUMS
HEAUME
ILLUME
JORUMS
LEGUME
MAZUMA
METUMP
NAHUMS
PNEUMA
PNEUMO
RESUME
RHEUMY
SCRUMS
SEDUMS
SERUMS
STRUMA
STRUMS
THRUMS
TRAUMA
VOLUME

•••U•M
VACUUM

••••UM
ACETUM
ACTIUM
ADYTUM
AECIUM
ALARUM
ALLIUM
AMYLUM
ANTRUM
ASARUM
ASYLUM
ATRIUM
BARIUM
BARNUM
BUNKUM
CAECUM
CERIUM
CESIUM
CILIUM
CIRCUM
CONIUM
CORIUM
CRINUM
CUPRUM
CURIUM
DICTUM
DORSUM
ERBIUM
FERRUM
FOLIUM
FRENUM
GONIUM
GYPSUM
HELIUM
INDIUM
IONIUM
KALIUM
LABIUM
LABRUM
LUTEUM
LYCEUM
MAGNUM
MEDIUM
MILIUM
MINIUM
MUSEUM
OMASUM
OSMIUM
PEPLUM
PHYLUM
PILEUM
PLENUM
PODIUM
POSSUM
QUORUM
RADIUM
RECTUM
SACRUM
SCUTUM
SEPTUM
SODIUM
SPUTUM
TALCUM
TEDIUM
TERGUM
VACUUM
VELLUM
WAMPUM

UN••••
UNABLE
UNBARS
UNBEAR
UNBELT
UNBEND
UNBENT
UNBIND
UNBOLT
UNBORN
UNBRED
UNCAGE
UNCAPS
UNCIAL
UNCLAD
UNCLES
UNCOCK
UNCOIL
UNCORK
UNCURL
UNDIES
UNDINE
UNDOER
UNDOES
UNDONE
UNDRAW
UNDREW
UNDSET
UNDULY
UNEASY
UNESCO
UNEVEN
UNFAIR
UNFOLD
UNFURL
UNGIRD
UNGIRT
UNGUAL
UNGUES
UNGUIS
UNGULA
UNHAIR
UNHAND
UNHATS
UNHOLY
UNHOOK
UNHURT
UNHUSK
UNICEF
UNIFIC
UNIONS
UNIQUE
UNISEX
UNISON
UNITED
UNITES
UNJUST
UNKIND
UNKNIT
UNLACE
UNLADE
UNLAID
UNLAYS
UNLEAD
UNLESS
UNLIKE
UNLIVE
UNLOAD
UNLOCK
UNMADE
UNMAKE
UNMANS
UNMASK
UNMEET
UNMEWS
UNMOOR
UNPACK
UNPAID
UNPEGS
UNPICK
UNPILE
UNPINS
UNREAD
UNREAL
UNREEL
UNREST
UNRIGS
UNRIPE
UNRIPS
UNROLL
UNROOT
UNRULY
UNSAFE
UNSAID
UNSAYS
UNSEAL
UNSEAM
UNSEAT
UNSEEN
UNSHIP
UNSNAP
UNSOLD
UNSTEP
UNSTOP
UNSUNG
UNSURE
UNTIDY
UNTIED
UNTIES
UNTOLD
UNTROD
UNTRUE
UNUSED
UNVEIL
UNVEXT
UNWARY
UNWELL
UNWEPT
UNWIND
UNWISE
UNWISH
UNWRAP
UNYOKE

U••N••
UBANGI
UGANDA
ULENCE
UNKNIT
UNSNAP
UPENDS
URANIA
URANIC
URANUS
URANYL
URINAL
USANCE

U•••N•
UNBEND
UNBENT
UNBIND
UNDINE
UNDONE
UNHAND
UNIONS
UNKIND
UNMANS
UNPINS
UNSUNG
UNWIND
UPLAND
UPPING
URBANE
URGENT
URGING
URSINE
UTURNS

U••••N
UNBORN
UNEVEN
UNISON
UNSEEN
UPTOWN
UPTURN
URCHIN
UTAHAN

•UN•••
AUNTIE
BUNCHE
BUNCHY
BUNCOS
BUNDLE
BUNGED
BUNGLE
BUNION
BUNKED
BUNKER
BUNKUM
BUNSEN
BUNTED
BUNYAN
CUNEAL
CUNNER
DUNBAR
DUNCAN
DUNCES
DUNDEE
DUNGED
DUNKED
DUNKER
DUNLIN
DUNNED
EUNICE
EUNUCH
FUNDED
FUNDUS
FUNEST
FUNGAL
FUNGUS
FUNKED
FUNNEL
GUNMAN
GUNMEN
GUNNAR
GUNNED
GUNNEL
GUNNER
GUNSHY
HUNGER
HUNGRY
HUNTED
HUNTER
JUNCOS
JUNEAU
JUNGLE
JUNGLY
JUNIOR
JUNIUS
JUNKED
JUNKER
JUNKET
JUNKIE
JUNTAS
LUNACY
LUNATE
LUNETS
LUNGED
LUNGEE
LUNGER
LUNGES
LUNGIS
LUNKER
LUNULA
LUNULE
MUNICH
NUNCIO
OUNCES
PUNCHY
PUNDIT
PUNIER
PUNILY
PUNISH
PUNJAB
PUNKAS
PUNNED
PUNTED
PUNTER
PUNTOS
RUNDLE
RUNINS
RUNLET
RUNNEL
RUNNER
RUNOFF
RUNONS

6

RUNOUT
RUNWAY
RUNYON
SUNBOW
SUNDAE
SUNDAY
SUNDER
SUNDEW
SUNDOG
SUNDRY
SUNKEN
SUNLIT
SUNNAH
SUNNED
SUNSET
SUNUPS
TUNDRA
TUNERS
TUNEUP
TUNGUS
TUNICA
TUNICS
TUNING
TUNNED
TUNNEL

•U•N••

BURNED
BURNER
BURNET
CUNNER
DUENNA
DUNNED
EUPNEA
FUNNEL
GUANIN
GUANOS
GUENON
GUINEA
GUNNAR
GUNNED
GUNNEL
GUNNER
LUANDA
NUANCE
NUDNIK
PUNNED
PUTNAM
QUANTA
QUANTS
QUINCE
QUINCY
QUINIC
QUINSY
QUINTS
RUINED
RUINER
RUNNEL
RUNNER
SUMNER
SUNNAH
SUNNED
TUNNED
TUNNEL
TURNED
TURNER
TURNIP

•U••N•

AUGEND
AUXINS
BURANS
BURINS
BUSING
BUTANE
BUYING
CUBANS
CUBING
CUMINS
CURING
CUTINS
DUENNA
DUGONG
DUPING
DURING
EUGENE
FUMING
FUSING
FUZING
GUIANA
GUYANA
GUYING
HUMANE
HUMANS
HURONS
JUPONS
JURANT
LUCENT
LUMENS
LUMINA
LUMINI
LUMINO
LUPINE
LURING
LUTING
MURINE
MUSING
MUTANT
MUTING
MUTINY
NUMINA
OUTING
PUISNE
PUKING
PULING
PURANA
PURINE
PUTONS
QUAINT
QUEANS
QUEENS
QUERNS
QUOINS
RUBENS
RULING
RUMINA
RUNINS
RUNONS
RUSINE
SUPINE
SUSANS
TUBING
TUNING
YUPONS

•U•••N

AUBURN
AUGEAN
AUSTEN
AUSTIN
AUTUMN
BUMKIN
BUNION
BUNSEN
BUNYAN
BURDEN
BUSKIN
BUSMAN
BUSMEN
BUTTON
DUBBIN
DUBLIN
DUDEEN
DUNCAN
DUNLIN
DUODEN
DURBAN
DURIAN
DURION
FULTON
FUSAIN
FUSION
GUANIN
GUENON
GUIDON
GULDEN
GUNMAN
GUNMEN
HUDSON
JUDEAN
JULIAN
JUSTIN
KUCHEN
LUBLIN
LUCIAN
LUCIEN
LUMPEN
MUFFIN
MULLEN
MUSLIN
MUTTON
NUBBIN
NUBIAN
OUTMAN
OUTRAN
OUTRUN
PUFFIN
PURLIN
QUEZON
RUNYON
RUSKIN
SUBORN
SUDDEN
SULLEN
SULTAN
SUMMON
SUNKEN
TUCHUN
TUCSON
TURBAN
TUREEN
TUSCAN
VULCAN

••UN••

ARUNTA
BLUNGE
BLUNTS
BOUNCE
BOUNCY
BOUNDS
BOUNTY
BRUNCH
BRUNEI
BRUNET
BRUNOS
CHUNKS
CHUNKY
COUNTS
COUNTY
CRUNCH
DAUNTS
DRUNKS
FAUNAE
FAUNAL
FAUNAS
FAUNUS
FLUNKS
FLUNKY
FOUNDS
FOUNTS
FRUNZE
GRUNDY
GRUNTS
HAUNCH
HAUNTS
HOUNDS
JAUNTS
JAUNTY
JOUNCE
LAUNCE
LAUNCH
LOUNGE
MAUNDS
MAUNDY
MOUNTS
MOUNTY
NOUNAL
PAUNCH
PLUNGE
PLUNKS
POUNCE
POUNDS
PRUNED
PRUNER
PRUNES
ROUNDS
SAUNAS
SHUNTS
SKUNKS
SOUNDS
SPUNKY
STUNTS
TAUNTS
TRUNKS
VAUNTS
WOUNDS
ZOUNDS

••U•N•

ALUINO
ALUINS
ALUMNA
ALUMNI
BLUING
BOURNE
BOURNS
BRUINS
CHURNS
CLUING
DHURNA
EQUINE
FEUING
FLUENT
GLUING
IGUANA
INURNS
MOURNS
SLUING
SPURNS
SQUINT
TRUANT
TRUING
UTURNS

••U••N

ACUMEN
ALUMIN
ANURAN
BHUTAN
COUPON
COUSIN
GLUTEN
HAUSEN
INULIN
LOUDEN
MOULIN
MOUTON
NEURON
PAULIN
REUBEN
SHUTIN
TAUTEN
TEUTON
TOULON
TRUMAN
YAUPON
YOUPON

•••UN•

ABOUND
AMOUNT
AROUND
ATTUNE
CAJUNS
COHUNE
DEBUNK
EDMUND
EXEUNT
FECUND
FLAUNT
GERUND
GROUND
IMMUNE
IMMUNO
JEJUNE
JOCUND
KORUNA
KORUNY
LACUNA
LAGUNE
OBTUND
OSMUND
PODUNK
REFUND
RERUNS
ROTUND
SECUND
SHRUNK
SPRUNG
TRIUNE
UNSUNG
VARUNA
VICUNA
YAMUNS

•••U•N

ALCUIN
AUBURN
AUTUMN
BEDUIN
BEGUIN
COLUMN
FRAUEN
IMPUGN
INTURN
OPPUGN
PAPUAN
RETURN
SATURN
SEQUIN
SIOUAN
UPTURN

••••UN

ADNOUN
OUTRUN
POPGUN
SHOGUN
TUCHUN
VERDUN

6

U•O•••
UBOATS
UBOLTS
UROPOD
UTOPIA

U••O••
UNBOLT
UNBORN
UNCOCK
UNCOIL
UNCORK
UNDOER
UNDOES
UNDONE
UNFOLD
UNHOLY
UNHOOK
UNIONS
UNLOAD
UNLOCK
UNMOOR
UNROLL
UNROOT
UNSOLD
UNTOLD
UNYOKE
UPBOWS
UPHOLD
UPMOST
UPROAR
UPROOT
UPROSE
UPTOWN
UTMOST

U•••O•
UNHOOK
UNISON
UNMOOR
UNROOT
UNSTOP
UNTROD
UPHROE
UPROOT
UPSHOT
UROPOD

U••••O
UNESCO

•UO•••
BUOYED
DUODEN
DUOLOG
QUOINS
QUOITS
QUORUM
QUOTAS
QUOTED
QUOTER
QUOTES
SUOMIC

•U•O••
AURORA
AUROUS
AUTOED
BUBOES
CUBOID
CUPOLA
CUTOFF
CUTOUT
DUGONG
DUGOUT
EUBOEA
EUDORA
EULOGY
EUROPA
EUROPE
FUCOID
FUCOUS
FURORS
HUMORS
HURONS
JUPONS
JURORS
MUCOID
MUCOSA
MUCOSE
MUCOUS
PUTOFF
PUTONS
PUTOUT
RUFOUS
RUGOSE
RUGOUS
RUMORS
RUNOFF
RUNONS
RUNOUT
SUBORN
TUMORS
TUTORS
YUPONS

•U••O•
AUTHOR
BUNCOS
BUNION
BURBOT
BURGOO
BURGOS
BURROS
BURROW
BUTTON
CUCKOO
CURIOS
CUSSOS
CUSTOM
CUSTOS
DUOLOG
DURION
FUGIOS
FULTON
FURROW
FUSION
GUACOS
GUANOS
GUENON
GUIDON
GUMBOS
HUDSON
JUNCOS
JUNIOR
LUMMOX
MUTTON
OUTFOX
PUNTOS
PUTLOG
QUAHOG
QUEZON
RUNYON
SUCCOR
SUITOR
SUMMON
SUNBOW
SUNDOG
TUCSON
TURBOT
TURCOS

•U•••O
AUSTRO
BURGOO
CUCKOO
DUELLO
JUDAEO
LUMINO
NUNCIO
PUEBLO
QUARTO
RUBATO
RUBIGO
SUBITO
SULPHO
TUPELO
TUXEDO

••UO••
FLUORO
FLUORS

••U•O•
BRULOT
BRUNOS
COUPON
CRUSOE
MOUTON
NEURON
STUPOR
TEUTON
TOULON
YAUPON
YOUPON
ZHUKOV

••U••O
ALUINO
FLUORO
FLUVIO
GAUCHO
GIULIO
PLUMBO
PLUVIO
POUSTO
STUCCO
STUDIO

•••UO•
LIQUOR
PEQUOD
PEQUOT
TOLUOL

•••U•O
AERUGO
ARTURO
BASUTO
CARUSO
COLUGO
ESCUDO
GLAUCO
IMMUNO
LANUGO
MADURO
PLEURO
PNEUMO
PSEUDO
ROMULO
STAURO
TENUTO

UP••••
UPASES
UPBEAT
UPBOWS
UPCAST
UPDATE
UPENDS
UPHELD
UPHILL
UPHOLD
UPHROE
UPKEEP
UPLAND
UPLIFT
UPMOST
UPPERS
UPPING
UPPISH
UPPITY
UPRISE
UPROAR
UPROOT
UPROSE
UPSETS
UPSHOT
UPSIDE
UPTAKE
UPTOWN
UPTURN
UPWARD

U•P•••
UMPIRE
UNPACK
UNPAID
UNPEGS
UNPICK
UNPILE
UNPINS
UPPERS
UPPING
UPPISH
UPPITY

U••P••
UROPOD
UTOPIA

U•••P•
UNCAPS
UNRIPE
UNRIPS
UNWEPT
USURPS

U••••P
UNSHIP
UNSNAP
UNSTEP
UNSTOP
UNWRAP
UPKEEP

•UP•••
CUPELS
CUPFUL
CUPOLA
CUPPED
CUPPER
CUPRIC
CUPRUM
CUPULE
DUPERS
DUPERY
DUPING
DUPLEX
EUPNEA
JUPONS
LUPINE
PUPATE
PUPILS
PUPPED
PUPPET
RUPEES
RUPERT
RUPIAH
SUPERB
SUPERS
SUPINE
SUPPED
SUPPER
SUPPLE
SUPPLY
TUPELO
TUPIKS
TUPPED
YUPONS

•U•P••
AUSPEX
BUMPED
BUMPER
BURPED
CUPPED
CUPPER
CUSPED
CUSPID
CUSPIS
DUMPED
GULPED
GULPER
HUMPED
JUMPED
JUMPER
LUMPED
LUMPEN
OUTPUT
PULPED
PULPIT
PUMPED
PUMPER
PUPPED
PUPPET
PURPLE
PUTPUT
QUAPAW
QUIPUS
RUMPLE
RUMPUS
SULPHA
SULPHO
SUPPED
SUPPER
SUPPLE
SUPPLY
TUPPED

•U••P•
CUTUPS
EURIPI
EUROPA
EUROPE
GUIMPE
JULEPS
SUNUPS
TULIPS

•U•••P
BURLAP
HUBCAP
MUDCAP
PUSHUP
TUNEUP
TURNIP

••UP••
COUPES
COUPLE
COUPON
DRUPES
ERUPTS
LOUPES

PAUPER
STUPAS
STUPES
STUPID
STUPOR
TAUPES
TOUPEE
YAUPED
YAUPON
YOUPON

••U•P•
CHUMPS
CLUMPS
CLUMPY
CRUMPS
EQUIPS
FLUMPS
FRUMPS
FRUMPY
GRUMPY
PLUMPS
SCULPT
SLUMPS
SLURPS
STUMPS
STUMPY
THUMPS
TRUMPS
USURPS

•••UP•
ABRUPT
CROUPE
CROUPS
CROUPY
CUTUPS
GETUPS
GROUPS
LETUPS
MIXUPS
OCCUPY
PINUPS
SCAUPS
SETUPS
SIRUPS
SIRUPY
STOUPS
SUNUPS
SYRUPS
SYRUPY
TIEUPS
TROUPE

•••U•P
METUMP

••••UP
BANGUP
BLOWUP
CATSUP
COCKUP
EYECUP
GALLUP
HANGUP
HICCUP
HOLDUP
HOOKUP
LARRUP
LINEUP
LOCKUP
MADEUP
MAKEUP
MARKUP
MOCKUP
PENTUP
PICKUP
PUSHUP
RECOUP
SANNUP
SLIPUP
STEPUP
TAKEUP
TEACUP
TITTUP
TOSSUP
TUNEUP
WALKUP
WARMUP
WIKIUP
WRAPUP

U••Q••
UNIQUE

•UQ•••
TUQUES

•U•Q••
PULQUE

UR••••
URAEUS
URALIC
URANIA
URANIC
URANUS
URANYL
URBANE
URCHIN
UREASE
UREIDE
UREMIA
URETER
URETHR
URETIC
URGENT
URGING
URINAL
UROPOD
URSINE
URSULA
URTEXT

U•R•••
UNREAD
UNREAL
UNREEL
UNREST
UNRIGS
UNRIPE
UNRIPS
UNROLL
UNROOT
UNRULY
UPRISE
UPROAR
UPROOT
UPROSE

U••R••
UMBRAE
UMBRAS
UNBRED
UNDRAW
UNDREW
UNTROD
UNTRUE
UNWRAP
UPHROE
USURER
USURPS
UTERUS
UTURNS

U•••R•
UDDERS
ULCERS
UMBERS
UMPIRE
UNBARS
UNBORN
UNCORK
UNCURL
UNFURL
UNGIRD
UNGIRT
UNHURT
UNSURE
UNWARY
UPPERS
UPTURN
UPWARD
USHERS
UTGARD
UTTERS

U••••R
UGLIER
ULSTER
UNBEAR
UNDOER
UNFAIR
UNHAIR
UNMOOR
UPROAR
URETER
URETHR
USURER
UVULAR

•UR•••
AURATE
AUREUS
AURIGA
AURIST
AURORA
AUROUS
BURANS
BURBLE
BURBOT
BURDEN
BURDIE
BUREAU
BURGEE
BURGER
BURGHS
BURGLE
BURGOO
BURGOS
BURIAL
BURIED
BURIES
BURINS
BURKED
BURKES
BURLAP
BURLED
BURLER
BURLEY
BURNED
BURNER
BURNET
BURPED
BURRED
BURROS
BURROW
BURSAE
BURSAL
BURSAR
BURSAS
BURSES
BURSTS
CURACY
CURARE
CURATE
CURBED
CURDED
CURDLE
CURERS
CURFEW
CURIAE
CURIAL
CURIES
CURING
CURIOS
CURIUM
CURLED
CURLER
CURLEW
CURSED
CURSES
CURTIS
CURTLY
CURTSY
CURULE
CURVED
CURVES
CURVET
DURBAN
DURBAR
DURESS
DURHAM
DURIAN
DURING
DURION
EUREKA
EURIPI
EUROPA
EUROPE
FURIES
FURLED
FURORS
FURRED
FURROW
FURZES
GURGLE
GURKHA
HURDLE
HURLED
HURLER
HURONS
HURRAH
HURRAY
HURTER
HURTLE
JURANT
JURATS
JURELS
JURIES
JURIST
JURORS
LURERS
LURING
LURKED
MURALS
MURDER
MURIEL
MURINE
MURMUR
MURRAY
MURRES
MURREY
NURSED
NURSER
NURSES
PURANA
PURDAH
PUREED
PUREES
PURELY
PUREST
PURFLE
PURGED
PURGER
PURGES
PURIFY
PURINE
PURISM
PURIST
PURITY
PURLED
PURLIN
PURPLE
PURRED
PURSED
PURSER
PURSES
PURSUE
PURVEY
SURAHS
SURELY
SUREST
SURETY
SURFED
SURFER
SURGED
SURGER
SURGES
SURREY
SURTAX
SURVEY
TURBAN
TURBID
TURBIT
TURBOT
TURCOS
TUREEN
TURGID
TURKEY
TURKIC
TURKIS
TURNED
TURNER
TURNIP
TURRET
TURTLE
ZURICH

•U•R••
AUBREY
AUDREY
BURRED
BURROS
BURROW
CUPRIC
CUPRUM
FUHRER
FURRED
FURROW
GUARDS
HUBRIS
HURRAH
HURRAY
JUAREZ
MURRAY
MURRES
MURREY
NUTRIA
OUTRAN
OUTRUN
PUGREE
PURRED

6

PUTRID
QUARKS
QUARRY
QUARTE
QUARTO
QUARTS
QUARTZ
QUERNS
QUIRED
QUIRES
QUIRKS
QUIRTS
QUORUM
RUBRIC
SUCRES
SURREY
SUTRAS
TURRET

•U••R•

AUBURN
AUGERS
AUGURS
AUGURY
AURORA
AUSTRO
BUCKRA
BUYERS
CURARE
CURERS
DUPERS
DUPERY
EUCHRE
EUDORA
FULCRA
FURORS
FUTURE
HUBERT
HUMORS
HUNGRY
JURORS
LUGERS
LURERS
LUXURY
OUTCRY
OUTERS
PUGGRY
PULERS
QUADRI
QUAERE
QUARRY
QUATRE
QUEERS
RULERS
RUMORS
RUPERT
SUBORN
SUBURB
SUDARY
SUGARS
SUGARY
SULTRY
SUNDRY
SUPERB
SUPERS
SUTURE
TUBERS
TUMORS
TUNDRA
TUNERS
TUTORS
TUYERE

•U•••R

AUSTER
AUTHOR
BUCKER
BUDDER
BUFFER
BUGGER
BUGLER
BULBAR
BULGAR
BULGER
BUMMER
BUMPER
BUNKER
BURGER
BURLER
BURNER
BURSAR
BUSTER
BUTLER
BUTTER
BUZZER
CULLER
CULVER
CUMBER
CUNNER
CUPPER
CURLER
CUSTER
CUTLER
CUTTER
DUCKER
DUELER
DUFFER
DUIKER
DULLER
DUNBAR
DUNKER
DURBAR
DUSTER
FUELER
FUHRER
FULLER
FULMAR
FUMIER
FUSSER
GUIDER
GUITAR
GULPER
GUNNAR
GUNNER
GUSHER
GUTTER
HUMMER
HUNGER
HUNTER
HURLER
HURTER
HUSKER
HUSSAR
JUDGER
JUICER
JUMPER
JUNIOR
JUNKER
KULTUR
LUBBER
LUGGER
LUMBAR
LUMBER
LUNGER
LUNKER
LUSHER
LUSTER
LUTHER
MUCKER
MUDDER
MUGGAR
MUGGER
MUGGUR
MULLER
MUMMER
MURDER
MURMUR
MUSHER
MUSTER
MUTTER
NUMBER
NURSER
NUTTER
OUSTER
PUCKER
PUFFER
PULLER
PULSAR
PUMPER
PUNIER
PUNTER
PURGER
PURSER
PUSHER
PUTTER
QUAKER
QUASAR
QUAVER
QUIVER
QUOTER
RUBBER
RUDDER
RUINER
RUMMER
RUNNER
RUSHER
SUBTER
SUCCOR
SUCKER
SUFFER
SUITOR
SULFUR
SUMMER
SUMNER
SUNDER
SUPPER
SURFER
SURGER
SUTLER
TUBBER
TUCKER
TURNER
TUSKER
TUSSAR
VULGAR
VULVAR
ZUIDER
ZUYDER

••UR••

ANURAN
AZURES
BLURBS
BLURRY
BLURTS
BOURGS
BOURNE
BOURNS
BOURSE
CHURCH
CHURLS
CHURNS
CHURRS
COURSE
COURTS
CRURAL
DHURNA
DOURLY
EXURBS
FLURRY
FOURTH
GOURDE
GOURDS
HOURIS
HOURLY
INURED
INURES
INURNS
KAURIS
KNURLS
KNURLY
LAURAE
LAURAS
LAUREL
LAURIE
LOURED
MOURNS
NEURAL
NEURON
PLURAL
POURED
POURER
PYURIA
SAUREL
SAURUS
SCURFY
SCURRY
SCURVE
SCURVY
SEURAT
SLURPS
SLURRY
SOURCE
SOURED
SOURER
SOURLY
SPURGE
SPURNS
SPURRY
SPURTS
STURDY
TAURUS
TOURED
USURER
USURPS
UTURNS

••U•R•

BLURRY
CHURRS
DAUBRY
EDUARD
FEUARS
FLUORO
FLUORS
FLURRY
GRUGRU
LOUVRE
OEUVRE
SCURRY
SLURRY
SOUARI
SPURRY
SQUARE
SQUIRE
SQUIRM
SQUIRT
STUART

••U••R

ABUSER
ALULAR
AMUSER
CAUSER
COUGAR
CRUDER
DAUBER
FLUTER
FOULER
GAUGER
GLUIER
GOUGER
HAULER
LAUDER
LOUDER
LOUVER
MAULER
MAUSER
MOUSER
NEUTER
OCULAR
OVULAR
PAUKER
PAUPER
PAUSER
POURER
POUTER
PRUNER
ROUSER
ROUTER
SAUCER
SAUGER
SOURER
STUPOR
TAUTER
TEUCER
TOUTER
USURER
UVULAR

•••UR•

ABJURE
ABSURD
ADJURE
ALLURE
AMOURS
ARMURE
ARTURO
ASBURY
ASSURE
AUBURN
AUGURS
AUGURY
CESURA
COLURE
DATURA
DECURY
DEMURE
DEMURS
ENDURE
ENSURE
ERFURT
FEMURS
FIGURE
FLEURY
FLOURS
FLOURY
FUTURE
HHOURS
IMMURE
IMPURE
INCURS
INJURE
INJURY
INSURE
INTURN
LEMURS
LIGURE
LUXURY
MADURA
MADURO
MANURE
MATURE
MOHURS

NATURE
NOMURA
OCCURS
ORDURE
PARURE
PENURY
PLEURA
PLEURO
RECURS
RETURN
SATURN
SCOURS
SECURE
SIEURS
STAURO
SUBURB
SUTURE
SYNURA
TENURE
UNCURL
UNFURL
UNHURT
UNSURE
UPTURN
VELURE
YOGURT

•••U•R
ARGUER
ISSUER
JAGUAR
LIQUOR
VAGUER

••••UR
ARTHUR
CONCUR
DETOUR
DEVOUR
GIAOUR
JAIPUR
KRONUR
KULTUR
LABOUR
LANGUR
MUGGUR
MURMUR
POSEUR
SAMBUR
SIDDUR
SULFUR
VELOUR
VIGOUR
VOYEUR
WILBUR

US••••
USABLE
USABLY
USAGES
USANCE
USEFUL
USHERS
USURER
USURPS

U•S•••
ULSTER
UNSAFE
UNSAID
UNSAYS
UNSEAL
UNSEAM
UNSEAT
UNSEEN
UNSHIP
UNSNAP
UNSOLD
UNSTEP
UNSTOP
UNSUNG
UNSURE
UPSETS
UPSHOT
UPSIDE
URSINE
URSULA

U••S••
UKASES
UNDSET
UNESCO
UNISEX
UNISON
UNUSED
UPASES

U•••S•
UNEASY
UNHUSK
UNJUST
UNLESS
UNMASK
UNREST
UNWISE
UNWISH
UPCAST
UPMOST
UPPISH
UPRISE
UPROSE
UREASE
UTMOST

U••••S
UBOATS
UBOLTS
UDDERS
UKASES
ULCERS
ULEMAS
UMBELS
UMBERS
UMBLES
UMBRAS
UMIAKS
UNBARS
UNCAPS
UNCLES
UNDIES
UNDOES
UNGUES
UNGUIS
UNHATS
UNIONS
UNITES
UNLAYS
UNLESS
UNMANS
UNMEWS
UNPEGS
UNPINS
UNRIGS
UNRIPS
UNSAYS
UNTIES
UPASES
UPBOWS
UPENDS
UPPERS
UPSETS
URAEUS
URANUS
USAGES
USHERS
USURPS
UTERUS
UTTERS
UTURNS
UVULAS

•US•••
AUSPEX
AUSTEN
AUSTER
AUSTIN
AUSTRO
BUSHED
BUSHEL
BUSHES
BUSIED
BUSIES
BUSILY
BUSING
BUSKIN
BUSMAN
BUSMEN
BUSSED
BUSSES
BUSTED
BUSTER
BUSTIC
BUSTLE
CUSHAT
CUSHAW
CUSPED
CUSPID
CUSPIS
CUSSED
CUSSES
CUSSOS
CUSTER
CUSTOM
CUSTOS
DUSKED
DUSTED
DUSTER
FUSAIN
FUSEES
FUSILE
FUSILS
FUSING
FUSION
FUSSED
FUSSER
FUSSES
FUSTIC
GUSHED
GUSHER
GUSHES
GUSSET
GUSSIE
GUSTAF
GUSTAV
HUSHED
HUSHES
HUSKED
HUSKER
HUSSAR
HUSTLE
JUSTIN
JUSTLY
JUSTUS
LUSHED
LUSHER
LUSHES
LUSTED
LUSTER
MUSCAE
MUSCAT
MUSCLE
MUSEUM
MUSHED
MUSHER
MUSHES
MUSING
MUSKEG
MUSKET
MUSKIT
MUSLIM
MUSLIN
MUSSED
MUSSEL
MUSSES
MUSTEE
MUSTER
OUSELS
OUSTED
OUSTER
PUSHED
PUSHER
PUSHES
PUSHUP
PUSSES
PUSSEY
PUSSLY
RUSHED
RUSHER
RUSHES
RUSINE
RUSKIN
RUSSET
RUSSIA
RUSTED
RUSTIC
RUSTLE
SUSANS
SUSIES
SUSLIK
TUSCAN
TUSHED
TUSHES
TUSKED
TUSKER
TUSSAH
TUSSAL
TUSSAR
TUSSIS
TUSSLE

•U•S••
BUNSEN
BURSAE
BURSAL
BURSAR
BURSAS
BURSES
BURSTS
BUSSED
BUSSES
CUESTA
CUISSE
CURSED
CURSES
CUSSED
CUSSES
CUSSOS
FUSSED
FUSSER
FUSSES
GUESTS
GUISES
GUNSHY
GUSSET
GUSSIE
HUDSON
HUSSAR
MUSSED
MUSSEL
MUSSES
NURSED
NURSER
NURSES
OUTSAT
OUTSET
OUTSIT
PUISNE
PULSAR
PULSED
PULSES
PURSED
PURSER
PURSES
PURSUE
PUSSES
PUSSEY
PUSSLY
PUTSCH
QUASAR
QUESTS
RUSSET
RUSSIA
SUNSET
TUCSON
TUSSAH
TUSSAL
TUSSAR
TUSSIS
TUSSLE

•U••S•
AUGUST
AURIST
AUTISM
CUBISM
CUBIST
CUISSE
CURTSY
CUTEST
DUDISH
DURESS
FUNEST
HUGEST
JURIST
JUTISH
KUMISS
LUTIST
MUCOSA
MUCOSE
MULISH
MUTISM
NUDISM
NUDIST
PUNISH
PUREST
PURISM
PURIST
QUEASY
QUINSY
RUDEST
RUGOSE
SUFISM
SUREST

•U•••S
AUDADS
AUDITS
AUGERS
AUGHTS
AUGURS
AUREUS
AUROUS
AUXINS
BUBALS

6

BUBOES
BUDGES
BUGLES
BUILDS
BULGES
BUNCOS
BURANS
BURGHS
BURGOS
BURIES
BURINS
BURKES
BURROS
BURSAS
BURSES
BURSTS
BUSHES
BUSIES
BUSSES
BUTTES
BUYERS
BUZZES
CUBANS
CUBEBS
CUBITS
CULETS
CULLIS
CULTUS
CUMINS
CUPELS
CURERS
CURIES
CURIOS
CURSES
CURTIS
CURVES
CUSPIS
CUSSES
CUSSOS
CUSTOS
CUTEYS
CUTIES
CUTINS
CUTLAS
CUTUPS
DUCATS
DUNCES
DUPERS
DURESS
DUTIES
FUCOUS
FUDGES
FUGIOS
FUGLES
FUGUES
FUNDUS
FUNGUS
FURIES
FURORS
FURZES
FUSEES
FUSILS
FUSSES
FUZEES
FUZILS
FUZZES
GUACOS
GUANOS
GUARDS
GUAVAS
GUESTS
GUIDES
GUILDS
GUILES
GUILTS
GUISES
GUMBOS
GUMMAS
GUSHES
HUBRIS
HUGHES
HUMANS
HUMORS
HURONS
HUSHES
JUDAHS
JUDGES
JUICES
JULEPS
JULIAS
JULIES
JULIUS
JUNCOS
JUNIUS
JUNTAS
JUPONS
JURATS
JURELS
JURIES
JURORS
JUSTUS
KULAKS
KUMISS
LUCIAS
LUCIUS
LUGERS
LUMENS
LUNETS
LUNGES
LUNGIS
LURERS
LUSHES
MUCOUS
MUFTIS
MULCTS
MURALS
MURRES
MUSHES
MUSSES
NUBIAS
NUDGES
NURSES
OUNCES
OUSELS
OUTERS
OUZELS
PULERS
PULSES
PUNKAS
PUNTOS
PUPILS
PUREES
PURGES
PURSES
PUSHES
PUSSES
PUTONS
QUACKS
QUAFFS
QUAILS
QUAKES
QUALMS
QUANTS
QUARKS
QUARTS
QUEANS
QUEENS
QUEERS
QUELLS
QUERNS
QUESTS
QUEUES
QUILLS
QUILTS
QUINTS
QUIPUS
QUIRES
QUIRKS
QUIRTS
QUOINS
QUOITS
QUOTAS
QUOTES
RUBENS
RUBIES
RUBLES
RUCHES
RUCKUS
RUFOUS
RUGOUS
RULERS
RUMBAS
RUMORS
RUMPUS
RUNINS
RUNONS
RUPEES
RUSHES
SUBAHS
SUCRES
SUEDES
SUGARS
SUITES
SULCUS
SUMACS
SUNUPS
SUPERS
SURAHS
SURGES
SUSANS
SUSIES
SUTRAS
TUBERS
TULIPS
TULLES
TUMORS
TUNERS
TUNGUS
TUNICS
TUPIKS
TUQUES
TURCOS
TURKIS
TUSHES
TUSSIS
TUTORS
TUTTIS
YUCCAS
YUPONS

••US••

ABUSED
ABUSER
ABUSES
AMUSED
AMUSER
AMUSES
ANUSES
BOUSED
BOUSES
BRUSHY
CAUSAL
CAUSED
CAUSER
CAUSES
COUSIN
CRUSES
CRUSET
CRUSOE
CRUSTS
CRUSTY
DOUSED
DOUSES
DRUSES
FRUSTA
HAUSEN
HOUSED
HOUSES
JOUSTS
KYUSHU
LOUSED
LOUSES
MAUSER
MOUSED
MOUSER
MOUSES
MOUSSE
NAUSEA
ONUSES
PAUSED
PAUSER
PAUSES
PLUSES
PLUSHY
POUSTO
ROUSED
ROUSER
ROUSES
ROUSTS
SLUSHY
SOUSED
SOUSES
TOUSLE
TRUSTS
TRUSTY
UNUSED

••U•S•

AGUISH
BLUEST
BLUISH
BOURSE
BRUISE
CLUMSY
COURSE
CRUISE
LOUISA
LOUISE
MOUSSE
SQUASH
SQUISH
TRUEST
TRUISM

••U••S

ABUSES
ADULTS
ALUINS
AMUSES
ANUBIS
ANUSES
AZURES
BAUCIS
BEULAS
BLUETS
BLUFFS
BLUNTS
BLURBS
BLURTS
BOUGHS
BOULES
BOUNDS
BOURGS
BOURNS
BOUSES
BRUCES
BRUGES
BRUINS
BRUITS
BRUMES
BRUNOS
BRUTES
BRUTUS
CAUCUS
CAULES
CAULIS
CAULKS
CAUSES
CHUCKS
CHUFAS
CHUMPS
CHUNKS
CHURLS
CHURNS
CHURRS
CHUTES
CLUCKS
CLUMPS
COUGHS
COUNTS
COUPES
COURTS
CRUCES
CRUETS
CRUMBS
CRUMPS
CRUSES
CRUSTS
CRUXES
DAUNTS
DEUCES
DOUBTS
DOUGHS
DOUSES
DRUIDS
DRUNKS
DRUPES
DRUSES
EDUCES
EDUCTS
ELUDES
EQUALS
EQUIPS
ERUCTS
ERUPTS
ETUDES
EXUDES
EXULTS
EXURBS
FAUCES
FAULTS
FAUNAS
FAUNUS
FAUVES
FEUARS
FLUFFS
FLUIDS
FLUKES
FLUMES
FLUMPS
FLUNKS
FLUORS
FLUTES
FLUXES
FOUNDS
FOUNTS
FRUITS
FRUMPS
GAUGES
GAUZES
GLUMES
GOUGES
GOURDS
GRUELS

GRUMES
GRUNTS
HAUNTS
HOUNDS
HOURIS
HOUSES
INURES
INURNS
JAUNTS
JOULES
JOUSTS
KAURIS
KNURLS
KRUBIS
LAUGHS
LAURAS
LEUDES
LOUGHS
LOUPES
LOUSES
MAUDES
MAUNDS
MAUVES
MOULDS
MOULTS
MOUNTS
MOURNS
MOUSES
MOUTHS
NEUMES
ONUSES
OVULES
PAULAS
PAULUS
PAUSES
PLUCKS
PLUMBS
PLUMES
PLUMPS
PLUNKS
PLUSES
PLUTUS
POULTS
POUNDS
PRUDES
PRUNES
RHUMBS
ROUGES
ROUGHS
ROUNDS
ROUSES
ROUSTS
ROUTES
SAUCES
SAULTS
SAUNAS
SAURUS
SAUTES
SCUBAS
SCUFFS
SCULLS
SCUTES
SHUCKS
SHUNTS

SKULKS
SKULLS
SKUNKS
SLUMPS
SLURPS
SNUFFS
SOUGHS
SOUNDS
SOUSES
SPUMES
SPURNS
SPURTS
SQUABS
SQUADS
SQUATS
SQUAWS
SQUIBS
SQUIDS
STUFFS
STULLS
STUMPS
STUNTS
STUPAS
STUPES
TAUNTS
TAUPES
TAURUS
THUJAS
THUMBS
THUMPS
TOUGHS
TRUCES
TRUCKS
TRUDYS
TRUMPS
TRUNKS
TRUSTS
TRUTHS
USURPS
UTURNS
UVULAS
VAULTS
VAUNTS
WOUNDS
YOUTHS
ZOUNDS

•••US•

ABLUSH
ACCUSE
ADJUST
AMBUSH
AROUSE
AUGUST
BEMUSE
BLOUSE
CARUSO
CAYUSE
CERUSE
CLAUSE
CREUSA
DEGUST
DISUSE
EFFUSE

EXCUSE
GROUSE
ILLUSE
ILLUST
INCUSE
INFUSE
INRUSH
LOCUST
MEDUSA
MISUSE
OBTUSE
ONRUSH
PERUSE
PROUST
RECUSE
REFUSE
RETUSE
ROBUST
SCHUSS
SPOUSE
THRUSH
THRUST
UNHUSK
UNJUST
WATUSI

•••U•S

ALBUMS
ALEUTS
ALMUDS
AMOURS
AMPULS
ANNULS
ARGUES
AUGURS
BABULS
BEAUTS
BEGUMS
CAJUNS
CLOUDS
CLOUTS
CROUPS
CUTUPS
DEBUGS
DEBUTS
DEGUMS
DEMURS
ENDUES
ENSUES
FANUMS
FEMURS
FIQUES
FLOURS
FLOUTS
FORUMS
FRAUDS
FUGUES
GAMUTS
GETUPS
GHAUTS
GHOULS
GIGUES
GROUPS
GROUTS

HHOURS
IMBUES
INCURS
INDUES
INPUTS
ISSUES
JORUMS
KNOUTS
LEHUAS
LEMURS
LETUPS
MAQUIS
MIAULS
MIXUPS
MOGULS
MOHURS
NAHUMS
OCCURS
PICULS
PINUPS
PIQUES
QUEUES
RAOULS
REBUTS
RECURS
RERUNS
REVUES
ROGUES
SCAUPS
SCHUSS
SCOURS
SCOUTS
SCRUBS
SCRUMS
SEDUMS
SERUMS
SETUPS
SHOUTS
SHRUBS
SHRUGS
SIEURS
SIRUPS
SNOUTS
SPOUTS
SPRUES
STOUPS
STOUTS
STRUMS
STRUTS
SUNUPS
SYRUPS
TENUES
TENUIS
THRUMS
TIEUPS
TOGUES
TOQUES
TROUTS
TUQUES
UNGUES
UNGUIS
VALUES
VENUES
VOGUES

VOGULS
YAMUNS

••••US

ABACUS
ACEOUS
ACINUS
ACIOUS
ADIEUS
AEACUS
AEGEUS
AEOLUS
ALDOUS
ANIMUS
ARIOUS
ATREUS
AUREUS
AUROUS
BANTUS
BAYOUS
BRUTUS
BYSSUS
CACTUS
CADMUS
CALLUS
CAMPUS
CANTUS
CARPUS
CAUCUS
CENSUS
CEREUS
CEROUS
CESTUS
CHIAUS
CHORUS
CIRCUS
CIRRUS
CITRUS
CLONUS
COCCUS
COLEUS
COLOUS
COMOUS
CORNUS
CORPUS
CORVUS
COYPUS
CROCUS
CRONUS
CULTUS
CYGNUS
CYMOUS
CYPRUS
DANAUS
DARIUS
DELIUS
DINGUS
DISCUS
ELBRUS
EPIRUS
EREBUS
ESTRUS
EXODUS
FAMOUS

FAUNUS
FEROUS
FICHUS
FLATUS
FOETUS
FUCOUS
FUNDUS
FUNGUS
GALLUS
GAMOUS
GENIUS
GENOUS
GEROUS
GRADUS
GYNOUS
HIATUS
HINDUS
HIPPUS
IAMBUS
ICARUS
IODOUS
IOLCUS
ITIOUS
JOYOUS
JULIUS
JUNIUS
JUSTUS
LAPSUS
LIMBUS
LITMUS
LUCIUS
MARCUS
MEATUS
MEROUS
MISSUS
MOBIUS
MUCOUS
NAEVUS
NESSUS
NIMBUS
OBELUS
OBOLUS
ODIOUS
PALPUS
PAPPUS
PAREUS
PASSUS
PAULUS
PELEUS
PEPLUS
PIERUS
PIGNUS
PILEUS
PILOUS
PINDUS
PLEXUS
PLUTUS
PODOUS
POILUS
POROUS
POYOUS
QUIPUS
RADIUS
RAMOUS

6

RECTUS
REGIUS
RHESUS
RICTUS
RIMOUS
RUCKUS
RUFOUS
RUGOUS
RUMPUS
SADHUS
SAJOUS
SAURUS
SCOPUS
SEAMUS
SEROUS
SETOUS
SHAMUS
SIRIUS
SNAFUS
STATUS
STYLUS
SULCUS
TARSUS
TAURUS
TELLUS
TEREUS
THYMUS
TOROUS
TRAGUS
TUNGUS
TYPHUS
URAEUS
URANUS
UTERUS
VALGUS
VENOUS
VERSUS
VILLUS
VINOUS
VISCUS
VOROUS
WALRUS
WAMMUS
WAMPUS
XYSTUS
ZETHUS

UT••••
UTAHAN
UTERUS
UTGARD
UTMOST
UTOPIA
UTTERS
UTURNS

U•T•••
ULTIMA
UNTIDY
UNTIED
UNTIES
UNTOLD
UNTROD
UNTRUE
UPTAKE
UPTOWN
UPTURN
URTEXT
UTTERS

U••T••
ULSTER
UNITED
UNITES
UNSTEP
UNSTOP
URETER
URETHR
URETIC

U•••T•
UBIETY
UBOATS
UBOLTS
UNHATS
UPDATE
UPPITY
UPSETS

U••••T
UMLAUT
UNBELT
UNBENT
UNBOLT
UNDSET
UNGIRT
UNHURT
UNJUST
UNKNIT
UNMEET
UNREST
UNROOT
UNSEAT
UNVEXT
UNWEPT
UPBEAT
UPCAST
UPLIFT
UPMOST
UPROOT
UPSHOT
URGENT
URTEXT
UTMOST

•UT•••
AUTHOR
AUTISM
AUTOED
AUTUMN
BUTANE
BUTLER
BUTTED
BUTTER
BUTTES
BUTTON
CUTELY
CUTEST
CUTEYS
CUTIES
CUTINS
CUTLAS
CUTLER
CUTLET
CUTOFF
CUTOUT
CUTTER
CUTTLE
CUTUPS
DUTIES
FUTILE
FUTURE
GUTTAE
GUTTAT
GUTTED
GUTTER
GUTTLE
HUTTED
JUTISH
JUTTED
LUTEAL
LUTEUM
LUTHER
LUTING
LUTIST
MUTANT
MUTATE
MUTING
MUTINY
MUTISM
MUTTER
MUTTON
MUTUAL
MUTULE
NUTLET
NUTMEG
NUTRIA
NUTTED
NUTTER
OUTBID
OUTCRY
OUTDID
OUTERS
OUTFIT
OUTFOX
OUTING
OUTLAW
OUTLAY
OUTLET
OUTMAN
OUTPUT
OUTRAN
OUTRUN
OUTSAT
OUTSET
OUTSIT
OUTWIT
PUTLOG
PUTNAM
PUTOFF
PUTONS
PUTOUT
PUTPUT
PUTRID
PUTSCH
PUTTED
PUTTEE
PUTTER
RUTILE
RUTTED
SUTLER
SUTRAS
SUTTEE
SUTURE
TUTORS
TUTTIS

•U•T••
AUNTIE
AUSTEN
AUSTER
AUSTIN
AUSTRO
BUNTED
BUSTED
BUSTER
BUSTIC
BUSTLE
BUTTED
BUTTER
BUTTES
BUTTON
CULTCH
CULTUS
CURTIS
CURTLY
CURTSY
CUSTER
CUSTOM
CUSTOS
CUTTER
CUTTLE
DUSTED
DUSTER
FULTON
FUSTIC
GUITAR
GUSTAF
GUSTAV
GUTTAE
GUTTAT
GUTTED
GUTTER
GUTTLE
HUNTED
HUNTER
HURTER
HURTLE
HUSTLE
HUTTED
JUNTAS
JUSTIN
JUSTLY
JUSTUS
JUTTED
KULTUR
LUETIC
LUSTED
LUSTER
MUFTIS
MUSTEE
MUSTER
MUTTER
MUTTON
NUTTED
NUTTER
OUSTED
OUSTER
PUNTED
PUNTER
PUNTOS
PUTTED
PUTTEE
PUTTER
QUATRE
QUITCH
QUOTAS
QUOTED
QUOTER
QUOTES
RUSTED
RUSTIC
RUSTLE
RUTTED
SUBTER
SUBTLE
SUBTLY
SUITED
SUITES
SUITOR
SULTAN
SULTRY
SURTAX
SUTTEE
TUFTED
TURTLE
TUTTIS

•U••T•
AUDITS
AUGHTS
AUGITE
AURATE
BURSTS
CUBITS
CUESTA
CULETS
CURATE
DUCATS
DULUTH
GUESTS
GUILTS
GUILTY
JUDITH
JUGATE
JURATS
LUCITE
LUNATE
LUNETS
LUXATE
MULCTS
MUTATE
NUDITY
PUPATE
PURITY
QUANTA
QUANTS
QUARTE
QUARTO
QUARTS
QUARTZ
QUESTS
QUILTS
QUINTS
QUIRTS
QUOITS
RUBATO
RUGATE
SUBITO
SURETY
TUBATE

•U•••T
AUGUST
AUKLET
AURIST
BUCKET
BUDGET
BUFFET
BULLET
BURBOT
BURNET
CUBIST
CULLET
CURVET
CUSHAT
CUTEST
CUTLET
CUTOUT
DUGOUT
DULCET
FUNEST
GULLET
GUSSET
GUTTAT
HUBERT
HUGEST
JULIET
JUNKET
JURANT
JURIST
KUWAIT
LUCENT
LUTIST
MULLET
MUSCAT
MUSKET
MUSKIT
MUTANT
NUDIST
NUGGET
NUTLET
OUTFIT
OUTLET

OUTPUT
OUTSAT
OUTSET
OUTSIT
OUTWIT
PULLET
PULPIT
PUNDIT
PUPPET
PUREST
PURIST
PUTOUT
PUTPUT
QUAINT
RUDEST
RUNLET
RUNOUT
RUPERT
RUSSET
SUBLET
SUBMIT
SUMMIT
SUNLIT
SUNSET
SUREST
TUMULT
TURBIT
TURBOT
TURRET

••UT••

BHUTAN
BRUTAL
BRUTES
BRUTUS
CHUTES
CLUTCH
CRUTCH
FLUTED
FLUTER
FLUTES
GLUTEI
GLUTEN
MOUTHS
MOUTHY
MOUTON
NAUTCH
NEUTER
PLUTUS
POUTED
POUTER
ROUTED
ROUTER
ROUTES
SAUTES
SCUTCH
SCUTES
SCUTUM
SHUTIN
SMUTCH
SMUTTY
SPUTUM
TAUTEN
TAUTER
TAUTLY
TEUTON
TOUTED
TOUTER
TRUTHS
YOUTHS

••U•T•

ACUATE
ACUITY
ADULTS
ARUNTA
BLUETS
BLUNTS
BLURTS
BOUNTY
BRUITS
COUNTS
COUNTY
COURTS
CRUETS
CRUSTS
CRUSTY
DAUNTS
DOUBTS
EDUCTS
EQUATE
EQUITY
ERUCTS
ERUPTS
EXULTS
FAULTS
FAULTY
FOUNTS
FOURTH
FRUITS
FRUITY
FRUSTA
GRUNTS
HAUNTS
JAUNTS
JAUNTY
JOUSTS
MOULTS
MOUNTS
MOUNTY
POULTS
POUSTO
ROUSTS
SAULTS
SHUNTS
SMUTTY
SPURTS
SQUATS
STUNTS
TAUNTS
TRUSTS
TRUSTY
VAULTS
VAUNTS

••U••T

AMULET
BLUEST
BOUGHT
BRULOT
BRUNET
CAUGHT
CRUSET
FAUCET
FLUENT
FOUGHT
KRUBUT
NAUGHT
NOUGAT
NOUGHT
SCULPT
SEURAT
SOUGHT
SQUINT
SQUIRT
STUART
TAUGHT
TRUANT
TRUEST

•••UT•

AGOUTI
AGOUTY
ALEUTS
ARBUTE
ASTUTE
BASUTO
BEAUTS
BEAUTY
CANUTE
CLOUTS
DEBUTS
DEPUTE
DEPUTY
DILUTE
DROUTH
DULUTH
EMEUTE
FLOUTS
GAMUTS
GHAUTS
GOMUTI
GROUTS
HALUTZ
IMPUTE
INPUTS
KNOUTS
MINUTE
PAIUTE
REBUTS
REFUTE
REPUTE
SALUTE
SCOUTS
SHOUTS
SLEUTH
SNOUTS
SOLUTE
SPOUTS
STOUTS
STRUTS
TENUTO
TROUTS
VOLUTE

•••U•T

ABDUCT
ABRUPT
ACQUIT
ADDUCT
ADJUST
AMOUNT
AUGUST
COQUET
DEDUCT
DEGUST
ERFURT
EXEUNT
FLAUNT
ILLUST
INDUCT
INDULT
INSULT
INTUIT
ISEULT
JESUIT
LOCUST
LOQUAT
MINUET
OCCULT
PENULT
PEQUOT
PIQUET
PROUST
RESULT
ROBUST
ROQUET
SCHUIT
THRUST
TUMULT
UNHURT
UNJUST
YOGURT

••••UT

ABLAUT
ALLOUT
BEIRUT
CATGUT
COBNUT
COPOUT
CUTOUT
DEVOUT
DIMOUT
DUGOUT
FAROUT
HAGBUT
HOGNUT
KRUBUT
LAYOUT
MAHOUT
MIDGUT
OUTPUT
PEANUT
PIGNUT
PUTOUT
PUTPUT
RAGOUT
RAJPUT
ROTGUT
RUNOUT
SPROUT
TRYOUT
UMLAUT
WALNUT
WAYOUT

U•U•••

UNUSED
USURER
USURPS
UTURNS
UVULAE
UVULAR
UVULAS

U••U••

UNCURL
UNDULY
UNFURL
UNGUAL
UNGUES
UNGUIS
UNGULA
UNHURT
UNHUSK
UNJUST
UNRULY
UNSUNG
UNSURE
UPTURN
URSULA

U•••U•

UMLAUT
UNIQUE
UNTRUE
URAEUS
URANUS
USEFUL
UTERUS

•UU•••

MUUMUU

•U•U••

AUBURN
AUGURS
AUGURY
AUGUST
AUTUMN
CUPULE
CURULE
CUTUPS
DULUTH
EUNUCH
FUGUES
FUTURE
JUJUBE
LUNULA
LUNULE
LUXURY
MUTUAL
MUTULE
QUEUED
QUEUES
SUBURB
SUNUPS
SUTURE
TUBULE
TUMULT
TUQUES

•U••U•

AUREUS
AUROUS
BULBUL
BUNKUM
CULTUS
CUPFUL
CUPRUM
CURIUM
CUTOUT
DUGOUT
FUCOUS
FUNDUS
FUNGUS
HUBBUB
HUMBUG
JULIUS
JUNIUS
JUSTUS
KULTUR
LUCIUS
LUTEUM
MUCOUS
MUGGUR
MUKLUK
MURMUR
MUSEUM
MUUMUU
OUTPUT
OUTRUN
PULQUE
PURSUE
PUSHUP
PUTOUT
PUTPUT
QUIPUS
QUORUM
RUCKUS
RUEFUL
RUFOUS
RUGOUS
RUMPUS
RUNOUT
SUBDUE
SULCUS
SULFUR
TUCHUN
TUNEUP
TUNGUS

•U•••U
BUREAU
JUNEAU
MUUMUU

••U•U•
BRUTUS
CAUCUS
FAUNUS
KRUBUT
MUUMUU
PAULUS
PLUTUS
SAURUS
SCUTUM
SPUTUM
TAURUS

••U••U
GRUGRU
KYUSHU
MAUMAU
MUUMUU

•••UU•
VACUUM

•••U•U
TELUGU

••••UU
MUUMUU

UV••••
UVULAE
UVULAR
UVULAS

U•V•••
UNVEIL
UNVEXT

U••V••
UNEVEN

U•••V•
UNLIVE

•U•V••
CULVER
CURVED
CURVES
CURVET
GUAVAS
PURVEY
QUAVER
QUIVER
SURVEY
VULVAE
VULVAL
VULVAR

•U••V•
HUELVA

•U•••V
GUSTAV

••UV••
FAUVES
FLUVIO
LOUVER
LOUVRE
MAUVES
OEUVRE
PLUVIO

••U•V•
SCURVE
SCURVY
ZOUAVE

••U••V
ZHUKOV

U•W•••
UNWARY
UNWELL
UNWEPT
UNWIND
UNWISE
UNWISH
UNWRAP
UPWARD

U•••W•
UNMEWS
UPBOWS
UPTOWN

U••••W
UNDRAW
UNDREW

•UW•••
KUWAIT

•U•W••
LUDWIG
OUTWIT
RUNWAY
SUBWAY

•U•••W
BURROW
CURFEW
CURLEW
CUSHAW
FURROW
GUFFAW
OUTLAW
QUAPAW
SUNBOW
SUNDEW

••U•W•
SQUAWK
SQUAWS

U•••X•
UNVEXT
URTEXT

U••••X
UNISEX

•UX•••
AUXINS
HUXLEY
LUXATE
LUXURY
TUXEDO

•U•••X
AUSPEX
DUPLEX
LUMMOX
OUTFOX
SUFFIX
SURTAX

••UX••
CRUXES
FLUXED
FLUXES

••U••X
CAUDEX

•••UX•
DELUXE

••••UX
ADIEUX
AFFLUX
BAYEUX
BIJOUX
EFFLUX
HALLUX
INFLUX
POLLUX
REFLUX

U•Y•••
UNYOKE

U•••Y•
UNLAYS
UNSAYS
URANYL

U••••Y
UBIETY
UGLIFY
UGLILY
UNDULY
UNEASY
UNHOLY
UNRULY
UNTIDY
UNWARY
UPPITY
USABLY

•UY•••
BUYERS
BUYING
GUYANA
GUYING
TUYERE
ZUYDER

•U•Y••
BUNYAN
BUOYED
RUNYON

•U••Y•
CUTEYS

•U•••Y
AUBREY
AUDREY
AUGURY
BUBBLY
BUNCHY
BURLEY
BUSILY
CUDDLY
CULLAY
CURACY
CURTLY
CURTSY
CUTELY
DUDLEY
DUMBLY
DUPERY
EULOGY
GUILTY
GUNSHY
HUGELY
HUMBLY
HUNGRY
HURRAY
HUXLEY
JUNGLY
JUSTLY
LUNACY
LUXURY
MULLEY
MURRAY
MURREY
MUTINY
NUBBLY
NUDELY
NUDITY
NUMBLY
OUTCRY
OUTLAY
PUDDLY
PUGGRY
PULLEY
PUNCHY
PUNILY
PURELY
PURIFY
PURITY
PURVEY
PUSSEY
PUSSLY
QUAGGY
QUALMY
QUARRY
QUEASY
QUINCY
QUINSY
RUDELY
RUNWAY
SUBTLY
SUBWAY
SUDARY
SUGARY
SULTRY
SUNDAY
SUNDRY
SUPPLY
SURELY
SURETY
SURREY
SURVEY
TUMEFY
TURKEY

••U•Y•
TRUDYS

••U••Y
ACUITY
BLUELY
BLURRY
BOUNCY
BOUNTY
BRUSHY
CHUBBY
CHUMMY
CHUNKY
CLUMPY
CLUMSY
COUNTY
CRUMBY
CRUMMY
CRUSTY
DAUBRY
DOUBLY
DOUGHY
DOURLY
EQUITY
FAULTY
FLUFFY
FLUKEY
FLUNKY
FLURRY
FOULLY
FRUITY
FRUMPY
GLUMLY
GRUBBY
GRUMPY
GRUNDY
HAULMY
HOURLY
JAUNTY
KNURLY
LOUDLY
MAUNDY
MOULDY
MOUNTY
MOUTHY
PLUCKY
PLUMMY
PLUSHY
POUCHY
SCUMMY
SCURFY
SCURRY
SCURVY
SLUDGY
SLUMMY
SLURRY
SLUSHY
SMUDGY
SMUGLY
SMUTTY
SNUFFY
SNUGLY
SOURLY
SPUNKY
SPURRY
STUBBY
STUFFY
STUMPY
STURDY
TAUTLY
TOUCHY
TRUSTY

•••UY•
TOLUYL

•••U•Y
AGOUTY
ARGUFY
ASBURY
AUGURY
BEAUTY
CLOUDY
CROUPY
DECURY
DEPUTY
FLEURY
FLOURY
INJURY
KORUNY
LUXURY
MAGUEY
OCCUPY
PENURY
RHEUMY
SIRUPY
SYRUPY
UNDULY
UNRULY

••••UY
CLIQUY
EXEQUY

PLAGUY

•UZ•••
BUZZED
BUZZER
BUZZES
FUZEES
FUZILS
FUZING
FUZZED
FUZZES
GUZZLE
MUZHIK
MUZZLE
NUZZLE
OUZELS
PUZZLE

•U•Z••
BUZZED
BUZZER
BUZZES
FURZES
FUZZED
FUZZES
GUZZLE
MUZZLE
NUZZLE
PUZZLE
QUEZON

•U•••Z
JUAREZ
QUARTZ

••UZ••
GAUZES

••U•Z•
FRUNZE

•••UZ•
MEZUZA
ORMUZD

•••U•Z
HALUTZ

VA••••
VACANT
VACATE
VACUUM
VADOSE
VAGARY
VAGINA
VAGINO
VAGUER
VAINER
VAINLY
VALERY
VALETS
VALGUS
VALISE
VALKYR
VALLEY
VALOIS
VALUED
VALUES
VALVAL
VALVAR
VALVED
VALVES
VAMPED
VANDAL
VANISH
VANITY
VANMAN
VANMEN
VAPORI
VAPORS
VARICO
VARIED
VARIER
VARIES
VARLET
VARUNA
VARVES
VASARI
VASHTI
VASILI
VASSAL
VASTER
VASTLY
VATFUL
VATTED
VAULTS
VAUNTS

V•A•••
VEADAR
VIABLE
VIALED
VIANDS
VIATIC
VIATOR

V••A••
VACANT
VACATE
VAGARY
VASARI
VEDAIC
VELATE
VICARS
VIRAGO
VISAED
VISAGE
VISARD
VITALS
VIVACE
VIZARD
VOCALS
VOLANT
VOTARY
VOYAGE

V•••A•
VALVAL
VALVAR
VANDAL
VANMAN
VASSAL
VEADAR
VENIAL
VERBAL
VERNAL
VERNAS
VESTAL
VESTAS
VILLAS
VIOLAS
VIRGAS
VISTAS
VISUAL
VITTAE
VIVIAN
VODKAS
VOLVAS
VULCAN
VULGAR
VULVAE
VULVAL
VULVAR

V••••A
VAGINA
VARUNA
VERONA
VESICA
VICUNA
VIENNA
VIMINA
VOMICA

•VA•••
AVAILS
AVALON
AVATAR
EVADED
EVADER
EVADES
OVALLY

•V•A••
AVIARY
AVIATE

•V••A•
AVATAR
AVOWAL
DVORAK
EVITAS
OVISAC
OVULAR
UVULAE
UVULAR
UVULAS

•V•••A
AVESTA

••VA••
ALVANS
DIVANS
HAVANA
INVADE
KAVASS
LAVABO
LAVAGE
LEVANT
LOVAGE
NAVAHO
NAVAJO
NEVADA
PAVANS
RAVAGE
REVAMP
RIVALS
SAVAGE
SAVANT
VIVACE

••V•A•
CAVEAT
CAVIAR
FOVEAE
FOVEAL
GAVIAL
JOVIAL
JOVIAN
LIVIAS
REVEAL
VIVIAN

••V••A
ALVINA
ELVIRA
HAVANA
NEVADA
NOVENA

•••VA•
CANVAS
COEVAL
CRAVAT
GUAVAS
LARVAE
LARVAL
SERVAL
SILVAE
SILVAN
SILVAS
SLOVAK
SYLVAE
SYLVAN
SYLVAS
VALVAL
VALVAR
VOLVAS
VULVAE
VULVAL
VULVAR

•••V•A
FLAVIA
LATVIA
OLIVIA
PRAVDA
SALVIA
SILVIA
SYLVIA
TRIVIA

••••VA
CASAVA
GENEVA
GODIVA
HUELVA
OTTAVA
SALIVA

V•B•••
VIBRIO

V••B••
VERBAL
VIABLE

•V•B••
OVIBOS

••V•B•
LAVABO

••V••B
ADVERB

V•C•••
VACANT
VACATE
VACUUM
VECTOR
VICARS
VICKYS
VICTIM
VICTOR
VICUNA
VOCALS

V••C••
VINCES
VISCID
VISCUS
VNECKS
VOICED
VOICES
VULCAN

V•••C•
VARICO
VELOCE
VENICE
VESICA
VESICO
VIVACE
VOMICA

V••••C
VEDAIC
VIATIC
VITRIC

•V•C••
AVOCET
EVICTS

•V••C•
AVOUCH
EVINCE

•V•••C
OVISAC

••V•C•
ADVICE
CIVICS
DEVICE
NOVICE
VIVACE

•••V•C
ATAVIC
PELVIC
SLAVIC

V•D•••
VADOSE
VEDAIC
VODKAS

V••D••
VANDAL
VEADAR
VELDTS
VENDED
VENDEE
VENDER
VENDOR
VENDUE
VERDIN
VERDUN
VOIDED
VOODOO

V•••D•
VIANDS

V••••D
VALUED
VALVED
VAMPED
VARIED
VATTED
VEERED
VEILED
VEINED
VENDED
VENTED
VERGED
VERSED
VESPID
VESTED
VETOED

VETTED
VIALED
VIEWED
VISAED
VISARD
VISCID
VISEED
VIZARD
VOICED
VOIDED

•V•D••

AVIDIN
AVIDLY
EVADED
EVADER
EVADES

•V••D•

AVOIDS
OVERDO

•V•••D

AVOWED
EVADED
EVENED
EVOKED

••V•D•

DAVIDS
DIVIDE
INVADE
NEVADA

••V••D

DEVOID
ENVIED
LEVIED
NEVOID
REVVED

•••VD•

PRAVDA

•••V•D

BRAVED
CALVED
CARVED
CRAVED
CURVED
DELVED
DROVED
FERVID
GLOVED
GRAVED
GRAVID
HALVED
HEAVED
LEAVED
NERVED
PEEVED
PROVED
REEVED
REVVED
SALVED
SERVED
SHAVED
SHOVED
SIEVED
SKIVED
SLAVED
SOLVED
STAVED
VALVED
WAIVED
WEAVED

VE••••

VEADAR
VECTOR
VEDAIC
VEERED
VEILED
VEILER
VEINED
VELATE
VELDTS
VELLUM
VELOCE
VELOUR
VELURE
VELVET
VENDED
VENDEE
VENDER
VENDOR
VENDUE
VENEER
VENERY
VENIAL
VENICE
VENIRE
VENOMS
VENOSE
VENOUS
VENTED
VENTER
VENTRO
VENUES
VENULE
VERBAL
VERDIN
VERDUN
VEREIN
VERGED
VERGER
VERGES
VERGIL
VERIFY
VERILY
VERISM
VERIST
VERITY
VERMIN
VERNAL
VERNAS
VERNIX
VERNON
VERONA
VERSED
VERSES
VERSOS
VERSTS
VERSUS
VERTEX
VERVET
VESICA
VESICO
VESPER
VESPID
VESSEL
VESTAL
VESTAS
VESTED
VESTEE
VESTRY
VETOED
VETOER
VETOES
VETTED
VEXERS
VEXILS
VEXING

V•E•••

VEERED
VIENNA
VIEWED
VIEWER
VNECKS

V••E••

VALERY
VALETS
VENEER
VENERY
VEREIN
VEXERS
VILELY
VILEST
VINERY
VIPERS
VIREOS
VISEED
VIXENS
VOLERY
VOMERS
VOTERS
VOWELS
VOWERS
VOYEUR

V•••E•

VAGUER
VAINER
VALLEY
VALUED
VALUES
VALVED
VALVES
VAMPED
VANMEN
VARIED
VARIER
VARIES
VARLET
VARVES
VASTER
VATTED
VEERED
VEILED
VEILER
VEINED
VELVET
VENDED
VENDEE
VENDER
VENEER
VENTED
VENTER
VENUES
VERGED
VERGER
VERGES
VERSED
VERSES
VERTEX
VERVET
VESPER
VESSEL
VESTED
VESTEE
VETOED
VETOER
VETOES
VETTED
VIALED
VIEWED
VIEWER
VINCES
VINIER
VIOLET
VISAED
VISEED
VIVIEN
VIZIER
VOGUES
VOICED
VOICES
VOIDED
VOILES
VOLLEY
VORTEX

V••••E

VACATE
VADOSE
VALISE
VELATE
VELOCE
VELURE
VENDEE
VENDUE
VENICE
VENIRE
VENOSE
VENULE
VESTEE
VIABLE
VIRGIE
VIRILE
VIRTUE
VISAGE
VITTAE
VIVACE
VOLUME
VOLUTE
VOTIVE
VOYAGE
VULVAE

•VE•••

AVENGE
AVENUE
AVERNO
AVERSE
AVERTS
AVERYS
AVESTA
EVELYN
EVENED
EVENLY
EVENTS
EVERET
EVERTS
OVERDO
OVERLY
SVELTE

•V••E•

AVOCET
AVOWED
AVOWER
EVADED
EVADER
EVADES
EVENED
EVERET
EVOKED
EVOKES
OVULES

•V•••E

AVENGE
AVENUE
AVERSE
AVIATE
EVINCE
EVOLVE
EVZONE
SVELTE
UVULAE
YVONNE

••VE••

ADVENT
ADVERB
ADVERT
BEVELS
CAVEAT
CAVEIN
CAVELL
CAVERN
CIVETS
COVERS
COVERT
COVETS
COVEYS
DAVEYS
DEVEIN
DEVEST
DIVERS
DIVERT
DIVEST
ELVERS
FEVERS
FIVERS
FOVEAE
FOVEAL
GAVELS
GOVERN
HAVENS
HAVENT
HOVELS
HOVERS
INVENT
INVERT
INVEST
KEVELS
LAVERS
LEVEES
LEVELS
LEVERS
LIVELY
LIVENS
LIVERS
LIVERY
LOVEIN
LOVELL
LOVELY
LOVERS
MOVERS
NAVELS
NOVELS
NOVENA
OBVERT
PAVERS
RAVELS
RAVENS
RAVERS
REVEAL
REVELS
REVERE
REVERT
REVEST
REVETS
RIVERS
RIVETS
ROVERS
SAVERS
SEVENS
SEVERE
SEVERS
TAVERN

UNVEIL
UNVEXT
WAVERS
WAVEYS
WIVERN
WIVERS
WYVERN

••V•E•
BEVIES
CAVIES
CIVIES
DAVIES
ENVIED
ENVIER
ENVIES
LEVEES
LEVIED
LEVIER
LEVIES
LIVIER
LIVRES
LIVYER
MOVIES
NAVIES
REVIEW
REVUES
REVVED
SOVIET
VIVIEN
WAVIER
WAVIES
XAVIER

••V••E
ADVICE
ADVISE
ALVINE
BOVINE
CAVITE
DEVICE
DEVISE
DEVOTE
DIVIDE
DIVINE
FOVEAE
INVADE
INVITE
INVOKE
LAVAGE
LEVITE
LOVAGE
NEVILE
NOVICE
PAVISE
RAVAGE
RAVINE
REVERE
REVILE
REVISE
REVIVE
REVOKE
SAVAGE
SEVERE

VIVACE

•••VE•
AGAVES
BEAVER
BEEVES
BRAVED
BRAVER
BRAVES
BREVES
BREVET
CALVED
CALVES
CARVED
CARVEL
CARVEN
CARVER
CARVES
CHIVES
CLEVER
CLIVES
CLOVEN
CLOVER
CLOVES
CONVEX
CONVEY
CORVEE
CORVES
CRAVED
CRAVEN
CRAVER
CRAVES
CULVER
CURVED
CURVES
CURVET
DELVED
DELVER
DELVES
DENVER
DRIVEL
DRIVEN
DRIVER
DRIVES
DROVED
DROVER
DROVES
ELEVEN
FAUVES
GLOVED
GLOVER
GLOVES
GRAVED
GRAVEL
GRAVEN
GRAVER
GRAVES
GRIVET
GROVEL
GROVER
GROVES
HALVED
HALVES
HARVEY

HEAVED
HEAVEN
HEAVER
HEAVES
HELVES
HOOVER
HOOVES
JARVEY
JAYVEE
KEEVES
KNAVES
KNIVES
LEAVED
LEAVEN
LEAVER
LEAVES
LOAVES
LOUVER
MARVEL
MAUVES
NERVED
NERVES
OGIVES
OLIVER
OLIVES
PEAVEY
PEEVED
PEEVES
PELVES
PLOVER
PRIVET
PROVED
PROVEN
PROVER
PROVES
PURVEY
QUAVER
QUIVER
REEVED
REEVES
REVVED
SALVED
SALVER
SALVES
SELVES
SERVED
SERVER
SERVES
SHAVED
SHAVEN
SHAVER
SHAVES
SHIVER
SHIVES
SHOVED
SHOVEL
SHOVER
SHOVES
SIEVED
SIEVES
SILVER
SKIVED
SKIVER
SKIVES

SLAVED
SLAVER
SLAVES
SLIVER
SLOVEN
SNIVEL
SOEVER
SOLVED
SOLVER
SOLVES
STAVED
STAVES
STEVEN
STEVES
STIVER
STOVER
STOVES
SURVEY
SWIVEL
SWIVET
TRAVEL
TRAVES
TRIVET
TROVER
TROVES
UNEVEN
VALVED
VALVES
VARVES
VELVET
VERVET
WAIVED
WAIVER
WAIVES
WEAVED
WEAVER
WEAVES
WEEVER
WOLVER
WOLVES
YAHVEH
YLEVEL

•••V•E
CORVEE
JAYVEE
LARVAE
LOUVRE
OEUVRE
PREVUE
SILVAE
STEVIE
SYLVAE
VULVAE

••••VE
ACTIVE
ALCOVE
ARGIVE
ARRIVE
BEHAVE
BEHOVE
CLEAVE
DATIVE

DERIVE
ENDIVE
EVOLVE
GREAVE
GRIEVE
GROOVE
INWOVE
MOHAVE
MOJAVE
MOTIVE
NATIVE
OCTAVE
RELIVE
REMOVE
REVIVE
SCRIVE
SCURVE
SHEAVE
SHELVE
SHRIVE
SHROVE
SLEAVE
SLEEVE
STARVE
STEEVE
STRIVE
STROVE
SWERVE
THIEVE
THRIVE
THROVE
TWELVE
UNLIVE
VOTIVE
WHARVE
WHERVE
ZOUAVE

V••F••
VATFUL

V•••F•
VERIFY
VILIFY
VIVIFY

••V•F•
VIVIFY

V•G•••
VAGARY
VAGINA
VAGINO
VAGUER
VIGILS
VIGOUR
VOGUES
VOGULS

V••G••
VALGUS
VERGED
VERGER
VERGES

VERGIL
VIRGAS
VIRGIE
VIRGIL
VIRGIN
VULGAR

V•••G•
VIRAGO
VISAGE
VOYAGE

V••••G
VEXING
VIKING
VISING
VOTING
VOWING

•V••G•
AVENGE

••V•G•
LAVAGE
LOVAGE
RAVAGE
SAVAGE

••V••G
CAVING
COVING
DIVING
GIVING
HAVING
HIVING
IRVING
LAVING
LIVING
LOVING
MOVING
PAVING
RAVING
RIVING
ROVING
SAVING
WAVING
WIVING

V••H••
VASHTI
VISHNU

V••••H
VANISH

•V•••H
AVOUCH

••V•H•
NAVAHO

••V••H
DOVISH
ELVISH

LAVISH
RAVISH

•••V•H
YAHVEH

VI••••
VIABLE
VIALED
VIANDS
VIATIC
VIATOR
VIBRIO
VICARS
VICKYS
VICTIM
VICTOR
VICUNA
VIENNA
VIEWED
VIEWER
VIGILS
VIGOUR
VIKING
VILELY
VILEST
VILIFY
VILLAS
VILLON
VILLUS
VIMINA
VINCES
VINERY
VINIER
VINNYS
VINOUS
VINSON
VINYLS
VIOLAS
VIOLET
VIOLIN
VIPERS
VIRAGO
VIREOS
VIRGAS
VIRGIE
VIRGIL
VIRGIN
VIRILE
VIRTUE
VISAED
VISAGE
VISARD
VISCID
VISCUS
VISEED
VISHNU
VISING
VISION
VISITS
VISORS
VISTAS
VISUAL
VITALS
VITRIC
VITTAE
VIVACE
VIVIAN
VIVIEN
VIVIFY
VIXENS
VIZARD
VIZIER
VIZIRS
VIZORS

V•I•••
VAINER
VAINLY
VEILED
VEILER
VEINED
VOICED
VOICES
VOIDED
VOILES

V••I••
VAGINA
VAGINO
VALISE
VANISH
VANITY
VARICO
VARIED
VARIER
VARIES
VASILI
VENIAL
VENICE
VENIRE
VERIFY
VERILY
VERISM
VERIST
VERITY
VESICA
VESICO
VEXILS
VEXING
VIGILS
VIKING
VILIFY
VIMINA
VINIER
VIRILE
VISING
VISION
VISITS
VIVIAN
VIVIEN
VIVIFY
VIZIER
VIZIRS
VOMICA
VOMITO
VOMITS
VOTING
VOTIVE
VOWING

V•••I•
VALOIS
VEDAIC
VERDIN
VEREIN
VERGIL
VERMIN
VERNIX
VESPID
VIATIC
VIBRIO
VICTIM
VIOLIN
VIRGIE
VIRGIL
VIRGIN
VISCID
VITRIC

V••••I
VAPORI
VASARI
VASHTI
VASILI

•VI•••
AVIARY
AVIATE
AVIDIN
AVIDLY
AVISOS
EVICTS
EVILLY
EVINCE
EVITAS
OVIBOS
OVISAC

•V•I••
AVAILS
AVOIDS

•V••I•
AVIDIN

••VI••
ADVICE
ADVISE
ALVINA
ALVINE
ANVILS
BEVIES
BOVINE
CAVIAR
CAVIES
CAVILS
CAVING
CAVITE
CAVITY
CIVICS
CIVIES
CIVISM
COVING
DAVIDS
DAVIES
DAVITS
DEVICE
DEVILS
DEVISE
DIVIDE
DIVINE
DIVING
DOVISH
ELVIRA
ELVISH
ENVIED
ENVIER
ENVIES
GAVIAL
GIVING
HAVING
HIVING
INVITE
IRVING
IRVINS
JOVIAL
JOVIAN
KEVINS
LAVING
LAVISH
LEVIED
LEVIER
LEVIES
LEVITE
LEVITY
LIVIAS
LIVIER
LIVING
LOVING
MOVIES
MOVING
NAVIES
NEVILE
NEVILL
NOVICE
PAVING
PAVIOR
PAVISE
RAVINE
RAVING
RAVISH
REVIEW
REVILE
REVISE
REVIVE
RIVING
ROVING
SAVING
SAVINS
SAVIOR
SOVIET
VIVIAN
VIVIEN
VIVIFY
WAVIER
WAVIES
WAVILY
WAVING
WIVING
XAVIER

••V•I•
CAVEIN
DEVEIN
DEVOID
DEVOIR
LOVEIN
NEVOID
UNVEIL

••V••I
NEVSKI

•••VI•
ATAVIC
CALVIN
CERVIX
CLEVIS
CLOVIS
FERVID
FLAVIA
FLAVIN
FLUVIO
GRAVID
JARVIS
JERVIS
KELVIN
LATVIA
MARVIN
MELVIN
MERVIN
OLIVIA
PARVIS
PELVIC
PELVIS
PLUVIO
SALVIA
SILVIA
SLAVIC
SPAVIN
STEVIE
SYLVIA
TRIVIA
WALVIS
WEEVIL

••V•J•
NAVAJO

V•K•••
VIKING

V••K••
VALKYR
VICKYS
VODKAS

V•••K•
VNECKS

•V•K••
EVOKED
EVOKES

•V•••K
DVORAK

••V•K•
INVOKE
NEVSKI
REVOKE

•••V•K
SLOVAK

V•L•••
VALERY
VALETS
VALGUS
VALISE
VALKYR
VALLEY
VALOIS
VALUED
VALUES
VALVAL
VALVAR
VALVED
VALVES
VELATE
VELDTS
VELLUM
VELOCE
VELOUR
VELURE
VELVET
VILELY
VILEST
VILIFY
VILLAS
VILLON
VILLUS
VOLANT
VOLERY
VOLLEY
VOLOST
VOLUME
VOLUTE
VOLVAS
VOLVOX
VULCAN
VULGAR
VULVAE
VULVAL
VULVAR

V••L••
VALLEY
VARLET
VAULTS
VEILED
VEILER
VELLUM
VIALED

VILLAS
VILLON
VILLUS
VIOLAS
VIOLET
VIOLIN
VOILES
VOLLEY

V•••L•
VAINLY
VASILI
VASTLY
VENULE
VERILY
VEXILS
VIABLE
VIGILS
VILELY
VINYLS
VIRILE
VITALS
VOCALS
VOGULS
VOWELS

V••••L
VALVAL
VANDAL
VASSAL
VATFUL
VENIAL
VERBAL
VERGIL
VERNAL
VESSEL
VESTAL
VIRGIL
VISUAL
VULVAL

•V•L••
AVALON
EVELYN
EVILLY
EVOLVE
OVALLY
OVULAR
OVULES
SVELTE
UVULAE
UVULAR
UVULAS

•V••L•
AVAILS
AVIDLY
EVENLY
EVILLY
OVALLY
OVERLY

•V•••L
AVOWAL

••VL••
PAVLOV

••V•L•
ABVOLT
ANVILS
BEVELS
CAVELL
CAVILS
DEVILS
GAVELS
HOVELS
KEVELS
LEVELS
LIVELY
LOVELL
LOVELY
NAVELS
NEVILE
NEVILL
NOVELS
RAVELS
REVELS
REVILE
REVOLT
RIVALS
WAVILY

••V••L
CAVELL
FOVEAL
GAVIAL
JOVIAL
LOVELL
NEVILL
REVEAL
UNVEIL

•••V•L
CARVEL
COEVAL
DRIVEL
FRIVOL
GRAVEL
GROVEL
LARVAL
MARVEL
SERVAL
SHOVEL
SNIVEL
SWIVEL
TRAVEL
VALVAL
VULVAL
WEEVIL
YLEVEL

V•M•••
VAMPED
VIMINA
VOMERS
VOMICA
VOMITO
VOMITS

V••M••
VANMAN
VANMEN
VERMIN

V•••M•
VENOMS
VOLUME

V••••M
VACUUM
VELLUM
VERISM
VICTIM

••V•M•
REVAMP

••V••M
CIVISM

VN••••
VNECKS

V•N•••
VANDAL
VANISH
VANITY
VANMAN
VANMEN
VENDED
VENDEE
VENDER
VENDOR
VENDUE
VENEER
VENERY
VENIAL
VENICE
VENIRE
VENOMS
VENOSE
VENOUS
VENTED
VENTER
VENTRO
VENUES
VENULE
VINCES
VINERY
VINIER
VINNYS
VINOUS
VINSON
VINYLS

V••N••
VAINER
VAINLY
VAUNTS
VEINED
VERNAL
VERNAS
VERNIX
VERNON
VIANDS
VIENNA
VINNYS

V•••N•
VACANT
VAGINA
VAGINO
VARUNA
VERONA
VEXING
VICUNA
VIENNA
VIKING
VIMINA
VISHNU
VISING
VIXENS
VOLANT
VOTING
VOWING

V••••N
VANMAN
VANMEN
VERDIN
VERDUN
VEREIN
VERMIN
VERNON
VILLON
VINSON
VIOLIN
VIRGIN
VISION
VIVIAN
VIVIEN
VULCAN

•V•N••
AVENGE
AVENUE
EVENED
EVENLY
EVENTS
EVINCE
YVONNE

•V••N•
AVERNO
EVZONE
YVONNE

•V•••N
AVALON
AVIDIN
EVELYN

••V•N•
ADVENT
ALVANS
ALVINA
ALVINE
BOVINE
CAVING
COVING
DIVANS
DIVINE
DIVING
GIVING
HAVANA
HAVENS
HAVENT
HAVING
HIVING
INVENT
IRVING
IRVINS
KEVINS
LAVING
LEVANT
LIVENS
LIVING
LOVING
MOVING
NOVENA
PAVANS
PAVING
RAVENS
RAVINE
RAVING
RIVING
ROVING
SAVANT
SAVING
SAVINS
SEVENS
WAVING
WIVING

••V••N
CAVEIN
CAVERN
DEVEIN
GOVERN
JOVIAN
LOVEIN
TAVERN
VIVIAN
VIVIEN
WIVERN
WYVERN

•••V•N
CALVIN
CARVEN
CLOVEN
CRAVEN
DRIVEN
ELEVEN
ELEVON
FLAVIN
GRAVEN
HEAVEN
KELVIN
LEAVEN
MARVIN
MELVIN
MERVIN
PROVEN
SHAVEN
SILVAN
SLOVEN
SPAVIN
STEVEN
SYLVAN
UNEVEN

VO••••
VOCALS
VODKAS
VOGUES
VOGULS
VOICED
VOICES
VOIDED
VOILES
VOLANT
VOLERY
VOLLEY
VOLOST
VOLUME
VOLUTE
VOLVAS
VOLVOX
VOMERS
VOMICA
VOMITO
VOMITS
VOODOO
VOROUS
VORTEX
VOTARY
VOTERS
VOTING
VOTIVE
VOWELS
VOWERS
VOWING
VOYAGE
VOYEUR

V•O•••
VIOLAS
VIOLET
VIOLIN
VOODOO

V••O••
VADOSE
VALOIS
VAPORI
VAPORS
VELOCE
VELOUR
VENOMS
VENOSE
VENOUS
VERONA
VETOED
VETOER

6

VETOES
VIGOUR
VINOUS
VISORS
VIZORS
VOLOST
VOROUS

V•••O•
VECTOR
VENDOR
VERNON
VERSOS
VIATOR
VICTOR
VILLON
VINSON
VIREOS
VISION
VOLVOX
VOODOO

V••••O
VAGINO
VARICO
VENTRO
VESICO
VIBRIO
VIRAGO
VOMITO
VOODOO

•VO•••
AVOCET
AVOIDS
AVOUCH
AVOWAL
AVOWED
AVOWER
DVORAK
EVOKED
EVOKES
EVOLVE
YVONNE

•V•O••
EVZONE

•V••O•
AVALON
AVISOS
OVIBOS

•V•••O
AVERNO
OVERDO

••VO••
ABVOLT
CAVORT
DEVOID
DEVOIR
DEVOTE
DEVOUR
DEVOUT
DIVOTS
ENVOYS
FAVORS
GAVOTS
INVOKE
NEVOID
PIVOTS
REVOKE
REVOLT
SAVORS
SAVORY

••V•O•
PAVIOR
PAVLOV
SAVIOR

••V••O
LAVABO
NAVAHO
NAVAJO

•••VO•
BRAVOS
CONVOY
ELEVON
FERVOR
FLAVOR
FRIVOL
REAVOW
SALVOR
SALVOS
SERVOS
VOLVOX

•••V•O
FLUVIO
PLUVIO

••••VO
OCTAVO

V•P•••
VAPORI
VAPORS
VIPERS

V••P••
VAMPED
VESPER
VESPID

••V••P
REVAMP

V•R•••
VARICO
VARIED
VARIER
VARIES
VARLET
VARUNA
VARVES
VERBAL
VERDIN
VERDUN
VEREIN
VERGED
VERGER
VERGES
VERGIL
VERIFY
VERILY
VERISM
VERIST
VERITY
VERMIN
VERNAL
VERNAS
VERNIX
VERNON
VERONA
VERSED
VERSES
VERSOS
VERSTS
VERSUS
VERTEX
VERVET
VIRAGO
VIREOS
VIRGAS
VIRGIE
VIRGIL
VIRGIN
VIRILE
VIRTUE
VOROUS
VORTEX

V••R••
VEERED
VIBRIO
VITRIC

V•••R•
VAGARY
VALERY
VAPORI
VAPORS
VASARI
VELURE
VENERY
VENIRE
VENTRO
VESTRY
VEXERS
VICARS
VINERY
VIPERS
VISARD
VISORS
VIZARD
VIZIRS
VIZORS
VOLERY
VOMERS
VOTARY
VOTERS
VOWERS

V••••R
VAGUER
VAINER
VALKYR
VALVAR
VARIER
VASTER
VEADAR
VECTOR
VEILER
VELOUR
VENDER
VENDOR
VENEER
VENTER
VERGER
VESPER
VETOER
VIATOR
VICTOR
VIEWER
VIGOUR
VINIER
VIZIER
VOYEUR
VULGAR
VULVAR

•V•R••
AVERNO
AVERSE
AVERTS
AVERYS
DVORAK
EVERET
EVERTS
OVERDO
OVERLY

•V••R•
AVIARY

•V•••R
AVATAR
AVOWER
EVADER
OVULAR
UVULAR

••VR••
LIVRES

••V•R•
ADVERB
ADVERT
CAVERN
CAVORT
COVERS
COVERT
DIVERS
DIVERT
ELVERS
ELVIRA
FAVORS
FEVERS
FIVERS
GOVERN
HOVERS
INVERT
LAVERS
LEVERS
LIVERS
LIVERY
LOVERS
MOVERS
OBVERT
PAVERS
RAVERS
REVERE
REVERT
RIVERS
ROVERS
SAVERS
SAVORS
SAVORY
SEVERE
SEVERS
TAVERN
WAVERS
WIVERN
WIVERS
WYVERN

••V••R
CAVIAR
DEVOIR
DEVOUR
ENVIER
LEVIER
LIVIER
LIVYER
PAVIOR
SAVIOR
WAVIER
XAVIER

•••VR•
LOUVRE
OEUVRE

•••V•R
BEAVER
BRAVER
CARVER
CLEVER
CLOVER
CRAVER
CULVER
DELVER
DENVER
DRIVER
DROVER
FERVOR
FLAVOR
GLOVER
GRAVER
GROVER
HEAVER
HOOVER
LEAVER
LOUVER
OLIVER
PLOVER
PROVER
QUAVER
QUIVER
SALVER
SALVOR
SERVER
SHAVER
SHIVER
SHOVER
SILVER
SKIVER
SLAVER
SLIVER
SOEVER
SOLVER
STIVER
STOVER
TROVER
VALVAR
VULVAR
WAIVER
WEAVER
WEEVER
WOLVER

V•S•••
VASARI
VASHTI
VASILI
VASSAL
VASTER
VASTLY
VESICA
VESICO
VESPER
VESPID
VESSEL
VESTAL
VESTAS
VESTED
VESTEE
VESTRY
VISAED
VISAGE
VISARD
VISCID
VISCUS
VISEED
VISHNU
VISING
VISION
VISITS
VISORS
VISTAS
VISUAL

6

V••S••
VASSAL
VERSED
VERSES
VERSOS
VERSTS
VERSUS
VESSEL
VINSON

V•••S•
VADOSE
VALISE
VANISH
VENOSE
VERISM
VERIST
VILEST
VOLOST

V••••S
VALETS
VALGUS
VALOIS
VALUES
VALVES
VAPORS
VARIES
VARVES
VAULTS
VAUNTS
VELDTS
VENOMS
VENOUS
VENUES
VERGES
VERNAS
VERSES
VERSOS
VERSTS
VERSUS
VESTAS
VETOES
VEXERS
VEXILS
VIANDS
VICARS
VICKYS
VIGILS
VILLAS
VILLUS
VINCES
VINNYS
VINOUS
VINYLS
VIOLAS
VIPERS
VIREOS
VIRGAS
VISCUS
VISITS
VISORS
VISTAS
VITALS
VIXENS
VIZIRS
VIZORS
VNECKS
VOCALS
VODKAS
VOGUES
VOGULS
VOICES
VOILES
VOLVAS
VOMERS
VOMITS
VOROUS
VOTERS
VOWELS
VOWERS

•V•S••
AVESTA
AVISOS
OVISAC

•V••S•
AVERSE

•V•••S
AVAILS
AVERTS
AVERYS
AVISOS
AVOIDS
EVADES
EVENTS
EVERTS
EVICTS
EVITAS
EVOKES
OVIBOS
OVULES
UVULAS

••VS••
NEVSKI

••V•S•
ADVISE
CIVISM
DEVEST
DEVISE
DIVEST
DOVISH
ELVISH
INVEST
KAVASS
LAVISH
PAVISE
RAVISH
REVEST
REVISE

••V••S
ALVANS
ANVILS
BEVELS
BEVIES
CAVIES
CAVILS
CIVETS
CIVICS
CIVIES
COVERS
COVETS
COVEYS
DAVEYS
DAVIDS
DAVIES
DAVITS
DEVILS
DIVANS
DIVERS
DIVOTS
ELVERS
ENVIES
ENVOYS
FAVORS
FEVERS
FIVERS
GAVELS
GAVOTS
HAVENS
HOVELS
HOVERS
IRVINS
KAVASS
KEVELS
KEVINS
LAVERS
LEVEES
LEVELS
LEVERS
LEVIES
LIVENS
LIVERS
LIVIAS
LIVRES
LOVERS
MOVERS
MOVIES
NAVELS
NAVIES
NOVELS
PAVANS
PAVERS
PIVOTS
RAVELS
RAVENS
RAVERS
REVELS
REVETS
REVUES
RIVALS
RIVERS
RIVETS
ROVERS
SAVERS
SAVINS
SAVORS
SEVENS
SEVERS
WAVERS
WAVEYS
WAVIES
WIVERS

•••V•S
AGAVES
BEEVES
BRAVES
BRAVOS
BREVES
CALVES
CANVAS
CARVES
CHIVES
CLEVIS
CLIVES
CLOVES
CLOVIS
CORVES
CORVUS
CRAVES
CURVES
DELVES
DRIVES
DROVES
FAUVES
GLOVES
GRAVES
GROVES
GUAVAS
HALVES
HEAVES
HELVES
HOOVES
JARVIS
JERVIS
KEEVES
KNAVES
KNIVES
LEAVES
LOAVES
MAUVES
NAEVUS
NERVES
OGIVES
OLIVES
PARVIS
PEEVES
PELVES
PELVIS
PROVES
REEVES
SALVES
SALVOS
SELVES
SERVES
SERVOS
SHAVES
SHIVES
SHOVES
SIEVES
SILVAS
SKIVES
SLAVES
SOLVES
STAVES
STEVES
STOVES
SYLVAS
TRAVES
TROVES
VALVES
VARVES
VOLVAS
WAIVES
WALVIS
WEAVES
WOLVES

V•T•••
VATFUL
VATTED
VETOED
VETOER
VETOES
VETTED
VITALS
VITRIC
VITTAE
VOTARY
VOTERS
VOTING
VOTIVE

V••T••
VASTER
VASTLY
VATTED
VECTOR
VENTED
VENTER
VENTRO
VERTEX
VESTAL
VESTAS
VESTED
VESTEE
VESTRY
VETTED
VIATIC
VIATOR
VICTIM
VICTOR
VIRTUE
VISTAS
VITTAE
VORTEX

V•••T•
VACATE
VALETS
VANITY
VASHTI
VAULTS
VAUNTS
VELATE
VELDTS
VERITY
VERSTS
VISITS
VOLUTE
VOMITO
VOMITS

V••••T
VACANT
VARLET
VELVET
VERIST
VERVET
VILEST
VIOLET
VOLANT
VOLOST

•V•T••
AVATAR
EVITAS

•V••T•
AVERTS
AVESTA
AVIATE
EVENTS
EVERTS
EVICTS
SVELTE

•V•••T
AVOCET
EVERET

••V•T•
CAVITE
CAVITY
CIVETS
COVETS
DAVITS
DEVOTE
DIVOTS
GAVOTS
INVITE
LEVITE
LEVITY
PIVOTS
REVETS
RIVETS

••V••T
ABVOLT
ADVENT
ADVERT
CAVEAT
CAVORT
COVERT
DEVEST
DEVOUT
DIVERT
DIVEST

HAVENT
INVENT
INVERT
INVEST
LEVANT
OBVERT
REVERT
REVEST
REVOLT
SAVANT
SOVIET
UNVEXT

•••V•T
BREVET
CRAVAT
CURVET
GRIVET
PRIVET
SWIVET
TRIVET
VELVET
VERVET

VU••••
VULCAN
VULGAR
VULVAE
VULVAL
VULVAR

V•U•••
VAULTS
VAUNTS

V••U••
VACUUM
VAGUER
VALUED
VALUES
VARUNA
VELURE
VENUES
VENULE
VICUNA
VISUAL
VOGUES
VOGULS
VOLUME
VOLUTE

V•••U•
VACUUM
VALGUS
VATFUL
VELLUM
VELOUR
VENDUE
VENOUS
VERDUN
VERSUS
VIGOUR
VILLUS
VINOUS

VIRTUE
VISCUS
VOROUS
VOYEUR

V••••U
VISHNU

•VU•••
OVULAR
OVULES
UVULAE
UVULAR
UVULAS

•V•U••
AVOUCH

•V••U•
AVENUE

••VU••
REVUES

••V•U•
DEVOUR
DEVOUT

•••VU•
CORVUS
NAEVUS
PREVUE

V•V•••
VIVACE
VIVIAN
VIVIEN
VIVIFY

V••V••
VALVAL
VALVAR
VALVED
VALVES
VARVES
VELVET
VERVET
VOLVAS
VOLVOX
VULVAE
VULVAL
VULVAR

V•••V•
VOTIVE

•V••V•
EVOLVE

••VV••
REVVED

••V•V•
REVIVE

••V••V
PAVLOV

•••VV•
SKIVVY

V•W•••
VOWELS
VOWERS
VOWING

V••W••
VIEWED
VIEWER

•V•W••
AVOWAL
AVOWED
AVOWER

••V••W
REVIEW

•••V•W
REAVOW

V•X•••
VEXERS
VEXILS
VEXING
VIXENS

V••••X
VERNIX
VERTEX
VOLVOX
VORTEX

••V•X•
UNVEXT

•••V•X
CERVIX
CONVEX
VOLVOX

V•Y•••
VOYAGE
VOYEUR

V••Y••
VINYLS

V•••Y•
VALKYR
VICKYS
VINNYS

V••••Y
VAGARY
VAINLY
VALERY
VALLEY
VANITY
VASTLY
VENERY
VERIFY
VERILY
VERITY
VESTRY
VILELY
VILIFY
VINERY
VIVIFY
VOLERY
VOLLEY
VOTARY

•V••Y•
AVERYS
EVELYN

•V•••Y
AVIARY
AVIDLY
EVENLY
EVILLY
OVALLY
OVERLY

••VY••
LIVYER

••V•Y•
COVEYS
DAVEYS
ENVOYS
WAVEYS

••V••Y
CAVITY
LEVITY
LIVELY
LIVERY
LOVELY
SAVORY
VIVIFY
WAVILY

•••V•Y
CONVEY
CONVOY
HARVEY
JARVEY
PEAVEY
PURVEY
SKIVVY
SURVEY

••••VY
GROOVY
SCURVY
SKIVVY

V•Z•••
VIZARD
VIZIER
VIZIRS
VIZORS

•VZ•••
EVZONE

WA••••
WABASH
WABBLE
WABBLY
WADDED
WADDLE
WADDLY
WADERS
WADIES
WADING
WADSET
WAFERS
WAFFLE
WAFTED
WAFTER
WAGERS
WAGGED
WAGGLE
WAGGLY
WAGGON
WAGING
WAGNER
WAGONS
WAHABI
WAHINE
WAHOOS
WAIFED
WAILED
WAILER
WAISTS
WAITED
WAITER
WAIVED
WAIVER
WAIVES
WAKENS
WAKIKI
WAKING
WALDOS
WALERS
WALING
WALKED
WALKER
WALKON
WALKUP
WALLAH
WALLAS
WALLED
WALLET
WALLIE
WALLIS
WALLOP
WALLOW
WALLYS
WALNUT
WALRUS
WALTER
WALTON
WALVIS
WAMBLE
WAMBLY
WAMMUS
WAMPUM
WAMPUS
WANDAS
WANDER
WANDLE
WANGLE
WANING
WANION
WANNED
WANNER
WANTED
WANTER
WANTON
WAPITI
WAPPED
WARBLE
WARDED
WARDEN
WARDER
WARIER
WARILY
WARMED
WARMER
WARMLY
WARMTH
WARMUP
WARNED
WARNER
WARPED
WARPER
WARRED
WARREN
WARSAW
WASHED
WASHER
WASHES
WASTED
WASTER
WASTES
WATAPE
WATAPS
WATERS
WATERY
WATSON
WATTLE
WATUSI
WAULED
WAVERS
WAVEYS
WAVIER
WAVIES
WAVILY
WAVING
WAWLED
WAXIER
WAXING
WAYLAY
WAYNES
WAYOUT

6

W•A•••
WEAKEN
WEAKER
WEAKLY
WEALDS
WEALTH
WEANED
WEANER
WEAPON
WEARER
WEASEL
WEAVED
WEAVER
WEAVES
WHACKS
WHALED
WHALER
WHALES
WHAMMY
WHANGS
WHARFS
WHARVE
WOADED
WOALDS
WRACKS
WRAITH
WRAPUP
WRASSE
WRATHY

W••A••
WABASH
WAHABI
WATAPE
WATAPS
WHEALS
WHEATS
WIGANS
WIZARD
WREAKS
WREATH

W•••A•
WALLAH
WALLAS
WANDAS
WARSAW
WAYLAY
WEIMAR
WHIDAH
WHYDAH
WIGWAG
WIGWAM
WILMAS
WITHAL
WOMBAT
WYSTAN

W••••A
WOMERA

•WA•••
AWAITS
AWAKED
AWAKEN
AWAKES
AWARDS
BWANAS
DWARFS
RWANDA
SWAGED
SWAGES
SWAILS
SWAINS
SWALES
SWAMIS
SWAMPS
SWAMPY
SWANEE
SWANKY
SWARAJ
SWARDS
SWARMS
SWARTH
SWARTY
SWATCH
SWATHE
SWATHS
SWAYED
TWANGS
TWANGY

•W•A••
AWEARY
SWEARS
SWEATS
SWEATY
TWEAKS
TWEAKY

•W••A•
BWANAS
SWARAJ
TWOWAY

•W•••A
RWANDA

••WA••
ABWATT
ALWAYS
BEWAIL
BEWARE
BYWAYS
COWAGE
COWARD
DEWANS
DIWANS
EDWARD
GAWAIN
HAWAII
HOWARD
INWALL
INWARD
KUWAIT
NAWABS
NEWARK
NOWAYS
ONWARD
OSWALD
REWARD
ROWANS
SEWAGE
SEWALL
SEWARD
SIWASH
SOWARS
THWACK
THWART
TOWAGE
TOWARD
UNWARY
UPWARD

••W•A•
BOWMAN
COWMAN
DEWLAP
ENWRAP
GEWGAW
HAWHAW
HOWDAH
INWRAP
PAWPAW
UNWRAP

••W••A
COWPEA
EDWINA
ROWENA

•••WA•
AIRWAY
AJOWAN
ANYWAY
ARAWAK
AVOWAL
COGWAY
DEEWAN
EARWAX
GALWAY
KEYWAY
LEEWAY
MIDWAY
NARWAL
NORWAY
ONEWAY
PAXWAX
PREWAR
RUNWAY
SCHWAS
SEAWAN
SEAWAY
SKYWAY
SUBWAY
TAIWAN
TWOWAY
WIGWAG
WIGWAM

••••WA
OJIBWA
OTTAWA
REDOWA

W•B•••
WABASH
WABBLE
WABBLY
WEBBED
WEBERS
WOBBLE
WOBBLY

W••B••
WABBLE
WABBLY
WAMBLE
WAMBLY
WARBLE
WEBBED
WILBER
WILBUR
WIMBLE
WOBBLE
WOBBLY
WOMBAT
WOMBED

W•••B•
WAHABI

•W•B••
TWIBIL
TWOBIT

••WB••
COWBOY
LOWBOY

••W•B•
NAWABS

••W••B
ENWOMB

•••WB•
BLOWBY

•••W•B
COBWEB

W•C•••
WICHES
WICKED
WICKER
WICKET
WICOPY

W••C••
WHACKS
WINCED
WINCER
WINCES
WINCEY
WRACKS
WRECKS

W•••C•
WHENCE
WRENCH
WRETCH

•W••C•
SWATCH
SWITCH
TWITCH

••W•C•
THWACK

W•D•••
WADDED
WADDLE
WADDLY
WADERS
WADIES
WADING
WADSET
WEDDED
WEDELN
WEDGED
WEDGES
WEDGIE
WIDDIE
WIDELY
WIDENS
WIDEST
WIDOWS
WIDTHS

W••D••
WADDED
WADDLE
WADDLY
WALDOS
WANDAS
WANDER
WANDLE
WARDED
WARDEN
WARDER
WEDDED
WEEDED
WEEDER
WELDED
WELDER
WENDED
WENDYS
WHIDAH
WHYDAH
WIDDIE
WILDER
WILDLY
WINDED
WINDER
WINDOW
WISDOM
WOADED
WONDER
WOODED
WOODEN
WOODSY
WORDED

W•••D•
WEALDS
WEIRDY
WIELDS
WIELDY
WOALDS
WORLDS
WOUNDS

W••••D
WADDED
WAFTED
WAGGED
WAIFED
WAILED
WAITED
WAIVED
WALKED
WALLED
WANNED
WANTED
WAPPED
WARDED
WARMED
WARNED
WARPED
WARRED
WASHED
WASTED
WAULED
WAWLED
WEANED
WEAVED
WEBBED
WEDDED
WEDGED
WEEDED
WELDED
WELLED
WELTED
WENDED
WETTED
WHALED
WHILED
WHINED
WHITED
WHORED
WICKED
WIGGED
WILLED
WILTED
WINCED
WINDED
WINGED
WINKED
WISHED
WISPED
WITHED
WITTED

WIZARD
WOADED
WOLFED
WOMBED
WONTED
WOODED
WORDED
WORKED
WORMED

•W•D••

SWEDEN
SWEDES

•W••D•

AWARDS
RWANDA
SWARDS
SWORDS
TWEEDS

•W•••D

AWAKED
SWAGED
SWAYED
SWIPED
TWINED

••WD••

BAWDRY
DAWDLE
HOWDAH
LEWDER
LEWDLY
POWDER
TAWDRY

••W••D

BAWLED
BOWLED
BOWSED
BYWORD
COWARD
COWLED
DAWNED
DOWNED
DOWSED
EDWARD
ENWIND
FAWNED
FOWLED
GAWKED
GOWNED
HAWKED
HOWARD
HOWLED
INWARD
INWIND
MEWLED
ONWARD
OSWALD
PAWNED
REWARD
REWIND
REWORD
SEWARD
TOWARD
UNWIND
UPWARD
WAWLED
YAWLED
YAWNED
YAWPED
YOWLED

•••WD•

CROWDS

•••W•D

AVOWED
BREWED
CHAWED
CHEWED
CLAWED
CLEWED
CROWED
FLAWED
FLOWED
GLOWED
GNAWED
MEOWED
PLOWED
SHEWED
SHOWED
SKEWED
SLEWED
SLOWED
SNOWED
SPEWED
STEWED
STOWED
THAWED
VIEWED

••••WD

SHREWD

WE••••

WEAKEN
WEAKER
WEAKLY
WEALDS
WEALTH
WEANED
WEANER
WEAPON
WEARER
WEASEL
WEAVED
WEAVER
WEAVES
WEBBED
WEBERS
WEDDED
WEDELN
WEDGED
WEDGES
WEDGIE
WEEDED
WEEDER
WEEKLY
WEENIE
WEENSY
WEEPER
WEEVER
WEEVIL
WEIGHS
WEIGHT
WEIMAR
WEIRDY
WELDED
WELDER
WELKIN
WELLED
WELTED
WELTER
WENDED
WENDYS
WERENT
WESLEY
WESSEX
WESTER
WETHER
WETTED
WETTER

W•E•••

WEEDED
WEEDER
WEEKLY
WEENIE
WEENSY
WEEPER
WEEVER
WEEVIL
WHEALS
WHEATS
WHEELS
WHEEZE
WHEEZY
WHELKS
WHELKY
WHELMS
WHELPS
WHENCE
WHERRY
WHERVE
WHEYEY
WIELDS
WIELDY
WIENER
WIENIE
WOEFUL
WREAKS
WREATH
WRECKS
WRENCH
WRESTS
WRETCH

W••E••

WADERS
WAFERS
WAGERS
WAKENS
WALERS
WATERS
WATERY
WAVERS
WAVEYS
WEBERS
WEDELN
WERENT
WHEELS
WHEEZE
WHEEZY
WIDELY
WIDENS
WIDEST
WIFELY
WIGEON
WINERY
WIPERS
WIRERS
WISELY
WISEST
WIVERN
WIVERS
WIZENS
WOMERA
WOOERS
WRIEST
WRYEST
WYVERN

W•••E•

WADDED
WADIES
WADSET
WAFTED
WAFTER
WAGGED
WAGNER
WAIFED
WAILED
WAILER
WAITED
WAITER
WAIVED
WAIVER
WAIVES
WALKED
WALKER
WALLED
WALLET
WALTER
WANDER
WANNED
WANNER
WANTED
WANTER
WAPPED
WARDED
WARDEN
WARDER
WARIER
WARMED
WARMER
WARNED
WARNER
WARPED
WARPER
WARRED
WARREN
WASHED
WASHER
WASHES
WASTED
WASTER
WASTES
WAULED
WAVIER
WAVIES
WAWLED
WAXIER
WAYNES
WEAKEN
WEAKER
WEANED
WEANER
WEARER
WEASEL
WEAVED
WEAVER
WEAVES
WEBBED
WEDDED
WEDGED
WEDGES
WEEDED
WEEDER
WEEPER
WEEVER
WELDED
WELDER
WELLED
WELTED
WELTER
WENDED
WESLEY
WESSEX
WESTER
WETHER
WETTED
WETTER
WHALED
WHALER
WHALES
WHEYEY
WHILED
WHILES
WHINED
WHINER
WHINES
WHITED
WHITEN
WHITER
WHITES
WHITEY
WHORED
WHORES
WICHES
WICKED
WICKER
WICKET
WIENER
WIGGED
WILBER
WILDER
WILIER
WILLED
WILLER
WILLET
WILTED
WINCED
WINCER
WINCES
WINCEY
WINDED
WINDER
WINGED
WINIER
WINKED
WINKER
WINNER
WINOES
WINTER
WINZES
WIRIER
WISHED
WISHES
WISPED
WITHED
WITHER
WITHES
WITNEY
WITTED
WOADED
WOLFED
WOLSEY
WOLVER
WOLVES
WOMBED
WONDER
WONTED
WOODED
WOODEN
WOOFER
WOOLEN
WORDED
WORKED
WORKER
WORMED
WORMER
WORSEN
WORSER
WOWSER
WRITER
WRITES

W••••E

WABBLE
WADDLE
WAFFLE

WAGGLE
WAHINE
WALLIE
WAMBLE
WANDLE
WANGLE
WARBLE
WATAPE
WATTLE
WEDGIE
WEENIE
WHARVE
WHEEZE
WHENCE
WHERVE
WIDDIE
WIENIE
WIGGLE
WILLIE
WIMBLE
WIMPLE
WINKLE
WINNIE
WOBBLE
WRASSE
WRITHE

•WE•••
AWEARY
AWEIGH
AWEING
DWELLS
GWENNS
SWEARS
SWEATS
SWEATY
SWEDEN
SWEDES
SWEEPS
SWEEPY
SWEETS
SWELLS
SWERVE
TWEAKS
TWEAKY
TWEEDS
TWEETS
TWELVE
TWENTY
TWERPS

•W•E••
AWLESS
OWLETS
OWNERS
SWEEPS
SWEEPY
SWEETS
TWEEDS
TWEETS

•W••E•
AWAKED
AWAKEN
AWAKES
SWAGED
SWAGES
SWALES
SWANEE
SWAYED
SWEDEN
SWEDES
SWIPED
SWIPES
SWIVEL
SWIVET
TWINED
TWINER
TWINES
TWOFER

•W•••E
AWHILE
GWYNNE
SWANEE
SWATHE
SWERVE
SWINGE
SWIPLE
TWELVE
TWINGE

••WE••
BOWELS
BOWERS
BOWERY
COWERS
DOWELS
DOWERS
DOWERY
FEWEST
HEWERS
JEWELS
JEWESS
LOWELL
LOWERS
LOWERY
LOWEST
MOWERS
NEWELS
NEWEST
ORWELL
PAWERS
PEWEES
POWELL
POWERS
RAWEST
ROWELS
ROWENA
ROWERS
SAWERS
SEWERS
SOWERS
TAWERS
TOWELS
TOWERS
TOWERY
UNWELL
UNWEPT
VOWELS
VOWERS

••W•E•
BAWLED
BAWLER
BOWLED
BOWLEG
BOWLER
BOWMEN
BOWSED
BOWSES
BOWYER
COWLED
COWMEN
COWPEA
COWPER
DAWNED
DEWIER
DOWNED
DOWSED
DOWSER
DOWSES
FAWKES
FAWNED
FAWNER
FOWLED
FOWLER
GAWKED
GOWNED
HAWKED
HAWKER
HAWSER
HAWSES
HOWLED
HOWLER
LAWYER
LEWDER
LOWKEY
MEWLED
PAWNED
PAWNEE
PAWNER
PEWEES
PEWTER
POWDER
POWTER
SAWYER
WAWLED
WOWSER
YAWLED
YAWNED
YAWNER
YAWPED
YAWPER
YOWLED

••W••E
BEWARE
COWAGE
COWRIE
DAWDLE
INWOVE
KEWPIE
NOWISE
PAWNEE
SEWAGE
TOWAGE
UNWISE

•••WE•
ANSWER
AVOWED
AVOWER
BLOWER
BREWED
BREWER
CHAWED
CHEWED
CHEWER
CLAWED
CLEWED
COBWEB
CREWEL
CROWED
DRAWEE
DRAWER
FLAWED
FLOWED
FLOWER
GLOWED
GLOWER
GNAWED
GNAWER
GROWER
KNOWER
MEOWED
PEEWEE
PLOWED
PLOWER
SHEWED
SHEWER
SHOWED
SHOWER
SKEWED
SKEWER
SLEWED
SLOWED
SLOWER
SNOWED
SPEWED
STEWED
STOWED
THAWED
TROWEL
VIEWED
VIEWER
YAHWEH

•••W•E
BROWSE
DRAWEE
DROWSE
PEEWEE

W•F•••
WAFERS
WAFFLE
WAFTED
WAFTER
WIFELY

W••F••
WAFFLE
WAIFED
WHIFFS
WILFUL
WOEFUL
WOLFED
WOOFER

W•••F•
WHARFS
WHIFFS

•W•F••
SWIFTS
TWOFER

•W••F•
DWARFS

••WF••
BOWFIN
LAWFUL
SAWFLY

W•G•••
WAGERS
WAGGED
WAGGLE
WAGGLY
WAGGON
WAGING
WAGNER
WAGONS
WIGANS
WIGEON
WIGGED
WIGGLE
WIGGLY
WIGWAG
WIGWAM

W••G••
WAGGED
WAGGLE
WAGGLY
WAGGON
WANGLE
WEDGED
WEDGES
WEDGIE
WEIGHS
WEIGHT
WIGGED
WIGGLE
WIGGLY
WINGED
WRIGHT

W•••G•
WHANGS
WRINGS
WRONGS

W••••G
WADING
WAGING
WAKING
WALING
WANING
WAVING
WAXING
WIGWAG
WILING
WINING
WIPING
WIRING
WISING
WIVING
WOOING
WOWING
WRYING

•W•G••
DWIGHT
SWAGED
SWAGES
TWIGGY

•W••G•
AWEIGH
SWINGE
SWINGS
TWANGS
TWANGY
TWIGGY
TWINGE

•W•••G
AWEING
AWNING
OWNING

••WG••
GEWGAW

••W•G•
COWAGE
SEWAGE
TOWAGE

••W••G
BOWING
BOWLEG
CAWING
COWING
HAWING
HEWING
JAWING
LAWING
LOWING
MEWING
MOWING

6

PAWING
ROWING
SAWING
SEWING
SOWING
TAWING
TOWING
VOWING
WOWING
YAWING
YOWING

•••W•G
BIGWIG
EARWIG
HEDWIG
LUDWIG
WIGWAG

WH••••
WHACKS
WHALED
WHALER
WHALES
WHAMMY
WHANGS
WHARFS
WHARVE
WHEALS
WHEATS
WHEELS
WHEEZE
WHEEZY
WHELKS
WHELKY
WHELMS
WHELPS
WHENCE
WHERRY
WHERVE
WHEYEY
WHIDAH
WHIFFS
WHILED
WHILES
WHILOM
WHILST
WHIMSY
WHINED
WHINER
WHINES
WHINNY
WHIRLS
WHISKS
WHISKY
WHITED
WHITEN
WHITER
WHITES
WHITEY
WHOLLY
WHOOPS
WHORED
WHORES
WHORLS
WHORTS
WHYDAH

W•H•••
WAHABI
WAHINE
WAHOOS

W••H••
WASHED
WASHER
WASHES
WETHER
WICHES
WISHED
WISHES
WITHAL
WITHED
WITHER
WITHES
WITHIN
WITHIT

W•••H•
WEIGHS
WEIGHT
WIDTHS
WORTHY
WRATHY
WRIGHT
WRITHE

W••••H
WABASH
WALLAH
WARMTH
WEALTH
WHIDAH
WHYDAH
WRAITH
WREATH
WRENCH
WRETCH

•WH•••
AWHILE
AWHIRL

•W••H•
DWIGHT
SWATHE
SWATHS

•W•••H
AWEIGH
OWLISH
SWARTH
SWATCH
SWITCH
TWITCH

••WH••
HAWHAW

••W••H
HOWDAH
JEWISH
RAWISH
SIWASH
UNWISH

•••W•H
GROWTH
YAHWEH

WI••••
WICHES
WICKED
WICKER
WICKET
WICOPY
WIDDIE
WIDELY
WIDENS
WIDEST
WIDOWS
WIDTHS
WIELDS
WIELDY
WIENER
WIENIE
WIFELY
WIGANS
WIGEON
WIGGED
WIGGLE
WIGGLY
WIGWAG
WIGWAM
WIKIUP
WILBER
WILBUR
WILDER
WILDLY
WILFUL
WILIER
WILILY
WILING
WILLED
WILLER
WILLET
WILLIE
WILLIS
WILLOW
WILLYS
WILMAS
WILSON
WILTED
WIMBLE
WIMPLE
WINCED
WINCER
WINCES
WINCEY
WINDED
WINDER
WINDOW
WINERY
WINGED
WINIER
WINING
WINKED
WINKER
WINKLE
WINNER
WINNIE
WINNOW
WINOES
WINTER
WINTRY
WINZES
WIPERS
WIPING
WIRERS
WIRIER
WIRILY
WIRING
WISDOM
WISELY
WISEST
WISHED
WISHES
WISING
WISPED
WITHAL
WITHED
WITHER
WITHES
WITHIN
WITHIT
WITNEY
WITTED
WIVERN
WIVERS
WIVING
WIZARD
WIZENS

W•I•••
WAIFED
WAILED
WAILER
WAISTS
WAITED
WAITER
WAIVED
WAIVER
WAIVES
WEIGHS
WEIGHT
WEIMAR
WEIRDY
WHIDAH
WHIFFS
WHILED
WHILES
WHILOM
WHILST
WHIMSY
WHINED
WHINER
WHINES
WHINNY
WHIRLS
WHISKS
WHISKY
WHITED
WHITEN
WHITER
WHITES
WHITEY
WRIEST
WRIGHT
WRINGS
WRISTS
WRITER
WRITES
WRITHE

W••I••
WADIES
WADING
WAGING
WAHINE
WAKIKI
WAKING
WALING
WANING
WANION
WAPITI
WARIER
WARILY
WAVIER
WAVIES
WAVILY
WAVING
WAXIER
WAXING
WIKIUP
WILIER
WILILY
WILING
WINIER
WINING
WIPING
WIRIER
WIRILY
WIRING
WISING
WIVING
WOOING
WOWING
WRAITH
WRYING

W•••I•
WALLIE
WALLIS
WALVIS
WEDGIE
WEENIE
WEEVIL
WELKIN
WIDDIE
WIENIE
WILLIE
WILLIS
WINNIE
WITHIN
WITHIT

W••••I
WAHABI
WAKIKI
WAPITI
WATUSI

•WI•••
DWIGHT
SWIFTS
SWILLS
SWINGE
SWINGS
SWIPED
SWIPES
SWIPLE
SWIRLS
SWIRLY
SWITCH
SWIVEL
SWIVET
TWIBIL
TWIGGY
TWILLS
TWINED
TWINER
TWINES
TWINGE
TWIRLS
TWIRPS
TWISTS
TWITCH

•W•I••
AWAITS
AWEIGH
AWEING
AWHILE
AWHIRL
AWNING
OWLISH
OWNING
SWAILS
SWAINS

•W••I•
SWAMIS
TWIBIL
TWOBIT

••WI••
BOWING
CAWING
COWING
DEWIER
DEWITT
EDWINA
EDWINS
ENWIND
ERWINS

HAWING
HEWING
INWIND
IRWINS
JAWING
JEWISH
LAWING
LOWING
MEWING
MOWING
NOWISE
PAWING
PEWITS
RAWISH
REWIND
ROWING
SAWING
SEWING
SOWING
TAWING
TOWING
UNWIND
UNWISE
UNWISH
VOWING
WOWING
YAWING
YOWING

••W•I•
BEWAIL
BOWFIN
COWRIE
GAWAIN
HAWAII
KEWPIE
KUWAIT

••W••I
HAWAII

•••WI•
BIGWIG
BREWIS
DARWIN
DIMWIT
EARWIG
GODWIN
GODWIT
HEDWIG
LUDWIG
NITWIT
OUTWIT

••••WI
MALAWI

•W•••J
SWARAJ

W•K•••
WAKENS
WAKIKI
WAKING
WIKIUP

W••K••
WALKED
WALKER
WALKON
WALKUP
WEAKEN
WEAKER
WEAKLY
WEEKLY
WELKIN
WICKED
WICKER
WICKET
WINKED
WINKER
WINKLE
WORKED
WORKER

W•••K•
WAKIKI
WHACKS
WHELKS
WHELKY
WHISKS
WHISKY
WRACKS
WREAKS
WRECKS

•W•K••
AWAKED
AWAKEN
AWAKES

•W••K•
SWANKY
TWEAKS
TWEAKY

••WK••
FAWKES
GAWKED
HAWKED
HAWKER
LOWKEY

••W••K
BYWORK
NEWARK
THWACK

•••W•K
ARAWAK

••••WK
MOHAWK
SQUAWK

W•L•••
WALDOS
WALERS
WALING
WALKED
WALKER
WALKON
WALKUP
WALLAH
WALLAS
WALLED
WALLET
WALLIE
WALLIS
WALLOP
WALLOW
WALLYS
WALNUT
WALRUS
WALTER
WALTON
WALVIS
WELDED
WELDER
WELKIN
WELLED
WELTED
WELTER
WILBER
WILBUR
WILDER
WILDLY
WILFUL
WILIER
WILILY
WILING
WILLED
WILLER
WILLET
WILLIE
WILLIS
WILLOW
WILLYS
WILMAS
WILSON
WILTED
WOLFED
WOLSEY
WOLVER
WOLVES

W••L••
WAILED
WAILER
WALLAH
WALLAS
WALLED
WALLET
WALLIE
WALLIS
WALLOP
WALLOW
WALLYS
WAULED
WAWLED
WAYLAY
WEALDS
WEALTH
WELLED
WESLEY
WHALED
WHALER
WHALES
WHELKS
WHELKY
WHELMS
WHELPS
WHILED
WHILES
WHILOM
WHILST
WHOLLY
WIELDS
WIELDY
WILLED
WILLER
WILLET
WILLIE
WILLIS
WILLOW
WILLYS
WOALDS
WOOLEN
WOOLLY
WORLDS

W•••L•
WABBLE
WABBLY
WADDLE
WADDLY
WAFFLE
WAGGLE
WAGGLY
WAMBLE
WAMBLY
WANDLE
WANGLE
WARBLE
WARILY
WARMLY
WATTLE
WAVILY
WEAKLY
WEDELN
WEEKLY
WHEALS
WHEELS
WHIRLS
WHOLLY
WHORLS
WIDELY
WIFELY
WIGGLE
WIGGLY
WILDLY
WILILY
WIMBLE
WIMPLE
WINKLE
WIRILY
WISELY
WOBBLE
WOBBLY
WOOLLY

W••••L
WEASEL
WEEVIL
WILFUL
WITHAL
WOEFUL

•WL•••
AWLESS
OWLETS
OWLISH

•W•L••
DWELLS
SWALES
SWELLS
SWILLS
TWELVE
TWILLS

•W••L•
AWHILE
DWELLS
SWAILS
SWELLS
SWILLS
SWIPLE
SWIRLS
SWIRLY
TWILLS
TWIRLS
TWOPLY

•W•••L
AWHIRL
SWIVEL
TWIBIL

••WL••
BAWLED
BAWLER
BOWLED
BOWLEG
BOWLER
COWLED
DEWLAP
FOWLED
FOWLER
HOWLED
HOWLER
MEWLED
WAWLED
YAWLED
YOWLED

••W•L•
BOWELS
DAWDLE
DOWELS
INWALL
JEWELS
LEWDLY
LOWELL
NEWELS
ORWELL
OSWALD
POWELL
ROWELS
SAWFLY
SEWALL
TOWELS
UNWELL
VOWELS

••W••L
BEWAIL
INWALL
LAWFUL
LOWELL
ORWELL
POWELL
SEWALL
UNWELL

•••WL•
BRAWLS
CRAWLS
CRAWLY
DRAWLS
DRAWLY
GROWLS
PROWLS
SCOWLS
SHAWLS
SLOWLY
TRAWLS

•••W•L
AVOWAL
CREWEL
NARWAL
TROWEL

••••WL
SCRAWL
SPRAWL

W•M•••
WAMBLE
WAMBLY
WAMMUS
WAMPUM
WAMPUS
WIMBLE
WIMPLE
WOMBAT
WOMBED
WOMERA

W••M••
WAMMUS
WARMED
WARMER

WARMLY
WARMTH
WARMUP
WEIMAR
WHAMMY
WHIMSY
WILMAS
WORMED
WORMER

W•••M•
WHAMMY
WHELMS

W••••M
WAMPUM
WHILOM
WIGWAM
WISDOM

•W•M••
SWAMIS
SWAMPS
SWAMPY

•W••M•
SWARMS

••WM••
BOWMAN
BOWMEN
COWMAN
COWMEN

••W•M•
ENWOMB

•••WM•
SHAWMS

•••W•M
WIGWAM

W•N•••
WANDAS
WANDER
WANDLE
WANGLE
WANING
WANION
WANNED
WANNER
WANTED
WANTER
WANTON
WENDED
WENDYS
WINCED
WINCER
WINCES
WINCEY
WINDED
WINDER
WINDOW
WINERY
WINGED
WINIER
WINING
WINKED
WINKER
WINKLE
WINNER
WINNIE
WINNOW
WINOES
WINTER
WINTRY
WINZES
WONDER
WONTED

W••N••
WAGNER
WALNUT
WANNED
WANNER
WARNED
WARNER
WAYNES
WEANED
WEANER
WEENIE
WEENSY
WHANGS
WHENCE
WHINED
WHINER
WHINES
WHINNY
WIENER
WIENIE
WINNER
WINNIE
WINNOW
WITNEY
WOUNDS
WRENCH
WRINGS
WRONGS

W•••N•
WADING
WAGING
WAGONS
WAHINE
WAKENS
WAKING
WALING
WANING
WAVING
WAXING
WERENT
WHINNY
WIDENS
WIGANS
WILING
WINING
WIPING
WIRING
WISING
WIVING
WIZENS
WOOING
WOWING
WRYING

W••••N
WAGGON
WALKON
WALTON
WANION
WANTON
WARDEN
WARREN
WATSON
WEAKEN
WEAPON
WEDELN
WELKIN
WHITEN
WIGEON
WILSON
WITHIN
WIVERN
WOODEN
WOOLEN
WORSEN
WYSTAN
WYVERN

•WN•••
AWNING
OWNERS
OWNING

•W•N••
BWANAS
GWENNS
GWYNNE
RWANDA
SWANEE
SWANKY
SWINGE
SWINGS
TWANGS
TWANGY
TWENTY
TWINED
TWINER
TWINES
TWINGE

•W••N•
AWEING
AWNING
GWENNS
GWYNNE
OWNING
SWAINS
SWOONS

•W•••N
AWAKEN
SWEDEN

••WN••
DAWNED
DOWNED
FAWNED
FAWNER
GOWNED
PAWNED
PAWNEE
PAWNER
YAWNED
YAWNER

••W•N•
BOWING
CAWING
COWING
DEWANS
DIWANS
EDWINA
EDWINS
ENWIND
ERWINS
HAWING
HEWING
INWIND
IRWINS
JAWING
LAWING
LOWING
MEWING
MOWING
PAWING
REWIND
ROWANS
ROWENA
ROWING
SAWING
SEWING
SOWING
TAWING
TOWING
UNWIND
VOWING
WOWING
YAWING
YOWING

••W••N
BOWFIN
BOWMAN
BOWMEN
COWMAN
COWMEN
DAWSON
GAWAIN
NEWTON

•••WN•
BRAWNY
BROWNS
CLOWNS
CROWNS
DROWNS
FROWNS
PRAWNS
SPAWNS

•••W•N
AJOWAN
DARWIN
DEEWAN
GODWIN
SEAWAN
TAIWAN

••••WN
DISOWN
IMPAWN
RENOWN
STREWN
THROWN
UPTOWN

WO••••
WOADED
WOALDS
WOBBLE
WOBBLY
WOEFUL
WOLFED
WOLSEY
WOLVER
WOLVES
WOMBAT
WOMBED
WOMERA
WONDER
WONTED
WOODED
WOODEN
WOODSY
WOOERS
WOOFER
WOOING
WOOLEN
WOOLLY
WORDED
WORKED
WORKER
WORLDS
WORMED
WORMER
WORSEN
WORSER
WORSTS
WORTHY
WOUNDS
WOWING
WOWSER

W•O•••
WHOLLY
WHOOPS
WHORED
WHORES
WHORLS
WHORTS
WOODED
WOODEN
WOODSY
WOOERS
WOOFER
WOOING
WOOLEN
WOOLLY
WRONGS

W••O••
WAGONS
WAHOOS
WAYOUT
WHOOPS
WICOPY
WIDOWS
WINOES

W•••O•
WAGGON
WAHOOS
WALDOS
WALKON
WALLOP
WALLOW
WALTON
WANION
WANTON
WATSON
WEAPON
WHILOM
WIGEON
WILLOW
WILSON
WINDOW
WINNOW
WISDOM

•WO•••
SWOONS
SWOOPS
SWORDS
TWOBIT
TWOFER
TWOPLY
TWOWAY

•W•O••
SWOONS
SWOOPS

••WO••
BYWORD
BYWORK
ENWOMB
INWOVE
REWORD

••W•O•
BOWWOW

COWBOY
COWPOX
DAWSON
KOWTOW
LOWBOY
NEWTON
POWWOW

•••WO•
BOWWOW
POWWOW

W•P•••
WAPITI
WAPPED
WIPERS
WIPING

W••P••
WAMPUM
WAMPUS
WAPPED
WARPED
WARPER
WEAPON
WEEPER
WIMPLE
WISPED
WRAPUP

W•••P•
WATAPE
WATAPS
WHELPS
WHOOPS
WICOPY

W••••P
WALKUP
WALLOP
WARMUP
WIKIUP
WRAPUP

•W•P••
SWIPED
SWIPES
SWIPLE
TWOPLY

•W••P•
SWAMPS
SWAMPY
SWEEPS
SWEEPY
SWOOPS
TWERPS
TWIRPS

••WP••
COWPEA
COWPER
COWPOX
KEWPIE
PAWPAW
YAWPED
YAWPER

••W•P•
UNWEPT

••W••P
DEWLAP
ENWRAP
INWRAP
UNWRAP

•••W•P
BLOWUP

WR••••
WRACKS
WRAITH
WRAPUP
WRASSE
WRATHY
WREAKS
WREATH
WRECKS
WRENCH
WRESTS
WRETCH
WRIEST
WRIGHT
WRINGS
WRISTS
WRITER
WRITES
WRITHE
WRONGS
WRYEST
WRYING

W•R•••
WARBLE
WARDED
WARDEN
WARDER
WARIER
WARILY
WARMED
WARMER
WARMLY
WARMTH
WARMUP
WARNED
WARNER
WARPED
WARPER
WARRED
WARREN
WARSAW
WERENT
WIRERS
WIRIER
WIRILY
WIRING
WORDED
WORKED
WORKER
WORLDS
WORMED
WORMER
WORSEN
WORSER
WORSTS
WORTHY

W••R••
WALRUS
WARRED
WARREN
WEARER
WEIRDY
WHARFS
WHARVE
WHERRY
WHERVE
WHIRLS
WHORED
WHORES
WHORLS
WHORTS

W•••R•
WADERS
WAFERS
WAGERS
WALERS
WATERS
WATERY
WAVERS
WEBERS
WHERRY
WINERY
WINTRY
WIPERS
WIRERS
WIVERN
WIVERS
WIZARD
WOMERA
WOOERS
WYVERN

W••••R
WAFTER
WAGNER
WAILER
WAITER
WAIVER
WALKER
WALTER
WANDER
WANNER
WANTER
WARDER
WARIER
WARMER
WARNER
WARPER
WASHER
WASTER
WAVIER
WAXIER
WEAKER
WEANER
WEARER
WEAVER
WEEDER
WEEPER
WEEVER
WEIMAR
WELDER
WELTER
WESTER
WETHER
WETTER
WHALER
WHINER
WHITER
WICKER
WIENER
WILBER
WILBUR
WILDER
WILIER
WILLER
WINCER
WINDER
WINIER
WINKER
WINNER
WINTER
WIRIER
WITHER
WOLVER
WONDER
WOOFER
WORKER
WORMER
WORSER
WOWSER
WRITER

•W•R••
AWARDS
DWARFS
SWARAJ
SWARDS
SWARMS
SWARTH
SWARTY
SWERVE
SWIRLS
SWIRLY
SWORDS
TWERPS
TWIRLS
TWIRPS

•W••R•
AWEARY
AWHIRL
OWNERS
SWEARS

•W•••R
TWINER
TWOFER

••WR••
COWRIE
ENWRAP
INWRAP
UNWRAP

••W•R•
BAWDRY
BEWARE
BOWERS
BOWERY
BYWORD
BYWORK
COWARD
COWERS
DOWERS
DOWERY
EDWARD
HEWERS
HOWARD
INWARD
LOWERS
LOWERY
MOWERS
NEWARK
ONWARD
PAWERS
POWERS
REWARD
REWORD
ROWERS
SAWERS
SEWARD
SEWERS
SOWARS
SOWERS
TAWDRY
TAWERS
THWART
TOWARD
TOWERS
TOWERY
UNWARY
UPWARD
VOWERS

••W••R
BAWLER
BOWLER
BOWYER
COWPER
DEWIER
DOWSER
FAWNER
FOWLER
HAWKER
HAWSER
HOWLER
LAWYER
LEWDER
PAWNER
PEWTER
POWDER
POWTER
SAWYER
WOWSER
YAWNER
YAWPER

•••W•R
ANSWER
AVOWER
BLOWER
BREWER
CHEWER
DRAWER
FLOWER
GLOWER
GNAWER
GROWER
KNOWER
PLOWER
PREWAR
SHEWER
SHOWER
SKEWER
SLOWER
VIEWER

W•S•••
WASHED
WASHER
WASHES
WASTED
WASTER
WASTES
WESLEY
WESSEX
WESTER
WISDOM
WISELY
WISEST
WISHED
WISHES
WISING
WISPED
WYSTAN

W••S••
WADSET
WAISTS
WARSAW
WATSON
WEASEL
WESSEX
WHISKS
WHISKY
WILSON
WOLSEY
WORSEN
WORSER
WORSTS
WOWSER
WRASSE

WRESTS
WRISTS

W•••S•
WABASH
WATUSI
WEENSY
WHILST
WHIMSY
WIDEST
WISEST
WOODSY
WRASSE
WRIEST
WRYEST

W••••S
WADERS
WADIES
WAFERS
WAGERS
WAGONS
WAHOOS
WAISTS
WAIVES
WAKENS
WALDOS
WALERS
WALLAS
WALLIS
WALLYS
WALRUS
WALVIS
WAMMUS
WAMPUS
WANDAS
WASHES
WASTES
WATAPS
WATERS
WAVERS
WAVEYS
WAVIES
WAYNES
WEALDS
WEAVES
WEBERS
WEDGES
WEIGHS
WENDYS
WHACKS
WHALES
WHANGS
WHARFS
WHEALS
WHEATS
WHEELS
WHELKS
WHELMS
WHELPS
WHIFFS
WHILES
WHINES
WHIRLS
WHISKS
WHITES
WHOOPS
WHORES
WHORLS
WHORTS
WICHES
WIDENS
WIDOWS
WIDTHS
WIELDS
WIGANS
WILLIS
WILLYS
WILMAS
WINCES
WINOES
WINZES
WIPERS
WIRERS
WISHES
WITHES
WIVERS
WIZENS
WOALDS
WOLVES
WOOERS
WORLDS
WORSTS
WOUNDS
WRACKS
WREAKS
WRECKS
WRESTS
WRINGS
WRISTS
WRITES
WRONGS

•W•S••
TWISTS

•W••S•
AWLESS
OWLISH

•W•••S
AWAITS
AWAKES
AWARDS
AWLESS
BWANAS
DWARFS
DWELLS
GWENNS
OWLETS
OWNERS
SWAGES
SWAILS
SWAINS
SWALES
SWAMIS
SWAMPS
SWARDS
SWARMS
SWATHS
SWEARS
SWEATS
SWEDES
SWEEPS
SWEETS
SWELLS
SWIFTS
SWILLS
SWINGS
SWIPES
SWIRLS
SWOONS
SWOOPS
SWORDS
TWANGS
TWEAKS
TWEEDS
TWEETS
TWERPS
TWILLS
TWINES
TWIRLS
TWIRPS
TWISTS

••WS••
BOWSED
BOWSES
DAWSON
DOWSED
DOWSER
DOWSES
HAWSER
HAWSES
WOWSER

••W•S•
FEWEST
JEWESS
JEWISH
LOWEST
NEWEST
NOWISE
RAWEST
RAWISH
SIWASH
UNWISE
UNWISH

••W••S
ALWAYS
BOWELS
BOWERS
BOWSES
BYWAYS
COWERS
DEWANS
DIWANS
DOWELS
DOWERS
DOWSES
EDWINS
ERWINS
FAWKES
HAWSES
HEWERS
IRWINS
JEWELS
JEWESS
LOWERS
MOWERS
NAWABS
NEWELS
NOWAYS
PAWERS
PEWEES
PEWITS
POWERS
ROWANS
ROWELS
ROWERS
SAWERS
SEWERS
SOWARS
SOWERS
TAWERS
TOWELS
TOWERS
VOWELS
VOWERS

•••WS•
BROWSE
DROWSE
DROWSY

•••W•S
BRAWLS
BREWIS
BROWNS
CLOWNS
CRAWLS
CROWDS
CROWNS
DRAWLS
DROWNS
FROWNS
GROWLS
PRAWNS
PROWLS
SCHWAS
SCOWLS
SHAWLS
SHAWMS
SPAWNS
TRAWLS

••••WS
ALLOWS
ARROWS
BEDEWS
BYLAWS
ELBOWS
EMBOWS
ENDOWS
INDOWS
INLAWS
MACAWS
OXBOWS
PAPAWS
PSHAWS
RENEWS
SCREWS
SEROWS
SHREWS
SINEWS
SQUAWS
STRAWS
STREWS
THROWS
UNMEWS
UPBOWS
WIDOWS

W•T•••
WATAPE
WATAPS
WATERS
WATERY
WATSON
WATTLE
WATUSI
WETHER
WETTED
WETTER
WITHAL
WITHED
WITHER
WITHES
WITHIN
WITHIT
WITNEY
WITTED

W••T••
WAFTED
WAFTER
WAITED
WAITER
WALTER
WALTON
WANTED
WANTER
WANTON
WASTED
WASTER
WASTES
WATTLE
WELTED
WELTER
WESTER
WETTED
WETTER
WHITED
WHITEN
WHITER
WHITES
WHITEY
WIDTHS
WILTED
WINTER
WINTRY
WITTED
WONTED
WORTHY
WRATHY
WRETCH
WRITER
WRITES
WRITHE
WYSTAN

W•••T•
WAISTS
WAPITI
WARMTH
WEALTH
WHEATS
WHORTS
WORSTS
WRAITH
WREATH
WRESTS
WRISTS

W••••T
WADSET
WALLET
WALNUT
WAYOUT
WEIGHT
WERENT
WHILST
WICKET
WIDEST
WILLET
WISEST
WITHIT
WOMBAT
WRIEST
WRIGHT
WRYEST

•W•T••
SWATCH
SWATHE
SWATHS
SWITCH
TWITCH

•W••T•
AWAITS
OWLETS
SWARTH
SWARTY
SWEATS
SWEATY
SWEETS
SWIFTS
TWEETS
TWENTY
TWISTS

6

•W•••T
DWIGHT
SWIVET
TWOBIT

••WT••
KOWTOW
NEWTON
PEWTER
POWTER

••W•T•
ABWATT
DEWITT
PEWITS

••W••T
ABWATT
DEWITT
FEWEST
KUWAIT
LOWEST
NEWEST
RAWEST
THWART
UNWEPT

•••WT•
GROWTH

•••W•T
DIMWIT
GODWIT
NITWIT
OUTWIT

W•U•••
WAULED
WOUNDS

W••U••
WATUSI

W•••U•
WALKUP
WALNUT
WALRUS
WAMMUS
WAMPUM
WAMPUS
WARMUP
WAYOUT
WIKIUP
WILBUR
WILFUL
WOEFUL
WRAPUP

••W•U•
LAWFUL

•••WU•
BLOWUP

W•V•••
WAVERS
WAVEYS
WAVIER
WAVIES
WAVILY
WAVING
WIVERN
WIVERS
WIVING
WYVERN

W••V••
WAIVED
WAIVER
WAIVES
WALVIS
WEAVED
WEAVER
WEAVES
WEEVER
WEEVIL
WOLVER
WOLVES

W•••V•
WHARVE
WHERVE

•W•V••
SWIVEL
SWIVET

•W••V•
SWERVE
TWELVE

••W•V•
INWOVE

W•W•••
WAWLED
WOWING
WOWSER

W••W••
WIGWAG
WIGWAM

W•••W•
WIDOWS

W••••W
WALLOW
WARSAW
WILLOW
WINDOW
WINNOW

•W•W••
TWOWAY

••WW••
BOWWOW

POWWOW

••W••W
BOWWOW
GEWGAW
HAWHAW
KOWTOW
PAWPAW
POWWOW

•••W•W
BOWWOW
POWWOW

W•X•••
WAXIER
WAXING

W••••X
WESSEX

••W••X
COWPOX

•••W•X
EARWAX
PAXWAX

WY••••
WYSTAN
WYVERN

W•Y•••
WAYLAY
WAYNES
WAYOUT
WHYDAH
WRYEST
WRYING

W••Y••
WHEYEY

W•••Y•
WALLYS
WAVEYS
WENDYS
WILLYS

W••••Y
WABBLY
WADDLY
WAGGLY
WAMBLY
WARILY
WARMLY
WATERY
WAVILY
WAYLAY
WEAKLY
WEEKLY
WEENSY
WEIRDY
WESLEY

WHAMMY
WHEEZY
WHELKY
WHERRY
WHEYEY
WHIMSY
WHINNY
WHISKY
WHITEY
WHOLLY
WICOPY
WIDELY
WIELDY
WIFELY
WIGGLY
WILDLY
WILILY
WINCEY
WINERY
WINTRY
WIRILY
WISELY
WITNEY
WOBBLY
WOLSEY
WOODSY
WOOLLY
WORTHY
WRATHY

•WY•••
GWYNNE

•W•Y••
SWAYED

•W•••Y
AWEARY
SWAMPY
SWANKY
SWARTY
SWEATY
SWEEPY
SWIRLY
TWANGY
TWEAKY
TWENTY
TWIGGY
TWOPLY
TWOWAY

••WY••
BOWYER
LAWYER
SAWYER

••W•Y•
ALWAYS
BYWAYS
NOWAYS

••W••Y
BAWDRY
BOWERY

COWBOY
DOWERY
LEWDLY
LOWBOY
LOWERY
LOWKEY
SAWFLY
TAWDRY
TOWERY
UNWARY

•••W•Y
AIRWAY
ANYWAY
BLOWBY
BLOWZY
BRAWNY
COGWAY
CRAWLY
DRAWLY
DROWSY
FROWZY
GALWAY
KEYWAY
LEEWAY
MIDWAY
NORWAY
ONEWAY
RUNWAY
SEAWAY
SKYWAY
SLOWLY
SUBWAY
TWOWAY

••••WY
SCREWY
SINEWY
STRAWY

W•Z•••
WIZARD
WIZENS

W••Z••
WINZES

W•••Z•
WHEEZE
WHEEZY

•••WZ•
BLOWZY
FROWZY

XA••••
XANTHO
XAVIER

X•A•••
XRAYED

X••A••
XYLANS

•XA•••
EXACTA
EXACTS
EXALTS
EXAMEN
EXARCH
OXALIC
OXALIS

•X•A••
EXHALE
EXPAND
EXTANT
OXTAIL

•X••A•
AXEMAN
EXTRAS

•X•••A
AXILLA
EXACTA
EXEDRA

••XA••
FIXATE
HEXADS
HEXANE
LUXATE
ROXANA
ROXANE

••X•A•
BOXCAR
PAXWAX
SEXTAN
SEXUAL

••X••A
MYXOMA
ROXANA

•••XA•
BIAXAL
COAXAL

•••X•A
ALEXIA
ANOXIA
ATAXIA

X•B•••
XEBECS

•XB•••
OXBOWS

•X••B•
EXURBS

X•••C•
XEBECS

6

•XC•••
EXCEED
EXCELS
EXCEPT
EXCESS
EXCIDE
EXCISE
EXCITE
EXCUSE

•X•C••
EXACTA
EXACTS

•X••C•
EXARCH
EXPECT
EXSECT

•X•••C
EXILIC
EXOTIC
OXALIC

••XC••
BOXCAR

••X•C•
MEXICO

•••X•C
ANOXIC
ATAXIC

X••••D
XRAYED
XYLOID

•X•D••
EXEDRA
EXODUS
EXUDED
EXUDES
OXIDES

•X••D•
EXCIDE

•X•••D
AXSEED
EXCEED
EXILED
EXITED
EXPAND
EXPEND
EXTEND
EXUDED
OXEYED
OXFORD

••X•D•
HEXADS
TUXEDO

••X••D
TAXIED

•••X•D
COAXED
FLEXED
FLUXED
HOAXED

XE••••
XEBECS

X••E••
XEBECS
XYLEMS
XYLENE

X•••E•
XAVIER
XRAYED
XYSTER

X••••E
XYLENE
XYLOSE

•XE•••
AXEMAN
AXEMEN
EXEDRA
EXEMPT
EXEQUY
EXERTS
EXETER
EXEUNT
OXEYED
OXEYES

•X•E••
AXSEED
EXCEED
EXCELS
EXCEPT
EXCESS
EXPECT
EXPELS
EXPEND
EXPERT
EXSECT
EXSERT
EXTEND
EXTENT
EXTERN

•X••E•
AXEMEN
AXONES
AXSEED
EXAMEN
EXCEED
EXETER
EXILED
EXILES
EXITED

EXOGEN
EXUDED
EXUDES
OXEYED
OXEYES
OXIDES
OXYGEN

•X•••E
AXLIKE
EXCIDE
EXCISE
EXCITE
EXCUSE
EXHALE
EXHUME
EXPIRE
EXPOSE

••XE••
BOXERS
FIXERS
LAXEST
MIXERS
TAXEME
TAXERS
TUXEDO
VEXERS
VIXENS

••X•E•
BAXTER
DEXTER
DOXIES
FOXIER
HUXLEY
NIXIES
PIXIES
PYXIES
SEXIER
SEXTET
SIXTES
TAXIED
WAXIER

••X••E
FIXATE
HEXANE
HEXONE
HEXOSE
LUXATE
MAXINE
MAXIXE
ROXANE
TAXEME
TAXITE

•••XE•
APEXES
CALXES
COAXED
COAXER
COAXES
CRUXES

FLAXEN
FLAXES
FLEXED
FLEXES
FLUXED
FLUXES
HOAXED
HOAXER
HOAXES
IBEXES
ILEXES
JINXES
LYNXES
MINXES
ORYXES

•••X•E
TRIXIE

••••XE
DELUXE
MAXIXE

•XF•••
OXFORD

•X•G••
EXOGEN
OXYGEN

••X••G
BOXING
COXING
FAXING
FIXING
FOXING
HEXING
MIXING
NIXING
SEXING
TAXING
VEXING
WAXING

X•••H•
XANTHO

•XH•••
EXHALE
EXHORT
EXHUME

•X•••H
EXARCH

••X•H•
SIXTHS

X••I••
XAVIER

X•••I•
XYLOID

•XI•••
AXILLA
AXIOMS
EXILED
EXILES
EXILIC
EXISTS
EXITED
OXIDES

•X•I••
AXLIKE
EXCIDE
EXCISE
EXCITE
EXPIRE
EXPIRY
OXLIPS

•X••I•
EXILIC
EXOTIC
OXALIC
OXALIS
OXTAIL

••XI••
AUXINS
BOXING
COXING
DIXITS
DOXIES
FAXING
FIXING
FIXITY
FOXIER
FOXILY
FOXING
HEXING
LAXITY
MAXIMS
MAXINE
MAXIXE
MEXICO
MIXING
NIXIES
NIXING
PIXIES
PYXIES
SEXIER
SEXING
SEXISM
SEXIST
TAXIED
TAXING
TAXITE
TOXINS
VEXILS
VEXING
WAXIER
WAXING

•••XI•
ALEXIA

ALEXIN
ALEXIS
ANOXIA
ANOXIC
ATAXIA
ATAXIC
ELIXIR
PINXIT
PRAXIS
TRIXIE

••••XI
BILOXI

•X••K•
AXLIKE

X•L•••
XYLANS
XYLEMS
XYLENE
XYLOID
XYLOLS
XYLOSE

X•••L•
XYLOLS

•XL•••
AXLIKE
OXLIPS

•X•L••
AXILLA
EXALTS
EXILED
EXILES
EXILIC
EXULTS
OXALIC
OXALIS

•X••L•
AXILLA
EXCELS
EXHALE
EXPELS
EXTOLS

•X•••L
OXTAIL

••XL••
HUXLEY

••X•L•
FOXILY
HEXYLS
VEXILS

••X••L
SEXUAL

6

•••X•L
BIAXAL
COAXAL

X•••M•
XYLEMS

•XM•••
EXMOOR

•X•M••
AXEMAN
AXEMEN
EXAMEN
EXEMPT

•X••M•
AXIOMS
EXHUME

••X•M•
MAXIMS
MYXOMA
TAXEME

••X••M
SEXISM

X•N•••
XANTHO

X•••N•
XYLANS
XYLENE

•X•N••
AXONES

•X••N•
EXEUNT
EXPAND
EXPEND
EXTANT
EXTEND
EXTENT

•X•••N
AXEMAN
AXEMEN
EXAMEN
EXOGEN
EXTERN
OXYGEN

••X•N•
AUXINS
BOXING
COXING
FAXING
FIXING
FOXING
HEXANE
HEXING
HEXONE
MAXINE
MIXING
NIXING
ROXANA
ROXANE
SAXONS
SAXONY
SEXING
TAXING
TOXINS
VEXING
VIXENS
WAXING

••X••N
SEXTAN
SEXTON

•••X•N
ALEXIN
FLAXEN
KLAXON

X••O••
XYLOID
XYLOLS
XYLOSE

X•••O•
XYSTOS

X••••O
XANTHO

•XO•••
AXONES
EXODUS
EXOGEN
EXOTIC

•X•O••
AXIOMS
EXHORT
EXMOOR
EXPORT
EXPOSE
EXTOLS
EXTORT
OXBOWS
OXFORD

•X••O•
EXMOOR

••XO••
HEXONE
HEXOSE
MYXOMA
SAXONS
SAXONY

••X•O•
SEXTON

••X••O
DEXTRO
MEXICO
TUXEDO

•••XO•
FLEXOR
KLAXON
PLEXOR

•XP•••
EXPAND
EXPECT
EXPELS
EXPEND
EXPERT
EXPIRE
EXPIRY
EXPORT
EXPOSE

•X••P•
EXCEPT
EXEMPT
OXLIPS

••X•P•
MIXUPS

•X•Q••
EXEQUY

XR••••
XRAYED

X••••R
XAVIER
XYSTER

•X•R••
EXARCH
EXERTS
EXTRAS
EXURBS

•X••R•
EXEDRA
EXHORT
EXPERT
EXPIRE
EXPIRY
EXPORT
EXSERT
EXTERN
EXTORT
OXFORD

•X•••R
EXETER
EXMOOR

••X•R•
BOXERS
DEXTRO
FIXERS
LUXURY
MIXERS
TAXERS
VEXERS

••X••R
BAXTER
BOXCAR
DEXTER
FOXIER
SEXIER
WAXIER

•••X•R
COAXER
ELIXIR
FLEXOR
HOAXER
PLEXOR

X•S•••
XYSTER
XYSTOS
XYSTUS

X•••S•
XYLOSE

X••••S
XEBECS
XYLANS
XYLEMS
XYLOLS
XYSTOS
XYSTUS

•XS•••
AXSEED
EXSECT
EXSERT

•X•S••
EXISTS

•X••S•
EXCESS
EXCISE
EXCUSE
EXPOSE

•X•••S
AXIOMS
AXONES
EXACTS
EXALTS
EXCELS
EXCESS
EXERTS
EXILES
EXISTS
EXODUS
EXPELS
EXTOLS
EXTRAS
EXUDES
EXULTS
EXURBS
OXALIS
OXBOWS
OXEYES
OXIDES
OXLIPS

••X•S•
HEXOSE
LAXEST
SEXISM
SEXIST

••X••S
AUXINS
BOXERS
DIXITS
DOXIES
FIXERS
HEXADS
HEXYLS
MAXIMS
MIXERS
MIXUPS
NIXIES
PIXIES
PYXIES
SAXONS
SIXTES
SIXTHS
TAXERS
TOXINS
VEXERS
VEXILS
VIXENS

•••X•S
ALEXIS
APEXES
CALXES
COAXES
CRUXES
FLAXES
FLEXES
FLUXES
HOAXES
IBEXES
ILEXES
JINXES
LYNXES
MINXES
ORYXES
PLEXUS
PRAXIS
TRIXYS

X••T••
XANTHO
XYSTER
XYSTOS
XYSTUS

•XT•••
EXTANT
EXTEND
EXTENT
EXTERN
EXTOLS
EXTORT
EXTRAS
OXTAIL

•X•T••
EXETER
EXITED
EXOTIC

•X••T•
EXACTA
EXACTS
EXALTS
EXCITE
EXERTS
EXISTS
EXULTS

•X•••T
EXCEPT
EXEMPT
EXEUNT
EXHORT
EXPECT
EXPERT
EXPORT
EXSECT
EXSERT
EXTANT
EXTENT
EXTORT

••XT••
BAXTER
DEXTER
DEXTRO
SEXTAN
SEXTET
SEXTON
SIXTES
SIXTHS

••X•T•
DIXITS
FIXATE
FIXITY
LAXITY
LUXATE
TAXITE

••X••T
LAXEST
SEXIST
SEXTET

•••X•T
PINXIT

••••XT
ADMIXT
UNVEXT
URTEXT

X•••U•
XYSTUS

•XU•••
EXUDED
EXUDES
EXULTS
EXURBS

•X•U••
EXCUSE
EXEUNT
EXHUME

•X••U•
EXEQUY
EXODUS

••XU••
LUXURY
MIXUPS
SEXUAL

•••XU•
PLEXUS

X•V•••
XAVIER

•X••W•
OXBOWS

••XW••
PAXWAX

••X•X•
MAXIXE

••X••X
PAXWAX

XY••••
XYLANS
XYLEMS
XYLENE
XYLOID
XYLOLS
XYLOSE
XYSTER
XYSTOS
XYSTUS

X••Y••
XRAYED

•XY•••
OXYGEN

•X•Y••
OXEYED
OXEYES

•X•••Y
EXEQUY
EXPIRY

••XY••
HEXYLS

••X••Y
FIXITY
FOXILY
HUXLEY
LAXITY
LUXURY
SAXONY

•••XY•
TRIXYS

••••XY
DESOXY
GALAXY

YA••••
YABBER
YACHTS
YAGERS
YAHOOS
YAHVEH
YAHWEH
YAKIMA
YAKKED
YAMENS
YAMMER
YAMUNS
YANKED
YANKEE
YAPONS
YAPPED
YARDED
YARROW
YASMAK
YAUPED
YAUPON
YAWING
YAWLED
YAWNED
YAWNER
YAWPED
YAWPER

Y•A•••
YEANED
YEARLY
YEARNS
YEASTS
YEASTY

Y•••A•
YASMAK
YEOMAN

YERBAS
YUCCAS

Y••••A
YAKIMA
YORUBA
YTTRIA

•YA•••
CYANIC
CYANID
CYANIN
DYADIC
EYASES
HYADES

•Y•A••
AYEAYE
AYMARA
BYLANE
BYLAWS
BYNAME
BYPASS
BYPAST
BYPATH
BYTALK
BYWAYS
CYCADS
CYMARS
CYRANO
DYNAMO
DYNAST
GYRATE
PYRANS
TYBALT
TYRANT
XYLANS
ZYMASE

•Y••A•
BYPLAY
BYROAD
CYMBAL
HYDRAE
HYDRAS
HYENAS
HYETAL
HYMNAL
HYPHAE
HYPHAL
LYDIAS
LYTTAE
MYRIAD
MYRNAS
SYLVAE
SYLVAN
SYLVAS
SYNTAX
SYRIAC
SYRIAN
TYMPAN
WYSTAN

•Y•••A
AYESHA
AYMARA
HYGEIA
MYOPIA
MYRICA
MYXOMA
NYMPHA
PYEMIA
PYRRHA
PYTHIA
PYURIA
SYLVIA
SYNURA
ZYGOMA

••YA••
ARYANS
BAYARD
BOYARD
BOYARS
BRYANT
DRYADS
GUYANA
KAYAKS
RAYAHS
RIYALS
ROYALS
VOYAGE

••Y•A•
AMYTAL
ANYWAY
CAYMAN
HEYDAY
KEYWAY
LAYDAY
LAYMAN
MAYDAY
MAYHAP
PAYDAY
PHYLAE
SKYCAP
SKYMAN
SKYWAY
STYLAR
WAYLAY
WHYDAH

••Y••A
CAYUGA
ELYTRA
GDYNIA
GUYANA
ODYNIA
PAYOLA
SCYLLA
ZOYSIA

•••YA•
BANYAN
BUNYAN
GALYAK
LIBYAN

MAGYAR
PLAYAS
SONYAS

•••Y•A
BARYTA
CORYZA

••••YA
KABAYA
MALAYA
NAGOYA
PAPAYA

Y•B•••
YABBER

Y••B••
YABBER
YERBAS

Y•••B•
YORUBA

•YB•••
BYBLOW
CYBELE
DYBBUK
HYBRID
HYBRIS
SYBILS
TYBALT

•Y•B••
BYEBYE
CYMBAL
DYBBUK
SYMBOL

••YB••
FLYBYS
KHYBER

•••Y•B
CORYMB

YC••••
YCLEPT

Y•C•••
YACHTS
YUCCAS

Y••C••
YOICKS
YUCCAS

Y••••C
YTTRIC

•YC•••
CYCADS
CYCLED
CYCLER

CYCLES
CYCLIC
LYCEES
LYCEUM
MYCETE
SYCEES
TYCOON

•Y•C••
EYECUP

•Y••C•
CYNICS
GYNECO
LYRICS
MYRICA

•Y•••C
CYANIC
CYCLIC
CYMRIC
CYSTIC
DYADIC
HYDRIC
HYMNIC
HYPNIC
MYOPIC
MYRMEC
MYSTIC
MYTHIC
PYEMIC
PYKNIC
PYTHIC
SYNDIC
SYRIAC

••YC••
GLYCOL
JOYCES
PSYCHE
PSYCHO
SKYCAP

••Y••C
AMYLIC
CHYMIC
PHYSIC
THYMIC

•••YC•
ENCYCL

Y•D•••
YODELS

Y••D••
YARDED
YONDER

Y•••D•
YIELDS

Y••••D
YAKKED

6

YANKED
YAPPED
YARDED
YAUPED
YAWLED
YAWNED
YAWPED
YEANED
YELLED
YELPED
YENNED
YESSED
YIPPED
YOWLED
YUKKED

•YD•••

HYDRAE
HYDRAS
HYDRIC
HYDROS
LYDIAS
SYDNEY

•Y•D••

DYADIC
HYADES
SYNDET
SYNDIC

•Y••D•

CYCADS
HYOIDS
SYNODS

•Y•••D

BYROAD
BYWORD
CYANID
CYCLED
CYMOID
EYELID
GYPPED
HYBRID
HYMNED
MYRIAD
XYLOID

••YD••

ABYDOS
CLYDES
DRYDEN
HEYDAY
HOYDEN
LAYDAY
MAYDAY
PAYDAY
WHYDAH
ZUYDER

••Y•D•

DRYADS

••Y••D

BAYARD
BEYOND
BOYARD
KAYOED
RHYMED
STYLED

•••YD•

FLOYDS
LLOYDS

•••Y•D

BRAYED
BUOYED
CLAYED
CLOYED
DRAYED
FLAYED
FRAYED
GRAYED
OBEYED
OKAYED
OXEYED
PLAYED
PRAYED
PREYED
SPAYED
STAYED
SWAYED
XRAYED

YE••••

YEANED
YEARLY
YEARNS
YEASTS
YEASTY
YELLED
YELLER
YELLOW
YELPED
YELPER
YEMENI
YENNED
YEOMAN
YEOMEN
YERBAS
YESSED
YESSES
YESTER

Y•E•••

YIELDS
YLEVEL

Y••E••

YAGERS
YAMENS
YCLEPT
YEMENI
YODELS
YOGEES
YOKELS

Y•••E•

YABBER
YAHVEH
YAHWEH
YAKKED
YAMMER
YANKED
YANKEE
YAPPED
YARDED
YAUPED
YAWLED
YAWNED
YAWNER
YAWPED
YAWPER
YEANED
YELLED
YELLER
YELPED
YELPER
YENNED
YEOMEN
YESSED
YESSES
YESTER
YIPPED
YLEVEL
YOGEES
YONDER
YONKER
YOWLED
YUKKED

Y••••E

YANKEE
YIPPIE
YVONNE

•YE•••

AYEAYE
AYESHA
BYEBYE
DYEING
EYECUP
EYEFUL
EYEING
EYELET
EYELID
HYENAS
HYETAL
MYELIN
PYEMIA
PYEMIC

•Y•E••

CYBELE
CYMENE
CYRENE
GYNECO
HYGEIA
HYMENO
HYMENS
LYCEES
LYCEUM
MYCETE
MYSELF
PYRENE
SYCEES
WYVERN
XYLEMS
XYLENE

•Y••E•

CYCLED
CYCLER
CYCLES
CYGNET
CYPHER
EYASES
EYELET
EYRIES
GYPPED
HYADES
HYMNED
HYPHEN
HYSTER
LYCEES
LYNXES
MYOPES
MYRMEC
OYSTER
PYXIES
SYCEES
SYDNEY
SYNDET
SYPHER
SYSTEM
XYSTER

•Y•••E

AYEAYE
BYEBYE
BYGONE
BYLANE
BYLINE
BYNAME
CYBELE
CYMENE
CYMOSE
CYRENE
GYRATE
GYROSE
HYDRAE
HYPHAE
LYSINE
LYTTAE
MYCETE
MYRTLE
PYRENE
PYRITE
PYRONE
PYROPE
SYLVAE
TYRONE
XYLENE
XYLOSE
ZYGOTE
ZYMASE

••YE••

BAYEUX
BUYERS
DOYENS
DRYERS
DRYEST
FLYERS
FOYERS
FRYERS
GAYEST
GAYETY
LAYERS
MAYEST
PAYEES
PAYERS
PRYERS
SAYERS
SHYEST
SLYEST
TOYERS
TUYERE
VOYEUR
WRYEST

••Y•E•

CLYDES
CLYPEI
DOYLEY
DRYDEN
ELYSEE
GEYSER
HOYDEN
JAYVEE
JOYCES
KAYOED
KEYNES
KHYBER
LAYMEN
MAYHEM
ORYXES
OXYGEN
PAYEES
RHYMED
RHYMER
RHYMES
SKYMEN
STYLED
STYLER
STYLES
STYLET
THYMES
THYREO
WAYNES
ZUYDER

••Y••E

ANYONE
CAYUSE
COYOTE
ELYSEE
GWYNNE
JAYVEE
PEYOTE
PHYLAE
PSYCHE
SCYTHE
STYMIE
THYRSE
TUYERE
UNYOKE
VOYAGE

•••YE•

BARYES
BOWYER
BRAYED
BRAYER
BUOYED
CLAYED
CLAYEY
CLOYED
DRAYED
FLAYED
FLAYER
FRAYED
GRAYED
GRAYER
LAWYER
LIVYER
OBEYED
OBEYER
OKAYED
OXEYED
OXEYES
PLAYED
PLAYER
PRAYED
PRAYER
PREYED
PREYER
SAWYER
SLAYER
SPAYED
SPRYER
STAYED
STAYER
SWAYED
THAYER
WHEYEY
XRAYED

•••Y•E

ALKYNE
ARGYLE
ECTYPE
ELAYNE
ENZYME
OOCYTE

••••YE

AYEAYE
BYEBYE
REDEYE

•Y•F••

EYEFUL

FYLFOT

•Y••F•
TYPIFY

•Y•••F
MYSELF

••YF••
DAYFLY
JOYFUL

••Y•F•
LAYOFF
PAYOFF

••Y••F
LAYOFF
PAYOFF

Y•G•••
YAGERS
YOGEES
YOGINS
YOGURT

Y••••G
YAWING
YOKING
YOWING

•YG•••
BYGONE
CYGNET
CYGNUS
HYGEIA
ZYGOMA
ZYGOTE

•Y••G•
SYZYGY

•Y•••G
DYEING
EYEING
LYSING
TYPING

••YG••
OXYGEN

••Y•G•
CAYUGA
ERYNGO
VOYAGE

••Y••G
BAYING
BUYING
CRYING
DRYING
FAYING
FLYING
FRYING
GUYING
HAYING
JOYING
KEYING
LAYING
MAYING
PAYING
PLYING
PRYING
RAYING
SAYING
SHYING
SKYING
SPYING
STYING
TOYING
TRYING
WRYING

•••YG•
SYZYGY

•••Y•G
LARYNG

Y•H•••
YAHOOS
YAHVEH
YAHWEH

Y••H••
YACHTS
YOOHOO

Y•••H•
YOUTHS

Y••••H
YAHVEH
YAHWEH

•Y•H••
CYPHER
HYPHAE
HYPHAL
HYPHEN
MYTHIC
MYTHOI
MYTHOS
PYTHIA
PYTHIC
PYTHON
SYPHER
TYPHLO
TYPHON
TYPHUS

•Y••H•
AYESHA
KYUSHU
LYMPHO
NYMPHA
NYMPHO
NYMPHS
PYRRHA
SYLPHS
SYLPHY

•Y•••H
BYPATH

••YH••
ANYHOW
MAYHAP
MAYHEM

••Y•H•
ERYTHR
GLYPHS
PSYCHE
PSYCHO
RAYAHS
RHYTHM
SCYPHI
SCYPHO
SCYTHE

••Y••H
BOYISH
COYISH
TOYISH
WHYDAH

YI••••
YIELDS
YIPPED
YIPPIE

Y•I•••
YOICKS

Y••I••
YAKIMA
YAWING
YOGINS
YOKING
YOWING

Y•••I•
YIPPIE
YTTRIA
YTTRIC

Y••••I
YEMENI

•Y•I••
BYLINE
CYNICS
CYRILS
DYEING
EYEING
EYRIES
HYOIDS
LYDIAS
LYRICS
LYRISM
LYRIST
LYSINE
LYSING
LYSINS
MYRIAD
MYRICA
PYRITE
PYXIES
SYBILS
SYRIAC
SYRIAN
SYRINX
TYPIFY
TYPING
TYPIST

•Y••I•
CYANIC
CYANID
CYANIN
CYCLIC
CYMLIN
CYMOID
CYMRIC
CYPRIN
CYSTIC
DYADIC
EYELID
HYBRID
HYBRIS
HYDRIC
HYGEIA
HYMNIC
HYPNIC
MYELIN
MYOPIA
MYOPIC
MYOSIN
MYOSIS
MYSTIC
MYTHIC
PYEMIA
PYEMIC
PYKNIC
PYOSIS
PYTHIA
PYTHIC
PYURIA
SYLVIA
SYNDIC
XYLOID

•Y•••I
MYTHOI

••YI••
BAYING
BOYISH
BUYING
COYISH
CRYING
DRYING
FAYING
FLYING
FRYING
GUYING
HAYING
JOYING
KEYING
LAYING
MAYING
PAYING
PLYING
PRYING
RAYING
SAYING
SHYING
SKYING
SPYING
STYING
TOYING
TOYISH
TRYING
WRYING
ZAYINS

••Y•I•
AMYLIC
CHYMIC
GDYNIA
GLYNIS
ODYNIA
PHYSIC
PHYSIO
PHYTIN
STYMIE
THYMIC
ZOYSIA

••Y••I
CLYPEI
SCYPHI
THYRSI

Y•K•••
YAKIMA
YAKKED
YOKELS
YOKING
YUKKED

Y••K••
YAKKED
YANKED
YANKEE
YONKER
YUKKED

Y•••K•
YOICKS

Y••••K
YASMAK

•YK•••
PYKNIC

•Y•••K
BYTALK
BYWORK
DYBBUK

••Y•K•
KAYAKS
UNYOKE

•••Y•K
GALYAK

YL••••
YLEVEL

Y•L•••
YCLEPT
YELLED
YELLER
YELLOW
YELPED
YELPER

Y••L••
YAWLED
YELLED
YELLER
YELLOW
YIELDS
YOWLED

Y•••L•
YEARLY
YODELS
YOKELS

Y••••L
YLEVEL

•YL•••
BYLANE
BYLAWS
BYLINE
FYLFOT
NYLONS
PYLONS
SYLPHS
SYLPHY
SYLVAE
SYLVAN
SYLVAS
SYLVIA
XYLANS
XYLEMS
XYLENE
XYLOID
XYLOLS
XYLOSE

•Y•L••
BYBLOW
BYPLAY
CYCLED
CYCLER
CYCLES
CYCLIC

CYMLIN
EYELET
EYELID
MYELIN

•Y••L•
BYTALK
CYBELE
CYRILS
MYRTLE
MYSELF
SYBILS
TYBALT
TYPHLO
XYLOLS

•Y•••L
CYMBAL
EYEFUL
HYETAL
HYMNAL
HYPHAL
SYMBOL

••YL••
AMYLIC
AMYLUM
ASYLUM
CEYLON
DOYLEY
IDYLLS
PHYLAE
PHYLLO
PHYLUM
SCYLLA
STYLAR
STYLED
STYLER
STYLES
STYLET
STYLUS
TAYLOR
WAYLAY

••Y•L•
DAYFLY
IDYLLS
PAYOLA
PHYLLO
RIYALS
ROYALS
SCYLLA

••Y••L
AMYTAL
GLYCOL
JOYFUL
THYMOL

•••YL•
ALKYLS
ALLYLS
ANKYLO
ARGYLE
ARGYLL
BERYLS
ETHYLS
GRAYLY
HEXYLS
JEKYLL
SIBYLS
SPRYLY
VINYLS

•••Y•L
ARGYLL
ENCYCL
JEKYLL

••••YL
ACETYL
ALPHYL
BENZYL
CHERYL
DACTYL
FORMYL
METHYL
PHENYL
PROPYL
TETRYL
TOLUYL
TROTYL
URANYL

Y•M•••
YAMENS
YAMMER
YAMUNS
YEMENI

Y••M••
YAMMER
YASMAK
YEOMAN
YEOMEN

Y•••M•
YAKIMA

•YM•••
AYMARA
CYMARS
CYMBAL
CYMENE
CYMLIN
CYMOID
CYMOSE
CYMOUS
CYMRIC
HYMENO
HYMENS
HYMNAL
HYMNED
HYMNIC
LYMPHO
NYMPHA
NYMPHO
NYMPHS
SYMBOL
TYMPAN
ZYMASE

•Y•M••
MYRMEC
PYEMIA
PYEMIC

•Y••M•
BYNAME
DYNAMO
MYXOMA
XYLEMS
ZYGOMA

•Y•••M
GYPSUM
LYCEUM
LYRISM
SYSTEM

••YM••
CAYMAN
CHYMIC
ETYMON
HAYMOW
LAYMAN
LAYMEN
RHYMED
RHYMER
RHYMES
SKYMAN
SKYMEN
STYMIE
THYMES
THYMIC
THYMOL
THYMUS

••Y•M•
ABYSMS

••Y••M
ADYTUM
AMYLUM
ASYLUM
MAYHEM
PHYLUM
RHYTHM

•••YM•
CORYMB
ENZYME

••••YM
ANONYM
EPONYM

Y•N•••
YANKED
YANKEE
YENNED
YONDER
YONKER

Y••N••
YAWNED
YAWNER
YEANED
YENNED
YVONNE

Y•••N•
YAMENS
YAMUNS
YAPONS
YAWING
YEARNS
YEMENI
YOGINS
YOKING
YOWING
YUPONS
YVONNE

Y••••N
YAUPON
YEOMAN
YEOMEN
YOUPON

•YN•••
BYNAME
CYNICS
DYNAMO
DYNAST
GYNECO
GYNOUS
LYNXES
SYNDET
SYNDIC
SYNODS
SYNTAX
SYNURA

•Y•N••
CYANIC
CYANID
CYANIN
CYGNET
CYGNUS
HYENAS
HYMNAL
HYMNED
HYMNIC
HYPNIC
HYPNOS
MYRNAS
PYKNIC
SYDNEY

•Y••N•
BYGONE
BYLANE
BYLINE
CYMENE
CYRANO
CYRENE
DYEING
EYEING
GYRONS
HYMENO
HYMENS
LYSINE
LYSING
LYSINS
NYLONS
PYLONS
PYRANS
PYRENE
PYRONE
SYRINX
TYPING
TYRANT
TYRONE
XYLANS
XYLENE

•Y•••N
CYANIN
CYMLIN
CYPRIN
HYPHEN
MYELIN
MYOSIN
PYTHON
SYLVAN
SYRIAN
TYCOON
TYMPAN
TYPHON
WYSTAN
WYVERN

••YN••
ERYNGO
GDYNIA
GLYNIS
GWYNNE
KEYNES
ODYNIA
WAYNES

••Y•N•
ANYONE
ARYANS
BAYING
BEYOND
BRYANT
BRYONY
BUYING
CRYING
DOYENS
DRYING
FAYING
FLYING
FRYING
GUYANA
GUYING
GWYNNE
HAYING
JOYING
KEYING
LAYING
MAYING
PAYING
PLYING
PRYING
RAYING
RAYONS
SAYING
SHYING
SKYING
SPYING
STYING
TOYING
TOYONS
TRYING
WRYING
ZAYINS

••Y••N
CAYMAN
CEYLON
DAYTON
DRYDEN
ETYMON
HOYDEN
LAYMAN
LAYMEN
OXYGEN
PHYTIN
SKYMAN
SKYMEN

•••YN•
ALKYNE
ELAYNE
LARYNG
LARYNX

•••Y•N
BANYAN
BARYON
BUNYAN
CANYON
CRAYON
GERYON
LIBYAN
RUNYON

••••YN
BOLEYN
EVELYN
SELSYN

YO••••
YODELS
YOGEES
YOGINS
YOGURT
YOICKS
YOKELS
YOKING
YONDER

6

YONKER
YOOHOO
YORUBA
YOUPON
YOUTHS
YOWING
YOWLED

Y•O•••
YEOMAN
YEOMEN
YOOHOO
YVONNE

Y••O••
YAHOOS
YAPONS
YUPONS

Y•••O•
YAHOOS
YARROW
YAUPON
YELLOW
YOOHOO
YOUPON

Y••••O
YOOHOO

•YO•••
HYOIDS
MYOPES
MYOPIA
MYOPIC
MYOSIN
MYOSIS
PYOSIS

•Y•O••
BYGONE
BYROAD
BYWORD
BYWORK
CYMOID
CYMOSE
CYMOUS
GYNOUS
GYRONS
GYROSE
MYXOMA
NYLONS
PYLONS
PYRONE
PYROPE
SYNODS
TYCOON
TYRONE
XYLOID
XYLOLS
XYLOSE
ZYGOMA
ZYGOTE

•Y••O•
BYBLOW
FYLFOT
HYDROS
HYPNOS
HYSSOP
MYTHOI
MYTHOS
PYTHON
SYMBOL
TYCOON
TYPHON
XYSTOS

•Y•••O
CYRANO
DYNAMO
GYNECO
HYMENO
LYMPHO
NYMPHO
TYPHLO

••YO••
ANYONE
BAYOUS
BEYOND
BRYONY
COYOTE
JOYOUS
KAYOED
LAYOFF
LAYOUT
MAYORS
PAYOFF
PAYOLA
PEYOTE
POYOUS
RAYONS
TOYONS
TRYOUT
UNYOKE
WAYOUT

••Y•O•
ABYDOS
ANYHOW
CEYLON
DAYTON
ETYMON
GLYCOL
HAYMOW
MAYPOP
TAYLOR
THYMOL

••Y••O
CRYPTO
ERYNGO
GLYPTO
PHYLLO
PHYSIO
PSYCHO
SCYPHO

THYREO

•••YO•
BARYON
CANYON
CRAYON
GERYON
RUNYON

•••Y•O
ANKYLO
CHRYSO

••••YO
ARROYO
DAIMYO
EMBRYO

Y•P•••
YAPONS
YAPPED
YIPPED
YIPPIE
YUPONS

Y••P••
YAPPED
YAUPED
YAUPON
YAWPED
YAWPER
YELPED
YELPER
YIPPED
YIPPIE
YOUPON

Y•••P•
YCLEPT

•YP•••
BYPASS
BYPAST
BYPATH
BYPLAY
CYPHER
CYPRIN
CYPRUS
GYPPED
GYPSUM
HYPHAE
HYPHAL
HYPHEN
HYPNIC
HYPNOS
SYPHER
TYPHLO
TYPHON
TYPHUS
TYPIFY
TYPING
TYPIST

•Y•P••
GYPPED
LYMPHO
MYOPES
MYOPIA
MYOPIC
NYMPHA
NYMPHO
NYMPHS
SYLPHS
SYLPHY
TYMPAN

•Y••P•
PYROPE
SYRUPS
SYRUPY

•Y•••P
EYECUP
HYSSOP

••YP••
CLYPEI
COYPUS
CRYPTO
CRYPTS
GLYPHS
GLYPTO
MAYPOP
SCYPHI
SCYPHO

••Y••P
MAYHAP
MAYPOP
SKYCAP

•••YP•
ECTYPE
POLYPS

Y•R•••
YARDED
YARROW
YERBAS
YORUBA

Y••R••
YARROW
YEARLY
YEARNS
YTTRIA
YTTRIC

Y•••R•
YAGERS
YOGURT

Y••••R
YABBER
YAMMER
YAWNER
YAWPER

YELLER
YELPER
YESTER
YONDER
YONKER

•YR•••
BYROAD
CYRANO
CYRENE
CYRILS
EYRIES
GYRATE
GYRONS
GYROSE
LYRICS
LYRISM
LYRIST
MYRIAD
MYRICA
MYRMEC
MYRNAS
MYRTLE
PYRANS
PYRENE
PYRITE
PYRONE
PYROPE
PYRRHA
SYRIAC
SYRIAN
SYRINX
SYRUPS
SYRUPY
TYRANT
TYRONE

•Y•R••
CYMRIC
CYPRIN
CYPRUS
HYBRID
HYBRIS
HYDRAE
HYDRAS
HYDRIC
HYDROS
PYRRHA
PYURIA

•Y••R•
AYMARA
BYWORD
BYWORK
CYMARS
SYNURA
WYVERN

•Y•••R
CYCLER
CYPHER
HYSTER
OYSTER
SYPHER

XYSTER

••YR••
THYREO
THYRSE
THYRSI

••Y•R•
BAYARD
BOYARD
BOYARS
BUYERS
DRYERS
ELYTRA
FLYERS
FOYERS
FRYERS
LAYERS
MAYORS
PAYERS
PRYERS
SAYERS
TOYERS
TUYERE

••Y••R
ERYTHR
GEYSER
KHYBER
RHYMER
STYLAR
STYLER
TAYLOR
VOYEUR
ZUYDER

•••YR•
SATYRS

•••Y•R
BOWYER
BRAYER
FLAYER
GRAYER
LAWYER
LIVYER
MAGYAR
OBEYER
PLAYER
PRAYER
PREYER
SAWYER
SLAYER
SPRYER
STAYER
THAYER

••••YR
MARTYR
VALKYR
ZEPHYR

Y•S•••
YASMAK

6

YESSED
YESSES
YESTER

Y••S••
YEASTS
YEASTY
YESSED
YESSES

Y••••S
YACHTS
YAGERS
YAHOOS
YAMENS
YAMUNS
YAPONS
YEARNS
YEASTS
YERBAS
YESSES
YIELDS
YODELS
YOGEES
YOGINS
YOICKS
YOKELS
YOUTHS
YUCCAS
YUPONS

•YS•••
BYSSUS
CYSTIC
HYSSOP
HYSTER
LYSINE
LYSING
LYSINS
MYSELF
MYSTIC
OYSTER
SYSTEM
WYSTAN
XYSTER
XYSTOS
XYSTUS

•Y•S••
AYESHA
BYSSUS
EYASES
GYPSUM
HYSSOP
KYUSHU
MYOSIN
MYOSIS
PYOSIS

•Y••S•
BYPASS
BYPAST
CYMOSE
DYNAST
GYROSE
LYRISM
LYRIST
TYPIST
XYLOSE
ZYMASE

•Y•••S
BYLAWS
BYPASS
BYSSUS
BYWAYS
CYCADS
CYCLES
CYGNUS
CYMARS
CYMOUS
CYNICS
CYPRUS
CYRILS
EYASES
EYRIES
GYNOUS
GYRONS
HYADES
HYBRIS
HYDRAS
HYDROS
HYENAS
HYMENS
HYOIDS
HYPNOS
LYCEES
LYDIAS
LYNXES
LYRICS
LYSINS
MYOPES
MYOSIS
MYRNAS
MYTHOS
NYLONS
NYMPHS
PYLONS
PYOSIS
PYRANS
PYXIES
SYBILS
SYCEES
SYLPHS
SYLVAS
SYNODS
SYRUPS
TYPHUS
XYLANS
XYLEMS
XYLOLS
XYSTOS
XYSTUS

••YS••
ABYSMS
ELYSEE
GEYSER
PHYSIC
PHYSIO
TRYSTS
ZOYSIA

••Y•S•
BOYISH
CAYUSE
COYISH
DRYEST
GAYEST
MAYEST
SHYEST
SLYEST
THYRSE
THYRSI
TOYISH
WRYEST

••Y••S
ABYDOS
ABYSMS
ARYANS
BAYOUS
BOYARS
BUYERS
CLYDES
COYPUS
CRYPTS
DOYENS
DRYADS
DRYERS
FLYBYS
FLYERS
FOYERS
FRYERS
GLYNIS
GLYPHS
IDYLLS
JOYCES
JOYOUS
KAYAKS
KEYNES
LAYERS
MAYORS
ORYXES
PAYEES
PAYERS
POYOUS
PRYERS
RAYAHS
RAYONS
RHYMES
RIYALS
ROYALS
SAYERS
STYLES
STYLUS
THYMES
THYMUS
TOYERS
TOYONS
TRYSTS
WAYNES
ZAYINS

•••YS•
CHRYSO
ENCYST

•••Y•S
ALKYLS
ALLYLS
BARYES
BERYLS
ETHYLS
FLOYDS
HEXYLS
LLOYDS
OXEYES
PLAYAS
POLYPS
SATYRS
SIBYLS
SONYAS
VINYLS

••••YS
ABBEYS
ALLAYS
ALLEYS
ALLOYS
ALWAYS
ANNOYS
ARCHYS
ARRAYS
ASSAYS
AVERYS
BARRYS
BECKYS
BELAYS
BENJYS
BENNYS
BESSYS
BETSYS
BETTYS
BIALYS
BILLYS
BOBBYS
BOGEYS
BONNYS
BYWAYS
CATHYS
CINDYS
CISSYS
CONEYS
COOEYS
COVEYS
CUTEYS
DAISYS
DANNYS
DAVEYS
DEBBYS
DECAYS
DECOYS
DELAYS
DENNYS
DOLLYS
EMBAYS
EMILYS
ENJOYS
ENVOYS
ESSAYS
FANNYS
FLYBYS
FORAYS
GERRYS
GERTYS
GLADYS
HARRYS
HATTYS
HENRYS
HETTYS
HOLLYS
HONEYS
INLAYS
JACKYS
JENNYS
JERRYS
JIMMYS
JINNYS
KATHYS
KENNYS
KITTYS
LARRYS
LENNYS
LEROYS
LIBBYS
LIMEYS
LIZZYS
MALAYS
MAMEYS
MANDYS
MARTYS
MATEYS
MICKYS
MILLYS
MOLLYS
MONEYS
MONTYS
MORAYS
MORTYS
MOSEYS
NANCYS
NELLYS
NICKYS
NOWAYS
PADDYS
PANSYS
PATSYS
PEGGYS
PENNYS
PERCYS
PERRYS
POLLYS
POPPYS
RELAYS
REPAYS
RICKYS
RODDYS
SALLYS
SAMMYS
SANDYS
SEPOYS
SPLAYS
SPRAYS
STACYS
STRAYS
TEDDYS
TERRYS
TETHYS
THADYS
TILLYS
TIMMYS
TOMMYS
TRIXYS
TRUDYS
UNLAYS
UNSAYS
VICKYS
VINNYS
WALLYS
WAVEYS
WENDYS
WILLYS
ZLOTYS

YT••••
YTTRIA
YTTRIC

Y•T•••
YTTRIA
YTTRIC

Y••T••
YESTER
YOUTHS

Y•••T•
YACHTS
YEASTS
YEASTY

Y••••T
YCLEPT
YOGURT

•YT•••
BYTALK
LYTTAE
MYTHIC
MYTHOI
MYTHOS
PYTHIA
PYTHIC
PYTHON

•Y•T••
CYSTIC
HYETAL
HYSTER
LYTTAE
MYRTLE
MYSTIC
OYSTER

6

SYNTAX
SYSTEM
WYSTAN
XYSTER
XYSTOS
XYSTUS

•Y••T•
BYPATH
GYRATE
MYCETE
PYRITE
ZYGOTE

•Y•••T
BYPAST
CYGNET
DYNAST
EYELET
FYLFOT
LYRIST
SYNDET
TYBALT
TYPIST
TYRANT

••YT••
ADYTUM
AMYTAL
DAYTON
ELYTRA
ERYTHR
PHYTIN
RHYTHM
SCYTHE

••Y•T•
COYOTE
CRYPTO
CRYPTS
GAYETY
GLYPTO
PEYOTE
TRYSTS

••Y••T
BRYANT
DRYEST
GAYEST
LAYOUT
MAYEST
SHYEST
SLYEST
STYLET
TRYOUT
WAYOUT
WRYEST

•••YT•
BARYTA
OOCYTE

•••Y•T
ENCYST

YU••••
YUCCAS
YUKKED
YUPONS

Y•U•••
YAUPED
YAUPON
YOUPON
YOUTHS

Y••U••
YAMUNS
YOGURT
YORUBA

•YU•••
KYUSHU
PYURIA

•Y•U••
SYNURA
SYRUPS
SYRUPY

•Y••U•
BYSSUS
CYGNUS
CYMOUS
CYPRUS
DYBBUK
EYECUP
EYEFUL
GYNOUS
GYPSUM
LYCEUM
TYPHUS
XYSTUS

•Y•••U
KYUSHU

••YU••
CAYUGA
CAYUSE

••Y•U•
ADYTUM
AMYLUM
ASYLUM
BAYEUX
BAYOUS
COYPUS
JOYFUL
JOYOUS
LAYOUT
PHYLUM
POYOUS
STYLUS
THYMUS
TRYOUT
VOYEUR
WAYOUT

YV••••
YVONNE

Y••V••
YAHVEH
YLEVEL

•YV•••
WYVERN

•Y•V••
SYLVAE
SYLVAN
SYLVAS
SYLVIA

••YV••
JAYVEE

Y•W•••
YAWING
YAWLED
YAWNED
YAWNER
YAWPED
YAWPER
YOWING
YOWLED

Y••W••
YAHWEH

Y••••W
YARROW
YELLOW

•YW•••
BYWAYS
BYWORD
BYWORK

•Y••W•
BYLAWS

•Y•••W
BYBLOW

••YW••
ANYWAY
KEYWAY
SKYWAY

••Y••W
ANYHOW
HAYMOW

•YX•••
MYXOMA
PYXIES

•Y•X••
LYNXES

•Y•••X
SYNTAX
SYRINX

••YX••
ORYXES

••Y••X
BAYEUX

•••Y•X
LARYNX

••••YX
COCCYX

Y••••Y
YEARLY
YEASTY

•Y•Y••
SYZYGY

•Y••Y•
AYEAYE
BYEBYE
BYWAYS

•Y•••Y
BYPLAY
SYDNEY
SYLPHY
SYRUPY
SYZYGY
TYPIFY

••Y•Y•
FLYBYS

••Y••Y
ANYWAY
BRYONY
DAYFLY
DOYLEY
GAYETY
HEYDAY
KEYWAY
LAYDAY
MAYDAY
PAYDAY
SKYWAY
WAYLAY

•••Y•Y
CLAYEY
GRAYLY
SPRYLY
SYZYGY
WHEYEY

•YZ•••
SYZYGY

•••YZ•
CORYZA

ZA••••
ZAFFAR
ZAFFER
ZAFFIR
ZAFFRE
ZAMBIA
ZAMIAS
ZANANA
ZANIER
ZANIES
ZAREBA
ZAYINS

Z•A•••
ZEALOT

Z••A••
ZANANA
ZBEAMS
ZENANA
ZONARY
ZONATE
ZOUAVE
ZYMASE

Z•••A•
ZAFFAR
ZAMIAS
ZEBRAS
ZIGZAG
ZILLAH
ZODIAC
ZOONAL

Z••••A
ZAMBIA
ZANANA
ZAREBA
ZENANA
ZEUGMA
ZINNIA
ZONULA
ZOYSIA
ZYGOMA

•ZA•••
AZALEA
AZAZEL

•Z•A••
AZRAEL
IZZARD

•Z•••A
AZALEA

••ZA••
BEZANT
GAZABO
HAZARD
IZZARD

JEZAIL
LAZARS
LIZARD
MOZART
SIZARS
VIZARD
WIZARD

••Z•A•
BEZOAR
FEZZAN
HAZZAN
PIZZAS
TAZZAS

••Z••A
ECZEMA
MAZUMA
MEZUZA

•••ZA•
BALZAC
BANZAI
BRAZAS
COLZAS
ELIZAS
FEZZAN
HAMZAS
HAZZAN
PIZZAS
PLAZAS
TARZAN
TAZZAS
ZIGZAG

•••Z•A
EPIZOA
PIAZZA

••••ZA
CORYZA
MEZUZA
PIAZZA
SFORZA
STANZA

ZB••••
ZBEAMS

Z•B•••
ZEBECK
ZEBECS
ZEBRAS
ZIBETH
ZIBETS

Z••B••
ZAMBIA
ZOMBIE
ZOMBIS

Z•••B•
ZAREBA

6

••Z•B•
GAZABO
GAZEBO

Z•C•••
ZECHIN

Z••C••
ZINCED
ZINCIC
ZINCKY
ZIRCON

Z•••C•
ZEBECK
ZEBECS
ZURICH

Z••••C
ZINCIC
ZODIAC

•Z•C••
CZECHS

•Z••C•
AZTECS

•Z•••C
AZONIC
AZOTIC
OZONIC

••Z••C
EOZOIC

•••Z•C
BALZAC

Z•D•••
ZODIAC

Z••D••
ZUIDER
ZUYDER

Z•••D•
ZOOIDS
ZOUNDS

Z••••D
ZEROED
ZESTED
ZINCED
ZINGED
ZIPPED
ZOOMED

•Z•••D
IZZARD

••Z••D
BUZZED
FIZZED
FUZZED
HAZARD
IZZARD
JAZZED
LIZARD
RAZEED
RAZZED
VIZARD
WIZARD

•••Z•D
AMAZED
BLAZED
BOOZED
BRAZED
BUZZED
CRAZED
FEEZED
FIZZED
FUZZED
GLAZED
GLOZED
GRAZED
JAZZED
PRIZED
RAZZED
SEIZED

••••ZD
ORMUZD

ZE••••
ZEALOT
ZEBECK
ZEBECS
ZEBRAS
ZECHIN
ZENANA
ZENGER
ZENITH
ZEPHYR
ZEROED
ZEROES
ZESTED
ZETHOS
ZETHUS
ZEUGMA

Z•E•••
ZBEAMS

Z••E••
ZAREBA
ZEBECK
ZEBECS
ZIBETH
ZIBETS

Z•••E•
ZAFFER
ZANIER
ZANIES
ZENGER
ZEROED
ZEROES
ZESTED
ZINCED
ZINGED
ZIPPED
ZIPPER
ZITHER
ZOOMED
ZOSTER
ZUIDER
ZUYDER

Z••••E
ZAFFRE
ZIZZLE
ZOMBIE
ZONATE
ZONULE
ZOUAVE
ZYGOTE
ZYMASE

•ZE•••
CZECHS

•Z•E••
AZTECS

•Z••E•
AZALEA
AZAZEL
AZINES
AZOLES
AZORES
AZRAEL
AZURES

••ZE••
BEZELS
COZENS
DIZENS
DOZENS
ECZEMA
FUZEES
GAZEBO
GAZERS
HAZELS
HAZERS
MAZERS
OUZELS
RAZEED
RAZEES
WIZENS

••Z•E•
BUZZED
BUZZER
BUZZES
COZIER
COZIES
DOZIER
FEZZES
FIZZED
FIZZES
FUZEES
FUZZED
FUZZES
HAZIER
JAZZED
JAZZER
JAZZES
LAZIER
MAZIER
MIZZEN
OOZIER
RAZEED
RAZEES
RAZZED
RAZZES
SIZIER
VIZIER

••Z••E
DAZZLE
ENZYME
EVZONE
FIZZLE
GUZZLE
LIZZIE
MUZZLE
NOZZLE
NUZZLE
PUZZLE
SIZZLE
SOZINE
ZIZZLE

•••ZE•
AMAZED
AMAZES
AZAZEL
BLAZED
BLAZER
BLAZES
BONZER
BONZES
BOOZED
BOOZER
BOOZES
BRAZED
BRAZEN
BRAZER
BRAZES
BUZZED
BUZZER
BUZZES
CRAZED
CRAZES
CROZER
CROZES
FEEZED
FEEZES
FEZZES
FIZZED
FIZZES
FROZEN
FURZES
FUZZED
FUZZES
GAUZES
GEEZER
GLAZED
GLAZER
GLAZES
GLOZED
GLOZES
GRAZED
GRAZER
GRAZES
GRIZEL
JAZZED
JAZZER
JAZZES
MAIZES
MIZZEN
PANZER
PRIZED
PRIZER
PRIZES
RAZZED
RAZZES
SEIZED
SEIZER
SEIZES
SMAZES
TETZEL
WINZES

•••Z•E
DAZZLE
FIZZLE
FOOZLE
GUZZLE
LIZZIE
MUZZLE
NOZZLE
NUZZLE
PUZZLE
SIZZLE
ZIZZLE

••••ZE
ABLAZE
ASSIZE
BELIZE
BRAIZE
BREEZE
BRONZE
FREEZE
FRIEZE
FRUNZE
IODIZE
IONIZE
SNEEZE
SNOOZE
WHEEZE

Z•F•••
ZAFFAR
ZAFFER
ZAFFIR
ZAFFRE

Z••F••
ZAFFAR
ZAFFER
ZAFFIR
ZAFFRE

••Z•F•
NAZIFY

Z•G•••
ZIGZAG
ZYGOMA
ZYGOTE

Z••G••
ZENGER
ZEUGMA
ZINGED

Z••••G
ZIGZAG
ZONING

••ZG••
FIZGIG

••Z•G•
SYZYGY

••Z••G
DAZING
DOZING
FAZING
FIZGIG
FUZING
GAZING
HAZING
LAZING
MAZING
OOZING
RAZING
SIZING

•••Z•G
DANZIG
ZIGZAG

ZH••••
ZHUKOV

Z••H••
ZECHIN
ZEPHYR
ZETHOS
ZETHUS
ZITHER

Z••••H
ZENITH
ZIBETH
ZILLAH
ZIZITH
ZURICH

6

•Z••H•
CZECHS

••ZH••
MUZHIK

••Z••H
ZIZITH

ZI••••
ZIBETH
ZIBETS
ZIGZAG
ZILLAH
ZINCED
ZINCIC
ZINCKY
ZINGED
ZINNIA
ZIPPED
ZIPPER
ZIRCON
ZIRONS
ZITHER
ZIZITH
ZIZZLE

Z•I•••
ZUIDER

Z••I••
ZAMIAS
ZANIER
ZANIES
ZAYINS
ZENITH
ZIZITH
ZODIAC
ZONING
ZOOIDS
ZORILS
ZURICH

Z•••I•
ZAFFIR
ZAMBIA
ZECHIN
ZINCIC
ZINNIA
ZOMBIE
ZOMBIS
ZOYSIA

•ZI•••
AZINES

•Z••I•
AZONIC
AZOTIC
OZONIC

••ZI••
COZIER
COZIES
COZILY
DAZING
DOZIER
DOZILY
DOZING
FAZING
FUZILS
FUZING
GAZING
HAZIER
HAZILY
HAZING
LAZIER
LAZILY
LAZING
MAZIER
MAZILY
MAZING
NAZIFY
NAZISM
OOZIER
OOZILY
OOZING
RAZING
SIZIER
SIZING
SOZINE
SOZINS
VIZIER
VIZIRS
ZIZITH

••Z•I•
EOZOIC
FIZGIG
JEZAIL
LIZZIE
MUZHIK

••Z••I
LAZULI

•••ZI•
BRAZIL
DANZIG
DIAZIN
LIZZIE
SEIZIN

•••Z•I
BANZAI
BORZOI

Z••K••
ZHUKOV

Z•••K•
ZINCKY

Z••••K
ZEBECK

••Z••K
MUZHIK

ZL••••
ZLOTYS

Z•L•••
ZILLAH

Z••L••
ZEALOT
ZILLAH

Z•••L•
ZIZZLE
ZONULA
ZONULE
ZORILS

Z••••L
ZOONAL

•Z•L••
AZALEA
AZOLES

•Z•••L
AZAZEL
AZRAEL

••Z•L•
BEZELS
COZILY
DAZZLE
DOZILY
FIZZLE
FUZILS
GUZZLE
HAZELS
HAZILY
LAZILY
LAZULI
MAZILY
MUZZLE
NOZZLE
NUZZLE
OOZILY
OUZELS
PUZZLE
SIZZLE
ZIZZLE

••Z••L
JEZAIL

•••ZL•
DAZZLE
FIZZLE
FOOZLE
GUZZLE
MUZZLE
NOZZLE
NUZZLE
PUZZLE
SIZZLE
ZIZZLE

•••Z•L
AZAZEL
BENZOL
BENZYL
BRAZIL
GRIZEL
PODZOL
TETZEL

Z•M•••
ZAMBIA
ZAMIAS
ZOMBIE
ZOMBIS
ZYMASE

Z••M••
ZOOMED

Z•••M•
ZBEAMS
ZEUGMA
ZYGOMA

••ZM••
GIZMOS

••Z•M•
ECZEMA
ENZYME
MAZUMA

••Z••M
NAZISM

Z•N•••
ZANANA
ZANIER
ZANIES
ZENANA
ZENGER
ZENITH
ZINCED
ZINCIC
ZINCKY
ZINGED
ZINNIA
ZONARY
ZONATE
ZONING
ZONULA
ZONULE

Z••N••
ZINNIA
ZOONAL
ZOUNDS

Z•••N•
ZANANA
ZAYINS
ZENANA
ZIRONS
ZONING

Z••••N
ZECHIN
ZIRCON

•Z•N••
AZINES
AZONIC
OZONIC

••Z•N•
BEZANT
COZENS
DAZING
DIZENS
DOZENS
DOZING
EVZONE
FAZING
FUZING
GAZING
HAZING
LAZING
MAZING
OOZING
RAZING
SIZING
SOZINE
SOZINS
WIZENS

••Z••N
FEZZAN
HAZZAN
MIZZEN

•••Z•N
AMAZON
BLAZON
BRAZEN
DIAZIN
FEZZAN
FROZEN
HAZZAN
MIZZEN
QUEZON
SEIZIN
TARZAN

ZO••••
ZODIAC
ZOMBIE
ZOMBIS
ZONARY
ZONATE
ZONING
ZONULA
ZONULE
ZOOIDS
ZOOMED
ZOONAL
ZORILS
ZOSTER
ZOUAVE
ZOUNDS
ZOYSIA

Z•O•••
ZLOTYS
ZOOIDS
ZOOMED
ZOONAL

Z••O••
ZEROED
ZEROES
ZIRONS
ZYGOMA
ZYGOTE

Z•••O•
ZEALOT
ZETHOS
ZHUKOV
ZIRCON

•ZO•••
AZOLES
AZONIC
AZORES
AZOTIC
OZONIC

••ZO••
BEZOAR
EOZOIC
EVZONE
KAZOOS
RAZORS
VIZORS

••Z•O•
GIZMOS
KAZOOS
MEZZOS

••Z••O
GAZABO
GAZEBO

•••ZO•
AMAZON
BENZOL
BLAZON
BORZOI
BRAZOS
EPIZOA
MATZOS
MATZOT
MEZZOS
PODZOL
QUEZON
SEIZOR

•••Z•O
AREZZO

••••ZO
ALONZO

AREZZO
REBOZO
SCHIZO

Z•P•••
ZEPHYR
ZIPPED
ZIPPER

Z••P••
ZIPPED
ZIPPER

Z•R•••
ZAREBA
ZEROED
ZEROES
ZIRCON
ZIRONS
ZORILS
ZURICH

Z••R••
ZEBRAS

Z•••R•
ZAFFRE
ZONARY

Z••••R
ZAFFAR
ZAFFER
ZAFFIR
ZANIER
ZENGER
ZEPHYR
ZIPPER
ZITHER
ZOSTER
ZUIDER
ZUYDER

•ZR•••
AZRAEL

•Z•R••
AZORES
AZURES

•Z••R•
IZZARD

••Z•R•
GAZERS
HAZARD
HAZERS
IZZARD
LAZARS
LIZARD
MAZERS
MOZART
RAZORS
SIZARS
VIZARD
VIZIRS
VIZORS
WIZARD

••Z••R
BEZOAR
BUZZER
COZIER
DOZIER
HAZIER
JAZZER
LAZIER
MAZIER
OOZIER
SIZIER
VIZIER

•••Z•R
BLAZER
BONZER
BOOZER
BRAZER
BUZZER
CROZER
GEEZER
GLAZER
GRAZER
JAZZER
PANZER
PRIZER
SEIZER
SEIZOR

Z•S•••
ZESTED
ZOSTER

Z••S••
ZOYSIA

Z•••S•
ZYMASE

Z••••S
ZAMIAS
ZANIES
ZAYINS
ZBEAMS
ZEBECS
ZEBRAS
ZEROES
ZETHOS
ZETHUS
ZIBETS
ZIRONS
ZLOTYS
ZOMBIS
ZOOIDS
ZORILS
ZOUNDS

•Z•••S
AZINES
AZOLES
AZORES
AZTECS
AZURES
CZECHS

••Z•S•
NAZISM

••Z••S
BEZELS
BUZZES
COZENS
COZIES
DIZENS
DOZENS
FEZZES
FIZZES
FUZEES
FUZILS
FUZZES
GAZERS
GIZMOS
HAZELS
HAZERS
JAZZES
KAZOOS
LAZARS
LIZZYS
MAZERS
MEZZOS
OUZELS
PIZZAS
RAZEES
RAZORS
RAZZES
SIZARS
SOZINS
TAZZAS
VIZIRS
VIZORS
WIZENS

•••Z•S
AMAZES
BLAZES
BONZES
BOOZES
BRAZAS
BRAZES
BRAZOS
BUZZES
COLZAS
CRAZES
CROZES
ELIZAS
FEEZES
FEZZES
FIZZES
FURZES
FUZZES
GAUZES
GLAZES
GLOZES
GRAZES
HAMZAS
JAZZES
LIZZYS
MAIZES
MATZOS
MEZZOS
PIZZAS
PLAZAS
PRIZES
RAZZES
SEIZES
SMAZES
TAZZAS
WINZES

Z•T•••
ZETHOS
ZETHUS
ZITHER

Z••T••
ZESTED
ZLOTYS
ZOSTER

Z•••T•
ZENITH
ZIBETH
ZIBETS
ZIZITH
ZONATE
ZYGOTE

Z••••T
ZEALOT

•ZT•••
AZTECS

•Z•T••
AZOTIC

••Z•T•
ZIZITH

••Z••T
BEZANT
MOZART

•••Z•T
MATZOT

ZU••••
ZUIDER
ZURICH
ZUYDER

Z•U•••
ZEUGMA
ZHUKOV
ZOUAVE
ZOUNDS

Z••U••
ZONULA
ZONULE

Z•••U•
ZETHUS

•ZU•••
AZURES

••ZU••
LAZULI
MAZUMA
MEZUZA

Z•••V•
ZOUAVE

Z••••V
ZHUKOV

ZY••••
ZYGOMA
ZYGOTE
ZYMASE

Z•Y•••
ZAYINS
ZOYSIA
ZUYDER

Z•••Y•
ZEPHYR
ZLOTYS

Z••••Y
ZINCKY
ZONARY

••ZY••
ENZYME
SYZYGY

••Z•Y•
LIZZYS

••Z••Y
COZILY
DOZILY
HAZILY
LAZILY
MAZILY
NAZIFY
OOZILY
SYZYGY

•••ZY•
BENZYL
LIZZYS

•••Z•Y
FRIZZY

••••ZY
BLOWZY
BREEZY
BRONZY
FLOOZY
FRENZY
FRIZZY
FROWZY
GROSZY
SLEAZY
SNEEZY
WHEEZY

Z•Z•••
ZIZITH
ZIZZLE

Z••Z••
ZIGZAG
ZIZZLE

•ZZ•••
IZZARD

•Z•Z••
AZAZEL

••ZZ••
BUZZED
BUZZER
BUZZES
DAZZLE
FEZZAN
FEZZES
FIZZED
FIZZES
FIZZLE
FUZZED
FUZZES
GUZZLE
HAZZAN
JAZZED
JAZZER
JAZZES
LIZZIE
LIZZYS
MEZZOS
MIZZEN
MUZZLE
NOZZLE
NUZZLE
PIZZAS
PUZZLE
RAZZED
RAZZES
SIZZLE
TAZZAS
ZIZZLE

••Z•Z•
MEZUZA

•••ZZ•
AREZZO
FRIZZY
PIAZZA